Film Reviews
1907-1980

A SIXTEEN-VOLUME SET,

Including an Index to Titles

Garland Publishing, Inc.
New York and London
1983

Contents

OF THE SIXTEEN-VOLUME SET

Film Reviews

1921-1925

VOLUME TWO

Garland Publishing, Inc.
New York and London
1983

© 1983 Daily Variety, Ltd.

All rights reserved

Library of Congress Cataloging in Publication Data
Main entry under title:

Variety film reviews.
  Includes index.

  1. Moving-pictures—Reviews.   I. Daily variety.
PN1995.V34   1982   791.43′75   82-15691
ISBN 0-8240-5200-5 (v. 1)
ISBN 0-8240-5201-3 (v. 2)

Manufactured in the United States of America

Printed on acid-free,
250-year-life paper

User's Guide

The reviews in this collection are published in chronological order, by the date on which the review appeared. The date of each issue appears at the top of the column where the reviews for that issue begin. The reviews continue through that column and all following columns until a new date appears at the top of the page. Where blank spaces occur at the end of a column, this indicates the end of that particular week's reviews. An index to film titles, giving date of review, is published as the last volume in this set.

1921

PASSIONATE PILGRIM.

Henry Calverly....................Matt Moore
Cecily....................Mary Newcomb
Madam Watt..........Julia Swayne Gordon
Senator Watt....................Tom Guise
Marjorie Daw....................Frankie Mann
Miriam....................Rubye de Remer
Esther....................Claire Whitney
Hitt....................Van Dyke Brook
Qualters....................Charles Gerard
Mayor McIntyre....................Sam J. Ryan
O'Rell....................Arthur Donaldson
Ammo....................Albert Roccardi
Listerly....................Bernard A. Reinold
Trent....................Charles Brook
Nurse Russell....................Helen Lindroth

In the first week of its third year the Rivoli offered Cosmopolitan's somewhat incomprehensively titled screen version of Samuel Merwin's story, "The Passionate Pilgrim" (Paramount).

It is singularly a combination of good and bad (not evil) that has come to the silver sheet in this or the past year. Moreover, it is one of those inevitable elements emphasizing more than anything else in a photoplay unit, those capabilities in direction—Robert G. Vignola's—which at times have the most satisfactory results, while in others sink to the level of utmost banality. Why is it that directors—Vignola and others—will not take to heart the first principle in art to seek and secure balance in their respective works? Instead they will take you momentarily to the peak, and with no other excuse than lack of ability ungraciously hurl you down.

Mr. Merwin's story has been badly damaged in the process of continuity by George Dubois Proctor, and its miscarriage in direction is hard to overlook. If the professional picture reviewer can be accredited with any ability to see beyond the surface of the present version of "The Passionate Pilgrim," then it appears that here was indeed a story—one which, with careful direction, might have counted.

Looking then beyond the surface of this vehicle there is an abundance of heart interest which it could have been invested with. Even in its present workmanship it shows a tendency of winning the interest, but never unfalteringly.

The scene calls for Miriam (Rubye de Remer) and Henry Calverly (Matt Moore)—she is or has been indisposed practically all her life and moves about in a wheel chair. To be a participant in the action when not wheeled in her chair she must be carried. Calverly is a well-known author, who, for valid reasons, is masquerading under an alias. He has served a term in prison, secures work on a newspaper, is fired, but is re-engaged to write the biography of the owner. The owner is the late father of the helpless daughter. Time passes. Both are consumed by an admiration which can only have one result. Time and again he has raised her in his arms and conveyed her to the spot where she is enabled to open the safe. He can no longer resist. Their lips meet in ecstatic approval of each other, and the helpless girl for the first time is able to stand. It is perhaps true that an inspiring influence of this kind may sustain momentarily what under ordinary circumstances would seem exaggerated. But your lay audiences will not swallow the bait.

The mere fact that the director's tactics are anticipated is not complimentary. Whereas, even if that incident is contemplated, no such criticism would have been given it by lay persons if it had been enacted in a manner to preclude any exaggeration.

The cut-back in the action which is one of the primary causes for the sequence of this story, wherein a confession is made by the woman who kills her husband, is too mechanically picturized to have human worth. The finale of the picture, in which the heroine introduces her future husband, is too theatrically portrayed. These and other instances lacking in the necessary human touch knock the bottom out of a picture that might have been.

What is arrestingly interesting in this picture is the character acting of Matt Moore, truly a triumph. The character itself is from the start sympathy winning, but it is the faculty of remaining in character that makes Moore the most valuable asset. It is difficult to pick any flaws in his performance for the simple reason that he holds the interest unwaveringly. Though not featured, he is supported by Rubye de Remer, and it is hard to recall when she performed to better advantage. Seldom has she appeared as advantageously, both histrionically and pictorially as she registers in this. It seems very strange and almost inexplicable how Claire Whitney's talents were invited or secured in a secondary role. She is a most able actress, possessing an infinite amount of screen intelligence, but she is absolutely out of place here, although what is required of her is done proficiently. The minor roles are well handled, with the exception of Julia Swayne Gordon as Madam Watt.

The production is worthy of its support in every respect, the photography is fair, although badly tinted in its nocturnal scenes. The title work is not exceptional, but comprehensive.

But will some one explain how it secures its title? Certainly it is a fine picture title, but wherein does it apply? *Step.*

THE BAIT.

Joan Grainger, the Bait....Hope Hampton
John Warren, the Fish....Harry Woodward
Bennett Barton, the Fisherman,
Jack McDonald
John Gordon, the Game Warden,
James Gordon
Dolly, the Hooked....................Rae Ebberly
Simpson, the Bait Catcher....Joe Singleton
Madeline, the Minnow......Poupee Andriot
Jimmy, the Bullfish.....Dan Crimmins, Jr.

The entire body of the story of "The Bait" is a flash-back. The picture itself arrests your attention the moment it starts. It opens with a fight in the dark between two men, shots are fired, and one falls dead. A girl rushes in, turns on the light, leans over the body, and when the police arrive there is every circumstantial indication that she is the perpetrator of the murder. The detective takes a close look at her and recalls having arrested her for shoplifting some years previous. As he is about to lead her away she begs permission to tell him her story in the presence of the man who has just declared his willingness to marry her. The story she tells is a flash-back occupying the remainder of the picture up to the "clinch."

It is an underworld tale in which she is accused of theft and found guilty. She had been framed by a band of crooks, who rescue her on the way to prison by an ingenious motor collision. She is shipped off to Europe, supplied with funds and groomed to attract a wealthy young husband. Her beauty is such that this is no difficult matter, and she falls in love with the young man who is attracted to her. She refuses to marry him because she loves him, but the chief of the band threatens to send her to jail on the old charge if she does not accept the young lover.

On the absorbingly interesting start right through to the finish there is a continual dramatic conflict which serves to hold the attention throughout. The direction is painstaking and artistic, the photography is exceptionally clear, and Miss Hampton's support competent to the verge of brilliancy. The beauteous Hope Hampton makes a step forward with this production in that she is given more opportunities for acting than in any of her previous screen efforts.

"The Bait" was adapted from Sidney Toler's play, "The Tiger Lady," scenario by Jack Gilbert and directed by Maurice Tourneur. It is a Paramount release. *Jolo.*

BUNTY PULLS THE STRINGS.

Bunty....................Leatrice Joy
Tammas Biggar....................Russell Simpson
Weelum....................Raymond Hatton
Rab....................Cullen Landis
Jeemy....................Cassön Ferguson
Susie Simpson....................Josephine Crowell

It is a question whether picture theatre audiences want their Scotch on the screen or in bottles with this production. Still, the great vogue that the play had may pull this entirely delightful and charming screen production of Scottish life into the hit class. It is a highly clever film presentation of a quiet comedy, and the chances are that while the picture will land in the better grade of houses and attract certain patronage, it is rather doubtful that it will appeal to the masses.

To Reginald Barker, who directed, a full measure of credit must be given for having transplanted to the screen a picture possessing real atmosphere, a number of exceedingly clever characterizations, with a story that unfolds charmingly with a laugh ever and again present.

Also to Leatrice Joy there should be credited a real hit. She is a most captivating Bunty. She possesses beauty and, that rarity in pictures, a screen personality. Raymond Hatton, playing opposite her, gave a really fine performance as Weelum, while Russell Simpson proved a delight as Tammas. Josephine Crowell as Susie should also receive a full share of credit for her performance.

The scenes are about equally divided between the interior of Tammas' house and exterior shots. The latter are truly a delight and the location man can pin a medal on himself for good work. Photography uniformly good. *Fred.*

'LAST OF MOHICANS.'

Magua....................Wallace Beery
Cora Munro....................Barbara Bedford
Uncas....................Albert Roscoe
Alice Munro....................Lillian Hall
Major Heyward..........Henry Woodward
Colonel Munro....................James Gordon
Captain Randolph..George Hackathorne
David Gamut..........Nelson McDowell
Hawkeye....................Harry Lorraine
Chingachgook....................Theodore Lerch
Tamenund....................Jack McDonald
General Webb....................Sydney Deane

Maurice Tourneur, as a unit of the Associated Producers, offers the old J. Fenimore Cooper classic of American pioneer days as this week's contribution to the program at the Strand.

Mr. Tourneur may understand the tale; so may those Cooper fans who read the book once a year or so as a point of conscience. To the ordinary screen spectator the results have become mere chaos; a series of episodes in which the warring forces are not always to be recognizable. There are battles between Indian and Indian and Indian and white man, but what they represent or their place in the story is not always apparent.

What Mr. Tourneur has made of the book is just a series of fights and scenes of violence. He has especially an eye to this phase of the tale. It was all right to feed the young American reader with these bloody episodes, but when they become transcribed to the literalness of the screen they become emphasized in their violence.

Probably for this reason Tourneur has shot most of his combats and Indian massacres in middle distance, where the figures are so small they lose much of the atmosphere of horror they might otherwise possess. This is another way of saying that Mr Tourneur has been working with one eye on the censor.

The hand-to-hand fight between Uncas and Magua at the cave is handled in this way, as are all the mass effects of the Indian massacre by the crew of drunken Indians after Montcalm's victory at Fort William. Tourneur has been for one thing embarrassed with too much material, as was to be expected, and has had to deal with a kind of material scarcely suitable to the modern American picture. His chief asset, and the one that ought to make his picture a commercial success, is the attraction of the title with the younger generation.

As part of his overplus of material the director subordinates Hawkeye the Leather Stocking who was hero of most of his tales and makes his outstanding figures Uncas, the Mohican; Cora Munro, daughter of General Munro, commanding the British forces in America against the French and their Indian allies, and Magua, the wicked Indian who conspires against the girl's virtue while pretending to be a friendly guide.

The backbone of the tale, as it was in the original, is the effort of the heroine to get from Fort Edwards to Fort William and the adventures attendant upon the trip. Magua deserts his charges and they are taken in hand by Uncas, the good Indian, and Hawkeye. Thereupon it becomes a progress toward a definite place, with a running fight between the Hurons and Magua and Uncas, just as in the Cooper tale. The girls are captured several times and escape in terrific conflicts, specific that between Uncas and Magua, a knife combat, done at a distance, and the French allies, the Hurons, for the possession of the Munro sisters. Upon their arrival in Fort William a British traitor discloses their weak position to Montcalm, and Monro surrenders on Montcalm's pledge for the safety of the women and children. However, someone gets quantities of firewater to the redskins and they take part in an orgy of blood and suggested rapine that was terrible enough in print, but becomes unspeakable as a picture.

Magua takes Cora as his price, but Uncas appeals to the justice of the Delaware tribe, which rules that Cora belongs to Magua, who shall have sanctuary until sundown. Under the Indian law Uncas may not pursue the departing Magua and the girl until sundown. Meanwhile the wicked Indian carries the girl off into the wilderness. She gets to the edge of a cliff and there are excellent trick photographs at this point with sensational fights between Uncas and Magua for her possession, ending in the death of all three. So it could scarcely be looked upon as a "happy ending."

Nevertheless the story delivers an outdoor picture of adventure which ought to draw the younger generation, although the work is far from adequate. The titles, however, are done economically and well by one who has made a conscientious study of the Cooper text.

THE CHARM SCHOOL.

With Wallace Reid, the Paramount's "Charm School" makes a satisfying Wallie Reid picture. Through the character of the subject matter, the feature will prove more of an inducement to the younger set. Budding children will like it very much, more so because of the views shown of a girls' school; it might be called a finishing school.

There are quite a number of laughs, some naturally through the story and others begotten by captions. There are an unusually large supply of captions, and this appears to be a recent manner of padding out a feature. "The Charm School" ran just 61 minutes at the Rivoli Sunday, at the first show.

James Cruze directed. He employed all of the scope given from the play this feature has been adapted from. The play was shown earlier this season on the New York stage. It was not a Broadway success, though dubbed a "sweet play." Last week it was produced in England (stage).

In burlesque (stage) for years the "Charm School" matter was known as "seminary stuff." That was when the tramp comedian or two of the company accidentally happened into a girls' school, donning women's dress to remain there. "The Charm School" takes another angle, polished up and smoothed off, but the basic scheme may still be seen. Mr. Reid as a lively auto salesman who is broke, suddenly finds himself heir to the Bevans School for Girls. The school has many useless courses. When the young man with a banking friend, who is capitalizing him, called at the school, the new owner decided the school needed another course to teach young women charm. As a part of that course and to provide room for it, he threw out natural history, inserting swimming, fencing and dancing. In this way is permitted a swimming tank, classical dances on the grass and delsarte.

The love end is the granddaughter (Lila Lee) of the banker, a student at the school, falling in love with the innovator, with the grandfather taking the young man into his employ, after a will has been discovered which dispossesses him from the school, passing it over to the oldest instructress.

If this is the Lila Lee (Cuddles) of the Lasky end, who was aimed for stardom, it looks somewhat peculiar to see her in support and not mentioned in the billing. Nothing about her performance to call for anything extra. In fact, there is nothing to any one's performance as a whole, excepting Reid's. He has it all. Edwin Stevens is the banker, looking and playing the role, but it's just incidental, as are all of the others.

It's strictly a Wallie Reid picture and a good one as a program release.
Sime.

NINETEEN AND PHYLLIS.

Andrew Jackson Cavanaugh..Charles Ray
His Uncle, Daniel Cavanaugh
...........................George Nichols
Mrs. Daniel Cavanaugh...........Cora Drew
Phyllis Laurin................Clara Horton
Judge Lee Laurin, her grandfather
...........................Frank Norcross
Jimmy Long.............Lincoln Stedman

There is no especial bid for it in "Nineteen and Phyllis," the latest Charles Ray-First National feature, presented by Arthur S. Kane at the Strand this week. An original scenario, not an adaptation from any play or book, by Frederick Stowers, it is a simple tale of youthful rivalry for the hand of the local belle of a little Southern village. Ray enacts a wistful, earnest, intense and fidgety youth earning $18 a week and tragically in love with the granddaughter of the judge of the community. His rival is the son of his wealthy employer. Not to be outdone he makes a deposit on a $500 diamond engagement ring and is at his wit's end to pay the remainder when he, by the merest accident, stumbles upon a hold-up men operating in that vicinity and for whom there is a reward of $1,000. Judged from the standpoint of plot or story, "Nineteen and Phyllis" is almost nil, but is more than worth while as a study in expressions on the part of the star, who has no peer on the screen as a delineator of earnest youth budding into manhood.

In the recent productions Ray has had a happy faculty for selecting first rate players for his support and this one is no exception. Joseph DeGrasse is responsible for the direction and can chalk it up as one of his successful efforts. There is

but one serious criticism to make—the sub-titles printed to conform to the night scenes are too indistinct to be read. *Jolo.*

GIRL WITH JAZZ HEART.

Kittie Swasher }
Miriam Smith }.............Madge Kennedy
Miles Sprague.....................Joe King
Tommie Fredericks....Leon Guerre Gendron
Miriam's Uncle............William Walcot
Miriam's Aunt..............Helen De Bois
Simeon Althoff............Robert Vaughn
Detective Quinn..................Emil Hoch
Camille.......................Lillian Worth

This week's attraction is a serio-comic, and thus for its comedy values it makes an appropriate offering for a holiday. "The Girl With the Jazz Heart" is a Goldwyn product, made from the original story by Robert T. Shannon and directed by Lawrence C. Widom, with Madge Kennedy as star.

The story swings both between city and country, and thus has excellent variety of background and types of principal characters. The story appears, for example, to deal on one hand with one of the severe sects scattered over Pennsylvania, such as the Moravians, and, on the other hand, with cabaret night life in New York. Here are obvious contrasts both in locale and in character. Both elements are used to advantage.

The story develops plausibly, and the motives which actuate are convincing both in their literary conception and realization in the actor's art, although at one point there is a false note when the heroine goes looking for a husband in a matrimonial journal which falls into her hands by accident. There is no sort of question but that the circumstance could have happened, but its happening takes away sympathy from the heroine. In its underlying effect on the story this detail has its result.

Goldwyn has given the picture an excellent production. The country scenes are well picked in local color to express the necessary atmosphere of a narrow-minded people such as would drive from them a high-strung person as Miriam Smith (played by Madge Kennedy) to escape an uncongenial marriage.

Miriam is a village heiress whose guardians seek to force her into a marriage with a local hobbledehoy for whom she has no regard and whose attentions are offensive, their expressed reason being to prevent her fortune from corrupting her soul, while the real purpose is to get control of her money.

Miriam picks up a matrimonial sheet dropped from a farmer's wagon. She gets into communication by this means with Miles Sprague, and he instructs her to meet him in the city. So she goes to New York's most elaborate hostelry. Her nerve fails her as the meeting approaches and she prevails upon Camille, the telephone switchboard girl, to masquerade for her until this new suitor is tested.

Camille is described as "the girl with a jazz heart," given to cabarets and generally cheerful and happy, holding a breezy outlook on life. She falls in with the plan. Miles appears and Camille takes him the round of the city's revels, accompanied by Miriam. However, Camille becomes interested with a frequenter of cabarets and leaves Miriam much in Miles' company. It is apparent that the pair have fallen in love.

Meanwhile the schemers at home have telegraphed to the New York police that a minor girl has run away and have sent instructions to bring her back. The police run Miriam down in a cabaret and rush her home, where she is locked up for the night, the local suitor on guard. The pair are to be married on the morrow. However, the village lover breaks into the girl's room, apparently not content to wait overnight.

Camille, Miles and the latter's cabaret sweetheart arrive on the

scene by motor car, to learn what is going on by the shadows on the bedroom window. They break in, and in a general rough and tumble the village lover is put to flight and Miles, the mail-order husband, carries the girl off, with their marriage in prospect.

THE LOVE LIGHT.

Angela ....Mary Pickford
Maria ....Evelyn Dumo
Joseph ....Fred Thompson
Mario ....Edward Phillips
Pietro ....Albert Frisco
Giovanni ....Raymond Bloomer
Tony ....Georges Rigns
Antonio ....Jean De Briac

"The Love Light" at the Capitol this week will not be recorded as one of Mary Pickford's "greatest." With any other star it might be classed as an exceptionally good program picture—provided that star had good support—but with Miss Pickford it is certain to suffer by comparison with her other pictures. She is a symbol of sunshiny girlishness, and does not fit well into a garb of mature morbidity.

Mary in motherhood is not Mary as the millions know—and want her.

Frances Marion, whose career is a story of intelligence intelligently exercised, is the author and director of "The Love Light." The story is not up to her standard; the direction, on the whole, is good, but weakens in spots. To her or to some clever location manager, however, must be given credit for finding locations · which, with the photography, form the chief assets. The photography is smooth all the way, and it is to be doubted if any picture ever offered more beautiful sea stuff. The lightings are splendid both exterior and interior, but the latter are chiefly in lowly fishermen's houses, which in small doses would be "artistic and picturesque." But in this they constitute an overdose and are tiresome.

If Miss Marion wrote the titles for this offering she did not do any better in that than in the selection of such a story for Miss Pickford. Ordinarily Miss Marion's titles vitalize a picture, and in the past they have been instrumental in saving many poor subjects. But here a thin, unhappy story is made even more so by soporific subtitles.

Mary does her best in "The Love Light" to be herself, but the dullness of the story is almost too much for her. Those exhibitors and photoplay fans who pretend to weary of Miss Pickford in "the same old stuff" will get the other extreme here. The girl whose curl-framed smile is one of the foundation stones of the picture industry shows in a tragical role that she can act, and she responds nobly to the calls made upon her by the role. But Mary Pickford as a maniacal mother whose mind is curtained through a series of sorrows is not a pretty sight, and it will leave audiences cold, as did the entire picture at the Capitol.

Another thing, Mary Pickford as an Italian girl in a fisher village on the shores of the Mediterranean is an anomaly; as convincing as would be Fatty Arbuckle in "Hamlet." Although Canadian born, Mary is to the public the sweet American girl. To make her otherwise is to trifle with the affections of her public.

There is not a "big moment" in "The Love Light," unless it be one where the villagers, led to her cottage by an Uncle Tom's Cabin bloodhound, almost discover her hidden husband, a German spy, masquerading as an American. She is informed a love signal he caused her to flash from a lighthouse has been the cause of her brother being killed in a U-boat attack, and denounces him after shielding him. But there the incident is closed, and he is led forth, submissive as a Charlotte Russe, while Mary fades from the picture.

The close-up boat scenes, of the water dashing into the cabin, were good, but the long shots were pathetically weak.

Miss Pickford's support was colorless, with the exception of a lovable infant and a chimpanzee, which supplied a comedy lift in infinitesimal flashes. The others were types and no more.

IRELAND IN REVOLT.

Here is an impartial record of present conditions in Ireland presented under the auspices, on a State rights basis of the Chicago Tribune and photographed on the ground by Capt. Edwin F. Weigle, the American Signal Corps officer who recorded the entrance of the Americans into Vera Cruz several years ago and who did much aerial photographing during the European war.

The captain has chosen his subject matter with all the impartiality of a conscientious newspaper reporter, although in the editing and assembling of the film there is apparent a slight sympathetic leaning toward the Irish Nationalist side. This, however, is not in the way of political propaganda, but rather artistic literary touches warranted to make a sentimental appeal to Irishmen of both sides of the controversy.

For example, there is some especially beautiful scenic material dealing with the lovely lakes of the south, with sentimental titles sure to appeal to the native of "t' Auld Sod." However, something of the same sort of stuff is presented of the north of Ireland. It would be but natural for an institution like the Tribune putting out a commercial proposition to make its appeal to the great majority of the screen public in America. It is estimated over 80 per cent. of the immigration to the U. S. comes from the south of Ireland and are passionately republican in their sympathies.

Nevertheless, this does not prevent the Tribune picture, which is in six reels, from maintaining an extraordinary degree of neutrality. The real value of the picture is its presentation of visual facts on a subject that has been so twisted and turned in written partisan reports that the public mind is hopelessly confused as to the merits of both sides of the controversy. There is no getting away from the camera report. The only way it could misinterpret would be to select the material which favored one side. There is no evidence of this.

The "Black and Tans" are pictured as bringing in a Nationalist prisoner in Belfast. One raid on a suspected Sinn Feiner house is shown but rather obscurely, since the camera appears to be turned away from the raiders' operations into the crowd looking on.

The dead line which separates the Sinn Fein and Unionist sections in Belfast presents a quantity of interesting material. But the best of the matter is disclosed in the ruins of houses wrecked and burned by Sinn Feiners for alleged brutalities by the Irish constabulary or vice versa. The titles which go with these views are singularly moderate and impartial. Shots within and without the "Black and Tan" barracks are interesting. The constabulary are so called, by the way, from the fact that since the armistice the force has been so greatly augmented by "Tommies" that the old-time black uniforms have been exhausted and khaki uniforms have crept into the ranks.

There is a good deal of titling in the film, as would necessarily be the case, but the phrasing has been well done and adds to rather than detracts from the interest in the views.

The incident of Mayor McSwiney's funeral is elaborately played up, together with the circumstance that the casket was draped in an Irish republic flag and many of the mourners carried the same emblem, although its display in Ireland is counted a crime. This impressive ceremony is made into a real spectacle.

The picture cannot offend Irish opinion in any particular and ought to be a sensational money maker in districts where there is a large population of Celtic origin.

As a business proposition, the film has all the marks of a winner. It should attract the interest of the Irish societies, a powerful element in its favor. *Rush.*

DAYS OF ST. PATRICK

Winfield F. Kelly presents this product of the gem of the Western World and, according to an announcer who preceded the film at the Lexington Sunday night, it was taken under difficulty, due to atmospheric conditions.

The players are all Irish, amateurs, none of whom received any financial remuneration. The film is a remarkable piece of work considering these factors.

The direction and photography "In the Days of St. Patrick" are excellent, and while the story was designed to appeal to a Catholic audience, it will interest any, regardless of race or creed.

The tale is a more or less faithful replica of the life of Ireland's patron Saint. The picture version shows the birth and early trials of this saint from the time he performed his first miracle until brought to Ireland by a famous sea king and pirate and sold into slavery.

After escaping from Ireland he returns to his home and enters a monastery, later going to Rome, where he was canonized a bishop by Pope Celestine.

Patrick returned to Ireland and began the conversions that brought the light of Christianity to the pagan isle. Persecutions by the king and his struggles from the first Church (in a converted barn) up to the magnificent Cathedral recently erected in his honor, are excellently reproduced, all of the numerous characters being intelligently portrayed and cleverly directed.

The picture took nine months to complete and shows few faults of direction, when it is considered most of the amateur artists engaged were making their first appearance before the camera.

"Memoirs of St. Patrick," which follows the picture itself, is a modern picturization of places made memorable by the former activities of the patron and the memorial edifices and scenes preserved in his memory. It terminates with an intimate study of the present Cardinal Logue, the 80-year-old successor of the ancient Patron Saint. *Con.*

INSIDE OF THE CUP

John Hodder, a rector..William P. Carleton
Eldon Parr, a banker......David Torrence
Alison Parr, his daughter.....Edith Hallor
Preston Parr, his son...........Jack Bohn
Kate Marcy, a salesgirl.Marguerite Clayton
Richard Garvin, a bank teller, Richard Carlyle
Mrs. Garvin, his wife......Margaret Sedden
Wallis Plimpton, a vestryman Albert Roccardi
Ferguson, a merchant......Frank A. Lyon
"Beatty," a butler...........Henry Morey
Kate Marcy's Friend..........Irene Delroy
Garvin's Child...............George Storey

In this newest Cosmopolitan production released by Paramount at the Criterion for an indefinite yet what seems a short engagement, "The Inside of the Cup" may be termed as the outcome of five principal sources, which, in the final analysis, are responsible for the screen version. Jesus of Nazareth is the inspiration. One of the first promulgators of His word is St. Matthew. The third is Winston Churchill, who, unquestionably founded the novel on the text of Matthew's interpretation of the words of Christ. The other two more practical forces are Albert Capellani as director and George Dubois Proctor, responsible for the scenario. Capellani is also coauthor of the continuity.

The production is placid drama, lacking in forceful and gripping movement, interesting only to the point it suggests faithfully a predominating moral, but is much overdrawn.

"The Inside of the Cup" is an exposition of present day Pharisees; even more than that. It is a picture sermon, with the main theme founded on the cleanliness or external man and the excess of rottenness which invests the inner man. The interpretation of the present-day Pharisees and their faults are laid at the door of wealthy men, who build churches by means of ill-gotten gains and worship in their self-financed house of God.

As this picture depicts it, there can be found little fault with Mr. Churchill's philosophy. It is Socialistic to the core. A picture of this kind is enough to make any conscience-stricken millionaire quake.

Parr, a millionaire, the boss practically of his home town, loses the esteem of his two children, daughter and son, who leave him. He is responsible for impoverishing a family, the head of which is an employe of his bank, while another victim of the millionaire's will is the fianced girl of the "working-class" whom his son loves. Characteristic of its other episodes is the further exposition of men of both power and influence whose heel of authority can crush all opposition. In its final episodes the banker is the victim of the crazed employe, the minister who has succeeded from a country parish to the sumptuous church of St. John's is to wed the banker's daughter, while his son is brought in happy union with his former love, both uncalloused by their experience in a harsh world.

Mr. Churchill's work may be said to serve some purpose and it will be curious to note how the picture is received elsewhere than the Criterion. There it was not hailed with acclamation of great or sincere gratification. But the story itself is not the best kind of material for a picture, primarily because it sermonizes too much, instead of offering dramatic action in the quantity that a fountain may spout water.

Mr. Capellani's art director achieves two striking pictorial effects in the interpretation of two episodes relating to Christ; the first in which a remarkable structure is erected to depict the incident with Magdalene, and the other in which Christ eschews the sinners in the temple. The interior of the church is very effective and artistically constructed. But Mr. Capellani's sets for the home of the millionaire, despite their lavishness, are gaudy, and I assert that people of wealth live or could live in them is venturing a great deal. The Garvin interior is a trifle exaggerated for a bank clerk. These are about the principal factors in structural design to be mentioned.

As for the individual efforts of the artists, scarcely one of the number can be singled out for any great merit. Mr. Capellani's greatest achievement in this picture is posing his groups and securing a close-up of facial gestures. These are in many instances admirable, one in particular showing the steel glare of the banker powerful enough to obviate the murderous purpose of Garvin. Perhaps the bit entrusted to Margaret Sedden as Mrs. Garvin is the most effective piece of acting in this sermon.

The photography has some high spots and is unique for its lighting effects, but in the main it cannot be called exceptional. The picture is permeated with too much titling, and this, more than any other element, invests it with the preachiness which film audiences may want to be freed from. *Step.*

GREAT ADVENTURE.

Priam Farll...............Lionel Barrymore
Henry Leek...............Thomas Braldon
Lady Sophia Entwistle.....Octavia Broske
Alice Challice..................Doris Rankin
Duncan Farll....................Ivo Dawson
Mr. Oxford.....................Charles Lane
Mr. Witt........................Jed Prauty
Lord Leonard Alcar.........E. J. Ratcliffe
Dorothy........................Maybeth Carr
Mrs. Leck................Katherine Stewart
The Two Young Leeks.................
..........Arthur Rankin and Paul Kelly

Probably the most thankless "job" in the world is the making of a screen adaptation of a popular novel. When the aforesaid "job" is made still more difficult by its presentation in stage form prior to the filming the director has but small chance to appease the indignation of the reader of the book and the observer of the play. They must know why this was altered, that bit deleted, and so on and so forth.

To an omnivorous student of Arnold Bennett the film adaptation of his brilliant comedy, "The Great Adventure," is a deliberate distortion of the subtle satire on England's reverence for Westminster Abbey and kindred institutions. To 90 per cent. or more picture patrons the Whitman Bennett production of the Arnold Bennett piece of literature, directed by Kenneth Webb, is, on the whole, a very satisfactory film feature, entertaining throughout as a high-class comedy. It is brilliantly acted (once more gauging it from the standpoint of commercial film production), intelligently directed and photographed, and the First National can safely assure its clients it will prove a satisfying feature to all exhibitors. At the Strand Sunday evening the audience was alternately absorbingly interested and audibly entertained by the comedy.

A comparison of the central characters as portrayed in the picturization by Lionel Barrymore and Doris Rankin might be interesting. Mr. Barrymore follows pretty much the characterization given to it in America by Lynn Harding, necessarily broadened for the screen. Neither Barrymore nor Harding brought it to the subtlety or ingenuous diffidence the author designed, and which was so vividly painted by Henry Ainley in the English stage presentation. Miss Rankin also follows the American stage presentation, depicting the part of Alice Challice along the lines laid out by Janet Beecher in New York and played as a cockney by Wish Wynne in London.

The strongest point to the satire of the original tale appeals only to the British and means relatively little in America. The Whitman Bennett production has wisely dodged this angle. Such details as the serving of tea during a serious—almost tragic—family discussion were wholly lost on an American audience, and which could only be appreciated by such of our natives who had visited England and know how nothing can interfere with this afternoon habit there.

Judging the picture from an American exhibitor standpoint, "The Great Adventure" ranks high in the list of present-day features. *Jolo.*

POLLY WITH A PAST.

Polly Shannon....................Ina Claire
Rex Van Zile..................Ralph Graves
Mrs. Van Zile..........Marie Wainwright
Clay Cullum...................Harry Benham
Harry Richardson.............Clifton Webb
Myrtle Davis...........Louiszita Valentine
The Cook.......................Myra Brooks

The word went out several weeks ago that Ina Claire had "put it over" in her first picture, "Polly with a Past," the latter produced by Metro, directed by Leander de Cordova, being a five-reel screen version of the stage play of the same name by George Middleton and Guy Bolton. The advance reports were correct. Taking "Polly" as a criterion, Miss Claire has everything necessary to success on the screen. She photographs particularly well, gets her points over without the slightest indication of over-acting and registers the varying shades of emotion requisite to making her characterization vital with ease and precision.

The first part of the picture has Miss Claire in the character of a maid, but the larger portion of the five reels presents her as a French woman, a character assumed through the exigencies of the plot. "Polly" in pictures follows the stage play closely in story, the scenario by June Mathis retaining all of the brightness of the comedy in its original form.

Miss Claire's support is excellent, Clifton Webb and Harry Benham showing to advantage in light comedy roles. Ralph Graves, another juvenile, plays opposite Miss Claire and give a highly intelligent interpretation of his role. Charles Eldridge shines in the minor part of an old top.., whose specialty is "getting reformed." Louiszita Valentine and Myra Brooks both contribute fine performances.

The general atmosphere of "Polly" is one of smartness, most of the action taking place in the environment of Long Islanć country clubs.

The exteriors have been chosen with an artistic eye and the interiors are likewise scenically effective. The picture holds an entertaining story, which is enhanced by the presence of Miss Claire and a faultless cast. Leander de Cordova's direction shows a skilled hand throughout. Miss Claire will doubtless establish herself as a first-grade picture star with "Polly."

Bell.

CINDERELLA'S TWIN.

Probably no story in the world has so general an emotional appeal as the Cinderella theme. This Metro "classic," with Viola Dana in the title role, has this strength in exceptional force. That alone would almost insure its success. But it has other values, not so potent, but of sure interest to a modern audience. There is a subordinate crook plot and society high life which makes possible big, impressive ballroom scenes, well handled by Director Ingraham. The society feature also makes effective contrasts to the more pathetic figure of Cinderella. It would indeed be strange if some of these features, if not all of them, did not strike response in a general public of fans.

Here is a commercial film based on an old idea brought up to date and made fresh by a novel sort of treatment, but which as its main appeal rests on a thoroughly human story simply told in direct fashion without alien incidents dragged in for their mere "movie" effect.

A study of the production is well worth the while of the whole trade for its general story scheme. It has its defects, but they are not inherent in the story or its treatment as to continuity. For example there are several errors in casting, notably the choice of Charles Sommerville as the hero, a modern Prince Charming. He is very theatrical in his methods and always impresses one as an actor rather than as a real personage. Miss Dana had a part to order to bring out her odd little comedy mannerisms.

Nell O'Neill (Viola Dana) is the cook in a fashionable residence, with a kitchen that works entirely by electricity—electric dishwashers, fans to dry dishes, electric stoves to smooth away her drudgery. One John Joseph Maudant, a democrat in spite of ancient lineage and social position, is a frequent guest of Nell's employers, and Nell worships him through the society columns of the newspapers.

The two are brought into contact when Nell is called upon to serve the dinner in the butler's absence. About the same time the Flints, a wealthy family in the social circle of Nell's master and mistress, are giving an elaborate ball to celebrate the birthday anniversary of one of the daughters. The newspaper talk given out by Flint describes the gifts as worth $100,000. Crooks plot to get into the pantry and get away with the fortune.

Upon their arrival in an auto reflecting wealth and social position, the girl crook picked to make the getaway retreats hurriedly because the detective hired to guard the jewels knows her and she cannot pass his inspection. An immediate substitute must be had, so the crooks pick up Nell, who is one of the worshipful bystanders in the street crowd, dress her up like the Fairy Godmother and send her in, telling her to open the window between the ladies' dressing room and the next room, for it is there the jewels are on display.

Nell follows all these instructions and as she goes into the ballroom crowd meets Prentice, who does not know her in this new environment, and the pair spend the evening in oblivion, falling in love. The crooks have meanwhile made off with the fortune. When midnight comes around Nell rushes out to the auto left for her by the crooks, losing a slipper which Prentice picks up. She goes back to apologize to the crooks for losing the slipper, in which one of the crooks had placed the key to their safe deposit box. The crooks threaten that Nell will be sent to prison if she does not recover the slipper.

Her efforts to get the slipper work around appropriately to bring her. Prentice and the family together just as the police are about to arrest Prentice for the robbery. She proves Prentice's alibi and the social lion and the Prince Charming of the story then and there announces that he and Cinderella will be married.

It's a rattling good story for all classes of fans.

THE DEVIL

Dr. Mueller	George Arliss
Mimmi	Sylvia Breamer
Marie Matin	Lucy Cotton
Her Aunt	Mrs. Arliss
Paul De Veaux	Edmund Lowe
George Ruben	Roland Bottomerley

"The Devil," produced by Associated Exhibitors and distributed by Pathe, this week at the Strand, has many points of excellence, but it unfortunately has an artificial, theatrical ending that goes a long way toward injuring the good impression sustained up to the very end.

That last impressions are the permanent ones, makes this particular defect especially detrimental. The screen playing of George Arliss is even better than would be expected of this fine artist, since it is his first big experiment in the screen medium. Mr. Arliss played the leading role in the stage version of the same work, which is followed pretty closely in the film translation.

The story begins at an art gallery exhibition in which the center of attention is fixed on a painting by Paul De Veaux symbolizing "The Triumph of Truth Over Evil." Everybody in the crowd subscribes to the truism that truth must always triumph over evil, but Dr. Mueller (Mr. Arliss), who impersonates the anti-Christ in this allegorical story. He listens, smiles a sinister smile and begins to plot the destruction of two young couples.

From this point on there is built up in detail a solid, physical story structure demonstrating directly and visibly the sinister power of evil. The point is that all the subtle evil plotting of the devil is visualized into actuality by convincing means. The evil Dr. Mueller pours subtle poison by suggestion and innuendo into the ears of the four people he seeks to destroy, until all his schemes are at the point of fruition.

Having erected this story fabric, when the devil is just about to triumph, one of his victims kneels and prays, and there falls between the devil and his virtual victim an illuminated cross of Calvary, symbolizing the power of good. Instantly the evil one is powerless and undone. The evil has been so painstakingly built up in terms of plausible actuality that this theatrical trick comes as an implausible hoax upon the spectator.

It is as though a giant but vicious prizefighter were matched against a slim, clean-minded youth. Suppose, then, the story went on to show the prizefighter training conscientiously for the battle, and the youth spending his time in thinking high and noble thoughts. On this foundation it was suddenly thrust upon the audience or reader that the high-minded youth rolled the evil giant in the dust by his physical prowess. You'd say the author of the story was taking a lot of poetic license.

That approaches the situation in this film. Still, the picture is interesting and the story, except for the cross incident, distinctly of the kind that compels attention by its succession of suspense and incident. Every movement of the characters comes as a surprise, and there are many points of deepest subtlety manipulated with remarkable ingenuity so as to get a delicate effect of meaning unusual in screen stories.

For example, the story is an allegory and must avoid commonplaces of details. For this reason the photography has been so used as to merge incidentals, such as dress and surroundings, in a way to tone down the realities and deftly suggest the mystic and superhuman. A good sample of this treatment is the group of girl dancers at the mask ball given by the wicked Dr. Mueller. The figures are merely shadow wraiths with the evil leer of Dr. Mueller staring out from the background.

Some wonderful bits of perspective are shown in Dr. Mueller's residence, where doors swing without visible means and open up wierd vistas of staircases and corridors.

As to the final scene, it could easily be eliminated, because the story stops with the reconciliation of the two lovers by the efforts of the honest wife. This symbolizes the victory of good in the human terms in which the creation of evil has been presented. It is sufficiently apparent that the honest wife has defeated the spirit of evil by her very honesty. Why add the superfluous detail picked up apparently from the story of "Dr. Faustus."?

Rush.

THE KID

The Man	Carl Miller
The Woman	Edna Purviance
The Kid	Jackie Coogan
The Tramp	Charlie Chaplin
The Policeman	Tom Wilson

Charlie Chaplin, after a long absence, comes back in "The Kid." It is a six-reeler, 5,300 feet long, and a corker. It will be called better than "Shoulder Arms" or "A Dog's Life," and is to be sent forth by Associated First National.

In this, the longest subject he has ever released, Chaplin is less of the buffoon and more of the actor, but his comedy is all there and there is not a dull moment, once the comedian comes into the picture, which is along about the middle of the first reel.

"The Kid," for which a year's labor is claimed by the distributors, has all the earmarks of having been carefully thought out and painstakingly directed, photographed and assembled. The cutting, in some places, amounts almost to genius. Introduced as "a picture with a smile—perhaps a tear," it proves itself just that. For while it will move people to uproarious laughter and keep them in a state of unceasing delight, it also will touch their hearts and win sympathy, not only for the star, but for his leading woman, and little Jackie Coogan.

It is almost impossible to refrain from superlatives in referring to this child. In the title role his acting is so smooth as to give him equal honors with the star. Usually Chaplin is the picture; but in "The Kid" he has to divide with the boy, whose character work probably never has been equalled by a child artist. Edna Purviance is attractive as the unmarried mother of the kid, but hers is comparatively a small role.

Chaplin indulges in the usual broad references where he handles a moist infant, and rather overdoes it. Some of this play could be cut out to advantage, and he might also eliminate the flash of the Savior bearing the cross, a piece of symbolism flashed on the screen to emphasize the burden of "the woman whose sin was motherhood," and, perhaps, to give the film tone.

Outside of these two spots, the picture is flawless in treatment and has so many good points, artistically and dramatically, it would seem the better discretion if the cited spots, potential points of attack, were discarded. The action is lightning-fast and the tempo never lags.

The picture, as is to be expected, does not have its action in regal splendors, but in tenements, police stations and back alleys. So there are no "sets" to it. But the photography is sharp all the way and the lightings, especially in the night scenes, are splendid.

There are characteristic "Chaplin touches." A fine instance of imagination is where he dreams of Heaven. His slum alley is transformed into a bit of Paradise, with everybody—including his Nemesis, the cop, and a big bully who had wrecked a brick wall and bent a lamppost swinging at Charlie—turned into angels. Here, with Satan doing a Tex Rickard, a cockfight between Charlie and the bully is promoted and pulled off and feathers fly freely. At another point, Charlie has "the kid," an infant, in a hammock with an ingeniously arranged coffee pot serving as a nursing bottle. Some of the best business is here.

"The Kid" starts with "the woman" issuing from a maternity hospital, bearing her child in her arms. She is distraught and, after scribbling a note, "please love and care for this orphan," abandons the infant in a limousine. Auto thieves get away with the car, unaware of its cargo. They drive to the slum district, where a wall attracts them to the child and they toss it in an alley. Charlie, ragged but debonair, finds the baby, and tries to get rid of it by putting it in a perambulator with another. But the mother objects and Charlie returns to leave it where he found it. A policeman makes him change his mind. He then hands it to an old man, but the latter drops it into the original perambulator. Chaplin is blamed and beaten by the woman, and forced to take the child to his garret house. Five years pass and the boy, devoted to his foster parent, is an enthusiastic assistant in his business, which is glazing. The boy breaks windows and Charlie, "happening" along at the psychological moment, repairs them.

Meantime, the mother of Jackie has risen to fame as an actress and when visiting the slums, gives the boy a toy without knowing it is her lost child. Subsequently, she holds the child in her arms after he has had a fight and urges Charlie to get a doctor. The latter sends the county authorities after the child, but they get him only after a terrific battle in which little Jackie wields a sledge hammer with all the delightful zest that Chaplin himself could have put into it. As the boy is carried to a waiting auto truck, Charlie flees over roofs, then drops into the truck and rescues the child. The doctor, who has taken the identification slip from Charlie, is at the house when the mother arrives. Seeing the note, she realizes Jackie is her own boy, and puts a reward offer in the newspapers. This excites the cupidity of the keeper of a lodging house where Charlie and the boy are asleep. He steals the boy and takes him to the police station, where the mother comes and claims him.

Chaplin wanders all night seeking the boy in vain and returns to his slum, worn out. It is then he has his dream of heaven. He is awakened by the policeman, who takes him to the home of the actress, where Jackie and his mother greet him and drag him into the house. This is th. end of the picture, the star's back being to the audience at the fade-out.

Chaplin, in his more serious phases, is a revelation; and his various bits of laugh-making business the essence of originality. No better satire has ever been offered by the comedian than the introduction of his ragamuffin kid seated on a curbstone manicuring his nails; and his instruction of the boy in table etiquet will register as one of the best things he has done.

PRISONERS OF LOVE.

Blanche Davis	Betty Compson
Her Father	Ralph Lewis
Her Mother	Claire McDowell
Her Sister	Clara Horton
James Randolph	Emory Johnson
His Mother	Kate Toncray
Martin Blair	Roy Stewart

"Prisoners of Love," produced by Betty Compson Productions, distributed by Goldwyn and directed by Arthur Rosson, marks Betty Compson's debut as a star. Miss Compson first attracted attention through her work in "The Miracle Man." This picture is in five reels. Catherine Henry wrote the story.

It is a sort of problem play, with the intent rather vaguely suggested. The plot treats of a young girl (Miss Compson) who inherits a tendency to flirt from her father. The latter is providing for an adventuress, who in turn has a younger chap as a "sweetheart." This fellow induces the father's female "friend" to shake him down for $5,000. The daughter discovers the father writing the check for the woman, the latter also being present, and there is a scene, in which the "shake-down" is ruined.

The father becomes angry on the daughter's discovery of his liaison, and she is ordered to leave the house. Going to 'Frisco, she becomes a stenog, falls in love with the junior partner, and is about to marry him when her father and younger sister arrive. The father has suffered a breakdown, and his physician has ordered him to the coast.

That's a nice, convenient way to get them all together, and is in line with the general mechanical construction of the story. Although they are all in the same city, and father and younger daughter visit the office older sister is employed in, the latter does not meet her relatives. Junior partner goes east with father, and is about to marry younger sister, not knowing she is related to girl he left in 'Frisco, when older sister appears and asks him what he is going to do about it. He turns her down.

Previous to that the father has given the junior partner a check (he's some check writer) for $10,000, to give to any girl who may have a hold on him. Of course, he doesn't know the girl who has the hold, and there is strong suggestion the hold is a heavy one, is his own daughter. The latter spurns the check, father learns all about it, and the older sister consents to the wedding, the younger girl apparently never learning of the relation existing between her husband and her sister. The latter scene is the strongest and best in the picture.

Miss Compson plays the older daughter in a restrained manner, but she only uses about three expressions, one of gladness and two of different shades of sorrow. This contributes to making for a sameness in her performance. Ralph Lewis is the father. He is inclined to overact at times, but on the whole plays well. Clara Horton, the younger sister, gives an average performance. Roy Stewart has little to do as the senior partner and does it competently. The younger partner is played by Emory Johnson, who gives a good suggestion f the weakness of the character he interprets.

The picture is interesting, but at no time rises above the average program feature. It looked a great deal better at the Capitol, with its lights, musical accompaniment and fine manner of presentation, than it probably will in the rank and file picture houses, lacking these attributes to set it off. *Bell.*

OUTSIDE THE LAW.

For weeks the billboards around New York have been plastered with paper reading "If you play cards on Sunday, you are OUTSIDE THE LAW," and other reading matter, with the law portion heavily displayed. Much of the paper held the initials P. D., commonly understood as standing for Police Department. With the Blue Sunday talk, the posted paper caught attention, causing talk at first, and then simmering down to waiting for the development. That is at the Broadway theatre this week, a Jewel-Universal feature, with Priscilla Dean starred.

"Outside the Law" is a Tod Browning picture all the way, written, directed and produced by him. Mr. Browning did the job well, very well, in all particulars, turning out a Universal that can stand up on the billing, most unusual for the U.

It's a crook picture, strictly underworld, but tense often and holding all the time. It starts with action and ends with action. There is little if anything in it that the censors may point to, and it carries a strong moral, which, in brief, is, that virtue or honesty has its reward. That honesty is the best policy is plugged at throughout the picture, spoken through a Chinese sort of all-guardian to the crooks of Frisco, who induces a very nice young couple, from crookland and children of crooks, to go straight.

Miss Dean is one of the very nice young couples and Priscilla Dean in this picture is a film revelation. She has acquired pantomime for the screen, in expression, which is the most, and in the knowledge of how to use it. While the picture is exceptionally cast, also for a U film, Miss Dean goes to the fore and remains there, although Lon Chaney gives her a strong race, also Wheeler Oakman, the other half of that nice young couple, though crooks. It isn't often when two thieving thieves, with one concerned in a murder frame-up that sent the father of his girl to prison, can gain the audience's sympathy as this couple do. That's heart interest with the interest very high. Chaney though makes his "Blackie" sneaky role so vicious he throws the house right into the young couple's laps.

There are fights that are fights, scenes of Frisco's Chinatown, a well set ballr.om, and a little blonde kid that are all of continued interest or excitement. And that kid is a bear. The director who made him alternately laugh or cry to win over Molly (Miss Dean) did some directing there, and he had the child to do it with.

As a crook picture the exhibitor can go as far as he pleases with "Outside the Law." It's real underworld stuff, of an educational sort, bringing out the inner emotions of thieves, especially when hiding from the police, the somewhat now prevalent belief there is always a chance for a crook to reform, and crookedness itself. The double double-cross at the opening of the film is worth while alone, while the battle between the crooks at the ending is a stirring scene of picture, but with suspense maintained to its finish. *Sime.*

THEIR MUTUAL CHILD.

"The Mutual Child" is a release by Pathe, a Jesse D. Hampton production made from a story by P. G. Wodehouse. Its stars are Marguerita Fisher and Nigel Barry. It has a cast of about 14, but to no profitable or praiseworthy purpose.

It is an ineffective, action and fun lacking comedy, and the impression it gave an (Stanley) audience was that its titles, taken from the text of Wodehouse, were funny, but that the piece as a feature comedy was beyond pitch as a mirth provoker. In direction the tempo has been entirely neglected, and whereas the spoken word might have given this piece some effect, the picture is without it. It is doubtful, too, if the theme of the hygienic child and the bringing of two perfect people together to produce the perfect specimen has not already outworn its novelty.

What Miss Fisher's film talents may be worth are to be judged in something different from "Their Mutual Child," for in this she does nothing beyond mere posing. Mr. Barry is lost similarly in the wilderness of nothingness. Also Harvey Clark, Joseph N. Bennett, Thomas O'Brien, Andrew Robson, Beverly Travers, Stanhope Wheatcraft and (Master) Pat Moore, really a delightful child to watch. But for the others they neither aid nor enhance a comedy whose flatness cannot be lifted, unless a line like this occurs, which is seldom: "Man's conceit is equal to the rooster's every time the hen lays an egg." *Step.*

BROADWAY — HOME.

There is nothing novel neither in the story nor the telling of John Lynch's work, but it is a fair picture. The continuity, by R. Cecil Smiths, runs with the rest.

"Broa way and Home," is nothing else than telling "The Mirage" (legit) over again. And "The Mirage" is nothing more than a rewrite of Bernard Shaw's "Mrs. Warren's Profession."

Certainly similarity in one or more of "Broadway and Home's," titles compared to the "lines" in "The Mirage," cannot escape observation. This transpires in the later episodes of the picture, when the mistress of the rich man, apparently thwarted in her purpose in seeking egress and happiness with the country youth, declares in effect that a promise was made that the bargain would end at a time mutually agreeable to her. "And now," she continues, "you want to stifle the first decent thing in my life." These few facts give concisely the vein of the theme in this feature.

There is a tragic end. The country lad, learning the definition of forgiving transgression (despite that he had been brought up in a minister's home), prepares to return to his wife and forget the past. Too late. He finds the wealthier man floored in a pool of blood. His wife is prone on the bed—hysterical. The reason is explained. She had been u willing to return as his mistress and had killed him. She dies later.

Superior to the story is the craftsmanship in production value and capability in direction. The director's na..e is not recalled. Through him the artists achieve gratifying results. At times the action may truly ' said to be absorbing. This was quite evident in digressing from a concentrated gaze on the feature and turning back to see how the audience took it. Within range of vision scarcely one could be called inattentive.

Mr. O'Brien may be said to achieve more in the lighter moments in matter of response than in the scenes calling for emotional ' vork." Pathos is not his strongest point. That he should fail to be responsive in the moments of profounder purpose, it seems in this instance, is due solely to the fact that his interpretation of those scenes are played without sufficient contrast. Played in one key, as Mr. O'Brien does, there is lack of depth. Ellen Cassity leads. She is a fair heroine. Her emotional work registers sufficiently to be sympathy win: . Mr. Losce plays masterfully and dominating in hi. way, and the impression is sustained throughout of the "type" which lends contrast to the more ethical purpose of the two lovers. Elinor Fair is entrusted with a bit. The roles of the two priests ~e left to "types," able ones, Frank Andrews and Warren Cook.

The photography is excellent throughout and the storm ..cenes at the conclusion of the picture offer some of the best "shots."

A great deal of interest, also at the conclusion of the feature, is centered on a rescue scene. *Step.*

FLAME OF YOUTH.

The William Fox studios offer this drama with Shirley Mason in the star part. It was at the New York theatre late last week as part of a double bill, the other feature being Lyons and Moran in a roaring farce, "A Shocking Night."

"The Flame of Youth" is so called for billing purposes in neighborhood houses. Its youth doesn't flame at all, but rather suffers in silence. The photography is fine and the selection of woodland background when such scenic locale is called for is extraordinarily beautiful.

The playing is only fair in several instances, although the Flower Girl (Miss Mason) stands out as a good, naive country girl in her characterization, playing the part with a wistfulness that gets over effectively.

The broad effect of the picture is that of a delicately shaded pastel. That is rather what the producer probably aimed at. He gets the effect for the most part, but the story is sometimes splashed with discordant heavy color patches.

Bebee is the girl flower seller in the village of Brabant, near Brussels, Belgium. Apparently the war has passed, although the struggle is never mentioned. Victor, a successful Paris painter and inveterate philanderer, visits the village. He is a bit of a lady killer in the picture, but plays the part with leering, simpering suggestiveness that would suggest the male vamp.

His approach to Bebee is almost laughable in this particular. Bebee, however, being a simple flower girl, falls hard for the Parisian artist, but Margaret, an old flame of Victor's, breaks in on the courtship and Bebee retires from the race, resigning him to Margaret. However, Victor won't have it that way. Margaret gives herself to charitable work in the village, and Victor returns to Paris, promising to send for the flower girl later.

Word comes from Paris that Victor is "heart-sick" for Bebee, and she interprets the letter to mean that he is really sick. She starts out for Paris, followed by her yokel lover of the village, and breaks in upon Victor in the midst of a studio revel marked by a swarm of ladies of the Latin quarter very much decollete and appropriately wild in their behavior.

Horrified by seeing Victor stretched out on a couch, where he receives the caresses of the wild women, she upbraids her lover and departs broken-hearted, but with the prospect that she will marry the village youth who followed her to Paris.

It's all "very sweet," as the women fans would say, but the whole thing is an unconvincing story, made purely for stage purposes and obviously artificial.

PAYING THE PIPER.

Barbara Wyndham.......Dorothy Dickson
Larry Grahame............Rod La Roque
Marcia Marillo.................Alma Tell
Keith Larne..............Reginald Denny
Gohn Grahame............George Fawcett
Richard Wyndham........Robert Schable
Mrs. Wyndham........Katherine Emmett

"Paying the Piper," the Paramount-George Fitzmaurice feature at the Rivoli this week, is an erratic, unwholesome concoction, bordering close to the edge of suggestion and unhealthy ideas. It has "blase" written all over it, and the plot, evidently designed to be ultra-modern and shocking, is the conventional, old-timey society melodrama.

Haughty society queen, ruined father, poor, but virtuous hero, rewarded; girl caught in wealthy rounder's rooms when jealous woman shoots him, etc., etc., etc.—all the time-worn situations are there, and their authorship credited to Ouida Bergere, of whom more originality is expected.

A questionable incident, but most likely the one that will be peddled as "the punch," and used as the big selling point of the picture, is that where the heroine, clad only in a nightgown and a clinging negligee, pays a visit to a man's room at night. Her visit is preceded by a discussion with her maid about lovers, and she tries her best to entice the young man. He instead proposes marriage and she spurns him. He thereupon locks his one door, climbs into bed and, so far as the audience can guess, leaves her free to use her own judgment. At any rate, she is in the room next morning, cuddled in a chair. This scene may be taken as the key to the thoughts of the heroine.

It will be gathered that "Paying the Piper" is not an entertainment to be recommended for children or adolescent boys and girls.

In the matter of settings, the production is typically Fitzmaurice, with commendable attention to fitness displayed in the richness of some. The gowning, too, of the women is noteworthy.

It may be a coincidence, but this picture, in its basic theme and in some of its big scenes—notably the cabaret—is strangely similar to the new Anita Stewart feature, "Harriet and the Piper," though the stories are entirely different. Comparison of the two, with the verdict in favor of "Harriet," is inescapable.

The cast is perhaps the best feature of "Paying the Piper." Miss Dickson, known to the public as a dancer, does not dance, but proves herself good screen material and a star who, with more experience, may go far. She is good to look upon—at most times—her facial expressions are good, and she has personality. She is cast here in a most unsympathetic role, that of a reckless, extravagant society girl, and gives to the type repugnancy which seems overdrawn, but probably is a true depiction of some isolated cases. It is a type which, by the way, may well engender class hatred.

George Fawcett, the sterling actor, has little more than a bit, but handles it convincingly. Alma Tell as a cabaret star who is 100 per cent. pure and has a nature as saccharine as 22-cent sugar, handles a difficult role exceedingly well. Rod La Roque, as a gay young devil whose chief aims in life are women and parties, seemed very artificial and strove for his effects. More easy in his work was Denny, who played opposite him.

The titles are for the most part good, and the most human touch in the whole thing was an incidental bit where Larry Grahame (La Roque) "picks up" a "chicken" and takes her for a ride in his new roadster.

George Fitzmaurice may be depended upon to direct cleanly and smoothly, and this picture is no exception; but the lightings on the star in some places could have been better. The shots at times detracted from her beauty very noticeably. Miss Dickson looks not unlike Louise Glaum and she has certain vampish mannerisms which recall the latter.

Mr. Fitzmaurice did the best he could, perhaps, with the hackneyed plot on which he had to work, but he was too sharp in drawing his contrasts. For instance, Marcia, the rage of Broadway, permits her beloved mother and little brother to live in the slums, and Larry, devil that he is, turns his father's mansion into a carnival dive, with be-tighted women, confetti, etc., as the high lights of his and Barbara's wedding party.

Whether it was the cutting or too fast a projection pace, the picture at the Rivoli was jumpy in spots and salient scenes swept by all too quickly.

The story opens up with a flock of rich children at play on the Wyndham estate. Barbara and Larry are a very sophisticated pair of urchins. Keith Larne is the son of the Wyndham gardener, and Marcia the singing daughter of an organ grinder. The parents of Barbara part and an over-indulgent father permits the child to grow up into a snobbish, daring young woman. She and Larry, who has, as a title says, become "a man of affairs, mostly with blondes," are engaged. Marriage is to them a formality, important if true. Keith, grown to be an architect, and Marcia, a Broadway favorite, have made successes of their lives. Larry amuses himself with Marcia, and Keith, called in to remodel the Wyndham home, supplies a new thrill for Barbara. The toys of these rich children take their attentions seriously—Larry going so far as to ask Barbara to marry him, Marcia so far as to expect marriage from Larry. Both are disillusioned. Larry and Barbara wed as a matter of course. Keith and Marcia wed for consolation. Keith sticks to business and so, when the fortunes of the elder Grahame and Wyndham are wiped out in Wall Street, Keith is able to offer Larry a job Barbara refuses to be reconciled to poverty and welcomes a chance to visit the apartment of a wealthy friend of better days. He "makes a play" for her and, in the midst of it, a jealous woman, using her own latchkey, comes in and shoots him. Barbara escapes via the dumbwaiter and goes home to repent and resign herself to poverty. A Christmas party at Keith's lodge introduces the elder Grahame as Santa Claus and caretaker for Keith and everything ends happily.

A SHOCKING NIGHT.

This is a Universal production with the old team of Lyons and Moran playing the leading parts. The farce is nicely produced as to its dainty interior backgrounds, but the story is ancient and stale, being built around the arrival of the benevolent old gentleman whose presence compels a young man and woman, sweethearts, to pose as man and wife, a situation which develops a hundred complications.

For purposes of the present tale the scenario doubles up the twists by making the unmarried pair take the place of a married couple who are their friends, and who want to put over a business deal. The married pair have gone broke, but hope to regain their finances by selling a mine to an old man investor who is about to arrive. To keep up appearances the married couple, who have discharged all their servants, become butler and cook, while the unmarried pair assume the position of master and mistress of the household.

This is the situation when the investor arrives. At bedtime he insists that everybody go to bed early. Of course this forces the unmarried man and woman into a long series of bedroom scenes meant to be funny. A few of them are laughable, but they weary presently with too much repetition. The tangle grows, dizzily, into one of those quick entrance and hasty exit farces. This sort of thing goes on indefinitely until the spectator is exhausted in patience, the situation always hanging on the edge of disclosure.

At length the tangle is made plain to the ancient investor, who takes the joke in good part and agrees to buy the mine and employ the man of the unmarried couple, on the theory that two men who had ingenuity enough to keep up so dangerous a deception must be quick-witted enough to be good business men.

ARE ALL MEN ALIKE?

Theodora Hayden, known as "Teddy"...
May Allison
Gerry Rhinelander West. WallaceMacDonald
Uncle Chandler.....................John Elliot
Mrs. Hayden...........Winifred Greenwood
"Gunboat" Dorgan........Emanuel Turner
Ruby Joyce................Ruth Stonehouse
Raoul Uhlan....................Lester Cuneo

For the period of about three months this (Metro) feature has been on the Loew circuit, but hasn't made much of a racket. It is far from being a good picture for many, the most important, it seems, is that it is utterly unbalanced in story value. It is not adept in action nor amusing, except for occasional "strokes" by the director, who is Philip E. Rosen.

In the first reel this picture spends all its power to entertain, and from then on slumps in the most awkward fashion, neither having a good pretext for continuity nor affording its numerous characters opportunity to show what mettle they are made of.

The principal reason for the entire subject, taken from Arthur Stringer's "The Iron Waffle," is that in the selection of a vehicle for May Allison, the star, it might have been deemed, as it was, advisable.

Mr. Stringer's story and the scenario from A. P. Younger make a brilliant start, both in titling and denouement. There are several touches that help to sustain interest. The introduction quoting Mr. Stringer's conception of life, and measuring it by the symbolic "iron waffle" in the jaws of which a babe forces the vise to expand and then, flowering into womanhood, attains absolute freedom. She then steps out in quest of independence. No sooner has she her way than the proverbial master—man—forces her backward until, forced to yield, resolves that subordination to well-meaning kindness is better after all.

Miss Allison bears the burden of the piece. There is scarcely an episode without her, and it is the buoyant manner in which she dominates the screen that makes the picture acceptable in whatever degree it can be accepted. The supporting cast for whatever it is asked to do does it, but no more. The fine "screen" features of the juvenile, Wallace MacDonald, stand him in good stead.

It is a question whether Mr. Rosen's direction of Miss Allison has not caused the latter to amplify the original estimate of the former in the continuity. Miss Allison "lays it on thick," so to speak, but to a good purpose. It is not overdone.

The titling is very well done, and conveys a certain amount of humor. Despite that, the overdrawn continuity does not insure a lethargic feeling. The photography of Mr. Ben Vail is fair but unexceptionable.

It would seem, in conclusion—and this may only be a guess—that if drama, tense, rigid in flavor, would have been the objective instead of farce comedy, the result would have been a materially greater feature. Perhaps artistically, too. Certainly the introduction warrants it. In its present version it is hard to recommend it other than possessing all the demerits of a regular release. Just one more. *Step.*

SOMETHING DIFFERENT.

Alicia Leo...............Constance Binney
Rosa Vargas.........................Lucy Fox
Don Mariano Calderon......Ward Crane
Don Luis Vargas...........Crane Wilbur
Calderon's Housekeeper... ......
Gertrude Hillman
Richard Bidgley.............Mark Smith
Mrs. Evans, Alicia's Aunt........
Grace Scudiford
Mr. Stimson, American Consul....
Wm. Riley Hatch
Spy...........................Adolph Millar

Constance Binney in Realart's "Something Different" isn't. It has no story warranting the expansion to its present length. It has no continuity (Kathryne Stuart) offering anything exceptional in episodical treatment. Its cast, while having some admirable artists, have nothing to do to excite one into speaking of any individual merit. Robert M. Haas' art direction is the best thing. H. William Neill as director will not shine over any accomplishments in this slow—oh, much too slow-moving—comedy. Withal the producers' idea in selecting Alice Duerr Miller's original story for Miss Binney's talents must have been along those lines that Charles Frohman selected pajama farces for Billie Burke.

The day is over in the legitimate theatre when a pajama-clad heroine is the center of interest because of a tendency to shock her aristocratic elders. Why should a lady in riding breeches with proclivities to shoot her boot-covered legs in the air and cavorting in pell-mell fashion be receptive to picture audiences?

Alice Lee (Miss Binney), preferring the invitation of a school chum in one of South America's imperturbable republics, leaves Long Island and a wealthy though objectionable suitor. In the strange land she is unknowingly made the accomplice of a revolutionary party. Imprisoned by a gallant captain and the usual "stuff," they fall in love.

Miss Miller's original story or novel is "Calderon's Prisoner." It was a popular seller, but not one of Miss Miller's best.

To single out any one in this dull comedy for any individual merit is to point to Ward Crane, who does some fine "straight" acting, with sufficient reserve in every scene to justify being mentioned. Lucy Fox, although scarcely sharing the number of scenes given to Miss Binney, does rival the star in pulchritudinous charm. This is a rare occurrence in any picture with a star.

Oliver Russell's photography is praiseworthy. Some of the titles are genuinely funny and you can't help laughing at the introduction to the American consul who seeks a post in any wet country. *Step.*

THE STAR ROVER.

Dr. Hugh Standing	Courtenay Foote
Faith Levering	Thelma Percy
Inspector Burns	"Doc" Cannon
District Attorney	Dwight Crittenden
Sergeant Andover	Jack Carlysle
Tubbs	Chance Ward
Mazie	Marcella Daley

"The Star Rover" (Metro-Shurtleff) has three of the most essential picture points—a good story, equally good cast and a finished production.

The late Jack London wrote the story. In a scenario succinct and well knit together by Albert Shelby Le Vino, it is largely dependent for its interest and endurance on the part of an audience, accepting facts that are to be coupled with the fantastic. For London's story is one of countless endeavors to prove the soul is ever transient, although it passes from the body after it is deceased.

There is a cut-back into two episodes as the result of a police "third degree" to wring a confession from a man. The methods employed are those of suspending him by the thumbs. And in the sub-conscious state, when the normal senses are numbed, the flash back is really the supposed conversation that the police chief hears through the dictograph, and simultaneously is the cause for the episodes. The continuity further embraces it is nothing more than a gentle, grave-grown old man, who is reading out of a book with the more vivid passages calling for the ensuing action.

The most interesting elements are the scenes of the Norsemen in action. Superior to that are the Chinese scenes, especially the floating gardens. They are a credit to Edward Shulter, art director, while excellent camera work is the contribution of Jackson J. Rose.

This may or may not be the picture debut of Courtenay Foote; but as for his ability to act few can find themselves his peer in this production. It is a triple role in addition, showing more than anything else the knack of being versatile in character. Thelma Percy is fair to look upon and her emotional work registered, although a little more of the Oriental make-up in those scenes would have brought more contrast to the part. A bit played with skillful reserve as the District Attorney was handled by Dwight Crittenden. It is seldom a player uses such discretion in a few scenes and still remains impressive enough to be spoken about.

The "boss" of Chance Ward was not sufficiently dominating to be convincing. As an inspector with old police methods "Doc" Cannon gives a very satisfactory performance. Miss Daly in a small bit was well cast.

The direction of Edward Sloman is able. *Step.*

THE LAND OF JAZZ.

"In the Land of Jazz" (Fox), starring Eileen Percy, a former Ziegfeld girl, is one of the numerous "over-night" productions this concern has literally circulated. Like many others, it has little merit.

The direction was by Jules G. Furthman from a story by Barbara Le Marr Deely. Neither holds anything to deserve mention, nor does the picture as a whole.

The heroine, on pretext of being insane, secures admittance to an "insanitarium," the presiding physician over which is the heroine's best friend and, although affianced to the "best" friend, is peeved over the latter's relationship to a French officer, whose kiss has a "heavenly kick."

The entire affair winds up in reel of shimmying for some obvious cause.

It is worth observing, however, the improvement in Miss Percy's pictorial efforts. From point of vivacity she may be able to do bigger things and certainly more worth while. It is all a matter of direction. *Step.*

HER FIRST ELOPEMENT.

A polite comedy with a shopworn theme.

Wanda Hawley stars. It is a Realart special adapted in a scenario by Edith Kennedy from a story by Alice Duer Miller and directed by Sam Wood. It runs through without a single "kick." The best place for such pictures is on the shelves.

An all-believing heroine who, under pretext of impersonating an adventuress, incidentally compromises herself with the man she is supposed to meet, but who has been too pre-occupied to make her acquaintance. She goes off on a yachting trip with him. Believing her to be the woman whom he can stall in her purpose of attaching his brother, he finally learns the truth.

It is curious to observe Miss Kennedy's idea in continuity in flashing on the screen the marriage license that the couple have procured to square the idea there may have been an illicit relationship. Technique of this kind has been passe for years.

The cast includes Jerome Patrick, Nell Craig, Ann Hastings, Lucien Littlefield, Edwin Stevens, John MacKinnon.

As a production the picture is expensive, rich in its interiors and settings. The photography is very good. *Step.*

THE GOOD BAD WIFE.

Vera McCord's production (independently released) of "The Good Bad Wife," has more bad (if one may use that expression) than good in it. It has been film-adapted from a novel entitled "The Wild Fawn," by Mary I. Taylor. The singular fact is that the subject is too much for Miss McCord's talent as a directress, and much beyond the starring efforts of Dorothy Green or the featured Sidney Mason.

It is doubtful if the book could have made good film material. Its application for a picture, it seems, needs the combined talents of a cast of truly big artists and a director worth his weight in gold. The task that would confront such a director under the pre-supposed circumstances would be to take the darling of the Parisian theatrical world, plant her in a Southern community, with all its combined elements of what it considers faith, religion, ethics, et al., and out of a clear sky, this Parisian lady shocks the community, causes the younger brother of her husband to shoot an alleged parasite whom she had divorced before her marriage. This is about the meat of the story.

Miss Green must dance in a manner nothing short of expert. This Miss Green fails to do, and the contention she is the darling of Paris and in her "coup de theatre," is enabled to stimulate the interest of the American is misrepresented from the start. On the face there is nothing in the action to show why this American should be entranced. These are but a few out of numerous incidents in the picture that cannot hold true, or if true, seem beyond reason as they are enacted.

The picture has been badly assembled. Its scenes are wobbly and, to add to the general demerit, the title work is permeated by matter which one can hardly forgive in these days of progressive picture making. The references to "never crossing the threshold of this home," has about exhausted its usefulness in both the picture theatre and the legitimate.

If the picture had been staged in the manner of the first opening scene showing the environment which surrounds Miss McCord's heroine actress, there would be something in a unit to commend. The continuity of Paul Price is poor, the photography of Abe Fried is inexpert.

It is not at all doubtful if this so-called "all-star" cast, including the featured members referred to, is highly exaggerated. They include Moe Lee, Leslie Stowe, Mathilde Brundage, Albert Hackett, Beatrice Jordan, Pauline Denkens, Wesley Jenkins, T. Thornton Barton, Erville Alderson and Bessie Stilson. The comedy work of the colored team has some good points, and what looks like an insignificant bit by Moe Lee, a Chinese girl, is effective. *Step.*

"ANNE BOLEYN" RATED IN CLASS OF "PASSION"

Second Big UFA Production Will Bring Rival of Negri.

King Henry VIII	Emil Jannings
Queen Katherine	Hedwig Pauli
Princess Marie	Hilda Mueller
Duke of Norfolk	Ludwig Hartan
Anne Boleyn	Henny Porten
Sir Henry Norris	Paul Hartmann
Lady Joan Seymour	And Egede Nissen
Marc Smeton	Ferdinand von Alten
The Jester	Paul Biensfeld

Berlin, Dec. 21.

Since the showing of Pola Negri in "Passion" at the Capitol, New York, the premiere of a new Ufa super-special must be of interest to the United States film industry. "Anne Boleyn" is up to every cent it cost (cost being upwards of 10,000,000 marks). The Ufa counts on the sale of this film in other countries for an adequate return on its investment, as the German market is insufficient. "Anne Boleyn" has the universal appeal.

A very free treatment of history, but the important things are action, color, consistency and sympathy—all achieved.

The film begins with Anne's journey from England to France and her innocent love affairs with Sir Norris; shifts to the court, showing Henry VIII's brutal but amusing character and that he is tired of Queen Katherine, his first wife, partly because she has given him no heir.

Then Henry's first meeting with Anne and his attempt to seduce her; she refuses, but Norris believes her guilty, and will have no more to do with her.

So to prove her innocence she accepts Henry's offer of marriage; he, against the order of the Pope, divorces Katherine, and at the same time founds the Church of England.

Then comes Anne's marriage and the unhappy bridal night. Henry retains his love for her only until her child is born, and that being a girl he begins his philanderings anew, now with Lady Seymour, who is to be his third matrimonial venture. Anne tries to win him back, but unsuccessfully, and Henry, hearing a false rumor that she has been untrue to him with Norris, has her tried and with evidence based on torture-wrung confessions, condemned to death, he himself signing the warrant. And so the block and the end of the film.

The action is developed with good crescendo and the captions are few and simple. Which simplicity is a welcome relief from the bunk philosophy, bunk psychology, bunk poetry, bunk economics, and, worst of all, bunk moralizing, which have become prevalent of late.

With all due respect to their other excellent qualities, De Mille and D. W. G. might do well to consider these captions carefully. When one reviews the downgrade from the splendid pantomime of "The Birth of a Nation" through the half-baked sophomoric philosophizing of "Intolerance" to the underdone moralizing of "Way Down East," there's stuff for thought.

Henny Porten, who has here a bigger following than Negri, is very good to look upon, somewhat in the Dorothy Dalton manner, and her Anne is a consistent performance, combining charm, power and a sympathetic appeal. She should do well in America. Emil Jannings' Henry VIII has a comic quality blended with the sinister. Paul Hartmann is an excellent juvenile lead of the Wallace Reid type. Ludwig Lartau and Ferdinand von Alten can be singled out of a generally adequate ensemble.

Ernst Lubitsch is an intelligent, competent director. He gives the scenario comparatively little hokum interladed. He handles his crowds well.

The whole production has a solid quality; the scenery and costumes recreate the reality of old England. The fete at the castle is quite a tremendous affair; huge floats sail by; nymphs in scant costumes flit through limitless gardens. Good stuff, yes; but no great display of imagination is involved.

And when will the Germans wake up to the fact that lighting need not come from all sides at the same time and that occasionally a blurred photographic effect is better than the clarity of an amateur snapshot? More imaginative scenery is already a reality, as witness Wegner's "Golem," and lighting will be modernized when the directors have the good sense to listen to their own scene designers (brilliant lighting effects are commonplace in the legitimate).

The big things in this film are a consistent well-handled scenario, the acting of Henny Porten, the stupendous quality of the sets (notably the marriage of Henry and Anne in the Cathedral and the fete) and the direction of the crowds. The fact of an unhappy ending in a historical film of this sort should not do it harm. It should do well for at least two weeks at one of the big Broadway houses.

HALF AN HOUR.

Lady Lillian..............Dorothy Dalton
Richard Carson..........Charles Richman
Hon. Hugh Paton..........Alfred Barrett
Dr. George Brodie...........Frank Losee
Earl of Dartmouth........H. Cooper-Cliffe
Susie, a slavey...............Hazel Tunney

Paramount's handling of Barrie's little dramatic gem, "Half an Hour," is another exemplification of what happens wher picture makers try to treat an author's product as a piece of elastic and stretch it out beyond its .ormal size. Written and produced originally as a curtain raiser, "Half an Hour" never was intended to be used as a three-act play.

'n its conceived form it runs about 30 minutes and is full of strong drama. As produced by Paramount, it is a draggy, dull, cheap thing, unfair to the author, to the star and to the public. The padding is all too evident, and the only things that save the production from utter ruin and desolation are the work of the leading players and the Barrie-written sub-titles.

Miss Dalton and Mr. Richman do as well as could be expected, and the others of the cast are good in flashes. But flashes are all, because they can only get on in flashes. The production does not indicate much care or expense in the matter of settings, there being only two of the latter worth mentioning—Miss Dalton's boudoir and the reception hall of her home.

HOLD YOUR HORSES.

Daniel Canavan..................Tom Moore
Honora Canavan...............Sylvia Ashton
Beatrice Newness..........Naomi Childers
Rodman Cadbury........Bertram Grassby
Jim James...........Mortimer E. Stinson
Horace Slayton.........Sydney Ainsworth

Anybody who is looking for a high grade comedy feature with real values in intelligent humor cannot go amiss in selecting this Goldwyn production featuring Tom Moore. The story is a screen version of Rupert Hughes' short story, "Cavanan," and is this week's attraction at th Capitol. E. Mason Hopper directed it. The program does not give the identity of the title writer. His or her (more likely a woman did the work) name ought to be in the electric lights, for no more sparkling set of film titles has made its appearance in a long time.

The story calls for no elaborate settings, but the interiors are adequate and the locations w ll selected. There are a few passages in the early part of the story which show extremely poor photography, these dealing with the humble home of the Canavans.

Tom Moore has one of the character parts of his life. It was made to order for him and he plays it with a grasp of its high comedy possibilities that no one else that comes to mind could equal. The story itself is rich in surprise and strongly shaded humor such as gets over most forcibly. The film version is an admirable translation to the pantomimic medium. Besides the story and characters have that basis of truth and fidelity to common life without which no really effective comedy can reach beyond buffoonery. The story:

Dan Canavan is a raw immigrant from Ireland puzzled and humiliated by his job as a street cleaner in New York and kept in utter subjection by a large and powerful wife, the latter delightfully done by Sylvia Ashton. Dan is always getting into the way of traffic and at length is knocked down by a high stepping team of the aristocratic Miss Newness. He comes out of the accident with only the imprint of a horseshoe on his "chist" as a sign of luck.

Dan gets another job with an excavating gang, and is detailed to halt traffic on Fifth avenue with his red flag whenever a blast is to go off. The experience of authority is a powerful tonic to Dan's self-respect. After bullying co hmen and nattily uniformed chauffeurs, he goes back and thrashes his own boss. The political potentate of the district sees this impudent performance and picks Dan for one of his lieutenants. "Now that I've got a good start," murmurs Dan, "I think I'll go home and lick the ould woman." He does and, as the admirable title says, "She falls in love with him at first sight," although she has been bouncing plates off his dome for years. In a few years the ex-white wings is the political boss and when the aristocratic husband of the former Miss Newness has got himself indicted on a crooked business deal Dan is appealed to to save him from the penitentiary. Dan does it out of gratitude for the horseshoe incident.

The aristocratic husband and Mrs. Canavan die and after a timid courtship on Dan's part the widow and widower are married. Coming back from a European honeymoon, the iceburg, aristocratic wife has repeated the performance of the late Mrs. Canavan in a different way and has Dan pretty well in subjection. In his absence rivals have undermined Dan's political throne.

He regains it in a fine free-for-all first fight (apparently in the Democratic Club), and then, realizing that he is '. the same situation as before, he measures it in the same words, "Now that I've got this good start, I think I'll go home and lick the old woman." This time he uses rather more subtle means, but they are just as effective, and at the **final fadeout the haughty wife murmurs "Come to dinner, Danny, and use any fork you like," and Danny is again master in his own house.**

Rush.

FORBIDDEN FRUIT.

Mary Maddock..................Agnes Ayres
Steve Maddock..............Clarence Burton
James Mallory..........Theodore Roberts
Mrs. Mallory.............Kathlyn Williams
Nelson Rogers.............Forrest Stanley
Pietro Guiseppe...........Theodore Kosloff
Nadia Craig...................Shannon Day
John Craig....................Bertram Johns
Maid ....Julia Faye

If picture producers required any further demonstration that the public will pay to see good productions one day's draw at the Rivoli, where Cecil B. DeMille's "Forbidden Fruit" is the attraction, should prove all that is necessary to convince them. The house, supper show included, played to standing room all Sunday, and at 7:45 in the evening the standees filled the back of the house and the lobbies, with a box office line extending for a block.

"Forbidden Fruit" is melodrama, and in less artistic hands could have been made a painful joke. But DeMille brings out with characteristic deftness every value put into the play by Jeanie MacPherson, and the result is a well told, smooth-running and skillfully developed romance.

While the story is strong and far above the average, it is dwarfed by the splendor of the production itself. The settings look what they are—the real thing, chosen with discrimination and arranged with taste. In keeping with the surroundings are the gowns of Miss Ayres and Miss Williams, each displaying a numerous and beautiful wardrobe calculated to drive the feminine audience into ecstacies.

In addition to telling his story superbly, DeMille has interpolated, as a sort of pictorial obligato, the story of Cinderella in a fashion probably never attained before. The photography here and all through the picture is flawless, the lightings exquisite.

The title seems far-fetched, and there is an evident straining to register the "forbidden fruit" idea in the mind of an audience. And at that "Forbidden Fruit" is a title with strong box office value. An example of the care the producer has exercised in giving his picture unusual touches is found in the subtitles. These, generally well written despite a leaning toward the obvious and a play on words, have color illumination.

The cast is most capable. Agnes Ayres, a young woman who has made marvelous strides since leaving Vitagraph, is given chief honors, and wears them well. She is a beautiful girl, with .poise and restraint, and portrays a many-shaded character excellently. Miss Williams has a more quiet part, but her beauty and charm never were shown to better advantage. Theodore Roberts is his usual splendid self, while Forrest Stan'ey, as the hero, and Clarence Burton, as the heavy, leave nothing to be desired In the case of Burton his interpretation at times, whether the result of the director's finesse or his own intelligence, is so sharp as almost to reveal the actual workings of his mind. Kosloff does a fine piece of work as the crooked butler, and Julia Faye puts over a tiny bit in her maid role convincingly.

"Forbidden Fruit" is high class society melodrama. It tells the story of Mary Maddock, a young seamstress burdened with a worthless husband. She is sewing in the home of Mrs. Mallory, whose husband is desirous of putting over a deal with young Rogers, an oil millionaire. To keep him in town a dinner is arranged. The girl chosen as Rogers' partner fails the hostess and she substitutes her seamstress, dressing her much like a modern Cinderella. The girl captivates the millionaire at dinner, but eludes his proposals and goes to her cheap flat house. The $20 the hostess had given her for playing "high society" her husband appropriates. He connects it and an orchid, gift of Rogers, as evidence the girl has come by it "the easiest way." But realizes if he drives her away, his "meal ticket" vanishes. Next day Mrs. Mallory visits Mary and asks her to return to the Mallory home as a week-end guest to keep Rogers interested, but the girl declines. However, when Maddock, in a fit of temper, kills her little bird because of its singing while he seeks to sleep, she decides to quit him and accept Mrs. Mallory's invitation.

That night the Mallory butler, a graduate of Sing Sing, frames with Maddock to rob one of the guests of her jewels. Maddock enters the house, goes to the apartment mapped for him and gets the jewels. As he starts to go he flashes his light on the sleeper, and discovers his wife. She awakens, screams, then tries to shield him. He starts to creep out of the house and is discovered by Rogers, who disarms him. The relationship between Mary and the burglar is revealed after he is relieved of his loot. Mary is sent away from the Mallory home. Back at the club Maddock and the butler concoct a scheme to blackmail Rogers, and with a forged note lure him to Mary's flat. There the husband demands $10,000 hush money. Rogers produces it and tells Maddock he will return in half an hour to get either the money or Mary. It is up to Maddock to choose whether he wants the money or his wife. Maddock decides for the money and starts to make his get **away, but is met at the door by the butler.** The latter proposes a dice game for the money. While they are tossing Mary gets the money unseen and escapes down the fire escape. Maddock loses, grabs the wallet and starts also for the fire escape. The butler shoots and kills him. Rogers, returning, hears the shot, breaks in the door and overpowers the murderer. Then he sees Mary in a faint at the foot of the fire escape. He goes to her and tells her what has happened.

The picture has a beautiful finale, with Mary back at the Mallory home and Rogers declaring his love anew.

THE SILVER LINING.

"The Angel"...................Jewel Carmen
Robert Ellington..............Leslie Austen
George Johnson...............Colt Albertson
Evelyn Schofield..............Virginia Valli
"Gentle" Annie......Julia Swayne Gordon
"Big Joe"...................J. Herbert Frank
George Schofield............Edwards Davis
Mrs. George Schofield.....Marie Coverdale
Billy Dean...................Gladden James
Detective.........................Paul Everton
Dancers..Carl Hyson and Dorothy Dickson

For downright cleverness and originality of story and treatment, "The Silver Lining," a Metro production, must be given high rating. It was written and directed by Roland West and is one of the most entertaining program pictures turned loose recently. The author-director has evolved a surprise finish that is a surprise and maintains suspense most ingeniously.

"The Silver Lining" is not a big picture, but it will hold its own with the better program product, not alone for its intrinsic value, but also because of the excellent portrayal of a girl crook by Jewel Carmen. It is one of the best things she ever has done and merits her a place among the leaders of the ingenue stars.

The story is a skillful presentation of the old argument—is criminality hereditary or the result of environment? The author says his picture story is founded on fact, and if it is, it is only another proof that truth is stranger than fiction.

It opens with three men seated in a balcony overlooking a reception salon in Paris. One man contends criminals are born, the other that they are made by surroundings and associates. They turn to the third man of the group, a secret service operative, who refuses to decide the question, but tells them a tale from his professional experiences with crooks.

An orphanage is revealed, with two little girls in the foreground. One, an ill-natured child, steals the doll of the other and throws it over the fence. The little one is forced to lose time retrieving it and thereby earns a tanning from teacher for being late in school. A wealthy couple come along to adopt a child. They instinctively turn to the abused one, but adopt the ill-natured one on the teacher's recommendation. The other, known as "the Angel," is adopted by a pair of crooks. Years pass and the favored girl is shown as a debutante, pampered and the fiancee of a rising young author. Angel is revealed in the home of the crooks, being taught thievery and revolting against it. But, through sheer fear of punishment, she becomes efficient. On an "L" train, on which Evelyn, the rich girl, is a passenger, Angel lifts the watch of a masher. A detective grabs her. The victim denies the watch is his, follows the girl from the train and reveals himself as a confidence man named Johnson. He proposes a business partnership with Angel.

Evelyn's engagement to the author is broken when he finds her kissing another man. He goes to Havana and there meets Angel and Johnson. The latter frames him for a $25,000 take on a race horse deal, "the lemon trick." The girl has been making herself agreeable to the novelist, Ellington. They fall in love with each other. When the time comes for her to get the $25,000 she cannot go through with it and confesses she is a crook. They are in his apartment. A knock interrupts them. He sends her out a side door, promising to meet her and Johnson in their apartment later. The interruptor is Evelyn, who has heard of Ellington's infatuation for Angel and has come to reclaim his love. He spurns her, then she recognizes Angel's picture as that of the "L" thief, and denounces her. But Ellington declares his intention of marrying the crook.

Entering her apartment, Angel sees Johnson's reflection in a mirror. It gives her an idea of how she may save Ellington from himself. She leaves her hall door wide open. When Ellington comes, he sees, in the mirror Angel in Johnson's arms protesting her love and ridiculing the author. He backs out. The girl faints and is carried to bed. Recovering, she repels Johnson, and he, realizing the girl actually loves Ellington and has sacrificed herself to save the author, goes to tell him the truth.

The picture cuts back to the three men on the balcony. The secret service man is telling his story.

"Well, what happened?" one of his companions asks. "You never can tell what a man like Johnson would do," he replies, and the picture fades into a scene showing the girl on the hotel balcony, watching a ship pull out to sea. She has had a note from Ellington saying he would be on that boat. As it passes from view, she collapses on a table. Suddenly a man's hand grasps her. She gets up affrighted. Then the diaphragm opens and Ellington is revealed. He has given Johnson his ticket and the latter has sailed to "go straight." Ellington and the girl embrace.

This seems the end of the picture, but the director, at the risk of an anti-climax, shows he is "different."

Cutting back to the three men again, one asks the secret service man if society accepted Angel. He looks down at the fashionable gathering in the salon. The guests of honor are Ellington and Angel, who greet him with sly winks.

"Yes," he says, "society accepted Angel."

"How do we know this is a true story—that it is not an invention?" one asks.

"Because," replies the secret service man, "my name for many years was"——

And the officer's face is transformed into that of Johnson, the crook.

BREWSTER'S MILLIONS.

Monte Brewster	Roscoe Arbuckle
Peggy	Betty Ross Clark
Mr. Brewster	Fred Huntly
Mrs. Brewster	Marion Skinner
Mr. Ingraham	James Corrigan
Barbara Drew	Jean Acker
Col. Drew	Charles Ogle
MacLeod	Neely Edwards
Harrison	William Boyd
Ellis	L. J. McCarthy
Pettingill	Parker McConnell
Blake	John McFarland

Dough, gelt, jack, kale, mazuma—money, all kinds of it, wads of it, bales of it—that's the all-pervading spirit of the screen version of "Brewster's Millions," in which Fatty Arbuckle is starred. It's a five-reeler, Jesse L. Lasky "presenting" Arbuckle by arrangements with Joseph M. Schenck. The picture is released through Famous Players-Lasky.

Mr. Arbuckle plays practically straight in "Brewster," wearing conventional business apparel and refraining from slapstick. He is successful in getting a considerable number of individual laughs without the aid of his baggy pants and butcher boy derby, but somehow the rolicking comedy spirit of the rough and ready "Fatty" of the Keystone days is missing.

The stage money handled all through the picture is treated in a comedy way, such as burlesque wheel shows have been doing for years. The farcical story of the book, by George Barr McCutcheon, and the play, by Winchell Smith, have been nicely welded for a scenario that holds plenty of dramatic interest, and is technically well construed by Frank E. Woods. Joseph Henabery directed and can be credited with an entertaining picture.

At the opening, through the means of some cleverly conceived trick photography, "Fatty" is shown as a baby in a high chair, and later as a five-year-old kid in Fauntleroy costume. There are some realistic scenes of a storm at sea that give the film a neat touch of the melodramatic.

The supporting cast is excellent. Betsy Ross Clark is the heroine. She makes a decidedly attractive and good acting one. The grandfathers are convincingly played by Fred Huntly and James Corrigan. Neely Edwards (Flanagan and Edwards), William Boyd and L. J. McCarthy are the three chums of Brewster. None has much to do, but each plays with ease and a sense of screen comedy values. Additional parts are handled by Marion Skinner, Parker McConnell, John McFarland, Jean Acker and Charles Ogle.

The whole weight of the comedy falls on Arbuckle. He is all through the picture, too much so. The titles are especially good, written in a slangy, breezy style, and securing laughs through that and their pointed humor. The yarn moves along with a speedy tempo, and there is no surplus footage or padding. The film has been expensively mounted scenically, and is up to the minute as regards lighting and other modern details. "Brewster's Millions" with "Fatty" should be a first-class box office card, even if Mr. Arbuckle is not quite as hilariously funny as his former "hokum" skits permitted him to be. For the exhibitor there's the "name" value of the play itself, coupled with "Fatty's" drawing power and a competently produced and consistently interesting story. *Bell.*

FLAME OF YOUTH

Beebe	Shirley Mason
Jeanot	Raymond McKee
Victor Fleming	Philo McCullough
John Forsythe	Cecil Van Auker
Antoine	Adlebert Knott
Lady Magda	Betty Schade
Old Bac	Karl Formes

Displayed on a double bill with "Hearts Are Trumps," and by far the lesser of the two features, "The Flame of Youth" (Fox) stood up considerably. The feature was meritoriously deserving of applause through Shirley Mason and Raymond McKee.

It is a picture whose subject is hardly sufficient to carry it over five reels. The theme of the flower girl of Paris who almost, but not quite succumbs to the charms of a Parisian artist has been overdone. But the knack of Howard M. Mitchell as director seems to rest in accomplishing almost the impossible with the inconsequential scenario of Howard Clark by securing the best out of the artists. The result has been something unique, for where a pale scenario counts for little, in this the acting stands out in bold relief against dullness with which this vehicle is profusely endowed.

In it Miss Shirley Mason shows more ability than what has been seen of her work in the usual order of Fox pictures. She has manifestly a capacity for tears, which no director has hitherto called upon her to evoke.

Sharing honors is R ymond McKee in a role calling for character work. It is that of a wood-chopper, although it may have been anything else so long as it was menial.

The titles are fair. A few art titles would not hinder the beauty of the production, manifest in the photography. As photographer, Friend M. Baker attains some illuminating and high spots in exteriors while his lighting effects are admirably executed.

A bit handled by Karl Fromes should be mentioned for merit. *Step.*

JUST OUTSIDE THE DOOR.

Madge Pickton	Edith Hallor
Gloria Wheaton	Betty Blythe
Edward Burleigh	Barney Sherry
Ned Pickton	Eddie Sutherland
Dick Wheaton	Arnold Gregg

"Just Outside the Door," a Weber production, released through Select, is one of those involved melodramas which were popular in 10-20-30 stock houses about the time Bryan tried to liberate silver. It is an adaptation of Jules Eckart Goodman's story, and the playwright will hardly count any new laurels as the result of this screen version.

Except for one or two spots, where some good night exteriors are brought in, there is little to commend the picture as a production. The director has taken Miss Hallor, a little star who seems to have talent and screen personality, and cheapened her miserably by making her and her brother the leaders in a cop chase which has been done much better in Keystone comedies. At that the chase, which was supposed to be full of tensity, got laughs. Miss Hallor and Sutherland, her screen brother, seemed to run for one entire reel.

Not only the chase, but the entire presentation of the story leaves one dizzy.

Miss Hallor, between sprints, did some very effective work at times, and so did young Sutherland, but the director permitted him to overact. Sherry, too, was guilty of acting in spots. Miss Blythe and Arnold Gregg were acceptable, but the very best work was done by the old lady who played Aunt Polly. Her name was not on the screen, but her work was, and it saved the picture from complete desolation.

LITTLE 'FRAID LADY

Cecilia Carnw	Mae Marsh
Giron	Tully Marshall
Judge Carteret	Herbert Prior
Saxton Graves	Chas. Meredity
Mrs. Helen Darrett	Kathleen Kirkham
Sirotta	Gretchen Hartman

Some producers seem to be saturated with the idea that a big ballroom scene, or a carnival, or a shipwreck makes a super-production. Robertson-Cole so label "Little 'Fraid Lady," featuring Mae Marsh, but it is far from a super-production.

The story, an adaptation of Marjorie Benton Cooke's "The Girl Who Lived in the Woods," is entertaining, and Miss Marsh is her own delightful self. There are some pretty woodland scenes and a fairly "penpy" reproduction of an artists' ball. But naught else. The picture is an average program feature and will get over through the popularity of Miss March, reinforced by some really good acting by Tully Marshall.

John Adolfi, who directed it, usually may be depended on to turn out a good work, and he does his part well here. He maintains the suspense and has caught some splendid exteriors. His lightings are generally good, especially in their relation to the star. All of her fine little arts are brought into play by Miss Marsh, her emotional shadings ranging from the depths of pathos to the heights of joy. The picture is not one that calls for massive sets, and the director has made up for this lack by beautiful sylvan shots.

"Little 'Fraid Lady" relates the tragedy of a young artist's life. She flees the city and takes up her abode in a woodlands lodge, barely existing by exchanging her little landscapes for supplies at the general store.

The director weakened his story considerably by injecting a coy lover's chase into the finish.

Miss Marsh was capably supported and some fine business was brought in with a dog.

TWO MOONS.

A Fox feature starring Buck Jones. Typical "Western"—a good one of its kind, with a fairly interesting story of the obvious sort, in which it is certain the hero will win the girl, despite she tries to kill him with a shotgun.

Jones is employed by the cattlemen to look after their interests in their conflict with the sheep herders. The girl belongs to the other crowd and resents his interference with what she regards as her rights. The cattle men have secretly hired a killer, but this sort of warfare is against the principles of Jones, who, being the hero, insists on "fair play." There is excellent Western atmosphere and a series of rough-riding fight scenes.

Buck Jones has a fine, strong, manly face and gives the impression of sincerity and naturalness which is magnetic to a considerable degree. Carol Holloway is the heroine—a fine looking, buxom type, physically suited to the role of a girl of the plains. She doesn't hesitate to permit herself to be roughly handled and does not sacrifice character for good clothes.

The story is by Robert W. Ritchie, scenario and direction by Edward LeSaint. The scenes are mostly exterior and the interiors merely "cabin" stuff. It will please in the majority of picture houses. *Jolo.*

HEARTS ARE TRUMPS.

Lord Altcar	Winter Hall
Michael Wain	Frank Brownlee
Dora Woodberry	Alice Terry
Lady Winifred	Francelia Billington
Lord Burford	Joseph Kilgour
Maurice Felden	Brinsley Shaw
Dyson	Thomas Jefferson
John Gillespie	Norman Kennedy
Brother Christophe	Edward Connelly
"Jake"	Bull Montana
Butler	Howard Crampton

"Hearts Are Trumps" is a Metro all-star production—an old Drury Lane English melodrama from the play of that name by Cecil Raleigh. It was scenarioized by June Mathis, directed by Rex Ingram, photography by John Seitz. It is a full six reels and relates one of those stories of high life among the titled aristocracy that is so dear to the hearts of the patrons of popular priced theatres which comprise the majority of picture patrons. English nobility is exhibited with all its "rottenness." There is enough plot for half a dozen ordinary film features. It starts off with Lady Winifred secretly married to her father's gamekeeper. Lord Altcar, her father, pledges her hand to Lord Burford and when he learns the truth he has the gamekeeper flogged and thrown off the estate. Michael staggers away, threatening vengeance, and returns 20 years later to wreak it. He has amassed a fortune in the goldfields of Alaska. A child is born to Lady Winifred, but she gives out it is her ward.

Meantime Michael has purchased a mortgage on the ancestral estate and in the midst of a house party turns everybody out, nobody knowing him as other than American but his wife. Later he learns the ward is really his own daughter and he devotes his energies to straightening things out and making the child happy with her fiance, who is an American artist.

The locations depicted are supposed to be rural England and Switzerland and these are exceptionally well reproduced. Details of direction are deserving of commendation and the picturizing of a blinding snowstorm with the aid of a little tinting is vivid to a degree.

The "all-star" cast is very near to being so in fact as well as in billing, and there is much to commend in the production, with but one unnecessary adverse opinion—its length. A few hundred feet devoted to atmosphere might be excised and quicken the action, of which there is a plentitude. *Jolo.*

A CONN. YANKEE.

The Yankee	Harry C. Myers
Sandy	Pauline Starke
Queen Morgan le Fay	Rosemary Theby
King Arthur	Charles Clary
Merlin, magician	William V. Mong
Sir Sagramore	George Siegmann
The Page, Clarence	Charles Gordon
Mark Twain	Carl Forms

Los Angeles, Jan. 26.

This William Fox special is being shown at Miller's here and now is in the sixth week of a run which seems to be bringing real money in the box office. However, the prediction of Edward Rosenbaum, Jr., and other Fox executives that the picture will run six months in New York seems a little far-fetched. Perhaps four or six weeks at a Broadway house if Fox is willing to pay the rental.

The full title is "A Connecticut Yankee at King Arthur's Court." It is a picturization of the Mark Twain satirical comedy of the same title. Of course, it has been modernized to a certain extent, and now flivvers and motorcycles play an important part.

To one viewing the picture there comes the immediate thought: "What a picture this would have made for Fairbanks!" And then, on investigation, when one discovers it was offered to Doug and turned down, all left to be said is some caustic comment on the lack of perspective on the part of some people. At that Harry C. Myers, who plays the role in the Fox feature, gives a highly entertaining performance and bids fair to cause Doug to step in time, providing he is given stories of this calibre right along.

The presentation at the Miller was staged by Norman K. Whisler, the producing manager of the California theatre. The picture itself was directed by Emmett J. Flynn, who kept the action and suspense in the foreground at all times. The screen adaptation was made by Bernard McConville, while Lucien Andriot did the shooting.

The principals in support of Mr. Myers are most capable. This is particularly true of Rosemary Theby, who does the vamp as Queen Morgan le Fay, and Pauline Starke as Sandy. The latter was a particularly pleasing ingenue. In the male support Charles Clary, William V. Mong, George Siegmann and Charles Gordon managed to impress most favorably. Mong's work as Merlin the magician is particularly worthy of comment.

There are some corking exterior shots and the interiors of the Court of King Arthur are very effective.

Fred.

813.

This somewhat cryptic title covers a multitude of sins in Robertson-Cole self-advertised super-special. It is nothing more than a poorly acted and utterly senseless version of the sequel to "Arsene Lupin." In this instance the French master-crook, reported dead, suddenly reappears. In a triple role he is first introduced as a Russian prince. Second as the first officer of the police. Third he personally reveals his identity as Lupin.

The plot is very zig-zaggy. Whereas it is supposed to hold its audience in suspense, there is not sufficient connection between the action and the final moral to give sufficient entertainment for the hour's time it takes up. It is only toward the end that the reason why Lupin turned up at all is explained.

Under the present version, unless a person is at all acquainted with Lupin's former history, that person may resolve himself from the start into absolute ignorance of what goes on until the finale.

The feature runs truer to the wild, uncanny purposes of the serial than vigorous melodrama. In the latter phase it touches lightly but insufficiently to warrant that classification.

The direction is not exceptional. It is dull albeit a certain action which few pictures possess excepting the serial type. But this is neither thrilling nor endowed with suspense.

The cast numbers over 12. None of the players appear to advantage. How can they in anything digressing so from every basic reason in motive? It is headed by Wedgewood Nowell, who is entrusted with the triple role.

Step.

The Truant Husband.

Except that this W. W. Hodkinson release gives three artists an opportunity to acquit themselves creditably in the interpretation of character types, there is nothing substantial in the way of plot, action, or story to justify the length of a full five-reel feature. Boiled down to one reel would have been quite adequate. And it might possibly have made the basis of a good one-reel comedy, in the better sense of comedy. And quite likely may have been a forerunner in showing numerous picture concerns the difference between boiling down a story and lumping it into something substantial in one reel, instead of wasting a lot of money on something that can't stand being stretched.

The story concerns a perfect husband wedded to a charming lady. Their marital existence occupies the space of six years. A former flame appears and entices this husband to seek the seclusion of a former forest rendezvous. In other words, the eternal feminine seeking to revive memories of youth. The couple take an accommodation train —by accident—and are forced to endure the humiliation of garlic smells and other inconveniences on a train of this character. It is a hot summer's day. There is no taxi from the station to the Inn. They must walk, and the lady wilting under the ray's of the sun and the "truant husband," no more comfortable for the experience, realizes his folly. The party ends up in a heated disagreement.

The picture features Mahlon Hamilton and Betty Blythe. In the cast is also Francella Billington. It is doubtful if women of Miss Blythe's pulchritudinous charms should undertake a part of this kind. But as it is played by Miss Blythe and permitting herself to become less beautiful by the melting paint on her features, there is a character touch that lends an abundance of humor to the role. Mr. Hamilton is very adept in the part of the truant through unerring husband. His best recommendation is to be found in the fact that it is good to see a man try to act on the screen instead of being a stilted figure. He scores his points with facial expression that are characteristically his own. The services of Miss Billington were well chosen by the director, who is Thomas Heffron. She has looks, a certain amount of charm and the contrast offered by her to the fickle widow shows good discretion in cast picking. A striking resemblance to Constance Talmadge registered itself when Miss Billington posed in what may be estimated as a three-quarter angle. This fact even startled the management of Loew's New York who seemed equally impressed. It is a good production, but the entire feature is scarcely good entertainment in its present length.

Step.

THE RESPONDENT.

Avice Milbrey	Claire Adams
Rulon Shepler	Robert McKim
Uncle Peter Bines	Joseph J. Dowling
P. Percival Bines	Niles Welch
Psyche Bines	Betty Brice
Mrs. Bines	Adele Farrington
Mrs. Athelstane	Virginia Harris
Mr. Milbrey	Tom Ricketts
Abe Trummel	Otto Lederer
Lord Mauburn	Harry Holland

This film is put out by W. W. Hodkinson and was set for its trade showing at an unreasonably early hour one morning last week. It deals with Wall Street from a romantic angle, yoking up the maneuvers of the stock market with the love affairs of a quartet, two feminine and two masculine.

Of course, this frame-up is bound to have its own story value, of reasonable interest, although the romantic features have more interest for the fans than the speculative evolutions. One element works back and forth with the other. The film is fairly well put on, but has no special value beyond that of an ordinary program picture.

The acting, without special distinction, comes up to the standards of the ordinary run of program films—that is to say, it is neither the extreme of excellence nor of mediocrity. The piece has several high lights, one a chorus girl dinner party, at which there are mild doings, and the other between the heavy and the hero, in which the hero douses the villain under a gasoline supply pipe after a lively struggle. Both of these incidents are good material for the neighborhood fans, the last described having comedy value in addition to the usual fight stuff.

There is also an excellent type in the shrewd old manufacturer who enters the Wall Street game and comes out victorious, a type of Americanism always popular.

Uncle Peter Bines wants the family to remain in the West, where he has his business interests. But Percival and Psyche, the grandchildren, insist on going to New York. Avice Milbury goes as the guest of the younger Bines. Psyche falls in love with a fortune-hunting nobleman, and this brings the old man East. Shepler gets the whole group involved in Wall Street speculation.

Old Uncle Peter has been busy on his own account in the financial plot. The double romance works itself out, and the old man brings the family home to their Western town financially rehabilitated and romantically in the best possible film condition, with the future promising wedding bells.

HARRIET AND THE PIPER

Harriet Field	Anita Stewart
Royal Blondin	Ward Crane
Tony Pope	Irving Cummings
Richard Carter	Charles Richman
Isabelle Carter	Myrtle Stedman
Tam o' Shanter Girl	Barbara Deeley
Nina Carter	Margaret Landis
Ward Carter	Byron Munson
Madame Carter	Loyola O'Connor

Exhibitors and the public will find little ground for complaint in "Harriet and the Piper," the newest Anita Stewart feature released by First National. It is not a world-beater, but it will class among the strong program features of the day, because it is a modern, well-made picture.

Miss Stewart has been surrounded by brilliant support, a cast that works smoothly in spite of the fact that three of its members—Richman, Cummings and Myrtle Stedman—have been featured as stars.

The picture is notable for its settings and its exterior shots, the director having displayed rare judgment in his groupings and lightings. The photography rates high, with especial emphasis on the interposes, cutbacks and close-ups of Miss Stewart. These, for the most part, constituted the best shots of the star, for in the regular course of the picture she at times seemed haggard and tired, as though overworked. The sweetness of expression for which Miss Stewart is noted was missing in many places, but her acting generally was far above her usual work.

"Harriet and the Piper" is an inoffensive "problem" story, following a prolog based on the old story of the Pied Piper of Hamelin, in which is pointed the moral that he —or she—who plays must pay the piper.

The story opens with a rush, showing Harriet Field and Blondin, a young rake, going through a free love marriage ceremony in a Greenwich Village resort. The girl he has cast off, played with strength by Barbara Deeley, witnesses the mock ceremony. She sends a message to the wealthy aunt of Blondin, source of his income, urging her to go to his studio. The aunt arrives shortly after Blondin has taken his "bride" in, but he gets rid of her. Harriet, in a bedroom, grows remorseful and tries to escape, but he foils her and the fadeout has her resigned to her fate.

The girl next is seen as the secretary of Mrs. Isabelle Carter, wife of Richard. Mrs. Carter is wooed by Tony Pope and after being found in her lover's arms at a masque ball, she flees with him. They later die in a motor accident abroad. Meanwhile, Blondin, who has been to India and now poses as an occult reader, appears and lays suit to Nina, the daughter of Carter. Harriet warns him away, but he threatens to expose their past relations. Harriet marries the elder Carter after shooing away his son and then is called upon to decide whether Blondin shall have Nina. She denounces him and he in turn tells of their "marriage." She prepares to leave the house, but Carter insists upon knowing the details of her life with Blondin. A fade-in shows that Harriet, after failing once to escape from his studio, had hurled a flower pot through a window, bringing a policeman and the aunt, who takes her away and disinherits Blondin.

The day after telling her story, Blondin comes for his final answer. Carter dismisses him with a $20,000 check as the price of his silence. But Nina intercepts him outside and insists on going away with him. As they enter his car, an avenging Hindoo stabs him as penalty for having betrayed a sacred virgin in India. The fadeout shows Harriet awakening to love of Carter, whom she had married only out of sympathy.

The honors of the picture go to Ward Crane, the heavy, but Miss Stedman and Mr. Cummings, although only in a few scenes, are very good.

The picture will stand up in any house.

ROGUES AND ROMANCE.

Against a background of exteriors taken in the heart of one of Spain's most picturesque districts is enacted a crude melodrama, the author, producer and director of which is George B. Seitz, with June Caprice as the star, Mr. Seitz again featuring himself in the billing as a participant in the cast, and directly under these two names is Marguerite Courtot. It is further embellished by a cast of able principals, that ability, however, being secondary to some good and alternately inadequate purpose in direction.

The impression in summary of Mr. Seitz's ambitious effort is that of a director whose direction in spots reaches the superfine, and at other times is mediocre.

He gives us a melodrama tinged with color, with some fair titling and photography that is never on the whole exceptional, but is now and then divided between very able and less effective results.

As a story, the material which he has provided for the talents of a cast of about 10 principals never runs true to purpose, but is ever crossing itself in that purpose, so that it is bound to react from a straight line. Had he given us instead the story in its straightforward, melodramatic style, concluding melodramatically instead of a comedy finale, its objective would have been more sustaining to public taste.

The individual merit of Mr. Seitz's direction is his ability to handle the mob and to encompass its pictorial value from at least 20 different angles. It is the best thing in this picture in a story which briefly concerns the infatuation of an American girl for a Spanish revolutionary, and her subsequent rescue by her American fiance. It is very hard to give any credence to the story itself, since Mr. Seitz's conception of the bad man defies all logic. A man who is entrusted with a revolutionary cause by a group of Spaniards could scarcely be the philanderer Mr. Seitz would have us believe. It may suit his purpose to the action and which ultimately brings him on the scene in the business of rescuing the fair heroine.

Miss Caprice's talents are a bit wanting, and so is Mr. Seitz's histrionic efforts. The real living figure in this picture when her style is not hampered by an affected prima donna or Carmanesque manner is Marguerite Courtot. Harry Semels is an exaggerated villain.

The picture is distributed by Pathe. *Step.*

THE TORRENT.

Velma Patton	Eva Novak
Anne Mayhew	Oleta Ottis
Lieut. Paul Mack	Jack Perrin
Sam Patton	Leonard Shumway
Red Calvin	Jack Curtis
Jud Rossen	Harry Carter
First Mate	Bert Apling

"The Torrent" (Universal's) will never succeed in making much of a noise as a feature offering. The biggest asset in the denouement of a story lacking in balance but somewhat profuse in gripping, tense situations is the cast, supervised by capable direction of Stuart Patons. Upon reflection the theme may be collated with the rankest of rank serials. There is little left of an element to subdivide it from the latter class.

The vehicle furnished by George Rix runs truer to fiction than reality and from the start is illogical. To believe that a millionaire husband may have aboard his yacht simultaneously his mistress and his wife is a little far-fetched even in rich circles. Rich men play, but never in the presence of their wives—not if they can help it. From the yacht where the youthful bride is accidentally yet objectively thrown overboard to escape the brutal personality of her husband, the scene shifts to a deserted island, and here an aviator-sportsman stops for lack of gas. The ensuing episodes bring into the picture several bootleggers, and, of course, there is the usual conflict for the "goil." From then on the play takes on all the ethics **of the serial, digressing toward the finale, which ends in the suicide of a paralyzed husband and the union of the happier two.**

The character work of Leonard Shumway, particularly in the opening scenes, are highly meritorious for the forceful manner in which they are depicted. The shot of the interior of the yacht rocking in raging sea is admirably executed. The rain storm of the exterior is colorful and imaginative.

Eva Novak (the star) is genuine in her pathos, while excellent support is offered by Jack Perrin as a mild hero. A few facile gestures of villainy that the camera caught just right of Jack Curtis as the villain are done effectively.

The photography is a trifle too dark in the nocturnal scenes, while some "shots" are really brilliant in their execution.

What the entire picture is worth in an era when the cry is for fewer and better pictures is left entirely to the imagination. *Step.*

FRONTIER OF STARS.

Buck Leslie	Thomas Meighan
Hilda Shea	Faire Binney
Phil Hoyt	Alphonz Ethier
Gregory	Edward Ellis
Ganz	Gus Weinberg
Mary Hoyt	Florence Johns

Thomas Meighan seems to do his best work in the role of an underworld hero, probably because of the character he played in "The Miracle Man." His Buck Leslie in the current feature, "The Frontier of the Stars," at the Rialto, belongs distantly to the same type, and makes a feature that ought to attract the feminine fans. It is presented by Jesse L. Lasky.

Its background is the tenement rooftops of the lower East Side, where the gangster and the "bull" fight their battles of violence and plot their campaigns. It furnishes a singularly romantic environment in the present tale.

Faire Binney is leading woman. She is a pretty duplicate of her sister, although in this picture she has rather a neutral, colorless part. The other principals are excellent types, and the big crowds are handled with unusual success.

The directorship, by Charles Maigne, is first-class, with numberless effective scenes at night and tricky use of shadows worthy of particular mention. Much of the action takes place after dark, and for this reason it must have required a good deal of ingenuity on the part of the cameraman to get a wide variety of tones, such as the star-lit roofs, the crowded sidewalks, haunts of the thieves and the like, a good deal more ingenuity than called for by plain darkness as it is usually interpreted by printing on blue-green positive film. The lighting of "The Frontier of the Stars" alone gives it interest. The story, by Albert Payson Terhune, is the real strength of the offering.

He uses a good deal of the usual thieves' plotting against police pursuit material, but he gives it new twists, such as making the family life of the honest policeman a vital element of the plot. And above all things, he has told an intricate tale in terms of the utmost simplicity so that the story advances logically and with ascending values to the climax of a tenement house fire, done with all the apparatus, rushing crowds and the paraphernalia of a firemen's spectacle drill. This passage is mighty effective melodrama.

Buck Leslie is the gang leader, more or less countenanced by the politicians because of his two-fisted control over his followers. **There is a raid on the crook's headquarters and the police chase Buck to the roofs for escape. The crook up there finds a curiously naive child, a wheel chair victim, who has made all her observations of the world from her far-away eerie. He first engages her assistance in gaining his escape by telling her it's a game and she must tell the police he has not been around.**

After the bluecoats are sent off on a wrong trail by the child the crook becomes interested in her artlessness and innocence. He even finds it impossible to lie to her. He makes innumerable visits to the housetop to talk with her and brings her gifts long before he learns that she is the paralyzed sister of the plainclothes detective who has been assigned to the special task of breaking up the "Leslie gang." The visits move Buck strangely within himself, and his regeneration begins when he determines to drop the gang and go to work in a steel mill.

His fellow crooks are angry at his supposed desertion, although the sleuth is still trailing him. The thieves frame up a plot on Buck. One of them, a clever chemist before he went wrong, gives Buck a chemical formula, in reality nitroglycerine, "soup" for blowing up safes, by telling him it is his new invention and will make a fortune for both by use in the manufacture of better steel.

Buck assembles the chemicals and takes them to the roof-girl with the tale of his triumph, when the detective brother makes his appearance and drives him away in a spirited bit of action across the roofs. The brother removes a plank bridge by which Buck used to reach that particular roof. Later the detective and Buck meet again and there is more fighting in and out of the streets, Buck working **always toward the girl on the roof.**

As he comes to the place where the little bridge used to be the paralyzed girl jumps from her chair and rushes to warn him that the span is gone and he must jump. The doctors long ago had said that only a miracle could restore the child's power to walk. The emergency performed the miracle. Buck is on top of the tenement when fire starts below. Although he has been wounded in the fight with the detective, he manages to carry the child down to a fire escape and drop her into the firemen's net, tumbling into the hands of the police via the same road.

Then it is straightened out, and with Buck in the hospital visited by the restored invalid, all is set for the happy denouement.

This crude summary does not indicate the deeper purpose of the story, which deals with mental and physical cures by the power of love, a theme which is well developed. Nor does it indicate properly the many romantic and tender passages that occur in the tale. The picture should be an exceptional moneymaker for Paramount, which is distributing it.

SOME ONE IN THE HOUSE.

Jim Burke, "The Dancer"	Edmund Lowe
Molly Brent	Vola Vale
"English"	Howard Crampton
Percy Glendenning	William J. Irving
Helen Glendenning	Clara Lee
Walter Hargrave	Lawrence Grant
"Deacon"	Edward Connelly
"Snowie"	Henry Miller, Jr.
Malone	Edward Jobson
Halloran	Thomas McGuire
McVeigh	Jack Levering

Metro's "Some One in the House," self-advertised as a "classic," is less classic than its melodramatic theme conveys. It is the conventional crook melodrama, offering very few if any new situations, from a scenario by Lois Zellner and Marc Robbins from the original script by Larry Evans, Walter Percival and George S. Kaufman.

Some of its scenes are paramount with melodramatic interest, its comedy episodes are forced both in the direction of John E. Ince as well as in the enactment, while any audience can be expected to bestow interest on the she-crooks to the end. The bitter end is never in doubt from the beginning. It is a situation contrived in no less an ingenious method than surrounding it with ornate theatricals. The hero returns with the valuable gems, to be forgiven by a heroine who had seen the honest light in his eyes, etc. Such incidents occur in the pictures now more than they do in the theatre. In the latter place of amusement they know better.

Three wise men like Evans, Percival and Kaufman, who could not shape better material than "Some One in the House" should be incarcerated in the library and be left to read Racine and Moliere for punishment, and if delinquent should be forced to read in addition "The Admirable Cracksman" or "Raffles."

An adequate and admirable production has been provided for this melodramatic vehicle, which is undoubtedly the work of the art director, name unknown. By far the best performance is a bit entrusted to Edward Connelly as the "deason." Edmund Lowe stands out with considerable attention as the master crook. Viola Vale is not at all satisfying as the ingenue. The subsidiary "bits" are well handled.

The photography of George K. Hollister is fair.

The title could well be "The Dancer." But there was one play produced on the legitimate stage, an adaptation from the Hungarian, with the same title. Perhaps that precluded the name of "The Dancer" in this picture. *Step.*

BEHOLD THE MAN!

The Father	H. O. Pettibone
The Mother	Sybil Sheridan
The Son	Richard Ross
The Daughter	Violet Axzelle

Time—Any Night. Place—Any Home.

(Principals of the Bible Story)

St. Joseph	M. Moreau
The Virgin Mary	Mme. Moreau
The Boy Christ	Le Petit Briand
The Adult Christ	N. Normand
Judas Iscariot	M. Jacquinet

By arrangement with the Messrs. Selwyn, Pathe, the French and American film producers-distributors, have taken the Apollo for the special showings of "Behold the Man!" on Sundays only. Before going into an analysis of the feature, its source is practically self-explanatory and is quoted as "A mother's story from the Bible adapted from 'The Life of Our Saviour.'" The initial presentation was made Jan. 9, two performances given in the afternoon and two in the evening. It will continue to be shown here on succeeding Sundays during the present month.

Possibly this is the third time within recollection that a picture version with Jesus of Nazareth as the central figure of interest has been projected before New York audiences.

In the present version Pathe's and in resume of its third showing on Jan. 9 before a slim audience, it may be said this is a passably interesting but unexceptional photoplay. It is doubtful in any event whethere any screen version of the episodic career of Christ, in the strict orthodox sense, can be made interesting to the vast majority of picture-goers. It must necessarily appeal to that class with reverence to use this religiously historic figure impersonated by a screen artist.

Mention is made of the cinemato**graphic value of bringing before the whole world the figure of Christ, whereas only "rich" pilgrims were enable to visit Oberammergau, the seat of the modern "Passion Play."**

In its continuity the movement of the religious story is augmented by a form of prolog and epilog in addition to a theme as a result of the two, by the adaptation of what is called a modern episode.

The religious episodes have been produced with a cast of French artists, while the modern episode has been made obviously on American soil. In the former is an admirable effort, well sustained to give the production a pictorial effect to conform with the thousands of illustrations which have been handed down to posterity. It is done in colors, and the most artistic are the scenes of Lazarus arising from the Tomb and the Last Supper. The production itself is admirable for the unity of purpose. Its background, to say the least, is picturesque.

N. Norman plays Christ. The Virgin Mary is essayed by Mme. Moreau, and Joseph is played by M. Moreau.

The photography in the modern episode is less harsh on the eye in comparison to the colors of the religious episodes. In the latter respect it has not in this case achieved a point where in the practicability of colors is advisable in motion pictures.

The special musical arrangement, with Harriet Lark, soprano; Elda Arlando Boyer, baritone, and choruses from members of the New York Opera and Oratorio Society, were lacking in the bigger requirements of artistic purpose. Throughout the performance there was a decided effort to maintain harmony with a limited (not augmented) orchestra, but the result was far from even. It was apparent that more rehearsals would have improved the effort.

The direction of the modern episode by Spencer G. Bennett was characteristic only for the lighting effects achieved admirably by a photographer not mentioned. The adaptation is made by Harding O. Martin, the titles by Arthur F. Warde, the art drawings by Maryan F. Broada. *Step.*

THE ROOKIE'S RETURN.

James Stewart Lee......Douglas MacLean
Alicia.............................Doris May
Dad ....Frank Currier
Henri ....Leo White
Gloria ....Kathleen Key
Mrs. Radcliffe ....Elinor Hancock
Gregg ....William Courtright
Tubbs ....Frank Clark
Mrs. Perkins ....Aggie Herring
Francois Dupont ....Wallace Beery

As a companion piece to "23½ Hours Leave," "The Rookie's Return" (Ince-Paramount), starring Douglas MacLean and featuring Doris May, made a bid for popularity for the first time in New York at the Rialto Sunday afternoon. It proved less popular than the preceding piece, although the prominence of the latter picture as a sequel is firmly implanted in the mind by the acquisition of MacLean in the leading role.

To sum it up is to pronounce it mildly amusing, and the biggest value that may be attached to it is a program release. It is not a rollicking comedy along the broad lines and undeniably funny situations that made the "Leave" feature the biggest comedy bet of the Paramount schedule for the preceding year. The present comedy seems less effective on the whole, and its situations are not commanding enough in their humor to obviate an impression of a loose story loosely put together.

The theme on which the rookie returns is based from the beginning on James Stewart Lee's (MacLean) homecoming from belligerent scenes. He starts out selling books, and by incident, uninvited, rides out to a country club. A golf ball in direct travel strikes him, introducing an apologetic heroine. The action subsequently sends him to his aunt's home, where a will is being read bequeathing her property to him. Some money is left to the servants who cannot secure it before six months' time. They propose to be discharged. While consulting some law books he meets unknowingly the heroine's father, who has come to the library to satisfy a craving for dime detective stories. The absent father causes concern to his family, while the hero proposes becoming a sleuth. The father, inspired by detective stories, hides and sends a note that he is kidnapped, and the finale melts out into the family being brought together.

To a client looking for refreshing entertainment, new ideas either in comedy or drama or a picture that will hold the undivided interest features like "The Rookie's Return" do not mean a continental. They only consume a deal of time better spent in other diverting fields.

About the best thing in it is the work of MacLean, himself, who as a silent farceur seems almost unlimited in the ability to register. His work is at all times pleasing, and the ease with which he projects his or the director's points are satisfactory in their effect. Miss Doris May could be counted on to subdue herself sufficiently to give the plum to her hero, and so the role is really secondary.

The story is by Arthur McMackin. The rest of the staff are omitted, since they are not on the Rialto program, and the fact that the screen flashes the other names too quickly to be noted is regretted. But of all, the title writer is entitled to a good bit of credit for the manner in which they have been edited, particularly when the action transpires in an automobile, the hero and heroine being blindfolded. Assuming that the darkness envelops them, much is left to the imaginative audience, and is amplified by titles in this effect: "James

do you love me?" 'a high soprano voice' utters. Effective? At least the audience showed it. *Step.*

THE SPENDERS.

This Jesse D. Hampton production, "The Spenders," with Miles Welch and Claire Adams, as a program release over the Pathe express, is superior to the average program feature—far above it. Yet not quite in the class of big features with a capital B.

It is a consistent story—one of the most consistently told in cinematographic fashion with artists, who, under the direction of Jack Conway, have put over a clean, well-constructed article that must perforce endure for its wholesome and sustained interest. There is in this feature, too, an element of comedy, subtle and boisterously affirmed, largely the response of clever title work. More than once an audience at Loew's New York punctuated the fleeting episodes by a hearty laughter that is seldom the reward of the silent drama from a receptive point.

The story is not new, but it's all in the matter of application in direction that makes an old theme stand out with scintillating brilliance.

In the introduction is told of a Western aphorism or truism, or whatever it is, that it takes three generations to pass from shirtsleeves to shirtsleeves. Following is the drama of beguiled and overwealthy youth struggling against the rugged ideas of an elder. Youth is determined to come to New York. It does, and blows its money in Wall Street under the sinister influence of one of the dramatic bears. The older generation saves the family fortune by playing the other end of the game.

This cast, if not entirely all-star, is better than the alleged all-star casts. The splendid thing about it is its conforming to a director's will that never seeks to overstep human limitations. Consequently the translation through a camera is as perfect as the camera can make it. The cast includes Miles Welch, Otto Lederer, Joseph Dowling, Claire Adams, Adele Farrington, Betty Brice, Robert McKim, Thomas Ricketts, Virginia Harris, Harold Holland, among others.

The production with respect to sets and exteriors is especially well balanced, yet the photography could be improved upon. The lighting in the hotel scenes strikes the onlooker as poorly handled. The art titles are excellent, the titling itself leaves little to be desired. *Step.*

LA POUPEE.

London, Jan. 7,
Wardour Film—Five Reels.

Up to the moment Wardour Films has been purely a renting firm, and its entry into the producing side with a screen adaptation of the famous comic opera by Edmund Adren is distinctly a disappointment. The production is scenically excellent, the acting is average, but the feature lacks grip and distinction. It soon becomes monotonous, a monotony relieved every now and again by some distinctly suggestive sub-titles. The story follows the lines of the opera very carefully, and a little inventiveness and imagination on the part of the producer, Meybrick Milton, would have worked wonders in putting some body into the work.

The cast is capable, although the monks might have paid more attention to their wigs; they look like so many lumps of unraveled tow. The greater part of the work rests on the shoulders of Flora le Breton, exceedingly good as Alesia. Her impersonation of the doll is excellent. In fact, her playing, and the

memories that the picture will awaken in older playgoers, are the only things that give this picturization of "La Poupee" a fighting chance of success. *Gore.*

THE FIRST BORN

Sessue Hayakawa gives a fine demonstration of screen pantomimic art in his performance of Chan Wang in "The First Born." The film version of Francis Powers' play of the same name supplies him with ample scope for portrayal of a series of emotions ranging from youthful happiness to poignant tragedy.

To those who do not recall the tale, it begins on the banks of the Hoang-Ho River in China, where Chan Wang, then a mere youth, loves and is loved by Loey Tsing. In the midst of their courting Loey is sold by her father to slave agent and brought to San Francisco. Meantime, at the behest of his honorable father, Chan Wang marries another woman, a discontented creature, who brings him little happiness. A son is born to them—the first born, whom Chan idolizes. They journey to America, where they expect to find gold on the streets. When the child is five years old Chan meets Loey once more, but only for a few moments. She is ordered back to her barred residence by the powerful merchant whose chattel she is.

Feeling a resentment against Chan, the merchant has the child spirited to his house, proceeds to abuse it—the child falls out of the window in attempting to escape a beating, is killed, and Chan here shows his inimitable art in portraying his inconsolable grief. How he plots and executes his diabolical grief and the Oriental cunning makes for powerful tragedy.

His suporting company is admirably handled by the director, Colin Campbell, and the production is atmospheric and most artistic. One seldom is regaled with such adherence to the most minute details.

Robertson-Cole have in "The First Born" a very high class feature. *Jolo.*

CHICKEN IN THE CASE

This latest Selznick program feature starring Owen Moore contains a story that bears down heavily on familiar comedy situations, but has been cleverly modernized with new freakish twists into one of the fastest and most entertaining of comedies.

Steve Perkins (Owen Moore) is suddenly made an heir to a large fortune through the death of an uncle. Stipulations in the will appoint a narrow, crabbed aunt as executrix of the estate, and another provision requires that Moore shall receive only an allowance until he is 40 years old.

He and his bosom pal, who has recently married, decide to outwit the aunt, and Moore borrows his friend's wife. Up to here the story is along familiar lines, but when the trio migrate to the new home of the newlyweds the complications are fast and furious.

Moore meets the right girl in a neighbor's daughter, and after his pal's young wife returns to Moore's apartments in the city, after their first quarrel, Moore stays in the country to press his own suit. The aunt arrives at the town headquarters and discovers Moore's supposed wife alone with Moore's pal. She drags them back to the country in time to introduce them to Moore's real fiancee and father, who are enjoying a betrothal dinner.

A wild night is spent at the house, with the married people trying to arrange to be together and auntie complicating matters by insisting upon tucking Moore and his wife into bed. The pal, surprised in his own wife's closet, dons female attire and passes the indignant female, going into the room Moore is in.

Moore, to shield his pal, trades duds with him and exits from the room in time for the aunt to form the worst possible conclusion. Another complication is the arrival of a certified check for Moore's share of the inheritance, but made payable to his wife.

Mutual explanations follow in the morning, with Moore wedding his real love in a stable, where all four are hiding, the ceremony being performed by a justice of the peace who has been summoned by the aunt to arrest Moore's pal.

A thoroughly capable cast took full advantage of the unusual opportunities for comedy, with Moore himself giving an intelligent light comedy characterization.

The direction, photography, lighting effects and continuity were on a par with the rest of the delightful comedy that will create comment and prove a welcome feature.

Con.

THE YELLOW CLAW.

London, Jan. 7.

Stoll.—Six Reels.

Strongest of strong sensational melodrama. The story, adapted from a popular novel by Sax Rohmer, is peculiarly weak and futile. Everything gives way to cheap sensationalism. Plausibility and even realism are sacrified to the upkeep of a mystery not unraveled when "the end" appears.

The staging is magnificent and the scenic side reflects the greatest credit on Rene Plaisetty. The scenes in the Chinese opium den are staged with utter disregard for expense. The scenes on the Thames during the motorboat chase are also very well done.

A dishevelled woman rushes into a man's room late at night and implores him to save her. She collapses. He goes for a doctor and on his return finds that she is dead. The doctor diagnoses her death as being caused by opium taking. All saw her strangled by a claw-like hand, but doctors are easily misled, especially in fiction and the opening scenes of a mystery film. Scotland Yard is baffled, and eminent French detective comes to their aid. He quickly obtains a clue—by now the murder trail seems to have given way to a search for opium traffickers and by pretending to be a dope fiend he gets into the elaborate den run by a mysterious "Mr. King," who is at the back of all this devilry. There the wife of the man in whose rooms girl No. 1 died is being kept and doped forcibly by means of a hypodermic syringe. After some adventures he bribes a man-servant and escapes back to the Yard. The police raid the place, but the principal villains escape by motorboat after the villainess, the "Queen of the Poppies," has stabbed their leader for whom she has conceived an unholy and undoubtedly jealous passion. The police pursue in another motorboat, and villainy eventually meets its end by drowning, the "Queen" being pulled under by a clutching and claw-like hand. The picture ends with this hand rising from the water, apparently in search of more victims, and the legend, "Who is Mr. King?" We don't know any more than the Stoll people seem to.

Chief honors go to Harvey Braban, who gives an excellent and natural performance as the detective (French). Stanley Seaward is officially stolid as his British colleague and gives quite a good performance. Many other male parts are well if not brilliantly played, the players having little opportunity for displaying histrionic talent. Kitty Fielder is excellent as the vampirish "Queen of the Poppies," and is responsible for a semi-disrobed scene in which she appears as Cleopatra or it may be Salome, probably to convey an impression of the joyful dreams dreamed by opium smokers. The best acting comes from Miss June as the terrified woman of the opening scenes, but she dies too young to prove if she could have kept it up.

"The Yellow Claw" will probably attract many not already satiated with morbid sensationalism. But Stoll, which produced a masterpiece in "Mr. Wu," while the firm was young, must look to its laurels—magnificent and extravagant staging alone will not create a super-picture.

Gore.

NUMBER 17

An assemblage of coincidences, melodrama, suspensive and intense conflict, winding up with the subtitle, "And our story ends as stories do that have lovers." It is from a novel by Louis Tracy, scenario and direction by George A. Beranger, starring George Walsh, a Fox production.

Walsh plays a fiction writer who familiarizes himself with the underworld in order to get first-hand impressions. The father of the girl he loves has incurred the enmity of the fanatical leader of the young Manchus through having meddled in their affairs in China. They are endeavoring to injure him through his family and make an effort to kidnap his daughter. All of which permits of the picturizing of a terrific battle between the two Tong organizations in New York's Chinatown and gives Walsh several splendid opportunities to enter into a series of fistic melees.

There are constant repetitions of explanatory sub-titles, designed to make the tale obvious, and it is a question if this idea has not been carried out at too great a length.

An interesting program feature.

Jolo.

THE MAD MARRIAGE

Jane........................Carmel Myers
Jerry....................Truman Van Dyke
Willie....................William Brunton
Mrs. Brendon...............Virginia Ware
Harmonia............Margaret Cullington
Althea............................Jane Starr
Christiansen...............Arthur Carewe
Bob.........................Nola Luxford
Mrs. Boggs..........Lydia Yeamans Titus

To facilitate the study of film acting and direction, why not compile a series of bits of business that must be strictly adhered to? For example, when you receive a letter, be sure to look inquiringly at the person handing it, then down at the envelope, before opening it. This is one of the numerous tricks of screen acting that never varies in picture directing.

"The Mad Marriage" is a story by Marjorie Benton Cooke, scenario by Marion Fairfax, directed by Rollin Sturgeon, produced by Universal. It is a silly yarn about a Greenwich Village artist who has so many women chasing him that in despair he asks his young housekeeper to dine with him, and on her refusal, says: "If you won't dine with me, will you marry me?"

So they get married that very night, and he looks upon her as just an efficient household machine. But she is more versatile. Besides darning his stocks, substituting for the leading role in his pageant in an emergency and presenting him with an heir, she writes a successful play, unbeknownst to him, and when she leaves him he discovers she is necessary to his creature comfort and is very contrite.

Carmel Myers has the role of the semi-wife, semi-slavey.

Just a five-reel picture. *Jolo.*

THE KENTUCKIANS

Boone Stallard....................Monte Blue
Randolph Marshall..........Wilfred Lytell
Anne Bruce.........................Diana Allen
Mace Keaton.....................Frank Joyner
Governor.........................J. H. Gilmour
Colton—Journalist...............John Miltern
Jake Stallard..............Thomas S. Brown
Boone's Brother..............J. W. Johnston
Constable......................Russell Parker
Young Keaton........................John Carr
Young Stallard.................Albert Hewitt
Ma Stallard.............Eugenia Woodward
Uncle Cadmus..............Wesley Jenkins
Mrs. Marshall..................Grace Reals

"The Kentuckians," this week's attraction at the Rialto, takes a whole paragraph for its lineage. It is presented by Adolph Zukor, is a Charles Maigne production, and was made into screen form by Frank W. Tuttle from the novel of John Fox, Jr. Monte Blue as the star gets the blackest type on the program.

The feature is an accurate picture of the locale which Fox knows and writes about so colorfully, and it must be said that this screen translation of the book reproduces to an astonishing degree the spirit of the novelist, both in character drawing and in settings. It carries complete conviction in its sincerity, and only falls down occasionally in minor details.

It must have involved a considerable outlay in investment, for there are numerous elaborate interiors and the producer has apparently set wide limits for his payroll. The photography is extraordinarily good. In the mountain scenes exquisite light and shadow effects and splendid forest scenes are noted, although there was a moonlight scene where the shadows were all wrong, casting crosswise with the moon (from the artificial lights) instead of straight away.

Monte Blue was happily cast as the mountaineer who comes down to the State Legislature to champion the cause of the hill folk against the oppression of the "grass country" aristocrats. There is a strong sympathetic appeal in the character of the crude mountaineer, a portrait doubtless inspired by an earnest study of Lincoln. Blue plays it with real intelligence.

One of the unfortunate defects of the picture is that common to most novels made into celluloid form: it is jumpy and wild in the confusing change from one locality to another. At one minute we are in the legislature, the next in the governor's home, and, zip, we are translated to a distant mountain cabin or a spot in the forest. These leaps are distracting and they spoil the orderly progress of the story. There is also present that additional picture defect which comes from filming novels, that there are too many characters, and it is actual labor to keep track of them in the bewildering shifts of narrative. Fourteen principal characters are listed, while about as many more personages appear several times and have to be identified by the spectator for a complete understanding.

The story has to do with the ancient clash of the wild, lawless Kentucky mountain feudists and the more orderly people of the grass country. An aristocratic legislator of the "settlements" tries to put a bill through rearranging the county lines so that the hill districts will be yoked to the plains and kept in order.

Boone Stallard comes to the legislature from the mountain districts to fight for his folks' freedom and falls in love with the daughter of the governor, becoming a rival of the aristocratic reformer. He tries to impose law and order on his own people as well, and goes so far as to prevent the mob rescue of his own brother, rightfully condemned for murder. In this connection there were several disagreeable scenes of a scaffold and the agonies of the condemned man just before the hour of his execution that might well be eliminated. The brother escapes death by executive clemency, the governor's daughter finally chooses the aristocrat after wavering between him and the mountaineer, and he goes back to his work of civilizing the hill folk. The finale is rather weak in drama, but has effective pathos. *Rush.*

THE BREAKING POINT

Ruth Marshall...........Bessie Barriscale
Richard Janeway..........Walter McGrail
Lucia Deeping...........Ethel Grey Terry
Mrs. Janeway...........Eugenia Besserer
Phillip Bradley..............Pat O'Malley
Dr. Hillyer....................Winter Hall
Mortimer Davidson.........Wilfred Lucas
Mr. Marshall...........Joseph J. Dowling
Mrs. Marshall................Lydia Knott
Camilla........................Irene Yeager

"The Breaking Point" is a J. L. Frothingham production distributed by W. W. Hodkinson. It was written by H. H. Van Loan from a published story and the filming was directed by Paul Scardon.

The story of a woman's sufferings under the cruelty of a drunken, philandering husband should make a powerful appeal to feminine fans. But in an effort to emphasize this phase of his story Van Loan has gone to lengths which are inexcusable. A description of one scene will suffice to indicate the fault of good taste.

The petticoat-chasing husband has just been summoned into the wife's room by the doctor to be told "It's a girl." The white uniformed nurse is by the bedside holding the little blanketed bundle in her arms. The husband gives the wife a casual glance, takes a coldly critical look at the little mite and then begins with his first show of interest and enthusiasm to "date up" the nurse.

In theory, of course, all interesting situations are dramatic material, but the whole field of drama must necessarily be governed by good taste and truth. Such an occurrence or such a husband and father as described might conceivably exist, but it is scarcely permissible to picture him with all the pitiless literal reality of the screen.

The story is sprinkled with incidents of like purport. At the climax the brutal husband throws his wife out of the house bodily, and puts his six-year-old daughter in the lap of his mistress with the words, "Here, you take her. You're to be her mother after this." This follows a series of scenes of revelry involving a crowd of drunken men and women of that extreme decolletage which goes with a society play. The child and the mother are in the same house, but in the nursery on an upper floor. The drunken husband goes to bring the tot into the scene of debauchery, and his mistress tries to make the child drink champagne. The episode likewise shows several scenes between husband and wife which are plain wife-beating.

Van Loan may argue that for the purpose of the story it is necessary to build up in advance a complete justification for the killing of the husband by the wife, which happens at the end; but other things are to be considered. This kind of lurid stuff cannot possibly do the industry or the picture art any good. Van forgets the censor just at a time when that personage seems mighty in the film business.

The production is a splendid one, and Bessie Barriscale plays the wife with really fine judgment. The settings are unusually good, particularly those in the palatial home of the Janeways. The direction is skilful, and as a sample of technical story structure Van Loan has achieved a directness and simplicity of method well worth the study of scenario makers. However, as pointed out, no excellence of craftsmanship could compensate for the disagreeable incidents of the picture.

Rush.

AN AMATEUR DEVIL

Carver Endicott..........Bryant Washburn
His father..................Charles Wingate
His sweetheart.........................Ann May
His valet......................Sydney Bracey
Farmer Brown................Graham Petty
Mrs. Brown................Anna Hernandez
A musical comedy star.....Christine Mayo
Her daughter..................Norris Johnson

"An Amateur Devil" is a five reel farce, produced by Famous Players Lasky and directed by Major Maurice Campbell. Bryant Washburn is starred. The picture is based on a theme similiar to that of one of Douglas Fairbanks' early pictures called "His Picture In the Papers." In the Fairbanks' picture the hero had to get his picture in the newspapers, in order to win a girl, get a wad of money or something like that. At any rate getting the publicity resulted in a series of comedy adventures.

In "An Amateur Devil" the idea is practically the same, only treated a bit differently. Mr. Washburn plays the part of a rich youth, whose sweetheart tires of his inactivity and general foppishness, and after throwing him over, tells him his only chance to be a regular fellow is to go out and do something disgraceful.

To her surprise he takes her at her word, and starts his career of "disgrace" by seeking a job as a farm hand, taking his valet with him. There's a flash or two of comedy here, but the fun gets a big boost shortly after when the youth secures a job in a restaurant peeling potatoes, from which post he is promoted to bus boy. As bus boy he meets a musical comedy actress, and frames matters so she will sue him for breach of promise.

The musical comedy actress has a daughter, however, who is sweet on the youth himself and she burns his letters to his mother, just as the suit is all set. A course of hard work, with attendant experiences of a comedy nature, gives the youth a knowledge of the world he had lacked before and the finish finds the girl ready to grab him and marry him any time he says the word.

Mr. Washburn makes a first rate light comic, standing out particularly in some funny comedy business in the restaurant scenes. Sydney Bracey plays legitimately the role of a dignified valet and Christine Mayo handles the musical comedy actress's part with ability. Chas. Wingate as the father, and Ann Mayo the girl have little to do, but get a lot out of the scenes they are in.

The settings are atmospherically correct and the photography excellent. "An Amateur Devil" averages as a good program picture, that should please any type of audience.

Bell.

GODLESS MEN

Black Pawl....................Russell Simpson
Red Pawl, his son..............James Mason
Dan Darrin.....................John Bowers
Ruth Lytton..................Helene Chadwick
Rev. Samuel Poor..............Alec B. Francis
Spiess.......................Robert Kortman
Mrs. Pawl.........................Irene Rich

"Godless Men," Goldwyn's Reginald Barker production at the Capitol, lacks many things that go to make a notable picture, but two most conspicuous by their absence are direction and actors. This director, rated sufficiently high to put his brand on a production as a box office draw, shows no finesse in this offering and turns out a picture with "cheap" written all over it. One cannot escape the conviction that Mr. Barker, intending that his own name should be the only one in lights, made "Godless Men" with one eye on the expense account and the other on the censor. The production is old-fashioned and totally lacking in technical or other novelties. It is distractingly slow in spots and lacking in suspense, chiefly for the reason that the director did not take the trouble to follow his story closely.

"Black Pawl," a hair-raising piece of fiction by Ben Ames Williams, formed the basis of "Godless Men." It was the story of a sea rover whose soul was embittered when he returned from a cruise with his young son to find his wife had fled with another. Forswearing Christianity, he instilled in his boy a hatred for all women and men, himself included. The tiger in the father was trebled in the boy and the enmity which grew between the two, where the father always was expecting his son to kill him, was a fearful thing to contemplate.

Years afterwards Black Pawl puts into a South Sea island for water, and Red Pawl, the son, leads a boatload of men ashore for it. There a missionary and a young girl beg to be taken aboard Black Pawl's schooner. Red Pawl, his lust aroused, agrees.

It is not until after Black Pawl and his son have fought over the girl that the man discovers, by a chance glance at a locket, that the girl is his own daughter. In the original she tells the story of her mother's fate. In the screen version this opportunity is passed entirely; nothing is shown to tell how the erring woman passed out. Only the main theme is followed on the screen, and that in a very sketchy fashion.

In its way "Black Pawl," as fiction, took rank with "The Sea Wolf"; and, for proper interpretation, should have had in its main character a Hobart Bosworth or a Theodore Roberts. In other words, an actor. For while it is a powerfully dramatic role, it is one easily destroyed. And the man Mr. Barker picked for it comes very close to annihilating it, either through poor direction or an uncontrollable desire to act all over the place.

James Mason, as Red Pawl, was more convincing; but the part should have been in the hands of a Rawlinson or a Tearle.

The producer reveals early that the girl is Black Pawl's lost daughter, and the audience only has to pass through a lot of slow motion to have its deductions verified. Other developments are similarly telegraphed in advance.

Ruth Lytton, in the story, was a girl of strong personality. Helen Chadwick, in the pictured role, is colorless. The same criticism applies to the character of Dan Darrin, her sweetheart, and the man who portrays it.

There is little to commend "Godless Men"—not even the advertising, for that is misleading and promises things which the picture does not contain. As, for instance, "A blow, a flash of a dagger, and hell spilled its furies on the decks of the Deborah." That line is a pledge of big action, a big scene. The scene is not there, the "hell spilling" consisting of three or four sailors semi-roughly rushing from the deck the man who stabbed Black Pawl.

THE SAGE HEN.

If this review of "The Sage Hen" sounds a trifle fullsome attribute it to the belief of this writer that Gladys Brockwell, its star, is the best all-around actress on the screen. It looks, when suitably attired in sartorial accoutrement and groomed with equal care, she strongly resembles (again this is the opinion of the reviewer) no less beautiful a woman than Pauline Frederick. When so handsome a woman will continually sink her individuality to properly interpret the character roles to which she is constantly assigned in the pictures, it means that she is an artist of the finest calibre. What other screen leading woman can you mention who isn't merely a type, always playing herself—nothing more. They may play slaveys or other nondress bits in a feature, but must always wind up gorgeously caparisoned to look their prettiest.

"The Sage Hen" is an Edgar Lewis production, released through Pathe, adapted from a story by Harry Solter. It is a very strong one that comes under the designation of "western." The picture takes its title from the name attached to women of doubtful character in mining camps.

It opens with a woman occupying a hut on the outskirts of a camp called Silver Creek. She has a child of perhaps three. No one knew from whence she came or anything about her. The other women of the community shunned her, not knowing why—probably because she never sought the company of anybody. By the ruse of giving the child some candy a crooked gambler is enabled to speak with her, but his overtures are not encouraged. That night he is caught palming extra cards, kills his accuser and takes refuge in her hut. She drives him out at once. He has been seen entering her home; the vigilance committee searches her place, and when the story of the gambler's visit to her is told the next day the local women's purity league stones her out of the community. She starts to walk 60 miles across the desert, is overtaken by one kindly young matron who has no child of her own. The human woman offers to relieve the friendless one of her child, but this is resented. She is given a horse and buggy to make the journey and told to unharness the horse at the end of the trip and that the animal will find its way back. En route a wheel comes off the conveyance; she is attacked by Indians. Wounded, she straps the child to the equine's back and sends him galloping back. She uses her shotgun effectively upon a couple of the redskins, is finally wounded, rolls down an embankment and the Indians leave her for dead.

The horse returns with the child; a searching party starts out to find her; she is carried to the home of a hotel keeper in the town of Keno. Recovering, she is asked by the hotel keeper to remain and take charge of the rearing of his motherless girl. She writes to inquire about her little boy and receives word the family owning the horse had moved to parts unknown, taking the child with them.

On the death of the hotel keeper she promises at his deathbed to guard the girl. She determines to sell the hotel and take the girl to more refined surroundings, but at this juncture there returns to Keno a trio of men she grub-staked, having struck it rich. They are, respectively, a Chinaman, a colored man and an Indian. The news of the gold strike reaches the outer world and immediately there is a rush for the spot. Among them come the cheating gambler-murderer and a stranger who consorts with the gambler.

As the gold strike is on government land a detachment of the U. S. army is dispatched to the spot to maintain order. It is commanded by a young lieutenant. He falls in love with the girl "she" is rearing, and is brought to the house and introduced as "Lieut. John Rudd." This is the name of the family that took over her child, and the scene in which she recognizes her son, grown to manhood, is a fine piece of facial transition and emotional acting. But she is constrained to reveal herself to her boy, fearing her "past" might blight his happiness.

She discovers the gambler in the act of killing the grub-staked Chinaman for his money; he threatens to proclaim her as a "sage hen" if she squeals; he demands the hand of the girl as his price of silence, and she is thus confronted with the dilemma of once more being driven out or telling her story. The stranger makes a slighting remark to the young lieutenant about the girl's "mother," is knocked down, the girl sees the fracas, the boy won't talk about it, the stranger dares him to repeat the remark and the girl rushes to tell her "mother" of the affair.

In a flashback "she" tells her story to the girl. The stranger was her husband, a drunken sot who staked her in a game of cards against a sum of money and when she refused to abide by the debt and go with another man he tried to take her child away. She shot him, and, believing him killed, she ran away with her child.

The "stranger" is determined to be revenged upon the lieutenant; "shoe" goes to him and tells him if he harms the boy he will be injuring his own son. Meantime the gambler has stunned the young man with an oar; the "stranger" comes to the rescue, is himself knocked out, placed in a boat which is sent over the rapids. He recovers consciousness, and, as the boat is speeding to sure death, fires half a dozen shots into the gambler.

Powerfully told, well acted, well photographed by Ben Bell, admirably directed by Edgar Lewis, who plays a minor part. Its chief asset is Miss Brockwell, whose enactment of the long-suffering mother is a triumph for her screen artistry.

Jolo.

PRIDE OF FANCY.

London, Jan. 7.

(Samuelson. "The Pride of the Fancy." Five reels.)

This picturization of George Edgar's story of the ring and showground is capital entertainment. The story is a good one, strong, dramatic, and is well told. It holds the interest firmly from the first reel to the last foot, although the introduction of several rather colorless subsidiary disciples of vice and virtue toward the end of the picture is somewhat confusing. The staging is a fine example of the effects that can be obtained by simplicity.

Phil Moran, an out-of-work ex-soldier, becomes a member of Professor Buston's troupe of athletes. Later he defends Kitty, his employer's daughter, from a roue. As a reward he is knocked out by a Negro pugilist in the blackguard's pay. He soon falls in love with Kitty, who is about to become a London chorus girl, and his love is obviously returned.

Ireton, the Negro's unscrupulous backer, wishes to marry Hilda, the daughter of Sir Rufus Douglas; but she loves Oswald Gordon. At the races Gordon's horse beats Ireton's, the latter losing a large sum of money. Ireton puts the screw on Sir Rufus and insists that Hilda shall marry him. Disgusted, she runs away to go on the stage.

Meanwhile Moran is making a success as a pugilist, and is eventually backed by Gordon to fight Ireton's man for the world's championship. Hilda becomes friendly with Kitty, but soon learns that the stage is not a bed of roses. The two girls live in the same house and manage to keep undesirable suitors at bay, although Ireton tries to force a manager to help him lure Hilda to ruin. The betting on the championship fight rises to a great height. Ireton fears the result, and knowing that Kitty and Moran are lovers, tries to decoy him by a forged letter. The plot is overheard by Hilda, who tells her father, and they go to the rescue. In the end Moran knocks the colored fighter out, after a splendid bout.

Rex Davis does most of the work as Moran, taking and receiving many a hard blow, but whether fighting or making love, he is an exceptionally manly and convincing hero. Daisy Burrell is a charming Kitty, although she is rather inclined to overact. Tom Reynolds presents a delightful character study of the old showman. Fred Morgan adds another picture of villainy to his already crowded gallery, and is excellent. Pope Stamper does what is required of him as Gordon quite well, and Dorothy Fane proves herself capable of good work by a sympathetic study of the persecuted Hilda. Many small parts are well played and the ensemble work is excellent.

Gore.

TIGER TRUE

"Tiger True" (Universal) reeks with melodrama. What is intended for suspense is too obviously incorporated in the story. Its underworld "stuff" has been done to death.

A millionaire sportsman discontent with the pallid existence of the social world seeks adventure in the underworld. He meets the girl he will eventually marry. His obstacles are first a gang of cutthroats, and last "The Baboon." This "baboon" is supposed to be invested with supernatural strength, and in addition is incog as "Whitey," a paralytic-stricken old man, to whom all of the underworld come for advice. This suggestion is not well carried out, but there is an item of interest in the manner that it is interpreted by the artist who plays the duo-role. He is not programed.

The direction of the piece is poor, and its introductory scene, in which the vision of the sportsman's tiger hunt is enacted, is tamely assembled. It is too noticeable for its mechanism. The extra people used in a street "take" are again posed with lack of contrast in the "dive" scene.

The principal parts are played by Frank Mayo (star) and Fritzi Brunette as the leading woman. The best that may be said about this mediocre production and inconsequential story is that the fight scenes are gripping. *Step.*

DIAMONDS ADRIFT.

Bob Bellamy.................Earle Williams
Consuelo Velasco........Beatrice Burnham
"Brick" McCann.................Otis Harlan
Don Manuel Morales..........George Fields
"Home Brew" Hanson........Jack Carlisle
Senor Rafael Velasco.........Hector Sarno
James Bellamy........Melbourne McDowell
Omar, the Cat........................Omar

The yearning of comedians to play tragedy and vice versa has its counterpart in pictures. Earle Williams, who probably has worn a dress suit more times than any man living, has tried for years to have Vitagraph feature him in comedy drama subjects, but his success in "The Christian" and other serious dramatic roles convinced the Vitagraph he was best in that class of work.

In "Diamonds Adrift," Mr. Williams seems to have put one over on the production manager, and he makes the best of his opportunity. He has a role divided 50-50 between light comedy and straight drama, and the change from his customary heroic casting is refreshing. The picture is not one of the biggest he has ever done, but, so far as his work is concerned, is one of the best, and will please his followers.

As Bob Bellamy, he is introduced "on the carpet" before his father, who cuts off his allowance and puts him to work on one of his coasting schooners as a supercargo at $50, meanwhile offering him a partnership when he can pay a $5,000 overdraft on his allowance. Bob tackles the almost hopeless task with a smile. Then he starts his sea career by knocking a husky sailor for a "goal." Next he wins, in a cribbage game, a fine Persian cat which "Home Brew," first mate, has annexed. Down in Mexico, he gives the cat to a senorita, and she gives him her love in return.

There is a bad hombre named Morales who has been awarded the girl by her father, but on the wedding night Bob and his shipmates kidnap the girl, knocking Senor Morales for a couple of "goals."

Morales is wanted by the U. S. government, so he is taken prisoner, and $5,000 reward falls to Bob. The cat is wanted by its owner in San Francisco, because a little boy has nonchalantly hooked his mother's $30,000 diamond bracelet around its neck. The senorita having brought the cat with her when she was kidnaped, Bob returns it to its owner and there collects another $5,000 reward. Then he weds the girl and his father forgives him.

The play was adapted from a short story by Fred Jackson, and makes splendid light entertainment. Williams, looking as good as ever, works as though he actually enjoyed it, and he has a bully supporting company, as the names in the cast indicate. Otis Harlan, Melbourne McDowell, Jack Carlisle and William Walling, who played the ship captain, are excellent. Miss Burnham is refreshingly pretty and naive, and the child in the case, Richard Heddrick, is a joyous piece of work.

Chester Bennett directed the picture and he did a good job in every department, not the least of his intelligence being the selection of Jack Mackenzie for the camera work, for the photography and lighting all through are smooth and well handled.

The picture will please in the largest or the smallest houses.

O'MALLEY OF THE MOUNTED.

O'Malley.................William S. Hart
Rose Lanier.....................Eva Novak
Red Jaeger......................Leo Willis
Bud Lanier....................Antrim Short
Big Judson....................Alfred Allen
Sheriff........................Bert Sprotte

William S. Hart blossoms out as an author in "O'Malley of the Mounted" (Paramount), directed by Lambert Hillyer, and the current at-

traction at the Rivoli. It's just another "Western" with all of the old sure-fires of that type. Hart is the hero, a member of the Canadian Northwest Mounted Police, appearing in that role early in the story, but later for the better part of the five reels, assuming his familiar "good-bad man" character, almost exactly as he has done in countless other films.

There's the usual hand to hand scrimmage with the villain played by Leo Willis, getting all the worst of it from Hart, numerous long shots of cowboys riding single file and in groups through mountain passes, beautiful mountain scenery and some excellent camp fire night effects. In several instances, however, tints have been used where night photography would have been much more artistic.

Scenes of a western rodeo with cowboys breaking wild bronchos, bull dogging steers and similar daredevil pastimes of the plains are nicely welded in. A bank hold up by Hart single handed and another by a gang of bandits is done in the regulation way, the gang holdup accompanied by much shooting. The inevitable chase after the bandits, with more shooting and some first rate thrills in the way of men falling from horses, etc.

Mr. Willis makes a corking heavy, Eva Novak is the girl and Antrim Short the "wanted man." Miss Novak looks pretty and handles the melodramatics competently. Mr. Short plays intelligently. An unprogramed man who does a bit, as the Canadian Police Chief stands out through the repressed method in which he characterized the part.

The picture will please the Hart following, but an actor of the latter's capabilities should not be wasting his time on stuff like this.
Bell.

HER PURCHASE PRICE

"Her Purchase Price," viewed at an Eighth avenue picture house catering to the tenement district of the middle west side, and probably not appearing in a large New York theatre, is interesting more for the manner in which it is exploited than for its merit or lack of merit as a screen production. It is a Brunton product distributed by Robertson-Cole, with Bessie Barriscale as the star. The title is rich in possibilities of suggestiveness from the street front to the lobby, where every sex slant is played up in frames of stills, but when one sits through the projection the story is entirely inocuous, merely a crude, stupid attempt at sensational drama done in the worst possible taste.

Here is an example of its atmosphere: A band of Arabs come upon a party of European tourists in the desert, and, in religious frenzy, kill all but a girl baby, because as the Arab says, "The child is a pearl of pure ivory, we will rear her and get a good price in the slave market." It is difficult to resist an impulse to trifle with the word "ivory" in connection with the heads that devised the cheap piece of sensationalism.

Whoever wrote the scenario probably had read Locke's novel, "Stella Maris," and been inspired by its tale of the girl brought up in the Orient and then suddenly introduced into formal British society. The flash of the main title was so brief the scenario writer's name was lost. So was the director's.

Miss Barriscale is too intelligent an actress to lend herself to this sort of product, which addresses itself to the least discriminating grade of film fans and lends itself to suggestive ballyhoo, while craftily out of the reach of the authorities. In this case the exhibitor is probably most to blame, but it cannot be denied that the producer gave him all the material to make an appeal to shock-seekers. This is just the sort of thing the National Association is seeking to prevent.

To make the matter worse, "Her Purchase Price" was offered as half of a double feature bill, the other half being "The Fall of a Saint," which at first glance promises pretty spicy material, but on examination is a very tedious picture. Just as the exhibitor emphasized the harem scenes of the Barriscale picture, individual scenes of "The Fall of a Saint" were seized upon for the lobby display.

There was one very immaterial passage between the heroine and the villain in the screening in which he kissed her. As it was projected the scene was over in an instant, and when it was inspected later in the lobby frozen into a still, the picture of an extremely decollete woman struggling in the arms of a man (the villian) gave an impression of nastiness altogether absent from the screen view.

It does not seem likely this lobby still was selected by accident. It seems reasonable to believe it was chosen deliberately for its effect in creating a morbid curiosity in passersby. It is exhibits like this which justify the National Board of Review in considering titles and stills in the grading of pictures and the National Association is using whatever means it can command to discipline offenders. This practice, mentioned elsewhere in this issue, encourages censorship and gives the film industry a bad name. *Rush.*

SILK STOCKINGS.

The producers of "Silk Stockings," from a story by Frank M. Dazey, must have been afraid the venture would not be accepted seriously, and hence resorted to a trick finish which is wholly unsatisfactory. The thing should have been done "straight" and given a chance to be accepted legitimately.

It is a pretty idea, well directed by Fred Niblo and released as a Thomas H. Ince-Paramount production.

A mannequin in a dressmaking establishment on Fifth avenue constantly reads romantic clothes, dreaming of a rich suitor. By a chain of very consistent circumstances she is called upon to appear at a fashionable reception given in honor of a foreign prince and for a signal service rendered the titled man, is rewarded with a beautiful jewel, and be further honors her by dancing with the little shop girl. Gunplays, etc., and all sorts of melodramatic situations, she is escorted back to the shop, where she is to discard the gown and ermine cloak, where her escort, whom she believes to be a lord of high degree belonging to the prince's entourage, tells her he loves her and is only a member of the U. S. secret service.

She seats herself in the shop and her friends, alarmed at her absence, seek her out, asking her what has happened. "I've been to the ball and danced with the prince." They tell her she's been dozing, and she replies: "I've not been dreaming. The prince gave me a beautiful jewel." She reaches down to get it from her stocking and the picture ends with a title telling the spectators to fight it out among themselves as to whether it was real or the girl had dreamed it.

The production is a gorgeous one in the matter of costuming and the ball. The picture will hold interest of any audience and is especially good stuff for the romantically inclined working girls. *JoJo.*

JUST OUT OF COLLEGE.

Ed Swinger.....................Jack Pickford
Caroline Pickering.........Molly Malone
Septimus Pickering....George Hernandez
Mrs. Pickering...........Edythe Chapman
Professor Bliss..............Otto Hoffman
Miss Jones......................Irene Rich
Herbert Poole.............Maxfield Stanley
Paul Greer.............M. B. (Lefty) Flynn
Genevieve....................Loretta Blake

Goldwyn has made a very creditable screen reproduction of George Ade's comedy, which was a stage success years ago, and Jack Pickford is more attractive than he has been for several seasons. Also, he is surrounded by a most clever cast, the work of George Hernandez being of a calibre to make him as strong a factor in the picture's success as the star himself.

This production, entitled to feature the best programs, is a striking example of story value. The play was written by Ade when the Indiana humorist was doing some of his best work, and its clean, natural comedy is a relief from the alleged comedy dramas of the present era. It is funny, but not flip, and, greatest asset of all, its characters are human beings.

The picture is exceptionally well made from the technical standpoint and has been so skillfully cut that not one foot is wasted. Ade's lively lines make bull's-eye titles and carry the action along rather than halt it, as most titles do. The Ade brand are living parts of the story, while the average title, used to explain things the camera should show, correspond to those long-winded descriptive parts of a book which a reader skips.

Credit is due the director for his intelligent directions of intelligent players and to the cameraman for clear, sharp photography and lighting. Less tinting at the start would help the night effect.

WAY WOMEN LOVE.

Judith Reynard............Rubye DeRemer
Ralph Barr.................Walter Miller
Schedd....................Thomas Magrane
Trent.....................Henry Pemberton
The Butler................Edward Elkas
A Detective...............Walter D. Greene

A Lyric Films, Inc., production in five reels, starring Rubye DeRemer, adapted from Herman Landon's novel, "Behind the Green Portieres," directed by Marcelle Perez.

The director had a hard time trying to tell his story and that he didn't quite succeed was probably not his fault. The tale, at best, is a confusing one, designed as a suspensive interest mystery story.

Two men love the same girl. One goes to the house of the other and says that unless he is given $50,000 he will kill himself and the other, with whom he quarreled the night before, will be accused of the crime. He points the revolver at his head, a shot is heard and he drops dead just as the girl knocks on the door. She finds the body and believes the surviving one, whom she loves, is a murderer. To save her lover she goes upstairs while the detective is investigating and fires a shot into a dark closet, bringing the revolver back, to make it appear as if there had been a battle and her fiance might claim self-defense.

In the end, after an intriguing series of happenings quite difficult to follow, it turns out the other man didn't kill himself, but was shot from behind the portieres by another man, and when she fired into the dark closet she wounded the murderer, who was hiding there. On his deathbed he confessed.

The detective's finger-print deductions on the revolvers are ridiculous, inasmuch as he also handled the guns and it is necessary to employ a great many lengthy sub-titles of an explanatory kind to keep up the interest.

Nothing in the acting to command individual praise, though all are competent in a mediocre way. The premise sought to be conveyed is the loyalty of a man's sweetheart in spite of her belief in his guilt. Just a program feature.   *Jolo.*

THE GOLDEN HOPE.

"The Golden Hope" is a Chatsworth production starring Edith Storey—a "western" with a very neat dramatic problem.

Story opens with man and wife in a lonely hut in the west. She is disappointed and lonely—he discouraged over inability to strike gold during his prospecting. It develops he absconded in the east and as he claims he did it for her, she sticks by him. She begs him to take her away to a village and accept a position. "We can't go to towns; I'd be recognized," but she craves human companionship, and they go.

In the village a young rancher-banker and friend of the under dog is fighting an avaricious land grabber, and there is a fight for private water rights versus government control. Husband is grubstaked by the hero, leaving wife behind. Banker-hero hires wife as his stenographer; hubby strikes gold. "Now I can take Kate away from this cursed country." But meantime Kate and Eric, the banker-rancher, have fallen in love.

Next day Eric and husband go to the gold strike, husband sees eastern detective and disappears. Feeling is created Eric had made away with husband—two reasons, to get entire control of mine and annex the wife. Searching party returns with shirt, etc., considered evidence of husband's death. Eric is arrested, charged with the crime.

Wife rushes to old hut to find her husband, and he in turn suggests to her they let Eric hang, so they will secure entire interest in the mine. When she refuses he charges her with loving Eric. She admits it. He decided to ride away and let Eric be executed. She takes a gun and shoots him, bringing him back dying across his horse, just in time to save Eric from being lynched.

For the "clinch" Eric and young widow are standing overlooking the new irrigation scheme laid out by ranger with the title "The golden hope at last a reality."

The problem offered for solution is, Should the wife let Eric be executed in order to save her husband, or vice versa. To save Eric she had to sacrifice her husband.

Well handled subject, adequately acted, with Miss Storey as the heroine and the man playing the husband acquitting themselves creditably.

Mostly exteriors, the production cost is minimum. But a good program feature.   *Jolo.*

THE ROMANTIC ADVENTURESS

Alice Vanni...............Dorothy Dalton
Her Mother..............Virginia Anderson
Her Father................Howard Lang
Louie Fitch...............Joe Dawson
Toni Maxwell.........Charles Meredith
James Cortright.........Louis Broughton
Signor Castelli...........John Ardozoni
Charles Robertson.........Robert Schable

If there is anything that will kill Dorothy Dalton as a star, it is pictures like "The Romantic Adventuress" (Paramount) a trashy story trashily produced. A few more like this one and Miss Dalton, one of the first flight film favorites, will be relegated to supporting roles, for the picture public does not blame the subject, it blames the star for a feature's failure to entertain.

This story, an adaptation from a magazine tale, is the kind of stuff that justifies censorship, because it treats of a matter which, if it does occur in real life, is isolated and kept out of view. A mother is made to abandon her sick husband and little daughter, and, in later years, when the girl grows to beautiful womanhood and success as a dancer, to use her as bait in blackmail schemes. This mother happens to have been an opera singer who had failed in her ambition on the stage.

Next to the Deity the mothers of this world have proved their right

---

to sanctification and worshipfulness. And the brain that conceives romance in one who departs from the rule, or thinks it fit material for screen entertainment, needs moral renovation.

Miss Dalton is totally unsuited to ingenue roles, such as she was called upon to portray here. She has a charm and beauty which are mature and her talent is for strong dramatics. Here she had little to do and she got all the worst of the deal from her director, Harley Knowles. In some places the lighting on the star was so atrocious as to give her a ghastly look. An attempt at "bigness" in some sets was evident, but they were no more convincing than the story. One place, the exterior of a gambling casino in France, offered an opportunity for real photography, but it was spoiled by a too liberal use of bluing, spilled with far more extravagance than a laundress would use in her work. This is supposed to be tinting, but it is daubing.

The picture stars who protect themselves by insisting upon a contractual clause that they may select or reject a film story for themselves are not so in. It might keep them some day from being "killed off." A star must have considerable box office strength to make that demand, but others who see their box office value in sight might be just as sensible in insisting upon it. This is the second Dorothy Dalton feature lately caught that had a funny look, for the men who pour barrels of money into feature production are fools.

THE KILLER.

Ruth Emory.................Claire Adams
William Sanborn............Jack Conway
Bobby Emory................Frankie Lee
Henry Hooper..............Frank Campeau
Artie Brower..................Tod Sloan
Ramon......................Edward Peil
Windy Smith...............Frank Hayes
John Emory.................Will Walling
Buck Johnson..............Milton Rose
Tim Westmore..............Tom Ricketts
Aloysius Jackson..........Zack Williams

The whole tenor of the production is along "different" lines. There is no handsome hero—just a regular human man who does a few heroic things but doesn't whip an entire army single-handed; there is a heavy who is always polite, loves music, hates birds, animals and children with an insane desire to kill every one and everything that irritates him and who so arranges his crimes that it is a difficult matter to lay them at his feet. For example, he takes his lifelong partner for an inspection of their ranch, accompanied by a suave Mexican. They are standing on the edge of a 500 foot mountainous cliff. The greaser's horse shies sideways, striking the partner and precipitates the victim into space. The macchiavelian villain has the daughter on the ranch, all evidence of her father's wealth in his possession, far removed from any outside aid, helpless and hopeless, and proposes marriage. He treats her with every courtesy, but she is, nevertheless, a prisoner. She is given time to think it over—she can accept his proposition or be handed over to the lecherous Mexican as a victim of his lustful desires.

In many respects it is old-fashioned melodrama—the papers, etc., but it is so thrillingly depicted, the plot is so suspensive, the character of the heavy is so sinister, the details of direction so brilliant and the acting of a consistently good cast so impressive, that the spectator is carried along on a wave of suspensive, intensive, absorbing interest.

In the hands of a specialist in the exploitation of special features "The Killer" might have been put

---

over as one of the big pictures of the year. It will stand up satisfactorily in any first-run or pre-release house in the world.   *Jolo.*

FOUR HORSEMEN OF THE APOCALYPSE

Julio Desnoyers.........Rudolfo Valentino
Marguerite Laurier............Alice Terry
Madariaga................Pomeroy Cannon
Marcelo Desnoyers........Joseph Swickard
Calendonio..................Brinsley Shaw
Karl von Hartrott...............Alan Hale
Dona Luisa................Bridgetta Clark
Elena....................Mabel Van Buren
Argensola...............Brodwitch Turner
Tchernoff................Nigel de Bruiler
M. Laurier..................John Sainpolis
Senator Lacour................Mark Fenton
Chichi..................Virginia Warwick
Rene Lacour...................Derek Ghent
Capt. von Hartrott........Stuart Holmes
Prof. von Hartrott.........Jean Hersholt
Heinrich von Hartrott........Henry Klaus
Lodge Keeper...........Edward Connelly
His Wife..............Georgia Woodthorpe
His daughter, Georgette.....Kathleen Key
Lieut. Col. von Richtoffen..Wallace Beery
Capt. D'Aubrey...........Jacques d'Auray
Major Blumhart.............Curt Rehfleld
French Butcher..........."Bull" Montana
Mlle. Lucette................Mlle. Dolorez
The German Woman..........Isabel Keith
Her Husband..............Jacques Lanoe
Conquest....................Noble Johnson
The Count.................Harry Northrup
Nurse ....Minnehaha
Dancer..................Beatrice Dominguez
Lieut. Schnitz.................Arthur Hoyt

In "The Four Horsemen of the Apocalypse" Rex Ingram has given to Metro and the world the super-picture, a masterpiece of motography. And for it this young director, hardly more than a boy in years, must be accorded a place alongside Griffith. His production is to the picture of today what "The Birth of a Nation" was. For a clear understanding of its artistic and pictorial superiority, comparison with the best of its predecessors becomes necessary. Therefore, be it said that "The Four Horsemen" is the equal of everything that was great in "Intolerance," "Cabiria," "Passion," "Hearts of the World" and "The Birth of a Nation."

To let the mind wander to lesser "great" pictures than these for comparison is to go mentally slumming.

It is a production that, in all its elements, comes nearer the ideal than anything which has gone before, and could, with proper handling, run a year on Broadway. Metro is seeking a New York theatre for its initial presentation to the public, and, while nothing is known of the plans for marketing the production, it probably will be put out in road shows, as Griffith has done with "Way Down East." The only way the company will get its money back is to adopt that method or to book it for long runs. Cities like Philadelphia, Boston and Chicago could handle it for three months, at least, while St. Louis, San Francisco, Detroit, New Orleans and cities of that class could easily pack them in for a month.

These guesses—and they are only guesses—are based on the entertainment value of the picture as a theatrical proposition, which it possesses in greater degree than many plays which have enjoyed long runs.

Every one who sees "The Four Horsemen" will thrill over it, but it will have special appeal to those who have read the book. Vicente Blasco Ibanez, in his capacity of a neutral observer of nations at war, wrote what has proved to be the greatest of the war romances. It must have been with reluctance and trepidation that he agreed to let it be filmed, particularly as it must be made from the English translation. This, while a magnificent piece of work, is said to have lost considerable from the original Spanish.

But whatever may have been lost in the translation has been restored by June Mathis in the screen phase, for this young woman has not "adapted" a great work to the screen. She has reproduced it and breathed life's animation into its people and its theme. Her work is probably the most magnificent instance of following a story that this reviewer ever has witnessed in a picture. There are some parts of the book which do not appear in the ten-reel production as privately shown at the Hotel Ritz—that part showing the hero as a young rider of the plans—but there can be little doubt it is somewhere in the 500,000 feet which were taken.

That lack, however, is a minor incident and is not mentioned in criticism, for there does not seem a place where derogatory criticism can be applied.

The magnitude of the "Four Horsemen" is staggering, and it is not hard to believe the statistics relative to the production. It is said to have cost approximately $800,000; director Ingram had 14 assistants, each with a cameraman; more than 12,000 persons were used, and 125,000 tons of masonry and other material employed; $375,000 insurance was carried on the art works, furniture, etc., used in the picture, which was six months in the making.

While the picture is a literary, artistic and technical triumph, the acting is perhaps the most striking phase of it. A mighty cast of 32 principals, some known to the screen public, others whose names have rarely appeared in print. To the latter class belong young Valentino, Alice Terry, Nigel de Bruiler and Virginia Warwick. And yet it is to be doubted if histrionism better than theirs ever has been seen on the screen. The spectator forgot they were acting, but followed them as living characters, an effect that is the quintessence of the stage art. This same atmosphere was with all the rest of the players, even to those in the ensembles. This cast most likely will take its place among the historic rosters and, perhaps, give forth a galaxy of real stars.

Nowhere perhaps is the lighting superior to that which is used in the Argentine dance hall, although lighting is the artistic heart of the whole picture. The groupings throughout are flawless, but attain their greatest power in the scene where the husband of Mme. Laurier discovers her in Julio's studio.

Ingram has taken the character of Tchernoff, a Russian philosopher, and, without seeming to do so, made him a symbolic Christus to such an extent that after his final speech, his head is left in a massive close-up covering the screen. His message is easily accepted as the climax. For the hero had been killed and the heroine had been eliminated earlier.

Grim in its lesson and the telling, the book carried little humor. Few as were the opportunities, Ingram has grasped them and presented them in such a manner as to afford plentiful comedy relief. His handling of a little monkey is one of the highlights.

Though a "war picture," its legend deals chiefly with events occurring in 1914 and 1915, a matter of six years ago. Even if it dealt with later events, the war and its agonies now are sufficiently removed to be gazed upon with a perspective different from that which obtained while the guns were still vomiting death and ruin.

Horror stalked grinningly bold through the book of Ibanez. Ingram has mercifully cloaked it with distance and delicacy of treatment. This is characteristic of the director's handling of the entire subject. It is a production of many nuances, shadings so artistic and skillful as to intrigue the mind of the spectator into responsiveness which is the zenith of dramatic construction. It is hardly necessary to add that the picture's tempo is perfect, with the narrative unfolding smoothly and consecutively, and the action moving along in rapid sequence to its climax.

The showing at the Ritz gave opportunity for introduction of a splendid musical arrangement and a beautiful staging, the latter done under the direction of Hugo Riesenfeld. He used "Patrie" as the overture, followed by the reading of a foreword, written by Dr. Frank Crane, and delivered by George Stuart Christie. Mr. Christie, possessed of a sonorous voice and garbed as the Apostle John, put the audience into the spirit of the picture and, as his voice died out on the last word of the introductory, the "Four Horsemen" started running. At the point where the crowd in a Parisian cafe is lifted to heights of patriotic exaltation by a singer holding aloft the tri-color, Mlle. Bertha Erza, a contralto, sang "The Voice of France." So perfect was the synchronization between her voice and the gestures of the screen character it almost seemed as if the latter were doing the singing. After the intermission, a symbolical character beating a slow measure on a kettledrum, passed before the stage and, as it disappeared through a side door, the audience, again swept into the mood of the author, was carried onward by the picture. "De Profundis," sung by a chorus, came at the closing.

FINDERS KEEPERS.

A curious title for a bad picture with few, if any, distinguishing characteristics. It is a feature which at first glance reminds you of ten or more years ago when the picture was still a crude product. It is announced to have been produced by Art-O-Graph and is a "Pioneer production" in the distribution sense.

Starring Violet Mersereau, it is directed with about the degree of skill attributed to immature directors. In photography, it is poor throughout. The theme is about ample for one reel, but not over that. The cast, with the exception of Miss Mersereau, holds nothing individually or collectively in acting honors. In Miss Mersereau's case much of her work is overdone, but in moments she seems to register the desired effect, which is one suggesting utter helplessness through oppression.

The story suggests the rural heroine "who sang in church until father died." Then she got a job in the Khedive gardens as cabaret expert. She charms one man, is admired by another who is less honorable, and is pursued by him until he finally plants on her some diamonds he has stolen. He forces the cops into the hero's home to search the heroine, who is suspected. The manner in which the latter has reached this stage of the action is through being rescued from a shallow stream into which she has flung herself. The rescue, of course, is accomplished by the hero—(but inexpertly). The usual finale in which virtue and righteousness clasps hands as the preacher makes the couple secure in holy matrimony.

The marked restlessness of an audience is one of the smaller theatres where this picture was seen is an argument against its entertainment possibilities, even in the smaller or neighborhood type of house. Any sort of re-issue of the more reputable sort is better than "Finders Keepers." *Step.*

BURIED TREASURE.

Pauline Vandermueilen......Marion Davies
Dr. John Grant...............Norman Kerry
William Vandermuellen..Anders Randolph
Mrs. Vandermuellen..........Edith Shayne
Jeoffrey Vandermuellen......Earl Schenck
Duc de Chavannes...........John Charles
The Captain................Thomas Findlay

A fanciful story of its kind, "Buried Treasure" (Cosmopolitan-Paramount), has as an added attraction the presentation of Marion Davies as her natural self, a blonde, and as she would have appeared as a brunette. Thus this handsome girl will get her admirers going and coming, for she is just as handsome with her Spanish girl's dark wig as with her own luxuriant blonde tresses.

Though "Buried Treasure" will be termed fanciful as a story by the skeptical, its basic scheme of reincarnation has many followers, and these will accept the tale as entirely plausible. Through that very thing it should provoke plenty of arguments which make good advertising.

The picture was finely directed by George D. Baker from the story by F. Britten Austen. It opened Sunday at the Criterion, as a special display, and caught capacity for the first afternoon show, an unmistakable sign Miss Davies is a standard film draw. Her individual work in this feature will please. It covers a range of much light and shade, with Pauline Vandermuellen (Miss Davies) as the stubborn-willed daughter of a wealthy and stubborn-willed father, called upon to step from light frivolity to extremely heavy dramatics. She steps gracefully, and although given a heavy acting impost, carries it particularly well.

The picture has been expensively produced and shows it. Preceding it at the Criterion is a specially set "Spanish Garden," full of Spanish types, singers and dancers. It leaves the spectator's mind in the land of the senoritas and that is where the story itself plunges.

The heiress is besought by a count and is beloved by a doctor. She naively confesses to the doctor his affection is returned, but the father selects the count for his title, with the only offset for the doctor to present, a bank account. To remove the daughter and reduce her stubbornness, for she refuses to marry the count, the father with his family included, sends the girl away on a splendid yacht, to the South Seas.

While aboard and reading of a Spanish pirate of old to her mother, the girl receives visions, following the trend of the story she is reading, and through these leads her lover to the pirate's buried loot, with the captain of the boat, being on the high seas, marrying the couple immediately after it is found.

The big scene is the switch back to the day of the pirate, when they fought and died on the main, to get or to save. William Vandermuellen (Anders Randolph) topically termed "The Pirate of Wall Street," in his Spanish masquerade at the ball in his home, afterward without change of costume or make-up became the pirate of the seas, faithful to the pirate's picture in the book. That was just a bit beyond reincarnation or anything else. And a fierce father he was, and a fiercer pirate.

The sea fight with the pirate is active all the time, with slashing and slaying, as one has often read about but seldom has seen, as well produced as this battle of old, even in the dreadful mellers that went in for that sort of thing only. Norman Kerry, as the doctor, gave a nice, even performance, and Edith Shayne, as the mother, in a small role, played with much intelligence. But the real subject, after all, is Marion Davies, the two Marions, light and dark, but always a delight to look upon. *Sime.*

THE SAPHEAD.

Nicholas Van Alstyne...William H. Crane
Bertle Van Alstyne, his son..Buster Keaton
Mark Turner.............Irving Cummings
Rev. Murray Hilton......Edward Jobson
Watson Flint...........Edward Alexander
Dr. George Wainwright....Jack Livingston
Musgrave ....Edward Connelly
Hutchins ....Jeffry Williams
Rose Turner..................Carol Holloway
Agnes Gates....................Beulah Booker
Valet ....Henry Clauss

Winchell Smith is given as the author of this Metro production co-starring William H. Crane and Buster Keaton, but old-timers will be unable to dissociate it from Bronson Howard's "The Henrietta," which gave Stuart Robson a starring vehicle 20-odd years ago. Also,

Mr. Crane, one of the stars in the celluloid version, appeared in it years ago. It's considerable of a kick-back for the average memory, but even so, and despite the modern interpretation given Bertie the Lamb, the plot remains the same and so does the comedy. Robson played Bertie as a monocled, "silly ass" type; Keaton makes him just as much the vacuum who doesn't know what it's all about, but reads and dresses him as a present-day Fifth avenue goldfish.

Metro has given the comedy splendid production, with sets and appurtenances in keeping with the supposed wealth of the main characters, and the direction is generally good. The author is credited with the personal supervision of the picture and his notions as to realism may have been responsible for the sparsity of close-ups and the overplus of long shots. But in a house the size of the Capitol, where it had its first New York showing, the action at times is so far away from the spectator as to make the scenes look like miniatures and the characters like pygmies. The lighting also was uneven, with its resultant effect on the photography.

The titles were good and the story well told, with the best part of the picture coming in during the action on the floor of the N. Y. Stock Exchange. Here the director and the junior star hit the high spots, with Buster's talent as an acrobat getting a full and legitimate play.

It is difficult to differentiate between the stars, because both were excellent in their roles. Mr. Crane, as the old Nick of Wall Street, who finds himself burdened with a mush-headed son, is a joy, and brings into his work all of his well known art as a comedian of the old school. Which does not mean that his methods are old, because they are as up-to-the-minute as those of his younger colleague. To see him on the screen is to enjoy a laugh at the expense of Father Time and his late ally, Dr. Osler. If the latter's chloroform theory had become a law, Mr. Crane would have passed out years ago via the etheric guillotine, and the picture generation would have been cheated out of a large part of its birthright.

As for Buster, a cyclone when called upon, his quiet work in this picture is a revelation. He is the personification of a mental minus sign in facial expression.

The supporting cast is acceptable, but the picture, after all, is a two-man proposition, and the fade-out which left only the stars together was the only logical finish. A novel touch has been given "The Saphead" through the introduction of the characters in silhouette, but it does not lift the production out of the fair program class.

At the Capitol the picture was introduced by a pantomimic prolog which meant little, if anything, to it.

EDUCATION OF ELIZABETH

Billie Burke is featured in this simple but interesting film story offered as a Paramount program feature. The production is away from the usual in that its unpretentious story is offered without any effort at dramatic effect, but depends upon the dainty comedy of the star. This is sufficient.

The picture demonstrates how a cleverly acted story, devoid of the sensational qualities and guiltless of anything like a sex or other lurid angle can be made into highly acceptable screen entertainment, just by its clever acting and a certain spontaneous comedy inherent in the character relations of its characters.

Miss Burke plays a "Follies" girl who is courted by the son of an aristocratic family, her entrance into the cold and formal household, there to be modelled into a worthy mate for the frigidly conventional suitor. The projection of a rough and ready chorus girl into such surroundings gives rise to countless amusing situations, all done in a spirit of high comedy and deftly played by this gracious comedienne.

She insists upon bringing with her her pet goldfish, "Mike," and when the other members of the establishment seem unsympathetic, and when she commits those unhappy faux pas which are inevitable, she always goes back to the goldfish for communion and sympathetic solace.

It chances that the suitor is called away on business, and the chorus girl learns to her astonishment that his bearded younger brother, who seemed to be absorbed in his books, is a regular human being. Whereupon the ingenious and ingenuous chorus girl transforms him into something like her ideal of a man of fashion and worldliness, beginning with a shave; contrives to alienate the affections of the elder brother, and by her own wit brings about a happy ending in her prospective marriage to the younger man.

It seems impossible that a picture utterly guiltless of a fight or a scandal could be made into a story that would interest, but the impossible has been accomplished in this case. The acting and the progress are entirely logical and natural and the settings are the same.

Certain scenes having to do with the intimacies of the "Follies" showgirls' dressing rooms have a touch of spice, but the bulk of the action takes place in the old mansion, presumably somewhere in Westchester County beyond the New York suburbs, of the blue blonde, an especially delightful background for the charming story and for Miss Burke. The old colonial interiors were splendidly suggested, and besides there were beautiful garden views and the splendid landscapes for which that section is famous.

The picture is not for the lower or medium class clientele of the fans, but a house bidding for the patronage neighborhood community would be likely to make a good impression with the feature. It is absolutely clean and thoroughly interesting in its unpretentious way. *Rush.*

THE EASY ROAD.

Leonard Fayne	Thomas Meighan
Isabel Grayce	Gladys George
Katherine Dare	Grace Goodall
Heminway	Arthur Carew
Ella Klotz	Lila Lee
Minnie Baldwin	Laura Anson
Laura	Viora Daniel

"The Easy Road" (Paramount), directed by Tom Forman and starring Thomas Meighan, is a five-reel picturization of Blair Hall's novel, "Easy Street," scenario by Beulah Marie Dix. It's a good program picture, made so principally by Mr. Meighan's screen personality and some excellent character work contributed by Lila Lee, with the story running secondary in importance to the acting.

The underlying idea is that a literary man does his best work under the spur of necessity, arising from poverty. While that has been true of many literary geniuses, it is far from a hard and fast rule. Mr. Meighan is the successful author in "The Easy Road," who marries a rich woman, and through lack of necessity to work after marriage becomes lazy with a consequent retrogression of his literary endeavors. The indolent society atmosphere in which he finds himself leads to drinking and neglect of his rich wife.

The wife, leaving her author-husband and going to Europe, gives the latter the final shove on the down grade, taking the action out of the society atmosphere and placing it in the slums. This gives opportunity for a realistically directed dance hall scene and several other atmospheric glimpses of the seamy side of life. The author (Mr. Meighan), through association with a waif (Lila Lee) whom he has rescued from drowning, when she was about to commit suicide, is awakened to his opportunities, stops drinking and pulls a "come-back" by writing the best seller of the year.

Reconciliation with the wife follows, despite the efforts of Arthur Carew, as a mild sort of dress-suited heavy, to frame the husband and win the wife away. The continuity is a bit jumpy at times, but the tale is unfolded with sufficient clarity to hold interest. Just why a good looking ingenue like Lila Lee should be cast for a character part of a near-blind girl, with heavy glasses all but disguising her, is a mystery. Despite the handicap, however, she stands out. In addition to those mentioned there are Grace Goodall, Gladys George, Laura Anson and Viora Daniel.

There are several effective night scenes in the picture, and the production end has been maintained in accordance with high class standards. The picture pleased the Sunday matinee audience at the Rivoli. *Bell.*

ROAD OF AMBITION.

Bill Mathews	Conway Tearle
Daphne Van Steer	Florence Dixon
Philip Colt	Gladden James
May Larrabee	Florence Billings
Monty Newcomb	Arthur Housman
Mr. Benson	Tom Brooks
Old Mack	Tom McGuire
Ole Olson	Adolf Milar

First rate "strong" story, with a wealth of robust action, expertly directed and interpreted by an entirely adequate cast. It bears the brand of Selznick Pictures and the direction is credited to William P. S. Earle from the story of Elaine Stern, made into a scenario by Lewis Allen Brown.

The picture has as one point of especial quality of excellence a fine contrast from its beginning in a steel mill and the environment of roughness to its later development in high society. The mill scenes have all the authenticity of an industrial subject showing the picturesque side of the steel factory and the additional value of having the drama unfold with the actual blast furnace as its background. Besides these passages have splendid photographic possibilities in light and shade. One scene deals with a thrilling hand to hand combat between the hero and a burly mill ruffian, while the heroine in her Paris frock (she is present as a sightseer) looks on in fascinated horror.

Here are many elements of drama drawn into one scene. The picturesque background, with its flaring molten metal, brilliant furnaces and black shadows, and the interesting relation of characters is the height of melodramatic action.

As the story progresses there is continuous interest in the rise of the hero from mill foreman to captain of industry and the play of character upon character as he enters society. First he becomes involved with an unscrupulous society woman, a hanger on at the fringe, and then his love affair with an aristocratic girl and his struggle to win her love. This is exceedingly well handled and its only defect is that the climax is revealed rather too far in advance. For example, there is a passage where the hero is told that the girl is at a distant hunting lodge alone with the hero's rival. The intimation is plain that the heroine has gone to the lodge purposely to keep a rendezvous, and the malicious gossip who makes the disclosure to the hero sums up the situation with, "If you have faith in her, you can prove it by not going to the lodge."

Here was a situation of capital suspense, but it was thrown away. An interested audience could have been kept at tiptoe of attention if the hero had been shown as in conflict with himself. Instead of which this element of suspense is lost when he does not hesitate, but jumps into his car and whizzes off. From that point the denouement is apparent. This, however, is a minor defect.

The picture proves the rule that the first purpose of a screen story is to sustain interest, and "The Road of Ambition" does this thoroughly.

ALL SOULS' EVE.

A Realart picture which reached Broadway not via the Rialto, Rivoli or Criterion. To the contrary its first Broadway showing was at Loew's, New York, Tuesday. In other words, it is obvious that the management of the three former theatres wouldn't risk it for a week's showing, and it is now on the Loew circuit. In consequence and in summary it is a fair program release with numerous distinguishing marks both from the standpoint of production and a cast which has been assembled to good purpose. It is in many respects a better offering than some of Realart's pictures which have endured for weekly runs; but many of its episodes are flat, uninteresting and altogether superfluous to the action.

"All Souls' Eve," is founded on the play by Anne Crawford Flexner, produced by Famous Players-Lasky at Maxine Elliott's where its run was brief. Persons familiar with the history of Famous' endeavor to enter the legit' may recall its brevity—that is of this play and the object of that concern to "control" the legit.' It is perhaps needless to add that the policy has been discarded.

The theme has been founded on the legend abounding in the phantasmagoria of superstition that the dead may visit us again if we believe firmly. It is all in the realms of fancy and possible credulity that the ensuing action may be of sufficient convincingness to interest its auditors.

The scenes calling for the character work of Lucine Littlefield might have been supplemented with more cause than a title. The work of Mr. Littlefield was overdrawn and therefore less convincing than it should have been. It is not an easy role.

The dual role of the Irish maid and the wife of the sculptor is enacted by Mary Miles Minter (the star). The parts are magnificent in their opportunity for contrast. This Miss Minter achieves with ease, as if it were effortless.

It is Carmen Phillips, as a woman of "unhallowed" passion who succeeds in attaining more convincingness than anyone else.

There has been a modification of the play as recalled in the scenario of Elmer Harris. It is not exceptional continuity which he supplies, but of a conventional and possibly a consistent order.

A g eat deal of credit must be given to the fade-in of the dancers on the cabaret-floor in which the comparison of numerous shimmyists suddenly reflect a herd of swine nudging each other in an enclosure. A few seconds interval and the fade-out again brings back in view the dancers. It was mirth provoking. *Step.*

LURE OF CROONING WATERS.

The George Clark productions will have to come better than this one if the noted English producer is to make much of a dent in the picture field here. The story is one of those old-fashioned dramas, with virtue triumphant, the type which went out with the crinoline. The heroine is one of those Salometic stage ladies who wears herself to a frazzle captivating London Johns and is sent to a rustic retreat, "Crooning Waters," to recover. But she vamps the lummux of a farmer at whose house she is staying, with the result another happy home is knocked for three bases.

Then she goes back to the city and Mr. Boob follows her, dressed just as he was when he was feeding the pigs on the farm. He tries to see the lady in her dressing room, but fails, so he trails her to a glittering devils' nest of a cafe. The heart destroyer gives him the air. He goes back to the wife and kiddies. Later the stage lady's doctor shows her a letter from Boob telling him his wife doesn't love him any more because he had gated her and the bairns for the plumed lure, so plumed lure beats it to the farm. She proves she is a real woman by staying up all night with a sick child, and this, for some reason, convinces Boob there is no place like home and nothing better than a good wife.

Guy Newall, who wrote the scenario, plays the farmer, and Ivy Duke the vamp. The former worked so slow he seemed becalmed. Miss Duke worked so fast it's no wonder she had the city and country vote counted before the polls closed. She is a most attractive English type and unsheathes a wicked calf at frequent intervals. There were some pretty instances of photography, especially the exteriors down on the farm. But the direction of the players was anything except smooth.

The picture is mediocre neighborhood stuff, a Stoll-Pathe release.

GIRL OF MY HEART.

Even the Fox people are experimenting with "mental science" these days. They have produced "Girl of My Heart," adapted from a story called "Joan of Rainbow Springs." It was put into scenario form by Frances Marion Mitchell and directed by Edw. J. LeSaint. Shirley Mason is starred.

The last male survivor of an aristocratic Southern family of musicians is told by his doctor that his only chance to live is to give up fiddling and go West. He places revolver on table, takes up his violin and plays "Good-bye." Having finished, places revolver to his head to kill himself when he is interrupted by orphan girl who had been "farmed out" and ran away from her cruel mistress.

Girl tells him that "love and faith meet every human need"—he adopts her—they go West, and after a series of incidents with a hermit the inevitable "struggle for honor" scene that seems to be so essential in all Fox pictures, and so on, the young man's health is restored and the girl says "yes."

An average Fox program release.

Jolo.

THE GREATEST LOVE.

Mrs. Lantini	Vera Gordon
Mr. Lantini	Bertram Marburgh
Francesca Lantini	Yvonne Shelton
Lorenzo Lantini	Hugh Huntley
Mr. Manton	William H. Tooker
Dorothy Manton	Ray Dean
Richard Sewell	Donald Hall
Mrs. Sewell	Sally Crute
Mrs. Murphy	Jessie Simpson

As a delineator of maternal emotion Vera Gordon stands pre-eminent. Having convinced the public of this in "Humoresque," Mrs. Gordon undertakes to duplicate the success with "The Greatest Love," a Selznick production, scenario by Edward J. Montagne, directed by Henry Kolker. Its principal fault, if such it can be called, is the length—six reels—which piles on the harrowing "emoting" of the star to unnecessary footage.

It is also possible the photoplay was "shot" for a Jewish characterization, and later the sub-titles were changed to make the star's role that of an Italian woman. This impression is gleaned from the absence of anything resembling a crucifix, the Virgin Mary or chromo of Garibaldi on the walls of the rooms in which she and her family reside on the east side. The atmospheric detail of a dance in the steerage on the boat in which the family comes to America is palpably Russian, which is one more basis for the impression.

All of which is of little consequence. The story is commercially artistic; that is to say, it has the elements that go to make for success in photoplay presentation. The star will live up to exploitation of the proper sort. She has the gift of bubbling over with maternial emotion and is given ample opportunity to do so in this picture. There is situation after situation of elemental melodrama, all calculated to indicate the torrential mother-love welling within the star's ample bosom.

A rather brilliant cast of players was recruited to support Mrs. Gordon, with an especial individual utterance of praise for Yvonne Shelton as the daughter who has been betrayed by the villain and indicates it without resorting to vulgar and unnecessary details.

To the public in general there is suspense, and the denouement comes to them as an unlooked-for surprise. "The Greatest Love" looks like a sure bet.

Jolo.

OLD SWIMMIN' HOLE.

Ezra	Charles Ray
His Pa	James Gordon
His Ma	Blanche Rose
Myrtle	Laura La Plante
Esther	Marjorie Prevost
Skinny	Lincoln Stedman
School Master	Lon Poff

For years the film psychologists—principally those abroad—have claimed the day would come when it was possible to project a full-length feature upon the screen without the aid of subtitles. The forthcoming Charles Ray release by First National, a film adaptation of James Whitcomb Riley's poem, "The Old Swimmin' Hole," is making the experiment, and the outcome should be watched with great interest. In some respects it is hardly a fair test, inasmuch as there is little or no story to the picture, merely a series of incidents in the life of a bucolic youth.

Ray plays a healthy, mischevious country boy, who is not much of a student at the local school house, and makes sheep's eyes at Myrtle, who is in the same school room and is an instinctive "vamp." He, in turn, is loved by Esther, but doesn't give her a tumble until he loses out with Myrtle, when he realizes Esther is a nice girl—especially as she shares her picnic basket with him, which aids materially in healing the heart wound left by the defection.

That's about all there is of plot—the remainder occupied with the pranks of a bunch of school boys and school girls.

It isn't necessary to employ subtitles to show a boy smoking his father's pipe and the ill result therefrom. Half a dozen still photographs would accomplish this.

The proposition, therefore, is producing pictures and showing them without the assistance of subtitles, remains unsolved, and if we never arrive at such a point in motion photography, we are at least moving closer and closer to it.

In most respects Ray is an ideal type of country bumpkin, depicting to a nicety the sincerity of youth and unsophisticatedness. His principal foil once more is Lincoln Stedman, the "fat boy" called "Skinny," and the remainder of the cast are carefully selected for character delineation.

Joseph de Grasse employed care and intelligence in the direction, and the production is mostly outdoor and relatively inexpensive.

Jolo.

BLACK BEAUTY.

Jessie Gordon	Jean Paige
Harry Blomefield	James Morrison
Jack Beckett	George Webb
Derby Ghost	Bobby Mack
Squire Gordon	John Steppling
Lady Wynwaring	Adele Farrington
John Manly	Charles Morrison
Black Beauty	Himself
Mrs. Gordon	Mollie McConnell

Vitagraph has done a novel and honest job with this story book classic, and if the Strand audience may be taken as a criterion every kid in the country will see the production before it has run its course. It deserves returns because the company spared no expense in making this a spectacular and thrilling attraction.

Stating frankly in its opening title the story of "Black Beauty," the autobiography of a horse, was insufficient, a romance has been skillfully fitted to the original and more skillfully presented on the screen. The production is two stories in one. Whenever the human element is introduced a curtain is lifted showing what is happening within walls while Black Beauty is living his own life afield. The effect of the curtain separating the two narratives is a clever thought, and craftmanship of high degree is displayed in the perfect blending of action in the two stories.

David Smith, brother of the Vitagraph company's president, directed the production and has done one of the finest things of his career. He is a man who seems to measure up to big pictures, though in lesser ones his results are negligible. Also, where animals are involved as in this and some older ones like "God's Country and the Woman" and "The Son of Kazan," he is always at his best. Here, he not only has handled his animals with exceeding intelligence, but maintained a smoothness in lighting, photography and continuity of action that is commendable. The tempo slows up in spots, perhaps due to the original story, which necessarily lags in the telling.

Jean Paige is pretty and appealing in a role that seems to have been inspired for her and, while Albert E. Smith gained a lovely wife by marrying her, Vitagraph is going to lose one of its potential assets if she retires. Miss Paige is only a young girl, and she has not had any the best of it during her brief screen career because she is an ethereal being who does not fit, temperamentally or physically, into harsh roles. Presenting her in characters similar to the one she portrays here, with stories suited to her, would be beneficial to the screen as a whole and profitable to Vitagraph as a company.

James Morrison, George Webb and Bobby Mack stand out in the cast supporting Miss Paige, and a refined and convincing portrayal was given by Mollie McConnell, who died shortly after finishing her work in it. Mollie, who was the widow of Will McConnell, was a beautiful woman in her youth and made probably the most beautiful grande dame on the screen.

While the story of "Black Beauty" is known to everyone who reads—and probably is fresher in the minds of the juvenile picture-goers than those of their elders—the treatment given it here is one that will appeal to all classes. Smith, in addition to telling his stories well, has given the picture some highlights, such as the big fox chase and the race between the villain and the hero (mounted on Black Beauty) that will compare with the big things of the screen.

"Black Beauty" will stand up with the best as an attraction.

STRAIGHT IS THE WAY.

"Cat" Carter, a young crook	Matt Moore
Aunt Mehitabel, a widow	Mabel Bert
Dorcas, her niece	Gladys Leslie
"Loot" Follett, a crook	George Parsons
Johnathan Squoggs	Henry Sedley
Constable Whipple	Van Dyke Brooks
Mrs. Crabtree	Emily Fitzroy
Bobby	Peggy Parr

Featuring Matt Moore and Gladys Leslie, "Straight Is the Way" (Cosmopolitan-Paramount), though erected on a slim and light story, comes out at the finish as a rather valuable laugh maker for a regular program release, unbilled as to its comedy angle. The snow-bound Sunday afternoon audience at the Rivoli, a small attendance through the sudden blizzard, was quickly thawed by some of the situations, with the biggest laugh centering around the use of an Ouija board.

The titling forced itself into the laughs. Captions were of a flippant variety and timed exactly to send the laugh along. Perhaps Frances Marion, who wrote the scenario, added the titles, though the program doesn't say so. One caption showed conclusively someone of experience had written them, though that particular caption sailed over the Rivoli's heads. It was about an antique store, very nicely set, and said the proprietors were in league with the best burglars of the world.

"Straight Is the Way," called in fildom a crook story, was adapted from the book, "The Manifestations of Henry Orth" by Ethel Watts Mumford. Robert G. Vignola gave it an attractive direction, calling for no intricate manipulation, with most of the scenes laid in a rural district.

The bucolic style of gowning was becoming to Gladys Leslie. She looked pretty and normal, helping her grandmother to defeat a rapacious holder of the mortgage on the old homestead. It sounded a bit wabbly when this mortgage thing started in, but Mr. Moore and George Parsons as the crooks, with the aid of the Ouija board, went to the rescue in a series of scenes that gave the spiritual board quite a little panning in a subtle way. Mabel Bert is the lovable aged grandmother, who turns to the supernatural to learn what "Uncle Henry" did with his money, before he died.

In these days a straight film release that can garner legitimate laughs should be worth going after. "Straight Is the Way," no matter what else it may do, will at least put any audience in a pleasurable frame of mind.

Simc.

RED FOAM.

Mrs. Andy Freeman	Zena Keefe
Arnold Driscoll	Huntley Gordon
Andy Freeman	Harry Tighe
Sheriff	Daniel Hays

Mrs. Murphy ....Peggy Worth
Matt Murphy ....Johnny Butler

All of us are good for something, some of us for many things, but it remained for Harry Tighe, erstwhile piano player, vaudevillian and musical comedy comedian, to register one of the genuinely "truc-to-life" characterizations of the season on the film. It is that of a blustering, back-slapping traveling salesman, the kind who tells suggestive jokes, buys the 'rst round of drinks ostentatiously, prates about how happy "the little wife" is at home, popular with "the boys," and usually a hit with the cheaper class of women—in short, a four-flusher, always making a grand stand play and without an ounce of sincerity.

Such is the role of the "heavy" in the Ralph Ince production presented by Lewis J. Selznick, entitled "Red Foam," from a story by William H. Hamby, picturized by Edward J. Montagne. All of the types are well selected for the story, an unconventional one about ordinary people—or at least people who would be normal human beings under ordinary circumstances.

Through a curious chain of happenings a young man and woman are facing death by lynching at the hands of a mob of infuriated inhabitants of a small town, believing they committed a murder. . How they got into the mess and finally escaped being strung up through the aid of a "surprise" twist, makes for a very interesting plot.

It is a fast moving rural tale. The picture is brilliantly cut as well as directed.

But of all things see the Tighe performance; it is well worth while.
Jolo.

THE FIRE CAT.

Dulce ....Edith Roberts
Gringo Burke ....Walter Long
Cholo Pete ....William Eagle Eye
Mother Alvarez ....Olga D. Mojean
Margarita ....Beatriz Dominguez
Pancho ....Arthur Jasmine
Ross ....Wallace McDonald

Universal five-part production, direction and story by Norman Dawn. Designed as a "romantic" tale of the Incas, it develops into a hidge-podge of bewildering zoological exhibits calculated to give the spectator delirium tremens without the aid of "hootch."

Dulce's mother has been murdered by a couple of bandits, and she, being a "fire cat," with a masquerade costume, swears vengeance. She goes to work as a dancer in a "dive" until she unearths the villain—and incidentally finds a lover —and then volcanic eruptions on the "cloud-kissed Andean plateaus."

There is an abundance of "cloud-kissed" subtitles intermixed with atmospheric scenes in the Andes Mountains, a number of exteriors "shot" in the night, and for good measure there is thrown in pictures of lizards, ant eaters, etc.

The whole thing, story, photography, action, animal exhibit, volcano eruptions, etc., are all jumbled into a heterogeneous mass of nothingness that would be annoying if it were not so ludicrous. *Jolo.*

MARRIAGE OF WM. ASHE.

Metro has done the best it could with "The Marriage of William Ashe," but the story which added lustre to the reputation of Mrs. Humphrey Ward as a novelist has not enough body to it to make it stand up on the screen. Edward Sloman, the director, has made up in production for a great deal that is lacking in the narrative, and this, with the fetching work of Miss Allison and a capable supporting company, will make it a pleasing program picture. But it is not a classic, and here Metro's brand is a misnomer. It will fit well into better class houses, but the bill will have to contain strong comedy or other features to support it.

In the main, Sloman has done well from a technical standpoint, but he gives the star some very bad lighting in many places, the rays being so strong in some spots as to make her actually ugly, while in others it is "o flat as to give her a vacuous look. His interiors are very good and so are most of his exteriors, though the Venetian canal shots are uneven.

Miss Allison is convincing as Lady Kitty and makes a gorgeous, if sensational, picture where she rides as Lady Godiva. And, for the benefit of the ultramarine filberts who regard feminine flesh as a horrible and disgraceful mistake which must be hidden, let it be said the graceful limbs of the star are a work of art, presented in a way that precludes censorial indictment.

Next to Miss Allison, the best contribution is by the veteran, Lydia Yeamans Titus. She is the most convincing member of the cast. Standing's English reserve fits well here.

THE SNOB.

Kathryn Haynes ....Wanda Hawley
Jim Haynes ....Edwin Stevens
Pud Welland ....Walter Hiers
Mrs. Haynes ....Sylvia Ashton
Capt. Bill Putnam ....Wm. E. Lawrence
Betty Welland ....Julia Faye
"Pep" Kennedy ....Richard Wayne

Elimination of a few hundred feet of needless bromidic sub-titles and extended still close-ups of the star would hav' made this Realart comedy drama one of real merit. The story is good, the star attractive, the direction acceptable and the acting generally fair, but too many titles take the edge off the production and slow it down.

The best work in the picture, not excluding that of the star, is done by Walter Hiers, and what little is permitted to Edwin Stevens, sterling actor that he is, is well done. Why a man like Stevens should be wasted in "bits" is beyond comprehension.

Sam Woods, who directed, brings his story out consecutively and has made a really sparkling comedy of the college type, but those inane titles, explaining and spoiling action which is perfectly clear to the audience, rob him of credit for skillful story telling. Woods has obtained attractive locations and fine lightings, has dressed his sets and his people with tastefulness, but he falters where he keeps his star in motionless clo.e-ups for periods which seem almost interminable.

The picture will please, but it also will tire audiences in its present form.

SHE COULDN'T HELP IT.

Nance Olden....................Bebe Daniels
William Latimer............Emory Johnson
Tom Dorgan.................Wade Boteler
Mother Hogan................Vera Lewis
Bishop Van Wagenen.....Herbert Standing
Mr. Ramsey.............Z. Wall Covington
His Wife...................Helen Raymond
Nellie Ramsey............Ruth Renick
Mag Monahan................Gertrude Short

This Realart is presented as "a new version" of "In the Bishop's Carriage," which in book form and on the stage scored as a neat comedy drama. As done on the screen it is piffle and a horrible example of what producers expect the public to stand for. The production, if such it can be called, is cheaply done, with the direction of a style which prevailed before the five-reel feature days.

That "new version" confession gives the producers an alibi for getting as far away from the original story as possible, but it does not excuse the antiquated, stereotyped structure that was permitted to find its way to a house of the standing of the Rialto. Nor is it fair to put a young star like Bebe Daniels into such a rickety vehicle at this stage of her bid for a place at the top. She may or may not have star qualities, but the answer will never be found in this picture, and unless Realart takes the trouble to find better stories and a real director for her a weary public will not wait.

There is nothing, technically or otherwise, to justify this film's presentation in a theatre charging 85 cents admission. With the exception of Herbert Standing and a little girl, Gertrude Short, who only has a bit, the work of the star and her support is stilted and unconvincing. Many of the sets are tawdry and there is no attempt at lighting or photographic excellence.

"WITCHING HOUR"

Jack Brookfield...........Elliott Dexter
Judge Prentice.............Winter Hall
Viola Campbell...........Ruth Renick
Frank Hardmuth...........Robert Cain
Clay Whipple...........Edward Sutherland
Helen Whipple.................Mary Alden
Lew Ellinger.................Fred Turner
Mrs. Campbell...........Genevieve Blinn
Tom Denning.............Charles West
Judge Henderson.............L. M. Wells
Colonel Bailey...........Clarence Geldart
Harvey....................Jim Blackwell

The William D. Taylor production of Augustus Thomas' play presented by Jesse Lasky via Paramount is not an especially happy translation from stage to screen. It is current this week at the Rialto. It is a painstaking effort in adaptation and as far as it closely follows the spoken play is understandable. But when the translator tries to interpolate touches of characteristic film comedy the effect is not good.

The play managed to cover up the newspaper exposure of the vengeful district attorney by Brookfield without going into details, but the screen must be very literal about it, filming the very newspaper text, headline and all. The newspaper that printed such an item as the one Mr. Taylor shows would have its editor in jail in half an hour, and the man who wrote the headline would have been fired "pronto" or sooner. Mr. Thomas used to be a practical newspaper man in New York. He never would have allowed such a faux pas. However, that's but a trifling detail.

More serious was the interpolated bit of having Lew Ellinger, presumably a person of some rank in the community and a white man, engage in a game of craps with a group of darky boy ragamuffins. The film people seem to be held in no restraint by any laws of probabilities. The crap incident struck someone as a comedy point and they went to it without reserve of good sense or good taste.

The story doesn't lend itself to picturization anyhow. There is too much explaining to do. That was a defect in the play. It was all argument and not much action as it was played on the stage, even with all the aids of dialogue. On the screen the task of covering the abstract subject of "mental telepathy" upon which the whole tale hangs is beyond the power of printed titles, be they ever so skilfully devised. It took all the art of Thomas, who had dramatic technique at his finger ends, to reconcile so intangible a theory to stage expression.

Without the illusion of living, speaking actors the screen story is not convincing, although the players who interpret the screen version are uncommonly sincere and genuine. Elliott Dexter was especially fitted to play the picturesque gambler, Jack Brookfield. It gave him opportunity for portraying a clear cut, intellectual hero, for which he is equipped in appearance, and a certain quiet dignity of method.

Winter Hall, as Judge Prentice, gave the part the nice touch of distinction in just the right shade of natural poise and forcefulness. The character stood out clearly, the actor was concealed. Few screen players have the nice judgment to get this effect.. Ruth Renick was a pretty heroine, therein fulfilling her entire obligation. Clay and Hardmuth were picked with a sure eye. The latter is an unsympathetic role and Robert Cain drew it appropriately. Clay, in the hands of Edward Sutherland, was perhaps a little too much the immature weakling, but probably that was the effect aimed at.

Added to the crap game and the newspaper passages, the filming of a negro cakewalk scarcely seemed to be in the atmosphere of the story, given as it was with such strong emphasis. Here again the dir tor was led astray in his effort to ject comedy interludes in a story which should not for a moment be permitted to relax in its tension. They had much better have stuck to the Thomas text. That at least had consistent dramatic values, whatever may be said for its plausibility, a subject that provoked wide debate when it was presented more than a decade ago on Broadway. In a faultless stage presentation the story was not too convincing. As a silent drama it is doubly hard to swallow.

Rush.

THE CONCERT

Augustus....................Lewis S. Stone
Mary, his wife............Myrtle Steadman
Dr. Hart..................Raymond Hatton
Delphine, his wife....Mabel Julienne Scott
Eva.......................Gertrude Astor
Poilinger.......................Russ Powell
Mrs. Pollinger.........Lydia Yeamans Titus

"The Concert" is a Goldwyn product, last week's feature at the Capitol. It is a debased version of the stage play of the same name done in a dainty spirit of high comedy by Leo Ditrichstein as a vehicle in the theatre of spoken plays, but here degraded to the cheapest sort of suggestiveness to catch the neighborhood "shock absorbers."

The scenes are bad enough and the coarse displays of undressed women worse, but the titles have disagreeable quality of "smart" cynicism that is utterly degrading. Nobody appears to have told the producer that there are censorship measures pending in 36 legislatures in the United States.

A sample of titling in this gem (which deals with the attitude of the girl who is about to write an anonymous letter to an injured husband): "None are so moral as those who are prevented from being immoral." That sweet sentiment is repeated a score of times. Spoken on the stage with all the palliating circumstances of shaded voice inflection and gesture these things might be endurable, but in staring print they have no excuse.

The whole thing bears the same resemblance to the play as would a deft French innuendo, translated into Ninth avenue barroom vernacular. This is not reading an evil meaning into what might have been intended as a mere comedy entanglement. The man who made the picture read the nasty slant into the story that could easily have been told without offense. That bathroom episode proves the purpose of the whole wretched affair. The woman had written a note informing the supposedly wronged husband that his wife had fled with the musician.

In the morning she (the writer) became frightened at the possible consequences of her act, but this thought did not strike her until she was in her bath tub. And the incident is shown with all the literalness of a plump young woman in a bath tub. What the director or scenario writer or whoever was responsible for the picture wanted was not a scene to make clear the essential fact that the girl regretted writing the letter. What he wanted was a startling revelation of a woman taking a bath, and that's what he got with all it implies. The intent is the whole point.

It is the same in the scene at the log cabin in the woods where the musician and the flirtatious wife make their rendezvous. The wife goes into the bedroom to change her clothes. Such a detail might have been managed with seemliness, but instead the thing is done with a wealth of detail and elaboration of lingerie that is all to the Polly Hyman. The figures on the screen made the situation sizzle sufficiently, but the leering inference bluntly emphasized by those nasty, cross-eyed titles were insufferable.

It was plenty bad enough to offer a picture which degraded practically every woman in it without adding those printed aggravations.

The picture is riddled with faulty direction. The only man in the story drawn as a real human being is a scientist. Imagine a scientist who wears a Norfolk jacket and belted in the back and wears it in his study. Raymond Hatton played the part of Dr. Hart. He was supposed to be a smooth, clever intriguer. The best he succeeded in getting over was an impression of being boisterously "fresh."

Rush

GUILE OF WOMEN.

Yal............................Will Rogers
Hulda..........................Mary Warren
Skole...........................Bert Sprotte
Armstrong....................Lionel Belmore
Captain Larsen.............Charles A. Smily
Captain Stahl.....................Nick Cogley
Annie............................Doris Pawn

Will Rogers in the role of a Swede sailorman is a long leap from the cow range, but he gets away with it in splendid style in this Goldwyn production, given its first New York showing at the Capitol this week. The story, written by Peter Clark MacFarlane, has real humor in it, together with a bit of pathos, and a surprise ending. Clarence Badger has done a creditable piece of work in its direction and, with actual locations in Frisco, where the action occurs, has been able to provide some very interesting shots.

While Rogers is the star of the picture, and all honors are due him, the story actually centers around the herone, and Mary Warren, a beautiful girl and an unusually intelligent actress, all but steals it away from the comedian. This is no reflection on Rogers, because he gets every ounce of value out of his part and is especially effective in the close-ups, where his facial expressions register strongly. Next to Miss Warren the best results attained by the supporting players are those of Bert Sprotte and Doris Pawn. The others are simply in the picture.

The story opens with Yal leaving Hulda and sailing for America to make his fortune. Later it is learned he has sent her $1,000 to come to him. But five years pass and he hears nothing from her. Meantime he has found another girl, Annie, and opens a delicatessen store with savings of $3,000, putting her in charge. When he seeks to draw it out and invest in a ship she laughs at him and, as he has nothing to show he ever had invested in the store, it is a dead loss. He becomes mistrustful of women. Then one day he sees Hulda on the waterfront. Between his love for the girl and his fear of women's guile he is in a quandary. But he surrenders to love. Hulda is living at the home of Captain Larsen, ship owner, but pretends to Yal she is a servant. When Yal has saved sufficient money to furnish a home they get ready to wed. But on his wedding eve he is shanghaled by hirelings of Armstrong, secretary of the late Captain Larsen.

Yal dives off the ship into San Francisco Bay, gets aboard a fishing boat and arrives back in town in time to be married. He is a barefoot bridegroom. Subsequently Armstrong's duplicity is revealed and Hulda, whom Yal believed to be double-crossing him, confesses she has been made sole heir to the estate of Larsen.

The interest in the story is well sustained and the narrative well told.

OFFSHORE PIRATE.

Ardita Farnam.................Viola Dana
Toby Moreland..................Jack Mulhall
Uncle John Farnam........Edward Jobson
Ivan Nevkova..................Edward Cecil

"The Offshore Pirate" will not be set down as one of Viola Dana's best, although it is an adaptation of a "Saturday Evening Post" story written by F. Scott Fitzgerald. The director, Dallas M. Fitzgerald, has tried to do something with it, but the story is too frivously fragile for a five-reel production.

It is one of those hidden identity yarns—hero posing as a daring criminal in order to win heroine—which was done so strikingly well in "The Mark of Zorro." There real purpose motivated, but here the author has only a "cute" piece of fluff.

Miss Dana is pretty and vivacious, wears some nice fluffy dresses and is stunning in her close-ups. Jack Mulhall is an agreeable hero.

The director has done well with his lightings and composition, but the outstanding feature of the film, all things considered, is the snappy style of title used. These may have been used to save the picture, but there was not enough solid matter involved to make the attempt rescue a worth-while undertaking.

The best portions of the picture are those where six black aces, first introduced as jazz band players, appear aboard the yacht of the heroine and, after some rough battling, engage the white sailors in a contest of skill with "Mississippi marbles." This crap game, in its variations, is good.

GIRLS DON'T GAMBLE

This is one of three of D. N. Schwab productions, made independently, by and with David Butler as the star. It has been sold independently throughout the country, and in New York is released through First National.

As a Loew's New York audience received it, there were evidently manifestations of pleasure in its more humorous passages, but the story is scarcely one of the pictures whose material has the requirements of lasting through five reels.

The plot is adapted from a Saturday Evening Post story, "Girls Don't Gamble Any More." The hero, with a penchant for machinery, leaves home, enters the employ of a department store as a chauffeur, comes in contact with a Cinderella-type of maiden, is "framed" by co-workers, foils them after they rob his ex-employer's department store, and receives the blessing of all.

The direction of Fred J. Butler is consistent and gives his namesake every opportunity to register. A stirring fight scene in the final episodes is the most salient point in action. The comedy between Harry Dodd and Butler in the second and third reel registered effectively. The cast is not distinguished except for Elinor Field as the demure, kitten-like sweetheart, and Elsie Bishop in a bit in the first reel. Rhea Haines, Alice Knowlton, Margaret Joslyn, Elmer Dewey, Rex Zane and Jack Cosgrave complete the cast.

A flash is given of "The Restless Sex," with a close-up of the title and magazine, just why is hard to explain.

The production in its entirety does not represent a large investment. The photography is excellent on long shots of rustic scenery.

A satisfying picture in the neighborhood houses.

Step.

WOMAN IN HIS HOUSE

Los Angeles, March 3.

Hilda...........................Mildred Harris
Sigurd.........................Gareth Hughes
Andrew Martin..................Winter Hall
Dr. Philip Emerson......Ramsey Wallace
Peter Marvin.............Thomas Holding
Bob Livingston............George Fischer
Baby.......................Richard Hedrick

For more than a year the Louis B. Mayer partizans, both salaried and otherwise, have been doing advance work for "The Woman in His House," stating that the picture was destined to be one of the greatest ever screened. It is the current attraction at the Mission here and on the night that it was reviewed there were any number of seats available, but there was a line held out of doors to give the impression that business was a turnaway. It wasn't, however, and it is doubtful if the picture will ever achieve that distinction, but it is nevertheless a good production that is capable of attracting business and entertaining in the first run houses. It is not by the widest stretch of the imagination a picture that will go in for a run.

John M. Stahl is credited with the directing of the production and the story is the work of Frances Irene Reels.

Its greatest asset is the work of and the sympathy that is attracted to Richard Hedrick, the little kiddie about whom the plot of the piece revolves.

Miss Harris plays the role of a sea coast maiden who is wooed and won by a famous physician. After they are wed she becomes "the woman in his house," the doctor becoming wrapped up in research work. A child is born to them, and when it is about four years old there is an epidemic of infantile paralyses. The doctor throws his heart and soul into the work of fighting the plague, and while working on a charity case his own child is stricken. On his return home he hurries into the sick room just as another physician pronounces the child dead.

The wife collapses, and then it is discovered that the child still lives, although there are indications that it will be a helpless cripple. The doctor decides not to inform his wife that the little one is alive until such time that he has restored it to complete health. While he is trying to achieve this the wife is drifting from him. There is a mutual friend who steps in at the opportune moment and saves her from falling victim to the villain, and as he has just been appraised of the fact that the child is still alive, he takes her home and into the rooms that have been set aside for the little invalid. Here mother love achieves what science has failed to accomplish and the child rises from its chair and walks.

There is an underlying current in the story that seems to shoot at a mental science target but somehow falls short. At one place in the picture there is a reflection on the wall that is supposed to represent the crucifix, and a mother, after making an appeal to the doctor to save her baby, because she knows he is the only one that can do it, has her attention directed to the cross and she offers a prayer, after which the child begins to get well. This touch and the later one of the crippled child walking both suggest faith healing.

Miss Harris is doing by far her best work of recent pictures in this production, but Gareth Hughes, in a character role of a crippled half-wit, and the kiddie run away with the acting honors. Ramsey Wallace as the husband and Thomas Holding as the family friend both gave studied performances that were acceptable from all angles, but George Fischer as the heavy did not seem to strike the proper note, either in his performance or in his manner of dressing the part. In a business suit he actually appeared slovenly, so ill fitting was the costume that he affected. There are technical touches that are not authentic. One showing the main dining room of the Hotel Ritz in New York, makes it possible to see the street and the crowds passing there on New Year's eve. If that many people ever got over on Madison avenue on that night it would have to be a fire to attract them. By the by, it is also the first time that the reviewer ever knew that one could see the street from the Ritz dining room, and also that the hotel management would keep the windows uncurtained in such manner as they were in the picture.

But other than that Mr. Stahl has done his work real well and there are but one or two other minor defects that can be easily remedied. They are principally titles.   *Fred.*

"MAKING GOOD."

Syracuse, March 2.

Created for the purpose of arousing interest in prison reform, to give the underdog a chance, Thomas Mott Osborne, distinguished "reform warden" of Sing Sing and commander of Portsmouth Naval Prison, has produced a wonderfully gripping film story in "Making Good."

The picture was given a first showing in Mr. Osborne's home city, Auburn, N. Y., two weeks ago, but made its first commercial appearance in Syracuse for a week's run at the Welting, February 23.

The scenario was written by Basil Dicky and produced under the personal supervision of Mr. Osborne and Edward H. McManus of the staff of Collier's Weekly.

Penal institutions, prison life and the heart throbs and the emotions that surround them have not been overlooked by producers. They have been woven in many screen dramas, but the "reform warden" has really given filmdom something new. He has drawn upon his years of study of prison life, analyzed as warden of two great prisons and as "Tom Brown," convict, in giving the outside world not merely an interesting picture, but food for study.

Filmed for the most part behind prison walls it is true to life there. He has insisted on accuracy of detail—from his point of view.

The story deals with two opposite types, the slum born and one born in the lap of luxury whose roads converge at the prison gate—and make them equal stone breakers. These characters, too, are true to life. They are types that Mr. Osborne has learned to know intimately, the rich man's son sowing wild oats, the low born son who was pushed into a life of crime, but both with the inborn germ of righteousness waiting to be brought to the surface to grow in the light of right living and right seeing.

The picture shows the old prison system with zebra uniforms, lock step, its solitary bread and water confinement and the nine-tail lash, the ball and chain and brutal guards. The double cross and counter double cross, subterfuge and intrigue back of the walls.

Then the new era, the Osborne way. The Mutual Welfare League and the honor system, the rebuilding of life's derelicts, salvaging the human wrecks, all in a gripping story.

So much for Mr. Osborne's picture and his sincerity, but beneath it all lies the great question, will it serve the purpose of its creation in the right way?

Already many students of criminology and punishment are questioning whether it will make for good. They declare that it is overdrawn, that it pictures the ideal, but fails to picture results as they work out in practice. Will the picture, playing upon the emotions of the public, give the right impression or build up a false state of mind regarding the nation's penal institutions? These students admit that the Osborne system has worked for

good in some respects and that it has its good points, in others it has failed. Escapes have been numerous. The beating of guards, yes, even their murder, has grown and is growing under the system which has tied the hands of prison officials to a great extent in dealing with cases where strict discipline is the only measure, they claim.

One sub-title of the picture perhaps explains the objections of those who see possible harm in "Making Good" as well as anything. The hero, returning to prison to find the new system installed, remarks: "It don't seem like being in prison."
                          Fahn.

THE CHEATER REFORMED.

Jordan McCall............William Russell
Dr. Luther McCall.........William Russell
Carol McCall................Seena Owen
"Buster" Dorsey..........Jack Brammall
Thomas Edinburgh.........Sam De Grasse
Mrs. Edinburgh.............Ruth King

This newest William Russell starring feature (Fox) has him doubling. This is about the salient point to this picture—its acting by Russell in widely contrasting parts; that of a rector and his twin brother, holdup man. The enactment of the two parts by the same man registers greater interest than the exaggerated story furnished by Julius G. Furthman. Scott Dunlap was director.

The photoplay belongs to that type of picture which has emanated from the Fox studios. The fault with the preceding pictures is similarly found in "The Cheater Reformed." It is a hurry-up job. No great care has been given to detail. Sequences in this scenario occur in many instances without sufficient preparation and here is an abundance of immaterial episodes which could easily have been eliminated. There is a tendency to clog up the action. In titles there are enough to make one forget that action is essential in pictures. The picture as a whole becomes so awkward that the characters who start out with lifelike semblance become vague and phantomlike.

The story could never stand the application of reason. Or at any rate in its present form it is barren of logic. The rector of a one-man-run-town is conveniently killed for a twin brother, a crook who steps into the shoes of the rector. The usurper after an ostensible convalescence finally reaches the point where he delivers his first sermon. Here the author asks the audience to believe that the departed brother's inspiring influence is sufficient to maintain the place he assumed. Moreover it does not occur to the authors that the departed rector's wife can be taken into the conspiracy as easily as the picture would have it. Conveniently no mention is made of this, but the authors ask the audience to swallow too much. The wife goes on believing that the twin brother is her husband. The picture goes on to show the crook's surrender to conscience and self-sacrifice, so that he exposes the "boss" of the town, in return is exposed by the former, but is forgiven by the community as well as his sister-in-law.

The acting is not of a high order in any case. Seena Owen neither in appearance or manner represents the appropriate type. A bit handled by Jack Brammall has some good points in character work. The photography is only fair. The interior and exterior are fair, but not strikingly artistic.   *Step.*

WHAT EVERY WOMAN KNOWS.

Maggie Wylie..............Lois Wilson
John Shand................Conrad Nagel
Alick Wylie...............Charles Ogle
David Wylie...............Fred Huntly
James Wylie...............Guy Oliver
Charles Venables..........Winter Hall
Sybil Tenterden...........Lillian Tucker

Comtesse de la Briere......Claire McDowell
Scotch lawyer..............Robert Brower

William De Mille's production of Sir James M. Barrie's "What Every Woman Knows," at the Rivoli, attracted interest by reason of its having been one of the truly great stage productions which Maude Adams made famous.

It is one of the best pictures directed by William de Mille, and proved itself delightful for the many ingredients of Barrieism which it disclosed in text and denouement. It follows the stage play closely.

It is likely that a younger generation will see "What Every Woman Knows" as a picture, although there will be a sprinkling — plentiful at that—of those who remember the legitimate version of the play. The distinct feature of the picture is that although it is based on a great play it stands up as a picture regardless of its stage fame. Unlike "The Admirable Crichton," Barrie's "What Every Woman Knows" has no twisted continuity or a remake into something "modern." Barrie in this latter picture is undiluted Barrie. His text is used freely and with discretion, and in not a single instance is it misapplied. It retains, therefore, a great deal of its original flavor, and that is very satisfactory.

"What Every Woman Knows" finds a new starring combination in Conrad Nagel and Lois Wilson. They are capital in their roles, and it is difficult to assign the major part of the credit to either one. It seems that both are in the foreground with equal number of opportunities, and both take advantage of skillful direction. It is all character work, and the Maggie of Miss Wilson stands out boldly for its repression and modesty to the pomposity of John Shand, played by Nagel. There is, in fact, so much that is delightful in their performance that when an element of shallowness in the work of the supporting cast asserts itself the duo (Nagel-Wilson) immediately lift the tempo.

A singular fact about this picture from the standpoint of continuity asserts itself in the instance that there are no big climaxes to be registered.

Olga Printzlau is the continuity writer on this occasion. The opening scenes depicting John Shand prior to his surreptitious entrance into the Wiley household could easily have been enacted with greater emphasis. A note of suspense, it seems, could have been registered.

In casting Mr. De Mille (assuming that he did cast) does not select his character for their true import and relationship to English society. In the case of Miss Tucker as Sybil better judgment might have been exercised. A type more distinct than hers was essential, it seems, to convey the reason for Shand's folly. The three Wylies, played respectively by Messrs. Ogle, Huntly and Oliver, were in substantial hands.

The art direction of Wilferd Buckland shows the latter's skill in maintaining unity of purpose in staging the piece and giving it the appropriate atmosphere. The photography is of a high order and the lighting effects are on an equal plane. The production is not expensive. It is a striking instance of absence of lavishness where it is unessential. The story in this case speaks volumes, the background is secondary, and the total absence of pretentiousness is one of the most welcome things in it.

What does every woman know? As Barrie proves it, every woman knows her husband's true capacity. That is her little joke—or "our," as she declares—but she is artful about not letting him (her husband) know that she knows so much.

The Rivoli audience applauded the picture at its conclusion, in proof of its excellent qualities to please.
                          Step.

THE NUT.

Charlie Jackson........Douglas Fairbanks
Estrell Wynn........Marguerite Delamotte
Philip Feeney..............William Lowery
"Gentleman George".........Gerald Pring
Pernelius Vanderbrook......Morris Hughes
Claudine Dupree.........Barbara La Marr

Exhibitors and others who have wished for Fairbanks in a "different" sort of picture realize their desire in "The Nut." For in it Fairbanks is less of the acrobat and more of the comedian than usual. For this reason it lacks the machine gun rapidity characteristic of Doug's features; but the hokum and an amount of burlesque, combined with giggle-breeding titles, put it over for a howl.

Ted Reed directed the picture and did a good job, technically, though he let it sag in several places, and the author provided a mixture of farce comedy and lurid melodrama which serves its purpose. But the story is somewhat like a slack wire —and about as important—used by a comic tumbler. It serves only as an excuse for the star falling off whenever he sees fit and indulging in slapstick, with the result laughs are sprinkled around like small shot at a trapshoot.

Doug has one good knockdown and dragout fight, with incidental comedy, but the big laughs come at four distinct places. First, the opening. He is in his bed, which automatically travels to the bathroom, dumping him in the tub. There an automatic arrangement of brushes scrubs him, followed by towels automatically drying him. Next he is automatically dressed. This is trick stuff, but loaded with laughs. Later Doug and the heroine, through clever photography, are shown climbing through the hot air pipes of a house and escaping via the furnace door. He is at his funniest in a wax works museum, whence he swipes several figures for outside comedy, and lastly, after the picture is ended, the audience is provided with a laugh by the introduction of a squirrel finishing a meal, the final title, "The End of the Nut," dissolving in for a last howl. A funny situation is where Doug loses a wax cop in the street and it is mistaken by autoists for a traffic officer.

Fairbanks' support is, as usual, ace high. Miss Delamotte is prettier and more charming, if possible, than she was in "The Mark of Zorro," and Gerald Pring, with a fair bit as a crook, registers strongly. Morris Hughes, playing a thinly veiled imitation of young Cornelius Vanderbilt, who is a reporter on the New York "Times," is a new one to this reviewer, but a corking good juvenile. He has pep and personality and acts with an intelligence that is refreshing. Somebody should grab this lad for feature roles.

At the Strand, where "The Nut" received its initial showing in New York, a subtle prolog is used. A quartet, with a group of wax figures mixed in, was used and sang old songs with tunes that had nothing whatever to do with them. It had the audience guessing what it was all about until the finish, when one of the singers provided the tip-off by grabbing a wax figure and dashing off stage with it.

MAN IN MILLION

Lupino Delchini.............George Beban
Flora Valenzi..........Helen Jerome Eddy
Mme. Maureveau.................Irene Rich
Clyde Hartley..............Lloyd Whitlock
Gustave Koppel...........George Williams
Mrs. Koppel....................Jennie Lee
The Belgian Waif.......George Beban, Jr.
"Bo-Bo" (the parrot)...........By Himself
"Toodles" (the dog)............By Himself

"One Man in a Million" is a Sol Lesser presentation distributed by Robertson-Cole, starring George Beban, who is also credited with the story and direction. The scenario is the work of Dorothy Yost and Ross Fisher, the cameraman.

While in many respects it is just another variation of "Rosa" and therein resembles the other Beban picture tales it is especially well done; in short, it is an obvious, sequential, cumulative, sure-fire plot. The main adverse criticism is its length, some 6,000 feet. A better result might be attained by closer cutting and the elimination of a few scenes not necessary to the progression of the tale until a full 1,000 feet had been excised.

Beban's is a lovable character, replete with his familiar exaggerated Italian gestures—a man who laughs when he loses his job, with a love for children, animals and all mankind. Through helping what he supposes is a tramp but is in reality a member of the Department of Criminal Investigation he secures the appointment of Pound Master (in charge of the local dog catching force), adopts a child, its mother turns up and is found to have been separated from her little boy during the Belgian invasion, he wants to marry the mother rather than give up the child whom he has learned to love, and so on. He, in turn, is loved by the office stenographer, an Italian girl, and it looks like a hopeless mix-up. But by an ingenious twist in the plot things are straightened out in a manner not readily foreseen, even by those more or less familiar with the rules of picture making.

Photography and direction are most workmanlike and the supporting cast is made up of a competent standard performers of a high order. "One Man in a Million" is above the standard of program features. *Jolo.*

THE GILDED LILY

Lillian Drake.......................Mae Murray
Creighton Howard..........Lowell Sherman
Frank Thompson..............Jason Robards
John Stewart..................Charles Gerard
Mrs. Thompson..............Leonora Ottinger

Mae Murray does the best work of her picture career as the star of "The Gilded Lily," a Robert Z. Leonard production, distributed by Famous Players, directed by Mr. Leonard and scenario by Clara Beranger. The story fits Miss Murray's personality perfectly, evidently having been especially written for her. It's a tale of the white light district, with real human beings for characters, impelled by human impulses and acting generally as people do in real life rather than going through the stilted motions of the puppets seen in the regulation program feature.

Introduced naturally and as a specialty there are several dances performed by Miss Murray. Whether it's the director or the camera men who should be credited with catching the real spirit of these bits of terpsichore and placing them on the screen in such a lifelike manner is beyond the knowledge of the reviewer, but whoever is responsible, and probably it was both, is entitled to high praise.

Scenes of New York night life, in cabaret and private dancing club, are depicted with fidelity to the original that convinces through lack of exaggeration. There is an interesting love story, well sustained action, plenty of conflict and a finish that stands out through being entirely different from what might be expected.

The picture has been mounted beautifully and Miss Murray's costumes should be an attraction in themselves for the women fans. Particularly fine portrayals are offered by Jason Robards and Lowell Sherman. Mr. Robards plays a weak-willed son of wealthy parents, making the character breathe because of its naturalness. Mr. Sherman, usually cast for the heaviest kind of villains, turns out to be the hero in the end, after giving the impression he is inclined to be at least a bit wicked.

Charles Gerard and Leonora Ottenger also lend real assistance in making the story intelligible and highly entertaining from a dramatic standpoint. As a program feature "The Gilded Lily" sets a standard for comparison that others might profit by in following values as regards general entertainment values. *Bell.*

CHICKENS.

Deems Stamwood........Douglas MacLean
Julia Stoneman..............Gladys George
Aunt Rebecca.................Clair McDowell
Dan Bellows...................Charles Malles
His Wife..........................Edith Yorke
Willie Figg..................Raymond Cannon

"Chickens" is a Thomas H. Ince production made from Herschel Hall's "Saturday Evening Post" story "Yacona Yillies," directed by Jack Nelson and with scenario by Agnes Christine Johnston.

It is an amusing film comedy painstakingly adapted from an interesting story, but the translation is less entertaining than the original. It was a difficult story to picturize for the quaint fun of the written version does not adapt itself easily to the screen medium.

The scenario writer and the director have tried to make the screen version a literal reproduction of the printed story and have dealt gently with the material. The trouble was this, as with so many stories taken from published fiction, that it is not well fitted to film presentation.

What was in its original form a sparkling little romance becomes in the picture theatre a rather homely bread and butter rural affair, more or less like "The Old Homestead" with all the drama left out and the comedy over developed. The original tang of flavor is absent.

This is no fault of the players, for Douglas MacLean plays the young city spendthrift with a good deal of spirited action, while Raymond Cannon, as Willie Figg, makes the intriguing country lad an excellent contract, and Gladys George plays the heroine in the right key of sweetness and charm.

The best laugh is MacLean's dream, one of those "chase" affairs in which the slow motion camera is employed to give a comedy effect. The hero in his dream is pursued by the man who holds a mortgage on his farm and while the best he can do is to float slowly through the air, the pursuer speeds along at double time by the use of the familiar camera trick. It was a capital laugh. The scenes at the country church bazaar was another amusing bit, with its character studies and the amusing contest of the two young men for the favor of the heroine.

The story deals with a young millionaire who tears into the chicken farm of a girl while out on a joy ride in a high powered car. He falls in love with the angry girl and decides to start a chicken farm next door to her. While the venture is hanging in the balance, the youth finds that his fortune has been dissipated by his guardian and he has to go into the chicken farm business in earnest to make a living.

Willie Figg is his rival for the girl and because he is a thoroughly capable business man and holds a mortgage on the city boy's farm, there is plenty of competition. The girl herself takes a hand in directing the courtship of the two contenders and brings about the triumph of the city boy, to the satisfaction of everybody but Willie.

The production could not have cost much for the cast is small and the settings simple. Most of the action is out of doors and the interiors are plain country farm house rooms and village stores and the church. *Rush.*

THE OATH.

Minna Hart.....................Miriam Cooper
Hugh Colman..................Conway Tearle
Irene Lansing....................Anna Nilsson
Gerard Merriam..................Henry Clive
Israel Hart.....................Robert Fischer

R. A. Walsh's latest production "The Oath" proves itself to be more than a worthy companion for its two predecessors of First National's "Big Five." Considered from every angle, it is one of the few real super-specials of recent release. An all-star cast, which for once lives up to its name, a production in which nothing is stinted, nothing introduced merely for effect, almost flawless direction, it has in addition to these things a big story founded on a vital human theme which has heretofore been neglected by the scenario writer and which ought to arouse discussion.

"The Oath" is the latest and one of the best arguments for the "director picture." Nothing seems to have been sacrificed to further any individual interest. Unhampered by the requirements of star or spectacle, the director has been able to tell his story with a sincerity that would otherwise be difficult. His minor characters are drawn as clearly as his leads and his people move through the lavish settings he has provided with an ease and naturalness which go far to make his startling climax altogether convincing.

Miriam Cooper, the featured player, gives a touching picture of the lonely Jewish girl whose love for the Christian, played by Conway Tearle, furnishes the theme of the drama. Her father is one of the wealthiest bankers in London; Hugh Colman, her lover, is paying the price of a dissipated inheritance by his poverty. Her lover's pride and her father's intention to have her marry a man of her own faith, whom she does not love, force the couple into a secret marriage.

For a short time they are happy together, but that happiness is soon threatened by forces beyond their control which gather with ominous swiftness. Idolizing him as only a woman of her type can who has sacrificed everything for the man of her choice and is prepared to go to any length to hold his love, Hugh seems to fail her in the hour of trial. To continue their stealthy married life together, when her faith in him is broken, is impossible and they decide to renounce all claim to each other in an oath which binds each never to reveal their marriage.

That night her father is murdered. The evidence points to Hugh as the guilty man. On trial for his life he redeems himself by his silence. No argument will move him and he is apparently bent on going to his death to keep his word with the woman whom he has broken forever. Torn by the conflicting emotions of pride and love, Minna attempts at the last moment to save him (he was in her room at the time the murder was committed) only to find her action forestalled by perjured testimony of another woman.

This is the big climax of the story and the building up of the suspense in the court room scene in which it occurs is a classic of this type of screen direction. Mr. Walsh has at this point picked up the threads of the plot in a neat and plausible manner holding the solution of a very complicated situation almost up to the very last scene.

It is in these latter scenes of the picture that Miriam Cooper does the best work of her career. Seldom has she appeared more appealing than in a scene where she contemplates putting an end to her life as the only solution of the tragedy in which she finds herself. There is at all times something more than great physical beauty and a display of gowns which will make even the mere male in the audience wonder what women will be wearing next season. There is a fineness of light and shade and real dramatic fire in moments of emotional intensity, which mark her one of the dramatic actresses of the screen to be reckoned with.

Anna Nilsson, while not as even in her characterization as Miss Cooper, is charming and her blond beauty sets off the suggestion of the Oriental in the Jewess to great advantage. Robert Fischer contributes an excellent characterization of the old banker and Conway Tearle in the male lead is both sympathetic and convincing.

Earle Browne is credited with the scenario. He has allowed himself a great deal of liberty in the adaptation of the original novel "Idols" by William J. Locke, but the general effect is that of strengthening the drama of the present version. There are a few things which might be bettered but these are insignificant beside the fact that Mr. Walsh has produced a picture with real artistic merit. *Jolo.*

LYING LIPS.

Blair Cornwall.................House Peters
Nancy Abbott.................Florence Vidor
William Chase.................Joseph Kilgour
Lelie Dodson.............Margaret Livingston
Mrs. Abbott.............Margaret Campbell
Mrs. Prospect.....................Edith Yorke
Horace Prospect..............Calvert Carter
John Warren.................Emmet C. King

"Lying Lips" is an absorbing story made up of combination of literary hokum plus the depiction of a feminine type that, while perhaps true to life, is not common enough to be familiar to the average fan and hence may not be generally understood. The tale was written by May Edington, scenarioized by Bradley King, directed by John G. Wray. It is a Thomas Ince special in seven parts, distributed via Associated Producers.

It is very elaborately "staged." Opening with a house party on an English estate, it switches to mid-west Canada, leading up to a most realistic shipwreck at sea—one of the most vivid picturizations of the sort ever offered. For good measure the producer follows this up with a bacchanalian revel that cannot be passed by without a word of special comment.

The crux of the tale is the depicting of the character of a girl reared in luxury, driven by her ambitious mother to accept the proffer of marriage of a wealthy man twice her age, to save themselves from bankruptcy. Before marrying him she insists on a trip to Canada to visit relatives, where she meets a virile young ranchman, named Blair, who is dreadfully poor, but loves her and for whom she conceives a reciprocal affection. While out in a canoe at night he rescues her from being swept over a waterfall, takes her in his arms in the moonlight and she is momentarily happy. Next day she accompanies him to his primitive hut, contrasts it with her luxurious existence in England and tells him: "I couldn't marry you—I couldn't live such a life."

Blair sells his ranch and books third passage on the steamer on which she sails for home. A stray mine blows up the ship, he climbs to the main deck to her rescue, and they are the only survivors left upon a section of the wreck. During a storm she fears the elements and clings to him saying "I want you to stay with me—I won't be alone."—"You mean you love me?" and she answers: "I'll have no one but you." There upon the open sea he goes through a crude marriage ceremony.—"I, Blair Cornwell, take thee, Nance Abbott, his wife," and she utters a similar declaration with respect to him—"until death do us part."

At the end of three days a ship is sighted—she pictures her future with the poor man and, unable to look forward to it, cries: "I couldn't, now that we're going to live—I couldn't—I couldn't be poor. I told you so."—"But you're my wife"—"I won't be found here as your wife. I'd die first." He looks her straight in the eyes and says: "We won't be found together." They pick her up alone and, conscience-stricken, she attempts to jump into the sea and is restrained. She cries: "I want to tell you"—but faints. Placing her upon the rescue ship they blow up the derelict and she goes through weeks of delirium.

Although it is later shown in a flashback how he is saved, this is somewhat improbably and inconsistent, but that's a detail of relatively little consequence. He falls heir to a fortune, comes unbidden to a party given by the man to whom she is betrothed and who is to announce the formal engagement on that occasion. Blair takes the name of "Charles Seaton," causing her untold agony of uncertainty.

Blair refuses to admit he is other than "Seaton" and she is left no alternative but to marry the wealthy, elderly man. When the ceremony reaches the phrase "Until death do us part" she goes into hysterics and cries out: "I can't. In the eyes of God I am another man's wife."

Blair sails for Australia, she learns of it from his lawyer and rushes to the vessel just as they are pulling up the gangplank, goes to his cabin and throws herself in his arms, not knowing he has fallen heir to a fortune.

The "classy" way in which this story is picturized—dialog, direction, production and excellence of acting, places it among super-features. It is provocative of argument with the film fan, and this should work to the advantage of the exhibitor. It stood up strongly at the Capitol last Sunday and should fare equally well wherever shown. *Jolo.*

GREATER CLAIM.

Mary Smith ....Alice Lake
Richard Everard...........Jack Dougherty
Abe Dietz.........................Edward Cecil
Richard Everard, Sr.....De Witt Jennings
Gwendolyn...................Florence Gilbert
Rosie..........................Leonore Lynard

"The Greater Claim (Metro), made by Wesley Ruggles, with Alice Lake as the star, is a strange mixture, with a hackneyed plot and conflicting technical elements, which make it only an average program picture. Izola Forrester and Mann Page are the accredited authors, with Bert LeVino as the screen adapter. None of those mentioned will gain any sustenance for their literary reputations as the result of it.

The story is antique in conception and construction, based upon the supposed unworthiness of all chorus girls. Why authors ignorantly and persistently slander this class of wage-earner, whose members slave harder than any other women workers, is hard to understand. Somebody, some time in the dim past, labelled the chorus girl as a mercenary and a chronic destroyer of morality and happiness. Since then every hack writer devoid of originality has followed the formula. In this particular story one good chorus girl is idealized as an exception to her class, when, as a matter of fact, the bad one is the exception. Chorus girls, as a class, are more sinned against than sinning, and writers who paint them otherwise only add to an injustice.

In "The Greater Claim," a father forbids his minor son to marry a chorus girl. The boy does it, anyway, and is kidnapped from a rustic retreat where they are having their honeymoon. He then is shanghaied at his father's order and taken to sea. The father maneuvers to have the marriage annulled, telling the girl his son consents. Son returns and finds his wife in a wild whirl of gayety, denounces her and departs for about three reels. A shyster lawyer arranges to have the father adopt the chorus girl's baby when it, in due time, arrives. Then the mother gets a job as the child's nurse. When the boy is three years old, the old man asks the lawyer to find the mother, and the shyster tries to ring in a woman crook on him. The real mother denounces them, but they stand pat. Then the son comes home and cleans that phase of the matter. But the crooks say the child is not Mary's, whereupon the author has the father resort to the old trick of matching money against mother love, with the result that the real mother spurns it while the imposter accepts the lucre.

The director seems to have started in a groove and remained there. He introduces some pretty woodland and lake exteriors in the beginning, with very artistic long shots, but seems to have forgotten there is such a thing as a three-foot line. Only one real close-up of the heroine is shown, the others being apparently shot from the 9-foot line. Also, for some weird reason, he photographs his star in long-shots most all the way through. His padding is so glaringly obvious that at times the star is kept holding a pose for so long it would appear she must fall over from sheer physical exhaustion.

Miss Lake's work was uneven, perhaps due to the directors' misconception of how her character should be played. Of the support, De Witt Jennings, who bears a striking resemblance to Tefft Johnson, provided the only acting worth mentioning. The remainder of the cast are machine-line in expression and interpretation.

The picture will please audiences of elementary minds, but not those which look for dramatic values on the screen.

WING TOY.

Wing Toy......................Shirley Mason
Bob.........................Raymond McKee
Lee Wong.....................Edward McWade
Yen Low........................Harry Northrup
White Lily........................Betty Schade
The Mole..........................Scott McKee

In "Wing Toy" Fox offers a Chinatown melodrama with the dizzying doors and sinister shadows usually associated with the section. As a study in "atmosphere" it does very well, but as an entertainment it is shy, and the star, despite her best efforts, is given very slender opportunity for breaking through to the attention of the audience. Shirley Mason is not to be blamed if the audiences do not like her in this.

As a story, the creation of Pearl Doles Bell is thin and totally lacking in the solids necessary to satisfactory screen drama. Briefly, it is a tale of a Chinatown boss who discards his white wife to marry a child that had been placed in his hands by a poor laundryman in whose care it had been left by a crook. Ultimately it is revealed the child is the daughter of a district attorney, from whom it had been stolen in revenge. For no reason at all a cub reporter falls in love with Wing Toy, and she, strangely for a girl reared to the restraints and suspicions characteristic of the Chinese, loves him at first sight.

Thomas Dixon, Jr., wrote the scenario and succeeded in giving the story a disconnected and jumpy presentation.

Such credit as the picture may deserve goes to the technical director, who has provided good interior sets and convincing exteriors. Also, Howard Mitchell, who directed the feature, merits commendation for his lightings and the handling of the players. Harry Northrup is strong as Yen Low, and good bits are contributed by Betty Schade, Edward McWade and Scott McKee.

As a whole, the picture is very lightweight.

COLORADO.

Frank Austin.....................Frank Mayo
Tom Doyle...................Charles Newton
Kitty Doyle........................Gloria Hope
Mrs. Doyle........................Lillian West
James Kincaid..............Charles Le Moyne
David Collins...............Leonard Clapham

When Augustus Thomas wrote "Arizona" he gave the stage an enduring American drama. When he wrote "Colorado," he gave the screen author a trapeze on which to practice tricks, for this Universal feature is the second attempt the same company has made to put it over. In 1915 it was put out with a version different from the one used in the present instance, and it cannot be said the Universal has succeeded in making a good entertainment. The Thomas story dealt with the old U. S. Army, and here the scenario writer has brought it "up to date" by having the army action occur after the A. E. F. returns from France. While he was about it, he should have brought the speeches up to date, as the old lines strike harshly in their new dress. What seems to have been done is, that the scenarist has taken the high light of "Arizona," were the hero suffers disgrace to shield the Colonel's wife, and transplanted it a bit north, over the Colorado line.

The acting and business throughout the picture are about as crude as have been seen in recent years, but Frank Mayo and Le Moyne, the only players who seem to know what acting is, are not to be blamed. They're victims of elementary methods of direction, made to work artificially and "stagey" all the way.

There is a big scene where the water floods a mine, but there is nothing new or sensational in this, having been done so often before—and so much better—an ennuied audience is more likely to laugh than to thrill over it.

BEAU REVEL

Billy Steel....................Florence Vidor
Bean Revel....................Lewis Stone
Dick Revel....................Lloyd Hughes
Alice Lathon....................Kathleen Kirkham
Rossiter Wade....................Richard Ryan
Will Phyfe....................Harlan Tucker
Fred Lathon....................William Conklin
Ma Steele....................Lydia Titus
Bert Steel....................William Musgrave
Butler....................Joe Campbell

"Beau Revel" (Paramount) at the Rivoli this week may be an original film script by Louis Joseph Vance with scenario by Luther Reed and directed by John Griffith Wray. Whether original or adapted, it tells a plausible story that involves a triangle, father and son, husband and wife, and a cabaret dancer (Florence Vidor). Miss Vidor is featured, and tells it with a pointedness that upholds the interest and with a naturalness of playing that reflects the greatest of credit upon Mr. Wray's direction. Seldom is the screen director found who so firmly implants a tale of this character in his mind that he can run it off, scene after scene, and repress his actors to the acme of perfectly natural playing, as may be seen in this picture, with the repression side stepping the all too open opportunities for high melodramatics that could include the rough stuff, from fist fights to scenery chewing. It's the direction of intelligence and understanding, with a mind that preconceives exactly how a story may be presented on the sheet and still keep its audience seated without the bluster. It's stage playing reproduced on the screen and made just as interesting. That's an accomplishment. Mr. Wray, whoever he may be or whatever he may have done in the past, should be entrusted with more important work.

"Beau Revel," even with that title, and no poorer one could have been selected, is going to leave an excellent impression as a release wherever exhibited. It's going to find more favor with the adult than the youth, but even youth will find much in it, while the adult will appreciate that a humane story is being unfolded. The story centres around Beau Revel (Lewis Stone), a middle aged man and evidently a widower, who has a son of marriagable age. They live together, father and boy, friends and pals, with the father standing for anything his son wants or does, meantime attempting to guide the boy through suggestion.

The father is an admitted chaser, a polished love maker with the wealth, poise and health to back that up—an ideal male vamp, and "A Male Vamp" could have been the title. The father plays no favorites. As the picture starts his current prey is a married woman, Alice Lathom (Kathleen Kirkham) with a drinking husband (William Conklin). Mrs. Lathom is swaying and on the verge through tiring of her husband's indifference and bestiality. Revel knows she is about to fall. They meet in the park. He professes his love. She is aware of his rep and stands him off. Says she will see when becoming convinced he can be faithful to at least one woman. Leaving her at the park's clandestine meeting, Revel goes directly to his club, where he stands as a boastful beau and tells his cronies there marriage is for no man—he can get any of them in 30 days and most of them in two weeks.

The son has grown enamored of the cabaret dancer. This picture makes Nelly Steele (Miss Vidor) a graceful dancer of the model kind, living at home with her aunt and a dissolute brother, meantime foiling the advances of the cabaret's manager and at the same time having naught but business relations with her male dancing partner.

It eventuates the father learns of his boy's infatuation for the dancer, and, believing the boy paramount to his own immediate affairs, decides to ascertain for himself to what extent the girl will go. Beau, as customary of his set, having but one opinion. He successfully urges his son to give him two weeks' time with Nelly, and, says the father, if Nelly is not at his (father's) apartment at midnight two weeks from the date the father agrees the son shall marry her. The son agrees with himself that if the girl is there he will kill his father, and on the night two weeks after the boy is watchfully waiting outside his home at midnight with a gun in his pocket. During the two weeks there have been scenes between father and son, with the son frequently restraining himself from striking his parent. It is such scenes as this throughout the picture, where violence would have been perfectly permissible, that Mr. Wray invoked that repression which does so much for the picture as a piece of fil mart.

The girl goes to the father's home at midnight on the fatal evening, but not for the purpose the son suspects. She was unexpectedly drawn there to save her brother on a criminal charge, the only illogical bit of the feature. The same afternoon the father had proposed marriage to the dancer, for she only, of all the women he had met, is the one he wants to marry. The father, aware his boy may be lurking about, is seized by fear and hides the girl as the son is about to burst into the room. The ensuing argument between father and son brings the girl back into the room. She denounces the father as loving no one, either herself nor the boy, only his own pleasure, and spurning both father and son returns to her cabaret dressing room, where the son follows, after placing the revolver on his father's table to acquaint him with what he had unintentionally missed. In the dressing room the young couple effect a reconciliation with the clinch finish that is an anti-climax, for the climax continues at home, with the father thinking it over. Nelly walking out on him in favor of his son wakes up the old man. It tells him he is growing old, that he will grow older, and his women will be of the past. He fondles the revolver, then thinks of the window as a more befitting ending, and after a talk with his butler over the mistakes all humans do and can make he topples backward to the pavement below.

It's not the usual finish, of course, but it's a bear for those who can get it.

Mr Stone takes the playing honors. He does the dandy in every way and makes almost a Mansfield Baron Chevral of the part, merely a few years younger. Miss Vidor is rather a pretty brunette, of much sincerity and with a chameleonlike face which the camera takes in several poses, each one different for the facial expression. Lloyd Hughes as Dick Revel, the son, played with a certain grasp and appeared to be the one who followed his director's instructions with the most fidelity. Miss Kirkham as Mrs. Lathom was convincing without stress, while Mr. Conklin as her soused husband conveyed his contrition as well as his drunkenness with no little artistic pantomimic effort. The scene where Mrs. Lathom is undressing to retire behind a latticed door drew her husband to her through a silhouette and was repulsed went forward in the most matter-of-fact way, as it should have beeen, although most directors would have worked that bit into a scene that the censors might have thrown out.

"Beau Revel" is more of a study than a big picture, but it's a good film, the best one along Broadway of the new ones this week, and as a well ; leced together bit of picturing with a nicely balanced cast it's a corker. But the public will see it as a picture release, good enough because it's holding, and perhaps the best thing about it the film fans of the neighborhoods will like will be the handsome sets. *Sime.*

THE MISTRESS OF SHENSTONE

Lady Myra Ingleby......Pauline Frederick
Jim Airth....................Roy Stewart
Sir Deryck Brand........Emmett C. King
Ronald Ingram............Arthur Clayton
Billy Cathcart..............John Willink
Margaret O'Mara...........Helen Wright
Amelia Murgatroyd.............Rose Gore
Eliza Murgatroyd...............Helen Muir
Suzannah Murgatroyd.Lydia Yeamans Titus

A quarter of a century or so ago the Laura Jean Libbey of England was Florence Barclay, who turned out romance after romance of the calibre known colloquilally as "housemaid's delight" tales. They were mostly about lords and ladies, dooks and dookesses, etc. "The Mistress of Shenstone" was one of them and has now been selected as a photoplay vehicle for Pauline Fredericks, who is starring under the Robertson-Cole trade-mark.

There isn't enough action in the tale to make of it more than a two-reeler, but it has been dragged out to a full hour's length by resorting to lengthened emoting scenes for the star, photographic reproductions of surging seas and so on.

As a matter of fact, the story is over the first 500 feet, wherein it is related that Lady Inglesby's husband has been killed at war, not in battle, but through an accidental explosion during an experiment with a new invention, and the widow says she doesn't wish to know the name of the man who made the fatal error, as she could not touch his hand. She goes to an isolated inn at a quiet seaside place and there meets and falls in love with a man who had just returned from the war and is writing a book. Need it be said, he is the very man who had accidentally killed Lord Inglesby? But it should be stated he turns out to be "a earl."

Despite the crudity of the plot and the certainty of the denouement, Director Henry King has brought to it a wealth of English atmosphere, with fine detail as to character types. The drawing-rooms, exteriors and selection of locations cannot be criticised adversely.

It was noticeable that, despite the brevity of dresses prevailing everywhere, Miss Frederick's gowns were all of most sedate length. As "the war" is spoken of, it is presumed this refers to the recent world conflict, and this is borne out by the modern attire of the men. The only other women in the cast were characters and no period was specifically indicated.

The whole thing lacks action.

Jolo.

SOCIETY SNOBS.

Conway Tearle courts professional suicide with both barrels in "Society Snobs" (Selznick) by acknowledging authorship and appearing as the star of the picture. Martha Mansfield is his leading woman. It is hard to believe that Mr. Tearle, a man of culture and experience, could have written the story accredited to him on the screen.

Tearle plays the part of a Ritz waiter who is introduced to a society girl by a discarded suitor as a Duke traveling incognito. The waiter has loved the girl silently and now, accepted by the heroine and her supercilious mother as a noblemen, he courts vigorously. He marries her, then tells her he is a waiter disguised. The rejected suitor sees to it that the story of the misalliance is spread all over the front page of a New York newspaper. The mother has the marriage annulled. Then, apparently, the erstwhile waiter turns out to be some sort of engineer and is given a big commission in South America. As he prepares to leave, love triumphs and the girl, evidently believing a good waiter a handy thing to have around the house, walks in on him and avows her undying affection. Curtain.

Aside from the fact the story is silly and a breeder of class hatred, it is totally lacking in virility and contains not one flash of comedy. It seems to promise something, but the promise never is fulfilled and the play ends with the spectator wondering what it's all about.

Tearle, one of the best actors and "troopers" on the screen today, is absolutely colorless here, slow-moving and seemingly witless. Miss Mansfield, reputed to be a beauty, gives not a semblance of ability and is so disappointing in her stiffness of expression, gesture and stride as to create wonder why she has been called to the screen for star honors.

"Society Snobs" lacks even photography to recommend it and, except for one or two close-ups of Miss Mansfield, mere portrait studies to display her pretty hair, has pictorial individuality. Unless Miss Mansfield has more talent than she displayed in this feature, she will not get far as a star, because the day of pretty faces masquerading as actresses has passed; and her promoters will realize that the make-up of a lasting star does not come in a paint box only.

The picture may get by on Tearle's name, but his reputation will suffer wherever it does.

THE FAITH HEALER.

Michaelis....................Milton Sills
Rhoda Williams..............Ann Forrest
Matthew Beeler..........Frederick Vroom
Mrs. Beeler..............Fontaine La Rue
Annie Beeler....................Mary Giraci
Uncle Abe....................John Curry
Dr. Littlefield..............Adolph Menjou
Dr. Sanchez..................Edward Vroom
A Mother..............Winifred Greenwood

"The Faith Healer," a George Melford (Paramount) production, is not screen entertainment. The thought is inescapable that its sole excuse for being is that somebody in the Lasky organization thought they had another "Miracle Man" and determined upon screening it in the hope of duplicating the earnings of the latter. It never will, because neither in dramatic appeal nor cinematographic quality does it approximate its model.

Adapted by Mrs. William Vaughan Moody and Z. Wall Covington from the play by Mrs. Moody's husband (also author of "The Great Divide"), "The Faith Healer" is a slow, cumbersome thing, so depressingly devout as to be damnably dull. No censor will snap and snarl at this offering, because there is nothing live enough in it to attract a censor's attention—unless a close-up of a babe feeding at its mother's breast runs afoul of the censorial idea of decency.

If Mr. Melford selected this story for production, his judgment of screen values is slipping; if he had it forced on him, he is a victim of misguided merchandising. Technically, Melford has done as well as could be expected with the material at hand. He has brought forth some sharp photography, good lightings and fair acting. But he has not produced drama, because there was none there to produce.

The main thought of "The Faith Healer" is so strongly similar to that of "The Miracle Man" as to cause speculation whether Moody got it from Packard, author of the latter, or vice versa. In the Packard play there were high lights and action, in this there is neither, nor is there the slighest comedy relief. The whole thing is the essence of triteness and solemn preachment. The titles overpoweringly leaden and sleep-inducing.

The "master mind" that figured this for a twin of "The Miracle Man" as a money-getter let his vision glide along the surface of things. He saw here a title, which would possibly suggest to the public another "Miracle Man;" a central figure who did exactly what the other did, except that in this case there was a young "healer" instead of a patriarch, and a chance to work in "love interest;" and an opportunity to assemble a concourse of limping, suffering humanity as was done in the other.

On the face of it, the parallel appeared complete. But the picker overlooked the fact that there were real psychology and human appeal in the picture which George Loane Tucker made, that Mr. Tucker had brought the high dramatic notes strong relief and had given the production touches and character, aside **from superb photography. These are the things which, with vociferous advertising, made the Tucker picture gross between $2,000,000 and $3,000,000. They were the elements that made it great.**

"The Faith Healer" lacks in psychology and punch, which is but a colloquial for human appeal. It has not one single strong character or characteristic, unless dullness be selected, and therefore it lacks the elements mentioned.

Dr. Hugo Riesenfeld must have been gravely impressed or sorely oppressed by "The Faith Healer," because he has set it in a most lugubrious frame. He opens it with a hidden choir singing "Rock of Ages," and, instead of providing a lively comedy to lighten up his program, has selected a tiresome scenic thing about "The Lone Indian." An Ollendorff Sketchograph gives the audience a few faint ripples of joy, but not sufficient to wipe out the funeral depression caused by the main feature.

MY LADY'S LATCHKEY

Annesley Grayle......Katherine MacDonald
Nelson Smith..................Edmund Lowe
Countess De Santiago.......Claire DuBrey
Lord Annesley-Seton..........Edward Gaye
Lady Annesley-Seton.......Lenore Lynard
Ruthven Smith............Thomas Jefferson
Mrs. Ellsworth..............Hellena Phillips

Katherine MacDonald in "My Lady's Latchkey," at the Strand for its initial run in New York, compared in the present production with her two previous pictures, "The Notorious Miss Lisle" and "Curtain," one notices a consistent progress toward greater poise, a surer command of herself and a well-defined as well as individual acting ability. There is still a monotony of expression and her familiar agonized look about the eyes. But she is so beautiful to look upon, photographically, and so modishly gowned—or comparisoned?—that she is, as always, a delight to the eye.

"My Lad's Latchkey" was adapted for the screen from "The Second Latchkey," by C. N. and A. M. Williamson, and is undoubtedly the last work to reach the screen by the famous collaborators, due to the recent death of C. N. Williamson.

It is a crook play, staged with a high degree of intelligence, and, therefore, will appeal to every type of mind among photoplay fans. It starts off absorbingly. The plot opens aboard an ocean greyhound where Ruthven Smith, the trusted international representative of a big diamond merchant, is guarding a rare collection of gems on their way to London. In the stillness of the night a shadowy figure mysteriously enters Smith's stateroom and after applying chloroform to the sleeper's nose departs with the precious jewel belt.

In London, Annesley Grayle, tired of a drab five years' existence spent in a house of gloom with her aunt, Mrs. Ellsworth, answers a newspaper advertisement for a traveling companion to an elderly lady; hopeful of breaking away from her present monotonous life. Awaiting the "elderly lady" in the Savoy Hotel, she is accosted by a young man, ostensibly an American, who, in apparent trouble, begs her to save him from an impending calamity by pretending to be his wife. She is, naturally, astounded by this proposal, but the man's distress appears so great that she agrees. The young man gives his name as Nelson Smith; the two young people depart for the girl's home, which is also the London home of Ruthven Smith. The latter, thinking Nelson is another robber, fires his revolver, the house is aroused, whereupon she declares they are engaged.

The affair enrages the aunt and she orders the girl from the house and the young woman is so bewildered she leans upon Nelson and accepts his hand in marriage. At a ball given after the marriage it is revealed to the young wife that her husband is a thief. She overhears his declaration to the thieving gang of which he is a member that he will go straight and that the proposed robbery of the house must not take place. It all ends happily with the redemption of the husband, who is really the star because his is the active and hers more or less a passive role.

Miss MacDonald is assisted by an excellent cast, including Edmund Lowe as the romantic husband; Claire DuBrey, a splendid heavy; Howard Gaye, Lenore Lynard, Thomas Jefferson, Helena Phillips.

The feature has been ruthlessly cut to make excellent speed and the settings and technical adornment all that could be desired. But the letter inserts are quite illegible. Why producers adhere to this form of annoyance to the picture-goers is one of those things not readily accounted for. The public would probably be much more pleased to have this sort of thing rectified than with the passage of censorship laws.

Jolo.

PLAYTHING OF B'WAY

Lola.........................Justine Johnstone
Dr. Jennings..................Crauford Kent
Pell..........................Macey Harlam
Whitney......................Edwards Davis
Dr. Dexter.....................George Cowl
Mrs. O'Connor..................Lucy Parker
The Patriarch...............Claude Cooper
Dr. Hastings...............Garry McGarry
Mrs. Ford...................Gertrude Hillman
Mrs. Slattery..........Mrs. Charles Willard

This new Realart feature with Justine Johnstone, is a symposium of nearly all the bad features that can be packed into a single film. It is made up of the cheapest sort of sloppy sentiment, but it has an intriguing title.

There are moments when the pathos of the heroine's sufferings are positively maudlin, as false and artificial as Miss Johnstone's glycerine tears and as forced as the star's acting. As a commercial picture it ought to be profitable in the rural districts, where such ballads as "There's a Broken Heart for Every Light on Broadway," and "You Made Me What I Am" and that school of so-called lyric writing are popular.

It belongs to that class. In addition the story is crudely handled in its translation from the story "Emergency House," by Sidney Morgan. E. Lloyd Sheldon made the scenario and the filming was directed by Jack Dillob, who divide blame for a poor product. The story is halting. It starts well enough and goes slowly to a climax that has long been foreseen by the audience. But then the film is too short to make a feature, so it begins all over and goes to three or four climaxes, each time laboriously working up a new preparation for a superfluous development.

Lola is a Broadway dancer on intimate terms with all the "Kings" of finance. The imagination is invited to go as far as it likes in elaborating what "intimate" implies. She entertains the captains of industry at their ultra-intimate "30 Club," where a couple of the money barons bet $20,000 that she cannot make a certain charitable doctor "fall" for her.

She sets out to do just that, but in the process has to become the doctor's aid in his settlement work. Anyone who has followed the strictly moral film movement will understand immediately that the butterfly's heart is touched by the nobility of self sacrifice and she is reformed into a saint. She cashes her bet to build a private hospital for the doctor. If that were worked out with any sincerity it might be made into a reasonably satisfactory picture story. But the regeneration is only the half-way stop. The scenario man has to introduce another chapter.

So he has a friend of the doctor tell the lurid life story of the dancer, including the bet. The girl is made to understand that she will ruin the doctor's career unless she disappears. She agrees to vanish but only after she has discouraged the doctor from loving her by having him attend a wild party at her apartment. This treatment is effective and besides permits the director to interject a touch of pep in the form of high life in the wicked city, such as is calculated to make quarters jingle in the box offices of Lafayette, Ind., and subordinate points.

The accomplishment of this narrative would make another complete story, but when it is told in the Realart picture, the film is still considerably short and they begin for the third time to devise new complications of counterfeit fiction, childish in their transparency and even more sloppy in sentiment, while a weary audience awaits with impatience to see what more agonies a heartless scenario carpenter will make the poor girl go through before he completes the invoiced 5,000 feet between the main title and the fadeout clinch.

There are plenty more heart throbs. A freckled boy is made to die to slow music, his mother is forced to go insane and gather a mob of tenement house matrons in a murderous mass meeting just as the heroine drives up in her disgraceful party decollete. They are about to tear her limb from limb when the doctor reaches the scene and saves her, damaged but still beautiful in her torn finery and a halo of glycerine. Laura Jean herself could go no further in mushy slobber.

Rush.

IF ONLY JIM

"If Only Jim" is a typical Universal western with Harry Carey featured. It is a maudlin piece of cheap melodrama, with three cheap sets in it. One set gives a view of the main street in a mining town, another shows the interior of a saloon and the third Carey's cabin. A dozen or so people appear in the picture, but Carey and Carol Halloway are the only ones that count. An "assistant villain" has a more or less feverish fight with Carey and there is a comical gun fight among the rocks around the hero's mining claim, but outside of these there is no action. For no reason at all, the hero, who get his sobriquet of "If Only" through his constitutional proscrastination, is made to pose as a preacher, this "church meeting" probably taking rank among the first worst pieces of business ever dragged into a picture by its heels.

$1 A YEAR MAN.

Franklin Pinney..Roscoe "Fatty" Arbuckle
Peggy Bruce..........................Lila Lee
Kate Connelly.........Winifred Greenwood
Tipton Blair, a Socialist......J. M. Dumont
The Prince...............Edward Sutherland
Colonel Bruce.................Edwin Stevens
General Oberano.............Henry Johnson

Jesse Lasky "presents" Roscoe ("Fatty") Arbuckle in the Paramount feature, this week's attraction at the Rialto. It is hard to classify, partaking of diverse elements of a Harold Lloyd comedy, trick photography, boisterous farce and romantic comedy. Perhaps the comprehensive name "picture comedy" would cover the ground.

Where it pretends to anything above the grade of slapstick it is dull, but there are passages of fantastic nonsense which are amusing, and from the first to the last a good many honest laughs are registered by rather clever, jazzy titling. All in all the title writer gets the lion's share of credit, although the rotund comedian is not without honor of his own. He has a breezy way of getting over rough stuff that is engaging, and in the present instance makes no pretense of legitimate intent.

It is just an unrestrained effort to make laughs by any device short of breaking crockery and spilling a custard pie around the cast. Walter Wood wrote the scenario, apparently under general orders to go as far as he liked, and James Cruze, as the director, took up the merry work from that point. The partnership was ingenious and in a work of clowning for laughs got over five passable reels with a whoop-hurrah finale in a free-for-all.

"Fatty" appears as a small-town laundry impresario who worked as an amateur sleuth during the war and bores his friends thereafter telling about his adventures. He makes a nuisance of himself in the yacht club and his fellow members put up a job on him. A foreign prince is about to visit the town, and the frame-up is to make "Fatty" believe he is to be kidnapped and lured to a haunted house. A parlor Bolshevist in the club is involved in the scheme, but he intends to kidnap the prince in dead earnest. Meanwhile all the younger set of the club makes court to "Fatty's" sweetheart, and "Fatty" gets into a jam with her papa, who is a real Secret Service man detailed to protect the visiting prince.

It turns out (wonder if "Just Suppose" inspired this) "Fatty's" sweetheart meets the prince and runs off with him on a motor escapade; "Fatty" is lured to the haunted house and the prince reaches the same rendezvous, where both the club jokers and the accomplices of the parlor Bolshevist are assembled. There follow all manner of ridiculous complications. The practical jokers seize "Fatty" and terrify him with all sorts of ghostly manifestations, such as self-opening doors, trap-doors that gape at his feet, weird noises and apparitions of faces in the dark.

When the nightmare is at its height the real Bolsheviks arrive on the heels of the prince and all forces plunge into a rough-house carnival upstairs, downstairs and in the garret, until the police arrive and capture the badly battered jokers and real kidnappers. "Fatty," victorious, departs with his sweetheart to be the guests of honor at the prince's royal banquet, sweetie's papa being at length reconciled to the good humored, bungling hero as a son-in-law.

The trick stuff in the haunted house is funny and so are several of "Fatty's" maneuvers to outwit his rivals, such as sending them off in his speedboat, after starting the engine and whisking the belle back to the dock as the boat sweeps out of control. It is fast, sustained nonsense, better adapted to the amusement of juvenile audiences than the adult crowd at the Rialto.

where the Monday evening showing was exceedingly slim. Another thing about "The Dollar a Year Man" is that it does not fit into a program with a two-reel comedy.

"The Jockey," an especially ingenious Fox comic with Clyde Cook, was the comedy in the bill and the two subjects made rather a lopsided show with no dramatic values to give it balance. *Rush.*

WITHOUT LIMIT.

Ember Edwards..........Anna Q. Nilsson
David Marlowe..............Robert Frazer
The Rev. Marlowe..............Frank Currier
Mrs. Marlowe................Kate Blancke
Clement Palter..............Charles Lane
Bunny Fish..................Robert Schable
Charley...................Thomas W. Ross
The Landlady............Nellie Anderson

"Without Limit" is a visualization of "Temple Dusk," a short story by Calvin Johnston, published in the Saturday Evening Post last October. Sawyer & Lubin produced and George D. Baker directed the picture, which is in six reels and distributed by Metro. In fictional form the story was notable for its charm, the authoritative manner in which its theme was treated, the convincing note of human interest that characterized its narration and the unusual qualities of entertainment it contained. It led the Post the week it appeared and caused considerable comment through the fact of its being "away" from the general run of tales of Broadway life appearing regularly in the magazines, most of them written by "authors" whose knowledge of the real Broadway could be written on the back of a postage stamp.

"Temple Dusk" was different, but it had one fault, and the picturization has the same—both hold so much material the action at times is abrupt. In magazine form this was due to the condensation into a short story of a plot that encompassed enough for a six week's serial. In visual form the story could have been better told in eight than in six reels. Not that "Without Limit" isn't a good picture. It is. But it could have been a better one even in the six reels it embraces.

The film follows the fiction version closely, bringing out vividly for the better part the human characteristics of the persons involved in the simple problem presented. The hero is a good-for-nothing son of a poor clergyman, the heroine a lazy grafter who permits her clergyman father-in-law to support her for four years on his slender pastoral stipend, and the villain a wealthy woman chaser. The dominant trait of these four is selfishness. Contrasted with the three "bad" people and one "good" one is a gambler—cynical, worldly and keenly intelligent, but with a philanthropical streak in his makeup that prompts him to take up the burdens of others. He's the real hero.

In his portrait of the gambler Charles Lane realizes the complete significance of the character, shading his work to a nicety and dominating every scene he appears in. Bob Frazer is the dissipated son of the clergyman, playing with ease and repression, and Anna Q. Nilsson is the girl, whose hasty consent to a hastier marriage causes a Gettysburg full of trouble. The naturalness of her performance is commendable. Robert Schable makes the villain lifelike, as does Frank Currier, playing the minister. Thos. Ross and Kate Blancke in contributory roles both play with case and distinction.

"Without Limit" has to its advantage that it tells a story of real depth, although a bit sketchily in one or two spots, but notwithstanding any slight shortcomings it may have it is head and shoulders above nine-tenths of the films supposedly depicting phases of Broadway life.

In a production way it shows evidence of a heavy financial outlay. The gambling house scenes are accurate, and while not holding anything of a startling scenic nature or lighting effects the general ensemble comes up to requirements. The picture was well received at the Capitol Sunday afternoon. *Bell.*

THE LOVE SPECIAL.

Jim Glover, railroad engineer.........
.........................Wallace Reid
Laura Gage.................Agnes Ayres
President Gage...........Theodore Roberts
Allen Harrison, director...Lloyd Whitlock
Mrs. Whitney................Sylvia Ashton
William Bucks.............William Gaden
Morris Blood..............Clarence Burton
Zeke Logan..................Snitz Edwards
"Gloomy"...............Ernest Butterworth
Young Widow..................Julia Faye
Stenographer..................Zelma Maja

Jesse Lasky, in presenting "Wally" Reid as a construction engineer in an adaptation from the novel, "The Daughter of a Magnate," by Frank H. Spearman, has provided the male star with a picture that may pass as an average program feature and be acceptable to the Reid "fans." It will never cause comment to arise concerning the merit it contains, either as to direction, action, interest or photography.

The scenario was done by Eugene B. Lewis, who evidently didn't give Frank Urson, the director, an overabundance of material with which to work. Either that or the original story lacked body as a novel. Certainly the cast, which comprises enough known ability, must have found it easy going in the making, as they have all gone through the identical action time and again, and it is in that respect, the repetition of many films that have gone before, where most of the fault will be found.

It's a railroad story, having to do with Jim Glover (Reid), a construction engineer of the road, assigned to guide the president's (Theodore Roberts) party over an inspection tour of a section of the line for the ultimate purpose of building a short cut that will shave five hours off the time to the coast. The party, including Laura Gage (Agnes Ayres), the magnate's daughter, his matronly sister and Allen Harrison (Lloyd Whitlock) a new director of the line.

Glover is told to hop on the special car after just returning from a 96 hours' job in damming a river and preventing the tracks from being carried away. The gathering stops off at a resort which is decidedly dull, and the daughter stages a charity bazaar to liven the place up. It looks like a flop until Glover puts across a fake hold-up that has the men redeeming their valuables at the stipulated sum stated by the instigator of the affair. This party, incidentally, allows for the only comedy and special interiors.

Immediately after the framed stick-up Glover is called away to direct the excavating of three men caught in a cave-in with the presidential party following up to offer congratulations when the work is successfully completed. The engineer then leaves the party for a few days, and during that time the daughter, Laura, discovers Harrison is making an attempt to jump her father's option on the land required to complete the proposed short cut and starts out in a blizzard to reach him at a town further down the line. Meets Glover at a station on the way, and as he's about to set out for the same destination aboard an engine, she accompanies him. The ride through the storm follows, in which there is a sad lack of suspense despite the supposed running into a snowdrift, another train coming against them and the raging of the elements. The windup is satisfactory, as Glover is on the spot with the option and grabs the girl.

Mr. Roberts, as usual, gave a sterling performance and runs Reid an even race for honors. Miss Ayres impresses with her photographing value, though not to the extent she did in "Forbidden Fruit," and played easily here in a part not calling for any especial effort. Others who showed to advantage were Mr. Whitlock as the heavy, Snitz Edwards in the key character, a rube farmer possessing the needed spur of land, and Julia Faye, who flashed on long enough as a widow during the hotel scenes, making a play for the railroad president, and succeeded in bringing to the role attention it might otherwise have missed, though entirely subordinate to the plot.

"The Love Special" shapes up as a fair feature for the better houses which will neither better nor injure Mr. Reid's prestige on the screen, but should make it easy going for his next release, if it should be superior to this one.

THE SCOFFER.

Hampered by a story of undue morbid character, "The Scoffer," a First National production featuring James Kirkwood, has as its main assets a capable cast and excellent photographic work. The director has wasted much energy on a story that will appeal to but a small portion of the picture-going public.

The tale centres around a young surgeon who is wrongfully sentenced to five years' imprisonment as the result of an illegal operation performed by a rival. Upon his release life holds nothing for him and he seeks solace in the west, however, scoffing at God and the world in general.

The inevitable occurs when a woman makes him see the light. There is considerable action, but the continuity is not always of the best.

Mary Thurman, playing the lead opposite Kirkwood, does some excellent work. This young woman is making rapid strides towards stardom.

Scenicly the picture has strength, but, regardless of its appeal in many ways, the story holds it back.

THE BIG PUNCH.

Buck ....Buck Jones
Hope Standish...............Barbara Bedford
Flash McGraw............George Siegmann
Jed, Buck's brother............Jack Curtis
Jed's Pals.............................{ Jack McDonald / Al Fremont }
Buck's Mother.....................Jennie Lee
The Sheriff.....................Edgar Jones
Dance Hall Girl..................Irene Hunt

It is rare that a cowboy hero can get away from his constituted character, but in "The Big Punch" (Fox) Buck Jones does it with unexpectedly good results. He appears here as a religious student and subsequently as a circuit rider, making a convincing picture of a clergyman.

The story is stereotyped in plot, being the narrative of a good brother who strives to save a bad one and gets a term in prison for his pains, only to come forth, redeem himself and claim the girl, who in this case happens to be a Salvation Army lassie.

Despite the antiquity of the motif "The Big Punch" is a satisfactory program feature and will be especially pleasing to the family theatres, where the audiences prefer their adventure sugar-coated. Jack Ford, who directed the picture, has done a neat job and maintains splendid atmosphere throughout. He introduces some fast action and faster riding in two or three places and has brought out the human interest phase of his story convincingly. This is especially true of the place where the pennyweight Christians turn up their noses and "walk out" on the new preacher simply because he has been a prisoner.

The comedy spots in the picture help it considerably and there is no dearth of pathos.

Buck Jones gives a capital performance, and the three men closely associated with him contribute some fine character work. The mother and the dance hall girl also are to be commended. The picture is smooth throughout, the photography and lighting being excellent.

THE UNKNOWN WIFE.

Just another of the numerous variations of the "Turn to the Right" plot. It opens with Donald Grant released from prison after serving his time, determined to go straight, is met by his two old cronies—comedy types just as were used in "Turn to the Right," and like the piece, he refuses to listen to temptation. He goes to a small town, falls in love with a nice girl, the New York detective recognizes him, but gives him a chance, the two pals continue their old life, one is captured and the other killed trying to escape, and so on. Obvious, elemental, mawkish twaddle, rather well played for popular appeal by Edith Roberts and Casson Ferguson in the leading roles. The feature runs less than an hour, but it seems like twice that amount of time.

It is a Universal, directed by William Worthington, scenario by Wallace Clifton, from a story by Bennett Cohen. *Jolo.*

ALL DOLLED UP.

At very rare intervals Universal turns out a good picture, and "All Dolled Up" is one of them. Its value lies chiefly in the personality and youthful spirit of Gladys Walton a young woman who gives every appearance of being destined for a big place in the sun of picture popularity. In addition to the star the story is ingenious and the direction of Rollin Sturgeon far above what is usually offered in a Universal product.

The story is a comedy melodrama, and Miss Walton is called upon to put up a couple of fights, which she does with all the vigor and pep of a Fairbanks. She is a little department store clerk, who saves a rich spinster from a pickpocket, and later is instrumental in thwarting a plot to blackmail the woman.

Under the capable hand of Sturgeon the play moves along with rapidity and sequence to its climax, where the only false note creeps into the story. That is the announcement by the spinster that she intends to give the heroine and her chauffeur sweetheart a million dollars—just like that.

Untypical of Universal pictures, this one has some attractive sets, and the photography and the lighting are above the average.

All classes of audience will like the picture, but it will make special appeal in the neighborhood houses.

JIM THE PENMAN.

James Ralston.............Lionel Barrymore
Nina Bronson....................Doris Rankin
Baron Hartfeld..................Anders Randolf
Louis Percival........Douglas MacPherson
Agnes Ralston.....................Gladys Leslie
Lord Drelincourt..............Arthur Rankin
Capt. Redwood.............Charles Coghlan
E. J. Smith..........................J. P. Laffey
Enoch Bronson....................Ned Burton

Whitman Bennett has turned the famous old melodrama into a screen story that interests but does not grip in the way the stage version did, at least to a theatregoer of ten years ago. The fault is not the producer's nor is it the star's, for Lionel Barrymore gave one of his polished interpretations, but, rather, the trouble is that the "punch" of the play does not thrill in its film form and all the exaggerations of the melodrama of a generation are over-emphasized in the screen medium looked at with a modern eye.

As a commercial attraction, however, it has fine possibilities as a box-office attraction. At the Strand, New York, Sunday the feature demonstrated its ability to draw. The afternoon and evening were mild and June-like, but the theatre was nearly filled during the "off show," between 5.30 and 7.30. The combination of the famous title and the presence of Barrymore doubtless was sufficient to arouse public interest.

These revivals of success from the past generation are seldom happy, anyhow. In the present case the characters of the old play are sadly unconvincing. The audiences of these days demand a good deal more realism in story and character than the Victorians. They demand to be convinced and are acutely alive to theatrical absurdities. They, too, are sophisticated in "crook" stories, thanks to a long and thorough education in underworld operations. Both the stage and magazine fiction have played their part to this end.

It was all very well for Jim the Penman to succeed in a long series of forgeries that brought him untold wealth, but just to be told he did so was scarcely enough. The audience wanted to know how it was accomplished.

It was a little too brusque to see Jim forge a "cheque" for $500,000 and then enjoy the ill-gotten proceeds. A modern scenario writer would have shown the whole process of ingenious accomplishment of the fraud. In the same way the old playwrights appear to have taken a good deal of license in making coincidence work for their peculiar purpose, such as the easy introduction of the detective into the household of the forger.

Still Mr. Bennett has dealt gently with the play. The structure of the original piece has been followed closely for the most part, especially as to the passages leading up to the big scene—the chain of evidence leading up to the wife's realization that her husband is a criminal. This classic bit of play construction has been quoted for a quarter of a century as a unique dramatic contrivance, a gripping passage in which there is scarcely a spoken word. On the stage it may have been tremendously effective, but on the screen, where drama seems to require a certain element of physical action, it does not hold.

Mr. Bennett has made some effort to bring the story up to date, as, for, example, where he has the young detective claim acquaintance with Lord Drelincourt on the score of having met him "in a German detention camp." But this modernity couldn't have been carried too far and Mr. Bennett has skillfully refrained from making it too modern. The styles of clothing are of no period or of any. There are no motor cars in evidence and in general the period has been quietly disregarded.

Mr. Barrymore's playing of the famous role is intelligent, as always. In the hands of a less polished player the whole thing might easily have been made absurd. Doris Rankin is an especially beautiful Nina, a part in which she is peculiarly at ease. She is beautiful in repose, but when demand is made upon her for expression she somehow fails to convince. Douglas MacPherson was rather a pale Percival.

The feature is offered as a First National attraction.

Rush.

SENTIMENTAL TOMMY

Tommy Sandys, an author..Gareth Hughes
Grizel, his sweetheart.........May McAvoy
The Painted Lady, her mother........
........................Mabel Taliaferro
Dr. McQueen...............George Fawcett
Corp Shiach.............Harry L. Coleman
Elspeth Sandys.................Leila Frost
Dr. David Gemmell.......Kempton Greene
Lady Alice Pippinworth.....Virginia Vaill
Gavinia....................Kate Davenport
The Little Minister.......Alfred Kappeler
Dominie Cathro...........Malcolm Bradley

It is a great pleasure to record that so fine a story as Sir James M. Barrie's "Sentimental Tommy" has been translated to the screen in a way to do credit to the author. Indeed, the achievement is more notable than this summary indicates, for two novels "Sentimental Tommy" and its sequel "Tommy and Grizel" have been compressed within the limits of a film feature and, marvel of marvels, tell a straightforward, simple, comprehensive tale plainly and adequately.

More than that the novelist's creation has been dealt with in a mood of reverence, so much so that there is in the picture translation much of the spirit of sincerity and a good deal of the delicate character drawing with which the Scotchman endowed the original work.

This screen adaptation is unique in these respects and too much honor cannot be accorded those who had a hand in its creation, namely, John S. Robertson, to whom the production is credited; Josephine Lovett, who "made the photoplay," as the program has it; Adolph Zukor who "presents it," and the four principal players who act the principal characters so charmingly, Gareth Hughes, Mabel Taliaferro, May McAvoy and George Fawcett.

The production is so good that the usual test of its commercial success ought not be applied. Rather its fate should be a test of the screen public. Critics of the film are not wanting in the assertion that the producers are giving the public pictures of a quality far below their wants. Producers who declare that they are giving the public what it wants are quite as numerous. Here the issue is fairly joined. Is the screen public educated up to Barrie in as near an adequate presentation of one of his best works as has come out so far? It will be interesting to see. The picture's beginning at the Criterion was auspicious. Sunday night at 8.30 the box office had the longest line of waiters noticed in several weeks. "Sentimental Tommy" is distinctly a picture that should have the support of the film enthusiasts of all tastes. It is a step forward toward sincere and intelligent adaptation of substantial novels.

The work of getting the substance of two novels to the dimensions of a feature must have been monumental, but the selection has been well advised. The story complete in its essentials as it is screened, gives a satisfying reading of Barrie's creation. Incidents and episodes have been eliminated ruthlessly. For example, the delightful scene of the essay competition is not touched upon, but there is a wealth of character touches ample to block in the queer human entity of Tommy that Barrie etched with such sympathetic vividness.

To this end the adapters have employed carefully chosen passages, such as Tommy's letter writing talents, specifically the note about the "weeping willows" that he walked three miles to see. Another is the leave-taking from Elspeth. So likewise are preserved Tommy's indulgence in emotional frauds; his uncertainties of mind and wierd conflicts with his own soul. The adapters have succeeded in a considerable measure by holding as closely to Barrie's text for their titles as possible. They must have been tempted often to devise their own short-cuts, but the results of deference to the original are worth the pains. For instance, Tommy cannot make up his mind whether or not to run away with Grizel and she upbraids him, he makes the illuminating reply, "How can I make up my mind, when I have so many minds." Nobody but Barrie could have put it so.

The real Barrie sentiment has been somehow conveyed through the camera, but only in part by means of the titles. The players have themselves gotten into the atmosphere of the author's people, and the producer has managed somehow to give the filming a background in settings that is thoroughly convincing. It would perhaps be too much to say that viewing the picture is as satisfying as reading the stories, but it is nonetheless true that to one who has read the book the picture will renew a delightful experience.

Rush.

THE WHISTLE.

Robert Evans..............William S. Hart
Henry Chapple..............Frank Brownlee
Mrs. Chapple.............Myrtle Steadman
Georgie ....Georgie Stone
Danny ....Will Jim Hatton
Baby ....Richard Headrick

For the first time in more than a year the Rialto exhibits the current week a William S. Hart special, the newest (Paramount) release by that hero of a hundred or more motion pictures with a background of western life. In "The Whistle," however, there is an absolute digression from the western locale. Instead, it has a theme involving the conflict, labor versus capital.

The title of the picture retains the original from the story by May Wilmoth and Olin Lyman. The whistle is symbolic of the clarion that arouses from slumber a myriad army of workers to renew their activity in one of a thousand mills where the call is for pressure and an apparent absence of humaneness under that pressure.

As this whistle affects Robert Evans (William S. Hart) he is introduced as the father of a motherless lad. The spokesman for less intrepid employes, he appeals to Henry Chapple (Frank Brownlee) to adjust some faulty machinery which might cost some one's life. The answer is a denial plus an argument that "they are late on orders." Adjusting machinery would take too much time. The lad is subsequently caught in the whirl of faulty machinery and dies, a bleeding picture of helplessness born in the memory of his father. So deprived, his vendetta is born. He saves the mill owner's boy from drowning, kidnaps him and subsequently brings him up as his sister's son.

The action passes on to a construction camp several years later. Here circumstances again brings the boy together with his real parents while his self-imposed uncle is recovering from a bullet wound. There is a bit of tense acting between Evans and Mrs. Chapple (Myrtle Steadman), the boy's mother, to whom thus far his parentage is unknown. A desire to acknowledge the legitimacy of the boy to the unhappy mother is frustrated by the relentless father, who is far from the humanitarian Evans deems fit for the bringing up of the lad.

The concluding episodes deal with the acknowledgment of Chapple to Evans that he was mistaken, his pledge that he will adopt the boy and brings him up to serve humanity. The confession follows, as well as the restoration of the boy to his rightful parents.

The picture as a whole falls short of the standard Hart has thus far created through individual acting and the numerous assets which he has become master of through the mediums enlisting him in the exposition of plainsmen's "ethics." By comparison with those he scarcely has an opportunity to "register" with that forcefulness that one is accustomed to in the work of this star.

With one exception there is an absence of violent action. There is an interpolated hundred or more feet depicting a fight, which for vigor and activeness is admirably effective. But its relation to the story is questionable, and whether the authors intended it or not the entire "shot" is incident, and therefore mechanically contrived.

In adapting the story Lambert Hillyer (also the director) did not possibly figure that the theme itself would be negative. Perhaps it never occurred to him that there are labor inspectors all over the United States keeping in close touch with every kind of a mill or factory. Rottenness in plant construction is something that the employer is quite anxious to adjust speedily because the government demands it. If the action of this story was coupled with the late 90's or the early 1900's it might be relevant.

The action of the first two reels combines the story's more salient points. Its opening scenes are well done, but the pace is never kept up as in the picturization of Hart and the scrapping lad. Hart's biggest scene is a debate with the mill owner, an attempt enacting certain scenes that might go very well on the spoken stage. Here they are lacking in screen effectiveness. The best acting is done by Miss Steadman as the bereaved mother. The role is outstanding for its sincerity, but it is hard to condone her extreme make-up. Mr. Brownlee is never suggestive of the callous mill owner, neither in attire nor personal features. The player was miscast. The three children act commendably.

As a production it is all that it should be in interiors and exteriors.

Step.

ROADS OF DESTINY

Rose Merritt.............Pauline Frederick
David Marsh.....................John Bowers
Lewis Marsh...............Richard Tucker
Ann Hardy.........................Jane Novak
Mr. Hardy...................Hardee Kirkland
McPherson.....................Willard Louis
Fate..............................Maude George
Colby..............................M. B. Flynn

"Roads of Destiny," a Goldwyn production, directed by Frank Lloyd, from a scenario by Channing Pollock, was suggested by the story of that name written by O. Henry. Instead of making the central character a man, as in the short story, Mr. Pollock has made the chief figure a woman. This was probably because of the fact that it presents a woman star, in Pauline Frederick.

In brief the gist of the story is that "what is to be will be." The fatalistic idea has been the basis of many pictures in the past, but as presented in "Roads of Destiny" it reveals hitherto unrealized possibilities. The dramatic element has been splendidly brought out in this production, due to the presence of an excellent cast as well as a scenario that possesses something deeper than the regulation type of scenarios.

In a production way the film has many outstanding features, such as the scenes laid in Alaska, depicting life in the rough and ready days of the gold rush, with its dance halls, gambling houses, etc. Another part of the film has the Long Island suburban cottage section for its background, with its wealth of picturesque scenery, furnishing atmosphere of the convincing sort.

The thousands who have read the O. Henry story will find in the film a splendid variation of the theme. A striking interpretation is given by

John Bowers, who incidentally bears a considerable resemblance to William Farnum. Richard Tucker, also shines in a role that permits of dramatic expression of the higher order. Jane Novak plays with her customary ease, and artistic portrayals are offered by Hardee Kirkland, Willard Louis, and Maude George.

Miss Frederick gets everything possible out of a role that calls for repressed emotion. The picture pleased when shown initially at the Capitol last Sunday afternoon. It should give equal satisfaction in any of the better picture houses.

Bell.

MAN—WOMAN—MARRIAGE.

Victoria	Dorothy Phillips
The Father	Ralph Lewis
The Mother	Margaret Mann
David Courtney	James Kirkwood
Schuyler	Robert Cain
Henshaw	J. Barney Sherry
Bobo	Shannon Day
Richard	Gordon Marr
The Wronged One	Jean Calhoun
Milly	Frances Parks
Jerry	Emily Chichester

Man's treatment of woman is the thesis of Allen Holubar's stupendous film production, starring Dorothy Phillips and released by First National. It runs 96 minutes, and in order to present it at the Strand Managing Director Plunkett found it necessary to eliminate all but the news weekly to keep the show within the two-hour limit. A brief prolog precedes the feature, handsomely produced, but quite as vague as the picture itself.

Emerging from the theatre Sunday evening the reviewer overheard a remark from a "flapper" which sums up the effect upon the audiences much more succinctly than a column of comment. It was as follows: "Every time it gets interesting she hits the pipe." This comment referred to the flashbacks showing "Woman" throughout the ages.

The story opens and closes in the present, telling of the Faith of Woman—that "Right must conquor Might," etc. Stripped of the cutbacks, which are magnificent, scenically and as specimens of the director's art, the story is elemental. These cutbacks alternate with the progression of the tale. They are a series of incarnations of Woman in the various ages, with nothing new other than the expensive manner in which they are produced before the camera.

The star and the supporting company are of fine quality as film artists—there is every evidence that a few fortunes were expended in the production, but the feature, taken as a whole, is tiresome. *Jolo.*

HER LORD AND MASTER.

A fragmentary slice out of the placid pages of life in society as lived here and in England is translated to the screen for Vitagraph by Edward Jose, director, from a story by J. Clarkson Miller entitled "Her Lord and Master." In it Alice Joyce is starred, and heads a cast of exceptionally able players — cast as desirably as anyone could possibly wish for—but, whose abilities are limited by a vehicle, which through direction, is lacking in action.

The story is not good picture material from the start, although it shows off the star to advantage. That, however, in addition to the able cast and a production carefully managed, is sufficient to warrant five reels. The element of suspense is lacking. The humor arising from a situation in which the heroine mockingly conforms to the modest ideas of an elderly and Victorian mother-in-law is not generously distributed to form a story in itself. Neither is it sufficient to make up for absence of action. Sequences between a youngish grandmother of the heroine setting her hook for an elderly and titled bachelor are amusing.

Its climax is weak, absent from any gripping force that otherwise would justify the preceding four reels. The star's most commendable bit of artistry is portrayed in several "shots," "registering" her happiness upon seeing her parents.

In all the total effect of the picture is equal to opening the pages of a picture book and getting no greater thrill from it than having observed some pretty faces in the foreground of rich surroundings.

The action is laid in the opening scenes in an autumn resort of a self made American millionaire. Here the heroine is wooed and won by the scion of an aristocratic English family. Before her marriage the heroine exacts a promise from her future husband that during their married life in the event that she displays self will, her husband is never to give in no matter how much he loves her. The subsequent scenes are laid in the home of her husband, and the climax is arrived at with a rebellious wife going out to dine with her parents on a Sunday evening, against the wishes of her husband who deems it improper for a lady to be seen in public on the Sabbath. The difference of opinion ends in a reconciliation the morning after.

In addition to Miss Beaudet, the character work of Ida Waterman as the mother-in-law and John Sutherland as the butler are two examples of fine screen acting, finished and polished in every degree. Marie Shotwell and Frank Sheridan as the parents have little to do. Holmes E. Hobart is typical of the cold, dominating English husband, while Eugene Acker has a bit.

The photography is even, well lighted and includes several excellent long shots commendable for their range and pictorial effect.

Step.

DUCKS AND DRAKES

Teddy Simpson	Bebe Daniels
Rob Winslow	Jack Holt
Aunty Weeks	Mame Kelso
Dick Chiltern	Edward Martindel
Tom Hazzard	W. E. Lawrence
Colonel Tweed	Wade Boteler
Cissy	Maurie Newell
Mina	Elsie Andrean

Bebe Daniels, the star, is the best thing in this Realart production which moved into the Rivoli March 27. The finest possible photography makes the most of her beauty, well fitted interiors and gorgeous gowns and lingerie, but when you have said this and spoken a word for aptly titled but scattered humorous scenes you have told the praiseworthy side of the matter. The story by Elmer Harris is slight and interminably extended. It makes a slow start, and Maurice Campbell in directing it failed at any point to tighten it up so it took a grip on the interest.

Teddy Simpson is a debutante who is engaged to Rob Winslow. She finds him a bore because he and her aunt are always in league to reprove her, and so starts a series of telephone flirtations. Winslow discovers fellow clubmen of his are the parties of the other part, but does not worry inasmuch as they are gentlemen. But suppose some bounder should get hold of the little girl? The clubmen combine to cure her. One calls when she is pretending to be ill. Another takes her automobiling and out to a secluded river shack, where the third pretends he is an escaped convict and stages a fake attack on her. The fiance comes to the rescue only to find she has made her own escape.

They are married but she rejects his attentions till he climbs into her room from outdoors. There's a laugh in the ending, but on the whole the picture is unconvincing though admirably acted. *Leed.*

"GHOST IN THE GARRET."

Delsie O'Dll, a poor relation..Dorothy Gish
Bill Clark, a secretary and hero........William E. Park
Gilbert Dennison, Delsie's uncle........Downing Clark
Percy White, a social secretary and villain........Ray Gray
Mrs. Gilbert Dennison..Mrs. David Landau
Dennison's butler.........Walter T. Lewis
Dennison's cook..................Mrs. Foy
Detective O'Connor..........Frank Badgley
Crooks......Tom Blake, Frank Hagney, William Nally, Porter Strong

That good old hoke classic, standby of burlesque and vaudeville in the variety days, when no show of that character was complete without an afterpiece, "Ghost in the Pawnshop" has been dug from the musty archives of the theatrical past, embellished, modified and modernized, and blossoms forth as "Ghost in the Garrett," a Fine Arts-Paramount, starring Dorothy Gish. F. Richard Jones directed and Wells Hastings wrote the photoplay.

It's a farce, and a capital one, with the laughs bunched in the latter part of the picture, cumulative action of the liveliest sort keeping the interest at fever heat through a thread of interpolated melodrama neatly blended with the farcical theme. The author knows his picture audiences and has succeeded in giving 'em "what they want."

The yarn unfolded is relative to a stolen necklace and a substitute paste affair, which suggests the author may have quite as good a knowledge of De Maupassant as he has of standardized farce and burlesque. Dorothy Gish plays a sort of "Peg o' My Heart" type, with a bulldog instead of a terrier, looks sweet and peachy and realizes the full meaning of the comedy situations she is involved in.

One of the pieces of business has Miss Gish sitting on a chair and pretending she is part of it by enveloping herself in the furniture cover. This is good for several wows and is capably handled by Miss Gish, a comedienne, incidentally, who registers every point with precision. The animated chair thing was old when Willie Collier made his debut, but it's apparently new to present-day film fans. In addition to the old afterpiece mentioned, which seems to have been the basis of the story, there is also a slight suggestion of "Seven Keys to Baldpate." The big comedy scenes—and there is a succession of nifties of the sure-fire sort, sufficient to "make" a couple of film comedies—take place in a haunted house, where Miss Gish goes in search of the stolen necklace.

A gang of crooks is making headquarters in the haunted house, and Miss Gish succeeds in spreading terror among them by utilizing draperies and various coverings, cavorting about the house as a supposed "ghost." There is a bit of a love story interwoven, conflict galore and a nicely sustained element of mystery.

That the story is based on an old idea and contains much familiar material means nothing, except possibly to strengthen the picture. As a whole the film is corking entertainment. The scenic investiture is up to the best standards, but the photography in several places is merely tinted, where "night photography" would have been more artistic. All the parts are well played, the chap playing the tough crook and the man doing blackface standing out in a comedy way. The leader of the crooks is also excellently interpreted. *Bell.*

THE SMART SEX.

Rose Darrow	Eva Novak
Fred Vaughn	Goeffrey Webb
Horace	Frank Kingsley
Danny O'Grady	James O'Neill
Papa Vaughn	C. Norman Hammond

Eva Novak is starred in this Universal effusion, which sub-featured at the Circle Tuesday—and amply proved the reason for the minor billing. It is just an ordinary Universal of usual U standard as far as production expense goes—which is kept at a minimum—and will do fairly well for the double jitney houses.

Miss Novak, as a member of a show troupe, is stranded in a country town where she happens along in time for an amateur contest at the local "opry house" and annexes first honors, winning the approval of the college crowd in general and Fred Vaughn in particular. The latter installs her at the Haskins farm, and in due time falls in love with her, although barred by the usual obstacles, such as a well-meaning female parent, who has already selected one of their "set" for her offspring's future wife, etc. Among other things, the hero leaves his home following a harmless gambling episode, and it is as a co-laborer with the heroine on the Haskins farm that he acquires a mate. For an attempted punch twist wherein some uncut diamonds are stolen, Rose falls under the usual suspicion, as is expected in such circumstances, but vindicates herself after a much ado about nothing situation.

The support is worthy, particularly Mr. Webb in the leading male role, and Frank Kingsley as Horace, the bespectacled, sedate personage.

Emma Bell Clifton perpetrated the story; Doris Schroeder the slow moving continuity, and Fred Leroy Granville is the accredited director of this Universal "special."

The role of Edith, the "smart" young lady who aspires to the honor of being the hero's wife, is sadly miscast and unconvincing.

Production expense, as stated before, is kept at a minimum, being mostly exteriors, with a theatre and a ball room scene betraying some trace of a loose purse string.

The title itself would not be considered as strictly descriptive of the exposition.

The star herself is acceptable all things considered.

GIRL WITH A MILLION

"The Girl with a Million" is a five-reel feature presented by Fred. W. Falkner, directed by Edwin Forrester, scenario by Germaine Dulac, and starring Suzanne Grandais.

The story follows rather closely "Peg o' My Heart" for the first four reels, and instead of finishing at the same point as "Peg," proceeds to a more serious situation.

Suzanne is a poor milliner's apprentice and loves a young artist who is her neighbor. They become engaged when suddenly she is informed she has fallen heir to a large fortune. Her fiance, in a burst of self-abnegation, renounces his right to marry her and tells her he has undergone a change of heart.

Meantime Suzanne has gone to live with titled relatives who scheme to marry her off to their son and thereby save the estate. Stung by what she believes to be a "throw down" on the part of the artist and dazzled by the pomp and importance of marrying a marquis, she contents to marry the profligate son, who plans to secure her fortune and squander it upon his mistress.

It is at this point Miss Grandais unloosens a wealth of emotional power. On the night her betrothal is to be formally announced she enters the reception hall and denounces the conspiracy to annex her fortune by marriage and returns to her former modest abode. There her bosom friend from the millinery shop frames with her to pretend she has lost her fortune, which has the effect of bringing the artist-lover to her feet once more, and all ends well.

A pretentious production, well directed and excellently acted throughout. *Jolo.*

OUT OF THE CHORUS.

Here again is the amplification of the theme involving the chorus girl married to a scion of a family with money and social prestige. Eager to do her share in the matrimonial contract and truly in love with her husband, she is slighted by a mother-in-law whose ambition is to see her son separated and her daughter-in-law in disgrace. An old admirer of her chorus girl's days whom she had turned down appears and tells stories of the girl's past. These are untrue, but enough to satisfy any dowager with a Van added to her name.

The mother-in-law goes on believing. The action culminates in the murder of the admirer by the ex-chorus queen's husband. The family is undetermined about helping the son. His chorus girl wife, accepts a two-a-day engagement at $2,000 per to pay the legal fees. She goes one better. She is willing to tell a jury that her husband had a right to kill this Ned. She is willing to confess guilt in the absence of real guilt to save him. The psychological moment occurs when the real murderer shows up. A confession that he is the uncle of the murdered man and had been "railroaded" to a lunatic asylum explains the reason. Several months later the family and the chorus girl are reconciled, but not until she has made a tremendous hit as a dancer at the "Winter Palace." Just why this had to be included in the continuity other than to show a magnificent set with Miss Brady as the central figure in diaphanous dancing apparel is hard to understand.

In this instance extravagance is entirely irrelevant, but still the extravagance goes on. Good drama is sacrificed to lavishness. The appeal to the eye means more than the appeal to the intellect.

The story's appeal and the drawing power of the star are the only commercial assets to the picture. The action of the story is too long drawn out. It does not follow a straight line, is padded, is lacking in suspense. It is also overcrowded with titles, so much so that where in the stage version of such a piece one would declare it talky.

The fault is not so much in the story itself as in its adaptation. No poorer example of continuity writing has been seen here in a long while as this by Coolidge Streeter.

A few scenes handled forcefully, convincingly and with the necessary touch of characterization are entrusted to Edith Stockton. For the number of scenes that she appears in she practically dominates the screen. Charles Gerard, Vernon Steele, Emily Fitzroy, Bigelow Cooper and Constance Berry complete the cast. They have been selected with discretion.

The lighting is exceptional and the photography very creditable to J. Badaracco. The art direction of Robert M. Haas adds much in the way of rich production. *Step.*

THE CABINET OF DR. CALIGARI.

Dr. Caligari	Werner Krauss
Cesare	Conrad Veidt
Francis	Fritz Feher
Jane	Lil Dagover
Alan	H. von Twardowski

The box-office value of the German-made "Cabinet of Dr. Caligari," brought to the astonished attention of local fans at the Capitol April 3 by S. L. Rothafel, is problematical in a nation letting "Passion" die in the sticks, but any consideration of that can properly be postponed till attention is centered on the artistic advance this picture marks. It is not only a step in a new direction—it is a misconception to call it a step in advance—but also in the way of direction and acting it is so completely and skilfully organized and handled as to compel attention and study.

It may catch the popular fancy, for certainly it is a mystery story told in the Poe manner and fairly prods the interest along at a high pace. But it is morbid. Continental creations usually are. The story is of a young man who is seen first relating to a visitor the peculiar reasons for the trance in which a young lady whom he points out appears to be. "She has been that way since—," we are informed by one of Katherine Hillaker's brief sub-titles, and then we are into the major portion of the story.

This relates how a faker—misspelled "fakir" on the screen—came to a fair at a small town and proceeded to enliven things by having a somnambulist who had been asleep for twenty-three years foretell the future. The faker called himself Dr. Caligari. A murder is foretold and a series of them occur. Finally the somnambulist, who commits them, fails to kill the young woman known as Jane, and throws himself over the cliff. Dr. Caligari is pursued to a neighboring insane asylum, where he is revealed as Dr. Sonnow, head of the institution. At this point we dissolve back to the young man, Francis, telling the visitor his story. Enter Dr. Sonnow. Francis promptly attacks him, protesting he is Caligari. That is the delusion of Francis, and now that he knows his delusion, the innocent Dr. Sonnow can cure him. The rest was a tale told by a madman.

Mr. Rothafel introduced the picture with a tableau and ended it in the same manner. All exhibitors cannot afford to do this, but the story is so unusual in its telling as to make it possible to say, without fear of successful contradiction, that any group of so-called cultured people who fail to see it are neglecting their education. To miss it is to include oneself among the insular and uneducated.

Of first importance is the direction and cutting. This has resulted in a series of actions so perfectly dovetailed as to carry the story through to its conclusion and answer at a perfect tempo, with due weight and no more given every item of which it is compounded. The director's name is Robert Wiene. Among the few pre-eminent in the world today he may justly be included because of what he has done with this story by Karl Mayer and Hans Janowitz.

He has made perfect use of settings designed by Hermann Warm, Walter Reimann and Walter Rohrig, probably members of the younger Munich group of independent artists. They have made—in black and white, of course—settings that squeeze and turn and adjust the eye and through the eye the mentality. This squeezing and adjustment of the mentality is of such a sort that soon the mind is attuned to the fantastic and mysterious quality of the story itself. Nowhere is there a shot of nature itself. Everything is designed and painted and there is everywhere a sense of the widening and narrowing of the attention. This is done not by irises, close-ups and other such familiar fowl that have prowled too long in the barnyard of the industry's infancy, but by new means, by the arrangement of spaces and values, by the laying of heavy lines in juxtaposition to ones lighter, and this new method deserves special and careful study by experts, with a view to making use of the basic notion in American productions.

Lastly we come to the acting. The settings are more important than the acting. They establish the mood for the acting. They maintain it inescapably, but with so much done for them the performers still do their share, and they have a great deal to live up to. If they did not live up to it their poor work would stand out glaringly.

The best performance unquestionably is that given by Werner Krauss as Dr. Caligari. He manages to lay in his part much as the settings are laid in. There is a suggestion of the cubist about his every attitude as Dr. Caligari and of the natural about his impersonation of Dr. Sonnow. The naturalness, of course, stood out as sane from the crazy background which suggested an insane asylum more surely than a real picture of such an environment could have done. The unpleasant somnambulist, Cesare, was ghoulishly made evident for every one by Conrad Veidt. Lesser roles were competently taken. The part of the girl, played by Lil Dagover, shows distinctly the difference in type appeal between this country and Germany. She suggests a dark model for Botticelli, where the head of a Raphael cupid on a girl's figure is nearer the American ideal.

But the settings were the main thing. As Willard Huntington Wright, America's most distinguished art critic, remarked, they were worthy of Picasso. Produced by a German scientist and professor as an independent venture, artistically this is the most interesting picture since "Broken Blossoms." *Leed.*

THE PASSION FLOWER

Acacia	Norma Talmadge
Esteban	Courtenay Foote
Raimunda	Eulalie Jensen
Norbert	Harrison Ford
Tio Eusebio	Charles Stevenson
Julia	Alice May
Their Three Sons	Herbert Vance H. D. McClellan Austin Harrison
Faustino	Robert Agnew
Little Carlosa	Harold Stern
Milagros	Natalie Talmadge
Old Juliana	Mrs. Jacques Martin
Francesca	Elsa Fredericks
Norbert's father	Robert Payton Gibb
The Padre	Augustus Balfour
Rubio	Walter Wilson
Dona Isabel	Mildred Adams
Acacia's father	Julian Greer
Bernabe	Edward Boring

It isn't often an established star, either in the legitimate or pictures, permits a member of the supporting cast to have a role of equal importance. It is comparatively easy to curtail a part that stands out too prominently, even after the picture is completed, through the medium of the cutting room. Norma Talmadge, however, has permitted Courtenay Foote, who has the role of Esteban, the step-father, in "The Passion Flower," to shine effulgently—so strongly in fact as to compete for first honor. The character of Raimunda, the mother, is also permitted to stand out. As a matter of fact there are so many good parts in the filming of the Spanish play, and they are all so excellently cast, one might set the production down as all-star.

"The Passion Flower" is probably the strongest piece Norma Talmadge has ever appeared in—an artistic achievement. Atmospheric, romantic and well directed, it follows closely the stage version shown here, but might have gone a little further by a couple of hundred feet of "clinch" to remove the taste of tragedy from it. This might not be so artistic but would be a sop to the proletariat and a bid for popular approval. First National can stand back of this release, guaranteeing exhibitors it will give complete satisfaction. *Jolo.*

CITY OF SILENT MEN.

Jim Montgomery	Thomas Meighan
Molly Bryant	Lois Wilson
Mrs. Montgomery	Kate Bruce
Oild Bill	Paul Everton
Mike Kearney	George MacQuarrie
Mr. Bryant	Guy Oliver

"The City of Silent Men" is a Paramount picture, presented by Jesse L. Lasky, adapted by Frank Condon from "The Quarry," by John A. Moroso and directed by Tom Forman. It has two excellent features, a popular star in Thomas Meighan and a title which piques interest. These two points probably explain the attendance at the Rivoli Sunday evening.

The two valuable assets mentioned are not supported by the film itself. The story is disjointed and rambling and as a screen production it is not, properly speaking, a story at all in the sense of a complete action. Rather it is mere narrative, a chronological record; not a dramatic unity. There is scarcely a moment in the tale when the audience is not well ahead of the developments. There is never a surprise and the element of suspense and of unexpectedness are entirely lacking.

The title, of course, refers to state's prison, in this case Sing Sing, where the hero is a prisoner, unjustly convicted of a murder on circumstantial evidence and railroaded. The conviction is unconvincing, as these screen happenings so often are. Jim Montgomery is a country boy, a mechanic who comes to the city for work, and is led into crime innocently by a gang of crooks.

They tell him they want him to do a repair job, and he goes along to a bank and stands outside while they take his tools inside and proceed to to blow open a safe. Interrupted by the watchman, they kill the guardian and escape, leaving the mechanic to fall into the hands of the police. It takes a good deal of credulity on the part of the spectator to swallow this labored, artificial set of circumstances, all of which is transparently contrived to make a theatrical situation.

The trial is just as implausible. As a matter of fact the whole intricate fabrication belongs to subject matter outside the real story and might better have been introduced in explanation after the prison life had been established. In Sing Sing Jim is befriended by an absurdly sympathetic fellow convict, an elderly crook who is a model of kind heartedness, although he is pictured as a confirmed criminal.

Old Bill, as he is called, helps Jim to escape and the convict is presently found re-established and prosperous in California. Here h[i]s is beloved by the daughter of h.s employer (a pretty close parallel of "Jimmie Valentine"), but haunted by the fear of being run down by the police. His pursuer is Mike Kearney of the New York police, who traces him by means of finding out who it was that ordered and paid for a tombstone for the grave of the escaped convict's mother. Jim's way of covering up this transaction is about as stupid as his actions in the safe-breaking, and leaves a wide open trail.

The detective catches up just on Jim's wedding day. Jim denies his identity, and to prevent detection by his finger prints, thrusts his hands into whirling machinery to mangle them. The detective is touched by this heroism and agrees to let Jim go free. Old Bill, however, has been released from jail in the meantime and runs down the real criminals just in time for a happy end. The whole thing is ridicuously theatrical and artificial and an unworthy vehicle for so satisfying a screen player as Meighan.

In a purely pictorial sense there are many striking "shots," particularly the night photography dealing with Jim's escape, and the directorshop throughout is painstaking. The trouble with the picture is that the story is basically all wrong in its form and material. It is depressing, particularly the harrowing passages of the death of the convict's mother and the gloomy atmosphere of prison life. It is a mistake to consider morbid gloom as "strong" drama. "The City of Silent Men" is an offering to be avoided as depressing and profitless.

Rush.

OUTSIDE WOMAN.

There is little to laugh at; there is little to smile with; there is little reason for the making of this Realart five-reel production entitled "The Outside Woman." Wanda Hawley is the star. Her principal business is to show off some distinctive creations in feminine apparel.

Intended as a comedy feature, it is devoid of comedy. Its situations were no more mirth provoking with a Loew's New York audience than registering five laughs, and not one that might be regarded as of the diaphram species. It is a disappointment from beginning to end. The piece never had a chance.

The play as a picture is from a scenario by Douglas Bronston from an early effort by Paul P. Sipe and Philip Bartholomae. Its situations are these: A newly-wed couple is entrusted with the care of a valuable antique, the value of which is unknown to them. The wife, with a penchant for exchanging things, gives the relic away in trade for a shawl. The shawl vendor in turn sells it to an artist living directly over the newly weds. Learning the value of the lost relic and discovering its whereabouts, the wife climbs the fire escape and encounters the artist. The latter's jealous wife returns in the interval and discovers the two. For safety the heroine locks the turbulent wife of the artist in a separate room. A policeman comes in and holds the scene until an ambulance may arrive for the outside woman. Explanations are offered in due time to clear the field.

One reason why this film comedy did not register with the audience was that the situations were explained by the sub-titles, and this had a great deal to do with wearing the edge off of its humor. In any event, this kind of material as furnished by the original authors hasn't a chance on Broadway.

The cast ranks as standard, but the members unquestionably miss the object as comedy purveyors. The players are Clyde Fillmore, Thena Jasper, Sidney Bracey, Rosita Martini, Misao Seki, Mary Winston and Jake Abrams.

Supplementing the film are the names of Paul Perry and Una Nixon Hopkins as having had the major part of the responsibilities in making this picture. The production is rich in settings and the photography is even. *Step.*

THE WAKEFIELD CASE.

This L. Lawrence Weber production cannot be recommended too highly as a picture offering with stellar merit, for the principal reason that the novelty of its theme, in which the hidden motive of its characters is bared in the finale. The idea has been used in pictures preceding it, and notably in "Seven Keys to Baldplate" and "Cheating Cheaters." There is a thrill in its tense and often exaggerated scenes.

As far as plot is concerned it is secondary. The action is spread over incidents involving a detective and his playwright son. The detective loses his life after an almost successful attempt in trapping two crooks, brothers, who are in possession of some jewels owned by the British Museum. An investigation into the killing of the detective leaves the clue that it may have been the "Breen girl," since her dagger is left near the victim.

The concluding drama is left to the playwright, who turns detective to avenge his father. He falls in love with the "Breen girl," who is unknown to him, while a passenger on the same boat is one of the crooks separated earlier from the jewels. The balance of the story is enacted in America. It is filled with the usual underworld atmosphere, with some dash and pep on the part of the hero, who is captured and eludes his persecutors. And again the usual titles explaining to an easily convincing hero that the master crook is from Scotland Yard. Worst of all is the desire on the part of the author to convince the audience that the "Breen girl" is the daughter of "Grayson" of the Secret Service and that the wounded soldier is also a Grayson. This is too much for any one's tired eyes.

The cast includes Herbert Rawlinson (featured), Charles Dalton, Jere Austin, Florence Billings, William W. Black, J. H. Gilmour, Joseph Burke, J. P. Wate. There is very little that one can say apropos of histrionic merit in any one's performance in that cast. If Charles Dalton could see himself in the role of a man waiting to poke out the eye of his victim with a hot poker projected in the flaming heat of a burner, and if the thought occurred to him that he gave one of the most masterful performances as the "Doctor" in "The Case of Lecky," wouldn't it seem equally absurd to him?

The direction is by George Irving, the scenario from an original by Mrs. L. Case Russell, the photography by Walter Young. *Step.*

THE LITTLE CLOWN.

Pat	Mary Miles Minter
Dick Beverley	Jack Mulhall
Colonel Beverley	Winter Hall
Mrs. Beverley	Helen Dunbar
Roddy Beverley	Cameron Coffey
Toto	Neely Edwards
Jim Anderson	Wilton Taylor
Connie Potts	Lucien Littlefield
Liz	Zelma Maja
Nellie Johnson	Lura Anson

Thomas Heffron has made a satisfying production of Avery Hopwood's "The Little Clown" for Realart, in which Mary Miles Minter is accorded starring honors, at the Rialto, New York, this week. It's a tale of the big top with the star personating the title role, that of a feminine clown in Jim Anderson's mammoth show. Enters the hero, Dick Beverly (Jack Mulhall) of Beverly Hall, Beverly City, Va., a refined "tramp," and secure a position with the circus as bareback rider. The romance quickly ensues, with his parents entering into the scene, inducing their offspring to return, and willing to accept his circus sweetheart on a six months' probation in which to prove her mettle. She leaves the Beverly home for the circus, the hero pursuing, and for a fade-out a church wedding scene, following a "title" which read, "After a year at a fashionable finishing school."

Nothing startlingly original here, yet altogether acceptable for a program feature. It is a case of story overshadowing the histrionic efforts of the cast. Even the star has little opportunity for distinguishment, her circus clown stuff being of the simplest, while a long distance view of her ground tumbling was evidently "double" by some expert. Yet on the whole, it is a well done job, cast direction, continuity and photography all considered.

Eugene B. Lewis did the adaptation and has done himself credit, for the continuity really is an interest sustaining affair. Faxon Dean's photography should not be overlooked either. He had some mellow shots throughout.

The support is worthy.

PARTNERS OF THE TIDE.

There are three incidents in the action of this picture filmed from the book of similar title by Joseph C. Lincoln which provide the major portion of the thrills. Otherwise it is slow in action. In fact, it drags and the loose titles and over-elaboration of detail do not help stimulate the interest but rather wear out the patience of the onlooker.

The element of drama leading to its pictorial climaxes has not been provided for with the interest concentrated on the three major incidents. And this has had a great deal to do with the lack of interest before the climaxes are attained. Director Irvin W. Willat announces from the start that "liberties" have been taken with the original. The wonder then is why he or L. V. Jefferson, accredited with the authorship of the scenario, did not build a more direct script. The picture gives the impression of padding with incident, when the need really is for more drama and romance.

The best that can be said for the picture in the matter of acting is furnished in the opening scenes. The hero, at first impersonated by Marion Faducah, is an orphan. He is on his way to two spinsters who adopt him. In the following scenes the acting by this youngster registers with sure appeal. Indeed, the merit of his work stands out in bold contrast to the acting by the rest of the cast. And none seems equal to the appeal that this boy exerts. The action then glides over a period of fifteen years. The hero is here disclosed in the role of a sailor, and afterwards as a diver. With another he is engaged in investigating the sinking of a schooner owned by his sweetheart's grandmother. The hero's fellow-workman plots his destruction and tries to lock him in the cabin of the submerged vessel. The hero is rescued, but the villain causes his rival's boat to catch fire.

A preceding shot of the sinking schooner is pictorially effective. The scenes below the water are well done. As a whole the picture might be regarded as a fair program release. At the New York it was used on a double feature day. It is released by W. W. Hodkinson through Pathe. *Step.*

THAT SOMETHING

This picture has been dedicated to the Rotary Clubs of the world by the Tacoma Rotary Club No. 8, of Tacoma, Wash. It is a production by the Hermann Film Corporation, directed by Margery Wilson, who also acts one of the major parts. The scenario has been supplied from W. W. Woodbridge's book of the same title.

The theme of the picture story is power of man's will over environment.

The action involves the self-indulgent youth of an irate parent, who, failing to arouse any of the better qualities in his son, orders him from his home, making it plain that the son cannot return until he shall have "made good.". The youth of polished manner and immaculate clothes is transformed into a tramp. He goes through every hardship, and the turning point in his career occurs just when he needs food the most. Applying to a stranger, he is rejected. Instead, the stranger hands him a piece of philosophy which sounds like this: "Young man, what you need is finding yourself. You must find 'That Something,' within you."

And from then on the psychological transformation takes place. He succeeds in getting his first job when the odds are against him, and the action compels him to move from place to place, winning greater consideration with each stepping stone. In fact, he meets the same man who once gave him knowledge instead of a 'hand-out.' That man is a silent partner in the concern which employs him. Later he is reconciled to his family, and the finale of the picture has him basking in the radiance of happiness achieved.

From a production standpoint, the feature has real merit. It is a fair program picture. It, nevertheless, profuse with technical faults and the continuity is choppy.

Apart from its commercial possibilities it is not unlikely that if the owners of this feature cared to exploit it, as industrial propaganda it might have it uses.

The acting is not of a high order with the exception of Charles Meredith, who measures up to the best artistic standpoint. *Step.*

CHARMING DECEIVER.

Together with "The Wakefield Case," this picture was used on a double-feature day at Loew's Circle. It is from the Vitagraph studios, starring Alice Calhoun, although there is scarcely any ground for starring her, judging from the present performance. The picture is adapted from an original script by Mrs. Owen Bronson, the scenario for which was completed by Fred Schaefer and the direction left to George L. Sargent. The photography is by Vincent P. Scully.

Dramatically it is a poor picture, offering scarcely anything in the way of a climax, and in its action moves listlessly, arriving at nothing more than a happy ending, which has been anticipated all along. Its continuity is often clogged by subtitles which do not lend, but detract, from what possibly might contribute something in the way of lifting the subject into a big moment. It is doubtful if the story could lend itself to that kind of action which is essential in pictures, and except for the acting of two principals there is little left to recommend.

"Charming Deceiver" has as its central character a girl deceived into marriage by a man who in the opening scenes is in jail. An invitation comes to her and a brother to spend the rest of their days with a grandfather, who earlier in life could not condine the match of their mother. The brother is recovering in a hospital, and she goes on alone, ultimately establishing herself in the home of the grandfather. Her husband in the interval escapes from jail and seeks the protection of his wife's home. He is introduced as the absent brother. The concluding scenes are taken up with the appearance of the legitimate brother. Due explanation is made. In the end the convict conveniently kills himself.

The cast includes Jack McLean, Eugene Acker, Charles Kent, Roland Bottomley and Robert Gaillard. Mr. Acker's performance, especially in the "drunk" scenes, were nothing short of wonderful, while the part handled by Charles Kent was amazing for a natural quality and interest attracted sheerly through personality.

Step.

DREAM STREET.

Gypsy Fair ....Miss Carol Dempster
Her Father ....W. J. Ferguson
James "Spike" McFadden...Ralph Graves
Billie McFadden ...Charles Emmett Mack
Sway Wan ....Edward Peil
Samuel Jones ....Porter Strong
A Police Inspector.......Charles Slattery
Tom Chudder ....George Neville
The Sayer of Old Truths (The Good
   Influence) ....Tyrone Power
The Trickster of the Streets (The
   Evil Influence) ......Morgan Wallace

D. W. Griffith's new picture production, "Dream Street," came to the Central Tuesday night, its opening having been delayed for several days. It is a typical Griffith screen creation, rich in deft touches such as he alone seems to be able to impart to film dramas, but at moments inept in its story telling method.

The defects are trifling, however, compared to the power of the melodrama and the sure instinct for compelling details, incidents and appealing character appeal. The good may safely be attributed to Griffith, the ill appears to be on the side of Roy Sinclair who made the scenario from two stories by Thomas Burke, who also wrote the original story from which "Broken Blossoms" was taken.

This new production will have its Broadway triumphs, although it may not reach the proportions of "Way Down East," but in less sophisticated communities, both in New York and elsewhere, its smashing melodrama will give it a following probably as great if not greater than anything the film producer has done. Its second half is tremendously absorbing with a succession of surprises and telling dramatic situations equalled by no straight-away film story that comes to mind.

Not that the picture is merely material melodrama. Nothing could be further from the truth. Griffith has made it his aim to express certain spiritual elements of real life in terms of melodrama. The terms of the story are perhaps theatrical, but its essence is of the spirit.

The theme of the play might be set down in its briefest form as this: We are all of us made up of good and bad and vague but strong forces are at work within us and about us to give direction to these raw materials of character. That being the thesis, Griffith makes his meaning plain in the story of two brothers, Billy McFadden, physically weak but spiritually fine, and "Spike" McFadden, a physical giant with a certain arrogance and almost brutal selfishness. "Spike" is the hard hitting leader of the neighborhood, the slums of London by the backgrounds, with a golden voice to aid him in his conquest of the girls. Billy is a gentle dreamer, no nightingale, but yearning to express a sense of beauty in making songs.

Out of these elements the two are to mould their characters. The test by fire comes when they both fall in love with the same girl, neither knowing of the other's passion. "Spike's" lust for conquest over women makes him a bold suitor after Gypsy Fair, a concert hall dancer. But Gypsy is no weakling and their courtship becomes a desperate battle of the sexes. Her resistance strikes sparks in "Spike" and the strength of will and body are converted into the finest kind of spiritual love.

Billy, made of different stuff, is a diffident lover. His weakness expresses itself in long distance wooing and he is soon outdistanced in the competition. When "Spike" wins Gypsy, Billy starts to shoot him, but his better nature, or perhaps Griffith means his sense of his own inferiority, makes him give up the design. A further growth of the pair in their relations comes when Billy kills a rowdy and he lets the stronger brother take the blame, shrinking from the ordeal of

pursuit and trial as one of his composition of body and spirit might be expected to do.

The stronger man's instinct to protect (a new development of his better side) makes him shoulder the blame and undergo the trial unshaken, until conscience drives the weaker to a confession and the release of "Spike" to Gypsy's arms.

That is the outline, but it is richly filled in with major and minor incidents. The love scenes between "Spike" and Gypsy are a mine of exquisite comedy and drama. That passage where the brute pursues the girl to her room intending to force her kisses, only to be overcome and shackled by her woman's wiles is a gem of deft and dainty high comedy. And the scene in which the man's awakened love sends him to the girl's feet in shame is a fine bit of poetry.

Griffith has done some effective creation in symbols to embroider his creation of the forces driving the two brothers. Whenever either of them is in the midst of a spiritual struggle there appear in the street close by either or both of two characters, personification of good and evil. The good influence is in the person of a "Sayer of Old Truths" as Griffith calls an itinerant street preacher (splendidly played by Tyrone Power). The evil force is typified by a street violinist, a weird and sinister figure, "whose strange face is beautiful, but whose stringed violin wails suggestions of evil," says a program note. These two, of course, represent the good and evil within the brothers.

Then there is another of those evil influences in the person of a vicious Chinaman with a deep lust for the music hall girl and evil ingenuity in plotting her downfall. Around this dreadful figure revolve some of the most thrilling episodes, colorful melodrama of the smashing sort, such as that in which he lures the girl to his luxurious den and seeks to bend her to his wicked desires. Another is the passage in which the uncanny Oriental betrays "Spike" to the police by the trick of springing a signal which brings them to the fugitive, as neat a dramatic surprise as could be conceived.

From first to last the scenic features of the play are flawless and the photography unmatched. One passage will serve as an index to this feature of the production. When the police are in pursuit of "Spike" after the killing, he races through the slum by-ways in the midst of a fog. These shots are wonderful. One sitting in the theatre almost gets a sensation of choking mist; the pavements shine with moisture and tiny globules stand out from the dark walls. No illusion could be more effective. These slum scenes are fascinating with their atmosphere of shadowy mystery and a sort of looming tragedy. No painter with brush and oils could make the effect more poignant than Griffith and his cameraman have done.

The players are splendid. Carol Dempster as Gypsy seems at first just a suspicion of too hard in her regular beauty, but misted portraits in the closeups correct this. Those faintly blurred closeups of a lovely face are new triumphs of portraiture. Miss Dempster gets over the essential quality of youth and femininity and creates an adequate characterization.

The other main character, that of "Spike," is done by Ralph Graves, who looks and acts like Maurice Barrymore of half a generation ago and makes one of the most striking screen characterizations in the Griffith repertoire. Morgan Wallace as the evil street violinist accomplishes an effect much like that of John Barrymore in "Dr. Jekyll and Mr. Hyde."

The picture at the Central Tuesday night ran two hours and a

quarter, approximately 10 reels, and is divided into two parts. The defect of the scenario or continuity is that the first half is rather tiresome, due to the over-elaboration of preparation and detail. The work of "planting" situations which are to come to fruit later is done too conscientiously, much as a certain brand of Sunday magazine story harps unnecessarily on detail in labored effort to build up an effect. The proof of the mechanical error here is disclosed in too many titles. The first half of the story at times seems to be told more in printed titles than in screen action.

However, when the work of preparation is accomplished it makes for a singularly powerful story from mid-way to end. It is a pity that the necessary preliminaries could not have been established with an art that would conceal the working of the technical machinery.

Rush.

QUEEN OF SHEBA.

The Queen of Sheba..........Betty Blythe
King Solomon ....Fritz Lieber
Queen Amarath, the wife of Solomon
   Claire De Lorez
King Armud, of Sheba...George Siegmann
Tamaran, a courtier of Sheba
   Herbert Heyes
Mentor, Sheba's Minister of State
   Herschel Mayall
Adonijah, brother of Solomon...G. R. Nye
King David ....George Nichols
Beth-Sheba ....Genevieve Blinn
Sheba's son, aged 4............Pat Moore
Nomis, Sheba's sister.......Joan Gordon
Olos, Sheba's giant slave...William Hardy
King of Tyre..............John Cosgrove
Envoy of King Pharaoh...Paul Cazeneuve
Princess Vashti ....Nell Craig
Captain of Adonijah's Army..Al Fremont
Joab, a soldier.................Earl Crane

Fox's third special feature now playing in New York opened Sunday at the Lyric before an audience that was aroused to an applause demonstration of acknowledgment at the conclusion of the first half of the film, and again at its completion. The reason for the first will be the outstanding characteristic of the latest Fox super whenever it is discussed, and it was worthy of the accord acclaimed—the chariot races which bring the initial stanza to a close.

Placed in an arena the visualizing of a sextet of chariots, each drawn by four horses, whirling around the track, affords action that is. Tom Mix is given credit, on the program, for "invaluable aid" in staging the races. He has done a corking piece of work and displayed some effects particularly noteworthy. The principal one was the overturning of a leading chariot, on a turn, with the remainder of the contestants going on, and over, the upturned vehicle. There were also numerous excellent flashes during the race between the Queen and her feminine rival which had the horses coming head on to the camera, at angles and from a distance. These also brought applause unto themselves.

Virginia Tracy authored the story based, mainly, on legend and tradition. The music was arranged by Erno Rapee. J. Gordon Edwards is scheduled as having done the actual directing, assisted by a corps of helpers. There is no stupendous sum stated as to the cost of production, but the picture looks money all the way with the lavish costuming, massive sets and the mob stuff, all of which have been handled nicely and recorded by photography that is worthy of more than passing mention, with John Boyle responsible for the camera men.

Cast honors go to Fritz Lieber, as Solomon, and Betty Blythe as the Queen of Sheba. Lieber stands out through his interpretation of the character of the wise man of all time. The main qualification for the leading feminine assignment seemingly was appearance, as the Queen, at no time, is unnecessarily overburdened with clothes, and Miss Blythe besides possessing the required visionary assets took care of her role acceptably and lent the required dignity associated with royalty. G. R. Nye attracted attention as the jealous brother of Solomon who finally turns on him in battle; Herschel Mayall as Sheba's chief advisor; Pat Moore as the little son of the Queen; George Siegmann as the King and tyrant over the land who abducts Nomis, the younger sister of Sheba, and whom the latter marries, in order to kill, and avenge her death.

The tale has been put together nicely with the continuity consistent and of enough strength to hold, though there are occasional lapses where the necessity of carrying the story on come to light. However, it is at the climax of the first half and in other words—the chariot races—that the picture reaches its pinnacle. Outside of that it is doubtful if the film would be big enough to warrant a special showing.

While "The Queen of Sheba" is a good picture, it is not a great one.

SMALL TOWN IDOL.

Sam Smith (Samuel X. Smythe).Ben Turpin
Mary Brown....................Phyllis Haver
Sheriff Sparks..................Charles Murray
Marcelle Mansfield..............Marie Prevost
J. Wellington Jones........James Finlayson
Martin Brown......................Bert Roach
Joe Barnum.........................Al Cooke
Mrs. Smith (Sam's mother).......Dot Farely
Bandit Chief....................Eddie Gribbon
Bandit Chief's rival.............Kalla Pasha
Director of "Two-Gun Sam"...Billy Bevan
Cameraman.....................George O'Hara

Mack Sennett's seven-part comedy this week at the Rialto has all the speed of a two-reel subject of the Sennett order a bit of sustained, ingenious nonsense revealing amazing resource for amusing nonsense. The Rialto on Sunday night gave a satisfying testimonial to the drawing power of the Sennett name, for even after the last night show had been going for 15 minutes the standees were five deep behind the rail on the orchestra floor. The film is put out by Associated Producers. Director, Earl Kenton.

The picture is set to make a record as a business builder, for the vogue is in the direction of comedy productions, and this one is a whale for swiftness and telling comedy. It runs nearly an hour and a half and does not weary. The story is a four-ring circus, with laughs scattered liberally throughout and an interesting element of the spectacular. In addition there is really skilful character drawing in a farcical way and a number of sensational "stunts." The picture has everything.

It tells a complete, although scattered, story, revolving around a ridiculous romance of the poor young man of the village in the person of the comic Valentine, Ben Turpin. The first whoop of the film comes in the introduction of Ben's mother, a sentimental character in the story who is twice as cross-eyed as Ben himself. You may think that Ben is the last word in knock-kneed optics, but you have yet to meet Ben's screen ma. She's a super-comedy all in herself.

The story is really in four two-reel chapters, although the units merge into a single whole. The first has to do with Sam Smith's (Ben Turpin) courting of the village belle, Mary Brown (Phyllis Haver) and his undoing by J. Wellington Jones (James Finlayson), the travestry villain who plots Sam's downfall and exile from the town.

The second chapter has to do with Sam's adventures in the film colony in Los Angeles, where he meets the queen of the films, Marcelle Mansfield (Marie Prevost, one-time Sennett bathing beauty), and rises to stardom on his own account.

Chapter three records Sam's return to his home town a hero and the local exhibition of his screen masterpiece before the townsfolk all present at the nickelodeon and with Sam modestly proud in a front seat.

The final episode resumes the romance and the counter-plotting of J. Wellington and brings the affair up to a finale, in which the villain is foiled and the hero and heroine go to a travesty lovers' clinch.

Holding up a travesty for seven reels is no small task, and what makes this production notable is the fact that it has been done uncommonly well. The first chapter would stand by itself as a two-reeler and the second has "production features" worthy of a serious spectacular affair. It shows the studio of the Soandso Film Co., where an oriental story is being filmed. Some of the ballets would pass at the New York Hippodrome for size and scenic effect and the camera shots of an enormous palace throne room are striking for their magnificence.

These incidents fill in the interest which usually goes with the Sennett Bathing Girls, for there were half a dozen dancing groups in the extreme of undress and several solo and small group dancing numbers of real beauty. Of course, Turpin as a comedy film actor was present in many of these studio scenes, playing a Roman in a heavy metal helmet, the visor of which kept slipping down at critical moments and gumming up the works.

Later on Sam, the hero, graduates to western melodramas and wins hero parts because he tries to commit suicide by doing stunts. It is with one of these roles that he returns home. The town gathers in the picture house, and the whole ridiculous travesty is screened—a film within a film. In this passage there are some of the funniest possible moments, and the situation of the self-worshipping hero may have been the means of Sennett slipping over a few slams at some of th serious-minded dramatic picture stars of the coast.

With the exhibition of the picture to Sam's fellow townsmen Sam is re-established and resumes his courtship of Mary Brown, but the villain, J. Wellington, plots anew. The rube hotelkeeper shoots himself by accident, and suspicion is cast on Sam because of his career as a screen gun fighter. J. Wellington works the townsmen up to the point of lynching him, and the last reel is an absurd chase, one of the most elaborate that could be staged, and a whooping burlesque on the life-and-death struggle between the familiar man-eating hero and villain.

They wreck a whole village, while the hero tries to save the g-i-r-l and the base betrayer tries to abduct her. There are horseback pursuits, fights over roofs and in and out windows and through attics and streets, until neither combatant has enough clothes to preserve the decencies. The end is a lynching party, with the goggle-eyed hero bravely awaiting his fate under the noose, just as the heroine arrives with proofs of his innocence and the militia rides up to complete the rescue.

The whole thing is done in a screamingly funny vein of seriousness which gives the travesty the keenest edge, especially to audiences well fed up on pompous screen drama. It's a pippin. *Rush.*

PROXIES.

Peter, the butler...........Norman Kerry
Clare Conway, the maid...............
Zena Virginia Keefe
Carlotta Darley..................Raye Dean
Homer Carleton.................Jack Crosby
John Stover....................Paul Everton
Christopher Darley.....William H. Tooker
Mrs. Darley....................Mrs. Schaffer
Detective Linton..........Robert Broderick

This Paramount feature, with a cast headed by Zena Keefe and Norman Kerry, came to the Rivoli April 10. Cosmopolitan made it. The story was written originally for that magazine by Frank R. Adams. George D. Baker made a scenario of it and directed the production, and so comes into the docket as the chief culprit.

For several years now the bated-breath boys have approached us all confidentially to confide that Mr. Baker was one of the first directors in the business, unusual in that he always made his own scenarios. No other director would have accepted the scenario for "Proxies" from anyone. To do so would have been to risk a reputation.

Based on this ill thought-out and careless piece of work, the story naturally gets a start like a slow freight. Over 2,000 feet have passed before it gathers headway at all. In the end it concludes without settling the interesting point as to why a man who has held up a crowd of people isn't arrested for his crime. Instead of disposing of that question, Mr. Baker leaves his butler-crook in the possession of a happy country home. This is an example of what he has done in this feature. His work is incompetent, nothing less.

His direction is little better. The story shows Peter and Clara, butler and maid in the Darley household. A politician named Stover calls. He is unwelcome and proposes to the head of the house a crooked financial deal. As he is ushered out, after telling his host that Peter is an ex-crook, he sees the daughter, Carlotta. Carlotta is engaged to a little man named Carleton, but she longs for a hero as tall as Peter.

This arouses the jealousy of Clare, but when Stover calls again the night of a big party he has with him a paper that puts the balance of power in his hands. So he is invited in to the party, after declaring his price is Carlotta's hand in marriage. To relieve Carlotta, Peter engineers a hold-up by which he gets and destroys the incriminating paper. He also puts Carleton in right with his girl by tipping him off in Portuguese, a language they both speak, to attack him and so pose as a hero. Later Peter rescues the little maid, Clare, by posing as a strange detective. The conveniences of the story are advanced by sending this out-of-town detective, who is unknown to the police at the home, instead of one of the local force.

Throughout what movement the story had was impaired by imperfect lighting. Very often it was difficult to get a clear view of the faces. A last smash tending to make the picture ridiculous was the wedding scene, where father and mother were seated in what appeared to be a stage box and bride and groom engaged in a long, long kiss at the altar, a breach of good taste that must have mussed up the wedding gown (why spare expense in a picture), but would occur nowhere else.

The acting was indifferent. Norman Kerry is seen on the screen too rarely. Here he was sometimes effective, but for the most part he was a leading man trying to appear like a butler. Miss Keefe was more natural. The role of the silly little daughter, who kept flirting with the butler, was played by Raye Dean. The part was against her, and the way she was directed tended to make her seem mostly a silly little bunch of fluff. Something redeeming should have been gotten into the characterization, but even in her song scene Mr. Baker let her use a series of impossible gestures that increased the farce impression. William H. Tooker, in the way he brushes his hair and the solemn massiveness of his expression, suggest more an animated statue than a humon being working at a job. Certainly the idea he got over didn't come anywhere near the public's notion of a man of affairs.

Paul Everton, as the crooked politician, did better, but, on the whole, the production seemed like a waste of good money. More competent handling could have made it entertaining, but as it stands it has only a few minutes while the hold-up is going on. The rest is wasted footage. *Leed.*

THE HIGHEST BIDDER

"The Highest Bidder" takes an odd twist, likely suggested by the "Prince and the Pauper" story, that intensifies the interest for a while, but the picture as a whole drops at other times through the mildness of the story. It's strictly a love tale with Madge Kennedy starred and Lionel Atwill in principal support.

Miss Kennedy's sympathetic appeal is very strong. Her role is that of a friendless girl who bargained with a designing woman that for maintenance by the latter, the girl would make a wealthy marriage. Mr. Atwill as Lester, a millionaire, seeks seclusion at Loon Lake in the Adirondacks in the hope of meeting someone who will be unaware of his wealth and like him for himself, falls in love with Sally Raeburn (Miss Kennedy). Sally's protector identifies Lester, however, through a society paper and informs the girl, who carries the affair to its conclusion, but rejects Lester when he proposes to her in his New York home on Washington Square, the girl telling Lester she had known of his wealth at all times.

Annoyed and disgusted, Lester has his butler dig up a bum from Washington Square park, gives him the name of Hastings, dresses him up and takes him to Lester's country home for a week-end, where Sally and some others are also invited. Hastings, washed, shaved and dressed, is a very personable young man. He is introduced as wealthy and just returned from the Orient. His instructions are to make a play for Sally, and Sally is informed through a catty divorcee who is angling for Lester that Hastings is worth twice as much as Lester.

Lester grows jealous of Hastings. Hastings' progress at love-making on short notice is too rapid for Lester to relish. He dismisses Hastings and gives him a check for $1,000 for his work thus far, but Hastings refuses to vamoose, saying he is going through with it and marry Sally. Threatening to expose Lester's connivance, upon insistence, Lester can do nothing. Hastings asks Sally to marry her, and is declined, but when Lester again broaches marriage, Sally confesses, will not listen to him and returns to Hastings, whom she now knows, and agrees to wed him, through both being adventurers and better suited to one another. Hastings turns her cold upon learning she is penniless, with Lester, of course, persuading her to marry him.

Miss Kennedy is the head of quite an important cast. In playing the company misses nothing. The cast's only blur is that Mr. Atwill somehow doesn't look the lover he professes. But as an actor of polish, he leaves no doubt.

The story must have been selected to give its star a feature in which she could handle herself most advantageously, which Miss Kennedy does, but the story after that, barring the one bit, is a little too vapid, without action and holding nothing beyond pretty scenes and settings. However, Miss Kennedy will hold it up as a release and the hackneyed all-star billing could almost be announced besides. *Sime.*

THE LAMPLIGHTER.

Gertie...........................Shirley Mason
Willie Sullivan.............Raymond McKee
The Lamplighter..............Albert Knott
Malcolm Graham......Edwin Booth Tilton
Emily Graham......................Iris Ashton
Philip Amory...............Philo McCullough
Housekeeper....................Madge Hunt

It may be a prerogative of any producer to make a brand of pictures with the minimum cost, with a production that looks "stock" all over, and a cast that does not compare favorably with those of competing productions. So it is with this new Shirley Mason vehicle (Fox), called "The Lamplighter."

The story is pale in sustaining interest. In production the sets look as if they had been thrown together hurriedly. In action the theme is interrupted by careless titling and the denouement of the story doesn't hold a bit of invigorating action.

"The Lamplighter" is taken from an original by Maria Susanna Cummins. Briefly it links a stranded waif with her parents, who have been separated through the uncompromising father of the bride.

Miss Mason is the waif, and acquits herself but fairly through five uninteresting reels. To ask a mature audience to swallow the story is almost an imposition. The direction is by Howard M. Mitchell, the photography by Glen McWilliams. *Step.*

MOTHER ETERNAL.

Alice Baldwin	Vivian Martin
Edward Stevens, Sr.	Thurston Hall
Dr. Emerson	Earl Metcalfe
Edward Stevens, Jr.	Jack Sherrill
Julia Brennon	Vivienne Osborne
William Brennon	J. W. Johnston
Mary Baldwin	Baby Ruth Sullivan
Mary Baldwin (25 years later)	
	Pearl Shepard
Charles Baldwin	Clyde Hunnewell

It wouldn't occur to most people that there was present call for a valiant champion of the proposition that motherhood is a praiseworthy institution, and mothers in general are supremely unselfish and self-sacrificing. Most people in the best circles accept it as a truism, so self-evident that debate is out of order. For this reason it comes as a surprise that Ivan Abramson uses up a seven-part photoplay to argue the matter with most astonishing earnestness and bad taste.

It is as though some one lavished passionate oratory on the novel contention that murder, theft and false witness were wrong. There's no one to argue against it. So what's the use or purpose or merit in the discussion? Hence "The Mother Eternal" is a bald rehash of platitudes, done into an absolutely uninteresting recital and plastered over stickily with sentiment of the most maudlin kind, emotional counterfeit that only cheapens a lofty subject. The Broadway screen has not seen such utter trash in many a day and it is hard to conceive of any community so simple minded as to take the wretched travesty seriously.

The picture, by the way, was shown first last Sunday night at the Casino, making a bid against six or seven other special films in the legitimate houses of the metropolis, posting a scale of $1.65 top. There can be small question of its fate on Broadway. Indeed it is not easy to believe that any grade of picture public would support it at any scale.

It doesn't deserve serious consideration from any viewpoint. Its story is stupid, its direction crude to the last degree and its acting on a par with the rest. There are moments when its serious scenes are pathetically comic, as for instance when Vivian Martin (the last screen actress in the world to play an old woman part) wears a makeup that might be transferred without abating a detail to a comedy character old woman. The black streaks under the eyes and streaming to the corners of the mouth must have been applied with a spoon. This is not exaggeration as proved by a titering audience. The whole production was as artificial and as forced as that unspeakable facial fresco.

The story has to do with an impoverished woman newly widowed who allows a doctor to substitute her newly born babe in the arms of a rich woman in the same hospital whose offspring had died. The needy mother yearns for her child for 25 years, during which time she is ill-treated by an older daughter who at length drives her out of her home to commit suicide by leaping into the river.

The long lost son, of course, happens to be on the dock and rescues her for the final reunion and the mother is safely ensconced in son's home of wealth. The hospital scenes and certain other passages in a doctor's office are fragrant with medical details dealing with obstetrics, although there were some interesting shots of babies here.

The crass sob stuff was laid on fearfully thick. A 30 or 40-piece orchestra, mostly violins with "D" strings, 'cellos and French horns started to wring the heart with their wailing at 8:30. Then a solemn elocutionist with a rich, moist baritone voice recited a fragment of verse lauding motherhood and mothers. A woman balladist took the strain up for a sentimental song in the same vein and then we had a tableau, showing an illuminated city at night and beyond the tiers of windows lighted by home fires, a symbolic figure of a mother brooding over a baby in her arms was revealed on a pedestal.

That was just the beginning. After that the screen story took the theme up and tore sentiment to tatters until 10:40. The proceedings were quite sufficient to make any efficient modern mother thoroughly indignant. *Rush.*

"SACRED AND PROFANE LOVE"

Carlotta Peel	Elsie Ferguson
Emilie Diaz, a pianist	Conrad Nagel
Frank Ispenlove	Thomas Holding
Constance Peel	Helen Dunbar
Mary Ispenlove	Winifred Greenwood
Lord Francis Alcar	Raymond Brathwayt
Mrs. Sardis	Clarissa Selwyn
Albert Vicary	Howard Gaye
Samson	Forest Stanley
Rebecca	Jane Keckley

"Sacred and Profane Love" is a Paramount picture, starring Elsie Ferguson, and produced by William D. Taylor. Before reaching the screen it appeared in the form of a novel, and during the season of 1919-20 was presented as a play, running for a considerable period in one of the Broadway houses. Arnold Bennett wrote the novel and play. The scenario from which the picture was made was written by Julia C. Ivers. Elsie Ferguson appeared in the stage version, playing the character of Carlotta as in the picturization.

The theme is a bit broad for general picture consumption. In brief, Carlotta, a young girl, attends a recital given by a celebrated pianist. She is of the impressionable type and the pianist, following a flirtation carried on during the recital invites her to his rooms. Time passes rapidly and apparently pleasantly, and after a bit of importuning the girl remains at the pianist's home all night. The girl, returning to her own home the morning after the night before, learns that her aunt, with whom she has been living, had died. The shock of the girl's absence from home all night, seemingly, having killed the aunt.

Carlotta has aspirations as an author and eventually acquires fame in that direction. Her publisher, a married man, falls in love with her. The publisher's wife, incidentally, is having an affair with another man.

The publisher's wife upon learning of her husband's feeling for Carlotta commits suicide by drowning. When the publisher discovers his wife's suicide he immediately places the blame on Carlotta, although Carlotta had not given him any noticeable encouragement in his infatuation. Having unburdened his mind to Carlotta, the publisher then proceeds to shoot himself. Rather an epidemic of suiciding.

Carlotta meets up with the pianist, Diaz, in Paris some time later, but Diaz is now an absinthe fiend and a mental and physical wreck. Through constant care and attention she regenerates Diaz, however, who makes a "comeback" as a pianist, and apparently they live happily ever after.

The incidents of the story relating to Carlotta's first affair with the pianist are very plainly brought out. But that was the story, and the director had no other recourse but to place it on the screen. The picture on the whole is an average program production. Miss Ferguson gives a likable performance as Carlotta, minus any great depth, but pleasing withal. The acting honors go to Conrad Nagel, as Diaz, the pianist, his sense and interpretation of the absinthe fiend being especially good. The rest of the cast are adequate. The picture has publicity possibilities. *Bell.*

DECEPTION.

Henry VIII	Emil Jannings
Anne Boleyn	Henny Porten

Directed by Ernest Lubitsch, the German producer who made "Passion," this came to the Rivoli April 17, sponsored by Adolph Zukor and Paramount. As entertainment it is slow going, but as a vivid historical document it is valuable.

The two hour progress of the film Sunday suggested the cutting had something to do with the way the picture dragged. Cutters who try to get in everything by shortening all themes instead of removing bodily the themes of lesser account, make a mistake. The best should be chosen and allowed to develop to the limit. Perhaps this picture was cut with a view to placing history before the masses, but history often is dull.

Nevertheless, it is as history this picture is valuable, but thanks to the acting, not the scenario. Emil Jannings (an American, by the way, who has studied under Rinehardt in Berlin), gave an amazingly capable portrait of the loose, merry, sensual Henry. Than his performance, nothing better has ever graced the screen. Equally effective was Henny Porten. The first view of her reveals a woman without much claim to beauty, but the distinction and power of her portrayal get to you. It is not her fault that she has not epitomized Anne Boleyn as her co-star has the king. The sympathy here is thrown to Anne. History's record hardly indicates she deserved it.

Photographically the portrayal could be little improved. There is, too, massed effect, great scenes, particularly those at the time of the coronation, that make for impressive effects and are well handled and arranged. Its success in anything but first run houses in larger towns is doubtful. *Leed.*

THE SKY PILOT.

The Sky Pilot	John Bowers
Gwen	Colleen Moore
Bill Hendricks	David Butler
The Old Timer	Harry Todd
Honorable Ashley	James Corrigan
The Duke	Donald MacDonald
Lady Charlotte	Kathleen Kirkham

A very pleasing atmospheric prolog was staged by managing director Joseph Plunkett for the introduction of "The Sky Pilot" at the Strand this week. Four male singers, attired as cowpunchers, and another dressed in ministerial garb, sang acceptably in front of a set cottage bearing across its shed the name of the saloon in the town in which the scenes of the feature are laid. "The Sky Pilot" is a filmization of Ralph Conner's widely-read novel of the same name, directed by King Vidor, produced by the Catherine Curtis Pictures Corporation and distributed via First National.

There is little in the story itself that differs from numerous other tales of college-bred young ministers who are assigned to ranch communities to preach the gospel and are compelled to fight their way physically, unless it be the rather far-fetched uplift lesson which it teaches—that sufficient faith will pretty nearly cure all physical ills. In this tale you are shown the heroine, pronounced by the physician a hopeless cripple who will never walk again. She is soon faced with the task of rescuing the minister from being consumed in the flames of a burning building. We see her drag herself to where he is lying, pull herself to an upright position and drag out a man twice her weight. It is a fine demonstration for the divine scientists and the rest of us who believe in the omnipotence of the Almighty.

The picture starts well—with two-fisted action. The day following the minister's arrival is Sunday and he attempts to hold services in the saloon. The ranch foreman resents the narration of the miracle of the loaves and fishes, refuses to be quieted and is ordered from the place. It becomes necessary for the athletic minister to administer a sound thrashing to the doubter, who thereupon becomes his friend and champion.

A really remarkable screening of a round-up is depicted, showing the hero standing over the prostrate body of the heroine and "shooing" the cattle to either side to prevent her being trampled to death. The steers are shown running apparently into the very eye of the camera, making the scene as vivid as is possible to photography.

The story runs along consistently and cumulatively, plentifully interspersed with comedy and leading to a satisfactory conclusion. The entire cast is exceptional, with excellent types, and admirably played by the three principals. John Bowers is the minister; Colleen Moore is the heroine and David Butler the ranch foreman.

Most of the scenes are exteriors of the "western" variety, with the inevitable rough-riding and red-blooded action. Direction, photography and detail are more than satisfactory. The feature won't create any sensation these days, but should please in the best cinemas. *Jolo.*

THE OTHER WOMAN.

There have been better feature picture offerings than this; there have been worse; but seldom has there been a combination of exceptionally high, individual spots which this "Other Woman" registers, balanced against a contrasting lack of interest.

The subject which Edward Sloman started to translate from the novel of the same title by Norah Davis strikes one as presenting many difficulties. The proposition was transplanting the different moods and stages in the progress of a man who felt his mind leaving him. Subsequently the individual finds himself another person, living a different life and all unconscious of what had taken place before. He finds himself in new surroundings, the husband of a woman, and not knowing anything of his former state until the thought of something in his past leaves him to contemplate the duality of persons in himself.

The story opens with the brief introduction of the relativity of small things to life, and points very significantly to the fact that if a certain individual had not followed a dog into a Chicago park, the story might not have been written. Under such circumstances, then, this individual is attacked by a ruffian, but is saved from further assault. The man thus saved suddenly finds his benefactor closely resembling an absent partner, and in addition the latter has been missing from his wife and child for a number of years. He denies his identity, explaining that he is John Gorham, instead of Langdon Kirven. What the author then wants to bring out is that Kirven and Gorham are the same, but that Gorham dominates this man's personality, because of amnesia, while at the critical moment Kirven asserts himself and returns to his wife, leaving all that he had built up in a Southern community and with just enough, explaining that he will return some day.

As Kirven he returns to his home, wife and child, living apparently in happiness at the reunion, although he does not understand and cannot explain his absence. But as Gorham he departs from the Kirven establishment, again returning to the Southern community where he is married. His partner, the same man whom he saved in the earlier episodes from assault, ultimately convinces him that Kirven and Gorham are one. It is at this point that the picture registers its profoundness more than at any other point.

Gorham returns to his home and importunes his wife for a decision, with the concluding episode that her husband is given his freedom to return to the Southern community, where a second wife has borne him a child. There is, of course, the explanation of the divorce that will follow and the fact that she will marry his partner is fully accepted.

What the picture fails to do, despite its interest in numerous episodes, is to project the note of convincingness in the duality of personalities in this leading character. The camera work in showing the transformation of this man is focused through a composite effect, and yet this fails to show the contrast. Or perhaps it is the lack of contrast in the interpretation of the role, as played by Jerome Patrick, that has materially to do with the inability to register more effectively. It is, in fact, on this very episode that the story revolves more than around anything else. And just at this big point it fails to prove what the director started out to prove. The interest had been keyed up with a tenseness that follows few pictures, but there was an almost audible note of disappointment as the scene unfolded and passed.

It is a suggestion, and nothing more, that the continuity of the picture should have given a greater contrasting note between Gorham and Kirven, until he is convinced that he represents both. It is assumed logically that two people have different standard and valuation of things, with concomitant values and mannerisms.

The acting in the picture is one of its biggest assets, and few scenes have had the dramatic force of the last episode, as played by Patrick and Helen Jerome Eddy. The direction in the main is good, and the rest of the cast have been selected with discretion, although there isn't very much for them to do. It includes William Conklin, Lincoln Plumer, Joseph J. Dowling, Jane Novak and Frankie Lee.

DOOR THAT HAS NO KEY

London, April 2.

Alliance Film Corporation. Six reels.

Frankly, this production, the second of the many promised by the "million pound" company, is about as grossly indecent as any ever seen. It has not even the virtue of covering its salaciousness with a strong story. The story, adapted from a novel by Cosmo Hamilton, is weak and the continuity is none too good, and this weakness may have led whoever was responsible for the scenario to make the most of scenes which surpass anything yet seen, publicly at any rate., in London, in suggestiveness.

"The Door That Has No Key" is mainly concerned with the lives of four people—the hero, a consummate prig who is forever boasting of his purity and honor, ("I want to take a clean body to a good girl" is one of his outpourings); a woman who has no purity and uses all her wiles to corrupt the hero, the woman he marries only to find that she refuses her wifely duties and shivers at the bare word "motherhood"—and it is children that the hero wants—and another woman who comes to him in his misery and is perfectly happy in yielding to his desire for ltle ones wthout apparently caring much as to the stigma which will rest on her offspring all their lives. These admirable people express their ideas very plainly, not only in the action of the play, but in copious sub-titles.

Coming down from college, Jack Scorrier joins his people's house-party. There he meets a notorious society "grass" widow known as "Blossy" who possesses neither virtue nor scruple. Their bedrooms are connected by a door—a strange arrangement in a country house—and one night the lady hears Jack prating to his chum Pat Mallory about his honor and purity. She promptly decides to make him hers and retires to bed in becoming but not excessive negligee. Mallory goes and the lady promptly rocks about and groans as though in pain. Jack overhears the strange noises and after a period of indecision enters her room and enquires as to what the matter is. She tells him perfectly plainly and he retires in scorn and agitation to his own side of the door. She is annoyed, but presently seeing the door handle move decides that he has thought better of it and is returning; therefore she snuggles down in bed. A figure enters, tip-toes to the bed and gently touches her. She springs round and with a joyous cry of "Jack!" flings her arms around—her own little son who is sharing Jack's bed that night and who has crept through the dividing door unnoticed by his grown-up and agitated friend.

Jack meets the "one girl" who unfortunately made Success her God. He is not yet sufficiently famous for her, so he goes to London to read for the bar. In no time he is called, appears as Blossy's counsel when her long-suffering husband appeals for divorce and wins the case for her. The divorce has made Jack famous and returning home he convinces the "only girl" that he is the forensic goods and marries her, while Ethel, the Vicar's grand-daughter, who has always worshipped him, presides sadly at the organ. On the first night of his honeymoon, his wife makes it clear to Jack that she has no intention of becoming a mother and locks him out of her room.

Time passes. Jack goes on becoming famous and more and more unhappy, his ambitious wife still keeping the door securely locked against him. Then England is in difficulties of some sort and the Cabinet decides that the inclusion of our paragon can alone save the situation. His wife is approached and consents to enlist him. That night she is very loving and promises to do anything he likes if he'll only go and join the Cabinet. He answers that he's on the Opposition and stalks back to his chambers in disgust and unhappier than ever. Then Ethel, the Vicar's grand-daughter, cheers him up and confesses that she is suffering too. We are mercifully spared the details of their start in housekeeping together, but it is not long before we find this good young man (with all his trouble, all his work and climb to fame, he has not aged a minute), and Ethel snugly settled down in a cosy little villa. Meanwhile human nature has begun to play a rough game with the wife—love has come to her and she shows this by looking longingly at and stroking the pillow next to her as she lies in bed. She makes up her mind to win Jack back and proceeds to the villa only to find she's "too late"—Ethel has already begun to provide the family she refused. Miserably she goes away, leaving them together. Then she gets a divorce, or dies, or something, but whatever she does, Ethel's wedding ring is the big thing in the final closeup. *Gore.*

MAGNIFICENT BRUTE.

Universal-made, with Frank Mayo starred, "The Magnificent Brute" will likely do well enough for the U trade as a melodramatic release. The story is set in the Hudson Bay country of the Canadian Northwest. Its outdoor scenic surroundings in the wintertime are attractive through the snowclad trees and ground.

The picture seemed to run short of five full reels when shown at the New York as half of a double bill. Its direction may be commended for the subject matter involved, excepting that Mayo's cabin in the woods when in close-ups appeared to be the only thing around there that the snow did not fall upon, for some studio reason.

Mayo is a trapper, in association with the representative of the Parisian company controlling the post. Other than that no French concern has any Canadian concession, that portion of the story fitted in because of the Frenchman who said he had come over to inspect the post and who fell in love with the daughter of the post trader. The trapper was also in love with her, but when the young woman returned to her far northern home after a visit to Montreal, she wasn't the girl the trapper had known three years previously. The rivalry between the two lovers brought a demand from the trapper for moneys due from the French company. To allay the demands, the Frenchman engaged a Canuck to kill the father of the girl. The Canuck jammed up the job and was caught himself through the detective work of the trapper, with the customary love finale following the expose of the Frenchman.

Mr. Mayo does very well in the film. He looked the role, that of a magnificent brute, and indulged in considerable action, in fights and scuffles with the roughnecks of the post.

Some knife throwing is shown and a tricky bit of photography for one bit of it worked out a fine illusion.

The U may be making capital of this picture as concurrent with the Stillman case and the Stillmans' placing of Three Rivers, Canada (half-way between Montreal and Quebec) as one of the principal points in that now notorious action. Taking Mayo's role as a replica of Beauvais, the guide, and the background of the scenery, with the types claimed to be the same that may be found up there (which would be true), the U should be able on that foundation to work this film up with advance stuff sufficiently to take it out of the double class at least.

The picture's best bet is Mayo, and Mayo looks like a good bet for any picture written to suit him. *Sime.*

PUPPETS OF FATE.

This is a "Metro" classic, featuring Viola Dana. And about the best thing in it is the sincerity in character portrayal with which Miss Dana endows the part. Otherwise the absence of drama is so outstanding that there is little to sustain interest. Briefly, it treats of the separation between two Italian peasants, with the subsequent journey of the much-in-love wife to America to find her husband. The incidents in the continuity bring in at the start some colorful backgrounds of Venice at Carnival time, and the principal characters are disclosed as vendors of the dancing Punchinello as a puppet. This, briefly, is the symbol on which the author, Donn B ne, has elected to write, and despite the absence of real drama in the story, carries his point convincingly that: We are more or less pup ts of fate.

The production as a whole shows a long drawn out series of scenes and sequences that does not make for drama, and the fault must be laid more at the door of Dallas M. Fitzgerald as director than Ann Baldwin and Molly Parro as the continuity expert writers.

The photography by John Arnold

is unique for lighting effects, while a lavish and substantial production in practically every phase of detail is a splendid achievement on the part of Sidney Ullman as art director. The acting is uniformly good. *Step.*

WANDERING JEW.

No, this is not a film version of the Sue tale, nor is it related in theme to the fothcoming Belasco production of similar title and based on the version by Matheson Lang. Instead, it is a European-made picture containing propaganda for the cause of Zion, and its incidents couple the life of Dr. Theodore Hertzl, the eminent exponent of that cause, and around whom are based various eventful happenings from the time when he gave up his career as a jurist until his death.

It is one of those curiosities in the trade that the film came from the European cinema market, finding its way to America, where it was shown to numerous would-be purchasers. But not until it was seen by a man who understood the Zionist cause and believed in the picture's value to Jewish audiences was it accepted. At that, for a song.

The first exhibition of this film took place in a 600-seat house in New York's ghetto. Beginning on a Wednesday morning it played through the end of the current (last) week and was retained for another. No day's patronage was under $600 and none over $800. That represents the absolute capacity from 10 in the morning until 11 at night.

The picture holds two prominent figures known to American theatregoers. The first, Rudolph Shildkraut, is now at the Jewish Art, while in a minor role his son Josef is now with the Theatre Guild in Molnar's "Liliom." The picture was made several years ago in Vienna.

Dealing with Zionism in the main and connecting the events in the life of Dr. Hertzl, the picture opens with an introduction relating the oft-discussed abuse and oppression of the Jew. A symbolic figure of a patriarch standing alone on the peak of a mountain with arms outstretched to heaven follows, and a supplication for deliverance from oppression brings in a dissolve of Moses followed by Dr. Hertzl, conceived in the script as the savior of Zion.

And from then on the most effective scenes in the picture are brought about with Dr. Hertzl as a jurist, is asked to change his faith, followed by meditation and an expression of faith in his nation. Taking up a book, obviously the history of the Jew, Dr. Hertzl reads, and the dissolves follow showing the triumphant Macabbeans, Bar-Kochba, etc.

What is left to Shildkraut, the elder, is the interpretation of that Jew oppressed by Tarquamada during the Inquisition and again in Russia he is the pathetic individual who loses all through the massacres, and wanders again in search of a new haven.

The picture caused a profound impression among its auditors, and as the scenes unfolded of a subject that has taken on a new significance with the arrival in America of two expounders of the cause of Zionism —Drs. Einstein and Weizmann—the interest assuredly was more than mere concentration.

The acting has the elements of a Continental style and the photography is as poor as anything that comes from most European cameramen, who have not yet attained the progress in that branch of the industry achieved by Americans.

The titling, by Dr. Goldberg (Ph. D.) and Charles Penser, is in the most lucid, comprehensive style that has been observed in a long time. The introduction, evidently by Dr. Goldberg, is masterful in construction. The picture is controlled in the United States and Canada by Charles Penser and Leo Fox. *Step.*

WHAT'S A WIFE WORTH?

As William Christy Cabanne undertakes to answer the question in pictorial form, he differentiates between the woman who marries in search of happiness and the other woman who marries for wealth and position, and is unwilling to assume duties of motherhood. Furthermore, his answer is quite clear, definite. The film runs over the usual number of reels and slides between maximum, par and the inevitable something that hinders most directors from smooth action and dissolves into platitudinous titles.

The biggest asset of the picture is its moral, and wherever an audience likes its "Way Down East" theme digested in another form, this picture should have great possibilities.

It is interpreted by a cast of artists selected with discretion, and act with capableness if not excellence.

The action covers the career of one woman, who, through self abnegation following conniving information by outside influences, leaves her newly wedded husband, that she may not hinder a marriage with one of "his own sort," as she is informed. The former marriage is annulled and the son enters into a new matrimonial partnership. A child is born to the neglected wife, or No. 1. No. 2 is reluctant to bear children, yet a child dies in infancy that is born of this unhappy union. The deserted wife abandons her child on the threshold of her husband's magnificent house. The same fate later on causes her to retrace her steps, with the result of a reunion, etc.

Mr. Cabanne personally directed and is also the author of the picture, which he mentions in the billing as "A Leaf from a Woman's Soul." That is not far fetched. In summary of the picture's merit Mr. Cabanne may be said to have achieved a meritorious drama. It can stand cutting, and the force of title writers and editors who were assembled does not speak well for the many cooks who spoiled a good pie.

The production is well mounted. The photography has its high lights. One "shot" in particular that recalls itself more prominently than anything else strikes the onlooker as being on an inimitable artistic plane. This is the lighting coupled with the effective response as a result focusing the camera at a three-quarter angle on the dead woman about the end of the third reel. The photographer is George Benoit.

Ruth Renick, Cassion Ferguson, Cora Drew, Howard Gaye, Alex Francis, Charles Wyngate, Lillian Langdon and Virginia Caldwell complete the cast. Among them Miss Renick, Miss Drew, Miss Langdon and, of course, Alex Francis, share honors. Given a "fat" part, Mr. Ferguson seemed less convincing in the central character of the husband than might be expected.

The picture is released through Robertson-Cole. *Step.*

A PERFECT CRIME.

Wally Griggs	Monte Blue
Mary Oliver	Jacqueline Logan
William D. Thaines	Stanton Heck
Richard Halliday	Hardy Kirkland

Monte Blue is starred in this new Allan Dwan-Associated Producers feature. It is adapted from Carl Clausen's Satevepost story and co-directed by Wilfred Buckland and Mr. Dwan.

Blue does a sort of Jekyll and Hyde role, which, discounting any queries as to the realism of certain situations and motives, proved an interesting creation. As Wally Griggs, a bank clerk, he is a pin-head (to quote the subtitles) and in love with Mary Oliver (Jacqueline Logan), also a bank employe. However, Wally in the evening blossoms forth in new regalia as James Brown and mixes with the president of his bank, Richard Halliday (Hardy Kirkland). He effects this satisfactorily by discarding his customary stoop—which in reality is a planned affectation through the medium of a specially padded vest—and ditto with his goggles. Any question as to his striking resemblance to the browbeaten Wally Griggs he always easily explains merely as a coincidence.

As James Brown he tells his newly found influential friends a number of Munchhausen stories of adventure which a publisher-guest decides to exploit. This incident proves very handy for a fade-out when the hero and heroine are shown opening envelopes filled with $5,000 checks as royalties. It is obvious by now the story is not strictly realistic, and one wonders whether that angle was not let go of purposely in sacrifice to its comedy values pure and simple. As such it is amply satisfying.

The hero recovers $25,000 among other things, discomfits an officious assistant district attorney and disports himself in an adventurous fashion throughout the five reels.

The support is worthy and on par with the star. As the feature attraction at the Broadway theatre this week, where it is showing for the first time in New York, it satisfied. *Abel.*

A TALE OF TWO WORLDS.

Su Sen	Leatrice Joy
Ling Jo	Wallace Beery
Newcombe	J. Frank Glendon
The Worm	Jack Abbe
Ah Wing	E. A. Warren

This is indeed a gratifying photodrama or melodrama to watch from every phase of production standards. It is effective in direction. Most essential of all, it has action of a kind that mingles suspense with smoothly moving episodes, while the titles, somewhat too profuse in explaining motive and incident, do not hurt the singular charm of the picture. It is enacted by a cast of Western World actors, yet who seem to have caught and sustained the characteristics of Orientalism.

Gouverneur Morris' story, supplied for this occasion, compares in theme to "East Is West." The outstanding fault with it, in its later episodes, particularly, is that it is too melodramatic in spots, although this does not detract from the interest. It does seem a trifle far-fetched that in these days the brain of a Chinaman should consider it necessary to employ in his home a machine that gives impetus to a moving wall, the crushing power of which is enough to snuff out the life of a half dozen.

The action involves at the start an outbreak by the Boxers, who clash with the border nations some time in '99. A child born to an American couple is rescued by a faithful native. He brings her up as his own, and in due time becomes a merchant in a Western city. A principal in the former incitement against the whites is now a rich gambler, slave dealer, etc., also living in this Western city. The action then concludes with the struggle between this gambler and an American who is in love with the girl.

The direction is by Frank Lloyd. The artistic direction and the photography embrace the very best. The production itself is scenically one of the best of its kind that ever came from the Goldwyn studio. In comparison to an earlier effort by Lloyd—"Madame X"—this is much superior.

In every sense of the word it is a first class feature. *Step.*

MADE IN HEAVEN.

Wm. Lowry	Tom Moore
Claudia Royce	Helene Chadwick
Elizabeth Royce	Molly Malone
Mrs. Royce	Kate Lester
Mr. Royce	Al Filson
Davidge	Freeman Wood
Lowry, Sr.	Charles Eldridge
Miss Lowry	Rene Adoree
Loland	Herbert Prior
Ethel Hadden	Fronzie Gunn
Mr. Hadden	John Cossar

This newest Goldwyn production, starring Tom Moore, is a saccharine morsel, frothy, light and pleasing, minus any serious "combatting of forces."

Billy Lowry (Tom Moore), doing a fireman role, rescues the heroine, marries her on the spur of the moment to avoid complications with an objectionable suitor, and then proceeds really winning her love. Of course, Lowry remains a fireman for only three and a half reels and toward the end he is in 'civvies" as a full-fledged, prospering business man, reaping the profits of an invention.

A funny thing happened with the sub-titles. According to the program, the hero's name is Lowry, while the sub-titles, which are very clever, by the way, continually insist on labeling him O'Gara. Whichever it is, Moore is continually "makin' spaches" in an Irish brogue, so it's an edge in favor of the O'Gara monicker.

Helene Chadwick proved a winsome opposite, while Rene Adoree (Mrs. Moore in private life) and Molly Malone also looked well in the picture, besides helping on with the sub-plot of making the quarreling couple kiss and make up. The balance of the supporting cast was accurate.

William Hurlbut wrote the story and Victor Schertzinger directed. A typical Tom Moore vehicle—light but pleasing.

PECK'S BAD BOY.

Peck's Bad Boy..............Jackie Coogan
The Man in the Case.....Wheeler Oakman
The Girl in the Case............Doris May
The Village Grocer........Raymond Hatton
Pa Peck ....James Corrigan
Ma Peck.................Lillian Leighton
Jackie's Pal................Charles Hatton
Jackie's Girl..................Gloria Wood
"Queenie" ....By Herself

"Peck's Bad Boy" as a picture will not go down in history as a great achievement. It is just a picture, and it is more than likely that the producers of it didn't expect to do more than present simply a picture. They had Jackie Coogan, and in figuring that he was enough they were probably right. Those who are familiar with the old "Peck's Bad Boy" plays will be disappointed if they expect to see any of the old-time fun in a grocery store. There is a grocery store without the comic storekeeper, the policeman, the pin-in the chair and the "take-one" on the basket of apples. This is a modern grocery store, with everything up to date, and is used as a hang-out for the kid, who takes things as he pleases with the permission of the storekeeper, who charges everything up to "the old man" as the boy takes it.

There is very little fun derived here and the action is a bit slow, as it is throughout the picture. The one big comedy bit is the scene in church, where the boy's dad begins to feel the effects of the ants which the boy has placed in his lumbago pad. This carries a good five minutes of continuous laughter.

Jackie is accompanied through the film by a half-breed mut that does very well, and if there is anything like grabbing off second honors they go to the dog. The animal several times shows signs of almost human intelligence and must go down as one of the very best of the animal actors. There is a little love story carried through the picture. It involves the Bad Boy's sister and a struggling young doctor. The latter becomes deeply involved in whatever plot there is through being suspected of stealing important papers, but it all falls back on the kid, who slipped the papers into his pocket as a joke.

He also gets into the big action punch at the finish. Jack steals a handcar and is off down the tracks before he can be stopped. The young Doc jumps on another handcar and overtakes the boy just before a train crashes into the car he was on, smashing it to pieces. This is worked up well and is a great thriller, especially for the children.

Those who saw Jackie Coogan in "The Kid" and predicted that he would be a star without Chaplin may feel reasonably assured after seeing "Peck's Bad Boy." Whatever any one may think of the picture, all will admit that this kid is a wonder. There may be other kids just as clever roaming about, but it is safe betting that they are few and far between. This boy goes about his work in a manner that would put the oldest and most experienced of screen stars to shame.

Not only is he the mischievous, fun-loving boy, but when a few tears are demanded, and there are one or two spots that call for the sob stuff, Jackie goes to it in the most natural manner. Many a tear he will bring with his touch of pathos when they are taking his dog off in the dog-catchers' wagon. All the time it must be remembered that he is only six years old. A baby, nothing more than that, may be the answer to his naturalness and his unassuming manner.

It does seem that a few more closeups of the kid could have been given, for the little fellow is so very small that, except in a closeup, it is hard to catch his expressions.

As we judge pictures today, "Peck's Bad Boy" is not a great picture, but it will please the grown-ups and be a real joy to the "kiddies."

HUSH.

Vera Stanford.......Clara Kimball Young
Jack Stanford...........J. Frank Glendon
Isabel Dane...............Kathlyn Williams
Hugh Graham...................Jack Pratt
Herbert Brooks..........Bertram Grassby
Grace Brooks...........Gerard Alexander
Maid ....Beatrice Le Plante
Butler ....John Underhill

A loose narrative play devoid of form or structure and disastrously overburdened with long, elaborate titles, is the starring vehicle of Clara Kimball Young, this week at the Capitol. It is sponsored by Harry Garson and the authorship is ascribed to Sada Cowan. A well-worn but interesting enough theme is worked out understandably, but the whole thing is artificial and mechanically theatrical. One never for a moment gets the illusion of real life in the characters or incidents. It is always a group of puppets moving through manufactured episodes at the behest of a moving picture director.

The fiction devices are transparent and the tools of the scenario carpenter are always in plain sight. Old man Fictitious Coincidence works overtime, while many of the discursive titles are so long they have to be put in such a small print that reading them is a strain from midway of the enormous Capitol. It is a question whether the story would be more complete if the action was dispensed with and the titles alone given, or the other way about.

Watching the film is almost like reading a book.

The title and the story hinge upon a woman, Vera Stanford (Miss Young), who before her marriage committed an indiscretion and whose conscience troubles her because she has not made a "clean breast of it" to her husband. The man in the case has married since the old affair, and by unhappy chance turns up at a seaside resort where Vera and her husband are spending a vacation. The chance meeting and the wife's harrowed conscience drive her to confess to the husband after a spiritual struggle, which is minutely set forth in the titles, together with the advice against her course by her women friends.

With the disclosure the husband's love grows cold. He insists upon knowing the identiy of the man in the case. The wife refuses to tell and the husband's suspicions are directed to the wrong man. He develops violent jealousy, mistreats his wife, accuses her of deceit and infidelity and drives her to rebellion. In these passages there is some pretty intimate by-play involving separate bedrooms and such details of the domestic arrangement. At length the pair separate, but are reconciled by the good offices of a woman friend, and apparently live happily thereafter, although neither one deserved it.

The moral' is "Don't tell," of course, and it is sent home by one of the few clever bits of the picture. Upon the reconciliation Vera is about to explain to her husband what she has been doing since their separation, but catches herself just in time when the parrot shrills "Hush!" The whole piece is done in the "society play" style, which in the pictures seems to mean demonstrations of nouveau art furniture and the display of good breeding by being rude to the servants. The interiors are so artistic and in such good taste that no one could possibly live in them outside a film studio, and everybody's manners are polished beyond perfection. But the costuming is undeniably beautiful and the photography excellent.

It should be mentioned that Kathryn Williams, as the woman friend of the heroine, gave a capital performance, playing a society woman with an air of ease and natural, unaffected poise such as you would look for in a woman of the world.

Sunday night business at the Capitol was unusually brisk, and all that has been said does not take away from the fact that Miss Young doubtless has a large and loyal following among the fans. It is also probable that the fans will be attracted by her latest picture, although it is not her best. *Rush.*

DIANE OF STAR HOLLOW.

Pat Scott.................Bernard Durning
Diane......................Evelyn Greeley
Orsini....................George Majeroni
Father Lorenzo............Fuller Mellish
D. Crispi.................George E. Romain
Harrison..................Freeman Wood
Hanscom.....................Al Hart
Sheriff................Louis J. O'Connor
Pietro....................Joseph Gramby
Carlotta..................Sonia Marcelle
Dr. Ogden..............Charles Mackay
Jessie....................May Hopkins
Jessie's mother............Julia Neville

The picturization of David Potter's famous story, "Diane of Star Hollow," is a new contribution to the screen and should jump into instant favor because of its being a subject seldom touched upon in the film world.

The director, Ollie Sellers of "When Bearcat Went Dry" fame, has gone in for thrills, believing the public wants action in pictures rather than atmosphere. And no doubt he is right, particularly in the case of Diane.

The story is of an army of black-handers being run to earth by a dashing young officer of the mounted police.

Diane's father, Orsini, was a man of fabulous wealth whose affluence and power surrounded him with a band of associates that was ever ready to follow his dictates. This band, including Orsini, was what is commonly known as the Black Handers. Sergeant Scott of the mounted police suspected Orsini. Diane, the daughter, arrives home from Paris to learn of the accusations against her father. She seeks out the sergeant in defense of her father, and her beautiful simplicity wins the love of the officer at first sight, but duty commands him to continue his investigation.

Through Hanscom, a mountaineer, a former member of the band, Sergeant Scott learns the truth about Orsini's crimes against society, and during a raid on his country home Scott is seriously injured. Orsini jumps into the river and supposedly is drowned, but safely reaches the opposite bank.

After the sergeant recovers from his gun wounds he seeks out Diane, thinking that her father is dead. He proposes marriage to Diane, and as the girl accepts him Orsini plunges through the door and covers the sergeant with a gun, threatening to kill him. When learning of the proposed marriage Orsini retires to his room and turns the gun upon himself, thus paying for his sins with his own hand.

The picture is a thriller in every sense of the word. Scenicly it is a gem.

Bernard Durning as Sergeant Scott is very acceptable, and Evelyn Greeley gives a refreshing performance as Diane. Great things may be expected from this little star.

George Majeroni is good as Orsini and Al Hart as Hanscom, the mountaineer, is splendid. "Diane of Star Hollow" should be a good box-office attraction. *Jolo.*

THE TRAVELING SALESMAN.

Bob Blake, a drummer....Roscoe Arbuckle
Beth Elliott.............Betty Ross Clark
Franklin Royce.............Frank Holland
Martin Drury...............Wilton Taylor
Mrs. Babbitt.................Lucille Ward
Julius......................Jim Blackwell
Ted Watts..................Richard Wayne
John Kimball...............George Pearce
Pierce Gill..................Robert Dudley
Bill Grabb.................Gordon Rogers

Lasky probably set himself back little more than $15,000 for this production, but it is adequate, nevertheless, with Fatty Arbuckle starring and holding up honors at the Rialto this week, with Charlie Chaplin in a revival of "The Floorwalker." The screen story holds faithfully to the main outline of the stage play by James Forbes, and what Walter Woods as scenario writer and Joseph Henabery as director have added by way of "business" is sure-fire screen stuff for Arbuckle fans. The story starts with three drummers on a railroad train and some amusing horseplay, with Fatty left at a railroad crossing in a rainstorm.

The next day he makes the big town and starts in selling his goods, not before falling in love, however. The victim of this woman hater's first affection is Beth Elliott, station agent at the town. She is somewhat leery of drummers, but in the end her sympathy is enlisted. Meanwhile the plot to rob her of some land she has to let go for taxes develops. It seems the railroad company wants this land for improvements, and Fatty, of course, saves the girl's fortune and wins her hand. So ends a series of laughs and a show with no mean love interest.

Much of the feature's success is due to the simplicity and straight-forward appeal of the cast. We have here the later Arbuckle, a regular fellow, though fat. His chief support is Betty Ross Clarke. Instead of trying to play a big-town cutie she made good as the kind of girl one really finds in the smaller towns, and she was particularly convincing in a shy, charming way when it came to playing the love scenes. Lucille Ward as an old maid held up the comedy end, and the minor parts were creditably handled.

Particular credit should go to Walter Woods for the way he developed suspense toward the end, though why a marriage should settle the question at issue when the girl signed the paper before she was married remains a question. *Leed.*

THE FREEZE-OUT.

This poker-title covers a Universal feature, with Harry Carey as the star. It has no excuse in a picture theatre accustomed to program features of merit, and as viewed by a Stanley audience failed to stimulate interest. The reason is only too apparent. The incidents in it are developed from a stereotyped plot. For a group of actors to participate in a picture that does nothing more than try to imitate some of the early Hart pictures that were put out by Triangle invites failure. "The Freeze-Out" is a western.

Its action covers the vicissitudes of a "stranger" who comes into a town unannounced and then makes a place for himself by threatening to build a new gambling palace, much against the wishes of the proprietor of the established one and against the wishes of the moralist ma'am, who hopes to exert a good influence on that particular town. The hero, becoming thoroughly imbued with piety, transforms his saloon into a library, bookcases and all, and appoints the town drunk as librarian.

The story and scenario are the result of an original effort by George Hall. The "art director"—why there should be any demand for one is hard to explain—is E. E. Sheely, while the photography is by Harry Fowler. Jack Ford is the director.

The cast includes J. Charles Le Moyne, Joseph Harris, Helen Ferguson, J. Farrell MacDonald and Lydia Yeamans Titus. Star or no star it was Mr. MacDonald who romped away with the acting honors as the town drunk. A better screen interpretation of a man saturated with wood hootch hasn't been seen in a long time. *Step.*

BOB HAMPTON OF PLACER.

Bob Hampton..............James Kirkwood
Dick.....................Wesley Barry
The Kid..................Marjorie Daw
Lieutenant Brant...........Pat O'Malley
Red Slavin................Noah Beery
Silent Murphy.............Frank Leigh
General Custer..........Dwight Crittenden
Rev. Wyncoop.............Tom Gallery
School Teacher...........Priscilla Bonner
Major Brant................Charles West
Sheriff.....................Bert Sprotte
Housekeeper.........Carrie Clark Ward
Willie McNeil.............Vic Potel
Jack Moffet..............Bud Post

There are about 12,000 inches of unnecessary footage in this latest production by Marshall Neilan for First National, now at the Strand. In addition, Marion Fairfax's continuity is tiresome evidence of how continuity writing has lagged in development while direction and acting have progressed. Badly arranged to begin with. Mr. Neilan has padded it to play up Wesley Barry, featured. This padding delays the action, and Barry's antics do not make up for the annoyance. And money! The way this director spends it in times like these makes the heart ache. Nor does he get results for his expenditures. Once so prolific of ideas, going forward all the time, Marshall Neilan has become guardian of a reputation acquired in the good old working days, who is buoying up that reputation on the deep green waters of money.

This picture won't do as a buoy. What might save him would be action on the part of his backers. Hand him $35,000 and no more. Tell him to make a picture with it. Then he would have to use his brains, not money. Then possibly we would get something again.

This particular picture is based on Randall Parrish's novel. There's a fair story in it. Captain Nolan fights with Major Brant over the former's wife, and the major is stabbed from behind. Once out of prison the captain takes the name of Hampton, becomes a gambler and finds himself with two wards, a girl and a boy. Action now is concerned with events leading up to and including Custer's last fight, which is shown.

Even in this mass action Neilan is lost. Never once does he bring events really to grips with the heart, though the design of this inept continuity here, for once in its course, approached what was needed. Money galore must have gone into this picturing of Indian tribes on the warpath and the cavalry in action, but even at the last Hampton and the kid are left dead but unscalped. Every schoolboy knows what happened at the junction of the Big and Little Big Horn in Montana, but Neilan—where Griffith wouldn't—overlooks the detail.

Of the cast Majorie Daw is her sweet, girlish self, while James Kirkwood makes an upstanding, effective gambling gunman. Character parts by Noah Beery and Frank Leigh were worked for their full effect. Wesley Barry and Carrie Clark Ward were supposed to supply the comic relief, but as their work was flung into the action wholesale and interrupted and delayed it to just that extent, it is difficult to write appreciatively of them.

A word should be said in praise of the realistic military work shown by the Tenth Cavalry and superintended by Colonel Wyncoop. Dwight Crittenden, too, deserves praise for faithful representation of General Custer. *Leed.*

THE HOME STRETCH.

Johnny Hardwick.......Douglas MacLean
Margaret Warren.......Beatrice Burnham
Mr. Warren............Walt Whitman
Molly.................Margaret Livingston
Mr. Duffy.............Wade Boteler
Gwen Duffy............Mary Jane Irving
Mr. Wilson............Charles Mailes
Mrs. Wilson...........Molly McConnell
Tommy Wilson..........Jack Singleton

Hi Simpkins...............Jo Bennett
"Skeeter".................George Holmes

Thomas H. Ince has not done as well as usual with this story adapted from Charles Belmont Davis' tale and current at the Rialto. It is billed as a Paramount product and stars Douglas MacLean.

The trouble is that it tries half heartedly to earn serious consideration as a likelike record and at the same time tell a story that would fit a frank melodrama without pretense to naturalness. So it is half way between the "action story" with a powerful punch, but little plausibility, and one of those "cross sections of life," realistic tales.

A carefully produced feature in either category deserves consideration, but the stories that try in vain to cover both specifications do not seem to get anywhere except occasionally when a picture has both "punch" and sincerity. But that happens only once in a while and results in the exceptional film.

In printed story form the author may have made the narrative progress naturally and concealed the mechanics of his fiction, but in the screen version the machinery of a contriving scenario writer is obtrusive. Motives are vague and conduct frequently out of character. The first horse race has its thrill, but the incident of the rescue of the child who wanders upon the course in the path of the galloping horses misses its "kick" because the auditor cannot but realize that it is invented for purely fictional purposes.

The progress of the story is frequently foreshadowed. When the villain enters a "ringer" in the county fair race it takes no agile imagination to predict that the hero is going to enter his world-beating thoroughbred and win the stakes. Hence a situation which, had it been more expertly built up, would have held suspense, brings up a lame second to the spectator's advance expectation. In the short story field O. Henry was master of the delicate art of suggestion without revealment, while Clyde Fitch had the knack in play technique. Both could prepare for coming events with a skill that did not prevent story progress from holding surprise. Some how the scenario makers do not catch the trick as a rule.

In the present case the only surprises come as bald coincidences. This is what happens when Johnny Hardwick's race track friend happens upon him. The same thing occurs when Johnny's old pals of the "Follies'" and paddock discover him at the county fair. If these two incidents are not actual abuse of coincidence they are close to it. It's rather slipshod method that has to call lucky chance so much to its aid in contriving situations.

These considerations are not nearly so academic as they appear. In "The Home Stretch" they interfere with the enjoyment of watching a story that might have been better told. A spectator feels resentment, whether consciously or not, in being thus crudely confronted with an arbitrary coincidence.

The two race scenes are neatly handled as straightaway action episodes and there is a fairly interesting romance between the racetrack hero and the village postmistress, which leads to a rather spirited happy ending, but the picture is lacking in character drawing and human touches, and the recital becomes merely labored manipulation of lay figures. Perhaps the titling, as uninspired an example of film captions as has been noted, have something to do with this result.

Douglas MacLean is not happily cast as the hero. Usually a likeable juvenile, he does not give a sincere reading of this hero, who could have been made another "Checkers" as Henry Blossom drew that entertaining person. Walt Whitman, one time Miracle Man, is in the cast,

but gets little out of a wooden part. The same might be said of the whole company—capable players hampered by a poor vehicle. *Rush.*

BUCKING THE TIGER.

At a time when picture magnates were trying to buck the legit by producing plays and then reproducing them in pictures along came Lewis J. Selznick, for whom a very industrious press department chronicled an association with A. H. Woods as the producers of "Bucking the Tiger." This by Achmed Abdullah and May Tully. Securing Larry Marsden to stage it, the piece took to the road, and there little encouragement swayed its further course. The management closed it after several weeks.

Conway Tearle and a cast were assembled to give it picture value. The result seems flat. Its situations are quite sterile as far as anything novel is concerned, and equally sterile of big, invigorating dramatic incidents. This is what it pretends to do, but does not pass beyond the boundary of pretentiousness. Its value as an offering for a program release seems to be entirely diminutive. The story is of five men practically stranded in an Alaskan hostelry, impecunious, will-paralyzed and all that. One in the group, apparently conscience stricken (always the hero in such cases) proposes a fund be contributed to one of this quintet. He is to live life to its fullest for one year. At the end the others are to become beneficiaries with the matriculation of an insurance policy. The one who is unfortunate enough to be nominated for this unique post is to eliminate himself at the end of a year. The others are to collect. The hero's motive is inspired by the heroine, who is a married woman with a disappointed husband and a mother who needs $1,000 to recover her health.

As far as can be estimated from the sequences in this story there is not enough material to cover five reels, and consequently there are numerous episodes in the filament which drag too much for the good of the picture.

Henry Kolker's direction in the main is very conventional, but now and then it is intersected with several fine points, one especially in the handling of the mob.

As for Mr. Tearle's acting, it is in the accustomed manner, varying little from his efforts in preceding picture dramas.

There is no cause here to single out any one as achieving anything above ordinary merit in the cast. The much pitied heroine seems to be much miscast, both as to looks and ability. On the other hand and by comparison the taller of the two principal women playing a secondary part acts rings around the glycerine-teared blonde.

The production is inexpensive. A snow landscape is used for the exteriors, while the interiors are of the conventional pattern, with a lobby of the hotel and the usual background of the saloon plus gambling palace. Photography fair. *Step.*

THE LITTLE FOOL.

Metro's adaptation of Jack London's story, "The Little Lady of the Big House," makes a capital feature. It has excellent feminine interest in a love story with a fresh angle and some of the finest scenic backgrounds and photography imaginable. Also it is a simple story, simply and capably acted, so that there are no side interests to

May 6, 1921

distract the spectator from the direct progress of the tale.

Milton Sills, always a likeable sincere player, has a part made to order; Frances Wadsworth is a lovely leading woman and Nigel Barrie fills out the essential triangle. The other figures are merely used to fill in the picture and never intrude. This is as it should be and serves the purpose of economizing attention and centering interest. Big casts only fog the story and scatter interest, although adapters of fiction seem to resist the idea.

Dick inherits wealth and runs it up to a huge fortune. He and Florence have been ideally married ten years when Evan, an old time pal of Dick's, appears at their luxurious California home. He accompanies husband and wife and their guests in their picnics and horseback excursions and gradually falls in love with Florence. Both friend and wife confess to the husband that they feel themselves drifting into a dangerous situation, but Dick laughs them off, declaring that they only imagine it.

The wife ultimately is forced to a choice between the lover and husband. While she is arguing with the lover, the husband appears on the scene and tells her she is at liberty to bolt. His view is that if she can't make up her mind after ten years of marriage, he will have none of her. There is a quick finale in which the wife begs forgiveness and asks to be restored to her husband.

The out of door shots are extraordinarily lovely, partly because of the fine composition of the views and partly by a tricky method of employing misted photography. The interiors of the fine mansion also are happily and artistically framed. In the first part there are a number of scenes showing the women of the house party bathing in a woodland pool that edges into the Mack Sennett bathing girl franchise, but the scenic setting is so lovely the union suited girl bathers strike one only as quite appropriate for an idyll.

A good "stunt" is done here. One of the girls as a bit of frolic rides her horse to a high cliff and drives it over the edge for a long dive into the water, a spectacular performance.

Altogether an interesting and likeable picture. *Rush.*

OLIVER TWIST, JR.

Designers of picture scenarios must be in a low state of imagination when they resort to a five-reel paraphrase of a standard book. In this William Fox story there is not a single change of material, not one detail of decoration added to the Dickens story of Oliver Twist. It is just a recital of the English work, translated to the American locale and to modern times.

Fagan is absent, but Bill Sikes is among those present under the name of Jim Cleek. So is Nancy and the Artful Dodger, nameless and modern, but the Artful Dodger as to occupation minus any distinguishing characteristics. Harold Goodwin plays Oliver, but it is a queer and unconvincing Oliver who stands half a head higher than the new conception of Bill Sikes.

A director should have known that the basic appeal of the Oliver Twist story is the childish helplessness of the boy. Without that element there is no sympathy. That was the reason of the tremendous appeal of the story as done some years ago with Marie Doro as the Dickens waif. Even in that case the sordidness of the tale of London

underworld life was a severe handicap.

What, then, is the excuse for a picture of the Fox sort, where the only convincing details are those of wretchedness and squalor? It is Dickens' "Oliver Twist" with all the beauty and sympathy left out and only the uncomfortable and harrowing portions emphasized. What's the use of spending money, time and energy for such a purpose. For the design seems to be to strip a great novel of all its beauty and burden it with all its original ugliness with a gratuitous addition of more of the same.

In addition to which the whole thing is done crudely. The crass device of the locket by which Oliver's identity is traced keeps cropping up at the most confusing moments. One would have to remember the book with extraordinary vividness to piece the tale together with any completeness from the film. In its taking or in its cutting the whole thing has been made unbelievably chaotic. The thing was not worth doing in the first place, and t) make it complete has been done badly.
Rush.

THE STRUGGLE.

An unrestrained melodrama with a wallop every hundred feet is the broad scheme of this five-reeler, offered by Canyon Pictures, under the sponsorship of William J. Selig. It is a model for a certain type of picture—the kind that addresses itself to a very wide section of the fan public which asks only to be thrilled with action episodes without inquiring too closely into the plausibility of the screen happenings.

This kind of picture serves the same purpose as the dime novel of western cowboy setting, but "The Struggle" does it very neatly, and for exhibitors whose clientele have a taste for that grade of story it will serve most satisfactorily.

The story opens with the hero (Franklyn Farnum), newly returned from the war, restless and given to rough-and-tumble exploits which disturb his parents. He finds a gang of rowdies persecuting women and young workers in the mills. He undertakes a campaign to drive them out, and this leads to a series of lively fist fights. The leader of the roughs and the hero come together at the factory gymnasium for a bare-knuckle bout in which the thug is knocked out. When it appears that he is dead the hero escapes through a window and takes a freight for the west.

City street warfare is translated into plains battles, the hero becoming an innocent member of an outlaw gang to hide his identity. The bandits become involved in a plan to rob the heroine, owner of a ranch, and the hero frustrates their designs after innumerable fights. There is a capital touch of comedy supplied by a pickaninny and a trick donkey, part of the personnel of the heroine's ranch.

There is no pretence to seriousness in the picture. It's just a rough-and-ready melodrama, with the "punches" scattered liberally throughout and no moral intent. Interest is sustained by fast action and there is no demand upon imagination. The screen does all the work and the spectator is not called upon to expend any energy in following the tale. *Rush.*

NOBODY'S KID.

Mae Marsh returns in this Robertson-Cole special, retitled and adapted from a novel called "Mary Cary," by Katherine Langley Boshon. Used jointly on a double feature day at the Circle with Milton Sills in "The Little Fool," both names proved a big draw. In its

denouement the Marsh vehicle rubs elbows with "Daddy Long Legs." Playing the role of an orphan and discovering that she is "somebody's kid" and not "nobody's" is practically the sense of the entertainment. The piece opens in an orphanage and the sequences couple the events in her life until she graduates from the tyrannical instructor to the loving arms of a relative.

The story itself is trashy and the script seems to have been manipulated by the continuity writers to offer action that is exaggerated with the object of covering the heroine with an abundance of bathos. It becomes a trifle saccharine.

The titles, from the original text, have a wealth of humor which was not lost upon the audience. Numerous scenes also offered a humorous touch.

The cast includes, in addition to the star, John Steppling, Anne Shaefer, Kathleen Kirkham and Maxine Hicks. While this is in no sense a first-run picture, it is adequate for program use. *Step.*

IN THE HEART OF A FOOL.

Atmospheric to an exceptional degree is the picturization of "In the Heart of a Fool," adapted from William Allen White's novel by Lillian Lucey. It is an Allan Dwan production for Mayflower, released via First National and featuring James Kirkwood and Anna Q. Nilsson.

The sub-titles are ponderously allegorical and their relativity to the unfoldment of the story rather obscure, designed to show that life is a loom and we are its myriad threads. They also refer to "the circumstance of chance and change." Preceding each series of scenes of actuality are shown flashes of the allegorical "weaver."

But, stripped of all this twaddle, there is a virile life story that is interesting, and the allegory serves only to retard the cumulative progression of a grim tale of life in a small town populated with flesh-and-blood beings, who sin and otherwise conduct themselves humanly. There is nothing especially in the story to require its narration in detail. Its personages live and suffer through the sins of sex, which are frankly set down through the medium of good dramatic action but minus any vulgarity and making little or no bid for sensationalism. To be sure, there is a mine explosion and fire, in which the hero is shown doing brave deeds. This is dragged in by the heels and has no direct bearing upon the tale. The story would be just as good without it. The director would have shone as brilliantly through the medium of a splendidly staged mob scene.

James Kirkwood gives a manly performance of a youth who falls for a scarlet woman through propinquity and suffers years of misery before he succeeds in winning the girl he really loves. Miss Nilsson **departs from her usual line of parts** with a vivid portrayal of the scarlet woman, while Lillian Thurman is pretty and sincere as the young girl who waits all those years for her lover to be rid of entanglements caused by his misstep. The screen fails to give the name of an elderly man who plays an old village doctor. It would be a pleasure to mention his name as a character actor of uncommon merit.

Excellent photography contributes in no small degree to the success of the feature. *Jolo.*

GYPSY BLOOD.

To the urge and sound of the moving operatic strains of "Carmen" First National brought to the Strand May 8 a film version of that opera made in Germany with the Viennese Pola Negri starred, and for the fourth time this season there was thrown on the screen here a major example of what can be done by pantomime in pictures. This Negri is amazing. She can do more with her face than most people can do with a sub-title. That is art in acting. As much cannot be said for the play. It is doubtful if it be commercially profitable, but this woman stepped into it after it had proceeded some 500 feet, caught it up and kept it moving—moving till the heart paused in inadvertent praise.

La Carmencita was a low-life, a tough little cigaret girl, a she-wolf in skirts. Negri makes her just that. And there is a passion, a dramatic clutching in her performance of the viewer's emotions that grips and moulds them, fairly forcing out a tendency to shout approval. But—and this is the big "but" about this picture—will America like it? It is sex—sharp, sure, terrific. It is never a sweetly smiling Marjorie Daw, for example, nor a Farrar, with a weather eye on the box office. Where our prima diva in her Carmen picture had a sweet old mother to set her off, Ernst Lubitsch has given Negri a hag with her lips to a bottle.

The story is well known. Carmen vamps Jose away from his sweetheart and makes a crook of him when he kills a wealthy officer and lover who comes to claim her. Later, off on the business of Egypt—gypsy work—she leads another officer to his doom and flirts with a famous matador. Riding at his left —a nice touch that—she goes to his greatest triumph, but soon Jose drops in on her, seizes her for the last time in his arms, stabbing her as she repulses him, and so, after a performance never surpassed here for sheer fire of womanhood as its most fundamental, Negri showed her Carmencita dying as she lived, the she-wolf enraged but unafraid, regretting the last great love unfulfilled.

Probably with wisdom, the picture was cut, but this precaution shears away the chance to do Lubitsch justice. Love scene after love scene loses full potency from the shears. The bull fight was clipped, too, and the full force of the climax lost, but professional observers, keeping their eyes on Negri, were held surely and certainly under a major spell.

For patrons of the best houses who want to see Carmen as Prosper Merimee imagined her (his name, by the way, was misspelled on the screen) this should be a sure-fire bet. A word should be said, too, for the able titling done by Myron Stearns, and still another word to directors shrieking for protection. From this sort of thing they and the world need it, but such acting is exceptional. It stands out mostly because it is unusual, and Americans do not attempt it. *Leed.*

THE LOST ROMANCE.

Mark Sheridan	Jack Holt
Sylvia Hayes	Lois Wilson
Elizabeth Erskine	Fontaine LaRue
Allen Erskine, M. D.	Conrad Nagel
Allen Erskine, Jr.	Mickey Moore
Librarian	Mayme Kelso
Butler	Robert Brower
Nurse	Barbara Gurney
Police Lieutenant	Clarence Geldart
Detective	Clarence Burton

"The Lost Romance" is the first of a series of original stories to be written for the screen by Edward Knoblock, to be produced by Famous Players. Everything known to the screen art up to the present time was done to the tale to make it important. The direction was placed in the hands of William De Mille, Olga Printzlau was entrusted with the making of the scenario, the three principal roles were allotted to Jack Holt, Lois Wilson and Conrad Nagel, not to mention Fountaine LaRue and Mayme Kelso in important parts. William De Mille's lavishness of production, some really remarkable photography, the uttermost care in the matter of details—in fact, everything of artistic value surrounds this tale.

The story starts off brilliantly, replete with smart titles, some philosophical observations on life in erudite verbiage, such as "the terrible commonplace is love's deadliest enemy," and so on; but when the unfolding is half way and headed for the home stretch it falls to the conventional and you know it is only a matter of another 2,500 feet of film when it will end with the uniting of man and wife.

Here it is in a miniature nutshell. Young man and wife have sort of soured on one another after half a dozen years of marriage, with one child the result of the alliance. She has a rejected suitor who returns from Africa, believes she loves him and they decide to tell the husband, who magnanimously offers to give her up. At this juncture their child is kidnapped and the couple turn to each other for consolation. It turns out the aunt of the husband had taken the child away to teach them a lesson.

A magnificent production squandered upon a trivial tale. If this is an average sample of what the standard playwrights will contribute to the screen in the way of "original" scenarios we can look for small relief from that quarter.

Jolo.

THE WILD GOOSE.

Diana Manners	Mary MacLaren
Frank Manners	Holmes E. Herbert
Mrs. Hastings	Dorothy Bernard
Mr.. Hastings	Joseph Smiley
Ogden Fenn	Norman Kerry
Tam Manners	Rita Rogan
Nou Nou	Lucia Backus Segar

This week's attraction at the Rialto is a Cosmopolitan production made from a Gouverneur Morris story under the direction of Albert Capellani, with Mary McLaren as the principal player.

It is a society drama with the domestic triangle elaborated into a five-sided complication and some of its "literary ethics" are rather strange. The only person in the play who transgresses the moral law appears to be the only person who does not suffer from consequences, and it takes an enormous length of titling to twist this circumstance about to fit the satisfactory working out of justice.

The name of Capellani guarantees a certain expertness of directorship, and the picture has some splendid examples of fine backgrounds, both out of doors and interiors. The lighting effects are notably fine throughout. The acting is good, although one bit of miscasting did a great deal to injure the effectiveness of the entire play. This was the selection of Joseph Smiley as the financier, a rotund, amiable person ill fitted to the role of a desperate hero.

The part of the wife is a particularly unsympathetic one. Diana Manners (Miss MacLaren) casts her husband aside in favor of a richer man, deserts him apparently without a regret and takes her baby daughter to the rich man's home. When the rich man is providentially killed she returns to her husband, repentent, but apparently none the worse for the episode. At least the prospect is that her husband is to receive her on the old standing.

The author disproves his own point. He takes the tradition that the wild goose choses its mate and remains true to the end of its life, the male bird seeking death before the hunter's gun when the female is lost to him. This bit of nature fakery is the text of a preachment on the marital fidelity and the tale is told to point the moral that love and faith can only be preserved by indissoluble marriage.

Frank Manners is a struggling artist with an extravagant wife. At the home of the Hastings Diana Manners meets a young millionaire from the west and at the same time Frank goes to California to execute a commission. During his absence Diana's infatuation for the millionaire develops into a liaison and upon his return she informs her husband that she wants a divorce in order to marry him.

Frank refuses to agree to this and Diana goes to her lover, taking her five-year-old daughter Tam. Half insane, Frank is about to seek out the lover and his wife and kill them, but Mrs. Hastings, who has loved Frank since childhood, defeats this purpose by drugging him. Her husband misunderstands her design and is about to interfere, but when he learns the real situation undertakes to work out a solution himself.

He goes to the millionaire's home and forces him at revolver point to accompany him back to the city in an automobile. On the way he deliberately plunges from a cliff, committing suicide and taking the home wrecker with him. On the screen this episode was a thriller, but nothing up to that time had prepared the audience to look for desperate action on the part of the portly, gray-haired Hastings. At this point there is nothing to do but reconcile the Manners. Mrs. Hastings says to the wife: 'You have wrecked your own and your husband's life and sent one good man and a scoundrel to destruction, but nothing counts except the child." This argument persuades her to return to her husband and all ends "happily," so to speak. Pretty artificial fiction, although it may have a certain appeal to feminine sympathies.

Rush.

BELPHEGOR..

London, April 20.

This is a film which will not reflect great credit on either the producing firm, Ideal, or the actual producer, Bert Wynne. The story is adapted from an old play produced at the Adelphi Theatre in 1851. It has ever since that date been a popular "stock" drama and feature in the weekly programs of most small repertoire companies. The original play deals with a "costume" period, but in the film version this seems to have been overlooked, or entirely ignored. Some of the characters certainly are in the period, but others, chiefly the principles are in modern attire, and such things as motor cars and revolvers are introduced, both of which are right out of the picture—one might just as well let Laertes depart for France in an aeroplane, while Hamlet got into wireless communication with his father's ghost.

Always a sloppily sentimental play, the film develops the "sob stuff," while managing to remain entirely devoid of atmosphere. It is doubtful whether audiences, many of whom have seen Belphegor since their youth at the minor drama houses and in the booths of the country and have wept over the woes of the nobleman turned traveling showman will crowd to the kinemas to see their unhappy hero screened. If they do it will be interesting to hear their opinion of this new feature. Scenically the production is very good. Some remarkably beautiful forest locations have been selected, and the scene in which the caravans cross a river is exceptionally well done. Throughout the photography reaches and maintains a high standard of excellence. The characters in the film as in the play are artificial, but a good cast makes the most of every chance.

Milton Rosmer gives a fine and powerful performance of the hero, although he fails to give one the impression of being a showman, even an unsuccessful one. Warwick Ward is the ordinary "twice nightly melodrama" villain as Laverennes. Margaret Dean, with an artistic performance of all-around excellence, almost makes Belphegor's wife human, and the rest of the players contribute good work. It is more than a pity that producers when dealing with old standard works of this sort do not consult some member of their company as to period before yielding to the temptation to introduce motor cars, etc., a temptation which appears to be the curse of film producers the wide world over.

Gore.

MR. PIM PASSES BY.

London, April 20.

As a stage play "Mr. Pim Passes By" was a success not only in the West End but in the provinces. In the smaller towns of the country it is still playing to excellent business. As a film its value is almost negligible, it is unconvincing and decidedly weak. Produced by General (Samuelson). The play depended almost entirely on the brilliant dialogue of A. A. Milne, while the cinema action conveys little or nothing of its humor or pathos. Its only chance of attracting will rest in its title, and those who are led to the pay box by the original play's fame will pass out of the cinema again sadly disappointed.

Returning from abroad Mr. Pim is given introductions to various people, among whom is George Marden, a fellow with old-fashioned ideas, who is married to a worldly wife. Pim mentions to the Mardens that he met a man called Telworthy on the voyage over. The fat is immediately in the fire, for Mrs. Marden has been previously married to a man of that name, but has believed him dead. If he is alive she has committed bigamy. However, Pim explains that Telworthy died through getting a fish bone in his throat. Then, Mrs. Marden, still very uncertain as to the legality of her marriage with George, refuses to be remarried until he has blessed his niece's union and becomes a little more modern in his own ideas. At last he agrees, and the happy ending comes when Pim drops in to explain that he's confused another man with Telworthy, who, he says, died years ago.

Not much of a story on which to hang a photoplay, and the frailty is somewhat emphasized by bad telling and lack of continuity. The whole feature is somewhat wearisome. It will doubtless be popular with those who seek the darkness of the cinema, there to sleep in comfort, undisturbed by telephone bells and callers. The cast is a notable one, but few of its members have any chance to distinguish themselves. Peggy Hyland is excellent in the leading role, Maudie Dunham is good as the girl, Campbell Cullen makes Pim a senile old fool, Henry Kendall overacts and the rest of the cast seem to have followed his example, developing theatrical exaggeration in its worst form.

The producer has found some pretty scenes in which to frame his story and the photography is excellent. This Samuelson picture should be yet another warning to those producers who, while screaming about the lack of original stories, fall over each other in their efforts to obtain the film rights of successful plays or books without giving a passing thought as to whether they are suitable for the screen or not.

Gore.

TEN-DOLLAR RAISE.

Wilkins	William V. Mong
Dorothy	Marguerite de la Motte
Jimmy	Pat O'Malley
Emily	Helen Jerome Eddy
Don	Hal Cooper
Bates	Lincoln Plumer
Stryker	Charles Hill Mailes

This J. L. Frothingham production released through Associated Producers and given a trade showing last week, is a Cinderella story, but instead of a girl, a man, William V. Mong, appears as Cin. Peter B. Kyne, its author, dedicates it to the "underpaid underdog." Albert S. Le Vino made the scenario and can always be depended upon to do competent, sure work. Edward Sloman directed and got in some neat details, as where the man falls through the door, but half the success of the production can be credited to the casting director, who provided a balanced, all together excellent collection of players.

The story is sure-fire hoakum and should go well most anywhere, for it has real sentiment and will hit the average picture crowd straight in the heart.

Wilkins has been promised a raise for 15 years and has never got it. This upsets his matrimonial plans. Bates, hard-hearted employer, has stood in his way, but is gradually overdrawing. His son is no good and sells Wilkins some lots that are worthless. Jimmy, helped by Wilkins, has been stung by bad boy Don in a gambling den and they trail him there, expose him and his Chinese gang, escape in a riotous scene and make for the lots, which are under salt water. While ducking Don, Wilkins finds there's oil there, so he becomes rich, marries the stenograper old-maid Emily, forgives his employer Bates, and everything ends happily, with Jimmy married to the daughter of the other partner.

William V. Mong made an excellent brow-beaten older man who has worn himself out as a bookkeeper, while Helen Jerome Eddy was as near perfect as it is possible to get as the old maid. A beautiful, effective picture type, Marguerite de la Motte, was her lovely, distinguished, well-dressed self, and Pat O'Malley, playing opposite, satisfactory.

An agreeable market production.

Leed.

IT CAN BE DONE.

Austin Strong	Earle Williams
Eve Standish	Elinor Fair

This is a mighty poor feature to be offered in good faith by the Vitagraph. Earle Williams is starred, and half the action at least must be given over to close-ups of him that serve no particularly good effect or to sub-titles reading "Later," "Next morning," "That evening"—you know the kind. It is a picture altogether impossible to take seriously.

The story is by Fred Jackson, though its lack of action makes that seem impossible. The direction is not credited. Perhaps that is just as well. It's all about a writer of detective stories who signs a 57-page contract binding him to write three exposes for a daily newspaper of three separate profiteers. Of course, he finds he can't expose his sweetheart's father. So he reforms the well dressed old thief in quite another way.

If there is anything recommending this offering as a buy at any price that something does not occur to the reviewer.

Leeds.

BLACK ROSES.

Yoda	Sessue Hayakawa
Blossom	Tsuru Aoki
Blanche De Vore	Myrtle Stedman
Benson Burleigh	Andrew Robson
Wong Fu	Toyo Fujita
Monocle Harry	Henry Hebert

Detective Cleary ....Harold Holland
Bridget ....Carrie Clark Ward

Well produced, but somewhat inconsistent story. Directed by Colin Campbell scenario by Richard Schayer, released through Robertson-Cole and starring Sessue Hayakawa.

Fine settings, giving the star ample opportunity for strong dramatic acting of the stolid variety. He is "jobbed" for a murder he didn't commit, serves a long jail sentence, escapes and brings the malefactors to justice along the "Monte Cristo" lines. A competent supporting organization, excellent photography and direction combine to make a most acceptable, high-grade program feature. *Jolo.*

THE ONE-MAN TRAIL.

Few pictures have been less insipid in story interest and few westerners have been made up as crudely as this "One-Man Trail" (Fox) with "Buck" Jones. Except for some redeeming features in the concluding episodes, in which Mr. Jones and a supporting cast distinguish themselves as heavy hitters—unsparing of person, with an indifference to their physical beauty that is quite admirable—there is little to recommend.

The feature was exhibited jointly with First National's "Love, Honor and Behave" on a double-feature day at Loew's New York. The story up to the concluding bit of fierce, aggressive action concerns the lone hero, who sets out on a "one-man trail" to find his sister, who obviously had absconded with a very wicked man.

For titles, plot, story, acting, the film is pretty much A. K. There are certain scenes, titles et al. that can stand cutting, and with so much pressure put on the censorship question in New York State and elsewhere to eliminate crime it somehow defies all logic why any picture like this should have been released in the first place.

The author of the story calls himself John Strumwasser, the scenario writer is William H. Howard, the director Bernard J. Durning. *Step.*

THE BLAZING TRAIL.

Universal five-reeler featuring Frank Mayo. The story, of little consequence, concerns the life of a hermit physician whose life is spent in the neighborhood of a small mountain village whose inhabitants to a great extent are illiterate.

The physician befriends the daughter of the village shopkeeper, supplying her with books. She becomes infatuated with him, although much younger, and the village becomes aroused at her frequent visits to his cabin.

A school teacher is sent to the town, with the physician falling in love with her and saving her life when she is stricken with blood poisoning. A villain tries to involve the younger girl with the M. D. and arouses the ire of the townsfolk, who go to lynch him. It is cleared up in the final rounds with the usual fadeout with the school teacher at the finish.

The Universal can turn out features of this order at a minimum of expense. It consists almost entirely of exteriors. The cast in addition includes Mary Philbin, Lillian Rich, Bert Sprotte, Verne Winter and Joy Winthrop. The players do acceptably, although the story provides them with little opportunity. To pad out a bill this might do, but cannot stand up alone as a feature on any picture program.

KEEPING UP WITH LIZZIE

The first showing was given privately Tuesday morning at the Stanley. A puzzling title, hinting more at farce than comedy, which it is, although delineated along very conventional lines, the whole thing as it stands is a fair and average program release. In no sense at all a first run feature.

A pamphlet distributed to the unknowing explains that it is the "first Irving Bacheller story to reach the screen." Like hundreds preceding it, it only proves magazine fiction for screen purpose has blown its last bugle note. The screen needs American magazine fiction, but of a different quality. It must be a human document, embracing action and mime essential to make cinematographic art a unit in itself. When this is lacking the result is nothing more than just another picture. The theme offers the ingenue daughter who is rushed off to a finishing school while her father, a slaving grocer, boosts his commodities to defray the expense of "finishin'" his daughter. The opposite angle is constructed of the following: The town's competing grocer has a son. He is shipped off to Harvard. The daughter comes back with the polish she started out to attain, and the son is quite useless. Added to this is a bogus count with whom the daughter is apparently infatuated. At the last moment the count contrives to make a getaway with the $10,000 dowry, is overtaken by the hero, knocked into splashing mud, and kiss—finale.

All this is not above the merit of a program release—there have been worse. One element that strikes the auditor as having real merit is the photography, and certain shots with Enid Bennett posed exhibit a certain hazy wistfulness that has demonstrated itself before in the work of the best cameramen.

In direction the very start of the picture is a glowing example of a director's ability in making his actors do something other than mere posing. The character of the grocer (Otis Harlan) is introduced and for this one scene his interpretation is inspiringly animated. But just this once. For the rest there is an appalling lack of action. Miss Bennett fills the bill as the ingenue, but the wish goes with it that she might really act now and then. A sympathetic part is entrusted to W. Landers Stevens, a rube lawyer, who makes most of it, while the count of Leo White had all the flavor of staginess. The rest includes Victory Bateman, Edward Hearn, Harry Todd and Lila Leslie. The feature is released by Pathe for Hodkinson and for the Rockett Film Corporation. Direction by Lloyd Ingraham. *Step.*

THE LURE OF EGYPT.

Filmed from a novel entitled "Once There Was a King," the sponsor for this feature is the Federated of California, releasing through Pathe, with Claire Adams as the star and heroine of a romance, with a background suggested by its title—Egypt.

Its lure is less as a story with active ingredients, but more in a succession of art titles that really give more color to the action than the drama. The producers were not aware of the fact that in suggesting Cairo as a locale, something would be needed to sustain the impression, if the filming couldn't actually be accomplished there. And so, the title was imprinted on a background of a scene of the city itself, while the action sped on to an interior. That's one way of doing it.

An archaeologist is at the end of his resources, and, unaided by the British Government, is at a loss to go on with research and experimental work that will unearth new treasures for civilization. A con-

niving Oriental prince comes along, becomes enamored of the daughter of this learned man, and the drama revolves around this triangle, with the customary ending. Flashes of spiritism are evoked through the introduction of an incarnate Egyptian monarch, while Oriental mysticism comes in the form of a bearded patriarch, not unfamiliar in this type of drama.

The picture falters in its interest at the start because its introduction is coupled with the appearance of new characters—too much in its way, so that when about half way through the real drama takes on speed.

For atmosphere, the picture itself sustains every vestige of interest, being filmed in the American desert. At the beginning an Oriental dancer makes her appearance in the center of the action gliding gracefully at an improvised ball for a selected few.

The cast is a large one, including Joseph Dowling, Zack Williams, Robert McKim, William Lion West, Maude Wayne, George Hernandez, Aggie Herring, Carl Gantvoort, Frank Hayes and Harry Lorraine. Perhaps Robert McKim, as the heavy, carries off the honors, being one of the few with any screen intelligence in this roster. But the uniform they gave him to show off a princely exterior must have been dug out of some California costumer's that was scarcely consistent with the character.

IDOL OF THE NORTH.

Colette Brissac..............Dorothy Dalton
Martin Bates.................Edwin August
Lucky Folsom.................E. J. Ratcliffe
Ham Devlin...................Riley Hatch
One-Eye Wallace..............Jules Cowles
A Soubrette ....Florence St. Leonard
Big Blond ....Jessie Arnold
Gloria Waldron..........Marguerite Marsh
Sergeant McNair.................Joe King

One of Dorothy Dalton's earlier screen successes was in "The Flame of the Yukon." Her present starring vehicle is "The Idol of the North," and the character of Colette is patterned as much as possible along the same lines. The tale is by J. Clarkson Miller, scenario by Frank Beresford, direction by William Neill; a Paramount production.

The locale is the picturesque Northwest, with no pains spared to create the proper atmospheric detail and one of the most carefully directed features of that kind ever offered the public. By this is not meant it is a very expensive production, but that intelligence and pains were exercised to visualize to a nicety the details of what would ordinarily be a commonplace production. As a consequence the picture is full of "life."

It starts with a speed that makes you hold your breath—breaks at once into action which never ceases, the story being unfolded in movement without having to resort to lengthy sub-titles or rhapsodical descriptions of life in the goldfields. Everything intended to be conveyed is shown rather than talked about. In this respect it is a well-nigh perfect specimen of dramatic construction. As a story it will hardly stand the test of too careful analysis, but for general cinema patronage is reasonably certain to satisfy.

None of the players, not even the star, does anything worth special commendation. Miss Dalton is called upon to play a young girl in the opening and doesn't look youthful enough. She is in the full bloom of youthful womanhood, both in face and figure. And, speaking of figure, she later appears as the star performer in a mining camp dance hall, with bare shoulders and abbreviated skirts. She shows her gorgeous back, shoulders and arms in a series of close-ups that are well worth while.

All of the characterizations are conventional theatrical types, well enough handled on the whole, but without distinctive individuality. But they are skillfully assembled and molded into a concrete, well-knit screen melodrama, calculated to please the general run of motion picture patrons. *Jolo.*

THRU BACK DOOR

Jeanne Bodamere...........Mary Pickford
Hortense Reeves..........Gertrude Astor
Elton Reeves...............Wilfred Lucas
Marie ....Helen Raymond
Jacques Lanvain.....C. Norman Hammond
Margaret Brewster..........Elinor Fair
James Brewster ....Adolphe J. Menjou
Conrad ....Peaches Jackson
Constant ....Doreen Turner
Billy Boy ....John Harron
Chauffeur ....George Dromgold

Offered by United Artists, this feature with Mary Pickford came to the Strand May 15 and started at once crowding them in. It is a market product—that's all—full of sweetness and light, a money maker and probably designed as such. The story is not credited. Marion Fairfax made the scenario and Jack Pickford and Alfred E. Green directed. Charles Rosher is responsible for as fine photography as it is possible to put on the screen. The cast, too, is excellent.

Jeanne Bodamere, stolen as a child by a Belgian peasant woman, is sent to her wealthy mother in America when the war breaks out. This mother is shielded from approach by a great establishment, and so little Jeanne with the two kids, orphaned, whom she brings with her, must be content to work as kitchen maid until she can make her identity clear. Before she does so she overhears a scheme to blackmail the head of the house and saves the day by exposing it. Of course, the young man next door falls in love with Jeanne while Jeanne herself reunites her parents.

Elinor Fair gives an unusual performance. She does not try to play the cutie, but looks good just the same and gets over the right notion of a designing young woman. As the mother Gertrude Astor gave one of those exceptional performances that cling to the memory. In picture fashion she had to be very haughty with the butler, but, nevertheless, she registered realistic hauteur and rose to the demands of developing situations which included a break with her husband over another woman and the recognition of her lost daughter after years. As this same husband, Wilfred Lucas was natural and convincing. John Harron as the young lover was for all the world that type.

A well rounded production, adequate for the market. *Leed.*

WOLVES OF THE NORTH.

"We all have two natures—the wild and the civilized." This is one of the subtitles in the Universal special, "Wolves of the North," written and directed by Norman Dawn, starring Eva Novak.

It is just one more of those program pictures, appealing to the "romance" of what was once the nickelodeon patrons who now pay 10 cents admission, including war tax.

A "refined" eastern girl resides in the northwest with her father. Along comes Wiki Jack, a native product, uncouth but withal a man—the kind who treats his women "rough." He strikes gold and spends his money freely at the local dive. He takes his liquor neat, accompanied by rhapsodial subtitles that mean nothing and sound "classy," such as "snow, snarling and crawling" and "pitiless crucible of blood and ice." (These are literal quotations.)

Wiki Jack takes a kiss from the heroine by force, and when her young eastern lover resents it he tosses the youngster down a snowbank. The cub falls for one of the saloon girls, the Wiki chap rescues the heroine from the clutches of a lecherous man with whiskers and later saves her life in a splendidly depicted snowslide, whereupon she has her sex aroused and sinks into the arms of the huski Wiki Jack, who gets a shave and dons a Norfolk jacket for the clinch.

A long-drawn out, feeble tale "romantically" picturized, palpably designed to pander to the flat-headed foreigners in mining and kindred communities and likely to give complete satisfaction to this type of "Americans." *Jolo.*

SHAM.

Katherine Van Riper	Ethel Clayton
Tom Jaffery	Clyde Fillmore
Monte Buck	Walter Hiers
Jeremiah Buck	Theodore Roberts
Aunt Bella	Sylvia Ashton
Aunt Louisa	Helen Dunbar
Bolton	Arthur Carewe
Uncle James	Thomas Ricketts
Clementine Vickers	Blanche Gray
Maud Buck	Eunice Burnham
Rosie	Carrie Clark Ward

The Paramount picture, "Sham," current at the Rivoli, puts forward Ethel Clayton in a romantic comedy, done in a neat way with faultless taste and holding a good average of laughs without resort to rough comedy device. The story is by Elmer Harris and Geralding Bonner, made into photoplay form by Douglas Doty and directed by Thomas Hefron.

Miss Clayton has a considerable following among the feminine fans, and this story ought to appeal to them for its atmosphere of "smart" society pictured in an intimate and convincing way and for its fine modern costuming, clothes being an element of screen presentation which carries a certain weight all its own.

The story is logical, compact, and progresses directly and simply to an entirely satisfactory romantic conclusion. Besides which its moral aspects are interesting and there is nothing in its characters or incidents that could possibly give offense. It's a clean, breezy, entertaining tale interestingly told by an uncommonly skillful group of screen players.

Katherine Van Riper (Miss Clayton) is an impecunious young fashionable left with an income much too small to satisfy her expensive tastes. Bill collectors besiege her home and she is put to the utmost of her resources to evade them, keep her credit from breaking and support a bijou apartment with a poor relation and a single maid. Escape from debt and nerve strain is offered by marriage with Monte Buck, son of a millionaire cattle king, but she loves the sturdy Tom Jaffery, an employe of Monte's father.

The story revolves about the proposition, Shall she marry Monte, fat and dull but with abundant money, or the handsome lover who promises happiness of a simpler kind? This theme is worked out in thoroughly expert story-telling style, with a wealth of clever comedy incident and splendidly sustained comedy suspense.

Theodore Roberts as the bluff cattle king, Monte's father, has another part that will go further to endear him to the film public. This fine character delineator seems to have the knack of taking small roles and making them stand out. He does so in this case. Jeremiah Buck undertakes in his crude way to stage manage the wedding of his son Monte, and interviews the ancient uncles and aunts of the heroine to that end. This passage is rich in the finest kind of character comedy. The cattle king does all that is humanly possible to make the match, but in the end Katherine comes to see herself as a grafting sycophant, and gives up the whole social bluff to throw her lot in with the handsome Tom.

Two excellent comedy scenes stand out. One of them is the scheme by which Katherine's maid intrigues to get chops for luncheon when Tom calls and has to steal them off the dumb waiter. The other is the comedy souse that Monte goes on when Katherine throws him over. Both bits could have been overacted into the last degree of vulgarity under unskillful handling, but in this instance they are genuinely funny and in good taste.

The excellence of the company contributes to this desirable end. Walter Hiers, who has done some first-rate character drawing in the fat-man comedy way on the stage, plays Monte; Carrie Clark Ward has a capital characterization as the maid, and the others are uncommonly convincing. Even the small parts are in capable hands. Sylvia Ashton and Helen Dunbar, the two rich, selfish aunts of Katherine, play with a skill that would justify roles of much more importance. It is not often that so uniformly good a cast is seen in an ordinary release.

The settings go with the splendid style of the presentation. The backgrounds, most of them interiors of fine homes, are especially real. The producer has struck an excellent middle ground between too much magnificence and too little. Katherine's little flat is the last word in dainty abodes and the Buck mansion is elaborate, but somehow impresses as a home for real people rather than a stage set. The titles are models of brevity, while still they get the color of neat comedy across. *Rush.*

GOOD WOMEN.

Katherine Brinkley	Rosemary Theby
Nicolai Brouevitch	Hamilton Revelle
Inna Brouevitch	Irene Blackwell
John Wilmot	Earl Schenck
Sir Richard Egglethorpe	Wm. P. Carleton
Franklin Shelby	Arthur Stuart Hull
Natalie Shelby	Rhea Mitchell
Mrs. Emmeline Shelby	Eugenie Besserer

This is unacceptable any way you look at it. Nothing so ineptly conceived has ever been so expensively mounted. It is really not a picture at all in the proper sense of the term. It is a novel (and a poor one) with illustrations, attractive ones, some of them, thrown in. There is insert after insert, subtitle after sub-title, and then pictures of people conversing. The only place there is any action at all is where Rosemary Theby, featured, dances at a cabaret, and this does not rouse the crowd. To cap the unsuitable continuity written by Gardner Sullivan, who is responsible also for the story, comes a climax touching the absurd. It was just possible to get it across, as it was possibly written, but Louis J. Gasnier, who directed, fails utterly to do so and has left his name as the maker chiefly responsible on this monumental mistake.

So expensive a mistake might be one in 100 and pass, but this is not the first time so inexplicable an offering has been shot at the public by Robertson-Cole. As a firm, none stands higher. Than Rufus Cole himself no executive in the picture business has a reputation more admirable for business ability, personal qualities and good sense, and yet apparently, he does not know pictures and has been ill advised. Witness "The Stealers," and even "Kismet," which should have been ten times the smash it was. "Good Women" is an offering for the ground-work of which C. Gardner Sullivan is responsible. Mr. Sullivan knows pictures. No one can deliver real drama better than he can if asked to, while Mr. Gasnier is capable of competent work. In fact, the scenes themselves in this special are adequately enough treated. The fault wherever it lies is a fundamental one of choice and policy.

Consider the plot and its presentation and what has been done is clearly enough a mistake to be avoided. First Miss Katherine Brinkley in her salon. Men are talking to her. She gazes longingly at a Russian pianist. She is warned against the pianist by a novelist. All this in conversation. Insert of the "World" telling of their elopement. Scene at their villa. Breakfast. Conversation—mostly unpleasant. They part. Scene at Monte Carlo with a reception and more conversation. Sir Richard Egglethorpe takes Miss Brinkley to a cabaret (but even this much action isn't shown). But, at last, at last. To shock people, Miss Brinkley does a dance, then Sir Richard takes her out and kisses her. Next see her at Naples. She becomes acquainted with Franklin Shelby, married but she doesn't know it. They read to each other. They converse. They see a former lover at the opera. Back come wife and mother and there are some 20 feet of action showing the wife kissing her husband. But the former lover spoils it all by telling the wife (more conversation), about Miss Brinkley. Shelby now goes to Miss Brinkley and they converse about the situation. She tells him she will give him up. Enter the wife and mother. Miss Brinkley tells them she has given up the husband, and then the mother returns (there's that much action), to tell the forsaken one that she is a good woman.

If this sort of thing, elaborately mounted, well photographed, makes a money-making special, everybody else has guessed wrong. Bad enough on the stage, mere conversation wrecks a picture. A great expert could, perhaps, have so cast this particular "conversazione" as to project vivid inner emotions dramatically, and so in a fashion scored, but Mr. Gasnier did not do this, nor did he apparently even sense the possibility. Rosemary Theby, a large, good looking woman, able to take care of herself, fails to catch the sympathy, while Hamilton Revelle really caricatured rather than presented a pianist of charm and ability, but loose morals. Irene Blackwell and Eugenie Besserer were dignified in minor roles, but Rhea Mitchell for sympathy-forcing purposes (that is to say, the box office), should have presented a stronger contrast, caught the sympathy, but in the effort to corral the interest for the star everything was literally lost.

A poor offering for any class of house. *Leed.*

BOYS WILL BE BOYS.

Peep O'Day	Will Rogers
Lucy	Irene Rich
Tom Minor	C. E. Mason
Sublette	Sydney Ainsworth
Judge Priest	Ed. Kimball
Bagby	H. Milton Ross
Sheriff Breck	C. E. Thurston
Kitty	Mae Hopkins
Mrs. Hunter	Cordelia Callahan
Aunt Mandy	Nick Cogley
Farmer Bell	Burton Halbert

This Goldwyn feature is true blue, and gets to you three-fourths of the way. The climax is mishandled and does not register for all it is worth, through the failure either of the cutter, or Clarence Badger, who directed, and E. A. Bigelow, continuity writer. These did not develop, as they should, the "fake niece" incident. The whole show is based on the Broadway play written by Charles O'Brien Kennedy from Irvin S. Cobb's story. Will Rogers is featured and scores all the way.

Mr. Cobb's stories about Judge Priest, of which this is one, are popular, and have been Saturday Evening Post features. Here we have the uneducated Peep O'Day, butt of the world from the day he came from the poorhouse, suddenly heir to a fortune. His reaction is natural. He wants to have that boyhood he has seen, but never enjoyed, and so he spends his money on the kids and in helping the pretty little school teacher who tried to educate him and was misjudged.

Naturally, such conduct looks crazy to Kentuckians who have never heard of psycho-analysis and couldn't pronounce the term if they had, so they readily fall into the crooked scheming of Lawyer Sublette, who thinks Judge Priest's brains "have been dead for 20 years." He brings a manicurist from Cincinnati who poses as Peep's niece and then tries to get a commission appointed and his estate given into her care. Seeing what a decent chap Peep is, this cutie in the end exposes the whole plot and everything is cleared up. Right here is where director and scenarist failed. If they had established clearly the changing in her point of view, they would have handed the crowd a bigger thrill and scored a marked hit.

As it was, the cast comes in for the biggest honor. All were good types, though nowhere was there exceptional work, Mae Hopkins, as the manicurist, being the one marked disappointment. But perhaps it was not her fault.

A good program feature. *Leed.*

HEARTS OF YOUTH.

Ishmael Worth	Harold Goodwin
Beatrice Merlin	Lillian Hall
Judge Merlin	Fred Kirby
Herman Brudenell	George Fisher
Mrs. Grey (formerly Hannah Worth)	Iris Ashton
Reuben Grey	Glenn Cavender
Countess Hurstmonceaus	Grace Goodall
Lord Vincent	Colin Kenny

The grown-up female members of

your family will probably remember Mrs. E. D. E. N. Southworth's hectic novel, "Ishmael, or Out of the Depths," from which the Fox feature, "Hearts of Youth," was adapted by Millard Webb, who also directed the picture. It has been brought up to date by the introduction of automobiles and present-day wearing apparel, but otherwise the story has been but little changed.

If you ask your "living ancestors" of the feminine sex about it they will tell you how they wept over the tribulations of Ishmael Worth, who renounced his young sweetheart because there was a stigma to his name, and how it turned out in the end his mother was really married to the man who was supposed to have wronged her—how his first wife, who was believed dead, turns up to confront him and how, near the end, it is developed she was a bigamist and the secret marriage held good and young Ishmael had a legitimate father and mother and could face Beatrice Merlin with an honest name, leading up to the clinch title, "Blossom time and love time."

It is rather well done in approved 10-20-30 fashion and should appeal to the proletariat. Harold Goodwin plays sincerely and with conviction, and with a story that is not wholly apparent after the first few hundred feet should be heard from. Lillian Hall, the heroine, is a sweet little ingenue and Colin Kenny as Lord Vincent, a villainous ladies' man, is a classy "heavy," an actor who would acquit himself creditably in any screen role requiring him to wear good clothes. The photography by Walter Williams is also worth commending.

SHELTERED DAUGHTERS.

Ivan Abramson or the Fox people might have made of "Sheltered Daughters" a seething, ebullient, foaming, sensational picture. The title alone should be sufficient inspiration for an offering calculated to appeal to the muckworm, the proletary and the clodhopper.

But Clara Beranger has made of George Bronson Howard's underworld story a scenario designed to teach a lesson to the Austere, intolerant parent, well worth proselyting. It is good propaganda in that it shows the necessity for showing growing girls the way of the world, instead of keeping them entirely sheltered—or apparently so. This insures them against gullibility and protects them from being led astray by conscienceless villains who prey upon the innocents.

The heroine (and star) is Justine Johnstone, a reincarnated Jeanne D'Arc, whose father, a police sergeant, has brought her up ignorant of the ways of the world. Full of enthusiasm she becomes the innocent accomplice of a bogus French soldier seeking to raise money ostensibly for the French orphans. In a quite plausible manner he persuades the girl to pose as his wife and make an appeal to the American public for funds.

There are a number of other unexaggerated types of the underworld, the whole making for an interesting melodramatic story that might readily have been highly colored and magnified into a lurid dime novel narration of hectic events.

Miss Johnstone is seen to her best advantage in "Sheltered Daughters," starting off in simple garb, running through plausibly to a display of sartorial art and concluding as a simple, but wiser, unsullied bride.

Riley Hatch is convincing as a stern but kindly father; Warren Baxter is a consistent reporter; Charles Gerrard is an unexaggerated heavy and so on. The tale winds up with the girl looking straight at her father and saying: "I didn't know—you never told me there were such men in the world."

The picture was well directed by Edward Dillon. It is a Realart release.

Jolo.

FIGHT OF THE AGE

A very cleverly arranged two-reel novelty in the way of a film attraction at this time, bringing to view Jack Dempsey and the handsome Georges Carpentier. Pictures of both the contenders for the world's championship July 2 are shown, in their proper person, in ring costume, in action and in measurements. The latter should prove important to the ring fan and as interesting to those who cannot see the fight or have not seen fighters, meaning women and children.

Comedy is introduced through some cartoon work by Gregory La-Cava. It is amusing and at the same time instructive.

The big punch of the film is its timeliness. The Pictures Trading Co. produced it. While pieced, and excellently so, the juxtaposition of the fighters on the screen at times leaves the impression they are actually engaged, though they are not.

It is announced as holding a "half million dollar" cast. That may be so, judging from the celebrities shown in connection, Al Jolson, Jim Corbett, Jim Jefferies, Tex Rickard and the managers of the fighters, together with Mrs. Carpentier.

Scenes of the training quarters of each fighter, their methods of training, illustrated measurements and cartoons on the effect of blows, besides some skillful boxing by Tom Gibbons and a sparring partner helps to compose a most interesting picture, though of short length, perhaps more interesting through that.

"The Fight of the Age" is current. It's good anywhere—up to the day of the fight."

Sime.

SCRAMBLED WIVES.

Mary Lucile Smith	Marguerite Clark
Larry McLeod	Leon P. Gendron
John Chiverick	Ralph Bunke
Bessie	Florence Martin
Beatrice Harlow	Virginia Lee
Connie Chiverick	Alice Mann
Dickie Van Arsdale	Frank Badgley
Mrs. Halsey	America Cheddister
Mr. Halsey	John Mayer
Mr. Smith	John Washburn
Martin	T. A. Braldon
Mrs. Spencer	Ada Neville
"Dot"	Emma Wilcox

The screen production of "Scrambled Wives" marks the advent of Marguerite Clark as an independent producer. The star-producer is making her releases via First National.

The vehicle is an adaptation of the play of the same name, written by Martha Stanley and Adelaide Matthews and was admirably directed by E. H. Griffith, who had no easy task to prolong interesting and amusingly a farcical plot that had enough in it to make a first rate, rapidly moving multi-reeler. That he succeeded in squeezing out of it a full-length feature is worthy of comment.

Miss Clark is the perennial soubret, and is as cute and pert as ever. It doesn't seem as if she will ever grow up. With natural ease and grace and rare judgment in the selection of clothes, she is not only a cute ingenue, but breathes "class." She is also wise enough to surround herself with good-looking women, every one of whom might qualify for a "Follies" show girl. Even the role of a stout school teacher is entrusted to a comely young woman—Emma Wilcox. There are not many with her avoirdupois who are young and pretty, and most of the stout parts in pictures are played by older women. The same sort of comment might be made upon the male support. They all look well and know how to wear their evening clothes.

There are a few flashes of color photography to visualize the color scheme in a fine ballroom scene. Unusual care and intelligence has been exercised in the making of Miss Clark's initial independent production.

Jolo.

2 WEEKS WITH PAY.

Pansy O'Donnell	Bebe Daniels
J. Livingston Smith	Jack Mulhall
Montague Fox	James Mason
Ginsberg	George Periolat
Mrs. Wainsworth	Frances Raymond
Chambermaid	Polly Moran
Hotel Clerk	Walter Hiers

This Lasky offering at the Rialto, with Bebe Daniels starred, makes a good entertainment, but brings up again the question as to just what the director's name is. On the program it reads Maurice Campbell, on the screen Major Maurice Campbell. Is the major a name or a title or what? The scenario is by Alice Eyton, who adapted Nina Wilcox Putnam's story of the same name. The cast itself is adequate and, as in all Paramount productions, the photography is A1.

The laughs are constant, though never side splitting. We see the star first as a salesgirl putting a hat over on an old lady, and next a man tries to vamp her, but when she is sent away to the fashionable Fairview Hotel for two weeks with pay to advertise her employer, Ginsberg, and his wares the real fun begins. First she meets a nice young man named Smith by way of a motor accident that lands them both in the mud, and mistakes him for a millionaire. Next she is prevailed on to pretend she is the picture star, Marie La Tour, only to learn she has to do a high dive. In addition a give-away is threatened by the man who tried to vamp her. But, of course, in the end all is well. The millionaire turns out to be a garage owner, and so they can marry happily and Marie saves Bebe from exposure.

But not from double exposure. Miss Daniels took both parts, and they were cleverly worked together. The star also did a clever back flop into the pool, and every one was happy.

A good hot weather feature.

Leed.

WOMAN GOD CHANGED.

Anna Janssen, dancing girl	Seena Owen
Thomas McCarthy, detective	E. K. Lincoln
Alastair De Vries	Henry Sedley
Lilly	Lillian Walker
Donegan	H. Cooper Cliffe
District Attorney	Paul Nicholson
Police Commissioner	Joseph Smiley
French Commissionaire	Templer Saxe

The device of telling an intricate story by means of fadebacks as various witnesses are brought to testify at a murder trial is used in the screening of this Cosmopolitan production (Paramount) offered this week at the Rivoli. It is the system made familiar to the show world by "On Trial," the technique having been adapted from the screen to the stage in that case.

The plan has the effect of holding a rather scattered tale together and gives it neat and unified form. Robert G. Vignola is the director. He has done a notably fine bit of work in the economy with which he gets his story elements before an audience. The narrative moves with utmost speed and has plenty of striking incidents and forceful action. The single feature amiss is the over-elaboration of titles. Probably this is a consequence of the form of the play.

The film starts with views of the courtroom and the preliminary situation is made plain by the exchanges of conversation between onlookers. The courtroom is especially convincing with its judge, lifelike jury and the opposing counsel. The prisoner, Anna Janssen (Seena Owen), is in the dock, a wistful figure.

A colored girl, former maid of the prisoner, takes the stand. She testifies (her testimony being shown in fadeaway action) how Anna abandoned a brilliant career as a dancer for the wealthy Alastir De Vries (Henry Sedley), and how the man-about-town tired of and abandoned her for another woman. A waiter from a restaurant testified how Anna found De Vries dining with the other woman, shot him and escaped.

The real story begins with the testimony of Thomas McCarthy (E. K. Lincoln), a police officer, who pursued the fleeing murderess to Tahiti, captured and brought her back to justice. The steamship is sunk on the way to the States. Captor and captured are cast away on a desert island. Thorugh various and colorful adventures the degraded woman is regenerated by her awakening love for the detective and comes to the bar purified. The jury, of course, urges mercy upon the court, and the verdict is that McCarthy marry the prisoner and keep her in custody for life.

The telling of this story is rich in interesting episodes. There is a dance hall in Tahiti where Anna is a performer. And there is a good deal of interest in the life of the pair on the South Seas island. One scene shows the honest detective coming unaware upon the girl as she is bathing, a glimpse which brings him to the sudden realization he is in love with her. The gradual awakening of the girl's conscience and her growth to a better spiritual state are well developed on the screen.

The cast is excellent. Miss Owen, both as the wild woman of the city night life, as the primitive woman of the wilderness and as the regenerated woman in the prisoner's dock, makes an appealing figure. Mr. Lincoln is entirely satisfactory as the manly hero and H. Cooper Cliffe is a convincing attorney for the defense.

As an illustration of the class of the cast, Lillian Walker has the small part of the woman who steals the affections of the rounder from

Anna, a role calling for only a few scenes early in the play. Joseph Smiley and Templer Saxe are other welll-known players who have unimportant parts and play them exceedingly well.

The feature ought to please any sort of audience. It is an interesting story, well played and produced in a signally dignified manner.

Rush.

GALLOPING DEVIL.

One of those hard-riding, quick-shooting melodramas of the west, done in the style of the old-fashioned dime novel. The hero is preposterously heroic, absurdly quick on the trigger and daring beyond human limits, but these things appear to find a large public among the fans.

Col. William Selig is sponsor for the production which serves its unpretentious purpose, which is to amuse as frank fiction. It has a wealth of action and a background of story sufficient to hold its episodes of man-to-man fights, both fist and gun, together. Franklyn Farnum is the two-gun cowboy, Genevieve Earl is the lovely plains maiden in distress and the occasion of "all the shootin'" is the ancient western feud between sheep herders and cattle men.

Col. Selig, whatever else he does, is always right on his types of wild westerners. There is a rather large cast involved in this canyon picture, but they are all convincing types, from the clean-cut cowboys to the unkempt sheep herders. And, as always, the out-of-door settings are splendid backgrounds for the story, with their broken landscapes of valleys, peaks and hillsides.

The tale has to do with a plot on the part of an unscrupulous sheepman to cheat a young woman ranch owner out of her property. A neighbor sends for a detective to upset their calculations, and he appears in the person of Franklyn Farnum, hired as foreman of the ranch and operating incognito. The herders invade the range with their flocks and by some juggling of land titles which is not always clear in its technique are on the edge of carrying out their design when the cowboy detective interposes.

The plotters lure him to a mountain cave and tie him up over a powder mine to which a lighted fuse is attached, but he and his trusty .44 are equal to the occasion. He turns the tables on the schemers and leaves them to be blown up. The explosion is screened sensationally. A neat comedy element is introduced in the story by making the hero a champion boaster and liar. He entertains the ranch force with lurid tales of his exploits, and they are enacted on the screen by the fadeback device. Some of them, such as the shooting up of a whole mining town, are exaggerated to the point of absurdity, but they get laughs and contain plenty of rough-and-ready action.

Another capital bit is the use of a five-year-old boy, son of the rancher, who gets himself in all sorts of scrapes in his efforts to imitate the habits of his elders. For example, his ambition is to roll cigarettes with one hand, and half a dozen times during the five reels he is shown studiously practicing the feat, always with amusing failure.

Of course, the detective falls in love with the girl ranch owner, saves her from kidnappers and, as the warfare with the sheepmen develops, the romance progresses to a satisfactory end.

Altogether a capital five-reeler designed for the unsophisticated film fan who wants his drama unadulterated with uplift or subtle problems. The exhibitor with an audience of this kind can't go wrong on it.

Rush.

SNOWBLIND.

Hugh Garth..............Russell Simpson
Bella ....Mary Alden
Pete ....Cullen Landis
Sylvia ....Pauline Starke

"Snowblind" was adapted for the screen from the story of that name by Katherine Newlin Burt. It is a Reginald Barker production, and distributed by Goldwyn. It relates an interesting story of melodramatic nature, with plenty of action featuring the plot. The locale is that of the Canadian North Woods. The production end has been amply taken care of, and photographically the film is up to the standard set by the better class of features.

Drama of the convincing sort features the unfolding of the story, which concerns a man who leaves England to seek seclusion in the Canadian wilderness, following a murder. There is a love affair between the refugee and a girl, who has been stricken with snowblindness. The refugee took the girl under his care, and in the natural order of things she should have stuck by him as a matter of gratitude. But she doesn't. Upon regaining her sight she falls in love with the refugee's younger brother. The finish is away from the conventional.

Russell Simpson, one of the best character actors on the screen plays the refugee. His performance is exceptional. Mary Alden also gives a remarkably fine performance as a nurse, who sticks to the refugee to the last. Pauline Starke, who plays the girl, who has been snowblinded, makes the character lifelike, bringing out its attributes in the fullest measure. Cullen Landis, plays the younger brother with smoothness and a complete knowledge of the part's requirements. The film should entertain picture audiences of the better sort, who are keen for a picture a bit away from the regulation type.

Bell.

LOVE'S PENALTY.

Janis Clayton................Hope Hampton
Sally Clayton.................Irma Harrison
Martha Clayton.........Mrs. Philip Landau
Steven Saunders............Percy Marmont
Bud Morgan ....Jack O'Brien
Mrs. Steven Saunders........Virginia Valli
Little Jack ....Douglas Redmond
Rev. John Kirchway..........Charles Lane
Mme. Natalie ....Mrs. L. Faure

"Love's Penalty" is practically bullet-proof—from a mechanical construction standpoint. It is first rate "hokum" melodrama, magnificently produced, ably directed and well cast. Written and directed by Jack Gilbert it makes a vehicle for Hope Hampton that will satisfy the average exhibitor and picture patron. The entire assembling of the necessary ingredients, from the camera work of Albert Ortlieb to the fitting of the star with a story that will show her off to proper advantage, has been intelligently worked out.

Miss Hampton is given opportunity the joy and innocence of youth to the uttermost depths of sorrow, emerging unsullied to what bids ity for the display of her visualization of the elemental emotions from fair to be a marriage of love and future happiness. In the interim, however, she is placed in a series of tragic situations not generally encountered by a sweet young maiden from the country.

Her sister has been led astray by a conscienceless villain and commits suicide, which is the direct cause of her mother's demise a week later. "Damn him! I'll make him pay, pay, pay!" and she starts out to wreak vengeance. Providence intervenes before she can carry out her revenge.

While not a big "special," the feature is good enough to play most of the better class cinemas. *Jolo.*

OLD DAD.

Daphne Bretton.....Mildred Harris Chaplin
Richard Wiltoner ....George Stewart
Jaffrey Bretton.............John Sainpolis
Virginia Bretton...........Myrtle Stedman
Sheridan Kaire ....Irving Cummings
Peggy Kaire....................Hazel Howell
Professor Pettigrew...........Edwin Brown
Claudia Merriwane........Loyola O'Connor
Ruth Pomeroy.................Bess Mitchell

One of the daintiest of the current year's crop of photoplays is the filmization of Eleanor Hallowell Abbot's story, "Old Dad." Despite its delicacy of treatment it is virile and teaches a moral without once being "namby pamby." It is a sweetly told tale, dwelling upon the relation of a father to his daughter—his aid in shaping her life, shielding her from harm and taking the place of the mother whose guidance she is deprived of.

The sub-titles breathe refinement and reveal the author as the possessor of a mind capable of setting down on paper her thoughts with a rare sense of literary values. Handled by Director Lloyd Ingraham, the situations are dramatically visualized in a manner to make for interesting photoplay acting, and the respective roles are entrusted to capable screen artists for depiction. In fact, all the essential ingredients are at hand, including a first-rate production and high-grade photography.

The wife of a wealthy man elects to take up an operatic career, sacrificing her home life and leaving the husband with a young daughter on his hands. He sends the child to an elite boarding school, and she is practically a stranger to her parents. Through a chain of wholly innocent circumstances the headmistress of the school finds her with a young man in her room at midnight, and she is expelled with a scandal which reaches the newspapers.

She comes to her father's home, tells him the story, he looks into her eyes and sees there nothing but innocence and truth. They become very chummy, he saves her from the clutches of a libertine and saves her for the young man who was found in her room in the school.

Mildred Harris Chaplin is the star of this Louis B. Mayer production, which is released by First National, and she visualizes the part of the boarding school girl to a nicety. From the standpoint of histrionic talent the star of the production is John Sainpolis as the father. In a lesser artist's hands it would be easy to overact by resorting to melodramatic intensity. In fact, all of the players conducted themselves quite humanly. Upon analysis, practically the entire story, which many times bordered upon the tragic, was told through the aid of comedy.

Photoplays of this sort are well worth while. Eleanor Hallowell Abbot always was a fine writer, and she always has something worth while to write about. *Jolo.*

THE MAN TAMER.

Kitty Horrigan ....Gladys Walton
Jim Horrigan ....Rex de Rosselli
Hayden Delmar ....William Welsh
Tim Murphy ....C. B. Murphy
Brad Caldwell ....Roscoe Karns

This Universal is a good little program feature, one of a first class series with Gladys Walton starred, an honor she deserves. Far from the typical cutie, she gets pep and punch into all her characterizations, and, given half a chance, shoves her every offering over. Harry B. Harris directed this one, got in some good circus stuff, realistic lion charging with injuries that looked sure enough, and a good 20-fisted battle for a finish. The yarn is credited to John Barton Oxford, but the main idea is the same as that in "A Question of Management" by Elizabeth Mercier, which appeared a number of years ago in "The Scrap Book."

With her father out from a lion bite, Kitty takes his act along alone. Delmar, who owns the circus, and young Caldwell both are crazy about her, she about neither. Caldwell's father, however, gives her a commission to tame the youngster, and she succeeds so well she falls in love with him, the final succumbing following his rescue of her from Delmar.

Mr. Karns made the youngster too much the inebriated fool, but Mr. Murphy's Murphy was a joy. The rest of the cast was adequate. A. P. Younger's scenario kept things moving and the titling was rich.

Cut to 4,500 feet this is a real program thriller for the average exhibitor. *Leed.*

WHITE AND UNMARRIED.

Billy Kane	Thomas Meighan
Andrea Duphot	Jacqueline Logan
Dorothea Welter	Grace Darmond
Chicoq	Walter Long
Marechal	Lloyd Whitlock
Mr. Welter	Fred Vroom
Mrs. Welter	Marion Skinner
Victor	Georgie Stone
Jacques	Jack Herbert

This is a first rate entertainment, ith everything from acting and irection to titling satisfactory. The rouble with most productions is hat somewhere along the line of ombined effort that enters into heir making there is a let down. his whether it be the titling, the ighting, some bit done poorly, erves to irritate and so make the pectator conscious of himself. Thus the picture's complete illusion spoiled. This tendency to break the illusion loosens the grip of many an verage film that would have scored, and while "White and Unmarried" is no more than average, it gets by because it is done competently and thoroughly.

Jesse L. Lasky presents it (Paramount) at the Criterion. Thomas Meighan is starred and gives one of his clean-cut performances with a sense of humor forever pleasantly apparent in his smile. He is adequately supported. Jacqueline Logan nakes a plump and attractive brunet heroine, and as the spoiled society girl who takes a chance in marriage with a rotter Grace Darmond looked sufficiently so. Walter Long came across with an ugly and villainous looking Apache and with Lloyd Whitlock's society weakling helped boost the score toward 100.

Tom Forman as director and Will M. Ritchey did their work—whatever discrepancies there were in the latter's continuity were amply bridged by clever titling—in such a way that nothing in it stuck out like a sore thumb provoking a whacking.

The whole was adapted from "Billy Kane, White and Unmarried," by John D. Swain. This tells how Billy Kane, a burglar, inherited a million and set out for Paris, where he was having a high old time until he met the little dancer, Andree, and fell in love with her, exciting the jealousy of Chicoq, who kidnaps the girl and holds her till Billy executes a thrilling rescue and returns to Paris for the final close-up, a kiss not so long as to annoy the censors.

Leed.

A WISE FOOL.

Jean Jacques Barbille	James Kirkwood
Carmen Dolores	Alice Hollister
Zoe Barbille	Ann Forrest
George Masson	Alan Hale
Sebastian Dolores	Fred Huntley
Gerard Fynes	William Boyd
Virginie Poucette	Truly Shattuck
Fille	Harry Duffield
Judge Carcasson	Charles Ogle
The Curate	John Herdman
Mme. Langlois	Mabel Van Buren

"A Wise Fool" is a George Melford production, presented by Jesse L. Lasky at the Rivoli this week under the trade-mark of Paramount. Sir Gilbert Parker adapted his own novel, "The Money Master," for a screen feature, featuring James Kirkwood as Jean Jacques Barbille, the wealthy first citizen of a small French Canadian village in Quebec.

Within the scope of film mechanics the production is splendid, but its story is sadly misshapen and staggering in its import. Is it a preachment on the dangers that beset a man too absorbed in the material things of life? Is it a sermon against selfishness? Or is it just a bit of literary invention without serious intent? It might be any of these or none. The story has moments of drama and certain sentimental values, but it is not clear what the author or the producer is trying to get at. This is not Sir Gilbert Parker's way when he is working in the familiar medium of pen and ink. Apparently he is a better novelist than film maker.

"Wise Fool" gets down to its actual story somewhere about the middle of reel two, about 1,500 feet having been taken up in such elaborate preliminaries and introduction as might be called for in a novel. It is all "atmosphere stuff" and makes pretty tiresome screen material. Even when the story does get to its essence it has little drama, as film fans comprehend drama. All these things make it an indefinite and unsatisfactory affair.

Jean Jacques is the wealthiest man of the village and the matrimonial catch of the province. He goes off on the grand tour, but tires of travel and takes steamer home. On the way he falls in with Carmen Dolores, daughter of a Spanish blackguard, falls in love with her and makes her his wife. Disappointment of the provincial maids on his return.

Carmen tires of Jean Jacques and his absorption in his business of miller and country financier, and the handsome figure of George Masson catches her eye. George is the master carpenter, who is building a flume for Jean Jacques, and the miller, learning of the intrigue, traps his rival in the water chamber. He is about to drown him when George wins his release by arguing that drowning him will be murder and will bring shame upon Jean Jacques' daughter. Thereupon George calls off the affair with Carmen. The wife, however, is too disgusted with Jean Jacques to remain under his roof, and runs away.

She is overcome by poverty and, broke, takes asylum in a Montreal convent, cared for by the kindly nuns. Meanwhile Jean Jacques refuses to permit his daughter to marry the man of her choice and she runs away. His mill burns down and his father-in-law steals his savings. Jean Jacques is turned out of his home and becomes a wanderer, his only possession Carmen's pet canary, saved from all his goods. By a startling series of coincidences he comes upon Carmen in the nunnery and they are reconciled. About the same time his daughter learns of his misfortune and returns to him with her now prosperous husband.

Small suspense in this recital of artificial events which do not illustrate any philosophy of life or carry any message. The title does not even bear any intelligible relation to the proceedings. Perhaps Jean Jacques was a fool for picking out a wife from the steerage of a trans-Atlantic liner, but wherein was he "wise"?

As a picture of rural Canadian life the film impresses one as sincere and atmospherically authentic. The outdoor settings are picturesque and the interiors are dignified and impressive. The interiors of the convent are especially well done. One of them, showing a reception room, was striking in its simple truth. However, realistic settings and convincing types and atmosphere do not alone constitute a screen drama. There should be some sort of orderly progress of happenings somewhere and leading to a goal more or less definite and significant. A record of a haphazard life may make a readable novel, illuminated by the story teller's interpolated comments, but stripped to its elements for screen pantomime it does not sustain interest.

Rush.

BLACK PANTHER'S CUB.

"The Black Panther"	Florence Reed
Sir Marling Grayham	Norman Trevor
Clive, Earl of Maudsley	Henry Stephenson
A Victim of Chance	Paul Ducet
Sir Charles Beresford	Don Merrifield
Lord Whitford	Henry Carvill
Faustine, the Empress	Florence Reed
A Butler	Louis Grisel
Mary Maudsley	Florence Reed
Jack, Lord Maudsley	Earle Fox
Hampton Grayham	William Roselle
Evelyn Graham	Paula Shay
Mr. Laird	Halbert Brown
A Stable Boy	Charlie Jackson
A Money Lender	Ernest Lambart
President Charity Ass'n.	Frank de Vernon
Count Boris Orloff	Tyrone Power
A Young Gambler	William van Braam
Mlle. Daphney	Mlle. Dazie
Apaches	Will Bourbon
	Eugene Breon
"Faustine"	Florence Reed

This is unexpectedly good as shown at the Capitol, though during its trade showing a month or so ago it took what seemed a year to get started. Now all the irrelevant stuff about Faustine is cut to the minimum and might better never have been included. The picture really starts later when Lord Maudsley is leading a little girl through the gate to his park. Emile Chautard is credited with the direction and W. K. Ziegfeld with the production, which he has mounted sumptuously. The story is Ethel Donoher's, adapted by Philip Bartholomae.

Despite dragging in Swinburne's majestic poem by the heels, an idea is in it, old as the hills, but still ideas are scarce. The Swinburne motif fails, however, because there isn't enough of it and could not be enough of it in a picture. There isn't room to give the sweep and breadth of the greatest lord of lyrics who has ever written in English. What remains—minus Swinbourne—is a plot, also old, but also always effective. This is what a mother will do for a child, handled recently in a story and later a film by William Allen White, and mishandled here. Mr. Chautard has made the mistake of letting the girl be rescued by her lover and other men. For a real thrill the rescue should have been performed by the mother, alone and unaided, and then the two saved by the others. Florence Reed, as an actress, was capable of making this count.

Miss Reed is such a competent actress, so thoroughly aware of every trick of the trade, so alive with vitality, that she makes every trick seem real; it would be hard to over-praise her. In this picture she plays mother and daughter, making both actual, succeeding where so many others have failed, or, worse, only half succeeded. An expensive and worth-while cast is in support. Henry Stephenson is English and a gentleman, just what he is meant to be. So is Norman Trevor, though Mr. Trevor's drawn face makes him look older than he is. Earle Fox as the young no-good likewise was effective.

The story shows a queen of the underworld giving her daughter to Lord Maudsley to rear. She disappears. With Maudsley's death, his no-account son steals some charity funds and the adopted daughter sets out to recover them by impersonating her forgotten mother as head of a gambling house. She is led into a rooming house kept by this same mother—then the rescue.

The story would have been better without references to Faustine and explanatory, allegorical cut-backs clogging the action, but it is, nevertheless, a good market offering as it stands.

Leed.

SCRAP IRON.

John Steel	Charles Ray
John's Mother	Lydia Knott
Midge Flannigan	Vera Stedman
Bill Dugan	Tom Wilson
Battling Burke	Tom O'Brien
Big Tim Riley	Stanton Heck
Matt Brady	Charles Wheelock
John's Chum	Claude Berkeley

It would be unfair to write a review of "Scrap Iron," as presented at the Strand this week, without making some reference to the prolog produced by Manager Joseph Plunkett of that house. An illuminated drop is shown, revealing the exterior of an iron foundry and giving the illusion of activity within. Lights are seen, smoke issues from the chimneys and the buildings stand out in the perspective, creating the idea of distance. A male quartet, attired as foundry artisans, harmonizes neatly, night comes, an illuminated trolley car glides up the hill, and the curtain closes, to reopen upon the feature itself. Very prettily conceived and executed and created the exact atmosphere of the photoplay following.

"Scrap Iron" is a Charles E. Van Loan story, adapted for the screen by Finis Fox. Charles Ray makes his debut in this picture as a director in addition to being the star. After viewing it the conclusion must be arrived at that a director for Ray is a wholly unnecessary luxury. Every detail has been worked out to a nicety. The foundry interior looks like the real thing, and the story, while obvious in a general way, is well sustained and gallops along to a satisfactory conclusion, ending at a point where the remainder is left to one's imagination.

Ray is a young workman in the foundry, supporting an invalid mother. He has promised her he would never fight, and in dodging physical encounters he earns the nickname "Yellow." He courts the girl next door, and when he refuses to mix it with a drunken fellow workman at a picnic she transfers her affections to a visiting pugilist, who knocks the souse down. Ray is discharged for being late, and secretly enters the local fight arena to get money for his mother. He doesn't expect to win, but fights for the loser's end of the purse.

The suspense during the progress of the fight, which continues into the fourth round before the professional pugilist is knocked out, is the most thrilling thing of its kind ever staged before a camera. Nor is this all. The hero rushes home finds his mother has suffered a relapse and is followed there by his trainer, who tells him the "pug" is dying and the police are coming to get him. Of course, it turns out all right, but in the interim the hopelessness of the situation is piled on until it becomes well nigh unendurable.

Ray does this sort of thing extremely well. His rapid change of facial expression, his visualization of pathetic helplessness are the acme of screen art. This, alternating with his depiction of boyish exuberance, carries him through his scenes most entertainingly.

As in all his productions, this star is no camera hog. He gives his support every opportunity to "play up" to his standard. The characterization of Battling Burke, the pugilist, is a fine delineation, as is also that of the girl he is courting, portrayed by Vera Stedman. All the others are equally competent, and each in turn is given occasion to contribute his or her best for the general good of the production.

"Scrap Iron" should satisfy wholly the most exacting exhibitor, who is generally more difficult to please than his patrons.

Jolo.

SONG OF THE SOUL.

The Messmore Kendall-Robert W. Chambers Co., releasing through Goldwyn, is the maker of the Vivian Martin starring feature, "The Song of the Soul," adapted from William J. Locke's story, "An Old World Romance." It was directed by John W. Noble.

If memory serves aright the original tale was purely descriptive, lacking in action. It is a harrowing narrative for picturizing and not an easy one to put into scenario form without introducing a lot of extraneous matter.

As picturized, a young boy is badly scarred about the face in rescuing a little girl from a burning house. He grows to manhood and the girl he loves writes him she cannot truthfully care for him. He decides to live alone, and takes up his abode in the Florida alligator swamps. A blind girl comes there to take up her home with an aunt, who promptly dies, leaving her unprotected. Realizing she cannot see his scarred countenance, he marries her; a child is born and they are very happy. A famous surgeon comes to the cabin on a hunting trip, offers to perform an operation on the young wife's eyes, she is permitted to see her baby for an instant, and when it comes time for her to see her husband she deliberately faces the glaring sunlight in order to make herself permanently blind, so she will never have to gaze upon her beloved husband's features. When he upbraids her for it, saying "Your happiness is everything to me," she counters with "And yours to me."

A flashback shows she is the child he rescued from the flames and had scarred himself in saving her life. John S. Stumar's photography and Noble's direction are the work of skilled artisans. Miss Martin is adequate as the blind girl, and Fritz Lieber is sufficiently harrowing as the lifeless, morbid, unhappy husband. The picture leaves a bad taste. *Jolo.*

MESSAGE FROM MARS

In picturizing Richard Ganthony's satirical classic comedy, "A Message from Mars," with Bert Lytell as the star, Metro has failed. Many producers have attempted to secure the screen rights to the English play, which made a fortune for Charles Hawtrey on the spoken stage. It is one of those plays that lends itself perfectly to the screen.

The film adaptation was entrusted to Arthur Zellner and Arthur Maude and the direction to Maxwell Karger. All three, together with the star, seemed inadequate to the task. It remained only for A. Martinelli, the cameraman, to distinguish himself.

The adapters have destroyed the subtle psychology which the author so clearly elucidated in his original manuscript. The star brings to it a characterization totally at variance with the stage portrayal and which Hawtrey delineated to a nicety. He is given to horseplay and exaggeration of the mannerisms of an Englishman of vast wealth and breeding. It seems incredible that a picture star who gave us such a fine portrayal of Charlie Steele in "The Right of Way" could possibly go so far wrong with the role of Horace Parker in "A Message from Mars."

Reverting again to the adaptation, the story was "modernized" and the main point brought out in the dream which the central character goes through, shows him reduced to such extremities that he steals a purse because he is hungry. Throughout he is disagreeably smug—never attractively and magnetically so, as was the stage counterpart.

The role of the messenger from the Martian world is also improperly portrayed. The man enacting it treats it humorously and flippantly, not investing it with the dignity of the spoken version; the comedy should arise through his "dramatic conflict" with the selfish, self-centered Horace Porter, who lives only for his own comfort and self-aggrandizement.

In the picturization of the London street scenes a great deal of care was evidently taken to secure proper detail, and after going to all this trouble the director permitted a sign to be shown on a street monger's cart offering his wafers at "6c." *Jolo.*

BEACH OF DREAMS.

This Haworth production has Edith Story as a featured lead and is released by Robertson-Cole. If not made in England it certainly exhibits the restrictions that keep American films top of the heap. The attempt to depict an aristocracy in this basically sound story by H. de Vera Stackpole approaches caricature, and so is often ridiculous. William Parke directed, and for some of the time his action is stilted. At others, out in the open, there is freer movement and a more convincing procedure. The story, perhaps, was too delicate for picture delineation.

It shows Miss Storey as Mlle. Cleo de Bomsart and one Jack Raft, a common sailor who will have no truck with common women. A sea accident leaves Mlle. Cleo marooned on an island with two sailors. One of them, played by Jack Curtis, who for once is seen in a heroic light, is lost in the quicksand. The other attacks her and she kills him. Then comes Raft (Noah Beery), lost in another expedition, and proves a real friend to her. But, of course, when they are rescued they cannot marry. Social caste prevents this.

So she buys him a boat and he sails away. The titling did not help these situations. It was affected and flowery, unconvincing. *Leed.*

DANGER VALLEY.

Pinnacle Productions, Inc., is responsible for the film, "Danger Valley," starring Neal Hart, and the three-sheet in front of the Circle carried the name of Independent Film Association as distributor.

Neal Hart is of the "rugged" type of western star. The feature is a very ordinary program picture. It starts right in to tell the story and succeeds so well that before it has progressed 500 feet you know the end. So much so is this the case that the conventional "clinch" has been omitted, it being totally unnecessary. A well-to-do man with a pretty daughter has invested all his wealth in a mine. The map showing its location has mysteriously disappeared. He sends for a mining engineer to aid him in trying to locate it. This engineer is a desert expert and his name is McBride (Hart). He goes west, saves the life of an Indian who is being manhandled and the silk-hatted villain is frustrated in his design to steal the girl and the mine.

There are such sub-titles as, "It takes real men to play the game of life," and others equally stereotyped. Just an ordinary western production, involving no undue expenditure—one worthy of playing the cheaper grade of houses. *Jolo.*

UNCHARTED SEAS.

Lucretia Eastman	Alice Lake
Tom Eastman	Carl Gerard
Frank Underwood	Rudolph Valentino
Robert Alden	Fred Turner
Old Jim Eastman	Charles Mailes
Ruby Lawton	Rhea Haines

The details of this unconvincing and conventional plot are drawn out to agonizing lengths, with no apparent object except to make it a six reeler. It might make a much better program feature in five spools, but even then cannot rank as a topnotcher. It is all about the wife "giving and forgiving," "sanctity of marriage," etc., in which a wife, after forgiving her weakling husband time and again, goes to the other man. After they are stranded on the ice in the arctic regions (where they went in search of the treasure of a sunken vessel) for days and days the hero is still smoothly shaven, although almost dead, and with both starving. Maybe they didn't eat the Gillette, and so he was able to bathe and shave with hot water while stuck on the ice fields.

There is, however, one episode worthy of favorable comment. The man and woman are stuck in their ship, awaiting the breaking up of the ice, for months and months. They are seated in the cabin. She is sewing and he is reading. With true feminine instinct she feels he is looking at her and that surging through his mind is the sex call. Without one caption this is pictured through vivid pantomiming. When it seems as if the picture would never end and that it should take no less than another 500 feet to come to a logical clinch it ceases abruptly and you are thankful.

The star and supporting company are competent enough, but their characters are so unnaturally drawn it is impossible to associate them with ordinary human beings.

Story by John Fleming Wilson, scenario by George Elwood Jenks, directed by Wesley Ruggles, photography by John Seitz. A Metro production. *Jolo.*

GET YOUR MAN.

This Fox program offering came to Loew's New York Friday with Buck Jones starred. An average story, written around the star as a member of the Royal Northwest Mounted Police, is by Allan Sullivan, while George W. Hill directed. Always sure to stage good rough and tumble stuff, Buck Jones is less happy with the stiff saluting of the Dominion police than in a role more natural to him, but on the whole his work is convincing and makes the fans who follow him feel as satisfied as ever. The directing is adequate though a strain is apparent in the effort to screen something novel as a final close-up.

The star is in love with the daughter of a smuggler, who strikes a bargain with an escaped criminal. Tracking this criminal is the first assignment of the newly made policeman. The fugitive, however, not only gets away, but takes the innocent girl with him and there is a long chase across the snows, through a blizzard and a final very bloody and convincing fight. Helen Rosson, Beatrice Burnham and Paul Kent, all were adequate.

Good stuff of its kind. *Leed.*

LOVE, HONOR AND BEHAVE.

His Honor, Judge Fawcett	Charles Murray
Milton Robin, a haberdasher	Ford Sterling
Mrs. Milton Robin	Phyllis Haver
Newlyweds	Marie Prevost George O'Hara
A Merry Widow	Charlotte Mineau
A Fake Lawyer	Billy Bevan
His Right-hand Man	Kalla Pasha
His Left-hand Man	Eddie Gribbon
The Judge's Wife	Fanny Kelly
The District Attorney	Billy Armstrong

"Love, Honor and Behave" is a Mack Sennett five-reel slapstick feature, directed by Richard Jones and Erle Jenkins, featuring Charles Murray and Ford Sterling. The plot is way above the average of knock-about screen farces in that it tells a human heart-interest tale—that of a pair of newlyweds appearing before a judge seeking a divorce. His honor (Murray) declares a recess and takes the couple to his chambers. The young bride exhibits as evidence a photograph of her husband holding a maiden in his arms and hubby explains it by saying he was helping her over a fence—that it was a frame-up, a camera was snapped and he was being blackmailed. Whereupon the judge says: "Let me tell you a story." The tale he relates makes for the body of the picture. It consists of a series of rapidly moving happenings that occurred to his honor years before, making for circumstantial and incriminating evidence.

These occurrences are of the most uproarious sort, tragic in plot, but worked out in a farcical way. It's main fault is its length. The pace set is so fast and furious that it is impossible to follow it without becoming utterly fatigued.

Murray throughout is so pantomimically expressive, and Ford Sterling is, if anything, funnier than usual. The remainder of the cast play up to these two comedians and there is a lot of novel trick photography, such as projecting Murray into a den of lions and having him struggle for his life.

When the scene flashes back to the judge's chambers, showing him relating this wild and wonderful tale, he says: "Never mind how I escaped," etc., and the young couple are reunited.

The picture would be ideal for a double feature day in a program house, following a heavy drama. *Jolo.*

REPUTATION.

Universal Jewel five-reeler from the story by Lucien Hubbard, directed by Stuart Paton, with Priscilla Dean as the star. The Universal in this has selected a story in which Miss Dean has many opportunities, the entire picture resting almost entirely upon her shoulders. She handles a dual role which demands greater character work than the average young picture star could possibly handle, with this young woman walking away with it on all occasions.

The story sets forth the life of an actress to whom success proves fatal. She becomes an opium addict in London, which causes her failure to arrive in New York for the opening of a new show in which she is to star. Her daughter, unknown to the management, masquerades as the star and plays the lead.

The mother returns to New York, threatens to kill the daughter for stealing her name and ends by taking her own life.

It is a gruesome subject. Other than the exceptional work of Miss Dean the picture has little strength.

The production end is above the average for Universal.

THE BUTTERFLY GIRL.

Edith Folsom	Marjorie Daw
Ned West	Ned Whitney Raymond
John Borden	Jean du Briac
Lorna Lane	Fritzi Brunette
Edward Van Horne	King Baggot
Mrs. Van Horne	Lisle Darnell

This Playgoers' production came to Loew's New York from Pathe with authorship and direction credited to John Gorham. The continuity suggests the amateur and a mind groping for more exact picture knowledge, but the feature is expensively mounted and has a certain program value. Its attempt is to enforce a moral lesson by showing the progression of a young girl's character from light flirtatiousness to deeper values, but it is told not in screen terms, but in those of a novel. The acting is fair enough. Miss Daw is pretty, extravagantly well dressed and Fritzi Brunette comes through with her usual solid performance. The two juveniles, du Briac and Raymond, unfortunately have something about them continually suggestive of the Gold Dust twins. King Baggot, now a stout, middle aged man, was fair enough as the banker-broker, while Lisle Darnell gave a dignified, reassuring interpretation of the banker's wife.

There is too much kissing, however, in this picture. Edith is forever kissing her boy friends, too general a habit since the war. She leaves her home town and a beau behind her and gets into a flirtation with a friend of Lorna's. Then she leaves a dance to joy-ride with a bounder and so forfeits Lorna's friendship, but after she has had some idiotic adventures as a business girl in Van Horne's office, she marries her boy and the banker's wife makes a real woman of her.

Before this happens the banker has fallen in love with the girl though Edith doesn't realize the significance of his declaration. His wife does, and meets the situation with true dignity. The way this is handled alone mocks censorship and justifies the feature's presentation, although its lack of grip can never carry it over the line far.

Some of the earlier sub-titles were clever, but many of them were ungrammatical and unintelligibly inexact, while the direction was meticulous (as Jolo would say) rather than comprehensive. *Leed.*

HEEDLESS MOTHS.

The Sculptor............Holmes E. Herbert
His Wife................Hedda Hopper
The Dilletante............Ward Crane
The Prey................Irma Harrison
The Sage................Tom Burroughs
Audrey Munson............{ Audrey Munson
{ Jane Thomas
"The Spirit of the Arch"....Henry Duggan

Audrey Munson is the star of "Heedless Moths," produced by (George) Perry Plays, directed by Robert Z. Leonard. All there is to this picture is Audrey's shape, undraped and unashamed. In the film as first presented last Friday night at the Greenwich Village theatre, as a special feature, the audience saw everything Audrey owned excepting the soles of her feet.

The film is called "A chapter from the life story of the queen of the artists' studios," with the king unnamed, but shape is also Audrey's ace so everything looked A. K.

This display of nude posing, with the added attraction of a couple of dimples near the small of Audrey's back, one on either side, is as bare as it is a bear. Hanging around the studios with not even an idea apparently about her, Miss Munson posed and posed, in all positions, one a darb that must have caught the censors dozing. But it was art even as it was artful.

Besides which was more artartifices of production. These ran to a prolog declaimer, called "The Spirit of the Arch," probably meaning the foot, and well though lengthily done by Henry Duggan, always in a green spot. Then there were views thrown upon the side lines, when the sheet was upraised, and for the finish of the first part a couple of the characters appeared in person on the stage, to exhibit how much more quickly a young girl may go to her ruin in the flesh than in photography. That was heartless.

Audrey Munson has been quite a figure in the show business and the newspapers. She started showing everything when young and is still keeping it up. Her shape has been seen in the studios, on the stage, on the screen and in the magazines. It's still bringing her the coin evidently, for it's only a few months ago that Audrey's wail from Syracuse about being broke lightened up a dull moment. It recalled that line from "The Gold Diggers" about a perfect back. Immediately Audrey's moan was heard, her coin popper got to work again, starting with a rave in the New York Sunday American Magazine, running week by week and very weak about her "studio experience," how and when to pose and what to show.

In this picture of "Needless Moths," Audrey is showing back, front and sides. It's a wallow of a story, about how Audrey escaped the wiles of the studios, psuedo, but how a companion fell, how Audrey felt enobled because a real sculptor allowed her to pose, and how Audrey saved the sculptor's wife. No one on the program stood for the story. Maybe Audrey wrote it herself, from an experience she would like to have had.

The production was said to have cost $125,000 but looks far this side of that amount. It is also short in footage, which is covered up by the extras and the stalling. It ran from 8.45 until 10.25, with an intermission besides the innumerable appearances of "The Spirit." The comedy of the film was the whiskers of The Sage. According to their looks, the Sage wasn't a day over 186.

Mr. Leonard did what could be done in the directing. He assisted Miss Munson in her efforts at modesty. Every time the studio door got a knock, Audrey went to a panic that she couldn't get a wrap over her shoulders in time, but didn't seem to mind the audience.

If the cops or the censors don't get to the nakedness of the Mun-

son film, it's a box office cinch, the farther away from New York the bigger the cinch, for the old home folks don't see as much often or even more so of what's inside a skirt as Audrey so frequently and abundantly displays in "Heedless Moths." May her shape never wither.

In a statement made by Miss Munson's mother in Syracuse last week, it was said Audrey Munson made but one appearance in the film, a single pose showing her head and shoulders only, with her face not seen at any time. That Miss Munson did none of the leading character's acting was recognized by those in front who knew the model. The program gave a double billing for "Audrey Munson" with the co-billed young women doing the actual playing. Who did the other bare posings around the studio set of the film is not mentioned.

The mother also stated her daughter had received but $1,000 for her picture services from Perry Plays, with which she is now in legal conflict.

The Munson "Studio Secrets" or "Life Story," appearing in the Hearst Sunday Magazine (Syndicate Service) gave the model $25 weekly it is claimed, for twenty weeks, instead of $800 weekly as reported. Alan Rock is said to have secured the screen rights to the published series, and it is from that "Heedless Moths" was adapted Rock interesting himself to that extent with Perry Plays. *'me.*

TOO MUCH SPEED.

Dusty Rhoades............Wallace Reid
Virginia MacMurran........Agnes Ayres
Pat MacMurran............Theodore Roberts
Tyler Hollis ....Jack Richardson
Jimmy Rodman............Lucien Littlefield
"Howdy" Zeeker............Guy Oliver
Billy Dawson............Henry Johnson
Hawks ....Jack Herbert

A pippin of a feature, A 1 summer entertainment, "Too Much Speed" was brought this week to the Rivoli with Wallace Reid starred. It is adapted by Byron Morgan from his Saturday Evening Post story and directed by Frank Urson. Helped by first-rate photography, the acting of the star, the inimitable Theodore Roberts, Agnes Ayres, who makes a pretty brunet picture, and the way minor parts were handled by Jack Richardson, Lucien Littlefield and Guy Oliver, it affected the imagination the way candy does a child. Credit, too, should be handed out liberally to the actors playing sheriff, judge and bailiff, who made bits count up a heavy score in the laugh column.

Dusty Rhoades is going to retire as an auto racer and marry Virginia, daughter of old Pat McMurran. Old Pat is against all racing since one of his drivers got hurt and his Pakro racer is benched for keeps. Dusty is driver for a rival firm, anxious to win the coming National races in order to impress a big buyer from Argentina. They need Dusty. In order to swerve him from his purpose the firm's manager gives him the dust on the road as he is riding in a limousine to his wedding, accompanied by his future father-in-law. Unable to stand the dust, Dusty climbs into the front seat and steps on the gas. Off they go, father-in-law bouncing around inside. The race ends in an accident, and old Pat declares the wedding off.

Dusty now picks up his bride and starts to elope, old Pat in pursuit, a chase that lands them all in jail when the sheriff with a camouflaged Ford catches them. A trick to bring Dusty back to racing is worked by Pakro's rivals, but Dusty is on, succeeds through daughter Virginia in hoodwinking old man McMurran into selling his Pakro racers and sails in, winning the National for his father-in-law-to-be and incidentally the South American order.

The racing scenes are immense. So is the handling of the continuity, which keeps things alive every foot. The net result is a feature so full of movement it is good for any type of audience or house, yet undeniably first class. *Leed.*

ONE A MINUTE.

Jimmy Knight............Douglas MacLean
Miriam Rogers............Marian DeBeck
Jingo Pitts................Victor Potel
Grandma Knight........Frances Raymond
Silas P. Rogers............Andrew Robson
Martin Duffey............Graham Pettie

Thomas H. Ince has turned out a highly amusing comedy for Douglas MacLean in this Paramount feature, handled along farcical lines and at times running almost into burlesque. The laughs are scattered liberally through its five reels to a climax in an absurd courtroom scene near the end. Side by side with the uproarious nonsense there is a neat little romance, and the whole thing is done in a likeable spirit of irresponsibility.

The story is by Fred Jackson, with scenario by Joseph Franklin Poland. Jack Nelson directed. The American small town makes the background of the action. Jimmy Knight returns from college to run the drug store left to him by his father. On the train he becomes acquainted with Miriam Rogers, daughter of the director of a chain of drug stores which has just entered Jimmy's town to compete with his old-fashioned establishment.

Jimmy is up against a tough problem to save his store from the cut-throat competition of a rival, and in desperation announces that he has discovered the great "panacea for all ills" left by his father. The "remedy" is Jimmy's own desperate concoction, made up of ginger, fuller's earth, charcoal and other hit-or-miss ingredients; but he calls it "Knight's 99," and puts it on the market with a bold ballyhoo.

The townsmen fall for the nostrum on the strength of Jimmy's bold claims for its virtues and because of their confidence and Jimmy's solemn certainty the dope works miraculous cures. Miriam's father has it analyzed, and causes Jimmy's arrest for violation of the Pure Food and Drug law, but the enterprising discoverer successfully defends his case, acting as his own lawyer. He argues that the virtue of the formula is its secret fifth ingredient, which he surrounds with complete mystery until the last minute. When the presiding judge is seized with illness in court, Jimmy offers him a dose of "Knight's 99," and the court is so impressed with its evil flavor that he is straightway made well, and directs a verdict in Jimmy's favor. The trial vindicates Jimmy and his remedy, and the chain store magnate offers him $1,500,000 for control of the formula. Meanwhile the syndicate head's daughter and Jimmy have made a match of it, and the business deal is closed at a breakfast at which all hands take part. Father demands the name of the mysterious fifth ingredient, and Jimmy, tucking the contract in his pocket, reveals that it is the faith of the patient, coupled with the awful taste of the medicine. The theory is that any dose that tastes so bad must have virtue. The final embrace is a matter of course.

The courtroom scene is true comedy, made ridiculous by the face of the hard-boiled judge, which reflects cynical disinterest as the witnesses come and go. Every time Jimmy's hopes are aroused by a favorable turn to his case and he expresses his delight there is a momentary flash back to that tough-featured, glowering judge, and the day is spoiled. The judge is not named on the program. He ought to be. That camera-cracking visage ought to make his fortune. Marian

De Beck makes a charming heroine, and there is a wealth of village types, all well drawn and provided with amusing relations and situations. The characters are neatly developed for comedy without for once getting into the cheap "rube" class. One of the things that makes the effort so effective is the fact that its people are always true to life in spite of the farcical character of the story. *Rush.*

FIGHTING LOVER.

"The Fighting Lover" is a Universal release produced by Fred Granville. It is founded upon an excellent Ben Ames Williams story that was, in its original form, a corking murder and robbery mystery.

In the filmization the director seemed to get himself into a muddle from which it was impossible to extricate himself. It starts off with great promise. Frank Mayo, the star, plays a young man about town. He wagers $5,000 with a friend that either or both of them will fall in love within a brief period "under the right conditions." He asks his wealthy aunt to aid him win the bet, and they advertise for three girls to be their guests at the aunt's country estate. The aunt's jewelry is stolen, the other man is killed, all three girls are under suspicion, but he refuses to believe one of them is guilty, though circumstances point to her guilt.

The girl he feels sure of turns out to be the daughter of the butler, well educated and gently reared, and she explains her apparent attempt to escape was only to telegraph the story to the newspaper she works for. And so on to the clinch.

A story well worth developing much more clearly and giving a first rate production. *Jolo.*

HOME STUFF.

Madge Joy	Viola Dana
Robert Deep	Tom Gallery
"Ma" Deep	Josephine Crowell
"Pa" Deep	Nelson McDowell
Susan Deep	Priscilla Bonner
Mr. "Pat"	Robert Chandler
Mrs. "Pat"	Aileen Manning
Jim Sackett	Phillip Sleeman

This Metro feature classic has been playing the Loew houses and is a good, workmanlike product with real heart stuff. Frank Dazey and Agnes Johnston wrote it and Albert J. Kelley directed, getting the thing billed as "An Albert J. Kelley production."

The star is Viola Dana, who knows how to put things over. She's a girl with a punch rather than tender beauty. Her supporting cast was adequate, and it was gratifying to note Josephine Crowell's appearance. As the old hayseed who hadn't smiled since he cheated a man on a cow deal, Nelson McDowell was particularly effective, and the whole thing gained from John Arnold's A1 photography.

The story shows a barnstorming troupe letting out Madge Joy as leading lady to make room for runaway Susan Deep, who has an admirer with a bankroll. Madge, without money, drifts into the employ of the Deep family, taking the missing daughter's place and getting engaged to the son, Rob, who has ambitions as a playwright. But when daughter returns "Pa" declares there's no place in his house for an actress. Madge wins the daughter a homecoming by giving up the son and killing his love (temporarily) by pretending drunkenness. They meet again as Broadway star and young, successful playwright.

The titling was amusing, but the continuity made room for it at times rather awkwardly. *Leed.*

WELCOME CHILDREN.

"Welcome, Children," a Drascena production, distributed by National Exchanges, Inc., featuring Elsie Albert.

Whoever wrote this scenario determined to throw into the mixture everything but the kitchen stove. It starts off with mawkish sentimentality, the center is made up of really funny kid comedy and the tale winds up with roaring melodramatic gunplay.

A young girl is the eldest of more than half a dozen orphans in a small village, the avaricious neighbors secure the property and she leaves for the city with her family, including a dog. She does this to avoid the decision of the neighbors to farm her out for her keep and place the others in the poorhouse.

Then for what seemed a dozen reels there is unfolded her efforts to secure accommodations in a city flat, finding always a prohibition against the admittance of children. Most of the titles sound like a campaign launched against apartment-house owners, with such sub-titles as "It's not the dog I object to—it's the children." A number of poetic sub-titles follow, with Tennysonian quotations, etc.

Any way, the kiddies are finally smuggled into a flat via the dumb-waiter, a young doctor discovers the girl's secret, the house is burglarized by three of its inmates, the girl is suspected, the secret of the children is revealed to the landlady, the kiddies are the means of unearthing the culprits, there is a terrific fight between the police and the robbers, the young doctor marries the girl and takes along with him on their honeymoon the ready-made family.

A cheaply made production, very long drawn out. *Jolo.*

BIG TOWN IDEAS.

Fan Tilden	Eileen Percy
Alan Dix	Kenneth Gibson
Spick Sprague	Jimmie Parrott
Deputy	Lon Poff
Molly Dorn	Laura La Plante
George Small	Leo Sulky
Show Manager	Paul Cazeneauve

"Big Town Ideas" is a rare combination of heart interest, violent melodrama and comedy, with most of the sub-titles written for humor. In other words, an intensely suspensive and absorbing melodrama is unfolded through the medium of comedy titles. For a program feature it is one of the best things, in its way, the Fox people have ever turned out. It is from a st[illegible] have John Montague, directed [illegible] Sara Harbaugh, with good cam[illegible] lequin)

by Otto Brautigam. Eileen Percy is the star.

Miss Percy is a waitress in a railway junction restaurant who yearns for the big city. The town is noted principally for its state prison. An innocent young man is brought in handcuffed; the waitress goes through a series of thrilling happenings in order to recover the stolen bonds and prove the young man's innocence, and so on.

May not sound like much in such a brief summary of the plot, but the story is worked out quite absorbingly and is replete with rapid-fire action. For example, she secures the "papers" by climbing to the top of a slender tree which bends over until she can enter the real crook's house via a second story window, makes a get-away, jumps upon the engine of a freight train, reaches the Governor's home just as he is departing in a motor car, runs after it, drops the "papers" while running, climbs over the back of the motor car, her dog picks up the papers and jumps into the auto, thereby saving the day and the innocent man, and succeeds in earning the $5,000 reward and a husband for herself.

Miss Percy brings to the role of the hash-slinger a well-drawn characterization, at once funny, but withal lovable and magnetic. Like all such melodramas, there are inconsistencies to the tale and numerous improbabilities, but it will serve to entertain for the 50 minutes of its footage in any but the high-priced first run picture houses. The direction, camera work, supporting cast and details are to be commended. *Jolo.*

IDLE HANDS.

Park-Whiteside production (Pioneer), of an ordinary story of a country girl wanting to see the big city, but enlivened in this picture through the number of "names." The names lead off with Mlle. Dazie, other than the featured players. Another specialist is Ted Lewis and his jazz band. They are in a cabaret scene in a restaurant called The Golden Dragon in Chinatown, New York.

Then there are Gail Kane and J. Herbert Frank among the players, a couple of more having their names on the paper.

The picture through its names and publicity possibilities should be good in the average release house that does not go in for big productions. This is not a big production in that sense. Most of the money spent on it went for salaries instead of properties.

Otherwise it is just so so. The country girl, leaving home to go on the stage, and breaking her mother's heart through her action, when in New York is enticed to Chinatown and held there a prisoner. After her mother's death back home, sister starts in quest of the lost one, interviews the mayor of New York, interests him, eventually shows up the chairman of the vice commission as the principal divekeeper of the city, and rescues her sister.

It's underworld all the way, told in a straightforward style, without much imagination by the writer or director. Mr. Frank had the brunt of the acting, as the suave, cool and cunning vice chairman. The others had walking parts.

As part of a double feature bill at the Circle Tuesday night, this one may have suffered, following "The Last Card," another crime picture, making the evening's entertainment very heavy.

In the houses that can use this type, "Idle Hands" can stand by itself. It tells nothing, however, that has not been told long ago, but it certainly shows that a Chinatown dump, properly managed, can give a cabaret program, the like of which has never been seen anywhere. *Sime.*

THE LAW'S OUTLAW.

"The Law's Outlaw" is a Roy Stewart feature released by the Film Distributors League, Inc. It is an intensive, melodramatic "Western." Stewart plays a deputy sheriff who runs for the office of sheriff and is beaten by a "pumpkin pusher," which is the contemptuous title given farmers. The election, however, turns out a frame-up. After bringing to justice the two men who feloniously assaulted and robbed the father of the girl, he is in love with, everything is smooth sailing for the rancher-sheriff.

Stewart has an attractive personality for this style of part, has

top" financially, [illegible] rides well days of industrial depression and unemployment.

triguing. In it the star deliberately "murders" a man in the presence of the district attorney, who rushes back to the town. It is believed he has gone "loco" and a posse start out to "get" him. He goes to Hawk's Nest, an outlaw district, apparently a nervous wreck, where they try to double-cross him by pretending they will hide him from the authorities, while in reality they seek his capture to claim the price put on his head. He rounds up the two culprits, brings them to the jail, and is himself incarcerated. Just as they are about to lynch him the sheriff shows up and when asked why he didn't appear sooner explains that he "got lost." This is a laugh on the newly-elected farmer-sheriff, who resigns in favor of the man whose election was defeated through fraud.

A competent company served to bring out the interesting points of a well-manufactured melodramatic plot, suited to a popular priced program. A few simple interiors and plenty of exteriors indicate the production is relatively inexpensive. *Jolo.*

THE LAST CARD.

Elsie Kirkwood	May Allison
Ralph Kirkwood	Al Roscoe
Freddie Kirkwood	Stanley Goethals
Tom Gannell	Frank Elliot
Emma Gannell	Irene Hunt
Sorley	Dana Todd
Chief of Police	Wilton Taylor

Bayard Veiller makes his initial bow as a director for Metro with "The Last Card," adapted from the story by Maxwell Smith, which appeared in the Saturday Evening Post under the title of "Dated." Conforming with Veiller's ability as a producer of murder mysteries for the stage, his efforts in this direction are equally convincing on the screen. The story takes a new angle on the jealous husband idea and is worked out graphically by the director. The plot hinges upon the murder of a young college student who is working his way through the university by taking care of furnaces in the town. The murderer finds him in the company of his wife on an unexpected visit to his home and follows the chap to the cellar of the home adjoining where he kills him, throwing the body in the rear, where it is immediately covered by a heavy fall of snow, which keeps the disappearance of the boy a mystery for several days. When finally located the owner of the home in which the murder took place is accused and brought to trial, the real murderer putting himself in as the defendant's lawyer. The weakness of the defense up until an adjournment of the court makes a conviction an assurance. During the adjournment, the wife of the accused plans to frame the lawyer, believing he is guilty of the crime, and arranges to bring him into intimate contact with phases of the case, which brings about a confession.

Veiller presents a series of pictures in this production that provide gripping moments, the suspense at all times holding up the interest. The story is convincingly told, the points being placed in an unmistakably satisfying way with the continuity of the story, one of the strong features of the production.

May Allison is the star of the piece in a young mother role and wife of the accused. Her one big scene in the exposing of the guilty is convincing, with the side business of the child throughout the picture providing the necessary heart stuff that brings forth a fine contrast to the gruesome murder idea employed throughout. Frank Elliot, in a heavy role, is the picture's hardest worker, in a part of little thanks. The remainder of the cast has been capably selected, with the production end well looked after.

LESSONS IN LOVE.

Leila Calthorpe ...... Constance Talmadge
Agatha Calthorpe .... Flora Finch
John Warren .... Kenneth Harlan
Ruth Warren, John's sister.. Florence Short
Robert, Leila's cousin..... James Harrison
Priestly, a lawyer......... George Fawcett
Henry Winkley, Leila's guardian, Frank Webster
Martha, a maid................ Louise Lee

Very entertaining is probably the best criticism one can make of "Lessons in Love," the latest Constance Talmadge starring vehicle. It is a film transplantation of Douglas Murray's comedy, "The Man from Toronto." There is nothing new in the basic plot—one of the oldest—but it is cleverly worked out in the matter of situations, brilliantly cast and intelligently directed by Chet Withey. The story might almost be found in any text book—two young folks who have never seen each other must marry by the terms of an uncle's will or the fortune goes to establish a home for old maids. To make it still more commonplace in plot, the girl pretends to be the parlor maid. Sounds almost like a comic opera libretto, doesn't it?

Only in this instance the uncle isn't really dead, but pretends to be, and there are other radical departures from the conventional unfoldment, such as a sister of the young man constantly discovering the girl, dressed as a maid, embracing the various male members of the household and denouncing her as a common hussy.

This sort of thing is exactly in line with Constance Talmadge's talents and her cute little ways of doing things that would be risque when performed by a less ingenious ingenue.

Kenneth Harlan plays the opposite-role in a serious, manly fashion, devoid of theatricalism and with rare naturalness. Two old guardians are capably enacted by such sterling players as George Fawcett and Frank Webster, while the role of a maiden aunt of the same name, mistaken for the young heiress, is played with unusual skill by that sure fire character comedienne, Flora Finch.

"Lessons in Love" is very entertaining. *Jolo.*

A VOICE IN THE DARK

A photoplay of Ralph Dyar's melodrama, "A Voice in the Dark," adapted to the screen and directed by Frank Lloyd, a Goldwyn feature, and this week's principal offering at the Capitol.

Admirably directed and well acted, it has an inadequate scenario, in that the suspense is broken too early, despite the brief footage of 50 minutes' duration. It is a murder mystery. Several people are suspected and circumstancial evidence points to each in turn. One of the suspects is in fact absolutely accused by a deaf woman who saw a young woman quarreling with the victim just a moment before, a shot is fired and the deaf old lady sees the young lady she accuses bending over the body with a revolver in her hand.

Later a blind man testifies to a conversation held below his window, and is sure he would recognize the voices if he heard them again. He does recognize them shortly thereafter—altogether too soon to break up the interest in the solution of the plot.

There are a series of improbabilities and inconsistencies—more than we are wont to accept in modern playwrighting. A very fine piece of cinema acting is shown where the victim and the accused quarrel for an extended period without breaking into it with a single sub-title, and yet you can understand exactly what is intended.

The cast is made up of such competent artists as Alice Hollister, Alec B. Francis, Ora Carew, Alan Hall, Irene Rich, Ramsey Wallace, William Scott, Richard Tucker and James Neill. It is a short thriller—all too brief. This is one of the rare occasions where additional footage might have helped. *Jolo.*

CHRISTINA McNAB.

This is one of the best features yet seen from a British studio (Gaumont), played by British actors and directed by a British producer. The legend "All British" in a renting company's announcements is only too often a danger signal and a more or less certain guarantee of mediocrity, but the exhibitor need fear nothing in offering "The Fortune of Christina McNab."

The story is a good one, full of humor and well told. The continuity is excellent. Clean, wholesome, without exaggeration or any attempt to force the humor, it is throughout a fine example of what a first-class photoplay should be.

Coming unexpectedly into a fortune Christina McNab decides to win a lordling for her husband. In this she is aided and abetted by her lover, a young mechanic, Colin McCrae. This youth calls upon a society woman who is, of course, impecunious. He claims a relationship with the lady—his grandmother's sister having eloped with her grandfather. Having explained the matter to her he eventually persuades her to receive Christina into her aristocratic household as a paying guest, and so the little Scotch girl is introduced into society. She is immediately much sought after for her wealth, and is also scandalized by the habits of her new friends and their dress.

A young Duke decides to marry her, his sweetheart standing docilely by, and Christina accepts him. Under the tutelage of one of her society friends she blossoms out and soon becomes as much sought after for her beauty as for her wealth. This friend, by the bye, is the girl the Duke was engaged to. Meanwhile Colin has prospered wonderfully, and it is through his strategy that the tangled skein is unraveled and happiness comes to both sets of lovers. The story is frail, but its slimness is lost in the excellence of its telling. Will Kellino is the producer.

The staging is excellent, whether showing the humble Scotch home of the heroine or the palatial residences of her new friends. The cast is unusually strong. Norah Swinburne makes an exceedingly good show of Christina and may be said to have arrived with this picture; Sara Sample (a well-known mannequin) appears as a society woman, the Duke's fiancee, and shows talent for acting as well as for exhibiting beautiful gowns. Archie Farr, of Farr and Farland, a well-known vaudeville turn, is excellent in a "silly ass" part. The rest of the company are all far above the average. The interest of the production is further added to by the fact that the producer has had the pluck to put all his sub-titles into broad Scotch. *Gore.*

SALVAGE.

An ambiguous title for this Robertson-Cole feature, starring Pauline Frederick, that ran 85 minutes at the New York Monday night. It has a direct appeal for women, with its "motherhood" foundation and a couple of small children, but is rather boring to the males watching it.

Miss Frederick is the disappointed mother who nearly lost her life through childbirth, with the wealthy father having the baby boy hidden, telling his wife the babe died, through the attending doctor informing the now father his offspring had a deformed leg and could never walk.

Another story runs through of a young man who loves his baby girl and his wife, though the wife is wrong and does not deem her child more than a bother. This father is sent to prison for knocking down a man who was escorting his wife home. The father would not disclose his identity to save the future of the child, so accepted the prison sentence, which seemed rather severe for the punishment inflicted.

The two-handed story is blended in toward the finish, with the tale then having Milton Sills as the former convict playing opposite Miss Frederick. Ralph Lewis is the wealthy husband who passes out, restoring the child, made normal by an operation, to the mother, and leaving his wealth to mother and son, with the assumption the mother will marry the ex-convict, since the latter's wife committed suicide due from drink, before the jail released him.

It isn't as morbid as it sounds, just an illustrated lecture on mother-love that never can be understood by a man but which seems to hold some sort of a charm for nearly all women, whether they are pro or con on the subject.

Nothing in the script called for exceptional playing, which left it easy for the seasoned principals. The drink-besotted female player, name unknown, had an awful make-up at times, when the character did not call for pallidness, while the lighting effects nearly as often gave Miss Fredericks a terrible aged look, though at other times and in the proper lights she was quite attractive. The children players were bright, but there was too much of them.

No novelty of direction was tried for. None was needed. It is just a straightaway story, plainly and directly told, with the 85 minutes making it seem twice as long, but still, though minus any action of consequence, "Salvage," with that title meaning nothing to the box-office or the picture itself, will pass along, particularly in the neighborhood houses. The Fredericks name will send it in likely and the story will hold it, with nothing else. *Sime.*

A PRIVATE SCANDAL.

Jeanne Millette................ May McAvoy
Jerry Hayes................... Bruce Gordon
Philip Lawton.................. Ralph Lewis
Carol Lawton............ Kathlyn Williams
Alec Crosby................ Lloyd Whitlock
Betty Lawton..................... Gladys Fox

When you see Hector Turnbull's name signed to anything look out for two-gun, regular stuff. He has scored again with "A Private Scandal," in which Realart presents May McAvoy at the Rivoli this week. Simple, straightforward, direct, moving the emotions with a rush straight to a heart-tight climax, and then making a quick, satisfying end, it's a smash right in the bull's eye. The little dark-haired star is like it. Unaffected, without pretense, a girlish, sincere, wholesome-appearing girl, she gets her points to you by entirely natural methods. She is more than welcome these days in these parts, and after some of the offerings seen here recently the play itself is worth a hallelujah.

And yet it is picture stuff in the market, anybody's candy sense of the word. This is thanks to Turnbull. The man knows realities and he knows drama. Best of all, he knows the screen. His subtle, experienced hand is everywhere apparent. By the use merely of the word "now," he left with those who saw his picture the impression that the injustice done the youngsters in those final scenes would be righted—eventually—and thus came the end of as near perfect a showing as it is possible to make in a program feature at the picture game's present stage of advancement.

Little Jeanne is a French orphan adopted into the home of the wealthy Lawtons. Lawton himself is interested in his race horses and neglects his wife. There is another man, Alec Crosby, and as the picture starts its pace you sigh and say here's another triangle, sex stuff, with the censor already aroused. But not at all. Three years later, when whisperings of scandal come to Lawton's attention, it is through his mother. She thinks it is the French girl, not Mrs. Lawton, who is attracting Crosby. All in a day the thing mounts to tragedy. Jeanne's beau, too, becomes suspicious. He is Lawton's trainer, and they are off to the track with the string when, remarks overheard arouse their suspicions. Who is guilty? Master and servant tear back to the home, where Crosby is about to elope with madame. He fails. Jeanne interferes, taking the blame herself when Lawton comes in, but before she can save Crosby her beau is after him. There is a regular fight, with Crosby out in the end and Mrs. Lawton explaining to the fiance that Jeanne is innocent.

This fiance, for Jeanne's sake, wants to tell the truth to Lawton, but for the sake of the couple's baby girl he is persuaded to hold his tongue. It required pantomimic ability of no mean order to put over these final scenes, with emotions tense, real—so honest that ordinary mugging would have made them ridiculous. It is praise enough to say that Miss McAvoy, Miss Williams, Mr. Gordon and Mr. Lewis made them anything but ridiculous. Mr. Whitlock also was a well-born bad egg, not some director or actor's idea of one, and that, too, is praise enough. In fact, Chester Franklin's direction and Eve Unsell's continuity were adequate throughout. The photography was up to the high Paramount standard. *Leed.*

A KISS IN TIME.

Sheila Athlone.............. Wanda Hawley
Brian Moore................... T. Roy Barnes
Robert Codman Ames........ Bertram Johns
Bertie Ballast................. Walter Hiers
Nymph...................... Margaret Loomis

An amusing Realart, current at the Rialto. Thomas Heffron has scored another punchy comedy in this screen version of Royal Brown's story "From Four to Eleven Three," published in McClure's, adapted by Douglas Doty and featuring Wanda Hawley.

The story has "class" in its characterization and in all its backgrounds, a highly desirable quality in a screen comedy where humor generally runs to grotesqueness, and it has a wealth of action. The five reels are as full of dashing auto chases as a two-reel western is of horseback galloping. The story is breezy, with amusing types of polite people, all of them young and of refreshing "niceness."

The settings when they are of interiors are of genteel homes and when they are in the open they picture landscapes of utmost loveliness of springtime country. The story itself grows naturally enough out of a basic situation and develops understandably.

Brian Moore has written a story and his publisher asks Shiela Athlone to illustrate it. Sheila objects that the tale is impossible—no heroine would let a man kiss her when she had known him only four hours—and Moore undertakes, without her knowledge, to prove she is mistaken. The author thereupon insinuates himself into the girl's apartment in the guise of a tradesman delivering goods, lures her into a stolen taxicab and rushes her into the country, where he makes absurd love to her in a lovely blossoming orchard.

Meanwhile Sheila's fiance starts in pursuit, aided by the police on the trail of the stolen taxi, and an amusing three-cornered motor chase ensues, leading to the loveliest imaginable roadhouse tucked in among the hills of rolling country that looks like Westchester county at its late May best, and back again.

The flight finishes in Sheila's apartment (Greenwich village or its equivalent somewhere else) where the author is about to be arrested for the taxi theft and is confronted by Sheila's finance. The theft he squares by showing that his father owns the taxi company and the kidnaping is set straight by Sheila's breaking her engagement and announcing that she will marry him because his knack of getting into and out of spectacular difficulties appeals to her Irish heart. Of coure she has to kiss the hero within four hours, and does so.

Miss Hawley's beauty is appropriately set in springtime woodlands and orchards, and there is no great demand upon her acting ability except that she look sweet and smiling, and she does this to the queen's taste. T. Roy Barnes, in a merry way, fills the bill as a hard-driving hero and lovemaker. Walter Hiers, in one of his fat-boy characters, gives the tale just the touch of subdued low comedy necessary to put zip into a screen comedy. The picture is rich in quick comic twists and in scenic beauties, and scores 100 per cent. as a light feature.

Rush.

PENNY OF TOP HILL.

A modern western comedy-drama in which motor cars take the place of galloping bronchos. It carries the trade-mark "A. J. C." as the producer, and features Bessie Love. Offered as half of a double feature bill at Loew's Circle, it proved a tame affair.

It is true beyond argument, of course, that the honk-honk has replaced the bray as a means of travel on Western ranches, but it's an annoyance to force the fact on romance loving film fans. Also dining in dinner coats in the ranch house, however modern the ranch house may be, does violence to all conceptions of fiction. It would be as fair to have the Hawaiian belle take her Saturday night in an open plumbing bathtub.

The story aims at arousing curiosity over a mystery, but succeeds only in irritating and annoying the spectator, and the heroine (Miss Love), who one is led to accept as a reformed crook, turns out to be nothing more intriguing than a film star trying to escape a pursuing manager with a contract of $2,000 a week. When the revelation comes the fan feels abused and hoaxed to provide a pleasurable pose for an egotistical picture actress.

The shrinking modesty of the producer in displaying its name on the title flashes leads one to suspect that the film was made by one of the principal manufacturers and then put out under an alias because it didn't register hopefully. It was good judgment to take it off a regular program, although the direction is good and a considerable amount of money must have gone into the production.

At the opening an airship drops from the skies and deposits the heroine in the middle of a western plain. She bids affectionate farewell to the air pilot and walks out of focus into the landscape. Back to the sumptuous ranch house, which looks more like a California millionaire's country place, and Joe, the cowpuncher, confides to the foreman that on his last trip to Chicago he fell in love with one Marta Sills, who confessed that she was a crook.

Next we find the air-riding heroine in the county jail, where the foreman finds her and brings her to the ranch chateau, where the cattleman's wife and family may reform her. The supposed girl crook goes through all the motions of being reformed, while the foreman watches over her and sees that she does not escape. Joe has been sent to a neighboring ranch on duty.

At the finish it is disclosed that the airplane passenger was the film star who had her brother bring her to the wilderness to escape the film magnate's pursuit with a contract. She found the real girl crook in the local jail and changed places with her. That was all. It's a queer sort of story. It proves that fictionizing fiction is no more interesting than burlesquing burlesque.

Arthur Berthelet is set down as the director. He did all he could with the impossible story. Its only virtue is the beautiful scenic settings for its absurd situations, and one or two spirited shots of horseback riding and horse breaking. The riding is for sport, by the way. When anyone wants to go anywhere, he or she takes an auto. And this in a western romance.

Rush.

THE MOTHER HEART.

Marion........................Shirley Mason
Edna..........................Peggy Elinor
Brewster......................Cecil Van Auker
Roberts.......................Edwin B. Tilton
Clifford Durant...............William Buckley
Jack..........................Raymond McKee

Fox program feature suitable to the market. Howard N. Mitchell wrote the original story and directed it from a scenario by Edward Frank Clark. All did competent work. Though this is entirely a hoakum bid for sobs and laughs it gets them. The mother of the two girls, Marion and Edna, dies from shock when the father is sent to jail on a technical charge of stealing food he was too poor to buy. One of the girls, Edna, is adopted into a wealthy home and shows herself an ungrateful snob. Marion is true blue. She takes care of her baby sister and wins old man Roberts' heart by acting as his housekeeper. As he is the man whose manager brought the charge against the father all turns out well when the manager proves to be a bad egg.

The acting puts the thing over. Edwin B. Tilton in his scenes with the baby gets onto the screen some well-shaded and effective pantomime. Raymond McKee also is called on for characterization that he realizes to the full. The rest is ordinary work but capably handled by a well-balanced cast. At Loew's New York the audience alternately laughed and wiped tears away—a good test.

The photography is exceptionally good.

Leed.

SOULS OF MEN.

The title is another of those flashy captions that have nothing to do with the story except to decorate the front of the theatre with an eye-catching phrase. The story is interesting in its genesis, but doesn't make good as it develops.

A sea captain returns home unexpectedly after a long voyage and finds his wife in the arms of another man, a pearl trader. Husband and lover exchange shots, both being wounded, and husband tells wife she is free to go off with his rival, but he will "get them" elsewhere where the law will not interfere with his vengeance. Thereupon the husband takes up his stand on a South Sea island where the pearl trader sooner or later is bound to appear.

Thus an interesting story is "planted." It would be fair to assume that a conflict would eventually occur, a straight-out issue that would settle the problem satisfactorily. But this does not eventuate directly. The pearl trader does appear, accompanied by the faithless wife, and the story goes through endless complications to an inconclusive end that satisfies neither ethics nor justice.

On the island the pearl trader attempts to make a conquest of a girl in the native hotel. In his designs he is backed by his lawless crew of sailors, while the girl is defended by the hero. It comes to an out-and-out contest, hero. vs. outlaws. As a solution the girl is permitted to choose her husband from the whole crowd, and picks the hero, who already has a wife, but accepts the situation to save the girl, with whom he is unconsciously in love.

The hero, of course, thirsts after the trader's life, but declines to attack him because he is crippled, the result of the exchange of shots back home. At the climax of the story the outlaws have the hero at their mercy and are about to kill him, when the trader is made to realize that he is alive only by the generosity of the outraged husband, so he lets him go free, clearing the way for his reunion with the island girl by announcing that the wife had divorced him and the trader and wife had been married.

A South Sea island tale that uses all this ingenuity to avoid a fight instead of devising circumstances to bring about a physical conflict is a novelty, but scarcely an interesting one.

The picture is a production of the P. & J. Company and is being distributed on the State rights basis. Its players are unknown. The featured player is Will Jefferis, a splendid looking leading man and a capable actor, entirely satisfactory in the role of the outraged husband. The adventurer also is convincing and many of the characters do well as types, but the women—there are only two—do not fill the picture.

Rush.

GOD'S GOLD.

Jack Cameron....................Neal Hart
Mary............................Audrey Chapman
Her father......................Charles Holly
Brighton........................James McLaughlin

The worth while and the worthless in this feature intermix and irritate, but on the whole at Loew's New York it proved a fair offering. Pinnacle Productions claim responsibility for it, and it is released by the Independent Film people of Chicago. Neal Hart, a whale of a man physically, is featured and makes his wholesale slaughter of the dozen or so roughknecks who periodically assault him all through the picture seem more or less convincing.

The good ship "Ocean Queen" has been lost at seat with a cargo of gold bullion. A bottle drifts ashore apprizing of mutiny and location. Mary's wealthy father sets out to save the crowd, buys a ship and wants a crew. But seeing Jack in rough clothes, Mary is unimpressed. She won't have him along as skipper, particularly as the society pet to whom she is engaged wants to boss the job. Turning Jack down, they go out and hire a crowd of roughnecks as crew—a likely thing! As soon as they sight land the crew mutinies, but Captain Jack, in love with the girl, has stowed himself on board and saves the girl and her fiance when the crew put off from the burning ship.

Of course, now they are marooned, Jack proves to be a man and Brighton a cad. But the gold isn't gold at all—it's pig iron gilded to deceive the insurance company. Escapes from headhunters figure now and a beating for the fiance for peeping when Mary takes a plunge in the all-together. Then comes a rescue ship and it turns out Jack is no roughneck but a millionaire and owner of a fleet of merchant ships

This might have been lots better in more capable and more careful hands. For one thing the photography varied badly. At times it was atrocious, at others very clear and attractive.

Leed.

THE MASK.

John Turner.....................Jack Holt
Kenneth Turner..................Jack Holt
Mrs. John Turner................Hedda ovaN
Kirolea.........................Fred Malatest
Little Jack.....................Mickey Moore

A first-class program feature with continuous action holding the interest. Col. William N. Selig produced it handsomely, with Hedda Nova and Jack Holt featured. The presentation is made by George H. Hamilton and the story is based on the novel of the same name by Arthur Hornblow. Bertram Bracken, who directed, is also partially responsible for an admirably effective continuity. Arthur Lavan is co-author. Criticism may justly be directed only at carelessness as to detail in the ship scenes. We get a full flash of a gray ship. Then a black ship pointed the other way is seen to blow up. They are supposed to be the same, and this inconsistency, of course, lessens the illusion of reality. The acting, however, made up. Mr. Holt is a great bet, manly and a gentleman; Mme. Nova sincere. The cast was close to life, too.

Kirolea, John Turner's partner, is in love with the latter's wife. He gets Turner to Africa, with a valet hired by Kirolea to betray him. Several schemes fall short, and in a raid, in which he is meant to lose his life, John Turner rescues his black-sheep twin brother. After a shipwreck, in which Turner is supposedly lost, the bad brother and the valet are rescued and the bad brother is persuaded to take his good brother's place, posing as Mrs. Turner's real husband. Only the little boy—cunningly played by Mickey Moore—suspects him noticeably. When the lad's real father comes back, physically sound but mentally dazed, the kid clings to him and is kidnaped. In an heroic finish the bad brother sacrifices himself for his twin, and we get a strong, natural finish.

Not a special, but an A1 program feature for all houses.

Leed.

DANGEROUS TOYS.

Referring to women, "Dangerous Toys," a Bradley production with William Desmond, runs through a fairly interesting story of considerable inconsistency and no especial merit. It tells of two wives who left their husbands when all were young because the husbands had not the money at that time to give the wives the luxuries longed for. The story is set in two periods, the wife of 20 years ago who did it and the other wife of today, with the first not returning through pride and the second returning through securing control of her common sense. It was the husband of the first wife who was responsible for the return of the second wife to the second husband.

The best thing about this picture is its start. Mayhaps it's because of that the ensuing portions appear weaker. At the opening Frank Losee as an aged banker, the deserted husband of the wife he loved in his youth, is having a party in his private flat with a couple of dames, one his own and the other anybody's. His aged wife calls, white haired, trembling, repentant, lovable and poverty stricken. Marion Elmore made this bit in her two appearances throughout the picture equally as eloquent as Mr. Losee did in his continuous work. The wife says she's lonesome, has been lonesome for the 20 years, ever since she left her husband and daughter, to look for the pretty things of life she never found and missed through walking out too soon. The aged husband looks at her with wrath in his eye and bitterness in his heart. He, too, has missed for 20 years, missed everything he wanted most, and it was her fault; but he doesn't say it. It may be seen in his face. He merely tells her he forced himself to forget, then leads her to the door of the dining-room so that she may see the sample in the two dames of what helped him to forget; then he leads her again, to the door, and once more she walks out of her home, back to the sewing machine she wished upon herself for a livelihood.

There's a punch. There isn't a man in front who isn't with the husband, and it's doubtful, though Miss Elmore was soul appealing, whether she gained the sympathy of the women at that time. Later, when the house saw her at her sewing machine, apparently with nothing left to look forward to but the undertaker, and her husband, still longing for that something he knew he had missed all his life, went to bring her back home, Miss Elmore swept the audience into her lap.

Still these were incidental sections. About all of the rest was handled by Mr. Desmond as the younger husband and Margaret Clayton as his wife, Miss Clayton having another unsympathetic role. Actual acting on the screen seems very meager nowadays, or at least in those pictures playing the Loew one-day stands on Broadway. So that the performance by Mr. Losee and Miss Elmore so far outshone everything else thereabouts that the really good playing by Mr. Desmond was somewhat indented through it. The rest looked like walking parts, as most of these picture roles appear to be, with every one seemingly picked for personality, looks or type.

"Dangerous Toys" analyzed isn't so bad as a story and the script in the reading must have convinced. Picturized, however, it's only fair, with the fault no one's—just happened, and could not have been bettered in any particular. *Sime.*

THUNDER ISLAND.

Isola Garcia	Edith Roberts
Juan Garcia	Edith Roberts
Pio Mendoza	Fred De Silva
Paul Corbin	Jack O'Brien
Sanchez the Loco	Arthur Jasmine
Barney the Mate	Fred Kohler

Looking up the pedigree of Edith Roberts, star of "Thunder Island," reveals that she was featured in such other Universal releases as "The Fire Cat," "The Adorable Savage," "Lasca," "The Unknown Wife," "White Youth," etc. She wades through a series of scenes that are full of activity, assuming the role of passive spectator so she may be taken into the arms of the hero for the inevitable clinch.

The story is by Beatrice Grimshaw, scenario by Wallace Clifton, directed by Norman Dawn. It is a tale of a Mexican girl who meets an American who is skipper of a sailing vessel. He comes to her rescue when her twin brother (she plays both roles) is killed by the henchmen of a villain who poses as the man who married her on what she believed was his deathbed. Suspense is secured through giving the audience the impression she is wedded to the villain, making for an insurmountable barrier between her and the young American.

Good atmosphere is created through the selection of suitable locale, but the make-ups of the white folks impersonating Mexicans are atrocious. An altogether impossible kind of a fight on board ship makes for "thrilling" action, and there are such sub-titles as "Morning came as calm and serene as the turquoise waters."

An inexpensively produced feature for popular priced consumption. *Jolo.*

DANTON.

Berlin, May 26.

The Woerner Film Co. presented "Danton" at the Ufa Palast am Zoo May 4. The film is a fair success and might do a paying business on the Riesenfeld circuit for one week; but that does not change the fact that, considered from an absolute critical angle, this production is a tragedy—a catastrophe—for here was a chance to make a film better than "Du Barry" (Passion), a film that should have gone down as one of the classics.

To begin with, the story was THERE! The character and life history of Danton are as sure fire as that of our Abe Lincoln—and more sensational. Danton is par excellence the man of the people—powerful, coarse, but full of a great pity, a great warm, glowing humanity. It was Danton who began the French Revolution and it was he who, until his death on the guillotine, stood firmly against the bloody policy of terror preached by Robespierre and his associates.

To anyone with half an eye for screen possibilities, this must have been clear at the Reinhardt premiere of Romain Rolland's "Danton" at Grosses Schauspielhaus, in February, 1920. Then Paul Wegener played the lead and played him as he should be played—a colossus, straddling the world, unshaken by the underhanded political intriguing of the Jacobins. And so, when he did fall, the effect was tremendous, rather as though the sky itself had suddenly collapsed upon us.

And for this film they had the brilliant Emil Jannings, practically the ideal man, one would think. But through incompetent direction and a diabolical scenario, an utter failure. What Dimitri Buchowetzki, the director and also fabricator of the scenario, has done is this: He has sentimentalized Danton into a wishy-washy poseur who sits about on film studio divans, reading dainty little volumes. Where there should have been humor, is only forced grimacing. Where there should have been power, is only grotesque spready gesturing. Where here should have been fire and magnetism, is only the meaningless close-up with the eye-roll and the lip-twitch.

As remarked before, the scenario is impossible—bad continuity lack of sustained tempis, and the introduction of ridiculous sub-plots, which only slow up the action. The direction, besides being inadequate, is often positively sloppy. The period is not sustained; exteriors and interiors have no possible connection whatsoever; scenes look new, when they should look battered, etc., etc. O, Lubitsch, where wert thou? And, American film directors, take notice, the Danton film has not yet been made!

THE GOLEM

Hugo Riesenfeld is set down as "presenting" the Paul Wegener produced feature "The Golem," with no reference as to its nativity, the program at the Criterion merely announcing that Wegener plays the title role and directed the picture, the remainder of the cast not being mentioned.

To hazard an appraisal of its value suitable for all localities is manifestly impossible, since the feature has an appeal mainly for the Jews and the more erudite public interested in history—legendary or otherwise. To those directly concerned in the picture industry there is also considerable interest, from the standpoint of production.

According to an old Bohemian legend the Golem was a clay figure of a giant which Rabbi Loew is supposed to have brought to life some 900 or so years ago, and which served him in good stead to ward off disaster to his people. The figure is said to have been buried in Prague alongside the learned rabbi and his 33 disciples.

The photoplay opens with a scene in the Bohemian ghetto in 1620, when Rudolph of Hapsburg issued an edict banishing the Jews from the city on the representation of his counsellors that they were directly responsible for a plague which swept the town. Rabbi Loew is a venerable and learned individual. In a secret dungeon he has carved the figure of a giant and lacks only the talismanic word necessary to put life into the figure of clay. During his astronomical studies he learns the stars foretell disaster to his people and the King's edict confirms his prognostication. Resorting to "the magic circles," he conjures up the essential word, writes it upon a piece of parchment, inserts it into a star and jams it into the chest of the clay figure of the giant, infusing life into the Frankenstein Hercules, which is his slave to command at will.

The bearer of the King's edict, a courtier, sees Miriam, the rabbi's daughter, and covets her. Although betrothed to Chilo, one of the rabbi's pupils, Miriam succumbs to the courtier, and while the rabbi visits the King to plead for his people Miriam spirits the courtier to her chamber, where he spends the night with her. Rabbi Loew is accompanied to the King by the Golem, and when the assembled court jeer derisively at the wonderful feat of magic which the rabbi conjures up, the King's palace crumbles and His Majesty's life is in jeopardy. In fear the King promises to recall the banishment edict if his life is spared. The Golem sustains the heavy girder which is about to drop upon the King, and the rabbi returns to his people to spread the glad tidings.

A call to prayers is blown upon the sacred horn, and Chilo runs to Miriam's chamber to take her to the synagogue to participate in the prayers of thanksgiving. As the Golem has served his purpose to obey only the will of the righteous, the rabbi has plucked the star from the giant's chest and the giant topples over an inert mass. Chilo is frantic, replaces the star, the giant is restored to animation and is directed by Chilo to break down the door of Miriam's chamber, throws the courtier over the ramparts, the giant drags Miriam by the hair out into the open, where she asks Chilo's forgiveness, which is granted.

The Golem encounters a group of children at play; they all rush away fearfully—all but one. He takes the child in his arms, the little one playfully plucks the star from his massive bosom and he is once more reduced to stone.

The production is an impressively dignified one and the scenes of mediaeval times are well visualized, with some magnificent mob scenes. The cast has been carefully selected with a view to the depiction of ancient types and are all excellent screen players.

So far as the layman can discover there is but one faux pas in the technical direction, when the rabbi adjusts a pair of what appear to be modern spectacles. *Jolo.*

LIFE

Tom Andrews	Herbert Druce
Grace Edwards	Nita Naldi
Bill Reid	Jack Mower
Wm. Sturvesant	J.H. Gilmore
Ruth Stuyvesant	Arline Pretty
Tom Burnett	Rod La Roque

A William A. Brady production, distributed by Paramount and directed by Travers Vale. It's at the Rivoli this week.

A caption slide says it's the adaption of "Life" as written some years ago by Thompson Buchanan and Mr. Brady. Just a plain melodrama of thievery and murder. Whatever results come from the picture must be redited to the directing. The story is knitted well enough, there is a snappy style of running it without scenes being unduly prolonged or dwelt upon, and there is a suspensive interest upheld to the last that will hold the spectator.

While the latitude of the picture permits of nearly everything melodramatic being woven in, other than the common meller thrills, the several threads are so filmworn that were it not for the manner handled it could hardly be hoped that this picture (with a title of "Life" that should cover more than a mere thrill in a meller) would attract much beyond passing attention.

Of the players, Rod La Roque, Arline Pretty, Jack Mower and Nita Naldi, of those programed, and in that order, stood up in the acting, while a role of a professional society dancer as taken by Effingham Pinto told a lot about the dancing restaurants' hangers-on. It's almost a pity the expose has happened so late. There are a number of other principals, of greater or lesser importance, like Dutch Joe, who did a crook role quite neatly.

Some ingenuity was evident in the direction, for instance, in the murder scene, also the escape of the prisoner condemned to death. That was a bit more ingenious than logical; likewise the introduction of the adventuress into the ballroom scene and her expulsion from it.

The story is of two good boys becoming bad, gambling, playing stocks and women, with a scheme to ruin the sweetheart-husband of the banker's daughter, the banker himself being the victim of the murderer when uncovering the real culprit, with the husband accused of the crime and sentenced to death, released when Dutch Joe, forced to a confession through a spiritualistic seance, tells the police the truth after having grown tired of hiding. The production is excellent and has class to nearly all of the scenes.

That snappy style of cutting a dramatic, as "Life" is, may be universally commended for any kind of a film. It keeps the picture leaping from one scene to another and with speed, without dropping the continuity. *Sime.*

APPEARANCES

Herbert Seaton, an architect	David Powell
Kitty Mitchell, a secretary	Mary Glynne
Sir Wm. Rutherford	Langhorne Burton
Lady Rutherford	Mary Dibley
Agnes, Kitty's sister	Marjorie Hume
Dawkins, a promoter	Percy Standing

Set down as a Donald Crisp production offered under the auspices of Famous Players-Lasky British Producers, Ltd., the English offshoot of the Zukor organization. It is the current at the Rialto.

The subject is a notably sincere effort with story by no less a personage than Edward Knoblock and a cast of English players who give an impression of highest dignity to the production. The direction, as far as its authority goes, carries out the effect of an earnest effort to screen a story in the finest style.

Everything has been done to make a notable production, but the story is lacking in the essential dramatic element. It is one of those polite British plays. In a stage version it might be interesting, but its drama is not sufficiently robust to be effective in the pantomimic medium.

David Powell is featured conspicuously in the billing. He is a splendid screen player, reminding one somewhat of John Barrymore. He is something of the same figure of high bred gentleman and plays with the same easy authority of method. Powell leans to the restrained method of expression, but he does not overdo the repressed style of acting and can, when the situation calls for forcefulness, tear loose and deliver the acting "punch."

Mary Glynn is the heroine, another welcome novelty to the American film fan who has become pretty well used to the native leading women of the screen. She is a fine actress endowed with a wealth of beauty and a style that is refreshing. All the players pitched their work in a minor key, taking their note apparently from the leading man, and it came as an agreeable variation from the aggressive methods of the American players. Just as a novelty it served nicely, but there is small danger that the British style of over-restraint will revolutionize our native method of more emphatic expression.

Restraint in emotional acting has had its day on the stage and American audiences have not been particularly impressed. On the screen it is unlikely to have any vogue.

The story of "Appearances" is typically British. Herbert Seaton (Mr. Powell) is a prosperous architect, in love with Kitty Mitchell (Miss Glynn), secretary to Sir William Rutherford, a wealthy peer given to literary research. The young people marry and overreach themselves in an effort to put up an appearance of magnificance. The cost of a too elaborate home and a too ambitious scale of entertainmont endangers the young husband's business.

Seaton plunges in the stock market, under the urgings of an unscrupulous promoter and gets further in the mire, while Kitty, in an effort to supplement their income does some special work for Sir William. The nobleman pays the wife with a check, and the husband raises it from 25 pounds to 500 pounds to save himself in a temporary financial emergency. He suspects that Sir William is in love with Kitty and out of these two story elements, the incriminating check and the unjust suspicion, grow the dramatic passages of the play.

The settings are splendid. The out of doors backgrounds show scenes in some fine English country estate and there are non finer in the world. The interiors are equally splendid and appropriate to the type of the story. But there is little action, as film fans understand the term. And therein the production fails in strong appeal. *Rush.*

WITHOUT BENEFIT OF CLERGY

Ameera....................Virginia Brown Faire
John Holden....................Thomas Holding
Ameera's mother....................Evelyn Selbie
Ahghan money lender....................Otto Lederer
Ahmed Khan....................Boris Karloff
Pir Khan....................Nigel de Brulier
Hugh Sanders....................Herbert Prior
Alice Sanders....................Ruth Sinclair
Michael Devenish....................E. G. Miller
Tota, at five....................Philippe de Lacey

This is a gorgeously, almost perfectly mounted adaptation of Rudyard Kipling's famous short story. The production is by Robert Brunton, but when you come to consider James Young's direction or Randolph C. Lewis' supervision of the picture it is difficult to determine what may justly be said about this week's feature at the Capitol. It cannot and will not satisfy the Kipling fans, but to do that with the irreprissible Anglo-Indian's first crashing bid for fame would have been next to impossible. On the other hand, it is a good market picture. Sheer tragedy all the way, it takes an hour to play its mournful course, and leaves you depressed. The tragic catharsis that worked in the story to the reader's benefit, sweeping from mind temporarily the dregs of day-by-day living, is here either not in evidence or nowhere near so effective.

The narrative itself is followed more or less faithfully. The prime absurdity of having a native marriage instead of none at all, as on the printed page, is committed. Otherwise it is as Kipling wrote it. Holden, an engineer, takes the native girl, Ameera, for bride, and she hopes to chain him to her by bearing him a son. The son's arrival has this effect, but death comes. In time the cholera sweeps Ameera, too, away, and rain ruins the love nest she and Holden lived in. So the story ends, a futile and yet a wonderfully touching thing because of the native girl's fear of the Christian women of Holden's own class who in the end would claim him. Mr. Young and Mr. Lewis have lost this out of their screen version. The poignancy of Ameera's dying cry: "Keep not a hair of my head. She will only make thee burn it!"—that, too, is lost.

The acting was satisfactory. Virginia Brown Faire wasn't pretty in our sense of the term, but certainly she made Ameera wistful, pathetic—one understood that around Holden's heart love wound silken cords. The native parts were played with faithfulness to detail and the kid role was charmingly interpreted by Philippe de Lacey. *Leed.*

SOWING THE WIND

Rosamond Athelstane....................Anita Stewart
Brabazon....................Ralph Lewis
Ned Annesley....................James Morrison
Baby Brabant....................Myrtle Stedman
Watkins....................William V. Mong
Petworth....................Josef Swickard
Cursitor....................Ben Deely

With Anita Stewart starred, Louis B. Mayer this week presented "Sowing the Wind" as a First National attraction at the Strand. It is adapted from the play by Sydney Grundy and directed by John M. Stahl. Unfortunately, it is one of those sex dramas, but it is handled with delicacy and good taste and gorgeously mounted. Miss Stewart herself does her best for it. She is delicate and charming, looks a well bred girl to her finger tips. Only at moments did she fail as she has not failed in the past. This was when she waved her arms—emoted, as they say. Somehow these moments did not seem real. Towards the last there was a regular debate of inserts, but this did not militate as the interest had been carefully built up to that point.

The supporting cast helped a lot. William V. Mong brought most of the comedy into the action, while Joseph Swickard and Ralph Lewis played straight roles with their usual ability. James Morrison made so young and adolescent a youth of the lead, it is a wonder a grown woman fell in love with him. Myrtle Stedman in an unpleasant role managed to bring out a degree of pathos.

This isn't exactly rollicking hot weather stuff as will be seen from a digest of the story. Brabazon's stage wife deserts him and follows the primrose path. Their daughter makes a success of the stage. Brabazon does not even know he has a daughter and so when his adopted son, Ned, falls in love with Rosamond, he does all he can to prevent the match, only to learn in the end the girl is really his daughter. He and she have fought for the boy. They end in each other's arms. *Leed.*

JOURNEY'S END

The Girl....................Mabel Ballin
The Ironworker....................George Bancroft
The Mill Owner....................Wyndham Standing
The Child....................Georgette Bancroft
The Uncle....................Jack Dillion

Hugo Ballin is the creator of "The Journey's End" (8-reel adaption of the story "Ave Maria") distributed by Hodkinson through the Pathe Exchanges Ballin presents the feature minus subtitles or captions, the picture being worked out entirely by the action derived from the story which is largely the reason for its length. Should subtitles and captions be used for explanatory purposes the production could be cut to five reels without affecting its dramatic value. In its present shape the story is well told, the continuity being well established at all times without a slip up on the part of the director in planting his points. The idea is novel with the production being credited as the first big dramatic picture of its kind, though Charles Ray made a comedy feature minus the captions. Ballin has taken a short cast. The story opens with a convent bred girl in Rome desiring to visit her relatives in America. The trip being made she arrives at the home of her uncle, which she finds far below what she expected. To secure her release from the houeshold she marries an ironworker below her station in life. The union results in the birth of a child some time later, with the wife also meeting the bachelor mill owner, who appeals to her due to his culture and refinement which overshadows her husband. The spouse seeing the situation switches his identity to a man killed in an accident, the wife believing herself free of her marriage ties, marries the mill owner, the couple leaving for Italy on their honeymoon. The first husband in the meantime shipped to Europe and had been installed in a monastery in Rome as a monk. The couple reach his place of refuge on a sightseeing tour and are conducted through the place by the ex-husband unknown to them due to a heavy beard. While in one of the lower chambers he makes known his identity and collapses after the effort, and the couple are free to proceed on their married way.

Although short in numbers the cast has been well selected. Mabel Ballin as the girl displays her best work in this production. She is the central figure of the story and continually on the screen and displays an adequate amount of expressive pantomimic ability. George Bancroft as the iron worker is a type of distinction for the part with Wyndham Standing as the polished mill owner working in well as a contrast. Standing's work at times contains a certain amount of stagieness that is not convincing. Georgette Bancroft in the child role and Jack Dillion as the irresponsible uncle are well cast. J. R. Diamond did the photography work in clever style, while the production end was well planned and convincingly worked out by the director. "The Journey's End" is a big picture in other ways than its length. It is a new departure in film making and for the initial production along these lines is commendable. It can hardly be credited as being big enough for a $2 Broadway house, but for the regular photoplay houses that can cram eight reels into their program without throwing their policies out of focus it can supply satisfying entertainment.

BEYOND PRICE

Mrs. Philip Smith....................Pearl White
Philip....................Vernon Steele
Vivaria....................Nora Reed
Weathersby....................Louis Haines

Fox program feature with Pearl White starred. As a whole this is skillfully devised to coax in the dollars. Paul H. Sloane too often keeps his story moving forward by the sudden introduction of incidents previously not even hinted at, but careful atention to detail by J. Searle Dawley, who directed, holds the interest and the result is a lengthy, but effective picture.

Mrs. Smith and her husband run a shoe store and the husband neglects his wife to center on shoe designing. She decides he must be wakened up to her need for attention. Enter a gypsy fortune teller who gives her three wishes. These come true. In turn she finds herself posing as the wife of a millionaire to get him out of a predicament resulting from his affair with Vicaria, the dancer, as the center of interest (manicured, so to speak, by every eye) at a fashion review, and lastly with a baby in her arms. It is someone's else baby, but having held it she realizes the glory of motherhood, goes back to her husband and everyone is happy. Humor and drama are skillfully intermixed throughout the telling.

As a program star, Miss White shows a tendency gained in serials to let action, rather than shaded pantomime carry her over, but in some hazy close-ups toward the end she registered well shaded emotion. Nora Reed as Vivaria is a dark beauty who should be seen more often. Louis Haines made an asinine old flirt of the millionaire with a leaning toward farce in some of his scenes, a fault Miss White also showed. *Leed.*

DON'T CALL ME LITTLE GIRL

Mary Miles Minter's success in her respective stellar screen vehicles can usually be gauged by the quality of the stories allotted to her. To say "Don't Call Me Little Girl" is a perfect vehicle for her is to record its huge success.

It is an adaptation by Edith Kennedy from Catherine Chisholm Cushing's play "Jerry," and was directed by Joseph Henabery for Realart. The other principals in the cast are Jerome Patrick in the male lead, Ruth Stonehouse, Fannie Midgely and Edward Flanagan. They are all excellent in the varying roles. Miss Minter exhibits an amount of ingenuish "pep" that somehow seems to have been lacking in her work of late. Like the naughty little girl with the curl in the middle of her forehead, when she is good, she is very, very good, etc.

The part of "Jerry" suits her to a nicety. She returns from school, aged 18, but wearing youthful clothes because her young widowed mother is seeking another matrimonial alliance and wants to pass as aged 28. Jerry's aunt, aged 30, is engaged to a nice young man who doesn't really love her and isn't overanxious to speed the ceremony. Aunt loves a more sedate, middle-aged man. Jerry promptly falls in love with auntie's fiance and determines to annex him. The daringly feminine wiles to which she resorts to secure him make for charming, youthful, sweet comedy.

With inexpensive yet tasteful settings, the feature has been admirably produced and should give complete satisfaction in any high class program cinema. *Jolo.*

DESPERATE TRAILS

Oh, that U! If it ever gets hold of anything good in a script you can gamble your last penny it will be somehow ruined. So with "Desperate Trails," with Harry Carey. As a western it's good all the way, a story out of the usual and well enough directed for the appropriation allowed, but everything about it is so cheap.

The U seems to go in for its own trade and probably understands its business best. Still, as part of a double feature at Loew's Circle the other evening that might prove that the U could bust into decent huoses if it doesn't want to tie up all the nickel joints left in the country. That's what its pictures are made for—the avenue places, mostly converted stores or hideaway picture places.

Seems too bad to see this Carey film just bump off through production. Mr. Carey played with force all the way. No startling stunts were tried for, no gun-play of any account—just an interesting picture of the western type, interesting through its twists and holding the pathetic figure of Irene Rich, in the feminine lead, as the deserted wife of a train robber, with a couple of kids hanging onto her skirts, waiting for Santa Claus at Xmas and wishing Carey was their daddy.

But Carey, who loved the wife, took a prison term for a crime committed by her husband, in order, as he thought, to shield the brother of a girl called Lady Lou in Rawlins. He liked Lou well enough to hook up with her as long as the mother in the hills could not be his wife. Lou said the bandit she hid in the closet was her brother, and Carey fell for that one. It was a neat bit of vamp work that must make more than one of the boys squirm when they see it, for what they have fallen for from vamps in their own past. Admitting the crime, Carey got 16 years, but was tipped off after three months in prison to the facts, and escaped, to get the girl and fellow in that same Rawlins that same night on a railroad train. This railroad train stuff was good direction in its way, when the trains were on the track, made misty in the photography with the engines' headlights played up, but the minute at that time or any other that the picture got into the 30-cent studio work one felt like yelling.

The finish was the real criminal jumping off the train to his death, with Carey, wounded by Lou in the Pullman, making a getaway, to be caught at his sweetheart's home. But a kindly sheriff had heard Lou's confession, so a pardon was forthcoming.

The picture seemed to run easily, a little below the customary length. Where a western is wanted or the heroic in its rough is liked, a chance can be taken on "Desperate Trails," always remembering it's a U.

Sime.

TWICE BORN WOMAN

The Man from Nazareth.....Albert Pasqual
Simon of Cyrene..............George Hugo
Marcus Petronius............Charles Chertier
Setna, the Egyptian..........Marcel Pallas
Judas Iscariot...........Edward Napoleoni
Mary Magdalene...............Deyha Loti

The display of "The Twice Born Woman" at the New York Hippodrome as a special feature, simply places another naught in the picture realm. Presented by Malcolm Strauss, the artist, with Eve Unsell and Mr. Straus credited with scenario, mostly in Palestine, that are brightened only by the ensembles. There were several of these ensembles, each one admirable in itself, although in many where the principals were prominent, little could be said of the acting that necessarily called for heavy pantomiming.

Acting seemed the most remote of anyone's thoughts. It was a matter of posing, studied posing and often, especially with Deyha Loti as Mary Magdalene, losing the attempted effect through distinctly unpleasant, though perhaps strictly foreign, makeup.

As a commercial proposition this picture holds no decided attraction, lest the biblical story, done so frequently in out of doors performances under other titles, draws biblical readers who may wish to see the tale worked out. Again, and commercially, it's problematical exactly how this pictured story will strike those same people. Because purely a commercial project robs it of any lure that might otherwise be contained, for when a person is charged $1.10 at the box office to witness a flight of film of a subject that should call for some reverence, the ticket buyer cannot be expected to view the picture other than per the box office impression given. Whether the feature is worth the price will be the personal opinion of those who watch it.

In detail, "The Twice Born Woman" keeps missing. At the first Hip showing, June 22, some present apparently familiar with the Scriptures alleged the quotations introduced as titles were quite faulty. But the titles told the story even if the picture failed altogether to do so. It ran as if an immense footage had been clipped, possibly through religious censorship or with an eye to future religious criticism.

Judged only as a picture there is nothing in it for film fans or others, as the twice born woman is a film-aged story, only the picture people have called her so often in the past the woman who found her soul or reformation.

The feature seemed to actually run about 85 minutes. Preceeding were views of Judea, a singing male quartet, and a classical dance mixture by Norka Rouskaya that found the Hip stage too big for it.

The film's promoters have rented the Hip for four weeks from Charles Dillingham, so Mr. Dillingham doesn't care nor does anyone else, or if "The Twice Born Woman" utterly flops as it is quite likely to do, there could be no excuse advanced. It was a gambling chance to commercialize this historical biblical tale, and as made it's an odds on loser.

Sime.

WEALTH

Mary MacLeod..............Ethel Clayton
Philip Dominick.........Herbert Rawlinson
Gordon Townsend............J. M. Dumont
Oliver Marshall........Lawrence W. Steers
Irving Seaton..............George Periolat
Mrs. Dominick ....Claire McDowell
Estelle Rolland...................Jean Acker
Dr. Howard..................Richard Wayne

The first thing striking you about this Lasky offering current at the Rialto is the frequency with which what story there is is advanced by inserts. It is based on an original by Cosmo Hamilton and the continuity is by Julia Crawford Ivers. William D. Taylor directed. Apparently its substance, purpose and idea can best be visualized by imagining its motto to be, "It is better to be poor than rich."

Ethel Clayton, who is starred, and a competent cast set out to prove it by showing Miss Clayton first as an illustrator who falls in love with a rich young man who forthwith marries her. They live with his wealthy mother, who proceeds to dominate them. A baby is born—then dies. In the meantime Mary asserts herself, pleading with her husband to go to work and make a home for them. Too late he realizes how much she means it. She has left him meanwhile, but he wins her back, and the audience is satisfied when the overbearing mother-in-law has a stroke of paralysis she has long dreaded.

Competently handled, this might have scored, but as it stands it is dressed up to conceal its defects. There are rich and costly interiors, a cabaret scene expensive in every way, and Miss Clayton's gowns to help.

Herbert Rawlinson and Claire McDowell stood out in the cast.

Leed.

CARNIVAL

Silvio Steno...................Matheson Lang
Simonetta........................Hilda Bailey
Count Andrea Scipione..........Ivor Novelle
Lelio..............................Clifford Gray
Baroness Ottavia..........Duchess D'Ansola
Nino Steno..............."Twinkles" Hunter

Harley Knoles' film production of "Carnival" is the only tangible evidence to reach America to represent the ill-fated Alliance Film Co. of England. It is being distributed here by the United Artists. If the Alliance had ever gotten into full swing with a series of such productions as "Carnival," it would have been a strong contender for first honors in the American film mart.

"Carnival" was presented here on the legitimate stage a year or so ago with Godfrey Tearle in the stellar role, and while Mr. Tearle scored a strong personal success, the piece proved a dire failure and was quickly withdrawn. Matheson Lang, a popular English actor, produced it in London on the spoken stage, where it enjoyed a prosperous run, and he is now in the same role in the film version, and Hilda Bailey, who created the leading feminine role in Matheson's company in London, is cast for the same part in the screen presentation.

While following closely the spoken version, the film adaptation is intensely absorbing melodrama of a high order. The film producer had the advantage of utilizing many more scenes than could possibly be shown on a stage, and for a background employed actual locations on the canals of romantic Venice, with its picturesque castles, gondolas, etc. It was also relatively easy for him to actually show a replica of a Venetian carnival, and for a number of these shots the film was artistically colored.

The story has in it a strong basis for tragic drama—that of a prominent Italian actor-manager, believing his wife guilty of infidelity, called upon to play the role of Othello on his stage to her Desdamona, winding up with the choking scene, wherein he is so frantic he actually tries to throttle the fair lady.

Mr. Lang is a typically stolid Englishman, and when he makes up for the Moor of Venice he looks the part to a nicety. A number of close-ups serve to bring out the fierceness of his jealousy, and the scenes in the theatre are not exaggerated or idealized. His screen performance is a fine piece of cinematographic mummery. Miss Bailey, however, does not fare so well. She fails to bring to the characterization the requisite "temperament" of a spoiled young wife who goes to the carnival attired as Bacchante with another man, merely out of pique because her husband is called away at the last moment and unable to escort her. She is not sufficiently convincing in her depiction of the consequences of her rash act. Mr. Lang, on the contrary, lives and suffers the role of Othello—or at least creates that impression.

The others in the supporting company are sufficiently competent for their respective parts, the photography is admirable throughout, and the entire production is a dignified and impressive one. It can be set down as a success of a high order. If this should turn out to be the case it will probably be the first British-made photoplay to win its laurels in this country.

Jolo.

SALVATION NELL

Nell Sanders...............Pauline Starke
Jim Platt......................Joseph King
Myrtle Hawes.............Gypsy O'Brien
Major Williams..........Edward Langford
Hallelujah Maggie..Evelyn C. Carrington
Sid McGovern...........Charles McDonald
Al McGovern....................Matthew Betz
Hash House Sal..............Marie Haynes
Giffen.................................A. Earl
Callahan.................William Nalley
Jimmie.................Lawrence Johnson

This is a serious picture for hot weather, but a good picture. Whitman Bennett is presenting it this week as a First National attraction at the Strand, and it leaves you better for having seen it. It is based on Edward Sheldon's well remembered play. Kenneth Webb directed competently and the mountings were adequate and in keeping.

Far above other considerations, the acting stands out. Pauline Starke never appeared to such good advantage. She was simple, direct, appealing. She outdid herself. Nothing this year has begun to approach Lillian Gish's performance in "Way Down East" as this has. She was well seconded by Joseph King, who in the latter scenes brought into his performance with pathetic charm a suggestion of the weakening of the roughneck and the growing of the better man, but the mind returns to Miss Starke to that moment of the fight when sheer terror took hold of her, to her rescue and the light falling on her face as she prayed, lastly to those final scenes when she struggled between the good and bad love, making clear the difference, the terrible inner urge that leads every woman worth a second's thought into the Gethsemane of all attractive girls.

Of the others who appeared it may be said that Evelyn C. Carrington made a bit convincing and effective by the simplest methods, while Mr. Bennett in his casting chose for his boy part a real boy who was neither angelic nor pretty, but a boy. As for the rest, they worked well in the ensemble.

Nell is the girl of a roughneck and can't keep a respectable job, as the man is always coming around while in drink. Finally, at work scrubbing floors in a saloon, she attracts the unwelcome attentions of the boss' brother and her own man defends her, killing the brother. For this he serves seven years. Coming back, he looks up his girl and their son and finds them happy in Salvation Army work. He himself has been tempted by a gang of thieves. In the final, moving, convincing scenes she saves him and herself and son, and all together they find happiness.

Leed.

HEARTS AND MASKS

Alice Gaynor...................Elinor Field
Galloping Dick..........Francis McDonald
Richard Comstock................Lloyd Bacon
John Gaynor ....John Cossar
Mrs. Graves................Molly McConnell

"Hearts and Masks" is a Federated production adapted for the screen by Mildred Considine from the novel by Harold McGrath. Elinor Field is the picture's leading light, possibly it being her first starring vehicle. Alice Gaynor (Miss Field), the ward of a rich, gouty uncle, is confined closely to her home, due to the puritanical ideas of her guardian. Her bubbling disposition causes uncle much worriment and brings about his sudden departure from home for a rest.

During his absence his niece takes command and assumes the role of a maid, making the servants the guests at the house, also informing a stranger that the house is a boarding place and that he may secure a room there. Uncle returns, finds the topsy turvy conditions, raises cain, and the boarder makes his departure. A love affair had sprung up between the lodger and the maid which was carried on after he had taken up quarters at a nearby hotel, they meeting at an affair at the country club in masquerade attire. They become mixed up with thieves working in the crowd, have several escapades, but end up with the customary close up.

The picture is a personal success for Miss Field if nothing else. She displays the winsomeness of a Pickford and the comedy ability of a Normand. A more appropriate role could not have been picked for her.

The picture in its general makeup had its production cost cut to a minimum. The interiors are the customary studio stock stuff, with not a flash displayed in the entire affair.

The cast in support has been sufficiently well selected, with each member honestly earning the money. William Seiter was the director, and although inclined to forget detail at times was provided with sufficient material in the McGrath story to bring forth a screen subject.

"Hearth and Masks" as a program picture has some value on the strength of the McGrath name and the work of Miss Field.

THE OLD NEST

Dr. Horace Anthon......Dwight Crittenden
Mrs. Anthon......................Mary Alden
Uncle Ned........................Nick Cogley
Hannah....................Fanny Stockbridge
Mrs. Guthrie..................Laura Lavarnie
Tom, age 13....................Johnny Jones
Tom, age 36..................Richard Tucker
Arthur, age 14..............Marshall Ricksen
Jim, age 10..................Buddy Messenger
Jim, age 22-32.................Cullen Landis
Kate, age 9...................Lucille Ricksen
Kate, age 21-31...............Louise Lovely
Frank, age 6................Robert Devilbiss
Frank, age 18..................J. Park Jones
Frank, age 28..................J. Park Jones
Emily, the baby..........Marie Moorehouse
Emily, age 12....................Billy Cotton
Emily, age 22...............Helene Chadwick
Stephen McLeod.........Theodore von Eltz
Molly McLeod..................Molly Malone
Harry Andrews........M. B. (Lefty) Flynn
Mr. Atkinson.................Roland Rushton

A goodly percentage of those present at the premiere of "The Old Nest" Tuesday evening at the Astor were members of the theatrical and film industry. They were pretty well agreed that the Reginald Barker production of Rupert Hughes' photoplay, made for Goldwyn, is more or less of a plagiarism of William Fox's "Over the Hill." Nevertheless "The Old Nest" is not a plagiarism excepting in the sense that every triangle drama is a variation of all the others.

"Over the Hills" is a photoplay about a venal, churlish, rapacious low-cast family showing the mother-love the one big thing in such surroundings, with one son so unfeeling as to permit his mother to go to the poorhouse. The father of the family is a horsethief as the culmination of a life of indolence.

"The Old Nest" depicts the married life of a sweet mother, the wife of a country doctor whose children grow up and marry, and in the carrying on of their own lives neglect their aged mother—never viciously, but unthinkingly, just as all of us—yes, even the best of us—are apt to do. It is a magnificent depiction of the inevitable existence, showing the love of a mother for her children, knowing their human frailties but loving them just the same. None of the children are especially good nor yet wicked—just ordinary, average children of any mother with an average husband. To be sure one of the youths hangs out in the village pool parlor and gets mixed up in a crap game and steals some money from the cash register of the village grocery store where he is employed. How many of us, placed in the same situation, wouldn't have taken the same chance to pay our gambling losses at that age?

What was more natural than for the mother to take the money the father gave her to pay the butcher and grocer and use it to buy her little girl a dress so she could go to a party?

The entire picture is full of just such human, natural touches. There are no villains, no sex problems, no triangle situations—just the life story of any family; not designed to teach anything but merely to remind us not to neglect our parents, especially our mothers.

It is all classily told without bathos or other mawkish sentimentality, admirably directed without having recourse to tremendous mob scenes or extravagance of production. The technical details are superb in their simplicity. *Jolo.*

SUCH A LITTLE QUEEN

Realart has picturized "Such a Little Queen" originally produced as a legitimate production by the late Henry B. Harris as the initial starring vehicle for Elsie Ferguson. Channing Pollack is the author, the screen adaptation having been made by J. Clarkson Miller and Lawrence McCloskey, with Constance Binney as its star. Although, as a matter of sentiment, the picture might have had Miss Ferguson as its star, a better selection than Miss Binney could not have been made. She has all of the charm which the role of a young queen calls for, and admirably plays the part, which provides the entire backbone of the production.

The story deals with the experiences of a dethroned king and queen. The couple, unmarried, are forced from their native lands by revolutionists and settle in America, where, regardless of misfortunes and lack of funds, find that true love grips them, and with their recall by their people they mount the throne together, connecting their two kingdoms.

It is a dainty tale neatly worked out, but not strongly enough fortified with action to place it in the front rank of feature pictures. To a large extent the production depends upon sub-titles and captions. These are most cleverly written and do not detract from the picture's value, although in continuous use.

George Fawcett did the directing and displays a competent hand in the development. Vincent Coleman is entrusted with the male lead, which he plays earnestly and with considerable ability. Roy Fernandez in a juvenile part, provides a dash of true American pep that is becoming, with two character roles well handled by J. H. Gilmour and Jessie Ralph, the latter handling a cook part for good comedy results.

Realart has done well with the production, and especially with the pageantry in connection with the court scenes. The detail has been well looked after in this direction. This latest version of "Such a Little Queen" should prove a draw on both the ability of its star and the interest derived from the story.

The original film version of the piece was made in 1914, with Mary Pickford as its star, after having been originally produced as a stage vehicle for Elsie Ferguson, and later as a musical comedy piece for Mitzi under the title of "Her Little Highness."

THE BRONZE BELL

"The Bronze Bell" misses, especially for the box office. It's a fine, big picture, splendidly set, yet it misses conviction, and through this becomes a feature film that once seen is shortly forgotten. The conviction is lost through the legendary story that carries implausibility so often with coincidence heavily entwined that the Rivoli audience Tuesday evening was moved to a light titter at a couple of points in the running.

It's really too bad. James W. Horne in directing has handled the story in a masterly fashion. He has huge mob scenes of Mohammedans, with much of the locale placed in India. It is that jumping back and forth from India to Long Island, with the characters congregating in that film dramatic way which knocks the conviction a tale such as this must carry.

There are discrepancies also in the story. Just why Har Dyal Rutton, one of the dual roles played by Courtenay Foote, would not obey The Voice of the Bell was not explained. It was set forth that the heir to the throne who became king upon his father's sudden demise when the son said he wouldn't obey, had received an English education or studied military science in that country. That might have been a hazarded reason. Had the story romped off to the son-king's love for an English girl, it would have been another story, of course, and possibly a more appealing one. Instead, Louis Joseph Vance wrote in a double, David Amber, an American, that called for any quantity of double exposure or trick photography that did not always seem true in the doubles, though if it were, it was excellent photography beyond a doubt.

The king, fearing the wrath of the Indian Bell, flees to Long Island, where the daughter of the Indian commandant has also gone, to visit her uncle, so these two people from faraway, unknown to each other and sailing on the same boat, locate within a couple of miles of one another near the Sound, to be in the same vicinity as the only man in the world who bears a resemblance to the king, minus some swarthiness. It's the double, Amber, who falls in love with the girl, while the king dies on Long Island after killing a courier of the Bell, who brought a message for the king to return and obey. Then Amber follows the girl back to India, is thrust forward as the king, undertakes the "ordeal" (of which much is made) of the Bell, and is rescued by the English troops just in time to stop an uprising of the Indians against the English.

It's a story with the world for the background, especially that impish, devilish India, and while the story remains in India, it is engrossing excepting the "Ordeal" proposition. In America, though, the tale becomes ridiculous through its illogical trend.

It's a Thos. H. Ince-Paramount, full of life, animation and color, with plenty of action and enough extras to suffice for any special, but nevertheless it is no more than an ordinary weekly feature release, although the production investment might have reached as high as the average special goes. *Sime.*

TRADITION

Res Madchuri.......................Carl Wagner
Tantara Bagha........................Paul Otto
Semena ....Marcella Halicz
Hodessa ....Erich Pabst
Wun-si ....Ralph V. Roberts
Dscham ....Max Zawislak
Old Tekki ....Emilie Unda
William T. Cunningham.....Hans Anderson
Eleanor ....Lotte Klinder
Arnold Cooper.................Arthur Schroeder

"Tradition" is another of the series of foreign film productions to which we are rapidly growing accustomed. It is impressive in the matter of its settings, not especially massive, but "dignified" as to atmospheric detail. Unlike some of the other Teutonic film productions, the types selected are not the most felicitous. Tom Bret, a local title writer, has made an American version of "Death and Love," written abroad by Paul Otto and George Jacoby. Mr. Otto is also the director and plays the principal male role.

The scenes are laid in Thibet and continental Europe. While the clothes of most of the principals are oriental, they do not simulate the manners of Mongolians convincingly. This is the main criticism. Next comes the inconsistencies, of which there are several, readily discernible to the layman.

Tantara, a prince of Manchuria, aids an European representative for a large corporation to secure an important concession. His sister, Semena, sees the European, Arnold Cooper, and falls in love with him. When the natives plot to kill Cooper, Semena rushes to Cooper's house to warn him and aids him to escape. She is seen entering and is strangled by the leader of the insurgents, who lays the blame on Cooper. Tantara swears vengeance, goes to Europe to search out Cooper, finds him engaged to marry Eleanor, daughter of the head of the big corporation he represents. Tantara plots to kill Eleanor, but falls in love with her. He tells her Cooper murdered his sister and that he means to kill Cooper. He gives her three days in which to accept his proposition to return to Manchuria as his wife or Cooper will die. If she warns Cooper of his danger and has him (Tantara) taken into custody this will not save her fiance, as the entire nation is sworn to carry out the vengeance.

After a series of melodramatic happenings Eleanor consents to go with him to save the man she loves. She mysteriously disappe rs from home, Cooper returns to Manchuria to carry on his work, sees Eleanor there, rushes to Tantara to find out what it all means, is confronted by the Mongolian prince on the day set for his wedding with Eleanor, the natives rise up against the prince, now ascended to the throne through the death of his father, an old Chinese servant tells who did the strangling of Semena, and, according to the traditions of his people, Tantara commits hari-kari after saving the lives of Cooper and Eleanor.

The entire cast seems to lack "temperament." The fierceness of oriental infatuation is missing, Eleanor is apparently inadequate to the demands of the great sacrifice she makes to save her lover, the native Mongolians are exaggerated types and the whole smacks of far-fetched improbability. The production just misses being a great one.

"Tradition" was added to the program at the Hippodrome last week, where "The Twice Born Woman" is now running. *Jolo.*

CONQUERING POWER

Eugenie Grandet	Alice Terry
Charles Grandet	Rudolph Valentino
Victor Grandet	Eric Mayne
Pere Grandet	Ralph Lewis
His Wife	Edna Demaury
Notary Cruchot	Edward Connelly
His Son	Geo. Atkinson
The Abbe	Willard Lee Hall
M. des Grassins	Mark Fenton
His Wife	Bridgetta Clark
Adolph	Ward Wing
Nanon	Mary Hearn
Cornoiller	Eugene Pouyet
Annette	Andree Tourneur

June Mathis, scenarist, and Rex Ingram, director, have done well with Honore Balzac's story "Eugenie Grandet." They have made of it for Metro a feature film that will likely meet with popular approval. Readers of Balzac will see in it a direct antithesis of what the famous French writer and philosopher sought to convey, but the director and scenarist have invested the tale with a "commercial artistry" that will be much more appreciated by the general run of photoplay audiences.

For the benefit of those who may not have read "Eugenie Grandet," the story in brief is: Charles Grandet is a "young blood" in Paris—the son of a wealthy Frenchman. While celebrating his twenty-eighth birthday with a wild party at his home his father returns, and it is shown his fortune has been swept away. He sends the young man to visit his (the father's) brother at Noyant, from whom he has been estranged for a score of years, giving the young man a letter imploring the brother to look after the nephew. The father then commits suicide. The brother is an old miser with a beautiful daughter, with whom Charles (the young man) falls in love. The old man frowns on the love affair, declaring: "I would rather see my daughter dead than married to Charles Grandet." He ships the young man off to Martinique and intercepts the letters between the young people, finally dying a horrible death in his strong room surrounded by the gold he has hoarded all his life.

In the original tale Eugenie gives Charles, her lover, her savings, and he squanders it in riotous living with other women, and Eugenie marries the son of the village notary, devoting her wealth and her life to doing good to the natives.

In the photoplay Charles is idealized, returns after he has made his way in the world, and the picture closes with the lovers locked in an embrace. It is also brought out that Eugenie is not his blood cousin, but the daughter of Pere Grandet's wife by her first husband. This makes of it a beautiful romance and not a depiction of sordid life.

For an American production the atmospheric detail has been admirably worked out. The acting is brilliant, but devoid of Latin mannerisms. Ralph Lewis as the old miser gives one of the best character delineations seen in many a day. He gives in this picture promise of ranking with the best of the present generation of photoplay character actors, of which Theodore Roberts and W. H. Thompson are the deans. Alice Terry, as Eugenie, is sweetly beautiful and beautifully sweet. It would be difficult to imagine any other screen actress who could look and play the part any better—or as well. Rudolph Valentino, who played the lead in "The Four Horsemen," by his performance in the present picture proves his right to stardom in motion pictures. The other roles are relatively small, but all of them are equally well played as the more important ones.

The photography (John F. Slitz) is wonderfully effective—especially the close-ups, many of which are softened to an almost Rembrandt effect. All indications point to an emphatic success for "The Conquering Power"—commercially and artistically. *Jolo.*

THE KISS

Universal's latest Carmel Meyers feature, taken from the story by Johnston McCully, adapted for the screen by A. P. Younger, with Jack Conway the director.

The story, of a Spanish trend, is laid in Southern California. The son of a Don, betrothed to a girl of equal aristocratic lineage, shows a preference for the daughter of his fathers' overseer. The girl's father, believing the boy's attentions toward his daughter are not of the right nature, makes an attempt to kill him. The girl protects her father and makes possible his escape when pursued by the Don's men, with the son sufficiently recovered to announce she is the only girl he loves and wishes to marry.

There is considerable action, worked out acceptably by the director. The picture displays adequate photographic value.

Miss Meyers gives a clever performance. The remainder of the cast, consisting mainly of types, has been carefully selected.

Universal should turn out a few more features of this caliber for the houses to which it caters.

FINE FEATHERS

Bob Reynolds	Eugene Pallette
Jane Reynolds	Claire Whitney
Dick Mead, a reporter	Thomas W. Ross
James Brand	Warburton Gamble
Mrs. Brand	June Elvidge

Eugene Walter's play, "Fine Feathers," was made into a film once before some years ago. Metro has attempted it once more, with a scenario prepared by Lois Zellner, directed by Fred Sittenham, photographed by Arthur Caldwell. Although in six reels, some of the footage must have been excised for its running on the American Roof Monday evening, where it was projected in considerably less than an hour.

It was just as well, as the action is slow, leading up to a single situation, tense enough to be sure, but still but one. You will recall the plot—a government inspector is bribed to permit the contractor for a huge water dam to substitute inferior cement for the quality called for in the specifications, becomes rich, goes broke, jail faces him and he commits suicide. That was the original play. In the present film version he kills the man who bribed him before committing suicide.

Rather well played throughout, especially by Eugene Pallette as the unfortunate inspector who falls for the bribery. His furtive nervousness and fear for the consequences of his dishonest act is capitally depicted. Claire Whitney is wholly convincing as his wife, and Warburton Gamble as the heavy is classily machiavelian in a modern way.

The original play enjoyed but a modicum of success. The present film version would seem to have a slightly better chance. *Jolo.*

I AM GUILTY

Connie MacNair	Louise Glaum
Robert MacNair	Mahlon Hamilton
Trixie Belmont	Claire DuBrey
Teddy Garrick	Joseph Kilgour
London Hattie	Ruth Stonehouse
Molly May	May Hopkins
Dillon	George Cooper
The Child	Mickey Moore

"I Am Guilty" comes dangerously near to being a sensational photoplay feature. It starts slowly and winds up with inconsistencies, incongruities and improbabilities. But the heart of the tale is as fine a piece of melodramatic suspense as can possibly be imagined. There is no reason why it could not be adapted into a spoken play and be equally arresting.

The story is by Bradley King, directed by Jack Nelson, photography by Charles J. Stumar—a Parker Read production released through Associated Producers. In it we have a lawyer seeking the identity of a mysterious woman who is believed to be a murderess, who turns out to be his own wife. Discovering her identity, he is then torn between his duty to his client and the mother of his little child.

Robert MacNair, a brilliant young attorney, is married to a former chorus girl. He is so absorbed in his affairs he has little time for his wife and child. Called to Texas for several weeks, Connie, the wife, is visited by a chorus girl friend and persuaded to attend a "party" at the home of a wealthy libertine, who holds her in the house by a ruse after the others have departed. He makes forcible overtures; in the struggle her back is badly burned by contact with a Chinese lamp and she suffers a butterfly scar. A burglar in the house hands her a revolver through the portierres, a shot is fired, she escapes and the burglar is arrested.

The burglar tells his story, but is unable to prove it, as there is no trace of the mysterious "Peggy LaMarthe." Her real identity is unknown to the others attending the party excepting her friend Molly May, the other chorus girl. Being a prominent criminal lawyer with a reputation for never having lost a case, it was within the range of probability that the crook's sweetheart should hire the husband to defend her lover.

The sequence of events are absorbingly interesting, winding up with a sensational trial—the crook found guilty by the jury—the wife declaring in open court she is the guilty one, with a "surprise" twist through the confession of the libertine's mistress that she shot him in a fit of jealousy—shown in a flashback.

Just a little more ingenuity might have been exercised in bringing about the denouement with more consistency. The feature starts slowly and the finish is interminably dragged out unnecessarily.

The direction and photography, on the whole, is admirable and the acting well nigh perfect. Louise Glaum is the star, enacting the role of the wife with an intensity of emotion that is gripping. Mahlon Hamilton gives a dignified, serious portrayal of the husband; Claire DuBrey an amusing character portrayal of the chorus girl friend of the wife; Joseph Kilgour is more lecherous than usual in his visualization of the libertine; Ruth Stonehouse is excellent as the cockney sweetheart of the burglar; George Cooper stands out vividly as the crook on trial for a murder he didn't commit, and May Hopkins gives a splendid performance of the jealous mistress.

It is all very fine—but it might easily have been one of the great pictures of the present day. The average cinema patron will probably have little fault to find with "I Am Guilty." *Jolo.*

THE RAIDERS

A Broadway picture house took a chance with this one in a double feature bill last week. It is one of the most amateurish melodramatic features seen.

The Canyon Picture Corp. stands sponsor for it, with Franklyn Farnum the star and Nate Watt the director. William E. Wing is credited with the scenario.

The story concerns Canadian whisky runners. It unfolds a tale of the mountains in which much of the old school melodrama is unearthed and a bit of a love story introduced, the lone woman of the cast being in love with three of the six men in the picture. Farnum was selected as her husband after the rest of the bunch had been killed off.

The picture in its seriousness is a scream. The audience laughed at all of the dramatic business. The production cost is nil. The action takes place almost entirely in the open. Studio work necessary could have been accomplished in an hour.

CONQUEST OF CANAAN

Joe Louden..................Thomas Meighan
Ariel Taber..................Doris Kenyon
Mamie Pike..................Diana Allen
Mrs. Louden..................Ann Egleston
Claudine..................Alice Fleming
Eskew Arp..................Charles Abbe
Jonas Taber..................Malcolm Bradley
Happy Farley..................Paul Everton
Nashville Cory..................Macy Harlan
Col. Flintcroft..................Henry Hallam
Judge Pike..................Louis Hendricks
Peter Bradbury..................Charles Hartley
Norbert Flintcroft..................Jed Prouty
Gene Louden..................Cyril Ring
Squire Buckelew..................J. D. Walsh
Mike Sheenan..................Riley Hatch

Great small town stuff!

This Paramount product is an adaption to the screen of Booth Tarkington's novel. Thomas Meighan is starred. About him is gathered a cast which is handled with judgment and distinguishes itself to an unusual extent. At the Rivoli this week it is getting to people strong and everywhere should make especially forceful appeal to those who have watched or suffered the indignities forming a part of life in a small town.

The story as told in the novel is preserved here. Joe Louden, because he acts like a natural human being, is more or less frowned on in Canaan, Ind., particularly by Judge Pike, the rich man of that vicinity. But little Ariel Tabor likes him. She is poor. When some money is left her she goes with her father to Paris and on his death, returns. During her absence, things have gone from bad to worse with Joe. To save his brother he has taken the blame for an escapade at Beaver Beach with a woman, then gone to Chicago, working days and studying law nights. When he returns to Canaan the town still hounds him and with his yellow dog he keeps to himself, his clientele the bad element from Beaver Beach.

A member of this crowd, Happy Farley, long suspicious of the attentions paid his wife by Nashville Cory, shoots before Cory can shoot him. Smouldering animosities break out. There is a riot, an attempt to lynch, but Joe saves him for trial and sentiment begins to turn toward Joe when they even pick on his dog. In the meantime, Ariel returns from Paris looking like our old college hope, a million dollars. She hunts Joe up. The trial is a success, with Judge Pike exposed as the real owner of Beaver Beach and Ariel shows her love for Joe in a neat final close-up.

There was great material here and the usual excellent Paramount photography made the most of what was set up for the camera. R. William Neil directed. The scenario is by Frank Tuttle and Tom Geraghty, an Indiana newspaper man himself, superintended the whole. He has turned out a good market product. The main regret is that he didn't do better, as well, for example, as was done with "Conrad in Quest of His Youth." The fault may have been in the cutting, but summed up, it consists in a failure to plant the earlier stuff on which the whole climax rests with sufficient solidity.

The characters, and especially Louden and Judge Pike, should have been developed less sketchily. Perhaps familiarity with the almost perfect workmanship shown in the book itself lessens the effect of the film. At any rate, artistically the production seemed less than it should have been, but if there was disappointment in this, there was far less to find fault with in the acting.

Paul Everton, as Happy, gave one of his classic performances. He is an exceptionally effective actor. Alice Fleming, Macy Harlan and Riley Hatch got over the underworld stuff in simple, convincing fashion. Small town types were also well done. Doris Kenyon made up for some earlier staginess and an unattractive way of doing her hair by the charming, winsome naturalness with which she played the latter scenes. Mr. Meighan, himself, got something wistful into his performance that was needed, but otherwise he was the upstanding young fellow he plays so well, rather than Tarkington's creation.

They are yelling for small town stuff. This should clean up.

Leed.

GOLDEN SNARE

Sergeant Philip Raine...Lewis S. Stone
Bram Johnson..................Wallace Beery
"Doug" Johnson...Melbourne MacDowell
Celie..................Ruth Renick
Black Dawson..................Wellington Playter
Pierre Thoreau..................Francis MacDonald
Baby..................Little Esther Scott

David M. Hartford and James Oliver Curwood have turned out a whale of an "action" picture such as the large majority of the fans demand and it ought to be a valuable property of the widest possible circulation. "The Golden Snare" (First National) is not always plausible. Indeed there are moments when its story edges toward the ridiculous under close examination, but even a hard boiled reviewer couldn't help but be carried along by its melodramatic story and be impressed by the magnificent Arctic backgrounds of limitless snowfields and bleak mountain peaks. It is this week at the Strand.

The story is the frankest sort of melodrama, as naively fictitious as a Grimm fairy tale, but it is as wholesome as a fairy tale and infinitely a better bit of screen art than the half baked "problem" stories that make large pretense of intellectual appeal. The one minor detail in which the production as it appeared at the Strand was lacking was a certain hardness and sharpness of photography. The effects were such stark black and white, without those softening tones that mark the best modern handling, that one got an impression of crudeness.

But the story is emphatically there, story in the sense of absorbing screen action. There is scarcely a hundred feet of film that has not a stirring fight of one sort or another; there is the romantic figure of the constable of the Northwest Mounted Police; there is a band of bad men who ravage the waste places of the Arctic, and finally there is the Homeric figure of the half-mad giant of the wilderness, Bram Johnson (Wallace Beery), and his pack of half-wolf dogs over whom he has the wierdest control and which he drives madly over the snow fields by word of mouth.

A curious musical setting contributes a good deal to the atmosphere of the screening, a wierd, mystic strain that repeats itself interminably during the scenes involving Bram.

Sergeant Raine is sent into the frozen wilderness to capture the outlaw Bram Johnson, who years before had killed ten men in a fight to rescue his father from the police after he had been unjustly convicted. Johnson has been traced by his habit of setting rabbit snares made of braided woman's blonde hair.

On his journey Raine falls in with a native trapper who has been frightened to death by the apparition of the ghost-like Bram and his spook dogs riding through the snow. Raine takes the trapper's baby along, and by virtue of the little one wins the sympathy of a lovely girl who appears miraculously out of the snow driving a dog team. She turns out to be a sort of ward of Bram and with her aid Raine is taken into Bram's cabin.

Black Dawson, leader of the outlaw gang further north, has seen the girl and covets her and here begins a series of terrific battles between the giant Bram and Dawson, one to steal the girl and the other to defend her. The inventive skill in keeping this contest boiling in ceaseless combat and warfare is the last word in resourcefulness, with fists, clubs and firearms, rushing dogsleds, snowshoes, the mysterious golden haired beauty and the most delightful baby all mixed up in a whirl of action.

The baby alone is worth the price of admission. It plays with half-wolf puppies and chuckles, and when the rough sergeant feeds it milk by means of a dripping handkerchief, there were squeals of delight from the women fans.

In the end Bram is killed in a smashing dramatic climax of a battle with Black Dawson and it is disclosed that the mysterious heroine was rescued by Bram years before when a band of Esquimo fell upon the frozen-in ship of an Arctic explorer and killed the whole party. Of course, there is a love story involving Sergeant Raine and the heroine, ending in the prospect of their wedding.

"The Golden Snare" is the goods. It promises to earn a place in film history with Neilan's "The River's End."

Rush.

A RIDIN' ROMEO

Jim Rose..................Tom Mix
Mabel Brentwood..................Rhea Mitchell
Highlow, the Indian......Pat Chrisman
Jack Walters..................Sid Jordan
King Brentwood..................Harry Dunkinson
Queenie Farrell..................Eugenie Ford

Authorship for this western thriller is credited to its star, Tom Mix, who has turned out for Fox one of his customary stunt pictures under the direction of George E. Marshall. The plot is very light and brings forth the familiar romantic cowboy character that is characteristic of features of this order. Jim Rose is a cowpuncher living alone in his shack, which he has fitted up with several ingenious contrivances for his own comfort, such as devices for cooking his breakfast and to feed his horse, etc., without it being necessary for him to get out of bed, all being worked from his bedside by levers.

The main trend of the story is along the lines of romance, Jim being in love with a neighboring ranchman's daughter, and although in the good graces of the girl finds her father a hard nut to crack, due to his having played several tricks on the old man some time before which brought about his banishment from the ranch. The story centers around a birthday party given by the girl while her father is away, Jim being one of the guests. While the party is in progress Pop returns and a general scramble ensues, after which Jim makes his getaway with the ranchman's clan at his heels. At this juncture a series of chases over the plain and through the mountains is introduced, with Jim always in the lead and capable of outwitting his enemies, and eventually he manages to patch things up and secures the girl, which was a sure bet from the start.

Mix can always be relied upon for trick riding of a high caliber, and demonstrates much of it in this production. He is untiring in providing action, and performs a series of stunts that places him in a class by himself. Rhea Mitchell plays the girl role and flits in and out of the picture without any trouble, always looking the part of the typical western girl. The remainder of the cast consists entirely of types all well chosen. The production end has no great cost connected with it, the great outdoors being used almost entirely for the development of the story. Benny Kline, the cameraman, has turned out some good photography, with the direction of George Marshal all that could be asked. "A Ridin' Romeo" is just another one of those western features that have a certain appeal to an audience not too discriminating.

THE HEART LINE

Fancy Gray..................Leah Baird
Francis Granthope......Jerome Patrick
Oliver Payson..................Frederick Vroom
Clytie Payson..................Ruth Sinclair
Big Dougal..................Ivan McFadden
Gay P. Summers..................Philip Steeman
Madam Spoil........Mrs. Chas. C. Craig
Blanchard Cayley..................Martin Best
The Child..................Ben Alexander

Frederick Thompson directed "The Heart Line,' a six-reel adaptation of the novel by Gelett Burgess, presented by Arthur F. Beck through the Pathe exchanges. The production was turned out by the Leah Baird Film Corp., with Miss Baird in the leading role.

The story of a spiritualistic nature centers around one Oliver Payson, who is entrusted with the care of his business partner's son upon the father's death. The boy is separated from his guardian in a railroad wreck and not located for several years, the guardian finally going to a medium to try to locate his whereabouts. Payson's daughter in the meantime had fallen in love with a palmist. This chap actually in love with the girl tries to mend his ways and is assisted by an admirer who, seeing his strong love for the other girl, decides to give him up herself.

The action is worked around in such a manner as to show the illegitimate workings of mediums and the disclosing of the fact that the young palmist is the lost boy, which brings about a marriage with his guardian's daughter.

Pictures of this nature have a certain appeal, especially to women audiences, the spiritualistic idea having gained a strong foothold in certain sections with stories of this character displaying the fallacy of the predictions of mediums, worth while in a moral way.

Thompson, apparently not overburdened with cash in the making of this production, has made the story stand up, which, together with a suitable cast, make the picture a fair possibility for the smaller picture houses.

Miss Baird, with her years of experience, can be relied upon for a good performance in practically any role. Her long term in stock with the Vitagraph gave her a schooling which cannot be credited to many now on the screen. Her work in this production carries the picture along in the right direction. Jerome Patrick, in the male lead, gives an intelligent interpretation of a role well suited to him. Frederick Vroom, Ruth Sinclair and Mrs. Charles C. Craig have been well cast.

"The Heart Line" has not been turned out to create a furore in filmdom, but for the smaller picture houses it can run along as a regular release.

THE BROKEN ROAD

London, July 6.

This adaptation of A. E. W. Masons's popular story falls very short of the novel in its gripping power, although it will doubtless prove popular and will provide perfectly healthy and not too exciting entertainment for thousands of picture enthusiasts. Rene Plaissatty, the producer, has done his work well from the scenic point of view and his Aghan scenes, native palaces and other oriental effects are among the best seen, but the picture is essentially a story of soldiering and soldiers and it is remarkable that so little regard for military detail has been paid. A subaltern commanding a punitive force makes a strong point of taking his men along the sky-line—they even pose there—a little matter which would have meant a court-martial and disgrace if he had come out of action alive, which in this case, as he is the hero, he of course does.

This is crass ignorance which might easily have been remedied by asking any member of the company who had soldiered what would be the best means to adopt on approaching an enemy who are notoriously sharpshooters. Again when the force advances it is as an unruly rabble, discipline seems absolutely absent. After watching the hero as a military tactician we will blame him instead of the producer. We were not at all surprised when a subtitle informed us that he had resigned his commission. He was exceedingly lucky to get off so lightly.

The story deals with three generations of the Linforths who, one after the other, have been engaged in making a great road from Kohara to the Hindu Kush. The natives are antagonistic and the first two generations are slaughtered in different risings. The third generation in the person of Dick Linforth makes a friend while at the varsity of Shere Ali, the native prince through whose territory the great road is planned to run. Shere Ali falls in love with a flighty widow who, having accepted his pearls, lets him know pretty plainly that "East is East, and West is West." Shere Ali returns to India and is followed by Dick, who has got the family road fever badly. The prince heads a rebellion and is defeated and captured after a display of remarkable military inefficiency on the part of Dick.

Later Dick pleads at the court-martial for his one-time friend, who therefore is only sentenced to banishment. The last we see of Shere Ali he is shifting strong drinks in a low Burmese inn. Dick returns to England and marries the one girl who will in due course probably provide another Linforth who'll have better luck in road-making than his ancestors. Dotted up and down the main story are spies, substitution of sham for the real jewels, an attempt to kidnap the widow, and a good deal of killing. Although the picture will please many it only fills us with more wonderment that the Stoll company with all its resources apparently cannot make first-class pictures. The producers are all men who have done brilliant work elsewhere, the staging is perfect, the photography of the very best, but there is always something missing. Can it be that the studio is being run as a factory in an endeavor to make art mechanical? The acting in "The Broken Road" is uniformly good and there is no straining to "get over." Tony Fraser, a colored actor, is a distinct find as Shere Ali.

PRINCESS OF N. Y.

London, July 1.

Famous-Lasky (British), seven reels.

This dramatic feature brings the British studios of the American firm several steps nearer their goal. The story by Cosmo Hamilton is a strong one, well told. It is also clean and does not depend upon the sensational for its punch. As it stands the picture caan stand a drastic pruning and when it comes through the operation of cutting, it will be a sound showman's proposition. Unfortunately, although we can see the reward of virtue, we do not see the punishment of villainy and can only hope that the crooks did not get clear away. The Princess of New York, called so because her father is the "Steel King," arrives in London with her chaperon. On the boat she has met and become friendly with Violet and George Marstham, "crooks" (the children of old Sir George Marstham, also a "crook") and Geoffrey Kingsward, a 'varsity man and "gentleman." Both men are in love with her, and for once Marstham's feelings border on genuineness, although he has an eye to the dollars.

The Marsthams persuade her to stay with them and soon hatch a pretty plot, although young Marstham has to be continually "gingered up" by his father and Violet. These nice people invite low friends to dinner and introduce them to the super-innocent Princess as members of the old nobility. She falls in eagerly and is dazzled, according to plan. Having been told by her old man to buy the town she sets off at a swell jeweler's and obtains much valuable jewelry on credit. Later on Sir George persuades her to let him keep her money for safety, and as usual she is as easy as possible. He backs a horse with it and the horse goes down. Meanwhile the Kingswards, father and son, are on the track of the Princess's friends real worth. Having lost the money old Sir George does a little more plotting on his own account while his precious children arrange to take the Princess into the country where they will be safe from the prying Kingswards. Old Sir George tells her a wonderful hard luck story about a dear old friend of his, the Princess again falls for it, falls also when he proposes that she shall pledge the jewelry which is not hers so as to save his friend. She does so and hands over the money.

Meanwhile the jewellers have read that the Steel King is ruined and hasten to retrieve their jewels, hasten also to tell Scotland Yard who, discovering that the Princess has pledged the property, come to arrest her. Luckily the younger Kingsward is at hand and after a struggle rescues the Princess. They seize the car which the "crooks" have hired to take her away in and drive off. Hotly pursued they hide all night in a wood. Morning finds them both in custody, later they appear at Bow Street, where the matter is cleared up and they are dismissed. Of course, the Steel King is not ruined, that was only a stunt of some New York newspaper man who had some space to fill, and the end of the picture comes when His Majesty tells the Princess to go on buying "li' ol' London" and marry the man she loves.

David Powell is again excellent as Kingsward. Ivy Dawson (also the art director), is very good as the younger Marstham, while George Bellamy is inclined to burlesque the crook baronet. Dorothy Fane comes up to the standard of beauty set for girl "crooks" and also plays well and easily. Mary Glynee in the title-role gives another proof of the hidden talent which her British producers have failed to discover. "The Princess of New York" should prove a big winner.

Gore.

IN HIS GRIP

London, July 1.

Gaumont (British Screencraft), featuring Cecil Morton York. Six reels.

Physiological studies on the screen are rarely successful. The development of a character in a novel can be traced through hundreds of minute episodes. On the screen there is no time for this. Much of the change is shown by curt sub-titles, and the actual changes are necessarily sudden and generally jerky. This quick transition is the great defect in "In His Grip."

Sir Donald MacVeigh wavering between good and evil, between honesty and crime, arrives at his decisions spasmodically. We have no chance of seeing much of the working of his tortured mind. In itself David Christie Murray's novel is a fine study of an unusual character, as a screen-play it is only moderately interesting and fails to convince.

UNCLE BERNAC

London, July 6.

A remarkably fine and interesting feature founded on Sir Arthur Conan Doyle's novel of the same name. Additional interest rests in the fact that although the big company is French, yet the leading man (Rex Davis) the author ,and the scenarist are British. This story of intrigue and romance in the great days of Napoleon Bonaparte has been excellently adapted and while adhereing to the legendary picture of the Emperor he is shown in a more human light than is usual; the iron will of the conqueror is there, but he is also a very ordinary being, a husband and who grumbles at his wife's dress-maker's bills, a man who loves a practical joke.

He does not spend all his time with hands clasped behind him scowling across the sea to where the white cliffs of Dover lie. Minute care has been taken to get even the minutest historical detail correct, and the producer presnts us to Ney, Savary, Lannes, Soult, Murat, Talleyrand, as they were in life. Scenically the whole feature is perfect, the camp at Boulougne, the Emperor's G. H. Q. and all the pomp and circumstance of war are fine examples of studio stage-management, while the scenes amid the dreary salt marshes inspire horror by their sheer desolation. The interior work and many other scenes are far above the average. One error the producer makes, an error due either to thoughlessness or bad "cutting":—we see the great planes of the wind-mill at Calvaine motionless but when the fisher-girl leads her uncouth lover into the mill the grinding machinery is all working—a sheer impossibilty.

Roughly the story tells how a young Royalist refugee in England goes to offer his services to Napoleon. By accident he learns of a plot aganist the Emperor's life and is captured by the plotters. His life is saved, however, by a mysterious individual who turns out to be his uncle. Bernac, a relative who has advised him to join the Emperor but whom he has never met. This fellow is a crafty old scoundrel who runs the hare and hunts with the hounds, and is really a sort of agent provocateur. He wants Louis de Laval, the hero, to marry his own daughter Sibiylle and storm clouds gather when the young man announces his intention of remaining true to his sweetheart whom he has left in England.

This decision although incurring Bernac's enmity gains the friendship of the girl who loves one of the plotters, who as time proves, is a worthless backboneless dreamer. After many adventures during which Louis gains the friendship of Napoleon, Uncle Bernac is done to death by one of his dupes, Sibylle finds a more competent lover in a young staff officer, and Louis gets the girl he loves together with promotion and the Imperial blessing. One other error the producer permits himself, the village of Ashford, Kent, is a typical French hamlet. The acting is extremely good on all sides. Messieurs Drain and Chawmont give fine studies of Napoleon and Bernac respectively, but chief interest will centre round the Britisher, Rev. Davis, as Louis de Laval. Davis is the ideal hero, and enjoys a "rough house" as thorcughly as do his audiences. He is manly, sincere, and can play the hero without effeminancy or the aid of highly burnished "Marcelle" waved hair, affectations which ninety-nine out of a hundred of cur film actors apparently cannot do without no matter what type of part they are attempting to get over. He can act, and it is a matter of regret that so few opportunities are found for him at home.

Gore.

CANDYTUFT

London, July 5.

The producing firm wisely withholds its name as does the actual producer while the renters (Cosmograph), will certainly gain nothing, financially or otherwise.

"Candytuft:—I Mean Veronica" is yet another example of the foolishness of employing expensive stage casts and thinking that their names, despite the fact that even they are unknown outside London, will get a thin, badly produced, poorly acted story over. This film is without interest, strength, or humor, although the latter element might be said to be represented by a comic servant and a backboneless clergyman. It is without appeal, but it will not cause a single blush to rise to the cheeks of the most maidenly of prudes.

Veronica was called Candytuft by her parents. Arriving at the age of maturity she married Anstruther and passed into a world socially above and alien to her former sphere in life. The course of true love did not run smooth. She had ambitions while her husband was devoted to his garden. At last in desperation she demanded a male companion and Anstruther, most complacent of men, found her one in his old friend Westlake, who came in the guise of a bookworm.

This was not quite what Veronica was after, and she was further annoyed when she found her husband paying attention to a pretty girl, in reality the masquerading Westlake's fiancee. What with boredom and jealousy Veronica was soon cured of her naughtiness.

The acting is equal to the story and serves to strike home a truism that stage artists are seldom able to show their ability on the silent screen. Mary Glynne does little but look pretty and the rest of an expensive cast do their best with the material. Perhaps the unnamed producer was overawed by the greatness of his players.

Gore.

SIGN ON THE DOOR

Mrs. "Lafe" Regan	Norma Talmadge
"Lafe" Regan	Charles Richman
Frank Devereaux	Lew Cody
Colonel Gaunt	David Proctor
Ferguson	Augustus Balfour
"Kick" Callahan	Mack Barnes
Helen Regan	Helen Weir
Alan Churchill	Robert Agnew
Marjorie Blake	Martinle Burnlay
Whiting, Dist Atty	Paul McAllister
Inspector Trefty	Lew Hendricks
Bates, Regan butler	Walter Bussel

The play of this name by Channing Pollock was a Broadway hit. This First National feature presented by Joseph M. Schenck at the Strand with Norma Talmadge starred follows closely the lines of the play and the result is a melodrama suited to the market. But it fails to loose your enthusiasm, to start the riot it should. Why? The direction. On the continuity Mary Murillo collaborated with Herbert Brenon and between them they managed at times to carry the action forward almost entirely by use of titles, a bad and irritating fault.

Mr. Brenon's direction is the sort of direction criticized in English film offerings, stilted, set, inelastic. He seems to feel himself constantly confined within the four walls of the speaking stage. His touch is apparent in the acting, too. Miss Talmadge's reputation rests on her naturalness, the simple, straight-forward wistful appeal she gets onto the screen. But, thanks probably to the directing, she is here at times so much the actress it is apparent to a skilled observer. The careless abandon that is life itself has given way to a trained, well thought out attempt to make a graceful picture. The attempt succeeds, but for popular purposes is regrettable.

What has happened in a far lesser degree to Miss Talmadge almost ruins Charles Richman's performance. One of the ablest leading men, in this picture he stalks, struts, is forever a reminder of the artificiality so necessary to avoid in artistic copies of the action of life. Lew Cody escapes the general feeling so noticeable elsewhere in this production. So does Paul McAllister, and little Helen Weir was a hugable subdeb all the way. As an example of what happened, take the comedy relief in the scene among the youngsters where the boy and girl quarrel. Miss Weir came through it safely, but Robert Agnew acted as if he had rehearsed it 100 times before he appeared sufficiently ridiculous to suit the production judge.

As a background to all these objections is the opinion of the backgrounds themselves. For a time inserts were made so "artistic," so much over-decorated it was hard to read the titles. Now producers are encouraging a new fault, "artistic" scene sets and photography. Many of the scenes in "The Sign on the Door" are so shaded, blended, faded, as to obscure the action. In those half lighted interiors it is difficult to guess, let alone know, exactly what is going on, but at the end when Mr. Brenon began concentrating on that final cross examination he showed marked skill, emphasizing each point up to the punch—the "I believe you" of the District Attorney. This scored.

The story is well known. Devereaux, son of a rich man, tries to take advantage of his father's stenographer. The result is something embarrassing to her when she attempts years later to rescue her stepdaughter from this same man. The big situation is when her husband kills Devereaux in self-defense not knowing his wife is on the premises, and the final action is a swift, tense clearing of the whole situation.

Leed.

WHO AM I?

Ruth Burns	Claire Anderson
Victoria Danforth	Gertrude Asbor
Jimmy Weaver	Niles Welch
John Collins	George Periolat
Jacques Marbot	Joseph Swickard
Wm. Zoltz	Otto Hoffman

Lewis J. Selznick production released through National Pictures, Inc., authorship credited to Max Brand, screen version by Katherine Reed, directed by Henry Kolker. Story centers around boarding school bred daughter of a professional gambler. Her father's identity is unknown to the girl until his death when she is made his sole heir and inherits his gambling establishment. This she endeavors to operate in order to repay her father's manager for an alleged loan made just prior to his death. A love affair springs up between the girl and one of the hangers-on around the establishment, the chap endeavoring to give her the right mode of operating the place. There are several mystery angles introduced with the main one, the real identity of the girl whose lack of knowledge of her parents keeps her asking questions continually as to her real identity. The story as originally framed has the girl the daughter of a recluse while as worked out in the picture version she is left the daughter of the gambler. The love story is worked out with the inevitable finish with the girl and sweetheart giving up the gambling business when married. Selznick has selected two practically unknown players for his leads. Claire Anderson, as the girl, is apparently lacking in experience to handle a leading role with Niles Welch in a juvenile lead having had somewhat greater experience, but is inclined to over act his part having a certain chestyness about his work that detracts. The remainder of the cast fits in well enough with their parts, although the picture is not heavily fortified in any of its acting. Kolker has directed it in a satisfying manner, making as much out of a weak story and a light cast as could be expected. The production end stands up nicely being the picture's main asset. "Who Am I?" can be termed only a fair program picture.

LITTLE ITALY

Rosa Mascani	Alice Brady
Antonio Tumullo	Norman Kerry
Marco Mascani	George Fawcett
Father Kelly	Jack Ridgway
Anna	Gertrude Norman
Ricci	Luis Alberni
Bianca	Marguerite Forrest

Realart presents "Little Italy," an interesting character comedy-drama, at the Rivoli this week. It is the work of Frederic and Fannie Hatton, starring Alice Brady, who makes a remarkably convincing Italian girl. George Terwilliger directed the production, while Peter Milne adapted the story to the screen.

The story is really a modern genre version of "Romeo and Juliet," set in an Italian colony, presumably in Jersey or Staten Island, and takes its principal interest from the amusing presentation of types. One of the best of them is done by George Fawcett as the father of the heroine, a new departure for that sterling actor.

The Hattons, who wrote "Lombardi, Ltd.," know their Latin-Americans, and this screen creation always has the stamp of authenticity and sincerity. Perhaps the backgrounds are a bit untidy and unpicturesque but the people themselves are very real and interesting and the story holds interest to the end, with several good dramatic moments and capital comedy incidents.

Rosa Moscani (Miss Brady) is a headstrong girl wooed by "The Fox," a political leader of the colony. Her family has brought to America a blood feud with the Tumillos, residents in the same suburban village. Antonio Tumillo returns a hero from the European war, and Rosa, disguised as a boy, attends a masquerade ball given in his honor. Antonio falls in love with Rosa, but she hates him with all the violence of a Latin feudist.

Because she refuses all suitors Rosa's father is about to drive her from home, when she vows she will wed the first man she meets. The man happens to be Antonio. They are married with the aid of a priest who hopes (in the manner of Friar Lawrence) to heal the feud. It's an unhappy household. Rosa refuses to be reconciled to her husband, who patiently hopes her bitterness will some day vanish.

Rosa, after a few months away, takes refuge with a cousin in the Bronx. Here her baby is born. Meanwhile "The Fox" secretly spreads the word among the villagers that Antonio has done away with Rosa, and a mob goes to Antonio's house to deal out justice. With the baby in her arms, Rosa makes up her mind that she really loves Antonio and is traveling back to him. She reaches the village just as the angry mob is closing in on Antonio.

The fight on the street is at its height when Rosa passes by in a village taxi and by her appearance alive rescues her husband. The happy finale thereupon comes about.

The picture is ultra modern and doubtless an intimate sketch of Italian life around the metropolis. There is nothing of the squalid immigrant atmosphere. All the characters are well off. The Moscanis are well-to-do florists and have their own cars. But the truck farming farmers are a dingy lot and there is little of beauty in the locale of the picture. This is its only defect, for the story is interesting and the character sketches clear cut.

Rush.

THE SILVER CAR

Anthony Trent	Earle Williams
Daphne Grenvil	Kathlyn Adams
Arthur Grenvil	Geoffrey Webb
Count Michael Temesvar	Eric Mayne
Earl of Rosecarrel	Emmett King
Pauline	Mona Lisa
Vicar	John Steppling
Hentzi	Max Asher
Colonel Langley	Walter Rodgers

The general run of picture-goers will enjoy the "suspense" of "The Silver Car," written by Wyndham Martyn, directed by David Smith—a Vitagraph production starring Earle Williams. To the sophisticated—that is those who patronize the better grade of first-run houses, the feature will be regarded as melodramatic clap-trap. An intenational crook with a reward of $25,000 on his head enlists under an assumed name. No one knows his identity as he always "works" alone. The son of an English Earl is also in the army in his uncle's regiment under an assumed name, having committed forgery. Both have been "sterilized" by the war. The young Englishman saves the life of the American crook, but at a moment when it looks as if both will die the American confesses his identity and the Englishman says the only one who knows his real name is his colonel.

Both are saved, the American seeks the English youth who knows his secret and holds his future in his hands, robs the colonel's safe to learn the name of his benefactor, meets the sister, falls in love with her; the Earl is compelled to seek retirement from public life because Count Michael of Malmatia holds a political paper; the American goes to Malmatia to secure the paper and does so after a series of impossibly daring ordeals; the mistress of Count Michael of Malmatia falls in love with the American and is shot for aiding him and in the end the American marries the daughter of the Earl. It might also be mentioned that her brother is suffering from shellshock and doesn't remember the American's confession.

The proletariat are sure to revel in the international political intrigues concerning "the papers" and the palpably fake overturning of an automobile, a terrific dive by the hero from a cliff into the water, and so on. But, as before remarked, in the more popular-priced cinemas the audiences will devour the story voraciously. It is all about people in "society" and the atmosphere of English "high life" is depicted as we fondly believe it is.

Earl Williams is his usual stilted self, cinematographically corect, immaculately clad, even when he disguises himself as a chauffer and his followers will continue to think he is "just grand" as the hero-crook. Eric Mayne as Count Michael, gives a fine portrayal of the haughty Malmatian villain; Kathlyn Adams is sweetly plump as the heroine, Emmett King is sufficiently dignified as the Earl and Geoffrey Webb is a pleasing juvenile.

The direction, settings, photography and lighting are of a very high order.

Jolo.

STRAIGHT FROM PARIS

Lucette	Clara Kimball Young
John Van Austen	W. P. Carleton
Robert Van Austen	Bertram Grassby
Ada Van Austen	Clarissa Selwyne
Claude Grenier	Thomas Jefferson
Doris Charming	Betty Francisco

This should go through the sticks and make them yell for more. Clara Kimball Young is starred in it by Equity Pictures and it was seen recently at the Loew houses here where it went over well. Sada Cowan wrote it and Harry Garson directed. It has everything melodrama should have to hit the masses right and Miss Young is like it. By the same token it is far removed from that austere improvement hoped for in pictures.

Lucette Grenier is a milliner and young Van Austen, member of the 400, falls in love with her. His family, of course, are opposed and the plot is off to a running start. In this picture, purity and general superiority of the milliner to the supposedly well bred members of New York's rich social set is proved by Uncle John who intends to force the acceptance of Lucette as his nephew's fiancee because he likes Lucette. The method he employs is neat.

He makes love to Lucette and she turns him down, thus proving her virtue and she is invited to a party at the Van Austens. Meanwhile, Robert renews his affair with a little chorus girl. At the party Lucette's grandfather comes in drunk to rescue his grand child from the wicked wiles of the 400. Lucette breaks her engagement only to be claimed in marriage by Uncle John who is a millionaire.

What more could exhibitors ask in the way of a story? They get in addition Miss Young's adept ability at screen work and her display of gowns. These are too low cut for a modest girl, but then people like that. The supporting cast, too, is excellent, Thomas Jefferson standing out by his portrayal of the old grandfather.

Leed.

UNWILLING HERO

Dick	Will Rogers
Nadine	Molly Malone
Hunter	John Bowers
Richmond	Darrel Foss
Boston Harry	Jack Curtis
Hobo	George Kunkle
Hobo	Dick Johnson
Hobo	Larry Fisher
Hobo	Leo Willis
Negro Servant	Nick Cogley
Lovejoy	Ed. Kimball

"An Unwilling Hero," made by Goldwyn from the O. Henry story, ing." at the Capitol, last week. ing." and current at the Capitol, introduces Will Rogers in one of the best comedy character sketches he has so far created for the screen. He plays a philosophical hobo, with a powerful distaste for work and baths, but a quaint outlook upon life and a gift for whistling. As a story the feature doesn't amount to anything at all, but with the inspired playing of Rogers and a certain deft handling of high comedy atmosphere, it stands out as a gem.

No other star or no other production comes to mind that has achieved any droller delineation of a comedy type than Roger's Whistling Dick in this production. It is high class portraiture, boldly drawn and deftly sketched and tinted. Clarence G. Badger is credited with the direction. He has made the slight story beautifully simple and direct, although its appeal depends upon its rich detail. There are only six characters identified in the cast and the light story is always clear cut and comprehensible.

Rogers himself wrote the titles and these printed interludes, with their amusing philosophy, neatly and tersely put, are a major part of the film. At the opening Rogers as Whistling Dick is ambling along a country road; ragged and lightly clad against the the autumn wind that blows the leaves about his half shod feet. A line of wild ducks flies past.

"Just to show I've got as much sense as a duck," muses Dick, "I'll go south, too."

He reaches New Orleans by the side-door Pullman with many sage observations by the way. Meeting up with a gang of yeggs in the outskirts of the Crescent City, he learns of a plot to rob a nearby plantation and leaves the company with no taste for such an adventure. On the road again his whistling of an opera air catches the attention of a girl driving into town and the dusty tramp and she strike up a humorous friendship.

It turns out that she is the daughter of the planter the yeggs plan to rob and Dick is instrumental in frustrating the holdup. He is accepted into the household as a hero and made much of. The conversation gives opportunity for many humorous titles in Rogers' best vein.

"Now that we have prohibtion," says one of the guests, "I suppose they'll stop tobacco and profanity next."

"While there is a prohibitionist left," replies Dick, "they cannot stop profanity."

Dick then is set for a life of prosperity as the planter's ward and protege. But they try to make him take a bath and promise him work. Dick awakes with the sun and looks from his bedroom window to see the happy farm hands go singing to their work. He slips into his old coat, stealthily drops from his bedroom window and the final fadeout shows him disappearing down the road, shuffling contentedly along and whistling.

The picture translates to the screen the very spirit of O. Henry himself in its quaint humor and deft human touches. *Bush.*

A BROKEN DOLL

"A Broken Doll" is an Allan Dwan production, scenarioized from Wilbur Hall's Saturday Evening Post Story "Johnny Cucabod"—an Associated Producers' release. Monte Blue is featured and Mary Thurman is the leading lady.

As a picture story it lacks action, being the study of a "sweet, simple" character, an orphan man who loves mankind, womankind and animalkind. It revolves around his love for a crippled child, the daughter of the ranchman for whom he works. Through an accident the youngster's doll is broken, he has no money to replace it and even goes so far as to steal from one of the other men to get her a new one. If he had been possessed of a semblance of ordinary intelligence he could have gone to either of the child's parents, explained the circumstances and they would have given him the money. But the character, as depicted, is nothing more than a simpleton—one might almost say half-witted. He accidentally captures an escaped convict, earns the reward and marries the rich sheriff's daughter. How so intelligent a young lady could take him for a husband isn't easy to figure out.

Monte Blue plays the role nicely with fine facial expression. If only the scenario gave him something "manly" to do that would stamp him as a picture hero one might forgive the draggy tale. His scenes with the child (who by the way is a good actress) are sweet and tender, but that isn't enough to sustain a full length feature. As it struggles along it degenerates into pathos and becomes monotonous. The direction, acting and photography are satisfactory, but the tale is twadol. *Jolo.*

COINCIDENCE

Billy Jenks..............Robert Harron
Phoebe Howard...........June Walker
Brent................Bradley Barker
Stephen Fiske..........Wm. Frederic
John Carter.............Frank Belcher
Dorothy Carter..........June Terry

This is a Robert Harron picture made over a year ago for Metro by Chet Withey and now being released. Howard E. Morton wrote the original story and Brian Hooker the scenario. Half the sting of the incredible mass of coincidences that go to make up the plot is taken away by the title which admits the fault and justifies it by a series of scenes in the beginning showing our hero as a bank clerk out of town. He comes to New York. A bank bill blown out of a window brings him in contact with the girl he is to marry.

There follows a fortune inherited, stolen, rescued. These coincidences rather take the breath away, but there is lots of pleasant action and Harron's charm and the capable support of June Walker and a competent cast help make the offering acceptable. *Leed.*

CHILDREN OF THE NIGHT

A first rate Fox program feature showing now around Loew's New York circuit. Max Brand wrote the story. Jack Dillon directed, showing especial competency for his job in the handling of some perfect fighting toward the end, every second of it crammed with action and really thrilling. The girls will like this. It is romance with a capital R, and action of the heroic sort.

William Russell is starred and shows to good purpose as the hero of the dream for this story spends most of its time telling the action of a dream. Russell is a clerk in a brokerage house and in love with the stenographer. To him it seems a prosaic sort of existence and he falls to imagining at his desk, seeing himself a wealthy man and the center of a scheme to rob him of his best girl. Beset by blackmailers, to save their lives she gives herself up to the gang. He goes to rescue her and is told an effective story by the head of the gang which parallels his own situation. Drugged by a cigarette while he listens, he is thrown into a cellar and recovers in time to save the girl in a peach of a row, full of suspense.

Action, romance at their best. Here is the better type of picture, sex stuff nicely camouflaged for the market. *Leed.*

DAUGHTER OF DEVIL DAN

Buffalo Motion Picture Co. production, featuring Irma Harrison and Kempton Greene. Regulation program feature with hackneyed tale. Just "listen" to this summary of its high spots. High-spirited daughter of Louisville gentleman with gray moustache and imperiale, married "Devil Dan" against her father's wishes and Dan is killed by a moonshiner. Young wife is seen on her deathbed, unforgiven by irate father. She gives villainous attorney "the papers" and her seven-year-old daughter. He steals the fortune and takes the child to the moonshiner's hut. Ten years pass. Child is young girl, uncouth and unkempt, but buxom. Dashing young revenue officer appears. She saves his life and escapes disguised as a boy.

Young revenue officer visits girl's grandfather (son of his old schoolmate stuff). They walk on street and find girl as newsboy in a fight. They take her home, old colonel wants to adopt her. She explores garret in colonial home, finds crinoline dress her mother wore, dons it, old colonel sees resemblance to his daughter, cries: "My search for my granddaughter has ended." Villainous lawyer and moonshiner kidnap girl and ride horseback with her to their hut in a few moments. One never knew before there were moonshine stills on the outskirts of Louisville. Young revenue officer to the rescue, villain-lawyer (who turns out to be hero's uncle) is shot in the melee, confesses and the clinch is finally arrived at after fifty-five minutes of footage that seems like ninety-five minutes.

The acting is on a par with the story, but the direction seemed far superior to the material given the megaphone man to work with. A pretty colonial interior was the only set of any pretension. *Jolo.*

THE SCARAB RING

Constance Randall..........Alice Joyce
Muriel Randall..........Maude Malcolm
Ward Locke...............Joe King
Burton Temple............E. Ph'lip
John Randall.........Fuller Mellish
Hugh Martin.............Claude King
James Locke...........Joseph Smiley
Mr. Kheres..............Jack Hopkins
Kennedy................Armand Cortez

A well wrought, suspensive melodrama with a surprise denouncement is "The Scarab Ring," scenario by Helen Gaylord, directed by Edward Jose, starring Alice Joyce—a Vitagraph production. But clever as it is, all connected with it overlooked a vital defect that, when brought to one's attention, makes one smile indulgently.

It opens with a respected banker on his death bed, asking his elder daughter's forgiveness for having been a blackguard and a thief and asking her to swear she would not reveal his secret to the younger daughter. She swears.

The younger girl, Muriel, is loved by a youth of her own years and the elder, Constance, by a young lawyer whose father is a great criminal attorney. Hugh Martin, a former business associate of the father, holds papers proving the double life the banker led and threatens Constance that unless she persuades Muriel to marry him he will give the story to the newspapers.

Martin is found murdered in his apartment one night and a scarab ring is found on the floor by the police. Constance is arrested charged with the murder, being unable to prove where she was that evening. Her lawyer-lover gets her acquitted at the trial by producing a duplicate scarab which even the Oriental from whom it was originally purchased is unable to distinguish from the genuine.

On Constance's refusal to marry her lover his father questions her and she tells (flashback) that she was in Martin's apartment and did kill him, but it is shown it was in self-defense and when the father puts it up to his son to decide if he will marry Constance whether she be guilty or not the noble hero says he doesn't care what she did—he has faith in her integrity, and all ends happily. In the flashback is shown Constance telephoning Martin for an appointment the fatal night. The first thing the police would have done—one of the first things at any rate—would be to examine the phone records for just such a call.

Miss Joyce sustains the role with a dignity and womanliness that commands admiration for her art. She never once overacts, avoids all "Oh my Gawds," etc., and conducts herself throughout like a human being—

a well bred lady. The supporting cast is fully competent and the direction intelligent throughout—with the one faux pas, the phone call. However could they let that pass?

An excellent program feature. *Jolo.*

DON'T NEGLECT YOUR WIFE

Madeline..........Mabel Julienne Scott
Langdon Masters........Lewis S. Stone
Dr. Howard Talbot........Charles Clary
Mrs. Hunt McLane..........Kate Lester
Mr. Hunt McLane.......R. D. MacLean
Ben Travers..............Arthur Hoyt
Mrs. Abbott..........Josephine Crowell
Holt....................Darrell Foss
Sybyl Geary.............Norma Gordon
George Geary...........Richard Tucker

Goldwyn puts this feature out, making great trumpeting of the fact that it is "Gertrude Atherton's First Original Screen Story." It is current at the Capitol, has Mabel Julienne Scott, Lewis S. Stone, Charles Clary, Kate Lester, et al., and was directed by Wallace Worsley.

"Don't Neglect Your Wife" is utter literary junk as far as its story is concerned, although no more painstaking bit of technical directorship has come upon the screen this long time. It is a grievous sin that so much effort should go into the filming of a tale so childish, so crude, so amateurish that without Mrs. Atherton's name it probably never would have got past the junior manuscript shock absorber in the Goldwyn scenario department. In her novels Mrs. Atherton is perhaps America's most finished dealer in subtleties. She writes in a vein of exquisite super-refinement. Her fiction is delicate embroidery, deft analysis and exposition of shades and tones of human emotion and impulse.

If "Don't Neglect Your Wife" is her mature work she has suffered a horrifying reversal of form, for the story might have been written by a schoolgirl of 18. It is so moistly sobful with sticky, syrupy juvenile sentiment it seems unbelievable that it could have been written by the novelist, of whom it has been said "she can pirouette on a needle point." Sunday night the audience at the Capitol giggled unrestrainedly during the picture's most moving passages. One guess is that somebody, whether with the connivance of the author, has resurrected a very early effort of Mrs. Atherton's and given it to the world.

Perhaps it was by design, perhaps by accident, that the Capitol management elected to put on the program a Mack Sennett-Ben Turpin comedy called "Love's Outcast," a shrieking travesty on the hyper-sentimental story. It might have been a deliberate burlesque of the Atherton film, it came so pat. If deliberate, it had all the elements of a dirty dig.

"Don't Neglect Your Wife" is set in San Francisco (where Mrs. Atherton has been living these many years) in the early '60s. The period gives it a certain interest as a costume play, the costumes and settings being done in a thoroughly painstaking and convincing way. Madeline is neglected by her club-going husband, Dr. Howard Talbot, and falls in love with Langdon Masters, the editor. Gossip goes the rounds and leads to disclosure. Discovered by the husband in a situation innocent but open to conjecture, and barred from divorce by the narrow-minded social prejudice of the fashionable set of the day, Masters and Madeline separate.

Masters leaves San Francisco and is next discovered in the squalor and vice of the Five Points, New York's lowest social level, where he seeks to drink himself to death. Madeline, still in San Francisco, decides she also will bump herself off by the fusil oil route. Husband tries to restrain her, but she threatens to throw herself to des-truct-ion from yonder window and he frees her to go her way. Presently she is a frequenter of "The Golden Gate," a San Francisco dive, putting three-star away at the speed limit, but, bless you, still pure.

Word comes that Masters is falling lower and lower in licker and degredation and she determines to "go to him," as Laura Jean says, e'en though he be in the Five Points. There are intermittent shots of Masters in his slum environment and he has indeed fallen low.

He consorts with the wild women of an unsavory dive called "The Bucket of Blood" and is a veritable cinema wreck, except that he continues to be a matinee idol for neatness. Realism slips a little here.

The denoument comes when Madeline tracks him down to this disgraceful resort and by her gentle presence regenerates him.

The record would not be complete without a recital of the "dramatic climax" which takes place in "The Bucket of Blood." Upon Madeline's entrance an unwholesome drab of the resort is making desperate love to the fallen editor and resents the apparition of the fine lady who would interrupt her wooing. Whereupon the two, Madeline, who previously was described as a "woman of exquisite delicacy," and the belle of "The Bucket of Blood" literally go to the mat with hair pulling and other violence.

At one point in the tale the editor is moved to exclaim, apropos of Madeline, "What a Woman." Some Woman is right. And by Gertrude Atherton! ! !

Rush.

MYSTERY ROAD

Gerald Dombey...........David Powell
Myrtile Sargot........Nadja Ostrovska
Christopher Went.......Pardoe Woodman
Lady Susan Farrington....Mary Glynne
Vera Lypasht...............Ruby Miller
Luigi...................Percy Standing
Jean Sargot..............Lewis Gilbert
Widow Dumesnel...........Irene Tripod
Pierre Naval.........Lionel D'Aragon
Earl of Farrington........Arthur Cullin
The Vagabond............R. Judd Green
The Priest...............Ralph Foster

Famous Players-Lasky British Producers, Ltd., made this feature from a story by E. Phillips Oppenheim and Paul Powell directed it admirably. Paramount is presenting it this week at the Rialto with David Powell and an exceptional cast interpreting it along lines laid down in the scenario by Margaret Turnbull. The continuity's fault is in allowing too much pictorial footage to explain the runaway girl. An insert saying she ran away because she didn't want to marry would have sufficed. As it stands the whole flow of the story is interrupted for 500 feet or so to establish this incident.

But this is perhaps carping. Anything Miss Turnbull or her brother touch gain in force and distinction from the contact and Mr. Powell's direction here bears out every promise. He handles his players with economy. That is, their abilities are presented in condensed form and so count for considerable. Also he had an unusual cast to work with. Mary Glynne in particular standing out. In this picture she is suppose to be an English aristocrat. She looks just that. Anything but a doll, she has brought to the screen a new type, charming, interesting, intriguing and yet distinguished all the way.

As a matter of fact, as we understand the term in this country and particularly in the picture world, there isn't a pretty girl in this feature, but it is doubly interesting for that lack. Nadja Ostrovska and Ruby Miller both gave performances that caught and held your attention while Percy Standing made his bit of blackguardism stand out. Again in Pardoe Woodman we have anything but a handsome man and yet the simplicity and sincerity of his performance stood out. David Powell plays an unpleasant role.

All together an unusual production based on a plot anything but the accepted thing in pictures. It starts off with a seduction bit as perfect in its screening as Griffith's birth scene in "Way Down East." Dombey is something of a libertine and so when he comes to marry Lady Susan she has her doubts. On the way to Nice to visit her, he picks up a runaway girl, takes her with him to Nice, dolls her up and presents her to his family. Went's interest in Lady Susan was previously suggested by a mere "Will Lady Susan be there?" and this counted for volumes. That is what people like the Turnbulls have brought to pictures—something different. The best tricks in literature they know, but better even than the eminent converts now fooling around out in Hollywood they know how to apply their knowledge.

Dombey, meanwhile, has started a new affair with the village girl with whom he started the picture. This ends in a row and when she is disposed of and Lady Susan prefers another, he is left to marry the runaway girl.

A different ending. No sugar sentiment. How will it go in the country. Possibly, being truer than Pollyanna stuff, it may catch on. Let us hope so.

Leed.

NOBODY

Little Mrs. Smith........Jewel Carmen
John Rossmore.......William Davidson
Tom Smith.............Kenneth Harlan
Mrs. Fallon...........Florence Billings
Hedges................J. Herbert Frank
Mrs. Rossmore..........Grace Studiford
Hiram Swanzey..........George Fawcett
Norton Ailsworth.........Lionel Pape
Rossmore's Secretary......Henry Sedley
Mrs. Van Cleek.............Ida Darling
Clyde Durand..........Charles Wellesley
Rossmore's Skipper...William DeGrasse
The "Grouch" Juror........Riley Hatch

Some years ago there was produced in vaudeville a sketch called "Circumstantial Evidence," wherein one of 12 jurors held out against 11 others, refusing to vote "guilty" on a prisoner whose life they held in their hands. In the end the "stubborn" one confesses he is the culprit and drops dead in the jury room.

Roland West has utilized a similar situation, having the husband of the guilty woman as the obdurate juryman, confessing after 30 hours and the members of the jury swearing to keep his secret. He has made of it an intensely absorbing photoplay for Jewel Carmen, which should give general satisfaction to First National franchise holders.

What happened before the trial is told in a series of flashbacks that include genuine scenes at Palm Beach, a millionaire's yacht, etc., all calculated to inspire open-mouthed awe to the proletariat, giving the already elongated arm of coincidence an additional wrench. Then, to add still more spice and mystery the flashback shows the crime was done by the young wife "prompted by her subconscious mind." She has been ravished by a lecherous millionaire, which resulted in an attack of aphasia, the following day starts for New York from Palm Beach, fails to recognize her home or her husband, eludes the nurse, goes to the home of the villain, fires half a dozen shots into his midriff, picks up her cloak, goes back home to bed, wakes up thoroughly normal and believes she dreamed the whole thing.

While the other inmates of the rich man's home attempt to break down the locked door the young wife calmly walks out of another door and it never occurs to any of the others to go to the door through which she made her exit. In spite of these inconsistencies it is a reasonably safe prediction that "Nobody" will satisfy 90 per cent of the picture attendance, who do not analyze so closely.

As a program film production "Nobody" ranks with the best of the drawing room melodramas. The photography is brilliant at times and the cast wholly satisfactory throughout. Miss Carmen has the difficult role of the aphasia victim and handles it intelligently. J. Herbert Frank stands out strongly as the butler accused of the crime; Kenneth Harlan is excellent as the young husband and William Davidson is natural and non-theatric as the defiling millionaire. Such sterling film artists as Riley Hatch, George Fawcett and others are cast for insignificant roles.

Jolo.

LURING LIPS

A Fox release with Edith Roberts, the story of a wrongly accused bank clerk, convicted and sent to prison for one year. His wife (Miss Roberts) during his imprisonment, vamps along the president or cashier of the bank, to the point where she agrees to elope with him to South America on the day her husband is released from jail. At the steamship dock they all meet, with the president hauled in carrying a bag containing the $50,000 the clerk was sent away for stealing, with the finish the clerk securing the cashier's job.

About the one novelty bit in the film is the reproduction of a picture show in the prison, wherein the husband-convict sees his wife meet the banker in Trinity churchyard, New York. That entails mental stress through jealousy and is the only imaginative point of the picture. In its scope, the entire direction may be mildly commended. Otherwise excepting for a little different twist to the story here and there, the thing has been done threadbare in pictures. There is nothing attractive about it or the playing.

"Luring Lips" was one-half of a double feature bill at the New York.

Sime.

GREAT MOMENT

Nada Pelham / Nadine Pelham ....Gloria Swanson
Sir Edward Pelham.....Alex B. Francis
Bayard Delavel...............Milton Sills
Eustace......................F. R. Butler
Hopper......................Arthur Hull
Lord Crombie.....Raymond Brathwayt
Lady Crombie..............Helen Dunbar
Bronson...............Clarence Geldart
Sadi Bronson...................Julia Faye
Blenkensop.........................Ann Grigg

"The Great Moment" (Paramount) is "presented by Jesse L. Lasky." Scenario is by Monte Katterjohn and direction by Sam Wood under the supervision of Thompson Buchanan. The picture is current at the Rivoli. Elinor Glyn contrived the story and it is typically in her vein of gusty passion, a bit labored in its literary devices, but nevertheless effective and it ought to be a first rate summer business getter, particularly among the women fans.

The production must have represented a large outlay of money. There are numerous massive scenes and throughout the settings look costly. One in particular is a midnight revel staged by a Washington millionaire spendthrift which called for a large number of people, much costuming and a studio tank water setting that probably represented a bill like a New York Hippodrome ballet ensemble.

The production throughout is thoroughly adequate and the money has been well spent. This is a case where magnificence of backgrounds is demanded by the story. It is an exotic idea of a young English girl, brought up in the austere atmosphere of her titled father's home but swayed by the gypsy blood of her dead mother.

The formula is distinctly Elinor Glyn's.

Nada's father, Sir Edward, selects as her husband her cousin Eustace to whom the entailed estate goes, a sappy looking, stolid British youth, but Nada gets a glimpse of Bayard Delavel, an American engineer, in a hurried visit to the estate to report on mining properties and falls in love. Delavel departs before she has met him, but later Sir Edward decides he must visit the mining properties and takes Nada with him.

The party goes on an inspection tour of the Nevada mine, wayward Nada, Papa, the handsome engineer and half a dozen others. Nada and Delavel become separated from the others on a mountain peak where Delavel has built himself a solitary shack, and here comes the kick—a very neat bit of tropical fiction.

Nada drops her glove and as she stoops to pick it up a rattlesnake strikes her in the chest somewhere below the decolletage line. Her life is in danger; the engineer must act in defiance of all the rules of convention. He must open the snake bite with his clasp knife. Nada shrinks away modestly; the situation is urgent and Delavel seizes her, tears her waist open, makes the incision and sucks the poison out, the catch-as-catch-can struggle involved going a long way to heighten the effect.

Delavel then carries the girl to his shack and applies the ancient remedy of pouring raw whiskey down her throat. The combination of alcohol and Nada's gypsy blood get in their insidious work and when the father and Eustace come up in search of the missing pair, they are in the midst of what has all the appearance of a loving embrace. There are misunderstandings and recriminations and Delavel is ordered forthwith "to marry the girl," which he proceeds to do.

Then the angry father and Fiance Eustace depart, disowning Nada the Shameless (as they suppose, although it is made plain that the whole chain of circumstances has been innocent). Delavel is conscience stricken, believing that he has taken advantage of a girl "while her senses were drugged," as the title puts it. He straightway secures an annulment of the hasty marriage, and Nada goes to live with friends in the British embassy at Washington.

But all the time she has been in love with Delavel and plunges into the dissipations of the capital's fast set to forget her sorrows. She becomes involved with a rich bounder and is about to marry him in pique, when the now repentant father sends for Delavel and they are reconciled.

Probably the one minor defect of the story is that it is rather scattered and diffuse and strung out too long by obvious trick and device. It is apparent long before the end that a reconciliation is in order and it would have been well to get to it promptly instead of inventing new transparent obstacles to the embrace when it was patently in prospect.

Nevertheless it is an absorbing story, particularly for the feminine public, with novel touches, very modern arguments touching the new woman's demand for freedom in choosing her mate and the story involves a first rate element of suspense. It is especially well acted.

Rush.

ROAD TO LONDON

Here's a whale of a novelty idea, conceived by David Skaate Foster and sponsored by Lee A. Ochs. Direction is by Eugene Muller and distribution in the hands of Associated Exhibitors, Inc., via Pathe. Bryant Washburn is the star. So much for statistics.

Briefly, the scheme is this. Devise a sprightly romance in which the rich young American visiting London is appealed to by a beautiful titled English girl in Picadilly Circus to save her from her aunt, the Duchess, who plots to marry her off to a worthless viscount. Bring about their flight together in a stolen auto and their pursuit by the aunt and viscount through all the most beautiful historic spots in Surrey. The net result is an interesting sublimated moving picture chase with comedy and romantic incidents and a wealth of suspense. As it works out Mr. Ochs has given us a travelogue strung along a romantic story. Burton Holmes could not have done the job better pictorially.

In all the five reels there is scarcely an interior and the only background that carries the slightest suspicion of a studio set comes at the end. The rest is made up of absorbing shots of historic London—Trafalgar Square, Charing Cross, Westminster, Parliament, London Bridge, Park Lane, and an exquisite series of views of the open country about the upper reaches of the Thames. It is hard to say whether the settings for the elopement comedy is subordinated to the story or the interesting story is subordinate to the capital record of a most interesting travel subject.

Both contribute splendid elements to the production. There are innumerable good touches of good comedy, deft character drawing, compelling situations and other good elements of screen values. For example, our hero at a critical moment in the escape (the stolen auto runs out of gas) finds that he has left all his money at the Savoy when he changed his clothes and he is hard put to it throughout the escape to bluff his way through. The Duchess is constantly losing her purse and delaying the pursuit and there is first rate humor in the phrasing of the titles, although there is an over-abundance of printed matter on the screen. Also as a virtue to American audiences, Yankee shrewdness and pep is pitted against British stolidity in a victorious contest.

The whole thing has the stamp of originality. The views of well known London points of interest are exceedingly well done and the production has a good deal of educational value, sugar coated and made palatable by the thread of romantic story. Everybody likes a chase and here is one continuous five-reel carnival of it with rich in incident and unflagging interest.

The story is skilfully put together so that suspense lasts until the final moment. The hero carries off the heroine and goes through 5,000 feet of narrow escapes from the pursuers, only near the end to rush her to a parson in Windsor where the marriage is performed, and then have her snatched away by the aunt and her unwelcome fiance. They hold her prisoner in their Park Lane mansion, while the discouraged husband, informed that the girl is a minor and the marriage is illegal, takes passage for home on the Olympic, the bridal suite having been engaged.

Arriving on the ship he goes to his cabin heartbroken, only to find his bride awaiting him as the ship heads **to sea, having escaped with the aid of her maid.**

A fine sincere effort, adequately and expertly registered on the screen. And also a distinct relief from the problem and sex play. *Rush.*

DANGER AHEAD

Tressie Harlow	Mary Philbin
Norman Minot	James Morrison
Robert Kitteridge	Jack Mower
Deborah Harlow	Minna Ferry Redman
Nate Harlow	George Bunny
Maj. Minot	George B. Williams
Dolly Demere	Jane Starr
Mrs. Della Mayhew	Emily Rait
Dora Mayhew	Helen Caverly

A machine-made Universal feature with Mary Philbon promoted to stardom. Story by Sarah Bassett, scenario by A. P. Younger, from Miss Bassett's novel "The Harbor Road," directed by Rollin Sturgeon. The director has done well with the material at hand, diving into U's excellent film morgue and utilizing the running down of a sailboat by a huge freighter in a fog.

Tressie is the ingenue in a small fishing village. Her aunt and uncle take in boarders. Juvenile comes to board and falls in love with Tressie. All this occurs in the first few hundred feet, so you needn't wait for the rest, unless you want to see the villain lure Tressie to his studio and attempt to ravish her. There is, however, a variation of the rescue. Instead of the lover arriving on time to save Tressie, the door is broken in by a female athlete who is smitten with the villain. She sees him with the "chicken," removes her dress (hers, not the chicken's) and proceeds to wipe the floor with said villain. When a woman friend of hers attempts to help out, she shoves her aside, saying: "You leave my man alone."

Tiresome even for a program feature. *Jolo.*

FRAGMENTS

Berlin, July 13.

"Fragments" (Scherben) the latest Rex Film of the Ufa, produced simultaneously at the U. T. Kurfuerstendamm and the Mozart Saal, is one of those exceptional films about which one can take one's hand off the critical throttle and open her up wide. Owing to the unrelievedly tragic nature of the story, however, it can expect no great international financial success; but as it cost next to nothing to make, a neat profit will be turned in. And from an artistic angle it is one of the big events of the year.

The scenario by Carl Meyer concerns a signalman (Bahnwaerter) whose daughter is seduced by an inspector of the railway company. While the Bahnwaerter is on his nightly rounds, his wife finds how things stand and rushes out of the house to throw herself at the foot of a wayside crucifix, where, as the time is winter, she freezes to death by morning. The daughter, refused marriage by the inspector, half madly tells all to her father, who strangles her betrayer and, stopping the next train, speaks the only caption of the film, "I am a murderer."

Thus briefly outlined, it does not sound over-original, but the simple, almost bromidic nature of the story leaves the director (Lupu Pick) free practically to do away with the caption and concentrate on character achieved through pantomime alone. Yes, actually, we get some real glimpse into the feelings and outlook on life of such people as this Bahnwaerter, living practically cut off from all civilization, tramping day and night, winter and summer up and down the same section of track. Just to give one characteristic example of how this note of eternal deadening monotony is struck. The film begins not with a shot of the Bahnwaerter going his rounds but with a two-minute close-up of track passing along before us as though we ourselves were walking it with eyes bent on the ground. In other words we are given things and events, not as they appear to us, the casual observers, but rather as they appear to such routine deadened slaves as inhabit the world of this film. And this revolutionary method is sustained throughout the entire five reels.

The handling of the acting ensemble is excellent. Werner Kraus here as the Bahnwaerter gives a characterization worthy to stand comparison with his Caligari; his work alone is worth the price of admission.

LIVE WIRES

Bob Harding	Johnnie Walker
Rena Austin	Edna Murphy
Mrs. Harding	Alberta Lee
James Harding	Frank Clarke
Slade	Bob Klein
James Flannery	Hayward Mack
Austin	Wilbur Higby
The Coach	Lefty James

The Fox News Weekly has been utilized for inserts in "Live Wires" story by Edward Sedgwick and Charles Emerson Cook, scenario by Jack Strumwasser, directed by Sedgwick.

It's a story about a manly college boy who starts in to run the family farm when his father dies suddenly. His mother signs a paper which is an option to sell the property for $1,000, on payment of $1,000. The villain who gets the option knows the railroad will pay $25,000 for it. But his sweetheart's father, who has been tricked and blackmailed by the villain, steals the option from the villain's pocket and the boy goes back to college to play on the football game. Without his aid his college team can't win. The villain has a bunch of thugs kidnap the youth, tie him up in a barn, he gets out and in order to arrive at the game in time, leaps from the roof of the moving train to a rope ladder suspended from an aeroplane, arriving at the dramatic moment.

The aeroplane stunt and scenes at the football game are palpably inserts from the News Weekly, ingenously interwoven with the progression of the melodrama, which is unoriginal and commonplace.

A cheap program feature.

Jolo.

THUNDERCLAP

Mrs. Jamieson	Mary Carr
Lionel Jamieson	J. Barney Sherry
Tommy	Paul Willis
Betty, the Baby	Carol Chase
Betty, the Girl	Violet Mersereau
Wah Leong	John Daly Murphy
Foster	Walter McEwan
Marian Audrey	Maude Hill
Gunga Din	Thomas McCann

"Thunderclap" is one of a new group of William Fox features put on in New York legitimate houses to succeed "Over the Hill," "A Connecticut Yankee" and "The Queen of Sheba." It opened July 30 at the Central. The scenario is by Paul H. Sloane and Richard Stanton directed the filming. Mary Carr (the mother in "Over the Hill") and J. Barney Sherry are featured.

As a picture it is a boisterous, unrestrained melodrama, matching in its implausibility the old Stair & Havlin thrillers at their worst. Its theatrical devices are labored and transparent to the point of absurdity and its characters mere stage mannikins jerked about by the director's strings without reference to anything resembling reality.

Its virtues are that it has two really arresting moments of "stunt" melodrama. One of them comes when the hero is tossed into a rushing torrent of a river and carried through the whirlpool rapids to the brink of a tremendous waterfall before he is rescued in sensational manner. The other is a capital horse race, with close-ups of the neck and neck struggle up the stretch to the hero jockey's victory by a nose. These two passages have excellent screen suspense, but the process of leading up to them is so crude and unconvincing they lose force as dramatic situations.

Both the writing of the story and the direction of the film have been handled in slipshod manner. Much of the action takes place in the luxurious gambling "palace" of the villain. From the outside the building is a small story and half bungalow, but the interiors disclose vistas of corridors, apartments and stairways that couldn't be packed into Madison Square Garden.

The tale is full of inconsistencies and absurdities. The hero is the product of a country orphanage and is disclosed as the dishwasher and man of all work in the gambling house, but by some miracle he owns and maintains a marvelous thoroughbred which he enters in the Century Handicap, the turf classic of the year. He wins the event, of course, with a pot of money which solves all the difficulties of romance and foils the villain.

This boy hero is brave, wise and powerful beyond all human reason. One day's work consists of an almost fatal struggle with the river rapids; the rescue of the heroine from a gang of fifty Chinamen who hold her in bondage, an auto race to the track and the winning of the handicap. Good as he is, the hero is not nearly so good as the heavy is bad. This villain is the champion hellion of the screen for all weights and distances. He is even more evil and sinister than the heavy in one of Ben Turpin's comedies. That reference expresses it. The heavy of "Thunderclap" is so venomously evil that he is comic. He is melodrama overdone into travesty. Mr. Sherry plays it with all stops open and heightens the unintended burlesque effect. There were occasional giggles from even the obviously friendly crowd at the initial Broadway screening.

Violet Mersereau is the heroine, the familiar curled and blonded doll type, while Mary Carr is her paralytic mother, whose business it is to distill tears for about 6,000 feet of film.

It will take a very, very unsophisticated audience to stand for such raw imposition as that of "Thunderclap"—either very, very naive or very young. The picture would address itself to about the grade of taste and intelligence finding its favorite reading in bad imitators of "Nick Carter."

Rush.

SHAME

David Fielding	John Gilbert
David	Mickey Moore
David	Franklin Lee
Jonathan Fielding	George Nichols
Foo Chang	George Siegmann
Li Clung	William V. Mong
The Lotus Blossom	Anna May Wong
The Weaver of Dreams	Rosemary Theby
Winifred Wellington	Doris Pawn
"Once Over" Jake	Red Kirby

Another Fox special film at $2, now at the Lyric. The idea apparently is to give Fox salesmen a talking argument when they approach exhibitors who should keep their eye on the amount of business done in New York as well as on the advertising value of such showings. This picture certainly isn't worth that top. Though money has been spent on it freely, it is no knockout and is open to serious criticism as it stands. To long drawn out, it could probably be worked over into a cohesive whole, for it has its moments. In between there's any amount of tiresome footage leading up to effective scenes.

George Siegmann's performance stands out. It is workmanlike and balanced. Doris Pawn, a new leading lady, proved sympathetic while John Gilbert was at his best in the conscience-stricken scenes. Otherwise there was little, save a bit by "Red" Kirby.

The story is by Max Brand, with the scenario by Emmett J. Flynn and Bernard McConville. Here the major fault lies. Effectively knit up and launched at the spectator—in, say, five reels—it would have scored, but in its present form it hesitates so between drinks the interest dies.

The story itself is all right. Mr. Brand tells of a boy born in China with whose woman attendant a powerful native, Foo Chang, falls in love. To avoid him she declares herself the elder Fielding's mistress and the child her son. In revenge Foo Chang brands the boy, kills the father, but is balked by the girl's own suicide, while faithful Li Clung escapes with the baby whose grandfather leaves him rich. Some lively action years later brings David and his future wife together. They are married and Foo Chang, as head of an opium ring, bobs up, demanding the use of Fielding's ships for smuggling. Refusing, David, is told he's a half breed.

He suffers agonies, a situation admirably conceived and acted. Finally, fearing social ostracism, he flees with his baby into Alaska, but his wife and Li Clung chase in rescue. Foo Chang, too, is on the trail and the final scenes show a fight with wolves, a hand-to-hand struggle with one wolf, temporary success for Foo Chang and then deliverance.

Great stuff, this, but screened without a true sense of relative values. The result is it never scores as it should. What should pack a terrific punch loses force through sparring for position. The photography, at times first class, at others lacks clearness. As for interiors, the old gentleman's parlor was ridiculous. It had the floor space of an armory. The lightings were unusually good, and the titling simple and grammatical. Someone who knows English wrote those inserts.

In fine, what this needs is an expert to clip it into a first run feature.

Leed.

OVER THE WIRE

Kathleen Dexter	Alice Lake
John Grannan	Albert Roscoe
Terry Dexter	George Stewart
James Twyford	Alan Hale

Barring the introduction of three or four minor characters in the filmization of "Over the Wire," there are but four principals and yet the story holds interest for more than an hour. The story is adapted from Arthur Somers Roche's "The Breaking Point," scenario by Edward Lowe, Jr., directed by Wesley Ruggles for Metro. Seldom is one regaled with an entire cast—even a small one—that is so uniformly excellent as artists. Nothing in the tale calls for any exceptional histronic art but the performance is even throughout, properly sustained and "holding."

Alice Lake is the star—a girl with a younger brother whom she mothers. The lad embezzles $20,000 from his millionaire employer and misconstruing the firmness of the kindly rich man for a threat to send him to jail, commits suicide. Kathleen (Miss Lake) determines to be revenged, secures employment in the man's office under another name, gives his stock market operations to another, which costs the rich man a million. Wealthy man falls in love with her, she tells him who she is after the ceremony, he is a "strong" man who gets what he goes after and wins her love and respect.

Albert Roscoe is the manly millionaire and conducts himself with a dignity that is convincing without being stilled or exaggerated. George Stewart is splendid in his depiction of the weakling, whining brother and Alan Hale makes a good modern heavy.

It is all very fine for an absorbing program feature, but for two details that seem to have escaped all concerned. In a fine scene with her brother, Kathleen says to him that she will give him the remainder of her fortune—all her securities—to repay the $20,000 theft, and writes out her check for the amount. Since when can securities be disposed of via check? But that isn't as serious an oversight as the fact that Kathleen is married to the rich man without her husband knowing her identity. This being New York state it was necessary to secure a marriage license and for the parties thereto to give their names. Did Kathleen marry the rich man under her assumed name?

Photography and lighting of a high order.

Jolo.

WHERE LIGHTS ARE LOW

T'su Wong Shih	Sessue Hayakawa
Chang Bong Lo	Togo Yamamoto
Tuang Fang	Goro Kino
Quan Yin	Gloria Payton
Lang Sco Bow	Kiyoshi Satow
Chung Wo Ho Kee	Misao Seki
Wong	Toyo Fujita
"Spud" Malone	Jay Eaton
Sergeant McGonigle	Harold Holland

At the Capitol the new Robertson-Cole feature starring Sessue Hayakawa and directed by Colin Campbell is disclosed as an interesting, picturesque Oriental romance set in San Francisco's Chinatown with an effective climax in a first rate finish fight between hero and heavy.

The picture presents the Japanese star in almost entirely native atmosphere and this is the background in which he is at his best. In his own environment the Celestial is interesting and picturesque, but no one has yet been able to make him a romantic figure in American or any other Occidental surroundings. In "Where Lights Are Low" (a title which does not mean anything), the Western settings and characters are very incidental, although Hayakawa does wear evening clothes. The essentials of the story involve Chinese settings and character relations.

Wong (Hayakawa) is a Chinese prince who refuses a princess as a bride whom he does not love in order to wed a peasant girl. He comes to America to study and the girl, Quan Yin, is spirited by Wong's aristocratic uncle to San Francisco, a "picture bride" to be sold to the highest bidder. Wong encounters her in the auction room of a Chinese marriage broker and bids successfully for her against a murderous hatchetman named Chang Bong Lo.

His relatives cast him off for contracting so plebeian a marriage and he cannot pay the purchase price. He undertakes to earn the money by manual labor; saves enough money to stake in a lottery and wins $5,000 for the marriage fee. As he is about to complete the bargain the hatchetman carries off the girl and the film ends in a spirited chase and hand-to-hand fight between the prince and the hatchetman. These melodramatic passages in Chinatown, with the queer doors, alleys and staircases and gorgeous Oriental settings, together with the fantastic flitting, shadowy figures, make good screen material. The picture holds attention.

Hayakawa must have a sturdy following among the fans, for the Capitol on Sunday evening at the early show had one of the best audiences of the season, probably within a third or a quarter of a full house. A remarkable good showing for midsummer on a warm night when the beaches and country invited city dwellers away from Times Square.

Rush.

MOTHER O' MINE

Robert Sheldon	Lloyd Hughes
Dolly Wilson	Betty Ross Clark
Fan Baxter	Betty Blythe
Willard Thatcher	Joseph Kilgour
Mrs. Sheldon	Claire McDowell
District Attorney	Andrew Robson
Henry Godfrey	Andrew Arbuckle

In 1917 Universal produced a Bluebird feature with the same title as Thomas H. Ince's present release, "Mother O' Mine," but not the same story. This one is adapted to the screen by C. Gardner Sullivan from "The Octopus," by Charles Belmont Davis. It was directed by Fred. Niblo, and is being distributed by Associated Producers.

While the production is an excellent one—from the standpoint of direction, acting, photography and settings—the story is a series of emotional absurdities, the big suspense having been done at least once before in pictures in a manner so similar as to almost elicit the statement that the current release is a duplication of what had been shown years ago. This refers to a race to save an innocent man from being electrocuted. The previous one was, if memory isn't faulty, more consistent in that the governor had signed a reprieve. In this instance it is merely the district attorney, who has no authority to halt a death sentence, rushing into the prison and calling off the festivities. There is the same chase in an auto, crashing through the "gates" lowered over a railroad track to indicate the impending passing of a train, with a new twist in that they cannot arrive in time, and so stop at the local power station and order the engineer to turn off the town's power temporarily. The inconsistency of this can be passed over, as it is within the wide range of possibility, if not probability.

Preceding all this comes the tale of a boy sent to the city by his mother with a letter to a financier, asking him to give the youth a position. It is the boy's own father, who had deserted the mother years before under a false idea of the mother's infidelity. The mother had told the boy his father was dead. In a quarrel with his father over business matters the father tells the youth he is a nameless mongrel and pulls a revolver from a drawer. A struggle ensues, the revolver is discharged, and the father is mortally wounded.

It seems a trifle far-fetched that the dying man would insist the boy had deliberately murdered him and to direct his mistress to so testify, she being the only witness to the tragedy.

The boy's mother, living in the country, strangely enough, reads not a word of the affair in the papers, and the boy elects to go to his doom without letting her know.

Mother, however, hears of it at the last moment through a young girl who loves the boy, which results in his being saved at the last minute, led up to by the race to save him.

It is a sordid, morbid tale, with the agony piled on by repeated showing of the electric chair and ultimately with the youth strapped in, the cap adjusted and the order to turn on the juice.

The star acting of the piece is that contributed by Joseph Kilgour as the heartless father, who seems to gain more distinction with each succeeding film portrayal. As a delineator of wealthy libertines he is without a peer among screen actors. Lloyd Hughes, as the son, acts with sincerity and conviction. The remainder of the cast is competent in a mediocre way.

"Mother O' Mine" is nothing more than a program picture, although shown this week at the Strand.

Jolo.

CARNIVAL

Chicago, Aug. 3.

Silvio Steno	Matheson Lang
Simonetta	Hilda Bailey
Andrea	Ivor Novello
Lelio	Clifford Gray
Nino	"Twinkles" Hunter
Ottavio	Maria de Bernaldo

Matheson Lang, English dramatic star and London matinee idol, is the star of this loosely put together foreign picture, made in Venice by a split company of Italians, Britons and Americans. American producers would do well to view this picture for plot and acting; both are splendid, but the photography is rather poor, the settings impossible and the direction, well—typically foreign. Matheson is cast as a cultured actor-manager contemplating the production of "Othello" at his own theatre in Venice. Absorbed in his artistic life, he neglects Simonetta, his bride and leading woman. Andrea, a young nobleman, the actor's best friend, becomes infatuated with the young wife and seeks her company. She does not care for him, but an incident on the Grand Canal is misinterpeted by her "black sheep" brother, Lelio, who extorts money from her. The actor sees her give Lelio money and his suspicions are aroused.

The situation works up to a climax on "carnival night" when Simonetta goes to the carnival ball with Andrea when Silvio is called to the death bed of his tutor. Of course he misses the train and learns of her escapade.

The punch comes at the opening performance of "Othello." Silvio, suspicious of Simonetta, plays the part of the jealous Moor like one in a frenzy. During the entre-act he forces a confession from Andrea and his wife. Then comes the death scene of the Shakesperian tragedy and Silvio stalks onto the stage as one in a dream. He unconsciously names Simonetta in his stage speeches instead of Desdemona and, at last, moves to the bed to strangle her. Frenzy seizes him and he twines his fingers about her neck to strangle her in earnest. The curtain is rung down and he is dragged away. Simonetta recovers consciousness and asks to be alone with him. Then she tells him just what happened and ends with a plea for faith, saying that if he does not believe her he can leave her. Silvio, still in the robes of the Moor, walks to the door, and calls her gondola. They are reconciled and return home together.

Miss Bailey, the leading woman, is certainly Italian, despite the name given her in the American version. She works well at all times, once rising to a point of splendor. Novello, playing Andrea, is the best-looking villian ever on the screen, anywhere. He acts his role in a sympathetic, understanding manner. Lang, as the jealous actor, is splendid. The rest of the cast is neglible.

MAID OF THE WEST

A Universal and so, trying to get away with a release that shows such little expense in the making exhibitors might sidestep it as notice to this producer that if it won't spend money to make pictures, it can't expect money to exhibit them. The locale is set in Texas and New York, ordinary studio sets for the interiors, most ordinary, and the outdoor stuff might have totaled $3, gross.

Eileen Percy is the feminine lead with William Scott opposite. Its story is light and rests wholly upon the captions, written in a comedy vein and containing several gags taken from vaudeville acts, such as "Everyone is liable to mistakes, otherwise it wouldn't be necessary to put rubbers on lead pencils." These get a titter off and on. They are so steadily flashed though and held so long on the screen as a footage killer that any audience will grow a bit tired of them. There is a laugh or so arising out of a situation. Even that comes from a well known farcial story, the theft of pearls, and the same subect matter has been used in serials, perhaps Universal serials. Like another picture maker in New York, that made a story the copyright had run out on. Believing because the story cost nothing it could be worth nothing, the concern cut 110,000 feet to picture house program size and thus threw away the best picture it had ever made, one that could have been turned into a special.

This "Maid of the West" is of a young Texan girl, consigned to her relatives. She falls in love with an aviator. Following are flying scenes, all inserts of course and quite scanty inserts at that.

Probably a good U release for the U class of business, but of no value for a regular picture house, unless on a double bill as the New York played it.

Sime.

THE INVISIBLE WEB

Practically the entire cast of "The Invisible Web" may be seen on any pleasant day leaning against the building that houses the pawnshop at Boadway and 46th street, New York City. And the production of "The Invisible Web" looks it. Written and directed by Beverly C. Rule, it is presented by Fidelity Pictures Co.

Just a cheap rehash of numerous mystery plots that have been seen so many times they would seem to have been written by machinery. The "suspense" is piled on by directly pointing the finger of guilt to four different people with circumstances pointing strongly to their guilt, one of them going so far as to confess the murder. Then, in the last reel another character is introduced—never before seen or spoken of—who proves to be the culprit.

The production is on a par with the actors and the plot—the home of a "wealthy banker" being depicted with tawdry settings. The inquisitor is a police commissioner who pounds his desk when grilling his witnesses, a stock broker is put in jail charged with the murder and when called before the commissioner emerges with his gloves in his hand as if going for a stroll along the "avenue," an elder sister tels how her younger sister "fell for his flashy clothes and flippant ways," the pretty female detective tells, in a flashback, how, alone and unaided she sat at a table in a cabaret with the blackmailer, ordering "hooch" in demitasses, which he drank while she surreptitiously spilled hers into a convenient flowerpot, the elderly, bewhiskered old banker's young, vampirish wife (weight probably 180 net), wearing a rakish sombrero, admits on cross examination she paid blackmail for fear the man who held her secret would tell her husband about her lover, with everybody, according to a sub-title "enmeshed in the web of circumstance." An audience at the Circle theatre received it derisively.

Jolo.

A HEART TO LET

Ordinary. A Realart production starring Justine Johnsone who needs mostly to study full face make-up. Her profiles are lovely and so far as acting goes she is fairly equipped though she hasn't much chance in this adptation by Clara Beranger of "Agatha's Aunt" by Harriet Loomis Smith. Miss Beranger uses too many titles and Gardner Hunting who supervised let her get away with them. Edward Dillon directed, the actual scenes showing skillful handling. The photography was exceptionally good.

The picture builds up at interminable length to some final situations in which there are real laughs. This is about all there is to this production in which a young man goes blind through malaria. Needing a country rest he takes up with an advertisement put in by Miss Agatha Keith whom he remembers from his boyhood as an old lady. Fearing they will not get him now Aunt Agatha is dead, her grand-niece impersonates the old lady and the laughs come when he recovers his sight, but does not let on, Agatha, of course, continuing the impersonation.

A heartless vamp who turns him down when he loses sight and fortune and then tries to get him back when he recovers both created the cross plot. Comedy relief was entirely out of keeping. We are asked to believe that Cousin Zaida, an old maid, is willing to choose for a husband between the two village hackmen. This was hardly in keeping with the aristocratic atmosphere.

What Miss Johnstone needs is stories suited to her personality. Trying to fit her with baby-girl, sweetness-and-light parts is all bosh. She could get somewhere with the stuff she knows how to put across.

Leed.

Moonlight and Honeysuckle

"Moonlight and Honeysuckle" was a comedy by George Scarborough, which had its premiere in New York late in 1919, with Ruth Chatterton starred. Barbara Kent wrote practically a new story for it for filming, for Realart, as a stellar vehicle for Mary Miles Minter. The picturization was directed by Joseph Henabery.

While the end may be readily anticipated directly the characters are introduced on the screen, Miss Kent has made of it an amusing comedy, at which task the original author failed. Miss Minter has materially advanced as an actress since she abandoned her "kid" characterizations and displays "weight" as an ingenue. She hung onto the child thing for a long time, but now that it is over she seems to have settled down to the serious art of acting. The principal male support is Monte Blue, who enacts an Arizona lover in a manner that carries conviction.

Incidentally if Mr. Scarborough will take Miss Kent's scenario and utilize it as the basis of a play it would probably fare much better than his original effort which Henry Miller accepted for Miss Chatterton.

Jolo.

THE MARCH HARE

Percy Heath is the creator of the story of this Realart production starring Bebe Daniels. Maurice Campbell did the directing with Elmer Harris supervising the production. The Heath story with a tomboy character as its central figue is well suited to Miss Daniels. It concerns the activities of the daughter of a Pacific coast millionaire who upon arrival in New York under the chaperonage of a girl cousin fails to notify the relatives she is to visit of her arrival entering into a wager with the cousin that she can live in New York for a week on seventy-five cents. This occurs in a cabaret where they are dining after leaving the train. To make good her bet the girl secures flowers from a woman in front of the restaurant and proceeds to sell them to the diners. The manager tries to eject her but she is befriended by a young Westerner who is dining with his family. A sob story brings about a temporary adoption and she finds herself taken to the home of the aunt she is to visit the other family being guests there. The chaperon in the meantime had been slipped a note and had taken up quarters in a hotel. The girl continues with her masquerading and finds that an imposter in her real place in the home, the butler having secured the telegram telling of her arrival a week later slips in an accomplice to put over a fake deal. This state of affairs puts the girl in the role of a detective to determine the whys and wherefors of the deception. A jewelry theft occurs for which she is accused from which she escapes upon the appearance of the chaperon and a general straightening out of the entire affair and the incidental winning of a husband. "The March Hare" is full of action well acted and has a corking production. Supporting the star is a capable cast with Harry Meyers playing the male lead. It provides a western character well suited to him. Other players include Grace Morse, Mayme Kelso, Frances Raymond, Melbourne McDowell, Sidney Bracey and Helen Jerome Eddy. As a program picture "The March Hare" is well balanced and up to the standard.

CRAZY TO MARRY

Dr. Hobart Hupp	Roscoe Arbuckle
Annabelle Landis	Lila Lee
Estrella De Morgan	Lura Anson
Henry De Morgan	Edwin Stevens
Sarah De Morgan	Lillian Leighton
Dago Red, a crook	Bull Montana
Arthur Simmons	Allen Durnell
Colonel Landis	Sidney Bracey
Mrs. Landis	Genevieve Blinn
Gregory Slade	Clarence Burton
Cement Man	Charles Ogle
Cupid	Jackie Young
Minister	Lucien Littlefield

To attempt to describe in cold, unfeeling print the story of a "Fatty" Arbuckle comedy is a well-nigh futile task. And if, perchance, some descriptive writing genius succeeded, he would only be spoiling a bunch of fun for those unfortunate to read it.

Arbuckle's newest pre-release is "Crazy to Marry," a Paramount five-reel production, written by Frank Condon, scenario by Walter Woods, directed by James Cruze. No effort will here be made to relate the tale, but it is only fair to state that it is one of the funniest "jazbo" slap-stick affairs ever conceived. Not only are the inimitably ludicrous mannerisms of the obese comedian uproariously funny, but there is a plot of no mean calibre. It is sufficient to make for a rip-roaring stage farce—one of those in-and-out-of-doors, fast-moving affairs originated by the French at which you laugh out loud and then feel like kicking yourself for not being sufficiently blase to restrain yourself.

Arbuckle has the role of an absent-minded surgeon with a pet hobby that he can cure criminals of their vicious tendencies by operating on their skulls. An ambitious newly rich mother "frames" him to marry her daughter, with resultant complications. The funniest is that of a criminal whose operation is postponed so the doctor can be married, who follows the surgeon right through, carrying with him the surgical instruments and pleading to have his skull opened. This is so funny that Tuesday evening at the Rialto the laughter was so loud as to give the impression the auditorium was being cannonaded.

There is a completeness of workmanship about the plot that differs materially from the average farcical picture plot. Every complication is carried through to a logical—or illogical, as the case may be—conclusion, all making for a rounded-out tale that signalized the craftsmanship of a master playwright. And then the funny bits of "business," without resorting to sub-titles, as, for instance, "Fatty's" attempt to raise a "one-man top" to an automobile is a driving rainstorm, culminating in the whole darned thing coming off and being blown away. Every amateur autoist who has been through it will hold his sides.

There is a splendid cast, with such seasoned legitimate players as Edwin Stevens in minor character roles. "Crazy to Marry" will make the whole world laugh.   *Jolo.*

NOT GUILTY

Albert A. Kaufman presents "Not Guilty" (First National), a rather confused and confusing film version of Harold McGrath's story, "Parrot & Co.," with Sylvia Breamer as star, capably supported by Richard Dix, a good looking hero of the Bushman type, in a double role. Except that the picture has the common fault of dramatized novels in that its appeal is diffused and scattered, the production is an interesting romantic melodrama.

The cut backs, fadeouts and iris-ins and iris-outs are present in profusion. The literary device of starting a story in the middle and then easing the beginning to the reader's attention, is employed and intensifies the puzzlement, but if you are equal to the strain of strict attention to the preliminaries, the story is interesting and has a number of gripping passages. One near the end is a spirited life and death battle between the hero and two hired assassins which has a fine punch.

The locale wanders all over the map of the world. It begins in New York, shifts apparently to the Andes mountains in South America and brings up breathless in Rangoon, Siam, after meandering around India. A number of Oriental settings are cleverly faked for these remote locales and the effect of realism is heightened by the splicing in of numerous shots taken from travel subjects, such as a trip down the Ganges and views of Hindu temples.

The photography is conspicuously good. It has none of those hard, sharp, stark effects of black and white, but runs to soft tones and misty effects that are artistic.

Harold McGrath splashes melodrama pretty thickly. The story starts with what appears to be a murder by a drunken man in a gambling house and his flight to his twin brother, an engineer in South America. The murderer is Arthur, the twin is Paul (both played by Dix). Paul takes the crime upon his own shoulders and disappears. He believes himself morally guilty, because when they were boys he accidentally shot Arthur and his (Arthur's) mind was affected by the wound. Arthur assumes Paul's identity, and by the coincidence so much employed by novelists, runs promptly into Paul's sweetheart, Miss Chetwood by name.

Arthur makes love to the girl and they are engaged, when Miss Chetwood makes a pleasure trip through the Orient. Coincidence goes to work again. In Rangoon Miss Chetwood, the fugitive brother and the only man in the world who knows the facts of the murder are thrown together on shipboard. The fugitive brother has a priceless diamond, the gift of a native prince in reward for freeing his province of the plague. A gambler named Craig plots to kill him and rob him of the gem.

He hires native assassins to do the job and this leads to the familiar film fight, a whopper of the kind. When the smoke clears, Craig is killed by one of his own hirelings and makes a dying confession that it was he and not Arthur who committed the murder and the way is opened for the fugitive Paul to return to his own and marry Miss Chetwood.

There are several bits of double exposure with a new kink. The rule

is that the two characters in a double exposure cannot touch each other, but somehow the difficulty has been overcome in the Franklin production. Several times when the two brothers meet they shake hands in a shot close enough to be examined closely. Both figures are facing the camera and a substitution seems out of the question. It's a clever bit of trick photography.

The picture has plenty of action and romantic interest and its settings are always picturesque. It will make good before the best of the neighborhood audiences as a first rate program feature.   *Rush.*

LOVETIME

A Fox release with Shirley Mason, directed by William M. Mitchell.

The tale of a country peasant girl in France, falling in love with the son of the Marquise, who owns the estate upon which her parents live. Her parents can't pay their rent but that is a detail. Nor does the girl know the artist she falls in love with is the son. But he knows she is the daughter of the peasants. But he doesn't know they don't have their rent.

The ground rules on estates are that the son of the owner can't fall for a daughter of a tenant. At least in France. Mrs. Marquise (as the last name can not be recalled) frames the boy to marry the daughter of a Count. The Count agrees and they make the announcement without either of the young folks being aware of it, when hearing it. This happened in the Paris home of Mrs. Marquise.

By that time of course the daughter of a peasant was there too. They had made her a dancer. They made her a dancer at Savoy, where was located the home of her non-paying parents. She went to Paris and the son followed. There's a villainous Count in the proceedings (the second Count of the film indictment) the general manager for the Marquise, who covets the peasant daughter, but not in marriage. When a priest at Savoy remembered the villainous Count had pulled the same stuff on another native maiden some time before, the parents without the rent agreed Paris was the only place for their daughter, for safety—a new thought in pictures.

And so it goes on. 90 cents' worth of production, 30 cents worth of acting, and action, nil.   *Sime.*

LIFE'S DARN FUNNY

Zoe Robert................Viola Dana
Clay Warwick............Gareth Hughes
Miss Dellaroc..............Eva Gordon
Gwendolyn Miles....Kathleen O'Connor
Prince Karamazov........Mark Fenton

There might have been a little more speed to this Metro Classic production, but lacking the speed it falls short of being a mighty clever little comedy drama. Originally published in the Satevepost as "Caretakers Within" it read much better than it played before the camera. Molly Parro and Arthur D. Ripley handled the adaptation and injected some funny bits of business but failed to retain the suspense of the original. Dallas M. Fitzgerald who directed held down the tempo to such an extent that the production is actually draggy at times.

Miss Dana has a role that she is capable of putting over without too much effort and Mr. Hughes playing opposite her proves an excellent foil. With a pair of shell rimmed glasses and boob facial expression he suggests Harold Lloyd.

These two carry the entire action except for a few minor roles. Mark Fenton as the Prince wore a flock of crepe hair entirely transparent to those who view the picture. Surely there are enough "types" on the coast that have the real thing in whiskers and who want a job! A producer does not have to resort to having his character people pin on a make up.

"Life's Darn Funny" has a cute story that will get by with any audience, and the picture should enhance Miss Dana's popularity.   *Fred.*

THE CALL FROM THE WILD

This is not "The Call of the Wild," showing what a change one word can make, not alone in title but in story. Still no adult can tell how this picture will affect children, for it has a boy and a dog in it. Both are featured. The boy is Frankie James; the dog is "Highland Laddie." The dog is a collie or shepherd. A nice dog too,

but they must have fed him just before he got caught in a trap where the dog had to remain for two days. Perhaps they fed him while he was in the trap for when the boy arrived at his side after two days, the dog didn't know whether to eat bread. According to the story the dog was accustomed to meat.

Neither can an adult say whether there will be a revulsion of feeling at some of the scenes, for children. There should be, for this attempt is to make a dog act like a wolf, ferocious like, tearing wild, chasing a man two miles up a gulley about three-quarters of a mile out of the town, but the idea was repellant, not because the dog didn't get the man, but because the man, knowing the wild dog was there, walked two miles in the woods and left his gun at home.

In the same way when the boy was lost and they found his coat on top of a cliff the first night, they voted the boy was dead because they found his coat. That is, the father did. When he got home the mother said the boy wasn't dead because God wouldn't let him die. Then as the boy wandered around the woods for two days, the father and mother sat home in the kitchen arguing whether God would save the child.

In other ways it's an educational, as other denizens of the forests were there, a rabbit, squirrel and skunk. They used the skunk for comedy, using both the boy and dog, which was enough to have made them both wild over the direction.

Wharton James wrote the story, directed the picture and acted in the film. If there's anything about the picture he deserves credit for, it's the direction, and that mostly through it being the best of the three which is not saying whether it was good or bad. The Pacific Film Co. is the maker.

It's not an expensively produced picture. There is no ballroom set nor jazz dancing and there is no mansion. The most important setting is a country notion store and a small shack. After that it's all outdoors, and all outdoors is a fine producing scheme when there is something to produce.

The picture was one half of a daily bill at Loew's New York. No exhibitor should play this picture without seeing it first, for there are too many gruesome thoughts concealed in it.

And remarkable as it may seem, when religion is rung in in a film for a "moral" or a "punch," it usually flops. The reason why is that it is not properly placed and since it flops so often, some day some one will get the idea it can't be properly placed, and if it can't be, it's only proper to suppose religion has no place in pictures, commercially. Mebbe so.   *Sime.*

WISE HUSBANDS

A most unusual plot for a feature picture is "Wise Husbands," story by Charles D. Isaacson, adapted for the screen by J. Clarkson Miller, directed by Frank Reicher. Lester Park and Edward Whiteside present the picture, distributed by Pioneer Film Co. Gail Kane is starred and J. Herbert Frank featured.

The picture is wrong from almost any standpoint viewed. The story is one that provides no opportunities for the star and, at best, is most irritating. It is not a drama of plot, but of sub-titles, there being comparatively little action. Just what the author desired to show is still an unsolved mystery to the reviewer.

A young man with no other apparent occupation than to be a constant attendant at his club is in love with a girl who devotes herself to Red Cross work. His mother thinks the girl is not good enough for him, and his father believes she is too good for the son. The father confides in a friend—an artist—and they conspire to break down the opposition of the mother by having the artist, who is a libertine, lure the mother into becoming interested and compromised in and with the artist. By this means the mother, realizing the girl isn't so wicked, consents to the girl becoming her daughter-in-law.

Here we have the proposition of the mother of a grown son visiting the artist in his studio, the husband being a party to the frame-up and the prospective daughter-in-law finding the prospective mother-in-law being wrestled with by the libertine artist friend of the family. When the artist starts to get familiar with the mother, she says: "You mustn't; I'm expecting my husband to call for me any minute."

Gail Kane, cast for the role of the Red Cross worker, has a purely receptive part. She shines most effulgently in so-called vampirish parts, where she can wear clothes and conduct herself as a worldly woman. A sinned-against role doesn't fit her. While Gladden James, as the young lover, contributes an intelligent piece of acting, his forte lies in "heavy" characterizations. **Arthur Donaldson has comparatively little to do as the father—that is, if one can say a man does little when he frames with a ~~friend to compromise his own wife.~~ Lillian Worth portrays satisfactorily the thankless part of the silly wife-**mother, while J. Herbert Frank has the really stellar part of the artist. But it is all so impossibly ridiculous that it is scarcely worth discussing.

Adequate production, direction and lighting for a most unsatisfactory feature.

Jolo.

THE MAN TRACKERS

Jimmy Hearn	George Larkin
Harry Morgan	Ralph McCullough
Molly's Father	Harold Holland
Hanley	Albert J. Smith
Jules, Half-breed	Farney Furey
Molly	Josephine Hill
Lizette	Ruth Royce

"The Man Trackers" is one of those old time melodramas, made of standardized materials and obviously built to suit the tastes of the type of fans who patronize the cheapest class of side street picture houses. It's a Universal, written and produced by Edward Kull, with George Larkin and Josephine Hill co-starred. The five reels are filled with theatricalism, with never a moment suggesting drama that convinces.

The story is laid in the Canadian Northwest, with one of the mounted coppers the hero, a local gangster as the chief villain and a young chap of the neighborhood a sort of secondary villain. It's a simple enough yarn, which like the locale and character has only been used a couple of thousand times for a picture story.

George Larkin, as the hero-cop is in love with Molly, the inspector's daughter. Ralph McCullough, secondary villain is also in love with Molly. This establishes conflict between the two, which results in a hand to hand clinch for the fair Molly's affections. It's a funny scrap, like a couple of South Street longshoremen mauling each other on a dull morning down on the docks. Hanley, the chief villain is sore on the hero-cop because being a gangster he naturally has no use for a harness bull in the first place. This dislike on the part of Hanley played by Albert J. Smith is flamed into hatred when Hanley discovers the cop is after the whole Hanley gang, including their leader for some trick they have pulled off.

While the hero-cop and Morgan are having their tussle, one of the Hanley crew socks the hero on the bean with a stick, knocks him cookoo, and while the cop is regaining his senses Hanley takes his gun away from him and fires a shot into Morgan, who has been knocked cold before that by the hero. The frame works, and Jimmy the cop is court-martialled and dismissed from the service. Molly's father, incidentally is the court-marshaller.

A half breed Jules (Barney Furey) sees the dirty work, however, and before he can tip off Molly's father how Jimmy was framed, Hanley makes his escape to the mountains, taking with him Lizette presumably his wife or sweetie, and a sister of Jules, the half-breed, who is not only a half breed but half witted. Before vamping away, Hanley knocks Jules, for a row of lamp-posts for talking out of his turn. That's scrap number two.

Scrap number three arrives when Jimmy, who has been handed a six months' sentence in the cooler, as well as being dismissed from the mounted force comes upon Hanley, following his discharge, and proceeds to rough it up with the gangster. Lizette, Hanley's side partner arrives just in time to slap the hero over the left ear with a handy bit of lumber, and the hero takes the count once more. While this is going on the half breed finally gets his story over of the frame up, and the hero's side kicks go out to look for him.

The hero regaining consciousness again keeps on the trail of Hanley and finally gets him, and gets him good, bringing him back to the local lockup. Finale a la mode with hero and heroine standing before pop with father extending his blessing. The parts are played satisfactorily. The picture has many exteriors of the familiar winter woodland type and has been cheaply put together.

The audience at the Stanley laughed in the wrong place once or twice at the crudeness of the meller situations. ~~An average Universal program fea~~ture on the whole.

Bell.

HER STURDY OAK

Violet White	Wanda Hawley
Samuel Butters	Walter Hiers
Belle Bright	Sylvia Ashton

In this Realart by Elmer Harris with Wanda Hawley starred and ably supported by Walter Hiers, is presented something amusing and quite different from the usual run. The question is, do men prefer clinging vines to efficient women? They do, Mr. Harris replies with amusing gusto, and Sylvia Ashton as the efficient lady lends emphasis to his view of the matter.

Belle Bright owns a ranch and fastens her heart on a fat and chubby poet whom she resolves to feed and house when he marries her, but as luck will have it a little cutie blows in and the engagement is off. Once married, Violet and Sam have a struggle, particularly after twins are born to them, but it all ends happily and merrily when Sam bucks up and proves he has manly qualities and can take care of his girl if he has to.

This type of a role is a change for Miss Hawley, but she was sufficiently clinging and certainly a contrast to the stalwart Miss Ashton. Walter Hiers' rotundity, like Fatty Arbuckle's, helps make fun, but isn't all Mr. Hiers offers. He has a good comedy method and under Thomas N. Heffron's direction put it over for results.

Well received at a Loew house.

Leed.

PLAYING SQUARE

This was caught at the Ideal over on 8th avenue and is offered by Realart Pictures Corp. with Gladys Hulette starred. The billing carries a line informing that the picture was formerly known as "The Shine Girl," but the print was in good shape and it doesn't look like an old picture. The cast is first class. There is a good climax and the uncredited direction is equal to all needs. The interiors were few.

The story is the sort of appeal to average audiences Miss Hulette appears as a little girl who does boot blacking and other shining in a shop and is hauled up for taking a plant before the judge of the Children's Court. He tells her it isn't square to take what doesn't belong to you. Becoming interested in her, during the summer he gives her a vacation at his mother's place in the country where she is finally adopted and grows to young womanhood.

A couple with a child have an adjoining place. The judge has known the wife before. She and the husband become estranged. The judge and wife are about to elope when the little city waif interferes, gets them to give each other up and then rescues the woman's little girl who has fallen over the cliff into deep water.

The picture ends with the city waif grown to young womanhood when the judge claims her in marriage.

Leed.

VIRGIN PARADISE

Gratia Latham	Pearl White
"Bob" Alan	Robert Elliott
"Slim"	J. Thornton Baston
Bernard Holt	Alan Edwards
Mrs. Holt	Henrietta Floyd
Constance Holt	Grace Beaumont
Ruth Hastings	Mary Beth Barnello
The Attorney	Lynn Pratt
Peter Latham	Lewis Seeley
Capt. Mulhall	Charles Sutton
John Latham	Hal Clarendon

The trouble with this Fox special now at the Park is simple. It isn't a special in the metropolitan sense of the term and can't possibly get over at $2 top. It is just another attempt to force the market and lift the price to exhibitors. But it is, especially toward the end, an effective melodrama. Pearl White, who stars, puts over a whale of a fight as a climax, and the title writer and the director, J. Searle Dawley, manage to get considerable laughs into the latter reels. Hiram P. Maxim's attempt to show what a lot of hypocrites people are is lost sight of, and the result is a mixture of roaring farce and melodrama.

The story begins with a brief, well managed attempt to place little orphaned Gratia alone on a South Sea Island with a lot of wild animals for friends and pets. Well photographed scenes of a volcano in eruption dispose of all other humans, and then, left heir to a fortune, Gratia, grown up, is rescued and taken back to civilization. What she does to civilization can be imagined. In fact her rebellion against clothes and the restraint of life in America is worth a lot of laughs.

Being an heiress, of course, she is aimed at in marriage, but she disposes of the villain in a rough and tumble engagement.

Crude, but roughly effective. Below the best standards.

Leed.

FIGHT FILM IN FRANCE

Paris, July 28.

A Paris evening journal is of the opinion the Carpentier defeat will handicap the renting in France of the film showing the match at Jersey City. "If the French boxer had been the winner the situation would have been quite different," the renting men are said to have declared to the reporter, who terminates his article by advancing another reason; "the owners of the films, basing their price on the colossal demand for the reel in America, are asking too big a price for foreign rights, a price which is causing the renters to reflect. However, it is probable the halls where the Dempsey victory is projected in France, particularly as they will be few, will do excellent business."

The reel arrived in England July 9 and in Paris July 12. It is stated 700,000 frs. will be asked for French, Swiss and Belgian rights, which sum will not be forthcoming.

EXPERIENCE

Youth	Richard Barthelmess
Experience	John Miltern
Love	Marjorie Daw
Ambition	E. J. Radcliffe
Hope	Betty Carpenter
Mother	Kate Bruce
Pleasure	Lilyan Tashman
Opportunity	R. Senior
Chance	Joe Smiley
Tout	Fred Hadley
Despair	Harry Lane
Intoxication	Helen Kelly
Good Nature	Jed Prouty
Poverty	J. Furey
Wealth	Charles Stevenson
Beauty	Edna Wheaton
Fashion	Yvonne Routon
Sport	Ned Hay
Excitement	Sybil Carmen
Conceit	Robert Schable
Temptation	Nita Naldi
Work	Frank Evans
Delusion	Frank McCormack
Crime	L. R. Wolheim
Vice	Mrs. J. M. Beatty
Habit	Agnes Marc
Degradation	Mrs. Gallagher
Frailty	Florence Flinn
Makeshift	Mac Barnes
Gloom	Leslie King

Without going into a discussion of the ethical side of making capital out of the display of pictures of the late Enrico Caruso as part of the Rivoli's Pictorial News this week, the fact that the management used a number of shots of the singer and heightened the effect with a phonographic reproduction of his voice, just prior to the showing of the feature of the bill had the effect of placing a damper on the audience.

With the house jammed to the back door at the final performance Sunday a sort of a choked sob from the audience followed the brief applause that greeted the first view of the tenor. It was showmanship of a quality that did not help the feature to any extent.

The feature was the Famous Players release of the George Fitzmaurice production "Experience" with Richard Barthelmess heading a cast of unusual length containing many players whose names should have a drawing power.

The Hobart play was adapted for the screen by Waldemar Young and fitted with a "down on the farm" prelude which planted the love interest and established the point from which Youth departed in company with Ambition to the marts of trade.

The story follows faithfully with the big scene being the cabaret known as "The Primrose Path." It is here that Youth in following pleasure meets with Beauty, Fashion, Excitement, Intoxication, Temptation, and the rest of the bright light characters and from that point his descent to crime and poverty is marked.

It is the cabaret set in which all the thrills come and Mr. Fitzmaurice is at his best when handling one of the scenes of this nature. In this one a flying ballet is employed for a brief moment that hardly justified the expense that must have been gone to, to secure the shot.

The lightings were unusual and the colored art titles also lent in a great measure to the tout ensemble.

As Youth Mr. Barthelmess gave a performance pleasing and studied. Marjorie Daw playing opposite as Love was a delight in the simplicity with which she endowed the characterization. But the wallop of the entire performance was that put over by Nita Naldi. This beautiful creation of God's handicraft caused everyone to catch their breath when she appeared on the scene and then the vamping bit that she did stamped her as an actress as well as a "looker."

One of the disappointments was the showing made by Lilyan Tashman as Pleasure. She screened poorly. Edna Wheaton as Beauty brought murmurs of admiration.

Of the men, John Miltern as Experience, E. J. Radcliffe as Ambition and Frank McCormick as Delusion gave finished performances.

"Experience" is a big picture that admits of endless exploitation on the part of the exhibitor and he should not be afraid to go strong on this end for it will draw and satisfy any picture audience. *Fred.*

BEAUTIFUL GAMBLER

"It's a Universal" is what flashed on the screen at the conclusion of this picture. "It's a Flop" would be appropriate.

Little Irving Thalberg, the head of the U west coast plant let William Worthington, who directed this production make about as neat a mess of this Peter B. Kyne story as has been seen in a long while. If Kyne ever got a look at the picture he must have groaned.

"The Beautiful Gambler" has G ce Darmond as the star and she is about the only thing in the picture with the exception of a district attorney bit that Arthur Millett played. Millett was the only one in the court room scene that deported himself with anything like naturalness. The balance of the cast with the exception of the male lead was quite bad and in these days of cut salaries on the coast, must have been bought for a little nickle. As a matter of fact the only expense that the picture had to amount to anything was the cost of the original story by Kyne and the raw stock used in the shooting.

Miss Darmond is "the beautiful gambler." Her father liked to play the wheel and as the head of the gambling house wanted to make the daughter the wheel was wired so that father had to eventually mortgage the house to indulge his passion and naturally he lost. Daughter consents to marriage to retrieve the family homestead, returning home after she has married with "them papers" only to find father has bumped himself off. From that point on it is life in a gambling hell for her with her husband making her double behind the wheel table and trim the come-ons. Among the latter there finally is a big cowpuncher, at least he is dressed up as one. He was turned out of his home in San Francisco a few scenes earlier dressed in evening clothes, but he walks into the gaming joint as a cowboy without any reason for it, so he must be a cowboy and that is all there is to it. He and the girl fall for each other and the gambling man gets sore.

His revenge takes the form of a frame to get the youngster's bankroll but the tool that undertakes the task is unsuccessful, whereupon the villainous gambler beats him up and casts him into the night right up against a convenient excelsior pile so that he can set the place afire. That fire stuff is the biggest joke of all. The flames rage and the smoke billows to the heavens for sufficient time to destroy a city but in the interior scenes that are cut in during the fire there isn't a bit of smoke visible; at least not until seemingly hours afterward. Of course, the gambler is supposed to kick off in this scene and so the "B. G." and the cowboy get married, settle down in a "big town," (maybe it was Los Angeles) and are residents in a swell hotel.

It is at this hotel that the supposedly dead gambler shows up and makes an inquiry at the desk. He is a mighty tough looking customer and might be an applicant at a ten cent lodging house, but the clerk and the house dick at this swell joint look him over and send him right up stairs without announcing him. A nice sort of a place that was!

Right behind him comes the other short card guy (the one who set the joint afire) and he walks right through the place and takes the fire escape route to the window overlooking the room where ex-husband is choking his former wife. Then the young and dashing cowboy hubby enters and the two go to it for a few shots of rough and tumble, during which the chap outside the window manages to fire a shot into the back of Husband No. 1, killing him. At that precise moment Husband No. 2 is down for the count and the pistol is tossed into the room so as to fall at his side. Naturally he is accused of the crime and on trial for his life. The wife wants to take the blame and at the moment that she is on the stand ready to perjure herself the real murderer is walked into the court room under arrest, makes a confession in time to let the hero and shero go to a clinch.

Story as adapted for the screen is highly improbable and as produced is totally impossible. *Fred.*

A MIDNIGHT BELL

Martin Tripp	Charles Ray
Stephen Labaree	Donald MacDonald
Abner Grey	Van Dyke Brooke
Annie Grey	Doris Pawn
Mac	Clyde McCoy
Spike	Jess Herring
"Bull" Barton	S. J. Bingham
"Slick" Sweeney	Burt Offord

If Charles Ray doesn't succeed in putting over the first feature of consequence without the aid of sub-titles, it won't be because he hasn't tried. He accomplished this feat with his film version of James Whitcomb Riley's "The Old Swimmin' Hole," but that was only a series of episodes in the life of a country youth and a comparatively easy stunt. Another producer essayed it with indifferent success. While Ray isn't offering a screen adaptation of the late Charles Hoyt's minus sub-titles, he utilizes very few of them and it is really marvelous how much story he puts over in the way of thrilling melodramatic action without a word being flashed upon the sheet.

Ray is once more his own director and, judging by the result, he has no use for one when he can secure such results. The tale has been brought up to date and old-timers who remember Eugene Canfield as the featured player would hardly recognize the characterizations. It is no reflection upon the original author of the spoken piece to state that the present version is more in keeping with modern stagecraft—or at least screencraft. Ray has made of the attempt bank burglary and its frustration by ringing the old church bell while tied to a chair a piece of dramatic suspense that will hold spellbound any kind of a picture audience, whether it be a first-run Broadway crowd or a nickelodeon attendance. And for his comedy, his inimitable portrayal of the "sick look around his gills" is a fine piece of laughable pantomiming. The cast, art direction and photography will hold up favorably under analytical inspection.

This First National release can safely be set down as a high class feature. *Jolo.*

AT END OF WORLD

Cherry O'Day	Betty Compson
Gordon Deane	Milton Sills
Donald MacGregor	Mitchell Lewis
Harvey Allen	Casson Ferguson
Terence O'Day	Spottiswoode Aitken
William Blaine	Joseph Kilgour
Uang	Goro Kino

Presented by Jesse L. Lasky and directed by Penrhyn Stanlaws, "At the End of the World" is a colorful melodrama with a wealth of picturesqueness and plenty of dramatic punch. It is from the play by Ernst Klein, adapted by Adelaide Heilbron, scenario by Edfrid A. Bingham. Thompson Buchanan had a hand in the editing.

Betty Compson is the star, heading a notable cast which includes Milton Sills, Joseph Kilgour, Spottiswood Aitken and others. With this array of seasoned players the acting takes care of itself and full value is given to powerful story elements. The tale has abundant action and settings of extraordinary interest, beginning with a turbulent cafe and gaming house in Shanghai and going thence to an isolated lighthouse somewhere in the South Seas, fitting backgrounds for a punchy drama such as Jack London might have written.

Although the production is offered as a vehicle for Miss Compson, it is really Milton Sills who has the star role, that of a writer and explorer seeking adventure in the Far East. Terrance O'Day runs the Shanghai cafe and brings up his daughter Cherry to look upon men as her victims to be used for her own purposes but keep at a distance. She flirts with them in the cafe just off the Bubbling Well road and sends them on their way when they cease to amuse her. MacGregor, a rough ship's mate, takes her flirtation seriously and tells her he will return in a year to marry her.

Meanwhile she falls in love with Gordon Deane (Sills), a casual wanderer who pays slight attention to her. Upon the death of her father, Cherry marries Blaine, manager of a Shanghai bank, but he casts her off. MacGregor comes back to claim her, while Deane passes through Shanghai on his way to take charge of the distant lighthouse. He recruits two derelicts, MacGregor and a boy ruined through speculation.

Cherry, learns of his purpose, without knowing that the sailor lover and the bankrupt boy are with him, and when her marriage is wrecked, starts for the lighthouse. Here's where the drama works up to its violent climax. Cherry is washed ashore on the rocky reef upon which the lighthouse stands, and MacGregor recognizes her as the woman he claimed as his wife. From long brooding he goes half insane, and regards the other two as dangerous rivals.

His jealousy grows to murderous hate until he and the bankrupt boy come to mortal combat on the lofty balcony outside the revolving mariner's light. A splendid bit of dramatic trickery is employed for this big scene. The two men are struggling each to toss the other over the rail, the fight being disclosed intermittently as the revolving light comes around to illuminate the scene for an instant and then to pass, leaving the straining figures in darkness. Fortune seems first to favor one and then the other, until the last flash shows the balcony rail broken outward and the heroine staring horrified through the gap into the dark below where the crasing sea is breaking at the base of the lighthouse.

The death of the two men leaves the way open for the embrace of the hero and heroine as a rocket in the distance promise the prompt arrival of the occasional relief boat. This bare recital gives small idea of the gripping incidents with which the story is richly provided and which keep the picture always at tip toe of suspense. It's a first rate adventure melodrama, sure to hold almost any kind of audience. *Rush.*

THE FIGHTER

Caleb Conover	Conway Tearle
Dey Shevlin	Winifred Westover
Blacardo	Arthur Houseman
Caine	Ernest Lawford
Jack Standish	George Stewart
Senator Burke	Warren Cook
Mrs. Hawarden	Helen Lindroth

A feature with the old thrill elements. It is a Selznick production that has Conway Tearle as the star and was directed by Henry Kolker. The story was written by "the R. Cecil Smiths," who turned out a rather matter-of-fact tale of the guardian and his ward, who fall in love with each other.

The manner in which Mr. Kolker directed the transference of the story to the screen reflects a great measure of credit to him. There is just sufficient love interest, a quantity of suspense and some fighting, so that the average picture audience gets just what it wants.

Caleb Conover (Tearle) is a self-made man. He has risen from the slums via an engine cab to be president of a roalroad. His ward (Winifred Westover) has just made her debut and broken the ice in the chilliest set in an exclusive suburban colony. Conover in addition to railroading is mixed up in politics and controls the legislature of his state to a sufficient extent to assure the passage of bills favorable to his line. Opposing him is Blacarda (Arthur Houseman), who mixes his social and business battles. His first step is to try to have Conover ousted from the country club social set because of his business activities. The latter, however, has enough on the board of governors to make them vote the right way at the right time. Then to continue the fight Blarcardo tips a story to the local press that the dead father of the railroad man's ward was a grafter. He gets beat up by Conover for this. To protect the girl the latter issues a denial of the story and shoulders the blame himself. The girl accuses him of hiding behind her dead father's back and leaves his home. During the separation the two discover that they love each other, and a reconciliation occurs, when the girl discovers the real reason for the story.

The real thrills and plot of the piece, however, center on a fight in the legislature with the appearance of everything being against Conover, who, in order to be present at the session, after the reconciliation, is forced to run one of his own locomotives as a special, which jumps a burning trestle and all looks to be lost, but the hero turns up in the lobby of the state house in time to defeat his enemies, and the picture ends in a business and heart triumph.

Miss Westover gives a corking performance opposite Tearle. She is pretty to look at and Tearle makes love to her with sufficient fervor to make one believe that she meant more to him than just an ingenue lead. Tearle is convincing in the picture, but at that he did not seem to particularly get the audience. Houseman made a good heavy while Ernest Lawford filed a minor role satisfactorily. *Fred.*

WOMEN WHO WAIT

Eileen Arden	Marguerite Clayton
Harold Van Zandt	Creighton Hale
Peter Van Zandt	George MacQuarrie
John Van Zandt	Thomas Cameron
Charlie Wing	Harold Thomas
Mary	Peggy Shaw
Baby Anne	May Ward

Here is a feature just like the California climate. One waits interminably for something to happen but it never does. It is a meller of the real "Shore Acres" type, with what the Playgoers Pictures Co. terms an all-star cast including Marguerite Clayton, Creighton Hale and George MacQuarrie. Philip Van Loan is responsible for the direction. The screen adaptation was made by Edward Russell. It is six reels in length and released by Pathe.

The story is a "Down East" tale of the fishing folk on the Cape. The elder Van Zandt is a fisherman who has a schooner of his own. His two sons help him in his work. Both boys are in love with the same girl and while the younger one is favored by the lass, the elder double crosses him and wins the girl. This is done while the younger son is in Bawston working for an uncle. When the latter returns the true state of affairs is revealed to the wife of the brother but it is too late to help an aching heart.

With the younger man remaining on the scene the love of the two is weakened but held in restraint. The older brother sees the trend of affairs and makes two attempts on the life of the younger. In the final attempt he brings about his own destruction by falling from the balcony of a lighthouse in a storm and sinks into the sea forevermore, which leaves the real lovers together for the final closeup.

The picture is a small time affair and just about fits in a double feature program with a fairly strong picture to hold it up. That is the manner in which it was utilized at the Circle where it was shown early this week. For some of the smaller houses of the 8th Avenue type it will manage to stand by itself.

Marguerite Clayton as the girl gives a fairly likable performance, but Creighton Hale walks away with the honors as the younger son. MacQuarrie as the heavy emotes all over the place until he becomes tiresome. Harold Thomas playing a Chinaman does so in decided occidental manner. A child part is very well handled by little May Ward.

The production for the greater part is exteriors. The interiors check up as three in number and their cost was mighty light. In trying to judge cost of production from the screen showing the picture figures as one that must have been made inside of $30,000. At that figure it should manage to show a nice profit for the producers when the returns are all in.   *Fred.*

THE BLOT

Professor Griggs........Philip Hubbard
His wife.............Margaret McWade
His daughter...........Claire Windsor
His pupil.................Louis Calhern
The other girl.........Marie Walcamp

This Lois Weber picture, the first release by the newly formed distributing concern, the F. B. Warner Corp., should clean up a tidy sum of money. It touches the heart. It is sensibly and intelligently put together, points a worth while moral without offensive preaching and is on a live topic. In addition, its technical qualities are high in standard. The cast, headed by Claire Windsor, who can act in a delicate and appealing fashion and is a great beauty besides, is adequate throughout, and the story, direction, photography and lighting please.

Miss Weber, who shares direction honors with Phillips Smalley gives us a story that is familiar to the average audience in all its details. The other kind of story, dealing with princes and lands beyond the sea, also succeeds, but this isn't one of them. The theme is the way university professors and teachers generally are underpaid. The author represents the professor's family as miserably underfed, perhaps an exaggeration, but not so great a one as to ruin the story.

Next door lives the family of a shoemaker who prospers at a trade,

The professor's salvation is worked out when the son of a wealthy trustee falls in love with his daughter and makes all his pals take lessons from the old teacher. A very human touch is the bringing together of the two families who have misunderstood each other. The climax and final fade-out is a gem. It ends on the disappointed lover, the young clergyman who bravely walks away. This is as it should be. The audience would wonder about him, not about the two who were happy.

Seven reels long and a good market bet.   *Leed.*

THE MAN WHO

Bedford Mills................Bert Lytell
Helen Jessop.............Lucy Cotton
Mary Turner...........Virginia Valli
St. John Jessop.........Frank Currier
"Shorty" Mulligan.....Tammany Young
"Bud" Carter...........Fred Warren
Radford Haynes........Clarence J. Elmer
"Bing" Horton.........William Roselle
Sarah Butler........Mary Louise Beaton
Jack Hyde...............Frank Strayer

Metro has attempted to filmize one of the best comedy stories that has appeared in the Saturday Evening Post this year, and only partially succeeded. The basic idea is a novel one, written by Lloyd Osborne, but the fault seems to be Arthur Zellner's, the adapter, if not that of director, Maxwell Karger. Instead of adhering more strictly to the original tale the adapter has attempted to jazz up its legitimacy by resorting to a number of "hokum" stunts, such as having a well-dressed man walk out of his home with a tailor's tag on his coat and having a man feigning illness dip the doctor's thermometer in a cup of hot tea to indicate fever. Such things were not in the author's original script and have no place in the scenario. Bert Lytell, the star, played the role with sufficient legitimacy but no actor can "play straight" a part jazzed up.

There are unlimited possibilities in a story that calls for a well-dressed man to walk down Fifth avenue minus shoes and stockings. Then not enough was made of the conflict in his mind as to which of the two dear charmers he wants to marry. In addition the tale is very slow in getting started and as a result there are six reels of what would make five more rapidly moving ones.

Production and cast on a high plane of excellence. Despite the drawbacks the feature will please in almost any picture house, but one can't help remarking that it might have been made into a rip-snorter.   *Jolo.*

THE GREATER PROFIT

Mel Brady................Edith Storey
Capt. Ward Ransome......Pell Trenton
"Nunc" Brady............Willis Marks
Jim Crawkins............Lloyd Bacon
"Gimp" the Hunchback..Bobbie Roberts
Creighton Hardage.........Ogden Crane
Mrs. Creighton Hardage.Lillian Rameau
Rhoda Hardage..........Dorothy Wood

Haworth production, released through Robertson-Cole, with Edith Storey as the star. Story credited to Clifford Howard and Burke Jenkins, with direction by William Worthington. Five reels in length. Mel Brady (Miss Storey), a girl of the underworld, is arrested for shoplifting. She is saved from prison by a society matron, who takes her in as one of her household, giving the girl a position in connection with a crusade against profiteers. The fiance of the benefactress' daughter becomes attracted by the newcomer. She is informed that the home is no longer open to her. The boy offers marriage, which she refuses,

due to differences in social standing. Before leaving she steals a paper which proves the woman's husband one of the country's most unlawful profiteers. The younger man had been offered a partnership with him. The girl shows the convicting paper to her admirer to keep him out of the concern and it is also used to influence the profiteer in bringing down the cost of foods. It ends with the customary "And they lived happily ever after."

As an every-day program feature, "The Greater Profit" will suffice. It has no outstanding features. The story is mildly interesting without embracing any new ideas. The casting has been done discriminately. The cost in this direction is not great, with the production end done on a moderate scale. As part of a double feature bill at the New York this production held its own.

WEDDING BELLS

Rosalie Wayne.....Constance Talmadge
Reginald Carter........Harrison Ford
Marcia Hunter........Emily Chichester
Mrs. Hunter.............Ida Darling
Douglas Ordway.......James Harrison
Spencer Wells.........William Roselle
Hooper....................Polly Vann
Jackson...............Dallas Welford
Fuzisaki.................Frank Honda

Chet Withey has turned out a corking light comedy production in "Wedding Bells," which has Constance Talmadge as the star. The picture is a First National release presented by Joseph M. Schenck, with Harrison Ford playing opposite Miss Talmadge and delivering a distinctly impressive performance.

Zelda Crosby is responsible for the adaption of the Salisbury Field play. She has prefaced the play proper with a succession of events that in their enactment do not quite compare in humor to the telling in the spoken version. There was a certain quantity of suspense in the play because of the fact that the meeting of the divorced couple was held under cover for some time and that aided the laughs. Also the character of Spencer Wells, as played on the stage by Percy Aimes, held a quaint humor that was entirely missing in the characterization by William Roselle. Mr. Roselle may not have been to blame for this, possibly the script failed to hold it for him.

The picture, however, is one that is sure to strike any audience as a mighty good entertainment. It is full of laughs through situation. The two principal characters are carried by Miss Talmadge and Mr. Ford (in the play they were enacted by Wallace Eddinger and Margaret Lawrence). In the screen version Miss Talmadge more than favorably compares with Miss Lawrence.

Dallas Welford, as the English butler, made a mark in the early section of the picture, with some exceedingly expressive grimaces.

It is to Mr. Withey that a greater portion of the credit for the making of a laugh producer of the picture must go. His handling of the story is all that could be asked for. He has managed to get some exceeding touches in lightings and settings and the bits with the little white poodle are sure to register anywhere.   *Fred.*

PERJURY

Circumstantial evidence and misdirected justice are the basic notes of this William Fox feature which has William Farnum as the star. Shown at the Park theatre Sunday to an audience of about 100 people of whom the greater part were "invited," the meller failed to make any marked impression. It is right along the line of the usual Fox program picture and

contains nothing that would warrant lifting it from the program class of production.

The original story was the work of Ruth Comfort Mitchell. Mary Murillo adapted it for the screen and Harry Millarde directed. The kiddie touches which the latter handled in the making of the production were far and away the most effective work that showed on the screen.

William Farnum plays the general manager of a manufacturing plant who is possessed of a violent temper. Gossip directed at his wife (Sally Crute) because of the fact that his employer favors him is the cause of his losing his temper, and his being accused of the murder of the head of the plant. He is innocent, but none of his family or friends believe it. He spends 20 years of a life term in jail, having been found guilty of murder in the second degree. Then the real murderer confesses and the broken man is turned out to weep all over the works. It is a great picture for weeps, everyone takes a hand at the crying ammonia bottle at one time or another.

Some day, perhaps, a picture will be made with Farnum as the star where he won't have to go to jail. He started in "Les Miserables" and seemingly the picture producers think that he must play parts of that nature forever more.

Sally Crute gives a corking performance as the wife and mother, while Gilbert Rooney and Alice Mann play the son and daughter respectively with lots of punch. Wallace Erskine is a lovable old man in the early period of the production. The other roles were also well played.

The picture has nothing that commends it as to sets or lighting and the camera work is of the type that will get it no extended comment.   *Fred.*

BIG GAME

Judith Baldwin......Mary Miles Minter
Tod Musgrove..............Monte Blue
Senator Baldwin...........Willard Lewis
Hallie Baldwin............Grace Goodall
Congressman Hamill........Guy Oliver
Robert W. Courtney......William Boyd
Mrs. Langley..........Mabel Van Buren

The practice of altering the psychology of a stage play when transferred to the screen is usually a debatable question, but when a film producing concern buys a stage play of no especial name value and then alters it so that even the original author couldn't recognize it, what's the sense of paying good money for such a story?

"Big Game," as a stage play, was written by Willard Robertson and Kilbourne Gordon. It bears no resemblance to the film adaptation made by Edward T. Lowe, Jr. Even the trio of principals has been so changed as not to be recognizable. As a consequence there is no suspense and the tale leads up to a single situation, the worth of which is discounted and destroyed by the woman in the case "framing" with the man to pretend to make love to her in order to make her husband assert his manhood and fight for her.

The stage play was not a success, but the filmization is many times worse. The titling is ridiculous, in that the "villain," who is a Canuck, starts off to talk good English, switches to a dialect and then reverts to scholastic utterances.

The lead is unnaturally drawn and the "heavy" altogether idiotic. To pass an opinion on their acting is, therefore, manifestly unfair. The feature was directed by Dallas Fitzgerald for Metro and he offered nothing unconventional.

"Big Game" is an unsatisfactory picture. *Jolo.*

THEY SHALL PAY

This is a Pickford production with Lottie Pickford starred, released through Pathe. The story is not credited, but Martin Justine is responsible for direction and continuity. Using many titles, he still manages to maintain the interest till the end—a bad end, by the way. Although a lot of fuss is going to be made about this unhappy ending, it is dragged in by the heels. Trust a picture producer. Where he should not have one, he has one, and vice versa, but all who go frequently to pictures know about that. In this case it was obvious the two should forgive and forget and give themselves up to love.

This feature has one merit in that everything technical shapes up to a fair standard, and the production is kept whittled right to the point of the story. There are 5,000 feet and nothing unnecessary. Finding her father has been ruined and sent to prison by his business associates, Margaret Seldon (Lottie Pickford) sets out to avenge him. She gets the chief conspirator by showing up his scheme to ruin his new business partners. The second she traps in an attack on her at a house-party. With the son of the third she falls in love, but clings to her scheme for revenge and they are parted.

The cast is adequate, including Lloyd Whitlock, George Periolat, Allan Forrest and Paul Weigle. Miss Pickford herself gives a restrained, competent performance. *Leed.*

THE OPENED SHUTTERS

Sam Lacey............Joseph Swickard
Sylvia Lacey..............Edith Roberts
Nat Morris...............Jos Singleton
Martha Lacey................Mai Wells
Judge Trent............Clark Comstock
John Dunham...........Edward Burns
Edna Durwent.............Nola Luxford
Thinkright................Charles Clary

A U program feature with Edith Roberts and acceptable stuff at a moderate price. There is a wholesome story by Clara Louise Burnham, well acted, and mostly exterior settings. William Worthington directed. Miss Roberts is here seen in a lighter role than usually falls to her lot and got away comfortably with the sweetness and light stuff, making displays of temper count at the proper times.

Left an orphan by her spendthrift, artist father, she goes on her way to her New England relatives only to be disillusioned when she finally encounters them, including in her dislike the young and handsome partner of the old judge, who ships her away to his farm on the coast where the overseer, known as Thinkright, makes his way of looking at life (Christian Science touch here) count for good. A young girl neighbor and an Englishman appear and give a chance to dress up in some summer scenes.

The closed shutters belong to the mill on the place and are symbolical of the local attitude of mind, but in the end the shutters are opened, everything gets straightened out and the right man gets the right girl. *Leed.*

THE WOLVERINE

An out-and-out "western," with no eastern character in it—mostly outdoor scenes and no pretense at anything bordering on so-called "production." "The Wolverine" is an adaptation from a novel of the same name and was made by Spencer Productions, Inc., and distributed by Associated Photoplays, Inc. The featured player is Helen Gibson and the male lead is handled by Jack Connell.

A straightaway, elemental melodrama with but a momentary flashback it runs along for about 70 minutes most entertainingly, principally from the fact that the details of ranch life, as visualized, are so unusually correct—never idealized for theatricalism. Some of the things shown are so technically western they are not so readily grasped by the tenderfoot and should be more fully explained in the sub-titles.

"The Wolverine' will please in the Grade B program houses. *Jolo.*

ONE WILD WEEK

Pauline Hathaway.........Bebe Daniels
Bruce Reynolds..........Frank Kingsley
Mrs. Brewster...........Frances Raymond
Angelica Jessop.............Mayme Kelso
Mrs. Dorn..............Edythe Chapman
Judge Bancroft.......Herbert Standing
G. Howitt Hertz..........Edwin Stevens

This is a thoroughly unfunny Bebe Daniels feature issued by Realart. No one in particular is credited with the story while the name of Major Maurice Campbell is compelled to plead guilty to the direction according to the screen.

Miss Daniels is the best selling bet Realart has on its flapper program, but it will only require a few stories like this one to place her stock on about a par with the others of the Realart string.

This story was manufactured (it couldn't have been written) with a view to capitalizing Miss Daniels' 10 days' free lodging which Judge Cox gave her in the municipal house in Santa Ana. But it is a very poor attempt at humor.

The star has the role of a flapper who at the age of 18 receives a legacy of $50,000 from her grandfather, his will, however, providing that she manage to lead a most circumspect life for six months after she receives the money, otherwise the coin goes to a rather vinegary aunt. The girl goes on a visit to friends. On the train a man loses his wallet. Bebe has it thrust upon her and as she emerges from the train is arrested as a pickpocket. Fearful the publicity that may follow the arrest would cause her to lose the $50,000 she refuses to give her name, or make any explanation, and is sent to a house of detention. After two days there she manages to escape and takes three other inmates with her. The aunt, who has been notified of her disappearance, arrives on the scene and corners the girl. The elder woman is congratulating herself on having stepped into a young fortune when the judge announces that the real culprit in the wallet case has been captured and thus the story ends. No one gives a whoop where the other 25 weeks of the six months were passed or whether the girl managed to keep her name out of print for that length of time and finally grab off the dough.

There is an effort made by allegedly humorous titles to get a laugh here and there in the picture, but it was fruitless.

"One Wild Week" is nothing to go wild about. *Fred.*

THE AFFAIRS OF ANATOL

Jeanie McPherson is resonsible for the scenario of Arthur Schnitzler's play that has attained considerable popularity. In producing the picture Paramount sought to achieve the foremost in film art by casting it with more stars than any picture of recent date has held.

In the array are Wallace Reid, Gloria Swanson, Elliott Dexter, Bebe Daniels, Monte Blue, Wanda Hawley, Theodore Roberts, Agnes Ayres, Theodore Kosloff, Polly Moran, Raymond Hatton and Julia Faye. Cecil De Mille directed, with the costuming and settings the last word in a material way.

But "The Affairs of Anatol" is not a good picture. Perhaps too many cooks tended to spoil the broth, or it may have been the scenario, or the general make-up might have lacked the necessary efficiency. The impression of the auditor as it unfolds is that situations are forced. It lacks spontaneity, suspense and comprehensive appeal, with the titling inferior. The titles retard this picture, more so perhaps because they were so essential in helping protect the intended satire, of which "Anatol" is almost wholly part and parcel.

The first and last locales are the home of Anatol. Mr. Reid, with scenes of his affairs, for Anatol, be it remembered, is a kindly cuss, where the female of the species is concerned, with his correct and spotless attitude toward them bringing him pecks of trouble. His first affair is with Emilie (Miss Hawley) not suspiciously played. She is of "The Green Fan" cabaret, Gordon Roberts, the wealthy and sinister, is seeking to sway her from the not so straight and not so narrow.

In the bucolic bit, Monte Blue, as Abner Elliott, and Agnes Ayres as Mrs. Elliott furnish the best acting, because it is the most natural.

Anatol's final escapade encircles Satan Synee (not bad vamp billing), who is a roof star in her own right—and left. The bits with her are very "voguey" and will hold the feminine eye rapt. Satan is all her devilish name implies in the matter of dress and undress. Bebe Daniels is Satan and as a vamp was vamping in her key. *Samuel.*

CAPPY RICKS

Matt Peasley .... Thomas Meighan
Cappy Ricks .... Charles Abbe
Florrie Ricks .... Agnes Ayres
Murphy .... Hugh Cameron
Skinner .... John Sainpolis
Capt. Kendall .... Paul Everton
Mrs. Peasley........Eugenia Woodward
Capt. Jones .... Tom O'Malley
Ole Peterson .... Ivan Linow
Swenson .... William Wally
Larsen .... Jack Dillon
Doris .... Gladys Granger

Offered by Adolph Zukor at the Rialto this week as a Paramount feature, this proved the sort of stuff people want to see Thomas Meighan in and should ride to a comfortable financial success. Founded on the novel by Peter B. Kyne and the play by Edward E. Rose, it was adapted by Albert Shelley Levino and Waldemar Young with direction by Tom Forman. The pair of continuity writers did more for this feature than the director, though the latter may have received an unwarranted slugging from the cutting room and also have been handicapped by the new efficiency supervisors on the Paramount lots.

However that may be, the picture, which gets a whale of a start and has your attention safely lashed to the subject, begins to slip half way through. The damage is fairly serious after the shipwreck scene. Apparently a model of a big ship on the rocks is used and the scene further loses color and value when the actual rescue is not shown. Again, in two cases at least, the acting could be improved. Agnes Ayres is nowhere near in this picture as appealing as she can be and Charles Abbe almost burlesqued his role. Still he got laughs, and that counts.

The story is fairly well known. When the captain of his ship dies, Peasley, as first mate, takes charge and comes to port, wiring the owner, Cappy Ricks, who sends on another man to take command. These two clash, and Peasley gets the best of the argument, taking the vessel to Frisco himself. But this displeases Ricks, who is further enraged when his daughter, Florrie, falls in love with Peasley. To separate them he sails with her for a long trip, but the ship goes on the rocks and is rescued by Peasley and a tug boat. Here was a chance for some real stuff, but the gap was plugged. That was economical, but will the public stand for it? The public is used, by now, to the real thing in pictures.

The photography is less sure and clear than is usual with a Paramount offering, but Meighan is a great commercial bet. He gets the money in almost anything. Even an efficiency man on the lot probably can't hurt him. *Leed.*

BURN 'EM UP BARNES

"Burn 'Em Up" Barnes....Johnny Hines
"King" Cole...............Edmund Breese
Madge Thompson........Betty Carpenter
An eccentric tramp.....George Fawcett
Whitney Barnes.........J. Barney Sherry
Ed. Scott..................Matthew Betts
Mrs. Whitney Barnes,
Julia Swayne Gordon
Stephen Thompson......Richard Thorpe
Betty Scott...............Dorothy Leeds
Francis Jones..............Harry Fraser
The Baby..........."Billy Boy" Swinton

A Charles C. Burr production introducing Johnny Hines in a picture of feature length, six reels in this case. The scenario is by Raymond L. Schrock and direction by Hines and George A. Beranger. The picture was screened for the trade this week, and disclosed an amusing story of fast and continuous comedy incident, considerable romantic strength and entirely free from the custard pie and slapstick school of comedy.

Its appeal is something like that of the Harold Lloyd output—intelligent fun without roughhouse and with a fairly cohesive story as a thread to hang the "stunt" incidents upon. Besides this it has a really notable cast, including Edmund Breese, George Fawcett, J. Barney Sherry and Betty Carpenter. A gathering of screen names which entitles the effort to attention.

The production has been made on a scale matching the excellence of the players and the titling is a model of treatment for this kind of a picture. There is a clever turn to the printed interpolations that goes a long way to enhance the picture, as smooth and snappy a sample of word juggling as has been done. The titles deliver almost as many laughs as the action itself. And the action is well supplied with amusing surprises and laughable twists.

Fawcett and Breese are picturesque tramps who become companions of young Barnes when he is blackjacked and thrown into a box car by automobile bandits who steal his car. Their exploits in grabbing food and luxuries from the countryside are especially entertaining.

The punch comes at the finish in an auto race in which the hero is really in pursuit of fleeing bank burglars instead of contesting for the speed cup. A thrilling episode in itself and neatly worked into the story finale, success in the race bringing a bride to the hero and solving a lot of complications.

"Burn 'Em Up" Barnes is the speeding son of a millionaire auto manufacturer. Father objects to speeding fines and in a dispute the boy departs in his machine to make his own way in the world. On the road he is knocked unconscious and his car stolen by thieves, who throw him senseless into a box car. He comes to when the train crew throw him off with a lot of tramps in Bedford, Pa.

Here Barnes falls in love with the heroine, is framed and jailed by his rich rival, but is located and freed by his father just in time to enter the local automobile race and foil the robbers, who had cracked the bank run by the heroine's father and entered the race to make their motor car getaway.

Rush.

FOOLISH MATRONS

Dr. Ian Fraser	Hobart Bosworth
Georgia Wayne	Doris May
Sheila Hopkins	Mildred Manning
Annis Grand	Kathleen Kirkham
Mysterious Woman	Betty Schade
Mrs. Eugene Sheridan	Margaret McWade
Lafayette Wayne	Charles Meredith
Chester King	Michael Dark
Anthony Sheridan	Wallace MacDonald
Bobby	Frankie Lee

This is a Maurice Tourneur production released by the Associated Producers. Although released throughout the country some months ago it received its first Broadway run at the Broadway theatre last week and is now being shown in the Loew houses. It was the feature attraction of the Sunday bill at the Circle, pulling as much business there as was noticed at a first run week stand house further down the avenue. As a matter of record business was not too good at either house.

"Foolish Matrons" is the work of Donn Byrne and called one of the "best sellers." The screen adaptation was made by H. Wyndham-Gittens. Maurice Tourneur and Clarence L. Brown are credited with the direction. To those who are in the "know" on the coast that announcement will be sufficient as to who handled the direction.

As a feature production "Foolish Matrons" holds interest. It is not to be classed as a special, although in a great many organizations it would have been released as such. It is, however, a picture that shows great possibilities in an exploitation sense and with such will pull money to any box office.

The theme of the story is marriage. Some women marry for love; others for ambition and still a third class "just to have a husband." Three married couples were selected for the book and picture exposition of Mr. Byrne's argument. The stories of two of the couples are interwoven; the third just happens for good measure. That one is the tale of the two small towners who arrive to conquer the big city. In this case the wife falls for a wealthy John and the last seen of her is leading "the gay life" at a cabaret table. The love tale is that of a well known actress who marries a doctor and rescues him from the "city." The third is the marriage of a newspaper woman to a poet whom she drives to drink and finally death by overindulgence, by her wifely negligence and devotion to her profession. The moral is that only love marriages are successful.

The three tales are run practically side by side and the telling on the screen is so handled as to hold interest. The sets and lighting are more than adequate and almost suggest "special."

There is one thing that Mr. Tourneur has arrived at in this picture and that is to get the value out of names on the screen one must have more than one in a production. He has coupled Hobart Bosworth and Doris May as his two biggest values in the cast. Mr. Bosworth enacts the role of the doctor who is made happy by the actress (Kathleen Kirkham). The role is not one that suits him particularly well and he seems rather too aged for it. Miss May in the role of the flighty little girl from the small town who married just to have a husband and through him satisfy her ambition for big city life, walks away with the honors of the performance.

Mildred Manning as the newspaper woman wife, handled herself nicely, while Wallace MacDonald as her husband was an acceptable souse. Charles Meredith played opposite Miss May and acquitted himself creditably, while Michael Dark as the heavy to this particular triangle was all that could be asked.

"Foolish Matrons" will get money for any exhibitor who goes out and gets the full publicity values of the production.

Fred.

MAN OF THE FOREST

Milt Dale	Carl Gantvoort
Helen Raynor	Claire Adams
Harvey Riggs	Robert McKim
Lem Beasley	Jean Hersholt
Al Auchincloss	Harry Lorraine
Bessie Beasley	Eugenia Gilbert
Les Vegas	Frank Hayes
Bo Raynor	Charlotte Pierce
Snake Anson	Charles Murphy
Jim Wilson	Frederick Starr
Lone Wolf	Tote du Crow

Produced by Ben Hampton from the story by Zane Grey, made into scenario form by Howard Hickman, Richard Scheyer and W. H. Clifford.

It's a frank western melodrama with plenty of shooting and riding and an abundance of thrills and a quantity of first rate incidentals with animals. A tame mountain lion is a novelty and a capital dramatic trick is worked by having the vicious looking cat leap upon one of the outlaws as he is about to shoot the hero from ambush. Of course, this is accomplished by some sort of camera legerdermain, but it is impressive. So is the device of having another of the outlaws pulled down by the hero's pet dog. It all makes interesting melodrama.

The story is a machine made affair, as most lurid melodramas are, and it requires too big a lot of explanatory titles to make it intelligible, but it has a wealth of robust action and that after all is what satisfies the large majority of fans. The playing is conspicuously good, but some of the direction is slipshod, as for instance, the interior of a cabin lighted by a candle at night, while the sun streams through the window.

Carl Gantvoort makes a likeable hero. He is a fine sturdy, manly figure and plays naturally without anything of the stilted posing of the film hero. Claire Adams' refinement of beauty recommends her as the heroine and she plays with excellent judgment. Robert McKim is his usual self as the heavy. Eugenie Gilbert is a strange choice for the scheming daughter of the outlaw-bootlegger in a rough cattle country village. Her youthful charm and grace would have been more fitting for a sympathetic character. Frank Hayes has another of his amusing character studies.

The photography is good, and the settings adequate, although there might have been more local color in the shots of the cattle range. The few glimpses of the herds might have represented at Katskill dairy farm more than a western ranch.

These, however, are details. The picture has the dramatic punch at the end. The heroine is held captive by a band of outlaws led by the bootlegger (pinch hitting in fiction these days for the old cattle rustler) and the hero goes to her rescue to fight the outlaw gang single handed. There is the tried and true device of showing the hero and heroine in dire straits and then a series of shots of the rescue posse riding desperately to their relief—here as always good for a thrill and the usual burst of applause.

Altogether a satisfactory picture for the grade of audiences that patronize the neighborhood house.

Rush.

DISRAELI

Disraeli	George Arliss
Sir Mitchell Probert	Edward J. Ratcliffe
Hugh Meyers	Frank Losee
Mrs. Noel Travers	Margaret Dale
Duke of Glastonbury	Henry Carvill
Duchess of Glastonbury	Grace Griswold
Lady Beaconfield	Mrs. George Arliss
Clarissa, Lady Povenacy	Louise Huff
Charios, Viscount Deerford	Reginald Denny
Mr. Lumley Foljambe	Noel Tearle

A screen production with George Arliss, in all respects worthy of that consummate artist and the honorable record of the play on the stage. Distinctly a credit to the United Artists who sponsor it. Mr. Arliss who plays his old part, Louis N. Parker who wrote the original and Henry Kolker who directed the picture version. It is current at the Strand and on Sunday night drew an audience resembling those at the house at the height of the season.

Business was improved all along Broadway Sunday evening, and probably the cool weather figured, but the loyal following of the star doubtless had a lot to do with the lobby filled with people waiting to get in and the five lines or so behind the orchestra rail for the last show of the evening. It is the kind of picture that will advertise itself by word of mouth and with anything like a weather break ought to show substantial returns as the week goes on.

The stage original has been dealth with reverently both as to its form and details, and players and director have managed to translate to the screen much of the quiet, suave, dramatic strength and deft comedy that characterized the play, an achievement that in itself recommends the production. Mr. Arliss is master of of a distinct style, a kind of bold economy in expression and gesture. He can get the most out of a telling situation without "acting." His method resembles that of a clever cartoonist who gets character into sketches with a few salient strokes and shuns embarrassing elaboration.

It is a tribute to his skill that it registers splendidly in screen pantomime. There was true drama in the scene in which the Prime Minister outwits Sir Michael Probert and saves himself and England from disgrace. There was also a fine bit of comedy in his management of the little love scene earlier in the story where Sir Charles takes his hurried departure from his sweetheart. The whole story is rich in nicely turned comedy incidents.

The character relations between Disraeli and his wife work a skillful touch of pretty sentiment into the pattern and the quick turn of tense situations from a thrill to a chuckle provide a succession of stimulating surprises. One loses sight of the theatrical fiction in the easy naturalness of the well made and well acted play—the final and supreme test of the artfully told story.

After Mr. Arliss, honors go to Mrs. Arliss as Lady Beaconsfield, a fine bit of unaffected playing. Louise Huff is lovely to look at in repose, but does not mirror emotion very successfully in the single scene that calls for more than graceful charm. Reginald Denny was the young lover, Sir Charles. He is handsome in a characterless way, but filled in the picture well enough. The younger pair merely an incident anyway. Edward J. Ratcliffe made a perfect Sir Micheal and the other characters fitted neatly into the picture.

The titles are a model of effective brevity and directness and the settings excellent. The Downing street interiors looked just that and the exteriors of English country places were thoroughly satisfying, at least to the American idea of what such scenic backgrounds should be. The costuming was well managed. The modes are of the middle 70's but were sufficiently modified to take the usual curse off Victorian hideousness as it usually looks to modern eyes.

Rush.

THE HELL DIGGERS

Teddy Darman	Wallace Reid
Dora Wade	Lois Wilson
John Wade	Alexander Brown
Calthrope Masters	Frank Leigh
Silas Hoskins	Lucien Littlefield
Siverby Rennie	Clarence Geldart

A Lasky production of Byron Morgan's Satevepost story of the same title scenarioized by the author and directed by Frank Urson. The story in screen form is told in a direct manner but the author in adaptation has failed to retain the suspense quality which his written effort contained. The result is that the production is a program picture and that is all. It is hardly worthy of a full week's run.

Wallace Reid plays the heroic role in a very matter of fact fashion, denoting that he is so sure of himself that it matters not what sort of a screen performance he delivers. A continuance of this attitude at this particular time and he will wake up some fine morning to discover the vogue he has enjoyed in the last few years has slipped away from him. He'll be high and dry on the lot.

Lois Wilson, who plays opposite him, manages to present a rather pleasing performance in a role that requires little. Frank Leigh as the heavy delivers with a wallop and a character role, played by Alexander Broun (Richard Bennett) is a real delight. Mr. Broun is an aged farmer about whose family the major portion of the plot revolves and he delivers himself forcibly in every shot in which he appears.

The story is that of a community of agriculturists who rise to do battle with a gold dredging company that has entered their territory and is laying waste the land they have depended on for their sustenance. Reid is the young engineer in charge of the work for the company. He has long advocated the use of a dredge that will resoil the ground broken in the search for gold. His company has looked upon his scheme as a useless one, but in the Cherry Valley operation he falls in love with the daughter of the leader of the farmers and finally throws his lot with them. They mortgage their lands to build his dredge and finally win out against the grasping corporation.

The scenes for the greater part are exteriors. There is one good fight staged before the camera that contains some thrills. Otherwise there is naught that is worthy of extended comment. *Fred.*

THE 3 MUSKETEERS

D'Aartagnan	Douglas Farbanks
Athos	Leon Barry
Porthos	George Seeigman
Aramis	Eugene Pallette
De Rochefort	Boyd Irwin
Buckingham	Thomas Holding
Bon face	Sydney Franklin
Planchet	Charles Stevens
Cardinal	Nigel de Brulier
De Treville	Willis Robards
Father Josephs	Lon Poff
Queen	Mary MacLaren
Constance	Marguerite de La Motte
Milady	Barbara La Marr
Louis XIII	Adolphe Menjou

Perhaps no other picture has been surrounded with the incidents that marked the opening of Douglas Fairbanks in "The Three Musketeers" at the Lyric Sunday evening Aug. 28. For an hour before the unwinding of the first reel a crowd lined the sidewalks on both sides and literally jammed 42nd street to Broadway. The magnet was the personal appearance of Fairbanks and of Mary Pickford, and, quite unexpected Charlie Chaplin and Jack Dempsey. There were demonstrations outside and they continued inside the theatre and throughout the showing of the film, the four celebrities occupying a stage box. Before the picture started Fairbanks was called for a speech, and again during intermission with a third requested at the conclusion of the performance. $2 tickets for the initial showing sold as high as $5.

The story of Dumas has been ideally approximated in the screen version, adapted by Edward Knoblock, directed by Fred Niblo and photographed by Arthur Edeson. The premiere contained a prolog provided by Knoblock and spoken by Stephen Wright. Aiding was a stage setting by John Wenger, with silhouettes of musketeers its main components. The program gives credit to Lotta Wood, scenario editor; Doran Cox, assistant director; Edward Langley, art director; Frank England, technical director; Paul Burns, master of costumes; Harry Edwards master of properties; Bert Wayne, electrician, and Nellie Mason, film editress.

The picture was in two parts, and reached the full length of an evening's entertainment.

It historically and dramatically contains the elements that made the play so successful with essential film elaboration. There is a flare and sweep about the film, with the assembling, cutting and continuity seeming spotlessly correct.

In the first views of the palace of Louis XIII there might have been padding with the usual form followed. In this case there is just enough to implant atmosphere. The entrance of D'Artagnan picks up the action with the ultimate reached in the climacteric moments. The boy from Gascony runs riot as befits the character reaching the heights of his ambition to become one of the king's musketeers, in natural sequence.

Fairbanks and D'Artagnan are a happy combination, the character providing the star with what will probably go down in film lore as his best effort, for Fairbanks is just a modern but of the mold of the Dumas hero. He must have toned up his fencing considerably for he displays work with the sword that has not been approached. In the incident where, with his three compatriots, Athos, Porthos and Aramis, the crack guards of the Cardinal are humbled, there is a flash of steel that cannot help but move the most casehardened. It is a befitting climax to the end of the first part and produced rounds of applause.

The concluding portion is worked up in that affair of Anne, where she seeks to recover the diamond buckle given her by the king and which she has given as a love token to Buckingham. It will be recalled that it was necessary for D'Artagnan to go to

England and return in a short space time with the jewel, to save the Queen's honor. It is accomplished here in an engrossing style with the romantic end never at any time cloying. One incident contains a leap from a boat that for sheer appeal is a bear.

Of the interpretations that of Nigel de Brulier as Richelieu developed a real creation, a magnificent delineated with the Cardinal. Excepting only the star he dominates the picture. Adolphe Menjou does excellent that the star he dominates the picture. Adolphe Menjou does excellently in a role not actor-proof by any manner of means. His Louis XIII evidences both sides of the king, gaining sympathetic response where in most instances the opposite is the case.

The companions of D'Artagnan, Athos, Porthos and Aramis found apt treatment by Leon Barry, George Seigmann and Eugene Pallette. Marguerite De La Motte is a sweet and winsome Constance. Mary MacLaren did not invest the queen with the poise expected leaving only a mild impression. The locales seem veracious, the sets and screens bringing the atmosphere of the France of old as it is regarded, with the costuming in keeping to the minutest detail.

"The Three Musketeers" is a splendid picture giving forth the Dumas story with a gusto and abandon. It is not marvelous though nor does it hold enough to be styled epoch-making, but as a super-production in the sense that term has come to be accepted, and with its star, it will strike universally, especially so in its appeal to younger folk, for the character of D'Artagnan is of youth and its enthusiasms. *Samuel.*

WET GOLD

The virility marking the directing and acting output of Ralph Ince, sticks out as companion excellence with the J. E. Williamson undersea wonders in "Wet Gold," a Goldwyn release, now circulating in Greater New York. Nothing more exciting or pictorially startling has found its way to the screen. Produced as a stage play even with only a few of its big effects realized in scenics, with real water of course, and the play would be a sensation. Why it isn't so in films must be answered by the mis-handling of publicity.

The author and inventor of "Wet Gold" got away from all prior submarine stories in a dramatic commingling of land effects with those shown beneath the surface of the sea. In its baldest interpretation it is a tale of stolen treasure buried in a submerged wreck at the bottom of the ocean, with two rival bands of adventurers in a race for the prize. The excitement reaches its height principally along the bottom of the sea, within the chambers of a pirate submarine, and in the waters, on and about a rusted old hulk concealing the fortune.

As a dramatic composition Mr. Williamson has accomplished a fine piece of work, regardless of the informing value that his undersea photography brings to the production.

Ince, the leading principal of the romance, also directed the picture. His role is one of a gentleman adventurer, a sort of wayfarer of the seas. The characters of the play are in the main well conceived and acted. The one who didn't fare so well was Charles McNaughton, as a gambling intruder. He overacted at critical moments. Aleene Burr as the heroine played with simplicity and real charm. John Butler, as her sweetheart, was bright and effective and a fine portrait of a southern gentleman of the old regime was contributed by Thomas McGrane.

A love story threads in and out through the composition, but it is rather in the big heroic moments of thrills, shocks and under-sea shudders that the main action centres, a final climax of these—the death of the unscrupulous intruder via the jaws of a shark—proving specially vivid in realism.

And now for the puzzle this splendid feature propounds: Why isn't this one of the talked-of productions of the year? Bristling with provocations to sensational advertising, why hasn't something of the picture's merits got into print somewhere? From all angles, it is an unusual production, its effects along the floors of the sea, its ocean graveyards, its revelation of submarine operation, its old wrecks related before the eye to a pulsating drama, all suggest ballyhoo.

The picture was opened in New York initially at the Broadway theatre without any splurge. Intelligently boomed all New York would want to see it. In its way it might easily have vied with the interest excited by feature productions held on Main Street for long runs.

Doesn't Williamson know what he's got? The market is choked with able, idle, film publicity men, who could make big money with this feature if put down as a show with all the circus trappings that a feature of its unusual sort demands to awaken the public to realize that "Wet Gold" isn't a mere passing program picture as its manner of manipulation classifies it.

Variety some time ago had occasion to express similar judgment and regret about a picture that, properly exploited—"The Killer"—should have proved a big box office magnet.

What is the matter with the present exploitation staffs of picture producers. *Jolo.*

SERENADE

Maria del Carmen........Miriam Cooper
Pancho....................George Walsh
Her Mother.............Rosita Marstini
Pepuso, His Father......Jas. A. Marcus
Domingo Maticas........Josef Swickard
Ramon, His Son........Bertram Grassby
El Captain Ramirez......Noble Johnson
Don Fulgencio..........Adelbert Knott
Juan....................Wm. Eagle Eye
The Dancer.............Ardita Milano
Pedro...................Peter Venzuela
The Secretary.............John Eberts
Zambrano.................Tom Kennedy

This is R. A. Walsh's initial release on his First National franchise. In it he has co-featured his wife, Miriam Cooper, and his brother, George Walsh. He has managed to turn out a picture that is almost of special quality, and a production that should be a box office attraction. Miss Cooper shows to greater advantage in this picture than in any recently, and George Walsh is a corking Spanish lover, although what seems to be a black wig makes him entirely different in appearance.

The story was originally a Spanish novel under the title "Maria del Carmen," and Miss Cooper plays the leading role. George Walsh plays opposite as the lead and Bertram Grassby as the heavy completes the triangle.

The scene is laid in a small Spanish town where Miss Cooper and Rosita Marstini, who plays her mother, are of the aristocracy, while Walsh is the son of the governor, played by James A. Marcus. The young people are in love, but when the new governor and his son (Josef Swickard and Bertram Grassby) arrive, the girl's mother prefers the new arrivals. The rivalry between the two young men leads to a duel in which the hero bests the late arrival and he has to flee for his life.

While he is away the new governor informs the girl that if she will marry his son and thus bring about his recovery from the wound he has received he will forgive her former lover.

She is about to make the sacrifice when Walsh reappears, refuses to be saved by the girl and gives himself up. But not before the son of the governor and he have another setto, during which the former undergoes a change of heart and is willing to have the young lovers escape. But the excitement causes a relapse and he dies. His father then swears vengeance and Walsh is arrested and condemned. The girl in an effort to save him tries to bribe the chief military aide of the governor, a former bandit, who has decided to loot the town and take the girl for himself. At the critical moment the hero escapes jail, friends come to his aid, they manage to defeat the bandits, and all ends happily.

Miss Cooper appeared stunning in all her scenes and gave a performance that is going to place her with the leading dramatic lights of the screen. George Walsh was the hot-blooded lover right down to the ground and managed to handle himself in the dueling scene, an earlier fight and in the escapes in a manner that will further endear him to the fans.

Messrs. Swickard and Grassby both gave clever performances, while Nobel Johnson as the bandit heavy looked and enacted the role to perfection. Ardita Milano handled a Spanish dancing bit nicely.

If "Serenade" is a sample of the class of the production that R. A. Walsh is going to furnish First National, the organization ought to congratulate itself. *Fred.*

PASSING THRU

Billy Barton...........Douglas MacLean
Mary Spivins............Madge Bellamy
James Spivins............Otto Hoffman
Willie Spivins..........Cameron Coffey
Silas Harkins...........Willard Robards
Mother Harkins............Edithe Yorke
Hezikiah Briggs..........Fred Gambold
Louise Kingston....Margaret Livingston
Fred Kingston..........Louis Natheaux
Henry Kingston............Bert Hadley

Douglas MacLean is happily suited in this Paramount feature by Agnes Christine Johnson, made into scenario form by Joseph Franklin Poland, and directed by William A. Seiter. It is current at the Rialto. The story has first rate, smooth comedy values, and its added interest comes from the use of a trained white mule employed cleverly in the action.

The character of Billy Barton, a good-hearted, over-generous youth, who has an unfortunate knack of getting in wrong, is especially likeable, a peculiarly congenial role for this young and agreeable comedian. The picture is one of those rare productions where the spontaneous laughs come frequent and regularly without esort to crudely slapstick and arise plausibly out of an interesting background of human situations. There is nothing grotesque in the tale, but it nevertheless sustains interest from first to last.

Billy is a bank teller in love with the daughter of the institution's president, Henry Kingston. Fred, his son, commits thefts from the bank's funds, and while the examiners are going over the books, appeals to Billy to accept responsibility for the defalcations, just for the moment, promising that he will make a clean breast of it after the examiners have gone. Fred refuses to make good and Billy is convicted and disgraced. He escapes a jail sentence and disappears, taking up his life anew in Colverton as a farm hand. He works for a poor farmer and agrees to take his wages in the form of a mule, owned by the farmer, Jim Spivins.

Billy is a good deal of a mouth organ performer. He charms the simple country folk wtih his playing and gets the mule to go through amazing maneuvers to the accompaniment of the harmonica tunes. Some of these trick mule passages are very laughable. Spivins and the local banker are at swords' ends over land litigation, and Billy must fall in love with the banker's daughter. While he is struggling to reconcile the enemies, the mule knocks the banker cold and Spivins is charged with attempted murder.

Meanwhile Fred Kingston is forced by a gang of crooks into whose toils he has fallen to attempt the robbery of the Culverton bank and the happy ending comes when Billy breaks in upon him while he is carrying away the spoils. Billy is knocked unconscious and locked up in the time vault and the happy ending comes about when the banker's daughter brings a yeggman from the nearby prison to crack the safe. The yegg isn't equal to the job, but Billy is rescued in an amusing manner by the trick mule in a hilarious climax and wins the beauty prize in the banker's daughter.

Billy, the trick mule, and the educated mouth organ make a refreshing triangle. They will amuse any sort of an audience anywhere. *Rush.*

MAN WORTH WHILE

Mary Alden..................Joan Arliss
The Child.............Lawrence Johnson
Herbert Loring..............Eugene Acker
Mrs. Ward...............Margaret Seddons
Andre.................Frederick Eckhart
Cecile........................Peggy Parr
Mrs. Forbes-Grey.......Herbert Standing
Miss Flo..............Vanda Tierendelli
The Judge...................Barney Gilmore
The Dancer..............Natalie O'Brien
The Parson..................."Tex" Cooper
A Lifer......................"Kid" Broad
The Doctor...............Emile Le Croix
Eddie Loring............Frank De Vernon
Percy.......................Burt Hodkins
The Sheriff...........Clarence Heritage
The Operator...........Ruth Buchanan
"Useless"...............Tammany Young
Napoleon......................Billy Quirk
Don Ward..............Romaine Fielding

Hillfield, Inc., presents "The Man Worth While," a screen adaption of the play, by Leopold Robbins. Romaine Fielding did the directing, also playing the leading role. The story, of a tensely dramatic nature, is nicely translated to the screen. It contains a human appeal graphically worked out. The action takes place in the Canadian Northwest. Don "Smiler" Ward, a ranger, is a well-regarded citizen in the locality. He makes known his love for Mary Alden, a local girl, and the marriage is about to take place. His love is known by the son of a rich lumber king, who tricks the girl into going to his lodge with him, where he forces her to go through with a marriage ceremony. He then deserts the girl.

The ranger learns of the affair, trailing him to the office. "Smiler" is arrested for attempting to murder the man, although the latter struck the first blow. A jail sentence is pronounced. The girl in the meantime has a child, who upon reaching a knowing age asks about his father. The mother goes to the home of the man who wrecked her life and demands that he give her recognition as his wife. A tussle ensues with the man falling dead. The "Smiler" at this time is released from jail and a happy termination of the story is brought about.

The Hillfield organization is apparently a new concern. It has turned out in this feature a picture that hits the mark for the average audience. It is a "sob story" to a certain extent with a direct sympathetic appeal. The cast is large and well selected as to types. The production end is not costly and for a Western picture shot in the East has been made realistic. For a regular program picture "The Man Worth While" is a satisfying film.

MAN AND WOMAN

"Male and Female" found wide popularity when directed by Cecil De Mille, with a superior cast. The returns were unusual.

Comes now the Jans Productions Co. with a picture that can be regarded in the comparative light of its predecessor, for it contains South Sea Island stuff and the title borders on "Male and Female" strikingly. It is about the twentieth of the sort since the Paramount feature was released. "Man and Woman" is a tedious affair even for a program offering. Diana Allen is starred in this tropic story that holds a cast evidently not particularly well acquainted with acting.

For their lapses, however, they can be forgiven for, as they are concerned in such proceedings, it is patent they could not help but be remiss.

The direction, credited to Charles A. Logue, may have accounted for some of the acting deficiencies. Always there is the background of sand stretches, palms and rippling waves, as in the other. Also cave men, cave women, the transporting of the heroine from one isle to the other, the fight in the last pool, and the attracting of the passing ship with the usual bonfire. "Man and Woman" is just a picture. *Samuel.*

BEYOND

Avis Langley.............Ethel Clayton
Geoffrey Southerne.....Charles Meredith
Alec Langley................Earl Schenk
Mrs. Langley.............Fontaine LaRue
Viva Newmarch......Winifred Kingston
Bessie Ackroyd................Lillian Rich
Samuel Ackroyd..........Charles French
Wilfred Southerne..Spottiswoode Aitken
Dr. Newmarch...........Herbert Fortier

"Beyond" is from the Henry Arthur Jones' story, "The Lifted Veil." Julia Crawford Ivers provided the screen version and William D. Taylor directed. Paramount is sponsoring the production. Ethel Clayton is starred. The theme is not novel, being that of the shipwrecked wife returning to her former home after spending a year on a desolate island, only to find her husband married to another. Distinctiveness is aimed at, however, in this film by having spiritual instincts move the characters, the premise being that some are distinctly swayed by a spiritual side while others are immune because of being too material.

In the reasoning out the director has lost sight of essential plausibility, causing too artificial an appeal, and making the action taut and blunt at times. This accounted for the audience at the Rivoli showing Sunday giggling audibly during serious passages. It is possible, though, that originally the proper concept was achieved, with inept cutting doing the harm.

"Beyond" has been mounted sumptuously, its interpretation is thoroughly in keeping, there is enough human interest to hold the spectator, and the psychic element saves it from being a "groove" affair, but the discriminating patrons will hardly display enthusiasm over it. As a regular program release for the less sophisticated, and for the smaller domains, it will perhaps gain favor. At the Rivoli it was dwarfed in point of esteem by a whale of a comedy called "Brownie's Little Venus," featuring "Brownie," the wonder dog, and the cutest feminine kidlet in pictures. *Samuel.*

THE BIGAMIST

London, Aug. 24.

This is, with the exception of "Carnival," the most ambitious British picture yet made. For some time past we have heard much of its wonders and it has been boosted in every conceivable way. That being the case let us say at once that we were sadly disappointed with the result. he production itself is magnificent, the sets being worthy of any studio in the world while the exteriors, made in and around Nice, are very beautiful, but the story is terribly weak and leans on the sordid side. It is also very much too long even for a "super" feature.

Pamela has been happily married for some years to Herbert Arnott and is the mother of two children. All is sunshine. Then one day a bomb bursts in the happy home in the shape of a letter from a woman who has a prior claim to Arnott and is in reality his legal wife. Pamela has been the plaything of a villain and her children are illegitimate. A scene follows but the upshot of the whole affair is that she consents to remain under his roof for the sake of the children but as "a wife in name only." In the midst of her unhappiness George Dare, who has always adored her, arrives, learns the truth and conquering his own passion stands by in the capacity of a faithful watch dog, a self-sacrificing role he sustains until the end. Cut off from domestic bliss by Pamela's decree Arnott casts his eyes elsewhere and soon finds solace in the caresses of the children's governess. Presently they elope. Eventually they are tracked down by Dare who finds that Arnott has become para'yzed, finds also that the real wife has been dead some time, and arranges then and there that the invalid shall make Pamela "an honest woman."

The end comes as Dare says farewell to the woman he loves and leaves her waiting for the priest who will presently unite her to the scamp who has wrecked her life. The best thing in the story is this determined get-away from the conventional happy ending, a'though it promises little happiness to Pamela and we very much doubt whether the bulk of picture-goers, trained as they are to having all obstacles cleared away in the last hundred feet or two and the uniting of hero and heroine will quite appreciate this state of affairs.

The acting is genera'ly above the average in British pictures although it is some distance from stellar distinction. Julian Royce plays well as Arnott, but is at times a little stagey. Ivy Duke is beautifu'ly statuesque as Pamela but shows more emotional power than her previous work had led us to suspect. Guy Newall, who is also responsible for the production, gives his usual portrayal of the immaculately dressed, perfectly mannered English gentleman, and is deserving of congratulation for his work throughout, whether as actor or producer. Comedy is introduced by Bromley Davenport as another type of Englishman—the one really created by the American producer, highly bred, perfectly mannered, but still just a bit of a silly ass. The rest of the company do all that is required of them well. "The Bigamist" is said to have cost over £51,542 to produce and has been boomed on approved American sensational methods by Harry Reichenbach. It is being shown daily at the Alhambra, but despite the theatre, the well advertised cost, the offer of a £100 for the best criticism, we very much doubt whether either the picture itself or Reichenbach's advertising methods will bring much of the money back into the coffers of the George Clarke Company. It might have been a great picture—it is not. *Gore.*

LONELY HEART

Lonely Heart................	Kay Laurell
Bartlett Goodale...........	Robert Elliott
Mr. Goodale................	Tom Burrough
Peter Blue Fox....	Escamillia Fernandez
Alvaro........................	Jack Dalton
Ossawami	Himself
A Grocery Boy............	Robert F. Hill
A Show Girl..............	Desacia Seville

C. C. Burr is the producer of "Lonely Heart" released through the Affiliated Distributors, Inc. Edgar Selwyn is the author with the screen version written by Anthony Paul Kelly. John B. O'Brien did the directing. Kay Laurell, the former Ziegfeld beauty, is the star, the picture being her third screen effort. The locale of the story is laid in the Oklahoma oil fields with the general trend of the tale dealing with the rivalry between the white man and Indians in that section. Lonely Heart (Kay Laurell), an Indian girl, falls in love with the son of an oil operator. Prior to this it was taken for granted that she was to marry one of her own race, one Peter Blue Fox, an educated Indian from the Carlisle School. The redskin in order to frustrate the efforts of his rival taps the leading well on the latter's land, stopping the flow of oil, which brings a decline in the price of the company's stock. This he buys in gaining the controlling interest. The girl, knowing of his plans, steals the stock certificates but is caught in the act by Blue Fox.

A struggle ensues in which he is stabbed by an unknown party, the girl being accused of the murder. In the trial following an Indian aide of the dead man confesses to the murder which releases the girl with the happy marriage with her white sweetheart at the finish. With the reputation Miss Laurell has as a beauty and a flashy stage dresser to step forth in a simple Indian maiden character is a novelty. It develops certain dramatic ability which is often unsuspected in a musical comedy star.

The supporting cast is made up from the general run of screen players. There is no outstanding feature other than the star. The story is entertaining with the production end worked out on a conservative basis. An ordinary feature that misses the mark on several occasions.

THE MIDLANDERS

Andrew J. Gallaghan produced "The Midlanders," a five reeler, starring Bessie Love for the Federated Exchanges. Charles Tenney Jackson wrote the story, which was published some time ago. The picture version of the story is not convincingly worked out. It is jumbled up considerab y with the continuity weak in several spots. The central figure is an orphan girl. She escapes from a convent and is adopted by a Mississippi river boat captain. She is sent by him to live with his brother, a squatter in a small town. She develops into a beautiful girl and wins a newspaper contest which brings forth an offer from a theatrical producer which is accepted. This move is frowned upon by her foster father as we l as by the other small-town folk. The girl rises to stardom over night, helps her benefactor financially, but upon her return to the home town she is looked upon with contempt by the neighbors. Anyway it ends with her marrying one of the home talent boys. There is a side bit with a hard-shell land owner which supp ies the melodramatic side of the picture. The picture was offered as part of a double feature bill at an Eighth Avenue house. It could hardly be classed as a suitab'e feature for the cheaper houses. The story was not well worked out in the film version. The directors have passed up detail and slapped in bits here and there to bring forth some kind of a story. The cast in support of the star does sufficiently well and is typical of pictures of this grade. The production end is on a par with the rest of the picture. Only a sma'l small timer.

ROOM AND BOARD

Lady Noreen..........	Constance Binney
Terrence O'Brien..........	Tom Carrigan
Ephraim Roach........	Malcolm Bradley
Desmond Roach........	Arthur Housman
Robert Osborne..............	Jed Prouty
Mary.......................	Blanche Craig
Ryan..................	Ben Hendricks, Jr
Leila......................	Ellen Cassidy
The Earl of Kildoran......	Arthur Barry

Light comedy, starring Constance Binney (Realart); story by Charles E. Whittaker, photographed by Donnah Darrell, direction by Alan Crossland.

Six reels make a lot of footage for a story so light and devoid of anything like drama, action, suspense, surprise or any other element except a mild interest in the development of a rather trifling romance involving hero and heroine. The characters are likeable people and the story is conspicuously without offense. In addition it has extremely picturesque settings. The background of an ancient Irish estate is most convincingly and beautifully reproduced upon the screen, and this scenic splendor is the redeeming quality of the production—indeed it is almost lovely enough (added to the demure beauty of the star) to make the film worth while in spite of its lamentably weak story.

The tale is practically without action, as the fans have come to understand the term in a screen way—that is to say action of more or less violence. There is to be sure, one short and conclusive exchange of fisticuffs between the hero and the scheming money lender who would evict the beautiful peeress from her castle, but that is small reward in the way of "action" when a fan can get an episode of a serial with two homicides, a train wreck and seven felonious assaults with lethal weapons for the same price.

Thus the feature assays as an agreeable enough little romance, too much spread out into footage, but offering interesting settings and nice people. Probably won't appeal to a very wide section of fandome, nor offer great opportunity for exploitation, but ought to please in a mild casual way. It cannot offend. There isn't anything in it of sufficient kick to invite criticism, win praise or hold attention. There are a few moments of fairly effective humor of the stagy kind, mostly sent over via the titles. But the only saving grace is the delightful shots of a dilapidated castle surrounded by lovely landscapes and with capital ancient interiors and the graceful presence of this dainty actress.

Lady Noreen is owner of the antique mansion loaded to the eves with mortgages and has to sell her thoroughbred hunter to make part payment of the estate's debts to escape eviction. A rich young American named O'Brien happens in the vicinity about this time and Lady Noreen diplomatically gets him to rent the place. She makes him believe that the owner is in France and she (Noreen) is the housekeeper. Meanwhile she is pursued by a sharper who schemes to marry her.

O'Brien learns early that the supposed housekeeper is really the peeress and he sends the schemer packing after knocking him out in a spirited fight. O'Brien's fiancee also gets into the proceedings and there are several amusing passages between the proud Irish lady and the rather vulgar guest, ending, of course, with the defeat of the fiancee and the embrace of Lady Noreen and O'Brien. It goes without saying that O'Brien has bought the mortgage and all is well. *Rush.*

CHARGE IT

Julia Lawrence....	Clara Kimball Young
Philip Lawrence......	Herbert Rawlinson
Tom Gareth.........	Edward M. Kimball
Millie Gareth................	Betty Blythe
Dana Herrick................	Nigel Barrie
Robert McGregor..............	Hal Wilson
Rose McGregor...............	Dulcie Cooper

"Charge It" by Sada Cowan is a Harry Garson production with Clara Kimball Young as the star and released through Equity Pictures Corp.

The story theme is that of the young couple who start out in life with the determination to live well within their income, but with the first gleam of success the wife falters from the path of thrift and starts a spending spree with charge accounts that finally ends in the family breaking up. Naturally there is "the other man" to the triangle, but in the end he is eliminated and there is a reunion.

Miss Young is the young wife, giving a performance not up to her usual mark. The story is partly to blame and atop of that, the lightings and camera work are such the star does not show to advantage. The lighting is particularly bad. It makes Miss Young look aged at times and decidedly hard featured at others. Shadows across her face and mouth have the effect of distorting her features. The same is true of Herbert Rawlinson who plays opposite her.

Betty Blythe as a heavy gives a corking performance and looks stunning at all times. Nigel Barrie as "the other man" romps away with a role that calls for a lot of dancing in which he excels. Hal Wilson and Dulcie Cooper play minor parts satisfactorily.

"Charge It" is just a program picture. *Fred.*

THE SHARK MASTER

Excellent memories these scenario writers. Universal has a feature called "The Shark Master," the plot of which revolves about a man shipwrecked on a desert island, living alone with a woman who is white and was reared by the South Sea Islanders, a child is born to them, his civilized fiance finds him, and the mother of his child leaps into the sea.

In this scenario by George Hall, however, he doesn't go back to civilization, but leaps into the shark-infested sea and rescues the wild woman who bore him a child, leaving his original financee to return home with her father. Frank Mayo is the hero and May Collins the hectic, undraped heroine, known as "The Flame Flower."

The only reason that can be imagined for the titling of the peace "The Shark Master" is that before cutting it contained some underwater scenes showing a fight between a man and a shark. If so, a'l that is left of such footage is the occasional cutting in of some resurrected pieces of Universal's "20,000 Leagues Under the Sea," showing a shark swimming lazily about.

Not a single interior set, the majority of the personages being "South Sea Islanders" in comic make-ups. The best thing about the production is the bunch of sub-titles. Boy, there are some hot ones, with poetry let loose with a vengeance. Leroy Granville directed. *Jolo.*

HABIT

Irene Fletcher..:..........	Mildred Harris
John Marshall........	William Lawrence
Mary Chartres.........	Ethel Grey Terry
Charles Munson.........	Walter McGrail
Richard Fletcher.......	Emmett C. King

The lithographs for "Habit" announce it as being presented by Louis B. Mayer, released by First National and that it was directed by Edwin Carewe. No mention is made of the star, Mildred Harris, nor is the name of the author given. It is a very good feature, modern in every respect—that is, in production, direction, interior details and in story. A good moral is taught—that of self-sacrifice.

The picture derives its name from the selfishness of a young woman of marriageable age who all her life has cultivated the habit of wanting things and not being denied till a doting father, who is in financial difficulties, is compelled to refuse. She upbraids him and rushes upstairs in a rage. She trips, rolls down and is picked up unconscious.

Bereft of her senses for 20 minutes she "dreams" a horrible series of happenings which come as the result of her selfishness and upon awakening throws herself into her father's arms and cries that she has learned her lesson. To the doctor who arrives she says it is not his services but will power she needs to combat the monster, Habit.

The dream is ingeniously concealed until the finish and comes as an agreeable surprise to the audience. Ably acted throughout and an intelligent avoidance of sub-titles wherever pantomine wi'l put over a thought. The feature should please anywhere. *Jolo.*

WIFE'S AWAKENING

A Robertson-Cole subject, shown in one of the lower priced neighborhood houses where it belongs. The story is by Jack Cunningham and the star is Fritzi Brunette. The tale is the familiar sort of the scheming, heartless, cruel husband and the loving, but persecuted wife. It takes a naive mind to accept the story at its face value. The trouble with these sob tales is that they approach dangerously close to travesty. The margin between drama and burlesque is so narrow the most careful handling is necessary to avoid the pitfalls of unexpected laughs.

This one travels a fairly safe path. It s full of impossible situations and the bromides come thick and fast, but there is drama of a sort in the telling—pretty stale and threadbare drama, but the crude elements of the theatrical stuff is there. Only it requires a most awful degree of simplicity in the spectator. The titles are stilted, in the old fashioned Family Story paper style. They express the meanings in florid language such as could never by any chance happen anywhere but in the pictures. The same is true of the character relations and the situations. As if the picture were not sufficiently artificial, Miss Brunette is the most mechanical and stagey of actresses and goes to intensify the unreality of the whole affair. It's just a picture make believe and never does resemble actuality.

George Otis (Sam de Grasse) is the heavy villain. He marries the heroine for her money. Nobody knows why the heroine marries him, because it is manifest during the entire picture she loves another man, John Howard by name. George is constantly in need of money, being a stock market speculator constantly on the wrong side. He tries to force his wife to borrow money from her old flame. Instead she gets the money from her mother. When George is short of cash again he repeats the maneuver. The wife rebels and he charges her with having secured the first bankroll from Howard "at a price," and having told the story about her mother to cover her "sin."

This is too much even for a film wife and she departs for mother's home. The ex-lover is called into consultation and during the three-cornered conference husband breaks in armed with a revolver. He attempts to shoot his wife, but the lover prevents him. Whereupon husband breaks down, sobs his repentance and departs to become a better man, leaving his wife, her mother and the former sweetheart in bandclasp tableau. Surely a curious and unsatisfactory ending. In the nature of a romantic stalemate.

A sample of the slipshod manner of direction occurs when George is facing ruin in the stock market and receives a telegram from his office warning him that all is lost because "We are forctd to cover on a falling market." George registered shock and anguish all over the place, although if there is ever a propitious moment to "cover," it is on a "falling market," as the director might have learned if he had taken the trouble to find out.

Not that a sloppy detail like that would mean anything to the sort of an audience that would be imposed upon by this variety of sentimental trash. *Rush.*

JUNGLE ADVENTURES

A picture of jungle life in the main, taken by Martin Johnson, with the captions stating Mr. and Mrs. Johnson invaded the innermost regions of unexplored Borneo, taking several months and many pictures. Mrs. Johnson in the pictures is heavily featured, and deserved to be if she underwent all the trials of the trip.

Opening views are of the preparations for the start, with following scenes up the inland rivers of upper Borneo, into the jungle, and back again. A caravan of native boats was the mode of transportation with much of the footage devoted to it, its composition, travel and camping place.

The actual jungle scenes are somewhat meagre for the length of the film. Three elephants are displayed, plenty of monkeys and an ape or two. One of the latter is shown flitting from tree to limb.

More is made of the picture in the lobby than on the screen. Outside the billing lean toward "jungle" and wild beasts. It may attract considerable through that. It's an Exceptional Film Co. product and creates a natural interest without sufficient of the natural history in its wild state, evident. *Sime.*

FOOTFALLS

Hiram Scudder............Tyrone Power
Tommy, his son............Tom Douglas
Peggy Hawthorne.........Estelle Taylor
Alec Campbell............Gladden James

A great special shown for the first time Sept. 8 at the Park by Fox. Its unusual quality, its exceptional value as artistry rests squarely on the story by Wilbur Daniel Steele, one of America's elect in the fiction field, but the producer deserves credit for allowing Director Charles J. Brabin to stick to the original conception and end it all unhappily. This gives it the cumulative power of Greek tragedy, but what is its market value? Probably it will surprise the wise ones for the public is tired of the conventional and wants the new, the real, the moving.

The public will get it here. The cobbler Hiram is blind, and when his only son, urged by the young girl he wants to marry, announces he must go into the world and make a fortune, the father is opposed. He cannot bear the thought of separation. Meanwhile the girl, to pique Tommy, flirts with Alec Campbell, but refuses to elope with him when he is about to make off with the payroll. Before he can get away with it, Tommy and he fight. The cobbler seeks to interfere, is shoved through the balcony and breaks his leg. Upstairs the house catches fire and an escaping figure, whose face you do not see, but whose clothes are Tommy's, seeks to get by the cobbler. In the end he does, but leaves the money behind.

The cobbler waits unendingly while the villagers mock him because he is so sure he can identify the murderer by his footsteps. And in the end he does. The man comes back, is caught by the cobbler and proves to be Alec, Tommy's body having been burned up in the fire.

Here was a real series of climaxes and close, intelligent cutting accentuate them. Perhaps the picture's fault is in overacting permitted by the director, young Tom Douglas being least guilty in this respect. Mr. Power strikes magnificent attitude, but is always too reminiscent of the speaking stage for the best effects. You are too conscious he is an actor, though an able one. Estelle Taylor never seemed girlish enough, and in her presentation of ideas there was frequently evident the command of the director rather than that naturalness which is so compelling.

Good use for emotional purposes was made of a dog, who went to summon help during the fight, which Mr. Brabin got a lot from, while exteriors, interiors, lightings and detail were all satisfactory. George W. Lane's photography was of the A1 variety. *Leed.*

CAMILLE

Camille......................Nazimova
Armand Duval.......Rudolph Valentino
Count De Varville..........Arthur Hoyt
Prudence................Zeffie Tillbury
Gaston..................Rex Cherryman
Duke..................Edward Connelly
Nichette......................Ruth Miller
Olimpe..............Consuelo Flowerton
Nanine......................Mrs. Oliver
Monsieur Duval......William Orlamond

The long-awaited production of Nazimova in "Camille" has arrived and it proves to be a modernized version of the story of "The Lady With the Camellias," which fact is welcome for the major part but not so felicitous as the conclusive parts of the Dumas film contribution are reached. For wonder of wonders, the director, in this instance Ray Smallwood, has entirely omitted the scene of Armand at the bedside of his beloved as she breathes her last. Perhaps this big moment was eliminated in the thought the picture fans, if unable to witness a happy ending, wanted one as happy as possible under the circumstances. Nothing could be further from the facts, if this observer has sensed audience demands correctly. People have come to associate "Camille" with its final boudoir incident in which Armand must of necessity be a central character. In the Metro screen document Marguerite Gautier passes away with only Gaston and Nichette present. Here indeed was arrant misconception!

Before and throughout the unfolding of the picture Nazimova had disclosed the finest acting with which the silver sheet has been graced. Those who were chary of her adaptability for the role sat in mute stupefaction as she totally immersed her own distinct personality into that of the famed heroine. Instead of the sinuous, clinging Nazimova, she appeared an actress almost new-born for the part. Her hair had been especially bobbed to aid in a chic, Frenchy aspect, her garments had been cut to give the appearance of diminutiveness, her mannerisms and facial play, in repose and when animated, were ever and anon as French as France itself. Her conception, too, approximated the niceties of delineation with marvelous finesse. And those eyes of Nazimova, as only she can use them, expressed first the wise, seer roguishness of the demimonde, later the gleam of love-contentment when her adoration seems sure and secure, and finally anguish and bitter disappointment as the utter dregs of despair suffuse her and diminish her stoicism.

In the gambling scene she reaches what may perhaps be termed the apex of her characterization. Swayed by the father of Armand to give him up, she has returned again to become the mistress of the Count de Varville. She encounters her lover as he has lost faith in her. Armand taunts her about her monetary affection, finally flinging a mass of bank notes in her face while stridently beseeching the crowd to note carefully the woman whose love was veered by gold. Into her countenance comes the play of almost every emotion and when she ultimately faints, a figure of abject pity, the thought occurs and recurs the acme of histrionic art has been reached. The end when poverty impends and her vitality is shattered brings regret commingled with pity. Her coughing remains a veracious incident but it is never disconcerting. It merely aids in the fidelity.

The surrounding company is excellent. Zeffie Tillbury, favorite of old, adds lustre to the part of Prudence. An impressive characterization is that of Duval, pere. But second to the star is the Armand of Rudolph Valentino. There are many opportunities for obtrusiveness in the role, but he keeps it correct to the minutest detail. And he looks Armand as no one else has in the past. It will do much to enhance his reputation. "Camille" will, it is safe to assume, attain wide popularity, holding as it does all the elements of success augmented by the mastery and superb artistry of Nazimova, transcending in her Marguerite Gautier many of the great roles of dramatic and screen history. *Samuel.*

3 MUSKETEERS

Queen Anne of France....Dorothy Dalton
Miladi Winters............Louise Glaum
Richelieu...................Walt Whitman
D'Artagnan................Orrin Johnson

The Alexander Film Corp., which holds a contract for the distribution of re-issued Triangle Pictures, took over the Manhattan opera house on a rental basis for two weeks, pending the opening of the San Carlo Opera Co., and began Monday night the exhibition of a five-reeler now entitled "The Three Musketeers," a new print of a production released in 1916 under the title "D'Artagnan," founded on the Dumas novel. Orrin Johnson is featured as the fiery Gascon hero and in the same cast are Dorothy Dalton and Louise Glaum.

The Alexander company is exploiting its picture to take advatage of popular interest in the story aroused by the showing of the Douglas Fairbanks screening of the same Dumas original, current at the Lyric, and apparently the Manhattan opera house engagement is designed to give it the prestige of a big "New York run."

The presentation is ambitious. Music is supplied by the former Rialto Symphony Orchestra of 50 musicians and this is featured in the billing.

Monday night, the opening, an invited audience was present, filled out by admitting pretty much anyone who applied, a crowd with a great many youngsters from the west side neighborhood, conspicuously lacking in "class" although attentive and orderly.

The picture is a first class production in all respects, although probably, inferior to the Fairbanks in point of elaborate spectacular effects. But the romance, the action and the picturesqueness of the original story are skilfully capitalized. As to excellence of cast, in acting and in name value, the Triangle company might be said to have edge on the Faibanks aggregation, with the exception, of course, of the star part. Dorothy Dalton and Louise Glaum have attained to stardom since 1916 and their advertising strength is considerable at this time.

The story version follows pretty closely the scheme used in the E. H. Sothern and other stage adaptations. It is compactly written and has a wealth of action. Besides which it is an altogether adequate recital of the novel. It details very elaborately the wild ride from Paris to the coast, with a dozen combats with the Cardinal's spies on the way; D'Artagnan's arrival in London and interview with Buckingham; the battle of wits with Miladi; the return to France by ship, including the momentary defeat by Rochefort; the escape by swimming and the closing episode at the Royal ball where the diamonds are presented in time for the King's inspection and the Cardinal's defeat. All this is done in a well-knit narrative without surplusage and with a wealth of hard riding and frequent interludes of sword p'ay.

There can be no question of the quality of the production, the objection of United Artists which is contesting the exploitation of the reissue is that it is "unfair competition" and an appeal has been made to the Federal Trade Commission to interfere.

The whoie question seems to hinge upon fair or unfair business practice in exhibiting the film without the announcement that it is a reissue and not a new production. The Trade Commission has put out the rulink that the showing of an old picture in such a way as to make it appear .. new one, constitutes "unfair practice." The ruling, as made public late in 1918, calls for the plain announcement in billing that a revived picture is a re-issue. This pronouncement has been disregarded in this instance except for the program listing as fo lows:

"7. Alexander Film Corp., presents Feature: "The Three Musketeers"

Formerly titled "D'Artagnan"

A Thos. H. Ince Production—featuring Dorothy Dalton, Orrin Johnson and Louise Glaum."

Except for the line "formerly titled D'Artagnan" there is nothing to indicate that the picture is not an entire'y new production. However, failure to follow the Trade Commission's dictum covering re-issue is not confined to this instance. It has been pretty well disregarded in the trade from the beginning.

During the evening Monday an unidentified speaker appeared on the stage of the Opera house at intermission and told the audience that "This orchestra, which made the Rialto theatre famous, is being prevented from making a living and is being locked out, by certain forces at work in your city," and begged that his hearers pass the word along that "it is a good orchestra." The speaker did not go into the facts of the trouble, merely touching on the "certain forces at work in your city."

The facts are that the Rialto organization is involved in the musical union's factional dispute. The musicians were members of the Insurgent Local No. 310, which is still locked out, while the new Locai No. 802, made up of the conservatives, is back at work. As soon as o d 310 contracts expire, jt is expected the 310 members will enroll in N 802.   *Rush.*

OUT OF THE DEPTHS

The Pioneer Exchanges are releasing this Art-O-Graph production with Violet Mersereau and Edmund Cobb featured. Otis B. Thayer did the directing. The story is of a Western nature and full of melodramatic features screened to appeal to a certain class of picture audiences. The tale centres around Chuckie Knowles (Violet Mersereau), daughter of a Western ranch owner. The theme involves the irrigating of the desert lands.

Two young engineers tackle the job. Both are attracted by the girl. One endeavors to do away with his co-worker to get her. This plan is frustrated and later it develops that the one plotted against is the girl's long lost brother. That makes it easier and brings about the inevitable happy ending.

There is a great abundance of atmosphere in this production. It is largely made up of exteriors, most of which scenicly are worth while. There has been no great outlay for production on this account. The cast in support of Miss Mersereau has been carefully selected and is largely made up of types. She possesses a winsomeness that is appealing, her work proving the picture's strongest

asset. A good Western picture that can be sold at a price for small houses.

WHEN DESTINY WILLS

Typical western melodrama produced by Redwood Pictures with Grace Davison starred. Story credited to A. L. Brunton and A. Rotheim. R. C. Baker directed

Girl and man she loves are caught in a storm, taking refuge in à cabin. The inevitable, with the man losing trace of the girl who feels he has deserted her. She becomes poverty stricken and tries to earn a living in a factory for herself and child, but is discharged, attempts suicide, is rescued and befriended by a rich lumber man. She marries him and makes her home in the west. He dies leaving her his sole heir.

The child's father is also in the lumber business and comes in contact with her when a big deal is pulled off. This brings about an explanation and the customary ending.

One of the cheapest. Story is told largely by captions. The continuity without the captions would have meant nothing.

A series of melodramatic effects, handled crudely. The casting displays cheapness with the entire production of inferior grade.

A very cheap rental must have been the bait to bring this into Loew's Circle as half of a double feature bill.

LORD FAUNTLEROY

Cedric (Little Lord Fauntleroy),	Mary Pickford
Dearest (his mother)	Mary Pickford
Earl Dorincourt	Claude Grillingwater
Bevis	Colin Kenny
Havisham	Joseph J. Dowling
Mrs. McGinty	Kate Price
Dick	Fred Malatesta
Hobbs	James A. Marcus
Minna	Rose Dione
Her son	Francis Marion
Rev. Mordaunt	Emmett Kin,
Mrs. Higgins	Mme. de Bodamere

From the novel of Frances Hodgson Burnett; directed by Jack Pickford and Alfred E. Green; scenario by Bernard McConville; photographed by Charles Rosher; music by Louis F. Gottschalk; presentation by Joseph Plunkett.

Offered as a high-priced attraction at the Apollo theatre (Selwyn's) with Miss Pickford and Douglas Fairbanks present at the opening performance, this interesting production was seen under ideal conditions and in the furore of tremendous enthusiasm, before a society audience. Police reserves tore their way through crowds on the sidewalk before and after the showing, as the stars entered and returned between their automobile and the theatre. Mary and Doug made speeches. She seemed truly nervous, and he was undeniably embarrassed.

But, to the picture:

Stripped of any extraneous and extraordinary personal factors, "Little Lord Fauntleroy" is a perfect Pickford picture. It exploits the star in dual roles, one them one of the immortal and classic boy parts of all times. Miss Pickford shows a range of versatility between the blue-blooded and sombre mother and the blue-blooded but mischievous kid, that is almost startling. She meets herself many times in double exposures, and she is taller than herself and different from herself, and incredibly true to each.

A strange and perhaps predominant factor is the influence of both Jack Pickford and Douglas Fairbanks in the finished product of their sister and wife, respectively.

Only Jack could have introduced the whimsical and always amusing touches of raw boyishness in the fighting, grimacing, scheming, lovable kid that Mary Pickford again turns out to be, but this time she is more boy than girl; heretofore her charm in boy parts has been her glorious girlishness; now it is her genuine youthful Tom Sawyer masculinity, a scrapping, two-fisted kid who tears off his laces and velvets and goes to it with the dirty-eared roughnecks.

At other times Doug's classic propensities are obviously exhibited. She jumps off high perches onto other boys' backs, she wrestles and does trick jiu-jutsus, she dodges and climbs and leans and tumbles and hand-stands.

Fauntleroy could scarcely have made a poor picture for any little star, least of all for Mary Pickford, who couldn't make less than a great picture of any ordinary story—anyhow, she never has within the observation of this amateur film reviewer. In this one she is transcendant. While Fauntleroy is not sensational, it is a human and appealing story, and, whereas it may not be Mary's foremost draw because it lacks any sex or important love interest, it is doubtful whether she ever made a finer picture or a more amusing, entertaining and charming one.

What Fauntleroy may lack in its punch appeal to the wise, it should make up in its manifold attraction for the youngsters. It helps to restore Miss Pickford to the innermost hearts of an audience, if she ever left those sacred recesses for more than perhaps an occasional mischosen subject.

Nobody can go wrong in booking "Little Lord Fauntleroy" in any house at any prices that any audiences will pay for any picture.   *Lait.*

WORLD AND WOMAN

A wierd one. It starts out on the fallen woman sentimental note with a Broadway backing, moves into "society" atmosphere of a kind, switches for a moment to down east country life, then steals pretty much the whole idea of "The Miracle Man" (except that the curer is a woman) and ends up with a happy reunion of lovers in a labored climax.

The star is Jeanne Eagles, whose training ought to have warned her to lay off this sort of stuff and Candler Pictures stands sponsors for the production. Miss Eagles first comes into view on a thoroughfare which a title indicates is Broadway, although the backgrounds suggest nothing of the sort. There is a party going on within a gaudy cabaret and one of the men through a window beckons the girl to join the party.

It appears that this diner has a country place and the housekeeper has asked the job to the girl and she—her name is Mary—takes it. When the reveller himself gets to the country house, he promptly makes advances to Mary and when she repulses him, roughs her up. She wanders away to the home of kindly country people nearby and is warmly received. The natives are having a party and the little girl of the household falls down stairs, sustaining injuries which threaten her life. But Mary, who has been purged of sin by suffering, is inspired to pray for the child's recovery and her faith works the miracle. This incident sets Mary up in the miracle business. The maimed and halt come to her from the whole countryside to be cured.

But (quoting the title) "There are men who so hate purity they would stamp upon a flower and crush a good woman's soul." Thus the rich man puts all other business aside and devotes himself to persecuting the poor girl. Unless she will agree to go back to the city with him, he will tell the world of her shameful past. What the past was and how he knew it is apparently none of the audience's business. He just tells the simple country people that "this woman has a past" and they shrink from her. All but one, a companion of the rich villain who promptly knocks him (the villain) down. There is a lot more of aimless narrative culminating when the hero, and the madman from the village meet in combat on a mountain peak and are to fight it out to the death when the hero is saved by the Miracle Girl.

Then it suddenly develops that the brave young man who smashed the villain, had a long time ago "wronged" the heroine. So he repents and they agree to marry. It is such fiction as the cheap magazines buy by the avoirdupois scale at $7.50 per 1,000 words. Still the magazines seem to prosper. If there's a reading public for this grade of matter, maybe there's a film fan public for it, too. They ran it in a Columbus circle picture house at the 35-cent scale and there was no indignation among the audience.   *Rush.*

BEATING THE GAME

"Fancy Charlie"	Tom Moore
Nellie Brown	Hazel Daly
G. B. Lawson	DeWitt C. Jennings
Ben Fanchette	Dick Rosson
"Slipper Jones"	Nick Cogley
Jules Fanchette	Tom Ricketts
Madame Fanchette	Lydia Knott
Bunk President	William Orlamond
Angelico, his wife	Lydia Yeamans Titus

This is Goldwyn's latest release, with Tom Moore as the star. It is a corking comedy drama more or less of the rural type along the lines of "Turn to the Right" and "The Fortune Hunter," but still different enough not to conflict. It has a corking twist at the finish and the suspense is maintained through the continuity until just before the final shot. That usually spells "good picture," and that is exactly what "Beating the Game" is for a regular program production.

Charles Kenyon, one of the Goldwyn regular staff writers, turned out the story, and he has fitted Mr. Moore with a role that he enacts to perfection. Victor Schertzinger directed the production and got all that could be had from the story.

Mr. Moore at the opening is a second-story worker in New York. He breaks into a place and after cleaning up runs across a kit of burglar tools. He believes that he has turned a trick on a brother cracksman and empties his pockets. All the while he's been working he has been under the eye of the owner of the establishmen, who stakes him to $1,000, directs him to a small town, and says that at the end of six months he will show up there, and if Moore has managed to establish a reputation for honesty in that time they will both be in a position to "clean up."

Moore is successful beyond his wildest dreams. The townsfolk are about to nominate him for Mayor, and in addition he has fallen in love. The latter is the reason that he has determined to go straight, and when the supposed cracksman from New York shows up and is ready to operate, he turns him down. Then it develops that his benefactor is really a State Senator, owns half of the town and is a crank on criminology. Of course, he has put the boy he is experimenting with through various tests, and finding him strong enough to "go through" with them all, he is willing to back him to the limit.

There are many little touches through the story that help along in making the picture one well worth while. Hazel Daly, who plays opposite Moore, is a cute ingenue lead, and answers all needs of the story to perfection. DeWitt C. Jennings plays the benefactor cleverly, while Nick Cogley is a corking old crook, but nevertheless a lovable one. Dick Rosson plays the heavy, doing very well with what is little more than a bit.

Fred.

FIGHTING STRANGER

A Canyon Picture featuring Franklyn Farnum is offered as half of a double feature at the New York. It is one of those elemental melodramas which have as their chief and only virtue a chain of swift action episodes the more violent and spectacular the better.

"The Fighting Stranger" fulfills this requirement abundantly. The blood and thunder incidents crowd upon each other's heels. The picture begins with an elaborate chase involving the robbers of a bank and the pursuit of a dozen policemen after as many thieves. The course runs over housetops, along the docks and into the water and has a punch a second with gunplay galore, a killing or two or three and eventual escape of the outlaws in a captured speed boat.

However, this is only a foretaste. After that the scene changes to the west and marine adventure gives place to hard riding, rope-throwing and the rest of the cowboy incidentals. Nobody rests for a moment and events happen as frequently (and with about as much plausibility) as in a chapter of a wild serial. Restraint in inventing situations is thrown to the winds. The villain puts the heroine's automobile out of gear so that it "runs away" without brakes down a steep mountain road and the hero saves her by hanging himself by his knees from a tree over the road and catching her up as she whizzes by.

Another villain lassoos her as she is galloping by and drops her over a precipice at the end of the rope while he stands at the brink and hurls rocks at her. The hero, who is in reality a detective posing for his own purposes as a leader of outlaws, first lassoos the villain, then goes across the chasm on his own lariat hand over hand and saves the distressed girl. Those two are merely samples. There are a score of spectacular "stunts" of equal excitement and they all go to making up of a story which should be interesting entertainment for the sort of audiences that like this sort of thing.

The picture is a crude dime novel grade of fiction, but it does not make pretension to be anything else and is offered frankly for just what it is. As a production in this class it is well done. It is straightaway melodrama and accomplishes its purpose of delivering a heroic thrill. These films have their field and their standards and are to be judged by their spectacular function. When they are well done, as this one is, they deserve credit. The objectionable picture, aside from ethics involved, is that which makes high pretense of intellectual appeal and then descends to cheap theatricalism.

"The Fighting Stranger" offers wholesome, simple romance and its action takes place in fine scenic mountain surroundings. The photography is excellent. The story has to do with the railroading of an innocent man by a rich and predatory blackguard and the efforts of his friends to secure his release from prison. The villain seeks to marry the victim's daughter and the rough and ready detective employed to free the father falls in love with the daughter (although he seems to be working against her) and thus a thread of romance is woven into the pattern.

Rush.

THE ROWDY

Made by Universal from the Saturday Evening Post story, "The Ark Angel," with Gladys Walton starred. Jack Cunningham wrote the scenario. It is an interesting little romantic comedy with picturesque settings in a fishing village. Some good comedy character relations give a certain agreeable flavor to the story and the whole thing is far and away above the Universal average for taste and intelligence.

Miss Walton, as the tomboy protege of an old lighthouse keeper, gives an amusing performance and does particularly well in the several passages where dramatic force is demanded. She has freshness of youth and a natural style of acting that registers clearly on the screen. The supporting company is excellent in an even way none too common in the output of this maufacturer.

In the catch-as-catch-can way of getting film data is thrown on the screen the names of the leading man and several supporting characters were lost although they deserve mention. In like manner the direction has been handled in workmanlike style with several capital tricks of light and shadow and the dramatic supprises are effective.

The story has to do with a baby cast up on the lighthouse beach and adopted by the lighthouse keeper and his wife. The child grows up among fisher folk, a rollicking tomboy. In behalf of a sorrowing wife Kit, as she is called, adventures into the cabin of one of the fishing fleet and breaks up a gambling game in which the husband is losing his earnings. The young man, owner of the boat, seizes her and is about to hold her captive. The girl pleads for a sporting chance and the gambler agrees that she may load one chamber of his revolver. She may pull the trigger twice and if he escapes, she may go free. Instead the girl points the revolver to her own temple and the gambler admits himself defeated. He thereupon falls in love with the brave heroine.

At this point two rich women appear and claim the girl as their niece. They take her away to their luxurious home across the bay to bring her up in a style appropriate to her new condition. The girl finds the stiff, conventional society people uncongenial as compared to the more sincere folk of the village and constantly returns to the scenes of her childhood.

In a trip back from the fishing fleet she is made captive by a young man in the cabin of his cruising boat and is only rescued by the prompt arrival of the young fisherman who loves her. There are some first-rate sea storms in this passage and a fine fight as a dramatic climax. In the end it turns out that the two old ladies are not her aunts at all. So she returns gladly to her own fisher folk and marries the young seaman.

Rush.

WHERE MEN ARE MEN

Vic Foster	William Duncan
Eileen	Edith Johnson
Frank Valone	George Stanley
"Dutch" Monahan	Tom Wilson
Laura Valone	Gertrude Astor
R. C. Cavendish	Harry Lonsdale
Sheriff Grimes	George Kunkel
Mike Regan	William McCall
Monty Green	Charles Dudley

A Vitagraph production adapted for the screen by Thomas Dixon, Jr., from the story "The Princess of the Desert Dream," by Ralph Cummins. William Duncan is the star, also credited with the direction. The story is of the west. The locale being the mining country. Vic Foster (Duncan) is accused of killing his partner to secure his poke. To clear his name he endeavors to locate the real culprit. This brings him into contact with the cabaret star of a mining camp saloon. Nothing is known of the girl other than she is strictly on the level. A friendship springs up between the two Foster aiding her to leave the place when she is threatened by the proprietor. She goes to a neighboring camp where he visits her after having been run out of the other settlement for beating up the saloon man who had drugged him and stolen the deed to his mine.

The girl proves to be the daughter of his dead partner masquerading under an assumed name in order to locate her father's murderer. To clear up the mystery it turns out that the saloon owner is the murderer which brings about his justified punishment and the serene finish for Foster and the girl.

For a western picture this is comparatively interesting. The general flood of pictures of this order has been noticeable of late in the cheaper houses. The old style melodramatic idea appears to hold a certain appeal for the middle class of picture goers. Vitagraph has outdistanced a number of the others with this production. Its story has sufficient interest to gain recognition. Duncan works extremely hard as a star and convincingly brings out his story in the directing. Edith Johnson, playing the leading female role, does some convincing work with the remainder of the cast largely made up of types. The production end has not been made costly through the action taking place in the open. The picture can be sold at a price at which it should bring returns.

WESTERN HEARTS

Cliff Smith produced "Western Hearts," a typical cowboy drama, released through Associated Pictures, with the New York rights held by Commonwealth. Smith also did the directing and is credited with co-authorship with Alvin J. Neitz. In addition to the customary thrills for a picture of this nature, "Western Hearts" presents a story in which several unusual angles are developed.

The theme is interesting and holds the attention without too much spectacular riding and holdups. It is true the production has its share of this sort of business but does not rely on it entirely. The scenes are laid on a cattle ranch. The foreman falls in love with an eastern girl visitor. The owner's niece loves him and endeavors to keep him from the other girl. After the latter's departure she holds up the letters of the two, giving the impression that neither one is sincere. This causes the chap to leave the ranch with the trouble maker marrying his successor as foreman, she remaining in hiding and writing to her uncle that she has married the foreman who resigned.

The eastern girl's father buys the ranch and, accompanied by his daughter, makes his home there. Upon his arrival he is informed that his daughter's former sweetheart had gone off and married the other girl. The man in question goes into the government service and is sent to the ranch to round up a band of cattle rustlers. There he meets the girl of his choice and manages to clear himself.

The husband of the other girl in the meantime is robbing the owner of his cattle. In order to escape he forces his wife to come in contact with the other man while his sweetheart is present, giving the impression that he is married to her. This causes further complications that are straightened out after several mixups with the rustlers and a general cleaning up of the entire affair. The inevitable serene ending follows promptly. It is almost entirely an outdoor picture. The ranch scenes in most instances are interesting, the director going a bit further with his work in picking interesting side bits. The cast includes Art Straton, Josie Sedgewick, Hazel Hart, Floyd Taliaferro, Edward Moncrief and Bert Wilson. All display adaptability to picture work of this order. A good cowboy picture.

RIP VAN WINKLE

Philadelphia, Sept. 14.

This celluloid version of a famous stage success will undoubtedly be a popular picture. That it is not a more artistic picture besides is a shame considering the traditions which go with it.

Thomas Jefferson in the role made famous by his father and played often by himself on the stage, gives a characterization that has many highlights, and the lack of some photodramatic subtleties will probably be overlooked by most audiences.

The scenes are a big feature. The picture runs about seven reels and is generally free from padding. Beautiful country sides, wind-tossed hill-sides, shady lanes and the rest are all photographed excellently, but Ward Lascelle, the producer, has made the mistake of omitting even a glimpse of the Hudson River. In this picture, the ancient hamlet of Kaatskill is an inland town which is a shame considering the fact that the spirit of Hendrick Hudson hung very closely over the Washington Irving classic.

The story of the drunken reprobate who fell asleep on a stormy night and awoke 20 years later, has been faithfully done. The stage version has been religiously adhered to, much too much so at times. A touch of slapstick comedy has been added, but it does not add to the effect. The scenes showing Rip being chased by the bear, Rip catching the rabbit, Mrs. Rip being chased by a bu'l and several others are rather out of the spirit of the picture.

On the other hand, the storm scenes, except for a very hose-like intensity of the downpour, were excellently done. The village scenes were realistic, and especially in the latter part, there were some excellent touches of atmosphere of the bygone day in shots of old houses, quiet streets and lazy, pleasant looking inns.

The best acting was by little Gladys Messinger as Meenie, Minna Davenport as Gretchen and Max Ascher as the inn-keeper. Some of the actors and actresses were inclined to overact, but as the who'e tenor of the production was a bit exaggerated, the acting was not out of place.

This picture is being run here as a big special at the Academy of Music. It seems in that auditorium a bit out of place, but it is sure to be a popular picture with the masses and ought to go great in smaller places.

HER WINNING WAY

This Realart production first obtained recognition as a novel and later as a play, now it is on the screen serving as starring vehicle for Mary Miles Minter. It is a pleasing little picture, but as one sits through it there comes the natural conjecture as to just how great a picture it would have been had Constance Talmadge, instead of Miss Minter played the lead. Not because Miss Minter does not fulfill the role within certain limitations, but just how much more Miss Talmadge would have drawn from the comedy situations.

Miss Minter plays the youthful book critic who tries to secure an interview from the author of books on women, with a certain amount of dash that is certain to entertain.

The story itself is prefaced by a South Sea Island touch that is amusing. It shows an island where the women have the right of courtship and they go after the boys in the most approved cavewoman style.

It then states that her more educated sister cannot employ the same methods but nevertheless she is the pursuer of man today. The young author-hero of this picture has been writing many works on women. He has a doting mother and mother has a girl all picked out for him. Then the little book reviewer steps into the works. The author has refused to be interviewed by her, so she takes an apartment in the same building, coincidence puts her in possession of a card from an employment agency which is left in the author's apartment by an applicant for the position of housekeeper. She makes use of the card and steps in on the job.

From that point on she decides to win the author for herself and she manouevers events in such fashion as to break off his engagement to the short haired dame that mommer has picked and then it is easy sailing for he has managed to slip the youngster a thrill or two while she was around the flat as maid of all work.

He learns just who she is before the final clinch and orders her out but when he comes back that night he finds her stretched out on his couch, covered just below the shoulders, with the suggestion that she is apparelless under the rug covering her. Of course, this is not so, it is just a very decollette evening gown, and the sap falls for her, hook, line and sinker.

However, it looks as thought the director, Joseph Henabery, was trying to suggest to the girls that if you want to cop a guy, all you have to do is to sneak into his apartment

and let him find you seemingly undressed on his couch when he comes home late at night. *Fred.*

I DO

A Harold Lloyd comic, at the Capitol this week. It's of the comedian becoming a married man, inviting some small relatives, one a boy and one a baby to his home, the ensuing consequences, caused mostly by the mischievous youngster, and the comedy results.

Sime.

THREE WORLD BRAND

Three World Brand
Governor Marmden .... William S. Hart
Ben Trego
Ethel Barton .... Jane Novak
George Barton .... S.J. Bingham
Bull Yates .... Gordon Russell
Jolly .... Ivor McFadden
Carrol .... Herschell Mayall
Jean....................... Colette Forbes
John Murray .... George C. Pearce
McCabe .... Leo Willis
The Twins .... By Themselves

W. S. Hart in "Three Word Brand" is the feature at the Rivoli this week, but even though Hart himself is in town and the dailies made more or less of a fuss over him, it remained for a little single reel cartoon comedy, "Out of the Inkwell," to overshadow the feature as the hit of the bill. From that the exhibitor can fairly well imagine just how much of a "wow" the Hart picture was.

It is one of those productions on which there was considerable cheating. The cost sheet on this bird must have had Hart's income tax for last year added on it to make it look like anything when he slipped it to the releasing organization to get his cost-plus turned over to him.

There is practically nothing but exteriors from one end of the picture to the other. Three interiors are used, one a bar room, the other the living room of a ranch house and the third the governor's office. All are cheap.

Lambert Hillyer wrote and directed the story which has a prolog laid in about 1865 showing Hart is a father with two twin sons, youngsters about six or seven years of age, crossing the country to the great west in a prairie schooner. An attack by Indians, the father sends the boys back to safety and leads the pesky reds a chase, finally blowing himself and a number of the Indians up—but the boys are safe.

Thirty years later the real story begins and it gives Hart a chance to play the twin brothers grown to man's estate. This makes three roles all exactly alike and all played just the same, for Hart.

Hart, as Three Word Brand, runs a ranch in a valley in Utah, while his twin brother who was adopted from the orphanage and reared under the name of Marsden has risen to be the governor of the state. A political clique is trying to secure the water rights to the valley and in the conflict that there is among the two factions Brand's partner is accused of murder and sentenced to be executed. At about that time the governor decides that he is going to look over the valley to ascertain for himself just why there is so much pressure from inner political circles in favor of the bill. He hits the county seat just as Three Word Brand is on the ground and after he rides off on his trip Brand gets into his clothes, hotfoots it to the capital, signs a pardon for the man convicted of murder and vetoes the water bill.

A skirmish at the finish of the picture brings Brand on the scene to save the governor and the two get together and all is forgiven by the governor because he feels that his brother could do no wrong.

There is a love story connected with action with Jane Novak playing opposite Hart in the Brand character as the sister of his partner, and from the manner in which the star shares his close-ups with her it is quite evident that she means more than just a leading lady to him and that there may be more than a rumor in the stories that they are to wed.

The detail in the picture is badly handled. In the prolog just things as the use of a repeating rifle in the 1865 period—which is the year that that gun was invented by Winchester, and it is hardly probable that a poor cross country emigrant would have in-

cluded so recent an arm in his outfit—seems to point to the fact that the general detail was let "go hang" so that this picture might be gotten over the plate as quickly and cheaply as possible. There is one mighty good close-up double where Hart as Brand puts his right hand over on the right arm of himself as Marsden. That is by far the best piece of business in the picture from the audience viewpoint. *Fred.*

THE INVISIBLE POWER

Sid Chambers............... House Peters
Laura Chadwick.............. Irene Rich
Mark Shadwell...... De Witt C. Jennings
Bob Drake............. Sydney Ainsworth
Mrs. Shadwell......... Jessie De Jainette
Mr. Miller............... William Friend
Mrs. Miller............... Gertrude Claire
Giggling Neighbor. Lydia Yeamans Titus

Just what the invisible power as defined in this Goldwyn production is hard to pin down. It is a question whether Charles Kenyon, the author, meant it for the cops, because they won't let the crooks "go straight," or the power of love that makes them want to tread the straight and narrow, or the fear that pre-natal influence might act on a child's later life being born while the father was in a a convict's cell, or the providence that guides the author's typewriter so that coincidence makes it possible for him to evolve a story that has a happy, altogether not an entirely probable ending.

However, "The Invisible Power," which was the feature production of the week's bill at the Capitol, might have any one of these as the meaning and still be right. It is nevertheless a fairly interesting picture despite the fact that it is mighty slow in action during the first couple of reels. The opening shots are fast enough.

A crook is released from stir, he rejoins his former playmates in the regular hangout and finds a former crony up against it because of the fact that he has contracted a cough which acts as a burglar alarm every time that he starts to pull a job. But when he decides to take his buddie to the country to cure the cough the rural tempo drags.

Later when the crook stuff again comes to the foreground the picture speeds up again and manages to hold the audience to the finish.

Frank Lloyd had the direction of the production and other than the aforementioned there is no fault that one can find with his work. Of course he should be held blameless for the touch at the finish where a mere fly copper can call up headquarters and have the couple of record cards destroyed, but at that cops do do funny things at times.

House Peters has the heroic crook role and manages to present a performance that contains his usual bit of pipe smoking, etc., but which nevertheless carries conviction. Sidney Ainsworth as his crook companion is more typical of the "mob." The best performance of the lot, however, was that of the characterization of the Central Office man as portrayed by De Witt C. Jennings. He was a "copper" right down to his heels, even if he did have to use a big black cigar to make it get over. Irene Rich, as the school-teaching rural maid who marries the crook and then tries to help him go straight, although the cops are after him continually, sounded a note of genuineness in several emotional scenes.

It looks as though the picture had its biggest sales point in the police expose angle, a sort of "you can't go straight even if you want to" ought to make it strong for neighborhood houses.

There is nothing in the way of production that stands out as being worth of extended comment.

Fred.

HEART OF THE NORTH

San Francisco, Sept. 28.

San Francisco's first finished offering to the film world in which Roy Stewart plays a dual role, supported by Louise Lovely and several non-noted players who show to good advantage. The picture is woven around the Royal Northwest police, showing Stewart as a mounted policeman and as a leader of a notorious gang of outlaws. George H. Davis is responsible for the city's initial feature picture, he having financed the enterprise which if weighed for merits as to what part San Francisco will play in the future of the film industry, may be credited a success. It is a Harry J. Revier production. Revier directed the entire "shootings".

In but one spot Revier has overdone the scene and filmed far too much. That is in the forest fire which starts poorly showing too much smoke escape for the size of the blaze and which runs for extra minutes, taking entire interest from the plot. The introduction is intensely interesting, likewise the finishing of the picture and but for the fire. The titles in which the Canadian-French dialect is used could be improved. The story is effective.

The book opens with the death of the father and later of the mother of infant twins. A French priest takes the babes to an orphanage where they grow up to their teens. One is adopted by Maupome, a leader of the outlaws, and the other by an officer of the mounted police. The former grows to manhood as "Bad" Maupome, a meaner man than his foster-father whom he succeeds at death as leader of the gang, while the other boy ages as John, a respected member of the mounted of which his foster-father is now a captain. Maupome's deadly raids on the villagers become so numerous a country-wide search is made for him at the head of which John and Sergeant O'Reilly set out to make the capture, John not knowing at this time of a twin brother. He learns during the chase from the kindly priest now old that a brother is still alive and is Maupome himself. The search continues until brothers meet in a rain-drenched forest. John, although wishing to be true to the mounted, gives Maupome a chance for his life by preparing for a pistol duel, one revolver being an empty one and the other loaded. Maupome in picking the gun up fingers the barrel and gets the loaded one which would have meant John's death, but resulted the other way when thunder and lightning cuts a tree which falls on Maupome.

Miss Lovely is the daughter of a police official and plays well. The characters of John and Maupome being drastically opposite give Stewart his chance for character contrast which he does excellently.

Truckee in Northern California was used for the snow scenes, likewise Marin county and Muir Woods for the forest sets. Golden Gate Park was utilized in several sections for background. All in all the picture reveals the wonderful natural resources San Francisco and the bay cities offer for picture use. Even the laboratory work is local.

KNOCK-NA-GOW

Mat Donovan..........Brian Magowan
Billy Heffernan..........Breffni O'Rorke
Maurice Kearney..........Dermott O'Dowd
Wattletoes..........Patrick McDonald
Pender..........J. M. Carre
Phil Lahy..........Arthur Shiels
Arthur O'Connor..........Fred O'Donovan
Henry Lowe..........George Larchett
Father O'Carroll..........Valentine Roberts
Sir Garrett Butler..........Charles Power
Mick Brian..........Donal Sullivan
Nora Lahy..........Kathleen Murphy
Mary Kearney..........Nora Clancy
Mrs. Kearney..........Peggy Casey
Mary Donovan, Mat's Sister, Sheila Rooney
Honor Lahy..........Brenda Bourke
Mrs. Brian..........Katherine Doran

"Knock-Na-Gow," is a picturization of Chas. J. Kickham's novel. The Film Company of Ireland made it. Director's name not disclosed.

A fairly accurate translation of "Knock-Na-Gow" is "Homes of Tipperary." The film was produced in Ireland and runs about six reels. From appearances the novel carried an interesting tale, with suspense, dramatic conflict and heart appeal. Efforts to place the story on the screens have been but mildly successful, due to lack of knowledge of modern picture making on the part of the director and a similar lack of screen acting requirements by most of the cast.

The technic of the picture is that of 15 years ago. The greater part of the scenes are acted square in front of the camera, giving the action a flat effect. The lighting is most ordinary. When night photography is called for, the scene is tinted. A fire scene is handled in the same old fashioned manner. Even the cutting and joining of the picture is rough and uneven. Nowadays when a character on the screen is supposed to be bearded, he grows the necessary whiskers. In this picture, however, recourse is had to the obvious crepe hair for beards.

A defect like that is trivial enough, and would not be noticed if there were not so many others. But it's the combined crudities, one piled on top of the other, that bring the picture so far below present day standards. A preliminary title seeks to anticipate criticism probably by stating there will be no stirring climaxes and the spectator need expect no thrills. The spectator didn't get anything approaching either.

The trouble with "Knock Na-Gow" is simple enough. Whoever made it had little or no knowledge of 1921 picture making methods. The story is laid in 1848, with the characters correctly garbed in period costumes. There's a hero, whom the villain frames with almost nothing shown on the screen that would indicate a motive for his hatred of the hero. That villain is a fiendish guy. One of those heavies, always washing his hands in invisible water, a typical hypocrite. There is nothing in the way of a title to indicate that the villain is English, although his make-up would suggest he is English rather than Irish. Were not the landlord's agents who evicted the Irish tenants in the Chauncey Olcott shows always Englishmen?

This villain is an evicter, and a devilish one, not only evicting but burning the house down as well. So why not be as frank as they used to be in the old Olcott plays?

There is a love story or two scattered throughout the picture, and some excellent acting by Brian Magown, as the hero. Patrick McDonald, also shows ability as a screen performer, handling a comedy role intelligently. Surely with all of the possibilities for real drama in present day Ireland, it does seem that there must be better screen material than this old fashioned story, which has been done so many times as to make it standardized. While there should be a direct heart appeal, "Knock-Na-Gow" never convinces. It's just "play-acting," all the way, with no illusion to make the spectator believe he is witnessing anything more stirring than a company of actors, impersonating human beings.

The film is in the Lexington, New York, for two weeks, beginning Sunday, Sept. 24, the presentation being made jointly by the Film Co. of Ireland and the Lexington Festival Orchestra, the latter composed of members of former 310 Musical Union.

Bell.

GREAT IMPERSONATION

Sir Everard Dominey, Leopold Von Ragastein, James Kirkwood
Rosamond Dominey..........Ann Forrest
Duke of Oxford..........Winter Hall
Duchess of Oxford..........Truly Shattuck
Princess Eiderstrom..........Fontaine LaRue
Gustave Seimann..........Alan Hale
Dr. Eddy Pelham..........Bertram Johns
Dr. Hugo Schmidt..........William Burress
Roger Unthank..........Cecil Holland
Mrs. Unthank..........Temple Pigott
Emperor William of Germany, Lawrence Grant
Prince Eiderstrom..........Louis Dumar
Prince Terniloff..........Frederick Vroom
Princess Terniloff..........Florence Midgely

Jesse Lasky presents this picture as a "George Melford Production." Mr. Melford directed this screen version of the E. Phillips Oppenheim story. He deserves the honor for the splendid double exposures he secured and the manner in which he handled James Kirkwood in the dual role.

Other than that there is naught to the picture in any way startling. The story is laid in the period prior to the opening of the world war in 1914. Its plot has to do with the tremendously overrated Wilhelmstrasse secret service that picture audiences are all too familiar with at this time. That the picture is to a certain extent a "war picture" may prove to be one of its principal drawbacks in general popularity.

Monte Katterjohn handled the adaptation cleverly and held the suspense to the last minute in the continuity that he prepared.

The cast was carefully selected. In addition to Mr. Kirkwood's splendid performance Winter Hall made a decided impression as his uncle. He is a finished artist and his work in this picture aids materially in holding the audience. Playing character roles Alan Hale, Bertram Johns, Cecil Holland and William Burress scored. This is especialy true of Burress as the German staff doctor. One gets so now that whenever the Kaiser is in a picture it is expected that Grant will play the role.

Of the women Fontaine LeRue as the Princess Eiderstrom walked away with the honors for looks and shared with Ann Forress the acting honors. Truly Shattuck appeared as a society dowager.

The actual photography is all that could be asked and from a technical standpoint there is almost an oversupply of atmosphere, especially in the South African jungle scenes. The lightings are fine and the big sets, of which there are at least a half dozen, show that the general idea was to have this production a special. It isn't that but it is a mighty good program picture that should get money providing the public haven't tired entirely of the pre-war spy stuff.

Fred.

THE IDLE CLASS

The Tramp, The Absent-minded Husband, Charles Chaplin
His Wife..........Edna Purviance
The Angry Father..........Mack Swain

"The Idle Class," Charles Chaplin's latest release, is one of those "hokum" slapstick two-reelers that you laugh your head off looking at and then walk out and say it isn't so good—it isn't artistic, and it isn't this and that. You never once admit that the picture accomplishes the purposes for which it was built—uproarious entertainment.

The picture has a semblance of a legitimate plot, in that the comedian plays two roles—that of a wealthy gentleman and a tramp. The scenes are laid at a summer resort. The rich man is an absent-minded husband who dresses immaculately to meet his wife. He is all dolled up but forgets to put on trousers. The wife arrives and concludes her husband has been drinking, so refuses to see him. Meantime, arriving via the same train, not on it but under it, is the tramp who bears a close resemblance to the husband. There is a masked ball, the tramp enters, is mistaken for the husband, etc. A most ludicrous scene is that where the husband dons a suit of armor for the ball, is about to take a drink when the visor drops and cannot be lifted. In this predicament he enters the ballroom, sees his wife stroking the hand of the stranger in the belief it is her husband, with nobody believing the husband is really the hubby, and so on.

Slapstick? Yes; Vulgar? Yes; but it is all done by the inimitable Chaplin, which counteracts all possible adverse criticism.

Jolo.

NE'ER TO RETURN ROAD

No. 12,896..........Wallace Beery
Mrs. Holt, the mother..Margaret McWade
Mr. Holt, the father..........Walt Whitman
The Girl..........Margaret Landis
The Stranger..........Jack Mulhall

To piece out the program at the Strand this week where the short Chaplin release is being shown, there is presented the Selig-Rork two-reeler "The Ne'er to Return Road," a strong drama, story by Mrs. Otis Skinner. There is enough plot in it for the average five or six reel feature and is a splendid example of how much story can be unwound in approximately 25 minutes.

Picture opens up with most intense melodrama—life convict escaping from prison and chased through the swamps by keepers and bloodhounds. Staggers to farmhouse door at night, exhausted; is fed by woman who is waiting for her son from whom she hasn't heard in years.

Grateful convict tells his story of how he killed a man in a brawl over a no-account woman and mentions the name of his victim—the woman's son. She takes up a gun to shoot him, relents, gives him a horse and aids him to escape, saying: "Somewhere there may be a mother waiting for you."

Cyclone; convict saves the mother, is recaptured, asks that the woman receive the reward for his capture and goes back to jail. Vivid characterization of convict by Wallace Beery; gripping performance of the mother by Margaret McWade and splendid visualization of the Girl by Margaret Landis. Picture is well worth playing.

Jolo.

RED COURAGE

"Red Courage" is a virile Peter B. Kyne "western" tale and has been picturized by Universal, with Ed ("Hoot") Gibson starred. Reaves Eason directed. The characters are so well drawn it would be well nigh impossible to miss with so straightaway a melodrama. Most of the scenes are outdoor, with one or two well staged fist fights.

A happy-go-lucky cowbuy buys the local paper in the town of Panamint, which is being run by a grafting mayor, whose niece the cowboy (Gibson) saved from a holdup.

Gibson cleans up the gang of grafters, is elected sheriff and wins the girl for a bride.

Suspensive and absorbing throughout, it is far better than the average popular-priced program feature.

Jolo.

AFTER MIDNIGHT

The Stranger (	
Gordon Phillips (	.......Conway Tearle
Mrs. Phillips	................Zena Keefe
Warren Black	.............Macy Harlam
Mock Sing	.................Charlie Fag
Toy Sing	.................Woo Lang
Harris	...................Harry Allen

Selznick production starring Conway Tearle from the story by John Lynch, scenario credited to Edward J. Montague. Ralph Ince did the directing. The principal feature of this Selznick production is its strength with a short cast. With but three parts of any proportions Ince has turned out a feature that provide sample entertainment in all of its five reels. The picture has in reality two stars, regardless of the fact that Tearle is given all the credit in the billing, the other being Zena Keefe. Miss Keefe is now one of the recognized Selznick stars but appears to have been passed up in the billing and press matter for this production. There is little doubt but that it would be advisable to co-star her with Tearle, her name in conjunction with his providing an added feature for the picture. The principal scenes are laid in the Chinese section of San Francisco. Gordon Phillips is a man about town who becomes involved with the proprietor of a Chinese hop resort. He is on the verge of death in the picture when his exact double is found in one of the outer rooms. In order to secure certain bonds in the home of the dying man the proprietor enlists the services of the stranger to take the place of the other. This accomplished, he is sent to the man's home where he remains undetected by the wife who occupies a separate room, due to the habitual drunkenness of her spouse. The family butler discovers that the masquerader is the twin brother of his employes but does not make known the fact to his mistress. It develops that the dying man had cheated his brother out of his rightful inheritance several years previous, causing him to take up the life of a wanderer. Upon his installation in the home the stranger refuses to aid the Chinese resort proprietor who endeavors to get him out of the way. A note is sent to have him go directly to the place as his brother was about to pass away. Upon his arrival there he is informed by a Chinese girl that they have tricked him there and that while he is absent from the home his brother's wife is to be kidnapped. This is accomplished, with the woman brought to the resort. A rough and tumble battle ensues with the weak brother dying. A general cleanup occures with the true story coming out and the usual happy ending between the wife and brother. Ince is largely responsible for the effectivness of this production. He works up his story to fever heat in several instances making the short cast stand up in capable style. Tearle plays a dual role as both of the brothers. Miss Keefe as the wife is effective. Macy Harlam in a heavy gives a convincing portrayal. The production end displays discretion on the part of the director and is substantial in its proportions. A good program feature fit for any house.

AUSTRALIA'S WILD NOR'-WEST

London, Sept. 10.

These travel pictures, the official record of the Nor-West Scientific Expedition, of Persth, Western Australia, belong to the category of things worth while. They are among the most remarkable and interesting ever seen. Not only do they show a portion of the Empire which is all but unknown even to Australians but they give a wonderfully clear insight into tribal life, customs, and the industries of that far off corner of the world.

They also prove that some of the much scoffed at statements of the late Louis de Rougemont were founded on fact and were not far-fetched stories of a mortal trying hard to out-do Ananias.

The pictures receive additional value from the descriptions of M. P. Adams, a member of the expedition, who, while frankly acknowledging he is not a fluent speaker, contributes a highly interesting, educational, often humorous, unvarnished story of the work done by the little party of white men.

Starting with some excellent scenes of events in civilised Australia the picture passes on to Broome and its pearl fisheries. Dugong Bay shows that peculiar mammal, the Sea Cow, and the mode of hunting her, which provides an unusual lesson in natural history, as does the section devoted to crabs, hundreds, thousands of them, scampering about on the sand.

Through ever varying scenes the picture arrives among aboriginals of wonderful physique and smashes the idea that the Australian native is a hideous person of stunted growth. Some of the men are giants, wonderful specimens, standing over 7 feet. Their women, clad very much in their birthday suits, reach a standard of ugliness in face and form which would be difficult to rival. Corrobborees and tribal rites are shown, also the remarkable anatomical disfigurments caused by rubbing dirt into open wounds—the more hideous the scars the greater the manly beauty.

The last reel shows Lacrosse island with turtles of all sorts and de Rougemonts story of riding on turtles, a feat he attempted in the London Hippodrome tank many years ago, proved at least to be founded on fact.

The whole series of pictures which have been splendidly "shot" by William Jackson should prove a valuable showman's proposition anywhere.

Gore.

DANGEROUS PATHS

With no pretence or attempt as expensiveness of production, the Berwilla Film Corp. has turned out a Ben Wilson production, starring Ben Wilson and Neva Gerber. It is released by the Arrow Company. The story and scenario are by Joseph W. Girard.

The picture is a splendid pattern of the moral preachment, designed to show the narrowness of small town life where the hypocritical inhabitants attend church on Sundays but fail to live up to the teachings of Christianity.

Ben Wilson plays a minister, in love with a young girl (Neva Gerber), who resides with her elderly father and a stepmother. The latter wants her to marry the richest man in town, but she rejects him in favor of the minister. Her father quarrels with his wife over the affair and the girl leaves for "the city" to earn her living. Securing no employment she is turned out by her landlady, is seated on the steps of an Episcopal church weeping, where she is picked up by a streetwalker and taken home. The big-hearted prostitute makes a position for her as housekeeper.

One evening they are walking along the main thoroughfare, when they are arrested, charged with soliciting. The rich man happens to be in the city, reads of the arrest, goes to court, pays the fine of the immoral girl, while the good girl is discharged. He takes the good girl to his hotel, promising to bring her home, but attempts to ravish her, is thrown out of the hotel, returns home alone and distorts the tale to make it appear that the good girl has gone wrong, offering the newspaper as evidence to substantiate his statements.

The minister throttles him, goes to "the city," brings both girls back and preaches a sermon in his church on the subject: "Let Him who Is Without Sin Cast the First Stone," tells the real story, denounces the male gossip, it is revealed the girl who went wrong is the daughter of the stepmother, both are taken home and the minister takes the good girl for his wife.

Mawkish sentimentality, to be sure, but admirably acted by a company that depicts bucolic types to a nicety. It is exceptional to encounter such a uniformity of high grade screen acting in a feature of such modest pretentions.

Jolo.

A TRIP TO PARADISE

"Curley" Flynn	..............Bert Lytell
Nora O'Brien	.............Virginia Valli
Meek	.............Brinsley Shaw
Widow Boland	........Unice Via Moore
Mrs. Smiley	............Victory Bateman
Mary	.................Eva Gordon

"A Trip to Paradise" is a film version of Franz Molnar's play "Liliom," adapted by Benjamin F. Glazer, scenario by June Mathis—directed for Metro by Maxwell Karger, and starring Bert Lytell.

The story has been Americanized, the scene laid at Coney Island, with the role of Liliom idealized both in dress and morals. Instead of him being a panderer who preyed upon servant girls and women in similar walks of life, the circus barker is depicted as an industrious young man who, when he finds the girl has been kept out too late to go home to her aunt's house, takes her to a hotel and registers as "man and wife." The clerk is suspicious, but he flashes his marriage certificate and everything is regular. It is not explained how he secured the certificate at one a. m.—a faux pas not often perpetrated in modern photoplay direction.

Instead of killing himself, as in the stage version, the barker steps in the way of the revolver shot intended for the man whose house is being robbed. He is seriously injured but doesn't die. He has a vision of Heaven while under the influence of ether on the hospital operating table; he recovers, isn't prosecuted, gets his job back and lives happily ever after with his wife and son. In other words the original Hungarian character study has been twisted into a conventional melodrama with a "happy ending."

The picture runs about 70 minutes, is carefully acted and directed throughout, but with nothing distinctive in any department to individualize it from an ordinary program feature.

Jolo.

HOME-KEEPING HEARTS

Cameo Classics produced "Home-Keeping Hearts" for Playgoers Pictures, releasing through Pathe. It is a screen version of the Charles W. Barrell story, "Chains," directed by Carlyle Ellis.

The story is described as a "romance of regeneration," the remaking of an ex-convict, worked out in the style of a rural drama.

Robert Colton (Thomas H. Swinton) serves a ten-year sentence, upon circumstantial evidence. During it, his motherless daughter is taken care of by skin-flint Squire Tead, a local political boss. Upon the father's release he is put to work in the Squires creamery which has a monopoly in the community. The farmers revolt against the institution, threatening to start a community creamery of their own. This enrages the owner who by bribery has the government inspectors condemn the cows of the instigators of the new idea. He is also mixed up in school matters by appropriating funds voted for the repairing of the school. At the local election he fails to secure his re-election and barely escapes with his life following a fight with one of the cow inspectors. This brings about a change of heart and all ends serenely. There is a bit of a love story interwoven with the ex-convict and the school teacher being together in the final close-up. The merits of this production are few and far between. Possibly in the smaller houses it will suffice. The convict idea is far from new with the twists in this story failing to supply sufficient strength to gain recognition. The cast in addition to

Swinton includes Mildred Ryan, Louella Carr, Edward Grace and Henry West. They fit their parts acceptably. The production end is far from costly. A cheap feature.

PILGRIMS OF NIGHT

Lord Ellingham	Lewis S. Stone
Christine	Rubye De Remer
Ambrose	William V. Mong
Lady Ellingham	Kathleen Kirkham
Le Blun	Raymond Hatton
Gilbert Hannaway	Walter McGrail
Marcel	Frank Leigh

The E. Phillips Oppenheim story, "Passers By," adapted for the screen and presented as a J. L. Frothingham production, directed by Edward Slomon, with the title changed to "Pilgrims of the Night." The picture is a fairly gripping detective tale that will please the average picture audience, although it is nothing to rave about. The Associated Producers release.

Mr. Slomon made the picture on the Brunton lot and he let himself run wild on at least two sets, both interiors, that must have cost a lot of coin in that studio. One of the sets wasn't at all necessary. It was the one showing the interior of the home of Lord Ellingham. Otherwise the picture seems to have had its expense held down outside of the cast, which was a capable one.

Lewis S. Stone plays the lead and carries it along convincingly. Rubye De Remer is his daughter, but in her case it cannot be said that the passing years have proven her camera proof. She has also seemingly passed up the matter of detail. In the slum scene she permited herself to be shot with a wave in her hair that must have cost at least $5, and she is supposed to be starving to death.

It is in the heavy section of the cast that the honors are handled to greatest advantage. Frank Leigh is most convincing and William V. Mong as a hunched-back organ grinder is a work of art. Raymond Hatton as a fastidious French fop detective pleased mightly and Walter McGrail playing the juvenile lead as an Englishman whose hobby is work among the criminal classes, got by.

The story is of a father who has permitted his brother-in-law to rear his daughter as his own, so that she might not know he was serving a prison sentence. When released the former compels his assistance in a number of crimes under the threat of informing the daughter. Finally the police capture the real criminal and the assistant makes his getaway. The girl is compelled to take an oath to hunt him down and bring about his death. But through the young English criminologist the truth is learned and she is restored to the arms of her real father.

Mr. Slomon was at fault on at least two occasions in editing and assembling his film. He permitted one of his characters to walk from one scene into another with a change of attire and later he uses a written title and a slip denoting an address when it was entirely unnecessary.

Fred

LUXURY

The name of the producing company of this Rubye De Remer feature could not be gained at the showing at the Stanley Monday night. Picture started by merely introducing the name of Marcel Perez as the author and director. Possibly the producing company preferred to remain in oblivion. It could hardly be termed a successful effort for any company. The theatre also failed to use any of the usual display paper outside.

The story is light and mediocre. The picture contains but one idea, the kidnapping of a young man on his bridal night. It is so worked out as to lead one to believe he has been taken away by a rival suitor. It is learned, however, his own stepbrother did the trick to secure more than his share in the father's will. Miss De Remer is the girl he is to marry. Her screen appearance is invariably a success but even her looks are wasted in this production. Walter Miller as the man appears to be a find. He should develop into a strong leading man. Other players included Fred Kalgren, Henry Pemberton and Tom A. Magrane.

The production displayed some attractive interiors. There is a great abundance of chasing around in automobiles and the introduction of a detective who marks himself so distinctly as a sleuth that most of the effect is lost.

A program picture that can fill in on off nights in some houses. The story is not worthy of the star.

ONE ARABIAN NIGHT

The Desert Dancer	Pola Negri
The Hunchback	Ernst Lubitsch

"One Arabian Night" is a film version of "Sumurun," made in Germany, as may well be guessed by the names of the two principal players in the cast. Those two names are the only ones programed. Others among the players are worthy of mention. Pola Negri is the star and Ernst Lubitsch, the director and principal support. In this picture he displays the fact that he is just as great an actor as he is a director and his characterization of the Hunchback is one that American character players can well study.

As shown at the Strand the picture runs 96 minutes. Joseph Plunkett has given the production a prolog with two solos and a dance in a Bagdad setting that leads one to believe that he is qualified to succeed Morris Gest as a producer of spectacles of the Far East. In a measure it approaches Gest's street scene in "Mecca."

The picture is worthy far greater publicity than was accorded its presentation at the Strand. It offers any number of chances to the exhibitor in the way of publicity and its presentation anywhere should be made an event, rather than a matter of fact program presentation. It is a picture that will pull audiences if they only know what to expect.

The American screen version of "Sumurun" was titled and cut by Leslie Mason of the First National forces who is given screen credit for the achievement. It richly deserves all of that for his titles explain the tale lucidly, yet with a certain colorful charm that at all times holds the audience in the poetic atmosphere of the East.

At the opening of the tale, of the "Thousand and One" of the Arabian Nights, a small caravan is shown approaching the city of Bagdad. In the wagon there is a quartet of players, the dancer, the hunchback, a juggler and an old hag who does snake charming.

Meanwhile, in the city, the mighty Sheik is having trouble in his harem. His favorite wife is in love with a merchant of the city and likewise she is loved by the only son of the Sheik. The latter suspects that all is not well and catches the favorite in what he believes a flirtation. She is tried and doomed to death, but the son intervenes and saves her life.

When recovering consciousness she is in the arms of the Sheik whom she spurns. He, tired of her indifference, harks to the tale of the slave dealer, who tells of a new beauty that has come to town. It is the untamed dancer of the player caravan. The Sheik sees and wants her. She is a woman who has loved and been loved, her lovers being in numbers, all serving in her mind to advance her, and she goes to the harem of the Sheik even though she has met the son and would be far more willing to become his mistress.

The poor hunchback clown who also loves her follows to the harem where in the coming of the dawn he steps into the chamber of the Sheik just as the latter kills her, after having discovered her in the arms of his son after she has risen from his side on the couch while he was sleeping. The merchant lover of the former favorite has been smuggled into the harem during the night and as the Sheik turns from the dead love to his former favorite he finds her in her lover's arms. The Hunchback avenges the dead dancer by killing the Sheik as is about to slay the merchant lover.

It is a tragic tale, spiced with amours, wonderfully well enacted and containing touches of comedy that only Lubitsch would and could have conceived. There is the scene at midnight, when the Sheik is about to take his ride in the cool of the desert and the dancer appears on the threshold of the harem. She lures him from his ride and the manner in which he dismisses his attendants and mount brought a howl from the audience.

The production is colorful throughout, the atmosphere of the East being perfect in detail and as before said the players present performances that are remarkable. Pola Negri is tremendous! That is the one word that describes her performance fittingly. She has fire and an allurement that is essential to the role assigned her, also she displays the fact that she is a dancer of exceeding cleverness.

Lubitsch, however, is the member of the cast that will create a historic mark as the Hunchback. It is impossible to recall a screen performance that equals his in this picture. The snake charming Hag is another player of note, as well as the young merchant and the two women, Haidee and Zuleika. The latter while not long on looks gives a corking performance.

One cannot go wrong in playing this feature no matter what the rental cost, for properly exploited, it would more than top the business "Passion" attracted.

Fred.

AFTER THE SHOW

Larry Taylor	Jack Holt
Eileen	Lila Lee
Pop O'Malley	Charles Ogle
Naomi Stokes	Eve Southern
Mr. McGuire	Carlton King
Lucy	Shanron Day
Vera	Stella Seager
Landlady	Ethel Wales

The picture system of distribution must have a big hole in it somewhere if the Rialto, New York, finds it necessary to play for a week a Paramount feature like "After the Show," and the Paramount finds it necessary to release the film on its regular programs to play week-stands houses like the Rialto. "After the Show" possibly could become a part of a double feature bill at one of Loew's houses for one day. Even, then it would be laughed at in its seriousness and walked out on as at the Rialto Sunday night.

Called an "all-star cast" and a William DeMille production, with story by Rita Weiman; scenario by Hazel McDonald and Vianna Knowlton, the best that may be said of this waste of film is that direction might have made a theatrical back stage picture of it, or possibly it was the fault of the scenario writers, or more likely the trouble is the mushy screen-old tale, of a chorus girl being lead to a flat instead of marriage; that, or the danger of that.

An old stage door tender (Charles Ogle is the self appointed guardian of the young chorus chicken (Lila Lee) that Larry Taylor (Jack Holt) starts in to make a play for. The thing tries to point a moral as between the love of lust and the love of purity, with the love of several other things intermingled, while for the love of almost anything else, every one has seen the same old stuff put over in the same old way or nearly so since the picture business got going.

No novelty, no action, no acting, nothing in fact but a foolishly inspired story that must be chuckling to think it's on Broadway. If the Rialto had to play this picture, that may be an excuse and if the Paramount had to release it, that's another, but the Rialto should have thrown it in the alley before putting it on the screen, provided that Paramount did not have common sense enough to throw away the picture before sending it out.

"After the Show" should be a record maker for both Paramount and the Rialto; giving Paramount a bigger dent in its rep than two "Paramount weeks" could erase, and for the Rialto, likely make this the poorest week's business it has ever had.

Sime.

THE RAGE OF PARIS

Joan Coolidge	Miss du Pont
Gordon Talbot	Jack Perrin
Mrs. Coolidge	Elinor Hancock
Mortimer Handley	Ramsey Wallace

Universal has a new star debutting in "The Rage of Paris." She is a Miss du Pont. For some reason or other, perhaps to make it more hcrlcate for the exhibitors, she is just Miss du Pont. Just how far this young lady is going to get along the starry path will remain to be seen, but it cannot be said that her first picture moves her beyond the beginning of the road.

The story is not one that seems to fit her very well. There are moments when she gets away with the work assigned to her like a veteran trouper, but at other moments she seems to lack everything, even to looks, that a screen star should possess.

Lucien Hibbard, head of the U scenario department on the Coast, provided the "Rage of Paris" for Miss du Pont, and Jack Conway directed the picture. Both have done better work in the past. The same might also be said of Ramsey Wallace and Jack Perrin who are Miss du Pont's principal supporting leads.

"The Rage of Paris" is nothing when compared to the rage of one man found who admitted he had paid $1 to see the picture at the Central, Broadway, where the U played it, although it also released the production to the Loew houses and Friday last week it played in opposition to the Capital at Loew's New York at 28 cents.

The story is that of a young girl forced into an unhappy marriage by her mother. The girl escapes from the husband when he proves a brute and makes her way to Paris where, by her dancing she becomes a local social favorite. The husband trails her only to find she has decided to join a former sweetheart who is head of an engineering job in Arabia. The husband follows, is killed in a sand storm by an Arab who seeks to steal his camel to escape the storm.

The picture is cheaply made and is just a fair program production, suitable for a double feature day at the majority of houses charging more than a dime admission.

Fred.

PARTED CURTAINS

"Parted Curtains" is presented by Warner Brothers, with Henry B. Walthall and Mary Alden starred. The story is by Tom J. Hopkins. It is a strong, elemental, melodramatic tale of self-sacrifice with a couple of inconsistencies, but nevertheless absorbingly interesting.

Walthall, "borrows" $2,000 from his employer's till to help out a "friend," who runs away and leaves him to bear the charge of embezzlement, for which he spends seven yars in prison. Emerging he faints, is carried into the home of an artist, gets on his feet again, falls in love with the sister of the artist's wife, becomes a genius at etching, finds the wife talking to the man who double-crossed him, asks her what it means: "He told me he would marry me and I believed him," and the villian blackmails her on threat of telling her husband.

When Walthall is caught wrestling with the villain who is robbing the house, he saves the wife by denouncing himself and saying the man is a detective. Artist doesn't press the charge, wife confesses to her sister, Walthall rescues the child from kidnapping, the villain is killed and the poor wife's secret is safe.

The role suits Walthall's sensitive face which is so capable of expressing suffering and the role of the wife is played by Mary Alden, who scored so strongly as the mother in "The Old Nest."

Feature is well directed and acted throughout.

Jolo.

THE INNER CHAMBER

Claire Robson .... Alice Joyce
Mrs. Robson .... Jane Jennings
Dr. George Danilo....Pedro de Cordoba
Edward J. Wellman..Holmes E. Herbert
Sawyer Flint ...... John Webb Dillon
Mrs. Sawyer Flint ...... Grace Barton
Mrs. Finch-Brown ...... Ida Waterman
Nellie McGuire ..... Josephine Whittell
Mrs. Candor ...... Mrs. De Wolf Hopper

This is a Vitagraph six-reeler that would have made a much better picture had it been a two-reeler. The story was originally entitled "The Blood Red Dawn," written by Charles Caldwell Dobie. The direction was by Edward Jose. In brief, the picture is one of those affairs permitted to wend its way through interminable footage all to no purpose to put over a slight kick at the finish. The result is that it is exceedingly draggy and drawn out.

The yarn drags through a series of episodes of the poor working girl with a sick mother whose boss tries to win her. The audience is far ahead of the story during this section for they have seen the selfsame things so many times on the screen. As the developments get down to the last two reels, there is really something stirring. The girl marries an Italian doctor, the best friend of the man she is in love with. After the ceremony the doctor discovers his wife and best friend have been acquainted in the past; his Latin blood runs riot, with the result he takes a shot at what he supposes is his wife but it is only her reflection in a mirror. Atop of that he shoots himself. In the end he dies and the lovers are reunited.

Alice Joyce gives a fairly interesting performance at certain points but the honors must be conferred on Josephine Whittell as a hick steno. She is there as far as the screen is concerned and invests her role with a quality of naturalness that should take her far in screen work.

Pedro de Cordoba and Holmes E. Herbert divide the male honors while John Webb Dillon is an acceptable conventional heavy.

Just what the title of "The Inner Chamber" means is a guess; surely there is nothing about the picture that suggests it.

The production is nothing out of the ordinary and is quite in keeping with the usual Vitagraph standard of old fashionedness.

Fred.

FOOTLIGHTS

Lizzie Parsons / Lisa Parsinova } ....Elsie Ferguson
Brett Page .... Reginald Denny
Oswald Kane .... Marc MacDermott
Etta .... Octavia Handworth

"Footlights" (Paramount) starring Elsie Ferguson and current at the Rivoli, makes an amusing comedy. The direction is in the expert hands of John S. Robertson, who handled the filming of "Sentimental Tommy" and several other notable productions and is extremely well done. The story needed careful, intelligent management, for it has certain moments where crude direction might have emphasized its artificial character.

Under its present treatment, however, its insincerities are masked by its agreeable high comedy atmosphere. Serious treatment would have spoiled the whole thing, but this error has been avoided. The bare plot has a certain effective humor, detailing with the experiences of a plain, small-town New England girl masquerading on the stage as a temperamental Russian actress with large pretense of serious art. This situation gives opportunity for several capital comedy moments, such as the scene in which "Lisa Parsinova" (who is really Lizzie Parsons) stages a fit of tantrums for the benefit of a roomful of pop-eyed hero worshipers.

Miss Ferguson is ideal for the role. She has a fine natural method of finely shaded comedy appeal and a peculiarly expressive face for the screen. Likewise she has the art rare among feminine stars of wearing gorgeous, exotic things in a natural way —as though they were her own clothes and not costumes supplied to an actress. This picture is a treat for the women in its sumptuous display of clothes.

The Rivoli has a queer idea of setting forth the names of the players in the cast. For some strange reason Octavia Handworth in the inconsequential role of a colored maid is identified on the program, but no mention is made of Mrs. Letty Ford, who does an exquisite bit as the grandmother in the early part of the picture. Mrs. Ford makes one of the most lovable old ladies of the screen and in this instance gives the production a charming fragrance as of lavendar and old lace.

The picture, in spite of certain implausibilities of detail, is done in a fine spirit of elegance, both as to acting and production settings. Probably Mr. Robertson is responsible for this touch. The story is by Rita Weiman and the scenario by Josephine Lovett.

It deals with Elizabeth Parsons, daughter of a Puritanical Massachusetts mother, who is aided and abetted in her ambitions for a stage career by her grandmother. She goes the familiar way of stage aspirants, and is found in the depths of discouragement, doing an act of impersonations on a small, cheap circuit, where she is discovered by a noted producer, one Oswald Kane (Marc MacDermott). Kane plans to pretend she is a noted Russian artist and trains her for two years to play that role before he springs her upon the metropolitan audiences. She is a great hit, of course.

Brett Page (Reginald Denny), a rich young man-about-town, falls in love with her and she with him. It at length breaks in upon Lizzie's mind that Brett loves her for her counterfeit personality as the Russian artist and not for her real self as Lizzie Parsons. So she goes rowing in a fog as Parsinova and disappears, so that her coat shall be found in the drifting boat. As Lizzie Parsons she gains the shore and by one of those screen coincidences immediately falls in with Brett, this time in her real character. Brett decides he loves her as much as Lizzie as he thought he did as Lisa and the way is paved for the happy ending with wedding bells in prospect.

The tale has stronger romantic and sentimental elements than this bald recital would indicate and ought to gain favor with the women film fans. Apparently the producing company thinks so, for the picture is set for a double week at the Rivoli.

The following of Miss Ferguson probably in itself would carry it through, but the story will help to this end.

Rush.

DANGEROUS CURVE AHEAD

Phoebe Mabee .... Helene Chadwick
Harley Jones................Richard Dix
Anson Newton .....M. B. (Lefty) Flynn
Mr. Mabee .... James Neill
Mrs. Mabee .... Edythe Chapman
Mrs. Noxin .... Kate Lester

Goldwyn has two people in this production worthy of stellar honors. They are Helene Chadwick and Richard Dix. Their screen performance here entitle their names to lights. The picture is by Rupert Hughes as author and E. Mason Hopper as director. The story begins as a domestic comedy and ends as heavy drama, interesting at all times, with sufficient comedy relief to please any type of audience.

Miss Chadwick and Mr. Dix are the young small town couple who come to the big city. The husband is successful as time creeps on and the wife might be construed as likewise, inasmuch as she becomes the mother of three youngsters and still looks like a chicken.

Eventually the social bug stings her and to be a success in that particular she accepts the invitation to dinner at a social leader's home, the nephew of whom was a former admirer of the girl and who is determined to "get her" sooner or later. On that particular evening one of the children is stricken with an illness and in the midst of the dinner the mother instinct overcomes that of social climbing and she creates a scene and leaves for home and her baby's bedside.

That is all that there is to the yarn, but the manner of telling and the capable characterizations supplied by the cast of players make the picture a delight. Miss Chadwick gives a really worth-while performance as the mother and Mr. Dix as the husband was most convincing. M. B. ("Lefty") Flynn, former gridiron hero, plays the heavy in a conventional manner with an ever-ready cigaret case.

Fred.

I ACCUSE

Francis Laurin......Monsieur Severin-Mars
Marie Laurin, his wife,
Mlle. Marise Dauvray
Jean, the poet.................Romuald Joube
Henri Lazare................Monsieur Desjardin
Angele..........................Little Angele

"J'Accuse" was originally filmed in France as the French cry for vengeance against the German enemy, a kind of Gallic "Hymn of Hate." Now it has been revised by Abel Gance, who occupies a high position in France as writer and film producer resembling the niche in America held by D. W. Griffith.

The first plan of the picture has been somewhat changed and brought up to date by revisions in the final passages which make it more a plea of international agreement for the limitation of arms as a means of preventing future wars, giving the picture a greater world appeal than a national appeal for vengeance.

This work has been skilfully done, and to a considerable extent takes away from the story the passionate partisanship of the French. For the American edition a message by President Harding in the furtherance of the arms parley has been inserted in the early part and the picture is dedicated to the American chief executive.

Much of the later scenes of war action late in the film also have an American flavor, showing operations in the St. Mihiel sector, some of the American advance toward Metz as part of the triangle up through the Argonne.

At the Strand the picture takes about an hour and a half to run and the rest of the show has been cut down to two musical interludes and the news topical. The usual comedy is absent. It could scarcely be introduced in this bill, anyway; any sort of comedy would be highly inappropriate in connection with this terrific epic of war. The picture has many dramatic moments, but the grim, harrowing happenings do not make for cheerful entertainment. Only its purpose of furthering the end of war could excuse its horrors. Some of the battle scenes are terribly real and the hospital shots achieve a realism that may be art, but certainly have an unhappy effect upon the spectator.

The episode of the death of Francois, the French husband, is a terrifying bit of shuddering realism. He is brought to the hospital dying from wounds and placed in the cot adjoining that occupied by Jean, the poet from his native village, whom he has suspected of being his rival for the affections of Marie, Francois's wife. The war woes of France have driven Jean insane.

After Francois's death Jean goes back home, still insane, and summons the widows and orphans of the village to a meeting at which he says he will give them news of their dead. These episodes consist of showing in double exposures and cutbacks troups and troups of the battlefield dead arising from their graves and returning home determined to learn whether the living have been worthy of their high sacrifice. As a device to drive this moral home, excerpts are printed on the screen from the verses written by the American Alan Seager under the line "We Shall Not Sleep in Flanders Fields." These passages occupy several reels and involve some powerful scenes in their grim message. But a "happy ending" is devised for the climax, showing Jean restored to reason and apparently happy with Marie.

The earlier chapters have to do with the stark tragedy of the war. Francois is intensely jealous of Marie, his young wife, and suspects Marie's former sweetheart, Jean. At the call to the colors Francois goes to the front, while Marie goes from Provence to the north of France to join her husband's relatives. There she is captured and deported by the enemy. Several years later she makes her way back to Provence, accompanied by a baby born of an enemy father. This fact is made plain in a series of cutbacks as Marie recites her experiences. She is shown crouching in terror in an underground room while the shadows of men in spiked helmets approach along the wall to within reach and are blotted out.

Marie fears her jealous husband when he shall learn of her tragedy and so leaves the baby in the care of Jean, home after being discharged for disability. The husband also returns on furlough and comes to believe that the child's father is Jean and the wife has been faithless. When he learns the truth he returns to the front, doubly determined to avenge his wrongs upon the enemy.

At each development of war cruelty one of the French characters repeats the formula "J'Accuse" ("I Accuse"), and for French purposes this was doubtless the message of the picture. Apparently the plea for disarmament has been an afterthought, although the revision has been skillfully done.

The picture is being released by United Artists, while the presentation at the Strand is sponsored by the American Legion. The subject is timely, inasmuch as the arms conference is to take place in Washington this fall, but it makes a pretty harrowing evening. *Rush.*

THE CASE OF BECKY

Dorothy Stone............Constance Binney
John Arnold..............Glenn Hunter
Dr. Emerson..............Frank McCormack
Professor Balzamo.........Montague Love
Mrs. Emerson.............Margaret Seddon
Mrs. Arnold..............Jane Hennings

The fact that this Realart production is playing the Rialto on Broadway for a week's run is one of the surest indications there is a shortage of good features in the picture marts. Even though this Realart production is far and away one of the best that has been turned out by the organization in some time, still it is not a Broadway picture.

There is something wrong with the entire Realart scheme of things. From a casual survey of the situation it would seem as though some one had given orders that only a certain type of production could be turned out by the organization. At present, of all their stars there is but one who is a real paying proposition, and that is Bebe Daniels. It is not because of the stars themselves, but rather because of the type of material that they are compelled to appear in.

As a case in point in this picture, Constance Binney proves she is a screen actress of unusual ability. She has looks, screens like a million dollars, and, above all, can troupe. But with all this she cannot pull the "Case of Becky" over on Broadway. With a few more like opportunities, with the picture built up around her, Miss Binney is going to make the majority of screen stars speed up to hold pace with her.

"The Case of Becky" is taken from the play of the same title, written by Edward Locke and originally produced by David Belasco. It is the story of dual personality brought about through hypnotics.

Miss Binney plays Dorothy-Becky, and gives a remarkable performance. Montague Love, finally cast rightfully, a leading heavy, gives Balzamo exactly its brutal touch. Frank McCormack played Dr. Emerson, with scientific reserve.

Chester Franklin, who directed, handled the picture nicely and achieved several effective night shots in which the lighting was especially good. Glenn Hunter, who played the juvenile lead opposite Miss Binney, gave a performance that combined subtle comedy with extreme earnestness.

The picture was made by Realart in the east. That may account for it being better than the usual run of pictures bearing this trade-mark, for the majority have been made on the coast. *Fred.*

FROM GROUND UP

Terence Giluley.................Tom Moore
Philena Mortimer.........Helene Chadwick
Mr. Mortimer..........De Witt C. Jennings
Mrs. Mortimer.....................Grace Pike
Carswell, Sr..............Hardee Kirkland
Carswell, Jr...................Darrell Foss

A fair comedy drama, very much of the type appealing to the juvenile mind. A sort of an Oliver Optic brought up to date, it is more or less of a surprise that Rupert Hughes should be guilty of the story. It has the appearance of a yarn ground out under pressure. It is just possible that R. H. is doing a little too much work to do full justice to all.

The picture does not seem to have sufficient strength to be utilized for a full week on Broadway at the Capitol, but as the Goldwyns hold control of the house as far as its features are concerned, there is nothing more to be said regarding the booking.

Tom Moore has the role of a ditch mucker on an excavating job. He is a happy-go-lucky lad, who plays the harmonica between shoveling. At the finish he is a contractor and builder with offices on the top floor of the skyscraper which he helped dig the foundation for. All this happens within a comparatively short time. Likewise, the man who originally promoted the building project goes down the slide as Moore goes up, and in the end the latter wins his daughter.

There are a few laughs in the picture, due mainly to the sub-titles. A thrill is afforded by Darrell Foss doing a drunken scene along the steel girders of the building while it is in course of construction. The building used for these scenes is the new Loew State in Los Angeles.

E. Mason Hopper directed the picture and managed to turn out a workmanlike job with the material at hand. The production does not show an unusual expense in any of the scenes, but at that it is as adequate as could be asked.

In the popular priced houses on a double feature bill it will get by, but that is about all. *Fred.*

EVERYMAN'S PRICE

Ethel Armstrong.............Grace Darling
Henry Armstrong...........E. J. Radcliffe
Bruce Steele.............Charles Waldron
Jim Steele.......................Bud Geary

The lights outside of the Circle Monday night told the story that Ethel Clayton in "Beyond" and Grace Darling in "Everyman's Price" were being shown. The other signs about the theatre substituted Grace Davidson for Grace Darling. Inside it was Grace Darling on the screen. The Ethel Clayton picture was a Paramount and the Grace Darling production is one released by the J. W. Film Corp.

Burton King is given screen and paper credit for the picture, the line being "A Burton King Production." That line will never get Mr. King anything nor will the picture, for that matter. It is about as poorly constructed and impossible a story as has been viewed in some time, and the direction is about on a par.

An utter lack of action at all times. The picture resolves itself into a series of semi-closeups that become tiresome as they continue without variation. The titling with which they are strung together is also exceedingly haphazard.

Here is a sample of the action. Closeup of girl's father; he sits and thinks. Closeup of girl; she sits and thinks. Closeup of district attorney; he sits and thinks. Closeup of girl; she has changed her dress, but still sits and thinks. Closeup of district attorney; he still thinks as he sits. As a matter of fact, there isn't even as much variation in the picture as there is in the written explanation.

As for the titles. The girl's father, who is a financier, must have been mighty glad his daughter was going to marry the D. A., for he told her so a couple of times. In the first reel it was "I'm glad you are going to marry Steele, for 'm going to make him the next Governor." In the next reel or so it was: "I'm glad you love Steele, for he is going to be one of the big men of the country." Atop of that when the girl speaks of the man to whom she is engaged to her father she is formal enough to mention him as "Mr. Steele."

As for the yarn itself. Charles Waldron as Steele is elected district attorney. The first day in office he reads there is profiteering in foodstuffs. He calls in his investigators to find out if it is true and then takes the afternoon off to propose to the girl. She accepts him, but later when the investigator reports that her dad is the food-hoarder and the D. A. is going after him she breaks off her engagement.

Whoever the author was his idea of legal procedure was all wet. He had the D. A. walk right into a jury trial and the food hoarder was turned out for lack of evidence. Not necessary in this picture for a Grand Jury to indict.

After he had the engaged couple parted the author had to bring them together again. The girl's brother gets into a jam for money. He goes to his dad for a check to help him cover his account with his broker (who happens to be the brother of the D. A.) Dad gives him a check, first stipulating the boy follow his instructions regarding it. When the check comes back to the maker he takes it to the district attorney and insists it was a forgery; that he will have to prosecute his brother for having cashed it. As the brother arrives and admits having cashed the check, the financier's son says he is equally guilty; then the girl walks in (sure a busy day in the criminal courts) and asks him not to go through with his action, whereupon it is disclosed it was all a frame by the father to bring the couple together.

As a picture "Everyman's Price" is so small that even the majority of nickel audiences will give it the raz! *Fred.*

AMAZING LOVERS

A. H. Fischer, Inc., presents "Amazing Lovers," starring Diana Allen, the former Ziegfeld "Follies" girl. Jans Productions is distributing. B. A. Rolfe did the directing with the story credited to Charles A. Logue. The story embraces several bits of antiquated melodrama, but is comparatively interesting in its screen version. Counterfeiting and murder are two of the leading themes. Counterfeiters operating in New York are making French paper money, backed by a private banker connected with it for the benefit he can derive from the low exchange rate the flood of imitation francs causes.

In order to ship an amount of the imitation stuff to France a girl representative is sent to New York to bring it back with her. She poses as a notorious Apache with one of the ring leaders falling in love with her. Meantime he kills the banker, but places the blame upon another who is made to believe he did the deed while in a drunken stupor. With this held over his head the latter is forced into a marriage with the girl so that she cannot be deported if branded as an undesirable alien, if detected as one of the gang's workers.

It turns out the girl is a secret service agent and causes the arrest of the counterfeiters. She was actually married to the man she was forced to take as her husband. Numerous twists, which should keep the average audience interested. Miss Allen has recently been elevated to stardom. She is of the blond engenue type that invariably appeals and is supplied with looks aplenty. Her acting should improve with each production. This one is a considerable improvement over her former efforts. Marc McDermott has the male lead as the master-mind of the counterfeiters. He gives the expected finished performance. The production end is adequate for a low priced feature.

"Amazing Lovers" is but one of the general run of cheaper grade pictures. *Hart.*

BLIND HEARTS

Lars Larson..............Hobart Bosworth
John Thomas..................Wade Boteler
Mrs. Thomas...............Irene Blackwell
Hilda Larson...............Collette Forbes
Julia Larson................Madge Bellamy
Paul Thomas..............Raymond McKee
James Curdy...............William Conklin
Rita.........................Lule Warrenton
James Bradley..............Henry Herbert

This Associated Producers' release starring Hobart Bosworth and produced by the corporation bearing the star's name, is sub-captioned as "a drama of a great hate," which for all its pessimistic appellation is paradoxically a beautiful epic on the love of Lars Larson (Mr. Bosworth) for his fellow man and justice. The story is a powerfully compelling thing credited to Emilie Johnson and adapted by Joseph Franklin Poland, who has concocted a masterful continuity. Rowland V. Lee, an associate of Thomas H. Ince was "loaned" by that producer to direct this feature, and the result is a credit to all concerned.

Where the Bosworth name is mentioned there immediately conjures up in one's mind a tawny, brawny he-man, sailor captain figure, and the expectation is satisfied from the start here as well, although the salt sea atmosphere in this instance is, but an incidental to the plot. Larson and John Thomas are partners in their Yukon gold mining enterprise and prosper jointly. The drama dates from the time the men's wives give birth to children, to Larson a girl and to Thomas a boy, which is exactly as they both wished it to be. In reality Larson's offspring is the male and Thomas' the girl, but an overzealous nurse purposely effected the exchange on their birth so that the men may be deluded into realizing their fondest expectations. However, a birthmark on the girl's shoulder similar to one on Thomas' body leads Larson to suspect infidelity on his wife's part (who dies shortly thereafter) and for 20 years Larson's affection and love for his old friend and business associate has become one of cool aloofness and sullenness. The children grown up are in love with each other, but Larson refuses his consent, with the result the boy endeavors to effect a reason therefor, and the following morning is arrested charged with the murder of Larson, who is supposed to have been murdered on his yacht and brutally cremated through the firing of the vessel. Larson in reality has gone back to Alaska, but learning of the boy's sentence to the gallows through an old newspaper he finds wrapped around some provisions, returns to the States to clear up matters, although he believes himself in turn to be guilty of a murder of another man. Everything turns out rosy for all concerned and the partners' 20-year-old promise that they would live to dance at their children's wedding is fulfilled. The balance of the story is meaty with interesting incidental situations which space prohibits reciting.

Bosworth is his usual compelling self in the dramatic scenes, exacting heavy toll in the way of "action" from mere stationary poses through facial contortioning and vibrant physical tensing of the limbs. In short Bosworth 's an excellent actor.

The support has been wisely chosen, all equally balanced in ability, with Raymond McKee's juvenile part standing out in the prison scenes, where McKee wisely foregoes the brave heroics of a wronged martyr going to his doom, but, on the contrary, affects a pathetically pleading, in fact almost cringing, pose in the protest of his innocence. That's realism that is worth a ton of the idealistic sham bravery.

It's a clean-cut feature that won a round of applause at its conclusion when exhibited at the Broadway this week. *Abel.*

EVERYTHING FOR SALE

A Realart release, story by Hector Turnbull, directed by Frank O'Connor, starring May McAvoy. Conventional tale, classily visualized. Girl brought up in boarding school, comes to live with her aunt, who frames a wealthy marriage for her, shunting off the girl's youthful lover, who is a poor architect. At the opening an allegorical title compares the aunt's scheming with the auction block of olden times when maides were sold to the highest bidder.

The wealthy man selected by auntie is a bachelor (Richard Tucker), whose theory of life is that everything is for sale—it is only a question of price. When you compare him with the penniless architect you really can't find it in your heart to blame auntie—that is, you wouldn't in actual life, though you might in romance. To show you how well fixed he is, he has a mistress, a yacht, is still young and good-looking, isn't a villain at all, has the manners of a gentleman, and is, from all angles, a desirable catch for any girl. He is also a business man par excellence, for he sends the young architect down south to build bungalows so the coast will be clear for his courting.

The bachelor is about to sail for Europe on business and persuades the girl, aided by auntie, to marry him in a week. On the day of the wedding the youthful architect returns, having already made enough money to want to propose to the girl. That's making one's pile pretty fast. Anyhow, he takes the girl out rowing to an island, where she tells him it is her wedding day—the boat drifts away and they are marooned over night—the wedding night. Finding his fiancee doesn't put in an appearance, rich man goes home and phones for his mistress, like a sensible man. When, the next day, auntie tries to renew negotiations for his marriage with her niece, he calmly tells her it is all off and turns to his mistress for consolation.

This leaves the coast clear for the girl and the architect to come to the inevitable clinch. Not a particularly inspiring tale, but it is well produced and competently played, with such admirable supporting players as Edwin Stevens as a sentimental uncle and Kathlyn Williams as the scheming auntie. A high-class program feature. *Jolo.*

HANDCUFFS OR KISSES

Interesting production—interesting as entertainment. It tells the public a lot of things about reformatories and should have a good effect upon young girls headed in that direction.

Story by Thomas Edgelow, scenario by Lewis Allen Browne, directed by George Archainbaud, starring Elaine Hammerstein—a Selznick feature.

Girl deprived of her father's estate by dishonest aunt who wants her own daughter to enjoy same—is made practically a slave in the household. Julia Swayne Gordon plays the aunt with sufficient villainy and Elaine Hammerstein excites your sympathy as the abused orphaned niece. When niece rebels she is railroaded to the reformatory, the scenes of which are either genuine or so well reproduced as to be natural. Here are shown some of the alleged abuses in such institutions, such as flogging, ice baths, etc.

The governor appoints a committee to investigate the prisons and the charming young assistant eventually marries the abused girl. There is apparently too much detail in the feature. They are fine enough, but carefully deleted and the action that much quickened, a better result might be attained and still have sufficient footage. *Jolo.*

German Pics

By C. HOOPER TRASK

Berlin, Sept. 24.

"SAPPHO"

This looks as though Pola Negri had done it again, for although the critics panned it, "Sappho" has been filling the U. T. Kurfuerstendamm nightly since its opening, And deservedly so.

The film lacks any artistic originality in direction, photography or scenery, but it has a well-constructed, swiftly moving scenario and gives ample opportunity for acting.

Sappho, queen of the women of pleasure, has betrayed Andreas, a young engineer, with his employer, George. Andreas finds it out and goes insane. His brother Richard is summoned to the lunatic asylum, and there vows vengeance against Sappho. He goes to the city to find her, but meeting her without learning her name they fall in love. She leaves George to go away with Richard to the seashore; she will begin a new life. George, however, follows her and tells Richard the truth of Sappho's identity. Furious, disillusioned, he leaves her and returns to his country home, where the sweetheart of his youth awaits him.

At the village church they are married, but at the wedding breakfast thoughts of Sappho surge over him. He cannot stand it any longer, and, dropping his glass, he rushes away to catch the first train for the city. At the same time at the asylum the mad Andreas, goaded by revenge, kills his keeper and escapes. These two swiftly converging threads give a breath-catching finale to the fourth reel.

In the city Sappho, learning of Richard's marriage, piqued, sets out for the great annual fancy dress ball. In a box, making a show of gaiety which she is far from feeling, Richard sees her. She flees up two flights of stairs, with Richard following, and in a private dining room their explanations quickly made, they are in each other's arms. The door opens and Andreas stands before them. George he has already murdered in his limousine while on his way to the ball. And now he has come for Sappho. With the cunning of madness he shoves Richard out of the room. Richard beats wildly on the door, shouting meantime for help. Up from the ballroom stream the thousands of masks; the door is broken in. But, too late; at the madman's feet Sappho lies dead.

Pola's Sappho is, taken as a whole, a superior grade of sex acting, and if it reminds you of Sumurun or Carmen or DuBarry, well, that only proves she isn't a character actress, which after all proves nothing in pictures. However, in the present film she fails on one or two occasions to register just the required shade of emotion, but as this is a thing which never happened under Lubitsch, it must be laid largely at the door of her present director, Buchowetski.

The support is adequate, with the Andreas of Alfred Abels a film masterpiece. Johannes Riemann as Richard always looks well and acts sufficiently. The George of Albert Steinrueck (the Rabbi of "The Golem") gets by, but why dress like an old clothes man?

Dimitri Buchowetzki, the director and scenario writer, deserves credit for a story of suspense and snappy, unobtrusive direction. No big feature should be intrusted to him (his botching of "Dant " proved that), but for ordinary program features he has a distinct place.

"ROSWOLSKY'S SWEETHEART"

The Ufa has here another release with evident American possibilities. Its assets include comedy, suspense and a happy ending. Asta Nielsen, one of its featured players, is not utterly unknown in New York and Paul Wegener, who plays opposite, will be remembered by his phenomenal "Golem."

The scenario after Georg Froeschel's novel, "Die Geliebte Roswolsky's," reworked by H. Galeen and H. Janowitz, is consistent and shows careful continuity work. It concerns Mary, a poor chorus girl, who loses her job because she will remain virtuous. She is saved from suicide (according to the modern scenario the only refuge of an honest show girl) by Roswolsky, the richest man of the city; indeed, he even goes so far as to give her a key to his garden, telling her to come and wander there at will.

This scene has been noticed, and next day an article appears in the papers linking her name and Roswolsky's. Credit pours in upon her; she is re-engaged at the theatre as star this time. Roswolsky, amused, does not deny the rumor.

One day in a box at the theatre Mary sees Count Albich, an African explorer, and falls in love with him. She follows him to Italy, and there, although he, too, comes to love her, he leaves her, believing her to be connected with Roswolsky. Returning home she is faced by unpaid bills, loaned money due. Thus for the first time she goes to Roswolsky.

At first Roswolsky had merely taken it all as a joke; at last the thing has become serious for him; he will have her for his mistress in earnest. Again her innate purity comes to the surface and she rushes madly away. Her delicate sense of virtue, however, does not carry her beyond preservation of her virginity, for she now decides to order a famous diamond necklace on credit and disappear with it. But already she has begun to be suspected and the police arrest her before she can escape. To the station house come both Count Albich and Roswolsky and the latter takes upon himself the payment of all the debts, saying that it was his duty to have contradicted the rumors at once. And as Mary and the Count start off on their honeymoon, the millionaire presents her with a bouquet of flowers in which lies concealed the diamond necklace.

As can be easily seen, a good modicum of hokum is present, but it is amiable hokum and the general tone of lightness gets it pleasantly by. Carl Drew's photography and Felix Basch's direction are more creditable for what they refrained from doing than for any definite plus achievement.

The chief burden of the film falls on Asta as Mary. From the acting angle she is there (her comedy being particularly commendable), but her face is a little hard and in certain lightings, unattractive. Paul Wegener lends a distinction and power to Roswolsky which justify his engagement for this comparatively small role. Max Landa as Count Albich is inadequate both as regards looks and acting.

THEODORA

Theodora Augusta	Rita Jolivet
Justinian	Ferrucio Biancini
Andreas	Rene Maupre
Antonina	Emilia Rosini
Belisarius	Adolf Touche
Marcellus	Mariano Bottini
Chief Executioner	Guido Marciano
Tamyris	Marie Belfiore
Buzes	Giovanni Motta
Mara	Leo Sorinello
Amru	G. Rosetti
Calcante	Luigi Rinelli
Philo	Alfredo
Eufrata	Rafael Bertoncelli
Conspirators	Giuliano Gardini Francois Renard Pietro Ferrari Alberto Belfiore

"Theodora" is another massive Italian production on the order of "Cabiria," only more elaborate, imported by Goldwyn and current at the Astor, New York, at $2 top. Goldwyn took it over and spent $50,000 in a preliminary city advertising campaign before it opened late last week. It has been a sell-out right along. Tuesday night Charlie Chaplin occupied a box, and the appearance was widely heralded. By 8 o'clock the box office stopped selling standing room.

The picture is a draw and will be a draw on its merits, because it satisfies a universal human craving for romance and melodrama. The film is a sumptuous revel in nervous shocks, melodrama that hits you between the eyes and at the same time fills the eyes with stunning pictures. The hugeness of the crowds and the vastness of the settings are sometimes distracting in their over-elaboration of background, but the story is gripping and the total is overpowering, both of drama and pageantry.

You leave the theatre bewildered, and it takes some moments to compose yourself to picking out the "smash" of the production, and then you are embarrassed by a confusion of choice, for there are so many big passages one must compromise by setting down a few of the many.

One scene shows the Roman hippodrome at Byzantium. Literally thousands of people are concerned and the effect is achieved of a countless horde. The mob is in revolt against Justinian, the Emperor, and surge inward from the banked circle around the royal box threatening and imploring; a wild riot of motion and massed crowd. The secret lover of the Empress has been seized as a rebel and is arraigned before the royal couple. To gain time the Queen gives orders that the lions be loosed in the arena to distract the king's attention, and the thing is done before one's eyes.

Here is **melodrama** trickily staged. The big cats slink up from their dens, slide through the barriers and appear to leap into the faces of the terror paralyzed rabble. How the thing is done is a mystery, but as a shocker it is 100 per cent. and high voltage. The lions are made to leap, snapping and snarling against the sides of the arena at the fleeing crowd. Half a dozen appear to fall back killed. And at the end attendants drag off a ton of convincing duplication of dead lions, if, indeed, it is not the real thing.

The scene goes so far as to show a closeup of one lion snarling into the very face of the hero, bound and helpless, with its claws sunk into his shoulders, while a lion tamer, a woman, actually struggles with the big beast and drags it away. It may be studio trickery, but what a sublimation of riotous melodrama. In all likelihood this is the "punch" that is registering at the box office. It appeals to the same human instinct that makes a street crowd stand by the half hour watching a steeplejack at work, fascinated by the possibilities of a tragedy. Leave it to the Freudians to analyze the impulse, but there it is and here it looks like a box office winner. Put it down for a natural human craving for an emotional adventure to break the monotony of monotonous existence.

Perhaps that's the big smash, but the two hours of projection has a host of subsidiary shocks. For one there is a glimpse of the Emperor's torture chamber in full operation. Ask David Belasco if torture chamber horrors are a commercial asset, and recall the success of "The Darling of the Gods." It isn't a month since an enterprising promoter cashed in on the Convict Ship, a ballyhoo side show moored at a Hudson River dock, by playing up the feature of "the black hole," where British convicts were tortured. It must go back to the same impulse that makes children beg for terrifying ghost stories at bed time. A giant executioner, a highly menacing bogey man runs through the picture and there is murder, rapine and intrigue galore from start to finish.

There are mob scenes a-plenty, staged with great vividness and realism; there are court scenes of the utmost magnificence, pageantry of stalwart, curiously garbed and accoutred soldiers; there are natural backgrounds (the program says the producers spilled the location over 100,000 square meters, including an Italian lake) that are lovely; and through it all there is a surge of a love story and a picturesque flavor of the Orient and bizarre atmosphere of antiquity, the events being placed in the sixth century.

Strangely enough, this dip into ancient events and surroundings does not come before one as artificial and an unreality. It will probably interest Arthur Hopkins and Lionel Barrymore to know that the tale in all its basic elements and in scores of details is identical with Henri Bernstein's "The Claw," which had its premiere Monday at the Broadhurst, and which deals in an analytical way with a social and moral problem of Paris and points east and west in Sept., 1921, to all intents and purposes. That ought to prove that the story of the Byzantian actress and courtesan who becomes Empress of the Roman Empire has within it the elements of universal appeal. Here is the same story in two forms, "The Claw" a brilliant, almost a clinical modern social study, and "Theodora," a tumultuous film melodrama, and in grip both recitals go step by step and shoulder to shoulder.

In both cases an oversexed, young, ambitious and unscrupulous woman in the early twenties subjugates a superior man approaching middle life and breaks him to her will. In the ancient story the woman is punished in obedience to a code of literary ethics that is defied in the modern French system. Bernstein has her emerge triumphant, at least in material things.

program note asseverates that the film production cost "15,000,000 lire, or $3,000,000." The translation to dollars is at parity and comes a little as a jolt, but the production must have cost a good deal of money. The costuming alone must have been a considerable item. Sumptuous describes it reasonably well, and it is convincing. The huge settings and the natural backgrounds are also impressive in illusion. The ancient interiors of palaces and villas are huge and often beautiful beyond adequate description.

The acting is astonishingly natural, perhaps because all the players are foreigners and unfamiliar over here, except Rita Jolivet, who plays Theodora. New, strange faces and figures help to hold the actors from the level of commonplaceness; they do not intrude New York, Los Angeles or Broadway upon the drama. Another way of saying the same thing is the statement that no actor could wear a toga on the stage without being ridiculous to his wife.

The story, of course, is adapted from Sardou's play of the same name and was produced by the Unione Cinematografica Italiana of Rome. The American presentation, which is severely simple and unadorned, is under the direction of S. L. Rothafel. Katherine Hilliker wrote the American titles, using fine restraint. At first she was rather prolix, but as the play approached the tense climax she penned some fine short, compact and telling lines.

The last was a model. As the desolated Theodora, kneeling beside her dead lover, bares her throat to the executioner's garrote, the title sheet reads: "Gorgia, be swift; I have a rendezvous." *Rush.*

PETER IBBETSON

Peter Ibbetson	Wallace Reid
Mimsi	Elsie Ferguson
Colonel Ibbetson	Montague Love
Major Duquenois	George Fawcett
Dolores	Dolores Cassinelli
M. Seraskier	Paul McAllister
M. Pasquier	Elliott Dexter
Mme. Pasquier	Barbara Dean
The Child Mimsi	Nell Roy Buck
The Child Gogo	Charles Eaton
Duke of Towers	Jerome Patrick

"Peter Ibbetson," picturized by George Fitzmaurice for Paramount and distributed by Famous Players, is an adaptation of the play of that name by du Maurier, which ran for the better part of a season on Broadway several years ago, with Jack Barrymore in the leading role. The screen version is the work of Ouida Bergere. Elsie Ferguson and Wallace Reid are co-starred. The film runs about eight reels.

Artistically the picture is entitled to high praise, not alone as regards lighting and mechanical details, but in the manner in which the elusive and deeply psychological story has been translated to the screen. That it will appeal strongly to the better class, that known as "carriage trade," goes without question. Whether or not the considerably larger number of fans making up the general run of film patrons will like it is a matter of speculation.

A particularly fine cast has been assembled to support the stars. Many a picture with far less claim to the billing has been trumpeted as an "all star" affair, an underline which "Peter Ibbetson" could readily sustain, through the presence of Montagu Love, George Fawcett, Dolores Cassinelli, Paul McAllister, Elliott Dexter and Jerome Patrick, each cast in a role that fits perfectly. Mr. Fawcett, for instance, never did better work in his long career than as the old soldier of the Napoleon Guard, shown at the age of 60, and twenty years later as a doddering old man.

In mentioning the cast might be noted two children who have not yet reached the heights of stardom, but who bear all the ear-marks of potential stars. The work of Charles Eaton and Nell Roy Buck is of such natural and sincere nature as to make their performances remarkable for their years.

While the tale unfolded is engrossing, it becomes decidedly depressing toward the end, which runs to extreme morbidness, piling on the gloom with cumulative thickness as it goes along, and terminating in an unqualifiedly "unhappy ending."

The fore-part breathes pastoral happiness, heightened by unusually pretty backgrounds, contrasting sharply with the dismalness of the prison environment in which the fanciful dream-weaving Peter is placed through later developments of the plot.

Mr. Reid gives a surprisingly authoritative interpretation of the central character, bringing out forcefully the depth of imagination that is the motivating spirit of the role. A few of the scenes have Mr. Reid more in accord with the modern type of roles with which he has been associated, but the greater part of the action calls upon him to sink his personality completely, a difficult thing for any artist to accomplish, but excellently done by Mr. Reid. Miss Ferguson plays with distinction throughout, depicting clearly the finer lights and shadows of Mme. Pasquier, and never making herself obtrusive.

The direction by Mr. Fitzmaurice is notable for the way in which the big dramatic moments are staged. A reproduction of a prize fight in the period when bare knuckles were the vogue is shown with touches of atmospheric detail that give the spectator the impression some rare old print of a London sporting club scrap of the vintage of 1824 has come to life. It also makes a likeable bit of comedy relief for the early action.

Quotations from Oscar Wilde's "Ballade of Reading Gaol," utilized for several of the titles, add to the interest. "Peter Ibbetson" is a "costume" picture, running through two generations, beginning about 1815 and until 1855. The action is in France and England, each locale offering splendid opportunities for incorporating scenic backgrounds of beauty.

The story, in brief, treats of a child orphaned at a tender age and brought up by his uncle amid roistering surroundings. The uncle slurs the memory of the boy's mother, and the youth, resenting the insult, attacks the uncle, who orders him from the house. The boy meets a childhood playmate, and the love of their early years is rekindled. The sweetheart of his childhood has married, however, their love affair being carried on through a mystic system of dual dreams—all rather highbrow and probably difficult to digest for the average fan.

A meeting with the uncle results in the boy killing him, with a death sentence following. This is commuted to life imprisonment, through the efforts of the "dream" lover. Various stages of the lifetime spent in jail by the boy, who finally dies with a vision of the dream lover beside him, makes for a tragic note that is brought out admirably and perfectly maintained to the final fade-out. *Bel'.*

BITS OF LIFE

Full length film subject consisting of four unrelated short stories, three taken from magazines and the fourth an original short comedy by Marshall Neilan himself. The following players are concerned in the different incidents, the characters not being programmed: Wesley Barry, Lon Chaney; John Bowers, Noah Beery; Teddy Sampson, Harriet Hammond; Dorothy Mackail, Anna May Wong; Edythe Chapman, James Bradbury, Jr.; Frederick Burton, Rockliffe Fellowes; James Neil, Tammany Young.

Marshall Neilan has put over a real novelty in his individual idea of making a full length feature out of a succession of detached stories, all of the utmost compactness and "punch." Here are six reels of picture drama that fairly vibrate with action, suspense and surprise. If Mr. Neilan started out deliberately to demonstrate that most multiple-reelers are sadly padded and could be boiled down into two-reelers, he has succeeded completely. There are at least two of the short pictures, notably "The Bad Samaritan" (from Popular) and a Chinese story from the Saturday Evening Post that most producers would never have been contented to let go inside of six reels of elaboration. Here in about two reels they are smashing, concentrated drama and comedy.

Mr. Neilan seems to have noted that performances of short playlets in groups of two to four for an evening of entertainment have been winning attention of late, and he has converted the idea to the screen. And it's a whopper. It's all right for Neilan to do, for he is singularly well equipped to select his material, to pick his players and to produce the plays. All these elements work together to make his first experiment an assured success. It wouldn't do to have too many film adventurers try to follow in his footsteps. The idea is good, but the execution through all the stages must be faultless.

The Bad Samaritan

The first playlet is "The Bad Samaritan," taken from Popular Magazine. It tells the story of a small boy, product of Chinese father and white mother, who is sold into slavery and ill treatment by the Oriental father. He grows up to be a shrewd and cruel crook who plays so cleverly against the police that he never is caught until his better nature asserts itself and he goes to rescue an apparently injured man. After escaping from deserved punishment for many real crimes, he is landed in jail as a result of his first act of kindness. A grim and cynical kind of humor, worthy of Kipling, but who shall not say true to life? The story is full of deft bits of high comedy and incidental surprises and finds its climax in a grand slam of a surprise. Wesley Barry plays the boy of the slums and Lon Chaney does the grown-up crook, both of them with splendid effect.

Man Who Heard Everything

This curious tale is taken from the Smart Set and is in the favorite cynical vein of that purveyor of fiction. It touches upon another grim jest of fate. Edward, the boss barber, is thrifty and contented in his simple mode of life because of the security of his love for his butterfly wife, Gertrude, whom he loves and who he supposes loves him. His only trouble is that he is stone deaf. But his affliction has cut him off from close contact with the world and saved him from intimacy with much of its sordidness and wretchedness. He reads the poets and loves the flowers and the trees.

A chance customer one day makes him acquainted with a new device for the deaf and he saves up the $50 necessary for its purchase a little at a time so that his indulgence may not interfere with the measure of luxury he has been able to provide his wife. The device arrives, he puts it in place and his ear's first experience is to hear the fag end of an obscene story which is being told in the shop. He goes home rather shaken at the new experience and, entering quietly, listens unobserved while the butterfly wife, Gertrude, discloses contemptuously in chat with her brother that she has been using "the dummy" for her own ends and unsuspected has been carrying on a fairly enjoyable career as a gold digger. Edward's life crumbles around him, but all he does is to shatter the ear device so that he may return to happy ignorance of a nasty, sordid world.

Chinese Story

Lon Chaney here plays another of those sensational roles of villainy. Sing Fat, a small boy in China, watches a succession of sisters arrive and meet destruction at the hands of a father who wants only sons to pray over his grave and insure his entrance into heaven.

He runs away, works in an opium factory and by theft of a passport reaches San Francisco where in a few years he becomes prosperous as proprietor of a chain of "hop joints." He meets a lovely Chinese girl and by pretending reform wins her. Once she is his he neglects her and, returning from a long journey, finds that he is a father. Sing Fat is about to congratulate himself when the wife tells him the child is a girl. He is struck with fury and beats the woman. In her distress the wife directs that her servant take a crucifix, received from the mission at her marriage, and nail it to the thin board wall so that she may pray to "Mr. God" of the Christians. As the nail is hammered through the thin wood the crucifix begins to drip blood. In terror the two women rush into the room beyond the wall.

The place had once been an opium den and Sing Fat, after the exertion of wife beating, had gone there to calm his nerves with smoke, resting his head against the back of the bunk, just where the nail came through. Here came another gripping surprise in an evening of jolts.

The Intrigue

The final playlet is a light trifle by Mr. Neilan. A young American is traveling in far places. He goes to play golf and is surprised to see a mysterious airplane deposit a beautiful woman and her servants in the open country out of the sky. They drive away in a waiting limousine. At dinner the same evening at the hotel the woman is greeted by a sinister foreigner as "Princess" and shows terror.

Apparently under some mysterious compulsion she accompanies the evil looking stranger who wears a turban and other odd Oriental trappings to another room. The American follows. The Princess appeals to the American who, as he draws his pistol is seized by huge Oriental soldiers while the stranger orders him executed on the spot. One of the soldiers plunges a knife into the American's breast—and the American wakes up in the dentist's chair, with the dentist holding a molar clasped in the forceps before his eyes. This, of course, is Mr. Neilan's backhand slap at cheaply artificial screen melodrama and its makers. Neilan is riding his own hobby, and the playlet is the weakest of the quartet, put last only because it is in the light vein—a sort of "happy ending."

Rush.

UNDER THE LASH

Deborah Krillet............Gloria Swanson
Robert Waring............Mahlon Hamilton
Simeon Krillet............Russell Simpson
Tanta Anna Vanderberg...Lillian Leighton
Jan Vanderberg.........Lincoln Steadman
Memke.....................Thena Jasper
Kaffir Boy.................Clarence Ford

Sam Wood, who directed this production, should be taken to task for having shot a single frame with the profile of Gloria Swanson showing. Miss Swanson is equally to blame, for she has been in pictures long enough to know her profile does not screen to advantage, and therefore she should avoid any close-ups or semi-close-up shots with herself in that position. Incidentally, that mourning costume Miss Swanson as Deborah managed to have right on tap for the morning after her husband's death, even though she was, in the midst of the South African veldt, would seem to indicate that she expected the bewhiskered Simeon to be bumped off at any minute. Judging from its style, it must have come from a very smart modiste's shop, and they don't have those "down at the corner" in the wilds of Africa.

Still in all, "Under the Lash," a screen adaptation by J. E. Nash of "The Shulamite," a novel by Alice and Claude Askew, and which was done as a play by the latter and Edward Knoblock, will prove an interesting program picture for the majority. The exhibitor can present it without fear his audience will demand money back.

The production is a Paramount, presented by Jesse Lasky.

Other than Miss Swanson, who, incidentally, gives a fairly passable performance, the cast contains Mahlon Hamilton as the lead. He does a more or less perfunctory young Englishman who falls in love with the wife of the old Boer. Russell Simpson is the husband, a religious old fanatic, who distorts the teachings of the Bible to meet with the needs of the moment as they arise in his life. He gave the character all that could be asked.

It remained for Lillian Leighton as his sister to walk away with the dramatic honors of the picture. She was a "tanta" to the word in action, and her scoldings were of the type one would expect. Myrtle Stead-

man's boy Lincoln played a young Boer in a stolid and even vein that indicates he is going to make a mark for himself outside of comedy productions, for his build denotes him as just the type for the "fat boy" roles. *Fred.*

WOMAN'S PLACE

Kay Gerson............Constance Talmadge
Jim Bradley..............Kenneth Harlan
Freddy Bleeker............Hassard Short
Amy Bleeker...............Florence Short
Mrs. Margaret Belknap..........Ina Rorke

Constance Talmadge is presented by Joseph M. Schenck in this farce by John Emerson and Anita Loos, who have managed to crowd a lot of laughs into their script and to tack a moral on besides. Their theory seems to be: Have something to prove, and prove it amusingly. With that as a working charm they have registered any number of market successes, and the attitude of the audience at the Strand Sunday indicated they have scored again with this. What they give you, though, is farce, not comedy.

In this we have the women's club offering the prettiest flapper in Fairfax the nomination for mayor. She can't speak, but when she hurts her ankle her opponent remarks, wisely, she has twisted one of her best campaign arguments, and the battle is on. Josephine is engaged to Freddy Bleeker, the town's rich young - know-nothing. But she breaks the engagement when she decides to run against him, and then proceeds to fall in love with the boss of the wicked political gang. At her home the women are holding a meeting, and a tough gang throws stones through the window. Hearing of their purpose, Bradley, their boss, rushes to the rescue, and Josephine falls in his arms. Loving her, his problem is to beat her.

She goes down to the Ninth Ward to a meeting, and he has his hoodlums demand a speech. Why isn't she home darning stockings? She can darn, she retorts, and shows them a darned heel. Riot! But the wives of the Ninth Warders turn against her, and she loses by 27 votes. But she captures Jim Bradley, and announces she is now the boss of the boss of Fairfax, and what they will do to the town would put a permanent wave in your hair. Get something to do, women, and you may capture a he-man, is the moral.

Miss Talmadge is pretty and engaging, and Kenneth Harlan supports her adequately, while Hassard Short puts over the mentally incompetent young heir with his accustomed skill. As the women's leader Ina Rorke gave a good imitation of Mrs. O. H. P. Belmont, and drew laughs, while Victor Fleming, the director, used minor characters for good effect, rounding off his work capably.

Light stuff, lightly amusing, and a best bet for matinees. *Leed.*

STING OF THE LASH

Dorothy Keith..........Pauline Frederick
Joel Gant...................Clyde Fillmore
Rhodes......................Lawson Butt
Ben Ames.................Lionel Belmore
Daniel Keith..............Edwin Stevens

No real dramatic wallop in this picture. There is, however, a real flogging with a blacksnake whip, with Pauline Frederick doing a Simon Legree and her no-account bootlegging hubby as the Uncle Tom, which was undoubtedly counted on as the punch, but it does not get to the audience.

The production is a Robertson-Cole release written by Harvey Gates and adapted for the screen by H. Tipton Steck. Henry King had the direction in hand.

The tale is a western meller that gives Miss Frederick a chance to do

some riding. Knowing the star's love of horses and her delight when mounted on a steed, it is easy to see why the story was picked.

Miss Frederick is the daughter of a New York financier who has gone broke, and the two "go west." On the trip dad passes out, and the girl lives with her uncle, who is the sheriff. She meets and marries Joel Gant, who has a claim staked out. While they are on their honeymoon the girl's uncle double-crosses them and sells it to the big mining interests. Thereupon the boy loses his nerve and slips from bad to worse. Finally he starts bootlegging, and the wife, disgusted with him and the life he is leading, strings him to the rafters of their shack and administers a flogging. Later he is sent to the pen for selling booze. While he is away she comes east and makes a place for herself in the business world. The husband, on being released, seeks her out and she shames him into trying all over again. In the end his regeneration is effected.

The picture does not seem to hit the fans, at least the audience at Loew's New York Saturday afternoon did not grow excited. Perhaps they are not in the habit of seeing Miss Frederick leaning over a tub and doing a slavey. Miss Frederick gives a corking performance, but the picture was not quite strong enough in story for her.

The direction of Mr. King was decidedly uneven and did not help the production. *Fred.*

NOBODY'S FOOL

Polly Gordon..............Marie Prevost
Mary Hardy................Helen Harris
Dr. Hardy.................H. Henry Grey
Artemus Alger.............Harry Myers
Housekeeper ....Lydia Titus

A rather pleasing comedy of no great pretentions, starring Marie Prevost—a Universal production. The principal merit is the characterization of a "woman hater" by Harry Myers.

Miss Prevost is a bespectacled boarding school pupil, whose tuition and maintenance are paid by a close-fisted aunt. The aunt dies, leaving the girl $400,000, whereupon she blossoms forth as a society bud; courted by fortune hunters.

Artemus Alger (Mr. Myers) writes a book called "The Unnecessary Sex," designed to prove the non-necessity of the fair sex—the two meet; he makes a fight for her against another suitor, who tries to compromise her, believing she is the wife of his friend. There is a very humorous clinch where he wades through a pond to take her in his arms. Both are projected into the water and they embrace as the water engulfs them.

The magnificent comedy pantomiming of Myers has much to do with the picture's success. A good feature for popular price houses.
Jolo.

HIGH HEELS

Christine Trever............Gladys Walton
Dr. Paul Denton.......Frederick Vogeding
Joshua Barton........William Worthington
Cortland Van Ness.........Freeman Wood
Laurie Trever.........George Hackthorn
Daffy Trever..............Charles Debriac
Dilly Trever..............Raymond Debriac
John Trever.............Dwight Crittenden
Robert Graves.............Robert Dunbar
Armand ....Jean Debriac

Here is an almost impossible story, lightwaisted and shallow, possible only through fairly good direction, "just another of those things" good enough for the cheaper houses or on a double feature program in the bigger neighborhood theatres. It's a Universal product, with Gladys Walton as the star, by Louise B. Clancy, adapted by Wallace Clifton. Lee Kohlmar handled the direction, and his manner of working Miss Walton in close-ups for a greater part of the picture is effective.

The story is that of a petted darling of a wealthy father who has been indulged with everything that her heart could desire. Then at the father's death she discovers that he has been on the verge of bankruptcy for some time. There are also a brother and two young children, and while a young millionaire is anxious to marry her she feels it her duty to remain with the family. In time she discovers the young man of money was far from being the person she should marry, and incidentally the family physician is the man she finally accepts.

The story is told on the screen in a manner draggy at times; but on the whole the production is far and away ahead of the usual run of U. features of this type. The sets and the lightnings have a certain quality that glosses the usual U. cheapness.

The cast supporting the star held Frederick Vogeding, who gave an interesting performance, with Freeman Wood as the juvenile lead rather overplayed in the later scenes of the picture. The two Debriac kiddies added an amusing touch to the picture. *Fred.*

KAZAN

This is a Selig production of the Canadian Northwest that is released through the Export and Import Corp. The picture, while not a recent release, has not been generally played and there is no record of it having been given any review in the trade press. Jane Novak is the star, and the supporting cast has Ben Deeley as the lead. The title of "Kazan" is obtained from the James Oliver Curwood story, on which the picture is based. Kazan was a dog which reverted to a state of wildness, mated with the wolves and led the pack, but which always was Johnny on the job whenever the sister of his former master was in need of help.

The tale, as far as it goes, is rather a disconnected one, with some three or four theme threads to follow all through the story.

Old Pierre Raddison is a trapper; his elder son is in the Canadian Northwest Mounted Police. A younger son and daughter live in the more sheltered regions. They, however, come north, and the boy turns out to be a weakling, spending his time drinking and gambling. The girl is left practically alone, and when the summons comes from the father that he is in his cabin in the hills and about to die, after the elder brother has been slain, the girl has to trust herself to the hands of a stranger to make the journey to her father.

The stranger is played by Deeley, who believes that the elder brother of the girl was responsible for the betrayal of his sister. His motive in helping her on the journey is to get the opportunity to wreak vengeance on the woman of the Raddison clan for the wrong done his sister.

When they arrive at the cabin, after having been chased by the wolf pack led by Kazan, the wild dog having recognized the woman's voice in time to drive off his followers and save her, they discover that the father is dead. The heavy of the picture cast having preceded them on the trail and stolen the evidence that would have marked him as the slayer of the girl's brother. This same heavy at the same time would have slain the father, but having found him about to die anyway; he simply opened the door and windows and permitted him to freeze to death. This much accomplished, the heavy doubles in his tracks and slips the Mounted Police the office that the man who accompanied the girl is the slayer.

The hero of the story is then arrested and the girl and her brother start on a journey. During the trip the father's watch opens and reveals a note which tells the real story, and the hero is saved from further imprisonment, but the heavy escapes. He finds the girl in camp alone and is about to attack her when Kazan leaps on him, bears him to the ground and kills him.

In story form Kazan and his life were played up and the human element made secondary. On the screen the animal stuff is placed in the background, but still there is sufficient of it to lend a thrill to the film version, which will get by in the cheaper neighborhood houses.

Fred.

DOUBLING FOR ROMEO

Romeo (Slim)	Will Rogers
Juliet (Lulu)	Sylvia Breamer
Steve Woods (Paris)	Raymond Hatton
Pendleton (Mercutio)	Sydney Ainsworth
Big Alec (Tybalt)	Al Hart
Foster (Capulet)	John Cossar
Duffy Saunders (Benvolio)	C. E. Thurston
Maggie (Maid)	Cordelia Callahan
Minister (Friar Lawrence)	Roland Rushton
Jimmie Jones	Jimmie Rogers
"Movie" Director	William Orlamund

At last something new in pictures! With "Doubling for Romeo," a Goldwyn production, Will Rogers has arrived with a satirical burlesque of the screen that is a howl from start to finish. It is a production that has all the more appeal if one knows anything about pictures at all. The more you know the funnier it is, and if you don't know a thing about them, it is funny anyway. It is Rogers' last picture for Goldwyn for the time being, at any rate, but it is far and away the best of the entire series that he has turned out under that contract.

Credit for the story is given to Elmer Rice, Will Rogers and Will Shakespeare. The two Wills share the greater part of the glory. Clarence Badger directed the production, and he managed to keep the action swinging along at a great rate of speed from the moment that the initial scene was flashed.

The sub-titles are a howl. Rogers is given credit for the modern titles and Shakespeare for the ancient ones. In some cases Rogers has improved on the Bard of Avon, but for another laugh Bacon and Shakespeare are asked to divide credit for the original "Romeo and Juliet" titles.

Rogers at the opening is disclosed a real, sure-enough cowboy herding cattle. When the boss decides to change over to sheep raising Rogers, with the rest of the boys, is let out. Just about this stage the girl of his heart has decided if he would win her he would have to learn to make love like they do in the movies, and she shows him a picture of Doug, whom she claims is the greatest lover on the screen. The boys from the ranch get together when Rogers announces he is going into the movies and dress him in the most approved screen cowboy style. With this regalia he makes his appearance at the Goldwyn studio, where he has a hard time getting past the door until the child star that is supporting all of his family in luxury, comes along and takes him in. Rogers is given a job of doubling for the villain and the hero, both in a serial, and this stuff is filled with laughs. But he flops and goes back to the old home town.

In the meantime the girl has read "Romeo and Juliet," and decided that Shakespeare's hero had it on Doug on loving. Rogers digs up a volume of the work from the parson and reads it in his room, going to sleep over the book and dreaming the ensuing action, which is the story of "Romeo and Juliet," with Rogers as the hero and the folk of his every-day life playing the other characters. It is a burlesque in the broadest sense, with Rogers enacting the role much after the dashing manner that Doug would have given it. When the awakening comes Rogers has learned his lesson and he dashes off, grabs the girl by force and rushes her to the parson.

The picture is a laugh from start to finish, and is the best out-and-out full length feature comedy that has been turned out in a couple of years as a regular program picture. It stacks up with any of the late Fairbanks pictures, with the possible exception of the "Three Musketeers," and should be a whale of a business getter for any house anywhere. The expose of the "inside of the movies" will get audiences no matter where it is shown.

The cast is all that any one could ask for, and their doubling from the straight roles they were playing to the characters of Shakespeare's story proves that they are troupers.

Fred.

TWO MINUTES TO GO

Chester Burnett	Charles Ray
Ruth Turner	Mary Anderson
Her Father	Lionel Belmore
"Fatty"	Lincoln Stedman
"Angel"	Trueman Van Dyke
Football Coach	Tom Wilson
Dean of Baker University	Francois Dumas
Professor of Spanish	Philip Dunham

Here at least is intelligent distribution. "Two Minutes to Go" is a football picture released for its first run in the height of the football season. Looks like finally some one has arrived in the picture business who thinks as to "time, place and picture" and links the three up. The production is one of the Charles Ray-First National series, presented by Arthur S. Kane.

In presenting it at the Strand, Joe Plunkett has prefaced the picture with a brief touch of college atmosphere. He has an "eleven" accompanied by the coach march through the audience onto the stage and run through a series of college numbers.

"Two Minutes to Go" was written by Charles Andres, produced and directed by Charles Ray, who is also the star.

The story is somewhat along the "College Widow" lines, as any football yarn must be. Ray naturally is the hero. The picture opens with a football game and closes with another. In the first Ray is shown in the stand. For several years he has been the backbone of the team, but this season he isn't playing and the team has been going down in defeat at one game after another. This has caused the star to lose his popularity with the boys, but there is one girl who sticks by him. His reason for quitting the game is kept secret by him about the college, but the audience is in on the fact his father has met with reverses and Ray is "running a milk route" to work his final year through college. That milk route calls for his being on the job at 3.30 a. m. and therefore he can't hit the field with the boys for practice each day.

Just before the big game of the season a rival for the favor of the girl accidentally stumbles onto the fact that Ray is a milkman in the wee sma' hours and faces him with the fact at a party. Ray denies it, but the next morning he is caught with the goods. Then the girl gives him the cold shoulder.

The appeal of the team for him to get into the final game has its effect, and at the end of the first half the score is 3 to 0 in favor of the opponents. Between halves Ray receives a note from the girl which gives him some added pep, and in the rest period before the final quarter a wire from his dad brings the news that he has rehabilitated his fortunes. Then with "two minutes to go" in the final quarter Ray makes a touchdown and wins the game. It may not be the best football, but it sure is good picture material.

The feature will prove mighty interesting at this time and should pull business in the better houses. There are any number of little picturesque touches and college pranks that lighten the drama of the story, and in all it is a good little comedy drama.

Mary Anderson plays opposite Ray and gives a corking little performance. Lincoln Steadman is the fat roommate of the star and gets a few laughs. A couple of professors, played by Francois Dumas and Philip Dunham, were a comedy relief to the tenseness of the game. Trueman Van Dyke was the cheer leading heavy of the picture and landed.

Fred.

THE CUP OF LIFE

Captain Brand	Hobart Bosworth
Pain	Madge Bellamy
Chan Chang	Tully Marshall
Roy Bradley	Niles Welch

A first-class picture, one of the best if not the best program feature in many a moon, offered by Associated Producers on the Loew circuit. Hobart Bosworth stars—really stars—and Thomas H. Ince supervised, while a nearly perfect scenario is credited to Joseph Franklyn Poland. Capable support rounds out an altogether satisfying screen contribution.

The story is plausible, full of the unexpected and not an inch is wasted in telling it. Captain Brand is a he-man and poaches pearls for the fun of it, not the money. He is in a hurry for home on the trip because his son, in ignorance Captain Brand is really his father, is on his way to Singapore. But a shark in the water delays the diver. In goes Brand himself and cuts the fish's throat. Coming out, he finds his diver about to swallow, as sure keeping for his theft, a magnificent pearl. Brand rescues it, announcing it is not for sale, but for a beautiful woman who cannot be bought in any other way.

Comes then a destroyer, and there is an amusing fake burial at sea to head off suspicion of poaching. The naval vessel looked American, but the officer wore a British uniform. Back in Singapore, Brand hunts Chan Chang, rich Chinese dealer and father protector to a little orphaned white girl now reaching maturity. The foster father wishes her to marry a Chinese. One pearl more is needed for her bridal gift, but it must be magnificent to match the others. One that would match it is Brand's, but the captain refuses to sell. Why? It is for a woman.

The son, known as Roy Bradley, meets little Pain and loves her. She shows him, innocently, the pearl string. From his father, whom he does not know is his father, he begs the pearl and adds it to the string, and old Chan, finding it, suspects Brand, suspects the worst, all unwittingly confirmed by Pain, who keeps silent to protect her boy lover.

Now things move fast to a climax in a darkened room, where the two men, unknown to each other, cunningly set in conflict by Chan, fight while Pain watches, afraid to cry because Chan will shoot the boy if she does. But in the end they break through a wall into the light, the boy falling unconscious, never knowing his father, who fights his way out, leaving a threat for Chan to take him to sea as a cook if he prevents the girl and boy marrying.

All this is played by Mr. Bosworth in stellar style, while Tully Marshall made a distinct and effective creation of the Chinaman. Madge Bellamy, with her lovely girlish features and her pantomime while the fight was going on, stepped forward as a picture possibility of no mean stature.

The technical accomplishment was good, though at times the handling of the lights produced more than the usual flatness. In resisting the plea for a happy ending, Mr. Ince staged something mightily effective with Brand sailing away in a churning sea leaving everything set for the lad he loved and never told.

Leed.

TO A FINISH

Jim Blake	Buck Jones
Doris Lane	Helen Ferguson
Bill Terry	G. Raymond Nye
Wolf Garry	Norman Selby
Joe Blake	Herschel Mayall

Fox presents "To a Finish," a Western five-reel thriller based upon the story by Jack Strumwasser. Buck Jones is the star, with Bernard Durning the director. While Strumwasser has turned out nothing particular in the way of a story the director has mapped out a corking Western feature based almost entirely upon his star's ability as a melodramatic hero. Fight after fight crowd the five reels, with Jones displaying himself as a nimble athlete and contender for the crown held by Douglas Fairbanks for this type of work. The story is practically forgotten with the abundance of action supplied by the star in the role of a typical Western hero.

As a fighter of the rough and tumble variety he stands out prominently, with his horseback riding displaying years of training. The theme is simple, having as its central figures a bad man, a cowboy hero and the girl. After the series of fights, mad dashes across the country on horseback and other incidental bits of melodrama, the hero rescues the girl in the bad man's home. All in all "To a Finish" is a fast running daredevil picture.

Its cast is short, with the star and Norman Selby the only players of any prominence. The latter is given little opportunity to display any of the fistic ability which he gained as Kid McCoy. As with the majority of Western pictures the production cost is slight. A great portion of the action takes place in the open. For audiences that like the Wild West stuff this should be a knockout. *Hart.*

DAWN OF THE EAST

Countess Natalya..............Alice Brady
Roger Strong..............Kenneth Harlan
Sotan..............Michio Itow
Mariya..............America Chedister
Sonya..............Betty Carpenter
Mrs. Strong..............Harriet Ross
Wu Ting..............Sam Kim
Liang..............Frank Honda
Kwan..............H. Takemi
Chang..............Patricio Reyes

Realart production starring Alice Brady. Story and scenario credited to E. Lloyd Sheldon with direction by E. H. Griffith.

Countess Natalya, a Russian refugee, secures employment as a dancer in a Shanghai cafe to support a sickly sister and herself. Disgusted with the life, the girl becomes entangled with Sotan, a Chinese royalist and plotter against the new republic. He promises to secure sufficient funds for her to leave the country if she will agree to marry a rich Chinese admirer.

The girl is given the impression the marriage ceremony is not binding, and escapes to America with the aid of the money secured as a dowry from her husband. This amount is divided by her with the plotter.

Shortly after arrival in America she marries an American diplomat who has been interested in the new Chinese Republic. The Celestian villain arrives, threatens to expose her as the wife of the Chinaman, which he claims will be held valid in international law, if she does not secure certain information her American husband has regarding the Chinese republic. This proving fruitless he brings over the Chinese husband, who, upon meeting the girl, is informed he was tricked into the marriage so that she could secure his money.

Believing her, he kills the villain and destroys all evidence of the marriage, and undoubtedly went back home, leaving things serene.

There is a certain interest in this melodrama that will hold the average audience. The Oriental settings are flashy and create an atmosphere that places the picture above the common program feature.

Miss Brady is admirably cast, with Kenneth Harlan short of opportunities in a leading man's role of but minor proportions. One of the most convincing bits is credited to Michio Itow as the villain. Next to Miss Brady his is the biggest part of a well done picture. *Hart.*

CLAY DOLLARS

Bruce Edwards..............Eugene O'Brien
June Gordon..............Ruth Dwyer
Sam Willetts..............Frank Currier
Ben Willetts..............Arthur Houseman
Lafe Gordon..............Jim Tenbrooke
Mrs. Gordon..............Florida Kingsley
Buck Jones..............Tom Burke
Peter..............Jerry Devine
The Village "Cut-up"..............Bruce Reynolds

This Selznick feature at Loew's New York, with Eugene O'Brien starred, is exceptionally good. The story and scenario are by Lewis Allen Browne and the direction by George Archainbaud. A simple enough yarn with all the old ingredients, you think at first, admiring the beautiful photographing, keen rural comedy touch and progressively interesting direction—and then you wake up. It is not the old story—quite. There's a new twist.

Bruce Edwards returns to find the property willed him by his uncle has been traded on his deathbed for valueless farm land. As the picture goes on you are led to believe the mud in the swamp is valuable for brick making, etc., and so is the villain who profited by the trade. Said villain's son is in love with the leading lady, whose mother suspects the worst about the deathbed trade, but can't tell because the villain has a mortgage. In the end a trade back is arranged because the villain is led to believe, as the audience is, that the property is valuable. He wakes up too late and Bruce has the girl.

Mr. O'Brien is always pleasant, an agreeable, well dressed, gentlemanly fellow. Ruth Dwyer, in support, is as charming and visually delightful a personage as you will encounter in many a day, and minor parts are developed faithfully for all screen purposes.

A first rate program feature, clean, wholesome, entertaining and with a fetch to it. *Leed.*

THE INFAMOUS MISS REVELL

Julien Revell }
Paula Revell }..............Alice Lake
Max Hildreth..............Cullen Landis
Lillian Hildreth..............Jackie Saunders
Mary Hildreth..............Lydia Knott
Samuel Pangburn..............Herbert Standing
Maxwell Putnam..............Alfred Hollingsworth

Alice Lake is starred in a dual role in this Metro Classic, directed by Dallas M. Fitzgerald. The story was originally done by W. Carey Wonderly and adapted for the screen by Arthur J. Zellner. It has no great picture punch and the production is one which while getting by with most audiences will undoubtedly seem slow and draggy to a great many. The story is told in the sub-titles rather than in action, which makes everything on the screen in a pictorial way slow, as the audience has to get to the titles to catch the advance of the story.

The twin sisters, played by Miss Lake, are concert stage singers who have flopped on their first tour. They have four young sisters and brothers to rear, so when a wealthy patron is willing to do a little providing for the family if one of the sisters will act as his companion through his declining years Julien decides that it is up to her to make the sacrifice. After a period of two years he dies while abroad, and when his will is read he has left all of his property to the girl during her life providing she does not marry. To his sister and her son and daughter he leaves $1,000 each. The niece schemes to separate the girl from her inheritance by getting the brother to marry her. In the development it is finally shown that Julien died shortly after her protector passed away, and Paula, her twin, impersonated her to receive the money "for the children's sake."

In the end the boy really marries her, so at least a third of the fortune remains in the family and the children are taken care of.

Pictorially the picture is far from being a wallop. The doubles are very much stilted and many better expositions of this particular form of trick photography have been shown. In detail Mr. Fitzgerald has also overlooked a few bets. One, for instance, is where the star writes four lines of a letter, and when the latter is shown it has more than a dozen lines on one page alone.

All in all, the 50 minutes that "The Infamous Miss Revell" occupies the screen were rather a bore than entertainment. *Fred.*

BRING HIM IN

All things considered, "Bring Him In" is a splendid program feature—not big enough to utilize in pre-release houses or anything of that sort, but one that will satisfy the patrons of picture palaces like the New York and the other cinemas on the Loew Circuit.

It is a Vitagraph production, story by H. H. Van Loan, scenarized by Thomas Dixon, Jr., starring Earle Williams, who is also credited with its direction in conjunction with Robert Ensminger. The story gets its title from the code of the Northwest Mounted Police, which is to bring your man in, dead or alive, and to live up to your oath of office under any and all circumstances.

The strength of the tale lies in the conflict between an officer after his man—the man saves the officer's life and he is thus torn between his duty and his gratitude. After giving the fugitive an hour's start the officer of the law starts after him, shoots in the air, the fugitive shoots the officer in the breast, and when the officer says, "I shot in the air, old pal," the other replies, "I wish to God I had."

Earle Williams plays the fugitive, who turns out to be innocent, of course, and Bruce Gordon the sergeant of the Northwest Mounted Police. In most respects Gordon's is the better role in that he is more romantically heroic. For example, when the fugitive brings him in wounded and apparently dying, he says to the others, "I shot myself," to save the man who rescued him from drowning. Williams' heroics are more or less dragged in without regard for the plot's progression, as in the case of his knocking down a halfbreed who is rough-housing the heroine within shouting distance of the hero's hut. The introduction of the halfbreed has no bearing whatsoever upon the plot. It is merely projected into the picture to give the hero somebody to knock down.

Williams is his usual self-complacent self, always to be depended upon to register in the direct range of the camera. Bruce Gordon carried off the acting honors as the police sergeant and Fritzi Ridgeway was wholly equal to the demands of an emotional heroine. The remainder of the small cast was quite competent. Direction and photography wholly satisfactory. *Jolo.*

SINGING RIVER

Lang Rush..............William Russell
Alice Thornton..............Vola Vale
John Thornton..............Clark Comstock
Grimes..............Charles King
Kane..............Louis King
Freud..............Jack Hull
Bert Condon..............Jack McDonald
Sam Hemp..............Arthur Morrison
Lew Bransom..............Jack Roseleigh

Altogether unoriginal plot is "Singing River," capably directed by Charles Giblyn from a scenario by Jules Furthman—a Fox program feature of the "western" type, starring William Russell. Star gets into a fight with a "bad man" and shoots him in self-defense. He runs away—but only a short distance, judging by the speed with which the other characters reach his cabin as the exigencies of the story require. He strikes "pure horn silver" at once, the sheriff's daughter (only female in the case) aids him in his temporary conflict with the law, and there is an inevitable conclusion to a straightaway melodramatic tale, without any flashbacks or other distracting elements or ingredients. The fist and gun fights are not very convincing, but the admirers of Russell should be pleased with his manly characterization. Vola Vale acts with sincerity the role of the swift-riding sheriff's daughter, and there are several western "types" adequately portrayed in competent stock company fashion. Not much opportunity for the director to exercise his imagination. Just a cheap program feature. *Jolo.*

EVER SINCE EVE

Celestine LaFarge..............Shirley Mason
Cartaret..............Herbert Heyes
Lorita..............Eva Gordon
Percy Goring..............Charles Spere
Mrs. Kerry..............Frances Hancock
The Stranger..............Ethel Lynn
Lieut. Gerald O'Connor..............Louis King

This is a William Fox short-length feature production. The picture does not seem to be more than four reels in length, judging from the time consumed in screening. What it is all about is going to be pretty hard to guess. It started out something like a mystery and then developed into a stereotyped guardian-and-ward-love story, where the end was in sight the minute the story was started. As a picture, however, it will answer on a cheap double feature program when there isn't anything else to be booked.

The story is by Joseph Ernest Peat, made into a scenario by Dorothy Yost and directed by Howard M. Mitchell.

At the opening there is a flash of a burglary being committed, a couple of shots being fired, a call for the police and the assignment of a detective to the trail. Then there is a flash to the studio of Cartaret, the artist. He is a wealthy bachelor and a woman-hater. His model is Lorita, who has a sneaky feeling for him and his dough. While Cartaret is in the midst of his work three other artists drop in just as a telegram arrives to the effect that Cartaret's daughter is coming home. This is a surprise to the trio of friends until there is an explanation that "the daughter" is a French war orphan that he adopted in 1915.

She arrives on the scene and there is the usual change of costume business which reveals the fact that she is a charming young lady, etc. At about this stage of the game Cartaret feels himself slipping, so it is necessary to work out a plan whereby it will be revealed later that the girl isn't the adopted daughter at all but an obliging cousin of the real adopted girl, who has since run off and married a second lieutenant of the A. E. F. When that is worked out then there is nothing left for Cartaret to do except marry the girl, and this is done.

Just at this point the audience discovers that the detective who has been trailing all through the picture *isn't in the story at all and never* had anything to do with it except to make it a little more difficult. As a matter of fact the picture is the veriest sort of soothing syrup bunk, and that is all.

Shirley Mason's performance was all that could be expected in a picture of this sort, the supporting cast as a whole being hardly worth mentioning. *Fred.*

ACE OF HEARTS

This is a recent release by Goldwyn, an excellent product from many angles. It tells an interesting story and accomplishes the high purpose of explaining away anti-colored beliefs, at the same time preaching a fine ethical sermon. The picture is done in splendid, dignified style and has as its featured actor, Lon Chaney, whose work ever since his playing of "The Frog" in "Miracle Man" has added to his reputation as an actor of utmost sincerity and skill.

"The Ace of Hearts" deals with a group of anarchists whose method of improving the world is to kill off malefactors of great wealth and vicious influence. Henry (Mr. Chaney) is a member of this group. They have singled out for death a rich man, described as "The Man Who Has Lived too Long," and they draw among themselves to designate the member who shall destroy him for the human good. For this purpose a set of cards is dealt around the circle, and whoever gets the ace of hearts must carry out the edict of death.

Both Henry and John, members of the group, are in love with a woman member, Lilith. John receives the fatal ace and starts off on his mission of death. But before he goes he marries Lilith (played by Beatrice Love). John is a waiter in the restaurant frequented by "The Man Who Has Lived Too Long," and it is his purpose to plant a time bomb under the table while he is at breakfast. When the time for the killing comes John observes that at a neighboring table there are two lovers who are certain to be killed in the explosion. His eyes being open to the understanding of love and life, it suddenly bursts upon him that the life and safety of the two lovers are of more importance than the death of "The Man Who Has Lived Too Long." Accordingly he declines to set off the bomb.

For this reason he comes under the doom of the socialistic group, who pronounce his death at a meeting at which Henry is present. While the anarchists are dealing the cards to determine by the ace of hearts who shall kill John, Henry sets the same bomb under the counsel table, and the climax comes when it explodes and kills off the group of anarchists, thus vindicating the theory that the regeneration of society must come from preservation of life and love rather than by the destruction of evil.

The picture story carries with it a fine love story and an uplifting moral of self-sacrifice. Whether its commercial success will be great or small is a question, but as an artistic achievement it assays 100 per cent. It belongs to the newer and better grade of picture standards.

Rush.

CONFLICT

Gwynne Ramalie	Priscilla Dean
John Ramalie	Ed Connelly
Miss Labo	Martha Mattox
Buck Fallon	Hector Sarno
Jevons	Herbert Rawlinson
Mark Sloan	L. C. Shumway

Universal undertook to put this feature over with a crash at their Central theatre on Broadway with the assistance of an exceedingly heavy advertising campaign. The picture, while a fairly good production of the U. program quality, manages to satisfy but does not by far hold up to the lengths that were gone to in exploitation for it.

Stuart Paton directed the picture, which has as its big punch a log jam. The story originally appeared in "The Red Book," from the pen of Clarence Buddington Kelland.

Priscilla Dean is starred in the production and gives a performance that has a few thrills in it. Her bit of work in the log jam scene is well handled, but it is nothing to rave about. There isn't the real suspense quality in this scene that there should have been. Had the picture been properly handled in the making this scene could have been as big as the ice floe stuff in "Way Down East." It is just another case where the U. system falls short in realizing on a real asset.

Miss Dean photographs like a million dollars all through the performance, and the director didn't overlook a chance to have her shot at every angle at which she appeared to advantage. Herbert Rawlinson, who plays the lead opposite her, gave a performance that will surely be liked by his fans, and makes him ready to resume starring with the U. L. C. Shumway as the heavy was all that could be asked.

Incidentally the presentations at the Central have improved during the last few weeks, and this picture is given all the opportunity that could be wished for it from an exhibition standpoint, but still this won't get it over with the wallop that the U. hoped for.

Fred.

SECRET OF THE HILLS

Guy Fenton	Antonio Moreno
Marion	Lillian Hall
Lincoln Drew	Kingsley Benedict
Francis Freeland	George Claire
Benjamin Miltmore	Walter Rogers
Mrs. Miltmore	Oleta Otis
Richard	J. Gunnis Davis

This Vitagraph mystery meller has enough action and plot to have been a twelve-episode serial. In action and story it resembles one of those blood-and-thunder affairs with which the screen reeked in the early days. It is a picture that will get over in great shape with the low-brow audiences and in the better class of houses where there is a change of bill daily it will do to fill in on a double-feature bill providing the companion picture is a fairly strong one.

From a production standpoint the picture was cheaply put on. It runs to exteriors to a great extent, and what few interiors there are do not represent any great expense.

The story is by William Garrett, having been adapted for the screen by E. Magnus Ingleton. Chester Bennett handled the direction, and although there were times when he permitted the story to get very much muddled he managed to advance the yarn in a fairly plausible manner.

Antonio Moreno, as the star has all the work to do, and he does it in the most approved Vitagraph style, which means the fashion in pictures of before the war. He dresses like a million-dollar fashion model, and although he is supposed to be an American correspondent for an American news service in London he is never without high hat and stick. Of course, Tony looks good with a topper and the cane helps dress him up some.

Of the support Lillian Hall makes a satisfying little ingenue lead, but that is all. She really has nothing to do in the picture. As a matter of fact, nobody except Moreno has anything much before the camera.

The story deals with sudden death, murder, kidnapping, buried treasure, secret cyphers and all the usual appurtenances of the serial thriller. The scenes are laid in London, one of the English shires and the hills of Scotland.

Miss Hall is the ward of a noted historian who has discovered that one of the ancient Scottish kings has buried the crown jewels, etc., and he has managed to discover the code that will make possible the recovery of the same. A gang of international crooks learn of his discovery and plan to get the information that he possesses and obtain the treasure. They kill him, but fail to obtain the map to the treasure. The young newspaper man, being lost in the London fog, stumbles into the house where the crime has been committed and convinces the ward that she should trust him and he will recover the jewels and capture the criminals. He manages to keep his promise, but the manner in which he achieves the desired end is so improbable that any adult audience with a grain of common sense will hardly believe it possible.

Fred.

NO VILLAINS

A Metro Screen Classic at Loew's State as the feature for the entire week under the auspices of the circuit. It is a crook play with a novel twist and plenty of surprises, and it gives Viola Dana wide opportunity to employ her characteristic feminine whimsies.

The material is perhaps rather scant for a full feature picture, but the story has certain odd twists which sustain interest, and the picture is well supplied with that magical quality—suspense. The denouement comes swiftly at the last minute and clears up a mysterious series of hero-and-heroine relations. Expert and judicious cutting in the midway passages might improve the picture as to its speed, but as it stands it holds interest, and has all the advantages of simple, although rather prolix story telling.

At the opening Rose (Viola Dana) returns to the district chief of the U. S. Secret Service and confesses that she has failed to get evidence against an opium smuggler after three months' effort. She says, however, that she suspects an association between Sada the smuggler and a waif named King, and asks that she be assigned anew to the case to work toward Sada through King.

From here the story develops clearly along romantic lines to a love affair between Rose and King, who poses as a wounded veteran of the A. E. F. Rose discovers that there are certain relations between the smuggler and the man she loves, but she refuses to furnish the evidence upon which he might be convicted.

The secret service chief threatens that he will put her on the witness stand and make her tell what she knows, and in desperation she hastens to marry King, the point here being that a wife cannot be forced to testify against her husband. The sleuths learn of the scheme by the record of a marriage license issued, and policemen interrupt the wedding, mid-way, which, however, is completed by an uncomprehending and indignant clergyman standing on the sidewalk while the couple take their positions at the window, the policemen being inside the building guarding the door of the apartment.

At the point where the story tangle is at its height, and as the secret service chief bursts upon the couple to arrest them both, the whole thing is cleared up by the revelation that King is a secret service operative assigned from the San Francisco office to run down the same gang of dope smugglers, unknown to the eastern secret service executives. Wedding bells—happy ending—wicked smuggler in bracelets—joy unconfined!

The film has many capital touches of incidental comedy and a fine flavor of romance. Certainly it will please the women fans, who, after all, are the ones who make or break a production.

Rush.

THE IRON TRAIL

Murray O'Neill	Wyndham Standing
Curtis Gordon	Thurston Hall
Dan Appleton	Reginald Denny
Eliza Appleton	Alma Tell
Natalie	Betty Carpenter
Dr. Gray	Lee Beggs
Tom Slater	Harlan Knight

This is the first of the Rex Beach productions to be released by United Artists. Production was made on the Whitman Bennett lot at Yonkers. Taking a picture of Alaska in Yonkers would naturally have its drawbacks, but one would believe that studio stuff could be shot most anywhere and the desired effects achieved for the screen. Such, however, does not seem to be the case in this picture. It is a good story that has been slaughtered by adaptation, direction, lighting, camera work, and last, but far from least, the cast that was selected to portray Mr. Beach's characters.

One is at sea to figure just why the Strand booked this picture. Surely it could not have been previewed by Joseph Plunkett, and if it were, then the picture mart must be in a mighty sorry state these days for him to accept it. "The Iron Trail" is the type of picture that might be expected on the screen of a daily change of program house, but hardly in a Broadway theatre where a full week's run is the policy. United Artists will be mighty careful before they accept the next Beach production if it is produced by the same hands that botched this one.

"The Iron Trail" was directed by R. William Neill, whose work leaves much to be desired. The cast is exceptionally bad with the exception of Harlan Knight, who plays a minor role. He was the only natural figure on the screen at any time. Wyndham Standing, who played the heroic role; Thurston Hall, the heavy; Reginald Denny, the juvenile lead; Alma Tell, the lead, and Betty Carpenter, the ingenue, were all so self-conscious that one would believe that their appearances in this picture were the first that they had ever made before the camera. Their actions were stilted and mechanical and the matter of detail was evidently entirely overlooked by the director.

There is one thing certain about Alaska, that will be of interest to the women folk, taught by this picturization of life in that territory, and that is that they have marvelous hair-dressers there. Both of the principal women figures have wonderful marcel waves in their hair at all times. One scene brings home this fact with particular force. The ingenue and the hero have been shipwrecked and the hero swims ashore with her, remarking on landing that he has been in the water for an hour and a half. He carries the girl to the home of her mother and stepfather, and the moment that she is carried into the room her hair changes from a damp bedraggeledness to a shimmering waviness that is simply wonderful. Incidentally, the hero is the first man we ever heard of able to swim for an hour and a half with heavy leather coat and his shoes on. Those little matters will give a general idea of the attention that was paid to detail in the direction of the picture.

The story deals with the opening of the Alaskan country to rail traffic, the battle being between two rival factions of railroad builders. Thurston Hall as the heavy is the crooked railroad promoter, while Standing is the upright engineer who wins out in the end and achieves fame, fortune and the girl of his heart. It could have been interesting, but it isn't.

Fred.

THE RIGHT WAY

The Father	Edwards Davis
The Mother	Helen Lindroth
The Rich Boy	Joseph Marquis
The Sweetheart	Vivienne Osborn
The Poor Boy	Sydney D'Albrook
His Mother	Annie Ecleston
His Sweetheart	Helen Ferguson
His Sister	Elsie McLeod
The Smiler	Tammany Young
The New Warden	Thomas Brooks
And 2,000 Others in Big Film	

This is the picture sponsored by Thomas Mott Osborne, leading advocate in America for prison reform and defender of the Mutual League, the association by which former inmates of New York State conducted their affairs pretty much on the honor system.

The film is a kind of propaganda for the Osborne method, but it is written and acted out in a thoroughly dramatic way. Except for a few titles arguing a certain point and except for the appearance of Osborne in the picture it might as well be a "crook play." As it stands, besides being an argument for a progressive prison system, it is a thoroughly interesting human story, with the play and interplay of character upon character and a crescendo dramatic effect up to the climax. The story stands by itself, the argumentative details interposed by former Warden Osborne are incidental. As a film story it is rather gloomy, but in a dramatic sense it stands on its own feet.

The film is described as personally supervised and sponsored by Thomas Mott Osborn and released through Producers' Security Corporation of 516 Fifth avenue, New York.

Amateur crusaders could not have done this dramatization, which has the professional touch throughout, both in direction and in technical picture handling. There are many tricky turns of theatrical effect in the story structure and many neatly done bits of light and shadow photography. In the same way the filming has the professional atmosphere, its acting is thoroughly well done, both as to the minor and the principal parts. Edwards Davis is in an inconsequential role, while Sidney d'Albrook has one of the most important roles. The picture is full of convincing types, none better than the warden under the brutal regime, a perfect sample of the policeman who rules by force.

Some of the mass effects, particularly those within the prison walls, carry conviction. The picture was presented at a trade showing late last week at which Mr. Osborne declared that the fictitious tale was founded upon fact.

It tells of two young men—one poor, one rich—who give way to temptation and are sent to prison. The poor boy steals in order to gain money to aid his sick mother. He goes through the jail under the regimen of the oppression. The rich young man goes to prison through a crime by which he sought to break away from association with an unworthy woman, and his experiences are under the reform method of prison administration. The poor boy has been marked for a career of crime by his adventures under prison brutality, and soon returns. But in the meantime the system has been changed and the two men are able, because of prison betterment, to bring to justice a real criminal for whom another is being punished. The dramatic elements in the story concern this latter phase, and it does make striking fiction. The whole thing, aside from its sociologic purpose, makes an extremely gripping story. *Rush.*

THE NIGHT HORSEMEN

Whistling Dan	Tom Mix
Kate Cumberland	May Hopkins
Joe Cumberland	Harry Lonsdale
Dr. Byrne	Joseph Bennett
Buck Daniels	Sid Jordan
Mac Strann	Bert Sprotte
Jerry Strann	C. Anderson
Haw Haw	Lon Poff
Marshal	Charles K. French

This is a whale of a western. It is a William Fox production, with Tom Mix as the star, that has a real story as its groundwork, and therefore has any number of legitimate reasons for the sensational stunts in horsemanship, fast shooting and other western feats which the star is so well qualified for. The picture is a rip-snorter of the type that will pull second and third day business to any house. In fact, the picture, which is being shown in the Loew houses where there is a daily change of program, is better qualified from the exhibition value standpoint to occupy one of the full-week Broadway houses than two out of four pictures that have had that prestige during the past three or four weeks.

"The Night Horsemen" is based on Max Brand's novel "Wild Geese," and is a sequel to "The Untamed," in which Mix also starred. The scenario and direction both were the work of Lynn Reynolds, who has acquitted himself in both departments in a capable manner.

Mix has always had the reputation of being one of the best of the interpreters of western roles, but in some of the stories he has been supplied with he often lacked a chance to appear at his best. In this instance, however, the combination of a good actor and a good story shows what is really possible with Mix properly fitted.

Whistling Dan, played by Tom Mix, is a wanderer on the desert when he is picked up as a youth by Joe Cumberland, a rancher, who rears the boy to manhood's estate. Dan has always been prone to "the call of the wild," and on the night before his marriage to Kate Cumberland he wanders off and is gone for months. At the home, old Joe Cumberland is shown wasting away because of the boy's desertion, and Dan is shown on his travels and adventures. He has developed into a man with an ungovernable temper when roused, and he wanders into a wild and wooly town on his way homeward just as the bully is on a rampage and mixes it with Mix, who is just a little too fast for him with a "gat."

The wounded man's brother decides to take up the fight, and in the event that his brother dies, he is going to hunt up Dan and have it out with him. Dan's reply is that no hunting will be necessary, as he will stay right on the ground awaiting events. At this stage of the story, Buck, Dan's buddie on the home ranch, arrives and tries to convince him of the necessity of going home to save his benefactor's life, for the old man will die unless the boy that he brought up returns. Dan refuses to go because of his promise to await the vengeance of the brother of the man he shot, and Buck finally angers him into chasing him home.

Once there, Kate and Buck manage to change Dan's views on a number of subjects, and finally he promises to give up wandering and fighting and settle down. But the brother of the man who was shot comes on the scene and another change of program is necessary. However, this fight winds up without a killing through the appearance of Kate in the nick of time, and the final fade-out finds the two in each other's arms.

May Hopkins as Kate is really a surprise on the screen to those who knew her in musical comedy. May looks and makes an attractive screen figure, as well as enacting a part in a manner that is most convincing. Had she started in films some years back she would today be with the top-notchers. Sid Jordan and Bert Sprotte, the former as Buck and the latter as Mac Strann, both give excellent performances. The others of the cast are also carefully selected types that can act.

Of course, Mix's horse and hound dog are also in the story, and the animal end of the cast can be judged from this as perfect. Some very pretty tinting of scenes in the open lend a lot of atmosphere to a picture that might better qualify as a special than some of the so-called ones that are on the market. *Fred.*

VENGEANCE TRAIL

"The Vengeance Trail" is an Aywon production, starring Guinn ("Big Boy") Williams, directed by Charles R. Seeling. It is released via state right and will serve as a good program feature in the popular-priced cinemas, especially where "westerns" are best appreciated. There are plenty of thrills in the form of expert cowboy riding, an aeroplane stunt, etc. The plot is all about cattle rustling, with the hero performing practically single-handed a few heroic feats that possess general appeal for the proletariat. Western atmosphere is well created with a series of outdoor scenes. On the whole, rather well played. The picture, which is in about five reels, will satisfy generally. *Jolo.*

WHITE OAK

Oak Miller	William S. Hart
Barbara	Vola Vale
Mark Granger	Alexander Gaden
Harry	Robert Walker
Eliphalet Moss	Bert Sprotte
Rose Miller	Helen Holley
Chief Long Knife	Chief Standing Bear

William S. Hart here appears in a Western romance one step above the old style dime novel, but it is packed full of action, has a fine free-hand story, with trick riding and Indians, and is a first-rate thriller of the plains.

Hart has a capital romantic character for him, first as a square gambler of the sort that Bret Hart used to create, and later as an Indian fighting horseman. In both characters he is always interesting, although sometimes his deeds of supercourage and wisdom are a little hard to swallow.

The story opens in the colorful surroundings of the Mississippi river steamboat gambling fraternity. His sister is traveling toward St. Louis unaccompanied, except for Mark Granger, who has tricked her into the appearance of a mock marriage. When the girl learns the truth of her position she attempts suicide by jumping into the water.

Word is brought to Oak Miller (Hart), the brother, a gambler in a border camp, and he swims on board, learns the situation, and the story thereafter becomes his pursuit of his sister's traducer. Granger, meanwhile, has entered into a plot with an Indian tribe, agreeing to deliver to the redskins a train of pioneers on its way further West. This plot is unknown to Oak Miller, who is in jail in the settlement on unjust suspicion of a killing.

The Indians close in on the white pioneers in a thoroughly thrilling, dramatic incident handled with a good deal of skill, with the red riders circling the caravan, which has fortified itself behind its little ring of wagons. The fight is going badly for the settlers, and unless aid can be secured from the distant camp, all is lost. One of the young men is sent for relief, but is treacherously shot by Granger as he creeps into the underbrush. At length the heroine bethinks herself of dispatching her dog for Oak.

The dog reaches the camp, delivers the written message tied to his collar to Oak and the gambler starts to the rescue. Here is a first example of dramatic tension, with alternate "shots" of the hard pressed settlers, and the sturdy horseman riding to their relief. Oak, single-handed, takes on and disposes of three desperadoes, and then, by taking prisoner the Indian chief, holds him as hostage and forces the tribe to give up the raid on the wagon train. It does seem a good deal to expect of one man, but if one puts oneself in the frame of mind of accepting this kind of fiction, it makes thrilling, absorbing entertainment.

There is a sort of subsidiary love story running through the main tale, having to do with the love affair of Oak and the sister of his friend. She is concerned in the Indian attack, and rescue of the settlers opens the way for the happy ending and romantic close-up. The feature is a typical Hart picture and serves its purpose nicely. It is bound to please the Hart fans.

Hart wrote the story himself; it was adapted to the screen by Bennett Musson, and the filming was directed by Lambert Hillyer. The picture was made by Hart's own company and is distributed by Paramount. *Rush.*

THE SWAMP

Wang	Sessue Hayakawa
Mary	Bessie Love
Norma	Janice Wilson
Buster	Frankie Lee
Mrs. Biddle	Lillian Langdon
Spencer Wellington	Harland Tucker
Johnnie Rand	Ralph McCullough

Robertson-Cole production, starring Sessue Hayakawa, with the story credited to the star. J. Grubb Alexander wrote the screen version, with Colin Campbell the director. The theme is one that has been done many a time in different styles, with the author in this instance adding a few new twists to make it up to date.

"The Swamp" is a name given the lower East Side section of New York. A deserted wife with her little boy is struggling for an existence. He sells papers to help support the household, the mother being incapacitated on account of illness. In the child's struggle to help matters he is befriended by a Japanese vegetable boy, who also offers his meagre financial support. The father of the child is located just prior to his marriage with a society girl.

This is broken up by the Japanese, who secures a position as fortune teller at the engagement party. A boyhood lover of the mother appears and asks her to be his wife, with the Japanese boy leaving for his native land to marry one of his own nationality.

Improbable in many respects, this picture has sufficient heart interest to warrant attention. The cast is a creditable one, with Hayakawa handling his role in his usual clever style. Bessie Love, as the mother, and Frankie Lee, as the boy, are admirably cast. The production end is good, with the direction all that could be asked. A fair program picture, but not the best this star has done. *Hart.*

ENCHANTMENT

Ethel Hoyt	Marion Davies
Ernest Eddison	Forrest Stanley
Mrs. Hoyt	Edith Shayne
Mr. Hoyt	Tom Lewis
Tommy Corbin	Arthur Rankin
Nalia	Corinne Barker
Mrs. Leigh	Maude Turner Gordon
The Queen (in fairy tale)	Edith Lyle
The King (in fairy tale)	Huntley Gordon

Before 500 feet of "Enchantment" have been unwound it is apparent to the most casual spectator that high comedy is the forte of Marion Davies in pictures. The story is a film adaptation of Frank R. Adams' "Manhandling Ethel," scenario by Luther Reed and directed for Cosmopolitan by Robert G. Vignola—a Paramount release.

Miss Davies has the role of a care-free, egotistical flapper, all wise, the pampered only child of doting parents of wealth, who deny her nothing and whom she winds about her finger at will. At the opening she spends her afternoons at tea dansants, assiduously courted by six Harvard seniors. She is afflicted with an acute attack of youth, beauty and self-satisfaction, certain of her influence with the male sex.

Ethel (Miss Davies) has her parents well-nigh frantic until one night they attend a performance of "Taming of the Shrew," whereupon it occurs to papa to hire the Petruchio to take the chestiness out of Ethel by making her fall for him and then walk out on her. "Remember," says papa, "it's only acting; you must walk out."

Ethel takes part in an amateur theatrical performance, playing the fairy princess to the professional actor's fairy prince, who must awaken her from a 100-year sleep by implanting a kiss upon her lips. The actor does so, but interpolates an ardent kiss, and in an undertone expresses his love for her.

Later the actor confesses he was hired by the father; there is a scene of denunciation on her part, and it all ends happily with her accepting the actor for a husband.

The superior "class" of the production, its artistic settings, admirable direction, splendid supporting cast and, above all, the breezy touch which Miss Davies brings to the role of the headstrong Ethel, makes for a highly entertaining photoplay.

Tom Lewis as the father is a revelation to the film world. He displays all the elements of a film star and gives every indication he could sustain a series of stellar two-reel comedy roles along the same general lines of the late Sydney Drew, or probably a cross between the late John Bunny and Drew. The other roles were all well sustained, but it is Miss Davies and Lewis who stand out.

A few more stories for Miss Davies as good as "Enchantment," equally well produced, will establish this star firmly and unmistakably. *Jolo.*

FACE OF WORLD

Thora ....Barbara Bedford
Dr. Mark ....Edward Hearn
Grandfather ....Harry Duffield
Duparc ....Lloyd Whitlock
Ivan Holth ....Gordon Mullen
Dr. Prahl......................J. P. Lockney
Gundahl ....Fred Huntley

This solid, substantial picture, with an heroic climax, was shown at the Loew houses last week, made by Irvin V. Willat and distributed by Hodkinson. It was adapted from the Norwegian Johann Bojer's novel by Dwight Cleveland and L. V. Jefferson, while John S. Waters assisted in directing. First class photography is credited /to Clyde de Vinna. The exceptional art work is by Harold G. Oliver. All together a worth while offering, it runs 65 minutes.

The story shows a young doctor curing a country girl's grandfather with a touch of chiropractic, but he is besides an able surgeon. Marrying the girl, they go to New York, where diversity of interests separate them, with Duparc entering as the villain who tries to tempt the girl by having her live a year as the guest of his wealthy uncle and aunt. Failing finally, he sets out in his motor to get Dr. Mark to divorce her, but is injured on the way and taken unconscious to the hospital, which catches fire while Dr. Mark is operating to save him, despite his prejudice against him as a home wrecker.

This fire scene—crowds watching daring rescues—is big stuff commercially, and the final reconciliation of husband and wife is prettily handled. Barbara Bedford, in the lead, is a dark, slender girl who handles her part with grace and appeal, while Mr. Hearn and Mr. Whitlock carry hero and heavy capably. Minor character roles are made the most of, with Harry Duffield scoring particularly in an old man role. *Leed.*

HAMLET

Pretentiously presented by Asta Films, Inc., at the Lexington, with an augmented orchestra and scenes from Shakespeare's play, this film featuring the Danish Asta Neilson opened Nov. 7. It is a mistake to play it as a special. Miss Neilson's abilities are exceptional, but they are not the type to enrapture the American public. Almost emaciated, she has command and distinction of movement. Her facial pantomime is of considerable range, but dead whites and blacks have to be used to overcome her physical deficiencies. She has as much chance of smashing the box office here as Walter Hampden would have in Denmark. What is interesting about this presentation is chiefly its clear presentation of the Hamlet legend, which intimates the prince was a girl, sex being concealed to save the crown for the immediate family. Much is made of a book setting forth this idea ascribed to an American scholar, Dr. Edward P. Vining.

Incidental and very effective music was provided by Herman Hand, who led an augmented orchestra, and the house was well filled. Signs in the subway and elsewhere have well advertised this presentation giving Georg Brandes' opinion. His name means nothing to Broadway, and Ernest Lubitsch's opinion but little more. The German director calls Miss Neilson "art itself." Well and good, but the German is continuing to bank his fortune on Pola Negri, who is a box office card if not so eminent a player. *Leed.*

THE FOOLISH AGE

Produced and written by Hunt Stromberg, this light comedy film should prove a suitable vehicle for Doris May, and will undoubtedly please her following among the "fans." The story is light and extremely thin as to probability, but provides for a sufficient number of comedy situations which brought forth many a laugh. W. A. Seiter directed, carrying the action along nicely up to the latter part of the story, where a let-down becomes evident. The photography is attributed to Bert Cann. The settings were up to the mark, with most of the action taking place in interior surroundings.

The story deals with a young school girl, engaged to be married, who gets the idea from the commencement speech delivered by the principal of the institution that she will uplift "suffering humanity." Follows the breaking off with her fiance, the aversion to the project of both him and her father, and the actual plunge into the social welfare game. The girl then secures offices and a secretary, of the "hard boiled type," who introduces her to his fellow "club" members, where she selects three others besides himself to elevate. The fiance of the girl meanwhile tries various means of queering the reform movement which meet with no success until he starts an organization for the out-of-luck chorus girls. That procedure, coupled with the actions of her subjects at a theatrical performance, concludes the girl's conception of her moral obligations to society which allows for the reuniting of the promised couple.

The work of Miss May in the picture will satisfy those who like her, while the appearance she presents, throughout, is particularly appropriate to the tale and highly pleasing to the eye. Opposite the star was Hallam Cooley, who offered assistance, as did Olin Howland in the role of the father. However, it is with "Bull" Montana that Miss May will have to share honors for her latest feature. As the "hard boiled" secretary, who forces himself into the job and becomes the self-appointed protector of his boss, Montana gave an excellent performance to the extent of outshining the other members of the cast and necessitating an equal rating with Miss May. *Skig.*

MORAL FIBRE

Marion Wolcott ....Corinne Griffith
Grace Ellmore ....Catherine Calvert
Nancy Bartley ....Alice Concord
John Corliss ....Joe King
Jared Wolcott ....William Parke, Jr.
George Ellmore...............Harry C. Browne

Vitagraph produced "Moral Fibre," a six-reeler based upon the story by William Harrison Goadby, scenarized by W. B. Courtney. Corinne Griffith is the star and Webster Campbell the director.

The Goadby story is a shallow piece of fiction, lacking a realistic punch and bordering on exaggerated melodrama of the thinnest kind. Jared Wolcott is the youthful proprietor of a country store. He lives with his 14-year-old sister with no parental protection. A coquettish matron from the city gains the boy's love without informing him of her marriage ties. The husband appears and the boy commits suicide from grief. The sister (she's only 14) vows vengeance. Time elapses. Girl becomes prominent artist. Is engaged to illustrate novel written by the coquette's husband. Her identity unknown, she pretends to make a violent play for author to have revenge for brother's death. The wife's brother, incidentally the girl's sweetheart, puts in an appearance, and, believing the love making with his brother-in-law is on the level, orders her out of the house. She goes. He follows. Explanations. Clouds pass over. Happy ending. Six reels for that. A very orginary program feature. Miss Griffith gets away nicely with the leading role. More discretion should have been used by her in the use of beaded eyelashes when playing the 14-year-old girl. Catherine Calvert and Wm. Parke, Jr., are worthy of mention. It cannot be possible that the scenario field is so barren that it is necessary to take a story of this kind for a six-reeler. *Hart.*

THE WAY OF A MAID

Nadia Castleton........Elaine Hammerstein
Thomas Lawlor.................Niles Welch
Dorothy Graham...................Diana Allen
Jimmy Van Trent........Arthur Houseman
Davis Lawlor...............George Fawcett
Mrs. Lawlor...................Helen Lindroth
Mr. Purcell...............Arthur Donaldson

Selznick production, based upon the story by Rex Taylor, directed by Wm. P. S. Earle, with Elaine Hammerstein as the star. The story of a light comedy nature calls for no serious effort on the part, with the director largely responsible for what satisfying effects the picture has.

Nadia Castleton is a society girl of wealth who attends a masquerade in the garb of a maid. In place of returning to her home after the affair she remains over night with a girl friend. Thomas Lawlor, the son of a wealthy candy maker of Peoria, in a liquored condition, encounters her in the hall, and noticing the dress, believes her a maid and requests that she bring him some towels. This fulfilled, time lapses until morning, when she is leaving for her home. The boy appears in the hall at the same time and she continues the deception. Under a fictitious name she gives him her home telephone number. He makes a hurried trip to Peoria and is informed by his mother that the family intends to go to New York so that she may accomplish her social ambitions.

Upon returning to New York he phones and arranges a meeting with the girl. He offers her a position as companion for his mother. This she accepts, the failure of a gold mine in the meantime having crippled her finances. Her villa in Newport is offered for rent and taken by the boy's family, who have no knowledge as to the identity of the girl they have engaged. One party in Newport and her identity becomes known, and the marriage with the candyman's son is assured.

There is a certain amount of interest in this picture for the younger set. The captions and titling has been well done. The cast fills the bill in good style, all being recognized film players. The production end has been well looked after, the interiors having a stamp of class upon them. A flimsy story made comparatively interesting as a picture. *Hart.*

THE SHEIK

Diana Mayo..........................Agnes Ayres
Sheik Ahmed Ben Hassan...............
.........................Rudolph Valentino
Raoul de Saint Hubert....Adolphe Menjou
Omair...........................Walter Long
Gaston.......................Lucien Littlefield
Youssef.....................George Waggner
Slave Girl..........................Ruth Miller
Sir Aubrey Mayo................F. R. Butler

Bad as this Lasky production now at the Rivoli and Rialto is, the public has nothing but the public to blame for it. Though by fear of censorship bled white of anything resembling human form, the popularity of Mrs. Edith M. Hull's novel on which this picture is based should carry it past the box office a winner. This same novel, preposterous and ridiculous as it was, won out because it dealt with every caged woman's desire to be caught up in a love clasp by some he-man who would take the responsibility and dispose of the consequences, but Monte M. Katterjohn's scenario hasn't even that to recommend it. He, in censoring, has safely deleted most of the punch, and what they missed George Melford managed by inept direction of the big scenes.

These occur toward the end. Lady Diana has gone—disregarding all advice—alone into the desert with a native guide only to be captured by the young sheik, Ahmed Ben Hassan. But does this youth force his attentions upon her in the forward fashion of the unleashed Oriental? By your grandmother's halidom, he does not! When he kisses her hand and she shrinks, he detains her in his palace of a tent, and that is all. There comes to visit them a Frenchman whom Ahmed knew in Paris, where he was educated, and this doctor and novelist in one convinces the sheik he should not detain Lady Diana. Naughty, naughty—uncivilized. The mere thought of something so uncouth, properly presented to the Arabian mind, works its neat effect, and Ahmed decides to release her. So painful is the decision, so heroic the renunciation, a great light breaks on him. He loves her. Not only loves her, but loves her truly, nobly, as great souls love. Ooh, la, la! Passion has passed; nothing remains but sweetness and light.

Alas, just at this climax the worst happens. Lady Diana is snatched away by a bandit and taken to his stronghold. But does the young sheik hesitate. He does not. He summons his trusty henchmen, and away they ride in a cloud of dust that must have obscured Mr. Melford's vision because here, with a chance to do something, he draws the veil, narrows the action down to a too easy rescue. Even how the rescuers got through the barred gates of the hostile city is left to the imagination. At any rate, they got in with ridiculous ease, and so what was left of this picture, which could easily have been something by building up this photographic action-full possibility, becomes nothing but an essay in film form on the sadistic urge, and a mealy, emasculated one at that.

The acting could not be worse than the story, but it is bad enough. Mr. Valentino is revealed as a player without resource. He depicts the fundamental emotions of the Arabian sheik chiefly by showing his teeth and rolling his eyes, while Agnes Ayres looks too matronly to lend much kick to the situation in which she finds herself. She has shown herself capable of much better things than this, and the fault is probably the director's. Besides, how could she live up to that finale with her hero discovered to be an Englishman after all and quite ready to marry her.

Minor roles were capably handled, particularly a slave girl, gracefully depicted by Ruth Miller. Settings, detail and photography reached the high Paramount standard, but if the public stands for this sort of diluted drama, it deserves censorship, and will get more of it. If it protests, it should protest to the censor and sharpen its pencils for Election Day. *Leed.*

WONDERFUL THING

Jacqueline ....Norma Talmadge
Donald Mannerby ....Harrison Ford
Catherine Mannerby Truesdale..Julia Hoyt
James Sheridan Boggs...Howard Truesdale
Laurence Mannerby ....Robert Agnew
Dulcie Mannerby Fosdick....Ethel Fleming
Lady Sophia............................Mabel Bert
Angelica Mannerby ....Fanny Burke
"Smooth Bill" Carser....Walter McEwen
General Lancaster ....Charles Craig

"The Wonderful Thing" is a screen adaptation of the play of the same name, written by Lillian Trimble Bradley and Forrest Halsey. It was scenarized by Clara Beranger and directed by Herbert Brenon as a vehicle for Norma Talmadge, a First National release. On the stage it was far from a success, but serves as a breezy "society play" for the screen star. The role is a relatively light one for Miss Talmadge, being mostly comedy, with a smattering of emotional display.

She plays the daughter of an American hog raiser who has amassed millions in the Middle West, falls in love with a titled young Englishman, learns from his sister that he hesitates to propose because he is poor; she impulsively pops the question to him and they are married.

The young bride hears her husband married her for her money and is heartbroken, but cannot understand why he won't use any of her wealth. It develops he did marry her for her money in order to save a younger brother from jail for forgery, but even then would not make use of his wife's fortune. In the end it all comes out right and the titled family which had sneered at her is humiliated by her generous impulses and anonymous financial assistance.

The production is high class in every respect—tho technical details, direction, lighting and uniformly excellent acting by the entire company. There is but one glaring error of direction—a scene showing the familiarity with which an English serving maid conducts herself in conversation with a member of the titled English family. Director Brenon knows, or should know, enough about England not to permit such a faux pas. It is the one wrong note in an otherwise acceptable photoplay feature. *Jolo.*

THE ROPIN' FOOL

"Ropes Reilly" .... Will Rogers
The Girl .... Irene Rich
The Stranger .... John Ince
The Foreman .... "Big Boy" Williams
The Medicine Doctor .... Russ Powell
The Sheriff .... Bert Sprotte

This is a Will Rogers two-reeler, written, produced by and starred in by Will Rogers. At the Capitol this week it shares the billing and lights with another two-reel feature, a Harold Lloyd comedy. That Rogers is currently personally appearing at the Winter Garden across the street from the Capitol in Shubert vaudeville may have had something to do with the picture booking.

"The Ropin' Fool" is an example of what Rogers wanted to do in pictures all the time he has been appearing before the camera, but which no producer would let him make. It is Rogers' vaudeville roping done on the screen, with a combination of the regulation speed camera and the slow motion effect. The picture is fairly amusing, principally through the titles, but there seems to be just a little too much of the roping stuff.

As in the case of "Doubling for Romeo," this picture pokes fun at the pictures, and in one of the final titles the sheriff when he discovers that he has been hoaxed by the film director, says: "Well, as long as it is a movie, go on and hang him; I'm in favor of hanging everyone in the movies."

The picture is short and snappy enough to be interesting, and the special titles at the beginning of it for the Capitol engagement add a great deal to the worth for the insiders of Broadway who will see it there. As a straight picture value in a comedy sense it cannot be said that Rogers classes with either Lloyd or Chaplin as a screen comic, but there seems to be a possibility he will build up into a real two-reel bet.

Clarence Badger directed.

Fred.

PEACOCK ALLEY

Cleo of Paris .... Mae Murray
Elmer Harmon .... Monte Blue
Phil Garrison .... Edmund Lowe
Alex Smith .... W. J. Ferguson
Hugo Fenton .... Anders Randolf
Joseph Carleton .... William Tooker
Abner Harmon .... Howard Lang
Mayor of Harmontown .... William Frederick
Mons. Dubois .... M. Durant
Toto .... Jeffrys Lewis
"Napoleon" .... By Himself

It may be safely ventured "Peacock Alley" is the best picture Mae Murray has ever done. In doing it the chances are that Miss Murray has also indulged in a wider scope of screen playing than hitherto has fallen to her share in filmdom. And on top of that "Peacock Alley" is a good picture, a very good picture, a picture that will do something for exhibitors, for its producers and, most of all, for Mae Murray's picture standing.

It's a Tiffany Productions, Inc., film, understood to be the first of Miss Murray's own production company's output. That "Tiffany" in the name stands up well in this production, that has class throughout, from some of the gorgeous mountings given the restaurant and home scenes to the magnificent wardrobe display by the star.

In playing and action the picture runs easily, holds and has a couple of twists as unexpected as they are nicely worked in and out. For instance, where the husband of the retired restaurant vamp is arrested for forgery, through patronizing his wife's expensive whims; that came with almost a shock, but it fitted in view of his distress at the accumulation of bills just previously shown.

Then there was his distress again, before they were married, and the country boy (possibly from Indiana) had walked out on his first love, the rage of the Parisian restaurants, believing it unbelievable she could lead her life and be on the level—the girl went to Normandy to the quiet of her family homestead, to pine and regret. He went there, too, unable to remain away, and because she had used her influence to secure his Indiana firm a French government contract. He saw her there, thanked her, told her how far apart they were, he was going home, and she said she was good, swore it on the cross of the church behind them, because she was and loved him.

There has been some fine manipulation of material in this scenario by Edmund Goulding, based on a Ouida Bergere tale. It may have been made strong in sentiment in the original. It is stronger in the picture.

The principals leap from the Peacock Alley of Paris to the Peacock Alley of New York, then to the home town of the late vamp. In that home town things commence to happen. Though the kid has made his company and the town through the contract, they leave him flat when, flashing his smart-looking wife, the company buys his stock and his uncle turns him out. Back in the city the bank account runs low, the young husband forges his uncle's name, is taken away to prison, and the misunderstood and misunderstanding wife, seeking for her husband's release, goes back to the restaurant in New York against her promise to him not to do so, but in order to make money and meet some one who can help her mate. She meets him, a lawyer, who invites her to his home after the restaurant performance, to assure himself she is right and not wrong. He is assured and promises his assistance, as the husband bursts in through a window. He was released when the uncle withdrew the charge, the uncle first informing the nephew his wife had gone back to the stage and was playing around with the restaurant's hangers-on.

After the compromising sight he saw in the lawyer's parlor the husband returned to Indiana and the girl to Normandy, but that didn't stop them from again getting together there at the finish.

Miss Murray played this girl of the restaurant as finely as it could have been done. She had the abandon and demureness shaded to a nicety. But will some one please explain how it was possible at moments for Miss Murray to look a bit elderly (unless it were the drop earrings) and at all other times to be about the prettiest looking girl a film could show.

Monte Blue as the husband may have played the role in a manner to leave a personal opinion. He didn't make it anything it was not, that's certain. It's too bad so many film leading men acquire a screen strut. It yells acting every time employed, and they all do it the same.

The types of Paris and Indiana drew laughs. W. J. Ferguson was the comedy hit in pantomimic expression. The cast is an excellent one.

Frederic and Fanny Hatton, who wrote the sub-titles, have done better, but still there were smiles for several. A special orchestration by Louis Silvers has a jazzy arrangement or two that will keep any house orchestra on its toes during the running of this film. That music was lively and appropriate all the while.

The direction by Robert Z. Leonard makes the film, with Miss Murray. There isn't a flaw in it nor has any one tried to save a dollar without throwing, either, a dollar away. The Paris restaurant scene is probably the best of that character that has been done in pictures, made so through Miss Murray's nifty dancing in it and the surrounding "business."

The picture was privately shown at the Hotel Commodore's ballroom one evening last week. A promiscuous manner of issuing invitations brought an overflow of friendly watchers. The film ran about the usual feature length, maybe a bit longer, but it held even that crowd until its end.

Mae Murray will be measured hereafter by her performance of Cleo of Paris until she excels it, and that is going to be some job—for Mae Murray or any one else.

Simc.

GIRL FROM GOD'S COUNTRY

Neeka LeMort } Marion Carlisle } .... Nell Shipman
Owen Glendon .... Edward Burns
J. Randall Carlisle .... Al. W. Filson
Pierre LeMort .... George Berrell
Old Inventor .... Walt Whitman
Otto Kraus .... C. K. Van Auker
Notawa .... Lillian Leighton

"The Girl from God's Country," a seven-part feature presented by W. H. Clune and released by the F. B. Warren Corp. proves one thing, and that is that Nell Shipman, the authoress and star of the production, should stick to acting in the future and leave the writing of her stories to some one better qualified. In direction Miss Shipman might also have had some one on the salary list qualified for that position instead of taking it on herself to do everything to be done.

She not only has written and directed, but played three parts in the story. Two of the parts were mighty important and the third was a bit in a single shot.

In reality "The Girl from God's County" is a serial that has been done as a feature. It has all the impossible thrill producing stunts that one would expect in a serial that is destined for the entertainment of the veriest lowbrows, but which seem entirely out of place in a feature.

The titling is also unworthy of boasting about and the picture might have been improved to considerable extent had intelligent brains been exercised in this particular regard.

It is a northwest yarn to a certain extent, but the threads of plot are so mixed up that one cannot figure just what it is all about. The heroine is supposedly an illegitimate child, who lives with her grandfather at a Canadian trading post. The hero is a French flying ace who has been blinded in action. This gives the impression the war is past and through with, but in the final reel the blinded ace with the aid of the girl makes a trans-Pacific flight in order to capture a Boche who is escaping with the plans of a new plane. With continuity of that sort no great imagination is needed to figure how loose jointed the story is.

At the opening a party of tourists come to the little post where Neeka is living, father, daughter and prospective son-in-law. Miss Shipman is playing Neeka as well as that of the daughter of the tourist. The grandfather of Neeka recognizes the name of the elder of the two men tourists as the same as the betrayer of his daughter and plans to revenge himself. Neeka saves his life, and she is taken back to California with the family.

Here through a series of impossible events she comes in contact with her real father, who is the demented brother of the tourist whom she saved. Her dad regains his sanity through a recurrence of the big quake in which he originally lost it, and all ends well, for after Neeka jumps out of a plane in the middle of the Pacific Ocean and kills a man to recover the stolen plans of the plane, is picked up again from the sea by the machine which is manipulated by a blind man, there is nothing left for them except to fly to Japan and be clinched in each other's arms for the fadeout.

Incidentally, that "quake" stuff won't be so forte to California audiences, especially if they are native sons.

As a picture "The Girl from God's County" is a laugh, and if it is to be taken as a sample of what the F. B. Warren Corp. is going to release that concern should first think it over. In the smaller houses on double bills it will get over, but there isn't any chance of it hitting in the first run league anywhere at any time. *Fred.*

STEELHEART

Frank Worthing .... William Duncan
Ethel Kendall .... Edith Johnson
"Butch" Dorgan .... Jack Curtis
Steve .... Walter Rodgers
Mrs. Freeman .... Euna Luckey
Vera .... Ardeta Malino
Dick Colter .... Earl Crain
"Old Tom" Shelly .... Charles Dudley

A typical "frontier" program feature, laid in another "Lost Valley." What the makers of "westerns" would do without these carelessly mislaid valleys it is hard to imagine. It is a Vitagraph release, scenario by Bradley Smollen, directed by William Duncan, who is also starred in the production. Despite its length of six full reels, the story is cumulative, piling up feats of courage for the hero that smack of the miraculous in the matter of luck. Photography and lighting are excellent for so unpretentious an offering—too much of the hero who stays days and days on the trail with a clean shirt and a stiff collar; the heroine goes with him, attired in an unruffled Central Park riding habit and immaculate blouse; there is a palpably posed scene at an up-to-date mining camp, with modern machinery; a landslide is unconvincing, and at the finish the wholesale slaughter of the villains borders closely upon burlesque. Obviously a machine-made program feature. *Jolo.*

THE SILENT CALL

Flash .... Strongheart
Clark Moran .... John Bowers
Betty Houston .... Kathryn McGuire
Ash Brent .... William Dyer
Luther Nash .... James Mason
Dad Kinney .... Nelson McDowell
Jimmy the Dude .... E. J. Brady
James Houston .... Robert Bolder

Made originally for the Associated Producers, "The Silent Call" is released by First National in the open market. It is labeled a Laurence Trimble-Jane Murfin production, presented by H. O. Davis. Larry Trimble directed the production and Miss Murfin adapted "The Cross Pull," a Satevepost story by Hal Evarts for the screen under the present title.

The real star is the shepherd dog Strongheart, a trained police dog which Trimble purchased in New York, it having been imported from Germany by a kennel owner. The work this animal does is not extraordinary to those aware of the capabilities of these dogs and know what they have done in field trials. But from an audience standpoint this dog will be a wonder. It is a good looking, upstanding animal and training has made him worthy of the starring honors. Mr. Trimble is to be congratulated on the work that he has done with Strongheart.

The picture is in seven reels at this time. Rather too long and can easily stand cutting in the early section. There is a little too much scenic and title footage in the first reel in an effort to create atmosphere.

The story is a Western, somewhat different from the usual run. In it Strongheart is supposed to represent a cross between dog and wolf, the latter of a type that was exterminated by a campaign of the cattlemen in an effort to protect their stock. He is taken as a pup and reared by a naturalist-author, and as he grows from puppyhood into maturity the call of the wild asserts itself when he is parted from his master. The silent call for the companionship of humans always reasserts itself and he returns to seek out his master.

It is the dog that is the main theme of the tale at all times, but interwoven there is a love story, a touch of the wild life of the range, with its cattle rustlers, etc., that makes possible the use of the dog in bringing the lovers together and the defeat of the outlaws trying to part them.

If the exhibitor is looking for something different this picture certainly fills the bill, and for one thing the star of the production is not the type of actor that is always trying to hog the camera lens. Seems as dogs have too much sense for that.

John Bowers plays the lead, with Kathryn McGuire opposite him. Mr. Bowers is convincing and handles the dog nicely. Miss McGuire was a pleasing picture and supplied a few thrills here and there in her battle with the outlaws. It is to William Dyer the majority of audiences will hand the palm. He plays the heavy and is forced into a couple of battles with Strongheart. Those not knowing shepherds will figure he must have been a mighty brave man to take a chance with the dog. *Fred.*

THE MILLIONAIRE

Jack Norman ....Herbert Rawlinson
Bobo Harmsworth ....Bert Roach
Simon Fisher ....Wm. Courtwright
Jimmy ....Verne Winter
Kate Blair ....Lillian Rich
Grandmother ....Margaret Mann
Delmar ....Fred Vroom
Mrs. Clever ....Mary Huntress
Marion Culbreth ....Doris Pawn
Evers ....E. A. Warren

It looks like the author of the story of this feature, Hulbert Footner, must have been bitten by the regular motion picture bug, for he has his hero, who is a clerk in a sash and door factory, fall heir to $80,000,000. That sounds just like motion picture money, doesn't it?

The picture is a Universal thriller directed by Jack Conway, who managed to put a lot of life into a couple of fights in the story. The feature, however, is one that will get by in the nickel and dime houses

where they wouldn't know how much $80,000,000 was anyway.

If Universal ever expects to get the full value out of Mr. Rawlinson from a star sales point they had better see that he is provided with better story material than this is. Rawlinson is a good actor, and has proven himself worth while playing leads opposite some of the biggest of the screen stars, but as a picture "The Millionaire" is about the cheapest millionaire that has ever stepped forth.

The manner of that money coming along is funny in itself. An aged recluse is bumped off by a band of crooks because he refused to pay them tribute to the extent of $1,000 a week. He leaves his money to the son of the only woman he ever loved and the crooks in turn go after the heir.

There is a house with secret passages and all the other necessary adjuncts to the old-fashioned screen mystery meller, and they are used to a fare thee well in this case. In the end the hero rounds up all the crooks with the aid of the police, and marries the little bookkeeper who worked in the sash and door factory with him.

There isn't a bit of class to the picture outside of the star and Doris Pawn, who plays the heavy. The rest is just cheap U. melodrama. *Fred.*

SERVING TWO MASTERS

Lee and Bradford present "Serving Two Masters," a screen version of the play, "Break Down the Walls," written by Mrs. Alexander Grossman. The Capitol Film Co. is distributing the feature, with no mention of this being made in the billing, the distributers in all probability preferring to remain in oblivion.

Josephine Earle is the star of the production. From general appearances it was made in England, or if not it is an antiquated American picture that has long remained on the shelf. The story is a simple one and not especially plausible. A man of wealth refuses to allow his wife to interest herself in his business affairs. He becomes entangled and is on the verge of financial collapse when his wife comes to his rescue with money made in a dressmaking establishment which she had started unknown to her husband and made a success of.

The cast supporting the star include Dalas Anderson, Pat Somerset and Zoe Palmer. No special merit is displayed in any instance, with the production end of the cheapest order. This feature must be offered at a price to have a look-in with any house manager. *Hart.*

MAN OF STONE

Conway Tearle stars in Selznick's "The Man of Stone," supported by Martha Mansfield and Betty Howe. The story has the North African desert as its setting, and gets some fairly effective bits of picturesque backgrounds and costuming from this fact, and the picture is reasonably entertaining in a Laura Jean Libbey sort of way, with a dash of Ouida's "Under Two Flags." It is a coincidence that it should come out just as the story of similar locale, "The Sheik," is attracting a certain vogue.

But the two stories are different. "The Man of Stone" need never disturb the censor. Its ethics are as pure as conventional fiction could make them. On the surface at least the picture could be shown in the First M. E. church of Moline, even if the hero, disappointed in love, does go on a solitary bat and drink himself into a touch of the D. T.'s and even if he is unduly familiar with a native girl. The D. T.'s are described in the titles as

an attack of tropical fever, and the native girl is the hero's servant. Thus the purity of the screen is protected. Maybe the censors haven't got the fifth largest industry buffaloed!

It's just cheap, florid fiction, but it ought to be interesting to the apparently large public that consumes this sort of literature, if the magazine output indicates anything. As a routine release for the neighborhood trade it probably will do well, although there are glaring inconsistencies in the telling.

Capt. Nevill Deering, a British officer, returns to England after a campaign in Egypt, where his deeds of daring have earned him the title of "The Man of Stone." His mission is to marry Lady Mary in London, but on arrival he finds that she has jilted him in favor of a richer man. Broken hearted he goes back to the desert on a government mission to the Moroccan tribes. Once among the palms he wrecks his health with drink, and in a drunken state wanders among a group of native travelers and seizes one of their dancing girls.

Instead of tearing him to pieces as they might be expected to do, the Arabs pick up the raving officer tenderly and carry him back to his cot. The dancing girl — Laila she is called—goes along as his nurse and saves his life. Capt. Deering has to go farther into the desert solitude to parley with the tribes, and takes Laila along. You can get this down with a gulp if you try, because Capt. Nevill is most circumspect in his relations with the girl.

Meanwhile Lady Mary's rich fiance has jilted her, and she travels all the way to the middle of the desert to make up with the captain. First she makes Laila believe she is the captain's wife and Laila departs for her own people. But when the captain learns of the situation he spurns Lady Mary and all her works and sets out in pursuit of Laila. The girl has been taken captive by bandits and there is a lot of desert fighting, with rushing horsemen and fluttering native costumes, but the captain wins and brings her triumphantly back to camp.

There is another battle around the camp between the captain's followers and the pursuing bandits, and Lady Mary is conveniently killed by a stray shot, so that the captain may suddenly find that he is in love with the native girl and the picture may end with an appropriate embrace.

It's all pretty far-fetched, but it's harmless and there are a few moments of stirring action amid the mass of inanities. *Rush.*

A PRINCE THERE WAS

Charles Edward Martin...Thomas Meighan
Katherine Woods............Mildred Harris
Comfort Brown ....Charlotte Jackson
Jack Carruthers ....Nigel Barrie
Bland ....Guy Oliver
J. J. Stratton ....Arthur Hull
Mrs. Prouty ....Sylvia Ashton
Mr. Cricket ....Fred Huntly

If there is any one anywhere that isn't able to tell the answer of "A Prince There Was" after the first few scenes are flashed on the screen then that person is ready to become an inmate of an asylum for the blind. As a play "A Prince There Was" was a hit while George M. Cohan played the title role; as a picture it becomes a very ordinary program feature, even though Thomas Meighan is starred in it. The fact that the production was turned out as a Paramount picture makes it all the more lamentable. By titling it might have been a picture worth while, but the titles are the most trite and matter of fact that have been screened in a feature intended for the better houses in some time.

The screen version of "A Prince There Was" is taken from the Cohan play, which in turn was based on the story by Darragh Aldrich entitled "Enchanted Hearts." Walde-

mar Young provided the scenario under the supervision of Frank Woods, and Tom Forman supplied the direction.

Neither scenario nor direction help the story.

The first couple of hundred feet of the picture were shot on Fifth avenue, New York, and the balance was shot in the studio. The studio street depicting a scene near Second avenue is altogether too apparent as studio stuff.

Meighan plays the young millionaire who has looked on the cup and permitted a manager to handle all of his financial affairs. Mildred Harris is the girl whose father was ruined through the manipulation of the manager of the young millionaire's affairs. Little Charlotte Jackson is the little slavey of the East Side boarding house who is the medium of bringing the two together.

In addition, the cast holds several players who manage to score. Nigel Barrie is in the picture for a bit that amounts to but little. Guy Oliver as a valet manages to extract some comedy from his role and pulls a few laughs from the audience. Arthur Hull as the heavy has but little, and Sylvia Ashton and Fred Huntly have minor roles which they characterize in a manner that gets them over.

The picture, however, is a very much hashed affair, with scenes badly matched up, continuity that is exceedingly rough, and titling that is bad.

On the whole, the picture is far from being up to Paramount standard for production. *Fred.*

UNSEEN FORCES

Miriam Holt.................Sylvia Breamer
Winifred....................Rosemary Theby
Clyde Brunton.................Conrad Nagel
Arnold Crane..................Robert Cain
Captain Stanley..............Sam de Grasse
Robert Brunton.........Edward Martindel
Peter Holt....................Harry Garrity
Joe Simmons.............James O. Barrows
Mrs. Leslie..................Aggie Herring
Mr. Leslie................Andrew Arbuckle
Henry Leslie..................Albert Cody

"Unseen Forces" is the initial feature produced by Sidney Franklin for Mayflower, released through First National. Carrying an all-star line in its billing the feature is to a large extent far more effective in the acting division than the average picture billed in this manner. The John Cort story has been substantially worked up by Franklin, who has turned out a feature that should have a direct appeal to the female followers of the screen.

The psychic ability of the leading character provides the fundamentals upon which the tale is based. Miriam Holt is the daughter of a country innkeeper. From childhood she has been able to foretell things which are about to befall her acquaintances, and in later years is brought to the city to display her ability, which she does purely for the benefit of mankind.

Early in life she falls in love with a young huntsman who stays at her father's place. Believing she loves another he drops her from his life. After a lapse of several years they meet again at a house party. She, meantime, has married. The old love springs up, especially when he learns she is unmarried. His wife, a shallow thing, has had an affair with a man whom she really loves but could not get and fell back upon the man she married to gain a social position.

The girl through her psychic ability diagnoses the case of the wife, brings her together with the man she loves, which in turn releases the choice of her own heart.

With Sylvia Breamer, Rosemary Theby and Conrad Nagel topping a long cast the picture is well fortified in acting. Director Franklin brings out the points to a nicety, with the production end displaying artistic ability.

"Unseen Forces" is a program feature of merit. *Hart.*

THE SPEED GIRL

This is a Realart production shown as half of a double feature bill at the New York Tuesday. It stars Bebe Daniels and is in effect a crude comedy dramatization of that actress' experience on the coast some time ago when she was arrested for auto speeding, and spent a few days in jail under more or less ridiculous circumstances.

The screen comedy-drama inspired by this adventure furnishes first rate entertainment for the infantile. It is scarcely conceivable that any film fan of a mentality more mature than that could be amused by the feeble invention. The story starts in a comedy vein, goes into melodrama, has a few moments of "stunt" thrills and then explodes in the wildest kind of cheap melodrama, and finally collapses prostrate in unintentional travesty.

The whole vapid rave might have been put on for no other purpose than to feed the vanity of the camera actress. Certainly it can have had no sincere purpose to amuse an audience of grown up people. If this kind of trash is salable why not have the stars write their own stories with no other end then self-exploitation and frankly let the public go hang. The idea would be to amuse the star who made the picture rather than the fans who pay to see it. That is the bald intent of "The Speed Girl."

The story concerns one Betty Lee (Bebe Daniels), a tomboy sort of person. Her horse runs away and she is saved by a Naval Ensign named Tom Something or Other. Presently Betty is grown up and a film star. She still loves Tom, but is courted by a blackguard named D'Arcy who has ruined and deserted a poor girl. The victim writes pathetic letters and D'Arcy plants them in Tom's coat pocket.

Tom entertains Betty at luncheon and misses the last train that will get him on his ship in time to start for maneuvers. He is in danger of court martial. Betty puts the officer in her car and drives at 80 miles an hour to catch up with the distant train. For this she is tried and sent to jail for 10 days.

In order to get rid of his victim, who has secured work as chambermaid in the hotel where he lives, D'Arcy has her convicted of bootlegging (honest to gawd, this is done seriously) and she is incarcerated in the same jail where Betty is doing her ladylike bit, and mourning over the supposed villainy of Tom, having discovered the planted note. Betty and D'Arcy's victim get chummy and when D'Arcy appears at the jail to press his courtship (we have gotten around to a strained sort of comedy by this time) the whole situation is laid open; Tom is recalled and forgiven and D'Arcy is arrested and punished on the spot because they find he has a silver flask on his hip and is in a measure a sort of bootlegger himself.

This sketch of the plot, tangled as it is, gives only a faint impression of the utter confusion of idea in the picture. It might have had a chance as a frank burlesque, but when the authors, director and actors take themselves seriously it transcends all bounds of weird fiction without meaning to. The whole futile thing is the last word in actor-made crudity. *Rush.*

LADYFINGERS

Robert Ashe ....Bert Lytell
Enid Camden ....Ora Carew
Justin Haddon ....Frank Elliott
Rachel Stetherill ....Edythe Chapman
Lieut. Ambrose ....DeWitt Jennings

If photography and lighting could put over a production into the special class, then "Ladyfingers," the latest Metro Classic release, with Bert Lytell starred, would be a special in every way. But such does not happen to be the case, for the story and direction play a big part in developing a special for the screen, and while the story in this particular instance could have been made a wonder if it had been properly handled, the direction would have slowed it up to such an extent that it would have been draggy.

That seems to be the particular trouble with the Jackson Gregory story, which was adapted to the screen by Lenore J. Coffee, and which was directed by Bayard Veiller. The feature is announced as "a Bayard Veiller production," and all credit is due Mr. Veiller if he was responsible for the photography and the lighting, but his exceedingly languid tempo in handling the action destroys all the credit that the former two artistic touches gain.

"Ladyfingers" is a story of a boy who has been forced into crooked paths, through having been adopted as a waif by a bank burglar. Originally of good family, he eventually drifts into the circle where his grandmother is active. She recognizes the family resemblance, and, although stories of the boy's past reach her, she refuses to believe them. Finally, when the boy has been tested and come through with flying colors, he personally makes a confession to the authorities and does his bit. On being released he does not turn to his wealthy grandmother, but decides to make his own way in the world.

Naturally, there was a girl behind it all. She is the ward of the grandmother, and after his release she seeks him out and throws her lot with him. Eventually there is an all round reconciliation and granny is seen with her two "grandchildren and their baby" just prior to the final scene.

A good story, to be sure, but slow and draggy through direction. As a matter of fact, Lytell stalls and scowls into the camera to such length that it is tiresome, and Miss Carew, who plays opposite him, seems entirely too mature for the role assigned her. Edythe Chapman easily walks off with the honors of the picture as the grandmother, and it would have been easy for her to have made as much of this role as Mary Carr did of the mother in "Over the Hill" had she been given the opportunity. This picture could have been built into one of those tear and dime compelling mellers had it been given sufficient attention in the making. As it is, it is a good program feature. *Fred.*

PLAYTHINGS OF DESTINY

Julie Leneau................Anita Stewart
Geoffrey Arnold.........Herbert Rawlinson
Hubert Randolph...........Walter McGrail
Claire......................Grace Morse
Conklin..................William V. Mong
Julie's Child.............Richard Headrick

Here is an Anita Stewart feature that has been released by First National and for some reason or other has been permitted to slip by all of the reviewing channels. The picture never saw Broadway, although it was announced by the First National back in July. Just what reason there is underlying all this is hard to say, for the picture is far from being an undesirable one, in fact, it is even better than some of the other Stewarts shown on the Main Stem.

It is said to be something like six reels in length, but the projection time at the 81st Street theatre this week belies that. The story was by Jane Murfin and Larry Trimble, while Anthony Paul Kelly furnished the working script, and Edwin Carewe directed.

The opening scenes are laid in snowbound Canada, while the final shots are supposedly neath the tropical glare of the Jamaica sun. Miss Stewart has a role that fits her completely, and her supporting cast is all that anyone could ask for.

She plays a little French Canadian girl who marries a young Englishman who is in the woods. Later, when another woman arrives on the scene and declares herself to be the wife in the absence of the husband, the young wife runs away into the storm. After searching parties are organized they fail to find her. In the meantime she is in the cabin of a timber reclamation patrolman who falls in love with her and asks her to marry. She consents as a measure of protection to her child which is to be born.

Five years later, in Jamaica, her husband has risen in the service of the government to sufficient extent to be a candidate for the post of governor-general of the island. He needs but the recommendation of a member of the nobility who is to visit the island on a tour of inspection. The latter is none other than the husband from whom the wife escaped in the Canadian wilds.

In the midst of a tropical storm, when the two are together in an isolated hut, the truth is revealed and later an annulment of the marriage agreed upon, which brings about a happy ending.

Pictorially the picture has much in its favor, and in comparison to some of the features that are being marketed today is well worth while playing. *Fred.*

COURAGE

Jean Blackmoore..........Naomi Childers
Stephan Blackmoore........Sam de Grasse
Angus Ferguson............Lionel Belmore
Bruce Ferguson...........Adolph Menjou
"Speedy" Chester........Floyd Whitlock
McIntyre...................Alec B. Francis
Stephan Blackmoore, Jr.......Ray Howard
Eve Hamish...............Gloria Hope
Oliver Hamish..........Charles Hill Mailes

"Courage" is based on a story by Andrew Soutar, scenario by Sada Cowan. Albert A. Kaufman presents it, and the distribution is handled by First National under the management of Joseph M. Schenck.

It is an intensely interesting melodrama, directed by Sidney A. Franklin, admirably produced with an excellent cast, in which Naomi Childers, Lionel Belmore and Sam de Grasse stand out.

The story takes its title from the sufferings of a man and wife, who go through the anguish of having the husband serve 18 years before he is released from a life imprisonment sentence for a murder he did not commit. The tale is laid in Scotland and the atmosphere of the locale is carefully reproduced. Scenes in a steel mill are undoubtedly genuine and the tale is cumulatively progressive. It holds interest for six full reels. *Jo'o.*

German Pics
By C. HOOPER TRASK

THE ROMANCE OF CHRISTINE

The two latest Decla films, as mentioned, the first to play in an Ufa theatre, are worthy of praise in that they attempted much, but the carrying out was far from completely successful.

The first, "The Romance of Christine von Herre," was both written and directed by Dr. Ludwig Berger of the State Schauspielhaus. The scenario concerns a countess who, to escape a brutal and faithless husband, has herself buried as dead and then escapes the tomb to wander the land in boy's clothing. The ending is happy—the husband dead and the countess united with her lover. The cast included Werner Kraus, Paul Hartmann and Adele Sandrock, all of whom did brilliantly. Agnes Straub played the leading role and although acting up to standard she is no film type, her face being too strong. The direction of Berger is very sensitive and atmosphere and beauty are finely sustained. But more action, more conflict! Dr. Berger is an intelligent man, as his stage work has shown, and perhaps his second production (for this was his first go at films) will be more pantomime and less pose.

THE TIRED DEATH

"The Tired Death," which followed "Christine," is considerably better film stuff. The scenario, by Fritz Lang, also the director, is called a German folk song and has somewhat the quality of "The Blue Bird." A young wife loses her husband on the marriage night and goes to Death to ask him back. Death tells her that it is impossible, but promises his return if she can save from death the life of one of three different persons who are about to die. She tries, first in Arabia, then in Renaissance Italy and finally in China, and fails each time. Then Death gives her one final chance, to bring him the life of another human being in exchange for her lover. All people refuse her request, but, rushing into a burning house, she is saving a baby left there, when Death stands before her. Here is her chance to win her lover back. But at this cost she cannot take him and, throwing the child to safety, she awaits in the burning cottage reunion through death.

Lil Dagover as the wife is decorative enough and Bernhard Goetzke as Death combines the sinister with the sympathetic. Fritz Lang's direction achieved some fine moments, but he seems to lack a final feeling for style, the whole being a bit confused.

SAILOR-MADE MAN

The Boy ....Harold Lloyd
The Girl ....Mildred Davis
The Rowdy Element..........Noah Young
Maharajah ....Dick Sutherland

Harold Lloyd's new four-reeler, release date and distribution plan not yet announced by Pathe. The story is by Hal Roach and Sam Taylor and the direction was in the hands of Fred Newmeyer; titles by Harley M. Walker.

The picture has plenty of laughs, all in the familiar Lloyd vein of comedy, and some good human touches, but the comedy does not compare with Lloyd's best. The comedian appears to be in the process of changing the spirit of his appeal. The transition so far is faint and scarcely discernible, but it is in the wrong direction.

Specifically, Lloyd is turning his characterization from the "boob" to the "wise guy." Instead of being always the victim of the joke he is the perpetrator. Instead of falling into the banana peel trap he sets the trap for somebody else, losing sight of the fundamental that the laugh goes to the banana peel victim and not to the joker.

In so far as the new picture obeys this rule, it is funny, and at all times the surprises are ingenious. Of course, the comedy punch is an elaborate chase. Picture making has not yet developed any substitute for this sure-fire device. The whirlwind climax is neatly led up to and is smoothly dovetailed with an amusing love story.

Lloyd is the rich boy. The Girl won't have him unless he "does something worth while." He goes into the navy. As a gob he goes to sleep and dreams he is an admiral. This is only an incident. The dream causes a fight with the ship's bully, a capital chapter, leading to the cementing of a firm friendship between the Boy and the Bully.

The ship anchors in an Oriental port and the Girl, on a yachting cruise with her father, comes to the same place. Girl goes ashore sightseeing, as gob also goes on shore-leave. The Rajah sees the American girl and kidnaps her. The Boy and his matey go to the palace in pursuit. Here begins the wild chase with a rich fund of comic detail. The Boy takes refuge in the bath of the harem, staying under water and breathing through the stem of on Oriental water pipe, which the Rajah lights so that smoke bubbles rise from the water. There is knockabout and roughhouse in abundance, ending in a carnival of clubbing and, of course, the rescue of the American girl.

The naval stuff aboard the warship is amusing and the chase is uproarious. The business on shipboard is said to be strictly according to Hoyle. Regular service men were employed for the scenes.

Rush.

FALSE KISSES

Jen..........................Miss du Pont
Paul..........................Pat O'Malley
Jim..........................Lloyd Whitlock

This is a commendable attempt by Universal to transfer to the screen the one-act play "Ropes," by Wilbur Daniel Steele. The scenario is by Wallace Clifton. Paul Scardon directed. The feature runs only a little over 4,000 feet, and its fault is mainly in the casting. Who is Miss du Pont, for example, and why this ridiculous designation? Surely the girl has a name. Entrusted with a role that demanded the dramatic ability of a Norma Talmadge, it is no wonder she fell short. In less exacting roles she should suit the type of exhibitor who buys the U product.

All Mr. Steele's conceptions are effective dramatically. This is no exception. Into a quiet fishing village Jen comes as a school teacher. For love of her two boy friends become bitter enemies. They fight. The worsted one she accepts and marries, while Jim goes away to return five years later, a lighthouse inspector. By that time Paul has lost his job and Jim gives him one as keeper of a remote island light. There Jen's second baby is born and dies. The scenes' possibilities are not realized.

The crux of the piece, with Paul gone blind, comes now, with Jim making love to Jen. To keep Paul's job she lets him kiss her, then kisses him because she wants to, only to be discovered through ingenious circumstances when Paul recovers his sight. That their long love and life together matters more than this indiscretion is the moral, adequately brought out.

Here was great material and the U did pretty well with it, but only pretty well. Mr. Whitlock, as usual, dominated the cast. He is one of the best heavies in the business, but the whole thing leaves you with the hope that more stories by Steele and his like will be bought. Fox and the U have both tried. Griffith and his like should, too.

Leed.

SIN OF MARTHA QUEED

"The Sin of Martha Queed" is a Mayflower production, written and directed by Allan Dwan, photographed by Tony Gaudio, distributed by Associated Exhibitors through Pathe.

It is a modern version of "Punchinello," carefully scenarioized to pass stringent censorship. It does not come up to the standard set for the better class of first runs, but for the general run of program picture houses it can be played up by exhibitors as a high-grade production and will please the patrons of such establishments. To a student of dramatic technique it is long drawn-out, with the agony and suspense piled on unnecessarily, but with, say, five minutes of footage cut from its present running time of 65 minutes, would make for a gripping melodrama, admirably directed and photographed, with a splendid cast.

Martha Queed, a school teacher in a mountain village, is in love with a "city feller," who is up there fishing, clad in riding breeches. He reciprocates her affection. She is worshipped silently by a hunchback and coveted by a middle-aged worthless relative.

Martha spends a perfectly innocent afternoon with the city chap in his bungalow, accepts his offer of marriage. The worthless one distorts the visit to the girl's father, and when she returns home he sends for a justice of the peace and forces her to marry the no-account. It is raining, and although the father gives the worthless one his daughter he refuses to lend him an umbrella.

When the hero hears of it the next morning he swears he will kill the no-account if any harm has come to Martha. Hero rushes to the hut, finds the no-account dead and the girl gone. He is tried for the murder and found guilty, with the girl's father in his capacity of district attorney prosecuting the hero.

The hunchback has spirited the girl away to his shack, where she lies ill with fever. Just as the hero is convicted the hunchback comes into the courtroom, whispers "In my cabin" to the hero, and tells (flashback) it was he who killed the worthless one, stabs himself to death, and in the hospital to which she is taken comes "love's fulfillment" in the form of a marriage ceremony with the hero, the "sin" having existed only in her father's mind.

Mary Thurman is featured as Martha, and Niles Welch as the hero, contributing excellent characterizations. But the outstanding hits of the filming are supplied by George Hackethorn, with the actual stellar role of the self-sacrificing, pathetic hunchback, Joseph J. Dowling, as the hard, unyielding father, and Frank Campeau as the repulsive relative who is shot by the hopeless and unhappy deformed "Punchinello."

"The Sin of Martha Queed" is far superior to the average example of program features. It will please all those not familiar with the elementary tutelage of story construction —that vast multitude which may best be designated as "the general public."

Jolo.

JUTLAND

Produced by Ideal and offered by Educational, "The Battle of Jutland" is part of the Rialto's program this week. It is fair, even fascinating, entertainment, but historically, as Billy Sunday would say, it is the bunk. In fact, British propaganda has never done anything quite so perfect or quite so awful. Here in small space you have set before you an example of what governments have to do to keep the masses (and their children and their children's children) in line behind the ruling, and very necessary, power. So give the author of this film, Gen. Sir George Aston, K. C. B., credit.

The battle of Jutland was fought May 31, 1916. Preceded by Admiral Hipper's flying squadron, the German High Seas Fleet came out that morning and were engaged that afternoon by Admiral Beatty, then commanding the English battle cruisers. These are lightly armored, heavy gunned ships of great speed. They did fairly well with Hipper, but encountering the heavier German ships coming up from the rear suffered a set-back. Beatty's own flagship, the Lion, went down with others, the British commander shifting his flag and heading north, leading the Germans after him till all came in touch with the advance of the Grand fleet. This advance was led by Rear Admiral Hood, who went down on the Invincible in the first charge.

Right here is an interesting point. The British after the battle complained of low visibility, but this film shows the German ships were against the light, though their commander may have figured the wind would blow obscuring smoke toward the British. In any case it was not long before Sir John R. Jellicoe British commander-in-chief, with all the dreadnoughts, goth the range, and Scheer, the German commander-in-chief, withdrew behind a smoke screen through which he sent his destroyers to attack the British line.

This torpedo attack occurred after seven that evening. The film quits here, merely stating Jellicoe moved to avoid this attack. Skipping several hours, it states that in the morning the Germans slipped through the whole British fleet into Wilhelmshaven. This is the first time we have ever seen it implied that the British fleet got between the German fleet and its refuge at Wilhelmshaven at any time during this battle. The Helgoland stronghold isn't shown in this film. Getting anywhere near it would have been difficult work for the British.

Meanwhile what really happened during those several hours skipped in the film? If memory serves correctly, the Marlborough was torpedoed and Jellicoe's movement was a "strategic withdrawal" to the north, which carried the great dreadnoughts far out of touch. Concerning this movement briefs have been filed both by British and American experts that ran in tone all the way from the bitter to the derisive. Both British and American critics have accused Jellicoe of running away. An American flag officer told this writer the wrong side got the better of the battle. Right here is where, and certainly as a result of this movement Jellicoe lost supreme command and Beatty succeeded to it.

Plenty has been said in defense of Jellicoe. He preferred to keep all that stood between the British empire and defeat in being as a potential menace, but if he had sailed in and won, the war would have been measurably nearer an end, the frightful issue decided two years earlier than it was.

As noted, the film did not picture this debatable maneuvre. It draws a veil over it. It ends with a picture of the King and an insert of his message to Jellicoe, in which he declares the Germans avoided the battle they had long prayed for, and so for purposes of propaganda the impression is perfectly created that the handling of the British Grand Fleet was all that it should be. From the King's statement it is inferentially evident why the Germans so criticised their own commander for failing to press the German advantage.

Furthermore, two more interesting points are left unexplained by this film. The Germans picked up British survivors after the contact in which the smoke screen was used. In the Skagerack, far to the north, German ships were sighted the following morning, June 1, by Danish lookouts. All this has been taken as presumptive evidence that the Germans followed the British all night and that Jellicoe retreated before them to the north, but the film neither asserts nor denies this.

For purposes of propaganda this is all right—in England. In England it is necessary to present that point of view; but in this country the exact truth, or nothing, should be presented, particularly in a theatre. The exact truth because this country is governed by popular vote; theatres and pictures form the opinions that direct those votes, and if they are wrongly directed, the country will suffer. The truth makes men free. It creates an intelligent body politic. It lessens mob rule.

Leed.

MOLLY O

Molly O.......................Mabel Normand
Tim O'Dair....................George Nichols
Mrs. Tim O'Dair...........Anna Hernandez
Billy O'Dair....................Albert Hackett
Jim Smith ....Eddie Gribbon
Dr. John S. Bryant...........Jack Mulhall
Fred Manchester............Lowell Sherman
Miriam Manchester........Jacqueline Logan
Albert Faulkner..................Ben Deely
Mrs. Jas. W. Robbins.....Gloria Davenport
The Silhouette Man.........Carl Stockdale
Antonio Bacigalupi.......Eugenie Besserer

A production that can be exploited into a box office attraction by the exhibitor. Not a whale of a picture, but one that is strong enough to permit of a campaign that will compel audiences to step up to the box office.

Mack Sennett is the producer and the picture has Mabel Normand, of "Mickey" fame, as the star. Sennett was also the producer of "Mickey," and it was a long while before that production got under way, for none of the regular releasing organizations of the time would take it, but finally when it was slipped over as a states right production it proved a veritable clean-up for those who took a chance.

"Molly O" was originally made for Associated Producers, but with the amalgamation of that organization and First National the latter stipulated that they were to have the right to accept or reject whatever they wished of the A. P.-made productions. They exercise the right to take "Molly O," and therefore it is being marketed as a First National picture.

It is on Broadway for a special run of four weeks at the Central theatre. The reason for that may be that the Strand, which is the First National franchise house, decided not to run the picture, or perhaps it may run it after the Broadway run has created a vogue for it. This seems rather doubtful, because the Central is only a stone's throw from the Strand and the most direct opposition to the big house.

The picture seems to have been chopped all to pieces as far as the last 1,500 feet are concerned. The fore part of the story is one of those sweet little Cinderella tales, somewhat of the "Irene" type, that is ended when the hero marries the little heroine, but in addition to this a couple of thousand feet have been tacked on that are totally unneeded.

It carries the story along after the marriage of the girl and the wealthy hero, and it is clipped in sections with the titles carrying the yarn. Incidentally that titling reflects credit on John Gray.

"Molly O" has the name role played by Mabel Normand, who is the daughter of a Tad family in a big town. Her dad is a day laborer, ma takes in washing to help along the cause, and Jim Smith has been picked to be Molly's hubby. He is a husky who works in the same ditch with dad. Molly, however, has other ideas, and she manages to capture the wealthiest young bachelor in town. He is a doctor, and they meet in a tenement where there is an infant ill. He takes her home in his car, and a few Sundays later they meet in church. He again takes her home and stays to Sunday dinner. Yes, a regular boiled one!

After it is all over, dad tells the wealthy young doc that he has been trying to raise a respectable family and that he'll be just as well satisfied if doc will forget the address.

But the church is giving a charity ball, and Molly steps in at the proper moment to lead the march with the young Prince (who is the doc) in place of the girl he is engaged to. The latter, who has been out on the balcony spooning with her real love and has missed the cue for the march, breaks off the engagement then and there, and Molly steps right in. But when she gets home that night dad is waiting for her with a strap and turns her out. She then turns to the doc, who marries her that night.

That logically should have been the finish of the picture, but the producer thought a few thrills were needed, and he padded out a few airship scenes and a couple of country club bits and little things like that. They weren't necessary at all, but they place the picture in the class of the big Drury Lane mellers, and as such will help the box office angle in the factory and tenement neighborhoods.

For the big houses it will be entertaining at that, for Mabel Normand does manage to get to the audience, for the role in the first part of the picture has lost none of the charm that the Cinderella theme ever has had.

F. Richard Jones, who directed "Mickey," is likewise responsible for "Molly O." There is nothing to rave about in direction in this picture and the photography hasn't a chance for medals, but the picture will get patronage. *Fred.*

FIGHTIN' MAD

Bud McGraw .... William Desmond
Peggy Hughes .... Virginia Brown Faire
Eileen Graham .... Doris Pawn
Nita de Carma .... Rosemary Theby
James McGraw .... Joseph J. Dowling
Francisco Lazaro .... William Lawrence
Howard Graham .... Emmett C. King
Amos Rawson .... Jack Richardson
Obadiah Brennan .... William J. Dyer
Micah Higgins .... Bert Lindley
Colonel Gates .... George Stanley
Captain Farley .... Vernon Snively

This Metro with William Desmond at the Rialto is a first-rate picture. Desmond's personality counts, H. H. Van Loan's story is straightaway and full of action, the climax gets you, and the photography is A-1. Joseph J. Franz directed.

Bud McGraw is sent to the border to enlist with the patrol, as he grows restless on his father's ranch. On the way he meets a girl under plausible and romantically exciting circumstances, and then hooks up in a fight, one, two, three, with his future cronies. From then on "Three Musketeers" stuff, "One for all, and all for one," making an amusing finale when the three kiss Bud's girl. Before then, in some convincing scenes, they save her from a Mex bandit, with a chase and a rescue along the approved lines.

Mr. Desmond's support is all satisfactory. The feature is a high-grade first run offering. *Leed.*

POVERTY OF RICHES

John Colby .... Richard Dix
Katherine Colby .... Leatrice Joy
Tom Donaldson .... John Bowers
Grace Donaldson .... Louise Lovely
Mrs. Holt .... Irene Rich
Lyons .... DeWitt Jennings
Stephen Phillips .... Dave Winter
Hendron .... Roy Laidlaw
Edward Phillips, Sr. .... John Cossar
John in prologue .... Frankie Lee
Katherine in prologue .... Dorothy Hughes

A woman denied the expression of maternal love is the basis of this feature, which takes as its theme the question of whether success in the form of business and social advancement is to be preferred to the wealth of a family with youngsters to clamber on one's knee and tiny hands and fingers to muss one's hair.

As a picture the feature will stand as one of those productions that can be handled either on a sensational scale—a sort of "Where Are My Children?" idea—or just as a feature that is slightly above the usual run of program features. Either way the picture is going to have its effect at the box office.

The Leroy Scott story, "Mother Love," was adapted to the screen by the author, and Reginald Barker was the directing force behind the filmization, and because of that "Poverty of Riches" carries the brand "A Reginald Barker Production" of Goldwyn release.

Ordinarily handled, the picture would have been just a program feature, but the manner in which the usual clinch is avoided at the finish, and the fact that the ending is not a happy one, pulls this from the rut of regular releases. Both story and direction are exceptional in those two particulars.

Richard Dix and Leatrice Joy, who play the leads, are first shown as children of about six years of age, boy and girl sweethearts. A brief prolog is employed for this purpose. Then they are shown on the day the heroine celebrates her twenty-first birthday. On the same day the hero is informed of his promotion in the iron works—the promotion that the pair have been waiting for that they might marry. With the promotion there comes the advice of the office manager that a young man owes it to himself to put up a front, appear a success if it takes his last penny, and the world will believe that he is successful. The hero takes this as his creed, and although his wife wishes for children to liven up their home, his attitude is that they must wait until they are on Easy Street.

When that time finally does arrive some four or five years later the wife is injured in an auto smash-up, and as a result of her injuries the possibility of a family is denied her.

Running parallel with the pictured life of this pair of people is that of another, the husband being a fellow employe. They have two children, and while they are not quite as materially successful, their existence is the happier in the end. The contrast is skilfully drawn and effectively shown on the screen.

The combination of Richard Dix and Leatrice Joy in the leading roles is a happy one. Dix has a leading role, which is almost a heavy, and therefore a difficult one for him, but he comes through with flying colors. Miss Joy is really a delight and acquits herself nobly. She has one of those speaking faces that are certain of success on the screen. John Bowers and Louise Lovely have the roles of the "other couple," handling them skilfully.

The balance of the cast is adequate and the photography and lightings excellent. *Fred.*

BAR NOTHIN'

Duke Travis .... Buck Jones
Bess Lynne .... Ruth Renick
Harold Lynne .... Wm. Buckley
Stinson .... Arthur Carew
Bill Harliss .... James Farley

A peach of a Western, Fox product starring Buck Jones, running 4,300 feet and every foot worth while. The story is by Jack Strumwasser and Clyde C. Westover, and the scenario by the former. Edward Sedgwick directed. Jones himself, with his faculty for seeming the real thing rather than an actor, stars for a fact, and the whole support pleased, Ruth Renick and Buckley particularly, which is one way of saying Arthur Carew was a satisfactory heavy.

The Lynnes have a valuable ranch which dishonest cattle people want. But rough and ready Duke comes to their rescue as foreman, sells their cattle, only to be lassoed and dragged to the desert. Meanwhile, the girl is persuaded he has run off with their money and is prevailed upon by Stinson to leave the country with her sick brother. Lost in the desert, Duke succeeds in roping a strayed horse, rides to the rescue, retakes the money, jumps from a bridge to the train and grabs Stinson. He jumps into the river, Duke after him. The fight can be imagined, with Duke getting the girl.

The best Western in an age. This Jones is a whale of a man, simple and natural besides, a genuine picture personality. *Leed.*

LADIES MUST LIVE

Christine Blecker .... Betty Compson
Anthony Mulvain .... Robert Ellis
Ralph Lincourt .... Mahlon Hamilton
Barbara .... Leatrice Joy
William Hollins .... Hardee Kirkland
Michael LePrim .... Gibson Gowland
The Gardener .... Jack Gilbert
Mrs. Barron .... Cleo Madison
Edward Barron .... Snitz Edwards
Nell Martin .... Lucille Hutton
Nora Flanagan .... Lule Warrenton
Max Blecker .... William Mong
The Butler .... Jack McDonald
Nancy .... Marcia Manon
Ned Klegg .... Arnold Gregg

Bearing in mind this is a Mayflower production, written and directed by George Loane Tucker, based on a novel by Alice Duer Miller, accepted for distribution by Paramount and shown at the Rivoli, it is undoubtedly the worst production offered the first run public in many a moon. It takes an interminable time to get started, at no time are you quite sure what it is all about, and it never proves its dimly apprehended point. Mr. Tucker, perhaps, had a moral in mind. Telling a story dramatically is what screen productions should do. What this picture might have had is a fashion display, but now that it is released all its fashions are out of date. Besides, the gowns are too low cut and in very bad taste.

What the production has is a cast. Betty Compson is named as star, but is lost in the shuffle, first honors going to Leatrice Joy. A minor characterization of an old roue always trying to buy women was superbly realized by Snitz Edwards, and the rest of the troupers are treated fairly enough when you say they did adequately with the absurdly conceived parts handed to them. Whatever Mrs. Miller wrote, it is doubtful her book is so full of caricature as this picture, which assumes society is made up of a lot of people who think of nothing but profitable marriages. This is the general assumption in "Ladies Must Live," but the story of it as told in the press book differs from the helterskelter tale told on the screen, arguing there was an orgy in the cutting room.

We see a little shop girl helped with $1,000 by the wealthy Lincourt. She is contrasted with poor little Nell, who is sent to jail because a man buys her a square meal. Once out, she gets a job as kitchen maid, but is pestered by the butler. The undergardener loves her, but refuses her, so she drowns herself. The body is carried into the living room and the scrubwoman points at all the well dressed women standing about and delivers herself of a series of moral precepts. Taking these to heart, these silk-gowned ladies all do the right thing forthwith. Before the tragedy an aeroplane has brought two men from the clouds to the house party.

Both are presumably wealthy, so the women set their traps for them. One of them is a roughneck, so grabs the lady he wants and rushes off with her in a motor, followed by Anthony and Christine. Anthony's idea is, of course, to prevent "the worst," but he has hard luck and ends up by having to spend the night in a mountain shack alone with Christine. At this point alarmed exhibitors will catch their breath—but no! The two come out as pure as they went in. In fact, there is enough purity in this film to suit a woman censor in Kansas—more than that, it is convincing. Who in this moral republic has sunk to low as not to believe that he (if he's a he) and she (if she's a she and beautiful as Betty Compson) would triumph over the promptings of evil if misfortune gripped them as it gripped these two young and noble souls in "Ladies Must Live."

However, while this picture may not suit the sophisticated, it is well to remember New York is not all America. In a country where novels by Harold Bell Wright sell to a million, "Ladies Must Live" may still make money—and the backwoods wonder what it's all about and if "sassiety" people are really like that. *Leed.*

ROUGH DIAMOND

Hank Sherman .... Tom Mix
Gloria Gomez .... Eva Novak
Manuel Garcia .... Sid Jordan
Pedro Sachet .... Edwin Brady
Emeliano Gomez .... Hector Sarno

In Tom Mix's latest Fox production, directed by Sedgwick, he perpetrates what is tantamount to a burlesque on his usual "Western" stuff. Although done seriously, with satirical, facetious sub-titles, it amounts to a take-off on the hackneyed plot of the gallant hero of the "Prisoner of Zenda" type who captures a throne and restores its former occupant to the highest office in the land, thereby winning for himself the beautiful princess. In this instance the mythical country is called Bargravia and is palpably meant for Mexico, with its revolutions and counter-revolutions.

It opens showing Mix working on a ranch—that is, he is being paid to work, but spends his time thrumming a home-made guitar. He is literally kicked off the place by the owner, taking with him his trick mule. Joining a circus, he once more meets the daughter of the deposed president of the aforesaid country, her father and her fiance, the latter a villain plotting to defeat the ex-president's efforts to win back his leadership and to steal the girl without giving the "old man" a look-in.

With the aid of his mule and a trick horse, Mix does a number of clever feats of horsemanship in the circus, is selected by the girl's father as the leader of his army bent on his restoration to the presidency, and Mix goes through a series of thrilling and romantic escapades before winning out for father and leading the girl to "the old hitching post."

Viewed from the standpoint of burlesque, the feature is very laughable, but there is a possibility that

Mix's admirers may resent his own refusal to take himself seriously, in which event the experiment might react on his future "dead straight" productions.

The cast, production, direction and lighting are on a par with Mix's other feature presentations. *Jolo.*

HUSH MONEY

Evelyn Murray ....Alice Brady
Alex. Murray ....George Fawcett
Bert Van Vleit..........Lawrence Wheat
Bishop Deems ....Harry Benham

"Hush Money" is a Realart production, written by Samuel Merwin, one of the leading short story writers of the day, and directed by Charles Maigne. It is a light story, but an interesting vehicle for Alice Brady, who wears some beautiful clothes and has an opportunity to prove that she can handle sentimental comedy neatly and convincingly.

The real star, however, is George Fawcett, who has a part made to order for his peculiar gifts as a character old man. Fawcett, who stands alongside Theodore Roberts in the portraiture of this type, plays one of those grouchy old boys whose bark is worse than his bite, and who always comes around after his tirades to agree that he is in the wrong and begs forgiveness. His part as the rich banker is an especially sympathetic and amusing one, and he gets all there is in it.

The cast is small and the story told simply and straightforwardly, but the production has been handled painstakingly. The backgrounds, most of them interiors in the heroine's luxurious home, are unostentatiously rich but still convincing. The usual studio attempts to picture modern palaces of the wealthy look just what they are, a make-believe film setting. These look real. The whole production has the air of genuine elegance. The acting is natural, easy and appropriate to the ensemble.

The story has to do with the adventures of Evelyn Murray, daughter of a sort of J. Pierpont. Driving in the city with her fiance, she runs over a waif named "Pipe" McGuire. The man insists that she run away and avoid arrest. She consents, but a garage mechanic learns what has happened and blackmails her father. The newspapers report that "Pipe" has been taken to the hospital badly hurt, but father forbids her to go to his aid, as she wants to do. Father has contributed a large sum to a church memorial to be devoted to settlement work, and Bishop Deems preaches a sermon on social service and the selfishness of the rich, while stirs Evelyn's conscience.

She appeals to the bishop with her troubled conscience, and he recommends that she go to the hospital and do what she can for her unintentional victim. Father learns of this development and berates her. So does Bert, the fiance. Evelyn breaks her engagement and runs away from home, taking refuge with the bishop and devoting herself to helping "Pipe" through his illness. For this the banker revokes his gift to the memorial.

Crusty old father misses the girl sadly and appeals to the bishop to find and restore her to his lonely home, but Evelyn holds out until dad comes to her terms, which are that he reinstate the gift to the church (more hush money) and live more unselfishly. Bert is also re-established as betrothed on condition that he receive "Pipe" into the family and be more human thereafter. All of which makes a satisfactory ending, with the Lady Bountiful in the middle of the picture and dad, the benevolent Santa Claus, looking on. *Rush.*

SHAMS OF SOCIETY

Helen Porter............Barbara Castleton
Herbert Porter..............Montagu Love
Milton Howard.............Macey Harlam
Mrs. Crest............Julia Swayne Gordon
Mama Manning...............Anne Brody
The Manning Sister........Gladys Feldman
Lucille Lee............Lucille Lee Stewart
Judge Harrington...........Edwards Davis
Reggie Frothingham.........Victor Gilbert

Robertson-Cole present a six-part photoplay, "Shams of Society"; story by Walter McNamara, scenario by Kenneth O'Hara and Mary Murillo, directed by Thomas B. Walsh. It is a pretentious affair, marred by several inconsistencies, despite an admirable cast, excellent direction, an elaborate scenic and sartorial investiture and splendid photography.

The story is somewhat involved, designed to teach a strong moral lesson. The principal situation is far-fetched, if not altogether unlikely. It purports to show that our so-called society is not the thing to be coveted, as it demands a hectic existence not founded on true happiness and genuine home life.

For the proletariat it reveals the inner workings of social life as something to be avoided instead of being coveted, and by such will be talked about, which makes for word-of-mouth advertising for the picture.

Barbara Castleton has a highly emotional role; Montagu Love is depicted as an impressive man of wealth; Macey Harlam, apparently a libertine, is in reality one of "nature's noblemen"; Julia Swayne Gordon is interesting as a hanger-on on the fringe of society, and the remainder of the cast all contribute to the generally good effect.

While the story will not stand the test of critical analysis, the production makes for pretentious program picture entertainment. *Jolo.*

THE SINGLE TRACK

Corinne Griffith, with Richard Travers as her leading man, manages to drive home this combination society and Northwest meller in great shape. The production is a Vitagraph release that was played this week as part of a double feature bill at Loew's New York. Splitting the bill with Betty Compson, another ingenue star, comparison of the work of the two was inevitable, with all of the honors going to Miss Griffith.

Miss Griffith, insofar as screen looks and acting ability are concerned, topped Miss Compson fully a hundred per cent.

She has the role of a society flapper who has never had a day of care in her life. At the time that the story opens she is in the midst of the season's round of gaiety. At that time, however, her guardian informs her that her income is practically nil and will remain so unless a project in Alaska comes through for the estate. The copper mines that they hold there have been worked out, but a new vein has been discovered about 40 miles further inland, and if the managers of the mines can complete a railroad to the new fields within a set period all will be well again. However, a rival company is offering strong opposition.

The girl, showing that despite all of her society associations she is still a chip of the old block, decides to go north to watch the working of the roadbuilding personally, although under an assumed name. She becomes a clerk in the company's store "in the field" and there meets with the engineer in charge.

Through her manipulation of one of the rival faction she manages to see that the job is completed on time, personally driving a locomotive over the road on a ride to rescue at the last minute, and when she has saved the day she reveals her identity. The love affair that has developed between her and the engineer comes to a happy conclusion in time for the fadeout.

The picture is well directed and contains a goodly number of meller thrills that will please any audience.

In the society stuff that takes up the greater part of the first reel Miss Griffith does a Salome that is an entirely new conception of what the dance is, but as she concludes it with a touch that gets a laugh, it can be passed up without criticism. She does look like a million dollars' worth of beauty at all times. Mr. Travers was a handsome and satisfying lead opposite her. *Fred.*

BONNIE BRIER BUSH

Lachlan Campbell............Donald Crisp
Flora Campbell, his daughter..Mary Glynne
Lord Malcolm Hay............Alec Fraser
Kate Carnegie...............Dorothy Fane
Posty..............................Jack East
John Carmichael........Langhorne Burton
Earl of Kinspindle......Jerrold Robertshaw
Marget Howe...........Mrs. Hayden-Coffin
Dr. William MacClure..Humbertson Wright

A screen version of Ian MacLaren's famous story adapted from the plays from the same source by James McArthur and Augustus Thomas and done by Famous Players-Lasky British Productions, Ltd., under the direction of Donald Crisp, is another admirable production in the same vein of sincerity as that other Scotch tale, "Tommy and Grisel," and on the showing of its opening day at the Rivoli last Sunday likely to meet the same sort of lukewarm reception. Sunday evening, with weather conditions all against attendance, the theatre was less than half filled at the early show. Business in the other houses was off, but not to the same extent. The State, for example, with "The Sheik," drew sturdily.

Here is a situation that seems to typify the artistic standards of film fans. "The Sheik," probably as trashy a screen story as has been screened by a representative producer in half a year, attracts them to the box office, and a screening of one of the tenderest and most beautiful idyllic tales in modern fiction goes neglected. If it is true that "the people get as good government as they deserve," it probably goes double that the fans get as good pictures as they want. The facts speak for themselves—they want "The Sheik" and they don't want "Tommy and Grisel," and probably "Beside the Bonnie Brier Bush."

The new production deserves a better fate. It is a fine translation from the printed page to the celluloid of an exquisite tale. Ian MacLaren's warm humorous character sketches come nearer to being alive on the screen than usually happens when familiar personages of fiction are filtered through the camera lens; the backgrounds are notably lovely, the picture having been made in the real Scotch hills, and the main thread of the story has been plainly and simply told. From first to last the quaint characters are played with utmost sincerity. There is not a false note in the production.

The book must have presented an embarrassment of riches to the scenario writer. Dr. MacClure, who was the outstanding figure of the novel, plays but a minor role in the film production, a shadowy shape that must have suffered severely in the cutting. Perhaps some day some one will make another picture with the rugged country doctor as its central figure. In this version there was no chance to stray aside for incidental character portraits. Margaret Turnbull, who made the adaptation, held closely to the romantic part of the original—the love story of Lord Malcolm and Flora, the humble shepherd's daughter—and the human oddities of the Scotch village merely passed in silhouette. Posty Macduff and John Carmichael appeared only as shadows of their real selves, but Lachlan Campbell, the stubborn father of Flora, was etched in with a good deal of care. Played by Crisp, it is a convincing bit of delineation. The scene between the dour old man and his daughter upon their reconciliation was a touching moment, a moment of honest sentiment that seldom comes upon the silver sheet where sentiment is too often maudlin.

The Scotch locale is refreshing to Americans, who have about been fed up on native locations. Some of the woodland meadow and village vistas are very beautiful. Even in the interiors of castle, cottage and "kirk" deliver real, convincing "atmosphere."

As a plain bald story the picture is trifling. It is only its deft touches that make it notable. The narrative structure is just conventional English fiction. The lowly Flora falls in love with the heir of "the castle folk," who returns her love, while the scheming Earl plans a rich marriage for his son. The woman the Earl picks is in love with the village minister and aids the young lord after many trials to wed the woman of his real choice. The time is two decades ago, and the period and place gives opportunity for a touch of picturesque costume. The wedding scene at the end has the women in crinolines and the men in kilts, with a small regiment of pipers on hand to furnish music for the wedding, which makes the happy climax. *Rush.*

CALL OF NORTH

Ned Trent..........................Jack Holt
Virginia Albret..............Madge Bellamy
Galen Albret....................Noah Beery
Achille Picard...........Francis McDonald
Graham Stewart.........Edward Martindel
Elodie Albret..............Helen Ferguson
Louis Placide...................Jack Herbert

Jack Holt makes his bow on Broadway this week as a film star, being presented at the Rialto by Jesse Lasky in the Paramount production, "The Call of the North." The picture is not likely to pull a great many first run contracts for the Holt starring series, for while a fairly interesting tale of the northwest, it has naught about it unusual or compelling from the box office standpoint.

"The Call of the North" is based on the Stewart Edward White story, "Conjurer's House," which was adapted as a play by George Broadhurst. Jack Cunningham adapted the story to the screen and Joseph Henabery directed.

There is a brief prolog, showing the manner in which the factors of the Hudson Bay Co. were wont to treat the trade invaders of their territory. They were usually attacked somewhere in the uncharted wilds and left without food or means of reaching the settlements. Usually they welcomed death when it overtook them in the snow wastes. In such manner did the father of the hero meet his end, and years later the son, following out an oath which he swore at the time he heard of his father's death, is also a free trader in the wilds trying to track down his father's murderer. He is also taken in hand by the chief official of the H. B. Co., the same man who caused his dad to be sent into the beyond, but in the case of the younger man a love affair develops between him and the factor's daughter, and the girl is the final means in saving him. Interesting in a mild way, but in the main weak when compared to other northwest thrillers.

Jack Holt plays the young hero. Madge Bellamy, who played the ingenue lead opposite the star, had little to recommend her for that distinction. Noah Beery and Edward Martindale were easily the outstanding characters, and the former especially seemed to walk away with the honors.

If the rental price is right the picture will do for the houses that do not play productions a full week. This is scarcely a feature of sufficient calibre for a full week's run.
Fred.

CHIVALROUS

Charley Riley..............Eugene O'Brien
His Uncle.................George Fawcett
Alice Sanderson............Nancy Deaver
Her Father.................D. J. Flanagan
Geoffrey Small.............Huntley Gordon

Clean, romantic melodrama, culminating in a hoax, is "Chivalrous Charley," a Selznick picture starring Eugene O'Brien. It was written by May Tully, scenarized by Edward Montagne and directed by Robert Ellis.

Charley Riley (O'Brien) is a romantic young man with a penchant for helping females in distress. His uncle, a politician, endeavors to cure him by framing up something that will teach him a lesson he is not likely soon to forget. The audience, however, is not let into the secret until the finish, which comes as a surprise denouement.

A dainty miss, fleeing from pursuers, makes her way into his apartment, remains all night, her supposed father arrives in the morning, points a revolver at him and demands that Charley protect the girl's honor by marrying her. (No provision is made for the marriage license.) After the ceremony the "wife" tells him a harrowing tale of persecution of her and her brother, who was lured into embezzling from a man who wants to marry her, and Charley gives her a check for $5,000 to repay the embezzlement. Later he receives a telegram telling him to call at a dilapidated house in the slums, where he is held captive. He fights a gang of "thugs," has a series of thrilling adventures calculated to hold any audience spellbound, is finally rounded up at his uncle's home, and then learns of the deception practiced upon him.

Meantime he is hurt to find the girl is a party to the hoax and appeased to find she really loves him. A fine stellar role for O'Brien; a dainty, witching part for Nancy Deaver as the young miss, with the remainder of the supporting characters in such capable hands as George Fawcett as the uncle, and so on.

The entire production exudes romantic action of the ultra-modern school, the footage is not prolonged one moment longer than necessary and when the surprise twist comes at the finish the audience is not annoyed by being fooled. A satisfactory program feature.
Jolo.

DR. JIM

Dr. Jim Keene...............Frank Mayo
Helen Keene.................Claire Windsor
Kenneth Ford...............Oliver Cross
Bobby Thorne...............Stanhope Wheatcroft
Tom Anderson...............Robert Anderson
Captain Blake..............Gordon Sackville

An unusually good Universal with photography of the exceptional sort credited to L. L. Lancaster. Stuart Paton's story and Eugene B. Lewis' scenario are satisfactory, and William Worthington's direction way above the program average. A clean picture for all classes, it strikes a high average. Frank Mayo and Olla Cronk, she of the lustrous hair and wonderfully clear-cut features, lend distinction to the acting, but the support is all capable.

The story deals with a young doctor's devotion to his child patients and his efforts to hold his butterfly wife. The action moves steadily and with a gathering interest up to a storm at sea, caught with considerable actuality and made very effective.

An unusually good Universal, worth booming.
Leed.

THE LOTUS EATERS

Jacques Lenol..............John Barrymore
Mavis.....................Colleen Moore
Madge Vance...............Anna Q. Nilsson
Mrs. Hastings Vance........Ida Waterman
The Dean..................Frank Currier
John Carson...............J. Barney Sherry
Jocko.....................Wesley Barry

This is offered at the Capitol this week by First National. Marshall Neilan directed. John Barrymore (with his hair curled) stars, and is ably supported. The whole is based on a story by Albert Payson Terhune. Despite these names, there's nothing exceptional to the picture. It aims at satire and falls short of it with the result it will probably satisfy no one. The general public will be vaguely dissatisfied by the barbed humor pricking their bubble of romance.

Jacques Lenol reaches the age of twenty-five without knowing a woman, due to an unpleasantness in his father's life, and so when finally he lands from the yacht he has inherited he falls for the first fair one he sees. This girl he marries, only to learn his income is cut for marrying before thirty. With a dissatisfied wife on his hands, he sets out on a mad ballooning expedition to China and lands on an isle in the Pacific. A bit of detail here alleging the over-world winds would aid a flight to China is a mistake. The winds blow the other way, toward us.

On this isle all is peace and plenty, every one does as he pleases, there is no money, and all is pure and holy. But Jacques longs for home and his frivolous wife, turning an unappreciative eye on the cutie in Greek costume close at hand. So they let him go back. In New York he finds friend wife has married a wealthier man. She must choose which husband she wants. Choosing a third, she elopes, and back goes Jacques to the isle of plenty of everything, including booze.

The most interesting thing about this picture is Barrymore and his performance. With long hair, it seems to the observer he must be offering a caricature of the old-type Shakespearean trouper, the kind who took himself and his "art" all too seriously. If not a caricature, the cynical fellow who began to show the beginnings of real ability will be missed, and what is offered in his place will be judged with the slight resentment of those who miss the expected.
Leed.

SIR ARNE'S TREASURE

"Sir Arne's Treasure" is the picturization of a story by Selma Lagerlof, made by the Swedish Biograph Co. of Stockholm, with Mary Johnson ("Sweden's Sweetheart") and Richard Lund as the stars. The picture has for its period and locale the Sweden of 350 years ago. It is quite possible the feature has been cut to conform to American regulation lengths and that in the process of excision much in the way of explanatory progression has been deleted. It was made two years ago **and directed by Mauritz Stiller.**

Judged wholly on what was offered at the Town Hall, Nov. 26, "Sir Arne's Treasure" is a fine production, well photographed and acted, interesting by reason of its difference from native output. It was offered as part of a specimen program of an entire evening's entertainment, which included scenics, educationals, a comedy and folk songs admirably sung by a Swedish prima donna. In Swedish communities in the northwest such an entertainment might prove successful, but the remainder of our populace would probably regard it as tiresome.

Sir Halmar, a fiery young man, is among the prisoners locked up for conspiring against the reigning king. With two others he escapes, and is shown deliberately assassinating Sir Arne and his entire family for robbery. The mysterious treasure chest of Sir Arne is mentioned in the sub-titles, but no explanation of its origin is vouchsafed. Again Sir Arne's wife is shown to be a psychic, merely by her having a vision of the impending murder, with no further mention of the subject.

The only member of the Arne family who escapes is little Elsa, grand-daughter of Sir Arne. She is taken in by a kindly fisherman's family, falls in love with her and the feeling is reciprocated. One night Elsa dreams that her murdered sister has led her to the kitchen of the local inn. Next day she haunts the tavern, where she overhears one of the assassins say: "Drink, Sir Halmar; make merry. We are not at the end of Sir Arne's treasure yet." Elsa tells her story to the scullery woman, who notifies the authorities; but Elsa repents denouncing the man she loves and runs to warn him to escape, to which he replies: "You betrayed me, giving me no chance to atone," and casts her away from him. She begs him to flee; the police arrive at the house; Sir Halmar uses Elsa's body as a shield and fights his way through them, she being stabbed to death.

The ship by which Sir Halmar was to have escaped is the only vessel that continues to be icebound, and the captain narrates a superstition that this is due to the fact that it is inhabited by an evil-doer. Sir Halmar has carried the body of the girl to his cabin in the vessel; the captain, on hearing of the whole affair, has Sir Halmar cast ashore; the titled murderer says: "It is God's will that we should pay the penalty of our crimes," is taken away by the police. the sea immediately opens and permits the vessel to depart.

They are a sad-looking people, these Swedes, with no joy in their faces; but they are most expressive in pantomime, so that there is necessity for fully one-half less sub-titles than Americans would employ to put over the same ideas. The conclusion must be arrived at that it is not for us.
Jolo.

FOR THOSE WE LOVE

This is a Betty Compson production released by Goldwyn with Miss Compson as the star. It was the last production Miss Compson turned out with her own producing unit. The reason that this was the final production the star made in the role of producer is easily apparent to those that view it. It is without doubt one of the most incoherent stories that has been screened in a long, long time.

Miss Compson has a corking company supporting her, which includes Lon Chaney and others of equal note, but even they cannot pull the picture through. Incidentally the cast also holds Walter Morosco.

The three Rossons were also active in the production of the picture, one as director, another brother in the cast and the third as camera man. The experiment of shooting the greater part of the feature in soft focus did not enhance the value of the picture.

The story is laid in a small town, with the principal characters being the sweet girl, her brother and father. This little trio all live together. Father is the bookkeeper in the sash factory, the boy is a pool room hanger-on who also likes to play stud, and the girl just keeps house. At the opening of the story the girl is rescued from the swimmin' hole by the town gambler, and after that he just naturally sticks around.

The brother gets cleaned in the Saturday night stud game and then goes home to turn off his old man for $80. That eighty is the whole story. As the result of the theft the father goes blind, the girl gets in bad with the town folks, for she is seen on Sunday to enter the stag hotel where the gambler lives to get the dough back, and the boy is accused of the theft of the money and in the end when he is accompanying the gambler and another hanger-on in the town to turn off the dive keeper he is shot and killed.

In the end the sap lover of the girl, who flopped on her while she was in trouble, finally wins her despite the fact that the gambler who stood the gaff and made it possible for her to win out is turned down. That part of the picture, at any rate, is almost true to life. How often do women turn on the men that are responsible for their success and pass them up in their hour of need for someone that cannot do a thing for them.

Trying to make the picture effective, the director took a chance at shooting everything in sight, even to a burning house to add a little pep to the production, but even that didn't help. There was also a speak-easy where you could get "it," but the comedy chances of this scene were entirely passed up.

The direction was draggy and wearisome from beginning to end and it did not move the story forward at all. There was an attempt to get the yarn over with titles, but these titles were such that they only made more of a puzzle of the story than the action itself.

This is a good one to pass up, except when one can make use of the Compson name at a price for a double feature bill.
Fred.

SCHOOL DAYS

Spec Brown	Wesley Barry
His Guardian	Geroge Lessey
His Friend	Francis X. Conlon
His Friend's Wife	Nellie P. Spalding
His Teacher	Margaret Seddon
His Sweetheart	Arline Blackburn
His Dog	"Rippy"
The Stranger	J.H. Gilmour
Mr. Hadley	John Galsworth
Mr. Wallace	Jerome Patrick
Miss Wallace	Eveline Sherman
The Valet	Arnold Lucy

In "School Days," an eight-reel film production based on the vaudeville playlet by Gus Edwards, Warner Bros. have turned out a screen story worthy of a verse creation by James Whitcomb Riley in its spirit of spontaneous, sympathetic humor. It promises to be the making of its young star, Wesley Barry, of the snub nose and opulent freckles, and the author, William Nigh, particularly, and in general of everybody concerned in its production.

The picture had an invitation preview at the Hotel Astor Dec. 1. The title is practically all that survives from the stage piece. William Nigh and Walter De Leon have written an original story around the school room bit, although the presentation is accomplished by a reproduction of the act with ten youngsters in a singing and dancing specialty, using the same children who appear in the film, accompanied by Margaret Seddon as the teacher.

Wesley Barry is featured by arrangement with Marshal Neilan. The novelty programs for the preview describe the film as produced by Harry Rapf, and directed by William Nigh, the scenario writer.

The film is a really notable achievement in development of effective, intelligent comedy and genuine sentiment. These two elements should carry it alone, and in addition it has extraordinary beauty of natural scenic background and astonishingly good acting by a score or more of youngsters from 8 to 14 years.

The one jarring note of the production is a defect in the story. It starts in the humble surroundings of a country school and shifts to the homes of wealth in an exclusive suburb of New York. There are two distinct stories, and the merging of interest is not well managed. This, however, is a minor shortcoming. The fine sentiment, the natural comedy, and the splendid sincerity of spirit that pervades the whole thing outweigh any other consideration.

The appeal of the poor country orphan boy is invincible. He is a sort of twin brother to Cinderella. Done by Young Barry, all the innate pathos and humor of the character is realized a hundred per cent. The picture has been drawn by Nigh in a tender spirit of fun, and the direction carries out the conception in an appropriate vein of unaffected sincerity. Nothing could be more touching than the parting of "Speck" and his dog "Hippy," and the reunion is quite as moving a passage. It would be a hard-boiled fan that could sit through some of these passages without moisture in the eyes. But there is always a sympathetic smile behind the shadow of a tear. This elusive quality of humor is the highest attainment of the picture art, and in this picture it has rare expression.

"Speck" is the country orphan boy farmed out by the asylum to a hard taskmaster in The Deacon, who overworks and mistreats him. He is a mischievous kid and gets himself in wrong with the school teacher by his pranks. The Deacon threatens to send him back to the asylum if he doesn't attend to his chores and his schooling, but just then a stranger appears on the scene to rescue him. "Speck" is invited to lunch in the mansion with the stranger, who turns out to be his uncle. Uncle, it appears, left the village when he was a youngster, deserting his sweetheart to seek wealth in the city. He got the wealth, but now lonely age is upon him and the wealth seems futile. Therefore he sends Speck to the city to learn that money is not all. In town, under the protection of Uncle's rich attorney, "Speck" comes in contact with fashionable kids who snub him properly and make him long for his old country pals.

When the lesson has been driven home that education is necessary to making his way in the world, "Speck" runs away from the city, back to the simple country, and the moral is complete. Upon this bare skeleton there is built a splendid story structure with convincing character drawing and interesting incidents that will keep any audience of youngsters and grownups absorbed. It's a safe prophecy that the picture will develop into a memorable one of the year. *Rush.*

QUEENIE

Queenie	Shirley Mason
Vivian	George O'Hara
Simon Pepper	Wilson Hummell
Quigley	Wilson Hummell
Aunt Pansy	Aggie Herring
Mrs. Mulliken	Lydia Titus
Mrs. Torrence	Clarissa Selwynee

The Fox feature with Shirley Mason starred is another irritating mixture of farce and melodrama. The story is by Wilbur Finley Fauley, and should have been either one thing or the other, preferably melodrama with comic trimmings. But this may be the fault of the scenario writer, Dorothy Yost. Howard M. Mitchell directed effectively, and George Schneiderman's photography was way above the average, very clear and very charming in its effects.

Queenie is a little girl dependent upon her aunt's charity. This same aunt she believes to be enormously wealthy, discovering she is only housekeeper for the eccentric millionaire, Simon Pepper, who closely resembles his butler, Quigley. The night he disappears Queenie wins his affection. Believing him dead, Quigley assumes his role and marries Aunt Pansy, but Pepper returns, unmasks the butler and saves Queenie from an unhappy marriage. The dual role was well taken by Wilson Hummell.

Two good women character parts got right over in the hands of Aggie Herring and Lydia Titus. As the young poet, George O'Hara appeared to be doing an imitation of Harold Lloyd.

Fair entertainment only. *Leed.*

ALL FOR A WOMAN

George Jacques Danten	Emil Jennings
Maximilian Roberspierre	Werner Kraus
St. Just	Robert Sholz
Camille Desmoulins	Joseph Rumich
Lucille, his wife	Charlotte Ander
Yvonne	Maly Deiscoft
Herault de Sechellus	Ferdinand Alter
General Westerman	Edouard Winterstein
Fouquier Tinville, public prosecutor	Frederick Kuhn
Henriot	Hugo Dublin
Little Babette	Hilda Worner

The acute crisis in the history of France—1793—the days of the bloody Revolution—are picturized in "All for a Woman," written and directed by Dimitri Buchowetzki, with Emil Jannings in the leading role, produced in Germany under the title, "Danton," edited for this country by Julian Johnson, and subtitled by Randolph Bartlett. It is presented here by Andrew J. Callaghan as a First National release.

Like its predecessors of German origin, "All for a Woman" is a massive production, and it is no exaggeration to go much farther by declaring it stupendous. Countless experienced actors have been employed to mingle with the mobs to secure "action" such as has probably never been seen before in a film production.

The biggest and most effective scene is a trial chamber with the tribunal in session, giving a "hearing" to four important personages of the French Revolution who have been arrested on warrants. At one end of a large auditorium is the judges' table, the accused stand in a "dock" in the centre, and at the other end a high gallery of perhaps 50 or 60 feet peopled by the proletariat clamoring for blood. Close-ups of the gallery reveal a spontaneity of "action" that is vivid to the verge of uncanniness.

The story of the photoplay is a phase of the Revolution—the tragic quarrel between Danton and Robespierre, the former the idol of the people, sympathetic and human, seeking to end the bloodshed of the guillotine, the latter cold, cruel, implacable.

At the opening Danton and Robespierre are at loggerheads, the latter constantly undermining Danton in his absence by intimating Danton is an enemy of the people, following it up with such suggestions as "If the Republic is to live, its enemies must die."

Disheartened by the constant thirst for bloodshed, Danton goes to the Palais Royale in search of recreation, there picks up a grisette, takes her to his home, has her bathed and cleanly dressed against her will, there to amuse himself, as was the fashion of the times. Camille Desmoulins, the poet, shared Danton's house, and on his way home rescues Lucille, the only survivor of an aristocratic family. He tells her that her only safety lies in marrying a "citizen," and offers her the protection of his name. Lucille becomes physically attracted to Danton through the sheer force of her character, and he treats her with the deference due a lady. Babette, the grisette, jealously protests against the homage Danton pays to Lucille, and Danton throws Babette out.

Babette denounces Danton to Robespierre for harboring an aristocrat, and the icy Robespierre employs this as a weapon to build up a barrier between Danton and the populace, culminating in Danton's arrest, trial and execution. During the trial Lucille enters the chamber, betrays herself, is seized and also convicted.

The four convicted men are called for execution—Westerman, de Sechelles, Desmoulins and Danton. Desmoulins is a physical coward and shrinks at the ordeal. Danton goes to him, looks into his eyes, braces his shoulders and imparts to the weakling the requisite courage to face the knife. When Danton is called Lucille throws herself into his arms and they indulge in their first and last kiss. As the executioners seek to tie Danton's hands behind him prior to dropping the knife on his neck he brushes them aside, crying: "Save the rope for Robespierre. Show my head to the people. It is well worth while."

Replete with romance, the story is gruesome in the extreme, but as a photoplay it stands alone. Dozens of character bits are employed, with the principals, headed by the inimitable Emil Jannings, proving themselves an assemblage of artists. This despite their Teutonic nativity, which is apparent in their features, and the consequent handicap in depicting the requisite French temperament. *Jolo.*

WALLINGFORD

J. Rufus Wallingford	Sam Hardy
"Blackie" Daw	Norman Kerry
Eddie Lamb	Edgar Nelson
Fannie Jasper	Doris Kenyon
Dorothy Wells	Billie Dove
G. W. Battles	W. T. Hays
Hon. Tim Battles	Horace James
Judge Lampton	Jerry Sinclair
Richard Wells	John Woodford
Gertrude Dempsey	Diana Allen
Mrs. Dempsey	Mrs. Charles Willard
Abe Gunther	William Robyns
Bessie	Patterson Dial
Mr. Dempsey	Mac M. Barnes
Harkins	Eugene Keith
Beilboy	Theodore Westman, Jr.
Mr. Quigg	William Carr
Wallingford's Valet	Benny One

Taken from George Cohan's legitimate stage production of the same name, Famous Players has produced a program feature of considerable merit. It includes abundant entertainment, as evidenced by the way received at the Rivoli, Sunday. Luther Reed provided the scenario for the screen version of this Wallingford episode. He has succeeded in laying out a series of scenes that builds up interest, secures all the comedy possible out of the story and it closes minus the usual "clinch" finish.

It's a type picture which Frank Borzage, who directed, has taken advantage of, resulting in several additional laughs through various bits of "business" before the camera allotted to the supporting cast that should go on record as on a par with the "rube" characters that inhabited Griffith's "Way Down East." Chester Lyons did the cranking and turned in a corking piece of work, while Joseph Urban is credited as having designed the settings. They called for nothing of the pretentious style until the conclusion. That allows for the "millionaire" house party and the extreme clothes of the "hit and run" boys, J. Rufus and "Blackie" Daw, taking a night view of the city they have built up.

The story, the most familiar of the Wallingford series, is laid in a "hick" village in Iowa, where the two promoters migrate, framing a corporation to manufacture carpet tacks which will match the material covering the floor. The proposition carries itself along until it looks like a bad jam for the high finance due, when the breaks start to come their way and the circumstances make the phoney business deal turn out on the level with all the prominent citizens of the town, who were on the ledger to be hooked, cleaning up and making a hero out of Wallingford, with he and his sidekick marrying two girls of the metropolis besides.

Sam Hardy, as Wallingford, put across a capital performance. If he can follow it up, Mr. Hardy seems likely to procure for himself a following among the picture goers, especially the fair sex. He lends plenty of personality to the screen, registers well, and if this work is any criterion will make a strong bid for honors as a light comedian of drawing power. Excellent support has aided materially in putting the picture across, with Norman Kerry, Edgar Nelson, Horace James and Doris Kenyon each making his or her bits stand out a bit more prominently than the rest.

There's little doubt this Wallingford film will connect. It's clean, wholesome, holds plenty of comedy, and with Hardy and his support contributing one of the best collective performances recently viewed, approval is bound to follow, but if there are any more of the episodes to come it's going to be tough to follow this one. *Skig.*

OUR MUTUAL FRIEND

Bella Wilfer	Catherine Reese
John Rokesmith	Peter Walton
Eugene Wrayburn	Albert Fenton
Mortimer Lightwood	Elvin Milton
Gaffer Hexam	Peter Anderson
Gaffer Hexam's Daughter	Katherine Casper
Rogue Riderhood	Evan Rostrup
"Ma" Boffin	Joan Nethersole
"Pa" Boffin	Alfred Miller
Mr. Venus	Charles Wilkens
Silas Wegg	Bertram Cross
"Pa" Wilfer	Charles Withey

At the Lyric, New York, in its second and final week, is the filmization of the last of the Charles Dickens novels, "Our Mutual Friend." Wid Gunning is presenting the picture, which is being released by his distributing company. He has had the house under lease for four weeks, first presenting "What Men Want" and following it by the Dickens film. Neither did much at the box office.

From a picture standpoint this film, which was made in Scandinavia by the Nordisk company, has some very fine points. It holds presentations of Dickens characters that are done wonderfully; its photography is likewise good and its titles make the story an interesting one even to those who do not profess to be followers of the works of the English author. It is a fairly good program production that will get past with the majority of film audiences, but there is one thing that might have been improved upon from a technical standpoint and that is the cutting of the film. In spots this feature is very jumpy and the action naturally suffers.

To those that are devotees of Dickens the film will undoubtedly be a rare treat, and the Dickens societies all over the country if gone after will undoubtedly support the picture wherever it is shown.

A complete cast of the players is available for this foreign made picture, a fact that is most unusual in itself.

However, there is no director named and therefore credit for some of the real work in the making of the production will have to go without name. Of the leading players Catherine Reese, an exceedingly pretty blonde ingenue of the Swedish type, played the role of Bella Wilfer perfectly, and Peter Walton gave John Rokesmith a really worth while characterization. The comedy characters such as "Ma" and "Pa" Boffin, Silas Wegg, Mr. Venus and "Pa" Wilfer were given their full value by Joan Nethersole, Alfred Miller, Charles Wilkens, Bertram Cross and Charles Withey respectively.

No credit is given for the titling, but the work to a large extent was done by Roy McCardell in this country. He is a New York newspaper man and writer of humorous stories as well as a scenario writer.

"Our Mutual Friend," while in no sense a special, certainly gives proof that the foreign producers can turn out pictures that for settings and atmosphere will make some of the American film makers step, and this picture, while it won't set the world afire, will undoubtedly be a money maker for the distributor and perhaps for the exhibitors. *Fred.*

THE LADY FROM LONGACRE

Sir Anthony Conway	William Russell
Isabel	Mary Thurman
Molly	Mary Thurman
King Pedro	Jean de Briac
Count de Freitas	Francis Ford

This is a Fox offering with William Russell starred. Victor Bridges' story and Paul Schofield's scenario give Mr. Russell plenty of chance to shine, but the offering itself after going three-quarters of the way loses ground because it shifts from melodrama that is convincing to farce that is less so. George E. Marshall directed competently, though he was inclined to let the actors assuming society roles handle those parts in burlesque. This detracts. Thugs and the well-born are the same in one respect at least: They are natural, because they have no reason to be otherwise, and naturalness is as effective dramatically as a ridiculous assumption of false dignity.

Sir Anthony is a young Englishman who rescues a girl giving the name of Isabel from some foreigners who are molesting her. Later he learns she is Princess Isabel of Livadia, who, to unite the royal factions in her own country and bring peace, is being forced to marry King Pedro. In exile the King has married Molly Moncke, the soubret, and so hesitates also to espouse Princess Isabel. Sir Anthony straightens it all out by substituting one for the other. They look enough alike. Thus he frees Isabel and she marries him.

Mary Thurman assumed the dual lead, distinguishing the two characters cleverly and yet leaving them alike. As de Freitas, Francis Ford did the most effective work of all.

The whole is fair entertainment for Russell fans. *Leed.*

FOOL'S PARADISE

Poll Patchouli	Dorothy Dalton
Rosa Duchene	Mildred Harris
Arthur Phelps	Conrad Nagel
John Roderiguez	Theodore Kosloff
Prince Talaat-Noi	John Davidson
Samaran, his chief wife	Julia Faye
Manuel	Clarence Burton
Briggs	Guy Oliver
Kay	Kamuela Searles
Girda	Jacqueline Logan

Jesse Lasky presented the Cecil B. DeMille production, "Fool's Paradise," at the Criterion, Dec. 9. As a "special" it is that in every sense of the word; as a production it speaks of unlimited expenditure in the making; as an entertainment it is wonderfully satisfying, and it should stand up with anything that DeMille has done heretofore as a box office attraction.

The Criterion run is to establish the picture, and if that $1.50 top, with $2.20 for Saturday and Sunday nights, isn't a little too much of a strain on the film fan pocket, then the picture should remain there a long while. At regular Broadway film house prices it would surely do that.

"Fool's Paradise" has a cast of stars featured in the production. They are: Dorothy Dalton, Mildred Harris, Conrad Nagel, Theodore Kosloff, John Davidson and Julia Faye; but Dorothy Dalton is the star of the picture. No one seeing the production will figure any one else, except as they are there to support Miss Dalton. She, as Poll Patchouli, has the finest role of her film career since she enacted Ethel Evans in "The Flame of the Yukon," the picture that made her a star of stars.

"The Laurels and the Lady," by Leonard Merrick, was the story that suggested the picture. Beulah Marie Dix and Sada Cowan provided the screen version. Mr. DeMille naturally handled the direction of the production, and while here and there a slight suggestion of overproduction slips in, the picture has so much in its favor that only those interested technically and from the standpoint of the finances will take notice of that point.

The story opens in an oil-boom town on the Texan border. Arthur Phelps (Conrad Nagel) is dead broke. He has returned from overseas with ocular trouble due to gases, a wound in his heart from a French girl and both of his oil lease ventures flivvers. The opening touches presenting the general atmosphere are corkingly done. There is the colored wash-woman and her bootblack husband, as well as the two picks of the family riding up in a high-powered touring car with a chauffeur, although only a week before they were working at their respective occupations. Oil did it, the same as oil made it possible for the Injun to move a player-piano into his tent, while his fat squaw rocked herself in front, and when she wanted to smoke, removed her corncob pipe from a jeweled chatelaine bag.

Poll Patchouli (Miss Dalton) is the principal vamp in a cantine on the Mexican side of the line, a short distance from the boom town. John Roderiguez (Theo. Kosloff) is the proprietor and an adept at knife throwing. He is in love with his establishment's vamp, but one night she crosses him when she interferes with the business of the establishment by preventing a wise guy from grabbing off a young girl he has brought to the place, and although she flees from his wrath, he sends his followers after her.

In making her get-away the first place she hits is the cabin of Phelps. It is love at first sight with her the moment she sets eyes on him. In this particular scene she is most convincing, for animal magnetism just leaps from her eyes as she looks the boy over. A couple of greasers try to enter the place, but are chased by the hero's little Boston terrier. The girl decides to stay for the night, but even though she conveys the suggestion she would just as leave have the tenant of the shack remain indoors, he decides to sleep on the porch.

Poll removes herself to the boom town's only hotel the next day and becomes the girl-behind-the-cigar-counter of the place. Her love for the boy is still uppermost, and she has formed an instinctive hatred for the woman that holds his affections, she having gathered that there was such a woman and just who she was from the numerous photographs of the noted danseuse, Rosa Duchene (Mildred Harris), clipped from illustrated papers tacked up about his shack.

Rosa, it happens, is making a tour of America. With her ballet she has been booked into the boom town and the tragedy of the picture is planted on the night she plays. Poll several days previous in a fit of pique has palmed off a trick cigar on the boy. The night the dancer is to appear he is standing before the stage door after having seen her into the theatre. Having a few minutes before curtain time, he takes the cigar from his pocket and lights it. When it goes off the smoke and fumes get into his eyes and injure them to such an extent he becomes totally blind later that evening, while in the theatre. Poll and her Castillian lover are seated in a box. At the conclusion of the performance she notes the boy trying to grope his way from the theatre, goes to assist him, and he tells her that if she ever speaks to or touches him again, he will kill her.

During the next few days Poll has become famous locally for her imitation of the French dancer's accented speech and a broad burlesque of her ballet about the hotel. The boy enters in the midst of one of these performances. Hearing the voice, he believes it is the dancer, calls to her and asks for a few minutes alone. She continues the mimicry. With its success the thought strikes her that as the boy will be blind for life, she will be able to impersonate the French girl and have him for her own. She goes to his shack the next day and tells him of her love. He, thinking that it is the girl of his heart, consents to the marriage which she proposes. After this Poll manages to eke out a livelihood for them by washing, until months later, when a noted surgeon arrives. She is torn between her love of the man and a certain selfishness of that love as to whether or not she will take a chance on having him cured and losing him. A cure is effected. At the same time comes the announcement a gusher has been brought in on the property adjoining his. He informs Poll he is leaving her, and takes up a chase around the globe to overtake the dancer.

He catches up with her in Siam, where she is being courted by one of the Princes of the blood. Here there is a clash between the two men, but through the frivolity of the girl they come to the realization that her love is all love of self.

It brings the boy to the realization he has thrown over a great love in the past, and he decides to return to it. In the time he was searching out the dancer his attorneys had arranged for an annulment of the marriage to Poll. When back, he discovers Poll has returned to the cantina and seeks her there. When she notes he wants her, the eternal woman asserts itself and she spurns him for Roderiguez. The boy refuses to abide by this decision. When Roderiguez bids him go on pain of death, he refuses unless the girl accompany him, with the result that at the crucial moment, when the knife is thrown, she steps between them in time to save her real love from the blow, and receives it herself. This leads to the natural happy ending of the picture.

The performance of Kosloff is the one that stands out next to that of Miss Dalton. He is reserved and quiet, but still carries a tremendous force. Conrad Nagel as the boy is all that any one could ask for, and the blind portions are very well carried by him.

Miss Harris is the one disappointment in the cast. Every one expected that she was going to burn things up from the advance reports, but this she failed to do. She was just a supporting player, and at that one without any distinction.

In sets and lightings the picture excels. The Siamese scenes are particularly effective, and one scene is a peach. The titling is exceptionally good and the suspense in the story is carried to the last notch in the celluloid.

Hugo Riesenfeld, who staged the presentation at the Criterion, gave the picture an unusual surrounding entertainment. A combination ballet and musical offering opened the bill. It is entitled "In a Doll Shop," and has about a score of people in it. It is a genuine delight and will be a draw for children's matinees during the holidays. In it Vera Myers as the "baby doll" and Ruth Matlock as "Colombine" were the outstanding figures, even though Mme. Victorina Krigher, a prima ballerina, had the principal role. Friday night her performance suffered through nervousness. This was staged and arranged by Josia Zuro, the choreography being by Paul Oscard. The settings, cleverly lighted and a distinct novelty, were by Herbert Schultze.

The ballet, together with the Criterion Magazine, which contained a color bit on gems by Prizma; a Chester scenic, entitled "Reel Riots"; a Fleischer "Out of the Ink Well" cartoon, and, best of all, the Goldwyn-Bray "Adopting a Bear Cub." The latter was the laugh punch of the film section. *Fred.*

THE LOVE CHARM

Realart released "The Love Charm," an Elmer Harris production, directed by Tom N. Heffron, taken from the story by Harvey O'Higgins, put in screen style by Percy Heath. It is the latest Wanda Hawley starring vehicle. The author employs the Cinderella idea for the working basis of his story. Ruth Sheldon (Wanda Hawley) is his leading character, she being the family drudge for an aunt and girl cousin, the latter about her own age.

The slavey attracts the attention of her cousin's suitor. This causes trouble in the family and necessitates her changing tactics by assuming the role of a vulgar girl known as a type the young man dislikes. This has the desired effect, with the girl leaving home. The chap, learning of the true state of affairs, locates her and the happy ending ensues.

An idea of this kind can invariably be relied upon for results. A new angle can usually be devised whereby it can be brought up to date, as has been done in this instance. The picture has a direct appeal with the star carrying her role capably.

The cast, comparatively short, has been well chosen, with the direction handled to a nicety. "The Love Charm" is a program feature that can hold up its end. *Hart.*

'AT THE STAGE DOOR'

Helen Mathews	Frances Hess
Mary Mathews	Miriam Battista
Mrs. Mathews	Margaret Foster
Mary Mathews	"Billy" Dove
Helen Mathews	Elizabeth North
Arthur Bates	William Collier, Jr.
George Andrews	C. Elliott Griffin
Grace Mortimer	Myrtle Maughan
John Brooks	Charles Craig
Mrs. Reade	Vivia Ogden
Harold Reade	Billy Quirk
Philip Pierce	Huntly Gordon
Alice Vincent	Katherine Spencer
Betty	Doris Eaton

An R-C special touring the Loew houses with Billie Dove, a dark damsel, who photographs like a summer moon, featured, and Doris Eaton walking away with the comedy honors. Some one should vote her a medal. What she does here is worth it. What the rest is worth is a question.

Sumptuously photographed, it tells a hokum story that should bring in money, but W. Christy Cabanne, who directed, and is the only person to get any credit, manages pretty much to jazz up at least his final effect. It was hard to credit his story as it was, but when he ended what should have been serious on a farce note, he went all the way toward dragging this expensive picture into the second rate class.

The story isn't new. Mary Mathews has been accustomed to giving up to her kid sister, Helen. Finally Helen steals her beau and Mary comes to the wicked city, where an old friend lands her a job in the chorus. But she's a good girl, and the wicked are hot after her till it reaches a point where only the opportune arrival of a rich young man in a limousine saves her from unwelcome attentions. He swings a hefty right, but otherwise is so gentle and well-behaved she accepts his attentions. At a bazaar some one suggests to Philip that he's playing round a bit strong for a man with a fiancee in Europe and that all chorus girls are alike, anyway. He proposes to assure himself and so makes a suggestion that would break the heart of any girl truly good and pure. Mary's heart forthwith breaks, and Miss Dove did this part as creditably and with as much reserve as the rest. From her depths of despair she is rescued by Phil's proposal of marriage. He's to come the next night with the ring, as she tells the girls who take her along on a rough party (she's always refused before) when he fails to show up.

And why did Philip behave as no film hero should? All a mistake. He'd sent a note around, explaining his real fiancee had arrived from Europe and he was busy explaining to her; but Mary hadn't got the note and so only another girl's interference by fetching Philip helped matters out. Needless to say, Philip arrived in time "to save Mary from a fate worse than death."

Such hokum is well enough for money-making purposes, but it is not well enough when the comedy shot into it burlesques its reality as this ending certainly does. There we see a comedy character who has been postponing his own wedding 15 years getting hooked up at a double ceremony with Philip and Mary! Philip is supposed to be a Fifth avenue aristocrat! At any rate, the rest is fair sob melodrama, competently acted by Huntly Gordon, Myrtle Naughan and the others.

The sets are the real thing and the photography exceptionally good.

Leed.

THE BEAUTIFUL LIAR

Helen Hayes / Elsie Parmelee	Katherine MacDonald
Bobby Bates	Charles Meredith
MacGregor	Joseph J. Dowling
Mrs. Van Courtlandt	Kate Lester
Gaston Allegretti	Wilfred Lucas

George Marion, Jr., is the author of "The Beautiful Liar," the latest Katherine MacDonald starring feature to be released through First National by B. P. Schulberg. The production was directed by Wallace Worsley, who has handled the star delightfully. Miss MacDonald appears to advantage, and with the exception of a few too many close-ups with her staring directly into the camera, with the eye make-up most evident, there is no fault to be found. From a box office standpoint the pictures will prove up to the average of the regular run of program features intended for the week-stand houses, although it is nothing startling or out of the ordinary.

The story is that of a scheming hotel manager about to lose his position, and who to save it threatens to wreck the plans for a charity bazaar by withholding the appearance of a stage comedienne, who the social lights at the resort are wild to have in their play. He is unable to get the star, but in the office of the brokers handling his market gambling there is a girl who is a double for the theatrical star.

Through the work of a bookkeeper in the firm, a canny old Scot who is after a free vacation, the girl is finally persuaded to double for the actress. At the summer hotel she meets with Bobby Bates, a customer of her firm and for whom she has long cherished a secret love. The boy meets and makes love to her in the play and later proposes, but at the last minute she runs away, for the real actress arrives on the scene.

At the office of the brokerage firm he again runs across the girl a few days later, and after explanations there is a happy ending.

Some clever comedy touches in the telling and the introduction of Lincoln Steadman as a former vaudeville partner of the actress is well handled as a bit. Joseph J. Dowling as the Auld Scot was a clever bit. Wilfred Lucas got all there was out of the role of the hotel manager. Charles Meredith, playing opposite Miss MacDonald, was a charming juvenile lead for her.

The sets are rather big and the hotel touches the principal scenes that called for an outlay. Nothing unsual in photography or lightings, but satisfactory in regard to both of these details.

Fred.

LURE OF THE JADE

A Robertson-Cole feature starring Pauline Frederick in a rather different kind of South Sea Island drama by Marion Orth. The smooth direction is by Colin Campbell. Offered at Loew's State first half of the current week it was disclosed as a skilfully written and splendidly acted story that should have sure appeal to women.

Miss Frederick wears a thrilling assortment of bizarre frocks and has opportunity for a lot of vivid emotional acting of the kind she can make thoroughly effective. It's all hectic melodrama, obvious and theatrical, but it does deliver a dramatic "punch" and its situations develop plausibly. Besides these qualities it has a good deal of the picturesqueness that goes with the locale.

In this case it is not a deserted island of the romantic South Seas, peopled by absurd barbarous natives, but a big naval base which has its own white society and a hotel of some magnificence. Hither come a naval officer and his wife, Capt. and Mrs. Copley, to meet the vengeance of Sada, now proprietress of "The Sea Gull," a tavern and gambling place. Back in America Sada was the daughter of an American admiral, who had been ruined by the scandal mongering tongue of Mrs. Copley. The gossip had killed Sada's father and driven her from the station, a wanderer.

Sada plots revenge. During the Captain's absence, she pursuades an English remittance man of good birth, who is in love with her, to trap Mrs. Copley by arranging a rendezvous in her (Sada's) bungalow, where she will expose her to the world as a faithless wife. The plan goes through, but at the moment when she is about to spring the trap, the victim's son, crazed by tropical fever, comes upon the scene and shoots down the Englishman whom he believes is his mother's betrayer. Sada, rather than have her vengeance fall upon the guiltless boy, assumes the burden of the crime, and the finale shows her going into the distance guarded by native police, presumably to silent punishment for the murder.

There are a few gaps in the progress of the story. For instance, it does not appear how the boy learns where his mother is, nor is any motive established for the shooting. In other places the threads are not neatly tied, but in unrestrained romancing of this sort of sentimental tale it does not do to examine details too closely. It is sufficient that the sentimental appeal is hammered home as it is here. As the presiding spirit of "The Sea Gull" Miss Frederick wears many gorgeous robes of an outlandish design but bizarre grace, and the settings are exceedingly picturesque.

Altogether a colorful story keyed to the appreciation of the less sophisticated fans, which is to say the majority. Why the title, "The Lure of the Jade," does not appear. It is just a label with an intriguing sound and has no conceivable bearing on the tale.

Rush.

R. S. V. P.

Richard Morgan	Charles Ray
Mrs. Morgan, his aunt	Flo ence Oberle
Benny Fielding	Harry Myers
Plimpton	Tom McGuire
Betty	Jean Calhoun
Private Detective	Robert Grey
Butler	William Courtright
Minnie Meadows	Ida Schumaker

A featur starring Charles Ray is always satisfying, and his latest, "R. S. V. P.," is not the least of them. The story is credited to Rob Wagner, directed by Ray, released via First National.

It is not easy to understand how Wagner, or any contemporaneous writer, can claim credit for the authorship of so familiar a story, but by the same token it is remarkable how so much clean, wholesome and amusing entertainment was extracted from so slight a variation of the elementary plot. Here it is in a few words: Two indigent young artists live in a studio apartment. Art connoiseur tells one (Ray) that what he needs is living models. He asks how they can be secured without money, to which the art critic replies they can't. Artist advertises for a model, promising payment and bonus when picture is sold. His childhood sweetheart calls after years of absence at boarding school. He fails to recognize her, mistakes her for model in answer to his "advert" and paints a fine picture of her without being aware of her identity.

The girl's father gives a reception in her honor and invites the artist; his friend wants to go along; there is but one dress coat between them, and the comedy arises through both going and taking turns in the dressing room of the mansion while the other disports himself at the party. Only recently there was presented a two-reel "comedy" with the almost identical story, but it was unfolded with the assistance of vulgar horseplay. Not once in the Ray production was such a method resorted to, yet it was equally uproarious and held attention for a full five reels. Perhaps it was the sub-titles, but it probably was the clever pantomiming of Ray and his able "runner-up" in the person of that all-round excellent screen actor, Harry Myers, who was the star of "A Connecticut Yankee," and who never failed to register a hit way back in the original Vitagraph days. Why doesn't somebody make a screen star of Myers? He would seem to be the surest kind of a bet.

A first-rate supporting cast, intelligent direction, admirable photography, etc., all contribute to the generally acceptable result. But the plot is a joke. It is Ray and Myers that count.

Jolo.

CONCEIT

William Crombie	William B. Davidson
Mrs. Crombie	Hedda Hopper
Hunt Kilstrom	Charles Gerard
Jeanette	Betty Hilburn
Barbe le Fleche	Maurice Costello
Bowles	Patrick Hartigan
McBain	Warren Cook
Indian Trapper	Red Eagle

This picture is the second release of the series of specials that are being marketed as the "Selznick Supreme Six." The story is by Michael J. Phillips, the screen adaptation being made by Edward J. Montague. Burton George handled the direction.

Banff in the Canadian Rockies is the location where most of the exterior shots of the picture were taken. Therefore the feature contains sufficient scenic stuff to stand off the admission price.

The story itself fails to stand up, principally because of the weakness that there is in taking a cad and coward as the heroic figure of the yarn. The fact that he is regenerated makes no difference to an audience, the bad taste of the early sections of the story will not wash out in the final reel with the regeneration sop.

William B. Davidson has the role of the caddish hero. It is a thankless job at the best, but Mr. Davidson does not add materially one way or another to the value of the charcter. He is a wealthy man who has managed to purchase everything that he wanted in life, even to a pretty wife. In addition to a cad he is also a braggart and when he takes a hunting party to his lodge in the Canadian Rockies to go after bear he lets it be understood that there never was a bear hunter such as he. The result is that while all of the others manage to make their kill he is unsuccessful, and their taunts drive him to remaining until he does get a bear. After the others have returned East he remains, and being unable to get a guide sets forth alone, becoming lost and finally bringing up at the cabin of a trapper, who has his late partner's daughter living with him.

The braggart on recovering from his scare due to a night in the wilds makes love to the girl, but when her guardian offers to fight him for the girl he welches. He then follows his friends East, only to discover that one of them has practically alienated his wife's affections, but he is too great a coward to retaliate.

Later he turns out to be a man after all. He goes out and takes a beating from an ex-pug who is running a gym, and that one walloping makes him turn around and lick the guy that copped his wife, kick him out of the house and then advise the wife to start divorce proceedings. But once started he is a glutton for punishment, so he returns to the woods to fight the woodsman who challenged him, and walks in on the scene just in time to save the girl from a heavy who has been trying to carry her off. And that night to top it all off when he returns to his lodge there is his wife, who has followed him to the woods to kiss and make up.

The story is pretty much a jumbled affair, but there are some places where it will manage to get by in pretty good shape.

In addition to William B. Davidson there is Mrs. DeWolf Hopper in the cast as the wife, Betty Hilburn as the ingenue lead, and above all the formerly famed Maurice Costello in the role of the heavy of the north woods. The latter proves himself still considerable of a screen actor and gets over with a wallop the little that he has to do.

Fred.

LOVE NEVER DIES

John Trott	Lloyd Hughes
Tilly Whaley	Madge Bellamy
Joel Eperson	Joe Bennett
Liz Trott	Claire McDowell
Jane Holder	Winifred Greenwood
Ezekiel Whaley	Frank Brownlee
Dora Boyles	Julia Brown

Sam Cavanaugh.............Fred Gamboal
Mrs. Cavanaugh............Lillian Leighton

A "somewhat different" picture story is "Love Never Dies," adapted from Will N. Harben's novel, "The Cottage of Delight," directed by King Vidor, featuring Lloyd Hughes and Madge Bellamy, photographed by Max Dupont, distributed by First National. Running 80 minutes. the spectator is intrigued through what is apparently the final "clinch" in the first reel, which turns out to be just the beginning of an absorbingly interesting and appealing heart-interest story.

Considerable ingenuity has been exercised in putting over the fact that the hero's mother is a woman of ill repute without likelihood of objection on the part of the censors.

John Trott (Lloyd Hughes) marries Tilly Whaley (Madge Bellamy). When her father discovers a stain on his son-in-law's parentage, he takes his daughter home. John goes to "the city"; there is a train-wreck en route; he is believed to have died in the accident; the girl's father persuades her to marry another man. John returns years later; the second husband tries to make way with himself by riding over the whirling rapids; John goes to his rescue; husband No. 2 does not survive, and the loving couple are reunited. Although Trott is the hero. it is a question to determine which is the "Gunga Dhin" of the tale—the second husband, who gave up his life, or the first one, who went to his rescue.

An extraordinary cast has been assembled for the enactment of the tale. They are so uniformly excellent that it is an injustice to the others to feature any individual. Lloyd Hughes is an attractive hero, with one criticism—he doesn't make up to look older and worn with the passing of time. Joe Bennett supplies a fine bit of characterizing as the second husband; Madge Bellamy is very pretty as the heroine and her excellent pantomiming enables her to express suitably the emotional characterization; Claire McDowell's work as the immoral mother stands out brilliantly, with the others equally competent. Photography and direction are all that could be desired.

An exceptional photoplay. *Jolo.*

DESERT BLOSSOMS

Stephen Brent.............William Russell
Mary Ralston..............Helen Ferguson
James Thornton..............W. J. Higby
Henry Ralston...............Willis Robards
Mrs. Thornton..............Margaret Mann
Lucy Thornton..............Dulcie Cooper
Bert Thornton...............Charles Spere
Mr. Joyce..................Gerald Pring

Kate Corbaley is credited as the author of this Fox feature starring William Russell, the screen version for which was written by Arthur J. Zellner. Arthur Rosson did the directing. The author has taken the familiar idea of having the college-bred son of a rich contractor turn out to be a weak-kneed individual who causes the downfall of his fathers' most trusted employe. The latter, in order not to cause the conviction of the son, takes a crime upon his own shoulders. He is disgraced, but after being confronted by innumerable obstacles clears himself when the truth of the affair is learned.

A love angle is brought into use, which, in addition to an abundance of melodramatic business, tends to make a half-way interesting program feature for the change-a-day houses. Russell is a capable actor for the line of work needed in this production, which has nothing in the way of opportunities to make the picture stand out above the general run of his productions. It will prove mildly interesting for screen audiences that clamor for the bromide melodramatics. Exteriors make up the production almost entirely. Russell's supporting cast has been well enough selected for the style of work demanded of them. No great expenditure has been made as far as production is concerned. It takes but one reel of this feature to know what it is all about. *Hart.*

RAINBOW

Rainbow Halliday...........Alice Calhoun
George Standish...............Jack Roach
Shang Jordan...............William Gross
Andy MacTavish..............Charles Kent
Denny Farrell...............Tom O'Malley
Rufus Halliday............George A. Lessey
Estelle Jackson..............Cecil Kern
Kid Short................Tammany Young
Joe Sheady..................Ivan Christie

Vitagraph feature made in the eastern studio starring Alice Calhoun, based upon the story by Harry Dittmar, directed by Edward Jose. The Dittmar story of a light texture centers around a young girl of the mining country.

She is the owner of property inherited from her father, who, in addition to his realty holdings, bequeathes to his daughter three male guardians, with whom she lives in the old homestead. The middle-aged foster parents treat the girl as their own. Her ownership to the property is questioned by a young prospector who believes, according to the will of his father, that he is its owner. An uncle of the girl by a bit of trickery had deprived this youth of his rightful property now in the hands of his own niece whom he has never seen. Uncle requests that she come and live with him in the city. The young prospector also puts in an appearance there and makes known his demands.

The girl seeing that the property does not rightfully belong to her, offers to give it up. He refuses to accept it, and she returns to the care of her three guardians. A thread of a love story has been worked up as the main idea which is developed with the finish finding the girl and the young prospector marrying. This leaves them as joint owners of the disputed property.

The picture is interesting. No attempt has been made to make it a big feature. It has been produced solely for the houses which change their features daily and offer them at an admission scale which attracts the economical and unsophisticated neighborhood fan. The cast is appropriate. Miss Calhoun, youthful, is well cast, with her co-workers equally successful with their parts. *Hart.*

DON'T TELL EVERYTHING

Cullen Dale.....................Wallace Reid
Marian Westover............Gloria Swanson
Harvey Gilroy..............Elliott Dexter
Jessica Ramsey..........Dorothy Cumming
Mrs. Morgan.............Genevieve Blinn
Cullen's Niece..............Baby Gloria Wood
Morgan Twins..........The deBriac Twins

A Paramount at the Rivoli featuring Wallace Reid, Gloria Swanson and Elliott Dexter, but the fact Thompson Buchanan supervised is the all-important consideration in making this a first class offering for all houses. It is clean, wholesome, well conceived character comedy with a society touch. It is knit together and gets to you as a whole, with every incident related to the central idea. This is the result, probably, of having someone of Mr. Buchanan's ability boss the works. Sam Wood directed, handling the actors competently. The story is by Lorna Moon.

She tells of two spoiled darlings who get married in a hurry and then quarrel temporarily over the advances of a vamp who doesn't know they have plighted their troth (as they say on the coast). They are reconciled up at the hunting lodge of the vamp in the mountains, to which Miss Swanson (as the wife) proceeded in the most extraordinary ermine wrap. This was the flashlight of costuming, the sort of thing no one in their senses would wear anywhere save at a masquerade—certainly never to go motoring in. Evidently this is one of the things Mr. Buchanan didn't supervise.

Outside of that, what Miss Swanson contributed was very much to the point. This comedy is mostly by-play, comedy touches. Miss Swanson managed them very well. So did Mr. Reid. Mr. Dexter had little to do, but did it acceptably enough. *Leed.*

A PARISIAN ROMANCE

"A Parisian Romance" is a Fox production, aimed for comedy and reaching boredom. As the other half of the bill at Loew's New York last Friday what was said about "Riding with Death" and the New York also applies to this miscue.

Marie Provost is the girl with a lot of men. The cast looks good enough if they had anything to do. It reads as though the laughs had to come from the captions, but the laughs didn't from those or anything else.

About the girl in Paris, a rave the Frenchmen are enthused over. Her cousin from America, a studio boob, is visiting her folks abroad. He is observing the girl to report to her grandmother back home. The girl, knowing he's going to report, becomes wild. Smoking cigarettes is her idea of that, and so it runs.

The mistake was in picking this story. *Sime.*

RIDING WITH DEATH

A Universal with Buck Jones. It was half the bill at Loew's New York last Friday, which usually tells the tale of a picture there before it is seen. If a film is worth while at all, this change daily house cant' afford to double it up.

"Riding with Death" is a western with a Mexican atmosphere, about a ranger, mortgage on the farm, Mexican villainy and so on, but not enough for a feature. They could have packed it within two reels. It is tediously padded, with irritating stalling. Some shooting action at the finish and a good fall by Jones, but the falling is all in the film; the fans will never fall for this kind. *Sime.*

STRANGER THAN FICTION

Katherine MacDonald stars in "Stranger Than Fiction," produced by MacDonald Productions, directed by J. A. Barry and released under the auspices of First National. The picture is in the new vein of satire and takes as its mark the flamboyant crook melodrama. But the producers display a curious uncertainty about burlesquing their subject.

From the fact that all the satire is in the titles and not in the action, one would almost suspect that the picture was made in all seriousness and the burlesque came as an afterthought when it was being edited and titled. It's curious to find the screen action done in a spirit of polite comedy while the interpolated titles are slangy travesty.

Toward the end the burlesque almost disappears and the film turns into a straight melodrama with spectacular "stunts" involving an airship chase with a surprise finish which discloses that it is a moving picture story within a moving picture story. This scheme is confusing to the auditor, who never is sure whether he should be amused or thrilled. The melodramatic climax is ingeniously managed and has plenty of "punch" and the titles are all brightly written, although they do take up a fearful total of footage.

Diana Masters (Miss MacDonald) is a society girl with a fad for making amateur films. At the opening she is screening her version of "Carmen" with herself in the title part, and her society friends, including the police commissioner, in the cast. The screening is shown together with the society audience in Diana's drawing room. Diana says she has made another picture which she will show. What appears to be a break occurs as she tells the projection machine operator to start the other film, and a new story begins.

The police commissioner is called to the telephone by headquarters reporting that "The Black Heart," a notorious criminal, has threatened to rob the Masters home that night. Suddenly the lights go out, and when they come on again the fashionable gathering has been "frisked." Dick, Diana's suitor, pledges that he will run the "Black Heart Gang" down, and from there the rest of the film is a crook-detective story done in the style of a lurid serial, with trick entrances through secret doors, pursuits through underground passages and all the other devices, with innumerable spirited fights and the rest of the tricks.

At the finish the crooks try to escape in an aeroplane. Dick, the hero, gets into the plane of the chief crook, and there is a thrilling hand-to-hand battle in the clouds, during which the plane takes fire and falls to the ground with the crook. Diana has given chase in her own aeroplane and as the crook's machine does a nosedive she throws the hero a parachute and picks him up as he floats in the air. This passage is skilfully done by studio close-ups of the airship battle and the heroine in her machine, alternating with cut-in sections of aerial stunts done for the news weeklies. This delivers a convincing thrill.

Even the crash of the burning plane is shown in a cut-in and a camera record of a nosedive shot from a falling machine is introduced. This same novelty was once exhibited as part of a "magazine" short subject. It all ends with the hero-heroine embrace, and then the scene shifts suddenly back to Diana's drawing room, and it is made clear that the wild proceedings have taken place in Diana's other film production. The idea makes an amusing burlesque, but some hint that it is a burlesque which might have been given in the action instead of being confined entirely to the titles. The scheme employed makes for confusion in the mind of the spectator. *Rush.*

THE FOX

Ol' Santa Fe..................Harry Carey
Sheriff Mart Fraser.........George Nichols
Stella Fraser..............Gertrude Olmsted
Annette Fraser...........Betty Ross Clark
Dick Farwell................Johnny Harron
Mrs. Farwell................Gertrude Claire
Rufus B. Coulter....................Alan Hale
K. C. Kid.......................George Cooper
Pard.........................Breezy Eason, Jr.
Black Mike.................Chas. Lemoyne
Rollins..........................C. E. Anderson
Hubbs......................Harley Chambers

"The Fox," a Universal production, story by Harry Carey, its star, scenario by Lucien Hubbard, directed by Robert Thornby, is about seven reels in length. It runs as if it had been cut from still greater footage after being finished, at which time it probably was decided that it was not destined to be much better than the usual run of "westerns" turned out by the U factory.

It is a good straightaway story, especially suited to the magnetic personality of the star, and with a higher calibre of direction and more liberal production expenditure, might have qualified as a big special. But when it came to big "mob" scenes and a battle between outlaws and cavalry troops there was an apparent skimping that left it in the general category of U releases.

The producer was given rare opportunities for exceptional heart interest situations between Carey and little "Breezy" Eason, Jr., the latter a wistful-faced urchin of no mean screen talent. There is presented the situation of an ostensible hobo rescuing the kid from the abuse of a gypsy animal trainer and adopting the child, the "hobo" sent to jail and taking the child with him, and so on. So little is made of this opportunity that it is small wonder that Chaplin saw in the same elemental idea enough to make of it a feature that appealed to the entire film-going world.

In the end it is revealed that the "hobo" is in reality a U. S. Secret Service man sent to the desert town to clean up a gang of outlaws, the head of which is the local bank president.

But U resorted to its conventional policy of utilizing rhetorical subtitles, as "frowning walls, bleak and baffling," and employing a handful of their Western riders to depict the cavalry troops. Perhaps the director was not to blame. It is just possible he was not permitted to spend the few additional pennies to make the battle with the outlaws look sufficiently pretentious. That, however, did not interfere with the excellent photography supplied by William Fildew. *Jolo.*

CHEATED HEARTS

Barry Gordon...........Herbert Rawlinson
Tom Gordon.................Warner Baxter
Muriel Beekman.............Marjorie Daw
Kitty Vanness......................Doris Pawn
Nathaniel Beekman..............Winter Hall
Col. Fairfax Gordon.........Josef Swickard
Ibrahim..................Murdock McQuarrie
Naomi................................Anna Lehr
Nil Hamed.........................Boris Karloff
Hassam.........................Al McQuarrie
Achmet..............................Hector Sarno

This is a pretty fair Universal feature directed by Hobart Henley, who undoubtedly is responsible for all that there is good about it. Herbert Rawlinson is starred, and in this instance the U. again has made the mistake of not giving this star material that is worthy of him. The combination of Rawlinson and Henley should, with picked stories, turn out some really worth while pictures.

"Cheated Hearts" is founded on the story "Harry Gordon," by William Payson, the screen adaptation having been made by Wallace Clifton, with Virgil Miller behind the camera.

In direction, photography and lightings the picture is far and away ahead of the usual run of Universal pictures.

The scene of action is laid in this country and Northern Africa. This gives opportunity for society and picturesque Arabian atmosphere that lends itself nicely to sets and exteriors. The studio exteriors are particularly good, and some of the night scenes done wonderfully well.

The story relates of two brothers both in love with the same girl. The father of the boys has been a liquor addict, and while the girl loves one of the boys, she is afraid that he has inherited his father's love for the cup that cheers, and so becomes engaged to the other brother in a moment of pique. Some time later her fiancee is held for ransom in Africa. Bedouin bandits and drunken brother go to his rescue and save him. The girl changes her mind and breaks off her engagement and throws her lot as her heart dictates.

Herbert Rawlinson plays the brother that wins out in the end, and handles it nicely. Warner Baxter plays opposite him, and seemingly is a newcomer before the camera; that supposition is ventured because of his work in this picture. Marjorie Daw, as the heroine, is all that the picture required, and more, too. Doris Pawn, however, did not appear to advantage; her make-up seemed bad.

In lesser roles Winter Hall, Anna Lehr, Murdock MacQuarrie acquitted themselves creditably. As a matter of fact Anna Lehr did not have enough to do in the picture; the audience would have liked seeing more of her.

Summed up, the picture is "a better than usual Universal." *Fred.*

A MAN'S HOME

Frederick Osborn...........Harry T. Morey
Frances Osborn..........Kathlyn Williams
Lucy Osborn.......................Faire Binney
Mrs. Sarah Hawkins......Margaret Seddon
Arthur Lynn.........................Matt Moore
Cordelia Wilson..........Grace Valentine
Jack Wilson..............Roland Bottomley

Ralph Ince has made an interesting picture out of the stage play by Edmund Breese and Anna Steese Richardson, bearing the trade-mark of Selznick and current at the Capitol. It is a modified crook drama, with certain sentimental sidelights on American society. Business at the Capitol Sunday night was big and the crowd showed plainly it was more than ordinarily interested by occasional applause at the dramatic high spots.

A first-rate cast has been assembled for the picture version of the work, containing half a dozen film names of importance. Probably the cast was the item that caused the initial draw. The picture ought to prosper by word-of-mouth advertising, for it has strong drama even if it is theatrical and obvious and elements of sentimental appeal to the women fans.

Its defects are innate in the play script and belong to the particular period of its stage production. At that time there was a wave of "crook" dramas, and in most the crook was the hero. If memory serves, the craze was started by "Alias Jimmy Valentine," which, oddly enough, is just now in a revival. Because of the temporary fad for underworld heroes the lady crook of this story is the "sympathetic character," while the respectable wife and mother of the tale is made to appear in a rather unworthy light.

The story revolves about the butterfly wife of the self-made Frederick Osborn, who goes gadding about New York and Atlantic City and makes the acquaintance of Cordelia Wilson and her supposed brother Jack, an underworld partnership which plays upon the new rich. Frederick summons his wife home to Toledo when he hears of her spectacular friends and at the same time has Pinkerton look up the Wilsons' records. Mrs. Osborn insists that her new friends visit her in Toledo.

When it appears that Cordelia had practically blackmailed Arthur Lynn, the fiance of Osborn's daughter Lucy (nicely played by Faire Binney), Osborn orders them from the house. This is the basis of a fine family row, made worse by the husband's stubbornness. In the end Cordelia is touched by the possibilities of the situation wrecking the girl's life, and bows out without shaking down the family, as she had intended. As she departs Cordelia preaches a sermon to the headstrong husband about sympathetic understanding of his wife, and at the end the prospect is that he will build a real home based on love and trust, the philosophy of the gifted lady crook.

It sounds rather stagey in the telling, but the tale is craftily built and becomes almost plausible as it develops bit by bit. The big dramatic passage is a clash between Cordelia's brother, who tries to blackmail Mrs. Osborn. It could have been made into a furniture-smashing fight, but is allowed to pass with a minimum of physical action but good dramatic tension, an effective climax. *Rush.*

MISS LULU BETT

Lulu Bett.........................Lois Wilson
Neil Cornish....................Milton Sills
Dwight Deacon...........Theodore Roberts
Diana Deacon...............Helen Ferguson
Mrs. Dwight Deacon......Mabel Van Buren
Manona Deacon.....................May Giraci
Ninian Deacon..............Clarence Burton
Grandma Bett........................Ethel Wales
Bobby Larkin.....................Taylor Graves
Station Agent.......................Charles Ogle

The only just way in which to pass judgment on the William DeMille film production of "Miss Lulu Bett" would be to forget having read the book or seen the play. From that viewpoint Famous Players has turned out a first-rate, non-sensational, program feature, from a scenario of the Zona Gale novel, prepared by Clara Beranger.

As is the custom in film adaptations of literature, the psychology has been so distorted as to be entirely lost, but there is no longer any doubt but that such a procedure is deemed to be essential to come with the mental scope of the general public. While the minority may protest at such "defilement," picture producers will tell you it reduces the percentage of business gamble. They add (generally with an admonition that it is not for publication) that they are not in the business for art's sake. Judging "Miss Lulu Bett," therefore, as an original scenario, it is a well-wrought, closely-knit, straightaway, cumulative domestic drama of rural life, well acted throughout, carefully produced and vividly atmospheric.

Lois Wilson in the name part is as nearly perfection as one could imagine. She brings to the role just the requisite pathos. A younger man cast for Dwight Deacon might have been more in keeping with the Zona Gale story, and an older, less vigorous woman, than Ethel Wales for Grandma Bett might have been selected, but both these players sustained their respective characterizations satisfactorily. All the others qualified pleasurably. *Jolo.*

THE HUNCH

J. Preston Humphrey.......Gareth Hughes
Barbara Thorndyke..........Ethel Grandin
John C. Thorndyke.......John C. Steppling
George Taylor.........Edward Flannagan
Sheriff Greene ....Harry Loraine
Minnie Stubbs.......................Gale Henry
Hodges ....William H. Brown

"The Hunch" was adapted for the screen from a magazine story by Percival Wilde. It is a Sawyer-Lubin film production, distributed by Metro, directed by George D. Baker. It has all the ingredients that go to make a good stage farce, and Director Baker has made of the story a corking filmization. There is a scene in a county jail that is screamingly funny on the sheet and sufficient action in it to make for an equally ludicrous third act of a ridiculous dramatic absurdity. It would be unfair to attempt a summary of the tale, but as acted before the camera it is ludicrous in the extreme and makes for good screen entertainment.

Gareth Hughes has the stellar role and sustains it well. His supporting cast is fully equal to the demands put upon them, the direction is of the best and the photography of a high order. "The Hunch" will satisfy wherever exhibited. *Jolo.*

THE NEW DISCIPLE

John McPherson.................Pell Trenton
Peter Fanning.......................Alfred Allen
Mary Fanning..................Norris Johnson
Marion Fanning..............Margaret Mann
Sandy McPherson............Walt Whitman
Mother McPherson..................Alice Smith
Frederick Wharton.....Arthur Stuart Hull
Daddy Whipple...............Walter Perkins
Jennings.......................Charles Prindley

"The New Disciple" is a feature picture offered at the Lyric by Federation Film Corporation and listed to stay two weeks. There was only a sprinkling of people in the orchestra at the opening, Dec. 18, and the film shows nothing calculated to draw them in. It has little entertainment value and even less value as propaganda. To say two plus two makes four is a very different thing from proving it interestingly. The photography is the best thing about it. Ollie Sellers' direction was without inspiration, and the story by John Arthur Nelson isn't convincing. What he attempts to prove is that the relations between capital an labor leave much to be desired by the laboring man. He goes back to wartime for his setting and then drags in "The New Freedom," by Woodrow Wilson, as the bible offering a solution.

The story itself is neatly joined. There is purpose and counter-purpose, but the acting is static and without inspiration. There is some good, homely sentiment. That's about all. Peter Fanning tries to squeeze the last penny out of his workers, but is caught himself when they strike, and he can't fulfill a time contract. Going broke, his competitors, who brought about the situation, try to buy in his mill at auction. The united farmers outbid the trust and the business goes on, co-operatively run. *Leed.*

VENDETTA

Marianna Paoli..........................Pola Negri
Antonio Paoli, her brother......Fred Immler
Count Musso Danella, her guardian....
Magnus Stifter
Lieutenant Gladwin Irving......Emil Birron
Lieutenant Edwin Alcott......Harry Liedtke
Lady Crawford...............Margaret Kupfer
Tomasso...........................Emil Jannings

Here is another Pola Negri picture, making the fourth that has been shown in this country in a year. The first three were First National releases, variously entitled "Passion," "Gypsy Blood," and "One Arabian Night." The current production is not released by that organization, but marketed in this country by the Howell's Sales Co., Inc. Heretofore the Howell's organization has been wholly identified with the foreign market sales, and as such handled the entire First National product outside of the U. S. and Canada.

Although "Vendetta" is playing the Strand this week, the picture is far below the standard set by the three previous Pola Negri starring features, and while the name of the star may draw, this production will hardly satisfy expectations.

Goldwyn makes a claim that "Vendetta" is really "Mr. Barnes of New

York." There does not seem to be anything in the picture that would suggest this. As far as the initial location of action is concerned, the picture would rather seem to be an infringement on the story of the same title written in 1886 by Marie Corelli.

The authorship of this feature is credited to George Jacoby and Leo Lasko. The former also directed the production.

The story, in brief, is that of a young Corsican noblewoman who on her brother's death in a duel, swears to be avenged on his unnamed slayer. Her guardian makes a pact with her to the effect that if he discovers who the slayer was she shall marry him. Later she meets a young Englishman whom she nurses through a fever during an epidemic and loves. After she has married him the guardian discloses that the man she married was the man that killed her brother. But instead of his receiving the knife intended for the husband it is the guardian who is slain at the end of the picture by the former servant of the countess' brother.

A very unsatisfactory story on the screen, and the star does not appear to advantage. Emil Jannings as the old servant managed to score in a character role. Harry Liedtke plays the lead opposite Negri in a rather matter-of-fact fashion and with an eye on the camera. A secondary lead by Emil Birron is fairly well handled, although both men are entirely too Germanic to suggest the English officers they portray.

James A. Creelman edited and titled for the American market, leaving much to be desired. *Fred.*

THE DEVIL WITHIN

Capt. Briggs.................Dustin Farnum
Laura.........................Virginia Valli
Dr. Philiol...................Nigel De Bruller
Hal...........................Bernard Durning
Scurlock......................Jim Farley
Wansley.......................Tom O'Brien
Crevay........................Bob Perry
Bevins........................Charles Gorman
Ezra..........................Otto Hoffman
Cabin Boy.....................Kirk Incas
Witch.........................Evelyn Selbie
Juvenile Witch................Hazel Dean

This Fox feature with Dustin Farnum starred is chock full of action, and carries an unusual story besides. George Allan England wrote it, Arthur J. Zellner made the scenario and Bernard Durning directed. He also played a part, but his direction in particular shows a nice feeling for successive effects. Starting off with heavy action, he ends up with the tale running along Christian Science and regeneration lines sure to bring money to the box office.

Capt. Briggs is a fiend at sea, an old-style, fist-swinging captain, but a Malay witch puts a curse on him. After he has retired and settled down the curse works itself out in his beloved nephew and heir, who is up to all sorts of deviltry before he is laid low in a riot after being stabbed with a poisoned krisr. One of two powders is the antidote. The old captain tastes one to determine whether it is the antidote or a deadly poison. This is the climax and a good one.

Farnum was good both as the fist-swinger and as the old man, and Durning ably seconded him. The rest of the cast did well. *Leed.*

1922

"ORPHANS OF THE STORM"

Henriette Girard..............Lillian Gish
Louise.........................Dorothy Gish
Chevalier de Vaudrey...Joseph Schildkraut
Count de Linieres............Frank Losee
Countess de Linieres.....Catherine Emmett
Marquis de Presle.........Morgan Wallace
Mother Frochard..........Lucille la Verne
Jacques Frochard.........Sheldon Lewis
Pierre Frochard..............Frank Puglia
Picard......................Creighton Hale
Jacques-Forget-Not............Leslie King
Danton.......................Monte Blue
Robespierre................Sidney Herbert
King Louis XVI..............Leo Kolmeri
The Doctor.................Adolphe Lestina
Sister Genevieve.............Kate Bruce

Griffith "showed it" Jan. 3 at the Apollo, on 42d street, at $2 top. It's "The Two Orphans" canned in the Griffith way, which means everything there could be in that story the Master Genii brought out. Some call Griffith the Master Genius of pictures, but as he is the only one among them all, let the Genii ride whether it's right or wrong.

The "Orphans of the Storm" is set in the days of France's Reign of Terror. There are the mob scenes of the Revolution, the French characters as mentioned on the program, the two little girls in the persons of the Gish sisters amidst all the pillage and plunder, and the picture has all the angles, all the detail and all the scenes that any one human could bring out.

What a break those two orphans got! About half-way through the film it looked as though their streak would be a tougher one than Nellie Revell has had. They were the so-near-and-yet-so-far-apart twins. Sobby? Wow! The guy that gets the handkerchief privilege in the lobby will win a fortune.

And yet between and among all the sentiment [and it's a super-sentimental picture that the women must adore], all of the fights (including a sword duel and knife battle), all of the galloping horses, all of the handsome scenes and equally beautiful photography, Griffith brought out a great thought that was not in the picture—it was in a caption. It opened the second part and said in effect that America might profit by the experience of France in not permitting fanatics to become leaders. That's pretty timely just now. And another brilliant thought was the momentary introduction of Capt. Napoleon.

Had Griffith lived in the darkened ages he would have been called a philosopher, as all of those days with advanced thought were called long after they were dead. For D. W. Griffith is the advanced thought of pictures—always has been. Griffith has never made his best picture. It's questionable if the public will ever permit him to. They know him too well; they expand everything he announces; they almost anticipate everything he does. And "Orprans of the Storm" is not Griffith's best to date, but it's among his best, and still leaves "The Birth of the Nation" in front.

But "Orphans" has a stronger human nature appealing force in the troubles and terrors of those two little girls that the Gish sisters play so perfectly than anything in a similar vein this picture creator ever before has done. That makes it its box-office attraction, if the rats in the cellar and the guillotine scene that is so suspensively prolonged do not interfere.

In film making and picture taking, over and above or below anything for or against, "The Orphans" is as fine an example of the picture art as may be seen, and after seeing it, if those stewed students of the drama again say there is no art in picturedome they must be off their nut. *Sime.*

Boston, Jan. 4.
It probably cost Griffith in excess of $25,000 to make his eleventh-hour title shift from "The Two Orphans" to its present pirate-proof title of "Orphans of the Storm," the chief loss being in paper prepared by the ton for a national release. The night that he gave the film its metropolitan premiere at the Tremont theatre, a German "Two Orphans" was being shown in Lynn at a four-bit top as compared with Griffith's $2 top to a genuine turn-away.

That Griffith has a bigger money-maker than "The Birth of a Nation" seems to be a certainty. He has tossed the two orphans onto the tempestuous sea of the French Revolution and is using the ride-to-the-rescue for a finale, with an orphan under the guillotine and "Danton five miles away." This scene is drawn out agonizingly but does not let down in any spot. The cavalry ride through the town, the storming of the moated guillotine gates, the last minute reprieve and the hesitating release trigger on the guillotine all make for a dramatic final reel with a Griffith thrill that will compensate those who are not won by the unbelievable fidelity of the entire film historically.

Apparently Griffith used France only for research work, leaning mainly on M. Louis Allard of Harvard and the Marquis de Tolignac of Paris. Mamaroneck was apparently the spot where the France of 1790 and the Paris of Louis the 16th were reconstructed.

The first portion of the film follows "The Two Orphans" quite closely, with credit being given to Kate Claxton, but after intermission the film swings into the French revolution, the storming of the Bastile and the wild period of political unbalance that followed, with special reference to the rise of Danton and Robespierre, and the Committee of Public Safety which guillotined everybody that did not think the way Robespierre did.

The plot in brief carries the two orphan girls, one blind, into Paris. Dorothy Gish has been given Kate Claxton's role of the blind girl, and this step from comedienne roles into a role of unlimited emotional possibilities, such as when the blind girl is thrown into the rat-infested cellar, reveals new capabilities in the less famous of the two Gish girls. The abduction of Henriette occurs, she is saved from ravage at the nobleman's festival, the blind girl falls into the hands of Mother Frochard and is sent out on the streets begging.

The climax of the first half is not based on spectacle, but is hung on the dramatic episode of the noblewoman learning that her daughter is the blind beggar girl, and with Henriette under arrest being led to the prison for fallen women just as she sees the blind girl being dragged away by Mother Frochard.

The picture then jumps directly into the French revolution, where Griffith begins filming with a lavish hand but with a historical fidelity that really constitutes a challenge to the foreign films which until now have been supposed to be the last word in historical re-visualizations.

Henriette is sent to the guillotine for harboring her noble lover, Madame Frochard's crippled son kills his brother and saves the blind girl from ravage, and then Danton, in an appeal to the populace, secures a reluctant reprieve for Henriette and her noble lover, after which comes the cavalry ride to the guillotine and the rescue. After the first night Griffith cut one of the guillotine decapitation scenes as too gruesome, although the entire film was passed by the censors, which was probably the main reason why Griffith gave Boston the picture ahead of the Apollo.

Griffith is using a clever play to get the interest of college and high school students by laying stress on the historical visualization of the picture as it concerns the French revolution, using the name and endorsement of Prof. F. Humphrey of Trinity College in the program.

His experiment with Joseph Schildkraut as a hot-blooded juvenile more than came up to his expectations. The entire cast is remarkable all the way through, but Lucille La Verne as Mother Frochard, Monte Blue as Danton and Sidney Herbert as Robespierre are the outstanding characters.

In curtain speeches made while he was here whipping the orchestra into shape Griffith spoke of the similarity of the conditions which prevailed during the French revolution and those in certain parts of the world today, indicating that the film is a strong weapon against Bolshevism. *Libbey.*

TOL'ABLE DAVID

David Kinemon........Richard Barthelmess
Esther Hatburn............Gladys Hulett
Iscah Hatburn.............Walter P. Lewis
Luke Hatburn..............Ernest Torrence
Luke's brother............Ralph Yearsley
Grandpa Hatburn........Forrest Robinson
Senator Gault..........Laurence Eddinger
David's father..........Edmund Gurney
David's brother, Allen...Warner Richmond
David's mother..............Marion Abbott
The Doctor ....Harry Hallam
Rose, Allen's wife...........Patterson Dial

Richard Barthelmess, in his initial release through First National, has turned out a program feature worthy of presentation in any of the more pretentious film theatres. It may be said "David" is a corking getaway for him on his First National career. Surrounded by a cast which lends particularly efficient support, Mr. Barthelmess plays a role that is in some ways similar to his "Way Down East" characterization. He does it convincingly, with an added appeal which makes this performance come pretty close to being the best effort he has ever made before the camera, "Broken Blossoms" included.

It's a tale of the Virginia hills, taken from the Saturday Evening Post story of the same title, written by Joseph Hergesheimer. Henry King did the directing and has turned in one of the best bits of work of the season, as demonstrated in the latter stages of the picture, with the possible exception of allowing the action to be tardy in getting under way. King brought the suspense up to a point where the house actually squirmed with the unfolding of the climax to the situation, bringing forth applause from the audience.

The narrative tells of David (Mr. Barthelmess), youngest son of the Kinemon family, wanting to undertake a man's responsibilities with special aspirations to his older brother's job of driving the hack which carries the government mail, but being held, due to his age, in subjection by his relatives. Nearby the Kinemons live the Hatburns, an old man and his granddaughter, who are forced to undergo an extended visit from three cousins. They have been in jail and are chased across the state line. The visit entails the killing of David's dog and the resultant crippling for life of Allen, David's older brother, by one of the visiting Hatburns, with the father of the Kinemon family passing away, due to a heart attack when about to begin the feud thence started between the two families. David, the only remaining capable male member of the Kinemons, is stopped from carrying out his father's purpose by his mother, and while later working in the village secures an opportunity to drive the mail hack. On the trip the convict cousins get the mail bag, which forces David into the house of the Hatburns, where he kills two of the visitors, while the third is chasing the granddaughter who has run away to secure aid for David. The fight between David and the last of the cousins, who returns from the chase when the girl faints, leaves him the victor, but barely able to get the bag into the wagon and back to the village, where a posse is about to start out, the girl finally having reached her destination with the news of the struggle.

There is considerable heart interest, emphasized at different points, but that which will probably attract the most attention is the fight between David and Luke Hatburn (Ernest Torrence), the "third cousin." It's one of the best battles, if not topping anything of its kind that has been screened around these parts lately. Direction and cutting have played no small part in the effectiveness of the struggle; especially so in the way the climax is reached—showing the dropped pistol under a bureau with both men striving for it; the switching to the scene of the girl reaching the village with her information; then back to the exterior of the shack where the fight is going on with the door slowly opening, closing and wavering open again to admit David, dragging the bag behind him. A smashing bit of business that, while not possibly original, was well enough executed to draw a substantial outburst of applause from the Strand audience.

Next to Barthelmess stands Torrence as the oldest son of the Hatburn cousins, whose hobby it is to destroy anything which crosses his path. His playing was strong enough to make the character positively repulsive on the screen—proof enough of the ability he lent to it. Others who made their efforts count were Edmund Gurney and Marion Abbott as David's father and mother; Patterson Dial as the wife of Allen, and Laurence Eddinger as the owner of the village store.

The photography is excellent, though no one either on the program or in the first few feet of film is given credit for it.

"Tol'able David" is a "sweet" vehicle for Barthelmess in which to inaugurate his campaign as a "name" in pictures, and should prove a means of strengthening his present following, which past efforts have gained him, besides opening the way for many another film production of his. *Skig.*

PARDON MY FRENCH

Polly ....Vivian Martin
Bunny ....George Spink
J. Hawker................Thomas Meegan
Mrs. Hawker.............Nadine Beresford
Zeke Hawker.............Ralph Yearsly
Countess Carstairs........Grace Studiford
Marquis de Void...........Walter McEwen
MacGillicuddy ....Wallace Ray

Messmore Kendall presented Vivian Martin in this feature film, a farce by Edward Childs Carpenter, at the Capitol Christmas week. Distributed by Goldwyn, it proved an amusing little venture with weakest points the titles by Irvin S. Cobb. While Mr. Cobb in the Saturday Evening Post and elsewhere has never proved a successor to Mark Twain, his mind would seem fitted for titling; but somehow he does not strike the necessary octave of humor. In his writing for the screen there is always a hint of digging up what suits him and forcing it into the picture.

Mr. Carpenter's story was a bright bit showing a barnstorming troupe stranded on the one hand, and some Kansas farmers who inherit a fortune on the other. The ingenue (Miss Martin) takes a job as a maid with the Kansans, who are trying to break in socially, and gets accused of theft for her pains. But she clears herself by unmasking the real crook, incidentally winning for a husband a famous actor she has always admired from a distance. All this was helped by the acting.

Miss Martin was bright and appealing, while Ralph Yearsly as Zeke got a laugh just from his looks. The photography was excellent. *Leed.*

MORALS

Carlotta	May McAvoy
Sir Marcus	W. P. Carlton
Pasquale	W. E. Lawrence
Mrs. Mainwaring	Kathryn Williams
Hamid Effendi	Nicholas de Ruiz
Stenson	Sidney Bracey
Antoinette	Bridgetta Clark

This Realart, directed by William D. Taylor and featuring May McAvoy, is just about a perfect picture. Based on "The Morals of Marcus Ordeyne," by William J. Locke, which Famous did once before back in 1915, each scene is given its proper value. The cutting is clean and effective, and the direction satisfactory in the best sense. Miss McAvoy seems to have the happy faculty of inspiring her directors to their best, and she certainly gives of her best. The cast is right with her in that respect, too.

Carlotta, daughter of English parents, is left an orphan and adopted and reared in his harem by Hamid Effendi, but when he comes to marry her to an old Turk she rebels and runs away with an English lad, who brings her to London only to meet with a deadly accident. In her dilemma she appeals in a public park to Sir Marcus Ordeyne, who is embarrassed and dumfounded. Lots of fun here, but gradually Sir Marcus yields to her charm, deciding to marry her. In the way is his former attachment for Mrs. Judith Mainwaring, separated from her husband. His free-and-easy friend, Sebastien Pasquale, also falls for Carlotta, and when Hamid threatens to recover her, persuades her, with Judith's help, that the life of Sir Marcus is in danger. So Carlotta elopes with him. But she soon learns his purpose, escapes and supports herself by sewing, returning to Sir Marcus, when Judith, repenting, seeks her out with the truth.

Effective acting and cutting fairly shot this story across. The principals gave their usual finished performances, but details were enlivened in particular by Bridgetta Clark. Mr. de Ruiz brought an Oriental dignity to his role and Mr. Bracey was the kind of butler they make only in England. *Leed.*

FIRST LOVE

A conventional story is "First Love," by Sonya Levien, a Realart production, directed by Maurice Campbell, scenario by Percy Heath and Aubrey Stauffer, starring Constance Binney.

But it is convincingly picturized—that is, convincingly for the proletariat. There is an anonymous bit of versification on file in the public library at Fifth avenue and 42d street, entitled "He had the nerve to bring her here to eat," which goes on, with another line running, "I seen him comin' half way down the street." It is the wail of a waitress in a beanery, called upon to serve as patrons the man who jilted her and his new sweetheart. This is, practically, the gist of the story of "First Love."

The chap with whom the waitress believes she is in love turns out to be a bounder, a type who tells every girl he encounters: "Honest kid, you're the only girl I ever loved." He takes the heroine's money, pretending to buy medical books with which to complete his schooling for the profession of doctor, and squanders it on other women. In the end she marries a rich man who really loves her, and all ends happily.

The sincerity with which Miss Binney enacts the role and the directness of the narration are pleasing to the patrons of houses who pay to see the so-called program features. *Jolo.*

SHADOWS OF THE SEA

Capt. Dick Carson	Conway Tearle
Shivering Sam	Jack Drumier
Andrews	Crauford Kent
Ralph Dean	Arthur Houseman
Dr. Jordan	J. Barney Sherry
Dorothy Jordan	Doris Kenyon
Molly	Frankie Mann
"Red"	Harry J. Lane
Capt. Hobbs	Wm. Nally

Selznick production starring Conway Tearle, based upon the story by Frank Dazey, from which the scenario was devised by Lewis Allen Browne. Alan Crosland did the directing. The author has turned out a script strongly resembling the dime novel type of story, not over effectively worked out as to details, but sufficiently interesting in a melodramatic way to prove entertaining to the average picture audience inclined toward that style of entertainment.

Capt. Dick Carson is a sailor of fortune who possesses a fast yacht in which he encircles the world and makes hair-breadth escapes from various ports just as he is about to fall into the hands of the authorities. Just why the authorities are after him is not made clear, but nevertheless there wouldn't be any story if they were not after him, so that is apparently the reason for it. After a quick getaway from Hong Kong he puts in an appearance on the California coast, where the coast guards are waiting for him. A battle ensues upon his reaching shore and a bullet cripples him, but not fatally. He finally makes his way to a doctor, who treats his wound.

Meantime the captain had seen the doctor's wife in another man's arms. To repay the M. D. he decides to make the trespasser pay. The latter tries to make a quick getaway, but is met at the dock by the husband, with a shooting following in which the doctor drops. The captain forces the woman and man into a launch and takes them to the yacht. He obliges them to share the same stateroom, with the woman pleading innocence, which she finally convinces him is the truth. A mutiny occurs on the ship, with the captain finally winning over a faction headed by one of his mates, with the finish having the girl in his arms, which was what was expected from the start. For the screen patron who does not desire a plausible story but plenty of action this picture will fill the bill.

A capable cast supports the star, with Doris Kenyon having the leading female role. Direction and production help to make it a satisfactory feature for the middle-grade houses. *Hart.*

THE LONELY TRAIL

The big wallop of "The Lonely Trail" is that Fred K. Beauvais, "the Indian guide" of the Stillman case, is the featured player. That is all there is to the feature, which has been cut so as to take up about 40 minutes in running time. If there is enough curiosity regarding "the Indian guide," the picture will pull in money, which it evidently did at the Shubert 44th Street Monday (holiday) afternoon, but it will not entertain.

As a picture it is one of the saddest bits of screen production shown anywhere near Broadway in a long, long time.

The story, at least that part of it that an attempt has been made to convey, is of a wealthy man and his daughter camping in the woods. Beauvais is their Indian guide, and saves the girl from the hands of the heavy. Finally, as the two part, the girl slips him a note telling him she loves him and that when he wants her she will return. Whether she ever did or not is still a mystery. However, the Indian had a good reason to want to square himself with the heavy, for years before the heavy ruined and deserted the Indian's sister.

The girl with bobbed hair must have been picked with an eye to resemblance to Mrs. Stillman, but it ends right there. As long as the program did not give her name it is just as well it remain a secret, as the names of the other four or five supporting characters can likewise remain dark. The heavy is about the poorest excuse for an actor ever, and hardly any one of the cast had anything on Beauvais when it came to trouping. As a "guide" Beauvais may be a world beater, but he was never cut out for the screen.

No one need rave about this picture, either in the trade press or the dailies, for if it is let alone it will die before the week is out.

JUST AROUND THE CORNER

Ma Birdsong	Margaret Seddon
Jimmie Birdsong	Lewis Sargent
Essie Birdsong	Sigrid Holmquist
Joe Ullman	Edward Phillips
The Real Man	Fred C. Thomson
Lulu Pope	Peggy Parr
Mrs. Finshreiber	Mme. Rose Rosonova
Mr. Blatsky	William Nally

Enter Sigrid Holmquist!

Here is a girl who is going to develop into one of the stars of the screen and, incidentally, she is going to make a number of star ingenues step to keep up with her.

In "Just Around the Corner," a new Cosmopolitan feature released by Famous Players, Miss Holmquist displays acting ability coupled with good looks, a pleasing personality, and an infectious smile. Incidentally this production of "Just Around the Corner" is not to be confused with a stage comedy of the same title produced about three years ago with Marie Cahill as the star. The film production is from a story by Fanny Hurst, adapted for the screen and directed by Frances Marion.

It is a story of New York's Ghetto, there being three principal characters that carry the tale, which in itself is almost as compelling sob producer as "Over the Hill." There are moments when the screening is rather draggy, but in the main the interest holds.

Margaret Seddon plays a widowed mother with a young son and daughter on her hands. The old lady is ailing and knows that her days are numbered. Her sole wish is to see that there is someone who will keep an eye on her offspring after she passes on. The boy, a husky youngster, works as a messenger boy. The girl has been working in a flower factory but later blossoms out as an usherette at one of the theatres. Here a flip young ticket spec starts rushing her about the cheap dance halls, and although the girl tries to get him to visit her home with her he always sidesteps.

One night when the mother is very ill he gets to the doorstep and again makes excuses. The mother has been waiting and the younger brother insists that the sister go after her "friend" so not to disappoint mother. The girl rushes forth, but she is unsuccessful in getting the ticket spec to return. She falls exhausted on the way home and is picked up by a young man who takes her back to her house, and on being told the situation poses as "Joe," making promises to the mother just before she passes out. This naturally paves the way for a happy ending as far as the young folks are concerned.

For detail the picture is as near perfect as it can be. The dance hall touches and the Ghetto stuff are all corking.

Lewis Sargent plays the young son and puts the role over with a wallop, a combination of real drama and comedy being his lot. Edward Phillips is the ticket spec sweetie, one of those "pineapple" cake-eaters to perfection. He could walk out on the corner of Forty-seventh street and Broadway and be "just the type."

Fred C. Thomson is the young hero for the final few scenes of the picture, looking the part, but not measuring full-up on acting. Peggy Parr as one of "the smart girls," also an usherette, who likes to step, got over nicely.

Miss Marion is to be congratulated on both her adaption of the story and the manner in which she directed it. It just falls a little short of being worthy of the title of "special." *Fred.*

HOLE IN THE WALL

Jean Oliver	Alice Lake
Gordon Grant	Allan Forrest
Limpy Jim	Frank Brownlee
The Fox	Charles Clary
Deagon	William De Vaull
Mrs. Ramsey	Kate Lester
Donald Ramsey	Carl Gerrard
Inspector of Police	John Ince
Cora Thompson	Claire Du Brey

Metro's screen version of Fred Jackson's play, "The Hole in the Wall," issued under the mark of the Metro-Classic series, makes a story of many points of appeal. For those of faith in spiritual manifestations it deals with the mystic in a serious sense and in an earnest way, and for the unbelievers it has interest in an expose of the methods of charlatans who prey upon the credulous. Over all this basic theme it has a gripping crook tale and a well-told story of heart interest.

Out of these many angles, merged into a direct and compelling narrative, it would be strange if pretty nearly any grade of audience should not find an absorbing element. The direction is excellent and the photography especially expert. It is appropriate to the subject to play up the mystic slant, and to this end first rate use has been made of misted photography. Those passages that take place in the establishment of the medium, Mme. Mysteria, showing the mechanics of the spiritualist faker, are particularly well done, with their weird light effects, trick cabinets and the other paraphernalia of the professional "seeress."

An exceptionally good cast has been assembled for the production. Alice Lake is an appealing heroine, playing quietly but effectively the part of Jean Oliver, driven unwillingly into an underworld career. Frank Brownlee as Limpy Jim has a striking role of a cripple, one of those parts with which Lon Chaney has been identified, and Brownlee plays it convincingly. Allan Forrest makes a fine, manly reporter-detective, and Charles Clary is handsome as the "gentleman crook."

The screen story has good suspense, as is commonly the case with adapted stage plays, and its combined underworld and mystic atmosphere is fascinating. The picture is designated a Maxwell Karger production and June Mathis is credited with the adaptation.

The story follows closely the stage version. Jean Oliver, newly released from Sing Sing, where she has served a term on an unjust accusation of theft, comes to the headquarters of a band of crooks operating under the leadership of Mme. Mysteria, a medium who learns from her clients where they keep their jewels, and tips off the thieves. Mme. Mysteria has just been killed in a train wreck, and Jean is prevailed upon to take her place.

Gordon Grant, a newspaper reporter specializing in the detection of crime, investigates the operations of Mme. Mysteria and her band, and at the climax learns that Jean is his former sweetheart who disappeared when her father, a Boston banker, fell into disgrace. The title comes from the circumstance that Jean, in the course of her "spirit readings" develops a strange spiritual power by which she at times can actually get occult mesages and an awed conviction comes upon her and Grant that actually there may be a "hole in the wall" that separates this world from the world beyond through which the departed may communicate with their loved ones still living.

The theory is dealt with in an entirely serious way, and the play is done with a good deal of sincerity and dignity. *Rush.*

FIFTY CANDLES

Mary-Will Tellfair.........Marjorie Daw
Hung Chin Chung.........Bertram Grassby
Mah Li.........Dorothy Sibley
Ralph Coolidge.........Walter Burns
Dr. Parker.........George Webb
Henry Drew.........William Carroll
Mark Drew.........Wade Boteler
Carlotta Drew.........Ruth King

A mystery tale of Oriental pride at times fascinating is this translation to the screen of Earl Derr Bigger's story from the Saturday Evening Post under the direction of Irvin V. Willat. The central idea deals with a proud, stoical Chinaman of good birth who is bound in virtual slavery to an unscrupulous American for 20 years; serves out his time in unspoken rage at the humiliation, and when the last day is over, murders his master in stealthy revenge.

It aims at "kid glove melodrama" with its creepy atmosphere worked up to a high degree of tension by tricky handling. The sinister passages of the murder have their setting in San Francisco during a thick fog and the camera record of drifting mist is weirdly effective. The whole atmosphere of mystery here is splendidly managed, building up a strong emotional shudder for the climax.

Bertram Grassby's work as the spooky Chinaman who moves through the story as a silent, shadowy figure adds a powerful element to the mystery quality of the story. The only detail that misses is the failure of the director to establish adequately the overpowering grievance of the Oriental against his master, a grievance which shall justify his smouldering fury. Nothing in the picture makes this plain. The big effect of sinister mystery is moving in its mere mechanics, but the preparation in story elements is faulty and for this reason the punch is weakened. The Chinaman's impulses and motives are vague, for as far as the picture shows the American master has been reasonably kind to his servant. One would be disposed to regard him as a weak and nervous old man rather than a persecuting demon.

Some of the scenes are puzzling. For instance, what did the episode mean in which the American reached for a weapon, picked up an ink well instead and smeared the ink all over his face? So striking a detail ought to have some significance. That nothing came of it was distracting to the spectator. This is not expert direction.

A mild little romance runs through the story, having to do with the love affair of a young man and a girl in the employ of the American. Some neat touches of comedy are worked into this sub-plot, but all the picture's excellences are injured by the failure of the director to reduce the tale to a clear, simple theme and work that out straightforwardly. So that all that remains of what might have been an absorbing mystery drama of the Orient is its theatrically gripping murder incident as it is worked up by ghostly "atmosphere." This may be enough to put the picture over, but it seems a pity the thing was not consistently worked out in its entirety. *Rush.*

THREE LIVE GHOSTS

Ivis.........Anna Q. Nilsson
Billy Foster.........Norman Kerry
Spoofy.........Cyril Chadwick
Jimmy Gubbins.........Edmund Goulding
Peter Larne.........John Miltern
Mrs. Gubbins.........Clare Greet
Miss Woofers.........Annette Benson
The Duchess.........Dorothy Fane
Briggs.........Windham Guise

What is evidently a foreign picturization of Frederick Isham's farce, "Three Live Ghosts," has been made by Director George Fitzmaurice during his recent visit to England—or at least those outdoor scenes showing the streets of London. Ouida Bergere has prepared an excellent scenario for the director and Paramount has supplied an adequate company of players—especially Cyril Chadwick for the role of Spoofy, which he played in the spoken version in New York. One of the outstanding hits of the stage presentation, Chadwick is even more prominent in the celluloid counterpart. Edmund Goulding has the role of the cockney "ghost," played here by Charles MacNaughton, but fails to get the same amount of humor out of the part. Norman Kerry is the third of the trio of "ghosts" and is sufficiently good-looking for the straight lead. Anna Q. Nilsson, featured in the billing, has little to do and picturizes with her usual set "Swede" smile. Clare Greet scored as strongly as Mrs. Gubbins as did Beryl Mercer, the clever character woman who created the part on the stage.

The sub-titles have been somewhat Americanized, probably to come within the mental range of the average American picturegoer. The direction is admirable and the feature is one of the few designed for laughing purposes that holds interest throughout.

"Three Live Ghosts" is the feature of this week's program at the Rivoli. It is separated by only a brief turn by a solo ballet dancer from Buster Keaton's latest comedy, "The Playhouse." As a result the Keaton comedy suffered. It is like having two comedy sketches follow each other in vaudeville—a ridiculous piece of booking. *Jolo.*

THE WOMAN'S SIDE

Mary Gray.........Katherine MacDonald
Theodore Van Ness, Jr.........Edward Burns
Theodore Van Ness, Sr.........Henry Barrows
Judge Gray.........Dwight Crittenden
Mrs. Gray.........Orra Devereaux
"Big Bob" Masters.........Wade Boettler

"The Woman's Side," Katherine MacDonald's newest production, made by Preferred Pictures and distributed by First National, comes close to banging the bull's eye of popularity. It is easily the best (in so far as regards its drama) story Miss MacDonald has had for a long time. It gives her exceptionally good opportunities to prove her worth as an actress, quite aside from her physical beauty. Not only does she contribute a portrayal of power and much dramatic intensity, but the others of the cast have chances for individual triumphs as well. It is one of the best all 'round acted screen plays that recently has reached the public, and is sure to add to "the American beauty's" popularity.

John A. Barry wrote and directed "The Woman's Side." The story contains much mystery, and not until the final scenes is it made certain the play will turn out pretty much as the average audience would have it. There are sudden twists and surprising turns to the unfolding that tend to keep the interest at a high tension and to baffle speculation as to the ultimate ending, although, of course, it is certain that Mary Gray, heroine, is going to triumph over the scheming politician who seeks to defeat her father by unscrupulous means.

Miss MacDonald has the role of a young girl, Mary Gray, whose father, Judge Gray, seeks gubernatorial honors. His opponent is a wily politician named Masters, who has been brought up in the school that holds everything is fair in the political game.

Mary meets Theodore Van Ness, son of the publisher of a powerful newspaper. It is a case of love at first sight. Young Van Ness' parent is against Judge Gray in his fight for governor, and when, at the eleventh hour of the political struggle, Masters seeks to have the Van Ness paper print a scurrilous story about the judge, a story that is sure to cause his defeat, Mary learns of the trick and visits Masters at his office. There is a highly dramatic scene in which the girl threatens to shoot herself if Masters follows his announced course. At that moment Judge Gray comes to Masters' office and at the point of a revolver makes the latter telephone to the Van Ness paper to kill the story. Then it develops that Mary is the daughter of Judge Gray's dead brother, and that, after all, there was nothing of a scandalous nature that truthfully could have been printed about him. It all ends happily with Mary and young Van Ness in each other's arms in the most approved end-of-the-picture fashion.

Photographically, "The Woman's Side" is a delight, some of the scenes being unusually beautiful. The work of Wade Boetler as Masters, the politician, is worthy of all praise. He offers a strongly drawn picture of the powerful political leader, gruff, domineering, arrogantly heedless of the rights of any and all that oppose him. Edward Burns is happily cast in the role of the young son of the newspaper publisher, and Dwight Crittenden, as his screen father, provides a characterization that is well sketched in its many details of light and shade. *Jolo.*

RENT FREE

Buell Arnister, Jr.........Wallace Reid
Barbara Teller.........Lila Lee
Buell Arnister, Sr.........Henry Barrows
Justine Tate.........Gertrude Short
Maria Tebbs.........Lillian Leighton
Count de Mourney.........Clarence Geldart
Countess de Mourney.........Claire McDowell
Betty Briggs.........Lucien Littlefield

The long arm of coincidence is pretty thoroughly stretched in unfolding the "plot" of "Rent Free." It is a story by Izola Forrester and Mann Page, directed by Howard Higgin—a Paramount release starring Wallace Reid.

Running but 50 minutes, it peters out as it approaches the clinch, and were it not for the uniformly high grade acting and painstaking direction would fail to hold interest half way through. As it is, you laugh heartily several times at the ludicrous situations, which would be well nigh impossible in actual life, but the moment your thoughts resume their functioning you realize how far-fetched it all is, and it becomes necessary to win you back all over again.

Wallace Reid is one of our most popular male picture stars, but he won't continue so unless he is given more consistent stories to appear in than "Rent Free," which is nothing but another variation of the "struggling young painter" plot. *Jolo.*

TRAILIN'

Starting with an old-fashioned stage coach hold-up, then riding to hounds in the effete east, and jumping back once more to the wild and woolly, is the curious admixture called "Tailin'," a Fox release starring Tox Mix, story by Max Brand, adapted and directed by Lynn Reynolds.

Anyone coming in after the picture started couldn't possibly figure out what it is all about. Besides, even if one is in at the jump-off, the scenario is so designed to lead up to a surprise finish.

Mix plays two roles, one of which is disposed of early in the footage, after which he is shown as a brilliant country-club horseman riding to hounds. When, later, he goes west, he is physically able to cope with the bad men of that section and always comes out the winner in fisticuffs and gun plays.

For the average program picture patrons "Trailin'" is an absorbing story, full of action, well played by a group of western types, all of them hard riders, even to the heroine, in the person of Eva Novak, who mounts her steed to ride to the rescue of her hero. In the popular-priced cinemas the feature will give satisfaction. *Jolo.*

MY BOY

The Boy.........Jackie Coogan
Cap'n Bill.........Claude Gillingwater
Mrs. Blair.........Mathilda Brundage

They say that Chaplin taught little Jackie Coogan to act before the camera. May be he did, and if so, Jackie hasn't forgotten. In "My Boy," a Sol Lesser production, directed by Victor Heerman and Albert Austin, released by First National, Jackie is the same wistful, lovable kid, still unspoiled, who looks directly into the eyes of the actors who play opposite to him.

There is a pretty, simple heart interest story. Jackie is shown as a lovable orphan arriving at Ellis Island via steerage, detained, but escaping and following an old sea captain who has been kind to him. When, later, Jackie comes into his own by being taken up by his wealthy grandmother, he insists that the old captain be included in the adoption or he won't stay. This is the basis for a series of alternately humorous and sentimental scenes between the two. All that is necessary to record in the way of praise for the feature is that Claude Gillingwater is cast for the role of the old captain. One would have to be without a heart not to be moved by the love of the "old man" for the child and its reciprocation.

"My Boy" will chalk up a hit with any kind of an audience anywhere in the world. *Jolo.*

GIVE HER ANYTHING

Rather an amusing comedy, this Fox five-reeler, although the principal character played by Eileen Percy is rather spoiled by inept acting. As the spoiled daughter of the rich broker who turns the business office of her fiance upside down, she is too utterly saccharine to be human. The quality of kittenish hoyden has to be intelligently balanced. Too much of it is cloying, and Miss Percy lays it on fearsomely thick.

The tale is one of those farcical stories which roll up complicated situations to a final tangled maze and then smooth them out in a minute. Enid is engaged to Henry and in order to be a helpful wife insists that she be given a position in his office so that she may be acquainted with his business problems and thus a helper during their married life.

Of course she throws a monkey wrench into the works. All the office help fall in love with what they suppose is the new stenographer and Henry has to fire most of them. Heads of departments become embroiled and resign and finally Henry's head clerk dates up Enid for dinner at a roadhouse. When Henry learns of this he gives chase.

At the roadhouse there are further complications. Everybody is mistaken for a crook and the jam is completed when the head clerk and Enid escape and become embroiled with the clerk's wife and six children. In the end Enid is taught that there is no percentage in meddling with business and all is well again. These tangles are skilfully turned and swiftly developed for laughs. The story deserved better acting than it got at the hands of Miss Percy and her supporting company, who were artificial and obviously screen actresses and actors, and the audience never could avoid the conviction that it was just fiction. There was no background of reality to carry the interest.

Rush.

THE UNKNOWN

The Unknown..............Richard Talmadge
Sylvia Sweet..................Andre Tournier
Parker Talmadge..............Mark Fenton
J. Malcolm Sweet...............J. W. Early

This is a first-class novelty for houses whose programs are not set to frame first runs. Phil Goldstone made it solely for the purpose of offering Richard Talmadge in something which would chiefly serve to pave the way, by showing his stunts, for feature stellar work. Talmadge is a stunt man who puts about everyone else in that class slightly in the shade.

The story deals with profiteers who are putting up the price of food. An Unknown is striking terror into their hearts and leading their detectives a merry chase, the chase giving the opportunities for sensational stunts. There are leaps, somersaults, a collection of stuff alone worth the price of admission, with the Unknown unmasked in the end as a hero, winning the girl in approved feature film style. The question is, Has Talmadge the personality for the finer shadings required by less regular out-of-door stuff than he is compelled to show in his athletic pyrotechnics?

It looks as if that part of him could be brushed up all right. Certainly from a first appearance he would seem to have as much to show in that respect as Tom Mix or Buck Jones had in the beginning, and Jack Dillon has charge of his next picture. This should settle the matter. Grover Jones directed this one competently.

Leed.

THE LANE THAT HAD NO TURNING

Madelinette ....Agnes Ayres
Louis Racine .... Theodore Kosloff
George Fournel ....Mahlon Hamilton
Joe Lajeunesse.................... Wilton Taylor
Tardiff .... Frank Campeau
Marie .... Lillian Leighton
Havel................................ Charles West
M. Poire............................ Robert Bolder
Governor General ....Fred Vroom

A Sir Gilbert Parker story, adapted for the Famous Players' screen and released through Paramount, featuring Agnes Ayres. Victor Fleming did the directing, with Eugene Mullin receiving program credit for the scenario and Gilbert Warrenton the photography.

The tale, as flashed upon the screen, is mediocre. While it may satisfy as a straight program feature, it will neither add to the laurels of Miss Ayres or Sir Gilbert. It tells of a girl, living in a French-Canadian province, who possesses a rich singing voice, marrying a young French lawyer of her community (who is in mortal dread of an hereditary affliction of becoming a hunchback), then going to Europe and realizing a vocal triumph, returning to find her husband deformed. She gives up her career in favor of the husband, and in addition discovers the legal right to the position which he holds in the province rightfully belongs to another, which leads to a complication, terminating in the husband accidentally finding proof of the situation, killing the man who has attempted to expose him and later shooting himself so as not to disgrace his wife who had tried to shield the knowledge from him by a plea to the man who was willed the position but did not need it. An anti-climax reveals the girl as having once more taken up her career with the ultimate proposal of marriage coming from the benefactor who had waived his rights to her former husband's legal place.

As in her previous picture, "The Sheik," Miss Ayres is relegated to a secondary position as regards prominence by another member of the cast. In "The Sheik" it was Valentine who outshone her, and in this release the honors go to Theodore Kosloff as the deformed husband. Kosloff has appeared on the same rollcall with Miss Ayres before, but generally as a villain, though always coming through with a creditable piece of work. This dancer, for such he was, has taken kindly to the film art, and since the days when he appeared under De Mille has continually turned in performances which brought p...icular attention, and with screenings oftener should threaten the reputation of Robert McKim as the best "dirty dog" of the films.

Miss Ayres lends a pleasing appearance, but is not called upon to do anything out of the ordinary during the script. It's mostly a matter of interiors, with not an overabundance of action within the sets. What interest there is centers around the husband (Kosloff), his dread of the affliction and his sensitiveness to it after it is visited upon him. The aftermath, of the girl remarrying, might have been done away with, but the proverbial rule of a happy ending evidently took precedence over a stronger finish which would have materially benefited a weak, as screened, theme.

Skig.

LOVE'S REDEMPTION

Jennie Dobson ("Ginger").Norma Talmadge
Clifford Standish................Harrison Ford
Frederick Kent.................Montagu Love
John Standish.....................Cooper Cliffe
Mrs. Standish...................Ida Waterman
Captain Hennessey.......Michael M. Barnes
Standish's Overseer...........E. Fernandez
Stewart of Club..................Fraser Coulter

There are many arresting novelties of romantic story involved in the new Norma Talmadge feature, current at the Strand. The tale departs in many respects from the orthodox love theme, and has as its central character a rather unusual heroine, "Ginger" (Miss Talmadge), a waif of the island of Jamaica, with a passion for mothering all the spiritual cripples that drift her way until a homesick English boy comes under her care and in helping him toward his reformation she wins his love.

A curiously sympathetic role is this part of "Ginger," which Miss Talmadge plays with a high degree of sincerity. There is nothing about the work of the cheap sentimentality that so often injures the screen plays of popular women stars. All the appeal is addressed to an intelligent characterization. There is no "talking down" to the supposed level of film audiences. The thing is direct and earnest, and all its sincerity registers. Miss Talmadge, by the way, has achieved a miracle of youthful slenderness, and makes her "Ginger" look the part of a girl in her early teens.

The direction is as simple and direct as the appeal of the tale; the tropical locale offers large possibilities for picturesque settings, and these incidentals have been skillfully managed. Finally the play has excellent contrasts in comedy touches, effective suspense, and enough of dramatic strength to sustain interest. Anthony Paul Kelly adapted the story from the novel, "On Principle," by Andrew Soutar, and Joseph M. Schenck stands sponsor for the offering which bears the First National mark.

Clifford Standish is one of those younger son British exiles running a plantation in Jamaica. Loneliness drives him to tippling, and he is rapidly going to smash, neglected and imposed upon by his lazy native servants. Jennie Dobson, "daughter of a Spanish beauty and an Englishman of vague identity," known as "Ginger" for her household efficiency, has been running the household of a roving sea captain, but his departure on a long voyage leaves her without an occupation. Straightway she goes looking for some other creature to mother, and the secretary of the Foreigners' Club puts her in the way of Standish.

She first makes his house clean and, armed with a revolver, hustles the servants around to their work. The bachelor establishment is reorganized on a capable basis. The next step is to break the boy's drinking habits, and the energetic "Ginger" goes about this task with the same cheerful courage. Standish's family has ignored him all this time, but the death of an uncle brings him fortune, and the fashionable family at home suddenly becomes interested in his welfare.

With his impending departure for home Standish suddenly realizes that he is in love with his little housekeeper, and they are married. The family in England has other plans for his social advancement, so when he arrives with Little Miss Nobody there is the inevitable clash between the bride and the young husband's women relatives. Here are some of the most interesting passages of the story. "Ginger" is the same efficient, capable, dependable creature in this new warfare and comes out on top in the clash, but at length becomes weary of the fight and is about to depart when Standish, with a sudden insight into the situation, packs up and departs with her, young romance stepping out together into a world of their own to work out their individual destinies together.

Miss Talmadge's supporting company is first rate, including Montagu Love as the heavy. Business at the Strand Sunday evening was big, a notable demonstration of the star's loyal following among the metropolitan film fans.

Rush.

FIVE DAYS TO LIVE

Tai Leung...................Sessue Hayakawa
Ko Ai...............................Tsuru Aoki
Chong Wo............................Goro Kino
Le (Mandarin).......................Misao Seki
Young Foo..........................Toys Fujita
Hop Sing.............................H. Konishi

Sessue Hayakawa stars in this R-C special. The story, by Dorothy Goodfellow, shows him as a young Chinese sculptor. The girl he loves is adopted daughter of the money-grabbing Chong Wo, and is overworked. Chong Wo resents Tai's attentions and attempts to marry the girl to a mandarin. She refuses this financial blessing and is locked up for her pains. Tai attempts a rescue, fails and the girl is dragged to the mandarin.

The punch is Tai's offer to the condemned Canton Wolf to take his place at the block in return for the bandit's cached wealth. With the wealth he buys off the girl, they are married and have five days before the execution. Tai departs to keep his part of the bargain, but the Canton Wolf is dead of cholera, the ends of justice served. Back rushes Tai, only to find his wife dreaming toward death from an inhalation she had kept with her to save herself from the mandarin. Fresh air revived her.

Norman Dawn directed and can be credited with excellent handling of individual scenes. The photography stood up, but the chief fault was unavoidable: How are you going to work up enthusiasm about a lot of Chinese characters? Not an American face! A secondary fault—had it been absent the picture would have been greatly improved—lay in the scenario, credited to Eve Unsell and Barrett Elsden Fort. These two seemed to be in a conspiracy to rob the picture of action. It got a slow start, given over to creating atmosphere. The Canton Wolf was inexpertly introduced; about as much action characterized the attempt to rescue the girl as is present at a pink tea, and the Griffith save-her-from-death ending was allowed to flop.

The acting was better, realistic and full of punch, though it would seem bad business to present Hayakawa and his wife in the same picture. That must have an effect on the choice of story. Moreover, dollars are going sadly to waste trying to make the Japanese star into a washed-out imitation of an American screen hero. The man has unlimited ability, particularly as a heavy. Why not let him loose on a lot of sweet Americans who foil him in the end? Make him a George Arliss of the screen. But perhaps Mr. Hayakawa objects.

Leed.

ANNE OF LITTLE SMOKEY

Some one must have suspected there was something all wrong with this picture before it was released, for there isn't the slightest indication as to who wrote or directed the production on either the film or the paper used in connection with it. It is a Wisteria production released by the Playgoers Pictures through Pathe. This week it served as part of a double feature program at Loew's New York in conjunction with "Burn 'Em Up Barnes." It is a lucky thing the latter was a fairly strong feature and thus balanced "Anne."

The shortcomings must be laid to the story. It wasn't really strong enough, and also poor direction. The cast is a rather good one as far as names are concerned, with two women featured in the production, Winnifred Westover and Dolores Cassenilli and a supporting cast headed by Frank Sheridan.

Draggy in the extreme is the story, going on and on forever and never getting anywhere. Laid in a mountain section of the country, a forest ranger is the heroic figure of the yarn. The territory of Little Smokey is the ground that he covers. Mr. Sheridan is the head of a family which considers the mountain as their personal hunting ground, with Miss Westover as his daughter. There is a love affair between the daughter and the ranger. It is love and duty about which the picture is built.

The father is caught poaching by the ranger and in the end is forced to choose between the girl and the law. The latter wins, but later the girl decides he did right.

Miss Cassenilli is a wandering gypsy dragged into the story by main force. If it hadn't been that her presence added another name to the cast and her work helped to fill in some of the rough spots, that portion of the story could have been eliminated.

Outside of the amount spent on the cast the picture seems to have been made rather cheaply, for the greater part the scenes are exteriors and those that are not are cheap interiors.

At a price the picture will do in the smallest houses, but that is all. It isn't strong enough to stand up even as part of a double feature bill in the bigger houses. *Fred.*

BLUE BLAZES

Doubleday Productions has turned out a five-reeler here which assays only fair in total, the score being somewhat reduced in the average because the story does not hold strictly to its main thread. Properly told it should be a plain cowboy romance, with a wealth of action and melodramatic incidents in abundance, but for no special reason the scenario writer has rung in the altogether extraneous circumstance that the cowboy hero is in fact a champion pugilist.

It's a curious thing about these frank melodramas that the makers thereof appear to be ashamed of them and veneer them with some pseudo-philosophical aspect. In this case the picture starts out with several long titles having to do with the artificiality of the city, with its "painted lips and false faces," and the contrasting nobility of life and people in the open plains.

To this end the champion is disclosed as the center of a lot of parasites in a cabaret. He becomes weary of their fauning and in a small riot casts them all aside, walks out and takes a train for California. Somewhere in the southwest he takes a walk while the train is waiting, is waylaid, robbed and left friendless, hurt and ragged in a strange world. Here the real story begins about the end of reel one.

From that the hero gets a job on a widow's ranch, learns that she is being ruined in a business venture by an unscrupulous neighboring ranchman and takes up her fight, assisted by a group of cowboy friends whom he becomes associated with. He is arrested, breaks jail, fights with the heavy and his cattle-rustling adherents and in the end wins out, being rewarded with the hand of the widow's beautiful daughter. This is all fine, vivid melodrama of the robust sort sure to make powerful appeal to the fans, capably directed for a maximum of dramatic effect, but with that carelessness of minor detail which the boisterous nature of the subject is generally accepted as permitting.

It is, of course, pretty unreasonable to have even the prize ring champion fight off nearly a score of husky cowmen in a barroom brawl and it seems a little unreasonable to have the prizefighter of the cities take command of a crew of cowboys in an expedition against cattle outlaws, but for the elemental purposes of this kind of picture it is perhaps allowable, because it is fair to assume that the spectator is in a mind to accept these things.

But if the idea is to do a riotous melo, why not do it frankly? Every pretense of moral precept or higher philosophical meaning destroys the frank romance. The thing should be one or the other.

Lester Cuneo plays the hero neatly. He has good appearance and a pair of shoulders that helps convince in the rough-and-tumble battles. Charles W. Mack handled the direction. The distributor is Irving M. Lesser. The subject was shown as half of a double bill at Loew's New York theatre, New York. It is for the lesser grade of houses, for whose purposes it will serve well enough. *Rush.*

THE CHILD THOU GAVEST ME

This is First National release, Louis B. Mayer produced and directed by John M. Stahl. An all-star cast is featured, including Barbara Castleton, Lewis R. Stone, William Desmond and the most precocious and natural screen baby yet unearthed for a child of his age which couldn't be more than three years old both actually and according to the film version. Perry N. Veckroff supplied a story that grips and is only handicapped by its lurid title that listens like one of Ivan Abramson's old "sex" pictures aimed primarily for the humpty-dumpty picture houses where such titles attract. For the intelligent patron and the regular picture theatre the title hints too much of hectic histrionics when as a matter of fact it is all "society" with a ton of human interest stuff via the kid.

Barbara Castleton, playing the heroine, almost jilts her fiancee (Mr. Stone) on the eve of the formal wedding ceremony. She has had a baby which her mother has led her to believe is dead, although in reality being kept with a poor family in the tenement district. Just after the ceremony the child shows up at his mother's home and her newly husband mistakes the situation, vowing to kill the father of the lad. He refuses her any opportunity at explanation in accepted screen fashion which must be delayed until the final reel, but this is plausibly smoothed over by Mr. Stahl's excellent direction. The husband makes her live the lie he has accused her of living when he first courted her. William Desmond personating the friend of the family is suspected by the husband as the paramour because of a former fondness each bore for the other. Jealous crazed, the husband shoots his best **friend, which is the cue for the wife's explanation of how it all came about.** In flash-back fashion she relates how in Belgium three years ago doing Red Cross service in the war hospital, she nursed back to health a Hun who was caught in the American lines and brought to the Allies' hospital on his statement he was really an American and was anxious to return to the States. His thanks for the nurse's samaritan efforts were typical of all the Hun's bestial practices, as a result of which a baby was born to the nurse which she did not know was alive until after she had married her husband. Of course, the punch is that the present husband really is the child's father, explaining that he was dragged away from his Alsace to fight against his own French people and marching with drink-crazed beasts, he, too, became one that night. He descends the stairs, stating that, now that he has found the father of the lad, he will keep his vow and kill him, meaning suicide, which the wife stays, saying she will try to forget the beast and

remember the man. It all ends happily, the mutual friend having sustained only a slight flesh wound.

Mr. Stahl's direction and the baby boy's wonderful antics more than make up for any plot inconsistencies. Of all the greatest film hokum what is there more sure-fire than ringing in a lovable child for the central character. Here it was done with a vengeance. The picture is worthy of bookings into first class houses. *Abel.*

HAIL THE WOMAN

Judith Beresford..............Florence Vidor
David Beresford..............Lloyd Hughes
Oliver Beresford..............Theodore Roberts
Mrs. Beresford..............Gertrude Claire
Van Higgins..............Madge Bellamy
"Odd Jobs Man"..............Tully Marshall
Joe Hurd..............Vernon Dent
Wyndham Grey..........Edward Martindel
Richard Stuart..........Charles Meredith
Mrs. Stuart..............Mathilde Brundage
The Baby..............Eugenie Hoffman
David, Junior.........Muriel Frances Dana

"Hail the Woman," at the Strand, is a Thomas H. Ince production, story by C. Gardner Sullivan, directed by John Griffith Wray, released by First National. It has a strong dramatic story built about the text "The sins of the father shall be visited," etc., and is powerfully played by a cast of extraordinary merit.

The absence of a star with a metropolitan following may have accounted for the indifferent attendance Sunday night. But the picture made sure appeal. It is done with unmistakable sincerity and some of its moments of pathos brought a flutter of furtive handkerchiefs from women's wrist bags. Real tears from a theatre full of Broadway film fans ought to be sufficient testimony to the strength of the photoplay.

It would be a daring prophet who would attempt to forecast the probable fate of the offering. It gets away from the direct romantic tale which is the accepted basis of film fiction and takes the rather feminist argument that tyranical man, specifically the unjust father, is responsible for unhappy marriages and old maids. The picture will be made or unmade by the women and the question is whether they will be interested in this departure from the story of direct romantic appeal.

Its sentiment is genuine in spite of many passages of frank theatrical device. The bringing together of the weak son, the disowned daughter and the hypocritical father in the home of the daughter's fiance is pure fictional contrivance. So is the climax when the spineless son meets his own child for the first time before the congregation of the country church. Here the hand of the playwright seeking a "situation" is too obviously disclosed. In like manner, the dramatist is too intent upon proving his point by one-sided argument. The men are all too bad and the women are all too good. All pure white on one side; all too black on the other. There is no convincing shading to give the people reality.

On the other hand, the drawing of Nan, the victim of an ill-advised marriage, is tremendously effective. It was during the moving scene of her death beside her crowing baby that the handkerchiefs came out. It's all old stuff, this death scene of the persecuted and outcast wife, but it is supremely well done by Madge Bellamy, who stands out as an emotional actress of exceptional gifts.

The picture is rich in fine touches of telling detail. The spirit of the story is outlined at the beginning in a sort of prologue showing a group of Puritans. One of the village maids smiles and blows a kiss to a passing youth and is punished for a Sunday flirt by means of the ducking stool. In the story proper, it is desired to indicate the protective instinct of the heroine's mother. The family row is on over the conduct of the heroine. The mother is fondling the household tabby and drops the cat to go to her daughter's defense against the bullying father. The cat symbolizes the whole situation by scuttling to her kitten. When the son is confronted with his child whom he has never seen, the baby's face fades out and in its place the sorrowful face of the dead mother appears as the father gazes, the screen dramatizing what is passing in the man's mind.

These are small details cited as

illustration of the excellent management of incidental effects which typify the spirit of the whole direction. The photography by Henry Sharp is notably fine. The misty effects are capitally handled, particularly in the sentimental scenes involving Nan, Miss Bellamy's wide-eyed, wistful type of beauty lending itself especially to this kind of treatment. The picture is full of beautiful rural scenes and the closing "shots" showing the heroine going through the farmhouse doorway into the fields have splendid "composition," as a painter would say.

The story has to do with Oliver Beresford, a hard and dogmatic New England farmer with severe religious ideas. His son, David, studying for the ministry, and the subject of the old man's ambitions, marries Nan secretly. Oliver learns that Nan is about to have a child by David, but, because Nan is true to her promise not to reveal the marriage, believes they are unmarried. He buys off Nan's father and Nan is cast off. She goes to the city, where she falls into evil ways.

Judith, Oliver's daughter, refuses to agree to marry a yokel picked out by her father and also is cast out. The two women meet in the city and Judith cares for Nan's baby when the mother dies from privation for the baby's sake. There begins Judith's fight for the recognition of the child until she forces the reluctant David to acknowledge his parenthood.

Florence Vidor as the emancipated woman makes a splendid heroine, forceful without forcing. It is enough to say that Theodore Roberts, best of the screen's character men, plays the father. Tully Marshall has his usual disagreeable bit as Nan's blackguard father. Lloyd Hughes is much too good looking and manly for his part of the weak son. *Rush.*

THE LAW AND THE WOMAN

Margaret Rolfe..........Betty Compson
Julian Rolfe..........William T. Carleton
Clara Foster..........Cleo Ridgely
Phil Long..........Casson Ferguson
Judge Thompson..........Henry Barrows
Aunt Lucy..........Helen Dunbar
Bates..........Clarence Burton
Detective..........J. S. Stembridge

A Penrhyn Stanlaws production presented by Famous Players at the Rivoli. Direction is credited to Mr. Stanlaws and complete supervision to Thompson Buchanan. The continuity was written with his usual skill by Albert Shelby Le Vino, who adapted Clyde Fitch's play, "The Woman in the Case," on a starring vehicle for Blanche Walsh. Photographic credit goes to Karl Struss, and credit is the right word. Despite so many cooks, the broth is excellent. The offering is frankly melodrama. Mr. Stanlaws and Mr. Le Vino have managed some throat-pumping suspense.

Julian and Margaret are just married, but Julian has had a previous affair with Clara Foster, whom he supported when other men weren't helping. Happy in his own marriage, Julian is horrified to learn that his ward, the wealthy young Philip Long, intends to marry Clara. Doing his best to prevent this, Julian is in a fight with Philip before he learns the two are already married. He exposes Clara, returning to his own house only to be arrested as the murderer of Long. He is saved from execution only at the last moment when his wife tricks, in dramatic fashion from Clara, a confession that it was she who murdered Long.

All this action shoots along without waste of footage and is helped by the acting. Miss Compson as a quiet little wife probably withholds all that is in her in the way of acting, and in the scenes the night of the murder her hair was done unbecomingly, but she still has her moments. Mr. Carleton, as always, was an extremely valuable addition to the personnel, while Casson Ferguson as Long raised high hopes of a successful future. He dresses like a well-bred man and behaves with a simple dignity that contrasts pleasantly with much of the posturing done by men in pictures or on the stage. Helen Dunbar as a busybody, the tale-bearing sort all families seem cursed with, kept up the comedy relief. *Leed.*

THE MAN FROM LOST RIVER

Barnes..........House Peters
Marcia..........Fritzi Brunette
Fosdick..........Allan Forrest
Rossiter..........James Gordon
Mr. Carson..........Monte Collins
Mrs. Carson..........Milla Davenport

A Goldwyn release of a Frank Lloyd production shown for the current week at the Capitol, New York. The picture is rather draggy at times, but for a lumber camp story it is fairly interesting, with the performance House Peters gives being the strong feature of the production.

"The Man from Lost River" was written by Katherine Newlin Burt and Frank Lloyd directed the screen version.

There have been better stories of the same type adapted to the screen and better lumber camp pictures have been seen, but this one will get by as one of the regular program productions without any special strength to it.

House Peters plays the role of the foreman of the lumber camp with Fritzi Brunette as the little orphan of the outfit. He is in love with her, but she falls for a "city feller" who, after marrying, deserts her and returns to the bright lights. Later when he is cast off by his wealthy uncle and discovers that the land which his wife owns is part of an oil field, he returns, only to fall a victim of an illness that sweeps the camp and brings about the death of a number of those there. After he dies the road is clear for the man who loves the girl and the two clinch for the final fadeout.

Peters and Miss Brunette carry their roles exceedingly well and Allan Forrest, who plays the young heavy, puts the character over in good shape. This trio has the three roles of the piece that are worth while and others are but bits.

About three small interior sets are used but the picture for the greater part has been shot outdoors, with the lumbering stuff counted on for the thrills. The felling of the giant trees and their toppling to the ground is highly picturesque.

The picture does not, however, rank in the class that is entitled to a week's run in the best of the Broadway picture houses. *Fred.*

THE LAST PAYMENT

Lola..........Pola Negri
Pedro Maurez..........Leopold von Ledebour
Henri Durand..........Albert Patry
Paul Durand..........Henry Liedtke
Jules Lambert..........Reinhold Schunzel

Pola Negri is once more before us for judgment as a screen actress at the Rialto the current week in "The Last Payment," a Ufa production released in this country via Paramount. It was written by John Brennert and George Jacoby, directed by the latter.

When one takes into account her work in all the pictures in which she has been shown in America, the conclusion must be reached that Miss Negri shines in roles depicting her as a woman of no morals—an unmoral rather more than an immoral screen female. Hers is not the doll type of beauty we worship in this country, and her acting is of the kind that demands "strong" roles visualizing women of the people. This limits her characterizations and debars her from enacting modern society women; and, as every one knows, the pictures that draw the most money in America are those portraying our heroines residing in mansions. Up to now, though, we have seen Miss Negri only in massive super-productions made in Germany.

In "The Last Payment" she is a conscienceless French model, who has had a string of lovers; marries a man who embezzles to pay for her extravagances; divorces him while he is in prison; marries a wealthy South American cattle man whom she hates; accompanies a wealthy young man to Paris when her second husband is killed; rejects the young man's offer of marriage so she can lure his father into her clutches, and so on. Her end is tragic, and the tale is altogether too foreign for general native approval.

The production is a massive one—not as gorgeous as "Passion," "Deception" or "One Arabian Night," but admirable in the matter of detail and with a Bal Tabarin fete scene that is a model of mob direction.

Besides her splendid performance, Miss Negri is supported by four actors whose names are mentioned in the cast heading this review, whose artistry is on a par with that of the star. In their respective roles they shine with an effulgence equal to that of the featured player, and they are not branded with the mannerisms usually characteristic of German actors.

"The Last Payment" will probably be acclaimed by the critics as a fine photo-drama, but it is not likely to enjoy popular appeal in our insular country. *Jolo.*

ACROSS THE DEADLINE

John Kidder..........Frank Mayo
Enoch Kidder..........Russell Simpson
Aaron Kidder..........Wilfred Lucas
Charity Kidder..........Lydia Knott
Ruth..........Molly Malone
Lucas Courtney..........Frank Thorwald
Old Abel..........Josef Swickard
Gillis..........William Marion

The melodrama is released by Universal, with Frank Mayo as star. It is meller pure and simple, so much so that a Broadway audience at Loew's New York laughed at it time and again last week, when it was part of a double feature bill. Jack Conway directed the feature, the story having been done by Clarence Budington Kelland and adapted for the screen by George C. Hull.

Conway has the knack of getting his productions pepped up with action, and this feature is not an exception, but the story is illogical at times, and that is where the wise Broadwayites got their laughs. In ordinary change of program daily houses the picture may get by with fair success.

Mayo has an unusual supporting cast for a Universal production. Wilfred Lucas plays the heavy, giving a good performance, while Russell Simpson in a character role also contributed to the acting success of the production. Molly Malone was the lead opposite the start, filling the role without doing much that is worthy of comment one way or another.

One set is big, but it is the U stock dance hall. Other than that there is nothing that speaks of expense. The majority of the shots are exteriors.

A corking storm scene and a couple of fights figure prominently in the telling of the story.

Lucas and Simpson portray the roles of brothers who practically own a town. The former runs the dance hall, while the latter is the church member of the family. He has a son (Mayo) who as a child was lured into the saloon-dance hall by his uncle. The boy's father makes the announcement then and there that a deadline divides the town, and if his brother ever lures the boy across that line again he'll kill him. Years later, when the boy has grown to manhood, he clashes with the uncle, who has taken a girl who was found in the woods by the boy during the big storm into the dance hall. The boy follows and rescues her, but his father turns him from the house because he has entered the dive. But in the end there is a reconciliation, and the boy and girl go home with the father after the uncle has been slain by a demented old man, whose granddaughter took the easiest way via the dance hall route.

Not a particular wallop for the better houses, but in the small neighborhood places it'll get by. *Fred.*

FLOWER OF NORTH

Philipp Whittemore..........Henry B. Walthall
Jeanne D'Arcambal..........Pauline Stark
Thorpe..........Harry Northrup
Pierre..........Joe Rickson
Blake..........Jack Curtis
D'Arcambal..........Emmett King
MacDougal..........Walter Rodgers
Cassidy..........William McCall
Sachigo..........Vincent Howard

"Flower of the North" is a Vitagraph special, the first of a series Vita has arranged to play at the Cameo, New York, for indefinite runs. It was adapted from James Oliver Curwood's novel of the same name, directed by David Smith, featuring Henry Walthall and Pauline Stark.

It is another of the "strong stories of the Canadian Northwest," and hence is mostly exteriors. Despite its continued melodramatic action, it is atmospheric to a considerable degree, due to the selection of a competent cast and made-up types. Made up of regulation situations, such as New York capitalists endeavoring to steal the right-of-way to a railway in construction by the hero, the wife who runs away with the villain and returns two years later with her child—and a locket—the faithful half-breed who dies in the end after bringing up the child, surrounding of the cabin by the villain's gang of thugs and their rescue at the eleventh hour by the honest Indians, who are warned by a signal fire lighted by the heroine—it is, nevertheless, thrillingly interesting to the program picture patron and makes for an interesting feature of that calibre.

Henry Walthall, with his expressive face, is convincing as the hero; Pauline Stark is interesting; Harry Northrup is sufficiently villainous as the chief rascal; Joe Rickson does not overact as the faithful half-breed, and the remainder of the cast are all competent film players. *Jolo.*

RECKLESS CHANCES

One good picture, offered by Playgoers Pictures through Pathe, with J. P. MacGowan starred and Dorothy Ward in the feminine lead. MacGowan is also put down as director and scenarist. He adapted a story by Anthony Coldewey, but would probably have done better to let some one with an eye more trained on the general effect. Despite virtues and sharp cutting, basically the motives of the story could have been better introduced and forwarded.

MacGowan himself has a forthright personality and, properly handled, could make most any type of part effective. His name isn't any too well known yet, but, properly advised, he should go far. Here he is seen as a railroad man. Thieves have been lifting gold ore shipments and through a mistake he is suspected of complicity. A running escape, cleverly conceived and pictured, follows. In the backwoods he rescues the daughter of the division superintendent, who gets him a job in the division yards. His identity with the escaped man is not discovered (a bit unlikely) till after he has eloped with the girl, but everything is cleared up in a final row in which the real bandits are caught.

This final action was a bit hard to follow. Either it was cut too close or caught from a bad angle to begin with, but as a whole the picture rings true and is a worthwhile bet.

Leed.

DON'T GET PERSONAL

Patricia....................Marie Prevost
Emily Wainwright.........Daisy Robinson
Horace Kane......................Roy Atwell
John Wainwright............T. Roy Barnes
Maisie...........................G. Del Lorice

A rollicking five-part comedy by Universal. The photography, by Milton Moore, is especially rich, and Clarence Badger's direction kept I. R. Ving's story moving at a fast comedy pace. Doris Schroeder made the scenario. Marie Prevost is featured, but certainly equal honors go to T. Roy Barnes, while a pet dog added to wholesome fun far away from the slapstick style.

Patricia, on a visit to the Wainwrights, starts out as a matchmaker. The village vamp, Maisie, has been making trouble with other girls' beaux and Pat sets out to reclaim them. In doing so her heart becomes involved and John Wainwright reciprocates. Jealousy stuff rules the roost from then on, with Horace Kane, Emily's sweetie, saved from a forced marriage by Pat, for which Pat gets no thanks, only, in the end, to win her heart's desire.

Clean fun. Up to the best house standards.

Leed.

FOOLISH WIVES

Andrew J. Hughes (U. S. Special Envoy to Monaco)..........Rudolph Christians
Helen, his wife...................Miss Dupont
Her Highness, Princess Olga Petschnikoff......................Maude George
Her Cousin, Princess Vera Petschnikoff...........................Mae Busch
Their Cousin, Count Sergius Karamzin, (Captain 3d Hussars, Imperial Russian Army)..........Erich von Stroheim
Maruschka, a maid.............Dale Fuller
Pavel Pavlich, a butler......Al Edmundsen
Caesare Ventucci, a counterfeiter..............................Caesare Gravina
Marietta, his half-witted daughter..............................Malvine Polo
Dr. Judd } "The couple { Louis K. Webb
His Wife } from home" { Mrs. Kent
Albert I, Prince of Monaco......C. J. Allen
Secretary of State of Monaco..Edw. Reinach

TECHNICAL STAFF

Assistant Directors.... { Edward A. Sowders / Jack R. Proctor
Architects.............. { Elmer Sheely / Captain Day
Technical Department. { William Meyers / James Sullivan / George Williams
Titles.........................Marian Ainslee
Chief Engineer (illumination and light effects)....................Harry Brown
Costumes and Uniforms.............................Western Costuming Co
Master of Properties...........C. J. Rogers
Scenic Artist....................Van Alstein
Assistant in Research...........J. Lambert
Sculpture........................Don Jarvis

After more than a year and a half of extravagant bally-hooing, "Foolish Wives" finally reached public presentation, Jan. 11, at the Central, New York, where it is now playing. According to the Universal's press department, the picture cost $1,103,736.38; was 11 months and 6 days in course of filming; six months in process of assembling and editing; consumed 320,000 feet of negative in the making, which footage was cut to 32,000 feet, and ultimately boiled down to 14,000, and employed as many as 15,000 extra people for atmosphere. The sets are announced as costing $421,000.

A simple operation in subtraction, using the U's figures at face value, would place the cost of director and actors' salaries, script, film stock, exploitation, etc., at $682,736.68. Sources of information outside the U.'s publicity bureau estimate the total cost at between $600,000 and $700,000.

Allowing for the usual bunk attending all published statements as to picture costs, there is no question but that the U. shot an enormous bankroll in producing "Foolish Wives." The picture shows it in the sets—beautiful backgrounds and massive interiors that carry a complete suggestion of the atmosphere of Monte Carlo, the locale of the story. And the sets, together with a thoroughly capable cast, are about all the picture has for all the heavy dough expended, for as Carl Laemmle probably realizes, it takes more than money to make a good picture. Serving a hamburger steak on a gold platter doesn't make the hamburger quail on toast. But comparing "Foolish Wives" to hamburger is a bit tough on the hamburger. Maybe chuck steak would be better, and tainted chuck steak at that.

Obviously intended to be a sensational sex melodrama, "Foolish Wives" is one of the funniest burlesque dramas ever screened. Mack Sennett at his farcical best never made a funnier one. Unintentionally funny, "Foolish Wives," however, is at the same time frankly salacious. So disgustingly so at times that if the rawest "turkey" burlesque show ever attempted anything like the scene where Erich von Stroheim, as Count Karamzin, sits beside the sleeping figure of Miss Dupont (Mrs. Hughes) and graphically depicts undisguised lust for the woman he has been pursuing, the reformers and vice suppression societies would descend on the show in jig time.

Postmaster General Will H. Hays, slated to leave the cabinet shortly and become the boss of the picture industry, and whose engagement as head of the National Association of the M. P. Industry at $150,000 a year includes, according to the big picture executives, the general uplift and cleaning up of the film business, would do well to take a peek at "Foolish Wives."

Erich Von Stroheim wrote the script, directed, and is the featured player in "Foolish Wives." Talk about hogging the show—Von Stroheim has every other author-actor-star beaten to a whisper. He's all over the lot every minute. His character, according to the program, is that of a Russian Captain of Hussars. That Russian thing runs for Sweeney. The uniform may be Russian, but von Stroheim's general facial and physical appearance clearly suggests the typical Prussian military officer, with extravagantly polished manners, an air of studied insolence, cocky, swaggering strut and repulsive leer as predominating characteristics.

He's a he-vamp of the vampiest kind in the picture. Not only does he pursue the wife of the American diplomat, but chambermaids, nurse girls and half-wits as well. As Count Karamzin, Mr. von Stroheim plays 'em all high and low; it makes no difference as long as they are women. The title is a misnomer. "Foolish Wives" is wrong anyway—there's but one foolish wife. **With the amorous Count chasing every woman in sight, a better title would have been "The Villain Still Pursued 'Em."**

The idea of a foreign gent, programmed as a Russian Count, but looking like a cross between a German officer and a waiter at one of the Broadway hotels, making a strenuous play for an American woman, with the latter apparently just managing to keep from falling for the foreigner more by good luck than discretion, isn't particularly edifying, and as carried out in "Foolish Wives" is revolting. That is to say, from an American standpoint; but probably "Foolish Wives" was produced with a view to distribution possibilities in other countries as well; certain European countries, for instance, where the weakness of the American woman depicted in "Foolish Wives" for a titled foreigner will be taken for granted as the usual thing among American married women.

And the husband of the woman, played excellently by Rudolph Christians. What a sap this husband is, and what a conception of an American diplomat, entrusted with an important mission to the Prince of Monaco, von Stroheim has of an American diplomat. Imagine a man of 41, no matter how raised or born in the smallest backwoods town of America, who, upon being presented to the Prince, doesn't know what to do with his hands, and who, as Mr. von Stroheim has conceived him, generally suggests a rube storekeeper, rather than a member of the diplomatic corps.

To be sure, Mr. Christians played him that way; but von Stroheim directed, and it is expected that if Carl Laemmle let Von shoot that million, Von also exercised jurisdiction over the characterization he wrote into the story. The same applies to Miss Dupont, who gives a vivid picture of the silly wife of the diplomat. She's struck on the Count, and doesn't make any bones about it.

The best characterization in the picture is offered by Dale Fuller, as a chambermaid, who makes the fact that the Count has betrayed her poignantly convincing. It's a minor role, this maid part, but Miss Fuller makes it stand out remarkably. Mae Busch and Maude George give splendid performances of two pseudo noblewomen; Caesare Gravina plays an old counterfeiter excellently and Louis K. Webb and Mrs. Kent contribute competent bits. The woman playing the old hag handles it perfectly.

But no amount of good acting could make the story stand up. There isn't a moment it convinces. It's just the regulation trash, such as the U has been grinding out since the days of the nickelodeons. A try for suspense is made near the finish, the betrayed chambermaid (doesn't that sound like burlesque drama?) setting fire to a house, to the tower of which the Count (von Stroheim) has lured the American diplomat's wife. The diplomat's wife and the Count are shown standing on the balcony, trapped by the flames. The scene is clumsily handled and misses by a mile.

The Monte Carlo fire department, with the firemen standing at attention before answering the alarm, and again standing at attention when they reach the fire, makes a picturesque series of scenes, photographically, somewhat similar to topical weekly stuff, only more beautiful. Some colored fire effects and night photography, showing the fire apparatus en route and at work at the fire, were particularly artistic. Scenes shot in a driving rainstorm were also marked with a fine sense of composition. The detail is faultless. More the pity in such a ridiculous yarn. Von Stroheim's management of detail comes to light particularly in the gambling house scenes. If the story were half as convincing it would be a knockout. Several big ensembles are also expertly handled.

In a scene near the conclusion, where Von, as the Count, is given the gate by his two female confederates, he meets a black cat and kills it with his cane. Later the Count is killed by the old counterfeiter while attempting to approach the bedside of the latter's sleeping half-witted daughter. [Another delectable scene for the attention of Mr. Hays.] Having killed the Count, whose intentions toward the counterfeiter's daughter were never in doubt, the counterfeiter tosses the Count's body into the street, picks up the dead cat and throws both down the sewer. Pretty!

The story starts with a flirtation between the Count (von Stroheim) and the American diplomat's wife, continues along with his obvious attempts to possess her, right under her husband's nose, and with the woman's evident liking for the Count's attentions, and winds up with the sewer burial business.

One of the scenes along the route has the Count beating up one of his women friends; another has him attempting to assist the diplomat's wife to disrobe. Still another has the Count using a hand mirror to peek at the woman disrobing.

With its two principal American **characters conceived as a pair of unadulterated asses by the author and the foreigners by contrast shown as smart slickers who make monkeys out of the Americans at every turn, "Foolish Wives" stands as a leering insult to Americans in general, and American womanhood in particular. If written by an American, it would be pretty rough, but when stuff like this is handed out by a foreigner (von Stroheim is an Austrian), it's aggravating.**

That the U should turn out such salacious junk as "Foolish Wives" isn't surprising. They've been specializing in junk ever since the days of the store shows. What is surprising is that the U spent so much money on "Foolish Wives." It could have been done just as well for the U's clientele for $200,000 or less, and with correspondingly better chances for a profit. Some he-vamper, that von Stroheim guy, if it was he who got the U to unbelt more than a million for "Foolish Wives."

That white slavery classic of the U's early days, "Traffic in Souls," and its more recent "moral uplift," "Where Are My Children?" were both produced cheaply, and both made slathers of money, not to mention "The Virgin of Stamboul."

Bell.

SATURDAY NIGHT

Iris van Suydam, a society girl	Leatrice Joy
Richard Wynbrook Prentiss, her fiance	Conrad Nagel
Shamrock O'Day, a laundress	Edith Roberts
Tom McGuire, a chauffeur	Jack Mower
Elsie Prentiss, Richard's sister	Julia Faye
Mrs. Prentiss	Edythe Chapman
Theodore van Suydam	Theodore Roberts
Mrs. O'Day, a washwoman	Sylvia Ashton

Another of DeMille's "society" tales backed by magnificent settings whenever the story calls for interiors of the van Suydam and Prentiss homes with the subtitles being equally embellished. The titles provide the usual amount of descriptive reading matter plus a certain amount of philosophy pertaining to the theme that deals with an engaged boy and girl "born to the purple" marrying their laundress and chauffeur, respectively. The social and domestic situation become impossible to both couples and the finale, jumping to "Seven years later," reveals that the working class duo have united. Another switch in scene discloses that the two members of the "400" have become re-engaged—though minus the proverbial clinch.

Incidental to tracing the destinies of the couples, DeMille has contrived amusing action which leads to the pairing off of the quartet, the reasons therefore and the ultimate progressive incidents that brings about the conclusion with its axiom of each to his kind, birds of a feather, blood will tell, or whatever you will. The picture has a couple of thrills through the incidents of the young heiress, accompanied by her chauffeur, driving her car across a railroad trestle only to be trapped by an oncoming train and being saved by her chauffeur. About three reels later the heroine again is the subject of a rescue from a tenement fire by her former fiance—her chauffeur husband having left her to see that the rich laundress wife, whom he is now driving gets to safety.

The remainder of the picture is taken up with the social Waterloo that Shamrock O'Day meets as the wife of Prentiss in a series of scenes that display DeMille's ideas of how a pretentious home should be decorated, and that shrieks extravagance. The path that Iris van Suydam has set out to tread as the wife of her former servant furnishes the counter plot.

Leatrice Joy and Conrad Nagel stand out from the cast in their roles of the wealthy couple, having opposite them Edith Roberts and Jack Mower who at times are not altogether convincing. Theodore Roberts is practically buried, being allotted scarcely 200 feet of film, if that, with the other members giving an average performance.

The story is credited to Jeanie Macpherson and is presented by Jesse Lasky through Paramount. There's no doubt the picture can take its place as a box office feature for DeMille's name and the lavishness with which he has done the home life of the "Ritz" characters, though somewhat reflective of former palatial residences as conceived by him, will satisfy. Also the pictorial narration of romance connected with the interclass marriage idea will always appeal strongly to the majority of the fair sex. *Skig.*

RULING PASSION

James Alden	George Arliss
Angie Alden	Doris Kenyon
"Bill" Merrick	Edward J. Burns
Mrs. Alden	Ida Darling
Peterson	J. W. Johnston
Carter Andrews	Ernest Hilliard
"Al"	Harold Waldrige
Dr. Stillings	Brian Darley

What a picture this is! Certainly, it pleased the Strand audience Jan. 22, when United Artists brought it there with George Arliss starred. From Earl Derr Biggers' Saturday Evening Post story Forrest Halsey has written a photoplay that is just that. You recognize a controlling hand in the whole that seems to have devised a complete play and not patched together pieces, and this recognition has a singularly satisfying effect. Harmon Wright is a young director who has made the most of specially advantageous circumstances afforded him by Mr. Halsey's story and a first rate cast, and Harry A. Fishbeck's photography and Clark Robinson's art work supplemented the rest very happily.

James Alden, overworked, is prevailed upon by his doctor and family to retire on his fortune, but enforced rest gets on his nerves and it is brought out amusingly that those who have worked, deprived of that main diversion, in effect a ruling passion, are precipitated toward their grave rather than saved from it. Mr. Alden is getting worse, not better, when an insurance agent suggests to him to get some small business as a hobby, a diversion. In leaving his big company, he said, "honesty was the best policy, that dishonesty worked its own loss," and now in a small way he shows why.

From the picture standpoint this was a change for the better. Bring your moral down to everyone's capacity to understand and you get a more real response than when you deal in millionaires and their doings, however gorgeously. Finding himself partner in a garage with a young man, both having been stung by one Peterson, Alden, under the name of Grant, takes his supposedly last $500 and with his young partner proceeds to open a garage on the state road opposite Petersen's new one. How they beat Petersen is interesting and equally so is the love interest, amusingly interwined with Alden's attempt to hide his real identity from his young partner and his family, particularly his daughter with whom the younger man falls in love.

Mr. Arliss's influence was felt all through the performance. His own restrained methods need no description. With the slightest means, he accomplishes much. Suggestion takes the place of elaboration and the cast followed suit. Doris Kenyon has charm, beauty, the air of a slender darling and her frocks were well chosen, setting her off to advantage. Ida Darling gave one of those rare performances that are delightful because you recognize in it a transcription to the screen of pleasant and agreeable traits you have met in life. Edward J. Burns was straightforward and attractive, but everyone's bit stood out.

Admirably cut, the picture furnished as pleasant an hour as possible at this stage of the screen's development. *Leed.*

TURN TO THE RIGHT

Elsie Tillinger	Alice Terry
Joe Bascom	Jack Mulhall
Gilly	Harry Myers
Muggs	George Cooper
Deacon Tillinger	Edward Connelly
Mrs. Bascom	Lydia Knott
Betty Bascom	Betty Allen
Jessie Strong	Margaret Loomis
Sammy Martin	William Bletcher
Mr. Morgan	Eric Mayne
Lester Morgan	Ray Ripley

A clean, wholesome picture, that would easily hold up at any first-run house for a couple of weeks. Instead, John Golden and Marcus Loew brought it to the Lyric Jan. 23 under the Metro trade mark for a special run. If, as reported, they paid $200,000 to Winchell Smith and John E. Hazzard for the screen rights to their stage success, the decision as to opening is understandable. Perhaps the name will carry the $1.65 top, but it remains, as described above—in addition, exquisitely done. Rex Ingram, who directed, puts the refining touch of the artist to his work. June Mathis and Mary O'Hara turned out a workmanlike scenario, and John F. Seitz's photograph was A-1 in grade.

From the stage showing the story is well known. Here again Joe Bascom is seen leaving home, the farm, his widowed mother and orphaned sister to make a fortune in the city wherewith to marry Elsie, Deacon Tillinger's daughter, the deacon opposing the match. In the city Joe turns to the left, takes up with the ponies, gambles, and in a year or so, on the verge of a big turnover, is nabbed for crime. Sent innocent to jail, he comes out resolved to turn to the right thereafter and makes his way home in time to save his mother from being cheated by the deacon. Two prison pals show up, and country influences reform them. Joe, too, in the end is vindicated.

The comedy, due to the crooks, is rich in this screen version. Harry Myers and George Cooper, as Gilly and Muggs, got an equal lot from their parts. Real laugh followed laugh, but the whole cast was excellent. Alice Terry was the ingenue, a very much younger part than in "The Four Horsemen," and Lydia Knott as Mrs. Bascom looks really like her enough to be her mother. The suggestion was inescapable. Clean-cut performances were offered by Jack Mulhall and others in straight roles, while William Bletcher assisted in building up the laughs. From sheer mastery Edward Connelly scored as the deacon. Eric Mayne, too, brought real dignity to his role.

The bass drummer sought to enliven the evening with interpretative discords, but with himself suppressed things should run smoothly. If any suppressing is done it also should include the program's blurb calling Rex Ingram "a young man conceded to be the genius of the screen." Youth will be served, but this silly piece of enthusiasm written by one young man about another is not only absurd. It is offensive, recalling Griffith, Neilan, Ince, Lubitsch—a half dozen of the illustrious. Ingram has a nice talent, discretion, above all a sense of form, being a sculptor, but this sense of form to an extent crimps the fullness of his work. It does not flow freely. It divides itself into groups, episodes of arrangement, and never yet has he caught the spectator in a compelling grip that forces out the thunder of heart-felt applause.

Nor could he do it at the Lyric opening. The claquers were busy, but by exaggerating the applause and applying it indiscriminately to every name flashed on the screen the audience kidded the claque—let us hope—off the payroll.

Meanwhile this is a first-rate commercial picture. It has tears and laughter, adequate mounting and finished charm. *Leed.*

HANDLE WITH CARE

Jeanne Lee	Grace Darmond
Ned Picard	Harry Myers
Phil Burnham	James Morrison
David Norris	Landers Stevens
Peter Carter	William Austin
MacCullough	William Courtleigh
Marian	Patsy Ruth Miller

A Rockett production, distributed by the Associated Producers through the Pathe exchanges. It is better than the ordinary run of program features and was the better of the two pictures offered on a double program bill at Loew's New York with the U. "Across the Deadline" being the other feature.

Grace Darmond, with her striking blonde beauty, is the star of the cast, which has several corking names in it, including Harry Myers and William Courtleigh. Philip E. Rosen directed from the script of Will M. Ritchie, Charles Belmont Davis having contributed the original story.

Other than Miss Darmond there is but one woman, Patsy Ruth Miller. All of the other roles are male characters with five types of men shown. The quintet woo the star and she selects one of them and after two years of married life decides she has made a mistake because her husband has forgotten to recall their wedding anniversary.

She upbraids her better half and he makes a strange pact with her, consenting to let her have a divorce if any of the four former suitors will agree to elope with her. This brings about a corking comedy situation well played up. In the end husband and wife are reconciled and take a second honeymoon trip.

The locations and sets are particularly good and the photography splendid, for which Philip Hurn deserves credit.

Myers and Courtleigh gave splendid performances with Myers having a shade the best. Landers Stevens playing the lead opposite Miss Darmond, while seemingly rather too old for the role, played admirably.

The exhibitor can go out after this picture with the all-star statement and get away with the claim. The picture will stand up anywhere for a couple of days. *Fred.*

THE GRIM COMEDIAN

Marie Lamonte	Phoebe Hunt
Harvey Martin	Jack Holt
Dorothy	Gloria Hope
Old Dad	Bert Woodruff
Gracie Moore	Laura Lavarine
Billie Page	Mae Hopkins
Geoffrey Hutchins	John Harron
Carleton Hutchins	Joseph J. Dowling

The Grim Comedian is none other than Life, "which turns the laugh on all of us," according to a title in this Goldwyn picture current at the Capitol. The story is by Rita Weiman, and the production is designated as Frank Lloyd's. It's a curious sort of story, filled with naive, almost childlike sentiment which sets up all kinds of objections in the mind of the grown-up spectator.

The character of Martin Harvey, played by Jack Holt, is an odd compound. He is an utter cad in the beginning of things, a spendthrift idler loafing about the musical comedy back stage. He provides a luxurious apartment for Marie Lamonte (Phoebe Hunt), a queen of the merry-merry, with motor car incidentals and the rest of the equipment, and lords it over this intimate domain. Marie has a daughter in the convent, and when the girl pleads to come home, Marie decides to revise her mode of life. Martin, who has always made cynical sport of Marie's maternal affections, becomes enraged at her determination to leave him and live with the girl. His attitude is that if there is to be any casting off, the privilege is his, not the woman who has been living on his bounty. Not a very agreeable person, this.

Nevertheless, when Marie's daughter does come home, disclosing herself as a charming young person, Martin falls desperately in love with her and pays secret court. He says it with anonymous flowers and jewelry. When Marie learns of the intrigue, she forbids the daughter to see Martin, who thereupon brings the girl to his apartment by a telephone message. Marie confronts the pair there and there is a clash between the woman and her former lover in which she wounds him with a pistol shot through the arm. Martin is cured of his infatuation and agrees to send the girl back to her young sweetheart. The strange part of the tale is that Martin, who is at first pictured in a most unfavorable light, is later presented as honorably in love with the younger woman, and the auditor's sympathy is invited to his pathetic situation.

If this were not sufficiently distorted fiction, the situation of a mother in conflict with her own daughter over the ownership of a cynical rounder is not particularly edifying. Of course, mother and daughter are not rivals for the man. The emphasis is entirely upon the older woman's instinct to protect her daughter from life's dangers; but there is about the whole situation an unwholesome flavor. This kind of oblique romance is all out of order. Some day some enlightened maker of fiction is going to set a clean, unstudied story of romance in the surroundings of the theatre back stage where a manly man loves a womanly woman and they get married. Somehow the locale of the theatre invites the imagination of the uninitiated to self-conscious inventions of lurid loves.

In the present case there is a labored effort to win sympathy for the no account hero. He is first introduced in a railroad Pullman, where a card game brings up a discussion of fate, and he recites the history of Marie Lamonte to illustrate his point that life is the grim comedian. At the end of the tale the scene fades back to the Pullman, and the listener to the story discovers from a scar on the teller's hand that he is the "man in the case." But the sympathy won't go down. For one thing the character of the rounder is pretty average rotten on the face of it, and any plea for him is utterly insincere even under the loose literary ethics of screen fictionists. Any theatre gathering would have to be altogether infantile in mind to accept the tale as anything but a travesty on life. The grim comedian in this case is not "Life," as the highfaultin' title writer would have it, but the scenario reader who failed to stand between the maker of the story and the fan public. *Rush.*

NO DEFENSE

John Manning..............William Duncan
Ethel Austin..................Edith Johnson
Frederick Apthorpe.........Jack Richardson
Milton Hulst..................Henry Hebert
Mrs. Austin..............Mathilde Brundage
MacRoberts. ....Charles Dudley

A Vitagraph production in six reels, adapted from the story "Pardon," by Clarence Davies; scenario by Graham Baker, directed by William Duncan, who is co-starred with Edith Johnson.

Another variation of the "Enoch Arden" tale, wherein a husband, supposed to be dead, returns home to find his wife married to another. In this instance he is accused of killing a man who is trying to blackmail the wife, stands for the conviction to shield the woman he loves, and so on, until it all turns out happily for the original husband, whom she loves, and herself.

The continuity runs along so smoothly that it makes for an absorbing photoplay, and it is still further made interesting through the artistic work of Jack Richardson as the second husband of the double-married woman, who is an unrelentingly ambitious politician and in the end permits the woman he married to return to the man she loves.

William Duncan is sufficiently melodramatic as the sacrificing hero, while Edith Johnson is adequately emotional in the role of the woman about which the tale revolves.

Excellent program feature. *Jolo.*

EXIT THE VAMP

The Wife.......................Ethel Clayton
The Husband..................T. Roy Barnes
The Father..................Theodore Roberts
The Vamp ....Fontaine La Rue

Paramount release, starring Ethel Clayton, based upon the story by Clara Beranger and directed by Frank Urson. This Lasky production was not built for the bigger picture houses. Shown at a pop vaudeville theatre, the picture section had to be bolstered by a strong comedy, which makes certain the fact that the feature is being sold at a moderate price.

The story will suit women. It has been designed along the proper lines for that. The old eternal triangle idea is its foundation. The slaving wife turns the tide by becoming a vamp and allowing her spouse all the leeway he wants in his attentions with another woman. This causes him to sicken of his new acquaintance, with the customary reconciliation at the finish.

It is a short cast production with a light story, done before in many ways. In this not over effectively. It has a slight homey appeal, but with little else to commend.

The cast does well enough with so light a vehicle. Few opportunities for the director to display initiative.

Picture exhibitors who demand bargain productions from the big exchanges are the only ones who will consider "Exit the Vamp." *Hart.*

RED HOT ROMANCE

Rowland Stone.......................Basil Sydney
Lord Howe-Greene.........Henry Warwick
King Caramba the Thirteenth..Frank Lalor
General de Castanet..........Carl Stockdale
Madame Puloff de Plotz.......Olive Valerie
Colonel Cassius Byrd......Edward Connelly
Anna Mae Byrd.................Mae Collins
Jim Conwell.......................Roy Atwell
Thomas Snow.....................Tom Wilson
Mammy ....Lillian Leighton
Signor Frijole ....Snitz Edwards

The authors of this burlesque are John Emerson and Anita Loos, with the former also assuming responsibility for the direction inasmuch as the picture, according to the screen, was directed by Victor Fleming under the personal supervision of Mr. Emerson. The story itself is nothing more than a broad burlesque of "The Soldier of Fortune" or "A Man's Man," with the burlesque for the greater part effected through a mass of sub-titles, and these not particularly funny.

Joseph M. Schenck is sponsor for the picture, although the screen informs the public that the Emerson-Loos combination presents it. Mr. Schenck made an arrangement with the Famous Players whereby he rented the Criterion for the presentation, so, although the production is a First National attraction it is not playing the Strand, which holds the first National franchise in New York for first runs.

Monday night, the second that the picture was being presented, the house for the two nightly shows could not have held over 250 people from a short time before nine until the final flicker. The Criterion heretofore has been playing a regular two shows a day policy, but the "Red Hot Romance" is being shown on a continuous plan. This change of policy might account for the lack of attendance at the late show, for surely the names of John Emerson and Anita Loos have been looked upon as of some box-office power in the film world, and both of these names were displayed prominently in lights in front of the theatre.

The cast in the production is a corking one, and the picture on the whole is well portrayed by the artists. Basil Sydney plays the lead. He is the gay son of a life insurance millionaire, whose dad has died and left a peculiar will. The boy is given the home and a spending account of $50 a week until he reaches the age of 25, then his father promises him something further. When the time arrives the endowment proves to be a job at $25 a week as a life insurance solicitor, with the proviso that if he makes good for a year the entire fortune falls to him.

He is in love with the daughter of a seeker after a political job. The girl played by Mae Collins and her father being Edward Connelly. The latter is not so sure that the boy can make good, and finally, when, as the result of a revolutionary plot, the father is appointed Ambassador to Bunkonia, he informs the boy that when he receives his fortune he can come there for the girl.

When the hero receives the news that he has to work for a year grabbing risks for his late dad's company, he choses Bunkonia as the scene of his soliciting activities, which brings him on the scene just at the moment that the revolution is going to break, and he manages to do the grand heroic all over the lot, defeat the conspirators and win the girl in time to have her in his arms for the final fadeout.

It is all presented in an exaggerated manner, with a battalion of colored marines arriving on the scene to handle the situation. That is presented in the light of burlesque, but it is doubtful if the audience south of the Mason-Dixon line are going to accept it in that light, especially when the colored boys start prodding the white about at the business end of their rifles. Incidentally there are one or two other touches of the color question that crop up in the picture that will be certain of censorship in the southern states, especially when the darky major domo of the hero is shown as the bailiff in a court room scene ordering the court to be cleared in the following language: "Get out 'er here, you miscolored white trash."

Other than that, for northern territories where the race question is not as decided as it is in the south, the picture is a fair burlesque comedy of the program caliber. *Fred.*

WHY MEN FORGET

Richard Mutimer............Milton Rosmer
Mrs. Mutimer....................Mary Brough
Alice Maud Mutimer.........Vivian Gibson
Emma Vine.....................Evelyn Brent
Kate ....Irene Foster
Adela Waltham..........Bettina Campbell
Mrs. Waltham...............Daisy Campbell
Hubert Eldon.............Gerald McCarthy
Mrs. Eldon.....................Haidee Wright
Daniel Cabbs......................Olof Hytten
Jim Cullen....................James G. Butt
Stephen Longwood.........Leonard Robson
Willis Rodman...............Warwick Ward
Keene ....George Travers
Cowes..........Thomas E. Montagu-Thacker

Robertson-Cole released "Why Men Forget," a screen version of the George Gissing novel, "Demos," written and directed by Denison Clift. The production was made in England with an English cast and released in this country under the "All-Star Cast" billing.

The screen version is not in many respects sufficiently interesting to hold the attention of the average American audience. The story has its effective parts, but in the screening loses in comparison with the American program picture.

The story deals with the acquisition of sudden wealth by a man of the working class, the money causing him to forget his former friends and to fall in line with other capitalists rather than to help the lower class as he had promised to do.

The success of a picture in this country is largely based upon the popularity of its players. It is in this respect that "Why Men Forget" will experience difficulty, as the cast, regardless of its value in acting, contains no players of any prominence over here, although known to a large degree in England.

"Why Men Forget" is a foreign picture of insufficient pretentiousness to gain recognition in this country. *Hart.*

WESTERN FIREBRANDS

Billy Fargo................Big Boy Williams
Mildred Stanton...............Virginia Adair
Lanning............................Jack Pitcairn
Pete.....................................Bert Apling
Red Feather.........................Helen Yoder
Robert Stanton..............William Horne
John Fargo.......................J. F. Needham

Released by Aywon and produced by Charles R. Seeling. With not much money spent on it, it could still have been good with better direction, cutting and photography. As it stands, it is one of those half-way failures. The story itself was all right, but arranged so it just failed to get you as it went along.

Lanning is up in the lumber territories trying to get the price of a mill down, so he can share on the rake-off. Bribing lumber-jacks to set forest fires, he starts Fargo on a still hunt for the perpetrators who have been burning and frightening his cattle. Robert Stanton, Lanning's boss, comes into the territory, and Fargo saves his train from wreck, winning Mildred's gratitude. She has been engaged to Lanning, but Lanning has been flirting with Little Red Feather, and, in the end, to further his schemes, kidnaps Mildred. The rescue is the punch of the picture and worth while. A glimpse of Red Feather bathing was another pretty touch.

The acting was unexpectedly good. Williams, a newcomer, has a wholesome, pleasant personality, and should improve with direction, and Virginia Adair was away from the usual and pleased, showing delicacy in her portrayal. Helen Yoder came through with some excellent pantomime and the men he-manned their parts satisfactorily. *Leed.*

THE SEA LION

No extended comment is called for in the case of this absurd rehash of Jack London's "The Sea Wolf" put out by Hobart Bosworth Pictures, with that star and producer in the principal part. Mr. Bosworth made his great screen success some years ago in a film version of London's powerful sea tale. This garbled invention adds nothing to his reputation. It is sponsored by First National. It was the current attraction at Proctor's 58th Street over on the East Side where a typical neighborhood audience declined to get stirred up by its crude fiction.

The data furnished by the billing is to the effect that the story is by Emelie Johnson, scenario by Joseph Franklin Poland and direction by Rowland V. Lee. Bessie Love plays the lead in the supporting organization. The players are excellent with first rate types of rough seamen and Bosworth would be his authentic self if the travesty of a tale would give him half a chance.

But how could any actor do in the part of a rough and cruel sea captain who is seriously referred to by the title as "The Sea Lion" and his ship casually introduced as the "sea lion's lair?" And that ain't the half of it. The story piles ridiculous detail upon mock heroics until the whole affair runs into unintended travesty. The film started out interestingly enough with some capital marine scenes about the three-masted whaler, with a real whale hunt, probably cut in from some educational subject. Interest was fairly well sustained when it appeared that the captain was an embittered man, his wife having apparently deserted him while he was at sea on a previous voyage, running off with another man.

On his arrival in San Francisco a new chapter opens. We are shown a gaudy cabaret (is there any dramatic film that does not somewhere get itself in a cabaret?) and the high flying young man, described as "a waster" is revealed at his revels. He is cast off by his family and in desperation ships with "The Sea Lion," on his next trip. Here's where the blow off comes. The Sea Lion is becalmed and the water supply runs out. The crew mutinies at its cruel master who takes all the remaining water, but he meets them all by squads and platoons and beats them down with his bare fists. Just then land is sighted. It seemed a little out of order that the Whaler should find himself in tropical waters, but such is the case.

In the offing lies none other than the well-known South Sea Islands inhabited by an old man and a beautiful bare legged girl, and we have as tense and serious drama the exact situation which Mickey

Neilan made into a rollicking burlesque in "The Lotus Eater." Only the Bosworth drama in its intensity is twice as laughable as the travesty. There are many adventures after the discovery of the island and its quaint dwellers, all leading up to the startling disclosure that the beautiful girl is the Sea Lion's own daughter. It appears that the Sea Lion's wife was kidnapped sixteen years before by an old suitor and carried off to sea while the Sea Lion (his name is John Nelson) was away on a cruise.

The kidnapper's ship was wrecked. All hands were lost (presumably a lot of rugged sailor men) and only the frail woman, about to become a mother and an old steward were saved. The baby was born on the island and grew up under the care of the ancient steward, although the mother, having served the scenario writer's fell purpose, perished. But sixteen years after this whole history is made known to Nelson by the written record of the wife in her family bible, which the beautiful daughter brings aboard the "Lair." That amazing detail ought to be enough to indicate the sort of trash this "Sea Lion" is. The rest doesn't matter. Some of the marine shots, particularly the approach of a violent storm across the water, and some spirited shots from the deck of the schooner showing the rushing billows, were extremely interesting. The photographer dealt kindly with the ocean. The rest of the picture is a total loss. *Rush.*

SKY HIGH

A few releases like this Western adventure story with Tom Mix as its hero will make up for a lot of mediocre, and worse, stuff from the Fox establishment. "Sky High," which bears the name of Lynn Reynolds as scenario writer and director, is a splendid action film, direct, unpretentious, but plausible and interesting in story and characters, and packed with truly sensational "stunt" material. It's a breath-taking tale in the gorgeous settings of the real Grand Canyon of Arizona.

Its backgrounds alone as a pictorial would be sufficient to hold interest, but in addition it holds a capital adventure tale and plenty of thrilling feats by the audacious cow-boy hero. Out of the opulent wealth of sensations, it is enough to describe the achievement of the hero, who is shown in an aeroplane flight over the actual canyon. The plane is seen in its soaring flights above the walls of the abyss, tipping below the rim of the awesome crater and as a climax apparently dropping the hero to the end of a long, trailing rope, from which he plunges into the river. Probably the landing is trick stuff, but it is so well managed that it would convince even the most sophisticated. To all intents and purposes it is a real feat.

A series of titles at the outset makes it appear that the stunt was done in reality, at least as far as the aerial flight was concerned, and there is nothing in the film to raise a doubt of the truth of the statement. If that aero thrill was not enough, Mix does a horseback dash up what appears to be miles of almost perpendicular, twisting trail, a hair-raising performance. Almost as thrilling were his many climbs on a slender rope up the straight sides of lofty precipices. Much of the action takes place on a narrow shelf of rock along the side of the cliff's face, surrounded by heights almost terrifying to behold even from the security of a theatre seat, and with the distant peaks as the heroic background of the simple but absorbing tale.

There are endless escapes and pursuits, with men on foot climbing the dizzy altitudes of the walls and sprinting about on perilous footholds with giddy distances stretching below them. Hardly a moment passes but has its thrill. It's as well sustained a Western melodrama as has been seen in many a day. Of its kind, the production matches anything that comes to mind as a program release.

The film has a brisk beginning. Mix rides into the picture from the surrounding forest in time to intercept a limousine speeding through the mountains. He holds it up, lining up at the roadside a group of what appear to be women tourists, but who are revealed as smuggled Chinese coming over the Mexican border. He is an immigration bureau agent sent to check the running of Chinese.

"The man higher up," the government learns, has concealed a whole army of Chinese in the Grand Canyon, awaiting a chance to get them into the States, and Tom is picked to run the band down. He gets himself employed by the runners by a clever trick and is among the fugitives in the canyon when the girl ward of "the man higher up," on the way to join her guardian, gets lost among the cliffs of the mountains nearby.

Mix finds her on a narrow shelf halfway up the wall and takes care of her until the outlaws learn his real identity and attempt to do away with him. Here is the beginning of the sensational fight and chase which runs through three or four reels to its breathless finish. To attempt to detail its incidents would be a task, but it provides an hour and a half of gripping adventure and action well worth anyone's time. Jane Novak is the pretty heroine, and there is a magnificent horse.

It's a picture for anybody's theatre. The marvel is that it was not held out as a special and given the exploitation it deserves. The picture is a credit to everybody concerned in its making, and that goes double for Mix, the best rough and tumble stunt film actor that ever took a chance. One picture hero like this is more credit to the business than all the sorrowful, introspective screen ladies that ever struggled with a broken heart or stubbed her toe on the Double Standard. More power to the breed! *Rush.*

KINDRED OF THE DUST

The most drastic adverse comment to be made with respect to R. A. Walsh's film production of Peter B. Kyne's story, "Kindred of the Dust," of which Director Walsh has made a special feature for First National, is that while he condensed the tale and yet followed the book in its essentials, he tried to encompass too much of the interesting details. As a result he submitted at a pre-view showing at the Ritz-Carlton last Friday evening (Jan. 20) 90 minutes of footage, which should be ruthlessly cut to seven reels, when he will have a splendid drama, well played, excellently photographed, admirably directed and full of romance and suspense.

The director has carried to great lengths the practice of allegorically visualizing the poetically descriptive sub-titles. The story would sound trite in its summary here, but as enacted by Ralph Graves as the hero, Miriam Cooper as the long-suffering heroine, Lionel Belmore as the stubborn father, and W. J. Ferguson as a comedy character, it makes for high-class picture entertainment. ***Jolo.***

LITTLE EVA ASCENDS

Roy St. George (Little Eva)..Gareth Hughes
Mattie Moore..............Eleanor Fields
Priscilla Price...............May Collins
Blanche St. George........Unity Via Moore
John St. George.............Ben Haggerty
Mr. Wilson...............Edward Martindale
Junius Brutus...............Harry Loraine
Mr. Moore....................Mark Fenton
Mr. Price.....................John Prince
Montgomery Murphy.........Fred Warren
Richard Bansfield............W. H. Brown

S-L (Sawyer-Lubin) Pictures produced "Little Eva Ascends" under the direction of George D. Baker for release through Metro.

The picture is an adaptation of the Thomas Beer story of the same title, published in the "Saturday Evening Post." The action centers around a barnstorming troupe playing "Uncle Tom's Cabin." The manager is a woman, whose two sons are in the company, the younger playing "Little Eva." His objection to playing the girl part causes trouble in the organization, the mother overruling his protest.

Reaching a small California town the father, deserted by his wife while the children were very young, is found to be the proprietor of the hotel. The younger boy, so he will not leave the show, is not informed the friendly proprietor is his father until after the performance, which ends in disorder, when the two boys are taken under the wing of their pater and given a home on his ranch, with a cash settlement made to the wife to have the boys remain there.

Gareth Hughes has been well cast for the juvenile lead, developing strong comedy. The supporting cast has been well laid out. As screened the story is draggy in spots, too much time being devoted to the performance of "Uncle Tom's Cabin." In other respects it is interesting and well mounted. *Hart.*

SHERLOCK HOLMES

The occasional fluke that hops up filmville with a dash of the wholly unexpected every once in a while has occurred again. The pictures made by Stoll of London haven't hit very high standards of concept or production since that enterprising Britisher decided to add picture making to his manifold other amusement outputs. Accordingly when some time since it was announced that the producer had evolved 15 of the Sir Arthur A. Conan Doyle adventures for screen consumption, the informed among the trade of his own and other countries somehow couldn't seem to whip themselves into any considerable degree of enthusiasm, this despite that the rich Holmes material was virtually all new soil for the camera. Stoll got crackerjack returns from London and British centres generally where he started to exhibit the results of about two years of studio and laboratory work on the Holmes material, but the smart ones outside the Stoll environs credited all the interest to the fame of the author and the backwash the famous Sherlock Holmes fiction series had created.

Attempts of agents on this side to open a market for the production failed. Prices offered were negligible. Just at about the time the Stoll folk had about decided there wasn't any more film business in America the Alexander Film Corporation, either very astute or very lucky lately in picking out dark horses, grabbed the 15 adventures. One has but to see the first five they have made ready for release, commencing Feb. 1, to discover this spread-eagling firm has put its clamps down on a real live buy, and that whatever the judgment of the American market has been regarding the Stoll productions, this Sherlock Holmes series must revise it.

The five subjects viewed comprise in their separate two-reel subjects a quintet of the most exciting mystery detective series thus far to find their way to the screen.

"The Man with the Twisted Lip" vibrates with the color and drama of the printed version, with the denouement startlingly effective when Neville St. Clair, gentleman, is revealed as a beggar with a trick of transforming his identity by old clothes and a distorted mouth.

"The Dying Detective," the Holmes adventures where a noted criminal undertakes to trap the detective, also follows the original in almost complete detail, suggesting "Alias Jimmy Valentine" in its police and underworld revelations.

"The Beryl Coronet" flashes its audience among London's drawing room elements, there to pit the wit of Holmes against a wily thief, same as in the story, with the stolen heirloom and its trail seeming infinitely more real in celluloid.

Perhaps the most tense of the first five is "The Resident Patient," the mystery of a strange invalid and his stranger death, told with a wealth of finesse in type, but here compacted with situations so electric with drama they must bring observers to right about attention.

Further variety of subject is offered in the filming of the famous Doyle tale of "The Devil's Foot," the mystery story of three strange deaths the criminologist undertakes to solve after professional crime experts have failed. **Few situations in films or the spoken drama have affected the reviewer more gruesomely than the sight of the three victims of the singular tragedy seen sitting bolt upright at a dinner, and each stone stark dead, killed by a tragic toxic pollen indigenous to Africa.**

Maurice Elvey, who directed the subjects, may plume himself confidently upon his success with the first five shown here. Eilly Norwood, as Sherlock, is an ideal selection. No alien or native player suggests so faithfully the grim, thoughtful physiognomy the public of this country is wont to identify with the character because of the portrait broadcasted here of William Gillette in the stage version of the same role. The photography is comparatively without flaw, the London and other British exteriors shown proving as interesting as a travelog. The spots cameraed are said to be actually those recorded in the Doyle stories.

The Alexander firm has dolled up the imports in native sub-title clothes, and here and there snapped up the original action by recutting. But the credit of the transfer of the adventures from the printed form to the screen expression belongs to Elvey and Norwood, not forgetting Stoll. The buy of the Alexander firm is advantaged by the new Holmes series Doyle has started with syndicate publications throughout the world carrying again the Sherlock advertising.

Although in two reels, any of the five shown is big enough drama to bill as a feature. If the productions are anything, they're box office stuff for fair.

THE ROOF TREE

Ken Thornton..............William Russell
Sally McTurk..............Florence Deshon
Dorothy Harper..............Sylvia Breamer
Caleb Harper..................Robert Daly
Bass Rowlett..............Arthur Morrison
Jim Rowlett....................Al Fremont

Fox program feature at Loew's New York last Friday, where it was part of a double feature program, though strong enough to stand up alone. Charles Neville Buck wrote it, Jack Dillon directed, and the scenario is credited to Jules G. Furthman. It runs about 4,500 feet and is a corking offering, well acted, with considerable emotional value lent to the whole by Al Fremont's performance and a running start that catches the interest at once.

Under an assumed name, Ken Thornton, wanted for murder, appears in the Virginia mountains, where he falls in love with Dorothy. His life is threatened for this, and he is finally shot, with the villain multiplying his troubles, but forced to stand up with him at his marriage. The loyalty of the mountain folk is well brought out when Ken

is taken back to stand trial for murder, but there his innocence is established by his sister's confession. She shot in self-defense.

Returning to his wife, he learns she has been pestered by Bass, and promptly Ken tackles him, Bass' own father turning against his son when he learns the extent of his betrayals. This made an effective climax just before the usual final clinch, and Mr. Fremont made it impressive. Miss Breamer was her usual attractive self and Mr. Russell up to his mark. In a few brief moments Florence Deshon contributed a lot. *Leed.*

JUDGMENT

Rialto Productions, Inc., is sponsor for this seven-reel dramatic spectacle based on Victor Hugo's story, "Mary Tudor," shown at a pre-release viewing in New York. The screen titles do not give any intimation of who produced the work, but it bears on its face all the marks of foreign origin. The star is Ellen Richter, the only player whose name is disclosed in the titles.

As a dramatic work it has powerful suspense, but its technical quality is full of flaws. The studio settings are obviously artificial and the principal characters are all theatrical. The make-up of Miss Richter alone would be enough to kill off any real illusion. She wears heavy black shadows under and around the eyes so startling as to suggest that she has a narrow mask across the upper part of her face. All these details injure the realism of the picture story.

But for strong dramatic valu s the play holds absorbing interest. It deals with plot and counter plot in the British court during the reign of Mary Tudor, the "Bloody Mary" of history. The costume features of the display are picturesque, and when the action goes into open-air settings the effect is convincing. Also there are numerous big mob scenes to give the story spectacular background.

The great virtue of the picture is the splendid way in which its smashing climax of suspense is craftily built up toward the end. The last reel and a half will hold any audience breathless, a fine, tricky bit of theatrical maneuvering. Leading up to this big "punch" the story has many interesting episodes and incidents, and it increases in intensity as it proceeds, climbs to its crisp climax and ends quickly without padding.

A handsome Italian adventurer, Frabino, an ex-convict, posing as a Spanish grandee, wins Queen Mary's love and becomes the power behind the throne. All his enemies he causes to be executed. The Queen takes his counsel and disregards the advice of her ministers until the people rebel and scheming politicians urge the succession of Princess Elizabeth. The counsellors are helpless until the Spanish Ambassador, who has learned of Frabino's amour with a commoner, Jane, betrothed to one Gilbert, a carver, takes a hand. The Ambassador reveals the faithlessness of the adventurer to Mary, and both Gilbert and Frabino are thrown into the Tower and condemned to death. While the Queen makes it appear that she desires the death of her faithless lover, in reality her love is still strong and she schemes to free him.

Here is where the tense climax gets its force. By the connivance of Jane she bribes the Tower jailers so that when the death warrant is signed Gilbert may be led to the execution block, his head covered in the black hood required by custom, and it shall be made to appear to the clamorous populace that Frabino is being executed, means being provided in the meantime for the escape of the adventurer.

By the skillful management of

scenes the audience, as well as the Queen and the girl, are left in the dark as to which of the two, Frabino or Gilbert, is led to the block, and this uncertainty leaves the spectator hanging in suspense until the last minute—as clever a surprise situation as has been noted on the screen in a long time. The effect is worked up with alternate views of the procession to the scaffold and of the agitated Queen, the public execution scene having well-handled mob incidentals. At the finale it is disclosed that Jane, in her love for Gilbert rather than Frabino, has double-crossed the Queen and sent the adventurer to his death, saving her real lover. English love triumphs over royal trickery. Long live the common people! Red fire! Major chord from the orchestra!

The film goes out as a territorial proposition, the Rialto concern having its own distributing machine in six centres and selling the others on the State rights plan. *Rush.*

TOO MUCH WIFE

Husband....................T. Roy Barnes
Wife.....................Wanda Hawley
Jane.........................Leigh Wayne

Realart farce featuring Wanda Hawley, superintended by Elmer Harris and based on a yarn by Lorna Moon. There are laughs of the hokum sort and a succession of incidents amusing in the broad sense. It should go better outside New York, where the Puck and Judge brand of humor still keeps the barber shop crowd in waiting.

The story is a rather crude treatment of the marriage question. The young wife has a hen-pecked father and a bossy mother, and resolves to do differently. She lets her husband do what he pleases, but insists on doing it with him. Desperate, he takes up business as a pleasure, but, missing his company, wifie descends on the office, fires the sentimental stenographer and goes to work there herself. The result is husband nearly goes crazy, and has to make an excuse of a business call to Chicago to get away on a camping trip his wife wanted to go on too. While camping he gets caught in a storm and washed up on an island where the stenographer also is marooned. With wifie tipped off, the results are imaginable. All is straightened out happily. Ordinary stuff.

The acting is better. Mr. Barnes is the type to succeed Bryant Washburn, and Miss Hawley is well known and invariably the same, sensibly efficient. Minor roles were capably handled. *Leed.*

BEYOND THE CROSSROADS

A Pioneer Film Corp. release, starring Ora Carew, featuring Melbourne MacDowell and W. Lawson Butt, directed by Lloyd Carlton.

The feature is in about five reels and gives the impression it had been cut from considerably greater footage, thereby destroying the continuity to a material degree.

The story is not new, but is of the kind that usually intrigues the patrons of popular priced cinemas—romantic melodrama, with oodles of suspensive interest.

The hero is a modern Monte Cristo. While prospecting in Alaska he strikes it rich, is called east to bond his mine, the villain runs away with his wife, she returns home to die at his doorstep, and he swears to be avenged. Villain has never met him; both change their names, and eight years later the villain is engaged to a sweet young girl, when hero comes upon his trail.

High finance, in which the hero pretends to be his friend in order to break villain financially—flash-

back in which hero narrates his story to the girl—the villain appears upon the scene. Hero says: "David Walton, I am James Fordham. I have told Leila all. You are a penniless beggar, for the corporation is bankrupt." And then, to the girl: "I will be waiting for you in my cabin," and she follows the hero.

The three principals are fully competent to hold interest to the finish. Miss Carew is the girl, Melbourne MacDowell is the heavy, and Lawson Butt is the long-suffering but finally triumphant hero. *Jolo.*

A CERTAIN RICH MAN

Molly Culpepper..............Claire Adams
John Barston................Robert McKim
Colonel Culpepper............J. J. Dowling
Henry Holmes...........John Gansevort

This is the film Ben and Bill had words about—harsh, bitter words—if memory isn't playing one of its tricks, as it sometimes does where the doings of Ben and the sayings of Bill are concerned. Ben, as you may have guessed, is Ben B. Hampton, once a hound on the trail of advertising contracts, later a magazine publisher, till Standard Oil took exception to a few remarks contributed by our esteemed critical co-worker, William A. Johnston, and more recently a maker of pictures and an uplifter of the screen. Bill, as you probably have not guessed, being interested in life and the show business, not in the movement to get more middle westerners to quoting Browning, is William Allen White. In the days before Sinclair Lewis slipped us the low-down on Main street, Mr. White had that same Main street saying a lot of high-faltutin' things in collegiate language about "a Balzacian novelization of profound truths" called "A Certain Rich Man." "A Certain Rich Man" was Bill's biggest. All Kansas cheered, and then into his paradise of praise entered Ben B. Hampton with a soft and stealthy tread.

Ben persuaded Bill (though doubtless coin played a part in the argument) to entrust the filming of this Balzacian commentary upon life as it is out west to "Ben B. Hampton and his co-workers," as the screen describes them. Bill fell. Since release the force of his impact can be measured by his words of denunciation. Hot words, sent broadcast.

One cannot blame him much. If the "movies" are to be hoisted into the empyrean of perfection we can only hope Will Hays won't let Ben Hampton undertake that task, with the assistance of William Allen White, for the fault, if the Emporia editor will but be at pains to see it, lies with him, not with Mr. Hampton, an earnest soul and one hep to picture necessities. These same necessities must have prodded him continually while he was at the task of transferring Mr. White's ideas to the screen when they belonged properly in the library.

Mr. White—who wrote "What Is the Matter with Kansas?" for his Emporia Gazette and attracted national attention—is an excellent newspaper man, but when it comes to writing a novel the virtues of his craft pursue him as relentlessly as they do Samuel Hopkins Adams. He hasn't the artist's instinct, the trick of condensation, the ability to seize upon moments of drama that sum up centuries of inheritance and environment, and so for dramatic purposes, as Mr. Hampton now doubtless realizes, are next to no good at all. This is obvious from this Hodkinson-released film, which takes almost 6,000 feet to reach its drama, and then is over with as ridiculous a piece of sentimental nonsense as was ever fed the American public.

To make himself rich the leading character almost gets all his friends into prison and forces a young girl into a loveless marriage. Years and some 4,500 feet intervene, and then because his wife is ill from unboiled water this same millionaire gives all his money to the poor and everyone is uplifted, saved and happy. The happiest of all must have been Mr. McKim and Miss Adams, who did as well as could be hoped for, though admirably photographed. The art inserts were good, but such trimmings do not sell a program to an audience.

Unentertaining, tiresome stuff. *Leed.*

ONE GLORIOUS DAY

Ezra Botts.....................Will Rogers
Molly McIntyre.....................Lila Lee
Ben Wadley.......................Alan Hale
"Ek".............................John Fox
Pat Curran..................George Nichols
Mrs. McIntyre...................Emily Rait
Bert Snead................Clarence Burton

Here is a distinct screen achievement, a story of whimsical humor and fanciful design, translated by the picture medium with a delicacy of treatment that would be possible in no other way. It couldn't be made into a play at all, and no written version could possibly convey it with anything like the vividness that is accomplished in the picture. The picture art can claim "One Glorious Day" as its own. It was written by Walter Woods and A. B. Baringer as an original work for the film theatre, and it has to acknowledge no source in novel or stage original.

The photoplay is a distinct novelty. In its way it has something of the flavor of Irving's quaint phantasy such as he crystallized in "Rip Van Winkle." There is a lot of the spirit of "Rip" in this dramatization, with Will Rogers as its star, a kind of modern fairy tale done in a vein of gentle and reflective, fantastic humor.

The title lead discloses James Cruze as the director and Arthur Woods as the maker of the scenario, but the Rivoli program does not indicate who deserves credit for some of the best camera trick manipulation that has come out in a long time. The old device of the double exposure is here employed for some delightful comedy effects, the film magic being used with surprising exactness for a lot of amusing surprises. Commonplace society in a small town is used as the background for the curious fairy tale.

Ezra Botts is an absent-minded, timid student of spiritualism and the modest shrinking butt of the town's humorists. The dishonest political boss names him as candidate for Mayor on the theory that he will obey orders. Ezra has been lecturing to a circle of friends, declaring that at 10 o'clock the following night he will appear among them in spirit while his body lies asleep at home.

In the meanwhile, the scene shifts to the abode of spirits not yet born, which is the "second turning to the right beyond the Milky Way," and we are introduced to the elfin "Ek," a restless sprite, who is determined to get himself born into the world in order to find an outlet for his bubbling energies. While the powers of the spirit world relax attention, he slips away and his flight through the universe is graphically pictured in the jolliest kind of detail, including a visit to the moon.

He arrives at Ezra's home in time to see Ezra's spirit leave his unconscious body to make good his promise. "Ek" forthwith takes possession of the vacant tenement, these developments being enacted by means of the double exposure. With its new spiritual tenant, Ezra's body is animated with a demon of aggressive enterprise and willful mischief. The apologetic Ezra invades a barroom, beats up the scheming politicians, goes on to a cabaret dance and fascinates all the girls. He finally rescues the girl whom Ezra really loves, although he is too timid to declare himself, and wins her in time to vacate Ezra's body and return it to him, enriched with a new reputation as a fighting fool and a public benefactor.

Picking Will Rogers for the part of Ezra was an inspiration. The role was made to order for his style of quiet, simple fun. Lila Lee, with her dark beauty, was splendid as the heroine of the sympathetic little romance that underlay the plot, and the half dozen other principal players were appropriately interpreted by an exceptionally even cast.

The picture represents screen comedy in its highest manifestation. It will make talk and it will amuse every type of audience; the higher grade the audience, the better the story will be received. *Rush.*

TWO KINDS OF WOMEN

Jackson Gregory's "Judith of Blue Lake Ranch" is the novel from which Robertson-Cole have supplied the latest film for Pauline Frederick featuring, it appearing under the title of "Two Kinds of Women," shown at Loew's State for the first half of the week.

It's a "western," but not the western of the old type, that of the rolling plains, the dead-shot sheriff and the types of the wild and woolly. It is set in the Sierras, with some picturesque long shots here and there and one lake scene that is a scintillating exception. That footage is a night scene, the lake surface being so softly pictured that it resembled glowing white satin.

Judith Sanford (Miss Frederick) arrives at Blue Lake Ranch, which is devoted to horse breeding, some time after the death of her father. She has traveled far and wide as surcease to her grief. But getting down to business, she has a pretty good idea that Bayne Trevors, the ranch manager, is not on the level. She believes with good proof that he has been selling colts to a favored company for a nominal price. So it's curtains for Trevors when she takes the reins. Some of the camp bunch vamp with the manager, but Bud Lee, the horse foreman, a college man by the way, sticks with the regulars.

Not being an old type western, this ranch house has most of the conveniences of a country show place. Judith's long residence in San Francisco makes it natural that she hold a dance, with guests from the coast cities. The ranch boys are invited, which permits a telling bit of comedy to be introduced. One of them writes to Sears-Roebuck for a mess of "evening dresses for men—assorted sizes—ages 20 to 60, everything complete from tail to horn."

There are three fight episodes through the five reels. One has Judith and Bud Lee hunting down some of the ex-ranch men, turned bandits at Trevors' orders. The payroll had been taken that, according to the story, is all-important to Judith, whose men would walk out if not paid off on the six o'clock bell. Money is secured from the bank in the meantime. The battle with the bandits takes the couple up and down rocky crags, with a successful but not especially thrilling action.

The second scrap is one in which Judith battles against a bestial guard, after having been decoyed and hidden away by the Trevors gang. The third has Bud Lee handing the villainous Trevors a lacing and extracting the promise of leaving the country. Judith resting at the ranch house after the terrifying ordeal in a shack under guard is waiting—for Bud and happiness.

Emotionally, Miss Frederick's fire is not given the opportunity of some of her other roles. Her Judith is a somewhat tired girl, even though there is undeniable determination in the character. The early scenes between her and Bud show the flint of skepticism on both sides. He tells her there are two kinds of women. She answers "Some that can and some that can't." Thomas Santschi builds a strong Bud, but a rather solemn one. That in a way matches Miss Frederick's direct manner. Charles Clary as Trevors is smooth, but always working in the background, as called for in the story.

"Two Kinds of Women" is a different kind of western and interesting. Colin Campbell has directed well. There are no lagging moments. Apparently the picture was retitled plentifully, some of the titles only being illuminated and holding the R-C seal. *Ibee.*

NANCY FROM NOWHERE

Nancy........................Bebe Daniels
Jack Halliday..........Edward Sutherland
Mrs. Kelly......................Vera Lewis
Mr. Kelly....................James Gordon
Mrs. Halliday.............Myrtle Stedman
Martha........................Alberta Lee
Elizabeth Doane...............Helen Holly
Mrs. Doane...................Dorothy Hagen

For those who claim the screen is badly in need of stories let it be said that they won't have to go much farther than this one to secure a glaring substantiation of the claim. Realart, responsible for "Nancy," has supplied Bebe Daniels with an extremely weak vehicle at a time when her film prestige is none too strong and which fact can be traced back to the continuous cause of her stories not holding sufficient merit.

It's been a considerable period since Miss Daniels has been the subject of a favorable scenario, and she is woefully in need of one. Whether some other feminine "name" could have accomplished anything with "Nancy" is doubtful, as the tale is far from convincing, lacks holding power and it's simply a matter of sitting there, watching the reels unfold with the audience not caring much one way or the other what becomes of the parentless waif.

At her best when handling light comedy roles Miss Daniels has been given a sequence of events to follow by Douglas Doty, who did the screen version of the original story by Grace Drew and Kathrene Pinkerton, which falls far short of providing mirth. They give evidence at times the wish of the director was that the theme be taken seriously. The picture is one of those betwixt and between affairs that rambles on without making noticeable headway. It flounders into a finale fadeout that labels it as "one of those things."

The story deals with Nancy, an orphan, dragging through an existence by means of doing the housework and chores for the Kellys, a ne'er-do-well husband and wife. The woman is continually beating Nancy and the man is casting longing eyes in her direction. She runs away to join the young society city chap she has accidently met. The young man gets himself into trouble through a would-be fiancee of his discovering Nancy in the palatial home. She wires the boy's father and sister to come home, which leads to the country girl's exit back to the dilapidated farm, there to be attacked by Kelly and saved through the young lover having followed her.

Chester M. Franklin, who directed, has either allowed a subject incomplete as to detail to be released over his name or the fault lies in the cutting the picture has received. From either angle it's hard to see how the film slipped by the projection room in its present state.

Outside of Miss Daniels, who simply walks through the entire film and gets a chance to appear at her best when dressed in the "sister's" clothes, James Gordon as old man Kelly predominates, and for actual work takes the palm away from the feminine star.

That someone had a pretty tough time arranging the continuity of "Nancy" and fared badly at it seems evident from two of the names of characters appearing on the program (Mrs. Halliday and Mrs. Doane) failing to show on the screen at all, while the boy's father, Mr. Halliday, takes up an average amount of footage but fails to be included on the programed cast.

The picture does not impress. Wherever shown it will hurt Realart, Miss Daniels and Franklin combined. *Skig.*

SHOULD WIFE WORK?

"Should a Wife Work?" featuring Edith Stockton, is a story by Lois Zellner, directed by Horace A. Plimpton, distributed by J. W. Film Corp. The title and idea were designed for sensational purposes but teach nothing, arrive at no conclusion and are not fair examples of life as it really is.

Two girls are about to graduate from a boarding school. One has visions of "a career," while the other pictures herself as a wife and mother. The one with a yearning for a career marries a struggling lawyer, has a child, the child dies and she is offered a position in a musical comedy at $150 per week, although she has never been on the stage. Her husband objects and it means the breaking up of her home. The other says to her: "Think what you are doing, Nina. You have a lot to be thankful for, and good men are hard to find." But Nina is firm, leaves hubby and moves to a Riverside Drive apartment.

The other marries a poor inventor and when he is pressed for funds she accepts an engagement to sing in church at $100 a month. The inventor also objects to his wife working, she, however, persisting, accepting engagements to sing at the homes of the wealthy, and through it is enabled secretly to finance his invention, whereupon he falls at her feet and kisses the hem of her dress, at which the audience at the Circle laughed derisively Tuesday evening.

At this stage Nina sends for her girl friend and weeps that she is out of work and cannot secure another engagement unless she submits to the advances of the theatrical agent. So the other brings her back to her husband for a reconciliation.

There is a subtitle at the opening propounding the query, "Has a wife the right to a career of her own?" The struggles of the two young wives are then visualized and you are left to figure it out for yourself. The two women enact their respective roles neatly, and the whole makes for a cheap program release. *Jolo.*

THE GUTTERSNIPE

Mazie O'Day.................Gladys Walton
Dennis O'Day.................Walter Perry
Mrs. O'Day......................Kate Price
Tom Gilroy.....................Jack Perrin
Sam Rosen..................Sydney Franklin
Lady Clarissa..............Carmen Phillips
Lord Bart.........................Ed Cecil
Angus...........................Hugh Saxon
Red Galvin..................Seymour Zeliff
Clarence Phillips.............Eugene Corey
Sally.....................Lorraine Weiler
Gregory...................Christian J. Frank

"The Guttersnipe" is a Universal production in a scant five reels, story by Percival Wilde, scenario by Wallace Clifton, directed by Dallas Fitzgerald, photography by Milton Moore, featuring Gladys Walton.

It is a travesty on romantic melodrama as imagined by a slum girl, who pictures life as revealed in the pages of "Sloppy Stories," a magazine to which she is addicted.

The girl rescues a young man in evening dress from a street fight and visualizes him as the hero of one of the "Sloppy" tales, seeing in him a strong resemblance to "Lord Lytton," of whom she reads. He turns out to be a clerk at a soda fountain. Seated on a park bench, they read the hectic magazine, and, with the aid of flashbacks, imagine themselves the players in the story.

Her hero is arrested for passing

counterfeit silver; she goes on the trail and finds he has been "framed" by his employer; She earns a reward for unearthing the band of counterfeiters, and the pair are thus enabled to take a honeymoon trip with the proceeds. It gets by neatly. *Jolo.*

BILLY JIM

"Billy Jim" is an Andrew J. Callahan production starring Fred Stone. It was directed by Frank Borzage, story by Jackson Gregory, scenario by Frank Howard Clark—a Robertson-Cole release.

One more attempt to make a picture actor of the musical comedy star. It will meet with no more success than the previous efforts. Stone doesn't photograph well. He has no magnetism before the camera, and the only thing that can possibly be attempted is to make of him a character performer.

In this instance he is revealed as a cowpuncher of the happy-go-lucky sort who loses his money with a smile, gets "lickered up" and goes about making the night hideous with ribald song. He falls in love at first sight with the rich mine owner's daughter, saves her father's property from being confiscated by a hand of claim jumpers and goes through the usual bag of tricks with obvious, unoriginal and ponderous comedy. After making a general nuisance of himself, somebody asks (meaning the apparent cowpuncher),

"Who is that man?" And the reply comes ,"He is the biggest cattleman in the West." So he wins the girl, and so on.

Millicent Fisher enacts the heroine and is scarcely more attractive on the screen than the star. Mostly exterior scenes, the production is lacking in class and will barely pass as an ordinary program feature. *Jolo.*

WHITE HANDS

Hurricane Hardy	Hobart Bosworth
Leon Roche	Robert McKim
Ralph Alden	Freeman Wood
Grouch Murphy	Al Kaufman
Peroxide	Baby Muriel Frances Dana
Helen Maitland	Elinor Fair

This is a typical C. Gardner Sullivan tale, and although laid in the African desert country, has all the thrills that were in his Klondike tales screened several years ago. Sullivan seems to have the screen angle first and foremost, and his manner of working out a tale of this kind cannot be improved on.

The production was made by Max Graf, with Lambert Hillyer directing and with Hobart Bosworth as the star. In the supporting company were an additional couple of names, including that of Robert McKim. The real star of the picture, however, is Baby Muriel Frances Dana, who seems just a little more than three years old on the screen, but who troupes with all the skill and expression of a veteran campaigner in front of the camera. Here is the kid find for the last two years. She is better even than Jackie Coogan, although in this picture she has not as much to do as he had in "The Kid."

Made on the Ince lot at Culver City, the picture does not look to represent more than a $50,000 outlay, but it has all the flash of a production that would have cost more than double that under ordinary circumstances.

As a production it has been judged strong enough to get 50 days in the Keith, Proctor, Moss combination booking around New York.

The story opens in Africa, with the heroine lost with her escort in the desert. She is the daughter of a missionary who has died, and the blacks are trying to take her to the coast, so that she may get a boat to take her to civilization. The party is found by Hurricane Hardy (Hobart Bosworth), a rough and ready sailorman who is the master of a schooner trading in African waters. He is a hard customer, feared alike by black and white. He covets the girl that he has found in the sands and takes her to the point where his vessel is moored. At the little dive of a hotel there is a young American, brought there through dissipation The girl and he fall for each other, and in the meantime Hurricane and the owner of the dive, played by Robert McKim, both are planning to win her. In the end the regeneration of Hurricane is brought about through the medium of the little baby who was in the dive, having been brought there after a wreck on the coast, she being the sole survivor. He, the baby and the boy and girl all sail for a happier land. *Fred.*

WHY ANNOUNCE YOUR MARRIAGE

Arline Mayfair	Elaine Hammerstein
Jimmy Winthrop	Niles Welch
David Mayfair	Frank Currier
Teddy Filbert	Arthur Houseman
Bobby Kingsley	James Harrison
Mrs. Gushing	Florence Billings
Mrs. Jerome	Marie Burke
Mr. Walton	Huntley Gordon
Gladys Jerome	Elizabeth Woodmere

This is one of those exceptional pictures that hit you, and hit you right, every once in a blue moon. Selznick produced it and put real money on his bet. The story—and it's a very important part of this picture—is by Lewis Allen Browne and Alan Crosland. Crosland also directed, handling his actors and arrangements with finesse and ability. He would probably have had a better picture if he had let the farce out of his final sequence, but even so it is class entertainment of the best sort. The objection is merely for artistic reasons. As a matter of fact, Crosland here achieves comedy most of the way where the stage grip on the same idea has always been too tight, invariably producing farce.

Arline, an artist, and Jimmy Winthrop decide to keep their marriage a secret and so avoid the troubles of marriage, but their attempts to be together lead to misunderstandings and malicious gossip. From the spectators' standpoint, of course, there is lots of comedy in all this, but it ends with the two routed from their bed by a burglar and exposed before a whole hotel, when out comes the truth and no harm done.

To the fun Arthur Houseman contributed in no small fashion. No such hit as his has been noted in many a day. He was applauded as he left the screen and as he came on, a thing almost unheard of in picture theatres. Without aping Chaplin, he achieved results as sure and final. It may be said without exaggeration that in the difficult field of film comedy he has achieved in this picture a success as distinguished as it is clever. It would have been easy to be simply an idiotic drunk. Mr. Houseman managed far, far more than that. He was a scream and an artist at one and the same time. Elaine Hammerstein, the star, was her usual well bred self. A wholesome, lovely girl, she is always an asset, and Niles Welch (with his hair curled) gives her able support. In fact, the cast was exceptional. When you see Huntley Gordon used only for a bit you know what to expect.

In short, this is the best comedy bet of the season, a clean, high-class, distinguished and well imagined film offering. *Leed.*

STAR DUST

Lily Becker	Edna Ross / Hope Hampton
Henry Becker	Thomas Maguire
Mrs. Becker	Mrs. Mary Foy
Jethro Penny	Charles Musset
Mrs. Penny	Vivia Ogden
Albert Penny	Noel Tearle / Ashley Buck
Antonio Marvelli	George Humbert
Daisy Cameron	Gladys Wilson
Bruce Visigoth	Charles Wellsle
Thomas Clemons	James Rennie

First National has released this screen version of Fannie Hurst's story, directed by Hobart Henley and featuring Hope Hampton. Anthony Paul Kelly's name appears as having adapted the tale for film presentation. He has accomplished about as much as could be expected with the subject in hand. The tale lends itself easily for picturization, though running pretty close to the conventional path with a story oft done before. Whatever credit the film will gather can be reasoned out as belonging to Mr. Henley for having held up the continuity of the theme and f supplying various bits of detail as the opportunities, which aren't many, presented themselves. A few elaborate interiors, revealing choice decorative staging, add tone.

The narrative relates how Lily Becker, having a natural talent for music, grows up under a tyranical mother to be forced into a marriage with one of the rich sons of the Iowa village. She eventually runs away from her husband to inaugurate a career in New York, becomes a mother, goes broke, attempts suicide, finally meeting a young composer who has gone through the same cycle of events. He gives her the confidence to go on until she makes her successful debut in operatic circles. The marriage of the two winds up the conclusion.

Mixed in are the incidents of the overbearing and under-cultured husband and his family, the death of the child, a "play" made for her by a theatrical magnate, the death of her husband in a railroad wreck and her premier performance in "Thais."

The smash-up of the trains is a gentle reminder of the train wreck pulled down at Brighton some time ago, when two engines were turned loose against each other with many a camera clicking as it happened and a general admission being charged to witness the event. Henley has worked up the situation to some suspense through coupling the night of the accident with that of the wife's initial stage appearance, interweaving snatches of the theatre and the confusion in the railroad's switch towers as the impending disaster approaches. The scenes showing the dead baby in a crib, with its hands folded, might be eliminated as it rather rubs the wrong way, and especially will it border on morbidness to women.

Miss Hampton will satisfy her following and the general run of fans as Lily Becker. The only instance in which the feminine star is liable to be found fault with is when informed her baby is dead. Beyond that there is nothing of the unusual called for, though her best appeal is made at the time preceding and following her marriage, previous to the running away. Noel Tearle gives a corking performance as the uncouth and gum-chewing husband, seeming to take special delight, as all Englishmen do, in bringing to light the repulsive features of America's choice habit. Tearle does it with enough gusto to make it close to audible, and if it doesn't do anything else, this one mannerism of the character should quiet down whatever chewers there are in the house. The cast lends able support, with Vivia Ogden, Mrs. Mary Foy and Thomas Maguire, allotted the small town roles of the immediate families, making the most notable impression. Gladys Wilson also made a brief chorus girl bit stand out for appreciation.

Showing at the Strand for the current week, "Star Dust" has the personal appearance of Miss Hampton twice daily to help the film, and the women were plentiful in the audience at the time she was to appear.

"Star Dust" will never be a record-breaker, but it should prove an intermediate feature for the larger picture theatres, and if compared to the films shown in the second and third run houses, it's a classic. *Skig.*

THE PRODIGAL JUDGE

Betty Malroy	Jean Paige
Judge Slocum Price	Maclyn Arbuckle
Solomon Mahaffey	Ernest Torrence
Bruce Carrington	Earl Fox
Col. Fentress	Arthur Carew
Charles Norton	Horace Braham
Gen. Quintard	Charles Kent
Hannibal	Charles Eaton
Bob Yancy	Robert Millasch
Cavendish	George Bancroft
Bess Hicks	Peggy Shanor

A Vitagraph production directed by Edward Jose, adapted from a novel by Vaughan Kester. About eight reels in length, "The Prodigal Judge" is endless, or apparently so. It is supposed to be a romance of the South in the early nineteenth century—the days f chivalry, when folks slapped each other with gloves and then went out into the woods with duelling pistols, first bowing profoundly. All of which wouldn't be so bad if related in a worth-while tale.

"The Prodigal Judge" is about a blustering, middle-aged man whose wife runs away with another, taking with her their child. The husband, Judge Price, promptly takes to drink and degenerates into a pest who "mooches" booze, etc., sinking in the social scale until he becomes a bum. This character is intended to be lovable and to be sympathized with. Instead he is a pest and, as Maclyn Arbuckle enacts him, it is more a burlesque than a characterization.

There is a young girl, played by Jean Paige, whose guardian plots to marry her and thus retain control of her vast estate. It turns out he is the man who eloped with the wife years before and he also tries to make away with the child, who also has a vast fortune coming to him. So the villain goes through the old-fashioned manouvres and machinations that we so dearly cherished in the palmy days of 10-20-30 and formed the basis of many a Drury Lane melodrama, many reaching these shores.

You sit through this drivel for nearly two hours, vainly striving to keep awake, and when it finally ends you breathe a sigh of relief. The picture is more a travesty on old-style melodrama than a modern film feature. *Jolo.*

MORAN OF LADY LETTY

Moran	Dorothy Dalton
Ramon Laredo	Rudolph Valentino
Captain Sternersen	Charles Brindley
Captain Kitchell	Walter Long
Nels	Emil Jorgenson
Josephine Herrick	Maude Wayne
Bill Trim	Cecil Holland
"Chopstick" Charlie	George Kuwa

"Moran of the Lady Letty," at the Rivoli this week, is designated a "George Melford production" from the story by Frank Norris; scenario by Monte M. Katterjohn, with Dorothy Dalton as star. It works into an interesting melodrama of the sea with a wealth of action, and has its dramatic punch in a man-to-man battle all over the deck of a three-masted sailing vessel and into the lofty rigging, ending with the hurling of the villain from the lofty main truck into the sea.

The marine scenes are splendid photographically and all the settings on board ship are tremendously realistic. The attendance was large at the Rivoli Sunday night, probably drawn by interest in the star and by Rudolph Valentino, who heads the supporting company. Miss Dalton appears in a new type of heroine. The sinuous frocks are gone. So are the vampish headdresses. With bobbed hair falling about her ears and in duck sailor trousers she looks the part of the girlish daughter of the Lady Letty's master. It's an astonishing transfiguration from the typical Dalton roles.

Whether the fans will accept Miss Dalton in an ingenue part of this kind is an interesting consideration. As translated to the screen "Moran" is rather a colorless person, the real star of the picture being Valentino as a rich young idler who is shanghaied and finds himself in the battle with a piratical skipper in shady trade between the California coast and West Mexico ports. As a rough-and-tumble fighting hero Valentino is a revelation. Physically he looks the part, but it comes as something of a shock, probably because he has so long been identified with roles of a daintier kind.

Ramon Laredo is a society idler, much sought after by the debutantes but bored by the artificialities of the gay world. He starts for his yacht moored at the waterfront, but his society friends have tired waiting and sailed without him. He enters into conversation with an old salt on the wharf and by way of a lark accompanies him to a waterfront drinking place. He is drugged and wakes up on the pirate ship at sea.

On the voyage to Mexico on some nefarious scheme the pirate ship finds the Lady Letty, whose cargo of coal is burning. All hands have been asphyxiated in the hold by coal gas, and Moran, daughter of the skipper, alone survives. She is taken aboard the pirate ship, where Captain Kitchell's designs upon her are frustrated by Ramon. Arrived at the Mexican port the plans of Kitchell to sell the girl into slavery to a native outlaw are discovered. Ramon organizes the crew, and when the Mexican bandits approach the ship there is a battle royal. This passage is a lively bit of staging as the outlaws swarm over the sides and are thrown back into the sea.

Kitchell stows away as the ship puts back to sea, homeward bound. Back in San Diego, Ramon hurries ashore to notify his friends that he is safe. During his absence and while the crew is away Kitchell leaves his hiding place and attacks "Moran" in her cabin. Ramon arrives among his former friends during a gay party. The debutantes renew their siege, but Ramon, who has new ideas of life after his experiences, is not interested in social butterflies. He returns to the ship and "Moran" just in time to save her from Kitchell. This is where the epic battle takes place. It starts in the cabin, takes in most of the decks and then goes into the rigging, ending when Kitchell crawls out to the end of a lofty spar and is thrown into the water, a 60-foot drop. Kitchell out of the way leaves the road clear for the finale embrace.

Rush.

WHERE IS MY WANDERING BOY TONIGHT?

Garry Beecher..............Cullen Landis
Silas Rudge............Carl Stockdale
Martha Beecher...Virginia True Boardman
Lorna Owens.........Ruth "Patsy" Miller
Veronica Tyler.............Kathleen Key
Stuart Kilmer..............Ben Deeley
R. Sylvester Jones....Clarence Badger, Jr.

Bennie Zeidman's initial effort as a producer of films, entitled "Where Is My Wandering Boy Tonight?" reached Broadway this week. It is at the Criterion, which the Equity Pictures Corp. has taken under a rental for three weeks. The picture has a story written by Gerald C. Duffy to fit the title of the old song

which was for years the punch in "The Old Homestead," but as a feature it isn't quite in the special class, although it will prove a fairly entertaining picture of the usual grade of program productions.

Its principal trouble at present is too long. The extra footage of a number of scenes give the picture a tendency to be draggy. With judicious cutting the value will be enhanced 50 per cent.

When one considers the title on which the story is based it seems rather a pity a great picture isn't the result. Surely with that material to work on another "Over the Hill" should have been the result. However, when it is taken into consideration that perhaps Mr. Zeidman and his associates had to work on a limited capital this effort must be rated as a rather worthy one.

Originally the picture was brought to New York and submitted to the First National. After a few months' time with no action by the Executive Committee regarding exhibition value that would meet with the approval of the producers the picture went into other hands.

One thing the producers did do was to pick a very fair cast. Cullen Landis, who plays the lead, is a clever juvenile and he makes the most of his opportunities. In the support Ruth "Patsy" Miller and Kathleen Key were the two girls who figured in the boy's life. The former was the little country miss delightfully, while the latter was the fly and flippant Broadway chicken. Virginia True Boardman handled the mother role very nicely and Carl Stockman was the small-town heavy. Ben Deeley as a rounder and Clarence Badger, Jr., in a minor role completed the cast.

The story is a tale of the small-town boy who comes to Broadway to make his way to fame and fortune, but does a Brodie and finally winds up doing a ten-year bit at Sing Sing after he has been crossed by the chorus girl vamp. In a jailbreak he saves the warden's life and for that is given his freedom in time to return to the old home town on Christmas eve to be greeted by a lonely mother and the real girl who has been waiting for him.

In detail the production has been badly handled, but seemingly J. P. Hogan and Millard Webb, who directed, cannot be blamed for this. The indications from the screen are that the picture was slaughtered in the cutting. That a chorus girl jumped to stardom within a week and other little things of that order seemingly mean nothing to whoever cut and titled the production.

Photographically the picture has some corking bits here and there. The prison break, with the convicts escaping on a locomotive and the final smash of that engine with another in a head-on collision, furnishes a real thrill. That locomotive smash, had it not been stock and had it been staged for this production alone, would have sent the production cost away up, but as the majority of picture goers of today have in all likelihood forgotten the original locomotive collision they may take this as a real wallop.

Fred.

JULIUS CAESAR

George Kleine is offering another Italian film spectacle, probably one more of the series of Cines productions, posed and executed in and about Rome. This one is titled "Julius Caesar," and is built around the life of the Roman dictator of that name. The leading role is played by Anthony Novelli, and from a spectacular standpoint the picture compares with the other film features which have come from that country. Like all the Italian screen productions, "Julius Caesar" runs to mob scenes, with a couple of ancient battle scenes that are probably correct in visualizing the costuming

and military tactics of those days.

The picture opens with Caesar, aged 20, in love with Cornelia, daughter of Cinna, who is the bitter enemy of Sully, then dictator of Rome. "Where is thy gratitude to me that thou didst marry the daughter of mine enemy."

After an exile of 20 years Caesar returns and offers himself as a candidate for consulship, aided by Calpurnia, daughter of the wealthy Piso. His marriage to Calpurnia occurs.

Step by step the rise of Caesar is traced through the intricacies and mazes of political intriguing and strife with such high spots as the famous battle between the Romans and Gauls depicted in detail—"I came, I saw, I conquered," etc. The Roman senate is magnificently pictured. As a lesson in history it would probably be intensely interesting to a classroom of students.

The production winds up with the city aflame with riot after the murder of Caesar by Brutus and others and the oration over his body by Marc Antony in the market place, wherein he concludes with, "Mischief, thou art afoot, take thou what course thou wilt," and showing Cornelia, his first wife, as his chief mourner.

As a film spectacle "Caesar" compares favorably with the other Italian pictures that have been brought to this country. If sensationally exploited it might attract more than ordinary attention. Without the booming, however, and offered simply on its merits as a picture it would probably not satisfy our cinema habitues.

Jolo.

LITTLE MISS SMILES

Splitting with U.'s "The Scrapper" on a double feature program, this film is directly opposite as to its characters and location. Where Universal's output deals with somewhat extravagant interiors populated by cast names dripping heavily with the brogue of Ireland, this Fox release has its locale on New York's East Side and unburdens itself of the woes of a Jewish family, including Shirley Mason as Esther, the only daughter.

The family includes the mother, father and older brother, who won't work, desiring to be a prize-fighter, always scrapping with the two younger sons and the daughter. Esther is the shining light, looking after all the members of the flat, later falling in love with the young doctor from the mission who is called in when the mother becomes almost totally blind.

The pugilistically inclined brother gets himself mixed up in a shooting affair when he lets drive at his proposed manager, whom he has heard insult his sister, which permits of the doctor taking unto himself the blame and makes way for the situation clearing up.

Miss Mason does nicely, but is somewhat cramped by the surroundings of the locale. The picture must have cost almost next to nothing. There is little beyond the tenement and poolroom interiors, while exteriors deal with ordinary street scenes.

Jack Ford did the directing and has turned in an average piece of work for the subject involved. Nothing to enlarge upon and little to be cut down; must have been pie for the director in turning out "Miss Smiles." It's a picture where the audience knows the finish and can guess all the incidentals after the initial 200 feet.

The cast is not called upon for any exceptional work. Attempts at comedy come to light at various intervals for relief, but the picture will run its natural course without being molested or causing any serious thought from those in front.

Skig.

BOOMERANG BILL

Boomerang Bill..........Lionel Barrymore
Annie..............Marguerite Marsh
Annie's mother..........Margaret Seddon
Terrence O'Malley........Frank Shannon
Tony, the Wop..........Matthew Betts
Chinaman..............Charlie Fong
Chinese Girl..............Harry Lee
Chinese Girl..........Miriam Battista
Chinese Girl..............Helen Kim

"He tried to build a house of love on a foundation of crime," says the sentimental plain clothes man to the youth who contemplates a career of crime. They are seated on a bench in Battery Park. A gangster had just left the boy after persuading him to enter upon "a job" that night. The detective had seen them together, and when the crook departs he approaches the boy and starts to read him a lesson.

At this juncture along passes a man, still young, led by a Chinese girl, but carrying himself like a person either blind or broken in spirit. "See that man," says the detective. "Listen to his story." The tale itself is then told in a cut-back.

It shows Boomerang Bill, otherwise Clark Street Bill from Chicago, a gunman from the Windy City, lately arrived in New York and a bit lonesome. He goes to a Bowery dance, rescues a girl from the clutches of Tony the Wop, a local gangster, runs into her afterward in a restaurant where she is cashier. They fall in love and he decides to go straight. The day before he is to go to work he takes Annie to the seashore, where she tells him she is worried about her mother, who must go to the country for her health.

Bill decides to do one more stick-up job to help his girl out of her dilemma, gets nabbed and is sentenced to a stretch. Realizing he did it for her, the girl promises to wait for him and writes him regularly. One day the girl visits him and tells him her mother is dying. Another man has the money that will save her if she will marry him, but she decides to remain true to Bill. He, however, declines to let her do so, sacrificing himself. Eventually

released from prison, Bill looks into the window, sees Annie surrounded by her mother, husband and baby, and goes back to the Chinese laundry, where the only other person who cared for him was a Mongolian child to whom he had been kind.

The picture flashes back to the park bench, with the noble detective pointing out Bill as an example of evil-doing, and as the shattered Bill fades out comes the sub-title "Verily I say unto you that whatsoever a man soweth that shall he reap."

A mawkish, old-fashioned tale, written by Jack Boyle, with an up-to-date scenario prepared by Doty Hobart, modern direction by Tom Terris. It is a Cosmopolitan production released by Paramount and starring Lionel Barrymore.

The star is altogether too "classy" for a gunman. It is not so much the clothes he wears but the unmistakable "distinction of good breeding" that marks him as anything but a personage of the underworld. Underlying his fine, rugged characterization, his gentlemanly mien obtrudes itself. Otherwise his performance is an excellent one. The only other character of any prominence is Annie, sweetly played by Marguerite Marsh. In the big prison scene, where she is tormented by her love for the man who went to jail to raise money for her, she strongly recalls her more illustrious sister.

Unmistakable care and attention have been devoted to the making of this picture, but there is nothing in the story to lift it out of the category of a program release. As such it should rank as one of the best of the present day.

Jolo.

POSSESSION

Lord Wheatley..............Reginald Owen
Constantine................Paul Capellani

Mouraki Pasha.............Max Maxudian
Hon. Dennis Swinton......Harrison Brown
Captain Martin...............Marcel Numa
Dimitri..................Salvatore Lo Turco
Spiro.......................Robert Mennant
Vlacho.......................Charles Vanel
Achmed.......................Carlos Colonna
Watkins.......................Louis Monfils
Lady Eyphrosyne......Malvina Longfellow
Francesca Stefanopoulos.................
Jeane Descles-Guitry
Panayiota.....................Miss Kassierri
Olga..........................Mme. Roland
Kertes the Strong.............Raoul Pasli

This is an adaptation of the novel "Phroso," by Anthony Hope, produced by Louis Mercanton and handled in this country by R-C Pictures. It has been showing aroun for three months now, and, while it is a corking special, it suffers from lack of a name with American appeal. Another trouble with it is Malvina Longfellow, who is disappointing as Phroso, but on the whole the seven reels make exciting, plausible entertainment. A better melodrama for screen purposes it would be difficult to imagine.

Lord Wheatley buys the island of Neopalia, but the natives resent the purchase, wishing to hold it for Phroso, and when Wheatley tries to take possession he encounters a united opposition. His difficulties are further complicated when he himself falls in love with Phroso and has to rescue her from a Turkish pasha. There is constant action, attack and defense, escape and capture, and always effective sea scenes. Photography and inserts were excellent.

Reginald Owen as a straight lead was attractive, but means nothing here as a drawing card. Max Maxudian made an effective heavy, while some first rate, natural comedy was supplied by Louis Monfils. Other roles were capably assumed, in particular by Raoul Pasli and Salvatore Lo Turco. *Leed.*

SIGN OF THE JACK O' LANTERN

Mrs. Carr.................Betty Ross Clark
Harlan Carr.....................Earl Schenck
Dick..........................Wade Boteler
Elaine.......................Zella Ingraham
Willie..........................Newton Hall
The Poet........................Victor Potel
Mrs. Dodd................Clara Clark Ward
Jeremiah Bradford............Monty Collins
Uncle Skyles..............Wm. Courtwright
Mrs. Holmes........Mrs. Raymond Hatton

Hodkinson state right release in six reels based upon the story by Myrtle Reed, the screen version of which was written by Lloyd Ingraham, also the director, and David Kirkland. The scenario writers have developed considerable worthwhile comedy from the Reed script, which in screen form has many valuable assets in the comedy line.

This is a rural comedy with the action taking place in an old New England homestead. The homestead has been left to the nephew of a man who during his life had been annoyed by his grafting relations, his beneficiary being one of the few who had not imposed upon him during his lifetime. Immediately upon the new owner taking possession, his relatives put in an appearance to take up their residence with no intent to pay their share of the expenses. This continues for some time with the owner finally declaring them out. Upon reaching this decision his dead uncle's lawyer presents a document which informs him that now that he has taken the action the dead man had wanted to take all through his life, but did not have the courage, he would receive $10,000 additional from the estate.

The comedy is largely developed by the number of types employed. In this respect the cast has been well selected with the two leads, Betty Ross Clark as the young wife and Earl Schenck, gaining the just returns with two straight roles.

No great cost was necessary in the making. The greater portion of the action takes place in a limited number of interiors, none of which have necessitated a large financial outlay.

Hodkinson can look for results with this state right picture, as it provides the proper comedy punch for neighborhood houses. *Hart.*

MAKING THE GRADE

Irving M. Lesser presents "Making the Grade," a David Butler production based upon the story "Sophie Seminoff," by Wallace Irwin, which appeared in the "Saturday Evening Post." The picture is being released through the First National exchanges but does not have the First National stamp.

The Irwin story misses in screen form largely due to the slip-shod manner in which the picture has been made. The story is made jerky and ridiculous at times in the screening. The director has made little attempt to turn out a finished product.

The theme deals with a wild young American who goes to Siberia with the army. While there he marries a Russian peasant girl. Returning to the States, he brings her with him. Upon hearing of the marriage his mother disowns him, with the father sticking, however, forcing the boy to go out and make his own way. This he does as a laborer.

David Butler Productions produced the picture with David Butler as its star and Fred J. Butler as director. Other members include Lillian Lawrence, Will R. Walling, Jack Cosgrove, Helen Ferguson, Alice Wilson, Otto Lederer and Jack Rollins.

Only at a 5-cent admission charge can this picture give film patrons their money's worth. *Hart.*

HEADIN' WEST

Bill Perkins......................Hoot Gibson
Potato Polly................Gertrude Short
Mark Rivers.............Charles LeMoyne
Red Malone.........................Jim Corey
Honey Giroux.......................Leo White
Ann Forrest...................Louise Lorraine
Barnaby Forrest.......George A. Williams
Stub Allen.....................Frank Whitson
Judge Bean.......................Mark Senton

A western comedy drama of the regulation Universal type, starring Hoot Gibson. Photographically it is far and away ahead of the usual U photography, and the direction makes for action right from the start. For these two items in the picture Alfred Latham is to be given credit for the former and William Craft for the latter. The picture made an impression at Loew's Circle, New York, where it served on a double-feature bill with the Fox release, "Any Wife," starring Pearl White.

The story and scenario were the work of Harvey Gates, who struck on a novelty for the opening of his picture. He has Gibson as a hobo stealing a ride on a mail aeroplane and dropping off via the parachute route at the point where he wants to land. This bit and the landing give the picture a thrill at the start and the follow-up is the usual ranch stuff with gun-play, bucking horses and a wild ride.

The scenes for the greater part are exterior on a ranch, the U back lot being used. Gibson shows up on the ranch where the owner has died but short time previously. A nephew of the deceased owner is the heir to the place, but no one suspects that the airplane tramp is he.

On a neighboring ranch there is a girl who has just returned from a fashionable school. She is the daughter of the wealthy cattle baron and she and the boy fall in love. Charles LeMoyne, foreman of the ranch on which the boy has landed and where he has been employed as a dishwa her, thinks it would be a great joke to palm him off as the heir on the "stuck-up girl" who has been passing up the rough cowpunchers since her return. But the boy at the last minute turns the tables and proves himself the real heir and there is the usual happy ending.

In direction Craft has managed to give the picture numerous touches that lighten it in a comedy way and two of the characters that aid materially in this are Gertrude Short and Leo White. LeMoyne makes a good heavy and at one stage of the picture puts up a corking fight with Gibson, but the hookup between the star and Jim Corey earlier in the story is the prize battle of the film.

Louise Lorraine makes a pleasing lead for the star and rides well besides looking pretty. *Fred.*

ANY WIFE

With Pearl White starring and Herbert Brenon as the director this production has at least two features worthy of advertising. But that about lets it out. Miss White does not make an extraordinary impression, and as a matter of fact is beginning to appear slightly mature, while Mr. Brenon's direction is naught that demands extended comment for its effectiveness.

The title of "Any Wife" is one that may have box-office value, but in the same breath the implication that the thoughts of any wife run in the direction the story suggests is a direct insult to the womanhood of our country. Even though the writer, director and producer have employed the time-worn expedient of the "dream" to "take the curse off," the fact the suggestion is there remains.

The story is that of a wife who is dissatisfied because her husband cannot give her all the attention she craves. The unfoldment of the tale is handled in such a manner the twist is given to the audience at the last minute. Up to that moment the action carried little but a heavy meller suggestion.

A successful business man lives in the suburbs. He has a wife and child. One morning he receives a wire that it is necessary to cross the continent to protect his business interests. He wishes his wife and son to accompany him. When reaching his office he discovers the plans necessary for him to take with him are not completed and so he asks one of his office executives to bring the plans to the house that night. This employe, one of the he-vamp type, takes it upon himself to arrive at the house prior to the arrival of his chief. While waiting he presents the wife with tickets for the dog show and requests her to permit him to escort her there.

After he leaves the house she has not determined whether or not to accompany her husband, and apparently decides not to do so. From then on the action indicates her running about with the he-vamp and the final return of the husband, who finds her in the arms of his employe. This leads to a divorce, with the husband taking the boy, a life of degradation with her seducer, although she is married to him, and at the end a leap from a bridge into the river.

At that point she awakes from the dream and immediately starts packing to accompany the husband on the trip.

It is the last few hundred feet with the comedy touch that saves the picture from utter condemnation.

Playing on a double feature bill at Loew's Circle, New York, with a Hoot Gibson Universal it failed to stir the audience until the laughs came during the last couple of minutes. *Fred.*

THE POWER WITHIN

Job Armstrong..........William H. Tooker
Mrs. Armstrong...Nellie Parker Spaulding
Bob Armstrong...............Robert Kenyon
Dorothy Armstrong..........Dorothy Allen
Count Cyril Bazaine.........Robert Bentley
Pauline.........................Pauline Garon
Little Bobby..............William Zohlmen

"The Power Within" is an Achievement Film Co. production, written by Robert Norwood, directed by Lem Kennedy, distributed by Pathe. It tells the old, old story of a successful business man, satisfied with himself and regarding himself as sufficient unto himself. This works out all right for years until a series of disasters befalls him, culminating with a breakdown in health. Until that time he finds no need for spiritual comfort, but is finally made to "see the light" through the beauty of soul of a little French peasant girl who comes to him as the widow of his son, bringing with her a grandchild.

Having arrived at the psychological moment when the old man's cup of bitterness is full to overflowing, the daughter-in-law is enabled to straighten out the problems confronting the unhappy old man—the whole designed to teach a strong moral lesson.

William H. Tooker gives an effective performance of the old man, visualizing his mental transition to a nicety, and Pauline Garen makes a sweet and wistful French girl. The remainder of the cast is reasonably competent. Adequately directed. A pleasing program feature. *Jolo.*

THE SCRAPPER

Released by Universal, featuring Herbert Rawlinson, with the screen version having been taken from the original story by R. G. Kirk, which appeared in the Saturday Evening Post. Showing at a second run house and splitting top honors for a "double feature day" the film satisfield, though failing to reveal anything of moment throughout.

For an Irish neighborhood house this picture is about perfect, perhaps constructed for that purpose. With the exception of two characters, who are the flies in the ointment and get their proverbial just desserts, the entire membership is cast in roles of Irish-Americans, with sub-titles in brogue.

Rawlinson as Pat Malloy, a young construction engineer who is assigned to a job of putting up a building that is to be completed upon a stated date, falls in love with the builder's daughter. He frolics through the theme, lending to the part a breezy assurance and appearance that should meet the feminine approval. There's not much else for Rawlinson to do besides whispering words of love in the ingenue's ear, all of which is flashed in detail on the screen. He does partake in a fist fight that clears up the labor trouble, permitting the building to be completed on time. This puts him in strong with the girl's father and he closes out to the usual clinch.

Gertrude Olmstead as the girl is pleasing in looks, though so far as work is concerned has little to do outside of sitting with Rawlinson and then having him chase her around the interior sets.

Direction and photography have been averagely taken care of, even if the story does fail to explain how young Malloy, recently graduated from college, is driving a corking raceabout and walks right in to boss the constructing of a steel skyscraper. That and his overcoming of the incidental delays in the work by means of the one fight seem to be the deficiencies in the scenario.

Appealing to purely an Irish clientele, "The Scrapper" should g t by if placed in conjunction with another feature to bolster it up. The film can't stand alone in other than the smaller houses.   *Skig.*

BACK PAY

Hester Bevins..................Seena Owen
Jerry Newcombe, her sweetheart......
....................................Matt Moore
Charles G. Wheeler, a millionaire......
....................................J. Barney Sherry
Kitty ....Ethel Duray
"Speed" ....Charles Craig
Thomas Craig................Jerry Sinclair

"Back Pay" is a slow plodding average feature, that barely passes, through paucity of story with acting and direction seemingl:· held down because of that. It's at the Rivoli, a Cosmopolitan-made film that is "presented" by Famous Players as a Paramount, that perhaps signifying the Famous Players made outright buy of the picture from Cosmopolitan. If so, F. P. got no bargain.

The best thing about "Back Pay" is its title, that having been made known in the Fannie Hurst story the play and picture were adapted from. The play, produced by A. H. Woods, had a short run on Broadway but has gone out again for the city week stand time. Its tale may have read well in type, but on the screen it drags along, that old-oaken bucket story about the country gal who goes to the big city and goes wrong along. Miss Hurst gave the stereotyped tale a couple of twists; the first the girl leaving the boob boarding house to look for lingerie, and the second, her regeneration, if that were it, when she quit the Riverside drive flat, put on her original little gingham gown and hiked back to her $25 a week job.

That Riverside apartment setting was elaborate enough to turn any girl's head, from a clerkship to an illicit courtship. And Hester Bevins (Seena Owen) got her lingerie although she didn't show any in the picture. Also she got remorse when her country sweetie, Jerry Newcombe (Matt Moore) came back from the front, blind. The doctors told Hester Jerry could only live three weeks. He still loved her and she had a hunch for him. Hester asked her gentleman friend with the gray hair and a bankroll if she could marry Jerry for three weeks, just to let him die happy, and, g. f. told her to go to it. So she did, moved Jerry from the hospital to her sumptuous apartment, told him it was a three-room affair and he died with that lie on his mind, along with the others he never knew of.

Which may bring out the moral of the story as the good die and the reformed bad live, to try it over again, if they wish.

There's never was any action. Much time is wasted planting the tale at the outset and much more along the way, in the mushy scenes between Hester and Jerry, their trysting place in the woods and their hospital meetings. The picture could still stand a 10-minute cut.

Frances Marion made the scenario and didn't over-work herself. It was about the same with Frank Borzage who directed, though the script of course held in the direction. Miss Owen only had to walk through the picture and she did only that, whether in the country or the city, while Mr. Moore did even less. The story called for no effort by anyone. Other principals hardly counted and seldom entered.

Notwithstanding there is the usual sentimental appeal to the love interest, but even here it seems to be risking any picture when the leading figure in a romantic tale is given a totally unsympathetic role, such as Miss Owen has, making Hester Bevins a gold digger in the country before she knows what gold digging means, and finishing up her education along that line when she reaches the city. It's a bad story for young girls to see.   *Sime.*

CAMERON OF THE MOUNTED

Corporal Cameron............Gaston Glass
Raven....................Irving Cummings
Mandy....................Vivienne Osborne
Little Thunder..........Frank Lanning
Potts....................George Larkin
Jim Haley................Joe Singleton

There are more "thrills" in the six reels of "Cameron of the Royal Mounted" than in half a dozen ordinary program features. It starts off with the raising of a check from 50 pounds to 500 pounds. The hero is accused of doing this to his own father, and, having been drunk, doesn't know whether or not he did it. Then his "thrills" only commence. He has a fist fight in a border saloon, is thrown out, and that is only the commencement. A jealous rival for the girl he is smitten with tries to brain him with an axe and succeeds in putting him in the hospital for weeks.

He becomes a member of the Northwest Mounted Police, chases one of the villains down a mountainside on horseback and over the rapids in a canoe; they have a terrific fight while clinging to a log in the water; they both reach land exhausted and the villain wants to die, admitting he raised the amount of the check. Does the hero let him die? Not yet. He literally carries him to headquarters and lets him confess before witnesses before permitting him to pass away.

And is that all? In rushes someone and announces the gal has been kidnapped. So he rides seven miles more for a fight with another villain, jumping on the bad man's horse and bearing him to the ground. Before he reaches the kidnapper, the captured gal says to her captor in the cave: "Why have you brought me here?" The stupid little minx, when said villain is the one who brained the hero through jealousy of her and who has made repeated efforts to embrace her. And, oh yes, there was a lot of bootlegging and a train hold-up by the villains, aided by the Indians, in order to capture the payroll. And how do you suppose they stopped the train? Naturally, you will say, by placing something across the track. Not so; they ran alongside it on horseback and shot at it, and when it slowed up they scrambled aboard. So the hero stepped out, jumped on the back of one of the gang's horses, and although they were right alongside him and many shot at him they "never touched" him and he rode furiously to the Royal Mounted headquarters and brought them back—and oh, there were many other such escapades, while the audience at the Circle Tuesday evening laughed derisively.

The name of this wonderful feature is "Cameron of the Royal Mounted," an Ernest Shipman production, released through Hodkinson. It was adapted from a story by Ralph Connor and directed by Henry MacRae. Really, there is "much too much" action, even for the most elemental audiences.   *Jolo.*

HER SOCIAL VALUE

Marion Hoyte........Katherine MacDonald
James Lodge...................Roy Stewart
Clifford Trent............Bertram Grassby
Bertha Harmon.........Betty Ross Clarke
Shipley........................Winter Hall
Joe Harmon..................Joseph Girard

"Her Social Value," a Katherine MacDonald starring feature, released by First National. It is a fairly interesting story evolved by Gerald Duffey and well directed by Jerome Strom. The production has a certain amount of value inasmuch as it has two starring names, Katherine MacDonald and Roy Stewart. The latter is not playing a westerner in this picture, but appears in regular store clothes. It is a story of a woman's sacrifice for her husband's career. In it Miss MacDonald does some of the best work that she has displayed on the screen in some time.

Miss MacDonald as Marion Hoyte is a girl of the middle class, who marries a man socially prominent; but he is unable to secure clients .. an architect because those who could assist him in a business way have passed him up socially because of his marriage. When the wife learns this she pretends to be in love with another, so that her husband will lea e her and be reinstated among the socially elect. He does leave her, but instead of moving back into society buries himself in a small town. His wife finally seeks him out and there is a reconciliation just about the same time that a fat commission arri es, his plans for a big railroad terminal having been accepted.

Mr. Stewart is a convincing lead opposite the star, and Bertram Grassby as the heavy does some excellent work. The minor roles are also well played.

Pictorially there are some very pretty interiors and one or two exterior locations that look well on the screen. The handling of the e rthquake is rather badly done, especially in the shot where a can of powder is set off to indicate that a landslide has wrecked a shack in the woods.

To the exhibitor it is just a question of how strong a drawing card the star is with his audiences. There is nothing particular about the picture that will draw, but it is an all around good program feature.   *Fred.*

CROSSING TRAILS

A Cliff Smith production released by Associated Producers. It is a cheap type of western feature that has Pete Morrison featured. The real star of the production is a kid actor who walks away with all of the comedy possibilities. As a picture it will serve on a double feature program providing the production shown with it holds sufficient punch to get the bill over.

Cliff Smith directed the production, holding for the greater part to exteriors for his shots. In several places he caught some picturesque scenes.

The featured player, Morrison, is rather a typical western hero, rides well and is handy with a gun, but other than that he seems to possess naught that will ever endear him to the hearts of film fans.

A simple story is employed for the purpose of parading a set of character across the silver sheet. There is the heroine, who is rearing a kid brother. She is made to appear as a circumstantial murderess. She escapes and settles on a ranch, the home of the hero and his mother. From that point on the events are discernible on the surface. Hero falls in love with her, heavy appears on the scene, tries to kidnap the girl, and finally is knocked off by the sheriff, with the usual happy ending.

Just "a western."   *Fred.*

TRUST YOUR WIFE

It's good advice, that title, but it doesn't make this a good picture, though it has a lovely woman as its star, Katherine MacDonald. And a lovely woman on the screen who can act should be superior to an ordinary story such as "Trust Your Wife" is. It's adapted from the play "Conscience," by H. S. Sheldon. There are two great titles to suggest a picture theme of magnitude for an original script. "Conscience" has been utilized for pictures and now "Trust Your Wife," stuck on a conventional, loses its film value for all time.

It's seldom a lovely woman is seen on the screen who can be anything but lovely. Miss MacDonald is not of the cutey nor the beauty type; she has just loveliness. It stands out on the film, it comes out and as a photographic subject, if her equal has been found, the other one should have a life contract if she has anything beyond looks.

Miss MacDonald has expression. In filmdom they say a player "registers." That registering is the biggest joke of the infant picture. You can register a yell on the phonograph disc, you can register emotions before the camera, but all the directors in the world can't make a player expressive. There is no such thing as a mechanic in that. The director's "register this" and "she will register that" may have been the sesame that got a bankroll out of someone, but it never made a picture star and never will. The personality of the voice or face can never be directed. Either may be cultivated or improved, but neither can be manufactured.

Which is recalled through having heard, "Katherine MacDonald is a bear of a looker, but that lets her out in pictures." The Katherine MacDonald Picture Co. presents "Trust Your Wife," released by First National. So she isn't out of pictures yet. Benjamin P. Schulberg is the president of the MacDonald Co. No one in pictureville ever said Schulberg was a simp. It should be pretty safe to back this combination.

There has been no better expression seen in a very long while on the screen than Miss MacDonald in her scenes on the yacht in this picture when resisting the advances of the man she had agreed to meet on his boat at night and alone. Nor could the expression of happiness and contentment as she rested in her husband's arms for the fadeout be simulated without the falsity of such simulation betraying itself. But it was a registration in part when Miss MacDonald tried to express fear upon first meeting her husband after the yachting episode. That was misdirection, of course, for why force a girl into unnaturalness when she has proven she can be natural?

Heigh-ho! And why rewrite the picture business?

So, getting down to the story, Miss MacDonald is the handsome wife of a good looking but needy inventor. Then the capitalist, with a girl of his own but an eye out for another, and that eye lamps Katherine. On or off, it would be the same. The capitalist schemes to win the wife and get the inventive husband out of the way. A yacht is one excuse. But the capitalist first takes a drink of booze he must have got in a Broadway cabaret. He couldn't wait. Before his guest could remove her wrap, cap started. She stood him off, professed helplessness and won out on his conscience, although the other girl, peering in through a window of the cabin, contributed her bit toward the conscience awakening.

The other girl put over other dirt. She phoned the husband where his wife was. As he reached the pier all the husband saw was the boat moving away. He went home and sat up all night thinking it over. When wife showed in the morning hot talk passed, with most of the captions in this picture evidently taken from the text of the play, they were so different. Husband wouldn't believe his baby or his eyes or ears until the cap came along, explained things, and then the fadeout.

The tale has been told in a hundred ways. Once or twice almost in the same way, minus the yacht but plus the finish. Still, there is Katherine—and she is there. This one is good enough where a lovely woman is bound to draw, but why not slip Katherine a regular story and see her put it over? *Sime.*

JANE EYRE

Hugo Ballin Productions (distributed by Hodkinson) has turned out a fine dignified transcript of the famous novel by Charlotte Bronte, with particular reference to its beautiful backgrounds and excellent acting. The exteriors give an astonishing effect of authentic English landscape and the interiors have done from first to last with utmost fidelity.

The production is always studiously careful and manages to reproduce with happy fidelity the atmosphere of the old story. A world of painstaking care is represented in this screen translation of the tale. It is considerable of a trick to crystallize the spirit of a novel such as this, surrounded as it is by the traditions of several generations. The picture version could easily do vast violence to preconceived ideas. That the film is an adequate presentation speaks volumes for the taste and intelligence of the adapters.

No small credit for the whole excellent effect is due to Mabel Ballin who plays the exacting part of Jane. Miss Ballin has a rare type of delicate beauty which lends itself perfectly to the early Victorian heroine. She could pose for a copy of Mona Lisa and her dark spiritual loveliness makes her ideal for the part of Jane. She plays in a quiet and natural vein which contributes greatly to the effectiveness of the whole work. A more energetic method might have spoiled the fine balance.

As an artistic achievement the picture is splendid, but as a commercial product its fate is open to question. Picture audiences have been educated to more robust drama than this photographic record of a phase of British life in a bygone day. Realistic common-places done with supreme fidelity (such as George Eliot's transcripts from life) may make literature, but the film followers seem to demand more sprightly romances than this delicate affair of lavender and old rose.

The picture deserves a large measure of success on its artistic merit. A painter would delight in some of its pictorial qualities. The exteriors of landscapes, gardens and vistas of rural roads are exquisite and have a convincing aspect of real English parks. In the same way the lofty rooms at Thornfield bear the stamp of actuality with their quaint furnishings and massive decorations. The handling of light and shadows has been remarkably well cared for. In the scenes where a creepy and sinister effect is desired —those having to do with the horrifying apparitions of the mad woman—this management of shadow masses is impressive.

These scenes, by the way, are managed with consummate craftsmanship and deliver a real thrill, the only drama the picture has. The rest of the story is rather colorless as it comes on the screen, although the romantic sentiment in the closing passages where Rochester has gone blind and Jane goes to him is sincere and affecting.

The casting of the picture is appropriate to the intelligence which directed the whole production. Norman Trevor plays Rochester in exactly the right spirit. A younger and handsomer lover might have been more impressive, but he would have done violence to the true translation of the story. Helen Poole (the titles failed to name the actress who played the part) sounded just the right sinister note and the other minor characters were absolutely in the picture.

The picture is a noteworthy accomplishment in the screening of a standard work of fiction and one is led to hope that it will not suffer the treatment of many fine books that lie neglected on the library shelves while cheap and shoddy current romance that satisfies the literary fads of the moment enjoy the shallow fancy of the public. *Rush.*

HOMESPUN VAMP

May McAvoy is the star of this Realart production released by Paramount. The story is an original by Hector Turnbull, adapted for the screen by Harvey Thew and directed by Frank O'Connor. The feature is a mighty good little picture, full of heart interest and not without a real comedy relief. Miss McAvoy is a charming little Cinderella heroine, and the fans that follow her will like her in this production.

The scene of the story is in a small town with the heroine the orphaned niece of two bachelors who are far from being spendthrifts. The girl keeps house for them, and they have set their hearts on her becoming the wife of the son of the lady blacksmith of the village. Just about at this stage along comes the hero, a writer, who is seeking out a lonely spot where he can complete "the great American novel." The town folk are suspicious of the stranger, and when the post office is broken into they start after him. In trying to escape he is wounded and falls in front of the home of the little orphan. Her uncles are away at the time and she hides the supposed robber, keeping him in the house over night.

In the morning the real culprit is captured, but then there is the scandal, for the uncles returning find the writer has stopped in their house over night and the girl has been there with him. No chaperon. A wedding is insisted on, the young man going through to protect the girl. Later he takes her to his own home, where his mother cares for her, while an action to annul the marriage is before the court. The decree is finally handed down, but a real love affair has been brewing in the interim. When the court's decision is handed down the hero announces he really loves the girl.

The picture is full of action which moves along swiftly. The cast has a number of clever character studies, not the least of which is the role of the hick boob that young Steadman plays. Charles Ogle and Guy Oliver as the pair of uncles also score.

On the whole it is a mighty good little comedy drama. ***Fred.***

A DOLL'S HOUSE

Torvald Helmer	Alan Hale
Nora	Nazimova
Ivar	Philip de Lacey
Emmy	Barbara Mafer
Bob	J. Ward, Jr.
Dr. Rank	Nigel De Brulier
Nils Krogstad	Wedgwood Nowell
Christina Linden	Florence Fisher
Anna	Elinor Oliver
Ellen	Cara Lee

Now we have the third film production of Henrik Ibsen's "A Doll's House." Originally the play was picturized by Universal as a Bluebird with Dorothy Phillips as Nora. That was in 1917. A year later Artcraft turned out a screen version of the same with Elsie Ferguson featured and now finally Mme. Nazimova comes to the fore with her version as her first independently made production released by the United Artists. With this picture it is just a question whether or not the coupling of the name of Mme. Nazimova with the Ibsen play in which she appeared on the speaking stage is to draw any money. As a film "A Doll's House" is entirely lacking in action to make it particularly worth while, and the hoydenish acting Nazimova can hardly be expected to put it over.

The Ibsen play is known too well for a resume of the story. That goes for exhibitors as well as playgoers for the former have undoubted seen either one of the other of the two previous productions.

As a picture even with Mme. Nazimova it is rather tiresome and old fashioned and this particular production is so handled to give it more the atmosphere of a foreign production.

Mme. Nazimova as the star, and her husband, Charles Bryant, as the director, have managed to pick Scandavanian types for the principal roles, and it must be said that the selection of Alan Hale for Thorvald was a most happy one, but Mr. Hale was undoubtedly overdirected, unquestionably he was compelled to overact in a couple of the scenes. This is what ends so much of a foreign production atmosphere to the feature.

Mme. Nazimova seemed at all times to be forcing herself in the playing of the role and it is doubtful if her interpretation of Nora will enhance her screen value to any great extent.

Photography is of the rather dark sort without any shadings as to lights. The sets adequate, although a couple of storm exteriors showed plainly that it was studio stuff that was used. *Fred.*

THE 14TH LOVER

Vi Marchmont	Viola Dana
Richard Hardy	Jack Mulhall
Clyde Van Ness	Theodore von Eltz
Aunt Letitia	Kate Lester
Mrs. Hardy	Alberta Lee
Mr. Marchmont	Frederick Vroom
Maid	Fornsie Gumm

The cold statistics of "The 14th Lover," a Metro Classic, run this way: A Harry Beaumont production, adapted by Edith Kennedy from Alice D. G. Miller's story; photography by John Arnold and A. F. Mantz, art director. Viola Dana is the star with Jack Mulhall as head of the supporting company.

The story itself is a light trifle, all the emphasis being on the side of comedy which frequently edges dangerously into farce. However, it's a cheerful story, bright and enlivening in all its characters and incidents and its only defect is the element so common to light comedy pictures of feature length, its tenuous recital is shamelessly padded with frivolous detail to pad out the necessary footage.

It requires a particularly meaty comedy story to sustain interest through the strain of attention required by something over five reels of flickers. So much depends upon the swift play of small incident and the interesting development of character that a frothy story has to be done much more expertly than a dramatic tale where the suspense of an ingenious plot grips interest. "The 14th Lover" illustrates this point. There are times when strict attention wanders because of the too elaborate detail which wearies.

Miss Dana has one of her familiar parts of the hoyden, a headstrong flapper who breaks through parental control and works out her own little romance in her own determined little way. The Metro star usually does extremely well with this kind of role and there are moments when she is effective here, but there is rather too much of the same thing and one becomes rather impatient with the repetition of her escapades. It is just a trifle too saccharine and cutie-cutie, this spoiled and imperious daughter of a rich and too indulgent father. It's rather difficult to sustain an hour and a half of sympathy for a spoiled darling and her adventures become rather cloying after a while.

The tale has to do with the love

affairs of Vi Marchmont who is pursued by 13 rich and handsome suitors of her own altitude of social eminence and who in revulsion against the trouble of making up her mind which one to accept, turns in desperation to her father's young guardian. To her utter astonishment when she practically throws herself into his arms, he displays no great enthusiasm, observing—and quite logically when you come to look at it—that he is looking for a helpmate and not a household ornament.

But Vi is not a bit disheartened. She continues her rather indelicate courtship until her aunt discharges the seductive gardener and then runs away from home and deliberately forces herself into the young man's home so that she will become compromised to the extent that he will be compelled to marry her. Some of the rough edges are taken off this situation by having the young man's mother act as the girl's accomplice in this design, her desire being to bring the two loving hearts together, but some how its a pretty tough morsel of fiction to get down as it comes before one on the silver sheet. The whole story apparently was inspired by an incident that was threshed out several years ago in the New York courts when a middle western millionaire waged a legal battle to free his daughter from a matrimonial entanglement of almost the identical sort. It was a good deal of a sensation at the time and it does seem that this is a pretty poor source to go for screen fiction.

As far as directorship goes, the picture is handled with skill worthy of a better scenario. It is full of clever little twists and deft-turns and its settings are extremely beautiful. The acting is capable, Miss Dana being likable for the most part. *Rush.*

TILLIE

Tillie.....Mary Miles Minter
Her Father.....Noah Beery
Jack.....Forrest Stanley
Doc.....Lucien Littlefield

Right at this time the name of Mary Miles Minter will have something of a box office value by attracting the morbidly inclined, for the association of the star with the late William D. Taylor is on the lips of film fans generally, and a number who have never seen her will want to give her the once over. "Tillie" is a picture that will gain her a lot of sympathy from audiences, and that is what she needs at this time. Incidentally, it is a fair program picture.

"Tillie" is the work of Helen R. Martin and Frank Howe, Jr., adapted for the screen by Alice Eyton. Frank Urson, who directed, turned out a story that on the screen is exceedingly draggy at times. It is a slow moving ponderous, affair that gets its tempo from the stolid Dutch folk, with which the story deals.

Miss Minter plays the daughter of a Pennsylvania Dutch farmer, the latter a stern master and not averse to utilizing his heavy leather belt to chastise his children. The little girl is at once haus frau and mentor for the other growing youngsters of the family. A neighbor who is of the Mennonite faith makes a will leaving $20,000 to the little girl providing she changes her religion and embraces the Mennonite church before she is 18. Otherwise the money goes to a nephew. A scheming lawyer in the village plans to get part of this money and discloses to the youthful postmaster his plan. The latter agrees to work with the attorney, and then goes to Tillie's father and promises the old man $1,000 on the day that he marries the daughter. The girl, however, refuses to become a party to the match and falls in love with a young writer who wanders into the town.

A runaway match and the two return to town, the elder of the Mennonite church expelling her, whereupon the husband announces the fact that he is the nephew and that she will receive the legacy after all.

The picture was shown last week at Loew's Circle, New York, as the strongest half of a double feature bill. *Fred.*

THE IDLE RICH

Samuel Weatherbee.....Bert Lytell
Mattie Walling.....Virginia Valli
Dillingham Coolidge.....John Davidson
Judge O'Reilly.....Joseph Harrington
Uncle Coolidge.....Thomas Jefferson
Mrs. O'Reilly.....Victory Bateman
Jane Coolidge.....Leigh Wyant
The Tailor.....Max Davidson

"Junk" was the original title of this story when it appeared in the Saturday Evening Post, with Kenneth Harris as the author, but as "written for the screen" by June Mathis it takes the title of "The Idle Rich." It is a Maxwell Karger production, with Bert Lytell as the star, released as a Metro classic. Perhaps the distributors were afraid of the original title for the picture, as there is so much "junk" on the film market at present. However, "The Idle Rich" is not a picture that is going to set the world afire, although it is fair screen entertainment of the usual run of program pictures. There is nothing about it that will lend itself particularly to exploitation, and except in the neighborhoods where Lytell has a following there is nothing unusual in the way of business to be expected from the picture.

The story in brief is that of a wealthy young society chap who is suddenly advised that his wealth has been wiped out. The fortune was originally accumulated by the boy's grandfather, who followed the gold rush to California and became a trader. The boy, shunned by his wealthy friends, becomes a junk dealer, and in time rehabilitates his fortunes and wins the girl who has stuck through his lean years.

Bert Lytell plays the hero, giving the role a certain characterization that pleases. Virginia Valli, his leading lady, is a pretty enough girl, but seemingly without personality. John Davidson played the heavy, fitting the type. The two most pleasing figures in the cast were Thomas Jefferson as an aged uncle and Victory Bateman, the former stock and melodrama favorite, in a character role.

Maxwell Karger has handled the direction in fairly lucid fashion, but in detail he was a little off at times. The photography was rather well lighted, although the one double exposure in the feature was poorly handled. *Fred.*

HER HUSBAND'S TRADEMARK

Lois Miller.....Gloria Swanson
Allan Franklin.....Richard Wayne
James Berkeley.....Stuart Holmes
Slithy Winters.....Lucien Littlefield
Father Berkeley.....Charles Ogle
Mother Berkeley.....Edythe Chapman
Mexican Bandit.....Clarence Burton
Henry Strom.....James Neil

A feature that shows considerable expense. There is enough in the way of sets on the screen to satisfy almost any audience. The story holds a number of thrills and considerable suspense. It is a Lasky production released by Paramount. The story is by Clara Beranger, with the scenario handled by Lorna Moon. Sam Wood handled the direction. Its principal wallop is that Gloria Swanson is starred and gives it good work. In her support are Stuart Holmes as the heavy and Richard Wayne playing the lead.

In action the story is a combination of a society drama and a western. Miss Swanson as the wife of Holmes is utilized by him to further his business interests. Through this he has managed to live in luxury and maintain a menage that bespoke of millions by the score, while in reality it was all part of a "front" on his part, a business asset, the same as his wife.

He is in need of money, and when Wayne as the returned engineer from Mexico, with a concession for acres of oil land appears on the scene, Holmes, after first refusing to see him, asks his wife to arrange to secure the returning engineer as a dinner guest. This accomplished, the wife is thrown into the guest's company by her husband in order that he may further his own ends. A trip to Mexico is suggested for the completion there of the necessary papers to close the deal. It is the husband's aim to get the engineer away so as to forestall other interests trying to reach him.

In Mexico the wife realizes she is falling in love with the engineer, and urges her husband to complete his business and leave immediately. This he refuses to do, she coming to the realization that she means nothing to Holmes except as a means to an end, with the result she is about to leave him, when one of the bandit generals arrives, and, seeing her, orders her seized for himself. In the fight that follows the husband is killed and the heroine and hero escape across the Rio Grande, with the usual flash of the U. S. Troopers coming to their aid.

The picture is well acted, with minor roles nicely played by Lucien Littlefield, Charles Ogile and Edythe Chapman. Clarence Burton as the Mexican General handled that role with decided capability.

In direction Mr. Wood for the greater part kept the action moving, although there were moments about half way where the story was a little draggy.

Sets of the bigger sort that were used held the attention. A cabaret scene at the opening was well done; also the society function later. Dance touches in both those scenes helped, as likewise did a dance in the opening of the Mexican scenes. The fight and attendant chase just before the close of the picture were the thrill stuff, although a puma that almost pounced on the star in the Lost Forest bit was an earlier touch that caused the audience to gasp.

The feature can be played up strong with exploitation and will get money anywhere. *Fred.*

PENROD

Penrod.....Wesley Barry
Mr. Schofield.....Tully Marshall
Mrs. Schofield.....Claire McDowell
Robert Williams.....John Harron
Sam Williams.....Gordon Griffith
George Bassett.....Newton Hall
Foster.....Harry Griffith
John Barrett.....Cecil Holland
Herman.....Sunshine Morrison
Verman.....Florence Morrison
Margaret.....Marjorie Daw
Marjorie Jones.....Clara Horton
Baby Rennsdale.....Peggy Jane

Were it not for its length (eight reels) "Penrod" would be one of the cleanest, healthiest and most wholesome feature picture ever turned out. With Wesley ("Freckles") Barry starred, it is an excellent picturization of the Booth Tarkington boy character.

Amusing to the highest degree, it somehow becomes tiresome through its over-footage and one cannot help thinking how preferable, if some of the simple incidents had been omitted. None of the scenes is prolonged but there are so many. It is like calling on friends and having the child of the house perform his little stunts. You are entertained for a time but after a while you long for the time to put the youngster to bed.

Little Barry gives a performance that stamps him as an artist. He is alternately wistful, humorous and mischievous. He is ably assisted by such seasoned film artists as Tully Marshall as the father, Claire MacDowell as the mother, Marjorie Daw, John Harron and a host of clever youngsters, the latter amusing you in spite of yourself until, as before mentioned, they become a bit tiresome.

The direction of Marshall Neilan and Frank O'Connor is all that could be desired, the scenario by Lucita Squier shows an understanding of the child mind, and the photography by David Kesson a fine piece of camera workmanship. First National should have no difficulty in placing this feature in the best first run houses at this time, when there is more or less antipathy or feeling against sex pictures. *Jolo.*

HER OWN MONEY

Mildred Carr.....Ethel Clayton
Lew Alden.....Warner Baxter
Thomas Hazelton.....Charles French
Harvey Beecher.....Clarence Burton
Flora Conroy.....Mae Busch
Ruth Alden.....Jean Acker
Jerry Woodward.....Roscoe Karns

Ethel Clayton is starred in "Her Own Money" (Paramount), taken from Mark Swan's play of the same name, with adaptation by Elmer Harris. The direction is credited to Joseph Henabery, with Thompson Buchanan in supervisory capacity. By the very nature of the story it should have strong appeal for women fans, dealing as it does in a sentimental way with husband and wife relations in the household situation of a newly married pair.

The topic is an interesting one, and is here treated in an engagingly frank way. There is a good deal of realism in the practical problems of finances of the young couple, with the ambitious husband spending in an open-handed way and the wife cautiously putting away small savings. The story is simple and direct and impresses by its direct sincerity. It might be the record of almost any couple.

It has no great dramatic strength, but makes its appeal upon a truthful transcript from life in its painstaking character drawing and in the working out of an every-day domestic situation. The weakness of all stories of this kind, of course, is that they lack "punch" in a melodramatic way, and probably its appeal will prove less broad and general than a story of more powerful dramatic elements, but it is a high-grade production in its conception and execution and reflects credit upon the author, director and players.

"Her Own Money" was unfortunately placed in the Rialto program this week because of the supplementary program which had a long Triart production called "The Young Painter," a rather trashy sentimental story in place of the usual news reel or scenic, and it rather overloaded the program with sentimental love stories. After one had sat through nearly three reels of this super saccharine romance the regular feature, with its domestic story of sentimental import, came as a little too much of the same thing.

Miss Clayton improves with each succeeding feature. In this she has some fine moments of easy restrained acting as the self-sacrificing wife, playing with a smooth, natural effect that registers at full value. The whole play is done in much the same tone, varied by more florid passages by Mae Busch, who makes an excellent contrast as the selfish butterfly wife.

The story deals with Mildred Carr, secretary to a big business man, who gives up the "slavery" of business for the "freedom" of wifehood with Lewis Alden, a young real estate operator. Lewis has plunged on a $5,000 option on a site which he proposes to turn over to Mildred's old employer at a big profit. Meanwhile he is a free spender in his plan to do big things in business, while Mildred is the saver of the partnership, all unknown to the husband.

The option is about to lapse and is only saved by Mildred's buying an extension with her savings. In order that Lewis may not be "humiliated," Mildred lends him the money in a round-about way through a neighbor, and misunderstandings arising out of the transaction separate the couple. Mildred goes back to her old secretarial post, while Lewis plunges into business more determinedly, and by hard work they re-establish themselves.

There is no impressive drama in all this, but it is interesting character drawing and makes a clean, attractive film subject. *Rush.*

CARDIGAN

Michael Cardigan......William Collier, Jr.
Silver Heels..............Betty Carpenter
Sir William Johnson....Thomas Cummings
Captain Butler.............William Pike
Lord Dunmore.........Charles E. Graham
Marie Hamilton........Madeleine Lubetty
Lady Shelton..................Hatty Delaro
Sir John Johnston...........Louis Dean
The Weazel.................Colin Campbell
Jack Mount.....................Jere Austin
Chief Logan.........Frank R. Montgomery
Dulcina ....Eleanor Griffith
Quider ....Dick Lee
Colonel Cresap.............Jack Johnston
Molly Brandt.............Florence Short
Patrick Henry.............George Loeffler
John Hancock...............William Willis
Paul Revere..................Austin Hume

Based on the novel of the same name by Robert W. Chambers, Messmore Kendall is presenting this screen feature directed by John W. Noble and backed with three camera men. The trio of "shooters" alleged to have been used in taking the picture sounds more pretentious than the celluloid product actually looks, for "Cardigan" will not cause any undue disturbance amongst producers and exhibitors. Reported as being corking reading matter, something must have been lost in transplanting the theme to the projection machine, as the story unwinds a mediocre piece of work prone to become melodramatic in its sub-titles.

"Buster" Collier has been assigned as "Cardigan," handling the title part for average results without lending that particular strength to the character called for through his various escapades of rescuing and being rescued. Besides the heroic incidents the story calls for young Collier to interpret the role as playing an important link in the chain of events leading up to the American Revolution, with the sequence of the picture having a tendency to reveal that the responsibility involved was a bit too much for him. Betty Carpenter is the heroine, with the remainder of the cast assembling a performance of average quality, having Jere Austin predominating somewhat above the others.

The story deals with the Colonial period and up to the beginning of the Revolution, including the friction that existed between the Colonists and Tories of the time, the probability as to which side the Indian tribes would support, and the love affair of Michael Cardigan and the girl termed "Silver Heels" by the redskins.

Noble, in directing, evidently allowed a substantial theme to slip through his fingers through subordinating the historical trend of the theme to the love interest, and having two principals unequal to the task of holding it up. On paper, "Cardigan," as a picture, must have looked like a great proposition, but the somewhat exaggerated escapes that the hero undergoes, the overdone sub-titles that read in one instance, "Michael, you shall not soil your hands with this man's blood; let him go"; the poorly handled mob stuff and the work of the cast, leaves the picturization of the ride of Paul Revere about the only kick in the film—and you've got to stretch your imagination a bit to get a thrill out of that.

The picture gets away fast and promises much between the intrigue that the Tories carry on and the showing of the Cayuga tribe (costumed as the old Biograph company presented their Indian characters) about ready to declare war, but the whole action slows up, with the love affair dwindling to almost nothing, besides losing the initial interest. As it stands, "Cardigan" should prove interesting to children through its historical relations, but it's more than doubtful if the older folk will enjoy it, though it may get some business at the box office from those who read the story. *Skig.*

THE LAST CHANCE

This is a Canyon Picture made by Selig with Franklyn Farnum starred. No other member of the cast is named, but an amazing jumble of a story was written by William E. Wing. So far as detail is concerned, Webster Cullinson's direction was fair enough. The picture can't have cost much (except the health of the actors pummeled by Farnum and his associates) for it is mostly made up of exteriors. It was part of a double bill Feb. 20 at Loew's Circle.

Farnum plays Rance Sparr, lackadaisical son of a Western ranch owner. His father is killed in a row but this doesn't spur Rance up much. He has all his cattle stolen and takes to drinking whisky. The saloonkeeper's daughter goes on a jag with him because she's sorry his own girl takes so little interest in his fate. Her influence is such that he wakes up and rehabilitates his fortune, taking to his heart the right girl.

Farnum would make a fair heavy and some of his supporting cast were all right. The story was so inadequately motivated, however, it was hard to follow, and left you mostly bewildered. Even the fights (they occurred so often the spectators laughed) didn't help. It was hard to determine who was who, and why they fought and what they wanted. *Lced.*

THE GOLDEN GALLOWS

A Universal feature starring Miss DuPont, who has been elevated to stardom since her work in "Foolish Wives." It is a story of back-stage life in the theatre that is about on a par with the usual screen versions of that phase of theatre, inaccurate with countless liberties permitted that never would be tolerated in any theatre. No author, director or scenario writer was given credit on the copy of the film that was screened at the Academy of Music on Monday of this week, where the picture was the weaker end of a double feature bill which included the John Barrymore starring feature, "The Lotus Eaters." However, it is a fair picture of the usual program type and if anything a little better than the average U. product.

Miss DuPont is starred with Jack Mower as her leading man and Edwin Stevens playing a bit in the early part of the picture. The balance of the cast is equally well picked and the playing of all the roles even to the minor bits are well handled.

The story has Miss DuPont as the heroine starting as an understudy who is made overnight. Mower, who is in the audience, falls in love at first sight and there are several others who do likewise. Stevens in the role of an old admirer who has been trying to capture the affections of the girl while she was in the chorus, changes his tactics when she is a star and becomes a loyal friend. When he is killed by a former sweetheart through jealousy it is discovered that he has left half his fortune to the new star.

His lawyer, who is also an admirer, tried through publicity of the will to kill off competition on the part of rivals for the girl's hand. He having a letter which was written by the dying man stating that he wanted the girl's name protected because their friendship was of a most platonic nature. He is successful in his effort for a while.

In the end, however, his tactics are disclosed and the lovers are reunited. *Fred.*

GIVE ME MY SON

A mother theme, six-reel independent production, distributed by George H. Hamilton, featuring Pauline Brunius and all-star cast. Shown at a special press exhibition at the Unity Pictures' projection rooms, it elicited mild interest as a feature. Miss Brunius works sincerely in her role, but to no striking purpose, impressing chiefly as being miscast. In age appearance about 40, personating a character of similar age, she is not altogether sympathetic as a "mother" character.

Bertha Brenner (Miss Brunius) married a young scapegrace in haste some 20 years before and begot a son of the union, her spouse dying in the Orient shortly after. The child is taken by Bertha's father and placed in an orphanage. Meantime she marries Richard Brenner, a wealthy shipowner, never disclosing her first marriage. All the 20 years she has been fruitlessly searching for her lost son until fate brings him, unconscious, reeling in at her very doorstep (so she thinks, because of a book in the boy's possession marked Howard Wall, able seaman).

The pseudo Howard is taken care of for several weeks by the Brenner family. An affection springs up between the boy and the Brenners' daughter Alice. Believing each to be half sister and brother to the other, the mother discourages the amour, the supposed punch twist being that the youth is not Howard at all.

The boy relates how Howard and he were chums from their orphanage days, growing up and running away to sea together. In flashback he recites of the accident through which the real Howard met his death. This boy is Paul Henning, the inconsistency of it being that, reared as a son for several weeks, his benefactors do not even know his name. True, the mother makes secret she harbored the thought he was her offspring, but she might have asked him his name to address him and introduce him to her daughter, Alice, and the guests of the girl's birthday party.

Such other inconsistencies arise. The titling of the production is replete with trite stock phrases such as "when dawn came," "that night," "the next morning," and then, too, there is an over-abundance of titles. The elimination of several could cut the picture down to five reels easily. The direction is jerky, employing too much flashback stuff. The production itself is cheap, employing a few interiors and lots of outdoor stuff. The cast makes the best of the weak story.

The pop price picture houses ought to provide a market for the picture if offered at a price. *Abel.*

THE ABLE-MINDED LADY

Breezy Bright..........Henry B. Walthall
Widow McGee............Helen Raymond
Daphne Meadows.............Elinor Fair

A fairly good little western comedy drama filmed from the Saturday Evening Post story of William R. Leighton. The production is another of the releases of the Pacific Film Co. handled by Julius Singer, in the independent market. Ollie Sellers handled the direction and managed to turn out a fairly interesting little tale on the screen, with Henry Walthall as the principal selling point for the exhibitor.

Walthall plays a rather whimsical character, a tramp ranch worker—whole-hearted, with a kindly thought for others, but always his own worst enemy. Helen Raymond, who carries the title role, walks off with all the comedy honors of the production. It is she who is the widow, with three former husbands under the sod, who owns the ranch. Aggressive and competent, she rules the place with an iron hand, so much so that her three ranch men walk out on her, and she manages to round up Walthall as the man of all work.

Her niece from the east has been sent to the widow to be cured of an affair of the heart, but the hero follows her westward, becomes a ranch man, and in the end wins out, while Walthall falls as victim No. 4 for the widow.

A well-told, fairly humorous tale that will be generally liked, although not exactly a picture to rave over. In a pinch it will fit almost in any of the smaller daily change houses and stand up on its own.
Fred.

THE GIRL FROM ROCKY POINT

Samuel Hoyden...............Milton Ross
Betty........................Ora Carew
Corrine....................Gloria Joy
Daniel Williams...........Charles Spere
Timothy Smith.............F. G. Davidson
Robert Gifling............Theo. Von Eltz
Mignon....................Verna Brooks
The Devil.................Walt Whitman

This is a light feature production released through the Pacific Film Co., which has its offices at Culver City, Cal., and handled in the east by Julius Singer. There isn't much to the story or the continuity, which was the work of Sherwood Mac-Donald, and much less contributed by the direction of Frederick G. Becker. As an independent production it will serve on a double feature program in the bigger daily change houses, providing that the accompanying picture is fairly strong.

The story deals with the simple fisher village folk along the Maine coast. There is an attempt in the latter part of the picture to introduce something of a Christian Science aspect, that bit falling to Walt Whitman of "Miracle Man" fame, but the thought comes rather too late to help the picture.

Types of village folk are drawn in the characterizations. There is the stern old sea captain with his two daughters; the hypocrite; the little crippled youngster and the "mystery man," who is termed The Devil by his neighbors. In the end he stands revealed as the most sincere devotee of the teaching of the Bible of them all. The hero is the society type, who is washed ashore from a wreck, and he in the end wins the heart and hand of the daughter of the stern old sea captain.

Had the story been handled in the proper manner and the direction and titling more carefully thought out, the feature would have been good program material, but in its present shape it is below the average cheap feature. *Fred.*

CHASING THE MOON

Dwight Locke....................Tom Mix
Jane Norworth...................Eva Novak
Milton Norworth.............William Buckley
Velvet Joe.......................Sid Jordan
Princess Sonia.................Elsie Danbrie
Prince Albert....................Wynn Mace

One will find considerable criticism, if one is exacting, with the incongruity of the story, but action in film plots excuses many things. So far-fetched and almost improbable is the theme one sort of expects it all to wind up with a fade-in showing the action up as a "dream." However, it is delivered straight, evidently meant seriously.

Mix is all over the lot in this Fox production, jumping off trains into autos and onto horses, etc. The title is aptly chosen, for the plot itself is really a "chasing for the moon" theme. Thinking he has drunk a poison which becomes fatal at the end of 30 days, he chases the only possessor of the antidote, a Prof. Sulphide, from America to Russia, into Spain.

Edward Sedgwick and the star supplied the story, the former also directing. Bennie Kline cranked the camera and Ralph Spence did the titling and editing, which is no small factor in the production. The captions are truly funny and in keeping with the zippy spirit of the theme. Spence has coined a couple of novel phrases, such as "beautleggers of 1922," referring to a chorus of coryphees.

Miss Novak is Mix's leading lady, although doing little in comparison to the star, who is literally all over the lot. Action is the only word to describe the plot. That predominates and to good purpose. It more than balances the incongruity of the plot. *Abel.*

LOVES OF PHARAOH

Pharaoh Amenes.............Emil Jannings
Ramphis....................Henry Liedtke
Theonis...................Dagny Servaes
Samlak, King of the Ethiopians........
Paul Wegener
Makeda, his daughter......Lyda Samanova
Sotis, architect.........Albert Basserman
High Priest.............Friedrich Kuehne
Menon, intimate to the king.Paul Biensfeldt

A German-made film production parallel in most respects to Goldwyn's "Fedora." It has much the same sort of drama, the same grade of impressive mass production, a like weight of pictorial magnificence upon which could be based an exploitation campaign. The film world knows what happened to "Fedora." It was tried in New York and made a sensational start. In Pittsburgh and elsewhere it began with like favorable auspices. But it never made good for the long pull. It was a quick flash and a prompt dieaway at high box office admission.

That seems to be the destiny of the elaborate foreign pictures brought to this side, and there appears nothing about "Pharaoh" to forecast any other fate, at least as a special at a high admission scale. It has a substantial background of dramatic appeal and it has in an unusual measure the value of spectacular mass effects. There are passages late in the picture which stand out powerfully for their mob effects, and throughout the film has picturesque qualities which make it interesting, but it is difficult to believe that it can be made into another world-beater like "Cabiria" or "Quo Vadis" Those two screen productions burst upon the American screen public as a novelty, but since then the fans have been made familiar with just plain enormousness of film dramatic proportions. Mere bigness of mob scenes do not impress any more. To get the spectacle over there must be some special quality of popular appeal to turn the trick.

At the dollar scale such as prevails at the Criterion, New York, where the importation had its first viewing and where it is still current, it looks like a draw. On the evening late last week when it was seen there was a capacity crowd for the first evening show, but the second was less than a full house. The picture had had all the advantage of a costly metropolitan advertising campaign.

Except for the huge crowds of supernumeraries the production does not look especially expensive. It obviously was designed for much more footage than in its present state. Toward the finish there has been drastic cutting, the story is jumpy and confused and there is a large amount of titling—usually the sign the film action has been cut severely. But its mob scenes are impressive, particularly in the desert fighting passages and in the assaults upon the city of Thebes. These bizarre scenes are tremendously effective, both because of the picturesque costuming and the romantic complexion of the story.

It is said to have cost between 16,000,000 and 18,000,000 German marks or between $70,000 and $80,-

000 in American money at the current exchange rate of .44 cents per mark.

The tale deals with the love of the Egyptian king Pharaoh Amenes for the slave girl Theonis, brought to his court by Samlak, king of the Ethiopians, when he comes to negotiate a truce, offering his own daughter in marriage as the means of binding the peace agreement. When the Egyptian makes the slave girl his queen and spurns the daughter of Samlak war breaks out between the two nations. Thebes is besieged and the destruction of the capital appears to be fated when the slave girl's young lover rallies the armies and, returning to the fight, drives the invaders off. The tyrant king is slain in the engagement, leaving the way clear for the happy culmination of the romance.

The picture is an Ernest Lubitsch production done in his familiar lavish way. It is put out under the sponsorship of the Hamilton Pictures Corporation and designated a Paramount release. It is given a fine, dignified but simple exhibition at the Criterion, preceded by a short dance by two girls in a dim temple setting, an exceedingly artistic bit of scenic embellishment. *Rush.*

LOVE'S BOOMERANG

Perpetua.....................Ann Forrest
Perpetua, as a child........"Bunty" Rosse
Brian McCree, an artist......David Powell
Russell Felton, a crook......John Miltern
Monsieur Lamballe.............Roy Byford
Madame Lamballe..........Florence Wood
Saville Mender..............Geoffrey Kerr
Stella Dainty.............Lillian Walker
Christian, a convict.......Lionel Daragon
Madame Tourterelle.........Ollie Emery
Jane Egg, a circus rider....Amy Williard
Auguste, a clown...........Tom Volbecque
Corn Chandler...............Frank Stanmore
Mrs. Bugle......................Ida Fane
Perpetua's Mother..........Sara Sample

One of those things, as the plot will tell. Made abroad by John S. Robertson, it was brought to the Rialto Feb. 26 by Adolph Zukor, with Ann Forrest and David Powell featured. The adaptation by Josephine Lovett is from the novel, "Perpetua," by Dion Clayton Calthrop. We first see a little girl coming to Brian McCree's studio to pose and later, when her mother dies, proposing Brian adopt her as his daughter, which he does. And how happy they are together! It is like heaven till the serpent enters in the person of Perpetua Mary's **real father, who is a crook and no end of a bad lot. But exhibitors must not lose heart. Mr. Robertson and his expert assistants (they include Tom Geraghty) see to it that everything works out right in the end for the characters in the picture and Mr. Zukor's pocketbook.**

But before the happy ending comes to pass, things look black. After touring foster father and daughter with a circus and getting a lot of good animal stuff into the film, Mr. Robertson brings them back to London, where a wealthy young man named Mender falls in love with Perpetua. But this young man is not only dying but, alas, he is also under the influence of Felton, a crook and the real father of Perpetua Mary. Needless to say, heredity plays no part in this film. None of father's wickedness has been inherited by Perpetua, in whom environment has triumphed over vicious antecedents. Goodness plays so big a part in her character, moreover, that she marries Mender to reform him, though really she loves her foster father and he her. Felton, meanwhile, for the sake of a fortune Mender has willed him, kills him with a poisoned drink, but the blame for this falls on Perpetua, not Felton. Felton gets his, though—never fear. Mr. Robertson knows the requirements of the picture market and he saw to that. You go away satisfied, because after Felton is disposed of, Perpetua and Brian are locked together in a kiss and a close-up and you are left

with the comforting idea that they lived happily ever after.

Ann Forrest appeared with Thomas Meighan once in a film with a somewhat similar plot, and her work here is not so good. Her make-up is inexpert and as a 15-year-old girl she was anything but convincing. David Powell is as he has been except that mannerisms are growing on him and he has adopted the slovenly manner of dress affected by the English, particularly since the war. Some of the circus scenes gave the actors concerned in them excellent opportunities of which they availed themselves.

This is the usual stuff, with a tried and true plot, adequately produced. *Leed.*

BEYOND THE RAINBOW

Edward Mallory.................Harry Money
Marion Taylor...........Lillian (Billie) Dove
Henrietta Greeley............Virginia Lee
Frances Gardener.............Dinna Allen
Louis Wade..................James Harrison
Count Richardo e Terrion......Macey Harlan
Mrs. Burnz...................Rose Coghlan
Dr. Ramsey....................Wm. Tonker
Mrs. Gardener.................Helen Ward
Mr. Gardener...............George Fawcett
Esther.................Marguerite Courtot
Inspector Richarson.........Edmund Breese
Robert Judson...............Walter Miller
Col. Henry Cartwright........Charles Craig
Virginia Gardener.............Clara Bow
Bruce Forbes..................Huntly Gordon

Robertson-Cole showed this ambitious feature to the trade in the projection room disclosing an unusually interesting feature. It has an impressive array of screen names and its story values are especially strong. There is a good romantic tale for the main plot and within the direct story a puzzling mystery develops such as will hold the attention of any audience of fans.

As against these points of excellence the story is slow in getting into its pace and in its introductory passages are confusing from the complexity of its threads and the number of persons involved in the action. The titling is rather crude also, but the good points of the production far outweigh the bad and the picture is bound to arouse interest.

The story is taken from Solito Solano's work, "The Price of Fine Feathers" and was adapted to the screen by Lolia Brooks and William Christy Cabanne who also directed. There are no less than 16 principal characters and the work of introducing them one after the other is laborious, but once the situation has been "planted" the narrative runs smoothly and understandably notwithstanding its complicated nature.

The feminine characters form a galaxy of beauty. Lillian (Billie) Dove has a wealth of brunet loveliness and makes an attractive contrast to the other two beauties, Virginia Lee and Clara Bow, both blondes and both beauty contest winners. An actress of no less note than Helen Ware has a minor part and Rose Coghlan has a bit. Marguerite Courtot also is in the cast as well as other well-known players. The list of men is even more impressive numbering Edmund Breese, Harry Morey, Macey Harlan, William Tooker and George Fawcett. A recital of the names is sufficient guarantee of the quality of the screen acting.

The story is too elaborate to stand more than a brief outline in this place and besides it would be a pity to disclose the surprise solution of its mystery, but the situation is based on the plan of a young society man to make his cold sweetheart jealous by bringing to a reception a humble stenographer. During the ball two mischievous children of the hostess, peeved because they are forbidden to take part in the festivities, distribute half a dozen letters to the guests, reading, "Examine your conscience! Your secret is known!" These notes are received with varying sensations and when the confusion is at its height the lights suddenly are switched out and a pistol shot stabs the darkness.

The rest of the picture (it is an **even six reels, cut from much longer footage) is devoted to an interesting solution of the mysterious pistol shot and the development of a pretty romance between the humble stenographer and a handsome young soldier. The denouement of the crime story is a splendid surprise and the love story, involving as it does the saving of the heroine's baby brother makes excellent screen fiction.**

The main story takes place in a luxurious home amid scenes of luxury and some elaborate settings are shown. The later passages shift to the Adirondacks where there are beautiful snow scenes. Altogether an interesting program picture with possibilities of exploitation as a special virtue of its "all-star" cast.

Rush.

FRENCH HEELS

Palma May....................Irene Castle
Lieut. John Tabor.............Ward Crane
Keith Merwyn..............Charles Gerard
Jarvis Tabor...............Howard Truesdale
Camp Foreman.............Thomas Murray

A Hodkinson picture at Moss' Cameo on 42d street, and a good picture. As a star it has Irene Castle, billed as "the best dressed woman in the world," which has something to do with its drawing power, but not all, for while Mrs. Castle, more than any other American, has what is most easily described in the French manner as chic, she has in addition that slenderness and grace of action, the short, bobbed curls, associated in men's minds ineradically with the American girl of the acceptedly popular type.

The story is only average, but the production, especially the photography, could with difficulty be made more elaborately rich. Taken from "Knots and Windshakes" by Clarence Budington Kelland, the production was directed by Edwin L. Hollywood (what a name for a megaphone commander!) and shows the marriage of a successful cabaret performer, Palma May, to the son of a timber king. Up in the forests there is trouble with the men, and father-in-law Tabor let the young people fight out their own destiny in the woods together. The climax, with young John Tabor being beaten up by infuriated drunkards, jams into too close action, and so is less effective. Spread out more the punch would have been increased, but the development till then is human and believable.

Mrs. Castle herself hasn't much range in expressing the emotions, but at her most restricted she has far more than the average picture queen to show, and she is besides so girlish a figure she is sure to appeal to those who prefer willowy youth to buxom maturity.

The support is capable. Mr. Hollywood got less from the rough crowd than should have been expected, but this came from considering them for camera purposes as a mass instead of singling them out, and developing them, then coalescing the whole into that much more effective a mob scene. Thomas Murray made the most of the lesser parts, while the others are little to blame if they did not, the lines laid down for them being so cut-and-dried and according to formula.

Leed.

GRAND LARCENY

Kathleen Vaughn...........Claire Windsor
John Anixter...............Elliott Dexter
Barry Clive..................Lowell Sherman
Franklin...................Richard Tucker
Thad..........................Tom Gallery
Harkness Boyd.................Roy Atwell
Emerson......................John Cossar

Goldwyn offered this production at the Capitol beginning Feb. 26, the picture having been elaborately advertised. The public response on Sunday evening turned out to be enormous. The house was crowded all evening by probably the most disorderly assemblage that has wrangled with film house ushers on Broadway for many a day. They accepted the picture mildly, but were tumultuously enthusiastic over the musical and dancing features of the program which were unusually interesting.

The picture itself is another forced effort to make a sophisticated problem play as contrasted with the straightaway romantic drama, and once again it fails of its purpose. These psychological social studies, labored clinical examinations of motives and intents of erring husbands and wives, are getting to be rather a bore.

This one is credited to Albert Payson Terhune as author, with Wallace Worsley as director. Mr. Terhune has always been identified with a more wholesome type of fiction, and it comes as a surprise to find him dealing in this sort of stuff.

Briefly the story covers this ground: John Anixter is committed to the austere principle that a thief must be punished, that anyone who deals with him on terms of mercy himself becomes an accomplice in a crime. In the working out of this belief he persists in prosecuting an employe who has stolen a sum of money. Subsequently Barry Clive (played by Lowell Sherman) falls in love with his (Anixter's) wife and the husband takes the position that he has committed the theft of her love. He allows her to secure a divorce and she marries Clive. Anixter lets her go, expressing in the presence of both the bitter conviction that a wife who can be stolen **from one husband can as easily be stolen from another and that a man who will steal one wife will be very likely to steal another. Thus he has planted suspicion and uncertainty in the minds of both.**

Subsequently Anixter meets his former wife, who, of course, is unhappy in her new marital situation with Clive, and the general question is argued at great length by printed titles. It all ends in the woman packing up her belongings and leaving Clive—to what end or purpose the audience is left to conjecture, for the film begs the question in a long title addressed to the women in the audience and reading in effect:

"Women of the audience, what do you think? Should she remain with Clive? Should she return to her first husband? Or should she decide to have nothing more to do with any man?"

This sort of thing doesn't teach any sort of moral and doesn't get anywhere. It doesn't reflect any kind of attitude toward life. It's just a cheap and lazy effort to start a sensational sex problem. It isn't easy to see where this accomplishes anything. If a playwright or a picture producer has no definite convictions on moral right and wrong, why enter into a discussion of this kind? A playwright who just asks questions and dodges the issue is merely a literary trickster where he should be something of a preceptor, or at least an enlightened recorder of life. Altogether the picture is a hoax and a disappointment. One leaves the theatre with a feeling of having been cheated.

Just as a pictorial play the thing has been rather well done. It reflects in a pictorial sense a dignified record of the physical aspects of the social life it deals with. The interior settings are very real and lifelike and its backgrounds are always convincing. In a mechanical way, such as its photography and its artistic composition (disregarding the literary quality of the story) it is an intelligent bit of work and its acting is excellent. The trouble with the whole work is that its story wasn't worth doing at all.

Rush.

WORLD'S CHAMPION

William Burroughs...............Wallace Reid
Lady Elizabeth...................Lois Wilson
John Burroughs..................Lionel Belmore
George Burroughs.........Henry Miller, Jr.
Mrs. Burroughs...............Helen Dunbar
Rev. David Burroughs.........Leslie Casey
Lord Brockington............S. J. Sandford
Butler.......................W. J. Ferguson
Mooney..........................Guy Oliver

In six reels Jesse L. Lasky, through Paramount, has released Wally Reid's latest based on the play, "The Champion," which shapes up as a pleasing light comedy feature for the better run houses. The film has not realized on the comedy value instances the show held, but on the other hand has come through for laughs where the stage presentation was unable to connect. The story is fitting for Reid, who ambles through without being called upon for any exceptional effort, though lending a deft touch to the character, possibly due to direction, that keeps the theme continuously amusing, backed, of course, by his appearance. Well dressed, having most of the action take place within interior sets, and nicely casted, the picture has the punch laughs placed down near the finish previous to a non-clinch ending which leaves a satisfactory and wholesome impression.

The story's locale is England with Reid as William Burroughs, the youngest son of a family whose father is a fanatical social climber. He ousts the boy from his home for not apologizing to a peer. The prodigal goes broke, with the succeeding film showing him sneaking his way on shipboard, accidentally meeting a fight trainer, caught by officers of the ship and set to washing dishes as a means of working his way to the States. Lost sight of for a while, in revealing what goes on back home, the next flash at young Burroughs is when he returns to the fold, unannounced, to see his mother, with the old boy still holding out and again ordering him away, with his second departure being stayed by a calling contingent of the mayor and a trio of nobles who have come to pay homage to the middle-weight champion of the world, "Gunboat William."

The father dotes on the social side and announces his pride in his son, insisting he stay and giving a stag dinner in his honor for all the male social leaders he can think of.

The climax comes when Lord Brockington calls to take away Lady Elizabeth, financially necessitated to act as private secretary to the Burroughs family. Recognizing in young Burroughs the boy to whom he gave a beating some five years previous, he challenges him to come outside for another trimming. The champ's preparation for the affair in taking off his ring and following out the door whistling, the carrying in of the lord on an improvised stretcher, with the action of the fight being shown by proxy through the facial expression of the butler, provide the laughs inserted into the film which lead up to the conclusion.

The fight wherein "Gunboat William" takes unto himself the middleweight crown is in the form of a switchback, not any too lengthy or convincing. It shows an outdoor ring, the attendant mob, the round in which the battle is won, and Kid **McCoy as the falling champion (very much overweight) and doing little but floundering around before taking the final dive for the count. The situation might have been worked up for much better results with possibly McCoy allotted some footage. He's of no little interest himself, remarks from men in the audience bearing out that statement. Despite McCoy is much heavier than when he taught a red-headed kid to swim, he certainly is deserving of the program or subtitle mention, which is conspicuous by its absence.**

The photography by C. E. Schoenbaum is adequate throughout. The supporting cast, outside of Lionel Belmore, who is prone to overplay the socially cringing father, upholds the action and lends valuable assistance to the interest of the story. Philip E. Rosen directed, carrying the picture along for good results though seemingly to have not developed the full possibilities of the tale, but maybe not entirely his fault, for J. E. Nash is listed as having done the scenario and Thomas Buchanan the supervising. The original story is by Thomas Louden and A. E. Thomas.

"The World's Champion" will not hurt Lasky, Paramount nor Reid. It is a program feature that doesn't infringe on the double-feature racket. It'll get over by itself and register for a society comedy the censors won't have to annex anyone about.

Skig.

WILD HONEY

Lady Vivienne...............Priscilla Dean
Henry Porthen..................Noah Beery
Freddy Sutherland.............Lloyd Whitlock
Sir Hugh.............Raymond Blathwayt
Joan Rudd.....................Helen Raymond
Wolf Montague...........Landers Stevens
Kerry Burgess................Robert Ellis
"Buck" Roper..............Wallace Beery
Liverpool Blackie...........Carl Stockdale
Repington.......................C. J. Frank

Billed as a Universal Jewel Special "Wild Honey" with Priscilla Dean as the star was brought to the Central Monday as the attraction succeeding "Foolish Wives." The latter was "the first $1,000,000 picture." Beside it "Wild Honey" looks as though Carl Laemmle must have let Von Stroheim spend all his money and there wasn't any left for anything else.

At present "Wild Honey" is much too long for the single thrill there is in it. That thrill is as good if not better then the log jam in which Miss Dean appeared a few months ago. In the present picture it is the blowing up of a dam and the rush of the waters down through a canyon in which a number of colonists are located. The hero and heroine are caught in the swirl and carried away, but later saved in time for the final clinch.

If anything makes the picture that thrill will do it. The title of "Wild Honey" may make some of the fans that are U regulars wonder what it is all about. The story originally appeared in the Ladies' Home Journal by Cynthia Stockley. The screen adaptation was made by Lucien Hubbard and Wesley Ruggles handled the direction.

No money has been spent in sets and the greater part of the picture runs to exteriors. In detail and lighting there is much left to be desired. Tinting instead of lighting seems to be one of the regular stunts as far as Universal productions are concerned.

There is one thing the lowering of salaries in Los Angeles has done and that is to make possible the gathering of mighty good supporting casts for Universal stars. This picture is noteworthy in that respect. Naturally Miss Dean has all the best of the scenes in the screen play but there is one point in the picture where Wallace Beery takes pretty much all that there is to be gotten in front of the camera. In some of the earlier scenes Noah Beery managed to handle a heavy in fine style. It was in this same portion of the picture that Helen Raymond also stood out.

Playing the lead opposite Miss Dean is Robert Ellis who did very well with a part that at its best was light-waisted. Others of the support worthy of mention were Lloyd Whitlock as a drunk, Landers Stevens and C. J. Frank. The latter was a heavy in the late scenes and impressed.

Other than the dam bursting episode there is absolutely nothing in the picture that shows a heavy expenditure. But that one bit is there. It shows the water comes thundering down the gap between the two hills with the hero and heroine running before the flood and finally the two are caught and drawn into the swirl, this being followed by some "tank shots" that help the illusion and the rescue bit is cleverly handled. There were several spots in the picture where the ardent love-making of Miss Dean brought a laugh from the opening night audience.

"Wild Honey" is not a special by any means but will be a good program production which when cut to the proper length so as to eliminate the draggy portion in the earlier part and as such should get money on the strength of the star and the water stuff. *Fred.*

THE GOLDEN GIFT

Nita Gordon	Alice Lake
James Llewellyn	John Bowers
Edith Llewellyn	Harriett Hammond
Leonati	Joseph Swickard
Rosana	Bridgetta Clark
Malcolm Thorne	Louis Dumar
Stephen Brand	Geoffrey Webb
Joy Llewellyn	Camilla Clark

Metro production directed by Maxwell Karger, with Alice Lake as its star, based upon the story by June Mathis, the screen version for which was supplied by Florence Hein. The Mathis story is a new development of the deserted child idea, having as its central figure a young woman deserted by her husband and forced to desert her child in order that she might earn a living as a cabaret dancer in a Mexican town.

Her husband had married her on the strength of her theatrical assets and deserted her when loss of voice occurred shortly after the birth of the child.

While serving as a cabaret entertainer she is discovered by her former vocal teacher, who believes that he can restore her voice. This he does by taking her to Europe, where he develops a finished opera singer in her. She returns to New York and is a success on the opera stage.

The child deserted five years before had been adopted by an oil operator in Mexico, who, in the meantime, had moved to New York. This man becomes acquainted with the opera singer and asks her to be his wife. At the crucial moment it is discovered that the child he adopted belongs to the woman he loves. He had expressed himself previously as having hated any woman who would desert a child.

The matter is straightened out satisfactorily and the serene finale enacted.

Metro has turned out an interesting feature in "The Golden Gift." Karger has laid out the scenes for the production in artistic style. The cast headed by Miss Lake has been well selected, with Joseph Swickard and John Bowers displaying polished work in support of the star. "The Golden Gift" can give satisfaction anywhere as a program picture. *Hart.*

A WIDE OPEN TOWN

Selznick production starring Conway Tearle, directed by Ralph Ince. This production has been made for program use with no attempt made to make it stand out prominently in the present-day crop of features. Whatever success may be gained by "A Wide Open Town" can be credited to Ince. The director displays rare discretion in his handling of a time-worn subject, for which the financial outlay was apparently placed at a minimum for a five-reel picture. The story of ancient vintage centers around a reformed gambler who rescues the daughter of the mayor from a gambling house just as her father is leading a raiding party on the place. The ex-gambler kills the owner of the establishment, who has enticed the girl there, and is given a life sentence for the crime. It is all squared in the end with the customary happy ending, with the ex-convict in an embrace with the mayor's daughter. The subject is one that has been rehashed time and time again ever since pictures were created. In this production it is worked out in a gripping manner. Tearle runs through his role with apparent ease, with no exceptional work demanded of him. Faire Binney plays the leading female role. Others in the cast are Ned Sparks and Harry Tighe. Both appear to advantage on the screen, to which they are comparatively new. With many detrimental points, "A Wide Open Town" has been made into a good program release on the strength of its direction. *Hart.*

The Light in the Clearing

Roving Kate	Eugenie Besserer
Sally Dunkelberg	Clara Horton
Barton Baynes	Edward Sutherland
Amos Grimshaw	George Hackathorne
Ben Grimshaw	Frank Leigh
Horace Dunkelberg	Andrew Arbuckle
Uncle Peabody	Arthur Morrison
Aunt Deel	Alberta Lee
Joe Wright	John Roseleigh
Mrs. Horace Dunkelberg	Virginia Madison
Squire Fullerton	J. Edwin Brown

If fine spiritual quality and lofty ideals were all that were necessary to make a picture this screen version of Irving Bacheller's novel, produced by the Dial Film Co., directed by T. Hayes Hunter and released via Hodkinson, would be a world beater. But apparently those elements do not insure a sensational success, for the picture was shown at Loew's New York only this week, although it was released around the first of the year. At that it was not deemed sufficient to carry the program alone, but was hooked up with a Triangle reissue in a double feature bill. It is worth mentioning in passing that the Triangle, which had Douglas Fairbanks in a capital acrobatic melodrama called "The Americano," is a first-rate picture, even if it was done more than five years ago and comes out now as a warmed-over subject. The two pictures represented high quality unusual in a dual bill.

"The Light in the Clearing" is an epic of small town commonplaces, preaching a pretty deep philosophy of life and good American citizenship. It has dramatic values in good share, but it is the finer quality of its spirit that really marks it as distinct and unusual. Of course, it has its source in a fine book, and the only credit the screen gets out of this lofty presentment of sentiment and truth to life is that some one in the picture business was attracted to it and that some one or some one else got it translated to the screen in as nearly an adequate form as is possible.

Maybe if the screen itself originated material of this quality it would be making better film plays. In spite of the moving passages the picture holds, individual scenes and chapters both dramatic and sentimental, it is a loose and scattered play. This is almost invariably true of filmed novels. It doesn't seem practical to translate to the screen the soul and spirit of a written work with altogether satisfying completeness.

Perhaps if the best scenario writers thought in as high terms as the best writers of books do they might make as good continuities as there are books might put, for example, as exalted a philosophy as Bacheller's book in compact, expert screen form that would display its real values. That is not true in this adapted novel, nor is it true in nine out of ten fine books put through the film-making machine. Once in a while a good, sturdy play is made into a satisfactory film feature, but that's another matter. The truth of it seems to be that the film people cannot make a good picture out of a good book.

This dissertation is inspired by impatience that so excellent a book has not turned out into a better film, although it was not utterly destroyed. The scenario man (W. R. Lighton is credited) has handled the material reverently, but, except for several of the mob scenes in the preliminaries of a lynching party and in several of the sentimental passages, such as the meeting between the mad mother and the heroic old lawyer, the film was wearisome. It had too much detail, its interest was diffused and it tried to do too much. Portions dwell upon the vicious results of greed and avarice; next we observe the young man in the making of his character by strong and right decisions. Another angle is the high purpose of the political candidate who declines courageously to compromise for the sake of office. There is nothing to bind these elements together except the title exposition that this is a record of life to teach that all striving is toward happiness and mere hoarding of possessions is a distorted concept of contentment.

The film has so many excellent points that one is averse to dwelling upon its deficiencies. Indeed it has material enough for several pictures. Maybe its defect is that it has too much that is individually good, but is poorly corelated. At any event, it is a genuine attempt to film a fine book; its tone is high-minded and its aim is right. And that ought to be enough to say of any film in these days when cheap sensationalism is exploited for profit and sincere and earnest effort "goes for the end book." More power to such pictures and may they get better and more numerous. The more there are of these and the fewer like "The Sheik," "Foolish Wives" and "The Loves of Pharaoh" the better name and public good the film industry will have and in the long run the bigger public it will appeal to. *Rush.*

DRAGON'S CLAW

Helen Nielsen	Mia May
Hai Fung, King of the Beggars	No name
Dr. Kien Lung	No name
Tsay Tsaih, a slave girl	No name
Ling Po, her sweetheart	No name
Benson, Danish Consul	No name
Ni, father of Kien Lung	No name
The Hermit of Kuan Fu	No name
Father Ambrosius	No name

The Rivoli and Rialto began this week the exhibition of its U. F. A. serial, "Mistress of the World," of which "The Dragon's Claw" is the first chapter. Three other installments, each of about five reels, are to follow. The film is presented by the Hamilton Theatrical Corporation, which was formed to handle the Famous Players importations. "The Loves of Pharaoh" at the Criterion is offered under the same auspices.

First the Hamilton Corp. presents the film, which is a Paramount picture. In addition it is copyrighted by Famous Players-Lasky and acknowledgment is made to U. F. A., to Carl Figdor, who wrote the novel; to Joe May, who directed it, and, on the American side, to Peter Milne and Ben De Casseres, who were among the corps of experts who cut and titled the work.

All of which is preliminary to stating that the picture is an exact counterpart of the typical American serial, except that it is administered in five-reel instead of two-reel doses, which makes it just that much harder to take. It is all infantile fiction, inexpressibly cheap and trashy in its story composition, but having great pictorial effects in its scenic elements. It must have been a homeric task to get the thing cut down to the limits of 20 reels, and the difficulties of the job are apparent in the enormous quantity of titling in this first episode.

The thing that stands out in consideration of the whole enterprise is that Famous Players has taken a long chance on the quality of shows for which the Rivoli and the Rialto have stood, and is risking the good will of the clientele of the two Broadway houses by this departure into dime novel literature. Serials have always stood for the small neighborhood house, while the two big Broadway houses have always tried, or pretended to try, to furnish a screen entertainment appropriate to the costly establishments and the fine musical and artistic programs offered there.

It scarcely seems possible that the sort of audience that would be attracted by Hugo Riesenfeld's splendid orchestras and by the concert features that usually go to the composition of a Rialto-Rivoli program can have the slightest interest in this serial, which is designed for the entertainment of childish minds. It it not even skilfully put together. As one watched the development of the first chapter it is almost always possible to keep about a jump ahead of the tale. The fiction is so crude that it discloses itself in advance, and one is always waiting for the story to catch up with itself. Suspense is defeated and one's emotions are principally impatience.

For some reason the only player whose name is announced is the woman star, Mia May, a statuesque blonde, who moves mechanically through the wild adventures that make up the tale. Even the screen titles are silent on these identities as well as the programs. Not that it makes any particular difference. As a matter of fact the story itself is not worth recounting. As fiction it doesn't mean anything more than the familiar serial—just theatrical invention piled on thick, a waste of time to create, a waste of time to watch and a waste of money and energy to picturize.

The only quality that has any merit is the picturesque settings in which the events of the story take place. The locale of the first installment is China, and so convincing are the backgrounds that one is at once persuaded that the scenes were taken in the actual Orient.

There is a vast amount of ingenuity in setting the stage for the action, and the scenes of native life are wonderfully picturesque and in a theatrical way interesting. Part of the first chapter had to do with the conspiracy of the King of Beggars to ruin a Chinese merchant, and the haunts of the mendicants within a fortified little city were picturesque. Other passages have to do with the rescue of the heroine from a riverfront house where she is held captive by the same King of the Beggars, and the curious craft and native workers were scenically interesting.

The mere atmosphere surrounding a Chinese execution was impressive for its staging and its mob effects, but these external excellences are nullified by the aimless events of which they are the settings. To get down on paper the elements of the tale is like writing one of those magazine summaries which deal with the story that has gone before and which nobody ever reads. But since the thing is just beginning and is going to run a month, perhaps some rough indication of what it is about would be handy.

Helen Nielsen is a Copenhagen girl student who has mastered the Chinese language. Among her father's papers she finds reference to a hermit in a Chinese temple who holds possession of a jewel within which is a diagram indicating the location of the forgotten treasures of the Queen of Sheba. Helen perceives that by securing this jewel and gaining the treasure she would be "mistress of the world" by virtue of fabulous wealth. She starts for China to find the Hermit of Kuan Fu, seized by the King of the Beggars and rescued by Dr. Kien Lung, a young Chinese student whom she had met on the steamer and who becomes her companion from thence on in promised further adventures. Somehow this idea of yoking a blonde Danish heroine with a Chinaman seems to be asking a good deal of an American public, but we'll see what happens. In the course of the first chap another aide is acquired in the person of the Danish consular attache in some Chinese city, a person of prodigious physical strength, Frederick Benson by name.

Up to date Benson has secured the jewel from the Hermit of Kuan Fu, but is lying injured in the Hermit's ruined temple, while Helen is held a prisoner in a missionary's home nearby just as a crowd of fanatical natives are about to attack. And there you are! The final title held out the alluring promise that when the affair is continued next week we will see the further adventures of Helen, the blonde heroine, among the cannibal savages. *Rush.*

THE SHEIK'S WIFE

Estelle Graydon................Emmy Lynn
Hadjid Ben-Khedin..........Marcel Vilbert
Cassin Ben-Khedin..............Albert Bras
Sir Thomas Powell........Gustav Bogaert
Charles Courtney..............Frank Medar
Ben El-Kebil.............Thomas Thornton
Kahlia ....Alice Fille
Mohammed Ben Karl..........Carl Fisher

A Vitagraph special at the Strand, New York, this week. The chances are it was selected principally because of its title and the success that marked the production of "The Sheik" when presented at another Broadway house about two months ago. At the best "The Sheik's Wife" can never come within a mile of being opposition to the other picture except as far as the title is concerned.

"The Sheik's Wife" is French-made, taken in Arabia. The screen and program give Henri Roussell credit. The lack of punch is principally due to the fact that little care was exercised in the selection of a leading woman. Had the girl selected to play the lead been of extraordinary beauty or even just good looking there might have been another story. As it is, hardly anyone can work up a thrill over the troubles of a girl one cannot become interested in.

The direction, judged from American standards, is entirely faulty and decidedly slow. Old-fashioned methods are employed.

It is a tale of an English girl who falls in love with the son of a sheik who has been educated at Oxford. She marries him after he consents to an agreement that she will be his only wife and that he will not bring any other to his harem. The two journey to the desert home of the husband where, after a time, a child is born. It is a daughter. The ancient custom of the tribe is that if the first born of the wife isn't a son, the husband shall take unto himself a second wife so that a son may be born to him.

The husband's father, who has at all times been opposed to an unbeliever in his family, insists the son shall follow the ancient custom of the tribe and orders the boy to take a second wife. This, coupled with that the English wife has constantly been breaking the tribal customs, brings about a breach, and she tries to escape with her daughter, only to be brought back by the husband. Later, when British troops are in the vicinity of the tribe's camp and a former suitor tries to see the wife, he is caught in the harem and the husband and he fight a duel to death. This is followed by an attack on the part of the Arabs on the troops, but they are defeated and the young sheik captured. He is released on his promise to go forth into the desert and create no further trouble. The final scenes show him and his English wife seated beside a stream with their child.

Just what reason there is for the story is hard to explain. There doesn't seem any reason for it, but the title should pull some money, although it did not seem to have that effect at the Strand Sunday afternoon when the house for the second show held only about two-thirds on the lower floor where standing room usually is at a premium at that time of the day. *Fred.*

THE SPLENDID LIE

Rather odd, that this feature film should have to be one-half of a double bill at Loew's New York on Tuesday of this week. It's a better picture in every way than three-quarters of the regular weekly releases playing any Broadway house. It is also somewhat over the usual feature (five reels) length, but no one will notice that unless timing the picture.

The chances are that no one reads these Variety reviews, so almost anything may be said of a personal nature or opinion, and it will still be a secret between the writer, his typewriter and the printer. But here's what is in mind, purely a matter of observation, so it doesn't mean anything anyway. "French Heels," the Irene Castle picture, played a week at the Cameo. The Cameo is the B. S. Moss' new house on 42nd street, of small capacity. Admit the presumed drawing power in a theatre of that size of the Castle name. The picture must have been seen before the Cameo accepted it. And it ran a week there. Today (Friday) "French Heels" will split a double bill at Loew's New York for this day only. This week at the Cameo is "Determination." It will run there a week. It's a sort of a nondescript with its history briefly outlined in a review by Fred on this or the next page. The real object of "Determination" going into the Cameo, according to accounts, is to secure a quick string of bookings for it through the pop vaudeville theatres in the east, or hereabouts. The Strand this week has "The Sheik's Wife," a picture, if of any value at all, only through the title's similarity to "The Sheik." It is said "The Sheik's Wife" is playing the Strand this week with no charge to the house, merely to exhibit there for the prestige in aid of bookings. The Strand, if forced, would give up a percentage for a feature that could draw which would return the feature as much as $12,000 or over for the week.

The Strand holds the First National franchise; Capitol takes the Goldwyn regular stuff; Rialto and Rivoli are tied up through the Famous Players' ownership; Loew's State and New York play what Marcus Loew orders into them. Those are the leading Broadway picture houses downtown.

If the Arrow Film Corporation is an independent concern, or producer or distributor, what chance has it got for a Broadway showing under the circumstances? The Arrow made or is distributing "The Splendid Lie." Or any other independent? How is Hays going to fix that? How is Zukor going to make himself or anyone else believe he can sew up the picture business through Hays or anyone else for the special benefit of Zukor? For all the Hays and all the Zukors can't prevent an independent producer from making a good picture. If they think that through Hays Zukor can iron out the renting proposition for the exhibitor so the exhibitor will finally pay what Zukor or other distributors in this commonwealth proposition Hays is thought to be able to eventually put over, a rent that will be agreeable to the distributor, not the exhibitor, that may be another side to it. Reams and reams of paper have been used to tell what Hays will do to the picture business, but not one line has been used to tell what the real people behind the Hays movement expect him to do. And first they must get the exhibitor—then all theatres, not only the first runs. And there are legit houses.

Which is pretty windy after all. And doesn't mean anything, not even that "The Splendid Lie" is as good a feature as one might suspect from the rave above, but it is strong on several angles. It has tremendous sentiment and a powerful holding story. Charles T. Horan, who wrote and directed the feature, wrote one of those nearly forgotten Laura Jean Libbey stories, but he wrote a dandy in this. There are so many ramifications to the plot of the victim of circumstances (Grace Davison) that they could not be recounted. But Mr. Horan turned out a genuinely human tale, one that may be easily followed with interest, and a story that runs as smoothly in its direction as it has been written. The direction is always good. It is intelligent from the actual work of the players to the selection of sets and locales.

Another pertinent or impertinent question might be aimed through this feature—why is the acting in an unknown picture of this description invariably better than that found in the placarded stuff, made by high price directors with high salaried stars or an all-star cast? Still, it's true, especially in this, "The Splendid Lie," and equally true of its companion half of the same bill, "A Wise Kid"—and the "Wise Kid" is a Universal at that.

There's an old man in "The Splendid Lie." His name was on a slide, but missed. He's as good a character player as Theodore Roberts, in fact whoever played that role might be said to be the leading old man character player of the screen. The casting throughout was as well attended to, in fact as a weekly release, just a feature as they call them now, and as against the sex and sensational thing, "The Splendid Lie" is splendid, splendidly done.

It's not a great picture; just one of those nowadays seen so seldom, but it's a feature release any exhibitor can take for as long as he wants it, with the knowledge it can't fall down, but will stand up instead in the ratio that he gives advance work to it. *Sime.*

A GAME CHICKEN

A lively little feature picture for the hour it runs; full of speed and action that bespeaks good cutting, with rum running, cockfights and love as the ingredients that make this Bebe Daniels' (Realart) stand up.

The Cuban cockfights may have suggested the title, "A Game Chicken." Bebe is the supposed game one at the finish, when she and the secret service operator (Pat O'Malley) confess their love on a torpedo destroyer that picked them up at sea.

The scene jumps from Havana to the Massachusetts coast. Miss Daniels is the daughter of the American head of the bootleggers on the island. She is a fractious girl, shying off the Spanish business partner of her father, who also wants to be his son-in-law, with the girl objecting. Dressed as a boy, she took her pet gamester, in the form of a rooster, and with a native son attended a cockfight at night, handling her own bird. She alleged the other handler threw pepper into her chick's eyes. A fight followed. Bebe's hair came down, wildly exciting the Cubans, who chased her off the lot, with the secret service man running after and escorting the unknown girl home.

The next day the operator hung around the docks, learned a loading boat was going to land the stuff off the New England shore, but he got into trouble before leaving the pier, as the runners became wise to him. They chased him then and got his credential card.

With the parents disagreeing over the girl, they decided to send her to the States and to an uncle in Massachusetts, the home end of the runners. He lived near the cove where the boats landed the illicit liquor. To that point went the booze in the sailing vessel, the girl by steamer and the secret service man by another, all meeting to have a fight on the rocks, the revenue men overpowering the leggers, but their chief escaping to the boat, taking along the girl and her sweetie official, the latter bound. For when the chief, who was the Spanish lover in Cuba, had found the girl and officer together on the shore, he showed her the credential card of her sweetie, informing the girl the secret service man only wanted to land her father as a rum runner. The girl fell for that, decoyed Rush Thompson (Mr. O'Malley) into their hands. But when on the boat she weakened, attempted to aid Thompson, who was ordered strung up, and in the ensuing mess Bebe set fire to the sailing vessel.

All on the burning boat jumped over the sides, with the two principals finally holding onto an upturned boat. Meantime the revenuers had signalled the destroyer through sky rockets, and as the naval boat neared the other it picked up the castaways.

Several fights, a great deal of youth in Miss Daniels' portion, whether climbing a tree or the side of the boat, and all rushing along in the most businesslike picture way that could be asked for.

What the principals had to do as players they did very well. Miss Daniels was just the type on looks and work. Nothing big or unusual about it, but as among the many ordinary weekly releases, this F. P. release should mean more than the ordinary. *Sime.*

SMILIN' THROUGH

Kathleen }
Moonyeen } ....Norma Talmadge

John Carteret..........Wyndham Standing
Kenneth Wayne }
Jeremiah Wayne }..............Harrison Ford
Doctor Owen..................Alce B. Frances
Willie Ainsley..................Glenn Hunter
Ellen ....Grace Griswold
Little Mary (Monyeen's sister),
Mirriam Battista
Village Rector..............Eugene Lockhart

Joseph M. Schenck produced the screen version of "Smilin' Through" as a starring vehicle for Norma Talmadge for release through First National. The screen adaptation of the Allen Langdon Martin play of the same name is credited to James Ashmore Creelman and Sidney A. Franklin, with the latter also the director.

"Smilin' Through" gained recognition as a stage success with Jane Cowl as its star. For the screen adaptation Miss Talmadge ably handles the leading role and gives to the production a stamp of class in the acting division that places it well up on the list of program features.

The theme is based upon love and hate. With these two valuable assets to work with, Director Franklin has turned out a feature with all the necessary heart interest to warrant its success.

The story centers around the life of John Cartaret. On his wedding day his bride is killed by a rival suitor. Years later his adopted niece falls in love with the son of the man who had committed the crime. Hate had predominated the life of Cartaret for all members of the family of the murderer. That his niece had fallen in love with the culprit's son sends his blood to a boiling point. Only after much persuasion is to make to see the light, with the story culminating in a happy romance for the young couple. Cartaret dies peacefully after having been won over to the other side.

"Smilin' Through" displays expert direction. The punches are landed effectively. A capable cast works up the big points, with Wyndham Standing and Alec B. Francis giving the star excellent support. The production end, not calling for a large outlay, is artistically worked out, with the director displaying discretion in his selection of exteriors.

The high esteem in which Norma Talmadge is held by picture patrons will not be impaired by her latest production. It will give satisfaction as a program feature. *Hart.*

DETERMINATION

Frances Lloyd.........................Gene Burnell
John Morton, Jr. }
James Melvale }..................Al Lincoln
"Lacky" ....Irene Tams
Lord Warburton.............Walter Ringham
Whitechapel Mary..............Nina Herbert
Dope Fiend ....Charles Ascott
Lord Dalton..................Barney Randall
Lady Dalton.......................Mabel Allen
Madge Daley..................Corinne Uzzell
Sport Smiler.............Hayden Stevenson
Putnam ....Maurice Costello

"Determination" is the feature the trade has heard about for more than two years in connection with the name of Capt. Stoll, who was the promotional factor behind the U. S. Moving Picture Corp., which made the picture. According to reports something like $800,000 was collected through stock sales for the picture, and recently there was considerable agitation over the disappearance of Capt. Stoll, his subsequent return and the amount of the expenditure in the making of the picture.

At present the picture is being shown at B. S. Moss' Cameo theatre, where the Lee-Bradford Corp. is credited with the presentation. Instead of looking anything like $800,000 worth of picture film it appears more like $8,000 worth of feature. There is a certain amount of advertising punch to the title and the picture may gather a certain amount of money, but right at this point it is pretty safe to say that it isn't going to gross anything like the amount that was sunk in it.

The picure is more or less of a haphazard affair, with characters constantly coming and going and seldom doing anything. There is an effort to justify the title of the production with a brief foreword to the effect that determination to do is the road to success, but then the picture story rambles on and on, and the only punch is at the finish, to the effect it is usually wise to have a father with a lot of money who will leave you a fortune.

Al Lincoln plays the principal roles. That is, he has the twin brother characterization in his hands. They keep him pretty busy. At first he is in London as a welfare worker. The scenes are in the Whitechapel district and the smart West End with its social activities. He has the good fortune to rescue a wealthy American girl from thugs, and she falls in love with him, but there is a fortune-hunting Englishman of title who is trying to win her, and when the latter discovers the double of the welfare worker in Paris leading a gay life and being the center of the sporting and gambling set, he makes up his mind the girl shall be informed her fiance is leading a double life.

From this point on there are plots and counterplots, leading nowhere, but finally the affairs of the twin brothers are straightened out, the two brought together and the girls in love with each are shown in a final close-up, clinched.

For punches there is a prizefight and a horserace scene. Just what they are supposed to mean is told principally in titles, and in the end it isn't clear what they were all about. A bet is supposed to be made on two events, the purse to go to the winner of both. The hero wins the boxing match, but the heavy manages to job the horserace, so each is the winner of one event, but the hero is supposedly the loser as far as the screen shows.

There are some corking London slum scenes, principally exteriors showing street stuff in the Whitechapel district that are very well done considering they are studio stuff. An English pub of the low order and a Parisian rendezvous of Apaches with the usual Apache dance included, are also counted on as wallops, but have been so much better done in other pictures that they fail to impress.

Mr. Lincoln is a dapper appearing lead, and he acquitted himesif creditably in both roles. The heavy of Walter Ringham left much. Gene Burnell carried the ingenue lead of the picture along fairly well, but didn't register at any particular time. Irene Tams as a slum product walked away with the women section. Bits here and there of character work were well done by Nina Herbert, Charles Ascott and Corinne Uzzell. Maurice Costello also played a bit and aided in the direction of the production.

The direction, editing and cutting were entirely faulty. These three factors combine to make the picture a rather old-fashioned melodramatic thriller of the old days. In the cheaper houses the picture will undoubtedly get over and draw some business, but it isn't sufficiently classy as first run material in the better houses.

Fred.

FALSE BRANDS

This Rialto production, released in the independent market, is one of a series of four pictures in which Joseph Moore and Eileen Sedgewick are co-starred. The production is a cheap type of feature, quite western in its atmosphere, and has been played in the Loew houses around New York as part of a double feature bill. It is hardly strong enough for that unless the accompanying feature is pretty good. Coupled with the Goldwyn release of the Max Linder comedy, "Be My Wife," the program proved decidedly weak.

The strength of the picture is in the coupling of Moore and Miss Sedgewick, who stand out as promising youngsters in this production. They can be built up into a neat little co-starring combination if provided with the proper material.

"False Brands" has Moore as a student at a co-ed institution. He is the son of a wealthy cattle baron. The girl is at the same school. She is recalled home because of the illness of her father, while the boy is sent home for a number of pranks committed. His father decides to send him away to one of his ranches, and it happens that it is the ranch on which the girl's father is the foreman.

Rustlers have been bu. in the neighborhood, and the ranch has been one of the sufferers. The boy finally runs down the cattle runners and wins the girl.

A fair type of story for the little houses, that is about all. *Fred.*

SIGN OF THE ROSE

While this picture is over a year old it has not been generally released because George Beban, its star, has retained it as a vehicle with which to make personal appearances. Mr. Beban and a company of three players who appeared in the picture with him have been doing this ever since the picture was completed. It was not until the current week he came into New York with his combination of silent and spoken drama, for this is exactly what he is presenting, having somewhat revised the original idea when "The Sign of the Rose" was presented as a play. At that time it was spoken drama with just flash of pictures; in the present form it is an hour of the screen drama presented with 18 minutes of the original vaudeville sketch on which both the picture and play were based, placed at an advantageous spot in the screen drama along about the fourth reel.

Mr. Beban made his New York appearance at Loew's State Monday. The combination of him and the picture seemed to be considerable help to the box office. Loew's State usually plays eight acts of vaudeville, giving four shows a day with six acts at each show, the schedule being so arranged none of the acts does more than three shows a day. For the Beban engagement two of the acts were out of the bill, which, with the added business he attracted as headliner undoubtedly showed a profit for the house, while his feature picture took the place of the usual feature length screen production shown.

In time "The Sign of the Rose" will undoubtedly be released as a feature, when the portion now played by the star and his little company in person will be replaced by film. Either way it is a mighty good screen entertainment for any house to play. The picture is one that has a real heart throb in it and is a production that women patrons are sure to like.

Beban plays his Italian who loses his daughter through an automobile accident and when he tries to purchase a single rose for her grave he is suspected of being a Blackhander, involved in a kidnapping case. There is a certain elaboration that has been furnished the theme by the star, and incidentally a happy ending has also been tacked on to the original story.

In the cast there is no one of note other than Beban and the little girl who plays his daughter. The kiddie he has employed in the screen version of this gripping drama is an exceedingly clever miss who handles herself with all the assurance of a veteran trouper.

There are but few settings and but one street scene. For the personal appearance a replica of the screen set of the florist shop is employed and the blending from the screen into the set is effectively handled. Beban as of old in the spoken portions of the sketch is effective, but the balance of his company while managing to get by on the screen would not stand up in a regular vaudeville production. However, being in the picture cast naturally gets them by.

The feature was produced by Harry Garson, who was associated with Beban in the direction of the production. The star takes the credit for the story and the scenario.

Fred.

PROPHETS' PARADISE

A Selznick distribution, made by Allan Crossman, with Eugene O'Brien starred. The O'Brien following will be satisfied with this program release, but it will hardly prove of much interest to others. For the picture populace the most attention may be secured by the street scenes of Constantinople. There are so many of these in the opening scenes that the picture at first takes on the aspects of a travelog.

It's an adapted tale from a novel and seeks to exhibit how the Turks might put over a gold brick game. In this instance an American traveler, tired with ordinary sightseeing of the town, is about to leave when a couple of Turks frame him to see before going the Prophets' Paradise, one of the real and inside sights; in fact, a slave market, with a caption here tending to leave the impression women are still sold at auction in that country. With instructions to be discreet, not to use English and dress as a Persian, the American is taken through sundry rooms and past sundry armed guards to a large inner room, where in the midst of merchants waiting to bid for women, he finally sees a princess placed upon the block "to save her father's honor for gambling debts." The traveler likes the girl, bids double the highest amount, and secures her for $60,000.

Then it comes out. She ain't no princess, but the daughter of another traveling American who seeks relics, while his daughter remains at home, with the other end of the frame shown, how she was inveigled into the same building and threatened with death if not obeying. That led her to the auction mart.

Outside the courtyard as the couple escaped after several adventures that involved a couple of fist and knife fights, each bungled for effect, they do not meet again until toward the end of the film, when they drive alongside of one another in open cars on Fifth avenue, New York, and on this, their second meeting, they decide to get married that day for the fade-out.

The scenes, setting and atmosphere of the picture are enough to carry it through. Everything else from acting to action is against it.

Sime.

A WISE KID

A Universal, directed by Tod Browning, that starts off as a comedy, diverts itself into serious lines and becomes melodramatic before concluding. And a good ordinary feature. For the U. it's a bear. Maybe that's Browning's fault. Certainly it doesn't happen often with the U regulars.

Gladys Walton is the star. All around could be heard: "Doesn't she look like Alice Brady?" Miss Walton takes her light role very lightly and her more serious moments are handled quite acceptably. There is more decent setting than is usual to "A Wise Kid." The title is merely fly. It doesn't enter with the subject matter, for Miss Walton in the film i anything but fly. She is the cashier in a restaurant and throws down the driver of a bakery wagon for a "swell" who turns out to be a bad villun. So bad he borrows $100 from t e girl he wants to marry the third time he sees her.

There is comedy between the girl and her sweetie; there is comedy in the captions, and though the captions, or some of them, hold laughs, of course, the U system holds them on the screen longer than necessary to take up the footage in that way. The manner in which some pictures stall on the footage through captions, their producers should have enough to be able to pay George Ade to write the sub-titles.

One of the scenes, a picture within a picture, holds some very real laughs. Another of a welfare dance, with two or three w. k. reformers supervising, was nicely devised.

The picture in its light and heavy sides makes entertainment sufficient to stand up alone in the medium houses, and for those that play the U stuff steadily, they can feature this one all over the lot. *Sime.*

BOUGHT AND PAID FOR

A Famous Players feature, of a poor girl marrying a wealthy man and taking a part of her family along with her. That much of the tale, with the title added, tells the entire story.

Much dragging out, little action and some dragged-in travesty playing that got a laugh here and there ran through the usual hour that ordinary pictures such as this take up.

Agnes Ayres, Jack Holt and Walter Hiers were the leading principals. Hiers did the comedy, rather well at times, "making" his role. There was little else for the others to do.

"Bought and Paid For" will please the tired shop girl and tire everybody else. At the Rivoli Sunday night it followed that awful second chapter, "The Race for Life," of "The Mistress of the World" serial. If Germany turns out another terrible thing like this and calls it a picture, there may be another war. It probably is the poorest made pretentiously-billed film attraction ever turned out, worse even than those manhandled four-reelers the Germans sent over here some years ago. Anything could have followed it at the Rivoli, where the German picture was laughed at, booed at and hissed at during its running. The only thing that kept the audience in the house was that "Bought and Paid For" was there, to follow it. *Sime.*

TRAVELIN' ON

J. B.	William S. Hart
Dandy McGee	James Farley
Susan Morton	Ethel Grey Terry
Hi Morton	Brinsley Shaw
Mary Jane Morton	Mary Jane Irving
Gila	Robert Kortman
"Know-It-All" Hashins	Willis Marks

William S. Hart's "Travelin' On," a typical Hart western, split the bill at the Rialto with the second episode of "The Mistress of the World," adding insult to injury. Forcing a trashy serial on Broadway is bad enough, but this Hart picture is positively dangerous.

The New York State censor having gone a long way toward scaring off the sex hounds in the production game, it remains for William S. Hart Productions to put on a feature that is bound to give offense to a large element of the church-going public. It's bad enough for cosmopolitan New York, but it's pretty likely to start something in the Methodist Episcopal middle west and south.

What can be said of a piece of fiction (the program credits the story to William S. Hart himself) which has a minister of the gospel resorting to all sorts of crookedness, including the holding up and robbing of a stage coach, to get money to build a church in a western mining camp? As if that were not sufficiently cynical, the minister is saved from the justice of the lynching party by the hero, a prideful and determined atheist. All this is done in Hart's gosh awful earnestness. In the name of all that is decent and considerable in social behavior and literary ethics, how do these birds get that way?

Here's the story, adapted and directed by Lambert Hillyer, photographed by Joe August, A. S. C., as the program has it. J. B. is a wandering prospector in Arizona in the '80s, who "don't believe in God and wouldn't trust anything but himself that walked on less'n four legs." Hi Morton is an itinerant preacher fired by the great zeal of a passionate missionary and accompanied by his beautiful wife in his journeyings.

Preacher and prospector came to Tumble Gulch and Morton determines to build a church there to fight the viciousness of a mining camp. Dandy McGee, dance hall and saloon proprietor and monopoly

of evil, plots to balk the invasion of the church by raising the price of necessities, chiefly lumber for the church, at the same time scheming to assail the preacher's pretty wife.

J. B. also has designs on the woman, but instead of underhand scheming he proposes to abduct her in a frank, bold way. Meanwhile Morton is having trouble financing the church construction job. He causes his wife to set up a booth near the saloon on which is printed a sign, "Buy the book every gambler ought to read—$5." Everybody buys a volume, which turns out to be a Bible. Everybody is hoaxed by the piece of mean trickery, including J. B. A title describes this turn in high finance as "a pitiful expedient to raise money for the church." As it comes on the screen it strikes one as a barbarous way to handle holy vessels.

But even the trick of salesmanship fails to build the tabernacle, and Morton goes forth to hold up the stage; does that little thing; takes $1,000 and is captured. Tried by a catch-as-catch-can jury, he is sentenced to be hanged, when the wife appeals to J. B. and he goes to the rescue. With his two trusty guns he holds up about three score tough citizens in the lynching party just as they are about to swing the minister. Then he declares it was he who robbed the stage coach and goes off alone.

We see him presently riding away across the desert while the minister, his church now completed, is tacking up a sign over the door announcing that this house of God was built by an unbeliever.

The point is that the figure of the **religious man is made mean and contemptible and that of the atheist bears a glorified halo of romance. The picture was probably inspired by a gross misreading of Bret Harte. Its ethics are all askew and its effect upon the spectator is unqualifiedly bad.** *Rush.*

THE SEVENTH DAY

John Alde, Jr.	Richard Barthelmess
Uncle Jim Alden	Frank Losee
Uncle Ned	Leslie Stowe
Donald Peabody	Tammany Young
Reggie Van Zandt	George Stewart
Monty Pell	Alfred Schmid
Aunt Abigail	Grace Barton
Betty Alden	Anne Cornwall
Katinka	Patterson Dial
"Billie" Blair	Teddie Gerard
Patricia Vane	Louise Huff

"It's a very old story, that's the best thing about it," reads one of the subtitles, and it states, approximately, all there is to be said concerning Richard Barthelmess' second starring vehicle. Inspiration Pictures, Inc., is presenting, releasing through First National, from the story by Porter Emerson Browne, under the direction of Henry King. It also marks King's second attempt in conjunction with the star, they having paired for "Tol'able David," shown early in January.

The tale opens in a New York club, where a mixed party of young society members are prevented from carrying out a birthday flask celebration of one of their members by the head waiter, with the suggestion the gang adjourn to his yacht. Those at the table, properly chaperoned, embark for a cruise which ends in the boat putting into a coast village for repairs with the necessary adjusting announced as needing a week.

The joy seekers are pretty much up against it, in a town minus a railroad or hotel, for amusement, with the story narrowing down to the love affairs, starting out as flirtations, on the parts of the "city" pair, Reggie Van Zandt and Patricia Vane, with Betty Alden and John Alde, Jr. (Barthelmess) of the village.

Included in the action leading up to the finish is the gambling, dancing and drinking of the party on board, a few atmospheric "shots" in

and about the village, and a couple of attractive scenes by the camera with the palatial pleasure craft as the subject. The seagoing yacht looks the part.

Barthelmess predominates and is in no danger of being overshadowed by any other member of the cast. Louise Huff proves a satisfactory society miss. George Stewart as Reggie has turned in a capable piece of work, also causing some favorable comment amongst the feminine onlookers for secondary honors. The remaining members flash nothing above the average.

"The Seventh Day" is somewhat indistinct in its sub-titling. It will suffer if compared to "Tol'able David." *Skig.*

MISTRESS OF WORLD

The second episode of the U. F. A. serial remains in both of the Famous Players Broadway theatres this week, although last week it had been decided to take it out of the Rivoli and keep it going only at the Rialto. As late as Saturday afternoon an inquiry at the company's home office brought the reply that it would hold forth only at the Rialto, and during the week the newspaper advertisements announced that plan.

The last moment decision appears to have been to force the issue, and the Sunday papers carried the announcement that both houses would carry the second episode, entitled "The Race for Life," supported by a regular feature. This program make-up compelled the elimination of the usual concert, specialty items and short subjects, all except the news reel, and made a rather heavy screen entertainment. At the Rialto William S. Hart in a typical western filled out and at the Rivoli the feature was "Bought and Paid For." Much drama and nothing to relieve it.

At the Rialto Sunday night business was brisk. There was the usual crush up to the beginning of the second night show, with the back of the house filled to the capacity of the taped lines. The question was whether interest was in the serial or in the Hart feature. A new Hart picture alone is usually considered a sufficient draw for the Broadway programs. Its introduction into the bill at the Rialto clouds up the issue of the Famous Players experiment with the Ufa chapter story, although the evidence would seem to have the force of a confession that the venture had started unsatisfactorily.

"The Race for Life," the second episode of "Mistress of the World," is not as good as the first chapter, "The Dragon's Claw." It lacks the picturesque scenic settings of the beginning and has all the crude story defects of infantile theatrical device that marked the opening installment. But it has this merit, worth considering by the exhibitor whose clientele is of the "serial grade": It gives promise of leading into a sensational Rider Haggard chapter next week and a pull is established for the return of serial fans. This is accomplished by bringing our adventurers into the wilds of Africa, where they discover a lost and forgotten City of Ophir where ancient tribes exist as in the times of the Queen of Sheba. At

the tail end of the second chapter the heroine and hero get their first glimpse of this weird community from a distance just as the "to-be-continued" title is flashed, but then about 100 feet of advance "trailer" is screened, giving scraps of the high points in the following installment. For the purpose of serial exhibitors the arrangement is shrewdly managed from a business viewpoint. If his customers see and enjoy the first two episodes they will be cinched for the rest of the tale.

Discussion of the artistic quality of the picture appears to have been covered pretty thoroughly last week by various commentators. "Artistic merit" and "serial" are irreconcilable. The two things can't be made to go together up to date. The only question involved in the venture is the wisdom of putting the serial on Broadway. The picture is just a serial for neighborhood serial houses and nothing else, and should have been restricted to that field.

It takes six full title sheets to cover the preceding story before the second chapter starts. Then the film goes back and the characters enact the last 150 feet or so of the first installment before the story goes on. Helen now has the mystic jewel with its diagram pointing out the location of the Queen of Sheba's buried treasure in the African city of Ophir. The trio—Helen, Dr. Kien Lung and Benson—take ship for Africa, and start with a native caravan for the interior. They have to cross the territory of King Makombe, a black cannibal chief. They present him with gifts (silk hat, gaudy umbrella and all the rest of the props) and all is well.

Malkalla, the witch doctor of the tribe, however, plots to destroy the white party and there is a running fight between the savages and the adventurers in which the mortality is high. The witch doctor and Dr. Kien Lung are killed during a pursuit in canoes, but Helen and Benson escape into a watery cave. They follow the subterranean waterway under the mountains until the tunnel is blocked by huge mortal portals. The Herculean Benson forces the gate. In the distant valley disclosed through the open doors is an ancient city teeming with life and—"continued in our next." It is then that the trailer starts, promising that the life of the city with religious rites, blood sacrifices, etc., is to follow, with quick flashes of appropriate scenes.

"The Race for Life" is poor stuff in itself, cheaply made, but it has a skillful climax for serial business purposes. *Rush.*

COME ON OVER

Moyna Killiea..............Colleen Moore
Shane O'Mealia..............Ralph Graves
Michael Morahan....L. Farrell MacDonald
Delia Morahan..................Kate Price
Carmody....................James Marcus
Judy Dugan............Kathleen O'Connor
Bridget Morahan............Florence Drew

A Goldwyn picture by Rupert Hughes, directed by Alfred Green and shown as a special St. Patrick's day offering at the Capitol this week, proves to be a feature that carries as much heart punch as "Over the Hill" or any of the big winners that counted on the love elementals as their theme. Mother love, love of home and young love all combine to make this feature a real box office attraction. Had Goldwyn taken this picture and given it a title that was more appropriate and run it on Broadway instead of some of the spectacles that they have shown for a run, they would have developed a distinct money maker. It has the universal appeal and that is what counts in film.

Rupert Hughes chose as his characters three generations of Irish and Irish-Americans. Their life stories are so told as to bring a tear and a laugh one right after the other.

The story opens in Ireland with but three characters showing. An aged grandmother left alone on the auld sod for years after her children have migrated to America. A lad of the neighborhood is about to follow in their footsteps and he is leaving his loved colleen to follow on when he sends for her.

In America he seeks out the son of the grandmother and makes his home with his family. A job comes but is lost soon after and a number of others follow. Meantime he meets with another Irish family consisting of father and daughter and, while the old man is a drunkard, the daughter is a fashionable

modiste with a Parisian nom-de-business. The girl achieves an affection for the young Irish lad, but he remains true to the girl on the other side.

The tales of Ireland told by the greenhorn to the Morahan family incites the son of the aged woman to return to Ireland to visit his mother, and when he gets ready to return to America he not only brings her along but also the sweetheart of the boy. It is to be a surprise, and when they arrive the girl walks in on a situation that puzzles her, for the boy is going to go to the priest with the girl of the other Irish family, she having gained the consent of her father to the trip. The little emigrant can think of but one reason for a visit to the priest and that is to arrange for the publishing of the banns. In reality it is to have the old man sign the pledge. With the complications straightened out it makes for a happy ending.

Colleen Moore and Ralph Graves, who play the leads, are splendid, but the balance of the cast also comes in for a goodly share of praise, especially Florence Drew, who plays the old pipe smoking granny, and her son, played by L. Farrell MacDonald. Kate Price also contributes a corking piece of character work.

In direction Alfred Green has done as splendid a piece of work as has been seen in a Goldwyn picture for a number of releases. *Fred.*

WOMEN'S CLOTHES

Jacqueline Lee..............Mabel Ballin
Barker Garrison........Raymond Bloomer
Rupert Lewis..............Crauford Kent
Mrs. Roger Montayne..........May Kitson
Joe Feinberg..........William H. Straus
Bessie Horowitz..........Aggie LaField
Ellen Downe..................Rose Burdick

Hodkinson release produced by Hugo Ballin from the story "The Luxury Tax" by Ethel Donoher. In addition to sponsoring the picture Ballin did the directing with Mabel Ballin as the star. The Donoher story contains several interesting angles as a screen subject. In the five reels of film devoted to it considerable action takes place with the story at times being slightly disconnected largely due to the fact that considerable cutting was necessary to bring the production down to the required length for a program feature.

The story centers around a girl of the show world. The closing of a traveling rep show of which she is a member throws her on the town. Unable to secure a position in the profession, she secures employment as a manikin in a modiste's establishment. While on duty she is sent to the home of a customer to return a gown. Being alone, she is tempted to put the creation on and is detected by the woman's nephew. He, believing her a friend of his aunt's, invites her to dinner in a restaurant. While dining they are met by a chum of the young man's who had seen her at the house while the other was dressing and knew her mission there. He discloses her identity to his friend. She explains her actions and is forgiven, being sent home alone after the meal.

Shortly after the young man with the wealth decides to give her the opportunity of having all of the money she desires in order that she may have the better things in life to determine whether or not wealth means happiness. He induces his attorney to notify her that she has been left a fortune by a woman in South America whom she had waited upon in the gown shop. Securing the money, she establishes herself in a sumptuous apartment and adorns herself to her heart's desire. A chance meeting with the young man who is helping her establishes him as a friend. Gossip among her former acquaintances is that a rich male friend is supply-

ing her with funds. A love affair springs up between the two which is shattered when the boy's chum informs her of what has been going on and who is her real benefactor. This causes her to disappear with her benefactor unable to locate her whereabouts for three years. A chance meeting after she has established herself as a star renews the love match with the customary close-up at the finish telling the tale.

Ballin has directed this production with his customary finesse. The points of the story are brought forth in a telling manner and landed with the proper punch. In Mabel Ballin he has a capable leading woman. She has all of the requirements of an ingenue star and possesses histrionic ability above the average. In support are Raymond Bloomer, as leading man, and Crauford Kent in the role of a heavy. Both creditably handle their parts. The remaining members of the cast have been selected with discretion.

The production end of "Other Women's Clothes" is one of its strong points. The director has selected attractive sets and has not skimped in any way. It is a corking picture for women and has all of the necessary qualities of a good program feature. *Hart.*

THE FOREST KING

Martin Webb..................L. M. Wells
Mrs. Webb..................Virginia Ware
Bob Lanier ....Reed Chapman
Evelyn Webb..................Dahlia Pears
Leslie Houston..............Lillian Hall
Eugene Stratton........Arthur Mallette
Steve Hawkin..................Joe Ray

This is another of the Pacific Film company's group of purchase pictures being offered in the state rights market at extremely moderate exhibition totals.

It goes without saying that it is second rate, but at the right price would be a buy. It is in five reels and, in general, has the quality of a fair melodrama of the "Blue Jeans" order. There are several effective punches, a forest fire, a fist fight between the hero and two heavies, and a third which marks the climax of the story an impressive explosion of dynamite which tears the landscape apart and deals oodles of poetic justice.

The interiors are rather poorly done, but for the purpose of this class of production reasonably adequate. There are, however, plenty of fine outdoor settings with the California redwood forests as a background, and for a picture of its class the photography is extremely good, including, as it does, some excellent examples of misted effects. The acting is mediocre, but acting in a story of this kind could scarcely be fine. The dramatic elements are too crude.

It's a so-so picture. Not good enough to be available for the best houses, and still not bad enough to be entirely without merit. The cheap state rights scheme appears to promise an equitable system for both buyer and seller. The story has to do with a doll-like blonde heroine, Leslie Houston, a factory worker who is the sole support of an invalid father. She is insulted by the foreman of the packing room and as she slaps his face a piece of jewelry falls from her throat into a parcel. She is discharged and falls upon poverty. Meanwhile, the package with its jewel comes into the hands of Bob Lanier, who is managing a logging camp for a lumber king to whose daughter he is engaged.

By the packer's slip in the parcel, Bob traces the forlorn heroine to return the jewel and falls in love with her. He prevails upon her to bring her father to the lumber camp where the open air may restore his health. The lumber king's scheming lawyer, who is trying to break up the match between Bob

and the lumber king's heiress, brings the latter to the camp and poor Leslie and her father are ordered out of the lodge by the jealous fiancee. They take refuge with an enormously fat Irish washwoman attached to the camp, who furnishes comedy relief of the good old fashioned kind.

Bob's jealous fiancee has the heroine abducted by one of the rough lumberjacks, but she is rescued in time. The scheming lawyer, his plans defeated, determines to rob the office safe and depart, after putting dynamite in Bob's desk, so arranged that a footfall on a loose board will set it off. Bob catches him there, together with the kidnapping lumberjack, and there is a royal fight in which the hero emerges victorious. After Bob has departed, the two heavies quarrel about the loot in the safe and during a clash one of them steps on the loose board. The whole landscape spouts up and the villains are done for, while Bob and the blonde heroine fall into the closing embrace. *Rush.*

GLASS HOUSES

A Viola Dana feature, issued and distributed by Metro. Not a bad feature of its kind, but yet not greatly above ordinary, with the story bringing out a couple of different angles during the action that heighten the interest. A couple of other intersections lessen the interest as well, so at the finish the story just about balances on an even keel that doesn't excite nor leave an impression either way.

As with other Metros, there's a ballroom scene and another society event or two. The Metro directors evidently thought when they started on their wild rampaging picture making anything "society" would get it over; the more social there was to a feature, the more certain. It doesn't look as if the plan worked out.

Miss Dana in this picture is one of two sisters who, losing their inheritance, must seek their living by work. One finds that to disguise her good looks she may find a job through an employment agency, and this one (Miss Dana) does so, given the position by a maternal and wealthy aunt of guiding her wayward young nephew into a righteous path. That was one of the intersections that knocked the kilter out of the logic. Another was that the nephew—if Miss Dana was as good-looking as every one seemed afterward to have believed—would have discovered her looks, even through a pair of rimmed glasses and a biddy hat. But maybe it was because Miss Dana had her hair bobbed. That bobbed hair has fooled more girls than it has made look girlish or youthful.

And so it ran, with a little comedy twist toward the finish, when Miss Dana, by this time the wife of the youth she was to have guarded, believes her husband is mentally unbalanced through his suspicions she is "Angel-Face Annie," a second story worker. The finish works out, and a check of $50,000 suddenly given the young couple by the aunt brought an unexpected laugh that could have been the summary of how the audience regarded the picture as a whole.

This picture will depress the heart of many a plain or homely girl who sees it. For that reason, that it will bring a heart-pang, as it surely will, it could be regretted. For there could be no more pointed illustration of the value of catchiness of good looks than this story unfolds—how the boy couldn't bear to look at his wife with her glasses on—how amazed he was, and how quickly he fell in love upon seeing her in evening dress and without the glasses—looks as against plainness, class against hickiness.

However, that doesn't prevent it being a fairly good regular feature release for the Metro standard, with average acting and somewhat better direction. But there's nothing in it to boost, excepting Miss Dana's name and perhaps her bobbed hair.
Sime.

QUESTION OF HONOR

Anne Wilmot..................Anita Stewart
Bill Shannon..................Edward Hearn
Leon Morse..............Arthur Stuart Hull
Sheb.........................Walt Whitman
Charles Burkthaler............Bert Sprotte
Stephen Douglas.................Frank Beal
Mrs. Katherine Wilmot (Anne's aunt),
Adele Farrington
Mrs. Elton, Morse's sister.......Mary Land
John Bretton.....................Ed. Brady
Parsons.........................Doc Bytell

A First National release, it stacks up as average alongside some of Anita Stewart's previous productions. Louis B. Mayer, as per usual, presents the star in a feature produced by her own company, the Anita Stewart Productions, Inc.

Edwin Carewe directed Josephine Quirk's adaptation of the Ruth Cross novel of the same name from the "People's Home Journal." To complete the credits, Robert B. Kurrle cranked the camera (and shot some nifty outdoor stuff), Wallace Fox was assistant megaphone wielder and William Darling art directed, whatever that means.

The picture didn't dent Mayer's bankroll to speak of. Plenty of outdoor stuff, laid in the Sierras with a dam building engineering feat as the central theme, nature has provided some beautiful but inexpensive locations. In fact, a hunting lodge interior and dance hall and a shanty ditto comprise the only indoor stuff recallable.

Anne Wilmot (Miss Stewart) is a flirtatious flapper who accepts Morse's invitation to accompany him in the chaperonage of Mrs. Katherine Wilmot, our heroine's aunt, to the Sierras. Morse is building a railroad through the mountains and desires the right of way to a tract of land owned by Bill Shannon (Edward Hearn), our hero, who has erected a water dam thereon as part of a fertilization project for the arid territory beyond. Shannon has ideals about this dam and is thinking of the future and what it might mean to the coming generations when they can reclaim the arid regions. Morse visits him, offering the engineer any price demanded. Shannon idealistically spurns the mundane offer, and from then on Morse is not above resorting to questionable means to obtain his ends. He has wired the ground to dynamite the dam, but Anne saves it by breaking the connection a second before the circuit is closed. It need not be recounted that Anne has become fond of Bill Shannon, although she had promised his rival, Morse, that she would give him an answer to his suit after they reach the Sierras.

The footage totals 6,065 feet and was screened in 73 minutes. While nothing spectacular in effects and situations it interested fairly throughout, a fight scene or something as forcible being interpolated at proper moments when there was danger of flagging interest.

The casting is adequate, Miss Stewart doing her flapper role faithfully and with due moderation. She presents a winning figure in her hunter's togs and puttees. Edward Hearn is a real he-man hero, Walt Whitman as "Sheb," his pal, lending the comedy contrast. Arthur Stuart Hull did not overdo his role of "heavy," although it could have been easily exaggerated in spots. Hull, while not exactly a newcomer, ought to be developed into a new type of screen villain, the semi-sympathetic kind, perfect for captain of industry roles and the like. Bert Sprotte also stood out with a character bit.

The title is a pip for the exhibitor to do stunts with. It's worth half of the picture. Release is due about March 25. *Abel.*

VERMILION PENCIL

Tse Chan (later called the unknown)..
.......................Sessue Hayakawa
His wife..........................Ann May
Pai Wang.......................Misac Seki

The Unknown..............Sessue Hayakawa
Li Chan...................Sessue Hayakawa
Hyacinth ....Bessie Love
Fu Wong.....................Sidney Franklin
Ho Ling...................Thomas Jefferson
The Jackal....................Tote Du Crow
Ma Shue....................Omar Whitehead

A typical Oriental story in the vein of previous vehicles for Sessue Hayawaka, capably done by R-C Pictures. Story by Homer Lea. scenario by Edwin Warren Guyol and Alice Catlin and directed by Norman Dawn. Bessie Love heads the supporting company.

The production holds to the average of the slant eyed actor. It has fair romantic quality and the usual impressive background of Oriental color characteristic of Hayakawa and his work, in short a feature altogether satisfying to the star's partisans of whom there are a very considerable number.

There is a certain genuiness about Hayakawa that attaches to no Occidental player in Chinese stories. He is probably the only actor who can create a complete illusion before the Oriental background, for the obvious reason that he is working in his native atmosphere. The film under discussion has numerous passages of crude theatrical material such as would go into a wild and unrestrained serial, but somehow the picturesque personality of the star colors the whole affair and gives it a certain plausibility. What would be childish fiction under the hands of a Western actor becomes somehow plausible by reason of Hayakawa's ability to build realistic atmosphere, an illusion that is painstakingly carried out in the surrounding detail.

His acting methods are natural and legitimate. In the present instance something of this asset is lost through the choice of an American actress Bessie Love, to play opposite. Her presence gives the play its only touch of unreality. The make-believe stares one in the face and comes near to spoiling an otherwise excellent bit of convincing story telling. The locale of the tale is China and the obvious Western personality of the actress stands away from the background like a widow's veil at a lawn party.

Hayakawa is called upon to play a double role, although one of the identities (that of an old man) is very foggy and unreal. The story deals with "the vermilion pencil," a red cylinder which a Chinese ruler lifts from a table as the ceremonial sign that a prisoner on trial is sentenced to death by torture. Tso Chan, a Chinese ruler (Sessue) pronounces this sentence on his wife whom he believes to be unfaithful. After she is dead he learns that his belief was unjust and he renounces his throne, sends his son to America in care of a tutor and goes into solitude to expiate his error.

Years after the son (also Sessue) returns as an engineer and while building a dam falls in love with the daughter of a humble basket weaver. The girl is abducted by a powerful mandarin and the young engineer goes to her rescue. He carries her off to a remote fastness near an active volcano where the pair are recaptured and are about to be executed under the doom of "the vermilion pencil," when the volcano bursts forth in eruption. All flee and the victims are set at liberty to complete their romance, the volcano destroying the former king as he prays that the evils that beset the son may descend upon his head.

The spouting volcano is trickily done with inserts probably from some scenic or news weekly inserted occasionally to give it verity and the picturesque Oriental backgrounds are exceptionally well executed. *Rush.*

SMILES ARE TRUMPS

Jimmy Carson...........Maurice Flynn
Marjorie Manning...........Ora Carew
John Slevin...........Myles McCarthy
James Manning........Herschel Mayall
Enrico ....Kirke Lucas
Martino............Norman Hammond

Looks as though William Fox had dug up a real bet in the line of a male star in Maurice ("Lefty") Flynn. Flynn made his name on the gridiron as a member of several of the Yale elevens, and in pictures looks as though he is going through for a goal. He is a husky individual with a corking personality and a winning smile, who can act and do stunts.

In "Smiles Are Trumps," a Frank L. Packard railroad adventure story, Flynn walks away with all the honors as the hero. Delbert Davenport, who prepared the script, gave him all the rough and tumble work possible for a star to handle and come up smiling, and the direction of George E. Marshall was such Flynn showed to full advantage.

There were touches of detail the director overlooked, such as having the star totally unmussed in a closeup after a big fight in a locomotive cab, but outside of that and a few other like minor touches, Marshall has delivered a program picture full of pep. During the week the feature shared a double program bill with Buster Keaton in "The Playhouse" at the Loew's New York, but it won't be long before "Lefty" Flynn will be able to stand on his own, providing the Fox script department provides him with story material of the right sort.

Flynn has the role of an assistant paymaster on a new branch line of an important railroad. The paymaster, played by Myles McCarthy (who incidentally makes a corking heavy), has had things pretty much his own way. Working with Martino, one of the section bosses, he has been getting a mint of graft by padding the payroll. Flynn discovers the crooked work, and the paymaster decides he should be put out of the way. Martino's gang is delegated to do the job, but the young assistant bests them and returns to clean up for the paymaster. In the fracas that follows the paymaster is knocked unconscious and Flynn, believing he has killed the man, starts for the sheriff's office to give himself up. The paymaster recovers and decides to put the assistant in dutch by taking $5,000 from the safe and accusing the young man of the robbery.

The train the assistant takes is the special on which the vice-president of the road is traveling. It is flagged by Martino and his section forces. They protest against being fired by the assistant paymaster. When they fail to receive satisfaction they attack the official with Flynn coming to the rescue. He is taken into the official's car and, arriving at their destination, discovers the road's detectives are looking for him, so he starts back to make Slevin, the paymaster, tell the truth about the robbery. Returning on a handcar, he is derailed by Martino, and when the vice-president and his daughter, with the train crew, return by locomotive, he isn't on the scene. As things look blackest Flynn arrives via horseback. Then Slevin and Martino join forces, force the road official's daughter into the cab of the engine and start off with her. Another locomotive goes in pursuit and a race between the two engines follows. This is the thrill, the two running on parallel tracks. As they come abreast Flynn leaps to the car with the crooks and bests them in a fight.

Ora Carew, who plays the lead opposite Flynn, has little to do, but shows up well. Norman Hammond as the second heavy looked the character, but somewhat overacted. Kirke Lucas as a boy registered nicely. *Fred.*

THE FIRE BRIDE

Lois Markham................Ruth Reneck
Steve Maitland.............Edward Hearn
Capt. Markham.............Walt Whitman
Capt. Blackton...............Fred Stanton
Atel ....Paki
Kalom ....Taura

This production is one of the so-called Entertainment Series that Wid Gunning, Inc., is releasing. It is the first feature that has been made in the South Seas, and, while pretty in spots, holds enough story and punch, together with a corking box office title, to put the production over in the average houses. W. F. Alder and S. M. Unander are the producers of the picture, which was directed by Arthur Rosson.

The scenes are laid on a tropic island and aboard a small sailing vessel. Capt. Markham has been shipwrecked on a small island and some years after charters a schooner to return there with his daughter to recover treasure that he has buried. The chartered boat is in command of Capt. Blackton, the heavy, and his first mate is Steve Maitland, a young man who is cruising the South Seas in search of the man that caused his sister's death.

When the schooner reaches the island where the treasure is buried Blackton has the elder sea captain slain and immediately after he kills the islander who did his bidding. He then tries to capture the affection of the girl, but prior to that he has wandered into the interior of the island and violated a holy cave of the islanders. This finally brings about his death at the hands of the tribesmen. In this much at least the hero is cheated of his revenge, for it was Blackton who caused his sister's death.

The photography through the picture is very good, while the direction carries sufficient punch to make the picture interesting, although there are a few details where the director has let things happen as they best might. A tropic storm and a shipwreck are very well handled.

Ruth Reneck and Edward Hearn, playing the leads, handled themselves nicely, while the heavy in the hands of Fred Stanton was tremendously well played. *Fred.*

BE REASONABLE

A Mack Sennett twin reeler released through First National. Although Sennett has turned out some better stuff, this slapstick effusion should satisfy as the comedy spice for any film program. Some of the lesser known recruits from the director's stock company are seen in this film, a particularly luscious peacherino standing out in the leading feminine role.

With such a heroine it is only natural that Sennett should open proceedings on the bathing beach. He eschews the bathing girl atmosphere which one always expects as soon as a beach scene was flashed.

The same fast tempo that pervades all slapstick comedy reels is maintained and of course the usual Sennett distinction of some semblance of story sequence, which concerns itself with the theft of a string of pearls. A chase by two score of coppers after the fleeing and long-suffering boob is nicely played up.

The discerning film fan has been educated to find new comedy bits and business in Sennett's stuff, for goodness knows they are all on the same rough and tumble order, and that is why this reel may not match up to par because of the familiarity of much of the business. *Abel.*

SHADOWS OF CONSCIENCE

Jim Logan.................Russell Simpson
Winifred Coburn Sherman,
                            Gertrude Olmstead
William Coburn..........Nelson McDowell
Alice Logan..............Barbara Tennant
Wade Curry....:.........Landers Stevens
Pedro.....................J. Bradley Ward
Winifred (at six years)..Ida Mae McKenzie

A real old-fashioned western melodrama of the ten, twent' type, evidently designed for the cheaper houses. It was the weak sister on a Loew's New York theatre double feature program, sharing the bill with Irene Castle in "French Heels." The story was written by Francis Powers and J. P. McCarthy, the latter responsible for direction. The latter is also old-fashioned, being slow and draggy throughout.

The first two reels are employed in planting the story. This is seemingly a waste of footage, for the story amounts to but little in the aggregate. A girl lured into a fake marriage is taken to a small western town. Her brother follows, and on his way runs across a slain miner with his little daughter. He takes the girl with him into the mining town. There he discovers that his sister has been tricked, and in the fight with her betrayer the girl is killed. The betrayer then accuses the brother of the crime, and he is compelled to leave the country.

Years later in another part of the country the two men again meet and clash. The little girl who was picked up on the trail has grown to young womanhood by this time. The heavy tries to win her, and almost succeeds, when he discovers who the man is that is posing as her father. He charges him with the murder of years ago, but in the end the truth of the killing is revealed by the conscience of the real murderer.

The picture is badly handled, the detail frightful and the mistake of tinting written titles makes it impossible to read them.

In the cheaper houses the production may get by, but it is hardly worthy of booking in the bigger daily change houses unless there is a strong picture to hold it up on a double feature bill. *Fred.*

TAKING CHANCES

A Richard Talmadge production, with Richard Talmadge the star, and called Richard Talmadge in his picture character. Not a bad scheme, this plugging the Richard Talmadge name steadily during all of the running, but it is hardly necessary with "Talmadge" on the screen, since there are other Talmadges on it much better known. As the others are girls, there's no possibility of an error in name.

This is a Phil Gildstone production, with no distributor mentioned. It was the daily feature at Loew's New York.

"Taking Chances" is strictly a stunt picture, with some comedy, some exaggerations and some nonsensicalities. The stunt stuff is carried to extremes, overshadowing a love interest in the story by Grover Jones that should have equalized the acrobatics of Talmadge's, if it did not predominate. For the class who will greatly prefer this good-looking young athlete will also want to see him in love scenes; the more the better they will like his athletics. But he can't fight a whole ship's crew and make an audience believe it; nor can he do a run-around with Mexicans chasing without causing it to appear silly, if carried as far as it was in this film.

The story is ordinary, young Talmadge starting as a book agent,

and through one of his stunts impressing a traction magnate who on the spot engages him as his private secretary. The magnate has a daughter; some schemers are after his road; then to Mexico; and it won't be hard for you to fill in or guess the rest.

The simplicity of the tale may be laid against the desire to exploit Talmadge by the stunt process, a la Fairbanks. Those two should have a stunt contest, with the odds most likely favoring Talmadge. But Fairbanks landed first and solidly.

A good stunt picture is this; an ordinary one otherwise, with the set acrobatics and athletics not well blended, although it may be said for Talmadge he did put up a couple of dandy fist fights, two-handed. They were superior to cleaning up mobs single-handed.

If Talmadge is given a romantic story that brings in his athletic energies harmoniously, he will do more than he ever can do in the haphazard style "Taking Chances" only offers. There seems to be a good deal to Talmadge in the picture way. He has many of the requisites. Now he needs to have **some judgment used in addition.**
Sime.

FAIR LADY

Countess Margherita........Betty Blythe
Caesar Maruffi.............Thurston Hall
Norvin Blake...............Robert Elliott
Myra Nell Drew............Gladys Hulette
Lucrezia ....Florence Auer
Gian Norcone..............Walter James
Count Modena..............Macey Harlam
Riccardo ....Henry Leone
Count Martinello..........Effingham Pinto
Uncle Bernie Drew.........Arnold Lucy

This is the second of the Whitman Bennett productions of Rex Beach stories. "Fair Lady," as the screen version is entitled, was originally "The Net" when presented in novel form by the author. It is a fairly good feature of the program type, containing a quantity of suspense and an exceedingly clever and handsome woman in Betty Blythe. As shown at the Strand this week, there was some room for improvement, which could be brought about by cutting. The mob scene chase stuff could easily be eliminated entirely or certainly cut to a degree where one scene would have been enough. The picture held the Strand's audience up to this point, but caught a laugh on the chase.

"Fair Lady" seems a title that should mean something at the box office, especially in connection with the good looking Miss Blythe, although she is not fair but of the decided brunet type. However, the title means nothing in connection with the story, which might have far better been called "The One Who Knows."

The direction was in the hands of Kenneth Webb, from the script by Dorothy Farnum. Mr. Webb has presented a corking entertainment up to the last reel, and then he falls down. Incidentally, it would have been better for the picture had there been a little more doubt as to the identity of the head of the Mafia ring. That the character of Caesar Maruffi (Thurston Hall), the Italian banker, is the real head of the ring is too apparent from the moment that the meeting in the office of the New Orleans mayor is held. That was a mistake. Suspicion should have been directed to a greater extent at Count Modena (Macey Harlam), who is in reality an Italian secret service agent. There was an attempt to do this, but it was not of sufficient strength to cover up the real offender.

The production is a pleasing one, with the exception of the use of tinting in lieu of lighting effects. That is one of the details that is seemingly beginning to get to audiences of the picture theatres at this time, especially when one looking from a lighted room sees someone in a garden in broad daylight when it is supposed to be night, and immediately after the reverse with the person standing outdoors looking into the house, seeing the person in the room that a moment before was brilliantly lighted, standing in the moonlight tint.

In sets there is nothing further that could have been asked from the producer and certainly a cast that was worth-while and assembled for the production. The one weak spot that showed was the lead as played by Robert Elliott. He lacked virility for the first half of the picture, but improved in the later scenes.

Miss Blythe walks away with the picture as far as the women are concerned, although Gladys Hulette as a southern girl makes a pretty picture at times. Florence Auer, as a Sicilian servant, was exceedingly good, although she seemingly overacted her first three scenes. Effingham Pinto, who appeared in the first reel, carried the lover role perfectly. Walter James, as a burly heavy, looked and acted the part with a punch. This was particularly displayed in a couple of fights that he had to put up in the story. A character bit of a souse by Arnold Lucy was well done.

While seemingly not containing enough wallop as a picture for a week in the bigger first run houses,

the picture will get by at this stage of the game in the regular program theatres. *Fred.*

MISTRESS OF WORLD

("The City of Gold")

Famous Players' serial, "Mistress of the World," passed into Broadway history this week with the showing of the final episodes, "The City of Gold," at both the Rivoli and the Rialto. At the last minute the scheme of pairing the last two chapters into one of about seven reels was resorted to, presumably to get the agony over with all possible speed. Originally the third episode had been cut to around four reels and the last one to a little over three.

Sunday evening the Rivoli was crowded, weather conditions probably having something to do with the attendance. The usual Sunday night crowd was on Broadway, and when it began to rain just after 8 o'clock the people scurried for shelter. The showing of the last chapter of "The Mistress of the World" developed into a merry kidding party in passages where no comedy was intended.

Helen and Benson were taken captive by the strange people of Ophir and were about to be sacrificed on the blood altar. When the high priest and ruler pronounced the doom on Benson, "The slaves are becoming restless. Let them have the man for a blood sacrifice," the crowd burst into hilarious laughter and there was tumultuous applause. But that wasn't a patch on their unseemly behavior when the screen recorded the fateful title "The end." It was the feature of the evening. Francis X. Bushman in a personal appearance never got any more enthusiastic applause than the announcement that the U. F. A. serial was over and out of the way.

From first to last the final episode was a lark. The Rivoli audience gave itself up throughout to the hazing of the picture. Its pompous dramatics called down a storm of sarcastic laughter and applause, and the gathering stopped just this side of disorderly conduct. It was a gleeful occasion for the crowd bent on showing its resentment against having the wretched thing slammed at them for three solid weeks. The attitude of that Sunday night gathering ought to be rich in significance to the Rivoli and Rialto director. It supplies a pretty definite line of evidence against that ancient dictum, "There's one born every minute and they're thickest on Broadway." That's something.

The last episode is introduced briefly with a series of titles of the utmost crispness, a model of clear-cut titling. Two title sheets sufficed. Then the picture started with a repeat of 100 feet or so of the preceding chapter. This episode has some very big spectacular effects, involving huge numbers of supers and a lot of expensive sets, showing the strange city of Ophir in the mid-African mountains. Upon the appearance of the strangers among the worshipers at the pagan shrine Helen and Benson (it is to be remembered that the Chienese hero was killed last week) are made prisoner.

Helen is about to be executed as a living offering to propitiate the deity when the high priest sees around her neck the sacred jewel taken from the Chinese temple in Chapter I and a duplicate of the sacred emblem of the temple. In the twinkling of an eye Helen is released and made queen of the City of Gophir, while the Broadway fans rocked in delight. Meanwhile Benson has been cast in prison with the black slaves. It is here that his destruction is ordered and it is here that the hilarity reached its first semiclimax, although the whole episode was a series of unintended climax.

In prison there is another white man, one Karpen, a scientist, who ventured into the wilderness and was captured when he entered the forgotten city. Benson is about to be sacrificed by the black slaves, but with his tremendous strength he overcomes the strongest of his captors and they with one accord make him their chief, obeying the ancient rule that the strongest shall lead them. Karpen and Benson thereupon begin to scheme escape. They go to the queen's palace, where Helén now presides, and there find a complete wireless outfit, brought years before when Karpen was captured, and preserved as strange magic.

Somehow the wireless outfit in the Queen of Sheba's throne room didn't get a giggle. Perhaps it made them numb for the minute. Anyhow Benson and Karpen construct a dynamo, using a sort of well-wheel arrangement driven by a couple of hundred black slaves to supply power to turn it. With this aid they broadcast a radio call for help. It is picked up by a European wireless operator, relayed to an enterprising newspaper editor and he dispatches a relief expedition in an airship in charge of a comedy trick reporter, who furnished the only intentional comedy, and didn't arouse a ripple.

The airplane alights in Ophir just as the adventurers have located the Queen of Sheba's ancient treasure. They load the plane with untold riches and are about to start when an earthquake rends the ground. A temple collapses and Benson is buried in its ruins. The others depart with their loot, and out of the odds and ends in the airship Helen manages to collect a perfectly fitting afternoon dress, coat and set of white fox furs, so that Karpen is bowled over by her beauty and makes love to her. The finish shows them on a ship, presumably back to Copenhagen, sweetly silhouetted against the setting sun and in affectionate embrace.

Up until the last moment the Rivoli had advertised "The Red Peacock," a new feature starring Pola Negri, as the supplementary attraction, but Betty Compson in "The Green Temptation" was substituted. The Pola Negri picture would have put four German film features in Famous Players' Broadway houses, counting "The Loves of Pharaoh" at the Criterion, two prints of the U. F. A. serial and the Negri film.

Rush.

GREEN TEMPTATION

Genelle / Coralyn / Joan Parker	Betty Compson
John Allenby	Mahlon Hamilton
Gaspard	Theodore Kosloff
Pitou	Neely Edwards
Hugh Duyker	Edward Burns
Duchesse de Chazarin	Lynore Lynnard
Dolly Dunton	Mary Thurman
M. Jounet	M. Von Hardenberg
Mrs. Weedon Duyker	Betty Brice
Mr. Weedon Duyker	Arthur Hull

The best thing about this Paramount picture at the Rivoli is the work of Betty Compson, reduced to a quite miraculous slenderness and making a particularly appealing figure as the wistful waif of Paris, associate of thieves and a thief herself, who is regenerated by her sufferings and newly aroused compassions as a nurse at the front in Flanders.

The story is adapted from "The Noose," a novel by Constance Lindsay Skinner, by Monte M. Katterjohn and Julia Crawford Ivers, and bears the name as director of William D. Taylor, who was murdered in Los Angeles last month. It was put into the Rivoli at the last minute, replacing "The Red Peacock," starring Pola Negri. A printed notice in the lobby made apology to the public for the confusion over the feature announcement. It is explained it was not certain up to the last minute "The Green Temptation" would arrive in time.

The news reel was out of the program this week in favor of a "Mutt and Jeff" animated cartoon. Certainly with the sombre mood of the Betty Compson picture and the depressing episode of the U. F. A. serial, "The Mistress of the World," some enlivening touch was urgently needed for the program. Probably the Bud Fisher subject, an unusually funny one, was good judgment, although the news topical was missed.

"The Green Temptation" is an interesting story, well handled and possessing a strong sentimental appeal, although it is guiltless of anything but superficial significance. It is just an intelligently managed crook melodrama with a touch of refinement and polish. It is satisfactory theatrical entertainment, a skilfully contrived illusion. The story has some of the defects innate in the adapted novel, chiefly an embarrassing abundance of material. There are moments when it is difficult to readily identify the characters, although this defect is not nearly so emphatic as usual in screened novels.

A picturesque beginning catches interest at the outset. Genelle is a dancer attached to a French circus giving street shows in the city as the disguise for the thieving operations of Gaspard, the master crook, whose hirelings rob the crowds attracted by the show. A Paris theater manager sees her dance and, forecasting a great future for her, has her trained in the schools of the capital. Presently we see her star of the Theatre des Beaux Arts in Paris and the rage of the town, playing at fashionable parties and taking occasion to rob the guests.

Her last coup of this kind, the theft of a fabulously valuable emerald which she dispatches to the thieves' den by carrier pigeon from a balcony, goes wrong and the police are on her trail. She escapes, but Gaspard is taken. Just then the war breaks out and she takes the uniform of a nurse to escape from Paris. By some turn she is sent to the Flanders front and there in service to the wounded she forgets her past and a new desire for self-sacrifice takes possession of her.

After the war she comes to America, meeting a rich American and an Englishman, both of whom she had nursed in hospitals. The American brings her to a lawn party given by his family and asks her to be his wife. At the same party is Gaspard, under an alias, and he demands that she join him in an effort to steal the same emerald, now in the possession of their hostess. She refuses and Gaspard denounces her as a former French crook. Gaspard gets possession of the jewel and is about to make off with it when the Englishman, who turns out to be a Scotland Yard detective, confronts him. In the battle which ensues Gaspard is killed. The rich American had withdrawn his offer of marriage when it appeared the girl was under a cloud, and she accepts the Englishman for the happy ending.

Rush.

THE CRADLE

Margaret Harvey	Ethel Clayton
Dr. Robert Harvey	Charles Meredith
Doris Harvey	Mary Jane Irving
Lola Forbes	Anna Lehr
Courtney Webster	Walter McGrail
Mrs. Mason	Adele Farrington

More or less of a "society" picture dealing with the problem of a young married couple who become divorced, marrying their second affinities only to once more remarry, due to their child having been unwelcome by both the step-parents and suffering a serious illness that brings the mother and father to the realization of their mistake.

Possibly made with the idea of sending a moral across the film, it falls somewhat short of producing that particular effect other than to make prominent its mother-love factor which predominates. The substance seems to be that which happens to a majority of stage plays when transposed to the screen, the losing of much of is value. "The Cradle" is no exception. However, it shapes up as an average feature possessing a theme not by any means new, though nicely done despite its tendency to revert to almost pure sobbiness for the major portion and the somewhat exaggerated thoughts and actions of a child around four or five years of age.

The presenting is by Lasky (Paramount) with the story adapted from the French play by Eugene Brieux. To wit, a young doctor finding himself not over successful in procuring patients becomes annoyed at his wife's continual petty economies and reaches a state of mind that when a call comes from the rich Miss Forbes, who has a failing for handsome physicians, the prescribed "fall" is not long in arriving. The wife accidentally finds out where the head of the house has been spending his time and gives him his divorce, with the decree stating each of the parents shall have possession of the child for six months of a year. Dr. Harvey marries his patient, while Mrs. Harvey accepts the proposal of Courtney Webster, lawyer and a former admirer.

The child, Doris, is an always present thorn in the flesh to Webster, who resents the reminder of his wife's former husband. At the conclusion of the initial half year Doris departs for her father's residence, where she meets with a discouraging reception from the former Lola Forbes, now Mrs. Harvey, and beginning to play about with another male prospect, which leads to her frightening the youngster into a nervous collapse that forces the doctor to take the child back to its mother.

The return of Doris to the Webster home and the presence of Harvey and his former wife, together, during their baby's illness brings about the realization to the parents that they should never have separated. Webster also begins to see the light and the following incidents reveal the recovery of Doris, Mrs. Webster reading of the separation of the Harveys and Websters offering to annul their marriage, leaving the child and mother embracing as the fadeout and to the imagination the logical reunited family conclusion.

Paul Powell did the directing and besides assembling a capable cast, has procured the maximum results with all the members stepping forth, at various times, to score personally and hold up the picture where the theme shows a tendency to let down.

It's very much of an "interior" offering, including one or two pretentious settings fully taken care of by the photography.

Ethel Clayton as Margaret Harvey is the devoted mother. Her name tops the billing.

The film permits of quite a few gowns to be worn by the feminine principals and leans towards a "dressy" classification on the parts of the men as well. Outside of Miss Clayton, who has little to do other than to sob for joy and sorrow, Charles Meredith stood out sufficiently to range equally on a par with the star and based on this performance he looks to be as good a male support for a feminine "name" as there is around.

Skig.

BARNYARD CAVALIER

"A Barnyard Cavalier," Christie comedy, directed by Al Christie and featuring Bobby Vernon, had its first screening this week as the feature of the Hippodrome. The picture was introduced to occupy the running time left open in the program by the termination of the Jack Dempsey engagement.

The comedy, sponsored by Educational Films, is a capital slapstick burlesque particularly adapted to the Hippodrome purposes for its appeal to the youngsters. It is a travesty upon "The Three Musketeers," lately put out by Douglas Fairbanks. Fort a short length subject it has extraordinary production features and is a slam-bang, rough-and-tumble comedy from start to finish, without a pause in the action. The youngsters at the Monday matinee found it amusing and showed it unmistakably.

The story starts as a "rube" comedy. Zeke, the farm boy, makes love to the rich neighbor's daughter and is ordered away by daddy. Disappointed in love, Zeke turns to his favorite novel for consolation. Falling asleep he dreams he is d'Artagnan and rescues the maid from a marriage forced by the father, who appears in the dream as the king. Zeke dreams himself into a feathered hat, doublet and hose, and makes himself a master swordsman before whom fall scores of the Cardinal's guards and the minions of the king in an endless battle up and down stairs and through the palace chambers.

The romantic dream passages dovetail into the love affair of today, when Zeke determines to make his dream real by riding boldly to his sweetheart's home and eloping with her under the father's nose. Dad learns of the scheme and is ready for the moonstruck Romeo when he arrives attended by three pals and all mounted on plow horses. The picture ends in a riot of knockabout low comedy, with Zeke riding off with his love while discomfited dad threatens in vain. Rollicking kid film, with its appeal confined to the juvenile fan.

Rush.

RIGHT THAT FAILED

Nothing the matter with this Metro-Classic, at the State this week, except the title, which suggests a travesty instead of a rather keen comedy. It is taken from a "Saturday Evening Post" story by J. P. Marquand, and Bayard Veiller is credited with the direction. Bert Lytell is the star.

The picture has a good deal of smooth comedy in its basic idea, although one would suspect that the written story was rather more whimsical than the picture. The screen comedy is obvious at times, as for instance the familiar British servant who instructs the roughneck American—a prize fighter—in the niceties of social conduct. The pictures with their necessarily broad effects do not lend themselves to delicate shadings of humor such as need the written word, but the general idea of the story somehow manages to register pretty completely.

Briefly put, the idea is that the modern butterfly society girls are not so strong for ultra refinement in the men they pick for mates, but look for a man with a kick in both mitts when they go choosing their life partners. The fun of the picture comes from the emotions of the prize fighter, Johnny Duffy, as he gradually finds this out in a chance adventure at a fashionable summer resort frequented by the wealthy.

Johnny is a comer in the prize ring. Early in the picture he is introduced in a spirited bout with the near champion, whom he knocks out in two rounds of fast fighting, a capital bit of film action. Walking across the park lawn he sees a policeman threatening to arrest Marjorie, daughter of wealth, for walking on the grass and cheeking the uniform. He rescues her and learns that she is leaving town the next day for Craigmoor. After his fight the same night the doctors tell

Johnny that he has broken a bone in his right hand and will have to lay off for three months. This is the opportunity to go to Craigmoor.

He falls in with a footman who worships him for his ring genius and takes him in tow, instructing him in dress and deportment. So he timidly begins the conquest of Marjorie, keeping his identity a secret. His campaign is interrupted by the arrvial of Marjorie's fiance, De Witt by name, who recognizes him and tries to expose him to the girl. De Witt sends for Johnny's father, his manager and the real champion, with whom Johnny is matched for a mill. Johnny manages to alibi himself and learns the real lesson when he observes how all the girls fall for the visiting champ.

Noting the hero worship of the flappers of the hotel veranda, he goes back to his servant-mentor and, observing "Who told you the society girls didn't admire fighters?" revises his plans. First he lures De Witt to a lonely spot in the garden and smears him up. Then he goes back to the girl and tells her what he has done, remarking casually that thereafter he stands ready to do the same for any other man who talks to her without his consent. Then he faints away, having broken his hand up, for good this time, in delivering the right swing on De Witt's alabaster brow. He wakes up to find Marjorie's arms about his neck and himself complete victor over the field.

An amusing character is the father of the girl, who stands aside while the two rivals are fighting it out for her hand, always putting in a good word for Johnny without seeming to do so, and pretending he doesn't know who he is, although he does from the first. His final speech over the lovers is, "I always thought the prize ring was a first-rate training for a business man."

The story is told in an engaging veing of drollery and sustains interest from start to finish. The supporting company is faultless in natural acting. Indeed the star is the least convincing character of the cast. The heroine is Virginia Valli, a lovely brunet with a fine light touch for graceful little comedies of this sort. *Rush.*

DON'T DOUBT YOUR WIFE

Rose Manning	Leah Baird
John Manning	Edward Pell
Herbert Olden	Emory Johnson
Mrs. Evanston	Mathilde Brundage
Marie Braban	Katherine Lewis

Leah Baird Productions, Inc., presents "Don't Doubt Your Wife" a five reel production released by Associated Exhibitors throug Pathe Exchange. Leah Baird in addition to appearing as the star is also credited with the authorship of the story

"Don't Doubt Your Wife" is a production depending largely upon its title for results. The name should prove a draw; the story is but a minor factor. The eternal triangle idea is the foundation upon which the tale has been built. John Manning becomes jealous when his wife receives attention from a former suitor. Accusing her of infidelity after a misleading affair with the other man in a road house, he secures a divorce. The woman is in love with her husband with what friendship she displays towards the other merely a matter of form. After separating she returns to the home of her mother. The third member of the triangle presses his suit and secures the consent of the girl to marry him. Learning that she is to become the mother of a child by her former husband he brings about a reconciliation and the couple are reunited.

All in all "Don't Doubt Your Wife" is an ordinary program feature. The short cast is comprised of moderate salaried people and the production end discloses nothing more than stock sets.

The production was taken by the Moss and Proctor interests for their local neighborhood vaudeville houses. The title and the price at which it was offered were the two outstanding reasons for its acceptance. *Hart.*

THE HIGH SIGN

Buster Keaton's latest Metro twin reeler is the comedy relief at the Capitol this week. Eddie Cline collaborated with the star on the story and direction, producing an interesting slapstick comedy.

Keaton has but to continue at the present rate and he will become a valuable adjunct to any film program. His stuff is original, and always consistent with the story thread he maintains. No haphazard bits for him, always ringing them in legitimately.

A secret society is out to blackmail August Nickelnurser for $10,000 or inflict capital punishment on him. Keaton is engaged by the victim as the bodyguard and by the secret society as their emissary in carrying out the death threat. He decides to protect him and double-cross the "dirty dozen" that comprise the Buzzards. A cross section of a house with numerous trapdoors and secret exits makes for some fast rough and tumble work. Keaton eventually annihilating the would-be assassins.

That old timer, Al St. John, is alloted a bit in the comedy. He is the only familiar in the support. St. John at one time was also Fatty Arbuckle's running mate in the corpulent comedian's two-reel output, later doing some feature work on the Fox Sunshine lot. He ought to be taken in hand by someone. He suggests untold possibilities.

Outside of that the comedy is all Keaton. The star predominates and to good purpose. *Abel.*

THE HEART SPECIALIST

This is a Realart with Mary Miles Minter as the star. The story is by Mary Morrison, Harvey Thew having made the screen adaptation. The direction was in the hands of Frank Urson. The feature is a comedy drama that sags considerable along about the middle of the story, but comes along with a wallop as it nears the finish. It was the best half of a double bill presented at Loew's Circle.

The picture while short cast, but five important characters, made it possible to give the star a corking supporting company. Noah Beery as the heavy does some excellent work in the picture and Roy Atwell contributes some corking comedy relief.

Miss Minter has the role of a newspaper girl. She is the editor of the advice to the love lorn column. Her managing editor wants to discontinue the column because a number of readers have written in to the effect that her stuff was "mush." She gambles with him that she can go anywhere within 40 miles of the office; if she makes good she is to have an extra month's salary; if she doesn't she loses her job.

From this point in the story, dear old picture coincidence steps in and takes the center. The girl takes a train to a town in Connecticut, in which there are two boys that have returned from the battlefields of Europe the day before. One is the heir to millions and the estate is shared between her and his cousin, who is married to an important Turkish official and lives in Turkey. A doctor, who was a friend of the young man's uncle, has had charge of the estate and has been helping himself to the funds. When the boy returns he has planned for a woman to appear on the scene, pretend that she is the cousin from Turkey and admit that she has been receiving money from the doctor. But the plant misses the train, and it so happens that the first assistant to Cupid is on that very train and gets off at the very station where they are expecting the lady from Turkey.

She steps right into the scheme of things, uncovers the plotters and manages to balk their plans, winning the heart of the millionaire at the finish.

Miss Minter made a pleasing screen picture as the writer and handled the role quite well. Her first appearance was greeted by chatter on the part of the Circle's audience anent her mention with the Taylor case. *Fred.*

THE GLORIOUS FOOL

Jane Brown	Helene Chadwick
Billy Grant	Richard Dix
Miss Hart	Vera Lewis
Head Nurse	Kate Lester
Dummy	Otto Hoffman
Jenks	John Lince
Senior Surgical Interne	Theodore von Eltz
Mr. Lindley Grant	Frederic Vroom
Mrs. Lindley Grant	Lillian Langdon
Al	George Cooper

Helene Chadwick and Richard Dix are again co-featured in a Goldwyn "eminent authors" release. Mary Roberts Rinehart contributing the story. The powers that be on the Goldwyn lot must be teaming this duo for some purpose, possibly as a future co-starring combination. They have appeared jointly together in several productions, and the forthcoming Gouverneur Morris story, "Yellow Men and Gold," will find them also featured therein.

"The Glorious Fool" (current at the Capitol) is a piquant paradox and should mean a lot at the box office, although after all is said and done it is just one of those human little plots, obvious from the first situation but spankingly produced. As soon as Billy Grant (Mr. Dix), who is expected to die on the morrow from an alcoholic heart and injuries sustained on one of his hooch sprees, and Jane Brown (Miss Chadwick), his nurse, marry to satisfy a dying man's whim, the story has been told. The audience knows that Grant is going to fool his nurse, doctor and the whole medical profession if needs be so that he and the heroine participate in the final clinch five reels later. However, since an audience likes the hero and heroine let off so sweetly, why worry? In truth they and the balance of the cast sell the plot so convincingly one does not realize the flimsiness of it all unless one reflects seriously thereon.

E. Mason Hopper directed. Hopper probably is Goldwyn's best bet as a megaphone wielder and has proved himself a winner time and again. J. G. Hawks, who adapted the story, has sub-captioned it a "dramatic comedy." That should make another good exploitation phrase.

The featured duo are perfect. Miss Chadwick is a winsome brunette and Mr. Dix brings to the screen a new type of hero who does more than look pretty. He helps carry a story than vice versa which also is indirect homage to the director.

Practically the whole action transpires in the hospital setting. It starts and ends there when our hero, fully recovered, is homeward bound.

One wonders, incidentally, whether Mrs. Rinehart did not get the germ idea of the plot from her husband, Dr. Stanley Rinehart, who is himself no mean writer. At any rate, the authoress has treated a human little situation masterfully (mistressfully to be prosaically consistent) and has elaborated on it and built it up in fine style. *Abel.*

BROADWAY PEACOCK

Myrtle May	Pearl White
Harold Van Tassel	Joseph Stryker
Rose Ingraham	Dora Eaton
Jerry Gibson	Harry Southard
Mrs. Van Tassel	Elisabeth Garrison

Fox release, starring Pearl White. Julia Talsova supplied the story, with Charles J. Brabin the director. Having selected Broadway night life as a subject for a starring vehicle for Miss White, the Fox forces have failed to supply her with sufficient worthwhile material to do her justice. As a story of Broadway night life it is interesting only to the unsophisticated hinterland.

Myrtle May (Pearl White) is the hostess of a Broadway cabaret. She acquires a monied sweetheart, who promises marriage. His finances are controlled by a straightlaced mother. The cabaret connections of his bride-to-be threaten to break the family ties and eliminate the ready cash. The boy attempts to release himself from the girl as easily as possible. At her home is a girl whom she had befriended. The boy meets the other girl, with Myrtle believing his coldness toward her is due to her. It finally turns out that way, Myrtle sticking to her hostess work, with the other girl accepted by his mother as a proper wife for her son.

Miss White furnishes what class there is to the production with her clothes. The short cast in support of the star suffices. At no time is exceptional acting demanded of any of the players. The cabaret scenes are effective, with the Nicky Goldman jazz band in evidence. *Hart.*

THE LEECH

Teddy	Roy Howard
Bill	Alex Hall
Dorothy Allen	Claire Whitney
Ruth	Katherine Leon
Joe Turner	Ben Gernard

"The Leech" is a Pioneer release that is an out-and-out propaganda production. It must have been shortly after the armistice was declared, when there was an effort to establish in the minds of the returning troops the worth-while facts regarding vocational training which the government was fostering.

As a picture production for straight entertainment purposes it is decidedly a sordid affair and hardly worth while the consideration of any exhibitor except those that are running the cheapest type of houses. Then at a price it might be used.

It is the story of two boys—brothers—who were the baseball idols of their home town. They enli . at the outbreak of the war; both are wounded. One returns with the loss of an arm, while the other has suffered from a leg that will remain stiff for the remainder of his life. The former takes advantage of training and obtains a position; the other decides that the country owes him a living for what service he has rendered, and also decides that he'll collect it without working. Part of the story is told in dream form, in an effort to take away from the sordid element in the yarn. This is not successfully done.

Miss Whitney plays the role of the heroine, who tries to straighten out the boy who is going wrong, and, after he has had disclosed to him in a dream the error of his ways, he marries her. The balance of the cast is not worthy of further mention.

Herbert Hancock, who handled the direction, has not turned out anything in this production that will place his name in the M. P. Hall of Fame. *Fred.*

DANGEROUS LITTLE DEMON

Betty Marmon................Marie Prevost
Gary McVeigh................Robert Ellis
Jay Howard..................Herbert Prior
Graham......................Jack Perrin
Denny.......................Anderson Smith
Harmon..............Edward Martindaale
Aunt Sophy..................Lydia Knott

Barring a fault of overacting on the part of several of the cast and the fact that the picture is a little draggy at times, this Universal feature is pleasing screen entertainment. The story by Mildred Considine and the script of Doris Schroeder hold fairly well and the direction of Clarence Badger helped the story considerably. The principal fault lies with the editing and cutting.

It is a society story with Marie Prevost starring in a typical "flapper" role. Miss Prevost manages to fill that role admirably, and Robert Ellis, who is her leading man in this picture, certainly stands out.

The yarn is that of a society butterfly who is constantly reaching for excitement. Her father believes she needs a steady hand, and is delighted when one of the more conservative of the younger set wants to marry her. Eventually he turns out to have been a fortune hunter, and the girl is in the arms of a "big brother" sweetheart" who has come to her father's aid in a financial difficulty at the close of the picture.

The photography and sets are all good, and Miss Prevost makes the most of a society dance bit that is sure to please picture audiences. She manages to display those physical charms that made her the "queen of the bathing beauties" in a nifty little soubret costume when she masks and appears at a social affair as "Mlle. Takoffski."

Edward Martindale as the father gave an interesting performance, but Jack Perrin and Miss Prevost at times overacted.

The picture served as half of a double feature bill with a Constance Talmadge reissue at Loew's New York. *Fred.*

GYPSY PASSION

Romany Kate, an old Gypsy.Madame Rejane
Miarka, her granddaughter............ Desdemona Mazza
Count de la Roque..........Jean Richepin
Ivor, the Count's nephew......Ivor Novello
Octavia, the Count's sister.Mme. Montbazon
Monsieur Chenal.............Marcel Numa
Louis ....Charles Vanel

The lurid title that this picture possesses is about all that there is to it from a box office standpoint. "Gypsy Passion" was made in France by Louis Mercanton and is being released in this country through Vitagraph. It is the second of that organization's foreign-made productions that has played the Strand within the last three weeks.

The story is a screen adaptation of Jean Richepin's story, "Miarka, the Child of the Bear," and the author plays one of the leading characters in the tale, adapting to himself all the technique of a veteran film player, getting as much of himself into the camera eye on all possible occasions. The real star is Mme. Rejane, who plays an elderly gypsy woman. She hasn't much in an acting way but does die for about 500 feet of the final reel.

Romany Kate (Mme. Rejane) is permitted to live in one of the ruins on the estate of Count de la Roque (Jean Richepin), an elderly Frenchman who is making a study of ancient manuscripts. He has secretly taken some books and writings which the old gypsy woman held and is trying to decipher them. With Kate is her grand-daughter Miarka, an orphan. Kate has read in the cards that her grandchild is to marry the King of the Gypsies and she prevents the marriage of the girl to the nephew of the Count. The young man and his uncle follow the trail of the elderly woman and the girl when they go on a pilgrimage and eventually it is disclosed that the body in reality is the son of the gypsy king who was murdered years before, the youth as a babe being left on the doorstep of the count's estate.

If you can dope anything passionate out of that tale, well and good. The picture is a long-drawn-out affair, extremely draggy at all times, and the cast overacts constantly to such an extent the audience tires of them. The Strand audience Sunday night laughed at the overdone death bit of Rejane.

It is said that the arrangement by which Vitagraph played the two attractions at the Strand calls for it to furnish the picture, pay the advertising and if the receipts gross in excess of $25,000 on the week, share in the amount above that figure. It looks like a fairly good arrangement for the Strand, but one of doubtful value when it is considered from the angle of building up patronage.

"Gypsy Passion" isn't, outside of the title, a picture that can stand a full week's run in one of the bigger Broadway houses. It is an ordinary program feature without the punch that the title suggests. *Fred.*

BEAUTY'S WORTH

By Sophie Kerr. Directed by Robert G. Vignola. Scenario by Luther Reed. Settings by Joseph Urban.

Prudence Cole..............Marion Davies
Cheyne Rovein..............Forrest Stanley
Amy Tillson................June Elvidge
Mrs. Garrison ....Truly Shattuck
Jane ....Lydia Yeamans Titus
Henry Garrison.............Halam Cooley
Tommy ....Antrim Short
Peter ....Thomas Jefferson
Aunt Elizabeth Whitney....Martha Mattox
Aunt Cynthia Whitney.....Aileen Manning
In Charades
Soldier ....John Dooley
Doll ....Gordon Dooley

This latest Cosmopolitan (Famous Players) starring Marion Davies at the Rivoli this week will give Miss Davies' admirers plenty of opportunity to see their favorite in many costumes and poses, from a demure Quakeress to a flashing beauty in bathing attire. If that were the purpose of the story it was kept well in mind by the director.

It is Miss Davies all the time, but she doesn't tire the audience, for with each change of dress, whether costume or gown, there is another angle to the Davies type, and in her bathing suit she is a peach, from her pretty head to her pretty feet. "Beauty's Worth" shows more of beauty likely than any picture of the famous film star's has within memory.

The story is light, with a dramatic touch here and there. Prudence Cole (Miss Davies), the youngest of an old Quaker family of which remain only two maiden aunts, has been bred by her elderly relatives strictly within the Quaker limitations. When Mrs. Garrison (Truly Shattuck) and Henry Garrison, her son (Halam Cooley) visit the Whitney home Mrs. Garrison's invitation to Prudence to visit her comes as a rift. At the Garrison home, though, Prudence is just Prudence, a nice little girl who wears a poke bonnet.

Hanging around the neighborhood is Cheyne Rovein, an artist (Forrest Stanley) with his heart in his art and a grouch in his mind against all society. The social set, aware of the artist's attitude, contrive to have Prudence request on their behalf that he stage charades for the society affair. The charades as presented are something of a novelty. Rovein has not been unmindful of the comeliness of Prudence hidden beneath the plainness of her garb. Hearing her sob she is painfully plain, so much so no one will look at her, and she wants one boy to look very hard (Henry), the artist consents, merely to bring out for his own artistic sense what the society folks have missed in the Quaker girl.

Her designed costumes and leading character of the charades cause the men about to fall over themselves in reaching Prudence first, with Henry in the van, until Rovein intervenes, with his opinions and definition of love. Prudence asks Henry what he thinks of love, and after that it's all Rovein for Prudence, especially as the artist mentioned he liked her best in her quaker dress. And as it thus ends Henry as nonchantly selects for his bride Amy Tillson (June Elvidge), another type of dark beauty in marked contrast to Miss Davies' fairness. That also marked Henry as a very versatile young man among the ladies.

No depth to this Cinderella-like tale (without the poverty). Just the blooming of a plain maid into a beautiful young woman, but interesting in a way because of that, and no doubt quite appealing to all women. Miss Davies seems to have a special appeal to women. If it's not direct it's a discussion as was heard at the Rivoli Sunday between a couple of girls near by, who talked it over whether Marion Davies is as beautiful as they say she is. It had not been decided by the time the picture ended, but that's the best kind of personal publicity.

Some of the captions carry laughs through glib comment, with the same spirit of the freshness of youth prevailing. "Beauty's Worth" is neither big nor small, but a first-class Marion Davies program release, and especially good for Miss Davies through her large part in it, the wholly capable support and the magnificent manner in which the picture has been produced. *Sime.*

WOMAN, WAKE UP

Anne Clegg................Florence Vidor
Monte Collins.............Louis Calhern
Henry Mortimer..........Charles Meredith

The domestic triangle here receives excellent comedy treatment, a welcome variation of the problem play or sex discussion, in which form the three-cornered story usually comes upon the screen. The picture stars Florence Vidor, with one of the best played parts she has had, and it put out by Associated Producers through Pathe.

In some respects the story employs many much used devices, but the screen treatment is neat and entertaining in spite of the threadbare theme of the quiet, timid wife who blossoms out into a wild woman in order to teach her husband a lesson. The thing has been done in countless vaudeville sketches, plays and stories and in this respect the elements of the tale are not promising, but it is handled in an agreeable vein of unaffected comedy and furnish capital screen material.

There is action all the time—whizzing automobiles, a couple of aeroplane flights, a trip in a speed boat and elaborate cabaret scenes. But the best feature is the humorous twist given to the triangle topic, and the other incidentals of skillful production merely serve to dress it up in attractive guise. Scenically the picture is notable. Much of the action takes place in a California bungalow, which furnishes some of the most attractive interiors. Marcus Harrison, the director, covers himself with credit for the composition of his stage pictures. The photography is conspicuously good.

There is some drama, but it always is developed trickily in order to supply a background for the play's humor. For example, the wife devotes her time to the Other Man, a family friend, in order to arouse the husband's jealousy, and by the breaking down of a motor boat is compelled to remain away from home all night. The furious husband and the family friend come together under circumstances which put the wife in a compromising position. Husband confronts them with a drawn revolver and wife falls into other man's arms, declaring he is the "man I love." Husband crumples up and departs stunned. The other man attempts to make love to the wife on the strength of her declaration and is rewarded with a hot blast of anger. She loves only her husband and made the speech to save him from committing a crime.

The film is full of Gallic drolleries of the same sort and the titling in this case is an aid to the amusing tangle with their crisp wit. There are passages in which padding has been done and a good deal of superfluous footage could be taken out to the betterment of the whole thing. The story properly reaches its climax in the scene just cited and should end soon thereafter. Instead the end is dragged out interminably. There are other cases of over-elaboration. Nevertheless it is a first-rate example of intelligent comedy.

There should be a field for this class of feature—a plausible story in high comedy vein away from the custard pie technique and at the same time a variation from the gosh-awful serious problem play. *Rush.*

THE ROSARY

Father Brian Kelly..........Lewis S. Stone
Vera Mather.................Jane Novak
Kenwood Wright............Wallace Beery
Bruce Wilton...............Robert Gordon
Widow Kathleen Wilton..Eugenie Besserer
Isaac Abrahamson............Dore Davidson
Donald MacTavisha.......Pomeroy Gannon
Captain Caleb Mather.........Bert Woodruff
Alice Wilton................Mildred June
Skeeters Martin.............Harold Goodwin

Col. Selig and Sam Rork combined forces and have remade "The Rosary" in feature length, issued by the First National. The original play by Edward E. Rose is utilized as the inspiration for the screen version, the work of Bernard McConville, while Jerome Storm directed the production.

It was presented last week at the Cameo, New York, for a week's run. Rather surprising this picture should have to go to the Cameo, when there is such a scarcity of real screen material for the regular Broadway houses. The title of "The Rosary" is rather old, but what of that? The present-day picturegoer scarcely recalls the old play as far as the big cities are concerned. In the smaller towns it is certain to be a hit for the reason those that have seen the play will go to see the picture.

It is wholesome as to story, well acted as to cast, with four names that can practically be starred, well handled in its direction, with photography that is as good as anyone could ask for.

What the picture does need is exploitation of the proper sort. It wasn't given that at the Cameo, consequently it did not draw, but nothing seems to draw at that house.

In the cast are Lewis S. Stone, Jane Novak, Wallace Beery and Robert Gordon as the foremost players. The supporting members all carry their roles well, and the entire cast is a happy selection.

In thrills the picture has a corking free for all fight, an explosion and fire scene, and a chase through a tremendous rain storm. All are well handled by Mr. Storm, whose direction carries the picture along with speed. It would have been an easy matter to let a rural drama of this sort sag, but the director has gotten away from this by cutting principally to quick flashes.

Stone as Father Kelley gave a well studied performance, while Miss Novak was altogether charming as the heroine. Beery handled the heavy in forceful manner, while the hero, by Robert Gordon, was satistory. Dore Davidson and Bert Woodruff in character roles scored with comedy effect, while Mildred June and Harold Goodwin carried on the secondary love interest nicely. *Fred.*

INVISIBLE FEAR

Louis B. Mayer puts out this Anita Stewart feature, played in Proctor's 23d Street without a first run showing in the major picture theatres on Broadway. It classifies distinctly as a second-class story with an appropriate production and a first-class star, the latter item depending upon how you regard the present standing of Anita Stewart with the screen public.

There can be no two ways of looking at the story. It is just rubbish, the kind of mechanical, obvious fiction that has its place in the cheapest magazines. It won't bear examination as a narrative, its dramatic devices are transparent and its people are foolish. You never are allowed to lose sight of the fact that this is mere make-believe, and all sense of illusion is lost. Just crude melodrama, all the cruder because it is dressed up and makes pretense to high import. What wonder that the players are stagey and theatrical! Sarah Bernhardt couldn't make the heroine a real person in this play.

The scheme has been to make a mystery with a surprise denouement, but it doesn't register because none of the people win the sympathy of the audience, and the solution of the mystery is obvious long before it is revealed. And when it is revealed it's only a fiction maker's contrivance. Altogether, a story not worth the effort of doing, and not well done on top of that.

The principal characters are: Arthur, blackguard; Randall, hero, and Sylvia, heroine. Sylvia and Randall are engaged, but Arthur finding himself alone with Sylvia in a remote hunting lodge, makes dishonorable love to her, and she fells him with a metal candlestick and leaves him for dead. She returns in a short time and finds the lodge burning and a man's body, seen indistinctly, in the midst of the fire. She returns home, keeping the whole affair, and in the course of time marries with the terror locked up in her heart.

She is now Mrs. Randall and hostess at a large party when Arthur, supposed to have been incinerated, turns up in the flesh. She greets him, chats with him, but continues to think he is a disembodied ghost, and in that belief is hypnotized by him to open her own safe while she is asleep (a Lady Macbeth sleep-walking scene here for pictorial purposes), and turns the jewels over to him. It takes a fearful lot of florid titles to get this over persuasively, and then it isn't convincing. Even so unsophisticated an audience as the 23d Street clientele giggled unresponsively.

Then it turns out by the confession of a Japanese valet that Arthur was not killed at all. While he was lying unconscious from the wallop from the candlestick the owner of the lodge happened along fortuitously to see who was occupying the place. The owner is the attorney who drew a new will by which Arthur's rich uncle disinherited him and Arthur had stolen the testament.

So Arthur kills the lawyer and sets fire to the lodge. He is about to take flight when the lawyer's Japanese butler appears and demands hush money. It was to finance these demands that Arthur tried to rob the safe, but Randall had detectives on the job, and they seized Arthur when he took the loot from Sylvia. It was then that the Jap spilled the story which comes on the screen as a fade-in. The thing doesn't knit together. In order to make it spectacular the conspirators pushed the lawyer's auto off a high bridge into a running brook to make it appear that his body had been lost. But the water is only about 50 feet wide and not deep enough to cover the overturned machine. You get the impression that the body couldn't have drifted out of sight.

Coincidences are always happening, and people are always so placed that they can overhear conversations which will get the playwright out of a tight place. The theatrical contraptions are childish. There is an enormous quality of unnecessary titling. Sylvia observes to her mother-in-law that she is to be married next week, and mother-in-law takes a whole title sheet to deliver herself of the following profound statement: "We shall never have the invitations out on time," which had not a thing to do with the proceedings.

The best thing about the picture was a horseback paper chase with an animated field of riders and a wealth of fine scenery. Here Miss Stewart, or a double (you couldn't tell which) did a remarkable fall from a running horse. *Rush.*

THE BIGAMIST

George Dare....................Guy Newall
Pamela Arnot....................Ivy Duke
Herbert Arnott...............Julian Royce
Richard Carruthers..A. Bromley Davenport
Constance Carruthers.........Dorothy Scott
Blanch Maitland.............Edith Ellison

R-C Pictures sponsors this made-in-England production credited to George A. Clark, Inc., and directed by Guy Newall, who also plays the hero. It's pretty poor stuff as to story, but it has beautiful scenic settings and its photography is splendid. Also it introduces to the American screen Ivy Duke, billed as "the world's most beautiful picture star." Miss Duke is lovely in a mature way and an actress worthy of a better vehicle.

"The Bigamist" is not a moving picture. Rather it is a story told in titles with screen action to illustrate the text. The whole narrative is disclosed by the printed word and the action is subordinated. The husband is seen to enter a room, chat with the wife for a string of footage and the titles blossom forth in 30-word gobs. Husband and wife, or husband and the Other Woman are revealed in earnest talk on a terrace overlooking a ravishing seashore view, and straightaway we have another lengthy flash of titles explaining what it is all about.

If you go to see a picture you want to see it in terms of film action. If you want to read you stay at home. This film could have been done almost as well with a stereopticon as far as screen action is concerned. This is the glaring defect, although the story itself is not an engaging one. The subject-matter opens up a very pertinent question that applies equally to mony of our American producers.

Why must the screen problem play degrade and debase all romance? Why must it do violence to every concept of ethics and good conduct? Here we have two couples, the supposed husband and wife on one side and the governess of their children and a young man friend on the other. Here might be the groundwork of a clean, simple, romantic story, properly ending in the bringing together of the unmarried pair and the satisfactory straightening out of the affairs of the supposed married couple after they had passed through the discovery that the husband had a previous wife still living.

Instead of that the wife trembles on the brink of a liaison with the young hero and is saved from moral lapse by accident rather than her own virtue, while the husband deliberately lays siege to the governess and is unconvincingly prevented from carrying out his designs by an accident which sends him to the hospital after he has run away from a disagreeable domestic situation. In the end the governess, described as a young woman of fine family but reduced estate, takes up her life in a low resort in Paris and the husband (the first wife having conveniently died) reweds the mother of his children in a legal way. The hero just walks out of the picture, regretted only by the heroine, who goes back to her husband unwillingly under compulsion of her children's welfare.

If that isn't poetic justice flat on its back, John Milton was a comic jazz songwriter.

Why will these producers pick stories written by bilious complainers against society? Courageous, successful romance is the most interesting and widest subject in the world and a cynical, sophisticated pose is the most boresome. These cynical pretenders who deal in anti-romance hold the shallow idea that romance necessarily deals with calf-love. They should study a few plays like "The Circle," which is romance itself under a camouflage of smart cynicism. *Rush.*

HILLS OF MISSING MEN

The Dragon................J. P. McGowan
Crando..........................Jean Perry
Li Fung.......................James Wang
Bandini....................Charles Brindley
Buck Allis..................Andrew Waldron
Hilma Allis................Florence Gilbert
Amy Allis....................Helen Holmes

The Associated Exhibitors released "Hills of Missing Men," a Playgoers Production, through Pathe. The picture is a fair western which has J. P. McGowan as star and director, supported by Helen Holmes and a fairly good cast. The story and continuity are by John B. Clymer, and the screen version tends to the belief there must have been much more of an idea behind the tale than what is shown.

As it stands at present there is a dreamer in the person of Crando who is recruiting a force of men to take over lower California and establish an empire with himself as the ruler. He is lining up ex-service men in his army and recruiting a number of daredevils from the bandit gangs in the west. He hears a noted bandit, known as The Dragon, has been worsted with the forces of the law. While his men were annihilated the leader is supposed to have escaped. He arranges a welcome for the bandit in the event he should appear at his stronghold. The Dragon does come and is disclosed as a secret service agent of the government. In his finish the entire scheme of Crando is exploded by the arrival of the U. S. Cavalry.

There is a love element through the story. Two sisters are involved. The elder is in love with Crando, who returns her affection until the arrival of her younger sister from the east. Then he wants the other girl. She prefers the bandit, Dragon. Her sister upbraids her for this but she remains true, although tipped off later he is really not what he seems.

Several corking fights with McGowan battling with three or four on each occasion. Also a quantity of gun powder burnt, reminding one of the old war pictures. The battle stuff is fairly well handled and has a thrill.

McGowan impresses in the heroic and Miss Holmes still retains a decided ingenuish appearance as she did in the days of the red-light railroad pictures. Jean Perry played Crando with something like a cross between Valentino and Lew Stone, the result being a fairly good heavy.

The picture is evidently designed for the cheaper houses where it will entertain and get some money. Loew played it at the New York last week as part of a double bill, with a strong Metro feature accompanying it. *Fred.*

THE BEAR CAT

The Singing Kid...............Hoot Gibson
Alys May.......................Lillian Rich

A Universal western with Hoot Gibson as the star. It was one of the features of a double bill at Loew's New York this week, doubling with "I Can Explain," a Metro release. Not a particularly strong feature, there being no new twists to the story. Edward Sedgwick, who directed the story, might well, if he continues to work with Mr. Gibson, try to curb the star's longing for close-ups. Too many of them in this production slow the picture to such an extent that one tires of it.

Gibson plays the role of a "bad man" who reforms. He wanders into a small American border town where he is informed by the sheriff that if he is going to stick around he wants to make up his mind to behave himself. Just then a runaway team dashes by with a girl in the rig and the bad man is off to the rescue. Of course it is the daughter of the local cattle baron and the hero gets a job on the ranch for saving her from injury.

The girl is engaged to a college chap from the east who has been a regular visitor during the summers, but visiting wasn't all that he did. There was a girl in the neighboring town that h was mixed up with and as she is in with a fellow who has blackmailing ideas they start to shake the boy down. Of course the Singing Kid gets wise to the game, but just about at the time that he can spill the beans he is accused of a shooting affray, and then a chase starts that lasts through about the two final reels, with the Singing Kid being wounded and cleared of suspicion in time for a close-up in the arms of Miss Cattle Baron.

Lillian Rich plays opposite Gibson, and as good as she was in a Harry Carey picture, reviewed elsewhere in this issue, she is bad in this. It must have been a matter of direction more than anything else, for with Carey she was very good indeed.

Fred.

TRACKED TO EARTH

Charles Cranner..................Frank Mayo
Anna Jones..................Virginia Valli
Stub Lou Tate..................Duke R. Lee
Shorty Fuller..................Buck Conners
Zed White..................Percy Gallagher
Dick Jones..................Harold Goodwin

An interesting and amusing comedy drama is "Tracked to Earth" (Universal), starring Frank Mayo, made into a scenario by Wallace Clifton from William J. Neidig's story in the "Saturday Evening Post." William Worthington directed.

The evidence accumulates that the screen has to resort to published fiction for its best material. In this case, as in four cases out of five, the story that has been revised by a magazine editor is better than the stuff created originally for the screen. That observation goes double for stage creations that have the stamp of production. The satisfactory original scenario is a rarity. There must be a reason for the fact that the screen is not self sufficient. Maybe starvation prices for scripts have something to do with it—maybe.

Here we have a plausible western adventure tale with riding, conflict and romance, all handled in a spirit of comedy and free from the pompous melodrama heroics that are the curse of average westerns. The comedy grows naturally out of the tale and is not in the travesty style so much in vogue since Marshall Neilan set pace in "The Lotus Eaters." This story has a capital novelty device. Part of the amusing little love story develops while the hero is buried up to the chin in the sands of the southwestern desert as a posse is hunting him nearby, intent upon lynching him for what has all the appearance of horse stealing. Here is a situation rich in comedy possibilities.

It turns out in the end that the supposed horse thief was really a railroad detective who lifted the horses of a band of train robbers in order to keep them helpless until they could be arrested. But in the meantime he is hard pressed to keep out of the hands of the outlaws and so digs in up to the chin, hiding his head behind a tumbleweed bush held in his mouth. In this helpless situation he is discovered by a rancher's daughter, who falls in love with his droll courage, although up to the end she continues to think him a criminal. However, she feeds him and brings about his rescue ingeniously when the bandits are about to run down his grave-like hiding place with dogs. Also she gives him her own horse and by means of the fresh mount he is able to escape during the night and bring back the marshal and his deputies, so that when he walks into the outlaws' hands the authorities are within reach and close in upon the bandits for a happy ending. *Rush.*

BOBBED HAIR

What Hector Turnbull may have written as a satire on verse libre poseurs and Greenwich Village nuts generally turns out a crude burlesque in this Realart-Paramount feature screened at the New York and starring Wanda Hawley. It's exceedingly thin material to spread over five reels. As a comedy it is not amusing enough to warrant first run honors in a first class house and it is too indefinite in its humor for the neighborhood theatre where comedy of a more robust quality is in demand.

It is the substance of Gilbert and Sullivan's "Patience," but Turnbull is no Gilbert. His creation of a 1922 model Bunthorne is rather a heavy-handed whimsy in the first place, and Harvey Thew's scenario doesn't improve it much, probably for the reason that the screen is no medium for the dramatization of such a subject. There is no real fun in the action, the only laughs coming from the titling.

The principal interest of the picture is in the pretty seashore scenes, in which most of the story is enacted. The action itself is a weary waste. The heroine is a lovesick, moon-struck girl who resents the matter-of-fact wooing of a rich young bonehead and runs away to a settlement of artists and other untrammeled souls, there to seek freedom and self-expression. She falls in with a sinister cubist poet, who wears Greek classic draperies and has a wife and two children.

He lures her to his house and is making dishonorable love to her when the wife returns unexpectedly and threatens to sue for divorce, naming the heroine as corespondent. In this dilemma the young sweetheart arrives, beats up the poet, and after reproaching the heroine is about to turn his back upon her for good when a girl friend brings them together for the happy ending. Justice is meted out to the poet when the wife rolls up her sleeves and wades into him.

It's all very dull. Nothing happens for hundreds of feet. Properly speaking, the story is over when the vicious Bunthorne is stretched on the floor by the hero's good right arm, but it must have taken half a reel to cover the anti-climax before the picture flickered out. That much footage was pure waste. The trouble is there is nothing to scale the burlesque against. The girl is plain fool; her young man suitor a flat head (by the way, this is the first picture on record that tries to glorify the tired business man type) and the other people of the cast are quite as removed from human sympathy.

Why devote 5,000 feet of perfectly good celluloid and something like an hour and ten minutes of precious time to the exploitation of the entirely indifferent doings of absolutely uninteresting epople? There isn't a genuine laugh in the whole proceedings. *Rush.*

MAN TO MAN

Steve Packard..................Harry Carey
Cahela..................May Giraci
Blenham..................Charles LeMoyne
Bill Royce..................Willis Robards
"Hellfire" Packard..................Alfred Allen
Terry Temple..................Lillian Rich
Yellow Barbee..................Harold Goodwin

This may be a suggestion that the U might use to pull themselves out of the hole on their lease of the Central—that is considering the Central proposition from the standpoint of straight show business and passing up the angle that the Universal can write off so much a week against the house for advertising.

Why not make it a real house of film novelty? Devote it entirely to westerns or some particular brand of features quite as different. The U cannot turn out a sufficient number of westerns to keep the house supplied, but there are others producing westerns that would be tickled to have an opportunity to show on Broadway in a theatre that specialized. All westerns, nothing else, except possibly a news weekly and let the house work on a grind. For ballyhoo for the first month or two a regular real western atmosphere out front ponies, lariat throwers, etc., and on the stage (as far as it is practicable) a rodeo.

There is no reason why a house of thrills for filmdom should not be established. The Grand Guignol of Paris is the sight-seers mecca because of thrills. What can furnish more thrills than films and the line "The House of Thrills" is submitted to Will Page and Bob Cochrane for what it will bring in at the box office with the usual picture percentage as the reviewer's rakeoff. Royalty on the idea for all westerns is hereby written off, because the Universal won't use it anyway.

Can you, with a little stretch of imagination, picture the Central as the only house on Broadway where as first run you could see Harry Carey, Tox Mix, Will Rogers, William Russell, Buck Jones, Dustin Farnum, Art Acord, Hoot Gibson and atop of all these, isn't it quite a chance that Douglas Fairbanks in "The Virginian" might be a possibility for a house that is all western?

"Man to Man" with Harry Carey as the star of the production is a Universal. U has lost Carey who is now going to Robertson-Cole. Harry Carey proved himself something different at the Central when "Man to Man" opened there on Monday night.

The picture is first and foremost a western. "Westerns" made pictures to a great extent when it was a baby in swaddling clothes. If that was what the public wanted a dozen, ten or eight years ago why doesn't it stand to reason it is what they want now. Tastes in amusements move in cycles (but the picture industry may be too young to realize that or take note of it) but the legitimate stage and its producers are fully aware of it and that is why there is ever again a reversion to type in the spoken drama and then someone says "why didn't I think of that."

"Man to Man" has a combination of South Sea Islands in it at the opening. The South Sea thing doesn't mean a darn except it lends atmosphere. Carey is a derelict on a South Sea isle, loving his liquor. There is planted in a title the fact he did a bit to save his father from jail, and when he stumbles up to the bar and sees a letter addressed to him, conveying the news his dad has died and that he is wanted back in the States to protect his own interests, he steps into the breech like a man. There are circumstances that make it difficult for him as the script was originally laid out, but in the making they are handled in such manner as to wipe them out without ever referring to them again, although they might have been made much of for love suspense.

He returns, manages to beat a hard-hearted old grandfather who believes him a crook and finally wins the girl of his heart. There is horsemanship, a couple of fights and a corking steer stampede in the story and Carey stands out as a million dollar bet in all of them. Atop of that Lillian Rich as a leading ingenue scores one hundred cents on the dollar, although she hasn't any too much to do. It might be a good idea for Carey to carry her with him wherever he goes for the girl is "there" when it comes to working opposite him.

In the cast are a couple of others most worthy of notice, namely Charles LeMoyne who plays the heavy and "mixes" with Carey in about five fights, and Alfred Allen as the stern old grandfather.

The fights named together with a cattle stampede (not as well done as one that was offered by Metro two years or so ago) were the real features of the picture. However, **it is a western with guts and after all that is what counts.**

Stuart Paton is credited with the direction and while there doesn't seem to be anything that a director can do to get a story or ordinary calibre over as far as western material is concerned, Mr. Paton nevertheless made this one interesting. *Fred.*

BENITOU

Paris, March 15.

The novel of Marie Thiery has been screened by A. Durec for the Eclipse Co., and recently tradeshowed here. Benitou occupies roughly 4,500 feet of film photographed by Emile Pierre and featuring Elluere, Jose Davert and Mlle. Solange Vlaminck. The work is good and the picture interests. Prosper, a young farmer, lives alone with his faithful man-servant, Benitou, long with his parents, now dead. He eventually engages a pretty young housekeeper and falls in love, proposing marriage. Benitou opposes the union, and to demonstrate his authority submits proof that he is Prosper's father. Enraged, the gentleman farmer destroys the proof of his mother's shame and turns the old man out of the home so that he may marry his new housekeeper.

The sets are in the Pyrenees and quite picturesque, which redeems certain shortcomings in Durec's production. *Kendrew.*

THE WITCHES

That seemingly is the title of a nine-reel picture brought here from Denmark. It purports to be a history of witchcraft among the ancients and the practice of sorcery in the dark ages.

In its present shape there doesn't seem any chance for the production, but it is possible that on a scientific basis it may be made valuable with the proper cutting and titling. There would, however, have to be a large number of eliminations from the present picture.

Whoever made the production spent a great deal of time in research work, going back a thousand years at least in witchcraft. Illustrations from old volumes and translations of the text of ancient writings are disclosed. The period of belief that witches were the concubines of the devil is extensively gone into, together with the days when the church in Germany was arrayed against witchcraft and conducted an inquisition against them. The trials and the tortures that the accused were subjected to and the punishment meted out are graphically portrayed.

There are many touches of a horrible and revolting nature shown, and nudity is thought nothing of from time to time in the picture, but withal there is something really gripping even as it now stands.

Whether it could ever be developed into a straight box office winner is something of a question, but there is no doubt that the picture, if with certain eliminations it could pass the censors, would prove a sensation for those in search of morbid thrills. *Fred.*

PARDON MY NERVE

Straightaway western action story with Charles "Buck" Jones, issued by Fox. The story is by W. P. White and direction by Reaves Eason. Altogether an interesting picture with its swirl of galloping horses, fine out-of-doors backgrounds and a couple of first-rate man-to-man fist fights. Besides which it has a well-told plot involving the unravelling of a detective tangle neatly and interestingly. The love motif is neatly woven into the melodrama.

This sort of unpretentious, candid fiction is infinitely better than the foggy problem play, with all its bunk of intellectual appeal (which usually turns out to be nothing more than sex exploitation) and pose of uplift. It delivers the diversion of a super dime novel. It has no other purpose than passing the time, but it doesn't leave a nasty taste.

"Pardon My Nerve" (the meaningless title is the worst thing about the feature) tells the story of a cowboy-drifter who breezes into a boom town in his journeyings from job to job. The pet dog of one of the dancehall girls snaps at one of the political bosses of the place, known as Nevada, and when it is kicked takes refuge under the protection of Racey Dawson (Jones). The bad man's pursuit of the pup brings him into a clash with Racey and a feud starts.

Nevada and an accomplice named McFluke are scheming to cheat a neighboring rancher out of his property, and Racey sets himself to defeat their purpose. In the course of this plan he is required to subdue McFluke in a fistic combat, made into a lively set-to, ending when the bad man is knocked out and left senseless. On Racey's departure the other conspirators murder McFluke as he lies helpless, and Racey is charged with the crime.

How justice is brought home to the really guilty man, how the same dog is made the instrument of detection and how Racey is exonerated make an absorbing film chapter that it would be unfair to reveal in advance. Thereafter Racey's intrigue to defeat the schemes of the crooks in cowboy style makes a thrilling climax, full of action. In addition to its hearty drama the picture has an engaging quality of natural humor, effective and unforced.

A curious little break happens. At the outset certain screen titles make it clear that it all takes place in the early western days "When men traveled by saddle instead of automobile," but near the end of a legal paper upon which the plot hangs is dated Jan. 14, 1922. The costumes are all modern, while the saloon business obviously antedates Volstead. Just a slip of the titler's pen in a generally excellent program release. *Rush.*

I CAN EXPLAIN

Jimmy Berry.................Gareth Hughes
Betty Carson................Bartine Burkett
Dorothy Dawson............Grace Darmond
Howard Dawson.............Herbert Hayes
Will Potter....................Victor Potel
Uncle Henry ....Nelson McDowell
Juan Pedro Gardez........Edward Wallock
Carmencita Gardez............Tina Modotti

This is an S.-L. production released through Metro. It has Gareth Hughes as the star, directed by George D. Baker. The story is by Edgar Franklin, who tried to construct something for the star that would establish him on the screen as the same type of light comedian that Willie Collier is on the stage. If it is the intention of those back of Mr. Hughes in this film venture to make him a screen type Collier they might well stop right where they are. Mr. Hughes will not land in this type of work. He is totally unsuited for it in many ways, and his greatest appeal is in roles that have more of the heavier touch of dramatics. Hughes is playing a young business man in partnership with a chap who is married and insanely jealous of his wife. That his young partner and the wife have a number of secret meetings enrages him, and he starts out with a gun. It is explained to him, however, that the meetings were of a business nature to help him out, and the legal papers are on deck to prove it. Later a complication arises that starts his suspicions anew and he decides to take his partner to New York and place him in charge of the firm's office there while he takes a trip to South America to establish a branch. At the last minute he plans to kidnap the partner and take him along, compelling him finally to stay in South America and look after the firm's interests there.

The wife, believing that her husband was sailing alone, decides that she will take the trip and disclose herself once they are at sea and square the row with her husband. This leads to further complications on board ship. In South America a series of comedy situations brings the realization of self-confidence in the younger partner, and he decides

to become aggressive instead of an "explainer," and begins to turn the tables on those that have been browbeating him. In this he is finally successful, returning home in time to discover that the girl that he was to marry is about to be joined in wedlock to another. He breaks up the ceremony and walks off with all the honors.

The continuity is rather badly done and the tale itself seems highly improbable, although for farce there are some things that are fairly allowable. Perhaps a player other than Mr. Hughes would have managed to get away with it, but as it stands at present it cannot be termed even a fair program picture. There are, however, a number of laughs in the picture that are secured by Keystoning to a certain extent.

Fred.

PAY DAY

The Toiler ....Charles Chaplin
His Wife......................Phyllis Allen
The Foreman.....................Mark Swain
The Foreman's Daughter.......Edna Purviance
A Mere Friend ....Sydney Chaplin

The next to final Charles Chaplin comedy to be made for First National is in Broadway first run at the strand. It is a two-reeler, in which Chaplin has incorporated revamped versions of many bits of business he has done in previous pictures. However, it is a corking two-reeler, but hardly enough to be played in lieu of a feature, as was done at the Strand this week.

Incidentally, he has also cleaned up his make-up somewhat. That may be a reaction from his last production, "The Idle Class," in which he was quite the dandy.

In this production he is a day laborer on a construction job. His first appearance is as a late arrival for work, and he slips the burly foreman a lily with a sweet little gesture. His first laugh comes with working in the ditch when he plants his pick in the stern of a fellow worker. From that point on his laughs come mostly through the employment of a hod elevator during the lunch hour, Charlie getting a free meal through the ups and downs of the contrivance.

When Saturday arrives he draws his pay and gets a few laughs out of the inability to figure correctly. Outside the job his wife is waiting, and Charlie figures a hold-out on the dough; but she catches him at it, and in a clever money-changing bit he manages to come off the victor.

After that the exterior of a saloon is shown with the workmen emerging after they have had their regular Saturday night spree. The barber-shopping takes place right outside the door, with the usual water thrown from above result. The breaking up of the part and a couple of bits with Charlie trying to board a trolley car are quite the funniest things in the picture.

For the wallop laugh toward the end he is employing the old gag where the husband is about to retire in the early hours and the alarm goes off, wakes the wife, and he gives her the impression that in reality he is just getting up. That was put over cleverly; but from that point on there wasn't much to the finish. Chaplin did some bathroom stuff, falling in a tub of water filled with soiled clothes and the final fade-out had him standing at a radiator in his undies trying to dry out.

In his support he has Edna Purviance, who plays but a small bit in the early section of the picture; his brother Sydney, who does a couple of bits with Chaplin in the drunk stuff with more or less of an "Ole Bill" moustache. Neither of these two has anything to speak of in the picture. Mack Swain as the foreman of the job manages to put over a couple of clever bits in the first reel, while Phyllis Allen as the wife got her share of laughs in the final reel. The picture runs 22 minutes. *Fred.*

YOUR BEST FRIEND

Esther Myers..................Vera Gordon
Robert, her eldest son......Harry Benham
Harry, her youngest son......Stanley Price
Aida, Robert's wife..........Belle Bennett
Her Mother...................Beth Mason
Morris, the family bookkeeper.......
......................Dore Davidson

A sure-fire hit from the box office standpoint that is bound to stand with the other winners that William Nigh has written and directed in the past. It is a Harry Rapf production released in the independent market by the Warner Bros. The picture was presented in the Grand Ballroom of the Astor at a special showing Monday night. The presentation was under the direction of Rapf, who provided the picture with

a brief prolog. The prolog and musical theme seemed to slow the picture to a certain extent as far as the first couple of reels were concerned. The production is about 6,600 feet at present, but it will be cut somewhat to speed up the earlier portion. That is the only criticism that is to be found. Vera Gordon is the star, and has playing opposite her Dore Davidson in the role of a faithful old family employe. He shares honors with the star to a certain extent.

Miss Gordon has another role of the type that made her famous in 'Humoresque.' It is one of those Jewish mother love stories, where the older generation strives for years so that their offspring may have ever, advantage, only to find that the youngsters take everything for granted and spread their wings and fly from those who provided for them in the early youth.

Miss Gordon as the self-sacrificing mother has a role such as she seems best suited to and the type that she has made stand up on the screen. But as a mother of this type she is in the foremost rank of those on the screen.

She rears two boys after the death of her husband. Sends one through law school, and at the opening of the story he is returning home after being made a partner in a law firm. He brings his wife and mother-in-law (two women of the advanced type) with him. They have decided that a home in a fashionable part of the town where they can entertain is the proper caper, and also that the mother is to live with them. Taken from the East Side to West End avenue, the mother proves to be a fifth wheel.

Finally when a crisis arrives in the family affairs the mother discloses the fact that she was the one that kept the expensive home going. She returns to the East Side, where finally the regeneration of the young wife is brought about, her mother, however, marrying a male butterfly and continuing on her way.

The story is full of heart throbs, and Nigh's direction is on a par with the story. He carries his theme along naturally, although he must have had something of a struggle to overcome the tendency to slow down the tempo of the action on the part of the star.

Belle Bennett, who is now playing the role Hazel Dawn originated in "The Demi-Virgin," plays the younger wife. She is a particularly striking blonde, and portrays the easily led young wife to perfection. But Beth Mason, who enacts the role of her mother, is a distinct find as a type. She managed to endow her role with an atmosphere that was apparent the moment she stepped before the camera in her first scene. Harry Benham plays the role of the older son nicely, while Stanley Price is the younger brother. Dore Davidson provided much of the comedy in the picture and at all times held his audience.

The production is nicely done, and the added Prizma color titles are effective. The picture looks like a $100,000 special. *Fred.*

THE RED PEACOCK

Violette ....Pola Negri
Alfred Germont....................No name
Clara Germont.....................No name
Mr. Germont.....................No name
Gaston Roy ....No name
Flora Lavelle ....No name
Count Girey ....No name
Violette's father ....No name

This U. F. A. production (Paramount feature) is current at the Rivoli. As with all Pola Negri starring productions made abroad, the Hamilton Theatrical Corp. (the F. P. L. subsidiary) "presents." This makes about the fifth or sixth of Miss Negri's pictures to reach Broadway for premier presentations and as has been commented on before, the brunette German star has yet to make a picture that will not suffer in comparison to her "Passion," the first foreign film to bring Miss Negri to the attention of American film fans.

Paul Stein directed from a story by Hanns Kraly originally titled "Poor Violette." Stein will not worry our domestic megaphone wielders to any great extent if this is a sample of his film product. Taking a story that winds up with a "Camille" fade-out (the heroine expiring from a racking cough, in her lover's arms) he has drawn out the theme unnecessarily, the audience at any time expecting its conclusion only to find a new sub-plot developing. It really does not begin to interest until the last half. At the beginning it gave rise to audible giggling, the business really hinting of travesty rather than realism. Some of the characters' "heavy dramatic" histrionics have been lampooned too broadly and extensively in America to command serious attention.

Violette (Pola Negri) has many affairs with her various benefactors. Rising from humble estate, first as a flower girl and then as a lady's maid, she is seen accepting the attentions and mundane assistance of Count Girey, a roue. After being discharged by Florette, her first mistress, the count takes her into his home for the night, offering temporary shelter and the position of maid in his household. The next fade-in finds Violette breakfasting in negligee with the count and being waited on by the butler. She is the peers' constant companion thereafter, mingling with his friends. Plainly she is his mistress, a relation which is not in keeping with the honorable love of Alfred Germont for the erstwhile flower girl. To recount the plot would uncover similar inconsistencies which raises wonder how the titler and editor overlooked them.

Famous Players has been trying some radical experiments at the Rivoli and Rialto houses of late. First it was that mediocre serial importation. Now it is the Pola Negri pictures. No doubt, at the current rate of exchange, F. P. L. must be paying very few real American dollars comparatively for these pictures and obviously the gain is attractive enough to warrant an attempt to force the market. But it looks like an uncertain undertaking. The audience giggled and tittered not once or twice but many times at some of the business.

"Passion" gripped on several points. Its stupendous mob stuff was an outstanding feature. None of this is present here. It is poor stuff as a society drama; men and women in evening clothes, with the women, as far as pulchritude is concerned, presenting decidedly unattractive appearance. The men on the contrary are convincing although the male lead at times also essays histrionics of a trite sort. The two hale heavies were adequate and compare favorably to the American conception of a society villain.

The production is handsomely mounted with evidently no restriction on the bankroll although Director Stein has a choppy, abrupt style of full-flashing the scenes and immediately thereafter irising-in the close-ups. It made for a ragged continuity and can easily be elided through the cutting of the introductory set flashes.

The star's personality in the dramatic scenes counts for not a little in distinguishing her, although, truth to tell, the native fan seems to prefer a "sweet 'n pretty" heroine to the other kind. *Abel.*

MAN FROM BEYOND

Star, Harry Houdini. Story by Houdini. Adaptation by Coolidge Streeter. Direction Burton King. Produced by Houdini Picture Corp.

The Man from Beyond............Houdini
Dr. Gilbert Trent............Arthur Maude
Dr. Crawford Strange.....Albert Tavernier
Dr. Gregory Sinclair........Erwin Connelly
Francois Duval...........Frank Montgomery
Captain of the barkentine....Louis Alberni
Milt Norcross................Yale Benner
Felice Strange..............Jane Connelly
Felice Norcross..............Jane Connelly
Marie LeGrande................Nita Naldi

This new production by the handcuff king had its first presentation at the Times Square Sunday night, the box-office scale being topped at $2.20. It is a five-reeler of about the grade of a serial built along lines of candid melodrama, but aspiring to higher appeal through its spiritual import, which deals in a rather stumbling way with the problem of the hereafter. The two things don't go together.

Taken as a frank melodrama it has a whale of a punch. Houdini does a sensational rescue of the heroine in the Niagara rapids, and it has a kick that would carry any audience with it independent of the rest of the footage. It is a veritable whale of a stunt and would have made the picture if the surrounding story had backed it up and led to it properly. The trouble is that the presumption of high literary meaning in the rest of the story is all bosh. So the net effect is pretty unsatisfactory. Serial melodrama and screen uplift won't mix, and disaster confronts anybody that tries the impossible.

The picture is offered as half of an entire evening's entertainment, the second half being a series of illusions and escapes by Houdini. Sunday night the illusionist did his needle-threading feat, a splendid bit of legerdemain; a cabinet disappearance with a girl, his straight-jacket escape and, finally, the Disappearing Elephant as the climax. The last-named is substantially the same as that performed at the New York Hippodrome, and makes an effective display—better in the small theatre than on the hugh Hippodrome stage.

There may be a grade of film fans that will take "The Man from Beyond" seriously, but the experience of "The Mistress of the World" leads one to the opinion that it won't do for Broadway. The story is raw melodrama. It opens in the arctic north, where a frozen explorer comes upon the ship of a former expedition ice locked for 100 years. Search of the wreck reveals the figure of a man frozen in a block of ice for a century. Simply as an illusion the passage here had a certain shocking realism. The scientist chops the figure out of its gelid casing, and the figure, in the person of Houdini, comes to life.

The scientist brings him to civilization as a discovery. It appears that the Man from Beyond had loved a maid in his former life, and when he is presented at the home of the scientist a wedding is going on. Who should the bride be but a reincarnation of the former sweetheart, and the Man from Beyond claims her, in spite of the protests of the bridegroom, one Dr. Trent.

Here's where the serial stuff starts. They send the Man from Beyond to the insane asylum, while Trent abducts the bride's father and locks him up in a rat-infested dungeon. Houdini escape from confinement, and the complicated rescue of the girl's father begins, piling wild melodrama upon wild melodrama until reason reels and totters. The end is the conventional embrace of Houdini and the heroine. One looked for some switch to make it all appear somebody's welsh rarebit dream, but the story stood "as is," without attempt to alibi.

It's a great pity that heroic swim by Houdini through the rapids couldn't have been a part of a more satisfactory picture. It is a true thriller. *Rush.*

SISTERS

Alix Strickland..................Seena Owen
Cherry Strickland..............Gladys Leslie
Anna Little..................Mildred Arden
Peter Joyce....................Matt Moore
Martin Lloyd......................Joe King
Dr. Strickland...................Tom Guise
Justin Little................Robert Schable
Colored Mammy..............Frances Grant
Colored Servant................Fred Miller

"Sisters" is the first International Film Service Corp. production the American Releasing Corp. has marketed. The production was secured some months ago from the Hearst interests and this week it opened at the Cameo theatre for a two weeks' stay. A strong advertising campaign with the serial story also running in the Evening Journal gave indications that the Cameo would have the best week's business in its short history with this picture. "Sisters" is a screen version of the novel by Kathleen Norris, produced under the direction of Albert Capellani, and it has three names in the cast that are worthy of featuring—Seena Owen, Matt Moore and Gladys Leslie.

The picture from the standpoint of story, cast, photography and editing is as good as any that has been seen on Broadway in weeks. It is well acted and the interest, even though the production is seven reels in length, never lags. It has a strong sex appeal and an absorbing situation. Two sisters living in one house and both in love with the same man, one of them being married to him and he believing himself to be in love with the other, is plenty wallop.

Seena Owen plays the role of the unloved wife, giving a worthy performance. She is a charming little actress and gets her points across with a punch. Gladys Leslie is the younger sister who almost succeeds in stealing the husband, while Joe King plays the husband.

A couple of minor roles are well played by Mildred Arden and Robert Schable, while two darky servant bits fall to Frances Grant and Fred Miller.

The direction of Capellani holds the story at an even pace, with lots of action making for interest. There are a couple of moments that might be considered slightly draggy, but on the whole the picture has been edited perfectly.

"Sisters" with a smash of advertising behind it is certain to be a box office winner. *Fred.*

MAN UNDER COVER

Paul Porter.............Herbert Rawlinson
Daddy Moffat.............George Hernandez
Mayor Harper............Wm. Courtwright
Jones Wiley..................George Webb
"Coal Oil" Chase..................Ed. Tilton
Holt Langdon.....................Gerald Pring
Margaret Langdon........Barbara Bedford
Col. Culpepper....................Willis Marks
The Kiddies.....Helen Stone, Betty Eliason

Herbert Rawlinson is the star of this Universal, which is released under that company's brand name of "special attraction." It is a crook story with the principal action laid in the oil fields, with the star giving a corking clean-cut performance as the reformed crook. The picture is an interesting picturization of a homely tale that is strong enough to stand on its own in the majority of daily change of program houses, although it was shown last week at Loew's New York as part of a double feature bill.

The story is by Louis Victor Eytinge, a "lifer" in the Arizona State Penitentiary. Harvey Gates provided the script and Tod Browning directed the production. All three contribute materially to the success of the tale.

Rawlinson has the role of a one-time crook, who with his pal played by George Hernandez, returns to his home town to find the cashier of the bank, a former intimate, in a jam and needing $25,000 to cover up a shortage in his accounts. The two plan to crack the safe of the bank to make it appear that the shortage occurred through crooks getting in. When they arrive, they see the cashier has beaten them to it and committed suicide. Then they make it appear that the bank has been "turned off" and the cashier has lost his life defending the property.

The younger crook decides to go straight and carries his pal with him. He buys the local newspaper from the dead man's sister and proceeds to operate it. Later he discovers that a couple of blue sky promoters are shoving oil stock in the town and collecting thousands of dollars. He frames a phoney well and gusher, gets the fakers to buy him out for all the dough that they have collected and run them out of town, returning the money to the victims and incidentally winning the girl from whom he bought the paper.

It is a well told film tale, full of interest and action and well handed as to direction.

In the cast supporting Rawlinson, Barbara Bedford has the lead and gives a winsome performance. Two heavies, enacted by George Webb and Edward Tilton, are also well drawn characters. Willis Marks in a character role manages to fill the picture nicely. An unnamed girl doing a "fat girl" bit comes in for the laughs at the finish of the picture. *Fred.*

RECKLESS YOUTH

Alice Schulyer.........Elaine Hammerstein
John Carmen....................Niles Welch
Mrs. Schuyler-Foster.......Myrtle Stedman
Mr. Schuyler-Foster....Robert Lee Keeling
Harrison Thornby..............Huntley Gordon
Mrs. Dahlgren...............Louise Prussing
Cumberland Whipple.........Frank Currier
Martha Whipple...............Kate Cherry
Chorus Girl..............Constance Bennett

Here is a corking box office title, coupled with the name of a well-known and liked star, a famous author who produced a worth while story, yet the result on the screen is a story that has been hurt through the tempo of its direction. It is draggy and wearisome to an extreme.

"Reckless Youth" is a Selznick production and has Elaine Hammerstein as the star. The story is from the pen of Cosmo Hamilton while Edward J. Montague provided the scenario. The direction was in the hands of Ralph Ince.

The story purports to show that suppressed desires in youth ofttimes lead the victim to eccentric behavior as an outlet for emotion. Miss Hammerstein has the role of the heroine, who is an orphaned child in the care of her grandparents, a pair of decaying aristocrats who are soured on the world at large because oncoming years have compelled them to cease their lives of social activity. They live in a prison like country place and when the girl arrives there after having been expelled from a convent school because of a slight infraction of the rules, the old people decide to teach her a lesson by holding her in seclusion. The result is the child runs away and marries the first man that she meets, luckily for her a well bred young chap with considerable of a fortune.

However, the girl undertakes the marriage simply as a means to freedom from her grandparents, and without any sense of the responsibilities that the step entails. The result is that in leading a butterfly existence she and her husband become estranged and she very nearly falls a victim to a he vamp. In the end, however, she and the husband are reconciled and all ends hapily.

Miss Hammerstein makes a charming heroine and Niles Welch as her leading man is of the type that fits perfectly in pictures. He is handling himself in the last few pictures with greater ease than heretofore. A bit played by Constance

Bennett stands out. She is a hick chorus girl type that figures for a moment in the story in a manner that gives the audience a thrill. She was in an auto accident and accompanied the hero-husband to his country place while the wife was in the city. It is inferred that they spent the night there with the hero sleeping on the sofa while the girl used his sleeping quarters. Her opening speech the morning after is "What an oil can you turned out to be."

"Reckless Youth," however, is at its best just a fair program production. *Fred.*

THE INTRIGUE

It becomes apparent why this Pola Negri five-reeler was not introduced via the usual medium of one of the leading week-stand Broadway houses and offered instead at the New York for a single day on its first run.

The picture, sponsored by Commonwealth and distributed by Howells Picture Sales Co., Inc., is pretty poor stuff. Even in the quality of its photographic work it belongs in the period of ten years ago. The pictures are flat black and white in great gobs of each, without intermediate toning.

The star, who under the best of treatment gives no effect of nymph-like youth, here becomes a hard-faced middle aged woman due to the atrocious photography and the backgrounds are spoiled in the same way. At this late day the least the fans can expect is decent workmanship from the cameraman. The mechanics of the film ought to be at the command of anyone and bad workmanship in this respect is unforgivable.

The story is an odd combination of old fashioned melodrama and inept problem play, transparently theatrical and forced, but it has one climax fairly effective in a stagey way. This is the passage where the French prefect of police enters the bedroom of the German woman spy who murdered his son and strangles her. It's a queer bit of fiction to come out of Germany, but properly handled by the camera man it would have been a "punch." The camera treatment here is especially bad.

Throughout, the melodrama gets a travesty twist from the dressing of the actors. In one scene, presumably a fashionable function in the Paris home of a government official, the women wear gowns that belong in a small village church sociable and comport themselves appropriately to that locale. A considerable footage shows the woman spy "vamping" the son of the French official, and the screen action here is of the type popular when the vamp screen type was at the top of its vogue in America, stilted and absurd beyond the worst offenses of our own Theda.

The picture reeks with sex stuff, ponderous in the German way and silly rather than risque. It all starts in a Paris gambling house run by a French woman and a German spy who is her partner. She tries to force her daughter to marry the German, but the girl loves a young French bank clerk, whom she is about to marry when the gambling house is raided by the prefect of police and the scandal ruins her chance.

Instead the girl (Pola Negri) swears vengeance upon the prefect and weds the German spy, who is in communication by wireless with Berlin conveying information that will be useful in case of another war. The girl is compelled to aid the spy. She secures a meeting with the son of the prefect who becomes infatuated and delivers his father's copy of the secret government code into her hands.

About that time the prefect is directed by the minister of state to search the spy's house. This brings him into contact with the woman and he also promptly falls in love with her. Having secured the code book the lady spy dismisses the boy who goes home and blows his brains out, leaving behind a note indicating that an un-named woman was the cause of his act and a scented handkerchief which later reveales her identity.

The prefect continues his affair with the woman spy, her husband having fled, and bit by bit comes to know that she was responsible for the son's suicide. Compelled at length to arrest the woman by pressure from higher officials, he enters her bedroom at night, apparently for a rendezvous and kills her. That's the climax, theatrically effective enough. But the whole thing is illogical, one of those fictions that depend for suspense upon every obvious trick of the stage and screen. *Rush.*

WOLF PACK

This is probably among the cheapest pictures ever produced, both from the standpoint of scenic investiture and cast cost. It impresses the observer as if Director William J. Crafts took the company of six out on location—a mountainous exterior—and shot the works in a couple of days. Joe Hammond (Joe Moore), a Northwest Mounted Policeman, is out to capture The Wolf, a notorious bandit. The Wolf has two henchmen and the N. W. M. P. have a similar number of allies, the girl (Eileen Sedgwick), and the heroine's uncle, who plays two roles. As Steve Lamont, he is killed by The Wolf in th. first half reel in an attempt to steal the old miner's treasure. The same man impersonates Lamont's brother for the rest of the action.

One thing is omnipresent—action and rough and tumble fighting at the slightest provocation. While always a commendable detail of any film production, it is overdone here to the extent it becomes oppressively noticeable. Some of the reviewer's neighbors at the Stanley, where this picture held forth last Friday, giggled audibly with each succeeding set-to. As a result, it evolved into a series of anti-climaxes, always delaying the punch which was nothing more than the capture of the bandit by our persistent hero. Said p. h. scraps fiercely, but is cruelly manhandled by The Wolf's henchmen, who, for some unexplained reason, inflict only corporal punishment on Hammond, but nothing f..el, explaining the Chief does not wish it so. Why, is an unexplained mystery, although the desperadoes seem vicious enough for anything.

The story could easily have been told in two reels. It was nothing but the drawing out of a serial twin reel episode two and a half times as long. Peerless Pictures produced and the Realto Pictures distributed.

Joe Moore, who is featured with Miss Sedgwick, is a scrapping lead who could do better with better scripts. Miss Sedgwick does her share capably riding hard cross-country and doing some active outdoor work. The heavy is almost farcical, with his ten-twent-thirt "villyun" personation.

One or two rough cabin interiors supplement the plentiful outdoor settings. For the exhibitor it looks like a cheap buy if his house is on the nickelette order. *Abel.*

THE RAGGED HEIRESS

Lucia Moreton...............Shirley Mason
Glen Wharton.................John Harron
Sam Moreton................Edwin Stevens
James Moreton..................Cecil Van Auker
Sylvia Moreton..........Claire MacDowell
Norah Burke................Aggie Herring
Lucia, age three..........Eileen O'Malley

"The Ragged Heiress" is a simple little story released by Fox with Shirley Mason as the star. As a matter of fact Miss Mason is worthy of better screen story material than this story by Jules Furthman proves to be. However, Harry Beaumont, who directed the picture, makes the most of the material at hand, and in the main the little feature appears to contain sufficient to interest the average audience in the general run of daily change houses. It was presented at Loew's New York this week as part of a double feature bill with a Goldwyn feature that but a week before had been at the Capitol as the principal attraction.

It is a story of two brothers, one a widower with a child and the other married to a grasping wife. The former is accused of a crime and sentenced to jail. He places his young daughter in the hands of his relatives, who treat her so cruelly that she runs away and goes to her old nurse. This fact is kept from the prisoner, who on his release goes west immediately and begins life over again, sending money regularly to his brother for the education of the girl.

She in the meantime remains with the nurse, who provides for her as though she were her own child, and on the death of the nurse, who the girl really believes is her mother, the little one starts forth to make her way in the world as a servant. Coincidence steps in and she obtains a position in the home of her uncle and aunt. It is discovered that she has used the references of the dead nurse, and is about to be turned out when word is received that the brother who has made a tremendous fortune in the west is coming to visit his daughter.

The uncle and aunt are in a quandary as to what they are to do when they decide to utilize the maid for the daughter. She is compelled to accede to the deception, and finally at the crucial moment she reveals the true state of affairs. The girl is proved to be the real daughter after all.

Miss Mason enacts her role of the girl cleverly, but occasionally lets a little flapper stuff slip that is not quite in keeping with the story. Edwin Stevens as the scheming uncle and Claire MacDowell as the grasping wife both give sterling performances. John Harron as the youth who falls in love with the girl is all that could be desired. He is a most promising type of juvenile lead, and with direction should develop to as great a screen artist as was his late brother.

Fred.

CRIMSON CHALLENGE

Five-reeler made from Vingie E. Roe's story, "Tharon of Lost Valley." Scenario by Beula Marie Dix. Directed by Paul Powell. Paramount picture, "Presented by Adolph Zukor."

Tharon Last...............Dorothy Dalton
Billy...........................Jack Mower
Buck Courtrey...........Frank Campeau
Ellen Courtrey.................Irene Hunt
Jim Last.....................Will R. Walling
Clive ....Howard Ralston
Black Bart................Clarence Burton
Wylackie.......................George Field
Anita......................Mrs. Dark Cloud
Confora..........................Fred Huntly

Dorothy Dalton introduces the two-gun woman to the screen in this melodrama, which has extraordinarily high blood pressure, hurried respiration and dangerously abnormal heart action. The curious inverted romance of a sweet young thing who can (and does) "draw" quicker than the desperado who has dishonorable designs upon her is a literary novelty that ought to attract some attention in the current releases.

At least it has plenty of lurid action. As a literary product it is rubbish, but as a screen play of the thrill-at-any-cost school, embellished by gorgeous scenery and played in a spirit of vigorous melodrama, it has effectiveness all its own. Miss Dalton, miraculously slender and youthful in knickerbockers and boots, is altogether delightful and the producers have surrounded her with a notable cast, chief among them being Frank Campeau, aforetime the cattle rustler in the Dustin Farnum stage play "The Virginian."

The feature will appeal to the big majority of fans with an insatiable thirst for action, movement, clash and conflict. It is five reels chock full of dramatic shocks of high voltage, and in that respect and in the respect that the whole thing is done well it is an excellent bit of theatrical entertainment. It is thought Belasco produced an artistic stage revival of "Why Girls Leave Home," with a cast headed by Margaret Anglin and E. H. Sothern. That combination would be sure to furnish a satisfactory entertainment out of any kind of dramatic materials, but you wouldn't be able to regard it, even in its most thrilling moments, entirely without a chuckle. That's the way it is with "The Crimson Challenge."

The movies never seem to be able to take a piece of fiction without injecting some hop into it. This novel was put out under the innocuous title of "Tharon of Lost Valley." That mild and colorless label wouldn't do for the screen. They had to pile the emphasis on thicker, and so we have the vociferous title "The Crimson Challenge"—candid dime-novel appeal to the infant-minded. But direct, unblushing appeal. Its frankness disarms impatience. Better this sort of childish simplicity than high-sounding pretence for something that is in reality cheap and vulgar.

The plot: Tharon Last, rancher's daughter in a remote cattle-raising community, is beset by a powerful desperado. She repulses him and he murders her father. Theron thereupon gathers the law-abiding citizens of the valley and leads them in warfare against the law-breaker, who is strongly entrenched in his evil business by association with the local sheriff and judge and followed by a horde of equally desperate characters.

Theron spends most of her time practising the "quick draw" against the time when she shall meet her persecutor face to face. She has the true sporting spirit. She holds up a whole barroom of tough customers to notify the outlaw that she'll "get him" and she does. The battle between the forces of evil and the good citizens goes in favor of the right side, but in such a way that the arch villain gets away and here arises the "punch" of the picture.

The heroine goes in pursuit of the fleeing outlaw and there is a running horseback duel in which the villain is disarmed by the superior markmanship of the heroine. She rides up to him, but can't shoot becauses he is unarmed, but when by the subterfuge of pretending faintness he reaches for a second concealed weapon, she is ethically free to wipe him out. Thereupon she crumples up and falls into the arms of her sweetheart, whispering that she wants someone to lean upon.

Rush.

THE GOOD PROVIDER

Becky Binswanger	Vera Gordon
Julius Binswanger	Dore Davidson
Pearl Binswanger	Miriam Battista
	Vivienne Osborne
Izzy Binswanger	William "Buster" Collier, Jr.
Max Teitlebaum	John Roche
Mr. Boggs	James Devine
Mrs. Boggs	Blanche Craig
Mrs. Teitlebaum	Ora Jones
Broadway Sport	Edward Phillips
Flapper	Muriel Martin
Specialty Dancer	Margaret Severn

Fannie Hurst has drawn an interesting story of Jewish life in "The Good Provider," which has been picturized by Cosmopolitan and presented by Famous Players at the Rivoli this week. Vera Gordon and Dore Davidson are featured at the head of a corking good cast, and Mr. Davidson in this production is shown in a role that gives him as great an opportunity as was accorded Miss Gordon in "Humoresque," and he makes much of the chance that was accorded him. In this role he earns the term "the Barney Bernard of the screen."

The direction was by Frank Borzage, who has turned out a screen version of the Hurst tale that holds the attention of the audience at all times. True, there is a moment or two when the action drags a little, but that is the fault rather of editing than direction. John Lynch turned out the working script, while the sets were the work of Josef Urban.

From a commercial standpoint this picture will not gross as much as "Humoresque," but it is an entertainment that will hit home, for it has a strong element of comedy that lightens it throughout. The homely sayings of the old Jewish father when his children try to make him a "smart setter" and steer him to a gilded New York hotel to live are out and out howls.

The tale opens with a struggling peddler who sells ginghams from a wagon at the time that his wife and two children whom he has not seen for a number of years are arriving at the small suburban town, where the father has secured a tumbled down shack for their home. From that point to the time that he has a plate glass front store on the Main street of the town life deals kindly with him. At that point, however, the children get the idea that the big city is the only place where they will have an opportunity, and finally their ideas bring the family to a hotel where the prices are more than a day's profit in the store, and at the finish the father is on the verge of bankruptcy. His salvation, however, comes in the young man that has fallen in love with the daughter, who is willing to invest for an opportunity in a small town, and the final fadeout shows the mother and father on the porch of the little country place where they started.

Miss Gordon plays the role of the mother, but loses out somewhat with the audience because of the fact that while she is sympathetic to a certain extent it is the husband role that sways the audience. Mr. Davidson has and holds all the sympathy from the start. William Collier, Jr., as the son gave a corking performance as the progressive youngster who is always trying for the big city idea in the small town. Vivienne Osborne as the daughter is not of the type that will stand for close-ups in photography, but she answered the requirements well enough.

Borzage's direction has lent a number of human touches, and the bits that Davidson had with the cat scored.

Fred.

WHEN ROMANCE RIDES

Lucy Bostil	Claire Adams
Lin Slone	Carl Gantvoort
Joel Creech	Jean Hersholt
Bill Cordts	Harry L. Van Meter
Bostil	Charles Arling
Holley	Tod Sloan
Dr. Binks	Frank Hayes
"Bootie" Bostil	Mary Jane Irving
Lucy's Chums	Audrey Chapman and Helen Howard
Dick Sears	Stanley Bingham
Thomas Brackton	Walter Perkins
Sally Brackton	Babe London
Van	John Beck

This Benjamin B. Hampton adaptation of Zane Grey's "Wildfire" is being released through Goldwyn. Showing currently at the Capitol, presumably to add prestige to it via a Broadway first run, it impressed merely so-so, further handicapped by a poorly laid out supporting bill. There was too much of the musical, ballet and vocal stuff in the fore section, minus any comedy throughout the program, to pave the way interestingly for the feature. When it did flicker into its plot it struck one as very average.

The situation of doping the rival nag in the great horse race scene dates from or before "In Old Kentucky," and seemed nothing new to the audience. The Zane Grey plot may have made interesting reading in book form, but its transposition to the screen was a mild affair. "Wildfire" is the pony which wins the great derby and around which the action is centered. The villain (Cordts) has a nag that looks certain to cross the barrier foremost unless some unknown added starter spoils his plans. The Bostil family at one time owned a prize-winning nag but it was stolen and they strongly suspect Cordts as being at the bottom of it. After the race, when "Wildfire," literally a "dark horse," emerged the winner, the heroine proves that Cordts' contender is really her former favorite equine excepting for the mane, which has been dyed. Lin Stone (Carl Gantvoort) is here introduced by Lucy Bostil (Claire Adams) to her father (Charles Arling). The romance develops from the second or third reel after the winning of the $5,000 derby, which is not the climax, as is to be expected. The story is dragged out, including a kidnapping of the heroine by a half-witted former employe who imagines himself wronged and the rescue of the girl by the hero—for the second or third time.

The Federated Photoplays of California produced the picture, adapted and directed by Mr. Hampton, although he acknowledges three assistants on the former end, and E. Richard Schayer and John Russell on the continuity. It looks like a case of too many cooks.

There is enough appeal in the picture for the average program but not enough for a really big house. The title may mean something at the gate. Even in conjunction with the metropolitan showing the Goldwyn people are aplurging heavy on subway and elevated three-sheets, showing the scene of a horse race.

The cast, very average, although satisfying in its entirety, has been made subsidiary to the story. And the story is average, tranquil screen continuity, lacking punch or power.

Abel.

WOMAN HE MARRIED

Natalie Lane	Anita Stewart
Roderick Warren	Darrell Foss
Byrne Travers	Donald MacDonald
Andrew Warfen	William Conklin
Mimi	Shannon Day
Muriel Warren	Charlotte Pierce
Richard Steel	Charles Belcher
Yosi	Frank Tokunaga

The First National release of the Louis B. Mayer production, "The Woman He Married," with Anita Stewart, was added to the Strand bill this week to bolster up the second week there of the Chaplin comedy, "Pay Day." The Chaplin production still topped the bill, while the Stewart picture was given a place of secondary importance in the billing and program matter as well as the running order of the show. The feature was in the position of closing the show with the comedy just ahead of it.

The "Woman He Married" is a Fred Niblo-directed production, written by Herbert Bashford. It is a mystery melodrama that is in itself an object lesson of what is wrong with the pictures and why the audiences are falling away from the film houses. At the Strand the audience Monday night seemed interested up to a point until the unraveling of the mystery began and then they started to laugh. Picture audiences are getting too wise in the better houses and the producers are not keeping ahead of them.

Miss Stewart has the role of an artist's model who weds the son of a wealthy father. The boy believes he can develop into a playwright, but his father cuts off his allowance after the marriage because he will not leave the girl, and the two are forced into a boarding house. The wife, when they are about at the end of their string, returns to modeling without the husband's knowledge, and thus keeps the wolf from the door. The father of the boy has her trailed, and finally decides it is time to report to the boy he is being tricked by the girl he married. The boy rushes to the artist's studio to find him lying on the floor unconscious and suffering from a gunshot wound. The attaches of the building send for the police. The boy is first accused and then cleared, after which the wife is found in a room. She is charged with the crime until a French model is discovered in still another room and confesses. But that does not account for the presence of the wife in the studio. This point is cleared up with the story of the young daughter of the wealthy father and sister of the boy. She was posing for her portrait which had to be finished that night so that she could give it to her father for his birth day, at least that was what the artist told her, but he had other ideas. The brother's wife is tipped by the former valet they had employed who was now with the artist, and so she went to the rescue of the young girl, she personally having had a pretty good idea of the manner in which the painter operated. Of course, that was enough for her daddy-in-law to forgive her and tell her to take the boy.

The story is draggy at times and the attempts at comedy to lighten it do not register.

Miss Stewart is supported by Darrell Foss, an acceptable lead, while Donald MacDonald is the heavy, playing the artist. Charlotte Pierce has the ingenue role and Shannon Day is the little Parisian who fires the fatal shot. She failed to register as she should and has seemingly lost a lot of that beauty that made her a favorite in the "Follies."

At the Strand they are terming this an all-star cast in the billing, but even that failed to pull any business Monday night; half a house at 9.30. The evening was exceedingly warm for this time of the year and also it was the beginning of Holy Week. It is possible the billing of the picture in this manner is to get over the starring of Miss Stewart alone, and so topping the director, the picture and then Miss Stewart and an all-star cast in the order named.

Fred.

REPORTED MISSING

Richard Boyd	Owen Moore
Pauline Dale	Pauline Garon
Sam	Tom Wilson
J. Young	Togo Yamamoto
Andrew Dunn	Robert Cain
Captain Ferguson	Frank Wunderlee

Lewis J. Selznick gave a special presentation of "Reported Missing," a five-reel comedy directed by Henry J. Lehrman, starring Owen Moore, at the Hotel Ritz Carlton, New York, last week. It is a whale of a laugh picture and undoubtedly will gross toward the half-million dollar mark as it stands, but if it were taken and re-edited and retitled the chances are that the picture would prove a second "Mickey" in the matter of gross receipts.

The story was written by the director, and it is a real thriller as a melodrama, but the meller is handled in such a slapstick manner as to make it a howling farce.

Moore plays the role of a wealthy youngster who has more money than brains and who has led a life that has been entirely along the primrose path. To please the girl he wants to marry he consents to purchase a gigantic shipping fleet that the United States Government has and is about to dispose of. Moore, as Richard Boyd, is the head of the directorate board that holds an option on the ships, but the Japanese shipping trust is also planning to lay their hands on the fleet. So their agent plots with a relative of the young man's to get him out of the way until his option expires.

From this point on the thrills start. Moore and the girl are on the way to the minister after he has delivered his ultimatum to the directors regarding the purchase of the ships, but instead they are driven to a wharf where they are set upon and taken aboard a yacht which is to keep them at sea until the option expires. The yacht is wrecked, the comedy that follows brings howl after howl from the audience. For the rescue a battleship is brought into play, and atop of that Moore starts off in a hydroplane for a chase after a sea-sledge in which the Jap conspirator is running off with the girl. Naturally, there is a happy ending, with Moore getting the girl and arriving on the scene in time to buy the ships.

Lehrman has taken that plot and dressed it with all the slap-stick hoke that one could ask for, and the general indications are that the picture is going to prove a clean-up for the exhibitor as well as Selznick.

Moore has a role that is difficult to say the least. He seemingly undertook to take all of the leaps and dives that the picture necessitated without resorting to a double.

Pauline Garon played the lead opposite him and managed to score nicely. But Tom Wilson, working in blackface, managed to clean up on the comedy outside of Moore. He was in all of the battle and took the flops and falls with a wow.

Five title writers are credited with having provided the reading matter. A number of them are daily paper columnists and humorists, but their titles failed to show any of the alleged humor that they are credited with being possessed of. It was the action of the picture that brought the laughs rather than the subtitles.

Fred.

"A POOR RELATION"

Noah Vale	Will Rogers
Miss Fay	Sylvia Breamer
Johnny Smith	Wallace McDonald
Sterrett	Sydney Ainsworth
Mr. Fay	George Williams
Scollops	Molly Malone
Rip	Robert De Vilbiss
Patch	Jeanette Trebaol
O'Halley	Walter Perry

"A Poor Relation" was made by Goldwyn, from the stage play of that name by Edward E. Kidder. Clarence Badger directed the film, in which Will Rogers is starred. It is a comedy-drama five reeler. The picture as a whole is draggy and uninteresting, Mr. Rogers playing a sort of Ezra Kendall role, that of a poor philosopher, who although poverty stricken maintains an optimistic spirit, meeting adversity calmly, and facing apparently unsurmountable difficulties with a smile and witty observation.

The story tells of the struggles of Noah Vale, an impoverished inventor, played by Mr. Rogers, to market a contrivance he has perfected and the ill-treatment accorded him by a rich relative. There is a commendable effort to mark the picture with a sort of Chas. Dickens atmosphere, carried out nicely in the scenes in the poor inventor's hovel. The photography also contributes materially in suggesting a likeable whimsical atmosphere.

Two children, a boy and girl, give excellent performances in the film. The other characters are incidental, George Williams making the rich relative convincing, and Wallace McDonald, playing the juvenile capably. Sylvia Breamer is an effective ingenue.

The situations are of the mechanically constructed sort, rather than of the natural type, that modern picture audiences have grown to favor. Scenically the film has been produced very well. The direction is satisfactory in every respect. Mr. Rogers makes the most of his opportunities, but the story does not give him sufficient scope to register more than passively.

"A Poor Relation" will do as a regulation program picture. Will Rogers should be provided with better vehicles, however.   *Bell.*

ELOPE IF YOU CAN

Story by E. J. Rath. Scenario by F. J. Poland. Directed by C. R. Wallace. Fox comedy production, starring Eileen Percy.
Nancy Moore..................Eileen Percy
Jazz Hennessy..........Edward Sutherland
Willie Weems...........Joseph Bennett
Elizabeth Magruder......Mildred Davenport
Mrs. Magruder.............Mary Huntress
Warren Holt..................Larry Steers
Mr. Magruder..............Harvey Clarke

There's no getting away from the chase as a comedy device. Nothing quite takes its place for a sure-fire laugh. In this picture it is handled in a highly ingenious manner, backed up by an amusing farcial situation and pointed with a lot of extremely clever and witty titles. Its trouble is that it has been carried along too far. It takes a tremendously skilful comedy to stretch out to five reels. The world is full of people who can get away with a gag, but a Mark Twain is born only once in a generation. And at that, a Mark Twain may be able to make scores of clever speeches, but he writes only one "Innocence Abroad."

Two reels appear to be the best length for comics, with an extreme range of three, but in this case they have shot the piece for six reels or thereabouts, injuring what would otherwise have been a smash. The length, however, hurts only the finale, for the story opens with a flying start and the action sets a fast pace right along. Only there can be too much even of speed. There are limits even to a fan's endurance.

This is all amusing slapstick and makes no pretense to be otherwise. It's a sort of sublimated chase, six reels long. The story opens with a hick actor and a soubret stranded and trying to beat their way home without paying fares. They get acquainted with a rich man in the parlor car who has just received a wire from his wife, informing him she will announce the engagement of their daughter in a few days to a young sap of whom the father disapproves. Father thereupon hires the *soubret to scheme for the defeat of the match.* The soubret is introduced into the fashionable

household in the guise of a maid, and her breezy slang and worldly philosophies make sparkling titles as she maneuvers to break off the match and bring about the elopement of the daughter and another man of whom father approves.

This involves intricate tactics, but the resourceful soubret is always there with the quick twist to make things go her way, aided by the faithful hick as an accomplice. The hick disguises himself as a taxi chauffeur and dumps the sap out on a lonely country road, while the girl sits in a distant hotel lobby waiting for him to appear with the marriage license. In the end the soubret jockeys the right pair to the altar, while the sap is herded in an attic, and has them married by a kidnapped clergyman, the ceremony ending just as the firemen arrive, and the climax is the stream of water business for a grand slapstick climax.   *Rush.*

MAN FROM DOWNING ST.

Five-reel mystery drama starring Earle Williams. Produced by A. E. Smith and distributed by Vitagraph. Directed by Edward Jose.

Rather an interesting mystery tale is this feature dealing with the British secret service in India. For a film story of the kind it is handled with conspicuous restraint and it has in ample degree the desirable quality of suspense.

Robert Wentworth is an English secret service man detailed by "Downing Street" to run down the traitor in Delhi who has secured possession of the British cipher code and is selling secret correspondence to foment a revolution.

Arrived at the military post in Delhi, Wentworth finds these people who comprise all the possibilities: A native Rajah, a lieutenant, a captain and his wife, a major and his daughter and a bazaar dancing girl known as Sarissa. Which one is guilty? Wentworth is disguised as a native, the only person in his confidence being the commanding officer of the garrison. One by one all the persons in sight earn the suspicions of the audience. First, the young lieutenant, but he is about to clear the mystery by telling the name of the guilty one when a pistol shot through the window lays him low.

The intrigues weave concentric circles until the quest seems to narrow itself down to the captain and the lieutenant. Wentworth arranges to have two messages sent from London. One will carry news of a new tax on jute, the other of a new tax on hemp. The message about hemp, he tells the commander, will get itself into the hands of the captain; the one about jute into the hands of the major. If the news leaks it will be evident among the native dealers in the bazaar and the traitor will be revealed. Neat theatrical device, arousing expectations.

Presently the commander brings word that hemp has risen amid great excitement and the captain is about to be arrested, when his wife, hearing the commotion, learns what has taken place and commits suicide. Quick shift of suspicion to the wife. The commander enters to demand what it's all about and is arrested as the real traitor—a development which would never have occurred to a spectator. The messages about the tax were never sent. The commander had tried to throw suspicion on the captain and thereby convicted himself.

All these are cleverly managed surprises. Then the commander is charged with murder and Sarissa, whose love affairs have played a considerable part in the story, stands forth as Ruth McAllister of the British secret service and gives the fatal evidence, having seen the commander fire the shot that killed the lieutenant on the instant of

disclosure.

The picture has a wealth of atmosphere and costuming and the native resorts in which Sarissa dances are interesting. Good program feature.   *Rush.*

THE SLEEP WALKER

This is a Realart production released through Paramount, with Constance Binney as the star. It is a stereotyped society drama that has as its heroine a sleepwalking school girl. Miss Binney plays that role, while opposite her Jack Mullhall carries the lead. The production was shown at Loew's Circle, New York, as part of a double feature bill with a Norma Talmadge production, which is about as definite an estimate as anyone would want of its strength.

The story shows the struggle a society woman will go through to retain her social position and surroundings when left penniless through the death of the family provider. This mother gets $10,000 worth of diamonds on memorandum and they depart for parts unknown after having converted them into cash. She is located a year later at a fashionable resort by the jewelry man, on the very day that her daughter is returning from a convent school.

The jewelry man proves the villain. He is all of that. He smokes cigarettes a la Desperate Desmond, flicks the ashes with a sort of a "curses" snap, and does all the usual m. p. heavy stunts. He threatens to send the mother to jail unless she produces coin she owes and also forces his attentions on the daughter. But the hero is right on the job, and he won't believe it true that the girl was seen going into the villain's room in her night robe until he discovers her behind a curtain. Then it is disclosed she walked in her sleep and he wouldn't believe that either. He was a most unbelieving hero.

But the following morning, when he sees the girl walking along the window ledge at about the fifth story of the hotel, he is convinced of the sleep walking and rescues her. After that she evidently walked in her sleep no more. The hero naturally straightened out mother's bills, slipping the villain a beating for interest and also administering a couple of wallops to the hotel manager who ordered the girl and mother from the hotel because of the finding of the girl in the villain's room.

It is a feature that will go in the cheaper houses with a daily change of bill. Miss Binney does not seem to have achieved anything in this picture that one would term exceptional. If anything, her appearance is neither youthful nor as beautiful as she has been wont to appear in the past.   *Fred.*

SO THIS IS ARIZONA

A western action drama with Mack Sennett custard pie comedy incidentals. Dull story with bad acting and poor directorship and without a redeeming feature unless it was the beautiful horses and the magnificent lanscapes which the movie business couldn't very well mess up. This picture and the others like it are one of the reasons there seems to be so much fact in Gus Hill's declaration that one out of five small town picture theatres has been converted into a garage.

The story opens with a fashionable young woman riding horseback, apparently in Central Park. In all seriousness she opens a wristbag and takes a timetable out to study. One immediately expected the worst. Young women equestriennes in Central Park don't ordinarily carry satin wristbags to the bridle-path. The fact that the scenario

writer needed the handbag in his business doesn't change the situation. Its purpose in the scheme was that it should be lost. The hero finds it, and that makes the story.

And such a story! One minute it is slapstick comedy and the next minute the playful hero is engaged in a fight for his life with all the strained seriousness of which a mediocre actor and a third-class scenario are capable, and that's a whale of a lot of seriousness. A sample of the comedy relief that goes into the film may be judged from this: The rich young man arrives in an Arizona town and goes to the hotel. At the same instant a "bad man" enters shooting right and left, and everybody gets under the table as the outlaw threatens the bartender with a gun. Only his back is visible as he appears to gulp down drink after drink. The hero approaches bravely and the bad man, it turns out, is consuming an ice cream cone.

It was a good enough idea when Lew Fields thought of it ten years ago, but where does it fit into a western drama? Later on the drama becomes intense. The workmen in a mine strike; two conspirators rob the hero; one of them kills the other; suspicion is turned on the hero, and the desperate miners are about to lynch him. At the same time the hero is beset in the underground passages of the mine where the outlaws have set three time bombs and the heroine is sitting in the mine owner's office with another smoking bomb in the cellar under her feet.

There is a lot of fighting and galloping horses, and at the end the heroine is saved, the hero is saved—everybody is saved. It seemed a pity.   *Rush.*

FASCINATION

Dolores de Lisa..............Mae Murray
Carlos de Lisa, her brother.Creighton Hale
Eduardo de Lisa, her father..Charles Lane
The Maequesa de Lisa, her aunt.......
.........................Emily Fitzroy
Carrita, a Toreador.....Robert W. Frazer
Ralph Kellogg, an American..........
.....................Vincent Coleman
The Count de Morera.....Courtenay Foote
Parola, a dancer...............Helen Ware
Nema......................Francis Puglia

"Fascination" is Mae Murray's second starring vehicle as head of her own producing unit, Tiffany Productions, Inc. As with "Peacock Alley," her first Tiffany picture, Metro is distributing this feature. The booking of "Fascination" into the Capitol necessitated the setting back for another week of Lady Diana Manners' Prizma color drama, "The Glorious Adventure."

"Fascination" is a great box office title, it seems, as was attested by the S. R. O. business Easter Sunday.

It is an original story by Edmund Goulding, which affords the star ample opportunity for display of her peculiar personality, pep and dancing, the action starting in America and winding up in romantic Spain. This is enough excuse for Robert Z. Leonard, the star's director-husband, to spread himself on the fandango and castanet hoke, and he has spread it on wisely and well. Taking the situation of Dolores' (Miss Murray) fascination for Carrita, the toreador idol of Spain, as the central situation, Leonard and the scenario writer have revloved a series of bizarre and colorful situations around it.

The action starts in America, where Dolores de Lisa, offspring of a Spanish pater and an American mater, is seen flirting, gyrating and syncopating outrageously with her many admirers to the jealous disgust of her fiance (Vincent Coleman). Dolores is just at that dangerous flapper age which her sedate aunt fears the most, berating old Eduardo de Lisa, the girl's indulgent father, for his easy-going attitude in regards to his son and daughter. (Creighton Hale is Carlos de Lisa, the son.) It is in the course of such merry-making that Dolores' fiance insists she come home and quit this prolonged revelry. She refuses and leaves with the other six or eight admirers for a round of the night resorts, explaining the next morning she had been to the Palais Royal, Club Royal, Rendezvous, Montmartre and the Plaza.

Her aunt decides to remove the girl from this jazz environment to Spain, where an affair develops between the matador and our heroine. For the finish Ralph Kellogg (Mr. Coleman) arrives to claim his fiancee, who demands one thing of him—to save her from "fascination." Somehow that tagline did not click so strong as it could have been, but made a satisfactory finish for a live and colorful production.

Miss Murray is supported by a high-grade cast, which by no means detracts from the star's individuality. Robert W. Frazer as Carrita portrays the matador in a sympathetic light, the audience seemingly disappointed at his fate in jail for an attempt to avenge his honor, which was falsely sullied by Parola, a dancer. Helen Ware as the dancer was perfect in the characterization, as was Emily Fitzroy as the aunt, another unsympathetic role.

The production represents real money. The costuming and settings are lavish and in keeping with the locale and action. The direction is even, although during the fore section it assumes a farce vein with some of Miss Murray's alleged flapper retorts.

For the exhibitor "Fascination" looks like a good box office buy.

Abel.

IS MATRIMONY A FAILURE?

Paramount picture billed as "all star" cast. From Leo Ditrichstein's adaptation of the play by Oscar Blumenthal and Gustave Kadelburg. Scenario by Walter Woods; direction James Cruze.

Arthur Haviland............T. Roy Barnes
Margaret Saxby......................Lila Lee
Mabel Hoyt.......................Lois Wilson
Jack Hoyt......................Walter Hiers
Mrs. Wilbur........................ZaSu Pitts
Mr Wilbur......................Arthur Hoyt
Martha Saxby...............Lillian Leighton
Amos Saxby..................Tully Marshall
Dudley King..................Adolphe Menjou
Mrs. Pearson..................Sylvia Ashton
Mr Pearson.......................Otis Harlan
Pop Skinner....................Charles Ogle
Mrs. Skinner.....................Ethel Wales
Bank President...............Sydney Bracey
Policeman.....................William Gonder
Maid..........................Lottie Williams
Silas Spencer......................Dan Mason
The Chef........................W. H. Brown
Marriage License Clerk......Robert Brower

Once again effective screen material has to make acknowledgment to the stage, adding another to the long list of good pictures made from tried plays and cutting down the average of original film stories. It would be interesting to have a dependable estimate of the ratio of successful play adaptations to successful scenarios created for the silent drama direct. At a guess it would represent three or four to one.

"Is Matrimony a Failure?" is a thoroughly enjoyable farce comedy, dealing in a droll but sympathetic way with the comedy side of the domestic situation. The tale has a mine of gentle satire aimed sometimes at the husband, sometimes at the wife, sometimes at both, with the wife the ultimate victor in the household battle for supremacy.

Probably in the whole range of humor there is nothing so sure of a laugh as the husband-and-wife conflict. Here the subject is exploited in sublimated form. No less than four couples are concerned in the frolic. There is some shrewd character drawing, all the couples representing a type. There is the too loving wife and the indifferent husband; the domineering wife and rebellious husband; the careless wife and the fault-finding husband and the selfish wife and her egotistical mate. It's a panorama of domestic wranges over undarned socks, competition for the mirror, personal liberty in the consumption of tobacco and control of the children.

It would be a rare husband and wife in any average audience that would not find some of their own eccentricities satirized, and therein will come much of the film's appeal. The whole thing touches real life at every point with an amusing angle that has no sting. This refreshing bit of tomfoolery is a vast relief from the desolate wastes of suffering heroines, pompous heroes, sex problems and piffle. Its crystallization into celluloid is a public service.

And it is exceedingly well done. A better cast could scarcely have been assembled. The whole company plays in the right spirit of natural comedy and the story develops to the accompaniment of explosions of delighted laughter, a conspicuous example of enlivening entertainment sustained through five reels without resort to slapstick or custard pie. The marvel of the whole thing is that a satirist could go so fast a pace of sophisticated funmaking without sounding one sour note. Superficially the comedy makes pretty short thrusts at the imbecilities of married people, but beneath there is an optimistic attitude toward the fundamental goodness of commonplace people and the essential happiness of everyday life. The immature critics that write most of our film plays could study "Is Matrimony a Failure?" with immense profit.

The story hinges upon the efforts of a bank clerk and the daughter of bickering parents to elope. The bridegroom goes to the county clerk's office for a marriage license, while the county clerk himself is away on a hunting trip and has delegated his duties to a deputy. The document is issued in due form and the pair steal away while the girl's parents are entertaining friends at their wedding anniversary. Before he goes the bridegroom takes his week's salary from the bank, leaving a note, "I've taken what is due me."

When the news of the elopement reaches the party a lawyer in the company declares the wedding is not legal, for the reason that the deputy county clerk who issued the license has never been sworn in. The young couple have motored to a near-by resort and the girl's parents telegraph to the hotel proprietor that they are not married, while the banker puts detectives on the clerk's trail. This leads to all sorts of amusing complications.

Upon their return home the girl's mother upbraids her. Everybody goes to the county clerk's office to investigate the affair. "Why," declares that grouchy official,"I've gone on a hunting trip every November for 20 years and my clerk has always issued marriage licenses." This starts all the dissatisfied husbands to thinking, and the quartet of husbands declare themselves free, all having been married in the eleventh month. They leave their homes and helpmates and declare themselves for a carefree life, but it palls upon them after one night of discomfort and boredom, and they return, penitent and anxious to resume the old yoke.

Rush.

CRIMSON CROSS

Independent six-reeler, produced by Fanmark Pictures. Story by George Everett. Direction by D. James Levett. Van Dyke Brooks is featured in the billing.

A poor, stumbling distortion of "The Miracle Man" idea, the story hinging upon the theme that miracles are worked by faith. The great Packard-Cohan story was worked out ingeniously into a plausible tale, while none of the copyists has been able to present the theory convincingly.

In this case the attempt is pitiable. Where the authors of "The Miracle Man" took infinite pains to "plant" their miracle, through the antecedent story of "The Frog," the writer of "The Crimson Cross" merely makes it happen arbitrarily. The result is that it won't go down and all effect is lost. The picture under discussion bears about as much resemblance to "The Miracle Man" as a "Nick Carter" dime novel does to Conan Doyle's "The Sign of the Four," all the difference between a masterpiece of mystery fiction and a machine-made, hack-writer's pot-boiler.

The story is jumbled and fogged by inexpert arrangement, and the climaxes are crudely devised. All the film has is hurry and bustle—mere motion as opposed to dramatic action. The characters make no pretense to actuality. Instead they are pure theatrical puppets, lacking in convincing motive and impulse.

The story has a hackneyed start in the finding of a foundling, abandoned on the steps of a police station, where it is rescued by Detective Billings, described as "a man infatuated by police work, although independently wealthy." Billings brings the child up and in due time he becomes the prize sleuth of the department, having certain mysterious hypnotic powers by which he is able to extract confessions from criminals.

That's one line of narrative. Another thread has to do with the welfare work of a benign old party. Call him Smith. He goes about among the convicts and oozes bromidic precept, such as "Live right, think right and all will be well with you." His preachings bring him into contact with an anarchist named Schultz.

These two strings come together when the young detective runs down Schultz and his wife. The wife is arrested, but Schultz escapes and plots vengeance against the detective. Meanwhile the detective's health has broken down, and Smith is called in to apply spiritual balm. While Smith is wrestling with the soul-demons in the detective's mind, who breaks into the scene but Schultz, revolver in hand, intent upon murdering the detective who jailed Mrs. Schultz. Here's where the miracle happens.

Smith closes his eyes and looks heavenward. Lo and behold, the desperate Schultz is overcome by some hypnotic power, drops his revolver, and proclaims himself beaten. In despair he drinks poison and is dying all over the interior setting in extreme agony, when Smith again goes into a trance, and he is quickly restored to health and peace. In gratitude the anarchist obligingly goes back to reel one and explains to Smith that the young detective is his (Smith's) son, and he (Schultz) stole him (the young detective) from the cradle in revenge against Smith, years before, because Smith had caused his (Schultz's) arrest in Paris. The situation is almost as obscure and tangled as the preceding sentence.

All this time and afterward there is nothing about "the crimson cross" which makes the title. It was probably chosen because it had a flossy sound. Certainly it has nothing to do with the story. The detective has a red birthmark in the form of a cross, which he shows every time he rolls his sleeve up, but it is not bearing on the story and doesn't figure in any of its developments. The picture has no reason for being and represents the low ebb of production.

Rush.

UP AND GOING

David Brandon......................Tom Mix
Marie Brandon..............Carol Holloway
Bonnie MacDonald..............Eva Novak
Albert Brandon...........Cecil Van Auker
Basil DuBois...............William Conklin
Louis Patie......................Sidney Jordan
Sergeant Langley.............Tom O'Brien

William Fox is presenting Tom Mix as the star of a corking Northwest Mounted Police story in "Up and Going." The story is the joint work of Mix and his director, Lynn Reynolds. For general interest and action it is as good a feature, as far as program productions go, as has been seen in weeks. At Loew's New York it shared a double bill with the Chaplin comedy, "Pay Day," although it was strong enough to have stood by itself.

The story is told in a prolog and play. The prolog is laid in Canada, where Albert Brandon, a "remittance man," is married to a French-Canadian girl. They have a son. When the boy is about eight, word arrives from England the father has inherited a title and an estate and he and his family go abroad. A year later the wife returns to the little Canadian village, the husband having divorced her and retained the custody of the boy.

Years later a few brief shots in England show Tom Mix as the boy grown to manhood's estate and an all-around sportsman. Being jilted by a girl, he decides to go to Canada, and later, in search of adventure, joins the Northwest Mounted. Assignment finally takes him to the little village where he was born and the action has him rescue his boyhood sweetheart from a rum-runner and incidentally discover his mother is still living, although he had been told she died while he was a youngster.

This tale is told in fashion that gives Mix several chances for rough and tumble fights, also to appear in dress clothes and polo costume, and he makes as good a screen figure in those as he ever did in cowboy costume. A couple of real thrills are furnished by his chase in a canoe after an escaping law-breaker and the fight that the two put up under water has a real wallop.

Miss Novak makes a charming lead opposite Mix, but the character performance that Carol Holloway delivered stood out above anything else in the picture. The heavy work done by William Conklin and Sidney Jordan also carried a touch of real artistry.

In handling the story Reynolds kept the action uppermost at all times and had his star up and going every second. The shots in the north woods are great from a scenic viewpoint and the camera caught all of the beauty in them. *Fred.*

PARTNERS OF THE SUNSET

Bert Lubin "presents" this five-reel western drama on behalf of Western Picture Corporation. Directorship is credited to Robert H. Townley. Allene Ray is the star, supported by Robert Frazer.

A strikingly excellent melodrama, full of surprises and thrills and at the same time logical and plausible. The story develops naturally, the principals play with restrain and unaffected poise, and from first to last the scenic features are splendid and the photography flawless. In all the feature scores 100 per cent. How it comes to be booked in the Stanley, an out-of-the-way, second-class house on the fringe of Times Square argues that somebody has been napping on the exhibitor end or the sales organization has been lacking in enterprise.

Compared to some of the stuff that has had the call at the leading picture palaces on Broadway "Partners of the Sunset" is a super-special. It has all a western melodrama ought to have by way of ingenious incident and thrilling surprise; the story is told in terms of straightaway, simple action and the titles are reduced to a minimum; the story is clean and absorbing, too, and the actors impress one as human beings. There is never a suggestion of the picture studio about them. There is only one minor defect—the picture gets rather a slow start and there are evidences of padding in the early passages. But this is more than redeemed in the whirlwind climax in swift riding and the rush of dramatic events.

Just to name over a few of the thrills: The hero (Frazer) engages in combat with two outlaws who seek to abduct the heroine (Miss Ray). He swings from an upper window of the ranch house and makes his way 30 feet above ground through the branches until he is over the battleground, then drops into the thick of it. He is disarmed, and after an exhilarating struggle regains possession of his dropped weapon. Then he steps into the forgotten loop of a lasso and is brought to earth again. The fortunes of war sway first one way and then another until the arrival of galloping rescuers.

At another time a desperado knocks him senseless as he is driving his auto through the woods, but as the car plunges into a rut the attacker is thrown out and dragged over a dizzy cliff with the car, which is shattered on the rocks below. Another smash near the finish is the pursuit of the villain up a perpendicular cliff, with both pursuer and pursued in momentary peril of their lives. If any of these effects are worked by a camera trick the thing is extremely well done, for the illusion is complete and the effect is breathless.

The details recited are in addition to a constant succession of thrilling horseback chases over the roughest kind of country and often up inclines that appear too steep for passage. The heroine, a splendid horsewoman, takes part in these animated passages. The comedy, of course, is subordinated, but there are numerous smooth touches of humor, as, for example, the homely cowboy wso is disappointed with his "six-bit" necktie because it doesn't make any impression. There are plenty of neat incidentals of this kind and capital details of animal life.

In the foreground of the melodrama there is a likeable romantic story of an itinerant "Windmill Man" who turns out to be in reality an oil-well driller, who puts down a line on the heroine's land and brings up a "gusher," defeating the scheming villains, who sought to rob the girl, and winning her love for a happy ending. *Rush.*

THE FIRST WOMAN

Carnation....................Mildred Harris
Paul Marsh....................Percy Marmont
Elsa Marsh....................Flora Arline Arle
Jack Gordon....................John Hammond

Mildred Harris is the star of this feature produced by the D. M. Films, Inc., and released through Robertson-Cole. Glen Lyons is responsible for story and direction. He has turned out a mystery tale with a bit of a surprise finish that will do well enough for the smaller daily change of program houses. The picture was the stronger of a weak double feature bill at Loew's New York theatre.

The tale opens with an author threatening to take his play away from a producer unless the latter changes his idea of the leading lady in the piece. From that the theme of the story jumps and a female burglar is captured in the house of the author. From that point on it is a trite tale that has been done a thousand times in vaudeville sketches.

At the finish there is the disclosure that the lady burglar is none other than the girl that the author turned down for the lead in his play on the grounds that she couldn't act. In the meantime she has been impersonating a Canadian waif at his home and he has fallen in love with her. Of course the period between the opening of the story and the final twist is filled with the wildest form of melodrama, and if those in front don't get the twist before it appears the picture will get over on the strength of it.

Miss Harris played the lady burglar quite naturally, although supposedly an unsophisticated girl of the Canadian wilds she could not resist a couple of very flapperish prances and mannerisms that the hero must have caught unless he was totally blind. She has not improved much as an actress despite her apprenticeship on the Famous Players' lot, and now discloses it was direction that made her stand out in a couple of the big features that she did in the more recent past.

Percy Marmont as the leading man acquitted himself exceptionally well and made a distinct impression. John Hammond and Flora Arline Arle in supporting roles managed to get by. *Fred.*

MONEY TO BURN

A Fox release, with William Russell. The story is not bad, taken from the tale, "Cherub Devine." Raymond W. Lee directed.

It's about an overnight millionaire youth, who gained his money in the stock market, buying a country place. Arriving there he finds it is occupied by the former tenants, grandmother and daughter. There is some ghostly business at the outset, to frighten him away, but when he doesn't frighten, the girl appears. He persuades the two women to remain as his guests. The younger woman was unfortunate in marriage, wedding a foreigner who turned out to be a gambler. When she hears Russell is in the stock market, she wants to walk out on him, but he induces her to say. To assure her gambling is not a habit with him, he remains away from business until an opposition stock crowd nearly breaks him.

The production is skimpy, but it didn't call for much. There is little excitement, but more humor aids, and it makes a pleasant enough, probably, weekly release for the Fox name. The picture distinguishes no one.

A bad error of commission—and it is happening often in pictures—was the young couple, after walking and driving in the open for four miles in a blinding rainstorm, suddenly appear in the parlor, as they arrive at shelter, both apparently perfectly dry. That seems to be caused by taking all scenes called for in one set continuously, without the director remembering how heavy he had made his rainstorm. It's a custom, though, that has endured. There seems to be different opinions about it. It certainly does tend to make picture acting quite mechanical, if it weren't always that, and if it won't be always that. *Sime.*

THE LYING TRUTH

The Eagle Corp. sponsors "The Lying Truth," distributed through the American Releasing Corp. The picture is billed as a Marion Fairfax Production. Miss Fairfax having directed it in addition to writing the story. The feature has a story of small town life not altogether new in its development but sufficiently interesting to hold the attention of screen audiences in houses for which it has been made.

The proprietor of a small town newspaper discovers his publication is losing prestige largely due to the lack of pep on his part and that of his employes. His death is hastened when his wayward son is discovered to be a drug addict. The paper is willed to his stepson who endeavors to put it over, notwithstanding the long list of creditors and the amount of back salary due the crew. He editorially attacks the town powers and becomes involved in various difficulties which terminate in having the paper blacklisted. In order to bring it back he decides to create news and frames a fake murder, offering $1,000 reward for the capture of the alleged murderer. At the time of developing his scheme a body is discovered and the finders demand the reward. He publicly makes known the supposed murder is a ruse, but upon discovery that the body which was located is that of his step-brother, he is held on a murder charge. The matter is straightened out when a note is discovered written by the dead man, stating he was about to commit suicide. A love angle is introduced here and there and is brought to the front in the final footage.

The cast displays the required strength. Pat O'Malley easily takes first honors, with Marjorie Daw playing the other lead creditably. Others are Noah Beery, Tully Marshall, Adele Watson, Clair McDowell, Charles Mariles and George Dromgold. Conspicuous among the players is Pete Schmidt, the press agent for the producing company, in a reporter role. The rural settings fill the bill in the production end.

"The Lying Truth" has been made to sell at a price. For houses that do not demand first-line attractions it will deliver the goods. *Hart.*

MAN OF COURAGE

William Gregory....................E. K. Lincoln
Stephen Gregory, his father....................
Spottswood Aitken
Morgan Deane....................Fred Bloom
Dorothy Deane....................Millicent Fisher
Mrs. Deane....................Helen Dunbar
Johnny Rivers....................John A. Eberts
Aquila, a bandit....................James Youngdeer
El Cholo....................George Gebhart

Here is a real bad boy and it is surprising E. K. Lincoln, the star, could have permitted himself to be presented in a story such as this is and with the direction he received. The picture is presented by Nathan Hirsh and is released through the Aywon Film Corp. The identiy of author and director is not disclosed, and it is just as well, for they could never get another job on the strength of the showing made here.

Whoever handled the cutting and the titling also did a job to be thoroughly condemned. On the whole the picture is about as badly a botched-up affair as has been seen in years.

In story it is an attempt at a combination of society drama and western. Lincoln has the role of a mollycoddle son of wealthy parents whose regeneration is brought about through being hit on the head and shipped off in a freight car in dress clothes. In this attire he hits a border town just at the time that his former sweetheart has been carried off a transcontinental train by a band of Mexican bandits, and he goes to her rescue, establishing his manhood when he manages to rescue her from the hands of the hold-up men.

Millicent Fisher plays the lead opposite Mr. Lincoln and looks very well when under sunlight, but fails to register under the studio lamps. In riding attire, with hat well down over face, she appears youthful and vivacious; in evening costume, however, she fails to stand out.

Mr. Lincoln's performance cannot be commented on in this picture with anything like justice to him. He has been cut in and out of the picture with such glaring disregard to detail that one wonders at times whether he is a protean artist. He is shot in dress and dinner clothes and walks from one scene to another with the clothes changing en route. Spottswood Aitken gives his usual studied character performance as his father, while Fred Bloom enacted the role of the heroine's dad. No mention is made of the identity of the heavy, who gave a good performance.

The farther away you keep from this one the better. *Fred.*

BACHELOR DADDY

A Paramount five-reeler, with Thomas Meighan as the star. A comedy-drama from the novel by Edward Peple, directed by Alfred Green and presented by Adolph Zukor.

Richard Chester	Thomas Meighan
Sally Lockwood	Leatrice Joy
Ethel McVae	Maud Wayne
Mrs. McVae	Adele Farrington
Joe Pelton	J. F. McDonald
Charles Henley	Laurance Wheat
Nita	Charlotte Jackson
Buddie	Barbara Maier
Toodles	Bruce Guerin
David } Donald }	DeBriac Twins

Thomas Meighan stands out like a house afire in this corking comedy-drama. The support that he receives from five juvenile actors, included among which are the DeBriac Twins, puts over this picture with a distinct wallop that is going to make itself felt at the box office. There won't be any rush that will break down the doors of any theatre, nor will the picture cause a sensation, but it is a production that that is sure to build up on word of mouth advertising where it is played for more than a single day.

The story holds a combination of society stuff, kid stuff, western and real love interest. It is handled in a manner on the screen that bespeaks for Alfred Green a distinct niche among the real directors of the industry.

Meighan has the role of a self-made millionaire who is about to marry a very aristocratic society favorite. A week before the date of the ceremony he is suddenly called to Mexico, where his mining properties are in danger of being ruined through the operations of a band of guerrillas. His former prospecting partner is the superintendent of the mine, a widower with five youngsters. As far as the family is concerned the partner must have got a very late start in life, but when the bandits raid the mine after Meighan's arrival on the scene and the partner is mortally wounded, the former pledges himself to take care of the kiddies.

His trip back to civilization in a Pullman with the five little mischief makers abounds with laughter that is gained from touches in direction that are almost slapstick and still quite probable. Of course, no society queen is going to take a husband who has a quintet of adopted youngsters, so when she slips Meighan the gate the private secretary that he has passed up during his earlier romance comes right into the picture and wins him and the babes.

It's a pip of a picture, and Leatrice Joy makes a very charming ingenue lead opposite Mr. Meighan. At the same time Maud Wayne as the society girl and Adele Farrington as her mother both give worthwhile performances. Laurence Wheat, a comedy foil for Meighan, delivered nicely, the two working together bringing a reminder of the old "College Widow" days in the long past. The three other kiddies were Charlotte Jackson, Barbara Maier and Bruce Guerin. It is impossible to distinguish which name fitted the smallest of this trio, but that baby certainly is a whale of a find. He seems (at least the role is of that sex) hardly more than three years of ago, but the manner in which he struts before the camera with his little arms held behind his back makes for great comedy.

Fred.

GREAT ADVENTURE

Five-reel melodrama done in color under the Prizma process for J. Stuart Blackton. Star, Lady Diana Manners, supported by a company of English players. Made in England.

Lady Beatrice Fair	Lady Diana Manners
Hugh Argyle	Gerald Lawrence
Stephanie Dangerfield	Alice Crawford
Walter Roderick	Cecil Humphreys
King Charles II	William Luff
Samuel Pepys	Lennox Pawle
Catherine of Braganza	Rosalie Heath
Nell Gwynn	The Hon. Lois Sturt
Barbara Castlemaine	Elizabeth Beerbohm
Rosemary	Flora Le Breton
Bulfinch	Victor McLaglan
Thomas Unwin	Rudolph de Cordova
Duchess of Moreland	Gertrude Sterroll
Humpty	Fred Wright
Lady Beatrice (as a child)	Violet Virginia Blackton
Solomon Eagle	Tom Heselwood

The picture with its seventeenth century costumes of rich hue is a riot of luxurious color and the story is a revel of romantic drama, with the climax in a sensationally filmed fire effect furnishing a lurid background in the Great Fire of London for a hectic melodramatic story. At the Capitol Sunday afternoon the picture won a reward of spontaneous applause an unusual demonstration of approval.

The billing sets forth that that is "the first drama in natural color," which is somewhat less than the truth. Kinemacolor eight or ten years ago did several full length pictures by that process fully as good in a pictorial sense as this. But irrespective of mere color quality, there seems no special merit in polychromatic films, especially in dramatic subjects. The color is uneven, and when the effects are striking they distract from story interest. This was emphasized in "The Great Adventure." The costumes are of eye-compelling tones such as salmons, rich scarlets and striking blues, and it frequently happened that a splash of color caught and held the eye and attention to the detriment of the scene in its story relation. Often effective dramatic passages lost their significance and were spoiled because the scenic features overshadowed the scene. The color plan seems to be pretty completely restricted to scenic or light comedy subjects.

The story here developed is a capital one. It has historic interest, heart appeal and a wealth of thrills, not to speak of fine suspense. The backgrounds are always refreshing to the American fan, who seldom gets a glimpse of any but his native locale. The same is true of the people. All are new faces, and the women selected for the principal parts are a revel in loveliness. Lady Diana is a real British beauty. Flora LeBreton as the maid, Rosemary, is of the bewitching blonde type. Some of the delicate tinting of the color process lends a special charm to the portraiture of the two actresses, but it works out badly in the case of the men. Charles II has a greenish pallor that could scarcely be intended, and the other men look unnatural. It seems the colors are not altogether under control.

The story deals with the reign of Charles II following the downfall of the Roundhead rule. Hugh Argyle is returning from distant wanderings in the Indies, and a crew of cut throats on his ship plot to murder him and claim his estates when the ship gets to England. One, Bulfinch, an outlaw, is chosen to commit the murder. He strips the hero of all his identification papers and throws him, supposedly dead, into the season as the ship nears England.

Roderick, leader of the band, represents himself as Hugh and makes court to Lady Beatrice (Lady Diana), but Hugh, who has swum ashore, appears in disguise to thwart his schemes. Out of this clash grows the dramatic conflict that runs through the tale. Lady Beatrice has been plunged deep in debt, and in order to defeat the arch plotter who would use this circumstance to force her into an unwelcome marriage, goes to Newgate, where Bulfinch is awaiting execution for the murder of Hugh. She marries the criminal. Under the English law this process would purge her of debt and the noose would remove Bulfinch the next day. But that night the great fire sweeps London, and all prisoners are turned out. Bulfinch seeks out the fair Lady Beatrice and carries her to the lair of the outlaw gang in the crypt of St. Paul's.

A jealous woman in the thieves' crew brings word to Hugh, and the hero rushes to the rescue. Events move swiftly to the climax, with the fire as a thrilling background of the struggle for the lady fair.

Rush.

ACROSS CONTINENT

Five-reel comedy drama with Wallace Reid. Story and scenario by Byron Morgan. Direction of Philip E. Rosen under the supervision of Thompson Buchanan (Lasky-Paramount).

Jimmy Dent	Wallace Reid
Louise Fowler	Mary MacLaren
John Dent	Theodore Roberts
Lorraine Tyler	Betty Francisco
Dutton Tyler	Walter Long
Scott Tyler	Lucien Littlefield
Art Roget	Jack Herbert
Irishman	Guy Oliver
Tom Brice	Sidney D'Albrook

A coast-to-coast auto race for the family honor and the love of a girl is deftly framed to provide one of the best moments of suspense the screen has ever designed. Monday night at the Rivoli there was an audible stir of excitement during the big passage, eloquent tribute to the skill of the people concerned in the presentation from author to actor.

It is worth noting that the author also made the scenario and few other names are disclosed as having had a part in the production. From this it is fair to presume that Byron Morgan had pretty much his own way in working out his theme. If all that George Randolph Chester says of the studio technique is true, here is an illustration of the good sense of one-man control.

The narrative opens out clearly and simply with good human character relations and grows naturally up to its vigorous drama although the play is constantly lightened with fine touches of comedy, not the usual sort of labored clowning, but real humor with its roots in every day character. To this end Theodore Roberts, best of character men, contributes vastly, although the principal players are all plausible.

John Dent is a maker of "Flivers," while Jimmy, his son is secretly ashamed of the humble "Tin Lizzy" and aspires to a road-burning "Fontaine," manufactured by the Tylers who hold the New York-to-San Francisco road record and put all kinds of ridicule on the Dent. Old Man Dent at length demands that Jimmy, since he is supported by the Dent car, shall drive one, and in the dispute Jimmy quits the factory. Angered Old Man Dent determines to go after the Fontaine transcontinental record with a special model of the "Fliver."

But the Tylers have protected their record by trickery. Every time another manufacturer goes after it, their agents manage to wreck the contending car. The Dent on this trial is ditched by the plot of a Tyler agent, and when Jimmy discovers their treachery and bum sportsmanship, he hangs up a $25,000 purse for an open across-the-continent race, observing to the Tylers. "You can't ditch 'em all in an open event."

Here begins the thrilling contest, Jimmy in the Dent and young Tyler in the speed demon Fontaine. To give the fight a romantic kick, the Tyler girl, Jimmy's sweetheart, follows the event from control station to control station by rail and in the same train is Old Man Dent and his girl secretary Louise. The Tyler car of course out-distances the Dent at first, but in the rain and bad going the lighter sturdier Dent closes the gap.

There is plot and counter plot on the long road and the struggle is worked up to a high nervous pitch until the little Dent passes the huge Fontaine on a heavy sand trail in the Mojave desert. Near the distant goal Louise learns of a final scheme to defeat the gallant Jimmy by unfair means and over the last lap she manages to insinuate herself into Jimmy's car in disguise and by her means the schemers are undone and Jimmy crosses the line in the lead.

Rush.

A WONDERFUL WIFE

Universal five reeler by Dolf Wyllarde, adapted for the screen by Arthur Stratter and directed by Paul Scardon. Miss du Pont starred.

Chum	Miss du Pont
Alaric	Vernon Steele
Gregory	Landers Stevens
Halton	Charles Arling
Diana	Ethel Ritchie

A story of English service life laid principally in East Africa. The tale does not seem to have any particular appeal to the general run of picture fans, who have seen stories of this type handled to greater advantage on the screen. It will do, however, on a double feature bill in the better daily change houses and serve as the sole feature in the smaller ones.

Paul Scardon handled the story rather well for what there was in it. Miss du Pont plays the role of a wife of a young officer in the British service. He is sent to an African post in charge of the government commissioner who has the reputation of being a man without a heart. She, however, finds the heart and he in turn decides that he wants her and so manages to send the husband on a mission that will practically insure his death, even though orders have been received to send him to another post.

The wife rescues her husband and thwarts the heavy's plans and the tale ends in the usual happy manner with the moral that wives had better not interfere in husbands' affairs.

Landers Stevens plays the heavy most acceptably, but it is to Vernon Steele the credit must go. He makes the lead opposite Miss du Pont fairly realistic, especially so when he is being "vamped" by Ethel Ritchie. Had Miss Ritchie gone in for vamp stuff in the days when that type of screen actress was the biggest box office draw, she would have been in a position to have given some of the best a run.

Fred.

KINGFISHER'S ROOST

A five-reel western Chaudet-Hurst feature starring Neal Hart, made by Pinnical Productions, and released by Commonwealth. Paul Hurst director.

Barr Messenger	Neal Hart
Betty Brownell	Yvette Mitchell
Bull Keeler	William Quinn
Betty's Mother	Adelaide Hallock
Sheriff	Chet Lyon

Neal Hart is a two-fisted riding fool in this picture, along the lines of the usual type of western that he appears in. The feature is one that is good enough for the smaller houses, or will stand up on a double feature bill in the bigger daily change houses, in fact, it is better than some that have served that purpose. The supporting cast is rather good, and there are a couple of corking fights in the action.

The story is laid in a small southwestern town near the Mexican border. The heavy, William Quinn, is known as Bull Keeler on the American side of the border, where he is seemingly engaged in a legitimate business, but across the line he is the notorious Kingfisher, bandit chief. He falls in love with a girl in the town, and as his rival has Neal Hart playing a cowpuncher. The girl is accused of stealing a sum of money from the firm where she is employed by Keeler, but he promises to overlook the loss providing she will forget her infatuation for Barr Messenger (Hart). Instead she escapes across the border and enters a small town on the Mexican side.

Near this town Kingfisher makes his headquarters.

After she has left Keeler manages to plant a charge of horse theft against Messenger and he also makes a getaway and finally winds up in the same town. Keeler in the role of the bandit chief also shows up later and Messenger and he mixed it a couple of times. Then the story of the theft is cleared up with Keeler admitting that he framed it to get the girl, and one of his henchmen gives up the inside dope on the horse stealing plant, thus leaving the hero and shero free for the final clinch at the fadeout.

The picture is spotty at times and the interior sets are not particularly well lighted, but the exterior stuff, especially the long shots, are well photographed.

From the standpoint of cost the picture appears to have been a fairly inexpensive one; however, that need not enter the question of bookings. As a feature it will pass muster in almost any of the smaller houses where they like westerns. *Fred.*

MY OLD KENTUCKY HOME

A six-reel semi-rural crook melodrama, original story by Anthony Kelly, produced by Pyramid Pictures under direction of Ray C. Smallwood. Released through American.

Virginia Sanders	Sigrid Holmquist
Richard Goodloe	Monte Blue
Conway Arnold	Arthur Carewe
Mrs. Goodloe	Julia Swayne Gordon
Col. Sanders	Frank Currier
Loney Smith	Matthew Betz
Steve McKenna	William Quirk

Here is a picture that is at once a combination of "In Old Kentucky" and "Turn to the Right," at least as far as certain essentials of the plot are concerned. It has as its hero the erring son who has been railroaded to prison for a crime he did not commit; a couple of crooks that have met him after he gets out of stir and who become his pals and reform, and a horse race scene for the thrill. It isn't a whale of a picture by any means, but it is a type of feature that should go out and clean up considerable money on a steady grind.

It was rushed into the Central, New York, this week without any great exploitation to put it over. The chances are that a campaign bein run in a daily paper against stock selling propositions which undertook to give the low down on the Pyramid Corp., which made this production, is one of the reasons for it being brought into New York so hurriedly. The Pyramid people wanted to show that they were really on the job of producing and that it had a picture worthy of being shown on Broadway.

"My Old Kentucky Home" looks as though it cost the Pyramid people just about what they claim, somewhere in the neighborhood of $80,000, with prints and advertising, and the production looks fully good enough to gross about three times that.

Sigrid Holmquist plays the lead, with Monte Blue as the hero. The two pair up rather nicely and the Swedish star manages to again impress in this production. Blue has a tendency to overact at times in the matter of facial expression. Arthur Carewe played the heavy in a matter of fact manner that neither impressed or detracted from the picture. It was William Quirk and Lucy Fox, however, that carried off the greatest honors of the production. Quirk was one of the crooks and Miss Fox had the role of a country girl. She is a rather pleasing little brunet, who photographs like a million dollars and who seemingly has the necessary to get over on the screen. As a matter of fact she looks like a real bet for the future.

Frank Currier, Julia Swayne Gordon and Matthew Betz in character roles managed to score nicely, especially Miss Gordon in the role of the mother.

The direction of Mr. Smallwood left much to be desired at times. His action was rather slow in the earlier portion of the story—and later he permitted small matters of detail to escape him. One or two of these were quite noticeable. But the photography is good and the locations and sets are all that could be asked. The horse race stuff is particularly well handled. *Fred.*

THE TRUTHFUL LIAR

Realart (Famous Players) release with Wanda Hawley in a morality story by Will Payne. The moral is threadbare in pictures. It is don't lie to your husband, or don't do what he would not want you to do, or don't be a butterfly or any one of the many don'ts picture writers thought of, long after playwrights worked them dry. But fine for the film fan.

Miss Hawley is the wife of an engrossed engineer. That permits her to wear many and handsome gowns in a very well furnished home. While her husband was away on business, she wanted to play and hearing about a gambling room, induced a nice young man to escort her to it, along with others of the whist party. The gambling house was stuck up, the women obliged to leave their jewelry. While the wife and escort escaped during a melee (that never would have happened under the circumstances), the wife had to leave without a couple of rings, one her wedding ring.

The next day her husband suddenly returned. Upon kissing her hand in true picture fashion, also in ditto fashion, he discovered his wife was without her wedding ring. The wife said she had sent it to the cleaner, but then, again, a policeman from headquarters called to say the commissioner had sent him with all of the seized jewelry for Mrs. Haggard to select what belonged to her. And so the husband wanted to know why she had lied to him.

But he was an agreeable husband and got over that. In haste though at the bawling out Mr. Haggard had given her young escort, finishing by calling him a yellow pup, Mrs. Haggard wrote escort a lettter saying hubby was all wrong, that she couldn't see escort at the house but would see him elsewhere. It was all perfectly innocent, for escort during the gambling house scrimmage, had been shot in the arm (pistol).

But this led up to a murder of a low down crooked politician, the same one who brought about the gambling hold up when the mustached young man who ran the joint wouldn't give up. The politician got hold of the letter through a maid at the escort's boarding house, which had a front that said it was anything but a boarding house, while the interior belied the front, but still the escort lived there in the picture. The maid copped the letter and sold it to the same politician.

When Mrs. Haggard went looking for the letter, she finally landed in the office of the politician with $7,000 in cash. He wouldn't take that for the letter but offered to take it on account. When the wife refused to give it up, he grabbed it from her but not before she had attempted to stab him with a pair of shears. The escort walking home that way, coincidentally, saw her leave the place, investigated, found the politician was dead, found Mrs. Haggard's pocketbook on the floor and believed she had killed him. He hurried to the Haggards' home, arriving there shortly after the police commissioner had called. The commissioner was there on business. He knew Mrs. Haggard had visited Mark Potts between 5 and 5.30 that afternoon; Potts was the politician and had been killed between 5 and 5.30 that afternoon; why did you kill him, Mrs. Haggard; I did not, said Mrs. Haggard, believe anything you want to about me but don't believe that, and Dave Haggard himself in person standing there all the time. But he was a nice agreeable husband and let that pass too.

Escort arrived, said he did the killing; then Vanetti happened in. Vanetti was a stool for the cops and a handy man for Potts; the commish knew Van, told everyone but Mrs. Haggard to hide and he overheard what Vanetti had to say; that he had a letter and would sell it to Mrs. Haggard.

Back came the commish, grabbed Van, told him to come through and Van confessed; said he should have taken the boat for Italy but wanted to sell the letter after killing Potts and copping the seven.

The commish turned over the expensive letter to Mrs. Haggard, wished them good luck and blew. Husband Dave around this time got out of the haze and asked the escort why he had confessed to murder. Because said the escort without a tremor of the sheet, he had found Tess' pocketbook on the floor of Potts' office. Tess was Dave's wife. You're a nice kid said Dave and come around often. That yellow pup stuff doesn't go any more. Then Dave asked Tess to show him the letter. She did with halting fingers. He looked at it, turned it over in true picture fashion, then burned up the horrid letter that only said anyway Tess' marriage had been a mistake. After looking at Dave Taggart wandering through the film and not knowing what it was all about, it did seem as though Tess had picked a flop for support at home.

There it is. A moral; either don't lie to your husband or don't wear a wedding ring.

Miss Hawley did look good in this picture. Besides looking well, she did some acting, about the only one who did excepting Potts. Tough guy, Potts.

The feature runs a bit over the usual length. Probably the moral won't stand any more cutting. It's an ordinary weekly release otherwise, interesting enough for the readers of the Sunday magazines. *Sime.*

THE MAN THAT MARRIED HIS OWN WIFE

A Universal five-reeler starring Frank Mayo. A society drama that holds interest, but rather peters out at the end. Directed by Staurt Paton.

John Morton	Frank Mayo
Mrs. Morton	Sylvia Breamer

Here is a real blood-and-thunder tale of the sort that one finds in the cheaper fiction magazines. The title, "The Man That Married His Own Wife," sounds as though it might mean something to the box office in the smaller towns, but at Loew's New York the picture shared a double feature bill early this week. The story has a lot of pep at the opening, but it slows down toward the finish, at the time where there was opportunity for some real screen suspense.

The wallop at the opening is the crash between a steam yacht on which a number of society folk are cruising and a sailing schooner commanded by John Morton (Mayo). Both boats go down, and out of the wrecks but three people emerge. They are Morton and his mate and Sylvia Breamer, who plays the heroine. Just prior to the crash Morton had been hit across the nose by the main boom and that feature shattered, marring his facial expression to a great extent. The society girl that is rescued by him becomes his wife, and during the war he becomes a factor on the west coast and finally the most powerful single factor in shipping circles.

When he has achieved his fortune he believes that his wife has ceased to care for him and he decides to pass out of her life, first arranging for a suicide plant to be effected.

Seemingly the story is quite palpable at this point, when one takes the title into consideration, but it takes a slight twist which brings added interest. Morton comes east, and while the general impression is that he is a roughneck, he really proves to be a gentleman's son who ran away to sea at an early age. Then plastic surgery restores his features to their natural appearance and he returns to the coast after a year. He has kept in touch with the executor that he appointed to look after his "widow's" affairs, and has learned that she is being robbed by a society friend who is managing the business and who is trying to marry her. On his return matters are quickly straightened out and the wife and husband are together in a clinch at the end of the picture.

Mayo gives a rather clever performance, but the nasal makeup is quite palpable on the screen. Miss Breamer is all O. K. until she tries to emote when she is informed of her husband's supposed suicide, then she flops. The direction does likewise in the last reel of the picture. *Fred.*

HER MAD BARGAIN

"Mad Bargain" is right. The bargain consists of a girl's accepting a gift of $50,000 on the spur of the moment from an artist under the supposed condition that she spend it in a year and then commit suicide in order that the artist may collect $75,000 on her life insurance. Her bargain is mad enough, but what of the artist who would survive and face prosecution for a conspiracy for fraud? The story is absurd because its foundation is false and implausible. Everything of characterization and incident that is built on the framework is ruined because the planting of the whole situation won't bear examination.

The whole thing falls down on this point. If you can accept this wild condition you can swallow anything and the rest of the picture will be interesting, but if you decline to acquiesce (and who wouldn't?) what's the use. All the preparation is crude. The heroine is forced to become an artist's model when the death of her benefactor turns her out into the world from a home of luxury to earn her own living. The artist is a cad and makes dishonorable approaches. She takes flight to another artist on the floor below, and he protects her from her pursuer. In a paroxysm of shame and discouragement she attempts to commit suicide by jumping from the studio window, and the second artist gives her the fifty grand. Of course, the year is up. Alice has a change of heart and agrees to marry Tom, the sensational giver-up, and they are married.

It's a pity the base of the story is so weak, for the picture has been very well done in all other respects. There are some splendid interiors, designed with utmost skill, and the light effects throughout are highly artistic. Also the players act easily and convincingly, and there are incidental touches that are highly effective. For example, there is a capital bit of sentiment in the use of an amusing youngster and several pet animals. All these points of excellence, however, are wasted for the central situation—the element from which the whole tale grows—sets up a resistance in the mind of the spectator that makes him absolutely refuse to accept the people or the incidents seriously. Sentiment gets a reverse twist, because it has its roots in a situation that is essentially farcical, and the drama takes its color of travesty from this absurd angle. *Rush.*

THROUGH A GLASS WINDOW

May McAvoy is the dainty doughnut dipping star of this Realart that is being released by Famous

Players. It is a corking little picture of New York's east side life as the audiences in the hinterland undoubtedly like to believe it is, and therefore the picture should be a pleasing one to that type of movie fan. The story is a cute tale that was evolved by Olga Printzlau, and Maurice Campbell directed the offering.

The production suffers from the common trouble with all Realart pictures. They have to be made within a certain figure, and therefore street scenes and sets that have seen service on other occasions must be called into use.

Miss McAvoy, however, makes a charming little head of the family for screen purposes. She is the doughnut wielder who lives with a widowed mother and younger brother, who sells papers. The kid gets into bad company, shoots craps and finally resorts to robbery, but only to get sister out of a nasty jam. He is pinched and sent to the reformatory, and sis in the meantime opens a doughnut joint of her own and takes all the business away from the man who formerly employed her and accused her of being a crook. The result is that she has a neat little business going by the time her brother gets out of the can and turns it over to him while she goes off and marries a wop vegetable peddler.

Raymond McKee plays the lead opposite the star with comedy effect. Burwell Hamrick, a youthful player, is her brother and manages to get over his points nicely. Carrie Clark Ward and Fannie Midgely both contribute character old women that held interest, especially the comedy work of the former.

In sets the picture does not show any expense; the big street scene, with the elevated road, etc., has been seen time and again and is as familiar almost as one of the real corners in the city. Perhaps in time out-of-town fans will come to New York and get lost trying to find the actual location.

Fred.

MAN FROM HOME

A Paramount feature presented by Adolph Zukor. Made abroad in England and Italy under the direction of George Fitzmaurice. "The Man From Home" originally was the play in which William Hodge achieved success. The authors were Booth Tarkington and Harry Leon Wilson, Ouida Bergere having made the screen adaptation.

Daniel Forbes Pike.......James Kirkwood
Genevieve Granger-Simpson...........
.......................Anna Q. Nilsson
Horace Granger-Simpson....Geoffrey Kerr
Prince Kinsillo............Norman Kerry
Princess Sabina.........Dorothy Cumming
Ribiere......................Jose Rubens
Faustina Ribiere..........Annette Benson
The King....................John Miltern
Secretary to the King........Clifford Grey

This is one of the foreign made productions by Famous Players in its London studios under the direction of George Fitzmaurice. It is a strong feature with a corking cast that could well be designated as "all star," but the picture does not contain the real humor of the original play. It isn't a picture that will pull unusual business but it will entertain nicely.

The original play was replete with a quaint homely humor that seemingly is missing entirely in the screen version. But there are so many redeeming features in the photography and from a scenic standpoint that audiences are certain to be interested.

A corking bit of atmosphere is achieved in the back home in Indiana" portion that opens the story. The scenes that were shot in Italy are beautiful. There seems to be a clarity of the atmosphere particularly conducive to sharp photography.

The pictorial quality, the real story had it been transferred to the screen with its comedy and humor, would have made this feature a world beater, but as it is there is just a good feature production.

James Kirkwood plays the Man from Home in a characteristic manner that scores, and Anna Q. Nilsson, opposite, impressed most favorably. Norman Kerry was the heavy, endowing the Prince with an "air" that scored. The cast had Jose Ruben as the fisherman and Annette Benson as his wife. The latter was a triumph. She has youth, verve and a personality that lands like a million dollars. John Miltern as the King was immense. If "The King" is ever screened he is the man for the role. *Fred.*

TOO MUCH BUSINESS

Albert E. Smith presents this Vitagraph five-reel comedy adapted from the Saturday Evening Post story by Earl Derr Biggers, "John Henry and the Restless Sex." Directed by Jess Robbins.

John Henry Jackson........Edward Horton
Myra Dalton..............Ethel Grey Terry
Amos Camby................Tully Marshall
Simon Stecker............John Steppling
Ray Gorham.................Carl Gerard
Mrs. Camby...................Elsa Lorimer
The Head Nurse............Helen Gilmore
Robert Gray.................Mack Fenton
Officer 16....................Tom Murray

Here is a capital comedy worked out with fine sense of character drawing and whimsical romance well acted by a cast of extraordinarily even quality. Tully Marshall in the person of an irascible old business man has a part of conspicuous drollery handled in that bland actor's best vein.

This scheme of weaving a romance in terms of bland fun is highly refreshing, as compared to the gosh awful seriousness of most screen love affairs. "Too Much Business" is characterized by deft touches of commonplace, every-day naturalness worked into an amusing play entertainment of unusually sustained interest. Some of the passages approach farce, but the appeal is always intelligent, and scenario writer and actors never descend to slapstick.

Amos Canby (Tully Marshall) is a hard boiled business man, given to peppery outbursts when things do not go right, but depending absolutely upon his girl secretary Myra and frowning upon any love affairs between his efficient aid and the men of the office. His ambition is to form a consolidation with Simon Stecker, a business rival, but Stecker is against the project until his automobile runs down John Henry Jackson, Camby's sales manager, and John Henry gives him an argument on the merits of the consolidation.

About the same time John Henry lays siege to Myra's heart in urging his suit as a pure business proposition by taking a 30-day option on Myra's hand, the consideration being that his income shall be doubled before he can exercise the privilege. Camby learns of the romance and, not knowing of John Henry's service in the business deal, discharges him flatly.

John Henry goes into business for himself, taking up Camby's threat that he will drive him out of town, establishing a "Hotelleries des Infants," or nursery for the children of fashionable mothers too busy to care for them. The enterprise prospers mightily. At the same time Stecker decides to come into the amalgamation, but makes it a condition that John Henry shall be the general manager.

Camby then is faced with the problem of persuading John Henry to forgive the past and rejoin the works, and this leads to an unroariously funny climax in the nursery, where Camby's wife becomes involved with her husband's plots, **gets locked in and has to telephone to Camby to rescue her. The last two reels make a splendid example of sustained fun with a satisfactory settlement for John Henry in Myra's arms and his defeated rivals defeated and undone.** *Rush.*

THE TRAP

Universal-Jewel five-reel feature of the Hudson Bay country with Lon Chaney starred, directed by Robert Thornby.
Gaspard........................Lon Chaney
Benson.........................Alan Hale
Thalie..................Dagmar Godowsky
The Boy...................Stanley Goethals
The Teacher....................Irene Rich
The Factor............Spottiswoode Aitken
The Priest...............Herbert Standing

Too much star in closeups every few feet makes this feature a very draggy affair. In the telling of the story of a long-lived hatred of a French-Canadian trapper this feature goes along slowly, without **delivering any punch until just a few moments before the finish. Then the supposed fight between the star and a savage wolf is left to the imagination. It seems doubtful if the picture is going to prove a money maker of unusual calibre, but classed with the ordinary program releases it will pass.**

Carl Laemmle presented the picture this week at the Central, which house is under lease to the Universal. It is possible it may be kept there for an extra week unless someone comes along with an outside production and offers to take the house on a rental.

In a certain sense "The Trap" is something of a freak, since it has little love interest. In a brief moment at the finish there is a suggestion the star is finally happiness, after he has been practically a victim of his own hatred **for years.**

Chaney plays a trapper who returns to his home in the spring after a winter on the trail and discovers that he has lost his sweetheart to a stranger. The stranger has located on a mine the trapper had started and, by filing his claim, has legal possession.

From that point Chaney schemes to injure his successful rival in devious ways, and finally contrives to have him sent to jail for a shooting. At about the same time the wife dies and there is a little youngster of five turned over to Chaney. It is his intention to wreak vengeance on the child, but instead he grows to love it. So great does this love grow that when he hears the father of the boy has been released from prison, he plans the wolf trap in his home, knowing the father will come there and believing that the wolf **will slay him and the child will remain with him afterwards. The trap is sprung, but it is the little fellow who walks into it. Chaney follows and kills the beast. Then the father comes and he and the little boy go down the river together, while the trapper starts to receive an education at the hands of a school marm who has come on the scene.**

The picture gives Chaney a chance to hog footage right along in close-ups. This becomes rather tiresome, as all the emoting he does does not carry the story forward at all. Alan Hale plays the stranger and Dagmar Godowsky is the unfaithful sweetheart. There are three names of value in the cast in Herbert Standing, Frank Campeau and Spottiswoode Aitken. Their roles, however, are of slight importance.
Fred.

LADY GODIVA

Pathe is releasing this Wistaria production (presented by Associated Exhibitors) of Lord Alfred Tennyson's immortal poem, "Lady Godiva." It is a period play, appropriately costumed. Whoever adapted and directed the picture made considerable of rather a threadbare theme.

Lady Godiva becomes the unwilling duchess of an unscrupulous Earl. Though his nominal wife she is not in spirit. The grim earl to wreak vengeance on her townsfolk edicts that if Godiva's amour, a fugitive architect, is not delivered into his hands within two days he will raze the town by fire. Godiva's plea for mercy brings the challenging retort, "You would not ache a little finger of your hand" (Tennyson), to which she replies in the negative. The Earl promises leniency on the condition, "Ride you naked through the town and I'll repeal it." Godiva tells the kinsmen of the condition. They promise to bar every door and window threatening death to whomsoever raises his eyes on their savior. "Then rode she forth clothed in her chastity," but the fugitive Dryer returns just then to shield her with his cloak from the rude gaze of the vicious Earl.

That's the big punch of the picture and as such should accomplish something at the gate. There are such things as censors to be considered but that obstacle is negligible. It is doubtful that even the original footage could have contained anything more than was shown at the Central, New York, where the film is for the current week. There seemed to be but little cutting, the shots of the undraped figure being flashes that satisfied the most minute gaze, the posing eliminating any suggestion of salaciousness. The motive and the choice Tennyson wording with variations by Dimitri Stephon, who did the titling, soothed the sting.

Minus the nude equestrian act, the picture for all its plot flimsiness interestingly developed.

The secondary wallop which serves as the climax is the extermination of the earl and all his tyrannical satellites through the collapse of the new castle which Godiva's architect-lover had designed before his imprisonment for a minor violation of his lord's severe hunting statutes. A neat twist is the incident where the Court Jester, who had instigated the folk to destroy at their own free will what they were compelled to build under duress, chants a hymn of regal destruction in semblance of his King's Fool character, which becomes real when the storming waves wash in the weakened foundation.

There are a number of deficiencies as well. The collapse of the castle looks too much like the papier mache erection it is, and does not suggest the foundation of the real fortress. The lighting was none too perfect either.

Lady Highbury, the earl's scheming paramour, particularly suffered thereby. In one scene her hair was raven black; in another chestnut brown. This alternated to a striking extent. Then the Earl would be shown meting out dire penalties for the slightest offences and yet, when he orders Godiva to caress him, and on her refusal orders any of his courtiers to taste her lips, a softer-hearted courtier is seen intercepting and escorting Her Grace out, while the Earl sits by, rebuked.

On the whole, the production is satisfactory. Costume plays are scarce enough just now to be a novelty although past performances of such type productions have not been any too lucrative. The one-sheets of Lady Godiva's riding forth clad only in her chastity will mean a lot. The Main Alley is flooded with them and a fair stag collection was waiting in the lobby before the first show.

The cast is accorded no screen mention although all are on the same average though satisfactory par. No program mention is made of the technical staff, but the film carries a few titles of scenario writer and director.

It looks like a foreign made picture judging from some of the character types although there is one thing to refute that. With the low cost of extras abroad, all importations have been heretofore distinguished by their huge mob scenes. Here they were somewhat skimped both through poor scene placing as well as insufficiency of numbers. Each extra meant an additional custom charge and that may account for it.

Abel.

WITHOUT FEAR

A Fox five-reeler of the society type with Pearl White as star. Directed by Kenneth Webb. Story by Paul H. Sloane.

Warren Hamilton	Charles Mackaye
Walter Hamilton	Robert Agnew
Ruth Hamilton	Pearl White
Billy Barton	Macey Harlan
John Martin	Robert Elliott

Just one of the regulation William Fox program features that may serve to pull a little money on the strength of Pearl White's name, but other than that there is nothing particularly recommending it as out of the ordinary. Loew played it as a double feature during the week he did the Big Seven revivals at his New York theatre.

It is just a case of Pearl White plays tennis; Pearl White rides horseback; Pearl White wears a number of stunning gowns, and there you are. Something of the story serves the purpose of permitting Miss White to do all of these things, but it is rather just a thread.

She is the daughter of a wealthy old society family and falls in love with a newly made millionaire. One of those fellows that must have made his money in pictures or something; maybe it was bootlegging; at any rate, her father objected to the young man. The girl persists in meeting the man, and finally a rival sees her enter his home. He imparts the information to father and then father insists the pair marry.

The only twist is that the girl refuses to be forced into a marriage and to obey her father's wishes, but at the last minute when she learns the man of her heart is going away relents and goes to him.

In titling the obvious is used all through, and one can guess the titles before they are flashed, at least that is what the New York Roof audience did last Friday night.

Fred.

'BEYOND THE ROCKS'

Theodora Fitzgerald	Gloria Swanson
Lord Bracondale	Rodolph Valentino
Lady Bracondale	Edythe Chapman
Captain Fitzgerald	Alec B. Francis
Josiah Brown	Robert Bolder
Morella Winmarleigh	Gertrude Astor
Mrs. McBride	Mabel Van Buren
Lady Ada Fitzgerald	Helen Dunbar
Sir Patrick Fitzgerald	Raymond Blathwayt
Lord Wensleydon	F. R. Butler
Lady Anningford	June Elvidge

Lasky production, starring Gloria Swanson, with Rodolph Valentino featured, based upon the novel by Elinor Glyn, placed in screen form by Jack Cunningham. Sam Wood did the directing, with the production a regular Paramount program feature.

"Beyond the Rocks" has the customary Glyn features. It has been mentioned as a sequel to "Three Weeks," and successfully develops the necessary action for a melodramatic love story. With the Glyn name behind the story and Valentino as the ardent lover, the production should have little difficulty in securing the necessary returns from the regular picture fans.

The story presents the eternal triangle idea with several punches. Theodora Fitzgerald (Miss Swanson), who has married for money, shortly after discovers her love for a heroic young nobleman. Her husband is considerably older, and her love affair with the younger man develops rapidly. It becomes so ardent they decide to break it off entirely to avoid trouble. The wife writes her lover to this effect and to her husband at the same time. The letters are switched by a jealous woman; the husband learns his wife loves another. He immediately leaves with an expedition to Africa. She follows, accompanied by her mother and the young lord. The husband's party is attacked by bandits in the desert and he is shot just as his wife's party arrives. On his deathbed he places her hand in that of the man she loves.

"Beyond the Rocks" has been built purely as a program feature. Its story should attract business. The cast has been well selected, with Miss Swanson and Valentino nicely suited. The picture may prove a matinee business getter. It has all of the requisites for the female picture fan.

Hart.

THE BEAUTY SHOP

Dr. Arbutus Budd	Raymond Hitchcock
Sobini, undertaker	Billy B. Van
Panatella, innkeeper	James J. Corbett
Cremo Panatella, his daughter,	Louise Fazenda
Coca	Madeline Fairbanks
Cola	Marion Fairbanks
Anna Budd	Diana Allen
Maldonado, a bad man	Montagu Love
Phill Briggs, attorney	Laurance Wheat

"Labored" is the whole sum of this comedy effort by Cosmopolitan (Paramount), at the Rialto this week. Everyone in the feature tries so hard to be funny, in their own way, whether as comedians or title writers. The labored effort ruins the effect, with the result remaining that if the names of this picture can not be played up for business, there won't be much business, beyond what any ordinary feature release might draw.

The names are those of Raymond Hitchcock, James J. Corbett and the Fairbanks Twins, besides Montagu Love for the picture fans, for any popularity or draw he may hold amongst them. Hitchcock and Corbett if plugged enough should mean something, together in one picture, but on the screen Corbett wears a wig and heavy mustache as a Spanish inn keeper. It doesn't present him in a favorable light and in acting, what Corbett does here will never be held for or against him.

Hitchcock and Billy B. Van with their methods of mime funmaking that smacks so largely of burlesque scenes, in Hitchcock's ruses to escape a duel with Maldonado (Mr. Love) and Van as the village undertaker urging Dr. Budd to go through with it, scarcely arouse genuine laughter. The fun is gone after so unmistakably mechanically as though laid out in advance by an architect that none registers. Even more labor was spent upon the titles. Everyone is aimed for a laugh and nearly all flop. But the title writers have the excuse of the material they were writing about.

The real comedy is in the story, that is the idea, of a beauty doctor in New York through using a picture of himself in a fanciful uniform on his advertising matter, becoming recognized in a foreign country as a long lost scion of a noble family, through the crest employed. A delegate sent by the country to reclaim the doctor, goes to America and finds the Doc about to be placed in bankruptcy by creditors. Promising him an inheritance the doctor accompanies the representative back to Bolognia, where Maldonadao, the tough man of the neighborhood, decides to put him away. If there is a laugh in Hitchcock's costume besides, that makes two laughs in all for "The Beauty Shop."

If anyone did anything worth while it was Mr. Love. He did seem fierce, as the ever-ready Spanish mangler.

It's worth while playing this in the usual way through the names, but it shouldn't be booked in for too long or too much dependence placed upon it as a comedy—the Hitchcock, Corbett, Fairbanks, Love thing may be promised for they will be there, but nothing else.

"The Beauty Shop" may be taken as the criterion by all picturedom as to the difference between the stage and the screen. Lauder found it out and others have in this picture, but Hitchcock is looked upon as a good enough name for Cosmopolitan to lately engage him for another feature. "The Beauty Shop" was finished some months ago but has been held back. With the scarcity of new productions for the summer, it may come in handy just now almost anywhere.

Edward Dillon directed the scenario made by Doty Hobart from the stage hit of years ago, written by Channing Pollock and the late Rennold Wolf.

Sime.

His Wifes Husband

Olympia Brewster	Betty Blythe
Henry Packard	Huntley Gordon
John Brainard	Arthur Carewe
Dominick Duffy	George Fawcett

"His Wife's Husband" was adapted from a novel by Anna Katherine Green. Society melodrama. The film version runs about 6,000 feet and was produced by Pyramid Pictures, Inc., with the American Releasing Corporation handling the distribution. Kenneth Webb directed and Betty Blythe is starred.

The picture is entertaining and has been well staged. The story is familiar, treating of a woman who re-marries in the belief her first husband is dead. The first husband through a twist in the yarn becomes the second husband's secretary. The three are thus under one roof. The first husband, however—he's the heavy—has been married before himself. His attempt to revenge himself on his second wife is thwarted by his first wife turning up opportunely.

Intermingled with this is the second husband's political ambitions—he is seeking the nomination for the governorship—and the desire of a political boss to sidetrack him. The story gives Miss Blythe many opportunities for emotional work. There is a likeable spirit of conflict in the plot that keeps the unfolding of it interesting.

Huntley Gordon's hero, the second husband, who incidentally turns out to be the first and legitimate spouse of the heroine, is manly and convincing. Arthur Carewe makes the heavy artistically sinister, playing quietly and effectively. George Fawcett does little more than a bit as the political boss and handles it with his usual skill.

The settings suggest considerable money was spent on the production. "His Wife's Husband" is not exceptional as feature pictures go, but it can more than hold its own with the rank and file, with sufficient to put it over in the higher priced film houses anywhere.

Bell.

QUEEN O' THE TURF

Roberta Morton	Brownie Vernon
Richard Morton	John Faulkner
Denis O'Hara	John Cosgrove
Jeffrey Manners	Raymond Lawrence
Dick Morton	Robert McKinnon
Myra Fain	Evelyn Johnson
Droone	Tal Orell
Toby Makin	Gerald Harcourt

Robertson-Cole feature produced by special arrangement with Lou Rogers. What the Rogers connection with the picture is has not been disclosed. It might be accepted he is the author or the director. No mention is made as to either of those persons. Brownie Vernon is the star.

As the title suggests, the picture has a racing story. It starts on a Kentucky stock farm and finishes up on a northern race track. Like other racing stories, villains who try to cheat at the races predominate.

A dishonest jockey is discovered just before the big race, and the girl owner is forced to ride the winning horse. The race is the big feature. When shown at the Broadway the picture was cut during the racing scenes and two horses took up the pace on treadmills on the stage.

The story leading up to the final race is of little importance; merely used for early footage.

Miss Vernon displays animation, one of the big assets. The supporting players do well enough with a story that means little. The production cost is nil. Exteriors almost exclusively.

"Queen o' the Turf" provides a horse race on the screen and nothing more. *Hart.*

SHERLOCK HOLMES

Alice Faulkner..............Carol Dempster
Madge Larabee..............Hedda Hopper
Terese..............Margaret Kemp
Rose Faulkner..............Peggy Bayfield
Dr. Watson..............Roland Young
Professor Moriarity,
Gustave von Seyffertitz
James Larabee..............Anders Randolf
Alf Bassick..............Robert Schable
Forman Wells..............William H. Powell
Sid Jones..............Percy Knight
Prince Alexis..............Reginald Denny
Count von Stahlberg..............David Torrence
Otto..............Robert Fischer
Dr. Leighton..............Lumsden Hare
Craigin..............Louis Wolheim
Billy..............Jerry Devine
Sherlock Holmes..............John Barrymore

E. J. Bowes, now one of the vice-presidents of Goldwyn, is the sponsor for this screen version of the former William Gillette stage success by Sir Arthur Conan Doyle. The production opened at the Capitol Sunday. While it seems to be one of those specials certain to make money because of the combination of names in it, there isn't much from a picture standpoint to recommend it. The story is badly handled, the continuity leaping along by fits and starts. There is, however, a cast of names bound to bring money into every box office.

The Gillette play is used entirely as the basis. Some of the scenes were taken in England, others in Switzerland and the interiors were finished in New York. Al Parker, who directed a number of Fairbanks' pictures and Clara Kimball Young, handled Mr. Barrymore in this production.

Mr. Bowes and his associates have not fully decided what channel they will release the picture through, but it seems certain the Goldwyn-First National arrangement will find this picture included.

Mr. Barrymore plays the detective-hero with plenty of dash, and while in stature he does not quite typify the popular conception of Holmes, he does endow the role with sufficient artistry to make it stand out. Gustave von Seyffertitz as Professor Moriarity, the heavy, gave the star a run in the development of his strong character role.

A number of real thrills as the story unfolds much after the fashion of a melodramatic serial. Punch after punch at times and all of the tricks are resorted to to put in the wallop. In the print at the Capitol there were times when the written titles and telegrams were a little short; this fault was also noticeable in several of the spoken titles.

No matter what the faults, the picture looks as though there was a real bet in the combination of John Barrymore and "Sherlock Holmes," especially when one realizes the names supporting the star. It certainly is a picture that can be truthfully billed as an "all-star production" without fear of a comeback, and it lends itself perfectly to exploitation.

Carol Dempster, who plays the lead opposite the star, does not get into the picture until about midway, but from then on she makes up for lost time. She is a pretty appearing and really clever heroine. Percy Knight, Hedda Hopper, Roland Young, Anders Randolf and William H. Powell all give praiseworthy performances. *Fred.*

TEN NIGHTS IN A BARROOM

Produced by Blazed Trail Productions, released by Arrow (State Rights). Film version of old melodrama of 50 years ago. Released in January.

Directed by Oscar Apfel.

Little Mary Morgan..............Baby Ivy Ward
Joe Morgan..............John Lowell
Fanny Morgan..............Nell Clark Kellar
Simon Slade..............Charles Mackay
Frank Slade..............James Phillips
Dora Slade..............Ethel Dwyer
Harvey Green..............Charles Beyer
Judge Hammond..............John Woodford
Willie Hammond..............Kempton Greene
His Aunt..............Mrs. Thomas Ward
Sample Switchel..............Harry Fisher
Mehitabile..............Lillian Kemble
Hank Smith..............J. Norman Wells
Mrs. Hank Smith..............Leatta Miller
Judge Lyman..............Thomas Vill
The Village Doctor..............Richard Carlysle
Foreman of the Mill..............Robert Hamilton

There are a few that never die. They have within some universal, basic appeal that makes them immortal. Among the conspicuous of the deathless plays are "Uncle Tom" and its companion "Ten Nights In a Barroom." Since its release nearly five months ago the seven-reeler has been doing real business. Its record is one of conspicuous drawing power.

The Tivoli, where the picture was reviewed, is a daily change establishment of the best class on Eighth avenue, just off the Times Square district and drawing from a middle class apartment-tenement population. It played there Monday and Tuesday to attendance, increased by an estimated 20 per cent. The outstanding feature of the picture's draw, according to the house management, was that it brought to the box office a very noticeable number of new faces, both young and old.

"They look to me," said a house attache, "Like people that don't go to a picture house once a month. Probably the elders are people who saw the stage play and were attracted to a screen version. The younger element, perhaps, had heard of the famous stage piece from their parents and looked in because the familiar name attracted them. From an examination of the crowd I should say there was a considerable percentage of church people that could not be classed as fans."

That's the box office angle. From the entertainment side the picture delivers the goods. There are half a dozen standard dramatic themes that never fail. First is the Cinderella story and its nearest neighbor is the theme that might be called "the comeback." In "Ten Nights In a Barroom" the "comeback" or "reformation" theme is powerfully developed. The story shows a man hammered down and down to the depths of shame, only to turn about, defeat the forces of evil, vindicate himself and reestablish his own happiness and self-respect and make good his better aspirations. That probably is the meat of the appeal of this indestructible classic.

The play is splendidly done in simple terms that cannot but register on any grade of intelligence. It is real drama, robust and vigorous in pattern and detail without any taint of the artificial, except as the melodrama is almost necessarily shaded with a certain theatrical intensity. It is honest drama—an interpretation of life if you like, although, perhaps, not quite an entirely realistic record. It is curious that this revival of a play conceived in the manner of the ancient school should make such a mark in a day when the stage and the screen are given almost entirely to fads of realism, sex theories and other eccentricities.

If this simple play that has stood the test of time can compete successfully with the modern screen fiction styles it ought to be worth a painstaking study to analyze the possibilities of the hosts of other old time standards. The libraries probably are full of honest old plays that can give a race to the day's best sellers. The old plays, perhaps because we, unthinkingly regard them as passé, always appear to us as they were done in the days when the stage producer dealt in cruder mechanical methods. "Way Down East," as Griffith screened it, is a fine illustration of an old play staged in the modern technique. The actual background of the big ice scene was a new theatrical trick (made possible only by the modern picture) which made "Way Down East" a brand new play in a theatrical sense. But its intrinsic drama was in the heart of the manuscript.

In the same way a tremendously effective denouement is achieved in "Ten Nights In a Barroom" by an exactly paralled device. The hero (splendidly played by John Lowell) goes into a river filled with grinding logs to rescue his hated enemy. The scene is done with a realism and effect that approaches that epic of "Way Down East." It furnishes a thrill that caps an hour of truly affecting sentiment.

The moral is that modern aids to illusion renew the strength of great works of another age and make them live again as they did in another generation. *Rush.*

THE AGONY OF THE EAGLES

London, May 1.

The Stoll Film Co. gave a private show of "The Agony of the Eagles," adapted from the novel, "The Old Guard," by Georges D'Escarbes. It was adapted and produced by Bernard Deschamps for Films de France. It is a magnificent production, too tragic in theme and too foreign in treatment for general American acceptance. The captions in the English version are verbose and the whole thing is more narrative than active.

A serious error was made in casting Severin-Mars for the double role of Colonel Montander and Napoleon. He is too tall for the Napoleonic role and not a bit like the histrionic type of the French Emperor.

The film winds up with the execution of the half a dozen heroes who sought to place the son of Napoleon upon the throne of France, and the audience departs with a bad taste in its mouth. *Jolo.*

WATCH HIM STEP

This might have been a corking comedy feature had it been properly titled and somewhat improved upon in the matter of direction. In the latter degree the principal fault is that the promoters behind Richard Talmadge as a star are trying to force him a little too hard. In their effort to make him a second "Doug" they are employing slapstick comedy methods. That is far from keeping him directed at the point they are trying to achieve. As the matter stands the picture is just an ordinary program release of the cheaper sort.

The story is the old one of the unwelcome suitor, with his final triumph over the objecting father. Talmadge plays the boy and pulls a number of thrill stunts, but they are too obviously of the slapstick type to get the laughs they should from audiences. His bounding acrobatics and flops and falls are done in a manner that shows careful preparation and that takes from their laugh producing value.

Ethel May Shannon as the girl whom he wants to wed is rather pretty and does her role effectively. She has a window climbing thrill. The heavy of Colin Kenny is worthy. He puts up a fight with the star in which he shows up better than the lead. How he ever got away with it is a question. Incidentally Kenny seemed to have the best of it when stacked up against Talmadge as to screen personality. The balance of the cast is fairly ordinary.

The production was shot principally out of doors and that naturally held down the costs. There were a number of office sets and the back drops used behind some of them were particularly noticeable because of the real shots from a balcony which had preceded them by a few scenes.

In the cheaper type of houses this picture will pass. It seems rather too bad that when some independent producer has a picture and perhaps a start he might develop into a real winner, that he doesn't go just a little bit further and have some real title writer and cutter handle his product after the shooting is finished. This one could have been improved a hundred per cent. in those particulars. *Fred.*

THE SILENT VOW

Richard Stratton }
"Dick" Stratton } ....William Duncan
Anne..............Edith Johnson
Ethel..............Dorothy Dawn
Elizabeth Stratton..............Maud Emery
"Doug" Gorson..............J. Maurice Foster
"Jim" Gorson..............Henry Hebert
"Bill" Gorson..............Fred Burley
"Sledge" Morton..............Jack Curtis
The Professor..............Charles Dudley

William Duncan has turned out "The Silent Vow" for Vitagraph, appearing in a dual role as its star and also doing the directing. Edith Johnson is featured, with the scenario credited to Bradley J. Smollen. With the bulk of the work in the production placed upon one man's shoulders, pretentiousness cannot be looked for. As it stands "The Silent Vow" is merely a series of views of the great outdoors, with an ordinary north woods story taking up the footage.

By having the star the director, Vitagraph has eliminated a large slice of expenese, and by having the production include practically only exteriors, the cost has been cut to a minimum. As it stands the picture cannot bring more than $15 daily rental for first run, and graded down from that according to its age. Even at the low rentals Vitagraph should secure a profit, as the Smith organization can't grind them out much cheaper than this has been done.

The story is based upon a feudal idea. It includes many chases through the mountains, fights and the like, all going to make up one of those outdoor pictures that appeal to a certain clientele.

The five and ten cent houses can use this production. *Hart.*

SHACKLES OF GOLD

Herbert Brenon directed William Farnum in this Fox feature, adapted from Henri Bernstein's "Samson." It is a society drama dealing with the Curb and Stock Exchange, employing a not entirely original idea for the climax—that of the hero forcing the stock market to a low margin in order to break his rival even though it means ruin for himself.

The action starts with a punch, literally in a fight scene on the docks, John Gibbs (Farnum) as a dock laborer preventing the removal of oil freight on his transport on a forged order. Ten years later Gibbs is a power in Wall street, and Hoyt, who opposed Gibbs on the docks 10 years earlier is similarly well intrenched. Gibbs is enamored of

Marie Van Trent, of society blue blood. She tells him it is a case of unrequited affection, but they become married on the behest of her mercenary mother because of her father's financial setbacks. Married in name only, the new Mrs. Gibbs seeks diversion elsewhere and accepts the invitation of Valentine, a man Gibbs had befriended through valuable stock tips, who proves himself a blackguard. Gibbs is supposed to have left town that evening on a business trip, but on changing his plans finds his wife has not returned and its after 1.30. Surmising whom she had been out with, after her confession and defiance, he forces the market on Callenda oil, in which Valentine has sunk his all, down to 80 to wipe away the latter's margin and though the market booms up to 120 again, breaking Gibbs as well as Valentine, the former is satisfied. And for the finish, now that he is a poor man again, the "heroine" decides to stick by and start all over again with him.

She is unconvincing to a degree in her part, although with her unsympathetic characterization little better could have been accomplished. A certain demureness and wholesome simplicity somewhat counteracts the lack of her physical charm and pulchritude.

Farnum in his part makes the most of his gift of expression in the dramatic scenes. He still retains that juvenile appearance, although inclined toward stoutness. As with most Farnum vehicles, since one can remember, there is always a "sad" ending, most of the times winding up with his going mad. That used to be the set Farnum fade-out, and this conclusion, in fact, is most optimistic comparatively.

The production has been nicely handled, and while not lavish it exceeds the usual Fox production limit considerably. Brenon has handled the situations nicely, the exchange shots looking realistic. The idea of shooting a street exterior from the doorway to include actual passers-by was effective. On the whole, it will interest as a program feature. The title should mean something also at the gate. *Abel.*

THE WIFE TRAP

Five-reel drama put out by the Hamilton Film Corporation (Paramount). Starring Mia May, who was the heroine in Famous Players' unlamented "The Mistress of the World" serial.

Apparently this is part of the lot of German film bought abroad last spring by Famous Players and put through the re-editing system, as was the Ufa serial. Peter Milne and Benjamin Decasseres are credited with the American titles.

It is apparent why the remote 58th Street house was chosen for the initial showing. The experiment of putting "The Mistress of the World" in the Broadway houses taught its own lesson. The idea appears to be to get what return is possible on the foreign job lot purchase in neighborhood houses.

This one is scarcely good enough for that clientele. It's the cheapest kind of mediocre melodrama, weak in conception and crudely acted. The settings and general direction belong to the period when the American production technique was young. Somewhere about the "Pop" Lubin level of 1910. The actors go through the whole play at a sort of jog. When the heroine engages in the business of crossing the stage she always trots, and one gets the idea that the whole play was a sort of Marathon canter.

The costuming (it is all modern society stuff where costuming has to approach perfection to stand the test) is sometimes almost comic. In one incident the heavy, who is passed off as a nobleman, has a rendezvous with the wife of a leading Paris banker, and he is disclosed lolling about in his gorgeous apartment dolled up in a musical comedy outfit, presumably a gentleman's lounging robe, which looks like a pierrot's outfit for a costume ball. That seems to be somebody's idea of the way the nobility orders things. Throughout there is apparent much of the same sort of naive striving to impress with sham magnificance. The actions of the personages of the story are no more convincing than the count's travesty lounge robe. It's all just infantile fiction, all burlesque to any adult intelligence. It would be an economy to scrap all this junk for the general good of the industry.

The play opens at the trial of the heroine, Louise, for the murder of her husband. She has refused to speak in her own defense, but the court confronts her with her child, and in order to save the little one from disgrace the mother agrees to tell her tale. The story then begins in the form of a fadeback. It might better have been told as a straight-away narrative.

Louise goes to the Hendricks' bank to draw an income from her father's modest estate. Hendricks has increased the income by clever investment and the girl visits him in his private office to thank him. Presently an adventuress suggests to the banker that he should marry, seeking to draw the proposal herself. Instead Hendricks goes to Louise with the proposal. Louise is really in love with an invalid artist and she marries Hendricks in order to provide money for her lover's cure.

Some years later Hendricks learns of the motive and is estranged from Louise, who, however, refuses to divorce him. Hendricks engages a detective to secure the record of Seminoff, a bogus nobleman and a blackguard. Once he has the count in his power he forces him to compromise Louise in such a way that he can cast her off. When Louise is lured to Seminoff's apartment and there, confronted with her husband, she sees the whole plot and stabs her husband to death.

The telling of the story before the court, of course, brings a verdict of "not guilty" in the familiar screen way, and just at the right moment the invalid lover turns up in the courtroom, restored to health in time for the embrace. In short, 12-year-old schoolgirl fiction. *Rush.*

WATCH YOUR STEP

Goldwyn picture of five reels offered as feature of the current Capitol program. Original screen story by Julien Josephson, not related to musical comedy of some years ago under the same title. Directed by William Beaudine.

Elmer Slocum................Cullen Landis
Margaret Andrews.......Patsy Ruth Miller
Russ Weaver................Bert Woodruff
Lark Andrews..............George Pierce
Lon Kimball.............Raymond Cannon
Jennifer Kimball...............Gus Leonard
Constable...............Henry Rattenbury
Ky Wilson...........................Joel Day
Detective Ryan............J. O. O'Connor
Henry Slocum....................John Cossar
Mrs. Spivey..............Lillian Sylvester
Lote Spivey......................L. H. King
Mrs. Andrews............Cordelia Callahan
Mrs. Weaver....................Alberta Lee

Goldwyn has turned out an uncommonly amusing comedy of small town American life, rich in shrewd character study and in story interest. The tale has something of the flavor of another "David Harum," although at no time does it encroach upon that famous novel. The reference is to a certain parallel in quality of appeal, not to subject matter.

It is a novelty to find the screen dealing with the small town character in terms of kindly humor rather than of burlesque. Mr. Josephson etches in his quaint people with a sympathetic understanding. The people of the play are human types, not transcriptions from the comic supplements. And for a background he has written a charming bit of idyllic romance concerning the love affairs of the young city man and the sweet daughter of the rural banker.

The cast is made up of a splendid group of natural players. None of them is a screen luminary. No name is forced forward for the familiar purpose of catching the attention of the dyed-in-the-wool fan, but the company has been intelligently picked with an eye to a smooth playing organization, and each player fits neatly into the pattern of the play. Cullen Landis as the young prodigal from the city who finds himself involved in the small town affairs of Greenville, is a fine manly young hero, playing naturally and convincingly without a trace of the self-satisfied pose of the film star. Of the younger men who have come to the fore lately he gives large promise.

Bert Woodruff in the delightful role of an eccentric country storekeeper has a gem of a character creation in Russ Weaver, the kindly but irascible Poo Bah of the village., and Patsy Ruth Miller is a refreshing new screen beauty. All the people are refreshingly natural and human, and nowhere is there a touch of the artificial illusion of life.

It's a delight to meet these quaintly amusing people of Greenville. One incident of the story may indicate the spirit of the comedy. Russ is out of the general store on some business when a telephone message comes that Ky Wilson wants him in a hurry and the store clerk sends his assistant to find Russ, adding, "I don't know what it's about, but you better take Russ' plumber tools along." Russ takes the message and starts on the mysterious mission, observing casually, "I guess that leaky bathtub of Ky's is in trouble again."

When he gets to Ky's cottage Ky meets him at the door, grinning broadly, and informs him, "Never mind, Russ, I got Doc Harrison instead. It's a boy." For a surprise laugh it was a whale, and the picture is full of the same sort of fresh and amusing touches. There is action aplenty, too. One episode is a fine spirited fight between the town bully and the down-and-out city boy that has a fine dramatic punch, and the picture starts out with a spirited passage of racing automobiles that has a thrill of its own.

Elmer Slocum is a high spirited, mischievous youngster who is always in trouble with the traffic cops because of his propensity for exceeding the speed rules. After one arrest his father warns him he must "watch his step" in the future. Elmer departs from the parental presence determined to be caution itself in driving, but at the first turn on the road he meets a doctor whose machine has broken down while he is on his way to an emergency case. Elmer takes the medico aboard and is urged to hurry. While Elmer's racer is doing 60 the motorcycle police take up his trail and are about to arrest him, when he trips the bluecoat, intent upon making his escape. The police falls on the hard road and lies still. Elmer fears he has killed the policeman and is forced to flight. A gang of tramps robs him and turns him loose upon the world, ragged and broke.

In this condition he flees to Greenville, ill and hungry. His condition arouses the sympathy of Russ, the kindly old storekeeper of Greenville, and Elmer becomes his clerk, still keeping his identity secret. In this capacity he meets Margaret, the village beauty, and the romance begins. Also the enmity of Lon Kimball, the village sport and rich man's son, is aroused, Lon being also a suitor for Margaret. The rest of the story is the contest between the prodigal and the village Lothario for Margaret. The scene in which the two boys, Elmer with a hired buggy and Lon in his trick flivver, contest for the honor of taking Margaret riding is a joy.

In the end the prodigal wins out. The policeman wasn't killed at all and the way is smoothed for the happy wind-up *Rush.*

MISSING HUSBANDS

Metro is distributing this French-made production, a five-reeler that was made from Paul Benoit's story, "L'Atlantide."

Antinea.................Stacia Napierkowska
Tanit-Zerga.............Marie Louise Iribe
Captain Morhange..............Jean Angelo
Lieutenant Saint-Avit.....Georges Melchior
The Antiquary....................Franceschi
Cegheir-Ben-Cheikh.Abd-El-Kader Ben-Ali

Jacques Feyder adapted the novel "L'Atlantide" of Paul Benoit for the screen. A French producing company made the production, but the version released here by Metro fails to give either the producer or the director credit. The picture is a highly fanciful tale of the type of Rider Haggard's "She," dealing with a lost continent and an imaginary Queen, who is the prize vamp. She loves for a short time and then her husbands usually commit suicide or die in some other fashion for love of her.

The trouble with the picture is that those who retitled and edited it for American consumption failed to realize the full possibilities of the film that they had on hand. The result is that what would have been a knockout feature has been so handled that it is just a little above the average Metro program production. The story is slow in getting started and there isn't any action until the two officers get into the apartments of the Queen of the mythical continent.

From that point, however, there is a flock of semi-dressed stuff that will certainly draw stag audiences. The vampish Queen shows just about everything that the law allows above the belt, and one of the maids in waiting also displays a mean undraped shoulder and thigh.

A French actress, Stacia Napierkwoska, plays the Queen, and to those who go in for the more voluptuous type of beauty she will appeal to. Marie Louise Iribe plays the role of principal maid in waiting, and to a great extent overshadows the lead. Jean Angelo, in the role of Captain Morhange, really the lead of the picture, is shunted out of the frame without any attempt at explanation of his passing. The last seen of him is when he has been struck on the head by his companion in arms at the instigation of the Queen because he wouldn't fall for her; but he is alive after the blow, so one cannot be certain whether or not he passed out. Georges Melchiro is the heavy, and to him is given the honor of closing the picture.

As far as sets and lightings are concerned the picture is a triumph, and had the story been skilfully handled in the cutting and editing here, the picture would have proved a terrific business puller. *Fred.*

NORTH OF THE RIO GRANDE

Bob Haddington	Jack Holt
Val Hannon	Bebe Daniels
Col. Haddington	Charles Ogle
Father Hillaire	Alec B. Francis
John Hannon	Will R. Walling
Brideman	Jack Carlyle
Briston	Fred Huntley
Lola Sanchez	Shannon Day
Belle Hannon	Edythe Chapman
Paul Perez	George Field
Glendenning	W. B. Clarke

Lasky has produced a fast western feature from the story, "Val of Paradise," by Virgie E. Roe, the scenario for which was written by Will M. Ritchey. The production co-stars Jack Holt and Bebe Daniels, with the direction, by Joseph Henebery.

"North of the Rio Grande" presents nothing new in a western story, but the production has been developed in such a manner as to get more out of it than is generally credited to a picture of this kind. The action includes the familiar chases, gun fights and the like, only in each instance the work is a bit better portrayed than in the general run of western features. The riding is a big feature. The horsemanship displayed at times is exceptional. The director often forgot to give a realistic touch to the riding by failing to have the horses tired or overheated at any stage.

The story centers around Bob Haddington, the son of a rancher. His father is killed by a horse rustler. The son seeks vengeance. He scours the country, ever seeking the slayer of his father. In his travels he meets the daughter of a wealthy ranch owner and is attracted by her. A horse thief has been operating in the neighborhood of her home, but fortunately her father has never suffered any losses. The ranchers of the vicinity determine to rid the country of the menace. They form a posse and start the hunt. It develops that the girl's father is the rustler. He is about to be captured when young Haddington takes his place as the hunted man for the sake of the girl. The real rustler is shot, but manages to reach home, where he dies. The girl immediately sets out and arrives at the proper time to keep the man she loves from being hung. She explains the circumstances of the affair and everything is serene at the finish.

Mr. Holt is the leading worker. He is included in practically every bit of footage. Miss Daniels gives the necessary punch to her role, although never ruffled, notwithstanding considerable breathless riding. Shannon Day, as a dancer, is the outstanding player of the supporting cast.

Director Henebery used discretion in his selection of locations. The western story is enhanced by the beautiful scenery. The action takes place almost entirely in the open. The few interiors employed have been well selected.

"North of the Rio Grande" should attract business in theatres playing standard program productions. *Hart.*

WESTERN SPEED

The title is no misnomer and with Charles (Buck) Jones in the stellar role it ought to appeal to wild west picture fans. It is a story of the West as it once was, in the latter half of the nineteenth century, when the wanderer could take possession of a forsaken shack and "nest" there—hence the sobriquet "nester"—and like as not incite the ire of the village natives for his pains to honor them with his presence. In this case, Ben Lorimer (John Lockney) and his daughter Dot (Eileen Percy) became the target of the village natives. Red Kane (Buck Jones) and his pal, Shorty (Walter Robins) are inclined to favor the nesters, but Dot shoos them away at the point of a rifle. He vows he will marry her in the end. He does—after a series of thrilling incidents, fast riding, snappy scrapping and the rest of the Buck Jones routine that makes for a very interesting program feature.

Action is the word throughout, Scott Dunlap and C. R. Wallace, the directors, accomplishing their purpose with a vengeance. The former also adapted the story from William Patterson White's story.

Its minimum production expense should make it attractive to the exhibitor on that angle alone. It is chiefly outdoors, excepting for the few log cabin interiors. An interesting western and a good buy. *Abel.*

PRIMITIVE LOVER

Phyllis Tomley	Constance Talmadge
Hector Tomley	Harrison Ford
Donald Wales	Kenneth Harlan
"Roaring Bill" Rivers	Joe Roberts
Indian Herder	Charles Pino
Indian Chief	Chief Big Tree
Mrs. Graham	Matilda Brundage
Judge Henseed	George Pierce
Attorney	Clyde Benson

The action of Constance Talmadge's latest First National release opens on a raft. A party of three has been shipwrecked. A triangle scene develops. The heroine's husband is delirious for want of water. She pleads with the guardian of the aqua supply to give her man her share. "I'm only a poor defenseless woman," Constance exclaims. Her delirous husband (Harrison Ford) chimes in "Zounds, if I only had my strength." The third party says he will not deprive either of them of anything so long as she is happy (even though his love for her is unrequited) and asking permission from the raving hero to kiss his wife a tender farewell, he jumps overboard so that the woman he loves remain happy with her chosen mate.

Of course, it's all travesty. The histrionics are so broad one suspects this is a hoke introduction. It develops to be the conclusion of Donald Wales' latest novel, "The Primitive Lover." It is propaganda for the caveman wooer and Phyllis Tomley (Miss Talmadge) is doubly affected considering that Wales, the author, has been reported lost in the African jungles. Wales (Kenneth Harlan) was Phyllis' favorite admirer until his disappearance. She has married Hector Tomley (Harrison Ford) meantime, and Hector has proved to be a docile sort of husband. An inventor, wrapped up in his work, utterly lacking in romance and the caveman spirit Phyllis so admires, there is a decided shortcoming by comparison to the wilful Wales who has returned meantime, explaining his "disappearance" and death notice was part of a publicity stunt to put over "The Primitive Lover," his latest novel. Phyllis is driven to the divorce courts, further spurred on by her husband's seeming indifference. He decides to step aside in order that she be happy. Poor Hector is altruistic to a fault and Phyllis again misunderstands. However, Hector, like every dog, has his day. He falls in with Big Chief Bluebottle, who teaches him a thing or two about taming wild squaws.

The result is that Hector stages a phoney hold-up, imprisons Phyllis and Wales in a cabin and tells the latter to put to practice some of his caveman propaganda. As one expects, Wales proves the tenderest sort of tenderfoot and Hector displays unsuspected caveman proclivities. Phyllis is enraged outwardly, but secretly elated at Hector's manliness, and when the news reaches her that the final divorce decree has not been granted her she treks for Hector's cabin for the fadeout clinch—despite her earlier threat he will crawl on his knees before he is forgiven.

The picture is light stuff of the well-known Connie Talmadge style, hybrid farce-comedy-hokum that should connect with picture fans all over. The showing up of the caveman bunk is great stuff for the city flippers who at one time or another may have been shortcoming of the caveman idea in the eyes of the flappers. Another appeal is the divorce court scene in view of the star's private little proceeding against the tobacco man.

Edgar Selwyn supplied the story, an original yarn, adapted by Frances Marion. Sidney A. Franklin directed in his usual finished style. David Abel's photography was perfect.

The casting is well taken care of, the character drawing being consistent excepting the court scene where Judge Henseed, the Reno jurist, leaves his bench in the course of trial to greet the charming would-be divorcee (Miss Talmadge). It served its purpose though for the laugh returns it was aimed at.

"The Primitive Lover" is showing currently at the Strand, being booked in at the last minute, replacing Marshall Neillan's "Fool's First," previously announced. *Abel.*

DON'T WRITE LETTERS

A. H. Sawyer and Herbert Smith present Gareth Hughes in the five-reeler from Blanche Brace's Saturday Evening Post story of the same title. Released through Metro.

A delightful comedy romance of youth done in a refreshingly novel spirit of good humor and with a neat turn of sentiment. The whole thing has a delightful whimsical twist such as Booth Tarkington might advise in his best sentimental moments, and behind its engaging fun there is a fine touch of tender humor. The tale pokes gentle fun at the youthful under dog of a department store clerk, but the undercurrent is kindly and gentle.

It's all very fresh and refreshing comedy that is free from slapstick, but always genuine in character drawing and natural in situations. The film starts with an amusing little prolog, pointing out by an incident of the stone age that letter writing leads to complications. The cave man lover chisels a tender missive to his neighbor's wife and gets his head broken by an indignant husband. For another illustration of the age-old truth, a medieval troubadour indites a billet doux and gets the same treatment from his lady love's hubby.

The truism being thus illuminated, the story gets down to modern days. Billy is a department store clerk when the war summons comes. He dreams of heroic deeds; but once in France the humble lot of cook falls to him, an ignoble substitute for opportunity to display valor. All the other boys get letters from the girls at home, but not Billy. He can't even get a smart uniform. The commissary issues him a 44-inch shirt to make him even more ridiculous. But within the wretched garment there is a note from the factory girl who stitched it, inviting the "hero who received it" to open correspondence. Ashamed of his small figure and his record as the butt of his regiment, Billy creates the fiction in his letters that he is a burly cow puncher. Thus the romance grows by mail.

When the war is over Billy returns to his clerkship; but meeting the girl of his dreams, he is forced to invent for her a fictitious war hero whom he describes as his pal and whom he declares was lost. The letter writing has apparently destroyed his romance. Conscience stricken at the girl's grief for her lost hero, he is compelled to produce a war veteran whom he meets; but the girl, meanwhile, has learned to care for the earnest little chap, and in the end the romance works itself out satisfactorily with a holiday to Coney Island, where Billy and his sweetheart at length find themselves and each other.

The smooth, bright titling contributes a great deal to the effectiveness of the pretty little tale, and the planning is handled in a splendid vein of restrained naturalness. The principal part was made to order for young Hughes, who scores with special effectiveness. The whole production is a conspicuous example of the best grade of light romantic story intelligently translated to the screen. *Rush.*

COCAINE

London, May 3.

This picture, obviously inspired by the present crusade against the drug traffic, is bad melodrama of the type which may attract the coarser class of patrons to the cheaper kinema. But if the patron expects scenes of debauchery and suggestiveness he will be sadly disappointed. "Cocaine" would be a good antidote for our grandmothers after an over-dose of Sunday school treat charades. The story, produced by Graham Cutts, is weak and unoriginal. It tells how the daughter of a straight-laced head of a dope ring meets an old friend who has become an actress and a dope addict. She falls in love with a young man and has a terrible row with her father, who catches them together. Running away from home, she goes to her actress-friend and is taken to a night club. There she is given cocaine by the Chinese manager, who also makes love to her. She enters heartily into the spirit of the thing, under the influence of the drug, of course, and her friend objects, her supply of cocaine and light-heartedness having run out together. The father, having been told where his daughter is by another Chinaman—a matter of revenge, this—arrives, shoots the informer and himself. The heroine is saved by the hero, who takes both her and the actress-addict to a nearby chapel, where the actress dies and a sub-title implores: "Forgive us our trespasses." The final close-up shows hero and heroine walking on the top of a hill arm in arm, so we suppose all is as it should be in a well-regulated melodrama. The redeeming feature in "Cocaine" is the photography. The acting is mediocre and suited to the story.

Hilda Bailey plays the actress-addict without conviction, although she smiles and is gay a second after receiving her issue of "dope," and writhes, shivers, and gnaws her hands when she hasn't got it. Flora le Breton might be anything as the innocent daughter of the leader of the gang. The best acting performance comes from Tony Fraser as a deformed Chinaman. The author, however, persistently refuses to give any player a sporting chance. It is remarkable that a woman of Hilda Bailey's reputation and position on the West End stage should associate herself with such a production however great the pecuniary gain.

GAY AND DEVILISH

A Robertson-Cole five comedy-drama by Charles Logue with Doris May starred. Directed by Wm. A. Seiter.

Fanchon Brown	Doris May
Martin Bennett	George Periolet
Peter Armitage	Otis Harlan
Peter Armitage 2nd	Cullen Landis

A corking comedy of the flapper type, sure to please any audience. It is a comedy drama that borders on farce at times, and the laughs come fast through the entire five reels of the story. In this respect the story is aided tremendously by up-to-the-minute titling that is so snappy that there is almost a laugh in every one of them. Although the picture was played as part of a double bill at Loew's New York this week, it is strong enough to stand by itself in any daily change house.

Doris May is the star, and her portrayal of a flapper type is really worth while. Cullen Landis plays opposite her, and manages to put over a pleasing performance as the juvenile. Otis Harlan, as a fat old man with his eye on the chickens, contributes to the comedy elements of the story.

That, in brief, has to do with two flappers, one the niece of a broker who is on the verge of going into bankruptcy. To save the day he proposes to his niece, whose fortune is also involved in the forthcoming crash, that she accept the suit of a business rival who can tide them over their difficulty. She accepts the task. A meeting is arranged at a summering place, and there the girl meets whom she believes is the man that she has been ordered to marry. Instead it is his nephew who bears the same name and, incidentally, is a much younger man. Finally, however, the difficulty is adjusted by the elder man falling in love with the girl's aunt, and the younger couple are left to their own devices.

There is missing money, sneaky coppers, a crook or two, a prize-fighter who poses for the flapper art bugs, and one or two others in the cast that make for real screen fun. The picture is decidedly worth while playing. *Fred.*

BOY WOODBURN

London, May 9.

This last George Clark picture, produced by Guy Newall, is essentially British in every way. A sporting subject, the story is slight and very ordinary and utterly subservient to the scenic beauty of the feature. "Boy" Woodburn is the charming daughter of an old race-horse trainer who acts for a wealthy young man, Silver. One day her father buys an old mare, who, after giving birth to a foal, dies. After the usual adventures to be found in sporting drama, including the burning of the stables which shelter the Woodburn runner, "Boy's" horse wins the Grand National, to the confusion of the stables' enemies. Then and not till then does "Boy" take Silver, who has been rendered a poor man by the failure of his bank, as a lover. The story is just sufficient to bind the fine scenic properties of the picture together, and what there is of it is well told.

A great feature of the film is the introduction of numerous animal actors, goats, dogs, horses, foals, all of whom show clever training and seem to enjoy their work. There is very little scope for acting, but the entire cast is remarkable for its naturalness. Ivy Duke plays "Boy." Given a good part she has every chance of becoming a genuine "star." She has repose, youth and uncommon beauty, without a trace of makeup. Everything she does is perfectly natural. The same can be said of Guy Newall, who impersonates Silver. The photography is perfect.

Among the scenes are some exceptionally fine ones of the Grand National taken in real Grand National weather, many exquisite rural "shots" and the burning of the stables is by far the best thing of its kind seen in a British picture. As a feature "Boy Woodburn" will not set the Thames on fire, but its charm and beauty of production cannot fail to raise the status of the British picture. *Gore.*

KISSES

Story by May Tully; scenario by June Mathis. Metro comedy starring Alice Lake. Designated a Maxwell Karger production.

Betty Ellen Estabrook	Alice Lake
Bill Bailey	Harry Myers
Thomas Estabrook	Edward Connelly
John Maynard	Edward Jobson
Norman Maynard	Dana Todd
Bessie Neldon	Mignon Anderson
Edward Neldon	John MacKinnon
Gustave	Eugene Pouyet

Five reels is a lot of distance for this light and inconsequential story to travel. It could have been told with all reasonable completeness in two reels. The rest of it is fluff. The point is that a young woman is suddenly reduced to making her own living, and with the assistance of her bright young sweetheart goes into the business of making candy kisses.

When the business has grown to large proportions a rival candy manufacturer opens negotiations to buy her out and great fuss is made in the bargaining about the "secret formula" of the girl's candy. When the manufacturer falls for the price of $50,000, the secret formula turns out to be the use of goat's milk, the private goat being tethered in the front yard.

As the point of a five-reeler in which very little happens, that doesn't deliver much of a kick. The story is fairly bright in comedy touches, but its character relations are conventional according to the magazine fiction school, and nothing in the idea raises it above the commonplace. Miss Lake is her old self, youthful and spirited, but disposed to overplay the kittenish hoyden. A very little of the frivolous schoolgirl stuff goes a long way, and for five reels it is rather cloying.

"Kisses" takes a good deal of footage in getting started as commonly happens in spreading out a two-reel idea into a full feature. However, the planting is done with amusing comedy incidentals, and when it does get into its pace it turns out to be a mildly interesting Cinderella theme with society settings. The picture probably cost considerably below the average to produce. There is only one elaborate scene, that of a charity bazaar, which calls for a hundred or more extra people.

For the rest simple interiors are used and the cast is a short one. Principal appeal will be for women with special reference to the better class neighborhood houses.

Betty Ellen Esterbrook comes back from college, the champion candy maker of the institute for higher education. Her father has been speculating and faces disagree for using the securities of his bank. He appeals to his friend, John Maynard, whose son, Norman, is engaged to Betty, but John declines to rescue him. The father dies and Norman squirms out of the engagement.

Meanwhile Betty has made friends with Bill Bailey, a young promoter, and appeals to him in her emergency to suggest how he can support herself and pay father's debts. Bill is there with the bright ideas and he undertakes the enterprise of marketing Betty's candy kisses. The business grows prodigiously, and so does Bill's love for Betty. Maynard also is in the candy business, and Betty's "kisses" are ruining his business, so he comes through with an offer to buy out the rival, never suspecting that the firm is the daughter of the man he abandoned.

This situation leads to the comedy climax, Bill conducting the negotiation whose completion paves the way for the romantic denouement. *Rush.*

PASTEBOARD CROWN

An independent production, presented by Nathan & Semerad under the Playgoers' Pictures, Inc., trade mark, released through Pathe. It's "A Travers Vale Production" adapted by Thomas F. Fallon from the novel by Clara Morris.

It's theme is hybrid. It starts in the Stock 'Exchange with the ruin of the heroine's father, takes the observer into "society" atmosphere and then develops into a common garden variety type of behind-the-scenes stage story. It may be that this shifting transition will carry the picture around the pop picture houses; each angle separately, particularly the stage story end of it which is the major portion of the yarn, could not stand up alone for 5,000 feet. There isn't sufficient meat. This padding, in fact, is commendable, although the interpretation is mediocre.

Sybil Lawton (Evelyn Greely), as the girl, who, having proved somewhat talented in amateur theatricals, takes up the stage as her life's career on the demise of her father, did the part in average fashion. She cannot stand close-ups. In spots, effective lighting camouflaged the tell-tale pouches under the eyes, but they showed up cruelly two or three times. Stewart Thrall (Robert Elliott) made an acceptable lead. In the role of the successful actor-manager (evidently addicted to Shakespeare in general and "Romeo and Juliet" in particular for his repertory) he befriends the penniless society girl.

Thrall is married to woman who admits she hoped to arrive on Broadway in that wise, but since her husband's belittling her histrionic ability she cares nothing for him. Her husband was a good judge of her acting, judging from her personation. An affair between Thrall and Sybil develops and Thrall's wife returns at just the right moment to tell him she had quietly secured a divorce in Paris during her European sojourn. That is a bit irregular, no indication of Thrall having been formally served with legal papers being made. The punch scene is where the misguided protector of the heroine shoots the hero from the audience as they are doing the "Romeo and Juliet" death scene. Of course, the hero survives the flesh wound for the final clinch.

The title is too figurative to be effective at the gate. It was one-half of a double header at Loew's New York last Friday, where it elicited mild interest. *Abel.*

ARABIAN LOVE

William Fox five-reeler written by Jules Furthman and directed by Jerome Storm with John Gilbert as star.

Norman Stone	John Gilbert
Nadine	Barbara Bedford
Capt. Fortine	Adolph Menjou
Thamar	Barbara LaMarr

William Fox has adapted a title for this picture and had a story written to order to fit into the craze started by "The Sheik." Incidentally he is introducing a star in the person of John Gilbert who stands out as a comer. The picture is a corking adventure romance of its type, and should please the greater part of the picture fans, especially the women. It is strong enough a feature to be played anywhere for as much as a couple of days, and seemingly will get money.

John Gilbert in a great many ways physically reminds of Wallace Reid, but coupled with this resemblance there is also ability to ride and put up a corking fight. Gilbert looks as though Fox had picked a good screen bet, and he should develop, provided that he is given the right material.

The strength of this picture, however, lies in the strength of its love story that carries a corking amount of suspense, and in its enactment two exceedingly clever women are involved. Barbara Bedford, who plays the lead, stands out wonderfully well, but the real punch is delivered by Barbara LaMarr, who screens like a million dollars in this production. Adolph Menjou, who plays the heavy, is in the picture hardly long enough for one to get a real line on his work, but what he does do he manages to get over to the audience.

The story is laid in the desert, with Gilbert playing a young American who has fled from the city and joined an Arab band after he has killed a French officer in avenging a wrong done his sister. Later, when the band attacks a caravan, he rescues the woman who is the widow of the man that he killed. The two fall in love, but neither has knowledge of who the other is. Finally the woman, on learning the facts, lays a trap for her lover, but before he is captured she learns the true story behind the crime and forgives him. His Arab friends arrive in time to rescue him from the troops intent on his capture, and the final fadeout shows the two lovers passing over a hill in the distance.

The production is skillfully handled by Jerome Storm, who managed to get a real atmospheric wallop in the film. *Fred.*

GLEAM O'DAWN

Gleam O'Dawn	John Gilbert
Nini	Barbara Bedford
Caleb Thomas	James Farley
Gordon Thomas, his son	John Gough
Pierre	Wilson Hummel
Silas Huntworth	Edwin Booth Tilton

A John Gilbert feature presented by William Fox and dealing with a story of love, jealousy and hate, pictured in the Canadian woods. O'Dawn is an artist, living in the woods. Huntsworth and his adopted daughter, Nini, live in the vicinity. Caleb Thomas and his son are representatives of the Hudson Bay Co. and they are endeavoring to rid the woods of the other couple. O'Dawn comes on the scene during a fight and pins the elder Thomas to the wall with a knife, thrust through his coat from a distance. A friendship springs up between the pair, but Pierre, a half wit, who roams through the woods fiddling, steps on the complication box and stits up a feeling of hatred in O'Dawn for Huntsworth by telling the former that Huntsworth is O'Dawn's father and had left his mother in want while O'Dawn was a youngster. O'Dawn decides to kill his own father, strange as it may seem. There is a scene where the shooting was apparently scheduled to take place, but instead the ghostly form of a woman enters, apparently meant for the dead wife and mother, and from thereon the picture took up film space in explanations and adjustments.

Mr. Gilbert is a good screen actor, registers the emotions clearly and looks the type. Barbara Bedford, however, instead of portraying the sweet little love child she was meant, looked as though ready to spring from the screen any minute and burst into a ragtime song. She looks more like a comedienne. Edwin Booth Tilton is a good character man, generously giving all the spotlight to Gilbert. Wilson Hummel as the half wit gave a good impression of the type with twisted face and bent up figure.

The photography is above the average and the direction is passably, but the director didn't have **much of a story, as unfolded in this picture, to handle. The close-up views are exceptionally good, but the story seems disconnected, giving the impression it has been chopped** through censorship or for other reasons.

It's just a fair feature, carried along by its views and titles. From the standpoint of interest it falls far behind the average. *Wynn.*

SECOND HAND ROSE

A five-reel Universal, adapted from the Shapiro-Bernstein popular song (by Grant Clarke and Jimmy Hanley) and directed by Lloyd Ingraham.

Rose O'Grady..................Gladys Walton
Isaac Rosenstein.........George B. Williams
Lillian Rosenstein..............Grace Marvin
Frankie "Bull" Thompson...Wade Boettler
Abe Rosenstein.................Max Davidson
Rebecca Rosenstein...........Virginia Adair
Rachael Rosenstein.............Alice Belcher
Terry O'Brien..............Jack Dougherty
Tim McCarthy..................Walter Perry
Hawkins..................Benedict Southard
Little Rosie....................Camilla Clark
Little Jake Rosenstein.....Marion Faducha
Jake Rosenstein...........Eddie Sutherland

This picture is bound to appeal to any neighborhood house where there is a Jewish-Irish parentage, notwithstanding the shortcomings in its direction, which could have shown better results with more discretion in the locales selected for the photography.

The story deals with an east side Jew who adopts an Irish child. He places his son in a shipping room with a silk firm. In taking the lad's lunch to him daily the girl meets his boss, an Irish chap. A love affair develops.

Meanwhile the son, whose habits are a bit loose, loses a bunch of papers, and the gang stealing them gets away with a cargo of merchandise. The boy is arrested. His father's heart is broken. The foster sister promises her heart to an elderly Irishman whose political influence procures the boy's release.

The boy vindicates himself and frames his companions into another theft, the police recovering the stolen goods and arresting the outfit. The old Irishman releases her from her pledge and she marries the choice of her heart.

Gladys Walton as the adopted child gives a very fine impression, and with the clever characterization of George Williams moulds a very sentimental story. The combination of Jew and Irish in real life has always been ideal, and this couple bring out the better natures in both types.

The photography is good, but there is nothing particularly sensational, although the midnight raid on the thief's holdout was evidently meant to be. This picture has the proper pulling power in metropolitan cities where the races are aplenty, but it's just an average program card on the whole, and while it will satisfy, it will never start any stampedes at the box office. *Wynn.*

THE YELLOW STAIN

Donald Keeth.........................John Gilbert
Thora Ericson....................Claire Anderson
Quartus Hembly....................John Lockney
Olaf Ericson...........................Mark Fenton
Dr. Brown.......................Herschel Mayall
Daniel Kersten.......................Robert Daly
Lyman Rochester.................Mace Robinson
Clerk..............................James McElhern

"The Yellow Stain," a Fox release, is somewhat of an innovation in the feature field. The production has John Gilbert as the star and Claire Anderson as leading woman, with an all-male supporting cast. Just how much a feature with but one woman included in a large cast will interest the average picture audience is problematical. Feminine charms have always been considered an asset to any picture, and in this latest Fox production the honors in the female division are left entirely to Miss Anderson. Jules Furthman supplied the scenario, with the direction handled by Jack Dillon.

It is a story of small town life. A young lawyer decides to establish himself in a town which is ruled by a monied tyrant. He becomes involved in difficulties with the latter, pulls the king down from the throne and marries the village belle. It has been told in different ways time and time again. The action takes place in a small town in the lumber district. This fact has not been made realistic by the director. Little of the big woods is brought into play. It is a studio picture.

The bulk of the work is entrusted to Gilbert as the young lawyer. He capably handles the role. Miss Anderson fits in here and there in light summery frocks, supplying sufficiently interesting efforts and looks for an ingenue lead. The remainder of the cast is limited to character parts, with which John Lockney and Robert Daly have the edge. The production makes no claims for pretentiousness.

"The Yellow Stain" is an average program release, the run of which should be limited to three days at the most, with a single day the most advisable. *Hart.*

NERO

A Fox production, made in Italy under the direction of J. Gordon Edwards. Presented at the Lyric, New York, for a run beginning May 22. Enacted by a cast of foreign players with the single exception of Violet Mersereau. Approximately 10,000 feet in length. The story is by Charles Sarver and Virginia Tracy.

Nero ....Jacques Gretillat
Horatius ....Alexander Salvini
Tullius ....Guido Trento
Otho ....Enzo De Felice
The Apostle........................Nero Bernardi
Hercules ....Adolfo Trouche
Galba ....Nello Carolenuto
Gracchus ....Americo De Giorgio
Garth ....Alfredo Galaor
A Roman General..............Ernando Cecilia
A Roman Captain..................Enrico Kant
Poppaea ....Paulette Duval
Acte ....Edy Darclea
Marcia ....Violet Mersereau
Julia ....Lina Talba
First Handmaiden............Lydia Yaguinto
Second Handmaiden.........Maria Marchiali

Presenting "Nero" to New York audiences, Fox has a note on the program to the effect he "does not care to state the cost of this production. He prefers to let the public judge 'Nero' on its artistic and dramatic merits, uninfluenced by any other considerations."

Fox didn't need that statement, but it could have been stated in lire and then forgotten to give the equivalent in American dollars. That would have made it look impressive.

However, "Nero" will bring back all of those lire J. Gordon Edwards expended in the making and more, for it is a worthwhile picture.

It won't be as big a money-making proposition as was "Over the Hill," for that picture cost "just a little nickle" as compared to what must have been the outlay for this. Although this may gross a great deal more than "The Hill," the chances are that the profits wont be as big.

Exhibitors in the regular run of picture houses need not start figuring on this picture until the Fox organization has managed to skim the cream off the entire country by playing special engagements. When it comes to them at prices that will make it next to impossible for them to make any money with the picture the exhibitors can have what is left. Providing the Fox people manage to arouse enough interest in the picture and again providing that they handle it right in the matter of the special road showings, it will be about six months or a year before it gets to the regular houses.

But in presenting the story of a period of the reign of Nero, the last of the Cæsars, on the screen Fox has done a work certain to reflect credit on the entire industry. It is at once a most engrossing picturization, teeming with dramatic intensity of a period of the history of the Roman Empire certain to impress even those opposed to the screen from any angle.

Just how much of the edge "Theodora" took from the sacrifice of the early Christians to the lions in the arena which is one of the real thrills of "Nero" is a question that can only be determined in time as the picture proceeds on its way. It it safe to assume the handling of the love story that runs through the Fox production will be enough to carry it. It is a story that holds the audience and makes it forget this is a spectacular costume film play dug from ancient history. In that particular this picture is far and away ahead of any of the out-and-out foreign productions imported to this country. That the screen story was compiled by two American writers and its direction was in the hands of an American, who, as a director of pictures, has obtained the greater part of his practical experience in this country, illustrates what those who have been a part of the advancement of the picture over here can do when they have at their disposal the tremendous architectural, natural scenic beauties and mob facilities of the European continent.

There are many who will say after viewing "Nero" that Edwards is the only director who has a legitimate claim as a rival of D. W. Griffith, basing their belief on "The Birth of a Nation" as Griffith's greatest. In reply, all that can be said is that Mr. Edwards has somewhat improved on the gathering of the Klans in his mobilization of the Roman army. One must wait and see what Griffith will do abroad, where he will also have unlimited facilities at a far lesser cost than in this country. The Griffith fans who really picked his greatest picture, which was "Intolerance," will see naught in "Nero" that Griffith did not present to greater advantage in that picture. That is about the point at which it may be well to let rest the question of the rivalry as to who is America's foremost director of pictures.

"Nero" is big; more than that, tremendous, and must be seen to be appreciated. At the Lyric it is in two parts. The first half, while interesting, contains no great thrills for the fans, but in the second half the production goes along at express speed. The burning of Rome, the slaughter of the Christians in the arena by the lions, the revolt of the Roman army, which concludes in the passing of Nero, and acclaiming of Galba as emperor, all crowded in.

The opening of the tale is a brief outline of the historical locations in which the action takes place. Follows the introduction of the plot of Poppaea to rid herself of her husband and become the favorite of Nero, and finally her arrival at the point where she shares his throne. The introduction of the love element comes with the sending of Horatius to escort Marcia, a princess of a conquered nation, who is sent to Rome as a hostage. Horatius wishes to forfeit his command to follow her but Galba insists he would appear to better advantage before Nero as a supplicant for the possession of the Princess, were he to return as a hero, and sends him to Spain to conquer the rebellion against the Roman rule which has arisen.

On his return from Spain a year later Horatius triumphantly enters the city at the head of his troops. Nero informs him that whatever there is in his power to bestow it is his for the asking. He requests the hostage Princess and she is granted him, but at the moment of her entry Nero sees and covets her, and asks that Horatius give him back his word. In the midst of storm that follows the hero and the princess make their escape, and the first part ends.

In the second part the city is burned and Poppaea, who has come to love Horatius, advises Nero to quell the populace by placing the blame for the conflagration upon the Christians, knowing the princess has adopted the faith and believing that with her death Horatius will turn to her. With the seizing of the Christians and their deaths in the arena comes the uprising of the army against the tyrant. He commits suicide after killing the empress who has led him into the greater part of his misdeeds.

Photographically the picture is a delight. Duo-tone scenes are used throughout. There is a white bordered trick utilized as a framing for several scenes and close-ups in a most effective manner.

Mr. Edwards has handled his mob stuff wonderfully. All of the spectacular elements are so effectively done they will thrill the most blase picture fans. He picked his artists for his Roman characters carefully and produced "type" in all. His story he carried forward with a quantity of genuine suspense that really makes the picture.

In the cast Nero is Jacques Gretillat, whose profile is that of Nero's as far as may be judged from pictorial conception registered on coins and other relics of the ancient days. As an actor he carried the role for the highest praise. Alexander Salvini, grandson of the great Salvini, is Horatius, and gives a most interesting and compelling performance.

Paulette Duval as Poppaea is also an artiste of tremendous capabilities, although she cannot register a smile effectively. Violet Mesereau as the Princess seems dwarfed amidst the rather statuesque ladies of Italy, but she manages to get over her role of the little hostage.

The others are also types true to history, and the repression that Edwards' direction forced on them must have been far from their liking. He kept the picture from being overacted, as so many of the foreign productions are.

For real thrills the lion stuff and a chariot race in the arena are 100 per cent., as is the entire picture from an artistic and interesting standpoint. The box office value yet remains to be decided, but the chances are decidedly in its favor.

Fred.

CROSSROADS OF N. Y.

A Mack Sennett six-reeler of a melodramatic thriller with strong comedy touches. Directed by F. Richard Jones.

Grace St. Clair	Ethel Grey Terry
James Flint	Noah Beery
Garrett Chesterfield	Robert Cain
Ruth Anthony	Kathryn McGuire
John D. Anthony	Herbert Standing
Michael Flint	George O'Hara
Press Agents and Promoters	William Bevan Ben Deely
Boarding House Mistress	"Dot" Farley
Her Humble Suitor	Eddie Gribbon
An Attorney	James Finlayson
A Jurist	Charlie Murray
A Wall Street Wolf	Raymond Griffith
A Waitress	Mildred June

This Mack Sennett production was made about a year ago and originally shown in Los Angeles at Sennett's Mission theatre under another title. It achieved indifferent success. Since, however, it has undergone some changes, and when shown at the Capitol Sunday it proved to be a knockout, sure to get the money anywhere from any type of audience. The Capitol's Sunday business on the picture was almost $7,000. No one is starred particularly, but there are several names worth while from exploitation standpoint.

Two people loom up as corking future possibilities. They are George O'Hara, the juvenile lead, who stands out as a distinct find. He is a combination of the Charles Ray-Richard Barthelmess type and troups and photographs like the mint. The other is the girl who plays opposite him, Kathryn McGuire, as sweet an ingenue lead as one could ask for.

The story holds just about everything. There is slapstick comedy of the usual Mack Sennett order, some real thrills, expected in a serial; a heavy vamp, a real "go-getter," and a business and society angle that stands up. There couldn't be anything else added without making the picture last all night.

The hero is a boy from the country who hits New York in search of his wealthy uncle. The kid's ambition is to "get a job with a uniform," and his uncle "fixes" it for him; but instead of being a resplendent mounted policeman he lands a job manicuring the boulevards. However, the "unk" has fallen for a stage vamp, who has him placed as an angel for her show, and in the finish, to escape a breach of promise suit, he runs away to Alaska, where later reports have him dead. The nephew is the only heir to millions, and the vamp then goes after him. He falls, but in the end the return of the uncle saves the day for the boy just as he is in the midst of a courtroom scene, where the girl is trying to separate him from a chunk of the money he has inherited.

Just when it appears the story is finished a new element enters in the matter of a business plot with a scheme to ruin the uncle in Wall Street, and this gives the hero a chance to come through to the rescue of the girl of his heart, her father and his uncle, which finally brings about the happy ending.

In addition to the two more youthful members, there must be vast credit given to Ethel Grey Terry, who handles the vamp role in a manner that is supreme, and to Noah Beery as the wealthy uncle. Then, too, "Dot" Farley and Eddie Gribbon walk away with low comedy roles in corking fashion, while Ben Deely and William Bevan as a couple of scheming press agents manage to secure laughs. Charles Murray is cast for a semi-serious role as a judge, and while he appears decidedly different to the type that audiences are most in the habit of seeing him in he makes the bit stand up.

Any exhibitor can go hook, line and sinker on this one and not be afraid that it won't get money for him. It looks like another "Mickey."

Fred.

THE REFEREE

"The Referee" is a Selznick "fight picture" that should draw the sporting element everywhere, besides the women and boys out of curiosity, if nothing else. It's an interesting picture of the subject, well directed by Ralph Ince, and the lead exceptionally taken by Conway Tearle, who is starred.

This is the picture it was reported the pugilistic fraternity had taken offense at as belittling that profession. The five-reeler as seen at the New York Sunday had nothing to offend any fight fan, fighter or promoter. The nearest was an expression employed as emanating from the audience over stalling tactics in a championship bout. Among the exclamations in disjointed alignment as a caption was "Throw out the bums!" not uncommonly heard around New York at the fights when stalling in the approved Madison Square fashion was indulged in.

The punch of the picture is where Honest John McArdle, the referee (Mr. Tearle), stops the championship fight in the second round, declares it no contest and all bets off. That a fight referee has the power to declare off all bets seems to have been forgotten by the official referees of New York state. There is not one tithe in this picture of the common talk about the fights held in New York. The worst here is a frame for the champ to foul his opponent in the third round. The promoters thought they had the referee with them, as they had asked him if a foul were committed early in the fight, what he would do in face of the rage of the fans in the event he gave a decision on a foul. The referee said there would be nothing left to do but to give that decision. Then they promised $5,000 as a bonus and believed they had the referee with them on the frame. But the referee wasn't. He had merely said he would do what was right for a referee to do.

The film has a couple of corking bouts. The first is where McArdle wins the championship. It is fast work, with Tearle showing up finely against an unnamed fighter. It's for the middleweight championship of the world. Following the fight McArdle breaks his arm, is forced to retire and opens a billiard room. He goes in for refereeing and becomes known as Honest John McArdle. The picture was adapted from the Red Book Magazine story of "John McArdle, Referee."

A year's absence from the ring by McArdle, with the championship bestowed elsewhere, brings on the second battle. This scene carries an immense crowd of regulation fight attendants and the atmosphere is made about near perfect. Among the characters known to fighters also seen are Joe Humphries, the announcer, and Tammany Young, familiar to all fight crowds. For phony fighting and expert stalling the two pugs in the ring in the final bout were experts.

Meanwhile a love story had been unwinding. Janie Roberts (Gladys Hulette), daughter of Steve Roberts, a sporting man (also well played), is in love with McArdle, but her father dissuaded McArdle after winning the belt from marrying her after they had become engaged. He sent Janie to Europe and John attended to his billiard business, though hard pressed for money and threatened with extermination as a business man through a $5,000 debt. The couple don't meet for a year until at the champ's training camp the day before the fight. That night at her home Janie again pleaded with her father for his consent. The father said he wanted her to marry a man on the level, that the fight the following day had been framed and John was in on it as referee. Janie repudiated the statement, said John would never go through with it and she would bet the $25,000 she had in her own right he wouldn't. The father accepted the wager, giving Janie 2 to 1.

When the referee stopped the fight and went home somewhat battered up in the ensuing melee his action had caused, Roberts called at his home to see him. John, with one arm in a sling, placed a gun in his pocket as additional protection, for he knew Roberts had bet a lot of money on the frame. But Roberts when greeting John appeared to be much pleased instead that he had found an honest man as his daughter's husband. The close was John and Janie in a clasp, seen through a shadow thrown upon an open door.

One of the best bits of propaganda in the picture is for fighting. McArdle said to Roberts, "Now, I suppose the game is killed," referring to the disappointed audience of the stopped fight. "No," replied Roberts, "it's better than ever, for it proves the game is stronger than the crooks in it."

Through the picture is McArdle's kindly mother. It shows their mutual love for each other, John's straight, clean life, and the mother stands by her son at all times. When churchly neighbors called upon her, speaking of fighting as disgraceful, Mrs. McArdle brought forth the Bible to quote from it that our hands and arms were given us to help defend ourselves.

A frame in horse racing or other professional sports is not unknown. It will always be where professional gamblers are permitted to intervene. All inside stories about fighting in New York state for the past two years have carried tales of the gamblers being on the winning end with some very peculiar decisions. "The Referee," if nothing else, should teach the fight commission and official referees that a contest and all bets can be declared off.

The fight crowd should plug for this picture—it's for them, not against them. And any exhibitor may play it with perfect safety, for it should draw with plenty of opportunity to work up advance stuff through the local sporting pages.

Mr. Tearle is the idealistic pugilist in appearance, and of course plays with a surety that makes naturalness. He's a strong star for a typical picture of its class.

Sime.

SILVER WINGS

Between six and seven reels. Drama featuring Mary Carr in a brand new angle of the "mother story." Screen plan by Paul H. Sloane. Producer, William Fox. Directors, Edwin Carewe and Jack Ford. Photography by Robert Kurrel and Ruttenberg. Offered as a special bill at the Apollo May 22, with special music by Erno Rapee.

PROLOGUE

Anna Webb	Mary Carr
John Webb, her husband	Lynn Hammond
John, Harry, their sons	Knox Kincaid Joseph Monahan
Ruth, their daughter	Maybeth Carr
Uncle Andrews	Claude Brook
The Minister	Robert Hazelton
Widow Martin	Florence Short
Her Child	May Kaiser

THE PLAY

Anna Webb	Mary Carr
John, Harry, their sons	Percy Helton Joseph Striker
Ruth, her daughter	Jane Thomas
George Mills	Roy Gordon
Little Anna	Florence Haas
Uncle Andrews	Claude Brook
The Bank President	Roger Lytton
Jerry Gibbs	Ernest Hilliard

Paul H. Sloane has written and Edwin Carewe and Jack Ford have produced for the Fox screen a simple picture as significant as anything the cinema has developed to date. In its intense and vital meaning it is as profound as "Hamlet," although perhaps in its visible manifestation it is just another picture. It reeks in spots with "comedy relief," it has touches of obvious screen trickery, but in its fundamental message it is as great a work of fiction as "Liliom." Not in the theatrical sense—indeed it may not be a commercial success, but there does not come to the recollection of this observer of the stage and the picture theatre a work so fraught with possibilities in radical human teaching as this seven-reel picture which came to Broadway without any particular fanfare and which created so little audible excitement Monday evening.

In social precept the picture is years ahead of the times, although the times are moving forward in this direction with di: .y speed, and one can't be sure it would stir something. The picture will engender in all probability a world of superficial tears from the unthinking; a wave of bitter sentimental revolt from the half-thinking; but from the analytical and sincere it ought to evoke an illuminating earful—or mindful, if you must have it—in "gnified terms.

And the whole thing is about nothing but a spoiled boy and a doting mother, but it's a remorseless dissection of the small genesis and the terrific consequences of family favoritism. Superficially it's just a sentimental story of mother love and maternal sacrifice; fundamentally it's a wrenching tragedy of family ruin and desolation. Translated into terms of the theatre it's just a tearful, emotional experience; translated into terms of real life it's an epochal revelation of human possibilities in the home.

There's a note on the program signed by William Fox. It describes the mission of the picture as "To provide clean, upbuilding entertainment for :every American family, 'Silver Wings' has a message for every one. If it is as inspiring to you as it is to me, it will do the world much good." Which is a mild way to put it. If nothing but the superficial meaning of "Silver Wings" gets across, it won't start much; but if its deepest significance gets into the open, it's going to raise a lot of noise.

It may go either way. It will be a pity if it dies without the widest kind of publication and public discussion. It's a thing about which educators and scientists might wage a mighty battle. It all depends whether it is forced to a widespread start. Its possibilities for ultimate service—not necessarily to the theatre alone—are limitless. If all knowledge, all understanding, all enlightenment are constructive in the long run, here is something that should not be lost.

The utter sincerity of the picture in its contention cannot be questioned. It touches human experience at every turn. The "mother story" has become a convention—a literary convention, than which there is perhaps nothing more fixed and unalterable in the world. In its theatrical form it harps upon the aged mother deserted, abandoned and in poverty—in all particulars a material tragedy. Here is the same thing done into spiritual terms. The family wrecked, the mother desolated, the sons abandoned to wreckage, all the product of good intentions. That's the poignant tragedy of it. All this waste and wretchedness grows out of emotions that have their roots in the ancient concept of mother love. And the crowning wrench of the whole epic tragedy is that the mother herself is the central victim, although around her is strewn the desolation.

It isn't pretty; a lot of its passages are far from sugared poetry; but who shall say it isn't true? *Rush.*

TROUBLE

A five-reel comedy drama, starring Jackie Coogan; produced by Sol Lesser; to be released by First National. Directed by Albert Austin, under supervision of Jack Coogan, Sr.
The Plumber.................Wallace Beery
His Wife....................Gloria Hope
The Boy.....................Jackie Coogan

Of course this won't be the knockout "The Kid" was with little Jackie Coogan and Charlie Chaplin in it, but it is a picture that will get a lot of money for the average exhibitor because it is a refreshing yarn that will appeal to the women particularly. It is the third of the series the juvenile star is making for Lesser, the first two being "My Boy" and "Peck's Bad Boy." This one holds up to the standard of either of the previous two.

A simple little human interest story is the background for the star. He is a runaway orphan, having quit the home because they wouldn't let his dog remain there. The home is out of funds, and a campaign is started to place the child inmates with families. Jackie is the last one to go, a plumber's wife selecting him. The husband is a wife-beater, and finally is sent to prison for a year, the wife and the adopted kiddie going back to the farm of her parents for a happy ending.

In the handling of the story the youthful star is given every opportunity to appear to advantage, and in a courtroom scene when he takes the witness stand he manages to put over a bit that would do credit to any of the much older stars of the screen. Wallace Beery makes the roughneck plumber a corking character study, while Gloria Hope is a winsome little housewife.

One of the real wallops is a fight that Beery and a cop put up in the latter part of the picture with the kiddie assisting on the side lines by hurling flower pots, etc. *Fred.*

GUARDED LIPS

London, May 11.
This exceptionally strong drama by the Swedish Biograph has all the excellence of the firm's previous features, but it, unlike the majority, bows to convention, inasmuch as it has a happy ending.

The story is exceptionally fine and is beautifully told. Of Russia and the late revolution the author and producer refrain from depicting horror or sensationalism, and beyond some wonderfully staged and photographed scenes showing refugees on the march leave the "penny dreadful" opportunities of such a catastrophe alone. Had the picture been full of brutality, floggings and assassinations it would not have one iota of the power it possesses.

The production work is of a very high standard, not a detail is slurred or missed, and the many great sets used convey no suspicion of the studio. Roughly, the story tells how the Princess Sonia saves a son of the people, Alexander Micheloff, from the political police. Years pass, and during the revolution he saves her and her family from his comrades. Years again pass, and he himself has to flee. He seeks shelter in the same country as the Princess. There he finds that the Prince, her father, is in the hands of a profiteering moneylender,

whom he also knows to be a traitor. Matters get worse with the refugees, and at last the profiteer shows his hand; he wants Sonia. She hears of this and of her family's indebtedness. Scornfully, she flings the family jewels to him as part payment, saying she will redeem them on New Year's night. He takes them, saying she will redeem them only with herself.

On New Year's day he is found murdered and she is arrested. Her advocate is Alexander Micheloff, but the case seems dead against her. In her cell while the jury is deliberating he confesses that he killed the traitor-profiteering, but should his name be connected with the "execution" hundreds, thousands of unfortunate peasants will suffer. Therefore Sonia, whom he loves, must be sacrificed. She gladly consents, but the jury return a verdict of acquittal, and the proud princess gives her future into the hands of the "son of the people." Throughout the acting is amongst the best ever seen. No matter the situation there is no straining for effect. The characters live.

Jenny Hesselquist gives a sterling performance as the Princess, her change from the proud patrician to the loving, suffering woman being shown with rare skill. Lars Hanson gives a fine performance as the young peasant lawyer and the entire cast is miles ahead of 99 per cent. of picture players. Particularly noticeable is the absence of apparent make-up. In this country "Guarded Lips" will be handled by Gaumont. *Gore.*

STEP ON IT

This Universal feature, written by Courtney R. Cooper, starring Hoot Gibson and directed by Jack Conway, is a typical Western. The story is of a girl trying to help a brother who is serving a term for cattle rustling. She accidentally meets a young ranch owner. They fall in love.

It goes on to tell how she, in trying to bring the guilty party to justice and free her brother, mingles with a band of rustlers who are stealing Gibson's cattle. Gibson searches for the rustlers, finds the girl in a cabin and upon asking her for an explanation of why with the rustlers, is captured. He escapes with the aid of the girl. While Gibson holds off the rustlers the girl goes for aid.

After an all night battle the rustlers capture Gibson through a trick, but he is again saved by the girl, who tricks the rustlers into being captured by Gibson's men.

The picture is well directed and should draw in the smaller houses. Barbara Bedford as the girl playing opposite to Gibson did her role flawlessly.

THE FACE BETWEEN

Metro feature starring Bert Lytell, showing the first half of the week at Loew's State. A Bayard Veiller production, adapted by Lenore J. Coffee from Justus Miles Forman's story.
Tommy Carteret, Jr. }.........Bert Lytell
Tommy Carteret, Sr. }
Sybil Eliot.................Andre Tourneur
Marianna Canfield..........Sylvia Breamer
Mr. Hartwell...............Hardee Kirkland
Mrs. Eliot.................Girard Alexander
Joe Borrall................Frank Brownlee
Jared......................Burwell Hamrick
Mr. Canfield...............Joel Day
The Doctor.................Dewitt Jennings

Bert Lytell's directors evidently are aiming for variety with each succeeding release. As far as can be recalled, this star has appeared in a crook meller, a prize ring yarn and a business romance story in his recent productions. This is out and out drama of the altruistic self-sacrificing school wherein the hero gives up his chance for happiness for the sake of another.

On the eve of the younger Tommy

Carteret's engagement, Hartwell returns in the middle of the night, accusing the younger man of having sullied his honor by making clandestine love to Hartwell's wife. Tommy, Jr., realizing that it was his father (also played by Mr. Lytell) professes willingness to make any amends possible. Hartwell edicts that Carteret bury himself in a forsaken backwoods section until he (Hartwell) dies. There, in the God-forsaken region in Kentucky, Carteret is almost driven frantic by the loneliness and the unsociability of his surroundings. Marianna Canfield (Sylvia Breamer) is one of the younger natives of the district. In warning Tommy of the corporal punishment about to be meted out to him by those who resent his intrusion locally, Marianna finds herself in a compromising position and tells her father and friends she is going to marry Carteret. Tommy dazedly agrees, but Marianna's jealous suitor kills her from ambush and wounds Carteret. Marianna thereafter haunts Tommy in his delirium and through convalescence under the care of his former betrothed, who has meantime learned the truth. Not until he again becomes unconscious in a mad plunge after the elusive phantom and again regains consciousness is he freed of this phantom fear.

It is pure theatrical drama, with no particular point admittedly, but it makes for excellent entertainment. It's a story that even though one might analyze as devoid of point and moral, is told well merely for the entertainment it affords. One has become so inured to deriving a lesson and moral from each picture—in fact, great pains are taken to drive it home with each caption—that where the purpose as divulged in the very first scenes and the rest of the action merely supplements and pads it out, it is more or less of a novelty.

Mr. Veiller has handled his puppets intelligently and to good effect. True, he has fought shy of the trick double exposure photography in the star's dual personation of father and son, but since that stuff is no longer a novelty, it matters little. The dramatics, it must be admitted, even in the introductory scenes, are so tense that one would hardly notice any scenes where father and son shake hands, etc. The casting has been excellently assigned from star down.

The exhibitor can make much of the alliterative "phantom fear," "son's sacrifice" captions for exploitation purposes. It may be added, a comedy for balance should be included in the program. *Abel.*

NO TRESPASSING

Mabel Colton...............Irene Castle
James Colton...............Howard Truesdale
Mrs. James Colton..........Emily Fitzroy
Roscoe Paine...............Ward Crane
Mrs. Paine.................Eleanor Barry
Dorinda....................Blanche Frederici
Lute.......................Charles Eldridge
Capt. Dean.................Leslie Stowe
Nellie Dean................Betty Bouton
Victor Carver..............Al Roscoe
Simeon Eldridge............Harry Fisher
George Davis...............George Pauncefort

Holtre production released through Hodkinson, scenario furnished by Howard Irving Young based upon the story, "Rise of Roscoe Paine," by Joseph C. Lincoln. Irene Castle is the star and Edwin L. Hollywood the director.

"No Trespassing" is not the type of story expected as a starring vehicle for Irene Castle. It is a homespun affair and distinctly away from the flashy style of production. The story is long drawn out in picture form and develops few real punches. The cast supporting the star includes a number of rural types, the majority well selected. Exteriors along the waterfront predominate with the interiors calling for no great outlay.

The Lincoln story is of the rural type, the action taking place in a small New England fishing village. The Coltons—mother, father and daughter—New York society people, take up their residence in Denboro, on Cape Cod, due to the ill health of Mrs. Colton. The daughter, Mabel, is a debutante, and the father a Wall Street operator. His transactions in the Street are of such importance that a private wire is installed in the Denboro home. He is endeavoring to put over a deal to secure the control of a mine adjacent to property he already controls. Other interests are trying to block his efforts.

A lane used by the fisherman which passes the Colton home, the noise from which annoys Mrs. Colton, is wanted by the operator. He is unable to purchase it, finding that it is owned by Roscoe Paine, a young man of whom little is known. Paine spends his time idling around the fishing village and taking care of his invalid mother. The daughter becomes acquainted with Paine and starts to show interest in him.

Just at the time that the big Wall Street deal is about to be consummated Colton is incapacitated and the entire proposition is put over with the aid of the daughter and Paine.

The latter, meantime, had sold the lane to Colton to secure $3,000 to help out the cashier of the local bank, who used the bank's funds for speculation. Paine is about to be run out of town by the fishermen for selling the property, when the true story comes out. The financier learns of the clever manner in which Paine handled his affairs and offers him a position in his firm, with the daughter included.

This latest Castle feature cannot be relied upon as a real moneymaker. Exhibitors will not find it productive. *Hart.*

ANGEL OF CROOKED STREET

Jennie Marsh...............Alice Calhoun
Schuyler Sanford...........Ralph McCullough
"Silent" McKay.............Scott McKee
"Kid Glove" Thurston.......Rex Hammel
"Cap" Berry................William McCall
"Mother" De Vere...........Nellie Anderson
Mrs. Phineas Sanford.......Martha Mattox
Mrs. Marsh.................Mary H. Young
Stoneham...................George Stanley
Dan Bolton.................Walter Cooper

Vitagraph production starring Alice Calhoun based upon the story by Harry Dittmar, the screen version supplied by C. Graham Baker. David Smith handled the direction. Compared with the general run of Vitagraph productions, "The Angel of Crooked Street" is no better nor worse than the average, although far from being a suitable picture for a theatre that has a following and does not depend upon floaters entirely for patronage. It has the stamp of a cheap five-reeler from start to finish.

The story centres around Jennie Marsh, who, due to the financial reverses of her family, is forced to take a position as a domestic in the home of a wealthy small town widow. She is wrongfully accused of a theft and sent to a reformatory by the woman. Upon securing her release she seeks revenge. She becomes associated with a gang of crooks, but does not enter into their ways of securing a livelihood. Instead she becomes acquainted with the son of the woman who wronged her and gradually gains his love. It goes along this way for some time, with the crooks having trouble with the police with gun fights ensuing, all of which is brought to a peaceful close by the girl actually falling in love with the boy she thought she would play for revenge.

The leads are handled by Miss Calhoun and Ralph McCullough. Of the two the former displays the better work. McCullough was miscast in the college boy role. The remainder of the cast consists of types. Cheapness marks the production end.

"The Angel of Crooked Street" was the Saturday feature at Loew's New York. The house plays a different program daily, and apparently the picture booker believes the house will draw business Saturday regardless of the attraction. A few minutes spent in the rear of the house Saturday night to hear comments passed upon this latest Vitagraph release would have convinced him a different policy should be employed. From the general trend of the conversations the audience left in a dissatisfied mood. They were justified, as the feature is one of ten-cent grade and never made for a showing on Broadway. *Hart.*

SILAS MARNER

Silas Marner..............Craufurd Kent
Sarah..............Marguerite Courtot
William Dane..............Robert Kenyon
Sally Oates..............Nona Marden
Elina Tempscum..............Ricca Allan
Jem Rodney..............Austin Huhn
Squire Cass..............Anders Randolph
Godfrey Cass..............Bradley Barker
Dunsey Cass..............Charles Coghlan
Nancy Lammeter..............Marie Edith Wells
Dolly Winthrop..............Alice Fleming
Dr. Kimble..............George Fawcett
Eppie ....{ Helen Rowland
                          { Jean Girardin
Aaron.......................John Randall

Adapted from one of the most popular books of former years, this picture is probably the most monotonous of recent years. Its story is disconnected, rambling along to the approach of a climax and then sheers off to entirely different channels, suggesting it had been cut with poor discretion or censored in a ruinous fashion.

The opening shows Silas Marner in the little village of Lantern Yard. Betrayed by his lifelong friend, Silas wanders off to other parts to begin life anew, leaving behind him the sweetheart. Whether one was curious as to Lantern Yard or the sweetheart or friend made little difference, Silas just ambled away, and Lantern Yard passed out with him.

In his new abode Silas is robbed some years later, and then more years follow and his adoption of little Eppie before the money is returned and the history of Eppie's life and birth unfolded. It seems Eppie was the daughter of the squire's son, who refused to admit his relationship to him, when her mother staggered up and fell dead from exhaustion outside Silas' cabin. Everything turns out all right for Eppie, she marrying a neighbor's child.

Although Silas' life is screened over a thirty-or-more year period, he didn't seem to age a single day regardless of his troubles and worries. The scenery selected for the locale was pretty and the camera work perfect, but when the direction and the manipulation of the feature's continuity are considered they run a bad last.

It's a seven-reel treat of tiresomeness. It's sole redeeming power and box office strength will depend on the title of the book, one that probably every school kid in America has read. *Wynn.*

THE BARNSTORMER

Joel Utility..............Charles Ray
His Father..............George Nichols
His Mother..............Blanche Rose
Manager ....Lionel Belmore
Leading Lady..............Florence Oberle
Emily ....Charlotte Pierce
Theatre Owner..............Gus Leonard
Her Pa.....................Lincoln Plumer

A Kane-First National six-reeler of the rural comedy drama classification featuring Charles Ray. The story by Richard Andres is a familiar theme of hokum and bucolic comedy, much after the style of the vaudeville act, "For Pity's Sake." Ray, who did his own directing, is handed the role of a stage-struck country youth who busts into show business via a road show that enlists his services because he can play a piano. His experiments with make-up and putty nose were good for a few laughs before he became an honest-to-goodness trouper. After joining the show he is the "Patsy" until a chance to shine as a real hero by sticking up the leading man, who, disguised as a robber, sticks up the audience, is arrived at. For this he wins the village druggist's daughter.

That's about all of the story with evidence of copious cutting discernible. The picture ran 65 minutes at the Broadway and could have razored to 40 without damage.

Several ancient "bits" were worked for laughs, as the prop snowfall with Ray aloft in the flies working the snow and dropping the container. Wilfred Lucas as a heavy legit leading man did well in a soft role, and Charlotte Price as the sweetheart was sweetly girlish.

Ray has established himself as a delineator of "natural" rural types. His latest effort is as "unnatural" as possible and will not stand comparison with any of his former efforts. It's low comedy at best. *—Con.*

OTHELLO

Berlin, May 12.

At a private showing the other morning a picturization of Shakespeare's "Othello," an Ufa film, under the direction of Dimitri Buchowitzki. The cast was excellent or, rather, looked excellent on paper: Othello, Emil Jannings; Iago, Werner Kraus; Roderigo, Ferdinand von Alten; Cassio, Theodore Loos; Desdemona, Ida con Lenkeffy.

Of these only Kraus and von Alten suggested anything of characterization, the Othello of Jannings being most disappointing, he having reached the overgrimace stage.

And the direction of Buchowitzki only proves again the stupidity of entrusting any big job to him. The whole picture is merely a stageplay which a camera happened to attend.

The dependence on caption to express the emotions of the characters is pitiful in its inadequacy. *Trask.*

WONDERFUL YEAR

London, May 23.

A very fine picture and probably the best ever made by a British producer in a British studio and with British players. The story is well told and relies entirely on its natural simplicity and truth.

It is a story of British rural life —"life in the raw," and its characters are those any one can meet in any little sleepy village. Its tragedy is the tragedy of many homes, its pathos devoid of slobbery "sob stuff," and, above all, its sentiment rings absolutely true.

Two brothers, one stern and morose, the other gay and happy, live together in a tiny cottage. The morose man falls in love and captures the heart of a village maid by sheer brutal assault. On the eve of his marriage he has an accident, and the result is paralysis. His brother and sweetheart look after him and fall in love, as is almost inevitable. On their wedding day the cripple curses them. From then on he gives them no peace. He is always lying on his couch, watching their every action.

Then the time comes when a child is to be born to the woman. The doctor fears the worst and the husband begs the paralyzed man to lift his curse. He refuses. A child is safely born, however, and it is the baby who brings peace and forgiveness to the household.

The production work is really fine, the director, Graham Cutts, having neglected no detail. His work is marked with a natural strength and freedom from straining after effect, which is seldom seen on the screen. This is his second picture, and before taking up the studio work he was a film traveler. Today he is probably the best and most truly artistic producer in England. The picture is also notable for the discovery of two artists who may well become our first two genuine British stars. Both of them were unknown before "The Wonderful Story" was shown to the trade.

Herbert Langley as the paralyzed man gives a performance which reminds one of the Swedish-Biograph, and through more than three-quarters of the film he is on his back and compelled to rely only upon his facial expression. Lillian Hall-Davis, the other newcomer, plays the lover, and is equal to Langley in power. Very few more gripping scenes have ever been screened than the one in which the paralytic struggling from his bed by sheer will power seeks to strangle her. Her one fault is that in the earlier scenes she looks rather like a society girl playing at being a milkmaid. The supporting cast, a very small one,

is far above the average and consists chiefly of Olaf Hytten as the brother and Bernard Vaughan as an old clergyman.

The whole of the scenic arrangements are laid among beautiful rural lanes and pasture lands, the interior "shots" being confined to a cottage living room. The photography is excellent. Up to now when turning out a "great British super film" we have invariably relied upon a servile copying of American grandeur and the inclusion of a cast of big stage names.

This picture is not a "super film"; it merely lives up to its title. *Gore.*

SONNY

A First National release, with Richard Barthelmess starred. The story is adapted from the play of the same title by George V. Hobart, Frances Marion and Henry King supplying the script with the latter directing. Story has a war angle.

Sonny ....} ....Richard Barthelmess
Sam Marden ....}
Mrs. Crosby ....Margaret Seddon
Florence Crosby..............Pauline Garden
Madge Craig..............Lucy Fox
Harper Craig..............Herbert Grimwood
Alicia ....Patterson Dial
Summers ....Fred Nicholls

A number of liberties were taken with the original play "Sonny" that was presented in New York only last season and failed to get much of a run, although on the stage it was a much better entertainment than it is on the screen. "Sonny" is a story that has its foundation on the war. It is going to be a question whether or not the public at large is willing to look at war stuff of this sort at this time and accept it as entertainment. They certainly did not seem ready in New York a few months ago. As an example, one of the girl ushers at the Strand (a widow of the war) became hysterical Sunday, when the picture was first shown, and had to be taken home.

As a picture "Sonny" is a corking feature, but the question the exhibitor will have to find out for himself is whether or not his audiences are willing to sit through a story where the son of a blind mother is killed at the front and a double in the same company consents to go back to his home and impersonate him for the mother's sake.

The war stuff, battle front, trenches, etc., are strongly played up in the first few reels. They are exceedingly well done from a pictorial and directorial standpoint. The lightings are particularly effective, especially the hand-colored bits with flashes of flame from bursting shells.

The picture is a corking one for Barthelmess, and he enacts the dual role with cleverness. The double exposure scenes in the early part as well as the vision bits later are masterly bits of photography, worked out very well to the advantage of the star. In support Margaret Seddon as the blind mother gives a fine performance, while Lucy Fox and Herbert Grimwood carry the heavy section convincingly. A lot of the comedy relief of the original play is lost in the manner in which the Lucy Fox role is handled in the screen script.

If the audience will stand for war stuff this is going to be a winner, but if not ready for it as yet around the country then the picture will draw fair business. Under ordinary conditions, however, it should be pretty much of a knockout. *Fred.*

THE ORDEAL

Paramount picture presented by Adolph Zukor at the Rialto. Adapted by Beulah Marie Dix from the W. Somerset Maugham story and directed by Paul Powell. A tale of self sacrifice on the part of an elder sister for her younger brother and sister. Agnes Ayres starred.

Sybil Bruce..............Agnes Ayres
George Bruce..............Clarence Burton
Dr. Robert Acton..............Conrad Nagel

Helen Crayshaw	Edna Murphy
Geoffrey Crayshaw	Edward Sutherland
Minnie	Ann Schaeffer
Gene	Eugene Corey
Mme. St. Levis	Adele Farrington
Sir Francis Maynard	Edward Martindale
Kitty	Shannon Day
Elsie	Clare Du Brey

A fairly good society story that has something of a punch, but pretty much along lines of similar self-sacrifice stories that have been seen in the past. There is naught that will take it out of the run of the program productions, as far as the Paramount standard of production is concerned. However, it looks to be a picture that can be played at most any of the week-run houses with the advance assurance of an average week's business if in a drop-in neighborhood. It is a picture that will not pull anything extraordinary in the way of box office returns.

The story is of a girl who marries for money so that she can educate and support her younger sister and brother. On her husband's untimely death he wills that she must remain a widow to enjoy his estate. She is in love with a young physician, but her belief that she still owes her relatives duty prevents her from accepting her happiness until she finally becomes aware that the money that she is holding through her refusal to wed is bringing about their ruin.

Miss Ayres gives a really clever performance and appears before the camera in a stunning series of gowns. In one particular dressing gown, when she informs the doctor that it isn't necessary that they be wed to enjoy love and he spurns her, one really wonders what is the matter with his eye-sight. Incidentally, this is one of the spoken titles that the censors are going to jump on. How it got by in New York is a mystery. Conrad Nagel, as the hero, is just about all that could be expected, while Edna Murphy and Edward Sutherland, as the ungrateful younger relatives, scored heavily. Adele Farrington and Eugene Corey provide the heavy element in the cast and do so to the Queen's taste.

In lightings and photography there is nothing to be desired. The direction of Paul Powell carries the story along at a speed that holds the interest at all times.

Fred.

MR. BARNES OF N. Y.

Mr. Barnes of New York	Tom Moore
Marina Paoli	Anna Lehr
Enid Anstruther	Naomi Childers
Gerald Anstruther	Lewis Willoughby
Antonio	Ramon Samanicgo
Tomasso	Otto Hoffman
Danella	Sidney Ainsworth

Goldwyn feature, starring Tom Moore, from the play of the same title by Archibald Clavering Gunter, placed in screen form by Gerald Duffy. Victor Schertzinger did the directing.

The production is a costume picture, the action taking place in the 80's. The director has followed closely the dressing of the times which for the average screen fan will not prove as interesting as the modern modes. The title role gives Moore few opportunities and could easily have been played by an inferior actor, although the Moore name will probably prove more of a draw than the title. Anna Lehr and Naomi Childers divide the honors of the feminine division, with Otto Hoffman playing a character role of considerable importance effectively.

The layout for the production has not reached a high figure. The plot is laid in Europe, with the exteriors and sets sufficiently well planned to give the proper European atmosphere. The photography reaches a good standard.

The story, starting with a duel between an English naval officer and Corsican of birth, has the greater portion of action in the early footage and the last moments. The Corsican being killed, his sister vows vengeance against his slayer. The latter is hunted throughout Europe. Mr. Barnes, a globe trotter, was a witness to the affair. Two years later he becomes acquainted with the officer's sister who, it is believed, did the killing. The Englishman in turn being in love with the Corsican's sister. The entire tangle is cleared up when the naval officer admits having loaned his gun to a fellow shipmate to take part in the duel, the latter in the meantime having died. This brings about the happy ending for the couple, who had been married before the disclosure was made and Barnes and the officer's sister make another match.

The production is not strong enough for over one day anywhere.

Hart.

YELLOW MEN AND GOLD

A Goldwyn five-reeler, presented at the Capitol. Directed by Irvin Willat.

Parrish	Richard Dix
Bessie	Helene Chadwick
Carroll	Henry Barrows
Carmen	Rosemary Theby
Lynch	Richard Tucker
Craven	Fred Kohler
Todd	Henry Herbert
Chang	Goro Kino
Jill	George King
John	William Carroll

"Yellow Men and Gold" as a feature picture has little to recommend it from the box-office standpoint. It is a good adventure story, but holds nothing that hasn't been presented on the screen at some time. There is an effort to condone its commonplace aspect through a "twist" finish, and that is the only thing that makes the picture at all possible to the audiences of the better class houses. In the regular run of daily change theatre it will get by nicely, but the week stands will not hold up in business on the picture.

The story is by Gouverneur Morris, who in writing it undoubtedly figured on the serial magazine angle for the yarn. But the magazine punch doesn't show on the screen.

Helene Chadwick and Richard Dix are featured, with a fairly strong cast behind them. Irvin Willat directed the story, and at times managed to keep the action going along at a fairly speedy pace, but on the whole the story is commonplace in the line of treasure-seeking yarns, and no doubt it was a task for the director to "get something" out of the script that wasn't in it, so as to make it different.

The story opens in a bungalow owned by a young author. He has had nothing but rejections on his stories for a time, and finally, when his mystery story comes back, he holds it in his hand and wonders what is wrong with it. From that point the screen version starts with the real story, although the audience is kept in the dark until the last few feet of the feature.

A murdered man, a map of an island where a Spanish treasure ship was sunk, a gang of crooks, the hero, a vamp and a girl heroine are the principal characters. There is the chase across the South Seas of two sailing ships to reach the treasure land first, a fight on the island, the defeat of the crooked gang and, finally, the victorious return. Then comes the twist, with the author standing in the position that he was in when the treasure hunt story started, with the fact revealed that it was the story that he was wondering about that has just been shown. However, in this case it wasn't a rejection, only a request for revision, and then he goes to the adjoining bungalow, where all of the characters that were seen in his story are in the life. They are his neighbors and are aware of the fact that he has cast them as the villains in one of his fiction yarns and are elated that he has finally sold a story.

In the cast Richard Dix, who is the author and the hero of the fiction yarn, gives a corking performance and stages a couple of fights that have a lot of speed. This boy is coming along like wildfire on the screen and looks like one of the few real bets that Goldwyn have. Helene Chadwick makes a very charming heroine, but Rosemary Theby as the vamp runs away with all the honors as far as the girl contingent of the cast is concerned. The advantage of having been a screen player from the old days stands her in good stead, and she certainly utilizes all of the tricks of the trade. Henry Barrows as the principal heavy gives a performance that registers, and the balance of the cast fills in most capably.

Fred.

DR. MARBUSE, GAMBLER

Berlin, May 12.

At the Ufa Palast am Zoo, April 15, the first showing of the first part of Dr. Marbuse, the Gambler," from the novel by Norbert Jacques, scenarized by Thea von Harbou. A good average popular thriller—dime-novel stuff in a $100,000 setting—but sufficiently camouflaged to get by with a class audience.

The story builds itself about the character of Dr. Marbuse, the great gambler, the player with the souls of men and women. He runs an underground counterfeiting establishment, and with this money starts all his enterprises. In the first reel of the film he appears as stock exchange speculator. He steals an important commercial treaty, which causes certain shares to fall; he buys. He lets the treaty be found again; the stocks rise; he sells. To get money out of a rich young man he sets Carozza, a dancer, on his trail; then he meets him and, hypnotizing him, wins large sums of money from him at his club. Marbuse meets Countess Told and desires her. He fixes the mark of cheating at cards on her husband, and in the ensuing excitement steals her away.

And so it goes on, a bit confusedly but generally with speed and life. The best moments are achieved by the conflict between Marbuse and the attorney, von Wenk, who is trying to uncover him. This first part ends with the stealing of the countess and the second and last (not yet publicly shown) with the finding of Marbuse, insane, in his own counterfeiting celler, where he has been trapped by von Wenk.

The film is somewhat hurt by the casting of Rudolf Klein-Rogge for the title role; he is physically too small and not a clever enough actor to make one forget this. Fritz Kortner would have been a far better choice. Paul Richter as the young millionaire and Bernhard Goetzke as Von Wenk do very nicely in their respective roles. And the Carozza of Aud Egede-Nissen, the Countess Told of Gertrude Welker are among the best pieces of film work of the year. Especially Miss Nissen is a fine type for America, as she combines great physical charm with some real emotional ability.

The interiors of Stahl-Urach and Hunte are sumptuous and tasteful, and Carl Hoffmann's photography generally adequate. The direction of Fritz Lang has moments—at last through the consciousness of the picture world is beginning to filter the idea that what you see is worth at least twenty times what you read. For instance, the handling of a scene in which Marbuse tries to hypnotize von Wenk and force him to play a card, the rest of the characters dim out, leaving only the face of Marbuse visible, and this becomes larger and larger, until it covers the whole screen. This is tremenously effective and film technique. This is the direction the film must and will go. It is my unfortunate duty to have to chronicle that Mr. Lang somewhat negated these good effects by twenty forty-word captions of a ludicrous unconciseness.

The film is doing tremendous business, filling the Ufa Palast twice nightly, and should, with some intelligent retitling, recutting and the aid of a good continuity doctor, fit neatly into any Broadway program.

Trask.

SUPPLY AND DEMAND

A new series of "kid" comedies have made their appearance with the release of "Supply and Demand," a J. K. McDonald Production in which Johnny Jones is starred. This youngster manages to make a favorable impression. The supporting cast is well selected and the juvenile players manage to pull any number of laughs.

The story of the first release has Jimmie Finn as the author, and if his initial effort is to be taken as a criterion of what is to follow it would appear that the McDonald productions have found another Booth Tarkington, for Finn in this picture seems to lay the groundwork for a "Penrod," if there is to be a second edition of that youngster.

It is a small-town story, with the kids, who have invested in a mail-order scheme and received a number of house traps, creating a demand for their wares after they have been unsuccessful in selling them. Well worked out and has any number of laughs.

Fred.

June 9, 1922

OVER THE BORDER

Dramatic feature (Paramount), "presented by Adolph Zukor," adapted by Albert Shelby LeVino from the novel "She of the Triple Chevrons," by Sir Gilbert Parker. Betty Compson starred, supported by Tom Moore. Designated as a Penrhyn Stanlaws production.

Jen Galbraith................Betty Compson
Sargent Tom Flaherty..........Tom Moore
Peter Galbraith........J. Farrell Macdonald
Val Galbraith.............Casson Ferguson
Snow Devil..............Sidney D'Albrook
Corporal Byng.............L. C. Shumway
Pretty Pierre.................Jean DeBraic
Inspector Jules............Edward J. Brady
Bord. ....Joseph Ray

One of the best examples of fine, clean, romantic melodramas the screen has seen in many a day. The film has everything—story, star, direction and gorgeous backgrounds in the snow-piled Rockies of Western Canada, not to mention the always dependable picturesqueness of the Royal Northwest Mounted Police.

What the film makers intimately call "the snow stuff" is wonderful. There is one passage involving a blizzard that is a knockout for effectiveness, and the whole picture takes immense interest from its white stretches and snow-covered forests, picturesque trading posts and wilderness types.

As to the story itself, there does not come to mind a film production in which the element of suspense is so skillfully handled. There are moments in which even the hard-boiled reviewer gets a thrill and the whole thing is convincing in its illusion. There is an apt contrast between "Over the Border" at the Rivoli and "The Woman Who Walked Alone" at the Rialto this week. The former is sturdy, simple romance; the latter is mere theatrical contrivance, counterfeit and artificial. The two pictures are as far apart as "Hamlet" and "Bertha the Sewing Machine Girl," although their materials are almost identical. And the difference amounts to nothing more than integrity of design, right in the first case, insincere in the second. Probably in the case of Parker, the author was inspired from a clear sense of romance; while John Colton, author of "The Woman Who Walked Alone," was just writing a story to sell. Both moods are indelibly written on the product.

In "Over the Border" there is the lure of far places and interesting people, notably the men of the Mounted, who will live as long as romance does as the ideal of courage, honor and adventure, types of rough and ready white men, Indians and half-breeds, all framed in the intriguing frame of the wilderness. Only in place of the bad white trader the plot revolves around traffic in whiskey and the liquor runners in their fight against the troopers.

Miss Compson, always an appealing type of heroine, has a splendid part as the daughter of a genial but scheming rum runner, in love with a sergeant of the Mounted (Tom Moore). In the early portion her role is rather pale, but it grows in action to a stunning climax. Moore is one of the few screen actors who can get a high comedy flavor into the most melodramatic scenes in a way that intensifies the drama without making it stilted. He never had a better character for the exhibition of this peculiar knack.

Peter Galbraith is a rum runner on a large scale, although ostensibly he is a tavern keeper a few miles north of the U. S.-Dominion line. Jen, his daughter, is deeply concerned for the dangers that this business involves for her father and brother Val, her attitude being complicated by her love for Sergeant Tom Flaherty of the Mounted, whose business is the capture of the dealers in forbidden liquor, the western province being prohibition as well as the United States.

Tom is in love with Jen and has applied for a discharge from the service, and as the climax of the interesting play approaches it appears that his release takes effect tomorrow morning at 8 o'clock. After that they will wed and buy a farm. Meanwhile Val, Jen's brother, has shot an Indian spy in the service of the Constabulary and the troopers are on his trail. Tom is ordered to carry orders for his capture to a distant post, but stops at the Galbraith home to make an inspection under orders from his commander, never suspecting that the sealed orders spell doom for the brother of his sweetheart.

Val's father alone knows what the official envelope contains. He drugs Tom to delay its delivery, but Jen steals the soldier's outer uniform as he sleeps and, riding through the storm, delivers the secret orders, not knowing their import, but anxious only to save her lover's honor. So the night passes. The brother has become lost in the blizzard on his flight to the border and returns home just as the troopers, acting on the orders received, catch up and make him prisoner. It is then lacking a few minutes of eight, when Tom is to be free of the service. How he stands fast to the code of the Mounted until the minute of release and then brings about the brother's escape, and how the whole tangle is straightened out makes the most exciting 15 minutes of tension anybody can imagine.

The picture ought to be a clean-up, and probably will be. As a romantic melodrama it holds a place well up among the best half dozen the screen has ever known.

Rush.

DOMESTIC RELATIONS

A First National release, presented by B. P. Schulberg, starring Katherine MacDonald. Just a fair melodramatic story, directed by Chet Whitney from the story and script by Violet Clarke.

Barbara Benton .....Katherine MacDonald
Judge James Benton...W. P. Clareton, Jr.
Joe Martin.......................Frank Leigh
Mrs. Martin..................Barbara LaMar
Sandy ....Gordon Mullen
Pierre ....George Fisher
Dr. Chester Brooks..........Lloyd Whitlock

Just another of the regular run of pictures in which Katherine MacDonald has been starred. It isn't any better or any worse than any of the others in which she has appeared. If anything, this one seems to have a little the better of it on direction, but even Chet Whitney seems to have been unable to stir the unemotional Katherine. Just a program feature release and that is all. It got into the Strand, New York, this week because "I Am the Law" was withdrawn at the last minute through the legal tangle over that picture for the present.

The title, "Domestic Relations," fits the story. The tale is of combat between husband and wife in high and low circles. Miss MacDonald plays the society wife, whose husband, a Judge, neglects her for his profession. Discovering her in a compromising position not of her own making, he immediately adjudges her guilty and turns her from his home. This follows a day in court when he has just sentenced a man to a year's imprisonment for having beaten his wife when he found her in a position very like that of the Judge's wife.

A year passes and Joe Martin is released from prison and in on his way to "get" the Judge. The latter's wife has made her home in the tenement district of the town and became acquainted with the wife of Martin, who runs to tell her of the plan of the husband that has just been released from prison.

There is a quick ride to the rescue, the Judge is warned by his wife of the impending danger, and Martin is caught. But the plea that the Judge's wife makes for the culprit in which she likens her own husband unto Martin in respect to brutality, has its effect and Martin returns to his wife, while the Judge begs forgiveness of his.

Miss MacDonald is entirely too stiff in enacting the role assigned her, but William P. Carlton, Jr., gives the picture a tone of sincerity that helps immeasurably. Frank Leigh as Martin gave a corking character performance, as did also Barbara LaMar as his wife. This latter girl certainly is a comer, although her working in this picture appears to have been done some time in the past, before she got opportunity to do some of the real good things that she has been seen in recently.

Chet Whitney has handled the picture with his usual skill, but he could not be expected to put anything into it that there wasn't in the script or within the range of the star's possibilities.

Fred.

FALSE FRONTS

Keith Drummond............Edward Earle
Helen Baxter............Barbara Castleton
John S. Lathrop...............Frank Losee
Marjorie Kemble...........Madelyne Claire

The Herolds Brothers produced "False Fronts" adapted from the story by S. Barrett McCormick and released through the American Releasing Corp. The feature is a non-star production directed by Samuel R. Bradley, featuring Edward Earle, Barbara Castleton and Frank Losee. The picture includes four roles of importance with Madelyne Claire the only unfeatured member of the quartette.

The Herolds Brothers produced the picture with backing furnished by Cleveland interests. They are newcomers in the independent field and confine their efforts as far as financial backing is concerned to the middle west city. For their initial production "False Fronts" should secure fair returns as an independent release. It is not a big picture, but contains sufficient interest to entertain audiences that are not too discriminating.

The acting reaches a fair standard with the greater portion upon the shoulders of the three featured members. The production fits acceptably with no great attempt made for pretentiousness. The photography displays the handiwork of a capable cameraman.

"False Fronts" has as its leading light a youth possessing a family name but no money. His main ambition life is to be in the social foreground. He makes no progress in a business way but marries a wealthy girl whose mother has social aspirations. His family name brings his wife and her mother into the limelight of society. He depends entirely upon his wife for support. Tiring of the life he leaves home to make his own way. He secures a position with an oil company in a distant town. Internal trouble in the company causes unrest among the employes all of whom own stock. His wife proves to be the controlling stock holder. She arrives upon the scene and discovers that her husband has been the one to save her interests. They are happily reunited he having made good in a commercial way.

Hart.

WOMAN WHO WALKED ALONE

Jesse Lasky presents a George Melford feature from the story, "The Cat That Walked Alone," by John Colton. Scenario by William A. Ritchey. Penwryn Stanlaws is credited with supervision and Thompson Buchanan with a hand in the production, starring Dorothy Dalton.

The Hon. Iris Champneys...Dorothy Dalton
Clement Gaunt...................Milton Sills
Earl of Lemister.............E. J. Radcliffe
Muriel Champneys..........Wanda Hawley
Marquis Champneys.......Frederick Vroom
Marchioness Champneys.......Maym Kelso
Otis Yeardley..................John Davidson
Sir Basil Deere...............Harris Gordon
Schriemann ....Charles Ogle
Hannah Schriemann......Mabel Van Buren
Jock MacKinney..........Maurice B. Flynn
Mombo ....Cecil Holland
Eaarl's Butler...............John MacKinnon
Muller, Iris' Maid.............Temple Pigott

English society play, which switches to South America, where it leaps from polite drama to artificial and forced melodrama. The story has some swift action and many real surprises, besides numerous tense situations, but always it is theatrical. Many slight incidents are extremely hard to swallow and the culminating weight of this forced staginess somehow destroys the illusion pretty completely and one can never get away from the feeling that it is just a fabricated story.

Motives are counterfeit and actions take on the complexion of dime novel invention rather than that of plausibility, not because of the acting, which is extremely good, but because the play itself is just a contrivance of fiction. It isn't entirely that the play is melodrama—nothing can be more entertaining than honest melodrama—but the thing doesn't ring true. In its making somewhere somebody has resorted to stage trick and device instead of depending upon an integrity of purpose. You might almost imagine that the author was "writing down to his audience" and nothing is quite so fatal to screen effect. The whole tale is cheapened and its sincerity destroyed. These undertones of insincerity register upon the audience as inevitably as if they were framed into titles and announced publicly.

To make the theatrical artificiality even more obvious, Dorothy Dalton, the star, wears a blonde wig. It would be interesting to know what dictated this curious twist. Miss Dalton's raven tresses are as familiar to the film fan public as Charlie Chaplin's toothbrush moustache. The minute she appeared in a blonde thatch a fixed and familiar figure was made different and unreal—an invitation at the outset to regard the whole affair as "just a story" and a blow at illusion.

Another thing that would be interesting to know is why they are constantly handing Miss Dalton a story with a twisted romance? Only recently she was a two-gun woman. This time she plays a part in which she is the aggressor in a courtship. First she leads her lover into a difficulty and then saves him, while he is merely the passive party to the wooing. Why is it that so beautiful a woman and so charming an actress cannot be cast for an old fashioned romance? These things are beyond explaining. Not so long ago, she played Aphrodite and was the talk of the town in that part. You'd suppose that such a circumstance would be tip enough for her producers to turn her out in strongly feminine roles. Instead they make her play rough and tumble masculine parts.

Hon. Iris Champneys (Miss Dalton) is forced into a loveless marriage to an old English nobleman in order to mend her family's fortunes. An emergency of travel brings her into casual contact with Clement Gaunt (Milton Sills), an American who "stayed on in England after the war" and is working as a chauffeur. Their ways part, Gaunt going on to South Africa in search of adventure and Iris becoming the nobleman's unloved and unloving wife. A blackmailer plots to exact money from Iris's sister and while she is trying to outmaneuver him she is caught in his room by her jealous husband, who divorces her.

Gaunt is working for a Boer in South Africa when the farmer's stupid wife tries to strike up a liason. The husband finds them in what looks like a compromising situation and the angry woman shoots him, throwing the guilt on Gaunt, who has to flee for his life. While he is in flight he happens upon a tavern where he seeks supplies, and, lo and behold! it is presided over by the disgraced and exiled Iris.

The South African Constabulary are on Gaunt's heels and Iris, without knowing his identity as Gaunt, but only as the supposed murderer, "Yankee Jim," delivers him to the troopers. By a chain of circumstances that puts a heavy strain on credulity, the troopers' leader make the pair marry. They try to escape, but Gaunt is recaptured. Meanwhile Iris has gone back to the Boer's wife and by playing on her native imagination forces a confession that it was she and not "Yankee Jim" that fired the fatal shot.

It is a long time since the screen put so severe a burden on Old Man Coincidence. *Rush.*

STROKE OF MIDNIGHT

Metro presents this feature at the Criterion (rented from Famous Players). It is a Swedish Biograph production written by Dr. Selma Lagerlof and adapted to the screen by Victor Seastrom, who also plays the star part.

David Holm..............Victor Seastrom
His wife..................Hilda Borgstrom
Edith Larssen..................Astrid Holm
Geller......................Tore Svennborg

The picture is murky with Scandinavian gloom. It is as depressing as Ibsen at his very worst and then some, but up to a certain point it has an impressive atmosphere of dignity and its brutal realism is undeniably compelling. This effect of strong drama lasts so long as the picture keeps to its pattern of humble tragedy, but somewhere about midway of the making of the picture somebody concerned in its manufacture must have said to himself or herself, "Here, we're making a commercial picture for the public, which likes a happy ending. We must have by all means a happy ending."

So they applied themselves to that end and wrecked the picture. After that it was merely theatrical, before it had been startling tragedy. The net result is much as though Ibsen had at the last minute decided that "Ghosts" must have a cheerful final curtain, had called in a wizard blood specialist and ended the play with a scene of happy, peaceful domesticity. Nobody would recommend "Ghosts" to a seeker after entertainment and you'd scarcely call it a popular success. But if Ibsen had given it a happy ending it would never have been heard of after the first production. The comparison is absolutely pat. Up to the middle the play is heart rending in its reality of human suffering; afterward it is a sort of pollyanna mixed with Dickens' "Christmas Carol." It starts out in funereal blacks and grays and ends in a bouquet of spring flowers. It can't be done.

Except for the wretched happy ending the play has the depth and proportions of Ibsen himself and a meaning as profound as almost anything the Norwegian wrote. Briefly its message is that evilly inclined humans must work out their own salvation or shoulder the consequences of their own crimes, and that sentimental souls, however well disposed, who seek to help them, only make them worse and bring down ruin on their own heads and the heads of other innocents. It's pessimistic, if you like, but who shall say it is not true? As much of the story as deals with this thesis is absorbing and entirely without artifice. Then the twist to the inappropriate happy ending and the whole thing goes to smash. Anybody that can endure the depression of the tragedy without rushing hence to a discreet bootlegger's would be proof against melancholy and the happy ending wouldn't penetrate to him.

We first meet David Holm on the eve of his departure from jail, an unkempt, burly, vicious brute, whose noxious influence has brought about a murder for which another pays the penalty. On reaching home he finds his wife, after suffering from his violence and neglect, has fled. He takes up her trail, vowing vengeance for the desertion "when he needed her most." His wanderings bring him to a Salvation Army salvage station, where a girl charity worker named Edith Larssen does her generous best to aid him to regeneration. He puts aside her good intentions with a curse.

Presently David, more unkempt and surly, wanders into a rescue mission where, unknown to him, his wife is present. Miss Larssen conceives that she should bring husband and wife together and pursuades the woman that her duty lies in helping her husband to re-establish himself. By her persuasion the pair are reunited in the neat, clean home the woman has built for herself and her children. A year passes. David has gone back to his old habits, drunk, surly, violent, and the neat home has returned to squalor and wretchedness. The consequences of a sentimental good intention pile up into a crushing mountain. David returns home drunk and abuses his wife again and she seeks again to escape, only to be balked and to relapse into hopeless uncomprehending submission to her fate.

The wretchedness she has wrought comes upon Miss Larssen as she lies on her deathbed and she sends for David and his wife, in a last effort to help the man reform. But it is New Year's eve and he declines to be distracted from his drunken revel (who but a pessimistic Scandinavian would have had the creepy ingenuity to stage the celebration in a graveyard?). David and his drinking companion get involved in a brawl and David is knocked unconscious and left for dead. Here's where they began to "plant" the happy ending. While David lies stunned he dreams a grisly dream of a ghost wagon driven always by a man who died at the stroke of 12 on New Year's eve, bond servant of Death, who must collect the dead. In the dream he is compelled to take this ghostly task and his rounds take him to his own home, where it appears the distracted wife is about to poison her two children and commit suicide. He awakens and rushes home to find that it was all a dream, and then and there, with many religious flourishes, resolves to reform and be a good husband. The finale shows them all a year later, re-established and comfortable.

To ask an audience to accept the solution that a mere dream would reform a creature so far gone in viciousness and guilt is too much. It leaves one cold and impatient. Some of the dream stuff (the audience doesn't know it is a dream until it's all over) is pictorially impressive and rich in quivering spookiness.

An attempt is made in the lobby billing to give the play some of the lure of a spiritualistic theme. "Do the dead really come back? Or is is all bunk?" says one caption. Without going into the merits of the subject matter of the billboard question, the attempt to capitalize the vogue for Sir Conan Doyle's theories just now current, all in order to exploit a moving picture, is "all bunk."

The picture has to stand on its merits. On the side of its moral teachings—and who shall say that a picture that mirrors and clarifies a real human problem is not as educational as a travel subject that shows the Louvre or "Native Life in Calcutta"?—on the side of its moral teaching the picture would be as valuable a contribution to the screen as "Ghosts" or "A Doll's House" if its original purpose had been sincerely carried to its logical conclusion. *Rush.*

THE GRAY DAWN

Milton Keith..................Carl Gantvoort
Nan Bennett..................Claire Adams
Ben Sansome..................Robert McKim
Calhoun Bennett......George Hackathorne
Krafft..........................Snitz Edwards
Casey..........................Stanton Heck
Charles Cora..................Omar Whitehead
Mrs. Bennett..................Claire McDowell
Mimi Morrell..................Maude Wayne
Sam ....Zack Williams
Mammy..........................Grace Marvin
Ned Coleman..................Charles Arling
King William..................Harvey Clark
Marshal Richardson.......Charles Thurston
Chinaman..........................Marc Robbins
Bill Collector..........Charles B. Murphy
Mr. Morrell..................J. Gunnis Davis

Hodkinson release produced by Benjamin B. Hampton based upon the novel of the same title by Stewart Edward White. The screen version was furnished by E. Richard Schayer and Marie Jenney with direction by Eliot Howe and Jean Hersholt.

This latest Ben Hampton production is the utmost in melodrama. It consists of a series of melodramatic bits linked together by a slight story which at no times reaches importance as far as the screen version is concerned. The picture starts with a shooting includes several hangings with fights thrown in for good measure. The action is heated any number of times with the picture the proper offering for houses where the patrons are dime novel readers.

The cast is long and includes no names of importance. Robert McKim in a character role, Carl Gantvoort and George Hackathorne take first honors among the men. Claire Adams is alone in her field. The handling of a number of atmosphere people has been well done. The production end displays discretion on the part of the director. A large street scene predominates the picture. It is a well devised set. The photography is on a par with the rest of the production. The print shown at the Broadway, New York, was exceedingly bad in spots.

The White story centers around activities in San Francisco about 1862. The city has a lawless and unscrupulous element that predominates the situation. Their activities become so great the respectable citizens are forced to form an organization known as the Vigilantes. The latter overthrow the city authorities and take the law in their own hands. Hangings, battles, etc., take place. A light love story is worked in with the melodramatics.

"The Gray Dawn" is 10-20-30 melodrama brought to the screen where is this instance it is only worth a dime. *Hart.*

FIGHTING STREAK

Andrew Lanning........................Tom Mix
Ann Withero..............Patsy Ruth Miller
Charles Merchant..............Gerald Pring
Jasper Lanning......................Al Fremont
Bill Dozier......................Sidney Jordan
Hal Dozier..........................Bert Sprotte
Chuck Heath..................Robert Fleming

Fox feature, starring Tom Mix, story by George Owen Baxter, adapted by Arthur Rosson, who also directed it. Lovers of western stuff and Mix fans will relish this picture, which contains some thrills, although not the best of the later Mix releases by a long shot.

An obvious effort to insert some new "stunt" punches is visible, as in a scene where the hero stops a team of runaway horses by vaulting onto the back of one. This and Mix's superb horsemanship were the high lights.

The story concerns a peaceful blacksmith in a western town who is bullied into a brawl by a bad man. The hero knocks him down and flees, thinking he has killed a man.

An eastern girl, the survivor of the runaway incident, has fallen in love with the horseshoer. Her eastern suitor offers the sheriff $5,000 to bring in the outlaw dead.

A series of "chases" with Mix exhibiting his horsemanship follow. He joins a band of outlaws, saves the life of the sheriff's brother after he has shot the sheriff, who refuses to accept his surrender on account of the reward, and finally wins his way back to civilization and the girl.

The story is far from original but suffices. Mix plays the lead in his usual stolid manner, getting most with "action." His attempts at emotional portrayal are vague, which necessitates close attention else the thread of the story is sometimes lost.

Patsy Ruth Miller, as the storm center of the warring passions, turned in a capable performance, registering lightly in the conventional ingenue role.

Good program addition. *Con.*

FATAL MARRIAGE

D. W. Griffith produced "The Fatal Marriage" several years back with Lillian Gish and Wallace Reid, both of whom had probably not reached the stage of stardom at the time of the making. Their names and that of the producer are the predominating features of the picture at the present time. As a present-day production it does not reach the usual standard of program releases. Notwithstanding this fact certain touches of the master hand of the producer which have predominated in some of his later productions are visible in this. The picture shows bits which have been developed materially by the director as his efforts reached a wider scope.

Cost of production was an important factor in the making of "The Fatal Marriage." The general layout called for no great expense with the possible exception of the sinking of a sailing vessel. A large portion of the action takes place on location, with the interiors of a simple nature. The cast is short including, besides the co-stars, Alfred Paget and Griffith himself in a minor role. The work of both Reid and Miss Gish has improved as time has gone on.

The story is based upon "Enoch Arden." It deals with the faithful wife of a seafaring man who refuses to wed an admirer of several years' standing, regardless of the fact her husband has not put in an appearance for several years. She finally succumbs to the entreaties of the admirer and marries. The husband returns but does not reveal his identity, allowing her to live peacefully. *Hart.*

THE CRADLE BUSTER

Five-reel comedy-drama, presented by Frank Tuttle and Fred Waller, Jr., written and directed by Frank Tuttle. Distributed by American Releasing Corporation. Star, Glenn Hunter. At New York Cameo, May 29

Benjamin Franklin Reed ("Sweetie")..
Glenn Hunter
Gay Dixon..............Marguerite Courtot
"Blarney" Dixon.......William H. Tooker
Melia Prout ....Mary Foy
Sally Ann Parsons..............Lois Blaine
"Cracked" Spoony..........Osgood Perkins
Holcombe Derry.........Townsend Martin
Mrs. Reed......................Beatrice Morgan

"The Cradle Buster" is a finely conceived and delightfully presented problem play done in a splendid spirit of sympathetic humor, a picture play of wholesome intent and purpose, and entertaining withal. Certainly the "movies" are awakening to a new sense of human values when so many new pictures touch upon universal experiences in so kindly and constructive a way.

"A problem play" used to mean invariably some twist of the eternal triangle, usually a reverse twist involving a scarlet woman in some capacity. The situations ordinarily were entirely theatrical and the circumstances far remote from everyday experience. Here is a problem play of commonplace life—nothing more highly colored than the struggle of a young man, too much pampered and petted by his household, who seeks to break away from crippling environment and make his own way in the world.

Nothing more startling than that, but it makes an absorbing tale, told as it is in gentle and kindly comedy.

Ben Reed (Glenn Hunter) reaches 21 bearing a crushing handicap in the nickname of "Sweetie," bestowed by a doting mother and worshipful family entourage of servants. Of course, he's the butt of the other boys, until in revolt and with the determination of establishing his sporting blood he visits a local cabaret and there falls in with Gay Dixon (Marguerite Courtot), the belle of the small town.

In jest Gay at first kids the boy along, conspiring with the other boys of the town, until she finds something real and substantial behind all his awkward male flapper exterior. Then she falls for him in earnest. Here begins a pretty little love story, rich in high comedy incident, leading to the plan of the pair to elope. They go to a fashionable hotel in a nearby big city where a celebration is going on. Ben hires a misfit dress suit in order to qualify for admittance, and about this detail is built up a lot of extremely funny (and equally touching) comedy. Ben's family trace the elopers and there follows the battle of the kid to stand on his own feet and fight out his own little individual battle. He goes down to temporary defeat, of course, but suddenly there arises a crisis. The girl's life is threatened and all the half-grown manhood of the youngster asserts itself in her defense. Young Ben saves the girl and wins her for the happy ending—happy in more ways than one.

It's a simple, almost trifling, story, except for the dramatic climax, but it has a real thrill of adventure to the sympathetic observer and it delivers the finest kind of a miniature etching of human experience that cannot but touch the great majority. The title is extremely pat after you have seen the picture, but it lacks something of pull in the lights before a theatre. It is too open to misinterpretation. Until one has followed the story the title doesn't mean anything.

A more descriptive title would help the picture a great deal, but the film itself is the best kind of modern screen high comedy and ought to make its way on merit.

Rush.

THE BLACK BAG

Five-reel feature in romantic vein taken from a story by Joseph Louis Vance and produced by Universal. Director Stuart Paton. Herbert Rawlinson starred, Virginia Valli opposite.

Billy Kirkwood	Herbert Rawlinson
Dorothy Calendar	Virginia Valli
Mulready	Bert Roach
Mrs. Hallam	Clara Beyers
Freddie Hallam	Charles L. King
Samuel Brentwick	Herbert Fortier
Burgoyne	Lou Short

Just a piece of entertaining film fiction without any special significance. The authorship of Louis Joseph Vance indicates sufficiently the classification of the picture. It is cheerful romance that amuses while it is on and forgotten on the way to the street. This sort of material has eminent virtues. It is light diversion and doesn't stir up any kind of emotion in the spectator —something like a frank detective. Pictures that don't evoke any special line of thinking are restful and serve their small purpose.

For its kind this film is neatly enough managed. It has action and speed and a couple of rough and tumble fights, but somehow the scenario writer (George Hively) has missed the suspense that should have been developed out of a mystery and its surprise climax. The hero steals a diamond necklace in order to protect the girl who, he mistakenly believes, is a thief. All the complications grow out of that planted situation. But the audience all the time knows perfectly well, and is meant to know, that the girl is not a thief at all, and for that reason when the revelation comes, it is no surprise.

Rawlinson has a jaunty rôle perfectly fitted to his style and capabilities. He is always a graceful player of these parts, a little obvious in his methods perhaps, but always getting his effects across. Miss Valli is rather in the background, with no opportunity to get into the center of interest, a pale part for an actress capable of much better things. Indeed none of the characters stands out except Rawlinson's. Everybody has been subordinated to the star.

For a film story adapted from a novel the picture has unusual coherence probably because detective stories of the sort by their very nature are fairly well concentrated. They usually follow a single thread from a generic situation to a conclusion without many side issues or discursive argument. The production is entirely satisfactory. The passages which are set in a summer resort with some shots at the beach and ocean are pretty and the bungalow sets are in excellent taste. A light, neat bit of entertainment, smoothly handled, that's all. *Rush.*

PAUPER MILLIONAIRE

London, June 1.

Another first-class picture from the Ideal studios. The story is an exceedingly well-done adaptation of Austin Fryer's novel. Its continuity is much better than is usually seen in British pictures. Deals with the adventures in London of an American multi-millionaire who through a chapter of accidents finds himself penniless in the Metropolis.

The production work of Frank Crane is excellent. He has paid great attention to minute detail; there are no mistakes. What exteriors there are, are either pretty rural scenes or well-known parts of London.

Hearing of his son's love affair with an English girl, Pye Smith the millionaire sets off, after a stormy scene with his son, to see the girl for himself. Immediately everything goes against him.

Things get worse and worse until at last he is driven to window-cleaning. While engaged on this he sees a newspaper announcing his own disappearance and in his excitement falls off the ladder. He is taken to the hospital where his son's sweetheart is a nurse and his troubles are soon at an end.

The picture leaves him wondering why on earth he didn't "ask a policeman" when his troubles started. The story is not a very probable one, but so well has it been treated it's improbabilities seem most natural.

The acting is of a very high order. C. M. Hallard, on whom all the work rests gives a finely thought out performance of Pye Smith, and his support is far above the home average. From the first foot to the last this feature reflects the greatest credit on its American producer, Frank Crane. *Gore.*

THE GODS OF ASIA

London, May 25.

The Regent Film Co., Ltd., held a trade show this morning of what is apparently a drastically cut spectacular film production, called by them "The Gods of Asia." It is a story of adventure among the wilds of the Far East, but the producer seems to have become somewhat mixed in his sartorial detail. While one of the central characters, a Maharajah, has some of his natives attired pretty much as Zulus, others affect the garb of Bedouin Arabs. The producer evidently wanted to be correct and took no chances, playing both ways.

From the angle of spectacle the production is a stupendous one with a dignity bordering on the ponderous, and with a relatively weak finish running up to a conventional "clinch." The cast is not mentioned nor is any reference made to the nativity of the production.

The story revolves around an Englishman who goes to the Far East to visit a local Maharajah who was a college friend of his in Great Britain. The titled Oriental falls in love with the Englishman's wife, and the Englishman becomes equally enamoured with the favorite dancing maiden of the Maharajah. This results in a number of sensational happenings that are more fanciful and impossible than one would be apt to believe, more especially the illogical escapes from death on the part of the hero and his wife.

The general run of program picture houses in America could play this feature, but it would not stand up as a first run in the big cities.

Jolo.

NANOOK OF NORTH

This is not the type of picture that that the title would indicate. In fact it is not a feature at all in the general sense of the usage of that word, but it is far better as an attraction than the majority of the regular run of program features released on the market in the last quarter. It is a freak such as occasionally crops up and the general indications are that it is going to be one of the real money makers.

"Nanook of the North" was secured by Revillon Freres from one of their Hudson Bay outposts and it is a true diary of the life of the average esquimaux family during a year. Interesting, educational, scenic and with all certain touches of comedy that are certain to make it entertaining.

For a hot weather picture it looks like a sure fire wallop. It has the ice, snow and storm of the northland as its background. These naturally lend themselves naturally to corking ballyhoo stunts for the warm term.

The picture depicts the life, customs, sports and methods of earning a livelihood on the part of the native of Labrador. The picture is the work of Robert J. Flaherty F. R. G. S. who must have spent a couple of years in obtaining the film shown at the Capitol this week.

There was one family selected to record the routine of their life before the camera. Nanook is the head of this little group and with him is his wife Nyla and three of their offspring. They are shown coming down to the trading post in the summer to barter furs for various odds and ends. They then return, the advent of the winter weather. With the freeze comes a shortage of food and the methods of spearing fish are shown. Later the capture of walrus and a seal are most effectively pictured while the building of an igloo and the home habits of the family are also set forth graphically.

"Nanook of the North" looks like it will have as great an interest to film patrons as did the famous pictures showing the South Pole discovery, which were a clean up as a special road show. This picture on the face of it could have duplicated that outside of the regular picture theatres, but in those houses the business will greatly depend how strong the exhibitor will go after it. A Pathe release. *Fred.*

GRANDMA'S BOY

Los Angeles, June 14.

A Hal E. Roach production for Associated Exhibitors starring Harold Lloyd and marking the last of a series of special comedies by Lloyd for Associated Exhibitors. Lloyd's next will be for Pathe.

The Boy	Harold Lloyd
The Girl	Mildred Davis
Grandma	Hannah Townsend
The Bully	Charles Stevenson
The Tramp	Dick Sutherland
The Sheriff	Noah Young

This is a picture that will get laughs from any type of audience. It is a knockout, clean at all times, and composed of truly funny situations. It is Harold Lloyd's best.

Entirely different from anything done by the bigger comedians for the screen. The story, an original by Jean Havez, Sam Taylor and Hal E. Roach, is a perfection of small-town life, showing Lloyd as a weakling who finally finds himself and becomes the hero of his town.

The supporting cast is excellent. Whoever was responsible for the casting deserves credit. Likewise the photography, which is above standard. Fred Newmeyer did a masterly job with the megaphone and can count this one as his big bet. The titles by H. M. "Beanie" Walker are more than titles. They help tell the story and supply plenty of laughs through their originality as well as to add spice to the program.

Hannah Townsend, although 79 years of age, is a find. On the strength of her showing in this comedy she fits right on the top row with the leaders. The bully could not have been handled any better than that of Charles Stevenson, while Sutherland as the tramp confirms the reason why all of the producers on the coast lots are after him for character bits.

In "Grandma's Boy" Lloyd not only shows his usual funny characteristics but does some surprisingly emotional acting. From the beginning to the end there are laughs with numerous pathetic scenes interwoven.

The story moves so fast it is impossible to guess the coming situations. It carries a good lesson, too, for the audience, showing that a man's success depends on his own ability.

The action finds the boy and the bully wooing the girl, who is somewhat inclined to lean toward the boy, although equally entertaining the bully. In their school days the boy always lost out in everything through his shy mannerisms and fear of the bully's strength.

A tramp is about town robbing stores and shooting those who attempt to catch him. Headed by the sheriff volunteers are chosen to capture the crook. Lloyd escapes being a member of this party by the shortage of deputy badges and is congratulating himself for his fortune when the bully pins his badge on the boy's coat. Lloyd runs home, fearing his own shadow and confesses to Granny that there isn't any use because "I am just a coward." Granny tells the boy a story about his brave (?) grandfather who captured an entire regiment singled-handed in the Civil War. Granny explains that grandfather's heroic deeds were the direct result of a good-luck piece given him by a witch. When you hold this charm, Granny explains, no harm can come to you.

Granny digs up the charm, which later develops to be nothing more than the handle of her old umbrella. Lloyd is inspired and so confident that he is free from all dangers, goes alone in search for the vagabond. After watching the sheriff's posse run from the crook, he captures him without the aid of a weapon. While the community watches in bewilderment the boy brings the crook to justice. Lloyd then proceeds to prove his success by soundly thrashing the bully. In the tussle with the bully he discovers it is his own power and not that of the charm which results in his victory. A five-reeler that is a corker and will pull business anywhere. It is having its premier at the Symphony, Los Angeles, where it is now in its fourth week of an indefinite run.

LIGHTS OF THE DESERT

William Fox five-reel comedy drama of the modern West, starring Shirley Mason. Directed by Harry Beaumont.

A straightforward, unpretentious romance with interesting character drawing and good atmosphere of the modern west. An altogether desirable program feature. May not pull much at the boxoffice, but will entertain them when they get in—in short the kind of picture that earns public good will. If there were more of the same sort the film business would be in better repute with the public.

The story has one capital comedy character, obviously borrowed from Harry Leon Wilson's Ma Pettengill in "Ruggles of Red Gap" and other stories. She is a self-sufficient fat woman who wears overalls when the occasion requires, hates the catty small town women with whom she is surrounded and is as independent of public opinion in thought and act as Lady Astor.

She befriends the stranded chorus girl from whom the other peanut minded women of the community shrink, goes to the aid of the hero with a shotgun across her arm and otherwise conducts unconventionally but in interesting manner. Some capital titles have been devised to express her practical philosophies.

When the heroine is in difficulties and on the brink of despairing tears, the old woman advises her "cuss a little, honey. It'll do you good." She manages a ranch and drives a car with equal nonchalance.

A theatrical troupe strands in a southwestern oil town. A foreman of the oil company has fallen in love with Marie (one of the chorus girls played by Miss Mason) and while the rest of the company are getting out of town as best they can, he asks her to stay and marry her. She agrees to remain at the hotel over night and consider it. The same evening she meets Tom, manager of the oil property, a one-time suitor for her favors who had previously offended her by his forwardness. He expresses his repentance and urges her to take a position in his office that will support her for the time being. She accepts and declines to marry the foreman.

The women of the town rise in war against this "chorus girl" invader and make it as disagreeable as they can. Also she is at swords ends with Tom the manager, until his workmen go on strike and threaten to tar and feather him. His danger inspires the girl to summon the old woman who has befriended her and they save him from the mob. The final embrace comes in a blossom ladened orchard when the girl confesses, on being asked why she saved Tom whom she apparently didn't like, "I find that you can't hate a man without loving him."

The direction is in accord with the nature of the story, simple and direct while the open air settings are splendid with picturesque natural settings as an appropriate background for the plain little romance. *Rush.*

SHATTERED IDOLS

A six-reel Frothingham production, distributed through the American Releasing Corp. Adapted from I. A. R. Wylie's "A Daughter of Brahma," directed by Edward Sloman. Marguerite De La Motte, William V. Mong, Ethel Grey Terry and Louise Lovely featured.

Sarasvati ....Marguerite De La Motte
Rama Pal.................William V. Mong
Lieut. Walter Hurst }
David Hurst }......James Morrison
David Hurst, the child.........Frankie Lee
Jean Hurst...............Ethel Grey Terry
The Judge.......................Alfred Allen
Diana Chichester............Louise Lovely
Colonel Chichester............Harvey Clark
Mrs. Chichester..........Josephine Crowell
Dick Hathaway...........Robert Littlefield
Ethel Hathaway.................Mary Wynn
The High Priest............George Periolat
The Rev. Doctor Romney..Thomas Ricketts

This production was originally slated for release by First National that had prepared the advertising matter, paper and other accessories for the picture, but at the last minute the American Releasing made an arrangement to take it over. It is a story of India full of thrills and is unusual in photography. As a program release it is somewhat above the average and can stand for a week in any of the first run houses, especially in these times when there is a shortage of pictures.

The story is a rather unusual one, and it does not end with the usual clinch of the lovers. That immediately is one point in its favor. The scenes are laid in India, with the uprisings of the natives and the constant efforts of the British government to keep order in that particular one of its colonies as the basis. The story opens with a young matron expecting an addition to the family, and the son is born on the night that the father, an officer in the British forces, is killed by the natives. That fact is marked on the child, who in his earlier days is a weakling. The mother, disappointed in her boy, displays it frequently. In the end, however, he proves himself a true hero by twice being the savior of the English. There is a lively love interest to the tale as well, with the boy first marrying an Indian girl, who is designated by the priests as "a bride of the gods" and betrothed to an idol. To counteract the effect of her death at the finish of the picture there is carried through the story the suggestion that there is an English girl who was his sweetheart in childhood who is waiting for him since he has proven himself a hero.

Direction plays an important part in the production, and Edward Sloman has handled the picture excellently. His Indian mob stuff is particularly well done. Scenically the atmosphere is well developed and the character touches in the minor roles are most decided.

Of the cast Marguerite De La Motte as the little Indian girl is most excellent, while Ethel Grey Terry and Louise Lovely also contribute considerably to the effectiveness of the ensemble. Miss Terry is particularly good in a most unusual type of role for her. The trouble, however, is that too many directors will want her to do character work after seeing her in this production, but she is still far too young and good-looking to go in for grande dames as yet. Of the men Alfred Allen stands out, but James Morrison as the son is rather weak for the lead. This would have been a wonderful role for Gareth Hughes to have played. *Fred.*

OUR LEADING CITIZEN

A Paramount feature presented by Adolph Zukor with Thomas Meighan starred. Written by George Ade, directed by Alfred Green.

Daniel Bentley, a lawyer..Thomas Meighan
Katherine Fendle, his financee..Lois Wilson
Oglesby Fendle, a capitalist..........
....................William P. Carleton
Col. Sam. de Mott, a politician........
.......................Theodore Roberts
Cale Higginson, Dan's friend.....Guy Oliver
J. Sylvester Dubley, a law student....
.........................Laurance Wheat
Hon. Cyrus Blagdon, a Congressman....
..................................James Neill
The Editor..................Lucien Littlefield
The Judge.........................Charles Ogle
Boots Monego..............Thomas Kennedy
Mrs. Brazey..................Sylvia Ashton
Eudora Mawdle................Ethel Wales

George Ade has developed a more or less modernized version of his great success of the past "The County Chairman" in "Our Leading Citizen." It is a fairly interesting story of its type which with the star and the author played up should manage to draw business. It isn't a picture that will turn 'em away or anything like that but it is a good standard program type of feature.

Meighan is supported by a corking cast which includes "name values" in Lois Wilson, William P. Carleton, Theodore Roberts, Laurance Wheat, James Neill and Lucien Littlefield. To some fans this will almost spell all star cast and it might be worked as that.

The direction is by Alfred Green who has managed to handle the story interestingly, carrying the yarn along logically. In titling the film has evidently had the advantage of Ade suggestion for some of them are quite humorous.

Meighan has the role of a young lawyer in a small town whose sole ambition is to go fishing his practice of law being entirely secondary and his monetary return therefrom about at zero. That is the state of affairs until 1917 when the U. S. entered the war. The hero enlists as a private and comes back a major, slipping off the back of the train to duck the welcoming party that is at the station to greet him. His first thought back in the old home town is whether or not the fish are biting and the official committee with a French dignitary who has come to pin the cross of the Legion of Honor on his breast have to call him in from the center of the river.

At this point Lois Wilson enters the scheme as the town heiress and she manages to fire the flame of ambition with the result that the hero goes out and makes a fight for Congressional honors and is elected despite himself.

Human and interesting in a style that is Ade's own with a moral attached to the effect that the man that is lazy is not always so inclined because of desire, but because he hasn't got the right job. Those that like Meighan will enjoy the picture tremendously. *Fred.*

MY WILD IRISH ROSE

Vitagraph five reeler adapted from Dion Boucicault's play "The Shaughraun." Scenario by C. Graham Baker and Harry Dittmar, directed by David Smith. Bill as a "special" and shown at the Strand, New York.

Conn, the Shaughraun........Pat O'Malley
Rose O'Neale..................Helen Howard
Claire Ffolliott..................Maude Emery
Moya ....Pauline Starke
Robert Ffolliott.................Edward Cecil
Captain Molineaux...........Henry Hebert
Corry Kinchella.................James Farley
Harvey Duff.....................Bobbie Mack
Father Dolan....................Frank Clark
Barry ....Richard Daniels

Vitagraph is presenting a melodramatic feature typical of the Irish plays of several decades ago in which Chauncy Olcott and Andrew Mack were wont to appear. The present production has all the real thrills for the Irish heart that usually are embodied in the beating of the hatred red-coated Britishers and the victory of the heroic Irish lad and his colleen. As a feature picture it isn't real material for the big first run week stand houses. In certain neighborhoods the picture will attract some attention, but it doesn't look like a real money maker unless there is considerable Irish element in the district.

At the Strand the picture was preceded by a quartet singing the various old Irish melodies and this created a certain atmosphere for the picture. It is the old story of the young Irish patriot who has been betrayed to the English and is sentenced to penal servitude in Australia for life. He escapes from the convict ship and returns to his home after some months in time to balk those who were scheming against his property and his sweetheart and sister.

Pat O'Malley playing the role of Conn which is really the title characterization of the old play was forced into a secondary position in the screen version and Pauline Stark as Moya was forced to the same position, the two however managed to outshine those playing roles that were given greater prominence. *Fred.*

THE DEVIL'S PAWN

Ufa feature, starring Pola Negri, presented at the Rialto, New York, June 11, by the Hamilton Theatrical Corporation (Paramount). Scenario is by John Brennert and John Kraly. Directed by Paul Ludwig Stein.

Lea, adopted daughter.........Pola Negri
Professor Stanlaws.....Adolf Edgar Licho
Demetri, a medical student..Harry Liedtke
Astanow, a student.....Werner Bernhardi
Ossip Storki.................Vikter Jansen
Dance Hall Proprietress...............
.........................Margarethe Kupfer
Vera..............................Marga Lind

For a while the second-class importations of the Hamilton concern were shunted to outlying theatres, where they would do as little damage as possible to the Paramount trade-mark, but this one must have looked better to some one. Why, does not appear on the surface. It is an exceedingly poor picture from all angles.

The story is jumbled and tiresome and the direction is no better. The whole thing is dingy. Some of the scenes of gaiety, such as the passages that deal with cabaret night life in Petrograd, are depressing. No such collection of dowdy women in makeshift costumes belonging to a long forgotten fashion has been shown on an American screen since the industry moved up out of the single-reel stage or the store show period of growth. These scenes alone would kill any picture on Broadway.

They had no less than five editors and title writers, all of whom, including Peter Milne and Benjamin De Casseres, receive title credit, to put the thing into presentable form, but the task was too much for even that galaxy of experts. The rambling tale isn't there with any human appeal and its pattern is indefinite. It is merely a cheap theatrical affair, the general effect being as though Victor Kramer tried to do a "Why Girls Go Wrong" in the style and spirit of Tolstoi. It wouldn't be Kramer and it wouldn't be Tolstoi. Indeed it wouldn't be anything.

Nothing is so trashy as a picture that tries to make pretentious drama out of shoddy melodrama. It misses on both counts as this film does. There isn't a natural touch about it—everything is stilted and pompous until the action trembles on the edge of travesty. They haven't missed a threadbare situation of the foundling girl and her sufferings when she grows up. She even gets herself caught in a den of vice—thinly veneered as a Petrograd dance palace.

The story takes place in Petrograd during the reign of the Czars. Lea believes she is the daughter of a kindly old Jewish scholar in a Russian village. At his death she goes to the capital to enter the university, but because she is not eligible as a Jewess she assumes the identity of a dead girl whose birth certificate comes into her possession by accident. She encounters Vera, habitue of the dance hall, and under her sponsorship is introduced to the night life of the town. By hard work, however, she wins high honors at the university, but the news of her achievement gets into the newspapers, and the brother of the dead girl comes to inquire who is using his sister's name. In Lea he discovers a youthful sweetheart, and all are happy. Then it turns out that the Jewish scholar was not her father at all. She was a foundling and he cared for her. Really she is the daughter of a professor at the university, separated from his wife almost at the altar by the objections of his family. The scene designed to deliver the punch comes when Lea, driven to desperation by the drunken attentions of the cabaret frequenters, leaps from a window, intent on suicide, and is taken to the hospital to be operated on by her real father.

Pola Negri does not shine in the "sweet simplicity" roles. Her work in this picture makes you think of Theda Bara playing Juliet. *Rush.*

A PAIR OF KINGS

A Larry Seamon-Vitagraph two-reel comedy full of corking slapstick hokum that is certain to get laughs. Seamon seems to have spent considerable on this production, which would be a corking comedy to show on the same bill with the "Prisoner of Zenda," as the comedian plays a double role in it that makes the comedy virtually a burlesque of the Anthony Hope tale.

Seamon plays the roles of one who has usurped the throne of a mythical kingdom and an emigrant country boy who has just arrived. The latter is brought into the palace in a coffin at the time that a group of plotters are planning to get rid of the king. The latter notes the resemblance of the new arrival and persuades him to change places with him.

From that point on the vases and crockery fly and the smoke bullets land all over the place. It is a slam-bang affair from beginning to end and the type of comedy production that is fast placing Seamon right at the top of screen comics with the only two ahead of him Harold Lloyd and Chaplin. *Fred.*

BLUEBEARD, JR.

Five-reel comedy starring Mary Anderson. Presented by James Livingston; directed by Scott Sidney. Distributed by American Releasing Corp.

A very old and much worn story is here made into an amusing modern farce. The "planting" and preparation are rather tedious and over-elaborate, but once the comedy tale gets into its stride it moves with high speed and interest. If it could have "picked up" more promptly, as they say of autos, it would have been a dandy comedy. Even as it stands it is excellent, clean entertainment.

The big laugh scene—probably what would have been the third act if the story had been told as a play—consists of about this situation:

A young man's uncle has agreed to give him $50,000 if he will demonstrate that he is a hard-working, conscientious youngster with a right sense of his obligations and a husband beyond criticism. Bob Beach, the young man, owing to certain accidental circumstances, is forced to invent a wife and a happy home to exhibit to the uncle's representative, who arrives on the scene suddenly and without warning.

In order to accomplish this he takes over another man's home. The other man's wife intrudes at the wrong moment and Bob has to commandeer her to pose as the wife. In the meantime Bob's own wife, in a jealous rage, reaches the spot. A third embarrassment is Bob's wife's girl friend, who was to have played the wife role, but who is projected into the complication as an outsider. In order to disguise the real situation from uncle's agent, Bob has to hide his diversity of wives in the various upstairs bedrooms and go to them to explain things and keep them quiet.

Uncle's agent becomes suspicious. He sees Bob come from one bedroom with a knife in his hand and (although the possession of the knife is entirely innocent) is led to believe violence has been done. In this he is confirmed in his own mind when he peeks into the room and sees a girl's form tumbled into a heap of coverings on the bed (really the girl had heard him coming and had covered herself up).

The agent sees Bob exist stealthily from another bedroom and makes another inquiry. This time the girl (Bob's own wife) hears him tip-toe in and hides in the clothes closet in a pose that makes the old boy think she has been hung or strangled. Thus it appears that Bob has committed several murders. It's all straightened out in the end, but it makes for hilarious fun while it is in process of winding up.

The story has served for a hundred plays. It even has been made the basis of several burlesque shows, always in much the same basic form and in like elements. Its virtue in this case is that it has been built up painstakingly in terms of everyday, natural life. It is full of delightful commonplace touches, small incidents that will touch the experiences of about everybody that would visit a picture theatre.

For example Bob's whole dilemma starts with a note from the landlord demanding a renewal of his rent at so high a price that he can't make it. What would strike a commoner chord in a crowd of spectators? Betty, Bob's wife, has to go house hunting and here develop a lot more experiences that anybody will recognize as familiar. They finally settle down for a moment in a tiny flat and a strained household situation develops that ought to get a reminiscent chuckle from anybody that has ever been married—either man or woman.

The story is Old Stuff, but done in a thoroughly modern way. The characters are human and natural in themselves and in their relations. There is about the picture play something of the same quality of sympathetic commonplace that has made a sweeping success of "The First Year" at the New York Little theatre. It's a good sign that playwrights and scenario writers are getting away from the ancient conventions of the theatre, of dealing with life in artificial make-believe, and both in comedy and drama dealing with things of life and problems of life in terms of human experience.

This inconspicuous little picture production is an excellent example of the modern tendency to try to make the theatre and the screen reflect and mirror real life and not a fictitious counterfeit of life. This may appear to be a rather ponderous way to discuss a rather trivial film comedy, but it is little things like this that mark improvements in an art. Today a comedy is done in a spirit of translating a phase of life—translating it as a rather broad caricature but still recognizable as an actuality. Ten years ago the thing would have been a knockabout, door-slamming farce, a crude buffoonery. If that much improvement has been made in ten years, it seems a fair prediction that the next ten years will find the picture art as much more improved. *Rush.*

ANNABEL LEE

A Joe Mitchell Chapple "heart throb" feature, which is termed a "fictionization of Edgar Allan Poe's 'Annabel Lee'." Script by Arthur Brilliant and directed by Wm. J. Scully. No release mentioned.

David Martin..................Jack O'Brien

This is an independent feature that has just happened. It was used this week as part of a double feature bill at Loew's New York, with a Talmadge reissue. There is nothing about it that would recommend it anywhere, but there is one thing it certainly does point out and that is the shortage of even fair pictures, for this one is below that mark.

The basis of the story is the famous Edgar Allen Poe poem, "Annabel Lee," which has been modernized and fictionized to a degree that must have caused Poe's ghost to walk. The adaptation is draggy and the continuity decidedly messy. One could hardly call it a continuity, it is just a series of events pieced together with titles, the latter being depended on to tell the story.

The cast hasn't anyone worthy of more than passing notice and the leading lady was employed more as a walking model than anything else. In direction the picture was a slaughter of film, there being more padding in it than there usually is in five regular program features. On the whole the picture proves to be a decidedly slow and draggy affair. *Fred.*

ROSE OF THE SEA

Production by Louis B. Mayer, starring Anita Stewart. Adapted from the book by Countess Barcynska. Directed by Fred Niblo. Distributed by First National.

Rose Eton....................Anita Stewart
Elliott Schuyler...........Rudolph Cameron
Peter Schuyler.............Thomas Holding
Vivienne Raymond........Margaret Landis
"Lady Maggie"...................Kate Lester
Roger Walton...................Hallom Cooley
Daddy Eton...................John P. Lockney
George Thornton.............Charles Belcher

This is rather a beclouded effort, with much to recommend it and a good deal in its disfavor. Adapted from a novel, it is scattered and disjointed. Instead of the concentration of interest which is the element of a play or a screen story it is discursive and rambling. Its theme addresses itself exclusively to women, and it probably will turn out to make a strong appeal to that division of the fan public. So much in its disfavor.

Its merits are that Fred Niblo has handled his material in masterly fashion. Technically, the picture is rich in good points. The backgrounds are always in splendid taste; the characters have been selected with a good deal of discrimination and the picture compositions are arresting. An important detail is that Miss Stewart does better and more natural acting than in any picture of hers for a year ar more.

The piece is a society comedy-drama and offers striking opportunities for scenes of broad magnificence in a pictorial and theatrical way. Its big effects, such as cabaret scenes, luxurious interiors in the homes of the rich and within and without a fine country home during a house party are lavishly done, and the production must have represented a considerable cost.

But when all's said and done the whole thing is just a piece of fiction without reference to common experience. The old school of fictionists escaped the real by taking refuge in the highly colored imaginary. That's the trouble with "Rose of the Sea." It is all theatrical parade of luxury, and nowhere does it touch upon the spirit of things, at least on the surface.

Rose Eton, from the country, works in a city flower shop, where she comes in contact with Elliott Schuyler, son of the aristocratic Peter Schuyler. Elliott is a pretty worthless sort of pup and lays siege to the rural beauty. He gets drunk, insinuates himself into her humble bedroom and starts a violent courtship. In the struggle he falls, striking his head on the table. Terrified lest he has killed himself, Rose goes to his father, Peter. The elder, recognizing her fineness of character, schemes to bring the young people together, thereby breaking off Elliott's environment of chorus girls, late hours and gambling.

The match is about to be made when one of the son's forged checks almost brings the boy to suicide. Rose saves him, but they are separated and he goes back to his chorus girl and marries her, while the father, learning of Rose's self-sacrifice, suddenly discovers that he loves her himself, and the rest of the story is concerned with bringing elderly Peter and young Rose together.

The picture has several excellent sympathetic characters, notably "Lady Maggie," an elderly aristocratic woman who devotes herself to aiding others, and Vivienne Raymond, a sophisticated chorus girl, who, in spite of her apparent hardness of heart, turns out to be a good sport. *Rush.*

GOLDEN DREAMS

A five-reel Goldwyn release, production is handled by Benjamin B. Hampton. A Zane Grey story of Lower California oil fields, having Claire Adams and Carl Gantvoort featured.

Countess De Elberca...Madame Rose Dione
Mercedes McDonald...........Claire Adams
Enrique McDonald............Norris McKay
Sandy Buchanan.............Carl Gantvoort
Althea Lippincott..........Audrey Chaoman
Countess De Elbercaa's Cousin...Idea Ward
Duke of Othomo...........Bertram Grassby
Don Felipe De Cristobal.......Frank Leigh
Pedro.......................H. Gordon Mullen
Big Bill ..The Foreman)..Pomeroy Cannon
Circus Clown.....................Frank Hayes
Strong Woman...................Babe London
Little Boy Clown.........Mary Jane Irving
Circus Manager..............Walter Perkins
Inn Keeper........................Harry Lorraine
Animal Trainer.................C. B. Murphy
Schoolmaster...........William d'Orlamond
Majordomo..........................D. Mitsoris

A stranded one-ring circus that is fitted in this picture is the touch that takes the production out of the rank of the commonplace. It also saves the picture from fitting right in with the ordinary everyday run of program releases.

A trio of directors are responsible with the footage so short on that particular title that it was impossible to record the name of any of them. However, it doesn't matter much, for they didn't do anything that would get them a place in the hall of film fame.

The story opens with one of those made-to-order plots. The widow of a Spanish grandee has adopted a nephew and niece. The latter is in love with the engineer, who is in charge of the mining properties and oil fields of the family. The advent of the heavy element at this time is in the person of a new arrival from Spain, a young Duke, who has come to visit his uncle and at the same time cast about for a marriageable heiress, and he picks on the niece.

The uncle, however, becomes aware of the fact that the engineer is the monkey wrench in the works of the scheme and he plans his removal in most approved Spanish fashion. The plan, however, goes wrong on two counts and finally there is an attempt to achieve by force what could not be accomplished otherwise, and then the day is saved by turning loose on the mob of the caged lions and tigers of the small circus in order to save the day. The ending of the picture is brought about rather abruptly at a time when it began to get really interesting.

The cast is a fairly good one and there are a number of fairly clever touches in the handling of small animal stuff in connection with the circus. A couple of real thrills are also furnished by the big cats.

A cast of unusual proportions is in the picture, with the honors principally going to Frank Leigh, who gives a really studied performance as the old Spanish uncle. The fact that he had been seen a few hours previously in another picture in a distinctively different character brought home his work all the more forcibly. *Fred.*

THE MAN WITH TWO MOTHERS

A Goldwyn five-reeler of the comedy-drama type, from the story of Alice Duer Miller, directed by Paul Bern. Mary Alden, Cullen Landis and Sylvia Breamer are featured.

Dennis O'Neill..............Cullen Landis
Claire Mordaunt............Sylvia Breamer
Widow O'Neill...............Mary Alden
Ritchie......................Hallam Cooley
Butler.......................Fred Huntley
Mrs. Bryan................Laura Lavarnie
Tim Donohue................Monti Collins

A fairly interesting program feature of ordinary calibre which seemingly has as its greatest asset the fact that Mary Alden, who played the mother in "The Old Nest," is in the cast. Played as part of a double feature bill at Loew's Circle, New York, with "Is Matrimony a Failure?" The mother theme is the strong punch of the story and a certain interest would be aroused by the title. In the regular run of daily change houses it appears to be a strong enough feature to stand by itself.

The story by Alice Duer Miller was adapted for the screen by Julien Josephson and directed by Paul Bern, with Percy Hilburn at the camera. It deals with the advent of a young Irish lad in this country to take charge of a tremendously successful junk business which was left him by his uncle. His widowed aunt is of the social elect and the mother of the youth who comes of the auld sod, does not seem to hit the pace that the Americanized aunt would like. There is an understanding the boy's mother is to return to the old country while the youth is to remain here as the son of the aunt by adoption. Instead of sending his mother back, the boy places her in an apartment and then begins to lead practically a double life.

In the end, however, he cleans up a grafting element in the junk yard, wins the niece of his aunt and there is the usual happy ending.

Miss Alden as the mother endows the role with an appealing winsomeness, while Cullen Landis as the boy and Sylvia Breamer as the girl both manage to score.

Laura Lavarnie as the aunt and Monti Collins in an Irish character bit both register effectively, while Hallam Cooley in a semi-heavy role manages to fit nicely.

The picture has naught that is unusual in photography or setting and there is no real thrill except that afforded by a rather stagey fight that Landis and a roughneck indulge in. *Fred.*

A VIRGIN'S SACRIFICE

A Vitagraph five reeler of the Northwest type with lots of snow and shootin' an' all that sort of stuff. Corinne Griffith is starred. Webster Campbell directed.

Althea Sherill..............Corinne Griffith
Tom Merwin....................Carl Nissen
Sam Bellows...........George MacQuarrie
David Sherill.................David Torrance
Mrs. Sherill................Louise Prussing
Jacques ....Nick Thompson

This is just another of those northwest stories on the screen. Just how many of them picture theatre audiences can stand for without tiring is a question, but it is a certainty with plots of the calibre of this one it won't be long before the whole kit and kaboodle of the snow and shootin' stuff will be taboo.

Loew's New York played this one Memorial Day (its regular double feature day) all alone, except that the Buster Keaton comedy, "The Boat," shared the bill. The production has Corinne Griffith as the star and was directed by Webster Campbell. From a box office angle it has nothing in particular to recommend it other than it is a fair program feature of the usual Vitigraph calibre and therefore playable in the smaller daily change houses.

In brief the story has a daughter taking the illegitimate offspring of her mother as her own, so that the father will not become aware of an outrage that has been committed upon his wife. In an effort to carry out the deception she enlists the aid of a forest ranger, who is a total stranger, to pose as her husband on the father's return. The heavy who raped the mother still has his eyes on the daughter. It was to protect the girl from him that the mother fell into a trap he set. Finally the villain kidnaps the girl. A battle between the forces of evil and good brings about the defeat of the former, the death of the villain and the revelation of the true state of affairs to the hero, who clasps the girl in his arms for the final fadeout.

All through the story the girl seemingly tries to create the impression she is a ruined woman. Oh, how she tries, but the hero tumbles blindly on in his belief in the girl. He can't see that ruined stuff a'tall. But how did the author expect any one in the world, even by the widest stretch of his imagination, to believe any mother would fasten her child, though illegitimately begotten, on her own daughter? 'Tain't bein' done this season.

Miss Griffith as the girl does give a corking performance and Carl Nissen, opposite, is at least passable. The others in the cast, other than Nick Thompson, who plays a half-breed convincingly, enact the characters they are cast for in perfunctory manner. In photography there are some clever exteriors, but it is just the same sort of snow and mountain stuff that has been shot in a hundred similar stories. The title is obviously for the box office, also for the censors and more so for reformers. Just why producers and distributors that don't try to protect their business expect it to be protected may be explained by this picked-out title. *Fred.*

RETRIBUTION

Lou Rogers, of the Rialto Productions, presented "The Story of Lucretia Borgia" at the Park theatre, New York, this week. It is an Italian production made by Camillo Innocenti from the script of Fausto Salvatori. A historical costume feature, about seven reels in length.

Caesar Borgia....Signor Enrico Placentini
Pope Alexander VI (Rodigo Borgia)....
Signor Eugenio Gilardoni
Lucretia Borgia..Countess Irene Saffo Momo
Rosa.....................Signorina Sangusto
Duke Alfonso of Aragon......Signor Troise
Jester..........................Signor Papa

Lou Rogers and S. J. Stebbins, of the Rialto Productions, have rented the Park theatre for the presentation of this feature, based on "The Story of Lucretia Borgia." The picture does not appear to have any chance in the better class of houses, but it should draw in neighborhoods where there is a strong Italian or other foreign element that might relish historic costume pictures. Otherwise there is naught about the production indicating any box office strength. At the Park Monday the management was under the handicap of a very bad orchestra, an exceedingly humid night, and a very dirty screen. All these angles are accounted for in reviewing the production.

"The Story of Lucretia Borgia" was produced in Italy with an all-Italian cast and under the supervision of an Italian director. It has all the earmarks of a mediocre foreign production that has not been edited or retitled any too well for presentation in this country. There is entirely too much footage at present, and this tends to make it exceedingly draggy from an entertainment point of view.

To those inclined toward historical research the picture might appeal, but the ordinary film fans will hardly relish this particular exposition of a very interesting period in Italian history.

There is a request from the management published in the program that the audience, to be in the proper frame of mind to receive the picture, would do well to imagine itself living 500 years ago. That's a long time back to remember history or anything else.

The handling of the story is typical of the usual Italian-made production that comes to this country. The types selected for the various characterizations are repulsive or too effeminate as far as the men are concerned, and as for the women, charity prevents any extended comment on either their beauty or histrionic abilities.

"Retribution" just won't do. *Fred.*

ACCORDING TO HOYLE

David Butler is starred in this David Butler Production, presented by Louis Burston and released by Western Pictures Exploitation Co. W. S. Van Dyck directed.

Butler as "Box Car" Simmons, knight of the road, is lolling lazily in a ditch when a lesson in a correspondence school course on how to become a success is wafted to him by the wind. He stretches his hand forth lazily to glance at it. There are three rules thereon about "don't be a piker, put up a bluff, think success and you'll be it, etc." and Simmons nonchalantly pockets it. He meets a girl and that's the turning point in his life. He decides to get shaved and during the tonsorial operation kids the barber about being a wealthy mining man from Nevada. The news spreads among the gullible townsfolk and Simmons clinches the bluff by giving away his last deuce to the barber for a $1.10 operation.

The rest of the action is a case of cheating the would be cheaters. A tract of land figures in the plot, owned by Doris Mead (Helen Ferguson), the heroine. The trimmers of this supposed wealthy come-on negotiate the sale of the land to Simmons for $12,000, although worth only $2,000. Simmons takes an option on the land for 10 days and then "salts" it with a piece of valuable ore with the result the avaricious land sharks are induced to repurchase the option for $10,000. Of course the tract is barren land and "Box Car Simmons," now B. Carr Simmons, is in a position to press his suit.

Obviously there are many plot inconsistencies. If audiences are as gullible as the natives in the picture are, well and good. It interests to a certain extent and as simple screen entertainment it suffices for one day picture programs or supplementing a vaudeville bill as in this case. *Abel.*

JOHN SMITH

Selznick feature of five reels, starring Eugene O'Brien in mystery tale. At Loew's 42d Street, June 13.

Excellent supporting cast and first-rate mystery story, with interesting romantic background. Besides the star the picture has George Fawcett, best of character old men, and J. Barney Sherry and a capital company. O'Brien has a part made to order, one of those jaunty heroes with a sense of humor, and he makes the most of it. A better title would not have been amiss. "John Smith" doesn't mean anything and gives no key to the play. The early passages have a quantity of neat comedy and the mystery develops later into a first-rate bit of suspense.

The comedy hangs upon the novel situation of a young business man being assigned to the task of running a rich old woman's household on an efficiency basis by reforming her servants. It is similar to the basis of the stage comedy "Adam and Eva" in this respect. The mystery develops when the young man (who has served a term in jail for a crime he did not commit) is made treasurer of a charity drive and the money is stolen by blackmailing crooks who know his record.

The spectator is left in the dark as to whether the hero or his enemies committed the theft, and the murder of a servant during the crime and the working out of this mystery gives the play its tension up to the last moment.

Nearly all the action takes place in interior sets, and they have been skillfully designed. The effect of reality is secured without over-elaboration. Even in a court scene this air of simplicity is maintained. The theatrical parade that usually marks trial scenes is agreeably absent, but the concentrated story interest is well managed. Another detail that marks this picture is the moderate use of the closeup of the star.

O'Brien is the star of the picture and his name is featured alone in the billing, but all the closeups go to the heroine (played by Mary Astor). This is unique and (augurs) a good deal of generosity on the part of the star and as much good judgment on the part of the director. Miss Astor is a brunet beauty, with eloquent eyes, and the enlarged portraits contribute greatly to the picture's appeal.

Tom Hilliard takes the blame for another's crime and is sent to prison under the alias of John Smith. A kindly probation officer (George Fawcett) become interested and secures his parole. Hilliard gets a job in a brokerage office, where his employer assigns him to the job of running his mother's household. He is so successful in bringing conflicting people into accord that a charity committee makes him treasurer.

Hilliard leaves the money in a strong box in the drawing room, and a band of crooks, knowing the circumstances from newspaper reports and being familiar with Hilliard's prison record, break in during the night, stealing the money, killing a servant during the robbery and throwing the blame on Hilliard. Hilliard is tried (the damaging testimony against him being shown in fadeouts) and the jury is about to bring in a verdict when the court is informed in a note that new evidence is available.

The story takes a new twist. During the trial the probation officer has been investigating the case on behalf of Hilliard, in whose innocence he believes, and has run down the real crooks. His acquittal establishes him in the good graces of his rich patroness and brings to a happy denouement his romance with her young girl companion. *Rush.*

GIRL IN HIS ROOM

Albert E. Smith presents this Vitagraph feature starring Alice Calhoun. Direction, Edward Jose. Circle, New York, June 13.

Marie Prevost in "Her Night of

Nights" was billed, but at the last minute the Vitagraph feature was substituted as half of the double bill, the print of the Prevost picture having failed to arrive. The other half was a Tom Mix five-reeler, "The Fighting Streak."

"The Girl in His Room" doesn't mean what you think at all; another sample of tricky titling. This sort of thing doesn't get anywhere. If a passer-by were attracted to the house by the display of such a title and would probably expect something with a kick of suggestiveness. When it isn't delivered, the patron is dissatisfied.

The picture is a transparent theatrical affair, depending upon one of those circumstances that couldn't happen. A young man who has been cheated out of his fortune and inheritance goes broke, and then suddenly remembers (as though such a detail might easily slip his mind) that in the wall safe of his former home he had left a large amount of bonds. So he turns Raffles and robs the house of his own property. The place is occupied by the daughter of the man who defrauded him and so, quite by accident, he carries in his pocket when he goes on the loot a letter from her father disclosing all the facts. It naturally follows that he would put the letter in his outside breast pocket with his handkerchief so he could drop it on the floor at the right theatrical moment. It goes without saying that he is a clumsy burglar, and makes enough noise to awaken the sleeping girl so they can meet and the rest one can imagine for oneself.

The picture is as artificial enough, but the people make it more so by their style of acting which is in the last degree stilted. The action moves haltingly and the titles are highflown and labored. *Rush.*

FREE AIR

W. W. Hodkinson release in six reels, from the story by Sinclair Lewis. Produced by Outlook Photoplays, Inc. Directed by Myron M. Stearns.
Milt Daggett...................Tom Douglas
Claire Boldwood...........Marjorie Seaman
Henry Boltwood..........George Puncefort
Jeffery Saxton...................Henry Snell

Here is a feature that looks as though it was a general advertisement for the beauties of Glacier National Park. It is "just a picture." The Sinclaire Lewis story was fairly interesting in the Satevepost, but the handling of detail in the screen production places the feature in the class dubbed "ordinary."

It is a tale of a Brooklyn flapper who with her father makes a tour of the National Park in their motor. They have a series of mishaps and a young native comes to their rescue. After they return to the hotel at the entrance of the park he follows at their invitation, only to find that the return to civilization and the meeting there with a devoted admirer has changed the general idea of the flapper's mind as to which of the two would be the more desirable for a life companion. This is worked out as the favored one shows a yellow streak when he and the girl are attacked by a tramp when some distance from the hotel, and it is the boy who again comes to the rescue.

There is something of a thrill in an auto race along the road leading to the top of the mountain, but that is about all there is in the production that can be commended. As a filler for double feature days at a price it will do, but other than that, except for the cheaper houses, there doesn't seem much of a chance for the picture. *Fred.*

EVIDENCE

Florence ....Elaine Hammerstein
Philip Rowland................Niles Welch
Judge Rowland..........Holmes Herbert
Jeanette ....Constance Bennett

Mrs. Bascom.................Marie Burke
Louise ....Matilda Metevier
Walter Stanley............Ernest Hilliard

In supplying the story for this latest Elaine Hammerstein feature, produced by Selznick, the author, Edward J. Montague, elected a subject often times worked out by novelists, dramatists and in everyday life. It is based upon the familiar idea of a youth with family connections marrying a girl of the stage. In this instance it is worked out harmoniously with the star handling the role of the stage girl.

George Archainbaud has again directed Miss Hammerstein and has turned out a creditable production. The star works up the stage story to a nicety with capable support furnished by Niles Welch, as the youthful husband, and Herbert Holmes. The one other role of importance is entrusted to Ernest Hillard who keeps it up to the standard of his co-workers.

In the production "Evidence" hits true. The director has selected well appointed interiors with lavishness predominating the majority of scenes. Taking a story combining society with the stage has necessitated an expenditure of considerable proportion. The lighting has been equally well carried out.

"Evidence" has as its central figure Florette a girl of the stage. She marries a youth of social prestige. His family fail to accept her. A former actor sweetheart tries to frame her and cause a split between her and her husband. He is discovered in her room by the husband's brother who is a believer in circumstantial evidence. The girl turns the tables by locking the brother in the room and convincing him that circumstantial evidence is not always true. He is convinced and establishes the proper understanding with the family. *Hart.*

OUT OF THE SILENT NORTH

A Universal attraction in five reels with Frank Mayo star. Story by Harry Sinclair Drago and Joseph Noel. Directed by William Worthington. A "snow" feature played by Loew in New York on double feature programs.
Pierre Baptiste................Frank Mayo
Marcette Vallois..........Barbara Bedford
Andrea Vallois..............Lionel Belmore
Ashleigh Nefferton...........Frank Leigh
Reginald Stannard..........Harris Gordon
Pete Bellew............Christian J. Frank
Jean Cour...............Frank Lanning
Mattigami..................Louis Rivera
"Lazy" Lester...............Dick Lareno

"Out of the Silent North" is just another "snow" feature with a fairly good story that runs about true to the stereotyped plot that the majority have. There is nothing in particular that will make any audience see it more than once, and most can tell the finish after the first reel.

Frank Mayo as the star impresses rather nicely, and from a photographic point the picture shows that the U. is going forward to an undeniable advantage in this particular. If the editorial and titling staff were only half as good as the production end the U. would make its regular run of program stuff stand up fairly well. However, for the average daily change house this picture will serve during the summer.

Mayo is a Canadian trapper in love with the factor's daughter. She returns the love, but on the arrival of an Englishman at the trading post seemingly falls for the polished chap. He has come in quest of a lost mine that his father has given him a map with which to locate. Another Englishman in the settlement steals the papers and plots with an Indian guide to make way with the prospector. A terrific snow storm and the wishes of the plotter are almost realized, but the factor's girl sends her sweetheart out in search of the lost one, which brings about his rescue.

The two form a partnership for the continuance of the search and finally they strike gold. At that point the heavy, with his followers, tries to take the claim by storm, but the trapper beats them to it. A happy ending with the Englishman returning to his promised bride across the seas and the trapper with the factor's daughter clasped in his arms.

Fairly good snow meller for the places where they like it. *Fred.*

THE DEPTH OF THE FURROW

Paris, June 10.
This is an exceedingly strong drama of the brutal type which some French producers glory in. It leaves life stripped naked and its morals are those of the farmyard. The story is powerfully told, full of realism to a point, but at the end it falls away altogether.

In his desire to keep original the producer has created a morality which is absurd and unnatural. Realism is the keynote of the whole feature, and a good deal of it could be deleted. Among the things which will repel any decent audience are the "first night" scene, when the drunken, lust-mad husband reduces his bride to a state of terrified collapse, and the equally nasty scene when he gives her a thoroughly good thrashing.

The story tells of three children adopted by an old farmer. Two are boys—one Bernard, brutal and a son of the soil; the other, Jean, an artistic weakling. The girl is Arlette. They grow up together, and Arlette loves Jean. Discovering this, the old farmer throws Jean out of the house and compels her to marry Bernard. From then on her life is unbearable.

Meanwhile Jean becomes a great artist. After a particularly brutal thrashing, an accidental meeting with Jean's benefactors puts her in touch with him. She begs him to come and save her. Bernard discovers what she has done and bides his time, plotting a lunatic to watch for Jean's coming. At last he comes and Bernard spirits his wife away to "the old farm." Jean compels the lunatic to tell him the truth, and is shot in the back by way of revenge. He, however, rides to the rescue, arriving just in time to save Arlette from another good thrashing. He attempts to go for his brother, and the result is his own death. Before he dies, however, he delivers himself of a philosophy which is altogether wrong. "The old man was right," he says. "She was for you, not for me. The farmer never makes mistakes; the artist often." This may be delirium, sarcasm, or merely the kinematographic straining for something new.

This gloomy story is beautifully produced and the acting is excellent. *Gore.*

ONE CLEAR CALL

A John M. Stahl Production presented by Louis B. Mayer, released by First National. Adapted from the story by Frances Nimmo Greene. Length about eight reels, running time 85 minutes.
Dr. Alan Hamilton...........Milton Sills
Faith ....Claire Windsor
Henry Garnett...........Henry B. Walthall
Maggie Thornton................Irene Rich
Sonny Thornton..........Stanley Goethals
Tom Thornton...........William Marion
Colonel Garnett (Henry's father)......
.....................Joseph Dowling
Mother Garnett (Henry's mother)......
.....................Edith Yorke
Phyllis Howard................Doris Pawn
Dr. Bailey..............Donald MacDonald
Jim Ware's daughter..........Shannon Day
Yetta ....Annette DeFoe
Starnes ....Fred Kelsey
Jim Holbrook..........Albert MacQuarrie
Toby ....Nick Cogley

There seems to be no doubt that this picture is a sure fire money getter at the box office. At the Strand, New York, where it is showing this week it opened strong on Sunday, with the drawing power seemingly being in the strong cast of names that the production has. The picture is a combination of everything that goes to make a successful screen production. It has a society element, some dive stuff, a measure of mystery, lots of love interest, a wandering boy and blind mother bit, comedy and a touch of Ku-Klux Klan that serves as a thrill. The cast will draw audiences and the picture will hold and entertain them sufficiently to send them out talking about it. The latter will not be because it is a tremend-out picture but is so far and away ahead of the usual run of feature production released in the last six months that the audiences will be compelled to say that here is a really good picture.

In the cast are Milton Sills, who plays the lead in a clever manner, carrying his role in a most convincing manner and turning from a successful surgeon to a souse with his regeneration being brought about when he has to operate on his youthful nephew to save his life. Claire Windsor who plays opposite Sills, portrayed the wife of the gambler king of the small city delightfully. She looked pretty and displayed a quality of reserve that carried her to the audiences from the screen. However, to that veteren Henry B. Walthall a full measure of praise is due. It was he as the gambler that really furnished the back-bone of the plot. Of a good family he strays from the path of righteousness, opens a gambling hell and disreputable hotel and dance place, causing a stern father to cast him off, the mother who has become blind, being informed that her son is dead. Walthall on being informed that he has but a short time to live tries to straighten out his accounts and right the wrongs he has committed and finally in an effort to bring happiness to his wife who has left him and is in love with his only friend he commits suicide.

Of the other players Irene Rich, Shannon Day, Doris Pawn contribute materially to the acting, especially Miss Rich, Joseph Dowling and Edith Yorke as the mother and father scored and little Stanley Goethals was corking. Annette DeFoe in a black face role managed to land, but there was a touch in her character that was not quite definable.

The story in brief is that Dr. Hamilton (Sills) is visited by his boyhood chum (Walthall) to be examined. He is informed that it is but a matter of weeks before his death must occur. He then starts a search for a girl who was entrusted to him by her father on his death and whom he defrauded of her legacy. A mystery woman who has appeared in the town with whom Dr. Hamilton has fallen in love strikes the audience as a possibility of being the missing person, but instead it later developes that she is the wife of the doomed man who left him when she learned of his occupation.

"The Owl" which is the name of the combined, gambling, dance and drinking place has so incensed the citizens of the town that the Klan finally issues a call for its destruction and the "getting" of the proprietor, but the doctor intervenes and saves the man on the promise that the place will be closed within 30 days. As a physician he is certain that there is only one thing that can occur to save his patient from passing on and that is the return of the missing wife of whom he has been informed, yet when he discovers that she is the girl that he is in love with he hasn't the courage to send her to her duty. In the end it is the gambler who clears the situation by an overdose of heart stimulant. In photography, direction and settings the picture leaves nothing to be desired. There are comedy touches here and there in the script that lighten the serious stretches and on the whole the picture is one that will pull no matter where it plays. *Fred.*

TOP OF NEW YORK

Paramount feature bearing the mark of Jesse Lasky. A William D. Taylor production story by Sonya Levien with scenario by George Hopkins. May McAvoy is starred.

Hilda O'Shaunnessey..........May McAvoy
Emery Gray..........Walter McGrail
Micky O'Shaunnessey..........Pat Moore
Gregory Stearns..........Edward Cecil
Mr. Isaacson..........Charles Bennett
Susan Gray..........Mary Jane Irving
Mrs. Brady..........Carrie Clark Ward
Mr. Brady..........Arthur Hoyt

The picture is a frank sentimental melodrama without pretention to anything else. The action is built up around the troubles of a working girl (a shop girl at that), and it follows in design a host of old fashioned plays and pictures that fall in the same catagory. It's frank, candid fiction without any subtle relation to life and so makes its appeal to the more elemental tastes of the film public. It is clean straight-away romance and serves its purpose satisfactory, even if it is not particularly significant in purpose and meaning.

The modern scenario writers have discussed these social problems in rather a more subtle manner than the melodrama writers of ten years ago when "Bertha the Sewing Machine Girl" was the type. Socialism and parlor Bolshevism have changed the terms and the technique somewhat but the material is much the same. In the present case the scenario writer and the director have reverted to the old style. Here we have the poor working girl struggling against the dishonorable plottings of her rich employer, trying to remain straight under the temptation of his proffered luxury. The problem remains fixed, only the medium of dramatic discussion has changed and this production comes on the screen as rather a crude and old fashioned affair. Dealing in old fashioned materials, it is only natural that Taylor made use of the old fashioned devices. For example his shop girl wears one of those short length, blonde wigs that used to be the trade mark of young beauty in distress; the heroine lives in squalor under the patronage of a drunken uncle and a bullying aunt and the surroundings are a tenement house in the slums.

All the paraphernalia of the melodrama of a generation ago is present. O. Henry was probably the first to take the shop girl out of the theatrical class and discuss her as an actual human unit and for the most part the picture writers and directors have followed his lead. In this case there is a reversion to the old convention. It remains a question whether it will make as strong an appeal as the new technique. Certainly this picture is extremely theatrical. Hilda O'Shaunnessey is a creature of the stage and the screen and the illusion of real life is pretty well blurred. That seems to be the principal defect in the picture. It's all family story paper type of fiction rather than the modern effort to reflect real life. The picture has theatrical force but it is eminently lacking in realism.

It is possible that a certain element of the fan public likes its drama in more or less childish terms, but the drift has been away from the obvious to the subtly realistic. We do not take our heroines any more as altogether, inhumanly good and our villains as unqualifiedly viciously worthless. We prefer some semblance of shading between good and bad such as everyday experience has taught us is the state of the world rather than the stage creations. We are being educated to move the actual theatre into the theatre rather than to symbolize an ideal world on the stage in terms that shall be unmistakable. This picture goes back to the old technique and it comes before as raw and unconvincing.

Hilda O'Shaunnessey works in a department story to support her invalid child brother, who spends his days in an invalid chair on the roof of a tenement. Next door there is a painter—disappointed in love by a selfish wife who abandoned him for a richer man—who lives in a bungalow built on the housetop. His daughter and Hilda's small brother strike up a childish friendship which is opposed both by the painter and Hilda's aunt who in her small minded way looks with suspicion on rich artists who befriend poor working girls.

Meanwhile the proprietor of the store lays siege to the young, unspoiled Hilda. Out of that situation it stands to reason that these three will sooner or later come together and the store proprietor will be disclosed as the man who wrecked the artist's home. Just that situation does develop and it leads to a rough and tumble fight between the two men—a pretty tame affair as film battles go—but it leads to the happy denouement in which the poor shop girl and the rich artist fall into each other's arms. *Rush.*

THE STORM

A Universal-Jewel Special in seven ree's based on the Langdon McCormick play of the same title. Has House Peters at head of all-star cast. Directed by Reginald Barker.

Dave Stewart..........Matt Moore
Burr Winton..........House Peters
Jacques Fachard..........Josef Swickard
Manette Fachard..........Virginia Valli
Kanteeka..........Frank Lanning
N. W. M. Police Sergeant...Gordon McKee

In "The Storm" Universal has turned out a picture that is a winner from start to finish. It has three great wallops. First, the great forest fire scene; then a great bit of river stuff of the shooting of the rapids in a canoe, and thirdly, a number of snow scenes such as haven't been shown in any of the more recent northwestern pictures. Incidentally, this one is a decidedly different picture of the territory where the action supposedly takes place. "The Storm" seems to be a special in the fullest sense of the word, and with a few draggy spots eliminated it will hit on all six for the fans.

House Peters as the hero manages to hit a stride which will start him on a new wave of popularity in this picture, and Virginia Valli, who is his principal support, is delightful. Matt Moore is a convincing heavy at times, while at others he flops just a little below what the picture audiences expect of the villain in an out-and-out meller of this type. It is these three that carry the story almost from beginning to end, although Josef Swickard manages to impress with the work he performed in the first couple of reels of the production.

Reginald Barker, who directed, is in a large measure responsible for the picture. He certainly managed to "get shots." Scenically, the picture is a beauty, and the action, except for a few scenes about two-thirds way along, where it drags, goes along at a great rate of speed.

The original play has been prefaced by several pieces of action that enhance it wonderfully. The meeting of Burr Winton (House Peters) and Dave Stewart, (Matt Moore) at a trading post hotel and the planting of a reason for their later friendship is well handled. Then the arrest of Jacques Fachard (Swickard) and his escape from the Mounted Police by jumping into a swirling torrent and his rescue by his daughter, who has followed the trail along the water with their canoe, is a real thrill.

In handling the fight for the girl through the long winter in the cabin of Winton, with him and Stewart as rivals for her after the father has died from a wound, is cleverly worked out and holds the interest of the audience. It is the forest fire, however, that furnishes the real big punch. Part of it may have been luck in getting a real forest fire, but if it was, then the manner in which the matching up of scenes is handled is wonderful.

It's a whale of a picture for thrills, and certainly different from any other northwestern that has been shown in more than a year. *Fred.*

SOUTH OF SUVA

Paramount feature presented by Adolph Zukor, starring Mary Miles Minter. Frank Urson directed from story by Ewart Adamson and continuity of Fred Myton. Supervision of Elmer Harris. Showing currently at Rialto, New York. Tale of South Sea Islands.

Phyllis Latimer..........Mary Miles Minter
Pauline Leonard..........Winifred Bryson
Sydney Latimer..........Walter Long
John Webster..........John Bowers
Marmaduke Grubb..........Roy Atwell
Karl Swartz..........Fred Kelsey
Alfred Bowman..........Lawrence Steers

Pleasant screen entertainment is afforded in this Mary Miles Minter Realart production allowing for a number of stagy novelties as part of the action. Set in its Fiji Islands locale anything from cannibalism and voodooism to primitive depiction of human existence can be made to conform to story requirements.

The action starts on board ship en route to New Zealand via the Fijis. Phyllis Latimer (Miss Minter) is due for the latter place to join her husband on a surprise journey. Pauline Leonard, her friend, decides not to join her guardian in the same place, but continues on to New Zealand with a man who professes affection for her, stating she prefers civilization to what she pictures as a place of unbearable crudeness. Phyllis enters Sydney Latimer's cabin and finds her husband booze-drugged and surrounded by a quartet of dusky native sirens. She agrees to stay and help him rise from the depths, but after two weeks of pretended virtuousness the copra and sugar trader is seen tasting forbidden fruit and liquor in one of the native's huts. She decides to leave and finds she has not sufficient fare to New Zealand. Missing the boat, Marmaduke Grubb (Roy Atwell) encounters her and, recognizing the "P. L." initials on her luggage, mistakes her for the Pauline Leonard his employer is expecting. She poses as such for a while until Latimer, embittered by John Webster's trade supremacy and driven crazy by hooch, decides to fetch Webster as a human offering to the native barbarians' heathen gods. Webster is away and Latimer forces his wife to accompany him back to the scene of the frenzied Fijian festivities. She is gaudily decorated for the cremation when Webster returns and in a tense moment accomplishes the rescue.

As a story it is a fanciful little thing, suitable for summer and all-weather entertainment. There is plenty of tropical outdoor stuff that makes a pretty setting. The casting is splendid. Walter Long as the heavy did a neat piece of work in a thankless role. John Bowers is a manly vis-a-vis for the star and can be made into a "name" if given the opportunity. *Abel.*

SEEING'S BELIEVING

Metro's latest Viola Dana starring vehicle produced by Harry Beaumont. The feature is an adaptation by Edith Kennedy of the Rex Taylor story. As a summer release "Seeing's Believing" is a good light picture. Beaumont made no attempt to make it a big picture but was satisfied with putting out a fast moving program release.

The star has been entrusted with a role which gives her many opportunities. She handles the part of a spirited miss with all of the necessary ginger. Her individual efforts are largely responsible for the speed. Allan Forrest is the male lead. He proved a good selection with Gertrude Astor as a young matron proving one of the best bets. Miss Astor is well suited for parts calling for the present day type of young matrons and can always be relied upon to build up her parts. Edward Connelly and J. P. Lockey come to the fore with character roles.

The scenes for "Seeing's Believing" are on Long Island. The majority of exteriors are on the grounds of an attractive estate. A satisfactory ballroom set is one of the predominating interiors. A small town hotel scene has been well worked out.

The Taylor story has as its central figure a boy and girl in their teens. The death of their parents brings them considerable money and the estate. They have as a guardian a youthful aunt. The girl becomes involved in several escapades, typical of a harem scarem miss but escapes unscathed, and finally wins the youth who earlier believed her of no account.

There are several angles to the Taylor story nicely developed. A twist here and there adds materially to the interest.

If it were not for the unexpected happening the production would lose most of its interest. *Hart.*

EVIDENCE

Five-reel society drama produced by Lewis J. Selznick. Elaine Hammerstein starred, supported by Nigel Conrad. Director, George Archainbaud.

A thoroughly enjoyable human interest story with an especially appealing and sympathetic role for Miss Hammerstein. The play is rather pretentious in a pictorial sense, but the director has managed to make his background appropriate without being too obtrusive. He has at least escaped the common fault of allowing the settings to overshadow the story. Here they are appropriate and convincing, but the progress of the drama itself is the center of interest rather than mere pictorial surroundings.

The play has one capital surprise twist that alone would insure it a certain prominence, a very deftly managed bit of dramatic trickery warranted to impress. Miss Hammerstein plays the part of a popular actress who marries the scion of aristocratic name and thereby earns the enmity of the small-minded women of his family and their social circles. An uncle is a successful lawyer and he constantly harps upon the fact that the "interloper" is an actress and by that fact alone they cannot expect to conform to the traditions of the high-bred family.

Husband and wife under the circumstances gradually grow apart and the husband is contemplating proceedings for a separation. At this point there intrudes himself an old sweetheart of the actress. He insinuates himself into her boudoir in such a manner that the uncle cannot but discover them under circumstances that make him believe she has been guilty of indiscretion. The intruder departs while the uncle lectures the wife on her stage antecedence and weaves a chain of circumstantial evidence that seems to condemn her. At this point the wife turns the tables on her prosecutor. She locks the boudoir door and announces that she will summon her husband, who is in another part of the house. The same chain of circumstantial evidence that the uncle has forged in the previous innocent situation will work out to his own appearance of guilt.

He admits himself defeated and goes to the husband, announcing that as far as he is concerned if there are any court proceedings he will appear for the wife and defend her against the husband.

This effective dramatic development is worked out smoothly and naturally and in a spirit of restrained unaffectedness that adds greatly to its strength. Miss Ham-

merstein can always be depended upon to give a certain earnest suavity to her roles and in this instance she does splendidly. A touch of theatrical insincerity might have spoiled the quiet effectiveness of the whole central scene, but it was handled in just the right degree of aplomb and delivered a powerful punch.

Aside from this "punch" episode the picture is as entertaining as could be expected of a story that depended upon one central, significant scene. Director Archainbaud has a knack for expressing subtleties in action that a less skillful manager would have to make plain by titles. In one passage the girl is divided in mind as to whether or not she will marry the young aristocrat. In nine out of ten cases her state of mind would be expressed in a title, but here the situation is neatly conveyed by the way the actress handles a bouquet of flowers just received from the young man. It is a capital example of a clever handling of a detail, a clever device to express in screen action a situation which ordinarily would call for title explanation.

The production will have a strong sympathetic pull among the women fans. It is one of the best in the series of this excellent young picture actress. *Rush.*

INNOCENT CHEAT

Roy Stewart and Kathleen Kirkham are co-starred in this independent production issued through Arrow under sponsorship of Ben Wilson. Broadway, June 19.

A rather florid problem play, maudlin at moments, especially in some of the lurid titles, but fairly interesting in a super-sentimental way. The play has to do with the marriage of a young woman to a battered old roue and, as the candid title puts it, "cheated of the boon of motherhood."

The hateful old party is given to gay parties on his yacht, the personnel being largely made up of girls from the "Follies" (symbol, of course, of gay wickedness). It is during one of these affairs, which serves the double purpose of pointing a highly respectable moral and at the same time treating a theatreful of highly respectable people to the sight of shapely girls in union suits, that the disreputable husband plots to maneuver the wife into a compromising situation with a hired man conspirator.

All this passage is displayed in the form of a fade-back when the husband's divorce case comes up, presumably before a referee. The court decides on the previous testimony that the husband shall have a decree and the custody of the child (a cute little girl plays the part), but then the outraged wife demands to be heard, and as she testifies the story is told by the fade-out device.

The suffering wife makes it plain that she wants a family, but has little hope of accomplishing her ambition under the circumstances. The ancient husband is constantly surrounded with showgirls, with whom he continuously carries on amours. To get rid of her he hires a spy to enter his wife's stateroom, where the frameup is witnessed. The wife thereupon departs from the yacht, going to her Canadian lodge (can this be a delicate suggestion of the scandal in high life that has recently been on view in the newspapers?). During a horseback ride her mount runs away and she is saved by the manly young engineer at work on a bridge near by. He accompanies the wife home and is forced to remain indoors during a violent storm.

The rich wife's yearning for motherhood is here made the motif for some pretty delicate dramatic handling, to the appropriate accompaniment of the crashing storm effects through the windows. The audience is left to understand that the pair pledge their love, the young man

departing in the belief that the woman is free to marry him. When he learns by a note that she is married he goes to pieces. Succeeding passages disclose his degradation in drink until at the finish his regeneration is worked out through the child. The woman's testimony on the stand is frankly to the effect that the father of the child is not her husband but the engineer, and when this set of circumstances is made plain the court reverses its decision, and in time the now degraded young man's reform is accomplished.

Of course, the story has a certain romantic appeal, but its working out is rather twisted and the moral is altogether oblique, but the situation is saved by creating a sympathetic atmosphere, however thin, around the wife and giving to the young lover a touch of romantic interest.

The drama is rather deftly worked out pictorially, with its seashore shots and wild country views and the luxurious interiors. The thing could have been made crude, but under careful handling it is not at all offensive. The play has some well-managed dramatic touches of a sentimental color, and probably would engage the sympathies of women fans, but the titles are too high flown. The effect could have been conveyed better in simple language. Flossy titling never helped a picture. Fine title writing always carries a suspicion of insincerity. It is the rugged and terse printed lines that deliver the kick on the screen even more than on the printed page.

This picture is for the neighborhood houses and the medium class clientele. A wiser grade of patronage would penetrate its Laura Jean Libbey sentimental bunk. *Rush.*

THE GLORY OF CLEMENTINA

An R.-C. five-reel production with Pauline Frederick starred. Story by Wm. J. Lock and script by Richard E. Schayer. Emile Chautard directed.

Clementina Wing.........Pauline Frederick
Quixtus ....Edward Martindale
Huckaby ....George Cowl
Billiter ....Lincoln Plummer
Tommy Burgrave............Edward Hearn
Etta Concannon...............Jean Calhoun
Vandemeer ....Wilson Hummel
Lena Fountaine.............Louise Dresser
Louisa Mailing.............Truly Shattuck
Sheila ....Helen Stone
Her Maid............Lydia Yeamans Titus

This seems to be rather an exceptional R.-C. program picture, and if Pauline Frederick draws the picture is certain to satisfy the fans. At this time it seems rather a point as to whether or not Miss Frederick has any drawing power at the box office. In the bigger week run theatres around the Times square section it is held that Miss Frederick has lost her power to attract there, but as against this the daily change houses maintain that she is as big a drawing card as ever for them. Perhaps her return to the stage during the coming season will alter the aspect regarding her box office attractiveness even to the big Broadway houses. This picture, however, was worthy of being run in any of the week stand theatres right on the Main Stem, especially in the view of the productions that the majority of those houses have been playing during the last three months.

Miss Frederick plays the role of a woman disappointed in mankind because of the fact that the man that she was in love with was vamped away from her. His death makes her co-guardian of his daughter with Quixtus sharing the responsibility with her. When she discovers that the vamp who stole her first love is about to ensnare Quix she decides to emerge from the dowdy cocoon that she has been affecting and emerge as a beauty. She does this and the result is that she proves to be the victor in the battle for his affections.

The story is well handled on the screen and Miss Frederick makes a

distinct impression. A juvenile love interest is carried by Jean Calhoun and Edward Hearn, while Louise Dresser, assisted by Truly Shattuck, furnish the heavy element. Edward Martindale is acceptable as the easily handled Quixtus.

There are a few spots about midway in the picture where the action drags a little, but with a little speeding here the direction would have registered perfect. *Fred.*

HATE

Loew-Metro picture featuring Alice Lake, with Conrad Nagel in support. A Maxwell Karger production from Wadsworth Camp's "Collier's" story. Skillfully adapted for the screen by June Mathis. Six reels, running about 65 minutes. Shown the first three days of the week at Loew's State, New York.

Discounting title appeal, star appeal, exploitation and the rest of it, this is a type of picture that once you get them in it will interest. Wadsworth Camp, a past master of mystery stories, has had none of his plot spoiled, if anything enhanced, by June Mathis' finished screen adaptation. It is primarily a plot picture (one of those the-story-is-the-thing productions) that would probably command attention with anybody in it. This is not derogatory to the sterling cast that makes each type so convincing, nor Mr. Karger's accomplished direction, but more to convince that the story is to the fore throughout. It gets started fast and moves rapidly from fade-in to fade-out.

Although certain situations are al-most too obviously planted in spots, that becomes necessary for the final unraveling. Babe Lennox, a chorister (Alice Lake) is the feminine angle of a quadrangle situation. Dick Talbot (Conrad Nagel), an assistant district attorney; Ed Felton (Charles Clary) and Dave Hume (Harry Northrup), rival gamblers, are each wooers for Babe's affections. Felton has been released on bail on a charge and promises to "get" Hume. The latter has been told his days are numbered to six or eight weeks at the outset because of a chronic ailment, although his robust physique rather belies this, and frames it so that his suicide looks like murder. Hume fatally chloroforms himself, using Felton's initialed handkerchief. Felton is innocent, but the overzealous assistant D. A., Talbot, secures a conviction on circumstantial evidence for murder, first degree. Felton is due for the chair on a Thanksgiving day, and the screen tension and attention is gripped as the audience watches the approach of zero hour at daybreak. It is all straightened out when Babe reminds herself to hand Felton a little devil effigy which Hume had once instructed her to present to his rival should the latter ever face legal execution. It is a written confession by the suicide. The tension is theatrically climaxed when Felton is shown entering the death chamber, with the electric chair silhouetted on the stone wall within. When the confession is read the district attorney, his assistant and the warden rush to the death room, the warden only entering and asking the others to wait outside. Young Talbot is seen chafing for what seems, and was intended, a long time, nervously fretting that possibly he has sent an innocent man to his death.

Further interest is secured through the audience's uncertainty as to which of the three the girl is favoring. She admitted it was not Hume, but stated to the condemned man at the final farewell that he was really the man. Her choice of the assistant district attorney was rather a surprise.

The technique from direction to lighting is skillful. The casting is excellent, Charles Clary, that screen veteran who has not been seen hereabouts for some time, doing the best piece of work. *Abel.*

WIFE AGAINST WIFE

A Whitman Bennett Production released through First National and featuring Pauline Starke. Adapted by Dorothy Farnum from George Broadhurst's play, "The Price." Society comedy-drama of Paris and New York Latin Quartier.

Gabrielle Gautier............Pauline Starke
Stannard Dole................Percy Marmont
Dr. Ethan Bristol........Edward Langford
Mrs. Dole......................Emily Fitzroy
Florence Bromley...........Ottola Nesmith

The title itself should hold up this picture. It ought to accomplish something at the gate even for hot weather audiences although as a feature it is a good one day release or used in combinations. Its Greenwich Village and Paris Latin Quartier locale is another angle to work on.

The story is a double repeat plot as one recognizes from the synopsis. Gabrielle (Miss Starke) is Stannard Dole's inspiration for a statue. Dole is married to a woman who will not release him. She thinks that the little French model has come between them when in fact love had died long before. Dole's heart attacks finally best him and he wishes Gabrielle happiness with Dr. Ethan Bristol who has long pressed his suit for the girl's hand. Gabrielle is happy with her medico-husband for three years although he too becomes wrapped up in his life work with the assistance of Florence Bromley. When the widow of Stannard Dole is taken into employment by the Bristols (on the doctor's sole request) as housekeeper because of her straightened circumstances, Mrs. Dole starts the green-eyed imp working on the young wife's conscience. A parallel situation develops, Gabrielle imagining the female student of medicine is weaning her husband's love away from her.

It is all straightened as all nice pictures generally are with the "catty" housekeeper ordered out of the Bristol household. Why this woman was taken into the family circle in the first place is weakly explained. However, if one is to analyze the plot too closely there would be no story.

Excepting for this situation, which is not made as plausible as perhaps it may have been in the original play, assisted by suitable language and possibly a more sympathetic looking opposing force, the rest is acceptable screen divertisement.

The support is well cast except Emily Fitzroy in the Mrs. Dole part. She is a bit too spooky and unsympathetic to make it all plausible even from the genesis of her marriage with the artist. Idealist that Stannard Dole was, one can hardly conceive his wooing this woman even a score years back.

The bankroll has not been skimped on although the picture displays no unusual production cost. *Abel.*

WHILE SATAN SLEEPS

Paramount picture presented by Jesse L. Lasky, starring Jack Holt. Written by Albert Shelby LeVino; suggested by Peter B. Kyne's Saturday Evening Post story, "The Parson of Panamint." Joseph Henabery directed. At the Rivoli this week.

Phil..................................Jack Holt
Red Barton.......................Wade Boteler
Sunflower Sadie..........Mabel Van Buren
Salome Deming............Fritzie Brunette
Bud Deming...............Will R. Walling
Chuckawalla Bill.............J. P. Lockney
Absolom Randall...............Fred Huntly
Bones..........................Bobbie Mack
Mrs. Bones....................Sylvia Ashton
Bishop.....................Herbert Standing

This picture is an interesting study in psychology—what influence a frank personation of a character will have on the inner self of the personator whose basic characteristics are directly opposite from what he appears to be. In this particular case an escaped convict, a son of a bishop, assumes the garb of a cleric to evade the law, with the result he finally "gets religion," decides to go back to jail to serve his penance, with the suggestion he will again assume his place on the pulpit on release. The hard-boiled, sophisticated film fan—he is usually not of the dyed-in-the-wool species—who will only go out of his way to see a muchly touted "super" picture will probably argue that such situation is not new and its development in this release must be pretty much obvious. All of which is true and readily granted, but its manner of development and the star's finely reserved character drawing deserve more than supercilious attention.

"Slick Phil" (Jack Holt) has made good his escape from jail and hides away in Panamint, where "Chuckawalla" Bill has just been elected mayor. Panamint is one of those western towns, presumably of the reconstruction period, where dance halls and its conveniences are wide open. Chuckawalla is proud of Panamint, and decides it deserves patterning after a metropolis like Los Angeles, including a school, church—and a parson.

"Slick Phil" hits the burg in his parson's disguise and a protecting moustache, and is duly elected shepherd of a willing flock—about half of the townsfolk, who follow Absolom Randall, a radical reformer, and unanimously voted a nuisance by the other half—the booze-fighting bunch haunting Bud Deming's dance hall. This paves the way for a couple rough-and-tumble fights to show off the "fighting parson's" pugilistic prowess. Salome Deming (Fritzi Brunette), the owner's daughter, thereupon becomes enamored of the Rev. and, strongly enough, influences him to confess his pedigree to his trusting flock. This is done while he is conducting the last rites for Sunflower Sadie, one of the dance-hall inmates, who had intercepted a bullet intended for him. An added twist is included where the Los Angeles bishop is advised from Davenport, Ia., upon his request, that there is no Episcopalian clergyman of the name Phil has assumed registered in the Iowa diocese. At the same time he recognizes the handbills offering a reward for the capture of the escaped Phil as his son. The bishop accompanies two detectives back to Panamint, where Phil is in the midst of his confession. The fadeout finds his father and Salome waiting at the prison gates as they swing open to release him, while back in Panamint, the town having prospered surprisingly, the leading citizens read of the bishop's son's release and remark it would not be a bad idea to have him back.

There is one thing in the story's favor—it's away from the infernal triangle thing and interests because it's different. That should mean most at the gate, although the title is a strong prop to build an exploitation campaign about. They liked it at the Rivoli and applauded it roundly, which is much comment and commendation as the star, cast, director and all concerned could ask for. *Abel.*

LOVE'S CRUCIBLE

London, June 17.

This is a remarkably fine Swedish-Bio. feature owned by Gaumont. Whether it is a good universal showman's proposition is quite an-other matter. The story and setting is mediaeval, as is the love interest, and the combination is likely to prove just a little bit too subtle for the minds of most picturegoers, educated as they have been on love, passion, lust, as a raw material.

The story is an exceptionally strong one and works up to a fine climax, the "ordeal by fire." Throughout the film the Sacred Image plays a very big part, and it was somewhat of a surprise that the scenes of the Image, such as the wounds bleeding until the guilty poisoner had expiated his or her sin, were passed. Inquiry elicited the information that the film censor (T. P. O'Connor, M. P.), does not object to the figure of Christ in itself but only to His impersonation by an actor.

Scenically the production is remarkable, the crowds, the types, the smallest detail being perfectly worked out. From a stage manager's point of view this film is a masterpiece.

The story is that of a young woman married to an elderly man although she loves and is loved by a young cavalier. Marriage made her hatred more intense so that when a wandering friar came selling trinkets, love potions, and deadly poisons she choose a ring and bade him fill a Borgian cavity in it with a poison. At an inn the friar tells the story which is overheard by the husband and the lover's father. The husband knew of his wife's intrigue and of her contemplated crime. That night he bade her bring him wine. Torn between temptation and fear she hesitated and in her nervousness the poison from the ring fell into the wine. She turned to find her husband dead. He had seen her handling the ring through a mirror and the shock had killed him. Her lover's father, believing her guilty, in his position as burgomaster put her to the test—he bade her drink from the cup. She refused and on her lover volunteering to drink the draught she dashed the cup from his hand. Later the page on guard around the old man's body noticed the wounds on the Sacred Image were bleeding and the news went forth that until the guilty person was discovered the wounds would continue to bleed. Condemned to the ordeal by fire she was saved by her lover, who was accepted in her stead. At the last moment, however, she insisted on taking her lover's place and was brought safely through the ordeal by the Sacred Figure who, becoming her dead husband, came down from the cross and led her safely through the flaming pyre to her lover's arms. As will be seen by this rough story there is no moral. The woman was a murderess at heart and her end was not the end, even mediaeval, which was painful of a murderess, but union with her paramour. If the scenic side of the production is superb so is the histrionic.

Jennie Hesselquist plays the part of the young wife with remarkable power. She gets over by sheer ability. Her make-up verges on the plain throughout, but she is a very pretty woman, hating intensely, loving madly. The rest of the cast is brilliant. To the film world these Swedish-Bio. productions are what the productions of Hare, Alexander, Irving, were to the legitimate as compared to the crude melodrama of their contemporaries. *Gore.*

WOMAN OF NO IMPORTANCE

British production with English players offered on this side by Select Pictures without credit to foreign makers. The director is Dennison Clift, reputed to be a protege of Cecil DeMille. At the Strand.

Rachel ....Fay Compton
George Harford..............Milton Rosmer
Gerald Arbuthnot........Ward McCallister
Hester Worsley.................Lila Walker
Sir Thomas Harford......M. Gray Murray
Lady Cecelia..................Hetta Bartlett
Rachel's Father..............Henry Vibart
Lady Hunstanton.........Daisy Campbell
Elsie Farquhar...............Gwen Carton

Oscar Wilde's ideas of social justice and the double standard were as daring in his day as George Bernard Shaw is in ours, but they come upon the screen at this late date as rather mild. "A Woman of No Importance" may have been rather startling to London of 20 years ago, but in this day and generation it hasn't a shock left, only a keen analysis of justice and a thoroughly interesting story.

It is easily the best British production that has come to this side from England, and in its technical development shows unmistakably the tutelage of DeMille. The photography is clear, and its action is natural and economical. There is none of the over-emphasis that has characterized the British studios, rather the whole thing is done in an intelligent spirit.

Its players are refreshingly new to the American fan. Fay Compton plays the heroine of a society drama without turning flipflops, and Milton Rosmer gives an intelligent interpretation of a difficult role as the philandering nobleman, a part that could easily be overdone. The backgrounds are always convincing and beautiful, and the argument of the story—the justice of the single moral standard for men and women—wholly plausible. Whatever may be said of Wilde, he was always a clear thinker in a literary way, and his screen adapters have done him fairly complete justice, at least in the lifelikeness of his characters. There is always something convincing in the way the English players do the high society types, and in this case they play them with an authenticity that contributes greatly to the building up of the illusion.

They give their scenes and actions a certain sense of real elegance, rather than an impossible grandeur such as that with which the American actors invest the type of nobleman and high-bred women. Some of the titles were probably adapted to the American exhibition, such as the noble sentiments expressed by the American girl in the latter part of the film, but that rather increases its value here and is a fair trick of nationalizing a foreign product. Altogether the picture will have an excellent appeal here and is a fortunate introduction of the better class British product in this market. It will especially gain the good will of the American women fans by reason of its argument.

The story is expertly framed for adaptation to the screen. Its drama is clean-cut and economical, with the possible exception that it is overtitled, and this perhaps is the fault of the American titler. But the action is crisp and significant. Those passages in which Rachel is made the victim of George Harford, the philanderer, are daintily played. The suggestion of his betrayal of the girl is made adequate, although not overdone, as probably would be the method of the American, and the sympathetic passages later when Mrs. Arbuthnot is confronted by her betrayer is not overdone, but the dramatic values are adequate.

At the Strand Sunday night, an evening of oppressive weather, there was a house somewhat short of capacity, but they displayed unusual liking for the picture, according it a really earnest burst of applause, something extraordinary in this house, where the clientele is rather apathetic as a rule. *Rush.*

THE $5 BABY

Five-reel comedy-drama adapted by Rex Taylor from the story by Irvin S. Cobb and presented at the Criterion, New York, under the auspices of Metro, which rent the house from Famous Players for the engagement. The subject is designated a Harry Beaumont production, and Viola Dana is starred.

Ruth	Viola Dana
Ben Shapinsky	Ralph Lewis
The Solitary Kid	Otto Hoffman
Larry Donovan	John Harron
Mr. Donovan	Tom McGuire
Bernie Riskin	Arthur Rankin
Esther Block	Marjorie Maurice
Isadore	E. Pasque

An engaging comedy-drama rich in heart interest, well played and skilfully devised, but there seems nothing about it to warrant this kind of Broadway exploitation with all the expense it entails and which must sooner or later come out of rentals.

The exhibitor idea appears to be that if there is inherent value in a picture, they are entitled to it in the first place, rather than having a huge overhead piled up on a picture through New York exploitation and paid off through the percentage plan of booking.

This is all irrespective of the picture under discussion, which has splendid sympathetic values in several directions, as well as several capital characters. The types are all native to New York City, however, and may not register so surely in other communities. For example, the venerable Jew pawnbroker (played with fine dignity by Ralph Lewis) is a character who will score 100 per cent. in the metropolis, but it is a question whether the sympathetic qualities of his character will have as great value elsewhere.

Another situation which is local to Manhattan is the fact the Irish and the Jewish elements of the communities mingle on the friendliest terms. That condition makes for first-class atmosphere in the big city, but probably will not be especially in favor of the film in the smaller cities.

As to the sympathetic quality of the picture, it ought to be sure-fire. The story is there a hundred ways, and represents Irvin Cobb's fiction work at his mature best. Its earlier passages have an exquisite human touch which represents Cobb at the apex of his writing career, and the latter portions of the story have capital romance with a comedy twist which cannot but evoke a warm response. It's a happy, cheerful story, and furnishes the best type of constructive entertainment. Certainly in a period of low ebb in high-class production it is an enterprise on the part of Metro that deserves a full measure of success. Whether it will be a draw remains a question; that it will entertain when the clientele has been attracted is without question, especially, as has been noted, in New York. It has all the tolerance, honest sympathy and warm humanity that are characteristic of Cobb, who is perhaps as typical of the highest class newcomers in the field of fiction as we have today.

The story naturally falls into two classes, the first dealing with the adoption of the foundling Ruth by the kindly old Jew and her childhood, and the scheming of a ne'er-do-well hobo who hopes to profit by her situation. The second division deals with her life when she has grown up to be a young woman of 18 and is courted by the youth of the neighborhood. There isn't a great deal of drama to the story, but it has a mine of interesting character drawing. There is one interesting passage in which a Jewish mother arranges the marriage of Ruth and her son Bernie, and around this incident there is woven a delightful romance. Bernie is in love with a schoolmate, Esther, while Ruth is drawn to Larry Donovan, son of the police sergeant who has been her guardian's old friend. This four-cornered romance appears to be blocked by the desire of Ruth's guardian and Bernie's mother to arrange a match and the apparent desire of the young people to obey their elders' advice. The happy denouement comes about when Esther and Bernie run away and wed with the connivance of Larry, and Ruth wins her real love in a typical tomboy Viola Dana scene. *Rush.*

MAN FROM HELL'S RIVER

Pierre	Irving Cummings
Marballa	Eva Novak
Lopente	Robert Klein
Padre	William Herford
Gaspard the Wolf	Wallace Beery

A state rights film by Western Pictures Exploitation Company, directed by Irving Cummings, who is featured. The story is an adaptation from James Oliver Curwood's "God of Her People," which probably explains the excellent "atmosphere." The tale concerns the love of a "Mountie," Canadian Northwest Mounted Police (Pierre) for Marballa (Eva Novak), the adopted daughter of a squaw man, who is a fugitive from justice (Robert Klein) and who is trying to forget his past buried in the north woods.

Gaspard the Wolf (Wallace Beery) comes into the country and becomes enamored of the girl. He uses his knowledge of her adopted father's past to wrest a promise of the girl's hand in marriage from the latter. She consents when the squaw informs her that refusal means jail for her father.

Pierre returns the day of the marriage from a man hunt. His sweetheart cannot tell him her motive on account of her father. He and Gaspard then wage the usual elemental battle for possession of the woman they love, with Pierre victorious after a series of incidents, which include a realistic looking fight, made thrilling by the intervention of Pierre's husky dog team leader, "Rin Tan." The latter is a typical Curwood touch.

The picture is melodramatic, but handled with the soft pedal on the gun throwing. Cummings gives a splendid performance in the romantic lead, adequately supported by an excellent cast. Miss Novak played and looked charming, while Wallace Beery made the most of his many opportunities. He is developing into one of the screen's most convincing villains.

A conventional story well produced, with an intelligent adherence to detail will make this an enjoyable feature to any program. *Con.*

AFRAID TO FIGHT

Universal feature made from the story of L. R. Brown, directed by William Worthington and played as half of a double bill on Loew's New York Roof, June 26. Frank Mayo the star, supported by Lillian Rich.

A good lively five-round prize fight, with plenty of action and a knockout as its climax, forms the basis of an interesting picture. Back of the ring battle and contributing to its genesis there is a capital heart interest and a sentimental story that bolsters the whole thing up into a first-rate program picture.

The picture is full of good sympathetic values, and the author has so framed his dramatic elements that deliver a high-power kick all the way to the climax in the prizefight scene. The picture is rich in popular appeal and ought to prove a cleanup. In all details it is candid sympathetic stuff, but neatly handled, and the product is well above the Universal average. The one objection is that the ring battle might have been shot at closer range and given more detail. Mayo strips down to an excellent representation of a clean-cut fighter and handled himself extremely well in the ring passages.

The sentimental value for the hero is built up deftly by making him a returned soldier with a pugilistic record overseas. But he has been gassed, and his promise to his mother removes him from the professional ring. It so happens that he has an invalid sister whose medical treatment requires a large sum of money. A great fight manager is trying with indifferent results to develop a second rater, and the pug treats a youngster unkindly. Hagen, the hero, takes the kid's part, and in a rough-and-tumble go gets the better of the second rater.

The great manager persuades the boy it is his duty to try for the professional title in order to finance his little sister's recovery. In pursuance of this plan Hagen is sent into the Rocky mountains under pledge to take part in no roughhouse and to devote himself to rest until his gassed lungs have been strengthened.

Here the romance develops. Hagen falls in love with the local beauty and his courtship is challenged by a rival, but Hagen cannot mix things under the circumstances. Later on he goes back to the city. The doctor pronounces his condition perfect and the title bout goes on. This bit of staging is nicely done, and as the battle shifts first one way and then the other a considerable degree of suspense is developed, ending, of course, in the victory of the hero.

Thus the situation surrounding the little sister's condition is provided for, and as an added kick Hagen makes tracks for the mountain village, where he was forced to decline battle under his sweetheart's eyes, where he makes a cleanup of his scoffers and enemies and wins the girl in a whoop hurrah finish. It's all frank but clean-cut romance, cheerful in character and the sort of a picture that leaves every one in a pleasant frame of mind. It has no great novelty, but it uses the familiar materials in excellent straightforward manner for the making of an altogether enjoyable screen entertainment.

The interiors are cheap but adequate, and some of the outdoor shots in the mountains are exceptionally pretty. Mayo, as always, makes a likeable, manly hero, and Miss Rich, although she has not much to do by way of pretentious acting, makes a trim figure and at all times looks the desirable sweetheart. *Rush.*

NINE SECONDS FROM HEAVEN

An independent release slipped into the Broadway for a full week in conjunction with the usual vaudeville played at that house.

The Rialto Productions is releasing the picture, made by the Peerless Producing Co. No cast is announced upon the screen, with the director and author also remaining in oblivion. It is to the advantage of all concerned that the secrecy be maintained, as the production would not prove an asset to anyone.

It starts as a comedy, gets a big mystery involved during the running, and returns to the comedy idea at the finish. It is long drawn out and uninteresting.

The production is nil and the photography is atrocious at times. From general appearances the picture would suggest having been made in England. The story is laid in that country.

At the Broadway the audience cheered at the finish, because it was over. Theatre seats have yet to be made that are comfortable enough to warrant anybody comfortably sitting through this one. *Hart.*

REAL ADVENTURE

Five-reel dramatic subject made from the novel of Henry Kitchell Webster, starring Florence Vidor, directed by King Vidor, and put out under the auspices of Associated Exhibitors. Arthur S. Kane is the producer. Presented as half a double bill at Loew's New York Roof, June 27.

Something always is to be expected from Mr. and Mrs. Vidor in their producing adventures. In this case they get away from the familiar style of story by beginning with the marriage and making the romance out of those readjustments which are worked out between men and women after the wedding. In the present instance it's quiet drama, with just an undercurrent of comedy, but in method and purport the story is that of "The First Year," the stage play which has been making history in the metropolitan theatre.

The whole thing makes a thoroughly interesting social study. It has some of the quality of young romance, but its point is rather beyond that as though one finished a sweetish Victorian novel and then constructed new and unpublished chapters. The experiment with an unusual literary style comes as refreshing and enlivening after the unending screen series of stories the elements of which are he-loves-her-she-loves-him-and-they-live-happily-ever-after. Certainly, "The Real Adventure" has points of reality that engage the attention and make the spectator think, besides providing momentary entertainment.

The production method recommends itself. Vidor has always been the advocate of simple emphasis rather than theatrical display, and this is a capital example of his style. There is nothing hectic about the play, but it has a sort of subdued force and grace. Most of the action takes place in interiors, and these have been constructed with an eye to simple effectiveness instead of the common method of making the background overshadow the drama. We have too many film plays anyhow which are merely a production splurge. In this case Vidor had what he conceived to be an interesting story to tell and he tried to tell it with as much self effacement as possible. The method recommends itself. Miss Vidor lends herself to this style of production. She has a high type of intellectual beauty as distinct from the flamboyant type, and she plays in a moderate key, a mode of quiet naturalness rather than emotional hysteria. Her comedy is moderate in the same degree, natural and recognizable without the usual flip-flop tricks of the screen comedienne.

In "The Real Adventure" she plays the high-spirited wife who becomes discontented because her husband, a young lawyer, keeps her apart during the serious occupations of real life and makes her a pet only in his moments of relaxation. She objects to being a plaything of his leisure and leaves his home in order to seek a career for herself. Her only asset being her beauty, she gravitates to the theatre where she becomes a chorus girl. In this capacity she develops a certain talent in the designing of dresses, and this knack brings her success, but sooner or later she realizes that her real sphere of happiness is the home, and when the husband reappears she gladly falls into his arms. The "Real Adventure" is not the mating in this case, but the final readjustment of husband and wife on a basis of mutual understanding and companionship. Who shall say that this is not as fine a type of romance as that of youthful courting. Certainly it works out into a highly absorbing screen story.

Perhaps the principal defect of the casting is the use of rather a too good-looking leading man (his name escaped in the business of catching the data from the title sheets). He looks too much the screen actor rather than the everyday man. Regular features are becoming less and less an asset to leading men while the discriminating fans are coming to demand character in their masculine types.

Rush.

ROUGH SHOD

Five-reel western from the William Fox establishment, starring Charles Jones. Story by Charles A. Selzer, scenario by Jack Strumwasser, directed by Reeves Eason.

"Syeel" Brannon............Charles Jones
Betty Lawson..............Helen Ferguson
Jo Hamilton................Ruth Renick
"Satan" Latimer............Maurice Flynn
Les Artwell....................Jack Rollins
"Denver" ....Charles LeMoyne

A typical Fox western melodrama, with a wealth of gunplay, abundance of swiftly galloping horses and gorgeous natural scenic shots. Direct and obvious melodrama addressing itself simply and candidly to that portion of the fan public which takes its entertainment in dime novel form. A good enough picture in its way, just as mediocre fiction is good enough in its way. They do no harm and furnish a certain amount of childish entertainment.

Grades for the daily change of program houses where they like their heroes most gosh-awful heroic and their heavies equally villainous. The picture has a number of excellent thrills, one of them a sensational fight between hero and heavy on the brink of a dizzy cliff and what looks like a sure enough plunge into the water below. Also the story has plenty of spectacular riding, and altogether is well up in its class of transparent theatrical melodrama, a little of which goes a long way.

All the ancient devices are there—including the cultured girl from the east, who starts by hating the rough and ready ranch foreman and ends by loving him; the cattle rustler and the brave cowboys, who ride to the rescue of the beauty in distress. Like any one of a dozen score of similar pictures, but, as observed, produced (manufactured is the better term) in workmanlike fashion.

Brannon is the foreman of Josephine Hamilton's ranch. Years before his father was murdered by a treacherous stranger, who shot him through the back, and Brannon is on his trail. There is much horse stealing in the district, and a rich rancher of the neighborhood is under suspicion. A posse captures a humble accomplice of the rich rancher and is about to lynch him when Betty, the eastern girl, accomplishes his escape. Later on "Satan" Latimer, the master horse thief, gets Betty in his power and abducts her while Brannon gives chase. The rescue, the fight between Brannon and Latimer, who turns out to be the murderer of Brannon's father (this is disclosed through a tattoo mark on Latimer's arm) and the happy ending make up the fast-moving remainder of the story.

Was mildly received as the feature of the New York theatre June 20.

Rush.

FOR BIG STAKES

William Fox feature starring Tom Mix, directed by Lynn Reynolds, with photography by Dan Clark.

"Clean-Up" Sudden...............Tom Mix
Dorothy Clark...........Patsy Ruth Miller
Scott Mason....................Sid Jordan
Rowell Clark....................Bert Sprotte
Ramon Valdez.....................Joe Harris

Tom Mix's latest Western thriller follows closely the lines of his other productions. Mix is the central figure and in the action all of the time. Few stars are given the opportunities this chap secures to carry their productions over. He is included in practically every bit of footage and individually provides the majority of thrills.

Ranch life again provides the ingredients upon which the story is based. All of the elements of life in the cow country are brought into play, and the attempts of desperados to play havoc with the herds are thwarted by the hero. There is such a great similarity in these western stories that the screen productions rely almost entirely upon the director and the star to produce new thrills. In all probability it is on this account that Mix has established himself as he has.

The stories are nil in the majority of his features, but audiences are always assured of a new stunt here and there by the star.

Supporting Mix is Patsy Ruth Miller, a youthful miss rapidly coming to the fore as an ingenue leading woman. She was a good selection to provide the necessary interest in the love angle of the story. The remaining members of the cast consisted entirely of the usual western types. There was no production cost to speak off, as the majority of the work was done on location.

Followers of western pictures should secure a thrill from this.

Hart.

THE DICTATOR

Famous Players (Paramount) adaptation of Richard Harding Davis's play originally done by William Collier, now made into screen form, with scenario by Walter Woods. James Cruze, director. Wallace Reid, star, supported by Lila Lee. At the Rivoli, July 2.

Brook Travers...................Wallace Reid
Carlos Rivas..............Theodore Kosloff
Juanita..............................Lila Lee
General Campos..................Kalla Pasha
Henry Bolton..................Sidney Bracey
Sam Travers.......................Fred Butler
"Biff" Dooley....................Walter Long
Sabos...............................Alan Hale

"The Dictator" is the same happy bit of nonsense on the screen it was on the stage, probably a little funnier, because the screen presentation has an elaborate scenic background which throws the humor of the action into more distinct relief. Comedy is largely a matter of contrasts. The best the stage production could do was to use the limited scenic equipment, but the screen version backs up its burlesque with what amounts to a pageant.

The pomp of South American officialdom in its settings of tropical loveliness makes a perfect background for the harum-scarum exploits of the matter-of-fact American hero. Half the fun of the whole affair is the burlesque of Latin-American politics, and the picture gives greatest scope to the building up of the ridiculous pretense of political magnificence. What could be funnier than the incident of a tough and commonplace New York chauffeur going through all the ceremonial of an execution by a squad of highly impressive and highly impressed soldiers of the trick republic of "San Manana," ruled by weekly revolutions, official and social ritual of the most imposing kind and the American banana trade. This execution scene was a delightful bit of broad travesty as it was handled by Walter Long in the character of the tough chauffeur, "Biff" Dooley, who followed the hero through all his adventures to collect a $60 taxi bill run up by the hero in a tour of the New York stage entrances.

The revolution itself is a riot of absurd spectacle, and the whole thing is surrounded by magnificent palaces and beautiful tropical scenery which give an added touch to a situation already comic. Reid plays the blundering young American with just the right touch of casual nonchalance to give point to its broad absurdity. Lila Lee makes a charming dark-eyed heroine, and the picture is rich in pictorial surprises.

The whole bill was framed to keep comedy to the fore. The two other items in the surrounding program were a whooping Mermaid farce with custard pie incidentals and a burlesque novelty. The latter was a scream from start to finish. They had taken a sentimental film melodrama of a past generation, "Mountain Laurel," and turned it into a roaring travesty by means of comic titles. The action was intensely serious (it is probable they used a reprint of the original one-reeler) and the titles were riotous. When the hero, hunting in the Adirondacks, mistakes his friend in the woods for a deer and shoots him, the title shows a pair of dice and makes a pun on the game of craps by saying: "He shoots a buck." The whole thing was full of like fooleries. In the case of the feature the title writing also contributed greatly to the comedy. The taxi chauffeur was always butting into thrilling situations with his demand that he be paid his "sixty berries."

In addition to the comedy flavor (again an interesting touch of contrast) they staged a capital patriotic display appropriate to the week of the 4th, with the audience standing for the national anthem while Susan Ida Clough stood posed as Liberty holding an American banner flanked by uniformed men at "present arms," representing the navy, marine and artillery divisions of the service, and sang "The Star Spangled Banner."

Rush.

GOD'S COUNTRY AND THE LAW

The billing sets forth "Arrow Film Co. presents James Oliver Curwood's 'God's Country and the Law.'" Directed by Sydney Olcott.

Marie ....Gladys Leslie
Andre ....Fred C. Jones
Dore ....Wm. H. Tooker
'Poleon ....Cesare Gravina
Oachi ....Hope Sutherland

As the title suggests, the picture is a hectic melodrama, very theatrical and made more so by its cumbersome and stilted titling. The picture would be rather ordinary except that it is saved by two conspicuously good qualities—the acting is spirited and the settings are gorgeous. Another item in its favor is a series of striking animal pictures, real moose feeding close by apparently in a wilderness pond, a close-up of an opossum, a lone wolf posed against a deep shot of what is apparently a wilderness landscape and a trio of tumbling bear cubs, pets of the heroine. All these details belong in the Curwood story of the Canadian north woods and supply a wealth of atmosphere.

Except for these things, the picture would classify as a rather trashy romance. It is full of literary artificialities; too many things happen at the behest of the dramatist and the long arm of coincidence is stretched to the breaking. Dramatic situations are well enough if they grow up naturally and the literary device is concealed, but in this case the hand of the playwright is too apparent. The climax which brings the villain to his punishment in the presence of all the persons he has wronged, assembled with more energy than skill from distant places, is exceedingly transparent. The wickedness of the villain is grossly overdone and his punishment (he goes mad in the lonely forest, apparently the victim of a bad conscience) is rather blatant melodrama. Curwood is usually better than this in his writings. He has a certain dignity and knack for creating illusion. This picture has done for his story about what Robert Service's verses do for Kipling. That is to say, the picture overdoes everything that is interesting in the original. The story:

Dore, a whisky runner in the Canadian borderlands, is driven to flight by the Mounted Police and takes refuge with 'Poleon, a white native. In return for the kindly woodsman's hospitality he attempts to dishonor his daughter, and is driven off. He strikes through the wilderness and takes asylum with Andre, a young trapper, and his beautiful wife, Marie. Their kindness he also repays by assailing the young wife. While Andre is away he abducts the girl, although how he proposed to carry a buxom young woman through the north woods would balk anybody but a scenario writer.

It balked Dore, anyway, because when Marie recovered consciousness she promptly escaped by leaping into the whirling rapids (the stunt would have been impressive if it had not been poorly faked), and Dore goes mad under the influence of the oppressive wilderness and his own evil deeds. Of course, Marie is rescued by the Northwest Mounted troopers and is brought safely home in time to put the frenzied Andre into raptures. Obedient to the technique of the "movies," Dore's crazy wanderings bring him straight to Andre's door, where he conveniently falls dead at the feet of the constables who have been ordered to catch him "dead or alive."

It takes a pretty naive picture fan to swallow it all, but the scenery was unquestionably exquisite.

Rush.

THE DUST FLOWER

A Basil King production made and released by Goldwyn. Directed by Rowland V. Lee. A "Cinderella" story in five reels that has appeal.

Letty .... Helene Chadwick
Rashleigh Allerton .... James Rennie
Steptoe .... Claude Gillingwater
Barbara Wallbrook .... Mona Kingsley
Judson Flask .... Edward Peil
Ott .... George Periolat

A combination of society and slum stuff with a little Cinderella type of girl raised from the dive by marriage to a wealthy man. The picture is prefaced by a title to the effect that the cynical will not believe it possible, but that it is romance. Nevertheless it is interesting and it looks as though the majority of audiences will like it, but it holds nothing unusual as a promise to the box office. Just a good program picture, but even they are few and far between these days. The production has Helene Chadwick as the principal player and her roles calls for her to be a habitual runaway. First she runs away from a cruel stepfather who wants her to become a cigaret girl in an all night cafe, then after the marriage to the wealthy young society man she makes two attempts to beat it from the mansion where she is installed before she is successful and finally on the third try she gets away. It doesn't sound thrilling but it is interesting.

Basil King wrote the story while he was one of the Famous Authors collection that Goldwyn assembled, therefore it is released as "A Basil King Production." Rowland V. Lee directed the story and handled it very well.

Miss Chadwick plays Letty, who on the death of her mother is left in the hands of her stepfather. The old boy likes the chickens and hangs around Ott's all night cabaret. Letty is supposed to go to work there selling cigars and cigarettes, but manages to make her escape on the advice of one of the girls in the place who informs her that the river is pleasanter even though a quicker death. She is about to take a leap from a bridge in Central Park when the hero, who has been just turned down by the girl that he has been engaged to and vowed that he would marry the first woman he met, walks in and carries out his promise. When he gets home with his bride he discovers that there is a note from a repentant fiancee-that-was and he immediately tries to figure a way out of his situation. However, he reckoned without his butler, who disliked the Mrs. Allerton that was to be and preferred the Mrs. Allerton that was.

In the end the hero turns down the haughty society girl who gave him the mitten and whips the wicked stepfather.

The picture does not appear to be of recent vintage, otherwise Rowland Lee has adopted rather old stuff in the parading of models in evening clothes as one of the tricks to take up footage. Judging from what the models wear on parade in the majority of motion pictures women evidently go around from breakfast to bedtime in nothing but evening gowns.

The cast has a quintet of outstanding figures. Miss Chadwick is most convincing at times, although overacts somewhat as the slum kiddie. James Rennie is an ideal hero in this case and Mona Kingsley fills the bill wonderfully as the haughty society deb. The character of the butler as depicted by Claude Gillingwater will endear him to the fans and Edward Piel as the heavy more than registered that. So much so that the Capitol audience Sunday night applauded the beating the hero administered, and when they do that on Broadway on a hot night it speaks well for the villain.

Fred.

THE GREAT ALONE

Produced by the West Coast Film Corp. under the direction of Jacques Jaccard, with Monroe Salisbury star. Presented by Isadore Bernstein. Five-reel northwestern snow picture, released by American.

"Silent" Duval .... Monroe Salisbury
Nadine Picard .... Laura Anson
Winston Sassoon .... Walter Law
Mary MacDonald .... Maria Draga
Bradley Carstairs .... George Waggoner
MacDonald .... Richard Cummings

A northwestern snow picture that must have been written according to Formula No. 6. It contains all of the stereotyped stuff usually seen in this particular type of feature. The particular fault is in the tempo, which at times takes on the aspect of a "slow motion" picture. In the regular daily change houses the picture will get by nicely, for it has everything that ever made a good northwestern, and therefore this one must perforce also be good; all the others were.

In direction there is an effort made to becloud the plot and create suspense, but all it does is to make the average auditor try to guess what it is about until just beyond the half-way point a series of cut-backs reveal what all the action has been for. Usually it is advisable to let the audience in on the secret, no matter how much the players may be supposed to be in the dark as to the causes for various happenings.

The story is that of a half-breed educated at college (refer back to "Strongheart") who because his full white brothers snub him decides to return to the land of his people. He is sent north by the head of a mining and trading company, who had been befriended by the boy's father, to investigate irregularities at a certain trading post.

At the opening of the film he is at the post, and it is New Year's eve. Word is brought in by an Indian guide the factor's daughter is snowed in at a cabin down the pass. The half-breed hero starts out to rescue her. A co-worker of the factor, who is responsible for the irregularities, sends two men after the hero to see he doesn't return. He outwits them and returns with the girl, leaving behind at the cabin his Indian companion to try to nurse back to life the man accompanying the girl. The latter is one of those who snubbed the boy at college.

When the girl returns to health and her lover is restored to her and the half-breed in the meantime has compelled the villain to walk out of the scene, he resigns from the company and in the final fade-out is at a cabin in the "alone" with a half-breed woman.

There are a lot of snow in the picture and some particularly good storm stuff. Also the usual dog sled, some shooting and a corking fight between the hero and the heavy. Salisbury overacts throughout and hangs onto the lens to the last fraction of a second, seemingly largely responsible through this for the slow action. Maria Draga, who plays the girl, does some clever emotionalism and scores. Walter Law as the heavy handled his role at about the same tempo as did Salisbury. In one scene in which the two men and Laura Anson, as the half-breed girl, appeared the action was so slow as to be painful.

Fred.

THE WALL FLOWER

A Goldwyn feature written and directed by Rupert Hughes, with Colleen Moore featured. "Cinderella" type of story with comedy relief.

Idalene Nobbin .... Colleen Moore
Walt Breen .... Richard Dix
Pamela Sheil .... Gertrude Astor
Prue Nickerson .... Laura Laplante
Roy Duncan .... Tom Gallery
Phil Larrabee .... Rush Hughes
Allen Lansing .... Dana Todd
Mrs. Nobbin .... Fanny Stockbridge
Mrs. Nickerson .... Emily Rait

The work that Colleen Moore does in this picture places her right in line to assume the screen comedy honors that once so well fitted Mabel Normand. She has a role giving her an opportunity as an eccentric comedienne and makes the most of it. The picture is a neat little comedy drama with the story along the usual "Cinderella" lines, with the poor, awkward little girl who has always been the wall flower developing into a real peach after a few months of association with social superiors and the aid of a few clothes. The feature is an entertaining picture that will please any audience.

Rupert Hughes was the author and also directed the production. He is very much present in the titles, but there are spots where little can be said for his direction, yet as a whole the picture is fairly well done. Hughes did handle the two automobile accidents rather well, and his working out of the youthful school stuff at the Junior Prom had detail. In the latter one rather strongly suspects his boy, Rush, more lately from school, may have had a hand in making suggestions.

(Sid: You want to catch this one and get a slant at Rush Hughes acting out.)

The cast that supports Miss Moore is ideal. Richard Dix is her leading man, and one wonders why after having started the pair in a series of productions as co-featured players there suddenly comes a twist through which Miss Moore is featured alone. She has shared billing honors with Dix in pictures where his role overshadowed hers by as marked a proportion as hers does his in this picture. Dix delivers all through the picture in what he is asked to do. The other youthful players in the cast also stand out especially Gertrude Astor and Laura Laplante. Fanny Stockbridge in a character role got a few laughs here and there.

The majority of laughs, however, come from the titling rather than the action. In sets the feature has one or two out of the ordinary and the lightings are particularly good.

In the next production Mr. Hughes directs he would be wise to watch his camera work a little more closely.

Fred.

GAS, OIL AND WATER

A Charles Ray starring production, directed by himself from the story by Richard Andres. In five feels and released through First National.

George Oliver Watson .... Charles Ray
Henry Jones .... Otto Hoffman
Susie .... Charlotte Pierce
Hobart Rush .... Robert Gray
Philip Ashton .... William Carroll
"Beauty" Strang .... Dick Southerland
Sanchez .... Bert Offard
Whiskers .... Himself

This Charles Ray production is about the poorest excuse for a feature picture this star has ever turned out. It isn't worthy even the consideration that would be tendered a fly-by-night production without star, producer name or director never heard of before. There is no reason, except that Ray appears in the picture, for the booking of it anywhere. Those who see it because Ray is in it will walk away from the theatre with the impression that the star has "gone back" 100 per cent. It is a cinch that it isn't a picture that will build up at the box office. If played for more than a day the chances are that the statement will show a decided drop in attendance.

There is no story, mighty little action, and Ray does nothing worthy of mention. In plain English "it's a flop."

In this production Ray is a Secret Service operative. After seeing him in it one might say that it sounds his cue to get back to the rural characters. He opens a gas, oil and water station near the Mexican border to watch smugglers (at least that is what the supposition is, there being nothing to indicate what he was after). There is nothing but people walking in and out of the set without rhyme or reason and without advancing anything like a story at any time.

There are also a number of automobiles chasing each other over mountain trails, a few scooting motorcycles and an almost love story, with Ray marrying the girl at the finish, but in all it's a lot of apple sauce that runs for the end book.

Fred.

YANKEE DOODLE, JR.

Comedy drama in screen action which runs to travesty in the comic titling. Cinart stands sponsor for the feature, in which J. Frank Glendon is starred. Jack Pratt is set down as the director. At Loew's Circle, July 4.

It is curious that this production should come out of the independent field just as Paramount's "The Dictator" is released. Both pictures are identical in farce-melodramatic spirit and both have young American heroes counterplotting during a South American revolution.

The stories differ considerably in detail, this one of Cinart's being rather crude in its burlesque, while the Wallace Reid picture has a smooth and mellifluous quality of humor. At that "Yankee Doodle, Jr.," ought to be an amusing subject for the medium-grade houses. It has plenty of broad comedy and an abundance of action. Some of the night photography is excellent, and the production has been handled with discrimination as far as settings are concerned. J. Frank Glendon has not quite the debonair style in the part the role calls for, being rather more in the obvious screen actor classification.

The whole story centers in the effort of an American business man to force his pampered son into a rough-and-ready job of selling fireworks. Jack, the son, picks the territory for his labors by spinning a globe and throwing a pen at it arrowwise. It hits in the South American trick republic of San Mariano, and hither the salesman takes passage, bearing an iron nerve and a sample case of fireworks.

He promptly becomes involved in a local revolution, led by one Mendoza, a traitor to the existing administration, in love with the president's daughter. Jack also falls in love with the senorita, and the theatrical clash of interest is all set.

The revolutionists are shown making their attack on the palace, where the President, his daughter and the American are on the defensive in rather a spectacular series of mob scenes, but then the story takes to the burlesque side, Jack conceiving the idea of meeting the armed revolutionary army with an attack of roman candles and firework bombs. The whole thing develops into a broad farce, with the rebels put to flight, the American hero in the embrace of the heroine and the American fireworks maker turning his plant over to fill a contract for munitions.

There are several good bits of action in rough-and-ready fights between Jack and Mendoza, who abducts the heroine, and numerous passages are interesting pieces of screen action, such as maneuvers of troops, breakneck horseback riding and the like. Neither the story, its production nor the acting is on a par with the Wallace Reid film adaptation of "The Dictator," taken from the Richard Harding Davis play of the same name, but it is an amusing, irresponsible bit of nonsense and makes acceptable program material.

Rush.

YOUNG AMERICA

This picture was started by Essanay some years ago, but only completed late last fall. It is presented by George K. Spoor, with the original cast of the Cohan & Harris play of the same name in it. The film was booked by the Peerless Booking Corp. (Moss-Proctor-Keith film bookings) for some of the Proctor houses the first half of this week (July 3-5), chiefly because of the patriotic appeal.

It is being distributed by Elk Photo Plays, Inc., who aver it is not a re-issue. The Peerless also says it pays a rental that exceeds that of a reissue. Arthur Berthelet is the director of the Fred Ballard play, in which George M. Cohan also had a hand.

Compared to present-day standards the direction, photography and, in fact, the entire production, is rather crude stuff. The flashing of the New Jersey 1918 license on the 'lizzie" gives away its antiquity, and certainly will not convince any sort of sensible film fan it is not a re-issue. What the picture needs is intelligent re-editing and cutting, although the Elk Photo Play Co. probably figures it's not worth it. It's just a pop house feature to be marketed at a price.   *Abel.*

WHEN DEVIL DRIVES

Leah Baird production made for Associated Exhibitors and released through Pathe. Leah Baird star and authoress of story. Paul Scardon directed. Five reels.
Blanche Mansfield...............Leah Baird
Grace Eldridge................Arline Pretty
John Graham.................Richard Tucker
Robert Taylor.................Vernon Steele
Nanette Henley...........Katherine Lewis

Despite that from the title it might be assumed the action was suggested by an automobile or a trolley car, such isn't the case. It is the devil that is the impelling force behind the actions of the characters. The picture is just a fair meller that will do anywhere in the daily change houses. It has Leah Baird as the star, with a good supporting cast, well directed by Paul Scardon. The tale deals with society and better class cabaret life, with the heroine a rather fast stepper for a time.

In representing the two social extremes in womanhood the authoress has her lady of the cabarets rather handy with a paper cutter when she learns that her lover is leaving her to marry another woman. The "other woman," a society girl, is very handy with a gat when she finally discovers her next-door neighbor is the girl who caused the postponement of her wedding by stabbing the groom-to-be. But naturally neither was responsible, for "the devil drove them to it." The story is rather well set forth with a regeneration of two women as the theme, to which is added the doctrine of "Peace on earth, good will toward all" when the contending factions flop in each other's arms on Christmas morning.   *Fred.*

TRIP TO PARAMOUNTOWN

Special two-reeler by Famous Players-Lasky to be distributed to the exhibitor gratis and shown by him in the interest of the coming productions on the Fall Paramount program.

Wallace Reid,	Julia Faye,
Marion Davies,	Rodolph Valentino,
Thomas Meighan,	Lila Lee,
Betty Compson,	Nita Naldi,
May McAvoy,	Dorothy Dalton,
Gloria Swanson,	Jack Holt,
William de Mille,	Cecil B. DeMille,
Bebe Daniels,	Leatrice Joy
Conrad Nagel,	Theodore Roberts
George Fawcett,	T. Roy Barnes,
Wanda Hawley,	Milton Sills,
Mary Miles Minter,	Tom Moore,
Betty Compson,	Bert Lytell,
Alice Brady,	Elsie Ferguson,

Here is a real all-star production, and the best part of it is that the exhibitor gets the picture free. It is part of the advertising campaign Famous Players is making direct to the public via the screen for the fall program of Paramount productions. It is a two-reeler cleverly ar-ranged with novelty photographic work. It shows the Famous Players' studios in Long Island City and Hollywood in the opening. This is followed by a trip through the studios, showing the various stars at work on the sets of the various productions that they have in the making, with references to their successes in the past.

To Dorothy Dalton goes one of the most interesting bits. Miss Dalton had the advantage of a quadruple exposure, she being shown in the screen in four different characters at one time. Another piece of trick photography is for Wallace Reid, who, while sitting on a chair, has himself, in miniature, drive up to the chair in a racing auto. Marion Davies is seen in dissolves and double exposure. While standing at a wardrobe trunk on one side of the screen, taking the gowns from the truck, she dissolves in on the other side clad in the gown.

Bebe Daniels stands at the side of a talking machine while in miniature she dances atop of the cabinet, also trick stuff.

Of the larger productions, directed by the two de Milles and George Melford, whole shots of the big scenes are shown.

It is an interesting picture and it should work out as a very successful business bringer for the exhibitor. It is certain never before has he been able to advertise so many real star names in one picture, and even though there is no story connected with this, the two reels are certain to interest the public who want to see how pictures are made. At that the picture doesn't let them in on too much of the inside stuff.   *Fred.*

FOOTBALL DAFT

London, June 27.

The producers describe this new British feature as a comedy of side-splitting tendency. They exaggerate, even for film producers. Comedy of a very weary kind it may be, but it certainly is not side-splitting. There is not a hearty laugh in it. In fact, so dreary is it that no one was surprised to discover it was made in Scotland by a Scotch producer with a Scottish company. Scots may probably see the joke if inspired by their own whiskey and patriotism, but no one else will.

Jock is a riveter who is mad on football and liquor. To cure him his wife, Aggie, persuades a temperance advocate to call. Jock returns from a football match very stewed, and he and Aggie quarrel. She goes out and Jock seizes the opportunity to hide a bottle of whiskey which he has brought in. This he does by camouflaging it as vinegar. The temperance man calls and is flung out when Jock discovers who is in. He meets Aggie, who insists on his coming back to tea. She gives him salad, plentifully drenched in vinegar as she thinks. The result is the collapse of the advocate, triumph of Jock and liquor and the usual reconciliation. It is all very bad.   *Gore.*

A BACHELOR'S BABY

London, June 27.

This latest Granger-Davidson picture is an excellent humorous feature, full of human interest and natural comedy. The story is well told and holds the interest throughout. A young naval officer finds a deserted baby. On his way to inform the police, having left the child at a cottage, he has a slight accident. He is attended to by, among other people, a girl, with whom he promptly falls in love. He also becomes aware of a romance between two of his more elderly helpers. He remembers the baby and returns for it, hoping by its aid to rouse sympathy. Then the complications beloved of comedy writers commence. He takes the wrong baby and becomes an object of suspicion. Then amateur detectives, thinking he is a child-thief, take the child.

The settings for this story are simple and possess a good deal of rural charm. The acting is above the average. Jaidee Wright is excellent, as is Tom Reynolds, while the main if junior romance is capitally played by Leigh Woodward and Malcolm Todd.   *Gore.*

THE FAST MAIL

William Fox release, from the Lincoln J. Carter melodrama. Prereleased at Strand, New York, this week. Directed by Bernard J. Durning. Eileen Percy and Charles Jones featured.
Walter West.................Charles Jones
Mary Martin................Eileen Percy
Lee Martin..................James Mason
Pierre LaFeite.............William Steele
Cal Baldwin...............Adolph Menjou
Henry Joyce.............Harry Dunkinson

"The Fast Mail" is a box office picture, so full of meat as a meller that for weekly release it measures up to super requirements. The picture will advertise itself anywhere upon opening and can stand any kind of advance booming.

As a thriller, and it is a thriller of the nth kind, "The Fast Mail" misses nothing. It has everything, even to fire engines with horses that should be one of the biggest novelties just now. But that is only a novelty. This Fox film goes in for thrills, the melodramatic kind that is, of every kind, from racing horses in rescues to horse races (steeplechase), to wild auto rides, dashing mail train, a thrilling leap to the engine of the fast mail from a hand car running alongside, and again from the same fast mail that won't slow up to another swerving auto on the other side; then to Vicksburg, and one of the several thrilling fist fights, and all this after a race down the Mississippi river between two river steamboats with one blowing up through high pressure of steam to escape the other.

Swift action! Boy, when that picture gets going it runs right overboard. There probably never has been a picture made with so rapid and continuous action.

The action surrounds a thrilling plot to throw the rider of the favorite in the steeplechase. They threw him and "they" were the brother of the girl he loved. That led to the murder of a gambler who stood in on the frame. His murderer started for Vicksburg in a car, while the hero chased the other fellow down the Mississippi, over the railroad tracks, into Vicksburg, busted with his car right into the Hotel Carrie and whipped his whole gang while the three-story wooden hotel kept on burning up.

Then it was quiet again, as it had been at the outset when Walter West (Charles Jones) and Mary Martin (Eileen Percy) called upon "Mammy Loo" to have their fortunes read in a tea cup. Mammy guessed it right. She said they would be happy, but they first would see trouble. Walter didn't have much faith in Mammy's tea leaves, but Mary got a hunch Mammy had inside info.

For a feature of this description the direction is superb. Mr. Durning never lost a second nor any part of the situation, while whoever cut the film knew his business, up, down and backwards. For the cast there wasn't one miss, even on appearance. Of the many villains, Adolph Menjou as Cal Baldwin played so perfectly there was no one who shaded him, for he will be more hated than even Mary will be loved or Walter will be liked.

The picture people will marvel at Fox producing this one, after all the others, the mellers, the westerns and everything else, to find that "The Fast Mail," following all the others, leads them all.   *Sime.*

IN NAME OF THE LAW

Emory Johnson five-reeler presented by P. A. Powers at the Cohan, New York, for four week's run. Released through Film Booking Office.
Patrick O'Hara...............Ralph Lewis
Mrs. O'Hara.............Claire McDowell
Mary (at age of 6 years)...Josephine Adair
Mary (at age of 18 years).......Ella Hall
Harry O'Hara (at age of 9 years)
                           Benny Alexander
Harry O'Hara (at age of 22 years)
                           Emory Johnson
Johnny O'Hara (at age of 8 years)
                           Johnny Thompson
Johnny O'Hara (at age of 20 years)
                           Johnnie Walker
Mr. Lucus....................Dick Morris

With really unusual exploitation, including a tie-up with the New York Police Department, P. A. Powers presented "In the Name of the Law" at the Cohan, New York, for a four weeks' run, starting Sunday. The picture is a sob-sister meller that lines up as a possible winner for the releasing company. If the exhibitor can work the picture as heavily through advertising and tie-ups as the releasing organization for its New York presentation, he may get some money, as the production, while not a world-beater in any sense, is a good commercial tear compeller.

The program states that the picture introduces "The Great American Family." If that is to be taken literally, then everyone in the country must have had a cop for a father. It is the story of a policeman in San Francisco, who, with his wife, two sons and an adopted daughter, make up the little home circle. The earlier scenes show the family at a time when the boys are eight and nine, and the latter scenes are when they are in their early twenties.

It is a picturization of the struggle the average American family of scant means makes to have its offspring better equipped through education for the struggle of life. In this case, it is the mother who by self-denial sends one of her sons through law school, while the other boy is a bank teller and the girl works as secretary to the treasurer in the same institution.

The boy in law school is the first care that comes to her. He is accused of theft, but later cleared. This accusation almost disrupts the family, threatens to bring about the downfall of the girl, the death of the other boy and finally his arrest on the charge of murder. In the end the elder boy, having graduated from law school, defends his younger brother, and through the suicide and confession of the real culprit he is cleared.

The manner in which the tale is developed on the screen will make the majority of screen audiences feel for the mother and also have great sympathy for the girl and the boy accused of murder.

In picturizing it the father is at times shown as a lovable, kindly character, and at others a hard enforcer of the law. He is a policeman, first and last and has no use for a crook, even though it be his own flesh and blood. He typifies "Once a cop, always a cop." Ralph Lewis plays the role remarkably well, while Claire McDowell as the self-sacrificing mother created an impression second only to that of Mary Carr in "Over the Hill." The grown-up youngsters were by Johnnie Walker, who gave a corking performance; Ella Hall as the daughter, and Emory Johnson as the elder son. As kiddies these roles were played by Josephine Adair, Benny Alexander and Johnny Thompson. Except in the case of Walker, the kiddie actors were better than those who took up the roles later on. *Fred.*

ALWAYS THE WOMAN

Goldwyn five-reeler, with Betty Compson as star. By Perley Poore Sheehan, directed by Arthur Rosson. Reincarnation story.

Celia Thaxter....................Betty Compson
Boone........................Emory Johnson
Mrs. Boone........................Doris Pawn
Reginald Stanhope..............Gerald Pring
Mahmud.......................Richard Rosson
Vaudeville Manager..........Arthur Delmore
Kelim Pasha....................Macey Harlam

This is the second picture Betty Compson has made as a Goldwyn star. It was completed about 18 months ago and has been on the shelf ever since. Incidentally, it brought about the parting of the ways between Goldwyn and Miss Compson's own producing company. As a program picture it is one that will interest the average audience, especially as Miss Compson has gathered considerable advertising since she switched over to the Paramount side. The support is good and the story at least different. It is based on reincarnation, with Miss Compson as a former Egyptian Princess back on earth as a small-time vaudeville dancer. She, with her "manager" is on a steamer bound for Cairo, and the action for the greater part takes place on shipboard. All of the principal characters, with the exception of one or two, figure in the reincarnation end of the story.

The little vaudeville dancer performs on shipboard and one of the natives, who believes he is the reincarnation of a priest of ancient Egypt who betrayed the Princess centuries before, sees her, declares she is the Princess come to life again and warns her of the attentions of an Egyptian Prince among the passengers, at the same time constituting himself her slave and offering to lead her to her original burial place, where she will find great treasure.

Before the party lands, it is disclosed there is a drug addict aboard who has been forced to the use of narcotics by a pleasure-loving wife who has married him for his wealth. He is supposed to be the reincarnation of the priest-lover of the ages agone. The "manager" is wished out of the picture when a globetrotter of the Prince's party proposes to the dancer and is accepted.

All start on a hunt for the treasure and the Prince reveals that in reality the globe-trotter was his tool and proposed to the girl only that she might go with the party without the manager "on the job," so that the Prince might have her. This disclosure comes after the girl has confessed that originally she and her manager had proposed to snare the globe-trotter into a proposal and then compel him to buy off her contract.

When the Prince discloses his real aspect, the dope fiend, who has been encouraged to pass up the hop, comes through 100 per cent. and rescues the girl after his wife and the Prince have both been killed.

The tale is a rather weird one, but it holds. Miss Compson gave a realistic performance as the little double-crosser, who in turn was crossed. Emory Johnson was the heroic drug addict, and Doris Pawn his wife. Both nicely delivered. Macey Harlam played the heavy effectively, while Arthur Delmore as the hick manager got a few laughs early in the picture.

The direction is rather fair, with some very good desert touches. *Fred.*

TENSE MOMENTS FROM OPERA

London, July 4.

Made by Masters and owned by Gaumont (British), these pictures are a fair example of trying to put a quart into a pint pot. The result is a good deal of disappointment. Although called "Tense Moments," an attempt has been made to pot the greater portion of each opera into the capacity of a one-reel film.

The operatic music is really the only excuse for these small features, which will probably form a useful "fill up" in kinemas where the orchestras are really good. In some cases the production work is not good, some of the "Rigoletto" scenes being very obviously affairs of batten and canvas. In other features it is quite good.

Throughout the acting is far above the material value of the pictures, and less expensive artists would have done quite as well as the well-known people who have been employed and given remarkably little chance of showing their histrionic ability.

The series consists of 12 pictures, and of those shown to the trade and press this morning Flotow's "Martha" is quite the best. It is well staged, well dressed, well acted by Dorothy Fane, Moyha Nugent, Alec Hunter and James Knight. Verdi's "Rigoletto" is not so well staged, but has some exceptionally good acting from A. B. Imeson and Booth Conway. "The Bride of Lammermoor" also is lacking in reality and power, although Olaf Hytten, Gordon Hopkirk and Vivian Gibson, the Lucy, get all they can out of it.

William Shaw's performance of the adventurer-lover of Lucy is bad. He neither looks a soldier of fortune nor anything else. There is very little pull in these short features, ambitious though the idea is. *Gore.*

IF YOU BELIEVE IT, IT'S SO

Paramount feature in five reels, with Thomas Meighan starred. Story by Pearley Poore Sheehan, directed by Tom Forman. Script by Waldemar Young. Regeneration story, slightly "Miracle Man" like in treatment.

Chick Harris, a crook....Thomas Meighan
Alvah Morley, a country girl.
Pauline Starke
Ezra Wood, a patriarch....Joseph Dowling
Sky Blue, a confidence man.
Theodore Roberts
Colonel Williams...............Charles Ogle
Tessie Wingate....................Lura Ansen
Frank Tine, a realty agent..Charles French
Bartender.....................Thomas Kennedy
Constable..............................Ed Brady

Thomas Meighan is the star of this picture, but it is Theodore Roberts who runs away with the acting honors and creates the best impression. The picture is a corking program offering, and Meighan stands out to advantage in it. In some touches it suggests "The Miracle Man," with Meighan as the big-town crook whose regeneration is brought about in a small country town through a girl. The general plot holds interest, while there is sufficient comedy relief to make the production good entertainment.

The action opens at the Grand Central station with a rube touched for his leather as he gets off the train. As the crowd gathers to hear his tale Meighan is among them. He follows the cop and the victim to the stationhouse, and after the latter's "squeal" is booked he takes him out to find a hotel. The old man's actions are so pitiful that Meighan finally turns over the wallet which he "lost," and on the strength of the old man's recital of country life he decides to "go straight" and get back to the soil.

As a peddler of soap he hits a small town and makes good to the extent of being offered a job in the local real estate and insurance office. As he is making his way, having fallen in love with the niece of the old colonel where he is boarding, one of his former crook companions turns up in the guise of an evangelist to "do the town good." The hero is between the devil and the deep blue as to whether he will let an old pal operate or protect those who have lately been his friends. He works this out satisfactorily and, incidentally, the small-town crook for whom he has been working is caught with the goods.

Pauline Starke plays the lead opposite, getting a country girl characterization over in nice shape. Charles Ogle as the old colonel scores.

The story is cleverly developed, with Tom Forman staging a corking fight scene between Tom Kennedy and Meighan in a barroom scene. The slum stuff in New York is rather well done for studio work. *Fred.*

SON OF THE WOLF

R-C northwestern feature, with a squawman theme, written by Jack London and directed by Norman Dawn. Five-reeler with Wheeler Oakman featured.

Scruff Mackenzie..........Wheeler Oakman
Chook-Ra.......................Edith Roberts
Father Roubeau......................Sam Allen
Ben Harrington..................Ashley Cooper
Malemute Kid.......................Fred Kohler
Chief Thling Tinner.......Thomas Jefferson

This Robertson-Cole feature is a little different than the average run of northwestern features as far as story is concerned. This one, authored by Jack London, is a saleable product for the exhibitor. The London name is the biggest box office asset. As far as action goes, it has all the usual snow stuff, the dog teams, a couple of fights and, of course, a dance hall scene. It is a picture, however, that will go into any of the daily change of program houses and satisfy fairly well. On Broadway it was at Loew's New York on a double feature bill, with Paramount's "The Spanish Jade" providing the other half of the entertainment.

The London story relates to a pair of gold prospectors in Alaska who return to a small camp after having been snowed in. One has a cabin furnished against the time he should find a wife. The daughter of the chief of a tribe of Indians has had his younger daughter reared from childhood by a priest. It is this girl one miner picks up and she returns his love. He makes a trip to Dawson to buy wedding finery and gifts for her father, but while there falls victim to the wiles of a dance hall girl, with the result that the Indian girl follows him down the trail to win him back. In the end she believes her fight is useless and returns to her tribe, the hero following, and finally bringing her back to civilization as his bride.

Wheeler Oakman is a fairly pleasing hero, while Edith Roberts makes her mark as the little Indian girl. Otherwise the cast contains few worthy of mention, except among the Indian characters. Here Thomas Jefferson as the chief and Fred Stanton as "The Bear" manage to make their respective roles works of distinction. Stanton puts up a great knife fight with the hero in one of the later scenes.

Scenically, the picture contains some very pretty shots, but there are one or two places where the editing is faulty and it should be either clarified by a title or snapped up in cutting. *Fred.*

THE UNDERSTUDY

R-C production, with story by Ethol M. Hadden; scenario by Beatrice Van. Directed by William A. Seiter. Joseph Dubray, photographer. Doris May star of society comedy-drama.

Mary Neil...........................Doris May
Tom Manning..........Wallace MacDonald

A very mild affair is this comedy-drama based on a story that would be second-grade magazine stuff, but with adequate interior settings in which practically all the action takes place. There is scarcely an out-of-doors location except for the passage, rather well done, of a rainstorm at night.

The trouble with the story is that it is based on the deception. The heroine gains entrance into the rich man's home under a dishonorable pretext, then develops untold beauties of character and thereby wins the love of the young millionaire. The two things don't go well together. It's all very well for the girl to undertake the masquerade in the first place, but thereafter it is difficult to accept the genuineness of her nobility. The other characters are pure fiction, especially the comedy father, who schemes to get his son married off to the masquerading actress. Otis Harlan shines at broad comedy effects, but in the present case the part is a misfit.

The best comedy role is held by Arthur Hoyt, as a decadent, sissified society "tame cat," played with a good deal of finesse. Wallace MacDonald is the young hero, played in rather too emphatic a key. The reality of the personage seldom registers. Always he is a film actor intent upon his pose.

Perhaps it is unfair to require any of the players to support a real illusion in a play so thoroughly theatrical, although Doris May, whose part is the most unreal of all, comes nearest to securing an effect of actuality.

Mary Neil is persuaded to impersonate a chorus girl who has ensnared a young millionaire, visiting his father's office to receive a check in settlement of the chorus girl's claim on the young man. The father is impressed with Mary's gentility, and requires that she come and live in his home in order that he may determine whether she will be a desirable daughter-in-law, the son meanwhile having packed off to Montana.

Mary wins her way into the affections of the elder couple, and the father becomes a schemer for a match with his son. He goes so far as to trick the young people to the marriage license bureau and a justice of the peace, and then hurries them by auto to a remote mountain cottage, where they are stranded until a new suitor, unaware of the marriage, comes in pursuit of Mary. The young people borrow his machine without his consent and return through a raging storm to the city, but their adventure has brought them really together, and the closeup shows them contentedly slumbering in the home armchair, exhausted by their journey. *Rush.*

SIE UND DIE DREI

Berlin, July 7.

"She and the Three," a five-reel film comedy, Ufa; scenario by Max Jungk and Julius Urgiss; directed by E. A. Dupont; interiors by Ludwig Kainer; photography by Helmar Lerski; first showing at the Ufa Palast am Zoo, June 23.

This farce, in which Henny Porten is the featured player, has besides her in its cast some 20 comedians, all with a reputation in Berlin, many stars. The following names will mean something to anybody who knows the German theatre ever so slightly: Hermann Thimig, Jacob Tiedtke, Hermann Picha, Oscar Sabo, Paul Graetz, Curt Vespermann, Blandine Ebinger, Hermann Vallentin, Leonhard Haskel, Max Adelburt, Hns Wssmnn, Willi Schaeffers, Carl Geppert, Anton Herrnfeld, Franz Gross, Paul Westermeier and Senta Soeneland.

From an advertising point of view, this has some worth, but the unfailing effect is to diminish the fun in proportion to the number of funmakers. Really effective humor anywhere out of variety or the revue (and here also the merely incidental is never the biggest laugh getter), really effective humor is culminative and builds itself on planted character or situation. But to get 20 Topsies into "Uncle Tom" or 20 "famous comedians" into one five-reeler you must of necessity leave them all merely sketches without vitality. And so it was.

The scenario remains merely a piece of manufactured goods. "She," a famous picture star, is besieged by suitors; she flees to a seaside resort to escape them. There follows her the "gentle one" (Der Sanfte), carrying with him a testimonial from a society of admirers of the film star. He tries vainly to get her, and at last, in desperation, steals the key to her hotel room and goes in. There she finds him, and, believing him a thief, raises a hue and cry. But he escapes. At the seashore she also makes the acquaintance of the president of the Vice Commission and a mysterious fat individual. On her return to the city the "gentle one" happens into her compartment in the train, and she, believing him to be a robber, pulls the alarm signal and the train stops. But again he escapes.

Then studio scenes showing the taking of a film called the "Child Murderess," in which "She" is being starred. Then "She" is arrested on the charge of having stopped a train without cause. A trial scene in court follows, in which the attorneys she has engaged to defend her do so badly she throws herself on the mercy of the jury, asking to be defended from her defenders. She gets a large fine or five days in jail; refuses to pay the fine and goes to jail.

There it turns out that the mysterious fat individual she met at the beach is the warden. He falls for her and has her cell elaborately redecorated. A party is given which all the prisoners attend. At length she gets permission to take scenes for her film in the courtyard of the prison, using the prisoners as supers. Meantime the "gentle one" has been learning pickpocketing in order to get into prison with her; he succeeds just in time to spoil the beheading scene, he believing it real. "She" captures him, but, on finding out that he is a count, accepts his offer of marriage.

The chief trouble with the above story is that it isn't funny, either from caption or action. It is suffering from the two diseases which beset almost all modern German production—over-looseness of the purse strings and Americanitis. The second requires some explanation. The best quality of German film of two years ago was an attempt to take a story of some reality and to carry it through consistently to its final conclusions; technically, there was much to be desired in the way of continuity, lighting, etc. Today the German has seen the American film and accepted, not its tremendous technical advances, but its machine-made, inconsistent character and plot development—in other words, the very things that have given the American film industry its big setback.

When will they learn that the way to make a good international film is to make a "good" film, not a bad imitation of an American picture?

This film is further handicapped by the casting of Henny Porten for the leading role; although a fine dramatic star, her comedy is as heavy as Thompson's pie crust. From the rest of the cast Hermann Thimig stands out as the "Sanfte" with nothing to do; he should have been a star long ago. Jacob Tiedke, Paul Graetz and Leonhard Haskel should also be mentioned. *Trask.*

TENSE MOMENTS FROM PLAYS

London, July 7.

This new Master Films series, one reel adaptations of famous plays, suffers from the same cause as do the other series. An attempt is made to cram too much material into far too small a space.

The chief attraction is Sybil Thorndyke's appearance as a film artist. Her voice, and the author's spoken word are missing, and as a mime she is inclined to sadly overact.

The series comprises "The Merchant of Venice," "Bleak House," "Jane Shore," "The Lady of the Camelias," "The Scarlet Letter," and "The Hunchback of Notre Dame."

In most of these the production work is excellent, although the producer has not been particularly careful in the detail of his periods. The sets are generally good and there is some beautiful exterior work in "The Scarlet Letter."

Beyond the "star," women have little to do, but the men are good: Booth Conway, Harry Worth, Annesley Hely, Ward McAllister, Ivan Berlin, Dick Webb and Tony Fraser. Several were well-known provincial legitimate players before the smash came. These little features will make good fillups. *Gore.*

YOUTH TO YOUTH

London, July 5.

"Youth to You," a film made by the Skandia Co. of Stockholm and released by Ideal, is exceptional in its human interest and artistic treatment. The action takes place in a Norwegian village during the sixteenth century. Story and setting are simplicity itself.

The first portion is pure comedy. Sofren, a young student, is on his way with his sweetheart, Mari, to compete with other clerics for a living which has become vacant through the late pastor's death. If successful he can marry. His humor when addressing the congregation as against the morbid ranting and solemnity of his opponents, wins the day.

All is well until the late pastor's widow seizes on an old law and announces her intention of holding to her right to marry her husband's successor. She is very old, but Sofren, being well primed with liquor, consents to the marriage and takes his sweetheart with him as his sister. Eventually the old widow learns the truth, forgives the deception, and treats Sofren and Mari as her children until she dies and is laid to rest beside her husband.

The acting is exceptional, especially on the part of Hildur Carlberg, who unfortunately died just after she had completed the film. *Gore.*

A SPORTING DOUBLE

London, July 6.

This Granger-Davidson sporting picture, made under the direction of Arthur Rooke, is excellent dramatic fare. The story is a good dramatic one, well told, and carefully leavened with wholesome humor.

Its big pull rests in the sporting scenes, the Derby, the Cup Final match, the big football event of the year here. Of these, the Derby, like all other horse-racing scenes in British pictures, gives little that is new. Racing scenes are as frequent in British films as cabarets in America, and they possess the same similarity. Having seen one you have seen the lot, although something new is perpetually being promised.

Throughout this feature the production work is excellent as is the photography.

Will Blunt, who holds an important job in his father's business, neglects his work through love of sport and is fired, his enemy, Phillip Hardy, stepping into his shoes. He loves Eileen Grimshaw and her father says that as soon as he comes to him with £1,000 he can have her. He meets a friend, a race-horse trainer, who tells him that one of his horses, Captain Cuttle, is sure to win the Derby and offers him a job in the stables so that he can help to train the winner. Will sees his chance of getting the money which will bring Eileen to him and promptly makes a double bet of £1,000 to £10—the town of Huddersfield to win the Football Cup and Captain Cuttle to win the Derby. Meanwhile, the rascally Hardy is laying siege to Eileen and threatening by proving that he committed a robbery at his father's office to send him to prison unless she marries him.

Terrified, Eileen agrees to break her engagement, but writes Will she is only doing so until his innocence is proved.

Meanwhile a little servant girl at the stables has fallen in love with Will. Her name is Aurora and out of pure kindheartedness Will is good to her. Aurora is responsible for foiling an attempt to get at the favorite, for which Hardy is responsible. Pursued by Will, the rascal jumps from a bridge onto a moving barge and Will follows. A terrific fight follows in which Will is victorious even to the point of making his enemy admit his villainy. The historic race is won by Captain Cuttle and Will and Eileen reach their predestined filmic end.

It is all sheer sporting melodrama, but the story is interesting and the producer has been able to use scenes of Huddersfield actually winning the Cup and of Captain Cuttle doing the same with the Derby.

The picture will not be a draw outside Great Britain and its great appeal will be in the midlands and north where football takes precedence over everything. The acting is quite good, although the cast includes no big names. This is one of the films to be released under the direction of the British National Film League. *Gore.*

A FOOL THERE WAS

The second screen production by William Fox of the Porter Emerson Browne play founded on the Kipling poem, "The Vampire." Directed by Emmett J. Flynn.

Gilda Fontaine................Estelle Taylor
John Schuyler................Lewis Stone
Mrs. Schuyler................Irene Rich
Muriel Schuyler................Muriel Dana
Nell Winthrop................Marjorie Daw
Tom Morgan............Mahlon Hamilton
Avery Parmelee......Wallace MacDonald
Boggs....................William V. Mong
Parks....................Harry Lonsdale

Back in 1915 William Fox released a feature picture under the title of "A Fool There Was," and introduced to the public Theda Bara, than whom as a vamp there was none vampier. It was the beginning of vamp types on the screen, a vogue, although considerably lessened in its appeal, still obtaining in the silent drama.

This week at the Strand William Fox is again presenting "A Fool There Was," remade under the direction of Emmett J. Flynn, according to the new plans and specifications as laid down to meet requirements of the various censor boards throughout the country. This "Fool There Was" seems entirely censor proof at present and still retains a corking wallop. It looks like a 100 per cent. picture on title for the box office and still retains the required entertainment value to please.

In the 1922 version of "A Fool" Fox introduces a new vamp for the part in Gilda Fontaine (Estelle Taylor), and the manner in which she ensnares John Schuyler (Lewis Stone) and her treatment of him shows she has been informed of all the tricks of the trade of "gittin' 'em and holdin' 'em." This girl is there as a vamp. If she had started after this style of part in the old days, there is no telling who would have come out on top, she or Theda. Of course, Theda was the voluptuous type of beauty, while Estelle is rather the slightly matured flapper type. Lewis Stone as the fool gave a corking performance, and if recollection serves right, it outshines the interpretation originally given on the screen by Edouard Jose.

The cast surrounding these two players is one that contains names that should draw, including Irene Rich, who stands out as the wife, while Marjorie Daw as the sister registers. Mahlon Hamilton, Wallace MacDonald, William V. Mong and Harry Lonsdale complete the cast.

In direction Mr. Flynn carried the action along at a pace that compelled interest. However, in detail he overlooked one bet—shooting Mahlon Hamilton at full length. No director should do that with this particular actor, for in every scene he entered in this picture a peculiarity of throwing one of his feet in a rather stumbling walk distracted the attention to that one mannerism. Otherwise Flynn didn't overlook a single bet to drive home the punches.

The boat scenes were particularly good, and the matching up of the New York skyline and the big Cunarder sailing was done perfectly.

It's a picture that will get money.

Fred.

MAN UNCONQUERABLE

Jesse L. Lasky presents the five-reel melodrama of the South Sea Islands, story by Hamilton Smith, scenario by Julien Josephson, directed by Joseph Henabery. Paramount production, supervised by Thompson Buchanan. Jack Holt starred. At the Rivoli this week.

Robert Kendall..........Jack Holt
Rita Durand..........Sylvia Breamer
Nilson..........Clarence Burton
Duenna..........Ann Schaeffer
Perrier..........Jean De Briac
Ricardo..........Edwin Stevens
Governor of Papeete..........Willard Louis

The picture has a lot of picturesque adventure stuff, but it falls down in its romantic aspect. The love story is entirely incidental as though it came as an afterthought to the main interest of film hand-to-hand battles between the Yankee hero and the foreign plotters. These battles really grow out of the rivalries of two pearl concessionaires with headquarters on a small island in the China sea, and the interest of the woman in the contest is subordinated. Of course, the romance should be the basis of the combat rather than its side issue. Probably it is this that weakens the story.

As an adventure tale the production has a powerful kick. One is the fight on the beach between a brawny seaman and the American heir to the pearling rights, as well staged a passage of film fisticuffs as has been screened lately. Another is a fight at sea between a crew of a pearling boat and the American hero, who goes against them single-handed in a small launch and sinks the larger craft with a machine gun.

The adventure story grows up to a smashing climax in a running fight between the hero and his enemies that must take up the whole thrilling fifth reel. Things move swiftly during this lengthy passage, with the fortunes first on one side and then the other uppermost, and the affair is first-rate theatrical melodrama. A novelty of the picture is that it employs most of the familiar situations associated with South Sea Island adventure, but instead of the people being rough and ready in appearance the men are marvels of sartorial perfection and the women wear the new st frocks from Paris. It's rather a shock to see a South Seas hero in knife-edge flannels and **the heroine in a dressmaker's dream. As far as the outward aspect of the people is concerned the whole affair might have happened in Bar Harbor during the season. Perhaps owners of pearl concessionaires comport themselves thus, but it is a shock to the orthodox film fan. Jack Holt is especially out of his element in this tailor-made atmosphere.**

The settings are neatly counterfeited and carry conviction, while the natives contribute to the picturesqueness of the story. One incident has a pearl diver going down in a diver's kit with a lot of interesting detail.

The story deals with the adventures of Robert Kendall of "Broad street and Gramercy square," who comes to the island to take over the pearl business of a deceased uncle. He finds his crews in mutiny. They have poached in the waters of a rival pearler, one Ricardo, and have robbed him of a collection of fabulously precious rose pearls.

On Robert's arrival, Nillson, leader of his own crews, is trying to dispose of the stolen jewels to a scheming trader who pretends to Ricardo's friendship. First Robert has to knock out Nillson in a spectacular fist fight. Then when Nillson goes into Ricardo's employ has to solve the mystery of the stolen pearls, which are returned to Ricardo. Nillson murders Ricardo to get them back and Robert is accused of the crime. He tracks the plotters to their hiding place and catches them in the act of dividing the spoils, but himself is captured. The heroine comes looking for him and is taken captive just as Robert escapes. From that on to the finale all the melodramatic tricks in the trade are employed to keep the shift of fortunes moving from one side to the other. They fight through underground passages, where first one side and then the other seems in reach of victory, and use every implement of combat from wine bottles to automatics until the climax justifies the hero. It's all very obvious **fiction, but in a naive way it is highly effective.**

Rush.

WOMEN MEN FORGET

Mollie King is starred in this United, presented by Hi Mark Film Sales Corporation. Miss King looks adorable, acts convincingly and charmingly, and has the honor of playing a human role in one of those rarities, a plausible and reasonable film story.

It is the old combination—the wife, the husband and the wife's best friend. With the exception of some strident vamp stuff, a touch overdone by Lucy Fox toward the end, it is intensely thrilling and believable in its simple unfolding of a triangle that everybody past seven knows of in every day life.

There isn't much to tell beyond that. No shots are fired, no melodramatic "punch" is offered, but the whole picture is easy to take and can be taken in the theatre and out into the home without a blush or an apology. Miss King's appeal is necessary to the plain composition, for she conveys a sympathetic quality that is wholesome and never maudlin. She convinced into enthusiastic approval a cynic who had never before seen her on the screen, but who judged her capabilities from musical shows in which she had been a light, fluffy ingenue. Miss King is an actress of talent and depth and superfine good taste. In a big role she will surprise those who are not already "sold" on her.

Frank Mills, as a friend who almost develops into a lover, was conventional; Edward Langford, as the husband, played excellently. John M. Stahl directed with extraordinary tact and dramatic sense of the best sort.

The cast is small in the main, but the shots are impressive enough to carry the "importance," and the story and Miss King will do the rest to make "Women Men Forget" an upstanding program release across the map.

Lait.

THE HALF BREED

Oliver Morosco production in six reels released by First National. Adapted from the stage play by Morosco. Continuity and direction by Charles Taylor.

Delmar Spavinaw..........Wheeler Oakman
Doll Pardeau..........Ann May
Evelyn Huntington..........Mary Anderson
Ross Kennion..........Hugh Thompson
Dick Kennion..........King Evers
Judge Huntington..........Joseph Dowling

Oliver Morosco returned to the picture producing field last year and made two screen productions. This is one. It has taken months of time to try to straighten out the picture to get it into shape for the screen, and finally it has been released but in such shape that it can hardly be said that it is a picture a pre-release full-week stand should play. In the daily change houses or in the theatres where it is presented in conjunction with vaudeville it will get by, but that is about all. The production has Wheeler Oakman as the star with a fair supporting cast. Charles Taylor directed and supplied the continuity, making a rather poor job of both as far as the results on the screen are concerned.

The story has to do with an educated half breed Indian who tries to win the affections of a society girl. The action is in the southwest, which gives a chance for range atmosphere and a corking cattle stampede. Lots of gun play and intrigue, but the story goes along aimlessly.

Wheeler Oakman in the title role gives a rather fair performance, but it is Ann May who runs away with the honors of the picture. She is a snappy little ingenue type, and although the better role of two was handed to Mary Anderson, Miss May outshines her.

In photography the picture is decidedly off, and there is a lot to be desired in the way of lighting. Hilation is visible in practically all of the scenes.

The cutting and editing of the picture also is rather badly handled, but it is likewise evident that whoever did this job had a mighty difficult task to get even the poor result that is shown.

Fred.

WORLDLY MADONNA

Harry Garson production, with Clara Kimball Young. States right picture.

Janet } Lucy }..........Clara Kimball Young
John McBride..........Wm. P. Carleton

Highly improbable story in which Clara Kimball Young plays a double role. The production was directed by Harry Garson, also sponsor for the feature. While not strong enough for a week in the better class pre-release houses, it nevertheless is a feature that will get by in most localities. There is an angle to the story that may offend in some territories where there is a particularly strong Catholic element.

Miss Young plays the dual role of twin sisters. One is a nun and the other a cabaret star. The latter is a drug addict and seriously wounds an admirer with a pistol. She believes that she has killed him. In fear of jail she goes to her sister in the convent and begs her to change places with her. This the sister does. That is the point where the story is highly improbable, and, incidentally, the point that might offend some of the Catholics in an audience.

The nun wears the erring sister's clothes, and is arrested for the crime. She is in jail until the man recovers, and he, being a politician, uses his influence to have her set free. Then another complication arises. The proprietor of the cabaret in which the sister appeared insists that she return there to work, under the pain of exposing another shooting affray that occurred earlier on the night that the politician was wounded.

The complications are cleared up and the nun goes back to the convent, while the former cabaret girl becomes engaged to the man she shot.

Were the story not so unbelievable the picture would have been a corker from the standpoint of direction, sets and photography. As it is, however, it is just a good program picture.

Fred.

WONDERFUL CHANCE

Selznick reissue, about two years old, with Eugene O'Brien as star. Rodolph Valentino featured. Written by H. H. Van Loan and directed by George Archainbaud.

Swagger Barlow } Lord Birmingham }..........Eugene O'Brien
Red Dugan..........Tom Blake
Joe Klingsby..........Rudolph de Valentino
Haggerty..........Joe Flanagan
Parker Winton..........Warren Cook
Peggy Winton..........Martha Mansfield

The reason for this reissue now by Selznick is that Rodolph Valentino appeared in it and at the time that the picture was made worked under the name of Rudolph de Valentino. Selznick has gotten out special paper for the reissue on which O'Brien is starred and Valentino featured in type equally as prominent. At that the picture is a fairly good one and has some real splendid double exposure photography, showing O'Brien in a dual role. It looks as though it was good for a single day here and there in the daily change houses.

The story is of a crook turned out of Sing Sing trying to go straight. A pal is wounded on a "job" and the crook turns one last trick. Through dear old coincidence he is mistaken for Lord Birmingham, a newly arrived Englishman, **and ushered into his apartment at the Ritz. The real nobleman was kidnaped on his arrival from abroad by a gang headed by Valentino, who is figuring on doing the impersonating personally.**

O'Brien plays Barlow and Lord Birmingham. The former in the guise of the latter is entertained at a summer place and falls in love with the daughter of the house. She returns the feeling. Valentino and his band, when they find they cannot pull one trick, decide to turn off the house, but are frustrated by Barlow, who discovers his pal in on the job. This pal gives him the low-down on the situation, and he goes to the hide-away and takes the place of the real nobleman, making a stipulation that the girl should not know who was who. But the crooks who wish to expose the imposter who spoiled their game take Barlow, believing him to be His Lordship, back to the scene, and then the expose occurs.

It's hokum, as far as the story is concerned, and full of improbable situations, but will do in the smaller places. *Fred.*

THE TROUPER

Universal five-reeler starring Gladys Walton, From the original story by A. P. Younger, directed by Henry B. Harris.

Mamie Judd.................Gladys Walton
Herman Jenks.................Jack Perrin
Frank Kramer.............Thomas Holding
Irene LaRue............Kathleen O'Connor
Neal Selden..................Roscoe Karns
Warren Selden...............Tom D. Guise
Mrs. Selden................Florence D. Lee
Mary Lee.....................Mary Philbin
Minnie Brown...................Mary True

A feature based on theatrical life with a barnstorming troupe of actors as the principal characters. If the acting the troupe contributes on the screen was of the standard the troupe delivered in the barns they played, then it is no wonder that they were on the verge of stranding.

The feature is presented by Universal with Gladys Walton as the star, written by A. P. Younger, and Harry B. Harris directed. Last week it was utilized on Broadway for a double feature bill at Loew's New York, with the audience giving it the laugh. The picture is played straight, but it would have been a far more marketable product had it been kidded and jazzed in the titles.

The story is that of a drudge with the company who finally turns out the heroine in a real situation. The company is playing a tank town where the leading lady starts to vamp the son of the local banker, a souse. She gets the boy to try to turn off the bank for her, but he goes only half way, and the heavy who acts as leading man and manager of the show, takes the keys from the youngster and turns the job himself. As he and the leading woman are about to make their getaway the kid is the cause of their being captured.

There is naught about the picture that could recommend it to any except the smaller daily change neighborhood houses. *Fred.*

HOPE

One of the series of Triart two-reel productions supposed to be relating the story of famous paintings. This one is based on the work of the famous painter, George F. Watts, which bears the same title as the film. Directed by Lejaren a'Hiller.

Lighthouse Keeper.............W. J. Gross
His daughter, Joan.............Mary Astor
Pierre......................Ralph Faulkner
Andre.........................Fred Gamble
Michel.......................Regan Stewart

This two-reeler has a brief prolog, introducing the character of the artist who painted "Hope," a model, who, discouraged with life, appeals to him for aid. He relates to her the story of how "Hope" came to be painted.

It is an engrossing little tale of Breton life, replete with dramatic qualities. The daughter of a lighthouse keeper loves and marries a fisherman. After he goes to sea a child is born; then a series of mishaps occur.

The girl's father dies; she is accused of neglect of the lighthouse, and finally her mother-in-law turns from her.

But through this adversity she retains hope, even on the day when her husband's fishing boat is sighted off short and afire. The rescuers who put off in a long boat return without her man, but she still retains that one bit of faith that he will return, and this he does.

The picture is very well done in story and direction and should prove an interesting short subject. *Fred.*

THREE BUCKAROOS

If this thing is meant seriously, it is a joke; if it is a joke, this thing is serious.

A Balshofer and one of the silliest Westerns ever conceived, with enough shots wasted to upset three Mexican governments, and one pretty girl, Peggy O'Dare, to give it flashes of interest. Miss O'Dare could interest anyone, any time. She is a beauty, with dimples that could steal a throne. And the riding is furious and amusing. But that story!

The Buckaroos are three idiots on horseback who have sworn for some unintelligible reason to serve the right and down the villains. The villains in this picture could have been downed by a Connecticut school teacher. But the Buckaroos rode a million miles and shot off a ton of blanks before they made it.

The story is absurd and the audience at Loew's Circle snickered and sneered aloud. The intellect of a three-year-old girl would have rebelled against this balderdash.

Should be cut to two reels, with comedy titles, and released as a burlesque on the oldest type of Western God-awfuls. *Lait.*

THE PALEFACE

This Buster Keaton two-reel comedy, released by First National, presents the comedian in a more or less laughable role. The picture, however, is not equal in real laughs to some of the others in which he has appeared.

Keaton is a big chaser who is captured by a band of Indians, tied to a stake and has a fire built under him. Asbestos clothes, however, save him from burning, and the savages think that he must be a god. They take him into the tribe as Little Chief Paleface. As such he manages to save the tribe from being trimmed by a bunch of oil well grafters.

There is a lot of chase stuff in the picture, with Keaton delivering a flock of falls and tumbles. A bit of business with him tied to the stake, he moving it from place to place as the Indians pile the brush to start a fire, is laughable.

As a filler it will get by, but it isn't strong enough to stand up without a fairly good feature with it on the bill. *Fred.*

THE KICK-BACK

First F. B. O. release starring Harry Carey. Usual western type. Story by star adapted by George Edwards-Hall, directed by Val Paul. Presented by P. A. Powers at the Capitol, New York.

White Horse Harry...............Harry Carey
Arron Price................Henry B. Walthall
Chalk Eye...............Charles J. LeMoyne
Phil Harris.......................Vester Pegg
Ramon Pinellos.................James O'Neill
Conchita Pinellos.....................Mignonne
Nellie.........................Ethel Grey Terry

While it may be flattering to Harry Carey as a star to have the first of his productions to be released through the F. B. O. (Robertson-Cole) shown at the Capitol, New York, it does not look like good business on the part of the distributors of the picture to place it there. It is putting Carey, who has always been a consistent money maker in a certain type of houses, into competition with the best in films, and even while that best is none too good at present, Carey in this present production does not profit by the comparison. He has made better pictures than the current offering, in the past with Universal.

"The Kick Back" is one of those pictures that undoubtedly make good with the Carey fans in the popular priced houses where they have a daily change of program, but it hasn't the class or speed for Broadway and the week run houses. That was reflected in the Capitol's business the first day of the week when the picture was shown.

The story is a western with Carey as the cowboy hero. He is about to marry one of the waitresses in the only restaurant in a little cow town. He owns a ranch and the only water hole for miles around. Others have their eye on the girl and the ranch and they frame him, so that he'll get into trouble with the Mexican authorities when he goes out to perform a job for the schemers, bringing horses across the border for them. The papers that they supply him are forged and the Mexicans are tipped off in advance. The result is that he is captured after he has killed one of the Mexes and sentenced to be shot. He escapes and returns to his home, to discover, meantime his ranch has been located on by others and his girl's mind poisoned against him. He goes out after one of the schemers and beats him up, with a feud declared which results in a shooting affray a few hours later. Harry gets his man but the law gets Harry and there is going to be a lynching in the town when the Rangers arrive and save him.

The next shot shows the happy ending. A man who has committed murder on two sides of the border evidently goes free because he gets married.

It's a thin story at the best and while the direction is fairly good at times it cannot save the tale or the continuity.

There is one thing the picture discloses, a girl who looks as though she is going to make her mark in pictures. Programed simply as Mignonne, she looks like a find in the role of a little Mexican girl. *Fred.*

MYSTERIES OF INDIA

Paramount feature presented by the Hamilton Theatre Corporation; distributed through Famous-Players. Directed by J. May.

Princess Savitri..................Erna Morena
Prince Ayan.....................Conrad Veidt
The Yogi....................Bernhard Gotzke
Myrra ....Lia de Putty
Carl Sargland........................Olaf Fonss
Laura Valmy...........................Mia May
Robert Allen.....................Paul Richter

The "Mistress of the World" series was generally supposed to have ended delving into foreign mystery melo-dramatic films. But with the release of this one it seems somebody is a bear for punishment and wants the film fans in on it. This picture, understood to have been made in Germany, holds many a similarity to its named predecessor, including lavish settings, improbable escapes from situation after situation, mediocre direction surmounted by a scenario emphatic in placing the leading cast members under perilous difficulties and extricating them through the means of a religious fanatic embodied with supernatural power.

Photography predominates as the most worthy asset. There are numerous callings for trick stuff (none of which hasn't been seen before) with the camera and showing occasional scenic exteriors of note with the best of the magi "shots" happening when the girl walks through a den of tigers, supposedly protected by him of the highpowered eyes. The cats are within a yard or two and then back away. Beyond that, the film simply grinds along to its finish minus any qualities making an audience care much just what happens. It incidentally chased a few patrons out of the initial afternoon show at the Rialto.

The story revolves around a pledge of friendship entered into by two Englishmen and the Prince of Eshnapur, while attending college. The picture's start has the Prince as a jealous husband of a wife, infatuated with one of the bonded trio, Robert Allen, now stationed in India. The remaining member is an architect living in Switzerland. Action starts when the head of the realm discovers the affair between his wife and friend, whereupon he decides to bury his wife alive, meanwhile calling forth the Yogi who buried himself before a temple and has been in a religious trance for weeks, to aid him in seeking something new in revenges. The most suitable choice is the burying of the wife alive, hence sending for the third member of the triumvirate who is to build a massive tomb as his donation towards upholding the pledge.

The "catch" comes with the designer also being tied with a financee who traces his mysterious departure from Switzerland to Eshnapur, where the Prince grabs her as a hostage when the boy friend refuses to build and carry out the prescribed happy burial thought. At the same time, members of the palace are chasing the odd angle of the threesome with orders to bring him in alive so that he won't miss any of the festivities to come.

The Yogi evidently sees no percentage in continuing under contract to a guy with such intentions. He switches his Conan Doyle influence to the opposition, and has sufficient to protect the engaged couple from harm, but makes no effort to save Allen when he is shown the way out through the tiger emporium. Which also takes both characters out of the picture and allows for not a bad brief bit of camera work in the attack of the animal upon the man.

The finale arrives when the architect and his fiancee frame to save the wife and get away over the mountains, where the inevitable pass-and-only-way-out is encountered. This scene has the man carrying the wife of the Prince over a rope bridge, with the other woman cutting the strands after they cross and just as the pursuers arrive. Whereupon the Princess casts one look at her master, decides there's been enough excitement on her account and takes a dive over the cliff.

The final dimming out had the Prince reduced to a beggar, either because of the incident or the price his former pal quoted on the tomb, which is finally built. The engaged couple coming down the steps stop to look the bedraggled figure that was once a Prince, shaking their heads while registering an "it's tough" expression. Mayhaps a fitting climax.

Whatever chance the picture will have is not enhanced by the title, which suggests a travelog or something on that order. Watching it will certainly not improve the impression.

With the scarcity of features this

summer and the mid-season's heat, it may have been thought feasible just at this time, to insert this foreigner into the Rialto, on the presumption that the smaller towns which in a way stood for "The Mistress of the World" in its several dull parts, will take this one, whole, in five reels and pay for it, on the further presumption it didn't cost much in the first place to bring over.

Skig.

HURRICANE'S GAL

Allen Holubar feature, with Dorothy Phillips starred. Adapted from Harvey Gates' story by Holubar, who directed. At the New York Strand, July 23.

Lola	Dorothy Phillips
Steele O'Connor	Robert Ellis
Chris Borg	Wallace Beery
Cap'n Danny	James O. Barrows
Phyllis Fairfield	Gertrude Astor
Sing	William Fong
Lieut. Grant	Jack Donovan
Mrs. Fairfield	Frances Raymond

Deep-sea melodrama with a whirlwind finish after a rather quiet start. Allen Holubar has packed an amazing amount of screen thrills into the second half of the picture, which promises to be a notable summer release on the First National list. Its only defect is that one common to adapted novels—it has two stories. From the opening to the fight with the revenue cutter is a pretty complete story. From the beginning of the action in San Francisco to the end is another.

But things move so swiftly toward the end that one forgets the story in absorption in the incidents. Some are rather hard to swallow, such as the swift conquest of the hard-boiled girl sailor by the stowaway and her sudden transition later to the ownership of a San Francisco gambling palace, but one hasn't time to object to these liberties with plausibilities. There's too much that's interesting happening on the screen.

The story opens on the three-masted schooner "Tahiti Belle," from Hong Kong to San Francisco, Capt. Danny in command, under the owner, Lola, daughter of the deceased Hurricane, one-time smuggler and hero of a thousand crimes on the high seas. Steele O'Connor, who later turns out to be a secret service man tracking smugglers, is a stowaway, and is almost drowned in a leaky compartment of the ship. On his release he is turned over to the brutal mate and well battered about until he fights back and knocks a few of the rough crew, including the mate, for a goal. At the same time Lola grows to love the stranger. All this deep stuff is interesting and includes a great deal of scenic beauty, in addition to the familiar rough-and-ready fighting associated with screen sailing ships.

Reaching San Francisco with a contraband cargo, the "Tahiti Belle" tries to slip through, but is checked by a waiting revenue cutter. A gorgeous fight ensues, in which Steele lines up on the revenue men's side and discloses himself as a secret service man. Somebody throws a firebrand into one of the hatches, and the ship burns to the water (probably a model was used for the purpose, but the trick was nicely turned).

Lola escapes and takes refuge in her San Francisco gambling place, another legacy from the late Hurricane, there to plot vengeance against the traitorous Steele, who, it transpires, is engaged to a society queen. Lying in port is the "Samoa Belle," sister ship to the "Tahiti Belle," and the property of Lola. She schemes to kidnap the society queen and take her to the South Seas in revenge.

Here's where the picture goes into high. The "Samoa Belle" gets to sea with Steele's fiancee before the revenue man learns of the plot. He puts a real navy destroyer on the trail, while he gives a chase in a navy hydroplane. Just out of port the same brutal mate (vividly played by Wallace Beery) decides to seize the two women and sail away to a desert isle in the China Sea, there to establish a kingdom. The women are trussed up and locked in separate cabins, and the mate goes below to attack Lola just as the black smoke of the destroyer and the roar of the aeroplane get into the picture.

The crew gives battle to the plane with anti-aircraft guns. A seeker of screen thrills will get an eyeful when the plane turns over half a mile in the air and does what has every appearance of a nose dive into the sea. This bit has a powerful kick and apparently is on the level as far as the plane plunge is concerned. The crew concentrates its fire on Steele in the water, but is distracted by the arrival of the destroyer, unquestionably a sure-enough government craft.

The destroyer comes alongside the "Samoa," with gobs and lawless smugglers fighting hand to hand in a highly realistic combat. The warcraft edges in until the gobs can leap aboard the schooner. Rough and tumble all over the decks, an exceedingly spectacular screen battle. These are the high lights, and they make a whale of a finish to an exciting picture. The swift chain of events starts with a storm at sea after the "Samoa Belle" has put to sea. This is perhaps the first time a deep-sea storm has been adequately screened. It may have been studio tank trickery, but the illusion of a terrifying storm at sea was complete and it delivered one of the biggest thrills of the thrillsome picture.

The production, particularly in its second half, stands out like a lighthouse among the summer releases.

Rush.

BORDERLAND

A Paramount five-reel feature with Agnes Ayres starred. Story by Beulah Marie Dix; directed by Paul Powell. Presented by Adolph Zukor at the Rivoli, New York.

Spirit / Dora Becket / Edith Wayne	Agnes Ayres
James Wayne	Milton Sills
William Becket	Fred Huntley
Francis Vincent	Bertram Grassby
Clyde Meredith	Casson Ferguson
Eileen	Ruby Lafayette
Mrs. Conlon	Sylvia Ashton
Jimty	Frankie Lee
Totty	Mary Jane Irving

A more or less imaginative story that professes to wander into the spirit realms, smacks somewhat of miracle stuff and preaches a sermon. Even with all of its touches of "the other world" there is enough of the materialistic in it to hold attention. But, as with all pictures where the author and director try to carry on three different themes at one time, the action is draggy and this production is no exception to the rule. It is a picture the exhibitor can put over with freaky exploitation, but not in hot weather. It makes an audience think, and the majority of picture house audiences don't want to think; they are more apt to want to forget, especially on the nights when the mercury is headed for the top.

Some money was expended, and the picture is done flashily, but still without heavy sets.

Beulah Marie Dix provided the story, which opens with a peek into the region supposed to separate this world sphere from the Pearly Gates. The region where those that have transgressed the laws of God are punished, and here a poor lost soul is shown wandering in a search, the fulfillment of which is to mark atonement for worldly sins. Back on earth the great-great-granddaughter of the wraith is passing through an experience that about parallels a tragedy occurring 70 years earlier. The spirit is permitted to return to the world to prevent a recurrence, and her success in this purges her of her sins and she is permitted to pass on to the higher sphere.

The modern touch is furnished by a quartet of players. Naturally, Miss Ayres, as she plays three roles, is one; Milton Sills plays opposite, and the others are the young son of the couple and the heavy, played by Casson Ferguson. The star takes the role of a silly young wife who craves outside admiration, which leads her into an affair with her husband's cousin. They plan to elope and she sends the young son to boarding school. On the night the runaway is set for she makes a rendezvous at her former family home. While there the spirit is shown returning to earth, and in an effort to deliver the message of warning a miracle is performed. An old servant who has been a paralytic for years is made to walk and recite to the erring wife the details that occurred years before under similar circumstances. This has the effect of awakening the woman to a realization of her duty toward her son, and she starts to the school where he is, arriving just in time to save him from a fall that would have meant his death. The father also, lonesome for the boy, arrives at the school, and a reconciliation follows.

It's a lot of improbable hoak, but dressed up in a way that a certain class of picture house patronage will like, but it is hardly a knockout picture for full-week runs.

Fred.

DEUCE OF SPADES

Charles Ray production (First National). Scenario made by Richard Andres from the story "Weight of the Last Straw" by the late Charles E. Van Loan. Ray director. Five Reeler.

Amos	Charles Ray
Sally	Marjorie Maurice
Jenkins	Lincoln Plumer
Bouncer	Dick Sutherland
Greasy Joe	J. P. Lockney

The picture is an amusing comedy in the familiar Charles Ray style with wild western settings, except that the usual rough riding is absent and the emphasis is put on the comedy role of the star. It's a good Ray part, strengthened by a multitude of well done Bret Harte types. Averages well in the Ray list for natural, wholesome comedy, centering on the bungling of a boob youth from the east surrounded by mining camp card sharps.

Amos sells out his Boston restaurant and goes to Montana seeking adventure and business opportunity. He stops in a hash house in Little Butte for a meal and is held up and robbed by the discouraged proprietor, who at gun's point makes him sign a bill of sale "to make it legal." Amos makes the best of it and with the aid of Sally the waitress reforms the hash house along Boston lines.

There are several very amusing passages in which Amos tries to marry off Sally to sundry tough characters, unconscious that he loves her himself. In a year Amos has saved enough to make a visit to Boston, but at his first stopping place he is fleeced by a couple of card sharps on the simple "deuce of spades" game—wherein the dealer's confederate pursuades him to bet that the dealer cannot pick the deuce out of the cut and shuffled deck.

Broke, he must go back to Little Butte, but the news of his fall has preceded him. When he gets to his restaurant the local jokers have plastered and festooned the place with deuces of spades and the whole town is laughing at him. He visits the Butte dance hall and is solemnly greeted although the jokesters are bursting with haw haws. Accompanied by suppressed laughter, Amos buys himself the wickedest looking 45s he can get and goes to practicing shooting at a deuce of spades. He can't hit the card from ten yards, but he sticks his finger through the pasteboard and the locals are impressed by the evidence of his marksmanship.

Thus encouraged by an atmosphere of respect that results from his trick, Amos is ready when the same two sharpers who robbed him appear in his restaurant. He holds them up at the point of his new five-shooters, makes them eat sandwiches made out of slices of bread with a deuce of spades between them and forces the return of his bankroll. Thus having established himself in the community as a person not to be trifled with, Amos takes courage and wins the beautiful Sally.

Arthur S. Kane sponsors the production. It is full of the small touches that help. There are numerous amusing character bits and atmospheric angles that contribute greatly to the total effect. Besides which the story is rich in capital comedy material, which has been preserved.

Rush.

FORGET ME NOT

A Louis Burston production in five reels released by Metro. Story by Henry R. Symonds, script by John B. Clymer, directed by W. S. Van Dyke. Presented at the Criterion, New York, for a run.

The Mother	Irene Hunt
The Father	William Machin
The Girl	Bessie Love
The Boy	Gareth Hughes
The Musician	Otto Lederer
The Other Girl	Myrtle Lind
The Dog	Queenie

A corking sob special which, if it is properly handled, may develop into a strong box office weep drama as "Over the Hill" did. It has that particular type of heart appeal sure to please the women, and the chances are the Metro's tie-up in New York with the orphan asylums will help to put over the production. The picture looks strong enough to go into any of the week stand houses and get money if exploited to its full strength by the exhibitor.

The cast is fairly strong, with Bessie Love and Gareth Hughes as the youthful stars of the picture. The two play the roles of orphans who are sweethearts while inmates of an asylum. They are parted when taken to different homes, but in time are reunited.

At the opening of the story the asylum is shown with Miss Love as one of the older inmates acting as a little mother to the other parentless kiddies. The boy (Hughes) and she are the last two youngsters left after a drive to find homes for the youngsters. He is finally adopted by the real mother of the girl, the latter being passed up by all of the child seekers because she is a cripple. Finally a supposed blind musician, who each day would give the kiddies a concert from the other side of the wall of the asylum, discovers her alone and sobbing and hears her story, which causes him to adopt her. In time she develops into a talented violiniste under his tuition and on the night of her initial concert is discovered by the boy.

There is a tremendous quantity of pathos throughout the picture and that will be its greatest appeal.

Fred.

TROOPER O'NEIL

A William Fox five-reel northwestern without snow, with Charles Jones starred. From the story by George Goodchild; script by William K. Howard; directed by C. R. Wallace and Scott Dunlap.

Trooper O'Neil	Charles Jones
Marie	Beatrice Burnham
Pierre	Francis McDonald
Black Flood	Claude Payton
Rodd	Sidney Jordan
Paul	Jack Rollens
Jules Lestrange	Karl Forms

Here is a northwestern mystery screen play that is a corker for suspense. In that regard it is different from the rank and file of northwestern tales in film form; also distinctive because it hasn't a lot of snow scenes. It has the Fox star, Charles Jones, as its principal player, with dainty Beatrice Burnham supporting him. The direction was capably handled by C. R. Wallace and Scott Dunlap. The picture looks good enough to play any of the houses that are running features from one to three days.

There are touches where the detail is slightly overlooked, but the incidents will not be caught by the average film audiences. Also Jones at times is prone to overact, but otherwise he looks like a corking bet for outdoor stuff.

The story is of a trooper of the Canadian Northwest Mounted who is sent out to investigate a murder. A rookie accompanies him. He visits the scene of the crime and makes his deductions, which are to the effect that the person who did the killing was wounded in the right side. Later when he has fallen in love with a girl of the neighborhood and embraces her, he discovers that she is wounded in exactly that spot. He arrests her. While taking her to jail the real culprit makes a dying confession and clears her. Prior, there was in the minds of the audience a doubt as to who really committed the crime. They had four people whom they might suspect, and the picture had them guessing.

That is where the direction counted most. Putting a mystery of this sort over on the film isn't an easy matter.

The opening of the picture has a corking fight in the mountains in which the star and Claude Payton, as the heavy, mix in great style. A couple of other fights also help out. The picture for the greater part is shot in exteriors with the photography fairly good. *Fred.*

THE HARDEST WAY

Society play of feature length made in France by Fannie Ward and marketed in this country by the Joan Film Sales Co. The supporting company appears to be made up of American and French players, including Red McDougall and M. Signoret. Story by Henry Kistenmaeckers. Half of double feature bill at Loew's New York, July 21.

Here is a first-rate exposition of the reason few films of French manufacture reach the American public. It has as its star an American actress of great experience and considerable drawing power, but the picture isn't there. It has breaks that no American director could allow to happen; its action moves haltingly and slowly, and worse than anything else, the story is dull and uninteresting.

The footage is padded out with every known device to eat up celluloid. Action is repeated without apology or reason, and the story development at times moves backward or forward erratically. As an example, just one of the big dramatic passages is approaching, the heroine goes from the steamship saloon to her stateroom, changes her wraps, goes up to the moonlit deck and spends 50 feet or more in looking over the water. Then she returns to her stateroom to change her wraps again and returns to the saloon. The action is mere crude padding. It has no relation to the story and might as well have been cut out in toto. The rest of the picture is filled with the same sort of stuff. There has been no effort to economize interest or footage, and before three reels have been projected the audience is weary.

The photography is technically splendid. So are the sets. But the French makers have not learned that these elements alone do not make a picture for the American market. It takes two reels of stalling and laborious planting to get the tale started at all, and even then nothing happens that could be called vigorous screen action. The picture is just aimless wandering.

The director and author, by way of illustration, couldn't be satisfied with introducing the hero as an American in Paris, but had to explain in detail that he was a banker and had a war record which is disclosed in numerous fade-backs. Everybody else has to be introduced with similar elaboration, and it becomes tiresome.

Ellen Olcott (Miss Ward), beloved by the hero, Jack, is the daughter of an American shipping magnate, and his social intimates are two French ship owners. Along about the middle of reel two it is disclosed that Father Olcott has ruined himself by a passion for gambling. He starts back for America on one of his own ships, apparently a luxurious passenger liner, although there are no passengers except Olcott, Ellen and one of the French shippers. Father and the Frenchman play for high stakes on the trip until father runs out of funds and gives his guest a check for $30,000, worthless because father knows he is bankrupt.

When the Frenchman goes to bed, father enters his stateroom armed with an automatic, determined to recover the check, but is prevented by Ellen. The French ship owner finds Ellen in his cabin, and, mistaking her purpose, tries to make dishonorable love to her. Father meanwhile has returned to his own stateroom and committed suicide with a hypodermic needle, although why a bankrupt for millions should be so disturbed over a $30,000 debt does not appear.

The girl orders the ship back to Havre while the Frenchman, basing his action on the girl's appearance in his cabin, determines to disclose the affair to her fiance, Jack. Ellen cannot clear himself, because her father had left a letter begging her not to reveal his guilty intentions against his guest. Back in Paris, Ellen goes to the Frenchman's home to plead with him not to tell her lover of the incident, and the Frenchman again tries to urge his dishonorable suit. There is a struggle, and a falling statue knocks him unconscious. The girl thinks she has killed him and is terrified with the prospect of arrest. In the end her innocence, both of the cabin affair and the injury of the Frenchman, are cleared up, one by the unintentional reading of the dead father's letter and the other by the recovery of the injured man and his admission that the blow that almost laid him low was accidental. *Rush.*

UP IN THE AIR ABOUT MARY

Farce-comedy featuring Louise Lorraine and Joe Moore in five reels. Put out by Associated Exhibitors. Story and direction by William Watson.

Mary	Louise Lorraine
Joe	Joe Moore
Mom	Laura La Vernie
Algernon Emptihead	Robert Anderson

Elaborate posters in myriad colors and of alluring design decorated the front of Loew's New York theatre as advertisements of the feature. They pictured a bewitching bathing beauty. Photographs indicated the same sort of subject and a caption promised "five reels of furious comedy."

Illustration and descriptive matter are false pretense. The picture touches new altitudes of vulgarity and stupid, infantile horseplay. The titles are full of atrocious puns and there are twice too many of them. The vulgarity is in the picture's wretched taste, not in the display of bathing girls, for there is only one short passage in which two or three young women extras stand about inconspicuously in their bathing suits, so inconspicuously, indeed, that one has to look closely to find them at all.

At a guess, one would suspect that somebody looked the negative over and figured that it would be a dead loss unless they put a pretty solid investment in good paper for front display. The posters would sell the picture without an argument—unless one happened to see the production itself. The lobby display ought to draw patronage. But the film will discourage a return visit.

The whole thing is just amateurish comedy, switching back and forth between polite farce and custard pie stuff. The acting is indifferent and the story might have been put together for a high school performance.

Mary runs away from home to escape a match with a sappy person, Algernon, picked out by her socially ambitious mother. She takes asylum with a friend on a farm, and there meets Joe, apparently a farmhand, but really a young millionaire. When Mary goes back home, Joe gets her chauffeur drunk and takes his place at the wheel disguised by the goggles. Mother decides to take Mary to the seashore, Algernon accompanying the party. Still Mary won't have anything of Algy. Mom plots to have her kidnapped by hired thugs so that Algernon may make a grandstand rescue, but Joe, who is still on the job as waiter in the resort hotel, gums up the scheme in counterfeit Mack Sennett fashion.

There's more Sennett material in Joe's business as waiter at the table occupied by Mary, Algernon and Mom, viz., spilling food on Algy and the like. But Mary doesn't know who rescued her, because she fainted just before Joe arrived at the kidnappers' lair. So when Algy, arriving after Joe has been disposed of, takes the credit, the nuptials are set with Algy. Just as the fatal words are about to be pronounced, Joe arrives in a dirigible, seizes Mary at the very steps of the altar and carries her off in his airship, hence the title, "Up in the Air."

This leaves out a lot of comedy detail, such as Joe's impersonation of a fake fortune teller, and other coy incidents, but the picture is so chaotic one can't remember its action 20 minutes after leaving the theatre. The picture didn't stand up on the double feature bill, even though the other feature was a distinctly mediocre Western comedy-drama, with Franklyn Farnum, entitled "The Angel Citizens." *Rush.*

THEY LIKE 'EM ROUGH

Metro Screen Classic comedy, starring Viola Dana. Harry Beaumont production. Story and adaptation by Rex and Irma Taylor. At Loew's State, New York, July 24.

An amusing comedy built to order around Viola Dana's screen personality. Not a pretentious picture, by any means, in production layout, but well fitted to the star and satisfying to her followers. At times it trembles on the edge of farce with the deliberate purpose of coaxing a she knows what it's all about he has landed her in the rough shack laugh even at the expense of plausibility.

Most of the action takes place in the open, and some fine scenic shots have been registered in and about a logging camp, with the wild forest as the background. The photography is excellent.

Miss Dana again is the spoiled darling of a rich and doting aunt. Dick is her playmate, a college youth whom she orders around with imperious self-will. After college Dick goes to manage one of his father's lumber camps. Out of sight is out of mind with this hoyden flapper. She writes only at long intervals to the exile, who remembers her fondly. Dick learns from a newspaper that his former playmate is about to marry a rich dub, and he hastens off to be at the wedding.

Meanwhile the girl finds that her guardians have been in favor of the match, and their opposition which inspired to accept the suitor was only counterfeit. In fury she runs away while the wedding guests are assembled, vowing she will marry the first man she meets. Of course, she encounters Dick as he leaves the train in his north woods working clothes. He has grown a beard, and she doesn't recognize him, but puts the marriage proposal up to him as he stands. He accepts, takes her before a justice of the peace, and the knot is tied.

After the ceremony the girl is for parting with her husband, but he adopts caveman tactics, and before of the lumber camp, ordering her to "rustle my grub and be quick about it."

She fights back like a wildcat, but there is no escape through the wolf-infested forest. I. W. W. agitators invade the camp and stir up trouble. The coterie of rebels is thrown out of camp by Dick, and in revenge they kidnap the bride, holding her prisoner in a remote cabin. Dick trails them to the hiding place, and there is a battle royal, in which Dick is stabbed. But the rescue changes the girl's attitude toward her caveman husband, even to the extent that when he is shaved she begs that he let his beard grow again.

Altogether an amusing program picture, with special appeal to women through star and story in spite of its far-fetched foundation. *Rush.*

PRISONER OF ZENDA

Metro-Ingram romantic drama adapted by Mary O'Hara from the Edward Rose version of Anthony Hope's novel. About two hours in length. Photographed by John F. Seitz. Production manager, Starrett Ford. At Astor, New York, July 31.

Rudolf Rassendyll / King Rudolf	Lewis Stone
Princess Flavia	Alice Terry
Colonel Sapt	Robert Edeson
Duke Michael (Black Michael)	Stuart Holmes
Rupert of Hentzau	Ramon Navarro
Antoinette de Mauban	Barbara La Marr
Count Von Tarlenheim	Malcolm McGregor
Marshall Von Strakencz	Edward Connelly
Countess Helga	Lois Lee

To say that Rex Ingram and a remarkably good company of screen players have made the very utmost of the possibilities of Anthony

Hope's story about sums up the premiere of the big, new Metro venture. In its day "The Prisoner of Zenda" was more than a vogue. It was an institution on both sides of the water, and if you took a poll today of the citizenry between 40 and 50 you'd find a enormous majority confessing to the recollection that in their late youth the tale touched the peak of fascinating romance.

In its revival for the screen it ought to repeat its first effect and become an extremely valuable piece of property. It is the kind of romance that never stales—fresh, genuine, simple and wholesome. Indeed this screen translation is more profoundly interesting than either the novel or the stage play. The silent recital captures the imagination and holds it by a completeness of illusion that the other two forms somehow did not achieve.

It is not too much to say that the producer has another "Four Horsemen" in this satisfying entertainment. Sophisticated Broadway may not flock to the perhaps over-sentimental play, but it will be unadulterated poetry to the women and to the new generation all over the country. They'll weep enjoyably into their cambrics and repeat the sentimental experience of their elders of twenty odd years ago. Translated into box office terms, that is money.

It's a long time since the screen has found story, players, director and the other elements in such happy accord. A lot of expert care has been lavished on the production. Its simple taste is a thing to be accomplished only with study and intelligence. In every detail the picture reveals high talent. One bit of overdone elegance would have spoiled it, for the story at times treads on over-abundance of heart throbs and superlative sentiment. But the picture never misses. Even so small a detail as the royal ball discloses a touch of novel realism. Give the average movie director a royal ball with unlimited exotic uniforms, a palace background and peers and peeresses without count and he would go forth with a rush of blood to the head and take on all the extras in Hollywood. The net result would be a sort of combination of a "Follies" number and Rector's before prohibition on a Saturday night.

Instead of that Ingram has built a spacious ballroom with an atmosphere of unobtrusive splendor where a score of couples have room to dance like human beings. For once you get the illusion that it is a royal ball and not a movie mob scene. This innovation alone entitles Ingram to a public vote of thanks.

The same restraint marks the whole. Not once do the players spreadeagle, although the temptation must have been almost overpowering. Quiet emphasis characterizes the action, and perhaps this is the charm of the whole affair. Another big scene is the coronation episode in the first part. It is big and impressive in its massive proportions and involves an enormous number of people. But Ingram has sidestepped the error of trying to make an impression by mere bulk. In the long passage there are only a half dozen views of the assembled crowds. They are merely an incidental background. The attention is centered on the development of the action in the hands of three characters.

Another bit of finesse was the choice of the hero and heroine, in Lewis Stone who makes no pretence to Apollo-like beauty, and Alice Terry who made a Princess Flavia of surpassing blonde loveliness in her regal robes. The story is saccharine enough without a male beauty to gild the lily, while a heroine of any sort can't be too lovely. Another neat trick of Ingram's; all the sympathetic characters on the male side are more or less homely, while the schemers are rather self satisfied in their perfection of countenance. There's a good deal of keen psychology in this choice. Nobody loves a handsome man except himself and his sweetheart. It's a wonder nobody ever thought of it before. Ingram is a pathfinder.

Of course the whole thing is a fairy tale. It couldn't possibly happen in real life. No more could a single hero fight off and defeat four practiced swordsmen. "Cinderella" couldn't happen in real life either, but it has survived the ages. Genuine romance carries its own license, and even if they do scoff to save their faces, the people do like their romance full measure and overflowing. It is for this reason that the picture ought to make a strong and universal appeal.

"The Prisoner of Zenda" has all the romantic elements, the mythical kingdom of Ruritania, a forest castle with a drawbridge and a mote, gold lace and trappings of pageantry and above all the opulent romance of chivalry. It couldn't miss. It probably would have been proof against bad direction, but done with perfect stage management and exquisite literary taste it is faultless.

Since the story deals in more or less poetic materials a special style of photography is employed. The close-ups of all the characters are done in a misty dimness that gives them a remoteness that inspires the imagination. Some of the landscapes are handled in like manner and throughout the photography is marked in its contribution to the dignity of the story. This treatment makes the difference between a well executed miniature and a snapshot photograph.

In the detail of costuming somebody has worked miracles. It would seem impossible to dress a husky man in a white uniform trimmed with sashes and decorations without making him look ridiculous, but these costumes have been modelled on modern lines and except that they look picturesque, they do not intrude on one's attention. In like manner the women's dresses have been made to combine modern smartness with still the vague suggestion of an ancient portrait so that they merge into the picture, leaving only a faint impression of interesting and picturesque oddity, quite in accord with the atmosphere.

It was a wise picture crowd at the opening performance and they fully appreciated some of the fine technical points. One of the best characters is that of Colonel Sapt in which Robert Edeson was thoroughly disguised. He is the rugged old soldier and looked like an impersonation of Bismarck on the screen, but a fine sympathetic character. There are two women besides Miss Terry, Barbara La Marr and Lois Lee, brunet beauties who furnished contrast to Miss Terry. But Miss Terry carried off the honors. Her final scene, the departure of her English lover, was a smashing good piece of pantomimic playing.

Rush.

HUMAN HEARTS

Universal-Jewel production. Story by Hal Reid. House Peters starred. At Central, New York.

A sob bucolic, with a rugged father, a blind mother, an idiotic son, an unfortunate marriage, a couple of murders and a jail. And yet withal a laugh here and there, a tear more often and a tenseness all of the while. If those ingredients make a picture, then "Human Hearts" is.

This Hal Reid story was originally a stage play, if recollection is working in high. On the screen it spreads out, not so much in territory as in scope. This U runs about 80 minutes. It starts wobbly, but races along pretty soon, and towards the finish it's traveling right to the heart strings.

It's one of those that cause you to say to yourself, "How can so much trouble come to one family?" But there it is, here right in the Logan assemblage, somewhere over yonder.

The scene is full of country types, from the mummified-looking figure driving the shivering Ford to that rugged blacksmith, Logan, who knew more than his son, who married the city gal. That city gal! A simp vamp who forgot to vamp and thought she loved the succeeding blacksmith. That was one of the sons (House Peters). The other and younger Logan started to chase a greased pig at a picnic, the grandstand fell upon him and he lost his mind. But Mrs. Logan, a lovely old woman, was blind all of the time.

The popular stunt in sentimental picturizing these days is to throw the strength of the characters into the mother. It has been well done here. The father warned his son before marriage to sidestep the gal, warned him afterward she was double crossing him, even after the baby came, and because "Paw" got rubbery in watching the daughter clandestinely meet a former crooked pal from the city "Paw" lost his life through a pistol shot and son-husband was convicted of the murder. Maybe the story is generally known. It develops from that into the son-husband receiving a life sentence, securing the good graces of the prison's warden through saving the latter's life, and after about four years in prison being freed upon the wife confessing her paramour had done the "Paw" shooting.

Her husband had remained in jail under the belief his wife had murdered his father. Freed, he went to her home and overheard the other man confess the shooting. In the same scene the other man, attempting to shoot the husband, killed the girl instead as she threw herself between them. And then back to the blacksmith shop, the peaceful ruralness and the anvil.

It isn't the story so much. Parts and all of it have been told in as many different ways on the screen. It's rather the blending or adaptation or scenarizing and direction that could cram the comedy with the pathos and hold an audience for 80 minutes straightaway, which audience filled the Central to capacity downstairs Tuesday evening.

That speaks rather well for Broadway and Forty-seventh street, a section blase and tough on pictures, and in Times square, where sentiment centers on the bankroll more than on unfortunates, for the section has enough unfortunates of its own, every kind.

"Human Hearts" will catch the human hearts, and for the inhuman at least it will show that there is still peace to be had in the country if you can keep your family away from the breaks.

As a feature it's a good U production, well if fervently played at times, and it is absorbing, for all of us, no matter how tough we may think we are, still have a heart while we can stand up. But "Human Hearts," away from Times square, will still be a bigger picture, an educational in its way, telling country yokels to stick to their own, making them city-gal-shy.

For as all the good looking girls in the country eventually go to the cities, so it should be taught that when good looking city girls go to the country, let the yokels hide in their own back yards.

But play "Human Hearts" because it takes in so much; it is clean and it is quite apt to do business in all communities, for there is the mother, and who can resist a mother, and who is so tough that a blind mother won't make him wilt?

Sime.

COUNTRY FLAPPER

Flapper	Dorothy Gish
Boy	Glenn Hunter
Other Flapper	Mildred Marsh
Boy's Father	Harlan Knight
Bashful Boy	Tommy Douglas
One Brother	Raymond Hackett
Other Brother	Albert Hackett
Sister	Catherine Collins

Dorothy Gish is presented here by Dorothy Gish Productions as a cross between "Mickey" and "Tom Sawyer," with spots here and there for suppressed emotional pathos of juvenile grief over puppy love. It is perfect casting, though far from a perfect picture. The same underlying principles, if applied with a bit more plot importance, might have made this a presentation of great merit. As it is, one can only credit it with being entertaining and amusing, and may deplore its being frivolous and smart-Alex.

There is no story to this film, and a title early in the showing warns of this. That is all very well, but it will scarcely make for a public interest such as comes when an intrinsically compelling moral or a situation of broad human appeal gives audiences something to take home with them and retail to others, in place of merely being able to say "It was a cute picture and Dorothy Gish was a darling."

Miss Gish, of course, is a comedienne of unquestionable genius and irresistible charm. But, especially since she has been identified with some powerfully absorbing roles, is it somewhat expected of her that she will contribute a clutch on the sympathies and the crave for seeing a girl who knows how to suffer and endure more poignant woes than those which come of the heartaches of a village flapper thrown down by the villainous druggist's boob son.

And where the story does try to have moments beyond those of juvenile love-troubles, the titles, trying desperately to be "clever," persist in making what is already a light story, flippantly facetious. The titles are by Joseph W. Farnham, who is blamed for them in the "credit." He should title Mutt and Jeff antimateds, but not Gishes. Miss Gish is a star and has so much human contact in every look and gesture that she should not be forced to drag the weight of tawdry stabs at wise cracks, even though some of them draw laughs, and even though some of them really hit. Their whole tone is detrimental and cannot be welcomed by the great body of film-lovers.

Richard Jones identified with several of Mabel Normand's conspicuous hits directed "The Country Flapper," and he is in part at fault for the generally thin texture of the tale, though he did wonders with developing the thoughts that he selected to emphasize.

The casting is good enough, though not important in any outstanding instance. The star is left to her own resources except for the accustomed brand of reasonably able support. The sets are very plain for the most part, and this does not appear to have been a heavily costly production, except for the star's hefty compensation.

At the Capitol this film held interest through Miss Gish's personality, even though the monotony of the story caused her to fall into repetitions of situation, mood and action time and time again. There were some hearty laughs, also. But there was very little to take out of the theatre after it was over, except to repeat that Dorothy is Lillian's very lovely sister, and that in "The Country Flapper" she is mighty winsome and deft. The name will draw, and those who come may not complain. But so much more might have been done and might yet be done if here and there a title with some sincere sentiment were substituted for the reel after reel of small-time observations on small-town romances.

Lait.

FOOLS FIRST

Crook drama produced by Marshall Neilan from Beatrice Fairfax's scenario based on the story by Hugh McNair Kahler. Distributed by First National. At Strand, New York, July 30.

Tommy Frazer................Richard Dix
Ann Whittaker................Claire Windsor
Denton Drew, banker..Claude Gillingwater
"Tony the Wop," leader of gang......
Raymond Griffith
Spud Miller, half brother to Frazer..
George Siegmann
"Blonde" Clark..............Helen Lynch
"Spider Webb"...........George Dromgold

Here is a clean cut melodrama full of arresting situations and surprises, ingeniously contrived and screened with admirable skill by this always dependable director. It takes a place in notable film works corresponding to the stage play of ten years or so ago by the late Paul Armstrong called "The Deep Purple."

The picture story is bizarre in its odd twists, but still absorbingly real and it has a curious sort of philosophy as a background in what at first has the tinge of bitter cynicism, but turns about in the startling climax so that all is cheerful and rosy. Neilan's pictures always have something of the unexpected. A new one takes on the complexion of an entertaining adventure. This one delivers the goods.

The story has two high power kicks, in a theatrical sense. The first is where a desperate gang is concealing a dead man just as the police knock at the door. They prop the corpse up in a chair at the poker table while one of the crooks takes a position kneeling at his side out of sight and using his arms to make it appear that the dead man is playing his hand.

For grisly, creep. suggestion the trick was a fine bit of dramatic effectiveness. The whole play is done with polished craftsmanship. The story builds up into compelling suspense, gathering force and momentum as it progresses. The big situation has the crook who is on the way to reform try to do a last job of bank robbing. He is aided by a girl employe of the bank whose motives are shrouded in mystery. The owner of the bank is another strange figure, an ancient financier and student who lives in a weird mansion where his butler swears at him and drinks with him at dinner.

At the same time the old gang of thieves which has thrown the hero out is engaged on the same safe cracking enterprise without the hero's knowledge. It's an electric situation and the solution is unguessable. When it does come, the surprise is complete. A minute before the mine is sprung one would have said the author had got himself into an impossible tangle, but the denouement smooths everything out and it is over in a twinkling. The solution is that the banker had served time himself and had made a hobby of reclaiming ex-convicts by allowing them to find themselves, directing their regeneration in secret and letting them work out their own destiny, aided by the girl, the daughter of a one time forger and the comedy butler, an alumnus of the lockstep too.

It's all gripping drama and its full value is secured by the excellence of the direction. Neilan has a unique knack for suggestion. One brief detail gives an illustration. The gangsters are gathered over the body of a member just "bumped off" by rival gunmen. They must **avenge him and get rid of the body before the police catch up.** The gang leader, a sinister Italian, calls up a woman confederate and directs her to entice the rival gang chief to the place. Then he calls another phone number. A change shows a ghostly apparition of a bald-headed demon in the smock of a surgeon, or maybe a butcher, answering the phone, and the title says "Spider isn't with us any more. We'll need you tonight." Presently the murderer is maneuvered into the gang's power. The Italian confronts him and with horrifying relish snips off coat and shirt buttons with a murderous knife, then he hits him a blow that sends him staggering into a closet masked by a heavy portiere. There are eloquent swayings of the curtain and the Italian comes out polishing his dirk. He goes to the phone and observes to the same nightmare figure at the other end, "We'll have two of them for you."

Where a less subtle director would have circused these highly colored incidents, Neilan strives to make them as casual and simple as possible. Of course, the simple directness gives them force and emphasis. His method is to apply kid glove melodramatic tempo to lurid characters and dime novel situations. The scheme is tremendously effective in this case.

In like manner when he undertakes the gradual regeneration of the young crook his skillful indirection is as interesting. Deft bits of detail are introduced, such as a holiday excursion into the country, where the crook deals tenderly with a lost and frightened child which point to phases of character development. The crude device of the verbose title never once comes into the building up of the desired effect. Indeed sometimes Neilan's technique is too fine. It takes a pretty alert spectator to absorb the full dramatic force of what is going on, and all pictures are not always that attentive. *Rush.*

THE SONG OF LIFE

John M. Stahl production released by Louis B. Mayer through First National. Bess Meredyth supplied the scenario with the direction by Stahl.

David Tilden.................Gaston Glass
Aline Tilden.................Grace Darmond
Mary Tilden..........Georgia Woodthorpe
Neighbor's Boy............Richard Headrick
District Attorney.......Arthur Stuart Hull
Richard Henderson......Wedgwood Nowell
Amos Tilden...................Edward Peil
Police Inspector................Fred Kelsey
Central Office Man..........Claude Payton

"The Song of Life" is the initial John M. Stahl First National release. The theme develops a mother idea with the customary sob material invariably linked with subjects of this order. The production includes what is usually termed an all-star cast, in other words, a starless feature. In this instance, as is often the case with mother pictures, a name is not essential. Georgia Woodthorpe in the mother role injects goodly sentiment and provides the necessary pathos. Gaston Glass is entrusted with the male lead with Grace Darmond handling the other role of importance.

Stahl has given the picture a satisfactory production. The interiors range from commonplace tenement quarters to more pretentious layouts all of which are effectively worked out. Street scenes supposedly on the lower East Side of New York are realisticly handled.

"The Song of Life" is but one of many sob pictures on the screen today. It fails to disclose a powerful story and is only fitted for the intermediate houses as a feature.

The story deals with the experiences of Mary Tilden who deserts her husband and baby to find the better things in life. After a lapse of several years she is located washing dishes in a restaurant in New York. She loses the position and is about to be ejected from her tenement when befriended by a young man and his wife who offer to give her a home in their flat. She later discovers the man is her own son whom she had deserted. His wife **is about to desert him as he had failed to secure the finery she demands. The mother tries to stop her with a shooting occuring shortly after, when the discovery is made that the younger woman is about to run away with another man. The latter is shot and the mother takes the blame. Usual finish.** ***Hart.***

OATHBOUND

William Fox semi-society crook feature, with Dustin Farnum starred. Story by Edward LeSaint, script by Jack Strumwasser. Directed by Bernard Durning.

Lawrence Bradbury........Dustin Farnum
Constance Hastings.......Ethel Grey Terry
Jim Bradbury...............Fred Thomson
Ned Hastings...............Maurice Flynn
Hicks.........................Norman Selby
Alice..........................Eileen Pringle
Gang Leader...................Bob Perry

An effort to make this a mystery melodrama. In effect it is a success. There is much mystery. The audience wonders what it is all about. It could have been made into burlesque melodrama had the picture been jazzed with comedy titles. Now it is simply a rather draggy program feature.

Dustin Farnum is a wealthy steamship owner, whose liners from the Orient are being despoiled each trip of part of their cargo. He sends his younger brother to trap the thieves. As a matter of fact the boy is in with the crooks. In the screen version the audience is led to believe the boy is on the level and those really working in the interests of the law are the crooks. That is the mystery element. In the end the audience is let in.

In cast the picture has its best selling points. There is a good supporting cast. Ethel Grey Terry gives a dandy performance. Maurice Flynn is a likable secret service man, and Norman Selby (Kid McCoy) characterizes a burlesque detective for laughable results.

No one is going to go crazy about this picture in its present shape, but it will do for the cheaper daily change houses. *Fred.*

THE BONDED WOMAN

Famous Players (Paramount) feature, starring Betty Compson. Adapted from John Fleming Wilson's story, "The Salvaging of John Somers." Scenario by Albert S. LeVino. Director, Philip Rosen. At the Rialto, New York, week of July 30.

Angela Gaskell..............Betty Compson
John Somers..................John Bowers
Lee Marvin....................Richard Dix
Captain Gaskell......J. Farrell MacDonald
Lucita..........................Ethel Wales

The third picture in a short time from the same producer having a girl skipper of a roughneck crew on a deep-sea vessel. They all run to South Sea Islands, and they're all rather silly. This one makes a new mark for absurdity.

The sweet heroine goes ashore in a satin skirt and silk sweater and high-heeled shoes. To make it more difficult when she is marooned in the good old deserted island she makes a change of costume to middy blouse and sport shoes. And all this time the audience is called upon to sympathize with her because the wild man whom she is trying to cure of the drink habit has brought her to poverty.

This is only one of innumerable violations of good sense. You can't hang such nonsense even on the sentimental film fans. Curing dipsomaniacs is in the closed season anyhow in America. Prohibition has made the curse of drink a comedy subject nowadays, and it is a mistake to use it as the basis of a sob story.

The picture has some excellent storm views, probably done in the studio tank, although they pass for the real thing. However, the episode of the heroine climbing the rigging and pretending to faint on the cross-trees so that the hero will have to rescue her was not so well counterfeited. A topmast on a pitching, rolling vessel ought to move, but this one is as motionless as the obelisk in Central Park.

Not that it mattered much, for by this time the accumulation of inconsistencies had alienated the audience. It was all so futile. John Somers didn't appear to need a rescuing angel. Even in his cups he was a perfectly capable first mate—good enough at least to save Angela's father from drowning when the old boy wanted to go down with his foundering ship. Besides he was perfectly well behaved when he came to Angela's house, lit up a little, but not more than enough to be good natured. At least that was the impression one gathered. It was Angela's father who wrecked the ship, and he was sober. John Somers, even if he was drunk, had sense enough to save the situation.

And so it didn't strike one as important that Angela chase half around the world to find John in Samoa. Of course John had a claim on Angela because he saved her father, but John also was under an obligation because Angela mortgaged her home to furnish a bond (hence the title) so that John could get a berth as skipper, and thus redeem himself. He made a gallant struggle to leave the stuff alone, but when he reached port his mate stole the ship's money, and everybody, including Angela, accused him of the theft.

What could he do but return to the South Seas and go to the dogs? Angela could have married a fabulously rich ship owner, but the title made it plain that while she could respect the saint her heart was with the sinner. She meets up with John in a waterfront dive in Samoa. He has managed to scrape up enough to buy a small schooner and intends to pay off Angela's loss, but Angela demands that he surrender the ship to her in payment immediately and sail the same night.

That's what they do. On the voyage John goes to drinking again, and Angela "plays her last card" by running the ship aground on an uninhabited island, sending the crew off in the only lifeboat after they had landed the stores, including many cases of whiskey. Angela once more "plays her last card," as the title has it, by pointing to the mound of hooch and declaring herself, "I'll talk to you when you have emptied those bottles." The picture makes a lot of the spiritual struggle John has with himself, but in the end he conquers his weakness and smashes the wet goods as sign and symbol of his surrender. All just in time for the arrival of the rescue ship picked up by the crew. ***Rush.***

HER GILDED CAGE

Jesse Lasky production (Paramount), with Gloria Swanson, based on the play by Ann Nichols. Scenario by Elmer Harris and Percy Heath. Designated Sam Wood production.

Suzanne Ornoff..............Gloria Swanson
Arnold Pell....................David Powell
Lawrence Pell...............Harrison Ford
Jacqueline Ornoff...........Anne Cornwall
Bud Walton....................Walter Hiers
Gaston Petitfils.......Charles A. Stevenson

A revel in gorgeous clothes and elaborate settings is this comedy of stage life, but it is pretty mild in action. The picture is all appeal to the eye and none to the sympathies. Miss Swanson outdoes herself in sartorial splendor, and the producers have matched the array of frocks with a scenic equipment as elaborate. If these accessories make a picture, "Her Gilded Cage" is an event.

Otherwise it's a rather tame affair. Suzanne is the daughter of an aristocratic French family in Paris which has fallen upon ill fortune. She is the sole support of a crippled sister and a doddering old uncle. She makes a living at first by teaching music. Then she becomes a model, and in that occupation meets and falls in love with a millionaire artist studying in the Latin quarter.

The artist makes love to her and she quits his employ. With her occupation gone Suzanne's family is in deeper difficulties until she unexpectedly gets an opportunity to sing in a small cabaret. An American press agent sees her performance and undertakes to boom her by circus publicity methods. First he fakes the story that she is "the favorite of King Fernando," making the tale out of a trifling incident in the cafe. The American artist visits the place and, hearing the supposed scandal which is the talk of Paris, leaves in disgust. Suzanne observes from the stage his expression of shocked dismay as he recognizes his shy model in the notorious Fleur d'Amour of the cabaret.

An opportunity presents itself for Suzanne to make a fortune on the American stage and she seizes it for the chance it will give to restore Jacqueline, the crippled sister, to health. Here comes the coincidence. The first person Suzanne meets in the States is a brother of the American artist. And to make the coincidence more binding the brother also falls in with Jacqueline, who is being cared for in the country.

Of course Jacqueline and the brother fall in love and, of course, Suzanne is invited to a gay and giddy party at the town house of the artist's brother just in time for the returning artist to meet her unexpectedly. He denounces her for a notorious adventuress whose affair with King Fernando is the scandal of Europe. Brother, being pretty well lit up at the party, takes umbrage, and asks Suzanne to marry him, and Suzanne agrees to do so in pique at the artist.

By some means which are not disclosed all the principals to this tangle next appear together at the country place where Jacqueline is being cared for, and the misunderstanding is all cleared up. The shock of the meeting jolts Jacqueline into perfect health on the instant, and without waste of time Suzanne falls into the arms of the artist and Jacqueline into the embrace of his brother. It's stretching credulity pretty tight all around.

But there are several striking bits of staging. The dinner party is an elaborate pageant, the guests being assembled in a huge bird's cage within which the dinner table is laid. The theatre scenes are also rich in production incidentals. Harrison Ford, as always, makes a manly juvenile, and from first to last Miss Swanson's gowns are eye filling. That's about as far as the picture goes. *Rush.*

THE LOVE SLAVE

Feature length, probably of foreign origin. Stars Lucy Doraine, who is described on the billing as "the famous screen beauty." Story by George Ohnet, author of the drama, "The Iron Master." Sponsored by the Herz Film Corporation.

Unfamiliar players and unfamiliar locations indicate that this picture is an import, probably from France. It adds further data to the explanation of why French pictures do not make much headway in this market. It was shown as half of a double bill at Loew's New York, July 28.

The picture has only one good point—some of its landscapes and backgrounds of lake country are very pretty, but that does not entitle it to a classification for any Broadway house, even of the daily change kind. It is poor screen material in all departments. The story is chaotic, stilted and implausible, the acting is exceptionally bad and even the photography is ten years or more behind the times.

In some of the shots the hero's face is an expressionless white blank because the mechanical work was inexpert somewhere from cameraman to printing. The direction is poor and never once does the screen action get anywhere near an illusion of reality. It commits the worst fault a director and a cast can be guilty of, it fails completely to arrest his attention at any point.

The story might make a trashy novel, but it couldn't be made into an interesting film. If it is French it is curious that the nation that leads the world in the art of fiction could produce so crude a picture play. There isn't a sympathetic character in the whole cast. The hero is a pompous tourist in Damascus, an artist traveling for local color.

Passing through a narrow street he sees a native sheik beating the heroine, a coffee colored girl, whom he has tied up to a whipping post. The European knocks the native down and goes on his way after freeing the girl. She follows him, and one is left to gather that a liaison develops. When the hero has to return home, he brings the girl with him, but doesn't introduce her to his family, setting her up in a villa, apparently on the Riviera somewhere.

She is piqued at this treatment and takes unto herself a new lover. The hero catches her and Sweetie No. 2 in a compromising situation in the girl's bedroom and shoots her. She recovers, but for the crime the hero has to serve five years at hard labor. He is shown at length in his noisome prison in much footage of adulterated Hugo. He escapes and becomes a teacher of painting in Paris.

One of his pupils, the greatest heiress in France, falls in love with him and they are married. Meanwhile the brown woman has prospered vastly and is proprietress of a luxurious gambling casino. By a series of made to order circumstances the hero is brought to the place. She threatens to deliver him to the police as an escaped convict and tell the bride the details of his career, and as the price of her silence demands that he come to her casino every night and spend the evening there in her company to the neglect of the bride.

It is apparent that she still loves him and desires him back and here begins a struggle between them, she to force him to infidelity and he to resist. In the struggle she goes mad and dies, while he reveals all to the bride and is forgiven. Sloppy, sentimental trash, all, and counterfeit melodrama, badly done at that. *Rush.*

THE NEW TEACHER

William Fox five-reel feature of New York life from the script by Dorothy Yost. Directed by Joseph Franz, with Shirley Mason starred.

Constance Bailey..............Shirley Mason
Bruce von Griff..............Alan Forest
Edward Hurley..............Earl Metcalf

A program melodrama of New York life from society to the slums that is interestingly portrayed on the screen. It is a picture that, while it hasn't any great punch, will please the majority. William Fox presented it last week in his own Academy of Music as part of a double feature bill, splitting the show with "Oathbound." "The New Teacher" is the more interesting of the two. In the regular daily change houses it will hold up with any of the regular program productions.

Shirley Masons is a little society girl who has consistently refused to marry the hero, played by Alan Forest. She has a desire to "do something in the world." The opening shows her with Forest above New York in a plane. He proposes and is again refused; the plane is forced to descend in the midst of the slums. Here she sees an opportunity to "do something," and becomes a teacher in a lower East Side school. The hero follows her, by obtaining an appointment on the police. A few months in the squalid atmosphere convinces her he is about as good a catch as she can make.

There are a number of clever little human touches with the East Side kids and wholesome comedy from schoolroom scraps.

In direction Joseph Franz has handled his kid stuff particularly well. The photography is also up to the standard, with the aeroplane stuff particularly well matched up to create the illusion the plane is sailing above New York, with cut-ins of the Manhattan skyline.

Earl Metcalf as the heavy gives a corking performance. *Fred.*

THE HEART OF A TEXAN

At Loew's Circle, New York, half of Monday's (July 31) double bill at 30c. top (regular house scale). Presented by William Steiner Productions; Neal Hart starred, story adapted for screen and directed by Paul Hurst.

The title says it's a western and it is, not unusual, not unconventional and not without a tiny bit of interest, even though a western all through, in dressing, locale and story. But good enough for the houses liking westerns that play the small-time feature stuff.

Inexpensive exteriors, mostly, with interiors of shack living-rooms. Extras may have counted up to 30 people, all men, with but two women in the picture, one mother and her daughter. The player of the daughter role seemed amateurish and was always posed, with one-colored screen in the living-room so muchly favored that after the daughter played it heavily behind her for close-ups, mother got in the same spot later.

The couple of points of interest were when Neal Hart, the Texan hero, made a couple of flying leaps from his horse, each time landing on the villain. The first was on the road, but the second held a little thrill, Hart making the leap as he and his horse jumped through a window into the cabin or shack.

Just what Hart's official capacity was, if any, in the place near the Mexican border, where the scenes were located, never became divulged. He may have been just a Texan. The lobby billing says a Texan is strong to protect women. Hart certainly did protect the daughter against Pete Miller, "a bad man on both sides of the border." Hart whipped Pete two or three times—in fact, every time he met him, and always with his hands, throwing away the guns and guarding himself from knives in various ways. Aren't those some of the Bill Hart stunts? At times Neal Hart was more reminiscent than in name only of the original Bill.

A rustlers' fight against the Texans wound it up, the Pete Miller gang having sent for assistance when hearing Hart had sent an Indian for more Texans to protect the Jackson home.

Not much other than those riding tricks and some poor acting, while all of the horses there could have ridden through the holes in the direction. *Sime.*

The title is the strength of the release. There is a lure in it. Otherwise the story is simply spun, with little that is exciting. It starts like a scenic. Then with scenes of tunnel-boring into a mountain of the Sierras, it takes on a dash of the educational. The dramatics are supplied through the schemes of a railway promoter to secure a right of way. Barring him is the construction of a dam that will supply the countryside with water during the arid season and make fertile the desert strip not far off. It is never made clear why the railroad must have the particular bit of scenery to work upon and why it cannot be attained by tunneling. The rail

BLOOD AND SAND

"Jesse L. Lasky presents Rodolph Valentino," the billing reads, "In a Fred Niblo production." Lila Lee and Nita Naldi head the supporting company. The picture is adapted by June Mathis from the novel by Blasco Ibanez and the play by Tom Cushing. At the New York Rivoli Aug. 6.

Juan Gallardo..........Rodolph Valentino
Carmen..........Lila Lee
Dona Sol..........Nita Naldi
El Nacional..........George Field
Plumitas..........Walter Long
Senora Augustas..........Rose Rosanova
Antonio..........Leo White
Don Joselito..........Charles Belcher
Potaje..........Jack Winn
El Carnacione..........Marie Marstini
Garabata..........Gilbert Clayton
El Pontelliro..........Harry Lamont
Marquise de Guevera..........George Periolat
Dr. Ruiz..........Sidney De Gray
Don Jose..........Fred Becker
Senora Nacional..........Dorcas Mathews
Fuentes..........William E. Lawrence

The picture started Sunday at the Rivoli with every evidence of public interest. The house front was profusely decorated with Spanish and American flags and the house attaches flaunted bull ring costumes of gay colors. Sunday afternoon the house sold out from mid-afternoon until the final show.

The attendance made it look like an extraordinary winner, but the behavior of the crowd in the theatre was peculiar. Along toward the middle of the screening they showed a disposition to scoff at the play. Some of the serious scenes, particularly those "vamping" episodes involving Juan the bull fighter (Valentino) and Dona Sol, the vampire widow (Nita Naldi) touched their sense of humor.

Joshing a matinee idol like Valentino is fatal. It's only a short step from public worship to public ridicule. The character called for more delicate treatment than Valentino could give. Ibanez matador needs deft handling. He is a creature of light and shades. Valentino was far from the mark. His bull fighter was just a movie hero. It was far from a satisfying performance, but the fans unquestionably were drawn to the theatre. Even at the "supper show" the lobby was nearly filled with waiting crowds Sunday and by 7 o'clock the press spilled over the lobby into Broadway. It was the same story up to Wednesday.

The picture has several effective passages. The scenes in the bull ring have a lot of thrill and the pageantry and parade won a spontaneous bursts of applause. The closing episode, the death of the matador in the chapel of the stadium also earned the hushed attention of the house. It was the struggles of the hero to resist the temptation of the siren widow that made them chuckle. The spectacle of the erstwhile sheik holding a beautiful woman at arm's length was too much.

Valentino's performance of Mrs. Hutchinson's "Shiek" fixed his status among the fans as a super-heated love maker and the sudden switch to a St. Anthony type comes as a shock. The essential moral conflict of the man never got to the surface. He was just a bewildered simpleton who made his gaudy clothes ridiculous. You can't make a character ridiculous and sympathetic at the same time. If you treat him seriously the audience provides its own burlesque, as it did at the Rivoli. The only way to defeat this tendency would be to give the hero himself a sense of humor and the screen treatment does not do this. It's all deadly serious, even to the moral reflections of the philosophical old party who acts a sort of Greek chorus to the story and occasionally breaks out into sub-titles such, "Passion is the devil's invention," which evoked a guffaw during the vamping episode. Straight theatrical heroing is Valentino's forte and he staggers when they take him out of the wild and unrestrained love-making environment.

The story has many picturesque elements but it is episodic and scattered. It seems to have no pattern. It starts with the theme of a humble shoe maker raised to eminence as a national hero of the bull ring and an idol of the people. Presently the problem is changed to the proposition, "What will be the fate of a man who lives by blood and cruelty?" Presently the conflict is the moral struggle between choice of the wife and the other woman and at the end the purpose appears to be an attack on the institution of the bull fight. "Poor matador; poor beast," says the benign philosopher, "But the real bull is out there (the crowd around the arena). There is the beast with ten thousand heads."

The production is confusing. The characters sometimes do not dominate the scenes because of the over elaboration of the settings. The wedding scene is a confused jumble of restless minor people. Always the principal people are befogged by their surroundings so you can't see the trees for the forest. And there is more confusion in the multiplicity of characters of whom there are 16 listed in the cast.

Rush.

JUST TONY

William Fox feature. Story adapted from Max Brand's novel, "Alcatraz." Directed by Lynn F. Reynolds. Tom Mix featured. The real star is Mix's horse, Tony. At the Strand, Aug. 6.

Tony....................By Himself
Jim Perris....................Tom Mix
Marianne Jordan....................Claire Adams
Oliver Jordan....................J. P. Lockney
Manuel Cordova....................Duke Lee
Lew Hervey....................Frank Campeau
"Shorty"....................Walt Robbins

This picture is unique in that it has the only absolutely natural actor of the screen. He is Tom Mix's horse, "Tony," and for delineation of horse character is a wonder. Nobody should miss this delightful novelty, especially the youngsters, although it is by no means a juvenile entertainment.

Tony is a dark bay beauty, the perfection of what horsemen call conformation, with a head and neck an artist could scarcely improve upon, a noble head and the style and fire of a thoroughbred. He is a find as a screen hero. How they managed to catch some of his accomplishments is a mystery.

The sub-titles constantly impute to the animal emotions and motives that are human, and then by some sort of legerdemain manage to make the animal express them. During most of the picture "Tony" 'is roving the plains at will, bridleless and without a human being in sight. The illusion that the horse is actuated by its own intelligence is complete. It opens gates to release a herd of saddle horses, leads them to freedom, appears to plot against cowboys who are sent to capture the runaways and does all manner of things in an utterly convincing way that seems to call for human intelligence.

The story starts with "Tony" as the property of a brutal Mexican, who tries to break his spirit. Jim Perris (Mix), a horse-loving cowpuncher, witnesses a whipping administered by the Mexican, and a fight ensues. Jim and the horse become friends. "Tony" gnaws his halter half through, and the next time the Mexican appears in the corral with his whip breaks loose and tramples his persecutor to death in an especially effective bit of trick action. A dummy is used, of course, but it looks like the real thing.

Then "Tony" leaps the barrier to freedom on the plains. Here he gathers a herd of wild horses around him and becomes their leader, defeating the efforts of a score of cowboys to capture or kill them. Jim has dedicated himself to taking the splendid animal alive. To this end he enters the employ of Marianne, owner of the ranch near the wilds where the free horses roam. Jim plants a "brush trap" and manages to get a rope over Tony's head. He saddles the horse after trying to make friends with it, but "Tony" won't be bent to the bridle. He bucks and rampages all over the lot until the exhausted rider is thrown, stunned, to the ground.

All these things are shown in detail and close at hand. How they ever kept a camera near the rough and tumble is hard to figure out. Even while "Tony" is leading his wild band in tearing gallops across the plains the camera kept close by. These running scenes match anything the screen h[illegible]ver shown in the beauty of a fine horse in action. The animals fairly fly over miles of deserted plain without a human being in sight and are a riot of tossing mains and speeding hoofs.

After defeating the cowboy "Tony" moves away reluctantly, looking back wistfully (the horse actually seems to express that emotion) at the prone rider, senseless in the brush. Meanwhile, the bad men of the ranch (they are really rustlers disguising themselves as the working force for the girl rancher) have plotted to steal all the stock and murder Jim. Jim returns to the ranch and falls into their wicked hands, while "Tony" follows cautiously behind, watching affairs from a distance. The picture finally grows into a chase. Jim and the girl, with whom he is in love, set off to the nearby town for help, both having escaped the plotters. The latter go in pursuit, hoping to catch and dispose of the pair before they reach safety. **"Tony" is galloping along in the rear, still watching the only man that was kind to him.**

Jim and the outlaws engage in a running gun fight, during which Jim's mount is shot from under him as he crosses a ford, and both hero and heroine take refuge on a mountain side. Here's where "Tony" comes in. He dashes to the rescue just as the outlaws are closing in. Heroine and hero leap on his back and he goes speeding away, carrying both over rough mountain places without saddle or bridle.

This is only a sketch of the story thread. It doesn't convey anything of the astonishing effect of "Tony's" performance, nor the surprises or thrills of the action. The riding feats would alone carry a picture, and there are frequent thrilling stunts, such as Mix's fall over a cliff, the throwing of "Tony" in full flight and other exhilarating performances. The acting is excellent. Mix is always a likable player in his familiar roles, and Claire Adams makes an attractive heroine both for beauty and grace of subdued acting.

Rush.

VOICES OF THE CITY

Underworld drama. Story by Leroy Scott. Lon Chaney starred. Director, Wallace Worsley. Produced by Goldwyn. At the Capitol, Aug. 6.

Georgia Rodman....................Leatrice Joy
"Duke" McGee....................Lon Chaney
Graham....................John Bowers
Jimmy....................Cullen Landis
Clancy....................Richard Tucker
Mary Rodman....................Mary Warren
Mrs. Rodman....................Edythe Chapman
Sally....................Betty Schade
Pierson....................M. B. "Lefty" Flynn
Courey....................H. Milton Ross
Garrison....................John Cossar

Interesting underworld melodrama with intricate plotting and counter-plotting by a master criminal and an abundance of gun play. A subordinate love story runs parallel and merges into the crook theme at the climax. The picture aims at swift interweaving of complications rather than realism and has the complexion of a dime novel. Rather elementary fiction, but neatly turned to develop suspense.

Lon Chaney, as always, gets the utmost out of the role of a powerful leader of lawbreakers. He has a gift for quiet emphasis in pantomime which fits nicely into this lurid tale. Leatrice Joy does exceedingly well as the lovely innocent who falls into his clutches and is rescued in the nick of time. It takes mighty good players to get the story over convincingly, for the incidents are pretty lurid, but they succeed in making the action convincing.

Jimmy, a young clerk, innocently takes his sweetheart, Georgia, to a restaurant run by "Duke" McGee on the way home from the theatre. McGee, the polished leader of the lawless element of the town, is struck by the girl's beauty, and directs one of his lieutenants to get acquainted with the pair.

While the lieutenant is seated at their table the police enter the place and a gun fight ensues. The lieutenant shoots a policeman and escapes. Jimmy and Georgia are held by the police as witnesses. The affair gets into the newspapers, and Georgia's mother upbraids the girl with such violence that she leaves home and, under advice of Jimmy, takes refuge with McGee, unsuspecting that he is evilly in love with her.

McGee plots to have Jimmy killed in a low dive under the pretext that the reforming district attorney will be there to accept a bribe. During these events Sally, McGee's sweetheart, becomes jealous of Georgia, and when she learns of the plan to have Jimmy murdered goes to the dive to warn him. She is too late. Jimmy is shot as Georgia looks on, and, supposing him dead, Georgia determines to be revenged on McGee.

In his capacity as gang leader McGee is giving a ball the same evening and has presented Georgia with an evening frock to wear to it. She dresses for the affair, but carries an automatic in her wrist bag. McGee from his seat of honor sees her enter the ballroom and invites her to be his partner in his only dance of the evening. After the dance the girl asks to be allowed to address the guests. She starts to deliver an expose of McGee's crimes and confronts him with the leveled revolver, but Sally, the abandoned, snatches it from her and fires the fatal shot.

All this sounds like pretty unconvincing fiction, but the chain of events is skilfully forged so that each step appears to grow logically out of the step before, and the mind is led along without opposition to the climax. The ballroom scene is rather implausible with its refined magnificence, but its pictorial effects are striking enough to cover up the inappropriate magnificence, which would be more fitting to a Newport society event than the function of a criminal ward politician.

Rush.

LILAC SUNBONNET

London, July 21.

Exceptionally good feature for a Sunday-school treat and would receive high commendation from an ultra-respectable mothers' meeting. The story, adapted from S. R. Crockett's novel, belongs to the days of cheap sentimentalism and is not even well told. Not a foot of it rings true.

Apart from the weakness of the scenario the production work is excellent and the producer is to be congratulated upon providing his poor story with a beautiful rural setting.

A young man is sent to a neighboring minister to study for the Scottish "kirk." He falls in love with a pretty girl, who lives with her grandparents. Another girl loves him and she goes out to make trouble. The boy is sent home in disgrace, but his sweetheart's grandfather compels the minister to take his part, for she is really the product of the good man's runaway marriage of long ago. Cornered, the minister goes to the boy's father and tells the truth. This story has resulted in five reels, and its only excuse is that it has given badly needed work to players.

The principal parts are played by Joan Morgan, Warwick Ward and Pauline Peters. S. R. Crockett has written many good novels, and doubtless in novel form "The Lilac Sunbonnet" is excellent reading—wholesome, and without any of those nasty incidents which train the young idea in the wrong direction. As a film it is another example of the British producers' slavish adoration of the alleged "best sellers" or—do English publishers make presents of the film rights of such stories in the hope of getting a free advertisement for a cheap edition to be sold while the picture is "now showing"?

Gore.

"SHERLOCK" BROWN

Bayard Veillier Production (Metro), written and directed by Veillier. At New Loew's, New York, Aug. 3.

A detective story, mildly interesting and often amusing, through the successful bungling attempts of an amateur detective to recover an envelope containing the formula of a high explosive badly wanted by the American Government.

Among the characters are the chief of the Secret Service, a General of Staff, statesmen and financiers, one of the latter proving to be the criminal who knocked unconscious an army lieutenant as he was about to deliver the envelope to a conference in Washington.

The story is melodramatic with some kindred action, but it is rather the skilful direction and cutting of a film working out such a simple story as this, for Veillier, that knits the tale so compactly without too much detail.

"A professional smeller," as the amateur (Bert Lytell) could be termed, gives the picture a different twist. Pooh-poohed by the chief when first presenting himself, the amateur, accidentally securing a scent of sandalwood of the woman crook, traces her to a cabin on an outgoing steamer, where he recovers the envelope, after the same woman had wheedled it from him the evening before, through his simplicity.

The story is held within 48 hours. While it doesn't overwell fit Lytell, he probably does as much with the boob bespectacled role as anyone would. It was well cast, with the sister of the injured lieutenant especially giving an excellent performance.

Sime.

QUESTION OF HONOR

Louis B. Mayer's latest Anita Stewart release through First National is not going to start anything. Just an ordinary feature with a story that can be counted in the group class—a tale of construction in the western mountain chain, the heroine crossing her admirer, saving the product of a young civil engineer and winning him for a husband.

Along Broadway it was reported the Strand was to get "A Question of Honor" but after screening it, did not exhibit, though First National was paid the rental as per contract. The feature certainly could not aid the Strand's class of show and if rejected as said, that was smart showmanship on the house management's part. Not that the picture is bad. It just hasn't the stuff.

man encourages a plot to dynamite the dam. The girl who has come west to a nearby pretentious lodge house with the railroad man's party, rushed to the cabin of the young civil engineer in the dead of night. She snaps a wire which was to have exploded the construction. The youth she aids misunderstands her motive, but added scenes make everything even that was promised at the start.

The lodge house provides some good long shots, there being no fault with the photography. Miss Stewart is pleasing as always. She isn't troubled and probably enjoyed the out of door work. The other players aside from the four leads, had thinking parts. A fight scene was good so far as it went, but hardly counted as important. Edwin Carew directed. *Ibee.*

THE LOADED DOOR

Universal feature with Hoot Gibson. Ralph Cummins wrote the story. Harry Pollard directed. Half of double features at New York theatre, Aug. 4.

An entertaining commercial grade film with this likable young western hero. All the old stuff, such as the girl left to the ownership of the ranch, a lease to the villain of the community and the accusation of the girl's brother of a murder. Enters into this situation the quick witted and hard riding and fighting hero, and clears up the whole tangle to the damage of the bad men and the rescue of the girl and her brother.

But it has one ingenious situation that makes all the rest of the footage worth while, a clever bit of theatrical trickery that works up an excellent state of tension.

The essence of it is this: The villains are nearly beaten and must flee from justice. It is known that the hero is riding to a deserted house far from the town. One of the bad men goes to the house and plants destruction for the hero by arranging so that the opening of a certain door will touch off a box of dynamite and blow the place and the hero to kingdom come. The hero arrives in due course and is several times about to open the fatal door, but each time is prevented. Finally, he goes away unscathed.

The leader of the gang does not know of the trap and presently he comes upon the scene in pursuit of the heroine. They struggle before the "loaded door," the girl seeking escape that way and the villain trying to drag her out of the house by another exit where the horses are. In the end the girl eludes him and escapes from the house. The villain is about to follow, but the appearance of the hero coming up in the distance restrains him. He goes back and by trying to get away he opens the wrong door and sets off the dynamite.

The picture has several other capital surprises, as where the hero is taken captive by one of the gang, but turns the tables by producing from his shirt front a second revolver, the weapon which he is preserving as evidence that the heroine's brother is guiltless of the crime of murder. Altogether it is a neatly framed western melodrama, so long as it sticks to straight melodrama. But somebody has demanded that a comedy slant be introduced into the action.

To this end two comedy tramps are dragged into the scenario. Their scenes and the titles that go with them must take up a third of the total footage and they have absolutely not a thing to do with any element of the story. If they had been wiped completely out of the action or cut out of the negative the picture would have been shortened 1,500 feet and the story left in all its completeness. The titles were particularly annoying in their labored efforts to be funny. At the New York they didn't get a ripple.

A melodrama is a melodrama. If its purpose can be aided and fortified with a comedy character well and good. The conventions permit and even encourage this pattern. But the arbitrary forcing of an alien character into sight distracts attention, injures the illusion of the drama and is an affront upon any fan who wants to be thrilled by action, not amused by travesty. *Rush.*

THE PRICE OF YOUTH

Produced by the Berwilla Film Corp. and distributed by Arrow. Described as a Ben Wilson production. Neva Gerber featured. Story by Wyndam Martin. Half of double bill Loew's New York, Aug. 4.

One of those Wall street battle-of-the-financial-giants stories with all the old stuff done in a second class way. Second class applies to the entire enterprise, with emphasis on the direction and the acting. It's a trashy story, cheaply done.

It starts out with the promise of a romantic melodrama, but acquires a mass of distortions as it goes along. For illustration, in the earliest planning of the story we learn that an unnamed blackguard has stolen the wife of Gregory Monmouth of Roanoke, Va., and at the same time ruined him financially. Almost on his deathbed Monmouth communicates these facts to his grown son and pledges the son to avenge the wrong. Immediately the son goes riding with a party of friends and is killed in a fall.

The daughter thereupon takes up the work of vengeance. The introduction of the son therefore was merely a bit of padding. A clearcut story would have started with the girl's status in the conflict. In any event the father dies promptly and the girl, Adela, comes to New York to study for the operatic stage. The first person she meets is Owen, son of the man who wronged her father, but Owen hates his father for breaking his mother's heart.

While Owen is out of town Adela gets a hearing before a grand opera impresario, but is rejected. As she is leaving the conservatory who does she run into but the father himself, although she does not suspect his identity. He is a Wall street broker named Treves, and by reason of the fact that he owns stock in the opera company he secures a new hearing for Adela. Her funds are running low and Treves pretends to invest her remaining money, $250, for her. Instead he hands her worthless stock and pays her expenses out of his own pocket. All this is a device to lay dishonorable siege to the girl, as appears when he makes the usual proposals.

Treves earns the enmity of a certain Wall street group at this time, and they seek his downfall for their own protection. Adela learns of their desire to keep him out of communication with the exchange for one day so they can raid his properties—"his Five Star stock," as the title has it. Adela pretends to accede to Treves' demand for a rendezvous. She borrows a Wall street man's "mountain lodge" (so the title says) and arranges a week-end with Treves there. The place is afterward referred to as "the place on the Sound" by a title writer who was unfamiliar with eastern topography.

In any event Treves is lured to the isolated country house. Adela takes him on a mountain climbing jaunt, and when he returns exhausted gives him every opportunity to fall asleep. When he is sound asleep she trusses him up on the couch with handcuffs and a mile of rope. This is Sunday afternoon. Treves remains a prisoner for 24 hours, or until the exchange closed Monday. In the interval the raid on his stocks is carried out in the usual frenzied scenes of the stock exchange, which in this case looks more like the lobby of the Mills hotel than the exchange.

Just as she releases Treves, Owen, who has been informed of the expedition by Adela's landlady, reaches the "mountain place on the Sound" and confronts his father. Father indelicately tries to make the son think the situation casts a shadow on the girl's good name, but the son declines to take this view, and it all ends with the wrecking of Treves' fortune and wedding bells for his son and Adela.

But the question that remains unanswered is this, What kind of a literary imagination conceives a romantic story that has as its motif the struggle of a honorable young man and his blackguard father for an innocent girl? Some things in the movies are too deep. *Rush.*

UP AND AT 'EM

Comedy starring Doris May. Sponsored by F. B. O. Director, William A. Seiter. Story by Lewis Milestone and scenario by Eve Unsell.

Five reels of slapstick comedy becomes wearisome, no matter how ingenious the devices to coax laughs. If this feature had been slightly roughened up and condensed into half the length it would have been a thoroughly amusing film. As it is, the vigorous comedy is pieced out with dull intervals and before it has run its length it becomes a bore.

The pattern is indefinite. There are times when it takes the line of a polite comedy story. Then it goes into the custard pie technique and back to drawing room comedy again until the spectator is bewildered. The good material is sacrificed by cruel padding and story interludes. If a picture is going to be Mack Sennett it should keep to that pattern. Mixed intent is destructive.

For this reason the production misses its purpose and falls into the daily change neighborhood classification. With better handling it could make a bid for regular playing dates. The knockabout stuff at times is genuinely funny. That passage in which the tomboy flapper, in pursuit of a band of society crooks, is thrown into a freight car inhabited by a quartet of tattered tramps had rich possibilities for Sennett travesty. Some of the comic complications are neatly framed for surprise. For example, the arraignment of the fashionable flapper and the tramps is timed to bring the heroine and her dilapidated company together, with the hero lover haled before the same rube j. p. on charges of speeding, a neat surprise twist.

A good deal of resourcefulness was expended in the swift action, that started with the first reel and kept going to the end. But the mere elaboration of entanglements of a travesty nature can't support 5,000 feet of film, and by the half way mark one is ready to quit. A dramatic story is capable of leading one from development to development, and holding up suspense so that the sense of time elapsed is lost, but multiplicity of absurd incidents soon palls. Here a double purpose spoils both angles. They try to make an elaborate crook plot, but the humorous interlude destroys any anticipation of a thrilling denouement.

Barbara is the tomboy daughter of a rich art collector. She first appears in jail for speeding and is rescued by her mother. Mother forbids her to go out and orders the chauffeur to go to the depot to meet father. Barbara dons the chauffeur's uniform and drives to the station for father. While she is waiting a band of crooks take possession of the auto and force the girl to assist them in a robbery on another art connoisseur's library. After the thieves have stripped the house of valuable paintings they are disturbed by the owner and escape, leaving the girl to be captured.

She proves her innocence, introduces the victim to her parents and a romance starts. Presently the thieves try to sell the stolen pictures to Barbara's father and she attempts to catch them. She trails the leader of the gang into a wax works, where there is a long scene of comedy stunts. Later the thieves kidnap her and throw her into a freight car with the tramps. At the same time they decoy the young lover out of town on a pretext, so that the couple come together in the court. They return home in time to find the chief crook bargaining with Barbara's father for the sale of the stolen masterpiece, and he is captured by a ruse for the romantic ending. Miss May's cutie-cutie mannerisms are rather cloying at times. Why is it that screen hoydens so often inspire impatient snorts rather than chuckles?

Rush.

A SON OF THE GODS

London, July 25.

If this is a sample of the majority of films which the Germans are sending into England, neither English nor American producers need be afraid for a moment. It is appallingly bad. A jumble of crude melodramatic absurdities, for the most part badly done. The story is utter rubbish of the cheap serial order. The continuity is the last thing the author or the producer thought of, and the characters hop from one place to another without the slightest explanation of how they managed it.

For instance, a small boy is tied to a tree by the villainous Japanese. This is in Europe, but having lost him for some hundreds of feet we find him in Japan. "Stunts" occur every hundred feet or so, but they are one and all as poor as the story.

Roughly—Marcco a music hall strong man, invents a wonderful explosive. His formula is stolen by Japanese. While attempting to recover it he is kidnapped. So is a ragged urchin who comes to his rescue. They escape, however, and Marcco chases the thieves to Japan, whither he has been preceded by his beautiful young girl assistant. She is kidnapped and driven to extremes of terror by being confined in a rat-haunted dungeon. This scene is obviously designed to permit her to show her legs and she makes full use of the opportunity. Ultimately she is rescued, the formula is saved by the ragged urchin, villainy dies in the ruins of a burning temple, and we hope Marcco marries the girl.

Much of the setting is cumbersome and gaudy, but there is an excellent reproduction of a Japanese garden. The acting is uniformly bad and the Japanese villain is an amazing example of wooden amateurishness.

The worst film ever seen becomes a work of art as compared with this "Wonderful Photoplay Full of the Glamour of the Far East." *Gore.*

FOX FARM

London, July 28.

The George Clark organization seems to pin its faith to simple stories set in beautiful surroundings, their present features being in marked contrast to the ornate splendor of the first big British superproduction, "The Bigamist." In the end they will probably find wholesome stories amid beautiful natural scenery more profitable.

Their latest feature, "Fox Farm," is worthy in every way of the very high standard they have set in their special class of production. The story is a good one, although they have had to go to a novel for it. It is well told and full of interest as well as natural pathos. The exterior "locations" are enough to make the city man loathe his drab surroundings and long for hills, glades and rippling streams, while the farm interiors are exceedingly well done.

Jesse Falconer is a farmer and also a fatalist, the two things running badly together. A married man, his wife thinks him a fool, but Ann Wetherell, daughter of a disreputable old scoundrel, is strongly attracted to him. One day while blasting a tree an accident occurs and he loses his sight. This drew Ann closer to him, but further estranged his wife. Ann obtains a situation at the farm and does much to comfort her blind master, thereby forming the eternal triangle. Then Mrs. Falconer employs Jack Rickaby to help her run the place. They soon fell in love and, discovering the intrigue, Ann boldly declares her love for her master. The end comes when Falconer leaves his home and is followed by the faithful Ann.

Both Guy Newall and Ivy Duke play parts somewhat out of their lines: Newall as the blind farmer, whereas he is generally seen in leading roles which are leavened by his own particular blend of light comedy; Ivy Duke, player of society women and sporting girls, as the cottage girl. Both are very excellent. Bromley Devonport gives a fine character study as the scoundrelly old father, and Barbara Everest is particularly good as the wife. The other parts are all well played. Well produced and told, "Fox Farm" presents a particularly efficient and interesting study of British village life. *Gore.*

"The Wee MacGregor's Sweetheart"

London, July 12.

The producing firm of Welsh-Pearson deservedly stand high at the top of the ladder where the British producing world is concerned. George Pearson makes one picture while other men make half a dozen, and has very little to say about his work at any time, but when he shows, he shows the goods.

This screen version of J. J. Bell's two books, "Oh, Christina" and "Courtin' Christina," reaches a very high artistic level and is thoroughly good entertainment of the highest class.

The simple story is very nearly plotless, but it is excellently told. It consists mainly in a film picturization of the courtship of the tomboy, Christina, by the now grown up "Wee" Macgregor and the attempts of Christina to get her aunt "off the shelf." The production work and the photography are alike perfect.

The acting of Betty Balfour as Christina and Donald Macardle as Macgregor is excellent, as is that of Minna Gray as the aunt.

Pictures like this revive the kinema and act as a sure antidote to the epidemic of melodrama under which England generally staggers. *Gore.*

QUALITY FILMS

London July 17.

These are short one or two-reel features and are designed to run the whole gamut of comedy, farce, drama and melodrama. The series will consist of 25, all adapted from short stories appearing in popular periodicals, such as "Pan" and "Truth." The four just shown are extraordinarily good, and if the rest of the series keeps up to the standard they should mark an epoch in British film productions. The stories are very well told and grip throughout. The action is rapid and devoid of padding. The production work is excellent but simple.

Of the four just shown, "The White Rat" is melodrama of the Grand Guignol order. The story is of a money lender who has a white rat as a mascot. A young man visits him to plea for time to repay a loan. This is refused and in a momentary fit of passion the caller strikes the usurer dead. His name is found among the dead man's papers and the detectives visit him. He can give no information and they are about to go when one mentions that a white rat, the dead man's pet, is missing. That is the rat's cue to pop its head out of the murderer's topcoat pocket. "A Question of Principle" is a delightfully told light comedy, chiefly remarkable for the introduction of a young actress, Joan Maclean, who will be heard much of. "Fallen Leaves," the adaptation of a short story by Will Scott, is a finely drawn human story, and "The Thief" is "spoof" melodrama of the highest order. No "stars," genuine or alleged, have been used in these productions and the result is a series of performances at least 50 per cent. above the average seen here.

The leading players are Mrs. Haydyn Coffin, Harry J. Worth, Sydney N. Folker, Frank Stanmore, Malcolm Tod, Jeff Barlow, Chris Walker and Joan Maclean. The producer is George A. Cooper. *Gore.*

THE TRAIL'S END

Drama from the W. M. Smith establishment. State Rights Market. Story by Arthur Summers Roche. Director, Francis Ford. In the cast are Franklyn Farnum, Peggy O'Day, Shorty Hamilton and Al Hare. Genevieve Burt also is listed in a minor part. At Stanley, New York, July 25.

The fourth or fifth release in this series, the company being substantially unchanged. The picture weighs in at about the Farnum average. It has a lot of helter-skelter action, muddled somewhat and marred by the very stagy playing of Farnum, who is beginning to make a pretty mature sort of rough riding Western hero.

They may preserve the heroics for Farnum and give him the center of the stage for heavy scenes, but all the honors of the production go to Hamilton, who has a capital natural comedy knack and a gift for neat character work. Al Hart as the heavy did rather well, although the part was somewhat indefinite and subordinate.

The Western scenery that served as the background for the familiar hard riding was strikingly beautiful and some of the scenic shots were arresting. But the picture has action aplenty and a good deal of interest as the complicated plot unfolds. The trouble is that it unfolds in hesitating fashion, so that it is not always clear who the personages are and what their motives. Of course, the mystery twist contributes to this effect, since the real situation is not disclosed until well along in the last reel. Probably the weakness of the picture is that it fails to generate the necessary suspense, and while waiting for the clearing up of the mystery one is not especially stirred. When the disclosure does transpire it is so laborious in its unfolding that the kick is dissipated.

The story opens with some fine shots of a cattle roundup. A stranger presents himself at the ranch house and asks for one Jack Frayne, a cow puncher of the outfit. Frayne disappears and goes into hiding—why, no one knows. On the heels of the stranger comes Mabel, also seeking Frayne. Mabel and Frayne are beneficiaries under an uncle's will, but any heir who has committed a crime is directed to be cut off. The stranger, it turns out, is a detective, commissioned by other relatives to pin a crime on Frayne.

Wilder Armstrong (Fanum) is boss of the ranch. He falls immediately in love with Mabel and pledges his aid to the finding of Frayne. Here starts a three-cornered chase involving the detective, Armstrong and the girl. Which will reach Frayne first and what will happen? The suspense of this is lost in independent incidents and episodes which cloud the issue.

When they do catch up with Frayne it turns out that he is not Frayne at all, but his half-brother, call him Dick. Dick was forced from his uncle's home on the suspicion that he had stolen certain property, although it was really Frayne who committed the crime. Dick and Frayne meet in a remote Western shack some time after and quarrel over the affair, and Dick is forced to shoot Frayne in self-defense. Then, to cover up suspicion, Dick lets his beard grow and assumes Frayne's identity. It's pretty complicated and foggy, but the screen version is reasonably clear, if one concentrates on it. It all ends up with the usual wedding bells, Armstrong and Mabel being the principals. Medium grade light program feature, with the rental figuring in its value. *Rush.*

MONTE CRISTO

William Fox special, approximately eight reels. From story by Alexander Dumas, adapted for the screen by Bernard McConville and directed by Emmett J. Flynn. At 44th Street, New York, Aug. 14 for a run.

Edmund Dantes, a sailor.... / The Count of Monte Cristo..	John Gilbert
Mercedes, Countess de Morcerf	Estelle Taylor
Caderousse, the inn-keeper	William V. Mong
De Villefort, King's attorney	Robert McKim
Fernand, Count de Morcerf	Ralph Cloninger
Albert De Morcerf, his son	Gaston Glass
Elder Dantes, father of Edmund	Harry Lonsdale
Morrel, ship-owner	Al Filson
Danglars, Baron Danglars	Albert Prisco
Baroness Danglars	Maude George
Eugenie Danglars, her daughter	Renee Adore
Haidee, an Arbian Princess	Virginia B. Faire
Benedetto, son of De Villefort	Francis MacDonald
Governor of Chateau D'if	Jack Cosgrove
Luigi Vampa, an ex-pirate	Geo. Seigmann
The Abbe Faria	Spottiswood Aitken
Napoleon	George Campbell
Jailor at Chateau D'If	Willard Koch
Surgeon	Howard Kendall

A great production, superbly acted by a great cast and capably directed, sums up the William Fox production of "Monte Cristo" which has John Gilbert as the principal player in the dual role of the feature.

As to the box office possibilities of the feature, it will be a big picture to say the least, but at a scale of $1 for matinees and $1.50 for the night performances, it does not appear to be a proposition that will play to big business.

In photography the picture stands out. That particular feature is the strongest in its favor, and alone will appeal to the picture fans.

The story on the screen does not seem to have the romance embodied in the book, nor does the interpretation by Gilbert hold the charm and delight in the performance of James O'Neill on the spoken stage. Still and all, undoubtedly sufficient of those even in this great unread country who have read the book will want to see the picture.

The presentation on the occasion of the initial performance in New York was somewhat marred by the faulty projection in the early reels. So badly did the operator or operators handle the machines that at least 400' feet of the story was dropped through the film breaking in several places. At one time this caused the audience in the upper lofts to revert to first principal as to picture audiences; they began to razz the operator by applauding. When the picture was resumed after a lengthy wait they handed the new sequence of the story a laugh.

The Fox organization cannot hold as much hope for this as for their "Nero." That is a real film achievement. This is just a picture, nothing more, even though it has been elaborately done and undoubtedly represents an outlay of tremendous money.

In direction there is one thing Mr. Flynn counted on to put his picture over and that was the use of the close-up almost continuously in the early sections. He was quite successful in it and held his audience. His general handling created an atmosphere of suspense but there was no real thrill. It was just suspense—a sort of "well, let's see what is going to happen next" idea.

In the supporting cast were at least three players who stood out to overshadowing advantage. They are William V. Mong, Robert McKim and Ralph Cloninger, while Francis MacDonald as the illegitimate son of de Villefort contributed a splendid piece of acting. Spottiswood Aitken as the Abbe Faria, the fellow prisoner of Dante's, was tremendous in his death scene.

Of the women Estelle Taylor was more or less matter of fact, at least as far as her later scenes were concerned, although she seemed vivacious enough a sweetheart earlier. Virginia B. Faire as the Arabian Princess scored the beauty hit and acquitted herself exceptionally well.

A slight comedy touch was well handled by George Seigmann as the ex-pirate attendant to the count.

The sets are unusually elaborate and massive. The port of Marseilles (evidently shot down at old Inceville above Santa Monica) looked particularly good. The lightings are superb and the photography remarkable. Some tinted shots are beautiful.

There is a chance that with the extraordinary advance publicity and fine exploitation that the picture has received, along with the tide, it could remain at the 44th Street to fair business for about four weeks, but the indications are that anything beyond that will be forced. The sooner this picture gets to the regular picture houses the better. It will make money for the exhibitors if they get it while its great publicity is still fresh in mind.

It is a picture for picture houses, not because of its screen value, but because of the value of the title and the publicity that has been given it since the picture production was started. *Fred.*

PRINCE AND PAUPER

A foreign made six reel production of Mark Twain's story, produced in Austria and Bohemia at Vienna and Prague under the direction of Alexander Kardo. American release not yet determined. At Capitol, week of Aug. 13.

The Prince / The Pauper	Tibi Lubin
Miles Hendon	Francis Everth
Jonh Canty	Francis Herter
Henry VIII	Alfred Schreiber
Hugh Hendon	Wilhelm Schmidt
Lady Edith	Ditta Ninjan
Isabel	Lilly Lubin
Lord Chancellor	A. D. Weisse

Through the medium of a film production of the Mark Twain story "The Prince and The Pauper," Austria and Bohemia enter into the world field of providing picture entertainment. The picture is in six reels. It tells the Twain tale consistently in well connected action. There are no dull moments and it looks as though the picture was certain of being a money getter. It is certain to have an appeal to all children, whether small or grown up, and the Twain fans who were so disappointed in the horse play that was indulged in in the screen version of "A Connecticut Yankee" will actually revel in this picture for it is Twain as written.

Well cast and played and exceedingly skillful was the direction of Alexander Kardo who is responsible for the picture.

At the head of the cast is a youngster by the name of Tibi Lubin who appears about eight or nine years of age. He is really a star. His work in this picture makes him a screen prospect for the future. In kid parts of this nature he stands out to greater advantage than some of the older stars that have been developed either abroad or here. His work in the double exposure scenes is simply great.

The supporting cast has a number of real clever players but it is the production itself that stands out as a world beater. Here the producers have a real human tale that is set in the early days of English history, with its massive castles and all the pomp and pagentry of the coronation of the King. They have overlooked no opportunity to use crowds of extra for the bigger scenes but still in all they manage to keep their principals well in the foreground of the story, which puts the picture over with a bang.

From the indications in observing this picture it looks as though the Austrian producers were in the field to give their German neighbors a run for their money in the picture producing field. In its own class this picture is as much of a revelation in foreign producing as was "Passion" and the fact that this is a story written by an American author of international appeal, gives indication that it will be 100 per cent. greater in its box office appeal as a film than was the first of the German made productions. *Fred.*

NICE PEOPLE

"Adolph Zukor presents a William De Mille production from the play by Rachel Crothers and screen play by Clara Beranger," reads the program. Wallace Reid, Conrad Nagel, Bebe Daniels and Julia Faye are featured in the cast. Current at the Rialto, New York.

The "flapper" theme at this late date after F. Scott Fitzgerald and other best seller authors have handled in several different angles must be pretty strong stuff to hold up nowadays. It is more to the director's and the featured players' credit than the author's that the piece got what it got before a rather lackadaisical attendance Sunday, although Miss Beranger in the screen metamorphosis has injected several masterful touches that add much to elevate the rather thin plot material. The screen with its wider range of latitude afforded the play limitless opportunity for elaboration and the lavish production so dear to William De Mille. Not one, but two ballroom scenes were included—the first a cabaret set and the other an American masque ball—all displaying nothing, not flambuoyant, luxury, applied with the fine Italian hand of De Mille. Those scenes, and all the interiors in fact, were soothing to a degree, bespeaking refinement and not shrieking or reeking with gaudy artificial display, for which there might even have been some excuse in the masque scene, for instance.

Yet, despite these assets, the plot material still impresses as rather "thin" on reflection, although interesting enough as the obvious theme is unfolded.

One knows that Theodora (Teddy) Gloucester (Miss Daniels) cannot keep up her wild gallavantin' and tearin' about without coming to a sudden halt, and that a change in her demeanor and a complete metamorphosis of existence must be consummated before the picture has run its course in order that she match up to the requisites of a really "nice" girl. Teddy comes of "nice people," and that probably excuses a good deal of her stuff that would be considered rather raw coming from other less privileged humans. So when Wallace Reid enters the rather notorious midnight "creep joint" an ex-captain, who wonders if this is the freedom they fought for in Flanders, and is muchly taken with the cynical wording on an undressed souvenir doll reading "The modern girl has as little in her head and heart as she has clothes on her back," why, it's plain as daylight Mr. Reid is gonna play an important part in making over Teddy's butterfly existence.

Things follow quickly—speed, by the way, is an important component of the action—and Teddy finds herself compromised through being forced by a rain storm to spend the night in a farmhouse with only Scotty Wilbur (Conrad Nagel), her escort. It so happens that Billy Wade (Mr. Reid) happens along while Scotty is sleeping off a hangover from the night before, and Teddy is really thusly chaperoned, although even Scotty does not believe it since Billy departed before he woke up, and Teddy is still in the dark as to her gallant's identity. So when "Town Tattles" starts dishing the dirt innuendo Teddy finds that all her "nice people" former friends are cutting her. She returns to her farm in Connecticut (or is it Massachusetts?) and starts rebuilding herself, dressed in puttees, with Billy Wade's assistance. Wade has agreed to "farm hand" for her and put the property on a paying basis and rebuffs Teddy's flirtatious attempts that will crop up periodically. However, the "back to the farm" stuff is really the making of Teddy, and when her heretofore indulgent dad, who at first was very much vexed by Teddy's embarrassing escapade, shows her a report from the War Department on Captain Wade's past performances, which mentions distinguishment for bravery, Teddy just takes matters in hand and makes Billy propose for the "clinch" even to the extent of almost doing a Leap Year herself to accomplish it.

There is no denying that the story interests in its unfolding. Miss Daniels effervesces pep, speed, energy—anything you want to call it—that is undeniable, but which again suffers proportionately on reflection. Such whiz-bang cutting up is not orthodoxically realistic; but then, again, who thinks about a feature more than once these days?

The casting has been excellently assigned. Miss Faye of the featured four is the least known possibly in comparison to the other three. She does a society deb that is a cross between an ingenue and a heavy, very friendly to the leading lady and at first appearing sympathetic, but really quite "catty" and spiteful. The conception is not new to any form of fiction, particularly the screen, but is handled differently, and capab'y, by Miss Faye. Mr. Nagel, too, does a similar counterpart, a hybrid juvenile and light heavy role that was deftly handled by him. Mr. Nagel impresses as a good bet for Paramount to build up for possible future starring purposes.

Claire McDowell's conception of the aunt role was superb. Edward Martindel as Teddy's father also took full advantage of all his opportunities.

"Nice People," compared to some of the stuff Paramount has been pre-releasing this summer at its Broadway twin weekly change houses, suffices as a one-week feature, although compared to regular fall and winter stuff it is just a good "society" program release. *Abel.*

THE MASQUERADER

Richard Walton Tully makes his debut as a picture producer with "The Masquerader" starring Guy Bates Post. The production is six reels in length directed by James Young and released through First National. Strand, New York, week of Aug 13.

John Chilcote / John Loder	Guy Bates Post
Brock	Edward M. Kimball
Eve	Ruth Sinclair
Fraide	Herbert Standing
Lakely	Lawson Butt
Lady Astrupp	Marcia Manon
Robbins	Barbara Tennant
Blessington	Kenneth Gibson

The long awaited screen debut of Guy Bates Post came this week with the presentation by Richard Walton Tully of "The Masquerader" at the Strand. The production is in six reels, full of action and coupled with the fact that it has been played by the star in practically every nook and corner of the country in the past five or six years, it should develop into a real box office attraction. The story is interesting and at times gripping. Mr. Post however doesn't seem to be fully at ease in front of the camera as he is on the stage and so there are moments when he rather over acts in the dual roles that he portrays. James Young who handled the direction has handled the subject rather well but the editing and titling gave the picture a rather uneven appearance at times.

In production the feature stands up with any of the better grade. The London scenes are well handled, even to the matching up of scenes shot abroad showing streets and crowds. The cast supporting the star is a fully adequate one that lends its best efforts toward making the tale interesting in action.

Mr. Post in the dual roles, John Chilcote, M. P., and John Loder, at times gave a performance that would have been worthy of Mansfield and still at other moments he seemed so fully aware of the camera that it was impossible for him to turn away from lense. On the whole however he acquitted himself very well indeed.

Edward Kimball as the old trusted servant also gave a corking performance as did also Ruth Sinclair and Herbert Standing.

Barbara Tennant in a slavery role was really one of the high lights of the cast, even though she had comparatively little to do. Marcia Manon in a vampish role made the most of it.

"The Masquerader" is a picture that while not standing out as a world beater is one that will surely turn the trick at the box office. It has a punch that it needed at this time to pull the public back to the picture houses. *Fred.*

EYES OF THE MUMMY

U. F. A. production with Pola Negri. Sponsored in this market by the Hamilton Co. (Paramount). At New York theatre, August 2-11.

Mara	Pola Negri
Radu	Emil Jennings
Albert Vernon	Henri Liedke

Another of those labored dime novel dramatic stories from the U. F. A. plant. The situations are an affront to adult intelligence, but might make a thriller for juvenile audiences. The release of so many films of this quality is a sure index of the poverty of current release material.

The picture is gaited for the daily change establishments of the neighborhood grade. Lurid billing probably will attract a matinee trade, but that's the extent of its appeal. It has some of the strained dramatic devices of the "Mysteries of India" kind.

An Egyptian religious fanatic pursues the heroine half way around the world, and leads one to believe that he seeks her death in revenge for her desertion. When he finds her one takes it for granted that he will satisfy his vengeance in a straightaway, violent Oriental way. Not so. The scenario writer has to go about it after the manner of Tom Sawyer and Huck Finn, who released Nigger Jim from the woodshed by digging a tunnel under the floor instead of pulling the latch.

Radu, the fanatic, breaks down the heroine's nerves and almost drives her mad by appearing before her like an apparition and then vanishing. He does this long enough to spread out the footage and then goes to the job with a dirk. As he is about to strike, however, this method appears too coarse. He changes his mind, for no apparent reason, and stabs himself to death instead, this providing a happy ending.

The picture has some rather effective desert wilderness settings and the passages in the Egyptian tomb, where the English scientist and the Egyptian girl, Marah, captive of the fanatic, come together. These passages are the best of the film. When the action changes to polite civilization, it is nowhere convincing. The woman extras are ludicrously dowdy in the presumably elegant ballroom scenes. The social events are supposed to take place in the home of an English nobleman, but the costumes look like a Greenpoint chowder party. Even so essential detail as the fit and style of the men's evening clothes run to comedy.

Pola Negri discloses unsuspected skill in dancing and her stage performance was interesting. Her acting was better than in most of the group of second rate films that have come out so far (this excludes the earlier samples). She looks the part of the Egyptian and the Oriental costuming helps her toward bizarre effects. Emil Jannings is always absurd as the terrifying bogey man, Radu.

Film fans by long practice get to accept almost any accomplishment of providential coincidence, but this goes beyond most extremes. But that's the kind of fiction it is. Mere crude make-believe.

Rush.

HER MAJESTY

Put out by Playgoers Pictures and distributed by Pathe. Co-stars, Mollie King and Creighton Hale. Directed by H. T. Rich; scenario by George Irving. At Loew's New York, Aug. 10.

Rather infantile sample of screen fiction with twin sisters who are each other's double as the basis of complications. Crudest kind of drama in material and construction. The story doesn't gather momentum until it is half completed and entirely new characters are still being introduced in reel three. The opening is especially dull. Double exposure occurs in frequent passages and is neatly managed, but all but the final scene contribute little, to getting on with the story.

One of the sisters is a poor but good country girl, the other is a sophisticated, scheming society flapper. The girls are orphans and their difference in station comes from the circumstance that they grow up separately, each with a guardian aunt. Susan's guardian is a humble New England woman, sister of the dead mother, and Rosalie lives with the rich sister of her deceased father.

They meet infrequently, and then on terms of coldness, until Susan's foster mother dies on the Down East farm, and she goes to the other aunt's luxurious Long Island home. Down on the farm Susan has been affectionately addressed as "Your Majesty" because of her love for playing childish games in which she poses as queen. In this simple country environment Susan meets a stronge youth named Ted Spencer, and they fall in love in their childish way. Ted subsequently meets Rosalie in the city, and when he turns out to be a millionaire's son the girl and her aunt let him go on thinking Rosalie is Susan.

Afterward when the two girls are in the same house Susan is kept in the background, while Rosalie is thrown at Ted's head. By accident Susan and Ted meet in the garden, but even then the boy never suspects the duplicity. He does propose an elopement and the girl consents to run away the same evening, although there is to be a Hallowe'en party.

Rosalie has become involved with a city slicker who wants to marry her for her aunt's money, and she makes an engagement (quite innocently, the titles would have us believe) to meet him in room No. 313 at a country roadhouse. Susan hears her make the date over the telephone, and, thinking Rosalie has grabbed off her elopement engagement with Ted, locks her in her room and goes to the roadhouse in her place, disguised in black domino. The city slicker tries to force the girl to marry him, but she eludes him and gets back home.

Meanwhile Rosalie has escaped and she appears in the roadhouse. The slicker is making love to her when another woman enters, revolver in hand, and declares she has a claim on him. Heartbroken, Rosalie returns home. The experience of man's villainy has instantly cured her of all her selfish habits, and she retires from the race for Ted's affections and bankroll in favor of the honest Susan. This is pretty hard to swallow, but no harder than numerous other theatrical situations. While Susan is in the city looking for employment (this is before she seeks asylum with the aunt) the evil son of her landlady makes dishonorable court to her and she is terrified. He accosts her on the street, and when she repulses him he gives her over to a policeman, declaring she had followed him. The policeman arrests the girl and brings her to the night court. She is released only by the appearance of her rich aunt, to whom she appeals in her extremity. The man just walks away when the policeman arrests the girl, a system of procedure confined to the screen. Presumably the cop who made the arrest testified to the magistrate that the girl annoyed him.

But this shrinking child of the country, when confronted with a smooth schemer in the bedroom of a spicy roadhouse has command of the situation, and with perfect poise laughs the schemer out of confidence.

Some of the theatrical complications toward the end of the film are ingenious, and for about a reel and a half things move swiftly if not convincingly, but the whole thing falls to pieces under examination as a mere device of trashy fiction. Mollie King as Susan on the farm looked pretty mature to be playing child's games. A knee-length gingham frock wasn't enough disguise.

Rush.

The Thinker

Done by Gaumont in France. story by E. Fleg, "inspired by Rodin's famous statue," as the title has it. Andrew Nox heads the company. Loew's Circle, Aug. 15.

A strained and labored dramatic effort which tries with awful seriousness to point the moral that one who delves too deeply into the human soul will forfeit sanity and life. At the opening the artist-hero is disclosed in the attitude of the Rodin figure, "The Thinker." The title discloses that he is dead in an insane asylum, and the rest of the story is in the form of a fadeback.

The hero is an artist. Dissatisfied with his work, he prays that he might have the insight into human souls that would make him another Vinci. In answer to his prayer he gets the message that if he will assume the pose of "The Thinker" (a copy of which stands in his studio) he will perceive the innermost thoughts of people.

The editor of a scandal publication sends him an anonymous communication suggesting that his wife loves one of his art students. The seed of jealousy and suspicion grows to an obsession. He sees evil where there is only innocence and good. The unearthly power of penetrating the human mask gives him an insight into all the hypocrisy and wickedness of society until he goes mad with cynicism. He falls ill and they send for a physician. The doctor declares him in a serious state. The artist falls into the Rodin pose and the screen fades to the reproduction of a doctor's bill for $1,500 and again to a view of the medico seated before a ladened dinner table. The artist and his wife go to a reception. The artist sees in a young couple about to wed nothing but the scheming of the young man for his fiancee's riches (indicated by his embracing a pile of money bags).

The artist looks into the mirror and sees himself murdering his wife and the young student. At her wits' end the wife coaxes him to go with her to church, and there before the altar (some good views of Notre Dame, in Paris, here) he is freed from his mania for the time being. But the damage has been done. His suspicions of his wife have destroyed her love and she turns to the young artist. The young man has been absent, traveling to forget her, but has now returned and sends a note to say that his regard is purely platonic and asking her to leave a light in her window if she will receive him on those terms.

The intent is rather foggy here. The wife apparently doesn't want the young man on any such conditions. She draws the curtains of her windows. The husband interprets this as guilt (the clairvoyant faculty revealing all her impulses), and in a long-drawn-out dramatic rave he kills her.

The idea sounds a good deal more interesting that it is as it comes on the screen. The devices are too transparent and the situations too grossly crude. The picture calls for an immense amount of suggestion rather than stark realism. The scenes that should be impressive are merely petty and theatrical, and long before the action has reached its peak the audience is bored. The fault is entirely in the direction.

Nox has an eloquent face and the other players are convincing at times when left to themselves. The leading woman has been handicapped with an unsightly wig for no purpose that is discernible, and throughout the direction is in the style of 10 years ago. Even the photography is poor, and one would imagine, except that the styles of dress are modern, that the picture was a reissue of an ancient original. Used as half a double in a daily change house. That's about its level.

Rush.

RICH MEN'S WIVES

Gasnier Production in five reels presented by B. P. Schulberg, distributed by Al Lichtman Corp. Story by Frank Dazey and Agnes C. Johnson; House Peters and Claire Windsor principals. Capitol, New York, week, Aug. 20.

John Masters	House Peters
Gay Davenport	Claire Windsor
Mrs. Lindley-Blair	Rosemary Theby
Juan Camillo	Gaston Glass
Mrs. Davenport	Myrtle Stedman
Jackie	Baby Richard Headrick
Estelle Davenport	Mildred June
Mr. Davenport	Charles Clary
Maid	Carol Holloway
Nurse	Martha Mattox
Reggie	William Austin

The first of the releases of the Al Lichtman Corp. to hit Broadway in one of the big pre-release houses. It is a picture that in itself runs along the usual lines of the society tales of a certain type. That of the wife neglected for business, discovered in a compromising not of her own making by the husband, the usual separation and reconcilation brought about through the little child. It is not a special. It is, however, a good program picture that should get money for the exhibitor on the strength of the title rather than the entertainment value. The production is presented by B. P. Schulberg and released through the Lichtman Corp. The story by Frank Dazey and Agnes C. Johnson, was directed by Louis Gasnier. The players that have the principal roles are House Peters and Claire Windsor.

In a measure the moral the story points is that business and social activities on the part of parents is not conducive to the education of children in a manner that will enable them to conduct affairs of life in a happy manner.

Miss Windsor plays the youthful girl graduate who returns to a home where the mother is busy half of the time with beauty specialists and the other half displaying that beauty at social functions; the father is 100 per cent business but has an ever ready checkbook for his daughters. A short time after the daughter is launched in society and marries. Her life goes along in the same channel as it did before marriage, with nothing to occupy her mind except the search for entertainment and excitement. A baby arrives but that serves only to give employment to a nurse. Finally the wife innocently steps into a trap laid by a society lizard which results in her and her husband separating. The latter retains the custody of the child, the mother being forbidden to see the little one. Sometime later amid a gay party she slips into the child's nursery at a time when the revellers decide that for a fountain of love they must have a Cupid, and the child is brought down into the water with the mother rescuing it. This brings the husband to a realization he must have been wrong in his suspicions and a reconcilation is effected.

Miss Windsor and Mr. Peters give a good performance as does Baby Richard Headrick, and Rosemary Theby stands out like a million dollars on looks as a vamp type. There is a bit of miscasting in the selection of Myrtle Steadman as the mother; she appears younger on the screen than Miss Windsor.

The direction is fairly even, although the "my baby stuff" by Miss Windsor seems overdone at times. In photography the picture is faultless, and clever art titles in natural colors lend class to the production.

Fred.

WHEN HUSBANDS DECEIVE

Designated as a "Leah Baird Production" presented by Arthur V. Beck. Story and scenario by Leah Baird who also plays the principal role. Wallace Worsley, director. Distributed by Pathe.

The title is just one of those catch phrases to arouse attention in the billing. It hasn't a thing to do with the picture. "A boxoffice title" they call it in this business, meaning a phrase that will attract the curious, however, foreign it may be to the subject matter of the story. This sort of thing must inevitably react to the damage of any producer or any theatre. You can't get away with such a hoax indefinitely, although some of the producers have been doing it a long time.

Women stars who write their own scenarios invite disaster as a rule, and certainly this instance adds another flop to the list. The whole thing is just cheap fiction and theatrical bosh, intense drama that trembles on the edge of unintentional comedy and sometimes slips over the travesty border. It is full of those mock philosophical titles by which uncertain scenario writers try to endow their weak efforts with counterfeit sentiment. If a story can stand on its own legs it needs only the simplest and most direct of titles. Stilted writing in titles is a poor device to cover deficiencies. "When Husbands Deceive" might have been written by a school girl.

Miss Baird is always convincing in dignified dramatic roles. That is probably why she framed this part of a kittenish young hoyden who was tricked into a marriage with a plotting schemer seeking only her fortune. Why will mature actresses persist in playing flappers?

The story itself is without distinction and full of the conventional devices. Dick and Rosalie are engaged, while John Martin, the girl's guardian and Dick's employer schemes to separate them. Dick is sent to the bank with $5,000 in bonds and Martin's woman accomplice, pretending to faint on the street, pursuades Dick to take her home in a taxicab. Dick is drugged in the cab, his securities stolen and his disgrace brought about. To make it more complete Martin shows Rosalie what purports to be a compromising letter written to Dick by another woman.

In pique, Rosalie marries her middle aged guardian. It' immediately becomes apparent that Martin has cheated her out of her inheritance ($1,000,000 in oil properties in the usual prodigal film way), and plots to rob her of her good name by maneuvering her into a compromising situation with Dick. Meanwhile Dick has turned his gifts as a painter to account and is paying off the lost bonds. By chance he meets Martin's woman accomplice in the street and under threats wrings a confession from her.

Martin's guilt is established and Dick goes to expose him to Rosalie. Rosalie receives him in her sitting room, being then dressed in a boudoir frock of the flimsiest. Martin listens to their conversation and, after locking them in, brings witnesses to confront them. Of course, he is speedily brought to terms by the heroic Dick, who forces a confession and then departs. Martin, desperate, tries to intimidate Rosalie with a revolver, but an enormous pet mastif dog comes to his mistress' rescue and the audience is left to understand that Martin is torn limb from limb by the animal, leaving the way clear for true love to run more smoothly than the continuity. Besides the trick dog the picture has a highly intelligent monkey which does more to advance the plot than the principal actor. It mischievously opens Martin's safe so that Rosalie may learn how he has stolen her fortune and otherwise contributes to the complications. The simian is the most interesting item in the story. *Rush.*

UNDER OATH

Myron Selznick production, presented by Lewis J. Selznick, starring Elaine Hammerstein. Mahlon Hamilton plays the male lead. Edward J. Montague story, directed by George Archainbaud. Shown at Loew's State first half (July 14-16).

Elaine Hammerstein was not exceptionally well fitted with this vehicle, which revolved chiefly about "Big Jim" Powers (Mahlon Hamilton). Shirley Marvin (Miss Hammerstein) learns that the long existent feud between the Marvins and Powers has resulted in a victory for the latter, who on the morrow, by hammering a certain stock controlled by the Marvins, will have pauperized the family. Shirley's betrothed, Hartley Peters (Niles Welch), an assistant district attorney, goes to Powers to effect some settlement, asking to let up on the Marvins. Old man Marvin has been seriously invalided by his financial setbacks and a complete wiping out would prove a fatal shock.

Powers, the vengeful, at first refuses any terms, but later agrees to make his rivals suffer the more by a certain proposition. It consists of a marriage between his scapegrace younger brother, who already is shown $14,000 in debt to a gambler and the Marvin girl. The D. A. leaves greatly incensed at this proposition, but Shirley is game. Powers is frank in stating his revenge will be greater by seeing the whole Marvin family suffer than by killing the old man off completely through the shock. At the actual ceremony Shirley's lips tremble in refusal of the "I will" acquiescence and faints before the consummation of the church rites. Powers in self-disgust releases her from her obligation, admiring her gameness, and lives up to his bargain in letting up on the Marvins. Of course, the romance between him and Shirley is inevitable from then on, although discernible as a final culmination of screen action.

The climax is not so punchy or dramatic as is usually expected. Powers is accused of having murdered his younger brother, whom he had ordered from the house in a fit of rage. The boy was really shot by the vengeful gambler who held the $14,000 I.O.U.'s. The murder was committed about one o'clock, ascertained through one of the bullets shatering the victim's watch at that hour, stopping it completely. Powers cannot alibi his whereabouts at the time, his servants testifying he left shortly before one but did not see him return. In reality, Shirley was with him then at Power's home to warn him of a trumped charge, but to save her any embarrassment the accused would not say anything beyond denying guilt. The punch is where Shirley visits her ex-betrothed, the assistant D. A. and in flashback fashion recites her whereabouts in Powers company at that hour.

The casting is well taken care of. Hamilton and the star naturally standing out, although the thankless role of Powers' younger brother was well handled also.

Good one-day program feature. *Abel.*

PUTTING IT OVER

"Phil Goldstone presents" is the only data furnished. The story and direction are credited to Grover Jones. At Loew's Circle Aug. 15.

Richard Talmadge is here the hero of a comedy written and played in the manner of Douglas Fairbanks, that is to say, Talmadge is constantly plunging by a headlong leap over obstacles into a clinch with the heavy and scrapping all over the lot. The information obtainable from the lobby billing is sketchy. A one-sheet liberally plastered about the front of the house says merely, "Who Is Richard Talmadge? Ask Douglas Fairbanks."

It's a very inexpensive production, except for one episode, a cabaret scene at the start which may have cost something, although it has been done economically. Even at that it's a waste of money. These cabaret spectacles must be well done to be impressive, and this is a half-way affair. It has no place in the picture anyway. The story is distinctly of small-town atmosphere and the principal scenes of the action show a background of a village street, a rural community that is at variance with a spectacular cabaret.

Talmadge is Bob Merritt, son of a political leader. A political campaign is on, the rival candidates being one Horton, supported by Bob's father, whose creature the candidate is, and Morton, the upright contender. Bob is sent electioneering for Horton, but switches his allegiance when he sees Morton's daughter and learns that his father is double-crossing Morton by means of bribing Morton's campaign manager to throw the election.

The town has been billed with banners with the device, "Vote for Horton." Bob merely paints the "H" into an "M" and the trick is done. The traitorous campaign manager then breaks into Morton's home and steals $2,000, a trust fund in Morton's keeping, in order that he may disgrace the rival candidate. Morton must raise $2,000 by that night to save his reputation, and here's where Bob makes the grandstand play. A champion pugilist is appearing in the town and offering $2,500 to anyone who can stay three rounds. Bob, of course, takes the challenge and the stage is set for the "big scene" in the prize ring.

Talmadge is a good looking youngster of fine physique, but the boxing exhibition is a good deal of a farce. The two men climb into the ring and maul at each other awkwardly. There's plenty of rough and tumble action, but it isn't a boxing exhibition. Anyway, Bob knocks the champ out and gets the $2,500 in time to rush it into Morton's hands just as he is about to confess that he has lost the trust fund. The messenger is the girl, Barbara, daughter of Morton and beloved of Bob.

Killing two birds with one stone, the same scene accomplishes the conviction of the robber, although the screen does not make it plain how he was captured. Some of the struggles between the hero and the various villains are spirited, particularly the fight in the dark when Bob tries to prevent the robbery, but the story is crude and the tale doesn't convince. Here used as half of a double bill. *Rush.*

DON'T SHOOT

James Harrington Court	Herbert Rawlinson
John Lysaght	William Dyer
Buck Lindsay	Wade Boteler
Mrs. Van Deek	Margaret Campbell
Velma Gay	Edna Murphy
Archie Craig	George Fisher
Jim	Tiny Sanford
Pete	Duke Lee
Mrs. Ransom	Mrs. Bertram Grassby
Police Officer	Fred Kelsey
Larry the Dip	J. L. O'Connor

This is a Universal starring Herbert Rawlinson from the story by George Bronson Howard, adapted by George Hively, directed by Jack Conway. It is a crook melodrama cooked up for popular consumption and will entertain the not too credulous.

The screen version covers an enormous amount of ground and at times becomes draggy before James Harrington Court, alias "The Possum," foils the gang of thugs and the crooked political boss who is trying to thwart the "Possum" in his determination to go straight after he has been forced into marriage with a society girl.

The "Possum" is about to rob the house of a millionaire oil man when he is surprised by the inmates. The oil king mistakes the crook for the lover of the girl, the secret correspondence of whom he has intercepted. He forces them to marry at the point of a gun. The crook attempts to effect a marriage between the girl and her lover, but the latter's ardor has cooled, so he takes her himself, determines to go straight, and they are next seen as professional dancers at a cabaret. The politician has him discharged, needing him to plant some incriminating papers in the safe of a reform alderman who is a bitter antagonist.

"The Possum's" refusal and the fight against the boss and his gang that follows was one of the high lights of the five reels. Befriended by the grateful alderman, the "Possum" outwits his enemies, wins the love of his wife and is well on the way to peace and prosperity before the final fade-out.

The direction is fair, considering the scope of the story. Nothing could prevent it from straining the credulity of an intelligent witness.

The cast is adequate. Edna Murphy looked pretty as the heroine, but fell far short of anything that registered in the emotional passages beyond a sweet ingenuish personality.

Rawlinson as the debonair good-looking pickpocket and safe-breaker of fiction made the most of a fat role. The rest of the cast maintained the general average. As a "special" the picture is just the average "crook" play, indifferently done. *Con.*

DOOR THAT HAD NO KEY

British society drama sponsored by A. Harley Knoles. Directed by Frank Crane. From original story by Cosmo Hamilton. Featured players are George Relph and Evelyn Brent. At Loew's, New York, Aug. 19.

One would expect something from the authorship of the story, but one is greatly disappointed. The picture is as bad as any of the British films that have reached this market up to date. Properly speaking, it isn't a picture at all, but a novel transcribed to the screen by way of long, verbose titles. The picture passages merely illustrate the titles. They could have almost eliminated the pictures altogether, and the titles alone would have given the gist.

The film is a perfect illustration of the wrong way to frame a continuity. It is full of unessential details worked out with annoying elaboration while really important developments are slighted. For example, it is made apparent that the adventuress will not marry the hero until he has made a success of his profession, and the story makes a great deal of his climb to eminence as a lawyer.

On the other hand, there is a vast deal of interest in the relations between the hero and the adventuress after their marriage and up to the point where they are estranged, but this passage in their lives is dismissed with a title, "Two Years Pass." The emphasis is on the trifling and the important details are slighted.

The theatrical devices are unutterably crude, and the titles with their pompous moralizing are unconsciously ridiculous. Jack is studying law in the office of an eminent London barrister. An important divorce case is about to be called for trial when the lawyer is injured in an accident. Jack thereupon conducts the defense. As his arguments come on the screen in the form of titles one begins to think it is some sort of a travesty with its Oliver Optic sentiment. The whole business is burlesque, and the New York theatre audience took it that way. They laughed at the false sentiment throughout.

The title comes from the fact that the mercenary adventuress locks her bedroom door on her wedding night and keeps it locked during the two years of her married life, while the young husband moons about in pantomimic suffering until he can stand it no longer. Then he gets a divorce by a single title to that effect, and marries the sweet daughter of the vicar; but this is not disclosed until the first wife tries to bring about a reconciliation (why, nobody knows) and is confronted with the new wife and a new baby, which the hero grandiloquently refers to as "My son and heir."

The only merit the picture has is **the lovely backgrounds of rural England. Some are beautiful, especially those dealing with a coaching tour that the hero takes when he is oppressed with his family troubles. But mere scenic quality cannot compensate for the absurd story and the silly action. One suspects that Hamilton's tale has been maltreated in the screen translation. He couldn't have perpetrated anything so awful.**

This picture and others of the imported sort seem to indicate the desperate need of the daily change theatres for material. It does seem that such stuff couldn't get a hearing if there were anything else available. "The Door That Had No Key" was half a double bill, the other being an American-made western drama of the usual sort. What is the virtue of a double bill, anyway, when it only doubles the weariness of poor entertainment? Two bad pictures at one setting are more than twice as bad as one.

Rush.

WEST OF CHICAGO

Fox release starring Charles (Buck) Jones in George Scarborough story; adapted by Paul Schofield and co-directed by Scott Dunlap and C. R. Wallace. Renee Adoree plays opposite the star, with Philo McCullough the "heavy." Sub-feature of double-header at Academy of Music, New York, Aug. 17-20.

George Scarborough, in conceiving the story, presumably banked heavily on the novel situation of a man really impersonating himself, unbeknown to the other characters in the narrative. It is worked out here in the case of Con Daly (Mr. Jones) first entering the scene under an alias, and then asked by the opposing forces to take sides with them in a scheme to do the real Con Daly out of an inheritance. Muchly taken with the newcomer's actions, John Hampton (Philo McCullough), the villain, asks Con Daly, known to him by another name, to impersonate himself. Con enters into the scheme, his accomplice being Della Moore (Renee Adoree), who personates the sister of Con, who, up to now, was supposed to be in a convent.

Miss Moore is forced into this subterfuge in exchange for enlisting Hampton's assistance to free her younger brother, Bud, charged with the murder of Con Daly's uncle. Bud really did not commit the crime, Hampton, the victim's superintendent, being the guilty one. His employer having discovered a falsifying of books was about to turn Hampton over to the sheriff on the morrow. Hampton intercepts the communication to the district attorney and frames the murder with Bud as the goat. To top it off, Hampton conceives the idea of having two accomplices personate the two sole heirs of the ranch, and thus make off with that. Bud having been indicted solely on Hampton's testimony, his sister asks the latter to retract it and thus possibly free the dupe of the situation. In return Hampton has exacted that she pose as Miss Daly.

There are a number of twists to the yarn, with the obvious culmination in the freeing of Bud, disclosure of Hampton's guilt, excusing the heroine for her questionable means employed to accomplish the noble end, and the coming into the hero's rightful inheritance.

Speed and action are the by-word, delivered in Jones' rip-snorting style. In a number of flashbacks he is shown more or less an irresponsible youth getting the ozone from restaurants, commandeering a milk wagon and hurtling its creamy contents at the pursuing minions of the law, which leads into his assignment to a ranch to "make a man of himself." He has done that in three years, the change from dress suit to sombrero and spurs denoting the transposition. His uncle's ranch is in the southwest district. Just before the murder Con has received a letter summoning him to take charge of things near his relative.

As a program release, this pars with the best of Buck Jones' past performances. *Abel.*

DANGEROUS LOVE

Yellowstone Productions present this screen version of the novel "Ben Warman," released through C. B. C.

An attempt has been made to make "Dangerous Love" a pretentious "western," with the effort having its shortcomings. Any success the novel "Ben Warman" may have secured is not brought forth in the picture. The latter is drawn out as to lose the effectiveness of the story. Anti-climaxes are crowded into the running, and when the final footage is reached the average audience has lost interest.

Pete Morrison heads what is termed an all-star cast. He is of a rugged western type, but lacks steam in his work. This is especially true in two fistic encounters intended for the real knockouts of the production. The first occurs in an early reel between Morrison and Walt Naylor. Its ineffectiveness can be overlooked, due to the early spot. The second is in at the finale, and equally poor. William Lion West is Morrison's opponent in this instance.

Carol Halloway plays the leading female role with a cetrain sincerity which is appealing. The other women are Ruth King and Zelma Edwards, both entrusted with roles of the vampish order. Other members include Jack B. Richardson, Harry Von Meter, Spottswoodie Aiken, Ralph Lee, Clair Hatton and William Walsh. The cast in general does creditable work, although given few real opportunities.

The production end has been well taken care of. Some mining scenes are well done and the western atmosphere is carried along in good style without being overdone. The picture is not one depending entirely upon wild horseback riding, but has the customary saloon and gambling house scenes. As a "western" "Dangerous Love" has its best assets in sets and exteriors.

The story is of the mining country. A young mine foreman is a well-known character around the town saloon. He is noted as a fighter, gambler and drinker. Meeting the right girl, he decides to change his mode of living, stakes a claim, and a thieving band endeavor to take it away. That causes action, but the hero wins out. How it is going to end is disclosed in the early footage. Many characters are introduced which mean little to the story.

Hart.

THE YOUNG DIANA

A Cosmopolitan production starring Marion Davies, directed by Albert Capellani and Robert Vignola, with settings by Joseph Urban. Presented by Famous Players at the Rivoli, New York, Aug. 27.

Diana May	Marion Davies
James P. May	Maclyn Arbuckle
Richard Cleeve	Forrest Stanley
Lady Anne	Gypsy O'Brien
Dr. Dimitrius	Pedro De Cordoba

The vogue of Marion Davies in screendom's realm will be augmented materially in the picturization of Marie Corelli's "The Young Diana," for which Luther Reed provided the scenario. The occult and metaphysical delvings of the novelist lend themselves admirably to film presentation and elaboration. In the thesis advanced in "The Young Diana" there occurs a vast fund for exploitation, advantageously employed.

The story background runs to the conventional. James May is an English social climber. His position is to be advanced by the marriage of his daughter, Diana, to Lord Cleeve. The night before the wedding a scientist, Dr. Dimitrius, enamored of Diana, overhears a conversation of Lord Cleeve and Lady Anne, who is a guest. Lady Anne is preparing through the good offices of Lord Cleeve to pay a visit to the captain of his ship, whom she married the week previous. Dimitrius, to further his own suit, advises Diana of their midnight departure under cover. She is shocked and faints as her lover departs with Lady Anne. During the fainting spell she has a weird dream. The dream takes up and makes for the greater part of the picture.

The Corelli reasonings are beautifully amplified through the artistic settings of Urban, odd and bizarre, as usual, especially in the dream portion. Diana dreams that her lover has deserted her. Her affections are crushed, utterly. There is a transition in which she has aged, her father has tired of her and is about to cast her out. She reads of the desires of scientist Dimitrius to secure the services of a mature woman to lend herself to an experiment requiring the utmost courage.

Through the scientific employment of light Dimitrius is convinced an elixir of youth can be achieved. Failure of the experiment means death, but its successful consummation will result in the attainment of youth in perpetuity.

Diana is unafraid. The experiment is successful, Diana regains her youth, but her heart is old, and it is weary. Even when she is the all-important cynosure during the magnificent ice carnival at Montreux, and is ultimately crowned queen, there is only the enshrouding cloak of unhappiness.

Later, in Paris, as the outstanding figure at the opera, feted and courted, there is within only the leaven of discontent. And, as she meets her old lover, it is piteous to note the old fires cannot be rekindled.

The reigning thought of Corelli always is that Love is Life, its warp and woof, its beginning and end, the real reason for being; all else is material, fleeting, the spiritual contrast used tending to implant the contention.

Miss Davies in "The Young Diana" plays with poise, surety and splendid artistry. In the transition from Youth to Age she surpasses the finer moments of Mary Pickford in "Stella Maris." Diana is her best role unequivocally.

Her support is excellent, the various characterizations having been allotted to competent artists.

With its superb photography, sumptuous settings and regal costuming "The Young Diana" shines forth one of the real regular releases of the year. *Samuel.*

KINDRED OF THE DUST

An R. A. Walsh production, released by First National. Story by Peter B. Kyne, scenario by J. T. Donohue, directed by R. A. Walsh. Shown at Strand, New York, week Aug. 27.

Nan of the Sawdust Pile	Miriam Cooper
The Laird of Tyee	Lionel Belmore
Donald, his son	Ralph Graves
Mrs. McKaye	Eugenie Besserer
Elizabeth McKaye	Elizabeth Waters
Jane McKaye	Maryland Morne
Mr. Daney	W. J. Ferguson
Mrs. Daney	Carolyn Rankin
"Dirty" Dan O'Leary	Pat Rooney
Little Donald	Bruce Guerin

Although the original Kyne story has been changed somewhat for the screen, the feature picture made by R. A. Walsh looks like it is going to be one of the consistent box office attractions of the year. The fact that the story when it appeared in "Cosmopolitan" and later in novel form was widely read has developed a certain clientele for the picture, and these with the regular film fans should make it a winner for the exhibitors.

The production is the second of the independents made by R. A. Walsh and is being released through First National. The sales appeal to the public will have to be made on the strength of the story, because there is no extraordinary name value in the cast, which nevertheless is a good one from a playing standpoint, with Miriam Cooper at its head.

The North Pacific lumber country is the scene of the story, with some very lumbering shots, but the scenic value is at all times held down to a minimum with the story in the foreground.

Miss Cooper is the little girl of Sawdust Pile, who with her grandfather, an old sailor, squats there, falls in love with the son of th' **lumber king and marries him after all sorts of tribulation and complications. Miss Cooper gave a corking performance. Ralph Graves played opposite and also scored, with the character role of the production going to Lionel Belmore as the Laird of Tyee. W. J. Ferguson played the confidential man to the Laird, and as the script held it down to just a minor role did very well with it. It was a far more import-**ant character in the story. The others were all the story characters to the type and gave adequate interpretations of the roles.

In handling the direction Mr. Walsh saw to it that the story went forward at all times. There were chances for spectacular stuff, but the direction held them only to flashes. The comedy spots fell just at the right minute to counteract the extreme tension of the heart interest.

There are a couple of corking fights in the story, one real rough and tumble affair coming about half way in the story, but the sensational punch in the story is a bit of under-water stuff that comes shortly before the finish. The bit comes after the Laird, who has taken a launch up the river by himself, gets caught in a log chute, his boat being sunk by one of the giant trees that came down the chute, and he has gone to the bottom of the river jammed in the cabin. His son, from whom he has been estranged, dives and brings him up, the picture showing the underwater stuff. This was a real novelty, utilized in the manner that it was presented.

"Kindred of the Dust" is just another proof that a good story makes a good picture when it is in capable hands in the making.

Fred.

THREE MUST-GET-THERES

A Max Linder burlesque of "The Three Musketeers," marketed through the Allied Producers and Distributors Corporation, the subsidiary of United Artists. Length about 4 reels, shown at the Strand, New York, Aug. 27.

Duke of Rich-Lou	Bull Montana
King Louis XIII	Frank Cooke
The Queen	Catherine Rankin
Connie	Jobyna Ralston
Walrus	Jack Richardson

Octopus....................Charles Metzetti
Porpoise....................Clarence Werpz
Bernajoux....................Fred Cavens
Bunkumin....................Harry Mann
Dart-in-again....................Max Linder

Max Linder completed this burlesque of "The Three Musketeers" some little time ago, but the release was delayed until this time until it was placed with a distributing corporation. The picture was secured several weeks ago by the Allied Producers and Distributors Corporation, and this week it was presented at the Strand more or less in the light of a half of a double bill program, sharing the billing with the First National feature "Kindred of the Dust." The picture will be a riot to those who saw the Douglas Fairbanks' production of "The Three Musketters." Several bits are sure fire for laughs. However, the titles are relied on as much as the action for the comedy. In classification the picture is just a comedy, not strong enough to be featured alone but great for double bills.

It is broad burlesque of the original with Linder starting to play Dart-in-again slightly lavender at first but breaking away from this after the first few scenes. After that he played the role broadly with a true burlesque sense. In his support he had Bull Montana and "The Three Musketeers" were members of the Metzetti troupe of acrobats which helped tremendously in one or two scenes. They should have been given greater opportunity to display their acrobatics and the chances are would have helped some in laugh action.

Jobyna Ralston is the one beauty touch, playing the maid in waiting to the queen and scoring as an actress. She looks like a find.

In sets the picture are a flash and the dueling stuff that Linder indulges in gets a laugh every few minutes. *Fred.*

VALLEY OF SILENT MEN

Cosmopolitan feature (Paramount) starring Alma Rubens. Picture adapted from story by James Oliver Curwood and directed by Frank Borzage. Scenario by John Lynch. At the Rialto week Aug. 28 during which Lew Cody, head of the supporting company, made personal appearances nightly.

Marette Radison, Canadian girl........Alma Rubens
Corporal James Kent, of the Royal Northwest Mounted..........Lew Cody
"Buck" O'Connor..........Joseph King
Pierre Radison, the father..Matlo Majeroni
Inspector Kedsty, of the Mounted............George Nash
Jacques Radison, brother...J. W. Johnston

The familiar romance of the Canadian wilds with usual romantic trimmings of Mounted Police—the stock melodramatic materials without special distinction as to story elements, but a picture elevated to real eminence by stunning mountain scenery and by the trickily handled episodes of daring mountain climbing by Alma Rubens and Lew Cody.

Without the authenticity of backgrounds the melodrama would be stagey, but impressive vistas of awesome mountain peaks in series upon series give a commanding atmosphere that overshadows the drama and compels a sense of reality. It is a curious case of mere settings creating a real illusion for a set of theatrical situations. The romance is in the environment rather than in the occurrences or the characters who never let you forget that it is all a story.

Even Mr. Cody, most artificial of screen heroes, takes on some of the glamor of the inspiring surroundings. And you can almost forgive Miss Rubens her Westchester-Biltmore get up, miraculously produced out of a dress suit case after she has come through from the Arctic wastes in a dog sled. No more could the tailor-made story fit itself together as neatly as author Curwood manipulated his incidents, but you can pardon the picture anything for those splendid views of the Canadian Rockies. There is a thrill in vast stretches of snow fields and yawning ice fissures that transcend fiction. Anything could happen in such surroundings. That's where the picture gets its kick—and it has a punch of the punchiest.

The scenic revel begins when Corporal Jim and the mysterious Marette start their flight from the Northwest Mounted Post where the third of a series of strange murders has just taken place and in which they are unjustly accused as accomplices. They take a flatboat down the river and almost into raging rapids where they abandon their craft to the terrific torrent and swim ashore. The pursuing constables believe they have met their death in the rapids, but the fugitives push on, with the aid of Indians, to take the trail over the high glacier.

Here is where the scenic carnival takes hold. Mr. Cody does a remarkable series of startling falls down precipitous snowslides and they have even caught an actual avalanche of snow at fairly close range. In the same passage Miss Rubens appears to climb down dizzy heights along an absolutely straight precipice. It makes one giddy, even on the screen. This passage alone ought to insure the picture. It is a real triumph of dramatic effect. How they manipulated the camera is a mystery. Certainly the effect is as though the cameraman was suspended in mid-air over thousand-foot plunges. If they used a double for the feminine star, the substitution was thoroughly concealed. It's a good guess that the star did the stunts herself.

The mystery is fairly well sustained. Two men have been murdered by being strangled with a strand of a woman's hair. A trapper is suspected and held in the police post. Corporal Jim believes himself to be dying from a rifle wound near the heart, and takes the guilt on his own shoulders to save the trapper whom he believes to be innocent and who had once saved his (Jim's) life. Instead Jim recovers. At the same time a mysterious woman appears at the post and makes it known that she is there to prevent the murder of the commanding officer. Of course Jim is held for the murder he has confessed under the shadow of death. And of course he and the girl fall in love.

Then the commanding officer is really murdered and Jim and the girl have to flee. In the middle of their hazardous flight they meet up with a dying man in a lonely cabin high in the hills. The Northwest mounted come up just in time to hear his confession. The three murdered men years and years before had killed the stranger's wife (why it not disclosed) and he has pursued them with vengeance ever since. It goes without saying that the mystery girl is the stranger's daughter, but the confession frees her and Jim, too, from suspicion and they allow them to go forward to "The Valley of Silent Men," pictured as a peaceful haven up under the Artic circle.

Why Jim wasn't arrested for desertion doesn't appear, but the scenery was wonderful. *Rush.*

A BILL OF DIVORCEMENT

London, Aug. 20.

The Ideal Company's screen adaptation of Clemence Dane's poignant play marks a big advance in British production. Denison Clift can be sincerely congratulated on his work. The staging is perfect and the attention paid to the most minute detail beyond all praise. The story of the play is faithfully adhered to, with the important inclusion that the marriage which ends so tragically is shown in its first happiness.

Fay Compton's performance as Mrs. Fairfield marks her, and she is very ably supported by Constance Binney as the daughter. The latter performance is full of charm and light and shade, the American actress rising to great heights when tragedy comes into her life. The rest of the cast is brilliant.

This is undoubtedly one of the finest pictures ever made in this country. *Gore.*

HER STORY

Second National production, featuring Madge Titheradge. The story by Dion Titheradge. Direction by Allyn B. Carrick.

"Her Story" has been produced for low rental purposes. In that class it stands up nicely. The story is consistent, worked out in good style by a small cast and includes sufficient genuine interest to hold attention.

Madge Titheradge as the leading member of the cast ranges in her work from an ingenue to a society matron. In the early scenes she acceptably handles the role of a young girl and later equally effectively that of a matured woman. She is the central figure at all times. The two male roles of importance are played by C. M. Mallard and Campbell Gullan, both furnishing satisfactory support.

The theme of "Her Story" is developed as a story being told by the wife of a millionaire in whose room an escaped convict is captured. She is involved in the matter and tells her husband the circumstances, which bring forth the discloseure she had at one time thought herself the wife of the escaped man. It was her belief she had legally married him in Russia. Later, after he had deserted her and she discovers he is a thief, the marriage is found to be a fake. She secures a position as governess in the rich man's home. He later marries her. While she is attending a masquerade ball at a friend's home in Ossining a prisoner escapes from Sing Sing and gains admittance to the house. He is taken for one of the guests in costume in his prison garb. It proves to be the man she believes herself married to previously. He had discovered her earlier in the day when an inspection of the prison was being made. Making his way to her room he forces her to conceal him. The police discover him there. The story as told brings forgiveness from the husband.

The prison, department store and newspaper plant scenes are well laid out. The production end has been well looked after for a moderate priced feature. The story takes care of itself, with the picture one to give satisfaction in the smaller houses with low admission scales. *Hart.*

THROUGH THE STORM

A Horace G. Plimpton Production, with Edith Stockton and Louis Kimball featured. Distributed by Associated Exhibitors through Pathe.

Helen Stone....................Edith Stockton
Dr. Bruce....................Louis Kimball
Lillian Atterbury....................Mary Worth
Jeremiah Blackstone..........Leonard Maudie
Sally....................Gladys Stockton
Samuel Drake....................James Cooley
Jack Henderson....................Regan Stewart

Any one seeing this picture is fairly certain at the beginning as to just what the story is and how it is going to end. At that it is a fair program picture, but that is about all. With the market, as far as the daily change of program house is concerned, short on material it will get by one single feature days at a pinch, but certain to hold up on the double feature days. On its title alone it may attract some business through the similarity to that of "The Storm."

The tale opens with a girl orphan sent out in the world to make her living. She is unsuccessful and meets another orphan on her way to make her home with a wealthy aunt whom she has never seen. The two are caught in an electrical storm, and the latter girl is killed by a flash of lightning, and the heroine decides to impersonate her. Later she is discovered, but by that time the wealthy spinster aunt of the dead girl has adopted her and is in love with her, so all ends well. Even the young doctor who is wooing her won't turn her down because of the deception she practiced.

There are several good storm effects and the settings are quite elaborate at times, but the action in the main is slow and draggy and rather old fashioned as to the manner of handling the story.

In the cast there are no outstanding figures, although both the featured players manage to handle themselves creditably. *Fred.*

LIGHT IN THE DARK

"The Light in the Dark," starring Hope Hampton, with E. K. Lincoln, Lon Chaney, Theresa Maxwell Conover and Dore Davidson. Scenario by William D. Pelley. Directed by Clarence Brown.

Buffalo, Aug. 28.

This Hope Hampton special was pre-released at the opening of the new Strand, Niagara Falls. Between the festive atmosphere of the occasion and the glamour of the star's personal appearance, it is difficult to gain an altogether fair and impartial estimate of the picture or to accurately gauge its box office value. The film is something in the nature of an experiment, inasmuch as it is in natural colors. In this respect, it possesses passages of real and rare beauty. If its story possessed half the merit of its technical equipment, it might have proved a world-beater. It doesn't, so it isn't.

A large and receptive first-night audience gave the feature respectful attention. The story is slow getting under way. It lacked coherence and direction and plainly bewildered the spectators.

Starting with the time-worn Cinderella motif, it turns abruptly into crook stuff and then suddenly launches into the highly spiritual depiction of the story of the Holy Grail. This is done through the theft by Chaney of a silver cup supposed to be the Grail itself, found by the hero (E. K. Lincoln) while hunting in an English forest. The cut-back showing the story of the Grail is done in beautiful and vivid coloring which brought acclamations. It is quite the best thing of the picture.

The return to the modern crook stuff is jarring and detracts immeasurably from the effectiveness of the story.

On the technical side, the feature leaves little to be desired. The art direction is superb, the interiors particularly showing originality, fine taste and discrimination. The coloring follows two general schemes. Most of the picture is done in flat blues, browns and greys which are highly effective and restful to the eye. The remaining passages in natural colors are gorgeously executed. The colorings are of a brilliancy and vividness which are superb. Unfortunately, by their very beauty, they stand out in violent relief from the rest of the picture and serve to detract attention from the general scheme. In this respect, the picture's main strength turns the spotlight on its own weaknesses.

Miss Hampton does her usual effective work in a role which varies from modern shop-girl to mediaeval lady of high rank. The story gives her a dozen or more negligees. There is more bedroom stuff in the film than in half a dozen Broadway farces. Lon Chaney is a somewhat more kindly crook than is his wont, and Mr. Lincoln struggles along in the fat but unconvincing hero role.

As a novelty, the feature has unquestionable box office value for the exhibitor in the better class of houses by reason of the unusual color work, combined with the high artistic standard of the entire production. Outside of this, and judged solely on the story, the film is merely another in the long line of "just program" features. *Burton.*

DESTINY'S ISLE

A W. P. S. Earle production, in six reels, from the story by Margery Land May, directed by the producer. Distributed by American Releasing.

Lola Whittaker	Virginia Lee
Tom Proctor	Ward Crane
Florence Martin	Florence Billings
Arthur Randall	Arthur Houseman
Judge Richard Proctor	George Fawcett
Lazus	Wm. Davidson

A rather fair tropical picture, combining society and desert island stuff, with some rather good aeroplane shots, litle stunt stuff, a speed boat and a couple of fights thrown in for good measure. Not a grade A picture, but a very fair production that will get by in the smaller daily change of program houses.

The story is one somewhat along the usual lines followed in tales of this type with a rather poor continuity. This at times rather slows the action. The director has used the natural beauties of Miami, Fla., where the picture was shot, to great advantage.

The southern winter resort is the scene of the opening of the story, with Judge Proctor (George Fawcett) trying to bring about an engagement between his nephew (Ward Crane) and his protege (Florence Billings). At the point where the boy enters the garden to propose to the girl he sees her in the arms of another, and in his disappointment dashes to his speed boat and starts out to sea, running into a storm. He is knocked unconscious and finally saved from the boat a day or so later by the girl, who is living with her dad on one of the little islands off Florida.

After her father leaves the two in charge of a colored servant while he goes to a neighboring island to attend a case of sickness, the uncle and the girl arrive on the scene, and to protect the miss who saved him the nephew states that he has married her. On their return to Miami the supposed wife realizes that it is best for the happiness of the boy that she leave him, which she does, and returns to the island home. He follows and a reconciliation takes place.

Virginia Lee, who plays the lead, was undoubtedly selected because she was a good swimmer and diver. There seems to have been no other reason. Ward Crane made a very acceptable male lead and a couple of heavy roles were well enacted by William Davidson and Arthur Houseman. George Fawcett gave the corking performance that is usual with him and scored heavily. *Fred.*

HEROES AND HUSBANDS

B. P. Schulberg production, with Katherine MacDonald starred. Written by Charles Logue and directed by Chet Withey, length about 7 reels. Release through First National.

Susanne Danbury	Katherine MacDonald
Walt Gaylord	Nigel Barrie
Hugh Bemis	Charles Clary
Martin Tancray	Charles Gerrard
Agatha Bemis	Mona Kingsley
Annette	Ethel Kay

This is really a good picture, better than some in which this star has appeared in on Broadway, although this production was not given a prerelease showing in any of the Broadway houses. It is a feature that has a story with a real twist bound to get to any picture house audience. The company is a corking one, with several screen names of value in support of the star, which, coupled with good direction and photography, places the picture in the class of being unusual.

An authoress (Katherine MacDonald) is in love with the illustrator of her stories. He is being vamped by the wife of the publisher. At a Long Island house party the writer arranged a play which is an exact duplication of the real life action, which finally results in the shooting of the publisher. When the facts are disclosed everyone who has been working at cross purposes realizes the error and the usual happy ending.

It isn't so much the story as the trick manner in which it is handled. Chet Withey did the direction most capably and got some real suspense at times.

Supporting Miss MacDonald, Nigel Barrie seemed a convincing lover who was ready to be vamped by almost anyone. It was Mona Kingsley as the wife of the publisher that landed most heavily. She is good to look at on the screen and can act. She did two or three very natural little things in the role that took whole scenes away from the star.

Even without a Broadway run "Heroes and Husbands" is a good enough feature picture for any house anywhere. *Fred.*

THE UNCONQUERED WOMAN

A Lee-Bradford production released in the state right market with Rubye de Remer starred. Shown at Loew's New York as part of double bill Aug. 29.

Rubye de Remer is the only name that one could gather from viewing this picture. The other principals were given the shortest possible name flashes or not named at all. The story is just fair as a meller of a certain type. With a real continuity writer, a titler and editor on the job it might have been whipped into such shape to make it fairly worth while for the cheap daily change of program theatres. That is about the class of the production. Miss de Remer cannot be expected to draw without a story behind her and a cast that registers. In this picture she has neither.

The story is a combination of Alaskan and New York scenes, full of highly improbable and impossible situations which should have been either glossed over by the editor or eliminated entirely.

In a mining camp the father of the story is in partnership in a general store. His son steals from the firm's funds to gamble. On the night that it has been discovered that he is a thief the girl goes to the gambling room and offers herself as a stake in a game of draw. There are four rough necks there at the time, one of them a half breed, who proves to be the lucky man, but at the point where he wins in steps the hero and offers to double the stakes, cut the high card for the roll and girl. Naturally he wins and the pair are married, or rather a ceremony is performed over them by a man they believe to be a parson. Later the wife discovers that he is an impostor, and at that time her husband has been off in the snows for months searching for the girl's missing brother. She believes that he has deserted her and comes to New York.

Here she meets a former music instructor, who proposes, and she marries him. Five years elapse and she is shown with a young son and a husband who is a dandy boy with the ladies. At one of his studio musicales her former husband walks in on the scene and gives her a satisfactory explanation of what really happened in the northwest, and as he has her brother to prove it she is convinced that he knew naught of the fact that the parson was phony. Then begins a struggle to release herself from the man to whom she is married. There is a child, of which the first man is really the father, and seemingly her marriage was really to provide the offspring with a name that she married. Finally the husband conveniently commits suicide and the pair are left for the happy ending.

The picture is fairly well handled as far as direction goes, but the titling is trite and really hinders the story. With re-editing this picture should be advanced at least 100 per cent. in value. *Fred.*

SISTER TO ASSIST 'ER

London, Aug. 17.

Made by the Baron Film Co., a hitherto unknown concern, this screen version of John le Breton's sketch so long played in English vaudeville by the late Fred Emney is a delightful comedy. There were doubts as to whether the sketch would answer as a film, so much in it relied upon the great comedian's voice and the book, but George Dewhurst, the producer, has overcome every difficulty and given his public really first-class entertainment.

The story is very slight, but it never flags throughout the five reels. Mrs. May is a char-woman with an aversion to paying her rent and a great love for gin. She is also of a boastful disposition, and has invented a rich relative, Mrs. le Browning. With this story and another about supposed savings she captures the heart of Mr. Harris, the fish hawker. They become engaged. She persuades her long-suffering landlady that pigs would be a good thing to keep in the back yard. The result is trouble with the neighbors and the authorities, for "the pigs smells all day and makes a noise all night."

Her wedding day approaches and she is discovered trying to sneak out with her luggage, one very battered basket. She is locked out and in her dilemma decides to impersonate her rich sister. She does this with the aid of a gown and outfit a friend "borrowed from her mistress when she left her last situation." In this guise she carouses with the landlady, and is not only successful in getting all debt remitted, but also gets a wedding present for herself. There are many really good incidents arising from the main story, and the subtitles would make the fortune of even a poor picture.

Mary Brough gives a brilliant performance as Mrs May, as does Polly Emery in minor degree as the landlady. The production work is excellent. *Gore.*

WAS SHE GUILTY

London, Aug. 16.

This Hollandia Film (Granger), written by Maurice H. Binger, the chief of the Hollandia directorate and produced by George A. Beranger, is probably the worst and most trashy drama made for many a long year. It never would have been made if Maurice Binger had not been the author. The story is sensational rubbish from the first reel to the last, and its unreal piled-up sensationalism of the penny novelette order defeats any chance the feature has of gripping the attention and winning success. It is practically indescribable in its crudity of continuity and production. Emotion and fear are portrayed by rushing about. All the female characters rush about when trouble overshadows them.

From a scenic point of view the feature is quite good. The exteriors are well done, whether studio or natural, and the interiors are often very beautiful as long as they deal with the wealthy, but the producer shows a very elementary knowledge of East End London, for public houses as he portrays them would never be licensed. In depicting poverty his brain never gets beyond public houses and Chinese dens. The latter are farcical.

Ruth Herwood adopts the girl child of a ruffianly cobbler and sends him to Australia after he has tried to burgle her house. Little Mary has a child sweetheart, Bobbie, and he, broken-hearted, sets out to face the world. Years pass. Mary grows to womanhood and thinks she is the Herwoods' daughter, her supposed father being apparently a third officer or something of a tramp steamer, although his home is a beautiful mansion. Then her real father returns home, accompanied by a woman, Palmira, who 'knows where he got his money." They take a low tavern in Limehouse and associate with a "lecherous, treacherous" Chinaman who runs an opium joint with a pantomime trapdoor entrance. Palmira finds out about Mary, and insists that Gometti, her real father, blackmail Mrs. Herwood, and makes the girl return to help in the bar, and so on.

The players include Gertrude McCoy, Zoe Palmer, Lewis Willoughly, Paul de Groot, Kitty Kluppel, W. A. Freshman and Pierre Balledux. They do their best. *Gore.*

FAITHFUL HEART

London, Aug. 6.

G. B. Samuelson was one of the men who in his youth made a fortune as a film producer. He took the first English film company to California, and coming back, announced he was going to produce there as well as in London. As far as London knows California is as yet free from the Samuelson Film Co. Later he became the pioneer of motor passenger traffic and, presumably having done well at this, returned to films with the declared intention of showing British producers how to do it.

Of his recent films "The Game of Life," reputed to have taken two years to make, is guaranteed to bore any audience stiff about half-way through its 10,000 feet, while "Brown Sugar" was good.

His latest film, an adaptation of the Royalty and Queens theatres success "The Faithful Heart," proves that having done all he has done he has not yet learned to cast a film or to turn a deaf ear to the cry of the "star" whose appeal is purely theatrical. He has gone all out on Owen Nares in this picture and the result would be ludicrous if it were not so sad.

Nares is essentially a good looking "matinee idol" but has not the slightest idea of this part. In the opening scenes his version of the rough, happy-go-lucky sailor who wins the love of a girl only to leave her, is an insult to sailor-men the world over and in the latter part when after many years he returns as the honored soldier to meet his own child, the result of the almost forgotten love affair, and to abandon his career for her sake, the pathos was ruined by his extraordinary make-up.

Apart from it "star" the Samuelson version of "The Faithful Heart" is remarkably well produced. Nares, on whom the firm undoubtedly depend to get the feature over, might be a good Romeo. The Creator never intended him to play men of sterner stuff at least not for some years. *Gore.*

TIT FOR TAT

London, Aug. 21.

This, the last picture made by the pioneer Hepworth company, which has since suspended operations, is quite up to the high standard set by the producers. It is excellent comedy of a high order, and the story is exceptionally well told. The whole production marks a great forward step in British comedy film producing, which up to now, with very few exceptions, has been remarkable for its crudity.

A young bachelor inherits an annuity of £1,000 a year and a house in Bloomsbury. Under the conditions of the will he is compelled to live in the house. His troubles soon start. He finds his housekeepers a terrible source of trouble. The first has a decided penchant for strong liquors and sees things. The next treats him to constant sentimental vocalism, and with the next he promptly falls in love. He also begins to see things. He indulges in dreams. As a knight in armor, mounted on a donkey which has to be urged forward with the aid of a bunch of carrots dangling from his spear point, he rides to the rescue of his lady love. Finally his exciting adventures are brought to an end by his crashing out of bed to the floor.

Henry Edwardes is at his best as the bachelor, and he is ably abetted by Chrissie White. The rest of the company is up to the Hepworth standard. "Tit for Tat" is a big argument that Cecil M. Hepworth and his associates should remain in the business. *Gore.*

A SOUL'S AWAKENING

London, Aug. 8.
This last shown Gaumont "Westminster" film breaks new ground for the producers. Whereas, previously the big majority of home-made Gaumont features have been set in high social circles and amid beautiful settings and surroundings this one shows the sordid side of low life and the gradual conversion of a brutal nature into something human. It is somewhat in the line of a "sob stuff" feature and sentimentality is written all over it. It also has the advantage of possessing a good deal of comedy.

Rackstraw, a brutal dog thief, lives mostly on the meagre earnings of his little daughter Maggie, a maker of artificial flowers and Jim, a newsboy. He brutally illtreats the girl. A neighbor, Sal, sticks up for the child.

One day a rich girl, Cynthia Dare, brings Jim home after he has been hurt. She offers to pay Rackstraw £2 a week as long as he is kind to Maggie. The plan works. Then Rackstraw buys Maggie a dog which is stolen by one of his old cronies. Maggie sees a dog which she thinks is her lost pet and brings it home with the result that her father is arrested for stealing it. Prison life completes the reformation and when he gets out he persuades the kindly Sal to become his wife.

The story is not up to the usual Gaumont standard and the fact that first money and then "time" led to Rackstraw's changed character is not a very good guarantee of his continued reformation. But it is the type of story that thousands of people swallow whole in this country and in others.

The production work is excellent. Flora le Brentor gives a really good performance as Maggie, and David Hawthorne is responsible for a powerful and well studied show as her brutal father. The photography is very good. *Gore.*

HEARTS DIVIDED

London, Aug. 7.
This is a Continental film of dubious origin, dubious morality. We are told it is French and it must go at that. The story is a tangle of marital and other infidelity; some of the women go "the whole hog," others are prepared to and even offer themselves to their lovers, and it is only the five-reel length that apparently prevents the wholesale consummation of desire. The "vamp" is the last word in courtesans and also in undress—a solidly built person who spends her mornings in her scented swimming bath, but has the decency to pull her bathing dress over her shoulders when her maid brings in her letters.

"Lola, the Heartless," was ruined and deserted by the Comte D'Amu-ry when a child; she therefore became a vamp and heartless, to say nothing of the rage of Paris. In the middle of her fame the Comte returned and joined up again, she accepting him for the sake of revenge.

In the country the Comtesse is loved by her husband's friend, a Marquis, but their love is platonic. A tour brings Lola near the D'Amuary's chateau, and her meeting with Hubert, her lover's son, gives her another idea. She plays father against son. Hubert has a fiance who is being chased about by his young friend.

The whole affair causes the Comtesse's ideas of morality to go wrong and she begs the Marquis to take her away. He refuses at first despite her passionate wooing. Hubert discovers the affair between Lola and his father and tries to shoot himself. He recovers, however, but his action brings everybody back to normal.

The production is about 200 per cent. better than the story or the acting. Many of the scenes are very beautiful, and the stage management and attention to minute detail is exceptional. The cabaret scenes, vulgar and sordid, are probably the most true to life ever made, there is no painting a "fast life" with gilt in these scenes of license and crude debauchery. *Gore.*

DUSK TO DAWN

Marjorie Latham ⎱
Aziza   ⎰ ....Florence Vidor
John Latham ....James Neill
Mrs. Latham ....Lydia Knott
Ralph Latham ....Truman Van Dyke
Philip Latham.............Jack Mulhall
Mark Randall.............Herbert Fortier
Babette ....Morris Johnson
Rajah Nyhai Singh...........Peter Burke
Marua ....Nellie Anderson
Nadar Gungi ....Sidney Franklin

An impossible story for the picture house trade is "Dusk to Dawn," adapted from "The Shuttle Soul," a novel by Katherine Hill. Its start will complex the average person, and especially the young, with its theoretical questions, and at the finish, for the story to pull itself out of the hole its impossibility plunged it in, the picture becomes ridiculous in its wildness. Aside from that, the barrenness of action and the absence of vigorous playing with a melodramatic theme without melodramatics remove whatever chance this film had for interest, entertainment or drawing power.

It's a King Vidor production, with Vidor directing and Florence Vidor starred. Miss Vidor assumes a double role, for no reason other than an economical one, as the dual role is totally dissimilar in make-up and appearance. One is of an American girl; the other a Hindu dancer, as far apart as the countries they are respectively in.

The theory is Freudism. Any two chapters or even one of Freud on dreams would have told more than the picture does. Then, again, it delves into theosophy in minor detail, with a question and the transmigration of the soul. It's too much, it's too high, it's too academic and too clinical for any audience in this form. Then what must it be for pictures and their audiences?

This scheme of making people think through popular pictures at popular prices is a Griffith one, and Griffith tired of it long ago. It can't be done. "Dusk to Dawn" might have strongly appealed to Mr. Vidor in its possibilities and opportunities. He has realized some of both, but the component portion, its backbone, the tale itself, was even more impossible. Strange that it did not so strike his mind in the first reading of the script.

Granting everything in the direction that the direction does—the excellently simulated locales through studio artificiality, the apparent genuineness of the Mohammedans and of the battle atop an elephant where an Indian rajah was killed by a program-called tiger (which was a leopard instead), there is nothing that can offset the weakness of the main thread of the double and divided soul, controlling two people, whether near or far. Yet this picture tries to make that positive on the American end and negative on the Indian end, a technical slip, however, that won't be noticed any more in a picture house than the entire thing will be seriously accepted there.

The American girl feels she is governed by an unknown force at the commencement; at the finish she has discovered it, even to the name of the Indian dancer, Aziza; where she is, who she is with and that the American girl's brother is the confidential adviser of the rajah. It's too much on the information received by her, while in jail, through a "spirit" message. That brought in spiritism, much too much. And the rest, the story of a vamp enmeshing the brother, who is accused of forgery and decamps, to wander into India with a full beard and to return to his sister in jail upon the call, still with the beard, after a long sea voyage, unless he also took the soul fleeting route.

The other little strain running through and across the main line is much better—that of the bank's president where the brother was paying teller informing the girl he would relent from pressing the charge against her brother if she would endeavor to wean away the banker's son from another vamp—a dancer. That lead the solicitous sister to jail, for as she was robbing her brother's vamp, vamp got her and called the police.

The soul releasing on the American side was accomplished through what will be one of the high lights of the feature, to those aware of the Hindu mode of mourning by widows, the widow of the rajah in this instance, and she being the soul mate of the American girl, going to her doom via a pyre following her husband's exit by the leopard finish. That released one-half of the soul, or otherwise made a whole soul for use alone by the American girl, so she was then free to marry the son of the banker, the brother was vindicated, the vamp was pinched and the light went out of the picture, with the ushers waking them up to go home. Too bad—a good effort wasted.

Mr. Vidor may make people talk if he will add another inscription to the opening titles, one as to whether the conscience is the soul, and if so, if it directs the soul; and if not, if the soul is the spiritual composition of the human, what then does compose it or how is it composed? Then let the local manager ask for answers, giving a couple of reasons why, after all, and after all theories and beliefs, it still may be possible that what has for ages been termed the soul is but the conscience. The picture needs something more than it has got and anything will do. *Sime.*

CHILD SHALL LEAD THEM

Colonel Lewis................Roger Lytton
Betty Lewis..................Peggy Shaw
Barbara ....Florence Billings
Frank Draper.............Ernest Hilliard
Bob Hale................William T. Hays
Mrs. Tyler.................Adelaide Prince
Ken...........................Niles Welch
Hannah ....Marie Reichardt

William Fox in his special screen productions can exhibit the most violent of contrasts, or, in sporting phrasing, a change of pace. At the Lyric, New York, last Friday (Sept. 1) was displayed "A Little Child Shall Lead Them." There certainly could be no wider range of topic from the special, "Nero," which just closed its exploitation metropolitan showing at the same theatre, unless it be "Silver Wings" and "Nero" or Fox's last season's opposites, "Over the Hill" and "Queen of Sheba." Contrast in releases or specials is likely a very definite plan of the producer and sounds like good business, designed to catch the entire range of film fans.

"A Little Child Shall Lead Them" in no sense is a biblical picture. It gets down to a phase of life pretty closely, touching as it does on married couples who are unhappy because childless. Pounded out is the moral that the woman who denies motherhood to herself denies the most divine thing of womanhood.

That factor will probably attract a large feminine clientele. It is the story above everything else in this picture, and it goes rather far afield in the telling. The author, "Mr. X," specializes on the adoption of orphans. From his conception that is more preferable to maternalism. His two sisters in the story are apparently normal young women and there is no explanation why one did not become a mother, while the other's child is kept from her for purposes of the story. Nor is there any explanation why a wealthy neighbor had brought up a promising lad to manhood, having secured him by adoption as an infant. Inability to achieve motherhood may be assumed in two cases, though no explanation is attempted.

Betty and Barbara are the daughters of wealthy Colonel Lewis. Barbara is married and lives in luxury. Her love for horses and dogs transcends all else and her husband is drifting away. Betty, in love with a young business man, is forbidden to see him, but the couple slip over to Jersey and are married. It is kept a secret, the girl returning to her father's home. The youth is killed and the story of Betty's impending motherhood becomes known to the Colonel. She is taken away. After the infant arrives she is informed it died. An old nurse places the child in an orphanage, but Betty finally learns the truth. She had meantime married the young man of the adjoining estate and, at the behest of her father, never divulged her secret. When the young husband discovers the situation he is for lighting out, whereupon the woman he thought was his mother discloses he too was a foundling. Barbara meantime re-establishes her household by adopting two children, to the delight of her husband. No one knows why Barbara didn't have her own.

There are frequent scenes within an orphanage; the other locales within homes and the grounds of an estate. The special was not costly in production.

Peggy Shaw as Betty is the outstanding character. She sweetly did a girl whose highest aim is marriage and motherhood. Miss Shaw is expressive and sincere. Roger Lytton as the stern parent of the motherless Betty and Barbara handled his job well. Florence Billings played the sister, cold to the entreaties of her husband until the lesson of the little children finally hit home. Ernest Hilliard looked very good as Barbara's husband. Niles Welch was personable as Betty's husband, and Adelaide Prince was excellently suited as the wealthy neighbor who devoted her interest to the orphanage. Kid actors, Florence Haas and Jimmy Lapsley, appealed as children in pathetic circumstances do on the screen. But a 15-months-old infant, supposed to be Betty's child, was a delight.

"A Little Child Shall Lead Them" had its first public showing at Tremont Temple, Boston, two weeks ago, where it opened for a run. At the Lyric a 16-piece string orchestra (12 violins, two cellos, bass and harp) supplied the soft music fitted to the film. A long run is not expected by the producer, for "The Shepherd King" is underlined as the next special. Yet "A Little Child Shall Lead Them" will supply a lot of food for thought to those whose homes are childless. It may even promote some such wives into adopting orphans.

J. Searle Dawley directed from Paul H. Sloane's scenario. Bert Dawley handled the photography. In spots, especially during the first section, the picture was fogged. That may have been faulty film. The picture consumes a little less than two hours, counting a 12-minute intermission. Admission, $1.50 top at Lyric.

Ibee.

BURNING SANDS

George Melford production made by Lasky and released through Paramount. From the novel by Arthur Weigall, adapted for the screen by Olga Printzlau and Waldemar Young. About 6 reels, shown at the Rivoli, New York, week Sept. 3.

Muriel Blair	Wanda Hawley
Daniel Lane	Milton Sills
Kate Bindane	Louise Dresser
Lizette	Jacqueline Logan
Robert Barthampton	Robert Cain
Mr. Bindane	Fenwick Oliver
Governor	Winter Hall
Secretary	Harris Gordon
Ibrihim	Albert Rooscoe
Old Sheik	Cecil Holland
Hussein	Joe Ray

This feature is billed as "the answer to 'The Sheik'." It may be just that, but it hardly shows it on the screen. That line, however, may make the picture a box-office winner, but it doesn't look on the surface as though it is going to touch "The Sheik" when the final count up is made. It is, however, a corking picture, almost worthy of being a special. It has a corking story, a great cast, beautifully directed, and the sets are really marvelous pieces of work. The title seemingly should have a great box-office appeal. That "answer to 'The Sheik'" line heavily used in the billing ought to have the power to bring the flapper element flopping into the theatres.

Egypt and the desert are the scenes utilized for the story. The opening takes place in Cairo at the residence of the British governor. His daughter has just returned from a school in England. A ball is in progress for her when the man from the desert appears. The daughter is played by Wanda Hawley, while Milton Sills is the desert man who accepts from the governor the commissionership to the Arab tribes. It is his indifference to the daughter that causes her to fall in love with and finally follow him into the desert when he goes to visit the tribe with which he formerly lived to prevent their being made a party to a revolution against the government.

He had been warned of the planned uprising by a little French dancing girl in one of the cafes (Jacqueline Logan), who also follows him to warn him of his danger of an attack within a few hours. He saved this girl from the attentions of an unwelcome admirer in the cafe on one occasion and in this case his playing of the chill for her feminine charms was also the reason for his conquest of her. The fact Mr. Sills in this sort of a role makes conquests should tag him as the "ice box lover," with Valentino the "incubator lover." Of the two types Sills should have the more universal appeal, for he doesn't offend the men in the audience as does the more romantic flapper idol.

At the oasis where the tribe makes its headquarters there is a corking fight, in which for a time the attackers are the victors, but in the end a squadron of British cavalry appears and drives out the invaders. During this attack it is disclosed one of the attaches of the governor's staff, who was a suitor for the hand of the daughter, was among the plotters, and when he discovers the girl present in the desert camp, he tries to take advantage of her. Here the little dancing girl, who arrives after the first attack, frees the hero, who steps in and bests the heavy and is holding the girl in his arms when her father and the relief forces appear.

It is a story with thrills and several corking fights, with Sills standing out throughout. Miss Logan, however, overshadows the work of Wanda Hawley and takes away all the honors. In the billing Miss Hawley has the preference, a place that on the strength of the work done should have gone to Miss Logan. Sills is second in the billing, with Robert Cain, the heavy, next. The balance of the cast is practically an all-star one, with Louise Dresser playing a rather prominent role in forceful manner.

Fred.

SLIM SHOULDERS

Irene Castle starring production, in five reels, made by the Tilford Studios, under the direction of Alan Crosland. A society drama written by Charles K. Harris. Released by W. W. Hodkinson. Capitol, New York, week Sept. 3, 1922.

Naomi Warren	Irene Castle
Richard Langdon	Rod La Rocque
John Clinton Warren	Warren Cook
Mrs. John Clinton Warren	Marie Burge
Count Guido Morriani	Mario Carillo
Jerome Langdon	Anders Randolph
The Crook	Matthew Betz

The chances are that the idea of the Fashion Show in conjunction with this feature is what sold the idea to Rothafel for the Capitol. Surely the picture alone, even though Irene Castle is the star was insufficient to get it a Broadway pre-release date at the biggest house on the street. At that the feature is as good as some of the Goldwyns that have played the house, but it is known how they manage to get into the theatre. In all it is a fair program production without great punch.

The Fashion Show angle is what pulls, still an exhibitor wants to be careful of that "Irene Castle's Fashion Show" line, for a lot of those who attend with the idea of seeing Miss Castle in person in the Fashion Revue are disappointed when they find she doesn't appear. It's a question whether or not the average exhibitor can afford to fool his public.

"Slim Shoulders" is a good picture for Miss Castle. It gives her **a chance to do everything. At first she is at Miami, doing a little horseback riding, some swimming and diving and finally chaufs a speed boat that really speeds, this, as well as doing some dancing. Fair enough for the first section.**

When the scene moves to New York she becomes a society deb, willing to do a little job of burglary to save the family name. The "Jimmy Valentine" stuff lets her slip into boys' clothes. Caught by the man of the house, she promises to go straight and get a job. That leads into a bit of modeling which she does when the man discovers her in a Fifth avenue modiste's shop. If that isn't running the gamut for a star so as to show her points, one wonders what would be. Miss Castle even has a chance to flash her pair of griffons and their ugly little faces are almost enough to get a laugh.

There is one find, however, the picture discloses, and if some producer doesn't grab Rod La Rocque and feature him in a couple of those red hot sands of the desert pictures and develop another Valentino he is overlooking a bet. This boy has everything that Val has as far as the eye tricks go, and it is that eye stuff that made the dancing boy a flapper king, only La Rocque seems to have something more behind the eyes.

Alan Crosland directed and kept the story moving as fast as it could, despite the rather trite and conventional material at hand. His handling of Miss Castle is to be admired. It is a better picture than her last starring vehicle.

As to the presentation at the Capitol, one was rather disappointed in the Fashion Show. At that show a clothes revue with only 10 girls is far from a flash.

Fred.

LOVE IS AN AWFUL THING

Anthony Churchill	Owen Moore
Helen Griggs	Marjorie Daw
Ruth Allen	Katherine Perry
Harold Wright	Arthur Hoyt
Porter	Douglas Carter
Marion	Charlotte Mineau
Superintendent	Snitz Edwards
His Wife	Alice Howell

This is a Selznick production and presentation, an acceptable Owen Moore farce and a good program picture. As a special it can scarcely have a stout enough appeal to justify its splash at the Criterion.

Scenically it is quite plain, and, except for the support of Marjorie Daw opposite Moore, in a role not especially exacting the farthest reaches of her talents, the cast is economical and undistinguished.

The story is an in-and-out-of-doors running thing, with baby-borrowings and unplausible mistaken identities and substitutions. It is the hackneyed tale of the young fiance who says he is married in order to get a vamp ex-sweetheart (a chorus girl, of course) off his neck, and what follows. There are laughs galore, naturally, and Moore humors them and keeps the action alive, assisted by a friend named Percy, whose identity is not disclosed on the program. Douglas Carter, colored, contributes some especially subtle Bert Williams touches of light humor that are most welcome.

In all this sums up as a good picture-house headliner for the usual program release period, with nothing inspired or extraordinary about it, yet solidly good amusement for the run of film patrons. It is a short film, apparently about five reels, and in that is a relief against the encroaching extensions in the fancy Broadway houses, where longer films are not uncommon.

Lait.

MY DAD

Robertson-Cole five-reeler of the Canadian Northwest, with lots of snow stuff. Story by Walter Richard Hall. Script by Cliff Smith. Released through Film Booking Office.

Tom O'Day	Johnnie Walker
Harry O'Day	Wilbur Higby
Mrs. O'Day	Mary Redmond
Dawn	Ruth Clifford
La Due	Les Bates
Rin-Tin-Tin	By Himself

Don't let them fool you, Mr. Exhibitor, with this one because it has had a Broadway run of two weeks. It is just a snow picture of program caliber, about on a par with the run of snow stuff the U was turning out a few years ago. The Robertson-Cole story is a little different, however, but the screen treatment makes it an ordinary picture. Continuity and titling are only fair, and this is where the picture falls down. The director isn't mentioned and there is evidently sufficient reason, as one can gather by viewing the production.

Johnnie Walker, who gained fame in a number of Fox productions after he had appeared as the boy in "Over the Hills," is the heroic figure. He gives a good performance, although it seems rather far-fetched to imagine Johnnie taking care of two husky roughnecks, either of whom is about twice his size, and Johnnie is supposed to handle both at the same time.

The story has Johnnie as a clerk in a trading-post store, where his father is the bookkeeper. He is in love with the stepdaughter of the factor. The latter, being a widower, wants to marry the girl. He has a hold on the boy's father because of the latter's belief the factor was a witness to a murder he thinks he **committed while under the influence of drink. When the factor informs him he will have to keep his boy away from the girl under the pain of exposure the father carries out the command.**

It later develops it was the factor who committed the crime, and it is through the efforts of the boy that evidence is secured. This hunt for the evidence is what really gives the picture its punches. One is the fight in a deserted cabin, in which a police dog acts as first assistant to the hero.

The direction is very poor at times. An example is the scene where the trading store is crowded with people to greet the inspector of the Northwest Mounted, and in the rooms above the factor is whaling away at a door with a heavy chair, while his stepdaughter on the other side of the door is screaming at the top of her lungs, yet nobody in the store below pays any attention.

Ruth Clifford as the girl gives a corking performance and looks particularly pretty. The mother, played by Mary Redmond, is also effective, while Les Bates, as one of the heavies, gives a fair performance. The role of the factor, the principal heavy, is well played, although the actor is unprogramed.

For the daily change houses this will prove a fair picture. In some of the bigger houses where a double feature bill is played for two to three days it is safe enough to play it if brought at the right price.

Fred.

THE WOMAN HE LOVED

Frothingham production in five reels starring William V. Mong, who also authored the story. Directed by Edward Sloman and released by American Releasing Corp.
Nathan Levinsky.........William V. Mong
Esther Levinsky.............Marcia Manon
Helen Comstock................Mary Wynn
John Comstock............Charles French
Max Levy....................Fred Malatesta
John Danvers................Harvey Clark
Jimmy Danvers...........Eddie Sutherland
Rosie Romansky...............Lucile Ward

William V. Mong is considered one of the greatest character actors on the screen, but this picture should prove to him he should stop authoring, at least when it comes to writing his own vehicles. This particular production in which Mr. Mong is starred is from his pen and it is about as bad a "bad boy" as has been seen in some time. It is a tale that might have been worth while with different treatment, but in the manner turned out it makes the feature only a cheap program production for the smallest houses.

There is too much Mong, too much of the real old-time surefire hoak and the long arm of picture coincidence is permitted to work overtime.

Mong is a thrifty Jewish peddler in Russia, cursed with a good-looking wife with a love of finery. The craze to spend for her own decoration almost causes them all to lose their lives. On the morning the husband and father had planned to start with his wife and child for the frontier and emigrate to America the Cossacks raided the village. They couldn't get away, as the wife had dipped into the savings for the traveling fund to buy herself a fur cape. Some years later they got to America and Mong became a street peddler, with the wife very much Americanized in garb. Finally she runs off with a crook, taking the child with her.

The crook is picked up by the cops in Chicago and the woman, fearing to return to her husband, places the child in an orphanage. He is adopted by wealthy gentiles.

From that point on it's all the old stuff. Naturally the father meets and recognizes the boy in later years but refrains from making known the fact that he is the dad, as he is in far better circumstances than the dad and he is engaged to marry the daughter of the millionaire owner of the neighboring ranch, who is a Jew hater. But in the finish everything is all squared up, but it is the manner in which it is squared that would make the picture a better comedy than a drama.

It really looks like Mr. Mong in authoring went after all the old ones with the idea of "The Peddler," the old Joe Welch play, and perhaps a bit of the "Music Master" idea back in his head. As a feature it just won't do a-tall. *Fred.*

BACK TO YELLOW JACKET

Ben Wilson production, starring Roy Stewart, distributed in the state right market by Arrow. Story by Peter B. Kyne, directed by Ben Wilson. Five reels. Loew's New York Sept. 3.
"Sunny Jim" Ballantyne......Roy Stewart
Carmen Ballantyne......Kathleen Kirkham
"Flush" Kirby................Earl Metcalf
William Carson...................Jack Pratt

This western started out as though it was really going to be something different; then it sagged into the ordinary, and finished a long-drawn-out, tiresome piece of screen padding that practically ruined what might have been developed into a real feature picture, worthy to travel in the best of company. As it is it is just a mediocre program feature, that may stand up on the double-feature bills in the better houses. The one sales point it has is that it is a Peter B. Kyne story. Other than that there is hardly anything in either the picture or the cast that will pull at the box office. In the houses where the crowds come no matter what the picture is it will get by, but where the exhibitor has to pull his audiences—nothing doing.

The directorial handling leaned too much toward cutbacks and visions, which naturally made for slow progress. The feature opens with reference to the gold rushes of California in '49; Alaska in '08 and the desert rush in 1907. It is here that the scene is laid. "Sunny Jim" Ballantyne is trying to win a fortune from the ground for his young wife, left behind in civilization. Finally she joins him in the mining camp, where the life is unbearable, and through his cruelty finally leaves him. He follows and continues a search over four years for her. In the meantime she has changed her mind after a day or two away from her husband and returns to the camp to await his return. When he comes back he has as a partner the man that his wife went to join, but who insisted that she return to her husband. The two have a claim together near Yellow Jacket, which is the name of the camp, and one night when supplies are needed "Sunny Jim" makes his first trip into the town and sees his wife in the dance hall working as an entertainer.

She is ill, and during her work faints and he carries her to their old shack across the road. There, while she is unconscious, he sees the picture of his partner on the mantel and immediately forms the opinion that he is the man responsible for the wife's condition and likewise for the youngster that is in the cabin. He returns to the mine to wreak his vengeance, but the wife, returning to consciousness, sees a note that he has left, follows him and prevents a murder.

Picture coincidence is working overtime again, but it will get by in the cheap houses.

It appears that Roy Stewart is getting a little too much forehead to be cast in the roles of heroic mould, and it looks that he is rather on tap for middle-aged character roles rather than the "win-the-gal" stuff. Incidentally there is but one role in this picture that gets any sympathy, and that is played by Jack Pratt. He is the cast-off suitor to whom the wife tries to turn after she and her husband have fought. The wife played by Kathleen Kirkham is decidedly an unsympathetic role, and the near-heavy of Earl Metcalf counts for almost nothing. *Fred.*

BULLDOG COURAGE

Five-reel western, released in the state right market by the Russel Productions. Made by Clinton Productions under the direction of Edward Kull from the story by Jeanne Poe. Shown at Loew's New York on double-feature bill.
Gloria Phillips.................Bessie Love
Jimmy Brent................George Larkin
John Morton...........Albert MacQuarrie
Snakey Evans...................Karl Silvera
Big Bob Phillips...........Frank Whitman
Sheriff Weber....................Bill Patton
Mary Allen...............Barbara Tennant

From the looks of this production it would appear George Larkin, who is starred, rather fancied himself as a leading man and, having more money than he knew what to do with, started to put Doug Fairbanks and Bill Hart into the discard. The manner in which the picture is laid out and the opportunities given to Larkin more than indicate this must have been the case. Otherwise there is no excuse for either the picture or Mr. Larkin in it. In the cheapest houses, where it doesn't matter what there is on the screen, the picture will get by, but that is about all it can do. It has no place in the race with even Class B program productions.

The story is a western, but the hero is a college youth who goes west at the behest of a rich uncle who promises him $50,000 if he meets and licks a man in a fair fight. The certain man is one who beat up uncle about 20 years before. The adventures of the rah rah youngster on the cattle range, where he gets a job as a puncher, his meeting the man that he is supposed to lick; a fight with the man and his final round-up of a band of cattle rustlers and the winning of the girl make up the story.

Bessie Love is the one bright spot. How a girl who has done as good work as Miss Love has would permit herself to get into a production and cast of this caliber speaks badly for production conditions on the coast. Mr. Larkin, who is the star, is utterly impossible, and as everything in the picture is subordinated to him one can guess the answer offhand.

Everything in the picture is done with an exaggerated touch that makes it almost a continual laugh. If it had been done as a comedy instead of straight, with the titles jazzed, it would have been a picture.

The "Bulldog Courage" comes in on the part of those who had the nerve to market this one and those sitting through it. *Fred.*

CHAIN LIGHTNING

Arrow feature, produced by Ben Wilson with Ann Little starred. Story supplied by J. Grubb Alexander and Agnes Parsons.
Peggy Pomeroy..................Ann Little
Major Pomeroy.........Norval MacGregor
Red Rollins................William Carroll
Colonel Bradley.............Joseph Girard
Bob Bradley...............Jack Daugherty

Horse racing is the predominating feature of this multiple reel independent release. As with the majority of pictures based upon racing there is a similarity in theme that tends to detract from the interest. In this instance the only difference from many other stories of this nature is that no attempt is made to poison the horse just prior to the big race. All of the other old standard bits are incorporated in it.

A southern-bred girl is the leading spirit, riding her horse in the big race to win enough to take father away to the mountains in order that he might regain his health. He in turn had been a good fellow by having taken a second mortgage upon the old homestead so she might continue in finishing school at Washington. A love angle is introduced and a well proportioned leading man brought into the story to keep the girl from hugging her pet horse through every reel.

Ann Little gallops through the lead role with little effort, easier when not upon the horse's back. She appeared ill at ease during the close-ups during the race scene. There is a possibility someone was doubling for her at the time. Norval MacGregor in a character role as the father handles it with deftness. Joseph Girard comes under the same classification. William Carroll plays the heavy with fair success. Jack Daugherty has the juvenile lead. Not overburdened with opportunities, he fails to gain much headway.

The production cost reaches no large figure. The interiors called for no great layout, with a small race track used for flashes and cutbacks.

"Chain Lightning" was included in a double feature bill at Loew's Circle. *Hart.*

WINNING A WIFE

This is an exceedingly good French racing picture. The story is by no means original, but has a great advantage over most racing films—the heroine does not ride the winner in place of the jockey who has been injured. The picturization of French racing stable scenes, the "pari mutuel" system of betting, race course crowds and training is exceptionally interesting. New, also, are the weird double-decked trains bearing the poorer class of race-goer to the course. The exterior work has been done amid exceedingly beautiful surroundings.

The renters make the usual English mistake in editing the film for the English-speaking market—although all the surroundings are obviously French, they have given all the characters English names, and whoever wrote the subtitles has completed ignored such a thing as punctuation.

Helen Ridder is the daughter of a race horse trainer and the beloved of the owner, Paul Marton. Helen's father, however, objects to the marriage. She has another lover, George Fairfield, whom she turns down. He plots against Paul and his horse, Pretty Polly, with a shady race horse owner, De Vries. Paul's entire future depends on winning a big race, but the villains get at his jockey and he is ruined. De Vries buys the Marton string, but so well does the Marton stable lad disguise Pretty Polly's true form that he thinks the horse is a "dud" and sells it back to the heroine. Of course when the next big race is run Pretty Polly wins, villainy is led off by gendarmes, and the aristocratic old man bestows his blessing on the lovers.

The principal parts are played by Louise Colliney of the Odeon theatre, Constant Remy of the Marigny and M. Angely of the Sarah Bernhardt. The supporting cast is excellent. The photography is of a very high standard. *Gorc.*

A GIRL'S DESIRE

Five-reel society drama made by Vitagraph. Story and script by C. Graham Baker and directed by David Devar. Alice Calhoun starred. Shown at Loew's Circle Sept. 3.
Elizabeth Browne............Alice Calhoun
Jones (Lord Dysart)..........Warner Baxter
"Lord" Cecil Dysart.........Frank Crane
Lady Dysart...............Lillian Lawrence
Mrs. Browne.............Victory Bateman
H. Jerome Browne...........James Donnelly
Miss Grygges.................Sadie Gordon

This looks like the average "factory grind" of society dramas that are turned out by the Class B League of producers of program pictures. It is one of those picture productions of the vintage of about five years ago. That doesn't mean the picture was made that long ago, only that it isn't any improvement over those then made. As a matter of fact, some turned out by this same company longer than five years ago were much better. This is just a program picture of very ordinary caliber and can just about get by in the daily change houses.

The story is of a family of social climbers, who have made their pile in oil. They get into the hands of a pair of English schemers, mother and son, who try to fleece them. The plan is to pass the son off as Lord Dysart, when he was only the stepson of the deceased holder of the title, marry him to the daughter of the oil millionaires, even though there is a real heir to the title living. This heir shows up on the scene in time to frustrate the plans of the schemers and marries the girl.

The story is slow moving on the screen without any action or pep at any time. The detail is badly handled, and in one instance night tinted scenes are utilized as the exterior of a house where an afternoon reception is being held, with a continuance of exteriors in the sequence of the action in full daylight.

Miss Calhoun makes a fairly neat little ingenue as the daughter, but the young woman is far from showing anything in this picture entitling her to stellar honors. Warner Baxter is an acceptable lead and Frank Crane a fair heavy of the wishy-washy sort. The true note sounded in the cast was delivered by Victory Bateman in a character role. James Donnelly, playing opposite her, made the father a low comedy Irishman, altogether out of keeping. It must have been the fault of direction to a great extent, however. *Fred.*

CREATION

London, Aug. 23.

This, the first production of the Raleigh King Co., shows promise. The producers have striven hard to find an original idea for a basis to their plot and have, to a point, succeeded. The story has much to do with a phase of spiritualism, but the producer has been unable to keep clear of social problems, which considerably lessen the wholesomeness of his work. Again he has not been too careful in some of his detail. The characters are supposed to belong to the higher walks of life and in such society one does not drink soup out of the point of a spoon nor does one throw match ends onto other peoples' drawing room carpets.

Zena Hammond is a devout spiritualist. She is also married to a man who is too good to be true. She believes if the paragon were to die his spirit would return to her in another man. The following day her husband is drowned. A doctor, Gannally, becomes her constant companion, but an adventurer, Evermore, learns of her fortune and also of her spiritualistic beliefs. By making use of one he determines to possess the other. He persuades her that her late husband's soul has entered his body and she marries him.

Gannally knows what a blackguard Evermore really is and mourns that Zena's belief should have carried her so far. Time comes when Evermore discovers he is really in love with his wife and he determines to become a decent man for her sake. He then discovers the dead paragon had a previous wife living and that, therefore, Zena was never really married. He pays the real wife to clear out of the country. Gannally tries to force Evermore to tell Zena the truth about himself, but hearing she is in delicate health the confession is postponed. Evermore has become thoroughly converted by his love and is working hard in the slums to brighten the lives of the outcasts. Again Gannally tries to force a confession but discovering that Zena is about to become a mother and is perfectly happy he agrees to let things remain as they are. The picture is well staged and the acting is up to standard, if without any special distinction. *Gore.*

THE VEILED WOMAN

"A Veiled Woman" doesn't mean a thing. An ordinary picture, made by the Reno Co., starring Marguerite Snow and taken from the story, "A Spinner in the Sun."

It moves along with nothing to impede it nor exhilarate it, doesn't stop moving and ends as it commenced.

There is plenty of No. 2 with the only thrill one of repulsion at seeing a heavily veiled woman (in white) continuously in it.

A slap at vivisection is tried for, but that won't get over, even with the mushy title that was thrown in to help, and the best that may be said for the release is that it was half of a double bill at the Tivoli. *Sime.*

THE GHOST BREAKER

Lasky-Paramount feature, starring Wallace Reid. Adapted by Jack Cunningham from the play by Paul Dickey and Charles W. Goddard; directed by Alfred Green. Shown at Rivoli, New York, week Sept. 10.

Warren Jarvis	Wallace Reid
Maria Theresa	Lila Lee
Rusty Snow	Walter Hiers
Duke D'Alva	Arthur Carewe
Sam Marcum	J. F. MacDonald
Aunt Mary Jarvis	Frances Raymond
Maurice	Snitz Edwards

This is one of those usual Wallace Reid starring pictures, fairly well done, with considerable comedy element that prevents the picture from falling into the classification of ordinary. To the Reid fans the feature will prove pleasing; to others it will be but mildly entertaining. As a box office attraction the draw depends whether or not the exhibitor's average audience is strong for the star. There is nothing in the production that will pull additional business.

Reid isn't present at all in the greater part of the first reel. That action takes place in Spain, where Lila Lee and Arthur Carewe are the principal characters in the story. Miss Lee is the daughter of a lately deceased Spanish nobleman; she and her very youthful brother are all that are between the title, the grounds and castle, a possible buried treasure, which is coveted by the cousin, played by Carewe.

A plan of the castle and its secret passages has been presented by the girl's father to an American, and the girl comes to this country to secure it so that she will be able to seek the treasure which is reported hidden in the castle. The cousin also makes the trip in an effort to forestall her.

In the meantime, Reid is shown as a New Yorker returning to the old homestead in Kentucky, arriving there in the midst of a feud. He is advised to return to New York pronto, refusing at first to take the advice, but after a shooting, in which he and the opposing faction battle it out, he decides to leave. The head of the other clan follows him to New York, and the two come face to face in the hotel elevator; both pull their guns and there is a shooting. Reid escapes unscathed, but dashes into the room occupied by the Spanish girl.

All of this action has used up about three reels of the allotted five, so that with the work of ghost breaking still to begin there is very little footage left for that portion of the story. However, Reid makes his get-away from the hotel the following morning in the wardrobe trunk of the girl and is placed aboard a steamer bound for Spain; the girl misses the boat and is finally put aboard from a hydroplane.

Once back in Spain, Reid readily breaks up the ghost business in the castle and shows up the aspiring and conspiring cousin as the man behind all the spiritual manifestations, winning the girl, who is the real treasure of the story.

If it wasn't for the work of Walter Hiers, who does a blackface valet to the star, there wouldn't be anything to the story. Hiers is the fat comedian, who, it is quite possible, is being groomed by Lasky to replace Arbuckle. His work in this picture polls all the laughs that there are.

The sets are elaborate and the photography good, but it looks as though Reid had made up his mind that he was going to do as little work in this picture as possible, and possibly conspired with the script writer and the director to help him out. Things of this sort are about as sure a road to oblivion, as far as the screen is concerned, as being involved in some unsavory scandal. *Fred.*

HOUND OF BASKERVILLES

R.-C. picture evidently made in England. Founded on the Conan Doyle story of the same title of the Sherlock Holmes series. Shown at Capitol, New York, week Sept. 10.

Sherlock Holmes	Eille Norwood
Dr. Watson	Hubert Willis
Sir Henry Baskerville	Rex McDougal
Osborne	Frederick Raynham
Dr. Mortimer	Allen Jeayes
John Stapleton	Lewis Gilbert
Beryl Stapleton	Betty Campbell

The combination of the Sherlock Holmes name, the title of the story and Conan Doyle is pretty certain to pull business, and in the case of this picture seemingly there is no exception. However, the picture itself is rather badly done, and it will not be of the entertainment value that the audience will expect in the bigger houses. At the Capitol Sunday night the picture pulled big, but the audience leaving after the first night show expressed its disappointment rather liberally. It is not a picture for the biggest houses, and the chances are that the Capitol must have been rather badly off for an attraction to have played this one.

This weird mystery tale of Sir Conan Doyle's would have made a whale of a picture in the hands of a capable American director and company. In this production the treatment of the story is very bad, and the producers trusted to night tints to carry the mystery end rather than working up the real suspense.

The direction was by Maurice Elvey, who followed the original tale in a matter of fact manner, letting the story develop on the screen as best it could. His work did not carry it forward with any great speed, nor was there any real element of suspense anywhere in the production.

As to the cast, Eille Norwood is featured as Sherlock Holmes, but, due to the adaptation for the screen, the honors should have gone to Rex McDougal as Sir Henry Baskerville, who held the center of the lens to greater footage than the character of Holmes did. Mr. Norwood does not measure up to the requirements of the Sherlock Holmes role when one weighs him with the characterization that John Barrymore gave in the recent Sherlock Holmes film in which he appeared. Betty Campbell is the only woman in the cast, and she manages to play a rather difficult role fairly well.

In sets the picture has nothing to boast of, and it is fairly noticeable the picture was rather cheaply made. *Fred.*

THE CURSE OF DRINK

A six-reel state rights production handled by L. Lawrence Weber and Bobby North. Produced by Joseph M. Shear and presented by Export and Import Film Corp. Founded on the play by Charles Blaney, modernized to meet Prohibition conditions.

Bill Sanford	Harry T. Morey
John Rand	Edmund Breese
Ruth Sanford	Marguerite Clayton
Ben Farley	George Fawcett
Baby Betty	Miriam Battista
Mother Sanford	Alice May
Sam Handy	Brinsley Shaw
Harry Rand	Albert Barrett
Margaret Sanford	June Fuller

Combination of a corking melodrama title and an all-star list of names in a state rights production that looks as though it was slated to get the money in the popular priced houses. The story is founded on the old meller that toured the country for years under the management of Charles Blaney. The play has been modernized so as to meet the present-day conditions brought about by the Volstead Act.

Outside of the fact that there is a good title to draw at the box office and a number of names in the cast, there is nothing about it that places it in the classification of unusual. It is just a good hokum picture that has been turned out to get the money.

The story is that of a railroad engineer, the best driver on the road, who has fallen to nursing a switch engine because of his fondness for the stuff they sell in blind tigers. His daughter is secretary to the president of the line, and his son is beginning to stoke a locomotive.

The boy and girl are in love with each other, but the former's father objects. The heavy is the division manager, who covets the girl. He has her father fired for drinking and the old engineer, inflamed with drink, seeks to take revenge on the president of the line. The latter is about to make a trip on a special and the old engineer boards the cabin of the locomotive, displaces the regular driver and heads for a washout down the line. The girl and the son of the president, boarding another engine, give chase, and the girl finally climbs from the cowcatcher of one locomotive to the rear of the other train, clambering over the roofs of the cars to her father in the cabin and brings the train to a stop, at the brink of the washout. Her reward is the consent of the road's president to her marriage to his son and the old man swears off drinking.

Harry Morey plays the old engineer with a real sense of sousing, while the heavy of Brinsley Shaw is of the type of villainy usually hissed in the old days. George Fawcett showed as a speak-easy keeper, who ran his joint to suit himself.

Miss Clayton, as the heroine, impressed, and there was a real thrill in the railroad stuff she did. Albert Barrett was an acceptable hero. Miriam Battista was really clever in the kiddie bit of the picture.

The production holds its thrill in the railroad chase which Harry O. Hoyt, who adapted and directed the picture, handled very well. *Fred.*

TIMOTHY'S QUEST

A rural drama produced by the Dirigo Films, Inc., released through American Releasing Corp. Adapted from the Kate Douglas Wiggin story of the same title and directed by Sidney Olcott. Seven reels.

Timothy	Master Joseph Depew
"Lady Gay"	Baby Helen Rowland
Miss Avilda Cummins	Marie Day
Samantha Ann Ripley	Margaret Seddon
Jabe Slocum	Bertram Marburgh
Hitty Tarbox	Vivia Ogden
Miss Dora	Gladys Leslie
Dave Milliken	Wm. F. Haddock

Two kiddies make this production stand out as a sure-fire money-getter for the average exhibitor. It is not a picture that one could play in one of the bigger pre-release houses, but in the regular run of theatres it will stand up with anything and pull business on the strength of the work that is done by Joseph Depew in the role of Timothy and little Helen Rowland.

The picture was made by a newly formed company which is going to devote itself entirely to a brand of Down East rural stories, with their producing center somewhere in Maine.

"Timothy's Quest" is right in line with the other adoption stories, such as "Forget Me Not" and "A Little Child Shall Lead Them," and while it does not lean to the tear stuff as strongly as the other two, its comedy angles are such that the production is certain to register.

A combination of tenement squalor and clean country life forms the background for the action. Timothy and "Lady Gay" are boarding kids in a tenement. When the woman who has had them in charge passes on, Timothy hears a couple of slatterns who are taking charge of the situation arrange how the kiddies shall be disposed of. He then takes little Lady Gay and runs off, beating a ride on a freight train which lands them in a little country town.

The youngster takes charge of the situation by making a house-to-house canvass to ascertain if anyone would like to adopt a baby. He manages to pick a house that he has fancied in dreams, and it is the home of his maiden aunt. She is a stern-appearing woman, who immediately notes the resemblance of the boy to her own young wayward sister, and later manages to check up this resemblance, proving to herself the boy is her nephew.

Eventually she decides to adopt both of the children, and the story closes with both tots assured of a home.

It is a cute story fairly well told, although there are spots where the continuity of the screen version of the tale could be improved on. But in the main the picture is a real good program picture for the regular run of houses.

The cast is one of characters, with Marie Day, as the stern aunt, registering most forcibly, while Margaret Seddon makes a lovely character of the spinster who passed up marriage to be with her girl friend in sorrow. Comedy relief is furnished by Vivia Ogden and Bertram Marburgh.

Fred.

THE BLOND VAMPIRE

It is seldom a picture so utterly lacking in merit gets as far as the screen. The work hasn't a redeeming virtue. Even its photography is poor, and when a film in these days of mechanical perfection hasn't at least clearness it is beyond all hope. "The Blonde Vampire" was made half of a double feature bill at the Eighth avenue neighborhood theatre, and by contrast with its companion feature, Arthur S. Kane's "The Real Adventure," suffered intensely.

"The Blonde Vampire" is so conspicuously bad it is difficult to pick out its special demerits. In the first place, the story does not hold together. The characters behave in the most extraordinary manner. A rich mine owner makes his hobby the visiting of poor tenement house dwellers to bring toys to the children. He falls down a flight of stairs and twists his ankle. He seems to make nothing of the injury, but, nevertheless, sends post haste for his butterfly daughter to convey him home.

Oddly enough, the strained ankle immediately turns the old party's thoughts to death; so he decides to make his will, leaving the Poppy mine to his daughter. He knows, or ought to, that his business associate, one Downs, is a blackguard, but in spite of this he makes Downs the executor in his will and the girl's guardian. In visiting the tenement the daughter, Marcia by name, ran over a child's doll with her car, and a young man of the district substantially threatens to strike her for the deed.

Marcia promptly falls in love with the young tough, attracted by his caveman attitude, so different from the behavior of the tame society men she meets. Here's where the plot thickens. Downs, with the aid of a political "master mind," who acts more like a cheap crook, schemes to have the young tough secure Marcia's signature to some sort of a document that will rob her of the mine and then do away with the old man by murder. Marcia is lured to a gaudy dinner party at Downs' home (one of those lurid affairs where everybody gets drunk and men and women fall into the swimming pool while a cabaret show is going on) and the young tough is thrown into her company.

Marcia's real sweetheart, a timid sort of chap, comes to the party and saves her from the plot by offering to thrash the tough, who suddenly turns virtuous and lets him get away with it. You'd suppose that with all this evidence the old man would have changed his will, but that wouldn't keep the story going to the fifth reel. Nothing so simple would do. Instead Downs sends a hired assassin to his home. For various scenario reasons the young tough, his sweetheart and a reformed crook happen at the mansion at the same time. The assassin is foiled and the guilt of Downs is exposed.

There is not the slightest effort to build up to situations. Things just happen fortuitously. One passage concerns the scheme of Downs to get the young tough in his power. It leads to a brisk bit of action, but because the way was not paved to arouse suspense the scene is reached and passed before any interest is awakened. The acting is as mediocre as the photography. The featured character of Marcia, who is the blonde vampire of the title, is absent from the action for a whole reel at a time, and she never for a moment engages the sympathies. None of the characters does for that matter, and the five reels are as tiresome and dull as any picture within memory.

Rush.

THE SIREN CALL

Famous Players-Paramount presented by Adolph Zukor, with Dorothy Dalton as star. Strong cast supporting has David Powell and Mitchell Lewis featured. Story an original by J. E. Nash, with Philip Hurn preparing script. Production directed by Irvin Willat.

Charlotte Woods..........Dorthy Dalton
Ralph Stevens..............David Powell
Beauregard...............Mitchell Lewis
Edward Brendt.......Edward J. Brady
Gore........................Will Walling

The general idea back of this picture was to turn out another "Flame of the Yukon," the picture that "made" Dorothy Dalton. In this respect the effort was a failure. However, a fairly good box office attraction has been turned out. It is a picture of the Alaska country that has at least two spectacular thrills in it, although the story itself has Miss Dalton a married woman in the first reel, and that is going to be objected to by some exhibitors and the screen fans to whom this star particularly appeals. That the marriage is a phoney one and the real love story and final happy ending are worked out won't make any great difference to them. Dorothy must be single at the beginning of the picture to make it a draw at the box office, according to the sharps that are serving the pictures to the public.

However, "The Siren Call" has everything that the usual run of Alaskan pictures of this type have. The dance hall, the snow, the mounted police, a dog team and all the regular stuff. Besides that, it has a real cast of names, with both David Powell and Mitchell Lewis as featured members. Powell is coming along in popularity with the women and Lewis is still the bold, bad heavy he always was.

There is considerable comedy relief in early reels of the picture during the dance hall scenes, with an Irish characterization by Lucien Littlefield contributing considerable of the laugh material. This helps the picture materially.

Miss Dalton has the role of the wife of the manager of the dance hall, the marriage of the pair being kept secret for business reasons, as she is the principal box office attraction that the place has. The marriage to the manager was a phoney one put over on the girl so that she would stay on the job and not be lured to one of the other places.

Out on the trail Mitchell Lewis has come across a man and woman who have frozen to death, but the little baby they were carrying is still alive. He picks it up and takes it to the dance hall, intending to win favor of the reigning queen by presenting it as a Christmas gift. She starts a bank account for the kid right there by selling kisses at a dollar a kiss, but Powell, who has come into the room, refuses to buy until she sticks him up with a gun, and then he pays double the amount to insult her again. She thinks it is going to be another kiss, but instead he bawls her out, stating she is unfit to care for the child.

Later, after the local Purity League has managed to burn down the dance hall and drive off the inmates, the girl, her supposed husband and the baby are seen in a small general store along the river. That was always the cherished dream of the girl. Powell is a neighbor. The husband, however, has had a lech for one of the other girls, who has returned to the states, so when Lewis shows up and tries to force his attentions the husband makes a deal with him to turn over the woman and the store for the pack of pelts which the trapper has. Left in the hands of Lewis, Miss Dalton defends herself by killing him, and Powell, walking in on the murder, starts out after the husband after hearing the story. He and Edward J. Brady (playing the husband) put up a corking fight on a raft floating down the river, and the hero of the story is worsted in the combat. The girl, however, comes to his rescue as the raft is about to go over the falls, and the two are shown taking the drop. Months later the pair are in a cabin when the mounted police show up and word is then received of the death of the husband, which leaves the pair of lovers free to bring about the happy ending.

The picture did not receive a Broadway pre-release showing because of the fact that the circuits around New York that have booked the Paramount output have been clamoring for the pictures, and the extended runs that the Rialto and Rivoli are playing made it impossible to present them there and hold to release schedule. However, it seems that the weaker sisters were the ones that were turned loose with the usual Broadway runs. But withal this picture will entertain and get some money on the strength of the Dalton and supporting cast names.

Fred.

THE GALLOPING KID

Universal western starring Hoot Gibson. Story by Wm. H. Hanby, adapted by A. P. Younger. Directed by Nat Ross. Loew's New York, Sept. 8, on double bill.

"Simplex" Cox..........Ed "Hoot" Gibson
Fred Bolston..................Leon Barry
Helen Arnett.................Edna Murphy
"Five Notch" Arnett.......Lionel Belmore
Steve Larabe..................Jack Walters
Zek Hawkins.............Percy Challenger

Just one of the usual type of westerns in which Hoot Gibson is generally starred by U. The role of the star in this picture, however, is one that he takes splendid care of. The picture will do nicely where the audiences like westerns, but a fairly accurate line is arrived at from the fact it plays on the double bills in the Loew daily change of program houses around New York.

The picture has some lighter moments. Gibson as Simplex Cox gets the job of acting as chaperon to the daughter of Arnett, who has a reputation as a gun man. His job is to keep Bolston away from the girl, who fancies she is in love with him. If he fails in the job Arnett threatens to shoot him.

The girl makes an appointment with her sweetheart and Cox follows, but the girl and Bolston stick him up and force him to climb a ladder to a cliff, after which they remove the ladder. Cox, however, manages to get down, and at the same time discovers a gang of crooks who have been mining platinum on the land belonging to Arnett. He rounds them up and at the same time manages to get Bolston. In the end he wins the girl and obtains forgiveness from her father for having failed once on the chaperonage job.

It is one of those regular stories of the west, with the usual horses, and while Gibson is a comer to a certain extent, this sort of material isn't going to take him out of the popular-priced class of western screen stars.

The direction of Nat Ross was all that could be expected with the material at hand.

Fred.

BLIND CIRCUMSTANCES

Northwestern drama with some snow stuff. Produced by the Morante Productions Co. under the direction of Milburn Morante, starring George Chesebro. Released by Clarke-Cornelius Co. for state rights.

Dick Hayden...............George Chesebro
Ruth...........................Vivian Rich
Capt. Erick Skag...........Alfred Hewson
Kelly...........................Harry Arras
Pierre..........................Frank Calfrey

Rather a weird northwestern made along lines intended to impress the audiences that must have their thrill no matter what the cost. It is a fair program picture of the cheaper grade that will do fairly well in the small daily change houses. Really no great punch to it, and the continuity and photography are pretty bad in spots. The direction is also nothing to boast about at any time.

George Chesebro is the star, with Vivian Rich featured. The balance of the cast matters little, with the exception of Alfred Hewson, who plays the heavy.

The story is laid in a sea coast town in Canada and later in the snow country. Ruth and Dick Hayden are sweethearts, with the heavy coveting the girl. The hero has a scrap with a man on a dock and knocks him out. A few minutes later a couple of the crew of the ship commanded by the heavy who has been assigned to shanghai the hero, pick up the other man by mistake, and the hero is then accused of murder. He makes his escape into the snow country and three years later rescues a man from the snow trail. Later it develops this man is a member of the Royal Mounted sent to find and bring him in. At the last minute it also develops that the officer is really the man supposed to have been murdered, the blow on the head causing a loss of memory, and he has since been under the assumption that he is plain "Bill Jones."

All this tends to a happy ending with the exception that the hero has lost his eyesight in a gun powder explosion. Underlying it all is the "Faith' 'doctrine of Christian Science that all works out to the general advantage of all concerned if they will only keep the faith. Thus the picture ends.

It is not a really happy ending of the conventional sort, and it leaves a doubt as to whether the hero had faith enough to get his eyesight back. However, for the houses that this one will play the audiences won't go into that any too deeply.

Fred.

WHEN KNIGHTHOOD WAS IN FLOWER

Henry VIII	Lyn Harding
Louis XII	William Norris
Charles Brandon	Forrest Stanley
Duke of Buckingham	Pedro de Cordoba
Sir Edwin Caskoden	Ernest Glendinning
Duke Francis	William H. Powell
Cardinal Wolsey	Arthur Forrest
Duc de Longueville	Macey Harlam
Will Sommers	Johnny Dooley
King's Tailor	William Kent
Grammont	Gustav von Seyffertiz
Sir Adam Judson	Charles Gerrard
An Adventurer	George Nash
Sir Henry Brandon	Arthur Donaldson
Queen Catherine	Theresa Maxwell Conover
A French Lady-in-Waiting	Flora Finch
Lady Jane Bolingbroke	Ruth Shepley
Mary Tudor	Marion Davies

The cast of "When Knighthood Was in Flower" reads like a composite of the leading drama and musical comedy of Broadway. It's a collection of names seldom met other than at a benefit. That is the indicator in its own way of the lavishness in money spent on this Cosmopolitan uplift in the film art.

At the Criterion, New York, when the picture opened for a run at $2 top the evening of Sept. 14 the premiere's scale was $5.50 on the tickets, but none were sold at that price. The showing was an invitation affair. Yet a desire had been created and enough people were turned away from the box office to have filled the rather meagre orchestra.

The theatre holds a glittering sign telling of Marion Davies and her picture, but the publicity of the advertising sign for the star and picture at the point of the Times square triangle (Broadway and 47th street) is worth nearly as much. That is on the downtown side of the old building that may easily be seen from 42d street and below, as it faces the entire square without obstacle intervening. All summer it has held the Ziegfeld "Follies" incandescents, with many conjectures why Ziegfeld should have taken that costly space for his w. k. show. Whether with design or not, the picture's ad is immediately under, with the wall reading in this wise:

Ziegfeld's "Follies"
Glorifying the American Girl

Marion Davies
in
"WHEN KNIGHTHOOD WAS IN FLOWER"

A magnificent film production that grips by its beauty of mounting and superbness of direction. "Knighthood" looks to have made of itself a compelling draw. Its romance and sentiment, with surroundings and players, stand out in picture-making. Reformers of the country —any country—will admit it is a picture of the character they are always yelling for—and recommend it.

The story, written by Charles Major, and the best seller of its day was dramatized long ago. In fact, it was first played on the New York stage, and at the very Criterion where the film is now located, in 1901, with Julia Marlowe as Mary Tudor, the loving but rebelliant sister of Henry VIII, England's notorious and chasing king. Henry has been in other pictures and plays so often and so different it may yet become necessary to dig him up to find out what he really looked like. And his chief sweetie, Ann Boleyn, but Annie is only here for an instant.

Mary just wouldn't marry King Louis XII of France, about the finest a. k. the world ever saw as played by William Norris. But Mary did marry him to save Charles Brandon, her beloved captain of the Guards, from the knife. And here is where direction stood up, also in marked contrast to the over-suspensiveness of a similar scene in Griffith's "Orphans." Robert G. Vignola snapped this scene over briskly and brusquely, with a tinge of an added thrill through the unseating of Ernest Glendenning, as Sir Edwin Caskoden, as Sir Edwin was riding to the Tower with a pardon in the form of Henry's signet ring.

Louis didn't linger long after marrying Mary. Mary with delectable foresight had secured a promise from her kingly brother she could choose her second husband. It was commencing to look squally for Mary in France. The universal opinion around the French palace seemed to be that Louis would kick off any minute. The Duc de Longueville (Macey Harlam) had been appraising Mary since she first came around. The Duc was in the line of succession to the throne, that he knew of, and to, as he thought, Mary. As Louis passed out the Duc tried to wrestle Mary, but Brandon arrived in time. They escaped after a chase that included a couple of cavalrymen and horses making dandy falls from a high bridge. When Mary next saw Henry in London she was Mrs. Brandon.

The picture is in 12 reels, running in two parts twice daily. The second set of reels has more action than the first part, making the ending lively. Throughout, the settings by Urban are a delight, the handling of the mobs a perfect picture, and the playing by most of the principals exactly what it should be; for the dignity of the production, not as massive or as heavy, even though magnificent as one might look for in English and French locales. And the photography! Anything may be said for it—there's not a word against it.

Miss Davies as the sweet, impulsive and loving Mary, emoted when that was called for, coquetted as nicely with her sweetheart, and sent the fierceness of her wrath when aroused out of the screen and over the footlights, while at all times making a charming etching, perhaps never more so than in the view as she kneeled before the Cross praying that Brandon should be saved, with the cut-ins showing Brandon awating the knife's drop. While this is a fine picture for all concerned, it is a finer one for Marion Davies, for "When Knighthood Was in Flower" implants this handsome girl right among the leading players, those who can act—something mighty few beautiful women of the screen ever accomplish.

Three of the men may be grouped for excellence of work—Lyn Harding for his King Henry, regardless of the looks; Mr. Norris for his never-forgettable King Louis, as fine a piece of character work as could be hoped for, and Mr. Glendinning, who gave a balanced performance with himself in the role as the hub of this entrancing romance, a role Glendining forced into prominence, perhaps mostly when he delightfully dallied with the guards at the gate of Louis's mansion as the loving couple completed their escape.

Forrest Stanley as Brandon looked the heroic role but had little else to do. He was only the hero to Mary. Pedro de Cordoba's Duke of Buckingham seemed slight as Mr. de Córdoba played it, in the tone of a sneering scowling countenance; Johnny Dooley, as the King's Jester, summed up all of his jesting in two falls when pushed over by the King each time, and if the original Tailor to the King was funny, William Kent failed to prove it in that role. But they showed the care with which the cast was selected, with George Nash hardly noticeable besides, while Flora Finch was there only for a bit and for a moment. About the single other mentionable is Gustav von Seyffertitz as Grammont.

Luther Reed did the scenario, a perfect one.

Cosmopolitan will gloat over this production—it may, though the film possibly won't return the production cost, for "When Knighthood Was in Flower" is a fine big and splendid mark on the not-so-long roadway of filmdom to date. *Sime.*

BROADWAY ROSE

Dramatic feature starring Mae Murray, produced and directed by Robert Z. Leonard. Story by Edmund Goulding based on the popular ballad of the same title. Distributed by Metro. At the Capitol, New York, Sept. 17.

Rosalie Lawrence	Mae Murray
Tom Darcy	Monte Blue
Hugh Thompson	Ray Bloomer
Reggie Whitley	Ward Crane
Barbara Royce	Alma Tell
Peter Thompson	Charles Lane
Mrs. Peter Thompson	Mary Turner Gordon
Mrs. Lawrence	Mrs. Jennings
Colored Maid	Pauline Dempsey

The story is in the atmosphere of Broadway and the theatre with which Miss Murray has always been so happily identified. Its drama is very forced, and Miss Murray is not as fortunate as of late in her role of the dancing divinity of the stage. She is a little out of her element, probably because the story doesn't ring true to the type this star has established for herself.

For one thing, it takes itself too seriously. Rosalie Lawrence hasn't a shade of that gay humor that belongs to the breezy stage type. She has moments of comedy, but they are dragged in. As the character was drawn Rosalie is a sort of feminine Corse Payton. She goes in heavily for emotional acting. When she is serious she is gosh awful serious, and when she is in lighter vein she reminds one of Eva Tanguay singing "I Don't Care." It's just make believe fiction and doesn't deliver the appeal of real character at any time.

The picture is painstakingly put on and expenditures have been made with a lavish hand. Some of the settings are impressive in a flamboyant way, and Miss Murray's costumes are a sartorial revel in six reels. The exhibition of stunning clothes and the display of Miss Murray's dancing, of course, are the real aim and purpose of the whole production, and, as always, they furnish excuse for it.

Besides which the locale of back stage seems to furnish its own excuse for all sorts of artificiality. Stilted acting that would be absurd in other surroundings somehow in the public mind is plausible in the atmosphere. As the butterfly of the "Follies" Miss Murray gets away with some posings that would be travesty in other settings. The picture has the virtue of freedom from any sex or other suggestive aspect. Here's one picture of Broadway life that could be shown to the Epworth League.

Monte Blue adds to his screen accomplishments by playing with fine, easy effectiveness the part of a dress suit country gentleman, a brand new departure for the fire-eating hero. He displays a splendid knack for polite characterization that has remained unsuspected till now. He wears a dinner jacket and performs in the drawing room with the best of them. Mrs. Jennings plays gracefully a sweet mother role, while Alma Tell fills the bill in the pale part of a designing society girl.

Rosalie Lawrence is a country girl who has attained eminence on the musical comedy stage. The guilded youth of the town are at her feet. She falls in love with Hugh Thompson, the polo-playing son of a Knickerbocker family, whose parents oppose his marriage to the star of the "Follies." Rosalie gives up Tom Darcy, owner of a stock farm near her childhood home, and secretly marries Hugh, who fears his rich father's wrath. Hugh's association with Rosalie becomes known through the spying of Barbara Royce, who schemes to marry him herself, and Hugh weakly permits his family to believe their relations are dishonorable.

This situation is disclosed to Rosalie, and in a tempest of fury she casts the rich husband off and falls into the arms of her girlhood sweetheart.

There's nothing especially original about the play, but its pictorial excellence may carry it along nicely. *Rush.*

MANSLAUGHTER

Daniel O'Bannon	Thomas Meighan
Lydia Thorne	Leatrice Joy
Evans, her maid	Lois Wilson
Gov. Stephen Albee	John Miltern
Judge Homans	George Fawcett
Mrs. Drummond	Julia Faye
Adeline Bennett	Edythe Chapman
Drummond, a policeman	Jack Mower
Eleanor Bellington	Dorothy Cumming
Bobby Dorset	Casson Ferguson
Dicky Evans	Mickey Moore
Butler	James Neill
Prison Matron	Sylvia Ashton
Brown	Raymond Hatton
"Gloomy Gus"	"Teddy"
Prisoners	Mabel Van Buren
	Ethel Wales
	Dale Fuller
Wiley	Edward Martindel
Doctor	Charles Ogle
Musician	Guy Oliver
Miss Santa Claus	Shannon Day
Witness	Lucien Littlefield

This Paramount, starring Thomas Meighan, features Leatrice Joy and Lois Wilson. The story is from the novel by Alice Duer Miller and also ran in the "Saturday Evening Post." The adaptation by Jeanie Macpherson adheres closely to the original script.

Cecil B. De Mille's direction carried several trade-marks, allowing for the De Mill[illegible] ensembles in a Caeserian touch showing the debauch of the ancient as compared to a modern version in a smart roadhouse. This set ran into money; in fact, the entire production looked lavish.

Miss Joy, the modern girl, who is being stifled by her environment, flashed a bewildering array of gowns and dresses that was a solo fashion show.

The story was ideally suited to the Meighan personality and virile manliness. It concerned a modern daughter of selfishness (Miss Joy), who is going to the bowwows. Meighan as Daniel O'Bannon, assistant district attorney, is in love with Lydia, and tries to dissuade her from her useless wasting.

Lydia is arrested for speeding, but bribes the officer with a diamond bracelet. The latter's wife learns of the bribe and persuades him that the honorable thing is to rearrest her and return the bracelet. Trying to carry out his wife's suggestion he follows Lydia, who is doing 60 in her roadster. She perceives the motorcycle cop in her mirror and skids into a crossroad. The cop, unable to stop, runs headon into the car and is thrown over the machine, mortally hurt. At the hospital he dies and Lydia is arrested, charged with "manslaughter." Her powerful friends immediately move heaven and earth to save her, but despite them she has to stand trial.

The district attorney prosecutes the girl he loves after a mental struggle between love and duty. Powerful influence and offers of political eminence fail to swerve him. The expected fine develops into a three-year sentence.

In prison Lydia meets her former maid, who was sentenced for the theft of jewelry from her mistress in order to send her sick boy to California. The maid and Lydia work out their own redemption. She comes out with a determination to devote her life and money to humanity.

The district attorney, following the sentence, resigns and becomes a victim of drink to allay his mental tortures. He sinks to the breadline, where he encounters Lydia serving the unfortunates. Her love for him has increased, for she realizes that he was the instrument responsible for her redemption. Her love and assistance help him in the battle to regain his manhood, and he eventually is a candidate for governor. The night before the primaries Gov. Stephen Albee (John Miltern), his political opponent, points out that an ex-convict cannot be mistress of the governor's mansion. The candidate by radio informs his constituents he will not be a candidate for governor, with the story ending in the usual embrace.

The photography is excellent. The entire picture has been staged with a liberal hand and a technical expertness that makes the romantic story a gripping series of events.

Meighan is at his best in it and Miss Joy, barring one or two insincere moments in a role that called for everything in the line of emotional display, was splendid. The rest of the cast are in keeping with the high standard set.

It's a feature that can't miss and will make Meighan's future releases objects of intense interest to the trade. The value of plot and originality is concretely illustrated in "Manslaughter."

Con.

ETERNAL FLAME

Norma Talmadge feature, adapted from Balzac's novel, "Duchesse de Langeais," by Francis Marion. Directed by Frank Lloyd. Distributed by First National. At the New York Strand, Sept. 17.

Duchessa de Langeais....Norma Talmadge
Duc de Langeais.....Adolphe Jean Menjou
Marquis de Ronquerolles, Wedgewood Nowell
General de Montriveau......Conway Tearle
Madame de Serizy..........Rosemary Theby
Princess de Viamont-Chaurray..Kate Lester
Vidame de Pamier........Thomas Ricketts
Count de Marsay.........Irving Cummings
Abbe Conrand..................Otis Harlan

The picture, which deals with the locale of Paris in Napoleon's day, is done on a scale of magnificence exceptional even for this star. Its costuming, settings and massed people in several scenes mark it as a costly production. The picture has notable beauty and pictorial force, but it is almost absolutely lacking in strong drama.

The nature of the story makes it so. It is mostly a succession of close-ups of Miss Talmadge and Conway Tearle as the centers of emotional scenes marking the progress of the distinctly sentimental story. It might better have been called "The Conquest of a Coquette," for that is the real basis of the tale, the gradual surrender to love of an embittered woman, told in the keenly analytical fashion of the great Frenchman.

It's all interesting, but it hasn't the grip of drama, particularly as it comes on the screen in pantomime. That passage where Montriveau abducts the Duchesse and threatens to brand her as his own has melodramatic values, but that is the only spot where the picture reaches dramatic force. Its final scenes have extraordinary emotional power, however, and it probably will be on the strength of the appeal here that the picture will create talk. It is here that the Duchesse, having been cast aside by Montriveau and having sought asylum in a convent, surrenders to the need of the spiritually broken man and returns to the world she had abandoned in order to restore him—the protective instinct of the maternal triumphant.

These scenes in the convent with their austere background and the striking lighting effects give the picture immense effect. Another smash in a pictorial sense is the passage of the grand ball, a whale of a spectacle, with apparently hundreds of dancers in the stunning costumes of the period in graceful ballroom maneuvers. The direction is always effective in a well-balanced way. The illusion of real life is splendidly maintained in spite of the artificiality of the surroundings, a result of both the directing intelligence and the fine acting sense of the players. Miss Talmadge brings great judgment to the aid of her special type of beauty and her eloquent face, and Mr. Tearle, one of the least actor-like of screen actors, achieves a real creation as the moody, woman-hating general.

One thing the adapter has been especially successful in achieving is a deft concentration of interest in the principal characters. Although nine roles are of sufficient importance to require listing in the cast, the attention is never diffused. It centers upon the two vital personages, which stand out clean cut as cameos. Miss Talmadge, as always, exhibits a ravishing assortment of frocks, an important production feature where this star is concerned. In other respects the production achieves innumerable excellences. The settings are an independent feature of the picture. Astonishing effects of space are secured in the interiors, which have an atmosphere of authentic reproductions. The ballroom scene must have represented a considerable investment. But all this magnificence merges into the ensemble unostentatiously, not as a revel in picture cost, but as an appropriate background for a colorful story.

The picture probably will be voted a little "fine" by the generality of fans, lacking somewhat in what is popularly called action, but pretty and "sweet."

Rush.

THE HANDS OF NARA

A Harry Garson production starring Clara Kimball Young, directed by Harry Garson. A story that is decidedly Christian Science propaganda by Richard Washburn Child. Released by Commonwealth. Shown at Loew's Circle, New York City in double feature bill.

Count Boris Alexieffs............Otto Orloff
Nara Alexieffs........Clara Kimball Young
Connor Lee.......................Edwin Stevens
Adam Pine........................Vernon Steele
Mrs. Yates...................Myrtle Steadman
Dr. Emlen Caveloux..........Elliott Dexter
Emma Gammel...........Margaret Loomis
Dr. Haith Caveloux...........John Miltern
Mrs. Caveloux...................Jessie Besserer

This picture is frankly and purely a bit of propaganda for the Christion Science faith. So much so that the title might better have been that of "The Miracle Woman" than "The Hands of Nara." The latter title means nothing, the former would have at least been in keeping with the story, and, further, it would have linked the picture with that great success of the past in filmdom, "The Miracle Man." The picture is a fair enough box office attraction for the medium classed houses, but it is far from being strong enough to stand the test of a real full week pre-release run anywhere. It is without a doubt one of the most significant lessons on how a star, that was one of the real top dozen in the point of box office strength may be permitted to slip without the right story material and proper direction in sufficient number of productions each year to keep her before the public. It isn't more than two years ago that a Clara Kimball Young picture was an event on Broadway, but in that short time she has slipped to such an extent that one of her new productions isn't even given passing notice.

The story has Miss Young as a Russian refugee who comes to this country and is sponsored by a wealthy widow who has the protege hobby, but the sham of the near Bohemian social set gets on her nerves and she seeks out a former friend of her father's who is a faker in the faith healing business. He sees great possibilities in the magnetic personality of this young woman and immediately starts her on a career as a faith healer. She has a tremendous success with her first patient, a waif of the slums, and from then on her vogue grows. While flitting with the social set, however, she has met a young doctor, whose father as well as himself are constantly showing up the fake healers and driving them from the city. The father, however, seeks the girl out when all scientific medical skill has failed and asks her to attend his wife. She is successful to a marked degree, but after the return of the son to the house and his informing her that she is an out and out faker with no extraordinary powers, she flees and returns to the tenements whence she came, only to be sought out later by the young doctor for the usual happy ending.

The picture is partly titled in color which is effective, but the contrast is so great when the ordinary titles appear that it takes from the entire production. The direction is not particularly good and there are times when the story is rather hard to follow. In the selection of the cast it seems rather unfortunate that Elliott Dexter should have been chosen as leading man to Miss Young because of his physical infirmities, which, though the director tried to cover them, showed glaringly through the picture whenever full length shots were shown.

The balance of the cast was not out of the ordinary, although Myrtle Steadman as a widow vamp with an Oriental room for her male proteges looked like a fast worker with all the appurtenances.

Fred.

MISSING MILLIONS

Alice Brady is starred in this Paramount picture, "presented" by Adolph Zukor. Based on two of Jack Boyle's well known "Boston Blackie" stories, adapted by Albert Shelby LeVino. Joseph Henabery directed. A "crook" meller. Current this week (starting Sept. 17) at the Rialto, New York.

The story carries this feature rather than the cast or star. It is a crook meller which A. S. LeVino has capably adapted from the Jack Boyle originals, a combination of two of the author's published fiction. "Boston Blackie's" yegg exploits are made subsidiary to Mary Dawson's (Alice Brady) motives, but nevertheless have a perverse way of creeping up and above the almost-honorable purpose that has been skilfully woven about the girl's personality, and at times even submerges everything. The breaking into the steamship's stronghold and rifling the rich gold bullion cargo is a breath-taking, enthralling situation that subjugates any and all interest in Mary's motives and her romancing.

Mary is the vamp of the outfit. She has gulled Dan Regan (George Le Guere) into entrusting the strong room's keys to her from which impressions were made. Mary goes across to London on the vessel in the guise of a bibliophile intent on purchasing some valuable first editions. The purser assures her of their safety on the return trip in the ship's hold and secures the keys from the captain to assure Mary thereof. The reason back of the larceny is Mary's motive to revenge herself on Jim Franklin, a figure in Wall Street, whose false accusation and treason had caused the imprisonment of her father which resulted in the failing man's death before the expiration of the 20 years' term. Franklin's creditors have been clamoring and the financier has been compelled to send to London for the bullion to satisfy their demands. The delay of its safe arrival before the first of the month would spell ruin for him and this is Mary and Boston Blackie's purpose. Blackie is Mary's sweetheart and a faithful Romeo who is twice called upon to return his spoils to satisfy the girl's whims. Rather an idealistic Raffles only to be found in fiction, but such inconsistencies are forgivable in the tale's interest. Surely, if one can obligingly forget how a man of Franklin's power and position should find himself in financial straits, so as to suit the story's progress, this is overlookable. The flicker excuse for this is not plausible enough, although it might have been in the story.

When the innocent purser is accused of complication in the crime Mary makes reparation in order to release him. She does this despite one of her henchman's objections. He insists on his share of the spoils, and Mary magnificently takes out her checkbook and notes the 24 odd thousand dollar balance. She gives him the 24 "grand" and keeps the change. Her marriage to Boston Blackie is only climaxed by the newspaper announcement, as they are exiting from the "Little Church Around the Corner," of Jim Franklin's suicide through financial distress.

Abel.

MOHICAN'S DAUGHTER

Full length feature presented by S. E. V. Taylor and distributed by American Releasing Corporation. Adapted from Jack London's "The Story of Jees Uck." Nancy Deever in lead, supported by Saxon Kling. At the Tivoli, New York, Sept. 16.

Exceedingly interesting Indian story with exceptional scenic shots of the Northwest Canadian wilderness. Especially well played and its direction commands attention. The only point in which the story misses is its character of monotonous narrative, quite lacking in dramatic progress.

The tale seems to amble aimlessly, an acceptable style in a novel but tiresome in a pantomimic presentation. The drama has no pattern, no proportions. There are none of those pauses and spurts, and the dramatic essential of progressive interest is absent. It's all a dead level of even recital. There are no climaxes, no half-climaxes to mark the climbing stages of interest.

The story is just as interesting in its last 500 feet as in its first reel, and no more. A dramatic story ought to grow and increase in tension. The introduction of high points of interest are introduced in rather startling manner. There is no preparation for the Indian woman's simple statement that blood stains on the tent prove the villain committed the murder and not the heroine. It comes out and is gone before one realizes its import. This is bad craftsmanship.

It was all right for Jack London's printed medium, but an ingenious continuity writer might have devised some introductory chain of events to lead up to the disclosure.

At another point the heroine is in the power of the villain and the hero is approaching his tepee. The situation ought to involve some suspense, but it doesn't. The hero simply meets a couple of Indians in the forest and they volunteer to introduce him into the tepee concealed in a bundle of leaves destined to make the marriage couch. This was so ineptly managed that it started a giggle all over the theatre and spoiled what had been up to then interesting. It was all mere awkward workmanship.

The picture lends itself to picturesque effects, what with Indian camp scenes with wierd campfire lighting and a wealth of really lovely scenery. The mechanical effects of light and shade have been skilfully managed, the errors have all been committed in the editorial work. Ordinarily white actors are ridiculous in Indian garb, but the principals in this picture create a real illusion. Perhaps the exceptional beauty of Miss Deever, an appealing wide-eyed type of dark, petite loveliness, works chiefly to this end. The other players were attractively natural and unaffected.

The film is something of a novelty. It gets away from the familiar love story triangle, and is fresh in its romance. Its settings in the open also recommend it and altogether its virtues vastly outweigh its demerits. It ought to appeal to the neighborhood clientele. It is built on simple romance and adventure and is proof against the objections usually brought against the screen.

It might have been written by Fenimore Cooper for the younger generation rather than designed for a modern screen scenario. The incidental score has some excellent passages, but they are spoiled toward the end by the introduction of "Tammany." Who ever thought to introduce a burlesque musical strain into a romantic Indian story?
Rush.

HEADIN' NORTH

A Pete Morrison western released by Arrow. Story by Bernard Furey, directed by Charles E. Bartlett. Shown at Loew's New York on a double feature bill. Released in New York State by Commonwealth.

Arthur Stowell.................Jack Walters
Madge Mullin..................Gladys Cooper
Bob Ryan......................Pete Morrison
Frances Wilson.........Dorothea Dickinson
Hank Wilson....................William Dills
The Boob......................Bernard Furey

Just another of those pictures which after seeing one wonders why the producers turn them out, and incidentally where the film bookers who handle the circuits get the nerve to play them. It is a real cheap western that as a feature seems to be .. great scenic; it will do for the cheap houses, but in the better class of the daily change theatres it's a flop. At the finish of the showing at the New York Tuesday this one got a horse laugh from the audience, and during the action there was many a laugh handed the picture.

What there is of the story has the hero starting out to trail a man who lured his sweetheart away from her prairie home with promises of a wonderful life in the big city. But the girl never reaches there, for on the night of the elopement the buckboard that she is in tumbles over a cliff and she is killed. The man, however, escapes and the hero starts after him. But when he meets him in a lumber camp later he fails to recognize his man, so there has to be another story altogether, with a different set of characters surrounding the heavy and the hero, to take up the footage. Another girl is brought into the story and the hero falls for her, but not until he is almost hanged for having held up the pay-roll wagon, a job that the villian did to get him in dutch.

The author played the character of a "boob" in the story as presented on the screen. It would have been more fitting had the producer played it, for that is what he was for having bought this story in the hope that he could get it across.

There is no one in the cast that amounts to anything and the two women playing ingenue leads are both rather bad.

This picture is one of a series of Pete Morrison released by Arrow for the state rights market, and if it is a fair sample of what the state rights market has to offer then it is easy to realize what is wrong with the independent field. *Fred.*

MARRIED PEOPLE

A Hugo Ballin production released by Hodkinson, with Mabel Ballin starred. Story by Neli Marie Dace, adapted by Hugo Ballin and George S. Heilman and directed by Ballin. About five reels, shown at Loew's Circle, New York City on a double feature bill.

Dorothy Cluer.....................Mabel Ballin
Robert Cluer.....................Percy Marmot
Lord Cranston.....................Ernest Hilliard
Timmy.............................Bobby Clarke
Mike..................................Dick Lee
Mary.................................Bertha Kent
Betty.........................Baby Peggy Rice

Did you ever ride in an automobile that was being driven by a fellow that was just learning to drive and almost have your head snapped off about a half dozen times by the fits and jerks that the machine goes through as he starts it and shifts the gears? Well, if you did, then you have a fairly good idea of how this picture runs. It goes and it stalls and it jerks and it almost snaps your head off if you are trying to follow the story. It is, in a word, a combination of poor continuity, direction and boasts of a collection of the tritest titles ever written. As a feature it classes with the second rate program material and that is about all.

Outside of the fact that it is a Hugo Ballin production and that Hugo Ballin directed it, there seems no reason in the world that Mabel Ballin should be the star of the production, or of any other. She can act and all that she does do is to wear a profusion of clothes. The best thing that she does is to change her costume and she seems to be doing that the greater part of the time.

It is the story of a girl who has been reared in the country and who develops an extravagant one when she marries and arrives in a big city. The husband wants babies and the wife wants a good time, so to cheat the husband and indulge her own whim she gets herself a lover. Finally, however, the lover is dropped out of the picture for no good reason and the couple adopt a couple of kids and all ends happily.

If someone really had to be starred in this picture it should have been the kid actor, Bobby Clarke.
Fred.

ME AND MY GAL

Obviously an English importation. Of short feature length, but longer than a two-reeler. Sponsored by Welsh-Pearson Productions. Betty Balfour featured. At the New York Tivoli, Sept. 16, half double feature.

This is a gem of a character comedy, dealing in a humorous but sympathetic way with the life of a coster girl and her romance with a London bobby. As a pure character sketch it excels in clean-cut portraiture. The hand of a real artist is discernible in the picture. Somebody concerned in its production believes that film comedy does not have to be made up of buffoons and bathing girls.

Here is a slice of life illuminated by imaginative sympathy and understanding. The scene between the bobby's mother and the coster flower girl is an inspired bit of delicious drollery. The older woman had been a cook before she married the bobby's father, who also was a London policeman. She takes the delightfully British lower class view that, as a matter of course, her son will also chose a cook for his wife. "Cooks and policemen are made for each other," is the foundation of her social code.

When learning in an unexpected way that the girl is a flower seller she explodes with righteous indignation. "She's not respectable. She never was in service at all," she moans. "She's a low flower girl." And the flower girl's fiery comeback is just as true and as amusing.

Betty Balfour, who ought to be known better in this country, plays the part for all it is worth. Here is an actress who can get delicate comedy across to a screen audience without doing a neck fall. Where have they been hiding this gifted pantomimist?

The rest of the cast is notably good. The characters all have the stamp of authentic London types. Even to one who takes his knowledge of England from reading there is no doubting the genuineness of the portraiture.

These English players are genuine actors. No more spontaneous and sincere bit of film creation has been shown in New York in a long time than this unnoticed subject introduced to New York via Eighth avenue. Of course, it's not the kind of picture to support a whole bill, but as an incidental it has a distinct and attractive flavor.

Rush.

THE CUB REPORTER

Richard Talmadge production presented by Phil Goldstone, directed by Jack Dillon. Five reels. Shown at Loew's New York on double feature bill.

Harrison Rhodes.........Edward B. Tilton
Mariam Rhodes..............Jean Calhoune
Dick Harvey.............Richard Talmadge

Phil Goldstone is still trying to make a Doug Fairbanks out of his star, Richard Talmadge, and this picture is just another of the series of productions in which he has been trying. Talmadge is a rather athletic youngster who registers on his acrobatic ability, but he is lacking in personality of the sort that registers with the picture fans.

"The Cub Reporter" is a very poor imitation of one of those Fairbanks pictures of the type that he turned out when he was with Triangle, and they, by a long shot, were about the best that Fairbanks ever did. As a feature it is in the Class B League for the cheaper houses with a daily change policy.

It is the story of a stolen jewel, taken from the eye of a Chinese idol. The heroine's father is a collector of Oriental jewels and he receives the diamond in his home in San Francisco. At the same time the brothers of the tong in the city receive word that the jewel from their temple is there and they start out on a hunt for it. At the same time one of the daily papers receives a tip that the jewel is in the town, and the cub is sent out on the story.

The tong manages to locate the jewel, and when they can't obtain it they abduct the daughter of the wealthy collector and hold her as a hostage for the stone. The cub manages to rescue her, and the usual happy ending results.

In action the picture manages to move along when Talmadge is in front of the camera, but at other times it's about as slow as running molasses on Christmas morn in Alaska.

Edward Tilton as the father gives a fairly good performance as the wealthy collector, but the daughter as played by Jean Calhoune is far from satisfying. Ethel Hallor is in the picture playing a bit. That is about all that she could have handled, judging from the manner in which she mishandled it.

Nobody is going to hang any medals on Jack Dillon for the direction that he gave this picture. There is only one stunt in it that registers, and that is where Talmadge does a leap from one automobile to another, landing in about four moving cars and finally on a trolley car in his progress. If one was judging this picture from a vaudeville standpoint the verdict would be, "for the small, small time only." *Fred.*

RAGS TO RICHES

Comedy-drama of feature length put out by Warner Brothers, starring Wesley Barry by arrangement with Marshall Neilan. Story by William Nigh and Walter De Leon, Designated a Harry Rapf production. Directed by Wallace Worsley. At the New York Capitol, Sept. 24.

Marmaduke Clarke...........Wesley Barry
Dumbell.........................Niles Welch
Mary Warde....................Ruth Renick
Sheriff.......................Russell Simpson
Sheriff's Wife......Mrs. Mina D. Redman
Blackwell Clarke...........Richard Tucker
Mrs. Blackwell Clarke.......Eulalie Jensen
Marmaduke's Governess.......Jane Keckley
The Wop......................Sam Kaufman
Bull..........................Dick Sutherland
Louis..........................Jimmy Quinn
Purist's League Members,
"Snitz" Edwards and Elaine Manning

"Rags to Riches" gives promise of being another "School Days," coming out under practically the identical auspices and having much the same merits and virtues. Young Barry is an absolutely natural kid actor with a distinct flavor of attractive comedy. It's a great film for the youngsters and an amusing one for their elders.

It's just a piece of artless fooling free from any serious intent, refreshing in its characterizations and incidents. It hasn't even a moral and is devoid of sensational appeal. A wholesome picture of this kind deserves support, and this one is likely to earn it on merit.

Wesley, the freckled, is the son of a fabulously rich father, spoiled and coddled by a society woman mother and yearning "to have some fun" with the other kids outside the high garden gate. He breaks bonds and has a glorious rough and tumble fight with neighboring urchins, but is promptly captured and returned to his prison round of butlers and music lessons.

It looks pretty gloomy for Marmaduke, when a fascinating burglar, member of the Zollani gang, breaks in on robbery intent. Marmaduke volunteers to help him burglarize the house, but the burglar is frightened off. Marmaduke goes in pursuit of the fleeing gang in his own miniature motor car and comes up with them in their rendezvous. The gang grabs him, their idea being to hold him for ransom, his scheme being to stick to the gang to escape from home.

The burglarizing member of the gang, known as Dumbell, takes the kid away, apparently unwilling to join the others in the desperate plan of killing him if the ransom doesn't come through, and they go to the country, where work is offered on a farm. A love affair develops between Dumbell and an orphan girl on the farm, adopted by the kindly farmer, who is also the local sheriff. Marmaduke, newly freed, makes a carnival of farm life, and in intervals helps on the romance of Dumbell and the girl. The hypocritical villagers get to knocking Dumbell, and when a detective appears and arrests him for kidnapping Marmaduke, they are accordingly delighted. Dumbell escapes for the moment, just as Marmaduke's papa and mamma arrive on the scene, but presently returns to straighten things out.

It appears that he was a federal secret service man all the time and was operating to run down the Zollani gang. So it all ends in a whoop-hurrah finale, with Marmaduke emancipated from the apron strings and the parents cured from making him a "sissy," all of which isn't such a bad moral when you come to think of it. *Rush.*

UNDER TWO FLAGS

A Universal-Jewel presented by Carl Laemmle, with Priscilla Dean as the star. Directed by Tod Browning, who also assisted in making the adaptation. Shown at the Strand, New York, week of Sept. 24.

Cigarette......................Priscilla Dean
Corporal Victor...............James Kirkwood
Sheik Ben Ali Hammed.....John Davidson
Marquis de Chateauroy......Stuart Holmes
Princess Corona...........Ethel Grey Terry
Rake..........................Robert Mack
The Sheik's Aide.............Burton Law
Captain Tollaire...............Albert Pollet

This is a remade picture. Originally it was done by William Fox with Theda Bara as the star in 1916. The present production, however, is a world beater for action and Priscilla Dean as Cigarette is wonderful in the role. Tod Browning who handled the direction has added little touches of color and atmosphere here and there that go a long way to enhancing the value on the screen. The feature is a special any way one looks at it. At this time it is keeping with the general run of all of the desert sands' pictures and in the matter of story this old tale shows that a lot of the present day writers must have delved into the past for their material. "Under Two Flags" looks like it will compete with any of the more recent desert pictures and more than hold its own.

In the matter of cast the U. spread itself on this production. James Kirkwood plays the hero opposite Miss Dean, while Stuart Holmes and John Davidson are the heavies. Davidson tries hard with the eyes to make his Sheik a Valentino, and to some slight degree he succeeds in putting it over in the harem scene with Miss Dean. Ethel Grey Terry plays the Princess Carona in a lifeless, detached sort of manner that does not register.

After all it is Priscilla Dean as the Daughter of the Regiment who is the center of the action. Kirkwood's performance qualifies but does not stand out.

Tod Browning did himself proud in the matter of direction. In the cafe scene at the opening of the picture he manages to introduce a number of types in short shots that are most interesting. Later his action stuff with the battle in the desert stronghold, the ride to the rescue are all well handled.

No exhibitor can go wrong in playing this one, for it has all the action that any picture house audience could want, and the story is a real one. At the Strand Joe Plunkett prefaced the feature with a corking prolog that was a real production. *Fred.*

DESERTED AT ALTAR

A five reel melodrama presented by Phil Goldstone, adapted from the old popular priced meller that played the combination houses years ago. Directed by Willam K. Howard.

Anna Moore....................Bessie Love
Tommy Moore...................Frankie Lee
Squire Simpson................Tully Marshall
John Simpson..................Wade Boteler
Bob Crandall..................William Scott
Nell Reed.....................Barbara Tenant
Marshal ....Les Bates

This looks like one of those pictures that has been made at a price but which will have an appeal in certain communities and get money for the exhibitor. There is a good cast, including Bessie Love, Tully Marshall, Barbara Tennant and Fred Kelso. The story is simply told with fair action. A distinctive feature is the uniformly excellent photography.

The title of "Deserted at the Altar" looks to be one that is going to have a certain amount of draw at the box office. In the old days it was one of the standard attractions on the ten-twent-thirt circuits presenting popular mellers. In film form it should have exactly the same appeal to the same class of audiences as the original play did.

The story is that of the orphaned sister and brother who are in charge of a rather hard shelled guardian. Through an automobile accident to the little boy, the girl meets the "city feller" with whom she eventually goes to the altar, only to have the ceremony interrupted by the arrival of the "woman with the baby." It is all a plant on the part of the heavy who wants to win the girl, and when this complication is cleared there is the usual happy ending.

Miss Love is altogether charming as Anna Moore the girl that is deserted, while Frankie Lee as her brother is one of the real stars of the performance together with the little dog, Queenie. Tully Marshall plays the old guardian, while the heavy his son is Wade Boteler. William Scott plays the hero and manages to give a rather satisfactory performance. Barbara Tennant as Nell Reed the woman who was wronged presented the usual weepy type that has survived for so many years of melodrama.

There is a lot of action in the picture and a corking mob scene is staged just before the finish. *Fred.*

PINK GODS

A Penryhn Stanlaws production (Paramount), featuring Bebe Daniels and James Kirkwood in bold program type and Anna Q. Nilsson and Raymond Hatton in lesser conspicuousness. A tale of the Kimberley diamond fields adapted from Cynthia Stockley's novel, "Pink Gods and Blue Demons," by Sonya Levien and J. E. Nash; scenario by Ewart Adamson. Current at the Rialto, New York, week of Sept. 24.

Lorraine Temple..............Bebe Daniels
John Quelch..................James Kirkwood
Lady Margot Cork.............Anna Q. Nilsson
Jim Wingate..................Raymond Hatton
Louis Barney.................Adolphe Menjou
Mark Eecher..................Guy Oliver
Col. Pat Temple..............George Cowl

If there is nothing else in "Pink Gods" as orthodox flicker entertainment to commend it, there are at least two things that will reimburse the observer for his hour's attention. One is Bebe Daniels' unsuspected attainments in rising to the dramatic heights and the other, the artistic Penrhyn Stanlaws' sense of artistry in the fancy production touches. However, it would take a greater director than Mr. Stanlaws to inject a sense of breathing realism into a theme that leaves one doubting from the first planting of the plot seed.

John Quelch, diamond mine owner of Kimberley and adjacent (South African) territory (despite Mr. Kirkwood's reservedly sincere personation) cannot bear out the scenario's title that the lust for diamonds is more pitiful than the inebriate's for alcohol or the drug addict's for "snow" and that he has yet to meet one woman whose very soul cannot be purchased for a few baubles of "ice." Of course, the plot development is quite obvious from the moment one flashes Mrs. Lorraine Temple's (Bebe Daniels) fascination for the diamonds Quelch is displaying to her and Lady Margot Cork (Anna Q. Nilsson). Quelch is a playful sort of codger (but a gentleman at heart, mind you) whose little idiosyncrasies run to leaving souvenirs in all his lady callers' gloves and thus gauge their varying states of temptation. Lady Cork very promptly returns the diamond thus placed in her glove and sees through the diamond king. Lorraine does ditto, but only after some strenuous intervals of writhing on the floor. That was her histrionic instructions to "get over" how the precious "ice" reacts on her. To her credit, one will not assume this interpretation was self-inspired but more likely director-perspired.

The story continues with Lady Cork's boy repeating ever and anon to his mother, "I like him" (the object pronoun italicized for emphasis) which refers to John Quelch. This is Lady Cork's guidance in her affair of the heart with the diamond owner. A formal engagement is finally arrived at, but broken after Quelch takes her to the diamond fields, displays his mastery among the Kaffirs, has some of the thieving laborers taken up to his specially prepared surgery, X-rayed, and the diamonds which they swallowed cut out of them. In Lady Cork's eyes, this stamps him a brute and the engagement is off.

Quelch turns his attentions to Lorraine whose husband has left town on governmental business. There's a lot of talk about Quelch's sumptuous "underground palace," his retreat, wherein stories have it, souls are bartered for diamonds. Lorraine is seen being vulgarly bedecked with strings and brooches of diamonds and on the verge of capitulating in exchange, when Quelch shakes an emphatic "nay" and explains he did this merely to show her where her lust for diamonds was leading her. At that moment, a vengeful ex-foreman dynamites the works, Lorraine's husband arrives on the scene as does Lady Cork with the fade-out showing Lorraine, blinded and deaf, monologing in a state of coma that "Quelch is a man and tell my husband I was true to him to the very end," etc. Quelch survives, however, for the clinch with Lady Cork.

There's a lot of picturesque stuff in the production which guarantees interest despite the incongruities. There is no doubting film fans will find this a compelling hour's entertainment, but on actual mental recounting it does sum up as somewhat far-fetched.

The excellent casting does much to convince and carry the tale. The photography is corking. *Abel.*

JUNE MADNESS

"June Madness" involves a good deal of production magnificence. It has two sets that measure up to the biggest in proportions. One is an elaborate staging of a church wedding and the other is a cabaret scene, both done with a lavish hand. But the story does not justify the cost of the picture. It greatly overdoes the cutie-cutie style of Miss Dana to the point where she alienates sympathy as the head-strong daughter of wealth.

There comes a point in the behavior of even a screen girl tomboy where bad manners and ill temper arouse impatience and Miss Dana reaches it in the tale of Clytie Whitmore, the spoiled daughter of riches. She throws things at her maid, treats her mother rudely, not to say violently. In general, this admirable heroine of Mr. Beaumont's story should have been put in a correction school instead of being coaxed and coddled. This idea occurs to one about the middle of reel one and from then on one's resentment grows.

The whole picture is flash and vulgar. Everybody who belongs in the environment of wealth and breeding, from the mother to the suitor for the girl, is made ridiculous, and the hero is a jazz orchestra leader in a roadhouse. Another character who wears evening clothes is a society spy who secretly contributes to a society scandal newspaper. Whoever wrote the story seems to feel that clean linen is a subject to burlesque. The attitude, by the way, is quite familiar to observers of the screen art. Does this sort of thing awaken a sympathetic response in the minds of the fans?

The mother has arranged a match between Clytie and a simpleton of wealth, but Clytie resists right up to the altar. The best man drops the ring, and while everybody is stooping under the pews to look for it Clytie dodges through the chancel and escapes. This is after she has fallen as she marches up the aisle and blackened her eye (the optic turns a fine grease-paint black in three seconds). This wedding party is broken up, but another is set and mamma places a husky housemaid at Clytie's bedroom door to prevent another escape. So she goes out the window on a rope made of her bed clothes.

She whizzes to Pennetti's roadhouse where Len Pauling, her romantic sweetheart, is leader of the jazz dance orchestra. The dancing star of the roadhouse cabaret has failed to make an appearance, and Pennetti (played by Snitz Edwards) is in despair. The society spy, who has followed Clytie, and is anxious to create a scandal, suggests to Pennetti that society's champion amateur dancer is in the place. Clytie is invited to take the absent dancer's place. She rips her evening dress apart until she has got down to the costume of daring "Follies" proportions and gives the performance. Len, meanwhile, has coached his musicians to turn all the lights out and make a noise in the dark. "It's a raid," shouts somebody and the crowd scrambles for the doors. Len seizes Clytie and hurries her to a nearby motor boat —"To escape the police," he says. He takes her to his bungalow, where the dancing star is being married, and then the runaways make a double wedding of it.

There are a few laughs in the picture, but Clytie's temperamental outbursts earn few of them. Miss Dana is a capital comedienne of a certain style, but you couldn't expect her to do much with a female rowdy of this sort. *Rush.*

THE FIGHTING GUIDE

A Vitagraph, with William Duncan and Edith Johnson co-starred. Directed by William Duncan from the script by Bradley J. Smollen. Shown at Loew's New York on double feature bill.

Ned Lightning...............William Duncan
Ethel MacDonald.............Edith Johnson
Lord Chumleigh Winston...Harry Lonsdale
Tubbs.......................William McCall
Grant Knowles...............Sidney D'Albrook
John MacDonald..............Charles Dudley
"Indian Bill"...............Fred De Silva
Mrs. Carmody................Mrs. Harry Burns

Here is a Vitagraph western that is decidedly different. Because of this fact it is strong enough to ride by itself instead of being played on double feature bills as it is being by the Loew Circuit. A western without a dressed up cowboy, or near cowboy, and still with just as much action and better riding stuff then the usual type of western has. William Duncan and Edith Johnson the the Vita's serial stars. They both qualify as feature stars and they should be kept so, providing they will continue to turn out pictures of the calibre of this one is. It is a picture that gets over the plate with a wallop.

William Duncan has the role of a guide in the northwest. The head of an English Syndicate engages him to guide him to the holdings of the company. Duncan decides to compel the titled one to change places with him and he walks into a mystery crime, clears it up and wins the girl, who is the daughter of his dad's former partner and who is accused of the crime.

It is a simple tale directly and simply told, but with a lot of action. Duncan handles himself wonderfully well, rides like a Comanche and pulls one trick in the riding stuff that is enough to make the picture. Miss Johnson shows a wealth of screen personality in this picture and handles her role exceeding well.

The production wasn't a costly one, but the picture is there with the action punch from beginning to end. *Fred.*

GIRL WHO RAN WILD

A Universal production of Bret Harte's "M'liss," adapted and directed by Rupert Julian, with Gladys Walton starred. Shown at Loew's New York on a double feature bill with Buster Keaton's "Cops."

Bret Harte's immortal "M'liss" is presented here under the title of "The Girl Who Ran Wild," which undoubtedly is the idea of the Universal executives as to a title that is sure fire for the box office. Maybe it is and then again maybe it isn't. Those that would be attracted by that particular title are going to be disappointed when they see the picture, and those who would come to see "M'liss" stay away from the theatre because they could not by the widest stretch of their imagination figure that "The Girl" title would be remotely connected with the Bret Harte story. It is barely possible, however, that U did not want this production confused with the Artcraft production of "M'liss" which Mickey Neilan directed with Mary Pickford as the star, released in 1918. That version of "M'liss" was a real picture; this version is just so much film. The Harte story was adapted and directed by Rupert Julian, who was far from getting either the spirit or the atmosphere of the story on the screen.

Gladys Walton, one of the younger U stars, suffers by comparison with Miss Pickford in the role by those who remember the performance of the latter in the picture, but she is a pleasing enough little harum scarum of the gold camp, with perhaps a slight tendency to over-act the tomboy stuff. The cast supporting the star is a fairly good one as Universal standards of casts go, and the production is about all that could be asked for in a picture of this sort that was evidently made inside of a low production overhead limit. .

It, however, is a fairly entertaining picture that moves along rather slowly as to action except for the dance hall barroom fight between the hero and the heavy. That is rather well handled by the principals involved. Otherwise there is nothing about this picture that takes it out of the U regulation program class, even though it might have been developed into a real special.

From a box office standpoint there is naught about the picture that one would bank on, except in the regular daily change of policy houses, where there is a steady grind and no one cares what is on the screen and the picture house just serves as a timekiller. *Fred.*

REPENTANCE

London, Sept. 15.

This, the first picture made by Geoffrey Benstead, with the "B. & Z." brand, is good dramatic entertainment. The story is an original one, written by Lilian and Edward R. Gordon, the latter having directed the production.

The story is of humble life, but although strong it is never sordid and the change of locale from the squalid east end to the fashionable west is well done.

Queenie has been kidnapped when a child and is "keeping house" for a good-for-nothing scoundrel named Dan Creedon. She has one friend, a flower seller, Toby Willis, and while chatting with him one night meets Frank Hepburn, a society man who is having a look around the slums. Returning home, she is assaulted by Creedon, who is arrested. The fellow, however, is only bound over and on his return home again assaults the girl. This time it is Toby who comes to the rescue.

In the subsequent fight he receives injuries from which he dies. Creedon is arrested for murder and Queenie is homeless. She is befriended by a charitable woman, who obtains a position for her as a mannequin. She soon becomes a success. She meets Frank again and he is once more attracted by her innocence and beauty. She falls ill and he has her sent into the country to his own home, but Queenie thinks it is the house of the doctor who has been called in. Creedon escapes and coincidence takes him to the house where she is. He forces her to write a letter exonerating him from guilt in the death of Toby. Later he calls on Lady Hepburn and tells her Frank has ruined Queenie. Lady Hepburn goes to the house and finding them together and with a baby Queenie is mothering believes the story. She disowns Frank at the same time, telling him he is only her adopted son. The tangle is ultimately straightened out when Dan Creedon, who has been mortally wounded while resisting re-arrest,

confesses his guilt and proves Queenie is really Lady Hepburn's missing daughter. Explanations regarding the true relationship between Frank and Queenie follow and the pair are happily united. The production work is excellent throughout and the settings are good.

Peggie Hathaway gives a very good performance as Queenie. Ray Raymond is capital, if a little highly colored as Dan Creedon, and a capital study of Toby Willis comes from Geoffrey Benstead. Many other small parts are well played and the east end scenes give scope for some capitally stage-managed crowd work. The British, French and some other continental rights in this film have already been disposed of. *Gore.*

DICK TURPIN

London, Sept. 13.

This latest greatly boomed and long anticipated Stoll film is a disappointment. Beyond the fact that it is historical, the central character is called "Dick Turpin," and the famous ride to York is featured, it might be anything. The story is merely the usual historical mixture of ladies in distress and cavaliers, wicked and otherwise, with the usual happy ending. The "doubling" in the ride is very apparent, not only on the part of Turpin but on the part of the Bow Street runners. Matheson Lang's name (no worse choice from a physical point of view could have been cast for the part) will probably bring some measure of success to the film in England, but that is its only chance.

The story tells how, on his way to Weston, near York, Ferret Bevis, who has jeered at highwaymen and wagered nobody could rob him, is held up by Dick Turpin. The braggart has his daughter Esther with him, the object of his visit being to marry her to the Earl of Weston, and with her Turpin promptly falls in love.

As a side line, he assists Luke Somers to recover his inheritance. Ferret Bevis now decides Esther shall marry Luke and in her terror the girl sends a message to Turpin, who is hiding in London. She implores him to come to her assistance. Turpin has been in the meantime captured, but Black Bess responds nobly to his call. Then comes the ride, with the pursuit close behind. Black Bess dies of a broken heart and Turpin arrives too late to prevent the marriage, but in time to kill her husband and restore her to the arms of her lover. The picture closes on Turpin, who has acquired another horse, a white one this time, drinking a sad toast to "Bonny Black Bess." The acting is good. *Gore.*

FIRES OF INNOCENCE

London, Sept. 11.

This is yet another picture put forward under the auspices of the British National Film League. It is an ordinary story marked by excellent production and much better acting than we are in the habit of seeing in native productions.

The story is one of village life and has for its theme the social battle between the vicarage and the big house of the aristocracy. Because the vicar's daughter dresses well she is looked upon by the village gossips as being "no better than she should be." The vicar calls on a widow, a stranger to the village, and immediately becomes the center of scandal. He is innocent, but appears so guilty that the bishop demands an explanation, which is considered quite satisfactory. Finding the bottom knocked out of their scandal-loving ideas the gossips

turn to the realities around them. The vicar's son has stolen jewelry from the local representative of aristocracy and his daughter has dared to fall in love with the son of the house. Eventually the gossips are hoist by their own petard and the vicarage family arrives at the conventional happy ending.

Joan Morgan is exceptionally good as the daughter, and the same can be said of Marie Illington as the aristocratic lady. The leading gossips are ably played by Madge Tree and Nell Emerald. *Gore.*

MAN WHO PLAYED GOD

Distinctive Productions feature with George Arliss. Made from the play by Jules Eckert Goodman founded on a story by Gouverneur Morris. Released by United Artists. Direction by Harmon Wright.

John Arden.................George Arliss
Marjory Blaine.............Ann Forrest
Carter ....Ivan Simpson
Philip Stevens.............Edward Earle
Mildred Arden..............Effie Shannon
A little girl..............Miriam Battista
A little boy...............Micky Bennett
A young woman..............Mary Astor
A young man................Pierre Gendron
An old woman...............Margaret Seddon
An old man.................J. B. Walsh

"The Man Who Played God" repeats the fine impression of "Disraeli," done under the same auspices and with the same star. It is first of all a thoroughly interesting picture and story and it is played in splendid style. The production element is 100 per cent., and finally the picture is eminently wholesome in material and purpose.

There is some pretty profound philosophy in this story by Gouverneur Morris, one of the best writers and thinkers in the American short-story field. The story makes the average screen recital seem cheap by comparison. It has dignity as one of its best points of appeal and something of the same high aim as "The Miracle Man." Not that it is "preachy," for it is not. It's a thoroughly absorbing human story told in strong dramatic terms and if it has a moral the precept is neatly concealed. Certainly it isn't forced on the audience. The one mischance in the screen version is its tendency to drift into saccharine sentiment, particularly in the scenes with the two kids. The sympathy stuff is laid on here pretty thick. But that's a small detail compared to many excellences.

In the film the preliminaries are a trifle tiresome. It takes a long time and much effort to get to the point. The preliminaries are over-elaborated in their painstaking "planting." John Arden is an eminent musician who is made deaf by an explosion when anarchists try to assassinate a European king at a command concert. He is devoted to his young wife and she to him, but the affliction which has wrecked his career makes him moody and capricious. He studies lip reading and becomes so expert that he can "read" conversation between persons at a great distance by observing them through field glasses.

Melancholy drives him to the verge of suicide, but he finds a new interest in life by studying the sorrows of his fellow men and helping to cure them. Seated in the window of his apartment, he can follow the conversations of people seated in the park across the street. He learns that a young husband is dying because he cannot afford to go to the country to regain his health. An old couple are crushed by hardships in the great city. He finances the young husband's cure and secures a home in the country for the old pair, losing his own sufferings in aiding others.

Meanwhile an ex-flame of his wife's has renewed his suit, arguing that she is wasting her life on a broken man. Arden learns of this situation, as he has learned the other affairs, by lip reading through his field glasses. He sees his wife put the lover's advances aside, declaring that she is bound by duty. Arden resolves to give the wife her freedom, not knowing that she really loves him. He goes to church to perform an obligation and while there becomes giddy and falls. The shock of the fall miraculously restores his hearing and brings the happy ending.

The settings of wealth are exceptionally good and a striking atmosphere of reality surrounds the whole production, to which the flawless acting of Mr. Arliss contributes much. *Rush.*

TRIFLING WOMEN

PROLOG

Zareda, a product of the Orient, with supernatural powers, meeting with great success in her assumed role of sorceress, succumbs to her vanity, and at the apex of her triumph pays with her life to learn for her sins.

Zareda..........Baroness Norka Rouskaya
Leon de Severac, the novelist...........Pomeroy Cannon
Jacqueline, his daughter..Barbara La Marr
Henri......................Ramon Novarro
Zareda, the fortune teller..Barbara La Marr
Baron Francois de Maupin..............Edward Connelly
Ivan, his son..............Ramon Novarro
The Marquis Ferroni............Lewis Stone
Pere Alphonse Bidondeau, innkeeper....Hughie Mack
Col. Roybet......................Gene Pouyet
Achmet.........................John George
Caesar.........................Jesse Weldon
Hasson.....................Hyman Binunsky
Hatim-Tai......................Joe Martin

The try of Metro to put over "Trifling Women" as a special at the Astor, New York, at $1.50 top, doesn't look feasible. The reason is that the picture doesn't approach the special class. Other than the Rex Ingram name attached, it will be fortunate to command attention as a regular Metro release. The title may mean something to the box office. It's a good title, much better than the film, now running in two parts and to short time for a special.

The main defect is that you are always looking for something to happen that doesn't. It's the story of a vamp, which doesn't back up the plural of the women in its name. The same vamping tale has been told before in many different ways. Here the main though meager interest is that the vamping one has a father and his son in tow, while the friend of the family marries her after all, and after the father had been killed by a poisonous drink he had prepared for the friend.

Mr. Ingram wrote and directed the story, the program says. He did this picture some years ago for Universal, under the title of "Black Orchids." The U's production, as usual then, was a cheap one, likely under $20,000, and its circulation meant nothing in those days to the picture business of now. The Metro's production looks like $250,000 or more. Mr. Ingram thought well enough of it, however, to reproduce the tale under another title and on a more elaborate scale. But it's not a picture to follow "The Prisoner of Zenda."

The film strings out like a book story, closely followed. Its big moment is at the finish, following a duel where the friend, Marquis Ferroni (Lewis Stone) was mortally wounded by the son, Ivan de Maupin (Ramon Navarro). The duel was watched by Zanella, the vamp (Barbara La Marr), a professional crystal gazer and wife of the marquis. Upon the doctor's informing the marquis he was finished, the marquis said he would live despite them until sundown, and he did. The ending of this series of events (it's a cut-back tale within a related story) brings the three together in a citadel where the husband throws his wife into a dungeon and, after killing the son, throws him in with her. He had been doing quite well for a mortally wounded man. After dispatching the couple, he gracefully died himself. This finale is not unlike the intrigue of Corelli's "Vendetta," and another scene in the picture suggested the Baron Chevrial of the late Richard Mansfield. This was the Marquis de Mapin as played by Edward Connelly. Mr. Connelly exaggerated the infirmities of the marquis until he was tottering. But the marquis died at the dining table, remaining there staring after all of the guests had departed. The scene was set in an attractive Parisian wine cellar.

A snatch of the war here and there is lightly brought in through the son going to Flanders. It is not prominent nor effective.

The picture looks to have been made abroad. Its chief feature is a trained chimpanzee. The animal had an eerie appearance as it frequently came into the scenes but did nothing sensational. A comedy bit was a cat always on the edge of a glass aquarium attempting to snare the gold fish within.

Other than Mr. Stone's playing there is nothing striking in the film's acting. Mr. Stone, when getting to the meat of his part, did stalwart playing. The vamp role presented no finer acting opportunities than the usual vampish roles, while Mr. Nevarre's part could also have been assumed by almost any juvenile of pictures.

The detail appears to be splendid, the direction makes no decided calls for action but lopes along nicely until reaching the duel, that was not brilliantly staged.

Sympathy will go out to Ivan, sympathy because he fell for a vamp and that he was killed for her, through his innocense, but he would have been a stronger character here if he had been Ivan the Terrible instead of Ivan the Sap.

The greatest difficulty this picture must overcome is the title, "Trifling Women," as the title is too big and encompasses too much for this film to stand up under it.

Sime.

FACE TO FACE

Mystery story produced by Playgoers. Marguerite Marsh and Coit Albertson featured. Main title does not give director or author. At the New York Sept. 29.

Picture was done at the New York as half a double bill. When new pictures come out in this way one looks for inferior quality, but "Face to Face" is somewhat of a surprise. The film has several good points. It is shrewdly constructed to mislead the spectator's imagination and then straighten out a mystery tangle in an altogether unexpected way. The effect in the picture is a minor one.

There is no reason in the world for making the feminine Sherlock Holmes an 18-year-old schoolgirl. It is all very well by way of novelty to have the mystery solved by a woman, but when the naive young thing of this story makes brilliant deductions, although it has been laboriously established that she is an inexperienced child, one rather revolts from the argument. She might just as well have been made a clever woman of the world, and then the story would have been plausible.

The direction slips in one particular. Fussy attention to small details makes one rather impatient. There was no ground for the endless footage to make it plain that the three men in the house were going to bed. Each in turn was shown in the elaborate process of undressing. It must have taken up more than 100 feet. A mere suggestion was all that was required. This is only one of many such passages. The director was overanxious to get his point set, so he planted it three or four times to make sure. This robs the picture of briskness and direct narrative.

Old man Hartley's business is on the brink of ruin when his son John brings word that he has negotiated a loan from the bank. Things are more encouraging until Martin, Hartley's brother-in-law, shows that in spite of the loan the crash is unavoidable. Everybody goes to bed except the old man, who prowls about nervously. A young ne'er-do-well, an amateur in crime, enters the house, bent on robbery. In the dark a pistol shot flashes and Martin finds the old man dead.

The young burglar is arrested. Meanwhile the daughter is summoned from school. She brings her chum, Helen (Miss Marsh), home with her. The burglar, a bewildered young drug addict, persists that although he fired a shot it was not at the old man. Helen believes him and goes sleuthing. When the accused is put on trial she appears in court and makes astonishing statements on the witness stand. She has discovered by close search that the young accused entered the house through a bathroom window. Starting for the bathroom door in the dim light he faced his own image in the door mirror and nervously fired. Helen brings the door into court to show the bullet hole.

Then who did fire the shot? All this time suspicion has been directed toward Martin, the brother-in-law. But he is able to show by a letter that the old man had committed suicide rather than face business ruin. With his quick solution of the mystery a brief passage suffices to indicate the marriage of Helen and John Hartley. The merits of the picture overbalance the demerits. Altogether it is as good as most of the like subjects trumpeted with a lot more exploitation.

Rush.

ON THE HIGH SEAS

Irving Willat production, presented by Adolph Zukor (Paramount-Famous Players). Starring Dorothy Dalton and Jack Holt. Story by Edward Sheldon. Scenario by E. Magnus Ingleton. At the New York Rialto week of Oct. 1.

Leone Devereux............Dorothy Dalton
Jim ....Jack Holt
Polack ....Mitchell Lewis
Aunt Emily................Alice Knowland
The Maid ....Vernon Tremaine
Captain ....James Gordon
Lieut. Gray, U. S. N.........Otto Brower
John Devereux..................Winter Hall
Dick Devereux...............William Boyd
Harold Van Allen............Michael Dark

Dorothy Dalton has another deep-sea romance, only this time they give it a comedy twist and lend to the feminine lead the prestige of a screen notable of considerable weight in Jack Holt. The two players receive equal prominence in the billing and the double star names ought to bring returns. The picture is one of the best of the marine romance series, principally because it doesn't take itself too seriously. The light touch helps on Broadway, but one wonders what effect it will have in the neighborhood houses, where they take their thrills straight.

The idea of an adventure romance with loads of shipwrecks and some astonishing effects, including the thrilling sinking of a big liner at night (probably done with a model in the tank, but presenting a wonderful illusion) and turning off into a comedy chase and a surprise wedding has a vast deal to recommend it.

The melodrama is top-notch stuff, and there is an abundance of it. There are some fine marine scenes of a majestic liner plowing through the sea—the real thing. The actual shots are so cleverly merged into the studio counterfeits that an expert can't tell one from the other, and the illusion is complete. The same is true of certain passages dealing with the adventures of the shipwrecked sailors and their girl companion, when they take possession of a two-masted schooner the crew of which has died off with plague. One episode is the rescue of the trio of characters from this vessel by a warship, which sinks the schooner as a derelict. The warship stands off and blows the little craft up with her guns, and one is convinced the performance is reality.

The picture has plenty of high-power kick in its development. Leone, pampered daughter of wealth, is returning on a liner from the Orient to wed a sappy individual picked out by her father. Fire starts in the ship's hold (some capital fire effects here). Leone is left behind in the panic, but is rescued by Jim (Holt) and the Polack (Mitchell Lewis), two stokers. They drift for days until they come across a deserted schooner, with all hands dead from plague. The Polack gets drunk and assails Leone, but she is rescued by Jim (spirited fight here). A storm comes up and the Polack is killed by a toppling mast. The schooner is sinking when an American warship sights her distress flares and they are saved.

Back home on the warship, and plans go forward for Leone's wedding. Jim has been lost in the shuffle of the arrival. As Leone is on her way to the church for the wedding she is abducted by Jim (an interesting auto chase here), who carries her to a fine mansion where another wedding party is assembled. It turns out that Jim is a person of wealth and was playing stoker on the liner for a lark. Wedding bells, the sappy bridegroom waiting at the church for a finale laugh.

Rush.

THE LONG CHANCE

Universal feature presented without an individual star but a strong cast, including Marjorie Daw, Henry B. Walthall and Ralph Graves. A Peter B. Kyne story, directed by Jack Conway. Five reels.

T. Morgan Carey..................Boyd Irwin
Harley P. Hennage.....Henry B. Walthall
Rob McGraw..................Ralph Graves
Donna Corberly..............Marjorie Daw
Borax O'Rourke.................Jack Curtis

Corking western without any wild riding stuff. Just a straightforward story that runs along rather speedily from the beginning until almost the end, but when it finishes there are several loose ends that have not been cleared up. The picture, however, has good entertainment value, and for the bigger daily change houses is strong enough to top a double feature bill anywhere. The cast has names that will draw 'em in, and the picture will please.

The story is told in the form of a prolog, and the real action takes place 20 years later. It gives Miss Daw a chance to play a double role, that of mother and daughter. Henry B. Walthall is the gambler of the small mining town on the edge of the desert. He is in love with the mother of the heroine in the prolog, and when her husband falls victim to the desert in the search for gold he protects the mother and watches the rearing of the daughter. At the mother's death he promises to watch over the girl, and in the end he finally gives up his life in the battle to assure her happiness.

Walthall gives a sterling performance, and Miss Daw and Ralph Graves ably support him.

The direction by Jack Conway was ably handled, there being some slight comedy touches that were evidently shot into the story at his hands.

Fred.

TRAIL OF THE AXE

Dramatic feature of the lumber camps. Sponsored by the Dustin Farnum Productions. Distributed by American. Director Ernest C. Warde, from story by Ridgewell Cullum. Dustin Farnum starred, supported by Winifred Kingston. On double bill at Loew's New York Sept. 29.

Picture is about the Dustin Farnum average, with the star doing one of those heroic roles as the chief of a logging camp. The action revolves about a battle between a righteous man and his blackguard brother, the two men struggling for the same girl. This is not a cheerful subject under any circumstances, and is mishandled here sadly.

The worthless brother is so unutterably wicked and the good brother is so gosh awful virtuous that one rather resists the contrast on the ground it is overwrought fiction. There was not the slightest reason for making the two men brothers, anyway.

The bad brother is addicted to hooch (no longer a melodramatic subject) and the good brother tries to redeem him by strong-arm methods. So the bad brother declines to reform, and instead plots the other's ruin. To this end he gets a discharged workman to dynamite the sawmill. When that scheme fails to destroy the property entirely the bad brother incites dissatisfied workmen to riot, and by plying them with liquor works them up to burning the camp.

All this time the bad brother's fiancee is staying at the camp, having followed him there in hope of helping toward his redemption. The ne'er-do-well treats her badly and thereby further angers the good brother, who is secretly in love with the girl himself. The ethics are confusing. After the bad 'un has tried his best to get the good 'un murdered, the drunken workmen turn on him, for no special reason except that a title makes the statement that the passions of mobs are fickle, and they want to lynch him. But the magnanimous good brother helps the bad one to escape, and then the girl falls into the good brother's arms.

All this is crude fiction, but the settings in a real lumber camp are interesting. Particularly the shots of huge logs scooting along flumes and throwing up pillars of water when they drop into the river are impressive. The forest scenes are lovely. Photography generally excellent, with some especially fine long views of row on row of misty mountains stretching into the distance. *Rush.*

FORTUNE'S MASK

A Vitagraph Earl Williams starring feature adapted from O. Henry's "Cabbages and Kings," with script by C. Graham Baker, directed by Robert Ensminger.
Ramon Olivarra............Earl Williams
Pasa Ortiz............Patsy Ruth Miller
Losada....................Henry Herbert
General Plair...............Milton Ross
Madame Ortiz............Eugenie Ford

O. Henry's "Cabbages and Kings" under the title of "Fortune's Mask" makes an ideal starring vehicle for Earl Williams. The picture is one of the type of "The Dictator," with a lot of Latin-American intrigue, revolutions and "shot at sunrise" stuff in it. As a feature this one is just about strong enough to hold up the weak end of a double feature bill in the daily change houses, but that is all.

Williams plays the role of the son of a former president of the somewhat mythical Central American republic who, after his father's death in a revolution, is sent to the United States to be raised. Those who planned his father's downfall and death have been in control of the country from the time that he was in knickerbockers until he grew to manhood's estate (that is the one false note). At the time of his return his trip is financed by the banana exporters, who are being taxed an extra ten cents a bunch by the controlling politicians, and they figured that the boy should be brought back into the country to rouse the populace against the grafters. He does that and manages to win the hand of the daughter of the keeper of the cantina, and there is the usual happy ending.

On the screen the story lacks speed, and Williams seems a little too heavy and mature for the role of the hero, but otherwise it is good picture material. The O. Henry humor of the story is permitted to slip into the discard, and it does not show until about the final couple of feet of the feature.

Patsy Ruth Miller is cute and manages to make much of the role of the little Spanish girl. The others in the cast were adequate. *Fred.*

TELL YOUR CHILDREN

London, Sept. 22.
This is terribly crude drama of the propaganda type. Its particular motive is to impress upon children, at an early age, the facts about sex relationship. The story, adapted from Rachel Macnamara's novel, "Lark's Gate," is not nice, nor is it well told. It is full of improbabilities. For instance, the innocent and ignorant hero is the only son of a stock-breeder and his father's right hand, yet he knows nothing about sex matters, and this ignorance leads to the seduction of his sweetheart. This young lady, daughter of a society leader, goes about the farm asking how young things come into being, and is told such information is not for little girls. Even the midwife at her confinement, a scene made too much of, is so ignorant of her business she says the child was born dead, at which the faithful old family nurse removes the little body from the sickroom to discover it is alive.

Rosny Edwards, daughter of Lady Sybil, an ambitious society leader, and her complacent husband, is sent down to a stud farm in the country for her health's sake. There she meets John, the farmer's son, and they fall in love. Both of them are absolutely innocent. A ban is put on their love, so they elope. They spend the night together in a ruined church. They are prevented from marrying by their youth. Rosny is sent to another part of the country, John to America. There he falls in with a wealthy American who first saves him from two girls by the simple process of buying them off. Meanwhile in England Rosny has become a mother. Through the midwife's mistake she is told the child is dead and her old nurse discovers the child to be alive. John has been adopted by his American benefactor, but still thinks only of Rosny.

Back in England the ambitious Lady Edwardes "sells" Rosny to the profligate Lord Belhurst. Four years of hell are ended by this gentleman being done to death by Arabs after he has insulted a native dancing girl. Rosny, coming upon the scene, finds him in the arms of a brave young Englishman who tried to rescue him. Who is this brave Englishman? Why, John! Again they separate, but not until she's had a final interview with him and told him of their dead child. After months of illness she returns to the old nurse, and on her way meets John with a little boy. Explanations come with great rapidity and we get the happy ending.

The only thing in this picture is its exterior locations, many of which are exquisitely beautiful. The acting is very patchy. Doris Eaton is "starred," why, it is difficult to understand. The producers could have found an actress equally unsuitable without recruiting from the Ziegfeld "Follies." The co-star, Walter Tennyson, will make a decent juvenile when he has had more experience, but at the moment, except for his appearance, he is not fitted for leading business.

These two young people are supported by a really fine cast who struggle gamely to infuse reality into the story. Margaret Halstan is the ambitious Lady Sybil, Mary Rorke gives a good show as the hero's mother, Gertrude McCoy has a small part as the hero's vindictive sweetheart, Maudie; Warwick Ward is good as Lord Belhurst, and Cecil Morton York presents a masterly character study as the farmer. This film is being released by Gaumont under the auspices of the British National Film League's program. *Gorc.*

THE MIRACLE OF LIFE

London, Sept. 22.
Tuberculosis and its treatment are the theme of a "triangle" drama. With the main theme goes a child invalid interest. The whole is as dreary and morbid as a picture could be and seems about twice its length of 5,000 feet. It comes from France.

Professor Harper, a famous tuberculosis specialist, has an assistant, Madge Newton. Madge is the wife of another man. She is also a mother. After forbidding her to associate with Harper and being promptly disobeyed, the husband follows her to the hospital and sees Harper kissing her, in a fatherly way, of course. He packs up and leaves home, taking their child with him. Madge seeks the consolation of tuberculosis bacteria and the constant companionship of Harper.

Then her husband calls and says her child is ill. It is tuberculosis. Madge nurses the child and for a time resumes marital relationship. Then she returns to Harper. Later she goes back again to her husband. Her child is kidnapped and she at last finds it in the Harper house. She thinks the professor has gone mad and is torturing the child; he has, however, completed its cure. After that she again takes up her life with the professor and together they write the great book. She discovers that on the completion of the book the professor intends to kill himself. She sends for her husband, who arrives just in time. They decide to make a commonwealth home and thus arrive at a happy ending. The acting and production is good. No distributor or producer given. *Gore.*

ONE EXCITING NIGHT

Boston, Oct. 10.
D. W. Griffith, inc., feature. Authorship credited to "Irene Sinclair, young Kentucky authoress." Filmed by Hendrik Sartov.
Agnes Harrington..........Carol Dempster
John Fairfax...............Henry Hull
J. Wilson Rockmaine......Morgan Wallace
The Neighbor.....C. H. Crocker-King
Romeo Washington..........Porter Strong
The Detective............Frank Sheridan
Mrs. Harrington...........Margaret Dale
Samuel Jones............Frank Wunderlee
Auntie Fairfax............Grace Griswold
The Maid..............Irma Harrison
Clary Johnson..........Herbert Sutch
The Butler....................Percy Carr

Griffith has taken a sock at the mystery play gold-mine on his own hook, after having found out that the picture rights to "The Bat" were around $150,000, with release not allowed until next spring.

It is a melodramatic hodge-podge of every mystery thriller from serial, dime novel, ten-twent-thirt, etc., right up to the modern "Bat" and "Cat and Canary." If the truth be told, however, it is probably more reminiscent of some of Griffith's old Biograph curdlers of a dozen years ago, particularly "The Lonely Villa," than a lift from any of the present-day mystery tinglers.

Although Griffith may take violent exception to the statement, it looks as if he wanted to make a little money for himself this time as a sort of a change from his "Orphans." The scenic investiture comprises one lavish interior, and a wow of a storm scene. Not more than 15 people are screened and his total payroll did not nick the old treasury as much as did the Gish sisters.

The plot starts off deliberately and prosaically, establishing minor plot incidents and characters almost to the extent of dragging. A baby, with mother dead, is left in South Africa in the care of a woman. Into America later comes a woman and grown daughter. The woman is in need of money and forces daughter to engage herself to wealthy middle-aged wealthy Southerner. She falls in love with hero, house party is arranged at his southern home, which has been unoccupied for some time and has been pre-empted by a prosperous (they all are) gang of bootleggers. A half million in bills in a satchel is hid in the mansion, one bootlegger is killed by the other (face concealed), and hero is blamed. Later the hero's chum is killed by the bootlegger, and the hero is blamed for this also. Everybody apparently is trying to find the satchel with the half-million, the audience is unquestionably bewildered, and ultimately the murdering bootlegger is unmasked and proves to be the wealthy Southerner. Counterplot proves girl and mother to be the South African baby and woman in whose care she was left. Mysterious neighbor turns out to be Scotland Yard detective and bedroom prowling negro proves to be South African native, who identified locket and prevented loss of big estate of baby. Such is the plot.

Hidden safes, sliding panels, masked figures, revolving bookcases, guns, knives, hidden hands groping out of doorways, all the old thrillers of Moreno and White, Blaney and Wood, Biograph and Vitagraph, are present.

The comedy is entirely in the hands of a frightened negro (Porter Strong), who has achieved a personal triumph. He is white, working under cork, and has been carried by Griffith for years in minor parts on spec. Formerly a cabaret singer, Strong shows real comedy, and bears out Al Jolson's predictions when Strong was a cabaret singer and was characterized by Jolson as "a natural comedian."

The storm is apparently an aftermath of last June's hurricane, which devastated Westchester County, where the Griffith plant is located. The toppling trees, blown-over buildings, flying branches and driving sheets of rain are shown with

convincing realism. The storm figures in the plot through the pursuit of the escaping mysterious murderer pursued by the girl and the hero, who is handcuffed. He saves her from death by a falling tree by pulling her out from the debris under which she is pinned.

The footage at present is around 11,000, having originally run around 14,000 feet when shown under no name in Derby, Conn. It was then shown at Montclair around 12,000 and was reduced to 11,000 at Newport. The first half will have to be ruthlessly slashed at once to speed up the action and reduce the time.

The mystery element is admirably sustained and while it will never achieve any fame for Griffith, it will probably bring him more real money in the next six months than some of the productions upon which he has spent young fortunes in producing. He is obviously cashing in on his prestige, and as the program puts it, "if our story has any merit at all, it is merely in the unfolding of the plot."

Libbey.

FACE IN THE FOG

Crook melodrama by Cosmopolitan (Famous Players-Paramount), featuring Lionel Barrymore, supported by Lowell Sherman, Louis Wolheim and Seena Owen. Made from the stories by Jack Boyle. Directed by Alan Crosland. At the Rivoli, Oct. 8.

Blackie Dawson, reformed crook.......Lionel Barrymore
Grand Duchess................Seena Owen
Count Orloff..............Lowell Sherman
Huck Kant..................George Nash
Petrus....................Louis Wolheim
Mary Dawson.............Mary MacLaren
Count Ivan.................Macey Harlam
Michael..............Gustav von Seiffertitz

This is a notable case of a kid-glove melodrama made for the screen out of a clever dime novel. It's a whale. Boston Blackie, the reformed crook, furnishes about an hour of breathless interest. There isn't a dull minute in his complicated maneuvres against the Russian Terrorists in a battle for the royal jewels.

If you can imagine a Nick Carter yellowback done in polished literary style, that would be about the equivalent of this five-reeler. It has the kick and the zip and its implausibility is so trickily veneered with splendid acting and skilful stage management that you follow the adventure with childlike belief in spite of yourself. The picture is a succession of third-act situations.

It all starts with a smash. Before the action is five minutes old your attention is nailed, and suspense never relaxes. The story opens with a blind beggar standing in front of a New York cabaret, half hidden in a thick fog. An auto drives up to the curb. A sinister, brutal face peers through the mist and the beggar is terrified. "Boston Blackie" sees the odd occurrence and stops to exchange a word with the beggar, who slips a packet into his pocket. The next instant the owner of the terrifying face looms out of the fog; there is a scuffle and the beggar is struck dead with his own crutch, Boston Blackie returning in time to pick up the broken shoulder piece of the crutch.

The scene shifts to Blackie's home, where the jewel packet is put in a mantle safe. Evil Face, we learn, is coming to take the jewels by force, while Blackie prepares for him and his gang of cut-throats by setting electrical alarms. But Evil Face is preceded by a secret service agent on the trail of the smuggled jewels. Detective and ex-crook together await the assault of the thieves.

Meanwhile another division of the crook band is in pursuit of the beautiful Russian Duchess, rightful owner of the Crown jewels, and the two chases are interwoven cleverly. The passage in which Evil Face breaks into Blackie's house by the basement door and advances gradually through the dark building toward the room where Blackie is awaiting him is a splendid bit of tension. So is the whole building up of the situation to the point where Evil Face forces Blackie to disclose the hiding place and the safe's combination, only to be made helpless when Blackie switches on the electric current as Evil Face touches the safe's dial.

There's a whale of a fight between Lionel Barrymore, as Blackie, and Louis Wolheim (he of "The Hairy Ape," of course), with the smashing of a lot of furniture, one of the most convincing combats the screen has had. In the end the explanation is that the beautiful Duchess brought the jewels to America to finance the restoration of the Russian throne and the blind beggar was her servitor, while the pursuing gang was a group of Russian Terrorists, intent on securing the fortune and defeating the political maneuver. This explanation calls for a fade-back to Russia, where the escape of Royalists is recounted, giving opportunity for a picturesque subordinate story. Lowell Sherman plays the Russian nobleman, faithful follower of the Duchess, who is rewarded with her hand by the benevolent conspiracy of Blackie, after he has turned the jewels over to the government. So the story has a capital element of romance as a background for its crook intrigue.

The whole action in all its remarkable complications takes a curious touch from the recurrence of the scenes in the fog which run through the whole picture, the entire happenings being confined in time to one evening. The program neglects to mention the continuity writer. He deserves mention, for the picture is a fine example of economy. The dramatic progress is perfectly maintained; there isn't an instant of digression, and in spite of its complex mechanism the story is absolutely clear at every stage.

Rush.

THE OLD HOMESTEAD

Paramount picture, presented by Jesse Lasky, adapted from the Denman Thompson play of the same title by Julien Josephson, and directed by James Cruze. An all-star cast with Theodore Roberts as Uncle Josh. Shown at the Capitol, New York, week Oct. 8. Eight reels.

Uncle Josh..............Theodore Roberts
Eph Holbrook.............George Fawcett
Happy Jack.................T. Roy Barnes
Ann ....Fritzi Ridgeway
Reuben ....Harrison Ford
Lem ....James Mason
Rose ....Kathleen O'Connor
Aunt Matilda....................Ethel Wales

Once again has the hardy perennial of rural melodrama been resurrected for the screen. If memory serves right this is the second film production of "The Old Homestead." But this one is a whale of a picture and fully worthy of being termed a special in every sense of the word.

Liberties have been taken with the original script, but only for the purpose of making the picturization more thrilling. Some of the old laughs have been left out, but the tale of the wandering Reuben and the self-sacrifice of his old dad back at the old homestead is as tear-compelling as ever. From the producing and distributing standpoint the picture looks like one of the big winners of the year, and from the exhibitors' angle there seems to be no reason why the picture shouldn't be one of the real business getters, providing, of course, that the prospective audiences are properly made aware of what the picture is.

With the original play of "The Old Homestead" as the background this filmization furnishes an excuse for a tremendous storm scene that in its effectiveness outrivals the ice scene of "Way Down East." Such a tempest of wind and water has never before been caught by the camera, and it certainly furnishes a real thrill for this production.

The handling of the direction of the story on the part of James Cruze leaves nothing to be desired. He advances his story logically, although there is a coincidental moment or two permitted to slip in the tale such as the meeting of Reuben and Happy Jack in a dive in China, and the meeting of Reuben and Rose on the street just as she is thrown from the backroom of a saloon. Outside of those two little touches in the script there is naught that can be taken exception to.

There will be those that will decry the selection of Theodore Roberts for the role of Uncle Josh, on the grounds that his personality is not just what they would have cared to see in the role. However, there seems to be hardly any one in picturedom at present that would be better suited to the role. True he does make Uncle Josh somewhat different from the characterization presented by Denman Thompson, but still he makes it a truly lovable old character. George Fawcett, who plays the grasping Eph Holbrook, lends true color to the role and the Aunt Tildy of Ethel Wales is a work of art.

Of the younger players the Reuben of Harrison Ford is fairly interesting, as is likewise the Ann of Fritzi Ridgeway and the Rose of Kathleen O'Connor. T. Roy Barnes is a real comedy relief as Happy Jack, and plants the character so forcibly he is given the honor of practically the final fadeout.

The picturization itself is a work of art. In photography there are some really beautiful shots. Especially those of snow stuff around the old farm. The studio staff did itself proud in some of the sets, but why the technical genius' of the Lasky lot permitted the old New York street with the elevated road in the distance, that has been used in any number of other productions to be repeated in this, is a question. It is all so familiar.

But to get back to the real thrill, that wind and rain storm. It alone is worth the price of admission. In it poor Harrison Ford is worked to death. It seems that all he has to do is to wade through the storm and bring women into the house. First it is Rose who comes back to the old home town with him and then he has to go forth and find Ann, who escapes into the storm to jump from Lover's Leap because she believes that Rose has been with Reuben all the years that he has been away from home.

In all, however, "The Old Homestead" is a really big picture, and when the current year's biggest winners are cast up at the end of the season it will be found with the big gross specials. That is certain.

Fred.

A WOMAN'S WOMAN

Densie Plummer.................Mary Alden
Harriet Plummer................Louise Lee
Sally Plummer.............Dorothy MacKail
John Plummer..........Holmes E. Herbert
Kenneth Plummer...........Albert Hackett
Dean Landbary..............Rod La Roque
Senator James Gleason....J. Barney Sherry

Another "mother" story, interesting and sympathetic, with a different turn in so far as the children (except the youngest) are not the heedless, thoughtless type, who inevitably implicate the family honor through force of circumstances or bad company, but just because they are naturally "cussed," ill bred, and heartless.

Densie Plummer is a mother who seems to get a great satisfaction in basking in the role of combination cook, scrub woman, valet, and seamstress, a combination that seems to be a favorite in plays of this sort. Kenneth Plummer, father, seems a perfectly normal specimen, possibly a trifle rude, and cannot be blamed for not being over-enthusiastic about mother, if only through the clothes she wears and her depressed air.

Harriet Plummer, the eldest daughter, who has graduated from the local school, listens to the serpent tongue of the principal of the school, who is one of the generally accepted screen suffragets, and departs for Greenwich Village to uplift her sex. Harriet is a girl of ideas and apparently no heart. Sally, the second daughter, is just as heartless, but has learned that this is an advantageous thing to hide. She adopted a routine that would make Cleopatra wince and practices it very successfully on father.

Kenneth, the youngest and the only human one in the home nest, is mother's only hope. So when she decides to open a tea room to help fortify the family exchequer (because daddy has spent it all on golf clothes and another woman he grew keen on because mother was so badly dressed) Kenneth stuck around Ma to see that no one got to the cash register.

This was a good thing, too, because after she found out about the other woman, Ma got wise to herself. She dressed up and took a flyer into politics. Meantime Sally has taken up with a questionable man about town, even if there was a perfectly nice boy who wanted to marry her. It was unfortunate for Sally, as the man (whose name was not on the program) did what everyone said he would, refused to marry her, though he had compromised her, so much so she takes poison at a most inopportune time, while mamma was in Washington at a conference with some Senators, one of whom had fallen in love with her and was patiently waiting for her to get a divorce from father. This she had decided to do when she found out about the other woman.

Kenneth, though 17 and the only dependable one at home, is apprised of Sally's predicament. He hurries to the hospital. Sally thinks she is dying and confesses. Kenneth starts at once for the man. Finding him at his apartment he tells the man he (Kenneth) is going to take him to the hospital, evidently with the intention of including a minister. But the man rebels. A fist fight ensues. The man shoots Kenneth, an act that must have chagrined the audience, as Kenneth deserved to die less than anyone in the cast. Mother is then summoned by long distance and returns, makes up with father, and decides to become the housekeeper once again.

The story had a few incongruous points in the telling; the way mother passed over the death of her favorite child, and the fact that although they lived in a very luxurious home there was a complete absence of servants. Even Densie Plummer could not have done the work while she was resting after waiting on the family and doing various chores.

It will be a relief to see a "mother" play that will allow mother to act like a mother.

An excellent cast included Mary Alden, Louise Lee, Dorothy MacKail, Holmes E. Herbert, Albert Hackett, Rod La Roque, who has been doing good work recently, and J. Barney Sherry. Miss Alden worked her handkerchief overtime and showed bad judgment in wearing clothes of an old period when the rest of the women wore ultra modern designs.

The sets were rich and in very good taste; the photography was also splendid.

Those two little clowns on the house drop that so cheerily introduce the feature and wave you a fond good night at the conclusion, gave their usual good performance.

THE BOND BOY

Inspiration picture starring Richard Barthelmess in the George Washington Ogden story, "The Bond Boy," adapted by Charles Whitaker, directed by Henry King. A First National release shown at the Strand, N. Y., week Oct. 8.

Joe Newbolt	Richard Barthelmess
Isom Chase	Charles Hill Mailes
Cyrus Morgan	Ned Sparks
Colonel Price	Lawrance D'Orsay
Lawyer Hammer	Robert Williamson
District Attorney	Leslie King
Sheriff	Jerry Sinclair
Saul Greening	Thomas Maguire
Mrs. Greening	Lucia Backus Seger
Alice Price	Virginia Magee
Mrs. Newbolt	Mary Alden
Ollie Chase	Mary Thurman

Richard Barthelmess, the star, and Mary Alden as his mother walk off with the honors as far as the acting is concerned. The picture is not an unusual feature, nor yet one that seemed to be cast in a regular mould at a factory. It is entertaining and interesting, and the action, as far as the direction is concerned, manages to forward the story in a natural manner that holds interest. There are one or two spots draggy, especially the swinging noose incident in the prison scene, but the feature should do business in the majority of the first runs where Barthelmess has any draft and in the regular houses it is sure to please.

"The Bond Boy" is rather an aged story and therefore perhaps good screen material without the necessity of very much fixing up, although the script writer did pick up a little touch of the "Tavern" in the titling writing. "What's All the Shooting For?" and a series of questions that followed suggested the handling of the lines in that show.

The star gave a corking performance in the title character of the picture, but Miss Alden was not far behind him. In the scene where the boy returns to her from prison she displayed a power of repression that was wonderful. Of the others Lawrance D'Orsay as a Missouri Colonel managed to stand out, as did Ned Sparks as a semi-heavy and Charles Hill Mailes, who played Isom Chase, the real heavy of the production. Virginia Magee and Mary Thurman in the roles of Alice Price and Ollie Chase, respectively, both scored. As a semi-vamp the latter added a real thrill to the picture in a couple of scenes.

For the greater part the scenes were exteriors, although what interiors there were held the atmosphere of the story. *Fred.*

REMEMBRANCE

Goldwyn production, written and directed by Rupert Hughes. A picture that defies ordinary classification. Practically an all-star cast.

John P. Grout	Claude Gillingwater
J. Pennock Grout 2d	Richard Tucker
Ethelwolf Grout	Dana Todd
Seth Smith	Cullen Landis
Mrs. J. P. Grout	Kate Lester
Elise	Nell Craig
Beatrice	Esther Ralston
Mab	Patsy Ruth Miller

Rupert Hughes, despite what a great many critics on daily publications may say, has in this production of "Remembrance," written and directed by himself, achieved a distinct step forward in the making of pictures. It is a picture that is so far away from the ordinary run of features in story and screen treatment it practically defies classification. Withal it is a plain tale of plain people that is plainly told. It is a picture that is going to please the older folk, amuse the younger ones and incidentally teach them a moral. As a box office picture it ought to rank mighty high, at least far above the regular run of the Goldwyn output.

"Pop" Grout is the real hero of the story. From an humble beginning he has developed into a big department store owner, but he has remained an humble, hard-working man, while his wife and two of his three daughters and a couple of sons have grown away from the old man and developed into selfish, self-centered beings who believe that all that their dad is good for is to shell out the shekels whenever they want money. The younger of the daughters falls in love with one of her

father's clerks, and the rest of the family, with the exception of her dad, come down on her like a ton of coal. Dad, however, when his wife insists that the young man be discharged, arranges to have him take over a small shop that has been offered to him.

Just as the details are about to be closed the old man suffers a breakdown and it is generally believed that he is going to die. Right here is where Mr. Hughes displays a master hand as a motion picture showman. Everyone viewing the picture will at this point immediately begin to dope the balance of the story, and the majority will dope it the wrong way. The author-director plants any number of little incidents that would suggest the further working out of the plot, and then he turns and fools his audience. That is real screen showmanship and that is what is going to make this picture stand out as an unusual feature.

With the old man ill in bed and a snug fortune planted in a sofa pillow one can see the battle that is going to ensue among the heirs when the old man kicks off, but he fools them all and gets well again. In the meantime the young clerk who has been fired manages to make a success of his little shop and the young love interest develops into a happy ending. But the real theme of the story is that the Grouts are brought to a realization of their own selfishness and are cured.

The tale is not told seriously, but is punctuated by any number of laughs and comedy incidents that absolutely counteract the sob that rises in the throat over the troubles of old Pop Grout, and it leaves a wholesome impression behind when it is all told.

Claude Gillingwater as "Pop" Grout gives a performance that is second to none in screen history. He is an actor first, last and always, but an artist of such caliber that one is never conscious of his acting. His support in this picture is a delight, especially the work of Patsy Ruth Miller as the younger daughter and Cullen Landis as the clerk. Richard Tucker as one of the sons, as sort of a heavy, also registers admirably.

"Remembrance" is a picture that will be remembered as a real feature. *Fred.*

MOONSHINE VALLEY

William Fox dramatic, directed by Herbert Brenon. William Farnum starred. Story by Mary Murillo. At the Academy Oct. 9.

The picture is a triangle so economically drawn that only three characters appear. They are the western prospector, his wife and the doctor, who is "the other man." Later on a baby appears, one of those clever youngsters, but her name is not given in the title. It should be, for she is the picture. The only novelty is the idea of putting a domestic triangle in the wild and woolly west during the 49's. The rest is just the simple plot, in this case taking a good deal of strength from its sheer simplicity.

The ending is rather unsatisfactory. The prospector's wife deliberately and without one plea transfers her affections to the other man and runs away with the interloper, believing he has killed the husband. The elopers have a child. Three years later the husband has gone to the dogs when his path crosses the paths of the pair who have wronged him. The child Nancy has become lost by the wayside and has been found by the unsuspecting prospector, who cares for her. She falls sick and the prospector, terror-stricken, rushes off for a doctor. Of course, he runs into his enemy and drags him to Nancy's bedside on threat of death.

The wife meanwhile has been left in a lonely cabin. Friendlessness and grief for the lost child have

driven her insane. She is nursing an imaginary baby while the child's father is bringing Nancy through her illness in the prospector's cabin at a distance. But the accounting between the two men is only deferred, despite the prospector's love for the little one.

When Nancy is restored to health the doctor tries to carry her off while the prospector sleeps. He awakes and the two battle, the doctor's revolver being discharged in the rough-and-tumble, killing the doctor. The prospector thereupon shoulders the body and carries it to the wife, dumping it at her feet with the speech, "I've brought him back to you."

But a film scenario couldn't well stop at that. There is a lot of sentimental titling with the tot saying her prayers and emphasis on "Forgive us our transgressions even as we forgive those who transgress against us," etc., leaving in prospect the reconciliation of the faithless wife and her wronged husband. The denouement is pretty hard to swallow, but the remarkably natural acting of the kiddie saves the picture. The tot is a wonder.

The faults are all inherent in the script. The acting is excellent in a florid way. Mary Mullins does a splendid bit of emotional pantomime as the wife and once again the kid is great. The direction is workmanlike. There are a number of good incidental touches. They introduce much animal stuff, a clever trained dog, for example. The picture has excellent pictorial effects. One shot was particularly neat. The husband has gone down in drink and neglect. The cabin is a wreck. It was inevitable, perhaps, that Farnum should be given the usual opportunity to overact, but the whole situation was made plain in an incidental shot, a bare, blackened pine tree disclosed through a broken window as the wind fluttered a tattered curtain. Holmes Herbert plays the home wrecker and gives a clean cut performance.

It's a neighborhood picture with special appeal to the women. *Rush.*

MAN SHE BROUGHT BACK

Playgoers picture, made by the Charles Miller Productions, Charles Miller being the director and Doris Miller the feminine lead. Distributed by Pathe. Story by James Ewing Brady. At Loew's Circle, Oct. 9.

All-around third-rate production. Story misses sadly, direction is crude and acting mediocre. The whole effort is amateurish. Action takes place in the wild northwest and the principals are Northwest Mounted men and outlaws. Picturesque snow scenes are the film's only virtue. The effort must have been made on a basis of strict economy. The Northwest Mounted post in the wilderness is commanded by a major, who apparently has only four constables under him, and all hands live in a 20-foot shack, if you believe the camera.

A sociable lot these grim guardians of the forest. When the major's daughter has a birthday the troopers make a party of it in the major's sitting-room, the major drinking with his men and being generally on the most astonishingly intimate terms with them. They all but slap him on the back. The newest rookie in the post makes love to the major's daughter, too, apparently with the major's indulgent approval. Somehow that doesn't seem right, nor does the major's habit of topping off an arctic bearskin coat with a white canvas cap for the northern blizzard.

The rookie's rival for the major's daughter (played by Doris Miller) is one Webster, the smuggler and leader of a gang of bad men. The rookie is the girl's accepted sweetheart and is looking forward to getting his chevrons, when we are encouraged to believe they will be married. Pretty uncomfortable situation for the major, with an en-

listed man as a son-in-law under his command, unless the idea is that the Northwest has gone Bolshevist since it got into the movies.

Anyhow, one of Webster's Indian rum runners has murdered someone and fled to the border. Naturally the newest rookie is detailed to bring in the slayer. Rookie is seized by the outlaws and sent back to the post handcuffed and humiliated. Of course, he's disgraced. Even the major's daughter is against him for his failure to obey the northwest dictum, "Get your man." So the rookie is turned out. He takes refuge with a picturesque hermit (a queer old party in buckskin, played, of all things, by Frank Losee). Under the encouragement of the hermit the rookie starts again after the outlaws and brings them in in pairs, the arch criminal Webster being one of them.

The rookie's capture of Webster was a fairly effective bit of action, involving a dramatic chase and combat in the snow. But one interesting chapter couldn't save this inept bit of film fiction. Its general aspect is too crude and unconvincing. They appear to have gone out of their way to invent mystifying angles. At one point we learn to our surprise that the hermit was one time the lover of the rookie's dead mother. This came out of a clear sky. It hadn't been mentioned until the hermit presented the rookie with his mother's photograph. After that nothing more was heard about it. The detail was as absurd and fruitless as though they had used a fadeback to show that the major had run a grocery story in Brooklyn before he became a major.

It is one of those pictures that inspire giggles in the wrong places, as it did at the Circle.

It should be set down that there were moments when Earle Foxe, the hero-rookie, gave the impression he could play a real part, perhaps on the Charles Ray order. *Rush.*

THE SPORTING INSTINCT

London, Sept. 29.

This last Granger-Davidson feature is excellent entertainment of its type. An original story by Arthur Rooke, who also produced it, holds the attention throughout and is an excellent addition to the growing list of pictures which are to be released under the auspices of the British National Film League.

June Crisp is loved by Jerry West but she swears she will only marry a sportsman. Jerry, who has been badly wounded in the war, resigns himself to her decree. Three of June's other admirers show their prowess in various sports, sculling, tennis, and cricket, while Jerry tries to forget his uselessness in kindly actions and the friendship of a crippled boy. The "sporting" scenes are rather vague and a stretch on the imagination. In the end the "sportsmen" are knocked out by Jerry's quiet heroism in giving his blood to save the life of his little friend. The cast is excellent. *Gore.*

WHY MEN LEAVE HOME

London, Sept. 29.

This is alleged comedy, and its only excuse is the appearance of the comedienne, Nellie Wallace, as a screen artist. It is pitifully crude stuff of the "stuffed stick" and eccentric order, and what little humor there is in it is obtained from the "star's" make-up and weird attire.

The story concerns a servant girl who wins a beauty competition and becomes a film star only to return at last to her domestic duties. Much could be cut out, notably the scantily clad girls in a badly worked dream scene. The studio scenes will give offense, and the portrayal of the film company's directorate is about as near libel as the screen has got. The acting is equal to the story. We don't expect to hear much more of this all-British comedy. An Anchor Co. production. *Gore.*

ROBIN HOOD

Chicago, Oct. 18.

Story by Elton Thomas. Directed by Allan Dwan. Photography by Arthur Edeson.

Richard the Lion Hearted....Wallace Berry
Prince John.................Sam de Grasse
Lady Marian Fitzwalter......Enid Bennett
Sir Guy of Gisbourne.........Paul Dickey
The High Sheriff of Nottingham........
                        William Lowery
The King's Jester............Roy Coulson
Lady Marian's Serving Woman.........
                        Billie Bennett
Henchman to Prince John...............
                        Merrill McCormick
Henchman to Prince John....Wilson Benge
Friar Tuck..................Willard Louis
Little John....................Alan Hale
Will Scarlett...............Maine Geary
Alan-a-Dale................Lloyd Talman
The Earl of Huntington, afterward Robin
    Hood................Douglas Fairbanks

Scenario Editor.............Lotta Woods
Supervising Art Director..Wilfred Buckland
Art Director................Irvin J. Martin
Art Director...........Edward M. Langley

The point about "Robin Hood" in Chicago is $2. That's the top at Cohan's Grand, where the latest Douglas Fairbanks special picture opened Sunday night. It opened to the best of this town's 400, and they will pay $2 or more for anything they want to see. But this town also has "Knighthood," at the Roosevelt, with a top of 60 cents. It is also a special, Marion Davies' latest as well, and while this is in no sense a comparative review of the two films, one can't get away from the fact of the prices, with "Knighthood" the first in here.

"Robin Hood," however, missed nothing in an exploitation way coming to this city, inclusive of the "400," quite a feat in itself, going with the rest of the publicity to the credit of Pete Smith and his assistants. But Mr. Fairbanks' "Hood" will have to prove itself in a picture house in this town, unless the dope reverses itself on the $2 thing.

As a picture, that comes in again. In Cohan's Grand it's $2, and you can't overlook that when watching the picture in review. It's a world-famous story made by a world-famous film star. Its settings are stupendous and elaborate, and there are the adventures of Robin Hood (Mr. Fairbanks), showing his home and lair, with the Fairbanks dare-devilry for his admirers, running along for 50 minutes. Before that, for 75 minutes the picture delves into a showing of Richard the Lion Hearted, his court and affairs. The people who pay are going to prefer the Robin Hood portion.

Which leaves the balance sheet in this wise: Fairbanks and Robin Hood for 50 minutes, together with perfect settings, costumes and playing, as against the price. *Loop.*

EAST IS WEST

Baltimore, Oct. 18.

Joseph M. Schenck presents Constance Talmadge in "East Is West," from the stage play by Samuel Shipman and John B. Hymer, as originally produced by William Harris, Jr. Directed by Sidney Franklin. First National Distributing.

Ming Toy..............Constance Talmadge
Billy Benson...............Edward Burns
Lo San Kee..............T. A. Warren
Charley Yong............Warner Oland
Hop Toy...............Franklin Lanning
Chang Lee..............Nick De Ruiz
Jimmy Potter............Nigel Barrie
Mr. Benson...............Winter Hall
Mrs. Benson............Lillian Lawrence
Proprietor of Love Boat.........Jim Wang

When "East Is West" made its debut on the speaking stage Baltimore witnessed its premiere. Comes now its advent in the movies, with Constance Talmadge doing her best with the Fay Bainter role. Baltimore witnesses the world's premiere of it, according to the management of the Rivoli theatre here, where it is showing.

This picture is an entertaining production, say what we may about it. But, all in all, much of the piquant charm and naive delicacy which Miss Bainter achieved with the rloe on the stage has been lost in the transition to celluloid.

As the play itself was largely a matter of skilfully strung together hokum, so the movie is, and where the play had a very good production, so the movie has. And just as the play toured the length and breadth of the country, so the movie will. And as Fay Bainter made a great name for herself in the role of Ming Toy, some thought that Constance Talmadge would.

But, speaking personally, we are much disappointed in the production as it revealed Miss Talmadge. She, an actress of undeniable charm in light comedies and school-girl stuff, seems strangely out of place as Ming Toy. Her facial make-up in no way suggests the Chinese characteristics. It is all very nice for the gentleman writing the sub-titles to excuse this by mentioning in one place that she looks like a white girl, but that is weak stuff. The others in the cast made up to look their parts, yet Miss Talmadge looks as much like an American girl as any other American girl as if she would but don a wig of straight black hair with a pig tail added.

Warner Oland, however, as Charlie Yong, quite carries the honors of the piece away, and although the oft-quoted lines, "Have a cigaret," in the stage play are left out here, some of the other big laughs are retained, and they go well.

Edward Burns is a good enough Billy Benson, but he will never set the world on fire with the ardor of his lovemaking, while Lo San Kee in the hands of E. A. Warren is quite the reverse. This aged Chinese character is treated most intelligently by the actor. Nigel Barrie as Jimmy Potter hasn't a great deal to do, but does that well. Why he wasn't put in the Billy Benson role we are not able to understand. The other characters are good enough, with no one making any understanding characterization with the exception of Oland and Warren.

It is only fair to say that the piece has a most excellent production accorded it, and the photography is always excellent, with the settings in good taste.

The thing that makes the picture entertaining is the story itself, and in almost any professional hand it would still be the same. Added to that is a most attractive setting given it on its presentation here, with the Rivoli orchestra of some 40 pieces playing music ideally suited to the action of the play. Bowers' "Chinese Lullaby" is used throughout the action of the film; in fact, it is the theme song, while the Danse Oriental by Cady and the Canzonetto of Godard come in nicely.

All in all, Miss Talmadge hasn't come up to expectations in this picture. There are those who will rave over her and will tell the world in no uncertain terms she has made her crowning achievement, but at countless other times and in comedies which outclassed this by yards she has done better.

As a program picture it is good stuff, guaranteed to draw by its name and reputation, but a person used to the movies must confess to being a little disappointed in the result of the work which has been kept so continually in our ears for the past six months. The press agent has overdone himself in announcing this film, but the leading lady hasn't. But, with all that, "East Is West" is nearly actor proof, but at that Miss Talmadge doesn't rise to the comedy heights that Miss Bainter did, or maybe the absence of the dialog may be blamed. *Sisk.*

A TAILOR MADE MAN

Charles Ray starring feature presented by Arthur S. Kane, adapted by Albert Ray from the Harry James Smith play of the same title. Directed by Joseph De Grasse. Released through United Artists. Shown at the Strand, N. Y., week Oct 15.

John Paul Bart............Charles Ray
Anton Huber.............Thomas Ricketts

Tanya Huber...............Ethel Grandin
Peter.....................Victor Potel
Abraham Nathan...........Stanton Heck
Mrs. Nathan..............Edyth Chapman
Miss Nathan...............Irene Lentz
Mr. Stanlaw...........Frederick Thomson
Mrs. Stanlaw.............Kate Lester
Corrinne Stanlaw........Jacqueline Logan
Theodore Jellicot...........Frank Butler
Gustavus Sonntag........Douglass Gerrard
Kitty Dupuy........Nellie Peck Saunders
Bessie Dupuy...........Charlotte Pierce
Gerald Whitcomb........Thomas Jefferson
Hobart Sears..............Henry Barrows
Russell ....Eddie Gribbon

Here is a Charles Ray picture that is going to do a lot toward reviving the popularity of that star, who, for a time, was considered to be slipping. It is a good story for the screen, just as it was a good play and Ray invests the character of John Paul Burt with sufficient interest to make the public sit through an hour and forty minutes of the picture without becoming the least tired of it. The adaptation added action to the play story and the direction went for speed at all times. The exhibitor who once had real Ray fans for big business can count on this feature winning them back.

One of the unusual points is that even though it has a cast of characters of unusual length and with all of the roles of real significance to the story, one viewing the film does not lose track of who and what the characters are at all time. That speaks for itself. Incidentally it speaks for the cast and whoever selected it. Because it was a long one they did not stint on expense in getting people. They got real names to support Ray, people who have picture reputations and they made good.

The tale of the tailor's assistant who virtually raves that clothes go at least 50 per cent. toward making the man, inasmuch as they give him entre, and then it is up to himself to make good for the balance of the road, is real comedy drama material. In this screen version the drama is practically permitted to take care of itself while the comedy is always in the forefront. Then there are the thrills. There is a chase in which Ray, as John Paul Bart tries to reach the shipyards before the hour that the strike is to be declared despite the attempts on the part of the agitating conspirators to prevent him. That is a real picture bit. Ray covers the ground like Fairbanks used to do, and he manages to put up a corking fight, finally diving from the masthead of a ship into the bay.

There is but one weakness and that is in the quartet of ingenue types. Ethel Grandin plays the lead opposite the star without registering to particular advantage and the trio of others, Irene Lentz, Jacqueline Logan and Charlotte Pierce all three failed to impress at any time. The director and camera man tried to be most kind to both the Misses Lentz and Logan with the aid of soft focus, but even that failed to help.

Ray's performance however will overshadow these faults and he will again make his mark in the ballot of popularity on the strength of this picture.

Character bits contributed by Victor Potel, Douglass Gerrard, Frank Butler and Eddie Gribbon helped toward the general success. *Fred.*

CLARENCE

Adolph Zukor presents the William C. DeMille production of Booth Tarkington's play, adapted to the screen by Clara Beranger. Wallace Reid in the name part created on the stage by Alfred Lunt. At the Rivoli, Oct. 15.

Clarence Smith.............Wallace Reid
Violet Pinney..............Agnes Ayres
Cora Wheeler...............May McAvoy
Mrs. Wheeler..........Kathlyn Williams
Mr. Wheeler..............Ed Martindel
Bobby Wheeler............Robert Agnew
Hubert Stem.............Adolphe Menjou
Dinwiddy ....Bertram Johns
Della ....Dorothy Gordon
Mrs. Martin.............Maym Kelso

The Booth Tarkington comedy makes a remarkably amusing screen subject, the translation being almost literal. The speaking version had a delicate shade of humor that must have called for extraordinary skill on the part of the film director. To say that he has risen to the occasion and made an adequate presentation is a real tribute.

There must have been a powerful temptation to "adapt" the odd appeal to its new purpose. In the passage where Clarence engages in fisticuffs with the fortune-hunting Stem, most directors would have followed the rough and tumble technique of the "movies," altogether abandoning the atmosphere of original work. Instead DeMille exercises admirable restraint. Instead of a thrilling combat he stages a comic episode well within the intent of Tarkington's original.

The picture is a demonstration of the fact that the screen can be the medium of fine character delineation and gentle humor and is not by any means restricted to horseplay and crude melodrama. "Clarence" is as neat a bit of foolery on the screen as it was on the stage, and that is saying a mouthful.

The character of Clarence is rather a departure for Reid. He does get into the spirit of the part, which calls for quiet effectiveness and absence of emphasis, no easy role for a pantomimist trained to flamboyant technique of the studio. The same comment applies to the others of a singularly excellent cast rich in film notables. All the care that went to the casting shows for full value. The company is an eminent example of what can be done in high comedy in the pictures. There was not a false note in the five reels.

The only departure from the dramatic original is a short passage of an automobile chase when Cora tries to elope with the designing Stem, but the whoop-hurrah is soft pedaled right up to the climax in the physical clash between the hero and heavy. Clarence merely gets an undignified hammer-lock on Stem in his amusingly awkward way and shakes him till his tongue rolls. Comedy for once triumphs over the "red-blooded battle" of the film tradition.

The episode with the saxophone, which made the comedy climax of the play, is extremely well managed with the utmost economy of footage and titles and is a capital bit of neat exposition. The sparing use of titles is notable throughout the picture. The printed word always delivers a laugh and the action is usually self-explanatory. Special credit is due to May McAvoy as Cora, the headstrong flapper; Ed Martindel, the harassed father; Robert Agnew, the petticoat-chasing son, and Agnes Ayres as Miss Pinney.

Rush.

NOTORIETY

A William Nigh production, presented by L. Lawrence Weber and Bobby North. William Nigh both author and director. Released through Apollo. Length, nine reels.
"Pigeon" Derring..........Maurine Powers
Ann Boland....................Mary Alden
Arthur Beal...............Rod La Roque
Batty ....George Hackathorne
Horace Wedderburn.......J. Barney Sherry
Tom Robbins............Richard Travers
Dorothy Wedderburn...........Mona Lisa
Van Dyke Gibson........John Goldsworthy
Theatrical Agent..........Anders Randolph
Mrs. Beal.............Ida Waterman
Hired Man...............William Gudgeon

Another William Nigh independently made feature which should be a knockout in certain sections. At present the production seems a little long in footage, but this can easily be snapped up. It is a typical Nigh picture, which should be enough to the average exhibitor, who knows that this director has turned out a number of money getters, and "Notoriety" should not fall behind the others. The story itself is a new subject for pictures, and it is well handled.

There is only one false note, the casting of Maurine Powers as "Pigeon" Derring. On the screen one cannot get away from the impression she is a child of about 14, and this cannot be reconciled with a man of at least 30 and a successful lawyer wanting to marry her. At 16 or 18, yes, but dressing as she does doesn't jibe with the other.

The tale hinges on the fact that notoriety never does any one any good; that reputations dragged into the public prints can never be patched up again. The heroine is a little girl of the slums with theatric ambitions. Boarding in the same house is a small timer who preaches that the way to become a headliner is through newspaper notoriety. One evening the kid creeps into the garden surrounding a mansion and witnesses a shooting, is arrested and charged with the crime herself.

Eventually she is acquitted, but the taste for notoriety lingers. She determines to win her way to the forefront of the stage through more of it. The lawyer who has become interested in her brings about a reformation in time.

It is a picture that has everything that has ever been screened. There is slum stuff, society, murder, court room, rural atmosphere and sex stuff. Nothing is left out that the average exhibitor will want in. On the title alone it should be a money getter for the average house.

The cast is a strong one, with Rod La Roque playing the lead opposite to little Maurine Powers. Mary Alden does some corking work and George Hackathorne as a "dippy" kid is fine.

One thing about Nigh when he does a picture, and that is that one can be almost certain he will grind out a box office product. Even with that he has turned out a picture in this that has certain artistic merits that will be enhanced with a bit of judicious cutting.

Fred.

TILL WE MEET AGAIN

Presented by Morris Kohn as the first of his new series of productions directed by Wm. Christy Cabanne. Released through Pathe by Associated Exhibitors. Story by the director and adapted by Edmund Goulding.
Mrs. Dorothy Carter..Julia Swayne Gordon
Arthur Montrose..........J. Barney Sherry
Marion Bates....................Mae Marsh
Henrietta Carter...........Martha Mansfield
Robert Carter...............Norman Kerry
Jim Brennan................Walter Miller

This is the first of the Dependable Pictures productions sponsored by Morris Kohn and directed by Wm. Christy Cabanne. It is a good picture. Just as good as a lot of those getting the big first runs. It is capably directed, well played and altogether interesting. The title seemingly is the only weak point about the picture from the box office standpoint.

The cast is a corking one, with Mae Marsh and Martha Mansfield featured. Miss Marsh runs away with the honors among the women, and Walter Miller, playing the secondary lead, does likewise with the men. Miller is a comer worth watching as a leading man.

The story is a society crook drama with action and punch. Miss Marsh is the ward of a crooked stock promoter who has her confined to an insane asylum in order to appropriate her legacy. He also has duped Mrs. Dorothy Carter, a wealthy society widow. The young girl escapes from the institution and takes refuge in a house that is the haunt of a gang of crooks, one of whom falls for her.

Later when the girl gets back to her own friends he is at the head of a mob that breaks in at the behest of the crooked stock promoter to obtain some incriminating papers. He finds the girl and also sees the photograph of his former captain in the army who saved his life overseas. He then turns on his own mob and falls fighting them. His final line is "till we meet again," delivered with a salute to his former officer.

The picture is effectively done with character bits contributed by Dick Lee and Tammany Young that stand out. The former does a "nance" crook that is a work of art. Cabanne has handled this portion of the picture most cleverly.

Fred.

MORE PITIED THAN SCORNED

C. B. C. production, produced by Harry Cohn, from the play of the same title by Charles E. Blaney. Directed by Edward Le Saint. About six reels.
Julian Lorraine............J. Frank Glendon
Josephine Clifford.........Rosemary Theby
Vincent Grant...........Philo McCullough
"Troubles" ....Gordon Griffith
Viola Lorraine................Alice Lake
Ruth Lorraine..............Josephine Adair

Here is a real old meller thriller that has the old "Hearts and Flowers" all through it from beginning to end. "More to Be Pited Than Scorned" should be a clean up in the neighborhood houses where there is a mixed class of patronage, not only on its title but on the strength of the picture itself. The old Blaney meller has been brought up to date considerably for the screen and it still retains all of its old thrills. It's a short-cast piece that tells its story in a straightaway manner, and that is one of the real necessities in pictures.

Harry Cohn, who produced the piece, got a fairly good cast together. He has a couple of names in Rosemary Theby and Alice Lake, both of whom stand out in the production. This is especially true of the former, who puts over about as mean a vamp heavy as has been seen in some time. Miss Theby is a real picture trouper, and she shows up like a million dollars in this picture. The men of the cast, however, do not keep up the pace, although they suffice for the needs.

The story of the enactment in real life of the plot of a stage play by the players themselves is a twist that will get to any of the small house audiences, and they are going to like it immensely. The production doesn't look like big money had been spent on it, but it is a good one. There are several bits, such as rain storms and a theatre interior, that are well done.

Fred.

THE LADDER JINX

Vitagraph in six reels of the comedy drama type. Story by Edgar Franklin, adapted by David Kirkland. Directed by Jesse Robbins. Shown at Loew's, New York, N. Y.
Arthur Barnes.............Edward Horton
Peter Stalton................Tully Marshall
Thomas Gridley.................Otis Harlan
Cheyenne Harry............Ernest Shields
James Wilour..............Wilbur Highby
Richard Twing...............Colin Kenny
Helen Wilbur.............Margaret Landis

Comedy drama built on the walking under a ladder superstition. Few laughs, but appears to be more of a slapstick two-reeler elongated rather than a six-reel feature. Perhaps it has strength enough to stand up in the small daily-charge houses, but it appears to be better suited to the double feature bills in the bigger houses which also make daily changes. There is nothing in story, acting or direction that takes the picture out of the small-time feature classification.

The story in brief is that of a bank clerk who is appointed to succeed a retiring cashier, even though the retiring cashier wanted his nephew to succeed him. The new cashier is engaged to the president's daughter and she is of a superstitious turn of mind. Learning that on the day that he received his appointment to his new post he walked under a ladder she insists that he find the ladder and retrace his steps under it before he call on her. In carrying out her commands he runs into all sorts of complications. First, he is charged with attempting to rob a house, and then arrested for breaking into the safe of the bank. But on being cleared he and the girl find happiness.

The only outstanding person in the cast is Tully Marshall, who has the role of the heavy. Neither Edward Horton, the lead, nor Margaret Landis impress.

Fred.

IMPOSSIBLE MRS. BELLEW

Jesse L. Lasky present Gloria Swanson in a society drama, done as a Sam Wood production. Scenario by Percy Heath and Monte J. Katterjohn, from the novel by David Lisle. At the Rivoli Oct. 22.

Betty Bellew..................Gloria Swanson
Lance Bellew......................Robert Cain
John Helstan...................Conrad Nagel
Jerry Woodruff...............Richard Wayne
Count Radisloff..................Frank Elliott
Alice Granville...............Gertrude Astor
Naomi Templeton..............June Elvidge
Rev. Dr. Helstan.........Herbert Standing
Lance Bellew, Jr., age 4.......Mickey Moore
Lance Bellew, Jr., age 6..............Pat Moore
Aunt Agatha....................Helen Dunbar
Attorney Potter......................Arthur Hull
Detective.....................Clarence Burton

A lot of money has gone into this mushy, sentimental picture, and still it's pretty trashy in the sense of the family story paper style of chromo literature. None of the characters behave except after the manner of screen puppets in order to make a movie. There isn't an incident that isn't infantile fiction, designed for gum-chewing schoolgirls. It belongs in a neighborhood picture theatre and not on Broadway.

The only thing about it that is high class is the clothes worn by Miss Swanson, and even the clothes are expensive rather than fine. It's a thoroughly parvenus movie, all surface flash and shine, and no substance that an adult intelligence can find interesting. It's phoney magnificence, like Woolworth jewelry, but the essence of it is vulgar.

Miss Swanson this time is a suffering mother, bereft of her chee-ild and sobbing through five reels all over gorgeous gown creations, the while plunging into the galeties of Deauville, as is the wont of rich and misjudged heroines on the screen. It's an innovation for the high-blood pressure emotional star of the Famous Players string. And not a happy choice. At the start Betty Bellew is a neglected wife, Lance Bellew, the husband, being addicted to other affinities.

Returning home rather the worse for a gay evening with one of his women friends, he finds a man neighbor visiting his home quite innocently, and, accusing the guiltless wife, kills the visitor in a fit of jealousy. Betty is heroically represented as saving her husband from the electric chair by declining to testify against him. She allows it to be made apparent that the husband shot in defense of "the unwritten law," whatever that may be. Betty seemed to like this doormat business, for the next step is her refusing to defend herself in a divorce suit.

The husband wins a divorce and the custody of the child. Betty kidnaps the youngster and gets him aboard the steamship Olympic (scenes aboard the actual ship are extremely impressive), but a police boat comes down the harbor and takes the child away from her on a court order. The honest-to-goodness police boat "Mayor Hylan" is used here and so is the big liner which is named. But that's the extent of the verisimilitude. Betty doesn't act like a human being at any point.

She goes on across and presently is in the thick of the life of the wasters at the gay watering place in Europe, as the title has it, "determined to be a social outcast." To this end she captivates one grand duke, or maybe it was a prince of the blood, and a famous novelist, the grand duke being pictured as a sinister sort of person who took dishonorable advantage of sad ladies looking for a little diversion, and the American novelist who loved honorably in spite of all appearances. Laura Jean never did anything more atrocious.

In the end the grand duke is made ashamed of his bad habits, and the noble young novelist wins Betty and her son, who is restored to her miraculously when the husband marries one of his affinities and the affinity absolutely refuses to have noisy kids around the house. It's a very long picture and the ending is a happy one. The production has some excellent views of animated and picturesque beach scenes, and a mardi gras revel given by the grand duke is quite impressive in a production sense. The backgrounds are in the best taste and the acting is as good as the absurd story will permit, especially the playing of two children, Mickey and Pat Moore, who do the child at the ages of four and six respectively.

The production department has spread itself on a picture that isn't worth the trouble. *Rush.*

ONE EXCITING NIGHT

The opening of D. W. Griffith's "One Exciting Night" occurred in New York Monday night before a capacity audience at the Apollo. Notwithstanding two other openings the same evening in the legit houses (one "The Music Box Revue") the Apollo, had a regular first night crowd.

The comedy of the picture, begotten by a colored character (Porter Strong) brought howls during the evening, although the veriest hokum as was much else in the film. The picture's reception however, on its comedy and dramatic values, made the regulars pass the opinion around "One Exciting Night" will make money for Griffith. That, of all the Griffith films, seems to be the sole object of this special feature, which was so ably and thoroughly reviewed for Variety in its issue of Oct. 13, last, by Len Libby of Boston, where the picture opened.

If Griffith can get away with this for real money, he deserves it, for of all the picture men who might be mentioned, Griffith would have been the last thought of to have put out "One Exciting Night." *Sime.*

HOW WOMEN LOVE

First of a series of four Whitman Bennett productions starring Betty Blythe. From the novel, "The Dangerous Inheritance," by Izola Forrester, adapted by Dorothy Farnum, directed by Kenneth Webb. Sold on states rights basis. Release in New York territory by I. E. Chadwick. Shown at Loew's American.

Rosa Roma.........................Betty Blythe
Natalie Nevins................Gladys Hulette
Mrs. Nevins............Julia Swayne Gordon
Nana.......................Katherine Stewart
Griffith Ames..................Robert Fraser
Ogden Ward......................Charles Lane
Count Jurka.......................Harry Sedley
Jacobelli........................Signor Salerno
Damitri Karee..................Harry Sothern

This feature is as good as the majority of pictures that get Broadway pre-release first runs. It is a well-acted, interesting story that has been handled skilfully in the matter of direction, and as a feature picture is going to interest any type of audience. Betty Blythe in this, the first of the series of four pictures that she is to do for the B. B. Productions, in which Whitman Bennett and Walter E. Greene are interested, proves herself a real star, and the picture itself is so good that if the other three she is to make hold up to this standard she will practically compel Broadway to accept her in the first runs.

The novel by Izola Forrester told of the fortunes of the daughter of a noted prima donna, who comes to America from Italy to make her fortune in grand opera. The family heritage is that the women love not wisely but too well, and Rosa Roma is no exception to the rule. Her vocal instructor manages to interest a wealthy patron of the arts in her and he on furnishing the finances exacts three conditions, namely, that she does not fall in love, that she does not disclose her real name until he announces her, and also not to sing in public. She lives up to the latter two, but that she fails in the first finally leads her to break all three. In the end she escapes the complications.

The picture is well done in cast and there are several outstanding performances, not the least of which is that of Katherine Stewart in a character role. *Fred.*

DO AND DARE

Fox Feature starring Tom Mix. Story by Marion Brooks. Directed by Edward Sedgwick. At the Academy, New York, Oct. 20.

This picture is a case of speed run riot. The five reels leave one a little dizzy and confused. One has to stay wide awake to keep abreast of events. The story starts as a modern western comedy; turns into a dime novel of the Indian days of the west; goes back to the modern comedy locale and proceeds to a Latin-American political revolution burlesque on the lines of "The Dictator." But all the while there is shooting, fighting and giddy riding stunts.

It takes a minute or two of adding and subtracting to decide that the film is a rattling comedy with a novelty twist and plenty of action "kick." This vogue for kidding screen melodrama is a new development and at times it is a pretty ticklish proposition. It all depends upon what grade of audience the producer proposes to address.

This "Do and Dare" is a good example. It is conceivable that it would be a first-class laughing comedy on Broadway, where the mock heroics of the brave Indian scout would get a giggle. But the audience at the Academy took the heroics in all seriousness and received the burlosque coldly. They seemed to be genuinely aroused when the brave Kit Carson rode out of the stockade and, single handed, bested the redskins. They got a real thrill from the dime novel incident. But when the story turned into a hilarious travesty they didn't know what to make of it. The custard pie stuff took them unaware and they probably resented it. Even the arrival of the soldiers, riding at breakneck speed with the Stars and Stripes snappin gin the breeze didn't get a ripple. This 14th street audience apparently likes its melodrama straight and its Mack Sennett the same way. The mixture gums both sides up.

All of which doesn't alter the fact that "Do and Dare" is an ingenious comedy of the sort. Mix plays a western boob, descendant of Kit Carson. He is present in the little village store when the oldest inhabitant is relating some of the exploits of his ancestor. The fadeback shows the incident where the heroine is kidnaped by the Indians and then is rescued by the scout-hero, who brings her back to the fort just as the redskins close in. The garrison is hard pressed and Kit has to ride desperately for relief, right through the hostile band. Here's a full reel or more of dead earnest melodrama, with wild riding soldiers and Indians. Then the action goes back to the country store, where Kit's descendant, inspired by the tale, goes on a rampage and is about to be treated to rough suppression by the townsmen.

He runs away to escape a hazing. In the woods he meets a mysterious senorita, who gives him a note to deliver to a revolutionary leader in a place called "Oilcania." She conducts him to an aeroplane and he is off. Here the story goes into frank burlesque. The plane is captured by the trick government and Kit is ordered shot as a spy, escaping with all the Mack Sennett trimmings of knocking his captors about. Then the revolution breaks and the American busts it up single-handed, saving the President's daughter and leaving the revolutionary leader suspended at the top of a flagpole. *Rush.*

PEACEFUL PETERS

Ben Wilson western starring William Fairbanks, directed by Lewis King from the story by W. C. Tuttle. Released by Arrow. Shown on double feature bill at Loew's New York.

Peaceful Peters..........William Fairbanks
Jim Blalock.....................Harry LaMont
Pete Hunter......................W. L. Lynch
Mary Langdon...............Evelyn Nelson
Sad Simpson...............Wilbur McGaugh
Cactus Collins..............Monte Montague

About four reels of the most awful junk seen around New York as an apology for a western picture in a long, long time. How the Loew bookers ever fell for it even for the double feature bills is a mystery. In the little store shows at a nickel or a dime it might get by, but then only if the audience slept through it. The portion of the title that says "Peaceful" is right.

It is a story regarding an old prospector who discovers a mine, but his claim is jumped by a crooked assayer and the keeper of the gambling dive in a small mining camp, who shoots the old man. He is left on the trail and along comes Peaceful and finds him. Just before he dies he says that his mine was the end of the rainbow and that Buddy's girl would have been glad. Then Peaceful buries him and utters a prayer that he may find the mine for Buddy's girl's sake. Let's hope he did. *Fred.*

ANOTHER MAN'S BOOTS

Real out-and-out western, with Francis Ford, former serial favorite, starred. Ivor McFadden production presented by the Anchor Film Distributors and released through Aywon. Shown at Loew's New York on a double bill.

The Stranger.......................Francis Ford
Ned Hadley........................Harry Smith
Nell Hadley...........................Elvira Weil
Injun Jim.........................Frank Lanning
"Sly" Stevens................Robert Kourtman

Here is one of the real old-fashioned thrillers. Old-fashioned in story, acting and direction, but withal an entertaining little production for the type of theatres where they like western stuff that is about half-way between being worthy of a first run and no showing at all. For small houses in neighborhood communities it qualifies as a "fair" picture. No director is credited with the job; likewise, the author of the story is also unnamed. It serves to bring Francis Ford back to the screen as a star with a fairly good supporting company. His leading lady is Elvira Weil, who, while not a knockout on looks, certainly has a world of magnetism that gets her over in good shape.

The story is that of two pals on a cattle range. One of the boys has been away from home for 15 years when receiving word his father has been stricken blind and his sister wants him to return to complete the necessary assessment work on a mining claim that they are about to lose. The pals part, but one is felled by highwaymen just out of sight of the parting place. The shot, however, brings his friend, and the victim, believing that he is going to die, asks the pal to take up the journey and impersonate him.

From that point it is clear sailing in advance as to what the plot is going to be. Those that are plotting the seizure of the mine accuse the impersonator of murder, and he is about to be lynched when the eleventh hour rescue occurs, and then the happy ending with the wounded man returning as evidence that no murder was committed, claiming his place in the home and the stranger winning the sister's hand.

Some wild riding, shooting and a flock of free-for-all, rough-and-tumble fights are the thrills in the production.

Ford does a fairly strong come-back, and it looks as though he might regain his place with the fans as far as the small theatres are concerned. *Fred.*

YOUTH TO YOUTH

Metro-Classic, featuring Billie Dove. Story from Robert Footner's novel. Directed by Emile Chautard. At the State, Oct. 22.

Another case of a fine cast wasted on an indifferent story. The story is just mediocre, labored fiction without a redeeming virtue. The characters move at the behest of impossible motives. Here is a young woman discovered in a country choir by a theatrical manager and made into a metropolitan star. Tawney, the manager, treats her with every consideration as far as the action shows, but when the girl hears two men gossiping in the hotel and hears one of them say "Tawney pays all her bills. These girls—." On the strength of this harmless innuendo, the girl abandons her career leaving behind all her magnificence. She wears the simple dress in which she had come to the city (they couldn't have left out this official detail).

This business of "escaping from shame" as the title puts it, is stretched out interminably with wearisome detail that seems never to end. They even take the fugitive heroine to a cheap restaurant to eat wheatcakes as sign and symbol of her deliverance from what they would have us believe is the false and shameful life of the city. Also she suffers all over the lot although what is on her mind is never quite plain.

She applies for a job in a floating theatre (the idea probably comes from Graham Phillips' "Fall and Rise of Susan Lenox"). There is a lot more of aimless detail in a misdirected effort to build up "atmosphere," but it's all mere tiresome twaddle. The picture is foolish, dull and uninteresting in its essence and gardens a long way below the high average the Metro output has attained in the last few months. In the cast besides Miss Dove are Noah Berry, George Bunny and Zasu Pitts, the latter wasted on a trifling bit that could have been left out without affecting the tale. ***Rush.***

WILDCAT JORDAN

Presented by Phil Goldstone with Richard Talmadge as star, produced by Richard Talmadge Productions. At Loew's New York, New York, Oct. 17, as one half of double bill.

This may be a new or aged picture with Richard Talmadge. The style signs say it is old, as the heroine is around in it with short skirts.

But that will never hurt or help Mr. Talmadge. So far the stories handed him seem enough. This one is like others, it starts off well, then blows up. Besides coincident being a near relative to everything in picture making, now they are adding implausibility.

Wildcat Jordan runs along somewhat entertainingly with Talmadge doing mild athletic stuff in it, until it commences to slobber. That's when it grows mushy. The tale becomes involved, a framed abduction becomes a real one, and the whole thing is left blank at the finish, while Talmadge and the girl on the first day they meet become engaged to wed.

The early part has to do with a ranch deal and young Jordan is the son of his father who sends the boy east to negotiate for the sale. There is a touch of double crossing among capitalists, with a listless lilt to the whole affair, until it picks up speed in the big city, where it also flounders.

No one is entitled to any special mention. The cast goes with the picture and story, that takes in settings and more so takes in the direction. It would have required little to have made this one stand up by itself instead of being used as a half of a double bill. If Richard Talmadge has any pull anywhere this may go for a short booking; otherwise patrons might wonder why it was booked at all. ***Sime.***

LITTLE WILDCAT

Vitagraph slum and society story starring Alice Calhoun. Written by Gene Wright and adapted by Bradley J. Smollen. Directed by David Davld. Shown on double feature bill at Loew's Circle.

Mag o' the Alley............Alice Calhoun
Judge Arnold..............Ramsey Wallace
Robert Ware...............Herbert Fortier
"Bull" Mulligan.............Oliver Hardy

One of the usual type of slum and society stories with a little touch of war in it. Fairly interesting feature of the variety designed for the 600-seat house at a price. As that it will get by nicely and entertain the audiences. It isn't a first-run for the big theatres and not designed as uch, but in it place it should please.

Alice Calhoun, the star, is a child of the slums, a deft dip and ready to battle with feet and fists when the occasion calls for it. Judge Arnold is a police magistrate, and his friend Ware an elderly man with theories. He is willing to back one that all women are good at heart and their state is a matter of environment. He is willing to back the theory with an experiment, so selects Mag from a line-up of prisoners in the Judge's court.

The girl develops into a society bud, goes overseas during the war and as a red cross nurse serves as a spy inside the German lines. There she meets the Judge, who as a Major has been captured and escapes. She finally aids him to get through the lines. On his return to his home he calls on his former friend and relates the story of the girl that saved his life, with the result that he finds it was Mag who once stood before him for sentence. Usual happy ending with the usual clinch.

David Davld, who directed, handled his slum stuff cleverly, but his resorting to the aged modiste shop stunt with the parade of models look like picture direction of five years ago. Otherwise there is naught faulty for this particular classification of features.

Fred.

BLAZING ARROWS

Doubleday Productions picture, starring Lester Cuneo, with Henry McCarty slided as author and director, and Chas. W. Mack as general supervisor. One half of a double bill at Loew's New York, New York, Oct. 18.

Toward the end of this picture is about the longest chase on record, Indians chasing bandits, and the bandits chasing the star. When all get together they commence shooting. Probably 300 shots are fired. At about the 290th shot one of the bandits fell over. It was the first fall and the bandits by that time were afoot. Perhaps he tripped. It shot the picture at the same time. And the house had a good laugh.

It was ridiculous direction, no question of that. A fairly interesting story up to then, perhaps a bit sparse for action in a western, the last reel murdered the previous four.

It's about an Indian boy, John Strong (Mr. Cuneo) who wasn't Indian, but thought he was; his sweetheart thought he was, and so they separated in the city to meet again in the wilds, near a place that Gray Wolf, a bad, bad bandit in the west and a crook in the east, had also picked for his camping ground. Gray Wolf was so bad that he cut a heavy iron ladder reaching many feet and held by rather a light rope for the weight, in order to kill the guardian of the girl rather than to give him a glass of hootch, for the guardian looked as though any exertion would have finished him. The guardian and the girl were then in the west.

But Mr. Strong, known to his Indian friends as Skyfire, finally got Gray Wolf and gave him a Dempsey beating. After that it came out he wasn't Indian and they were married, probably, but before that she had said she would marry him, Injun or no, so everything was strictly on the up and up.

For the small picture time "Blazing Arrows" may do, principally because it will be comparatively inexpensive, but it's a pity to waste film like this, for, at the least, Mr. Cuneo did made a good-looking Indian.

Sime.

BROADWAY LIGHT

Universal crook drama with an all-star cast in which Lois Wilson and Jack Mulhall are featured. The story is by Harvey Gates and Geo. Pyper with the former doing the script. Direction by Irving Cummings. Shown at Loew's New York on a double feature bill.

Nora Fay......................Lois Wilson
Detective Marks............Wilton Taylor
Daniel Shyer............Robert M. Walker
Shadow Smith................Ben Hewlett
Joel Morgan..................Jack Mulhall
Peter Fay...................Ralph P. Lewis

A fairly good crook melodrama that holds interest. The cast is a well selected one, the story logical, and the direction rather good in spots and fair in others. The picture has name possibilities, as the two featured members and the director can all be played up. A lot of action and Miss Wilson does stand out on the strength of her performance. In the houses where there is a daily change this picture is strong enough to go it alone without the aid of another feature for a double bill.

The story in brief is that of the daughter of a man who is serving a term for a land swindle. He is mixed up with a gang of crooks and they are keeping tabs on the girl while the old man is away. They plan a shakedown to be **manipulated on a candidate for public office who has a wild son.**

Needing a girl, they inform the convict's daughter the father of this boy was responsible for her father being in jail. She is ready to go through and when they bring in a young man whom they believe to be the son, she marries him, only to find he isn't the boy picked as the victim.

Three years later, after her father is released, the crooks pull him in on a job again. The daughter learns of it and warns her f ther it is another frame-up on him, when the old man turns and kills the crook campanion. The crime is committed in the house of her husband, who comes in in time to save her from the police. But they find the body of the murdered crook and the next day the true story comes out, the girl's father, who has been wounded in the battle, making a dying confession.

Miss Wilson gave the role of the daughter a performance that ranks her with the best. In one scene she had the advantage of a corking and novel piece of direction. She was supposed to be standing at the doorway of a room witnessing a struggle between her husband and one of the crooks, with her face varying expressions as the battle progressed. It was well done and registered.

Jack Mulhall has improved greatly in the last couple of years, and as the youth that marries the girl while on a souse in this picture he slips over a worth-while performance. The balance of the cast was uniformly good.

Fred.

WOLF LAW

Outdoor picture with a thrilling horse race not on the track. Made by Universal with Frank Mayo starred. Story by Hugh Pendexter adapted by Charles Sarver. Directed by Stuart Paton. Shown on double feature bill at Loew's Circle, New York.

Jefferson De Croteau..........Frank Mayo
Francine Redney..........Sylvia Breamer
Etienne De Croteau..............Tom Guise
Enoch Lascar...........Richard Cummings
Simon Santey.................William Quinn
Samson Bender.................Nick De Ruiz
"Dandy" Dawson............Harry Carter

Outdoor story, laid in Missouri after the Civil War, so in a sense it is a western. In type, it is a melodrama that has a lot of kick for the average small house audiences. There are a number of real thrills, including a thoroughbred horse race in the open and a lot of good outlaw stuff in the mountains. Frank Mayo gives a corking performance and will please his fans in this one. From a money standpoint, it is an average box-office picture of the usual Universal type in which they star Mayo. The picture was directed by Stuart Paton, who went after action all the time.

"Wolf Law" as a title hardly applies to the story, which is laid in the Ozark Mountains. Frank Mayo plays the role of the son of a wealthy rancher who likes to gamble, race horses and lead the hard, fighting life of the period in that country. His father has placed him in business with a mutual friend. The boy has a thoroughbred horse and has been challenged by another horse owner to a race. On the day of the race he leaves his employment to make a deposit at the bank for his employer on the way to the course, finds the bank closed, and after he has won the race he doesn't get time to place the money in safe-keeping. That night at a celebration of the victory he fights with the owner of the beaten horse, and when the latter tries to shoot him he wrests the gun from him and in the struggle the challenger is shot. The boy makes his escape and places the money he was to deposit in the hands of a fellow clerk to return to the boss.

In his hiding place in the mountains with a gang of outlaws, he discovers that he was charged with the theft of $25,000, so aiding two hostages to escape he returns and gives himself up, facing his accuser compels him to tell the truth. The two who were held prisoners in the outlaw den were father and daughter and later the girl and boy figure in the usual happy ending.

Mayo is good, while Sylvia Breamer playing opposite has little to do. Two character performances in the feature stand out. They are portrayed by Harry Carter and Nick De Ruiz.

Fred.

THE CRIMSON CIRCLE

London, Oct. 5.

Produced for the Kinema Club by George Ridgwell, scenario, from Edgar Wallace's story by Patrick Mannock, photographed by J. Rosenthal, Phil Ross and H. Kingston, and played by "the largest number of British players who have ever appeared in a film play," this latest Granger Exclusive comes after much preliminary boosting. Even the old adage that too many cooks spoil the broth does not hold good in this case. The picture is an interesting mystery melodrama. It is well produced without any attempt at lavishness, the big Arts Ball scene being an example of clever stage management rather than expense.

The story tells how various people are threatened with death by the "Crimson Circle," a blackmailing organization. Two of the threatened are James Beardmore and Harvey Froyant. James Beardmore has a son, Jack, and Froyant a pretty secretary, Thalia Drummond. They are lovers, but Thalia will not yield to Jack's entreaties to marry him, but she won't tell him why. We know, however, it is because she is an agent of the Crimson Circle. An attempt is made on Beardmore's life and Jack calls in Scotland Yard; Froyant being in fear enlists the services of a private detective. At the Arts Ball a trap is laid for the criminals who escape after drugging the private detective and stealing the money entrusted to him by Froyant. After this Froyant enlists the aid of the French police, discovers who the criminal is, but is mysteriously murdered before he can inform the chief detective, Inspector Parr. Thalia is arrested on the evidence of an unwelcome admirer, but the mystery is cleared up by the arrest of the private detective and the discovery that Thalia is really Parr's daughter, who has been put on the job as a decoy. Except in one case the acting throughout is excellent.

Fred Groves is very good as Parr, and the same applies to James English, Clifton Boyne, Sydney Paxton, Lawford Davidson, Harry J. Worth, Eva Moore, Norma Whalley and Madge Stuart. Rex Davis, one of the best British actors, is out of his element. Minor parts and "extras" include many of the best-known names in British filmdom: Olaf Hytten, Arthur Walcott, Betram Burleigh, Thelma Murray, Knighton Small, Eric Albury, Henry Welton, Mary Odette, Joan Morgan, Victor McLaglen, Sir Simeon Stuart, Henry Victor, George Dewhurst, Henry Vibart, Jack Hobbs, Flora le Breton, Kathleen Vaughan, Pollie Emery, Cyril Percival, Kate Gurney, Malcolm Todd and Eille Norwood.

The picture was made with the assistance of I. B. Davidson and Screen Plays who lent their studios, Kodak, Ltd., who gave film stock; the Star Publicity Co. for titles, Knighton and Cutts for process blocks, Messrs. Berman, costumes and accessories, and many others who came to the club's aid, financial and otherwise. The Kinema Club should become a powerful co-operative producing concern. This, its first attempt, is 50 per cent. above the standard of most British melodramas and the wealth of well-known names has little to do with its success.   *Gore.*

ROB ROY

London, Oct. 12.

Despite rumors to the effect that this picture had been damaged by injudicious cutting and crude subtitling, the trade showing of this latest Gaumont feature gave every evidence that the firm had succeeded in making what it had promised—one of the finest British pictures ever screened. Will Kellino is the producer. The story is set in one of the most romantic periods of Scottish history, and although pedantic historians and "high-brows" may quibble at certain things, the public will have no fault to find in an entertainment which is full of punch and grip.

The story tells how Rob Roy, chief of the Clan MacGregor, goes to Stirling to seek alliance with the Duke of Montrose. There meets Helen Campbell, upon whom Montrose has his eye. They fall in love and elope. Orders are given by the Duke for the ruining of the chieftain. By a crafty plot Rob Roy is robbed and the eviction of his clan is ordered. The village is burned and Rob Roy is declared an outlaw.

For ten years he is hunted. His son is kidnapped and he himself is eventually captured. Saved by a faithful servant, he gathers his scattered clan together and they attack the castle which Montrose has built upon the site of the sacked village. MacGregors are victorious and all is well. Rob Roy, who lived between 1671 and 1734, is made a heroic figure, whereas he was an outlaw who levied toll upon the countryside in return for alleged protection. Scenically, the production is good, and great attention has been paid to detail in wardrobe and accoutrement. The fights, however, are much too obviously rehearsed affairs. In the main the acting is good, the principal parts being played by David Hawthorne, Gladys Jennings and Sir Simeon Stuart.
Gore.

RUNNING WATER

London, Oct. 5.

Produced by Maurice Elvey for the Stoll Film Co., this picture will bring British productions no nearer the popularity pleaded for by Sir Oswald Stoll at a recent meeting of his shareholders. Adapted from a popular novel by A. E. W. Mason, it is just ordinary dramatic entertainment of the secondary grade. The story has been well adapted, the production is good scenically, and the acting is neither better nor worse than the majority of pictures adapted from "best sellers" turned out by these studios.

Through an accident in the mountains, Wallie Hine, an illiterate young fool, becomes heir to a fortune. Hine is in the clutches of Jarvis, a money-lender, who, hearing of his fortune, proposes to persuade him to insure his life for £100,000. At first the lad refuses, but on being offered a loan, consents. Sylvia Thesiger hates her life with her cold mother and decides to go home to her father, who is known as Garrett Skinner. Skinner is really a crook and conspires with Jarvis to rob Hine, who is trying to become a gentleman. Sylvia arrives in the midst of the crooking and threatens to upset the gang's plans. One of her first acts is to get in touch with Hilary Chayne, her old lover at Chamonix. Hine falls in love with her and his infatuation helps the gang.

Soon she learns the truth about her father's character. Jarvis comes to Skinner with a proposition—let Hine have a fatal accident, and they'll go "fifty-fifty" on the insurance. Chayne calls on Sylvia, but they get no chance of a talk alone. Everywhere they are spied on. Hine is plucked by his so-called friends, who leave without knowing of the more villainous scheme. Chayne proposes to Sylvia, who thinks he's asking her to marry him out of pity. He assures her it is not so, but she says she must stay to protect Hine. Skinner's first attempt on Hine's life is through the medium of an old duelling pistol; it fails. Chayne tells Sylvia her father is out to murder Hine, but he can't prove it. He persuades her to run away with him and get married, which she does. They return only to find the house empty; Skinner has taken Hine to Chamonix. They follow, and Chayne is in time to save Skinner from committing murder.

The Alpine scenes are very fine and the other sets and locations all that could be desired.

The great fault of the picture is that it is obviously machine-made and lacking in sincerity. The company is a good one. Julian Royce is excellent as Skinner; Lawford Davidson is far above the average British film hero, Madge Stuart is good as Sylvia, and an exceedingly good study of Hine comes from George Turner.   *Gore.*

A GIPSY CAVALIER

London, Sept. 20.

The "starring" of Georges Carpentier is the big thing in this new J. Stuart Blackton picture. The story, adapted from John Overton's novel, "My Lady April," has no great originality, but it lends itself to beautiful staging and dressing, a point which the producer has taken full advantage of. Locations and sets are very fine, and the big crowd scenes show careful and expert stage management.

The picture leads up to a great stunt on the lines of Griffith's. Its flood scene is most sensational and should make the fortune of the picture even if it had no other merits. The "head on" scenes of horses galloping are not so effective and could do with pruning.

The story tells of the romance between the gipsy, Merodach, who is of high birth, and Dorothy Forrest. Merodach is really Valerius Carew and is called upon to take up his right position in the world. Fashionable life fits him well and he is soon famous as a fop, but, unknown to his new friends, he still wanders abroad and when opportunity offers as the fighting gipsy. In this guise he is one night waylaid by ruffians, whose object is to make him unable to enter the ring for a big fight. He is, however, rescued by Dorothy, who is being pestered by a bailiff. Merodach knocks the fellow down and he ultimately becomes the good friend of the lady and her cavalier. Merodach wins the big fight. Dorothy is abducted, but promptly rescued by Merodach, who thrashes the abductor, his worthless kinsman. He is pursued by Bow street runners, who want him in connection with the death of Sir Julian Carew. After a big struggle he escapes and seeks shelter with his old friends the gipsies. Meanwhile Dorothy and her maid are hastening to bring the proofs of Merodach's innocence. Caught in a flooded river, the flood being caused by the gipsies blowing up a dam. Dorothy is almost drowned when her lover swims out and succeeds in rescuing her. His innocence established, Merodach is united to the "beauty of Bath," and everyone is satisfied. The production throughout and the photography are as near perfection as it is possible to get.

Georges Carpentier is somewhat disappointing from an acting point of view, but he makes up for everything by his fights and athletic stunts. Flora le Breton is charming as Dorothy, and the rest of a long cast is excellent. The film is a great improvement on "The Glorious Adventure" and should prove a winner anywhere.   *Gore.*

A Rogue in Love

London, Sept. 15.

Adapted from a novel by the late Tom Gallon, this is an excellent feature. Like many of Gallon's stories, he was the nearest thing to Charles Dickens, comedy is mingled with pathos and his settings are taken from scenes of poverty and squalor. There is no exaggeration in the pathos of this feature, and even if the comedy is at times a little sudden and exuberant the producer can be forgiven.

A jailbird called Badgery persuades another ex-convict to aid him in a robbery on the very night of their release. The other man is shot, but before dying confesses he robbed an old man of a fortune he was expecting from a brother in New Zealand. The brother dies and the man gambles away the money. He begs Badgery to explain. In a cheap lodging house lives Keeble, who is still waiting for the fortune his youngest brother has promised him, and Joe Bradwick, an impecunious journalist. Keeble is expecting his only daughter home from school, and she believes he is a rich man, whereas he is very poor. Unknown to him, Bradwick and she are in love. Badgery arrives at the house, is unable to tell the truth, and the old fellow thinks his dream is at last coming true. Pattie arrives from school and is persuaded into believing the story as well.

The little family meet a worthless man about town, who takes a fancy to Pattie, but bides his time. Every night old Keeble puts on his old dress clothes and says he's going to his club, whereas he is a waiter in a cheap restaurant. Badgery finds this out. To keep up the fiction of coming riches Keeble gets more and more involved until at last he's at the end of his tether. That night he gets fired from his job for incivility. Meanwhile Pattie's rich admirer has learned the secret and with the help of a shady lawyer has made her believe the fortune has arrived and the dingy rooms have been refurnished on the strength of it. He insults her and is ordered out, and also knocked down by Badgery. In revenge he has the rooms stripped and tells Pattie there is no fortune, no rich uncle. However, he is wrong. The rich uncle is not dead —in fact, he was one of the customers that Keeble insulted in the restaurant. Pattie marries her journalist and every one is happy at last, even Badgery finding solace in the love of the slatternly little servant at the boarding house.

The picture is well produced. Some of the scenes, notably those of bank holiday on Hampstead Heath being exceedingly good. The acting is above the average. Frank Stanmore gives a capital performance as the rogue Badgery, while the Keeble of Fred Rains is among the best performances we have seen. Betty Farquhar is admirable as Pattie and Ann Trevor proves herself a clever comedienne as Eudocia. Gregory Scott is excellent as the journalist and the rest of a big cast is up to the standard set by the principals. "A Rogue in Love" should prove a good proposition anywhere.
Gore.

ROBIN HOOD

Story by Elton Thomas, directed by Allan Dwan and photography by Arthur Edeson.

PLAYERS

Richard the Lion-Hearted..Wallace Berry
Prince John....................Sam de Grasse
Lady Marian Fitzwalter......Enid Bennett
Sir Guy of Gisbourne...........Paul Dickey
The High Sheriff of Nottingham........
.........................William Lowery
The King's Jester.............Roy Coulson
Lady Marian's Serving Woman........
.........................Billie Bennett
Henchmen to Prince John.............
......................Merrill McCormick
.........................Wilson Benge
Friar Tuck.....................Willard Louis
Little John...........................Alan Hale
Will Scarlett......................Maine Geary
Alan-a-Dale ....Lloyd Talman
The Earl of Huntingdon, after Robin
Hood ....Douglas Fairbanks

Scenario Editor.................Lotta Woods
Supervising Art Director..Wilfred Buckland
Art Directors..........Edward M. Langley
..........................Irvin J. Martin
Costumes Designed by.............Leisen
Research Director........Dr. Arthur Woods
Technical Director........Robert Fairbanks
Film Assembly by............William Nolan

Archery, and when knights were bold while villians were cold, and that is "Robin Hood" at the Lyric, where it opened Oct. 30, plus the tremendousness of its settings, a slow first part and a fast second half, appearing more so by contrast, and plus Douglas Fairbanks, who is a fetching picture himself and more so as Robin Hood, besides a splendid cast and the most admirable of direction.

"Robin Hood" is a great production but not a great picture. It's a good picture and just misses being great through that slow long opening, in the days of Richard of the Lion-Heart and his first crusade. But it's good enough to draw at $2 and when "Robin Hood" reaches the picture houses, they will mob it.

Archery may be new or old to the screen, who cares? And the archery, trick or otherwise, of this picture, who cares how it's done? But the prettiness of the sets of Robin Hood's lair in the Sherwood Forrest, the picturesqueness of his band of outlaws who were for their King and aganist his villianous brother, Prince John; the breadth of the settings throughout, the stunts by Fairbanks when he got going, and when he gets going, how he can go; the superb supporting cast, that castle, that drawbridge, that banquet room, that convent, that long stretch of everything and that lovely photography which brought all so close nearly all of the time and glimpsed it often enough to let you see the massiveness meanwhile, with that likeable Robin Hood right in the centre—that's "Robin Hood" and why it is a good picture. It holds you tense in the "Robin Hood" portion and lets down badly when it's about Richard, for unless Fairbanks is in action, he isn't Fairbanks, but all film lovers will want to see this one.

At the Lyric at the premiere (first performance) Monday night the audience passed up the first section with perfunctory applause, not even that, but at the finale of the picture they remained to applaud. Some may have known Fairbanks and his wife were back stage. Anyway he appeared in person, said he was pleased and introduced Miss Pickford who mentioned her pleasure through saying "Robin Hood" was Doug's best, then Allen Dwan was dragged forth and wouldn't remain, with others who evidently had been in the wings, escaping before they could be dragged.

No distributor or presenter was program mentiond, though the program told everything else.

"Robin Hood" breathes money in production and yet the uniniated will not believe the sets of this film were studio-possible. But they were and they are remarkable, perhaps almost as much so as the inconsistencies that may be inserted into a picture of this magnitude and yet pass without criticism. Which means that it's the effect, not the detail in current picture making.

Many minutes could be cut from the first part and those lost minutes may become valuable time when the Fairbanks film reaches the picture houses. The less of the first part, the better, though it is absorbing in its historical narrative style.

Sime.

THE TOWN THAT FORGOT GOD

William Fox special directed by Harry Millard from the story by Paul H. Sloane claimed to be based on fact. Length about six reels. Shown at Astor theatre, N. Y., Oct. 30 for a run.

David ....Bunny Grauer
Eben ....Warren Krech
Betty Gibbs......................Jane Thomas
Harry Adams..................Harry Benham
The Squire..................Edward Denison
His Wife.........................Grace Barton

For sob stuff this feature appears as though William Fox had a successor to "Over the Hill." Perhaps it is not quite as sobby as "Over the Hill," but with all its sentimental stuff it has a terrific storm and flood scene, which Harry Millard has directed in such a manner as to outstrip any storm that has been shown on the screen. He even out-Griffiths Griffith's storm in "One Exciting Night" and tops the one in "The Old Homestead." That storm is really the picture. It is built tier upon tier and just as it begins to become tiresome there is a new thrill in it. The picture is short in footage as far as running it as a special attraction in legitimate theatres is concerned, but built perfectedly for the picture theatres. On the opening night in New York it ran just a trifle longer than an hour and a half and, at that, there are about 15 minutes of the epilog that might just as well be cut from the picture when it hits the regular film theatres.

As far as the audience is concerned, the story is ended when the storm is over and the boy and his companion wander away from "The Town That Forgot God," and come upon another town where all is peace and happiness. Whatever else is tacked on to the picture after that time means absolutely nothing. The orphan boy's troubles are ended when he escapes from the bondage of adoption and makes his way into the world and that is all the audience wants to know.

The scene of action is laid in a small town where the local carpenter is in love with the school teacher, but she marries a surveyor and a year later they have a child. The carpenter fashions the cradle for the baby and then wanders forth into the world with broken heart and a mind unbalanced. Within a few years the school teacher is widowed and returns to teaching. Later she is dismissed from the position because her youngster is the brightest boy in the school and favoritism is charged. She fails in health and dies and the boy is adopted by the squire, because the adopter will receive the money from the sale of the home of the orphan.

Abuse is the lot of the boy from the time that he enters the squire's home, although the carpenter who has returned to the scene becomes his champion. The son of the squire, a boy about the same age as the orphan, taps his Dad's till and the adopted one is accused of the crime, threatened with arrest and his fear is so great that he utters a prayer that he may be taken to the Beyond to be with his mother. Seemingly in answer to the prayer, the storm breaks forth with terrific fury and the bursting of the dam practically wipes the little town from the map. The boy escapes from the house and seeks refuge with the carpenter. The two are saved. Then, in answer to another prayer from the little chap, quiet comes with the dawn and the two wander away to new fields.

In the epilog, the boy is shown grown to manhood's estate and a banking power, who believes in a square deal to the working man and empowered by his monied associates with the right to negotiate the points of difference with the workers. He is married and in his splendid home the old carpenter is working on the plans for another cradle.

In the matter of cast a happy selection has been made all around. Bunny Grauer is the orphaned boy and the performance he gives is a wonder. William Fox is going to find a real asset in this youngster and this picture will undoubtedly make him. Warren Krech is the carpenter and gave an exceedingly clever characterization. Jane Thomas as the teacher and Harry Benham as the husband, both delivered strongly, the former having the more important role of the two. Edward Denison played the hard-hearted squire, and Grace Barton was the wife.

In photography Joseph Ruttenburg has done a wonderful piece of work, not alone in the storm and flood scenes, but in the double exposure stuff early in the picture, and the lightings were perfect. The production as a whole does not look as though it cost a million dollars, although the flood, with the breaking dam and the wiping out of the town that was built especially to be wrecked, must have been a considerable item on the cost sheet.

"The Town That Forgot God" looks like a sure-fire picture with the masses, and those that believed Harry Millard would not be able to follow "Over the Hill" are going to be considerably mistaken, for this picture appears to be a logical repeat.

Fred.

THE SIN FLOOD

Dramatic feature from the Goldwyn studio. Made from Henning Berger's play, "The Deluge," produced on the speaking stage by Arthur Hopkins. Film version directed by Frank Lloyd. At the Capitol Oct. 29.

Billy Bear.........................Richard Dix
Poppy......................Helene Chadwick
O'Neill......................James Kirkwood
Swift..........................John Steppling
Frazer.............................Ralph Lewis
Sharpe........................Howard Davies
Stratton..........................Will Walling
Nordling..................William Orlamond

Typical translation from stage to screen in more respects than one. As usual, the title was twisted into a more hectic label, while the story itself was pretty severely censored. The title was edited up to make it promise more while the play was edited down to make it deliver less. The object in the former case is to make the picture sell better and in the latter case to make it censor-proof.

All of which does not change the fact that the work has been skillfully done. For its changed purpose the picture is excellent. The bitter cynicism of the play is greatly modified. There are touches of comedy that lighten the gloom, and in the end romance triumphs for Billy and Poppy; instead of going their several ways (Poppy back to the streets and Billy to the game of financial cut-throat gambling), they hie them to the license bureau and the wedding bells are in prospect.

This isn't what the play's author meant. Instead of a problem play it becomes a romance shining in a world of gloom. The difference is good business. Its fidelity to life is less, but its appeal to the sentimental picture fans (which means selling it to its new public) is undoubted.

The screen acting is splendid. The wistful beauty of Helene Chadwick is enormously effective here and has been cunningly employed by a shrewd director to furnish the high light of the production. Poppy is kept cleverly in the background and soft-pedalled most of the time, but brief glimpses of her plaintive figure, done in exquisite misted photography, gives the whole picture a background of sentimental motif.

Most of the play's wilder hysterics have been deleted—such, for instance, as the marching about of the drunken flood prisoners singing—and the business of drinking to drown terror is greatly modified. Nevertheless, the main incidents of the play are recorded faithfully.

As in the stage version, the same group of characters are caught in a basement saloon in a Mississippi cotton town when they believe the levee has burst. They close the flood doors when the telephone warning comes and prepare to face death by suffocation. Confronted by death, all the hard and cynical people soften toward each other and a revel in brotherhood and good will lasts until they unexpectedly learn that the flood has gone down. Then each returns to his own selfish life; grudges, hates and rivalries spring up again between business antagonists, and the Golden Rule goes by the board.

The bursting of the levee (as it is pictured in the minds of the victims) is cleverly reproduced, probably with a model, and some striking flood scenes (apparently cut from various news weeklies) give a big effect of reality. *Rush.*

MAN WHO SAW TOMORROW

Paramount picture starring Thomas Meighan. Adapted from the original story by Perley Poore Sheehan and Frank Condon; adapted by Will Ritchey and Frank Condon. Directed by Alfred E. Green. At the Rivoli week of Oct. 29.

Burke Hammond..........Thomas Meighan
Capt. Morgan Pring.......Theodore Roberts
Rita Pring.......................Leatrice Joy
Jim McLeod....................Albert Roscoe
Sir William De Vry............Alec Francis
Lady Helen Deene.............June Elvidge
Vonia.................................Eva Novak
Larry Camden..............Laurence Wheat
Prof. Jansen.....................John Miltern
Bishop.........................Robert Brower
Botsu..........................Edward Patrick
Maya.....................Jacqueline Dyris

Thomas Meighan's last Paramount feature, "Manslaughter," ran three weeks at the Rivoli and a fourth week at the Rialto. This may or may not have caused the sudden release of "The Man Who Saw Tomorrow." It's a cinch the latest won't duplicate, for it is constructed around a story that is incredible and preposterous.

The picture has received a production and cast that deserve a far better plot tha the unconvincing "Oriental mysticism" theme about which the story rotates.

Mr. Meighan does splendidly in a role chuck full of opportunities for all sorts of heroics and meller melodramings. The story starts convincingly, but wanders into difficulties from which it never survives.

It shows Meighan as a Lothario, with two women seeking to marry him. One is an English noblewoman (June Elvidge), the other a rum runner's daughter (Leatrice Joy). He is about to become ensnared by the former when coming under the influence of an authority on Oriental mysticism (John Miltern).

The Prof. goes into a mind-controlling trance, allowing Meighan to visualize his future as the husband of each of the females. As the husband of the English woman he has a loveless existence, but climbs political heights until he is the Viceroy of India. He has a love affair with a Russian Princess whom he is tricked into deporting from England as Home Secretary. Eva Novak was a beautiful, beguiling sorceress in the role.

His dual experience with the beach comber's daughter was replete with thrill and perils after marriage. A rival with murderous intentions was ever present and ever repulsed. This experience included a trip on a bootlegging sloop, a mutinous crew inspired by the thwarted rival and several good fight shots.

The dual idea was carried out by

jumping from one "vision" to the other so that one reel would show the hero surrounded by pomp and splendor while the other had him on a South Sea isle and in the close-to-nature environment. The story covered more ground than an atlas.

The "trance" allowed the authors much latitude, but the entire illusion was destroyed by the impossibility of the construction. To expect a modern audience to take the "trance" thing seriously is going beyond the reasonable. Every cut back to the "trance" scene showing Meighan and the mystic slumbering was greeted with laughter.

Despite the weakness of the story it is not a bad picture, through the excellent cast and the splendid photography and production. The Durbar scene in India is a colorful flash. The picture is crammed with splendid bits of acting, corking exteriors, lavish interiors and interesting situations that were discounted by the mushy structure of the whole story.

Had the adapters the perception to treat the "future" seeing portions as a comedy subject, the picture would be accepted in the proper spirit. But the palpable effort to make it credulous defeated its own ends so that the entire film was received as a light comedy subject in the face of its obvious efforts to qualify as melodramatic.

It will bring no new fans to the star and will offset the good reports from "Manslaughter."   *Con.*

SHADOWS

Tom Forman production presented by B. P. Schulberg, with practically all star cast. Adapted by Eve Unsell and Hope Loring from Wilbur Daniel Steele's prize story "Ching Ching Chinaman."

Yen Sin	Lon Chaney
Sympathy Gibbs	Marguerite De La Motte
John Malden	Harrison Ford
Nate Snow	John Sainpolis
Daniel Gibbs	Walter Long
"Mister Bad Boy"	Buddy Messenger
Mary Brent	Priscilla Bonner
Emsy Nickerson	Frances Raymond

A decidedly grim and morbid tale, directed and presented without any lighter relieving moments. Deals with the conversion of an Oriental who is left to die in solitude by his Christian fellows after he has acknowledged their faith. In a sense it is an interesting feature, but hardly an attraction that will draw big money or prove entertaining to the average picture theatre audience. In its grimness it at times approaches Griffith's "Broken Blossoms" and were it done with as fine a sense of the artistic, it would still have to suffer the fate of that production as a real box attraction.

The unfoldment is draggy and the present film version will have to be edited and cut considerably before the feature will ever approach a semblance of holding the sustained interest of an audience. The special showing and the manner in which the preliminary heralding of the production were handled for the trade, gave it a glamor and dignity worthy of a really worth while achievement in filmdom. This alone accentuated the disappointment the picture proved to be a feature of just ordinary weekly release calibre.

"Shadows" has its locale in a small fishing village. Here the admiral of the fishing fleet lives with his charming little wife. He is a brute and when he fails to return from a cruise after a storm, the widow accepts the attentions and finally weds a young minister who has come to town. The local banker and owner of the drug store, also a suitor, while seemingly taking his defeat in good grace secretly plans revenge. After a year he starts blackmailing the minister indirectly by letters supposedly written by the first husband of the minister's wife. The storm in which he was lost also washed up on the shores of the little hamlet a Chinaman, who opened a laundry. The minister tried to convert him but failed, although he succeeded in making a loyal friend of the Oriental. It is the Chinaman who finally solves the mystery of the blackmail plot and on his death bed brings a confession from the offender, making possible a happy ending to the troubles that beset the minister and his wife.

Lon Chaney as the Chinaman gave a corking performance and successfully withstood the strain of dying through about 2,000 feet of film. Marguerite De La Motte was the leading lady and gave a corking performance, as did also Harrison Ford as the minister. Walter Long, as the first husband, and John Sainpolis, the unsuccessful suitor, furnished the heavy element. Both gave faultless performances. Buddy Messenger carried a kid part nicely.

It may have been that Priscilla Bonner was the name of the girl with a baby in her arms in the beach scene after the storm. If it was she, then she is to be congratulated on a remarkably fine piece of screen work in a short close-up flash that was given of her.

The production is adequate and the lights rather good.   *Fred.*

QUEEN OF THE MOULIN ROUGE

A Ray Smallwood production founded on Paul M. Potter's musical comedy. Adapted by Garfield Thompson and Peter Milne. Length, seven reels. Released by American Releasing Corp. At the Cameo, New York, for a run starting Oct. 29.

Rosalie Anjou	Martha Mansfield
Tom Vaughan	Joseph Striker
Louis Rousseau	Harry Harmon
Jules Riboux	Fred T. Jones
Gigolette	Jane Thomas
Moozay	Tom Blake
Albert Lenoir	Mario Carillo

In adapting the "Queen of the Moulin Rouge" to the screen considerable liberty has been taken with the original, undoubtedly to make the picture censor proof. As a matter of fact, there isn't a thing of the original story left in the picture. To be sure, the title has been retained and the Parisian locale is also still present, but that is about all. However, there is a fairly interesting little feature picture worked out which, with the glamor of the title to lure at the box office, should manage to draw some money for the exhibitors.

In the original the heroine and hero were the children of royalty in neighboring principalities, whose parents had betrothed them while they were both students in Paris schools. The children are advised that the premiers of their respective countries are coming to arrange their wedding, and both escape and meeting in the Moulin Rouge fall in love and bring a happy ending.

The picture, however, has the hero a student of the violin in Paris; the heroine a little country girl who comes to Paris to become a dancer and falls into the hands of a clique in an Apache dive. In escaping from them she falls into the studio of the violin student. He is being taught by an old master who believes that the boy will be one of the violin geniuses providing he suffers a broken heart, so noting his interest in the girl he arranges with her to accept a position in the Moulin Rouge to dance and earn sufficient for the boy's tuition. When the boy finally discovers what the girl has been doing on the night that she is crowned queen of the resort he leaves her and wanders about the town until his master finds him and imports the true story. Then a search for the girl brings them to the edge of the river, with the boy arriving just in time to rescue the girl from a watery grave.

The picture is well handled from the point of direction and production. The winding streets of Paris have been exceedingly well done, and the chase after the girl over roof tops and her final battle to escape are a real thrill. The Moulin Rouge scene is also well done with the unveiling of the models.

Martha Mansfield as the "Queen" gave a fairly satisfactory performance, with the boy played by Joseph Striker fully adequate. Jane Thomas makes a flashy looking underworld queen that registers.   *Fred.*

YOUTH MUST HAVE LOVE

Fox release from the story and scenario by Dorothy Yost, directed by Joseph Franz, starring Shirley Mason. Length, short five reels. Shown at Loew's New York, N. Y., on double feature bill.

Della Marvin	Shirley Mason
Earl Stannard	Wallace McDonald
Frank Hibbard	Landis Stevens
Austin Hibbard	Wilson Hummel

A highly improbable story only fairly well done. It is a feature that with Shirley Mason as the name can go along in the small houses and interest. It is semi-western and society, with a murder, false accusation and a jail-break as its principal features. The early part of the picture shows Miss Mason in a rather nifty one-piece bathing suit doing some fancy diving and swimming stuff that should give some of the lowbrows in the small houses a thrill.

The scene of action is laid in the west, with the father of Della Marvin in the power of Frank Hibbard for no reason that is made clear. However, he is in need of a bankroll and the two call on the uncle of Hibbard, a wealthy recluse. They arrive on the scene just as Earl Stannard has had a fight with the old man because the latter has trimmed Stannard's father on a cattle deal. In a struggle the old man is knocked cold and the boy goes after water to revive him. While he is gone the nephew, who with Marvin has been watching the fight, enters the room and steals money and securities, but just as he is about to escape the uncle revives and the nephew shoots him. On the return of young Stannard he is accused of the crime, but makes his escape.

Hibbard compels Marvin to stand by him and keep the real story of the crime a secret. Stannard in escaping has been wounded, and falls from his horse near the spot where Marvin's daughter is swimming, and she assists him and hides him from his pursuers. On the strength of his threats Hibbard tries to compel Marvin to make his daughter consent to marriage, and the girl, overhearing it, informs her father that she is already married to Stannard, with the result that the father divulges the true story of the murder and the young couple are clinched for the happy ending.

It is a commonplace feature but the title ought to draw business. Miss Mason gives a fairly consistent performance, but the unprogrammed actor playing her father is particularly bad. Landis Stevens as the heavy delivered nicely, while the lead opposite the star is capably handled by Wallace McDonald.   *Fred.*

THE WHITE HOPE

London, Oct. 20.

Walter West can reasonably claim to be the foremost producer of British sporting films, and this production is quite up to the standard he has set. On this occasion boxing instead of horse racing provides the basis of the feature. There is little originality in the story or the manner of its telling, the whole thing being merely a vehicle to introduce a big fight between a white man and a negro at the National Sporting Club.

Jack Delane, training for his fight with Crowfoot, the negro heavyweight champion, accepts an invitation from Durward Carisbrooke, a sporting squire to train at his country place. The squire's sister, Claudia, is being wooed by the Duke of Dorking and retires to the same place to think things over. The aristocratic lady and the fighter meet and fall in love. Her aunt, however, persuades the fighter to give her up. After this Delane begins to lose faith in himself and his trainers tell Claudia the truth. She puts the heart back in to him; he fights, wins and gets the girl.

Slight as the story is, it is further hampered by slowness and a preponderance of padding. The acting is quite good. Stewart Rome and Violet Hopson are excellent in the leading parts and the support is good.

Any success "The White Hope" gets will come from the splendidly stage-managed fight and the popularity of the leading people.   *Gore.*

THE YOUNG RAJAH

Jesse Lasky presents Rodolph Valentino in a drama from the play by Althea Luce and the novel by John Ames Mitchell, the latter having enjoyed a vogue 20 years ago. Directed by Philip Rosen. Scenario by June Mathis.

Amos Judd	Rodolph Valentino
Molly Cabot	Wanda Hawley
Amos Judd (as a boy)	Pat Moore
Joshua Judd	Charles Ogle
Sarah Judd	Fanny Midgely
Horace Bennett	Robert Ober
Slade	Jack Giddings
John Cabot	Edward Jobson
Narada	Joseph Swickard
Maharajah	Bertram Grassby
Tehjunder Roy	J. Farrell MacDonald
General Gadi	George Periolat
Prince Musnud	George Fie'd
Miss Van Kovert	Maude Wayne
Stephen Van Kovert	William Boyd
Dr. Fettiplace	Joseph Harrington
Caleb	Spottiswoode Aitken

This mystic tale loses something in the telling on the screen. The novel was a lot more plausible. The screen version savors of camera trickery and the whole thing loses in sincerity and conviction. The device of having a luminous spot appear on the brow of the hero as he goes into a trance strikes one as a crude arrangement. It brutally reminds one that the whole affair is a piece of fiction, this to the sad damage of the illusion.

The book was infinitely more persuasive in its appeal to the imagination. The screen is much too literal, even to the flashbacks which show the Hindoo uprising and political plottings in India. They were faintly suggested in the novel, but on the screen they are mere theatrical display, having some value as a series of spectacles, but exceedingly stagy and unreal.

It's not an especially fortunate part for Valentino. His successes have been made in roles which called for hectic romance with a dash of paprika in their flavoring. This one is a milkshake after the cocktail of "The Sheik" or even of the Toreador of "Blood and Sand." Nevertheless, the star has a pull, as testified Monday night when the Rivoli was well filled in spite of the rain. The picture probably won't repeat "Blood and Sand," but it should be a satisfactory entertainment and a profitable release. It's nearly 20 years since the popularity of "Amos Judd" in no form and the name probably doesn't mean much.

The flashbacks to the Oriental part of the story make violent and disturbing contrast to the modern American locale, and the finish has been twisted into a happy one to the damage of the work, although there is no disputing the good judgment in a commercial way of the arrangement as a general rule. If memory serves, the novel finished with the death of Amos, while the film takes him back to India, restores him to the throne of his native principality and gives a hint of future wedding bells.

The story opens in the Connecticut home of Caleb Judd. To the farmhouse come two mysterious strangers and a boy, bearing a letter from Caleb's brother, a merchant in Calcutta. There has been a revolution in a native state, the ruler has been slain by the successful pretender and his son has escaped and is to be brought up by Caleb. The strangers are high officials of the former royal court. They give a vast fortune in money and jewels to Caleb in trust for the boy, who remains in ignorance of his origin.

He grows up and enters Harvard, becoming a leading athlete and leader of the wealthy set. He is regarded with suspicion by the other youths because of his foreign air and a strange gift of seeing into the future. He falls in love with Molly Cabot, who is divided in her affections between him and an American youth who turns out to be something of a bounder. At length Amos' suit triumphs and the wedding day is set, but Amos has a vision that he will die before the marriage day.

There is a fadeback to India. The usurper is a tyrant over the people,

who are suffering. He learns (this disclosure through an American newspaper is pretty hard to swallow) that the rightful heir is alive, and he sends a crew of assassins to America to put him out of the way. But other forces assemble to protect the prince. A mystic religious leader with powers of clairvoyance has a vision of the danger to the young Rajah and he sets out to prevent injury to the prince. The usurper's hirelings capture Amos and are about to do away with him when the priest and his followers appear, killing the leader of the assassins and conducting the prince back to India, where he is acclaimed by the people as their savior and restored to his throne after the pretender has committed suicide.

The epilog shows the Rajah in his garden, mourning for the love which he had deserted at the call of duty, but the vision of prophecy, which has never been wrong appears to show that ultimately they will be reunited. *Rush.*

VILLAGEBLACKSMITH

A William Fox Special, founded on Longfellow's poem, with the screen script by Paul H. Sloane and directed by Jack Ford. It is rural melodrama in about six reels. Presented at the 44th Street theatre for a run, opening Nov. 2, 1922.

John Hammond	William Walling
The Blacksmith's Wife	Virginia True Boardman
Alice	Virginia Valli
Alice, as child	Ida Nan McKenzie
Bill	Dave Butler
Bill, as child	Gordon Griffith
Johnnie Brother	George Hackathorne
Johnnie, as child	Pat Moore
Ezra Brigham	Tully Marshall
Squire's Wife	Carolina Rankin
Anson	Ralph Yeardsley
Anson, as child	Henri de la Garrique
Asa Martin	Francis Ford
Rosemary Martin	Jessie Love
Rosemary Martin, as child	Helen Field
Doctor Brewster	Mark Fenton
Gideon Crane	Lon Poff
Aunt Hattie	Cordelia Callahan
A Village Gossip	Eddie Gribbon
Flapper from the City	Lucile Hutton

A real weep-inspiring melodrama that has trials and tribulations piled one on the other until the final scenes, when all the complications work out for the ultimate happiness of the Village Smith and his family. It is a picture that the majority of picture house audiences will love and rave over. It has almost all of the tear-compelling strength of " Over the Hill" and it is well enough done on the screen to make it a really worth-while feature from the standpoint of the big pre-release theatres.

The picture is presented in the form of a prolog and main story, there being about a 50-50 split in the two themes, with the opening portion holding the greatest interest. Because of the division in the story it is necessary to have two sets of fplayers for the smith's children, those that appear in the prolog having supposedly aged considerably when the second portion of the tale is told. In matching up the players for these characters splendid work was done.

Being founded on the Longfellow poem will undoubtedly prove something of a draft in a box office way for the picture. The poem is utilized in the sub-titles from time to time as the melodramatic action develops in keeping with it.

The story opens showing the smith at his force under the spreading chestnut tree, and his family of wife, two sons and daughter are introduced in their home and school life. In opposition is the family of the squire, who was an unsuccessful suitor for the hand of the girl that married the smith, he in turn having married a vinegary cousin who has led him a wretched life, and therefore he has harbored a grudge against his successful rival through all his years.

It is the squire's son that eggs on the youngest of the smith's brood to climb a tree from which he falls and cripples himself. This accident inspires the older brother's ambi-

tions to become a great surgeon, so that he may cure his kin. The accident is the second of the family's trials, the first being the death of the mother. Then as the story develops the elder brother is almost killed in a train smash, which incidentally is counted on to be one of the real thrills of the picture, but so badly done that it got a laugh from the first night's audience. The daughter is accused of the theft of church funds, after her father has suspected her of being unduly friendly with the son of the squire.

In the end, however, the girl is cleared of both suspicions; the elder brother recovers from his accident and operates successfully on the younger, and the picture ends with the marriage of the youngster and the daughter as well, while the smith and his elder son look on pridefully.

William Walling plays the smith with much feeling and scores heavily, while as the squire Tully Marshall manages to warrant hisses for his villain. Of the other adult characterizations those enacted by Francis Ford, Carolina Rankin, Mark Fenton, Lon Poff, Cordelia Callahan and Virginia True Boardman were worthy more than passing mention. The village gossip bit of Eddie Gribbon's was a fine piece of character work. He is coming along in great shape as a character actor.

In the two sets of characters for the children the first comprised Ida Nan McKenzie as the daughter, Gordon Griffith the elder son and Pat Moore as the younger. The latter immediately won a place for himself in the hearts of the audience, and as far as he was concerned the audience felt that they did not want him dropped from the cast when the prolog ended. The squire's son was played by Henri de la Garrique.

In their second stage of development these characters are played by Virginia Valli, Dave Butler and George Hackathorne as the smith's family, while the son of the squire is Ralph Yeardsley, who developed into a real heavy. Miss Valli's performance, however, was the prize piece of work. She has improved greatly in her screen work in the last year and certainly appears to be starring material at present.

The production is an adequate one, and in keeping with all the late pictures that have come along it has a storm scene. It seems as if all the directors are trying to outdo each other with the wind and rain stuff, and had this picture appeared before the others—"The Old Homestead" and "The Town that Forgot God," not forgetting "One Exciting Night"—the storm scene would have been a wallop indeed.

In all, "The Village Blacksmith" looks like a feature that will clean-up as strongly as did "Over the Hill." It gets an audience in the throat at the beginning and never releases its grip until the final minute. *Fred.*

TO HAVE AND HOLD

A George Fitzmaurice production, presented by Adolph Zukor. Mary Johnston's famous novel has been scenarized by Ouida Bergere. This Paramount picture is current this week at the Capitol, New York, with the following cast:

Lady Jocelyn Leigh	Betty Compson
Captain Percy	Bert Lytell
Lord Carnal	Theodore Kosloff
Jeremy Sparrow	W. J. Ferguson
King James I	Raymond Hatton
Patience Worth	Claire Dubrey
Red Gill, a pirate	Walter Long
Lady Jane Carr	Anne Cornwall
Paradise	Fred Huntley
Lord Cecil, Jocelyn's brother	Arthur Rankin
Duke of Buckingham	Lucien Littlefield

The costume play is enjoying quite a vogue. Here's another with sword play and all that sort of thing prominent throughout. Whether by design or accident it follows Douglas Fairbanks' "Robin Hood" on the market, permitting the latter to pave the way.

The Mary Johnston novel is familiar to almost everybody. In type it

thrilled with its romantic climaxes depicting the trials and tribulations of Lady Jocelyn Leigh (Betty Compson) and Captain Ralph Percy (Bert Lytell) in winning their happiness and the dissolute King James I's patronage. The monarch is intent for four and a half reels on rewarding his favorite, Lord Carnal (Theodore Kosloff), with the hand of the fair lady. The latter would not have it, and sails to the Virginias to become the bride of some settler. Captain Percy marries her out of pity at her plight to prevent her return to England. Lord Carnal follows with a king's warrant for her return. She is imprisoned; her lover dungeoned; escape, strategy, sword play and lots of other things follow. The suspense is maintained even until the actual scene of the forced marriage between Lady Leigh and her unwelcome Lord Carnal. Enter Captain Percy for a duel for the lady's hand (their marriage was annulled by court decree), and in besting the most expert sword in England wins a reprieve.

There are a number of interesting details in the production. Of course, the court masque scene of King James could not have been anything so Hollywood-esque as depicted despite the monarch's w. k. love of regal revel. Here, however, Kosloff is given a chance to do a couple of his Russian whirls and dizzy spins that have been neglected since posturing before the camera. A battle scene between a pirate galleon and a king's vessel was a thriller, with another storm scene standing out.

It is lavish production throughout, with the cast intelligently deporting itself in keeping with the action. In addition to Miss Compson and Mr. Lytell, the central figures, W. J. Ferguson does a neat character bit. Kosloff and Raymond Hatton as King James I stand out in the support. *Abel.*

OLIVER TWIST

A Sol Lesser production, with Jackie Coogan starring, in a screen version of Charles Dickens' "Oliver Twist." Directed by Frank Lloyd. Presented at the Strand, New York, two weeks beginning Oct. 30.

Oliver Twist	Jackie Coogan
Fagin	Lon Chaney
Nancy Sikes	Gladys Brockwell
Bill Sikes	George Siegmann
Mr. Brownlow	Lionel Belmore
Mr. Bumble (the bedale)	James Marcus
The Widow Corney	Aggie Herring
The Artful Dodger	Edouard Trebaol
Charlie Bates	Taylor Graves
Noah Claypole	Lewis Sargent
Charlotte	Joan Standing
Mr. Grimwig	Joseph H. Hazleton
Sowerberry	Nelson McDowell
Rose Maylie	Esther Ralston
Mrs. Bedwin	Florence Hale
Monks	Carl Stockdale
Toby Crackit	Eddie Boland

Jackie Coogan in a costume play. That about sums up the production of Dickens' "Oliver Twist" as presented by Sol Lesser. It is a series of characterizations from the pages of Dickens, but hardly enough of Jackie Coogan to please the picture fans. Just how the picture will appeal to the majority of fans is a question. Of course, there is a certain element of non-fan Dickens lovers who will be attracted to the theatre by this picture.

Although there are a number of names with picture value in the supporting cast, there is hardly anything in their performances that stands out. They appear to be rather lacking when weighed against some of the stage characterizations that have been presented of the better known roles of the Dickens work. This is particularly true of the interpretation of Fagin presented by Lon Chaney and the Bill Sikes of George Siegmann.

As to the picture itself, Dickens without the lines seems to be something other than Dickens. Jackie Coogan manages to endow the role of Oliver with real youth, and one perhaps feels more for the youngster than one would for a more mature girl playing the role, as has been the case in the past; but still and all it isn't a Coogan picture in the full sense.

There is this, however: the production with the coupling of the names of "Oliver Twist," a standard classic, Charles Dickens and Jackie Coogan makes a rather imposing combination for the average picture theatre, and it is on the strength of this combination that the picture will have to be sold to the public. It won't sell itself by word-of-mouth advertising by those that view it. The exhibitor will have to go out and create the demand, otherwise he cannot look for an unusual box-office return.

From a production standpoint the feature is well done, and Frank Lloyd, who directed the work, is to receive no small measure of credit. In lightings and the sets reproducing the old London streets the picture is superb. *Fred.*

ALIAS JULIUS CAESAR

A Charles Ray production, released through First National. Written by Richard Andres, directed by the star. About six reels.

Billy Barnes....................Charles Ray
Helen....................Barbara Bedford
Harry....................William Scott
Tom....................Robert Fernandez
Dick....................Fred Miller
Nervy Norton....................Eddie Gribbon

This is a typical Ray comedy, with more laughs in it than any picture that Ray has turned out for more than a year while he was making productions for First National release. It was one of those pictures that in the old days made Ray a favorite and one of the type which he failed to make for a long time.

It is a laugh producer of rare quality, with the starring honors such that they should have been divided between Eddie Gribbon and Ray himself. Gribbon is there forty ways with the tough hick stuff as the crook in this picture. He is the foil for Ray all the way and makes possible the laugh-getting that the star does. Without Gribbon there would have been fewer laughs for Ray.

The story is one that was palpably manufactured for the screen. Ray has the edge on three other young men in the affections of Helen. He deserts a golf foursome to be in her company and the three others decide to even things up with him. They get him into the locker-room and stage a race for the showers. Ray is the first in, and then the others steal his clothes and lock him in so he can't attend a dance that night. Ray, however, makes his escape clad in a shower sheet, and is pinched as a nut who is parading as a Julius Caesar. In the jail house he is clad in a discarded cop's uniform, and the coon janitor of the place believes him an officer, leaving the cell open so that he and the crook who works society affair.. (Gribbon) can make their escape.

As soon as the crook gets loose he starts operations and turns up at the very dance where Ray goes to square things with the girl. The action from that point is all at the society function, with Gribbon wandering through and cleaning up all the jewelry in the place and slipping it to Ray, whom he has pressed into service as an accomplice. Finally the real cops arrive, round up Gribbon and leave Ray to work out his salvation with the girl.

Barbara Bedford plays opposite the star and manages to impress nicely. But all the way through it is a Ray-Gribbon picture, which for laughs would be hard to beat outside of an out-and-out Chaplin or Lloyd slapstick comedy. *Fred.*

ADVENTURES OF "CAPTAIN KETTLE"

London, Nov. 7.

Made by Austin Leigh, this series will probably achieve some popularity by virtue of the popularity of the stories in novel form and the name of the author, Cutliffe Hyne. Beyond that they are merely picturesque melodrama. The production work is good, but the producer wants to re-edit drastically and delete all his hymn sub-titles. They are not humorous and will cause offense. The first of the stories, "How Kettle Became a King," tells how, when down on his luck, the fiery little sailor is engaged to command a gun-running expedition to America. On his way he quells a mutiny, rams a submarine, and generally has his fill of adventure. He eventually lands his contraband cargo and is asked to become king. This is too good a chance for more trouble and he promptly accepts. The trouble comes along in plenty and he soon loses his throne. He and his employer escape with their lives with the help of a pretty native girl who has fallen in love with the sailor. Then to level things up properly she shoots his enemy.

The great charm in the picture rests in some of the "shots" and the scenery of the Canary Islands where it was made. The ship scenes are excellent and the mutiny is well stage-managed. The cast is good, but the calling of the actor who plays the title role "Captain Kettle" is without reason and a throw-back to the days when the heroes of sensational dramas were wont to adopt fictitious naval and military titles. *Gorc.*

TESS OF THE STORM COUNTRY

Mary Pickford, star, produced by Mary Pickford Company. Directed by John S. Robertson. Released through United Artists. At Strand, New York, week Nov. 12.

Tessibel Skinner....................Mary Pickford
Frederick Graves....................Lloyd Hughes
Teola Graves....................Gloria Hope
Elias Graves....................David Torrence
Daddy Skinner....................Forrest Robinson
Ben Letts....................Jean Hersholt
Ezra Longman....................Danny Hoy
Dan Jordan....................Robert Russell

The Mary Pickford fans will revel with her in "Tess of the Storm Country." It's Mary Pickford all of the time, throughout the entire picture that seemed to run bit over the usual length. Those of the picture clan not so wild perhaps over Miss Pickford will lean more in her favor after seeing the "Tess" performance. Miss Pickford acts with her head, hands and feet in this film; she pantomimes and plays the part all of the while, with the titles often lending an addition but quiet though effective amusing touch.

"Tess" is a Pick'crd remake, which explains why the program says, "By arrangement with Adolph Zukor." Miss Pickford first did "Tess of the Storm Country" for Famous Players a'.ut eight or ine years ago. The Grace Miller White book story fitted her perfectly then; it does now. Which is likely the reason for the remake. Speaking of remaking the story in modern picture style sounds like the bunk, as there isn't anything modern to be made out of "Tess." It's probably the cheapest picture ever made by Miss Pickford, eight years ago or now, and especially now. The scenario doesn't call for lavish outlay and it's all right just as it is, or was, with Pickford in it.

Before "Robin Hood" with Fairbanks opened in New York, the film bunch repeated they had heard, "'Robin Hood' is all right but Pickford's 'Tess' is better." Pickford's "Tess" isn't better than "Robin Hood" as a picture, but for those who like Miss Pickford "Tess" will be preferred above "Robin Hood" by those who like Fairbanks, for in "Tess" you have Pickford all of the time and she is Mary Pickford, whereas in "Robin Hood" you get Fairbanks as Fairbanks for but a little while. Besides the difference in the cost!

Merely as an off-side expression—if Mary Pickford spent on her pictures what her husband does on his, who could surmise where Mary Pickford might go to as a picture star? Now she's the popular favorite of the screen, a mighty fine film actress in the lighter vein and a girl who thoroughly understands any art there is to picture playing or picture making. Miss Pickford's asset in the trade, however, may be that a Pickford doesn't call for a valuation of a million or more.

The "Tess" story doesn't need retelling, even if it did call for remaking. The title will inform the uninformed. It has everything in the sob line, offset by Tess' impetuosity that is just as natural with Tess as Mary Pickford is natural in her playing.

Naught to be said against the least item in the film. Everything has been done well, particularly the photography by Charles Rosher, and the direction overlooked nothing.

Among the players and after Miss Pickford the fine performance was that of Ben Letts by Jean Hersholt. Mr. Hersholt made his villainous character real, of the seafaring sort, shaggy and bearded, uncouth and rough, the exact kind of a fellow Ben Letts must have been. In contrast was the Teola Graves of Gloria Hope, carrying a misery whining countenance that could not bring her sympathy in a sympathetic role. Lloyd Hughes made Frederick Graves, the father, an upstanding role, and David Torrence gave a likable performance as the juvenile.

"Tess" with Pickford should be a box-office bear for the exhibitors in the Pickford precincts. *Sime.*

ANNA ASCENDS

Paramount feature starring Alice Brady presented by Adolph Zukor. Adapted from the play by Harry Chapman by Margaret Turnbull. Directed by Victor Fleming. Shown at the Rialto, New York, week of Nov. 12.

Anna Ayyob....................Alice Brady
Howard Fisk....................Robert Ellis
The Baron....................David Powell
Countess Rostoff....................Nita Naldi
Count Rostoff....................Charles Gerrard
Siad Coury....................Edward Durand
Bessie Fisk....................Florence Dixon
Miss Fisk....................Grace Griswald
Mr. Fisk....................Fredrick Burton

In this picture Alice Brady is at the head of practically an all-star picture cast. In support are David Powell, Nita Naldi and Robert Ellis. The picture is a screen version of the play "Anna Ascends," in which Miss Brady first achieved stardom on the stage in New York several years ago. It is a combination slum and society melodrama, certain to appeal to a definite set of picture fans. As a feature it ranks about with the average Paramount product.

Miss Brady is the little Syrian immigrant girl who develops into the author of a best seller. Mr. Ellis has the lead opposite her as the young reporter, son of the publisher of a big New York daily paper. Mr. Powell is the semi-heavy as keeper of the Fifty Club, a resort where he operates two ways at one time, deals in food and entertainment on the surface, while underneath he disposes of jewels smuggled into the country by international confidence workers. Miss Naldi is a Russian countess, the heavy, operator for the crooks and associated with her as her brother is Charles Gerrard. The two score heavily.

From a pictorial standpoint the film is very well done with some of the best and oddest shots of lower New York that have ever been screened. The picture has sufficient punch to get by most anywhere, although it must not be expected that it is going to draw record business. *Fred.*

WHITE HELL

A state righter by Charles E. Bartlett Productions, starring Richard C. Travers and a special cast. Released several months ago, but just getting around in this territory. Distributed by the Aywon Co. Story by Leola Morgan. Director, B. C. Seibel.

A mediocre independent production characterized by crudities in story and playing. "White Hell" is the designation of a town in the distant north. The titles make a great fuss about its remoteness, but much of the action takes place in a house furnished with the appurtenances of civilization. Instead of an overpowering effect of snow, the ground generally is barely covered, although one or two shots, taken in drifted hollows, have deep snowbanks.

The characters act as they do merely to make a scenario and not under plausible compulsion. The heavy forces the honorable father to consent to his daughter's marriage on threat of disclosing a family scandal. The scandal apparently consists in the fact that the father's brother married a squaw. In a rude northern settlement such a circumstance wouldn't constitute grounds for any kind of blackmail. The whole picture has similar unconvincing details. Besides, the story is confused by multiplicity of characters, none very clear cut or human.

The best of the picture is a thrilling fight or two between the hero and the heavy, but a few feet of physical roughness in a feature picture is pretty poor return for the footage. The acting is only fair, except for the interesting performance of a freckled boy and his fox terrier dog, who at least are natural. The heroine is a doll-faced blonde, who is merely a lay figure, and the whole thing classes merely as cheap fiction for the daily change houses, for which it probably was aimed.

Dave Manley (Travers) and Conley, the heavy, clash over rivalry for Helen the beautiful daughter of Allen, but Conley threatens to expose Allen's brother's disgrace unless he (Allen) promises Helen's hand. Conley and Manley fight it out on the barroom floor and Manley, of course, wins. Conley trails him in the dark and shoots him down from behind. But Waurna, a beautiful Indian girl and the daughter of Allen's brother, rescues Manley from the snow and nurses his wound.

Meanwhile Conley has shot his wife and thrown suspecion on Manley. Manley is about to be arrested by the Northwest Mounted constable, when all is straightened out by the convenient death-bed confession of Conley and Manley resumes his courtship of the beautiful Helen.

The picture would have to be offered pretty cheap to be a bargain for any but the minor daily change houses.

Rush.

TABLE TOP RANCH

William Steiner production, starring Neal Hart. Written and directed by Paul Hurst. A five-reel western, shown at Loew's New York, N. Y., on a double feature bill.

John Marvin }
William Marvin }....................Neal Hart
Falque Powell....................William Quinn

An out-and-out western based on the hatred of the cattle men for the sheep raisers. A good-enough feature of its type for the smaller houses, where they like the western type of stuff. Neal Hart plays a double role, his first character being shot in the first couple of reels. He next appears on the scene as the avenging brother and gets his man. There is the usual wild riding chase stuff, and the picture is fairly interesting.

Table Top Ranch in Texas and vicinity is the scene and the cause of the trouble. The cattlemen of the locality who have an association have agreed to let a girl raise sheep on the table top, because the flock would not wander down into the valley and graze on the cattle lands Palque Powell, a suitor for the girl's hand, is refused, and he takes a stand before the association that the sheep should be driven out of the country. Hart as John Marvin defends the girl, and the association votes to let the sheep remain. Powell hires an assassin to knock off Marvin, and has his wish fulfilled. Then the brother of the murdered man appears and takes up the trail and finally pins the crime on Powell, but not before he has had various narrow escapes. Naturally he wins the girl in the end and the sheep with her.

There are a couple of corking fights in the feature, and Hart as the hero walks off victorious in all of them.

It is a fair small feature that will do on the double bills in the larger houses and serve alone in the smaller theatres. *Fred.*

THE YOSEMITE TRAIL

A Fox five-reeler, western, starring Dustin Farnum. Story by Ridgwell Cullum, scenario by Jack Strumwasser, directed by Bernard Durning. Shown at Loew's New York, N. Y., on double feature bill.

Jim Thorpe.................Dustin Farnum
Eve Marsham.....................Irene Rich
Ned Henderson..............Walter McGrail
Jerry Smallbones...........Frank Campeau
Peter Blunt....................W. J. Ferguson
Sheriff.........................Charles French

Dustin Farnum is here the hero of a real western that has a story of logical quality behind it as the ground work for a number of real fights, some wild riding and the usual western atmosphere. Farnum has with him in this picture as one of the heavies Frank Campeau, his Trampas of "The Virginian." That is enough of a combination to get any story over. Walter McGrail as the other heavy also plays an important role in the proceedings. The heroine is Irene Rich, who looks pretty and is the third angle of the triangle of the tale.

Dustin Farnum plays the role of Jim Thorpe, who takes his nephew, Ned Henderson, into his home and shares his all with him. Both are in love with the same girl and Jim beats Ned in a trial of skill with revolvers, which at the beginning looks as though it was going to be a duel, but which develops into a target shooting contest, and thus earns the right to propose first. Ned double crosses the winner, asks the girl and is accepted. The loser takes himself off on a trip to South America and on his return finds that Ned is abusing his wife and has become mixed up with Jerry in several stage hold-ups. On his arrival Jim is made the victim of the accusations of Jerry, who states that he was the stick-up man, and Jim, in order to prevent Ned being accused and thus bringing greater sorrow to Eve, keeps his peace and is about to be lynched when the truth becomes known through the confession of Ned, who has been shot on the road by an aged sage who has had the happiness of Jim and Eve at heart.

It is a good western of its type and with names enough to stand alone on the programs of the regular daily change houses. *Fred.*

COWBOY AND LADY

Paramount production directed by Chas. Maigne featuring Mary Miles Minter and Tom Moore. Adapted by Julien Josephson from Clyde Fitch's play. At the State Nov. 6-8.

The production cost is probably one of the lowest ever expended on a Paramount picture. It is all outdoors, with a few crude interiors that look very easy on the F. P. exchequer. Nothing skimpy about it necessarily, only complying with scenic requisites. The "cowboy" end of the title gives away the Western atmosphere, although the title itself sounds very much to the Buffalo Bill. It may prove a hindrance at the box office accordingly, although the story itself and its presentation are rather interesting if not elevating.

The Clyde Fitch opus which Nat Goodwin undertook in legit for a short run has been faithfully adhered to. It concerns Mrs. Jessica Weston (Mary Miles Minter) and her scapegrace husband (Robert Schable). She decides to give him another chance to prove himself and starts for her Wyoming ranch. Ted North (Tom Moore), a dude rancher, enters the action as the Westons' neighbor. He pulls a couple of hero stunts (disproving his foppish handicap) which Weston does not make much of, being wrapped up in an amour with the village soda fountain siren. This is Weston's weakness, resulting in his death at the hands of Ross, the girl's former steady. Ross is Mrs. Weston's ranch foreman. Circumstantial evidence points to the Weston-North-Weston triangle with the heroine accused. The obvious happy conclusion develops.

It is an interesting Western romance minus the rip-snorting rough riding and more of the staid society atmosphere with "roughing it" trimmings. The picture missed a week's run at the Rialto, New York, through Lionel Barrymore's "Face in the Fog" being held over. *Abel.*

IF I WERE QUEEN

Romantic comedy starring Ethel Clayton. Scenario by Carol Warren from the novel, "The Three-Cornered Kingdom," by Du Vernet Rabell. Directed by Wesley Ruggles. At the Circle, New York, Nov. 11.

Story deals with one of those mythical Balkan principalities where the royalty may wear modern tweeds and behave in the manners of 1922 society or get itself into operetta uniforms and coronation robes and conduct itself after the colorful manner of the romantic era. Handy situation for the scenario writer and desirable state of affairs for a producer who puts out a film on the heels of "Prisoner of Zenda."

Obviously the picture is designed to capitalize the "Zenda" vogue, and it does that nicely. It is handsomely produced and well acted. The outdoor settings are magnificent and some of the interiors are fine samples of dignified backgrounds.

But the story is a pale affair compared with "Zenda." There is little of the dramatic clash that gives the Anthony Hope novel its thrill. This is rather an insipid society play.

Miss Clayton makes a jaunty heroine, and Warner Baxter is a handsome hero, albeit stagey at times. The rest of the cast is made up of satisfactory players of minor note, chief among them Victory Bateman in a character comedy part, done in her always amusing style.

Ruth, an American girl, and Oluf, princess of a little Balkan trick kingdom, become friends in a French school. The princess must go home to wed a neighboring prince for political reasons to save her people from invasion or something like that; but she loves another whom she may not marry for reasons of state. This romantic tangle is presented to Ruth in a letter. Ruth starts to join the princess in her troubles. On the way the train is wrecked and by a series of misadventures she finds herself a virtual prisoner in the house of the hostile prince, marooned there by a flood.

The prince mistakes her for Princess Oluf because of a jewelled order presented to her by Oluf. He falls in love and the affair creates a delicate situation in the court for political reasons which are rather foggy, but serve well enough. Ruth tries to escape by an underground passage disguised in one of the prince's uniforms, but is captured and returned. The prince thereupon arranges a royal marriage without Ruth's knowledge, and she is led to the altar, knowing nothing of what it means. This passage had a lot of picturesque trimmings of military pomp and display and a touch of dramatic force.

In the end there is a general clearing up of the misunderstanding, with the American girl in the prince's arms. Picture may win the women by its romantic appeal and pictorial beauty. *Rush.*

THE CROW'S NEST

Sunset production having to do with the west, starring Jack Hoxie and directed by Paul Hurt. At a Loew house, New York, Nov. 14.

Very much of a wild, wooly and hectic western with not so much gun-play but predominating in situations where Hoxie overcomes from four to a dozen men like they roll off your (or my) knife. It's practically all outdoor "shooting," with the camera having plenty of the rolling hills for a background and tons of horseflesh up front. Hoxie gets out of more predicaments than Houdini ever thought of, besides showing glaring deficiencies in his greased facial make-up when approaching too near the camera. And he wears his hair long.

Whatever honors the cast may take unto itself should be centered upon an Indian squaw, the foster mother of the supposed half breed. Evelyn Nelson played opposite the featured member as the daughter of the ranch owner, returned from an eastern finishing school. Beyond that tip off as to the proverbial sequence of the early westerns there is "the paper" proving just how white the hero is, the villainy coward with illegal possession of his cousin's inheritance, the outlaw and cohorts after the gal and the final cleaning up.

Some of the methods of "turning the tables" were so grotesque that they drew laughs from the witnesses, also revealing members of the bandit crew stalling to give Hoxie time to complete his evolutions and make bums out of 'em.

There's many a remembrance incorporated into this one, and while all the "Convention Halls" in the country, with a minor aged patronage, will probably dote on it, for the somewhat more particular customers it just won't do. In addition the photography is somewhat off, and splitting a double bill it came far from holding its own. *Skig.*

THE LOVE CHILD

London, Oct. 23.

Artistically Swedish films are probably the finest in the world, but scarcely a trace of humor or lighter material appears to tone down their footage of morbid gloom. It seems as though Sweden is a land of tragedy, where happiness and laughter come as accidental. Strong simplicity, sincerity, and brutal frankness mark most of the country's productions, and this latest Palladium film is no exception.

The story tells how a young middle-class girl is seduced. A child is born and is put out to nurse. Presently a genuine love comes into her life and she is married. But the memory of that previous lapse from virtue kills her happiness. Her secret is well kept, however, but her mother, thinking to make doubly sure, writes to tell her the child is dead. She is broken-hearted at the news and seeks to drown her sorrow in drink. Then the mother, thinking that she is going mad, confesses she lied; that the child is alive and well. The girl brings it home and tells her husband the story of her past. He casts her off, but his own mother tells him she herself sinned in her youth. This causes a revulsion of feeling on the husband's part and all is well.

Seduction, drink, deceit, are the keynotes of the story, which has been carefully produced with excellent settings. The photography is excellent. The acting is not generally up to the Swedish standard, but the work of Astri Torssell as the girl-wife is excellent. *Gore.*

ONE WEEK OF LOVE

Dramatic feature starring Elaine Hammerstein and Conway Tearle. Produced by Lewis J. Selznick, directed by George Archinbaud. Myron Selznick also is mentioned as producer. Story by Edward J. Montagne and George Archinbaud. Edited by Harold J. McCord. Trade showing in the Ritz-Carlton ballroom Nov. 3.

Beth Wynn............Elaine Hammerstein
Buck Fearnley...............Conway Tearle
Francis Fraser...............Hallam Cooley
Mrs. Wynn, Beth's aunt.........Kate Lester

Interesting and well-done romantic picture with dramatic appeal well sustained, splendidly acted and skilfully handled as to backgounds and locale. In apportioning the credits for this story it is well to keep in mind that it comes pretty close to an absolute parallel to "The Great Divide," which by many has been held as one of the best dramas of American production.

The pattern and spirit of the stage play are reproduced practically without disguise. The film differs only in detail and incidentals; much of the essence is there, although perhaps the melodramatic details introduced to heighten the popular effect of the picture somewhat cheapen the tale. Put another way, the picture puts a soft pedal on the spiritual problem discussed in the play and emphasizes its purely theatrical aspect.

Disregarding the picture's apparent source, it should make a popular release, for it strikes an effective romantic chord and holds several distinctly absorbing passages. Chief among them is a wonderfully reproduced railroad wreck and flood. The wreck is a convincing bit of camera trickery the technique of which is so true to life one is convinced it really happened. A real train is shown rushing toward a lofty trestle. A terrific storm and cloudburst is reproduced for the camera, and the trestle (it looks 150 feet high and 300 yards across) is seen to crumple as a train sweeps upon it. The train is seen (from a considerable distance) to plunge from the gaping breach in the trestle into the raging waters. Even if you presume the effect is a studio model as you watch the episode, the effect grips you in spite of yourself.

There are some capital bits of melodrama dealing with the struggle of the wreck victims in the whirling rapids, ending with the rescue of the heroine on the brink of the plunge. These highly colored details are shrewdly pieced into a direct and clearly unfolded story and the dramatic punch is capitally worked up.

Miss Hammerstein does a capital bit of quiet acting that has telling force. She is rapidly crystallizing a position as one of the most engaging of film stars by her intelligent playing, earnest and without pose or pretense. Tearle is a happy choice for the opposite part. He comes as near as possible to an ideal screen hero for much the same reason as Miss Hammerstein is notable, his direct naturalness and freedom from staginess. The title is a better commercial label than a name for the story. The tale isn't about a week of love at all, but deals with a woman's surrender to a dominating man even in spite of herself—just as it did in "The Great Divide."

Beth Wynn is a spoiled darling of wealth. The story opens with her birthday party—a characteristic bit of hectic film display, with elaborate production and spectacular incidentals such as one-piece-suit bathing girls and cabaret dances in Beth's swimming pool. Beth wagers with her fiance, Frank, she will beat him in an airplane race, and they start off. Beth is lost in the fog and comes down across the Mexican border, where she alights in the hut occupied by two Mexican desperadoes and Buck Freamley, renegade American engineer. The "greasers" claim her as their property and win her at cards from Buck, but the American buys them off and takes the girl his prisoner to his isolated shack in the mountains. The Mexicans follow, on robbery bent, and in a revolver battle Buck kills them both but is wounded severely and has to be nursed back to life by Beth. But the girl declares her hate for her captor and lives in rebellion for eight days.

A dove is blown into the shack during a storm and is tended by the girl. She gives it its freedom, but it returns, the inference being that this also is her state of mind in relation to Buck. Buck at length rides to the nearest town and communicates with Beth's people. Frank comes to get her, and Frank and Beth start home. Here is where the screen story departs from the play, to the detriment of the film. The railroad train is wrecked, and this brings Beth and Buck together again. The meeting thus is accidental rather than the deliberate act of the woman returning to the man she loves, which is the whole point. However, it makes a thrilling "movie" climax, which, of course, was the desired end.

The photography is splendid and the scenic features are especially fine. *Rush.*

WHEN DANGER SMILES

Albert E. Smith presents this Vitagraph western subject starring William Duncan. Supporting company head d by Edith Johnson. Story by John B. Clymer. Director, Mr. Duncan. At Loew's New York, Oct. 28.

Familiar type of western melodrama with usual trimmings of galloping horses and rough riding hero, but in this case having an additional element of romance. The locale is New Mexico or some such part of the Southwest, where there is a Spanish population. The romantic element in the story gets some pictorial quality from the Spanish (or maybe it's Mexican) heroine played splendidly by Edith Johnson, a conspicuously beautiful actress with a knack of screen pantomimic eloquence.

Duncan is the conventional type of the western story formula, that is to say, an impossible super-man. The picture is full of passages in which he single handed gets the better of half a dozen husky villains and assistant villains, all of them armed to the teeth and the hero having only his miraculous wits and his bare hands.

After a few of these incidents the performance of the heroine when she shoots a rope to pieces at what looks like a distance of a quarter of a mile with one shot from her trusty .45 is merely a casual incident in a welter of impossibilities, although it did get an incredulous giggle at the showing on the New York roof Saturday evening. These westerns seem to satisfy a certain class of fans who like their melodrama done with a scoop shovel instead of a trowel and for that clientele the picture does well enough.

Duncan is the mining engineer traveling through the west and dropping in for diversion at a village dance. Stepping aside from the festivities, he encounters in the woods the daughter of a rich Spanish rancher, barred by her aristocratic standing from mixing with the boys and girls of the cattle range and holding a solitary dance all by herself. Here starts the romance. There is a holdup near the scene, Duncan is suspected and we get a reel or so of pursuit. Meanwhile, the senorita's papa has betrothed the girl to a prosperous American rancher, but the girl protests that she loves only the stranger of the woodland dance episode.

Duncan and the girl meet again, but he does not recognize her and in pique she plots his murder. By mistake the assassin's blow falls upon an innocent party. Again Duncan is suspected of the crime and there is more chase, ending in his capture. He is about to be lynched when the girl, her attitude changed toward the hero by understanding the situation, brings about his release.

Some of the complications are ingenious in a crude way and the story certainly moves swiftly. That's about all that can be said for it. *Rush.*

WOMAN WHO FOOLED HERSELF

Edward A. MacManus' production, written and directed by Charles Logue, with May Allison and Robert Ellis featured. A melodramatic offering in five reels, shown at Loew's New York, N. Y. Released through Pathe by Associated Exhibitors.

Eva Lee	May Allison
Fernanda Pennington	Robert Ellis
Don Fernanda Casablanca	Frank Currier
Cameron Camden	Robert Schable
Eban Burnham	Lewis Dean
Padre	Rafael Arcos

This is the first of a series of Edward A. MacManus productions being made in Porto Rico. Because of the locale of production the first story which Charles A. Logue developed is laid in New York and Central America. As author and director Logue has done a worth-while job. The picture has May Allison and Robert Ellis as the featured players of a good cast. The subject is one that will stand up anywhere under any conditions and it is strong enough to be given more than a single day run. As a matter of fact, it could well have stood up with some of the pre-release productions that are getting the Broadway showings in the big houses.

In photography and action it is far and away ahead of the general run of pictures that play the Loew houses without first having had a pre-release showing. And in story there is nothing that the average motion picture fan could ask for that isn't in the picture. Possibly a slight comedy relief might have been added to the other good qualities.

Miss Allison has a corking role as the showgirl out of work who lends herself to a Central American trip as a star dancer for one of the big cafes to snare the grandson of a wealthy old Spanish rancher, so he will sell his interest in the estate to a large American exporting combination. Robert Ellis plays the young man who is to be the victim of her wiles, the thread of the story hinging on the fact that the girl really falls in love with the man she is supposed to vamp to his ruin, with the result that after he has signed away his share of the land she wins back the papers for him in time to prevent the company taking over the lands.

Frank Currier plays the venerable and excitable old Spaniard to perfection, and the two heavies of the cast are done by Robert Schable and Lewis Dean, both of whom give finished performances.

Miss Allison looked decidedly pretty on the screen and showed to great advantage in the dancing scenes, she as least stepping when it was necessary to do so. In the emotional portions of the story she was equally at ease and handled herself capably.

From a production standpoint the picture looks as though considerable money had been spent on it, there being two or three rather big scenes that stand out. It is a picture that you won't go wrong in playing. *Fred.*

THE JILT

Universal mystery-dramatic feature, starring Matt Moore. Story by R. Ramsey. Loew's American, Nov. 13.

"The Jilt" is far away from the style and aim of Universal product. Instead of a rip-roaring action drama we have a psychological problem play, quiet in its acting and with all the dramatic force in the under-the-surface progress of the story. In some unexplainable way the play is intensely gripping, with suspense maintained at the high point for the ingenious climax. The trouble is that the preparation of the central situation is rather tiresome.

The photography is supremely fine, with splendid landscapes, bits of rural roads, and interiors of a picturesque Southern mansion, all done in the best pictorial manner. The acting is as good as the backgrounds. Even the most trifling episodes are done in an impressive naturalness of manner that goes a long way to establish the illusion of reality.

An inexcusable error of judgment was the device of making the heavy a returned soldier of the great war. He might just as well have been a scientist made blind by a laboratory accident or anything else. The expedient of making the vengeful villain a blind veteran gains nothing and arouses resentment. It is only a matter of titles, anyway, and may have been made so in the editing of the film. If it was an afterthought it was a mighty bad one and should be corrected before the picture goes any further.

George (Moore) is the blind soldier, in love with Rose (Marguerite de la Motte) but bitterly morose at his affliction, a bitterness which gets into his relations with his fiancee, whom he is constantly nagging at her imagined neglect due to his helplessness. He is torn by groundless jealousy, charging the girl with keeping up correspondence with Sandy, a former sweetheart. Rose has been drawn to the war victim by sympathy which she has mistaken for love, and decides to break off the engagement. Just at this time Sandy returns from Coblenz, and the betrothal having ended, Sandy and Rose are much together. George, apparently reconciled with the broken engagement, goes abroad. Rose learns from a friend in Paris of a wonderful surgeon who has worked miracles on the blind and writes to him, describing George's case, asking if there is a chance for him.

George returns home unexpectedly and the three young people, George, Rose and Sandy, continue their friendly relations, George and Sandy going on long country motor excursions together. During one of these Rose becomes worried with a premonition of evil and this grows to active terror when they have not returned late at night. The atmosphere of impending evil here is splendidly worked up.

At length George returns alone, describing a mysterious assault upon Sandy as they were stalled on a lonely country road, he (George) being forced by his blindness to sit quietly in the car while thugs attacked Sandy and carried him away. This recital is capitally screened with occasional fadebacks to show the events as George tells them, and the mystery grows tense. But at this juncture Rose receives a letter from the Paris surgeon explaining that he had operated on George a month before and restored his sight. The deception of the embittered man is disclosed in an instant, and the happy ending is brought about by the reappearance of Sandy, wounded but alive, and the perspective of the young people restored to each other, while George departs broken and disgraced. *Rush.*

CALL OF THE EAST

London, Nov. 6.

This International Artists' film, a Bert Wynne production, is of the type which makes one wonder why anyone ever went to the expense of making it. It is very ordinary in story, in production and in acting. Its great charm in the eyes of people who do not care for entertainment too heavily doped in tragedy and problems will be its setting, much of which is excellent, and includes a good sand storm effect.

Jack Verity, meeting an old friend, Burleigh, in Egypt, learns how an accident the latter has had in the hunting field is responsible for times when he is not responsible for his actions, but that he has married for companionship in spite of his mental instability. Verity returns the confidence by telling of an affair he has had with a girl whom he loved, but left on finding she was married. Of course this girl is his friend's wife. They meet and find that love is by no means dead. This love leads to Burleigh attempts to shoot his wife, whom he suspects of an intrigue with his friend. Then in remorse he creeps out into the desert, dies in a sand storm and leaves the lovers to find happiness. The scene in which the demented Burleigh shoots at his wife's reflection in the mirror, thinking it is she, is the best thing in the picture.

The photography is universally good. Neither Doris Eaton or Walter Tennyson show much greater histrionic ability than they did in "Tell Your Children." Both of them are stiff and amateurish. The rest of an economical cast does its best.

International Artists seem to have a penchant for "problem" films of one sort or another, but they forget that getting such material over requires a hundred per cent. better acting and production than does the ordinary story. Genius alone can excuse nastiness, and not often then.

Gore.

BRIDGE OF SIGHS

London, Nov. 7.

The Unione Cinematographica Italiana can always be relied upon for good films of strong entertainment value. This is no exception to the rule and has the advantage of showing Italy's pet strong man actor in quite a new type of role and period. The story is somewhat complicated but is well told and the climaxes are well worked up. If the film has a fault it is that the producer, having started off with his hero as a gallant of the period, suddenly remembers his reputation for "stunts" and put them in ad libitum. This, however, will only serve to increase the value of the picture with the popular audiences it is intended for. Sansonia is still the Sansonia they know, whether in modern attire or in sock and buskin.

Roland the Strong marries Leonora, the daughter of Dandola, but is soon imprisoned on suspicion of having killed Imperia, the lover of a Venetian courtesan. This is part of a plot to make Fodcari Doge instead of the strong man's father. The plot is successful. After five years' incarceration Roland escapes and sets off in pursuit of vengeance. Leonora in the meantime has married Roland's rival, Altieri, but her heart is still faithful to her first husband. In the end Roland is avenged on all his enemies who die various unpleasant deaths and is reunited to Leonora. Many of the settings are very fine and attention has been paid to well-known Venetian landmarks, such as the Doge's Palace, the Campanile of St. Mark's, the Bridge of Sighs, etc. The crowd work shows skilful stage management.

The acting is not so good as usual in Italian films. *Gore.*

PRIDE OF PALOMAR

Cosmopolitan feature (Paramount) co-starring Marjory Daw and Forrest Stanley. From the novel of Peter B. Kyne; scenario by Grant Carpenter and John Lynch. Directed by Frank Borzage. At the Rivoli, Nov. 19.

Don Mike.................Forrest Stanley
Kay Parker..................Marjorie Daw
Pablo.....................Tote De Crow
Father Dominic..............James Barrow
Don Miguel................Joseph Dowling
John Parker..................Alfred Allen
Conway.....................George Nicholls
Okada.........................Warner Oland
Mrs. Parker..........Mrs. Jessie Hebbard
Butler.........................Percy Williams
Caroline.............Mrs. George Hernandez
Lostolet.......................Edward Brady
Mrs. Supaldio..............Carmen Arscella
Nogi..............................Eagle Eye
Alexandria.......................Most Mattoe

The whole picture has as its single object the exploitation of the Californian's bogey man, the menace of the Japanese on the Pacific coast. Peter B. Kyne, the novelist, has all the patriotic fervor of the native son, and the producer is William Randolph Hearst, whose attitude toward Oriental immigration, and especially Japanese landowners in California, is well known.

It would not be at all surprising if the State Department made some comment on this production, although the war-time situation which brought a protest over a similiar subject put out by Pathe no longer obtains. But the anti-Japanese feeling is here expressed in pretty raw terms. One of the big scenes of the screen play has a scheming Jap, defeated in an underhand transaction, make this declaration: "You won't sell me the land now, but some day I'll come with a Japanese army and take your damned ranch." At his elbow as he speaks stands a marble bust of George Washington, and with the speech the Jap scratches a match across the face to light his cigaret. What happens to the Jap immediately thereafter is ample.

The story doesn't look or listen like Kyne as it comes on the screen. One gets the impression it has been doctored in the producing process. Usually Kyne has a fine sense of dramatic sincerity and a good deal of honest humor. This thing is forced and unconvincing. Its melodrama is crude and nobody with a lively sense of fun could deal with the enormous sums of money without a grin. The penniless hero has to raise $300,000 in a year to pay off the mortgage on the ranch; he wins a Kentucky turf classic with his pet horse, which goes at 100 to 1, and then he gets $2,000,000 for the property.

For no good reason except that it makes a scene for the movies he disguises himself as a Mexican when he goes to the track, and there are a lot of other jarring artifices in the piece.

But one thing about which there can be no adverse comment is the scenic beauty and splendid photography of the production. In its direction the play is perfect and the old mission atmosphere of southern California gives it an enormous charm, a picturesqueness of which the cameramen has taken full advantage. Some of the views around ancient mission churches are lovely and interiors and exteriors about a venerable Spanish ranch house are as delightful. But the story itself is as artificial as the backgrounds are convincing in their loveliness.

An eastern capitalist plans to foreclose on a mortgage on an old ranch property and turn it into a Japanese colonization operation by an irrigation project. The owner dies while his son is in France with the A. E. F. But the son, Don Miguel (Forrest Stanley) returns in time to halt the plan. The war moratorium gives him a year's grace against eviction. The capitalist's daughter, Kay Parker (Marjorie Daw), conspires with Don Mike, while the conspirators are opposed by Okada, a Japanese agent, partner in the colonization scheme. Okada summons his secret agents to plot against Don Mike, and one of them shoots the soldier down from behind, but not mortally.

Don Mike is supported by a picturesque old contractor, Bill Conway, amusingly played by George Nicholls, and an ancient servant of the household, Pablo, played by Tote de Crow. The contest goes on through six reels or so and has some effective bits of screen melodrama—such as the passage in which Pablo ropes the Jap assassin and drags him across the country, and a horse race; but its all pretty forced and an unconvincing theatrical play without much sympathetic appeal for the eastern audience to whom the Japanese menace is pretty remote. *Rush.*

EBB TIDE

George Melford production presented by Jesse Lasky with practically an all-star cast. Adapted by Waldemar Young from the novel by Robert Louis Stevenson and Lloyd Osbourne. Shown at the Rialto, New York, week Nov. 19.

Ruth Attwater...........................Lila Lee
Robert Herrick............James Kirkwood
J. L. Huish................Raymond Hatton
Captain Davis..............George Fawcett
Richard Attwater..............Noah Beery
Tehura....................Jacqueline Logan

This started out as though it was going to be a whale of a picture, but simmered down, lost its punch and finished as one of the usual run of program features that the Paramount are releasing. Nothing out of the ordinary about it that will lift it above the class of the fair calibred box-office attractions, although it seemingly could have been turned into a sure-fire commercial hit.

There is one thing about it that is saleable and that is the South Sea Island dance that Jacqueline Logan does. Of course as a South Sea dance it doesn't hold a candle to any of them that Gilda Gray does, but in those parts of the country where they won't ever see Gilda the Jackie Logan wriggle will serve as a fair imitation, providing of course the censors don't break loose on it.

James Kirkwood and Lila Lee might be picked as the two featured members of the cast. But with them are such clever players as George Fawcett, Raymond Hatton and Noah Beery. That alone is a five-name film combination hard to beat. The performances of Fawcett and Hatton are gems of character work and stand out.

The direction is capably handled and the miniature sailing sloop in a tropical storm is well inserted, although in the cuttin and editing there are a couple of shots shown supposedly days apart of the boat in sunlight that are identical, markedly so because of the wonderful manner in which the shadows fall upon the sails. That's bad detail in editing.

Noah Beery plays the role of the heavy, who holds an uncharted pearl island as his kingdom, after he has slain his wife and his closest friend because he suspected them of having an affair. The daughter is held by him on the island and the natives are his subjects. To this island the storm-driven craft comes manned by its motley crew. Here James Kirkwood as Robert Herrick is regenerated through his love for Lila Lee, playing the daughter, and in the end after a couple of deaths by violence, the burning of the boat and some corking under-sea pictures, the couple are found clinched in each other's arms for the final fade-out.

The dance of Miss Logan as a native islander and the under-sea stuff are the best selling points that the exhibitor has in the picture, in addition to the cast of names.

Fred.

GOLD GRABBERS

W. M. Smith production apparently with a stock company headed by Franklyn Farnum and with "Shorty" Hamilton, Al Hart and Genevieve Berte in the cast. Western story by William Wallace Cook. Director not credited. At the New York Stanley, Nov. 21.

This is another in a series put out by the same people. They all have been bad, but this is the worst. It hasn't even reasonably good photography and, in this day of technical perfection, bad photography is inexcusable. The film has scarcely a merit. Its titles are long and wearisome and several of them contain grammatical breaks, such as the heroine's declaration, "The mine rightfully belongs to my father and I."

This stock company appears to have gone in for mass production. They are using the same locations and it seems at times they are using the same script with minor changes and a new title. Like at least one of the others, this story is based on the struggle for a mine and a battle between the new manager and a gang of claim jumpers. This is economy and efficiency gone to the extreme.

The picture is machine-made. Whenever fertility of story runs out, four or five bad men jump out of the bushes and the hero single-handed lays them out cold. Farnum, one of the least appealing of wild western heroes, fights in all styles in this picture. One of his battles, however, has some stunt angles. He rolls down a steep cliff into a swiftly running river and continues the combat in midstream. There was a touch of thrill in this episode, but after he had manhandled a dozen or so huskies it began to pall.

There was no following the intricacies of the story of shifting mine ownership. First the heroine's father bought an option. Then he was cheated out of it and it fell into the hands of a Denver promoter, who hired Farnum to operate the property. The original option holder and his daughter somehow managed to support a gang of hirelings to prevent the profitable running of the mine and these forces were the ones that the new superintendent had to face. They shot at him from trees, rocks and from the corners of houses, but never hit him and always had to close in and take a thrashing.

In the end the heroine let Farnum in on a secret ledge of fabulous richness, but why she spilled the secret to her family's enemies wasn't plain. But it worked out fortunately. Farnum sent for the Denver sharper, but when he arrived he turned against his own superintendent and tried to kill him. Almost succeeded, too. But when Farnum recovered and gave the Denver man a talking to on the subject of mine business ethics, he was ashamed of himself and immediately signed over a half interest in the property to Chiquita, the heroine. Then the hero and the heroine got married in the ordinary course of events.

The acting is as bad as the production and photography, with the single exception of Shorty Hamilton, who always is a genuine sort of player, although his part was reduced to a mere bit in this picture. *Rush.*

WEST IS EAST

Sanford Productions sponsors this independent Western distributed by Arrow. Pete Morrison is starred. Story by Marcel Perez. At the New York Stanley, Nov. 17.

Crude melodramatic story addressed to juvenile fans and suitable only for the most unsophisticated of audiences. Made according to the dime novel formula of plenty of action regardless of plausibility.

As illustrating the type of story, it may be related that the villain, who is scheming to get control of a western ranch, puts a spy in the household of the owner who reports to his chief via a radio outfit hidden in a discarded trunk in the garret. The villain sitting in his Chicago office receives the aerial reports without getting up from his desk. When the villain wants to communicate with his spy he merely unhooks a telephone transmitter from his desk and goes to it.

There is a complicated plot having to do with a will which deprives the present ranch owner of his property and puts it possession of a poor girl whom he befriends, but how it got into the villain's hands is not clearly shown. There are other confusing angles. The real owner is discovered as a servant in the house of an adventuress who tries to marry the ranch owner during a visit to Palm Beach, but how this was brought about is a mystery. It was also a confusing detail that the servant is on strictly business terms in a cap and apron at home, but goes bathing with the family and their guests on a basis of social equality.

The picture is full of raw breaks of this sort. For the finish all hands are on the ranch—adventuress, villain, hero and the poor girl—but how they got assembled is not disclosed. By some scenario magic the villain had possession of a deed to the property and he got the heroine into a remote shanty, where he tried to force her to sign some sort of a paper for a vague purpose. When she wouldn't sign he struggled all over the place with her. Nothing more came of this scene until the hero arrived, whereupon the hero and the heavy clinched for more business of struggling. When it was all cleared up it appeared that the heroine owned the ranch and the hero had no right to it. So the heroine tore up her deed, or maybe it was a will, and they got married.

That much was satisfactorily plain, but the intermediate stages by which they achieved this desirable situation were badly confused. It isn't often they make 'em quite as bad as "West Is East." The title, by the way comes from the fact that the Western hero travels as far East as Chicago to engage in the contest over the property. They didn't seem certain about the title at the Stanley. The main screen title called it "West Is East," which is pretty similar to the new Constance Talmadge picture from the Fay Bainter play, "East Is West," but it was billed outside the theatre as "East Against West." Not that a little discrepancy in titles means anything to a picture like this. *Rush.*

RIDIN' WILD

Universal western comedy-drama featuring Charles (Hoot) Gibson. Story by Roy Myers, direction by Nat Ross. At the New York, Nov. 21.

"Ridin' Wild" departs somewhat from the typical western pictures with which Gibson has been identified. It has a rather neat character angle. Instead of the hero being a rough-and-ready cowboy who fights by choice, he is a Quaker lad in a cattle town who is peaceable by nature, but is forced to fight by force of circumstances, and goes into the melee unwillingly. But, once in, he sticks to the finish and, of course, wins his battles and the girl.

The story has some rather strained situations, but the whole production serves as one of those commercial products that have no special virtue but fill the modest purpose of amusing the unsophisticated fans in the neighborhood houses—audiences whose demands are moderate, except that they must have action at any cost. At least the picture has some scenic beauty and is sufficiently clear and simple to be intelligible.

The Henderson family is in the hands of mortgage sharpers, but the father raises money to take up the obligation through a friend. He goes to pay his note and becomes involved in a violent argument with the lender. They have a harmless tussle, but old man Henderson is a Quaker and peaceable on principle. He pays his debt and departs. Scarcely has he gone when the schemer's partner in doubtful enterprises, a crook named Jordan, enters the office and an argument arises. They clinch, and in the struggle a revolver is discharged and the sharper is killed.

Old man Henderson is blamed. He is arrested protesting his innocence and lodged in jail, while Jordan busies himself in working up the town's prejudice against Henderson. Carl Henderson, the son, played by Gibson, is a mild youth and the butt of the town for his unwillingness to quarrel. He runs afoul of Jordan and in a fist fight bests him. Then Jordan stirs the citizens up against the Henderson family. Fearing his father will fail to get justice, Carl kidnaps the sheriff's daughter and carries her off to a lonely shack to be held as hostage.

The girl puts him to shame and he turns her free, but before she can get back to the protection of the settlement she falls into the hands of Jordan and his hirelings, and then it is a struggle between Carl and Jordan for the girl, the hero finally winning the contest and in the end the hand of the heroine. There is a neat little comedy finish, with a committee of citizens presenting the Quaker lad with a pearl-handled revolver and his mild old mother protesting that he is not promising to be much of a Quaker, but he is a first-rate son. Jordan, of course, is forced to confess the killing of the loan schemer earlier in the story, and justice is satisfied all around.

The picture is made of the familiar materials, but furnishes a fairly interesting feature. *Rush.*

HEART'S HAVEN

B. B. Hampton production, released by Hodkinson. A straight out and out Christian Science feature. Story by Clara Louise Burnham, directed by William H. Clifford, Eliot Howe and Jean Hersholt. Shown at Loew's Circle on double feature bill.

Joe Laird	Carl Gantvoort
May Caroline Laird	Claire McDowell
Vivian Breed	Claire Adams
Adam Breed	Robert McKim
Gladys Laird	Betty Brice
Bobbie Laird	Frankie Lee
Ella Baird	Mary Jane Irving
Henry Baird	Jean Hersholt
Pynch	Frank Hayes
Mrs. Horehan	Aggie Herring

This picture is designed purely and simply as a tremendous piece of propaganda for the Christian Science faith. "The Miracle Man" was not a bit stronger than this picture in that particular direction. Yet it is a simple story that is well told on the screen in an interesting fashion that holds attention and entertains. It is a fair little feature that will answer the purpose in most houses of larger capacity where there is a daily change without carrying an added feature with it.

The story is semi-society and a picture of middle-class life as well. Joe Laird has been a clerk in the traffic department of a big railroad system. He is married and there are two children. His wife is a slovenly type of woman, one who prefers novel reading to housewifely duties. Suddenly the husband is elevated to the position of secretary to the president of the road, and with his family he moves to a cottage on the grounds of the president's estate. At the same time he sends for his mother to join his household and discovers that she has lost the old home, and mother is then to remain with him forever. She is the one that is the Scientist, and it is her faith that cures the crippled limb of her grandson. This cure is brought about through prayer after the daughter of the president has had her back injured in a fall. When her father hears of the cure of his secretary's son he visits the mother and asks her to pray for his daughter, whom the biggest specialists in the country have said would never walk again. Needless to say her cure is effected.

There is comedy element in the picture furnished by Frank Hayes as a patent medicine fiend, who is also converted when he witnesses the cure wrought on the young mistress of the house.

All of this is strong stuff in favor of the Christian Scientist faith, but with it there is an element of love that carries the story along. The wife of the secretary deserts him and he falls in love with and finally captures the president's daughter. The president himself proposes to the boy's mother, who, it turns out, was a boyhood sweetheart of his, and the butler proposes to the housekeeper.

The picture is well cast, with the honors for clever work going to Betty Brice, who handled the role of the slovenly wife and walked away with it. From the first flash on the screen she established her character and registered just what she was going to do before the finish of the story. Hayes, as the butler with a yen for pills and pain killers, also contributed a clever piece of work. Gantvoort as the lead failed to impress, particularly as he held to the background in a large measure. Robert McKim gave his usual sterling performance. Claire Adams played the ingenue lead as the president's daughter and Claire McDowell scored heavily as the faith healer. *Fred.*

LOVE IN THE DARK

Metro screen classic from the magazine story, "Page Tim O'Brien," by John Moroso, made into film form by Jack Hawkes. Directed by Harry Beaumont, and designated a "Harry Beaumont production." Viola Dana starred, with Cullen Landis heading the supporting company. At the State, Nov. 20.

Viola Dana is here provided with one of the best sympathetic roles that has fallen to her lot in a long, long time. The orphan girl, Mary, is rich in humor, but a gentle, tender sort of fun. It has a healthy laugh, but the suspicion of a tear isn't far away from the giggle. As a coworker she has one of the cutest baby actors, a two-year-old boy, who doesn't get on the program, but ought to.

The story doesn't amount to much, but a story isn't especially necessary to a character sketch like this. It is sufficient without the help of anything like a dramatic support. Mary is a scrappy kid in an orphanage. A well-dressed woman applies for a girl who can take care of a child, and she looks over the candidates for the job. Mary doesn't wait to be chosen, but audaciously maneuvres the situation for herself.

It turns out that the woman is Tim O'Brien's wife, and is too indolent to care for her youngster. She urges her husband to go after easy money since he is the victim of a rare affliction called "tyctalopia," which makes him blind in the sunlight, although his vision is keen in the dark. She practically demands that he take up a career of crime to provide her with luxuries, and in the meanwhile she has an affair with a crook. Mary falls in love with the O'Brien youngster (who wouldn't with this chubby babe?), and when Tim's occupation gets him into trouble with the police and he has to disappear, she assumes responsibility for him, getting a job as companion to a wife of a kindly old minister. Mary has taken little "Red," as the baby is called, to the movies, and she goes movie mad and handles her commonplace, every-day experiences as though they were great climaxes of a drama. The minister's son has got into the clutches of gamblers, and in a desperate effort to recoup his losses has taken money from the old man's trust funds.

At this juncture Mary sends for Tim, and together they conspire to rob the gamblers and restore the stolen money to the girl's benefactor without anybody knowing. In this they are successful; Tim reforms; his ex-wife is killed in an auto accident, and the way is paved for a happy threesome of Tim, Mary and the kid on a farm.

The picture is a fine, human comedy, bound to amuse any type of audience, as it did that at the State Monday evening, when the end of the picture brought a demonstration that seldom greets a screen comedy in a house of that sort. Altogether, it is one of the best things of the kind Metro has turned out this year. *Rush.*

THE GIRL FROM PORCUPINE

Melodrama with romantic interest produced by Pine Tree Pictures, Inc., and distributed by Arrow. James Oliver Curwood wrote fiction story from which film was adapted and also furnished his own scenario. Faire Binney starred and Dell Henderson directed.

"The Girl from Porcupine" is an average program picture with very little action in the first two reels, but melodramatic incidents in the last three reels which more than compensate for the slowness of the first section. Faire Binney, one of the prettiest ingenues on the screen, has a sort of Cinderella-like role that fits her perfectly. Buster Collier in the opposite boy role also gives a thoroughly satisfying performance.

The atmosphere is divided between the Klondike mining region along the Yukon and a girls' boarding school. There's a tale of two old miners who have acted as foster fathers for Miss Binney (Girl from Porcupine) and Collier, their own parents having been killed in a mining saloon brawl.

The Yukon portion offers opportunity for mountainous scenic effects which the camera man made the best possible use of. Scenically the film is excellent.

The story itself is convention, but carries more than enough interest to please the neighborhood fans. Photographically the film is of an average.

A stage coach hold-up and considerable shooting of fire arms in the film are well staged effects. Usual happy ending with the hero and heroine in fade-out clinch. Strictly a neighborhood house picture. *Bell.*

JOCELYN

Paris, Nov. 14.

The poem of Lamartine has been produced for Gaumont by L. Poirier and now released as a Gaumont-Pax film. The photo is praiseworthy, as usual, for this French company, but the text is somewhat frequent, the only criticism to be made.

When Jocelyn was a youth he entered a seminary kept by monks, abandoning his portion of the family estate for the benefit of his sister, that she could marry with a suitable dowry. The French revolution broke out and the seminary was invaded by a crowd, the young priests and older monks being murdered. Jocelyn managed to escape, and, guided by a shepherd, he found a safe shelter in the mountain grotto. Some days later he found a youth in distress, whose father had been killed by the revolutionary troops. His name was Laurence, and after a time an affectionate friendship was established between them. Laurence had an accident in the mountains and was carried unconscious to the grotto, where Jocelyn opened his jacket to dress a wound. The breast of a young girl was revealed, and Jocelyn realized the situation, a tender love now filling their hearts.

One evening the shepherd, whose nephew was working in the Grenoble prison, brought a letter to Jocelyn. It was from his former bishop, now condemned to death by the revolutionary tribunal. The priest begged him to come before he died, and Jocelyn, leaving a note to explain his absence, stole away while Laurence was asleep.

The bishop was anxious to see Jocelyn in order to ordain him as priest so that the people of the district would not be left without a qualified religious leader. Jocelyn confessed his love for Laurence and his desire to marry her, but the prelate impressed the former seminarist of the necessity of sacrifice, so the latter fell on his knees to be ordained. The bishop was executed, being the last victim.

Laurence, after remaining alone some days, journeyed to Paris, and it was there Jocelyn met her. Due to misfortune and temptation the poor girl had been leading a dissipated life in the capital. Bowed down with grief, Jocelyn returned to the mountain village where he had been appointed priest.

Weeks passed, until one day Jocelyn in his religious capacity was called to the village inn to give absolution to a dying traveler. There he found the unhappy Laurence, who before passing to another world wished to see again the scene of her former love. Laurence died with her hand clasping that of the young priest.

Long years after when he also closed his transitory existence they buried him near the grave where the only girl he loved (but as a priest could not marry) had been laid to rest.

Such is the story told by Lamartine in his famous poem and forming the scenario of a good Gaumont picture. Armand Tallier plays the title role, with Mlle. Myrga as Laurence and Roger Karl as the bishop. *Kendrew.*

QUINCY ADAMS SAWYER

Baltimore, Nov. 29.

At the New theatre, Baltimore, week beginning Nov. 27, world premiere coincident with showing in Washington, D. C. Metro Pictures Corporation producers, with Clarence G. Badger as director.

Quincy Adams Sawyer	John Bowers
Alice Pettengill	Blanche Sweet
Obadiah Strout	Lon Chaney
Lindy Putnam	Barbara La Marr
Abner Stiles	Elmo Lincoln
Mandy Skinner	Louise Fazenda
Nathaniel Sawyer	Joseph Dowling
Mrs. Putnam	Claire McDowell
Deacon Pettengill	Edward Connelly
Betsy Ann Ross	June Elvidge
Hiram Maxwell	Victor Potel
Samanthy	Gail Henry
Ben Bates	Hank Mann
Mrs. Sawyer	Kate Lester
Bod Wood	Billy Franey
Cobby Twins	Taylor Graves, Harry Depp

An excellent picture of its kind, with the "homey" atmosphere accentuated. But in the long run the thing which marks its from the rest is that it contains more hokum than every other picture produced this year.

And yet, with all its hoke and its palpably theatric devices, it is entertaining and at times thrilling. It is the type of picture a critic could pick to death, yet nine-tenths of the population of this land will find it vastly amusing.

The story is true and seems devised merely to show off the physical powers of John Bowers and Elmo Lincoln and to give opportunities to sling the rural comedy on thick.

Quincy Adams Sawyer is a young Boston lawyer, one of the rising type, who is induced to come to Mason's Corner, Mass., in order to assist Deacon Pettingill in the settling of an estate. The estate is that of Mr. Putnam, who left behind him a widow of the usual type and a vampish daughter, Lindy Putnam, who is played by the rather voluptuous Barbara La Marr. Lindy is beloved by Obadiah Strout, a local attorney, who is doing his best to win Lindy, but on the side he has been annexing a considerable portion of the Putnam estate to his own exchequer. Strout and Abner Stiles, the village blacksmith, who sings bass and wields a hefty sledge, resent the presence of the young lawyer, especially since Lindy has taken great pains to win him for herself.

Rumors reach Sawyer's ears the gossips of the town resent his boarding at the Putnam home, so he moves over to the residence of Deacon Pettingill. There is the deacon's blind niece, Alice, who by chance he had met in Boston. Her memory lingered with him and his memory stuck to her. So the romance starts, the plot curdles and the dirty work begins, and it's thick and fast.

First it is a street fight which Abner starts with Sawyer as he is out riding with the blind girl. The whole village turns out and sees the lawyer give the blacksmith a sound trouncing. But the crafty Strout coaxes Lindy and Stiles into a plot to rid themselves of the lawyer and Alice. The plan is to cut the cables on the ferryboat which swings across the river, which is one of the rivers with rapids, falls and thrills. The plan works. Alice, however, is on the boat alone, and the thrills in the play come when Sawyer rides like mad down the bank of the river, jumps fences on his horse, and finally falls into the river from a precipice which gives way under the weight of the horse. Then he swims to the boat and rescues the girl just in time to prevent them from being swept over the falls, and, as he tells her he loves her, they clinch.

Blanche Sweet makes her reputation all over again as the blind girl, and John Bowers adds to the lustre he gained in "Lorna Doone." Lon Chaney and Elmo Lincoln do good work as the villains.

But it seems that the good work of nearly everyone in the cast, which is as near all-star as one can assemble, is overshadowed by the fearful hokum purveyed in the story. *Sisk.*

THIRTY DAYS

Newark, Nov. 29.

Paramount production presented by Jesse Lasky and starring Wallace Reid. Scenario by Walter Woods from the play by A. E. Thomas and Clayton Hamilton. Directed by James Cruze. Five reels. At Loew's State, Newark, Nov. 27.

John Lloyd	Wallace Reid
Lucy Ledyard	Wanda Hawley
Huntley Palmer	Cyril Chadwick
Judge Hooker	Charles Ogle
Giacomo Polenta	Hershell Mayell
Rosa Polenta	Carmen Phillips
Mrs. Ledyard	Helen Dunbar
Marcel	Kalla Pasha

By some unexplained freak of fortune Loew's State, Newark, secured this picture for what is apparently a world premiere. It is merely a program picture of average merit. If Wallace Reid is satisfied to continue in pictures of this type he will soon join the stars of yesteryear. Not that his acting is bad, but he seems to think it sufficient in some scenes if he merely makes a "personal appearance." Despite a few typical Reid touches most of his work is commonplace, and mediocrity neither makes nor maintains a star. Furthermore, he seems at times to think he is Harold Lloyd.

The story itself is an amusing conception, but utterly misses fire in the telling. John Lloyd is suspected by his sweetheart, Lucy Ledyard, of being too susceptible to the charms of her sex. She finally agrees to marry him if he keeps free from entanglements for 30 days. His engagement greatly disappoints his solemn rival, Huntley Palmer, but the latter, encouraged a bit by Lucy, stays around waiting for Lloyd to fall. While doing welfare work with Lucy, Lloyd is found in a compromising attitude with Rosa Polenta by her husband, the leader of a secret Italian order. The rest of the picture is taken up with Lloyd's attempts to escape the vengeance of the Italian. The complications that ensue should be amusing, but generally fail to arouse more than mild interest. One exception is a genuinely comic scene in which Palmer, Judge Hooker and Lloyd await the arrival of Polenta, who has run amuck with a carving knife. Their fear and their attempts to gauge the size of the knife are admirably expressed. In an effort to save Lloyd the judge sentences him to 30 days in jail, where he will be secure, as his pursuer sails to Italy before the end of that time. But Polenta meets him in jail and when Lloyd is released she follows him home.

The climax, though an essentially clever conception, is spoiled by as crude a piece of business as ever disgraced a serial. Lloyd, with the help of two ex-prisoners, entraps and binds what he supposes is the Italian (but who turns out to be the judge) dismisses the prisoners and while he is telephoning in triumph. Polenta steals upon him with a stiletto. Just as he is about to strike he is stopped by Lucy with a gun. She appears from nowhere without rime or reason; apparently the author was stuck but had to save his hero.

Reid's support in general is excellent. Cyril Chadwick walks off with first honors, closely followed by Charles Ogle and Hershell Mayell. As the warden, Kalla Pasha hardly equaled his work in "The Dictator." Wanda Hawley had no chance to act and carefully avoided taking any.

The titles are mediocre, the production adequate and the photography generally good. The direction is uneven. Several gags quite extraneous to the real plot are introduced to little point. Even the old story of the drunk giving up his seat in an empty car to a lady makes its appearance.

A capacity audience Monday night manifested but mild interest in the picture. *Austin.*

HUNGRY HEARTS

Goldwyn comedy-drama made from the novel by Anzia Yezierska. Titles written by Montague Glass of "Potash and Perlmutter" fame. Directed by E. Mason Hopper. Featured players Bryant Washburn, Helen Ferguson and Rosa Rosanova. At the Capitol, Nov. 26.

THE CAST

David	Bryant Washburn
Sara	Helen Ferguson
Abraham	E. A. Warren
Hannah	Rosa Rosanova
Rosenblatt	George Siegmann
Gedalyah Mindel	Otto Lederer
Mishel Mindel	Millie Schottland
Cossack	Bert Sprotte
Sopkin	A. Budin
Judge	Edwin B. Tilton

"Hungry Hearts" among other things demonstrates that five reels is pretty broad territory on which to spread a thin human interest story. This sentimental record of an immigrant Jewish family from Russia in their adventures in America has many touching passages and a wealth of sympathetic character sketching. It has an authentic touch and a lot of fine, gentle humor, but it is entirely devoid of dramatic action and one is constrained to fear that its appeal will be limited.

It's a pity, too, that the production could not have been converted into a more compelling drama, for it has the elements of a novelty in that it gets away from the time-worn screen topics and the familiar character types and it deals with some recognizable and very human people.

Here's a big subject—the theme of the Americanization of an alien family delivered raw in New York from the oppression of Russia. But out of this rich material it does seem the incidents that have been picked are petty. Certainly they are inadequate for a feature length picture.

The best they have been able to do is to elaborate a mildly amusing short story into a five-reel picture with some moments of bright human comedy spaced out by long periods of dullness. The best of the film is the character work of Rosa Rosanova, whose Jewish immigrant mother is a companion piece of acting to Vera Gordon's creation in "Humoresque." This is a fine bit of authentic acting by a gifted screen player, done with splendid subtleties of meaning. But it stands alone. There are a few telling character bits of Ghetto types, chief among them by Otto Lederer and A. Budin. It was a grave error to cast Bryant Washburn as the young lover. Here was a play of foreign flavor, and they chose for its romantic foreground an actor who is familiar to all fandom as a smart modern hero, entirely out of the atmosphere of the story and production. Helen Ferguson was much better. She looked the part and played it sympathetically.

Abraham is the impractical scholar and teacher of ancient learning in his Russian village. The Cossacks break up his little school, and the wise and efficient Sara, mother of the brood, schemes to get to America, the land of promise. By manifold privations they reach New York—the steerage scene as the ship passes the Statue of Liberty is a touching episode. But in this new land there are more troubles. The East Side tenement with its grime is a sore trial to Sara's soul. By pinching she manages to finance a revel in white paint to give it "beautifulness," to do honor to the engagement of the daughter and David, nephew of the grasping landlord, Rosenblatt.

This Rosenblatt is an alien who has prospered and he opposes violently the alliance of his nephew with these "nobodies." To break up the betrothal he imposes $10 more rent on Sara for her "painted up" kitchen and here comes the explosion. Sara goes insane at the injustice and wrecks the kitchen with a cleaver. For this she is hailed to the police court, but so sincere is her appeal to American justice that the case is dismissed, the wicked landlord is punished and "justice for the poor is vindicated in this new America." The final scene has Sara installed in the country home of David and Sara, where she can revel in white paint, and the flowers in the garden are so beautiful "it looks almost like a cemetery. The title is close in name to the U.'s "Human Hearts." *Rush.*

THELMA

Chester Bennett Production released by the F. B. O. Adapted from the Marie Corelli novel by Thos. Dixon, Jr. Directed by Chester Bennett. Six reels. Shown at Loew's State three days, Nov. 27.

Thelma	Jane Novak
Britta	Barbara Tennant
Lovissa	Gordon Mullen
Olaf	Bert Sprotte
Philip	Vernon Steele
Lorimer	Peter Burke
Sigurd	Jack Rollens
Dyceworthy	Harry Clark
Lady Clara	June Elvidge
Lennox	Wedgewood Nowell

Chester Bennett has turned out a rather fair feature, but his manner of handling the Marie Corelli tale is a little slow as to tempo and therefore rather tiring before it finishes. Otherwise it is a picture good enough to play the better part of the split week houses, especially where there is a double feature policy or vaudeville as an added attraction. It is sure fire for the daily change houses along the line.

The cast has sufficient in names to make it worth while from an advertising standpoint, especially if the exhibitor cares to pound on the Mrs. William Hart angle. That might bring a little money along for the house. But Barbara Tennant and June Elvidge are also among the women, which makes for a flash.

The story is a tale of London and Norway, with the society element in it to a certain extent. Sir Philip, being turned down by a girl, starts on a yachting cruise and meets the daughter of a direct descendant of the Vikings of old, marries her and returns to London. Here the trouble makers start to get busy. They lead his wife to believe Sir Philip is a trifler. She returns to her home, to be followed by the husband, who effects a reconciliation, proving his innocence.

There is some picturesque camera stuff shot outdoors and some very clever lightings. A couple of brief thrills, but they do not linger in the memory. *Fred.*

SINGED WINGS

Paramount, presented by Adolph Zukor, co-starring Bebe Daniels and Conrad Nagel. Directed by Penryn Stanlaws. Story by Katherine Newlin Burt, adapted by Edfird A. Bingham. Five reels, shown at the Rivoli, N. Y., week Nov. 26.

Bonita della Guerda	Bebe Daniels
Peter Gordon	Conrad Nagel
Bliss Gordon	Adolphe Menjou
Don Jose della Guerda	Robert Brower
Emilio	Ernest Torrance
Eva Gordon	Mabel Trunelle

This production appears to be a real novelty in screen entertainment. It isn't a picture, however, that will break box office records, but it will attract a nice even business and please. It is especially suited for children's matinees during the coming holiday period. From the latter, however, it mustn't be judged a kid picture, because it isn't. It is simply a corking story with a short costume prolog as part of a dream of the heroine. The co-starring of Bebe Daniels and Conrad Nagel should have some box-office value.

The story is of the granddaughter of a famous old Spanish grandee whose family was once a power in California. The girl's grandfather and she are the sole surviving members. They are in poverty and the girl is dancing in a water front cafe in San Francisco. She has attracted the attention of a society man, who tries to win her for his mistress.

At the opening is a dream in which the girl is a princess and the hero of the tale a devoted knight. They love, but she is slain by the jealous court jester. Her grandfather informs her, when she tells him of the dream, that that has been the fate of the entire family, their end is always foretold in visions of that nature. A half-witted clown who secured the position in the cafe for her is her protector from the attentions of the rougher element and the society men who try to flirt with her. Of all of the latter the one who makes the greatest impression is Bliss Gordon, played by Adolph Jean Menjou. He makes it a corking heavy. Securing engagements at social functions for the girl as part of his campaign, when his wife calls in her nephew to assist her in breaking up the infatuation, the dancing girl recognizes him as the knight who appeared in her dreams. Although she loves him she bids him go, in fear he will mean her death.

Gordon's wife in an effort to regain her husband's waning affection takes up dancing, and at a social affair substitutes for the dancing girl. The half-crazed clown, believing the girl has fallen in love with Gordon, trails her to the affair. As she is finishing her dance he fires a shot through a window and apparently kills her. It was the wife of Gordon who was the victim. At the finish the girl and nephew are clinched for the final fadeout.

The picture is well handled in direction, especially the trick stuff in the dream episode, where Stanlaws has employed the fairies and witches as aids to his story, which part will please the children.

Fred.

WHAT FOOLS MEN ARE!

Production by Pyramid Pictures, Inc., from Eugene Walters' stage play, "The Flapper," adapted by Peter Milne and directed by George Terwilliger. Fair Binney featured. Distributed by American Releasing. At the Cameo, New York, Nov. 26.

Peggy Kendricks..............Faire Binney
Ralph Demarest..............Joseph Striker
Bartley Claybourne........Huntley Gordon
Kate Claybourne..........Florence Billings
Olga..............................Lucy Fox
Horace Demarest..........J. Barney Sherry
Bayard Thomas..............Templer Saxe
Steve O'Malley.........Harry Clay Blaney

Eugene Walter built up a play of bitter pessimism and unadulterated ugliness, and then the pollyanna movies took it up and sugar-coated it. The result isn't satisfactory. "The Flapper" was a disagreeable treatise on the selfish, unscrupulous female of the younger generation. Walter's may have been a distorted view, but at least it was a real attitude and it went to a reasonably logical conclusion.

The film version is nothing at all. The indictment of the unprincipled young person of the feminine persuasion is presented with painstaking care and in its exposition is convincing. Then the play takes it all back and we are treated to a counterfeit "happy ending" that simply won't go down.

Peggy wrecks a couple of homes as she goes her self-indulgent way, and is about to deliberately wreck the life of the young man who marries her, when she suddenly experiences a change of heart, and in a twinkling is as angelic as before she was vixenish. They took limitless care in building up the wicked character, but the paragon was the makeshift task of one short scene and a couple of titles. The net result was the Little Miss Hyde stuck and the Little Miss Jekyll was dismissed as phony. **Any audience would feel imposed upon by the patent hoax.**

The ethics of the play are all wrong, anyway. The heroine is an intensified Becky Sharpe without any of the graces or wit of the Thackeray heroine. She spends half her life in the play in making other people miserable and then the rest of her fruitless existence in achieving her own happiness. To be sure she regrets some of her misdeeds mildly, but it doesn't bring her any special unhappiness, and altogether she presents a queer study in literary moralities. The whole thing is just a makeshift and was never worth the doing either on stage or screen, the reputation of Walter's for doing worthwhile things to the contrary notwithstanding.

Peggy is a parasitic daughter of luxury living in the home of her sister and wheedling her brother-in-law for costly clothes and jewels. She takes advantage of the husband's feeling that he is neglected by his wife, who is preoccupied by her literary work. When the wife finds that Peggy has a wardrobe full of expensive clothes paid for by the husband, and learns from a scandal society paper the two are seen in company sufficiently to cause gossip, she taxes husband with being in love and goes off to Reno.

The husband insists upon marrying Peggy when his wife wins her decree, but Peggy turns him off in favor of a younger and richer man, Ralph Demarest, never suspecting that the marriage will cause Ralph's disinheritance. When old man Demarest refuses to support the young pair, Peggy has no compunction in taking a bribe of $25,000 to discard her new husband at the demand of his father. She takes the money and agrees to divorce him, being supported by her companion of many flirtations, Olga, her maid until they trod the primrose path together. The money is paid, the agreement signed and Peggy is on her way back to the carefree life of the cabaret lounger when she suddenly reverses hers'f for no visible reason except that it made a better commercial movie.

So she spends the last reel in bringing her sister and her divorced husband together again in a passage meant to be prettily sentimental, returning to her own saphead husband and receiving the blessings of the rich father, who came in just in time for the sugary finish with his benediction. Apparently she lived a life of content thereafter. An old age of poverty and toil would scarcely have been too severe a penalty for her acts of reel one to four, something like Becky Sharpe's, say.

Even so fresh and dainty a young actress as Faire Binney can't save the character from vulgarity. An excellent cast of players is wasted, including Joseph Striker as the young husband, Huntley Gordon, J. Barney Sherry, Florence Billings and Templer Saxe. The production was in the best style of the up-to-date studio and the photography first-class.

Rush.

DRIVEN

Feature length drama by Charles Brabin. Story by Alfred Raboch; scenario by Mr. Brabin, who also directed. Principal parts by Charles Emmett Mack, Emily Fitzroy, Burr McIntosh and Elinore Fair. Invitation screening Nov. 23.

An admirable bit of dramatic staging and screen story telling, but the story is gloomy and depressing to an extreme degree. There are powerful passages of almost tragic import, but the tragedy has a sordid quality that leaves an ugly impression.

It deals with brutal people of the Tennessee mountains, creatures without a redeeming grace or a saving touch of humor or picturesqueness, a sordid, dingy lot, whose ugly lives form the background of the play, which has not an enlightening contrast. Violence and blood and hate enter into the tale as its only motif, and the whole thing makes an unlovely picture.

Why is it that dramatic "realism" plays constantly upon the nasty side of life? It is doubtful if this kind of material has any appeal for the picture fans. Indeed, it does not seem to prosper, especially beyond the limited audiences of the so-called "new theatre," and its possibilities for the screen are negligible. The picture is well enough done, but the question is one of choice of material with which to address a special public, and Mr. Brabin is at fault in attempting to present a heavy, gloomy tragedy through the screen medium that lends itself to romantic treatment pretty exclusively.

The story centers in the Tolliver family of moonshiners, a brutal father and three equally brutal, snarling, drunken sons, the quartet seemingly being in a conspiracy against a younger brother, favorite of the brow-beaten, toil-worn mother, a pathetic slave of poverty and wretchedness. A pretty little love affair develops between the boy Tommy and the sweet daughter of the neighboring Hardin family, little Rose. The elder and worst of the three older brothers looks upon the child with eyes of desire, while the silent mother vainly tries to aid her favorite's suit.

Rose's father opposes the older brother's surly courtship, and is shot down in the back in revenge while the daughter is taken into the Tolliver household believing that **"the revenuers" killed her father. The brothers' rival claims upon the girl are put to the crude mountain code—if Tommy is to have the girl, he must be man enough to lick his elder brother, and this leads to one of the most disgusting exhibitions of violence the screen has ever shown.** The boy is no match for the stronger brother, and is pounded to helplessness in a one-sided fight that makes the flesh of the spectator crawl.

By the issue of this fight the girl's fate is decided. She is to be forced to marry the elder brother at the next visit of the parson. Meanwhile the mother and Tommy strive for some escape. Money to get away from the mountains is Tommy's hopeless goal. The day before the expected arrival of the parson and the marriage the mother in desperation steals away to a distant cabin where a revenue officer is located, and in return for $100 discloses the hiding place of the Tolliver moonshine still. The revenue men close in on the whiskey plant while the father and three sons are at work and a fine dramatic battle is staged here, while the mother at the cabin is arranging for the departure of the girl and boy for happiness beyond the mountains.

The father escapes from the revenue men, and in a series of short scenes is shown hastening toward the cabin, working up suspense for a final clash, the previous action having disposed of the three brothers at the hands of the armed revenue men. The climax is not effective. The father reaches the cabin after the young people have departed, but is prevented from interfering with them by the mother's threat to shoot. Husband and wife meet in a clash of wills after she confesses it was she who sold out to the revenue men. The only logical ending would be the death of either one, but the scenario writer's nerve must have deserted him at the last moment. He has the husband giving way and agreeing that henceforth they shall live in mutual partnership. A hopelessly unconvincing solution and a feeble anti-climax.

Emily Fitzroy's performance as the backwoods mother is a remarkably strong bit of dramatic acting. Burr McIntosh contributes fine work as the father. The scenic features are excellent and the photography first-rate, but the story almost precludes any substantial record at the box office.

Rush.

THE TOLL OF THE SEA

Technicolor production, released through Metro. Story by Frances Marion. Chester M. Franklin, director. Photographic direction by J. A. Ball. At Rialto, New York, week Nov. 28.

Lotus Flower..................Anna May Wong
Allen Carver....................Kenneth Harlan
Barbara Carver.............Beatrice Bentley

It was chancing it to place a Chinese "Butterfly" on the screen at this date for that kind of tale wherever set. It hardly called for Miss Marion to write it. Thousands of them must have been thrown in the basket ever since there were pictures. Though, coincidentally, "East Is West" is released about this time as well.

The sad and tragic romance of Mme. Butterfly passed through made it once, and enough. There are others sadder and more tragic nearer home. Let the scenario writers open up their imaginations, if possessing them, not to water the stock of others.

Here it is no different, other than in the locale, the nationality and a baby boy, with the Chinese girl-wife rescuing her husband from the sea as he floated in at the opening of the picture, to win and lose him as he forgot his chink wife, the baby to come and the sea. And she, after vainly waiting, in Hong Kong, to again have the husband and his latest American wife return, to give him and the boy up for her, the American, and the Chinese girl, alone with her sea, walked into it and to her death, for the finish.

Someone recognized this story needed something else, even beyond the extraordinarily fine playing of Anna May Wong, who is an exquisite crier without glycerine, or Baby Moran, as darling a boy (if not a girl) as the screen owns.

So it was a color process Technicolor gave to the filming that seemed to run quite short of the regulation five reels. Nothing in a moving picture story can rise superior to the story. Coloring never will, never has, and doesn't here. The coloring runs without streaks, the camera catching the natural colors aparently, although what seemed something of a freak in this process is that the pallid color given to the complexion of the Chinese extended to the faces of the Americans as well. Perhaps white cannot be taken by this camera with its pallid shade enveloping all faces, white being open to question as a color or for coloring in specific connection. But it was a noticeable defect in the coloring scheme.

Still, though, the natural colors or the coloring in this Technicolor product is attractive, as it brings out the foliage or strikes the colorful dress of the Chinese, but, as with all devices tried for in pictures as something new, other than story, direction or settings, the newness becomes part of the picture almost immediately, and thereafter is accepted, with the story remaining as the main thread or holding power, if there is a story such as here, and not a display of flowers or some particular objects to accentuate the colorings.

Which causes "The Toll of the Sea" to be gauged as strictly a weekly release plus what novelty the coloring may contain, aided as it may be by advance publicity. There are those who will continue to prefer the plain black and white, for, with a good strong tale, nothing more is required for the sheet.

But this picture will gather to itself advocates among those who like the romantic, the drear of love, and may wish to engulf themselves with hatred for Allen Carver, that American who could not but be hated in his despicable role, and was played in a matter-of-fact way by Kenneth Harlan.

As a matter of record, on the Rialto's program this week is a short reel named "The Mirror." It gives the history of aviation from the days of 1908, when the Wrights, Curtiss, Farman and Bleriot did their missionary work at the risk of their lives. It is set down pictorially and statistically in a way to the present day. As an interesting picture less than one-third the length of "The Toll of the Sea" (a misnomer in its title, by the way), it is vastly more interesting to children or adults.

But "The Toll of the Sea" will do on the regular programs if too much is not looked for from it. *Sime.*

ARE THE CHILDREN TO BLAME

The moral values of this picture are perfect, but in all other particulars it is as bad a production as ever gets within walking distance of Times square. The story is a crude transcript of "Silas Marner," with such variations as making the weaver a blacksmith named David something, placing the action in a nondescript place and in a time when people wore clothes of about 1899 and rode in autos of about 1916 model.

The continuity is disordered, the story void and without form. As soon as one gets acquainted with a set of characters they disappear and a new set comes on. One episode starts and finishes independently, and then the story takes a new hold and begins again. Here's a sample:

Robert is a college student. He marries secretly, fearing his father's wrath. His wife dies; her baby dies; the wife's sister gets somebody else's baby and schemes to blackmail Robert. All this is set forth in two scenes and three titles. Then they waste 100 feet or more in picturing the agonies of conscience that the blackmailing sister suffers for her crimes. And the jest of it is that these agonies don't lead anywhere unless it is to the sage moral in a title copied in full and here preserved to posterity: "Uneasy in mind and heart is the woman who would deceive." The moral is plain—it is all wrong to blackmail timid husbands, if you get the point.

The acting and direction are on a par with the rest of the junk. In one scene—it was where the blackmailing sister dies in the blacksmith's home, if a stunned and staggering memory serves—one of the characters starts to exit registering sorrow. When he takes three steps he observes that his course is going to lead him between the hero, also in an appropriate attitude of dejection, and the camera. So he starts, retraces his way and decorously walks off behind the hero. The passage was worthy of Mack Sennett.

The featured player is a child, Em Horman, who was poorly coached. Of course, the little one had a dog, but the chance was lost. It wasn't a movie dog at all, just a natural brindle pup, and it was obviously unnerved by all the fuss and noise of a movie lot. The blackmailing sister threw it out of a window along about reel two and the pup's value was out for the rest of the production.

Joseph Marquis played Robert, and besides resembling Wally Reid gave evidence of acting ability.

Rush.

GRIFFITH'S "BIRTH OF A NATION" REMAINS "THE DADDY OF 'EM ALL"

Initial Special, First Shown Eight Years Ago, Has Everything—Revival for This Week at Selwyn, New York—Ku Klux Klan Konnection

Eight years old, and still the daddy of 'em all!

It's showing over at the Selwyn, New York, for a week's run, produced identically, with the possible exception the crinoline usherettes are missing, as was the initial performance for New York, which occurred at the Liberty during the first week of March, 1915.

It looks very much as if this were the standard film for all time. No matter how often seen, there's always that "kick" or thrill involved that no other special feature or general release has held.

And it always causes a panic among the censors or societies of one sort or another. There's never been a picture that drew more "repeats" in attendance than this one. That's definite. Nor has there ever been an evening's entertainment on the screen produced to compare with this first 12-reeler which inaugurated the $2 picture playing in a legitimate house.

The recent and present publicity regarding the Klan situation made it problematical as to just how the house would receive "Birth" Monday night, and the general conception had it about right. Every early appearance of a Klansman on the screen was a signal for half the audience to burst into applause along with minor hissing. It continued so until the gathering seemed finally to realize that the Klan the picture was telling of had no connection with the organization of today. Whence they quieted down and let the film proceed without prejudice.

The two-day controversy between Griffith and the state picture commission, settled by the producer saying a title would be inserted to the effect that the management disavowed any connection with the present Klan, or an announcement would be made, concluded in the title being flashed. It was not a slide, but incorporated into the film. It stated that after the reconstruction of the South, following the Civil War, the originators of the Klan put away their uniforms and disbanded the organization forever. This wording was flashed at the completion of the story. It might have saved considerable annoyance if it had been shown at the beginning of the second half, or, at least, previous to the activities of the Klan, which takes up such a major portion of the concluding footage.

The "Nation" is the masterpiece of the screen. You can't get away from it. It has everything. Devoted to that part of American history which is the most romantic and picturesque, it has pathos, suspense, anti-climaxes, climaxes, detail, unison in the cast, big production (called tremendous when first shown), capably cut and titled, Griffith directing, Thomas Dixon's story, mob scenes to make it almost a continuous spectacle, a musical score by Joseph Carl Breil that for appropriateness has never even been approached, and excellent photography. Also, as to the camera work in this picture—granted there has been vast improvements made in securing various effects since the "grinding" on this film was done—nevertheless, there's not a camera man who has since turned out a finer piece of work than did G. W. Bitzer when he "shot" this production. Not forgetting that this was the initial bit of night photography to be projected as well.

As to the cast, Mae Marsh has yet of *$500,000, which is generally rerated at $300,000 as the actual sum spent on the film. It would be interesting to compare that expenditure of money with that which Fairbanks cut loose with for "Robin Hood," or for "Knighthood," "Four Horsemen," etc. Though what the "Nation" would cost today to produce cannot be estimated.

As to the fact, Mae Marsh has yet to equal the performance she gave here, which borders on a classic, as the young sister of the Cameron family; Lillian Gish has sobbed and fought through many a "special" since; Henry Walthall worked up to this effort through the old Biograph days and has since slowly faded away; Wallie Reid has never had a more realistic fight than the barroom battle he takes part in; Spottiswoode Aiken, George Seigmann and Miriam Cooper are still in the films. Besides which directors and other luminaries have sprung from others of the cast, which includes Maxfield Stanley, Ralph Lewis, Elmer Clifton, Mary Alden, Walter Long, Raoul Walsh, Donald Crisp, Josephine Crowell and Bobby Harron, passed away.

The picture itself remains the same, including the backstage effects, and, in some instances, is showing a few additional scenes that must have been deleted after the first few performances eight years ago. Certain bits eliminated in the Chicago showings are also now included, though, if rightly recalling, the midwestern screening was somewhat more generous than the New York performance. A special "run" Tuesday morning for the authorities may have done away with a few specific episodes, though that didn't seem necessary.

D. W. Griffith, himself, has yet to surpass this effort. That includes "Intolerance," "Hearts of World," "'Way Down East" and "The Two Orphans." Many a director has taken material from "Nation" for the specials they did make or are making, which, possibly, can't be helped, because this picture holds so much—but let it be said that Griffith did his best with this one. And they've never topped it.

Reverting to the Ku Klux Klan affair in connection with "Nation" at the present time, it's the belief of any number of people this very picture with its spectacular and thrilling white masked costumed riding Klansmen, as they were in long years ago, suggested to a little crowd of coin-getters in the south, located principally at Atlanta, that the moment was opportune for a revival of the Ku Klux Klan. From that commencement, it is thought, comes the present Klan and its consequent agitation, the Klan growing beyond the money crowd, spreading all over but still remaining partially under the domination of its recreators. However, that is but a side light on "The Birth of a Nation," although the Klan's animosity against the picture brought forth the conclusion. *Skig.*

DOWN TO THE SEA IN SHIPS

Boston, Dec. 6.

Feature length drama fathered by the Whaling Film Corporation of New Bedford, Mass. Produced by Elmer Clifton. Scenario by John L. E. Pell. Raymond McKee carrying lead. Balance of cast includes William Walcott, William Cavanaugh, Leigh R. Smith, Marguerite Courtot, Elizabeth Foley, Thomas White, Juliette Courtot, Clarice Vance, Curtis Pierce, Ada Laycock, Clara Bow, James Turfler, Patrick Hartigan, J. Thornton Baston, Capt. James A. Tilton. Special score by Henry F. Gilbert and photography by Alexander G. Penrod.

Despite its amateurish cast, its indifferent photography, its crude plot and its obvious attempt to attain historical fidelity at any sacrifice of entertainment, this whaling film has displayed entirely unexpected drawing powers. Booked into the Selwyn theatre at a $1 top as a local-interest picture during a three-week gap in the legitimate bookings caused by the flop of "It's a Boy," it drew real money from a field not ordinarily invaded by feature films.

Its name, while apparently a cumbersome handicap, is apparently an asset, as a study of the faces at $1 per at the entrance indicated that the pull came from that type of citizenry who recognized Psalm 107:23-24: "They that go down to the sea in ships, that do business in great water; these see the works of the Lord and His wonders in the deep."

The film is backed by a group of ship owners, bankers, mill owners and business men in New Bedford, Mass., a historic old Massachusetts city formerly the headquarters of the world's whaling industry. The whole city was placed at the disposal of Clifton, including every historical curio in the possession of the famous Dartmouth Historical Society.

The story creaks with historical accuracy and with its methodical story of the stiff-necked Quaker ship owner of a century ago, his eloping son who is cast away on a desert island, with the baby adrift on a raft, to be recovered by the captain on one of the Quaker's whalers. The Quaker's daughter's sweetheart is unable to marry her until he kills a whale, is shanghaied aboard a whaler, saves the ship, kills his whale, locates the shipwrecked brother of his bride-to-be and returns to New Bedford just in time to battle his way through a storm and frustrate the wedding of his sweetheart to the villain. To those who love old New England of nearly a century ago and to those who love stories of the sea, and there are myriads of both, the picture will pull.

Its real novelty, however, is when the action goes into the Carribean Sea and the actual killing of a big sperm whale is portrayed with startling realism. The harpooning, the mad race of the towed whaleboat, the attack of the whale upon the boat with its ultimate upset in a shark-infested sea, are genuine thrillers, and if there is much faking, it is incredibly clever. The pictures of the approaching storm, while merely a quiet touch to the picture, gets over to applause, something that perhaps a group of clouds has never done before in a picture house. The filming of the cutting up of a whale, the slicing of the blubber, and the spectacular picture of the kettle fires burning on the decks of the whaler at night and lighting up the sky for miles with a roseate glow against a background of smoke are also unbelievably interesting.

The average film fan will remember the picture for its whale fight and for its close-ups of a dead whale and how whales are actually stripped of blubber, the sperm oil baled out of the head, and how the whale bone is hewed out of the massive mammal. It's a safe bet that nine out of ten normal fans will criticize the picture because it doesn't kill more whales and show more about how they were harpooned in the olden days, before the whaling gun and other modern safer methods of killing came into vogue.

With better photography ashore, probably missing for lack of studio facilities, and with a cast that would do some semblance of justice to the picture and to McKee, and more of the life aboard a real old whaler with a real old crew, the picture would have been a knockout. As it stands it is still a good feature film, unrolling its story as might some maritime Yankee-born Charles Dickens, ponderously, accurately, convincingly, and holding the interest of anybody who was ever held by Dickens or Gibbons or the story of the Pilgrim Fathers.

It will be interesting to see how New York takes it. *Libbey.*

HUNTING BIG GAME

San Francisco, Dec. 6.

The premiere presentation of the Snow African Expedition pictures entitled "Hunting Big Game In Africa With Gun and Camera" occurred here last week at the Century, opening that house under its new picture policy and registered an emphatic hit. This house seats 2,000 and the picture is getting $1 top.

The success of this remarkable film is the result of word of mouth advertising, for audiences repeatedly show their enthusiasm by bursting into spontaneous applause in different thrilling sections of the film. The credit for the exploitation belongs chiefly to Jack Brehany, acting for Eugene Roth who controls the film. William McStay is publicity director.

The film starts with scenes of the arrival of the Snow Expedition on the African coast with a few shots of whale hunting. Almost at the very beginning bursts a scene that brings gasps of astanishment. It shows the stamping ground of the "Jackass Penquins" with literally millions of them on every hand. Then follows a scene as the birds in their clumsy way make a mass movement into the sea.

Practically every specie of animal known to haunt the African plains and jungles are shown in their native surroundings. Many excellent closeups obtained by means of the telescopic lens give the audience a comprehensive idea of these creatures. Plenty of comedy, due chiefly to the title-writer. Scenes showing the chasing of herds of wild animals with a flivver brought many a laugh. Then there is the stalking of vicious lions and leopards and the final destruction of them with a rifle shot. One scene reveals a bull rinoceros charging the camera, head on. Thousands of baboons are revealed, trooping from the jungle to the water hole and returning like a battalion of soldiers.

The picture closes with scenes of the discovery of a herd of wild elephants in an extinct volcano crater. These huge beasts are of the killer type with the enormous ears. Some remarkable "shots" of the animals are obtained and the hunters finally bag a mammoth specimen.

There is an exceptional quality to the photography. Most of the film was developed and finished in a laboratory on wheels in the jungles of Africa. The musical score is excellent, the work of Gino Severi.

It is expected that the film will have a long run in San Francisco, after which it is to be road-showed.

OUTCAST

Famous Players, presented by Adolph Zukor, starring Elsie Ferguson; adapted from the play by Hubert Henry Davies by Josephine Lovett. Shown at the Rivoli week of Dec. 4, 1922.

Miriam....................Elsie Ferguson
Geoffrey Sherwood..........David Powell
Tony Hewlitt..............William David
Valentine Moreland........Mary MacLaren
John Moreland...........Charles Wellesley
Nellie Essex...............Teddy Sampson
De Valle....................William Powell

If recollection serves, Miss Ferguson appeared in this vehicle on the screen, as well as on the stage, at some prior time, and that this production then would come under the classification of a recreation for the picture houses. Anyway, "Outcast" is a good picture, cleverly handled to get by the censors, which the original story of the play would not have done, and supplied with a few added thrills certain to please picture house audiences.

In adapting for the screen Josephine Lovett has wiped out all the suggestion the hero and heroine lived together for a period of time after she is brought in from the streets to the bachelor apartment, where three of the boys are knocking over a few tall ones. Instead she has her in from the streets within a few hours after she decided to lead a life of shame and before she has had time to fall. Instead of being in the same apartment as a mistress of the hero of the tale she is the business partner who has brains and is making enough money to furnish her own apartment on Park avenue.

All of this is fair enough as far as the picture goes, but it is also the direction of Chet Withey and the playing of David Powell opposite Miss Ferguson that get over the picture. Powell is coming along like a house afire in his last few pictures, and if ever any one was ripe for starring honors in the male division, he appears to be the logical candidate at this time.

The balance of the cast as far as the real action is concerned amounts to little. Mary MacLaren as Valentine Moreland tries to assume that blase inertness that Katherine MacDonald affects, and loses out by it. It is only a couple of years ago that this girl looked like the biggest bet that the screen had had in some time, but evidently association and an aptitude of assimilating mannerism through it seemingly has stopped her from going forward as she should have. Teddy Sampson handles a bit in the picture rather cleverly; William Powell is a fairly good bet as a South American. *Fred.*

LORNA DOONE

R. D. Blackmore's famous romance, done into screen form by Maurice Tourneur. Released by First National. Directed by Tourneur. Photography by Harry Sharp. At the Strand, Dec. 3.

Lorna Doone...............Madge Bellamy
John Ridd.....................John Bowers
Sir Ensor Doone.............Frank Keenan
"The Counsellor"..........Jack MacDonald
Carver Doone...........Donald MacDonald
Ruth ....Norris Johnson
Lorna, as a child...............May Giracci
John, as a child.............Charles Hatton

If there is anywhere in the whole scale of literature an idyllic romance of young love, it is this simple, honest, unsophisticated tale. Done into screen form with a fairly adequate presentation, its fate takes on special interest, for it puts to the test the argument of many commentators on the picture against sensational sex and problem plays. If the fans want poetic romance in its most colorful form, here it is in large proportions, in a work of fiction that has stood the test of time and supported by generations of romance lovers of all ages and varieties.

Pictorially, the film is a splendid effort, although it has most of the faults of dramatized books, principally that it is episodic in its dramatic unity and is loosely knit. The story is jumpy, with disconcerting leaps from the village of the robber Doones to the peaceful valley nearby, thence to 17th century, London and back again. These transitions are trying enough, but there is ample compensation in the thrill of separate episodes, such as the battle of the yeomen and the robbers, the spectacle of the Royal christening and others.

Tourneur has managed to achieve a dignified and convincing atmosphere of romance in ancient times. The accoutrements strike one as authentic and the spirit of the production creates a satisfactory illusion, no mean feat in realizing for the eye a story that has lived until now only in the imagination. But the issue before the film public is more than production methods. The question is how will it respond to a poetic love story typical of the old-fashioned school.

The picture is well acted. Madge Bellamy has just the right wistful quality of beauty for Lorna, daughter of the nobility, abducted and forced to live among the brutal robbers, and Frank Bowers realizes fairly well the Blackmore hero, John Ridd, strongest and bravest of romantic heroes. The histrionic honors, however, go to that best of character portrait makers, Frank Keenan, as Sir Ensor Doone.

The scenic features of the picture have been splendidly managed. The stage coach inn might have been lifted from an authentic print of the times. The spirited passage of the coach robbery on the seashore is a smashing bit of pictorial emphasis and the action in the robbers' village is scenically impressive. So is the ceremonial pageantry of the royal christening and the marriage of the hero and heroine in the village church. Misted photography is used to fine effect and the backgrounds are always beautiful. *Rush.*

A BLIND BARGAIN

Goldwyn production, starring Lon Chaney and directed by Wallace Worsley. Barry Pain is the author, with the scenario having been adapted from a story of his. At the Capitol, New York, Dec. 3.

Dr. Lamb / The Hunchback ....Lon Chaney
Robert.......................Raymond McKee
Angela.....................Jacqueline Logan
Mrs. Lamb..................Fontaine LaRue
Mrs. Sandell.......Virginia True Boardman
Bessie..........................Aggie Herring
Angela's mother...........Virginia Madison

Another addition to the "horror" situation so prevalent in fiction, theatre and on the screen for the past year. The script is shy of originality in plot and in telling, seemingly having borrowed numerous instances from at least one novel, as well as a stage production which has only been out of New York about three weeks. Somewhat fantastic, it takes a bit of stretching of the imagination to swallow this story, and beyond the work of the star himself there is nothing to raise this film above the average feature.

It deals with a prominent surgeon who is a fanatic on prolonging the life of man, and to this end carries on secretive experiments with human subjects. A hidden operating room, paneled passages and iron barred cells, where the subjects of previous failures are kept, are all included in the screening. The main topic is of a young former A. E. F. sergeant, made destitute by the war, offering his services to the surgeon without knowing what he is getting into in compensation for an operation which will save his mother's life. One of the results of Dr. Lamb's experiments, a hunchback, who has reverted back to the half ape stage of development, is kept at the house as an assistant. The wife and this half animal constantly attempt to frustrate the doctor's plans.

The ex-soldier is pulled away from a charity ball by the surgeon and taken to the house for the fulfillment of his bargain. Morning is to see the operation performed, but the hunchback reveals to the youngster the predicament he is in, though being discovered in the act, and the mad physician decides to go through with it immediately. It leads to a struggle, with the youngster being overpowered and strapped to the table, after which the doc goes into the alleyway between the cells to get the hunchback. The degenerated human pushes a spring which releases a crazed physical giant, another specimen that failed, who attacks the surgeon and kills him by brute force.

The latter scene is the kick, revealed in flashes of the struggle and by the facial expressions of the hunchback. Love interest has been interspersed through an affair between the former "doughboy" and a girl with the concluding footage, showing the mother entirely recovered, the boy and girl married and a publishing company accepting the story of the actual experience.

Chaney, doubling as the doctor and the hunchback, gives a creditable performance and allows for some double photography that is by no means unworthy of mention. Always at his best in a grotesque make-up, Chaney predominates in the character of the man-ape, using the ungainly lope of the supposed animal as a means of locomotion throughout the interpretation of the character. Other than that the cast is just ordinary and lends no noticeable support. The production runs almost entirely to interiors, with the scene of the charity ball being the most lavish so far as settings are concerned. Colored photography is used to enhance the scene, though it is questionable if it helped materially the picture as a whole.

The Sunday night audience at the Capitol, generally demonstrative if the feature is to their liking, accepted the "Bargain" calmly, minus an applause finish. *Skig.*

LUCKY DAN

Phil Goldstone production, starring Richard Talmadge, released by Capital Pictures. Story by W. A. Levey, directed by Wm. Curran. A western shown at Loew's New York, N. Y., on double-feature bill.

Lucky Dan.....................Richard Talmadge
Rose Chapman.................Dorothy Woods
Buck Chapman.................G. A. Williams
Slim Connor......................S. E. Jennings
Slippery Joe..................Ernest Van Pelt

One of the usual type of Richard Talmadge westerns, not better or worse than the others designed for the small houses where the nickel and dime admission prevails. At Loew's New York it was the weak sister on the program, which held "What's Wrong With the Women?"

The author chose formula No. 1 for his picture—the old rancher with a daughter and a mortgage on his ranch. The heavy holds the mortgage and wants to marry the girl. The hero has no dough, but gets wealthy in time to save the ranch for the girl's father and the girl for himself.

It's the old, worn and thousand-times told tale without a single new twist to make it different in the slightest, and to the New York's audience the picture seemed like a comedy. There were at least three different touches in the picture that would have been good sight gags for any comedian in films.

Talmadge does all his usual tricks, such as leaping to the back of a horse from the ground and into moving automobiles and out again in the self-same manner that he has done in any number of other pictures. At best he is just a fair imitation of Fairbanks when he did that western stuff in the old Triangle days, and Talmadge is far from being even a good imitation. With better story material he might stand a chance of developing a following in the bigger and better daily change houses, but with what they are handing him for production he can't get started.

There is a lot of riding stuff and three or four fights. It seemed that whenever the director got to a point where he didn't know what to do next he would either have Talmadge whip three or four other members of the cast or else jump on a horse's back and lead them a chase.

The matter of production did not call for any great expense. Three interiors are all that are used. All are cheap one-room sets and all the other scenes were shot outdoors.

Fred.

THE SUPER SEX

Frank R. Adams production from the Cosmopolitan story of "Miles Brewster and the Super Sex" by Adams. Adapted and directed by Lambert Hillyer. Distributed by American Releasing. Shown at the Cameo, week Dec. 4, 1922.

Miles Brewster Higgins......Robert Gordon
Irene Hayes..............Charlotte Pierce
Mr. Higgins................Tully Marshal.
Mrs. Higgins..................Lydia Knott
Grandma Brewster.......Gertrude Claire
Cousin Roy............Albert MacQuarrie
J. Gordon Davis..........Louis Natheaux
Mr. Hayes...................George Bunny
Mrs. Hayes...................Evelyn Burns

After viewing this picture one wonders how and why the young American Releasing Corp. secured it, when the older and perhaps bigger distributing organizations in the field are clamoring so loudly for good picture productions. This one is a good one, no matter from what angle you look at it. It is better than some of the early real good Charlie Ray pictures and a production of the same type. It is cast perfectly, it is directed finely, and it is a picture good and strong enough to play any one of the big pre-release houses and not only satisfy audiences but pull business, because it is a picture that will get word of mouth advertising.

In it Lambert Hillyer seemingly has done something for pictures which in its way is almost as great as the close-up. From this time on one can expect to get a follow up on his idea of splitting action with a spoken title by almost anyone of the directors, for it is a real advancement and the only one that has come along since the close-up. Talking pictures? No, not in the fullest sense of the word, but as near talk as one can get without the words actually beign uttered.

Hillyer takes his characters and starts them on a speech. In the centre of it he givs the spoken title, following it with the character concluding the speech. And you don't have to be a lip reader to get what is uttered even before the title is flashed, so well do the speeches fit into the action.

Incidentally in Robert Gordon, who plays Miles Brewster. Hillyer seems to have picked a boy destined to land as big as Ray did in the matter of personal popularity, providing he has in his next couple of pictures, direction as capable as that which he had the advantage of in this picture. The Irene Hayes contributed by Charlotte Pierce is likewise as clever a piece of work as that which Gordon does. How Booth Tarkington will love both of these two young people on the screen and figure how much he would have liked to have had them characterizing his youngsters of fiction.

As for the story it is one of those that they rave about but seldom get. Clean, wholesome with a delightful vein of comedy, a cleverly handled love story of youth, in a wonderful background of small town home atmosphere.

No matter where your theatre and less matter the kind of theatre it is, from the highest and smartest to the smallest and cheapest, you can't go wrong with this one, your audiences will love it. *Fred.*

DAUGHTER OF LUXURY

Adolph Zukor presents Agnes Ayres in "A Daughter of Luxury"; adapted by Beula Marie Dix from the play, "The Impostor," by Leonard Merrick and Michael Morton. Directed by Paul Powell. At the New York Rialto, Dec. 4.

Mary Fenton....................Agnes Ayres
Blake Walford................Tom Gallery
Ellen Marsh......................Edith Yorke
Bill Marsh................Howard Ralston
Loftus Walford.........Edward Martindel
Mrs. Walfrod................Sylvia Ashton
Rod Conroy..............Clarence Burton
Mary Corgrove......................Zasu Pitts
Charlie Owen...............Robert Schable
Winnie........................Bernice Frank
Genevieve Fowler.........Dorothy Gordon
Nancy...........................Muriel MacCormic

A society comedy-drama is here presented neatly. It has a capital thread of romance, an agreeable flavoring of comedy and character drawing and telling comedy complications. The defect is that it is a talky play in the first place and here is struggling with the unhappy medium of pantomime.

The result is little action and long passages of draggy developments, most of which are disclosed via titles. However, it does build up to a satisfying climax and the last reel is the best of the five, leaving a pleasing final effect in the happy working out of a tangle of misunderstandings. A lot of rather trifling people are concerned in the principal incidents, the only sympathetic characters being the young lover and the heiress out of luck, who really are subordinated to the parallel story of a domestic mixup that really should form the basis of a farce instead of a polite comedy drama.

The progress of the romance is constantly interrupted and overshadowed by the introduction of extraneous matter, and in the summing up it seems that the love story has been slighted in favor of a society satire in which the young lovers are not vitally concerned. The young people are interesting. The elders are not.

Mary Fenton, so the story runs, is reduced to temporary poverty by a law suit over her inheritance. She has just been evicted from her hall bedroom for non-payment of rent. The Walford family are nouveau riche, a little vulgar and selfish in their precarious wealth. The young son returns from cow punching in the west, a wholesome unspoiled youngster, who declines to agree to his parents' plan to marry him off to a rich wife, sister-in-law of a cousin who married for money.

Mary walks the streets homeless and in famished desperation strikes up an acquaintance with the cousin at a fashionable hotel entrance. She is invited to dinner, and being seen in the cousin's company is palmed off as his wife's sister. From this start, Mary is presently installed in the Walford home, more by force of circumstance than her own scheming. Papa and Mamma Walford plot to throw Mary and the boy together for the benefit of the family fortune. The son falls in love, but is restrained by the girl's supposed wealth and his own poverty and things are at an impasse when the real sister-in-law appears on the scene.

The instant the son learns that their now unwelcome guest is penniless he makes violent love and is accepted just in time to learn that she is in fact disgustingly rich. There is an episode of a jewel robbery, of which Mary is accused, and this adds to the complications and heightens the surprise twist which is rather violently brought at the end. The long arm of coincidence is pretty well worked throughout the piece, and there are times when one becomes a bit dizzy keeping up to the astonishing happenings, such as the husband picking out two strangers to rob his house so that he can collect the insurance and the circumstance that the chief robber is a rooming house friend of the heroine and comes in pat at the right minute to save her from the police.

These screen coincidences have to be gulped down quickly or they choke. That's the kind of picture it is. It won't bear close inspection, but if you don't examine its plausibility too closely, it passes for entertainment. *Rush.*

KENTUCKY DERBY

Universal-Jewel production adapted from the play by Charles T. Dazey, "The Suburban." The scenario is by George Hull; photography by Victor Milner; directed by King Baggott; at B. F. Moss' Broadway, Dec. 5.

Donald Gordon.............Reginald Denny
Alice Brown...................Lillian Rich
Col. Moncrief Gordon........Emmett King
Ralph Gordon.............Walter McGrail
Helen Gordon...............Gertrude Astor
Col. Romo Woolrich........Lionel Belmore
Joe Rance..............Kingsley Benedict
Newcombe...................Bert Woodruff
Topper Tom......................Bert Tracy
Bob Thurston................Harry Carter
Capt. Wolff...................Wilfred Lucas
Jensen...........................Pat Harmon
Mrs. Clancy..............Anna Hernandez
Timmy Clancy...............Verne Winter

This is a pip of a meller featuring Reginald Denny, who is crashing into prominence through the medium of athletic scenarios and a clean, manly personality. The scenario from the old melodramatic play, "The Suburban," allows the director ample scope for action, hinged around the universally appealing horse race and thoroughbred.

The screen version follows the play somewhat, but shakes off the restrictions of the speaking stage when the hero is shanghaied and kept prisoner aboard a sailing vessel for three years. A pair of villains aided and abetted by a sea captain (muchly resembling Jack London's famous sea bully, and also named Wolf) succeed in estranging Donald Gordon from his father, Col. Moncrief Gordon, a Kentucky breeder of thoroughbreds.

The crooks steal $20,000 from the Gordon safe, throwing suspicion on young Gordon, who has just been disowned by the Colonel for marrying the girl of his, and not his father's choice. Gordon is kidnaped after being blackjacked in a sailors' lodging house in New York, and kept on the sailing vessel for three years. His young wife doesn't despair, and is finally awarded when Gordon escapes after saving Wolf's life in a shipwreck. On his death bed on an island in the China Sea Wolf confesses his duplicity to Gordon. The latter returns in time to frustrate the schemers who bribed the jockey named to ride the Colonel's horse in the Derby.

Gordon switches jockeys at the last moment, after appealing in vain to his father and informing him of the plot. "Duke Charles" wins, saving the Colonel from financial ruin. The crooks are arrested on a warrant from the New York police at the psychological moment.

The story has several discrepancies which will not be noticed by the average picture fan. It is an interesting tale, splendidly cast. Gertrude Astor was almost too beautiful to be so villainous, but gave a convincing performance. Lillian Rich was sweet and appealing as the young wife, and Denny was manly and virile as the center of the maelstrom of the connivings of the confidence gang that had wormed their way into his father's favor by posing as distant cousins.

The photography was excellent, the race being exceptionally well blended. A real race was taken with frequent cut-backs to show "Duke Charles" and "Twilight" fighting it out neck and neck for the $10,000 wager. The splicing was masterly.

It's a sure coin getter for the pop priced picture houses. As a program release it achieves special feature proportions. *Con.*

WHAT'S WRONG WITH WOMEN

Produced by Daniel Carson Goodman for Equity and released in the state's rights market. Story and script by D. C. Goodman, directed by R. William Neil. Six reels. Shown at Loew's New York, N. Y., on double feature bill.

James Bascom..............Wilton Lackaye
Mrs. Bascom..........Julia Swayne Gordon
Elise Bascom...........Constance Bennett
James Belden................Montagu Love
Jack Lee......................Rod La Rocque
Janet Lee...............Barbara Castleton
Baby Lee.........................Helen Roland
Mrs. Neer.......................Hedda Hopper
Lloyd Watson..............Huntley Gordon
John Matthews..............Paul McAllister
A Friend.........Mrs. Oscar Hammerstein

One flash at this production and it is easily seen that Daniel Carson Goodman started out to make a super-special. In this he failed, but he did turn out a whale of a program picture that in entertainment value stands out. The exhibitor that takes this picture can either do a lot of business or none at all, just on how he handles the exploitation. It is a picture that offers untold opportunities in an advertising way, especially in the small towns and cities, and there is where it ought to clean up.

The story deals with the unrest among the women of today. Their constant quest of a thrill, no matter if they are among the wealthy or among the middle class, their general dissatisfied frame of mind over their own status in life, which eventually leads to the breaking up of homes and unhappiness. In a sense it is a sermon, but on the screen the theme is carried out interestingly.

In cast the producer has gone the limit in the matter of names, and here certainly is a picture that one can bill practically as all-star. In production he has not stinted, and the picture shows that there was a lot of money spent on it.

Jack Lee (Rod La Rocque) is a young architect employed in the office of Bascom (Wilton Lackaye). His home life is ideal, his wife being a good helpmate until she gets in with a grass widow who lives in the same apartment house. Then she starts moving in a fast set and the family goes to smash. Lee's employer, a $50,000 a year man, has no better luck in his family, and in both cases it is the women folk of the family that are the cause of the trouble. Through it all there is a carpenter who lives in the basement of the apartment house of the Lees who portrays a character akin to Jesus, and in a quiet way he is the factor in straightening out the affairs of the Lees, while the Bascom family likewise comes to see the light, and all ends happily.

The cast without exception is good, and La Rocque, Barbara Castleton, Lackaye and Hedda Hopper all score. Mrs. Oscar Hammerstein, the widow of the theatre builder and grand opera impresario, did a bit as a souse that landed. In introducing the characters, however, there is nothing to indicate who is playing the various roles, and this makes it rather difficult to the average picturegoer to distinguish who is who.

Fred.

ALTAR STAIRS

This Universal feature has Frank Mayo looking like a mirror reflection of Wallace Reid. Seemingly all that U. will have to do is to furnish Mayo with a line of Reid stories and they will develop this star to an extent where he will be in line to steal all of Reid popularity at the box office. This picture is an interesting one that will please the majority of audiences in the daily change of program houses, but not strong enough to make the grade on three-day or week run.

It is a story of the south seas with Mayo the captain on a trading schooner. He is employed by a company that operates from one of the principal islands. On the island that is the home port there is a girl with whom the captain falls in love and although she seemingly returns his affection she refuses to marry him. The reason being she has been secretly wed to a chap who has developed into a bad boy. Through picture coincidence this husband is one of the crew the captain has on board his ship slated to act as the company's agent on one of the islands.

On this island a parson has set up a church and convinced the natives they should embrace Christianity, they accepting his teachings until the trading post man takes up his residence on the island. He informed the chief that he might just as well return to his former mode of life and take unto himself as many wives as he cares to have and to eat, drink and be merry, in the meantime copping a native girl for himself. This leads to his undoing, for on the night that there is a celebration over the return to former conditions, the trading boat arrives and the captain ascertains what has been done and that the cause of the general disturbance is also the no account husband of the woman he loves. A fight follows in which the captain is worsted and the offender makes his escape, only to be tracked by the native who was turned down by the girl when the white trader made a fuss over her.

There is some corking sea stuff in the picture and a couple of native island touches that make the picture worth while. Dagmar Godowsky makes corking looking native vamp, who goes about her business as though she enjoyed it.

The title "Altar Stairs" refers to the fact that the heroine of the picture left her husband immediately after they were wed. With his death she naturally takes the second trip to the altar with Mayo. *Fred.*

STREETS OF N. Y.

A Burton King production, which has no bearing whatever on the title, selected undoubtedly for its attractiveness, other than through the introduction of a number of sectional views of Greater New York, which precedes the unfolding of a weird, almost impossible melodramatic yarn, and one that is neither interest-bearing nor sensational, except, possibly, near the finale. Then a rather good flood scene is shown with the principals struggling in the water in an overturned shanty, which tumbles down a falls, ending the story and adjusting the complications.

Just why the streets of New York, Coney Island, Ellis Island or any other portion of the metropolic was selected for the title and shown in chopped views is problematical.

The story deals with the history of a crooked banker, who saves bankruptcy and ruin by lifting $100,-000, placed in his hands by a sea captain. Immediately after banking this sum, the captain returns and demands it, but upon being refused, conveniently dies of heart disease.

The banker and his chief clerk have the secret between them, the banker keeping the money and the clerk the receipt for it, which he deftly lifts from the dead man's pockets.

Years later, we see the banker's daughter grown up, a charitably-inclined girl, pretty, etc. Also the sea captain's widow and crippled boy, crippled in an auto accident in which the banker's daughter was the passenger. The mother is a weak, haggard old woman, who scrubs floors for a living. The director has her placed in the banker's office. Then dispossess proceedings. The boy, a street violinist, meets the banker's daughter, a love affair and the flood scene, which culminates in their marriage and the straightening of the banker's business deal, the son getting his father's money, of course, while the banker and his chief clerk rush to their death over the waterfall.

It is a penny thriller, and a poor one at that. What acting is offered is of the average type, with the girl shining in this department. The interior scenes are all of the conventional sort, well set, but nothing exceptional. As a feature picture,

this is just one of those passing things that fill a program, but mean nothing at the gate.

Its title, misleading, of course, shows the producer's sagacity, for such a title carries some value as a magnet, even though it has no relation to the subject pictured. It failed to arouse any enthusiasm at Loew's State Monday and beyond the water scene has nothing to recommend it. *Wynn.*

THE BEAUTIFUL AND DAMNED

Presented by the Warner Brothers from the novel of the same name by F. Scott Fitzgerald. Olga Printzau did the adapting for the screen and William A. Seiter directed. At the Strand, Dec. 10.

CAST

Gloria	Marie Prevost
Anthony	Kenneth Harlan
Dick	Harry Myers
Adam Patch	Tully Marshall
Muriel	Louise Frazenda
Dot	Cleo Ridgeley
Mr. Gilbert	Emmett King
Hull	Walter Long
Bloeckman	Clarence Burton
Maury	Parker McConnell

Probably will have some drawing power at the box office because of the novel, but the picture isn't there. It screens as mostly a catch-as-catch-can presentation of the story, neither covering the territory which the bound edition did nor is it as interesting. Besides "The Beautiful and Damned" is not generally conceded to be Fitzgerald's best work. Additional attention to detail might have helped the adaptation as a picture, but it simply flicks along, causing no undue interest at the beginning and soon settles itself into an average feature. The title is the film's best asset.

It's a free translation, from the print to the screen, much having been deleted and a few liberties taken with the script. Not advantageously. Kenneth Harlan does nicely, so far as appearance goes, as Anthony Patch, the youthful idler. Marie Prevost, opposite, as the social butterfly who marries and then ruins him through extravagance, is appealing to the eye, though her work would hardly be called convincing. Whatever honors there are go to Tully Marshall, always dependable, as the grandfather, and Harry Myers as a serious novelist with a decided leaning towards his liquor. Louise Frazenda and Walter Long are also included in the line-up for small bits.

The picture is unquestionably standard, so far as photography and settings are concerned. Some of the interiors and the action are almost entirely indoors.

The story follows the career of young Patch, who won't work and merely is stalling until his wealthy grandfather sees fit to pass away. The old gentleman is obstinate on this subject, and when cornering his grandson as to just what he meant to do, the boy says he intends to write a history of the world. As a means to this end he marries Gloria. Thereafter starts a regularly formed habit of "stew parties," concluding in the young married couple moving to the country in an attempt to get away from their willing guests. Anthony actually does some work for two months on his proposed history edition, when the girl suggests one of the old parties to relieve the monotony. It's framed up and in full sway when the grandfather happens in, takes one look and goes out to return home, and, shortly afterwards, dies. The hilarity witnessed ruined whatever chance "Tony" had with his old relative and the will leaves him a blessing and a dollar.

The edict forces the young couple back to town, where most of their remaining financial means are thrown into a law suit to fight the will. Meanwhile, Anthony spends the surplus for booze, and Gloria, finding herself up against it, starts to do some work around the house. It all clears up, before the youth actually becomes a drunkard, by the law suit breaking the will and the conclusion sees the couple on a steamer bound for foreign lands.

Seiter, in directing, has done nothing out of the ordinary with this release. He seemed to pass up one or two instances in the book which might have made good material for the camera. But, then, that may also have been the fault of the scenario writer. Either way, the film won't be conducive to Fitzgerald for future subjects of his that might be screened, though it does

seem that his "This Side of Paradise" would have made a better subject, because of the logical finish of that story, if nothing else.

As a money-making proposition, "The Beautiful and Damned" is a possibility because of the circulation the novel had, but it's almost a surety the picture won't drive anyone into a bookstore to procure the story in its original form. *Skig.*

BROKEN CHAINS

Allen Holubar production, story by Winifred Kimball, presented by Goldwyn. Reviewed at Capitol, New York, Dec. 10.

Peter Wyndham	Malcolm McGregor
Mercy Boone	Colleen Moore
Boyan Boone	Ernest Torrence
Hortense Allen	Claire Windsor
Pat Mulcahy	James Marcus
Mrs. Mulcahy	Beryl Mercer
Slog Sallee	William Orlamond
Butler	Gerald Pring
Burglar	Edward Peil
Gus	Leo Willis

This is the scenario that won the Chicago "Daily News" contest, which carried a prize of $30,000, according to the advance publicity given "Broken Chains." If this be "de trut" it's a soft racket. No wonder the average human feels that he has within him the talents for potential greatness as a screen author.

Either the author or the director is responsible for one of the most preposterous and ridiculous fight scenes on the sheet. It occurs between the hero and heavy in a cabin on a mountain and lasts for oceans of footage. After tossing the hero through a window at the end of a wild battle the villain sinks exhausted upon a bed, only to sit up a moment later with eyes popping as his recent adversary staggers back in the room via the front door.

During this mad scramble, embellished with all the tricks of realism up to a certain point, the heroine, a child-wife of the "brute," is forced to watch the struggle between her lover and brutal spouse while chained to the floor. Her effort to reach a gun discarded by the villain was particularly well done and her emotional responses to the tide of battle almost saved it from ridiculousness, but not quite.

A bridge leading to the mountain retreat was the director's downfall in this instance. The bridge had been sawed off and tampered with by the villain, Boyan Boone (Ernest Torrance) in such a manner that by stepping on a certain board the whole structure fell into a mountain stream beneath.

The cowardly youth who had regained his manhood in his own lumber camp, Peter Wyndham (Malcolm McGregor), had destroyed the bridge after removing all chances for escape and after he had wrestled with his cowardness, inspired by love for the girl, but determined to die at the hands of her brutal husband, letting the law avenge him and liberate the girl.

At the conclusion of the terrific battle between the rivals the director has them break the world's "rolling" record by rolling what appears to be an eighth of an mile down hill to arrive at the edge of the stream. The hero wrestles the villain over the edge to a watery grave and turns to embrace the girl, who has broken the links which bound her.

Another incongruous touch was a "money" bit. The girl, who has made an ineffectual attempt to escape from her captor, tells Wyndham the story. She has an aunt in Nebraska to whom she could go. Wyndham tells her he has $10,000 in a local bank. He makes an appointment to meet her next day. This is overheard by her husband's partner in crime, who informs the bandit. Wyndham appears at the rendezvous with five grand, the balance being in the bank. The husband takes the money away from the wife after forcing Wyndham to give it to her. To make it more even, the bandits rob the bank and are chased by a posse to their mountain retreat, where another battle is staged. Five thousand fish is some carfare, even in Nebraska.

The picture is excellently cast. Colleen Moore as the girl-wife rose to unusual heights emotionally. Her touches were sure and flawless. Torrence as the bearded ruffian was splendid. William Orlamond as the lumber camp vagabond was the comedy relief and scored repeatedly. McGregor as the cowardly rich boy who overcomes his early environment was convincing. His athletic prowness during the "fight" was high class.

The story runs along conventional lines until the lumber camp episode, which destroys whatever chance it has for a successful dramatic conclusion. A large Sunday night audience at the Capitol "kidded" the fight stuff and the last shots of what started out to be a corking picture.

Nick Carter, the James boys or Dick Merriwell in their palmiest days never staged a more preposterous battle. *Con.*

THIRTY DAYS

Jesse L. Lasky presents this feature starring Wallace Reid. Adapted from the play by A. E. Thomas and Clayton Hamilton by Walter Woods. Directed by James Cruze. At the Rivoli, Dec. 10.

John Floyd......................Wallace Reid
Lucille Ledyard..................Wanda Hawley
Judge Hooker.....................Charles Ogle
Huntley Palmer................Cyril Chadwick
Polenta........................Herschell Mayall
Mrs. Floyd......................Helen Dunbar
Carlotta.......................Carmen Phillips
Warden...........................Kalla Pasha

Wallace Reid makes a sad affair of this nondescript picture. The story never makes up its mind whether it is going to be a comedy, a travesty, a farce or a Mack Sennett burlesque. For screen treatment the thing should have been done in a spirit of farce and with another star, for Reid is no farceur. Probably the man they should have had was Harold Lloyd. He could have done something with the picture. Reid merely went through a set of motions as dictated by a director, and his performance is without spontaneity or vigor.

It is a case of a player out of his element. Reid has gained his position on the screen for the handling of breezy, slap-dash romantic parts with a tang of daring and plenty of zip. Here he is a helpless sort of timid boob, the victim of circumstances over which he has no control—in short, a made-to-order part for Lloyd.

The producer several times goes off at a tangent. The story opens as a polite romantic comedy, and, although it is dull enough in these passages, the picture is in the Reid style. After that it goes into the broadest farce, with several incidents that are nothing more than Mack Sennett comedy chase bits, toned down somewhat in deference to the polite background of the story. The net result is that the picture isn't frank knockabout on the one hand, and it isn't high comedy. It's just a clumsy combination of both without the honest appeal of either. And, besides, it has the unforgivable defect that it is dull.

John, the inveterate flirt, is accepted by Lucille on condition that he swear off flirtations for 30 days. To keep him occupied she busies him with the role of assistant in her settlement work. John attempts to comfort a tenement house woman and is caught in what appears a compromising situation by her high-tempered Italian husband, who threatens horrible murder. To avoid arrest for a stabbing affair the Italian has to take refuge in a quiet job, and as luck will have it, secures the situation of butler in the home of John's mother.

Terrified by the threat of Mafia vengeance, John takes the advice of Judge Hooker, a family friend, and gets himself committed to jail for 30 days, by which time the affair will have blown over and the Italian will have sailed, but the latter gets into trouble and is incarcerated in the same jail. An idea of the farcical complications laboriously erected may be gained from the fact that Lucille's uplift work brings her to the same jail where our hero has to think fast to explain the situation and at the same time ward off the attacks of the Italian.

The complications in the latter half of the picture are ingeniously managed and for a time the top is kept spinning, thanks to the employment of custard pie technique, but things taper off to a mild and tepid finish.

Its four reels of uncertain effort are rewarded by one reel of knockabout and half a dozen thin laughs, which, by the way, is usually the final count on a five-reel farce. Why a multiple-reel farce, anyway, for use on a program that customarily has a two-reel comic anyway?

It is so at the Rivoli. Snub Pollard is the hero of one of those slam-bang two-reelers. It's coarser but funnier than the Reid effort, and contains as much meat in less than half the footage. A mild five-reeler can't compete with a two-reeler of the same kind and on the same bill, and that's about the trouble this picture is going to have during its natural life. *Rush.*

PAWNED

Production by J. Parker Read, Jr. Distributed by Select. Story by Frank L. Packard, author of "The Miracle Man." Picture directed by Irvin V. Willat. Tom Moore starred with Edith Roberts opposite. At the New York, Dec. 8.

"Pawned" is a high class romantic melodrama with all sorts of ingenious twists and surprises, and it is all done in a capital spirit of neat comedy, without pretence or bunk. The play develops casually and naturally, with high suspense, and ends in a whale of a melodramatic climax well worth the five reels of attention. The picture has pretty nearly all an adventure film play should have; romance, stirring incident, real and interesting characterizations; a beginning that nails attention and a whale of a finish. That makes a score approaching 100 per cent.

The story begins in the South Sea islands, but is quickly on the wing. Bruce, a gentleman adventurer and soldier of fortune, is down on his luck. He engages to undertake an investigation of a chain of gambling clubs in America on behalf of the owner, who happens at the time to be on the other side of the world. That ends the South Seas chapter.

Arriving in New York, he starts to play the wheel in one of the clubs. Another player goes broke and tries to borrow a stake from the manager. The manager won't lend money, but he suggests a "Trip to Persia," a mysterious catch phrase that leads to developments. Bruce declares himself broke, and is also invited to the "Trip to Persia," which turns out to be a visit to a trick pawnshop rigged up in a traveling taxicab, the presiding genius of which is pretty Claire. The bizarre experience and the pretty face catch Bruce's fancy and he follows the girl to her home. Becoming involved in a street fight, he is wounded and takes refuge in the girl's apartment, maintained by her supposed father, barred by an unjust conviction from running a licensed pawnshop and forced to the taxi expedient.

Bruce is dangerously wounded and in a way to die, when Claire calls in a drug fiend surgeon to tend him. The doctor agrees to save the stranger's life only on condition that Claire become his wife. This is the least plausible incident in the play, although it is skillfully smoothed over by the argument that the girl has fallen in love at sight with the agreeable stranger. The surgeon, a renegade and social outlaw, has long laid seige to the girl.

When Bruce has recovered the struggle begins—Bruce to win the girl for himself and save her from the drug fiend, and the surgeon to compel her to keep her pledge. It would be unfair to unfold the plot. Enough that its swiftly moving turns and twists make a brisk and thrilling five-reeler of underworld plotting and intrigue and a heroic defense and counter plot. There is one clever incident built around the hero's capture by the crooks who force him to act as decoy for the rich club owner, summoned from half way across the world, his scheme to defeat the plan by the use of a chemical ink that comes out only when touched by salt water.

The people are made extremely real. There is one dandy character, an old cab driver, an honest old fellow, but with a soul in pawn to drink. He serves to give the climax an additional punch. The finish is a whale of a dramatic surprise. The cabman has the villian and the heroine (who is really his own daughter) in his taxicab, taking them, as he supposes to their wedding. As they are waiting at the ferryhouse he makes the resolve that the marriage shall not take place. So he drives off the ferry slip, cab and all, and the final close-up has the hero rescuing the heroine while the old cabman is shown in a tricky close-up (done by means of a glass tank) holding the villian under water in the cab. It's a high-powered kick to a colorful picture play. *Rush.*

MIXED FACTS

A William Fox production starring William Russell. Story by Roy Norton; adapted by Paul Schofield; directed by Rowland V. Lee. A short five-reeler. Shown at Loew's, New York, on double feature bill.

Judge J. Woodworth Granger..........
..........................William Russell
Jimmy Gallop...............William Russell
Miss Sayre.......................Rene Adoree
Murray McGuire..........De Witt Jennings
Mrs. Sayre..............Elizabeth Garrison
Mr. Sayre....................Charles French
Mrs. Molly Crutcher........Eileen Manning

A rather fair program feature in which William Russell plays a dual role, which has him as a rather up-stage self-important candidate for political office and then as a flip traveling salesman given to practical jokes. The combination works out rather well in an interesting manner in the development of the story, for while the Judge wins the political office he is after, the salesman wins the girl that was engaged to him. After all, that is what matters to a moving picture audience, who gets the girl and why he gets her.

This is a comedy-drama of small town stuff and as such it will get by anywhere in the daily change houses. It isn't strong enough for a longer run than that anywhere.

Rowland V. Lee handled the direction rather cleverly and with his camera man has the girl walk through a double exposure in which he has Russell on one side of the picture as the Judge and on the other as the salesman, with the girl walking away from the former and going to the arms of the latter. That was a clever piece of trick work done, and it is done almost so smoothly that the average picture house audience won't get the dividing line.

Russell and Rene Adoree walk away with about all there is to the picture, although DeWitt Jennings makes a corking political boss. *Fred.*

BULLDOG DRUMMOND

London, Nov. 28.

Produced by Oscar Apfel from a scenario by B. E. Doxatt-Pratt, this film version of "Sapper's" great melodrama is one of the finest pictures screened in this country. In the 6,700 feet there is no superfluous footage. The continuity excellent and the thrills, of which there are many, are effective.

Although made in Holland with an international company for Astra, the English atmosphere has been wonderfully preserved.

The story tells how Captain Drummond, bored by post-war inactivity, inserts an advertisement asking for a job which has some excitement in it. It is answered by Phyllis Harden, whose uncle is in the grip of an international gang of crooks who run a bogus nursing home. Drummond agrees to help her. The gang have kidnapped Hiram C. Travers, an American shipping king, and by torture are trying to make him sign away an enormous sum of money. Ordered to forge Travers' signature, Phyllis' uncle shoots himself. The plot thickens and Drummond is soon on the trail.

Then, through countless thrills and breathless situations, the story develops until the gang is vanquished and Drummond gives up his craving for excitement in his love for Phyllis.

Not the least of the attractions of this fine picture are the subtitles. These are always concise and witty. The casting is far above the average and the acting brilliant throughout. Carlyle Blackwell is excellent as Drummond, although of an extremely different type to the original Sir Gerald du Maurier. From first to last he never loses his grip, and whether he is fighting, bluffing or making love, his characterization lives. Horace de Vere, a Dutch actor, gives another brilliant performance as Peterson, and the same may be said of Warwick Ward as the villainous doctor, while all the other male parts are splendidly played. Evelyn Greely is a fine Phyllis, pretty and charming. Over-acting would kill the part, but she never offends in this respect. Dorothy Fane as Irma Peterson is also exceptional and presents quite a new idea of female villainy. Oscar Apfel can be sincerely congratulated on "Bulldog Drummond," his players and his own work. The picture is rough melodrama through and through, but it is sincere and will be a winner anywhere. *Gore.*

'CONQUERING THE WOMAN

Society melodrama ascribed on the house billing to Pathe (there is no display of regular "paper"). Florence Vidor is starred and her husband, King Vidor, directed. Story by Henry C. Rowland, writer of sea tales for the magazines. At the American, Dec. 11.

It was a pity the main title came and went too rapidly to permit the grasping of all the data concerning the genesis of this picture. Everybody who had a hand in it should go on record, for it is a shining example of the vulgarizing of a story in its translation to the screen. The whole subject is the cheapest kind of appeal to the feeble-minded and the infantile.

To start with the hero is a boor. The heroine is an upstart new rich American girl and her father is held up to admiration principally because he has rotten table manners. The picture must have been made for waterfront consumption, for it glorifies stevedore habits and drunken sailor behavior. One of the sweet episodes has a sailing vessel skipper deliberately spit a mouthful of tobacco juice upon the shoulder of the heroine's immaculate white polo coat as part of the girl's education into the rough and ready life of honest, hardworking people, designed to cure her of her social aspirations.

That is perhaps the worst bit of vulgarity in the five reels, but the spirit of the whole production is scarcely more elevating. The story takes the attitude common to a lot of cheap people that a clean collar and decent observance of the rules of conduct—with special reference to dinner table demeanor—are the marks of a snob, and that bad manners are the sure marks of sterling virtue. The marvel is that a Rowland story could have been twisted into this line of trash and that so intelligent a director as King Vidor would have anything to do with it or allowed his wife, Florence Vidor, who has done some notably excellent things, to be associated with it.

There isn't a flicker in the whole affair that a censor would object to. They even go so far as to take distant shots of a group of bathing girls so that there shall be no feminine display, and the utmost ingenuity has been employed in close-ups of Miss Vidor in a bathing suit to keep her legs out of view. But the whole picture fairly **revels in a trashy vulgarity that is almost degrading.**

The thing isn't even mechanically reasonable. The hero and heroine are shanghaied aboard a sailing vessel bound for the South Sea Isles, and a title gives the impression they are in mid-ocean. Almost the next view brings a nearby shoreline into view, when the vessel rolled and the camera accidentally swept the horizon.

David Butler is the cowboy hero and his heroics are unintentional travesty. His dainty love scenes are a thing to marvel at. Probably he is the only leading man playing polite leads on the screen whose acting methods are designed for comedy relief.

Judith is a society girl, daughter of a millionaire shipping magnate, who wants to marry a French count. Nothing is alleged against the count, who behaves better than the hero (and is a better actor), but the whole five reels are devoted to making him ridiculous. The girl gets herself engaged to the count during a yachting trip, but on her return trip papa has her kidnapped aboard one of his own vessels in company with the cowboy hero and deposited alone on a South Seas Island, the idea being that close association with the boob cowboy and the tobacco chewing sailors on the ship will show her their superiority over the count.

Of course, the count (rather implausibly) discovers them in the remote place, but is sent packing, for the girl has fallen in love with the cowboy during their trip back to nature. One sweet little touch by way of dainty sentimental stuff happened. They stressed the fact that the pet cat arrived alone on the island with the young couple, but presently kittens are all over under their feet. Also they emphasized the vital statistics of the henyard, but the young people themselves were supremely circumspect. The picture is absolutely chaste—and supremely vulgar. *Rush.*

AS A MAN LIVES

Produced by Achievement Film, Inc. Directed by J. Searle Dawley. Distributed by American Releasing Corporation. At Cameo, week Dec. 10.

Sherry Mason	Robert Frazer
Naida Meredith	Gladys Hulette
Dr. Ralph Neyas	Frank Losee
La Chante	J. Thornton Baston
Henri Camion	Alfred E. Wright
Mrs. John Mason	Kate Blancke
Babette	Tiny Belmont

"The eyes are the windows of the soul." That is the predicated quotation upon which this title is erected and the story, in part, founded. "As a Man Lives" is full of action, in the dramatic and melodramatic style, not novel nor even modern in this feature, but is still action, which, with the story, makes it a picture worth while as a release, but with no visible sensationalism nor special box office draw. The title, though, should pull a little on its own.

The story at the outset bears promise for the film fan, of perhaps a new picture theory, to be worked out. It gets away from that path, however, to become a straight drama, blending into melodrama toward the finale.

The high meller lights are an Apache scene in the Montmartre section of Paris, the murder of his woman by an Apache, the transformation of the devilish leering face of the Apache to one sufficiently angelic to carry a Salvation Army cap above it, and later to the west in the U. S., where an explosion crumbles down a mountain side in fairly effective fashion, killing a couple of the villains, revealing real gold which saves the fortune of the girl and brings out a wild youth as a tamed man.

The youth, Sherry Mason (Robert Frazer) is the start of the tale, a careless only son of wealthy parents who quarrels with his father, and when drunk goes home to his mother. He falls in love with the daughter of a bookstore keeper. She is Naida Meredith (Gladys Hulette). Naida loves the boy, but sees something in his eyes which informs her he is not living the life of a future husband for her. She tells it to him. He goes away, to Paris, with the representative of his father's firm over there. The Paris rep schemes to engulf him in trouble or eventually lose him. Just why didn't come out. But the lead to Montmartre, where the boy indulged in a free-for-all to save the Apache's girl, and the Apache, to notify the young woman to stop dancing with him, playfully threw a knife at her. It killed the girl, although the audience only got the suggestion of the knife throwing.

After that the "gendarmes" came and the murderer escaped to go to Dr. Neyas (Ralph Losee), who, although not a beauty doctor, did change the face as a skillful surgeon might, if skillful enough. This was another pair of soul gazing eyes, so the doctor told the Apache if he wanted to reform, his visage would tell, for if he flopped, the old evil countenance would return, otherwise he could go on his angelic way deceiving the world, although an Apache and a murderer and wanted by the police. Rather a nice old doctor. He should locate in Times square and be kept busy.

Then the ends commenced to weave toward the center, the parties got together in unsuspected places, and the end duly arrived, amidst **some excitement and many angel faces.**

It is interesting, though. Mr. Dawley's direction made it that. He did quite a lot with oft-time meager material. The philosophic vein running through won't mean a thing in the picture house, but it won't hurt either. All of the principals played well, with Mr. Losee and Kate Blancke as the mother in striking-looking roles through their white hair.

The cabaret scene was made a pretty tough hang-out for an American youth under guidance. It was tough; so tough that a Chink seated opposite a besotted white woman was in the picture.

The American probably picked "As a Man Lives" for its action and its players as making it a reliable release, which it is. Steady ones of this character would do more for any distributor than the many in and outers they have for regular releases.

But it's a horrifying thought to believe your record may be gauged from your eyes. That's worse than wearing your heart on your sleeve. Although the unnamed author of "As a Man Lives" says in a caption, or the title writer said it, that everyone knows what his heart believes. Another conscience twist.

Sime.

FLAMES OF PASSION

London, Nov. 11.

Made by Graham Cutts for Graham-Wilcox productions this long super production which had its premiere at the New Oxford, Nov. 10, by no means approaches the art or value of the same producer's **"The Wonderful Story."** It can however be voted capital entertainment and will doubtless be exceedingly popular.

The story is a somewhat ordinary one, well told but by no means strong enough for 10 reels. As the title implies sex has much to do with the picture—as a matter of fact sex predominates everything. The subject is well and carefully handled and there is little to give offense although the killing of the baby by its brutal and degraded father will be found just a little too strong and realistic for some stomachs.

Arriving home from school Dorothy Forbes, the daughter of a wealthy man, finds herself very much left to her own resources. She strikes up a friendship with her father's chauffeur, a married man called Watson. Very soon "sex" conquers the man and Dorothy finds herself in that condition supposed to be allowable only to "wives who do truly love their husbands." She confides her trouble to a worldly-wise aunt and retires to the country for the birth of her child. It is put out to nurse and she returns home. But she pines for the baby and it is brought from its original foster parents and put into the care of Watson's wife.

Watson meanwhile is becoming more and more besotted and degraded. Hawke, "the hangman barrister," a famous K. C., falls in love with her, she with him, but the past is between them. Again she goes to the worldly aunt for advice. The result is that Dorothy keeps her secret and marries her lover.

In a fit of drunken fury Watson murders the child. Hawke is retained by the Crown for the prosecution. Then comes the big **moments of the picture.** Mrs. Watson pleads with Dorothy to save her husband. Dorothy goes to her husband and tells him she has something to tell him. He is overjoyed at first, thinking she is about to tell him she is expecting to become a mother. Then he learns he is about to prosecute the father of his own girl—wife's illegitimate child. Duty must be done and he puts Dorothy in the box to prove motive. Her evidence given, he tears off wig and gown and retires from the legal profession.

The last scenes show the sorely tried couple in a rural retreat, happy in their love and family. The production is masterly, and the photography brilliant. The murder of the child is a realistic bit but repulsive. The use of the Prizma color process in photographing a fancy dress ball and also in the final scenes detracts from their beauty. Color photography is anything but perfect yet, and there is little excuse for its use in this feature.

Throughout, the acting is fine. Chief honors go to Herbert Langley for an exceptional study of the chauffeur, Watson. With him ranks Hilda Bayley as the brutally ill-treated wife who however loves him through everything with a doglike devotion.

An earnest band of scattered friends greeted every introductionary subtitle with applause and the end of the screening was the signal for the demonstration resulting in speeches.

"Flames of Passion" was preceded by a prolog realization of Dante's Inferno chiefly remarkable for the nakedness of the ladies concerned and the number of lycopodium pipes used in producing the necessary hell flames and fire. *Gore.*

IN ARABIA

Comedy-melodrama from the William Fox studio, featuring Tom Mix. Story by Tom Mix and Lynn Reynolds. Reynolds directs. Titles by Ralph Spence. Supporting company headed by Claire Adams. At the Academy, New York, Nov. 30.

This picture is a whale. It has everything. There is some western stuff at the opening, mild as to its drama, but neatly flavored with comedy and strengthened with wonderful scenery and a thrill or two. The scene is switched to Arabia, where the acrobatic star does some more dizzy horseback stunts and for a finish there is a dramatic free-for-all that calls for suspended breathing, except when it has a laugh. As for speed that touches only the high spots, "In Arabia" is there.

It gets under way with a rush. The first 50 feet have a kick. Mix appears at the peak of a lofty mountain peering over the perpendicular side that gives upon a vast panorama of Rocky mountain scenery. Half way down the dizzy precipice a mountain lion is snarling and spitting in what looks like sure enough close-ups. Mix swings over the giddy brink of the chasm on a lariat, drops another rope over the cat, and presently is seen putting the animal in a bag (so realistically done you never figure it is any other than the wildcat of the mountain side). But that's just a foretaste.

Tom runs a tourists' ranch and has to entertain a scientist's party on a camping trip. He is invited for his horsemanship to accompany the scientist on an expedition to Arabia, but declines, although the scientist's daughter (Claire Adams) is an attraction. They depart and the story takes up the affair of the scion of an Arabian ruler, now in an American college, but threatened with an unwelcome recall home to prevent marriage with a "Follies" beauty. The college youth flees from the sultan's agents in a racing auto, meets Tom as he rushes through the ranch, and hires him to take his place to lead the pursuers astray. Tom jumps at the adventure and there starts an auto chase that leads through highly colored incidents to a climax when Tom drives full tilt into the Pacific. He is captured, the sultan's agents still believing Tom is the heir, and they take him aboard ship bound for Arabia.

The scientist and his daughter have reached the desert land and are deep in research among the antiquities when Tom comes on the scene. The tale takes a new start. The local ruler is a pretender who has usurped the throne to the rightful sultan. He conspires to seize the scientist's daughter and in pursuance of that plan the party is attacked in the desert by outlaws, captured, and the girl held in the pretender's palace against her will.

Through all these adventures in the picturesque surroundings of the desert and with the background of oriental characters, Tom plays an energetic part. He rides his horse at a thrilling pace down shifting sandbanks, scales high palace walls and gains access to the inner chambers of the pretender's palace, where the gorgeous fight takes place. The elaborate fight runs through about all of the final reel and it never pauses. Tom is always swinging from one perilous balcony to drop into a tangled row; crawling from window to window, apparently 100 feet in the air, or tossing the pretender's hirelings into the bathing pool. At the end there is a battle royal in the palace courtyard between the pretender's outlaws and the army of the rightful prince which brings the rescue and th happy ending.

It's boisterous and elemental and

anything but highbrow, but for its kind it's one of the best things that have been done and it's bound to be a clean-up, particularly when it gets around to the neighborhood houses where the youngsters make a good proportion of the audiences.

Rush.

THE FLAMING HOUR

Universal, starring Frank Mayo; no director or author credited. Shown Dec. 12 at Loew's Circle on double feature bill, though scheduled for release next month.

John Danby..........Melbourne MacDowell
Lucille Danby..............Helen Ferguson
Richard Mower..............Charles Cleary
Bruce Henderson...............Frank Mayo

This picture shows the U. seemingly going ahead with Mayo to make a Reid successor out of him. But the Universal stride of making cheap pictures is evident. They relied on their big wallop from the firing and blowing up of a fireworks factory where the hero at one time was the production manager. It would have been a cheap flash had it been handled instead of manhandled. The picture, however, is certain to do nicely in the small cheap admission houses. Mayo after all is the only thing that there is in the production.

The story has Mayo as a hot-tempered youth who, as production manager of Danby & Son, is in love with the daughter of the head of the firm. The general manager and heavy, Charles Cleary, likewise wants to marry her. The elder Danby is as quick tempered as his production manager, and after one of their clashes the latter is fired, but the daughter tells her father that she is the promised bride of the discharged man and is going to accompany him.

At a later time, when the father is willing to consider a reconciliation, the heavy gums up the cards so that the young wife leaves her husband and returns to the home of the father. The husband becomes a tramp, discovers the grade of blasting powder Danby & Son are turning out is of an inferior grade, goes back into the plant in a menial position and discovers that the heavy and others in the plant are in a conspiracy to rob and ruin Danby.

Then comes the big flash. The heavy sets fire to the factory after imprisoning the head of the firm and his daughter in a powder vault, and the hero rescues them in the nick of time.

In the matter of casting the U. likewise held back on the money question. Helen Ferguson hardly fits as the leading woman for Mayo, while Cleary's heavy did not register particularly well.

The direction was choppy, and whoever handled the story was seemingly too willing to let picture coincidence take care of the details.

Fred.

HER HALF BROTHER

A production made by the Certified Pictures Corp., with no one credited with either authorship of story or direction. A western with Ester Ralston and Edward McWade featured.

Paul Preston......................R. Lee Hill
Dan Hallett............William A. Lowrey
Lee Wong.................Edward McWade
Nina.........................Ester Ralston
Black Bill...................Jack Patterson

This picture is advertised as made by the Certified Pictures Corp. No reviewer can certify it, however, for any exhibitor, no matter how cheap a house he runs. At the Stanley Monday night those who saw this film atrocity looked upon it in the light of a good joke, but it is a cinch that the Stanley management didn't play it with that in mind.

No author or director is credited, just as well. The picture looks like one of those productions turned out by fly-by-night picture companies about 15 years ago. It had all of the faults that pictures of that period had.

The leader title describes it as "A drama of Love, Hate and Revenge." It opens with a desert scene showing a down and out prospector with his burro coming cross the horizon. In the distance a gang of rustlers are shown, then another prospector. The latter has struck a mine, but is ill and about to pass out. But he doesn't, which was too darn bad. The rustlers see him and a couple go over to stick him up, and down and outer goes to his assistance. Just then the rangers arrive and chase the gang. The sick egg promises that he "shall be well repaid for his assistance."

Three years, or maybe its months, later the two are shown ta the exterior of a shack about to ride into town to see the rodeo (the latter comprises two rope tricks by a cowboy), and there the heavy gets in his work. He is Lee Wong, half Chink and half white. He has been trailing the older of the two mining partners for years; the older was the sick guy and who should have died the first reel, but didn't. Wong has a white girl working with him, and he sics her on the partners.

For the next couple of reels he tries to croak them in every way possible under the censorship laws, but does a flop, and in the finish when he has the object of his vengeance where he wants him, he tells him he had followed him because he was the man who deserted his half-sister, who was all white when he found out that he had a Chink half-brother and the girl that did the vamping was the sick miner's own daughter that he left with the wife when he deserted her. But in slipping this over the plate the Chink talked too much, for the other guy almost gets away, and after the struggle for a knife for a couple of hundred feet, more or less, the Chink finally knocks the miner cold with a prop club, while the rescue party looks on without doing anything. In the end the miner, who is toppled into the rapids, is rescued by his partner, and the agony, happily for the audience, is over.

Fred.

DAWN OF REVENGE

Nathan Hirsch Production starring Richard Travers, who also directed. Distributed by Aywon.

Ace Hall...................Charles Graham
Alicia......................Florence Foster
Nelson Miles...................Louis Dean
Judson Hall..............Richard Travers
Sherry Miles................Ethel Kingston
Aldene........................May Daggett

If this picture wasn't made ten years ago it should have been. At that there must be a market or they would not be on the market at this time, but where the market is is also something of a question, for at the Stanley, near 42d street and Broadway, with a 25-cent top admission, the audience walked out cold on the picture. This house from past and future bookings noted is cheating with a production of this sort once or twice a week and relying on the stronger pictures to keep its clientele coming. The house caters to a great extent to the shift workers in the restaurants and hotels in the neighborhood who want to kill time during the hours they have a "swing," and evidently come into the theatre rather than hang around the streets.

There seems to be hardly a question in the mind of one who sees pictures as a pretty regular thing that this picture must be a reissue or has been on the shelf for years and lately resurrected.

It is a weird tale of the discovery of a silver mine by a man who is then crossed in love and his desire for revenge which leads him through years of strife and struggle, a couple of kidnappings, the formation of a private Ku-Klux, and a final triumph when he believes he has forced the marriage of brother and sister of the man and woman for whom he has an intense hatred. But this is short lived as he destroys himself and the one other heavy in the piece by setting off a blast just at the moment the heroine and the hero are informed by the latter's mother and father (the boy having been kidnapped as a babe) that his wife was in reality their adopted child. That was enough complication to drive 'em out.

Fred.

BARRIERS OF FOLLY

Russell Productions. George Larkin starred, supported by Eva Novak, Winifred Lucas and Lillian West. Story by Theodore Rockwell. Directed by Edward Kull. At the New York Nov. 24.

Crudest kind of dime-novel melodrama, cheaply and inexpertly done. Some of the scenes pretend to elegance, but miss by a mile. The heavy is supposed to be a polished manipulator of capital, but his behavior suggests a tough hick.

The incidents are absurd and the incidents mechanically contrived for ten-twent-thirt effects. The heroine is abducted and carried to a den kept by a Chinaman master-mind criminal surrounded by scores of henchmen, all in the pay of the heavy for the carrying out of his criminal designs, which consist of cheating the heroine out of her ranch.

Anybody who could hire that number of things for the hero to fight with wouldn't have to scheme for anything less than a kingdom. The picture has impossibly childish scenes, such as the abduction of a screaming, struggling heroine in an open automobile through a crowded street, the hiding of the hero in the tonneau of the car without the others being aware of his presence, and similar trash.

If it had been twisted into a comedy it might have made some headway, but it is all so serious it becomes wearisome when it isn't unintentionally laughable. The whole picture is done in the ragged manner of the early single-reelers, and hasn't an excuse at this stage of picture development. How it ever got into the New York, even half a double bill, is a mystery.

Rush.

KICK IN

Crook drama, designated a George Fitzmaurice production under the auspices of Adolph Zukor (Paramount-Famous Players). Adapted for the screen by Oulda Bergere from the stage play of the same name by Willard Mack. At the New York Rivoli, Dec. 17.

Molly Brandon..............Betty Compson
Chic Hewes.....................Bert Lytell
Myrtle ....May McAvoy
Bennie ....Gareth Hughes
"Frou Frou"..............Kathleen Clifford
Mrs. Brandon.....................Maym Kelso
District Attorney Brandon....John Miltern
Whip Fogarty..................Walter Long
Jerry Brandon.................Robert Agnew
Jimmy Monahan....................Jed Prouty
Diggs Murphy..................Carlton King
Delaney ....Charles Ogle

First class underworld melodrama with a multitude of kicks and a heavy cast including Betty Compson, Bert Lytell, May McAvoy, Gareth Hughes and others. This cast means a lot to picture fans and ought to draw them in. The screen story will hold 'em and the play should build up on long engagements by word of mouth advertising.

The screen version has lost something of the speed of the play, but it has strengthened the romantic interest and comes to a more definite end in the marriage of the hero and heroine, all of which was merely suggested in the stage version. "Kick In" has the always interesting plot and counter plot of underworld characters and police and by contrast the elegance of society locale. By way of giving it added "class" they introduce an elaborate cabaret scene without which no picture these days is complete. This one is splendidly handled. It gets over its effect of splendor and hectic gaiety without fussy detail; it is brief and intrinsically dramatic, for all the incidents belong in the story and the passage has not been dragged in as usual to make a director's opportunity.

For the scenes in the home of the rich district attorney they have used the exterior of the Charles M. Schwab mansion on Riverside drive. The interiors are on a similar scale of splendor and extent. Miss Compson has rather a passive, colorless role with only one real action scene, but the proceedings are lively enough with the others. The story accumulates in intensity as a well balanced screen play should, so that the last two or three reels have a high degree of suspense. The passage where the reformed crook is compelled to hide stolen jewels and the body of his brother slain in the robbery from the pursuing detectives, is packed with thrills and the swiftly moving incident of getting the dead man away is a tricky bit of screen management for its melodramatic kick.

The incidental comedy is neatly introduced and is natural and not over-done except in the scene of "Ducky's" boudoir, where it is laid on a little thick. The several episodes of the police "third degree" are handled better than this particular standby of the stage and screen have ever been done before. The picture takes the rather absurd attitude that all crooks are really well intentioned persons, but this is innate in the underworld story and here is no worse than the rule. As a super-dime novel entertainment the picture scores.

Rush.

HEROES OF STREET

Harry Rapf production, presented by the Warner Bros., with Wesley Barry starred. Adapted from the play of Lem Parker, directed by William Beaudine. Shown at the Strand, New York, week Dec. 17.

Mickey Callahan..............Wesley Barry
Betty Benton..................Marie Prevost
Howard Lane....................Jack Mulhall
Gordon Trent..............Philo McCullough
Mike Callahan..................Will Walling
Mrs. Callahan................Aggie Herring
Symes ....Wilfred Lucas
Arthur Graham.........Wedgewood Nowell
The "Kid"..........................Phil Ford
"Peaches" Callahan...."Peaches" Jackson
Joe Callahan......Master Joe Butterworth
Baby Callahan.........."Bumps" Beaudine
Dog ...."Cameo"

This melodrama that for years served to get money in the popular priced combination houses has been developed into a pictûre that seemingly will have the same qualities. It is a melodrama pure and simple, a story of life in New York of the type that was sure to please the middle class of theatregoers that were wont to cheer the hero and hiss the villain. As a picture it seemingly will please to a certain extent in the better houses, where it will draw because of the star, Wesley Barry, and when it plays the regular houses after the pre-release dates have been filled it will be a clean-up.

Harry Rapf, the producer, selected a corking cast to support young Barry, placing Marie Prevost, Jack Mulhall, Wilfred Lucas, Philo McCullough and Wedgewood Nowell in the company. Will Walling plays the copper and Aggie Herring opposite as an Irish mother scored.

The script cannot be said to have planted the mystery story about which the real yarn revolves any too strong, but it does suffice to carry the tale along fairly well.

Wesley Barry is the eldest of four youngsters in the family of a patrolman of the New York police force. He wants to follow in father's footsteps. This early section is principally given over to comedy touches up to the point to where the story reaches Christmas Eve, when the father is shot and killed by a notorious criminal known as "The Shadow." That practically wrecks the little family, but the boy gets a job as "props" in a theatre where a society man is the angel for the show. A kidnapping is planned to gain publicity for one of the girls of the show. It is about fifty-fifty, as the angel in reality is "The Shadow," and he plans to use the girl in a blackmailing scheme that he has framed. Props gets suspicious of the backer and on trailing him finds the girl. In a struggle there is a shooting and one of "The Shadow's" men accidentally kills him, afterwards disclosing the fact of the dead man's identity.

Not a story to particularly rave over, but it is a picture that will lend itself to freak exploitation and should easily be worked as part of propaganda for police benefit funds in every town that it plays first runs.

Fred.

BIBLE PICTURES

Special arrangement in 10 reels of the 52-reel production of Old Testament passages produced by Armando Vay by a subsidy arrangement with the Italian Government. The whole work is said to have cost the equivalent of $3,000,000. Direction is ascribed to Pietro Antonio Gariazzo, and the characters are enacted by professional Italian studio players. The whole work is offered for non-theatrical purposes by National Non-Theatrical Motion Pictures, Inc. (Harry Levy), either in single reels, five-reel groupings, or in its entirety at $10 a reel. It is proposed to make three versions for use of Catholic organizations, Protestant and Jewish, the difference being that ecclesiastical committees of all three denominations shall approve the different titling to accord with their several doctrines.

This 10-reel version comprising the high spots of the entire narrative was shown publicly for the first time in the Columbia University School of Journalism, New York, Dec. 15, before a gathering of teachers, with addresses by several clergymen and by Burr McIntosh, representing the screen art.

The magnitude of this undertaking, its dignity and sincerity are manifest even in this abridged form. Outstanding is that here is a serious educational effort made in a reverent spirit, but at the same time putting emphasis upon the human interest of the Bible story. The endeavor has been directed toward bringing out the pictorial appeal and letting the theology take care of itself.

Popularized Bible stories perhaps is the apt description of the series, but the screening has been done expertly, obviously by workmen who know the camera art and mechanisms and the technique of the studio. Still the popularizing has been done with a moderate hand. The facts have been popularized, but never vulgarized in the process. The mark of scholarship is evident.

The picture is rich in pageantry and spectacle. It is said 10,000 people were used in some of the scenes, and the statement is credible after viewing some of the passages, such as the flight from Egypt, the setting up of the Golden Calf, and like episodes. In elaborate spectacle scores of scenes go far beyond the biggest feats of the recent foreign productions, both as to number of people concerned and in massiveness of background. The statement that the picture cost $3,000,000 to make sounds moderate in view of settings such as those for the Tower of Babel passage, the destruction of Sodom and Gomorrah, and scores of other incidents.

In the form of 10 reels the screening is unquestionably wearisome, principally because it is disconnected and episodic. Individually all the incidents are immensely interesting, but just as one becomes absorbed in the Tower of Babel episode, for instance, that chapter ends and one is required to shift attention to an entirely different set of personages and interests.

There is close upon two and a half hours of steady projection in the 10 reels, enough in itself to set a severe strain on attention and the shifting of interest is additionally exhausting. It is understood, however that there is no intention to push the 10-reel version, which is merely for the purpose of introducing the whole subject to educators. Put out in serial form at two to five reels in a group, the picture will be an extremely valuable contribution. The film is available in any grouping from one reel to five.

The picture has some of the technical defects of most foreign output. Its photography is rather hard and sharp at times and lacking in tone delicacies compared with the best work of the American photography, but it is at all times clear and sharp. The sets are remarkably elaborate and ingenious, with great richness of detail. The chapter devoted to the Tower of Babel shows a collection of building machinery such as crude rustic winches and such barbarian building tackle with the picturesquely garbed workmen toiling at enormous blocks of stone. Models of the tower are not particularly convincing, but the smaller scenes showing bits of minor action are powerful in literal suggestion.

Most of the story is unvarnished narrative, but the last two reels have a big punch in dramatic interest. These sections begin with the judgments of Solomon and carry through to the death of the Shulamite, and tell a big tale of love and intrigue in the king's harem. It might be a sensational costume production for its lavish Oriental settings, costuming and spectacle.

The subject starts with the first chapter of Genesis, with flashes of an undraped Adam and Eve that may give the censors a good deal of study. Indeed, the whole picture is a hard nut for the censors to crack. Under the rules of Pennsylvania, for instance, the historic Cain and Abel homicide would have to be cut to a title, although it is here shown in actuality. It is difficult to see how they can discuss the Sodom and Gomorrah episode with delicacy and the intrigue of Solomon's alien wife is sex stuff that could scarcely pass muster under any other circumstances.

Rush.

ENTER MADAME

Equity production starring Clara Kimball Young, presented by Harry Carson. Adaptation of the play of the same title by Frank Beresford. Directed by Wallace Worsley. Short seven reels, distributed by Metro.

Lisa Della Robbia....Clara Kimball Young
Gerald Fitzgerald..............Elliott Dexter
Mrs. Preston..................Louise Dresser
Archimede ....Lionel Belmore
Doctor ....Wedgewood Nowell
Bice ....Rosita Marstini
Miss Smith....................Orra Deveraux
John Fitzgerald...............Arthur Rankin
Aline..................Mary Jane Saunderson

Enter Clara Kimball Young, actress! In this picture Miss Young is giving a performance better than most she has done in the past two or three years. The reason for it is pretty much the tempo at which she was forced along at, there being speed instead of the usual slow, draggy performances that she has been giving, and the result is surprising.

Surrounding is a capable cast and the story itself has been well done under the direction of Wallace Worsley, with the result that "Enter Madame" is a feature that will stand up with the best of the better program productions. There may be some question whether or not the audiences in the small theatres will get the finer points of the picture, but they will be entertained whether they do or not. The audience on the American Roof (Loew's) in New York got a lot of laughs out of the picture that a Broadway audience would not get and muffed a number that would be sure fire with a high-class audience.

The feature is best described to the exhibitor as a society comedy. The plot deals with a grand opera prima donna who practically deserts her husband to follow her career, even though she loves her better half. While the pampered pet of a suite of servants and receiving the homage of operatic mad foreigners, she believes he is sitting at home in Boston immersed in his work. Instead he has fallen for a designing widow and has about decided to divorce his songbird wife. When the latter comes to a realization of this she hurries back to the husband's native land and immediately begins to exert her emotional wiles to win him back, but he does not react as she expects. In the end, however, she emerges victorious.

The story is well screened, and Miss Young takes the role of the emotional and tempermental prima donna to her heart as though she had been doing that sort of thing all her life. It is a distinct triumph for her. Elliott Dexter plays the husband, and the third angle to the triangle is furnished by Louise Dresser, whose blonde beauty proves an excellent foil for the brunet C. K. Y.

The youthful love interest in the hands of Arthur Rankin and Mary Jane Saunderson is capably handled and a bit of character work that is rendered by both Lionel Belmore and Rosita Marstini is perfect.

In sets and atmosphere the production is all that could be asked for, and Wallace Worsley has turned out a picture in which the star is really handled as she should be.

Fred.

BULLDOG DRUMMOND

Screen version of the stage play of the same name by Cyril McNeile ("Sapper") played in America and still running in London. Carlyle Blackwell starred in the role of Hugh Drummond, supported by Evelyn Greeley as Phillis Benton. Directed by Oscar Apfel. Distributed in this country by W. W. Hodkinson. Produced by the Hollandia Film Co., of Haarlem, Holland, and first released abroad. At Fox's Academy, New York, Dec. 17.

The screen play is as much a mystery as the stage version. You can't tell whether the audiences take it seriously or enjoy it because it hits them on the funny bone by its hectic melodrama. You could argue either way from the behavior of the crowd at the Academy.

They applauded vociferously at the bland heroic passages and the finish of the delirious action brought a burst of applause, but for the rest of the evening (it was a double bill) that audience was out of hand. They laughed at the wrong places in the serious little picture that followed and generally were in a kidding frame of mind, presumably in excess of exuberance at the "Drummond" play.

The film arrangement is a faithful and adequate transcription of the stage play. It has all the extravagances of a dime novel in its high-flown and pompous episodes, but it certainly does move swiftly even if implausibly. This work has been the amazement of two hemispheres. How one can look at it seriously is the marvel, but they do. Once the hero has accomplished the liberation of the millionaire Potts, there is no reason in the world why he shouldn't call up the police, have the master criminal pinched and go home for a rest. Instead of which he walks back to the den of thieves and gets himself involved in all sorts of painful experiences. The whole affair is in the spirit of Nick Carter or more so. You wouldn't think it could get past an audience of school children, but the adult crowd at the Academy were about evenly divided, if the audible evidence was to be depended upon, between those who were genuinely amused and those who were sincerely thrilled. Laugh or thrill the picture delivers abundant emotional appeal and anything that gets out of the rut of screen dullness is a find. That seems to be the length and breadth and thickness of "Bulldog Drummond." For the simple minded it has a kick and for the sophisticated it has a more or less subtle laugh. So everybody's pleased.

The picture is well done. All the emphasis is on quick shock, quick surprise and swift action. Automobiles are dashing back and forth through all five or six reels. The hero is constantly getting himself involved in seemingly inextricable situations, only to turn the tables on his torturers in a surprise twist. He is such a jaunty, breezy, self-confident hero and the arch criminals are such intensely wicked, craven, sinister demons, one can't help being drawn toward both sides. It is so seldom we get heroism and villainy in such pure, unadulterated gobs, it's an engaging variation of indefinite pale characters that are both good and bad. Here are villains you can hiss with a whole heart and no such hero has walked the boards or slithered across the screen since the days of Charles E. Blaney. More power to them both.

The production is an attractive background to the hilarious story. No serious society drama ever had more painstaking production in settings and props and the players carry out the dead serious illusion in a spirit of earnestness that is positively massive. You have to be mentally alert and agile to keep track of the conviction that it is all being done in a spirit of sublimated travesty while playwright, director and players work their bag of tricks. The slaying of the diabolical doctor by one of his own engines of torture was a gem of shrewd stage management. So much happens and it all happens so swiftly that one is torn between a desire to laugh and an impulse to enjoy the naive thrill of it all.

Rush.

I AM THE LAW

Released through Affiliated Distributors, Inc., and presented by C. C. Burr. Edwin Carewe, director, with Robert Kurrle, camera.

Snow stuff, Royal Northwest Mounted, good story, excellent direction, clear photography and a sweet cast that registers all the way. The picture is not exceptionally new, having been showing for some weeks, but whether recent or not this film rates above plenty that have been lately screened in the Broadway first run houses.

The cast includes Noah Beery, Kenneth Harlan, Rosemary Theby, Alice Lake and Gaston Glass. Not a bad line-up, and their work reveals the class it contains. Especially do the men predominate. A full hour and a half is consumed in the running time, but it is not noticeable, due to the story which grips and continues to hold.

It tells of two brothers, one older and very much on the level, with the younger having a decided leaning towards liquor and women. Both members of the Mounted. The youngster is making a play for the wife of the sergeant who is in charge of the post. The woman is fed up with the bewhiskered trappers, the life she is leading, and her husband. So it's a setup. The booze thing gets him into a jam and he's ordered to report to his brother, a corporal, at another barracks of the force. En route he stops at a cabin where he finds the member of his family, Bob, by name, escorting a feminine school teacher to safety, Bob having rescued the girl from a Chink joint.

The youngster takes one flash at the gal, registers the me-for-you babesie idea, and slips the corporal the transfer order. The non-com has to start on his jaunt, leaving the kid brother to see the girl to the post from which he was ordered. The commanding sergeant personally likes young Fitzgerald, so the return is easily squared, but it's a smooth working routine the boy starts using between the wife and the schoolmarm. Bob finally comes back, elated at the thought of seeing the girl again, only to learn his brother has been beating his time and the two are engaged. He bows out until he chances to overhear the youth swinging into action with the wife. An argument ensues with both "cheaters" telling him to lay off.

The boys live in an adjoining hut to the sergeant, hence when the searg. starts off on a trip the red-coated Don Juan hops right across the way to frolic with the spouse. The usual forgotten incidental brings the husband back, where he discovers the carryings on taking place in his household. The boy gets him in the shape of a dog whip, during which he sneaks the sergeant's gun and shoots and kills him.

Bob hears the shot, rushes over, knows the situation and realizes he must "get his man." It leads to an all-night chase through the snow, concluding in the murderer finding refuge in his fiancee's shack, where he tells her she must hide him. Bob flounders in, seeking information and to grab a warming beverage, during which he sees his brother hiding behind a trunk through a mirror. No intimation of the discovery, so when young Fitzgerald is about to continue his runaway he opens the door, looks at a gun with his relative behind it and hears the "I arrest you in the name of the king for——"

It's a case of pneumonia for Robert right then. When he lapses into unconsciousness the youth thinks his relative dead and himself free. His rejoicing reveals to the girl she never loved him, and the engagement is over. A mere detail to the kid, who thinks he has dodged the gallows and still has the widow, anyway. He exits and the girl finds Bob still alive, which means a siege of nursing him back.

Meanwhile the scamp of the Fitzgerald family has reported to the new commanding officer his brother had killed the late sergeant and was now himself dead. It clears up the case, so far as the department is concerned, until a trapper relates he has seen Corporal Fitzgerald alive. The youngster is sent for and ordered to arrest his brother on his own information. Not to be daunted he goes through with it, charging the other boy with the murder.

Meanwhile the school teacher and Bob are about to be married, but the imprisonment calls off the ceremony. The natives, previously incensed at the cowardly way in which the sergeant was killed from behind, start out to lynch the alleged murderer. The jail has only young Fitzgerald in charge. It's a small matter for the mob to grab the corporal and start hiking to the nearest tree. The school teacher finds what is about to occur and rushes over to the widow to ask her to tell the inside stuff on the case, but she won't. A fight between the two women ends in the widow being dragged through the snow to the scene, where she arrives in time to free Bob from the gang. Not to be thwarted, the residents start back to get the guilty brother, only to discover he's beaten them to it by poison.

Carewe has turned out a corking picture without overplaying the dramatics where it would have been so easy. Mr. Harlan as the older brother and Gaston Glass as the weakling hog the footage, both because of their conspicuousness in the story and their work. And the Beerys are the Beerys, though it's mostly the teamwork of the cast that is the outstanding feature.

The picture is a splendid northener and will satisfy in any theatre.

Skig.

FORSAKING OTHERS

Universal comedy-drama, story by Mary Lerner, direction by Emile Chautard. In the cast Colleen Moore, Cullen Landis, June Elvidge, Sam De Grasse and David Torrence. At the New York Dec. 8.

Universal misses on this subject, principally because it is not fitted to screen use. The argument of a mother who interferes with the mating of her favorite son and almost spoils his life, might be made into an interesting satirical short story, or even a novel with delicate play of humor, but it all makes exceedingly dull screen material.

The meaning doesn't get over in pantomine and the whole screen significance of the character relations are principally revealed by means of titles. Its another case of the picture being an illustration of the reading matter instead of the dumb acting being the center of interest and the titles subordinate. The thing never gets into action.

The actors and director have done the best possible with the matter at their command. The trouble is that the materials and story treatment don't fit. The story deals almost entirely with a conflict of motives which can be expressed only in words and not in actions. When the mother pretends to fall ill and requires a change of scene, it takes a lot of titling to make it evident that she is merely scheming to separate her son and his sweetheart for the selfish reason that she wants to keep her son with her.

They go to a fashionable resort, where the boy, driven by ennui, gets himself involved in what threatens to become dangerous scrape with a married woman. Mamma changes front and appeals to the deserted sweetheart to help her out of the situation. The surprise twist that makes the unexpected climax is neatly turned, but it was not worth the footage of a dull five-reeler to get to it.

The same subject matter might make a real picture if its meaning could be expressed in action. Fox's "Silver Wings" dealt with material of somewhat similiar import—that is to say a mother and son situation—but there it was handled as a rather tragic, or at any rate dramatic, problem, with the emphasis on the sombre aspect. And besides the Fox picture discussed the situation in terms of action. The clash there was a physical and violent one. Here the contest is masked behind an exterior of comedy and the whole treatment is fogged up and lost. Nothing happens except in the titles. It isn't a picture play at all. Its just illustrated reading matter and you don't go to the picture theatre to read a book.

Rush.

THE FRESHIE

Kerman Films production presented by Frederick Herbst, starring Guinn (Big Boy) Williams and Molly Malone. Written and directed by W. Hughes Curran. Shown at Loew's Circle, New York, on double feature bill.

Charles Taylor..Guinn (Big Boy) Williams
Violet Blakley..............Molly Malone

This is a semi-western with a lot of college atmosphere. The picture is a small time program feature that hasn't any particular punch but which will suffice on the double feature bills where there is a fairly strong attraction played with it. At Loew's Circle this one has the Goldwyn production, "The Sin Flood," as its running mate.

There were times when the Circle patrons Tuesday night started to razz, so it was evident it was the Goldwyn picture that drew them and they were just tolerating this one.

In this story there is very little beyond the pranks of a number of college youngsters in hazing a freshman, and in the main it makes for good slapstick fun. A cowpuncher makes the friendship of a college professor during the latter's vacation and is embued with the idea that he wants a college education, so by dint of hard study and saving he starts out in the autumn to acquire book learning. He arrives at the small-town school and is immediately set upon by the sophs as their meat for hazing. During one of the stunts he manages to capture a gentleman burglar and wins the belle of the college town by so doing. A simple tale that is rather directly told without any particular frills.

Guinn Williams plays the cowboy student and manages to get away with it in fairly good shape, while Molly Malone, who is co-starred with him, is a pleasing enough ingenue lead. The direction is fair.

Fred.

DANGER POINTS

Dramatic feature sponsored by the American Distributing Corp., six reels. Story by Victor Halperin; directed by Lloyd Ingraham. Starring Carmel Myers, J. J. Dowling playing an incidental part. At Loew's Circle, New York, Dec. 16.

Interesting dramatic story framed on the domestic triangle with several good points of modern middle class and at least two capital screen "punches." One of the latter is the burning of a big oil tank and the other a cut-in of a realistic train wreck, both of the stunts working into the body of the story neatly.

The picture would be none the worse for judicial cutting, but as it stands it has a fair degree of dramatic suspense and it develops naturally and convincingly to its forceful climax. The presence of J. J. Dowling of "Miracle Man" fame was capitalized in a religious twist that must have been an after thought. Certainly it is extraneous. The business of planting the antecedent story is rather laborious, but the full development of the characters pays later on when the story gathers speed, for it is in the accumulation of details that the narrative has its main interest.

Unless you can get interested in a sympathetic way with the people of the play the story is weak, and for this reason the elaboration of their characters and motives pays abundant returns. There is nothing particularly novel in the dramatic material which is made of age-old stuff, but it is a sincere and simple version of the neglected wife, the pre-occupied business man husband and the former sweetheart.

The husband's absorption in his affairs piques and arouses the wife, who is hard pressed by the former sweetheart, although she keeps him at as far a distance as she can without exposing his attentions to her husband. While she is battling with the suspicion that her husband no longer loves her a fire breaks out in one of his oil tanks. The wife is just calling him on the phone as the news of the fire reaches his office, and a clerk replies to the woman: "He can't talk to you now." Not knowing the circumstances, the wife breaks down at this seeming affront and determines to leave her home. The former sweetheart happens to be calling on her when she makes this decision and she begs him to help her to the train with her luggage.

He pretends to bid her good-bye at the car entrance, but instead jumps on the car behind as it moves off. The dramatic high spot of the picture comes later. Flashbacks of the flaming oil tank and the struggle of the fire-fighting husband appear from time to time, while the action of the flying train proceeds. The wife retires to a drawing room, and when the other passengers have gone to their berths the sweetheart forces an entrance and makes violent love. The wife has left a note of farewell at home and her blind uncle and guardian, knowing of the situation, is seen in prayer that the unhappy affair may end fortunately.

The train is wrecked and the injured passengers brought back to the wife's town, where the waiting husband gradually learns from an examination of the victims that his wife and her former suitor were on the same train. The wife is uninjured, but the lover is mortally injured. In a dying statement he confesses his treachery and absolves the wife, paving the way for a happy ending.

The direction is intelligent and the acting even and natural. Excellent program feature, particularly for the houses with a large percentage of women fans in its clientele.

Rush.

BUTTERFLY RANCH

William Steiner Productions, Neal Hart starred. At Loew's Circle, New York, Dec. 11 (day only), one half of double bill; other half, Carmel Meyers reissue with Valentino co-starred on new paper.

Neal Hart looks like a nicolet star. This picture of western life, like his others, is of ancient type in story, and Hart appears to follow a formula for this kind of outdoor film work. Here, as in the last picture seen in which he appeared, Hart is injured through being shot in the head by bandits, and also here, as before, he jumped off a high rock onto the back of a moving horse, to do battle with its rider.

There must be a market for these kind of pictures, otherwise they could not be continuously produced, but in metropolitan sections anywhere they are nil, so the nicolet, otherwise the fives and tens, must have a call for them.

Hart's support is no better than himself when acting; the direction, of course, is wretched, and there is nothing whatsoever appealing in the picture unless it is Hart's horse. His leading lady, whoever she may be, will be better off if advising the cameraman to stop taking close ups of her. In trousers and at a distance she looks quite nice. That is the way it should be.

The story is of easterners crossing the plains in the good old way, all alone, and reaching the Steve Saunders' range. Saunders (Hart) acts as their guide. A strain of gold is located on the range by the head of the eastern family, but meantime the younger easterner in love with the girl gets too gay around her. That's when Steve butted in. When the zealous easterner engaged the bandit chief to kidnap the girl Steve frustrated the plan, and very simply, too, even to the point of making a couple of bandits keep on looking the other way while he made off with the gal. And then the eastern father and mother discovered the bandit chief was their long-lost son, so they thanked Steve for uncovering that as well.

This picture was on the wrong side of Columbus circle. On the opposite side and in the Park theatre, where a weekly change of burlesque show is given, the Hart "photoplay," if adapted for burlesque, would have been a scream. However, in the picture house, it was only a flop. *Sime.*

MAKING A MAN

Presented by Jesse L. Lasky, released through Paramount and starring Jack Holt. An adaption by Albert Shelby LeVino from the original story of Peter B. Kyne. Joseph Henabery directed with Faxon Dean the photographer. Showing at the Rialto, New York, Dec. 17.

Horace Winsby....................Jack Holt
Jim Owens....................J. P. Lockney
Patricia Owens....................Eva Novak
Henry Cattermole..........Bert Woodruff
Shorty ....Frank Nelson
Bailey ....Robert Dudley

Extremely backward in getting started but from about the third reel on it picks up to supply amusement. The comedy has H lt mentally transformed from a snob to a regular fellow, but wastes far too much footage in "planting" that part of the narrative concerned with the character's self-satisfied attitude. The story takes the action from California to New York to Atlantic City and back to New York, where it concludes. The picture sponsored various outbursts of laughter before a matinee audience that was more or less surprising after the handicap imposed by the initial 20 minutes. It looked as if nothing could save it.

The film starts out along the lines of the usual hectic westerns, revealing the star (Jack Holt) as Horace Winsby, a sugar beet king and owner of the entire valley, extremely wealthy and hard hearted as regards foreclosing mortgages of tenants on his property. Eva Novak is the neighbor's daughter just returned from an eastern school and in time to establish herself in the argument between the two men. The scene switches to the east when one of the farmers attempts to shoot up Winsby and the manager of the offices (with the firm for 50 years) tells the boss to blow until the situation quiets down.

With the arrival of Winsby in New York, the picture actually starts its purpose. The abrupt departure has necessitated only one suit of clothes and a grip; hence the arrival at the Plaza and a demand for a suite of rooms is received skeptically by the boys behind the desk. Never having been in New York and unacquainted, the small town luminary spends a week-end alone in Atlantic City, revealed a single "shot" at the Boardwalk, where he gets a touch of ptomaine poisoning and has his wallet lifted by a couple of dips. The return to the 59th street hotel brings the bill for the week and no coin to meet it. The management won't guarantee the wire out home for cash and Winsby is escorted to the door by the house detective.

A siesta in one of the downtown parks with the rest of the boys who are laying off at the time, strikes up an acquaintance with a bum. The two stay together until they happen on jobs as a dishwasher and waiter in the same establishment. The chef gets sore at the manager for hiring Winsby in place of the fired union waiter, frames the new tray carrier which leads to a fight.

Meanwhile the California neighbors have come east, registered at the same establishment, made inquiries and told of the identity of the man they bounced. It leads to the discovery of Winsby and his new found boy friend just as they dash out of the restaurant, where the scrap has taken place. It ends with the whole party including the tramp and wife planning the return home, Winsby getting the o. k. from the girl on at last being "reg'ler" and he wiring to have his superintendent call off the hard hearted business routine.

Holt gives a good performance and is an excellent "straight" during the rough element episodes. The only noticeable support comes from Frank Nelson, as the tramp, who made the role predominate.

The camera work is standard and Henabery evidently did wonders to bring the picture back after such a mediocre start. That may have been his fault or of the scenario, but there was considerable redeeming to do. He did it, however, so whatever credit is due must go his way. Other than that, this feature should be acceptable to the Holt fans and will amuse if they'll stay to see it through. *Skig.*

A DANGEROUS GAME

Universal comedy-drama starring Gladys Walton. Story by Louis Dodge. Direction by King Baggott. Half of double bill, Fox. Academy, New York, Dec. 17.

Designed as a simple pastoral romance of childhood, the picture develops into a bare-faced theft of footage. There isn't enough material in the five reels to make a reasonable two-reeler. In fact, there isn't material enough in the story to make a picture of any kind.

In a frenzied effort to stretch it out into the regulation length they project close-up after close-up of the star, in which she does nothing but register concentrated thought and does it for minutes at a time. The story is chaotic. It starts out as an idyll of childhood and presently it has an expose of spiritualist fakery, finishing up with a trifling love angle. Its comedy is as indefinite as its drama.

Gret'n Ann is a dreamy little girl in the country, seeing visions of fairies which are shadowed in by double photography. Her father dies and she is taken in charge by a hard and unsympathetic uncle and aunt. They mistreat her and she runs away, climbing on a freight train where she becomes acquainted with a kindly brakeman named Kelly. Kelly takes her to his home, where there are already ten little Kellys, and Gret'n Ann fearing she will be a burden upon Kelly, departs, walking into the household of a farmer suddenly made rich by the discovery of an oil well, and announcing that she wants a place to live and has chosen this one.

Pete, the farmer, is in the hands of spiritualistic fakers, who seek to swindle him. He takes Gret'n Ann to a seance and the child unintentionally exposes the fakers, saving Pete from their clutches. She is sent away to school and returns three years later a fashionable young woman. Pete has fallen in love with the child, but, overhearing a lovers' conversation between Gret'n Ann and the young son of the Kelly household, resigns his courtship, leaving the field to the young man. This provides for the happy fade-out on a romantically satisfactory situation.

Where the title "A Dangerous Game" applies does not appear on the surface, unless it bears on the perilous business of swindling farmers by clairvoyants. *Rush.*

THE INNER MAN

Syracuse Picture Corp. feature made for Playgoers and released through Pathe. Wyndam Standing starred. Shown at Loew's Circle, New York, on double feature bill. Directed by Hamilton Smith.

Thurlow M. Barclay, Jr..Wyndam Standing
Margaret Barclay.........Kathryn Kingsley
Thurlow M. Barclay, Sr..J. Barney Sherry
Jud ....Gustav von Seyffertitz

This is a mixed society and mountaineer story, absolutely spoiled by titling and editing. Seemingly, the director shot some fairly good footage, but whoever had the assembling of the picture afterwards ruined the chances of what would have been a mediocre program picture. As it stands now, it is a haphazard sort of an affair that the audience cannot make head or tail out of.

The story has as its hero the namby pamby son of a wealthy mine owner who would rather teach school than devote himself to the interests of his father; then, suddenly, for no reason at all, he decides to undertake a trip to father's mine. There he meets and falls in love with the untamed child of one of the mountaineers and discovers that there is a scheme on foot to fleece his father out of the mine. He bests the schemers and wins the girl.

All of this is told in some six thousand feet of film that shoots off at all angles in the telling of the story.

Wyndam Standing gives a fair performance, but the real star of the piece is the little mountain girl who played opposite him. She reminds one of Edna Purviance some years ago; has the same type of blonde beauty and severe manner of dressing her hair, and with it all she does troupe.

Other than that, there is mighty little in the picture that amounts to anything that would make playing it in any but the cheaper admission priced house worth while. On a double feature bill it was the weak sister of two bad pictures. *Fred.*

ONLY A SHOP GIRL

Newark, N. J., Dec. 16.

Melodrama produced by C. B. C. Film Sales Corporation. Scenario and direction by Edward J. Le Saint. Seven reels. At the Strand, Newark, N. J., Dec. 15.

Mame Mulvey....................Estelle Taylor
Danny Mulvey....................William Scott
Josie Jerome....................Mae Busch
Charles Black....................James Morrison
Josie's Sister....................Josephine Adair
James Watkins....................Willard Louis
His Assistant....................Tully Marshall
Mrs. Watkins....................Claire DuBrey
James Brennan....................Wallace Beery

The Strand secured the world premiere of this picture which turned out to be a good piece of work. It neither makes nor has any claims to greatness. It will please the average audience without arousing any wild plaudits. The exhibitor can't go far wrong with it as the name itself ought to draw.

The story, said to follow Blaney's melodrama closely, is simple. Mame Mulvey, a clerk in a department store, is led astray by her wealthy employer, Watkins, who attracts her more by his money than person. To get rid of her brother (Danny) Watkins frames him and when he is released, tries to do so again. Danny escapes and vows to get even. Watkins, tiring of Mame, discharges her and Danny learns of his sister's shame.

Apparently to wreak vengeance on Watkins, Danny goes to the department store at night. In Watkins' office he sees the manager making advances to Josie Jerome, Danny's sweetheart. To the same place come Mame and Mrs. Watkins, without the knowledge of the other, and they also watch the scene. Watkins presses his attentions upon Josie, who is virtuous, and she struggles against him. A few minutes later Watkins is found murdered. Mame and Danny have escaped, Mrs. Watkins is released and Josie arrested for the crime. Danny casts suspicion upon himself and is arrested and confesses. Meanwhile Mame has been caught by a fire in the tenement house in which she lives. She rescues Josie's little sister, but is mortally burned herself. On her deathbed she admits that she killed Watkins.

It is understood that for Newark consumption some cuts were made in the picture. A gruelling third degree used on Danny was entirely eliminated.

The picture is frankly melodrama but aside from the exigencies of the plot it is in no way handled as such. The director has treated it as straight realism. Even the titles are matter of fact and save for the final warning that all shop girls should be good, they read as though they were impartially elucidating a stern transcript of life. For this treatment the director deserves all credit but it is a debatable question whether the story has intrinsically the worth to stand up under such handling.

Aside from several gorgeous gowns worn by Estelle Taylor the production is not elaborate but it is adequate. The scene in an East Side dance hall and one of the sales floor of the store are not entirely convincing, although they serve their purpose. High lights are a joyous rough and tumble in the dance hall, the fire is a reasonable thrilling combination of a studio blaze and a real one, and the scene with cut-backs where Mame tells her brother of her downfall.

The casting is good, but it is a shock to see an actor with Tully Marshall's reputation appear but for a flash. Miss Taylor does well as the erring shop girl. She works hard, is sincere, and is not unattractive—in fact so good—one wonders why she is not better. Mae Busch scores with a clean cut characterization of Josie. William Scott leads for the men with a convincing sympathetic portrayal of Danny. Watkins was no doubt played as directed by Willard Louis, but girls must be willing to overlook a good deal to fall for this type of villain. But department store seducers should have their trousers pressed. Josephine Adair walked away with a kid part as did Wallace Beery in a character bit. *Austin.*

STREETS OF NEW YORK

Out and out melodrama produced by Burton King for the Arrow and released by that organization. Adapted from the play of the same title by Loeta Morgan. Shown at Loew's Circle, New York, on double feature bill.

Gideon Bloodgood..........Anders Randolph
Badger ....Leslie King
Capt. Fairweather.........Arthur Donaldson
Jennie ....Kate Blancke
Paul Fairweather..............Edward Earle
Lucy Bloodgood...........Barbara Castleton
Sally Ann....................Dorothy Mackaill

One of the old standard mellers that play the pop-priced combination houses for years transferred to the screen in a haphazard manner that is far from making it a picture that anyone will rave about. In the cheaper neighborhoods it will suffice as fair entertainment and the out-of-town exhibitor can play it up as a rubberneck trip around New York, showing all the points of interest. But it is a cheap picture intended for the cheaper audiences.

Burton King in the matter of direction has failed to a great extent to hit on anything that would make the picture show the slightest class.

The early shots shown depict the streets of New York from the Battery to Riverside Drive, with shots of Wall street, the lower east side, Fifth avenue and other busy thoroughfares. They were news shots rather than connected with the story but they did create an atmosphere for the tale that was to follow.

However, looking at the picture was just like looking at one of the old melodramas that played the American theatre or the Grand opera house 25 years ago. There was no effort made to modernize it in any way and the story would have lent itself to modernization beautifully. The result is just a picture, that's all.

Edward Earle plays the lead in the production and manages to register fairly well with what he had at hand to do. Barbara Castleton was the principal woman of the cast. Anders Randolph and Leslie King furnished the heavy work and Arthur Donaldson was the victim. Dorothy Mackaill furnished a slight comedy touch, and by a long shot was the most effective player of the cast. *Fred.*

FOOLS OF FORTUNE

Five-reel comedy presented by Louis A. Chaudet Productions and handled by American Distributing. In the cast, Tully Marshall, Marguerite De La Motte, Jack Dill, Russell Simpson. At the Tivoli, New York, Dec. 15.

The task of making a five-reel comedy is again demonstrated to be the toughest proposition in the whole production business. This time it is less successful than usual. "Fools of Fortune" is impossible. It hasn't even sufficient substance to make even a good two-reeler, and when its poverty of material is spread out over more than twice that length it reaches supreme heights of dullness.

They were not even resourceful to devise enough slapstick hokum to make the distance, and trifling incidents are stretched out to unbelievable lengths. One of the incidents has to do with four cowboys, one of them disguised as an Indian, traveling from the ranch to New York. A reasonable amount of knockabout comedy was perhaps excusable for the situation of disposing of a bogus Indian in a Pullman car, but without exaggeration they filled a whole reel of footage with clumsy buffoonery that hadn't a laugh in it.

In order to piece out the picture into the arbitrary feature length the producer has padded unmercifully with titles. There are stretches of film that amount to almost a monolog. One scene had the cowboys getting on the train. There were no less than ten titles involved in this trifling action, representing what the cowboys said to the conductor and what the conductor said to the cowboys. Most of them are crude gags and puns, meant to have a laugh in them. The trouble is the comedy is absent.

Another incident hung on the arrival of the cowboys in New York and had them hiring a taxicab. This episode was elaborated into several hundred feet with titles where all its purposes could have been accomplished in a tenth of the space. There are a hundred faults in the picture, but its chief defect is that it isn't funny in any particular, and an unfunny comedy that runs upward of an hour is suicidal.

This Tivoli is a neighborhood house on the fringe of a rooming house and tenement district just off Times square. It gets both neighborhood and drop-in trade, and besides playing independent pictures like "Fools of Fortune" gets the best of the releases on second run. For example, it lists among its features for this week (Dec. 17) "To Have and to Hold" and "The Man Who Saw Tomorrow." It has played such pictures as "Way Down East" and "Blood and Sand." It is reasonable to suppose that the house bids for an intelligent clientele, and one wonders what effect a picture such as this will have on customers.

The Tivoli lately has been going in for "double feature" bills, and the one with "Fools of Fortune" on it is a sample. The other half is an old Dolores Casinnelli release called "The Challenge," almost as bad in its way as the Chaudet picture. Exhibitors of the Tivoli class seem to work on the theory that if they book one inferior picture in a bill the situation is saved by bolstering it up with another inferior film, whereas the result is the contrary. What is the probable effect on a neighborhood following of a strikingly poor entertainment slipped in between bookings of the best the film market affords? Whatever the Tivoli saved in rentals on this double booking must ultimately prove a pretty costly economy in its effect on the house's good will.
Rush.

THE MONEY MONSTER

Peerless Pictures Corporation presents. Presumably English made. No billing other than title on paper. First two slides carry technical information. At Stanley, New York, Dec. 19 (day only).

"The Money Monster" has the earmarks of an English-produced picture. It is mostly notable for its character types, all British. For a single day's run such as the Stanley, New York, employs, this picture will do as well as any other.

Among its players three are outstanding. Foremost is the woman playing the old caretaker of the Burley mansion. Another is old Burley himself, before he dies in an early reel, and the other is the Dr. Nicholson player.

In screen acting, although taking this as a single example, the English seem to be beyond the American, because they are more natural pantomimists. The player of Dr. James Calvert, the juvenile, was an example. His pantomime in facial expression especially was most effective. It wasn't "registering" as the untutored American screen actor has been taught to do; it was acting.

Yet on the reverse, the inferiority of the direction could not fail to be observed. As, for instance, when the father of the doctor spoke to his wife he continually looked in another direction instead of at the girl, without the camera showing anything else he could have looked at. It was as bad as the poor guesswork on a double exposure might have been.

Otherwise in direction there is an economy here the director could complain of. The scenario was written or rewritten to hold down the production expense. When it was not an exterior setting, the interiors were all of one set, and once a small furnished room, built in the studio like they built them over here 15 years ago.

But the types take the film along. They are different to start with, and cover a gamut of English characters, some heard or read about. They gather when an advertisement appears in the papers calling for the legal heirs of John Calvert Burley to appear at the office of the solicitor of the estate for a settlement of his estate of 12,000,000 pounds. Whoever the author of the story was he made that estate no piking one. All the Burleys of London and the provinces seemed to think they were legal heirs. They covered a multitude of Burleys and types.

The story started with promise, but petered out, as though the best of the tale having been complicated in four and one-half reels, why bother with the rest?

"The Money Monster" as the theme was a streak in the Burley family; the more money they got the more they wanted. James, the grandfather, in getting his bankroll, had been an out-and-out villain, so much so that his son disowned his father and changed his name to James Calvert. His son, the grandson of the millionaire, wrote himself into the story through marrying a girl with good ideas but a poor actress. When marrying her, father-in-law told the young woman that if her husband ever found out who he was and how much money he stood to inherit, to steer him away from the coin.

When the grandfather was informed his son was dead he mentioned changing his will so the grandson would go wrong, understanding the frailty of the family; then granddad died himself, right on the spot. With no will found the grandson stepped in as his wife stepped out when he refused to sidestep the coin. Just as the young fellow was growing accustomed to going insane over money the will was found and it left everything to charity.

About the same time the wife returned to her husband, after he had had a fit and became sensible. He gave up the money for love, having decided he would have to give it up.

For the fade-out the man and wife were out canoeing on a very pretty sheet of water in a very pretty but large canoe.

This picture in total might be good enough to take a chance on to bill it as English-made, on the assumption that such pre-advertising might excite curiosity to see how they made pictures abroad. Certainly any exhibitor may bear down hard on the statement there will be characters in this film seldom previously seen on the American screen.
Sime.

THE GREEN CARAVAN

London, Nov. 23.

Starring Catharine Calvert, this feature is scarcely worthy the player or the publicity it has had. The story, adapted from a novel by Oliver Sandys, is very penny novelettish and improbable. The continuity is good, but the watcher is apt to get somewhat mixed up by the love affairs which run through it.

Lilias Vesey, a beautiful but intensely selfish girl, runs over a dog belonging to a traveling showgirl, Gipsy. Angered at her coldness Gipsy curses her. Lilias throws over her lover, Hugo Drummond, for his cousin, Lord Instow. In his despair Hugo leaves her and joins the traveling show, very soon consoling himself with his new friends.

On the eve of his wedding Instow is killed and Hugo comes into the title and estates. He leaves the circus and proceeds to London to take up his old social position again. Lilias promptly tries to win him back, but his heart is with Gipsy. Gipsy decides to come to London. She and Hugo meet again and become engaged. Lilias agrees to chaperon Gipsy, and in order to break off the engagement plots with a rascally artist, who has previously attempted to assault Gipsy, to ruin her character. She then tells Gipsy a tissue of lies which take the girl to the artist's house to obtain some letters he is supposed to be holding over Lilias' head. She is caught by the artist, but is rescued by Hugo.

After seeing her to her car Hugo returns to the studio and is told there is no need for him to marry his sweetheart. In proof of her frailty the artist exhibits a large nude portrait of Gipsy. Maddened, Hugo binds the rascal to a chair and then destroys the picture. Thinking her lover believes the worst of her, Gipsy decides to earn her own living. She is befriended by a chorus girl whom the late peer threw over to become engaged to Lilias. Having failed to win Hugo, Lilias marries a wealthy American, and the true woman in her comes into being when a child is born. The child contracts diphtheria, but its life is saved by Gipsy, who possesses the peculiar powers attributed to wandering nomads. In return Lilias tells the truth and the lovers are reunited.

The whole thing is unconvincing, but the acting is good. Miss Calvert is excellent as Gipsy, and on her the success of the feature depends. Mlle. Valia is capital as Lilias, and in the small part of the chorus girl Sunday Wilshin betrays lack of experience. Gregorey Scott is not well cast as Hugo. All the other roles are well played.

"The Green Caravan" will be handled here by the House of Granger and will be one of the features in the British national program.
Gore.

1923

SURE FIRE FLINT

Presented by C. C. Burr, with Johnny Hines at the head of an all-star cast. Story by Gerald Duffy, directed by Dell Henderson. Shown at the Cameo, N. Y., week of Dec. 31, 1922.

"Sure Fire" Flint	Johnny Hines
June de Lanni	Doris Kenyon
Johnny Jetts	Edmund Breese
Anthony de Lanni	Robert Edeson
Mrs. Anthony de Lanni	Effie Shannon
Flint's Father	J. Barney Sherry
Dibley Poole	Charles Gerrard

"Sure-Fire Flint" is a sure-fire audience picture. It has thrills, laughs and action from the start to the finish, and with it all a love story that, while a little far fetched, seemingly serves its purpose, that of the happy ending.

Johnny Hines is coming along at a pace that will place him with the few other comedians of the screen who can do feature length comedies and get away with it. In this picture Hines, while slightly given to overburlesque, still holds himself in check, so that there isn't too much Hines. It must also be counted that Edmund Breese, Doris Kenyon and Robert Edeson in his supporting cast added materially to the general worth. In action the picture has everything that could be asked for. In old hoak for laugh purposes not a bet was overlooked, and the titles are as big a comedy asset as anything else, including the star.

Gerald Duffy, who wrote the story, must have had an intimate line on the star's capabilities, otherwise he would not have worked in that very clever piece of pool shooting stuff that gets over so well.. He also had a line on the hoofing abilities of Hines, for he supplied the situation that called for a touch of dancing in which Hines got away with the floor stuff in great shape.

Hines plays the character of Flint, who, after his return from overseas duty, gets a job as a taxi driver, is fired, becomes a bus boy in a high-class cafe, is fired, and finally in company with Breese, who got both positions for him, and a little war orphan they are rearing, takes to the open road. They get to a town where the steel mill is owned by a man in whose coat Flint discovered a large sum of money. The purpose of the journey is to return the money rather than utilize it for their own use, although they were broke and had to bum their way.

The reward for this honesty is a position for them in the works. This results in the almost overnight rise to the position of manager on the part of Flint, who in the end wins the hand of his benefactor's daughter.

This simple outline does not give any idea of the thrills. Hines proves himself a go-getter with motor cycle driving, auto racing, a leap from a moving train into a river, another leap from a locomotive to a moving train. All of this is done by him more or less in a comedy vein that makes it possible for the audience to take easily.

In the support Mr. Breese stood out, as did also the kiddie, unnamed, but on first flash every bit as clever as the Coogan kid. Miss Kenyon was an altogether pleasing leading woman who has improved if anything since last in pictures. Others in the all-star aggregation are Effie Shannon, J. Barney Sherry and Charles Gerrard, who is an altogether acceptable heavy. *Fred.*

DR. JACK

Dr. Jackson	Harold Lloyd
Sick-Little-Well-Girl	Mildred Davis
Her Father	John T. Prince
Dr. Ludwig von Saulsbourg	Eric Mayne
The Lawyer	C. Norman Hammond
His Mother	Anna Townsend

"Dr. Jack" is Harold Lloyd's second five-reeler. It's slapstick farce of the old school, dependent for comedy principally on a bunch of gags that antedate the well-known infancy of the pictures. In construction "Dr. Jack" likewise follows ancient lines with a general technic strongly reminiscent of the hoke single and double reelers of the early General Film period.

The business of knocking a dignified middle-aged man's high hat into a plate of soup, the decrepit comedy bit of a comic sitting down on a piece of embroidery that contains a needle, business end up, and another that has a doctor walking out of a house with the seat of his trousers torn out as the result of a flank attack by a bulldog, gives a pretty good idea of the conventionality of the film's comedy values.

Summed up the appeal of the humor of "Dr. Jack" is distinctly juvenile. As that is about on a level with what the average picture fan considers screamingly funny, however, "Dr. Jack" may please the general run of picture audiences, whether juvenile or adult.

Harold Lloyd, admittedly a good light comedian with a flair for handling low comedy in a manner that stamps him as an expert, should be fitted with better stuff than this. Many of Lloyd's old two-reelers were far funnier, and more than one outdistanced "Dr. Jack" in speed, novelty, thrills and all-around entertaining qualities.

There's a sketchy story in the film. A young M. D. (Lloyd) manages to horn himself into a case that is being handled by a high-priced specialist. The specialist has been treating a young woman (heroine) for something or other for three years, and doing little for her, but collects regularly. Lloyd, engaged as consultant, decides to give the patient a style of treatment that calls for ridiculous comedy antics principally, with a routine that has the patient's house in an uproar.

Mildred Davis makes a pretty heroine, who works well with Lloyd; John T. Prince, C. Norman Hammond, in two contributory parts, give good performances, and Eric Mayne handles the specialist's part competently.

A couple of unprogramed children figure in several scenes that add greatly to the entertaining values of the picture. *Bell.*

BACK HOME AND BROKE

Paramount production, starring Thomas Meighan. Picture based upon the story of the same title by George Ade, with screen adaptation by the author. Directed by Alfred E. Green. At the Rivoli, New York, week Dec. 24.

Tom Redding	Thomas Meighan
Mary Thorne	Lila Lee
Otis Grimley	Frederick Burton
Eustace Grimley	Cyril Ring
H. H. Hornby	Charles Abbe
Olivia Hornby	Florence Dixon
Aggie Twaddle	Gertrude Quinlan
John Thorne	Richard Carlyle
Mrs. Redding	Maude Turner Gordon
Billy Andrews	Laurence Wheat
Horace Beemer	Ned Burton
The Policeman	James Marlowe
The Collector	Edward Borden

A genuinely amusing starring vehicle for Tom Meighan, screened from the story of the same title by George Ade. The author provided the screen version and did it to a nicety. With the possible exception of some of the early footage, largely devoted to introductory business, the picture runs at a fast clip well filled with laughs and offering opportunities in abundance for the star. It is a sparkling satire on small town life, ably aided by a well selected number of character players who furnish strong support for Meighan.

The story is typically rural, the scenes being placed in a town where even the traffic cop is not on the job. The leading manufacturing plant is owned by Redding & Son. Redding Sr. dies and his financial affairs are in a chaotic condition. His son Tom leaves town to discover oil on land his father had leased years before but thought valueless. He succeeds, but prefers to return home as if broke to determine his real friends, and does not disclose the news to the home folks. By arrangement with a friend he manages to buy practically the entire town under a fictitious name. When the time comes for the wealthy stranger to put in his appearance the supposed ne'er-do-well appears upon the platform of the private car as the train pulls into the station.

Forgiving all the slurs thrown at him in former days, he establishes himself as the town's leading citizen and benefactor of the community. A neat love story is worked up just to make the subject that much more agreeable.

Lila Lee ably leads the feminine division, with James Marlowe and Gertrude Quinlan taking the honors among the character workers. Marlowe as a comedy cop captures a couple of the biggest laughs. The general direction of the picture and its continuity stand in its favor.

"Back Home and Broke" was selected as a Christmas week attraction at the Rivoli. It should have little difficulty doing business there all week and can stand up for that length of time in any of the big program picture houses. *Hart.*

SOLOMON IN SOCIETY

Potash and Perlmutter type of story presented by the Cardinal Pictures Corp., starring Wm. H. Strauss. Produced under the supervision of Whitman Bennett, distributed by American Releasing. Shown at Cameo, New York, week of Dec. 25.

I. Solomon	Wm. H. Strauss
Rosie Solomon	Brenda Moore
Mary Bell	Nancy Deaver
Frank Wilson	Charles Delaney
Orlando Kolin	Fred Jones
Mrs. Levy	Lillian Herlein

Here is a real Potash and Perlmutter type of story by Val Cleveland, developed into a rather fair program picture. It is possible that with Wm. Strauss as the star the organization can lay the groundwork for a series of pictures with Solomon as its principal character. The "In Society" part of the title would indicate that that might be the idea. The present story is a tale of the ghetto and society with Solomon and his wife Rosie. There is one thing lacking to make this a bang-up picture, and that is comedy both in action and in the titling. In that respect the Goodman-Glass touch was shy.

Strauss plays the role of a kindly hearted east side tailor whose aptitude for designing modes finally leads him to a position where he has a Fifth avenue establishment patronized by the elite. His wife somewhat younger, falls a victim to a designing blackmailer, but Solomon, believing her happiness requires a divorce, arranges for a separation. At the last moment both realize they are acting foolishly and a reconciliation is effected. A secondary pair is composed of a laundry girl who becomes a motion picture favorite and a young lawyer who is without a client at the opening of the tale, but later is a leading legal light. This quartet are together in poverty, and together they rise to wealth and position. It is the little laundry girl who when a screen star assists the Solomons in their marital difficulties.

The tale is rather well told, though the direction in spots is a little slow in tempo and Strauss is rather prone to overact. He is not a Barney Bernard as yet, although he somewhat resembles that player. If there is to be another of the "Solomon" pictures a little more attention should be given to his work and he should be toned down. Brenda Moore as Rosie, his wife, gave a rather pleasing performance, while Nancy Deaver as the shirt-shining screen star handled what was allotted to her in a rather good way. Charles Delaney plays a juvenile lead.

In the popular-priced houses this one is bound to go, and for New York on the lower east side it is sure fire. *Fred.*

ONE WONDERFUL NIGHT

Released through Universal and featuring Herbert Rawlinson, this melo should prove adequate in topping a program for the intermediate picture houses. Lillian Rich heads the women in the cast and plays opposite the hero. Having nothing much more to do than to walk through her role, Miss Rich, nevertheless, presents a pleasing appearance. It's about all that is necessary.

The film carries along in an average manner as regards continuity in its tale of the heiress due to marry a title because of her father, but who is rescued by the youth she had met two years previously in China, same being accomplished by holding a ceremony of their own. Meanwhile the titled gentleman is the head of a gang of crooks, which leads to various scenes with the police. The hero is suspected of a criminal attack, and it all clears up with the innocent suspect leading the police raid on the gang.

The settings are well enough presented, there is more or less comedy, photography is par and Rawlinson aptly handles his share of the burden. It's not the best Universal that has ever been screened, nor is it the worst, and for those who have a leaning toward hectic mix-ups this picture will satisfy. *Skig.*

THE POWER OF A LIE

Universal All-Star Attraction, directed by George Archainbaud, from the story by Johann Bojer, adapted by Charles Kenyon. Shown at Loew's New York, N. Y., on double feature bill, Jan. 2, 1923.

John Hammond	David Torrance
Jean Hammond	Maude George
Betty Hammond	Mabel Julienne Scott
Mrs. Hammond	Ruby Lafayette
Richard Burton	Earl Metcalfe
Lillie Cardington	June Elvidge

Here was a great idea from the story standpoint, capably cast, that seemingly was permitted to slip into the caliber of the ordinary feature through faulty direction. The tempo at which George Archainbaud handled the direction made it tiresome o sit through. That is really a pity, for the story was a corker, showing the tremendous amount of complication that can arise from one lie through a series of circumstances.

The action takes place in New York, where a contractor has risen to success through having applied his wife's fortune with his own in his business. The wife, a haughty society woman, takes exception to a young man who is paying attention to the contractor's sister, and forbids her husband to make a loan to him so that he can launch a new business project. But the husband agrees to sign a note providing another indorsement can be obtained. Later the young man succeeds in getting a wealthy man-about-town to agree to lend his signature, and calls his prospective brother-in-law, arranging an appointment. The man-about-town arrives with a string of friends who have been at a wild party. Both the contractor and the other friend sign the note, and the former leaves immediately.

However, a fire occurs in the studio while the party is in progress, and the man-about-town and a society woman are locked in a room through a prank. They are rescued by the host, who gets them to a window, and the woman is carried down the ladder by the firemen and then disappears, the man, however, falling from a window and is killed. This breaks the story in the papers and the young man is turned down by his fiancee.

He starts drinking, and finally the contractor, through a situation brought about by his wife, who delivers a social snub to the wife of a banker, is compelled to deny his signature. The punch comes with the trial of the young man for forgery. A general confession at the finish cleans up the tangle in a manner that is only fairly satisfactory.

The production end of the picture as well as the cast is all that could be asked for, and had direction been worthy the picture should have been a knockout. *Fred.*

SALOME

Nazimova's production of "Salome," presented at the Criterion, N. Y., Dec. 31 1922, for an extended run under the direction of Charles Bryant. Released through United Artists.

Salome, daughter of Herodias....Nazimova
Herodias........................Rose Dione
Herod, Tetrach of Judea....Mitchell Lewis
Jokanaan, prophet.........Nigel de Brulier
The Young Syrian, captain of guard....
Earl Schenck
The Page of Herodias......Arthur Jasmina
Naaman, executioneer.....Frederick Peters
Tigellinus, young Roman......Luis Dumar

A highly fantastic "Salome" is that which Nazimova is presenting on the screen. It is far from the "Salome" Oscar Wilde penned, and decidedly different from the "Salome" generally expected.

As it is, "Salome," the play as adapted by Peter M. Winters, is a picture that none of the censors can harp against. The picture is done with a decidedly modernistic touch, so much so, in fact, it is going to be a question whether audiences will accept it. It seems rather doubtful they will. Picturesquely it is very pretty as to lightings, setting and photography, but there ends about all that can be said in praise. "Nazimova in Facial Expressions," with Salome as the background, would have been much better billing for the picture.

On the occasion of the opening performance the screening was preceded by a spoken prolog written by Louis K. Anspacher and followed by Nazimova dashing on the stage in the costume she wore in the earlier portion, in breathless manner, as though just finishing 100 yards, to inform the audience they all had a great time making the picture.

Other than the facial contortions indulged in by the Madame there is little to the picture, likewise little to her costume, which, however, was all that the law required and a bit more, so the box office won't get any great draw because of any lack of dress on the part of the star. The adoption of the Aubrey Beardsley modern idea in art for the screen does not appear as though it were going to cause any tremendous furore, especially as the heroic figures were given a decided appearance of effeminacy and the slaves of color were beefy instead of muscular.

The settings, however, were well worked out and made a really worth background for the action, such as it was.

"Salome" as a picture is going to please a few who are Nazimova devotees, a few that like higher art in all its form perversions, and then its box office value will end, unless a tremendous advertising campaign is put behind the picture to make the public believe they are going to see a "Salome" such as they have never seen before. *Fred.*

THE HEADLESS HORSEMAN

Based on "The Legend of Sleepy Hollow," by Washington Irving, and featuring Will Rogers as Ichabod Crane. Presented by Carl S Clancy, distributing through Hodkinson Pictures. Edward Venturini directed. At the Capitol, New York, week Dec. 24.

Ichabod Crane......................Will Rogers
Katrina Van Tassel...........Lois Meredith
"Brom" Bones.........Ben Hendricks, Jr.

Undoubtedly meant for comedy, Rogers' latest release is picturesque. It reveals splendid photography, but this schoolroom classic lacks the sustaining power on the screen to make it vital. It should be pie for the children who have read or are reading the story, but it doesn't seem as if their elders will become enthusiastic over this spectacle.

Rogers is the ungainly school teacher, destitute of funds and attempting to capture the belle of the valley because of her father's wealth. The action is entirely in costume. Though the picture is pleasing as an illusion, the finish is indecisive, the tale is but a legend and it's odds that the modern movie spectator will watch it, enjoy the settings, get two or three smiles out of it, then shrug his shoulders and let it go at that.

The narrative has its foundation on the supposedly headless horseman who rides the valley at night and is reported to be a former Hessian soldier looking for his head, shot off by a cannon ball during the Revolutionary War. The film starts out with the arrival in the small township of the new Yankee schoolmaster, Ichabod Crane. One evening going homeward, when half way across the haunted bridge, he sees the Headless Horseman. A deviation from the general conception of the legend has the Horseman with his head under his arm. An abrupt halt, reverse and away is in order, with the supposed ghost in pursuit. The chase concludes in the pursuer throwing his head at the fleeing Ichabod, registering a bull's-eye and knocking him from his horse, with the last flash of the school teacher revealing that he is still running. The picture concludes in a title explaining one of the villagers states he has seen Ichabod in Nieu Yorke, though his sudden, mysterious departure is the favorite ghost story of the community.

Ned Van Buren, who was behind the camera, has turned out an excellent piece of work, especially in the scenes involving Ichabod's discovery of the Headless Horseman. It's of the silhouette type and as nice a bit of cranking as has been recently witnessed. *Skig.*

THE TELEVIEW

Laurens Hammond's invention "The Teleview," a device for making certain kinds of pictures more stable and magnifying the projection, was given an initial showing at the Selwyn Dec. 27.

The house seats were equipped with the new device. It is attached to the sides of the chairs and can be folded back out of the way. "The Teleview" in use is brought up to the proper height and stays in place automatically.

It is a device which resembles the old-fashioned stereoscope which used to adorn the parlor tables of our grandparents, used for looking at snow scenes and views. The result is similar. It is explained that the glass used in the "Teleview" is ordinary window glass, the effect being obtained by a revolving shutter arrangement operated by a small motor concealed in the instrument. The hum of it is plainly heard.

The instruments are worthless as far as the ordinary picture is concerned through the necessity for a double exposure. The "Teleview" pictures are taken by a camera with two lenses. When viewed by the naked eye they are blurred and vague. Through the machine they are remarkably clear but seem restricted to small projection space.

The program opened with an ordinary picture followed by "Teleview" studies. The studies consisted of "A Bottle of Rye," "A Hole in Space," "Circles" and "A Dragon." The subjects were increased and diminished in size at the will of the projector, giving an effect of distance and proximity, unusual in a picture house.

Scenic studies next in natural colored "stills," with views of Hopi and Navajo Indian life in motion pictures, followed by an ordinary picture, viewed without the instrument.

A Shadowgraph dance by Jeanette Bobo, Helen Cronova and Elly Roder was staged behind a white drop in "one." The effect obtained was novel. The silhouettes seemingly came right out over the audience when viewed through the "Telescope."

"Mars," a "Teleview play" taken with the special camera and featuring Grant Mitchell and Margaret Irving in their picture debut, proved a fanciful comedy, draggy in spots. Miss Irving screened like a million dollars and should have no trouble in this field should she care to continue. Mitchell betrayed his lack of picture experience at times. He is a young inventor who "dreams" he has achieved radio communication with the planet Mars.

On the Selwyn showing the "Teleview" is a distinct aid toward a versatile and entertaining straight picture program. Whether the initial cost of installation—said to be $30,000 for this house—and the special cameras necessary and patents of the same company will prevent the other houses from restricting themselves to this particular program is problematical.

To install "Televiews," take their program and also show the ordinary house programs would run into considerable money. The effect is "in" now. *Con.*

Thorns and Orange Blossoms

Preferred Pictures feature release by the Al Lichtman Corp. Directed by Gasnier. Taken from the novel of the same title by Bertha M. Clay, adapted for the screen by Hope Loring.

Rosita Mendez..............Estelle Taylor
Alan Randolph.............Kenneth Harlan
Barnes Ramsey..................Arthur Hull
Violet Beaton..................Edith Roberts
Colonel Beaton..............Carl Stockdale
Pio Guerra....................Evelyn Solbie

There is a certain amount of class attached to this B. P. Schulberg production bearing the Preferred Pictures trade mark. It is a program release with much color and artistry added. Director Gasnier selected his locations to a nicety, giving the story of Spain and the South a colorful background. The natural facilities of Southern California as the locale for a Spanish picture have been used to the best advantage, the story depending largely upon the manner in which the director has worked out his selection of location. The interiors are equally artistically done.

Estelle Taylor takes first honors of the cast. She gives a genuine touch to the role of a Spanish singer with Kenneth Harlan carrying the role of hero with little difficulty. Of the remaining members of the cast, Edith Roberts stands out nicely in an ingenue role.

The story centers around a young American, who falls in love with a Spanish singer. He is engaged to an American girl, and leaves Spain without notifying the Spanish girl. She comes to America on a concert tour and confronts him in New Orleans. He then tells her that he is about to wed another. She is furious. He immediately marries the other girl in order to solve the difficulty. While visiting the singer at her hotel he informs her he will not marry her. She threatens him with a pistol, and she is shot when they struggle. He is accused and put in prison on the singer's testimony. She later repents upon learning his wife is to have a child and secures his release from the toils.

Program house patrons will enjoy "Thorns and Orange Blossoms." *Hart.*

SMUDGE

First National production, presented by Arthur S. Kane, starring and directed by Charles Ray. Story by Rob Wagner. Shown at Proctor's 23d St., New York, for three days, commencing Dec. 23.

Stephen Stanton..................Charles Ray
John Stanton............Charles K. French
Mrs. Clement.................Florence Oberle
Marie Clement.......................Ora Carew
Purdy ....J. P. Lockney
Mrs. Purdy ....Blanche Rose
McGuire.........................Lloyd Bacon
Regan....................Ralph McCullough

"Smudge" is but a second-rate Charlie Ray feature, accountable for its failure to secure a metropolitan showing at the Strand. Rob Wagner, the author, has failed to deliver a subject containing ingredients for an interesting screen story. His main idea deals with the orange-growing industry of California. To this is linked a wishy washy newspaper tale. As worked out, the combination proves weak.

Ray took a heavy task upon his shoulders in trying to direct and play the leading role and turn out a real feature with what he had to work with. The supply of ideas provided by the author proved woefully weak from the general layout of the story. Ray in one of his customary juvenile roles romps through the production and at no time is really given the opportunity to display any genuine work. The members of the supporting cast are used practically only for bits with Ora Carew, entrusted with the only other role of importance.

The title is taken from the custom employed in the orange belt of California to ward off damage to the trees from frost. Smudge pots which throw off heat and an abundance of smoke are used to keep the groves at the proper temperature. The smoke from the pots blackens the surrounding country and annoys the inhabitants, especially those not interested in the orange growing. Two factions are formed in the town of Citrona, one for and one against smudging. The two local papers are divided on the subject. The owner of the orange growers' sheet turns it over to his son. The latter is won over to the other side, much to the annoyance of his father. The young editor wins out by inventing a pot that will supply the necessary heat and will not throw out the annoying smoke. A goodly portion of melodramatic business is involved as well as a love story. The story depends largely upon auto chases and other incidents of the old school of picture making.

"Smudge" is one of the tailenders among Ray productions. It can do business only on the strength of the star's name. *Hart.*

PHANTOM

Berlin, Dec. 7.

This film, produced at the Ufa Palast am Zoo, is taken by Thea von Harbou from Gerhard Hauptmann's last novel of the same name. Poor Hauptmann! But then, after all, one mustn't feel too sorry for him, for it isn't such a great novel after all.

But when Mrs. Harbou gets through with it it looks like a collection of Duley's bromides, written for "Merton of the Movies." All the old junk from the picture attic is present.

The story is supposed to concern a clerk who sees a young girl driving a wagon drawn by white horses, and who then goes slightly "nuts," steals, almost murders, because he finds a prostitute whom he believes looks like his "dream girl of the white horses."

Then he goes to jail. Then he comes out of jail. Then he writes all about his life. Then he rushes down to the orchard, where the peach trees are in bloom, where his wife is waiting for him—his wife who waited for him all those dreary 20 years that he was in jail, and yet did not get a year older, etc.

This may sound a trifle crude as

thus told, but it is really cruder, and, what is more, technically, in casting, direction and photography, the film is not up to the standard of those made 10 years ago in America.

Alfred Abel, in the leading role, is all wrong. He plays, or one should rather say he overplays, the role, so that it is unsympathetic. It was essential the audience feel sympathy for him from the very beginning.

The direction of F. W. Murnau is without ideas. He never gets one of those little effects—one might almost say inspirations—so necessary to keep a film alive. His handling of the part of the old mother of the clerk is typical. She is kept always with the same gloomy, depressing mien, always "so sorry for herself."

But the extraordinary thing about this film is that it seems to be a popular success here in Germany. There must be some vague type of sentimentality which it touches. It is to be hoped, however, that they won't ever be so stupid as to waste any time trying to sell it to America.

Trask.

WHEN LOVE COMES

A Ray Carroll production, starring Helen Jerome Eddy. Written and presented by Ray Carroll, directed by William Seiter. Released through F. B. O. Shown at Loew's New York, N. Y., Jan. 2, 1923, double feature bill.

Jane Coleridge.........Helen Jerome Eddy
Peter Jamison.................Harrison Ford
Aunt Susie Coleridge......Fannie Midgeley
Marie Jamison.................Claire Dubray
Jim Mathews.......................Joseph Bell
Rufus Terrence..............Gilbert Clayton
The Coleridge Twins......Buddy Messenger and Molly Gordon
David Coleridge..................J. Barrows
Ruth ....Fay MacKenzie

A rather slow-moving rural melodrama that has as its big punch a rushing river scene and a rescue from the stream. Another angle that is somewhat different is a hand-to-hand battle between two women over the hero. For the regular daily change houses the picture will serve nicely, averaging up fairly well with the regular run of program features.

The story is laid in a small town where the daughter of the local banker is in love with a young engineer who has evolved a plan for utilizing the water power and making the town the industrial center of the state. The girl's father has sunk considerable money in the hope that the project will go through, but the town's council turns it down. The boy decides to seek his fortune in new quarters and proposes to the girl, asking her to accompany him. She makes up her mind to do so, but on starting out discovers that the disappointment of the failure of the project has caused her father's death, and the boy, who is awaiting her, goes on his way believing that she preferred his rival.

Later he returns to the town with a little girl, his daughter. During the five years that he has been away the girl has remained a spinster. His return is brought about with the final decision to put the water power project through. On arriving he learns that the family of the banker have been in hard straits since the death of the head of the house and that the girl has supported them through teaching.

On the day that the dam is to be dedicated the wife that had deserted the engineer puts in an appearance and claims that he deserted her for his former love, and he and the girl are in disgrace. As the maters are unleashed the wife and child are in their path. The girl rescues the babe first and then returns to help the wife, and the latter finally makes a confession, which brings the happy ending.

Both Miss Eddy and Harrison Ford, who plays the lead opposite her, manage to score fairly well, but there was naught about the picture to tax the capabilities of either. The direction was rather draggy in spots, which made the picture more or less tiresome.

Fred.

BOSS OF CAMP 4

William Fox production starring Charles Jones. Story by Arthur B. Haskins, adapted by Paul Schofield, directed by W. S. Van Dyck. Shown at Academy of Music on double feature bill.

Chet Fanning ....Charles Jones
Iris Paxton ....Fritzi Brunette
Dave Miller ....G. Raymond Nye
Dude McCormick................Francis Ford
Warren Zome........................Sid Jordan
Andrew Paxton ....Milton Ross

A melodrama of a labor camp with Charles Jones as the hero. The picture is an outdoor story, fairly interesting in its rough-and-tumble fights with Jones the boy taking on all comers, anywhere from singles to scores, and cleaning 'em up with speed and dispatch. Of course there is a love story which carries along and Jones wins the daughter of the contractor by whom he is employed. As a feature it is just an average program production that will get by nicely on the double feature bills, perhaps a little better than the usual type of outdoor pictures presented at these bargain shows.

Jones is a lately discharged veteran of the A. E. F. who has been policing the Rhine since the armistice. He arrives in a small city where there is a special advertisement for road laborers. He walks into the employment office just as a bully is cowing the other applicants, and he takes him in hand and whips him. An offer of a job is immediately forthcoming, but the ex-trooper refuses until he gets a flash at the boss's daughter, and then he makes up his mind to join out. Once at the camp, he frustrates the plot of a gang trying to impede the completion of the road building contract, and incidentally saves the life of the girl.

In all of this Jones fights about five or six rough affairs, victorious in all. This one feature alone will appeal to audiences liking action.

Fritzi Brunette as the leading woman to the star gives a rather pleasing performance, and the balance of the cast is all that could be asked for.

Fred.

SHIRLEY OF THE CIRCUS

Fox program feature starring Shirley Mason. Story and scenario by Robert M. Lee. Direction by Rowland V. Lee. Shown at Loew's New York as the secondary picture of a double feature bill Dec. 23.

Nita ....Shirley Mason
Pierre ....George O'Hara
James Blackthorne..........Crauford Kent
Max ....Alan Hale
Blanquette ....Lulu Warrenton
Susan Millbanks ....Maude Wayne
Mrs. Millbanks.........Mathilde Brundage

No great pains were taken with this Shirley Mason starring vehicle, produced by Fox. It is a commonplace production with no outstanding punch to sanction it for a worth while program release. The value may be judged by the fact that it was in a double bill at Loew's New York. When two features are played at that Loew house each is bought at a price. This Fox production was booked for but one day by the Loew interests, the New York being the only house it was scheduled to play for them. Possibly the price was the reason the picture was shipped in there at, as it was a surety the other feature of the bill took the greater portion of the day's appropriation.

Robert M. Lee, the author, provided a story of simple design based upon circus life. The circus idea is of several years' standing. This picture has nothing more interesting or attractive in its circus scenes than were in similar features before it.

Miss Mason's supporting players have practically as many opportunities as the star herself. Crauford Kent, Alan Hale and George O'Hara divide the honors in the male division. Hale and O'Hara experience difficulty at times in displaying their acrobatic ability, many of the circus scenes calling for difficult work, which is faked to a large degree. The star appears as a young miss wearing a wig to cover her bobbed locks during convent scenes in the early footage. The picture calls for little acting by her.

The story starts with its locale in France. An acrobatic trio of two men and a girl travels from town to town, performing in the streets for returns from passing the hat. The girl is befriended by an American artist, who sends her to a convent to be educated. The head of the trio secures an opportunity to join a circus in America and tries to induce the girl to leave the convent. She runs away and goes to America, appearing at the artist's home, and is there befriended by his fiancee, who takes her home. Her acrobatic partners arrive from Europe and she is finally located. In love with the younger of the two, she finally agrees to return with them. The other chap, through jealousy, allows his partner to fall while performing a trick in the hope he will kill himself so he may marry the girl. He fails in his attempt and she marries the other acrobat.

Hart.

THE MAN AND THE MOMENT

A foreign-made product from an original story authored by Elinor Glyn. It smacks very much of the English. After viewing this picture it's not hard to fathom the reason why American-made films are in demand on the other side. No American director would ever release such a vehicle as this behind his signature.

The picture is flagrant in its cheapness of production, the story is unendedly drawn out, photography is but fair and the cast is a distinct reminder of the melodrama screened about 15 years ago. Identical sets are repeatedly on view; the same clothes of the principals are continually worn despite any jump in time the story may take, and most all of the action is interior while placed in one scene of a large room of a castle that has closeups of different sections of the same building as its main diversion in scenery. The film carries a Playgoers Pictures, Inc., trade-mark.

Relating a society drama, it tells of a young member of the peerage allowing himself to become entangled with a married woman on the verge of divorce, with his only means of escape an immediate marriage. An American heiress who won't receive her legacy until she marries is sightseeing in the castle of the peer; they meet and decide on a marriage of convenience. But it becomes a bit more than that. The girl disappears, and both fall in love with the memory of each other. The remaining footage is taken up in the bringing together again of the hastily married and separated pair.

Vast padding takes away whatever merit the script may have had as also does the superfluous reading in the form of sub-titles, a film-footage-saving scheme which seemingly crop up at every 10 feet.

Showing at a middleclass house, the outside billing gave no indication as to the nature or make of the film other than to reveal the title, banked by "With an all-star cast" line, which leads to the impression it must have been exceedingly foggy in England while they were grinding out this one.

Skig.

THE FLIRT

Universal-Jewel Production, from the Booth Tarkington story. Directed by Hobart Henley. At Rialto (Famous Players house), New York, week Dec. 24.

Papa ....George Nichols
Mama ....Lydia Knott
Cora ....Eileen Percy
Laura ....Helen Jerome Eddy
Hedrick ....Buddy Messenger
Jimmy ....Harold Goodwin
Della Fenton..........................Nell Craig
San Fenton ....Tom Kennedy
Valentine Corliss............Lloyd Whitlock
Richard Lindley..............Edward Hearn
Wade Trumble ....Bert Roach
George Carroll ....William Welch

That this Universal made feature, "The Flirt," is playing at the Rialto, New York, this week must have denoted to those of the trade that through a pre-showing to the F. P. people it was deemed a good picture. So F. P. allowed the U. to take the Rialto on a guarantee by U. for Xmas week. And it is a good picture, with a peach of a title for big or little cities or big or little towns. There's no place so small it hasn't its flirt, and in most of the towns this picture will pay there's one of the Tarkington kind on every block. This makes its title a peach because there is a picture back of it to back it up, thanks to the splendid direction by Hobart Henley, so splendid it cannot be overlooked by anyone understanding anything about pictures.

"Flirt" is a comedy and a drama and a comedy-drama. Its laughs and its interest balance, as odd as that may sound for a picture nowadays. Its cleanliness helps the laughs which are begotten by such simple expedients, aided to some extent by bright, incisive titling, that the very simplicity is a part of the superior direction.

It's not a simple matter to bring forth an involuntary outburst of laughter from a picture audience expectant of a semi-drama, and to repeat it as frequently as it is repeated here, but the Rialto audience on Christmas night, an over-capacity house, burst into joyous laughter at least 20 times, and toward the finish wiped a tear or so away as it watched the wreckage accumulate with its consequences by the designing flirt. "The Flirt" may have been written by Tarkington as a screen play, or it may be a new title for one of his adapted books.

The picture runs somewhat over the customary feature length. It was 90 minutes running off at the first night show. But there isn't a minute left to cut out. It's all meat, with its locale "Capital City, Indiana," and its types or characters blending in with what would be that city if there is, and there may be.

The Flirt is the pretty daughter of James Madison, the father of a considerable family and in the real estate business, substantial, but worried over money matters that the size of the family causes, mostly through Cora, the flirtatious one. One of the sons is a plumber and married; he needs money and asks his father; another son has gone away, got into bad habits, needs money and calls on father, who helps them all, going to the extremity of mortgaging the family homestead.

Cora frames a routine she regularly goes through, of becoming engaged, asking the engagement be kept secret, and continuing to flirt with every strange man hitting the burg. She finally winds up against one Valentine Corliss, an oily oil promoter, who returns to his home town to pluck it. Seeing how easily Cora is falling, he induces her, under promise of a world-wide tour, to persuade her father to become secretary of his company, to make the plucking move faster. When Cora can't obtain her father's signature, she forges it to his consent to become the secretary. On the strength of that Corliss quickly secures $6,000 through stock sales and as quickly vamps, leaving the irate townsmen to visit old Madison, ac-

cuse him of fraud, and swear out a warrant for his arrest for obtaining money under false representations.

Cora, getting wind of the brewing trouble, marries Wade Trumble in a hurry but not soon enough to prevent her enduring sister, Laura, from obliging her to return home, confess the forgery, and bring about a family reunion, completed when Jimmy, the former erring son, arrives just in the nick of time to square everything. While the oil promoter did ruin the father, he left Cora alone, so the only chance for dirt was thankfully overlooked.

And now for the comedy part. The Madisons' youngest son, Hedrick (Buddy Messenger) was an impish cut-up. His flirting sister made him sick; he told the family so. "The way she lured on the goofs" was the reason. Hedrick was short and dumpy, an inquisitorial kind of a kid, always in mischief, with his own comical ideas he worked out for his own laughs, and always jamming up something. It's this kid and the way he has been handled, his slant at things in general and his comment, his didoes and his mischieveness that will make you laugh, whether you are five or 75.

There are other types and other laughs, and some reflection. Laura Madison, as played by Helen Jerome Eddy, is a sympathy-compelling role. She is the other sister, not so good-looking, not so flirty, and taking all the slaps for the benefit of her sister. But when she got started over her father passing out, what she did to Cora!

The flirt part was written for Eileen Percy, and if it wasn't it could have been. Miss Percy played it just that way, from the wave in her hair to the kick in the shins she gave her little brother. She was the small-town flirt all over. In fact, there wasn't a mar in the cast, and the casting director can take a bow on his or her work.

This picture is going to travel and do business, amusing and interesting while it does. Its moral, if any, will be realized only by the flirts. Whether it is a lesson to them is beside it, for they will grow flirts faster than they can make pictures.

The production is ample for its needs, which are small, and with excellent photography there's nothing missing here—even if it is U. No one could ask for better film entertainment, and without flare, extravagance in production or wasted footage—just straightaway good fun in a good story with a peach title. If U. would have stood for the necessary production cost "The Flirt" could have been made into a super-special.

Perhaps this will be an incentive for the U. No doubt it will surprise that organization to find it has a hit the censors are not watching, to know it can put out a success without being a freak sex draw, to find out a decent-looking feature picture may be made within a maximum of limited expense, and to play one of its features for the first time in a regular first run house on Broadway. *Sime.*

STRANGERS' BANQUET

Presented by Marshall Neilan, co-directed by Neilan and Frank Urson and distributed through Goldwyn. Story by Donn Byrne, with D. Keeson and M. Fabian the photographers. At the Capitol, New York, week Jan. 1.

Shane Keogh	Hobart Bosworth
Derith Keogh	Claire Windsor
Angus Campbell	Rockliffe Fellowes
Al Norton	Ford Sterling
Jean McPherson	Eleanor Boardman
John Trevelyan	Thomas Holding
Mrs. McPherson	Eugenia Besserer
John Keogh	Nigel Barrie
Prince	Stuart Holmes
Uncle Sam	Claude Gillingwater
Bride	Margaret Loomis
Bride's Father	Tom Guise
Bride's Mother	Lillian Langdon

Quite a pretentious feature from whichever angle you may choose to gaze at it. The picture runs better than an hour and a half. Also, the program revealed a printed cast of 30 names, as did a flashed title.

For the story itself little need be said. While not exceptional, neither is it uninteresting, and the way it has been handled suffices for any deficiencies. Probably whatever skepticism this film will invoke will revert to the running time. Exhibitors and picture men in general will no doubt find numerous instances that might be eliminated without doing any material damage to the narrative, but such a procedure would cut a wealth of detail and business from a feature that thrives on just such. Neilan's hand is very much in evidence all the way. And how!

They've lifted a gag line, generally credited to an author of stories concerning knights of the prize ring, to follow a fighting character's individual scraps and, besides, jump a "stag" story to the screen, somewhat cleaned up, of course, for an honest laugh from those who have heard the tale and a snicker from those who haven't! But it all helps. The picture, in addition, shows some handy work in the deft art of splicing, for at one time the scenes switch so fast it's hard on the eyes to follow. However, it lasts less than a minute and is simply used to present four characters, in pairs, saying identical things.

Rockliffe Fellowes is the outstanding member of the ensemble. A corking performance he gives. The remaining 29, as well, take note unto themselves, with it, perhaps, being but fair to mention Claire Windsor as running only second to Fellowes for top honors. Both hold the roles around which the story revolves, though that fails to be the main reason for their predominating.

The narrative has mostly to do with a capital and labor problem, having its setting in a large shipyard plant on the west coast. Shane Keogh is the owner of the works, and when he dies he leaves the responsibility of carrying on to his daughter, Derith. Angus Campbell, an adopted son of the old gentleman, has worked himself up to the post of general manager and is in love with the girl, though afraid to state his case because of her position. John Keogh is the rightful son, but somewhat of a weakling. His marriage to a coin digging young lady and the aftermath, ending in the death of the girl in a wild automobile ride, practically give the picture a double story to relate.

Following the death of the father the workers in the shipyards are subjected to a siege of red flag propaganda, fall for it and walk out on strike, all the time urged on by a Bolshevik fanatic made so through his marriage having been stopped at the altar through its being revealed he has no legal father. Hence, he's out to ruin the world in general and society in particular. Angus, the fighting general manager, who doffs his glasses as a sign that he is going into action (and it's a whale of a piece of "business"), has disagreed and quit with his sweetheart boss because of her leniency in dealing with a walking delegate's demands. But he comes back when it looks like a general outbreak. Same is averted by the girl and Angus making an appeal to Trevelyan, the fanatic, who is shot by one of the inside red workers with the bullet intended for the returned general manager. He, however, speaks to the massed workers before passing out and the strike is off. The finale has Derith proposing to Angus, as the lad continues to be a bit backward on the subject.

The picture is another mark for Neilan and a credit to Urson. Not forgetting Ford Sterling, splendid in the role of a chap who never takes anything seriously. The photography is at all times beyond reproach, though the lighting in one instance might be termed questionable. One peculiar interior effect was that of two figures, both on a parallel line, with one showing in soft focus and the other sharp and clear. Whether or not the lighting did it or the effect was intentionally produced, the illusion was most unusual.

The "Banquet" is a fit subject for any of the first run houses, and if the latest Harold Lloyd release ("Dr. Jack") cost the $300,000 or more reported, who can guess the total this one hung up. For, if nothing else, it looks money. *Skig.*

MY AMERICAN WIFE

A Jesse Lasky production, starring Gloria Swanson, directed by Sam Wood. Script by Monte Katterjohn, based on the story by Hector Turnbull. Shown at the Rivoli, New York, week Dec. 31, . 722.

Natalie Chester	Gloria Swanson
Manuel La Tassa	Antonio Moreno
Don Fernando De Contas	Josef Swickard
Carlos De Grossa	Eric Mayne
Pedro De Grossa	Geno Corrado
Donna Isabella La Tassa	Edythe Chapman
Hortensia De Varela	Eileen Pringle
Gomez	Walter Long
Horace Beresford	F. R. Butler

An altogether interesting feature production has been developed from what seemingly was a story without any involved plot. Its simplicity alone makes it a pleasure to watch the unfoldment of the story on the screen. From the box office standpoint there is naught in particular about the picture, which can be pointed out as holding extraordinary appeal, but the picture is an all around satisfying entertainment.

The cast is a good one, with Gloria Swanson starred and Antonio Moreno as her leading man. Moreno appears to better advantage in this production than he has in a great many of the pictures in which he was starred. Had he had so capable direction and general atmosphere surroundings in the past productions he would now be a star who would practically top the list of screen favorites. That is one thing that the Famous Players-Lasky can do for the player to bring them to the top of their profession.

The Hector Turnbull story has its scene of action laid in South America, and while no country or city in particular is named it is quite apparent that Buenos Aires, Argentina, is intended. Two families are represented as the principals in action. One, an all powerful political power, is using its office to further its own schemes and promoting measures that reek with graft. The head of the house of the other family, who holds a seat in the parliament, refuses to enthuse over politics, but goes in for sport and maintains an extensive racing stable. His entry for the big race of the year is defeated by an entry from the United States, and when he seeks out the owner to offer congratulations he discovers that it is an American girl.

At a dinner in celebration of the victory that night the son of the political leader insults the American girl and the defeated horseman becomes her champion, whereupon a duel is arranged. Through the employment of a gunman the horseman is shot from ambush as the duelling pistols are fired. The American girl nurses him back to health and he proposes, but his mother intervenes, and the girl then turns to uncovering the plot which brought about the shooting. In this she is successful, and finally marries the hero, who deserts his sportive ways and turns to politics and his country's call.

For picturesque values there is nothing left to be desired. There is a corking horse race scene, a beautiful fete of flowers and action at all times.

Miss Swanson, however, does not seem to register as effectively in this production as she has in the past. In several scenes her style of hair dressing seemed to detract from her face, and in the early outdoor scenes lines and shadows in her face marred her beauty. Moreno was splendid, and Josef Swickard proved himself once more a most capable screen character man. The heavy of Geno Corrado was fair in its enactment, but the burly gunman contributed by Walter Long, was a real piece of work. Loyal Underwood, playing a jockey, managed to slip into several scenes and take them away from some of the heavier guns of the cast. He is a clever chap. *Fred.*

WOMEN MEN MARRY

Production by Edward Dillon, put out by the Genius Productions Corp. Story by Adelaide Heilbron, adaptation and direction by Edward Dillon. E. K. Lincoln featured, with Florence Dixon heading the supporting company. Picture is a society drama. At Proctor's 125th Street Dec. 2.

The picture has some excellent production points, the settings for the fashionable drawing room scenes being in really notable good taste and with impressive atmosphere, The backgrounds are always convincing.

How so much good taste and intelligence could be expended upon the staging of the picture and so much crude bad judgment in the selection of the story and its development before the camera is a matter of complete puzzlement. The thing is full of dramatic crudities.

For instance, the director at one time goes through an elaborate scene of the wife getting her things on for the street, taking leave of her husband with a subtitle "I'm going out to tea. You don't mind, do you, dear?" and then departing. We are thus prepared to find that some important development hangs on this incident, but it has not the slightest bearing on the proceedings.

It is rather a shock to have the husband die in almost the next scene, although we have been led to expect that the husband is to be the main figure of the whole story. The hero plays almost a minor part. He does not appear until nearly the middle of the picture, and then in anything but a heroic role. His introduction to the heroine comes when he happens to find her pet pup. The nearest thing to heroic action on his part is his mere presence when her automobile is wrecked and he brushes her face with a handkerchief. For these small services he is rewarded with her hand in the final closeup.

The dramatic values are all awry. The story is really about Amelie, a rather vulgar new rich American girl who schemes to capture a worthless Englishman with a title but is defeated by her foster father, and after she has tasted poverty for a few months turns to the young American engineer whom she encountered while he was a stoker on an ocean liner.

One becomes impatient at this spoiled child of fortune. Why is it that the ideal of a movie aristocrat is a man or woman who behaves offensively to the servants? And why does a foreigner with a title have to conduct himself like an eccentric comedian in a musical comedy? The unworthiness of the girl's fortune hunting suitor could have been indicated with less raw crudity. And it was a pretty brutal theatrical scheme to transplant the young American hero from the liner's stokehold directly into the job of second man in the heroine's home and then into that of her father's confidential secretary. A few jolts like that make one turn from the screen in disgust. There is a limit to this sort of thing.

The picture probably is an old one that has waited for release a long time. All the dresses of the women are a foot and a half from the ground, in the fashion of nearly two years ago. *Rush.*

HUNTING BIG GAME

Heralded from the Coast as the greatest animal pictures ever taken, this 10-reeler opened at the Lyric, New York, Monday night showing just cause as to the why of the advance complimentary mouth-to-mouth publicity it received. The picture is educational and historical without, at any time, becoming boresome and what is more, it is entertainment.

No story has been attempted. It's simply straightaway shooting of what the title implies, "Hunting Big Game in Africa With Gun and Camera." Eugene H. Roth is responsible for the presenting with H. A. Snow and his son, Sid, having done the actual work in the taking of the picture. The showing at the Lyric is in two parts, runs a little short of two hours and carries a good-sized orchestra rendering a special score. The business end of the project is under the direction of J. J. McCarthy and Theodore Mitchell. The price scale reads $1.65 top at night and $1 for matinees.

Information, concerning the picture, gleaned from other sources than the program, narrated it was over two years and a half in the making; the expedition was financed by a corporation located in Oakland, Cal., through means of a stock subscription of which the University of California holds the controlling interest. It cost $288,000.

The expedition started out with 10 camera men and came back with one. Around 125,000 feet of film were exposed, needing six months to assemble. Snow slipped one over on all previous photographic efforts of the jungle in developing, while sweltering in the terrific heat, by doing his work late at night or in the early morning hours instead of waiting until the return to this country. The photography shows it. Some of the scenes, made through both the ordinary lense and the telescopic arrangement, are as clear and concise as the average exterior witnessed in a general release.

Beyond the merit comes the titling. Whoever did it revealed excellent discretion with a sense of humor that gets away from the preverbial wording in this type of a screen attraction, that simply states facts, data, more facts and then additional data—just to make it good. Incidentally the writer has included a complimentary phrased title that mentions the Paul Rainey expedition.

The film is bound to draw applause from any audience. Inside of five minutes after the start applause came with the screening of thousands upon thousands of penguins lined up on a beach and making for the sea, some specie of antelope which takes a leap while running (30 or 40 feet in actual distance) and which is most spectacular the chasing of a number of giraffes across a plain with "close ups" following and the charging of the camera by a rhinoceros and the elephant herd, used as a finish, which is remarkable.

The two latter episodes are th thrills, disclosing the natives edging away from the camera as the animals advance and concluding in everybody running for it and shooting as they go. There is comedy in the subject of a Ford chasing all sorts of animals across the plains. It's very funny to watch. One or two of the animals became so tired of galloping ahead of an object that won't quit that they stop, turn and attack it. Which puts the "lizzie" into reverse. A close up of some sort of a wart hog, exhausted, following his encounter with the machine, screened a facial expression that shrieked, "What is this, a gag?"

That this picture is paramount as an educational feature is without question and as a box office attraction it seems safe to say it will land, for it certainly has all the requisites. Interest, thrills, comedy, photography, titling and the censors can't bother it. The chances are it will receive an amount of publicity through the talking of those who have witnessed it. *Skig.*

SECRETS OF PARIS

C. C. Burr presented this screen version of Eugene Sue's novel, famous a century ago, "Mysteries of Paris." The adaptation is credited to Dorothy Farnum. Direction is by Kenneth Webb, with the production credited to Whitman Bennett. Distributed by Mastodon Films. The all-star cast is being featured for the special engagement at the Cameo, beginning Jan. 7.

Prince Rudolf	Lew Cody
Mayflower	Gladys Hulette
The Schoolmaster	Montague Love
Lola	Dolores Cassinelli
The Chancellor	J. Barney Sherry
The Strangler	Walter James
Francois	William Collier, Jr.
The Owl	Rose Coghlan
Madam Ferrand	Effie Shannon
Hoppe (the hunchback)	Harry Sothern
The Hindu	Bradley Barker
Margot	Jane Thomas

The picture is frank melodrama; it's all "old stuff" of thieves' dens, subterranean chambers where victims are "drowned like rats" and the rest of the props; but it's extremely vigorous melodrama and it does keep you on the edge of your chair.

The whole thing is theatrical and elemental, but it has it over the thin-bodied material of the modern kind of fiction. It has the genuine punch proved by generation after generation of readers of robust romance and heroism. The old stuff is the best after all. This picture is wildly melodramatic, but it progresses with a sweep of action that is beyond and above realism, and it creates its own illusion. This is an odd thing. Nothing could be more artificial than the plot, but the illusion is there because the story has that touch of antiquity which invites credulity. It is somewhat the appeal of "The Two Orphans" in its play form, which remained for generations one of the hardy perennials.

There was an unwonted briskness about the Cameo Sunday night, one of the coldest of the winter. The statement that the day totaled better than $1,100 and is the best Sunday for two months is believable to one who attended the evening show, which had the crowd filling the lobby out to the street box office. No large advertising appropriation could account for the attendance, nor had the picture any previous chance to gain by repute since this was its premiere. Probably the preliminary advertising in newspapers would be covered by less than $1,000.

The best explanation of the unexpected draw was the cast, which has eight eminent names of the stage and screen, aided probably by a capital title that intrigues the imagination. The Sue name may also have carried weight, although the famous novel is not so much read as in other generations.

A very neat treatment is given the old tale. At times the backgrounds are of the ancient period, but the costuming is always smart and modern. They have apparently to keep the picture out of the costume story class by merely ignoring its time. The scenes in the Rat's Hole, as the thieves' dark resort is called, have a touch of ancient atmosphere. So have a number of street scenes. These give the picture a certain venerable flavor. But all the costuming is modern, and they even use an automobile as the vehicle of an abduction. The thing has been trickily handled. The ancient atmosphere is hardly glimpsed, but the character of the story belongs to another age, suggested only in its robust spirit, while its physical telling is accomplished in modern and therefore more easily understandable terms.

The narrative moves in bing-bang style. There is no elaborate leading up to effects. The tale has native strength enough to go right into it. And it has an astonishing amount of meat and punch. It starts with the pretty little romance of the maid of the people and Prince Rudolph. But this is short, and within a few hundred feet we are in the midst of the thieves' gang, with the Strangler, the Owl, Mme. Ferrand, the sinister old hag and the Schoolmaster who ruled the outlaws and directed their crimes.

Here is an imaginary underworld that lays all over the modern, pale sort. There is a fight between Lew Cody and Montague Love, one a convict and the other a king in disguise, that is a pippin, and through it all there runs the sympathetic story of the two waifs, Mayflower and Francois, to give it pathos. The adaptation has been splendidly done. The finale has the hero and heroine trapped and being drowned in the fiends' trap, while the brigands are off looting the king's residence. The flashbacks from the adventure of the crooks to the slowly rising tide about the victims and the approach of the boy rescuer is a fine bit of thrilling melodrama.

The picture is bound to be a draw, for it is the best kind of rugged melodrama that will appeal to all strata of fans. *Rush.*

THE THIRD ALARM

P. A. Powers presents a seven-reel melodrama dealing sentimentally with the life of the fireman. Story by Emilie Johnson, production by Emory Johnson Productions, with Emory Johnson directing. Charles Watt, assistant director. Ralph Lewis is starred. Distributed by the Film Booking Office. Opened at the Astor, New York, at a scale of $1.10 top, beginning Jan. 8.

Dan McDowell	Ralph Lewis
Johnny McDowell	Johnny Walker
June Rutherford	Ella Hall
Mrs. McDowell	Virginia True Boardman
Dr. Rutherford	Richard Morris
Jimmie, a newsboy	Frankie Lee
"Baby"	Josephine Adair
"Bullet"	Himself

The picture has plenty of thrills and moments of genuine sentiment, but it is cheaply made if one excepts the possible cost of fire department aid for the climax, an effective fire scene with a capital backing of dramatic action and a shrewdly devised handling of the romantic element.

But whether it will get much of a play at the $1 top appears doubtful. It hasn't a star name to attract fan attention; it is a good picture, but not big enough to command a clientele and coax them from the regular film palaces of Times square, especially at a scale above those of the leading cinemas. These excursions into legitimate theatres don't exert the pull they did once. The business has tried to put over too many mediocre pictures by that medium and the public is shy. A picture has to make a lot of noise to attract, especially without the guarantee of a screen luminary.

Tuesday night (weather bad) there were about 150 people on the lower floor, and they were lukewarm in audible demonstrations. The finale got a patter of applause, but it was perfunctory. There is a false note somewhere in the picture, hard to put one's finger on, but probably it is an overplay on sentimentalism that at times becomes maudlin. It's a pity they struck this false note, for some of the passages have honest and genuine sympathetic appeal.

Parsimony is evident in the handling of settings as well as in the absence of star names that represent any considerable total on the payroll. The appropriation probably was pretty well used up in securing the services of fire department apparatus and filming the fire scene at the finish. This has a fine thrill and works neatly into the sentimental story, but it is not backed up by any force of production elsewhere. For example, one of the subordinate roles is that of a world famous surgeon who rides about in a high-priced sedan, but when they come to show his home one is forcibly reminded of a modest Harlem flat. The only other backgrounds are a few interiors showing the cottage of Dan, the veteran driver of the racing horses of Engine No. 7. The outlay here is small.

The story has to do with Dan's great love for his prize team and his grief when he is retired because he cannot fit himself into motorized fire engines. The script is better than the production, instead of the reverse, as happens nine times out of ten. Dan is made a lovable character bound up in his five splendid horses, and especially the big white "Bullet," a beautiful animal and a first rate actor. Dan has been the department's prize driver for 30 years when they introduce motors. His leave-taking of "Bullet" is a touching scene. Dan can't put his son through college on his pension and he sorrows at inaction. "Bullet" is no more happily placed as a cart horse with a brutal owner.

Dan gets a laborer's job working on the streets, and when the driver abuses "Bullet" there is a free-for-all in which the old man is bested, but rescued by his sturdy son, Johnny. The same night "Bullet" in the contractor's stable hears the engines go past and breaks loose to follow. An urchin (same kid that played the cripple in "The Miracle Man") captures him and leads him into Dan's woodshed out of harm's way.

They arrest Dan for stealing the horse and he is in jail when the big fire starts. His case comes to the attention of the Chief and he is promptly released. From there the action is superlatively melodramatic. Dan goes to the fire by force of habit; finds that his son Johnny has been pinned under burning wreckage in an effort to rescue his sweetheart. Dan dons coat and helmet and goes to work. The saving of Johnny and the girl depends upon moving an iron safe that holds them down as the fire creeps toward them.

"Bullet" has sniffed the excitement from afar, and, breaking his harness, rushes to the scene. All but a few heroic firemen remain to struggle with the safe, but they cannot move it. During these action scenes capital cutbacks are shown of the approach of the galloping 'Bullet," until he rushes on the scene in time to find Dan amid the flames, ready to hitch him to the tackle and drag the hero and heroine clear.

The picture has a wealth of popular bits involving a group of clever kids and effective side scenes of dumb animals, such as the flight of the firehouse cat when the new auto engine begins to backfire. All well done and contributing to the sum total.

The presentation is cheap and shabby. A two-reel Carter De Haven comedy precedes the feature. Thereafter follows an act, the National (male) quartet in a firehouse set confined to a back drop. They sing a routine of songs, including the old boys like the one beginning "The cows in the meadow, they moo—" At the finish of the old style harmony there is a back drop effect showing a distant fire, the sounding of the gong in the regulation "double 3" taps, and the main title of the feature flashes on. The orchestra is small with a lot of emphasis on the brasses and drums, and appropriate sound effects run through the picture.

The big fire scene is at times realistic on a big scale, but there are shots that look extremely fakey. The falling of the walls has a thrill, but shots at massed flames do not altogether convince, perhaps because of the difficulties in getting right flame color values into a black and white film. *Rush.*

DARLING OF THE RICH

Dramatic feature by B. B. Productions, starring Betty Blythe. Story by Dorothy Farnum. Directed by John Adolfi under the supervision of Whitman Bennett. Supporting company headed by Montagu Love. Others in the cast, Charles Gerard, Gladys Leslie, Julia Swayne Gordon. At the New York Dec. 6.

A naive and ingenuous melodrama in which pretentious situations and childish incidents are mingled in utmost confusion. The big scene of the story has the pure heroine, an artless young thing from Long Island, playing hostess for a society monarch of untold wealth and wearing a Cleopatra costume of truly Ziegfeldian daring.

Our pure heroine has a crippled brother at home and has to finance a costly operation, so she takes advantage of the society fete to auction herself off in marriage to the highest bidder. One captain of industry bids a million, but the social giant goes him one better with an offer of half his entire fortune. At the end the heroine turns down both offers in favor of a young financier whom she truly loves.

Mixed up in this tangled fabric of absurd fiction is a struggle for so gross a thing as a patent for a rubber-making process, deep schemes by polite and rough underworld characters and other outlandish elements. It all leaves the spectator rather stunned and dizzy.

The physical production is in the highest taste. The Bennett studios have provided a number of rich settings for the action, but the story doesn't command serious attention at any point. Its only virtue is that it is so childish it wins a sort of indulgence by virtue of its very naivete. Its heroics are scaled so unreasonably high, the money and jewels are in such huge amounts and its emotions are so terrific one gets to accept them smilingly. The story in its ridiculous complications might have been contrived by a 14-year-old child. Certainly it has no relation to life. It is just unrestrained fictionizing, and probably will have a certain appeal to that section of the fan public which loves to have its romance laid on good and thick.

It is strange to see so crude a story produced with such splendid backgrounds. Many of the interiors would have been appropriate for a Pinero problem play. The settings for the home of the society millionaire were especially convincing. The costuming is gorgeous and Miss Blythe is always a beautiful if an implausible figure. *Rush.*

IN CALVERT'S VALLEY

Fox production starring John Gilbert. Based upon the story by Margaret Prescott Montague, adapted for the screen by Jules Furthman. Directed by Jack Dillon.

Page Emlyn...................John Gilbert
Hester Rymal.............Sylvia Breamer
James Calvert ....{
Eugene Calvert...........}Philo McCullough
Judge Rymal..............Herschel Mayall
Widow Crowcroft..........Lulu Warrenton

From general appearances Fox is making no attempt to produce program features of any great value. Apparently this producing organization is devoting its energy upon large features and letting the regular program five reelers come along to be used as fillers wherever a picture of that length is needed. "In Calvert's Valley" is a good example of minus quality. It is a cheap feature and the story means nothing. That it was used in a double feature bill at Loew's New York for one day suffices.

The author turned out a mystery story along standard lines around a murder. The hero until the final footage appears to be the guilty man and believes it himself as he had been under the influence of moonshine at the time the crime was committed.

To bring the tale to an end the blame is placed upon the shoulders of a half-wit which paves the way for the formerly accused to win the girl of the murdered man.

Discriminating picture audiences will not take to the story. The cast does comparatively satisfactory work. Gilbert appears to have the ability to do better things. Philo

McCullough in a dual role is another asset.

Some picturesque exteriors help out to a certain degree. *Hart.*

WHILE JUSTICE WAITS

Fox production directed by Bernard J. Durning, with Dustin Farnum as the star. Story credited to Charles A. and Don A. Short. Scenario by Edwin Booth Tilton. At Loew's New York, Jan. 9, part of double feature bill.

For the picture fan who still maintains a liking for western thrillers this Fox release with the robust Dustin Farnum in the stellar role will hold some interest. Exhibitors wanting a western at a price can use this. It is just a degree better than the big percentage of pictures of this type being turned out at the present time.

There appears to exist a feeling among producers that audiences for which these thrillers are made are not discriminating. This does not ring true, as many who patronize the houses playing the less expensive screen productions are critical to an extreme. To the majority western dramas are not new. It is that style of feature which came to the fore when pictures secured their first foothold. Many of the patrons of nickelodeons of former days are patronizing the 15 and 20-cent admission houses today, and it is there that the western picture gets its biggest play and the returns for the producer.

Regardless of these facts the majority of western dramas are stereotyped and rest almost entirely upon their laurels as scenic productions. The players in few instances are called upon to do any real acting and suffice in their efforts as long as they can remain seated upon a horse.

"While Justice Waits" is a short cast production, with the roles of importance in support of the star handled by Irene Rich, Gretchen Hartman and Earl Metcalfe. Although the continuity is allowed to dwindle at times, the story proves comparatively gripping and sufficiently interesting to hold attention. It reverts to type at all stages, bringing in the familiar bar room scenes, gun work and fast riding. It discloses a certain amount of acting a bit beyond the usual requirements of the standard low-priced western program picture. The four roles of importance are handled expertly, each of the four players being of the old school and well up on what is needed for this type of production.

The authors start their story with the leading character successfully locating a gold mine in Alaska. He had prospected for some time and had left a wife and baby back in Nevada. Attaining success he decides to return. Just prior to his arrival his wife is induced to leave her home by a new male acquaintance who promises to protect her as a gentleman, the country being full of bandits. His true desires are learned upon her arrival with the child at his camp. It is learned he is a notorious bandit. She escapes after he steals the child, which is placed in a mission. The husband, returning home, learns of her apparent unfaithfulness and seeks his revenge. He scours the country and gets his revenge at the finish, when all is forgiven and the family reunited. *Hart.*

SNOWSHOE TRAIL

R-C production, released through the Film Booking Office. Story by Edison Marshall, placed in screen form by Marion Fairfax. Directed by Chester Bennett.

Virginia Tremont................Jane Novak
Bill Bronson...................Roy Stewart
Harold Lounsbery............Lloyd Whitlock
Kenly Lounsbery............Herbert Prior
Mrs. Bronson...................Kate Toncray
Herbert Lounsbery.....Spottiswoodie Aitkin
Mah Lung......................Chai Hung

A production featuring snow scenes, the greater portion of each reel being devoted to the snow-covered outdoors. Every once in a while a picture of this type crops up, and in most instances does nicely scenically, but that is about all that may be said for it. That is the case with "The Snowshoe Trail." It is long on snow scenes, many really picturesque, but as a gripping picture falls short largely, due to the familiar lines of the theme.

Taken all in all, "The Snowshoe Trail" means little other than the snow and outdoor scenes disclosed. It has Jane Novak as its star and one of its best assets. Miss Novak has made a reputation for herself in these outdoor pictures. It seems a pity that more worthwhile stories cannot be supplied, as she puts all the genuine feeling into her roles to insure their success. Roy Stewart is the featured male member. Stewart is the type for this style of picture. He is rugged and improving greatly in his acting. He has appeared in several slipshod productions, but now appears ready to step into a role in which he can gain some standing. This R-C proves only a stepping stone to something better, as it is little more than a very ordinary program feature.

The story is based upon the lost gold mine idea with the sons of the two prospectors who discovered it hunting for the mine in later years. One is the right sort of a chap and the other the wrong. Both want the same girl, and the right one wins her.

They do a lot of tramping around in the mountains, fall about in the snow, and from general appearances experience few hardships, although captions would lead one to believe they do. One of the chaps is a trapper. According to the picture he must have been exceedingly prosperous, as he had attractive cabins all along his trap line, a unique state of affairs for any kind of a trapper. In real life the majority are glad to have a lean-to here and there in which they can sleep overnight.

The director made the mountain life a bit too luxurious to be realistic, especially as it was supposed to be in the gold country in the Rockies, where it really is wild. It would not be difficult to find some wilder places in the Adirondacks, where a lot of this snow stuff is shot every year.

One day is all that can be looked for in any type of house for this feature. *Hart.*

GIMME

Distributed through Goldwyn. Rupert and Adelaide Hughes co-authors, with Mr. Hughes director. J. J. Mescall, photographer. At the Capitol, New York, week Jan. 14.

Fanny Daniels............Helene Chadwick
Clinton Ferris............Gaston Glass
Mrs. Roland Ferris............Kate Lester
Clothilde Kingsley......Eleanor Boardman
Claude Lambert............David Imboden
Mrs. Cecily McGimsey........May Wallace
Miss Annabel Wainwright.............
...................Georgia Woodthorpe
John McGimsey............H. B. Walthall
Lizzie...................Jean Hope

A six-reel light comedy episode on the modern girl the Hughes have turned into a screen attraction which will satisfy an audience in any of the better houses. The title may sound objectional to some because of its slang interpretation incorporated as the heading for a first-class production, though at the same time let it be understood "Gimme" does not imply a gold-digging flapper but the present-day wife who dares to insist on an equal sharing basis so far as the financial means of the family is concerned.

The picture looks to be another sendoff for Helene Chadwick, heading the feminine contingent. This girl has turned in a corking performance which dominates anything else the film may hold, and it's far from shy on assertive attributes. Miss Chadwick is, literally, all over the screen, and besides presenting a potent appearance registers, for this release anyway, as being above the remainder of the film ingenues who flicker back and forth in the top features.

Outside of Miss Chadwick, the director has produced a refreshing effort that is, in its settings, artistically presented, has splendid photography with which to show it off, is delightful in various scenes between the youthful couples, and is not without merit in the titling. There's many a smile in the various wordings.

Possibly intended to point a moral for the young married couples, in that the money question should be an open topic instead of an embarrassing situation, the film tells of a young girl taking up interior decorating as a source of revenue, meeting and marrying a young son of the rich. Having made good at her job but being somewhat backward in funds, the girl borrows $500 from her boss, on a note, with which to procure her trousseau. The mother financially cuts off her son upon his marriage, but it's o. k. until hubby innocently hands his spouse a blank check at the time her former employer demands the money due him.

The head of the firm, in love with the girl, offers to tear up the note if—but it's "cold," along with a wallop on the head, delivered by means of a telephone transmitter, and the check leaves the husband almost null and void at his bank. It leads to a demanded explanation, thought most unnecessary by the wife, followed by a separation. She takes residence in a friend's home, where she receives an opportunity to go back to work for her former boss.

A wealthy widow, acquainted with the mother-in-law, has met the girl, likes her and tells the firm they can't have the contract for redecorating the house unless the young miss is declared in on it.

Hence the purely business proposition from the former loving boss. The girl accepts and goes to the house to see what must be done. Mr. Boss is there with the same persistent routine, which, incidentally, allows for some of Mr. Hughes' philosophy.

Meanwhile the husband hears of his wife's whereabouts, accidentally meets his mother and both migrate to the scene of action, where they expect to find a compromising situation, but find their imaginations are working too fast. It clears up when the boy allots a half interest in the bankbook to the wife.

A well selected cast plays the

story capably. The added momentum supplied by the direction and captions takes the picture along easily to more than qualifying results. *Skig.*

DRUMS OF FATE

Famous Players production presented by Adolph Zukor featuring Mary Miles Minter. Adapted by Will M. Ritchey from "Sacrifice," by Stephen French Whitman. Directed by Charles Maigne. Shown at the Rialto, New York, week Jan. 14, 1923.

Carol Dolliver............Mary Miles Minter
Laurence Teck............Maurice B. Flynn
Felix Brantome............George Fawcett
Cornelius Rysbroek............Robert Cain
David Verne............Casson Ferguson
Hamoud Bin-Said............Bertram Grassby
Native King............Noble Johnson

This might have been a wow of a picture had Famous put anyone except Mary Miles Minter in the principal and only woman role. Placing Miss Minter in the picture lets it in under the classification of a program production of the usual caliber turned out by Famous Players. No better than the average and likewise no worse.

Miss Minter is not wholly to blame. Charles Maigne who had the direction, must also be charged with a certain portion of the failure. His handling of the African jungle stuff was far from convincing, even though he had swarms of blacks. Also in his early rushes he should have caught that trick mustache of Maurice Flynn's and ordered it off and retaken the first couple of shots that had the leading man wearing it. That would have made considerable difference, for no one cared whether Flynn got or lost the girl after they had one flash at that Chaplin upper-lip decoration.

The story is a corking one as far as the chances that it offered for screening. Miss Minter is a young heiress, an orphan and the ward of a wealthy eccentric. The latter has a crippled musician whom he is sponsoring and there is a hope in the guardian's mind his ward will fall in love with the composer. Another suitor for the girl's hand is a wealthy young man about town, while the successful one is Flynn as a young mining engineer who has been representing his company for years in Africa. On his return he arrives on the occasion of the girl's 21st birthday, her guests at the party being all the men that have ever proposed to her. Here there was a chance for character comedy stuff entirely overlooked. It is the hardy adventurer who has been in the heart of the girl while he was refusing all the others, and when he proposes marriage is accepted. A brief honeymoon and his company calls for him to return to Africa for a final trip that is to last but a few months. One of the rejected suitors has already preceded him to the Dark Continent and as the two at the head of a small army of natives go into the wild country they are attacked and routed, with the husband being taken prisoner. At home, however, it is believed that he has lost his life, and the guardian after a time prevails on the girl to marry the musician.

The husband, obtaining his release finally, comes to America and is led to believe that his wife is very much in love with her second husband, and so returns to Africa, where the king of wild jungle tribes wanted him to remain as a full brother. The printed stories of the affair cause the death of the musician husband, and the wife, accompanied by one of the servants of her first husband, goes in search of him. Her guards are killed or captured and she is taken a prisoner and brought before the king, finding the object of her search there.

There was a chance of a lifetime for a director to have planted a name for himself with this, providing he had a real actress for his lead. The men were all good, especially George Fawcett as the elderly guardian and Robert Cain as the heavy.

"Lefty" Flynn made good as the lead after he had a shave. *Fred.*

THE MARRIAGE CHANCE

Produced, written and directed by Hampton Del Ruth; photography by Del Clawson. Released through American Releasing. At Cameo, New York, Jan. 14 week.

Eleanor Douglas............Alta Allen
William Bradley............Milton Sills
Dr. Paul Graydon............Henry B. Walthall
Timothy Lamb............Tully Marshall
Mary Douglas............Irene Rich
The Mute............Mitchell Lewis
Martha Douglas............Laura La Varnie
Uncle Remus............Nick Cogley

Just what an experienced picture man like Hampton Del Ruth was driving at in this "Marriage Chance" feature or what he started out for is hard to determine. Whatever it was, nothing came out to denote it. The casting might explain the weakness of the story. There are some names among the players that could be made use of in the advance work, and they hold up on the screen, according to what they had to do, but that is all. Outside of a possible legitimate reason for "all-star" billing, this feature has nothing else.

The film runs as though the intent was to have a "sweet story." Upon concluding the sweetness wasn't strong or big enough for a feature; it was switched over to melodramatics, without much time left and all the dramatics compressed into a few minutes, afterward excused by the "dream," in this instance a faint. It may require a medical opinion to say whether a person in a faint can "dream" as Eleanor Douglas did.

And to start with, Eleanor Douglas (Alta Allen) in a finishing school did not look the childish young girl such young women pupils usually do. Miss Allen has a great pair of eyes; so have other picture players. Eyes have sent more people onto the films than anything else excepting prettiness of looks, which may explain why there are so many poor panto players of the screen.

"The Marriage Chance" may be a good title to attract the elderly maidens who lost or missed their chance. Here it is a very nice young woman, quite the best actor of the picture, Irene Rich, playing Mary Douglas, engaged to marry Dr. Paul Graydon (H. B. Walthall), but Dr. Graydon continually postponed a definite marriage date through his preoccupation in vivisection. That "vivisection" thing seems a popular background on the coast for miserly scenarios.

Eleanor is engaged to the district attorney (Milton Sills), and their marriage is set. Eleanor tries to maneuver between Mary and Dr. Graydon, with the result that while nothing much happens while this is untangling, as Eleanor is about to be wed, with the minister and guests assembled, she properly faints. Then the picture, without explanation, goes into an ordinary series of melodramatic views, gloomy and dismal, that Eleanor thought could have happened and which never did. Even her "dreamy faint" is left for the audience to decide.

It's a very ordinary picture for an independent or any other description of production for nowadays. Stuff like this only makes it better for the big distributors.

The one chance here is the cast, and that's a bigger gamble than "The Marriage Chance." *Sime.*

WHILE PARIS SLEEPS

Maurice Tourneur production, distributed by the W. W. Hodkinson Corp. Released Jan. 21, 1923, shown in projection room. Adapted from the Pan's "The Glory of Love."

Henri Santados............Lon Chaney
Bebe Larvache............Mildred Manning
Dennis O'Keefe............Jack Gilbert
His Father............Harden Kirtland
Father Marionette............Jack F. MacDonald
Georges Morier............F. Farrell MacDonald

This feature looks as though it was an old boy that had been lying around for some little time, finally patched up and released to salvage whatever could be got from it. It has all the appearances of a picture that might have been made three or four years ago. Its box office value will be more or less a problem, but the title is one that should pull at the little window in the cheaper admission houses. The best that can be said of the picture is that it is of the type usually the weak sister on the average double feature bill.

The story is weird. It has as its heroine Mildred Manning, a girl of the Louise Glaum type, who is an artist's model in Paris. One of her employers wishes to possess her, but she holds him off and falls in love with a young American. The latter's father opposes the match and prevails upon the girl to pass the boy up for his own happiness.

The artist-suitor, however, has arranged with a half demented manager of a wax works to make away with the American. The latter is trapped and about to be put to death when he is rescued. In a hospital his life is despaired of until the girl for whom he is constantly crying arrives. His health returns and the father consents to the marriage.

Lon Chaney plays the heavy and from the role it is quite evident it must have been shot long before the day he started starring. But Chaney is better in this picture than he has been in some of his more recent efforts. Jack Gilbert is a conventional leading man. *Fred.*

FINGER PRINTS

Presented by G. H. Wiley through the Hyperion Pictures Corporation. J. Levering directed the story, authored by Alton Floyd, which features Violet Palmer.

Splitting a double-header at one of the Loew houses, this film could hardly be said to have held up its share of the burden. It's a mystery story, reaching the solution of its murder problem in a manner far from definite as regards those in the audience. The film holds no explanation as to just how the juvenile secures a clew to the slayer of his fiancee's father and tracks him down. A statement to that effect is supplied. You accept it—and like it, figuratively speaking.

The picture has been cheaply produced and the direction it receives falls far short of being able to overcome that handicap. Even though such instances have been accomplished, as witness Marshall Neilan's "Fools First," which that director is reported to have claimed was the cheapest film in the making he ever released, but, nevertheless, ranks with, or at the top of, any program feature screened in the past two years.

In its narration the "Finger Prints" story has a string of valuable pearls as the cause of the murder of the banker, who is about to make a present of them to his homecoming and motherless daughter the next day. The daughter arrives to find her father dead and his financial affairs in a chaotic state that leaves a stain upon his name.

The remaining footage is taken up with the lover hot on the trail, the murdered man's friend also seeking a solution while showing the opposite angle of the crook who framed the robbery and was in the house at the time of the shooting, but who swears his innocence of the crime.

The crook's love for an orphaned child left in his charge also takes up a good deal of time, with much padding revealing superfluous "business," commonly termed cute, by the little girl. The proverbial butler, who has been "with the family for nigh on to 30 years," has been planted with such an abundance of action to make him suspected of the deed that the only sure thing in the picture is that he didn't do it. And the finale acclaims that he didn't.

The cast is decidedly mediocre and why Miss Palmer is featured might be another mystery. *Skig.*

LA ROUE

Paris, Jan. 1.

The latest serial, "La Roue" ("The Wheel"), produced by Abel Gance and trade showed here by the Pathe Consortium, is frankly listed as a remarkable French super-film in six episodes. Focused amidst railroad people it is emblematically a reference to the wheel of life.

The first two episodes are somewhat monotonous, notwithstanding some splendid views, particularly of locomotives and landscapes, but thereafter the action increases, and finally reveals one of the best productions put out by a French company, worthy of the author of "J'Accuse."

The scenario explains how Sisif, an engine driver, rescues a little girl, Norma, during a railroad accident, and adopts the child, bringing it up with his own son, Elie, and letting the world imagine both are his legitimate offsprings.

Fifteen years later Norma is a beautiful girl, loved by her supposed brother Elie. Sisif, a widower, becomes jealous of his son, being violently in love with his adopted daughter, but, being a straight man, he tries to forget by having recourse to alcoholic drinks. Norma, mistaking the bad habit of her father and attributing it to poverty, accepts the proposal of marriage of Hersan, a prominent engineer in the company.

Sisif drives the engine of the train which takes Norma to the city where her marriage is to take place, and in a fit of despair, hoping to kill himself and his supposed daughter, he puts on full steam, with the intention of causing a catastrophe. This is prevented by the stoker.

To repent for this act of folly Sisif becomes a model employe, while remaining unhappy at the separation from the girl to whom he has devoted his life. But the supposed brother Elie is the most miserable.

When some time later he learns from the family register that Norma is not his sister he bitterly reproaches his father for having hid the secret whereby family reasons forbade him expressing his passion for his beautiful sister. Had he known sooner he could have married the girl he loved.

At this period Sisif met with an accident, being almost blinded by an exploding steam pipe. The superintendent, when obliged to relieve the driver from duty on his beloved engine, which he has named Norma, discovers a part has been willfully damaged, and Sisif is traced as the culprit. In view of his former long good conduct in the company's employ he is not discharged, but given a position on a mountain funiculaire, with a hut for himself and his son Elie to live in. Both continue an existence amidst the snow far from another habitation, mutually thinking of Norma. But all communications with the girl have been stopped by Sisif.

The wheel of fatality revolves. During the summer Norma and her husband, Hersan, visit the region. The former accidentally meets her supposed brother. She visits the hut during her husband's absence, spending hours with Elie. The young man hides his passion, while Norma still believes him to be her brother. They resume the intimacy of their childhood until Hersan returns suddenly from Paris. The two men meet as rivals, and the husband, knowing the truth of his wife's birth, declares that one of them must disappear.

They climb higher up the snow-covered mountain to a platform, where they decide to fight it out, each trying to throw the other over the edge. After a long struggle neither is vanquished, both falling into space, but Elie is able to hang on to a shrub.

Meanwhile Norma, remaining in the hut, has guessed the drama; with Sisif she hastens to find the rivals, arriving too late to save Elie.

The engine driver accuses his adopted daughter of being the cause of the terrible tragedy, and she flees from the district. Sisif has now become totally blind, and remains in the mountain hut, the man who replaces him on the funiculaire bringing his food daily. On the anniversary of Elie's death Sisif wanders toward the platform up the mountain, guided by his dog. Another person is already there. It is Norma, a poverty-stricken widow. She hides, and then follows him back to the hut, taking shelter therein after Sisif is asleep. She prepares his breakfast next morning, but when the old man awakens he is furious and orders her away.

Norma persists in her attentions, transforming the miserable hut into a comfortable home, always working while Sisif is out or asleep, until finally he realizes her kindness and takes her in his arms.

The poor woman again feels the love of a father, but only for a short time, for with a smile of happiness he dies the next winter while Norma is attending an annual dance of the local guides.

The main feature of this serial, as explained, is the mountain scenery and railroad life. The late Severin Mars terminated the role of the engine driver before he likewise passed into another world, this picture, as a matter of fact, having been filmed two years ago.

Yvy Close plays Norma, with Pierre Magnier as Elie and Gravonne as the husband, Hersan. The local critics consider "La Roue" of Abel Gance his best production, but it is a bit long and needs prudent pruning to make it a big film.

Kendrew.

THE SCARLET CAR

Universal starring Herbert Rawlinson. A Richard Harding Davis story, adapted by George Randolph Chester. Directed by Stuart Paton. Shown at Loew's Circle, N. Y., on double-feature bill Jan. 16, 1923.

Ernest Peabody	Edwin Cecil
Jim Winthrop	Tom McGuire
Violet Gaylor	Edith Johnson
Billy Winthrop	Herbert Rawlinson
Jerry Gaylor	Marc Robbins
Beatrice Forbes	Claire Adams

A fair average Universal program feature—just about strong enough to go around New York in the bigger daily change houses for double-feature bill purposes. In the smaller day-to-day-change houses in neighborhoods it will get by nicely by itself. There are times when the story is rather draggy and the action might have been snapped. There is some fairly good comedy at the opening that pulls a laugh or two, but unfortunately it is not continued.

The story is that of a small-town campaign for mayor, with the heavy as the reform candidate. He is the type who hates himself and feels that the country is going to call him for its president one of these days. Incidentally he is a double-crosser, a grafter and a despoiler of women. That's pretty good for a reform candidate. He has managed to con his way into the good graces of the local poobah who runs the bus line system, is editor and owner of the local paper and the town's power, and got him back the campaign for office on certain promises, and then sold out to the rival bus company for $10,000, promising to give it the sole franchise for the use of the city street

and thus double-cross his benefactor.

But the benefactor has a son. The son is in love with a girl and the girl has turned him down for the candidate for the local city hall seat. It is the boy who discovers the real caliber of the reformer through the aid of a girl who has been jilted and the boy who is in love with her. So at the finish, the day before election, the bad boy is exposed and his chances for election ruined, and he personally beaten up by the father, the son and the boy who was in love with the girl that was crossed.

The handling of the story by Stuart Paton will not win him a place in the directors' hall of fame and the picture itself will never be named with the hundred best of the year—any year.

Herbert Rawlinson, however, gives a rather snappy performance and puts up a couple of pretty good fights. Tom McGuire as a backer of a reform movement (that's a laugh to the Broadway bunch that know Tom) manages to ooze in and out of focus with a laugh every now and then and gets away with the role fairly well. But it was not a role for the man that is the first one to play a screen detective without the aid of a cigar. Both women screened well, but that is about all that can be said for them. *Fred.*

BROTHERS WERE VALIANT

Loew-Metro production from Ben Ames Williams' story, Irvin V. Willat directing. Jullen Josepson adapted for the screen. Billy Dove and Lon Chaney featured. Malcolm McGregor plays opposite Miss Dove. At the State, New York, Jan. 15-17.

A whaling story, although not exactly a whale of a story, sufficing as average program feature entertainment. Without star, story or title draw—the title is anything but titillating—the production must depend on the program for the market.

"All the Brothers" were valiant concerns the motto of the lineage of the family Shore. Capt. Mark Shore (Lon Chaney) is the idol of the seacoast village in connection with his whaling activities on the schooner "Nathan Ross." His younger brother Joel (Malcolm McGregor) is lorded over and condescendingly patronized by the captain-brother. Capt. Mark embarks on a new expedition, but the vessel returns minus its chief, with the report he was lost on an island, having landed in an intoxicated condition and not found after a fortnight's search. The ship owner does not promote the chief mate, but installs young Joel in the captain's cabin. All goes well until Mark, for whom Joel has gone in search in conjunction with the whaling activity, returns and incites mutiny on board. Joel puts him in irons after much difficulty, but in a free-for-all fight aboard ship he is being bested by some of the mutineers. His brother Mark, chained to a stay, is appealed to by Joel's young wife (Miss Dove) to save her husband. The bond of relationship proves supreme. Mark breaks his bonds, rescues his brother but is bounced off the ship by a pulley block propelled by the treacherous first mate. Despite Joel's attempt to rescue, a shark gets him. Capt. Joel makes another notation in the diary of the family Shore that "all the brothers were valiant." A tiff between his newly-wed bride is patched up, and curtain.

Obviously not much to it and insufficiently stirring, it has been tellingly woven together by Director Willat into a rather interesting screen yarn. With practically all the action transpiring on water, the Metro bankroll was not decreased to any noticeable extent. The production cost probably represents a new low mark for the Metro people.

Miss Dove was a revelation on personality and smile, although really a "just pretty-pretty" actress. If properly developed to bring forth any latent histrionic ability she could make an ace card. Mr. Mc-

Gregor was a manly opposite when occasion called forth, and successfully uncertain and "kiddish" in the fore part, as plot demanded. He reminds of Dick Barthelmess and shows possibilities. Chaney appeared straight for once, minus character make up, and did well with a hybrid sympathetic and negative role.

Abel.

THE CHRISTIAN

Goldwyn production adapted from the Sir Hall Caine novel of the same title, directed by Maurice Tourneur. Special preview at Capitol, N. Y., Jan. 23, 1923. Nine reels.

John Storm	Richard Dix
Glory Quayle	Mae Busch
Brother Paul	Gareth Hughes
Polly Love	Phyllis Haver
Lord Robert Ure	Cyril Chadwick
Horatio Drake	Mahlon Hamilton
Father Lampleigh	Joseph Dowling
Lord Storm	Claude Gillingwater
Parson Quayle	John Herdman
Liza	Beryl Mercer
Rev. Golightly	Robert Bolder
Maton	Milla Davenport
Mary	Alice Hesse
Lady Robert Ure	Aileen Pringle
Faro King	Harry Northrup
Doctor	Eric Mayne
Coroner	William Moran

Here is a picture! A real picture with a corking story, a great cast and finely produced. It should be one of the biggest box office winners of the year for the exhibitor, but if it isn't then no further proof is needed that pictures, good ones, and this is one of the best, won't draw. However, it seems hardly probable that this one will fall down at the gate.

Sir Hall Caine's story was a real tale for the screen. It was made about nine or ten years ago by Vitagraph. Goldwyn secured the American rights from it. This version should be able to go 'round the world.

The cast selected presented a performance that needs a new adjective to express their work. That goes for everyone, but the performance that stands out as a gem is that by Richard Dix, who, as John Storm, presents a characterization without compare. After witnessing Dix's performance in this picture, the Goldwyn people need not worry as to who should play the lead in "Ben-Hur" for them. Dix has undeniably won the right to it for his performance of John Storm.

Next to Dix, Mae Busch is entitled to a full measure. This girl has delivered a hundred per cent as Glory Quayle, and then some, but at the same time Phyllis Haver as Polly Love, on the strength of the death scene alone, is entitled to all that the critics can give her in praise.

To the many others a great deal of credit is due, especially Cyril Chadwick as the heavy, and Mahlon Hamilton.

In production, nothing has been left undone. The company, at least a part of it, was taken to the Isle of Man, England, and the original scenes as described by the author were utilized for the picturization. The direction could not go wrong with the story laid out as it was, and with the cast. The handling of the mob scenes was excellent, especially in the final reel of the picture. In lighting the photography is perfect.

The answer is that if "The Christian" doesn't get money for any theatre at its picture scale, then that theatre might just as well look around for a change of policy.

Fred.

PEG O' MY HEART

Laurette Taylor in her famous play written by J. Hartley Manners, done into a Metro-Screen Classic under directorship of King Vidor. Screen adaptation by Mary O'Hara. Miss Taylor plays the part she created on the stage. At the Capitol, New York, week of Jan. 21.

Margaret O'Connell (Peg)	Laurette Taylor
Sir Gerald Adair (Jerry)	Mahlon Hamilton
Jim O'Connell	Russell Simpson
Ethel Chichester	Ethel Grey Terry
Christian Brent	Nigel Barrie
Hawks	Lionel Belmore
Mrs. Chichester	Vera Lewis
Mrs. Jim O'Connell	Sidna Beth Ivins
Alaric Chichester	D. R. O. Hatswell
Margaret O'Connell (Peg) as a child	Aileen O'Malley
Butler	Fred Huntly

Peg on the screen isn't the full, rich, racy character she was on the stage, but still stands head and shoulders over almost any pantomimic comedienne the screen has. Miss Taylor does a unique piece of work here. New to the camera she has mastered that pitiless instrument by sheer naturalness and abandon.

She looks 20 and acts 16 with an exquisite grace that is memorable. Except for her deft and dainty comedy the picture might be pretty tepid. It took Miss Taylor herself to get the production over. If the action had been in any other hands but hers the humor would all have been in the titles. But this consummate actress makes the little imp of O'Connell live and breathe.

There can be no question of the box office value of "Peg." It is almost in the "Ben-Hur" class as a draw, for it played from one end of the country to the other with half a dozen actresses in the name part for more than 10 years, and was in the "Way Down East" class as a repeater. It is one of the dozen or so titles that will appeal to the whole public, for it is as standard as "David Copperfield." Miss Taylor's presence gives it prestige, and the result as far as the box office is concerned is "in."

Metro and Mr. Vidor have done **handsomely by the production. It has some exquisite settings, authentic scenic background taken abroad, and interiors done in the best form of the best modern practice. The picture couldn't have cost an enormous amount to make, for most of the sets are simple. But they are real.** The rooms of a well-appointed home are just that, solid, honest, plain but rich and without frippery. For once they don't drag van-loads of furniture to force an effect of elegance down your throat, and for once an English hall could be put in Madison Square Garden.

The playing is in the same mood of restraint. The butler is just an uneasy and embarrassed servant instead of a clown, and Mahlon Hamilton makes his Jerry a wearied man of the world with posing in the familiar lackadaisical, studio manner. Michael was a bit disappointing. He ought to be a disheveled bundle of rags, but the one they employed for the picture was too plump and actually a smug pup—not the real Michael at all. Perhaps the trouble with the picture is that they have taken liberties with the play.

It was inevitable perhaps that there would be changes, but it is not easy to see that it was necessary to resurrect Peg's father and drag him through nearly a reel of picture at the start and bring him back for the finale. Peg gains sympathy from being an orphan. What was gained but footage to give her an absent but protective father? Half the pathos of the girl's position was her helplessness and her gallant fight not to be a lady against overwhelming odds. One has somewhere in the back of one's head all the time at the picture that Peg was a fool to stay and be annoyed. Why not chuck it up and go home?

S. L. Rothafel has mounted the production nicely at the Capitol, with a striking bit of scenic setting showing the Irish moors, and a musical score of Irish melodies that is irresistible. *Rush.*

OMAR, TENTMAKER

Richard Walton Tully production, adapted from the stage version as also produced by Tully with Guy Bates Post the star of both. Directed by James Young. Released through First National. At Strand, New York, week Jan. 21.

Omar, the Tentmaker	Guy Bates Post
Shireen	Virginia Brown Faire
Nizam ul Mulk	Nigel de Bruliere
Shah's Mother	Rose Dione
Little Shireen	Patsy Ruth Miller
Hassan	Douglas Gerrard
Little Mahruss	Will Jim Hatton
Imam Mowaffak	Boris Karloff
The Christian Crusader	Maurice B. Flynn
Omar's Father	Edward M. Kimball
The Executioner	Walter Long
Zarah	Evelyn Selbie
Mahruss	John Gribner
Emissaries of the Shah	Gordon Mullen, George Rigas

There are sufficient elements in "Omar" to make it sure fire as a box office picture in the general release way. It may not be unwise to predict that "Omar" will shoot the gross ahead of the usual release, for this is a spectable of a film production as well as holding a story set in curious climes for the native American.

Accepting that the widely played "Omar" of the stage failed to show before the majority of the film fans, this picture is complete in itself. For the women it has a certain appeal through the love making of Omar with Shireen in the first reel; an element removed from the "sex" thing and still strong enough alone with its suggestion to linger in memory. Guy Bates Post never missed a thing when he hugged Shireen after their marriage. He was still hugging and kissing her the next day, while Shireen herself was some little kisser after she got started, but of course she waited to pick her spot—Omar.

According to the picture they did treat 'em rough in the Harem of the Perisian Shah. Women meant nothing to the eunuchs. And Shireen when torn away from her husband and sent to the Shah as the next addition to his Harem collection, was thrown into a dungeon when informing the Chah she loved another. In a later reel Shireen in the dungeon had a babe. Since the Shah had forgotten Shireen following her consignment to solitary imprisonment, everybody but Omar seemed to know Omar was the kid's pop.

The Shah ordered the mother and child placed in a bag and thrown from a cliff. But the Persians were gyppers as well. They threw a dummy for Shireen, for the mother had arranged to have the child conveyed to its father, and then they sold poor Shireen into desert slavery.

So the story runs, familiar to so many. In the lapse of 17 years, the child (daughter) has grown up; the Shah has died and in his place reigns another; all interesting and growing more tense as the film unreels.

There are mobs, tribes, denizens of the underworld, fights, and the Christian Crusader, made a stalwart figure by Maurice B. (Lefty) Flynn, of invaluable assistance to this picture toward its finale.

In the early part it might be said the story doesn't hold well; it's too legendary, but there is the always attractive production to offset it. The production and its picturesque people will make many forget the story until the latter reaches its absorbing portion.

Amidst it all is Omar with his philosophy, guarding his own child whilst believing its father to be another. 'Tis romantic and grows sympathetic as mother and daughter find one another and huddle together, to finally escape to save their husband and father. This view of the two women is not unlike the touch of the two sisters in "The Orphans."

James Young will get an awful lot of credit for direction in this picture, an awful lot for he has done an awful lot of directing. But Young may have to stand some criticism in the choppy manner at times the film ran at the Strand. It looked as though the Strand had done its own cutting to keep down the running time, as "Omar" ran but 70 minutes Sunday afternoon, whereas, it had been reported "Omar" held 9,000 feet in the original. If the Strand didn't cut whoever did, made the early section often too abrupt.

Mr. Post played better as the youthful lover than as the aged and grieved husband and father bereft. Virginia Brown Faire "registered" well enough as Shireen but it seemed more registration than playing. The Shah of Norah Berry's is peculiar. The Shah was senile, as a caption mentioned, but Berry made him worse than that. And the captions were nothing to boast over at anytime.

"Omar" came near approaching a special. It is of super range in production and for Mr. Tully's second film production ("Masquerader" first), he may also look upon it with great pride. *Sime.*

DARK SECRETS

Paramount picture presented by Adolph Zukor. Features Dorothy Dalton in story by Edmund Goulding, with Victor Fleming directing. At Rialto, Jan. 21.

Ruth Rutherford	Dorothy Dalton
Lord Wallington	Robert Ellis
Dr. Mohammed Ali	Jose Ruben
Mildred Rice	Ellen Cassidy
Biskra	Pat Hartigan
Dr. Case	Warren Cook

Nothing inspiring about this feature, which, incidentally, signalizes Miss Dalton's return after a somewhat prolonged absence. It is a society picture, migrating from this country to Egypt, having as its foundation the mystic power of an Arabian doctor accomplishing the task of making the social belle walk after she is, supposedly, permanently crippled. The familiar aftermath bargain between the patient and the physician is alco an issue.

The film is minus outstanding opportunities for Miss Dalton to the point where it must be simply a matter of routine with her. Robert Ellis supplies even support in the role of the fiance, with the others of the cast doing no better, or worse, than the average players in a general release. Fleming has turned out an indecisive sequence of events from a manuscript that at best is woven from exceedingly light fabric, so perhaps it isn't entirely his fault. The photography and settings may be termed standard.

Ruth Rutherford is the society miss betrothed to Lord Wallington, whom she has previously met in Egypt. The film opens for an interior of the marriage proposal under the eastern moon, thence immediately switches to this country with a garden party and Ruth showing the wedding present from her fiance, which is a pair of Arabian horses. The girl scoffs at the warning that one of the animals is unbroken and that she shouldn't attempt to ride it in the forthcoming horse show. The effort leads to her being thrown and forced into a wheel chair. The Arabian doctor is present at the time of the accident and offers to attend the injured girl, but Wallington refuses his services on the ground that he (Wallington) exposed the practioner in Egypt in a political frame-up and does not trust him. American doctors can do nothing for Ruth, so she tells Wallington their engagement is broken, and he returns to Cairo, where he takes to drink.

The deplorable condition to which he allows himself to descend forces his service companions to send for the girl, who upon arrival realizes that her willingness to marry is the only thing that can save him. To this extent she makes the bargain with the Arabian, who is also on the scene, and he begins his cure. She is finally able to walk, but it leaves her under the mystic force of her benefactor's willpower. The situation culminates in the brown-skinned doctor's demand that Ruth pay her debt with the usual "No, not that," a fight and the physician being stabbed by the girl's attendant. He lives long enough, however, to place a curse of Allah on her that forces her back to the wheel chair. The moral supposition she is under keeps the spell unbroken until the faithful attendant feigns an attack on Wallington, which brings the girl out of the chair to warn her lover—and finis.

For those who are very much in favor of Miss Dalton this picture may register for a fair amount of approval, though it is unlikely it will impress the average film fancier as other than an ordinary effort. *Skig.*

MILADY

Henri Dimant-Berger production, made in France under the direction of Dimant of the sequel to "The Three Musketeers." Distributed through American Releasing. Shown at the Cameo, New York, week Jan. 21.

D'Artagnan	Aime Simon-Girard
Constance Bonacieux	Pierrette Madd
Milady de Winter	Claude Merelle
Cardinal Richelieu	Monsieur de Max
Athos	Henri Rollan
Porthos	Monsieur Marintelli
Aramis	P. de Guingand
The Queen	Jeanne Desclos

The heavy vamp gets the axe at the end of about the seventh reel after she has gone through the picture vamping, poisoning and sticking daggers into people. It would have been just as well had the axe fallen in the first reel and ended the whole affair right there. The picture is a sequel to Alexandre Dumas' "The Three Musketeers," made in France with a French cast under the direction of a French director and perhaps for French audiences, where they insist on their Dumas screened according to the original text. Perhaps this picture is what audiences over there want, but in the U. S. A. they want things a little different and are not the sticklers for the original text. That's why a Doug Fairbanks "Musketeer" is worth about a whole gross of others.

The D'Artagnan of Amie Simon-Girard in this picture hardly figures. There would have been a better effect had Henri Rollan, who played Porthos, been chosen for the leading male role. In one scene with Milady he showed a certain fire and ability that would indicate that he would have been a better selection.

In sets, effects and in some spots photography this picture is good, and for the cheaper admission houses it will do, but it isn't a big picture in the scene of the Broadway application to "a special."

There undoubtedly will be something of an audience for it in spots, for the fact that the exhibitor can bill it as a sequel to "The Three Musketeers" will have box office value, but in entertainment it is lacking. This is partially due to the editing and titling that has been done for it, for it is far from setting forth the story clearly, and in this production one has to rely on the titles to tell the tale, for the action is far from doing so.

The chances are that the picture was originally worked out abroad as an exposition of the love affairs of D'Artagnan, that much is at least suggested in one of the earlier reels with the musketeer in the apartment of Milady, where the two are vamping each other at cross-purpose. If this was a fact there must have been a bit of cutting to get the American version past the censors. That in itself may have hurt the picture considerably. *Fred.*

THE FLASH

Produced by Russell Productions in conjunction with Clinton Productions. George Hively wrote the story, directed by William Craft and featuring George Larkin.

Much ado about a newspaper office, political boss, the chief of police, his daughter and the star reporter. It's considerable melo and entails all the incidentals of such that combine for a hectic conglomeration of automobile chases, fights and hurrah titling which produced more laughs than many a comedy can brag of.

The picture even includes a rowboat and water rapids incident with the gal deserted by the villain, in mid-stream, the hero going to the rescue, finally getting the girl to a

rock which they can't hold on to, drift further with the current and finish by climbing out on the rock they previously missed. How, only they know.

The directing and continuity all through are far from average. There is a woeful lack of attention to detail. An automobile chase revealed the cars going in the same direction, taking the same curves in the same way, whether going or coming—and how many times can a machine go around the same curve while headed in one direction? The boys must have chased up or down road for weeks when they were filming this one.

The story tells of the head of the police department starting on a campaign to clean up a city, arousing the ire of the gambling and political element; the frame to get the daughter involved to make the chief lay off and the boy reporter always thwarting the enemies of noble ideals. The lead-off caption had something or other to do with greed and honesty. What titles followed, and they were many, became more dramatic as they progressed.

Scenes in the newspaper "editorial department" will never make any scribe who turns in copy for a daily burn up with envy. George Larkin as the lead reporter is pictured skipping into the copy room with a scoop, a big "inside" yarn, and tears it off on less than half a sheet of paper. The editor uses a typewriter that couldn't be more than a thousand years old as a means of strutting his stuff. The howl of the film comes when the star member of the staff knocks his employer "cold," messes up the political boss, ruins the department's furniture in general, and when the editor comes to he points to the door and states (title) "You're fired."

Splitting a double feature program, "The Flash" impressed as being just about the type which keeps a number of people out of picture houses.

Pictures were made better than this release 10 years ago. Added to which the cast screens as extremely stagey along with a flagrant tendency to exaggerate. Ruth Stonehouse, as the daughter, seemed the only one who had any idea of how to work when the film was being taken, and, although never a star, this girl certainly deserves a better fate than to be in such surroundings.

Which doesn't lessen the fact that someone, with a sense of humor, could have made a great comedy out of this picture.

Skig.

THE GREAT NIGHT

William Fox five-reeler starring William Russell. Story by Jos. F. Poland. Directed by Howard M. Mitchell. Shown at the Academy of Music, N. Y.

Larry Gilmore	William Russell
Molly Martin	Eva Novak
Pepita Gongales	Winifred Bryson
Robert Gilmore	Henry Barrows
Jack Denton	Wade Boteler
Simpkins	Harry Lonsdale
Green	Earle Metcalf

This feature started out big as a comedy, but was allowed to slip, so that the verdict at the end of the fifth reel is that it is just a fair program production.

A bundle of laughs in the first couple of reels, with William Russell the hunted young man, with a flock of women intent on marrying him.

It is a rather old story, that of a young man who must marry by a certain date to obtain his inheritance. He has 30 days, and the girls are determined to get him after the newspapers publish the story. To avoid them he hides his identity and becomes a member of the police force through the kindness of the head of the department, who is his friend. On his beat he sees a girl in a lunchroom and falls for her, managing to wed her just as the clock was ticking off the time limit.

Russell makes the role of the hero fairly convincing, and as a copper has a chance to get in a couple of good rough-and-tumble fights. Eva Novak, his leading woman, is charming. The balance of the cast held Winifred Bryson as a heavy vamp, with Earle Metcalf as her companion in crime.

Had the pace that the picture started with been held to it would have been a winner for laughs, but after the second reel passed the picture slowed down into an ordinary mush tale without anything to redeem it.

Fred.

PAWN TICKET 210

William Fox production starring Shirley Mason founded on the play by David Belasco and Clay M. Green. Directed by Scott Dunlap. Length 5 reels. Shown at Loew's New York, New York, double feature bill, Jan. 23, 1923.

Ruth	Shirley Mason
Chick Saxe	Robert Agnew
Ruth Sternhold	Irene Hunt
Abe Levi	Jacob Abrams
Mrs. Levi	Dorothy Manners
Harris Levi	Fred Warren

A human interest story of old New York, nicely produced and rather cleverly played, with the principal sympathy going to the character taken by Fred Warren. Shirley Mason is appealing in the role of the adopted waif whom the pawnbroker takes into his home and rears, giving the mother who cannot care for the child a receipt in the form of a pawn ticket, from which the picture gets its title. The picture is one that will fill in as the top of the average double feature bill in the big houses and is strong enough to stand by itself in the small houses off the main stem.

The story in brief is that of a father and son who conduct a pawn shop. The wife of the latter deserts him and on the same night a mother comes in who cannot care for her child and the deserted husband takes it and cares for it. After a lapse of years he is anxious to give the girl the benefit of other surroundings and arranges for her to live with an influential friend of his. At the finish he discovers the friend is not all he seems and that the boy of the neighborhood who is in love with the girl is far more worthy of her. The mother also reappears after 15 years to claim her child. So there is an all-around happy ending.

The picture will have an appeal in certain neighborhoods that will be greater than in others. That is, the neighborhood houses will get the greater benefit out of it. Robert Agnew makes a pleasing juvenile opposite Miss Mason, while Fred Warren gives the role of Harris Levi a characterization that is decidedly worth while.

Fred.

WORLD'S A STAGE

Perfect Pictures production, starring Dorothy Phillips. Story by Elinor Glyn, placed in screen form by Colin Campbell, who also directed. At the Broadway, New York, week of Jan. 22.

John Brand	Bruce McRae
Wallace Foster	Kenneth Harlan
Richard Bishop	Otis Harlan
Jo Bishop	Dorothy Phillips
Cy	Jack McDonald

Elinor Glyn is responsible for the story of "The World's a Stage," supposedly dealing with the life in the film colony of Hollywood. It hardly compares with several stories turned out by this authoress, and as a feature it is mediocre. Its only chances as a money-maker are the publicity which can be derived from the Hollywood connection and the name of the author. The cast is short and consists of capable people, but the entire idea of the piece is weak and as an entertaining feature it misses.

The story starts with the experiences of a fly-by-night theatrical troupe playing one-nighters in California. A picture director running into the troupe in an out-of-the-way town informs the leading woman he believes she would be successful on the screen, and tells her to come to Hollywood. The road tour is curtailed and the screen career starts. It proves successful immediately. She marries a man in the orange growing industry. He is a wild youth and irresponsible; their life is turbulent, due to him. The idea of the story is to show that the real trouble-makers in Hollywood are not the film people, but those in other lines who have acquired money and come in contact with the picture colonists.

There is little to recommend in this, other than a good cast.

Hart.

WATCH MY SMOKE

Fox western featuring Tom Mix, with Lillian Rich heading the support. Story by James B. Ames. Picture directed by William Beaudine. At the Academy, New York, Jan. 23.

Western melodrama of thrills and stunts, good in quality as are most of the Mix films, and having a special interest through the presence of Mix's educated horse, Tony. The animal is a big asset to this picture, which has a wealth of wild and exhilarating riding. Among the stunts worth mentioning are the performance of a mounted horseman leaping, horse and all, from a high cliff and doing several turns in the air before striking the water; a fight on a moving train between Mix and a band of desperadoes which goes several times all the way from the caboose to the engine and back again; and that of racing Tony up to a moving train and jumping him off the ground through the door of a box-car. There may be other feats that escape memory, but these serve for a five-reeler.

The story is of the usual kind involving a weak and shrinking maiden, owner of a ranch, beset by scheming cowboys in her employ who are trying to heat her out of her property. The outlaws kill off all the punchers who are loyal and then try to make the girl sign her ranch away to them. Happens along just at this time Bob Sutton, the real owner of the ranch. He is about to claim it when the girl's position appeals to him and he signs on in her employ. Then starts the battle of wits and brawn, horsemanship and marksmanship, to defeat the evil designs. The hero wins the contest and the girl.

Altogether, rather above the ordinary film of the sort, made so largely by Tony.

Rush.

DOWN TO SEA IN SHIPS

Dramatic special produced and directed by Elmer Clifton through a company formed at New Bedford, Mass., and financed with New England capital. Story and scenario by John L. E. Pell. Cameraman, Alex G. Penrod, assisted by Paul Allen. Picture 8,900 feet, to be distributed by W. W. Hodkinson as a special, probably under some percentage playing arrangement. At trade showing in the Hodkinson projection room, Jan. 22.

Charles Morgan	William Walcott
"Scuff" Smith	Leigh R. Smith
Patience Morgan	Marguerite Courtot
Baby Patience Morgan	Elizabeth Foley
Thomas Allen Dexter	Raymond McKee
Baby Thomas A. Dexter	Thomas White
Nahoma	Clarice Vance
The Town Crier	Curtis Pierce
"Henny" Clark	Ada Laycock
"Dot" Morgan	Clara Bow
Jimmie	James Turfler
Jake Finner	Patrick Hartigan
Samuel Siggs	J. Thornton Baston
The Captain	Capt. James A. Tilton

Here indeed is a fine bit of realism, tinged with splendid romance and fascinating adventure on the deep seas. It is not too much to say that the picture has something of that epic of sea romance as Dana's masterpiece, "Two Years Before the Mast." It has thrills of adventure, thrills of romance and a dramatic climax that will hold any audience breathless. Here is embodied most of the qualities the screen needs in wholesome, robust melodrama. It's a pity it couldn't have had a Broadway presentation to advertise its merits.

Here are dramatist, scenario writer and producer-director in happy accord. The story is direct and simple as "Treasure Island" and works from a brisk beginning through faster and faster pace to a stimulating finale. Between the two there are views of whaling men at work in distant seas. The whole picturesque and dangerous life has been caught and recorded with the utmost vividness and economy. The actual harpooning and capture of a whale is presented in every detail. How they worked it is no concern of the spectator. It is there in utterly convincing form, with the spearsman throwing his harpoon, the rush of the sea mammoth, with the frail boat's crew hanging to the line for dear life as the tiny craft rips through the broken water. Indeed the super thrill of the picture is the wrecking of a whaleboat by a leaping whale—all convincingly done on the screen.

These realistic feats are woven into a colorful romance and backed by some of the finest bits of picture composition the screen has seen in many a day. The backgrounds of Quaker settlement of the whaling port on the Massachusetts coast are flawless in beauty and atmosphere. One never gets the effect of a bit of staged action. It all comes before one as reality. It is seldom that illusion is so forcefully secured and maintained, especially where the subject has a touch of "costume play" and belong to a bygone era (this is set about 1850).

Clifton bought a real whaler and manned it with a crew of real whalers besides the acting cast. The players are undoubtedly convincing, and the whole work holds together and maintains suspense.

A sketch of the last reel indicates the type of action:

The hero has been kidnapped and carried to sea on the whaler, in order that a scheming blackguard with a touch of "orient" in his blood may plot to wed the heroine. The hero has been at sea for months of mutiny and bloodshed, during which he achieves practical command of the ship with villain's aid in chains. They are homeward bound, the blot against the heroine having been disclosed. Meanwhile the action proceeds ashore. A stubborn father is gradually driving the heroine to marry the "yellow" schemer, while she mourns her absent sweetheart.

Here's where the crafty damatist and director do some of their best work. The ship is approaching the shore while the heroine is gradually being dragged to the altar. Which will win? There is real suspense, which is emphasized by the tricky shift of scene from shipboard to land and back. You know the hero will triumph, but to save yourself you can't escape the thrill. There are fights galore, ashore and at sea; a terrific storm in which the fine old square rigger fights her way. Back to the land. They have gotten the heroine to the meeting house itself just as the cutter grounds on the beach in a thundering hurricane. Its tiptoe excitement, and it lasts to the minute when the hero breaks through the church window and confronts the villain in time to prevent the bride's final word of the ceremony.

The picture is rich in capital details such as dock scenes in the whaling port, the sailing of the ships, life in the picturesque village, "cute" babies, and Marguerite Courtot makes the sweetest kind of a Quaker maid heroine.

Rush.

NOBODY'S MONEY

Lasky-Paramount starring Jack Holt. Adapted by Beulah Marie Dix from the William LeBaron play of the same title. Directed by Wallace Worsley. Shown at the Rialto, New York, week Jan. 28.

John Webster....................Jack Holt
Grace Kendall..............Wanda Hawley
Eddie Maloney..................Harry Depp
Carl Russell..................Robert Schable
Frank Carey..............Walter McGrail
Mrs. Judson..............Josephine Crowell
Annette ....Julia Faye
Gov. Kendall......................Charles Clary
Briscoe ....Will R. Walling
Kelly ....Clarence Burton
Prue Kimball..............Eileen Manning
Miller..............................James Neill

Jack Holt makes a greater impression in this picture than in any recently. It is his first comedy. He is a go-getter sort of a hero and in that capacity manages to impress himself on his audience. The story itself is, in a large measure, responsible for this, for it shapes into a picture that has suspense. There is one angle on which the audience is kept in the dark until practically the last minutes and it is the twist that serves to bring about the conventional happy ending. "Nobody's Money" will go a long way toward establishing Holt in the spot that his sponsors want him to occupy with picture fans. The picture is mighty good entertainment and will make good in any type of house. That isn't to say that it will break box office records, but if you can get 'em to see it they will be satisfied.

Holt first appears in the guise of a book agent in the town where the lumber mills of the Webster interests are located; later it is developed that he is the heir to the plant and his posing as a book seller was to secure evidence that those supposed to be looking out for his interests were trimming him. He runs into a pair of writers who, while under contract to one publisher, are writing stuff jointly under a pen name and when the Federal authorities come down on them for the income tax for that person they are forced to produce someone to pass as the famous writer. They seize on the book agent and he takes advantage of the situation and practically runs the town, as well as the writers, and becomes the head of the committee that runs the Governor's campaign, finally defeating the ring and winning the hand of the daughter of the Governor. Then it is that he discloses his true identity.

A comedy romance runs along with the principal theme that also brings laughs. The pair of players handling this are Harry Depp and Julia Faye, both of whom contribute considerably to the enjoyment of the picture. Wanda Hawley plays opposite Holt effectively.

The picture has Robert Schable and Walter McGrail carrying the opening portion as the two scheming writers rather successfully, but as the finish arrives they are rather lost in the general scramble.

It's a good comedy drama of politics that will get over. *Fred.*

POOR MEN'S WIVES

Preferred Pictures production distributing through the Al Lichtman Corporation. Presented by B. P. Schulberg, with Agnes Johnston and Frank Dazey the authors and Gasnier directing. At the Criterion, New York, Jan. 28 week.

Laura Bedford...........Barbara La Marr
Jim Maberne.........................David Butler
Claribel........................Betty Francisco
Richard Smith-Blanton.....Richard Tucker
Apple Annie...........................Zasu Pitts
The Heavenly Twins....{Muriel McCormac / Mickie McBan}

Unfolding a conventional tale, ofttimes screened, Preferred evidently has an average feature here that can make use of all the prestige the pre-showing as a special at the Criterion may give it. At the Criterion the film is succeeding a brief first part that includes two comedy subjects and a Prizma reel.

Gasnier has turned in a likely piece of work from a subject much worn at best, while the cast is fairly adequate as a whole. The narrative it relates is the film's worst enemy, if because of nothing else than the abundant footage which has been "shot" on other releases of a similar type. This particular picture sticks pretty close to its knitting without revealing any new angles. The usual screen audience will guess the sequence of events after the initial 500 feet.

As to production the picture holds an "Artists' Ball" episode that comes in for a considerable display and looks money, though there is nothing else hinting of pretentiousness in the settings. Karl Struss is the photographer, and has done nicely with his assignment. Some credit should be allotted to those who are responsible for the cutting of the film, as it is a smooth-running presentation despite its flagrant obviousness. Gasnier's best bit seems to be in an amusement park's roller-coaster ride which has the cameraman in the front of the car grinding on the couple in the rear seat throughout the dips and whirls.

The domestic tragedy takes off with two girls, employed in a class dressmaking establishment, in love with Jim Maberne, a taxi driver. Claribel, the favored one, meets a society youth. It's all off between her and her affianced chauffeur, which allows the girl friend, Laura, to step in and keep house for the knight of the wheel. Claribel finally gets the fastest stepper of the social set (Richard Blanton) as her own, after which it's a cross-fire between the two lives the girls are leading, with neither seeming to get a break.

The moneyed miss induces Laura to slip away for the Artists' ball, with the clothes problem overcome by procuring them "on approval." During the affair Claribel's husband "makes a play" for Laura, is discovered by his wife, and Laura spontaneously exits. It looks as if everything is to be o. k. until Laura's two children get the evening gown the next morning and proceed to cut it to pieces. The family bank finally squares the ruined outfit, though it all comes to light when Jim wants the money to buy a new taxi. He orders his wife out of the house. She appeals to Richard, who won't come through except on condition, and ends with Jim, who has followed her, letting the "percentage" husband have it on the jaw.

Barbara La Marr's characterization keeps her in calico and gingham most of the time. After Miss La Marr, Zasu Pitts takes whatever honors there are. *Skig.*

WORLD'S APPLAUSE

Paramount picture presented by Adolph Zukor. William DeMille production, featuring Bebe Daniels, Lewis Stone and Kathlyn Williams in story by Clara Beranger. At the Rivoli, New York, week of Jan. 28.

Corinne d'Alys.....................Bebe Daniels
John Elliot..........................Lewis Stone
Elsa Townsend.................Kathlyn Williams
Robert Townsend, her husband.......... Adolphe Menjou
James Crane.....................Brandon Hurst
Maid to Corinne................Bernice Frank
Secretary to Corinne............Maym Kelso
Valet to Townsend..............George Kuwa
Valet to Elliot......................James Neill

"The World's Applause" is a screen treatise on theatrical publicity and exploitation with a twist that a certain theatrical personage's craving for newspaper "notices" and the desire to be the talk of the town boomerangs viciously when she is indirectly implicated in a murder mystery.

The theatrical personage is Corinne d'Alys (born Cora Daly), who has "taken the Rialto by storm," but who is counselled by her manager-lover (Lewis Stone) to cease her craving for the world's applause and deal seriously with her work. This is momentarily disparaged by her with ensuing developments taking the audience rather interestingly through the usual five-reel span.

It starts with Robert Townsend, an artist who has "arrived" (Adolphe Menjou), becoming enamored with the favored and favorite footlights beauty and honoring her with painting her portrait for the annual Parisian exhibition. Townsend is married to the sister of John Elliot, the impresario, and a parallel situation develops of Townsend slighting his wife for Corinne, and Townsend interposing himself between the actress and her suitor, Elliot.

At a studio party in Corinne's honor to which Townsend did not invite his wife, the latter enters through the private studio door and, enraged at her husband's nonchalance, slashes the portrait and stabs the artist fatally. She telephones for her brother, who also enters unbeknown to the guests in the outer rooms. Both slip away, but not without being seen by a newspaper publisher, whose testimony implicates Elliot, who shields his sister. Elliot is arrested on first degree murder charges, but is absolved when his sister confesses to Corinne. The sister runs away, and there is a suggestion she commits suicide via the watery route.

Not much to the story, but rather deftly handled by DeMille in his customary pretentious manner—never lavish but always in good taste. The captioning is pithy and bright, and such leaders as "the public always believes the worst about an actress" is good lay propaganda for the profession.

Miss Daniels sports a nobby collection of clothes to excellent advantage. Mr. Stone is a sincere opposite, who also has the ability of really acting when called upon. Miss Williams, too, accounted for herself handily.

The picture pleased at the Rivoli. *Abel.*

MILLION IN JEWELS

William B. Brush presents this five-reel detective story. Directed by J. P. McGowan, who also plays the leading role of a Federal agent. Helen Holmes, McGowan and Elinor Faire featured. Picture taken last fall in Cuba. Distributed by American Releasing. At the Cameo, New York, Jan. 28.

Helen Morgan..............Helen Holmes
Burke...........................J. P. McGowan
Sylvia Ellis.........................Elinor Faire
Jane Angle........Nellie Parker-Spaulding
George Beresford............Charles Craig
William Abbott...............Leslie J. Casey
Morgan...........................Herbert Pattee

Rather better than a fair program picture. It has action, some suspense and a brisk final reel. The picture has some crudities, but there are neat twists to the story development.

Something is the matter with Miss Holmes' character or the way she plays it as the leader of an international gang of jewel thieves who are trying to run the crown jewels through the U. S. customs. There was no good reason why she should be made to appear in love with the secret service agent, sent to track them down. This is the first time in years McGowan and Miss Holmes (who is Mrs. McGowan) have worked together.

If it had been merely a sportsmanlike battle of wits between the woman crook and the detective all would have been well, but a false note comes in when they tack a sentimental, romantic angle on the situation and mistakenly try to give the woman crook a sympathetic part. It was here that the story fell down. It made a fool of the hero and spoiled the punch of the whole affair. On so small a detail did the difference between a pretty good picture and an ordinary program release hang.

The scenes taken in Havana harbor with the crooks signaling from steamer to shore and old Morro Castle in the background were excellent. So were shots, apparently in Florida, at the luxurious mansion of the crooks. It is here that the rapid fire climax comes about. Burke, the secret service man, has trailed the crooks to Cuba and back, but they have outwitted him and smuggled the jewels through. In consequence Burke has been dropped from the service. He determines to redeem himself, breaks into the crooks' mansion, cracks their safe and secures possession of the jewels as they close in upon him.

There is some tricky melodrama in the passage in which Burke passes the jewels to a girl aid and holds the gang off in a running fight all over the house. Some equally good bits of surprise in the schemes by which the crooks get the jewels through the customs.

The picture just misses excellence. *Rush.*

IT HAPPENED OUT WEST

Independent in the Franklyn Farnum series. Half a double feature bill at Loew's Circle, New York, Jan. 29.

Just a piece of film junk. Picture hasn't an excuse on any ground. Probably was made several years ago, judging from the women's dresses and has taken this long to get a showing. Put on in the cheapest possible manner. The only settings are a ranch house sitting room and an abandoned shed or two. Dame nature furnished the other backgrounds.

The picture is so bad it hasn't even decent photography. One or two shots in half lights are fairly well made, but the scenes in white sunlight of the southwest are about of the quality of an amateur kodakist. The story is as poor. It rambles on and on without getting anywhere and the only ingenuity displayed is a certain resourcefulness in grabbing footage.

At one point a Chinaman presents the hero with a letter in Chinese hieroglyphics. The hero turns it all four ways with knitted brows and shakes his head. After this business they need a three line subtitle reading "No Wong, I'm sorry to say I cannot read Chinese." This detail illustrates the quality of the production. It must have been constructed with the idea that it was to go before feeble minded audiences. They have half a dozen fights, but they don't even exert themselves to make them realistic. Farnum merely lunges out lazily, first with one hand and then with the other, and two bad men do a neck fall.

Shorty Hamilton is in the cast, but for the first time doesn't get anywhere. The picture would kill any actor. The production hasn't billing. How it got into the Loew bookings is a mystery. *Rush.*

ONE STOLEN NIGHT

Albert E. Smith presents this Vitagraph Oriental drama featuring Alice Calhoun. The main title specifies it is taken "From the Magazine Story, 'The Arab,'" with scenario by Bradley J. Smoller. Half double bill at Loew's Circle, New York, Jan. 29.

There may have been a magazine story called "The Arab," but this picture is a shameless lift from "The Sheik." "The Sheik" was a second rate picture and this is a second rate imitation, cheap in cast and production outlay, and shabby in character and spirit besides. To make it harder it is only moderately well played.

Its virtues are that it has some picturesque desert stuff with good pictorial effects of dashing Arab horsemen across the sands or silhouetted against the sky. While Vitagraph continues to turn out these mediocre pictures it would show better taste to lay off federal suits charging competitors with conspiracy to keep its pictures out of the best first run houses. "One Stolen Night" belongs to the neighborhood establishment of the second grade.

The play progresses almost episode for episode with "The Sheik," sloppy, maudlin sentiment in all. It is the same love sick American girl tourist who ventures out on the desert alone on a moon light night, after visiting an arabian camp in disguise as a native woman. They work in the Oriental dancing girl here just as they did in the screen version of Mrs. Hull's tale.

Out on the sands the heroine (her name is Dianith, if you must know) falls in with an Arabian horseman and there are hectic love scenes, interrupted by desert outlaws who leave the horseman for dead and take the girl captive to their camp. Here her virtue trembles in the balance at the mercy of an ogre of a fat, black chieftain. Funny how these woman-made melodramas always have the pure heroine's purity at the mercy of some horrid brutal brute and funny how they revel and slop over at the situation. This sheik is no Valentino, however. He's a big, moist looking person with terrifying eyes that open round and wide and bode our shrinking heroine no good.

Here the "Sheik" technique is shifted. Instead of the swarthy chieftain turning out to be a white man in disguise, the horseman left for dead out yonder, suddenly comes to life after the naive technique of a 10-20-30 melodrama of 20 years ago, and rescues the heroine, against a horde of pursuing tribesmen These wonder horsemen of the sands are never more than 100 feet from the fleeing hero and heroine, but they never are able to close the gap although the hero and heroine are on one horse in the soft sand. Ain't nature wonderful!

It turns out that the first horseman of the love scene, is not only a disguised white man, but the very man the heroine was engaged to several years before, but never recognized in a harem veil. He appears at her hotel in European kit the next morning to introduce himself, but Dianith will have none of him in regular shirt and pants of civilization. So he has to go back and change into his disguise, while Dianith gets into her trick native clothes and they go forth into the desert for a regular sentimental wooing. That's the kind of sentimental slop it is from start to finish. The billing didn't say who the leading man was and the main title worked too fast for a single handed writer in the dark to get all the dope, but it doesn't matter. *Rush.*

A WESTERN MUSKETEER

Tfuart western featuring Leo Maloney. Written and directed by William Bertram.

Tom Willkes	Gus Suvall
Ranger	Leo Maloney

A hoakum western designed for the 600-seat neighborhood house where they don't care what they look at. For the double feature bills in this type of house this one will answer, but that is about all.

It is the old, old yarn that usually serves the purpose in westerns, but slightly rehashed for the purpose of grinding out another 4,500 feet of good Eastman stock. The usual ranger played by Maloney, and he has the usual old mother that he takes care of. The girl is the daughter of the impoverished and aged prospector, who still holds faith in a hole in the ground that he has dug. The bold, bad heavy is the general storekeeper, whose advances have been repulsed by the girl. To get even he first tries to blow up the old man and fasten a murder on the favored suitor, who is the ranger.

There is the regulation chase stuff that has its horse features, its automobiles and what was intended for a real thrill, the heroine making her way down a log chute to be in at the death. Not a single touch of chase stuff has been overlooked, except the airplane.

At the finish is the usual fadeout with the hero clasping the heroine to his manly bosom. However, there is a possibility disclosed in the picture for comedy purposes. She is a Mex gal about as broad as she is tall, that they must have picked up in Cholo town over in the east end of Los Angeles. Despite her size she has a youthful face and a pathetic pair of eyes, and every time she rolls them because of unrequited love it is good for a scream from any audience. Even those on Eighth avenue saw that she was funny. *Fred.*

THE FIRST DEGREE

Universal feature starring Frank Mayo. Based on "The Summons," by George Patu. Adapted by George Randolph Chester. Direction of Edward Sedgwick. Shown at Loew's Circle, N. Y., on double-feature bill, Jan. 30, 1923.

Sam Bass	Frank Mayo
Mary	Sylvia Breamer
Will Bass	Philo McCullough
Sheriff	Geo. A. Williams
District Attorney	Harry Carter

A feature that might have been the rip-roaringest meller ever screened had not Frank Mayo given a really corking performance. It would have been easy, too, for the director to have slopped over, but in this instance Eddie Sedgwick broke away from the Universal method and turned out a program picture that will convince in the popular neighborhood houses. It doesn't show Mayo at his best, and after having seen him in some lighter things one realizes that he would be far more effective in comedy-drama than in straight meller stuff.

The story is a semi-western, as far as locale is concerned. Mayo is living on a small farm and is unexpectedly called before the grand jury to give testimony in a sheep-stealing case. He does not know just what he is wanted for, but an uneasy conscience leads him to make a confession of having killed a man a few days before. His recital of the events leading up to the killing compose the picturization, which in reality is presented in more or less of the flash-back method.

His recital tells of his being falsely accused of being in on a bank robbery in his home town and having served a year in jail, drifts to another town to start life anew. He is followed here by his half-brother, who was his rival for the hand of a girl and the one first accusing him of the crime. In the town where he is starting all over again the half-brother is again successful in raising popular opinion against him, and he again drifts on. Finally he settles on a small farm and starts raising sheep. His half-brother again shows up on the scene and tries to blackmail him.

In a fight that follows Sam believes he has killed the half-brother, and when the call from the grand jury comes he relates this story, only to find at the end that they really wanted him to testify in a sheep-stealing case, and the prisoner is brought into the room, it being the man that he thought he had killed. For the finish the sweetheart, who came from the home town, arrived to furnish the happy ending.

In photography the picture stands out as something unusual, being particularly sharp and clear. The direction sends the story along nicely and holds the interest, the suspense being maintained to the end. Philo McCullough plays the heavy, while Harry Carter is very acceptable as the district attorney. *Fred.*

KINGDOM WITHIN

Producers Security Corp. production having the Victor Schertzinger trade-mark. Story by Kenneth B. Clark, directed by Schertzinger. At Loew's State, New York, for three days, commencing Jan. 29.

Caleb Deming	Russell Simpson
Danny West	G. Walt Covington
Amos	Gaston Glass
Emily Preston	Pauline Stark
Will Preston	Hallam Cooley
Krieg	Ernest Torrence
Dodd	Gordon Russell
Connie	Marion Feducha

Considerable heart interest is developed in this rural drama. Although a story of the woods the greater portion of the production is studio made. This is largely due to the fact that the picture sponsors some genuine acting and does not rely upon the regulation styles of outdoor work to gain headway. There are times in the production when a bit of spectacular work could be used to advantage with the picture's big asset as it stands.

The action is in a small town in the timber country. The village blacksmith had wished from the early days of his marriage his wife might become the mother of a boy. The mother dies in child-birth and the boy is born a cripple.

The main topic of the town is the experiences of two partners in the lumber business. One had been convicted of robbery and sentenced to prison. His sister remained alone in the town completely ostracized by the rest of the natives on account of her brother. She is later befriended by the cripple boy who has reached twenty. Just at this time her brother is released from prison and his former partner is killed by a lumberjack. In making his escape the woodsman stops at the girl's house for food. She learns he has committed the crime. Upon discovering her knowledge he threatens to return and kill her if she gives him away. To save her brother, who has been accused, she gives out the information.

The lumberjack returns and attacks the girl, the cripple arriving in time to save her life. He is badly beaten by the big man who grabs him by his paralyzed arm and pulls it into its natural position, thereby giving his body a normal appearance. After a few minor angles are ironed out the story ends with the girl in the former crippled boy's arms.

The picture features Russell Simpson, Pauline Starke and Gaston Glass. Ernest Torrence is equally deserving with others of that distinction. Torrence makes his character role one of the big features of the picture. The other members are effectively cast with the production in this division well looked after. The continuity at times is rather hazy with the general ideas forcibly put over by the director.

Pictures of this nature have a direct appeal. "The Kingdom Within" has dramatic value and for the general run of audiences will give full satisfaction. *Hart.*

THE GHOST PATROL

Universal program picture of five reels. Story by Sinclair Lewis. Scenario by Raymond Schrock. Ralph Graves starred. Bessie Love head of the supporting company. At Loew's Circle, New York, as half of double bill, the other feature being "Bulldog Drummond," Jan. 27.

Mild comedy-drama with excellent sentimental values and pleasing romantic angle. The picture is based on the efforts of a young loafer in the slums to redeem himself and his success through the good offices of a kind-hearted old cop. Light story, not very strong in drama, but with interesting character study and sentimental passages to compensate for the lack of "punch."

Worst pictures have been depended upon to support a program, but this one is tucked away and hidden under the billing for "Drummond," and on a Saturday evening at that, when almost any kind of a bill draws capacity in this neighborhood. The ways of film bookers are beyond understanding. Here we find "Drummond," which has been regarded as a sufficient single feature and a pleasing five-reeler besides. The next time the double feature will consist of two pieces of junk. Some sort of conspiracy ought to be worked out in the double feature proposition. It's a gamble for the fans as they run it now.

Dorgan has policed the "Little Hell" beat until his hair is gray. He knows the people by name and nature and he does his duty on the theory that a bit of kindness is worth more than a lot of rough discipline. He helps rather than punishes. Jerry had been a typical loafer until he fell in love with Effie, daughter of a German store keeper. He starts to mend his ways; gets a job and tries to win the girl by exemplary conduct.

Effie's austere old father, however, warns the girl she must have nothing to do with Jerry and he won't be moved from his decision, although Dorgan does his best to pursuade the old man that through their marriage lie happiness for Effie and self-respect for Jerry. The old man is obdurate. He separates the young lovers and in despondency Jerry takes a couple of drinks, gets into a bar-room brawl and, as a consequence of a hasty blow, goes to prison for a year, leaving Effie to mourn.

Meanwhile there has been a political change. The new police commissioner orders Dorgan retired and replaces him with a spruce but alien young cop, who wields a stern night stick over the district, while the sorrowful Dorgan dons his old gray uniform a-nights and secretly patrols the neighborhood as of old, bringing help to the troubled and mild reproof to the mischievous and misguided.

Jerry is released from bail, but on his return is jobbed by an unscrupulous politician and beaten up. Dorgan finds him senseless in the street and takes him in to recover, bringing Effie to care for him. For his unofficial interference he is summoned before the police commissioner and, trembling, admits his fault, only to receive his commission and commendation as the "best cop on the force." The finish brings the young people to each other's arms and the finish finds everybody happy at their first Christmas party. *Rush.*

SOUTH OF NORTHERN LIGHTS

William Steiner production, with Neal Hart as the star, author, adapter and director. At Loew's Circle, New York, on double bill Feb. 5, 1923.

Jack Hampton..........................Neal Hart
Corp. McAllister........James McLaughlin
Chick Rawlins........................Ben Corbett
Jane Wilson........................Hazel Deane

Just a western built by a star to suit himself. Directed with the same idea in mind, with the result it is a picture that will fit in in the cheapest houses, where they like 'em real wild and woolly. A general idea may be obtained from the fact there is no love interest until about the last 100 feet or so. Prior it is rough-and-tumble stuff, with the story told with the aid of a series of cut-backs, long-drawn-out posing by the star in close-ups and about the most draggy action caught in a long while.

Hart has the heroic role of a nothwestern rancher falsely accused of murder by a gang that wants to obtain possession of his ranch because gold has been discovered on it. He makes his escape and crosses the line to Canada. There he has the Northwest Mounted after him as well as the American sheriff, who crosses the line to assist in the chase. It seems the gang after the rancher operates on both sides of the line. They are respected citizens on the American side and criminals on the Canadian side of the line.

Their leader, Chick Rawlins, runs a dump at a trading post in partnership with another fellow, and the Canadian authorities have sent a woman into the camp to get evidence against them. This woman shows up in the last 200 feet. Captured by the crooks, she has been imprisoned in a cabin in the mountains. Her escape from there and a long chase on the part of the crooks on one hand, the hero on the other and the sheriff and mounted on a third take up a great deal of the footage. Finally Hart, in a hand-to-hand battle with the leader of the crooks, manages to best him and save the girl. At the same time the leader manages conveniently to fall on his own hunting-knife and mortally wound himself, confessing before passing out that he was the one that framed the murder charge on the hero. That leaves it dead open and shut for the lady detective and the hero to fall in love within 50 feet of the fade-out.

It was the weak sister of the Circle's double bill, and just a hoak picture that even the Circle patrons, case-hardened as they are to poor ones, laughed out loud when the dying crook saw a vision of the Grim Reaper in a double exposure which impelled him to make his confession. *Fred.*

FABIOLA

Chicago, Feb. 7.

Fabiola Photoplay Corporation production, made in Italy, based on the story by Nicholas Cardinal Wiseman. Special music composed by Alexander Henneman, of Washington, D. C. At the Auditorium, Chicago, two performances daily, with prolog features.

Fabiola ....Elaine di Sangro
Agnes...........................Adelaide Poletti
Afra...............................Ninette Dinelli
Cecilia.............................S. Sanfilippo
Fulvius.......................Anthony Novelli
Sebastian..........................L. Pavenelli
Euroatas...............................M. Paola

A photoplay which will easily secure the endorsement of religious organizations, especially Catholic societies, as it shows the contest of Christianity with Paganism in a very effective way. It is divided into two parts, each having a prolog. Half a dozen singers and a dancer pay homage to Caesar and the gods for the Paganism part, and a male quartet and a girl at the Cross lent atmosphere to the second part, which is Christianity.

The performance opens with pictures giving a splendid idea of the Rome of ancient days; maps showing the Roman empire, and with views of the present day, which give an idea of the buildings erected to give grandeur to imperial Pagan Rome. Throughout the performance has an air of propaganda which there is no attempt to conceal, since there is a program announcement that the seeing of this picture is not "time lost," nor does it mean filling the mind with "frivolous ideas." The announcement concludes: "Rather let it be hoped that some admiration and love may be inspired by it of those primitive times, which an overexcited interest in later and more brilliant epochs of Christianity is too apt to diminish or obscure."

It is not the style of picture which gives opportunity to players. Fabiola, daughter of a wealthy pagan patrician, although having the title role, figures but to a small extent in the picture and is important only that she is first a selfish, heartless, cruel woman, who later sees the faith of the "Teacher of Nazareth" triumph over the treachery, hate and greed of the world she had known and believed unshakable, and finally becomes a convert. Agnes, her cousin, is the principal feminine role, and Adelaide Poletti is a pretty girl who plays it effectively. Fulvius is the heavy to the finish, when he, too, is converted, and is well played by Anthony Novelli (the John Barrymore of Italy), though the part is not of a kind that will give movie fans a chance to enthuse over. There are several other roles quite as important to the story as those named on the program that are omitted, including characters of the boy, Pancratius; the mighty Quadratrus and the son of the prefect, Corvilus.

The photoplay has enjoyed good business because of the interest worked up in religious societies and is well spoken of. There was no applause, excepting for prolog numbers on the night witnessed. Many things remove the possibility of popular applause. A blind girl is stoned to death, much time is given to the burial of Agnes, the most lovable character, and there is torturing of Christians, including the casting of the boy, Pancratius, into the arena of the Coliseum and turning loose a panther. This scene is badly done.

There has been much money spent in reproductions of homes of wealthy patricians of the fourth century and in showing the magnificent buildings of that day.

VOICE FROM THE MINARET

Joseph M. Schenck-First National attraction starring Norma Talmadge. Adapted from the play by Robert Hichens by Frances Marion. Directed by Frank Lloyd. Shown at the Strand, New York, week Feb. 4.

Lady Adrienne Carlyle....Norma Talmadge
Andrew Fabian...............Eugene O'Brien
Lord Leslie Carlyle...........Edwin Stevens
Bishop Ellsworth..................Winter Hall
Secretary Barry......................Carl Gerard
Countess La Fontaine.......Claire Du Brey
Lady Gilbert................Lillian Lawrence
Saleim.............................Albert Presco

"The Voice from the Minaret" will give the Norma Talmadge fans entertainment. It seems a trifle lengthy, but nothing in it needs speeding.

The locale is in India, Africa and England. It is in India where Miss Talmadge as Lady Adrienne, wife of the Governor-General, falls in love with the young Englishman who is going into the church. In Africa they discover their love, and finally in England, after the wife has returned to the husband, on the latter's death, the couple are left to work out their life's happiness.

In the opening is a corking polo game in which Eugene O'Brien plays an important role. Also several big scenes as far as the number of people used are concerned in the early reels. After the polo game is a reception in the Governor-General's gardens, where there is trick photography to permit a Hindoo fakir to do a couple of tricks. The African scenes are well worked out with an eye to atmosphere.

Playing the heavy is the late Edwin Stevens, who, as the husband, put over a role that in spots was as wonderful a piece of work as anything that was ever done by Mansfield on the stage.

The direction is good, Frank Lloyd keeping the story moving. His close shots held action instead of being mere posings. *Fred.*

THE DANGEROUS AGE

First National distributing production by Louis B. Mayer from the story of Frances Reel. Direction John M. Stahl. At the Strand, New York, week Jan. 28.

John Emerson............................Lewis Stone
Mary Emerson, his wife......Cleo Madison
Ruth, their daughter.........Edith Roberts
Gloria Sanderson................Ruth Clifford
Mrs. Sanderson...............Myrtle Stedman
Bob..................................James Morrison

Stahl and Stone will be allotted the major share of credit for this release. Both have made an average tale not only presentable and likable, but as good a feature as any of the first run houses have held within recent months. The film looks as if the director had taken the script in good faith, adding numerous touches sufficient to lift it above and beyond the average.

Philosophizing on the danger age of a man in marriage (placed at 40), the picture takes its subject seriously while including comedy to the extent of two or three honest outright laughs, a neat bit of suspense that is splendidly worked up, sustained interest and a touch of pathos for those inclined to view, romantically the screened narrative. Further than that the film will be attractive to the women, whether because of the title or after actually seeing the version. And its odds on men will take kindly to it, if for nothing else than the idea of witnessing a man 20 years married wanting to step out for himself, doing so and the blame placed on the wife. The theme may offer various angles on a new alibi for the "hooked" boys, at that. In fact, the picture will be duck soup for both ends of the dinner table.

Lewis Stone as John Emerson, the husband (but not Equity's boss), has given a superb performance. It is questionable if Mr. Stone ever has done anything finer. And he always has been of the most dependable among the male leads for merit of work. The role would easily have lent itself to overplaying. A deft touch of refinement and certain mannerisms that are terrific in their power to register the idea desired across total a piece of work Mr. Stone has succeeded in making human.

On the other end John M. Stahl supplied tasteful settings for the action, which he definitely carries along to the conclusion without overdoing any of the stressed points or becoming flabbily sentimental. A night race between an automobile and a train, seen mostly by the lights of each conveyance, is a corking piece of production and camera work, bound to cause comment. Neither does the casting director seem to have been lax in choice outside of Ruth Clifford, who illusioned as offering a somewhat colorless effort.

The theme takes Mr. and Mrs. John Emerson as the personalities. They possess a daughter of 20. Emerson, the husband, hungers for companionship and a touch of romance. The wife is too busy taking care of her household to allot any serious thought to her spouse's youthful reflections. When she refuses to accompany him on a trip to New York it's the beginning of a continuous gay panic for him, mostly caused by the meeting of a miss, the same age as his daughter, who is on the train going east with her mother.

Everything is strictly on the up and up—no badger game or frame lurking in the offing. It's simply a matter of a neglected husband stepping out from the sheer joy of seeming to have regained the lost environment of his youth. Led on by **the girl, who does just a wee bit of cheating herself (for she has a fiance), Emerson becomes obsessed with the idea he is about the best around. He writes his wife asking for freedom—and then finds the girl always regarded him as a father. It's a wallop to the iron-gray haired man's vanity. But he hasn't much time to think it over, for there's the letter to the wife, enclosing the request to call everything off. That must be recovered. An attempt to beat the epistle home fails when he misses the train, which allows for the race between "gas" and steam. After finally catching the limited it's** not over, for there's still a possibility of the letter reaching the wife—and it does.

The homecoming is on his daughter's wedding day. He had muffed the wire demanding his presence for the occasion, so that constitutes a "break," but it takes a few feet of film to square the pen and ink ultimatum.

A cleverly presented film this, that will draw to the box office from that type of advertising sometimes termed "mouth-to-mouth." Hence, as said before, Stahl and Stone can both take bows on this one. *Skig.*

THE BOHEMIAN GIRL

English-made production by Harley Knoles (American), who also directed. Adapted from "The Bohemian Girl," light opera. Stars Ivor Novello, Gladys Cooper and features Ellen Terry, Constance Collier and C. Aubrey Smith. Distributed through American Releasing. At Cameo, New York, week of February 4.

Arline ....Gladys Cooper
Thaddeus ....Ivor Novello
Buda ....Ellen Terry
The Gypsy Queen......Constance Collier
Devilhoof ....C. Aubrey Smith
Count Arnheim..................Henry Vibart
Count Florestein.......Gibb McLaughlin

"The Bohemian Girl" should be a sure-fire drawing card as a regular release. To what extent an exhibitor may make it draw will wholly depend upon the exhibitor. There is much to exploit in this picture, and on the exploitation will depend the business, with the picture standing up under the most flamboyant advance work that sticks closely to the facts.

First, there is Ivor Novello, that much heralded expected supplanter of Valentino, and who is now over here to appear under Griffith's direction. Then there is Gladys Cooper, acclaimed as England's best looker and foremost actress on the legitimate stage. After that, Ellen Terry, who really should be first through it all, but is made secondary in the billing, even on her first screen appearance and in an English-made picture. There is no limit of latitude for the Terry connection. And after that, Constance Collier, the American actress, who appears in this picture produced by another American in England, Harley Knoles, who also directed.

Besides for curiosity may be cited what the American, Knoles, did with a picture made abroad as against what the English make themselves. Yet for further attention is the piece itself, an adaptation of "The Bohemian Girl."

Possibly the present generation is not familiar with the standard light operas of the everlasting past, and it should be future, as it would have been without the jazz. "The Bohemian Girl" ranked with "The Light Hussar" among the classical light operas.

And still again, what girl has not felt an answering thrill to the lyric of "I Dreamt I Dwelt in Marble Halls," almost the theme song of "Bohemian Girl," and a classic that even time cannot efface from the world's most favored numbers?

There is almost too much for the rewrite man in this picture. Nevertheless, it is there, and the picture is there with it. Mr. Knoles must have given a punch to the English directors when they saw his output. He made it on American film lines.

Mr. Knoles' best is the handsome visualization of the "Marble Halls" song on a moving platform, with a palace set of simple but highly efficient effect, that has a throne on the extreme end and an art gallery sprinkled throughout with marble objects. To the throne, on which sits the queen, come the many claimants for her hand, but Arline (Miss Cooper) rejects them all in favor of Thaddeus (Mr. Novello), who is the Prince of her dreams as well as her Prince at the picture's finale. There is a heart throb in this for any girl. Accompanying, of course, by the house orchestra is the operetta's favorite strain.

This scene, as studio made, equals any seen on this side in its prospective, simplicity and effectiveness. The moving floor is again utilized for a coming out party in an English castle, with the dancing couple doing it in the English way, a pleasing departure from the "Greenwich Village" thing or the "midnight cabaret."

The adapted story lends itself to picturesqueness, and it has been taken advantage of. There are gypsies and a gypsy camp, the latter somehow never made really real through an undetectable fault. But the gypsy camp, however, contains a fetching romantic scene on the night of Thaddeus' declaration of love for Arline, when they meet outside Arline's wagon by the light of the moon, to be discovered by the gypsy queen (Miss Collier), who is the villainess (and excellent with her Spanish strut). This scene is sweetly **poetical, as is the gypsy betrothal ceremony immediately following.**

It's a nice, sentimental story of holding value and interesting to those knowing the opera as well, but the importance of the personages in it overshadows the tale.

In photography the picture does not always run true. It is also a matter of camera work and lights as to the looks of Miss Cooper and Mr. Novello. Miss Cooper is a handsome girl in the English style, and this style should never allow an American to see the profile of an English beauty. For seldom h what the English consider a pretty girl a likeable profile to the American idea.

Novello will be the subject of most attention by picture fans, particularly the American girls. He's a manly looking fellow, of good appearance, but there is no telling how our girls will see him. The men will like him as a good looking average picture actor. Professionals will recognize his brunet type when it is said he looks much like Fred Niblo did 20 years ago, without Novello being as good looking as Mr. Niblo then was.

Miss Cooper plays "graciously," which means nothing. Miss Terry as the nurse had an opportunity or so. Mr. Smith made his Devilshoof character devilish in looks and was splendid. Gibb McLaughlin as Count Florestein had an Austrian makeup that might be true to the country but it looked burlesquey.

"The Bohemian Girl" attests to Knoles' work in a strange land. It should do a great deal for him in England. *Sime.*

JAVA HEAD

Presented by Jesse L. Lasky (Famous Players) from the novel of Joseph Hergesheimer, releasing through Paramount. George Melford production, with Waldemar Young adapting for the screen. At Rivoli, New York, week Feb. 4.

Taou Yuen	Leatrice Joy
Nettie Vollar	Jacqueline Logan
Jeremy Ammidon	Frederick Strong
Gerrit Ammidon	Albert Roscoe
William Ammidon	Arthur Stuart Hull
Barzil Dunsack	George Fawcett
Edward Dunsack	Raymond Hatton
Kate Vollar	Helen Lindroth

A few current reports waiting about lately have carried the idea that a campaign is about to start or is under way to exploit either Leatrice Joy or Jacqueline Logan for permanent big type in screen billing. It isn't exactly recalled which girl is to be on the receiving end of the drive. As far as this picture is concerned it really doesn't make much difference, for each will gather a host of admirers on the strength of her performance.

The picture is splendid and the two girls run away with it amidst a well selected cast. Whatever "edge" there may be between the two women goes to Miss Joy. It's difficult to recall when has been seen such a wistful performance as this girl gives as a Chinese princess brought to this country as the wife of a young seafaring captain. She has succeeded in spreading a personal appeal across the screen that is most emphatic. To say Miss Joy is charming might possibly sum it up. Miss Logan, too, is cast in a role abundant in its capacity for gaining the sympathy of the spectators, though she has failed to realize on it as did her counterpart.

George Melford has accomplished creditable directing in his subject. It's a costume picture, with the time placed in the late '40s and having most of the action in a town along the New England coast, other than the episode in Shanghai. That permits of the princess' entrance into the tale.

Not having read the novel, it is beyond saying just how closely the film version follows Hergesheimer's story, but the screening does impress as though it should be a credit. Everything is conservative but not necessarily meaning by that cheap. It is tasteful, while the action has been toned down and kept down, where it would have been so easy to become melodramatic.

The film story tells of an engaged couple, Nettie Vollar and Gerrit Ammidon, kept apart by a feud between the boy's father and the girl's grandfather. While away on a voyage to China he rescues a Manchu princess (Taou Yuen) from an attack and marries her to save her life, thence bringing her home with him. Meanwhile, the relatives have patched up the family feud, but the effect on the youthful pair is nullified by the foreign wife.

The family accepts her (no dramatics here), as does the town, following the example of the household. It's a delicate situation until the princess learns of her husband's love for the other girl, when she takes an overdose of opium and dies.

Close to an hour and a half is consumed in the presentation. Much footage is taken up at the beginning in planting the tale and registering the atmosphere, with the exteriors of the small town (supposedly Salem, Mass.) looking to be authentic. Lengthy or not, the picture had no trouble in holding a Sunday night assemblage at the Rivoli until 11.40.

Those in the cast, besides the two girls, to stand out were Albert Roscoe, George Fawcett and Frederick Strong as the husband and the grumpy old elders, respectively, while Raymond Hatton demanded attention in a "dope" characterization.

Having a foundation of an excellent story embossed by an excellent sense of production, "Java Head" is picturesque and entertaining to the point where it actually grips, while surmounted by the performances of Misses Joy and Logan, to which the former has added a touch of pathos that is as neat a piece of work, or art, as a lens has gleaned in projection for these parts in months.

It is also of note the captions are minus any trick phrasing on the Chinese girl's utterances (she speaks English) and is, additionally, shy of the usual "cute" business generally allotted to such a character. Hence, it may be understood that there are no superfluous scenes involved, every incident has a direct bearing on the story, and it's straightaway "shooting" to register a corking feature that connects purely on merit. *Skig.*

HEARTS AFLAME

Metro special presented by Louis B. Mayer, produced by Reginald Barker. Adapted from the novel, "Timber," by Harold Titus. Scenario by J. G. Hawks and L. G. Rigby. Frank Keenan in lead, Anna Q. Nilsson opposite. At Rialto, New York, week Feb. 4.

Luke Taylor	Frank Keenan
Helen Foraker	Anna Q. Nilsson
John Taylor	Craig Ward
Bobby Kildare	Richard Headrick
Black Joe	Russell Simpson
Philip Rowe	Richard Tucker
Jim Harris	Stanton Heck
Aunty May	Martha Mattox
Charley Stump	Walt Whitman
Ginger	Joan Standing
Thad Parker	Ralph Cloninger
Milt Goddard	Lee Shumway
Lucius Kildare	John Dill
Sheriff	Gordon Magee
Jennie Parker	Irene Hunt

Excellent melodrama with several splendid thrills, much fine scenery, first-rate comedy and dramatic interest in spots. But it falls down for some reason. The trouble is not on the surface and is difficult to point out. Probably the picture goes awry because the producers have distorted its romantic appeal in order to make it a vehicle for Frank Keenan as an old man. The affairs of the young hero and heroine are subordinated to the character sketch of the hero's father, a rugged old lumber king, and the thing won't hold together. Interest is dissipated instead of being economically directed along a simple line of narrative.

First, because he is the only good actor among the principal characters, and, second, because every effort is made to hold him in the center of the story, attention is attracted to and confined to Mr. Keenan, playing old Luke Taylor. He engages interest and attracts sympathy and understanding. Once he has attracted, you want to see him prominent in the vital development. Instead of which all the heroic action revolved about the young couple. John is victor in a rough-and-tumble fight. Helen wins a victory over those who plot against her to cheat her of her timber lands. It is John and Helen who drive the locomotive through a raging forest fire and save the hemmed-in villagers, but all the time you have the feeling (because of the way emphasis has been placed on the Keenan role) that all this is secondary. Since the old man's part has been italicized, you have the sense that all that happens that is to be vital and significant must have him **as the central figure. Hence the edge is taken from the real action because he is not concerned in it.**

Here is a case where bad technical dramatic work has spoiled what should have been a capital picture. The "stunt" stuff is great. In one scene, the hero and heroine build a dam in order to back the water up until it will float enormous mountains of cut logs, then blast the dam away and send the timber rushing and tumbling down a mountain torrent, with lumberjacks skipping giddily over the tossing logs. It must have been a big job to arrange the effect, but it's worth it. The other "punch" is a big forest fire—a rushing, thrilling passage of melodrama, accomplished with stunning scenic effects.

The whole picture is a revel in scenery of the noble forests, but its story is scrappy and jumbled and confused. Values are disproportioned, probably because a novel nearly always has too much material for a film unless wise selection is made. For example, the incident of the death of a settler's wife bears but obscurely upon the main story, but it is played out at interminable length and with tiresome detail. A mere title would have covered the passage adequately. In a dramatic version all this action would have happened off stage and been made known in a line or two of dialog. There are other similar scenes all of them reacting against a simple, cohesive story.

The comedy is excellent. Russell Simpson has a capital part as the husband who hasn't spoken to his wife except through a third party for 20 years. Joan Standing does a neat bit as a "hired girl," and Ralph Cloninger handles a low-comedy role as a sporty hick with nice judgment.

There are a lot of arresting shots of wild animals, such as wolves and deer fleeing before the forest flames and one of a big black bear tumbling down a tall tree as the fire approaches. The utmost care and pains have been taken over these incidentals, but the main point of concentrated attention has been neglected, and the work falls to pieces in spite of its many excellencies. *Rush.*

EINSTEIN THEORY

Educational subject of feature length, explaining in non-scientific terms Dr. Albert Einstein's theory of relativity. Prepared under the auspices of the scientist himself and arranged for American presentation under the direction of Prof. Garrett P. Serviss. Drawings and animated diagrams by Max Fleischer, maker of the "Out of the Inkwell" series of animated drawings. Special showing for educators at the Rivoli, New York, Feb. 3. Announced as part of the Rivoli program next week.

The picture occupies just 40 minutes and doesn't hold for that stretch of time. What inspired them to book it into the Broadway film house, is a mystery. A title quotes Einstein as saying that only 12 scientists in the world are capable of understanding the theory. That ought to be enough to keep it from boring a mixed lay assemblage of Valentino and Swanson fans and the army of women who do their popular science reading in May Manton and the Butterick publications.

The film isn't even illuminating in a popular way. It doesn't explain anything that wasn't already clear. It seems a waste of footage to create elaborate and intricate diagrams to demonstrate that if you step off the earth's surface there is no such thing as east and west; that there is no meaning to the conception of large and small unless you establish some fixed standard of comparison, and that fast and slow don't mean a thing except in relation to something else. It's just a labored exposition of the obvious. The picture toils through a morass of these elemental matters and then gets down to the abstruse substance of Einstein's theories.

The conception of bent space and bent light rays is illustrated by elaborate diagrams, but they give no enlightenment. They use up an immense footage to demonstrate that if a man walks toward the stern of a moving boat at the boat's exact speed forward, he is standing still in relation to the shore, but moving backward in relation to the boat itself. A title would have covered that. But when they come to deal with the bending of light they merely declare the principle and let it go at that.

The diagrams are extremely ingenious to elucidate obvious things, but when they get Einstein into the rarefied atmosphere of pure scientific reasoning they are baffling and the spectator is befogged. The thing is meaningless and gets down to the mere juggling of words. They establish the meaning of measurements by the yardstick of "time space," and then describe the mysterious "fourth dimension." If the three known dimensions are up and down, right and left and near and far, the fourth is "soooner or later."

The whole thing is about as clear and useful as this description of it, and it will probably bore the film fan stiff.   *Rush.*

CAPT. FLY-BY-NIGHT

A romantic tale of the early days of California—days before the gold rush and the film stampede, when the Spanish ruled and the men were dashing horsemen, with gay trappings and a ready knife and gun. In a sense this picture is a romance, still in another it is almost a comedy. It is the sort of picture that will get by nicely in the smaller daily change houses.

Capt. Fly-by-Night was one of the most famed bandits of the early days. This picture is of his escapades, although the picturization does not profess to be a true tale—just an excuse for a film feature. It won't pull 'em in, but it will help them pass their time once they are in the seats.

Johnnie Walker is a fairly lovable hero, although there is an effort early in the action to place him in the light of the heavy. They couldn't get away with that at all. Johnnie was spotted as the hero the moment he got within range of the lens. Shannon Day makes a very acceptable heroine, and the balance of the cast is quite good, especially Eddie Gribbon as a swashbuckling Spanish soldier.

The direction is fair and the photography decidedly good.   *Fred.*

Foreign Films

THE VIRGIN QUEEN

London, Jan. 23.

Apparently Stuart Blackton is beset by two obsessions—the pull of the aristocracy, from a box office point of view, and the glories of his Prizma color photography. Bereft of these two he can turn out excellent features, as witness "The Gypsy Cavalier," but when social ambitions become paramount he fails badly.

For weeks past the trade journals have published ornate inserts boosting this picture and the lay papers have been flooded with press stuff.

However, "The Virgin Queen" is only a super film from the angle of the elaborate staging it has received. To this end the producer has gone far in his search for locations and impressive interiors.

It is not even conspicuous for good acting. Extremely doubtful is the likelihood of its drawing business to the Leicester Square house and its attractiveness, as regards the provincial kinemas, is nothing above that of any other well advertised feature.

The story is that of Queen Elizabeth (The Virgin Queen) having an enemy in the Countess of Lenox, who wishes her son to become the husband of Mary, Queen of Scots, with the object of placing the young couple on the English throne in place of the present ruler.

The story is not strong and is disjointed. This feature is in dire need of drastic cutting.

Of the cast, the less said the majority the kinder. A. B. Imsson does nicely as the Spanish Ambas-

sador, and Carlyle Blackwell gives an average performance as Lord Dudley. Lady Diana Manners offers a splendid appearance, but cannot be said to fulfill the "queenly" requirements of her characterization as Elizabeth.

It might also be added that the inserted color in idents are not brilliant and impress as a long way from approaching perfection.

THE STEINACH FILM

Berlin, Jan. 17.

This long-awaited film, officially authorized by Dr. Steinach himself, the discoverer of the process for making the old young again, is really much better than was to be expected from such a venture. The putting of anything scientific on the screen for the general public seems almost a hopeless task. Yet, although the present film is open to many objections, still it teaches much more than was to be expected.

This film could never be circulated generally in America, even though it was cut from six to two reels. If leaving anything which would make sense, the American censors would be after it. If it had a hard time getting by the German censors (who are very liberal, as children under 16 are not allowed to enter film theatres except to see certain fairy films, Cooper's Leather Stocking Tales, etc.), then you can imagine what a chance it would have getting by on your side. To put it frankly, the whole film is about the sexual life and organs of man and beast, and shows how Steinach, by experimenting on rats, achieved a method whereby he made old rats young and energetic again. From this it goes on to show how the same method, slightly varied, was applied to man. The film is very discreet, in that it does not pretend that the fountain of youth has been found, but merely that so far the present process seems very hopeful.

There is no doubt about it that if this film were discreetly cut (much of the evident material about copulation among the animals and about homosexuality should go at once) it should be good for colleges and, perhaps, even for selected lecture public.   *Trask.*

MONNA VANNA

Berlin, Jan. 20.

"Monna Vanna," a new monumental film shown lately at the Marmorhaus, is called a tragedy of the Renaissance. It is certainly a tragedy, but not of the Renaissance. This film will be probably sold to South America. Has there ever been a film that hasn't been sold there?

But it has seldom been our misfortune to be present at a more deadly hodge-podge of bad scenery, tawdry costumes and impossible acting.

This is all the more extraordinary when one considers that Paul Wegner, one of the finest heavies now in captivity, plays the role of the Governor of Pisa. And how badly he does play it! Yes, the responsibility for this atrocity must rest directly on the shoulders of Helmuth Ortmann and Olga Alsen, the scenario writers, and those of the director, Richard Eichberg.   *Trask.*

DER FALSCHE DIMITRY

Berlin, Jan. 20.

"The False Dimitry," a film taken from Russian history, has had a successful showing at the Ufa Palast am Zoo. The scenario by Hans Steinhof and Paul Beyer is far from being a model of its kind, as it is much too spready. Instead of concentrating on a few characters and

making us either sympathize or hate, it takes in so many that we can really know none of them perfectly.

It begins with the death of Ivan the Terrible, who puts his son Fedor by his third marriage as the successor. But the boy is not of age, and in the meantime Boris Godunoff rules in his stead. When the boy dies before coming of age, Godunoff has Dimitry, the son of Martha, Ivan's seventh wife, murdered, and takes the throne himself.

Peter, a young boy, playmate of Dimitry's, has escaped and later gives himself out as the real Dimitry. With the aid of the Poles he conquers Godunoff, and for a short time is Czar. The Russians do not like to see the Poles in power. Dimitry is ousted and shot.

Many of Germany's best actors are in the film, and they generally do their best; only the Boris Godunoff of Eugen Klopfer is really bad, while the Peter of Paul Hartmann and Friedrich Kuhne in a small role are excellent.

The direction of Steinhof and the scenery of Walter Reimann are competent throughout, but, as remarked before, the effect is chilling, as no personal touch is established with the characters.   *Trask.*

ADAM AND EVA

Cosmopolitan feature starring Marion Davies and distributed by Paramount. Scenario adapted by Luther Reed, from the stage play by Guy Bolton and George Middleton. Directed by Robert G. Vignola. At the Rivoli, New York, week of Feb. 11.
Eva King....................Marion Davies
Adam Smith................T. Roy Barnes
Mr. King.......................Tom Lewis
Uncle Horace...................Wm. Norris
Lord Andy.....................Percy Ames
Clinton DeWitt..............Leon Gordon
Julie DeWitt.................Luella Gear
Dr. Delamater.............Wm. Davidson
Lord Andy's Secretary.....Edward Douglas
Eva's Admirers........ { Bradley Barker
                       { John Powers
Gardener....................Horace James

A distinctly promising photoplay and one of the best light comedy roles this star has ever played. The picture has the charm of gay youth and makes an appropriate setting for Marion Davies' blonde beauty and her knack of carrying off breezy comedy parts with a certain jaunty chic.

The adaptation from stage to screen has been shrewdly managed. The picture version puts all the emphasis on the humorous side of the story of a spoiled daughter of luxury who meets adversity with the sporting spirit and carries on to triumph. It's a story of American social life that is modern and "smart" and yet hasn't a dry twist. It's atmosphere is happy and cheerful. The whole production puts on a smiling front and is an altogether refreshing entertainment.

The soft pedal is on the sentimental angle with the whole appeal toward comedy and romance. For picture purposes the changes in the original are all for the better. For example Eva has cajoled Adam into permission to give "a little party" which turns out to be an elaborate and costly Venetian fete. It is in the midst of these gaieties that Adam breaks the news of the family's financial crash. That frightens off the false fortune seeking lover and paves the way for the regeneration of the entire group of society wasters.

The party, of course, gives capital opportunity for the introduction of striking costumes and carnival pageantry and it also gives point to the dramatic action of the family ruin. In other ways the script has been altered for its new purpose. In the play Eva was at times forced to the background while here the action centers in her character development, a change that is an unqualified improvement. Eve is ever the main interest, from the Garden on down the stretches of time. Thus several new passages have been devised. Adam and Eva share the secret of the stolen jewels, instead of Adam alone committing the theft. Again when they all go back to the old farm to work for a living, it is Eva who solves the financial problem by driving off in the town car and coming back with a bankroll and a flivver.

The picture is plentifully besprinkled with wholesome laughs. Eva's shopping tours will hand the woman fans a giggle anywhere. So will her high handed bullying of her real and her counterfeit father. And the single sentimental passage of the five reels—Eva's emotional greeting of her supposededly impoverished father—will surely make a strong appeal. Miss Davies has never handled a pretty bit of sentimental acting with more sincerity and conviction. The picture, both as to its comedy and its drama, is managed with admirable restraint. The humor is genuine, intelligent and never condescends to the supposedly crude tastes of the fans. And it has something all new in the film laugh line, in a cow-milking scene.

A first rate company surrounds the star. T. Roy Barnes makes a quiet, manly Adam while Percy Ames has several effective moments as Lord Andy. Tom Lewis brings all his portly aplomb to the role of the real father and William Norris is a credit to the rich part of Uncle Horace.

The direction is always sure and capable and the settings notable examples of artistic judgment and sound taste. The atmosphere of the farm is especially good and the romantic closeup at the finish is a neat and picturesque touch, with Eva sending an affectionate hint in a note floating down a jolly little forest brook to the disconsolate Adam mourning below in solitude.

"Adam and Eva" is far from "Knighthood" in character and production, yet Miss Davies will not disappoint the horde of new admirers her superb performance as Mary Tudor won for her in that most remarkable production of all the screen; "When Knighthood Was in Flower." "Adam and Eva" will bring to those who have seen Miss Davies only as the fiery Princess another side of herself, and just as charming. *Rush.*

FURY

Inspiration Pictures' production released through First National. Has Richard Barthelmess starred with Dorothy Gish featured. Story is by Edmund Goulding, and the direction the work of Henry King. Length about 7 reels, running an hour and 36 minutes At Strand, New York, week Feb. 11.

"Dog" Leyton....................Tyrone Power
Morgan, First Mate..........Pat Hartigan
"Boy" Leyton........Richard Barthelmess
Looney Luke...............Barry Macollum
Mr. Hop.................Harry Blakemore
Yuka..........................Adolph Milar
Zece...............................Ivan Linow
Miss Matilda Brent..........Emily Fitzroy
Tillie.....................Jesse May Arnold
Minnie, Waif................Dorothy Gish
Mrs Ross..............Lucie Backus Seger
Looney Luke's Girl..........Patterson Dial

Here is the best picture that Richard Barthelmess has appeared in since "Tol'able David." It isn't as great a wallop as "David" was, but it is a picture that is going to do a whale of a business. It is the first picture that Edmund Goulding has done for this star since he adapted the "David" tale and that may account somewhat for the punches that there are in it. Goulding seems to know how to fit Barthelmess, and seemingly this current attraction and the previous one that this writer did for him are the proof of the pudding. The coupling of Miss Gish with the star is also bound to develop a certain pull at the box office. In addition "Fury" is a great story as screened, coupling a corking touch of humor here and there through a story that is replete with action and heart interest.

"Fury" has a little touch of the strength of "Madam X" in it, only in this instance the boy discovers his mother who was lured away and tackles the man who seduced her. The ending, however, comes rather abruptly, but suffices the needs of the story.

The tale is laid in the Limehouse district of London and the wharves of Glasgow, with the star on board the "Lady Spray" as second mate, his father being the master of the craft. The father is embittered at the world due to the fact that his wife deserted him for another man. The opening scenes disclose the life on board ship and plants the types perfectly. The master of the ship stern and unforgiving, without love of a single soul on earth; the first mate a bully of the roughest type; the master's son an easy-going, lovable boy with a shrinking spirit. The other ship board characters are also skillfully drawn.

Then on shore there is revealed the girl in the person of Miss Gish. She is her same flip, half humorous, half pathetic, self as of yore. A waif who is employed as scullery maid in a sailors rest in the water front district, with the first mate of the Lady Spray and the master's son both trying to win her. The latter is one that she favors and finally she consents to go to Glasgow to meet him there and marry. It is on that trip along the coast that the father dies and places into the hands of his son the task of finding the man responsible for his mother's downfall with an oath that will wreak vengence on him. In Glasgow he finds the mother and in turn discovers that the first mate is the man responsible, and the fight wallop of the picture occurs here, with the boy being worsted in the battle. Later, however, on ship board he manages to carry out his task when during the course of the second clash between the pair the burly mate who has been made master on the death of the former captain tumbles over the side during the conflict.

Through it all Barthelmess as the boy carries with him a certain wistfulness bound to appeal, especially with Miss Gish acting as an excellent foil for his work. Miss Gish gets the laughs in the picture, she again easily qualifying as being absolutely alone in her particular style of work on the screen.

In direction the picture holds the interest all the way. There isn't a moment that drags anywhere in the picture, although it is more than the average feature length, and Henry King and the script of Goulding is to be credited with having accomplished this. In detail the picture seems perfect, and the square rigged schooner that was used for the ship scenes adds much to the picturesqueness of the production. *Fred.*

THE LAST HOUR

Presented and directed by Edward Sloman distributing through Mastodon Films Inc. Adapted from Frank R. Adams' "Blind Justice" with Max Dupont, photographer. At the Cameo, New York, week Feb. 11.

Steve Cline........................Milton Sills
Saidee McCall...............Carmel Myers
Philip Logan..................Pat O'Malley
Tom Cline.........................Jack Mower
Reever McCall..................Alec Francis
William Mallory.............Charles Clary
Red Brown........................Walter Long
Governor Logan.................Eric Mayne

A crook story supplemented with an imposing cast that fails to sum up as anything more than an average feature while typifying the "blood and thunder" release every so often. The players comprise a list of established names that certainly should secure better results than the finished product reveals. Perhaps it's the fault of the direction of the story itself.

Milton Sills and Carmel Myers hold the leading figures and neither has outdone themselves in this presentation. One or two slips in continuity were noticeable while the working up of the finale unfolds a few overly imaginative instances that make it hard to reasonably digest.

The narrative covers a period of about six years which gives Steve Cline (Mr. Sills) a chance to return from South America after making a fortune, and Saidee McCall (Miss Myers) the necessary time to reach womanhood besides permitting the insertion of a few feet of film on the late war. The one battle flash pictures, an over-the-top instance that has a flag-bearing individual leading the assault, will probably bring a snicker from the average witnesses. The charge was a distinct reminder of previous Blue and Gray engagements as generally produced before the camera.

The picture is projected by means of average photography with most of the sets running to interiors; one or two of which might be termed pretentious if compared to the majority of scenes it includes.

Relating of the Cline brothers, famous safe crackers, the story opens with the return of Steve on the day the papers carry scare heads on a bank robbery. Tom, the other brother, is responsible for the crime with the brothers meeting in the flat of Saidee McCall and her father who are forgers. The cops blast in. During the ensuing mixup Tom is killed, after which Steve gets the girl and her father away.

A jump to France shows the girl as a nurse tending to a boy who relates how he was saved by his pal. The boy friend is, of course, Steve, though Saidee doesn't learn that until after the return to this country where her patient is fully recovered and is now insistent in his demands for marriage.

The suitor's father is governor of the state. At a dinner to the executive Steve, Saidee and the detective whom they gave the slip the night of Tom's death but who is now a political boss, meet. The copper is wise. When circumstances leave the girl without anyone to escort her home it leaves an opening for the usual proposition under threat of exposure. The situation concludes when the father calls for his daughter and shoots the "bull." Leaving Steve to again get the couple out of the "jam" which he does by taking the blame for the murder.

Sentenced to be hung, all the action pends until the final 24 hours when the girl takes a 400-mile trip to the governor and back, misses the prison in time with her secured pardon, but the trap on the scaffold sticks which just makes it convenient for the father to entrance, confess and then pass out, through having been hit by a machine on his way to square matters.

If you think you can arrange things more conveniently than that, try and do it. *Skig.*

THE LOVE LETTER

Universal starring Gladys Walton. Story by Bradley King, adapted by Hugh Hoffman. King Baggot director. At Loew's New York, Feb. 9, 1923.

Mary Ann McKee...........Gladys Walton
Kate Smith...................Fontaine La Rue
Red Mike........................George Cooper
Bill Carter......................Edward Hearne

A trite and commonplace tale as far as the twisting of the triangle is concerned, but a feature picture sure to go in factory neighborhoods. Its combination, slum underworld and rural, with a certain amount of appeal. In it Gladys Walton looks more like Alice Brady than ever.

The story starts off with an idea used in a fiction story several years ago, only that instead of overalls a shirt was used, with a factory girl sending a letter in the pocket of one of the shirts she finished in the factory. The reply was the means of her wedding a chap in a small town and living happily ever after.

However, the slum stuff was effective, except the author is unaware that in these days in the neighborhoods near the Bowery there aren't any gangs that are run by the Irish boys. It's the wops, Hebes and Greeks who run the works these days.

Miss Gladys Walton has the role of a worker in the overall factory, where the girls place mash notes in the finished product and the replies that they get are good for laughs.

The small town and the blacksmith hero are the next points of interest. The gang leader shows up after the girl has been happily married and a mother and then the smash of the story comes along with the wife willing to sacrifice her own happiness to save her husband's life, when the gang leader insists she accompany him back to the big town.

It's the old, old hoke, and not a good picture for anything except the real small houses. *Fred.*

THE FLAME OF LIFE

Hobart Henley-Universal production starring Priscilla Dean. Based on Frances Hodgson Burnett novel "That Lass O' Lowrie's," adapted by Elliott Clawson. Shown at Loew's State, New York, Feb. 12-14. Seven reels.

Loan Lowrie.....................Priscilla Dean
Fergus Derrick...................Robert Ellis
Anice Barholm...........Kathryn McGuire
Dan Lowrie.....................Wallace Beery
Spring ....Fred Kohler
Liz ....Beatrice Burnham

The Universal seems to be coming along in the matter of class in production, at least as far as the pictures that Hobart Henley directs are concerned. In cast this picture holds its own with any of the productions turned out by what are classed the better program producers and in direction there is nothing that can be asked for.

The picture, however, is not going to hold the box office strength of Mr. Henley's "Flirt." This is a period picture, laid in the worst period, as far as dressing goes, that there is for picturizing. It is 1870 with its hideous attire for women and men, although as far as the women in this story are concerned they are all with one exception employed in the coal pits of a Lancashire mine, so dressing for them doesn't matter.

"The Flame of Life" carries as its real thrill the coal mining scenes, the explosion that wrecks the mine with its accompanying fire and flood. In addition, it has a corking fight in one of the earlier scenes. In these scenes in particular the direction carries the picture along. The story is a sordid tale, but Henley has lightened it here and there in skilful touches with "kiddies," and again shows he can handle youngsters to perfection before the camera.

Miss Dean has a terrific role for a star to uphold. It is rather surprising that she would consent to do it. She is one of the pit girls at the mine working through the entire picture, except for a brief moment just before the final fade out, and does not appear except with a smudged face, for the greater part of the time with a shawl tightly drawn across her head. One thing the picture does do for her however and that is to establish her as a character actress of no mean ability.

Wallace Beery as the heavy gives a fine performance of the brutal father of the star. Robert Ellis is acceptable in the heroic character although he seems entirely secondary in the part. *Fred.*

CRINOLINE AND ROMANCE

Metro feature starring Viola Dana. Story and script by Bernard McConville. Directed by Harry Beaumont. Shown at Loew's State, New York, Feb. 8-11.

Col. Cavanaugh........Claude Gillingwater
Emmy Lou Wimbleton.........Viola Dana
Mrs. Wimbleton..........Lillian Lawrence
Betty Biddle...............Betty Francisco
David Gordon..................John Bowers
Augustus Biddle.............Allan Forrest

A romantic comedy drama evidently designed to order for Viola Dana. A picture that has considerable comedy in its action, and one that is certain to please the Dana fans. For the ordinary run of picture houses it will serve nicely, but it isn't a feature that any of the better first runs would want to show. Directed by Harry Beaumont, the story by Bernard McConville holds the interest to a certain extent, with the laughs coming from the manner in which the director handled his situations.

Miss Dana had the role of a Southern lass, whose grandfather has kept her secluded from the rest of the world on his plantation in the mountains, his reason being that his daughter, the girl's mother, had eloped and made an unfortunate marriage, and he seemed determined that the grand-daughter should know naught of the outer world and thus avoid the pitfall that her mother fell victim to. The result is that the girl finally runs away to visit an aunt on her father's side of the family, and there she meets two young men. Both fall in love with her, and finally both follow her to her home in the hills. She cannot determine which of the two she prefers, and finally when they start to battle and the grand-dad suggests a duel she makes up her mind.

The story in itself is simple, and the half-kidding performance that the star gives, assisted by flip titles, are the things that put the picture over for whatever it gets from an audience. Miss Dana is perfectly **at home in the picture, and the writer and director managed to give her a chance to appear in the altogether for a brief minute in an under-water swimming bit, and that perhaps is counted on to give the thrill quality to the production. The contrast between the star in ante-bellum and the modern flappers in their costume of the day also serves to furnish a laugh or two.**

John Bowers is fairly satisfactory as leading man, but did not seem to develop the punch in this picture that he has had in productions in the past. A semi-heavy played by Allan Forrest was convincing. The star performance of the picture, however, was contributed by Claude Gillingwater as the old Colonel. *Fred.*

THE SPEED KING

Presented by Phil Goldstone, featuring Richard Talmadge. Adapted from "Hail the King" under the direction of Gordon Jones, with photography by Arthur Todd. At Loew's New York, Feb. 8.

Much melodrama revolving around two Balkan musical-comedy countries that has Richard Talmadge doubling for the king of one of the fatherlands and straightening out the diplomatic contingencies after having been backed up against a wall before a firing squad. It holds an abundance of action that takes the star from this country, as a motorcycle speed king, to the foreign shores, where he battles through the national army and a group of Apache hounds to win the princess.

The director has carried along his subject fluently. One situation swiftly follows another, with each provoking some sort of a fight or a chase. It keeps Talmadge on the jump away out of proportion to any one man's physical prowess. The picture nevertheless entertains with its consecutive action and the rough and tumble stunts the male lead performs. The photography is par at all times, and the cast, including Virginia Warwick, as the princess, supplemented by the usual number of soldiers of the king, peasants and cabinet, is satisfactory.

The narrative tells of Jimmy Martin (Mr. Talmadge), monarch of the **motorcycle speed boys, induced to sail to a foreign port for the purpose of racing, which turns into the cash offer being considerably raised if he'll double for the king, of whom he is an exact replica. It's a frame to turn a portion of territory over to the rival country with the plotters making Martin believe everything is all right until he suspects something phoney about the deal.**

Thence starts the unraveling of all he has done, the saving, by him, of the real ruler, and the switch of the king rescuing Martin as the loyalists are about to execute him from impersonating their ruler.

Talmadge in dual role f the young American and the king offers a nice appearance while running wild through the picture. It should be fair enough amusement for those who crave seeing a youthful stalwart continuously besting gangs of five and ten. The film has been adequately produced and illusions proportionately as to backgrounds and settings.

Just straightaway, fast-moving melodrama that should suffice for its assignment in the intermediate picture theatres. *Skig.*

ONE-EIGHTH APACHE

Ben Wilson Production starring Roy Stewart, written by J. Grubb Alexander. Semi-western and society drama. Released through Arrow. Shown at Loew's Circle, N. Y., double feature bill, Feb. 13, 1923.

Charlie Longdeer.........Wilbur McGaugh
Tyler Burgess............George McDaniel
Apache Joe Murdock......Richard La Reno
Brant Murdock................Roy Stewart

One of those regulation program pictures ground out by the producing mill in order to fill in whenever a gap occurs in the bookings here and there, in the hope that some day it will eventually return its cost and possibly a little profit. There is nothing about it that means anything to the box office, either in the way of star, story or direction. However, if a theatre is doing business anyway, and they come in no matter what the program is, then this is one that the exhibitor can afford to cheat with.

It is a combination western and society story. Didn't cost very much to produce, for the majority of the scenes are exteriors. One fair interior sequence of scenes supposedly laid in a Long Island country home. **However, the story has one distinction, it is a western, without a horse.**

Roy Stewart has the role of the son of a wealthy cattle man who became many times a millionaire when oil was discovered on his land. The son for the greater part has been living in the east since his dad became wealthy. He is the result of an affair his father had with an Apache squaw in the early years of his wife in the west, though unaware of his Indian blood. At the opening he has made a trip west with his father and two women, mother and daughter. Both of the latter broken society folk with the daughter offered in the marriage mart. The heavy is a society man who is in love with the girl, and who has also taken a trip west to seek a fortune so that he may be able to support her. It's a funny thing, but if pictures were true there wouldn't be any society folk it seems that had any money at all.

Of course, the heavy learns the secret of the hero's birth and the taint of Indian blood, but not in time to prevent the marriage. Instead he waits until the marriage is consummated and then tries to shake down the boy's father to keep the secret. He almost succeeds, only the boy learns the truth and refuses to stand for the blackmail. In a row which follows the father is shot and killed by the heavy, whose plea that it was self-defense makes it possible for him to beat the case. The bride's feelings are much shattered by the scandal which follows and the airing of the fact of her husband's parentage, and she moves to have the marriage annulled, after a settlement is fixed for her. Then she marries the heavy, only to find that she got the wrong man after all, and in the end she realizes that it has all been a mistake. Then comes the task of getting rid of the husband, which is nicely accomplished when an Indian bumps him off and leaves the road clear for the usual happy ending.

There are a couple of fairly good fights in the picture which will make a certain appeal in the cheaper priced admission houses. The Circle's audience, however, which is far from being highbrow, gave it the laugh razz. *Fred.*

THE HOTTENTOT

Ince presentation adapted from the stage success of the same name, featuring Douglas MacLean. Directed by Del Andrews and J. W. Horne, and distributed through First National. At the Strand, New York, week of Feb. 18.

Sam Harrington.........Douglas MacLean
Peggy Fairfax...........Madge Bellamy
Mrs. Carol Chadwick...........Lila Leslie
Mrs. May Gilford...............Truly Shattuck
Ollie Gilford..................Martin, Best
Swift.......................Raymond Hatton
Major Reggie Townsend.Dwight Crittenden

Having been screened out of town for three or four weeks previous to the New York showing, the reports had this picture favorably received at the box office in the middle west, although closer proximity to the Atlantic seaboard demonstrated nothing unusual so far as receipts were concerned. Either way it made little difference to the Sunday matinee gathering at the Strand for the assembled multitude, and they were there to standing room, seemed to draw forth an abundance of entertainment from this comedy vehicle.

The film is noteworthy for the action it contains, if nothing else, while the directors have inserted a series of surprise laugh instances that hit the witnessing throng between the eyes. Some actually brought howls. The camera man, or men, receive no program nor title mention, but the photography is worthy of it. Corking effects have been secured during the steeplechase race that illusions as having been "shot" from every angle possible, even unto phoney close-ups of the riders in action, while the celluloid translation of the saying, "Gone in a cloud of dust," was a bit of camera work that provoked a spontaneous gale all over the theatre both times used.

Ince has given the production adequate presentation, and the cast surrounding Douglas MacLean is on an equal basis. The story of Sam Harrington, who is deathly afraid of horses, but through circumstances consummates an enviable reputation as to horsemanship, has been permitted a much wider scope on the screen than when bounded by a full stage set. The titling, at times, reads as verbatim from the original book, and is inclusive of numerous laughs on its own.

MacLean gives a splendid performance as the yachtsman forced to unwillingly straddle horses, and on the "Hottentot" in particular, the wildest animal in the stable. Madge Bellamy is opposite to carry on the love theme which is made entirely secondary to the principal object of laugh procuring. Dwight Crittenden and Raymond Hatton also registered for attention.

Whether the MacLean name means anything at the gate or not, this picture seems certain to favorably impress, with the logical follow-up being his next release will draw on the strength of this one. It's a whale of a script that has lost nothing in the migration to the screen, and may possibly be termed to have surpassed the footlight staging. *Skig.*

OTHELLO

Ben Blumenthal presents this film version of Shakespeare's tragedy, with Emil Jannings starred. Directed by Dimitri Buchowetzski. Released by David P. Howells for U. S. and Canada.

Othello..........................Emil Jannings
Iago..............................Werner Kraus
Rodrigo.........................Ferdinand Alten
Brabantio.....................Frederick Kuhne
Montano..........................Magnus Stifter
Desdemona.........................Ica Lenkeffy
Emilia.............................Lya de Putti

Several months ago Will H. Hays and Augustus Thomas at a dinner got together on the suggestion that the "Hamlet" of John Barrymore should be filmed and shown throughout the country. It wasn't done, and it probably won't be, but from Germany there has come a screen version of "Othello," presented by Ben Blumenthal. The picture was shown to an invited audience at the Century Roof theatre Sunday night and will open at the Criterion next Sunday.

From an artistic standpoint the picture is a triumph. The Moor of Emil Jannings, who is starred, is a superb piece of acting, and the production is about all that could be desired. However, it is a question just how the public will take the picture. To the Shakespearean scholars the production will make a terrific appeal, but it is hardly possible that the rank and file of motion picture fans will flock to see it.

The picture was made in Berlin last summer with the great Russian director, Dimitri Buchowetzki, in charge of the production. Jannings, famed in Europe for his Othello on the speaking stage, was engaged to head the cast, while Werner Kraus, who was the original Dr. Caligari, was cast for Iago. Desdemona was played by a young Hungarian actress, Ica Lenkeffy, who proved a delightful surprise, for generally in these foreign productions the leading women run to beef. In this instance a blonde of the ingenue type in appearance and an actress of ability was shown. Lya de Putti in the role of Emilia, wife of Iago, scored on appearance, her decided brunet appearance being an excellent foil to the blonde beauty of the leading woman.

In the matter of production seemingly nothing was spared to make the sets stupendous. They carry the suggestion of massiveness, and there are any number of mob scenes **in which the foreign director delights and handled capably.**

It does not seem likely that "Othello" will cause the furore that the first of the big German productions, "Passion," did. It is a question whether or not the general run of the public want Shakespeare on the screen. If they do then this should be a clean-up, but from indications of the past, when the production of "Hamlet" made by a Scandinavian company was shown in New York, it does not seem possible that they will take kindly to the classics of the famous Bard of Avon.

With a great deal of plugging along educational lines, teachers, schools, etc., there should be business enough for the picture on the high spots of the country for a couple of weeks each, but that is about all that can be predicted for it. *Fred.*

RACING HEARTS

Famous Players production starring Agnes Ayres, with Theodore Roberts and Richard Dix featured. Adapted from Byron Morgan's story by Will M. Ritchey. Directed by Paul Powell. Shown at the Rivoli, week February 18, 1923.

Virginia Kent..........Agnes Ayres
Roddy Smith..........Richard Dix
John Kent........Theodore Roberts
Fred Claxton..........Robert Cain
Jimmy Britt........Warren Rogers
Silas Martin..J. Farrell MacDonald

A rather light little comedy drama of the automobile world. It carries as its big punch an automobile road race which should be satisfying enough for the most blase seeker of thrills. In cast it is fairly strong on names, having both Theodore Roberts and Richard Dix as featured members under the name of the star. There is nothing, however, about the picture that is going to cause any unusual jam at the box office, although as entertainment it is fairly satisfying.

Richard Dix has the role of the son of the owner of one auto manufacturing plant. He is a go-getter type of youth who believes in advertising stunts and his father sanctions his wild splurges for publicity. A rival company is headed by Theodore Roberts, and the star appears as his daughter. She is also a believer in advertising, but her father is a conservative and won't go in for racing or any of the usual stunts that are utilized to popularize a car.

In an effort to obtain publicity for her father's machine the girl drives it at 65 miles an hour through a town where the magistrate is noted for sending speeders to jail in the hope that if she is sent to the hoosgow she will get her name and that of the car in print. It is in this town that the rival auto shops are located and the son of the owner is acting as a motor cop temporarily, he persuading the judge to discharge the girl because it would appear as though his father's firm was behind the pinch as a sort of spite rivalry.

The next day the boy gets an assignment from his father to obtain a position in the rival plant to make a survey of conditions there, as it is known that they are pinched for money and it is possible that the plant will shortly be on the market. Once on the job he is given the task of designing a racing car under the direction of the girl. Her father in the meantime having left for London to close a foreign deal for his cars. The girl has written into the set of instructions that her father left a command that a racing car be built.

Then comes the day of the big road race, with the usual crooked driver stuff and the girl jumping in at the last minute and winning the race, although she manages to cross the line with the assistance of a bump from the rival company's car, which was driven by the son of the owner. Of course prior to this the girl has discovered his identity and accused him of spying, but the finish of the race finds them clinched in each other's arms.

There are some fairly good comedy moments in the picture but it is the race that will get to the fans. That feature was well handled in direction. *Fred.*

WOMAN CONQUERS

B. P. Schulberg is the producer of this First National feature, with Katherine MacDonald. Directed by Tom Forman. From the story by Violet Clark. Notable cast includes Bryant Washburn, June Elvidge, Mitchell Lewis and others.

The picture starts out ominously, with a New York society setting, accompanied by the usual counterfeit atmosphere of heavy society stuff as they see it in the studios. But presently the locale moves into the far North and the picture more than redeems itself, with picturesque settings in the snow country and melodramatic action that is fast and gripping. The final impression is altogether satisfactory.

Katherine MacDonald's pictures always start with a big advantage—the flawless and persuasive beauty of the star. If they would only make it an unalterable rule to give her sympathetic roles it is difficult to see how she could go wrong. This picture is an illustration. At the beginning Miss MacDonald is a bored and querulous society queen, "tired of this sham and pretense," and especially tired of the attentions of Freddie (Washburn), a social butterfly, who pays casual court to her.

You can't like two such people. They bore you as much as they pretend to be bored by themselves. That supercilious attitude alienates any audience, especially when they lay it on as thick as they do here. And they do overplay the grand society stuff unreasonably. When Miss MacDonald is introduced she is just waking up in a bedroom set that couldn't be duplicated outside the royal chamber of the Czar of all the Russias. And the heroine wears a nightie that looks as though it were made of embroidered velour. From these details one wouldn't be surprised to have the picture turn out a comedy-burlesque. The impression is emphasized when we switch to the hero's bedroom and he is disclosed in pajamas that look as thought they might be hand painted. You can't get any illusion of reality out of such naive exaggerations, and you can't help but put a low estimate on such people.

But when the heroine's uncle leaves her an inheritance of a furtrading business in the Canadian wilderness and she goes to inspect it the situation changes and the mimic characters come near to becoming real people. The society masquerade disappears and a rather neat romantic tale begins. It has no special novelty in idea, but in the snow-covered landscapes, the dashing dog trains and the picturesque trappers one finds a colorful background for the love story. Besides Miss MacDonald is an infinitely more beautiful figure muffled up in furs than in silly figured nighties.

The trading post is ruled by a giant bully (Lewis), who tries to make love to the heroine, and so comes in conflict with Freddie. The pampered society butterfly and the rough giant come into death grapple in the midst of a realistic arctic blizzard for the big scene of the story. The society man is bested, of course, but his display of courage captivates the girl and leads to the satisfactory closeup, while the familiar Indian guide whom the heroine had befriended disposes of the ruffian.

The blizzard scenes, which run through more than a reel, are wonderfully effective, and all the wilderness passages are convincing, even to the interiors of the traders' huts. *Rush.*

WOMAN IN CHAINS

Amalgamated Exchanges of America (independent) present this five-reel problem play, taken from the novel "The Madonna in Chains," by Edward Owings Towne. Directed by William P. Burt, under the supervision of Harry Grossman. Cast includes E. K. Lincoln, Mrs. Rodolph Valentino and Martha Mansfield. At Loew's Circle, Feb. 20.

Society drama has outstanding merits in its production, the interiors being especially impressive. A cabaret scene also is extremely well done as to its setting and stage management, but they waste enormous amounts of actionless footage and then, when they want the story to progress, they make it leap forward with titles. You get the effect of climbing a hill by going three steps up and two back.

The faithless wife deserts her husband and child and is next shown at the height of her prosperity as a cabaret dancer. They linger on the dance hall scene indefinitely (perhaps because it exploits the former Mrs. Valentino—Jean Acker—in a scene like that in which Rodolph figured in "The Four Horsemen"). Then, when they have to go on, they reduce the woman to poverty and mortal illness without any explanation.

The picture is full of similar crudities. It has no clear theme. You don't know who to sympathize with—the lover who sacrificed himself for the woman and served four years in jail to protect her from shame; the artist who married her and was cast away when the lover was released from jail, or the husband's jilted sweetheart, to whom he returned when the other woman left him. They're a queer assortment of characters and they go through a perplexing series of theatrical experiences.

The dancer woman deserved nothing better and the husband she double-crossed deserved no more. There seems to be nobody to be honestly sorry for, and that's not good fiction. If the husband were the hero—as you would suspect from the circumstance that the part was played by the star, E. K. Lincoln—he made a sorry figure. He took his wife's desertion in favor of another man much too tamely. All he did about it was to deliver one blow, and it was not an especially convincing blow at that, even if the lover made a lot of business as of being knocked senseless. Nothing would adequately have met the film situation short of a rough-and-tumble fight all over the lot. But they let the opportunity pass, and you couldn't help but feel that the husband was a poor fish.

After that he went back to Martinique, where he had left his fiancee waiting without a word of encouragement for five long years or so. And she greeted him rapturously, made him understand that she still loved him by letting him read her diary, and it ended sweetly happy with a romantic close-up. Only the romance, after all that had gone before, wouldn't jell. *Rush.*

LOVE'S OLD SWEET SONG

Independent dramatic feature, Helen Lowell and Louis Wolheim heading the cast. Produced by Norca Pictures. Oscar Lund director. Credit is given to J. L. Molloy, composer of the famous old song. At Loew's New York, Feb. 16.

Mother	Helen Lowell
The Wanderer	Louis Wolheim
Eunice	Helen Weir
Charlie	Donald Gallagher
Babs	Baby Margaret Brown

The picture has one good melodramatic stunt in the blasting out of a quarry hillside, the rock seeming to crush a shanty, throwing the hero and the baby into the river. Its second virtue is the remarkable performance of Baby Margaret, a captivating youngster of four or five who acts with jaunty naturalness and does an astonishingly good bit of acrobatic dancing.

That lets the picture out. Its story is rubbish. In the explosion scene, Charley rescues the baby from a watery grave, is arrested, released and goes to meet his sweetheart. In this lapse of time his hair has not had time to dry, but the real villain of the drama has confessed and the victim of his plotting has been released from jail and come home. But this sample of crudity is no worse than a lot of other details.

One minute we meet a rich banker. Ten minutes later his directors have discovered irregularities in the books of his cashier. Do they pinch the cashier? They do not. They lug the bank president off to jail, apparently without the formality of a trial. Indeed the detective who makes the arrest seizes a roll of money the banker was about to give his son.

The picture has some odd legal twists. When the banker is in jail, a Children's Society agent tears the baby from its home, casually explaining to the housekeeper that "the house has been closed by a sheriff's attachment and we must send the baby to a home." That's why the baby and her adult brother run away and hide.

The story is about a marble quarry owned by a widow. The wicked bank cashier tries to ruin the widow so he can get possession of the quarry, although the details of his schemes are foggy. After the president has been jailed (they don't even explain what for), it seems odd that the bank goes right along doing business so that the cashier can (heaven knows how) get possession of the widow's notes held by the bank.

A tramp called The Wanderer and a very unsavory looking personage, is introduced early in the proceedings. When it looks blackest for the widow, the bank president and the baby, the tramp turns out to be an agent for the Department of Justice who has been on the trail of the wicked cashier all along. His plottings are unmasked and he is well beaten up after all the excitement, so that the widow and the exonerated banker can have a mushy love scene. Even so easily satisfied New York roof's casual crowd of transient drop-ins laughed at the absurdities of the story. The company is worthy of better things. *Rush.*

MONEY, MONEY, MONEY!

First National release, starring Katherine MacDonald. A Larry Evans story adapted by Hope Loring, directed by Tom Forman. Six reels. At Proctor's 23d St., Feb. 19-21.

Priscilla Hobbs	Katherine MacDonald
Geo. C. Hobbs	Carl Stockdale
Mrs. Hobbs	Frances Raymond
Lennie Hobbs	Paul Willis
Mr. Carter	Herschel Mayall
Mrs. Carter	Brenda Fowler
Caroline Carter	Margaret Loomis
J. J. Grey	Charles Clary
Reggie Grey	Jack Dougherty

Just a fair program feature that started out as though it were really going to be a good picture, but simmered down. The picture was rather badly handled in the cutting and editing, which made the continuity rather jumpy at times. It is possible that the leading man selected to play opposite Miss MacDonald in this production might have had something to do with the lack of interest on the part of the audience in the proceedings on the screen. Jack Dougherty was the lead opposite the star. He is entirely lacking in personality and failed to get over with the audience at all. Miss MacDonald is still her striking good looking self as of yore, and that is about all.

It is a story of social ambitions in a small town, with the daughter and son of the little manufacturer of farming implements striving to move with the real fast set of the little town. They are vexed at their dad for his old-fashioned ideas and his desire to remain in the old home instead of moving to the more fashionable section. Finally they do manage to crash the gate in the social set, but only when those at the head of it believe that the Hobbs have fallen into a lot of money. When the truth becomes known as to the amount of the legacy that was left Mrs. Hobbs, it is discovered that the father will have to lose his business to protect a note that he signed at the insistence of his women folk when they believed that they were to receive a bundle of wealth.

At the last minute the head of the farming implement trust, who was anxious to take over the business decides that instead of letting shark bankers fleece his old competitor he will take a half interest in the business for his son. The son has been around the little town looking the situation over and has fallen in love with the rival manufacturer's daughter. It was the close proximity of the crash that brought the girl to her senses and to a realization that money wasn't everything and friendships that had to be purchased were not worth having.

The story is told in a rather disconnected and haphazard manner that fails to hold the audience. *Fred.*

THE MAN ALONE

Morris Schlank presents Hobart Bosworth in this dramatic feature. Directed by William H. Clifford. Produced by Motion Picture Utility Corp. and released through Anchor Film Distributing, Inc. At the New York, Feb. 20.

Aimed as a human interest story with sympathetic values, there are passages where the unintentional humor takes command. One such episode happens near the beginning, and thereafter it is difficult to take the story or the leading character seriously.

Hobart Bosworth plays Ben Dixon, a rough and ready mine owner of great wealth, who falls in love with a society girl. At their betrothal dinner Ben pulls some rough stuff with a knife and fork and the terribly refined fiancee is so shocked and horrified with his manners that she calls off the engagement. Ben, to tell the truth, was pretty crude, and you couldn't very much blame the girl, but the incident stopped Bosworth cold from getting serious attention for his subsequent heroics.

So it turned out just a mediocre program release, and rather second class at that. It's a weak story, although it has a certain amount of vigorous action on shipboard. But the theme of a middle aged man in love with a young girl has to be flawless to engage a sympathetic hearing—as good, for example, as "When We Were Twenty-one"—but that was a long way back. But an indifferent story of the sort is hopeless. Ben is rather a ridiculous figure in his heart broken melancholy, and when he sacrifices his heart and gives the girl to a younger and poorer man, you can't work up any great tear duct activity.

The action is rather theatrical and much of the material is aside from the vital issue. For instance, when Ben is dismissed by his fiancee he goes mooning down along the water front, and just manages to save the life of a despondent girl about to commit suicide. He befriends her and helps her to reclaim herself. But nothing comes of this expenditure of footage, for it doesn't lead anywhere. At the finish the girl is entirely forgotten. Maybe they meant to have the hero marry her as a substitute for the girl who passed him, but changed their minds after the picture was well along. Anyway, it leaves you wondering.

There are some rather good shipboard scenes, but it all seems to have been forced in because Bosworth always has been identified with deep sea action. He is shanghaied by his financial enemies, who somehow have his estate auctioned off so they can buy it cheap, but he turns up at the sale and throws them all into confusion, besides knocking his principal enemy cold with the famous Bosworth short arm hook. It is then he finds that although the society queen loves him devotedly, she loves his former social secretary more. So he ma! s the pair's fortune and departs, with a final closeup of Ben philosophizing into his pet horse's ear. All pretty juvenile stuff, unworthy of so sterling and vigorous an actor as Bosworth. *Rush.*

THE GRASS ORPHAN

London, Feb. 7.

Every picture Frank H. Crane makes enhances his reputation here and goes to prove that his specialty is to make good features from poor stories. The story of "The Grass Orphan" is very weak, but the picture has a high entertainment value, for which the production work and a very good acting cast are responsible. The St. Johns are a young coupe living on an allowance of £12,000 a year given them by an uncle they have never seen. They have one child, whom they neglect. One day they receive news of the uncle's bankruptcy and discover they are penniless. St. John cannot even get a job at a pound a week.

In the midst of their trouble comes an old lady who offers them £5,000 a year if they'll give up the child. They almost consent, but the mother love wakes at last in Mrs. St. John's heart, and she runs away with the child. Later she gets a job as a mannequin, while St. John drives a hansom cab. When they have been punished enough a vulgar auctioneer's valuer reveals himself as the uncle. Of course, he was never ruined and merely did it to teach them a lesson.

There are some exceptionally good sporting scenes and the interiors are excellent. The photography is very good and great attention has been paid to the lighting. As Mrs. St. John, Margaret Banneerman shows a good deal of ability. Her performance is the best thing she has done yet. Joyce Gaymon is excellent as her friend. Reginald Owen is responsible for an easy, finished performance as St. John, and Douglas Munro is capital as the masquerading uncle. *Gore.*

PATSY

Truart release starring Zasu Pitts with Wallace Beery and Marjorie Daw featured. A melodramatic comedy in five reels, directed by John J. McDermitt. Shown at Loew's Circle, New York, Feb. 13, 1923.

Patsy	Zasu Pitts
Crook	Wallace Beery

This would have been a big picture had the story been a little differently handled and the melodramatic portion jazzed a little in a comedy vein instead of seriously. Then with some real direction and a cast a picture could have been made of it that would have been able to go along in real fast company. As it is, however, just a mediocre independent program feature is the result. It is a picture in its present shape that can go along in the cheap houses and deliver fair entertainment value.

It is a story of an orphan who runs away from a woman who has adopted her with an idea of making her a "man of all work" on the farm. She starts tramping it and heads for California. When within a day's ride of Los Angeles she crashes her way aboard the limited and lands in the tourist mecca of Southern California.

Here she runs into no end of adventures, masquerading as a boy. On the train a kind hearted passenger has paid her fare for the trip into the town when the conductor wanted to throw her off the train. A young woman and her mother who were aboard offer her a home, but she misses them at the station and in her wanderings about the town meets an aged scientist, who takes her to his adobe shack, believing her to be a boy at first. He lives in a tough neighborhood and she has to fight her way into "the gang," which she does so successfully as to become leader.

Finally she manages to defeat the aim of several crooks, who frame to use the old man as their tool in a swindling scheme, and reunites the old scientist with his long-lost family. There is a lot of picture license taken and coincidence plays a tremendous part in working out the story, but as it is all in fun one cannot take the producer to task for this.

In direction there are three or four bits of comedy that are the things that save the picture from being an out-and-out meller of the rawest sort.

Zasu Pitts puts over the masquerading waif in pretty fair shape and gets any number of laughs. Wallace Beery is himself as the heavy. The balance didn't amount to very much, with Marjorie Daw playing a role far from important. *Fred.*

PADDY, NEXT BEST THING

London, Feb. 5.

This latest Graham-Wilcox production is an excellent screen version of the play which ran at the Savoy for such a long time. In every way it is a fine feature. For once the story has obtained additional power from the screen instead of losing it.

The exterior locations are exceptional, notably those of a hunt meet, and the interiors possess all the ornate grandeur of the American school. Among them is a beautiful but somewhat incongruous ballet on the grand staircase of an ancestral hall.

The photography by Rene Guissart is some of the best seen here.

The story opens with a yachting episode in which Paddy very nearly gets drowned. Rescued, she meets Laurence Blake and conceives an imaginary dislike for him. This grows when she discovers her sister, Ellen, has fallen in love with the immaculate young man. This love is not returned, and when she discovers Blake loves herself there is a row which drives Blake into exile.

Jack O'Hara is also in love with Ellen and goes abroad to seek his fortune. The death of the girl's father breaks up the home. When Blake returns he finds Paddy working as a dispenser for her uncle in London. He again declares his love without success, but later, after he has been knocked out in a street row, Paddy realizes she does love him. Jack O'Hara returns with a fortune and is accepted by Ellen. Paddy returns to Ireland, and feeling out of all the happiness, wanders off alone into the hills. She is reported lost and Blake heads the search party. He sinks into a morass where Paddy already is, and the situation brings the usual happy ending.

Graham Cutts has done his work admirably. Mae Marsh as Paddy is at her best, doing all the heroine's many moods with art and realism. The strong supporting cast includes Nina Boucicault, Haidee Wright, Marie Ault, Sir Simeon Stuart, George K. Arthur and Darby Foster.

The film is preceded by a short playlet by Jack Wilcox, entitled "The Banshee," in which Miss Boucicault and Herbert Langley appear, while Langley opens each show with the prolog from Leoncavallo's "Pagliacci."

This is one of the best British films yet made.

A WHITE BARBARIAN

London, Feb. 8.

Although this picture has not yet been shown, trade reviewers saw it privately. The feature is practically the record of the Baron-Bartholomew big game hunting expedition in equatorial Africa, into which a melodramatic story has been written. Three white men and two white women play the leading parts and are supported by natives from half a dozen different tribes.

As well as acting, the whites had to turn to and do other jobs, the most important of which was providing the meat food daily for the camp and watching that tribal quarrels did not break out among the mixed crowd of natives. The picture itself was actually made with rifles close at hand. For some time the late Captain George Outran was the guide and chief hunter, and it was shortly after leaving the expedition that he met his death through being almost torn to pieces by a wounded lion after he had gone to the rescue of a native boy.

The story concerns a legend of the Songora tribe, who possess a white royal family, supposed to have sprung direct from some wandering Carthagenians. An English hunter falls in love with their princess and compels her to free some slaves she is about to sell to an Arab caravan. She threatens him, but he has fallen in love with her and follows her into her own country. Here the adventures start and gradually work up to the burning of a entire native village. In the end the hero gets his princess.

The locations used are of exceptional interest, one being the top of a mountain which has the head of the legendary king of the Songora, M'Jintu, carved on its face. This head is supposed to keep watch over the tribe, and it is said that no man had ever trodden the summit of the mountain before. Another fine series of shots show the Nairobi falls and rapids. The photography is excellent considering the climatic conditions. The members of the company were John L. Baron, Herbert Leonard, Daphne Wynne and Leal Douglas. An almost human chimpanzee which attached herself to the men of the party returned with them to England and is now in the Zoological Gardens.

As a proof of how the government authorities help the film industry in England it is interesting to note that the negative was hung for months while the owners filled in forms proving that they were British, and when they did get their property it was discovered that the zealous customs officials had scratched their signatures in many places, choosing for preference important scenes or the faces of the players. *Gore.*

THE PRODIGAL SON

London, Feb. 5.

In this production of Sir Hall Caine's novel A. E. Coleby has proved that a big film can be made in England, or rather by an English company. The thing now is, will the Stoll Film Co., responsible for the production, keep it up or return to mediocre melodrama and penny novelettes?

Despite its inordinate length, the trade show lasted something over four hours and a half, the picture is full of interest and held the packed house throughout.

If it has any great fault, it rests in the remarkably generous supply of sub-titles, many of which could be dispensed with. Much of the work has been done amid the bleak scenery of Iceland a..d the photographic representation of bleak moorland, storm-battered coasts and mighty glaciers is fine and effective, while other scenes have been made in different parts of the Riviera and in Paris. The photography is exceptionally good.

Coleby's idea has been to present the novel as it is; hence the mileage of the feature, and with the aid of his copious sub-titles he has left nothing untouched. Sticking carefully to the book, he tells the story of Magnus and Oscar Stephenson and of the theft of the elder brother's sweetheart by the younger; of the hate which filled Magnus' heart and of his oath that should Oscar ever cause Thora pain he would kill him. Inevitably Oscar does cause Thora pain and leaves to make his fortune. The young wife dies and Magnus rears and tends her child. Anon Oscar returns rich and famous and in time to atone.

The acting is exceptionally good and the cast has been much more carefully chosen than is usual in native pictures. Henry Victor and Stewart Rome give two very good performances as the brothers; Colette Brettel is excellent as Thora, as is Edith Bishop as her rival in Oscar's affections. Frank Wilson and Mrs. Hadyn-Coffin are alike good as the parents, and many small parts are capitally played.

When "The Prodigal Son" is shown publicly it will be in two sections—the first, "The Prodigal Son"; the second, "The Return of the Prodigal."

ENVIRONMENT

Principal Pictures production, distributed on a state's rights basis. Based on a story by Harvey Gates. Produced and directed by Irving Cummings. Six reels. Shown at Loew's Circle, double-feature bill, Feb. 27, 1923.

Steve MacLaren..................Milton Sills
Sally Dolan......................Alice Lake
"Willie Boy" Toval..............Ben Hewlett
Grandma MacLaren.........Gertrude Claire
"Jimmie" MacLaren.......Richard Hedrick
"Diamond Jim" Favre........Ralph Lewis

Here is a real blood-and-thunder thriller, done in corking style, that has crooked Chicago and the straight and narrow of the farm as its plot. It has a couple of real thrills in a fire and rescue, a couple of fights, a murder and a love story in which the honest lad from the farm wins and reforms the beautiful confidence queen of the Chicago slums. What more could any exhibitor ask for than to have a plot like this dished up to him in sets that include a Chicago dance cabaret, a fire scene, with the smoke and flames pouring forth, and the engines dashing, and as an extra touch a chance to see the heroine of the cast in an old tin bath tub down on the farm, with an undraped shoulder and a dimpled knee showing. The majority are going to say here's the picture for us, and in the average first and second run neighborhood houses it is just going to be the thing, for they will have a couple of names that they can feature in Alice Lake and Milton Sills, and there are going to be enough punches in the feature to please their audiences.

Alice Lake plays "Chicago Sal" Dolan, formerly a cabaret dancer, but more lately turned confidence queen, working with a band of wire tappers. On the way south from Chicago in a machine with "Willie Boy," the head of the mob, he decides to stop off and turn a trick at a lonely farmhouse, with the result that she is nabbed while he makes a getaway. Her case comes up in the local court, and Milton Sills, who is the big-hearted and honest farmer, doesn't want her sent to jail, but is willing to take her home to "help ma with the cooking," so that the $300 that was stolen is to be repaid with work, and the court thinks that it's a pretty good idea.

But "Willie Boy" gets back to Chi and tells his tale, and "Diamond Jim" makes him take a return trip to ascertain if Willie's story is on the square and to give "Sal" a chance to make a getaway. Sal, after a month on the farm, is far from loath to get back to her old haunts, but she insists the $300 be made good. Before going she makes it a point that the farmer gets her Chicago address.

Back in the big town she is the lure in a wire racket, and the cops are on her trail. The farmer, who has fallen like a ton of coal, walks in just before the cops show, and while he manages to let her make a clean break, he is grabbed. He gets three months for refusing to squeal, and in the meantime the girl looks up the grandma and youngster that he brought to Chicago with him and takes care of them. His release from jail finds him at the door of "Diamond Jim's" place. He makes a bid for her to take to the straight road, although in his mind he has a doubt of the relationship between the girl and Jim. Jim is knocked off a few minutes later by "Willie Boy," who has a grudge, and then Sills, after hearing the story from Jim of the true state of Sal's affections, dashes after her, to arrive on the scene just as the apartment in which she has placed his mother and little youngster is in flames, so he does the big heroic and rescues them both, and the quartet go back to the farm. 'Tis a pretty thing.

But it is well done in true melodramatic form, with Irving Cummings handling the direction in great shape and slipping up in only one or two minor details. For state right picture in the popular-priced houses this one is there. *Fred.*

THE PILGRIM

Charlie Chaplin's four reel comedy, released through First National. At the Strand, New York, week Feb. 25. Programed as having been written and directed by Charles Chaplin.

The Pilgrim................Charles Chaplin
The Girl....................Edna Purviance
Her Mother..................Kitty Bradbury
The Deacon......................Mack Swain
The Elder...............Loyal Underwood
The Boy.........................Dinky Dean
His Mother........................Mae Wells
Her Husband...............Sydney Chaplin
The Crook.................."Chuck" Reisner
The Sheriff.......................Tom Murray

"The Pilgrim" is not sensationally funny, not as much so as expected from Chaplin in four reels. There are laughs; a number of them and brought together in two reels, they would have based a corking comic film.

In the story Chaplin is an escaped convict. It brings him later into contact with another crook. While Chaplin is made to appear heroic, although this is a picture comedy, somehow the groundwork brings about a mental clash.

After escaping with a reward of $1,000 offered for his capture, he secures a clerical dress and picking at random a small Texan town, goes there to be secure in his liberty. The town's church is expecting a new minister. Chaplin is mistaken for him when met at the train by a delegation, rushed to the pulpit for his first service and later installed in one of the parishioner's homes, presided over by a widow and her daughter.

A small boy called Dinky Dean on the program but said to be the son of Chuck Reisner (who appears as the other crook) is responsible for considerable of the fun. He is a little kid, looking about five and has been taught some rough tactics for laughs. They are out and slapstick Dinky slaps the minister in the face, slaps his father's and mother's faces and also shoves a sheet of sticky fly paper over his father's map. That "fly-paper" and "slapstick" still seem to be standards.

The best hit the boy started was the placing of his father's derby over a plum pudding as it stood upon a plate in the kitchen. Chaplin decorated it with white frosting and attempted to cut it in the parlor as the father commenced looking for his hat.

The nearest approach to genuine humor is when Chaplin with a paid for ticket to Texas but in fear of detection, tries to ride on the bumpers of the passenger coach. Ordered out by an observing conductor he displays his ticket and is taken inside the train, next seen sitting there as his neighbor flashes a paper toward him with its outside page carrying an advertisement of his picture and the reward.

Later in church there is some rough fun, illogically done in very broad if not uncouth style and the remainder runs spasmodically.

The picture will draw on the Chaplin name according to its start at the Strand Sunday, when it was filling up the house before 2:30. Fan payers may be satisfied with the number of laughs it provides in 45 minutes.

Sydney Chaplin as the father of the boy did well enough in his small chance, as no one but Chaplin himself gets much of an opportunity in any of his pictures unless he points them for it as with the kid here. Loyal Underwood held a laugh in his make-up as the Elder.

This is Chaplin's final First National release under his contract with it. *Sime.*

MINNIE

Marshall Neilan presenting and co-directing with Frank Urson. Released through First National, featuring Leatrice Joy. At the Capitol, New York, week of Feb. 25.

Minnie ....Leatrice Joy
Newspaper Man..................Matt Moore
Minnie's Father............George Barnum
Stepmother ....Josephine Crowell
Stepsister ....Helen Lynch
Chewing Gum Salesman..Raymond Griffith

Rather a conventional feature contains two or three good laughs, but in no way approaches the pretentiousness or actual entertaining qualities that Neilan and Urson turned out in their previous effort, "The Stranger's Banquet." Carrying a Cinderella-like theme the story is dead open and shut as to its conclusion. The various comedy incidents scattered through the continuity suffice to hold up the interest.

The picture seems to reach its zenith with the trio of instances wherein "Minnie," the ugly duckling of the town, falls for the auto ride gag, walks back twice and the third time takes her walking shoes along. It's a sure-fire piece of business exceptionally well handled and secured heavy returns in each instance before a Sunday night audience at the Capitol.

Other than that Neilan has gone in for brief philosophy that with the pictured examples and reading matter must come close to 500 feet of film before the story to be related is given its sendoff.

The script tells of Minnie, very much neglected and spurned because of her unbeauteous qualities finally spreading the impression of a heavy lover through sending herself impassioned missives along with flowers and candy. Discovered and threatened with exposure by her step-sister, a newspaper item of an unclaimed body in the morgue prompts the "out" only to lead to complications when a reporter trails the item to play up as a story. The scribe, no raving beauty himself, falls for Minnie. It's all over when her father finally succeeds in perfecting his electrical invention sold to a company of which the reporter's uncle is president. The finish has a surgeon changing the facial expressions of the couple for a return to the home town in triumph.

Leatrice Joy clicks regularly and sincerely as Minnie. A continuation of such performances as this girl has recently been turning in should very soon see her established beyond a doubt. Matt Moore, opposite, in as the absent minded reporter, lends capable support and George Barnum was worthy of attention as the father. Neilan has inserted a dance floor flash, a la "Fools First," with Raymond Griffith as the principal figure. As a traveling salesman and one of the auto ride instigators he protruded at every opportunity afforded.

Neilan is credited with being the author of the story, which, according to a title, is based on facts in its early episodes. The camera work is above the water line although there are no extravagant light effects employed due to the action which supposedly takes place in a small town hotel. The settings are appropriate to the atmosphere.

A First National attraction in the Capitol, a Goldwyn house, may cause some comment amongst picture people. No matter the distributor it would seem as if all the Broadway picture houses are starting their features too late at the last shows. Running 10 minutes over the hour "Minnie" went on at 10.21. It is getting to be nothing unusual for the final evening projections to terminate anywhere between 11.30 and midnight. The cause is easily attributed to the length of the vocal and tab portions of the programs. Good or otherwise the film houses are just letting out when most of the legit theatres have already become dark. *Skig.*

ADAM'S RIB

Society play of about eight reels presented by Jesse L. Lasky (Famous Players-Paramount), designated as a Cecil B. DeMille production. Story by Jeanie Macpherson. Five names featured in the order given in the attached cast. At the Rivoli, New York, week Feb. 25.

Michael Ramsay..................Milton Sills
Prof. Nathan Reade.........Elliott Dexter
M. Jaromir, King of Morania.........
..........................Theodore Kosloff
Mrs. Michael Ramsay.....Anna Q. Nilsson
Mathilda Ramsay...........Pauline Garon
"The Mischievous One".........Julia Faye
James Kilkenna..........Clarence Geldart
Minister to Morania..........George Field
Hugo Kermaier.............Robert Brower
Kramar..................Forrest Robinson
Lieut. Braschek..............Geno Corrado
Secretary to Minister...Wedgewood Nowell
Cave Man.................Clarence Burton

A silly, piffling screen play, dealing with husband and wife sex subject in a peculiarly crude and obvious style, but a picture that probably is destined to make a lot of money. As early as the evening of its first day on Broadway the title and cast appeared to have attracted attention, for the Rivoli was filled before 7 o'clock and jammed half an hour later with the lobby filled and an overflow spilling out over the sidewalk. It looks like another case of "The Sheik." Only this story is even more foolish.

There are half a dozen places where the complications would stop cold if any one of half a dozen characters had common sense. It is only possible to keep the story moving by making its people do unreasonable things. A woman of 40 keeps a rendezvous with a nobleman at his house, deliberately planning to elope with him. Her daughter follows, determined to prevent a scandal, and is discovered in compromising circumstances by both her father and her fiance. The fiance agrees to marry the girl forthwith in order to save her good name, and the girl accepts him. Ten words to the bridegroom would have explained the whole affair, but the girl allows him to depart on a foreign mission, heart-broken and disillusioned. Just crude theatrical device.

But that's the least of the crudities. What can be said for a modern play which seeks to engage sympathy for a 40-year-old flapper-matron, with a marriageable daughter, who "yearns for romance and life" to the extent of bilking her loyal husband in favor of a comic opera king from one of those trick Balkan states? Of course, she's just a plain fool, but she hasn't a thing on her husband. The fact that they picture him as an able wheat pit manipulator doesn't save his face. He knows all about his wife's affair with the comedy king, but he spends $7,000,000 in gold (honest, they show you some of the gold) to put the king back on his throne and so get him out of the way.

But the plan miscarries and the middle-aged kitten is about to bolt with his majesty, when the husband interferes and prevents the elopement. Although it is made to appear that the king has compromised his daughter, what does this Napoleon of the wheat pit do? Kill the miscreant in a film rough-house? Nope. He musses up his kinglet's hair and tie and tears his collar, then goes mournfully away from there. It was woefully inadequate, but more is to come.

Presently frivolous mamma comes home and confesses all, handing the outraged husband .. revolver to kill her with. But the husband couldn't see a good idea when it was forced on him. You were left to suppose he seized her in his strong arms and loved her to death. Anyhow, we presently find the family dead broke, with $7,000,000 worth of Balkan wheat and nowhere to put it. Under the circumstances you'd think the situation called for tact and discretion on the wife's part. She might at least have kept out of the way. But, no, here she is in the center of the picture, and of all things, she is playfully urging on her indulgent better half that they "leave all this and go off on a second honeymoon." The old girl was going to have her romance if hell froze over. But it didn't. The northwest wheat belt froze over instead and European spot No. 2 red wheat jumped to $1.20 a bushel f. o. b. Black Sea ports. So the picture ends with husband peddling wheat to clamorous "shorts" on the Chicago Board of Trade while romantic mamma makes eyes at him from the visitors' balcony and he simpers back. Milton Sills, best of movie leading men, saved his reputation at this point by looking sheepish as though he was ashamed of the exhibition.

The production is extremely elaborate and must have cost a lot of money. *Rush.*

FLAMING HEARTS

Presented by Franklyn E. Backer. Distributed for State Rights by East Coast Distributors. James B. Warner starred. Story by Frank Howard Clark. Shown at Loew's Circle, New York, double feature bill Feb. 27, 1923.

Combination society and western that has a never ending list of characters in it. The picture is presented by Franklyn E. Backer, who must think that he has a logical successor to Wallace Reid in James B. Warner, whom he is starring in it. Warner is a fairly snappy looking young fellow, who seems all out of place in afternoon attire and equally ill at ease in rough-and-ready cowboy costume later.

Outside of that he is likable enough and if properly coached in the matter of dress may go along in pictures and make a spot for himself.

This offering, however, looks like it was "just one of those things." There isn't much to the story, although it looked for a time as though there must have been a real idea behind it, and the shooting of it was so arranged every possible little thing that could be caught out of doors without any production cost was in the footage. It's just a picture intended for the little low admission priced houses.

Warner plays a society tame cat in the early part of the picture who has his spirit roused by a girl, the social secretary of one of the middle-aged flappers he dances attention on. He determines to take her advice and "go west, where men are men," etc. He mixes with a couple of hoboes in a box car, and all three are kicked off the train, steal a handcar, and while the "dude" does all the work the other two argue over the division of the spoils of a recent robbery, with the result the dude pumps them back to the scene of their crime and they are grabbed, while he is made a hero of and given a job.

Right there it looked like the story was cold and any one could guess what the answer was going to be, for the wealthy rancher, his daughter and the glowering foreman of the hands were all on the job. But the author slipped a surprise under the belt of those in front. He had the hero of the tale rescue the girl and then put her in the arms of the ranch foreman and take a run out. Girls were too much for him. Right after that at a carnival he wins the lottery, the grand prize of which is a kiss from the pretty daughter of the sheriff, and he runs out on that, but she gets him at the finish.

It's just hoak of the old kind dished up a little differently. That is what is going to make the low-brow audience hate it, for it is away from the regular formula, and it isn't good enough for the middle-class houses. *Fred.*

"IF WINTER COMES"

The William Fox filmization of the novel of the same name by A. S. M. Hutchinson. Scenario by Paul H. Sloane. Directed by Harry Millarde. Announced length, 14 reels. Photographed by Joe Ruttenberg.

Mark Sabre	Percy Marmont
Hapgood	Arthur Metcalf
Twyning	Sydney Herbert
Harold Twyning	Wallace Kolb
Rev. Sebastian Fortune	William Riley Hatch
Lord Tybar	Raymond Bloomer
Young Perch	Russell Sedgwick
"Humpo"	Leslie King
Old Bright	George Pelzer
Coroner	James Ten Brook
Nona, Lady Tybar	Ann Forrest
Mabel	Margaret Fielding
Effie	Gladys Leslie

Springfield, Mass., March 7.

"Over-direction" is one of the faults of "If Winter Comes." Hutchinson's novel has its good and its weak spots. The same is true of the film version. Perhaps this is because the story has been treated respectfully in placing it in celluloid form. There is no question as to the fidelity of detail and plot being transplanted from words to the screen.

Percy Marmont plays Mark Sabre, the quixotic hero of the story; a man upon whom the temptation of an affair with the women he loves, the discouragement of unfriendly business partners, and the odium of scandal fall, and who still has the mettle fine enough to meet his troubles manfully. Returning to "over-direction," it is well evidenced in the acting of Mr. Marmont. His forced smile—at time when it seemingly is uncalled for—actually becomes boresome. If heaving chest and labored sighs are the means of expressing emotion, especially in a man, on the screen, then Mr. Marmont is graphic. His motions in dramatic scenes caused giggles at one viewing of the picture. In the lighter moments the work of Mr. Marmont is pleasing. One of his biggest dramatic scenes is in the coroner's court at a hearing concerning the death of Effie and her baby. But here the words of the hero are substituted right out of the book and the frequent flashing of the words "look-here" become monotonous and spoil an otherwise effective climax.

Ann Forrest is a splendid Lady Tybar. Her confessing to Sabre of her husband's infidelity and her own unhappiness is a splendidly done passage. Her restraint from making the character "weepy" and hysterical and her pantomimic force are deserving of high praise.

The big emotional scene is that of the death of Mrs. Perch. Upon hearing the news of her son being killed in the war, she is seen dying. The son, by means of double exposure, appears and beckons to the spirit of his dying mother, which joins him. The most cold-hearted feminine contingent will be moved to tears. Mr. Millarde, by the way, has not "over-directed" this scene. He has made the most of it in every way.

In picture form, the story lacks comedy. High Jinks and Low Jinks, the maids in Sabre's home, get a few laughs in two or three scenes, but that really is the only comedy relief throughout the picture.

William Riley Hatch, as the Rev. Sebastian Fortune, makes a unique character. Mabel, the wife of Sabre, in the hands of Margaret Fielding, is most unlikable. She keeps well within the bounds of the calling of her character. Raymond Bloomer portrays a husband who delights in tormenting his wife, but Mr. Hutchinson has redeemed him through his service in the war. Effie is portrayed by Gladys Elsie in a satisfactory manner.

The scheming, selfish Twyning, is adequately enacted by Sydney Herbert. The other minor characters are played in satisfactory manner.

The shots of the trenches are brief, another item worthy of commendation for Mr. Millarde. Some of the scenes in the little English town will give American theatre patrons some conception of how the announcement of war was received.

In one scene Sabre is seated on a bench overlooking the water. He throws a straw hat he has been wearing into the water. There is a brief flash to another scene. When Sabre is again shown he rises from the bench and places a soft hat on his head. Another is where Sabre is given a letter by a postman as he arrives in front of his home. He reads the letter and places it in one of the outside pockets of his coat. He enters the house and meets his wife, who asks for the letter. He thereupon withdraws the letter from an inner pocket of the coat.

The film had its world premier at Mr. Fox's theatre in Springfield, and it will not be shown again until September, it is said, when it will open in a New York theatre. *Cliff.*

MAD LOVE

Goldwyn presentation of U. F. A. picture featuring Pola Negri, made in Germany. Film has been retitled for America by Katherine N. Hilliker and H. H. Caldwell. Originally titled "Sappho" in Europe. Directed by Dimitri Buchowetzki. Shown at the Capitol, New York, week March 4. Cast not published.

Without the publicity built up about Pola Negri's presence in the United States and the engagement of the star to marry Charlie Chaplin "Mad Love" would have been set down as "another of those imported clucks." But, thanks to the press agenting, they crowded into the Capitol Sunday night. Goldwyn scores a neat bit of showmanship; but what will be the kickback on Famous Players' forthcoming Negri production?

The picture, in design and appeal, is about the grade of a Universal program with Ivan Abramson trimmings; in technical quality it is below the grade of American pictures of 10 years ago. It is just a trashy sex tangle, crude in idea and absurd in execution. The only thing the picture has is some massive settings and a few mob scenes. Its drama belongs in the Family Story Paper class, which is two steps below the ten-twent-thirt grade.

If you can imagine a thoroughly vulgarized version of Daudet's "Sappho" that is the brutal sex angle alone and devoid of the literary niceties that mark that novel you get some idea of the picture. They dress up a sordid Parisian gold digger in phoney romance and try in vain to engage your sympathies in her fictional love affairs and final destruction. The net result is they achieve the realistic atmosphere of New York's old Haymarket, but the romance is sadly lacking in conviction. It is all heavy-handed, make-believe melodrama, and no point do you get an illusion of real people and real events.

Nothing is quite so cheap as pretentious vulgarity, and this picture abounds in that commodity. Its appeal is to the feeble-minded who can get a thrill out of stagey suggestiveness. The scenes in which the wicked adventuress "vamps" the millionaire are designed to furnish a spicy kick; but they are so badly overdone they provoke derision and amusement instead. Pola Negri, with her atrocious German make-up on, may be the Berlin idea of an irresistible siren, but her work is too coarse for Broadway. All she does is to reproduce the Theda Bara type that America grinned off the screen some years ago. These "spicy" episodes never would get by any one with the sophistication of a schoolgirl.

The story is rather muddled and unnecessarily complicated. Liane (Miss Negri) vamps a young engineer, then double crosses him in favor of a rich manufacturer. The engineer thereupon goes insane and has to be put in a padded cell.

Pierre, his cousin, comes to Paris to attend, to the lunatic's affairs and meets Liane, supposing that it was another woman who had ruined his kinsman. Liane falls violently in love with the young man and they are married. During the honeymoon at some French watering place the manufacturer runs them down and acquaints Pierre with the real history.

Pierre casts Liane off and returns to Paris; but, still infatuated, seeks out the girl, who is trying to forget in the gaieties of the Odeon. The mad engineer makes a timely escape from the asylum, and all three come together in a private room of the amusement place. Pierre is thrown outside by his maniac cousin. He summons the crowd from the dancing floor and they break in, to find that the madman has strangled Liane. The mob scenes at the end of the picture are at times effective, and some of the marine backgrounds have a good deal of scenic beauty. *Rush.*

MR. BILLINGS SPENDS DIME

Paramount release presented by Jesse L. Lasky with Walter Hiers starred and Jacqueline Logan featured. A. S. LeVino adaptation of the Dana Burnet story. Directed by Wesley Ruggles. Shown at the Rialto, New York, week Mar. 4, 1923.

John Percival Billings	Walter Hiers
Suzanna Juarez	Jacqueline Logan
Gen. Paolo Blanco	George Fawcett
Captain Gomez	Robert McKim
Priscilla Parker	Patricia Palmer
Estaban Juarez	Joseph Swickard
John D. Starbock	Guy Oliver
White	Edward Patrick
Diego	Clarence Burton
Manuel	George Field
Martin Green	Lucien Littlefield

This is the first starring production for Walter Hiers, groomed by Jesse L. Lasky to replace Roscoe Arbuckle as the funny fat man of the screen. "Mr. Billings Spends His Dime" does get a few laughs here and there, the best one coming just before the finish of the picture, which while intended as broad comedy is really a romantic little tale, well done on the screen and a type of picture that is going to eventually bring Hiers a great measure of popularity. He has been in pictures for a great many years and is fairly popular, but not as a star.

To make him a star it looks like Paramount will have to flood the country with his pictures and they won't be able to do that very well as long as they hold him at Wallace Reid prices. He isn't at this time the draw Reid was and as long as the producers are looking to the exhibitor to build a star for them they should give the theatre men some slight opportunity to get a little the best of it for the time being until Hiers is established as having a definite box office value.

In casting this picture the producer surrounded Hiers wth players that have names, in fact, there are one or two who are as well if not better known than the star. The list includes George Fawcett, Jacqueline Logan, Robert McKim and Joseph Swickard. That quartet acquitted themselves most creditably.

"Mr. Billings Spends His Dime" was originally intended to be a Reid starring production, but at the time of his illness the production plans were changed and Hiers was selected to replace him. One can readily see how this would have been an ideal story for the late star, but still played in the broader comedy vein is equally suited to the somewhat heavier Hiers.

Hiers is a picture fan according to the screen version of the "Mr. Billings" tale and in a news weekly sees the daughter of a Central American republic on the occasion of the celebration of the failure of the latest revolution. How he loses his job that same week because he is overstaying his lunch hour time to get an extra peek at the girl on the screen, and finally he becomes involved with the conspirators through the spending of his last dime to buy a cigar that has the girl's picture on the band is set forth in interesting if not extremely comical fashion in the feature. He steps into affluence through spending the dime to make it possible for him to take a trip to the Republic and on the same steamer again runs into the conspirators. In the end he acts as an agent for them and unwittingly is the means of frustrating their attempt to gain control of the little nation. Of course he wins the hands of the President's daughter and then comes back to the old store and buys it out, making the floor walker who fired him the manager. This final touch is the best laugh wallop of the entire picture.

Miss Logan as the President's daughter makes a charming picture while Mr. Swickard as the father is an imposing figure. Messrs. Fawcett and McKim as the principal conspirators have a couple of clever pieces of business that they might have worked out a little more effectively, especially the little money bit which they repeat three times. That should have been a bigger howl on each repeat, but it didn't seem to get over.

Perhaps Wesley Ruggles, who directed might be to blame for this to some extent, but on the whole his direction of the picture was good, for the unfoldment did hold the interest. *Fred.*

THE WHITE FLOWER

Paramount production starring Betty Compson, presented by Adolph Zukor. Written and directed by Julia Grawford Ivers. Five reels. Shown at the Rialto, New York, week Feb. 25, 1923.

Konia Markham	Betty Compson
Bob Rutherford	Edmund Lowe
John Markham	Edward Martindel
Ethel Granville	Arline Pretty
Mrs. Gregory Bolton	Sylvia Ashton
Mr. Gregory Bolton	Arthur Hoyt
David Panuahi	Leon Barry
Bernice Martin	Lily Philips
Edward Graeme	Reginald Carter
Sorceress	Native Hawaiians
Kuhuna	Native Hawaiians

The novelty, if it can any longer be counted as such, is that the picture for the greater part was made in Hawaii. It is a story that has its locale laid there and deals with the superstitions of the natives of the island. As a feature film it is atmospheric in one extreme, while actionless to the other. It is far from the type that can be counted on in the fullest sense of money getters in the pre-release houses. As a program picture of ordinary calibre it will get by but that is all; it won't pull any extra business anywhere.

While not particularly interested in the cause of its lack of punch from the box office angle, it might be well to state in passing this is an author directed picture. That may account for it, and again it may not. It is true, however, that about two reels at the opening of the feature are spent in laying the atmosphere of the islands as the back ground to the story.

The punches counted on to put the picture over are a couple of Hula-Hula dance scenes with Betty Compson as the dancer and a surf boat riding bit. Neither new to the regulars at picture houses, nor done particularly well in this picture.

Miss Compson does some of the best work she has more recently shown and scores as the little half-blooded heorine of the story. She has the character of the daughter of a wealthy American planter, whose wife was a native islander. Possessed of all the superstitions of the native half of her blood she believes that the priests and sorceresses of the island have the powers to fortell the future and to cause death by their prayers. At the opening of the picture she has just been informed by a seeress that she is to wed one who is to come to her and present her with a white flower. The plot thus far has been laid by a wealthy native who has the seeress in his pay and figures as appearing on the scene with the floral gift. However, a young American who has just arrived on the island to manage a plantation beats him to the presentation and the girl accepts him as her fate.

Their love progresses until the fateful day when the man's fiancee accompanied by her aunt and uncle arrive from the states. The little islander's heart is broken. However, in the working out of the tale she manages to get the r an she loves with the American girl renouncing him.

One remarkable thing about Edmund Lowe's lead opposite was his resemblance to John Barrymore in some of the pictures that he did some years back. Lowe incidentally gave a really clever performance and one that registered with the audience. The heavy contributed by Leon Barry was also effective. Arline Pretty played the American fiancee, getting past nicely, but putting on a very bad make up in her illness scenes. This showed particularly in the close-ups. *Fred.*

PLAYING DOUBLE

Independent western melodrama by Prairie Productions, also described as a Dick Hatton production after the star. Billing carries the name of the Western Picture Exploration Co. Story by J. Stewart Woodhouse and direction by Dick Rush. At Loew's Circle March 5, half of double feature bill, the other half being a Select reissue with Constance Talmadge.

A rank outside independent bearing many marks of the amateur. None of the people in the cast have screen reputations and their work indicates they may be amateurs. The leading woman is Ethel Shannon, and she alone gives promise. She has at least a large endowment of beauty and some natural camera knack.

Dick Hatton has no special qualifications for stardom. He is just a nice-looking young man without any particular distinction and no gift for acting at all.

The picture probably represents the absolute minimum of expenditure. It has only one interior showing, a lawyer's office. The rest of the action takes place out of doors. The item of setting represents a row of goose eggs in cost, and they are not particularly impressive at that, beng mostly flat prairie lands, occasionally broken by an economical hill. So horse and actor hire represent the negative cost.

The story probably was made up on the lot as they went along. It has not the slightest pretentions to dramatic form. There are no climaxes and no surprises. There was a time they could have framed up a situation, but they missed the opportunity. This was where the lone hero was creeping upon the bandits who had abducted the heroine (no special reason for the abduction—just a whim on the part of the boss outlaw). At the same instant the sheriff's posse was riding pell mell for the same spot. Of course, any movie fan knows that the hero should have fallen into the bandits' power just in time for the posse to turn the tables, the action leading up to the climax by alternate shots of the hero in desperate straits and the galloping posse.

Instead of that the sheriff arrives only after the hero has knocked all five desperadoes senseless, although the hero is unarmed and all five bandits have pistols. It took a lot of screen hand-to-hand fighting, but the blows were not convincing. The fighters just pushed each other around. So the sheriff's posse just stood around looking foolish as any lot of cowboy actors would busting in like that on an anti-climax. That was only one sample of an unusually inept picture production. *Rush.*

KINDLING COURAGE

Universal comedy-drama featuring Hoot Gibson. Story by Leet Rennick Brown; direction by William Worthington. At the New York Stanley, March 3.

Hoot Gibson is being supplied with a first-rate line of comedy-dramatic stories lately. This one fits him splendily and makes good light entertainment. It has another virtue in that its cost must have been inconsiderable, probably representing the very minimum. But the story value is there. It starts briskly, develops character clearly and immediately engages the sympathies of the spectator for the modest hero. The action is simple and straightforward, with good comedy and a variety of surprise situations that register for full force.

The feminine interest is a little pale, although there is a thread of romantic adventure running neatly through the narrative, but the heroine is passive throughout.

Gibson has another of those amusing roles where he is the hard luck victim most of the time and only wins his vindication at the climax. This is rather an unusual formula for a film plot but it is capable of infinite elaboration and works out most satisfactorily. A hero who is introduced by means of a series of situations in which he plays anything but a heroic role catches the interest. You can't help but like a well meaning bungler who always gets the worst of it, as this one does from the outset.

He is made the butt of a practical joke and loses his job therefore. He drops into the small town billiard parlor and the local bully picks on him, plastering his face with an ice cream cone and chasing him out of town on a freight train. The boy is terror struck at the prospect of a fight and avoids it rather cravenly. Taking refuge in a box car, he runs into a pair of bank robbers making their getaway, and without meaning to do so is instrumental in bringing about their capture. In recognition of his supposed bravery the sheriff of a distant town makes him a deputy and dispatches him to round up a desperate gang of outlaws. The sister of one of the bandits, knowing nothing of her brother's criminal business, asks the hero's aid in locating him.

The deputy blunders into a lonesome house where the bandits are hiding and in a series of skilfully managed thrills and surprises kills them all off and delivers their bodies to the authorities, all by dumb luck and a sort of desperate courage, inspired by the presence of the girl with whom he has fallen in love. The situation is much the same as the genial but bonehead hero of "The Cat and the Canary," who shivers but goes ahead nevertheless.

Having tasted the sweets of courage, the boy resolves to go back to his home town and square the account with the local bully who drove him away. This is a splendid bit of comedy, with a curious thrill of satisfaction for the sympathetic spectator. Our hero goes back to the billiard room and pays back the ice cream cone with a custard pie and then wipes the floor up with his former tormentor. Then he carries the heroine off to the nearest license clerk.

The picture is a succession of laughs and has several ingenious thrills.

Rush.

NIGHT LIFE IN HOLLYWOOD

F. E. Maescher production distributed for state rights through Arrow. Written and directed by Fred Caldwell. Shown at Loew's Circle, New York, on double feature bill March 6, 1923.

Pa Powell	J. L. McComer
Joe Powell	J. Frank Glendon
Carrie Powell	Gale Henry
Ma Powell	Elizabeth Rhodes
Wayne Elkins	Jack Connelly

Leonora Baxter..............Josephine Hill

Just a cheap attempt to "cash in" on the notoriety that Hollywood has received. The title is the best evidence of that.

Imagine what "Night Life in Hollywood" means in front of the theatre in Jasbo Center, Sap Crossing or Simptown.

In a word, this is an attempt to whitewash Hollywood and its motion picture colony. But it is not sponsored by anyone of note or standing in motion pictures. If the screen folk wanted any sort of vindication it would have paid them to have gotten together and had a good director make a picture from a probable yarn or excuse that would have shown Hollywood as it really is.

In this feature there is an attempt to handle the introduction as a comedy. The Powells are a family in Hickville, Ark., who have read of the wild doings in Hollywood. The son slips away to the coast, lured by lurid visions that his mind conjured up in dreams after reading the bunk about the fast life there; then the daughter does likewise, and finally Ma, Pa and a younger girl go west to seek out the erring ones to return them to the fold.

There must be a thrill or two, so they permit the hick hero to go to sleep in the lobby of what is supposed to be the Hollywood Hotel and dream a couple of hundred feet of women dancing.

For the sister's contribution there is all the old hoke stuff of hearing a couple of professionals rehearsing a melodramatic scene in the next room and taking it on the level. That and a few more like it and you have an idea of what the picture is.

It's the bunk, all except the title. That is the only thing about the picture that is worth paying for.

The exhibitor using it will be lucky if his patrons don't demand the return of their money after seeing it. *Fred.*

THE HERO

B. P. Schulberg production, directed by Louis Gasnier, released by Al Lichtman. Special cast. Adapted by Eve Unsell from the play by Gilbert Emery. At 58th St., Feb. 26-28.

Oswald Lane....................Gaston Glass
Hester Lane..................Barbara LaMar
Andrew Lane..................John Sainpolis
Sarah Lane...................Martha Mattox
Andy Lane......................Frankie Lee
Bill Waters.....................David Butler
Martha...........................Doris Pawn
Hilda Pierce..................Ethel Shannon

A corking picture that should have been put over on Broadway before it reached the circuit houses. It is an effective feature production based on a play still fresh in the memory of Broadway theatre goers, well directed, and acted by a capable cast.

It may not have any great big smash in any one particular scene, but if it wasn't for the censors there are a couple of scenes in it that they could have put an awful punch in, and leave it to Gasnier to do it, too, if he had the chance.

The wallop of this feature picture is in its story which while not a tremendous outstanding success on the spoken stage when produced by Sam H. Harris in New York still was sufficiently compelling at the box office to pull a lot of money. The screen version, naturally, contains much more punch than did the spoken drama.

It still seems that had "The Hero" been taken and walloped over on Broadway, and by that we do not mean one of those casual two week affairs at the Criterion, but plugged with a purpose and a punch, its value would have been enhanced at least ten fold in the neighborhood houses.

As it stands now it is just a good program picture unless the unusual is attempted for it in any first run house that it plays. It means work for the exhibitor, but he can feel pretty certain that his audience will be thankful to him for the exhibition of the pucture. It is a pretty human tale after all and that is what the public does want.

In casting it one has to give Ben Schulberg credit for having placed the various roles in capable hands, although it looks as though Martha must have been cast by the director. Barbara LaMar as the wife of the plodding Andrew Lane, played to perfection by John Sainpaulis, was a delight. She was everything that anyone could have wanted on the screen or off of it for that matter and she managed to put over some very heavy emotional stuff without over acting it. Gaston Glass was the holder of the titular role (or was the heavy cast for that role; there has always been a doubt in the writer's mind, feeling that Andrew was "The Hero" after all), but Glass did very well with it. He was the no good younger brother without sense of responsibility or gratitude to perfection, a despoiler of women and a general cad, who acted in heroic manner on impulse only. Martha Mattox in a character role, as the mother of both boys, manages to register in one brief scene in the kitchen when she bawled out her daughter-in-law. Frankie Lee and the mixed breed Boston terrier also hit a responsive note, and Doris Pawn as the poor little ruin refugee from Belgium had a couple of moments in which she showed a real dramatic flash. *Fred.*

THE PIPES OF PAN

London, Feb. 20.

A long and wearying presentation did all in its power to kill this Hepworth feature. This was the work of the Margaret Morris school of dancing, and for something like half an hour the audience at the Alhambra was bored stiff by grotesque movement and immature seminudity. This type of art requires a special education, and a trade show is not a good school. When we did get to the picture we found it like most other Hepworth features—a thin story well told, but conventional, set amid magnificently beautiful forest and rural scenes and perfectly photographed. Nobody in this country can beat this firm's photography, and it almost seems that everything else in one of its pictures is subservient to the demands of the camera.

The story tells how the daughter of a traveling tinker meets a young widower who has become a recluse. The meeting is brought about by his young son, who wanders into the woods to hunt for fairies. Love soon dawns. The tinker invents a metal polish which makes him rich, and he goes into society. Later the secretary of his company bolts with the profits, ruining him. He returns to his nomadic life, and the death of the little boy brings the girl and the recluse together.

The acting is excellent on the part of Alma Taylor as the girl and John McAndrews as the tinker. The rest of the cast is good. "The Pipes of Pan" is excellent as a technically perfect subject, but it has no drawing power whatever.

THE PRISONER

Universal, starring Herbert Rawlinson. Adapted from the George Barr McCutcheon novel, "Castle Craneycrow," by Edward T. Lowe, Jr. Directed by Jack Conway. Shown at Loew's, New York. Double feature bill March 2, 1923.

Philip Quentin..........Herbert Rawlinson
Dorothy Garrison..............Eileen Percy
Lord Bob.......................George Cowle
Lady Francis...................June Elvidge
Dickey Savage...........Lincoln Steadman
Prince Ugo Riccardi......Bertram Grassby

The real hoax in meller. Just another of those fiction tales with the scene laid in a mythical kingdom with the American hero saving one of his countrywomen from a marriage with a designing prince whom the mother is anxious to have for a son-in-law. It's just a flock of the regular formula incidents that go to make up a fair program picture.

Herbert Rawlinson is the hero, supposedly a globe-trotting American who has grown sour on the world because the girl he loved turned him down. Eileen Percy is the girl, and she is the one about to marry the Prince Ugo Riccardi. When they meet at a reception in the Prince's native land the girl tells the former admirer that she has made up her mind to become one of the nobility. In the Prince the American recognizes one who under another name was mixed up in a scandal in South America, where a prima donna was slain by the angel who backed her opera tour. The Prince and the angel are the same. But the Prince smells a mice and frames to have a noted duelist at a stag party he is giving and to have him and the American clash so that there will be a legitimate excuse for knocking him off. The American sidesteps the duel stuff and the girl, who has heard of the row, brands him a coward.

At this point it seems about certain that the chances of the American are slim. But he comes back with a little kidnapping party and takes the girl out of the church just as she and the Prince are before the altar and about to hear the fateful words making them one pronounced, and in the end she consents to marry the American.

Rawlinson isn't at his best in the picture. His role should have been played with a laugh all the way to have gotten the most out of it. The balance of the cast fits well enough, but the direction of Jack Conway is such that the picture is extremely draggy. The sets also looked as though someone was trying to overdress this one to get it by as a big production. *Fred.*

GREAT EXPECTATIONS

Nordisk production made in Denmark of Charles Dickens' work. Presented in this country by Hopp Hadley. Shown at Loew's Circle, N. Y., double feature bill, March 6, 1923.

Little Pip........................Buddy Martin

Foreign made production of a Charles Dickens work. There is considerable effort made to class a youngster named Buddy Martin with Jackie Coogan. This might well be possible if the Martin youngster ran all through this picture as Coogan does through "Oliver Twist." The kiddie is a born trouper, and when it comes to real pathos seems to have the edge on the Coogan offspring. Perhaps if he were brought to this country, where he would have the advantage of American direction, he might develop as a screen idol.

It is the foreign direction and acting that is the drawback to this picture. At least that would have to be the conclusion reached after witnessing the manner in which the Circle's fans accepted the picture. They howled with laughter at the most serious moments of the story. Each time that a murder or any other form of death was apparent on the screen it was the signal for another roar.

The editing and titling left the story very much up in the air. It was a disconnected effort at its best.

There was, however, some semblance of the Dickens tale left for those who want Dickens on the screen. The characters all bore the names of those in the original, and in spots the language of the titles was that of the author, but for the greater part it was simply motion picture titles inserted to fit the action.

All in all, this is just another reason why the American market fights shy of foreign-made pictures.

BRASS

Harry Rapf production, presented by the Warner Brothers from the novel of the same name by Charles G. Norris. Adapted by Julien Josephson, with Sydney Franklin directing. Norbert Brodin the photographer. At the Strand, March 11.

Philip Baldwin.................Monte Blue
Marjorie......................Marie Prevost
Wilbur Lansing................Harry Myers
Mrs. Grotenberg.................Irene Rich
Frank Church ....Frank Keenan
Rosemary Church.........Helen Ferguson
Lucy Baldwin...................Miss Dupont
Roy North....................Cyril Chadwick
Mrs. Baldwin..............Margaret Seddon
Harry Baldwin.................Pat O'Malley
Judge Baldwin..............Edward Jobson
Mrs. Jones........................Vera Lewis
George Yost ....Harvey Clark
Mrs. Yost ....Gertrude Bennett

What was true of the novel is similarly so of the picturization; its tediousness. One hour and 33 minutes allotted to the pitfalls that are strewn along the pathways of marriage is a considerable stretch to digest—favorably. Void of any specific action, the subject is practically all story to the point where the work of the cast, production and photography (which is excellent) cannot overcome the handicap thereby imposed.

The transplanting of this Norris brain-child to the screen may mean something to a ticket window, due to the more or less "talk" the book invoked upon its release, which, in turn, was obligated to its predecessor, "Salt," by the same author, for the attention which it received at the time. But "Brass" is far from a great picture. A fair picture, yes, and that mainly due to the deft handling which may be credited to Franklin, the director. The original work, also guilty of being overburdened as to length, has been fluently cut, revamped and revised for the screen presentation; and decidedly "cleaned up," too, if we remember rightly.

For the book, if memory serves, was inclined towards being risque in various of its passages. Not even a resemblance of such remains in the celluloid narrative, however. In fact, it seems as if many liberties had been taken with the author's script. Which may, or may not, have enhanced the value for screen production. It seems not.

Elimination was undoubtedly the most necessary requisite in preparing this work for the camera, and along with that which the scenario editors evidently deemed advisable to do away with went much of the effectiveness of the bound edition. Of a surety is it that the projected version is lacking in the force to get over as a reality and to bring out what advantageous qualities this ode to the discrepancies of marriage possessed when in type.

The locale of the story centres around San Francisco. Philip Baldwin is the eldest son of a fruit rancher's family, who is scheduled to take as his wife the daughter of the lifelong friend of his father. City girls of the poorer class, who spend their vacation earning money by picking fruit on the various ranches, attend the Baldwin acreage in that capacity. This permits of the meeting of Philip and Marjorie. The parental warning of his mother "to make sure" goes unheeded by the boy, and the marriage to the girl from the metropolis follows. Up against a nagging and mercenary mother-in-law, whom through circumstances he is forced to board with, and a wife who continually craves excitement develops into an impossible situation culminating in the young wife's choice to side with her mother. Divorce proceedings shortly succeed the birth of their son.

The young father turns the care of his child over to Mrs. Grotenberg, who was also a former boarder in the unsettled household but who now is established in a cottage of her own. (The picture here fails to mention just wherein the widow, or divorcee, procures the essential funds with which to move into a moderate homestead after previously having been a boarder—but the book made no bones about it.) A socially ambitious sister attempts to frame Philip into another marriage with a miss of the town's elite, but he will have none of it, realizes his love for "Mrs. G" and arrangements are commenced for their wedding.

At this point the former wife returns, calls on the newly intended Mrs. Baldwin, states she realizes the mistake she made (after having married and been divorced again) and Mrs. Grotenberg departs for localities unkown and for reasons as obvious.

It leaves Philip very much nonplussed when he arrives to take his fiancee to the ceremony, but his former spouse never enters into the question and the finale has him back at his parents' home, who are downstairs celebrating their 35th wedding anniversary, putting his baby boy to bed. The child offers **a prayer that "Mama G" will come back to them and Philip states he knows she'll come back.**

In other words, better than an hour and a half of picture to finish on a supposition.

The conclusion to be drawn, from the numerous subtitles, is that the wife is the responsible party in either making or breaking a marriage and the term "Brass" refers to the quality to which the wedding ring reverts if the venture is not successful.

The cast, as a whole, is adequate and may be said to have accomplished a combined creditable piece of work. Monte Blue in the role of Philip improved in effort as the film progressed and will not suffer with those patrons who are partial towards him. Marie Prevost and Irene Rich are the outstanding feminine members both because of the prominence of characters they play and the caliber of their respective performances. Harry Myers, placed as the boy friend of Philip, frolicked through the assignment, which was emphatically rewritten from the book to supply comedy, and made good with it.

Thence, to sum up, is to wonder if the producers didn't make a mistake in picking this particular edition of Norris' work instead of his previous effort, entitled "Salt." It seems as though the latter novel held many more possibilities for the screen than the completed photographed manuscript of "Brass" reveals.

However, and as is, "Brass" is a picture that will need an abundance of publicity, paid for or otherwise, to aid it for results in the average film auditorium. *Skig.*

JAZZMANIA

Tiffany production, featuring Mae Murray, in story by Edmund Goulding. Directed by Robert Z. Leonard, with Oliver Marsh, photographer; released through Metro. At the Capitol, New York, week March 11.

Ninon	Mae Murray
Jerry Langdon	Rod La Rocque
Captain Valmar	Robert Frazer
Sonny Daimler	Edward Burns
Prince Otto of Como	Jean Hersholt
Baron Bolo	Lionel Belmore
Josephus Ranson	Herbert Standing
Marline	Mrs. J. Farrell MacDonald
Julius Furman	Wilfred Lucas
Colonel Kerr	Herbert Frank
Gavona	Carl Harbaugh

With a story nothing more than an excuse, the producers have given this picture a production so lavish it may carry the film to the class A feature mark. What this release would have done if it had been cheaply, or even averagely, put on is in the catastrophe class. The men behind the camera have overcome one of the most negligible pieces of writing ever in a Broadway first-run house. The script means practically nothing.

Mayhaps Miss Murray's personality offers obstacles in selecting a story in which she may be properly presented. If "Jazzmania" is the criterion it's certain that she has, is now and will continue to appear in pictures woven of the lightest scenario fabric that only cost of production and the ingenuity of the director can hope to surmount. Obviously there is no aid to be gleaned from the narratives. Then, too, there may be the question of whether Miss Murray's ability rates the selecting of a theme which possibly has some semblance of reality or actual literary digestive qualities connected with it. Possessing almost entirely a physical appeal as her principal assertive claim, this luminary of the screen continuosly flickers in flounces of gowns, dances in abbreviated costumes and is backed by a display of settings that classify her productions as the musical comedies of the screen.

Not that this picture is an absolute "bust." Quite to the contrary. Miss Murray gives a corking performance as the queen of an imaginary European monarchy besides which she is given passable assistance by the majority of her supporting cast. And then comes to attention the staging, which supercedes the star's contribution, illusioned to a most appropriate degree through means of excellent photography.

In this supposed country where the action is located they serve revolutions with coffee. All the pomp and ceremony of the interior of the royal palace couldn't take place in a season of Broadway light musical productions staged by four Ziegfelds, two Erlangers and one Lew Cantor. Griffith's Klansmen never got the entrance music the cabinet of the queen is alloted when they officially hold council before their ruler in this picture. A flash at some of the instances contained in this film should make some of the producers with established reputations for lavishness, find new means of strutting their stuff.

The plot-Ninon is queen but in danger of taking "air" because of a revolution on tap that has Prince Otto as its principal instigator. The only way the Prince will call his party off is if her nibs will enter into an "until death do us part" routine with him. The alternative bores the feminine ruler profusely hence Otto opens his mental offspring in full stage and the panic is on.

Much parties and jazz dancing by the incognito queen, who "goes off her nut" every time a "hot" band wails, comprises the routine.

But the gay life terminates for Ninon. She calls her boy friend and **in words that would portend as "pull up a chair and learn something" states her case to the effect their affair is cold.**

Robert Frazer made the role of the captain of the guards stand out and take unto itself all it was worth while Lionel Belmore did nicely with his assignment.

The picture is null and voil as to objective, but it provides sufficient material for Miss Murray to frolic, wear clothes and look good. The film is easy on the eyes, is haphazardly entertaining and should be a money maker. And so? *Skig.*

THE LOVE GAMBLER

Fox feature with John Gilmore and Carmen Meyers. Story by Lillian Bennett Thompson and George Hubbard. At Arena, New York, one-half double daily change bill March 8.

A typical Fox western that has confined most of the Fox output to its own houses and those film places where Universal once reigned supreme.

This is on a par with a Universal in its production and story may have been selected through its economical angle.

John Gilmore is in the picture and featured as the western young and romantic youth with will enough to tame wild horses and a woman. Carmel Meyes is also there as the woman but not featured.

The story takes quite a twist toward its finish that is only made a bit of whereas the twist was enough in itself to have erected an entire feature around it. It also will hold up this picture as a passable western where they are still liked.

In the twist of the ordinary tale, Gilmore as the westerner, altruistically marries a woman expected to die, to give her child a name. It **is at her request after she had been shot by her supposed prior husband as he aimed at the westerner. The latter at the time expected to wed the daughter of a ranchman. When the daughter arrived at the hotel where the finale occurred to wed her sweetie, he informed her of the other marriage just earlier. They had about agreed to await events, the doctor saying the sick woman would not recover, when the child, overhearing the lovers converse, informed her ill mamma who with much consideration, forthwith committed suicide.**

All exteriors when not interiors of shacks. Acting doesn't count, nothing counts; just a western. *Sime.*

ROMANCE LAND

William Fox production starring Tom Mix. Story by Kenneth Perkins; directed by Edward Sedgwick. Shown at Fox's Academy, New York, double feature bill March 12-14. Five reels.

"Pep" Hawkins	Tom Mix
Nan Harvess	Barbara Bedford
"Scrub" Hazen	Frank Brownlee
Counterfeit Bill	George Webb
White Eagle	Pat Christman

William Fox made a screen version of "A Connecticut Yankee" and scored heavily with it, so when this story came along that combined a touch of the Mark Twain, together with a chance to star his principal western player in it, they evidently grabbed it on the coast. Altogether, even short in length, having a running time of 45 minutes, it played to a whale of a number of laughs. It's the kind of a picture the public craves. It kids the romance of the west to a certain extent, but it still has a constant action wallop that makes them want more of it. One thing about it as a picture for a double feature bill, it is there. It has a star name that is known, action **and laughs and doesn't run too** long.

The action **is all set in the west, with Mix a cowboy who has gone** cookoo over the King Arthur period. He has armored suits, the lance and all the other necessary trapping to go with the outfit. At the same time the girl, Nan Harvess, is living on a ranch nearby. She owns it, but her uncle is running it for her under the will of her departed parents. Within a few weeks she is to become of age and an accounting of the trusteeship of her estate will have to be forthcoming. The uncle, who has not administered any too well for the girl's good, is afraid of the result of his accounting and therefore is trying to select as a husband for her someone that he can manage. That sets the plot.

Naturally Mix is not the husband selected, but the one that the girl wants and he wants her. She is of a romantic nature and to appease her desire for a romantic thrill a rodeo is arranged, a feature of which will be a chariot race. The girl consents to marry the victor of the three principal events. Naturally she figures that her loved one will carry off all three and therefore agrees to the arrangement. It is here that the thrills come with the racing in four-horse chariots, the pony express race, and finally all-vehicle race. Mix is the victor in the end, and then just as the wedding ceremony is about to take place, the uncle has the bride-to-be kidnapped and a mad chase follows with Mix doing some tall wall scaling and a few free for all fights.

As picture stuff it is great. It's action from the first bell to the final punch, which is a laugh finish. The titling is particularly good for laughs throughout the film. *Fred.*

STORM SWEPT

Presented by R-C Pictures releasing through Film Booking Offices. Story by H. H. Van Loan, featuring Noah and Wallace Beery. Robert Thronby directing. At Loew's New York, March 10.

Possessing no one explicit quality to raise it above the average intermediate house feature, "Storm Swept" impresses as an inactive vehicle for the Beery brothers. Either of the men has oft times rendered more creditable performances than are gleaned in this instance. Fault of direction or of the script, the fact remains there is a dearth of inaction and little to uphold the interest.

Two inserts, evidently taken from a news reel with one a likely "lift" from the German submarine pictures, provide the only episodes which tend to make it worth while.

Of the two featured men, Wallace seemed the least at home in the surroundings, although struggling with his role of a dejected wanderer made so through a faithless wife. Besides which the tale is anything but convincing. It tells of a deserted husband (Wallace) drifting down to the wharves of a city where he rescues a seaman (Noah) from drowning. The latter, Moran by name, and captain of a lightship stationed miles off shore, offers a job to the wanderer, who is bent on getting away from his fellow-men.

Thence onward the action is entirely centered upon the abode of the self-sacrificing men who "stand to their posts that others may live." The daughter of the captain of the supply tender which makes occasional trips to the floating beacon is the means of the love interest included in the film. Previous to the time whence the faithless wife is found drifting and brought to the ship the principal means of eating up footage is through the watching of one of the crew slowly lose his reason, and a storm during which the maniac succeeds in his attempt to smash the signal lights of the ship. Herein is included the inserts with the scenes on board the lightship, during the tempest, none too well faked.

The coming of the wife on board is the cause of a rupture in the friendship of Moran and his rescuer, although the woman informs her former provider she has had her divorce for over a year. That, of course, sets everything for the second wedding of the disillusioned individual and the departure for the festivities closes out the picture.

Running ten minutes over the hour, this screen attraction is continually handicapped by its dragginess, especially so throughout the early reels. An overabundance of reading matter is a conspicuous liability.

Virginia Brown Fair and Arline Pretty, as the young fiance and the deserting wife, are the only women while the single other supporting member to secure attention is Jack Carlyle in his bit of the mindless member of the ship's crew.

As far as is known, this is the first time the Beery brothers have been featured together, although they have often been included in the same cast of a picture. The combination should have some drawing power at the box office, for certainly the Beerys have possessed a degree of prestige when in support. However, it will take stronger scenarios than "Storm Swept" to establish the two men if the joining is to become a business proposition. They're capable if given the material. *Skig.*

SUPREME PASSION

Playgoers Pictures production, released through Pathe. Florence Dixon and Robert Adams featured. Written by Robert McLaughlin and Chas. T. Dazey. Show at Loew's Circle, New York. Double feature bill, March 10.

A long drawn out, wearisome melodrama that is laughable, so impossible is it in the manner in which the action is made to conform to written titles so that the picture might be utilized at all. It looks as though this production has been made some little while ago and was chopped, re-edited and worked over time and again until finally in despair someone said: "We'll have to make the best of it."

The best about the picture is the title. For the five and ten-cent houses that might be a business getter, but when one thinks that the screen feature comes from a story suggested by the Tom Moore poem, "Believe me if all those endearing young charms, etc," that screen title is just about as laughable as the rest.

In length the picture seemingly is between six and seven reels. The story starts in Ireland, travels to New York and for the finish goes back to Ireland. It is the tale of a retired Irish contractor who is living with his wife and daughter in fair circumstances. The girl is loved by the son of a neighboring lawyer, whose father objects to the match. A former friend of the contractor, who has been in America and amassed a fortune, returns to the old country for a visit, sees the girl and also falls in love with her persuading the mother and father to come to America with him and bring the daughter. The young lover follows and is on the job when it is time to balk the plans of the schemer, who is figuring on wrecking the father financially so that the girl will have to marry him.

The girl is about to go through the ceremony when a friend and the family physician decide on a plan that may present the sacrifice. The girl is to pretend to be burned by her bridal veil and her beauty of face destroyed for all time. The plan is carried out and the bridegroom to have been refuses to go through with the ceremony. The girl and her mother return to Ireland where prayer and the wishing well will restore her good looks. This gave the young hero another chance to make an ocean voyage and he arrives on the spot just as the girl reveals it was all a plan.

In direction the picture is a horrible mass of mishandling and it is just as well that no one is credited with having been responsible for it.
Fred.

SECOND FIDDLE

The Film Guild, Inc., presents Glenn Hunter and Mary Astor in this dramatic feature, written and directed by Frank Tuttle. Distributed by Hodkinson. At the New York, Feb. 23.

Once in a while they get two satisfactory features on a double bill, and this is one of those lucky breaks. The Tuttle picture has excellent human interest, finely drawn character studies and a well handled dramatic story. Young Glenn Hunter makes an appealing hero in a kind of "Patsy" role such as Charles Ray plays, and the story is skillfully laid out to bring the sympathetic quality of his playing to the fore, in a story that has the Cinderella theme, only converted to the boy's side.

Jim is the younger son of the family. He stays home and works in his garage while his brother Herbert goes to college. When Herbert comes home for his vacation, surrounded with all the glamor of the college boy, poor Jim sinks into obscurity, while Herbert makes love to Polly, Jim's sweetheart, and generally lords it over the whole household. The countryside is aroused over the murder of a humble girl of the neighborhood by her madman father, who has broken out of jail. A posse is formed to hunt the killer down. Polly remains at the Bradley home under the care of Jim and Herbert while the posse searches the countryside. The two boys have a shotgun for protection, but when the murderer prowls around the house Herbert goes off to summon help, leaving Jim with the gun but by an oversight carrying off all the shells in his pocket.

The criminal gets into the house, but because of the unloaded gun he escapes from Jim, and the boy is made to appear a coward, Herbert concealing the fact that it was his carelessness that was responsible. Polly discovers the real truth and is on her way to expose Herbert and exonerate Jim, when her auto breaks down and she sends for Jim to help her. A storm comes up and she takes shelter in a lonesome cottage where the mad fugitive also has taken refuge. Both Jim and Herbert go to the deserted house, neither knowing of the madman's presence. Herbert runs away ignobly, but Jim puts up a courageous fight to save Polly, and, although he is beaten, he saves the girl. Then the affair of the shotgun is straightened out and Jim becomes the hero, while Herbert has to slink off in disgrace.

The scenes in the deserted house have a fine thrill, with some trick camera work that puts a touch of horror to the episode, although these violent passages are neatly suggested rather than portrayed in a horrifying manner of realism. The murder of the child is an excellent example of suggestion, the brutal attack taking place out of sight but in a way that makes it entirely evident.

Miss Astor is a splendid player of the young ingenue type, handling the role with refreshing naturalness and a pleasing absence of pose. There is only one defect in the direction. Much of the action takes place during a terrific rainstorm, but the rain is mechanically imperfect, coming down in scattered streams in such a way as to compel the idea that it is all artificial. The photography is generally first rate and the settings are convincing, although they represent no great amount of investment. For the money outlay the picture delivers high values in interest. *Rush.*

CANYON OF FOOLS

P. A. Powers production. R.-C. trademark. Released by Film Booking Office. Taken from the Saturday Evening Post story by Richard Matthew Hallett; scenario by John W. Gray. Director, Val Paul. Harry Carey featured. Marguerite Clayton in support. At the New York, Feb. 27.

A gripping action story with at least one ingenious spectacular flood thrill has been injured by too much footage. The picture just measures up to a program release in general effect, while in better knit form it might have been much more worthwhile. At the New York it was half a double bill, commonly the mark of price concession.

Adequately managed the story should have been a succession of surprise developments to a fine climax, but the progress was so adulterated by repetitions that the spectator is wearied when the real punch comes. There are long passages toward the middle of the five or six reels that remind one of the hokum dramatic serials of bygone fashion. At one point the hero and heroine are overpowered by the outlaws and dragged into a mine shaft, where they are left tied up and helpless.

Both escape three or four times, only to be seized and trussed up again. This sort of stuff is laying the crude melodrama on too thick and it kills interest and illusion. Besides the repetitions balk the progress of action.

A lot of the plot developments are foggy. Why did a gang of outlaws running for their lives with bags of loot load themselves up with half a dozen or so machine guns? How did the pursuers get possession of one of the guns? Why did the hero order the dam broken when he was about to enter the mine shaft that was sure to be flooded? These are only a few of the perplexing points, and picture audiences quickly tire when they are forced to solve puzzles and keep track of an intricate story at the same time. There were none of these misunderstandings in the printed story as published serially.

But for melo-spectacle the flood scenes are impressive. Water torrents always are and in this case there is a lot of fast action. The hero and the heavy have a death struggle in the swirling tide that pours through a sure enough break in a dam; the heroine is carried off in the stream and has to be rescued, and at the same moment the sheriff's posse rides up and engages hand to hand with the gang of bandits. It makes a bewildering climax, but much is lost because the attention has been overtaxed up to that point.

The story has a good romance, neat turns of comedy and an interesting story, but these merits have been negatived by footage and by crudities in the continuity. The action all takes place in the desert lands of the southwest and lacks scenic beauty in locations. Besides which the strong light has injured the photography in places where it is too light and "flat"—with shadings or pictorial quality.

Carey does nicely with a fat part, handling his heroics with a good deal more judgment than is commonly find in a western hero. The sheriff is a neat comedy part, but the other characters are just magazine fiction puppets.

It's a neighborhood picture, where more skillful handling might have put it in a higher class. *Rush.*

GENTLEMAN FROM AMERICA

Universal comedy of feature length, featuring Charles ("Hoot") Gibson, supported by Louise Lorraine and Tom O'Brien. At the New York, Feb. 23, as half a double bill.

This amusing picture is an extravagant bit of nonsense in which a couple of American doughboys in France after the armistice clean out the camp at a crap game and go adventuring by mistake into one of those fabulous principalities like that of "The Prisoner of Zenda." The absurd contrast of two bonehead A. E. F. soldiers stumbling about in situations of hectic romance is a delightful bit of fooling, and it works out into a gorgeous comedy idea for five reels.

Private O'Shea (Gibson) and Private Kelly (O'Brien) are broke when their furlough comes, but they remedy that by making a score of right passes with the dice and start off on the railroad for what they fondly think is Paris. Instead they land up in a place called "Cardonia," a mythical principality over the Spanish border, where everybody wears comic opera clothes and live comic opera lives. The heroine is about to be forced into a marriage with the overlord of the place when Private O'Shea falls in love with her.

The people of the state appeal to the duke against the tyrant overlord, who rules that they shall all assemble in the market place and vote for a new local ruler. O'Shea thereupon gets himself a lot of native finery, dresses up and announces himself a bandit from the mountains, but rightful ruler of the community. The people all rally to his standard and the tyrant is voted out of office in favor of the doughboy.

There is a lot of first-rate rollicking in the courtship of the soldier and the heroine, leading up to their pompous, elaborate marriage when the hard-boiled top sergeant of O'Shea's company appears on the scene and takes O'Shea into custody as A. W. O. L. for a final surprise laugh.

The whole affair is a rollicking burlesque and gets its humorous kick from the situation of a blundering, commonplace doughboy set in the midst of absurd and extravagant story-book romance. It's a good deal like Mark Twain's rich travesty of "A Connecticut Yankee whole thing is managed in a spirit in King Arthur's Court." It's a laugh from start to finish. The of intelligent fun, working out into a rich burlesque. *Rush.*

COVERED WAGON

A Paramount Picture presented by Jesse Lasky. Adapted from the Emerson Hough story by James Cunningham. Directed by James Cruze. Opened at the Criterion, New York, March 16, 1923, for run.

Will Banion............J. Warren Kerrigan
Molly Wingate....................Lois Wilson
Sam Woodhull....................Alan Hale
Mr. Wingate....................Charles Ogle
Mrs. Wingate....................Ethel Wales
Jackson ....Ernest Torrence
Bridger ....Tully Marshall
Kit Carson....................Guy Oliver
Jed Wingate....................John Fox

"The Covered Wagon" has been months in the making with its cost said to have been in the neighborhood of $800,000. The plan for its general distribution is to hold it back until the beginning of next season. Uudoubtedly in addition to the Broadway run at the Criterion Theatre they will present the picture in other cities for extended runs. They can do that safely for in a great many respects it is the biggest thing the screen has had since Griffith made "The Birth of a Nation." That is not saying that this picture is a "Birth" but it is about as close to it as anyone has come since the first smashing big picture that there was.

Like the "Birth" it is based on historic fact. It is American and it carries any measure of thrills, a love story that is pretty, and several notable pieces of character acting that would in themselves be enough to carry any screen production anywhere. When all is said and done about "The Covered Wagon," producer, author, director and all concerned with the picture should take their hats off to Ernest Torrence for having done one of the absolutely finest pieces of work in character playing that the screen has seen. He steals the picture from the time that he first hits the screen right down to his final bit of business.

Emerson Hough, who wrote "The Covered Wagon" for the "Saturday Evening Post," disposed of the picture rights for $8,500, so that makes the most important part of the production, the story, cost just a trifle more than one per cent. of the production. He chose for his subject our great American Empire builders, those pioneers who left their farms and safe-guarded homes in the territory east of the Ohio and started in prairie schooners for the Pacific Coast in 1847, before the discovery the California hills contained the glittering metal that was to be a tremendous lure in 1849.

This particular wagon train, which has some 300 vehicles, started for Oregon. It was the combination really of three trains. They split up on the banks of the Platte, and later there was a second division when word came of gold in California.

Through it all a very pretty and simple love tale runs, as well as an element of intrigue that lends an added interest, which together with the thrills that have been devised makes this production a real picture of pictures.

The thrills, big ones that an audience will remember and go from the theatre to talk about, are three. First and foremost is the fording of the Platte by the wagons of the train. This scene is one that keeps the audience on edge as much as though they were a party to the task the pioneers endured and triumphed above. Then there is the Indian attack with a corking battle staged and finally a prairie fire that has a punch with a corking rescue scene.

As to the cast one must first mention Ernest Torrence for his characterization of the plainsman of frontier days. His work was a consummate piece of acting. Later in several of the scenes Tully Marshall, as a guide and freighter of supplies across the uninhabited wastes, with his couple of Injun wives waiting for him at the fort, lent an admirable touch.

The return to the screen after several years of absence by J. Warren Kerrigan is marked with this production. He plays the lead and does so admirably—as a cashiered officer of the United States Army, turned out because he took cattle to save his detachment from starving and later accused of being a cattle thief. With Lois Wilson, the leading woman, Kerrigan supplied the love interest with Alan Hale as the heavy. Hale also gave a performance that stood out.

In direction James Cruze turned out a picture that will live down through the ages as a triumph that he can always pridefully point to. In picturesqueness there has been nothing on the screen in five years that touches "The Covered Wagon."

It is only a question of how hard making of the picture. In New York it has established it to a certain ex- Paramount is going to go after the tent, but it must drive home from one end of the country to the other that this is the biggest thing that the screen can boast of having had to offer the public in a decade.

Fred.

MIGHTY LAK' A ROSE

Edwin Carewe, six-reel production through First National. Story by Curtis Benton. Directed by Edwin Carewe. At the Strand, March 18.

Jimmie Harrison............James Rennie
Jerome Trevor ....Sam Hardy
Bull Morgan...............Anders Randolf
Rose Duncan..............Dorothy Mackaill
"Hard Boiled" Mollie.....Helene Montrose
"Slippery Eddie" Foster.......Harry Short
Humpty Logan...............Paul Panzer
Mrs. Trevor.............Dora Mills Adams
Jean, the dog...............By Herself

A picture of sentimental hokum. The story revolves around a blind girl violinist who is a combination of Little Eva and Oliver Twist and its passages of pathos are pretty syrupy. The Oliver Twist angle comes from the fact that the child falls among thieves and through her innocent purity work their regeneration. Only the process was too swift and too arbitrary to be convincing.

When they're bad, they're very bad and when they're good they're gosh awful unnatural. The only really sincere part is played by a beautiful collie. You could understand the dog's motives, but the feelings that impelled the people were foggy. One or two of the underworld twists by which a crook escapes from pursuing police are neat surprises, such as the chase in the Grand Central station in New York, and the robbery in which the dog is employed to carry off the loot under the policemen's eyes has a novel turn.

A great musician discovers a musical prodigy in Rose, a child in an Ohio asylum, and has her sent to the big city to be educated. She is waiting for her uncle in the Grand Central station when Bull Morgan, the "terror of Murderers' Alley" and leader of a gang of thieves, takes charge of her in order to cloak his escape from pursuit. She is accordingly taken into the band as their innocent tool. The young crook, Jimmy, a creature of circumstances, is impressed with her beauty and her violin awakens in him a better nature.

Bull commands that Jimmy use the girl in the commission of a crime. The two engage in a desperate fight over Jimmy's refusal and in the mix-up Rose is struck down by Bull unintentionally. Remorse over injuring the child brings Bull to a better mind and he resolves to go straight. There remains "Hard Boiled" Mollie, the lady crook. She holds out against the appeal of Rose's violin, but finally sees the error of her ways, although by what means is not satisfactorily shown. This benevolent trio determines that Rose must be cured of her blindness and to raise $1,000 for an operation Jimmy undertakes a last "job," the robbery of a factory. He succeeds with the help of the dog, but is captured and sent to prison for five years, while Rose is told he is dead.

Just as Jimmy completes his sentence and is released, Rose, who has been found by the great musician, is about to make her concert debut. Of course, Jimmy mingles in the crowd at the concert hall and, again through the intelligence of the dog, he and the girl are brought together for a happy ending and the finish comes on a picture of almost pastoral peace, with Bull and Mollie married and a cooing baby in the background and Jimmy and Rose embracing in one of those misted closeups and the organ crooning "Mighty Lak' a Rose," the musical theme of which runs through the picture. Just an artificial, theatrical affair spread thickly with heavy sentimental jam that will please the very unsophisticated.

It runs 90 minutes and becomes pretty tiresome toward the end.

Rush.

LOST AND FOUND

R. A. Walsh produced-directed, running 63 minutes at Capitol, New York, week March 18. Story by R. A. Walsh with atmospherical prolog by Sam Rothafel (for Capitol only).

Captain Blackbird...........House Peters
Lorna ....Pauline Starke
Lloyd Warren.............Antonio Moreno
Baby Madge............Mary Jane Irving
Madge ....Rosemary Theby
Faulke ....George Siegmann
Skinner ....William V. Mong
Waki ....Carl Harbaugh
Kerito ....David Wing

It does look as though in "Lost and Found" R. A. Walsh has turned out a box office feature. The "South Sea Romance" carded with the title in nearly all billing appears to lend immediate interest. In the picture Mr. Walsh has taken pains to found that descriptive matter with little South Sea touches, some ever so close to nature, though but flashes, and others popularly known as the "wiggle" dancing by the tribes.

The story itself would have meant but little excepting in the handling as Walsh, the director also, did it.

There are tribal dances with the women shimmying just awful but not for long, there are everglades where the barbarians go swimming and sneaking, and there is a battle between the tribes, which became a real war scene almost. The latter a feature of the film, is nicely worked out with water scenes of one tribe rowing to the island of another and in the sequence of a logical strain in the tale calling for it.

The picture is all atmosphere. To aid it Mr. Rothafel produced a very pretty little singing prelude called pretty little singing prelude, introducing through it an exceptional baritone, Bruce Benjamin, with a full melodious voice. Dorma Lee sang with him. It gave the picture a splendid start and would be worth copying by the larger houses playing this feature.

The cast holds a number of picture names in the leading role way. In performance Pauline Starke took the lead. She has quite a range to cover and did it all well, from looks to playing. **Besides at one time Pauline showed in an everglade pond with her shoulders bare as though in bathing au naturel, this effect heightened by the terrible Waki intensely watching her from amongst the glades. That seemed to settle with Waki that Lorna must be his bride. Escape by her from the snare thereafter became most of the scene with Antonio Moreno** having a light and love interest he did little with.

House Peters played a seafaring captain of a sailing schooner which must have been a rum runner. Rosemary Theby was his wife early and also later, dying two days before Captain Blackbird finally found her daughter on Pango Island, a near neighbor of Moa. William V. Mong is excellent as the villain. The House-Mong scene when Mong was revealed as the seducer of Blackbird's wife through Peters reading the inscription on a wedding ring Mong gambled is a finely staged bit, for its repression in the first part and action in the ending of it. Few directors could have resisted the impulse to have made Peters act all over the lot at the disclosure.

The story receives a bad kick because of lack of sustenance, the excuse for it all being vague and improbable, but once it gets going, it keeps going with action and mainspring. That a wife with her baby could be lured or kidnapped to the South Seas by a stranger from her home in the states, to verify jealous suspicions aroused by the stranger, is too implausible. Other bits are reminiscent, such as the scenes on the schooner, but the photography in this and other minor matteers stands them off to some extent.

Playing the South Seas for a money getter is the best idea and this Walsh did. He gave them just enough of all that they want mostly to see, but sufficient to make them forget the story and talk about the scenes outside the theatre.

The Capitol Sunday afternoon for the second show, with Broadway packed with promenaders on the first fine Sunday afternoon of the spring, was capacity. That either spoke for the billing or the theatre. for in "Lost and Found" itself, as a name, by itself, there is nothing to draw, although the picture will.

Through the cold, flat title heavy exploitation should be given.

Simc.

TRAIL OF LONESOME PINE

Paramount picture presented by Adolph Zukor, starring Mary Miles Minter. Adapted by Will M. Ritchey from the story by John Fox, Jr., and play by Eugene Walter. Directed by Charles Maigne. Shown at Rialto, New York, week March 18. Five reels.

June Tolliver...........Mary Miles Minter
John Hale..................Antonio Moreno
"Devil" Judd Tolliver.....Ernest Torrence
"Bad" Rufe Tolliver.........Edwin Brady
Ann.........................Frances Warner
Buck Fallin.................J. S. Stembridge
Dave Tolliver.....................Cullen Tate

Although there is a picture on view at the Rialto this week with the title of "The Trail of the Lonesome Pine," professedly an adaptation of the play and story of the same title, it isn't "The Trail of the Lonesome Pine" at all, although the characters bear the same names and the action is laid in the hills of Tennessee. There is, however, a picture that is a rewritten tale into which some of the characters of the old story have been placed. The picture itself is far below the original which the Lasky company made in 1916, with Charlotte Walker in the role Mary Miles Minter now plays. It is a toss up whether or not Theodore Roberts wasn't better as "Devil" Judd Tolliver than Ernest Torrance is in the present production. However, Roberts had more of a part in the other version.

It is just another instance of what prohibition has done to us. In the original story the mountaineer feud was secondary, with the moonshining as the outstanding feature of the tale. Now that they couldn't have moonshine in the picture, although we have it in the home, the feud was brought to the foreground. It doesn't make as good a story.

"The Trail of the Lonesome Pine" is just an ordinary program picture machine made and ground out without any idea of getting anything artistic on the screen. Well remembered is the opening that William de Mille had for the original. It was a work of art, that tall, lonesome pine and the introduction of his characters. In this Charles Maigne has fallen down. He has gotten some action, but there is not one bit of suspense that is calculated to make the audience watch and wait with expectancy as to what is going to happen next.

Miss Minter is a colorless June Tolliver, and Antonio Moreno gets little or no chance to show what he really can do in this picture. Cullen Tate, from a character standpoint, gives one of the best performances in the production. *Fred.*

STRAUSS' SALOME

Produced by Malcolm Strauss. Diana Allen featured. At Loew's New York one-half of double bill for day, March 20. Running time, 64 minutes. No releasing connection mentioned.

Salome with bobbed hair and a Broadway glide! A typical moving picture miscast. That means the best acting you get is out of the titles. They do need titles in this picture. There are plenty of them, but maybe not enough.

Malcolm Strauss' "Salome" was probably made some time ago. Strauss appears to be producing himself out of pictures as a producer. He should produce or direct for others, with the technical details, casting included, left to those who make a business of that. Strauss is an artist. He displays it in his own work, but there seems to be no support for him by others.

To see players struggle through this rather expensive picture is a pity. "Salome," if it needs anything, needs actors. With good actors or properly directed actors, some skimping could be done on production.

The whole "Salome" story is there, perhaps a bit different from the others, possibly a little more romantic, and that doesn't hurt. But Diana Allen as Salome realized it as much as her Queen Mother did her role or King Herod his, both picturesque only, in this story.

Miss Allen did her dance of the veils without veils and got an encore from the banquet mob, an encore gotten in the picture she never would receive elsewhere with that dance.

The Prince of Egypt displayed about as much emotion in his many scenes calling for it as Tut, who may have been one of his ancestors, did when lately discovered. Whatever emotion the picture emitted came from the audience. It was inclined to titter now and again, although this picture has a certain holding quality as produced that, despite its defects, earned respect for it.

It is too good a scenic or sight picture to be cast away in a half of a Loew double bill. At least there is enough to make it stand up on the title for the medium grade houses for one or two days. One flash of the Princess taking a bath when called by the King should do that. It's quite a flash and, to see it properly, use field glasses. It threatened for the moment as though Miss Allen intended to skip to the King forgetting her bathing gown.

The mob scene with The Wanderer was badly cut, but it was a well placed mob scene with hundreds of persons in it. More could have been made of the Egyptian camp, for there were material and atmosphere there, but long before that poor direction and bad acting had ruined "Salome." *Sime.*

WONDERS OF THE SEA

J. E. Williamson's undersea picture, releasing through the Film Booking Offices of America. At Loew's New York, March 15.

Featuring the device by which the negative was secured this educational film, for upon such it borders, holds few entertaining qualities until during the last reel. At that time two men in the full regalia of divers go overboard. The spearing of a dangerous fish, which resembles an eel, and the catching of a shark close out the "kick." These instances were sufficient to draw meagre applause at the finish from an audience which had found nothing to provoke enthusiasm up to that time.

A vast majority of the footage is taken up in revealing the construction of the patented device by which the photographer is permitted to rest under the surface in safety and the diving of a girl to swim before the two-inch glass behind which the camera man grinds. The underwater gyrations of the miss are too often repeated while enacting a degree of similarity that lessens the value of the incident. A slow-motion bit is also inserted at the time the girl is before the submerged lens.

Other than that the film is taken up with the different formations of coral, plants and the odd types of the smaller species of fish to be found in the locality whence the pictures were taken, off Nassau, in the Bahamas, to be exact.

The photography is clear and concise throughout, but the emphatic tendency to drag, which the film possesses, is too flagrant a liability for the registering of the picture to be other than a moderately interesting and amusing program episode. *Skig.*

THE QUEEN OF SIN

Presented by Ben Blumenthal, with the program announcement, "Europe's Greatest Screen Gesture," with an added line, "The Spectacle of Sodom and Gomorrah." Produced by Sascha in Austria. Directed by Michael Kertess. Lucy Doraine featured. Shown at the Lyric, N.Y., for an indefinite run March 25, 1923. Time, 92 minutes.

Jackson Harber .... George Reimers
Edward Harber
A Goldsmith from Galilea .... Walter Slezak
Miss Mary Conway
The Wife of Lot .... Lucy Doriane
The Queen of Sin
Mrs. Agatha Conway, her mother .... Erila Wagner
A Priest Tutor ot Cambridge .... Michael Varkonyl
The Unknown Wanderer
Harry Lighton, A sculptor
Lot .... Kurt Ehrle

Ben Blumenthal took over the Lyric, New York, on a rental and, beginning Monday night, presented the European film spectacle entitled "The Queen of Sin," founded on the Biblical tale of Sodom and Gomorrah, the latter its German title. The film was preceded by an elaborate masque and pantomimic offering, entitled "The Green Song," presented by Ned Wayburn, the program crediting its conception to Ben Ali Haggin. The combination of the masque and the film spectacle made an interesting evening's entertainment, even though the modern angle of the story which is utilized to bring about the exposition of the Biblical tale, failed to hold anything for the American public. However, the destruction of the ancient city and the scenes of revelry leading up to it were magnificently done and the settings were tremendous in the magnitude. This feature alone is enough to make the picture worth while for any house, especially when one takes into consideration the terrific wallop that the title "The Queen of Sin" should be at the box office.

The principal fault with this picture, as with the majority of foreign-made productions, is the fact that the film fans of the continent must have a lot of beef as far as the leading women are concerned, and Lucy Doraine fills that requirement fully. And as far as their leading men are concerned, the foreigners have a queer conception when measured with American standards in this respect. Their leading men are all heavy, pouchy individuals of over 50, while their juvenile leads, it seems, must have been recruited from the cradle, so immature do they appear, both in stature and in histrionic ability.

"The Queen of Sin" has all these faults, yet with them it is a picture that as a spectacle ranks with any of the bigger foreign-made productions that have been brought to this country. The titling that was done on this side of the ocean evolved a story that in its language is entirely American, to say the least. Originally the production was in 18 reels and the current picture is in eight. That the original must have been decidedly interesting from an erotic standpoint is indicated by that portion of the film utilized in the American presentation.

The story opens in the studio of a young sculptor who is in love with a society deb, posing for a masterpiece he is at work on. They are in love with each other, but the sculptor isn't wealthy and the girl has been groomed by her mother for a marriage which will rehabilitate the family fortune. A financial power desires the girl, and as he holds the mother in his clutches through her having forged his name to a check, the proceeds of which she utilized to keep up the family position, the girl is to be sacrificed to his lustful desires.

The engagement is to be announced at a fete which as it proceeds rivals in its excesses and abandon the wild orgies of the ancients. The father has caused his son to be brought from his school to be present.

The son, of about 18, arrives with his father confessor and teacher. The latter views the scenes that occur before him with alarm and tries to have the boy leave. The jilted sculptor puts in an appearance, and when the girl that he loves refuses his advances, although refusing to disclose she has consented to be sacrificed to shield her mother, he tries to commit suicide.

The young priest is called to administer to him spiritually, and the supposed to be dying man exacts a promise from the holy man he will use his influence to save the girl. The latter meanwhile has conceived a revenge that will in its scope embrace the man who is compelling her to marry him and his son. She lures the younger into making love with her and makes a rendezvous with him in a pavilion where she is to meet the father at an appointed hour. She figures to arouse jealousy in both and set father against son and vice versa.

But the young priest, who has discovered the son and the girl in an embrace, takes the boy aside and relates to him the tale of the Biblical queen of sin of Sodom and Gomorrah. This gives leave for the introduction of the first portion of the ancient Biblical lore and shows how a wicked queen ground her own people under her power in the desire to achieve tremendous riches in gold and silver, and ending with the turning of the people against the queen, their uprising and the sacrifice of a young man of the country who would believe no ill of her, and finally when he has been instrumental in saving her from the infuriated mob, she turns on him and through her accusation has him thrown to death from the tower heights.

This portion of the picture is finely done, but as magnificent as it is it serves but as a forerunner for what is to follow in the second half.

The second half finds the dream theme used in order to utilize the story of Lot and his wife and the destruction of Sodom and Gomorrah. The heroine of the tale when she has arranged her rendezvous with father and son retires to her chamber to rest prior to the ordeal and the working out of her revengeful plans. She falls asleep and dreams the father is slain by the son and she is arrested as guilty of the crime, condemned to be punished with death. On the eve of her execution she calls for the priest, and the young priest of the story enters. Her plea is that she cannot die and leave the world and its pleasures. He turns and utters a prayer that his lips may be empowered to tell the tale of Lot, so that this girl can visualize it.

Then follows the second period of Biblical material, ending in the destruction of the cities and the turning of Lot's wife into a pillar of salt. If the earlier portion of ancient history was magnificent, this is tremendous. The destruction of the Temple of Astarte beggars description.

Through both the modern and the ancient themes the same players appear in the characters. Thus the leading woman plays three roles—the young society deb, the queen of sin and the wife of Lot. The men likewise double in their roles.

In face, form and dramatic ability it would seem that Miss Doraine might prove a strong runner up to Pola Negri, providing she was brought to this country and given the same opportunity and training the Polish star is now having. In this production she does not appear to advantage in the matter of dress, according to the American idea. In the undraped, or, rather, slightly draped character, she is far more pleasing to the American eye, even though inclined to weight.

Of the men, Michael Varkonyi as the priest is far and away the outstanding figure. The others practically mean nothing.

"The Queen of Sin" is not going

to prove a screen sensation, nor is it going to prove tremendously successful as a "road show" in the event the idea to send it out as an attraction is gone through with, but in the regular picture theatres it should pull big business.

A special score was provided by Sigmund Romberg, who directed the opening night. Mr. Romberg seemingly has not the knowledge of the requirements of the screen musically and failed to accentuate the big scenes when a huge musical punch was called for. *Fred.*

SOULS FOR SALE

Goldwyn special production, written and directed by Rupert Hughes. Shown at a special preview Capitol, New York, March 26. Time, 90 minutes.

Remember Steddon.......Eleanor Boardman
Robina Teele.......Mae Busch
Leva Lemaire.......Barbara La Marr
Frank Claymose.......Richard Dix
Tom Holby.......Frank Mayo
Owen Scudder.......Lew Cody
Jimmy Leland.......Arthur Hoyt
Caxton.......David Imboden
Arthur Tirrey.......Roy Atwell
Lord Fryingham.......Wm. Orlamond
Rev. John Steddon.......Forest Robinson
Mrs. Steddon.......Edith Yorke
Pinkey.......William Haines
Spofford.......George Morgan
Abigail Tweedy.......Dale Fuller
Hank Kale.......Snitz Edwards
Assistant Cameraman.......Auld Thomas
Company Electrician.......Leo Willis
Company Prop Man.......Yale Boss
Company Grip.......Walter Perry
Company Violin Player.......Sam Damen
Company Melodeon Player...R. H. Johnson
Motion Picture Heavy.......Jack Richardson
Second Cameraman.......Rush Hughes
Lady Jane.......Aileen Pringle
Velma Slade.......Eve Southern
Mrs. Sturges.......May Milloy
Mrs. Kale.......Sylvia Ashton
Quinn.......Fred Kelsey
Doyle.......L. J. O'Connor
Magnus.......Jed Prouty
Boss Canvasman.......Charlie Murphy
Leva Lemaire's Mother...Margaret Bourne

A big picture.

It is big in a great many ways and certain to be big at the box office. It is going to have an unusual attraction for the average film fan.

Really "inside stuff" of life in the big studios in Hollywood, where they grind out the film fodder that the millions of fans the country over eat up every day. It is at once what "Merton of the Movies" is to the speaking stage and all of the fan magazines rolled into one, but whereas "Merton" deals with the Hollywood life in a comedy sense, with its romance as an underlying motive, "Souls for Sale" shows the romance of the workers of the screen and of the making of screen's reflections.

It is the biggest thing Rupert Hughes has done, either as author or director, since identified with the picture industry.

It is also a remarkable piece of propaganda for Hollywood, the picture industry as a whole and its clean-living acting people as well.

There is a cast as long as your arm and there are a score or more stars of the screen shown, whose names are not mentioned. They fill in as bits here and there, some sitting around the cafeteria on the lot, others working on their own sets, etc.

This is a picture Goldwyn could have taken and shown for a run in some legitimate house on Broadway during the coming summer, and put it over for three months at least. It is a picture every visitor to New York from every part of the country where a picture was ever shown would want to see, just as sure as all interested in films and screen players are certain to want to see "Merton." It is a fan picture that combines as much fan food as all of the fan magazines rolled into one.

When Mr. Hughes started working on "Souls for Sale" he went to work with the intention of evolving something that would give the picture-going public something to look at; give them an insight into the workings on a big production lot and help to wash out the bad taste in the mouths left by the string of scandals the industry has had. He has succeeded in applying a real coat of whitewash, and in such a manner no one will realize it is propaganda for the industry.

The story is simple, compelling, full of romance and abounds with thrills and touches of comedy.

The heroine is a small-town girl, daughter of a minister, who marries an affable stranger in the little town. The couple are on a train carrying them on their honeymoon journey when the girl realizes she has made a mistake and leaps from the observation car as the train stops at a watering tank in the midst of the desert. Her husband continues on his way and finally hops off the train at a town, where a couple of cops recognize him as "wanted," but after they get the cuffs on him he makes an escape. He is described in the circular asking for his arrest as a bluebeard, who marries, insures and then kills off his wives.

The girl, wandering in the desert, is found by a picture company working on location. They care for her and give her a few days' work as well as an offer to return to Los Angeles with them. But pictures and the theatre spell Satan to her, according to her teachings, and she instead takes a position as a waitress in a small hotel on the desert. When that resort closes for the season she decides to go to Los Angeles and look up her picture friends.

On arrival, after being buffeted about from one studio to another, she finally meets with her friends, gets a test and a job, and from that time on her rise to stardom comes rapidly. The leading man and her director are both in love with her, but she refuses them both because the husband whom she deserted is hanging over her head, and she has heard a scandal is fatal to the career of a screen favorite, man or woman.

Finally the husband shows, and after causing her some uneasiness is most conveniently bumped off by backing into a wind-making machine. It leaves the little star free to choose which of her two admirers she would prefer, and she, wise girl, takes the director instead of the handsome leading man.

The half-dozen outstanding characters are played by Eleanor Boardman, Mae Busch, Barbara La Marr, Richard Dix, Frank Mayo and Lew Cody. The first may not mean very much to the average fan or exhibitor, but after this picture the name of Eleanor Boardman is going to mean a whole lot, on the screen and in the box office, for if there ever was a screen find she is one. Miss Boardman plays the lead, and Mr. Dix, opposite, is the director. Mr. Mayo is the good-looking leading man of the company, Miss Busch his leading lady whom Miss Boardman replaces when forced out of the production through an accident, and Mr. Cody is the heavy who marries 'em and knocks 'em off for what they will bring in insurance.

In production the picture has everything that could be asked for. Its final big punch is the wrecking by fire and storm of a big top in which a picture of circus life is being enacted. That furnishes about as much thrill as anyone would want.

Rupert Hughes as a director has topped everything he ever did, even as an author, in this picture. *Fred.*

CHURCH AROUND THE CORNER

Warner Bros. production adapted from the Charles E. Blaney play by Olga Printzlau, directed by William Seiter. Shown at the Strand, New York, week March 25, together with "Bell Boy 13." Time 55 minutes.

Iella Morton.......Claire Windsor
David Graham.......Kenneth Harlan
Morton.......Hobart Bosworth
Hex.......Walter Long
Hetty.......Pauline Stark
Rev. Bradley.......Alec Francis
Mrs. Graham.......Margaret Seddon
Jude.......George Cooper
Doc Graham.......Winter Hall

The showing of "The Little Church Around the Corner" as presented at the Strand, New York, showed that the picture ran 55 minutes, although the feature is supposed to be 6,300 odd feet in length. That seems to indicate that considerable footage was clipped for this house. However, it is a fair type of melodrama of the ten-twent-thirt school and as such will have a certain appeal, but hardly in the bigger first run houses like the Strand.

In making the screen adaptation certain liberties were taken with the original play, perhaps in an effort to make it stronger. The adapter evidently did not care where the strengthening ideas came from so long as they helped the picture. It is possible that an author or two of some Broadway's current plays (one in particular "The Fool") might look at the picture and find that some of their thoughts have found the way to the screen in perhaps a slightly different guise.

As "The Little Church" now stands it is a preachment in behalf of faith. Faith in the works of God and the power of cure; faith in mankind to the end that aims may be achieved without needless strife and violence. That is all set forth in a story that begins in a coal mining town where an orphaned youth has been adopted by the local physician. The boy's father lost his life in a mine accident. The boy on Sunday's holds a church of his own with a soap box as a pulpit.

At this period the owner of the mine steps in and decides to give the boy an education for the ministry, then the story jumps to a time when the boy has been ordained. He returns to his benefactor's home and falls in love with the daughter. His affection is returned and the two are to be wed. The miners appear and make a demand that the mines be safeguarded against the possibility of a cave in. When their request is refused in the presence of the young minister, he sees that after all he belongs to the miners and he returns with them to their town instead of taking over the wealthy church he is to be assigned to.

There is a mine disaster on the day of his arrival. He leads the rescue crew and finally saves the mine owner and his daughter from attack. The attack is warded off through the medium of giving the angry mob a concrete example of the power of faith in making a dumb girl speak.

Therewith the story practically ends, without one grasping which of either the two girls the minister finally wed. It is shown in the earlier portion of the story he was engaged to the mine owner's daughter. Still there is something of a doubt at the conclusion of the picture following the miracle of the return of speech to the dumb girl whether or not he favors her.

In the matter of production the Warners did not limit William Seiter the director. Some of the scenes, as a matter of fact, are overdone, as an instance the fully fifty foot deep bedroom of the young society girl. Yet there seems to be but little about the picture that would enable one to pick it as a picture above the usual run of high grade program productions. *Fred.*

GRUMPY

Adolph Zukor presents this Famous Players (Paramount) production by William De Mille, from the play of the same name by Horace Hodges and T. Wigney Percyval. Screen version by Clara Beranger. Theodore Roberts featured in multi-star cast. Running time, 70 minutes. At the Rivoli March 25.

"Grumpy".......Theodore Roberts
Virginia.......May McAvoy
Ernest Heron.......Conrad Nagel
Chamberlin Jarvis.......Casson Ferguson
Keble.......Bertram Johns
Ruddock.......Charles Ogle
Dawson.......Robert Bolder
Wolfe.......Charles French
Susan.......Bernice Frank

"Grumpy" makes splendid screen entertainment and furnishes the best vehicle up to date for Theodore Roberts' talent in character portraiture. In return for the opportunity Roberts makes the new play a valuable piece of property for Famous Players. The cases where a picture makes a star are plentiful, but this instance is unique in reversing the process.

Not that it isn't a strong story, for "Grumpy" is all of that, but Roberts by sheer force of interpretation stands out and throws the story interest into the background in a summing up of the elements of entertainment value. No better piece of pantomimic delineation has come on the screen in many a day. It's a triumph of high comedy that fits in with the atmosphere of the play to perfection. This happy conjunction of actor and story makes an offering conspicuously worth while for clean, intelligent screen entertainment.

The picture is singularly free from all the familiar tricks of the trade. It is guiltless of cheap sex appeal, melodramatic bunk and comedy hokum, and De Mille has preserved all the human interest appeal of the original stage presentation. For once a stage play has been translated to the screen without being mangled.

The appeal of the stage "Grumpy" was that it was a straight detective story done in a spirit of smooth and natural comedy, while at the same time preserving all the suspense of a thief chase and the dramatic kick of solving a mystery. The film version in a remarkable degree retains the same balance of comedy and drama, and the success of the scheme is largely dependent upon the playing of the main character by Roberts, who for once is permitted to express moods and tenses without a prop cigar.

De Mille has given the piece a splendid production. The whole background is appropriately simple and unobtrusive, including the other players. The rest of the cast fits in smoothly, achieving nice balance for the whole without exploiting any one detail. May McAvoy is pretty and graceful, and Conrad Nagel is manly and wholesome looking, but the romance of their courtship merely gives a touch of color to the background without intruding directly upon the absorbing story of Grumpy himself.

In short, one "Grumpy" and one Roberts are worth a dozen "Sheiks" and "Adam's Ribs." *Rush.*

SUZANNA

Mack Sennett production, starring Mabel Normand, with the producer the author. Releasing through the Allied Producers and Distributors' Corp., directed by F. Richard Jones, with Ray Grey assisting. Time, 60 minutes, At the Capitol, New York, week March 25.

Suzanna.......Mabel Normand
Don Fernando.......George Nichols
Ramon.......Walter MsGrail
Dona Isabella.......Evelyn Sherman
Pancho.......Leon Bary
Don Diego.......Eric Mayne
Dolores.......Winifred Bryson

A likely feature to signalize the more or less return of Mabel Normand to the screen. The film will never cause a stampede, although it is a light comedy vehicle, capably handled as to its technicalities and revealing Miss Normand in a distinct "cute" classification. It amused and satisfied a capacity Sunday afternoon gathering at the Capitol.

The picture is entirely in costume, with the locale and period set in an old Spanish colony of California. The illusion has been nicely carried out by settings, with a few of the exteriors gaining particular attention because of their appeal to the eye. To wit, the cameraman has turned in a notable piece of work throughout the entire footage. An appropriate cast has been chosen that screens as a worthy combination in support of the star.

Of Miss Normand, it may be said that she is a much more refined damsel during this episode than she oft has been in her previous pictures. And not eliminating all the tomboy mannerisms, either. But the general trend in the direction seems to have been under the motto, "tone down," and such procedure sums up as far from detrimental. Miss Normand's personal performance is a worthy feature of this release, as is the placing of the title of the picture over the star's name whence introducing her in the role by means of a caption.

The story is lightly weaved around Suzanna, a peon girl, beloved by and in love with Ramon, the son of the ranch owner. Their marriage is considered impossible because of their different stations in life and the boy forcibly becomes betrothed to Dolores, the daughter of Don Diego. Ramon is resigned to his fate until from the church where his ceremony is to take place he sees Suzanna marching to another altar with Pancho, the toreador. Whence follows a flying pick-up from a horse and the ensuing chase.

Meanwhile there is the revelation made that Suzanna, and not Dolores, is the true daughter of Don Diego, which permits of the happy ending.

As a comedy minus any potential strength this Sennett production will undoubtedly please. It's simply a matter of a few chuckles, every so often, picturesquely presented. If nothing else, it brings Miss Normand before the filmgoers once more in a release that will be beneficial for anything that is scheduled to follow with her. *Skig.*

BELL BOY 13

Thos. H. Ince production, starring Douglas MacLean. Written by Austin Gill and directed by William A. Seiter. Released by First National. Shown at the Strand. New York, week March 25, together with "Little Church Around the Corner." Time, 44 minutes.

Harry Elrod..............Douglas MacLean
Kitty Clyde..............Margaret Loomis
Uncle Elrod..............John Steppling

Straight comedy picture in short four reels. For that reason it was evidently picked for the Strand's bill for the current week in order to bolster up the showing there of "The Little Church Around the Corner."

As a comedy it is just fair, especially after MacLean in "The Hottentot." This picture, however, may have been made before the "Hottentot" and therefore is being used to gather patronage on the strength of the racing comedy. This is a mistake, at least, if one was working for the best interests of MacLean in the first run houses. It makes it appear as though "The Hottentot" was an accident, and this one or more of the regular type of comedy that MacLean was apt to do. It may break down the impression he created for himself in the longer picture.

The story in this tale is a simple one. MacLean plays the role of a non-working nephew of a wealthy uncle. He is in love with an actress and is trying to obtain uncle's consent to the marriage. Uncle refuses and the boy plans to elope with the girl. Uncle overhears the plan and tries to prevent the runaway match. The boy finally gets out and follows the girl to another town where she turns him down because he failed to obtain uncle's consent, and the boy, broke, goes to work as a bell hop. Uncle comes on the scene and there is some farcial horseplay which eventually brings about the desired "bless you" speech.

The one bit that really gets laughs is the automobile ride through town by the boy with a fire chief's hat on his head and the entire fire department following him. MacLean's work personally is good but the story isn't there. *Fred.*

THE LEOPARDESS

Paramount picture, presented by Adolph Zukor and starring Alice Brady. Adapted from the story of Katherine Burt by J. Clarkson Miller, with Henry Kolker directing and Gilbert Warrenton at camera. Time, 56 minutes. At the Rialto, New York, week March 25.

Tiare..............Alice Brady
Captain Croft..............Edward Langford
Scott Quaigg..............Montagu Love

Whether or not the story lost anything in its adaptation for screen usage, the fact is outstanding this picture neither carries weight as entertainment nor will it enhance the popularity of its chief luminary, Alice Brady. At various passages the continuity actually is boring. So deplorably weak is this feature it would hardly cause attention in any intermediate class house. The tale is a dead open and shut proposition after the initial reel.

Miss Brady does not convince in her role of a girl of the South Pacific islands whom an American millionaire attempts to tame. Other than presenting a pleasing appearance, after the return to civilization and running around in tight and scanty garments previous to that, there is little for the star to do beyond registering fear every time her would-be boss threatens.

The burden passes on to Montagu Love as the purely outdoor specimen of American manhood, interested mainly in hunting wild game and taming women. The only variation from former similar situation for him is that he has to marry this girl to use his system.

Mr. Love, with his playing of the "heavy," could not lift the release from out of the ordinary class. It doesn't seem possible for any one to have saved this screen effort. Edward Langford failed to gain any rooters as the sympathetic captain of the millionaire's yacht, who finally gets the girl. Beyond those characters the playing was divided into bits mediocrely handled.

Technically the film is "pretty" with some of its exteriors with a framed storm at sea being included. The interiors are average with the main source of action based upon a captured leopard whom the hunter turns loose in his home.

Narrating of Tiare, the island belle, who is a daughter of a renegade Scotchman and brought up under the influence of all the islanders' superstitions the theme jumps to the arrival of Quaigg's yacht. He sees the girl, she defies him; he forces her into marriage and begins the process of taming through taking advantage of her superstitious fear. The captain of the craft takes an opposing view and tries to convince the girl of her foolishness but gets into a fight with Quaigg and is thrown overboard before he can accomplish his purpose.

Back at Quaigg's home on the Hudson the return from a hunting trip is signalized by the girl having overcome her moral submission but still antagonistic to her husband. Having already by mistake shot her friend and benefactor, Croft, who has returned from the sea and preceded the owner into the house, it gums things up further when he of the savage instincts lets loose the leopard with the intent the animal shall kill his wife. The spotted cat turns on its captor and all ends with Tiare and the captain back on the islands.

It's probably the longest 56 minutes in any of the Broadway houses for months. *Skig.*

FIRPO-BRENNAN FIGHT

Picture taken at Madison Square Garden March 12 of Firpo-Brennan heavyweight boxing bout promoted by Tex Rickard. At Moss' Broadway, New York, week March 26. Running time, 25 minutes.

The picture of the Firpo-Brennan bout fought March 12 at Madison Square Garden is unquestionably genuine of the actual fight. Numerous inconsequential details which a technical director would overlook, the entire fight itself, with Firpo ever using the "rabbit" punch and the knockout, in addition to the ringside spectators and the scenes following the knockout, stamp the picture as genuine.

The promoters have themselves to blame for the stories circulated to the effect the picture was taken after the fight. The delay between the time of taking and exhibiting to the public, the secrecy with which the cameramen worked from the exit box, the long-distance photography and the lack of any comment in the dailies about pictures being taken gave wide circulation to the reports.

The writer saw the fight and the picture, and will stake his reputation on the genuineness of both. A few points of proof are the reproductions of round 10, when the referee walked over to Firpo's corner and ordered Jimmy De Forrest to leave the ring. De Forrest had been violating the 10-second warning, or "seconds out," until the crowd got after him. After Brennan was dropped as the count proceeded, Brennan raised himself to his knees and began to crawl toward the ropes. One of the spectators, frightened at the glassy stare in Bill's befogged eyes, half-raised out of a ringside seat to get out of his way. The picture reproduces this perfectly. Numerous other details prove its genuineness.

No one who saw the 12th round and Brennan beaten to the floor from a volley of "rabbit" or "occipital" punches could be hornswoggled by any picture reproduction, any more than a trained observer would fail to detect minute difference of movement in a picture "cut back."

The picture will appeal to fight followers through the interest in Firpo, who is being groomed by Tex Rickard for a killing in South America. Firpo will be carefully nursed, with a Dempsey bout in view.

The photography is very bad throughout, the features of the men being at times so blurred as to be almost unrecognizable. In the actual encounter Firpo was as slow as a truck horse. The speed of the camera version makes him appear as fast as a bantam.

Firpo's overhand right hook, which has been called the "rabbit" punch, and which was in use by ringsters before Firpo was born, is very much in evidence. This punch has been ballyhooed as a Firpo creation, but the announcer who accompanied the pictures at the Broadway was roundly raspberried when he said, "In the next round you will see the knockout from the 'rabbit blow,' which Firpo first introduced." After the razzing had subsided he added, "In this fight." Even then he was wrong, for Brennan used it throughout.

On its merits as a piece of photography the Firpo-Brennan fight picture is mediocre. Firpo's personality and the legion of boxing fans created during and since the war by national recognition of a wonderful sport will give it considerable value at the box offices of New York state picture houses. *Con.*

QUICKSANDS

Howard Hawks production, directed by Jack Conway. Story by Howard Hawks. Helene Chadwick and Richard Dix starred. Distributed by American Releasing Corp. Reviewed in projection room. Time, 70 minutes.

The Girl..............Helene Chadwick
The Boy..............Richard Dix
Ferrago..............Alan Hale
"Silent" Krupz..............Noah Beery
Colonel Paterson..............J. Farrell McDonald
Matt Patterson..............George Cooper
Sergeant Johnson..............Tom Wilson
Cupid..............Dick Sutherland
Farrell..............Hardee Kirkland
Bar-fly..............Lou King

A border story, timely, inasmuch as it deals with the smuggling of narcotics into this country across the Mexican line. Its cast of 10 names means something to the regulars. This, together with some real thrills and a couple of corking fights, as well as a wild ride to rescue by a regiment of United States cavalry, should put the picture over with a wallop with almost any type of audience, from the bigger first run houses to the little daily change theatres.

The story is strong in its romance and adventure and still has sufficient comedy relief.

Helene Chadwick is the daughter of one of the investigators of the U. S. Customs Service. She is assisting her father in uncovering the organized band which is bringing drugs in. Richard Dix is a young officer at a border army post. He falls in love with the girl. Later when he is sent into Mexico accompanied by two Mexican officers on a mission of investigation of a canteen, suspected of being the headquarters of the dope smugglers, he is puzzled by the resemblance of a girl that he sees there to his sweetheart. Especially when on his way home he makes an investigation of an old smithy and discovers a girl's clothes and wig, as well as his croix de guerre, which he presented to the girl. That leads him to the conclusion the girl that he is betrothed to is in league with the smugglers. He is about to resign his commission when word comes that the girl's father is held a prisoner by the gang and that the girl is trying to effect a rescue. The boy obtains leave to go to their assistance, unofficially.

At the finish the trio—father, daughter and lover—are all in the hands of the gang with the U. S. troopers riding to the rescue and arriving just in the nick of time.

The picture is well done in production and direction, as well as the cast, and should give general satisfaction. *Fred.*

THE GIRL I LOVED

Chicago, March 28.

Charles Ray production, presented by the United Artists, from the poem of James Whitcomb Riley and dedicated to Riley's memory. At the Barbee Loop, Chicago, March 24, 1923.

John Middleton..............Charles Ray
Mary..............Patsy Ruth Miller
Willie Brown..............Ramsey Wallace
Mother Middleton..............Edyth Chapman
Silas Gregg..............William Courtwright
Betty Short..............Charlotte Wood
Minister..............Lou Roff

A typical Charles Ray production with Ray doing the country lad, which is his best. It is quite as good as anything he has done from a standpoint of sentiment and the only thing that would make previous productions more attractive to the exhibitor is the comedy—there is a little comedy early in this photoplay when Ray is pictured as a boy, but little to bring laughs when he attains manhood. The subtitles are mostly lines from the poem.

It makes an interesting story, gripping, tear-bringing to those who cry easily. Charles Ray has no superior in pictures when it comes to portraying the unassuming, gawky, country lad.

In this picture he fails to get the girl of his choice. There are scenes where it looks for the time like he had told the girl (his adopted sister) that he loved her more than a brother and had fought the successful rival in her affections, but both turn out to be dreams. These two injected ideas bring sensation into the film. This quality is strengthened by a storm which the crowd fears will be a cyclone and a runaway team with Ray and his adopted sister in the spring wagon.

The scenes are all in the country. The costuming is in line with the period the poem was written. Ray's mother had the only organ in three counties. It is employed at a husking bee, interesting and entertaining, without given major comedy value.

Patsy Ruth Miller plays the girl charmingly. Ramsey Wallace is satisfactory as the successful rival. Edyth Chapman is excellent as the mother. *Loop.*

ENEMIES OF WOMEN

Special production from the novel of Vincent Blasco Ibanez. Much of the filming was done in France and on the Riviera by Cosmopolitan Productions. Directed by Alan Crosland. Multi-star cast headed by Lionel Barrymore, supported by Alma Rubens. Projection time, 2 hours, 10 minutes. Many sets by Urban and with special musical score by William Frederick Peters. Presented at the Central, New York, March $1 for an indefinite run.

Prince Lubimoff	Lionel Barrymore
Duchess Alicia	Alma Rubens
Her son	William Collier, Jr.
Atilio Castro	Pedro de Cordoba
Vittoria	Gladys Hulette
Spadoni	Garath Hughes

Others are Mario Majeroni, Paul Panzer, Betty Bouton and Ivan Linow.

"Enemies of Women" sets a high mark for sumptuous production and therein is its high spot of appeal. Its scenic gorgeousness is matched by some of the finest ensemble acting the screen has ever seen and there is an effectiveness of dramatic trickery that delivers half a dozen high power thrills. In addition the picture has a piquant title and the tremendous prestige of the Spanish author's name. These various elements of strength add up to a total that should assure wide public interest and clinch the box office success of the undertaking.

The one uncertain factor is the probable attitude of the feminine public toward the story itself. There are times when it strikes a false note, generally for two reasons, one a strained effort for merely theatrical effect as opposed to dramatic illusion and the other the character of the inverted romance.

One of the big scenes shows the Prince sardonically angered by the desertion of his friends who seek the companionship of women and ordering an elaborate festival in which he proposes to show them "the way to attract women." This episode develops into a sumptuous orgy or revel in the portico of the Prince's villa on the Mediterranean and pictorially and theatrically a magnificent bit of stage pageantry. But in the midst of the scene the Prince loads huge masses of jewels in a fountain basin and scatters them among his half naked women guests by an explosion under the collection. Much as you might be interested in the story situation, the very prodigality of the incident and its staging forcibly make you think "it's just a movie." It's a case of piling on fabulous detail until the illusion of it is spoiled if one has a sense of humor.

It is this quality of the picture that takes away from its power the tense and strained striving for theatrical effect that shall be more sensational than anything done before. Much of actual dramatic strength is missed for this very reason. They haven't time or footage to develop the story, so busy are they with making spectacles. For example there is a splendid play or story in the detail of the heroine being torn between the emotional conflict of choosing whether she shall confess that she has a 16-year-old son, or shall suffer under the unwarranted suspicion by her suitor that she is entertaining a young lover. This angle of the novel is scarcely touched upon, although it has all the elements of an exceedingly interesting play all in itself—probably indeed, a better play than the one they have chosen which deals with the adventures of a noble Russian libertine.

Most of Ibanez work has this curious attitude toward romance. This one takes a strangely cynical slant up until the finale when as a mere afterthought it is suddenly twisted into a mushy "happy ending" that fails utterly to convince.

The picture then will have to rest upon its splendid acting and upon its stunning scenic and pictorial beauty and these two factors probably will be ample. As indicated, the pageantry is wonderful and the scenic features—such as the settings at Monte Carlo and other places in the south of Europe—are marvelous in splendors of background and picturesqueness of settings. The scenes at the gaming tables were taken in the Casino itself and that the Prince's villa and gardens of the story are the properties of the Prince of Monaco himself, as the program states. It is easy to believe this is so for the villa scenes are marvelous beyond description.

The action take place during the 1914-18 period and a quantity of thrilling war shots have been cut in. Once again the program is convincing when it declares these pictures—sinking of ships by submarines, burning of air craft and battle scenes—have been taken from the archives of various governments. They have a world of kick.

Lionel Barrymore plays with his acknowledged authority the sinister princely wrecker of women's lives, but the palm of the picture goes to Alma Rubens as the Duchess Alicia. She has several emotional scenes—notably her reunion with her son and several passages with the Prince toward the end of the story in which she achieves some of the most eloquent pantomime of screen history. These few moments took hold of the auditor and accomplished the miracle of making a false and theatrical presentation something resembling a human document. Genuine emotional expression is rare in the picture medium and these gems of acting are therefore especially noteworthy.

Mr. Barrymore had a fine melodramatic moment to himself in a duel scene earlier in the evening, a splendidly mounted episode backed by a real situation, when he meets the Cossack brother of one of his victims and they fight it out with sabres in the snow-covered palace courtyard surrounded by the trappings and company of a fashionable ball. Another stirring episode was the fight between the Prince and a horde of Red Terrorists after the Russian revolution, another finely mounted directed scene with a high powered punch. *Rush.*

ONE NIGHT IN PARIS

French-made feature by Play-goers Pictures, released through Pathe. At Arena, New York, as one-half of double daily bill March 8.

"One Night in Paris" or a bad picture made worse might be a better name.

This is probably the champ chump among foreign made films, not worth express charges to send it over here. There's nothing in it, acting, direction or actors; just a jumble of junk.

A sad attempt to stand off the badness by English titles (written over here) only made the whole thing sadder.

If this is a usual sample of French-made pictures it might well be said that not only is the industry in its infancy in France; it even hasn't yet been born over there. Pathe must have taken it blindfolded. *Sime.*

SAFETY LAST

Harold Lloyd's latest release, comedy, with production by Hal Roach, distributed by Pathe. Billed in seven reels, picture running 6,300 feet in 61 minutes. Six shows daily for firm at Strand, New York, week April 1, with usual weekly Joseph Plunkett bill surrounding feature, consisting of Overture (1) with "Apple Blossoms" melody and tableaux, "Kiss in the Dark," Eldora Stanton, soprano; (2), short films billed as "Odds and Ends"; (3), orchestral and vocal numbers listed as "A Barnyard Episode," the house (a) orchestra opening with Dawn, (b) "The Rooster," Anatole Bourmann; (c) "Chick," Mlle. Chabelska, (d), "The Flapper," Mlle. Hermann (four performances daily); (4) Topical Review; (5), Madeleine MacGuigan, violinist, in three numbers; (6), feature; (7), Bray comic, "Col. Hoeza Liar, Burglar"; (8) Organ solo, Percy J. Starnes, Ralph S. Brainard, organists. (Mr. Plunkett produces entire program as presented and arranged at Strand.)

The Boy	Harold Lloyd
The Girl	Mildred Davis
The Pal	Bill Strother
The Law	Noah Young
The Floorwalker	Westcott B. Clarke
The Kid	Mickey Daniels
The Grandma	Anna Townsend

To one who has failed often to see the many Lloyd comedy films, it's just as easy to talk about him and his methods of fun making as it is to say that in "Safety Last" Hal Roach has a Harold Lloyd bear-cat for laughter or the box office.

This picture could open, say, in a city the size of Buffalo Sunday afternoon and before six o'clock Sunday evening everybody in town will have heard of it. That's the kind of a comedy it is. It's another kind besides, a money maker for its exhibitor as well as its producer.

For the reason that Goldwyn's "Souls for Sale" should be played by every picture house in this country because it sets forth Hollywood in its proper sphere, exactly so should "Safety Last" be universally played, for it will make all of the nation laugh.

This Lloyd high-class low comedy has thrills as well as guffaws, and the latter often happen in shrieks. At the Strand Monday night some children in the audience just screamed above the laughter of the entire capacity audience. Lloyd's worst enemy will have to laugh at some of the scenes. The picture's business in the laugh way is all new, adroitly worked in and of logical sequence, a story carrying the full film. It leads up to the big shrieks through Lloyd apparently climbing the outside wall to the top or 12th floor of a building, probably in Los Angeles. This bit, full of yells and "hows" as the photography turns toward comedy or danger, is chockerblock with trick camera work but so skilfully done or pieced it's questionable if versed picture people will detect all of it.

The comedy business of the department store where Lloyd is clerk nearly equals the remainder. There are so many bits in it that make laughs that two fun totals result about equally divided.

Lloyd as a small town boy leaves his sweetheart in the country, going to the city and obtains a $15-a-week position as a counter jumper. Back home the girl receives a little cheap piece of jewelry and believes Lloyd has made the great success he said he would in the big city. Upon the advice of her mother she goes there, to see that Lloyd doesn't squander all of his money on such baubles. Reaching the store, Lloyd, in an attempt to have her think he is the boss instead of a clerk, wanders into all kinds of complications, meanwhile cutting up didoes for the comedy side. It leads up to the building climbing, a plan suggested by the clerk to the general manager as a means of obtaining publicity for the firm. He gains a reward and the girl for a wife through successfully accomplishing it.

Lloyd, through this seven-reeler (although it may have been true of any of his others) looks like a picture staple in the comedy line for all time. Regardless of the script or scenario, Lloyd plays cleanly, without crudeness or uncouthness, for laughs, though it is low comedy. He also gets his effects without straining for them, working in quick laughs that are not builded up to. Whether it is Lloyd himself who does this or his director or writer, he is doing it here, and it's bound to hold him in the front ranks of all screen funny men, for there is nothing better on stage or screen than to be funny and clean. *Sime.*

WHERE THE PAVEMENT ENDS

Metro production by Rex Ingram based on the story, "The Passion Vine," by John Russell. Adaptation by Rex Ingram. John F. Seitz, photographer. Projection time, 70 minutes. At the Capitol, New York, week April 1.

Pastor Spener..............Edward Connelly
Mathilda..........................Alice Terry
Motauri........................Ramon Novarro
Capt. Hull Gregson..........Harry T. Morey
Napuka Joe........................John George

Now that Rex Ingram has done a South Seas tale it may be set down the last word has been said in pictorial beauty for the subject, and still much remains to be desired. The exotic story somehow doesn't convince. A handsome young native makes tropic love to the beautiful daughter of the missionary for five reels and she responds with romantic ardor for a like stretch of footage and then discards him, and in a minute romance goes bla. If the original intent was to make the wooing hectic it missed its purpose for the flawless but frigid beauty of Miss Terry defeats such an end.

The locale calls for vivid passion, but the mood of this whole picture is poetic romance and the two won't mix, do what Mr. Ingram will in photographic and scenic splendors. If the purpose has been to build a thrilling melodrama pure and simple the intent has somehow gone wrong. The forces of the story are mixed. In the end the powers of evil prevail and love fails to find a way. All of which turns romance inside out and leaves an unsatisfactory feeling. It isn't easy to see how it could have been made otherwise, for an ancient convention forbids a completed romance between a white heroine and a native of darker hue. It has been done in fiction, but the popular prejudice bars it from the screen.

But the director of "The Four Horsemen" has done theatrical and scenic marvels with his materials, however impossible they may be for story purposes. Some of the water and beach bits are exquisite, and the close-up portraits of the heroine are stunning in their soft and misted photography. Notable among the details are a series of under water shots showing the hero diving for pearls and almost within touching distance of a business-like shark as big as himself. However the trick was turned, it is thrillingly convincing. There is the hero and there is the shark. How they did it is something else again.

There are beautiful love passages with a frothing water falls as the backgrounds and a thrilling climb down the face of the waterfalls by the two lovers vainly seeking escape from the island. There is a spirited battle between the hero and a rum-sodden white trader also that has a kick, but the gloomy end of the picture in the suicide of the native lover leaves a disagreeable impression—an impression that negatives all the romance of the tale.

For another thing, the recital does not make plain the impulses which compel the girl to change her attitude toward the handsome son of the jungle. She accepts his wooing and responds to it. The mental and emotional processes by which she is alienated are not even hinted at. For all we know she cast off the boy by a mere whim. Ramon Novarro would be rather too conventionally and spiritually good-looking for a regular hero, but in these surroundings he is a picturesque figure, and his slim, boyish type furnishes effective symbolic contrast to the burly figure of the drunken trader who represents the evil influence of civilization among the primative people.

If sheer beauty of production can carry a production this one will make its way far but its story interest is likely to be mild. *Rush.*

GLIMPSES OF THE MOON

Allan Dwan production presented by Jesse Lasky, with Babe Daniels and Nita Naldi featured. Adapted by Lloyd Sheldon from the novel by Edith Wharton. Shown at the Rivoli, week April 1. Time 66 minutes.

Susan Branch.......................Bebe Daniels
Ursula Gillow..........................Nita Naldi
"Nick" Lansing...................David Powell
Fred Gillow.................Maurice Costello
Mrs. Ellie Vanderlyn......Rubye de Remer
"Streffy" (Lord Altringham)..Chas Gerrard
Bob Fulmer........................William Quirk
Grace Fulmer....................Pearl Sindelar

"Glimpses of the Moon," an outstanding novel, failed to make a picture. It is a long drawn out and exceedingly draggy story as told on the screen. Even though the cast is strong on names, there is a lack of punch to the feature. In the matter of sets the picture is almost overdone; it is almost all sets and no action. In direction Alan Dwan left much to be desired.

There is one thing interesting and that is, it has given Broadway a chance to glimpse one of the earliest stars of the silent drama in Maurice Costello who plays the much abused husband. Nita Naldi has the heavy vamp portion, while Bebe Daniels is the poor relative who finally wins the struggling young author, played by David Powell.

All the sympathy is in the Daniels role and the little star made the most of it. Miss Naldi vamped all over the place and overacted considerably. Rubye de Remer's blonde beauty was happily selected for the "cheating wife" and was the correct contrast to the brunet Bebe and Nita.

The story is an out and out society affair. Susan Branch is the poor young society relative, tolerated by her wealthier relatives and given their cast off frocks to wear as long as she acts as a buffer for them. She is in love with and loved by a young author, likewise poor but of the socially elect. Ursula Gillow with whom Susan is living also loves the young writer and utilizes Susan to cover her attentions to him, because she has a husband who is a good provider, with the result that when Susan marries the writer Ursula is furious. Later upon the death of her husband she tries to make a deal with Susan to give up her husband to her for a consideration that will make Susan independent for life. A divorce is arranged. At the last minute husband and wife realize they are still in love with each other and decide to struggle along even though they will have to do so in comparative poverty.

Seemingly with the material at hand a much better screen version of "Glimpses of the Moon" could have been provided. Now it just ranks with the ordinary program feature. *Fred.*

CAN A WOMAN LOVE TWICE?

Problem play with melodramatic trimmings in five reels. Produced by Robertson Cole and released by Film Booking Offices. Running time, 70 minutes.

"Can a Woman Love Twice?" stars Ethel Clayton. It's a mixture of good and bad, like most program pictures of its type, holding an appeal sure for neighborhood houses. War stuff arriving along about the middle, and just enough to make it interesting, adds life where it is needed. A child actress, Muriel Dana, as a little boy, gives the always desirable touch of heart interest. This little girl has a future.

The story treats of a boy supposedly killed in the war returning to find a woman has passed herself off on his father as his widow. A convenient similarity of names permits of the deception, the woman being the widow of another soldier who was killed. The woman's real husband has folks who are ritzy, and they readily believe a tale about the woman told them by a private detective. The woman's real husband's parents want to get possession of the child, and that's the reason the woman practiced the deception.

The plot is clear enough and carries until the end, when the usual apple sauce arrives. An explosion of dynamite adds a thrill near the finish. Al Hart is the father of the supposedly dead soldier and plays well. Malcolm McGregor is the answer to the query which constitutes the title, "Can a Woman Love Twice?" She can, according to the picture.

The Laura Jean Libbey title is an asset, which should mean money at the box office. Direction satisfactory without anything standing out. *Bell.*

FOOTLIGHT RANGER

William Fox production, starring Charles Jones. Story by Dorothy Yost, direction by Scott Dunlop. At Loew's New York, N. Y., double feature bill, March 27. Time, 50 minutes.

Bill Moreland......................Charles Jones
Janet Ainslee...................Fritzi Brunette
Al Brownley.........................James Mason
Nellie Andrews...............Lillian Langdon
Miss Amelia..........Lydia Yeamans Titus
David Marsh.....................Henry Barrows

This is just another one of those stories the fillums love. A tale that tries to prove Broadway is all bad and to succeed on the stage a girl must part with everything. In the end she goes back to the little rube town on the same train with the honest hard-working young feller who rescues her from the angel-villain's arms at the precise moment he wanted to collect in advance for backing a show that was to make her a Broadway star. It's the old, old hoak, done again, and as it was good in the past it is just as good today as far as the smaller houses are concerned.

The story was written by Dorothy Yost, who seems to have the faculty of putting over thread-worn originals at the Fox plant. It was directed by Scott Dunlop, who did about as good as could be expected with the material.

Charles Jones has the sympathetic role of the poor but honest lad in a small town who parts with his dogs to get the money to carry a stranded troupe of show girls back to their home town, and is so inspired by the glowing picture of the big town painted by one of the girls he decides to follow. He does, and gets a job as a structural steel worker. This affords the only thrill. Two girders are being hoisted and there is a man astride each. The chains holding one slip, and Jones, who is riding the other, swings over and effects a rescue at a cost to himself which means a stay in the hospital. While he is lying injured on the street his actress friend sees him, and after that she starts sending flowers to the hospital. When he recovers he calls at the theatre to thank her and is informed that he has been taking her too seriously.

That same night the angel takes her to a questionable road house for dinner in a private dining room, but the stage veteran roommate of the girl seeks out the poor but honest admirer and has him on the ground in time to save the day.

There is nothing about the picture that will start any box office riots, but it is one of those little safe bets that fits on a double program. *Fred.*

BRAWN OF THE NORTH

First National production presented by Laurence Trimble and Jane Murfin, photography by C. B. Dreyer. Proctor's 23d Street, New York, March 31.

Marion Wells............................Irene Rich
Peter Coe.........................Lee Shumway
Howard Burton.................Joseph Barrel
Lester Wells........Roger James Manning
The Missionary................Phillip Hubbard
The Missionary's Wife..........Jean Metcalf
The Vamp..............................Lady Silver
Brawn...............................Strongheart

Conventional story of the north draped around the police dog "Strongheart." The picture is probably the cheapest from an expenditure angle First National has produced, consisting in mostly outdoor shots and a few interiors.

The dog and a pack of about five trained wolves provide whatever merit this feature possesses. The story itself is a stereotyped unfolding of the experience of Marion Wells (Irene Rich) after she journeys to the northland to join her sweetheart and brother who have prospected a gold mine.

The fiance for no reason at all unless it is the cold, turns villanous, maltreating the dog and cutting up generally. A fight between the two men results in the drowning of the brother who staggers about a half a mile, backwards, before he topples overboard. This bit was ridiculous. The villian is rolled into the water in a thrilling fight with the dog but turns up later for more villiany, none the worse for the immersion. The first part is heavily padded and lacks interest but the shots in which the wolves are visible, are real thrillers.

Marion and her reformed cave man husband (Lee Shumway) start for the settlement with their baby. They are "mushing" it with a log team. The trio are pursued by a pack of famished wolves, made bold through hunger and a lean winter. An attack by the wolves on the sleeping camp of the travelers was realistic.

"Brawn's" reversion to type and seeking his mate, a full grown female timber wolf, with the ensuing love making, will interest all dog lovers. His rescue of the baby from the pack of wolves, after the parents had been diverted elsewhere, was another high light.

The photography was excellent with exteriors of snow scenes and winter stuff. This and the splendid performance of the police dog will insure "Brawn of the North" as an interesting photoplay. *Con.*

FOURTH MUSKETEER

Walker-Caldwell production releasing through Film Booking Offices. Story by H. C. Witwer, featuring Johnnie Walker with W. K. Howard directing and L. O'Connell cameraman. Time, 65 minutes. At Proctor's 58th Street, March 26.

Taken from Witwer's story in the Cosmopolitan magazine, this film is of the sporting type, narrating the family woes of a prize-fighter. Somewhat rearranged from the original story the picture shapes up as having more than an equal chance of getting across if not too adequately prolonged. It is understood there are more screen presentations to come from this author's pen. The tendency to "dog it" is this particular release's own worst enemy.

Generally framed for comedy, the transposition to the screen is minus the phrasing of Witwer upon which his stories are so dependent. It is surprisingly so that the subtitles read as being not of his originating. Were he to write his own captions, and if he does, to thence cut loose a bit more, it would seem a valuable addition to these episodes, although the producers may figure Witwer's literal expressions too fast or too wise for the average screen patron. Certainly they would provide many a laugh where the opportunities are now lacking.

Assisting Walker are Eileen Percy and Eddie Gribbon. The latter stands out in his characterization of the popular conception of just what a manager of a battler should be. The picture is neatly produced with the camera work up to scratch.

The tale has to do with Brian O'Brien, pugilist, married and about to embark upon his final ring scrimmage to obtain sufficient money to buy a garage, as per instructions from his wife. His opponent, made desperate by a failing mother, makes advances to O'Brien to "lay down" in the scrap, which our hero refuses to do. After scoring a knockout, O'Brien calls around and slips the defeated rival his own winning percentage of the winner-take-all receipts, and the garage thing is off until the garage owner, figuring a guy who would do that may be trusted, says he'll take his note.

Prospering as a mechanic, O'Brien's wife begins to carry on with herself and dives in for the social side, much to the chagrin of her provider, who is strong for the idea of children. She figuratively leaves him flat until he can get his picture in the dailies, which makes the opening for his defeat of two stick-up men and the recovery of the lost pearls. Spurning a reward from the society matron, from whom the jewels were taken, O'Brien (always obsessed with Dumas' "Musketeer" tale) kneels and kisses her hand, which gives the newspaper boys present the "hunch" for a story and the negative on the front page, with the photo bringing the wife back.

Taking more time to run than the average features consume in the first run houses, this picture loses value and some 15 minutes or more might be deleted. The work of the cast is efficient with Walker lending a neat, youthful appearance to the role, besides playing it capably.

Skig.

THE TENTS OF ALLAH

Encore Production presented by E. A. MacManus. Story by Charles Logue, who was also responsible for direction. Monte Blue and Mary Alden featured. Shown at Loew's New York, New York, double feature bill, March 27. Distributed by Associated Exhibitors. Time, 72 minutes.

The Girl....................Mary Thurman
The Berber Caid....................Monte Blue
His Mother....................Mary Alden
Sultan of Morocco....................Macey Hallam

A long drawn out desert story that finishes without a real ending. One is in doubt at the final fade out what it is all about. That is rather unfortunate, for the first picture this little producing organization turned out in Porto Rico proved highly enjoyable. This one, however, does not come up to the standard of the previous production, either in the matter of story or direction. Incidentally at this late date desert stuff has had its vogue and the features with the racing Arabian steeds and grains of sand no longer have the appeal. As a picture for the regular run of picture houses that change daily it will get by, but that is about all. The feature is altogether too long; both the story and action are exceedingly draggy.

The scene is laid in Tangiers, where the niece of the American Consul commits a breach of etiquette on a feast day of the natives and incurs their anger. A desert rider rescues her from the mob about to do her harm. Later she is kidnapped by some of the natives and taken into the desert. Her uncle cables for a battleship and the marines are sent into the desert to effect a rescue. The Sultan gives his consent because he recognizes the commanding officer as one who years before took a woman from his harem.

In the desert the camp of the Berbers is discovered, the girl rescued and the young Caid guarding her taken prisoner.

Then the big disclosure—the captured Berber is none other than the son of the American officer. The latter, instead of permitting the Sultan's troops to put the prisoner to death, allows him to escape and resigns his commission, for the mother of the boy appears on the scene and discloses his identity.

The finish is brought about through the Sultan offering the exnaval officer command of a sailing vessel. Once he is aboard, makes him captive to torture him. The Berber son being apprised of the situation comes to the rescue of his father and mother, but the father dies within a few minutes after he is saved from the Sultan's hands. At the finish the boy and his mother ride into the desert again as the picture closes.

A notable lack of love interest is apparently one of the most glaring faults of the picture. The sets indicate that considerable money must have been spent on the production, but sets do not make a picture these days.

Fred.

NOBODY'S BRIDE

Universal society-crook melodrama starring Herbert Rawlinson, with Alice Lake featured. Story by Evelyn Campbell. Directed by Herbert Blache. Shown at Loew's Circle, double feature bill, April 3, 1923. Time, 52 minutes.

Jimmie Nevins....................Herbert Rawlinson
Doris Standish....................Edna Murphy
Mary Butler....................Alice Lake
Morgan....................Harry von Meyer
Charlie....................Frank Brownlee
Smithy....................Sidney Bracey
Cyrus W. Hopkins....................Phillips Smalley
Uncle Peter....................Robert Dudley

Fairly interesting society-crook melodrama that will satisfy the fans in the average daily change of program houses, especially those where the double feature programs are in vogue. Otherwise to describe it would be to say that it is a little better than the average type of Universal program feature and that it fairly bristles with action.

Herbert Rawlinson is starred, and in his support as featured player is Alice Lake. The latter gains practically all the sympathy in the story, playing a woman crook whose love dreams come to naught, and she finally suffers death at the hands of a crook admirer, who shoots her.

The story has Rawlinson as a young society man, who, through the loss of money by his father, is forced to forego his more wealthy friends and become a tramp. He is on the verge of starving when the lady crook of the story takes him into her apartment and feeds him offering him the use of the apartment while she is away for a time. Later he is pressed into service to drive a car for the crooks, who have planned to make away with the wedding presents at a social May and December union. He is waiting outside the house to run the car for the lady crook, whom he believes to be an artist who has been engaged to sketch the bride, when out walks the girl who was to have been wedded and to whom he was engaged in his more prosperous days. She is carrying the grip in which the crooks had parked their loot and, of course, he has to take her on her way.

Believing that they had been double-crossed the crooks hoof it back to their apartment and to their surprise their car is standing before the door. Then when they discover that the bride that was to be is also their guest they make a demand for ransom, after they have knocked the hero cold. In the end, however, he manages to bring about a settlement of their demands and just as the money is to be paid over the coppers make a round-up of the whole party with a little gun powder being spilt.

It's the type of film fodder that the middle class type of fans like and it will get by with them.

Fred.

TRUXTON KING

William Fox production starring John Gilbert. Adapted by Paul Schofield from the George Barr McCutcheon novel of the same title. Directed by Jerome Storm. Show at Fox's Academy, March 29-31. Time 64 minutes.

Truxton King....................John Gilbert
Lorraine....................Ruth Clifford
Count Marlanx....................Frank Leigh
Prince Robin....................Mickey Moore
Hobbs....................Otis Harlan
Count Carlos von Enge....................John Miller
John Tullis....................Richard Wayne
Olga Platanova....................Winifred Bryson
William Spanz....................Willis Marks
Baron Dangloss....................Mark Fenton

One of the Graustark series of stories and ranks about on a par with any of them adopted to the screen. As a costume production it holds an unusual romantic interest and it is will played and directed. John Gilbert who is starred plays the role of the American who mixes into politics in Graustark and saves the boy king from the plans of the revolutionists, who plan his overthrow. The feature is a slight shade better than the average Fox program production and it will interest any type of audience in almost any locality.

In handling the direction Jerome Storm takes his story along with a purpose that holds the interest at all times. He has not permitted his sets to overshadow his story and the action is at all times consistent.

Gilbert gives an interesting performance that will please the fans and Ruth Clifford is charming playing opposite him. Mickey Moore as the boy king gives really a decidedly worth while performance going after his role with a seriousness of purpose that makes it stand out.

The balance of the cast was carefully selected and Otis Harlan was very much among those present getting some comedy out of his role.

Fred.

MAN FROM GLENGARRY

Ernest Shipman production distributed through Hodkinson. Made from a novel by Ralph Connor; adapted by Faith Green; scenario by Kenneth O'Hara; directed by Henry McRae; editing by Elmer McGovern. In projection room March 15.

Big MacDonald....................Anders Randolph
Renald MacDonald....Warner P. Richmond
Rev. Alexander Murray.....Harlan Knight
Kate Murray, his daughter..Marion Swayne
Louis Lenoir....................E. L. Fernandez
Eugene St. Clair....................Jack Newton
Mamie St. Clair....................Pauline Garon
Frank De Lacey....................Frank Badgley
Colonel Thorpe....................William Colvin
Kerstin McLeod....................Marion Lloyd

Smashing melodramatic action picture of the northern logging camps, with magnificent scenic features, but losing something of its force through an unconvincing story management. As long as the story is confined to the outdoors and the lumber camp locale it is intensely interesting, but it goes to pieces when they ring in the city and polite characters. Then it becomes merely a mushy, naive moral preachment.

Ralph Connor somehow manages to make his sermons plausible when he is writing, but this translation to the screen loses his virility of style and his sincerity. He is best outdoors among rough, rugged men, and this departure into Ottawa and business intrigue is piffle.

The story interest centers in the affairs of "Big" MacDonald and his son, bosses of a big Canadian lumber camp, hard fighting Scots, but reined into tight control by their domgatic religious beliefs. A renegade French-Canadian bully, boss of a Godless neighboring camp, is consantly inviting "Big Mac" to a frolicsome fight and "Mac" is restrained by the preacher.

Lenoir, the bully, finally forces a fight on the Scot, and in the melee "Mac" is killed, leaving a blood feud upon his son. Meanwhile the winter supply of logs has been assembled and the drive down the river to Ottawa is about to begin. Lenoir gets away first, and by the time "Young Mac," who has avoided a fight due to the pleadings of his sweetheart, daughter of the minister, reaches the lower river it has been blocked by the mischievous Lenoir.

The rival gangs have been spoiling for a battle to settle old scores, and here is the opportunity. The combat is splendidly worked up for dramatic effect, and when it comes it's a whale. It takes place in the middle of the broad river, with the bobbing logs as the only footing, and pictorially it has high voltage. To give it added kick the heroine is brought to the scene, and in an effort to get to the struggling men and prevent a murder she falls between the grinding logs as they draw near a boiling torrent of water. Alternate views of the white rapids and the progress of the girl toward destruction work up fine tension, until the hero rescues the girl just at the brink of the whirlpool.

That is the high point, and it is abundant for punch. There are two more reels of anti-climax dealing with the schemes of a lumber king to force the hero to aid him in a crooked deal, his virtuous refusal and a thoroughly unconvincing reformation of Lenoir, which isn't especially important anyhow. The film ought to end as soon after the big fight as possible. Every foot thereafter adulterates its kick.

Rush.

THE TIGER'S CLAW

Paramount release, featuring Jack Holt and presented by Jesse L. Lasky. Joseph Henabery the director, Jack Cunningham credited with the story and Faxon Dean at the camera. Time, 55 minutes. At the Rivoli, New York, week March 18.

Sam Sandell....................Jack Holt
Harriet Halehurst....................Eva Novak
Henry Frazer Halehurst...George Periolat
Raj Singh....................Bertram Grassby
Chamell Brentwood....................Aileen Pringle
Sathoo Ram....................Karl Stockade
George Malvin....................Frank Butler

Nothing much more than an average feature serving as a fair to middling vehicle for the star. It is standard in all respects as concerns the usual fundamentals of photography, settings, directing, etc.

A couple of thrills are included by means of a tiger's attack, first upon Jack Holt and then Eva Novak towards the end. Both incidents are favorably handled. Also the blasting of a dam which permits of rushing water over much foliage.

Nothing specifically to be commended; neither anything to be flagrantly condemned. Hence, it may be classified as the parallel of a first-run house headliner.

The story is that of Sam Sandell, an American, supervising the construction of a dam in India. The long sojourn brings about his marriage to a half-caste following a misunderstanding with his fiance back home. Harriet Halehurst, the girl, eventually goes to the locality for the main purpose of smoothing over the breach but runs into the marriage situation and tries to make the best of it.

A conspiracy between a Hindoo magician, who sees his power over the natives waning, and a brown-skinned youth, previously in love with the American's native wife, results in a plot to destroy the construction work and let loose the waters, along with the death of the white girl and her father. To gain this objective the initial move is to place Sandell under the influence of a drug which keeps him in a continuous mental daze.

The former sweetheart takes it upon herself to arouse Sandell from the influence under which he has fallen and coincidentally aided by a timely attack from a tiger, with the engineer the rescuer, achieves her purpose. The discovery of the plot and the saving of the girl and her parent follows along with the death of the half-caste from a shot intended for Sandell.

The cast does adequately and for those who like Holt his playing will appease. *Skig.*

THE BOLTED DOOR

Universal starring Frank Mayo. Story by George Gibbs, script by George Randolph Chester. Directed by William Worthington. Shown at the 42d Street Theatre, N. Y., double feature bill, March 19, 1923. Running time, 53 minutes.

Brooke Garriott..............Frank Mayo
Oliver Judson..............Chas. A. Stevenson
Natalie Judson..............Phyllis Haver
Rene De Land..............Nigel Barrie

One of the eternal triangle affairs, handled somewhat differently, and as presented the continuity carries a certain suspense that will hold almost any audience. Frank Mayo, starred, gives his usual sterling performance, while Nigel Barrie as the heavy handles the action opposite him effectively. Phyllis Haver is the leading woman and fills the picture nicely.

The story is that of a young society girl who carries out her uncle's wishes in regard to marriage to obtain the fortune he has left her. She stipulates her husband must leave her immediately after the ceremony. That accounts for "The Bolted Door" title. After a time, especially when word is received she has lost her fortune, she makes a comparison between her society friends and her husband, and concludes the latter is more desirable.

Mayo does the husband effectively and puts up a corking fight with Barrie, which is one of the principal action points.

The direction is such as to hold the suspense from the beginning. The society stuff is especially well handled. *Fred.*

THE MIDNIGHT GUEST

A Universal starring Grace Darmond. Story and script by Rupert Julian. Directed by George Archinbaud. Shown at Loew's Circle, double feature bill, March 17, 1923. Five reels.

Gabrielle..............Grace Darmond
John Dryden..............Mahlon Hamilton
William Chatfield..............Clyde Fillmore
Monk..............Pat Harmon
Aunt Sally..............Mathilde Brundage

One of those stories like a hundred others. A guttersnipe type of crook, a girl, is caught in a wealthy man's home at midnight, becomes a lady in a day, wears a million dollars' worth of clothes and has everyone fall in love with her. It is the usual old-fashioned bunk, good for the 5-10 houses.

Not only is the story trite and old-fashioned but the acting is likewise. Grace Darmond, who plays the lead, does a fashion parade all by herself, and that is about the best thing that she does do in the picture. Mahlon Hamilton acted as though he didn't know what to do when he was supposed to characterize a drunk and that seemed strange for him. The only one in the picture that gave a performance that was at all away from the ordinary was Clyde Fillmore.

The direction also was just of the ordinary caliber. In sets, however, the picture looked like a lot of money had been spent in an effort to get a story over that wasn't "there."

There is just one word that is necessary to classify this production—"ordinary." *Fred.*

'NTH COMMANDMENT

Cosmopolitan production, adapted for the screen by Frances Marion from the Fannie Hurst story. Directed by Frank Borsage. Released by Paramount. Shown at the Rivoli, N. Y., week of April 8. Time, 80 minutes.

Sarah Juke..............Colleen Moore
Harry Smith..............James Morrison
Jimmie Fitzgibbons..............Eddie Phillips
Angine Sprunt..............Charlotte Merriam
Max Plute..............George Cooper

This production starts out as a corking comedy drama, but becomes draggy as it proceeds, and finally rather wearisome. It seems as though in an attempt to make something of the story that looked like a point a shooting of footage was continued until there was just too much footage and not enough story. However, the comedy touches in the early section will go a long way towards putting it over. There is no one starred, but Colleen Moore makes a fairly interesting character out of Sarah Juke. The balance of the cast is also very well selected.

The tale is based on the fact that occasionally in every one's life a situation arises that isn't covered by the Ten Commandments, and, therefore, the Nth Commandment, which is to suffer and sacrifice for love, is called in to meet the situation.

It is a story of love in the basement of a department store, with Sarah Juke as the girl selling corsets, in love with and loved by Harry Smith, behind the wrapping counter. Jimmie Fitzgibbons, the song demonstrator, also has a crush on Sarah, but she marries Harry and goes to live in a little flat. Harry develops the "con," and Sarah has to go back to work to support her husband and baby. The husband, according to the doctor's orders, must be taken out of the New York climate before the snow flies. The wife finally turns to Jimmie for help. Jimmie has made his mark as a song writer and has coin and a letch to "get" Sarah, but Sarah gets him for $300 and Harry is sent to California, where Sarah and the baby join him later for a happy ending to the story.

In the direction the punches are the comedy scenes in the basement of the department store, the roller skating rink and finally the big cabaret scene. There are laughs in all of these three sections, but the roller rink is the strongest. Nothing is overlooked in the way of flops and falls to get it over.

James Morrison plays Smith and gives a corking performance, while Eddie Phillips is "the he flapper" heavy and contributes much. He is the type and perfect. Charlotte Merriam slips over a clever conception of the gum-chewing type of salesgirl who becomes a Broadway show girl.

As a box office picture "The Nth Commandment" is not going to show any heavy results, but as passing entertainment it will serve nicely. *Fred.*

THE GO-GETTER

Cosmopolitan production (Paramount), made from the Saturday Evening Post story by Peter B. Kyne of the same name, being one of the "Cappy Ricks" series. Scenario by John Lynch. Director, E. H. Griffith. Projection time, 64 minutes. At the Rialto, New York, April 8.

Bill Peck..............T. Roy Barnes
Mary Skinner..............Seena Owen
Cappy Ricks..............William Norris
Charles Skinner..............Tom Lewis
Daniel Silver..............Louis Wolheim
Jack Morgan..............Fred Santley
Joe Ryan..............John Carr
Hugh McNair..............Frank Currier

A first-class comedy-drama, with fine human interest, a wealth of cinema action and good romance. The humor is neatly turned, and something of the flavor of the story is retained in the transcription to the screen. For one thing, it is the best work T. Roy Barnes has ever done before the camera. There is a world of charm about the character of Bill Peck, the courageous go getter of salesmanship, although the scenario somehow misses its sentimental import.

That passage of the story that went into the wartime morale and the recital of Bill's fine old military chief, who replied to orders, "It shall be done," is absent, but in its place there is an effective substitute in a post-war hospital that is truly affecting when Bill takes farewell of his wounded buddies.

As a straightaway action picture with comedy slants the picture does well. It is one of those stories where sentimental values are masked under a comic exterior which intensifies the sympathetic quality and heightens the humor at the same time.

The situation of the rather "fresh" salesman sent off on a wild goose chase is absurd. But the spectacle of the lame veteran who carries on in the face of weariness and distress, even on a ridiculous job, commands honest sympathy. A screen hero with a background of comedy is a cheerful innovation. You can't help but like him.

The story values are proof against some spots of indifferent direction and poorly managed mechanics. One passage—Bill's flight in an airplane —was obviously faked, and there are scenes in a railroad train where the photography of lighting is crude. But the human interest of the chronicle outweighs the imperfections and carries the picture triumphantly. It is such a refreshing experience to find human beings in pictures!

William Norris played Cappy Ricks as a farcical type of bewhiskered old man and worked all the old props. His staginess was an irritating false note throughout; but Tom Lewis, as Skinner, Ricks' grouchy general manager, was a joy throughout. Lewis is a comedy find. Seena Owen was only a graceful, easy leading woman.

Bill Peck is discharged from the army hospital and goes in search of a job. Cappy Ricks hires him and gives him the toughest job he can find. Bill gets away with it, but in a way that displeases Cappy. So Bill is fired, but hired again. Cappy needs a strong business man for a China post, and by way of testing Bill gives him the task of buying a certain blue vase, having planted a hundred difficulties in the way.

Bill starts blithely to execute the mission, but the vase is stolen and Bill has to knock out two thugs to get it back. Then he has to get an airplane and catch up with a railroad flyer to deliver it in time, only to find that he has been hoaxed. But he wins out on the job and thereby wins Mary, Skinner's daughter. And the telling is a mighty interesting and amusing affair. *Rush.*

TRAILING AFRICAN WILDS

Martin Johnson travel picture made in Africa. Released through Metro. Shown at New theatre Baltimore, Md., week of April 15, 1923. Time, about 80 minutes.

Baltimore, April 18.

"Trailing African Wilds," the Martin Johnson travel film, now on view at the New theatre, is the most interesting camera excursion into the jungles ever witnessed in this city. The Snow picture, "Hunting Big Game in Africa," which recently made a sensation in New York, has not yet visited Baltimore. Those who have seen both films, however, declare that the Johnson film rivals it in excellence and predict that it will rival it in popularity.

Although the Johnson film proceeds in a rather leisurely fashion, it holds one's interest throughout and offers many moments of entertainment of a highly informative nature. Many strange animals are introduced by name.

Among the interesting bits of information imparted by the film are: Ostrichs don't seek refuge by poking their heads under ground; about 40,000,000 healthy zebras are residing in East Africa; the Grievy zebra is more aristocratic than the common variety because he dresses in stylish narrow stripes, while the more lowly classes go in for "loud," broad stripes; the giraffe is a long-distance drinker and often attains the height of 18 feet, and the tick bird is regarded with great friendliness in African circles because it proves such an efficient instrument for housekeeping among the larger beasts of the jungles.

Leon Victor of the Metro is exploiting the picture. It opened Monday night to a capacity audience which included some of the most representative men and women of Baltimore.

For two years the Johnsons, accompanied by a large number of very black and very undressed natives who formed the "sofari," braved the dangers of endless deserts and even more endless forests for the purpose of making a photoplay of big game. It is said that many of the species caught by their cameras are even now verging toward complete extinction. Doubtless Mrs. Johnson's omnipresent cuteness even in the face of a charging elephant scared half of them to death. Writing without exaggerating, Mrs. Johnson doesn't seem to know what the word "fear" means. In the film you see her astride a lion much as if the king of beasts were no more than a humble donkey. What is more, you see her chasing a herd of hungry elephants half way from the Cape to Cairo, taking an afternoon stroll with an upper class zebra, shooting a tiger from her tent door, much as a thousand and one other things which no sensible woman has any right to do.

More than 100,000 feet of film were exposed during the period the Johnsons sojourned in British East Africa. Every known and unknown kind of wild animal was photographed. Of this tremendous footage only six reels have been retained. In consequence the photoplay contains what are perhaps the most vivid and exciting scenes of animal life that have ever been obtained. That Mr. and Mrs. Johnson are alive to tell the tale must remain one of the world's great mysteries.

Nairobi, in British East Africa, was the starting point of the expedition. Then over swamps, on deserts, through territory rarely visited by human beings, until the goal, Lake Paradise, was reached.

Here the climax of the picture, the elephant hunt with the tremendous beasts charging straight into the camera, was photographed, and it's a thriller. This scene alone is worth going to the New theatre to see. In its own particular way it is just as exciting as Harold Lloyd's climb in "Safety Last" to the top of that twelve-story building, and a good deal more believable. There are times when truth is stranger than fiction, after all. "Trailing African Wild Animals" is one of these.

A fine picture—interesting, informative and exciting. *Sisk.*

BELLA DONNA

Famous Players production. Pola Negri starred with Conway Tearle, Conrad Nagel and Lois Wilson featured. Directed by George Fitzmaurice. Adapted from the Robert Hichens novel by Ouida Bergere. First American made production presenting Negri, with her last screen display over here, "Mad Love," German-made. At Rivoli, New York, week of April 15. Running time, about 60 minutes.

Bella Donna....................Pola Negri
Mahmoud Bardoudi........Conway Tearle
Nigel Armine................Conrad Nagel
Mr. Chepstow...............Adolphe Menjou
Dr. Meyer Isaacson..........Claude King
Patricia........................Lois Wilson
Ibrahim.......................Macey Harlam
Dr. Hartley..................Robert Schable

A simple tale for simple people but certain to fill the eye and mind of the usual picture house patrons. That makes "Bella Donna" good for the box office, although Pola Negri seems to have some peculiar draw over here. Whether it was lately gained through publicity or that the sex-mad public believes Negri is symbolic of the diabolical is just guesswork.

The Hichens book was to book-readers what "The Sheik" was to the flapper. "Bella Donna" got a big rave among the novel buyers with its tale of the desert. If the **picture does it justice or an injustice could be stated by a reader of the book, but without having read it the hazard is the story is not nearly as strong in its picturizing as the book was in print.**

The trade matter of note is that this American-made production gives Negri what she never before has had, a production and a personal presence. The Famous Players has dressed up Negri. When that foreign girl first saw this complete picture with herself in the centre of it she must have been paralyzed with delight, after thinking back to what she got as a production in Germany.

They have improved upon Negri in appearance, that through make-up and clothes but they didn't improve upon her methods of registration. As in "Mad Love," Negri still registers like a taxiclock, either too fast or not at all. Her scheme for anguish appears to be a line drawn across her cheek and a drop of glycerine under the left eye. One-eyed criers are new over here.

But as a vamp in "Bella Donna," Pola will make you forget the others, although the male vamp in the same picture, Conway Tearle as the Egyptian mogul, does her dirt at the finish. Walking out on her English husband and turned down by her lover, Bella Donna goes into a row boat, rows over to the desert and flounders along through some nice new sand until a tiger or a jackal sees her. What a tiger or jackal or Bella was doing in that part of the desert just then is picture stuff, but the animal must have gotten Bella out there in her semi-evening clothes, for the screen shut off right there. The whole scene looked suspiciously like Coney Island Creek just before the kids break up the sand dunes, but of course it wasn't Coney whether phoney or not.

The best part of the film is where Mahmond Baroudi (Mr. Tearle) refuses to accept Bella Donna as a plaster; he tells her he isn't in the business of wife-stealing, especially from the English, and this after he had vamped Bella to the limit, and sent her back home in a sand storm while he lolled around the parlor's fireplace. There must have been three or four barrels of sand used for the storm. Also one camel. And Pola knows how to get off a camel even if the picture doesn't show her getting on.

The story has been hashed up in a hundred ways but maybe in the woods it isn't the apple sauce it looks in Times square.

The Fitzmaurice direction prevented any flaws in that particular although there are a number of scenes abruptly cut off as though that were a better scheme than retakes. Some of the Egyptian scenes were elaborate and some of them had Little Egypts in them. Tearle became the commanding figure with his Sheik role and matter but if that will make the women love him more than they do now, it won't be his fault. Lois Wilson as the fiancee of the English sap who married Bella made the sweetest picture, the only relief from the villainy of Bella and the smartness of Baroudi.

If the Famous is out to make Negri the star vamp of pictures, this feature will give her a big start as a Famous star. Once in a while they might allow her to follow her own notions in acting, now that she has been over here for some time and should have a fair impression of the American idea. *Sime.*

DADDY

First National feature presented by Sol. Lesser, starring Jackie Coogan. Directed by E. Mason Hopper. At the Strand, New York, April 15, 1923. Time, 60 minutes.

Jackie Savelli (afterwards Jackie Holden), Jackie Coogan
Paul Savelli.....................Arthur Carewe
Helene Savelli...............Josie Sedgewick
Cesare Gallo.....................Cesare Gravini
Eben Holden....................Bert Woodruff
Mrs. Holden....................Anna Townsend
Impresario.......................William Lewis
Valet..................................George Kuwa
Mildred................................By Herself

Jackie Coogan is back on the screen again in his bedraggled little sweater, oversized panties and his battered cap at a rakish angle over an ear in "Daddy." It is Jackie Coogan that made his mark in "The Kid" that has come back to pictures instead of the Jackie that appeared in the Dickens stories. The youngest of screen stars in this picture is back to where he belongs and where he will endear himself again to thousands of kiddie film fans and their elders.

The couple of pictures young Coogan did based on Dickens subjects did not do exceedingly well at the box office. This one, however, should bring the youngster that wave of popularity which greeted his co-appearance with Chaplin. It's a made-to-order story for the youngster. He has a chance to work for comedy in innumerable places, and there are at least a score of corking big laughs in his work. Together with that he is also given opportunity to display some of the weep-compelling tricks that he did in his first picture.

After the groundwork of the story is laid, with Jackie represented as a babe in arms in the earlier scenes, a lapse of six years brings the star in for his first appearance—he's milking a cow and feeding the milk via the bottle route to a suckling pig. From then on it is pathos and laughter all the way to the finish.

Jackie's dad in the story was a **well-known violinist. Mother was jealous of his attention to pupils and walked out on him. She goes back to the home town and is taken in by poor farmers, who were friends. She dies and Jackie remains with the old couple until they are forced out of their home and into a poor farm. Jackie runs away and comes to the big city, where he meets a street violinist, who takes him in. The old man teaches Jackie to develop his natural talent for the violin, and finally the boy's dad and he come together for a happy ending.**

It stands as a story with the old Horatio Alger tales; it is as full as it can be of convenient coincidences, but it is great picture material for the kid star.

E. Mason Hopper handled the direction of the youngster almost as well as he was handled in "The Kid," and he got about all that he could get out of the story for the screen.

In the supporting cast Arthur Carewe carried the principal role, although the character touches contributed by Cesare Gravini, Bert Woodruff and Anna Townsend were decidedly worth while and went a long way to building up the sympathetic side of the picture. *Fred.*

PRODIGAL DAUGHTERS

Jesse L. Lasky presents Gloria Swanson in a Sam Wood production. Scenario by Monte Katterjohn, from the novel by Joseph Hooking. Projection time, 63 minutes. At the Rialto, April 15.

"Swiftie" Forbes..........Gloria Swanson
Roger Corbin.................Ralph Graves
Marjory Forbes..............Vera Reynolds
J. D. Forbes.............Theodore Roberts
Mrs. Forbes...............Louise Dresser
Stanley Garside............Charles Clary
Lester Hodges..............Robert Agnew
Connie........................Maude Wayne
Juda Botanya................Jiquel Lanoe
Dr. Marco Strong............Eric Mayne

The picture presents an unfortunate mishandling of Gloria Swanson which injures it in many ways. The fan public has been long accustomed to see Miss Swanson in a certain type of heroine, a woman of sophistication and the wearer of the last word in modes. This time they have made her a giddy flapper, and the result is a disappointment.

The fatal thing about the effort is that the star loses the interest of startling dresses. In trying to make her a butterfly young thing they have adapted her frocks to the character, and generally the whole affair is off the key. Miss Swanson doesn't look herself, and from the way she plays she must have felt out of her element.

Theodore Roberts, who, by experience and ability, ought to be proof against miscasting, is in no better situation. Placed to play a millionaire father out of sympathy with the modern "emancipated" young woman, he is wooden and uninspired. Roberts generally gives color and shading to anything he undertakes, but here he might be an ordinary makeshift screen actor picked haphazard to play an unimportant bit, and playing it without zest. The screen has no player who can draw character old men more vividly than Roberts, and coming as it does upon the heels of his splendid creation in "Grumpy," the contrast between J. D. Forbes of "Prodigal Daughters" and the old grouch of "Grumpy" is startling.

There is no reason why a fine, strong picture couldn't be made out of the clash between the modern younger generation and its parents. The dramatic appeal of the subject is self-evident, but they have not made it stick in this case. For one thing, the author's attitude is not sincere. He pictures the youngsters as a lot of flippant, fox-trotting fools, and the father (as representing the older generation) as a weak and uncertain objector to their habits.

Altogether you can't like either the youngsters or the oldsters, and for that reason there is no particular kick in their clash of wills nor in the issue of their contest. When the father practically shows the daughter the door because she insists upon going golfing on Sunday instead of going to church you wonder if the author and the producer are not trying to put over a travesty on cheap melodrama, particularly when the girl wants to go golfing in a costume from the "Follies," consisting of an armless shirt waist, pleated Scotch skirt above her knees, rolled down stockings and a military cap.

She'd have been arrested on the street before ever she got to the clubhouse. That's a sample of the excesses that make the picture ridiculous. Instead of being a representation of real things, it's just a badly done make-believe—a piece of cheap movie fiction. In the same mood is the incident of the rebellious daughter becoming a department store sales girl, and, in another passage, setting herself up in a Greenwich Village bohemian studio. This treatment might have served for a frank comedy, but the picture pretends to hold dramatic interest, and its absurdities are irritating.

Some of the big ballroom and party scenes are managed with a good deal of skill for stage effects, particularly the lawn fete at the opening, but the dramatic force of the story and the playing of the principal characters fail to register, and the picture weighs in as distinctly inferior. *Rush.*

A BILL OF DIVORCEMENT

Ideal Production, made in England. Distributed through Associated Exhibitors. Adapted and directed by Denison Clift from the stage play of the same title by Clemence Dane. At Fox's Academy, New York, April 15-18, on double-feature bill. Time, 61 minutes.

Margaret Fairfield............Fay Compton
Sydney Fairfield..........Constance Binney
Hilary Fairfield..............Malcolm Keen
Hester Fairfield..............Dora Gregory
Gray Meredith..................Henry Victor
Dr. Alliot.........................Henry Vibart
Rev. Christopher Pumphrey............Fewlass Llewellyn
Kit Pumphrey....................Martin Walker

It seems rather tough luck that Associated Exhibitors should not have been able to have those who book for Broadway pre-release runs to see the value of this English picture. It also speaks rather badly for the two bookers for the independent Broadway pre-release exhibitors that they were unable to see the punch, especially when it is considered the type of pictures in both houses during the last six months or so. This production was and is 50 per cent. better than a great many that have been shown at either the Strand or the Capitol, and likewise at either the Rialto or Rivoli, but they, for that matter, can't be counted, as they are devoted solely to the Paramount output.

Here is a picture that in direction ranks with the best of society plays that have been given on the screen here, and in the matter of acting overshadows most. In lightings and settings it is as good as anything that has been done in this country. Was it passed up solely, then, because it was English made? If so, why? Or was it because that here finally came an English-made picture that could stand up and do battle with anything of a like caliber that has been turned out in America? England has been a mighty consumer of the American-made product, and when a picture that has been made there comes up to American standards and requirements is sent across the Atlantic, America should be big enough to acknowledge it. **To see "A Bill of Divorcement" one had to journey to Fox's Academy, on 14th street.**

There isn't a single house that plays pre-release week runs anywhere that can't afford to play this feature. It is a 100 per cent. good production, and there are numberless American directors who might take a lesson from the direction of Denison Clift as to the manner of getting to the meat of his story without wasting footage in planting. Clift gets his plot over in a few deft scenes, and then goes on into the balance of the tale, at all times carrying the story forward surely and straightly to the point. The story follows the play rather closely and hasn't overlooked any of the punches.

With the acting there is hardly a fault to find. Fay Compton was superb as Margaret Fairfield, and Constance Binney likewise was a delight. It is, however, to Malcolm Keen, only on in the prolog and in the final scenes as Hilary Fairfield, the husband with insanity in his family, that the palm must be handed. His characterization was a distinct triumph, and that of Miss Binney only second to his with the closing scenes considered.

In the cast were several character bits, Henry Vibart scoring in one, Dora Gregory in another, with Fewlass Llewellyn in a third. Martin Walker played the juvenile lead cleverly as a foppish English youngster, and scored with it.

The verdict on the photography is fine, with the sets and outside locations beautiful. It's a corking good picture, despite made in England, and has the indication that if it is the type of picture that they are going to turn out over there it is only a matter of time before they'll be able to sing "Britannia Rules the Screen." Wot d'yer think of that?

Fred.

HAS THE WORLD GONE MAD?

Equity release. Story and script by Daniel Carson Goodman, directed by Searle Dawley. Shown at Fox's Academy, New York, April 15-18. Double feature bill. Time, 60 minutes.

Mr. Adams	Robert Edeson
Mrs. Adams	Hedda Hopper
Their Son	Vincent Coleman
Mr. Bell	Charles Richman
Mrs. Bell	Mary Alden
Their Daughter	Elinor Fair
Cabaret Dancer	Lyda Lola

This should have been a whale. That it isn't is in casting and direction. There was a real story behind, a story dealing with the unrest that is seething in social conditions of the day. The author dug a real theme and was wise enough to confine it to a short cast, thus driving it home with greater effect. Had the direction been as simple and straightforward, there would have been something the showman could have gone after with a sort of a "your home and mine" idea.

Atop of this, one looks at a cast that has names, names that mean something in the picture world, but when it is said Hedda Hopper ran away with the picture and that people of countless stage and screen successes fell by the wayside, such as Robert Edeson, Mary Alden and Charles Richman, it seems conclusive there must have been something wrong with direction. However, it measures a little above the average independently released program picture, and as such it contains a fair entertainment value for the shorter run theatres. It is not by far a week-stand picture in a first-class neighborhood house.

The story is of the unrest that there is in one family of wealth, where the mother craves the freedom of Bohemia, even though she has a son who is old enough to vote, and decides to live her own life in a modern studio apartment. In that same apartment there is another family. Here the wife and husband are of about the same age and have a daughter. The daughter is engaged to marry the son of the far more wealthy family. The wife of the former, now on the loose, and the father of the latter meet. An affair develops, with the daughter finally discovering who the woman is that is causing her father to break his home ties. The woman in the case at the same time, realizing that this is the girl her son is betrothed to, sees the foolish figure her search for freedom has led to. An expose of the father to a certain extent brings about the happy ending for three couples, each forgiven and forgiving, two wives and husbands and a young couple.

In sets the picture is all that could be asked, but it hasn't got the punch that it might have had.

Fred.

CRASHING THRU

Harry Carey-F. B. O. production adapted from the story by Elizabeth DeJeans by Beatrice Van. Directed by Val Paul. Shown at Loew's New York on double feature bill, April 17, 1923. Time 74 minutes.

Blake	Harry Carey
Allison	Chas. LeMoyne
Saunders	Vesta Pegg
Kid Allison	Cullen Landis
Morelos	Jos. Harris
Gracia	Neil Craig
Celia Warren	Mrytle Steadman
Diane Warren	Vola Vale
Uncle Benedict	Chas. Hill Mailes

This is not a particularly strong western, at least for Harry Carey. The story isn't particularly strong and extraordinary lengths are taken to pull the suspense angle along through the yarn. The thrills are badly done and the stampede scene that undoubtedly was counted on as the big punch fails to get anything from the audience. It is just a western that will get by perhaps on the strength of the star's name in the daily change houses on double feature bills, but that is about all that can be said for it.

The story in brief is that of two ranching partners, one of whom risks his life to save the other and is so injured that for years he is unable to use his legs. The invalid is a widower with a son who turns out to be in league with a gang of horse thieves. The partner who was rescued from death, played by Carey, has been doing the housework, until he decides that the ranch needs more attention to prevent all of the livestock from being stolen, so he advertises for a wife. The reply that comes decides him on sending for the woman, but when she arrives, though she is comely, she has brought her daughter with her, a daughter that she has not hinted about in her letters. So the matrimony is off for the time being. Later, however, the star falls in love with the daughter and the invalid partner, whose health is restored through love, wins the mother. There is a murder mystery that plays the suspense angle to the limit. When it is cleared up the gang that the boy is traveling with are discovered as guilty, and the boy is shot and killed in a round-up of the crooks.

Nothing there that is startling, and likewise nothing in the screen telling of it that will cause an audience to go wild with joy.

Fred.

HER ACCIDENTAL HUSBAND

Belasco production (not David Belasco), from the story by Lois Zeliner, directed by Dallas M. Fitzgerald. Released through C. B. C. Shown at Proctor's 23rd St., New York, for three days, commencing April 16. Time, 65 minutes.

Rena Goring	Miriam Cooper
Goring	Mitchell Lewis
Paul Dupre	Richard Tucker
Gordon Gray	Forrest Stanley
Mrs. Gray	Kate Lester
Vera Hampton	Maude Wayne

Melodrama of the old school is the basis upon which this Belasco production is developed. It is the tale of a New England fishing village, with all the melodrama the briny deep can give worked into the story. The producers have taken a short cast of experienced picture players, surrounded them with a rather hackneyed story and an unimpressive production, and demanded a feature of 5,000 feet or over. Fitzgerald, the director, had people of experience at his command, and, with something real in the way of a story and some worthwhile sets in which to develop the plot, would have produced a picture. A large portion of the story is worked up at sea—a portion on a fishing boat and some on a private yacht. To call the yacht used a fishing boat would be giving it too much credit. As far as the fishing boat was concerned it fitted the bill, although there was little fishing going on at any time in the story. There have been a number of productions with stories of this nature. This is but a weak-kneed effort in the division. It is not realistic. The melodramatics are far-fetched and not well staged. The cast stands out, due to the producers being able to secure capable people, as there were but six parts.

Rena Goring and her blind father operate a fishing boat. During a storm at sea she locates a man in the water and dives overboard to rescue him. Towing him back to the boat, he is pulled aboard, and her father falls into the ocean and is drowned. The newcomer is blamed for his death. The girl forces him to marry her and continues to operate the fishing boat, which was her father's wish. This continues for six months, when he finally persuades her to go to his home, he having been a youth of wealth. At his home she is taught the traits of a polished lady. Her husband had been engaged to a girl whom he thought dead. His wife meets the girl at his home. Through the efforts of a photographer who had met her as a fishing girl she is led to believe her husband loves the other woman. She returns to the little village. The photographer follows, and later comes the husband. The two men battle and the girl is finally convinced her husband loves her.

"Her Accidental Husband" is a cheap picture. A discriminating buyer would not touch it except for the cheaper grade houses.

Hart.

A NOISE IN NEWBORO

Harry Beaumont production, distributed by Loew-Metro. Adapted for screen by Rex Taylor from story by Edgar Franklin. Photography by John Arnold. Five reels. Loew's State, April 13. Time 70 minutes.

Martha Mason	Viola Dana
Ben Colwell	David Butler
Anne Paisley	Eva Novak
Buddy Wayne	Allan Forrest
Letia Wayne	Betty Francisco
Eben Paisley	Alfred Allen
Harry Dixon	Malcolm McGregor
Dorothy Mason	Joan Standing
"Dad" Mason	Bert Woodruff

A stagey picture that gives the impression of a lot of actors working before a camera. It isn't the actors' fault, but the picture fails to hold the mirror up to nature—it's mainly the story itself, and to some considerable extent the direction.

Starting with small town school room types that plant the rural atmosphere, it is passably interesting for the first 1,500 feet or so. It's in the second section it wanders in a rambling fashion into the far-fetched realms of farce.

Viola Dana is starred. She is in gingham in the forepart and silk in the latter portion. She's a small-towner with an ambition to become an artist. After seven years in the big city the girl returns to the small town and renews the love affair started when a kid. He's the town lawyer now, and she expects him to marry her. He has grown pompous with success and plays the chill for his childhood's sweetheart. Incidentally, the girl had planned giving $5,000 to the local school board as a remembrance. When the pompous one gives her the air the girl becomes peeved and seeks revenge.

It happens in the form of the reporter from the local paper. He, scenting a yarn to discredit the town lawyer, who's on the opposite side of the political fence from his boss, the editor, ribs up a wild pipe about the gal wanting to give $50,000 to the school board and the lawyer turned it down. Not very clear in the film—the lawyer turning it down—but the reporter makes him a horse thief and worse because the reporter feels that way about it.

This part is preposterous farce, full of hoke. The reporter is a slick looking guy, too. The rap in the paper doesn't get such an awful rise out of the rube lawyer. That town lawyer character, by the way, is another thing that makes the picture unnatural and stagey. He's at a swell reception, the only one there with white socks and a dress suit. If that town was such a rube burg as the story otherwise would indicate, all the rest of the guests wouldn't look like fashion plates that stepped out of the Ritz. Funny the lawyer should be the only yap in the village.

Miss Dana does well as the artist, handling it as convincingly as an artificial part like that can be. Bert Mason makes the small role of the girl's father stand out, and Hank Mann is wasted on a comedy character that belonged in a slap-stick farce. Good comic, but his good line of hoke only added to impression of unreality.

Some good night scenes with photography soft and pleasing. Picture is a bit below average program stuff, and must depend for drawing power on Viola Dana's name.

Bell.

VENGEANCE OF THE DEEP

South Seas romance produced by A.B. Berringer, who wrote story and directed from the scenario by J.L. Lamothe and Agnes Parsons. Photographers, Paul Ivan, William William McGann and Homer Scott. Released April 18 by American Releasing. Projection time, 52 mins: footage, 4,752 feet. Trade showing, April 13.

Captain Musgrove	Ralph Lewis
Ethel Musgrove	Virginia Browne Faire
Jean	Van Mattimore
Frederico	Harmon McGregor
Tagu	William Anderson
Native Chief	"Smoke" Turner
Kiliki	Malda Vaio

Acceptable commercial picture with plenty of startling action in its underseas photography and a fair amount of romantic interest. The story has its weak spots and the acting averages no better than fair, but the extraordinary scenic features carry the picture to a triumphant ensemble effect.

It is the novelty and spectacular features that put the film over rather than the acting personnel, for Virginia Brown Faire and Van Mattimore are the most unconvincing of lovers. But there is no getting away from the thrill of some of the exploits of the pearl fishers. In one episode there is a battle between a native fisher and what looks like a sure-enough shark shown partly above and partly below the surface by a submarine device.

There is a lot of the subsea stuff. It is not so clear as the Williamson films, but it is genuine and highly impressive for its dramatic quality. The pearl divers are shown at work surrounded by the weird growths and the strange creatures of the depths. Some of the shots are of divers in the clumsy contrivances as they grope along the bottom, and some of the natives who go to the bottom without the apparatus.

One of the big scenes is the capture of a diver by a giant shell fish and his escape by clinging to the ship's anchor line as the hook is drawn up. Another good bit of adventure stuff is the finding of a pirate's treasure chest on the bottom and the running down of a pearler's canoe by a fishing schooner. All the water scenes are well managed and convincing, and it is only when the people have to act out obviously theatrical scenes that the illusion is injured.

The scenic background is beautiful, especially the deep-water and beach scenes and those aboard the schooner. The reality of these settings helps the action. On land the company is not so successful, especially as the story has its rough places. We never do learn what became of the treasure chest, and it was not made plain why the captain's daughter fell so violently in love with the beach comber. But the whole story is naive, unpretentious melodrama, and these niceties do not particularly matter. All the story is meant to do anyhow is to provide an excuse for the impressive undersea exploits, and it serves this purpose adequately.

Rush.

TRIMMED IN SCARLET

Universal feature adapted by Edward T. Lowe from the William Hurlburt play of the same title. Directed by Jack Conway. Shown at Loew's New York (New York) double feature bill April 13, 1923. Time, 54 minutes.

Cordelia Ebbing

Mme. De La Fleurʃ ......Kathlyn Williams
Revere Wayne..................Roy Stewart
Faith Ebbing...............Lucille Ricksen
David Pierce...............Robert Agnew
Charles Knight............David Torrence
Peter Ebbing...............Phillips Smalley
Fifi Barclay...................Eve Southern
Duroc.........................Bert Sprott
Molly Todd...................Grace Carlyle

Universal gathered a cast full of names for this picture and then went out and made a production that is old-fashioned as far as the story is concerned. Undoubtedly in the days agone, when William Hurlburt wrote this play for one of the stage stars, the situations must have been fairly new, but the general idea has been used over and over again so often in pictures that one knows what the story is going to be before it gets fairly under way. However, Jack Conway handled the direction nicely and turned out a picture that will hold its own in the houses where there is a daily change of bill, with the names in the cast being counted on to pull a little money for the exhibitor's box office.

The story is that of a wife that deserts her husband because he is on the loose. Later His daughter also leaves her home because she refuses to remain there with the woman that has been chosen as her stepmother. A brief time later, while working in an office she steals $5,000 to protect her mother from a blackmailer. The mother in turn takes a chance of appearing in a compromising position in the eyes of a former admirer, who has returned to her side, in order to protect the daughter and to obtain the money to cover up the shortage in the office funds. Eventually a happy ending all around.

It is the cast that makes the story at all possible, and Miss Williams does her full share toward carrying the tale over. *Fred.*

DOLLAR DEVILS

A. Hodkinson release from a script by Louis Stevens. Directed by Victor Schertzinger. Shown at Loew's New York, N. Y., double feature bill, April 13, 1923. Time, 61 minutes.

Zannon Carthy.............Joseph Dowling
Hal Andrews.................Miles McCarthy
Mrs. Andrews................May Wallace
Amy............................Eva Novak
Bruce Merlin.................Hallam Cooley
Jim Biggers..................Cullen Landis
Mrs. Biggers.................Lydia Knott
Helen Andrews...............Ney Farrell

Just an average program production, containing no particular dramatic punch, but a story that is fairly interesting in entertainment value as it progresses on the screen, the performance of Cullen Landis bring about the outstanding feature of the picture. It is just one of those productions that the average daily change exhibitor can play and get away with without harming his house, but, at the same time, without giving his audience anything that they are going to rave over.

It is a little tale of a New England town that goes wild because a smart city feller comes along and discovers oil. All the inhabitants, with one exception, sees visions of millions of dollars in their hands and John D. working for them. This one character seeks investments in other directions, and in the finish, when oil has been discovered only to have the wells run dry in a week or so, he is vindicated, and the town again resumes its natural way through life. There is a love story that runs through, with Eva Novak and Landis as the principals, that helps to fill in the picture.

Just a program picture, without extra frills or wallops. *Fred.*

GOLDEN SILENCE

Independent designated a Sylvanite Production, released through Richard Kipling Enterprises. Paul Hurst, director. Production Ebbing, 65 minutes. Hedda Nova and Paul Perrin featured. Half double feature bill at Loew's New York, March.

Average program western production in all respects. Investment small by reason of action taking place exclusively in the free outdoors. Has brisk riding episodes and the usual spirited fights—this time in a mountain snow bank—between hero and heavy. Simple, well-told narrative of the familiar style of mining camp intrigue. Played satisfactorily by an average cast. In fact, every detail about the production is in the medium ground of "good enough," but nothing particularly stands out.

There are many bits of excellent scenic effect, apparently the joint work of a clever cameraman and a good location picker. Much of the action takes place in lake country and beside lovely water courses, and the landscape composition has been neatly worked into the picture for picturesque backgrounds.

Sam Corwin, stage line owner and camp bully, makes unwelcome love to Polly, daughter of an old prospector. The old man drives him off the place at gun point and Sam conspires to have the old man sent to prison. He stages a fake hold-up, leaving the old man's hat on the scene. This is managed with the connivance of one of Sam's stage drivers. By one of those far-fetched coincidences of the screen the whole plot is unfolded to a stranger in those parts, and he impersonates the hold-up artist, double-crossing the plotters, vindicating the old man, overthrowing the villains, and in the end winning the girl.

The suspense, principal mainstay of such stories, is rather well sustained up to the end, when it is disclosed that the hero is not the cowboy wanderer he appeared, but a U. S. secret service operative gunning for the mail robbers operating under direction of Sam. The title arises from the laconic habits of the sleuth. Pleasing light program feature for the daily change houses.
Rush.

LOST IN A BIG CITY

Providence, April 18.

The latest of the old-time melodramas to be converted to the screen is "Lost in a Big City," which had its first showing at the Rialto (Providence) last Monday. John Lowell and Baby Ivy Ward, who starred in "Ten Nights in a Bar Room," appear in person all week.

Lowell fits into the character of the strong, virile and at the same time lovable Harry Farley. Others in the cast are Miss Ward, Evangeline Russell, Charles Beyer, James Watkins, Charles Robins, Jane Thomas, Leatta Miller, Edgar Keller, Anne Brady, Edgar Phillips and Whitney Haley.

"Lost in a Big City" is a fast-moving melodrama, adapted from the screen version of S. C. Woods' famous play by L. Case Russell. It carries much action, punctuated with romance, pathos, adventure and good comedy relief. New York's East Side slums, Broadway, and finally the Adirondacks serve as a background, coming in logical sequence.

The story relates the adventures of Harry Farley, a prospector, who returns from Alaska and finds that his sister's husband has deserted her and that she has sold the old farm and gone with her blind child, Florence, to New York. Richard Norman, the missing husband, believed to be dead, has, under the name of Sidney Heaton, married Blanche Maberly, the daughter of an old friend of his father. Dick Watkins, an old pal of Heaton, who has been paid to report his death, threatens to blackmail him.

To raise money Heaton joins a gang of bootleggers in the Adirondacks. Watkins demands more money for his silence, but Heaton cannot agree with him and as a last resort decides to kidnap his

daughter, Florence, and hide her in the mountains. Meanwhile, Helen, his first wife, dies, and Watkins, fearing that he will be cheated out of his money, turns the tables on Heaton by telling Farley the whole story. *Gravalese.*

THE BRIGHT SHAWL

Inspiration Pictures, Inc., presents Richard Barthelmess, with Dorothy Gish, in the story by Joseph Hergesheimer, adapted by Edmund Goulding, directed by John S. Robertson, and distributed by First National. Projection time, 64 minutes. At the New York Strand, April 21.

Charles Abbott........Richard Barthelmess
Andres Escobar........Andre de Beranger
Domingo Escobar..........E. G. Robinson
Carmenita Escobar.......Margaret Seddon
Narcissa Escobar.............Mary Astor
Vincente Escobar.............Luis Alberni
Cesar Y Santacilla.......Anders Randolf
Caspar De Vaca............William Powell
La Clavel....................Dorothy Gish
La Pilar.....................Jetta Gondal
Jaime Quintara...........George Humbert

Here is an all-'round fine contribution to the screen, especially fine in its production rather than in the subject matter of the story. It is an atmosphere and costume play done in a splendid, artistic style. It gives Richard Barthelmess the best romantic role probably he has ever had, and it furnishes a picturesque character type for Dorothy Gish which displays that charming young woman in an entirely new aspect as a dark-eyed Cuban dancing girl.

The picture was taken in Cuba, and the atmosphere is conspicuously convincing. Instead of obviously phoney studio sets they have picked out odd native corners and fronts of buildings that make especially satisfactory backgrounds. One shot shows the heroine and hero entering a church. Almost any church entrance would have done, but this one is eloquent in its appearance of age. Another incidental scene takes place on a parapet overlooking Havana Bay, with Morro Castle in the background. A few scenes in the country have the tropic landscape and vegetation, and the mob scenes have authentic people.

On its romantic side the picture is excellent. It takes place in Havana in the 70's or thereabouts. Barthelmess wears the stovepipe silk hat, stock and tight trousers of the period and makes a strikingly handsome figure. The women are equally picturesque in their crinolines and tight waists. The costuming has been most cleverly handled, with designs that carry the force of actuality and, the whole picture carries an air of authority that ordinarily is missing from attempts at costume effect. Ancient dress is usually makeshift and awkward. One usually thinks, "How silly these people look!" Here one gets the feeling that one is viewing a beautiful painting or print of another generation.

The one defect in the picture is that its story is a little gumbled, especially at the beginning, when the characters are being introduced and the situation is being "planted." This state of affairs seems to be almost inseparable from the adapting of a novel. There is so much material that it becomes an embarrassment in the economical technique of stage or screen. Here it becomes necessary to set the stage for a complicated story of plot and counter plot, shifting intrigue and political maneuvering, and the story requires so many characters that it becomes unwieldy.

It deals with intrigue in Cuba under the Spanish rule, when the natives were oppressed by arrogant Spanish officials and crushed under the oppression of a tyrant overseas. It is a splendid subject, especially for the American audience. Into the intricate political situation is introduced a rich young American (Barthelmess), who, out of sympathy for the oppressed people of Cuba, acts as the agent of the revolutionaries.

He learns the moves of the Spanish colonial rulers through La Clavel, the dancing girl, who is their plaything, and communicates the tyrants' moves to the insurgents.

La Clavel falls in love with the American, while he falls in love with the sister of one of the revolutionists. There is a wealth of movement and dramatic action to a satisfactory romantic ending. The picture will have an especially strong appeal to women. *Rush.*

FAMOUS MRS. FAIR

Louis B. Mayer production with Fred Niblo, its director, starred. No player featured. From play by James Forbes, produced on stage by Henry Miller. Adapted for screen by Frances Marion. Distributed by Metro. At Capitol, New York, week April 22.

Mrs. Fair	Myrtle Stedman
Jeffrey Fair	Huntly Gordon
Sylvia Fair	Marguerite De La Motte
Alan Fair	Cullen Landis
Dudley Gillette	Ward Crane
Angy Brice	Carmel Myers
Peggy	Helen Ferguson

Buddies—Lydia Yeamans Titus, Dorcas Matthews, Frankie Bailey, Josephine Kirkwood, Muriel Beresford, Eva Mudge, Kathleen Chambers, Peggy Blackwood.

Soldiers from Coast Artillery Corps, Fort McArthur.

"The Famous Mrs. Fair" on the screen is a very nice and polite feature picture. Its strength for the box office lies in a new twist given to an old story, with this one dating from war times to shortly after peace. It's one of those dependables for the exhibitor and does not appear to suggest that Fred Niblo, director, believed he had more than that in the material.

James Forbes when writing this piece that Henry Miller stage-presented, did it with a Broadway slant. It might hold true of New York or Chicago (and Sid now says that Chi is the widest open town on the U. S. map. The kid should know). It is this very slant with its decorous handling that grips the attention. The something big that may be waited for won't arrive—it isn't there, never was.

The Fair family is wealthy and healthy with the wife the pivot of it. Father, mother, son and daughter. And war arrives. And the boy goes. And the mother, to look after the boys over there while the father becomes a Dollar Man for the government. That left the daughter alone but then she was growing up. Still she was alone at that time and it is important in a way.

With the armistice back came the wife and mother, now as the Famous Mrs. Fair, decorated, in uniform, for she did everything a woman could do over there, from nursing in a hospital to driving an ambulance under fire.

The father and son also came back. Although the town turned out to greet the famous one, she just wanted to be home with her folks. And the folks wanted her, for she was a dandy wife and mother, a great one the way Mr. Forbes wrote her, the kind you find in every 1,000,000 women—once.

Then the interviewers and the film news men, also a lecture bureau and for the latter Mrs. Fair succumbed to a tour at $30,000 gross, despite her husband's objections and for the purpose of turning the money over to an orphan fund.

When the mother left to lecture, the family went all to pieces. Either any or all could have made the jump to be with her on a week-end but they didn't, nor did she return home for over two months. Had the natural course been followed there would have been no story, and the Laurajeanlibbyish tale of no mother to guide her could not have been hung onto the daughter.

The son was a minor. He only fell into gambling and love with a phone switchboard operator who finally landed him through making him promise to quit playing cards at 10 p. m. to take her home. So he was harmless, any 10 p. m. gambler is.

The husband and father, perhaps through pique but also perhaps through lonesomeness, started to step. A neighborhood lady, Mrs. Angie Brice, grew attentive—a lively blonde, and very good-looking, too. Mr. Fair held his evenings open for her. That left Sylvia Fair, the daughter, looking at the pictures on the wall for pastime in the hotel suite.

Then the daughter commenced to slip. An oily booking agent for lectures, the one who got the contract for her mother, started to escort Sylvia around until "Chicago" was the only tune she wanted to dance and die by.

Mother ran into an open week and decided to spend it at home. When she got home nobody was there. But they came in and started the busiest day the Fair family ever will have. The son married the operator, bringing her home; the daughter eloped with the lecture agent, and father confessed to mother about his relations with Angie, almost before mother got off her hat.

It's a very fine bit of educational work for husbands Mr. Niblo devised about that confession. It should be great for the male picture patrons. In effect it says, "Don't talk too much." Mrs. Fair got a slight hunch her hubby, Jeff, had been stalling around with Mrs. Brice. Angie had taken a chance, calling up the apartment for him, with Mrs. Fair answering the phone. Angie gave her right name and that was a tip off.

While Mr. and Mrs. Fair were on the sofa Mrs. Fair, out of uniform and again a woman, sort of snuggled up to Jeff, and, trying to be cutey, wanted to know if she wouldn't do as well as Mrs. Brice, only for a flip remark. And Jeff, the big slob, said he had just fixed Mrs. Brice, and so he had, as a previous flash had him giving her a check in settlement.

Then the famous Mrs. Fair again disclosed she was a woman by mentioning a divorce. On that remark Sylvia based her elopement, but the son, after a very phoney race between auto and train, got her before the deceiver did, brought his sister back, and there was a family reunion on mother's promise to waive the divorce proceeding.

It's the manner in which the different incidents are visualized that helps the picture. A laugh or so is held by the titling, but that is not exceptional in whole by any means. "The Buddies," as programed, are funny for a moment, with Niblo giving Lydia Yeamans Titus, Frankie Bailey and Eva Mudge, among the others, a chance in it. Which shows that even a director has a memory.

Myrtle Steadman played Mrs. Fair in an understanding way; she was snappy in khaki and lovable in skirts; while Marguerite De La Motte (despite her name) nicely did the daughter, although, perhaps, the Capitol's orchestra played "Chicago" as well as anything else connected with the picture.

An evenly balanced, well-produced picture, without a punch. *Sime.*

YOU CAN'T FOOL YOUR WIFE

George Melford production presented by Jesse Lasky. Story and script by Waldemar Young. Directed by George Melford. Leatrice Joy, Nita Naldi, Lewis Stone and Pauline Garon featured. Released through Paramount. At Rialto, New York, week of April 22. Time, 64 minutes.

Edith McBride	Leatrice Joy
Ardrita Saneck	Nita Naldi
Garth McBride	Lewis Stone
Vera Redell	Pauline Garon
Dr. Konrad Saneck	Paul McAllister
Jackson Redell	John Daly Murphy
Lillian Redell	Julia Swayne Gordon
Russell Fenton	Tom Carrigan
John Yates	Dan Pennell

This isn't a special, but a mighty good program picture as pictures go. It is built to order by the author for the picture houses, has all of the elements that the various types of film fans want, with the heavy vamp stuff played as the ace from beginning to end. Incidentally, seeing Nita Naldi "do her stuff" in this picture one wonders somewhat why the heavy hand on Pola Negri. Pola can't have everything on Nita when it comes to making 'em fall, for Nita is "there" 150 per cent. on flopping them over.

The story first and foremost has a society atmosphere with its scenes laid in New York, Miami and Nassau. Secondly, it feeds the fans what they like to believe New York society is like, every one out grabbing every one else's wife. It feeds it to them in a dressing of bathing girls, a midnight bathing pool, an airship ride to the British West Indies, a bootleggers' ball at the source of the hard stuff supply, and finally gives them a thrill in the last minutes before the final happy ending.

It must be said, however, that Waldemar Young managed to "borrow" the situation that he utilized for his thrill. It is the situation where the noted surgeon has on the operating table before him the man whom he believes is his wife's lover. That was done in Paris in a play a couple of years ago, and also in this country not that far back. In this picture, however, it places the punch in the spot where it is most needed, right in the final reel.

From a title standpoint this picture has a wallop. "You Can't Fool Your Wife" sounds intriguing enough to pull money most anywhere. Lewis Stone, a successful Wall Street operator, playing the husband doesn't put it over on Leatrice Joy as his wife. Miss Naldi is the vamp that fascinates him. She is the wife of the noted foreign surgeon who goes out with the preconceived plan that she is going to interest the Wall Street man first in herself and then in her husband's work. The latter is carrying on costly experimental work, and his wife conceives the idea that if she moves in the right set she might receive subscriptions that would assist her husband.

The McBrides (Mr. Stone and Miss Joy) and Ardrita Saneck (Miss Naldi) have mutual friends in New York through whom they meet, and a party is arranged for a month in Florida during the season. Garth McBride immediately falls for Ardrita, and as the days in Florida pass there is considerable of a flirtation progressing between the two. One morning on the sands the vamp expresses a desire for a ride in the flying hip. McBride consents. They are compelled to make the trip across to the British islands. Missing the return trip, they stay on the island over night, and while away the hours at the bootleggers' ball. Returning in the mooning over the small transgressions of his son in the manner of a fussy mamma we are disposed to utter, "Oh, sugar!" and let it go. The drama here is that kind. It's the strained and forced fiction kind. People do things that couldn't happen except in the mind of an amateur dramatist and then suffer through rods of celluloid. For example, two reels of the picture deal with the father's fruitless search for the son after the son has been released from prison. Father didn't know where son was for the simple reason that father didn't write to the boy during the three years he was in the cooler. If the old man was such a fool he didn't keep track of his beloved son's record in the hoosegow he deserved to suffer.

That's a minor sample of the twisting of human action to suit the purpose of a movie scenario. All the people all the time act on impulses that couldn't exist outside yellow covers or in an open market picture studio. It's just six reels of juvenile moonshine, without a relieving gleam of humor. *Rush.*

FOR YOU, MY BOY

Open market feature by Rubicon Pictures in about six reels. William L. Roubert, director and producer. Projection time, 76 minutes. Trade showing April 19.

Grant Melford	Louis Dean
His Wife	Jean Armour
Jack Melford	Matty Roubert
John Austin	Ben Lewin
Jack Austin	Schuyler White
The Girl	Gladys Grainger
The Girl's Father	Franklin Hanna
George Harvey	Scott Hinchner

A picture of hokum sentiment, with the sob stuff laid on thick. Attractive enough in its photography and exterior backgrounds, but revealing extreme economy in its interior sets. Apparently a cheap production for the daily change houses. For this clientele it ought to be fairly satisfactory. But its appeal is pretty well limited to the class of patronage to which the smaller, low admission establishments cater.

The story is written in the heavily emotional style of "Over the Hill," except that the hero is a father instead of a mother. It is scarcely necessary to point out that dealing with father in a moist and tearful way is dangerous. It is conceivable that a genius of the screen could sneak the Old Man across in a sentimental attitude, but it would have to be done with delicate shadings of comedy. The attempt to do it in a strictly emotional way is perilous. A sentimental papa is too easy to josh. The Old Man has his sentimental side, of course, but it can't be dramatized in terms of stilted theatrical emotion. It's just a conventional taboo.

Thus, when we have an old man morning, McBride finds that his wife has decided to return to New York, leaving him flat and refusing to listen to his explanation.

McBride follows his wife north, and in turn the vamp follows him. Back in the city one of the enemies of McBride arranges he shall have an "accident" in front of the house of the husband of the vamp, he having already disclosed to the surgeon the reports that he has received from a private detective agency which has been watching the Florida romance for him.

Then comes the big moment when the doctor is informed whom he has on the operating table. He brings his wife into the room to look upon the man she was supposed to be in love with, and although she protests the accusations are false and pleads for his life, the surgeon seems certain to carry through his plan to wreak vengeance on the man whom he believes despoiled his home. Then there arrives a nurse, hurriedly summoned from a registry. It is none other than McBride's wife. When she states she believes the protestations of the vamp the doctor is also convinced and a happy ending all round ensues.

Paul McAllister plays the surgeon with a clever touch of characterization and a makeup that reminds of old Bill Brill, the A. P. war correspondent. A comedy touch is contributed through the Redells—mother, father and daughter, played by Julia Swayne Gordon, John Daly Murphy and Pauline Garon. This trio, especially Miss Garon, lent the lighter tone to the more somber shades of the picture.

In direction Mr. Melford left naught to be desired. *Fred.*

ARE YOU A FAILURE?

A Preferred Pictures production, presented by Ben Schulberg. Story by Larry Evans, adapted by Eve Unsell. Directed by Tom Forman. Released by Al. Lichtman Corp. Shown at Loew's Circle, N. Y., double feature bill April 23, 1923. Time, 64 minutes.

Phyllis Thorp	Madge Bellamy
Oliver Wendell Blaine	Lloyd Hughes
Killdevil Brennon	Tom Santschi
Gregory Thorp	Hardee Kirkland
Aunt Emily	Jane Keckley
Aunt Charlotte	Myrtle Vane
Emmet Graves	Hallam Cooley
Thaddeus Crane	Samuel Allen

The outstanding fact about this production from a producer's angle is that in Lloyd Hughes there seems to have been uncovered another Charles Ray. From an exhibitor's angle this is a picture that audiences are sure to like. It has a human note that registers, and for a thrill has a corking log jam that is sure to get over. Incidentally, the picture has Madge Bellamy, who is a good bet on looks and ability both. It is a picture that can go in anywhere and stand up with any program production no matter of what brand.

Lloyd Hughes plays the role of Oliver Wendell Blaine, the last of a long line of river lumber men, but far from being a follower in their rough-shod footsteps in the early portion of the story. He has been reared by his two aunts, who have made a mollycoddle of the boy, and instead of permitting him to follow the drifting logs for a living he is forced to clerk in the village general store. Madge Bellamy, as the daughter of the lumber king, is the heroine of the story, and she is the only one that looks upon the last of the Blaines as anything other than what he appears to be on the surface.

She has just returned to the little town from a finishing school and brought an admirer from the city with her. This admirer and the river boss of her father's camp are rivals for her favor, but she in turn would rather have the mollycoddle, providing he can prove himself to be what she really believes him.

Then comes a period where self-suggestion works a miracle for the youth. He sees an ad of the mail order variety that asks the question, "Are You a Failure?" and he subscribes to the course that is to set him on the right path. The lessons, all four of them, arrive one at a time. The first comes at a moment when he needs its advice to the effect we are to conquer the thing that we are most in fear of. It looks for a moment as though the youth were on his way to lick the bully of the town, the river boss. But he doesn't get that far. That at least was good direction, for most directors would have made the lightweight kid the victor in a scrap with a heavyweight. Later, however, he does mix it with the bruiser, and except for the interference of others he would have been in for a beating.

The kid does finally come through and assert himself in a pinch and thereby steps into the job of river boss and wins the girl.

It's a mighty interesting and entertaining story that is well told on the screen. The cast is good and both Lloyd Hughes and Madge Bellamy score. Tom Santschi puts over the heavy river boss in great shape and the two character bits of the boy's aunts are also capably handled. It's a picture that has everything, romance, comedy, drama and a thrill. *Fred.*

THE DRUG TRAFFIC

An Irving Cummings production, presented by Sol Lesser. Story by Harvey Gates. State Rights. Starring Gladys Brockwell and Barbara Tennent. Shown at the Tivoli, N. Y., April 23-24. Time, 56 minutes.

George Wallace .... ?
Dr. Steve Maison .... ?
Mary Larkin .... Barbara Tennent
Edna Moore .... Gladys Brockwell
Willie Shade .... Bob Walker

This was a rush order in production to beat all the other drug pictures to the market. It isn't anything extraordinary from a production standpoint, but on the strength of the title and the foreword regarding the traffic in narcotics it looks as though it would be a money getter in the neighborhood houses. Right now when all the dailies and the magazines are going after the drug evil there is no doubt that the picture-going public in the houses where there is a policy of changing every few days will give a strong box office drag to this picture. At the Tivoli, which is a neighborhood house on Eighth avenue, New York, charging 30 cents top there were standees at the back of the house

for the final show on the first night the picture was shown.

The biggest part of the drug traffic is in the foreword. The action of the picture itself details the story of a successful surgeon, who, trying to burn the candle at both ends through keeping up his professional activities and also keeping abreast of his social obligations to please his fiancee, resorts to a drug to stimulate him as he is about to perform an operation. This leads to a shot now and again, and soon he is an addict, giving up his profession and sinking to the slums, until he is thrown into jail. He escapes and returns to his humble abode, burglarizes the hospital where he was formerly an attache to obtain a supply of drug, and then when he is brought to a realization of the uselessness of it all he puts up a fight to get away from his habit, but although he spends a night of terror fighting off his desire his victory against the drug brings death.

In reality there is naught of the drug traffic shown, although the title might imply that the picture was to be an expose of the methods employed to gain recruits. It is nothing of that sort, however. There is a moral, "The wages of drugs is death."

The cast fail to make any impression because there is nothing for them to do. There is one set that looks like anything at all. Otherwise the scenes are shot against a black drop or in little sets that amount to nothing.

With a strong show around this and some strong exploitation it will get money in certain neighborhoods. *Fred.*

IS MONEY EVERYTHING?

A Lee-Bradford production, starring Mariam Cooper. Written and directed by Glen Lyon.

John Brand .... Norman Kerry
His Wife .... Mariam Cooper
Sam Slack .... Andrew Hicks
Rev. John Brooks .... John Sylvester
Mrs. Justine Pelham ..... Martha Mansfield
Roy Pelham .... William Bailey
Phil Graham .... Lawrence Brooke

"Is Money Everything?" is one of those titles pulled out of the ether for box office purposes. There is an attempt at a preachment to the effect than money is not everything, but, on the contrary, the pursuit of the almighty dollar leads but to discord and unhappiness. In that respect the story is consistent, but it is one of the most wearisome and long-drawn out screen affairs of some time. As a feature it is strong enough in the matter of title, and with the playing of the couple of worth-while names in the cast to play the houses where there are two or three changes of program a week.

The action of the story leads from a small country town to New York, and in the latter place has Wall street and a society angle for its big punch scenes. The usual line of society stuff, week-end parties at a country place, with a phoney hunt scene; a reception with a dance bit, etc. The earlier section rings far more true in the matter of screen atmosphere than do the later reels.

John Grand (Norman Kerry) is a farmer with hopes that he may eventually reach the pulpit. A local merchant convinces him he would be a greater success commercially, and he becomes his partner. Everything predicted in regard to commercial life comes to pass, with the result that in gathering the coin John Brand is the greatest ever. He comes to New York to take a try at the stock market, and within less than six months has the powers of the street practically begging for mercy. Meantime his wife sees a change in him that worries here. His quest for money has blunted his senses to the righteous things in the world, and finally she plans with his financial enemies to bring about his ruin in Wall street in order that his soul may be saved.

Mariam Cooper plays the wife effectively, while Martha Mansfield handles the role of a vamp, wife of one of Brand's rivals, who want her to entangle the new financial power so that she can obtain his secrets and disclose them to her husband and his associates. Instead, she falls for Brand. In handling the role Miss Mansfield acquitted herself quite well. The others of the cast mean little or nothing to the story.

Direction has been handled with a view to getting in every little detail that can be utilized to use up footage, and it seems that of this time at least 15 minutes could be edited out of the picture to the enhancement of its value with the average exhibitor. *Fred.*

THE CUSTARD CUP

A William Fox production, starring Mary Carr. Story by Florence Bingham Livingston; adapted by G. Marion Burton. Directed by Herbert Brenon. Shown at Fox's Academy April 9-11, 1923. Time, 81 minutes.

Mrs. Penfield .... Mary Carr
Gussie Bosley .... Myrta Bonillas
Lettie .... Miriam Battista
Crink .... Jerry Devine
Thad .... Ernest McKay
Lorene Percy .... Peggy Shaw
Mrs. Percy .... Leslie Leigh
Jerry Winston .... Frederick Esmelton
Frank Bosley .... Henry Sedley

Here is a cross between "Mrs. Wiggs of the Cabbage Patch" and "Over the Hill," dealing with the theme of mother love. However, as a picture it doesn't come within a mile of "Over the Hill" and as a story it cannot be considered with "Mrs. Wiggs." It is just a fair melodrama that will do in the neighborhood houses, but that is about all. Herbert Brenon is far from living up to his reputation as a producing director. It is in seven reels running a little more than 6,100 feet. In the house where they want a lot of footage and a few names and don't care much about story as long as there is some action this one will get by.

It seems rather too bad that a man of Brenon's undoubted talents should have been wasted on the direction of a story as mediocre as this, for Brenon has had the reputation of being able to turn out a picture of real box office proportions with a camera, raw stock and a bank roll.

"The Custard Cup" refers to a group of tenements that have been built in an oval. Mary Carr as Mrs. Penfield, who lost her husband and children during the flu epidemic, is in charge of the houses, getting her living quarters in a remodeled barn in payment for her service. There she lives with three adopted children, taken by her to soften the loss of her own.

There is a melodramatic element in the story dealing with a gang of counterfeiters who are working in the neighborhood, shoving the queer and using the unsuspecting caretaker from time to time as their tool. The big thrill is supposed to be supplied by a burning excursion steamer (a la "The Regeneration," another Fox production several years ago, but not so well done), at which all the inhabitants of the "Custard Cup" are the guests of the alderman. The boat is set afire by one of the gang leaders in destroying the phoney money he has on his person when he thinks he is about to be captured. As the finish there is a round-up of crooks, and the little caretaker is arrested with them, only to be cleared by the advent of a U. S. secret service man who has posed through the picture as one of the crooks.

Mary Carr delivers everything in the way of a real performance that is asked of her, as does also little Miriam Battista, but the balance of the cast failed to contribute much. The heavy of Harry Sedley was far from impressive and somewhat over-acted. The picture could easily have been a four and a half reeler. *Fred.*

THE STORM GIRL

Anchor production, presented by Morris Schlank. Directed by Francis Ford. Peggy O'Day starred.

Francis Ford, the film original of the Valentino sideburns, is the director-lead of this film feature which has Peggy O'Day as its star. The feature is just one of the ordinary cheap type of melodramas that has no particular punch, but which will serve as a filler-in in the smaller type of houses.

There was an attempt to get a real idea into the tale, but it wasn't planted in the earlier part of the story and when it did develop as the real reason for the plot and the title of the feature there was not a bit of wallop to it. Peggy O'Day plays the role of a scullery maid in a cheap lodging house and through a good patron has a Cinderella rise to the position of prima donna at the head of a stock burlesque company.

Whoever titled the story failed in so far as their knowledge of the stage is concerned and it is the titling that is about the faultiest portion of the picture. There was enough action on the screen to have been worked into a fairly logical melodrama that would have gotten by somewhat more effectively than this one does in its present shape, but the editing and titling only aided making something that was bad worse.

Miss O'Day does not seem to impress to any extraordinary extent, nor does Francis Ford in the role of her leading man make any particular impression. Seemingly Ford would have better been cast for the heavy with the young man playing that role (who incidentally looks as though he might be a younger brother or even a son of Ford's) cast in the lead. It would have been more consistent at any rate for youth to fall for youth.

In direction Mr. Ford also failed to distinguish himself and as a matter of fact was decidedly off in matters of detail throughout the picture. Some of the scenes were handled so over-melodramatically as to bring a laugh instead of a thrill. *Fred.*

MAN'S SIZE

William Fox five-reel feature starring William Russell. Story by Wm. McLeod Raine; scenario by Jos. F. Poland; direction by Howard Mitchell.

Tom Morse .... William Russell
Jessie McRae .... Alma Bennett
Bully West .... Stanton Heck
Angus McRae .... Charles K. French
Carl Morse .... James Gordon
Whaley .... Carl Stockdale

Another of those red-blood-he-man melodramas in the familiar vein of William Russell, this time with the locale among the splendid pine forests of the northwest. Scenically the picture is a beauty, dramatically it has plenty of action and melodramatic punch with a climax in a hand-to-hand fist fight between hero and heavy that delivers.

One agreeable circumstance in these Russell-Fox productions is that you never are in doubt of what it's all about. It's plain candid blood-and-thunder and makes no pretense beyond that appeal. It's much better than those cheap melodramas that introduce philosophical fluff via the stilted titles in a transparent effort to give the picture class and tone, but which cheapens rather than elevates. This is a simple thriller and lets it go at that.

But it has one novelty. It is placed in the Canadian Rockies and not a single Mounted Police constable appears, although the force is mentioned. They pack a lot of story into these five reels, but it is well handled and is always plain and understandable.

There are practically no interiors, as commonly happens in the Russell series, which serves two purposes—the natural settings help the illusion and the outlay by Mr. Fox is materially reduced. Russell is an attractive homely hero and he has as his leading woman a raving beauty in the dark Alma Bennett. Action starts early and keeps up at a fair gait to the finish, although the final clinch is somewhat delayed after the principal line of action has run to its climax.

Tom is the young nephew of a northwest trading magnate, off on his first trip to learn the business. Jessie, the ward of an old Scotch trapper, steals upon the expedition and shoots holes in their barrels of whiskey being carried into the wilderness to bribe the Indians. She is pursued to the trapper's home. A fade-back shows how the Scotchman kidnapped the girl in babyhood to revenge her father for his supposed theft of the Scot's wife, and has treated her cruelly for years.

She tells Tom of the wickedness of giving whiskey to the Indians, and Tom decides to stop the practice of the trading companies. When he returns after a trip to the trading company's headquarters, he is made post manager and discharges Bully West, the boss. West, about to leave the country, buys the girl from the Scotchman and departs. Tom learns of the old trapper's cruelty and sets off to rescue the girl and punish West. They come together in the deep forest for the big fight and the picture's climax. Then it turns out that Jessie is really the old Scotchman's own daughter and not his enemy's, as he supposed. This prepares for the final embrace and wedding bells.

Good average melodrama for the daily change houses. *Rush.*

THE DEVIL'S BOWL

William Steiner Western, starring Neal Hart. Story by Phil Le Noir; script and direction by Neal Hart. Stanley, New York, April 20, 1923. Time, 54 minutes.

Helen Hand	Catherine Bennett
Jim Sands	W. J. Allen
His Wife	Fonda Holt
Sam Ramsey	Neal Hart
Sergt. Jerry O'Neil	William McLaughlin
Andy Walker	John Beck
Mery Walker	Gertrude Ryan

Of all the hoak, slow, wearisome and entirely slipshod Westerns, this one takes the palm. It is the worst bit of screen material that has come along the pike in a couple of years, at least.

Perhaps there was a story when Phil Le Noir wrote "The Man Who Wouldn't Take Off His Hat," but when the star, director and script-writer combination represented by Neal Hart got through with it it wasn't anything. The feature as a picture isn't even suited to the nickel houses, if there are any of them left. How the Stanley, right off of Broadway and 42nd street, where they get a 25-cent admission, ever played it is a question. The house has a great drop in play that comes no matter what is on the screen, and that may account for it.

There is one bet in the picture, however — Catherine Bennett. At present she can't act, but if there is some one looking for a different type of blonde who screens well and will have the patience to teach her something, she should develop.

The reason for the draggy tempo is the same as with every production where the star is permitted to direct himself. All stars like themselves, and Neal Hart isn't any exception, so he figures that in any picture that he makes he will give the public just as much as possible of himself. He does it in this picture until one wearies of seeing a great big hulk of a man trying to emote all over the lot.

Hart plays a ranch foreman engaged to a girl visiting the owner. She has a jealous disposition, and when he receives a letter in a woman's handwriting she becomes furious and leaves. He quits his job and starts out in response to the letter. This letter and the mission he undertakes are counted on for the suspense. In the end it is disclosed the girl who wrote it was his sister. Hart starts out to rescue her from the Mexican bad lands, where her husband, a horse thief, has taken her. The husband gets the drop on brother, compels him to change clothes, and then brother is grabbed and branded as the thief.

Later, when he is getting out of the country with his sister, the husband picks the girl off from the brush, and brother is held by the Mexican authorities and accused of the crime. But he gets his man and squares it with the girl.

The titling is particularly bad. The phrases, "can't understand," "won't understand" and "wouldn't understand," are used a score of times. *Fred.*

THE TOWN SCANDAL

Universal starring Gladys Walton. Story by Frederick Arnold Kummer, script by Hugh Hoffman. Directed by King Baggot. At Loew's New York, New York, on double feature bill April 20. Time 57 minutes.

Jean Crosby	Gladys Walton
Toby Caswell	Edward Hearne
Avery Crawford	Edward McWade
Bill Ramsey	Charles Hill Mailes
Samuel Grimes	William Welsh
Lysander Sprowl	William Franey
Mrs. Crawford	Anna Hernandez
Mrs. Sprowl	Virginia Bordman
Mrs. Grimes	Nadine Beresford
Mrs. Ramsey	Louise Reming Barnes
Effie Strong	Rosa Gore
Trixie	Margaret Morris

Corking little light comedy drama that should send the averange film audience away pleased. Almost any exhibitor of the smaller towns and houses can play it for it ridicules the small town busy bodies always legislating for blue laws. Even though the little production contains this propaganda it is mighty good entertainment that has any number of laughs.

A chorus girl goes back to her home town for a summer vacation. After there for a short time rehearsals are called and she returns to the city. All of the "big men" of the town drift down to the city from time to time and all try to "date her up." When she goes back again to the home town the following summer and tries to get a job, they're all off of her, until she does go to work on a small paper that has been started by an enterprizing young man and begins to write the "Life of a Chorus Girl." It is veiled blackmail in the eyes of the old boys and they try to buy her off, but she refuses a bankroll and tells them that the second installment of the story will give them all something to really talk about.

They band together and try to Klu Klux the young editor but the girl bursts in at the right minute and saves the day and her script, tearing the latter into shreds when they all promise there will be no more blue laws in the town.

Gladys Walton, who is getting to look more like Alice Brady on the screen is a charming and vivacious heroine and makes a corking little number leader with a cute shimmy dance in the musical comedy stuff. Edward Hearne with little to do does more than well as the editor hero. The balance of the roles are in the majority exaggerated characterizations built for laughs and get them. It's a worth while little program feature. *Fred.*

Foreign Films

BLAZING AIR WAY TO INDIA

London, April 5.

In 1922 Captain Geoffrey Malins, O. B. E., the man who made the photographic record of the German front and "shot" the worst fighting on the Somme, Captain Macmillan, M. C., and another officer set off from Croydon Aerodrome to circle the world by aeroplane. They only succeeded in blazing the way to India, where in the Bay of Bengal they had to come down with their Fairy hydroplane.

For three days and three nights Malins and Macmillan stuck to one of the floats of their machine—the other man had been taken ill and left them at Calcutta—until today they were taken off by a destroyer which had been searching for them. Before then they had been sighted by a boat commanded by a native skipper, who, however, sailed by. On being apprehended by the authorities this man said he understood that if the men on the float were dead he knew he would have to keep their widows and families; if alive, he would have to keep them. It is pleasant to note that this humanitarian was deprived of his "ticket" as a sailing master. Having been rescued, both Malins and Macmillan spent some time in a hospital and then came home. The hydroplane has never been discovered; the aeroplane on which their 10,000-mile journey was accomplished is in the University Museum of Benares, having been purchased by the faculty when put up for public auction at the Queen's theatre, Calcutta.

Toward the end of the summer Malins and Macmillan will take up their circle of the world. Starting from Calcutta, they will make Vancouver via Japan; from there on to Winnipeg, New York and home. This portion of the journey Malins looks upon as easy on account of civilization. He reckons the worst part of the trip will be over the Northern Pacific to Vancouver, but on the beginning of the journey he hopes to do 500 miles a day from Calcutta to Vancouver before meeting the rough stuff. For this second trip of the airmen a boat will be sent out previous to the flight and its crew will establish food and petrol dumps at a distance of 200 miles apart. These will be left in charge of armed men, who may be on duty for months absolutely alone. Such guards are necessary in order to protect the valuable stores from fur and seal poachers.

The actual time of flying from Croydon to Calcutta occupied 112 hours. Eight days were required to do one-third of the circle round the world.

The picture, which was shown today before members of the Royal family, distinguished soldiers, sailors and politicians, was remarkably interesting on account of its obvious sincerity and truth. While the simplicity of Malins, who talked with it, and the sub-titles did much to convey the danger of the trip, the picture is by no means without humor even when things seem desperate and the most is made of every chance. Among the most remarkable views are those of Mount Vesuvius in erection with the machine skimming the lip of the crater, the different far-away outposts of empire with soldiers who do not look exactly like going on parade with every button bright, a cloud mirage of mountains at 7,000 feet, Macmillan's take-off on a road in India almost too narrow to let the aeroplane's wings get past, and the pictures taken while flying through the clouds over India during the monsoon season. Not the most remarkable feature in the picture is the solid friendliness of all races to the aviators, whether in France, Italy, Greece, Persia, Arabia or Hindustan, where they always found mechanics and helpers. The only person who seemed to have failed them was the native skipper, who feared if he saved their lives he might have to keep them.

At the special show Malins, in the union of the Air Section of the Legion of Frontiersmen which he founded, was left alone to face the public. Macmillan, who should have been with him, has just finished blazing a new air track from Britain to Serbia, and was hung up by snow storms on the return journey. Before starting on their new trip one of the officers will personally lecture at each showing of the picture, which should be one of the biggest box office propositions going. *Gore.*

LAND OF OUR FATHERS

London, April 6.

This picture, made by George Layton, once a vaudeville "star," is a fine example of how not to do it. It takes the watcher back 10 years. The story is crude and full of the long arm of coincidence, without ever once giving even a trace of reality. If the authoress, Diana Torr, and the producer, Fred Rains, had gone out deliberately to weave a network of improbabilities they could not have succeeded better.

Take a famous violinist who vanishes after achieving a concert and turns up only a few miles from his home, is taken care of and given another name, his memory having gone—that might have been plausible enough 200 years ago, but today there are many newspapers, even in Wales, and such a disappearance would have been far too good "copy" to miss. This is but one of the absurdities with which this picture, "passed for Universal exhibition by the British Board of Film Censors," abounds.

David Morgan, a famous violinist, loves Dilys Colwyn, and is loved by her. His rascally cousin plots to have him kidnapped, and this is done after he has created a furore at a great concert. Dilya mourns him as dead, but her mother puts sleuths upon the scent. Meanwhile David has been washed ashore and taken care of by the Lady Gwenneth, "the proud daughter of a haughty race," and her father, the earl. Without knowing anything about him, the Lady Gwenneth goes out to capture her treasure trove, and pursues him to the extent of marriage. On their honeymoon David hears a hotel orchestra play "Land of My Fathers" and collapses. Later he discovers he is a musician and begins to neglect her for his violin. Seeking solace, Lady Gwenneth invites her best friend, who is, of course, Dilys, to come and stay at the ancestral hall. At the sight of her David remembers everything and clasps her in his arms. The earl does not seem to worry much, but Gwen is a little peeved. As David and Dilys get more and more on their old footing, this peevishness becomes anger, and the proud beauty pushes the other girl over the edge of a cliff. Of course, she does not fall far and is easily rescued, but, thinking she is a murderous, her ladyship commits suicide. The reunited couple then sail away, according to a sub-title, on a "sea of happiness."

The "locations" include some fine examples of Welsh scenery. Generally, the acting is up to the story. Seldom have so many wooden people ever been gathered together in one picture. The one redeeming part is the performance of Fred Rains as "Bad Bill." He is a very fine actor, but his production work almost amounts to crime.

Prior to this five-reeler the trade audience was harrowed by a comedy "Our Aggie." The one redeeming feature about this was the whispered information the lady who put the money up and starred as Aggie used to come down in her own car, which was loaded with bottles of champagne, port and whisky, with which to reconcile the company to its fate. Seventy-five per cent. of the people appearing in these two films should be prevented by law from ever trying to do it again. As for the pictures themselves, they are not worth the electricity required to project them.

THE BLUE LAGOON
London, April 3.

This film adaptation of a de Vere Stacpoole's novel is one of the best pictures ever made by a British company. The adapter has handled his subject with great skill and the many scenes which might have been made simply an excuse for sensuality and nastiness have been handled with a delicacy which removes any trace of lasciviousness. This cannot have been an easy matter considering the story and the almost complete nudity of the leading players. The scenes on board ship are realistic, and a fire scene has been done with an effective suggestion of deadly peril which is far and away superior to the usual elaborateness which generally marks such episodes. Most of the scenes have been made on a tropical island and all of them are very beautiful. The fight with the octopus is well done and has a great semblance of truth. The novel has been fairly well adhered to.

Two children, Dick and Emmeline, are cast away with an old servant, Paddy Button. They land on the desert island, as in the book, and Paddy takes up his job as nurse. Presently, through a discovery of rum, he drinks himself to death. The children grow up without any idea of sex until the awakening is brought about by a chance blow. The child is born and the young couple are discovered by the parent of the boy and guardian of the girl who has never ceased to search for them. Then, going away from the novel, they are once more left alone in their island paradise.

The acting is exceptionally good. Mollie Adair and Arthur Pusey are excellent as the boy and girl. Dick Cruickshanks gives a fine performance of Paddy Button, and the support is very good. This picture, the first of a new series of African Film Productions, marks a great advance in British photoplay art.

WONDERLAND OF BIG GAME
London, April 10.

This film, personally made and described by Major A. Radcliffe Dugmore, is anything but a good showman's proposition. At the outset of his lecture Major Dugmore damages his own cause by apologizing for his photograph, for the fact that his pictures were not as good as they might have been. This apologetic beginning has become the fashion at the Polytechnic Hall, where this picture was shown, and at the Philharmonic, and has badly damaged more than one picture of this kind. True the photography is anything but good but there has been much worse and the pictures themselves are not very interesting although many wild animals are shown on their native heath and taken under circumstances requiring great patience and pluck. Pictures are shown of a family of rhinoceroses, of herds of great elephants including giants of the species who came to within eight feet of the hidden cameraman, of buffalos, of giraffes and zebras. There are also some fine and unusual pictures of bird-life.

During the great war Major Dugmore, after being gassed and wounded, was sent to America on a special lecturing mission. Unfortunately his present program with its very many colored "magic lantern" slides partakes too much of the nature of a Sunday School entertainment to be much of a pull for the general public.

AUX JARDINS DE MURCIE
Paris, April 10.

The picture version of this French play from the Spanish drama of Feliuy Cadina, entitled "Maria del Carmen," and given in English as "Spanish Love," has been completed by Louis Mercanton (Avery Hopwood and Mary Roberts Rinehart adapted the Spanish play for the American stage in 1920). It is one of his best productions, mainly photographed in North Africa, where some splendid effects have been secured. The acting is excellent, and the story is more fully explained than in the stage version.

The scenario of this fine picture commenced with the daily disputes among the inhabitants of the plain of Murcia, known as the Huerta, relative to the irrigation, the farmers of the upper country being accused by the lower land of retaining the waters for their own uses.

The "highlanders" looked on Xavier, son of Domingo, a rich farmer, as their chief, while the "lowlanders" were led by Pencho, a disputatious youth who is betrothed to Maria del Carmen, the prettiest girl in the region.

One evening the "lowlanders" detect the "highlanders" in the act of closing the sluices and thus changing the stream to their own advantage. The two sides come to a pitched battle, Xavier and Pencho withdrawing to a secluded spot to fight it out. After a desperate duel Xavier falls seriously wounded and is afterwards found unconscious by his father and companions. The father also picks up Pencho's knife, a formidable weapon, known throughout the Huerta because of the inscription engraved on the blade:

*"For her to see, my eyes;
For her to keep, my steel."*

On the pressing advice of his friends, and after a last painful interview with his sweetheart, Maria, Pencho escapes to Africa to avoid being arrested. Anxious days follow, both for the parted lovers and for the father of Xavier who watches over his wounded son. In order to appease Domingo's anger and particularly to enable Pencho to return safely to her in the Huerta, Maria del Carmen offers to assist in nursing the invalid. The unhappy father accepts, hoping her soothing presence will facilitate his boy's convalescence. This anticipation is fully realized and Xavier slowly but surely gains strength, at the same time becoming sincerely attached to his gentle nurse.

The gossipers of the village, judging by appearances as usual, spread the report that selfish interests have alone inspired Maria's conduct, and the proverbial cupidity of her parents enhanced the supposition, so that Pencho's faithful friend Pepuso writes to him in Africa, explaining the situation and the infidelity of his sweetheart.

Meanwhile the inevitable happens, and believing himself completely cured, Xavier confesses his love for Maria, asking her to be his wife. She frankly explains she is engaged to Pencho, but Domingo, thinking only of his son's future and desirous at any cost of fulfilling Xavier's desire, has little difficulty in convincing Maria's parents of the benefits they may all derive from such a union. Maria's inflexibility is ultimately stifled by the knowledge that the father has positive proof of Pencho's guilt. To enable her former lover to return to his home without danger of arrest and to be near her, she finally accepts the offer of marriage.

On receiving Pepuso's letter, and despite the risk of being denounced, Pencho hastens back to claim his betrothed. Maria hears his serenade at her window, and goes out to greet him. She explains the true conditions and begs him to flee again for a time, as she has plighted troth to Xavier and is soon to be married.

Pencho refuses to act on such counsel and fearlessly appears the next day at a local festivity known as the "accordailles" where all the village is assembled and there publicly denounces himself as having attempted to kill Xavier. The latter insults his rival and offers to renew the duel. Pencho, however, is arrested and detained by the sheriff in the house of Domingo while he hastens to the nearest town to fetch the guard. At nightfall Domingo offers him his freedom, but Pencho refuses, remembering he has accepted to fight Xavier at the first opportunity.

As soon as the father has gone, leaving the door open, Xavier enters the cellar where Pencho is detained. On their way out they overhear a conversation between Domingo and the doctor who has been attending Xavier. The medical man has ultimately considered it his duty to warn the distracted father that his son is beyond permanent recovery and his days are already numbered. On hearing this sentence Xavier faints and Pencho fraternally supports him. When the invalid recovers his senses he begs his rival to kill him, whereupon Pencho taking pity on the poor fellow, declares he no longer counts him as an enemy.

It has already been arranged that Maria would elope with Pencho, and she now appears prepared for the journey. Xavier feels the separation keenly and would fain prevent their departure. Nevertheless, he realizes on the selfishness of such opposition and facilitates the lovers leaving, the two young men, with a simultaneous movement cordially embracing one another at the last moment.

Then, while Pencho and Maria del Carmen hastily disappear in the distance, Xavier, crushed with dispair, picks up a flower left behind by the girl and presses it passionately against his heart.

Kendrew.

MOSCOW KAMERNY THEATRE
Paris, April 6.

Tairoff is in the French capital with a troupe of Russians prior to a would-be tour of the world. It is not in the Russian version of Lecocq's operetta, "Girofle-Girofla," that we can judge the suitability of an Anglo-Saxon engagement.

As a curious show for vaudeville it might go if cut from three hours to 20 minutes, but as a serious dramatic performance we want to see more before giving a definite opinion.

Fancy a number of persons conversing in Russian, without scenery worth mentioning, but replaced by traps, ladders, platform and collapsible furniture, the scenic manipulation being set (according to Tairoff) to the rhythm of the play. The manager of the Kamerny Teatr claims this French musical comedy done in his own vernacular has "enfranchised the actor from the tyranny of dress." He states he founded his theatre in 1914 "as the humble servant of the dramatist, while remaining an autonomous and self-sufficing art, for which a new school of actor had to be created." This may be very beautiful, but is far beyond the average playgoer in France, and elsewhere, except, perhaps, in Moscow, where the audience fully understands every line of the script.

The text is a pretext for introducing the "new" theatre, humorously dubbed as acrobatic. When a table folds up and a rocking chair appears in its place, constituting a new set, we can safely consider we have reached the acme of mad stage craft. That Russian art is superb we all acknowledge, but the sample presented at the Theatre des Champs Elysees by Tairoff and his company is not of the sort to suit outside its own country, particularly when adapted to a foreign work which is almost a household word in France.

Had Tairoff given an original Russian piece with his curious settings it would have met with a better reception, and he has been unwisely counseled in presenting Russian versions of French plays under such conditions, particularly in France.

Kendrew.

WITHIN THE LAW

First National release starring Norma Talmadge, presented by Joseph M. Schenck. A screen adaption of Bayard Veiller's play of the same title by Frances Marion, directed by Frank Lloyd. Shown at the Strand, New York, week April 29, 1923. Time 81 minutes.

Mary Turner............Norma Talmadge
Joe Garson......................Lew Cody
Dick Gilder....................Jack Mulhall
Aggie Lynch..................Eileen Percy
Edward Gilder..............Joseph Kilgour
Demarest...................Arthur S. Hull
Helen Morris..............Helen Ferguson
Cassidy ....Lincoln Plummer
General Hastings........Thomas Ricketts
Irwin........................Lionel Belmore
English Eddie................Warde Crance
Darcy..........................Eddie Boland
Gilder's Secretary........Catherine Murphy
Burke.....................DeWitt Jennings

This is the second time that a screen version of the Bayard Veiller play, "Within the Law," has been made. The first was turned out by Vitagraph about six years ago, with Alice Joyce in the principal role. On this occasion Joseph M. Schenck is the sponsor for the picture Norma Talmadge is starred in. The question is, Will Miss Talmadge pull sufficiently at the box office to overcome the fact that a number of people have previously seen the picture? At the Strand Sunday afternoon any casual observer would have immediately answered, "Yes." But any one who watches the Strand business closely would wonder, for at the performance that started at 4 p. m. there were plenty of seats available, and from then on until 5:45, when the picture ended, there were no standees at the back of the house. That isn't the regular story at the Strand, but perhaps the fact that daylight saving for the summer became effective at 2 a. m. Sunday may have accounted for this to a certain extent, for a majority of the people in the big town forgot to change their watches in accordance with the law.

This version of "Within the Law" is particularly well done, and Norma Talmadge is a particularly effective **Mary Turner, while Eileen Percy is admirable as Aggie Lynch, but much of Aggie's effectiveness was in her flip speeches, and these to a great extent were of necessity omitted on the screen. However, there is a little fault to find with the fact that Lew Cody was chosen** as Joe Carson. Cody is far too well identified to the fan mind as a heavy to have him accepted as a heroic crook figure. It looked as though the Strand audience was waiting at any moment to see him do an about face in his role and try to knock off the hero. Incidentally Jack Mulhall was all that could be desired as the younger Gilder.

The cast supporting these principal characters is a lengthy one and fairly bristles with names that are well known on stage and screen, and this should be an asset to the picture. *Fred.*

THE NE'ER-DO-WELL

Adolph Zukor presents Thomas Meighan in an adaptation by Louis Stevens of Rex Beach's novel of the same name; directed by Alfred Green. At the Rivoli April 29.

Kirk Anthony............Thomas Meighan
Chiquita..............................Lila Lee
Edith Cortlandt.............Gertrude Astor
Stephen Cortlandt..............John Miltern
Andres Garavel...............Gus Weinberg
Ramon Alfarez......................Sid Smith
Clifford.......................George O'Brien
Allen Allan......................Jules Cowles
Runnels........................Laurance Wheat

The picture is bound to make good if only on the strength of Meighan's presence at the head of the cast. That one best bet of Famous Players has a following loyal enough to support him in almost anything that will pass muster. This production is only so so. It adds nothing to Meighan's reputation, but it makes a satisfactory enough vehicle for an established "name." The story has strong points, notably a swift and absorbing denouement, but its earlier stages are draggy.

It does seem that this defect is **almost inherent in adapted novels which present a troublesome problem to the adapter, who is ordinarily faced with an embarrassment of material. It takes as much resourcefulness and perhaps more sound judgment to turn a novel into a picture than it does to create an original play.** In this case the introductory passages by which the basic situation is planted are a bit tiresome, but a certain ingenuity of treatment makes some compensation.

For example, it is necessary to lay a foundation of character for the reckless hero. This is done by way of an enlivening incident involving a wild party of college football players in a Broadway hotel in which they capture the whole chorus of a restaurant revue and carry them off to a private dining room. This has a good value as spectacular display as well as the familiar "cabaret" flash, and likewise introduces an element of comedy. Altogether, it gets the picture well started.

When it is in full swing, the scene shifts to Panama, and we go to plot-planting all over again for a momentary halt. However, when the new situation is established the complications gain speed and vigor in South American political and romantic intrigue and interest is sustained to the end.

Meighan is not at his best. Something of his old ease and spontaneity seems missing, but the reason is not apparent on the surface. The production is a fine one in technical details with real backgrounds in Panama and well managed "atmosphere" which registers as authentic without conscious effort. *Rush.*

GOOD-BYE GIRLS

William Fox production starring William Russell. Story by George Foxhall, adapted by Jos. F. Poland. Directed by Jerome Storm. Shown at Fox's Academy, N. Y., April 29-May 2, 1923. Double feature bill. Time, 49 minutes.

Vance McPhee............William Russell
Bill Jordan.....................Tom Wilson
Florence Brown...............Carmel Meyers

Corking comedy, built solely for laughs. On the screen it gets them one after the other. The story is one of the mystery affairs handled somewhat after the manner of "Seven Keys to Baldpate," that has as its only weak point the finish. However, for laughing purposes the picture is certainly well worth playing in the smaller houses, and in the bigger theatres it will fill in on the double-feature bills to take away the sting of any heavy drama that might be shown.

William Russell is the author of popular fiction, on the verge of a nervous breakdown, who is ordered by his physician to take a rest. An aunt lately deceased has left him a country home, and he decides that that is just what the doctor ordered. On his arrival there the negro mammy servant informs him that a sailing boat in the bay is owned by a young lady who either wants to buy or rent the house. The young woman is being pursued by a gang of roughnecks who are seeking to obtain a box that she has in her possession. For the balance it is nothing but a succession of fights, shots, housebreaking, automobile chases and other mysterious stuff all worked out for laughs.

In the finish the doctor appears on the scene and pronounces his patient cured by the rest that he has had. A finish to the story that would have brought a laugh would have **been the confession on the part of the doctor that he had arranged the whole affair to give his patient physical excitement, instead of the rather old-fashioned story of the girl to the effect that the mysterious box contained the plans for a submarine that her father had evolved** and the pursuers were agents of a foreign government trying to secure them.

Russell as the author-rest seeker worked hard and scored, but not to any greater extent than did Tom Wilson, working opposite him as his servant in blackface. Carmel Meyers was the little lady of the plot who had the mysterious box and did all that was required of her. But why the title, "Good-Bye Girls." She is the only girl in the picture, and he doesn't say good-bye to her, for the final fadeout has the usual clinch. *Fred.*

MAIN STREET

Los Angeles, May 2.

Warner Brothers' production from the novel of the same name by Sinclair Lewis. Adapted for the screen by Julien Josephson, with Harry Beaumont the director and Homer Scott the photographer. Time, 1.46. At the Mission, Los Angeles, week April 25.

Dr. Will Kennicott..................Monte Blue
Carol Milford..................Florence Vidor
Erik Valborg......................Robert Gordon
Adolph Valborg........................Noah Beery
Miles Bjornstam.......................Alan Hale
Bea Sorenson......................Louise Fazenda
Dave Dyer..........................Harry Myers

Advertised to be shown in 10 reels, the picture is far too lengthy to ever install itself in the program houses as a satisfying feature, due to the time consumed. But that was at its initial presentation, and there will be undoubtedly some drastic cutting.

For those who read the book and enjoyed it the celluloid version will disappoint. While it may follow the script more or less closely, the action jumps to such extremes and so much of the original text has been omitted the picturization must suffer in comparison.

A consensus of opinion would indicate that the producers took a long chance on making a picture out of the story, for the book's principal attribute was the penmanship of the author in drawing his characterizations of the small-town inhabitants. That left little action upon which to build interest for filming. The projecting emphatically revealed this fact. It is certain the picture lacks the staying power to make it entertainment for a consummation of the one that approaches the "special" class.

The novel looks to have been probed of all its resources for the screen, and the directing seems to have woefully drawn out the presentation through an overabundance of unnecessary closeups. Besides which the actual tale lacks that underlying quality of body. Deletion will help, and with the draw at the box office through the title, this feature may get by, although to say it is a good picture is to stretch a point.

The tale is that of a small-town doctor who marries a city girl and brings her to his home town, where she immediately inaugurates a personal campaign to revolutionize the community's mode of living. Finding the life she has selected flagrantly droll, besides failing in her efforts to awake the town folks from their years of lethargy, she becomes innocently embroiled in an affair with a local youth of big league ideas. It is in the climax of this situation wherein the picture makes its only bid for high attention.

Other than that it is simply a matter of revealing the routine the Gopher Prairie locals indulge in, and it shapes as a procession of types before the camera more than anything else. The finale is reached when the wife realizes she is beaten and resigns herself to the situation.

The playing permits Monte Blue and Florence Vidor footage to the point where they overshadow everyone else. Both impress as having struggled valiantly with their burdens of the rube doctor and the wife. It is but fair to give Miss Vidor an "edge," so far as actual results are concerned. Beyond that and other than Louise Fazenda, who made a Swedish servant girl stand out, the cast is pretty much jumbled and buried in the ensembles, so that the full value of the names listed is lost.

Scenicly it holds nothing, with perhaps the best shot a snowstorm view, looking down the main thoroughfare of the village. The photography may be said to average with that percentage gained through a minority of excellent bits at close range upon Miss Vidor. At one point the lighting is in distinct contrast with that of the immediate preceding scene.

Hence it is to wonder what the producers of this vehicle will do with "Babbitt," another of Lewis' works, and on their schedule for screening. The last-named novel received much adverse criticism and is narrated to hold even less material for the camera than "Main Street." Then there is the author's angle, who will, or has, viewed the screening of his work with what must be some misgiving, for "Main Street" doesn't deliver as a picture. *Skig.*

BACKBONE

Distinctive Pictures Corp. production, featuring Alfred Lunt and Edith Roberts. Adapted from the Sat. Eve. Post. story by Clarance Budington Kelland. Directed by Edward Sloman. Released through Goldwyn. Shown at the Capitol week April 29. Time, 74 minutes.

Yvonne.............................Edith Roberts
John Thorne..........................Alfred Lunt
Colonel Tip.......................James D. Doyle
Bracken.........................William B. Mack
Doc Roper...........................Frank Evans
Andre..............................L. E. La Croix
Ken.................................Charles Fang
The Indian........................Frank Hagney
Mrs. Whidden....................Marion Abbott
When the romance began in France hundreds of years ago.
Yvonne de Chausson.........Edith Roberts
Andre de Mersay..................Alfred Lunt
Minister of State........George MacQuarrie
Captain of Guards............J. W. Johnson
King...............................Hugh Huntley
Robert de Chausson.......William Walcott
Jailer..................................Adolf Miller

This is the first of the Distinctive Pictures that Goldwyn is releasing. It is a program production of a little better than the average quality. It is a snow story, with the scenes laid in the north Maine woods. Incidentally the picture marks the screen debut of Alfred Lunt, who scored so strongly in Booth Tarkington's "Clarence" on the stage. Edith Roberts is co-featured with him in the picture. "Backbone" does not rank as a special in the sense of the word that Broadway accepts special screen productions, but it will look all right to the smaller houses.

"Backbone" as a title might mean Kitty Gordon as much as it means anything in the picture. As a matter of fact, it is seemingly exactly what the picture does lack.

The one outstanding bit of the tale is the flashback into ancient France for about a reel or so, showing the reason for the advent of the family that is carrying on the modern tale in the Maine woods of today. That is a bit that was well handled. This bringing together of a combination of costume stuff and a snow picture stands out.

The outdoor shots in the real snow were great, the studio set of the exterior of the home of the de Mersays, also covered with snow, showed clearly that it was shot indoors. That sort of stuff isn't expected in pictures that are presented in Broadway's pre-release houses.

The story of "Backbone" tells of a family that has lived for several centuries in the Maine woods and won a fortune from the forests of that state. They are lumber people. The sole survivor of the male line is Andre de Mersay and his sole blood relation living is his granddaughter, who at the opening of the story is abroad. He has his late sister's adopted son handling his business affairs, and discovers that he is robbing him. As he orders the younger man from the house he is stricken with a heart attack. The younger man returns with his companion, a doctor, who has been without a patient in the town because none of the inhabitants would trust themselves to his care, knowing that originally he was a horse doctor. The two plan to keep the old man from all of his friends, and when the elder de Mersay died during the night they continue the deception, even after the return of the granddaughter.

Then comes a period where a stranger enters the scene and takes over a lumber tract and starts to develop it. The foster son of the de Mersays and his doctor companion start a long fight to prevent his working the timber. But finally he manages to beat them at their own game, and it is disclosed that he was a descendant of the opposite side to the ancient romance that started in France.

The principal trouble is that it is not a production that one can come in late on and witness the latter reels and then see the preceding portion. For the element of suspense that goes with the deception of the continued illness of the head of the house and the mysterious spirit-like singing that is supposed to break down the will of one of the criminals are such that, once they are disclosed, the interest in the picture ends.

Mr. Lunt, however, displayed the fact that he is destined to be one of the real vigorous heroic types of screen leading men of the future, and it seems certain that he is destined for bigger things in pictures. Miss Roberts, on the other hand, failed to fill the requirements of her role.. Her matchless beauty referred to in the story was far from being apparent. Major Doyle in a comedy role, that of a retired vaudeville artist who returned to his native town and became the hotel keeper, brought many laughs. The Maje proved himself 100 per cent. for the screen, and when the picture hits the neighborhood houses the Major should obtain a tremendous vogue in the personal appearance field.

Fred.

VANITY FAIR

Hugo Ballin production of Thackeray's "Vanity Fair" with Mabel Ballin as star. Directed by Hugo Ballin. Released by Goldwyn. At the Capitol, New York, week May 6, 1923. Time, 78 minutes.

Becky Sharp	Mabel Ballin
Marquis of Steyne	Hobart Bosworth
Rawdon Crawley	George Walsh
George Osborne	Harrison Ford
Capt. William Dobbin	Earle Fox
Amelia Sedley	Eleanor Boardman
Joseph Sedley	Willard Louis
Sir Pitt Crawley	Robert Mack

If ever the screen presented a most consummate piece of butchery of a masterpiece of literature in an effort on the part of a director to make a complete series of close-ups of his star-wife, this is the instance.

This feature should not have been titled "Vanity Fair." That is a reflection on Thackeray. It should have been entitled "A continuous close-up of Mabel Ballin in many reels."

Never in several years at the Capitol has the writer ever heard so great a volume of voiced condemnation come from an audience during the screening of a picture and on the way out of the house as was listened to last Sunday evening at the last performance. Several women earlier in the evening wanted to know how any one could tell what the picture was all about. It is certain that if even Thackeray saw it he wouldn't know, for he **wouldn't recognize his brain child in the film footage that Hugo Ballin turned out with the label of Thackeray's story on it.**

The Capitol management itself cannot be blamed for running the picture, for it is a Goldwyn release. But if the business starts falling off there, there is one thing to be blamed and that is the type of features that have been shown at the theatre for the last two weeks. No house can stand up under this type of entertainment for its patrons and continue to hold patronage. The Goldwyn people should be the first to realize that pictures of this type and calibre are going to do inestimable harm to their brand name, if they continue to foist them on Broadway audiences at the biggest theatre of its kind in the world.

The picture has a cast of names in support of Mabel Ballin, but they can't do anything to counteract the interminable close-ups of the star. Miss Ballin, however, isn't bad to look upon, and if given a chance to have played Becky Sharp she might have done so, but that would have meant the director would have had to have shot something that might have resembled a continuity of story, which would have spoiled his close-up gorging.

"Vanity Fair" is too replete with faults to go into them in detail. It isn't "Vanity Fair," and not only that, it isn't even a fair picture of ordinary program quality. *Fred.*

THE DEATH LEAP

London, April 24.

This Astoria picture is frankly sensational rubbish and is funnier than any comedy. Re-subtitled from the proper angle, it would be worth a fortune to a showman who had an intelligent public. The story is sheer tripe, badly told and without any continuity, the only idea of the producer being to make his "star" accomplish weird stunts every other minute. These stunts are put in haphazardly and have nothing to do with the story. Neither is there any excuse for the title.

The little Princess Renee has been abducted by the Grand Duke and is being held a prisoner in the slums, where she is compelled to beg. A rich engineer rescues her and is aided by Albertini, "the strongest man in the works." The engineer's daughter falls in love with this uncouth laborer, but he has little time for romance. His occupation consists of jumping onto express trains, climbing high steeples, chimneys, diving into rivers, fighting as many men as the producer can afford and generally behaving in a manner which no man ever has done, not even in a nightmare. In the end the little Princess sits upon the throne and Albertini wins the love of the wealthy engineer's daughter. There is no production and no acting. The whole thing is rubbish.

SCARS OF JEALOUSY

Thos. H. Ince production with Frank Keenan starred. Lloyd Hughes and Marguerite de la Motte featured. Story by Anthony M. Rudd, directed by Lambert Hillyer. First National, distributor. At Strand, New York, week May 6. Time, 65 minutes.

Coddy Jakes	Lloyd Hughes
Colonel Newland	Frank Keenan
Helen Meanix	Marguerite de la Motte
Jeff Newland	Edward Burns
Zeke Jakes	James Mason

While this story sounds original in its subject as far as known, unfortunately it has been too familiarly set. And then again it is a little too much of a narrative and too little of a picture. Intertwined, though with the tale are some bits of action, the best a couple of fist fights, and there is a forest fire fairly well done. But in total "Scars of Jealousy" hardly reaches beyond an average weekly release for the better houses, and in some of the better houses may not reach that high.

One bad setback, becoming more evident as the film proceeds, is that there is scarce conjunction between the title and the subject. Scars of jealousy is accepted as meaning of the heart rather than the face, if one facial scar left remaining from a fist fight is accountable for the title. Otherwise there seems no reason for the present name of the picture. This will disappoint all of those whom the title may attract.

It starts with a sort of prolog in the days of Louis XIV of France telling how the king chased one of his nobles off the lot into New France as then known, now called America by the drys (only). The new sect appeared to settle in the moonshine country among the hills of Maryland, Virginia, Tennessee or Kentucky, wherever they have hills and moonshiners. According to this script, moonshining is an aged business.

The new settlers, called the Cajons, stood so well no one bothered them and everyone thought less than that of them. On the other side of the hill and not so far away was an old Colonel of the "yes, suh" brand, with a dissolute son. Skipping the detail, the father threw the son right out of his house and family, and, to make it harder, lured a crude youth of the Cajons to his home, builded him up into new clothes and intelligence, then lost him when the Cajon discovered he was only subbing.

After that the story winds in and out on the thread with the fights and the forest fire, and the Cajon going back after making a man out of the son, and incidentally copping the son's girl.

The sub and the son put up a dandy fight, two of them, either much better than the captions, for the captions in many spots were little short of terribly conventional.

Frank Keenan has the star part but isn't the star. Maybe that hurts too. Lloyd Hughes as the Cajon youth runs away with the film, with Edward Burns as the son close up, while Marguerite de la Motte as the ingenue is or isn't, according to the way you see and like her.

That also covers the general opinion this picture will create—some will and some won't like it. Many will get in and under its story, liking that in preference to its film manner of working out, and then again most of the picture fans will take it as it is superficially presented, an ordinary film meller.

Sime.

THE LITTLE GIRL NEXT DOOR

Produced by Blair Coan. Made in Chicago at the Essanay plant. Directed by W. S. Van Dyke. Six reels. First shown at Orpheum, Chicago.

Mary Slocum	Pauline Starke
Jim Manning	James Morrison
Milly Amory	Cramel Myers
Tug Wilson	Mitchel Lewis
Hank Hall	Edward Kennedy

Fifty cents top for this picture requires some nerve. The emphasis in the billing that it is an expose of spiritualistic tricks may justify the high price, which at the Orpheum and under the circumstances suggests something exceptionally notable in film productions. "The Little Girl Next Door" is very ordinary. There is no one in the cast who commands special attention and nothing in the acting or story to stand out. The strong point of the photoplay is the expose of spiritualistic tricks, only incidental.

This is a revamping of a white slavery film made when Barrett O'Hara was conducting a campaign in Chicago. Instead of that theme dope has been substituted. The picture has a young man fall into evil instead of the girl, as in the original picture, but he is rescued through the inborn virtue of the girl, who is wise beyond any reasonable expectations.

The fact that the picture was made in Chicago had little value here, as it was difficult to recognize the scenes. There is a fight which may carry some appeal to lovers of blood and thunder, but this is overbalanced by the opposition that the film may create on the part of those who think pictures have a greater purpose than to portray the evil of great cities.

Pauline Starke plays the country **girl very well. James Morrison is a nice looking leading man, though his work is not always convincing. Carmel Myers is the female heavy and puts beauty on the side of Satan. Mitchel Lewis is the male heavy and all that the term means.**

Loop.

SPAWN OF THE DESERT

Ben Wilson production starring William Fairbanks. Written by William Tuttle, directed by Ben Wilson. Shown at Loew's Circle, double feature bill, April 9, 1923. Time, 54 minutes.

Duke Steele	William Fairbanks
Sam Le Saint	Al Hart
Silver Sleed	Dempsey Tablor
Luck Sleed	Florence Gilbert

A western with all the usual stuff. A cheap western without much of a story that would keep an audience other than those of the smaller houses at all interested.

The opening has a wagon train (2 wagons). Perhaps that is going to be the regular thing in all westerns now that "The Covered Wagon" has caught on. From that point on the story has an association between an old desert wanderer and a young guide. The elder man has been searching for 18 years for his wife and daughter, stolen from him by his partner. The younger man accompanies him on his search because the elder's trusty rifle saved his life with a timely shot at the hands of the old man.

They wander into a mining camp where Silver Sleed is the boss. He runs the gambling house and the town. The old wanderer recognizes him as his quarry, and the girl falls in love with the young man. From that point, all apple sauce. Same old stuff done in the same old way with the villian finally disposed of and the father of the girl also dying, leaving the young hero to tear up an I. O. U. for $47,000 he won from the heavy at stud poker, so that the girl will have small change enough to go to school with.

Here is one thing that this type of picture does and that is help the poor shirt makers along. There is a fight between the hero and the heavy and the usual shirt tearing is done to perfection. The boys simply must bare their manly chests to thrill the film flappers it seems, and the shirt manufacturers are the gainers by their vanity.

In detail the picture, even as bad as it is, leaves much to be desired. The day of crepe hair is past as far as appearing before the camera with it is concerned, but one wouldn't think that to look at this production. The made to order whiskers stick out all over it. That goes for story as well as characters. *Fred.*

MASTERS OF MEN

Vitagraph production, presented by Albert E. Smith. Two other Smiths are concerned in the technical end of the picture, David Smith directing and another of the Smith clan "shooting" some corking photography. Adapted from the late Morgan Robertson's novel by C. Graham Baker. At the Cameo week of May 13. Runs 78 minutes.

Lieutenant Breen............Earle Williams
Mabel Arthur..................Alice Calhoun
Dick Halpin...................Cullen Landis
Bessie Fleming...............Wanda Hawley
"Pig Jones"..................Dick Sutherland
Sawyer......................Charles E. Mason
Mr. Thorpe.........................Bert Apling
Captain Bilker.....................Jack Curtis
"Nigger".......................Martin Turner

Sea stories are having their inning along Broadway these days. At the Cameo "Down to the Sea in Ships" held forth for about three months to very profitable business, and the Strand currently has a sea feature. This may account for the unusual number of nautical looking men seen around in this particular theatre.

The Morgan Robertson story has been pleasantly visualized. It is far from subtle in its denouement, but, for the average film fan, that commends it, if anything. The suspense is not maintained any too long, and the observer sits back with a contented feeling in the subconscious knowledge that everything will turn out hunky-dory for the principal quartet of sympathetic characters.

The scenario maker follows the course of least resistance in his unfolding of the tale. The very first title, following the usual credits, refers to Mr. Robertson, the idea being conveyed that a visualization of the book will be unfolded. The audience, if it does become lost in the realism of the story, is intermittently reminded by references to the author. Thus, after a couple of reels have run their course, a title flashes, reading something to the effect: "We now come to what Mr. Robertson calls the Iron Age."

The story is divided into four "ages"—stone, iron, barbarism and civilization. In sequence the stone age deals with the experiences of the youthful Dick Halpin (Cullen Landis) at school to shield the erring brother of Mabel Arthur (Alice Calhoun), with the result he is accused wrongly of stealing the school's athletic funds, a crime committed by Mabel's brother. It results in the boy's running away to sea (iron age), where Dick has become quite adept with his fists and earned the interest of Lieut. Breen (Earle Williams) of his vessel. Breen's sweetheart is Bessie Fleming (Wanda Hawley), but a screen complication that would and could have been easily explained in real life estranges the twain. The crew is enjoying a week's shore leave along with the officers, Dick cutting up considerably in returning to pay back to his cowardly schoolmates a thrashing they inflicted upon him after the missing athletic fund's episode.

Dick decides to desert, and changes his sailor regalia for "civvies" with Lieut. Breen, also sans uniform, seeking him out in the slums for the purpose of dissuading him. A stop in a gin-mill for the purpose of administering alcoholic first aid to Dick results in both being fed "k. o. drops" and shanghaied.

The third episode of the tale, the age of barbarism, recounts the duo's experiences aboard a vagabond vessel. A broad discrepancy becomes apparent to most all of the audience here, resulting in comment from neighboring spectators. Lieut. Breen, immediately on being kicked back into his senses by the none-too-gentle officers, says: "I demand to be put ashore. I am an officer of the United States Navy." Later, when Halpin salutes and "sirs" Breen as his superior officer, the latter says he has lied; that he is a valet in civil life because as an officer they would not dare allow him shore leave for fear of communication with an American consul.

However, through force of habit Breen gives himself away in assisting the outlaw captain of the ship in the flag-signalling. Captain Bilker queries: "How did you know which was the right flag to answer with?" and Breen recourses to physical action to take command of the ship in the name of government, reading the distant warship's signals that war has just been declared with Spain (all the action led up to the 1898 period) and that the ship is now part of the U. S. N.

The age of civilization finds Dick Halpin promoted to officership after distinguishing himself in naval strategy in trapping the Spanish commander, Cerverez's, fleet almost single-handed, with the duo's affairs of the heart becoming straightened out satisfactorily.

The film is pleasing entertainment, and should deliver in any grade picture house. Its quaintness of costume is fetchingly charming. The women's regalia is particularly contrasting to present-day modes.

The cast is well balanced. Dick Sutherland as "Pig" Jones has a phiz that rivals Bull Montana's. Truly, his face is his fortune, if not for leading man purposes. *Abel.*

ISLE OF LOST SHIPS

M. C. Levee presents a Maurice Tourneur production, adapted from "The Isle of Dead Ships," by Crittenden Marriott, personally directed by Maurice Tourneur and distributed through First National. Projection time, 75 minutes. At the Strand, New York, May 13.

Dorothy Fairfax............Anna Q. Nilsson
Frank Howard........................Milton Sills
Detective Jackson..........Frank Campeau
Peter Forbes.....................Walter Long
Patrick Joyce..................Bert Woodruff
Mother Joyce..................Aggie Herring
Captain Clark..............Hershall Mavall

Rather a top-heavy melodrama, its bizarre complications in the end become rather staggering as though author and film producer sought to outdo Jules Verne in their accumulation of startling and outlandish dime novel incidents. Nevertheless, the picture has many elements of striking ingenuity.

The locale is a weird spot in the unknown seas, where all the derelicts have congregated, from ancient Spanish galleons to the ocean grayhound of modern commerce, and the conception is that these lost craft have become entangled to form an island. To this strange spot come the hero, a convicted murderer being brought back from Central America to face justice in the States, and the heroine, a rich young American tourist.

Their ship is wrecked and deserted by passengers and crew, leaving them alone on board. Instead of sinking the big ship drifts to the isle of lost ships, which is found to be tenanted by about 50 other persons, all desperate characters. The sudden introduction of the beautiful young woman into this community of brutalized men is pretty daring fiction for screen purposes, but there is something of a punch in the battle between the murderer and the self-appointed ruler of the "island" for her possession. It's all rather a brutal romance, but not without its power, particularly when the fist fight is one of the most violent and realistic filmed in many a day.

So much of the story is none too plausible, but when the recital goes further and stages the escape of hero and heroine in a submarine one is inclined to blink and draw back from such dime-novel imaginings. That is the picture's principal defect—its fictioning runs amuck in search for effect and the structure draws an obstinate grin instead of a gasp. It's all just a bit too feverish and strained, and the dime novel story balks interest at a certain point.

It's a pity, too, for the producer has employed a good deal of skill in achieving some of his effects. The scenes of storms at sea are remarkably vivid and impressive, and only a resourceful picture maker could have secured the bizarre effects of the weird island of stranded ships. These are studio sets, of course, but they convey an astonishing effect of reality.

The submarine episode has been elaborately managed. The scenes in the subsea craft are absolute in their actuality, and at the finish the adventurers do actually come to the surface in a real sub just as a real torpedo boat destroyer comes up from the distance blowing clouds of smoke. The film must have cost a considerable sum, and its production standard is high, but there are points where the story overreaches itself. The cast is a notably excellent one, with the always satisfactory Milton Sills in the heroic role, the beautiful Anna Q. Nilsson as the American girl and Walter Long playing the vicious ruler of the outlandish community. *Rush.*

60 CENTS AN HOUR

A rural comedy drama by Frank Condon, adapted for the screen by Grant Carpenter and directed by Joseph Henabery. Starring Walter Hiers. Shown at the Rialto, N. Y., week May 13, 1923. Time, 85 minutes.

Jimmy Kirk, a soda jerker....Walter Hiers
Mamie Smith, his sweetheart...........
Jacqueline Logan
William Davis, Jimmy's rival...........
Ricardo Cortez
James Smith, a banker........Charles Ogle
Mrs. Smith, Mamie's mother...........
Lucille Ward
Storekeeper.......................Robert Dudley
Three Crooks.................................
Clarence Burton, Guy Oliver, Cullen Tate

This is the second of the Famous Players-Lasky features starring Walter Hiers, and this picture goes in for a little broader boob comedy than the first did. Perhaps the adaptation of the story, made by one who has a knowledge of picture values of the fat comedian, has something to do with the fact that here is a picture that really has some laughs in it. Playing opposite Hiers is Jacqueline Logan, who also contributes a fair share to the proceedings. The picture, however, is a little too long as it now stands and could easily be cut 10 or 15 minutes.

The story is one of those tales that are only too true in southern California, where a great realty boom is in progress. The action takes place in a town that has sprung up practically overnight. James Smith is the banker of the town and the heroine, his daughter, is also the cashier and the works of the banking institution. Next to the bank is the original shack around which the town was built, and here Jimmy Kirk gets a job as soda jerker at $7.50 per. He seemingly is the only one that is not cashing in on the town's wave of prosperity.

Of course, he is in love with the banker's daughter, and so also is William Davis, a speedy young real estate broker. The latter works fast and becomes engaged to the girl. And finally she lets the soda clerk take her for a flivver ride to break the news to him that all is over. The night before, however, the bank has been robbed, and the crooks have been using one of those "60 cents an hour rental and drive it yourself" flivvers, and the fat boy of the tale gets the same fliv to take the banker's daughter riding. The crooks, however, had not paid off on the car yet and were only storing it for a few minutes, having left the biggest part of the loot in the car. Then the old motion picture chase starts. The father and sweetheart of the girl are hunting the pair, believing that the fat boy committed the robbery and kidnapped the girl. The police are looking for him for both crimes and the crooks are also on the trail to get the dough in the car. The boob, however, turns the works on them and captures the real crooks and finally wins the girl's forgiveness and her hand as well.

Incidentally a "joke lease" that he has had put over on him on four feet of ground between two buildings turns out to be the means of his getting considerable fortune, for the lease is for 99 years and the bank itself encroaches on his property to the extent of three inches.

The picture might have some of the chase stuff clipped to advantage.

Fred.

DEAD GAME

Universal five-reeler, featuring "Hoot" Gibson. Story by Edward Sedgwick, who also directed. Projection time, 54 minutes. At Loew's New York, April 24.

Regulation western, following the ancient formula pretty closely, but taking a good deal of interest from its rough riding. Gibson is always a likable cowboy hero, and in this subject does some rather wonderful feats of horsemanship. One is falling down the face of a steep cliff mixed all up with the mount and another is the feat of capturing a bridleless horse, mounting it in an open desert and riding it bucking furiously across the field of vision. This latter performance was a conspicuously thrilling bit of filming.

The story is weak in its artificial staginess, one of those things with the will-the-hero-arrive-in-time or where - is - the - mortgage-on-the-ranch things. Gibson is working with a new leading woman. She doesn't figure in the billing, and this reviewer wasn't quick enough on the trigger to take it from the title on the fly, being a little stunned by having to inhale a double feature bill at one sitting. She is rather a colorless actress, pretty in face but rather awkward in bearing.

The picture has all the official stuff of the hero who braves and bests a whole gang of outlaws by force of quick wit. It isn't explained how he escapes from the watchful eyes of the desperadoes long enough to get miles away and capture the heroine by holding up the stage. You just have to take it on faith. Indeed, you have to take most the whole story on faith, but the swift riding and the melodramatic finish in which the mounted hero dashes on horseback right to the altar rail, snatches up the bride and carries her off from the clutches of the designing villain who wanted to marry her to get possession of her property, was unquestionably thrilling in its crude dime novel, melodramatic way and effectively staged to deliver a maximum kick such as the neighborhood audiences revel in. That's about the picture's grade. It was done at the New York as half a double bill.

Rush.

BAVU

Universal-Jewel production. Based on the play by Earl Carroll. Adapted by R. L. Shrock and A. G. Kenyon. Directed by Stuart Paton. Shown at Fox's Academy, New York, April 29-May 2, on double feature bill. Time, 67 minutes.

Felix Bavu	Wallace Beery
Princess Annia	Estelle Taylor
Mischka Vleck	Forrest Stanley
Olga Stropik	Sylvia Breamer
Prince Markoff	Joseph Swickard
Kuroff	Nick De Ruiz
Piplette	Martha Mattox

This is straight drama that was written for the screen more than it was for the stage, although it had a stage presentation in New York in the theatre that is controlled by the author. It is screen drama at its best, there is punch after punch in the story as it proceeds, and as the action narrows down to practically four people after the first flare of excitement it is easily followed. Yet with the action confined to practically one room and carried on by a quartet of characters the suspense is so great that it virtually keeps the audience on the edge of its seats.

For a Universal it is an exceptional picture, and for any one else it would have been better than the average. There is but one fault that can be found with it, and that is the title. True, it is the name of the character of the heavy in the story, but it means nothing until after one has seen the picture. Any exhibitor that plays this one and who happens to have a Russian or a Yiddish section in his town wants to plaster it with paper in the native language. It is a story of the beginning of the Russian revolution, and as such is a whale of a tale, not only for those Russian-born, but for every one. It is gripping, intense and thrilling.

The story in brief is that of a comrade of the newly formed Soviet force, who, for love of his Princess, aids her to escape from the mob incited to violence by the Treasurer of the revolutionists, who knows that with the looting of the city he will be able to fatten his own coffers. After the uprising the brute Treasurer plans to escape the city with the girl who has incited him to plunder and theft, accompanied by his two servants. It is, however, necessary to obtain passports from the rescuer of the Princess, and when the request is made of him he plans to escape across the border with the passports that have been stamped by the Treasurer, who believes that they are being made out to him. He cannot tell the difference because of his inability to read or write. Finally after several reels of action, in which both factions are working at cross purposes, the hero and the Princess escape and cross the border as the heavy in pursuit sinks through the ice with his team of horses and sleigh.

The direction is perfect. The early action with the mob scenes has thrill after thrill, and the burning of the city, evidently done in miniature, is so handled as to appear as though a real city was being destroyed. In the chase stuff a number of falls on the part of horses was well done, although there appeared to be a suggestion of hobbles on some of the animals.

In casting the picture seemingly the best possible types were secured. Wallace Beery as the heavy Bavu was really a screen sensation. His performance can be marveled at, so gripping is he in his work, and the duel between him and Forrest Stanley as Mischka is a corking bit of work. Stanley was the heroic figure that looked and managed to act the part in a convincing manner. Estelle Taylor endowed the Princess with a human as well as an imperial atmosphere, and Sylvia Breamer as the sweetheart of Bavu contributed a clever performance.

"Bavu" is a picture well worth the playing anywhere for any class of audience. But it is one that the exhibitor will have to go out and work up, because the title does not suggest either the story or the theme.

Fred.

YOUR FRIEND AND MINE

S. L. Pictures Production. Distributed by Loew-Metro. Adapted by Winifred Dunn from playlet by Willard Mack. Directed by Clarence Badger. Photographed by Rudolph Bergquist. Special production. Five reels. Running time, 65 minutes at Loew's State, New York.

Patricia Stanton	Enid Bennett
Hugh Stanton	Huntly Gordon
Ted Madison	Willard Mack
Mrs. Beatrice Madison	Rosemary Theby
Victor Reymier	J. Herbert Frank
Andrea Mertens	Otto Lederer
Marie Mertens	Aileen Ray

Willard Mack's sketch "The Rat" played by Mack in vaudeville several years ago formed the basis of "Your Friend and Mine." It classes with the better sort of films pointed for the first run houses, with the usual padding out of a story that while familiar has been capacity handled in its transition to the screen.

It's the world-old triangle with the picture carrying a sort of message to husbands that wives should come before business. That's been done before in pictures and stage plays, but it's one of those things that's always good if presented right.

All pictures are supposed to have good photography and lighting nowadays, but all don't. This is one that carries a real big time atmosphere, not only in its lighting but in the convincing staging given it.

The film is also fortunate in its cast. Enid Bennett plays a weak willed wife in a natural easy way that makes it stick. Mack has a contributory part and also plays with a likeable ease.

One thing about the film that makes it decidedly unusual—its hero is not the central character, that being played by the heavy, J. Herbert Frank. And he plays it as it should be for pictures, with a leer, a trick waxed mustache and cigaret that recalls the heavy villians of the old melodramas, but not overdoing it.

The tale sweeps along for the better part and holds interest. A bit of hoke here and there has been dragged in, but its good hoke and registers.

A thunder and lightning storm for the climax scene is a realistic bit of picture production, nicely timed with the tempo of the story.

Others appearing include Rosemary Theby, Otto Lederer, Aileen Ray and Huntley Gordon, each a good type for the role and playing in an experienced way. And as a clincher there's that message to husbands to keep tab on their wives, and not let 'em play around with heavy villains, with or without waxed mustaches and cigarets. That never failed to get a picture audience and probably never will.

Willard Mack and Enid Bennett should carry drawing power. *Bell.*

A FRONT PAGE STORY

A. E. Smith presents the Jess Robbins Production. Story by Arthur Goodrich, adapted by F. W. Beebe, directed by Jess Robbins. Projection time, 74 minutes. Edward Horton and Edith Roberts featured. At the New York as half a double bill, April 24.

Here is a case where an amusing scant five-reeler was wrecked by expanding it into a total of around seven reels. The story has a certain interest, but it simply won't spread over that unreasonable length. The inconsequential episodes are elaborated to the last degree of tediousness, and by the end of the third reel one's attention is stretched to the breaking point.

There isn't a spot in the picture that is not logical, convincing and neatly done, but nothing happens but commonplaces, and you can't concentrate on commonplaces for an hour and 15 minutes without feeling drowsy. The acting and direction are faultless, and the story is well thought out but without dramatic action, and with a quiet vein of comedy it just bores. Edward Horton, whose name strikes unfamiliarly on the ear, has possibilities for a style of comedy resembling that of the late Sidney Drew, whom he closely resembles in facial appearance. He has, besides, a first-rate equipment of smooth comedy style. Maybe it will mean something to this producer to recall that the Sidney Drew comedies were always confined to two reels. If this picture had been about cut in half and the comedy situation reached promptly and knitted up economically, it would have been a splendid subject.

The characterizations are skillfully developed. Two old men, one the mayor of a small town and the other its newspaper editor, have been devoted enemies. In one of their quarrels the rich mayor determines to ruin the editor by destroying his business and getting possession of his outstanding notes. There arrives in the town at this time an adventurous youth (Horton), who forces the editor to give him a job and later admit him to partnership in the paper.

The young man starts a violent publicity campaign against the mayor in the paper, against the wishes of the editor, and by overdoing the attack brings the loving enemies back to friendship, winning the editor's beautiful daughter (Miss Roberts) in the meantime. The young stranger's trick flivver and the fury of the mayor as one after another a dozen different people call his attention to the newspaper attack both made good comedy. So did the battles of the two old men. But the good points were smothered by quantities and quantities of dull material.

Rush.

THE PURPLE DAWN

Charles R. Seeling production, presented by Nathan Hirsch, released by Aywon. Story, script and direction by Seeling. Bessie Love starred. At Loew's New York. Time, 53 minutes.

Red Carson	Bert Sprotte
Bob	William E. Aldrich
Quan Foo	James B. Leong
Wong Chang	Edward Peil
Mui Far	Bessie Love
Mr. Ketchell	William Horne
Ruth Ketchell	Priscilla Bonner

One of those weird melodramas turned out every so often by one of the independently operating producers. One of those pictures that any self-respecting audience takes exception to, for it is an insult to the intelligence of those that patronize even the cheapest type of neighborhood houses.

Why any one should permit an ingenue lead star of the type of Bessie Love to appear in a story that is as utterly impossible and far-fetched as this one is a question.

Charles R. Seeling is the author, script writer and director of this picture. He has dedicated the film version to the city of San Francisco. That city will never mention it.

The plot, such as it is, revolves about stolen cans of hop, worth $120. They were brought to San Francisco Bay on a small boat, the skipper of which is Red Carson. He has aboard with him a youth by the name of Bob, whom he has browbeaten. This youngster he sends ashore with a package to be delivered to a Chinese, Wong Chang. The boy makes the initial delivery and then returns on board ship with the money and a note. The latter calls for an additional consignment, and the boy makes a second trip ashore, only to be seized by a couple of Chinks who have trailed him. They knock him over the head, steal the hop and then dump him into an automobile, which carries him into the country. When he comes to he goes to the village store and immediately gets a job there, also falls in love with the daughter. Meantime the skipper, robbed of $120 in hop, has the Ching tong send a searcher broadcast to find the culprit. When he is pegged another auto is sent after him, and he is again knocked on the head.

Then, in the headquarters of the Tong, he is beaten and asked where the hop it. When he can't tell further punishment is administered until he is finally unconscious. Then he is placed into charge of the tong leader's daughter, who is in love with him, having seen him once in the old man's place and fallen like a ton of coal. She finds out where the boy has been and the girl that he has fallen in love with and slips across the street into a place that has been planted earlier in the picture as a house of ill-fame, and phones into the country making a date for the girl to "meet me at the Federal Building." A few scenes later both are disclosed walking into each other in the office of the inspector. Then there is a trip in a motor boat with three Federal men, who arrive on the scene just in time to prevent the hero from meeting his death at the hands of a Chink strangler, who is doing his work even though another Chinaman who has been accused of the crime has been killed for it just a few feet ahead of this.

We are now at the point at which the picture gets its title. About a hundred feet of film have been tinted a light purple, and that is "The Purple Dawn," with the Chinese heroine walking out into it and leaving the boy she has braved all the dangers for in the arms of his white sweetheart.

The foregoing, as told on the screen, made the audience at the New York laugh. The direction is draggy in spots and jumpy in others.

In all the picture might well be termed a piece of junk. *Fred.*

LOVEBOUND

A William Fox production starring Shirley Mason. Story by George Scarboro, adapted by Josephine Quirk and William Furthman. Directed by Henry Otto. Shown at Loew's New York, N. Y., double feature bill May 11, 1923. Time, 52 minutes.

John Moberly....................Al Roscoe
Belle Belwyn...............Shirley Mason
Belwyn........................Joseph Girard
Paul Meredith..............Richard Tucker
Stephen Barker...........Edw. Martindale
Fred Hahn....................Fred Kelsey

Just a fair little dramatic program offering that will get by nicely in the daily change houses. The story is one that could have been built up in the picturization to greater dramatic strength, but it is an interesting little tale that will please most audiences. Incidentally it also gives Miss Mason a chance to show her figure in a bathing suit, even though it had to be dragged in by the heels.

In Al Roscoe a strong leading man was given to the little star, and he carried the picture fully as much as she did. The balance of the cast was good.

The story deals with a young girl who has managed to become the secretary of the District Attorney. The latter falls in love with her, proposes and is accepted. The father of the girl is a reformed crook, and one of his former pals, on being released from prison, calls on him and, learning of the affair between the daughter and the D. A., forces the girl to assist him in a crime on pain of exposing her father.

There is considerable suspense in the manner in which the girl escapes detection though more than a year after the crime, as she comes in contact from time to time with those that were either the victims or pursuers of the crooks. Finally the girl, who has by this time married the D. A., makes her confession through shooting the crook who tried to blackmail her, and he is killed by a fall while trying to escape from the house. The husband then makes restitution to the jeweler and the story ends happily.

The continuity is well handled, and the direction is fair throughout the picture for the calibre of program production that it is. *Fred.*

A CALIFORNIA ROMANCE

Burlesque melodrama, with John Gilbert starred, presented by William Fox. Story and script by Charles Banks, directed by Jerome Storm. Four reels.

Don Patricio Fernando.........John Gilbert
Dolores........................Estelle Taylor
Don Juan Diego...........George Seigmann
Don Manuel Casca.........Jack McDonald

It is hard to believe that this picture was made with the intention to burlesque. It looks as though it had been shot straight and after it was completed some one decided that the best thing to do was to kid it through the medium of titles. Whoever suggested that had the right idea, and the idea was carried out cleverly. To anyone who has seen any of the real romantic thrillers this picture will be a delight, providing, of course, that they have a sense of humor. It is a short subject, for it runs less than four reels.

The tale is that of a guitar-playing young Spaniard in the early days of California. He is in love with a girl who is also of Spanish extraction, but she spurns him because he will not take up arms against the American invader who is coming to take their California. The heavy of George Siegmann is a swashbuckling type who promises to lead the native sons to victory, but in reality he has a deal on with an outlaw band by which, when he is in possession of land grants of the natives, they are to sweep on the scene and kill off the men and grab off the women. In the midst of this attack the U. S. cavalry, with the hero at their head, arrive on the scene and the day is saved.

It's hoak pure and simple, and good for a laugh anywhere. *Fred.*

GOSSIP

A Universal starring of Gladys Walton. Story by Edith Barnard Delano, script by Hugh Hoffman. Directed by King Baggot.

Caroline Weatherbee........Gladys Walton
Hiram Ward.............Ramsey Wallace
John Magoo.................Albert Prisco
Robert Williamson.........Freeman Wood
Mrs. Boyne...............Carol Halloway

Here is a picture that not only fails to live up to the title that it bears but proves to be a very wishy washy sort of screen affair without any particular punch that could recommend it to the public in the smaller houses. It is just a lot of the old hoak somewhat rehashed in the hope if the public liked it once they are certain to like it again. That seems to be more or less of a general trouble with screen productions these days.

For the average exhibitor running a daily change house where he has to have something to fill in on a double feature day it will serve well enough providing he has a fairly strong picture with it and can get it at a price.

It is a capital and labor story for a short distance and drops off in something else and finally just is a picture, that's all. A factory town with the third generation in charge of the works. His dad and granddad have been the idols of the workers; the young successor is a hard task master and refuses to treat with the workers when they make a demand upon him. At that point a Southern girl comes to his home. She is the niece of the girl that the young man's father wanted to marry, but the two were parted by their parents. The girl is an orphan, and when the young man is about to turn her out, his secretary takes charge of the situation.

Once in the home she not only wins the heart of the younger Ward, but also wins him over to the point of treating with the workers and ending a strike. In the end there is a proposal and a happy ending.

Not much in that to rave about. There isn't anything in the production either in acting or direction that is more worthy than the story itself. *Fred.*

BREAKING HOME TIES

E. S. Manheim presents the six-reeler via Associated Exhibitors and Pathe. The billing and main title are silent as to writer and history of the piece, except to say that the story was inspired by "Eili Eili." In the cast are Lee Kohlmar, Richard Farrell, James Thomas, Betty Howe and Rebecca Weintraub.

The play is all atmosphere, character sketch and has very little drama. The dramatist was so anxious to make a graphic picture of Jewish family life that he forgot to have his people do anything that would constitute an interesting story. That he has made a picture that reflects Jewish family life vividly is true. So much might have been well worth while to set up an interesting background against which dramatic action would have receive heightened effect—such, for example, as the case of "Humoresque"—but the atmosphere alone is not sufficient.

The picture probably was as much inspired by "Humoresque" as by "Eili Eili," for its central figure is a Jewish mother. She appears in a number of finely wrought sympathetic passages, and the character is smoothly played by Rebecca Weintraub; but, as before observed, nothing happens in the picture of weight enough to engage one's interest. There is never any suspense or uncertainty as to what is going to happen. The nearest approach to tension is the episode early in the picture where the son's best friend is caught in a compromising position with the son's fiancee and the two men fight it out.

David, the son, thinks he has killed the other man and flees to America, the family being Russians. Presently David is a prosperous American lawyer, holding a position of responsibility with an eminent firm and looking forward to a partnership and a marriage with the daughter of the firm's head. This change of status is brought about rather brutally in a few titles, the object of the scenario writer being otherwise than tracing the romance of David, the young immigrant.

David's father and mother back in Russia have sold their small belongings and come to America, but David, being a fugitive, has not disclosed his whereabouts, and as they search for him they suffer bitter privations in the strange land. As David advances step by step the old folks descend gradually to poverty and end in a home for the aged. There are touching details to the story of hardship of the loving old couple, but, as usual, the sob stuff is laid on pretty thick.

In the end, of course, David finds them out by accident and all are happy. One of the troubles with the picture is that the scenario writer has confused his purpose. There are times when he seems intent on David's romance and times when his main purpose seems to be a sympathetic picture of the aged father and mother. Confusion results. The best thing about the picture is the fine, artless playing of the casts, who give the Jewish characters a convincing air of authenticity. *Rush.*

THE BUSTER

William Fox production featuring Dustin Farnum. Story by William Patterson White; director, Colin Campbell. Projection time, 62 minutes. At Loew's New York.

Dustin Farnum is still trading on the reputation he acquired in the dramatic version of Owen Wister's "The Virginian," probably the best cowboy story ever written. "The Buster" is a crude effort on the same formula. It aims at something of the same order of comedy and fresh characterization and if the purpose is to furnish simple entertainment to simple people it serves fairly well.

The objection to this particular picture that must strike any observer is that its production details are careless, as though the director figured the film was going, before an unsophisticated grade of film fans and small details didn't particularly matter. One trifle illustrates the point. The modern flapper from the city is suddenly introduced to the rough and ready ways of the wild and woolly west. She is represented as the last word in modernity, but when her baggage is jolted out of the buckboard her suitcase bursts and the most conspicuous article of its contents is a harness-like corset of the vintage of about 1910, an item of wardrobe that no city girl would be found dead with in these days.

That's a sample of slipshod male directorship, but the whole picture abounds in similar defects. One isn't always sure why the people do as they do, or how they get away with it. It is asking the audience rather too much to picture the gently bred city girl as taking the wild western community by storm seizing a team of half-wild horses and driving them at break-neck speed over the countryside. In the same way she attempts to ride a wild horse and all but gets away with it.

On the other hand, when the purpose of the scenario writer demands it the heroine is just a poor, weak woman. The story is uncertain in its theme. The planting of the situation is not sure and definite. When we meet the capable city girl and are given to understand she will enter into a conflict of wills with the cowboy, the preparation all seems to be toward having her the victor, whereas it turns out the other way about. One gets the feeling of being hoaxed.

Gilbert Holmes is introduced in a low comedy role, a crude counterpart of Jeff of "The Virginian," but the humor is knockabout and rough, and so is some of the comedy business portioned to Farnum. Doris Pawn is the leading woman, a personable young player and considerable of a horsewoman, unless some one doubled for her in the wild horse episode. By a curious coincidence Miss Pawn played opposite Herbert Rawlinson in another picture by Universal, "Fools and Riches," which filled out the double feature program. *Rush.*

GIRL WHO CAME BACK

B. P. Schulberg feature, produced by Tom Forman and released through the Al Lichtman Corporation. From the play by Charles E. Blaney and Samuel Ruskin Golding, adapted for the screen by Evelyn Campbell. Shown at Proctor's 23d Street, New York, for three days, commencing May 7. Time, 70 minutes.

Sheila......................Miriam Cooper
Ray Underhill.................Gaston Glass
Norries....................Kenneth Harlan
Convict 565.................Joseph Dowling
Valhays......................Fred Malatesta
Belle Bryant..................Ethel Shannon
Anastasia Muldoon.............ZaSu Pitts

In "The Girl Who Came Back," a stage play of a decade ago is brought back to life on the screen. One of the old standby melodramas of the stage, it should be equally effective with a certain class of picture patrons. A certain demand for productions of this order exists throughout the country. This has been disclosed by the selection of plays by stock company managers as well as film bookers. It is apparent the old style melodrama has its followers both among the picture fans and legitimate theatre-goers.

This latest Schulberg production cannot be taken as the best or worst of pictures of this class. It is melodrama of the old school from start to finish. It lacks the polish in many instances of the more modern film story, but nevertheless holds a punch in every reel.

Sheila, a country girl, comes to the city and secures a position in a department store. With some of her co-workers she attends a dance hall and meets a young chap whom she marries shortly after.

Immediately after the ceremony he is arrested as an automobile thief. She is placed under arrest at the same time as an accomplice. Her term is short and she is released before him. He escapes with his cellmate, who had been convicted of swindling but who is willing to make amends for his misdoings. The husband is arrested shortly after in the girl's room, he in the meantime telling her where money his cellmate had hidden is located. She goes there, encounters the other convict and, knocking him out with a chair, makes her escape with the cash. She leaves immediately for South Africa. The money she secured was sufficient to give her every luxury. Later she meets and falls in love with a rich young diamond mine owner. He asks her to return to the U. S. with him as his wife. She agrees, believing her own husband dead. The new husband proves to be the first's cellmate. Both keep their identities hidden. The first husband puts in an appearance and complications arise. The true state of affairs is made known and their happiness assured when the first husband and another crook are killed.

The story moves swiftly and were it not for its melodramatic punches would have little value. The production meets requirements nicely with the cast suitably selected.

For melodrama patrons "The Girl Who Came Back" will furnish a thrill. *Hart.*

THE SIGN OF FOUR

London, May 2.

This new Stoll picture, shown at the Alhambra, is one of the best screen melodramas this firm has made. Keeping well to Sir Arthur Conan Doyle's story, the film runs smoothly and is full of grip and thrill. Maurice Elvey has seized every opportunity the story gives and the result is a "Sherlock Holmes" story which is fine entertainment of the strong, sensational type. In his production he has several novel effects, the best, perhaps, being the race between Sherlock Holmes in a motor boat up the Thames and the vallains trying to reach the coast by motor car. During the race the progress through London of the two parties is shown alternately, and some unusual views of Thames-side and greater London are shown, while all the time the excitement is working up.

No less effective are the scenes when, the villains' car having beaten the launch, Holmes takes to the open sea in pursuit of the yacht. Few more thrilling scenes than these have been seen in screen drama. Another effective innovation is when the detective is explaining things to his friend Watson, the explanation aided by "ghost" effects instead of by the usual irritating "flash backs."

Some new camera effects are also used for the first time, including a great improvement on the usual "fade out." Stolls and Elvey are alike to be congratulated upon this feature. Eille Norwood, who has been playing the great detective in George Ridgewell's two-reelers, is excellent as Holmes, and the support is very good. *Gore.*

THE QUEEN'S FAVORITE

London, May 1.

This was the first picture handled by Adolf Zukor and is said to have formed the basis of the now great Famous Players. After many years the death of Sarah Bernhardt has caused it to be unearthed from the vaults of Wardor street, and it is being exploited for all it is worth, which is little, according to modern standards.

The story is poorly told, the production crude and mechanical, the great tragedienne making her first entrance in a cloak which looks remarkably modern. Throughout the crowd and small part people seem to be working by numbers.

What story there is tells of Elizabeth's love for the Earl of Essex, of his for the Countess of Nottingham and of the latter's vengeance.

In the height of her infatuation for the courtier Elizabeth gives him a ring, saying should he ever be in trouble its return will save him, no matter his fault. Anon his liaison with the countess is discovered and he is sent to the Tower. The queen sends the countess to get the ring, but her vengeful husband takes it and flings it away. Thinking Essex too proud to ask for clemency Elizabeth signs his death warrant. Later, having learned the truth, she dies of a broken heart.

Great though Bernhardt was as a legitimate tragedienne she proves hopeless as a screen artist, and probably her fame caused the producer to talk to her about such things as make-up. Lou Tellegen manages to get something of romance into his Earl of Essex. The rest of the cast does not matter. *Gore.*

SCHLAGENDE WETTER
("EXPLOSIONS")

Berlin, May 6.

This film produced by the Stern Company and directed by Karl Gruner, is one of the very best seen here for some time. The director really seems to have caught some of the American spirit, and the film works up to a fine climax.

The story centers around Marie's affair with Georg, a mining engineer. She has a child. Her father turns her out when he finds that Georg has disappeared, and she goes wandering off, finally falling down from exhaustion and want of food. There she is found by Thomas, a worker in the mines, who takes her home to his parents. There the good-natured giant falls in love with her, and although she does not really love him she is so grateful to him for his kindness to her that she readily agrees to marry him, but on the wedding night Georg appears, and the husband feels that something is wrong, although he is not sure just what it is. Later on, while he is down in the mines, Georg comes to the young wife and attempts to seduce her again. Thomas is told that he is there, and he comes home and finds them together. Georg escapes, but Thomas has seen him and vows to take vengeance on him. From this time on Thomas is careless about his work and is threatened with discharge. One day in the mine Thomas comes upon Georg, who is employed as an engineer. He chases him and Georg lets his lamp fall and ignites the gases in the mine. Then come terrific scenes, with explosions, rushing of human beings and the falling of great masses. Thomas is freed of Georg, as he is killed by a falling mass of coal, and Marie, disguising herself, gets down into the mine, meets her husband and asks forgiveness. He takes her in his arms, but it seems too late, for they are cut off from the exit by another terrific explosion. Terrible days of waiting follow, while the rescue parties get nearer. Will they find them before it is too late? One headed by Thomas' father almost goes by where they are, as Thomas is too weak to answer his father's pounding. But they are rescued, and all ends happily.

The direction is first rate throughout, the scenes in the mine being particularly well handled, especially from a technical angle. The photography is satisfactory, except for certain interiors, which are lighted much too indistinctly as regards the faces, and thus much good facial expression is lost.

The acting throughout is superior, even the bit of Marie's father being perfectly played by Hermann Valentin. Thomas' father is made a humorous gem by Leonhard Haskel, and Liane Haid fulfills the promise she gave in the title role of Lady Hamilton. But the best performance of all is the giant slouching, good-humored and yet pathetic Thomas of Eugene Klopfer. *Trask.*

EIN GLASS WASSER
("A Glass of Water")

Berlin, May 1.

Just as one has about decided that the Germans never were going to make another decent film, along comes Ludwig Berger with his adaptation of Scribe's old farce. This is one of the very best atmosphere pictures ever done anywhere; a mood, a period of history is created and sustained throughout with marvelous definiteness.

Queen Anne's England lives before us again and over it all is thrown a delicate veil of fantasy that keeps everything out of touch with the every day. The photography also, a very rare thing in German pictures, helps remarkably to sustain this illusion; many of the shots are as beautiful as anything we have seen anywhere—all of which goes to prove that good photography can be gotten here if only trouble enough is taken. It is not new to find interesting and well-designed architecture in German films, but nevertheless the designers, Hermann Warm and Rudolph Bamberger, deserve credit for the absolute completeness of their work.

The story is well known, but merely to outline it briefly, it is concerned with Masham, an attractive young boy, who catches the fancy of both Queen Anne of England and of the Duchess of Marlborough, the leader of the war party and the power behind the throne. The boy really loves Abigail, a little girl employed in a jewelry shop.

Lord Bolingbroke, the head of the peace party, now out of power, learns of this infatuation for Masham and uses it to make the Queen jealous of the Duchess of Marlborough and to get her thrown out. The boy is to marry Abigail.

Ludwig Berger has himself adapted this rather slight story for the film and the additions he has made have always been tasteful and never harmful. He adds, for instance, a festival and play at a castle belonging to the Duchess and gets many charming scenes between the Queen and the boy.

The cast, with one exception, was excellent. Lucie Hoeflich, as the Duchess of Marlborough, has not enough lightness for the role, and Agnes Straub, who played the role on the stage, should have been used. But the Queen of Mary Christians, the Bolingbroke of Rudolph Rittner and the Masham of Hans Brausewetter are all performances of first rank.

It is true that such a film would not have a big transcontinental appeal in America, but it should do well around the better-class theatres of the East. *Trask.*

THE LONELY ROAD

Benjamin P. Schulberg production, distributed by First National. Kathryn MacDonald starred. Directed by Victor Schirtzinger. Adapted for screen by L. Zellner. At Proctor's 23d Street, New York, for three days, beginning May 21. Time, 65 minutes. Cast: Kathryn MacDonald, Eugenie Besserer, James Neill, Leila Meade, Orville Caldwell, Margaret Campbell, Chas. French, William Conklin, Frank Leigh.

A tale of every-day folk depicting their joys, sorrows and problems for the better part of the five reels in an interesting manner. It's a comedy with a touch of sentiment and a flash of the dramatic here and there. The story does not carry quite the distance of the footage. It starts out entertainingly with the yarn laid in a rural atmosphere that is convincing. Along about the beginning of the fourth reel the interest sags somewhat, but picks up again around the end of that chapter, continuing interestingly to the finish.

There is no villain. The principal male character is that of a stingy husband. An unqualified sap who permits his mother to pick out the furniture for his home when he marries and generally administrates his domestic affairs like a first-class bromide. There are a number of scenes of family life that will strike a responsive chord. Plenty of good human interest stuff included in the action.

The story is clearly told and the direction is adequate. "The Lonely Road" isn't exactly gaited for the big first-run houses, but it will make a very good feature for the second runs. *Bell.*

THE WHITE ROSE

D. W. Griffith production, directed and written by the producer, with Mae Marsh and Ivor Novello in the leading roles. Shown at the Lyric, New York, commencing May 22 for four weeks. Time, 2 hours and 10 minutes.

Bessie Williams "Teazie"	Mae Marsh
Marie Carrington	Carol Dempster
Joseph Beaugarde	Ivor Novello
John White	Neil Hamilton
Auntie Esther	Lucille La Verne
Apollo	Porter Strong
Cigar Stand Girl	Jane Thomas
An Aunt	Kate Bruce
A Man of the World	Erville Alderson
The Bishop	Herbert Stutch
The Landlord	Joseph Burke
The Landlady	Mary Foy
Guest at the Inn	Charles Mack

For his latest production, which inaugurated his sixth season as the producer of feature pictures of a pretentious nature, D. W. Griffith has cast aside the idea of spectacle and has produced a feature of true dramatic value without the spectacular and massive elements which have been associated with some of his earlier productions. His latest is a drama of life. It is devoted to youth, with the characters carefully drawn. It is a story that grips, is realistic in all its angles, and as screened should prove a powerful factor.

The subject-matter upon which the story is based brings forth a new idea. It introduces a man as an equal sinner with the woman he wrongs. It is worked out with a tenseness that grips from the start. Bessie Williams leaves an orphan asylum possessing a creditable record. She secures employment in a small winter resort in the south. Her duties consist of handling a cigar stand. Under the tutelage of her predecessor she proves an apt scholar, and soon learns the many tricks of the trade and the little pleasures enjoyed by girls in her sphere of life. Joseph Beaugarde is the son of one of the foremost families of the south. His inclinations are towards the ministry, with Marie Carrington, of equal social standing, considered from childhood as his future wife. During a vacation from the theological seminary Beaugarde decides on a trip to learn of the lives of the people whom he is to help. He travels under an assumed name, and while stopping at the inn where Bessie, known as "Teazie," works becomes acquainted with the girl. Their affair reaches a serious pitch, and he leaves suddenly after a night out of doors with the girl. On departing he believes his affair but one of many in her life. A child is born and the girl is ejected from her home. She tries to secure employment but, due to the child, in vain. She unknowingly comes to the home of the girl the man who had wronged her is engaged to marry. She is turned away by a servant. Befriended by the colored nurse of the other girl, she is taken to the former's cabin and given shelter. Little hope is held out for her life, with Beaugarde, who has since been ordained, called in during what is expected her last moments of life. He has since learned of her innocence prior to meeting him, and with their meeting at the critical moment a reconciliation is brought about and a marriage performed immediately. The other girl to whom he was engaged is married to a former sweetheart, who has made his way in the world from a low start.

Griffith has assembled a capable cast. The picture bares the Griffith stamp of genius and is a personal triumph for Mae Marsh. Ivor Norvello in the leading male role plays effectively. His work displays the expertness of the direction. Carol Dempster plays the second feminine role of importance. Her work is on par with that of the two leads. Neil Hamilton is given several opportunities in the early reels for capable work. Lucille La Verne and Porter Strong take first honors in the character roles.

The production cost of "The White Rose" is probably less than that of any other Griffith special feature. It adequately fits the story with the photography, an outstanding feature of every reel.

"The White Rose" is up to the Griffith standard and carries a dramatic punch, together with a smile in every reel. *Hart.*

GIRL OF THE GOLDEN WEST

Edwin Carewe production, distributed by First National. Adelaide Heilbron made the screen adaptation. Edwin Carewe directed. At the Strand, New York, week May 20. Time, 65 minutes.

This is the second time David Belasco's famous play of early frontier life has been screened. Lasky produced it about 10 years ago, with Geraldine Farrar starred and a supporting cast that stood out prominently. It was a notable picture in every department in its day.

The current version of the "Girl" by Edwin Carewe lacks considerable of the finesse that marked the Lasky film. In the matter of cast the Carewe picture suffers possibly the most, although in the production end it also falls quite a way below the first one.

The big scene of the play was the one which had the hero-heavy lying on a cot in a sort of improvised garret in the "girl's" cabin, with blood dripping down on the sheriff who had come to take him to the lockup. This misses somewhat in the Carewe picture. Not altogether, but somehow it doesn't just grasp the complete significance or dramatic value of the scene.

Another striking scene from the play was the poker game, in which the girl matches her wits against the law and wins her lover's life. The Carewe version handles this much better than it does the garret scene.

The film rolls along smoothly in the early section, with sufficient entertainment to keep the house interested until the big scene is reached.

Several shots of the western mountain country are scenically beautiful. The lighting of the interior scenes is also artistic.

Among the cast Rosemary Theby stands out above the others in a secondary role, that of the villainess. Miss Theby makes it a hard, sneering type of female heavy, without resorting to overacting. Every foot of film she occupies means something.

Sylvia Breamer's conception of the "girl" is satisfactory. It's along conventional lines, however, never reaching above an ordinary level. Russell Simpson is the sheriff. He plays the part intelligently. J. Warren Kerrigan is the hero-heavy, handling it well.

The "Girl" should find a ready market at present, since Westerns have come into their own again with the advent of the "Covered Wagon." Had the Lasky film never been made this one would have created plenty of comment. As it is, it can travel over the best first run houses and hold its own, as the Lasky picture is too far in the past to interfere as far as present day audiences are concerned. *Bell.*

SOUL OF THE BEAST

Metro release, produced by Thomas H. Ince Corp. from C. Gardner Sullivan's story. John Griffith Wray directed. Madge Bellamy featured. Running time, 67 minutes. At the Rivoli, New York, week of May 20

Ruth Lorrimore	Madge Bellamy
"Oscar" the elephant	By Himself
Paul Nadeau	Cullen Landis
Caesar	Noah Beery
Jacqueline	Vola Vale
Silas Hamm	Bert Sprotte

The action opens under the big top of Silas Hamm's circus. The title is derived from the actions of Oscar, the elephant, around whom much of the story revolves. Following a reel of interesting circus "shots" Oscar is introduced and put through his paces by Ruth Lorrimore (Madge Bellamy), the stepdaughter of Silas Hamm, the miserly owner of the outfit. Judging by its size (a two-ring affair), its proprietor is given no cause for his extreme cruelty and frugality, which went so far as to half-ration the "skinny man" for fear he lose his distinction. The "wild woman from Borneo," in private life a Mississippi wench, objects to Hamm's culinary offerings despite her reputed fondness for wild meat, and hands in her notice. Hamm elects his stepdaughter for the wild woman side-show attraction and locks her in her cage after fitting her up with the prop tusks and the grass skirt.

The long threatening storm breaks and the big top takes fire. Ruth is imprisoned in her cage, which has been locked by a very practical lock. She calls to Oscar for assistance, with the pachyderm responding by pushing the wheeled cage out from under the canvas and out of danger, following which he releases his mistress from her involuntary captivity. This is the first actual display of the mammoth's super-intelligence in protecting his friends and avenging their wrongs.

The action thereafter is centered in Canadian territory, where Ruth has sought refuge. The "bull" is ever nigh. Oscar from then on is the real punch of the production. With Noah Beery, the villain, pursuing the hero and heroine through the rest of the footage, the pachyderm interjects himself at strategic moments to foil the heavy's nefarious purposes. Cullen Landis is the sympathetic lead who enters the action at this point. He is cast for a rather fragile characterization, that of a lame youth with a fondness for his violin. Ruth is Paul's idol, when Caesar suddenly awakes to the charms of the girl. This is a forerunner of Caesar's decision to make things generally miserable for the hero, starting with the shooting of Paul's pet rabbit and forcing its owner to eat the roasted animal. Paul and Ruth's escape leads to a rather gripping canoe chase by Caesar, with the former's craft wrecked. Climbing to safety, Paul is met with Caesar's onslaught in a dirk fight, with the hero placed in a dangerous position and only saved by the advent of the mammoth. Caesar's mortal fear of the "bull" gives wings to his feet with the animal enjoying several hundred feet of combat by dousing the heavy by means of his trunk. Caesar is half drowned before Ruth decides to call Oscar off. The story concludes with the couple blessed with an addition and Paul's return from Montreal heralding the loss of his lameness, thanks to a surgical operation.

There is plenty of outdoor stuff from the middle on, which makes a pleasing natural background for the action. Judicial selection of types also adds to the general scheme of things. Comedy is derived from flashing titles of the pachyderm's speech as interpreted from his actions, which in themselves are mirthfully diverting. Oscar should appeal to the juvenile fans and should be accordingly featured in the press matter.

Miss Bellamy, a "comer," is still maintaining her pace as in her past performances. Cullen Landis is limited by his characterization for distinguishment. Beery was a most effective "heavy." *Abel.*

THE GIRL I LOVED

Sponsored by Charles Ray Productions, Inc., and presented by Arthur S. Kane, United Artists' Corp. release. Adapted from James Whitcomb Riley's poem, scenarist not mentioned. Joseph De Grasse directed. Runs 68 minutes. At the Capitol, New York, week of May 13.

John Middleton	Charles Ray
Mary	Patsy Ruth Miller
Willie Browne	Ramsey Wallace
Mother Middleton	Edyth Chapman
Neighbor Silas Gregg	William Courtwright
Betty Short	Charlotte Woods
Neighbor Perkins	Gus Leonard
Hired Man	F. B. Phillips
Minister (Circuit Rider)	Lon Poff
Hiram Lang	Jess Herring
Ruth Lang	Ruth Bolgiano
The Judge	Edward Moncrief
The Organist	George Marion
A Spinster	Billie Latimer

James Whitcomb Riley's poem makes rather thin story material for Charles Ray's initial United Artists' release, shown at the Capitol, N. Y., last week, but it has been skilfully woven and developed by the director through the injection of a number of local color touches to sum up as an interesting and gripping production. The star displays genuine histrionic ability that becomes markedly evident and impresses the most casual observing lay people. His facial "registering" of the various moods and emotions evinced considerable comment, the picture being more of a personal triumph for Ray than the production itself.

Favored with a good box office title, it is handicapped (or, strictly, may prove to be handicapped) by the lack of a "happy ending," to the average audience's way of thinking. The action revolves around the country boy's deep love for the girl his mother adopted in infancy. Both having grown up as brother and sister, Mary (Patsy Ruth Miller) cannot interpret John's (Charles Ray) affection other than that of a relative. When, after the barn dance, John takes Mary home, he starts to impart a secret to her. Mary insists on telling hers first—that she has just become betrothed to Willie Brown (Ramsay Wallace), which chokes John's proposal. Slouching down listlessly in his seat on the old-fashioned buckboard vehicle, the horses run wild. John sustains a broken leg and Mary is thrown unharmed from the wagon in a thrilling scene of the runaway team.

John, helpless and incapacitated because of the injured limb, is almost driven frantic every time Willie calls on his betrothed. Melancholia takes possession of John's being. A hectic scene shows him speaking his love for Mary and frantically kissing the hem of her skirt, the twist being the old dream idea—it was just John's wild imagination. In a scene where John is depicted accusing Willie in a melodramatic fashion, "You have stolen the girl I loved," and committing murder and a couple other crimes from that down, again it develops to prove but an hallucination. This was a bit too much for the audience. Several of the neighbors felt as if they were being toyed with. Unconsciously one prepared himself for a possible third attempt at the same sort of thing, but the action proceeded with the preparations for Mary's marriage. The actual ceremony concluded with all the guests exiting light-hearted and John slumping in a pew in the church.

The flashing of the "finis" title did not seem to please some of the patrons, judging by the mild "ahs" of disappointment. The happy "clinch" between the sympathetic male character and the girl of his desire was lacking. Not that Willie was not also sympathetic. He made a manly lover for Mary, with every outlook of the "happy ending" for him which for John seemed so dolefully lacking.

The direction was all that could be desired as regards the bucolic theme and settings. The picture, on the whole, seemed to please. *Abel.*

GARRISON'S FINISH

Adapted from book of similar title. Picture directed by Arthur Rosson, supervised by Elmer Harris. Distributed through Allied Producers and Distributors' Corporation. Jack Pickford starred. At Capitol, New York, week May 27. Running time, 73 minutes.

Billy Garrison	Jack Pickford
Sue Desha	Madge Bellamy
Colonel Desha	Charles A. Stevenson
Major Desha	Tom Guise
Mr. Waterbury	Frank Elliott
Crimmins	Clarence Burton
Sue's Friends	Andrey Chapman
	Dorothy Manners
Lilly Allen	Ethel Grey Terry
Judge of Race Course	Herbert Prior
Col. Desha's Trainer	Charles Ogle
Billy's Mother	Lydia Knott

"Garrison's Finish," with Jack Pickford, has enough, with Jack Pickford, to carry it along in any house. A meller from the outset and right up to its ending, the feature, well made and directed, catches hold on the sentimental side.

It's the horse racing story, probably first made into picture form several years ago. As remade it's a new picture. The story is of a young jockey living with his widowed mother. The boy is doped by the trainer of the favorite he is to ride in the Melville Handicap at Belmont Park. Making a suspicious ride and losing, the boy is ruled off. Later the same day he is struck on the head in a barroom melee. Losing memory the boy is taken by tramps to an estate in Kentucky, the tramps having found a girl's card in his pocket.

The young woman on the Kentucky estate recognizes him as a youthful jockey who attracted her attention through his good looks while she visited New York and Belmont. Believing it was unsportsmanlike to rule him off without a hearing, the girl receives the uncouth-looking lad when led up to her door, rewards the tramps, and finding his memory gone, gives him a new name in the hope she will win her father over to allow him to ride his "Rogue" in the Kentucky Derby.

It works out that way with Billy Garrison (Mr. Pickford) becoming reinstated through a confession from the trainer's paramour in a fit of jealous rage. He wins the Derby on Rogue—and marries the girl after having his mother restored to him.

It's full of villainy and tricks, race tracks and horses, romance and sentiment, crookedness and righteousness. And the sentiment is first. When Billy gave the trainer a good beating, breaking up a dinner party to do it following the confession, the final show's audience at the Capitol Tuesday night broke into involuntary applause. It was a good fight but better directed sentiment that had been accumulating throughout the running.

Some slight applause followed the finish of the picture at the Capitol, this at 11.30. It was somewhat remarkable in its way as evidencing the hold the picture had taken upon the slight remaining crowd at that time.

It was more remarkable in view of a peculiar condition on the Capitol's program that same evening. Previously in the Fox News had been an excellent taking of the recent Kentucky Derby that "Zev" won. That pictured race was bound to remove the edge of anything likened to it that might follow, and here in this picture were two races. Notwithstanding, the "Garrison" picture got over, but it would have been better protection for the feature to have held out the Fox News insert, despite its current news value.

Pickford is giving a good performance, making up nicely when suffering from asphasia through smearing his face. It seemed he was doubled for in the races if there were actual races taken. The effort to stand that off merely accentuated it. But his fight was realistic enough to atone for everything else.

For the affection of the audience Madge Bellamy won right out. She looked and played the role of the young girl who liked the jockey and mothered him when he didn't know he had a mother of his own. A very likable girl, Miss Bellamy, on the screen. Lilly Allen as taken by Ethel Grey Terry made a fine opposite for Clarence Curton as Crimmins, the bad trainer, who did well despite a tendency to exaggeration of the role when in polite society. Charles Ogle as another trainer in Kentucky did a contrasting part to Burton's that was just nice by comparison, although not as prominent.

The story is well carried forward, the direction is always with intelligence, much more so than some of the rough captions, and in all, here is a meller with class that in the present day of the shying off that stuff in the best houses will just fit in right where the others can not go.

Sime.

FOG BOUND

Famous Players production, presented by Adolph Zukor, with Dorothy Dalton starred. Designated an "Irving Willat production." Projection time, 70 minutes. Story by Jack Bechdolt; scenario by Paul Dickey. At the Rivoli May 27.

Gale Brenon	Dorothy Dalton
Roger Wainwright	David Powell
Mildred Van Buren	Martha Mansfield
Deputy Brown	Maurice Costello
Sheriff Holmes	Jack Richardson
Mammy	Mrs. Ella Miller
Deputy Kane	Willard Cooley
Gordon Phillips	William David
Revenue Officer Brenon	Warren Cook

A story and production of fine pictorial quality, but injured somewhat because it puts the star in a role that gives her small opportunity. Miss Dalton is an actress of great appeal, both from her beauty and from her acting sense, but she requires special surroundings. Here she is a simple country girl, and the flashy passages go to Martha Mansfield. Miss Mansfield's role is an unsympathetic one, but it is the one that compels attention, and this rather takes away from the star.

The story has many capital moments of drama, most of them dealing with the hunt through the Florida swamps for a supposed murderer. These scenes, all take place in a thick fog, and the effect of the gathering mists gives the whole thing an effective atmosphere of thrill. There is a mystery turn to the story as well, leading up to a surprise finish, although this detail is rather theatrical and crude.

Gale is the daughter of a Florida sheriff in love with her neighbor, a rich northerner playing the gentleman farmer and wasting his time with the gay set of idlers in the vicinity. The society people go on a wild party to the Casino just as the sheriff is organizing a raid on the place in search of bootleggers. The hero wins a large sum at the roulette tables, and the gamblers scheme to rob him of his takings. He is sleeping in a side room when one of the crooks steals upon him. There is a fight and the hero fires at his assailant.

The shot goes through the door, but is harmless. However, when a bootlegger confederate murders the sheriff the shot through the door is used to make it appear that he committed the crime.

The hunt is organized and the heroine is brought into it, not understanding that it is her lover who is pursued. When she learns the truth there is a fight between her desire to avenge her father and her love for the accused man. This brings into the story the shooting heroine, with which Miss Dalton seems always attached. There are numerous spirited passages in the chase, with bloodhounds bringing on the ascending climax, in which the truth comes out.

Maurice Costello has a heavy role played especially well. He is the bootleggers' accomplice who actually committed the murder and has a tense scene of high suspense during the chase. Mrs. Ella Miller does a good bit supplying comedy relief in the character of a fat colored "mammy." The picture drew well at the Rivoli, Miss Dalton having an especially loyal following among the women, but the first warm weather of the late spring was against it. It should make a substantial but not a sensational attraction..

Rush.

SLANDER THE WOMAN

Allen Holubar production, released by First National. From the novel by Jeffrey Deprend, adapted by Violet Clark and directed by Allen Holubar. Dorothy Phillips starred. At Strand, New York, week May 27. Time, 67 mins.

Yvonne Desmarest	Dorothy Phillips
M. Duroacher	Lewis Dayton
Dr. Emile Molleur	Robert Anderson
Nanette	Mayme Kelso
Scarborough	George Siegmann
Indian Girl	Ynez Seabury
Father Machette	Herbert Fortier
Tetreau the Guide	Geno Corrado
The Stranger	William Orlamond
M. Redoux	Robert Schable
Mme. Redoux	Rosemary Theby
Marie Desplanes	Irene Haisman
M. Lemond	Cyril Chadwick

This is about as prize a piece of haphazard film producing as has come to a Broadway pre-release house in a long time. It is a joke for producers to believe that they can turn out this sort of feature and get the audiences that frequent the better houses in the bigger towns to fall for them. The Strand audience Sunday afternoon gave this picture the laugh in more than a dozen places where the director must have thought he was getting away with tense melodrama. Of course, Allen Holubar gave Dorothy Phillips, the star, every chance possible to show what she could do, but what she did do was far from being enough to carry this picture. In a word, it is a real bad boy.

The story is from a novel that has its scene of action laid in Montreal and the portion of Canada further to the west. Miss Phillips is a Montreal society girl whose good name is besmirched through a scandal in which she is the victim of circumstantial evidence. After living down the harm that wagging tongues have done she goes into the woodland, where her father formerly had a hunting lodge. Here she remains with her old nurse and later is found by the judge who denied her the right to clear her name. He has learned she was unjustly the victim of circumstances and he has come to inform her that he stands ready to make any amends possible.

Just to make it more intricate, there is also a murderer hiding in the neighborhood, and he is cleared by the judge at the same time. However, not before the murderer plugged him, so that there would be some excuse for the judge to stick around and be nursed by the heroine.

A "nut" character reminded of the one in "The Tavern," and in this particular case he might have well asked, "What's all the shootin' for?" for seemingly whenever there wasn't anything better to do some one else was shot in the picture.

As a snow picture it isn't much, as a society picture it is less, as an excuse to have Dorothy Phillips before the camera for any number of feet it just is enough to get by.

Fred.

THE MAN NEXT DOOR

Vitagraph production presented by Albert E. Smith. Written by Emerson Hough, author of "The Covered Wagon." Directed by Victor Schertzinger. At Cameo, New York, week May 27. Time, 73 minutes.

Colonel Wright	David Torrence
Curley	Frank Sheridan
Jimmie	James Morrison
Bonnie Bell	Alice Calhoun
David Wisner	John Steppling
Mrs. Wisner	Adele Farrington
Catherine Kimberly	Mary Culder
Tom Kimberly	Bruce Boteler

All that Vitagraph needs here in conjunction with the names this feature has is a real picture, and then it would be a clean-up.

The story was written by the late Emerson Hough, who wrote "The Covered Wagon." One of the character roles here is played by David Torrence (perhaps similar enough to that of Ernest Torrence, who walks away with the principal character role of the "Wagon," to be coupled with the title of the latter) will be utilized by some shortsighted exhibitors to "get the money." However, "The Man Next Door" is going to send audiences that may be lured to the theatre through advertising of this sort away as knockers for the house. It is just a mediocre feature of the cheaper program type.

In directing it Victor Schertzinger failed to turn out anything to win any particular credit. The direction is slow moving and the story lags at all times. There isn't a single moment where the audience will get a thrill nor is the interest sustained enough to keep them on edge at any time.

The story is a combination society and western, and the only thing of account is some of Miss Calhoun's work.

At the Cameo early this week the audience passed it up completely.

Fred.

TRIFLING WITH HONOR

Universal production from William Slavin McNutt's story. Adapted by Raymond L. Schrock. Direction Harry A. Pollard. At the Broadway, New York, in conjunction with vaudeville, week of May 28.

"Bat" Shugrue	Rockliffe Fellowes
Ida Malone	Fritzi Ridgeway
Kelsey Lewis	Hayden Stevenson
Jimmy	Buddy Messinger
Lute	Fred Stanton

Handicapped by a ten-twent-thirt meller title, the picture impresses as but fair, although possessed of possibilities sadly neglected. Probably intended for realism, the picture somehow does not ring true. Sympathy is misapplied, and the observer will have naught of some of it.

Bat Shugrue, the Babe Ruth of the Pacific Coast league, is introduced first as "the gas-pipe kid" released on parole from a San Quentin stretch. His response to Ida's waiting is frigid. Although he is shown beating up a landlord for dispossessing a tardy rentpayer, the sympathy is almost lost. For one thing, the tenant, a male of bleary aspect, looks much like he has drunk up the rent, if he ever had it, and the brutal assault by the Kid is going it a bit too strong.

The gas-pipe gent is arraigned in Night Court, but makes a successful desperate escape.

Five years later finds Shugrue a mighty king of swat and idol of the Los Angeles fans. Kelsey Lewis of a syndicate news service seeks an interview with the new public favorite for the purpose of writing an "autobiographical" life story over Shugrue's signature. In Lewis' office is employed Ida Malone, the girl who waited so long for the Kid. Lewis is not blind to Ida's charms, and declares himself. Ida is the steno assigned to type the Shugrue life story, illustrated with photographs, and recognizes the new idol as her former beau. The reporter has piped a wishy-washy yarn about how good to his mother Bat was in his youth; his abstainance from smoking, drinking and swearing, and altogether glorifying the 30-minute egg he really was.

The same judge from whose court the Kid escaped is shown doing a Benlindsey to a pair of juveniles, reading extracts from the Shugrue newspaper serial, which seems to impress the youths. It also has a good effect on Jimmy, Ida's kid brother.

The punch of the story is an important game between the Angels and Vernon, with a gambling coterie holding the information over Bat's head that the knew of a certain "Gas-Pipe Kid" who ran out of a court during trial. Shugrue takes "sick" suddenly. The ninth inning finds the score 2—0 for the Vernons. The Angels pull a last-inning rally and get two men on first and third. That's the cue for Shugrue to heed the insistent fans' demands for his pinch hitting. The obvious circuit clout results and its an Angels' victory by 3—2.

The Kid decides to visit the judge's home and confess, with the jurist magnanimously saying something about "better one Shugrue free than in jail." The Kid confesses his affection for Ida hasn't waned, and the picture admits "Looks like I've struck out."

The flashes of the baseball games have a certain thrilling effect. The casting is adequate, but the production doesn't click just right. The attempts at the introductory comedy with the landlord and hallowe'en carnival are painfully artificial. The leading male role is not drawn just right, although forcefully played by Rockliffe Fellowes. Miss Ridgeway did well opposite, and Buddy Messinger, the kid brother, is his usual bonnie self. That kid should be taken in hand and plugged for stardom. He ranks with the best of the youngsters. *Abel*

JEALOUSY

London, May 15.
Produced by Victor Seastrom and shown privately by the Ideal last week, "Jealousy" went into the program for a run at the New Oxford May 14. It is strong drama of the "triangle" type. The story is powerful and well told, while the production is as near perfection as such things can be. The production has an added pull as far as London is concerned, by the fact that Matheson Lang is "starred."

The story tells how the skipper of a ship carrying munitions woos and weds a girl. He takes her to sea with him, but, unfortunately, signs on one of the girl's old lovers as mate. The "eternal triangle" being thus completed, it takes only small incidents to arouse the spark of jealousy in the skipper's breast and fan it into a dangerous flame. One little thing leads to another until their mutual hatred culminates in a fight between the two men, which is followed by mutiny on the high seas and brutal murder. One day the skipper loses all control of himself and knocks his young wife overboard. Maddened, the mate fires the magazine and the whole ship is blown up, but not before all the leading people have escaped. The terrible events they have passed through lead the three sides of the triangle to a better understanding and happiness.

There are but three people of any importance in the cast—Victor Seastrom, Matheson Lang and Jenny Hesselquist, the Swedish dancer. Although playing a brutally heavy part, Seastrom takes everything from Lang, the "juvenile man," and out-acts him from the beginning, gradually taking all the sympathies of the audience. Lang is merely the tutored hero of melodrama; Seastrom is volcanic, unconventional and, with it all, perfectly natural and in the picture. Jenny Hesselquist gives an excellent rendering of a difficult part as the wife.

AN OLD SWEETHEART OF MINE

Metro production, featuring Elliott Dexter and Helen Jerome Eddy, directed by Harry Garson. Screen adaptation by Louis Duryea Lighton, based upon the poem of the same title by James Whitcomb Riley. At Loew's State, New York, for three days commencing May 29. Time, 60 mins.
John Craig, as a boy............Pat Moore
John Craig, as a man.....Elliott Dexter
Mary Ellen Anderson, as a girl.........
    Mary Jane Irving
Mary Ellen Anderson, grown up........
    Helen Jerome Eddy
Stuffy Shade, as a boy.......Turner Savage
Stuff Shade, grown up .....Lloyd Whitlock
Irene Ryan................Barbara Worth
Frederick McCann.............Arthur Hoyt
William Norton.............Jean Cameron

Harry Garson has turned out a genuinely interesting and wholly refreshing feature for Metro in the screen adaptation of the James Whitcomb Riley poem.

The adapter for the screen has worked out a story worth while in its general texture, with the heart interest kept up to a high voltage in every reel.

The story carries its leading characters from childhood to maturity, with the interesting sidelights on kid life among the most interesting bits of the production. Garson has selected some capable youngsters for the work in the early reels. The scenario gives him ample opportunities to bring them to the front in a worth-while manner. At times the action as far as the kids are concerned is a bit stagy. This can be overlooked, however, on the generally good impression made. In the latter portion, when the characters of the earlier part have matured, the story is equally effective. The adapter has added a melodramatic element in order to give the picture the necessary action. It has been well done, although the idea is not one that can come under the heading of original.

The juvenile roles in the early footage are entrusted to Pat Moore, Mary Jane Irving and Turner Savage. The youngsters are well handled, with their own ability displayed capably. Elliott Dexter and Helen Jerome Eddy share the honors with the leads. Dexter has a part of considerable proportions and works it up to a good average. Miss Eddy proves a most capable country sweetheart, with her slight emotional scenes among the production's worthy moments. The remaining members of the cast have been selected discriminately.

The production needs call for much of the simple, small-town atmosphere and none of the garishness invariably linked with screen productions of today. It is a simple story told in simple settings, but told with a telling effect. The production from all angles is worth while. It is a picture for the whole family and a good buy for any exhibitor on that score.

The story has as its leading characters John Craig and Mary Ellen Anderson, childhood sweethearts. As they grow up their love grows with them. John becomes the owner of a small-town newspaper. He is poor but a valuable asset to the community. Stuffy Shade, a boyhood friend, returns to the town with an oil-promotion scheme. He convinces John it is worth millions and secures his co-operation in exploiting it in the newspaper. The people of the town bring in their ready cash to finance the project on the strength of John's say-so. When the oil well is about to be tapped he is informed the scheme is a fake. Just at the critical moment it is found the property does contain oil and the investors are assured big returns, with the promoters frozen out. *Hart*

PLAYING IT WILD

Vitagraph feature, with William Duncan and Edith Johnson. Story and scenario by C. Graham Baker, directed by Duncan. At Loew's Circle May 27. Running time, 62 minutes.
Jerry Hoskins.................Wm. Duncan
Beth Webb...................Edith Johnson
Old Man Webb............Francis Powers
Sheriff Gideon.............Dick La Reno
Wetherby...................Frank Beal
Bill Rucker.................Frank Weed

Very satisfactory western comedy melodrama, with the accent on the comedy. If Vitagraph will continue to turn out this grade of material it ought to stage a comeback promptly. The picture probably cost less than even most westerns, for it is practically all done in natural locations. This is in Duncan's familiar style, and there is much to be said for the formula aside from the money involved, for nothing contributes so thoroughly to creating the illusion as a natural background.

The story is amusing with first-rate surprises and a lot of well-handled titles with a funny slant. Character development is natural and convincing, and although the incidents are mostly in a humorous vein they have a certain dramatic support. For example, the hero and heroine are brought together in a highly realistic runaway accident, in which the girl is rescued by the hard-riding Duncan after he leaps from his own galloping mount to one of the runaway team, a trick that appeared to call for a good deal of nerve.

The only bit of hokum is the constant gunplay, but that seems to be necessary to the western type of tale. Still it does seem a bit ridiculous to have control of a situation three or four times as one gun-toter after the other "gets the drop" on the rest. It's getting to be stale stuff.

Miss Johnson makes a charming heroine, playing quietly and without the syrupy sweetness that goes with most screen heroines. There are a number of good character bits, all well handled.

At least the story gets away from a fight for control of a ranch or a mine, and the familiar type of "bad man" does not figure in it. Instead a ne'er-do-well drifts into a cattle town and in a card game wins a local newspaper. He conceives the idea of using this unfamiliar instrument to work out the moral and political regeneration of the community. In the process he falls in love with the former editor's daughter. He finds gross mismanagement in the office of the sheriff, and works out a campaign to defeat the present sheriff and put in an efficient successor.

To accomplish this he has to make believe he is a desperado and work all sorts of tricks on the sheriff, including the exploit of pulling his nose. By this he makes him ridiculous before the natives and carries the day for his own candidate with a capital surprise ending, although the finale is rather slow in arriving and pauses just a bit too long before the "Finis." Nevertheless it makes a good, amusing, light feature. Here presented in a daily change of bill house as half a double bill, the other half being "The Leopardess," with Alice Brady. *Rush.*

FOOLS AND RICHES

Universal society drama with Herbert Rawlinson and a cast of important players. Story by Fred J. Johnson, directed by Herbert Blache. At Loew's 42d Street, May 28.
Jimmy Dorgan..........Herbert Rawlinson
Nelly Blye.............Katherine Perry
John Dorgan.............Tully Marshall
Bernice Lorraine............Doris Pawn
Dick Mason.............Arthur S. Hall
Fransconi.............Nicolai de Ruir

A picture shrewdly made for the neighborhood trade. It has a certain flash of high life, but the sympathetic scenes go to a plain and homely hero and heroine. It has a world of hokum such as went into the tried and true old melodramas, but for the Universal line of trade it is sure fire.

The manly young hero is tricked and tripped by the society moguls and stripped of his fortune, only in the end to turn the tables against his enemies, aided, of course, by the gingham heroine, and comes out winner. In short, it's a Cinderella theme with a male Cinderella and society schemers for the stepmother. The same formula could be worked infinitely and indefinitely and could hardly miss under reasonably expert handling.

The story points a moral—no less than the world old one of the prodigal son—indeed, the hero is a modern prodigal who wastes his inheritance and only wins his way back after he has been forced to menial labor as a waiter in a restaurant. Virtue wins, vice is punished, and at unusually brief intervals the fans burst into applause when old-fashioned justice is meted out by the scenario writer.

Rawlinson has a better part than most of his recent ones, and he plays it with his accustomed naturalness and absence of posings. Playing opposite is Miss Perry, who deserves more prominence than she has been given in filmdom. She has in a high degree the appeal of simple womanhood, a type of beauty that is sweet and yet has character. She could be made a strong screen name with right exploiting. Tully Marshall has a splendid bit as "Pickhandle" Dorgan, Jimmy's father, who by his shrewdness brings about Jimmy's reformation and rehabilitation after he has had his foolish fling, the trick being turned by tying up his fortune and letting it go to the boy only after he has had his lesson.

In the early part there are some fine settings, and the society scenes and fashionable restaurant episodes are managed with telling effect. *Rush.*

IS DIVORCE A FAILURE?

Associated Exhibitors, Inc., production, presented by Arthur F. Beck. Pathe release. Leah Baird featured and also credited for authorship of adaptation and continuity from play "All Mine," by Dorian Neve. Chief in support are Richard Tucker, Walter McGrail, Thomas Santschi and Alec Francis. At Loew's New York, May 26.

A little over a year ago Paramount marketed "Is Matrimony a Failure?" with the answer in the negative. "Is Divorce a Failure?" contrarily, is answered in the affirmative. The story, which the staf-authoress has adapted from the "All Mine" play is developed with that object in view, the action starting with a Reno divorce between Carol Lockwood (Miss Baird) and David Lockwood (Richard Tucker). The story continues, with each essaying a vacation on mutual counsel's advice, with the attorney "arranging" the passage bookings. As a result the Lockwoods, unbeknown to each other, sail on the same boat, as does a "friend" (Walter McGrail) of the newly-divorced.

The steamer is wrecked somewhere below the equator and the trio find themselves cast on a volcanic island, geographically unknown to the outside world. A fourth member, Smith (Tom Santschi) joins the triangle. Smith was a deck steward on the shipwrecked steamer, and his presence on the island is for no good purpose. His forced attentions on Carol reach a climax when the three men embark to a nearby island to forage some herbs for the purpose of alleviating the feverish Kelcey's delirium. Smith is manning the boat, and after landing Lockwood and Kelcey, leaves them stranded there and returns to Carol. Lockwood successfully manages to swim back, despite the threatening sharks, just in time to foil Smith's treacherous purpose. Smith is trussed up for a time, but manages to free himself of his bonds for another fisticuff encounter with David, and is on the verge of besting the latter when Carol is instrumental in halting the onslaught.

In the background of the human happenings the seething volcano is flashed in its intermittent eruptions, with the lava oozing down the slopes. At the psychological moment it attracts the attention of a specially chart.red y.cht sent to search for the Lockwoods, with a rescue being effected and everything turning out as expected. Back in the States Carol and David decide to go it once again in harness and thus fulfill the affirmative import of the title, "Is divorce a failure?"

The production is inexpensive, with much of the action on the tropical isle, although the sinking steamer and its panic-stricken passengers fighting for safety makes an appreciable flash. For a story that is credited to its star for authorship, it has pleasantly sidestepped an overdose of close-ups or general construction of a "fat" stellar part.

Miss Baird manages exceptionally well in what she does. Richard Tucker, opposite her, is adequate, although at times given somewhat to considerable heroics. The balance of the cast was effective.

The picture is a good daily change feature. *Abel.*

TEMPTATION

C. B. C. production based on the story by Lenore Coffee. Directed by Ed J. Le Saint. Carries all-star cast billing. At Loew's Circle, New York, May 26, as part of double feature bill. Time, 65 minutes.

Jack Baldwin.........Bryant Washburn
Marjorie.........Eva Novak
Mrs. Martin.........June Elvidge
Frederick Arnold.........Phillips Smalley
John Hope.........Vernon Steele

The producers of "Temptation" selected an enticing title, backing it up with a story often told before, but in this instance given a twist or two in order that it might not prove identical with pictures that have gone before.

The basic idea has wealth as the cause of most evils. Husband and wife are overcome by their sudden acquisition of means.

The story is rather well worked out, considering the idea is of such ancient vintage.

In addition to its old story, the photography would fit a production of 15 years ago. There is little of the footage that reaches any kind of a satisfactory average in this direction.

The cast is short and of seasoned players. The leads are Bryant Washburn and Eva Novak. Washburn takes first place in the running, with no great opportunities offered him. Miss Novak is a blond miss who handles with comparative ease the ingenue lead. June Elvidge in a widow role is an important factor in the story. Her work is that of an experienced player, with Phillips Smalley and Vernon Steele coming under the same classification. The sets provide a flash at times. The picture's greatest weakness is in the photography.

In working out the story many of the old standard melodramatic bits are employed, with an automobile race and a raid on a roadhouse being brought forth for the punches of the production. *Hart.*

THE LAST MOMENT

J. Parker Read, Jr., production, distributed through Goldwyn, from Jack Boyle's story. Henry Hull, Doris Kenyon and Louis Wolheim have the three major roles. Runs 62 minutes. At the Broadway, New York, in conjunction with vaudeville bill.

How this picture escaped a Broadway showing is something to wonder about. While not a sensational film, it has all the ingredients that usually make up a feature booked at one of the mammoth palaces along Main street and is a good deal more interesting than many seen within the past several weeks. Possibly its general reminiscence of something heretofore produced has something to do with it.

The episode of shanghaing the leading characters parallels that in Morgan Robertson's "Masters of Men" at the Cameo this and last week. The introduction of the hybrid monster with the form of a gorilla and the destructive vengeance of a human brute was the big punch of another Goldwyn release some months ago ("The Blind Bargain," with Lon Chaney), which played the Capitol, Goldwyn's assured Broadway stand.

The story opens with Hercules Napoleon Cameron (Henry Hull), a bookish young man who finds his heroic inspiration between book covers despite his given names. Alice Winthrop (Doris Kenyon) is the girl. Following one of Alice's parties the girl insists on accompanying Napoleon (Nap for short) to the Red Lamp, a waterfront dive periodically frequented by Pat Rooney, the sire of the young bootblack who visits Nap periodically and swallows Cameron's imaginative exploits much to Nap's secret gratification. The slumming tour results in the girl, Nap and a third male acquaintance being shanghaied on a tramp vessel bound for the South Seas.

The action aboard ship is interspersed with the skipper's brutal manifestations, the timid Nap shrinking in physical fear of the burly Finn's physique. Louis Wolheim makes the character realistically vivid. The Finn has in his possession this unnamed monster, which a scientific expedition had discovered and which the Finn had taken unto himself in the knowledge that scientists back home would pay handsomely for it.

The punch of the story is the escape of the monster, with its subsequent wreaking of destruction on everybody and everything it comes in contact with. The brutal captain hides in mortal fear, while Napoleon, in a pinch, becomes endowed with truly napoleonic mental domination in facing the beast and subduing it much on the order of a lion tamer who faces the king of beasts and dominates it. In view of the prepossessing figure of the monster that is a bit hard to swallow, but it is deftly smoothed over in the scenario transition. The monster has not been wholly subdued by Nap, however. After strangling the Finn he lies in wait for Nap. Land is sighted and Alice and Nap decide to swim for it, with the monster following. It is the hero's intention to put into action an idea that has stuck with him through the years from his book learning that a pigmy can keep a giant under water and both can drown. That is his purpose, but it does not become necessary when an abalone, a submarine shellfish, grips one of the monster's paws and holds it until its captive succumbs.

Nap rejoins his sweetheart on shore, and the third friend, heretofore boastfully disdainful of Nap's obvious heroic shortcomings, comes rowing from the boat, where he has been in hiding in the storeroom.

As film fare it has the fact that it is entertainingly diverting to commend it. The cast takes care of its roles perfectly. *Abel.*

THE SHOCK

Universal-Jewel production, featuring Lon Chaney. Directed by Lambert Hillyer; author unnamed. Projection time, 67 minutes.

Picture is an underworld story, with Chaney cast as a cripple, and the effort apparently was to give it some touch of the atmosphere of "The Miracle Man," in which Chaney came into fame almost overnight in the part of the "Frog." The subject misses by a wide margin the high aim of the other vehicle and degenerates into a cheap shocker.

The punch is a mechanical reproduction of the San Francisco earthquake and fire, designed as a bit of sensational melodrama, but failing in its kick because there is no time when it is not evident to the spectator that the whole business is mere studio trickery. The display is accomplished by burning an open-air set, the flames appearing against a night background. Smaller incidents of the conflagration are cut in, and the whole effect is artificial and phoney.

There are evidences that the cutting has been done with a heavy hand. The point of the story is that the cripple, Wiltse Dilling (played by Chaney), is miraculously made whole when he is crushed in a falling building while engaged in an effort to rescue the heroine from a band of criminals. The plausibility of the incident is spoiled by its inexpert management. We merely see the cripple under masses of fallen debris and then are informed that he can walk. The effect is substantially as though all the important passages of a play took place off stage and the audience only heard them talked about. The system makes for unsatisfactory drama.

The story deals with a "queen of the underworld," played by Christine Mayo, who dispatches one of her spies, a cripple with a twisted mind, played by Chaney, to accomplish a mission of vengeance against a banker who had caused her to be sent to prison. The cripple instead falls in love with the banker's daughter (Virginia Valli) and refuses to carry out his bargain, actuated by her good influence. The "queen," failing in her scheme of direct vengeance, plans to punish the banker by the ruin of his daughter and lures her to San Francisco.

There are numerous passages of heavy melodrama concerning the plotting of the crooks and the counterplotting of the cripple, reaching a climax in the earthquake, which defeats the criminals in their schemes and opens the way to a happy ending, with the cripple restored and in happy embrace with the heroine. A picture graded for the daily change houses, resting upon crude melodramatic device, although Chaney has several effective passages. *Rush.*

CROSSED WIRES

Universal production, directed by King Baggott. Gladys Walton starred. At Loew's 42d St. May 25. Running time, 65 minutes.

This is just one of those things. Obviously made for the second and third-run houses, it succeeds, however, in rising above the commonplace several times. The titles are unusually good throughout, incidentally. The good old Cinderella plot is utilized and dressed up a bit, with Cindy a "woiking gal" who wants to crash into society.

Some of the characters are well played, notably the "Tad" father by William Robert Daly. The fellow playing the "hick" boy friend of the heroine is inclined to overdo the part. He's "hick" to the life in appearance, but overacts too frequently.

There's a dancing contest, one of those social club affairs, that's very finely staged. Perfect types and atmosphere. A swell society function by contrast is also excellently done. The latter part of the film runs to farce.

A free-for-all scrap, taking place at the social club's racket, was another scene that reflected credit on the director. Story contains a good idea, but flickers out as it gets toward the middle of the fourth reel. The sets are well built and indicate considerably money was spent for production. It is possible, however, some of the backgrounds may have been standing in the studio and utilized for this picture.

Gladys Wilton makes a pretty telephone gal, with a yen for society, making her role convincing throughout. Kate Price pleases as the mother. Good photography, with nothing out of the ordinary required to unfold the story.

A program picture with flashes much above the average that fits nicely for a double-feature bill. *Bell.*

THE LEOPARDESS

Paramount production starring Alice Brady. Adapted for the screen by J. Clarkson Miller from the story by Katherine Newlin Burt. Directed by Henry Kolker. Shown at Loew's State, New York, for three days, commencing May 21. Time, 70 minutes.

Tiare.........Alice Brady
Scott Quaigg.........Montague Love
Captain Croft.........Edward Langford
Angus McKensie.........Charles Kent

No outstanding feature to recommend this Paramount release, which frames up as an ordinary program picture. It contains a story of the South Seas mixed with the life of a barbarous individual from civilization. The production is not an achievement for Alice Brady as a picture star. In the role of a girl brought up on an island, on which she and her father are the only white people, and her later experiences as the wife of an arrogant creature of wealth, she is given no great opportunities to display her known histrionic ability. In the early footage Miss Brady displays herself scantily clad as a native of the South Seas. In the later reels as a woman of culture she appears to advantage in attractive creations.

The acting at no time shows her at her best. In this division Montague Love comes to the fore. As a husband who trains his wife the same as he does an animal he displays some finished work. Charles Kent and Edward Langsford handle the other two roles of importance satisfactorily. Natives and extras used as a ship's crew furnish the background for the four principal players.

The production includes numerous exteriors and several scenes aboard a yacht. Some interiors of a Westchester home frame up nicely. In no departure has an attempt been made to make this a big picture. It is a production which will prove but a cog in the wheel and never make a name for itself.

Angus McKensie, a Scotchman, and his daughter are shipwrecked on a South Sea island. The girl is brought up as a native, her father being of little account. When she has attained womanhood a white traveler of means reaches the island. He wishes to take the girl, but is forced into a marriage by her father, who secures a case of whiskey for his permission. The girl is taken to her husband's home near New York. There he treats her in the same manner he does a leopardess he had captured. He brags to his friends that his method is the only way to handle women. The girl had learned to care for the captain of her husband's yacht, whom she believed had been drowned when thrown overboard by the latter on their trip to New York.

The captain puts in an appearance later, and considerable confusion takes place, which ends in the husband meeting his Waterloo when the animal which he had kept in a cage in his home leaps upon him and causes his death, leaving his wife free to accept the captain. *Hart.*

WHAT A WIFE LEARNED

A Thomas H. Ince production. Scenario by Bradley King. Directed by Ince. Released by First National. Time, 70 minutes.

Jim Russell.........John Bowers

Rudolph Martin................Milton Sills
Sheila Dorne.......Marguerite De La Motte
Esther Russell..............Evelyn McCoy
Tracy McGrath................Harry Todd
Maggie McGrath...........Aggie Herring
Lillian Martin..........Francella Billington
Terry..................Ernest Butterworth
Maxfield...................John Steppling

A conventional story unfolded in stereotyped manner by a cast of good players of whom none stood out but Marguerite De La Motte. This girl runs away with whatever honors the roles embrace. She is convincingly emotional as the literary school teacher who is torn between love and a career. Coming west to acquire "atmosphere" while teaching school, the story tells of her struggle after marrying Jim Russell. Russell is a western product with secret yearnings to build bridges, etc. He promises not to interfere with his wife's career. She writes a novel which becomes a best seller; it is to be dramatized and she must collaborate with the playwright, Rudolph Martin (Milton Sills) and move to the city.

Her husband doesn't mix with her new friends, but secures employment as a truck driver rather than live on his wife's bounty. Her new circle of friends are surprised at dinner one night by the entrance of the truck driver. When one of them laughs he bounces the crowd. From then on they go it alone until the husband returns to his ranch and completes the building of a dam which has been started years before and abandoned. The bursting of the dam and the rescue of the playwright, who has followed the authoress west, is the big thrill of an otherwise featureless tale that is heavily padded and draggy toward the latter portions. The story solves itself when they decide they are builders and that the creative instinct can be practiced in double harness.

The picture is an ordinary program release and becomes tedious before the last embrace. Milton Sills did well in a colorless role and John Bowers was intense if unconvincing as the transplanted westerner. Marguerite De La Motte must be credited with saving the release from absolute mediocrity. Her work was high grade throughout. *Con.*

THREE JUMPS AHEAD

Fox Film Production, starring Tom Mix. Written and directed by Jack Ford. At Fox's Academy of Music, New York, Tuesday, May 22. Time, 55 minutes. Cast: Tom Mix, Francis Ford, Buster Gardner, Edward Teil, Joseph E. Girard, Virginia Boardman, Margaret Joslin.

This is a western of the machine made sort. Cut and dried situations galore in the early part of the picture, with the big punch arriving in the final reel and making up for the drivel that has preceded it. Punch is leap on horseback made by Mix across chasm that looks to be mountainous in height and possibly 20 feet in width. Maybe more. Whatever the exact dimensions, it's a darb of a leap.

Story is built up slowly, first part dragging. Usual bandits, cow hands, tough guys, mountain scenery, and a chase toward the finish. It's the sort of stuff they used to fill the dime novels with years ago, and evidently aimed to please the kids. Lots of apple sauce, with hero (Mix) outwitting bandits and rescuing sweetheart's father from cruel clutches.

A title mentioned something about "Old Hokum Bucket." Looks as if title writer had been reading Variety. Great riding stuff. One stretch of film has Mix doing a wild chariot ride on remains of stage coach that has gone over the cliff. That's the kind of film it is, "over the cliffs with 'im, boys."

Mix is excellent in role that means nothing, making it important through sheer force of personality. He deserves better vehicles than junk like this. Rest of cast good, including ingenue, whose name is not mentioned in cast because Academy doesn't give out programs with casts, and film was run off so swiftly name could not be caught from screen.

Photography average. Picture would make great two reeler. As it is there's a nice long sleep between reels one and five. Punch is worth waking up for, though. That riding by Mix and bandits, and Mix's leap would make any picture. Would have made this a big timer had rest of it been any way near it in point of interest. For the smaller houses it should be a great card, especially matinees for the children. Lacks class for the big houses, but should make an excellent half of a double feature bill. *Bell.*

SNOWDRIFT

William Fox production starring Charles Jones. Directed by Scott Dunlap from James B. Hendryx's story. Runs about 55 minutes. Half of a double feature at Loew's New York.

This is the forerunner of the usual avalanche of Arctic subjects so prevalent during the torrid months. The title gives away its frigid locale.

The story is one of those stock formulas about the white daughter of rather veiled origin; the gambler-hero; the "the Queen of the Yukon" and the boss of the Bonanza dance hall who insists on making the heroine an inmate of his Dawson rendezvous.

The period of the action is vaguely denoted as around the gold rush time. Charles Jones is only identified by the soubriquet of Ace-in-the-hole because of his unusually lucky poker activities. Heralded by a title as a college graduate and an engineer, he is introduced on one of his stud rampages. Later tables turn and Jones becomes and is accused as being a "bum" by the "Queen of the Yukon."

Ace is led to reform and cure himself of the grip of hootch by his stoic Indian good man Friday. He "mushes" north to again develop his mine which purpose is conveniently lost sight of in Ace's wooing and winning of "Snowdrift" (Dorothy Manners). She is the daughter of the McFarlands who entrusted her as a babe to an Indian (or is it Esquimo?) squaw—it is not made clear—who places Snowdrift in a convent and leads all to believe the girl is her offspring from a hybrid mating of questionable origin.

Ace having conquered drink trails Claw (the heavy) to his Dawson City dance hall where he has kidnapped Snowdrift and in a truly gripping fight amid flames effects a rescue and the convenient demise of the villain in a mortal combat in self-defense. That's the big punch of the picture—that fight—and tops off the release effectively.

It is produced with the usual Fox production economy with plenty of outdoor stuff and a couple of crude log cabin interiors. Probably a pop price rental release and should please in the small daily change houses.

The star gets in some effective work. Miss Manners is an unknown quantity and fell below the mark in the little she was called upon to do. For that matter all the women did nothing distinguishing excepting the Indian squaw. Irene Rich as the dance hall queen was given few opportunities. G. Raymond Nigh as Claw, the heavy, was effective. *Abel.*

THE RAGGED EDGE

Distinctive Pictures Corp. production released by Goldwyn-Cosmopolitan. Adapted by Forrest Halsey from Harold MacGrath's novel. Directed by Harmon Weight. Alfred Lunt and Mimi Palmeri featured. Running time, 81 minutes. At the Capitol, New York, week of June 3.

Howard Spurlock..............Alfred Lunt
Ruth Endicott.................Mimi Palmeri
Ah Cum.......................Charles Fang
The Doctor..................Wallace Erskine
McClintock..............George MacQuarrie
O'Higgins..................Charles Slattery
The Wastrel................Christian Frank
Prudence Jedson............Grace Griswold
Angelina Jedson.................Alice May
Hotel Manager.................Percy Carr
Rev. Dalby...................Sydney Drew
Mrs. Dalby...................Hattie Delaro
The Aunt........................Marie Day

A South Sea Island picture with different angles is here presented. It has an attractive romantic flavor. Most of the South Seas hokum, such as undressed native maidens and heavy atmosphere, is missing. Instead the picture rests on the sure foundation of a clean-cut story and well-drawn characters, with a picturesque backing of ancient China.

It is seldom a novel is transcribed to the screen in so satisfactory a manner. It progresses logically from scene to scene and character to character with remarkable economy and logic. It has cleverly knitted bits of comedy, such as the Chinese guide, who introduces himself as Yale '16, and rescues the hero by a native trick, explaining that the hero (who also is a Yale alumnus) is "a blood brother of my tong."

The picture is a little long, but it is packed full of meat and the length never becomes wearisome. There are other angles. Suspense is skillfully introduced by the device of having a detective from the States pursue the hero for some vague crime. In the end it turns out that his friends at home were merely trying to get track of him to tell him his supposed crime was all imaginary. But the pursuit gives the whole story a mysterious turn and furnishes motives for the whole tale.

The Oriental touch is especially vivid. The hero in Pekin goes on a lonesome spree, and under the influence insists upon visiting the native quarter in spite of warnings of danger to foreign devils. He forces his way into a native gambling place, buys a "sing song" girl to free her and escapes because the superstitious natives think him mad. The scenes inside the gambling place and in the streets, with their weird Chinese crowds, are impressive bits of pictorial punch, and the whole atmosphere is convincingly accomplished.

Out of his experience with hooch and mental complexities the hero breaks down, and is nursed back to health by a missionary's daughter. A benevolent doctor secures a job for him on a distant island in the South Pacific, and on the eve of departure he marries the girl. Here the story takes a rather unsatisfactory twist. The young man, believing he has committed a crime back home, resolves he will not claim his bride until he has reestablished himself, although she makes it plain she loves him and is pained by his coldness.

It's all straightened up by the appearance of the detective with explanations that his theft of money has been forgiven and his family welcomes him back. To put a satisfactory romantic finish to the story, a drug fiend who has been pursuing the girl is introduced, and the clash between the derelict and the hero wins the young man's self-respect and brings him to his wife's arms.

One of the picture's charms is that most of the cast is comparatively new to the screen. Alfred Lunt is a splendid natural actor, and Mimi Palmeri makes a likable heroine, partly because she is a variation from the insipid beauties we have become accustomed to. *Rush.*

THE EXCITERS

Famous Players-Paramount production, presented by Adolph Zukor. Bebe Daniels and Antonio Moreno co-starred. Adapted from Martin Brown's play by John Colton and Sonya Levien. Directed by Maurice Campbell. At the Rivoli, New York, week June 3. Time, 64 minutes.

Ronnie Rand....................Bebe Daniels
Pierre Martel...............Antonio Moreno
Rackham, the lawyer........Burr McIntosh
Ermintrude.......................Diana Allen
Roger Patton......................Cyril Ring
Hilary Rand................Bigelow Cooper
Mrs. Rand..........................Ida Darling
Della Vaughn..................Jane Thomas
Mechanician..................Allan Simpson
Minister......................George Backus
"Gentleman Eddie"............Henry Sedley
"Strangler Louis"............Irvil Alderson
"Flash".............................Tom Blake

Here is a fast-moving, entertaining light comedy melodrama sure to please film house audiences. It has a rare combination of a clever co-starred pair of players, a good story, a number of thrills and a great little love theme. What more can any one ask for? But with this it is going to be up to the exhibitor to pull his audiences in, with the assurance that they will be entertained once in the theatre.

The screen offering was adapted from Martin Brown's play of the same title. It deals with the fast-moving flapper of the upper social set who is out in search of thrills. In her adventures she marries one whom she believes to be a burglar, only to discover in the end that he is in reality an avenger who has given himself to the task of tracking down a gang of crooks who had wronged a friend of him.

In picturizing the events as above Maurice Campbell has handled the task with a perfect understanding of the dramatic value of suspense. The public is unaware of the real status of the hero until the final few feet of the story.

Bebe Daniels incidentally is proving herself something of an actress in this picture. She is no longer affecting the drooping eye and the Cupid's bow lip make-up that she was wont to present to the camera is also a thing of the past as far as this picture is concerned, and, therefore, there is practically a new Bebe Daniels on the screen and a much better actress than the former Bebe was. Antonio Moreno makes an altogether convincing hero. The balance of the cast matters but little, except for a small character bit played by Irvil Alderson as a strangler. He was enough tto give one the shivers when his hands started working. Jane Thomas and Cyril Ring also contributed cleverly to the ensemble background for the two stars. *Fred.*

A MAN OF ACTION

A Thomas H. Ince-First National production, starring Douglas MacLean. Story by Bradley King, directed by James W. Horne. Shown at the Strand, New York, week June 3. Time 59 minutes.

Bruce MacAllister.........Douglas MacLean
Helen Sumner....Marguerite de la Motte
Harry Hopwood..........Raymond Hatton
Spike McNab..................Wade Boetler
Dr. Sumner.....................Arthur Millett
Andy......................Kingsley Benedict
Eugene Preston.......Arthur Stewart Hull
The "Deacon"..........William Courtright
"Frisk-O" Rose...........Katherine Lewis

This is a farcical crook story, ideal for warm weather programs. It is a laugh yarn from beginning to end and as a picture offering comes as better follow up material to "The Hottentot" than the one picture with MacLean as the star that was released since. In this the young comedian handles himself particularly well and the comedy action with several eccentric crooks wandering through the story brings scream after scream of laughter.

MacLean is depicted as a young man born with a silver spoon in his mouth, roused by the desires of his fiancee that he become a man of action. A newly appointed director of his estate tries to fleece him of a shipment of diamonds. This leads to a series of complications that really tax the young man to all the action that his being is capable of.

The story is handled in a snappy farcical manner, that almost borders on slapstick at times, but it is delightful hoak that the audiences will eat up. MacLean handles himself cleverly and is stepping into the position of the foremost light comedian of the screen today. Raymond Hatton and William Courtright as a pair of underworld characters scored heavily as did Katherine Lewis as their companion in crime. *Fred.*

THE HEART RAIDER

Famous Players production, with Agnes Ayres starred. Scenario by Jack Cunningham, from a story by Harry Durant and Julie Herne, directed by Wesley Ruggles. At Rialto, New York, week June 3. Running time, 54 minutes.

Muriel Gray, a speed girl......Agnes Ayres
John Dennis, a bachelor..Mahlon Hamilton
Gaspard McMahon, an insurance clerk, Charles Ruggles
Reginald Gray, Muriel's father, Frazer Coulter
Mrs. Dennis, John's mother...Marie Burke
Jeremiah Wiggins, captain of yacht, Charlies Riegal

A breath of the whole outdoors that just fits in for the summer time and with Agnes Ayres looking as well as playing the impetuous self-willed young woman makes "The Heart Raider" a pleasing hour as a regular weekly first-run release.

The title is derived through Muriel Gray (Miss Ayres) having decided to have John Dennis (Mahlon Hamilton) for a husband. She goes after him willy-nilly and gets him. To accomplish that she drives her car wildly to Palm Beach, breaking down fences, killing chickens en route and finally landing in jail for overnight along with her father, who was the only passenger, as a result of her reckless driving. But she got to Palm Beach in time to meet Dennis, who didn't know she was there, he having arrived on his yacht.

When Dennis sought to escape the very pretty and likeable girl no other man would have resisted, she dove from a bulkhead and swam to his boat, then went ashore in a huff at him, but, relenting, again chased him, and this time in a motorboat that was doing 35 (and a dead ringer, Sid, for the old one), the complications inclusive of a southern typhoon culminating in their eventual marriage, when one of the best captions of the evening came forth. Muriel, looking at John, said: "I wonder if I will have as much trouble in holding you as I had in getting you?"

A side story intermingled and for comedy was the father insuring himself against his daughter's escapades with the insurance company, fearful through the accumulating damage demands of victims of the daughter's car, sending a representative (Charles Ruggles) to marry the girl or lose his job. The policy provided the company's liability ended upon the daughther's marriage. Ruggles probably did as well as anyone could with the role, a purely fanciful one, as was the policy incident, but he won a few laughs. But the light texture of the entire story gives it an amusing angle continuously.

The picture's best bet, however, is Agnes Ayres, that rare type of a good-looking athletic girl who is both, the kind of a girl everyone likes. Miss Ayres never let it be forgotten she's the sort that gets what they go after. It's this dominant spirit of the girl, always manifest, that brings to her admiration despite her leap-year methods and strict attention because she's apt to do anything at any time.

The adaptation by Jack Cunningham is excellent, equaled by the direction of Wesley Ruggles. Just whether it was Mr. Cunningham or Mr. Ruggles or the cutter who passed up the details of getting the folks out of jail in Atlanta of course isn't known, but that detail stuff elided as it was might be observed by any director as a distinct advancement in useless waste of time and celuloid.

This picture will please the patrons for the exhibitors and do a lot for Agnes Ayres. You leave the theatre with that vision of a healthy young girl in your mind, and the vision is still with this guy, some hours after. *Sime.*

THE TIE THAT BINDS

A wishy washy melodrama, presented by "The Tie That Binds" Co. Adapted from a sob ballad of years ago by Pearl Keating. Directed by Joseph Levering. Shown at Loew's New York on double feature bill, June 5. Time, 73 minutes.

Daniel Kenyon..........William P. Carlton
Charles Dodge..............Robert Edeson
David Winthrop...............Walter Miller
Mary Ellen Grey..........Barbara Bedford
Flora Foster...............Mariam Swayne
Mrs. Mills....................Effie Shannon
Lieia Brandt.........Julia Swayne Gordon

This picture is one of the reasons that the exhibitors are complaining that features are too long and take up too much running time in their shows. It is just a fair program melodrama that will get by in practically all of the daily change houses, but at the same time it is a picture that could have been delivered in five reels as well as six or seven. The feature contains naught that has not been seen time and again as far as situation goes, nor has it any particular punch that is going to send it over with audiences. It's just a picture, and while it is pretty fair when viewed from the angle of a state's rights offering it doesn't go beyond that.

Originally "The Tie That Binds" was one of those sob ballads that delighted the hearts of those close harmony fiends of a score or more of years ago. As a picture it is somewhat different than the theme laid out in the song. For screen purposes a murder mystery, a ruined girl and all the other little necessary touches that would eat up footage have been added.

The cast, however, is a fairly good one, with Barbara Bedford the outstanding figure in the enactment of the drama. She is the private secretary to a toy manufacturer, who wants to marry her. Instead of accepting she weds one of the organization's staff and he is discharged a few weeks after the ceremony. For several years after that he is employed but intermittently, and devotes his time principally to working out a toy novelty in a tiger that springs. The wife, finally worn down by his lack of progressiveness, returns to her old position, living apart from her husband, who retains their only child. The old employer tries to have an affair with the wife and attacks her in the office on a night that the husband has followed her. The wife, trying to protect herself, pulls a revolver; her husband also has one, and a mysterious shot is fired. Each believes the other has done it, and the husband goes to jail. It finally develops that the night watchman, whose daughter was ruined by the boss, fired the shot.

The principal angle of note in the picture was the baby that was utilized, which seemingly could be made to laugh or cry at will.

There are any number of good names in the cast, but for the greater part they have nothing to do. *Fred.*

BURNING WORDS

Universal romantic melodrama of the Northwest Mounted, starring Roy Stewart. Story by Harrison Warren Jacobs. Directed by Stuart Paton. Projection time, 52 minutes. At Loew's New York, June 1.

David Darby..................Roy Stewart
Mary Malcolm.............Laura LaPlante
Rose Darby...................Harold Goodwin
Mrs. Darby.........................Edith Yorke
Mr. Darby........................Alfred Fisher
John Malcolm...............William Welsh

Some of these story makers and directors must think the human race is extremely obtuse. They are never content to picture emotion, sentiment or action in convincing proportion. Everything has to be superlative. If a scene is tinged with pathos they pile the agony on until an ordinary mortal with average sensitiveness revolts. If you over-emphasize an emotional quality far enough what you accomplish is to awaken in the back of the spectator's mind the thought, "Oh, sugar! It's only a picture." The illusion is gone and with it sympathetic interest.

That's what happens in "Burning Words." Not content with working up a situation of moderate pathos—briefly, the meeting in a cell between a condemned murderer and his aged mother—they work endless variations on the theme, such as having the mother asking the boy to repeat a childhood prayer learned at her knee, etc. The idea presumably is that emotional appeal must be spread on so thick that it will bore through the densest grade of fans. If it is Universal's deliberate campaign to specialize in pictures for the lowest class of audiences, this is the way to go about it. Only it's rather a cynical notion that the majority of fans are boneheads.

Except for this tendency to slop over in sentiment the picture isn't a bad one on its technical side. Some of the locations are exceptionally beautiful in a scenic way and the photography is consistently fine. But always the overdoing of the dramatic and sentimental stands as a bar to interest. The story has to do with two brothers, both in the same troupe of the Northwest Mounted Police. The younger brother is a weakling, the elder a moral and physical hero. When the younger brother, as the climax of his career of petty vice, commits a murder, nothing would do but the elder brother be sent into the wilderness to capture him. Such a situation couldn't happen except in cheap fiction.

When the youngster is put on trial the elder takes his guilt upon his own shoulders, another threadbare device of second class fiction. The introduction of the old mother and the stilted scene in the cell of the condemned is the last straw.

To make it worse Roy Stewart is an unconvincing hero in a straight role, just a screen actor in every pose and gesture, while Harold Goodwin, who plays the younger brother, is a thoroughly human and natural young player.. Your sympathies go out to the better actor, and as it unfolded on the screen the story seemed to contradict itself. The romantic element is practically absent. They do drag in a love scene from time to time, but it is never convincing, and at the fadeout of the hero and his bride you have a feeling the whole affair somehow is unsatisfactory. *Rush.*

LOVE, LIFE AND LAUGHTER

London, May 24.

This new Walsh-Pearson film is exceptionally good entertainment. A mixture of romance and fantasy, the story is well told and the continuity is excellent. As far as the story itself is concerned the keynote is simplicity, but scenically the picture is more ornate and extravagant than any other British production, but this elaborate staging is necessary to give the point to the simplicity of the story. Throughout, George Pearson's production work is remarkably good and he succeeds in making his characters live as few British producers have done. His staging is admirable whether showing the squalor of a tenement house or the glories of the fashionable West End. The interiors of the auditorium of a big theatre are the best seen and his "behind stage" scenes are real. There are many shots of London by night and throughout the photography is beautiful.

The story tells how a boy and a girl, both lonely and living in squalid lodgings, become sweethearts. He is an unpublished story writer, she an illiterate chorus girl. At the moment she is promoted to be leading lady in the No. 2 company of the revue he gets the news, his first story has been accepted. That night he reads a novel to the girl. It is the story of their own lives. She becomes a great music hall "star," but he sinks to the lowest depths. She is loved by a rich man, but her heart is always with the boy. They have decided on a reunion in two year's time, but when the hour comes it brings her news of his death. This is the end of his story, but the girl insists upon it having a happy ending. They must both achieve fame and fortune.

Although the story gives every opportunity for it there is an entire absence of the suggestive or the nasty. The cast, without being of the so-called "star" class, is very fine. Betty Balfour gives one of her best performances as the girl, and a newcomer to leading parts on the screen, Harry Jonas, is excellent as the boy. Frank Stanmore gives a fine character study as an itinerant toy seller, the Optimist, Annie Esmond and Nancy Price are exceptionally good as his wife and her friend. Gordon Hopkirk is natural and good as A Gentleman, and Aubrey Ridgewell presents an excellent study as a girl in love with the boy. This impersonation from the point of view of sheer histrionic ability is by far the best performance in the picture. Many small parts are very well played.

As has become common nowadays the feature had a prolog, but up to the moment of writing no one knows what it was about or why it was staged. Cut drastically, "Love, Life, and Laughter" will make a fine showman's proposition. *Gore.*

CRIQUI-KILBANE FIGHT

Made under the auspices of the Polo Grounds Athletic Association and are claimed to be exclusive. At the Broadway this week. Running time, 20 minutes.

This film should be of great interest to close followers of boxing, but as it stands now is too long and technical to offer much enjoyment or excitement to the average picture audience. At the Broadway it ran for 29 minutes, even though it was reeled off at a much greater speed than the actual action. Women, children and a good many men are bound to find this round-after-round stuff boring, particularly if no music is played, as at the Broadway.

The picture starts with stills of the contestants and the promoters, followed by some views of the crowd entering the Polo Grounds. Then there are six of the eight rounds of the Curtin-Sharkey prelim, only the second and fourth being omitted. This is where the film lags and should be cut. It is a particularly uneventful scrap and two or three rounds would have been plenty to establish Curtin's supremacy. Besides, the focus is rather blurred, but the camera man evidently eliminated this trouble before the start of the main bout.

After Joe Humphreys introduced the principals and the defending champion is shown to be the favorite with the crowd the big fight begins. It is slow and productive of few real wallops, with Criqui having a shade the better of it all the way. It is interesting to notice how

Kilbane, full of confidence at first, gradually loses the look of scorn and native superiority and becomes more and more worried under the Frenchman's provocative little jabs until the middle of the fatal sixth round.

The sudden right to the jaw is so unexpected it is impossible to anticipate it even when warned beforehand on the screen. With it comes the one big thrill of the picture, but it's a genuine thrill, far superior to the staged climaxes in the regular film dramas.

The picture is enlivened with a few well-taken bits of the crowd, cheering, eating hot dogs and generally amusing themselves. It hardly looks as if 20,000 were present, though, judging from the empty seats.

THE STRANGER OF THE HILLS

Farra Production released by Anchor in the State rights field. Features Edward Coxen, Ethel Richie and Charles Farra. Shown at Times Theatre, New York, a 600-seat house on Eighth avenue, with a 20-cent top scale, on double feature bill, June 1. Time, 60 minutes.

This is just one of the usual hoak Westerns, with a fairly well centered story that is designed for the cheaper type of houses. As such it will get by. There are four principals that stand out; three form the usual triangle and the fourth provides comedy. The cast of principals holds the girl, the killer, the ranger captain and the sheriff. With the quartet of characters to work from, a tale that is interesting is worked out. The direction and photography are rather poor, and the print shown at this house was decidedly "rainy."

There is one thing that the picture does bring to the fore, and that is a possibility in Ethel Richie. Here is a girl that seemingly has everything that goes toward the making of a successful screen artist, and if some one does not pick her for a real picture shortly they will be overlooking a bet.

"The Stranger of the Hills" is just what it was intended to be, a cheap picture for the cheap houses, and as such, answers. *Fred.*

Foreign Films

GRAND GUIGNOL

Paris, May 28.

We have another show to chronicle at the little Grand Guignol, in the ville lumiere, which is well mixed with the accustomary doses of farce and drama, but this time it is not a credit to either this famous chamber of horrors or the city of Paris.

The first number is a one-act drama "Le Devoir de tuer" by Rene Berton, posing the problem whether a physician has the right to kill a patient when he knows the victim is past recovery, but may continue to live a time in terrible agony. The author shows us the practician has not only a right, but it is a duty.

A poor fellow is dying slowly from a cancer on the liver and begs to be put out of pain. If he dies before a certain date his wife loses her claim to a pension, but the sympathetic doctor in connivance with the wife changes the morphine for strychnine in the syringe. Who would convict for such a deed?

We blame M. Choisy a great deal more for having mounted "J'veux voir Virginia," one-act farce by Jose de Berys. This Frenchy production is the yarn about a false American artist paying a big price to a janitor for the privilege of watching his niece in a state of nudity. The exhibition is supposed to be held in the adjoining room, and the amount paid in a false check. The police arrest the generou spectator, who is an escaped lunatic in the form of a false art student. Indeed the entire act is false.

M. Arquilliere, the actor, has turned playwright and given a two-act drama "Nevrose." An Oriental Countess is desperate at the idea of being separated from her young lover by the return of her husband. She suggests to a former admirer that he should put the legitimate intruder out of the way, but the former favorite, not blind to the truth, and having nothing to gain, declines.

The husband challenges the younger lover to a duel, whereupon the wife tries to disarm her lawful companion by a night of voluptv. As a matter of fact, the husband is killed in the duel, to the visible joy of the wife, but the former admirer takes the law into his own hands and shoots the unnatural woman. This drama is played in sombre scenery, to create an atmosphere of halucination, the action being rapid and ably constructed.

It is followed by "La Jalouse," one-act piece by Michel Brega and Georges Hoffman, explaining the troubles of an author possessed with a jealous wife. The dramatist is flirting with an influential actress, his only object being to have his piece accepted, but owing to the interference of the spouse who declines to see her nose put out of joint, the poor author loses the only opportunity he ever had of getting a play produced.

On the whole the new program of the Grand Guignol has proved a slip. *Kendrew.*

AUX DEUX MASQUES

Paris, May 29.

The little theatre known as the Deux Masques, a sort of competitor to the Grand Guignol, under the direction of Marcel Nancy, has also treated its habitues to a new mixed show.

There is nothing much to report. Starting off with the smutty sketch of "L'Impossible Aveu" already mentioned and for which a substitute could have been easily found, we have a two-act drama, "Le Chien qui hurle" by Rene Wisner, a pastoral of peasant ways and means. Harbois has refused to sell a plot of land to his neighbor, Fromont, both cunning farmers, so the latter insinuates to the good-for-nothing son of Harbois that his father is suffering from heart disease and when he quits this earth all his fortune will belong to the disreputable lad. During the night the dogs are heard barking (hence the title), in a manner that indicates a calamity according to local folk-lore.

In the morning young Harbois calls to tell Fromont his father has died, whereupon the crafty old cultivator declares without going into details that he is able to testify relative to his neighbor's unhealthy physical condition, thereby supposing a natural end, if the heir will give (not sell) the plot of land he wants. In this drama the audience has all the impression of a wicked crime without knowing any details, and as such it is an interesting effort.

There is another two-act drama "Une Main dans l'Ombre," by Pierre Palau and Jean Velu, a sort of echo of the war. A German general is tempted in a moment of fear to confess to a Dutch journalist that he assassinated a mother and violated her two daughters while billetted in a French mansion. His companion, having by a subterfuge got the other visitors out of the way, flies at his throat and strangles him. The newspaper man from Holland is a Frenchman in disguise; he is "The hand in the shadow' tracking down unpunished war criminals.

"Mon Frere de Lait," two-act farce, also by Pierre Palau, is a bit near the knuckle, with an unexpected denouement. A man is flirting with his cook; she tells his wife who persuades her t sleep in the spare bedroom while the lady takes her place. But a friend from the colonies pays a visit and the husband decides to put him up for the night, generously suggesting he shall join the cook.

The colonial foster brother (vide title) willingly accepts. Meantime, the repenting cook, hearing of the situation, warns her master when it is too late, and the husband is seen fretting at his own stupidity. However, the friend, a bit off color had declined the favors of the supposed cook, it developed. The farce is well acted, and quick in movement, constituting a really comic sketch of the poet Chaucer style, but totally unfit for modern export.

In spite of a few laughs and a passing shudder, the new program of the Deux Masques proves a slip likewise. *Kendrew.*

L'EMBRASEMENT

Paris, May 29.

A separate group of dramatic enthusiasts calling themselves the Oeuvriers (workers) were given hospitality by Lugne Poe at the Maison de l'Oeuvre for a matinee and presented a remarkable three-act piece, "L'Embrasement" ("Conflagration"). No regular playhouse has had the privilege of producing a work of the same power during the entire season, now almost ended. The author has attacked a delicate subject in a proficient manner.

A married couple watching themselves grow old have retired to a small country town. The man is a painter of a certain talent and his pictures have brought him mild notoriety. The woman is reconciled to the role of housewife and is the companion of her husband at the fireside, without any anticipated change to break the monotony. But the husband, well turned 50, feels the oppression of provincial dullness and is bored to death, notwithstanding he has his art to occupy the time if he could only muster energy and inspiration to paint.

Then into this dreary existence a young girl appears as a beacon. She is an orphan, taken into the home as general servant, although her refinement and education are far above those wont to accept such a menial occupation. It appears, however, she preferred domestic service in the country to the temptations of the capital, and so sadly but confidently entered the painter's household as she would have taken the veil in a nunnery. Her presence, full of youthful charm, quickly alters the dreary aspect of the artist's daily life. She fills the place with sweet gaiety. The man's ardor is rekindled despite his 55 years, and he seeks to be continually in the company of this young creature, whose charm and chastity inspire him to resume his painting.

The maiden becomes keenly interested in her master's work, and on his supplication consents to become his model for a study of the nude. She is quite pure in her intentions, only admiring and respecting the artist, who is old enough to be her father. But is it a genuine inspiration for true art on the part of the man or an excuse to satisfy his craving desire to contemplate the perfect lines of this refined, healthy maiden within his clutches? The elderly artist dare hardly put the question to himself, and will only acknowledge in his own mind that the presence of this innocent, confiding girl has fired him with renewed energy to paint, such as he has never before experienced.

Then, as the picture progresses, the virgin doubts the purity of her own soul, for she begins to fear the growing affection and warm admiration she feels for her employer and benefactor are the reticence of a deeper sentiment that may lead to a violent passion followed by possession at the first opportunity.

The wife visits the studio one day and discovers the canvas on which the painter has expressed the voluptuous exuberance he has not yet dared to openly declare to the model. She immediately sizes up the situation, taxes her husband with forbidden and evil designs and recalls him to his duty. As the moral man he is, the artist realizes the sin he was about to commit, for he is now sure the servant girl loves him. He promises to renounce the flesh and the devil, but would certainly have ultimately failed, despite his honorable endeavors, were he not assisted by his former model, who, to spare grief to the wife and shame to the husband, accepts an offer of marriage made by the gardener. It is true she gives herself to the young laborer with the same spirit of resignation as an incurable would commit suicide.

Fortunately the gardener is a straight, sensible, intelligent, hard-working fellow, capable of winning a woman's esteem and assuring her a lasting happiness. And the evening of her departure for another village with her husband the young woman laughs as freely as when she first entered the house. When she has gone the artist sadly shuts the door, more than ever feeling the weight of his age and thanking the great Architect of the Universe for sparing him from eternal remorse.

This painful tragedy of unrequited secret desire is unfolded in an impressive style of dramatic art by a young author giving his first effort to the public. He has succeeded beyond his own hopes. It is as good as a church sermon and just as effective. Many men will see themselves reflected as in a mirror. It draws one of the great dramas of human nature. There are many honest folks who have thus suffered, and it behooves all of us to refrain from throwing a stone of contempt at a guilty neighbor.

Kendrew.

CORDELIA THE MAGNIFICENT

Samuel Zirler production starring Clara Kimball Young, released by Metro. From the story by LeRoy Scott adapted by Frank S. Beresford, directed by George Archainbaud. At Loew's State, New York, June 11-13. Time, 73 minutes.

Cordelia Marlowe	Clara Kimball Young
D. K. Franklin	Huntley Gordon
Esther Norworth	Carol Halloway
Gladys Norworth	Jacqueline Gadson
Jerry Plimpton	Lloyd Whitlock
James Mitchell Grayson	Lewis Dayton
Jackie Thorndyke	Katherine Murphy
Francois	Mary Jane Irving

This is a society mystery play with Clara Kimball Young as the star; a Clara Kimball Young, however, that seems to be fighting hard to retain her hold on the picture fan public; a Clara Kimball Young who is taking on weight to an alarming degree and whose face carries more or less of a worried expression, and a Clara Kimball Young whose work in this picture is far from the best she has offered during her screen career.

In this production of LeRoy Scott's story "Cordelia The Magnificent" Miss Young is a society girl whose family's fortunes have been shot to pieces to such an extent that she must seek employment and so becomes a confidential outside operative for a legal firm, which thrives on blackmailing the social elect. It is a story that will appeal to the fans in the majority of houses and the star's role is a sympathetic one. However, her leading man Lewis Dayton, and Jacqueline Gadson, who must be somewhat of a new comer to screen activities, and who plays the female heavy in this picture, walk away with the production, at times leaving the star stranded before the camera.

The story is the main attraction. It is a yarn full of interest that holds the audience to the last and were the star at her best this should have been a whale of an outstanding production for her. The direction was admirably handled and mystery element sustained until practically the last moment.

The action at all times is keyed perfectly and the audience's interest can be measured by the fact that at the big situations with the hero coming forward at the precise moment when he was suspected of being the heavy and aiding the heroine who is in a tight corner there was unusual applause at Loew's State on Monday night. That there was the twist in the character of the leading man from supposed heavy to the real hero of the situation was novel and that as much as anything brought the approval of the audience.

As a picture for picture houses "Cordelia the Magnificent" will get by in great shape, but as to Miss Young adding anything to her reputation as a film star her performance here won't accomplish it.

Fred.

A FRIENDLY HUSBAND

William Fox production. Directed by Jack Blystone. Loew's Circle, New York, June 12-13. Time, 60 minutes.

The Husband	Lupino Lane
The Wife	Alberta Vaughan
The Mother-in-law	Eva Thatcher

If Lupino Lane could get a succession of Benda masks and take them off and put them on by cue, each registering a different expression, he might justify the faith that Fox had in him and pay back all the money invested in him. Lane is a tumbling, comedy "business" comic of far beyond average star merit—from the collar-button down. But his face has two "changes"—the dizzy, staggering imbecile and the blank idiot.

"A Friendly Husband" is a lengthy slapstick that will land with a bang in the 30-cent houses, for its has falls, somersaults, trick props and speedy action. It is the busiest comedy since Harold Lloyd's early efforts. But it lacks both a thought and a thrill, and therefore will be rated funny, but not passed along as beyond being missed.

The piece de resistance (and a great idea, too) is a Kozy Kampers' outfit, a trailer to a flivver, with beds, stove, shower bath, dishwasher and other weird and amusing gewgaws. The usual boob bridegroom takes the conventional ex-bathing-girl bride camping, and her stereotyped man-eating mother and the rest of her relations horn in, making the husband the sap of the family tree.

Out in the woods he stumbles over everything; the various "improvements" fall out and slide in, etc., and he is chased by the stock bear and licks the huge heavy, who drags off the cutie bride. Whenever he is passing out under the succession of strains he gets a kiss from her lips, and that hops him up. Everything is overdone, of course, except by Miss Vaughan, who really puts some human moments into her absurd positions as a lollypop to a lunatic.

The most interesting element, of course, is Lane, about whom there have been conflicting reports and many speculative arguments. Lane as a single star appears in this film to be wanting, though as the comedian of a light story he would be immense. He will never gather admirers solidly about him, for he is quite devoid of screen personality and is dependent entirely upon violent, though often convulsing, calisthenics and acrobatics.

There is no subtlety anywhere—no sympathy, no change of tune; it is all fall-down and bounce-up, knock-down and yank-up, with only the mechanical trailer and the flivver to give variety. In close-up Lane registers negative. And he is not establishing a "character," even to the extent of Lloyd's spectacles, Chaplin's feet or Turpin's eyes. He seems set for the second-class houses, and "A Friendly Husband" will set him there pretty.

Lait.

SLIPPY McGEE

Oliver Morosco production based on the story by Marie Conway Oemler, directed by Wesley Ruggles. Features Colleen Moore and Wheeler Oakman. Shown at Proctor's 23d St., New York, June 11-13. Time, 70 minutes.

Slippy McGee	Wheeler Oakman
Mary Virginia	Colleen Moore
Father De Rance	Sam De Grasse
George Ingelsby	Edmund Stevens
Madame De Rance	Edith Yorke
Howard Hunter	Lloyd Whitlock

When Morosco turned out this production for First National he made no attempt to make it a first-class picture. It is slipshod with many of its short-comings of such a gross nature it is hardly conceiveable the realeasing corporation would tolerate it. It is quite apparent the production is being given little consideration by exhibitors and is not worthy of being brought forth as one of the regular First National program releases.

Few productions of the present day sponsored by recognized companies have words spelled wrong in the captions and mix up the names of their characters such as here. The story as unfolded on the screen is jerky and disjointed with an unsatisfactory ending. The author in all probability turned out a readable tale. It touches upon a subject always interesting if well done. Her work from a screen point of view hits a very low average with the producing company to a large degree responsible.

The story is one of regeneration. Slippy McGee is a cracksman of the first order. He is thrown from a freight train and his leg badly injured. Befriended by a priest and taken to his home, wooden leg is secured and his mental condition improved. From cracking safes he goes to collecting butterflies. It is quite a contrast but it was necessary to stick to the story. Love springs into his heart upon meeting a young miss. Later when she is in trouble and her reputation is at stake he comes to her rescue by stealing some letters from the safe of a man who tries to degrade her sister. After establishing her character will remain unsoiled, Slippy, known as John Flint is his new environment, looks out into the beautiful horizon and the picture abruptly ends.

The continuity would suggest the work of an amateur. There is no smoothness to it. The story jumps from one angle to another with nothing between to harmonize. This is one of the causes for its lack of interest.

The short cast does comparatively well. Wheeler Oakmar as the regenerated Slippy is given the most opportunities meeting few obstacles although the production largely due to faults other than his own will never add much credit to his work. Colleen Moore fills the bill as the girl. Lloyd Whitlock has a role of importance which is in his line.

The production end is ordinary. It is a cheap picture and shows it.

Hart.

DESERT DRIVEN

P. A. Powers production, starring Harry Carey. Released through F. B. O. Directed by Val Paul. Shown at Loew's New York, N. Y., double-feature bill June 12, 1923. Time, 62 minutes.

Dr. Otis Graydon	R. Waggoner
Tim Leary	Chas. Le Moyne
Assistant Warden	Ashley Cooper
Bob Grant	Harry Carey
Sam Brown	Dan Crimmins
John York	Alfred Allen
Mary York	Marguerite Clayton
Gee Gee Graydon	Buddy Johnson

This is a rip-snorter of a western that keeps the interest at almost fever heat through the picture. Harry Carey is still a corking western star and this picture puts him a bit ahead of where he has been recently in his screen efforts. The picture, although shown on a double feature bill, is strong enough to stand by itself in the majority of daily change houses.

The story is a prison tale with Carey as the hero serving a life sentence for a crime he did not commit. He escapes and after a series of adventures in the desert is forced to seek assistance for a wound he received while making his getaway. The ranch he picks out is conducted by the Yorks, father and daughter, and the girl falls in love with him. In the neighboring ranch house lives a family whose son has been a prison physician, a man who trafficked in drugs among the prisoners. He is discovered in his criminal operations the same night the life prisoner escapes and is forced to resign.

Of course he appears on the ranch scene and falls in love with the girl. When she turns him down he discovers that his rival is the escaped prisoner and immediately starts things moving for a recapture. Although recaptured, Carey again makes his escape and is again in the desert with the man trailers after him when a former assistant warden who befriended him arrives in time to save him with a confession from the real murderer. He has been wounded and at the fade-out it is difficult to tell whether he dies or recovers from his wounds, although the inference is that the former was the case.

Charles LeMoyne is a corking heavy in the picture, playing a brutal deputy graphically, while Marguerite Clayton is a sweet ingenue type of leading woman.

It is a picture with some real thrills, the escape stuff early in the feature being very well handled.

Fred.

RAILROADED

A Universal, with Herbert Rawlinson starred. Story by Margaret Bryant, adapted by Charles Kenyon. Directed by Edmund Mortimer. Shown at Loew's New York, N. Y., June 12, on double-feature bill. Time, 67 minutes.

Richard Ragland	Herbert Rawlinson
Joan Dunster	Esther Ralston
Hugh Dunster	Alfred Fisher
Judge Garben	David Torrence
Foster	Lionel Belmore
Corton	Mike Donlin
Jessie Kent	Virginia Ainsworth

This is a somber prison story that holds considerable interest at first, but soon develops into just a program picture of the Universal type. For the regular run of daily-change houses it will do well enough, especially in those where they play a double-feature bill. Herbert Rawlinson is the star and his usual screen self in this picture. Rawlinson must wear dress clothes at some point in every picture he does.

Seemingly there was an attempt to place the locale of this story in England, but there certainly was a lack of English atmosphere in the picture as it appeared on the screen. It was more like small-town midwest than London. That was due most likely to a desire to keep the figures down. The picture showed it.

The story is by Margaret Bryant, and Charles Kenyon is credited with the adaptation. Rawlinson is the son of an English judge who breaks from his father's restraint and becomes a society outlaw in rebellion. He is first shown in jail, where he and a partner were sent after one of the gang squealed. The partner has just died, and Rawlinson takes an oath to the widow that he will square accounts with the betrayer when he gets out. He makes his escape and is tracking his man, going so far as to attend a dinner at the home of a bishop. Here his father is also a guest, and he insists that the boy accompany him home. Once there, the father proposes that the boy undergo a period of punishment by being confined to a country home for the period of his sentence. The boy agrees, and his father places him at the home of a friend. The latter's daughter returns unexpectedly from college, falls in love with the young prisoner and he with her. And there you have the story. Of course, the crook companions insist on his keeping his oath to avenge the death of his companion in crime, but at the last minute it's a question of love or oath, and love wins out.

Esther Ralston makes a very fair leading woman for the dress-suit star, but the balance of the cast doesn't figure very strong. Mike Donlin, the "Babe Ruth" of almost a score of years ago, makes good in a character role.

Fred.

THE SNOW BRIDE

Adolph Zukor presents Alice Brady in "The Snow Bride" (Paramount), by Sonya Levien, from story by Miss Levien and Julie Herne. Henry Kolker directed. Current at the Rialto, New York. Runs a little over an hour.

Annette Leroux	Alice Brady
Andre Porel	Maurice B. Flynn
Gaston Leroux	Mario Majeroni
Indian Charlie	Nick Thompson
Paul Gerard	Jack Baston
Padre	Stephen Gratton
Pierre	W. M. Cavanaugh
Leonia	Margaret Morgan

Outfitted with but an average story, a frigid locale and passable support and production, the final judgment of this Alice Brady release is summed up in the adjective "mild." The continuity flickers through its allotted sixty-odd minutes in transitory interesting fashion, but makes no lasting impression in the course of the screening, which diminishes immediately on departure from the theatre.

The story has been endowed with a romantic title to link it with the Arctic setting, and should have a cooling reaction on ardent picture fans in the torrid days to come. They will see unfolded a story centred in the fur trading post of La Croix with Miss Brady as Annette, the daughter of Gaston Leroux, keeper of the local inn and a fur trader given to shady receipt of questionably obtained skins. Indian Charlie, who is shown filching from others' traps, disposes of his loot to Leroux. A physical encounter over the division of spoils between Leroux and the renegade Indian chief of the adjacent tribe results in the latter's death, with Paul Gerard, the heavy, stumbling into the scene and deciding to keep the murder a "family secret" with Annette as the means to make t possible.

Andre Perol, the sheriff ("Lefty" Flynn) is the sympathetic male lead, and the obvious choice of Annette. The girl acquiesces to marriage when apprised of the situation, but immediately following the ceremony decides to take the poison route out of a loathsome union. She mixes the deadly liquid with wine and writes a note pledging her love to Andre. Gerard, in drunken festal stupor, invades Annette's room as the unwilling new bride is saying her final prayers and drains the poison wine.

Annette is accused of willful poisoning, the alibi of the farewell letter being nullified through its loss by the hand of a jealous claimant for Andre's smiles. Conviction of murder and sentence to the gallows follows with the sheriff placed in the peculiar situation of guarding his amour and leading her to the hangman's noose. The intermittent stressing of the simple folks' primitive belief in the Supreme Deity is climaxed when the frantic father dramatically ascends the gallows, announces his guilt and pleads to the Heavens, "Take me! Take me!" with the threatening snow-laden mount nearby becoming agitated and avalanching Gaston Leroux in its thunderous path. The simple folk and their religious leader see in this a manifestation of the Lord's will and purge Annette of any further suspicion of guilt with the scheming Leonia announcing her destruction of the suicide note to further clinch the alibi.

A blatant discrepancy is apparent in the direction. Annette is shown filling the poison glass to the brim with wine. She has it lifted to her mouth (close-up), which makes the detail the more apparent. She halts to write the note and say her final vespers. When Gerard interrupts and lifts the wine glass, hesitating a moment before he drains it, the tumbler is only half full. A bit of grim humor is injected with the gallows bearing the inscription, "God's Gate," thereon. To commend the direction is the complete elision of any flashes of a court room scene or the local jurymen, the trial and conviction being denoted by three iris-in titles in immediate succession.

The production represents a minimum investment as compared to other Paramount releases. With most of it snow country, the interiors are few and crude, sufficient for the purpose thereof, but economical to a degree. The story, because of its many shiftings of interest from one situation to another, sustains the interest which the average balanced cast handles well, but, as previously noticed, the final summing up is only mild. For the hot spells, this will hold up on the daily change bills with any of the other frigid-setting releases.

Abel.

SHRIEK OF ARABY

Mack Sennett comedy starring Ben Turpin. Directed by F. Richard Jones. Released by the Allied Producers and Distributors Corp. Shown at the Capitol, New York, week June 10. Time, 46 minutes.

The Shriek	Ben Turpin
The Girl	Kathryn McGuire
The Magician	George Cooper
The Arab Prince	Ray Grey
The Chief of Police	Louis Fronde
The Bandit	Dick Sutherland

Five reels of Ben Turpin looking two ways at one time proves tiresome. What this picture is doing at the Capitol is another one of those things that are going to go down among the great unsolved mysteries of the film industry. In the little hoak houses the picture will undoubtedly be a "wow," but for the bigger pre-release theatres it is hardly the type that will get anything either at the gate or from the audiences in the way of appreciation.

To the "insiders" in the business the fact that the picture was made more than a year ago immediately on the heels of the tremendous hit Valentino achieved in "The Sheik," and is only being released at this time will speak volumes. The reason is just about what they will figure it. It is one of those comedies that because of an attempt to stretch it into feature length fails to hit. As a two-reeler it would have been good enough but as a five reel feature it's a flop. There are laughs in spots, but the spots do not arrive often enough for five reels.

As to story, that is simple enough. Turpin is the bill-poster at a little picture house where "The Sheik' is playing. The ballyhoo is a good looking fellow riding about the town made up as "The Sheik" but the impression he creates on the minds of those who should be flocking to the theatre is that they would rather follow him about the town. All the flappers fall for him, seeing in him the real hero of the story. The house manager perceiving the situation fires the "Sheik" and puts his bill-poster a-horseback with the balance of the picture working out as a dream that the paste bucket guardian has while riding around the town asleep.

During the dream he is transported to the sands of Sahara, where the manager is the villain, and the real Sheik is the ballyhoo man, who permits the bill-poster to replace him for a time. The adventures in the desert make up the balance of the footage until the bill-poster is finally awakened by mounted cop.

Kathryn McGuire is the heroine who finally falls for Turpin in his dreams but hands him the laugh in real life. Turpin does everything that he ever did and does it time after time during this picture until one actually tires of him. *Fred.*

ONLY 38

William De Mille production, presented as a Paramount picture by Adolph Zukor. From the play by A. E. Thomas, adapted by Clara Beranger and directed by William De Mille. The Rivoli, New York, week of June 10. Time, 63 minutes.

Lucy Stanley, a college girl	May McAvoy
Mrs. Stanley, her mother	Lois Wilson
Professor Charles Giddings	Elliott Dexter
Hiram Sanborn	George Fawcett
Bob Stanley	Robert Agnew
Mrs. Newcomb	Jane Keckley
Mrs. Peters	Lillain Leighton
Sydney Johnson	Taylor Graves
Mary Hedley	Ann Cornwall

Just every so often a real picture comes along. This is one of the occasions where there is a real story that has passed in successive stages from a short story by Walter Prichard Eaton to a play by A. E. Thomas, and in turn to the screen through the combined work of Clara Beranger and William De Mille, the former as adapter and the latter as director.

Yet from a picture standpoint there is a fault. It is a fault exhibitors will most generally find, and that is the title of the feature. "Only 38"? What does it mean? Exhibitors as a whole may guess it is a "perfect 36" gone wrong. But no matter what they think, it is a corking picture, one that is going to interest the snappy young high school flapper and cake-eating set as well as the middle-aged and older folk, especially the latter.

In its appeal it is going to hit hard with all sorts of picture fans who see it. The theme is such that they cannot escape its appeal, which is the love story of a young widow of "only 38," who has two children of 20. The latter feel that a mother must be kept in her place as a mother and not permitted to become frivolous, even though she was originally married to man much older and of stern principles regarding life. Thus, when romance finally comes to the mother in the form of a genuine love on the part of a professor of English in the school where her children are pupils the son and daughter are not only shocked and angered, but oppose the affair with every weapon at their command. This is especially true of the daughter, who at 20 has a sincere admiration for the professor herself. The final outcome is a victory for the mother through the children being won over by the professor.

The manner in which the screen continuity has been worked out for the story makes it a real interesting and sustained tale. In its enactment the four featured players stand out. May McAvoy as the daughter, Lois Wilson as the mother, Elliott Dexter as the professor and George Fawcett, who appears only in a few scenes in the early part of the story, as the father of the mother of the story, are the quartet. Robert Agnew and Taylor Graves, the former as the son and the latter as the school admirer of the daughter, lend true value to their characterizations of the typical young college boys.

In production the picture has everything that will lend atmosphere, and William De Mille's handling of the story is deft and clever.

The matter of title, however, is one that it is going to be up to the exhibitor and his exploitation staff to overcome. It is, however, a picture that is going to be well worth while for the summer programs, especially in vacation centres. *Fred.*

BUCKING THE BARRIER

William Fox feature featuring Dustin Farnum. Story by George Goodchild; scenario by Jack Strumwasser. Colin Campbell, director. Projection time 52 minutes. At Loew's Circle, June 4

"Bucking the Barrier" is a promising runner up in the competition for the year's trashiest picture trophy. It's a combination of Bertha M. Clay and a dime novel and for crude and amateurish fiction it is unique. Things happen at the unbridled whim of the author and mere plausibility is cheerfully ignored. The acting is governed by the standards of 10 years ago and even the photography is inferior.

Any director is liable to the tough break of having a sloppy scenario wished on him, but in these times of mechanical progress there is no excuse for bad photography. These views have that blurred yellow tinge and that flatness that characterized the work of a decade ago.

It's a story of the Yukon and England and the action hinges on a will in the favorite manner of the old ten-twent-thirt school. Kit Carewe (Farnum) and his partner are prospecting in Alaska when the partner, one Cavendish dies, leaving a will by which Kit is his sole heir, presumably of a small property in England.

Kit goes to England to claim his bequest. There are three Cavendishes, Luke, Cyril and Claudia. Luke hires thugs to meet Kit at the steamer and do away with him. They lure him to a deserted waterfront place and blackjack him, but Kit comes back and single handed knocks out all four husky desperadoes and tumbles them into the Thames. Then he hires them to plot against the Cavendishes, against whom he plans revenge. The younger Cavendish wins 24 pounds from Kit at cards and raises the check to 2,400. Kit is about to expose the brothers, when he is suddenly introduced to Claudia (Arline Pretty). He falls in love with her and all idea of reprisal is off. The story is now set for wedding bells and a happy ending, but it begins all over again in a series of misunderstandings. Claudia is waiting at the church while Kit is at the lawyer's office learning that the Cavendish estate is worth "a million pounds."

What he's doing at the lawyer's is left unexplained, but he stays there so long that Claudia becomes indignant. When she finds him, logically enough she shoots him, just like that. But Kit is a patient soul. With the blood dripping from his brow, he smiles wanly and signs documents giving Claudia all the million pounds.

A year passes in one brief title and without warning we are in Alaska again. Kit is lost in the blizzard and stumbles upon an unknown cabin. Who should be dwelling there but Luke, Cyril and Claudia. What more logical? Luke comes home in a dog sled in a state of high intoxication as the two lovers meet. Of course he tries to shoot Kit, but is prevented. The two lovers talk it over and become involved in deeper misunderstandings. Claudia has hidden from her brothers that the fortune is hers.

Kit departs sadly while Luke goes to the neighboring barroom to get drunker. Kit finds him there among the merry natives and lugs him away determined to abduct him up into the Yukon country where he will have to work for a living. They are caught in their dog sled in another blizzard. There is a clash of wills and Kit is victor until he suddenly goes blind (Claudia's bullet has made him subject to such fits) and Luke steals the dogs and deserts him.

When he reaches home Claudia learns what has occurred and promptly goes into the blizzard to find Kit. This turns out to be an astonishingly simple matter, so the happy ending is accomplished with cheerful dispatch, making welcome way for the one-reel comedy.

Rush.

DAUGHTERS OF RICH

Preferred picture presented by B. F. Schulberg; distributed by Al. Lichtman Corp. From the Edgar Saltus novel of the same title; directed by Louis Gasnier. At the Capitol, New York, week of June 17. Time, 63 minutes.

Maud Barhyte..............Miriam Cooper
Gerard Welden..............Gaston Glass
Mlle. Giselle..............Ethel Shannon
Sally Malakoff..............Ruth Clifford
Count Malakoff..............Stuart Holmes
Barhyte, Maud's father.....Josef Swickard
Mrs. Kandy, Sally's mother..........
..........................Truly Shattuck

Missing one big punch, this latest Schulberg feature just misses being a big picture. But it holds several kicks, without a direct one, in the story There are twists, the tale suddenly doubling around a couple of times after an interesting start. This holds the strict attention, and Louis Gasnier, its director, employed no unnecessary footage for useless detail.

The story takes a peculiar angle when an American heiress of mild temperament is forced into a marriage by her mother with a Duke, abroad, and a marriage she never consummated, becomes a knave herself to obtain the young American she loved.

To accomplish that end her beloved countryman and his betrothed, another American heiress, had their future nearly wrecked. The former Duchess, after her deceitful marriage, was uncovered and she conveniently committed suicide. The suicide resulted in her husband being suspected of her murder and imprisoned. The first betrothed in her American home revealed the actual facts in a letter received from the wife just before destroying herself.

"Daughters of the Rich,' as a title, is made to fit, but it doesn't mean much else otherwise. The play is a straightforward narrative with holding complications. That is what it may be depended upon to do, hold and it will hold the younger element more easily than the skeptical, who never can be convinced any Amrican girl would have married the caricature Stuart Holmes made of the Duke character.

Ruth Clifford ran away with the picture for what running there was. Miriam Cooper had a "sweet" role without the part permitting much. Miss Clifford was the Countess. Truly Shattuck played Sally's mother, a small bit for which Miss Shattuck suited. Gaston Glass made the heroic role upstanding.

In production Mr. Gasnier hit it off rather well. There are several well-displayed sets with two or three lively scenes, particularly his bachelor dinner bit, where 12 girls did a high school dance around the horseshoe table in the stable, where the Duke held his farewell single blow-off. A bathtub bit with Ethel Shannon in the tub looked quite good from the front and several interiors were sumptuous. A duel scene was given as a scanty long shot. One of the scenes in which an East Side family is getting its red-hot scandal from a Sunday newspaper magazine was used in somewhat similar manner in another picture such a short time ago the two must be a coincidence.

A picture that plays as well as this does for an hour should have a punch. That it hasn't is the fault of the story; there didn't appear to be any opening to insert the punch the picture lacked. But it will do as a feature; it's interesting and well made, while those twists keep the action at a swift tempo.

Sime.

WOMAN WITH FOUR FACES

A Herbert Brenon production presented by Jesse L. Lasky (Paramount), featuring Betty Compson and Richard Dix. Screen adaptation by George Hopkins from Bayard Veiller's story. Running time, 60 minutes. At the Rialto, New York, week of June 17.

Elizabeth West, a crook....Betty Compson
Richard Templer, district attorney,
Richard Dix
Judge Westcott................George Fawcett
Jim Hartin, a conviot...Theodore von Eltz
Judson Osgood, a narcotic peddler,
Joseph Kilgour
Morton ....James Farley
Warden Cassidy..................Guy Oliver
Ralph Dobson........Charles A. Stevenson
The Boy......................Gladden James
The Mother....................Eulalie Jensen

This picture should make money for every program from all angles. It has a good box office title, two good featured players and is a gripping screen meller that includes all the old tricks of hectic dramatic writing without becoming cheap and tawdry. It is ten-twent-thirty stuff in dress clothes and mighty interesting screen fare for the warm days or any other time.

Besides, it has the "dope" element to make it timely. Betty Compson as Elizabeth West, a crook and reformed burglar, is in the title role. The "four faces" seemingly refers to her introduction in burglar's mask, herself, as a pseudo-old woman and in her reformation period. The story starts with a whizz with Elizabeth West shown on the outer ledge of an apartment hotel several stories in the air, making her entrance through the window and stealing a prima donna's jewels. Elizabeth has the room adjoining, and after changing to pajamas, first disposing of her loot and the burglar's outfit by dropping it through the window to an accomplice in the street, she raises a hue-and-cry that she, too, has been burgled. A veteran detective recognizes the young adventuress, but she is acquitted at trial for lack of evidence. Here Richard Templer, the district attorney, is introduced as after a narcotic dope ring, the "Big Five." A signed paper of mutual protection in the matter of smuggling drugs into this country is the object of the D. A.'s particular quest. The judge refuses to issue a search warrant without further proof of the existence of such paper, disregarding a dope fiend's statement of having seen it.

Templer decides to resign and run down the ring himself. He recognizes the brains of the clever girl crook and calls on her as a possible ally. He takes her to a hospital, and the adventuress decides to turn against her clan and run the drug runners down—just like that. The cleverest safe-cracker in the country is at present a guest of the state in a penitentiary, so the first plan is to secure his escape. Elizabeth makes up as the young cracksman's mother, and quoting a Bible Psalm tells him to "look up to the west, my son," or something on that order.

The day of a prison baseball match, an aeroplane, guided by Templer and borrowed from an army buddy, descends low over the prison grounds, Jim Hartigan making his escape by the swinging rope ladder. However, later he fears a "frame" and refuses assistance.

Elizabeth and Templer decide to burgle Osgood's safe on their own, this being successfully accomplished after a couple of twists. The document in their possession, the dope ring evidently is put out of business. Templer confesses his love for the erstwhile adventuress and a zippy hour of screen entertainment closes.

Brenon has wielded his puppets wisely and well. Miss Compson is the centre of the story and very capably deports herself as required. Richard Dix was his usual reserved self, carrying the male lead with dignity and not overacting, even where there might have been some excuse for it. The support is top-notch.

In the hot first Sunday matinee the audience roundly applauded the picture.

Abel.

THE LAW OF THE LAWLESS

Paramount picture presented by Jesse Lasky with Dorothy Dalton starred. Adapted from the story of Konrad Bercovici by Lloyd Sheldon and Edfrid Bingham. Directed by Victor Fleming. Shown at the Rivoli, New York, week of June 17. Time, 67 minutes.

Sahande, a spirited Tartar maid......
........................Dorothy Dalton
Sender, a faint-hearted musician.....
........................Theodore Kosloff
Costa, a gypsy chief......Charles de Roche
Ali Mechmet, a money lender.........
........................Tully Marshall
Osman father of Sahande....Fred Huntley
Fanutza, a gypsy.........Margaret Loomis

Although Dorothy Dalton is the star, there are a trio of feature players in Theodore Kosloff, Tully Marshall and last, but far from least, Charles De Roche, the imported player whom the Lasky organization believed would succeed to the honors left vacant by the desertion of Valentino. That latter might have been a fond dream, for from this picture it appears far from ever becoming a fact.

But "The Law of the Lawless" is a fairly interesting love and adventure story of the type that the earlier film fans were in the habit of liking. There are a few real thrills, and from an all around standpoint it will do in the general run of houses, although it does not seem a strong pre-release feature. The exhibitor can make it look like a lot for the money in playing up the names of the four leaders of the cast and go after Roche as the new Valentino.

The scene is in the eastern part of Europe with the two opposing factions, the Russian Tartars and the Gypsies. The former have a daughter coveted by the Gypsy King who purchases her for his wife. She is in love with a song-maker After the wedding ceremony she demands ten days' grace from her husband before becoming his wife in fact, hoping that her lover will come and rescue her through a hand-to-hand battle with the man who purchased her. The husband agrees. On the tenth day the lover does appear, but not to do personal battle. He has taken advantage of the fact that all men, except the King, are absent at a fair, and with 30 of his friends attacks the camp that has but one man to defend it. The Gypsy King is taken captive, the camp looted and in the midst the girl rides off to summon the Gypsy tribesmen. They come to the rescue of the chief, and with naught but their whips beat the Tartars into submission, with husband and wife finally reunited in loving embrace.

In direction the picture is well handled, with the detail in production likewise well looked after. There is atmosphere throughout that interests, but the hero does not seemingly lend himself to the character with sufficient strength to make him outstanding. Miss Dalton as the heroine is far and away the best. Kosloff does the song-maker lover weak, and Tully Marshall's role is hardly noticed.

Fred.

MARY OF THE MOVIES

Film Booking Office of America release, produced by Columbia Productions, subcaptioned "Gems of the Screen." Directed by John McDermott. Idea conceived by Louis Lewyn and Jack Cohn. Joseph W. Farnham did the titling. In addition to following principal players, flashes of a number of screen notables are incorporated. Shown in conjunction with vaudeville bill at Proctor's 125th Street Theatre June 18-20. Runs 70 minutes.

Creighton Hale.........................Himself
Mary of the Movies............Marion Mack
Oswald Tate...............Raymond Cannon
Joseph Seiler............Francis McDermott
Jane.......................Rosemary Cooper

This is probably the cheapest production made in view of the auspicious cast of screen players included in brief scenes and whose names on the F. B. O.'s press sheets are probably boldly featured. The picture is on the order of Rupert Hughes' "Souls for Sale," and because of the Goldwyn's prior release this production must necessarily suffer odious comparison.

It is a tale of Hollywood, naturally, with Mary, hailing from Barston, Ariz., a jerkwater town, trekking westward as a last resort to raise funds necessary for a brother's operation, which would save him from life-long incapacitation. This decision follows the local money man's refusal for a loan despite old man Tate's son, Oswald, having called regularly on Mary. Ozzie seemingly is not made for enduring love, for he readily acquiesces to his father's proposal to give up Mary and acquire a Ford he has been yearning for.

Several titles about "movie madness" sets the atmosphere, all of this preceding the actual sojourn in Hollywood, where Mary, as a screen novice, is initiated into studio mysteries. This, of course, is interesting audience stuff. Her arrival in Hollywood finds her mistaking Bryant Washburn's car for a Hollywood jitney. She remarks he looks like Washburn, and the latter admits knowing the celebrity, alighting Mary at the Hollywood Hotel, where Washburn introduces Mary to Louise Fazenda, Alec Francis, David Butler, Anita Stewart, et al. The hotel says its rate is $12. Mary, learning it means a day, not per week, immediately deserts the hostelry.

Jane, a screen extra, befriends Mary and introduces her to Creighton Hale, the latter acting as leading man thereafter. Mary naively congratulates Hale that he was "wonderful" in "Way Down East." The story continues with Mary sending money home periodically, lending the impression she is a celebrity when in reality she must recourse to a waitress' job after the movie bubble bursts. However, her resemblance to Norma Winters, a star who is taken ill in the midst of a production (with the boss of the outfit complaining the picture has cost him $200,000 to date and will set him back $5,000 a day during his star's illness), gives Mary her chance. Mary makes good, of course. In a desert sandstorm on location, during the filming of a "sheik" sort of play, she is rescued by Hale. They arrive in Mary's home town while the old farm is in the process of being auctioned off, with the usual happy ending closing.

Messrs. Lewyn and Cohn, who "conceived" the production, have been identified with a "Screen Snapshots" release showing intimate closeups of the screen folks' daily life. Some of the scenes of the celebrities and their homes may be cut-outs from the "Snapshots" and others are not. Flashes of J. Warren Kerrigan, Rex Ingram and Maurice Tourneur directing; Edward J. Le Saint, Rosemary Theby, Johnny Walker, Barbara LaMarr, Gaston Glass, Herbert Rawlinson, Stuart Holmes, Elliott Dexter, et al., are included, some as being introduced to the heroine and others as obliging by signing Mary's autograph book. In a casting office scene a flash of Craig Biddle, Jr., the scion of the prominent Philadelphia family, is shown encouraging Mary, stating, "I've been thrown out of every studio in Hollywood," which may or may not be so. Flashes of the Pickford-Fairbanks "home," Chaplin's, Hayakawa's and a shot of the scene where the motion picture exposition will be held are also included.

The production is an ingenious routine of travelog, "behind scenes" stuff and fiction to make it appeal to film fans generally. To resort to the "Souls for Sale" comparison, "Mary of the Movies" might be said to have the general mob appeal and the Hughes' production a class appeal.

Abel.

BLACK SHADOWS

Travel picture presented by the World's Tours, Inc., and released by Pathe. At the Broadway, New York, week of June 18. Time, 38 minutes.

Although the title rather suggests one of the usual society mellers, the picture in reality is a travel subject that has considerable interest. It is a pictorial record in motion of the scenes visited by the Edward G.

Salisbury expedition into the South Sea Islands.

It is a record by slow stages from the world civilized into the spaces where savagery and cannibalism still reign and the use of the title undoubtedly comes from the map that is utilized in marking the course that the expedition took. On this map the civilized islands are indicated by all white circles, while those where the natives are still in an uncivilized state, and possibly cannibals, are indicated by circles that are half black.

The expedition starts from Los Angeles, and its first stop is Marquesas Islands, and thence to the Samoan, Fiji, New Hebrides and Solomon islands. In the various islands the natives and their customs are shown. In the last set of islands the thrills occur. These islands are inhabited by head hunters. For the benefit of the camera they make an attack on a neighboring island and stage a battle. This was done in a rather realistic manner, and it wouldn't be at all surprising if some of the stuff that was shown was rather real, for it is quite possible that one of these half-wild natives might have lost track of the fact that a camera was grinding and that he was acting and "accidentally" slashed off the head of one of those that were opposing his forces. At least it appeared as though some of the warrior men on their return were carrying heads with them.

In some of the scenes there were shots of dancing girls that would put Gilda Gray at her wildest to shame for the girls wore less than Ziegfeld undresses his "Follies" beauties in, and these girls were in their own way just as much beauties as those that are on the Broadway stages.

It looks like a good enough picture for summer, especially if there is a long vaudeville show, or another feature shown with it. There is a lot of interesting data of the South Sea Islands for any audience, and as the Los Angeles producing group grinds out any number of South Sea Island stories, it might be a good idea to let the audience see how the things really are.

Fred.

THE WANDERING JEW

London, June 4.
With this last Stoll picture Matheson Lang has established a right to be regarded as a screen star instead of just a legitimate player who has been persuaded to join the studio ranks purely on account of the value of his name from a publicity angle. His performance is one of the best we have seen on the screen, and throughout his screen impersonation of the Jew, condemned to wander through the ages, arrogant, proud, though broken-hearted, ever within reach of happiness, but always overtaken by disaster just as he was about to grasp his heart's desire, is as masterly as his stage performance in Temple Thurston's play.

The story follows the play fairly close. In the opening scenes we see the Jew, Mathias, and his lover, Judith, his reviling of the Saviour on His way to Calvary and the dreadful outlawry which sent him into the world a wanderer. Thirteen hundred years pass and he is among the Crusaders; again a lovely woman loves him, but again fate stands between him and happiness, and so the story goes down the years until at last the Inquisition gives him the peace and eternal rest which before have always been denied him.

Spectacularly, the production is very fine and the subject has been treated with great reverence by Maurice Elvey, who in this picture does some of the finest work he has yet done. The figure of Christ in the opening scene is never seen, but the whole of the walk to Calvary is

wonderfully suggested by the shadow of the cross. Equally well done are other Biblical scenes.

The cast is a big one, the leading people supporting Lang, who only appear in one episode each, being Hutin Britton (Mrs. Matheson Lang), Winifred O. Izard, Florence Saunders, Malvina Longfellow, Isobel Elsom, Hubert Carter, Lionel D'Aragon, Shayle Gardner, Lewis Gilbert, Gordon Hopkirk and Jerrold Robertshaw. Many smaller parts **are well played and the crowd work** gives proof of clever and patient stage management.

"The Wandering Jew" is a picture which the producing firm and everybody concerned can be sincerely congratulated on. *Gore.*

PETER THE GREAT

Hamilton Theatrical Corp. presents this foreign subject featuring Emil Jannings whose "Othello" was shown some time ago under the same auspices. A German product acquired under Famous Players' blanket purchase. Directed by Dimitri Buchowetzki. Story and scenario by Sada Cowan. Production editor Julian Johnson. Projection time 75 minutes. At the Rivoli New York, June 24.
Catherine ....Dagny Servaes
Menchikov ....Bernhard Goetzke
Alexis ....Walter Janssen
Czarina Eudoxia..........Cordy Milovitch
Aphrosina ....Alexandra Sorina
Peter the Great............Emil Jannings

With the revival of "Passion" at the Capitol and this foreign subject at the Rivoli it looks as though the big Broadway houses are seeking to fill in the dull warm weather period with low cost foreign features in order to save more valuable material for better times.

There is much to be said for this Jannings picture in spite of its mechanical crudities. It sticks to the German formula of spectacular crowds and heavy mass effects and it has long and discursive passages that make the action drag but in the main it furnishes a document of historical romance with a good deal of human appeal.

There are cumbersome passages of labored and stagy drama, the thread of narrative staggers and wanders, but in the summing up the producers (presumably it is Ufa, although the main title does not specify the source) have made a living portrait of the great Russian Czar, and have drawn a convincing picture of rude times of empire building.

The acting method of Jannings is not subtle, but his style serves admirably for the portray of the epic figure of Peter, the bull dog monarch, man of a thousand contradictions, passions and cruelties, but of one consuming patriotic purpose—to build a great nation. It's not an especially admirable portrait, but it does strike one as an authentic record, insofar as the principal character is concerned. Nobody else in the cast is more than a theatrical puppet. The German style of makeup robs the women of any semblance to reality and the bizarre costuming of the period heightens the effect of artificiality.

The Ufa system has always put the emphasis on feverish theatrical effect and goes a little further here. Emotion is expressed in facial contortion and huge crowds seem a necessary background to the dramatic high spots. These crowds are well managed and the massive backgrounds have a certain effectiveness, but indifferent photograhy lessens and weakens the punch. For example there is a tremendous bit of mob manipulation in the scene showing the return of Peter from the Swedish wars. Viewed all together it was impressive, but the detail is blurred and the toning is crude.

In the same way the scenes of royal ceremonies in the palace overreached themselves. They never are content to suggest masses of people as Rex Ingram did in "Zenda," clearly and adequately, but must jumble the whole picture by trying too much. There is a banquet scene that is spoiled by attempting too much. They have crowded so many people into the picture that the tiny figures look only jammed and petty and the regal effect is lost. In like manner, where they try for an effect of a battle, they try to take in the whole countryside and one gets an impression of sham spectacle instead of the real conflict. The failure of Ufa's mob effects is that they depend upon raw realism and neglect the art of suggesting the whole by the adequate presentation of a significant and typical detail. A literal crowd is strictly limited while a suggested mob is bounded only by the capacity of the spectator to vision infinity.

The defects of the picture are on the technical side. The story and

the conception are fine. There is high romance in the love of Peter for Catherine, refugee, waif and camp follower. There is the strongest kind of drama in the rugged determination of the Emperor to rule with a rough hand, defying the patriarchs of the church, the plotters in his household and the superstition of an ignorant people and there is compelling sentiment in his struggles to make his unworthy son Alexis fitting successor to the throne. The picture is an irritating combination of good and bad, judged by American production standards.

One would guess it was a fine literary effort gone wrong in the studio execution. *Rush.*

DIVORCE

F. B. O. release, presented by Chester Bennett at the Rialto, New York, week June 24. Story by Andrew Bannison; directed by Chester Bennett. Jane Novak star. Running time 63 minutes.
Jane Parker.....................Jane Novak
Jim Parker....................John Bowers
George Reed................James Corrigan
Mrs. George Reed........Edythe Chapman
Gloria Gayne..........Margaret Livingston
Townsend Perry.............Freeman Wood
Withrop Avery..............George Fisher
"Dicky" Parker............Philippe DeLacy

Despite this picture was given a pre-release run at one of the Paramount's Broadway houses, it proves to be but a program picture of ordinary quality. In direction and lighting the picture is excellent, the fault lying mainly with the story, which is a repeat of a tale that has been told on the screen hundreds times.

The title is going to be counted on as the big box-office punch to the production. Perhaps it will serve to draw at the box office, but those that see the production, if they are regular film fans, will recall having seen the same tale with the same situations time and time again.

I brief, the story is that of a young husband who achieves success in business too rapidly and falls for a vamp. They part, but as soon as he loses his influential job all of the fair weather friends give him the go-by and then there is nothing left for him except to return to the wife and child, and she forgivingly takes him into her arms and all is well with the world again. He even gets his job back, for the president of the big iron works was the wife's father. Same old stuff, with the same old moral, told in the same old way.

There are some redeeming features in the cast of the production and not the least of these is Jane Novak, the star of the picture, who, with a role that so many other stars have played, must be forced to stand for comparison. Miss Novak fortunately is no worse than any of the others that have played the same type of role. If anything, she is a little better. John Bowers, playing opposite her as the husband, also scores. But the vamp of Margaret Livingston was just about as overdone a piece of screen portrayal as has been seen in some time. Freeman Wood, as one of the first assistants to the vamp, and Tom McGuire, working with him, both put over several clever minor pieces of business. James Corrigan and Edythe Chapman in character roles proved likable, although when George Fisher was paraded as Miss Chapman's No. 2 in the matrimonial stakes he was a laugh.

In "kiddie" actors the picture carries a corking youngster in Philippe DeLacy, who just about walked away with one-half of the picture, he being in all of the principal scenes and getting the eye of the camera like an old trouper. This youngster will bear watching in this day of kid stars. *Fred.*

PENROD AND SAM

J. K. McDonald presents Booth Tarkington's sequel to "Penrod" via First National.

Scenario by Hope Loring and Lewis Leighton. Direction by William Beaudine. Projection time, 62 minutes. At the New York Strand, June 24.

Penrod Schofield..............Ben Alexander
Sam Williams.............Joe Butterworth
Rodney Bitts............Ruddy Messinger
Georgie Bassett..............Newton Hall
Marjorie Jones..........Gertrude Messinger
Herman......................Joe McCray
Verman......................Gene Jackson
Father Schofield..........Rockliffe Fellowes
Mother Schofield..........Gladys Brockwell
Margaret Schofield..........Mary Philbin
Robert Williams............Gareth Hughes
Deacon Bitts................Wm. V. Mong
Maurice Levy.............Bobbie Gordon
Duke (Penrod's dog)................Cameo

Another chapter in the adventures, both jolly and sentimental, of a real American kid, done in Tarkington's happiest vein and transcribed to the screen with a wealth of unassuming charm and in a spirit of refreshing simplicity. Perhaps the note of childish griefs is a thought too insistent, but the thing is done with an appealing tenderness that disarms and wins one's sympathetic response.

The picture is rich in chuckling comedy. Nothing could be funnier than the inquisition conducted by Father Schofield and Father Williams over the hazing of the unpopular fat boy by Penrod and Sam or the solemn ceremonies of the whole gang of kids, including the ebony Vermaan, named to his own disadvantage.

Here are mere commonplaces of everyday life touched with color and illuminated with sympathetic understanding to make a thoroughly enjoyable hour of artless amusement. The story has a master's touch. It has diverting comedy guiltless of vulgar buffoonery; a deft sort of drama in the relations of people in a small-town community, and it has sympathy and tenderness that isn't built on sex triangles, neglected wives or the rest of the studio hokum. Nothing could be finer in delicate handling than the episode of the return to Penrod of his lost playground in the vacant lot as dad escapes from a scene that is getting rather too sentimental for him, and turns it into the hands of the mother, who had unobtrusively brought the happy occasion about.

This Tarkington household is the only happy and affectionate family the screen has had in many a long day, and it makes a jolly variation from the established scenario formula. A happy family that is also interesting is a substantial achievement in picture making. But it has a score of delightful attributes besides. Item one is the remarkably convincing acting of the whole group of youngsters, led by a handsome freckled kid named Ben Alexander and backed up with the astonishingly natural acting of his homely pal—Joe Butterworth in real life.

If anything could be more faithful to life than the kids themselves it is a cocky fox terrier, property of Penrod, called Duke, a pup that has attained the highest achievement of art—utter absence of self-consciousness. The elders of the cast are amazing in their simple naturalness, as though they caught the cue from the children. Nothing quite so naive has been done since the Sidney Drew comedies. The cast has been carefully assembled, a trifling part going to so well known a young juvenile as Gareth Hughes.

There isn't any plot that could be set down. Penrod and his lieutenant Sam organize a gang, leaving out the nasty fat boy and a mollycoddle brat. The parents of the excluded pair—people of importance—force Pen and Sam to admit them, and that starts trouble for all hands. The fat boy's father buys the playground lot from Penrod's father, and then Penrod's dog is killed by an auto and ceremoniously buried in these hallowed precincts. The boy's heart breaks when he is driven from his playground and alienated from his gang, until his mother makes the situation plain to uncomprehending dad, and all is set straight by the repurchase of the lot and its formal conveyance back to Penrod. It is astonishing that such simple things as these can be made so moving, but they held a summer audience spellbound Tuesday evening.

The picture is a better picture than "School Days," which was a cleanup on a similar theme. It probably didn't cost a tenth as much as an ordinary feature, and it ought to make a fortune on its merits.

Rush.

FACE ON THE BARROOM FLOOR

Fox production based on the story by C. Marion Benton and directed by Jack Ford. At Loew's Circle, New York, June 26, for one day as part of a double feature bill. Time, 63 minutes.

Robert Stevens........(.Henry B. Walthall
Marion Trevor................Ruth Clifford
Dick Von Vleck..........Walter Emerson
John Pussy..............Frederick Sullivan
Lottie......................Alma Bennett
Governor Rankin..........Novel McGregor

A fairly interesting picture has been made out of this melodrama of a decade ago. As a picture it holds the attention and presents a story well told. The producer has made no attempt to place the feature above the program class, with its possibilities in that division comparing favorably with pictures made by the same concern. Few of the old-time melodramas have proved as interesting on the screen as this version of "The Face on the Barroom Floor." The picture is credited with having been made from an original scenario by C. Marion Benton. He has unfolded his story neatly, without any hitches, with the dramatic element well sustained from start to finish.

From a direction standpoint it hits a fair average. Jack Ford at no time shows flashes of class but has worked out the story in a sufficiently convincing style to make it satisfactory for the medium class of picture patrons. The cast headed by Henry B. Walthall does all that is asked of them, with some of the tough barroom characters a little overdrawn, which possibly can be overlooked considering the type of story. Walthall makes his work stand out. In every reel he does hard work, with the real returns of the picture being credited to him. Ruth Clifford plays the feminine role of greatest importance, although much less important than Walthall's. She is given really no opportunities in the production. Walter Emerson plays a callow youth role with ordinary intelligence. The others hit a fair average. The production cost is of minor importance, nothing of an expensive nature being called for.

An artist is the central figure of the play. He is broke and an outcast on account of a woman. He appears in a barroom to spend his last dime and incidentally tells his life's story to the hangers-on. Through someone who had seen him enter the place the girl, who had accused him of infidelity years before, is told of his innocence and, rushing to the barroom, brings him to realize life and start anew.

The old title should draw a certain class, with the picture sufficiently interesting to hold its own in the pop price houses. *Hart.*

MAN AND WIFE

Arrow release in States' rights field. No producer or director credited. Shown at Fox's Academy, N. Y., double feature bill June 24-27, 1923. Running time, 51 minutes.

Caleb Perkins............Maurice Costello
His Wife....................Edna May Spooner
Dora........................Norma Shearer
Della..................Gladys Leslie
Dr. Howard Fleming.........Robert Elliott
Walter Powell..............Ernest Hilliard

No author, director or producer credited for this picture. It was produced principally outdoors, with a story unusual enough to have been taken from life. In the cast there is one old star favorite in Maurice Costello, a stock favorite in Edna May Spooner, and a screen possibility in Norma Shearer. From a State rights standpoint at a price the picture looks as though it will get some money, although it is rather crudely produced and directed and badly titled and edited.

The story starts with the old lure of the city for those in rural communities. Down on the farm live Caleb Perkins, his wife and two daughters. One of the girls runs away when the father wants her to marry the hired man. Several years pass and a noted brain specialist, broken in health, seeking a quiet spot to rest, applies for board, falls in love with the younger daughter and marries her. During the time he is at the farm there is disclosed by the vision route the fact he had married the older sister, who had run away, and that he believed she lost her life in a restaurant fire while he was absent from the city attending a patient. In reality a distant relative whom he commissioned to entertain the wife in his absence was in an automobile wreck with her, and several doctors informed him she was hopelessly insane because of injuries to her head. The relative, in fear, had her committed to an asylum, and there she remained until after the marriage of the doctor to her younger sister.

Then the relative comes forward with the real story and the doctor has two wives on his hands—sisters, and one insane. He has his first wife removed to his own sanitarium, where he performs an operation on her that restores her sanity, and wife number two returns home to her parents to have a child. The first wife, after a time, also returns home to suffer a nervous breakdown and die, which leaves the road clear for the doctor to return for the younger sister and his child.

It's a wild tale, wildly done on the screen, but it had a great element of melodramtic suspense.

The cast was a short one, and there was very little studio stuff, so that the production did not entail any great financial outlay.

Fred.

ALICE ADAMS

Presented by Associated Exhibitors. Story by Booth Tarkington, directed by Roland V. Lee; Florence Vidor, star. At Loew's New York, New York, June 23. Running time, 73 minutes.

Alice Adams................Florence Vidor
Virgil Adams..........Claude Gillingwater
John Russell..................Vernon Steele

This story looks as though Booth Tarkington in writing "Alice Adams" started out to slip over the inside stuff on how the girls set out to trap the unsuspecting male when they make up their minds that they want any particular one for a husband. Roland V. Lee, in directing the picture, started with an idea of getting the spirit of Booth Tarkington on the screen, and there were some instances during the picture where he did it, others where he relied on the sub-titling to do it for him. However, on the whole it is a very interesting program picture that will have a great deal bigger box office drag in the small towns than in the bigger cities.

Three outstanding members. First, Florence Vidor, starred in the titular role; Vernon Steele, opposite her, and Claude Gillingwater, seemingly great at times as the father, and at other points overacting.

It's a small town story. One of those small towns where everybody started even in the race after wealth and position in life. Some stood still and others made their pile. Of the former type was the father of Alice Adams, the heroine of the story. He was a drudge, a henpeck, and finally forced by his family, principally his wife, to do things that revolted his honest old soul. In the end matters straightened themselves out for the old man and for the daughter as well, for the girl manages to snare the "catch" of the town whom she had set her mind on as a husband.

One of the best scenes is the preparation for and the dinner at the Adams home on the night that the favored suitor is to call. The director got both comedy and pathos over in that scene to a surprising extent. One felt for the screen characters, especially the father and the daughter. The poor old dad in his dress suit and the girl trying to keep up appearances to make an impression were well handled in this portion of the story.

There are some real laughs and room for a good deal of thought in the picture. *Fred.*

MERRY-GO-ROUND

Universal Super-Jewel, directed by Rupert Julian, presented by Carl Laemmle, at the Rivoli, New York, week July 1. Authorship not credited. Running time, 91 minutes.

Count Franz Maximillian von Hohenegg,	Norman Kerry
Agnes Urban	Mary Philbin
Sylvester Urban	Cesare Gravina
Ursula Urban	Edith Yorke
Bartholomew Gruber	George Hackathorne
Shani Huber	George Seigmann
Mariana Huber	Dale Fuller
Mrs. Aurora Rossreiter	Lillian Sylvester
Minister of War (Gisella's father),	Spottiswoode Aitken
Komtesse Gisella von Steinbrueck,	Dorothy Wallace
Nepomuck Navrital	Al Edmundson
Rudi (Baron von Leightsinn),	Capt. Albert Conti
Nicki (Baron von Nubenmuth),	Charles L. King
Eitel (Prince Eitel Hogemut)	Fenwick Oliver
Gisella's groom	Sidney Bracey
Emperor Franz Joseph	Anton Vaverka
Madame Elvira	Maude George
Jane	Helen Broneau
Marie	Jane Sherman

Universal is releasing this Super-Jewel directly to the picture houses without giving it one of those forced prerelease runs in a legitimate theatre. It is wise showmanship by Universal in so far as this picture is concerned. It isn't a picture that could stand for the road showing in legitimate houses in these days, and the exhibiting world at large knows the forced runs in legitimate Broadway theatres are only for the purpose of tilting the rental price, and in increased rental the exhibitor has to stand for what the producers lose in one of those engagements.

But if "Merry-Go-Round" is not a road show picture, it certainly is a whale of a picture for the film theatres. That Universal got into the Rivoli with it speaks somewhat for the production. It is real screen entertainment.

Incidentally, it is more than that. It is a star maker, for in Mary Philbin Universal has uncovered a real camera find through her work in this production. It has added tremendously also to the histrionic laurels of George Seligman, George Hackathorne, Dorothy Wallace, Norman Kerry and Cesare Gravina. This quintet, together with Miss Philbin, dominate the story, and their performances are largely responsible for the gripping interest that the picture contains.

Although not credited with having anything to do with this picture, it is known the production was started for Universal by Erich von Stroheim. Recently a Universal executive stated that while it was true von Stroheim had started the picture so little remained of what he had done that it wasn't noticeable. In observing the picture as screened there are the unmistakable signs of the von Stroheim handiwork present in a host of scenes.

"Merry-Go-Round" is a simple story of a love affair between an aristocrat and a peasant girl, well told amid a setting of Vienna's Coney Island (the Prater), the palace of the Emperor Franz Joseph, the war, and finally back to the Prater again.

Symbolic in a measure is the title, for the "merry-go-round" of life proceeds no matter come what may. That is the story.

In Vienna, prior to the fateful days of 1914, lives Count Franz Maximillian von Hohenegg (Norman Kerry), a captain of the Royal Guards and attached to the emperor's suite. Like all of the young men of the court, he is a free and easy living chap, with an eye for a lass and a taste for a glass. His emperor has decreed the young count shall marry the Komtesse Gisella, daughter of the minister of war. She frankly tells her father she desires the young count as he appeals to her physically.

In planting the character of Gisella, the direction shows her in one of the earlier scenes returning from her morning ride, and on entering the stables draws a groom into a dark corner, letting her affections have full reign, but strikes him with her riding crop when he would likewise express his roused passion. Grisella was a great little girl at that, for immediately thereafter she returned to her own chambers and, lighting a big black cigar, threw herself on a couch and telephoned to her fiance.

At the same time on the Prater, there is the brutal Shani Huber, who owns the big merry-go-round and likewise the Punch and Judy show. The little organ grinder for the merry-go-round is Agnes Urban (Mary Philbin) whose father is the manipulator of the puppets in the little show for Huber. The next concession is owned by Mrs. Aurora Rossreiter (Lillian Sylvester) who has Bartholomew Gruber, a hunchback (George Hackathorne) on the front, spieling for her. Among her principal attractions of the ballyhoo is a huge monkey.

These characters enact a little tragedy all their own up to the time the Count enters the life of the little organ grinder. The brutal Shani has a lustful desire for the girl and the little hunchback loves her. Shani attacks the youngster at one time in front of the monkey's cage with the animal showing he resented the blows rained on his friend. But the count visits the playground with two women and a couple of male companions in civilian clothes, makes love to the little organ grinder and poses to her as a necktie salesman.

With him it is seemingly passing fancy; with the girl it is an epoch in her life. Then later comes the chance meeting between the Count and the girl, on the day after her father has been arrested for attacking his employer, because the latter was trying to assault his daughter. It is the Count's influence that has the father released and he and the girl start working for the concession next door.

The advent of Urban as a clown at the concession adjoining Shani's attracts all his juvenile trade. He becomes revenged by dropping a huge flower pot on the old clown's head, but the same night is repaid for his action when the monk escapes his cage and strangles the brute in his room while he sleeps. While the old clown is in the hospital nursed by his daughter, the Emperor pays a visit to the institution. It is here the girl realizes her necktie salesman is of the nobility. Prior to this she in her belief of his protestations of affections has given her happiness into his hands. When the Komtesse Grisella claims him as her husband it breaks the girl's heart.

Then the beginning of the war. This portion is admirably handled with the conflict held entirely secondary to the story itself, while it would have been all too easy to have let it overshadow the real interest. There are a few shots of feet marching on and on; a few scenes of a shattered army returning in defeat, a story all too plain and complete to need anything more than the brief flashes of the principals who are involved in it.

The Count reported dead, little Agnes consents to wed the hunchback in the spring. Their ceremony is set for the opening day of the season at the Prater, when the Count looms on the scene again. He is a widower and with the monarchy wiped out no longer of the nobility; free to wed as he will. But the girl refuses although her heart would have him; her promise to the hunchback is first in her mind. In the end, however, the two are in a close up embrace for the hunchback has sent her to the man she loves.

It is a tense tale of conflicting emotions that will hold any audience. In producing it Universal spent money rather lavishly. Detail is outstanding and direction carries the story along without a hitch or a break.

To the artists must go a full share, especially to Miss Philbin, for that little girl proves herself a wonder of dramatic ability and a remarkable actress. Mr. Kerry as the Count is a true picture of the square-head nobility of Central Europe. To Dorothy Wallace as Grisella also a full measure for what she has to do she does well.

In "Merry-Go-Round" the exhibitor will find a picture that his audiences will not only enjoy but praise, providing he goes out and really makes them believe the picture is as big as it is. *Fred.*

HUMAN WRECKAGE

F. B. O. (Film Booking Office) presents Mrs. Wallace Reid (Dorothy Davenport) in "Human Wreckage" at Lyric, New York, opening June 27 as special in legit house at advanced scale for run, playing two shows daily. Story by C. Gardner Sullivan. Names of technical staff concerned not on program but flashed on slides.

Ethel MacFarland	Mrs. Wallace Reid
Alan MacFarland	James Kirkwood
Mary Finnegan	Bessie Love
Jimmy Brown	George Hackathorne
Mrs. Brown	Claire McDowell
Dr. Hillman	Robert McKim
Mrs. Finnegan	Victory Bateman
Steve Stone	Harry Northrup
Dr. Blake	Eric Mayne
Harris	Otto Hoffman
Dunn	Philip Sleeman
The Baby	George Clark
Ginger Smith	Lucille Ricksen

"Human Wreckage" is strictly a commercially-made drug expose film. Like many others preceding it, there is no merit to any part, from story to acting. Its drawing powers will depend upon the Mrs. Wallace Reid billing and the drug notoriety of late in the dailies. That should compile a draw at the box office, as the sad ending of Wally Reid and the reams devoted to the evils of narcotics should have left a curiously inclined public in all towns and cities who may want to see the widow of Wally Reid if not particularly desirous of knowing more about drugs.

As an educator for the purpose of suppressing the drug habit, "Human Wreckage" isn't. It is more of an enlightener. The young can see here things they should not know, for it's naturally a morbid film, since its subject is entirely sodden. In its propensity to expound the effects, there appears to be an error. Morphine is utilized by a lawyer as a stimulator for a deadened mind. Morphine deadens instead of exhilarating; cocaine is supposed to be the stimulator. That, however, is no great import, since drugs seize as their prey only those who likely would be seized by something else if drugs didn't get them. The morbidity of the film is heightened through a majority of its locales placed among the lower classes.

There is little new in the picture, excepting the trend of the story, that has not been exhibited in other film exposes of the past two decades. None did any material good, since the drug habit is not screen welfare work, as it goes directly to the non-users probably much more so than the users.

The best impression left by "Human Wreckage" is that of a ghostlike hyena stalking through every scene where drugs come in to wreak their worst. This was frequent. A title said the hyena is the ugliest of animals, inferring the drug habit is the ugliest of the diseases. There is another disease in these United States that has spread far more rapidly, that is much more deadly and dangerous and under less control than the dope habit, since the war ceased. The government and pictures could better concentrate upon the isolation and suppression of that vicious but slow killer which attacks both sexes than for picture makers to splurge for commercialism upon drug films that at the most only inform the unknowing.

"Human Wreckage" as a picture is a self-player, as all drug pictures

have been; it's perfunctory and futile, written no better nor worse than the others, and hardly could have been written in any other way, played about the same and with the same result—nothing.

No reference is made in the picture or in the pre-announcements by Mrs. Reid to her husband, his fate or the cause.

The picture at the Lyric is given in the usual picture show style, some short reels running ahead of the feature, that takes up but little over an hour and that caused through heavy padding, which drags the picture badly. *Sime.*

THE CHASE
IVAN THE GREAT

The Capitol, New York, a Goldwyn-booked house, featured the two above named pictures this week in lieu of a regular running release. Both of the pictures are of short length, with "The Chase" the longer, and both should properly be classed as travelogs.

Last week the Capitol played a return of "Passion," with Negri, without gratifying results. It may have been the heat gamble and the Fourth for this week which induced Rothapfel to take no chance on his current program for expense.

The entire Capitol bill this week could be looked over by those who believe a cut-up show of short films and turns might be the solution instead of the extra drawing card. (if there is an extra drawing card anywhere for a picture house outside of pictures). The bill of 10 numbers is not overinviting, particularly as there is no especial life to the named specials. "Ivan the Great" seems to be a cutdown travelog of the Far North (Alaska), with too much attention given to the bear species of that country. The bears look like grizzlies. There was too much titling and too little action, with as much more footage wasted in a "love scene" of possibly reindeer or moose, perhaps musk-ox or maybe antelope, whatever they were, with the feminine end of the triangle. It was exactly what the caption mentioned—a "love scene," not worth the celluloid given to it, as the three animals in a single flash would have sufficed. New Yorkers are not that sentimental. Harold McCracken's Alaskan adventure picture is a sub-title for it.

"The Chase" is of skiing, presented by Jacob Fabian, and announced as the first American showing. "Europe's most amazing cinema novelty; a tale of Alpine thrills," says the program. The program says too much. Five minutes of this film would have been enough. The remainder of the 25 or 30 minutes is a succession of skiing repetition. Very pretty, graceful and attractive is this skiing over the untracked vastnesses of snow, but twice would have been as good as 50. The skis kept right on, making their plunges, walking, skidding, sliding or jumping. A story linked the picture, but there's nothing in the story other than the excuse to pad it out. Not big enough to stand by itself or as one-half of any bill.

Another of the short reels was "The Cuckoo's Secret," a Bray nature, and scientifically excellent, no doubt. It is the first screen record of a cuckoo's life, also her program, and as far as the screen is concerned on Broadway it could have remained a secret there, too.

A couple of other bits were divertissements, nicely enough staged, but not enlivening. *Sime.*

WANDERING DAUGHTERS

James Young production presented by Sam E. Rork. Adapted from the story by Dana Burnet; directed by James Young. Released by First National. Shown at the

Strand, New York, week July 1. Running time, 60 minutes.

Bessie Bowden.....Marguerite de la Motte
Will Bowden, her father..William V. Mong
Annie Bowden, her mother
Mabel Van Buren
Geraldine Horton..........Marjorie Daw
Charles Horton, her father....Noah Beery
John Hargraves.............Pat O'Malley
Austin Trull.................Allen Forrest
Servant in the Bowden home..Alice Howell

A decidedly slow moving, badly produced, poorly edited and but fairly directed production that is far from being up to the standard to merit a pre-release showing at any of the bigger Broadway houses. Nevertheless it is the attraction at the Strand for the current week, and the business the house did from 7:30 to 9:15 on Monday night seemed to tell the story completely. There was less than 50 per cent. of the lower floor occupied. In the regular run of daily change houses of the better class where double features are the policy a couple of times a week the picture will serve as entertainment, but in a de luxe house where the better class of presentations are in order it doesn't belong.

The story is a small town tale of the effect that the modern "jazz spirit" has on the younger generation. Seemingly, according to the story, any girl that stays out until midnight with a young man that the family does not approve of is a "wandering daughter," but if she stays out until dawn with the young man that they like, and comes home in his car, sits in front of the house and stops the milk man and baker for drink and food and sits complacently munching the rolls and buns dressed in a Hawaiian dancing costume, it is all right.

The girl is a small town vamp of poor but honest parents who treasure her highly. She falls in love with the hero, who as far as the screen would indicate is a real estate salesman, a newspaper reporter and what not.

Of course the story has a heavy. He is just a country club dancer, heavy sheik lover and an artist that paints nudes on the side. He steps into the country vamp's life and starts her sampling kisses, has her visiting his studio and a few little things like that. Incidentally he is the guy that keeps her out until midnight one night and when she returns daddy asks her to "tell him all."

That's all there was; there wasn't any more. At least not until daddy decided that the daughter needed a more modern atmosphere at home so that she could compete with the country club set in the matter of entertaining. He blasts into the family bankroll to revamp the house and through the experiment he manages to marry off daughter to the hero, stalling off the installment men who want to move the trick furnishings out of the house while the wedding ceremony is being performed.

The picture leaps from pillar to post on the screen, there being about the worst continuity of events shown as could be imagined. There are scenes seemingly dragged in by the roots, such as a parade of models with gowns, a swimming pool scene at the country club (this, by the way, was a little different through having illuminated swings over the water in a night scene), and a lot of jazz dancing stuff that is of the toddle type that passed out a couple of seasons back.

Marguerite de la Motte as the heroine showed nothing that will win contracts for her, Marjorie Daw in a secondary role topping her in every scene in which they both appeared. Pat O'Malley was a lukewarm hero and a patent leather-haired heavy was contributed by Allen Forrest. *Fred.*

THE LAMP IN THE DESERT

George M. Davis presents screen version of Ethel M. Dell's novel. Script authorship, director's name and that of the cast unavailable. Released through C. B. C. for state rights. At Fox's Academy, N. Y., July 1-4, on double feature bill. Running time 60 minutes.

This screen version of Ethel M. Dell's novel is just "one of those things." There seems to be no reason for the title, likewise no reason for the picture. It is just a cheap hodge podge of a story of India the like of which has been done hundreds of times on the screen and incidentally much better.

The production bears all the earmarks of having possibly been done abroad, at least it is disconnected enough in the matter of story to have been. For the cheaper grade of houses where there is a daily change it will get by on a double bill, and for the rest it will pass nicely for the audiences who do not care what it is as long as there is something in motion on the screen.

The story as near as it is possible to ascertain starts out with a women's knocking club at the English army post in India. They are panning a girl who has come all the way from England unchaperoned to visit her brother. The youth is popular at the post, and therefore the cutting of the girl does not take place in the open, but behind her back the married hens peck her to pieces. In self-defense the girl accepts the attentions of the lady killer of the post and marries him. The brother and his closest chum disapprove of the match. After the ceremony has been performed the brother's chum receives a letter from England, where his brother is a prison chaplain. The latter requests that he look up a certain Ceptain Darce, as there is a woman prisoner at the institution who claims him as her husband, she having alleged in her own defense when brought up on a charge of forgery that her husband by his refusal to support her had driven her to crime. It was this same Captain Darce that the young English girl had married.

Then the chum sets out to put matters right. He follows the honeymooning couple and places the fear of God into the bridegroom by showing him the letter from England and informs him that he had but two ways out of the situation, one was the suicide route and the other to disappear. This latter he decides is the easier.

The brother's chum then returns to the wife and informs her that an accident had occurred and her husband is no more, a few months later proposing and marrying her himself. That was fast work for a girl in a picture — two marriages in three reels.

In the end the husband No. 1 returns to the scene, but is conveniently knocked off in a native uprising, and there is the usual happy ending.

Hardly any reason for it all as far as the screen is concerned. As for the acting, the less said the better about that end of the picture, for every one in the cast, and none of them could be recognized on the screen as having ever been seen before, acted all over the lot.

Fred.

THE BROKEN VIOLIN

Atlantic Features production released by Arrow. From the story by George Rogan, directed by Jack Dillon. Shown at Proctor's 23d St., in conjunction with a five-act vaudeville bill for three days commencing July 2. Time, 75 minutes.

Jeremy Ellsworth...........Joseph Blake
Thomas Kitterly............Warren Cooke
James Gault..................Henry Sedley
Dr. Mason....................Sydney Dean
John Ellsworth..............Reed Howes
Constance Morley.........Dorothy Mackaill
Beatrice Ellsworth...........Rita Rogan
Jules Davega...................J. H. Lewis
The Governess.................Zena Keefe
Phil Carter }
Floyd Watson }............Gladden James

Melodramatics are the stock in trade of this production, with the story bringing forth only old bits in this line to create interest. The tale has a flimsy love angle weakly told, with the theme in general falling short of holding attention. The story is long drawn out, the rough and tumble action being well separated by great lengths of film in which little action or interest is developed.

The producing company has stuck quite closely to studio work with this production, the sets coming in the classification of ordinary. What exterior work is brought into play is not spectacular. The big scene of the picture is a race between a motorboat and hydro aeroplane. It is far from convincing. A fight scene, where the hero single-handed tackles a tough gang, is another of its punches. The rough and tumble work is poorly done. As the fight went on the cooler the combatants became.

The cast has Zena Keefe as its only name, the others being from the rank and file of picture players. Miss Keefe's role proved of little value to her, its opportunities being very limited Reed Howes did the bulk of the work. Gladden James and Henry Sedley were kept comparatively busy.

The story is of an imposter endeavoring to secure the millions rightfully belonging to another. His ruse works for a time, but the rightful heir finally comes into his own and incidentally wins the girl which the other had also attempted to secure.

These long drawn-out melodramas are pretty tough on summer-time audiences. *Hart.*

SHOOTIN' FOR LOVE

Universal production starring Hoot Gibson. Story by Raymond Schrock and Edward Sedgwick; script by Schrock and Albert G. Kenyon. Directed by Edw. Sedgwick. Shown at Loew's New York, on double feature bill June 28. Running time, 61 minutes.

Duke Travis......................Hoot Gibson
Mary Randolph..........Laura La Plante
Jim Travis.....................Alfred Allen
Bill Randolph...............William Welsh
Dan Hobson.................William Steele

Smashing good little feature of the western type with a couple of good thrills. Even though it opens with a war atmosphere and has a little battle stuff, there isn't enough to worry anyone.

The scene for the greater part is in the open country and there is a lot of good riding. For audiences where westerns are liked this one is sure to stand out. The story is simple and not too involved. Hoot Gibson makes an altogether acceptable hero.

Gibson has the role of a sergeant in the A. E. F., from Texas. On the other side he suffers shell shock and the slightest unexpected noise drives him looney. Back in Texas, while the boy is abroad, his dad and the nearest neighbor start a war of their own over the water supply for the cattle.

On a train speeding home at about the same time are the boy and the daughter of the neighbor. They recognize each other, a childhood romance is revived and the result is by the time they reach the home town they are practically engaged to marry. But the two dads meet them at the station and tear the fond lovers apart.

Gibson's dad says the boy has to take up the fight against the father of the girl he loves, and the girl's dad informs her that should he ever become aware she has spoken to the boy he will disown her. At about this stage the heavy gets busy and starts to lay suit to the girl's heart, without success.

The heavy finally tries to get the girl into his arms by main force. Escaping, she makes for the forbidden lover's home. His dad, not aware the boy is suffering from shell shock, believes him a coward and the two have come to a parting of the ways. The arrival of the girl sends Hoot on the war trail after the heavy, with the result he is badly beaten up. This pleases his father as an indication his son wasn't afraid.

At the finish the boy gets a third and final "shock" from the explosion the heavy sets and blows up the dam of the water works. This brings the boy back to normal and he starts after the heavy, who has kidnapped the girl. Of course he catches him, pulls him from his horse, trims him and rides back in glory with the young woman.

It is a little western "Romeo and Juliet" that will get over with the majority of the film fans. Gibson puts over the shell-shocked boy nicely and his jump from a horse at full speed and the tumble he and the heavy take were thrills.

Fred.

THE RAPIDS

Ernest Shipman presents "The Rapids" by Alan Sullivan, produced by the Saulte Ste. Marie Films, Ltd., released through Hodkinson. The story was adapted for the screen by Faith Green with David M. Hartford, director. Shown privately by Hodkinson June 14. Time, 60 minutes.

"The Rapids" is a Canadian production carrying the name of the Sault Ste. Marie Films, Ltd., a company organized by Ernest Shipman and promoted by Canadian capital. The picture is one of many promoted in the same manner several of its scenes being taken in the section where the money was raised for the producing company. Few pictures made with this style of financing have reached a high mark. This latest Shipman production is about on a par with the rest. Its story is so laid out as to bring several local scenes into use a number of which are interesting from an educational standpoint. As screened the story oversteps the bounds of regulation fiction, so far fetched in many instances as to be ridiculous.

In setting his producing organization together Shipman selected players of a medium calibre and an acceptable technical staff with David M. Hartford the director. Harry T. Morey was assigned the lead with Mary Astor taking the leading role in her division. Walter Miller carried what bordered on being a juvenile lead. The remainder fitted in satisfactorily, the outstanding work of the minor roles being that of Frank Andrews. The only cost of any consequence was the cast. Little studio work was necessary with a number of exteriors including river scenes taking up the footage. Several of the pulp wood mill and steel mill shots were exceedingly interesting and well done.

The story is laid in a small Canadian town. For years it is dormant regardless of natural advantages. Robert Clarke appears and sees its possibilities. He secures backing and transforms it into a thriving pulp mill center. Not content with the development he learns iron is in the vicinity and erects large steel mills.

Together with the commercial side is a love angle helped along by a child with the finish having the creator of the city an unsuccessful lover with his right hand man winning the girl both had been after.

It is a very simple tale. Were it not for the educational tinge the picture would have little value.

The big drawback is that none of the characters with the exception of the child mature as the story progresses, notwithstanding the tale is spread over a term of years. That the huge mills spring up as if over night is also a bad feature. The story intends the impression be given the buildings are erected with great speed but not as miraculously as the film would lead one to believe.

"The Rapids" is just a picture. It may please the people in Canada who put their money into it but it hardly meets the requirements of a regulation screen audience. *Hart.*

RUPERT OF HENTZAU

Lewis N. Selznick's screen version of Anthony Hope's novel of the same name, written as a sequel to "The Prisoner of Zenda," and involving the same characters. Scenario by Edward J. Montagne. Director, Victor Heerman. Billed as produced under the supervision of Myron Selznick. Projection time, 98 minutes. At the Strand, New York, July 8.

Queen Flavia	Elaine Hammerstein
Rudolph } Rassendyll	Bert Lytell
Rupert of Hentzau	Lew Cody
Countess Helga	Claire Windsor
Colonel Sapt	Hobart Bosworth
Count Fritz	Bryant Washburn
Rosa Holf	Marorie Daw
Bauer	Mitchell Lewis
Count Rischenheim	Adolphe Menjou
The King's Forester	Elmo Lincoln
Lieut. von Bernenstein	Irving Cummings
Mother Holf	Josephine Crowell
Herbert	Nigel de Brullier
Paula	Gertrude Astor

"Rupert of Hentzau" necessarily invites comparison with "The Prisoner of Zenda," since both concern the same characters and are done in the same romantic spirit. "Rupert," then, is a good picture, but far below the level of "Zenda" both as to story interest and artistic production quality.

The weaker story interest probably goes back to the novel itself. There was always something false and artificial about "Hentzau." The reader couldn't quite get it out of his mind that the whole romantic history was a bit of a literary hoax. Indeed the same thing is more or less true of nearly all "sequels" to successful stories. They seem to be written, not from inspiration, but because the profit of the first successful book invited a like venture. It is particularly so with "Hentzau." It is hard to consider with sympathetic interest a series of romantic and dramatic situations which are based on a woman's foolish letter to a former sweetheart and the political consequences that follow its capture by the enemies of Queen Flavia. You're more likely to be impatient with the queen than absorbed in her sorrows. Since the very foundation of the tale has this suggestion of being phoney, so every development built upon that foundation takes on a like color, and the whole thing has a touch of insincerity.

But the Selznick organization has achieved some fine artistic effects. The passage showing the royal wedding is a splendid pictorial effort, with big mass effects and compelling quality of regal dignity and ceremonial. The settings are enormous, showing the magnificent perspective of a cathedral nave with the chancel and surpliced choir in the distance. The wedding procession also is finely managed to bring out the dignity of the ceremony without messing the screen up with fussy detail.

Numerous other passages are as skillfully handled. It is desired to put emphasis upon the loneliness of the mismated queen, and this effect is subtly secured by having her move about a small solitary figure in trailing gowns in huge interiors. There are many such fine effects, but there are other details where directorial mismanagement strikes false notes. Some of the constructed street scenes are obviously make-believe, and it was a mistake to show the whole Palace of Zenda. Rex Ingram got his effects by showing only portions of the palace that suggested the scale of the whole building, such as the drawbridge and palace portals. Here they picture the whole castle, and, although it is a huge setting, its effect is inadequate, almost puny compared to the imaginary picture conjured up in the imagination from one of Ingram's details.

For the most part, the designs are drawn on an impressive scale of simple dignity, but one scene (that in which the head huntsman reports to Flavia that the King will spend the night at the hunting lodge) is so cluttered up with furniture and decorations the people are lost in the confusion of detail. There is another false note here. The situation is tense. The presence of the King at the hunting lodge threatens to involve the Queen in a scandal, but her loyal followers, Count Fritz (Bryant Washburn) and Lieut. Bernenstein (Irving Cummings) find time to be amused at the awkwardness of the huntsman.

The picture's costuming is brilliant in its pageantry and the playing is as near flawless as it could be made. There are no less than eight names that have been starred, and they work out into a compact, smooth-running playing organization. Elaine Hammerstein does some of the best work of her screen career. She gets over the feeling of regal dignity by the sheer simplicity and naturalness of her bearing and commands in situations where a hint of "acting" would have wrecked the character.

Lew Cody in the dare-devil Rupert has a role made to order for his peculiar style. There is a sinister touch about the character, relieved by a cynical gallantry, that fits Cody like a glove. His big scene with Lytell, a furious sword duel, ending with Rupert's game acceptance of mortal defeat, is a splendid bit of high romantic melodrama. *Rush.*

CHILDREN OF JAZZ

Jesse L. Lasky presents the production screened from the play, "Other Times," by Harold Brighouse. The adaptation is made by Beulah Marie Dix and direction is in the hands of Jerome Storm. Projection time, 67 minutes. At the Rialto July 8.

Richard Forestall	Theodore Kosloff
Ted Carter	Ricardo Cortes
Clyde Dunbar	Robert Cain
Babs Weston	Eileen Percy
Lina Dunbar	Irene Dalton
John Weston	Alec. B. Francis
Adam Forestall	Frank Currier
Ullivens	Snitz Edwards
Deborah	Lillian Drew

"Children of Jazz" is done in strict accordance with an established formula, the design in this case being the exploitation of the supposed dissipations of the American rich, with a lot of racy sex stuff thinly disguised and absurdly elaborated "society spectacle."

The first part is a succession of scenes familiar to the fans as "cabaret stuff," only here they are supposed to be Christmas parties and New Year's revels. All this material deals with trivial make-believe people, and as a picture of real life is about as convincing as a scene from the "Greenwich Village Follies."

The people aren't even likable. The hero is a bully and a good deal of a cad, just a self-satisfied braggart. The pretense that he is a sort of Richard Harding Davis soldier of fortune doesn't go down. The heroine is worse yet, a half-naked young fool who goes from one affair to another with the sweethearts and husbands of her intimate friends and spends her time accumulating engagement rings and consuming synthetic gin. It's a sweet picture of American life to go abroad.

The tale is never convincing, and in its screen form is on a par with some of the most trifling of the magazine fiction that is fed to the juvenile consumers of print. A drunken party of young people slip away from a New Year's eve party to "go to Havana for breakfast" via airplane, although the party appears to be held in New York. The picture has some bright titles also. A steamship is pictured approaching the Brooklyn Bridge, and one of the characters shrewdly observes, "We will be landing soon."

Theodore Kosloff has been handed an impossible role. This intelligent actor does exceedingly well with roles of a certain kind, usually with a slightly foreign and bizarre kind; but here he doesn't come through in any capacity as the "cave man" master of the society butterflies. It's the unsympathetic role of a thoroughly objectionable person.

The production must have represented a considerable outlay. Large numbers of extra people are used in the party scenes, which involve elaborate sets and costuming; a real airplane is wrecked and a four-masted schooner with a good-sized crew is used for several passages. These things and the big cast cost more money than the picture is worth.

Richard Forestall, an adventurer, falls in love with Babs Weston, a society girl, and on his hasty departure she accepts his engagement ring and pledges her word to wait for his return. Later Richard comes back, to find Babs engaged to two other men, one of them not yet divorced, and he upbraids and repudiates the girl and all she represents of frivolous indulgence.

To drown his sorrows he undertakes an expedition to aid a revolution in San Sebastian, wherever that is, and presently is seen piloting his ship through a tempest at sea. These storm scenes are exceedingly graphic. The New Year's party has broken up meanwhile for the Havana air trip, and by one of those screen coincidences the ship and airplane party fetch up on a strange, mythical island, presumably in the Caribbean somewhere.

Richard's eccentric father and his lordly household are the only inhabitants. The father's hobby is to reproduce on the island the life of a century ago, with middle 18th century costumes to match, and it is into this odd atmosphere the adventurer and the young jazzists are introduced. Richard takes command of the situation, forcing the jazz girls to cooking and household work and making the society men labor at daily tasks. Likewise he makes persistent love to Babs after knocking both of her fiances about. In the end one of Babs' lovers gets up courage to make a fight of it and beats Richard in a rough-and-tumble combat. This convinces the superman that he has reformed the jazzists, and he prepares to go along with his San Sebastian affair. But at the chip's side there is a mushy, sentimental reversal of the relations of all hands. Babs declares her love for the adventurer, while her young defender sails away to carry out the revolutionary plan of Richard.

All cheap fiction designed for 12-year-old intelligence. *Rush.*

SUCCESS

Murray Garson production released through Metro, featuring Brandon Tynan. Story written and adapted by Adeline Leitzbach and Theo. A. Liebler, Jr. Directed by Ralph Ince. Shown at the Capitol, New York, week July 8, 1923. Running time, 63 minutes.

Barry Carleton	Brandon Tynan
Jane Randolph	Naomi Childers
Rose Randolph	Mary Astor
Sam Lewis	Dore Davidson
Willis Potter	Lionel Adams
Gilbert Gordon	Stanley Ridges
Henry Briggs	Robert Lee Keiling
Nick Walker	Billy Quirk
Ruth	Helen Macks
Joe	Gay Pendleton
Treadwell, the Peasant	John Woodford

Here is a picture that should make Brandon Tynan "The Music Master" of the screen. It is a story of the theatre, but a different type of story than is usually found in screen versions of theatrical life. Perhaps the fact that the son of an old producing manager of the legitimate theatre was partly responsible for the story is in a measure accountable for the fact that this is more or less a true revelation of the life that the people of the profession lead. At that there was one character, that of the former burlesque manager who achieves to better things in the theatre, that was possibly overdrawn. As a picture, however, this is certain to appeal to most any type of audience. That paternal love appeal that this story abounds in is certain to get to the heart and the tear ducts of the average picture fan.

At the Capitol Monday night the picture seemed to interest the audience intensely, but the outstanding fact of the entire feature was the tremendous impression that Mr. Tynan made as the broken-down star of Shakespearean repertoire in "the good old days." There is no question that his interpretation of the role on the screen ranks with that created by David Warfield in "The Music Master" on the legitimate stage. It was a role that was written along the lines of the same sympathetic appeal.

In brief, the story deals with Barry Carleton, a matinee idol and Shakespearean star of several decades ago. The action opens with the final night of his New York season in repertoire. The company arranges a banquet as a farewell surprise. At the same time the formation of a co-partnership between the artistic manager of the company and the more commercial aspirant from the field of burlesque is announced and Carleton refuses to sign a contract with the new combination unless his leading lady, who is to become his wife, is co-starred with him. The commercial manager decries the fact that the matinee idol is to take a wife, for, as he puts it, no matinee idol should have one.

As the years passed Carleton slowly sank from the heights of stardom. A little too much of the cup that cheers and hail fellow well met companionship, and finally his wife deserts him, taking with her their daughter. Some 15 years later a huge Shakespearean revival is projected. A new star is to have the principal roles; his leading lady is to be the daughter of the old actor. The company is being backed by a financier who has an eye on the girl, and the role of acting as dresser for the star. On the opening night the angel presents the girl with a string of pearls and the star, who loves her, goes out and gets drunk, with the old-timer impersonating him and carrying off the most triumphant acclamation of his career. There are but two aware of the secret, the star and the former manager. The girl the next 'day becomes aware that it was her father who saved the opening performance, and there is a reconciliation effected all around.

Naomi Childers plays the leading woman to the star of long ago and is the mother in the modern episodes of the picture. In the later scenes, however, she appeared young than in the earlier ones. Dore Davidson as the former burlesque manager walked away with the comedy bits of the picture. Stanley Ridges as the star of today suggested one of the Barrymores slightly in his expression at times. There was one scene that suggested rather forcibly how fights are apt to start in a theatrical club, with the suggestion that the men of the profession are just as gabby about "dirt" as any of the womenfolk.

Ralph Ince handled the direction of the production rather well, sending the story forward practically at all times. There were only one or two moments that were permitted to drag a little. *Fred.*

THE SCARLET LILY

B. P. Schulberg presents this production, starring Katherine MacDonald, released through First National. Victor Schertzinger directed from Lois Zellner and Florence Hein's adaptation of Fred Sittenham's story. Ran about an hour, concluding the program at Proctor's 23d St., New York, in conjunction with vaudeville.
Dora Mason........Katherine MacDonald
Lawson Dean........Orville Caldwell
Jessup Barnes........Stuart Holmes
Beatrice Milo........Grace Morse
Mollie Mason........Jane Miskimin

Trixie........Adele Farrington
Mrs. Rosetta Bowen......Gertrude Quality
Tubby........Lincoln Steadman
Mrs. Barnes........Edith Lyle
Lawrence, her brother......Gordon Russell

The paradoxical title refers to Dora Mason (Miss MacDonald), who has accepted the hospitality of a married man's apartment in all innocence and then finds ensuing circumstances reflecting on her character because of the purely innocent itinerary in the Jessup Barnes suite. Barnes, a married man, commissioned the interior decorating firm which employed Dora to fix up a new apartment for him. Miss Mason is the one assigned to the task, and Barnes commits a bad break at the installation night's party. Dora leaves in a huff, returning to her squalid hall bedroom to find her ailing sister, Mollie, on the ebb. The landlady, objecting to anything happening in her house, demands possession of the room, and Dora faces a tough situation because of her depleted exchequer. (She has lost her position meantime.) Comes a note from Barnes inviting her to use the apartment for a month in his absence out of town, which Dora is forced to accept in view of her sister's plight.

The situation becomes complicated with the intervention of Mrs. Barnes and her private detective on Barnes' return at an unfortunate moment, and Dora Mason is publicized as a co-respondent. In a country retreat Lawson Dean, a promising political figure, renews acquaintance with the heroine, having come up to recuperate from severe eye-strain. Her marriage to the lawyer, who has announced his candidacy for District Attorney, ruins his political chances when Mrs. Barnes recognizes the newly-wed bride as the supposed "other woman." The usual situation about the husband's suspicions and disbelief and her efforts to establish her innocence follow, with the final fade-out satisfactory all around.

There is considerable story to the picture and it interests all the way. Director Schertzinger has wielded his puppets wisely and well, shifting attention from one situation to another without overplaying any particular point. Opportunities for pardonable stressing presented themselves at divers times, but footage probably limited any such desire.

The star acquitted herself intelligently. Mr. Caldwell as the male lead had a few opportunities, but was generally limited until half the picture had run its course. Stuart Holmes was his usual suave light "heavy," and the balance of the support was satisfactory. *Abel.*

HER FATAL MILLIONS

Metro production from the story by William Dudley Pelley; adapted for the screen by Arthur Statter. Directed by William Beaudine, with Viola Dana as the star. Shown at Loew's State, New York, for three days in conjunction with a vaudeville bill, commencing July 9. Time, 65 minutes.
Mary Bishop........Viola Dana
Fred Garrison........Huntley Gordon
Lew Carmody........Allan Forrest
Louise Carmody........Peggy Brown
Amos Bishop........Edward Connelly
Mary Appleton........Kate Price
Landlady........Joy Winthrop

Metro has turned out a genuine summertime picture in "Her Fatal Millions," a starring vehicle for Viola Dana. Not a big picture in any sense of the word, the production will come up to the requirements of the average exhibitor of program pictures and should prove a satisfactory selection for houses of that type. It is a comedy-drama, with emphasis on the comedy, its dramatic value being null and void. The story gives Miss Dana ample opportunities to display her ability as a comedienne, which she ably does, displaying a winsomeness and piquancy in some of the comedy scenes which prove the production's biggest assets. With the buxom

Kate Price as a comedy foil, the star brings forth a number of genuine laughs. Huntley Gordon is allotted the male lead, being featured in the billing. Gordon is not over-burdened with opportunities, but runs through the several reels in a convincing style. Edward Connelly in a character role was next in importance, with Allan Forrest doing a fair heavy part.

In the production end "Her Fatal Millions" comes up to the general standard of Metro features. Nothing pretentious in the way of sets, with those brought into play convincing. William Beaudine in his direction has worked out a light story in the proper comedy vein. His work is creditable.

The story has as its leading figure Mary Bishop, a young girl who wishes to give her former sweetheart the impression she is worth millions. By borrowing clothes, jewels and an automobile, she is well on the road to success when an automobile accident breaks up her plans, causing innumerable complications, which are finally cleared away, allowing her to marry the chap who she had thought already wed and who had figured her as having already stepped into matrimonial harness. *Hart.*

STEPPIN' FAST

William Fox feature, starring Tom Mix. Written by Bernard McConville. Directed by Joseph J. Franz. Shown at Fox's Academy, New York, June 24-27, 1923, double feature bill. Running time, 57 minutes.
Malvern........Tom Mix
Quintin Durant........Tom Guise
Fabian........Donald McDonald

A feature that for action has everything. The story is a wild one, but the action is there with gun fights, fist fights, hard riding, automobile racing a couple of steamship races across the Pacific, mystery murders by Chinese in Los Angeles, a hidden treasure in the mountains, a map hidden in a ring, and a hero and heroine to be involved in all of the foregoing. Could any picture fan ask for more?

Tom Mix is the hero and at the opening is leaving his little ranch in the hills to visit his mother in the city. On the way he runs across Quintin Durant, an elderly scientist who is being attacked by three men. Mix rides to the rescue, and the two continue to the city together. Arriving there, Mix is invited to the scientist's house, arriving just in time when the old man is being attacked by the same three men that waylaid him on the road, their forces having been augmented with a couple of Chinese. Mix drives them off, but not before the old man has been fatally stabbed. As he is dying he gives Mix a note and the map ring. Both are to be taken to Durant's daughter in China.

The plotters are tipped off that Mix has the note and go to his mother's home to secure it. The mother dies from shock and Mix's pet hound is also killed by them. That gives the hero an incentive to track down men. However, they trap him in a Chinese den and knock him over the head, casting his unconscious body into the bay, from which he is rescued and taken on as one of the crew, working his way to China in the stokehold. The plotters, however, have taken a fast steamer and arrive in port a few hours ahead of him, and one with the note impersonates Mix, luring the daughter of the scientist into a dive to obtain the ring from her, the girl and father both having had copies of the map to the treasure. The plotters get away with the ring, but the Chinese joint in which they were operating is wrecked by a gang of American sailors. Then with the aid of a kindly old friend of the Durant family a race back across the Pacific is staged, the old friend loaning his yacht so that the crooks can't get away with the girl's treasure.

On arrival in America Mix drives a racing automobile across country to the mountains, where the treasure is located just in time to prevent the three crooks from getting it, he bringing about the death of all three of them via the rope route, thus avenging the death of his mother, the girl's father and his own dog. The final fadeout finds the usual close-up clinch.

There are a couple of bits of action stuff that are corking, one especially with Mix driving the racing car in the desert and cornering a horseman. That was well worked out.

The picture is as good a feature as Mix has been seen in for some time. Claire Adams was a fair enough leading woman for the western star as far as what she had to do was concerned. *Fred.*

THE LOVE PIKER

Cosmopolitan production, released by Goldwyn-Cosmopolitan. Story by Frank R. Adams, starring Anita Stewart. Director, E. Mason Hopper. Projection time, 64 minutes. At the Capitol, New York, July 15.

Hope Warner	Anita Stewart
Peter Pan Huisen	William Norris
Martin Van Huisen	Robert Frazer
Archie Pembroke	Carl Gerrard
Professor Click	Arthur Hoyt
Edith Cloney	Betty Francisco
Willie Warner	Winston Miller
Mrs. Warner	Mayme Kelso
Mr. Warner	Frederick Truesdell
Butler	Robert Bolder
Maid	Cornelia Callahan
Judge	James F. Fulton

Production method rather than scenario material probably is the trouble with "The Love Piker." The substance of the story is the regeneration of a new rich snob by her love for a poor young man, but the difficulty is that she is objectionably snobbish for nine-tenths of the story and sympathetically yielding for so short a tenth that the count up is nine to one against her at the end.

Director Hopper makes his points crudely. When he is sentimental he is too utterly mushy. His comedy is no more delicate nor subtle. Altogether his effects are achieved with a heavy hand. Plainly he doesn't believe a fan audience is capable of fine shades of expression. He never suggests; he insists upon spelling it out so there may be no possibility of misunderstanding.

Altogether a picture made for the literal and matter-of-fact people who would rather laugh at the banana peel fall than be gently nudged into a chuckle. That's one kind of film, of course, and pleases its own kind of audience. So in its way it is an admirable effort, but it doesn't spell screen success at any point.

Neither is it calculated to win Anita Stewart a clentele among the discriminating Broadway regulars. Worse yet, it doesn't picture true and recognizable characters, and, worst of all, it doesn't present interesting or likable people.

The heroine starts as a snob, and a particularly exasperating one, and remains a snob until it's too late. What defense can a director make for a young woman who reluctantly gives up a rich suitor for a poor young man and then all but sneers at the size of her fiance's engagement ring? The author couldn't conceal by any romantic device the fact that the poor young man had let himself in for a lot of trouble at the wedding. That wife of his would give him a lot of trouble later on—but that would be after the end of the picture. Still, it stuck in your mind that the ending wasn't in reality a happy one.

The film is a collection of unpromising people, with the probable exception of the heroine the person of Robert Frazer, a young man not much noted until now, but who makes love gracefully and is genuine even in a wooden straight part.

One reason Hope was reluctant to marry Martin was Martin's humble Dutch father, who lived in a queer neighborhood, smoked a corncob pipe (the corncob seems rather out of key with a Dutch father), and went moistly sentimental about his late spouse at Hope's first visit. There was some justification for Hope. It must be trying to have your future father-in-law get your georgette waist all damp the minute you enter the place. That probably was Hope's reason for declining to invite father to the wedding, although the scenario alleged the pipe. However, at the last minute she saw that keeping the old man away was out of order. So she left all the wedding guests waiting for more than half an hour while she rushed to the shack in her limousine, being then all done up in her bridal veil and the other appropriate scenery, told the old man (she called him "Peter," which was pretty fresh for a daughter-in-law-to-be and ordinarily would have brought swift results from a Dutch father) she was sorry and brought him along to the wedding then and there. Peter remained undisturbed this time, even though they told him his bride had run away with another man. When she returned he told her he knew she would do the right thing by the old man all along. Martin was the better part, and properly the film should have had a man star for the part.

The comedy is all hokum, including the familiar somersaulting butler, who is constantly making love to a disdainful parlor maid and dropping china. They forgot very few of the hardest worked comedy props, remembering the vulgar society-climbing mamma, a gushing flapper sister, cissy boy brother and toy lapdog, which was rapidly passed from one guest to another until it brought up in the butler's arms and he transferred it to the simpering parlor maid. Stock company farce producers will find a lot of old friends here.

In short it's a machine-made picture without any spontaneous spirit, built on the mistaken idea that "they like the old stuff best."

Rush.

A GENTLEMAN OF LEISURE

Paramount picture presented by Jesse Lasky. From the play by John Stapleton and P. G. Wodehouse, adapted by Jack Cunningham and Anthony Coldeway. Star, Jack Holt. Directed by Joseph Henabery. Shown at the Rivoli, New York, week July 15. Running time, 56 minutes.

Robert Pitt	Jack Holt
Sir Spencer Deever	Casson Ferguson
Molly Creedon	Sigrid Holmquist
Sir John Blount	Alec Francis
Lady Blount	Adele Farrington
Spike Mullen	Frank Nelson
Big Phil Creedon	Alfred Allen
Maid	Nadeen Paul
Chorus Girl	Alice Queensberry

A year or so ago, when the Famous Players-Lasky organization issued its schedule of productions for the year which ends next month, "The Gentleman of Leisure" was to have had the late Wallace Reid. His unfortunate demise made this impossible. So, having discovered that Jack Holt in his last release made a considerable impression in the lighter form of comedy, they cast him for the principal role in this comedy drama of society and crooks.

It is mighty good hot weather entertainment. Not too fast, still not too slow—just a medium-paced vehicle, in which the star acquits himself fairly well and is helped out considerably with titles in the matter of securing laughs.

The story opens in London and then shifts quickly to New York city and then to Bay Shore, L. I. There are several scenes in both of the latter locations that are entirely too studio in atmosphere. Park avenue, New York, as set in a studio in Los Angeles is far from convincing, and Bay Shore, L. I., is far from having palm trees that are two feet in thickness. Outside of that every little thing seems O. K.

Holt plays a dashing young American millionaire who on his return from Europe meets with several boon companions in a Broadway cafe for luncheon, remarking that since his return he hasn't seen a pretty girl. However, there happens to be one right across the dining room, and he bets that he'll win a smile from her before she leaves the room. Failing in this, he makes another bet that he'll have a picture of her within 24 hours that will be inscribed "With Love," figuring that he will be able to lift one that she has been displaying to her friends that bears exactly those words.

In this, however, he is also unsuccessful. That night in his rooms a burglar appears, and when he captures him he decides that the two shall make an attempt to enter the girl's home and steal the picture therefrom. Here he is frustrated again, but manages to talk his way out of what looks like a sure arrest. The following day at the home of the Deevers' at Bay Shore he boldly makes an appearance, and Sir Spencer Deever, a young Englishman who is being forced by his aunt and uncle to propose to the American girl, hails him with delight, finally losing the girl to him. Through this all runs the complication of the crooks, a couple of strings of phoney pearls and a number of heavy-footed coppers.

Playing opposite the star is Sigrid Holmquist, the beautiful young blonde from one of the trio of Scandinavian countries, who has improved 100 per cent. in her acting since last seen in a picture that Cosmopolitan produced. In this production she runs the star a race whenever she is on the scene with him. Alec Francis and Adele Farrington, as the uncle and aunt, handled themselves nicely, but Casson Ferguson seemed badly cast for the young Englishman. Frank Nelson in a crook low-comedy character got a couple of real laughs.

The direction carries the story along rather well. *Fred.*

STORMY SEAS

Co-starring production for Helen Holmes and J. P. McGowan, released through Associated Exhibitors. Directed by J. P. McGowan. Shown at Loew's New York, N. Y., on double feature bill July 17, 1923. Running time, 65 minutes.

"Storm" Weems	Francis Seymour
Mary Weems	Helen Holmes
Capt. Morgan	J. P. McGowan
Steward	Gordon Knapp
Capt. George Tracy	Leslie Casey
Angus McBride	Harry Dalroy

This is a story of the sea and a souse. A sort of a real blood-and-thunder meller that will go in the popular-priced houses, and while the picture is somewhat draggy in spots, due to direction, there is sufficient suspense toward the end of the tale to make it stand up with the average audience that frequents the smaller houses. The regular run of exhibitor playing a daily change can run the picture and get away with it in good shape.

It is the tale of an old ship owner in San Francisco, a sort of a Cappy Ricks type, whose only daughter is his pride and joy. He has two men in his employ, both of whom he showers his affections upon as though they were sons. One is the son of his former partner, who died because of heavy drinking, and the other is just in the picture without any explanation other than the old man thinks as much of him as he does of the other. The son of the drunkard is about to become the son-in-law of the ship owner, and his last cruise before the marriage is to take the newly launched pride of the fleet on a trip. He does, and runs into a storm, starts drinking despite he has made a promise not to do so, and finally wrecks the magnificent ship. All trace of him is lost then, and several years after, in a small Central American port, he is picked up and brought aboard the ship that was his command before he wrecked the new boat, to be returned to his native country under pain of sentence of 15 years in the quarries.

His old friends aboard conspire to make a man of him through hard labor, and they finally succeed in bringing out some of his former manhood. In the finish he does the self-sacrificing thing and permits the other man to take the girl, who has awakened to a new love through the weakness of the man who was pledged to become her husband.

Those that love sea stories will like this one, for the picturesque touches that are given the wreck stuff are great. Undoubtedly some weekly news pictures of a real wreck were secured, and these are so well fitted to the picture that it stands out as a remarkable piece of work. A burning pleasure yacht is also an effective touch, and it brings the suspense at the minute when the picture was beginning to die. There are also a couple of fairly good deck fights.

Helen Holmes, while not overburdened with the role assigned her, manages to give a good account of herself, and McGowan as the souse was all that could be expected. Forceful at times and weak at others, it is a good touch his sacrifice at the end of the story, for where is the girl that would want him in preference to the handsome chap that was his rival. It would have just been another of those "Bill" Hart things if it had turned out the other way. Leslie Casey as the rival gave an exceedingly good account of himself and should shine in the future as a sort of genteel semi-heavy. *Fred.*

BROKEN HEARTS OF B'WAY

Irving Cummings production released via state rights. Suggested by James Kyrle McCurdy's play, written for the screen by Hope Loring and Louis Duryea Lighton. Directed by Irving Cummings. Reviewed in projection room. Running time, 74 minutes.

Mary Ellis	Colleen Moore
George Colton	Johnnie Walker
Bubbles Revere	Alice Lake
Barney Ryan	Tully Marshall
Lydia Ryan	Kate Price
An Outcast	Creighton Hale
Tony Gudio	Anthony Merlo
Barry Peale	Arthur Stuart Hull
Frank Huntleigh	Freeman Wood

A corking picture for the state rights market. It will fit the smaller towns and the neighborhood houses where the title and the cast, which has a half dozen names of good screen value, and should prove to be business pullers.

The picture is being sold on a $100,000 quota basis for the entire country, so that won't place any too great a burden on the various territories. From the general appearance of the picture it appears to be one of those productions that if given the proper amount of hurrah publicity it should clean up for the small exhibitor. The box office value is there, it only remains for the man that is playing the picture to get it out of the public, and that shouldn't be a hard task with the "Broadway" title and the cast that he has to work on.

The story is really in the form of a prolog and the tale itself. It is to the effect that Broadway has to take you and break you before it can make you. That is the philosophy uttered by an old Bright Lights cab driver who has turned private chauffeur for a popular Broadway star and her husband, whose trials and tribulations he relates to a down and out playwright who is about to throw up the sponge.

With the beginning of the real tale a country girl, burning with ambition to become a great actress, invades New York and goes to a boarding house, where she occupies a room with a gay little gold digger, and the room above is tenanted by a struggling song writer who is trying to get a hit over the plate. It is the romance of the latter and the little country girl that hold the foreground of the story. They have hardships and trials and have to steal their breakfasts from the front stoop before they finally hit upon an idea that carries the girl to stardom and makes the boy the writer of a successful play on Broadway.

Before all this arrives there is a period where the girl is working in the chorus of a show and is fired because she turns down the advances of the angel John, while her room mate seeks the easiest way, only to become the central figure in a murder trial when her affianced lover appears on the scene and knocks off her protector. The boy likewise plays piano in a dump to get his cakes and has a fight with the Chink owner because he would not permit one of the guests to insult one of the girl performers and is fired.

It is all there, all the regular hoak that the small towners believe of Broadway, and it is fed to them in liberal doses. It is what they expect of Broadway, and this picture won't disappoint them in any of their expectations.

Colleen Moore plays the role of the little heroine from the country, and does it effectively, while Alice Lake is the "gold digger" that jumps from the chorus to a star, dressing room by being "nice" to the friend of the angel. Johnnie Walker is the hero of the ivories, and Tully Marshall is the philosophical old cabby, with Creighton Hale as the down and outer.

The action is well directed and for the greater part of the story is advanced with fair speed. There are one or two spots that are slightly draggy, but these can easily be remedied. It should be a money maker for all concerned in it.

Fred.

McGUIRE OF THE MOUNTED

Universal northwest mounted picture, starring William Desmond. Story by Raymond L. Schrock, script by Geo. Hively, directed by Richard Stanton. Shown at Loew's New York, N. Y., July 6, 1923, on double feature bill. Running time, 53 minutes.

Bob McGuire.............William Desmond
Julie Montreau............Louise Lorraine
Bill Lusk....................Willard Louis
Katie Peck.......................Vera James
Andre Montreau..............P. J. Lockney
Major Cordwell...........Wm. A. Lowery
Mrs. Cordwell..................Peggy Brown
Henri.........................Frank Johnson
Sergeant Murphy.............Jack Walters

One of the usual type of northwest mounted pictures that has as a principal redeeming feature no snow. It is cut to the usual pattern of this type of story. As a feature it will fit only in the cheaper houses where the most ordinary calibre of program feature is acceptable to the audiences.

The story is a badly hashed up affair. The entire action starts with a smuggling plot lost sight of long before the story finishes. In place of this a couple of murders and a drugged marriage take up the thread of the tale. At the finish the entire affair is unravelled through the death confession of the heavy's woman assistant.

William Desmond plays the Northwest mounted cop detailed to break up the smuggling band.

Just a regular formula hoak Northwestern.

Fred.

HOLLYWOOD

Chicago, July 25.

Paramount production with James Cruze director. First shown at the Orpheum, Chicago, July 21, where the photoplay opens a remodeled house for a run. Running time, 90 minutes.

Angela Whitaker..............Hope Brown
Joel Whitaker...............Luke Cosgrove
Lem Lefferts.....................G. K. Arthur
Grandmother Whitaker.....Ruby Lafayette
Margaret Whitaker........Eleanor Lawson
Horace Pringle....................King Zany

A picture that can be exploited by the use of the claim there are a large number of stars in it. While the players proper are not well known, at some time or other for a moment or two in the picture the majority of the better known stars of filmdom are introduced. The list includes:

Cecil B. DeMille	Pola Negri
Wm. S. Hart	Jack Holt
Walter Hiers	Jacqueline Logan
May McAvoy	Nita Naldi
Charles de Roche	Wm. de Mille
Owen Moore	Jack Pickford
Baby Peggy	Lloyd Hamilton
Viola Dana	Will Rogers
Anna Q. Nilsson	T. Roy Barnes
Thomas Meighan	Agnes Ayres
Betty Compson	Lila Lee
Leatrice Joy	Lois Wilson
Theo. Kosloff	Noah Beery
George Fawcett	Alf. E. Green
Bryan Washburn	Anita Stewart
Hope Hampton	Ben Turpin
Eileen Percy	J. W. Kerrigan
Bull Montana	Ford Sterling

The story is cleverly conceived. It concerns a pretty girl in a small town who thinks that she should be in the movies and who is urged by her friend to enter. She is of a poor family and has an ailing grandfather. Using the need of a change of air for her grandfather, she visits Hollywood on funds provided by the sale of the lot on which the family home has just burned, a donation of the grandmother, who is certain the girl will succeed.

Having nothing but beauty in her favor, she cannot get a chance; but the grandfather, being a type, is practically forced into film work by runners for producers. He takes on airs, is an honored guest at the homes of the stars, while the girl who expected to prove a sensation in pictures depends upon him for her living.

The old chap becomes so gay the girl writes home without making her letter plain. The grandmother and an old maid of the family rush to Hollywood on money the old fellow sent home. They are both nabbed as types and get into pictures. The girl finally marries, and her twins are commandeered for pictures. Every one connected with her gets into pictures but she, herself.

It is an amusing idea, good comedy, and the fact that the inside life of Hollywood is shown with many notable stars appearing for a moment makes it a capital draw. Every one will want to see it.

The girl meets Mary Pickford, to whom she delivers a dress. Mary calls Doug Fairbanks out that the girl may meet him. Other stars appear equally as briefly, but they appear.

Loop.

THE 11TH HOUR

A Lincoln J. Carter melodrama, adapted for the screen by Louis Sherwin and directed by Bernard J. Durning. Shirley Mason and Charles Jones featured. Presented by William Fox at a special showing at the 44th Street theatre, New York, July 20, 1923. Running time, 65 minutes.

Barbara Hackett..............Shirley Mason
Brick McDonald..............Charles Jones
Herbert Glenville.............Richard Tucker
Prince Stefan de Bernie..........Alan Hale
Dick Manley...................Walter McGrail
Estelle Hackett..................June Elvidge
Submarine Commander.........Fred Kelsey
Mordecai Newman.........Nigel de Brulier

A red-hot, rip-snorting melodrama that is going to pull the audiences right out of their seats. It is a picture that has everything in the way of thrills in it except the kitchen stove. In fact, it is a serial jammed into five reels, and while it may not have everything that "The Fast Mail" had it is there with punch after punch that is going to delight the average picture audience. One has to hand it to Lincoln J. Carter when he sets out to thrill, for he writes every twist and turn possible into his works. On the screen these days they can do so much more with one of his real mellow mellers than they could on the stage that the screen versions of his works have the punch plus.

"The Eleventh Hour" is one of those mystery thrillers with the heroine a girl whose guardian-uncle has squandered her fortune and who doesn't know it. The uncle is in the hands of the heavy, who wants to marry his ward, and the two are in a plot to evolve the most powerful explosive in history. A mad prince learns of their object and is aware of the fact that they have finally solved the question, and he plans to seize the formula. He starts his secret society members after the formula.

He has a submarine, a secret wireless cabinet and all the other aids that a first-class villain should have. In his employ as commander of his forces he has a sturdy young fellow who, after traveling through the greater part of the story in the guise of a heavy, finally emerges as the hero and happens to be a member of the Secret Service.

At the finish he rescues the girl from the clutches of the villain and all ends happily.

In addition to the submarine there are aeroplanes, fast motor boats, automobile chases, a den of lions and trap doors galore to furnish thrills and the manner in which the story is worked out certainly supplies all that could be asked in the way of punches.

Shirley Mason is the youthful heroine that takes a number of chances, and Charles "Buck" Jones is the athletic hero who pulls all the stunt stuff imaginable.

Bernard Durning, who directed the picture, made it a wizz-bang for speed. This is one of those affairs that you don't want to look at if you have high blood pressure, but audiences are just about going to eat it up.

Fred.

LAWFUL LARCENY

Allan Dwan production. Presented by Adolph Zukor. Adapted from the play by Samuel Shipman by John Lynch. Featuring Nita Naldi, Hope Hampton, Conrad Nagel and Lew Cody. Directed by Allan Dwan. Shown at the Rivoli, New York, week July 22. Running time, 59 minutes.

Marion Dorsey..............Hope Hampton
Andrew Dorsey...............Conrad Nagel
Vivian Hepburn.....................Nita Naldi
Guy Tarlow...........................Lew Cody
Sonny Dorsey................Russell Griffin

Here is a whale of a picture for entertainment purposes. The story is a high-class society melodrama taken from the Samuel Shipman play in which Lowell Sherman appeared last season and which is serving the A. H. Woods star as a vaudeville vehicle for the summer.

In the screen version much has been added to the original which lends a delightful comedy relief. Lew Cody's playing of Tarlow is in itself a work of art and adds tremendously to the screen value. Incidentally this picture again shows Allan Dwan back in his directorial stride at his best. As a picture "Lawful Larceny" is sure-fire for any type of audience in any type of house from the highest to the lowest.

The featuring of four names—Nita Naldi, Hope Hampton, Lew Cody and Conrad Nagel—gives the picture more value at the box office for the exhibitor. The wise theatre men will also take advantage of the fact that Gilda Gray is in the production with her famous South Sea Island dance that she does in the current "Follies" and make advertising capital out of it.

The story is that of a wealthy young husband who is left in New York to amuse himself while his wife is abroad. He falls into the clutches of a heavy society vamp who is running what is on the surface a society club, which in reality is nothing but a crooked gambling house, and who has for her silent partner a society man about town who has a good name but is short on dough. The two manage to "take" the young husband for all that he has and then in addition get him to sign a note for $100,000 on his firm.

That is the condition of affairs when the wife returns and obtains a confession from her husband. She then lays plans for the recovery of the money and the note. She starts out by vamping the society steerer and finally by using a cheating cheaters idea manages to attain her object.

Miss Hampton plays the wife, with the soft focus lens in use for every one of her close-ups. Miss Naldi was the heavy vamp to perfection, and she looked wonderfully well in the prolog in a Cleopatra role. Mr. Nagel was all that could be asked as the young husband, but the honors of the picture must be handed to Mr. Cody for his playing of the part that Sherman originally created on the stage. He walked away with the picture.

The director deserves credit for getting all of the punches possible and never permitting the story to lag for an instant.

Fred.

THREE WISE FOOLS

Goldwyn production, directed by King Vidor, from the stage play by Austin Strong. Running time, 78 minutes. Seen at Capitol.

Findley.........................Claude Gillingwater
Rena Fairchild...........Eleanor Boardman
Sydney Fairchild........Eleanor Boardman
Hon. James Trumbull....William H. Crane
Dr. Gaunt.............................Alec Francis
John Crawshay.................John Sainpolis
Benny the Duck...............Brinsley Shaw
Gray.................................Fred Esmelton
Gordon..............................William Haines
Douglas...........................Lucien Littlefield
Mickey..................................ZaSu Pitts
Saunders...........................Martha Mattox
Poole..................................Fred J. Butler
Clancy............................Charles Hickman
Young Findley...............Craig Biddle, Jr.
Young Trumbull..............Creighton Hale
Young Gaunt...............Raymond Hatton

There have been squawks innumerable—and many bitterly just—of screen "versions" that perverted and distorted the brain-children of playwrights. But Austin Strong should say a prayer of thanksgiving to the folks who executed his "Three Wise Fools" in the silent form, for they have caught all his subtleties, preserved all the finesse of his amiable tale, and added to it those possibilities of distance, outdoors and rapid shifts of locale that only the films can afford.

For fidelity to an original, the Vidor production is a model. One who sees the picture at the Capitol has seen the play as done by John Golden. But he who has only seen the play has not seen "Three Wise Fools" until after witnessing the picture. That is the apotheosis of screen adaptation.

It makes an acceptable, pleasing feature, not thrilling and not even important. But it is clean, humorous, romantic, sane, plausible and capable of holding continuous concentration without boring or giving the onlooker any creeps or jumps. It is, for the main, a "parlor" story. The brief flashes afar into the underworld alleys, the counter-atmosphere of the story, are no more than relief.

The love portions, too, are daringly light. And the kiss between the youngsters takes place half-way along instead of being tortuously preserved for the tag, as is the orthodox method, against which few directors dare rebel. The interest is not in any measure ruptured or even spotted thereby.

The photography is of the modern type of the best—sharp, clear and fine. The settings are mainly devoted to the interior of the home of three old gentlemen who loved the one girl, with an acre of living room and a great shot upstage to a staircase that permits of plenty of running up and down without getting outside the focus. The direction is simple, straightforward and human. For a production that cost comparatively little, as costs are reckoned in this prodigal age, the entire effect is rich and impressive.

In the acting Eleanor Boardman easily stands forth, with Claude Gillingwater as one of the trio of monkey-glandless Romeos taking next honors. William H. Crane, the unctuous veteran, is prominent but not brilliant. ZaSu Pitts has the merest sort of a meaningless bit, as have Creighton Hale and Craig Biddle, Jr. (the last of these the Philadelphia "scion" who is breaking in), and these interesting personalities go for incidentals. William Haines makes a colorless young hero.

"Three Wise Fools" will do anywhere. It is good enough to play up, as it will please and entertain, and it should be well within the price of the average exhibitor for a program feature on the apparent economy of the investment; not that it is done cheaply, but it is done as well as it could be done, and still finds no occasion for lavish outlay.

For a sound, sweet picture that will never hit anyone hard but should react on many people pleasantly, it is a success. *Lait.*

MIND OVER MOTOR

Los Angeles, July 25.

"Mind Over Motor," produced and directed by Ward Lascelles, starring Trixie Friganza. Distributed by Principal Pictures Corporation. Running time, 60 minutes. Hill Street, Los Angeles.

This Mary Roberts Rinehart story, published in "Saturday Evening Post" as "Tish" and scenarized by H. Landers Jackson, proved a happy selection for Trixie Friganza's screen debut. Letitia Carberry, also known as Tish, fits into the story like a glove.

Miss Friganza should encourage the vaudeville star to film more of Miss Rinehart's stories.

The continuity and the direction are not so good and the lighting in spots is also off, with the cast, though not holding any other names of note, still is good. Just why Tish was not incorporated in the title is not clear, as the present title is of little consequence.

The story evolves Larry Steers as Ellis, fake race promoter, inducing Tish to innocently finance a fake motor race in which three of the drivers are fixed. The fourth, Ralph Graves as Jasper McCutcheon, is in love with Clara Horton as Bettina Bailey, and enters the contest, but near the finish of the race is pocketed and injured.

Tish, realizing unless the race is won she would be arrested for conspiracy, jumps into the racing car and wins.

Tish taking the wheel is the punch and draws applause.

Bennett Copen and Landers Jacksons supplied good laughing titles.

Others in the cast are Carolyn Rankin, Ruth Hanford, Grace Gordon, George Guyton, Pietro Sosso, with Eddie Hearne acting as official starter.

The picture has many redeeming features and is above the usual conventional program features. *Josephs.*

THE PURPLE HIGHWAY

Kenma production released by Paramount. From the play "Dear Me," by Luther Reed and Hale Hamilton, adapted by Rufus Steele. Star, Madge Kennedy. Directed by Henry Kolker. Running time, 69 minutes. At the Rialto, week of July 22.

April Blair..................Madge Kennedy
Edgar Prentice (Edgar Craig)...Monte Blue
Dudley Quail...............Vincent Coleman
Joe Renard.............Pedro de Cordoba
Mrs. Carney.................Emily Fitzroy
Mr. Quail.................Wm. H. Tooker
Mrs. Quail...............Winifred Harris

Manny Bean................Dore Davidson
Shakespeare Jones........John W. Jenkins
Mr. Ogilvie...................Charles Kent

Just a light breezy story of "two fellows and a girl," with the right fellow winning out is the substance of this feature, judiciously released for late summer or early fall production, prior to the time more composite and impressive subjects are placed on view.

Madge Kennedy is introduced as a slavey and goes along until achieving success as a musical comedy star. The burden is placed on Miss Kennedy, who struggles, in some instances against the odds of negligible direction, to do the best she can toward making the picture entertaining.

The balance of credit should go to the title writer.

The cast seems to move in a listless, nonchalant manner, taking or being given little opportunity to register in what should be dramatic and comedy moments. Blue, opposite Miss Kennedy, straggles through as though just part of the usual day's routine. Vincent Coleman, as the indulgent son of rich parents, desirous of winning the prima donna, gives a similar colorless interpretation. Dore Davidson, as the theatrical manager and producer, strives to be realistic, but appeared held in "leash" to enable Blue to stand out. Davidson's showing is greatly enhanced by the title speeches he makes.

The story tells of the establishment of a home by a millionaire for literary and artistic failures to commemorate the failure of his son, who left home to become a playwright. The entire duty of the inmates of the home is to eat, sleep and recreate. Most of the latter they get through the good nature of April Blair, daughter of a musical genius, who had left her homeless, and to the mercies of Mrs. Carney, the housekeeper, who installed her as maid of all duties.

The majority of the shots are indoors, with an endeavor made to be spectacular in a ballroom scene, where a flying ballet is used, and in a sunken garden, where a pageant is enacted, after which a pyrotechnic display blazes out the name of the girl.

The theatre scene is cheaply staged, with just a few chorus girls used.

As the picture appears now it can be placed in the group of fair program releases, with nothing to recommend it outside of the name of Kennedy.

OUT OF LUCK

Universal feature starring Charles ("Hoot") Gibson, supported by Laura La Plante. Story and scenario by Edward Sedgwick. Projection time, 62 minutes. At the Broadway, New York, July 23.

Another light comedy with melodramatic trimmings such as have furnished Gibson with his best vehicles. In this case, although the story is western in its background, there is no cowboy-riding stuff. Oddly enough the best of the material has Gibson as a gob, struggling laughably with navy discipline. There are some good laughs here, although they do rather overplay such business as the hero struggling to walk a boom and get himself stowed in a sleeping hammock.

From the plains to the deep sea is a novelty, and here it works out for capital effects. Gibson is always likable, especially in this release, which shows him at his breezy best. This star has conferred a great service to the fan public in putting the josh into westerns, even if he has killed the locale for straight heroics.

The combination of melodrama and nonsense is well done. Comedy has the upper hand; instead of the old method of putting the emphasis on the straight stuff and introducing comedy by way of relief it's the other way round. The comedy is the backbone of the story and the melo-

drama insinuated for change of pace.

Hoot is a regular cowboy, but even in that capacity he never gets a leg over a horse. Instead he rides a bicycle to keep tryst with his sweetheart. Nellie is willing, and just as they become betrothed Nellie's papa, the bully of the community, enters and knocks the interloper cold for daring to kiss the girl. He is about to commit further assault and battery upon the suitor when Hoot picks up the poker and lays him out. Thinking he has killed the old man, Hoot beats it by way of the freight route to the nearest seaport.

The eating is not so good, and starvation and luck finally bring him to a naval recruiting station, where he is regularly introduced to the trick pants and the rest of the paraphernalia. Meanwhile Nellie's father recovers and, recognizing that the mixup was all his own fault, advertises for Hoot to return. There is a bit here—detailing Hoot's ingenuous explanation to the petty officer that he has resigned and is going home—that is as full of laughs as a Harold Lloyd gag. Instead Hoot is shipped off to sea.

There is capital stuff aboard a real man-o'-war. Hoot is so sick they send him to the bav. There he meets up with a crazy seaman, whose bug is that he must murder the captain. Meanwhile Nellie has left the old place to live for a while with her rich aunt. Hoot saves the captain's life and is made a special messenger for the skipper by way of reward. Returning to port the crazy seaman escapes, while the captain takes Hoot home with him.

Crazy seaman makes tracks for the captain's home, and it turns out that the captain's wife is none other than Nellie's aunt, but Hoot doesn't know it yet. The meeting is brought about when Hoot discovers the murderous maniac in the house and again save his skipper's life. That leads to the happy clinch.

Throughout the joke is always on the hero, which makes it all the more amusing to fans fed up on stilted screen actors. Capital five reels of solid amusement. At the Broadway the end of the picture brought a burst of applause seldom heard in a picture house. *Rush.*

LEONARD—TENDLER

Shown at B. S. Moss' Broadway July 25. Produced by Cromwell A. C., Inc. Direction Leon D. Britton. Released through Penscr Productions. Length, 30 minutes.

The Leonard-Tendler fight pictures at the Broadway are productions of the 15-round championship bout staged July 23 at the Yankee Stadium, in which Leonard outpointed Tendler and retained his title.

The pictures are the best fight shots ever seen around New York. The entire 15 rounds are shown, as well as some interesting preliminary shots of the Leonard and Tendler camps.

No views of the huge throng were shown, due to the late hour. This helped the film rather than elsewise, confining it to actual fighting, which is what the mob at the Broadway wanted to see.

Slow motion shots of two rounds were shown in rounds 12 and 13. The pictures also refute the claim that Tendler went down in one round from a punch. It can be plainly seen that Tendler missed a swing and went down from loss of balance.

The pictures will interest every one, but they don't show the superiority of Leonard as the actual contest warranted on account of the angle shot from. Many of Leonard's punishing body blows and uppercuts are missed on account of the speed of the camera. This occurs also when one fighter has his back to the camera.

The one-minute rest periods between rounds are supplanted by captions commenting upon the fight and the crowd, all well written and

interesting. Sidelights of the fight are shown in shots of the scribes working in the press stands, Damon Runyon being prominent. A battle royal staged at Leonard's camp for charity was interesting. A flock of kids whaling away at each other is then shown with slow motion effect. Leonard's sportsmanship in allowing Tendler to recover his balance after missing punches and diving into the ropes is shown on several occasions.

The pictures should be a draw, for the fight itself was one of the most interesting contests ever staged between lightweights and one that lends itself to photographic reproduction admirably. *Con.*

TRILBY

Richard Walton Tully presents a new screen version of George Du Maurier's famous novel, starring a new French star, Andree Lafayette. Directed by James Young. Distributed by First National. Projection time, 82 minutes. Projection room July 20.

Trilby.....................Andree Lafayette
Svengali..............Arthur Edmund Carew
The Laird................Wilfred Lucas
Zouzou...................Maurice Cannon
Durien......................Gordon Mullen
Mme. Vinard..............Martha Franklin
Rev. Bagot...............Gilbert Clayton
Impresario...............Edward Kimball
Little Billee................Creighton Hale
Taffy.......................Philo McCullough
Gecko...................Francis McDonald
Dodor........................Max Constant
Miss Bagot.............Gertrude Olmstead
Mrs. Bagot.............Evelyn Sherman
Laundress....................Rose Dione
Jeannot.................Robert De Vilbiss

Richard Walton Tully has filmed an especially satisfying version of "Trilby," notable in respect to the playing of two roles—Mlle. Lafayette and the Svengali of Arthur Edmund Carew. It must have taken a good deal of courage to make the essay, for "Trilby" was not written for the screen. It has high dramatic qualities, but they depend intimately upon mood and atmosphere in a peculiar degree.

This production is appealing because it does get over something of the color and shading of the original, a background of picturesque studio life in Paris of the 80's, a far more delicate thing to manage than the mere presentation of the narrative.

The original has been treated reverently, although changes were unavoidable. The delightful Christmas party is filmed with a good deal of agreeable detail, but it is here that Bagot and Little Billee's mamma break into Trilby's romance instead of later on. The picture is particularly generous in the picturizing of small incidents. Very little of the material has been elided—the incident of Little Billee's sketch of Trilby's foot, Gecko's fight with Svengali, Trilby's job as "blanchisseuse de fin," etc. The life and soul of the story lies largely in these side lights, and the screen version takes life and color from their use.

The picture appears to have been made principally on this side, although there are a number of shots taken in Paris and matched up here. Generally the work has been well done. There are views from the studio of the Three Musketeers of the Brush, with the city in the background. For these the placing of the American characters by way of foreground shots is skillful and convincing. The big scene of Svengali's death was done in the studio, of course, but real bits of the actual Circue de Paris, with an enthusiastic audience in appropriate business, gave the incident immense force.

The screen version holds to the original ending. A manufactured happy ending would have been a crime, and although perhaps the death of the heroine is not the best ending for a picture, it was here inevitable.

Andree Lafayette is an ideal

Trilby in face and figure. She is best in the comedy passages, such as the camaraderie with Taffy and the Laird, and she has a knack for sentimental scenes, but her management of the more emotional moments was not so convincing. The scene where Little Billee finds her posing in the altogether before the art class (neatly and discreetly done as far as suggesting without revealing too much of the girl's undraped figure) was not very strongly acted. But the lighter scenes are delightful. Creighton Hale's Little Billee is pale and indefinite, and Wilfred Lucas, smothered in beard, is not very impressive as the Laird. Philo McCullough was uneven as Taffy. But the performance of Carew as the sinister Svengali is ample compensation for the deficiencies of the others. It is a great bit of playing. *Rush.*

SAWDUST

Circus story by Courtney Riley Cooper, featuring Gladys Walton. Universal production, directed by Jack Conway. Half a double feature bill at Loew's New York June 19. Runs about 60 minutes.

Nita Moore (Janice Wentworth)........ Gladys Walton
Phillip........................Niles Welch
"Bull" Gifford..............Frank Brownlee

There's a certain basic similarity between "Sawdust" and a recently released Paramount, "Soul of the Beast," that is bound to create comment from fans who see both. Both are circus stories and both yarns revolve about a young circus performer who tires of the big-top existence and runs away from the circus.

This general similarity becomes specific when the situation of the "Soul of the Beast" tale, which has the "heavy" in the guise of the heroine's stepfather, is paralleled in "Sawdust," the villain being the heroine's foster-father. Thereafter both are worked out differently. Doubtlessly this is just one of those coincidences that has been known to occur in any creative work, for C. Gardner Sullivan ("Soul of the Beast" author) does not have to borrow from the popular Courtney Riley Cooper, and vice versa. However, when "Sawdust" plays the New York on Tuesday and "Soul of the Beast" is boldly displayed and heralded with a replica of an elephant in front of the theatre as the coming Sunday-Monday's attraction, the regular patrons are bound to comment because of the brief interim between the two.

The circus is labeled Delmar's Combined Shows and is playing a southern town. Nita Moore's parents having died in a circus wreck, she is following the family tradition under the brutal, though none the less effective, guidance of "Bull" Gifford, her foster-father, who is ringmaster. The girl is a feature of the circus, and, in addition, has her worries in keeping two booze-fighting clowns out of the ringmaster's sight to avoid immediate dismissal. During one of the clown Tip's "jags" Nita dons the clown's costume for the emergency, which culminates in her meeting Phillip, a young local attorney, who was seeking the show manager to adjust an irate client's claim of having his property unlawfully plastered by bill "snipers."

Colonel and Mrs. Wentworth are introduced as regular patrons of every incoming circus or carnival, hoping to find their daughter, who, the parents believe, had been kidnapped by show people. This is the cue for the friendly, short-changing ticket seller to frame Nita as the Wentworths' long-lost daughter. Nita, tired of it all and wanting a home, acquiesces in the subterfuge and makes the old couple truly happy for a while, assuming the name of Janice Wentworth.

The advent of another spring season and the circus brings back "Bull" Gifford, who has been hunting for his runaway foster-daughter ever since her escape. Rather than return, Janice, after confessing to Colonel Wentworth that she is really not his daughter, attempts suicide via the neighboring creek, with Phillip effecting the rescue. "Bull" Gifford is shown being chased off the premises by the former clown "Tip," now one of the Wentworths' gardeners. It is not made clear why Gifford so calmly acquiesces to a departure when at first he was intent on getting Nita back under the big top.

There's plenty of circus atmosphere included with "shots" of the performers, although the "audience" is depicted only as a handful of extras in one section of the mammoth tent. The story progresses easily and smoothly, and is passably pleasing summer entertainment. It was coupled here with a rather good Fox program release, both features holding up.

The star is consistent in her characterization, the hoyden in her, a heritage of the circus rearing, becoming manifest in her occasional lapses, such as using her boudoir chandelier for trapeze purposes, the four-poster bed for acrobatics and the bedspring for flip-flops. Niles Welch has few opportunities because of the story limitations, but does his bit rather well. Brownlee was a villainous "heavy" and made the role vivid.

The picture should hold up alone in the small daily-change houses. *Abel.*

THE FOG

Max Graf production released through Loew-Metro. Adapted by H. H. Van Loan from William Dudley Pelley's story. Scenario prepared by Winifred Dunn. Directed by Paul Powell; photography by John R. Arnold. Runs about an hour. At Loew's State, New York, in conjunction with Loew vaudeville July 23-25. The cast:

Madelaine Theddon.........Mildred Harris
Millie Richards............Louise Fazenda
Mrs. Theddon..............Louise Dresser
Edith Forge...............Marjorie Prevost
Carol Gardner.......................Ann May
Mrs. Forge...................Ethel Wales
Nathan Forge...............Cullen Landis
Jonathan Forge...............Ralph Lewis
Si Plumb......................David Butler
Caleb Gridley................Frank Currier
Gordon Ruggles...........Edward Phillips

Several valuable box office names included among the cast as witness above and they should mean something at the gate. The interpretation is consistently intelligent and the direction rather good. Yet somehow the sum total does not ring true. The basic genesis of it, as transferred to the screen, presents a rather flimsy groundwork. It may be this is one of those unusual instances of too much story. A recounting of the plot details this, but at the same time it would ordinarily tend to belie the assumption that the story was to blame. Possibly what it lacked was a master's hand in wielding the puppets. A sneaking idea persists that if a Griffith had manipulated the mechanics the story might have resulted in a truly unusual picture. There is enough character material to allow for some unusual interpretations. As it is, it's a passably fair production, mildly interesting when one is inclined to loll back and let the screen have its hour of flickering and when it's all shown and done with, one reflects and concludes what a flimsy idea to base a romance on.

It may be that having become inured with saccharine romanticism this deviation from the ideal does not jibe with one's expectation. But again it is refuted when it is considered that originality is also appreciated and approved.

The action is set in Paris, Vermont. Jonathan Forge, a narrow-minded bigot who horsewhips his juvenile offspring, Nathan, for mingling with girls at a harmless children's picnic is introduced. Nathan, grown up and harboring a secret desire to write, has been lost in an ideal of "a girl without a name" who from her carriage sympathized years ago with the lad who was being cuffed and kicked down the road by an outraged father. On this abstract "girl without a name" idea is built a romance starting with the local gazette printing a poem of that title by Nathaniel Forge. The hick town paper seemingly has a wide circulation for in a distant girls' finishing school is the young lady who, as a girl, was so sympathetic to the then young Nathan. Nathan is shown working in a tannery; winning the interest of dour old Caleb, the proprietor; becoming the part owner of a paper box factory; losing out with a girl and marrying one of the shop girls who on the next day after the marriage is not averse to receiving a former suitor in her home in her husband's absence; the ensuing divorce; the hunt for the "girl without a name" and the final finding of her in Siberia during the war where she is in the service as a Red Cross nurse and he as a private. That covers considerable territory and only briefly touches on the incidental sub-plots—and there is much of that too.

The casting was really high grade. Cullen Landis as Nathan, was sincere and Mildred Harris was a sympathetic feminine lead. Louise Fazenda lent some comedy interest and David Butler, who looked like a "comer" a couple of years back, only figured with a small bit. Ralph Lewis as the father was superb. *Abel.*

THE VICTOR

Universal production and release. Directed by Edward Laemmle from Gerald Beaumont's fight story, "Two Bells for Pegasus," retitled as above for the screen. Scenario by E. Richard Schayer. Herbert Rawlinson starred. Half of a doubleheader at Loew's New York theatre, New York, July 24. Running time approximately 60 minutes. The principal players as caught from the screen are:

Hon. Cecil Fitzhugh Warring.......... Herbert Rawlinson
Teddy Walters............Dorothy Manners
Esther.........................Esther Ralston
"Porky" Schaup.............Eddie Gribbon

Universal seems to have a penchant for sporting stories, and probably the success of H. C. Witwer's "Leather Pushers" series has determined a policy of doing more of this sort of work. The twin reel series has been generally popular, and already U. has released a full-length feature with a baseball theme as the central motive. This is a ring yarn again, and from the typewriter of one of the best of present-day sports story authors, Gerald Beaumont.

If Beaumont's series of racing, ring and other athletic yarns have not been garnered by some producer they have been overlooking a sure-fire bet. Beaumont, as an ink-slinger who knows the sport proposition from the middle out and has the knack of mixing the realism with genuine literary ability, is in the late Charles E. Van Loan class. He has been among the demand writers in the "Red Book" and similar type periodicals for years, and this story probably first saw publication there.

The romantic and society interest is thrust prominently to the fore to relieve the boxing scenes for the punches, but the latter are by no means relegated to the background. They merely add novelty to the idea of a scion of Lord Cecil Fitzhugh Warring essaying the "leather pusher" game as a profession.

The younger Warring (Herbert Rawlinson), despite the flutter he is heralded as having created in the American marriage market, is shown flat broke, despite his immaculate attire of cutaway, silk topper and swagger stick. Similarly situated is Teddy Walters, actress (Dorothy Manners), who is breakfasting sumptuously in the park on 10 cents' worth of doughnuts. The couple realize each other's financial predicament, and for about a reel and a half the suave but penniless peer is shown "conning" his and the girl's way through a fashionable hostelry.

Finally forced to look for a "position," he cannot even get a "job," and accepts employment as waiter in a cheap eatery. There he spoofs "Porky" Schaup, a pugilist, who is a regular patron of the dining place. Porky takes offense and also the k. o. when the lord-waiter plants a perfect haymaker on the pug's button.

That starts Warring's ring career and ends the contemplated marriage of a chewing-gum king's daughter to the impecunious lordling. Esther could stand for anything but a common leather pusher. Warring determines to quit the game, but accepts a final match with the same "Porky" for the middleweight title, and annexes it after a thrilling three rounds. He formally proposes to Teddy, and everything ends happily.

Rawlinson did some exceptionally good work in and out of the ring, and particularly in the squared circle stood for some realistic punishment, also giving more than a fair share in return.

The picture should hold up alone in the daily change houses, although it was half of a double bill here. *Abel.*

YOUTHFUL CHEATERS

Glenn Hunter starred in this Film Guild production released through Hodkinson. Frank Tuttle directed from Townsend Martin's story. Fred Waller, Jr., credited for photography and general supervision. Ran an hour as half of a double feature bill at Loew's New York theatre, New York, July 24.

"Youthful Cheaters" as a title suggests its flapper theme, a rather worn-out thesis at this late date, but always more or less interesting. The exposition in this instance would have the audience believe that life on a Long Island estate is a continuous marathon of careless abandon, carnival, revelry, party and insouciance rolled into one, interspersed with not a little indulgence in intoxicants. And the young folk hardly over 25 years of age on an average!

The action is first introduced with a flash of MacDonalds, father and son, in the far east, bringing medical relief to the heathen tropical natives. It shifts immediately to the Long Island district, where the vessel has cast anchor in the sound. Edmund MacDonald has contracted what later develops to be malaria (or was it cholera?) and his son Tad (Glenn Hunter) has arranged for the periodical visits of a physician, who comes over in a rowboat.

Martha Mansfield, the female lead as Lois, is shown in the midst of a bacchanalian lawn revel which winds up in her determination to take a spin in the motor launch. She invites herself onto the MacDonald schooner and is marooned for a number of days when the visiting medico determines to quarantine the vessel. Her life on shipboard permits for the romantic development.

Tad is invited to Lois's home and the few weeks on shore metamorphoses him from a barefooted man to a syncopating, self-indulgent cake-eater. Lois and Tad become engaged but seem not to take it very seriously. MacDonald, Sr., eventually enters the scene and brings the youth to his realization. Lois, the pleasure-loving, has expressed her unwillingness to confine herself to a shipboard existence with her betrothed, but contributory circumstances in which the sleek "heavy" and one of his former amours figured also in the means of bringing out the stern stuff in her and it all ends happily.

There was too much of the party stuff, indoors and out, but probably made necessary by the meagerness of the basic plot. Stripped of all the fol-de-rol, the story could be packed into two or three reels easily.

Hunter's work was also convincing, as was that of the actor personating his father (name not caught from screen). Miss Mansfield's characterization was uncertain and undefined and accordingly the sympathies were not always centered in her favor. The chap doing the heavy sufficed, but also did not ring true. His sleek artificiality cried out that in real life there ain't no such animal.

In the small daily change houses the picture could hold up by itself, although for double feature purposes it shouldn't miss. Chiefly commending the production is the fact it is consistently diverting. *Abel.*

THE EMPTY CRADLE

Burton King production, presented by Truart, with Mary Alden and Harry T. Morey featured. Adapted from the story entitled "Cheating Wives." Directed by Burton King. Shown at Fox's Academy of Music, New York, June 17-20, on double feature bill. Time, 67 minutes.

John Larkin.................Harry T. Morey
Alice Larkin................Mary Alden
Buddy Larkin...............Mickey Bennett
Frankie Larkin.............Edward Quinn
Samantha Adams............Marcia Harris
Ethel Lewis...............Madelon La Varne
Robert Lewis...............Colt Albertson
Lawyer.....................Lew Storm
Martha Blake...............Rica Allen
Louise "Lewis".............Helen Rowland

The idea behind the original title is that wives who fail to bear children to their husbands are cheating the latter out of their just fruits of married life.

Perhaps "Cheating Wives," if it could have passed the censors, would have been a better box-office title for this picture than "The Empty Cradle."

The picture is one of those rather wishy-washy melodramatic affairs that seem to please the majority of the picture house audiences. This picture is no better nor worse than hundreds of others that come along every year and a great many of which play pre-release runs on Broadway. Perhaps with the "Cheating Wives" title this might have had a chance on Broadway, too.

It is the story of a small town, where the rich live on the Hill and the middle class of workers on "the road." Those on the Hill are the social elect and the mentors of the town. Those on the Road are the drudges and the wage-earners, who make it possible for the other half to live on the Hill. Mary Alden is of the Hill set, but she falls in love with Harry T. Morey as John Larkin, a "poor but honest blacksmith" of the Road. They marry, and Alice Larkin is cast out by her relatives on the Hill. Through years of poverty and want she remains happy in her three children—two boys and a baby girl.

The baby girl is the punch. Christmas comes and there is no Santa Claus for the Larkin home; but at the same time a lawyer approaches Alice Larkin and makes a proposition that he will give her $50,000 for her baby and assure her that it will have a home of plenty and be educated as a lady. Seemingly she accepts the offer. The girl baby is taken into the home of the Lewis family. Here the wife has lost her husband's affection because she has not brought a family into the world.

Robert Lewis, incidentally, was a great admirer of Alice before she left the Hill. His wife is not only planning to win him back with a child, but at the same time figures to be avenged on the woman she has always looked upon as a rival. The $50,000 offer for the child is made at the time when John Larkin has been blinded while experimenting with an invention, and the wife seemingly accepts to get a specialist to restore his eyesight. When he has recovered he is shown as a jealous husband, fearing his wife's association with the Lewises as a cover for Lewis to again become friendly with her, and in a rage he fires a shot at Lewis, which strikes the child that the latter is holding in his arms.

Right here is the weakest part. The mother awakes and finds that it is all a dream, but at the same moment her wealthy aunt walks in on the scene with a lot of Christmas presents for the kids, and all is jake for the finish.

It's a lot of old-fashioned hoak, with that dream-ending thing having been done to death time and again; but after it is all over it's no worse than others have done it. Miss Alden gives a corking performance as the wife, and Morey is the "true but honest" type to perfection. The kiddies are the best of the picture. *Fred.*

SPIDER AND THE ROSE

Principal Pictures present "The Spider and the Rose," a B. F. Zeidman production from the story by Gerald C. Duffy, directed by John McDermott. Shown at Proctor's 23d St., New York, June 25-27, in conjunction with vaudeville. Time, 85 minutes.

Paula........................Alice Lake
Don Marcello.............Richard Headrick
Don Marcello.............Gaston Glass
The Governor............Joseph J. Dowling
Mendoza..................Robert McKim
Maitre Renaud............Noah Beery
The Secretary.............Otis Harlan

Seven reels are devoted in telling the story of an uprising against tyranny in California when Mexico governed the district. Just why all of the footage was necessary is a question. The story could have been told more briefly and with more satisfying results. It has been done in one way or another in pictures before and in most cases more convincingly than here.

It is apparent the producer realizing he had recruited a cast of considerable strength determined to make an attempt to create a big picture. He did not take into consideration the story. It is such a simple tale told in so many ways before it could hardly be expected to prove engrossing when drawn out to seven reels. As it stands the production lacks interest due to its length. The story twists and turns losing interest with every wiggle.

Alice Lake and Gaston Glass head the cast. The Glass role far outdistances that of Miss Lake's. The picture is built around his character with the Lake role insignificant in comparison. Glass goes in for some Fairbanks acrobatics which he accomplishes with but a fair degree of success. There is no reality to this work, Glass apparently lacking the grace for this style of acting. Some of the supposedly sensational scenes of the production in which he is the leading figure are ridiculous. Robert McKim comes in for some generally good all around work in a villain role. His work adds much to the worthwhile side of the feature with Noah Beery and Otis Harlan displaying their usual ability in roles of less importance. Joseph J. Dowling handles a weak part acceptably.

In the production end the picture contains all of the necessary atmosphere for a Spanish tale of this order. The country in which the picture was taken undoubtedly is the same as the locale for the story. The direction in all probability experienced little difficulty in picking locations. The studio work is of minor importance.

The story centers around Don Marcello, the son of the Mexican governor of California. The governor through the efforts of Mendoza, a double-crosser in everything he attempts, rules with an iron rod. The people are planning to fight the oppression when the son joins their ranks. His love for a girl forces him to tell her of the plans. She unintentionally lets the secret out which results in the arrest of the conspirators. From then on it is one battle after another with Mendoza appointed governor through trickery. The youth turns the tables by releasing the prisoners from jail after he had been thrown from a cliff and been thought dead. With the return of their leaders the people gain control of the situation and the old governor is reinstated and everything is serene with the love angle also brought to happy ending.

Stories of this nature were used for two reelers in the old days. *Hart.*

HOMEWARD BOUND

Paramount feature presented by Adolph Zukor; Thomas Meighan star. Adapted by Jack Cunningham and Paul Sloane from Peter B. Kyne's "The Light to the Leeward." Directed by Ralph Ince. Shown at the Rialto, New York, week July 29. Running time, 74 minutes.

Jim Bedford...............Thomas Meighan
Mary Brent.................Lila Lee
Rufus Brent................Charles Abbe
Rodney....................William T. Carleton
Murphy....................Hugh Cameron
Capt. Svenson.............Gus Weinberg
Mrs. Brannigan......Mary Turner Gordon
Rufus Brent, Jr.............Cyril Ring

This current starring vehicle for Thomas Meighan is far from comparing with the last three or four features turned with this real box office star. Undoubtedly the story was selected because of its possibilities in a "Cappy Ricks" sense, but it doesn't touch that series by a long shot. It is just a fair program picture for Paramount that will undoubtedly pull because Meighan is a favorite, but that is about as far as it will go.

The action is laid in a small Maine seaport and on the high seas. Meighan is the first mate of a tramp freighter, who saves the vessel in the midst of a storm when the captain, who is in his cups, turns yellow and wants to abandon ship. When the freighter gets in the captain is himself again and takes all the credit.

The ship owner has purchased a yacht for his daughter, and as a reward assigns the captain to take her out on the first cruise. The mate, who has loved the girl since childhood, forces the captain to resign the assignment and replaces him. The love between the pair develops on the cruise, and when on their return to the home port the father threatens to make the girl take a trip abroad or remain and see her lover thrown into jail for piracy the two elope and marry.

Having purchased a half interest with his wife's father in an old schooner, the mate, now promoted to rank of captain on the schooner, starts on a cruise with the boat, not knowing that the wife has stowed away aboard. Her father gives chase in the yacht, and in a terrific storm at sea both boats are almost wrecked; the schooner, however, saving the yacht. This brings about a happy ending for all concerned.

There is nothing except the storm at sea that really counts, and there is so much of this that it slows up the action and makes the picture drag at times.

Meighan gives his usual perfect performance and Lila Lee is a charming lead opposite him. The balance of the cast has Charles Abbe as the crabbed ship owner and Hugh Cameron in a corking comedy character. *Fred.*

BROADWAY GOLD

Independent comedy-mystery feature starring Elaine Hammerstein. Story by W. Carey Wonderly, adapted by Kathlyn Harris. Directed by Edward Dillon and J. Gordon Cooper. Distributed by Truart Film Corp. Projecting time, 75 minutes. At the Cameo, New York, July 29.

Sunny Duane..........Elaine Hammerstein
Jean Valjean..........Kathlyn Williams
Eugene Durant...........Elliott Dexter
Elinor Calhoun..........Elois Goodale
Cornelius Fellowes.........Richard Wayne
Page Poole...............Harold Goodwin
Jerome Rogers...........Henry Barrows
The Driver..............Marshall Neilan

An interesting picture of many angles. Perhaps it has too much material in it and a clear story thread would make it easier to follow, but as it stands it holds attention with its well sustained suspense. In the first place the tale has the lure of backstage life and people, which always is an asset; it has a good love story and a mystery angle that is puzzling, and, finally, it gives the screen two bits of extraordinarily well played parts, those of Miss Hammerstein as the innocent chorus girl and Kathlyn Williams as Jean, the hard-boiled, sophisticated gold digger.

Jean is a mine of screen laughs

in a part played smoothly and with a good deal of subtlety instead of the crude burlesque that usually goes with the type. There are a few moments when the action threatens to become machine made and the mechanics of it creak, but it is so well done in the direction and staging that its defects do not count against it.

The photography by J. R. Diamond stands out as a perfect sample of the best modern technique and the backgrounds (art direction is credited to Cedric Gibbons) come nearer to creating an illusion of real places than any independent that has come to attention in a long time. They even do a bit of cabaret stuff that looks more real in its bizarre way than is commonly the case. The sets are all of pictorial beauty and there are a number of interiors that achieve an effect of magnificence without overdoing it all. The final scenes, supposed to be in a Long Island country home, are exquisite scenic settings with a house of fine colonial architectural lines and beautiful gardens.

Sunny Duane (Miss Hammerstein) is the innocent newcomer to the chorus, while Jean is the disillusioned chorister who takes the "kid" under her wing. Sunny has a mild affair with a young man of no means, and Jean holds out his gifts of flowers and trinkets, to obtain which he commits forgery. But when the desirable Durant comes along, Jean schemes to throw the couple together.

They meet at a gaudy party, but become separated and a man about town takes Sunny home. They stop at his apartment en route, innocently enough, and while there the man about town is murdered in an adjoining room. Sunny escapes as the police enter the scene of the crime. Meanwhile Durant has been badly injured in an automobile accident. He is anxious that his fortune shall not fall to worthless relatives, and on what he supposes is his deathbed sends for Sunny, who has caught his amiable fancy. He proposes that they get married merely to cheat the objectionable heirs, and under the mercenary promptings of Jean the ceremony is performed.

The two girls go to Durant's country place, there to await his death and Sunny's prosperous widowhood; but, instead, Durant improves. The police have learned of Sunny's presence in the apartment of the man about town and are expected momentarily, when Sunny's young suitor turns up and is revealed as the real criminal. Sunny is exonerated and the complete recovery of Durant paves the way for the romantic finale.

Rush.

LEGALLY DEAD

Universal melodrama with Milton Sills starred. Story by Charles Furthman, script by Harvey Gates. Directed by William Parke. Shown at Loew's Circle, New York, on double feature bill with "The Fog," July 30. Running time, 68 minutes.

Will Campbell	Milton Sills
Mrs. Campbell	Margaret Campbell,
Minnie O'Reilly	Claire Adams
Jake Dorr	Edwin Sturgis
Jake's Sweetheart	Faye O'Neill
Malcolm Steele	Chas. A. Stevenson
District Attorney	Joseph Girard
Anarchist	Albert Prisco
Judge	Herbert Fortier
Governor	Charles Wellsley
Detective	Robert Homans
Doctor	Brandon Hurst

Milton Sills is about the only thing that is connected with this picture that will mean anything. It is intended as a melodramatic thriller. It could have easily been switched into a melodramatic farce, for the greater part of it is exactly that, at least as far as the story is concerned. At the Circle, New York, where the audience isn't too particular as long as they are entertained, they laughed at a great deal of the melodramatic action. However, as the weak sister on a double feature bill it may get by in the cheaper neighborhood houses.

The story is the weakest point, while the work Sills offers is the best thing about the picture. The balance of the cast means nothing as far as the box office is concerned, and none of those included in the rather lengthy list of names will draw a nickle.

The basis of the tale is rather far-fetched. The hero is a reporter assigned to cover the criminal courts. He is of the belief that many innocent men are sent "up the river" because of the strenuous efforts of the average prosecutor. One morning after three men have been sentenced to the death penalty he voices his opinion that one was innocent, and it is suggested that he do a "stretch" himself to sound out his principles among those doing time. A few hours later when he reaches home and has a row with his wife he walks out and goes to another city. There a short time afterward the theory of spending time in a state prison as a regular inmate as an experiment decides him to commit a crime, for which he is sentenced. In the pen he is made a trusty, and later paroled for good behavior, and goes to a small town, following a girl, who was also a prisoner, sentenced for shoplifting.

She helps him to a position in a bank, where in a short time he becomes receiving teller. An escaped convict hits the same town about a week later and decides to stick up the bank, but the detectives are on his trail, and when cornered he kills one. The new bank clerk is accused of the crime and convicted on his record and sentenced to be hung. His picture appearing in the papers is recognized by a former doctor friend, who has been experimenting in restoring life successfully on animals, but wants a human subject. At the prison he makes an attempt to have the warden promise to turn over the body of his dead friend, but is refused.

When the Governor telephones an order to stay the execution about 10 seconds after the hangman's trap has been sprung and the innocent victim of the law pronounced dead by the state's physicians, the warden readily consents to the doctor friend trying out his experiment on the dead body, with the result that life is returned.

There is a little romance through all this, with the girl convict and the man who was dead found finally in a clinch when he discovers that the wife he walked out on has divorced him.

Next to Sills, the only real actor in the cast was the warden, who, although unprogrammed, was easily recognized as Tom McGuire.

Fred.

LITTLE OLD NEW YORK

Cosmopolitan production, with Marion Davies starred. Adapted by Luther Reed from stage play of same title by Rida Johnson Young. Directed by Sidney Olcott, with settings by Urban. Original score by William Frederick Peters and house orchestra under direction Victor Herbert (and his orchestra). Distributor reported in controversy, with Goldwyn-Cosmopolitan claiming rights, disputed by exhibitors who allege holding contracts for "Little Old New York" from Famous Players (Cosmopolitan later withdrew from Famous, combining with Goldwyn). Opened new Cosmopolitan theatre (formerly Park), New York, Aug. 1. Running time, about two hours.

Patricia O'Day	Marion Davies
Patrick O'Day	Steve Carr
John O'Day (her father)	J. M. Kerrigan
Larry Delevan	Harrison Ford
Robert Fulton	Courtenay Foote
Washington Irving	Mahlon Hamilton
Fitz Green Halleck	Norval Keedwell
Henry Brevoort	George Barraud
Cornelius Vanderbilt	Sam Hardy
John Jacob Astor	Andrew Dillon
Mr. De Puyster	Riley Hatch
Reilly (Larry's servant)	Charles Kennedy
Bunny (the night watchman),	Spencer Charters
Bully Boy Brewster	Harry Watson
The Hoboken Terror	Louis Wolheim
Delmonico	Charles Judels
Ariana De Puyster	Gypsy O'Brien
Betty Schuyler	Mary Kennedy
Rachel Brewster	Elizabeth Murray
Chancellor Livingston	Thomas Findlay
Mrs. Schuyler	Marie R. Burke

Marion Davies is to "Little Old New York" what Times square is to all of the country—the centre of attraction. Her performance will sell this film when it reaches the picture houses. At that time the picture will be freely cut to meet the exhibitors' time requirement. Cutting will be no task, either in the first or second part, from its two-hour run at the Cosmopolitan at a super-special top, $1.50. Sliced to a proper size, the film on its own will better stand up.

As a historical reminder of the early Manhattan days, with the program full of the best-known names in New York through the money their ancestors accumulated, "Little Old New York" was a quaint village, like a thousand other villages that have been cameraed or passed through. It hasn't the punch expected there, but it does give a kick when Fulton's "Clermont" is sent on its sidewheeling way up the Hudson.

Fulton's sidewheel scheme of water locomotion has endured. So has the "Star-Spangled Banner." As the "Clermont" unfurled the flag the Victor Herbert orchestra broke into the national anthem and every one stood up, applauding. It may have been a first-night idea, or it may be in the picture's score, although it never would be called a clean hit by itself as thus theatre-employed.

The big effect is a prize fight in a firehouse with a serio-comic bout that brought many genuine laughs, with this running into a whipping-post scene. Both were extremely well directed by Sidney Olcott and as well handled.

A novelty bit is of Miss Davies as the boy entering a room where men are telling a story, with a commanding picture device causing a deepening blush as she stands motionless to sweep over her face.

It's probably the single Marion Davies picture not characterized by "clothes." "Little Old New York" is not a fashion display. It may be an antique exhibit and interesting on that end, but there was no Fifth avenue in those days and they didn't wear "clothes" in the part of Ireland Patricia O'Day (Miss Davies) hailed from.

That may be one of the reasons why Miss Davies' dual playing here attracted such strict attention to herself—that and her acting. There was nothing to distract from it, not even the playing of the remainder of the unusually capable cast Marion Davies heads so well.

Patricia O'Day was the sister of her brother, Pat., named the heir to the fortune of an uncle in America. On the way over Pat dies aboard. Her father obliges Patricia to become Pat to obtain the inheritance. The deception ousted Larry Delevan (Harrison Ford) from the prospective estate that otherwise would have gone to him within a few hours after Pat arrived. But as Patricia and Larry married at the ending the estate remained in the entire family.

It's just a good picture house picture as a story, produced to the limit, as all Cosmopolitans have been, but there's a length in the first part that sets an audience viewing a "special" evening's picture to wondering what it's special about. The second part, almost starting with the prize fight, picks up and is strong enough in all of its points to fade the earlier section from memory.

It is here where Miss Davies glistens and glows, both as the boy and girl. She shades everything she does and draws tears through her tears from nearly all of the house. Miss Davies is in a wider range than "Knighthood" gave her, and gives a far better all around performance than her Mary Tudor, as excellent as her Mary Tudor was.

The old Park, now the Cosmopolitan and Hearst's, is a new theatre, inside and out, with nothing spared in the transformation, although the seating capacity seems less than before. All of the boxes are on the balcony floor.

Sime.

THE SPOILERS

A Jesse D. Hampton production, released by Goldwyn, from the Rex Beach story, first done into pictures in 1914 by Selig. No star other than name of author. At Capitol, New York, week of Aug. 5. Running time about 80 minutes.

Roy Glennister	Milton Sills
Cherry Malotte	Anna Q. Nilsson
Helen Chester	Barbara Bedford
Joe Dextry	Robert Edeson
"Slapjack" Simms	Ford Sterling
Broncho Kid	Wallace MacDonald
Alex McNamara	Noah Beery
Marshall Vorhees	Mitchell Lewis
Attorney Wheaton	John Elliot
Struve	Robert McKim
Captain Stevens	Tom McGuire
Landlady	Kate Price
Matthews	Rockliffe Fellowes
Burke	Gordon Russell
Tilly Nelson	Louise Fazenda
Judge Stillman	Sam de Grasse
Mexico Mullins	Albert Roscoe
Bill Nolan	Jack Curtis

After all, "Action" is the biggest thing the screen can have. When there is Action with a capital A, such as "The Spoilers" possesses, and a full-blooded story that holds on its active as well as romantic side, along with such superb production and direction as Jesse D. Hampton has given to this picture, there isn't an exhibitor in the country who needs think twice.

It's great work; it's intelligent work; and while it may be said the story is there, which it is, one cannot gainsay at the same moment that the worth of a story must be brought out in the celluloid. That's what Hampton has done. He has made that Beach story stand and dance. It never lies down. That's why it's Action and that's why Action is the film's best seller.

Rather difficult with the many pictures since, to clearly recall the first "Spoilers" film of nine years ago, that Selig made in 1914, and which opened the Mark Mitchell Strand, New York. Peculiarly, too, S. L. Rothafel was the first manager of the Strand, and he is now at the head of the Capitol, where the Hampton re-make is this week. But even the dim recollection notes the advance of picture making in setting, action and cast. Take the big fight scene of "The Spoilers" as the example; in the Selig picture that fight as done by William Farnum as Glenister, and Thomas Santschi as McNamara, the wily politician, was conceded to have been the best screen fight up to its time. Farnum and Santschi battled all over the place, breaking everything in sight while doing it. It was the wreckage as much as the battle that made the Beach famous line, "I broke him with my hands," align itself with the struggle preceding.

In the Hampton picture the fight is between Milton Sills as Glenister and Noah Beery as McNamara. Boy, that is a fight! It's remarkable either one or both didn't go to the hospital. They broke little furniture, but went after each other like a couple of tigers. When it was over and Beery "out" on the floor while Sills was gasping for breath, those two battlers looked as though they had been through a real mill. "Pulling punches" or rehearsing, no matter what it was, there is no one in the heat of the fight they put up who could remember everything. It's the corking fight of all time on the screen.

And again! Variety's review of the Selig picture written by *Mark* (no longer with the paper) mentioned but few players named on the Strand program. Among the missing was Slapjack Simms, foreman of the Midias mine. In the Hampton picture the foreman, Slapjack, is Ford Sterling. Ford Sterling is still funny. In the midst of the most serious situation, when he moves, there is a laugh. He did a peach comic bit in trying to piece up a broken sluiceway with the water pouring over him.

While not attempting comparison, excepting to note the advancement, it cannot but be remarked that there is hardly any comparison between the splendid performance of now by Anna Q. Nilsson as Cherry Malotte, the music hall girl, with that of Kathlyn Williams of the years ago, while Miss Nilsson in the Hampton picture made her role so strident and forceful that Barbara Bedford, playing Helen Chester, could not keep pace. Bessie Eyton played Helen in the Selig film.

Another point of improvement that maybe Hampton shouldn't receive undue credit for is the absence of dance hall scenes. Selig's went to the dance hall thing, but there have been so many westerns with them that Hampton might have concluded there was nothing new to show in the Alaskan setting. Colin Campbell directed for Selig; Lambert Hillyet is the director of the current Hampton's "Spoilers."

The Beach story went into the early gold rush days at Nome, with the politician, McNamara, having his own U. S. Circuit Court judge appointed to jump the gold claims. Glenister and Joe Dextry (Robert Edeson) held the leading Midas mine which the invaders immediately jumped, forcing out its owners and eventually having Judge Stillman (Sam de Grasse) issue warrants for their arrest, to be later arrested himself for contempt in failing to obey an order of the court obtained at San Francisco by Glenister's attorney.

The love story running meantime between Helen Chester and Glenister with Cherry as the forlorn figure in the triangle is very feelingly set out. Sympathy must go out to Cherry during it. Miss Nilsson makes the role poignant in its sincerity; Wallace MacDonald as the Broncho Kid has another well-played role.

The cast contains many names, several very well known, and all generally exceptionally cast, for instance, the steamer's captain as done by Tom McGuire—just a bit, but made constrained and relieved at the finish by McGuire with a laugh.

"The Spoilers" (Hampton) opened first at Chicago, where it had a run in the middle of the summer that bespoke its drawing qualities. It's one of those self-advertisers and sure-fire for money. *Sime.*

CIRCUS DAYS

First National feature, presented by Sol. Lesser. Jackie Coogan star. Adapted from James Otis' story, "Toby Tyler." Directed by Eddie Cline. Shown at the Strand, New York, week Aug. 5. Running time, 69 minutes.

Toby Tyler....................Jackie Coogan
Ann Tyler....................Barbara Tennant
Eben Holt....................Russell Simpson
His Wife....................Claire McDowell
Luigi....................Cesare Gravini
Jeannette....................Peaches Jackson
Lord....................Sam De Grasse
Daly....................De Witt Jennings
Fat Woman....................Nellie Lane
Human Skeleton....................William Barlow

Toby Tyler's experiences while ten weeks with a circus have developed into a mighty good screen vehicle for the presentation of Jackie Coogan under the direction of Eddie Cline. This is a picture everybody will like.

There isn't a constant effort to shove little Jackie into the foreground of the action until he is compelled to do things that no kiddie of his age could accomplish. Therefore it is plausible as well as entertaining.

For the little kiddies it is going to be a veritable delight, for where isn't there a kid who hasn't either played circus in the back yard or at some time or another wished that he or she could run away from home to join one of the shows?

But Toby stands out as a hero in this picture. He is spanked by the uncle at whose home he and his widowed mother are living, and runs away to get a job with the circus. He starts as the "lemo" kid and finally develops into the comedy trick rider, doing a burlesque of a bareback act, and becomes the star of the show at "$75 a week and cakes."

Of course he goes back to the humble farm and rescues his mother from the hands of her cruel brother-in-law and ends the picture by driving away with her in a "high-powered Ford."

In direction the picture is carried alone nicely. The circus atmosphere which predominates is well handled. There are any number of comedy bits on the circus lot that are going to be sure fire with audiences. The show itself is a "wagon show," carrying a small menagerie, but as the lion has died they have one of the coon roustabouts wearing his skin and impersonating him in the cage into which Jackie bounds to escape the wrath of the lemonade stand proprietor for whom he is working. It is a thrill and then a laugh. The picture abounds with just this type situations.

Little Jackie Coogan has personally improved 100 per cent. The youngster is no longer working by rote, just doing the things shown him by imitation. Now, judging from the expressions on his little face he is thinking of what he is doing, and the facial expressions he contrives to achieve are little short of remarkable when one takes his youth into consideration.

The supporting cast is a corking one, and as an all around picture "Circus Days" should be extremely satisfying to any audience and all exhibitors. At the Strand for the night shows Tuesday there were more than two score kiddies of various ages in the house accompanied by their parents, conclusive proof there is a special draw to the Coogan pictures. *Fred.*

BLUEBEARD'S EIGHTH WIFE

Paramount, presented by Jesse Lasky, founded on the play of the same title by Alfred Savoir, translated by Charlton Andrews and adapted for the screen by Sada Cowan. Gloria Swanson starred. Shown at the Rialto, New York, week Aug. 5. Running time, 61 minutes.

Mona de Briac....................Gloria Swanson
John Brandon....................Huntley Gordon
Robert....................Charles Green
Lucienne....................Lianne Salvor
Marquis de Briac....................Paul Weigel
Lord Henry Seville....................Frank R. Butler
Albert de Marceau....................Robert Agnew
Alice George....................Irene Dalton

Sex stuff that goes as far as it can before the camera without the censors getting after it. That is what picture-house audiences want, according to the exhibitors—sex stuff that will go the limit, keep the audience on edge and still be censor proof. In "Bluebeard's Eighth Wife" they have got exactly what they ordered, the goods being delivered by a competent cast in a photographic setting that is interesting. The more the pity that the director who turned out the picture isn't given program credit for his work.

One touch, however, those who witness the picture are most certain to remark, and that is the fading pep and beauty of Gloria Swanson. After witnessing her go through the role of Mona one cannot help to remark how much she has progressed as an actress and likewise what she would have done to that role from an alluring standpoint had she played it in the same manner in the full flush of her beauty. Huntley Gordon as the American millionaire, playing opposite, practically walked away with the picture.

The story, that of an American millionaire who has divorced seven wives and takes unto himself an eighth, the latter only discovering after she is married how many have preceded her in her husband's affections, is deftly handled on the screen.

The opening scenes show the broken-down members of the French nobility hoping that the young daughter of the family will ensnare the American millions. She consents to the marriage, as she is in love with the American, but after discovering she is No. 8 on his list defers the honeymoon until such time as she is convinced her husband's protestations of love are genuine and not surface indications, as they must have been in his previous marriages.

Miss Swanson plays capably. The three or four subterfuges employed to rouse her husband's jealousy and to compel him to grant her a divorce are deftly delivered. In the supporting cast there is a clever piece of work by Paul Weigel in a character role, while Robert Agnew answers very well as a juvenile. Irene Dalton, however, in a revengeful vamp bit, walks away with the honors as to looks in the production. She appears to be headed for a "heavy vamp" future.

No one need be afraid of this picture; it is going to deliver at the box office for the exhibitor. The title, in the locations where they know anything of what a stir the stage version caused when it first hit Broadway, is going to be sure-fire for the box office. *Fred.*

SALOMY JANE

Paramount picturization of the famous Bret Harte story, featuring Jacqueline Logan, George Fawcett and Maurice Flynn.

Salomy Jane....................Jacqueline Logan
Yuba Bill....................George Fawcett
The Man....................Maurice Flynn
Gambler....................William Davidson
Madison Clay....................Charles Ogle
Col. Starbottle....................William Quinn
Red Pete....................Raymond Rye
Mrs. Pete....................Louise Dressler
Larabee....................James Neill
Rufe Waters....................Tom Carrigan
Baldwin....................Clarence Burtin
Mary Ann....................Barbara Brower
Steve Low....................Milton Ross

Baltimore, Aug. 8.

Quite a few years ago "Salomy Jane" received the initiation into the celluloid realm, and, if memory serves, Vera Michelena was the heroine. In its day it wasn't so bad, although that has been eight or ten years ago.

The new picture, with Jacqueline Logan as the heroine, and with the excellent support of George Fawcett as Yuba Bill and Maurice Flynn as The Man, the film takes on new values which line it up as a good card for the intermediate houses. Whether it could hold up in a first-class first-run house is problematical. At all events it is pleasant entertainment and the cast is excellent throughout, Charles Ogle being among those present.

The story of western desperadoes, of Salomy Jane, the daughter of Madison Clay, of the Vigilantes and The Man who rides home with Salomy Jane in the sunset and who marries her, is clearly told, the continuity of the film being remarkable. The subtitles, too, it might be added, make no painful attempts at flippancy, much of the dialog being taken from the covers of the book.

Miss Logan, aside from a tendency to curl the eyebrows with every glance and to work the facial expressions overtime, makes a good heroine. Her face is fresh and not overly sophisticated, so that she hasn't the appearance of being an Eastern millionaire's daughter out on a movie holiday. Of George Fawcett it can be said that he is great—as he nearly always is. Maurice Flynn makes the stranger's role appealing, while the others fit into their parts neatly. The film itself makes a good program picture, and is not drawn out nor too long. *Sisk.*

SIDEWALKS OF N. Y.

Lester Park presents this screening of a story built around Charles B. Lawlor's famous song. The plot and scenario were manufactured by Willard King Bradley. The main title has the information that the cast is from the Reel Town players and workers. Lester Park directed. Sixty-four minutes projection time. At the Broadway, New York, Aug. 6.

Lester Park bursts upon us practically a stranger, and his introduction is far from felicitous. This five reels or so of film has about as high a percentage of rank vulgarity and cheap hokum to the running foot as commonly comes within the observer of Broadway picture goers. That goes double for the neighborhood establishments for big and little towns.

The cast has several capable players, notably Hanna Lee, one of our most engagingly earnest kid players, and Bernard Siegel, who does an old man character part neatly. Templay Saxe has done some good work, but here he has an impossible role.

It is enough to tell of the story that the sweet, romantic heroine—one of those yearning maids who sobs moistly when she is turned away from home because she will not marry the man of her dear father's choice—is at other times a lady prize fighter.

Some of the absurdities of the tale may be imagined when it is related that this young woman saves her dear old dad from eviction and a sheriff's sale of his cherished violin by winning the "ladies' world championship" in a three-round bout. They didn't even take the trouble to dig up a girl who could handle herself with boxing gloves. The feminine prize fight (seriously done and led up to in all sincerity as a dramatic punch) was a staggering clawing and hair pulling match within the limits of 14-ounce gloves.

Mack Sennett could do much with the idea of a lady prize fighter lifting the mortgage on the Old Place. It's a great idea, but what does Charley Lawlor think of it? His name isn't mentioned, by the way, in "The Sidewalks of New York." At that he couldn't collect damages for the omission, which leaves him on the debtor side.

The whole thing is unspeakably bad in every department. It is padded out with close-ups, interminable shots of street scenes on New York's lower east side, and scores of other unnecessary details which don't belong but didn't cost anything.

The Broadway tried valiantly to sell the picture. The front of the lobby was plastered with gaudy painted canvas and the orchestra played a medley of old songs before and after the projection, running through the list from "After the Ball" to "Tammany." The further "The Sidewalks of New York" plays from the sidewalks of New York the better the chance it will have. It may be a riot among the Australian bushmen, where perhaps prizefighting ladies are romantic.

But on Broadway——! *Rush.*

LUCK

States' rights production sponsored by C. O. Burr, with Johnny Hines starred. Produced by Mastodon Films, Inc. New York state's rights controlled by the Commonwealth Distributing Co. Story by Jackson Gregory; adapted by Doty Hobart and titled by Ralph Spence.

Bob Carter....................Johnny Hines
Sylvia Templeton..........Violet Mersereau
Alan Crosby..................Edmund Breese
Judge Templeton............Robert Edeson
Fighting Miner..............Matthew Betts
Dumb Dora......................Polly Moran
The Plumber...............Charles Murray
His Girl........................Flora Finch

A typical, breezy Johnny Hines subject, generally irrelevant, with not much attempt made to counterbalance it with a pretext at being anything otherwise. The "Luck" title is introduced in an episode at the Essex Country Club on Long Island.

Alan Crosby, a self-made captain of industry, who is not averse to admiring his maker, derides the attitude of the young blue-bloods in matters of sports, etc. It results in Bob Carter (Hines) deciding to enter a cross-country match at the last moment, and he accidentally wins the race because of his fear of a pursuing elephant. The bull was previously introduced when Carter h: lifted a golf ball into the adjacent winter quarters of the Walter L. Main circus (so labeled), with the elephant refusing to give up the small pellet he was playing with.

Simultaneous with the start of the race the mammoth is frightened by a field mouse and tears away from his stake. This contributes to Carter's accidentally winning the marathon and results in Crosby wagering the wealthy young idler a small matter of $100,000 that he couldn't earn $10,000 the first year without the assistance of his private fortune, but starting as he is. It so happens he is attired in running trunks an: a bathing suit, his friends contributing a hip flask and Crosby a small cigar lighter, which always refuses to light.

So oddly arrayed, Carter hitches on a passing auto, encounters Sylvia Templeton at the railroad station; cons his way through a rail trip to the town of Templetonia, Pa., over which Sylvia's father, the judge, presides, in the heart of the mining district. Arrived there, Carter is greeted as a visiting pugilistic champ and agrees to a match which develops into a farce exhibition, he emerging victor and explaining the mistaken identity.

The rest of the acton is concerned with Carter's promoting the town of Sylvania, named after Sylvia, after the citizens of Templetonia have refused him support. Considerable opposition makes itself evident, but on the last day of the year Carter is given $10,000 as his first year's salary as president of Sylvania, Inc.

The comedy by-play is interesting and well suited for weather of the present sort. It's a good summer picture with every member of the cast seemingly keeping the weather limitation in mind and gauging his or her efforts accordingly.

The presence of such comedy sure-fires as Charles Murray, Polly Moran and Flora Finch doesn't hurt either, and sounds more like the old Mack Sennet days. *Abel.*

THE CRITICAL AGE

Independent melodrama, adapted from Ralph Connor's novel, "Glengarry School Days." Directed by Harry McRae. Distributed by Hodkinson. Shown at Loew's New York, N. Y., on double feature bill with "A Man of Action," Aug. 7. Running time, 68 minutes.

Peter Gorach.....................Harlan Knight
Tom Finley.....................James Harrison
Mrs. Finley..........................Alice May
Margaret Baird.................Pauline Garon
Bob Kerr.........................Wallace Ray
Senator Morgan Kerr........Raymond Peck
Senator Baird...................William Colbin
Mrs. Baird.......................Marion Colbin

Interesting melodrama set amid rural surroundings having a schoolboy love affair for its main theme and political intrigue for its counterplot. The love affair between Tom Finley and Margaret Baird is planted in the early reels. So is the comedy, introduced in the schoolroom scene, with the mischievous youths playing the usual pranks upon the rural teacher. Young Finley's self-sacrificing nature and love for his dog has made him the idol of the small boy. Tom, who is a diamond in the rough, finds the competition of Bob Kerr, dapper son of Senator Kerr, too much for him and is about to give up hopes of winning fair Margaret, when fate intervenes. Bob and Margaret are upset in a canoe and the girl is brought to shore by Finley after a thrilling rescue, which provides the best action of the picture. Young Kerr waddles his way to shore, lamenting the fact that he has lost an opportunity to shine as a hero.

Although a commonplace story, it has action, good continuity and will make a good feature for the smaller picture houses.

SKID PROOF

Charles Jones Series presented by William Fox. Story by Harvey Gates. Directed by Scott Dunlop. At Academy of Music, New York, on double feature bill, July 26-28. Running time, 54 minutes.

Dutton Hardeman..................Fred Eric
Lorraine Hardeman....Jacqueline Jadstone
Tyler..........................Earl Metcalf

This is one of the type of auto race thrillers that went a long way toward establishing the reputation of Wallace Reid as a screen favorite. The Fox organization is releasing it as one of the series of seven outdoor pictures to star Charles Jones. It doesn't give him much of an opportunity in the early part of the picture, but once he enters the action he is the whole works. It is a picture that is designed for popular consumption, and in the houses where they like thrillers it will please.

The story has as its basis a transcontinental auto race between two rival manufacturers for a $50,000 side bet. One of the manufacturers has insisted on the bet because his rival in business has managed to win the affections of his wife. He has figured on beating him in the business race and breaking him financially at the same time. Both automobile men cross the continent via aeroplane at the same time that the cars are covering the roads. The heavy, when he sees that his car is about to lose the race, swoops down in his plane and wounds the driver with pistol fire. The driver was one who replaced the regular driver at Painted Falls, near Los Angeles. He was an ex-champion racer who was running the garage. His losing the race makes him determined to be revenged on the man that wounded him, and he finally beats him out in the motor sweepstakes.

Jones is the ex-champ driver at the garage. He handled himself well in this picture, although he maintained a rather serious mien throughout, an occasional smile would not have hurt. The cast in general is fairly well selected, with the possible exception of Fred Eric, whose work at times was quite laughable. He was the wronged husband, and he showed in this picture just how it is possible to almost wreck a picture through the miscasting of a single character.

Fred.

REFUGE

Katherine MacDonald starred in this B. P. Schulberg production released through First National. Directed by Victor Schertzinger from story by Lois Zellner; scenario by Florence Hein and edited by Eeve Unsell. Runs about an hour.

One of those passably interesting romances of a mythical kingdom, a righteous princess, a usurping ruler, the long lost heir to the throne and his final discovery and marriage to the princess, who has been the victim and object of desire of the usurper.

With the signing of the Armistice, a sort of Three Musketeers trio is disclosed in Belgian Louis, French Jean and British Dick. Also introduced is the locale of "Marivania" and Prince Ferdinand (Arthur Edmund Carewe), the usurper. The action develops with Princess Nadia (Miss MacDonald) fleeing across the border to Paris, where she hopes to find the rightful ruler; agreeing to a mock marriage with the weary French soldier, Jean, to assist this purpose, and after a series of thrilling escapes, etc., finding that Jean is the long sought for Prince Eugene.

The plot skeleton is rather slim, but its recounting has been dressed up with considerable gold braid and formality to make it interesting to the average audience. The development is breezy and the familiar musical comedy trick of having the butler and maid dialog and give the plot away, is paralleled here with the maid and chauffeur characters, by means of pithy tales.

The royalty hocus-pocus is not spread on too thick despite the courtly atmosphere, although it was inevitable that one ballroom scene with many distinguished looking people floating around should be dragged in.

Miss MacDonald is her usual beautiful self and takes care of her opportunities to fullest measure. Mr. Carewe was a reserved, but spiteful heavy and the hero (real name not caught from titling) did his little share in accepted fashion.

Should make a good daily change program feature with the "Refuge" title lending itself to heavy stressing in several features on the exploitation. A flash of the posters with the court scenes and regal costuming should also be counted on. *Abel.*

THE LOVE BRAND

Universal production starring Roy Stewart. Story by Raymond L. Schrock, adapted for the screen by Adrian Johnson. Directed by Stuart Paton. Half a double feature bill at Loew's New York, July 31. Projection time, 56 minutes.

Don Jose O'Neil..................Roy Stewart
Peter Collier....................Wilfred North
Frances Collier...............Margaret Landis
Charles Mortimer...............Arthur Hull
Miguel Salvador...........Sydney De Grey
Teresa.............................Marie Wells

The conceptor of the plot of "The Love Brand" must be a most thorough reader of magazine stories, as the tale adapted for the screen here bears a marked resemblance to a serial story printed in a national magazine last winter. The locale, instead of Mexico or New Mexico, is transplanted to Lower California, and instead of the conspirators acting in behalf of a Japanese syndicate to accomplish a certain purpose they do so for themselves. Nevertheless, the story is a good western drama and one, even though constructed and produced along conventional lines, will please the followers of Roy Stewart.

Stewart dominates the picture from the moment he comes into sight until the last foot is projected. His smile and personality are always in evidence and seem to atone for a few dull spots.

Margaret Landis, a petite blonde, who plays opposite him, has a rather difficult role which she makes impressive.

There are some very good outdoor shots, especially a stampede of a herd of cattle driven off by cattle thieves and a chase of the thieves. Only a few indoor scenes are taken, but are adequate.

The direction, considering the story, is exceptionally good. The titles, of course, as in all pictures of this type, are the most important and well written and spotted. In the smaller daily change houses this picture will hold its own easily.

FIRES OF FATE

London, July 27.

Adapted from Sir Arthur Conan Doyle's novel, "The Tragedy of the Korosko," this new Gaumont picture has been awaited with more than the usual interest. Except for a few ordinary interiors the whole thing has been made in Egypt. Shepherd's Hotel plays a prominent part, so does the Nile, the pyramids and many other famous places. The effect of this, together with the sub-titles, is apt to give certain portions of the film a guide book appearance which detracts greatly from the story, which only begins to grip toward the end when good use is made of the Camel Corps and Soudanese troops generally.

Judicious cutting, it runs close on two hours, will add greatly to its entertainment value and the episodes with a crucifix, and the attempt to make his Christian prisoners accept the Koran, should come out bodily. The very sudden return to health of the dying man is almost farcical, and kills the end of an otherwise genuinely artistic production.

The story is mediocre. Colonel Egerton is told by an eminent specialist he has only a year to live. To fill in the time he joins the doctor's party for a trip to Egypt. There he meets Dorinne Adams, a beautiful American whom the Prince Ibrahim desires. Egerton and Dorinne are mutually attracted, but knowing of his approaching end he cannot speak. However, when he saves her from Ibrahim, the truth comes out, and she decides to "stay with him 'till the end." The party is almost annihilated by Bedouins, who takes the survivors prisoner. Ibrahim gets busy, and arranges to buy the girl from her captors. Before his desire can be consummated, however, the marauders are annihilated by the Camel Corps, and Dorinne is restored to the arms of her doomed lover, again announcing her intention of staying with him to the end. Here the picture could well- have finished, but with the customary slavish pandering to convention, Egerton is instantaneously restored to health by the specialist who originally condemned him, and we get the final "close up" as we have had it thousands of times since kinematography was invented.

Tom Terriss, the producer, has been very lucky in his choice of locations, and scenically the whole picture is exceedingly beautiful. Those who find the far-fetched story tedious, will find joy in the production as a fine "travel" feature.

The leading parts are played by Wanda Hawley and Nigel Barrie, obviously with the intention of making the show palatable to the American taste. They do well but except for the American market being in view, dozens of British players would have done just as well. Pedro de Carboda is excellent as the Prince, and Percy Standing gives a very good show as Stephen Belmont, an American business man who dies very gallantly. The rest of the company includes Stewart Rome, Arthur Gillen, Douglas Munro, Cyril Smith, and Edith Craig. The big "star" of the picture is undoubtedly the Camel Corps. In combination with the beautiful scenery the army will get this expensively made picture over.

Gore.

WATCH YOUR STEPS

London, July 27.

Made by Hepworth, this is a short series of one-reelers showing how popular dances should be danced and how they should not. The movements are shown in the ordinary way, and then by means of the Ultra Rapid camera. The first four of the series are "The Fox Trot," "The One Step," "The Waltz," and "The Tango." The executants are Alec Ross, of the Purcell School of Dancing, who won the World's Exhibition Dancing Championship at the Queen's Hall toward the end of last year, and Eileen Dennes, a member of the Hepworth stock company.

There is nothing new in the idea, and the little features are not helped by the fact that the dancers do their job with about the same amount of happiness they would wear when going to the funerals of their nearest and dearest. The producer is "Q," the nom-de-screen of Gaston Quieriebett, a Hepworth regular producer.

These features owe their chief claim to recognition from the fact that one of them was chosen by H.R.H. the Princess Mary (Viscountess Lascelles), for the big charity matinee held at the St. James' Kinema, July 26. *Gore.*

UNINVITED GUEST

London, July 27.

Made in Germany by George Dewhurst with an all British company, this picture is out of the producer's usual run. As a rule he goes in for comedy pure and simple, or delicate fantasy, but on this occasion he has produced a good sound red-hot drama. His story is exceedingly good and well told, but certain scenes will doubtless be considerably cut before the picture goes to the public.

Steele, a financier, is in monetary difficulties. His daughter is loved by Denton, who is the co-trustee with him in a fortune, the heir to which is missing. On the night of his daughter's birthday party Steele is surprised by the entrance of a delapidated stranger, "the uninvited guest." He persuades the man to pose as the heir and dresses him for the part. Denton soon sees through the trick, and sees also that the girl, Mavis, is falling in love with the newcomer. He tries to put the screw on, but fails. He then traps Mavis in his flat, and attempts to forcibly seduce her. She is rescued by the stranger who thrashes Denton. Later Denton brings the lawyer who knows the missing heir. His idea is to expose the other man, but the bottom falls out of his plot when the lawyer recognizes the "uninvited guest" as being the genuine article. The conventional happy ending brings the picture to a conclusion.

The production work is very good. The players have been carefully selected and present one of the finest combinations ever seen in a British picture. Madge Stuart as the girl gives an exceedingly good performance of a part which in the later scenes must have been a severe nerve test. The same applies to Cameron Carr as the villain Denton. Their bedroom scene is the last word in strength, and handled with less skill, would have been merely nauseating. Stewart Rome plays well as the "uninvited guest," and Cecil Morton Yorke is excellent as Steele. Various small parts are admirably played.

Taken on a whole, this feature consolidates the reputation achieved by George Dewhurst with his "A Sister to Assist'er" and the features he made for the Hepworth company. *Gore.*

DER ABSTURZ
(THE DOWNFALL)

Berlin, July 5.

One of the best films Asta Nielsen has made for some time, but it is sad to have to add this, unfortunately, does not mean much.

Within the last year she did a film version of Strindberg's "Fraulein Julie," totally unsuited to the screen and in which she had to play for a long time a girl of 15, which was an impossibility. The present production gives her an excellent chance to display her acting, and this Swedish star still must be reckoned as one of the very strongest personalities before the camera.

The present is merely the conventional film story and does not rise for a moment above the conventional level. It tells the story of a beautiful stage star mixed up in a crime, her lover serves a prison sentence, she goes through everything with the hope that when he gets out she can marry him. When that does not take place she goes down and down, and in the last act plays an old woman.

And in this last act as the old broken-down woman of the streets she gives a performance which could not be surpassed by any single actress on the screen.

From the rest of the cast only Wassmann and Gregori Chamara are adequate. The regie by Dr. Wolf is quite impossible. Of course, he may not have cut the film himself, but if he did that is another point against him.

The present film is interesting, but does not seem to have quite the right appeal for an American success. *Trask.*

DER SCHATZ
(THE TREASURE)

Berlin, July 5.

This is one of the best films produced in Germany for some time. It is taken from a novel by Hans Bartsch, and very cleverly, too.

The tale concerns a treasure buried years before by the Turks when they invaded the country. A house stands on the foundations of an old mansion, and in these foundations, so legend says, a treasure was buried.

In the house of the present lives an old bell maker, his wife and daughter, and an old servant. Into this household comes a young man from the city, an artist who has been commissioned to do the decoration on a newly-ordered bell. He hears from the old servant the fable, and with the aid of the girl sets out to find the treasure.

The servant is also seeking it, but with the aid of a willow wand, which he has charmed and believes will point to the buried hoard. The young fellow, however, using the methods of modern science, measures the walls to find out where a treasure might possibly be concealed.

After many nights of searching the young fellow finds the treasure, but the servant comes upon him during the latter part of his search and tells him not to look any further; that he will tell the master bell-maker about it.

The young fellow and the girl leave for a walk. Meantime the three old people dig out the treasure and make themselves very happy about it.

When all are quite drunk the young people return and the servant demands as part of his share the hand of the girl in marriage. This the girl does not want. She and the young fellow rush off, leaving the old people with their gold, while they have their happiness. Then the old servant in drunken excitement rushes down to the cellar, and in searching for the gold digs away one of the most important pillars that holds the house. It falls in, burying the three.

It will be difficult to imagine any of the five roles better played. Especially desirable is Werner Kraus as the old servant. The half-mad craftiness of the man is perfect. It is the best playing Kraus has done in several years. Hans Brausewetter has improved tremendously and now is an acceptable film juvenile. Albert Steinruck as the old bell maker, Ilka Gruning as his wife and Lucie Mannheim as the daughter are fitted.

E. L. Papst, who directed, has never before had a chance at direction. With this considered, it is really extraordinarily well handled. He seems to be one of the few directors who understand.

The photography should not pass without a word of praise. It is artistic, but at the same time never fails to be clear, a very exceptional thing in Germany today.

The present film has a distinct American appeal and should do nicely as a better class feature in America. *Trask.*

THE GREEN GODDESS

Presented by Distinctive Pictures Corp., releasing through Goldwyn-Cosmopolitan. Adapted from William Archer's play of same name by Forrest Halsey, starring George Arliss and featuring Alice Joyce. Directed by Sidney Olcott, with H. A. Fischbeck photographer. Special musical score composed by Joseph C. Breil. Opened at the Sam Harris theatre Aug. 14. Projection time, 106 minutes.

The Rajah of Rukh	Mr. Arliss
Lucilla Crespin	Miss Joyce
Major Crespin	Harry T. Morey
Dr. Basil Traherne	David Powell
The Ayah	Jetta Goudal
Watkins	Ivan Simpson
The High Priest	William Worthington

Distinctive Pictures may not have an unusual special with this screen adaptation, but there is little doubt "The Green Goddess" will suffice as an excellent program feature. The performance of George Arliss alone is enough to make it that.

Opening at the Harris Tuesday night for what is becoming a habit with the producing organizations [at the slightest suggestion they've "got somethin'," a pre-release run] the film clicked regularly and often before a friendly audience. But despite that fact it may be said that the picture is "there."

Olcott, in directing, adhered closely to the stage presentation, with the sub-titles (at least 50 per cent. of the entertainment's qualities) being lifted directly from the original script. Arliss far overshadows any other contributing member, some of whom were with him during the run of the play. In this respect Ivan Simpson, valet to Arliss, comes in for special mention because of a meritorious effort which ranks him second to the star.

Photography and lightings are splendid and the sets appropriate if not elaborate. Olcott did nicely with a meagre amount of mob stuff, possibly overtaxed his climax a bit, but inserted as neat a shot of an airplane squadron in flight as can be imagined. A corking bit, that.

The story tells of a Major Crespin, his wife and Dr. Traherne falling into the kingdom of Rukh due to a mishap to the doctor's plane. As three brothers of the Rajah (Arliss) are about to be executed by the English authorities the moment is opportune for revenge, and so demanded by the populace.

Mr. Arliss' highly educated and serenely satirical Rajah, who possesses an extraordinary sense of humor, is fully equal to his stage characterization. And to those who saw the play there need be nothing further said. Harry Morey as the Major was perhaps permitted too much freedom as the constantly liquored major and husband, with the result he has greatly overdone the strutting, quick-tempered and braggart type.

On the other hand, David Powell, as the doctor and lover, can be classified as of the modest, retiring and shy sort in comparison. Too much so, probably, and falls short of equaling Cyril Keightley's performance in the same stage role.

Miss Joyce, heralded in the program as returning to the screen for this special effort, lent a charming appearance and tone while making her role of the wife a quiet and subdued one, but convincing.

The picture may suffer in a regular program house for those who happen to walk in on it failing to catch the initial viewpoint of the Rajah. But in the pre-release theatre, where everyone is seated at the start, the film entertains with its dramatics and cynical sub-titles.

It's another mark for Arliss on the screen. They can take all their previous Sheiks, Sultans and Rajahs and put them in the bag. For Mr. Arliss as the wise-crackin' Rajah, who regards women as strictly business while preferring to work on percentage, is the pay off. *Skig.*

LITTLE JOHNNY JONES

Produced by the Warner Bros., with Johnny Hines starred. Film version of Geo. M. Cohan's play, adapted by Raymond Schrock. Directed by Arthur Rosson and

Johnny Hines. Shown at the Strand, New York, week Aug. 12. Running time, 72 minutes.

Johnny Jones....................Johnny Hines
Earl of Bloomsburg.....Windham Standing
Johnny's mother..........Margaret Seddon
Sir James Smythe.............Robert Prior
Edith Smythe...................Molly Malone
Robert Anstead..................George Webb
His jockey.......................Mervyn LeRoy
Chauffeur..............................."Fat" Carr
Lady Jane Smythe...........Pauline French
Brownie......................The Wonder Dog

Dear George M. Cohan:

Whatever you do, don't go to the Strand this week. It has advertised a screen adaptation of your famous play, "Little Johnny Jones." Unless you want to set yourself for one of those things, keep away from that picture. There is about as much of "Little Johnny Jones" in the Warner Bros. picture as there is of "Hamlet," although it is nearer the latter, for it is a tragedy.

They have just taken the title and some of the characters, incidentally leaving out some of the most important ones, and turned out a slapstick hoak picture that isn't anything except a very mediocre second grade feature, good for the cheaper grade of houses.

How the Strand fell for it is a mystery, George. But digging into **inside stuff the Warners always manage to get into the Strand, somehow or another.**

When one remembers "Little Johnny Jones" of the Liberty and later the New York, where it ran for so long, George, and starts for the theatre remembering you, your mother and your dad, Billy Meehan, Tom Lewis, Patsy Mitchell, Eadie Gervan and the rest and starts into the Strand prepared to have the memory of those friends refreshed with a pleasant hour and witnesses what is supposed to be "Little Johnny Jones," it makes one want to turn the picture business back to 1910.

I'm just warning you not to go near the Strand this week, for the Friars need their Abbot.

What Schrock has done to your story is a "shreck." What Johnnie Hines has hoaked the story with is all the old junk he has seen in slapstick pictures since they started making them, and some of the stuff that he is using was in the first one ever made.

All the rest of it is "just a high hat," George.

With fond memories of "Flo," "Yankee Doodle Dandy" and "Give My Regards," Yours, *Fred.*

MARRIAGE MORALS

Produced and distributed by L. Lawrence Weber and Bobby North under direction of Will Nigh. Eighty-five minutes projection time. At the Central, New York, week Aug. 15.

Cast: Tom Moore, Ann Forrest, Florence Billings, Shannon Day, John Goldsworthy, Charles Craig, Edmund Breese, Harry T. Morey, Tom Lewis, Little Russell Griffin, "Mickey" Bennett.

A picture with a box office title, but one that will disappoint the discriminating in story. Will Nigh is credited with the conception, which is drawn out in spots. While the excellent cast do some splendid work, the development of the story and the "dream" ending leave the audience in a quandary as to what it is all about.

The picture attempts to moralize, but the author, in his effort to provide the usual hack happy ending, resorts to that oldest of stage and screen tricks, "it was all a dream."

Tom Moore as a youthful dissolute wealthy spendthrift falls in love with Ann Forrest, a beauty shop employe. They marry and he takes her to his magnificent home to live. The girl doesn't fit in her new environment, out of sympathy with Moore's boozing friends.

His promises to reform are broken time and again until she decides to cure him by apeing his friends. She walks in on a wild party and drinks and smokes. He knocks down a mutual friend who makes love to her and takes her home. Bestially drunk he smashes the statue of "purity" which he had presented to her on their wedding night. She leaves him, returning to her sordid home surroundings.

She meets a former admirer who is married to a slattern and decides to return to her husband. Upon her return she finds him lying in bed with an injured spine. He will never walk again. She realizes her love and after preventing him from suicide wakes up in her own home to discover she isn't married. She had been reading a book entitled "Marriage Morals," by J. C. Black. Black is a friend of her wealthy suitor. In her dream he is a sort of an allegorical Satan whispering bad advice to the principals in the drama.

The improbability of the story is not alibied by the "dream" ending, for the latter doesn't occur until the picture has played for over an hour.

The excellent cast with numerous "names" did well in their various roles, while the production is high-class throughout, also the photography and direction.

The shots of the millionaire's home and Monaco's cabaret where he stages his wild parties are the big flashes aside from the cast. Given a consistent and reasonable continuity this would be an unusual picture, one with all the elements of bigness. It is written about a subject that has universal appeal, but before many hundred feet have been unwound it achieves inconsistency and becomes maudlin in its melodramatics. So much so that it will strain the credulity of the average picture audience.

Buyers will get a cast, a flash and a title. *Con.*

TIPPED OFF

Presented by Harry A. McKenzie and released by Playgoers Pictures through Pathe. Story and scenario by Frederick Reel, Jr., and produced under the supervision of William Matthews. Shown at the Circle, New York, Aug. 14. Running time, 56 minutese.

Chong Wo..........................Noah Beery
"The Fox"......................Tom Santschi
Anthony Moore.................Harold Miller
Sidney Matthews.............Stuart Holmes
Mildred Garson.................Arline Pretty
Rita Garson.........................Zella Gray
"Pug" Murphy...............Thomas O'Brien
Chinese Maid....................Bessie Wong
Chuck Morrison...............James Alamo
Baldy Bates.....................Jimmy Truax
Detective Sergeant...............Si Wilcox
Major Domo......................James Wang

This picture possesses every ingredient of a thrilling melodrama of intrigue and adventure, but its assemblage was so handled, probably by the cutters and title writers, that its purport proved to be vague and incomprehensive.

The author probably started off with the idea of injecting thrills and escapades into the time-worn theme of "double crossing," but those who supervised or directed its supervision lost all track of continuity and plausibility, and simply turned out what can be construed as a series of cheap episodes of thrills.

No fault can be found with the cast. They did their best and went through their scenes as directed. All in all the film bears a marked savor of amateurishness and haste to turn out a product regardless of the consequences.

The story deals with Mildred Garson, who is secretary and fiancee of Anthony Moore, a playwright, looking for a certain type of leading woman for a new play. Mildred suggests the part to be given her and when turned down plots with her brother and sister to demonstrate that she is fit.

Arline Pretty as the girl has some hard stunts to perform, but manages to achieve her purpose and convince the audience she has done her best. Noah Beery as Chong Wo gives a realistic Chinese role. Santschi played his cold villainous role in a manner that impresses. Harold Miller was among those present and excited no interest. Stuart Holmes as a confidence man had a rather short part but registered with his efforts. The balance of the characters were incidental and created no furore.

"Tipped Off" can be summed up as a cheap, gaudy, and unpretentious melodrama.

THE MYSTERIOUS WITNESS

Belasco Productions, Inc., sponsors this five-reeler. Author and director omitted from credits, which may be fault of Fox's Academy of Music, New York, in projection room. The film was run through in 50 minutes and showed signs of cutting, besides being screened in fast tempo. Robert Gordon and Elinor Fair have leading sympathetic roles. Half of double feature August 9-11.

If this production was produced as unreeled at the Academy the director is fully justified in wanting to keep his identity secret. It is no credit to his directorial skill. However, it is more likely it was amply slashed by the house projectionist, although the editing and continuity at times suggests being at fault from inception.

There is little to commend in the picture, half of a double-header at this house. The mother theme is the basic idea, and its manner of exposition approached the maudlin at times. The hero is not altogether sympathetic, according to manly standards, and the whole structure does not ring true throughout. The villain and his subordinates could hardly be so mean in real life, and his sudden capitulation towards the conclusion seems insincere.

Johnny Brant (Robert Gordon) is shown leaving his aged mother to make good. He connects at a ranch run by a crooked and bullying foreman, Ed Caney. Johnny sends home all his monthly earnings to his mother regularly and paints vivid word pictures of his affluence and kindly interest from the foreman when, as a matter of fact, he is given the "dog" assignments in patrolling the extensive ranch. Caney has a crush on the boss rancher's daughter, Ruth Garland (Elinor Fair), and the opposition is heightened when Johnny is effective in saving the girl's life and earning her favor, much to Caney's disgust. Johnny, because of his Scotch proclivities in nursing his earnings, has won for himself the soubriquet of "miser" and is generally disapproved by his ranch confreres.

The hero becomes involved in a murder charge, but is eventually cleared, involving Caney and his henchmen. The mother, who has suffered through the foreman's rifling the hero's money letters to the old woman, enters the scene for a happy ending.

A fight scene towards the finish between Johnny and Caney finds the former victorious, with Johnny giving him an extra lacing despite his acknowledgment of defeat. This is not in keeping with the accepted movie standards of letting the villain off easy, and was probably the director's idea to satisfy the audience's secret desire to see the villain get an extra measure of assault and battery. The idea is good, but it was not skilfully developed.

It's a fair release for the small daily change houses, although it has nothing particularly to commend it. It is not fast and full of action, and, contrarily, rather passive, nor is the direction and acting anything distinctive.

The title only applies to one incident in the courtroom scene of the hero's trial. *Abel.*

DRIFTING

Universal-Jewel presented by Carl Laemmle, with Priscilla Dean starred. Adapted from the John Colton play of the same title. Directed by Tod Browning. Shown at the Capitol, New York, week of Aug. 19. Running time, 70 minutes.

Cassie Cook / Lucille Preston..............Priscilla Dean
Capt. Arthur Jarvis............Matt Moore
Jules Repin...................Wallace Beery
Murphy...................J. Farrell McDonald
Madam Polly Voo...............Rose Dione
Molly Norton...................Edna Tichener
Dr. Li........................William V. Mong
Rose Li......................Anna Mae Wong
Little Bruce......................Bruce Guerin
Mr. Hepburn...................William Moran
Mrs. Hepburn.................Marie de Albert
Chang Wang....................Frank Lanning

This picture is an adaptation of the play in which Alice Brady appeared in several seasons ago in the role of Cassie Cook. The screen version is as different from the play as day and night. All the "guts" that the play contained have been removed and the story switched considerably to make it censor-proof.

The result is a rather wishy-washy picture that relies on its Tod Brown effects to get it over. It is a good enough feature for the average split week policy house, but hardly strong enough to stand up under a pre-release run in one of the bigger houses. In the daily change houses it will get by in good shape.

In the screen version the Cassie Cook of Priscilla Dean is a lady opium smuggler instead of a lady of easy virtue, as she was in the play. The screen Cassie Cook of the Yellow Sea hasn't the punch of she on the stage. There are moments, however, when she manages to get a little fire into the role. The opening scenes in the Shanghai cabaret with Cassie selling off her clothes and the race track scene, in which she gives the local police the run around are light laugh touches that get over. There is missing in the character, however, the touch of regeneration in marked contrast to her past life that comprised the wallop of the play.

During the latter part of the picture the attack on the little Chinese village by the hill men is graphically portrayed. Here Browning is at his best in the direction of the attack and the burning of the village with the ultimate rescue through the arrival of the native cavalry.

Matt Moore makes a rather light role of the lead opposite the star, while Wallace Beery hasn't enough to do to make him stand out. William V. Mong as a sinister Chinaman manages to impress, but the real star of the performance is the little Chinese girl, Anna Mae Wong, who walked away with all the honors ,and who handled a death scene magnificently. *Fred.*

THE SILENT PARTNER

Jesse L. Lasky presents this Charles Maigne production, featuring Leatrice Joy, with Owen Moore and Robert Edeson in support. Story by Maximilian Foster, published in the "Saturday Evening Post" and adapted by Sada Cowan. Projection time, 62 minutes. At the Rivoli August 20.

Lisa Coburn.......................Leatrice Joy
George Coburn...................Owen Moore
Ralph Coombes...............Robert Edeson
Harvey Dredge...............Robert Schable
Cora Dredge.................Patterson Dial
Jim Harker ....E. H. Calvert
Gertie Page ....Maude Wayne
Mrs. Nesbit ....Bess Flowers
Mrs. Harker........................Lura Anson
Owens ....Bert Woodruff
Chas. Nesbit ....Robert Grey

A modern story about real and interesting people, done in a smooth, easy vein and guiltless of hokum or bunk. In brief, a neat comedy drama produced and directed in the best mode of the modern studio. The women will love it, for it has Leatrice Joy in a series of startling gowns that overshadow Gloria Swanson's sartorial flights. Besides which this same Leatrice Joy is a mighty persuasive actress in a particularly appealing role.

Owen Moore hasn't had so excellent a role in a long time. It gives him abundant scope for a neat high comedy knack, and, by way of contrast of light and shade, for some first rate tense situations which he carries off effectively.

A picture that can support five reels of story and still remain quiet and casual is an achnevement. This story never has to resort to the worn out stage tricks and the stereotyped devices of fiction. It's all as natural as life, but its interest never flags because its people and their problems strike a natural human note.

George Coburn and Harvey Dredge are neighbors in a modest apartment house and both work in Wall street brokerage offices. Harvey makes a coup in a lucky speculation on the side, and they depart on a short but merry life as spenders. The itch to make a strike himself attacks George, but Lisa, his wife (Miss Jay), argues against it, preferring a working to a gambling husband. Harvey goes broke and sinks to the bottom, while George becomes a successful plunger on the ticker. But to overcome Lisa's objection he has to agree that winnings shall be 50-50.

Coombs, a millionaire stock operator, falls in love with Lisa when they enter society on George's winnings, and plans a campaign to ruin George, working on the theory that as soon as George is broke Lisa will desert him. Here is an excellent bit of stage management. The director has chosen wisely to pass up the **pandemonium of the Stock Exchange floor as the scene of George's ruin and has the action take place, quite adequately but simply, in a broker's customers' room.** George's catastrophe is pictured much more graphically on the broker's quotation than would be possible with the usual mob scene on the floor, and the treatment gets away from a hackneyed screen device, disclosing a director who isn't bound by the "follow the leader" rule in the studio.

The finish is a little delayed, but comes in a neat surprise. Lisa has collected her half of the winnings and hidden it by making her own clothes and forging stunning dressmakers' bills. So when George goes smash she is $100,000 to the good. But George, believing she has fallen for Coombs, casts her off. She is brought to understand the situation and puts it all straight for a happy ending.

Altogether an intelligent comedy-drama, done in the best manner of the up-to-date screen producer.

Rush.

MIDNIGHT ALARM

Bearing the Vitagraph brand and designated a David Smith production. Made from the story by J. W. Harkins, Jr., screen adaptation by C. Graham Baker. No player featured. Running time 75 minutes. At the Rialto, New York, Aug. 19.

Sparkle	Alice Calhoun
Capt. Harry Westmore	Percy Marmont
Chaser	Cullen Landis
Silas Carringford	Joseph Kilgour
Aggie	Maxine Elliot Hicks
Mr. Tilwell	George Pierce
Mrs. Tilwell	Kittie Bradbury
Springer	J. Gunnis Davis
Mrs. Thornton	Alice Calhoun
Susan	Jean Carpenter
Mrs. Berg	May Foster
Bill	Fred Behrle

This is the first Vitagraph feature to get pre-release showing in a Famous Players Broadway theatre on the reported arrangement for the discontinuance of Vita's suit against the big company, alleging restraint of trade. The picture has points of appeal, but its whole style and spirit are away from lines laid down for the Rialto and Rivoli under the Famous Players regime.

"The Midnight Alarm" is a candid melodrama, with the meller laid on good and thick. It has several florid passages in the Charles E. Blaney style of heroics, but it is not for Broadway. Rather its legitimate field is the second run program houses where this sort of thing is **in demand. The Rialto reacted against the picture pretty conclusively. Monday evening the place was not a third filled at the end of the 7.30 show and it was the most undemonstrative gathering noted in that house for a long, long time.**

The story gets a quick start. Ten seconds after the main title there is a murder, after the manner of the old dime novel that started "bang, spoke a pistol in the dark and Frisco Ed, king of the underworld, was no more." It's not very subtle, but it does nail attention. Unfortunately the story does not build up from that point. It lapses sadly for many yards of film, but does wake up for another thrill when the heroine is rushing on an express train toward an open draw bridge while the villain gloats. She is saved in the nick of time by the hero, but presently is again in the villain's clutches, this time locked in a time vault on the sixth floor of a burning building.

Once more the hero to the rescue in the guise of a fire battalion chief expert in the use of the acetyline blow torch. In their lurid way the two big scenes are effective, being built up with and elaborate incidentals, such as a fight between the heavy and the young man doing comedy relief. The only thing against the picture is that it is modelled on the old fashioned blood **and thunder drama that went out of style a decade and a half ago and now excites giggles rather than gasps from sophisticated Broadway.**

The continuity is crude. For example the heavy is chasing the heroine across country. He stops to ask the way of the draw bridge keeper who seizes the occasion to explain the mechanism of the draw. Hot on the heavy's heels comes the hero, who also stops and chats with the bridge keeper, explaining that before he became a fire fighter he also ran a draw bridge. Thus the way is paved for the big scene, but the trouble is the audience is tipped off long ahead by this elaborate preparation and knows just what is going to happen. Surprise is absent and the situation loses its kick.

The same is true of the fire scene. Nothing more indirect occurred to the author than having an accomplice of the heavy throw a lighted cigar in a pile of papers. Knowing the hero was a fireman and the girl was in the villain's power in the deserted building, it required little guessing to construct the story's finish before it happened. However, the episode was played out with shooting flames, rushing fire engines, ladders and nets and all the rest of the paraphernalia to inspire a bit of a thrill. But it isn't what the Rialto clientele has been used to.

Rush.

ASHES OF VENGEANCE

First National picture, presented by Joseph Schenck and starring Norma Talmadge. Directed by Frank Lloyd, from the script of H. B. Somerville, with Tony Gaudio the photographer. At the Apollo, New York. Projection time, 111 minutes.

Yoeland de Breux	Norma Talmadge
Rupert de Vrieac	Conway Tearle
Duc de Tours	Wallace Beery
Catherine de Medici	Josephine Crowell
Margot de Vaincorie	Betty Francisco
Margot's aunt	Claire McDowell
Comte de la Roche	Courtenay Foote
Father Paul	Forrest Robinson
Paul	James Colley
Charles IX	Andre De Beranger
Duc de Guise	Boyd Irwin

A pretty picture not emphasized with action but held up by the work of Miss Talmadge and Conway Tearle. Split into two parts the film is at the Apollo as a "special showing."

The film is another costume effort and picturesque if nothing else. One interior of the upper strata of mediaeval France attending a ball at the King's palace was worthy of note, and as it is used to put the story under way it becomes doubly effective.

Many of the outdoor scenes are attractive with the remainder of the interiors appropriate and upon occasions, lavish.

The picture lacks nothing in production with the photography giving it full value except in one instance where the lighting is extremely bad. That is when Tearle is in bed, with Miss Talmadge watching over him.

Lloyd, in directing, seems to have obtained all the results possible from the story. It is always pleasing to the eye and in a drowsy manner that would be perfect to watch were one installed in a loge chair at the Capitol.

The story deals with a lifelong feud between the Vrieac and Roche families. Rupert de Vrieac (Tearle) engages in a duel with the Comte de la Roche, who succumbs to his mercy, but Rupert allows him his life as a result of an outburst of satirical generosity. The same night the attack upon the Huguenots is launched and the Comte returns the favor by saving Rupert, an avowed member, and his betrothed from the mob under condition that the Vrieac representative will become his servant for a period of five years.

The bondage becomes effective immediately with the meeting of Yoeland de Breux (Miss Talmadge), the Comte's sister, and Rupert coming as a matter of course. While in the role of servant Rupert learns of his fiancee's marriage to another. Numerous heroic deeds have endeared him to Yoeland and the finale is reached when the Comte prematurely gives him back his freedom as a reward and the sister and Rupert declare their love for each other.

The cast has turned in a nice piece of work, but it is Miss Talmadge and Mr. Tearle who predominate. Wallace Beery as the cowardly Duc de Tours is the only other member to gain particular attention and this he does emphatically.

Skig.

CHILDREN OF DUST

Arthur Jacobs presents a Frank Borzage production. Story by Tristam Tupper. First National, distributor. Projection time 64 minutes. Featured in the cast are Johnny Walker, Pauline Garon and Lloyd Hughes. At Proctor's 58th Street, Aug. 23.

This story is thin stuff to spread over more than five reels. It has some agreeable light comedy touches, but there is no substance to the whole. The work belongs in that class of pictures which try to make their principal appeal on what should be incidentals. It is all well enough to elaborate upon a good story with side lights and interesting detail, but they only heighten the effect of a good story—they cannot make the story itself.

Intrinsic interest is the essential, and that is the element absent from this effort. It is conceivable that "Children of the Dust" might have made an entertaining novelette, but it is a distinctly dull picture because it has not enough suspense or action. You could boil the five reels down to the bare statement that it is the history of a poor boy and a rich girl who overcome social obstacles and make a happy love match, helped on by a humble old gardener.

In the screen telling there are several touches that are remindful of O. Henry's literary tricks. They are humorously managed and make excellent side lights, but the story itself doesn't hold together in convincing fashion. The first two reels deal with the childhood of the principals. Young Terwilliger is the ward of a drunken truckman. He breaks into a private garden to get flowers for his mother's grave and is seized and beaten by the old gardener. Little Celia Van Houghton, daughter of an aristocratic family, witnesses the beating and goes to the waif's defense. The two children become fast friends, and young Terwilliger is given free use of the garden and becomes the fast friend of the ancient gardener. It is indicated that the children are childish lovers, but Celia is supposed to be pledged to another young aristocrat, last of the wealthy Livermores.

Celia has a gold coin which the trio bury while playing pirate. Subsequently the treasure is missing from its burial place and suspicion falls upon both boys. Terwilliger's dream is to have 50 express wagons, each drawn by a horse named Celia.

We pass over the years to the youth of the children, when the war breaks out. Terwilliger never dares hope for Celia's hand, and in order to further the wedding of the girl and his rival confesses to the theft of the gold coin. The war breaks out and both boys enlist. There are some mediocre passages of trench fighting and Terwilliger is believed to be killed.

Livermore returns home to find the old gardener grieving for the supposed death of Terwilliger and they try to comfort him. The gardener is troubled by the suspicion of the boy's theft and plants a coin near the same spot to clear his memory. But in digging up the gardener's gold piece they come upon the original coin, which absolves Terwilliger from blame. At the same time Terwilliger himself comes home, but no satisfactory explanation of his reported death and resurrection is ever made.

At any rate, the declaration of love comes promptly, and for the finish they add a dream of the old gardener's, in which he bluffs his way into Paradise by reciting to St. Peter a history to show that sometimes to lie is saintly. This touch is a graceful bit of comedy, but the story it is designed to set off is trivial and dull.

Rush.

DAYTIME WIVES

Presented by F. B. O. and written by Lenore Coffee and John Goodrich. Directed by Emile Chautard. Photographed by Lucian Andriot. At the Central the week of Aug. 26. Running time, 80 minutes.

Ruth Holt	Derelys Perdue
Elwood Adams	Wyndham Standing
Francine Adams	Grace Darmond
Michael O'Shea	Mickey O'Ban
The foreman	Eddie Hearn
His wife	Katherine Lewis
Larry Valentine	Kenneth Gibson
Perry Martin	William Conklin

Mediocre pictures that try their hardest to be entertaining are sometimes excusable, but mediocre pictures that endeavor to moralize have committed one of the most heinous sins of filmdom. No audience wants to be bored and rebuked at the same time. "Daytime Wives" does just that, and, to make it worse, the sermon it preaches is a very half-hearted and unconvincing one.

With an elaborate production and the best to be had in direction and casting, something might have been accomplished with this film, as its story holds inherent possibilities. But any original twists or ideas in the plot have been buried under the limitations and handicaps that bind the typical third-rate production. The direction is ordinary at best, the acting uneven and the continuity and sub-titles, both important factors in a picture of this description, particularly bad.

A "daytime wife," we are informed, is a working girl, not married at all, whose duty it is to look after her employer's affairs, as all good business women should. The reason for the queer appellation is never made quite clear, but the point evidently is to contrast her with the gilded butterfly of a regular spouse whose sole ambition seems to be to spend the money earned with great effort and struggle by the husband and his "daytime wife" assistant. In this particular story it is the secretary that takes the erring wife's place when a crisis arises, and it is this same secretary that brings the now repentant wife back to her forgiving husband. Naturally the business girl hates to relinquish the man she loves, but she is comforted—and here is the most glaring inconsistency of a horribly inconsistent picture—by landing the "progressive young banker" whom she has met for the first time that evening and to whom she drops an unmistakably insinuating hint about marriage.

As a side plot there is introduced the troubles of a building foreman and his wife, the kind who patronizes the delicatessen store before every meal. A de Mille or a Neilan might make an extremely effective bit of human interest business out of this, but in "Daytime Wives" it dwindles away into a trite and artificial nothingness. Physically, the film holds two fair thrills—a fight on the top of structure for a skyscraper and the caving in of the latter after the beams become loosened. Some masterful photography is shown at this spot.

A little sandy-haired, pug-nosed devil of some four or five years and bearing the bright green name of Mickey O'Ban runs away with the acting honors. Not a Jackie as yet, but as cute looking in his own mischievous way, and certainly a worthy runner-up to the one and only Coogan. Derelys Perdue is absolutely colorless as the heroine. She is pretty, but if she is a good example of the independent, resourceful business woman, most men will prefer the petted darlings of the powder puff. Wyndham Standing does well as the husband, and Grace Darmond, wearing lovely clothes, makes the most out of her ridiculous role of his wife. A newcomer named Kenneth Gibson is the best looking villain to be imagined. He tries hard to be mean and churlish and smokes innumerable cigarettes, but his handsome face, particularly because it lacks the symbol of all movie desperados, a mustache, puts him in line for decent, upstanding parts instead of nasty ones. The rest of the cast, including Craig Biddle, Jr., as a workman, have little to do.

Discriminating filmgoers will balk at this one, but with the sensational played up it will probably get by at the cheaper neighborhood houses.

TO THE LAST MAN

Lasky presentation and Paramount picture featuring Lois Wilson and Richard Dix. From the story of the same name by Zane Grey, adapted by Doris Schroeder with Victor Fleming the director. Photographers, Jean Howe and Bert Baldridge. At the Rialto, New York, Aug. 26. Running time, 75 minutes.

Jean	Richard Dix
Ellen Jorth	Lois Wilson
Colter	Noah Beery
Gaston Isbel	Robert Edeson
Blue	Frank Campeau
Lee Jorth	Fred Huntley
Daggs	Edward Brady
Simm Bruce	Jean Palette
Guy	Lenard Clapham
Bill	Guy Oliver
Mrs. Guy	Winifred Greenwood

A well made, feudal, western that should click on the strength of its story and the work of the cast. Authenticated as having been actually "shot" in the Tonto Basin, Arizona, where the tale in bookform was located, the exteriors seemingly not only bear out the claim but are of intrinsic value for their beauty.

Fleming, in directing, has trailed pretty close to the narrative as laid down when a novel and outside of permitting a few overly dramatic subtitles to get by has turned in a creditable piece of work as his bit. And the photographers have well taken care of their end.

The story is that of a family feud, between the Isbels and Jorths, transplanted from Texas to Arizona and carrying on until only the boy and girl are left as representatives of their native kin. The clinch finish calls off the strife after much gun play, horsemanship and picturesque falls off high mountain ridges.

There can be no wail because of a dearth of action in this one for the film teems with it. Individual combats, a bar-room gunplay free for all, chases, and a well executed avalanche give some idea of what goes on during the 75 minutes the picture is on. Neither is that to say that the film is wild and hectic. It's not. The action carries along nicely, gaining momentum on the way to reach its conclusion without having lost a member of the witnessing audience.

The feature is "pie" for all the younger picture theatre-goers throughout the country while the older members should also get a "kick" out of this fast moving vehicle.

Richard Dix, as Jean Isbel, records favorably as the youngest, fighting halfbreed son of the family with Miss Wilson in the role of Ellen Jorth neatly taking her share of the burden. Others to stand out in the cast are, Robert Edeson, Noah Beery and Winifred Greenwood who made a small bit stand out for all that it was worth.

Skig.

THE CHEAT

Presented by Adolph Zukor under the Paramount banner, starring Pola Negri and featuring Jack Holt. The story, by Hector Turnbull, adapted by Ouida Bergere, with George Fitzmaurice directing. Arthur Miller, photographer. At Rivoli, New York, Aug. 27. Running time, 78 mins.

Carmelita de Cordoba	Pola Negri
Dudley Drake	Jack Holt
Claude Mace, alias Prince Rao-Singh	Charles de Roche
Lucy Hodge	Dorothy Cumming
Jack Hodge	Robert Schable
Horace Drake	Charles Stevenson

Another mark for Paramount so far as production is concerned, but it doesn't mean a thing for the star. Pola Negri fails to convince in her characterization of a South American heiress. Point the arrow toward the boys which has the underline, "Go Get 'Em," set up a camera, and this foreign belle is able to produce with intelligent direction founded upon a sustaining tale.

But this particular release is minus the necessary value in story to carry it through, and has only the work of Jack Holt to redeem it. Fitzmaurice's presentation illusions he has attempted by sheer strength of settings and clothes to put this one across, and while the lavish interiors impress and the clothes of Miss Negri make the women talk, it doesn't alter the fact that a Monday night audience at the Rivoli laughed at it.

The wilful, thoughtless and spoiled characterization Miss Negri was given would seem to have been somewhat beyond her registering powers. Where the role should create a sympathetic atmosphere there is none, with just the opposite becoming more true than otherwise. Miss Negri throws upon the screen a distinctively hard personality, which, when she is vamping, is foolproof, but when it should create pathos there is a direful lack that in roles of this sort is courting disaster.

Along the usual "society" lines is the story, bounded on one side by a fake Hindu prince loaded with pieces of eight who continues to chase the girl after her marriage, and on the other by a poor, American husband who must wait for "an important deal" to go through before he can give his wife her accustomed luxury. Between the two the tale skips from a few interiors of South America to Paris, to New York and thence Long Island. It's of little interest outside of the star's flash costuming and a sincere effort on the part of Holt to make the conglomeration realistic.

A courtroom scene caused a gale of laughter which swept the house. There's one of those included in the continuity, a plea of guilty by the wife to release her husband, who would shield her, the branding of the girl by the Hindu, who retaliates by shooting him, not fatally, and the riot in court when the wife reveals the brand upon her shoulder which sets the mob upon the phoney prince. The latter incident was the laugh.

Outside of Holt the remainder of the cast hardly qualifies, although Charles de Roche is allotted special billing but doesn't rate it. *Skig.*

SHATTERED REPUTATIONS

Released by the Lee Bradford Corporation and starring Johnny Walker and Jackie Saunders. This is all the information given during the film or on the advertising sheets. At the Circle Aug. 21 as half of a double bill with "The Untameable." Running time, 51 minutes.

The director and author may be flattered on their judgment if their names have been purposely left off the billing. To be associated with it in any way is a left-handed honor, because it is a lemon. Usually there is some redeeming feature, but in this case even the least critical will search in vain.

The story, decrepit with age, is of the loving sister shielding the erring, misguided brother in order not to bring grief to the father who worships his only son as above sin.

A sordid bit is near the end, when the brother and the villain who has taught him to steal fall over a cliff together after a struggle and are shown lying mangled at the bottom.

The scenes supposed to be snapped at a fashionable summer beach look like Hoboken on a nasty day. Subtitles and attempted bits of local color are equally dull. The escape of the brother from the prison chain-gang is one of the crudest pieces of action ever filmed. There are no shots that show any photographic originality. Everything is uniformly bad, and the acting is no exception.

Jackie Saunders plays the lead. Miss Saunders would be smarter if going in for character stuff. Johnny Walker does not make an appearance until the film is half over, and then he is utterly miscast as the righteously indignant hero. The rest of the cast is fully down to the general standard of the picture.

LOYAL LIVES

Whitman Bennett production, featuring Faire Binney, Mary Carr, Tyrone Power and William Collier, Jr. Whitman Bennett directing from the script by Charles Rich. Projection time, 63 minutes. At Proctor's 23d St., New York, Aug. 27-29.

One of those indefinite independent pictures. In this case the producer has assembled a notable cast, but the story is weak. It is devoted to the exploitation of humble, faithful workers in the American postal service—a sentimental and sympathetic tale of humble, commonplace lives, but without any striking situations.

The punch of the picture is a fight in a railway mail car, in which young Collier battles with a brigand, throwing him through the car door as they are crossing a trestle and leaping into the water for a life-and-death struggle in defense of the mail bag. Except for this melodramatic incident the story is drab and dull.

Long passages are devoted to the humble life of the faithful letter carrier, O'Brien, and his family, which remains poor but contented in Uncle Sam's service, while O'Brien's pal, Mike Brady, goes into the mail order business and piles up a fortune.

Postal thieves rob the mails of Brady's remittances, and one of the marked stolen bills comes into O'Brien's possession. He is suspected of thefts and is arrested. In the meantime his son, who has followed the old man's footsteps in the postal service, performs his act of heroism, and for a finale they have O'Brien visiting Postmaster-General Harry New in Washington to receive from his hands the praise that is the only reward for a faithful servant of the government.

They show the postoffice building in Washington for this episode, and really get Posstmaster-General New to pose for the short shot. That is the picture's closing surprise.

The special purpose may be disclosed in the quotation from the New York postoffice front, "Neither storm nor rain nor gloom of night stays these couriers from the swift completion of their appointed rounds," and frequent dissertations on the worthiness of the hard-working postal carriers and the meagerness of their reward.

All of which is true; but it does not help to make a commonplace screen story especially thrilling to the general public which demands a thrill and a kick in its screen material.

Rush.

DON'T MARRY FOR MONEY

B. P. Fineman production released by L. Lawrence Weber and Bobby North. Story by Hope Lorning and Louis Duryea Leighton; directed by Clarence L. Brown. Shown at the Central, New York, week of Aug. 19. Running time, 63 minutes.

Pete Smith	House Peters
Marion Whitney	Rubye de Remer
Edith Martin	Aileen Pringle
Crane Martin	Cyril Chadwick
Rose Graham	Christine Mayo
The Inspector	Wedgewood Nowell
Amos Webb	George Nichols
An "Explorer"	Hank Mann
Alec Connor	Charles Wellesley

This is one of the stereotyped society dramas with a little of the underworld element thrown in to make it effective. All of the regulation tricks and bits of business that have proven successful in the past are included so that the picture is in reality comprised of a series of scenes that have proven themselves surefire in the past, and therefore cannot go wrong. The result is a picture that is certain to please the average dyed-in-the-wool movie fan in the majority of houses.

It is the story of the good-looking girl who weds wealth, falls in the clutches of the smooth heavy, who is in reality trying to compromise her so that he can pin a shake-down on her. The husband walks in on the scene as the heavy is getting in his strong work, but instead of rushing in and beating him up he takes other means to revenge himself and to make the home-wrecker look foolish in the eyes of the wife. The success of the scheme makes the heavy determined to get square through the medium of a little gun play, but his accomplice, a girl blackmailer, struggles with him and the gun goes off killing him. Then the wife and husband both walk in, and each believing that the other committed the crime, take the blame on their own shoulders, with the result that when the real cause of the death is discovered there is a reconciliation at the final fade-out.

Regulation meller hoak fairly well presented. *Fred.*

HARBOR LIGHTS

Produced by the Ideal Films, Ltd., with Tom Moore starred. Film version of the English drama by George R. Sims and Henry Pettitt. Presented by Associated Exhibitors and distributed by Pathe Exchange. Directed by Tom Teriss. Shown as half of double feature bill at Loew's New York, Aug. 21. Running time 59 minutes.

Lieut. David Kingsley	Tom Moore
Dora Nelson	Isobel Elsom
Lina Nelson	Annette Benson
Capt. Nelson	Gordon Begg
Mark Helstone	Gibson Gowland
Mrs. Helstone	Mary Rorke
Frank Morland	Gerald McCarthy
Nicholas Morland	Percy Standing
Solomon	Jeff Barlow
Tom	Judd Green
Detective Wood	A. B. Imeson

Tom Moore appears in an English production surrounded by an entire English cast. It is a thrilling tale of passion and intrigue with the right out on top as usual. From the start one feels that they have already guessed the incidents which lead to the climax, but they are quickly fooled when the story through able direction takes a sudden twist which practically holds the audience in suspense throughout. The production is not gigantic nor big but will pass muster.

Moore has the typical part and shows the English cinema folks a trick or two in speed and action. His effervescing smile is always in evidence, whether the situation or scene be one of love, despair or anguish.

Isobel Elsom, as Dora Nelson, gave an unusually capable performance in an emotional role. She had several heavy dramatic scenes. Annette Benson had no easy task as the betrayed sister who strove to have her lover redeem himself with her while he was seeking conquest with her sister.

The story is of a young girl smitten with a naval officer and prepared to marry him when his ship comes to port. At that time the lover of her sister after hearing that the girl about to be married has inherited a fortune decides he will get her into his clutches and retrieve the fortune he has lost through dissipation.

Most of the scenes are interiors, with the outdoor shots being taken in a beautiful natural setting which will draw marked attention, especially the panoramic views of the cliff and the swirling seas.

THE SUNSHINE TRAIL

Thomas H. Ince production starring Douglas McLean in William Wallace Cook's story, screen-adapted by Bradley King and directed by James W. Horne. Ran 60 minutes, as half of a double feature coupled with a Selznick-Norma Talmadge reissue at Loew's New York, New York.

From start to finish the picture satirizes and burlesques the Pollyanna theme. While at first thought one might opine that the travesty could have been meted out in broader doses, its restraint is commendable on reflection.

Jimmy McTavish (Douglas McLean) is the central character. His one motto in life is "scatter seeds of kindness," etc., a guiding slogan conned from an illustrated post card. And so like all well-meaning humans who plan their kindnesses with purpose aforethought, his good intentions go astray and involve him in several embarrassing complications while he is traveling the "sunshine trail."

The picture starts with a rough and tumble fight between two burly westerners, the victor of the fisticuff engagement admonishing his conquered opponent, "that'll teach you not to use my safety razor" and

which effectively plants the general idea of the production. Enters Jimmy McTavish announcing his intention to return to his home town in the east.

While practising one of his Pollyanna principles at a way station in minding a young child, he finds himself with the lad on his hands and so must continue his journey with a juvenile burden. Also, with the best of intention to assist an "eloping" couple who are in reality heads of a band of crooks, he effects the criminals' escape at the expense of the arresting officer although later he is solely responsible in foiling their hold-up on a bank and capturing them single-handed.

The girl is June Carpenter (Edith Roberts). She becomes engaged to the son of the richest man in Jimmy's home town against her own inclinations and only to oblige her mother. She has a basic affection for the "Sonny" McTavish of her childhood years and when the latter makes his identity known to the townsfolk they suspect him an imposter there to claim a fortune of $50,000 left by an old friend (or relative — distinction not made clear). June is the only one to recognize him but when the hero spies her engagement ring he denies his true identity for altruistic reasons. Among other things he is jailed as a villain a half hour after having been hailed a hero but the wind-up finds him escorted from the hoosegow with a brass band, once more village idol.

Much of the picture is screen persiflage but is interesting throughout for all its careless fun. Probably written to reflect a real situation humorously, the director at times has lapsed into farce and unrealistic hoke. The admixture all told is funny however.

Were the story taken seriously for instance, a flashback at a birthday party among 12 year olds wouldn't find the stocky McLean in knickers and furbelows doing the "kid" part, personally, instead of a juvenile substitute.

In addition to the principals, Muriel Francis Dana as the kiddie deserves worthy comment. The youngster could stand some attention as a kid star possibility on the order of Baby Peggy. *Abel.*

BLINKY

Universal, starring Hoot Gibson. Story by Gene Markey, adapted and directed by Edward Sedgwick. Shown at Loew's New York, N. Y., on double feature bill Aug. 17, 1923. Running time, 58 minutes.

Geoffrey Islip	Hoot Gibson
Mary Lou Kileen	Esther Ralston
Mrs. Islip	Mathilde Brundage
Col. "Raw Meat" Islip	DeWitt Jennings
Priscilla Islip	Elinor Field
Bertrand Van Dusen	Donald Hatswell
Major Kileen	Charles K. French
Husk Barton	John Judd
Lieut. Rawkins	William E. Lawrence

Fairly interesting comedy romance, in which Hoot Gibson is given a role of a type somewhat different from those he has had, and in it he makes a decided impression. The story is of Washington society and the Mexican border. There are many possibilities for laugh material, and they are made the most of in the direction of the screen version.

It looks like a picture that exhibitors in almost any class of theatre, except possibly the big pre-release houses, can run and rest assured that their audiences will be entertained. There isn't much to the feature that will pull to the box office unless Gibson has a following in the neighborhood.

Gibson has the role of a rather namby-pamby son of a retired army colonel. The mother wants the boy to have a commission. Dad fixes it for him, but instead of getting him a swivel chair job dad frames for the boy to be sent to his old outfit on the Mexican border. Here they eventually make a real man of the boy and he wins the daughter of his

commanding officer after rescuing her from the clutches of bootleggers.

Esther Ralston, DeWitt Jennings and Charles K. French acquit themselves admirably. The army post riding stuff is particularly well done in direction. *Fred.*

MINE TO KEEP

Ben Wilson production, presented by Samuel V. Grand and released by the Grand-Asher Distributing Corp. Author not caught from screen and the names of the three assistant directors to whom Ben Wilson acknowledges credit for their efforts also passed up in hasty screening. Ran an hour at Proctor's 58th Street theatre, New York, in conjunction with vaudeville, August 20-22.

Victor Olney	Bryant Washburn
Constance Rives	Mabel Forrest
Carmen Joy	Charlotte Stevens
Mrs. Rives	Kate Lester
Clint Morbray	Wheeler Oakman
Mrs. Joy	Laura LaVarney
Joy Children	Peaches Jackson / Mickey Moore / Pat Moore

The very first titles start out with a discourse on the marriage theme and the third of the lengthy leaders concludes with something like this: "Our advice is, etc." This stamps the production right off the bat, although it does not become too preachy, which is something to be thankful for, anyway.

The premise that a union based on a tissue of falsehoods is insecure is demonstrated with Victor Olney's and Constance Rives' marriage. Olney, identified as a wealthy clubman, engaged Carmen Joy, "the toast of the Winter Garden," to do her wire dancing specialty at his bachelor dinner. The dancer is smitten with Olney, although the latter knows naught of it, and even the audience is given no intimation of the fact until a title breaks the information on them suddenly. While doing her stuff aloft an enthusiastic guest proposes a toast to the bride. Carmen becomes dizzy and falls from the wire, resulting in a serious spinal injury. Olney effects a $5,000 settlement with her.

The couple are married, and thereafter Olney's peculiar jealousy causes a rift between the two. Clint Morbray's entrance further complicates matters. Clint was a former admirer of Mrs. Olney. Morbray has become reckless in his mad motoring and airplaning following Constance's marriage and the latter feels somewhat responsible. This adds coal to the fire. The couple separate. Constance has been falsely informed of her husband's alleged "affair" with the Winter Garden dancer, and it all becomes straightened out when the latter personally admits she has had a childish "crush" on Olney, the latter being totally in the dark all the while. Carmen's back has become strong under Constance's care, and it all ends happily.

Some of the titles do not ring true and are little less than flowery phraseology thrust in the mouths of the characters to progress the debate.

Wilson evidently started out making Morbray a sort of sympathetic "heavy," but spoiled it by permitting him to do some nasty lying in true villain fashion. Much of the picture strikes a false note, although Wilson tried hard to dress it up neatly. The night race between auto and train was a minor punch. A nice touch was the dancing to radio music.

On the other hand, some of the sepia tinting did not jibe well with Miss Forrest's blonde beauty. Charlotte Stevens appeared miscast at first in the indoor shots, due to the bad lighting. In the outdoor scenes she showed off to better advantage. The casting otherwise was adequate. Bryant Washburn was sincere throughout, and Wheeler Oakman gave a good account of himself. The balance of the support took care of their parts nicely.

It's a "society" picture of the sort that usually appeals to the average neighborhood house fan and should make a good buy for the daily change theatres. *Abel.*

ROUGED LIPS

Metro picture starring Viola Dana. From the story "Upstate," by Rita Weiman. Adaptation and continuity by Thomas J. Hopkins. Directed by Harold Shaw. Photographed by John Arnold. Subtitles by Clyde A. Bruckman. At the State, Aug. 20-22. Running time, 62 minutes.

Norah MacPherson	Viola Dana
James Patterson III	Tom Moore
Mamie Dugan	Nola Luxford
James Patterson II	Sidney de Gray
Mariette	Arline Pretty
Mr. MacPherson	Francis Powers
Mrs. MacPherson	Georgie Woodthorpe
Billy Dugan	Burwell Hamrick

The thousands of Viola Dana fans will see in this film something of the Viola Dana of a few years back—the elfish, wistful flapper of "A Chorus Girl's Romance," "Head and Shoulders," "The Off Shore Pirate," and others of the Scott Fitzgerald type at which she excels. In her more recent pictures Miss Dana has tackled other sorts of roles and consequently has lacked her customary piquancy and appeal. Here she has a part that fits her like a one-piece bathing suit—a fiery, resourceful daughter of a Scotch father and an Irish mother.

The picture is a slight little thing, attractive, and a welcome relief from the heavy divorce and intrigue stuff cornering the screen of late. It is one more eloquent plea against the destructiveness of that insurmountable "no less than an hour running time" law. Were it to last 45 minutes it would be an ideal program attraction, but that extra quarter of an hour causes it to drag unmercifully toward the finish. Rita Weiman has written a story without an ounce of originality, but with pounds of humor and tons of human interest.

Norah MacPherson is left alone in the world after the death of her parents, who have striven for years to instill into her the qualities of their respective native lands. Thirty-five a week in the chorus of the Summer Garden looks good to her and she accepts a job as a chorine.

Along comes James Patterson III, who "knows every bootlegger and chorus girl on Broadway" and "whose main ambition is to yawn without stretching." From then on it is Norah's task to force this gilded youth to the point where he realizes that it might be a good idea to get out and work for her. She is successful eventually, but in doing it she gets in and out of all sorts of scrapes herself. The punch comes when she decides to conquer her inherited Scotch thrift and buy herself some clothes that will make Jimmy proud. He misunderstands and it takes a long time before he is convinced that some other man is not "daddying" her.

Next to Miss Dana's acting, the subtitles are the best. Written by Clyde A. Bruckman. The direction is also splendid and the camera work above criticism.

The opening night at the Summer Garden is done without all the artificiality usually attending such scenes in the films. Some delightful touches are woven, as when the two old bucks in the baldhead row look around cautiously and whisper, "I hope there's nobody here from Utica." The dressing room scenes are intimate and spicy, but need not fear any censors. Some good double exposure shots are used to show the Scotch and Irish spirits advising the heroine at various times.

Miss Dana is pretty, as usual, but she looks thinner than ever and unnecessarily stresses the title of the film by having her lips too heavily coated. Tom Moore has never done better work than as the lovable loafer of a hero. No villain is introduced, to Miss Weiman's credit, but Arline Pretty plays a ritzy show girl with a nasty disposition and does it well.

THE UNTAMABLE

Universal picture starring Gladys Leslie. Directed by Herbert Blache. Story by Gillette Burgess. Photographed by Ben Kline. At the Circle Aug. 21 as half of a double bill with "Shattered Reputations." Running time, 55 mins.

Joy Fielding....................Gladys Leslie
Chester Arnold..........Malcolm McGregor
Dr. Frederick Copin.........John Sainpolis
Ah Moy...........................Etta Lee

A preposterous little affair but one that will not harm nor bore. Gladys Leslie has appeared in ridiculous pictures before, but never in one with as moonstruck a plot as this holds. It lives up to its evident purpose—to amuse and to provide a few little spine ticklers. An inexpensive film to produce, it will doubtless prove a good, stable moneymaker for the Universal.

The central theme is hypnotism, which causes the heroine to be a sort of Dr. Jekyll and Miss Hyde. A sweet, demure girl when not molested, she becomes awfully naughty when under the spell of the wicked physician, who hopes to get both her and her money by subjugating her to his psychic powers.

The worst part is that when under his spell she not only turns into a veritable fury but abandons all modesty and maidenly reserve. So she runs around very much in dishabille, petting all the men, tearing her gown from her shoulder and even coaxing the virtuous hero into the sanctityt of her boudoir.

She marries the villainous doctor one day, and the next, when free from his hypnotic trance, weds the rising young architect. Complications follow like machine-gun bullets, but at last the doctor is torn to pieces by the fierce dogs he has mistreated in the evening, the girl is free from his machinations, and the final clinch comes with a rush.

All this action transpires in an exotic looking mansion scented by oriental incense. The story is more weird and impossible than is apparent on paper. Direction and photography stress the imaginative side and add to the general atmosphere of make-believe.

A heavy burden rests upon Miss Leslie and she does surprisingly well. In her sane scenes she exhibits a reserve and girlishness that are most appealing. But when supposedly hypnotized she misses by being too much the impish gamin of her earlier pictures rather than the victim of a subconscious force. John Sainpolis as the physician adds another notable performance to his long list. Malcolm McGregor is a handsome, virile hero, and Etta Lee outstanding in a Chinese maid bit.

A FRONT PAGE STORY

Vitagraph special presented by Albert E. Smith. Made from the story by Arthur Goodrich; directed by Jess Robins and a Jess Robins production. Seen at Loew's Hippodrome, Baltimore.

Rodney Marvin..............Edward Horton
Mayor Gorham..............Lloyd Ingraham
Matt Hayward..............James Corrigan
Virginia Hayward...........Edith Roberts
Don Coates.................W. E. Lawrence
Tommy ....Buddy Messenger
Mrs. Gorham...........Mathilde Brundage
Suzanne Gorham....................Lila Leslie
Jack Peeler......................Tom McGuire

This film makes pretensions of being out of the ordinary, yet, in the final analysis, it is an ordinary piece of work, being without novelty in theme or development and acted out by a fair to middlin' cast which makes no special claim to distinction, the Press Sheet to the contrary.

It is a pleasant warm weather tale of a newspaper and of its owner-editor, played by James Corrigan, and of the usual brilliant young reporter (Edward Horton), who, in the course of the five reels, meets the boss' daughter, takes time out for a couple of reels to pick up lunch at Childs' and then goes out and pulls the big scoop of the year, arriving back in Dad's house in time to propose to the beautiful daughter and work things around to the place where that old Latin word (Finis) of infinite comfort can be flashed.

In the course of all this, Mr. Horton displays a good sense of comedy and quiet humor much like that of Johnny Hines, he of "Torchy" fame, and also permits the public to gaze at one of the most remarkable flivvers which ever walked its way across the silver sheet.

A local critic remarked that it did everything but stand on its hind legs and bark.

The film is good for the neighborhood houses and is pleasant entertainment for the undiscerning, but for a dyed-in-the-wool movie fan, this film isn't going to ring the bell. Its just that sort of a picture. Looking at it from another angle, it is merely another film in that long succession of films which have tried to give newspaper work some degree of truthful presentation before the people — but like its predecessors, it has failed miserably. The fault with most of them is that they must introduce a love interest, the boss' daughter and one of these screen variety of brilliant cubs to make the film stand up.

They omit much of the real excitement and lose all the real atmosphere of the offices where copy paper ofttimes gets ankle deep around the city editor's desk and where the old copy readers still maintain their individual spittoons.

Sisk.

THE MIRACLE BABY

R-C production, starring Harry Carey. Distributed by Film Booking Office. Adaptation by Bernstein-Jaccard from story by Frank Pierce. Directed by Val Paul. William Thornley, photographer. At Loew's New York, Aug. 9.

Neil Allison.........................Harry Carey
Judy Stanton..................Margaret Landis
"Hopeful" Mason.....Charles J. L. Mayne
Hal Norton..................Edward Hearn
Violet..............................Hedda Nova
Dr. Amos Stanton..............Alfred Allen
Sam Bradford.....................Bert Sprotte

Program picture of average merit, with the sort of stuff they like in the pop price houses. Considerable action in the five and half reels, including a murder with the hero believing he committed it until the heavy is disclosed the culprit; a hand-to-hand scrap between hero and heavy; chase over the snow-carpeted mountains which winds up with the heavy going over the cliff to his death in good old melodramatic style, and the rescue of a baby from a burning cabin.

The heart interest is provided for, and there is comedy relief here and there. There isn't a great deal of suspense as most of the incidents comprising the plot are over familiar through frequent usage. But the big scenes have been compactly put together and where punches are supposed to be—they're there, with a certain element of speed characterizing the more important dramatic scenes.

A mining camp atmosphere with realized opportunities for some first rate mountain exteriors forms the scenic background for most of the happenings. No great artistry in the directing or acting is discernible nor expected in this grade of picture, but the direction is satisfactory, and the acting qualifies to the extent that the dramatics are made convincing and the story intelligible.

Harry Carey in this is just Harry Carey, a typical blue-shirt lead as he has been in innumerable other pictures in which he has starred. Edward Hearn makes a good heavy and Margaret Landis, although having little as the heroine, does that little acceptably. Hedda Nova is convincing as the villainess, and Chas. J. L. Mayne as a character role interesting. In general the cast should be credited for not over-acting. Pictures like this never cause any great commotion, but they're necessary to fill a definite demand for the second and third run houses. This one classes as good for its type.

Bell.

Foreign Films

HUTCH STIRS 'EM UP

London, Aug. 10.

Frank H. Crane and the Ideal Company have reputations for good work which they fail to quite live up to in this their latest shown picture. It is melodramatic hotchpotch in which Charles Hutchison, specially brought over, attempts to get over some of the stunts and rough stuff which have made him a popular serial "star."

The somewhat weak story, adapted from a novel, "The Hawke of Rede," is packed with fights, fires, villainy of a very desperate sort, gliders, patrol boats and all the things which go to make a serial, but here we have the whole collection in five reels. Only in the beautiful setting and locations is Crane's art apparent.

Hutch, after 15 years as a cowboy, returns to his native village and promptly falls foul of the insane and tyrannical squire. This worthy loves to live in the days of feudal glory and seeks to bend the villagers to his will. He desires to possess Joan Armstrong, who fears and resists him. Saved by Hutch from his embraces, she falls in love with her rescuer. The Squire, madder than ever after several accidents to his plans, at last captured the daring Hutch and then trapped Joan. Full of mediaeval cruelty, the Squire had Hutch tortured in the girl's presence in order to make her yield. She consented to become his, but was again rescued after a terrific fight. They escaped by means of a tunnel to the open. Putting Joan in a place of safety, as he thought, Hutch returned to settle things with his enemy, who, however, once more kidnapped the girl and put out to sea with her. Hutch pursued on a glider and arrived in time. The Squire met the reward of villainy and hero and heroine found that of virtue.

The picture was made down amid the beautiful scenery of Devon and many of the shots are of great beauty. Charles Hutchison gives an excellent performance as himself, and rides, fights, makes love, falls into traps, flies, swims and does all the things which have made him famous. Gibson Gowland is responsible for an excellent performance as the maniacal Squire. Malcolm Tod is easy in a "walking juvenile" part. Joan Barry is out of the picture as the girl and seems rather bewildered by the rush of events. She does this without conveying for a moment that she is terrified. Sunday Willshin has little to do but look pretty, which she does to everyone's satisfaction. She is quite one of the prettiest women in the British screen world and deserves better parts. Many small parts are well played.

Hutchison's name will get this feature over, and there is no doubt its "thrill a minute" business will make it popular with many audiences.

Gore.

PEACE AND QUIET

London, Aug. 7

Produced at the Comedy last night by Benrimo, "Peace and Quiet" proved very light fare, a comedy tinged with conventional and unoriginal melodrama, which could not be taken very seriously. All that mattered really was that the author, Horace Hodges, had written himself an eccentric character part something after the style of "Grumpy," which he played admirably. Hodges was co-author of "Grumpy."

A middle-aged hypochondriac in search of a rest-cure prescribed by his doctor for an attack of nerves, finds himself in the midst of deep dyed villiany at a farmhouse recommended to him by his cousin Grant. Through the clumsy overturning of a flowerpot in the dead of night, the honorable, if unromantic, hero discovers Grant has eloped with the farmer's daughter, a sweet young thing who is the village belle, and knowing his cousin to be something of a scoundrel, he sets out to overtake the runaways. He tracks them down at an empty house just as a mock marraige ceremony has been concluded, and exposing the trickery compels the couple to return. Needless to say he finally wins the girl for himself and speedily forgets his fancied ailments.

With the exception of Tom Reynolds as the father of the eloping girl, the cast is worse than mediocre. The average school of acting in America could have recruited a much superior aggregation.

Jolo.

LOVE-INTRIGUE-PASSION

London, Aug. 3.

If super pictures were judged by their inordinate length and gorgeous setting this feature would be a super. Unfortunately, something more than these things are required, and this requirement puts "Love-Intrigue-Passion" among the "also rans."

Of Teutonic origin, it is a first-class practical joke, the joke being emphasized by the most clumsy subtitle probably ever seen. It is melodrama of the problem type, enlivened by such literary gems as "Shows a man in search of his soul" and "When Destiny cannot get a man it sends a woman to get him." For some hours it gave the jaded film [illegible] years since they laughed so much or so heartily.

A woman of easy virtue lives in a palace about twice the size of Buckingham. She has a battalion of servants, whom she reviews. She gives a big fete. Mistaking a cowled figure for that of the man who is at the moment her favorite, she leads him into her private apartments. He turns out to be an escaped convict. She promptly decides he is desirable, and when an army of police arrives she secrets him. He repays her by stealing her diamonds, but leaves a notte extolling her beauty. "Through the dark hours she waits, confident of his return." He returns all right, but nothing more is said about the diamonds; instead she welcomes him in one of the scantiest chemises ever seen. After this she keeps him.

He meets a "pure young girl," who gives him the glad eye, with the result his keeper shows him the door. He contemplates suicide, but is prevented by an emasculated individual in an effeminate costume which more than suggests his real character, who begs him to "spare one hour from a life he would waste." He accompanies this thing, and is then shown love, passion, intrigue in many different lands and always with himself and the lady who has just kicked him out as affinities. The result is he decides to work and books his passage from America, taking the "pure young girl" with him.

As one delighted critic said when "Finis" came on the screen it is to be hoped they had been married before they took their cabin. Used to tripe as we are in this country, the story of this picture beats anything yet seen. The production is on a magnificent scale and the crowd work is very fine. The players' names, with one exception, are denied us, which is lucky for the players. The exception is the woman with a capacity for love, Lucy Dorinne. She is described as the beautiful Franco-Slav actress. If beauty be judged by bulk she has the prize.

Acting is apparently of little account, but she is an authority on stripping down for it. *Gore.*

WITCHCRAFT

London, Aug. 6.

Swedish and Danish pictures easily hold the palm for morbid realism, and in many cases for brilliant acting and production. "Witchcraft," made by Benjamin Christensen, leaves all the others beaten. It is in reality a pictorial history f black magic; of witches; of the Inquisition, and the thousand and one inhumanities of the superstition-ridden middle ages. Many of its scenes are unadulterated horror.

The story tells how a young man lies sick. A priest passes over his body a ladle full of molten metal. This is then cooled in water, and the shape the cold metal assumes prove the patient is under the spell of a witch. An old woman beggar is accused, and the girl wife comes under suspicion. All are haled before the Inquisition and the torture is applied. In her agony the old beggar confesses and implicates the other woman in the sick man's household. They are condemned to the stake. The priest has conceived a guilty longing for the young wife, and submits to a ghastly flagellation. She is accused of bewitching the priest and forced into a confession. She is executed.

Many of the scenes are remarkable, especially those in which the girl wanders stark naked in a world of imaginative horror. Devils and other horrors rise around her. She awakes to find herself in bed, but nerve-shattered. Hysteria is mistaken for witchery, and she is condemned. Wonderful though this picture is, it is absolutely unfit for public exhibition, and it is very unlikely any firm will take it up for such a purpose, at any rate in England. *Gore.*

HUNCHBACK OF NORTE DAME

Film adaptation of the Victor Hugo story, presented by Carl Laemmle as special attraction at Astor (legit) New York, Sept. 2, for run. Lon Chaney starred. Directed by Wallace Worsley with adaptation by Perley Poore Sheehan. Running time about 120 minutes. Universal picture.

Quasimodo....................Lon Chaney
Clopin....................Ernest Torrence
Esmeralda....................Patsy Ruth Miller
Phoebus....................Norman Kerry
Mme. de Gondelaurier..........Kate Lester
Jehan....................Brandon Hurst
Gringoire....................Raymond Hatton
Louis XI....................Tully Marshall
Dom Claude....................Nigel de Brulier
Monsieur Neufchatel..Harry L. Van Meter
Godule....................Gladys Brockwell
Marie....................Eulalie Jensen
Fleur de Lys....................Winifred Bryson

The programed statistical recordings say this picture cost U over a million; that it called for tons of materials and hundreds of people, all sounding truthful enough (except the cost) after seeing it and the total achieved seems to have been a huge—mistake.

"The Hunchback of Notre Dame" is a two-hour nightmare. It's murderous, hideous and repulsive.

The "sex" angle is meagre and it [illegible]ot on that score the picture will [illegible] panned; it's the repulsiveness even in the massiveness that repels.

Hugo's tale is immortal; Laemmle's picture is fragile as a film house commodity. In an inserted preamble in the "souvenir" program signed by Carl Laemmle in his Spencerian signature occurs the following: "I doubt that he (Hugo) had ever even heard of Hollywood."

Mr. Laemmle could have made the statement that Hugo had never heard of Hollywood without qualification. But there is certainly some doubt if Laemmle ever heard of children.

No children can stand its morbid scenes, and there are likely but few parents seeing it first who will permit their young to see it afterward.

Lon Chaney is starred on the program and in the billing for the Astor, but in the preliminary slides detailing manufacturing information, Mr. Chaney is featured. A change of opinion about the billing must have occurred between that same Hollywood and Broadway.

Mr. Chaney's performance as a performance entitles him to starring honors—it makes him for ever more on the screen, but his make up as the Hunchback is propaganda for the wets. His misshapened figure from the hump on his back to the deadeyed eye on his face can not stand off his acting nor his acrobatics, nor his general work of excellence throughout this film. And when the hunchback dies the manner in which he is killed is not left to the imagination; you see Jehan (Brandon Hurst) stab him not once but twice, and in the back or in the hump.

Knives were plentiful in the reign of Louis XI., A. D. 1482, in France. So were the tramps with Clopin (Ernest Torrence) as King of the Bums making the misery of the picturized version stand up and out.

"The Hunchback of Notre Dame" is misery all of the time, nothing but misery, tiresome, loathsome misery that doesn't make you feel any the better for it. As witness the only involuntary applause breaking our during the running of the picture when the King's Guards galloped in view, to put down the uprising of the bums who were storming the Cathedral. The audience didn't want the bums, it didn't want the misery, it didn't want the gruesomeness, not even the "invited" audience that walked in at the premiere with tickets stamped $10 each.

And with tickets at $10 each on the opening night the single way to get a program was to pay 25 cents for it in the lobby. A big time picture with small time manners!

The preamble related much of the "gore" of the Hugo tale had been overlooked, but sufficient was retained. It's gory nearly all of the way with the only laugh moment when the deaf hunchback was testifying in court before a deaf justice with such ensuing comedy in the midst of a "$1,250,000 production" as might be expected in a Columbia burlesque show.

Patsy Ruth Miller is the Esmeralda, a sweetly pretty girl carrying her troubles nicely enough for the heavy work thrust upon her and with the absence of heavy emoting not so noticeable through her opposites not being always as emotional as they should have been either. Norman Kerry is the gallant Phoebus and a lukewarm lover at times, although Mr. Laemmle may have decided lukewarmness was in vogue in A. D. 1482.

Hurst's Jehan as the dirty villain had much character, although Torrence's was well balanced and evenly handled in playing as was Chaney's role. Raymond Hatton's Gringoire is well conceived in its poetic leanings and faithfully done.

Just what an exhibitor may expect from this U special is problematical. It has the name of Victor Hugo for an extra attraction and through that U got the benefit of a story calling for no royalty nor price-for-story with the latter a possibility for the error in judgment in bringing "The Hunchback" to life in motion.

Produced as it is, "The Hunchback of Notre Dame" may become a detriment to the box office it plays for, other than on main thoroughfares in the larger cities similar to Broadway in the largest.

Let the matter of direction and cost be decided by personal observation. *Sime.*

ROSITA

Mary Pickford production based on "Don Ceasar de Bazan." Holbrook Blinn featured with the star. Screen adaptation by Edward Knoblock. Direction by Ernst Lubitsch. Opened at Lyric theatre, New York, Sept. 3. Running time 96 minutes. Distributors, United Artists.

Rosita....................Mary Pickford
The King....................Holbrook Blinn
The Queen....................Irene Rich
Don Diego....................George Walsh
The Prime Minister.....Charles Belcher
Prison Commandant........Frank Leigh
Rosita's Mother..Mme. Mathilde Comont
Rosita's Father..........George Periolat
Big Jailer....................Bert Sprotte
Little Jailer..............Snitz Edwards
Serving Maid........Mme. de Bodamere
Rosita's Brothers....................
Philip De Lacey
Donald McAlpin
Rosita's Sister............Doreen Turner

Enter Mary Pickford, actress, as Rosita in a screen production of the same name directed by Ernst Lubitsch. A Mary Pickford different and greater than at any time in her screen career; a Mary Pickford with her hair done up, pretty as a picture and displaying acting ability few thought her capable of.

In "Rosita" she tops the splendid work of "Stella Maris" the greatest picture she ever made until the current feature.

"Rosita" is going to mark an epoch in the career of this star. It is one of the biggest pictures of the year, and if any screen entertainment is worth $2 admission as entertainment, this picture is it.

The production also marks the debut of Ernst Lubitsch as a director in America. There is no question but that he in a measure is responsible for the splendid work Miss Pickford does as Rosita, as he is also responsible for the turning out of a production replete with infinite detail delightful atmospheric touches, consummate characterizations by a cast of players that fairly bristles with names of box office pulling value. His direction is so skilful one sits through the hour and a half it employs in screening and at the finish wants more. The story has been done with deft craftsmanship and is revealed with a perfect continuity.

Holbrook Blinn, featured with Miss Pickford, gives a performance that not only vies with that of the star, but in spots overtops her work. He is the artist at all times. His conception of the Spanish monarch will go down in history as the equal of his Napoleon of "The Duchess of Danzig." Blinn is the King to the manner born, a King that despite his love of loving, was altogether lovable.

"Rosita" is defined on the program as "A Spanish Romance." It is exactly that, but still a romance full of thrills and dramatic intensity that makes it a joy to look at on the screen. Miss Pickford plays the title role, a Spanish street singer with whom the King falls in love and desires as his mistress, but she in turn loves a nobleman whom she had seen on the streets, and whose sword was unsheathed in her behalf when the troops would take her to jail for singing a treasonable ditty she composed while in wrath because the passing of the King drew the audience away from her while she was singing to them in the streets.

The nobleman is likewise placed under arrest and sentenced to death. The King conceives the idea of bestowing a title on his latest love through her marriage t. the condemned man prior to his execution. The twain are blindfolded during the ceremony, but at its completion Rosita tears the masks aside and discovers her husband is the man of her heart. She rushes to the King to plead for his life, and is successful to all appearances for the King gives her an order that calls for a mock execution.

Later he countermands it and orders that the execution go through. It is his Queen that finally foils him, for she feels that with the little street singer married to a man she loves, the King will have to look elsewhere for romance and he will be safe for the time being at least.

Then comes the tragic moment. Rosita has been permitted to spend the night with her husband in his cell. With the morning light come the executioners, and he is led forth to his doom. She watches him go with light heart, believing the mock execution is to take place, but with the report of the guns she is informed the King recalled his order and her lover is now dead.

Here is Mary Pickford in a mad scene that rivals anything that has been done on either stage or screen by the greatest of actresses. At this point everyone believes "Tosca" has been reenacted in a different setting, but later it develops the Queen stayed the King's order and the guns of the firing squad contained blanks.

To do justice to the work of the cast in review one would have to mention all, for each does the best. George Walsh as the young Don loved by Rosita, gives a remarkably clever performance, and Irene Rich as the Queen does likewise. Mme. Mathilde Comont as Rosita's mother is a delight, and Snitz Edwards as a bloodthirsty little jailer is a scream.

"Rosita" is going to go down into screen history as the picture that made Mary Pickford a real actress, or at least, revealed her as one.

In production, settings and direction it is a decided work of art.

To Lubitsch full credit must be given. He seemingly inspired his cast and compelled them to give greater performances most people thought beyond them, and his work in this production is a revelation as to what the picture industry may expect from foreign directors when they are given the material to work with that American directors have. *Fred.*

THE SILENT COMMAND

William Fox production, without star or featured player. Written by Rufus King and directed by Gordon Edwards. , At the Central Theatre, New York, for run starting Sept. 2. Running time 91 minutes.

Captain Richard Decatur.....Edmund Lowe
Hisston....................Bela Lugosi
Menchen....................Carl Harbaugh
Cordoba....................Martin Faust
Gridley....................Gordon McEdward
Admiral Nevins..............Byron Douglas

Admiral Meade.........Theodore Babcock
Mr. Collins............George Lessey
Ambassador Mendizabal.....Warren Cook
Pedro...................Henry Armetta
Jack Decatur.............Rogers Keene
Butler, Decatur's Home...J. W. Jenkins
Mrs. Richard Decatur........Alma Tell
Peg Williams.........Martha Mansfield
Her Maid.............Florence Martin
Dolores................Betty Jewel
Mrs. Nevins...........Kate Blancke
Jill, Decatur.......Elizabeth Mary Foley

This is one of those "Columbia, the Gem of the Ocean" pictures. Full of the "Star-Spangled Banner," patriotic to the 'nth degree with the navy floating all over the screen. A real hero, a vamp, and a flock of thrills.

In a measure it might have been a revamp of the old "Man o' Warsman" brought up-to-date and as the public in general, especially in the smaller houses, is sure to like that melodramatic patriotic stuff, it will have a vogue.

William Fox over his signature in the program says that the "picture was made with a purpose—to entertain." He may be right, then again he may have decided that the manner in which to get the selling punch behind it was to get the U. S. Navy to work its recruiting staff in conjunction.

That is going to be good business in the spots where the exhibitor figures recruiting for the "Join the Navy and See the World" idea will get by with his audience. Otherwise it's just a red-fire, flag-waving picture that relies on the real old sure fire hoke to get over.

Whoever Rufus King is or was, he must have been around some time or another in the company of George M. Cohan, who is the king of all of those flag waving guys.

Still and all, it is good Americanization stuff and in that it will undoubtedly have the backing of the Government as well as the Navy and with the combination of the two may get some money for the average exhibitor—not the first run man, but the regular neighborhood house where they come anyway, no matter what the picture is. It is a case where the house manager will have to make his audience believe it before they get into the theatre.

The story is of a naval "four striper" attached to the staff of the Governor of the Canal Zone who completes a plan for the mining of the Canal and its approaches. He does it behind locked doors in the Administration Building in the Zone. The night he finishes the building is broken into by foreign agents and their attempts to get the document lead to fire and a couple of attempts at murder. The document is destroyed in the flames. To frustrate another attempt to get them the naval attache is sent to Washington to make his report and to redraw the plans.

The foreign agents had dictaphones in the Administration Building and their spies were also on the job. When the attache starts home the spies are on another boat. In Washington they get a vamp on the job to snare the officer. That is where the "silent command" comes in. It's a case of the naval officer making his report to the department and the Chief of the Naval Intelligence Bureau swearing him in as a member of the "secret service" staff. His orders are to work with the plotters, his wife is not to know what he is doing, and then for a period it appears as though he is untrue to his trust to his nation, wife and self. In the final twist it is shown that he has been acting under orders of the "silent command" and there is the usual happy ending.

In the cast are a lot of names that sound imposing but they really amount to little. Edmund Lowe is the heroic naval officer, his wife is Alma Tell, the heavy vamp is Martha Mansfield and they are the three principal figures. The rest is an effort to play on the patriotic stuff. Lowe stands out for his performance, although somewhat overdone at times; Miss Tell is conventional, and Miss Mansfield as the vamp handles herself well, but needs "lighting" before the camera. In her natural stuff she is fine, but there are times when the camera man let the shadows creep in, and that injured her chances, especially so because it was in the scenes she was to do her "heavy vamping stuff."

There is a juvenile love interest carefully designed to make an impression in the Latin-American territory; a youthful graduate of Annapolis and his fiancee, the daughter of a representative of a Central or South American country. In this Betty Jewel as the Spanish girl was very attractive. She is evidently a newcomer to the screen, but looms as a possibility, especially in light ingenue roles.

As a thrill provider where they want that sort of entertainment the picture is there. Otherwise it's just a meller. At the Central for the opening performance all of the naval dignitaries were present, with gold braid all over the place. The Annapolis scenes as well as those of the fleet (the latter regulation news weekly stuff) were certain applause. It is a point that the exhibitor in towns where there is a navy yard or a naval station of any sort may remember with profit to himself.

There is a little "inside stuff" attached to this picture. Wells Hawks, once publicity promoter for the U. S. N. (sorry, should have said Lieut. Commander Wells Hawks), was later attached to the publicity staff of the Fox organization. Mayhap that is, or rather was, the reason for U. S. N. co-operation in the making of the picture. And in addition the fact that this picture was shown in Chicago at Barbee's Loop theatre (now Monroe) and the running time there was 73 minutes as against 91 minutes in New York, is possibly another argument for an exhibitor's right to cut film if necessary. The Fox organization controls both houses.
Fred.

THE FRENCH DOLL

Tiffany production released through Metro starring Mae Murray. Presented by Robert Z. Leonard, who supervised the picture. At the Capitol, New York, Sept. 3.
Georgine Mazulier............Mae Murray
Wellington Wick.........Orville Caldwell
Pedro Carrova.............Rod La Rocque
Madame Mazulier.............Rose Dion
Monsieur Mazulier........Paul Cazeneuve
Joseph Dumas...............Willard Louis

"The French Doll" is ultra-obvious picture making. It is never imaginative, lacks suspense, heart interest and even naturalness. The titles, too, deflect it in the wrong direction, attempts at comedy in them being very visibly strained.

The theme is that of scheming parents and a financially interested advisor, who would capitalize the heroine to their own advantage. Eventually she does marry the man of their choice, but not before they receive many pangs of regret.

The opening scenes are in Paris with America the concluding locale.

As the French girl, Georgine, Miss Murray gives forth examples of her histrionic attainments as familiarized screenically. Of course, she dances.

Miss Murray will need something or two of them to efface the unsatisfactory impression of "The French Doll." *Samuel.*

WHY WORRY

Harold Lloyd comedy presented by Hal Roach, released by Pathe. Story by Sam Taylor, directed by Fred Newmeyer and the author. At the Strand, New York, week Sept. 3.
Harold Van Pelham.........Harold Lloyd
The Nurse............Jobyna Ralston
Colosso......................John Aasen
Herculeo...................Leo White
Jim Blake.............James Mason
Mr. Pipps................Wallace Howe

Harold Lloyd's latest comedy secured the Labor Day week assignment at the Strand with the engagement announced for two weeks. Announcing a picture for two weeks at one of the regular Broadway weekly change houses at the start of the first week is out of the ordinary. When a production is held over the regulation seven days in the majority of instances the announcement it will be retained a second week is generally withheld until several days after the opening with the holdover reported, due to big business.

Not alone the Lloyd name, but also the class of comedy productions this comedian has turned out in the past warrants it. He rarely misses with his feature comedies and the latest is no exception. It is a production made for laughs and secures them. As with other Lloyd pictures it is full of genuine comedy ideas. The creative ability of the comedian asserts itself with credit also due the author, who likewise aided in the direction for some of the comedy ideas.

The thread of the story is practically nil, so there is every possibility Fred Newmeyer, who wrote it, was responsible for considerable of the comedy by-play.

The scenes for this latest Lloyd production are laid in a South American country with pronounced Spanish atmosphere and the usual rebellions for the comedy material.

The theme is of the lightest texture. Harold Van Pelham, a youth overburdened with wealth and always under the impression he is ill, leaves the whirl of the large city to find peace and quiet in the small South American town.

Upon his arrival, accompanied by a nurse and valet, the town is the scene of a battle between two factions trying to secure control. The revolutionists are headed by a renegade American.

This leader, upon seeing the girl, immediately desires her for himself and makes every attempt to complete her capture, she finally being forced to disguise herself as a boy. The over-monied youth with the weak heart wanders around the town, coming in contact with both factions at various times, and while endeavoring to locate the hotel where he had sent the nurse and valet lands in jail. He is placed in a cell with the giant. With the latter's aid he gets out of a window with his accomplice following. Gaining their freedom they completely demoralize the two battling factions. The giant overawes both armies and proves a faithful follower of the rich youth. The latter, learning his nurse, for whom considerable heart interest had been aroused moonlight nights enroute on shipboard, was being molested by the renegade, he immediately sets out to vanquish that individual and does it very effectively, the giant in the meantime cleaning up the rest of the community. The final footage discloses the youth, girl and giant completely demoralizing an entire army. The love angle is then brought to a proper close.

Employing a giant as a comedy assistant to Lloyd proves immense. John Aasen handled the role. It is reported it was originally intended to have the late Capt. Auger, for some time in vaudeville, do it, his sudden death causing Aasen to get the part. He is a big chap appearing on the screen as well over nine feet. A great comedy contrast is created in Lloyd's work beside the big fellow. Although of average height the comedian appears exceedingly small with the size of others in the cast being even more pronounced through the selection of some on account of smallness.

The big hits are given over to Lloyd and the giant. They work together almost continually and are fortified with sure comedy ideas. The battle scenes are always certain of a laugh with the work all done on the lot without mechanical effects being brought into play for comedy purposes. It is all rough and tumble stuff and highly amusing.

Jobyna Ralston play the girl, the only feminine member, the others being only atmosphere extras. James Mason plays the heavy and takes some rough treatment in the final chapters. Wallace Howe, as the valet, is lost as the picture progresses. Leo White does a desperado character acceptably.

The picture practically in its entirety was made in one lot set, that of a village. It was pretty well mussed up at the end, but served its purpose nicely for the business needed.

Lloyd feature comedies are looked upon as box office winners. The latest will live up with ease to the reputation of its predecessors and may be relied upon to produce.
Hart.

THE GOLD DIGGERS

Warner Brothers' production starring Hope Hampton with Wyndham Standing and Louise Fazenda featured. Adapted from the Avery Hopwood stage play of same title staged by David Belasco, who is above the title in the picture as presenting in arrangement with the Warners. Adapted for screen by Grant Carpenter. Directed by Harry Beaumont. At Rialto, New York, week Sept. 9. Running time, around 80 minutes.

Jerry La Mar..............Hope Hampton
Stephen Lee............Wyndham Standing
Mabel Munroe..............Louise Fazenda
Sopsy St. John..............Gertrude Short
James Blake..................Alec Francis
Barney Barnett..................Jed Prouty
Eleanor Montgomery..........Arita Gillman
Trixie Andrews...............Peggy Brown
Mrs. La Mar...............Margaret Seddon
Wally Saunders.............Johnny Harron
Violet Dayne................Ann Cornwall
Dolly Baxter...............Edna Tichenor
Gypsy Montrose..............Frances Ross
Sadie.........................Marie Prade
Cissie Gray................Louise Beaudet

It doesn't seem that much more than the title of "The Gold Diggers" is required at the box office of picture theatres for this Warner Brothers feature. It sews up the women of the country immediately, the gold diggers and all of the others—one to see if it is done right and the other to see how it is done.

But on top of that the Warners have turned out an entertaining film of its character and kept it within bounds, even passing up the chance, against the possible temptation, to do anything in it that would bounce back against the stage or screen. That is most commendable from the trade viewpoint.

This picture is as much of a preachment for the stage as "Souls for Sale" or the others are for Hollywood. Every chorus girl in this picture is a working girl as far as disclosed by the story and most become engaged to marry before the picture concludes.

The Hopwood story has been rather well readjusted for the screen. The piece has plenty of laughs in the action and in the subtitles. Louise Fazenda plays it well up all of the time in the principal comedy role while Hope Hampton does a surprisingly good performance as Jerry La Mar, with Louise Beaudet the soap selling former "toast of Broadway" (played in the original stage version by Pauline Hall).

Miss Fazenda, figuring the panto and absence of dialog in the original role, does just as well here if not better than Jobyna Howland did in the similar part that established Miss Howland. And that's going some for this girl of the screen, as there was never a fatter role written for a woman in a spoken piece.

In the screen play it revolves around the love story, made double during the running, of the two sisters, with one taking the chance of wrecking her perfect reputation in order that her sister shall marry the man she loves. Miss Hampton in the drinking (souse) scene perhaps did not have the scope taken by Ina Claire, but for the picture audiences it will do as well; also Miss Hampton's Spanish "Carmen" dance that wasn't exactly as wild as she may have thought it.

Wyndham Standing as Uncle Steve played and looked the part, with Jed Prouty nicely caring for the Barney Barnett role. Johnny Harron is a likeable and good-looking juvenile without a load on his shoulders here.

The picture opens with Hopwood's definition of a "gold digger." That definition is the spiciest thing in the entire picture without it being at all naughty—merely suggestively spicy, like the milk.

Even the prudes will like the way the Warners have done this picture and the Warners have done it well.

Sime.

POTASH AND PERLMUTTER

A motion picture produced by Samuel Goldwyn founded on the play of the same name. World premier at Rivoli, Baltimore, week Sept. 10.

Abe Potash.................Barney Bernard
Morris Perlmutter.........Alexander Carr
Mrs. Potash (Rosie)..........Vera Gordon
Ruth Goldman............Di Sacia Movers
Miss O'Brien............Martha Mansfield
Boris Andrieff....................Ben Lyons
Irma Potash...............Hope Sutherland
Wide-Awake Salesman.......Lee Donnelly
Feldman...................Edouard Durand
Mark Pasinsky...............Lee Kohlmar

"Potash and Perlmutter" has been rounded into a good movie comedy, far better than one would expect, and by dint of a fairly elaborate production and good use of the subtitles much of the attractiveness of the play, lost by the enforced absence of dialog, is retained. Barney Bernard, Alexander Carr and Vera Gordon are featured, and to this list should be added Edouard Durand, who does a good performance as Feldman, the crooked lawyer.

The story is familiar to most of the movie trade. It deals sympathetically with a pair of Hebrew partners in business, their trials and tribulations and their friendly spats. Its humor is founded on the funny page humor usually applied to their race and much of it is forced but all surefire as movie audiences go. In Baltimore it is drawing packed houses daily.

It turns out to be good movie material. Good for laugh after laugh. A touch is a reproduction of a cabaret in which the Tiller girls are performing. Throughout the setting photography and acting are up to par and in some spots above it.

Bernard walks away with the film and Carr is second, although he doesn't show up as effectively as his comrade. Vera Gordon has a prosaic part of the Jewish mother and fulfills it, while Durand plays Feldman to the hilt. The others are sufficient unto their parts.

RED LIGHTS

Clarence Badger Production presented by Goldwyn. Adapted by Carey Wilson from Edward E. Rose's play, "The Rear Car." Shown at the Capitol, New York, week Sept. 9. Running time 72 minutes.

Ruth Carson................Marie Prevost
Sheridan Scott...........Raymond Griffith
Blake.......................Johnnie Walker
Norah O'Neill......................Alice Lake
Roxy...................Dagmar Godowsky
Luke Carson.........William Worthington
Kirk Allen.......................Frank Elliott
Alden Murray................Lionel Belmore
Ezra..........................Jean Hersholt
Porter ....George Reed
Henchman..............Charles B. Murphy
Conductor..................Charles H. West

"Red Lights" just misses being a wow of a comedy mystery melodrama. The fault is with the script, the direction, and finally the cutting. The script did not handle the story clearly; the direction was given too decidedly to middle length shots, so that the audience failed to get the drift of what was going on on the screen, and in the cutting the titles were too short, a fault likewise present in the showing of writing and telegrams in the feature.

At that, the Capitol audience got a laugh or two out of the picture, principally because of the performance by Raymond Griffith. Possibly in smaller theatres, where the audience is more apt to be close to the screen, the picture will stand a better chance of getting over for its full value; but at the Capitol it was lost.

Most effective in the entire production is the trick coloring of lights and the rushing of trains through the night. The story on the screen is so terrifically jumbled that it is difficult to repeat more than the barest outline of it. A railroad president has been informed that his daughter, who was kidnaped from his home years before, has been found in Los Angeles, and he is rushing westward to meet her. On the coast there is a scheming lawyer representing the father who wants to marry the girl. She, however, loves a boy with whom she was "keeping company" at the time that her real identity was discovered. There is a crime deflector in the story.

This is the Raymond Griffith role. It is a new type of detective who circumvents crime because of advance knowledge of it. Played in a comedy manner it scores. The rest of the story is just a series of thrills, trick doors and hoak. In reality a sort of a combination of "Seven Keys to Baldpate" and "The Vagabond" in style.

Had the picture been played with a view to giving the audiences a more intimate insight as to what was happening on the screen it would have undoubtedly been the comedy wallop of the new picture season.

Fred.

MOTHERS-IN-LAW

B. P. Schulberg presents a Gasnier production under the Preferred Pictures (Al Lichtman) mark. Story by Frank Dazey and Agnes Christine Johnson, with adaptation by Olga Printzlau. Projection time 75 minutes. At the Cameo Sept. 9.

David Windgate..............Gaston Glass
Vianna Courtleigh............Ruth Clifford
"Mom" Windgate..............Edith Yorke
Newton Windgate.........Joseph Swickard
Alden Van Buren...........Craufurd Kent
Nina Phillips.....................Vola Vale

A lot of conventional material is here employed, but the familiar situations have a "different" twist. The result is often confusing and one gets a blurred, foggy idea of the whole purpose and intent of the picture. Whatever may be said of the literary quality of the production, and much of it is unsatisfactory, the technical work is remarkably fine.

There are whole passages of stunning pictorial effects, arising from the composition of the scenes, the delicacy of the lightings, tonings of shadows, arrangement of backgrounds and exquisite photographic handling. The technical work is the picture's leading feature. It has splendid acting too, but the confusion arising from its violence to tradition somehow dulls interest.

The story follows the beaten path up to the introduction of the hero's mother into his new home, her ferreting out of the young wife's apparent infidelity and her determination to save her son from the unworthy bride. The familiar theme from this on should be the battle between the two women, but here the conventional story is turned about so that the mother-in-law schemes rather to defeat the dishonorable suitors for the young wife and save her from herself.

It's an audacious idea, but it doesn't convince. When, for instance, the old mother catches the runaway wife in the mountain lodge of her lover with the husband approaching, it strikes one as pretty poor logic that has her strive to make the meeting seem innocent so that the son shall be deceived. Likewise, it is pretty hard to accept the scene of the trapped wife refusing to accept this settlement of the situation and insisting on the spot that her husband know the truth. These are radical departures from the conventional path, and nothing is presented to make them plausible. So you get the impression of an author who persists in being different from mere perverse whimsy. His people do not shed new light upon familiar character relations; they merely confuse recognizable type characters by eccentric and unintelligible acts.

There is a novel turn to the theme of a fond mother who tries to act the part of a real mother to her daughter-in-law, but this scenario doesn't go direct to the development of that theme. Rather it leads one from the start to look for an avenging mother-in-law and the preparation is all in that direction. When the surprise comes the spectator resents it because he has been deliberately led in the wrong direction by a score of unmistakable leads. For instance, there is no possible doubt but that the young wife actually intends to elope with her lover. It is made plain that she is unworthy of respect when she returns tipsy from a party that looked more vicious than gay and enters the room where her baby is sleeping in the grandmother's arms. On the count of the suggestive clothes she wears alone the young wife is no better than she should be. There you have about five reels of tearing down the wife's character, and then all is made straight in a few hundred feet of implausible "happy ending."

Edith Yorke as "Mom" Wingate was as persuasive as the part could be made. She is a perfect "mother" type in appearance and plays with a fine intelligence. Ruth Clifford is rather too flashy a person to play the young wife convincingly. Gaston Glass is a handsome young leading man and entirely satisfactory in an altogether conventional part.

Rush.

RUGGLES OF RED GAP

Jesse L. Lasky presents the James Cruze production of "Ruggles of Red Gap" adapted by Walter Woods and Anthony Coldeway from the play and novel by Harry Leon Wilson. Projection time 65 minutes. At the Rivoli, New York, week Sept. 9.

Ruggles....................Edward Horton
Cousin Egbert.............Ernest Torrence
Mrs. Kenner.....................Lois Wilson
Emily Judson..............Fritzi Ridgeway
Jeff Tuttle......................Charles Ogle
Mrs. Effie...................Louise Dresser
Mrs. Belknap-Jackson..........Anna Lehr
Mr. Belknap-Jackson.......William Austin
Ma Pettingill...............Lillian Leighton
Earl of Brinstead..........Thomas Holding
Hon. George...................Frank Elliott
Herr Schwitz....................Kalla Pasha
Sam Henshaw...............Sidney Bracey
Senator ....Milt Brown
Judge Ballard......................Guy Oliver

It has taken a long time for "Ruggles" to get to the screen, but the result is altogether satisfactory and satisfying. Here is a great comedy novel made into a delightful feature picture in a translation that is entirely adequate. Everybody gets a share in the credit.

The adaptation is literal in that it reproduces the effect of the original story with no forced interpolations and a full use of the material. The acting is a triumph of team work. Ernest Torrence's Cousin Egbert is a gem, a bit of comic characterization that hasn't a suspicion of clowning. Cousin Egbert is epic from the moment of his delivery into the hands of Ruggles in Paris to his final triumph in getting the outlawed Mrs. Kenner married to the English earl. An actor that can make a screen character funny apparently without intent, and even with the appearance of doing it in spite of himself, has achieved something in the way of unconscious art. That's what Torrence does and it makes him almost unique in screen annals.

Edward Horton's Ruggles is a fitting companion piece. This most British of British valets is almost as good fun in the films as he was in the book. Not quite, for that would scarcely be possible without the written word. But he was genuinely human and amusing, and always by legitimate means.

One of the things that go to make the whole picture delightful is the absence of hokum. Ruggles is as far from the familiar comic picture of the English valet as could be. He is just an embarrassed automaton hedged about by his own class consciousness and prejudices and stunned by the strange people he is thrown among. He is actually a likeable human being. The scene of Ruggles' betrayal into a Paris spree by Cousin Egbert and the introduction of the staid servant in a state of liquor to the merry-go-round is an uproarious bit of nonsense.

The cast is heavy with screen names. Lois Wilson plays "the Kenner woman" with her invariable charm while Louise Dresser, now become a handsome matron, is abundantly convincing as the formidable Mrs. Elfie, wife and general manager of Cousin Egbert. Fritzi Ridgeway is rather too much like Miss Wilson to have been cast as Emily. There are nearly a dozen other parts in the cast, all played smoothly.

This is the third film feature now current on Broadway having the name of James Cruze as director, the other two being "The Covered Wagon" and "Hollywood." The first named is of course the screen winner of the year in its appeal to America, but it is not going too far to venture the comment that this "Ruggles" in its genuine humor is as truly native to these United States as "The Covered Wagon" a good bit of Yankee fun such as Mark Twain himself would have been glad to acknowledge.

Rush.

THE GUN FIGHTER

William Fox production starring William Farnum. Story by Max Brant; script and direction by Lynn F. Reynolds. Shown at Fox's Academy of Music, New York, Sept. 9-12. Running time 54 minutes.

Billy Buell.................William Farnum
Nellie Benchley.................Doris May

Fairly good feature of the stereotyped program calibre that will appeal in the regular run of cheaper admission houses. It is a melodrama with a lot of gun powder and in certain localities sure to be liked. William Farnum as the star seems to be carrying a little too much weight for the heroic character who wins the heart and hand of the slim young heroine, but his personality carries him past this on the screen.

The story is one of those feud affairs, told in practically a prolog and play itself. It is the tale of two families in the unsettled country, the Camps and the Benchleys. The younger men of the two are friends, both marry on the same day at a double ceremony and they live together in the same cabin for over a year.

The wives both have daughters at the same time. One of the children dies. Benchley who has been left at the house to attend to the women while Camp rides for a physician, switches the children, for it was his daughter that passed away.

Years later when he is hurt in an accident and about to die he confesses to Camp, who retells the confession at the funeral of Benchley. The Benchley clan refuses to believe the story and retain the child, over whom the feud wages for years and years.

It is when the child has grown to young womanhood that Farnum rides into the picture. One of the Camps after trying him out in shooting and riding retains him as of their clan to cope with the leader of the Benchley faction. He undertakes to fight it out single handed with the Benchley leader, but through a double cross loses the battle which was to have marked the end of the feud. He learns of the double cross while in the Benchley cabin and makes his escape, kidnaps the girl and makes for the Camp headquarters.

Then the Benchleys following, start a pitched battle which must have eventually meant the wiping out of practically all the participants on both sides, only that Buell and the girl halt the proceedings by announcing their engagement, with the marriage to follow which is to make her a Buell and take her out of the name of either Benchley or Camp.

The story is fairly well told in action with Farnum doing some corking riding stuff. A well handled bit is a knife fight in the dark between the star and the double-crossing heavy, the lighting in this particular section being an important feature.

It was not an expensive picture to make and for its class is good enough to get by especially in the neighborhood houses.

Fred.

THE RIP-TIDE

An Arrow production, featuring Stuart Holmes and Rosemary Theby. Second feature on double bill at Circle, New York, Sept. 11. Projection time, 50 minutes.

Aside from a feeble attempt to dress a morality play with picturesque costumes of the Far East and the splendid acting of its featured members, "The Rip-Tide" has little to recommend it. Possibly the weakest of weak sisters among screen drama, or at any rate the weakest the reviewer has glimpsed this season. Just what may have influenced Arrow to transfer such an actionless story to the screen can readily be listed with unanswerable conundrums.

The story utilizes the moral that the rip-tide of hatred has dashed many a man upon the rocks of despair. In this instance it is particularly aimed at a young Hindu prince who has renounced his early religious teaching to embrace the cloth of an Episcopal clergyman. He is betrothed to his father's ward, a Hindu princess. A mission calls him to the Far East, and when his father learns that he is about to return to his own people for the purpose of converting them to Christianity he disowns him.

The story is soggy with drama, has neither comedy relief nor any real action, with the exception of a rescue in the early reels. Rosemary Theby is a likeable princess, while Stuart Holmes lends inimitable finesse and eloquent touches of villainy as the Russian. J. Frank Glendon also contributed his quota of splendid acting as the Hindu clergyman. Yet neither of the parts were worthy of their delineators.

An in between feature in the third-rate houses at best.

THE WHITE SISTER

Henry King Production presented by Inspiration Pictures, Inc., starring Lillian Gish. From the novel by F. Marion Crawford. Shown at the 44th Street theatre, N. Y., for run beginning Sept. 5. Running time, 2 hours 41 minutes.

Angela Chiaromonte............Lillian Gish
Captain Giovanni Severi....Ronald Colman
Marchesa di Mola...............Gail Kane
Monsignor Saracinesca....J. Barney Sherry
Prince Chiaromonte...........Charles Lane
Madame Bernard.......Juliette La Violette
Professor Ugo Severi...........Sig. Serena
Filmore Durand............Alfredo Bertone
(By courtesy of Teatro Constanzi, Rome)
Count del Ferice............Ramon Ibanez
Alfredo del Ferice.......Alfredo Martinelli
(By courtesy of Unione Cinematografica Italiana)
Mother Superior...............Carloni Talli
General Mazzini.........Giovanni Viccola
Alfredo's Tutor.............Antonio Barda
Solicitor to the Prince...Giacomo D'Attino
Solicitor to the Count.......Michele Gualdi
Archbishop ....Guiseppe Pavoni
(By courtesy of Unione Cinematografica Italiana)
Professor Torricelli......Francesco Socinus
Bedouin Chief...............Sheik Mahomet
Lieutenant Rossini............James Abbe
Commander Donato......Duncan Mansfield

A more or less wistful, yet intensely, dramatic performance at times on the part of Lillian Gish in the titular role of "The White Sister," and a production that makes clever use of the natural facilities obtainable in Italy with photography that is a delight to the eye, are the salient features of this production.

Still it is a picture extremely tearful and depressing, with action that drags through endless reels of suffering and finally culminates in an eruption of Mt. Vesuvius. The latter scenes are very well handled and are the best action shots in the entire production.

From a straight picture standpoint, "The White Sister," in its present shape, is too long for the regular picture houses and the action in the first part will have to be snapped up considerably before it is released in that type of house.

Taken from the standpoint of a "$2 picture" it cannot be said to be "there," for in this day of screen liberties with the script it would have been just as well had the producers of the screen version undertaken to lighten the story somewhat with some slight comedy.

The chances are that with intensive publicity the Inspiration people will manage to keep the 44th Street theatre crowded during the two or four weeks the picture is to stay at the house. There are a few minor corrections that might be made in the spoken titles to the advantage of the picture. One in particular is about the "church enslaving women that should be wives and mothers" might react.

Miss Gish lends a wistfulness most appealing and the sorrows of the heroine, who forsakes the world and dons the robes of sisterhood when she believes that her bethrothed has been slain by Arabs in Africa, will give those of the women who enjoy a good cry a real chance, so in that respect there is certain to be a considerable patronage for the picture.

The heroic figure is played by Ronald Colman, a most convincing characterization of the dashing Italian army officer. He is a comer for the screen. Gail Kane as the Marchesa di Mola, the elder half-sister of the heroine, presents an interesting performance of the heavy. J. Barney Sherry is the Monsignor who keeps entirely in the atmosphere of the character.

A number in minor roles were enlisted from the Italian screen in studios in Italy and they showed that they accepted direction from Henry King in comprehensive manner.

The picture will rely mostly on its scenic shots for general appeal. Those connected with the organization who selected the outdoor scenes for the production should have a full measure of credit for their work, for it was splendidly done.

This is one picture finally that was taken abroad with a reason, and the reason shows plainly in the exteriors.

Fred.

HER REPUTATION

First National Picture, a Thomas H. Ince production, featuring May McAvoy. Directed by John Griffith Wray. At the Chicago Theatre, Chicago.

Jacqueline Lanier.............May McAvoy
Sherwood Mansfield.........Lloyd Hughes
Jack Calhoun............Casson Ferguson
Andres Miro....................Eric Mayne
John Covert Mansfield........Winter Hall
"Dad" Lawrence..........James Corrigan
Madame Cervanez........Eugenie Besserer
Consuelo......................Louise Lester
Ramon Cervanez............George Larkin
Clinton Kent................Brinsley Shaw
Petita..........................Jane Wray

It has never been possible to produce a play built on the getting out of a newspaper that has proven much of a success. For this reason there must have been some hesitancy on the part of picture makers to found "Her Reputation" on the work of reporters, the position of men in close contact with the owners of publications, the owners themselves and the printing of a big paper. The photoplay makers have chosen the imaginary "San Francisco Tribune" as their chief factor and "New Orleans Star" as a secondary publication.

The story concerns a star reporter who is intent upon a story and lets nothing stop him; the son of the owner of the publication, who falls in love with the girl whose reputation the star reporter is destroying; the owner of the publication, who loves his son and hates women because his wife abandoned him years before, and a girl just out of a convent.

May McAvoy is the convent girl, adopted into a family of cabaret performers and dancers. This possibly suggested her for the star role, as she is in her element in a cabaret scene.

There is not much of the cabaret stuff, but it is important. Instead of the hardened performer, Miss McAvoy's role is of a modest beginner who resents having a man see her shoulder. Brinsley Shaw plays the star reporter, Lloyd Hughes the young reporter (son of the owner) and Winter Hall the newspaper owner.

The girl picture reviewers of Chicago emphasized that this photoplay sets the newspaper business in a wrong light, but that is either one of their illusions or a play they are making to other newspaper folks who know more than they do about real newspaper work. There is an organization in this paper which is determined to provide what the people want, and stops at nothing, and another organization that has a heart. The big boss divides his attention between the two and shifts from one to the other as he sees fit. Finally, in this picture, the newspaper owner does what is "right" at the expense of an edition of his paper and this is not asking more of a publisher than it is reasonable to assume he will perform.

The newspaper touch is ideal. Everyone will like it, excepting those who for some reason or another wish to build up false impressions of the press. The playing is capital. The scene where the levees break down south are very good and it would be interesting to know just how they were obtained.

The girl is about to marry a rich man whose intention is to have a marriage in name only so that she can inherit his fortune. She consents with a view of contributing to the happiness of his last days. A fellow in love with her forces himself upon her just before the marriage and shoots the man she is to marry and then herself.

There are front page articles telling of the crime and two-page spreads speculating as to whether or not this girl is the world's worst vamp. Without any real foundation they destroy the reputation of a girl whom the film story lets the audience know is blameless.

THE KNOCK ON THE DOOR

Johnnie Walker presents Eddie Polo as star. Directed by Wm. Hughes Curran. Shown at Loew's Circle, New York, on double feature bill Sept. 10. Running time 46 minutes.

Possibly Johnnie Walker makes his debut as a producer with this picture. If it is the same Johnnie Walker who is acting in pictures then after viewing this sample it is suggested to him that he had best stick to working before the camera rather than being the bank roll behind it. "The Knock on the Door" is just a hoke picture.

Eddie Polo, who is starred, seemingly wore his welcome out with the day that saw the passing of the serial as sure-fire entertainment in the better houses. In this picture he pulls all the serial tricks he was noted for, especially the throwing out of his chest and the thumping of it in self-satisfaction. Outside of the star there is no one in the cast that even has any chance of being a draw.

The story is one of those impossible dream things that is just a joke. However, the Circle's audience did manage to get a few laughs out of the highly improbable and impossible situations in the yarn.

As a picture "The Knock on the Door" is a knock against free lance produced features.

Fred.

RAMBLIN' KID

Universal Western subject featuring Charles ("Hoot") Gibson. Story by E. W. Bowman. Edward Sedgwick, director. Laura La Plante and Carol Halloway in support. Projection time, 60 minutes. Broadway, New York, Sept. 3.

Done in a scant five reels this story makes a pleasing addition to the western series in which young Gibson has figured. He is the most natural and least actor-like of the screen cowboys and has an ingenuous grin that gets to your sympathies.

The high points of the present subject are a spirited horse race, a beautiful horse, and a barroom fight of the most energetic kind of realism. The horse race is especially well done, with good, clear shots of the fortunes of the race from start to winning post, and side excursions into the grandstand boxes, where the plungers are worked up to hysterics at the changing fates of the contenders.

The story is a composite of the oldest of old stuff, but it is so naively done and so easily played out you are persuaded to forgive the ancient situations. Besides it has in generous proportion those open country scenic settings that go so fa to take the curse off screen make believe. A wild horse known to the cowboys as "the gold dust maverick" figures in the tale, and some fine views have been taken of the magnificent animal in graceful motion, apparently alone on the wide plains.

The stereotyped story recites the arrival of the rancher's pretty niece from the east just as the cowboy hero comes into town on a (supposed) spree. Cowboy, here the Ramblin' Kid of the title, rouses the girl's ire by his crude behavior. The annual rodeo is only a few weeks off.

The local bully has been winning the big sweepstakes for years with a horse called Thunderbolt, and the boys of the Quarter Circle ranch despair of beating the whirlwind until the Kid pursues "the maverick" and brings her into camp captive. The chase, by the way takes place during a violent storm and these views are particularly good.

The day of the race comes around. Thunderbolt's owner and the boss of the Quarter Circle bet their last asset on their favorites. Meanwhile the heroine has made friends with Maverick. The town villain manages to drug the Kid. You expect the finish to be that the girl rides the horse to victory, but they give it another twist.

Instead, the Kid, drugged and reeling, manages to drag himself into the saddle and get to the start, half in and half out of the saddle. Close-ups of the galloping horses convey the meaning that the Kid gradually recovers under the excitement of the race and the rush of air as he speeds along, until at the last minute he comes to himself and rides a Garrison finish to win by a nose. The camera has been made to record a tricky series of shots of the big chestnut Maverick moving up through a spread-out field that will get any normal person.

After the race the Kid searches out the man who drugged him, and the fight follows. The end is a little delayed by the Kid's belief he has killed his enemy and running away into the hills, but it all comes right for the closeup.

The picture has an abundance of good incident, such as the hero's rescue of the heroine caught in quicksand, and plenty of hard riding. *Rush.*

ADVENTURES IN FAR NORTH

Lee Bradford Corporation presents. Half of double bill at Circle, New York, Sept. 5. Running time, 48 minutes. State right picture.

A consistent digest of the travels of Captain and Mrs. Kleinschmidst through the inner passage to Alaska, which extended over a distance of 5,000 miles from Seattle and return.

The picture does not burden the audience with looking at one subject or scene too long. The titles are cleverly handled with the caption reading that the incidents and scenes have been taken from a diary kept by Mrs. Kleinschmidt on the tour. It was a good idea and convincing.

The trip was made on a former submarine chaser, which Capt. Kleinschmidt now calls the "Silver Screen," with him supervising the work of several camera men who made the picture. The trip began in May, 1922, and lasted seven months.

Scenes in Glacier Bay show the breaking up of a 40-foot sea wall and the huge waves caused by the collapse, the capture of a school of whales and the disposition of their carcasses at the whaling station. Also salmon fishing. There are also views of sea lions, polar bears, walruses, brown bears and other animals found in the Arctic.

A thrilling scene is where Capt. Kleinschmidt, his wife and a camera man are adrift on an ice floe and forced to seek refuge on the top of a giant iceberg. Other thrillers are the endeavor to capture a brown bear and a hunt for silver foxes. A battle between these animals is also shown.

The scenes depicted are clear, with most of the film in natural colors, with other parts colored and tinted.

TEMPORARY MARRIAGE

Sacramento Film Corp. picture released by Principal Pictures Corp., directed by Lambert Hillyer from the magazine story by Gilbert Patten. Starring Kenneth Harlan and Mildred Davis. At Proctor's 23rd St., New York.

Robert Belmer..............Kenneth Harlan
Hazel Manners..............Mildred Davis
Mrs. Hugh Manners......Myrtle Steadman
Hugh Manners..............Tully Marshall
Preston Ducayne............Stuart Holmes
Olga Kazanoff..............Maude George

Here is a picture that is a triumph in cast, direction and story, holding the interest for more than an hour, unravelling a corking tale of a 40-year old wife who refuses to grow old and is about to divorce her equally middle-aged spouse, only brought back to her senses by the murder of a social adventurer with whom she is having a flirtation.

The story has strong melodramatic moments, is tense and active at all times but never for a second wonders from the path of plausibility.

Kenneth Harlan as a young lawyer who takes the responsibility for the murder is the only member of the cast inclined to be stagey. Maude George as the Russian mistress of the adventurer and the real murderess turns in a dramatic performance that could serve as a copy for many of our emotional heroines. Hazel Manners as the daughter was young and flapperish but didn't deserve featuring above any of the women in the picture, being outdistanced by both Myrtle Steadman as the errant 40-year old butterfly, and Maude George. Tully Marshall as the wealthy old husband and Stuart Holmes as the "blackmailer" were far above the average.

The strength lies in the direction and casting. The story, while plausibly told and interesting in theme, could have been badly smeared in less capable hands.

A costume ball given to "divorcees" by the frivolous wife was a colorful triumph without a single jarring note. A court room scene was another. A scene in Ducayne's (Holmes) rooms in which his mistress accumulates a jealous souse is a gem of a bit of acting, natural enough to give one a thirst.

The unravelling of the murder with its surprise denouement of the scarlet one, is convincingly unreeled and flawless in detail. At the finale the jealous mistress of the philanderer confesses to the crime in a dramatic scene in the court room after she has been tricked by the lawyer-husband of the middle-aged butterfly.

The picture is intensely interesting for women, giving as it does intimate back stage glimpses of the battle against time constantly being waged by the woman trying to hang on to a slipping youth. In one scene the "sleeping mask" and other time-annihilating accessories of the boudoir are exhibited.

The picture has all the necessary elements required as a feature and is as far superior to the average feature as Jack Dempsey is to Al Reach.

It's a natural for the deaf and dumb racket. *Con.*

MODERN MATRIMONY

Lewis J. Selznick presents Owen Moore starred, with Alice Lake chief in support and featured. A Victor Heerman production and adaptation from story by Sara Y. Mason. Released through Selznick Distributors, Inc. At Proctor's 23d Street, Sep. 10-12 in conjunction with vaudeville. Runs an hour.

A little more restraint, a little more heft to the yarn, a little less incongruity and with a better than just average director this might have been made a whale of a picture.

It's one of those human interest propositions, dealing with a just-married pair and their trials and tribulations in making good with a home, their unsympathetic parents and with their job. Some day somebody will take just mundane ingredients and mold them into screen epic.

The workaday movie fan is all wrapped up in sidelights on "society" plays and costume or historical romances, but how much more appealing might a recital of every-day folks prove if properly portrayed. There's romance in the most unassuming of human existences, and for every society recounting there are thousands to be found among the masses.

"Modern Matrimony" (a good box-office title, by the way) starts where the other stories usually end, and is so captioned, with the marriage of an impecunious investment broker's assistant and the daughter of rich folks. Their leasing of a country home from the Swampus Realty Co. (one instance of pre-intended burlesque) and its subsequent complications with the installment furniture and rental office pople are entirely human. Chester (Owen Moore) inve.. his $800 commission check in closing a waterfront property option in his employer's absence. The latter looks with disfavor on the clerk's initiative and results in the hero's loss of employment. Worse, the check was counted on to settle for the household expenses and the rent; and this is the date it is due. Mother-in-law visits the following day and departs angrily when her unwelcome son-in-law is dispossessed.

Meantime, the sire of Chester's wife, who has been a sympathetic old gent but for the mother's intervention, is worrying about the same option on the waterfront property. He controls a number of small concerns dealing in investments, the one for which Chester worked being among them. The wealthy old boy learns of his son-in-law's foresight and this proves to be the silver lining amid the fast encircling gloom.

A number of human touches throughout makes the picture delectable. From a production standpoint it is acceptable in view of the material. As an investment it was light on the bankroll without seeming so.

Moore and Alice Lake were capably supported by Kate Lester and Mayme Kelso among others. *Abel.*

ITCHING PALMS

F. B. O. release, taken from the story "When Jerry Comes Home," by Roy Brant. Scenario by Wyndham Gittens and Helmer Bergman. Directed by James W. Horne and photographed by William Marshall. At the Stanley, Aug. 30. Running time 64 minutes.

Jerry..............................Tom Gallery
Jerry's father.............Hershall Mayall
Virginia........................Virginia Fox
MacDonald......................Tom Wilson
Obadiah Simpkins.......Joseph Harrington
The village yokel..............Victor Potel
Grandma....................Gertrude Claire
Doctor Peak..................Robert Walker
Judge Barrett.................Tom Lingham
Constable Coman.......Richard Cummings

A picture billed "Itching Palms" with an all star cast sounds pretty foreboding. This one does not turn out to be a pleasant surprise. It's worse than its name and that makes it very bad.

The "all star" stuff has been associated with so many poor films the picturegoing public has learned to steer clear of it as often as possible.

In "Itching Palms" a weak story and inefficient direction are made worse by a dearth of good acting.

Were certain portins intended as rural travesty they would be startingly clever. But these are the serious parts presented on the screen, as stark drama.

For instance, one of the scenes the director probably intended as the most dramatic shows the old grandmother stealing out of the house at night, creeping to the orchard and climbing the high tree to search for hidden fortune. The villian comes along. After taking away the ladder, he tells the old girl she can't come down until telling him where the money is. All this is done in the most serious manner imaginable.

This is only one of the incongruous bits. The locale is supposed to be a small town of presumably some population, and yet there is only one doctor in the entire village. Nor can another physician of any description be found for two days.

While the heroine's life is hanging by a thread, her bed room is the scene of innumerable fights, heated arguments and scuffles, and about a dozen people are buzzing in and out the door constantly.

Immediately after the serious operation that saves her life has been performed and before the surgeon has taken off his white robes, she is shown half sitting in bed, chatting gaily and kissing and petting the hero generally.

The story is the usual type of pathos, interspersed with obvious local color that one finds treated in custard pie fashion by Mack Sennett. The fortune is hidden in the old well and the hero nearly loses his life and his girl before he can outwit the villian and deliver it to his old, tree-climbing grandmother. The worst distortion of probability comes with the introduction of the deaf and dumb town bumpkin, who, in spite of his handicap, is seen wandering around the village playing the flute and the jews harp. Victor Potel plays the role, and suggests the total imbecile rather than the simple yokel. It finally develops that he is not a moron nor a hick at all, but a secret service agent on the trail of the crooked doctor.

The players either overact or do not seem to know the rudiments of screen portrayal. Tom Gallery, as the hero, is handsome and shows some promise, but Virginia Fox is a totally insipid and lifeless heroine. Gertrude Claire as the grandmother, Tom Wilson as a bo' and Robert Walker as the villainous doctor are all exaggerated types. The best name in the cast is Hershall Mayall, and he dies before the film has run ten minutes.

Exhibitors can only risk this one coupled with an especially strong feature or supported by a fine program. No audience, no matter how believe it an adequate picturization of country life.

urban, is going to really enjoy it or

SECRETS OF LIFE

First of what is planned as a series of popular science subjects, using a new "cool light" process discovered by Louis H. Tolhurst for microscopic motion pictures. Sol Lesser produced these three single reelers and showed them to the trade at Town Hall, New York, Aug. 30.

The three single-reelers, offered with a view to having them put out as part of some "Screen Magazine" feature by way of finding out how the public will receive them, deal with microscopic views of the bee, the spider and the ant, each subject being about 1,000 feet long, including titles.

They are capital popular science subjects ideally adapted for magazine compilations, but it is doubtful if they can be pushed in the market as individual subjects, not because they are not interesting, but because the exhibitor mind seems to stand aghast at "educationals" irrespective of their quality. Fifteen minutes of insect study might create a break in a picture program, but as a short fragment in a mixed reel, some of this material would be admirable.

For instance, there is a capital incident in the ant reel, showing an ant lifting a piece of wood on a miniature apparatus which would represent in comparative power the lift by a man of a log weighing something like 280,000 pounds. This is an ingenious little derrick with pulleys and threads for rope complete in all details.

The ant views are particularly absorbing. They have arranged an ant-hill so that a cross section is exposed with a horde of the little workers on a construction job in the tunnels. The gangs of excavators are shown, backed up by the carriers and refuse removers. They have even created an "ant engineering problem," the tunnellers coming to a twig that blocks progress. They organize in squads, dig around the fragment of wood and finally drag it away to the surface. An explanatory title says the moving of the twig represents the man-job of moving a log 15 feet in circumference and 300 feet long, a distance of 80 miles.

The series is full of similar interesting details. In the spider picture a miniature spindle is rigged up, and as the spider spins his web it is taken up on a reel at the rate of 230 feet in two minutes. By comparison with the spender thread, a human hair equally magnified looks as thick as a lead pencil. The bee exhibition is equally interesting in a popular way. The insect's stinger is magnified to the size of a drum stick and the process of sucking honey from an orange blossom is illustrated in magnified views. Other details of the curious life and social habits of the bees make absorbing passages, and throughout witty titles relieve the severe scientific phase of the subject. It would be a splendid work for school use in connection with natural history studies, but until the experiment has been made, it seems a reasonable forecast that its appeal to the public would be limited to fragmentary bits in mixed magazine reels. In that form it should fill a definite need in a field that is capable of considerable development. *Rush.*

OUT TO WIN

London, Aug. 27.

Adapted from the play by Roland Pertwee and Dion Clayton Calthrop, this latest Ideal picture is frank melodrama. The story gives the producer every opportunity for a strong gripping feature full of punch and thrill and Denison Clift has left no stone unturned to get good results. He has succeeded admirably, and there can be no doubt but that this picture will prove a popular winner. The settings and locations are excellent.

Anthony Barraclough attempts to leave London to claim a valuable radium field situated in the Balkans. He tries to get out of England by the Thames, by car, by aeroplane, but is stopped by the enemy at every point. Eventually his friends find a double—a man of birth and education ruined by the machinations of Barraclough's enemies, who are also after the radium. So close is the "double" even Barraclough's own sweetheart is taken in.

Annoyed at what she considers her lover's desertion she goes over to the enemy. The "double" is kidnapped while Barraclough succeeds in getting clear away. The "double" is tortured but holds out.

Meanwhile Barraclough has secured his concession, is escorted to the frontier, and promised an airship to convey him safely home. One of the gang is suspicious, however, and tracks the real Barraclough to his mother's villa in Brittany. Barraclough again escapes the trap laid for him and gets to his dirigible, which, however, has a member of the gang aboard.

During the night there is a fierce fight, during which a revolver shot explodes the petrol and the airship is soon a mass of flames. Barraclough escapes by parachute. He sets off for London in a car, pursued by the gang's emissary who has also escaped.

Things are bad with the "double," and Barraclough's sweetheart is sent to "break him down." She soon discovers the imposture, but falls in love and helps him to escape. Barraclough's car is wrecked, but he is taken up by the other car and brought to London. The "double" again falls into the hands of the gang. The gang now decides on extreme measures, and fearing for her lover she divulges the location of the radium. Barraclough arrives in the nick of time to save the situation and the "double" finds his reward in the arms of the somewhat treacherous girl.

The motor wrecks and airship sensations are particularly well done. The cast is a large and distinguished one, headed by Clive Brook and Catherine Calvert. The latter, in this part, at least, shows little right to her international stellar position and does little more than look beautiful. The support, which includes the Marchioness of Queensberry in a small part, is uniformly good.

Gore.

DEMPSEY-FIRPO FIGHT

By Sime

Jack Dempsey-Luis Angel Firpo battle for the heavyweight championship of the world at the Polo Grounds, New York, Sept. 19. Produced by Leon M. Britton. At Moss' Broadway, New York, opening Sept. 15 and continuing for nine days. Running time, about 20 minutes.

The best picture of a prize fight ever reproduced on a screen. This is so because the first round, pictured in the usual way, is repictured by the slow motion process.

There is not a move nor a punch of the fighters missed in the slow motion section. The disputed point as to how Dempsey got through the ropes, whether punched or pushed by Firpo, is clearly shown. He was pushed by a blow to the side of the head. But previous to that even Dempsey must have been surprised when seeing this picture at the ease and frequency with which Firpo hit him.

In the slow motion Dempsey looks to have been "out" on his feet. After having knocked Firpo down several times, with Firpo taking the count of nine the time before the "push" happened, any one must have concluded Firpo needed but another punch to go completely out.

It seemed Dempsey was wholly unexpectant of Firpo's come-back. Firpo, upon arising, caught Dempsey with a full right flush upon the jaw. Firpo then backed Dempsey over to the south side of the ring and rained a shower of blows upon Dempsey's face, any one of which, if properly aimed, should have put Dempsey out. Instead, with the "push" blow Firpo appeared to land it and keep it tight against the side of Dempsey's head, shoving with all of his power and literally shoving Dempsey between the ropes into the press stand beneath.

Dempsey regaining the ring, Firpo started to rush him, but the champion clinched and stalled through the few remaining moments before the bell, doing damage meantime to Firpo at the close quarters.

At the opening of the second round Dempsey went after Firpo, having weakened him in the infighting at the end of the first round. He caught Firpo with one of his short blows, sending him down, and the next blow Firpo got put him out.

This picture will bewilder fight fans as to how Firpo could manage to land his lunging right, while at the same time they will be unable to catch, even in the slow motion portion, the swift, lightning-like short blows delivered by Dempsey that had a world of strength behind them, felling Firpo almost every time they landed. Firpo knows nothing of infighting and little else except swinging.

The picture clearly brings out the extraordinary action of the fight, with its 11 knockdowns inside of four minutes. Firpo was knocked down nine times, and Dempsey went to his knees, also out of the ring.

In this fight of the two Americas a shiver will pass along the spine of many a North American who sees the picture as he watches Firpo battering up Dempsey, who looked helpless after that awful right hand to his jaw. It was odds-on then for Firpo. A featherweight with a head and a left hand (which Firpo needed but couldn't use) under the circumstances would have put Dempsey away. That Firpo did not merely means Firpo is just a puncher, really the bull he has been called, and it is unlikely he ever can be anything approaching a boxer.

The chances are if the same two men met again to-day Dempsey would put Firpo out for the full count within two minutes. Dempsey went into this contest full of confidence and to make a quick finish of it. The affair was running according to schedule when Firpo got in that one unexpected blow. It may have been unexpected blows that carried Firpo, the veriest novice in boxing, to a match with the champion, and they were enough. But any one who can whip Firpo right the first time should be able to "kill" the South American the next time, for he has but one style, and that is no style at all.

Leon M. Britton, who made this fight picture, has done an excellent and interesting job. The actual fight is prefaced with scenes of both fighters in their training quarters, the principals, their backers and trainers, and the work, including training bouts.

It is said Dempsey sold his picture rights under the impression the fight would not go long enough to make the picture of great value. These two rounds or less of this fighting are just as valuable as 20 rounds would have been. In fact, there is more of a thrill in the picture than there was in the fight.

Entitled "The Battle of the Age," the picture will draw the males to the last man or boy wherever exhibited.

By Ibee

There was so much confusion at the Polo Grounds last Friday night when Jack Dempsey successfully defended his world's heavyweight championship title against Luis Angel Firpo, of Argentina, that the moving pictures of the great contest were immediately recognized of vast importance even to those who witnessed it.

The film started showing at the Broadway Saturday and is continuing throughout the week. Sunday and Monday it started grinding at 10 a. m. and is proving a bonanza.

The battle lasted but one and one-third rounds. The first round was so spectacular and sensational the going of that session alone gave the bout the rating of the greatest contest on record.

It is certain that a majority of the crowd on the field never saw but part of the hectic action. People jumped to their feet, then mounted the benches. Those not within a few rows of the ring could see the action of the battle only in flashes. Bedlam broke loose and conditions were chaotic. Many fans knew in a vague way what was going on from the frenzied shouts and yells of the fight-mad crowd, but just what blows were struck they could not learn until reading the papers. Even then there was no uniformity in the reporters' chronicles.

For that reason almost every man who attended the history-making event will want to see the pictures to clear up the differences of opinion.

Many fans were in the Broadway Monday night, and it is likely many out-of-towners who attended the contest and who were still in the city over the week end visited the house, as the pictures may not be exhibited in other states because of the prohibitive law against interstate shipment of fight pictures.

The pictures show clearly how close Dempsey came to losing his crown in the first round. His narrow escape came after he had knocked Firpo down six times. A right punch by Luis lands on Jack's jaw. His head goes back and his knees sag. He moves away but Firpo comes on hitting with his right eight times. Dempsey appears unable to escape the punishment. Only one of Firpo's blows strikes the back of the champion's neck, and when he straightens up a wallop to the jaw sends him through the ropes. Just before is shown how Dempsey went to his hands and knees for a fraction of a second.

The detail of how Dempsey got back into the ring is not shown. Another portion not shown is Dempsey's hitting Firpo after the bell rang. That could not well be judged from the picture, although there is some mix-up depicted with Referee Gallagher going in between the men.

The second round and the quick knock-out coming shortly after Firpo took a short count is quite clear. There are parts of the picture, however, that leave the bout open to further discussion.

The fourth knock-down of Firpo is one point. Two viewings of the film left the question of whether Firpo was really on the canvas 10 seconds still a question.

Over the Radiophone Firpo was counted out but the announcer then said it was a mistake. Gallagher's arm is raised and just about to descend when Firpo arises. The picture clearly proves, however, that Dempsey committed a breach of the rules by rushing at Firpo and knocking him down hardly before the Argentine was straightened up.

There was a slow motion picture of the first round. That, too, proved Dempsey's haste after the fourth knock-down. When the film was run at regular speed a split second watch showed elapsed time of 10 seconds once and 11 seconds the second trial from the time Firpo dropped until he got on his feet, indicating he missed being counted out by a hair. His ability to come back after being punched off his feet several times after that and then slam the champion through the ropes is certain proof of his lion-heartedness and enormous strength. But that Dempsey could knock such a glutton for punishment to the mat so often is evidence of the champion's far greater socking powers.

The slow motion pictures (technically the high speed camera) though expected to clear up that fourth knock-down fails to do so. The referee did not pick up the count until Firpo was flat on his back. Gallagher is seen looking over at the time-keeper and tolling the count, but where he picked up the count cannot be discerned. He may have started at two or three. His right arm is seen to drop eight times, which does not go with the split second watch, while the difference in time caught by the watch may be accounted for by a difference in the speed the picture was projected. The tap of the time-keeper cannot be checked because Dempsey walked to a neutral corner and leaned on the ropes, being in direct line with the camera and shutting off view of the time-keeper.

Leon D. Britton produced and controls the picture, as true of several other big bouts in New York within the past year or so. The training camps of both fighters are shown with the men in action with their sparring partners. Dempsey boxes Farmer Lodge, Jack McAuliffe and Jeff Clark, while Firpo takes on John Lester Johnson, Bob Fitzsimmons, Jr., and Joe McCann.

The weights announced were incorrect. Dempsey is down for 189 as against the 192½ pounds announced at the ringside. A picture of a bull's head which faded away into a Firpo pose was bad.

As fight films go this one rates very well, the photography being clear except in the slow motion footage.

There is so much difference of opinion about the fight that as a box office attraction it is a whale.

SCARAMOUCHE

Washington, Sept. 19.

Rex Ingram production, presented by Metro, starring Ramon Navarro, Alice Terry and Lewis Stone. From the novel of Rafael Sabatini. Shown Shubert-Belasco, Washington, D. C., for run beginning Sept. 15. Time, 2 hours and 28 minutes.

Andre-Louis Moreau.......Ramon Novarro
Aline de Kercadiou...........Alice Terry
The Marquis de La Tour d'Azyr, Lewis Stone
Quintin de Kercadiou......Lloyd Ingraham
The Countess Therese de Plougastel, Julia Swayne Gordon
The Chevalier de Chabrillane, William Humphrey
Philippe de Vilmorin........Otto Matiesen
Georges Jacques Danton..George Siegmann
Le Chapelier.............Bowditch Turner
Challefau Binet.............James Marcus
Climene Binet.................Edith Allen
Madame Binet.......Lydia Yeamans Titus
Polinchinelle....................John George
Rhodomont..............Nelson McDowell
Maximilien Robespierre, De Garcia Fuerburg
Jean Paul Marat..............Roy Coulson
Louis XVI.....................Edwin Argus
Marie Antoinette...........Clotilde Delano
The King's Lieutenant....Willard Le Hall
A Lieutenant of Artillery, Napoleon Bonaparte
Count Dupuye............Lorimer Johnston
A Minister to the King..Edward Connelly
Viscount d'Albert...........Howard Gaye
Monsieur Benoit...........J. Edwin Brown
Madame Benoit........Carrie Clark Ward
Jacques.......................Edward Coxen
Gamekeeper....................William Dyer
La Revolte........................Rose Dione
A Student of Rennes......Arthur Jasmine
Keepers of the Paris Gate, Tom Kennedy and Kala Pasha

Rex Ingram's latest picture, "Scaramouche," should be classed as one of the big features of the year. Comparisons cannot be made with his "Four Horsemen," as it is an entirely different type of story. It will possibly not have the general appeal of his former success due to the lack of a predominating love interest. There is evident the same remarkable ability of Rex Ingram in the handling of his mob scenes and many new angles are developed in these phases of the picture, some actually startling as well as most effective.

Those exploiting the picture did something when they arranged the premiere showing in conjunction with a benefit for the Red Cross relief fund for Japan. Those out front seemingly brought the pages of the diplomatic and social lists of Washington into life.

The selection of Rafael Sabatini's story of the French Revolution leaves an opening for the questioning of the desirability of another picture along these lines, particularly with Griffith's "Orphans of the Storm," so vivid in the memories of theatregoers. The familiar characters of this epoch in French history are faithfully produced in the Ingram picture. The many close-ups of types and the remarkable minute details of make-up are going to be one of the biggest winners for the picture.

The first half discloses an apparent impression of jumbled hurriedness, so much to tell in an allotted footage. There is much switching backward and forward of scenes with an overabundance of titles. The second portion runs considerably smoother. Throughout there is no great suspense, but, nevertheless, the interest holds to the last minute. It has been said of the book that it was too talky, but Ingram has taken some liberties with the novel.

Adhering closely to historical fact, the story tells of a youth in love with a titled lady, also sought by a marquis who holds domination over that portion of France. The boy, returning from school, has absorbed through his chum much of the doctrines of "justice and right." This is fanned into a desire to strike the rich when his friend denounced the marquis because of the death of an old beggar who had been killed on the estates of the marquis. He saw his chum murdered in a duel by the marquis, the only explanation being given the boy was that his friend, who was studying for the clergy, could talk too well.

The story then carries the boy through the various stages of French history up to the breaking of the revolution in Paris. He leaves his uncle's home, and after addressing a mob in the public square is sought by the soldiers of the aristocrats. Finally he finds refuge with a band of strolling players. It is with them, because of his wit and ability as a writer that, through the players catching on in Paris, he is again brought face to face with the marquis.

The progress of the love affair always brings the girl before the eyes of the boy with the marquis, his jealousy adding to his desire to further the cause of the people. After one of those meetings he proposes to a girl member of the players he is with, only to have her meet the eye of the marquis and spend an entire night in a carriage with the marquis.

The boy plans a denouncement from the stage, only to have the mob spirit he has aroused quelled by the police and the titled lady of his affections forced into the arms of the marquis for protection.

The progress of the story is rapidly advanced from this point. Andre, the boy, is brought into the French Assembly (a most impressive setting as conceived by Ingram), first, because of his swordmanship to stem the tide of the killing off the deputies of the people by the aristocrats through the process of duels following debates. It is here that Ingram makes many truly worthwhile long shots, the galleries filled with the bedlam, the white-wigged aristocrats and then the deputies of the people. A duel finally takes place between Andre and the marquis after the boy has despatched numerous members of the opposition, during which he wounds the marquis. Another view of the girl in the arms of his rival, she having come there because of fear for Andre, leads him to accept a mission into the south of France for his compatriots.

While away the outbreak occurs in Paris. On his way back Andre stops at the home of his uncle, learning that his mother is the countess with whom Aline, the girl, is visiting and who had come to endeavor to have him forsake the duel with the marquis. He returns, and through a letter from Danton gets the girl and his mother safely out of the city. Not, though, until he learns that the marquis is his father. Forgiveness is brought about between the two men, and the marquis with his son's sword goes out into the mob to make a hopeless fight to safety out of Paris.

The uprising of the mob, their march and attack on the palace are excellently done. Ingram has demonstrated genius in the several bits of detail to create his main picture. There are flashes of comedy timed just at the proper moment and many characterizations that will create new laurels for the established stars featured in the picture.

This feature will put Roman Navarro; whose development in the past year has been from an unknown "poser" to a finished artist, in the place left vacant by Valentino because of the latter's inactivity. Navarro's performance has a sincere boyishness which, coupled with his natural good looks and ability, will do for him what "The Four Horsemen" did for Valentino.

Alice Terry not only is beautiful in the white wig and gowns of the period, but she gives a capable performance as well. Lewis Stone as the marquis here gives the best portrayal of any of his many successes. George Siegmann as Danton made himself felt though with but brief flashes being allotted him. Julia Swayne Gordon as the mother-countess could not have been improved upon. Among the remaining members of the lengthy cast the work of Lloyd Ingraham, William Humphrey, Otto Mattieson, James Marcus, Edith Allen and Lydia Yeamans Titus stand out because of exceptional worthiness.

The picture is worthy of Ingram in every way, and that it is a costume affair rather enhances than detracts from it. The photography of John F. Seitz is among the best yet seen; it is truly beautifully done.

Assisting Mr. Ingram were Willis Goldbeck, adaptation; Curt Rehfield, production manager; Grant Whytock, editor; O'Keane Cornwell and Evamay Roth, designers of the costumes, which were executed by Van Horn.

The musical synchrony of Ernst Lutz is a brilliant bit of work. Chester W. Smith conducted the orchestra very capably. The projection of the picture here was under the direction of Lester B. Isaac.

Meakin.

ZAZA

Allan Dwan production presented by Adolph Zukor with Gloria Swanson starred. The play of Pierre Barton and Chas. Simon adapted by Albert Shelby LeVino. Shown at the Rivoli, New York, week Sept. 16. Running time, 66 minutes.

Zaza.........................Gloria Swanson
Bernard Dufresne............H. B. Warner
Duke de Brissac......Ferdinand Gottschalk
Aunt Rosa..................Lucille La Verne
Florianne......................Mary Thurman
Rigault..........................Riley Hatch
Stage Manager...................Roger Lytton
Apache.............................Ivan Linow

Here is a picture that looks like a real bet. It has title that means something to the box office, it has entertainment value for the audience after they get into the theatre, and it has a star in an actor-proof role she manages to sell 100 per cent. "Zaza" is a screen adaptation of the play that made Mrs. Leslie Carter famous on the speaking stage under the Belasco management. The screen version would do the same for any unknown, but as it is it proves a world beater of a role for Gloria Swanson.

Supporting the star is a cast that might be termed all-star. It contains H. B. Warner as her leading man, Ferdinand Gottschalk, Lucielle La Verne, Mary Thurman, Riley Hatch and Roger Lytton. Allan Dwan in directing has turned out a feature always fast in action, but still contains all the meat of the story.

Zaza is the name of a soubrette type of French girl who falls in love with a man whom she believes unmarried, but finally becomes aware of the true state of affairs and renounces her right to happiness, although the man would divorce his wife. In later years, after the death of the wife, the two meet again with the usual happy termination of their tribulations.

In making the adaptation Albert Shelby Le Vino has modernized the play somewhat, put in a slight war touch, but not to an extent where it matters much.

As Zaza, Miss Swanson will win a new host of friends. She puts a snap into the role that will make any audience love her, still she handles the more serious moments toward the end of the story perfectly. As the fiery, devil-may-care soubret who stands ready to battle all womankind for the love of her man, she interjects a comedy value that is delicious. Mr. Warner as the leading man scores, as does Miss La Verne in a character role.

It's a good picture for the box office and the screen.

Fred.

SIX DAYS

Charles Brabin production presented by Goldwyn. Story by Elinor Glyn, adapted by Ouida Bergere. Shown at the Capitol, New York, week Sept. 16. Running time, 1 hour and 22 minutes.

Laline Kingston............Corinne Griffith
Dion Leslie.......................Frank Mayo
Olive Kingston..............Myrtle Stedman
Lord Charles Chetwyn........Claude King
Clara Leslie (Gilda Lindo)...Maude George
Pere Jerome...........Spottiswoode Aitken
Richard Kingston.............Charles Clary
Hon. Emily Tarrant-Chetwyn.......... Evelyn Walsh Hall
Dion Leslie (as a child of six)......... Robert De Vilbiss
The Chef.......................Paul Cazenova
Guide..........................Jack Herbert

If the name of Elinor Glyn authoress of daring novels and the title of her book "Six Days" mean anything to the film going public then from the box office standpoint the picture should be a draw.

Outside of that it is the bunk as far as picturization goes. It is choppy and jerky, as if an effort was made to cut and then cut some more to get the footage down to reasonable length with the result the yarn moves along in a series of flashes.

Those that go to see the picture with the expectation of seeing anything salacious, suggestive, dirty or daring are going to be sorely disappointed. There is but one scene that might mean anything. That is after the entombed young couple have been married, where the young husband starts to make love to his wife and then turns and snuffs out the candle. That brought a laugh, although it may have been the title that followed hard on the scene which read "thus ended the first day." The title of the second day also brought a titter. From that point the picture resolved itself into a six-day walking match with the hero wandering about in the underground passages of the deserted mine, trying to find an out for himself and his young bride.

The cast for the production was decidedly well selected and the work of Corinne Griffith is little short of remarkable. Here is a girl that looks like a million dollars and troupes all over the place. She is "there" in this picture if she ever was in anything. Frank Mayo is decidely convincing as the young lover and Myrtle Steadman also manages to create a most favorable impression as the society mother. Claude King as the titled lover is also convincing.

Pictorially there are some very pretty shots in the English hunting scenes, the others are merely of the stereotyped order. In detail there are some bets that the director overlooked, and in a measure he is responsible for the laugh which greets his love scene. To make it possible for the candle snuffing bit he has the lighted wick placed right at the hip of the hero, so that in the picture it appears that he is in danger of scorching his trousers in the midst of his heated love scene.

Fred.

MARRIAGE MAKER

Zukor presentation and Paramount picture featuring Agnes Ayres and Jack Holt. A William de Mille production adapted from "The Faun" of Edward Knoblock. Photographer, L. Guy Wilky. At the Rialto, New York, Sept. 17. Running time, 65 mins.

Alexandra Vancy............Agnes Ayres
Lord Stonbury..................Jack Holt
Sylvani..................Charles deRoche
Cyril Overton..............Robert Agnew
Vivian Clarke..................Mary Astor
Mrs. Hope-Clarke.............Ethel Wales
Fish.......................Bertram Johns

Just another deMille myth with the usual demilling nymphs scampering hither and yon over the screen and Chester deRoche leading them. Anyone three or four drinks to the good and in a sentimental frame of mind will perhaps "go" for this picture but for those who are witnessing minus stimulant and possessing a desire to be amused, this feature is going to become fearfully boresome long before it terminates.

"More sinned against than usual" is Jack Holt, who is cast in a role that means less than nothing to him. Either the parts he is accepting lately or the mediocrity of the pictures are certainly doing him no good.

Especially is this noticeable following so close upon his having been included in the cast of the last Negri film. And the same might be said of Miss Ayres so far as this individual effort is concerned.

DeRoche in the title role runs away with this epic of fantasy and the screen evidence relates that he has struggled manfully with a characterization of the "God of Love" type, etc., that comes extremely close to being "nansy-pansy." But at least he saved it from that, although the essential requirements to place this narrative upon a sound basis are beyond the powers of any one man. DeMille is the only one who might have proffered a helping hand but he seemingly was more willing to indulge in legend to the point where the tale is not even interesting, let alone plausible.

It deals with a financially embarrassed member of the British aristocracy who is about to sell himself in marriage to an American heiress despite that he is in love with a cold blooded lady of his own set. The faun (deRoche) comes upon Stonbury (Holt) as the latter is about to take his life. The half-beast half-human person tells the would be suicide he can recover his losses at the racetrack for him by picking the winners through "smelling the horses' hoofs." Which makes him a member of the household, immediately, whence he also takes it upon himself to bring the Lord and the Lady together in wedlock. He's a strong advocate of natural impulse with the playing of the pipes, conversing with animals and abhoring the self control that humans place upon their feelings.

The finale has the faun accomplishing his object after which he discards the tuxedo he has been harnessed in to return to his native haunts scantily attired in skins and to frolic with the nymphs.

Neither the story nor the adaptation means anything to the members of the cast who have done little with it although it's hardly justifiable to place the blame on the players when handed such a burden as this. The settings and photography are both adequate but it seems the one great mistake was to have ever made a picture out of this piece of writing at all.

Skig.

A WIFE'S ROMANCE

Harry Garsson presents Clara Kimball Young in this Metro release adapted from H. W. Roberts' story. Thomas Heffron directed. New York state rights controlled by Commonwealth Distributing Co. At Loew's State, New York, Sept. 17-19 in conjunction with vaudeville. Runs 65 minutes.

This is the sort of production and story Harry Garsson should outfit Clara Kimball Young with if the star would maintain her standard. Her past couple of entries were a bit off.

A Spanish-locale picture, it jibes with Miss Young's personality although much of it does not ring true on retrospection and even in the course of the screening lacks conviction. If the romance between the neglected wife of an American attache and the dashing Spanish bandit-cavalier is intended to win sympathy, there is always the drawback of the audience's knowledge the heroine is in love with her husband. Film fans prefer their leading characters' romances to point towards a definite clinch and the knowledge that Joyce (Miss Young) is merely conducting a temporary affair with her fiery and amorous model builds up an unsatisfactory atmosphere from start to finish.

Joyce's husband is too wrapped up in his work with negligible details to pay much attention to his wife. She is a painter of some reputation and her current work is a portrait of a true Spanish type. Her model is selected from among a band of highwaymen who divest her of her jewels. The bandit chief gallantly returns the loot, poses for the painting, confesses noble extraction and among other things conducts the heroine to a polyglot Spanish dive. The gallant's courtship becomes too persistent for a while with a fiery declaration of his love being overheard by the neglectful husband which brings said n. h. to his realization for a happy ending.

The production is colorfully in keeping with the Spanish atmosphere. The casting suffices. Miss Young's work is impressive throughout, ever the centre of attraction.

Where the C. K. Young name is popular it should do for two or three days. Otherwise for the daily changes it's a good buy.

Abel.

DULCY

Joseph M. Schenck production, First National release, from the play by George Kaufman and Marc Connelly; directed by Sydney Franklin; continuity by C. Gardner Sullivan. Presented at the Strand, New York. Running time, 72 minutes.

Gordon Smith....................Jack Mulhall
Mr. Forbes...............Claude Gillingwater
Mrs. Forbes........................May Wilson
Billy Parker.................Johnny Harron
Angela Forbes..............Anne Cornwall
Vincent Leach...........Andre de Beranger
Schuyler Van Dyke........Gilbert Douglas
Blair Patterson..........Frederic Esmelton
Matty, Dulcy's companion. Milla Davenport
Dulcy....................Constance Talmadge

One of the sweetest, most amusing and continuously delightful high-power low comedies of recent unveiling, with Constance Talmadge head and shoulders above anything she has ever revealed before in her electric person and her delightful talents. She shares the success of "Dulcy" with many, however; for the adapter, the director and the title-writer all finish well up in the money, all having caught the spirit of the satiric comedy and all having executed the screen version with snap, understanding, sparkle and discretion.

Surely here is one instance where stage authors may not harangue against the incredible stupidity of studio staffs. They contributed a fine and fleecy comedy to the boards. The wonder is that the screen edition of it was so quickly and completely conceived, with so few changes in the important points yet with so many alterations of the actual narrative.

The well-meaning Dulcinea, flapper bride who burns to be a help to the husband she worships, and the complications and complexities she causes thereby, is expressed in Connie's acting and the continuity and execution of the picture even more pointedly yet more broadly than within the limitations of the stage. Every fine shade is preserved, every humorous underthought is cherished and nursed, and the slapstick added is not out of keeping or out of order.

The young Miss Talmadge, in addition to appearing more fetching and nifty than in the past, strikes one as having cut with deeper etching into her action and characterization. She "gets over" in every mood, in every foot of film; never loses the sympathy, makes herself adorable as the blundering well-doer and sustains the unbroken interest and suspense every second because the audience is wrapped up in her—what will happen to her, what she will do and say, where she will go, how she will wiggle out; not what will happen to the others she has all tanglefooted up, but what the others will do to Dulcy when they find out.

That is about the highest accomplishment an ingenue can achieve in farce in any form, and Miss Talmadge makes it from first to last.

The story of "Dulcy" is very slightly altered in the main. The scenes employed are rather elaborate, the husband being elevated to owning a mansion in California, but that makes good picture stuff. The photography is sharp and clear and perfectly lighted. The direction is brisk without being rushy and impatiently chasing "punches"—it has poise and repose enough, though not too much.

Here is a picture that pleases and holds and enthuses an average gathering. It has class, action and wit and a spanking good plot and theme, and it has a whizz of a star who couldn't miss with a dyspeptic landlord.

Lait.

THE UNBLAZED TRAIL

Adventure Production directed by Richard Hatton, featuring Richard Hatton and Vivian Rich. At the Circle, New York, Sept. 18. Running time, 58 minutes.

"The Unblazed Trail" brings to the screen a new director and a new actor, Richard Hatton. In both capacities he shows promise, although handicapped in his endeavor to be a film hero by a decidedly unromantic appearance. He is the faithful secretary of the wealthy John Miller, power in the financial world. Accused of a theft committed by his employer's worthless son, and the circumstantial evidence being strong, he is sent to jail. His wife dies and his baby girl is sent to a home.

Three years later Miller's son is killed in an auto wreck, but before he dies he clears La Grange. Miller and his daughter Doris adopt the baby and set out for the west to find the secretary, who has buried himself in seclusion to live down the stain of the stripes.

Doris gets off the train for a moment as it stops in the great unblazed regions and in her hurry to catch it as it starts slips and plunges over a cliff into the water below.

It happens La Grange has established himself just around the corner and he is Johnny-on-the-spot.

Besides coincidences, there are death struggles, scandal, horse whipping, attempts at abduction, more fights, and finally the joyous meeting of Miller and his daughter and, not to be outdone, La Grange and his daughter, too. It's a pretty hectic hour.

Vivian Rich is a pretty heroine, who spends day after day in the same old shirt and trousers of La Grange's, and the worst part is that she sleeps in them, too. The rest of the cast is adequate, with the exception of Donald McCollum as the villain, with dime novel mannerisms. The photography is hazy in spots but the shots of the western canyons and wastes are well taken.

Compared to many of the films seen in the cheaper houses this one is good, because, though it strains probability, it holds interest throughout.

MONNA VANNA

William Fox presented this German made spectacle of Maurice Maeterlinck's play, directed by Richard Eichberg, at the Central theatre, N. Y., for a run Sept. 23. Running time, 103 minutes.

Giovanna (Monna Vanna)........Lee Parry
Guido Gurlino..................Paul Wegener
Piero Luigi ....Hans Sturm
Genezzano ....Paul Graetz
Tonio ....Hans Hurka
Frederigo Fondalo...............Emil Rameau
Pater Coelestin ....Dr. Max Pohl
Machiavelli ....Toni Zimmerer
Andrea Buonacorsi ....Alb. Steinrueck
Maddalena Pazzi.........Lydia Salmonova
Vitellozo Vitelli......................Olaf Fjord
Paolo ....Viktor Gehring
Rimuzzio........................Fritz Kampers
Burgli ....Hans Sturm

"Monna Vanna" as a spectacle on the screen, with huge surging mobs, the German hausfrau types in the women roles and the usual over-weighted past middle-age men that one sees in the foreign made product. It is one of those pictures that may have some slight vogue in certain sections of the country because there seems to be a demand on the part of the public for costume stuff, otherwise there is little about the picture to recommend it. It is badly directed, decidedly over-acted by a cast that seemingly believes that constant "mugging" is the only manner in which they can convey their roles unto celluloid, but it has got a couple of mob scenes, where the armies of Pisa and Florence clash in which they must have used the entire German army when it returned from the wars. From the spectacle standpoint it is big, at least in the number of persons that are employed in the picture, but from every other viewpoint is just another of those German pictures.

One advantage that William Fox has in this picture over an American made super-spectacle that is running at another Broadway theatre is that this one did not cost him over $1,000,000 and the chances for what the picturization of "Monna Vanna" cost in marks is that he won't have to go after a big gross to get his money out of the picture.

The best selling value that there is in the picture are the sets that in some respect remind of the big scenes that D. W. Griffith had in "Intolerance," with "Monna Vanna" suffering by comparison. Director Eichberg handles his mobs in a mechanical fashion that fails to get a punch into his big scenes. Incidentally his mob workers went at their work as though it were a huge joke and fought their way through endless battles with laughter, this showing up particularly on the part of some of those prominent in the foreground.

Of the cast Lee Parry had the role of Monna Vanna and what she did to it was plenty. She just naturally emoted all over the screen and then some, but even then she wasn't as bad as was Paul Wegener in the role of Guido Gurlino as the "Lion of Pisa" who rolled his eyes every few minutes and "mugged" every chance that he had to get the center of the lense and that was about every minute that he could be there. Olaf Fjord playing the lead of Vitellozo Vitelli looked as though he would have been an apt candidate for a job as a chorus man in one of the Winter Garden shows of a couple of seasons ago. The character of Maddalena Pazzi, daughter of Machiavelli, was played by Lydia Salmonova who proved herself little of a screen actress and very much shy on looks.

In Italian neighborhoods it is quite possible that the picture will be a draw as a freak, but outside of that there seems to be little that would warrant the average picture house playing the feature. *Fred.*

CALL OF THE WILD

Hal Roach picture, releasing through Pathe, featuring Jack Mulhall and Walter Long. Adapted from the original story of the same name by Jack London and directed by Fred Jackman. At the Cameo, New York, Sept. 24. Running time, 70 minutes.

Another dog picture that is weak in its titling, and outside of the actual work performed by the featured St. Bernard species of canine contains little. In book form the story had a terrific sale, and although first published a number of years ago it can still be remembered by those who ever read it. The picture reveals that much of this gripping force of the narrative has been lost in the transplanting to the screen.

In location the film is mostly made up of snow exteriors which, outside of the views of the dog teams breaking trails through the deep snow, hold nothing of the unusual. The film is minus any human love interest, although the finish reveals "Buck," the dog, with his wolf mate and a new-born brood of pups.

Walter Long portrays the heavy, who is eventually killed by "Buck," while Jack Mulhall is the prideful owner for whom only the dog will do anything. An attempt at comedy has been introduced through having a tenderfoot trio start out on a sled journey, which lacks much and only serves to pad out the gross time consumed.

Various bits as done by the St. Bernard are neat pieces of work, although the general impression gained is that the dog is too obviously under instructions. A decidedly halting manner in which he works is the cause for this.

The general action might be improved with some selective cutting, for the film has a tendency to drag. But at that, this feature will undoubtedly please the children, while the dog should prove to be capable of holding the interest of a majority of an adult audience that is witnessing.

At the Cameo it looked as if "Buck" pleased, while at the same time the patrons didn't think so much of the picture. *Skig.*

HIS LAST RACE

Phil Goldstone production (independent), directed by Phil Goldstone; no author mentioned. Directors, Reeves Eason and Howard Mitchell. Projection time, 57 mins. Frank melodrama, with its climax in a horse race. Released some time ago and witnessed at the Tivoli, New York, Sept. 24. Features Gladys Brockwell.

Dick Carlton............Rex (Snowy) Baker
Mary.......................Gladys Brockwell
Stewart.......................William Scott
Denny............................Harry Depp
Denny's Wife................Pauline Starke
Tim Bresnahan..............Robert McKim
Packy Sloane....................Noah Beery
Mr. Strong.....................Tully Marshall
Boomerang ....Itself

Snowy Baker is an Australian daredevil rider and stunt man who is here capitalized in a wild melodrama which addresses itself candidly and unashamed to that grade of fans who take their screen entertainment in that familiar form. It is without pretence to intelligence, but has many well-managed thrills, such as the rather convincing trickery of the hero leaping from an airplane in full flight, dropping into a lake and then riding the wonder horse miles and miles across country just in the knick of time to get into the crucial race that shall make a fortune for the hero and accomplish the undoing of the heavy.

There are rough-and-tumble fights galore and a lot of fine horsemanship by the Australian astride the fine white animal who is as much the hero as is Baker. Also there is some rather strained acting by Gladys Brockwell. But aside from the melodramatic thrills the picture is nonsense and rather awkward nonsense at that. Of skill in story construction it makes no excuse. The story is scattered and diffuse and what on paper looks like an imposing cast is entirely wasted on foolish characters. For instance so genuine a character man as Tully Marshall merely strolls in and out for a few inconsequential scenes where any sort of an unknown would have served as well. Noah Beery has a small part that is entirely unworthy of his capacity for deep, dark villainy. Neither Gladys Brockwell nor Pauline Starke figure in any important capacity, and indeed the whole picture outside of Baker and his horse might have been played quite as adequately by a second-rate stock company.

There are a lot of society preliminaries dealing with the marriage of the heroine to the wrong man that might as well have been omitted. Then the story begins, with a striking chase and capture of the wild horse by Baker, who takes a high dive from the cliff and mounts the animal as it swims, with a series of thrilling feats of horsemanship.

There is a lull while they start an entirely different story which has to do with an unscrupulous capitalist, all leading up to the familiar situation of the framed race and the victory of the hero, whose entry in the stakes comes in a winner in spite of the plotting of the heavy. Just as mechanical stunts it has much merit, such as a chase of the horse thieves in an airplane and the daredevil riding of Baker.

But as anything but a lowly dime novel screen it doesn't call for much consideration. *Rush.*

WHERE THE NORTH BEGINS

A Harry Rapf production, releasing through Warner Bros., and featuring "Rin-Tin-Tin." Directed by Chet Franklin, with Claire Adams, Walter McGrail and Pat Hartigan in the cast. Now in second week at Metropolitan, Baltimore.

Baltimore, Sept. 26.

Here is a cracking good film for almost any audience. A film packed full of the old heroic stuff and having as its leading character a dog actor, "Rin-Tin-Tin," who bids fair to walk away from his competitor, "Strongheart," in this particular line. It has a good love story, plenty of snow atmosphere, the customary masculine looking heroes and an excellent production in its favor. And what is even more important, it furnishes real entertainment of a certain kind.

In Baltimore it opened unheralded. Playing uptown in the northwestern section of the city in the new Metropolitan, which is dependent exclusively upon a large residential district for its draw, it is being held over for a second week after it is estimated that more than 32,000 people saw it last week. And the Met is about a 1,500-seat house with a 40-cent top at night. It caught on like wildfire.

It has the conventional hero and the conventional heroine, but Rin-Tin-Tin is the show. In the film he reforms after running with a wild gang of wolves, exposes a vile plot against his master, rescues the heroine from the villain and tosses the aforementioned villain over the rocks, then gets married, and before the picture runs its course has raised a family, and is still so happy with married life that he does a billing and cooing fadeout with his mate at the finals. A good many closeups are given the dog, and in all of them he holds the attention of the audience closely for a good many facial expressions are gained of him.

The supporting cast works well and fits in nicely with the yarn, not strikingly new, but which serves the purpose nicely. The dog, incidentally, is a police dog and a good actor. *Lisk.*

A CHAPTER IN HER LIFE

Universal-Jewel production presented by Carl Laemmle, adapted from Clara Louise Burnham's story, "Jewell." A Lois Weber production. Jane Mercer in "Jewel" role with Claude Gillingwater also featured. Run an hour at Proctor's 23d Street, New York, in conjunction with vaudeville, Sept. 13-16.

A saccharine Pollyanna theme that may appeal to the matinee children and women but is rather tepid for average consumption, even for the daily change houses. "U" should exploit this picture among the educational institutions such as schools, churches, clubs, etc.

There is no punch or drama to the whole affair although Lois Weber has managed to turn out a fairly finished production. Jane Mercer as "Jewel" distinguishes herself as a child actress. She appears to be about 11 or 12 years, doing a similar role, although some of the titles ascribed to her sound precocious without any other suggestion in that direction.

The youngster spreads goodness all around her, among other things winning over an aloof grandpa and a "cold" cousin. Jewel is the daughter of a rich man's son and his "working girl" wife. Her father and grandfather have been enstranged, a visit becoming necessary to Grandpa (Claude Gillingwater) because of a business call by the child's parents to Europe. Handicapped before her arrival, Jewel discourses considerably about the house being a Castle of Discord, and citing other similes in the name of altruism, finally winning over everybody.

It's too sweet for words. *Abel.*

HER REPUTATION

A Thomas H. Ince production featuring May McAvoy. Directed by John Griffith Wray. From a novel by the late Talbot Mundy and Bradley King. A First National attraction. Shown at Rivoli, Baltimore.

Jacqueline Lanier.............May McAvoy
Sherwood Mansfield...........Lloyd Hughes
Jack Calhoun..............Casson Ferguson
Andres Miro.........................Eric Mayne
John Covert Mansfield..........Winter Hall
Dad Lawrence..............James Corrigan
Madame Cervanez........Eugenie Besserer
Cosuelo...........................Louise Lester
Ramon..........................George Larkin
Clinton Kent.................Brinsley Shaw
Pepita.................................Jane Wray

Baltimore, Sept. 26.

"Her Reputation" seems like propaganda against the newspaper profession. If it isn't directed against the entire press of the country, it is at least a slap to the "yellow" journals and their methods of ruining the lives of "innocent" ladies.

And in the making of the picture the producers have shown an admirable disregard for newspaper methods, for they have based their whole theme on the assumption that any newspaper in the country can print anything it likes about anybody and get away with it. They forget that there are laws of libel and that nine-tenths of the papers in the world go to a great deal of trouble to verify any questionable story. Added to the intimate knowledge displayed of libel laws and their usage is a neat little error in another newspaper practice, for this film shows a linotype operator setting type on a local yarn from proof. The scene of the composing room foreman bawling out a compositor for throwing away the type from which the proof was taken is omitted. And one more criticism as far as the newspaper office end of it goes: An editor's desk is shown, a nice, neat mahogany desk, with not a proof or cut or pair of scissors anywhere in sight, while the editor has his coat on all the time.

As a "hoke" picture of rather wishy-washy sentimentality this one is good enough and is well produced as far as the mechanical end of the work goes. Miss McAvoy, in the lead, proves herself once more to be a very good and attractive little actress, while her supporting cast throughout is capable. As the story concerns her in the role of a cabaret dancer, some elaborate and beautiful shots of a cabaret are made, the most beautiful being obtained with lighting effects on the dancers.

The story is that of a dancer who is supposed to be a notorious woman. In reality she is as sweet as the essence of saccharine and as pure as snow. Her only failing is that she is in love with a young newspaper reporter whose father owns the sheet. However, in New Orleans some false scandal leaks out about her and she is forced to leave the town because the newspapers there printed sensational stories without a foundation. (In the ads. of the picture her face is shown peering through the front page of "The Picayune.") So she moves on to another city, San Francisco, and here "The Tribune" is located. It is "The Tribune" which is owned by the father of her sweetheart, Sherwood Mansfield. She is booked into the El Toro cabaret as "Conchita." But a news sleuth gets wind that "Conchita" is none other than the notorious Jacqueline Lanier, and on to the story he hops.

Following a raid on the joint the girl learns that a story on her is in the newspaper office and there she goes, whereupon the editor, still in his coat and with his desk unlittered, has no mercy, even when he finds out that his son loves her, and the order is sent to let the paper go to press. To protect her from a reporter who is seeking to identify her an old friend sends her to his cabin in the mountains, and here the sleuth follows; but his car runs over a bank and burns up, while he is rescued by her sweetheart. After much excitement the presses are stopped and the lovers united.

That's the story, and a good enough one for all the dramatic moments it affords. But as propaganda against the newspapers of the country it is so silly that any one who knows anything about the methods employed by the reputable papers of the land will regard the whole film as a rattling good comedy meant to be otherwise.

To those who are wont to look upon newspapers, as instruments through which scandals are created all will be well and the picture will prove a delight. However, it should be a good box office draw, for it has excitement and suspense as well as a capable company. *Sisk.*

THE SIX FIFTY

Universal production with all-star cast. Directed by Nat Ross. Photography by Ben Klein. Story by Kate McLaren. Scenario by Harvey Gates and Lenore Coffey. At Circle, New York, Sept. 12, as half of double bill. Running time, 54 minutes.

Another rural comedy-drama frequently in the cheaper houses. The theme of this one is discontent—the yearning of a placid young farmer's day-dreaming wife to get away from her humdrum existence. Same old story but there are one or two new twists and it is a plot that holds interest and that will strike home in many cases.

It is not the story that keeps this film from belonging in the first class. Similarly it is not handicapped by acting or photography, uniformly good. It is the lack of seasoned, expert direction that is mostly keenly felt. Nat Ross, the director, is a young man who has had only a few pictures to his credit, and no important or noteworthy productions. For a beginner Ross has not done a bad job, but it would be a bigger proposition than he is capable of just yet to lift this film above the level of hundreds of others in the same class.

Renee Adoree, heretofore best known as the wife of Tom Moore, does splendidly as the young wife. Miss Adoree is a beauty. At times she shows a sophistication and urban carriage entirely away from the role of a simple country girl.

The husband is well played by Orville Caldwell, the young giant described by Elinor Glyn as "the perfect lover." Niles Welch as the "he vamp" is the best known name and weakest performer in the cast. Bert Woodruff contributes another of his fine characterizations as the surly but lovable old "gramp."

A WOMAN OF PARIS

Special presentation by Charles Chaplin, written and directed by himself, released by United Artists Corporation, to open at Lyric, New York, Oct. 1, for a run, with prolog; assistant director, Eddie Sutherland; editor, Monta Bell; photography, Rollie Totherch, Jack Wilson; running time, 80 mins. Seen privately in projection room.

Marie St. Clair	Edna Purviance
Pierre Revel	Adolphe Menjou
John Millet	Carl Miller
His Mother	Lydia Knott
His Father	Charles French
Her Father	Clarence Geldert
Fifi	Betty Morrisssey
Paulette	Malvina Polo

The chief interest lies in the first dramatic output of Charlie Chaplin; in fact his first direction and conception without his own appearance. If anyone imagines that Chaplin did it to express his "versatility," in the same spirit in which Eddie Foy sighs to play Hamlet, this illusion will be knocked edgewise when "A Woman of Paris" is viewed. It is a serious, sincere effort, with a bang story subtlety of idea-expression in many instances entirely new to film dramatization, a thoroughly workmanlike production and a candidate for honors and dollars entirely independent of the drawing power Chaplin built up in other fields.

If the sentimental Charlie made one outstanding error he did it in casting Edna Purviance, his leading woman of many classic comedies, for the central and stellar role in his first legitimate picture. Miss Purviance fails to realize the obvious prediction so often uttered when she shone so brightly in Chaplin's support that here was a girl who would some day be a sensation in a straight picture. She is not a sensation. She looks and acts well enough, but she falls short of the fine pace set by the rest of the endeavor. She is a good ingenue but a light star.

However, this is entirely critical and not a conspicuous drag on "A Woman of Paris." Were she an unknown she would be hailed as a find, but being so well known she adds little to her past accomplishments. Chaplin, on the other hand, straying far from his haunts of yore, comes forth as a new genius both as a producer and a director.

His broad and keen farce touches, which stood his comedies out from all other comedies and have defied imitation or competition in their own school, are just as effective when applied to lighter humor and to drama—even to tragedy. Every hundred feet or so something is done that no one else but Chaplin would think of and in a manner no one else except Chaplin would employ.

The finish is as brilliant and as memorable as the Mexico-line finale of "The Pilgrim." After the girl has gone through all the vicissitudes of Paris high and low life, her rich exlover, driving in his Rolls-Royce in the country where she has become a welfare worker passes her on the road as she sits on the back of a farmer's cart with a little orphan. He just whizzes by—that's all. And it tells more than if he had the conventional breakdown just then or about anything else that anyone could contrive. It bites, it burns, it shows life as Chaplin, the razorblade psychologist who has made millions laugh or cry with a kid or a dog or a sausage or a tin can, knows it and can sell it and demonstrate it.

The synopsis of "A Woman of Paris," as written by himself, tells the story about as well as it can be told:

"Marie St. Clair is a victim of the environment of an unhappy home life in a village, somewhere in France. In the hope of finding love and solace with her village sweetheart, John Millet, she decides to elope to Paris and be wed.

"On the eve of their elopement, Marie having secretly left her home to talk over plans with John, finds on returning that she has been locked out by her tyrant father. Then she is refused the hospitality of her lover's home by his parents and the couple decide to run away that night.

"Marie, waiting at the station while John returns to his home to gather his belongings, becomes impatient. An interrupted telephone conversation with him causes her to believe her intended husband has changed his mind about the elopement. This belief and the timely arrival of the midnight train prompts her to go to Paris alone.

"Time brings many changes, and in a few short months life has made of Marie St. Clair 'A Woman of Paris,' the beautiful toy of Pierre Revel, the wealthiest man in the gayest city in the world.

"At the height of a luxurious life the engagement of Pierre to a woman of social and financial prominence is announced. The brings a rift between Marie and Pierre. He insists that their life as it is will not and must not be interfered with, while she demands for herself a home and genuine love.

"In the course of events Marie is invited to join a studio party in the Montmarte. Not having the correct address she accidentally knocks on the door of her one-time sweetheart, John, whose studio is in the same vicinity and who has gone to Paris to continue his art studies.

"This surprise meeting and the [illegible] **finds the two in an embarrassing situation. Formality covers their real and mutual emotions, and it is arranged that Marie pose for her portrait. In the meantime the old love, still smoldering, bursts into renewed flame.**

"John again proposes marriage, still loving her devotedly in spite of everything. Marie, overjoyed, loses no time in telling Pierre that they must part. Making all preparations to give up her life of loveless luxury, she returns to John's humble studio, which to her means love and happiness. Entering, she overhears a conversation between John and his mother, in which John is saying he does not intend to marry Marie; that he proposed to her only in a moment of weakness. This fact hurls her back onto the mercies of Pierre.

"Remorse and despair control the fate of John Millet. His love for his village sweetheart becomes an obsession. He follows her everywhere until he becomes possessed by a mania to end his life. He decides to kill both Marie and Pierre, but weakens. Distracted by his emotions, he follows them to a cafe, sending a note to Marie in the hope of clearing their misunderstanding. Pierre invites John to join them. Words and hasty tempers bring on the inevitable fight. John is ejected from the cafe and left standing under the brilliant lights of the entrance, **where a sparkling fountain with its nude statue, symbolic of a woman of Paris, seems to mock him. In utter despondency John ends the struggle of his seared soul."**

"A Woman of Paris" will be a money picture because it has everything in production, clothes, mechanical and physical properties that the average picture reveals, besides having always over it the flicker of a soul far beyond that of the average picture-maker—that of Chaplin, the prodigy.

The story is fair and provides enough substantial elements to keep suspense alive. The acting is good enough, with Miss Purviance holding her up end, even though not elevating it, and Adolphe Menjou doing brilliant dramatic and comedy strokes that will draw applause and laughs. Before an audience the comedy will be more easy to judge, but in the cold silence of a 42d street projection room it drew audible howls at times and titters whenever the seriousness was relieved.

One may safely say that if Chaplin could afford to give his time to the drama on the screen he would run away with it as surely as he did with the comedy. In "A Woman of Paris" he hits hard without ever leaving his plot for a second.

The picture looks like a cinch for the biggest houses. *Lait.*

SECOND HAND LOVE

Fox production starring Charles Jones. Directed by William Wellman. Story by Shannon Fife. At the Circle, New York, Sept. 12 as half of double bill. Running time about 60 minutes.

Seth Podgins	Frank Weed
Angela Trent	Ruth Dwyer
Andy	Charles Jones
Johnny Walker	Charles Coleman
Scratch	Harvey Clark

The former "Buck" Jones now blossoms forth with the dignified "Charles." Unfortunately, his pictures do not seem to have kept stride with the advance of his name. "Second Hand Love" is a harmless, not exactly boring, second-rate program attraction. Its star's name might just as well have been "Buck."

Undoubtedly Jones has a following among the 10-20-30 variety of filmgoers. He is a big, likable sort of chap with what his admirers might term "a kind face." His acting is quite adequate, although he has a tendency to become entirely too grave. His role in this film is a fat one, and with a Meighan or Harry Myers it would be a striking characterization. Jones is an M. D., "Doctor of Mending."

A roving, never-worrying vagabond, he comes to the little village in time to mend fences and houses and even the heroine's heart. But that he can do the opposite of **mending is shown when he almost breaks the villain's face.**

Jones does not do a bad piece of work, but it lacks spontaneity and bubbling irrepressibility. It's a unique character, and with better handling might have lifted the picture above the ordinary.

The villain is a bootlegger, not necessarily villainous because of his liquor-selling activities, but because of his brutal treatment of his pretty young wife. He has framed her innocent brother, and "it's the woman who pays," and then appeals to the wandering doctor of mending to fix up her affairs. His fight at the end is one of the most ferocious ever seen. The men battle on the limb of a tree over a bed of quicksand. When the villain finally falls he is engulfed by the all-powerful moving earth.

Some lively photographic shots of rustic scenes. The direction is draggy at times and the innovations that enliven a film are at a premium. Only at one place, the assembling and drill of the local fire department, are the attempted bits of rural comedy successful. The supporting cast is satisfactory with an interesting looking newcomer, Ruth Dwyer, as the maltreated wife.

"Second Hand Love" won't hurt Jones' reputation with those who have liked him for some time, but it won't bring him many new admirers.

THE FIGHTIN' STRAIN

William Steiner production, written, adapted, produced by and featuring Neal Hart. Photographed by Harry McGuire. Stanley, New York, Sept. 13. Running

time 52 minutes.
Bess Barlow................Beth Mitchell
Jim Black.................William Quinn
Jack Barlow....................Neal Hart
John Canfield.................Burt Wilson
Miss Canfield..............Gladys Gilland

Neal Hart has again tried his hand at the "jack-of-all-trades" stuff with the inevitable results. He tried hard, but the product of all his efforts is a puerile story, badly adapted, atrociously directed and only fairly acted. It has all the earmarks of a film made in a rush. It is not so bad that there is not room for it on the bills of the cheaper houses, but it is poor enough to deliver a body blow to whatever prestige Hart has obtained as an all-around film executive.

Once again the "frozen North" is the locale, but the Canadian Mounted Police is unimportant and there are no faithful Eskimo dogs.

Hart as Jack Barlow returns from the war laden with honors to find his sister has married and gone off with a scoundrel who informed her he (Barlow) had been killed in France.

Barlow finds his brother-in-law is a swindler and has gypped the father of his girl with some fake mine stock. He rushes to Canada, nails the crook, marries the girl and has the satisfaction of seeing his sister engaged to the brother of his fiancee, a former buddy in the trenches.

When Barlow comes to aid his imprisoned sister and sweetheart he finds himself facing, single-handed, four husky Canadian woodsmen.

He outfairbanks Fairbanks and outmixes Mix. The most ridiculous part of this scene is that, although his ally, the girl's brother, is in the same hut tied up during the battle, the two girls, left unmolested, do not make a move to free him to help Barlow, but hug each other in terror.

Actual scenes of Armistice Day in different countries and of American doughboys returning to this country are shown. They fail to rouse appreciable enthusiasm, not because of the sluggish patriotism of the audience, but because they are poorly selected and not adapted to cause thrills. The war shots are only one example of the padding.

Hart's acting in the man-to-man, virile scenes is acceptable, but his love making is all wrong and caused laughs. The exterior shots of the great Canadian outdoors are decidedly inferior to those seen in most pictures of the North. There is practically no comedy relief, another sign of the general weakness.

Because of the never-ending appeal of titles and stories of this description the film will probably make money in the cheaper houses. But few will really enjoy it and every one will trust that Hart does better in the future

THE POWER DIVINE

Independent release, produced by Premium. Mary Wynn and Jack Livingston featured. Directed by Howard Moody. At Stanley, New York, Sept. 14. Running time, 50 minutes.

Kentucky hills, with their feuds and stills, contribute a picturesque background for this latest Premium production. Although rampant melodrama of a familiar school, it is spotted with action, has some good color photography in its early reels, and unravels an exhilarating, yet sterotyped, love yarn.

The power divine—is love. In this instance it combats the hatred of the Kentucky feudists for the lone survivor of a mountain clan, who, unaware of the existing hatred in the hills for his ancestors, returns to appraise their land upon which he strikes oil.

Fate further complicates matters by having him yield to the charms of the winsome little schoolmarm, only to find that she also has vowed to avenge her father's death upon the first member of her lover's clan that sets foot on the hills.

The villainous bully who had previously set his cap for the schoolmarm noses around the effects of the young engineer. He learns the purpose of his presence and that he is a member of the hunted clan by ancestry, if nothing else. He loses no time in carrying these facts to the folk of the hills. It naturally precipitates another feud.

Everything ends well. The visitor is haled as a pseudo Wallingford who has come to turn the barren lands into money. The villainous one is run out of town. Matrimony calls a truce between the lover-feudists.

All old stuff, but interesting enough for an in-between feature in the smaller districts. Continuity is good and the feudal scenes sufficiently thrilling.

Mary Wynn and Jack Livingston give good accounts of themselves as the central characters, although neither is given much opportunity to act.

THE REEF OF STARS

London, Sept. 6.

Made from an adaptation of a novel by H. de Vere Stacpoole, this picture is a mixture of piracy, blackguardism, murder, sensuousness, sudden death and rubbish—mostly rubbish. African Film Productions has made fine pictures, mostly from the works of Rider Haggard, but lately it adopted melodrama at its worst, and of the results of the new policy this is an example.

It is also a good speciment of the solid and immovable inconsistency of the British film censor, for it carries a "Universal" certificate. Features like "The Leather Pushers" only carry an "A" (adults only) because the prize-fighters are stripped to the waist.

Macquart, a thorough-paced blackguard, is in love with Chaya, a beautiful Batavian waif. She, however, loves Lant, the skipper of the boat of which Macquart is mate. He is in prison on a charge of piracy. Macquart and the crew rescue him, kill the guards and steal a boat which has come into the harbor loaded with gold. Chaya accompanies the pirates and the mate marries her to Lant.

Two years later they are on a desert island, where the gold is buried; Chaya has become a mother, the crew become mutinous, Macquart and Lant kill the lot, then Macquart kills Lant. Chaya swears vengeance, promising her infant daughter as wife to the man who will hunt down the murderer and kill him with the dagger which killed her beloved. Things are rotten for, all eyes are on him and he bolts.

Twenty years after, etc.

The whole story is crude and rubbishy. The continuity is conspicuous by its absence and the scenario was probably written overnight or to meet the amount of film stock in hand.

The photography is beautiful, but, unfortunately, cameramen cannot make a picture on their own.

Molly Adair, who gave a beautiful performance in the "Blue Lagoon," has gone off considerably. Her performance in the dual role of Chaya and Moya is stereotyped and mediocre. Roy Gowthorne, as Houghton is something in the nature of a find as a juvenile. Harvey Braban has all the fat as Macquart and makes the most of it. Dick Cruickshanks is excellent and Finch Smiles puts over a fine character study of a man who is trying to drink himself to death. Much of the best acting in this picture is by small-part people who do not get the program credit. *Gore.*

SCARAMOUCHE

A Rex Ingram-Metro picturization of the Rafael Sabatini novel. Alice Terry, Lewis Stone and Ramon Novarro featured. 44th Street, Sept. 30, 1923. Running time, two hours.

Andre-Louis Moreau.......Ramon Novarro
Aline de Kercadiou.............Alice Terry
The Marquis de La Tour d'Azyr......
.............................Lewis Stone
Quintin de Kercadiou......Lloyd Ingraham
The Countess Therese de Plougastel...
.....................Julia Swayne Gordon
The Chevalier de Chabrillane........
.....................William Humphrey
Philippe de Vilmorin.........Otto Matiesen
Georges Jacques Danton..George Siegmann
Le Chapelier..............Bowditch Turner
Chalifan Binet..............James Marcus
Climene Binet.................Edith Allen
Madame Binet........Lydia Yeamans Titus
Polichinelle.....................John George
Rhodomont................Nelson McDowell
Maximilien Robespierre...............
.....................De Garcia Fuerburg
Jean Paul Marat..............Roy Coulson
Louis XVI....................Edwin Argus
Marie Antoinette..........Clotilde Delano

The Rex Ingram Metro super feature, "Scaramouche," had its New York presentation at the 44th Street last night, before what might be aptly termed "a hand-picked audience." The picture did not have to be shown to any selected assemblage, however, to make good. It is a faithful visualization of the book that has been most ably directed by Ingram. The cast is one that handles the characters of Sabatini's novel with a touch of realism that makes one believe that they have walked out of the pages of the book itself. There is one thing certain, and that is that on his arrival here the author will be unable to take exception to the manner in which his work has been picturized, for the feature is the book itself.

Ingram has done himself proud in this picture. He had a task before him when he was assigned the book, but he had the good sense to know that he had a good story and he left it alone, not trying to have a picture written from it. He may not have previously been placed on the same plane as the greatest director, but he certainly stands with the best that there is in the industry after this, and there are only two or three that can be mentioned in the same breath.

Alice Terry looked wonderful and managed to score heavily, but Lewis Stone stands out as the biggest figure in the picture. His finish, after having been the heavy all the way through, is heroic. Ramon Navarro as the young lawyer, actor-duelist hero of the story is made for the future.

The picture is being shown in two parts. The first of these is merely a planting of the story, and it is in the second half of the picture that the real thrills arrive. After seeing the manner in which Ingram handled his mob in this production one need not think that the foreign directors can teach him anything. He proved himself a master in this particular.

"Scaramouche" is a picture that is going to make a lot of money for Metro, no matter what it cost. Being run in one house with the spoken play in the other within the next few weeks is going to work out a box-office novelty that should be a help to the spoken and the unspoken drama on about a 50-50 basis, for seeing on will make you want to see the other. *Fred.*

THREE AGES

Joseph M. Schenck presents Buster Keaton in another feature length comedy, directed by Keaton and Eddie Kline. Story and titles by Jean Havez, Joe Mitchell and Clyde Bruckman. At the Rivoli, Sept. 30. Projection time, 56 minutes.

The Boy.......................Buster Keaton
The Girl.....................Margaret Leahy
The Villain....................Wallace Beery
The Mother................Lillian Laurence
The Father......................Joe Roberts
The Emperor......Horace "Cupid" Morgan

Keaton has achieved something in making a five-reel straightaway low comedy, knockabout film and the secret is that it's fun is so varied it never has a chance of becoming monotonous. This desirable effect is secured by having the story progress along three distinct lines each involving a different epoch with its change of pace and atmosphere.

The three periods are the stone age, the pompous days of Rome and the modern. The first two furnish rich possibilities for travesty clowning while the modern section makes for contrast and the whole design works out into screaming farce.

On the Sunday night aspect of attendance the picture will get a big public following and it should, for it is first class screen amusement by a distinct personality and one of the best legitimate comedians we have, either for screen or for the stage.

The new picture disposes of the argument that a knockabout comedy can't be interesting for over two reels. "Three Ages" is a continuous laugh for nearly an hour. The film is full of surprise laughs and for continuous amusement stands in a class by itself.

There is another well placed angle. The character played by the star is always getting the worst of it, although he is the character toward whom all the sympathy is directed. It's pretty, shrewd showmanship to create a lovable, glorified fool against whom the fates seem to be engaged in a conspiracy. That's the basis theme.

The three parallel stories are held together by a brief foreward explaining that although customs and times change, lovemaking and loving are always the same. Then the screen goes to illustrating the truism. First we have the young lover of the stone age up to a certain point in his courtship; then the Roman dandy up to the same point, and finally the modern swain in a like cross section of his love affair.

In all three cases the situation is about the same—a humble, but faithful lover (Keaton) struggling for his lady fair against the unscrupulous unworthy adventurer (Wallace Beery) and in his efforts stumbling into all sorts of scrapes.

Some of the settings are rather pretentious, particularly in the Roman episodes and the stories are worked out with the most ingenious incidents. They show a burlesque chariot race with the background of a section of the Coliseum and other backgrounds look impressive.

A few of the details perhaps will indicate the quality of the humor. In the Roman story The Boy has failed in his suit and goes to a soothsayer to have his destiny read. He is required to cast a die, just as the Ethiopian slaves of his sweetheart are passing, and the dignified visit to the augur degenerates into a crap game.

There's a lot of rich fun also in the stone age incident of The Boy in a sentimental mood dictating to a stone age stenographer armed with a chisel and hammer, also in The Boy's scouting trip on a dinosaurus. At another time the Roman heavy throws the hero into a lion's den and he saves his life by remembering that some traditional hero made friends with the lion by doing something to his paw (Androcles who extracted the historic thorn); so he manicures this particular lion and they part good friends.

The modern instance where the hero pursues his sweetheart into an up-to-date cabaret is a mine of a knockabout comedy and the wedding scene is packed with solid laughs. *Rush.*

THE ETERNAL THREE

Marshall Neilan production, distributed by Goldwyn. Program credits Marshall Neilan with story. Directed by Neilan and Frank Urson. Capitol, New York, Sept. 30. Running time, 70 minutes.

Dr. Frank R. Walters....Hobart Bosworth
Mrs. Frank R. Walters....Claire Windsor
Leonard Foster...........Raymond Griffith
Hilda Gray.......................Bessie Love
Bob Gray.....................George Cooper

Tommy Tucker................Tom Gallery
Miriam Barnes................Helen Lynch
Dr. Steven Browning..........Alec Francis
Owner of Hacienda (Dr. Walter's friend),
          Wm. Orkmond
Butler...................Chas. H. West
Maid....................Maryon Aye
Old Roue................William Norris
Governor................James F. Fulton
Governor's Wife...........Irene Hunt
Governor's Child...........Peaches Jackson
Mrs. Tucker..............Victory Bateman
Mrs. Tucker's Friend........Billie Bennett

A fine cast makes this rather ordinary triangular story a good program picture. Mostly made of familiar stuff, with the heavy getting away with everything he tackles for quite a while, but with good old virtue triumphant in the final dash for the post.

Good for evil is the motif and it's nicely carried out to a logical conclusion. The events that transpire in the unreeling are pretty trite when they're analyzed, but competent direction, together with intelligent acting, lends an air of reality to more than one scene that would have seemed pallid without such aids.

There's a terrific amount of booze consumed in the filming. Twice the heavy starts a campaign to capture women, and once he does, but each time he utilizes the seductive lure of wine or red-eye to help bring about the gals' downfall. He'd have captured both of 'em, too, only he was careless in walking along the street and met with an accident. A truck smacked him, and his foster father, an eminent surgeon, was called upon to perform a major operation. Now the heavy happened to be rushing his foster father's wife, and the M. D. knew all about the little affair.

With that knowledge rankling in his mind the doc wasn't in any too keen a humor to lend his professional services toward saving the heavy's life. But ethics prevailed and the doc did his stuff.

The staging of a couple of Bacchanalian parties was excellently done, and the whole film shows intelligent direction. The sets are up to the best standards throughout. There are several glimpses of an operating room that are authentic and marked with atmosphere without being repulsive.

The titles are few and far between. That's one of the picture's several good points.

Hobart Bosworth plays the M. D. He gives his usual virile performance, never overacting. Bessie Love has the wronged girl role and makes it distinctive. Raymond Griffith is a good heavy of the modern type, playing with ease and a certain smoothness. George Cooper has a bit and handles it for real results. The part of the doctor's wife is also well done.

This mixture of problem play and melodrama will probably never break any house records, but it will furnish average entertainment for any type of picture house.

                                        Bell.

DEVIL'S PARTNER

Independent feature produced by Iroquois, featuring Norma Shearer. At Loew's Circle, New York, New York, on double feature bill Oct. 2. Running time 50 minutes.

The title of this picture is intriguing to the extent one readily accepts it as a caption for another one of those sex films. Instead it is a commonplace story of the Northwest with the familiar melodrama ingredients such as the browbeaten father urged by a villainous gent to give him his daughter in marriage or else he will expose his secret.

In this case the villain sets his cap for the pretty Jeanne in the opening reel and spends the other four trying to keep her and her more youthful lover from achieving matrimony. But it can't be done in the movies.

After being mauled and hauled through five reels the girl finds her much needed haven of rest in the arms of her lover. At the same moment the unlikable gent is perishing in the flames of his own hell.

Norma Shearer is always charming. She manages to retain this asset in the portrayal of the hunted heroine. Charles Delaney portrays the youthful lover, while Edward Roseman does his villainous best to make the pursuer hateful.

Whatever prompted them to call this film "The Devil's Partner" is a conundrum. "And the Villain Still Pursued Her" would have been far more explanatory.

THE MAN BETWEEN

A Finis Fox production: story and direction by Fox; produced by Associated Exhibitors from Lois Zellner's scenario. Pathe release. At Stanley, New York, Sept. 27.

This has a fairly interesting story that lends itself well to economical production, but the sum total could have been more effective in better directorial hands.

Allan Forrest personates two roles, not twins, but of similarly resembling characters. They are Jules and Pierre, the former a wealthy scion whose affluence leads to his life imprisonment for murder. Pierre, a sympathetic character, is also committed to prison on a false larceny charge. Pierre swears vengeance on Dick (Philo McCullough), who framed him.

Jules asks Pierre to personate him and visit his aged mother. The close resemblance makes this possible. Pierre is believed by Jules' wife to be her husband, but he maintains honorable relations until the situation is straightened out. It includes Jules' escape from prison and his meeting with Dick, the heavy. Both die in a cabaret brawl over a cabaret performer, Rosie Beautiful (Viola Vale), which makes Pierre's union with Jules' wife possible.

It sounds a bit involved, and its depiction could have been better. Capably handled it would have proved a snapper.

Edna Murphy as Jules' estranged wife had little to do but did it well. Miss Vale as the other woman is a strong possibility although little known. Forrest was satisfactory in the dual role.

The picture is a little above the average usually shown at the Stanley, which is a drop house off Times Square with a policy that anything will draw 'em.

                                        Abel.

THE CLEAN UP

Universal starring Herbert Rawlinson. Story by H. H. Van Loan; scenario by Raymond L. Shrock, Eugen Lewis and Harvey Gates. Directed by Richard Fryer. Shown at the Stanley, New York, Sept. 29, 1923. Running time, 65 minutes.

Montgomery Bixby......Herbert Rawlinson
Phyllis Andrews...........Claire Adams
Mary Reynolds............Claire Anderson
Robert Reynolds..........Herbert Fortier
Mrs. Reynolds............Margaret Campbell
Amos Finderson..........Frank Farrington

A picture showing a good idea gone wrong. What an awful time there must have been had with the making of the story can be judged from the fact that there are three names credited with having had a whirl at the preparing of the script. That in itself tells a whole story. The finished product is one that runs by fits and starts. There are two laughs in the picture, both secured through the medium of titles. Had the idea been properly put over there should have been a succession of laughs from the beginning to the end of the picture. As it is at present it is just a mediocre feature, and hardly that.

The scene of the story is laid in a small town in New Jersey, where the grandfather of the hero, Monty Bixby, has just died and left a will whereby he bequeaths $50,000 to each one of the born and bred natives who are living in the town at the time of his death. To his grandson he gives $1, but asks that he remain in the town for 30 days after his death. As soon as the natives receive their legacies they then knock off work and let the town go to pot. The disinherited youth who was his grandfather's secretary seizes the opportunity and starts to run the town. Of course the girl that he is engaged to at the time that he is cut off in the will passes him up and the secretary replaces her in his affections and at the end of the 30 days the lawyer shows up and informs him that he is to receive $2,000,000 which the old boy has left him providing that in the month's time he should have taken the object lesson provided for him to heart.

Rawlinson goes through the picture in a matter of fact sort of way that doesn't get him anything as far as creating an impression is concerned. He does manage to put up a fairly good fight in one of the scenes, but the pulling of punches on the part of both contestants is so palpable that it almost compels a laugh. In the supporting cast there is no one that stands out other than Claire Adams, who handles a light lead fairly well.   Fred.

DARK ALLEYS
(DUNKLÉ GASSEN)
Berlin, Sept. 17.

This film in which Battling Siki, the negro boxer, is featured is one of the most extraordinary hodgepodges ever seen.

The scenery is designed by a German, Robert Neppach, but many of the exteriors were taken in Paris. The direction is by Jack Wortling, who sounds like an Englishman; the scenario by C. Lyn, probably a Frenchman.

Most of the actors are German, although some of them are undoubtedly French, and the photography by Stefan Lorrant, whose first name is German and whose second is quite evidently Gallic.

And it is just as bad as it sounds. It seems that the director had been looking at American films and tried to find out what made them successful. He evidently thought tempo and suspense were the chief points, but he forgot that if the whole thing appears ludicrous you don't get any suspense, and that mere speed means nothing.

The story is really too ridiculous to recount, but it seems to have been something about a rich girl whose cousin tried to have her murdered by a Chinese because he wanted to inherit her money. However, she was only knocked cuckoo and is found by a Chinese dock worker who worships her as a goddess.

Then there is her faithful servant, Jimmie Low (played by Siki), who rescues her and becomes a famous boxer. While he is in the ring the wicked cousin comes to kidnap her again and we have cut-backs to the fight and back again to the house with the Chinese breaking in. Before anything can happen to her she is, of course, rescued, and marries the poor boy who loves her.

The only good thing in the film is a real scrap between Siki and another negro boxer named Baker, evidently new stuff sandwiched in. Siki's personality is impossible. The only people in the cast who distinguish themselves are two Chinese, not named, and Robert Neppach, who has designed some excellent scenery which is well lighted and often brilliantly photographed.   Trask.

THE LOVE TRAP

A Ben Wilson production; written by Evelyn Cunningham; presented by Harry Asher featuring Bryant Washburn and Mabel Forrest. Released through Grand-Asher Distributing Co. Directed by John Ince. Ran 65 minutes at Loew's New York Sept. 27.

A crude production, inconsistent, non-gripping, wandering and maudlin at times in its admixture of pathos and bathos. It is surprising that a house like the New York should have recourse to stuff like this.

A brief recital of the yarn will point out its inconsistency. A daughter of a judge is announced married to a young blood, Grant Garrison (Wheeler Oakman), the heavy. Joyce Lyndon (Mabel Forrest) is lured to a roadhouse by Garrison, where the latter meets his death at the hands of an abandoned wife. The girl accidentally becomes acquainted with Martin Dexter (Bryant Washburn), who announces himself impecunious despite his cozy apartment. One blatant discrepancy in this scene, where the heroine is put up for the night in Martin's apartment, becomes evident. The place looks roomy and Martin is shown ascending the stairs, yet the girl is made to repose on a couch and the hero makeshifts on the sink or washtub in the kitchen. Seemingly there wasn't a real bed in the place!

The heroine fears implication in the murder. The roadhouse owner attempts blackmail; the hero saves the day and the girl recovers the incriminating handbag left in the place through a ruse of a cheap melodramatic order. To make it perfect, that old standby of mystery and detective stories—the dictograph—is introduced to frame the real murderess. And for good measure the guilty one admits she was a former show girl.

The story wanders, there is no direct purpose, the society stuff is literally dragged in by the teeth, the direction never convinces, and the actors deport themselves as if they feel they are guilty of something. There is absolutely no conviction to the whole production which rings false from the very first title. It starts off with a long leader setting forth some high-sounding premise that is immediately lost sight of and completely forgotten.

Then, too, the roadhouse keeper is made up for an Hebraic part of the unsympathetic, gesticulating school, and then, at the last moment, for fear it might offend the exhibitors and the customers, the Semitic appearing individual is labelled with an Italian name as an effort to take the curse off it.

Washburn at one time had some standing. If he has been appearing in pictures like these for any length of time, it is surprising he has survived oblivion thus far.

An economical buy for the nickelodeons. *Abel.*

STRANGERS OF NIGHT

Louis B. Mayer presentation and a Fred Niblo production; also directed by him. Releasing through Metro. Adapted from the stage play of "Captain Applejack," by C. G. Sullivan. Showing at the Capitol Oct. 7. Running time, 75 mins.

Ambrose Applejohn............Matt Moore
Poppy Faire..................Enid Bennett
Anna Valeska..............Barbara La Marr
Borolsky......................Robert McKim
Mrs. Agatha Whatacombe,
Mathilda Brundage
Mrs. Horace Pengard.........Emily Fitzroy
Mr. Horace Pengard..........Otto Hoffman
Lush.........................Thomas Ricketts

Thrills, laughs and a whale of a picture. So much so it drew spontaneous applause at various intervals from a close to capacity matinee gathering and seems destined to receive that most valuable means of advertising, by word of mouth. For they're bound to talk about this one if the manner in which it was received at the Capitol Sunday afternoon is any criterion.

The picture deserves it. It is a superb effort upon the part of the director, Fred Niblo, and a cast that combines to make this film rank with or even surpass any program feature at the Broadway houses this season.

The adaptation is abundant with those two characteristics, suspense and comedy, whilst probably marking the best effort Matt Moore has ever given before the camera.

In doing this Moore has not outdistanced the remaining contributing members, for Enid Bennett and Barbara La Marr closely follow for personal honors; but at the same time it is Niblo's picture.

Moore as the rather meek and mild Ambrose Applejohn, who suddenly craves romance and excitement and gets it all in one night, gives a splendid performance. The story, once under way, never lets up. Whether due to the excellence of the narrative or otherwise, Niblo has sustained the suspense and interest to hold an audience within the last 25 feet of film, when the proverbial clinch terminates.

Meanwhile there is the comedy, which hints at satire, and were the subtitle, "Who's All the Strangers?" injected it would not be hard to imagine it another edition of Cohan's "The Tavern" picturized, even though somewhat different in script.

The picture looks money. Some of the interiors may even be said to illusion as extravagant, but that does not indicate the fault of overdoing. The absence of just such a thing is one of the picture's commendable features. Of the photography the same might be said, which would include two neat pieces of "faking." Both production and the camera work (the photographer getting neither screen nor program mention) are also adequate during the interlude of the pirate ship and its buccaneers, which takes place in the form of a dream.

The picture is unquestionably "there" and would seem the tipoff that Metro is going out after its regular program release schedule with as much attention as it gives the specials.

"The Green Goddess," with George Arliss, is receiving lobby billing as next week's attraction, but it is unlikely the Capitol will house that home office vehicle until the week of Oct. 21, for if ever a picture gave indications of a sure holdover, "Strangers" did Sunday afternoon. *Skig.*

THE SPANISH DANCER

Herbert Brenon production, starring Pola Negri. Presented by Adolph Zukor. Adapted for the screen by June Mathis and Beulah Marie Dix from the play, "Don Cesar de Bazan," by Adolphe D'Ennery and P. S. P. Dumanoir. Shown at the Rivoli, N. Y., week of Oct. 7, 1923. Running time, 1 hour 28 minutes.

Maritana, a gypsy dancer......Pola Negri
Don Cesar de Bazan, a nobleman,
Antonio Moreno
King Philip IV. of Spain....Wallace Beery
Queen Isabel of Bourbon..Kathlyn Williams
Lazarillo, an armorer's boy..Gareth Hughes
Don Salluste, a courtier....Adolphe Menjou
Marquis de Rotundo..........Edward Kipling
Don Balthazar Carlos..........Dawn O'Day
Cardinal's Ambassador..Chas. A. Stevenson
Juan, a thief..................Robert Agnew

This is a picture that will serve as a feature that is somewhat better than the ordinary run of costume pictures, but which, however, falls short of being entered in the category of specials. It will suffer by comparison with the Mary Pickford feature, "Rosita," also based on the story of "Don Cesar de Bazan," and which was previously shown in New York.

There is this that the exhibitor will have to count on, and that is that when his opposition plays "Rosita" he can play "The Spanish Dancer," or if he controls two big houses in his district it might be a good idea to play them in opposition to each other for the controversy it will create. It isn't often that the exhibitor gets a chance such as this, a screen battle between two of the greatest stars of the screen, both in the same role, and he should capitalize on it.

This production is handled from an entirely different viewpoint in screening than was "Rosita." Where that picture was romantic this is rather historic, where Pickford was wistful and charming, Pola is fiery and flashing, and Pickford must be said to have had considerable the better of it in as far as the "mad scene" is concerned. There is also the fact that in having the support of Holbrook Blinn as the King she fared better than did Pola with Wallace Beery in that role. Antonio Moreno as the dashing young Don is reminiful of Doug in "The Three Musketeers," and there are moments when one would almost swear it was Doug at a distance. Kathlyn Williams as the Queen made an impression, but her role was far differently conceived than it was in "Rosita."

Frankly, "Rosita" is far the better of the two pictures in the mind of this reviewer.

The matter of direction in the two cannot be compared. Herbert Brenon, who handled the Negri production, did his work skillfully and in workmanlike manner. He does not, however, approach Lubitsch when it comes to a matter of detail and delicate touch. However, his picture is strong enough to hold interest as a straightforward tale. There is lacking, however, a comedy relief in the picturization that was present in that directed by the foreigner. *Fred.*

THE BAD MAN

A First National production adapted from the Porter Emerson Brown play of the same title. Shown at the Strand, N. Y., week of Oct. 7, 1923. Running time, 67 minutes.

Pancho Lopez...............Holbrook Blinn
Gilbert Jones....................Jack Mulhall
Morgan Pell..................Walter McGrail
Mrs. Morgan Pell..............Enid Bennett
Red Giddings....................Harry Myers
Uncle Henry...............Charles A. Sellon
Jasper Hardy....................Stanton Heck
Angela Hardy.................Teddy Sampson
Captain Blake.................Thomas Delmar
Indian Cook....................Frank Lanning
Pedro......................Peter Venezuella

If it wasn't for Holbrook Blinn "The Bad Man" at the Strand this week would be very poor material for the screen. In the titling there is a tendency to overplay the dialect thing. As a picture it appears that it will get by principally on the strength of Blinn, but it will at the best be only a fair feature production for the box office. In the Southwest country it will perhaps get over better.

The play originally had Blinn and he made it a work of art. There were moments in witnessing the picture when one could almost hear Blinn hiss words through his teeth, words that would have the Mex dialect, instead of the half French, half Canuck, that appeared in the written titles.

Last night at the Strand did not show anything extraordinary in the way of business, but then the Rivoli on a check-up seems to be doing the business of the street this week with "The Spanish Dancer."

In the cast with Blinn are Jack Mulhall, who handles the young rancher rather well, and Enid Bennett as the woman, seemingly overacting in a great many of the earlier scenes but in the final shots when all was serene and peaceful her charming self photographically. Harry Myers over-played his comedy and Teddy Sampson was just "flapper." Walter McGrail as the heavy was all right, while Charles A. Sellon as Uncle Henry got away to great advantage.

From the standpoint of direction Edwin Carewe turned out a picture that could have been better. In detail he was decidedly forgetful at times. A little thing like a revolver leaping from the floor to the holster of the hero unassisted, to be there at the needed moment meant nothing to the director, editor or cutter.

There are some corking exterior shots and a whale of a rainstorm. That is the best that there is from a photographic viewpoint.

TEA WITH A KICK

Halperin feature, made for Associated Distributors, released through Pathe. Written and produced under personal supervision of Victor Hugo Halperin. Shown as feature at Tivoli, New York, Sept. 26. Running time, 60 minutes.

Jim Day........................Ralph Lewis
Bonnie Day.......................Doris May
Aunt Pearl..................Rosemary Theby
Art Binger....................Creighton Hale
Napoleon Dobbings..........Stuart Holmes
Drainy Jones......................ZaSu Pitts
Chris Kringle.....................Harry Todd
Oscar Puddleford...............Snitz Edwards
Birdie Puddleford...........Louise Fazenda

Undoubtedly one of the best comedy releases that has been "framed" by an independent this season. Has a wealth of good comedy, is superbly cast and actually exceeds the speed limit for action. The story also is commendable. It blends everything that is anything in the way of rollicking entertainment and moves with a pleasurable gusto. A melodramatic introductory plants the incentive for the ensuing escapades, but when comedy takes hold one almost entirely forgets the imprisoned father of the heroine until we learn in the final reel that he has been pardoned.

Jim Day, the father of Bonnie, had been made the scapegoat by stock swindlers. He was framed and sent to prison. Plucky Bonnie wants to quit the fashionable finishing school she has been attending, to raise funds to appeal her father's case. A scheming aunt has other plans. She would marry her off to Napoleon Dobbings, a small-town capitalist. Through the marriage Aunt Pearl sees a way of bringing money into the family to fight for the release of her brother. But Bonnie has a mind of her own—also a young man. He is Art Binger, the bucolic barrister.

Bonnie also does some quick thinking, capitalizes the headline of the papers, "Tea with a Kick," and stages a cabaret revue with the stranded choristers. Success comes in bunches. When at the height of prosperity with her tearoom she also gets word that her father has been pardoned, this being brought about by the untiring efforts of young Binger, the legal light and lover.

Doris May gave a likable delineation of Bonnie, bringing to it a delicious touch of piquancy and at the same time crowding in some remarkably good acting. Creighton Hale was also superb as young Art Binger. Stuart Holmes is less villainous in this picture than in preceding ones. His Napoleon Dobbings gave him more opportunity for laughs than any role he has ever had. In fact, the entire cast added their mite toward making the picture enjoyable and a worthy addition to the screen.

In conclusion, it may well be said that "Tea with a Kick" has all the ingredients that appeal to lovers of the cinema play, and as a feature it cannot fail to hit.

EAGLE'S FEATHER

Metro all-star production with James Kirkwood and Mary Alden. Based on the story by Katherine Newlin Burt; scenario by Winifred Dunn. Directed by Edward Sloman. Shown at Loew's New York, New York, Sept. 26, 1923. Running time, 72 minutes.

Delila Jamieson..................Mary Alden
John Trent...................James Kirkwood
Jeff Carey.......................Lester Cuneo
Martha.............................Elinor Fair
Van Brewen...................George Seigman
Parson Winger.....................John Elliott
The Irishman..................Charles McHugh
The Swede...................William Orlamond
Wing Ling...........................Jim Wang

A western and different, so different it just falls short of being a great picture.

It should have been and would have, had the direction been equal to the story itself. As it is, it's a fair feature that will go in the daily change of program houses anywhere. It has all the thrills that the average western has and goes just a little further than most of them. There is a corking cattle stampede in the production. The cast is a good one with three capable players at its head in Mary Alden, James Kirkwood and Elinor Fair.

The story is one of those "after the war" affairs, with Kirkwood playing the role of a returned soldier who has been hunting a job for a couple of years. Finally fate plays him the trick of being chased off a freight on which he is stealing a ride at a small western town. There he lands a job at $40 a month and is found on the ranch operated by Delila Jamieson, who is known as "the biggest man" in the county. She is a middle-aged spinster who lives with an adopted niece. With the advent of Kirkwood as general handy man the ranch woman falls in love with him and pictures in her dreams his proposing to her. So intent is she on this mentally that when he starts to tell her of his love for her niece she takes it for granted that it is she that he means, but on learning the truth she turns and it is the old story of "Hell hath no fury, etc.," orders her ranch hands to take him to the bunk house and administer a flogging, after which he is to be turned out into the night; likewise she sends the girl forth. In the end, however, she relents and goes forth into the snow-storm which is raging to find both the man and girl and bring them back, consenting to their marriage.

It is a brisk story with a different twist than most westerns have and Mary Alden endows the role of the spinster with a performance that is one of the best things she has done in some time. Kirkwood is at ease at all times. Lester Cuneo plays a heavy that doesn't shine particularly. The balance of the cast was selected for types, and there are a couple of spots in the picture where the director has used them to advantage. George Seigman gives his usual finished performance as a real roughneck rancher. *Fred.*

GOING UP

Encore Picture, presented by Associated Exhibitors, Inc.; directed by Lloyd Ingraham; adapted from the musical comedy by Otto Harbach, after the farce by James Montgomery, "The Aviator."

Robert Street	Douglas McLean
Hopkinson Brown	Hallam Cooley
James Brooks	Arthur Stuart Hull
Jules Gaillard	Francis McDonald
Sam Robinson	Hughie Mack
John Gordon	Wade Boteler
William Douglas	John Steppling
Bellboy	Mervyn LeRoy
Grace Douglas	Marjorie Daw
Madeline Manners	Edna Murphy
Mrs. Douglas	Lillian Langdon

If this was designed as a special, it came out a little undergrade; if it was aimed as a programmer, it resulted a little above the average.

The natural amplification of "Going Up," the great musical show, in film treatment, is the flying part. This comes in at the end of the first reel and during most of the last. The first part is only to plant the hero's terror of sky-wagons, when he, as the author of a novel about an airman, is coaxed in as a passenger by his press-agent. The machine turns on its nose before leaving the ground, and he hurts his knee. This is the end of that episode and he runs off to a Berkshire resort to get away from promotional annoyances—but, as always necessary in farces, he takes with him the chum; the bird who "fixes" things.

He falls in love with a flapper and the friend makes a hero of him by saying he fell 25,000 feet from a plane and is a great aviator and hero. A real bird-guy, a French ace, also in love with the girl, comes in out of the ozone. A match flight is framed. The hero is shamed into it because the girl is wild over heroes. So he calls in a comedy instructor and there is a good scene where he takes an indoor aviation lesson.

After every effort to get out of it, he at last is pushed into a powerful machine and his crazy flight wins him the contest, the girl and the title of the greatest birdman in the world.

This is a great opportunity for trick stuff. But it is not entirely realized. The stunts are either so genuine and legitimate that the observer is sure the hero is not piloting, or else they are so far away and so rapid that the planes look like cardboard marionettes worked mechanically.

The close-ups show MacLean in the driver's seat, but only a few feet on any side of it, and he is so motionless that they at times remind one of the Coney Island snapshots for postal cards, where the visitors put their heads through dummy autos, airplanes, etc., painted on little canvas flats.

It is dubious whether a child, seeing "Going Up," would leave with a suspicion that MacLean had ever left terra firma.

Had this important element been carried out like Lloyd's dizzy climb in "Safety Last," this would have been a hair-raising feature. The faking is far from perfect, however, being patchy and at no time carrying the watcher away or causing a gasp. There are many spontaneous laughs at that, for the stunt flying is obvious comedy stuff, having inherent value but little applied strength as affecting the interest in the hero or story.

It is a polite and light story with some excellent incidental action, and qualifies as a good comedy. Marjorie Daw, as the heroine, slows it up. Had she played a hero-mad flapper instead of the diffident, serious girl, the amusing qualities would have been greatly enhanced and the speed would have been accelerated. In some of her close-ups she was Madonna-like in spirituelle appeal and in all of them she was subdued and sad-like, which slacked the slapstick story up considerably.

In production "Going Up" is not lavish, being mostly outdoors and in no magnificent sets when indoors. The photography is of Grade A order, and the direction stands up remarkably well in the portions where one might look for dullness, though it doesn't measure all the way up in those where one could demand tension. The subtitles are smart and help the spirit, but a few could be eliminated as superfluous.

Lait.

THE BROKEN WING

B. P. Schulberg presentation released by Preferred Pictures as a Tom Forman production, the latter supplying the scenario and directing. The picture is based upon the play of the same title by Paul Dickey and Charles W. Goddard. At the Rialto, New York, Oct. 7.

Philip Marvin	Kenneth Harlan
Inez Villera	Miriam Cooper
Capt. Innocencio Dos Santos	Walter Long
Celia	Miss Du Pont
Sylvester Cross	Richard Tucker
Bassilio	Edwin J. Brady
Luther Farley	Ferdinand Munier
Quichita	Evelyn Selbie

"The Broken Wing" slipped into the Rialto, a Paramount house, for a week, and just what was the reason for the booking is difficult to determine. There is no great strength **to the production and no apparent reason why it should take the place of some Paramount production in one of the recognized Broadway weekly change houses.**

It is not up to the standard set by some of the past Schulberg pictures. No great pains seem to have been taken in outlining the scenario from the original play. The play was far superior to the picture, and is still creating some interest as a stock bill.

Tom Forman, who designed the scenario, failed to take his work seriously from general appearances. As much can be said for his direction, which at times is distinctly ragged.

The **story should** have been built **into an interesting picture.** It is comparatively interesting in its general makeup and needed only occasional flashes to make it stand up.

The action practically in its entirety takes place in Mexico. An American flyer who comes to grief is nursed back to health by the daughter of a Mexican ranchman. A revolutionary leader had claimed the girl for himself some time previous. He expresses considerable hate for his rival, who completely wins the girl. With all the hate there is little action, and the story wanders along, ending up in the usual manner.

The cast is headed by Kenneth Harlan and Miriam Cooper. Harlan does little to make his work stand out, with Miss Cooper doing somewhat better. The remainder of the cast consists of types, the majority having been well selected.

"The Broken Wing" cost little to make. One banquet scene in the **first reel shows a bit of a flash, but that apparently was used for many other productions. The remainder of the footage takes place on the desert.**

"The Broken Wing" is lacking as a picture. *Hart.*

GOLD MADNESS

Screen adaptation of James Oliver Curwood's novel, "Man from Ten Strike," starring Guy Bates Post. Produced by Perfect Pictures Corp. Shown as principal feature on double feature bill Loew's Circle, New York, Tuesday, Oct. 2. Running time, 60 minutes.

James Kendall	Guy Bates Post
Olga Kendall	Cleo Madison
Scotty McGee	Mitchell Lewis
Margaret Stanton	Grace Darmond

Gripping drama, suspense aplenty and countless intriguing situations characterize this latest James Oliver Curwood yarn to find its way into the realm of flicker drama. The story is written in the best Curwood vein and, like all of his contributions, is laid in the gold regions, where men are men and women—are faithless. Moreover, it gives us Guy Bates Post in another masquerader role, just the sort in which this sterling actor revels and at the same time excels.

As the prospector-husband of a woman who has married him while under the influence of gold madness Post gives his usually finished performance, played in a tone that readily gains sympathy of the auditor and at the same time establishes a solid rock contrast to the gayer personage in the latter reels, whose quick-wittedness not only accom**plishes revenge upon his faithless wife and the man for whom she forsook him, but leads him into the arms of a woman who appreciates him.**

In the story Curwood has attempted to demonstrate to what lengths one will go when hypnotized by gold madness. In this instance he emphasizes his point through the faithless wife. She has entered into marriage with the prospector not because she loved him but for the possibility that he would strike a vein and give her the comforts and luxuries she craved.

But, unfortunately for her, she kicks over the traces and makes off with her lover at the same moment the husband has struck gold. Upon learning of her flight he joins the Alaska police and is assigned by his superiors to bring back a man and woman swindler, who eventually turn out to be the runaway wife and her lover.

While Post's acting overshadowed everything else the other principals gave splendid accounts of themselves. Cleo Madison was superb as the wife. Mitchell Lewis was also in his element as McGee, the mine swindler and third member of the triangle. Grace Darmond as the stenographer who later becomes the wife of the millionaire mine owner also gave a performance worthy of honorary mention.

The feature has been well directed, continuity is good, and its substance matter is sufficiently interesting to satisfy the most critical devotee of the screen play. With the additional **popularity of the star it should not have any trouble registering in the better class houses.**

SO THIS IS HOLLYWOOD

R-C picture releasing through F. B. O. From the pen of H. C. Witwer, and directed by Mal St. Clair. Running time, about 30 minutes.

Probably a fight series for R-C by the author who wrote the "Leather-pushers" in script, later transplanted to the screen.

The send off for this serial is decidedly weak considering the importance of "planting" such an undertaking. It shortly develops into nothing **more than an ordinary** chase comedy and nothing of the fight game in the episode other than to reveal a picture of "Six Second Smith" (George O'Hara) adorning the cover of a sport magazine. Albert Cooke is cast as the fight manager and Mary Milford plays the girl of the story.

O'Hara presents a nice appearance although it remains to be seen how he has handled the actual ring stuff. Beyond revealing his arrival in California by means of a freight train this particular episode gives little opportunity for O'Hara to step out other than a couple of prop battles inserted in the chase things.

The series will need a fluent spice to pick up interest on the next edition for it's away to a poor start and even the usual punch of the Witwer subtitles is missing. *Skig.*

DESIRE

Louis Burston production distributed by Metro. Story and continuity by John B. Clymer and Henry R. Symonds. Directed by Rowland V. Lee. Photographed by George Barnes. Art director, J. J. Hughes. At Loew's New York, Oct. 4. Runs about 80 Mins.

Ruth Cassell	Marguerite de la Motte
Bob Elkins	John Bowers
Madalyn Harlan	Estelle Taylor
Jerry Ryan	David Butler
Bud Reisner	Walter Long
Mamie Reisner	Lucille Hutton
Rupert Cassell	Edward Connelly
DeWitt Harlan	Ralph Lewis
Oland Young	Chester Conklin
Mrs. DeWitt Harlan	Vera Lewis
Patrick Ryan	Nick Cogley
Mrs. Pat Ryan	Sylvia Ashton
Mr. Elkins	Frank Currier
Best Man	Lars Landers

The all-absorbing theme of marriage between persons of different **social** scale is treated with not as cleverly as in De Mille's "Saturday Night," but with a good interest, dramatic artistry and color. The wedding of a girl born to the purple and her chauffeur always commands attention whether described in the papers or portrayed on the stage and screen.

Madalyn Harlan and Bob Elkins, children of the wealthy, are engaged to be married, but are unable to go through the ceremony because they really do not love each other. Bob's further romance may be quickly disposed of by telling that he falls in love with the little granddaughter of an old violin teacher.

Madalyn falls head over heels over her big handsome chauffeur. **She** secretly marries him. Visiting **his** poor uncouth parents, it strikes **her** forcibly a life of lowly drudgery **would** be just as unbearable. Deciding to choose social ostracism **rather** than give up her love she denies her parents and goes to her **Jerry. His** mother, fearing the influence of this strange woman on **her son's** life, drives her away by **telling her Jerry is** through with **her.**

Madalyn, all hope gone, takes poison in a private room of the cabaret in which she had formerly spent so many carefree, happy hours. She is carried out and placed in the taxi driven by Jerry. Believing his fare is just another drunken woman, he takes her to a hotel. There he learns she is his wife. In a hysterical fit of grief he drives his cab with its cargo of tragedy into the river.

The plot has elements of power. The ending is undoubtedly a bit different, sordid and incisive. Perhaps the authors saw no other way out. But if all present day films carried stories with as much heart-tug and human interest, the screen would be on a much higher level.

As box office material "Desire" is one in a hundred if properly exploited. A short, sexy name is the first big draw (although there is nothing in the picture objectionable to anyone). Added to a good list of names in the regular cast, there are on the press sheets and advertising posters the names of several other well-known screen players. Chester Conklin was visible for a few instants, but Noah Beery, Frank Currier and Hank Mann, all billed, must have appeared in the parts cut before the film was readied for exhibitors.

Estelle Taylor, John Bowers and David Butler did well in the respective roles of the wealthy couple and the chauffeur. Marguerite de la Motte as the fourth of the quartet appeared to be simple and sickeningly sacherrine instead of innocent and sweet. Edward Connelly and Walter Long were their usual selves in character parts and the rest of the cast was adequate.

The director staged the lawn wedding and Casa Diablo cabaret scenes as lavish and rich-looking without too thickly spread on.

DAUGHTERS OF TODAY

Syracuse, Oct. 10.

Produced independently by Rollin Sturgeon. Author and scenarist not given. Presumably original story. At Strand, Syracuse, N. Y., Oct. 6.

Lois Whittall	Patsy Ruth Miller
Ralph Adams	Ralph Graves
Mabel Vandegrift	Edna Murphy
Peter Farnham	Edward Hearn
Reggy Adams	Philo McCullogh
Dirk Vandegrift	George Nichols
Ma Vandergrift	Gertrude Claire
Dick	Truman Vandyke
Flo	Dorothy Wood
Leigh Whittall	Phillips Smalley
Lorena	Zazu Pitts
Calnan	H. J. Hebert
Mrs. Mantell	Fontaine LaRue
Maisie	Marjorie Bonner

If the current movie season produces a poorer and trashier picture than "Daughters of Today," which had its premiere at the Syracuse Strand Saturday, it is yet to be presented in these parts.

"Daughters of Today" is not from start to finish. Sturgeon, responsible for it, has sold his screen birthright for a mess of box office pottage. How the picture ever managed to secure approval from the National Board of Review is a question that only the board can answer.

Sturgeon, in his lurid billing, calls his picture "a slice of life." If life is as bad as this picture paints it, you can't blame those poor souls who turn to self-destruction to escape it.

"Daughters of Today" is, to take Sturgeon's claim at face value, presumed to answer the question, "what's your daughter doing?" Sturgeon's answer is that she's either shooting craps for "pash" garters, playing strip poker with her boy friends, getting pie-eyed daily and nightly and living a free and easy existence generally.

It is of those things that Sturgeon has builded his impossible story. And to make it more impossible, Sturgeon gives it an American university setting. The picture would have you believe that college life today is one cocktail and "night out" after another, with the girls leading the boys a merry chase for the public intoxication and jazz crown.

As the story starts, there's a party at the country club where the young set are celebrating the clo ng of the summer vacation. The opening shows a couple mixing a cocktail with the girl draining her friend's flask. From there, the story moves rapidly to introduce a crap game with the girls playing for their garters, and later, the strip poker episode, staged in one of the rooms of the country club.

The action next shifts to the American university where high jinx are the favorite course of study. Inasmuch as the college is located in New York, you may take your choice as to whether Columbia or the College of the City of New York is the target. There, the story has it, the boys and girls occupy living quarters in the same building, and are more or less in each other's rooms.

Drinking is the rule by both sexes, and those who don't wield cocktail shakers are armed with sideboards stocked with pre-Volsteadean stuff. When Thanksgiving blows around, the young folks start off on an all-night party, which is the forerunner of grim tragedy—the mysterious killing of Reggy Adams, one of the gay young blades who, although he sizes up as about 30, is still a college student.

Suspicion falls upon Lois Whittall because she happened to be overall-clad at the party. Enter the clever detective who uses a dictaphone and, from a conversation between Lois and Mabel Vandegrift (the latter the traditional sweet little country girl who has fallen for the jazz stuff) learns that it was Mabel whom Reggy was attacking in his room after plying her with liquor.

But, to prolong the misery, Mabel avers that the last she remembered was seeing the face of Peter Farnham, the boy friend left down on the farm when she went to college, in the window. Peter walks in, but professes his innocence, and says he entered the place just in time to see a woman's form fleeing through the doorway.

Ralph Adams, the finale hopper and parasite cousin of the dead man, who is very much in love with Lois, comes in to announce that he's been working with the newspaper boys all night, and that they're closing in on the slayer. And to prove it's only too true, the chief of police calls up to advise his detective to drop the case, because the maid has confessed she did it.

A very much peeved pater familias, Leigh Whittall, drops round to express his opinion of his flapper daughter. Manly Ralph tells him a few plain truths. Dad, it seems, has been overly chummy with a blonde divorcee of rather dubious morals and antecedents. Which paves the way for the inevitable clinch for Lois and Ralph who both pledge reformation.

That's "Daughters of Today" in a nutshell—an impossible story told with impossible characters, including co-eds who might be drafted from the Mutual Wheel chorus ranks and male students who measure up as first class lounge lizards.

It's doubtful whether Sturgeon is a college man. If he should be, he'll have a sad day of reckoning with his alma mater, for "Daughters of Today" is a libel per se against American colleges. Bahn.

THE MAN WHO WON

A Fox production, featuring Dustin Farnum. Directed by William A. Wellman and photographed by Joseph August. Scenario by E. Adamson. At New York Oct. 9 as half double bill. Running time, about an hour.

Zip	Ralph Cloninger
Jessie	Jaqueline Gadson
"Lord" James	Lloyd Whitlock
Wild Bill	Dustin Farnum

For several years Dustin Farnum, who in the days of "The Littlest Rebel" and other shows of 10 years ago gave promise of becoming one of our great American actors, has been appearing in unimportant pictures that have brought him down to the class occupied by our second-rate film players.

In "The Man Who Won" his assignment is even worse, for though he is billed as the star his part is secondary and the main action revolves about the wedded couple played by Ralph Cloninger and Jaqueline Gadson.

Farnum has at best a doctored part that seems to have been thrust into the scenario. The little he has to do is accomplished well and gives further proof he might really make good if given the proper chance with the right company and director behind him.

He is Wild Bill, a two-fisted and two-gun gambler, as hardboiled as they come. The wife of Zip, his pal, tired with her life of squalid poverty and work, runs away with the villainous leader of a gang of robbers. Bill draws the highwaymen away from their ranch by driving a coach laden with gold, and while they are gone Zip goes and persuades his wife to come home for the sake of the children. Bill fights off the bandits, but is mortally wounded, and after strapping himself to the driver's seat drives into town lifeless, but with the money safe.

A ridiculous incident occurs during the fight scene, when Bill is distinctly shown to kill two men with one bullet. Otherwise the direction toes the mark. Ralph Cloninger, a new name, gives a stirring performance in the important role of Zip. His wife is well played by the pretty Jaqueline Gadson and Lloyd Whitlock is a sufficiently dastardly villain. Two small children, unbilled, provide most of the comedy relief which too often seems forced.

The picture is okeh for the neighborhood houses.

THE MIDNIGHT FLOWER

Hirsh feature in five reels, distributed by Aywon, featuring Vola Vale and Gaston Glass. At the Circle, New York, on double bill Oct. 9. Running time, 50 minutes.

This feature may or may not have been patterned after that meller classic "Pet of Poker Flat." Nevertheless both have much in common. The waif of the gaming den is there but the "chance parlor" has been shifted further east.

Myra, the central character derives the titular sobriquet because of her penchant for doing a wild dance atop the gaming table at the stroke of midnight.

A young Spaniard, violently in love with the girl, wants to rescue her from the den. He stages a stick-up at the most profitable table but is winged on the get-a-way. Before dying he passes the twelve grand booty and bids her beat it. But the cops are too quick and she is jugged instead.

While in prison she is converted to the straight and narrow by a young evangelist and upon release attempts to help him at the mission but scandal-mongers wag tongues and she next runs into the profligate nephew of the most influential family in town.

It later develops that she is their long lost daughter who had been stolen in childhood.

The commonplace story is overshadowed by the splendid acting of the featured members. Vola Vale gives a charming interpretation of the waif and later contrasts it equally effectively as the refined society girl. Gaston Glass is capital as the young evangelist of the slum district.

As a one-day feature in the daily change houses it may appeal.

A WILD PARTY

Universal production starring Gladys Walton. Story by Marion Orth and direction by Herbert Blache. At the New York Oct. 9 as half double bill. Running time 56 mins.

Leslie Adams	Gladys Walton
Scissors Hogan	Lewis Sargent
Stuart Furth	Robert Ellis
Bess Furth	Esther Rawlings
Jenkins	Sidney Bracy
Mrs. Cartwright	Doris Reviere
Horace Cartwright	Sidney de Grey

Starting in as a story of newspaper life with its attendant bustle and hustle, this picture develops into a most hilarious and frantic bedroom farce. Miss Walton is the cub reporter who in trailing down a divorce case gets herself, the man she loves and everyone else in a jam.

Doors are furiously slammed, disclosing quaking transgressors in pajamas hiding behind them, and the conclusion sees the entire company including jealous husbands, worried parents and flirtatious young wives lodged in jail on a charge of having participated in a pajama party with plenty of liquor on the side.

Up to its wild ending it has been a nice enough little program picture with Gladys Walton her usual kittenish self. A swimming pool scene gives her a chance to display a thoroughly trim figure in a one-piece affair. More than that it demonstrates her to be an excellent diver, for if the eye does not deceive it is the star herself and not a double.

The direction by Herbert Blache is capable, and if the story drags too often it is not his fault. Unfunny subtitles that aim to be humorous and the injection of some entirely unnecessary and stupid bootleg comedy are the two things that fail. Robert Ellis does well as the much persecuted leading man and Doris Reviere is a most enticing vamp. The rest of the cast hold up with the exception of Sidney Bracy, who instead of playing his famous butler role is miscast in the impossible role of the bootlegger.

Miss Walton has many admirers and they are sure to enjoy this film. Others will not be bored or disgusted with it and will probably get their admission's share of enjoyment during the bedroom scenes at the end.

THE HUNTRESS

Baltimore, Oct. 10.

First National Production starring Colleen Moore. Story by Hubert Footner, adapted by Percy Heath and directed by Lynn Reynolds. At Rivoli, Baltimore, Oct. 1.

Bela	Colleen Moore
Sam Gadding	Lloyd Hughes
Big Jack Skinner	Russell Simpson
Joe Hogland	Walter Long
Black Hand Frazer	Chas. E. Anderson
Musquoosis	Smitz Edwards
John Gladding	Wilfred North
Mrs. John Gladding	Helen Raymond
William Gladding	William Marion

"The Huntress" is an out and out western feature of high order, minus the usual shooting and rodeo stuff, but possessing a story which, if it is trite, is also interesting and full of action. It has been excellently produced and while it will not become very famous, just now affords an excellent evening's entertainment that will justify its exhibition in most any of the big houses of the country. It also marks the promotion of Colleen Moore to stardom.

The story deals with Indians and the old theme of the girl who thought she was a member of the red skins but who found out later that some careless parents had deserted her. And with the discovery that she isn't an Indian comes a desire to capture a white husband.

The husband she sets out to capture is one of the bashful New York boys, reared in the atmosphere of Fifth avenue and high society. Tiring of the high society and its accompanying bores, he sets out to the land of open spaces where mountains are tall and where gopher hills are not entirely unknown. Here Bela, the girl brought up by the Indians, sees him and straightway she sets her cap for the handsome Easterner, who, away from the influence of subways and yellow taxicabs, finds her very interesting, so much so that they become married, which causes Bela's expulsion from the tribe of Indians. After a rough and tumble fight with a villain who is pursuing his wife, the two start their love making all over again and work toward a happy fadeout.

From her work in this film Miss Moore deserves her promotion to stardom. Her supporting cast is excellent, too, and the production is given a fine setting, both in the eastern and western scenes. And the fight scene in it, incidentally, is very good and although not as long and as highly feature as the famous screen fight in the recent production of "The Spoilers," is exciting and realistic.

It drew well here and also got good notices, the film being vote an agreeable entertainment. It is not distinguished but at least better than the average run of films boasting a big star. For a house of fairly well established patronage, "The Huntress" will prove satisfactory and will hold up its end of the bill.

Sisk.

ALIAS NIGHT WIND

Five reeler featuring William Russell, produced by Fox. On double feature bill at Circle, New York, Oct. 9. Running time, 50 minutes.

Bill Russell is in his element in this Fox feature, having one of those roles which suits him.

As Bingham Howard, the broker's clerk, whom they are trying to frame for a theft of bonds he gives a gem of a performance. But when confronted with the reality of being victimized and possibly sent to prison he throws repression to the winds, becomes the Bill Russell of old and bowls any that would block his path to freedom.

Although the feature lacks the action synonymous with Bill Russell features, the star is given opportunity in several spots for daredevil feats.

The film from a story standpoint means little. Whatever demand created will be mainly due to Russell. Even at that it is just a mild feature.

Foreign Films

LIGHTS OF LONDON

London, Oct. 10.

Starting with the statement this is a film version of the Drury Lane drama whereas the play was produced by Wilson Barrett at the Princess', this latest Gaumont film, produced by C. C. Calvert, is a disappointment throughout.

George R. Sims, the author of the play, gave abundant material in his original for any picture which is purely melodramatic without the producer's elaboration, over elaboration, which does much to kill the humanity of the well known story. His introduction of the Oxford-Cambridge boat race is forgivable, but in most approved modern style of film drama he can hardly produce an exterior scene without making much use of motor cars, motor boats and the other approved methods of using up footage, while few of his interiors are without the all-necessary telephone.

Nor do his characters ring true, they possess none of the human essentials of the originals.

The Louis Stevens-C. C. Calvert version of George R. Sims story starts with the Oxford and Cambridge boat race. Oxford is the favorite and Harold Armytage is "stroke." His crook cousin, Clifford, has heavy bets on Cambridge, and drugs the Oxford "cox." Oxford, however, wins and Harold knocks Clifford down, having learned of the doping while the race was actually in progress. He returns home to find that Clifford has been before him with stories as to his, Harold's, gay life. These, coupled with Harold's determination to wed Bess Marks, the daughter of his father's steward, cause the hero to be disowned. He and Bess marry and are soon up against the "lights of London."

Under the promise of marriage, Clifford has seduced Hetty, the daughter of Seth Preene, but he always puts off the promised wedding. After a year of London with nothing better apparently than a wonderful motor engine to subsist on, Harold takes Bess home to ask forgiveness.

Scenically there is nothing remarkable in the production, although there are some beautiful shots of London by day and night. The producer utterly fails in his fire scenes. This, however, is not his fault so much as the authorities who vetoed his plans at the last moment. The motor boat chase is nothing and has been much better done a dozen times.

There are several excellent performances. Nigel Barrie gives an ordinary straight forward show in the Wilson Barrett part of Harold Armytage; Cecil Morton York is really good as his father, and Warburton Gamble is by turns debonair and blackguardly as cousin Clifford. Harding Steerman gives a beautifully proportioned performance as Marks, while H. R. Hignett and John Harris are capital as old Jarvis and his son, Shakespeare. The latter will probably make a find for some producer of eccentric comedies. Wanda Hawley is good as Bess as is Mary Clare as Hetty. Mary Brough gives one of her customary sound performances as Mrs Jarvis. Several other parts are well played. The fame of the old play will doubtless help to get it over, apart from that it is very ordinary and mediocre drama.

Gore.

GUY FAWKES

London, Sept. 17.

The second of what might be called the Stoll "Great Scoundrels Canonized" series.

Maurice Elvey has put some of his best work into this feature which should prove a fine business proposition. All the children will want to see it on account of the gunpowder plot story and all the women will want to see Matheson Lang once more consumed by a hopeless love.

The story has been deftly handled, fact-mingled-fiction cleverly, and the result is an entertainment of exceptional value.

Anything sordid or wilfully bloodthirsty has been ignored and the interpolation of a pretty love story gives the right touch of pathos to a character whose infamy has lived down the ages and whose effigy is still burned on Nov. 5 to commemorate the frustration of his dastardly plot.

In the opening scenes is an inquiring child who asks Lang to tell him the story of Guy Fawkes. He does so, sticking to the historical story as we know it.

The edict of King James against the Catholics; their plotting and the hiring of a soldier of fortune, Fawkes, to blow up the houses of Parliament on their reopening.

The betrayal of the plot by one of the conspirators and the capture of Fawkes, his torture, and subsequent execution. As a side issue runs the love story of Viviana, the daughter of Radcliffe, for an exile, Catesby, the villain in the piece, who wishes to make Viviana his, tries to force her into a marriage, from which she is saved by Fawkes, who marries her himself. In the end, while on the rack, he obtains a pardon for the lovers.

The production is very fine and one has never seen better sets than those of the Houses of Parliament, the vaults, and the singularly dignified and beautiful interiors. There are some fine exteriors. Care has been paid to detail and the few anachronisms which do occur will pass unnoticed in the general interest of the story.

It is however somewhat of a bad faux pas to introduce a very modern and vaudevillian Spanish dancer into a Dutch tavern of the period.

Throughout the film the acting is exceptionally good. As Guy Fawkes, protector of virtue, swashbuckler, hero, and martyr, Lang does the best he has done on the screen. His conception of the part is a cross between Raresby the Rat and D'Artagnan and the mixture is very effective. Lionel D'Aragon gives a fine performance as the Earl of Salisbury, Hugh Buckler is excellent as Catesby and all the other male parts are well played. As Viviana, Ninna Vanna is merely a foil to show off the gallantry of Fawkes and the blackguardism of Catesby. In this capacity she is excellent. A more mature and "actressy" player would have damaged the sympathy centreing in the main character.

The feature would be improved by the deletion of the nursery episodes and the kick off right on the story of the would-be wholesale murderers but if the nursery must be kept in, the story would finish artistically on the gradually closing of the nursery door on Matheson Lang's exit, a natural finale.

The "shot" of the Houses of Parliament as they are now together with the information, which every English school-boy knows, that the vaults are always searched before the opening of Parliament, and the Brock's Benefit which closes the picture, constitute an anti-climax and are unnecessary. *Gore.*

THE WOMAN WHO OBEYED

London, Sept. 26.

A British picture given a trade show at the New Tivoli. The conditions of this house will not make it popular with producers and renters, who realize the people present for business purposes like to do their work in comparative comfort. There is no comfort or very little at this kinema. Seating space is reduced to the minimum per seat, and when the picture starts it is only by contortion one can see the whole screen. The rake from the circle is vile.

"The Woman Who Obeyed" is triangle drama, strong and gripping, but handled with much more delicacy than generally characterizes such features. Roughly the story is the hackneyed one of the self-made wealthy man who runs his household and his wife by a time table. His money forces her into society where she meets an artist who is also a roue. Constant trouble with her husband over petty details throws her into this man's way. He attempts to seduce her but fails. The husband, who is an arrant snob, believes the story of the artist's cast off mistress, and turns her out. Attempts at reconciliation fail, and it is not until their little son runs away to her and is knocked down by the husband's car that "the proud man is humbled" and happiness returns to the household.

On the whole the production work is admirable. There are many fine sets, and exteriors form beautiful rural pictures. The big dance at the aristocratic Wessex House was anything but aristocratic, most of the elite dancing with the jazz vigor of a "sixpenny hop." These scenes were not helped by being handpainted, although the colored searchlight effects were good.

The character of the woman's son, aged five or six, was not true to life. No child of that age consumes "David Copperfield" and understands the tragedy of Little Emily, yet this abnormal, feminine-looking child made much in sub-titles of Peggoty putting a light in the window to guide the erring Emily home. When running away from home he leaves a beautifully written note couched in language no child would use. This insufferable little prig, although true son of his narrow-minded snobbish father, is the only real error in the production.

The acting is exceptional. Stewart Rome makes the man alive, but is at his best in the latter scenes where he alternates between rage and grief. He has never done better work than in this picture. Hilda Bayley gives an excellent show as the wife, and touches real depths of emotion. Henri de Vries gives a particularly fine study of the lovable old sea captain, and Gerald Ames is easy as the scoundrelly artist, although the villainy is chiefly portrayed by sub-titles.

The picture will prove a winner.

Gore.

CHU CHIN CHOW

London, Sept. 24.

In this screen adaptation of Oscar Asche's enormously successful play Herbert Wilcox has made the finest spectacular picture yet produced by a British firm. There is very little story, the whole thing being a dramatic rendering of the pantomime theme "Ali Baba and the Forty Thieves," but what there is has been deftly handled and provides the producer with every excuse for gorgeous settings and Oriental scenery.

The exteriors, which were made in Algeria, are excellent and the interiors give still further proof of the vastness of the German studios and the competency of their organization. In producing the picture Wilcox has throughout used a remarkable restraint and has determinedly kept clear of anything appertaining to the sensual or unwholesome.

The first half of the story tells little beyond the fact that Zahrat is beloved by Omar and is seized on her wedding day and conveyed to his fastness by Abou Hassan, the robber chief. Her lover is also captive. They escape. The second half is the story of Ali Baba and the Forty Thieves, and is very well done working up to the killing of the wicked Abou by Zahrat.

Apart from the settings and photography one of the finest things in this feature is the management of huge crowds.

Betty Blythe as Zahrat makes the most of her physical charms and also infuses the character with a good deal of sincere drama. Eva Moore gives a finely finished performance as Alcolom.

The men are more than excellent. Every character even to the smallest is a cleanly cut cameo, chief acting honors going to Judd Green as Ali Baba and Jeff Barlow as Mustafa. Herbert Langley is, if anything, too Western looking as Abou, but gets over well in many disguises, notably as the character from which the story takes its name. Olaff Hytten gives a clever study as the auctioneer, Mucbill.

The minor parts of which there are many, are well played. *Gore.*

CLIMBING MOUNT EVEREST

London, Sept. 24.

This latest travel and interest picture to be shown here is one of the best. The pictorial record of the expedition headed by General Bruce with the object of crossing Tibet and conquering the world's highest mountain. The approach was through the forbidden lands of Nepal and Tibet and permission had to be obtained from the Dalai Lama before the attempt could be made.

The picture takes the audience from Darjeeling to the Jelep Pass where prayer flags mark the Tibetan mysteries and religious ceremonies.

The highest altitude at which "shots" were taken was 23,000 feet above sea level and at that height the cameramen, Capt. J. B. L. Noel, F. R. G. S., stayed for four days and nights to get the desired results.

The picture is being released in weekly instalments. *Gore.*

FIGHTING BLADE

Inspiration Pictures, Inc., Charles H. Duell, president, presents Richard Barthelmess in "The Fighting Blade," a romantic drama of Cromwellian England of 1640 by Beulah Marie Dix, scenario by Josephine Lovatt. Designated a John Robertson production. First National attraction. Projection time 61 minutes. At the Strand, Oct. 14.

Karl....................Richard Barthelmess
Earl of Starversham.........Lee Baker
Lord Robert Erisey.....Morgan Wallace
Watt Musgrove..........Bradley Barker
Oliver Cromwell......Frederick Burton
Viscount Carisford..........Stuart Sage
Lord Trevor..................Philip Tead
Bob Ayskew................Walter Horton
Thomsine Musgrove....Dorothy Mackaill
Charlotte Musgrove..........Allyn King
Joan Laycock..............Marcia Harris

The screen seems to be in for a cycle of romantic costumed dramas. More power to them if they come up to the pace set by this story and production. In power of incident and in climacteric punch "The Fighting Blade" has much that neck-and-necks with Dumas; the big moment is shrewdly built up and the melodrama holds a world of suspense. Barthelmess is at his best.

Of course there are numerous inconsistencies, there always are in these romantic hero plays, but the very boisterous melodrama carries its own excuse. You can't analyze a 17th Century plot and situation in the light of reason. Rather you turn your imagination loose and let it revel on what comes before it in pictorial exaggeration. What these romantic plays do is to typify modern strife without its stark realism.

Barthelmess plays a sort of modified D'Artagnan, only he is a Dutchman named Karl Van Kerstenbrook, come to England during the Cromwell-Roundhead struggle intent upon avenging the betrayal of his sister by an Englishman.

He butts into numerous adventures at Oxford where the royalists are holding a revel. To the same center of gayety comes Thomsine, country heiress, to visit her guardian, the vicious Earl of Starversham. The Earl schemes to marry the girl off to his worthless son. In the whirlpool the girl falls into misadventures and is rescued by Karl, known as the greatest swordsman in Europe.

Karl is seized by Cromwell who is hovering around the Royalist jamboree for his own purposes and the Savior of British Parliament takes him into the anti-Royalist service, with instructions to secure a plan of Starversham castle. Karl secures entrance into the castle service under the guise of a military mercenary, but his identity as the Oxford swordsman is exposed and he is thrown into irons as a Cromwell spy and condemned to hang in the morning.

He escapes from his dungeon and accidentally reaches Thomsine's room. She hides him in her bed until his escape can be effected and he returns to Cromwell. There is a lot of theatrical maneuvering here, but the story holds water. Karl returns to Cromwell's camp and volunteers to lead a force against the Earl's castle and is given the commission.

Thomsine has fallen in love with Karl and refuses to marry the Earl's heir, whereupon the Earl himself attempts to force her into a marriage with him. She goes through the form under cumpulsion and plans to make a declaration at the wedding feast that she never spoke the words of the ceremony and is not a wife.

Here's where the theatrical trickery comes. Karl with his soldiers is galloping toward the castle while the feast is on. Views of the armored knights pounding through the night and the wedding feast are alternated, a tricky effect to work up tension, ending of course with the timely arrival of Karl and her rescue. A lot of the effects are old stuff but the surest kind of surefire.

Dorothy Mackaill, playing opposite Barthelmess, is extremely effective in a role that just suits her frail beauty. She is an actress who is more than beautiful, for she has a face of supreme feminity, something like the quality of Maude Adams in appearance, and her pantomime is fluent and natural. The rest of a long cast works smoothly and well.

The production is elaborate, but one rather gets the idea that the producer tried for more than he could accomplish. The period atmosphere is made to create a vivid illusion and the costuming is exceptionally well treated, but there are settings that altogether fail to suggest the intent, such as interior rooms that look cramped. A good deal of the action, particularly in the castle, takes place through the corridors and on the stairways, and these are always good, particularly in respect to tricky light and shadow effects.

But these are minor matters, the outstanding fact being that Barthelmess has what gives every promise of being another winner on his string. *Rush.*

ETERNAL STRUGGLE

Louis B. Mayer presentation, Reginald Barker production and adapted from G. B. Lancaster's novel, "The Law Bringers," by J. G. Hawks and Monte Katterjohn. Releasing through Metro. At the Rivoli, New York, Oct. 14. Running time, 65 minutes.

Andree Grange.................Renee Adoree
Sgt. Neil Tempest..........Earle Williams
Camille Lenoir............Barbara La Marr
"Bucky" O'Hara...............Pat O'Malley
Barode Dukane................Wallace Beery

Ordinary Metro program release far short of the "class" recent pictures of this distributing company have held. Late in reaching Broadway, this particular epic of the Northwest has been playing out of town for at least a month and could have stayed away altogether, for it won't do Metro any good where the clientele is inclined to be fussy.

The story is out-and-out melodrama, cheap at that, with the cast over-acting and the photography so off in lighting the contrasts flashed in this respect are actually hard on the eyes.

It has to do with two members of the Northwest Mounted, pals, becoming rivals for the hand of a girl who believes herself guilty of murder and runs away, to be followed by both men, one with the purpose of bringing her back, due to a sense of duty, and the other to aid in getting her away.

The sergeant (Earle Williams) is the straight and stern type, while "Bucky" (Pat O'Malley) screens as a love-making Irishman who breaks the girl's heart, but finally succumbs himself, and all is well upon the return that discloses another had committed the killing. The slight twist is that the Irishman is the one who insists on bringing the girl back.

The subtitles are boring with their abundance and attempt at being "cute," for every advantage has been taken to insert something, no matter at what interval, to purvey the idea of the lilt in "Bucky's" love-making and the broken English of the French-Canadian girl, "Andree" (Reneé Adoree).

O'Malley and Miss Adoree turn in the best work, although each has done, or should do, better. The remainder illusion as sincere enough in their efforts, even too much so, to the point where some of the action totals as nothing more than either violent gestures or posing.

Some picturesque exteriors are included, as also a wild canoe dash down a water rapids that is a corking piece of work; but it is insufficient to lift this release out of a mediocre classification. Hence, the "Struggle" illusions as being about right for the smaller houses, but fails to impress as a major attraction. *Skig.*

FIGHTING BLOOD

The second of F. B. O.'s promised series of 12 of the H. C. Witwer short stories adapted to the screen. Done in length between two and thre reels with projection time of about 30 minutes—that is to say, nearer three than two. The story was adapted by Beatrice Van from Witwer's short story published in "Collier's" under the title of "She Supes to Conquer." Directed by Henry Lehrman. George O'Hara is the featured player, supported by Mary Beth Milford and Louise Lorraine. At the Stanley, New York, Oct. 15.

The short subject is billed over the five-reeler which makes up the double bill, a William Steiner production called "Below the Rio Grande," and it should be. It has snap and action and, above all, a wealth of low comedy. That would recommend any picture, and this one looks like a clean-up. Any picture that can make a film audience laugh right out loud so you can hear 'em on the sidewalk is in a way to returns.

At the start they work up a serious situation built around the Roman Christian martyrs, and as quick as it catches hold of attention the camera switches to show the film director working the situation. From that on it is screamingly funny Roman travesty, pure hoke, but tremendously funny. The hero is instructed in the next scene to step into the arena as a lion crouches to spring upon the pale, blonde heroine, and choke the lion to death. It is urged by a nancified lion tamer that is is perfectly safe. They release the lions and for 400 feet or so it becomes a lion chase equal to the classics in some of the earlier Sunshine subjects put out by Fox.

That passage finished, the story goes on to tell that the leading woman of the picture, and an heiress who aspires to screen stardom, are both seeking the hero's favor. O'Hara is cast as an exchampion of the prize ring. He invites both girls to a fight, and when one of the contenders in the star bout fails to put in an appearance, an open challenge is made on behalf of the fighter in the ring, one "Lightning" Kelly. O'Hara wants to get some "fighting blood' out of his system, so he accepts the challenge. Then they stage a lively two-round fight that has plenty of goodlooking action. The rest is dull, merely the formal courtship of the scrapping actor and the heiress.

Another funny passage had O'Hara on the street in a hurricane storm, on his way to call on the heiress and not a taxi in sight. An old woman leading two poodles by strings against a wind that made them stand straight out behind her like a child's balloon was also a strong laugh. *Rush.*

WIFE IN NAME ONLY

Pyramid production, directed by George Terwilliger. Distributed by Selznick. Adapted by Adele Hendricks from a story by Bertha M. Clay. Photography by A. L. Mariner. At the Stanley, Oct. 12. Running time, 64 minutes.

Philippa L'Estrange......Mary Thurman
Victor Harwood........Arthur Hausman
Norman Alleigh..........Edmund Lowe
John Dean................William Tucker
Madaline Dornham.......Florence Dixon
Mrs. Dornham.........Edna May Oliver
Dornham.....................Tyrone Power

Another picture with a super-sex title that turns out to mean nothing. It gets its name from the fact that the young wife leaves her husband the day of their marriage because she feels he does not love her, and lives apart from him until matters are cleared up. There is no rough stuff pulled in connection with the conjugal relations, or rather lack of relations, as in several films bearing milder titles.

The plot, taken from a story by Bertha M. Clay, obsolete writer of trashy, shop-girl novels, is melodramatic and impossible, but adaptable for the kind of photoplay enjoyed by the majority of American filmgoers. Interest and dramatic suspense do much to atone for the crudeness and ineptitude of the general idea.

Philippa L'Estrange, confident of winning the handsome young Norman Alleigh as her husband, drops a few gentle hints to him at a party. To her surprise and dismay, he tells her that he regards her only as a sister and is waiting to meet his ideal before he thinks of marriage. Philippa's love changes to hate. Striving for revenge, she arranges it so that he falls in love with and finally marries Madaline Dornham, a girl who comes up to his ideals. On the day of the wedding Philippa writes to Norman and tells him the woman he has married is the daughter of the burglar who years before murdered his mother.

It looks dark for the happy ending for a while, but in the end everything turns out well when it is learned that Madaline's mother was married twice and the young bride is not the murderer's daughter after all. Considerable dramatic intensity has been squeezed out of this story by the director and adapter. The photography and titles are also up to the mark.

The featured name of the cast is Arthur Hausman, who has won some little following for his work in previous films as a polite society "souse." In this picture he has only a minor role, playing a lounge lizard suitor of Philippa's. The latter is well portrayed by Mary Thurman, who does better than might be expected with a difficult and not wholly unsympathetic part. Edmund Lowe is his usual suave self as the hero, and Edna May Oliver contributes a notable bit as the girl's mother. The girl herself is played by Florence Dixon, who is pretty but far from being a good actress as yet. Tyrone Power is seen for only a couple of minutes as the heavy.

With generally capable acting, efficient direction and an appealing story, the film should be a moneymaker when not exhibited to audiences of too marked discrimination.

BELOW THE RIO

Open market subject produced by William Steiner Productions, Inc., featuring Neal Hart. Western story with Mexican border locale. Part of double bill, with a 2½-reeler of the F. B. O.—Witwer series billed above it. Projection time, 50 minutes. Taken from story material and adapted by H. Halburt. No director designated. At the Stanley, New York (daily change), Oct. 15.

Just a western melodrama with Mexican trimmings, fast action and good variety, but the worst photography seen in a long time. From the quality of the camera work, especially in interiors, one would suspect it was a reissue from 'way back.

The picture commits one serious fault. It was made at low cost, evidently to be addressed to the least sophisticated, simple-minded fan public; yet there are times when its story becomes so confused that Henry James himself couldn't understand it. It ought to be a matter beyond argument that if one deliberately addresses a picture to a juvenile-minded public, he ought to be as clear and simple as possible. The story falls down hard in this particular.

One Pierre Jacques, a French-Canadian and a fugitive from justice, rules a remote town on the Mexican side near the border. Chuck Watson is his confederate in horse and cattle thieving. Chuck frames King Calhoun, Texan cowboy, on a cattle-running charge, but King persuades the sheriff he can prove his own case and also bring Pierre to justice if he (the sheriff) will accompany him (King) on an expedition to Texas. Oddly enough, the sheriff agrees. Meanwhile the Northwest Mounted are notified of the location of Pierre and the Mexican Rurales are after the outlaw, and here starts a three-cornered chase that ends in the capture of the bandit and the liberation of his supposed daughter, who turns out to be the lost child of the old desert prospector who guided the King-sheriff party to the bandit. But the expedition called for a large quality of desperate rough-riding and fights innumerable, tall heroics and the rest of the western hokum. The picture was made at very little cost, probably, and should return a generous profit, for there is a vast public for this kind of dime-novel screen material that would sleep through "The Miracle Man."

Rush.

MEN IN THE RAW

Universal picture, featuring Jack Hoxie, and an adaptation from a magazine story, authored by Bert Foster. George Marshall the director, with Harry Fowler at the camera. Splitting double feature day at the Circle, New York, Oct. 16. Running time, 50 minutes.

A very ordinary "U" release that looks like one of those things they shove through that factory regardless. They turn 'em out like Fords, anyway.

Hoxie is featured as the champ liar of the world, with the picture mainly viewing his miraculous and weird experiences. It's too asinine to ever mean anythng. Not only will it do Hoxie no good, but it will undoubtedly keep more people away from picture houses than anything else. For those who wail, moan and dote on "panning" the silent drama this one is a pip, with nary a comeback.

The picture is a Western which gives Hoxie a change to ride a score or more of horses, although how he ever bulldogs a steer while wearing spurs is something those who were there may explain.

Marguerite Clayton is the girl in the story struggling valiantly with poor material.

Hoxie? He must be used to it, as this particular reviewer has yet to see him in anything that resembles a good picture.

Either he's a bear for punishment or Universal is too optimistic concerning its public, as "Men in the Raw" fails to even rate the honor of splitting a double-header at such a house as the Circle, while it will never go down in history as much entertainment in the cheapest of houses.

Skig.

BRIGHT LIGHTS OF BROADWAY

B. F. Zeidman Production, released through Principal Pictures Corp. Scenario by Edmund Goulding. Adapted from a story by Gerald C. Duffy. Directed by Webster Campbell, starring Lowell Sherman. Shown at Loew's New York Oct. 10, running about 90 minutes.

Randall Sherrill............Lowell Sherman
Irene Marley................Doris Kenyon
Tom Drake..................Harrison Ford
Rev. Graham Drake.........Edmund Breese
Mrs. Grimm.................Effie Shannon
John Kirk..................Tyrone Power
El Jumbo..................Charles Murray

Chorus girls from New York Hippodrome. Sixteen Tiller Girls from Ziegfeld's "Follies."

Webster Campbell, who directed "The Bright Lights of Broadway," has crowded in all the suspense hokum possible, from the chase in automobiles and trains to saving the innocent hero from death in the chair at the last second. Perhaps the best thing about the picture is really its cast, worthy of a much better story than this.

The film brings the perspiration to the palm of the hand and the fingernails to the mouths of the more nervous. Therefore, it's a success.

The story is of a country girl lured to New York by promise of a career. This promise is almost fulfilled and she marries the villain before realizing what is happening. Her country sweetheart comes to rescue her and is framed for murder by the villain, the latter being the guilty

party. The rest concerns the saving of the boy by the villain's wife through securing a confession, and the death of the scoundrel.

Lowell Sherman is, as usual, the most hateable villain possible. Doris Kenyon has the audience suffering with her in her tribulations and loving her in other moments Harrison Ford is quite an acceptable juvenile, and Edmund Breese, Tyrone Power, Effie Shannon and Charlie Murray have but bits to do.

The 16 Tiller Girls and the Hippodrome chorus are used in a cabaret scene which has been lavishly staged.

UNSEEING EYES

A Goldwyn-Cosmopolitan production written by Arthur Stringer and adapted for the screen by Bayard Veiller. Starring Lionel Barrymore, with Seena Owen featured. Directed by E. H. Griffith. Shown at the Cosmopolitan theatre, New York, for a run commencing Oct. 21, 1923. Running time, 1 hour 48 minutes.

Conrad Dean.............Lionel Barrymore
Miriam Helston............Seena Owen
Laird.....................Louis Wolheim
Father Paquette.....Gustav von Seyffertitz
Dick Helston.............Walter Miller
Arkwright................Charles Beyer
Mrs. Arkwright...........Helen Lindroth
Trapper.................Jack Johnson
Eagle Blanket...........Louis Deer
Singing Pine...........Frances Red Eagle

Last winter and early this spring the trade in general heard a great deal about a picture that Cosmopolitan was making in the far north that was scheduled to be a whale of a snow picture. Reports came back of the company that remained in the far north weeks and weeks after the production schedule had them slated to be finished, but still they worked on and on, and everyone thought that surely a great picture was forthcoming. During the production days the picture was known as "Snowblind," but last Sunday night it opened at the Cosmopolitan theatre under the title of "Unseeing Eyes."

Frankly the picture as shown leads one to believe that there must be a lot of "unseeing eyes" in the picture end of the Hearst organization to permit this picture to go on the market bearing the Cosmopolitan brand, which in itself has only been building for the last two years, since the advent of "When Knighthood Was in Flower." In a word, it is a cheap meller.

This one will please neighborhood fans, but in the houses that the producer must count on to get his money back out of an investment such as this picture represents "Unseeing Eyes" hasn't much chance. It would have been better for Cosmopolitan to have shelved this one and stood the whole loss, or to have sold it in the outside market and let someone release it either as a state right picture or through some small releasing organization without the Cosmopolitan name attached.

As a snow picture this one is no different from a hundred others of the same type, except that it might be worse than the majority. Its story is weak, the adaptation of it bad, and the direction amounts to almost nothing. That makes it 100 per cent in the red on the ledger.

The original story was by Arthur Stringer, Bayard Veiller adapted it for the screen, and if the director followed his script then it must be said that Veiller turned out an extremely bad piece of workmanship; if the director didn't follow the script, it simply adds to the burden of what blame is to already be laid on his shoulders.

"Unseeing Eyes" is laid in New York and in the north country. The start of the picture shows a deserted mine in Canada that has been shut down for several years because of the lack of labor during and immediately after the war. A lawless band that has been organized by one Laird is working the mine and getting the gold ore out. Then the New York home of the boy and girl who have inherited the mine is shown. The girl, a social butterfly, is about to start to Quebec for the ice carnival and her brother decides to also go north, but his purpose is to go to the mine and reopen it.

While the girl is enjoying herself in Quebec the boy is set upon by the band at the mine and severely wounded in a fight with their leader. An Indian in the band picks him up when he is left to die in the snow and takes him to his cabin. This Indian's daughter has been taken as a squaw by the gang leader and the father has sworn vengeance, but stands in deadly fear of the brutal

Laird. He proposes to nurse the boy back to health so that the latter may accomplish his vengeance for him. It is the Indian that sends a message to the sister at Quebec to the effect that her brother has been injured and she decides to go to his aid. The trains, however, are snowed in, and when one of her admirers proposes that he take her in an aeroplane she consents.

The two set out, but before reaching their destination the machine is forced to alight because of engine trouble, and while the man is seeking help a blizzard sweeps down and the girl is snowed in. After waiting for a time she decides to try to follow the man but loses her way and spends the night in a deserted cabin. The man in the meantime has reached the cabin of two prospectors where he remains for the night. In the morning both again set out from their shelters and eventually both fall into the hands of the outlaws.

From then on it is but a series of escapes and rescues, built along the familiar lines of melodramatic thrills. In the finish all are safe and sound and back in New York for the final clinch.

From a direction standpoint there are a couple of little things that may be granted as clever touches, but it is a question whether it was directorship or just good camera work. The scenes showing Seena Owen and Lionel Barrymore in the plane supposedly soaring over the ice and snow-clad mountains is very cleverly done, only there is much too much of it. Also in a couple of fights there is fairly good handling of the material, but that is about all.

Lionel Barrymore wasn't at all impressive in anything that he did in the character. Seena Owen did not shape up any, too well either. She failed to get any punch into anything that she did. The picture, as a matter of fact, was seized by Louis Wolheim. He as the heavy Laird had everything his own way from beginning to end of the picture, and despite the fact that the sympathy was entirely with those opposed to him he walked away with the feature. As a heavy it is a relief to see someone else besides the Beery family doing the rough stuff. On the coast they must only have the Beerys, for one sees no one else except them in the heavy roles. Wolheim makes them both look like beginners with his work in this picture. In it he is hairier than the "Hairy Ape." The others in the cast had little to do and consequently amount to but little.

Fred.

RICHARD, THE LION-HEARTED

Presented by Associated Authors, Inc., and releasing through the Allied Producers and Distributors' Corporation. Adapted from Sir Walter Scott's novel, "The Talisman"; a Frank E. Woods production; directed by Chet Withey; featuring Wallace Beery, with Joe Walker the photographer. At the Strand Oct. 21. Running time, 86 minutes.

More than likely made on the strength of the impression Beery left after the initial showing of "Robin Hood," in which he did King Richard. Some still believe he actually took that special "Robin Hood" film away from Fairbanks, but either way here is Beery, again in the same role, and with a trio of inserts from the "Hood" picture, each of which reveals Fairbanks. This current registering of another episode of the English Crusades should suffice as a program feature if deleted as to length. There's sufficient action to hold it up for around an hour, but the extra 26 minutes inclined toward overdoing.

Beery, as Richard, predominates, with the action revolving around what occurred to the King, while Robin Hood was safeguarding England. It's a cinch portrayal for Beery, and he does nicely with it, although when brought immediately to the front he loses some of that significance which was so prominent, when placed secondary, to Fairbanks.

The men in the cast far overshadow the feminine contingent, albeit Marguerite de la Motte does acceptably in heading her division. There is an abundance of sword play, horse-riding and some comedy to carry the narrative along, and it is pleasing without calling for any undue amount of attention with which to mentally follow the script.

In reproduction the film offers a couple of castle view fakes, fairly done at that, with the general staging being up to scratch if nothing more. The film will not cause any undue stir among the picturegoers and seems just about able to fulfill the purpose for which it was meant—a follow-up of Beery's "Hood" characterization. *Skig.*

MICHAEL O'HALLORAN

Hodkinson production, directed by James Leo Meehan. Taken from the novel by Gen Stratton-Porter and produced under her personal direction. Photographed by Floyd Jackson. At the Stanley, New York, Oct. 17. Running time, 72 minutes.
Michael O'Halloran..........True Boardman
Peaches..................Ethelyn Irving
Nellie Minturn...............Irene Rich
James Minturn..............Charles Clary
Nancy Harding...........Claire McDowell
Peter Harding.........Charles Hill Mailes
Leslie Winton...........Josie Sedgwick
Douglas Bruce..............William Boyd

"Michael O'Halloran" is a screen adaptation of one of the five highly sweetened Gene Stratton-Porter novels that have sold considerably over a million copies each. Its success on the screen will not be as proportionately great, but it should find favor with both kiddies and grown-ups because of its irresistible appeal. Miss Porter brings to the film field an experienced and workmanlike knowledge of those small but vital things in everyday life that tug at the heartstrings and bring tears to the eyes and lumps to the throat.

"Micky" is a newsboy of 12 years, an orphan who manages to maintain the wretched home in Sunshine Alley left him by his mother as a home. Seized with pity for a little crippled girl who has also been left alone in the world, he brings her to his room, adopts her without formalities of any sort and christens her "Lily Peaches." By his devoted attention and loving care of his "family" he sets an example for every one around him. The Minturns, a society couple, whose life together has been one long tragedy, are reunited, and together they set about caring for their heretofore neglected children. Through the little newsy's influence the affairs of another family, the Hardings, are set straight also. Finally "Lily Peaches" is cured, and everything ends in a halo of neighborly love and unselfishness.

The average filmgoer is going to enjoy this picture wholeheartedly. He or she is not going to stop to consider that such a boy as Michael O'Halloran never existed. This would have been a more artistically realistic film if Micky were shown occasionally indulging in one or two boyish pranks of mischief. But Mrs. Porter's boy is perfect at all times, so much so certain of our little Penrods and Tow Sawyers, when viewing the picture, will be inclined to mutter a contemptuous "Sissy!"

The title role, a fat one, is entrusted to True Boardman, son of the film heavy of the same name who died several years ago. Aside from a trace of self-consciousness, especially when smiling, and a delicacy almost unbelievable in a newsboy, young Boardman does very well. A seven-year-old girl, Ethelyn Irving, new to pictures, is amazingly sweet as Lily Peaches. Little Miss Irving has more charm than prettiness and is a welcome relief after all the doll-faced baby stars.

The balance of the cast are satisfactory in subordinate roles, with Irene Rich the outstanding name. Her usual sterling performance is contributed by Claire McDowell as a hardworking farmer's wife.

Efficient continuity and sympathetic direction are other assets. Jeannette Helen Porter, daughter of the novelist, is credited as being the assistant director. There are several lovely exterior shots, some of which are done in color, and the photography as a whole is exceptionally fine.

"Michael O'Halloran" should prove a box office picture. It is claimed Miss Porter's total readers number high in the millions. This should assure the success of a film version of one of her most popular novels, particularly when it is as well done as this.

YOU ARE GUILTY

Masterdon Production presented by C. C. Burr, released by Commonwealth. Story by Roy Middleton. Directed by Edgar Lewis. All-star cast. Shown at Loew's New York, N. Y., Oct. 19, 1923. Running time, 62 minutes.
Stephen Martin.............James Kirkwood
Silky Smith.................James Kirkwood
Annapolis Angle..........Wm. A. Williams
Mrs. Grantwood...................Mary Carr
Theodore Tennent............Robert Edeson
Alice Farrell..................Doris Kenyon
Her Son.....................Russell Griffin
Judge Elkins...............Edmund Breese
Murphy...................Wm. Riley Hatch

Here is a meller that started out as though it were going to be an "Over the Hill," but then it stopped dead in its tracks. The reason was the weakness of the story. Had the story been a little stronger the all-star cast that Charlie Burr put in the picture should have put it over as a real winner. However, as it is, it will just about get by in the cheaper houses.

It is a small-town story. There are two boys, step-brothers, the mother liking her own son not one bit more than the one that her second husband brought to her from a former marriage. The latter boy is a straightforward, hard-working youngster and is in love with a town girl. The two become engaged, when the stepson discovers that his half-brother is in reality a crook, and, fearing that it will break the mother's heart should her own boy be accused of the crime, he takes the blame and leaves the town.

As the story opens he has been a tramp for a year, and as he nears his own town memories as reflected in the waters of a wayside stream crowd upon him, and the opening of the story is told. Then he discovers that the girl he was engaged to married his employer, who since died, and she is again back in the town with her young son. This youngster he manages to rescue from the burning house. On the same night he had an appointment with his half-brother, whom he wants to straighten matters out. He leaves the brother, and the latter is stabbed to death for the roll that he is carrying. The tramp is arrested and charged with the crime and placed on trial for his life, but it seems that even though he has been away from the town for only five years there is no one that recognizes him and he won't talk to save himself. In the end, however, the fact is proven that he was at the fire rescuing the baby at the hour that the crime was committed, and there is the usual happy ending.

James Kirkwood doesn't impress particularly as the lead, but Doris Kenyon is fairly good in the role assigned her. It is only a fair picture at its best. *Fred.*

MODERN MATRIMONY

A Selznick production written and directed by Vic Herrman. Shown at Loew's New York, N. Y., on a double feature bill Oct. 19, 1923. Running time 63 minutes.

Chester Melville Waddington.Owen Moore
Patrica Flynn..................Alice Lake

Here is a picture that started out like a house afire and kept to the pace for a little more than two reels and then flopped, dragged along until it completed the full five reels that are required to have a production called a feature, with the result that the good impression created earlier in the picture was lost and the whole was summed up as boresome. At the beginning this looked like it was going to be one of those delightful domestic comedies that one got in the days that Mr. and Mrs. Sidney Drew were turning out two-reelers for Metro. But it didn't continue that good.

Vic Herrman wrote and directed the picture and it is a pity that he could not mantain the pace that he set for himself in the first couple of reels.

His story was that of a promising youth in a real estate office who meets and marries the daughter of a wealthy family. The result is that he wrecks the plans of the deb's fond mamma and naturally the latter is sore on him, However, the couple have been married and decide that they will get a home of their own. Stepping into one of those dollar down establishments they pick a bungalow, furnish it and start housekeeping, the boy feeling perfectly safe that his commission check is going to cover the installments as they fall due.

However, when the check comes along he decides to use it for the benefit of the office that he is working by taking an option on a piece of property, but the office manager, jealous of the fact that anyone in the establishment except himself should have sufficient foresight to make a deal, tells the boy that his option is not wanted. Result, the moving man backs up and the real estate man gives him the order to get out. Just then, however, father-in-law arrives and asks about the option, finds out that it is still in force and congratulates his daughter on having picked a smart man for a husband, and all is forgiven, even mamma asking the children home again.

There are some laughs in the early portion of the picture and in the houses where double features are the rule this will stand up with a heavy drama on the bill if bought at a price. *Fred.*

LIGHTS OUT

R. C. production distributed by F. B. O. Adapted from the stage play by Paul Dickey and Mann Page. Directed by Al Santell. Scenario by Rex Taylor. At the New York Oct. 23 as half a double bill with "The Eleventh Hour." Running time, 80 minutes.
Foster Payton..............Harry Fenwick
Bull Decker................Fred Kelsey
Ben......................Hank Mann
Egbert Winslow........Theodore Von Eltz
Walter Sebastion..........Walter McGrail
"Hairpin" Annie..........Ruth Stonehouse
"High Shine" Joe..............Ben Deely

A screen adaptation of the comedy of the same name by Paul Dickey and Mann Page, which lasted only two weeks at the Vanderbilt a year ago last August. At that time it was spoken of as having filming possibilities. This promise has not been fulfilled. The picture is a pretty dull, possibly because of inefficient acting and poor adaptation, but more likely because the story, itself lacks too many of the elements that appeal.

The play was in three acts and the film version sticks pretty closely to the same locales, an observation car on a trans-continental train, a hotel room in Hollywood and a picture studio. The plot concerns a gang of crooks led by a vicious, eccentric individual known as "High Shine" Joe. "Hairpin" Annie and Walter Sebastion two of the members decide to go straight but first they want revenge on Joe who has double-crossed them on the last job and jumped to Brazil.

The plot holds some interest but

---

for some reason, pans out into a very slovenly picture. Ruth Stonehouse does well as "Hairpin" Annie and Walter McGrail is not bad. But the rest, particularly Hank Mann, appearing in blackface as a porter, and Ben Deely as the hated "High Shine" are all unconvincing.

Some of the scenes at the filming of the serial with its attendant excitement when the real villian appears are good for laughs.

The film can get by in any of the houses except the very best.

THE COMMON LAW

Myron Selznick production from the story of Robert Chambers, adapted by Edward J. Montague, directed by George Archainbaud. Shown at the Strand, N. Y., week Oct. 28. Running time, 80 minutes.

Valerie West....................Corinne Griffith
Louis Neville....................Conway Tearle
Jose Querida....................Elliott Dexter
Henry Neville....................Hobart Bosworth
Burleson....................Bryant Washburn
Stephanie....................Doris May
Cardemon....................Harry Myers
Lily Neville....................Miss du Pont
Rita Tevis....................Phyllis Haver
Samuel Ogilvy....................Wally Van
Mazie....................Dagmar Godowsky

A picture that as far as all-star casts go has that asset. Just how far the all-star players will go toward pulling box-office returns remains to be seen, but it must be said there was something about this picture that pulled tremendously the first day of the week (Sunday) at the Strand, when the picture did around $8,700 on the day.

The picture taken from the story, cast and production angle looks to be the type that will suit almost any gathering of film fans, whether in a first or a tenth run house.

Originally "The Common Law" was done from an entirely different angle by the Selznick people about seven years ago. At that time Clara Kimball Young played the lead and Conway Tearle was opposite her. This version, however, differs entirely from the former one and also from the original in book form, but it is good picture stuff. In making the adaptation Montague added a couple of characters and rewrote the story to suit himself. Of course, the censorship restrictions in various parts of the country that have sprung up since the first screen version of the Chambers story was made may account for the rewriting.

George Archainbaud, who directed the picture, took the material he had to work with and handled it well. He took great care with the nude scenes in the artist's studio so that no one can take exception to them. He made a great piece of work of a cabaret scene with a New Year's Eve party in progress. It was colorful and full of action.

It seems the production end is a bit overdone as far as the studio sets are concerned. They look large enough to be hotel lobbies, an expense that was totally unnecessary to the picture.

Conway Tearle is again in the same role he did in the original, but instead of Clara Kimball Young there is Corinne Griffith opposite. Both deliver. Miss du Pont, incidentally, was very disappointing. The majority of others in the all-star aggregation were principally used for bits.

All in all, "The Common Law" looks like an uncommon box-office attraction. *Fred.*

WOMAN PROOF

Adolph Zukor presents Thomas Meighan in "Woman Proof," a comedy by George Ade. Direction by Alfred E. Green (Paramount). Projection time, 70 minutes. Lila Lee, leading woman. At the Rivoli Oct. 28.

Tom Rockwood....................Thomas Meighan
Louise Halliday....................Lila Lee
Milo Bleech....................John Sainpolis
Wilma Rockwood....................Louise Dresser
Dick Rockwood....................Robert Agnew
Violet Lynwood....................Mary Astor
Cecil Updyke....................Edgar Norton
Uncle Joe Gloomer....................Charles A. Sellen
Bill Burleigh....................George O'Brien
Celeste Rockwood....................Vera Reynolds
Col. Lynwood....................Harde Kirkland
Wistful Wooer....................Martha Maddox
Isaac Dirge....................Bill Gonder
Foreman....................Mike Donlin

George Ade has written a first-rate high comedy of American life out of the threadbare materials of the ancient device of a will that requires the beneficiary to marry before a certain date on pain of losing a bequest of $1,000,000. The plot is old, but the treatment is new and characteristic of Ade, even to the MORAL (as in the Fables), which provides the tag line.

The direction is splendid in its taste and settings, and a splendid cast has been assembled to do the star and author justice. All of which results in a different style picture and reflects high credit on everybody concerned.

Ade knows the real American types, particularly those of the prosperous, or wealthy small-towners, and he alone (except Tarkington) has chosen to deal with them in a vein of fairness and sympathetic understanding. More than that, his understanding is touched with gentle humor that makes him and his fiction people exceedingly real and human. Everybody else in the modern school of novelists either burlesques or analyzes or attacks the American small-towner. Ade takes him seriously, as some of the English authors regard their own class of about the same level; that is to say, with seriousness touched with mild and harmless satire.

There are little heroics and as little drama in "Woman Proof," but there is refreshing incident and enjoyable situation in plenty, **and it makes for a desirable deviation from the usual.**

The effect is aided by a directorship that is skillfully hidden, but moulds the production into faultless taste in action and setting, and by an extraordinarily capable cast, with Lila Lee as leading woman and Louise Dresser playing gracefully a grande dame part. Charles A. Sellen and George O'Brien make two comedy characters worthy of Mark Twain, and Mike Donlin has a good straight bit.

The story is scarcely worth the telling in type, but its framework has to do with one Thomas Rockwood, who founded the town of Rockwood and accumulated a million for each of his four children; "but he had to work nights to do it," as the title has it. His will provides, foolishly enough, that they must all be married by June 30, four years hence, or the money will go to a home for the aged. The two girls and one of the boys straightway fall in love, but Tom has become so interested in a water-power engineering work that he neglects society. The whole plot rests upon his reaching the altar before the 30th. He becomes so disgusted with women who try to attract his attention that he takes asylum on the engineering job and all females are warned off.

The three other children do their best to bring him to the altar, while two old bachelor friends try to save him from matrimony.

It looks like the inheritance of all is off, when he accidentally meets the ward of the lawyer who is seeking to divert the money to the old folks' home, of which he is designated manager at a big salary. The girl proves hard to win, and the lawyer is constantly blocking their marriage in secret; but in the end they fall into each other's arms aboard a liner at sea, are married by the captain, and the wireless does the rest at the last moment.

Good deal better picture to watch than read or write about. Probably one of the surest sure things Famous Players-Lasky has put out this fall. *Rush.*

TEMPLE OF VENUS

William Fox production. Written by Catherine Carr; directed by Henry Otto. Mary Philbin featured. Opened at the Central, N. Y., for a run Oct. 29, 1923. Running time, 80 minutes.

Dennis Dean....................William Walling
Moria....................Mary Philbin
Micky....................Micky McBain
Peggy....................Alice Day
Nat Harper....................David Butler
Stanley Dale....................William Boyd
Constance Lane....................Phyllis Haver
Phil Greyson....................Leon Barry
Venus....................Celeste Lee
Thetis....................Senorita Consuella
Neptune....................Robert Cline
Juno....................Marilynn Boyd
Jupiter....................Frank Keller
Echo....................Lorraine Easton
Diana....................Helen Virgil

A few touches about this picture that talk of the box office; there are a few others that are a knock; still others that don't count at all.

The trouble is it did not have the right kind of editing and titling. Had that end of the production been given careful consideration there is no doubt that a corking box office attraction for the medium admission-priced neighborhood houses would have resulted.

A wise Broadway audience gave the picture the laugh in a couple of spots Monday night. Those laugh-compelling spots will doubtless be removed, and then the picture will get by.

It looks as though the production was a patched-up affair. It has the appearance of some one taking two different productions, each of which might have been shelved, and piecing them together with a few extra shots and filling in with a lot of sea nymph stuff that may have been around the Fox plant from the days when they had Annette Kellerman as a star and Herbert Brenon was shooting that particular kind of stuff for atmosphere.

At any rate, there is a lot of jazzy stuff in this picture that is going to be sure fire for the box offices in the small towns. The gal stuff is what is going to put the picture over in the little places.

The story is a combination of real sob sister, down-by-the-sea meller, and a touch of jazzy high life, with evening gowns without any backs, that are stripped off, showing the society dames in bathing suits that will give the average hick audience an awful kick. There are legs all over the screen, sometimes in the water and most times out of it, but legs at all times.

It revolves about a little cottage in which a fisherman lives with two daughters. There is the city chap, a couple of them. One is an artist who comes to the seaside to paint and falls in love. Of course, the fascinating widow back in the city tries to win him back when he returns home by giving a "Pepper Box Ball" for him, but the ball and the antics thereat of the "Smart Set" serve only to send him back to the demure little girl by the seaside. The widow follows with all of her friends and stages a beach party that is another pippin for undress stuff, and at the finish goes back home with the villain of the story to console her, while the artist and the **beach girl are together for the final clinch.**

Two things brought out are that William Boys makes a corking leading man for the screen and Micky McBain is a find among kid actors. Mary Philbin was a disappointment. She did not register with 50 per cent. of her strength in the "Merry-Go-Round."

The next time that Henry Otto directs a picture he should be compelled to stick to the jazzy stuff wholly and let melodrama alone. With the proper sort of story picking for him or one specially written this director should turn out a whale of a Broadway jazz story that would stick him into a class by himself, a producer of jazzy screen revues of the "Follies" type. *Fred.*

THE COUNTRY KID

Warner Brothers production, starring Wesley Barry. Adaptation of story by Julien Josephson, directed by William Beaudine. At Rialto, New York, Oct. 28. Running time, 90 minutes.

Ben Applegate....................Wesley Barry
Joe Applegate...................."Spec" O'Donnell
Andy Applegate....................Bruce Guerin
Mrs. Grimes....................Kate Toncray
Hazel Warren....................Helen Jerome Eddy
Mr. Grimes....................George Nichols
Arthur Grant....................Edward Burns
County Judge....................George C. Pearce

"The Country Kid" should make an excellent picture for the neighborhood houses throughout the country. It's one of those old fashioned comedy dramas made of sugary ingredients with such sure fires as three orphan kids, a hard hearted uncle who tries ineffectually to get the kids' inheritance away from them and considerable human interest.

The hoke is laid on in slathers. While there is no particular finesse in the way the picture is put together the scenes in which the three kids figure hold a definite appeal for the countless thousands with a soft spot for homely sentiment.

There's an incident for illustration in which two of the kids raid the kitchen and stuff themselves with a conglomeration of food that includes canned salmon, chocolate, dried apples, molasses, etc. They suffer from an aftermath of the glutinous adventure and there's many a human touch in the administering of the medicine that naturally follows.

While Wesley Barry is starred as the eldest of the three orphans, a little chap named Bruce Guerin who appears to be about four years old or younger pretty nearly takes the picture away from Barry. Most children are self conscious when acting either in oral or screen stuff but this kid Guerin isn't. A wonder in his way who plays like a veteran.

The third kid "Speck" O'Donnell is satisfactory, but also needs direction to make him forget he's facing a camera.

The film does not indicate a large production outlay. There's a sub-motif of a love story that never grows very important.

The part of the hard-hearted uncle is handled perfectly by George Nichols, an experienced actor.

Although its appeal is chiefly for children there's plenty to interest the grown-ups.

A little too home-spun for the big first run possibly, but holding unquestionable drawing powers for the houses catering to family trade. *Bell.*

WHY WOMEN REMARRY

A drama in six reels adapted from story by Van A. James, produced by John Gorman Productions, and distributed in this territory on a state right basis by Commonwealth. Directed by John Gorman, and starring Milton Sills. Half of double bill at Loew's New York, Oct. 30. Running time, 78 minutes.

Another one of these "Why" films.

And like most of the others doesn't show much in attempting to deal with a sociological question. The material isn't handled well. Good sentimental hokum should draw a tear or so and at least strike a semblance of reality. But not in this film.

The story concerns a murder—the murder of a man named Talbot, who leaves behind him a wife and two kids. The son of a rich politician is arrested and the rich papa doesn't even know him, for knowing him would hurt his chances for higher office.

That makes momma mad, for mamma loves her little boy.

The wife of a crook, Ted McKinnon, is at the same time fussing with her husband, for hubby doesn't dance and his wife is a tango stepper for fair.

Enter quarreling couple No. 2. And then enter Dan Hannon, the policeman, big of heart, pure of soul and smokes a pipe. This part is Sills'.

And that is "Why Women Remarry."

The film is long and drawn out, cheaply put on and has no good acting in it aside from Sills, wasted on an inconsequential part. It was played at Loew's New York as half of a double bill, Tom Mix in "The

Lone Star Ranger" holding up the other end well. *Sisk.*

A MILLION TO BURN

Universal comedy feature featuring Herbert Rawlinson. Story by Mary Whiteside. Director, William Parker. Projection time, 56 minutes. At the New York, New York, Oct. 26. Run as half a double feature, the other half being First National's "Trilby."

Universal is commonly supposed to address itself to an unsophisticated class of fans. The audiences to enjoy this slapstick horseplay would have to be more than that. Indeed, the best results probably would be secured from an audience 100 per cent feeble-minded.

Except for the buffoonery of a lot of servants in a hotel seeking self-expression in nature dancing, female impersonations and such, nothing happens. The comedy is stretched out endlessly to make footage.

Besides which, if Universal is going after the patronage of the humble masses, has nobody in the huge organization the sense to see that the very worst thing they could do would be to ridicule and travesty the things the humble of the world believe in? That's exactly what this picture does. If you want to set up a humorous argument that if working people are poor and shiftless it's their own fault, the place to address that conception is at the annual banquet of the National Bankers' Association at the Plaza, not in a picture patronized in the generality by working people. Every incident is a slam at any worker below the grade of railroad president.

Tom (Rawlinson) is an idealist, just out of college, working for the present as a waiter in a summer hotel, badly mismanaged by a resident manager, the owner being a New York financier unknown to the hotel people. The working people of the place constantly are at odds with the manager, who mistreats them. Nevertheless, the place manages to prosper. Along comes the owner and discovers the mismanagement. He discharges the manager and puts Tom in his place to run it according to his ideas.

Tom's idea is that to make humans happy and contented in humble work they should be allowed time and opportunity for self-expression; that is, given a chance to do the thing they like best to do. There is no question that this is a modern and reasonable theory, but the picture from that point goes into a crude system of ridiculing it to the point of crude travesty.

The scrubwoman goes in for nature dancing; the burly porter rehearses an impersonation of Julian Eltinge; several of the waiters try ludicrously to train themselves as acrobats. Almost half the footage is made up of this sort of stuff.

The owner returns and finds the experiment has caused the hotel a loss of $6,000, and is about to "can" him when Tom is suddenly informed that he has received an inheritance of $1,000,000; so he buys the hotel himself and continues the experiment in self-expression until he goes broke. Thereupon the former manager reappears. Tom tells him the experiment has failed so the old manager remarks he will buy the old place back and let Tom run it now that he has come to his sense and knows that you can't make a silk purse out of a scrubwoman's mop.

There is a subordinate love story, but it is so exceedingly subordinate you suspect it was introduced during the filming. All the way through the picture has the earmarks of having been conceived by some one (could it be a filium magnate?) with a heavy bankroll and supreme contempt for all creatures below his fortunate estate. *Rush.*

HALDANE OF THE SECRET SERVICE

Released by the Houdini Pictures Corporation and starring Houdini. At the Stanley Oct. 24. Running time, 60 minutes.

The name Houdini is supposed to carry a strong box office draw. Therefore, it may or may not be surprising that when reviewed there was a slim crowd at a house which usually is packed to the doors. Perhaps the renown of Houdini is fading, or more probably the Broadway filmgoers were wise to how bad a film this one is.

Houdini seems to be endeavoring to act the dashing young juvenile in the picture. With all due respect to his famed ability for escapes, the only asset he has in the acting line is his ability to look alert. He does this for over an hour through the tedious monotony of another Chinese counterfeit plot. The picture is infested with an over-abundance of subtitles and cutbacks.

The pity of it all is that the film is reputed to have cost a good deal of money. But it is the company's own fault, because, added to the weak plot, they have inefficient direction, poor acting and carelessness of detail. London and Paris as well as other places in Europe were visited in an effort to achieve something, but nothing is accomplished except for two or three fair shots of Westminster, the Eiffel Tower and other points of interest.

The billing outside the theatre leads one to think that some of Houdini's miraculous escapes from death are to be featured. There is only one, and that is a poorly staged affair showing the star free himself from a giant water mill. Some earlier scenes reveal him swimming around in the New York Harbor; but there is nothing spectacular about them. Instead of going in for his specialty Houdini waltzes around in a tuxedo and dress suit, the handsome and virile Haldane of the U. S. A. One fight scene at the end is particularly unconvincing and stagey.

Gladys Leslie plays a much persecuted heroine with her usual mixture of diffidence and sacharrine. The balance of the cast holds unfamiliar names, with the acting at its best but ordinary and at its worst atrocious.

'Way out in the sticks they may flock to see this one because of the name Houdini. But they won't like it.

THE DRIVIN' FOOL

Regent Pictures Corp. production released through W. W. Hodkinson. Featuring Wally Van. H. H. Van Loan adapted from "Blue Book Magazine" story by W. F. Sturm. Directed by Robert J. Thornby; assistant director, Emil De Ruelle. Titles by Walter Anthony. Photographed by A. J. Stout and Steve Rounds. At the Cameo, New York, for a week, starting Oct. 28. Runs 62 minutes.

John Moorehead	Alec B. Francis
Sylvia Moorehead, his daughter	Patsy Ruth Miller
Henry Locke	William Taylor
Hal Locke, his speed-mad son	Wally Van
Richard Brownlee	Ramsey Wallace
Howard Grayson	Wilfred North
Horatio Jackson Lee St. James	Jesse J. Aldriche
John Lawson	Kenneth R. Bush

There are plenty of credits for this picture. The ordinarily least important mention at times carries the picture. That goes for the titling and the photography.

The story is lightweight and could be boiled down, although much thinner stories have also been previously extended through 5,000 feet.

When the business executives in San Francisco learn the railroad strike halts the mailing of a $500,000 check to a Wall Street power in New York by a certain date it is obvious that Hal Locke, the speed-mad son, whose constant violations of the traffic laws have made him notorious on the Pacific Coast, will undertake the task and prove his mettle to a doubting father and an antagonistic prospective father-in-law.

The check must reach the greatest financial centre in the greatest city in the world by noon Oct. 7 or else the Wall Street powers will take over a huge west coast project which is just getting back into sound financial waters. The eastern faction realizes this, and would rather they did not get the paltry half million, since they have a buyer for the works for $2,000,000.

Anyway, the big money makes it all sound better.

Young Locke (Wally Van) has seven days to navigate 3,000 miles from coast to coast. He does it with a half minute to spare. The cross-country drive takes up most of the footage, with the hero's battling against obstacles maneuvred by the Wall Street emissaries. (The trip by car has been done in less time.)

Van dominates the picture through being in practically every foot of the picture. Except for occasional "shots" at a pair of worried business men and a trusting heroine, Van at the wheel of a saucy roadster is constantly to the fore.

The picture is pleasing, that's all. Sufficient for the daily change houses. *Abel.*

YOUNG LOCHINVAR

London, Oct. 8.

Will Kellino's first picture for Stoll has all the ingredients necessary for a big spectacular feature and should be a success. The famous poem appears to have been ignored and the synopsis announces the film as adapted from the story by J. Preston Muddock.

It is a pity the poem was not adhered to. Everything from hoary castles to dark lochs were at the producer's hand, and although the main incident of Lochinvar's kidnapping his bride is there, we miss the poetry and romantic glamor of the escape. Throughout the production is very fine, and the interior settings have rarely been excelled, while the exteriors are many of them strikingly beautiful. The crowd work is admirable and the fights have a rare touch of realism.

Much of the acting is very good, but why Owen Nares was cast for the part of a braw Highland chief is a mystery. His name has a certain box office value, but he is anything but heroic. With sword and buckler in hand the audience have the comfortable feeling his enemies are quite safe.

Cecil Morton York is extremely good as Johnstone of Lockwood; Dick Webb is excellent as Musgrave and would have done much with the stellar part. Lionel Braham and Bertie Wright provide a welcome comic relief. Nelson Ramsey is good as Graeme of Netherby. Gladys Jennings is singularly sweet and natural as Helen, and Dorothy Harris **is good as Cecilia, as is Charles Barrett as Alick.**

It is a great pity the author should have allowed these two very important parts to peter out. Taken as a while, there is no doubt that this picture is yet another proof of the Stoll determination to raise the standard of British productions. *Gore.*

THE AUDACIOUS MR. SQUIRE

London, Oct. 18.

Save for a certain unevenness in the cast this is an excellent screen comedy. In fact, it is one of the very few good comedies, long or short, turned out of a British studio and it augurs well for the new policy which Edward Godal is inaugurating for British and Colonial Films.

The story is an excellent one, adapted from a play by Eliot Stannard and Sydney Bowket. It is on the time-honored comedy lines which insist upon one or two rooms and a staircase—the rooms having the requisite number of doors for the quick "trap" work necessary and the staircase for listening in purposes.

The screen adapters have done their work well and the picture is built steadily up to a highly diverting finale. The two blots on the presentation are the performance of Russell Thorndyke as an old man, which he plays in a manner that entirely kills the character, and the other flaw is photography, of which the exterior work is excellent, but much of the interiors of an inferior quality seldom seen these days.

The story tells how two old men quarrel over the ownership of a piece of land. Smallwood's daughter, Connie, loves Howard's son, Edgar, but the feud forbids their union. However, they marry secretly. Tom Squire, a character akin to Raffles, burgles the Smallwood house with a view to stealing some priceless objects on the night the young couple return to their respective homes. An alarm is given; Howard, who is stealing an interview with his wife, escapes, but Squire is captured. Taking advantage of a conversation he has heard between the lovers, he bluffs and lies in the true Hawtrey manner, and is at last accepted as a brother "collector" by old Smallwood, who orders the "Pink Room" to be prepared for the young couple. Squire does everything he can to get away, but is always stalled.

Meanwhile young Howard has been wounded by the party after the burglar and is brought to the Smallwood house, where he is recognized. Connie's younger sister gives the whole thing away by screaming out, "Connie, Connie, they have killed your husband!" In the end Squire escapes with the aid of friends who pose as detectives, the two old men are reconciled, and everybody is happy.

The setting is adequate. With the exception of Thorndyke as Smallwood, the cast is excellent. Jack Buchanan, already a popular revue and musical comedy favorite, is a find as Squire. No light comedian on the British screen has so light and unexaggerated a touch and he never gets out of the picture. **The acting show of the film is that of Sydney Paxton as John Howard. His performance is a delightful one and classes him among the leading screen players of the day. Malcolm Tod is excellent as his son, Edgar. Mlle. Valia is capital as the secret wife, Connie, and Dorinea Shirley does everything possible as the sister. Many small parts are well played. This picture deserves to be and probably will be a success.** *Gore.*

LA GUITARE ET LE JAZZ BAND

Paris, Oct. 9.

A picture version of the story of H. Duvernois by the above title has been made by Gaston Roudes. It is a creditable production, with some excellent acting by Camille Bardou, Devalle and Mme. France Dhelia, but a rickety sort of story. Here is the scenario as unfolded: Martine, a lady launched into the fast set of Paris (the jazz band), meets her faithful and constant dancing friend Denis during a society party and informs him her husband Maxim is called away to Morocco, so that she will be obliged to spend the period of his absence at her father-in-law's home in the country.

The two lovers then scheme how they can see one another in a small provincial town without raising suspicion of their intrigue. Martine explains her father-in-law, rich gentleman farmer, dislikes her, but they can possibly win over her sister-in-law, Estelle, who is fond of playing the guitar, as a confederate to their love rendezvous.

Thus, it is arranged Denis shall take the same train, but alight at a station before the town where Martine is to reside. The husband accompanies her to the depot, and we see the railroad trip, with an ultimate squabble between Denis and a stranger named Hupont over a seat in the restaurant car. The latter is unnoticed witness to their farewell kiss when the train stops, and he tries to speak to Martine before she joins her husband's family at the station. She shrugs her shoulders.

During the next few days Martine smiles her sweetest on her sister-in-law, teaching her to dance and proposing a visit to the local casino. Denis is advised to be there and to pay court to Estelle. While waiting in the casino the fellow called Hupont accosts Denis and seeks a further explanation concerning their quarrel in the restaurant car, but the latter fibs and hastens to greet Martine when he sees her arrive, being introduced to Estelle as a casual friend from Paris. He quickly wins the heart of the simple country maiden and is invited to spend a few days at her father's home.

Martine has thus attained her end when Denis is installed in a small cottage at the end of the garden. Here he is joined by Martine the same night. After the visit, when Denis has returned to his hotel, he discovers he prefers Estelle and is struck with remorse. He then writes to Martine informing her of his intention of asking Estelle to marry him, but the sudden appearance of his mistress changes his intention. They decide to return to Paris.

Meanwhile Estelle is heartbroken at the departure of her beloved Denis, and at midnight talks to the blinking stars of all her imaginary troubles. She is smitten with the young puppy and feels miserable at his neglect.

Next morning she decides to pay him a visit, for shame will be better than uncertainty. She learns Denis has just left for the station with Martine. She hastens after the fugitives, searches through the train, scrutinizing each passenger. Denis and Martine, who have hidden themselves in a compartment, are finally detected by Estelle, who stretches out her arms in despair as the train starts. She jumps on a step as the wagon moves, falls on the track and faints.

The official stops the train while Denis rushes to Estelle's assistance. When she recovers she finds herself in the arms of the man she dotes on. He takes her back to her father and probably the wedding bells are set a-ringing. Martine has understood the feelings of her fickle sweetheart and returns alone to Paris to await her lawful husband.

A feature of this film lies in the fact that it has been executed in the mansion and park of the property at Orly recently acquired as the home founded by the picture industry in France for aged members of the trade. *Kendrew.*

SUN WORSHIPPERS

London, Oct. 8.
Apart from the interest mathematicians, astronomers and scientists generally may take in this picture, its value as a showman's proposition is negligible. We are informed the owners, United Theatres and Films, Ltd., are hopeful of getting it shown under the auspices of the All-British Film Week, but being a feature made by American scientists from the Lick Observatory, its chance of being included in the national program it remote. As a feature it has little interest for the general public, and it shows practically nothing of interest to the average man or woman, however interesting it may be to scientists.

It is purely the record, not too well photographed, of Dr. W. W. Campbell's expedition from the Lick Observatory to Wallal in Northwest Australia. There is nothing particularly beautiful in any of the "shots," and the haphazard introduction of a few native dances and customs cuts little ice. The actual eclipse is only of interest to the scientific mind, and the statement the cameraman took 900 shots of it will be looked upon as a sheer waste of time by the layman.

This film is one for the Royal Society and not for the general public.

"LANDRU," BLUEBEARD PICTURE, SHOWN BEHIND BOLTED DOORS

Film of Zest and Crime First Exhibited to Police, Then to Variety's Reviewer—Will Pack House if It Can Pass Censors

LANDRU

London, Oct. 24.
No one outside Germany could conceive such a picture as "Landru" which, after being shown to police officials, was screened behind bolted doors for "Variety." The picture is without a fictional story, being nothing more or less than a kinomatographic reconstruction of the crimes which thrilled the world some time ago. No players' names are mentioned, and the producer is anonymous. The production work is excellent and nasty, though, the story of the seduction of more than 11 women and their subsequent murder must necessarily be, it has been handled with a great deal of discretion.

The whole thing has been compiled from official records starting from the point when a woman complained to the Chief of Police in Paris that her sister was missing. From then on the story of the crime is worked up from clue to clue, each of the eleven love stories is taken from its base and analysed. The perplexity of the police is vividly shown together with their apparent impotence. Then comes the recognition of Landru by the friend of one of his "wives." After this the action becomes swift. Arrested, he is brought to trial after three years' cross-examination. The actual trial is more gripping than any fictional story and has been remarkably reconstructed. Throughout there is no sign of acting; the camera might have been in court. The evidence is piled up remorsely until the only verdict possible is given.

The famous stove and many of the articles figuring in the case are used as "props." Much time is spent in determining whether the bones dug up and found among the ashes of the stove are human or animal, still more in determining the sex, and much more in lengthy quotations from legal arguments and evidence.

Throughout the names of actual people concerned in the case are used and several of them are understood to be actual players including Mlle. Segree, the minor vaudeville artist with whom Landru was really in love and who believed in his innocence to the end.

An attempt will be made to put this picture out for the public in a modified form. If it passes the censor and is permitted for public exhibition there is little doubt but it will pack any building in the cheaper and more popular parts of the country, cities and towns.
Gore.

HIS CHILDREN'S CHILDREN
A Sam Wood Production presented by Adolph Zukor. Adapted for the screen by Monte M. Katterjohn from the novel by Arthur Train. Directed by Sam Wood. Shown at Rivoli, New York, week November 4, 1923. Running time 86 minutes.

Diana	Bebe Daniels
Sheila	Dorothy Mackaill
Lloyd Maitland	James Rennie
Rufus Kayne	George Fawcett
Claudia	Katheryn Leas
Larry Devereaux	Mahlon Hamilton
Mercedes	Mary Eaton
Dr. Dhal	Warner Oland
Florian	John Davidson
Mrs. Wingate	Sally Crute
Uncle Bill McGraw	Joe Burke
Lord Harrowdale	Templar Powell
Mr. Pepperill	Lawrence D'Orsay
Mrs. Rufus Kayne	Dora Mills Adams
Krabfleisch	H. Cooper Cliffe

This is the second of the pictures of Paramount to be given a "demonstration run." The production opened at the Rivoli on Sunday to rather light matinee business, but did very well at night. The picture itself doesn't seem particularly to be one that will pull unusual business on Broadway, but it looks like a box office whale for the smaller cities. West of the Hudson River they love anything that is a slam at New York and this picture certainly does slam the present mode of living in the metropolis, especially among the socially elect. That is why this picture seems like sure fire any place outside of New York. It is a society story that has been printed in popular fiction magazine, has been published in book form, which is enough to give it some pulling power over the country in general. Then with a picture cast that has a lot of fairly good names the question of the box office should be cinched.

To begin with Sam Wood in directing this production must have spent a lot of money, possibly a couple of hundred thousand more than it should have cost, for to get what he shows on the screen there must have been about $400,000 sunk on the production, which in reality is a good $150,000 picture.

The cast has Bebe Daniels, Dorothy Mackaill, James Rennie and George Fawcett as the four featured members, but there are an additional half dozen names all of which have screen value. These are also going to be a box office asset in the smaller stands.

The story deals with the old Biblical teaching that "the sins of the father's shall be visited upon the children," with the action opening at a time when the founder of the Peter B. Kayne fortune is about to pass out of the picture at a ripe old age, his son is 56 and has a family of three daughters. When the old Peter came to New York he hooked Wall Street as his game and won a tremendous fortune, his son with the father's millions behind him achieved social distinction, and now the three young daughters are social butterflies.

One has married an English nobleman who is making her unhappy, a second has turned out to be a girl among the boys and the youngest is a veritable flapper who is jazzing around with a lounge lizard and following a foolish cult, as well as taking an occasional hop pellet for her tired nerves. Along about that time dad gets entangled with a couple of theatrical managers who framed him with a vamp, grab a loan of a couple of million on their theatre and then threaten the old boy with the Mann Act and exposure if he presses the collection of the notes.

With that the board of directors of the bank of which the father is president ask for his resignation and the payment from him of the notes he had endorsed, the first of the line dies from shock when the big pile of stone that he built on Fifth Avenue has to go under the hammer to meet his son's obligation, but the girls seemingly wake up to the fact that it was all for the best as far as their lives are concerned.

Its a story with a moral, plus a lot of jazzy atmosphere and a laugh here and there. The coming out ball of the youngest daughter of the family is full of real punch stuff for the hinterland, what with society flappers smoking and drinking, rolling their own and leaving their almost corsets in the retiring room, it may be termed "hot stuff." Woods has some corking touches of detail and atmosphere in this particular scene, as well as in a Greenwich Village scene, and a couple of theatrical parties. His hotel stuff, with father and the actress and the actress as part of an Atlantic City party, is very deftly done.

If audiences want sexy stuff this one has it, and it should be a box office clean up away from the blase Broadway.

Dorothy Mackaill as the youngest daughter makes a distinct impression in the picture. Bebe Daniels is herself and that is all. Mary Eaton does a nifty bit as the vamping show girl that gets over in great shape. James Rennie impresses as the lead opposite Miss Daniels, while George Fawcett and Hale Hamilton, playing father and son, score heavily. *Fred.*

HOSPITALITY

Buster Keaton comedy. World's premiere at Warfield, San Francisco, Nov. 3. Cast includes Buster Keaton, Jr., Natalie Talmadge (Mrs. Keaton) and Joseph Keaton, father of the comedian-star.

San Francisco, Nov. 7.

Buster Keaton's latest comedy is replete with trick stuff and comedy stunts that have been likened to those of Harold Lloyd. The star hangs over cliffs hundreds of feet in the air, rides a log down a seething rapids and manages to save himself at the brink of the waterfall, which looks a mile high. This scene particularly is a real thrill and kept the audience on edge, gasping with fear one minute and laughing the next. The trick stuff is very realistic and cleverly managed.

"Hospitality" concerns a feud between two families in Kentucky, starting in 1810. The opening melodramatic scenes plant the feudal theme and the action jumps 30 years later, showing Broadway and 42nd street, New York, as it looked in 1840. A farmhouse and cowpath are on the site of the now notorious crooked square. Title reads, "Scene reproduced from an old photograph."

Keaton, a baby in the opening scene, is now grown up. Over 500 feet are devoted to showing his railway journey from Times square to Kentucky, an actual railway train of that day being reproduced. The engine is named "Rocket," and three cars resembling stage coaches on wheels comprise the train. This portion of the picture was a riot at the opening performance, packed with comedy and the big smash of the entire picture.

Keaton, as the sole surviving heir of the McCay family, goes to Kentucky to claim the estate. He meets The Girl on the train and they are attracted to each other. The Girl is a daughter of the Canfields, it develops, with whom the McCays are in deadly feud.

Keaton discovers that his "estate" consists chiefly of old tumbledown shacks. He accepts The Girl's invitation to dinner, and when the latter's family discovers Keaton's identity as a McCay the Southern code of honor saves him from being harmed while under the Canfield roof. The fun consists at this point of trying to get Keaton out of the house so that they can take a shot at him.

He finally escapes and the ensuing chase makes possible the thrill stuff, with Keaton shooting the rapids and climbing cliffs. The obvious conclusion of his marrying the girl and burying the feudal hatchet follows.

The supporting cast, in which Buster, Jr., Natalie Talmadge and Joseph Keaton (comedian's father) are to the fore, is consistently good. The picture is also enhanced by some striking photographic effects. *Rivers.*

THE MONKEY'S PAW

An English made production from the story by W. W. Jacobs, directed by Manning Haynes. Distributed by the Selznick Co. Shown at the Stanley, N. Y., Nov. 2. Running time, 63 minutes.

This English made feature is a mystery play, and that goes as to why it was made. In the first place, while there is a good story behind it, there isn't the slightest bit of love interest in the tale, and, after all, that is what American audiences want for their screen fare. It is an out-and-out tale of English life in a small town, with the principal figures two old people in the neighborhood of 70, with their grown son, who is their mainstay in life. These three characters, together with a returned soldier who has spent years in the Far East, carry the entire tale. None of the cost is named on the screen, but the father and mother are played by people who do some excellent character work.

The picture may be of the type that the English audiences like, but it will hardly get over in this country, even in the smallest picture houses. The English director's idea of a motion picture is evidently to have something moving on the screen, and that is all. This picture is utterly lacking in action and is only carried along by the tritest sort of titles telling the story.

With a mystery tale of this character to base a good screen story on it would be rather a novelty in the hands of an American director, who, with a lot of trick camera stuff, could turn out a picture that would be a real thriller. This one, however, hasn't any thrills. Its one outstanding feature is the fact that it has suspense, but from the story rather than from direction. *Fred.*

DAVID COPPERFIELD

A film version of the famous Charles Dickens novel, made by the Nordisk Film Corporation, of Norway, and released by the Associated Exhibitors. Directed by A. W. Sandberg. Reviewed at the Cameo, New York. Running time, 67 minutes.

CAST

Little David	Buddy Martin
David Copperfield	Gorm Smidd
Agnes	Karen Winther
Aunt Betsey Trotwood	Marie Dinesen
Mr. Micawber	Frederick Jensen
Uriah Heep	Rasmus Christiansen
Dora Spenlow	Karina Bell
Peggotty	Karen Caspersen

Although heavily advertised in a leading national weekly as an authentic version of the famous Dickens novel, the "David Copperfield" film of Scandinavian origin shows itself to be a distinct "movie" version in that much of the original theme has been subordinated in order to bring out the elements of the story suitable for the screen. Because of this, the film does not live up to the advertisement, for much more is made here of the Copperfield loves in later life than of his early vicissitudes.

It is true that they are portrayed, but in an unsatisfactory fashion. There is too much in the novel for an ordinary length film to tell completely, and this production has attempted to do this and has fallen short.

It is a thoroughly serious effort, however and as such is way ahead of many other features, but to Dickens lovers and students it will prove a disappointment because of its failures in some spots and its achievements in others. In a word, it is uneven. Where Frederik Jensen does an excellent piece of work as Micawber, Rasmus Christiansen does not nearly approximate a portrayal of the fawning Uriah Heep. And Barkis—he who made "Barkis is willin'" a by-word—is given one short flash and out, never to be heard from again.

The story concerns young David Copperfield, born after the death of his father. His mother later marries a man who treats him unkindly and he is left friendless upon her death. As a young boy of 10 he is sent to wash bottles in a London warehouse and to lodge with Mr. and Mrs. Micawber. And the pompous Mr. Micawber, good at heart, but a spendthrift, is soon packed off to the Debtor's Prison, and David trudges 50 miles to see an unfriendly aunt, who later becomes attached to him. So once more his fortune turns and he is sent to school in London, and there dwells with the Wickfields, where he falls in love with their daughter.

But when he finishes school and writes a successful novel, he marries another girl, who shortly afterward dies. By this time Uriah Heep, a crooked clerk in the Wickfield counting rooms, has stolen money, which ruins the Wickfields and Copperfield's old aunt, whose money was in their care. Micawber enters again as the one who shows up Uriah Heep and restores the family fortunes. For this he is sent away to Australia, the land of opportunity, according to Charles Dickens and the sub-titles. And David finally marries the girl who has been waiting for him.

In reality it is supposed to have been the life story of Charles Dickens and is disclosed as such at the end of the picture. The characters are all fairly well taken, but Jensen in the Micawber part so far outshines the rest that he deserves the electrics for his performance.

The backgrounds throughout are of the best, and apparently some little care was taken with the technical end of the production. The photography is good and the adaptation slovenly. The sub-titles are like the well-known bishop's well-known egg—good in spots.

"David Copperfield" as a film now has a distinctively limited draw which will come principally from the more intelligent movie-goers. It appears that if more care had been given to the adaptation of the story its appeal would have been twice as great and business possibilities thereby widened. It isn't strong enough for the big first run houses if they expect to send their patrons away happy, while the smaller houses can get away with it nicely as a classy flash. *Sisk.*

FOOLISH PARENTS

Associated Exhibitors presents this British-made Ideal Films production with an "all-star cast." Released through Pathe. Ran 64 minutes at the Stanley, New York, Nov. 6. Adapted from I. A. R. Wylie novel. Other credits not caught. Principals include Margaret Bannerman, Reginald Owen, Peter Deare (juvenile), and Douglas Munro.

An obvious story, obviously told, and on a par with the general run of British productions that reach this side. From this, probably not the worst of English-made features, it is easy to understand why American films are more popular in Britain than the native product.

The cast is not to blame, and even the story, in a scenario adept's hands, could have been made more convincing. The direction as far as it went is also sufficient. That probably is the answer to why the English pictures don't impress. They go so far and no further. It is merely a lack of sufficient advancement in the British film industry.

The St. Johns are a pair of wealthy idlers, made so through the convenient allowance of a $50,000 annuity to the master of the household. The mistress is so busy spending it in elaborate social fetes that she seldom sees her husband much less her young son, Archie (Peter Deare). The youngster is the motif for the "foolish parents" title. When St. John decides to write his uncle in South Africa, whom he has never seen, that an extra ten "grand" would come in handy, the latter comes to London, has his solicitor announce he is bankrupt, the allowance immediately curtailed, with a sympathetic complication of testing the parents' inherent love for the child.

The parents come through heroically and everything is patched up again, the allowance increased, and the couple return to their former state of social ease and luxury.

In between it is demonstrated that Cecilia St. John, who formerly was a very valued client of Lucile's, is not averse to accepting a position as a sartorial model. Also that Heathcoate St. John, who paid fancy prices for thoroughbred horses, is not above to driving a not so thoroughbred behind a hansom.

That's carrying it a bit too far. An American director would probably have made the financially straightened lady still retain her social gentility by assuming a position with the women's apparel establishment whereby she would attract the social elite. That's a bit more distinctive than being mannikin before a host of former social equals. In real life that would be the least likely position to choose.

The title sounds all right for the daily changers on the order of the Stanley, for which grade theatre the picture suffices. *Abel.*

"ISLE OF VANISHING MEN"

Los Angeles, Nov. 7.

"The Isle of Vanishing Men" (William F. Alder Explorations, Inc.) was given a world premiere at Clune's Broadway, the film as well as the lobby display of curios and specimens from the cannibal country receiving favorable comment. The picture is in seven reels, and is said to be positively the last that ever will be made with real, honest-to-goodness man eaters.

The Dutch government, it is explained in a title, has forbidden any more cameras in the jungle country. The fact, too, that the cannibals are rapidly diminishing as a race is also proof of the film's rarity. Alder has obtained some very fine "shots," showing in an intimate way the life of the uncivilized citizens of Dutch New Guinea. The picture is in many ways another "Nanook of the North," but is lacking in thrills. It is probable it will run three or four weeks at the local first-run house. *Krieg.*

YOU ARE IN DANGER

A six-reeler produced by Blair Cohan, featuring Carmel Myers. Shown on a double feature bill, with William Farnum in "The Gun Fighter," at the Circle, New York, Oct. 31. Running time, 68 minutes.

Jim Manning	Jimmy Morrison
Mary Slocum	Pauline Starke
Hank Hall	Edward Kennedy
Tug Wilson	Mitchell Lewis
Milly Amory	Carmel Myers

This feature seems to have been premeditatively framed for the countryside. If we've guessed it, it's an ace. But if the director was not altogether tongueing his cheek during the making and meant it to be an honest-to-goodness big town smash his calculations were anything but proportionate.

Its best chance is with the country folk, who will gape in bewilderment at the intrigues resorted to by the criminal band who waylay the boyish hero. Neighborhood audiences also, especially the type that likes its melodrama lurid, will find compensation in this crook melodrama.

Devoid of newness in either theme or treatment, the film has action, and plenty of it, thereby redeeming the slower early reels that are spun off to plant an introductory.

The story is the old angle of the small town chap who gets too big for his native berth and makes for the city to roll up a fortune and return to reclaim his local sweetheart. Instead he goes broke and falls in with a gang of smugglers. Later learning the true status of his connections, he tries to shake them off. It is too late. He knows too much about their operations. And dead men tell no tales.

He lives to become infatuated with Milly Amory, the vampish gold digger of the gang, but the romance is checkmated by the arrival of his rustic Juliet. The remainder of the film occupies itself with making the paths of the lovers as perilous as possible.

Carmel Myers, featured, gives a splendid delineation of the vamp. The role permits a wide range for contrast, and more than once she achieved stellar heights, particularly in the final reel, where she slays the gang leader. Mitchell Lewis makes the latter character deliciously despicable. Jimmie Morrison contributes a likeable characterization of a weakling who later finds strength of character. Pauline Starke is all an unsophisticated country lass should be.

The picture should go big as a lead in the smaller houses and can stand on its own as an in-between feature anywhere.

HEARTSTRINGS

London, Oct. 24.

Founded on a novel by Mrs. Gaskell entitled "The Manchester Marriage," this latest "British and Colonial" picture is excellent if conventional. It is another version of the story of Enoch Arden, and the screen adaptation is probably more gripping than the Victorian original, although in those days when such matters as sex and childbirth were only whispered of, it doubtless made something of a sensation. The production work is good and there are many interesting scenes of Liverpool docks and Manchester cotton mills, together with some beautiful "shots" of the Thames valley and the Karsino. This latter pleasure resort, or anything like it, was certainly unknown when Mrs. Gaskell wrote her novel. The interiors are good.

Frank Wilson, first officer of a tramp vessel, leaves his wife, who is expecting to become a mother, on a voyage which is to be the last before getting his command. The boat is reported lost. The child is born a cripple. Years of hardship, running a Manchester boarding house, culminate in Alice, the wife, marrying the "star" boarder, a Manchester merchant. A child is born, but in the midst of Alice's new-found happiness Wilson turns up. He has been shipwrecked and a prisoner of savages. He is at first furious at the news he learns, but the faithful servant shows him the sleeping children and explains what his return means to them. He goes away. Later some jewelry is missed. Another maid tells of the visit of a strange man. The faithful servant hurries to Frank to warn him. Meanwhile the jewelry is found, and on the merchant's going to acquaint his faithful servant with the fact Frank is discovered dead. He has committed

suicide sooner than wreck Alice's happiness. The truth comes out, but it is decided to say nothing for the sake of Alice and the children.

Once more "B. & C." risk success by bad casting. Russell Thorndyke is nothing like a strong, stern Lancashire mill owner who has worked his way up from the bottom. He has neither the facial nor physical appearance for such a part and is throughout most unconvincing. Given a light comedy part or a juvenile role he would be quite all right but he is unsuited for leading business. Victor MacLaglen gives a fine show as Frank Wilson and rises to great heights on the discovery of his wife's remarriage.

The women are all sound. Edith Bishop is responsible for a beautifully toned portrait of Alice; Gertrude McCoy is good as the faithful servant, a part which carries the big acting of the picture, and Kate Gurney gives a really good study of Wilson's mother. Little Cathleen French is excellent as the crippled child, and other parts are well played by Sydney Farebrother, George Bishop, Kate Stafford and Gray Murray.

This is the second picture under the new producing-renting scheme of the company, and it should make good. *Gore.*

THE BELOVED VAGABOND

London, Oct. 23.

Conjure up an experienced picture actor who has for years had to submit to the dictates of a director and a business department that scrutinizes expenditures. Place a bankroll at the disposal of a film star, with power to expand it as he sees fit. In 99 cases out of 100 the actor will turn out a "feature picture" of abnormal footage with himself occupying the centre of the stage almost continually, interspered with close-ups showing his "marvelous facial expression.".

That is what happened in the case of Carlyle Blackwell in his "sole supervision" of the film adaptation of William J. Locke's novel, "The Beloved Vagabond," directed by Fred Leroy Granville, art direction by E. P. Kinsella, photographed by William Blakely, edited by S. K. Winston, with musical arrangement by DeGroot. The United Kingdom rights to the picture are controlled by Astra-National Productions, Ltd.

They do say that more than three reels were cut from the feature only a few days before its opening at the Palace last night, yet the picture ran for practically three solid hours, with only a ten-minute intermission. The deletion of from three to four thousand more feet would undoubtedly vastly improve the commercial value of the production.

Locke's novel is almost entirely descriptive and narrative writing, which is always extremely difficult to transfer to the screen. For the benefit of those who do not know the story, it is the tale of a young man who agrees with a wealthy nobleman not to see or communicate with his fiance for a period of two years, in consideration of the rich man saving the girl's father from bankruptcy and imprisonment. The girl, not hearing from her lover, marries the rich count; whereupon the young man becomes a vagabond, earning his living by playing his violin on the road and passing the hat, incidentally growing a fierce and profuse adornment of facial foliage. In the picturization it is a sort of Quixotic characterization, with his ramblings entourage augmented by a boy, a girl and a dog.

Despite the star's persistent occupation of the centre of the picture, the outstanding hit is that of the boy, as played by Albert Chase, said to have never before been on the stage, which is doubtful. The lad

would make an ideal Penrod. The girl is well enacted by Madge Stuart, Miss Sydney Farebrother plays in her usual fashion, which is most acceptable, a bibulous washerwoman; Owen Roughwood is extremely competent as the heavy, while Phyllis Titmuss is exceedingly unattractive as the heroine. The photography is generally good and the direction atrocious, especially in the handling of ensemble scenes.

Two or three spools could easily be clipped from the first part and easily one more from the second. Opening at 8:30, it was a generally disgruntled crowd that filed out of the theatre at 11:30 the opening night. *Jolo.*

THE BAREFOOT BOY

A rural comedy drama by Wallace Clifton, based on the John Greenleaf Whittier poem. Directed by David Kirkland. Presented by the Mission Film Corp. at a special showing in the Palace, New York, Nov. 10. Runs 70 minutes.

Dick Alden	John Bower
Mary Truesdale	Marjorie Daw
Millicent Carter	Sylvia Breamer
Rodman Grant	George McDaniel
Deacon Halloway	Raymond Hatton
Tom Adams	Tully Marshall
Si Parker	George Periolat
Mrs. Drake	Virginia True Boardman
Josiah Blake	Brinsley Shaw
Bill Hawkins	Harry Todd
Wilson	Otis Harlan
Dick Alden, as a child	Frankie Lee
Mary Truesdale, as a child	Gertie Messinger

This is one of the usual type of rural picture plays that are of the comedy drama type bordering on melodrama. There is a good, strong cast in the picture that will help to pull it out of the class of ordinary program features, but if it weren't for that it would be just another one of those things. With the cast that it has, however, it can play the split week houses in the better neighborhoods and get away nicely. It isn't what a great many would try to make one believe —that this is a picture worthy of playing the bigger pre-release houses.

That section of the film that is most interesting is the portion where the action is carried on in the main with a juvenile cast. Here little Frankie Lee and Gertie Messinger carry off all the honors.

The scene of action is a small village that relies on a single manufacturing plant for its life. In that village there is a little chap whose widowed mother has married again, and the lad's stepfather is a brute. The boy is one of those lovable, freckle-faced youngsters who is made the town goat. Everything that happens is blamed on him, until he finally he runs away from home. Returning years later, when he has made his mark in the world, he decides to have his revenge on those that made his youthful days miserable, but at the crucial moment his sweetheart of childhood days sways him from his purpose.

John Bowers, as the youngster grown up, carries the heroic role, with Marjorie Daw as the heroine.

In the picturizing of the story there are a couple of thrills—one the runaway of a team hitched to an open carriage, with the little barefoot lad acting as the rescuer of the daughter of the town poobah's daughter; a school fire, and finally the blowing up of the works —are counted on as the big wallops of the picture. Of the three the first one is the best handled and gets over most effectively. *Fred.*

HELD TO ANSWER

A Metro production with House Peters starred. Written by Peter Clark MacFarlane; adapted by Winifred Dunn; directed by Harold Shaw. Shown at Loew's New York, New York, Nov. 10. Runs 67 minutes.

John Hampstead	House Peters
Marian Dounay	Grace Carlyle
Hiram Burbeck	John Sainpolis
Bessie Burbeck	Evelyn Brent
Rollie Burbeck	James Morrison
Mrs. Burbeck	Lydia Knott
"Red" Lizard	Bull Montana
Maid	Gale Henry
Judge	Thomas Guyse
Organist	Robert Daly

A fairly good program feature that will get by in the general run of houses. It is a story along the lines somewhat of "The Christian" that is rather effectively if somewhat slowly told. If it weren't for the draggy spots the picture would create a greater impression. At the New York it seemingly displayed rather strong box office value, even though the name of House Peters was the only one displayed outside. In the daily change type of house it is surefire, and it has strength enough to stand up in the half-week runs where there is anything like a floating population.

The story is a simple one, that of

an actor who deserts the stage for the pulpit. He makes his way to the pastorate of a church, and a woman who was a fellow player in his theatrical days, and loves him, tries to win him back. Failing in this, she tries to ruin him by planting a crime at his door. Through this crime he is not wholly held to answer in court, but those at the head of his church request his resignation. Foremost among those who want him to resign is the father of the boy who really committed the crime, and whose confession the minister has, but which he refuses to disclose to save himself. At the crucial moment the boy tells the truth and the minister is cleared.

The action is rather deftly handled at times and there is considerable suspense created. House Peters carries the actor-minister role rather well, supressing almost a natural desire to overact in certain sections of the role. Evelyn Brent plays the lead opposite rather effectively in an ingenue manner. Grace Carlyle is the heavy. *Fred.*

THE ROYAL OAK

London, Nov. 4.

Adapted from a Drury Lane melodrama by Henry Hamilton and Sir Augustus Harris, this is an excellent picture. The story is good and well told, while the period gives the Stoll company's principal producer, Maurice Elvey, opportunity for spectacular display. He misses nothing, but spectacle is not allowed to interfere with the drama proper, and it is doubtful whether any previous British picture has been made with such sincerity on the part of every one, from star to super.

It is the story of King Charles and his historical flight. After much fighting the King gets away and hides in the oak tree, while the Roundheads are searching the woods. His sweetheart's little brother is shot protecting the King, and the whole party returns, while the fugitives are once more hidden in disguise. To gain further time the girl disguises herself as Charles and is captured. After being brought before Oliver Cromwell the truth is quickly discovered. The little party of royalists are condemned to die, Charles having in the meantime escaped. At the last moment, however, Cromwell relents and all is well.

Scenically the production work is **fine. Elvey's studio interiors have rarely, if ever, been bettered on the screen and carry a touch of realism and solid stonework which is most commendable. The battle of** Worcester is cleverly managed, and a few private quarrels are well fought out.

The acting is very good. The greater portion of the work rests on the shoulders of Henry Victor as King Charles, and he gives a fine performance. Clive Brock is also very thorough as the young loyalist lover, while Henry Ainley does well as Cromwell. Betty Compson, fully dressed, is good as the girl, although the authors are relying on the credulity of their audience in making her masquerade as the King.

If finance allows Maurice Elvey to go on improving his work British pictures will soon arrive. *Gore.*

MARK OF THE BEAST

Authored and directed by Thomas Dixon. The cast comprises Robert Ellis, Warner Richmond, Madelyn Clare and Helen Ware. At Loew's New York Nov. 13. Running time, 69 mins.

A mediocre composition for the screen dealing with the human mind and its reactions to subconscious suggestions. Both cheaply produced and but averagely acted, this film vehicle fell somewhat short of up**holding its share of double-feature day billing. To a witnessing house it gave evidence of meaning less than nothing.**

The delving into the gray matter for a scenario, at least in this instance, provides the excuse for a doctor's fiancee to know it beyond herself to resist a second-story burglar because he resembles her deceased father. The physician, doing research work of this order, follows the couple when they elope, and is present at the time of the struggle, when the criminal reveals himself for the brute he is. It leads up to the conventional ending.

An angle upon the culprit's mother is included for little of the desired effect, and serves only to prolong the consumed time, which is probably 15 minutes beyond a natural stop. There is not an interior of note throughout the picture and, in fact, is an obviously cheap production.

Robert Ellis secures what billing there is, and as the doctor gives an average performance. Others in the cast come under an in-and-out classification which is incapable of saving this episode as an attraction except in the most minor houses.

Skig.

CROOKED ALLEY

Universal production directed by Robert F. Hill. Adapted by Adrian Johnson from the story "The Daughter of Crooked Alley," by Jack Boyle. Photographed by Harry Fowler. At the Circle Nov. 7 as half double bill with "Monna Vanna." Running time 50 mins.

Boston Blackie	Thomas Carrigan
Norine Tyrell	Laura La Plante
Judge Milnar	Tom S. Guise
Rudy Milnar	Owen Gorine
Kaintuck	Albert Hart

The current season has had its share of underworld, crook melodramas, but there does not seem to have been as many as in other years. This type of picture generally has occupied a warm spot in the affections of the picturegoing public.

"Crooked Alley" will help to fill the void considerably. **It is a moderately absorbing, sufficiently impossible and particularly well acted story of the inhabitants of such a street as the name signifies.**

Another box office point to be chalked up is that it is adapted from one of the "Boston Blackie" stories by Jack Boyle. These sketches carrying as a central figure the kindly, whimsical and yet lawless master crook were immensely popular when running in a magazine some years ago. Since then several films built around the stories have met with considerable success.

In this case the Boston "Raffles" fixes it so that a hard old judge is brought to see the light. This judge has refused to release a dying criminal who begs to be able to breathe his last among his friends and not within prison walls. Blackie and the young daughter of the old crook join in a pledge to revenge themselves on the judge.

They decide to drag his son and the pride of his heart down to crime. The girl almost jams the works by falling for the intended victim. In the end the judge's son doesn't steal but gets under the skin of his father and wins the girl.

Blackie, who also thinks a whole lot of her highness, is left to think what a noble thing is sacrifice.

The suspense holds until the finish, particularly as to which one the girl is going to choose. Most of the audience, particularly the women, will claim she finally picks the wrong one.

One reason for the latter viewpoint is because Thomas Carrigan gives by far the most appealing performance of the two heroes. Owen Gorine, a newcomer, heralded as a European find and brought to this country by Laemmle, is too wishy-washy, foreign in his mannerisms and appearance for American audiences. Laura La Plant, for some time leading woman with Hoot Gibson, is the girl, and discloses one of the prettiest profiles in pictures.'

The balance of the cast does exceptionally well, and direction, photography, continuity and technical details are all efficiently handled. Too much lingering posing and a distractingly long drawn out scene of pathos, when the girl is told of her father's death, are the only outstanding faults.

THE LONE FIGHTER

A five-reeler adapted from the Keene Thompson story, "Certain Lee," presented by A. J. Xydias, with J. B. Warner as star. Released by Sunset and directed by Albert Russell. Shown as the feature at the Stanley, New York, Nov. 7. Running time, 60 minutes.

Harvey Bates	Vester Pegg
Rose Trimball	Josephine Hill
Macklyn Vance	Joseph Ryan
Patrick Trimball	Jim Gamble
Certain Lee	J. B. Warner

Just another hokum westerner that wastes five reels on a story scarcely worth two.

Ostensibly patterned as a starring vehicle for J. B. Warner, it gives him little opportunity to display athletic prowess except in two brief flashes. Warner essays Certain Lee, a ranger who has gained that sobriquet because of his ability to get anything he goes after. If the producers should send him out to sell this film he'd find it a tougher assignment than bowling over western bullies.

Lee's rep as a go-getter is built up in captions before he enters upon the scene. When he does there is little left to do except take the bows.

The story is an inane mixture of long since stereotyped screen yarns. The villain-horse thief frames the lover to get the gell. He is sentenced to the penitentiary. Certain Lee arrives and also has a yen for the trusting sweetheart. The imprisoned lover escapes, returns to find his lady in Certain's arms. Later he is conveniently discarded in a cliff struggle with the villain, so as not to interfere with the happy climax.

It is of the sort that causes unrest among the local grocery Mertons, who, after glimpsing screen entertainment of this type, wants to cast their three square a day and pad at night to elevate the movies—by writing better scenarios.

THE FAIR CHEAT

Burton King production. At the Circle, Nov. 13, as half double bill with "Hold to Answer." Running time, 72 mins.

John Hamilton	Wilfred Lytell
Morgan Van Dam	Edmund Breese
Camilla Van Dam	Dorothy Mackaill
Rutledge Stone	William Robbyns
Gloria Starke	Marie White
Floman Ziegler	Bradley Barker
Sam Hiller	Jack Norton
Bunk Willis	Tom Blake

The sort of picture Viola Dana and certain others of the chickenish stars delight to play. There is the usual compound of Park avenue and Broadway, with Park avenue given as they imagine it on Second avenue and Broadway shown as it is believed to be out in the sticks.

If you prefer your film preposterously light, imaginative and entertaining you are bound to like "The Fair Cheat."

For that reason it looks promising as a box office attraction since it is mildly amusing and the mental strain on the spectator is negligible.

Camilla Van Dam (Dorothy Mackaill) wants to marry John Hamilton (Wilfred Lytell), a poor clerk employed by her enormously wealthy father (Edmund Breese). The latter believes his daughter to be a little spendthrift and fears that if she marries Hamilton she will never be happy or satisfied. To put her to a test he arranges to leave her on her own for a year while he is away on a cruise. Camilla has the makings, however, and it is not long before she is established as a musical comedy favorite.

Miss Mackaill, heralded far and wide as one of the few promising newcomers of Hollywood, gives a workmanlike if not striking performance. She has an appealing type of beauty and is a relief after reels and reels of doll faces. In a midnight show scene Miss Mackaill dances with surprising pep and vivacity in a yard of silver cloth that might be called a costume.

Breese chalks up one more completely satisfactory performance and the hero is convincingly played by Wilfred Lytell. The rest of the cast is adequate as are the photography, settings and important points of the direction.

THE MASK OF LOPEZ

Independent state right production being handled by Monogram Pictures Corp. Starring Fred Thomson. An original story and script by Marion Jackson. Directed by Albert Rogell. Produced by Harry J. Brown. Running time 65 minutes. Shown in projection room, Nov. 13, 1923.

Jack O'Neil	Fred Thomson
Richard O'Neil	Wilfred Lucas
Angel Face Harry	David Kirby
Doris Hampton	Hazel Keener
Steve Gore	Frank Hagney
Lopez	George Magrill
Matron	Dot Farley
Silver King	Himself

Mighty good little western, evidently made at a price and with the purpose in mind of cheap sales. It is strong enough to play any of the daily change houses and the better double feature houses.

It seems as though the producer has something worth while in Fred Thomson, who is starred in this picture. **All that he wants for this athletic star is real stories.**

Jack O'Neil is the son of a warden in a western state. Doris Hampton is the orphaned daughter of a wealthy ranchman who has always been known to give ex-convicts a lift. The daughter after her dad's death decides to keep up the work of her father and makes arrangements with the warden, and the latter's son, seeing her, decides to be an ex-con so as to get a job and be near her.

Thomson's athletic stuff is particularly good and he does not try to force himself too much. Hazel Keener was an acceptable ingenue lead opposite him.

Fred.

THIS FREEDOM

Springfield, Mass., Nov. 21.

"This Freedom," the screen version of A. S. M. Hutchinson's novel, which had its world premiere at Fox's here Monday, concerns the perplexing present-day problem of the sort of woman who sways between the momentous question of juggling in the scale, pans her home and family against a life of business in Lombard street, London, the money market of England.

Fay Compton, English actress, is in the lead role of Rosalie Aubyn, the daughter of an impecunious clergyman. After witnessing her older brother lording it over the girls of the house she becomes possessed of a hatred for men, but later, upon coming into contact with Harry Occleve, a young lawyer, love enters her life and she becomes his wife.

Though married now, she still retains a yearning for a business career, in which world she had proved a distinct success in a responsible position with a London banking establishment previous to her marriage.

She determines to continue her business life after she is married, turning over her children to the care of a governess. As a result they are neglected and denied a real mother's care and devotion. It follows the book in the end.

Miss Compton essays the heroine role of the "foolish woman" who makes the double mistake of selecting a business career and simultaneously being directly responsible for the wrecking of her home and children. Hers is a splendid characterization of the part.

Two "big" scenes are registered by Miss Compton which call for special mention. One is the courtroom scene, when her eldest son is sentenced to prison, and the other at the bed of her daughter, who refuses to recognize her mother, and fails even to call for her. In both cases her restrained emotion reaches the heights as she puts over the mother love for child.

The supporting cast is composed entirely of English actors and actresses and is adequately satisfactory. John Stuart, as the son grown up, and Nancye Kenyon, as the flapper daughter who falls into disgrace, lend color to the picture, while the performance of Baby Bunty Fosse as the daughter at six years augurs well for future promises of brightest hues.

At present a little pruning is needed at the introduction, when lengthy captions tend to explain too much what is about to follow, thus detracting dramatic effect from subsequent scenes. This, however, should be easy to erase and an attractive box office attraction seems assured for the Fox people.

The film was pictured in England and directed by the American director, Denison Clift. It will run here the rest of the week and then be sent to New York for showing. Hatty Gray Barker, editress-in-chief, and Charles Sarver of the Fox production department, attended the premiere. *Callaghan.*

STEPHEN STEPS OUT

Famous Players-Lasky production starring Douglas Fairbanks, Jr. Original story by the late Richard Harding Davis was titled "The Grand Cross of the Crescent. Edfrid Bingham made the screen adaptation and Joseph Henabery directed. At Rivoli, New York, Nov. 18. Running time, 75 minutes.

Stephen Harlow, Jr.. Douglas Fairbanks, Jr.
Stephen Harlow .... Theodore Roberts
Muley Pasha .... Noah Beery
Harry Stetson .... Harry Myers
Dr. Lyman Black .... Frank Currier
Prof. Gilman .... James O. Barrows
Mrs. Gilman .... Fannie Midgley
Virgil Smythe .... Bertram Johns
Osman .... George Field
Rustem .... Maurice Freeman
Sultan .... Fred Warren
Sultan's son .... Pat Moore
Secretary .... Jack Herbert
Hotel Proprietor .... Frank Nelson

Of all of the late Richard Harding Davis' stories, and he turned out a lot of great ones "The Grand Cross of the Crescent" was about the weakest choice that could have been made in supplying the basis of a picture vehicle for Douglas Fairbanks, Jr.'s debut as a screen star.

Re-titled "Stephen Steps Out" the story may be helped somewhat commercially by the new monicker, but it's decidedly ordinary stuff and distinctly old-fashioned aside from the title.

Young Fairbanks is 13. He looks about 16 and screens well enough, but the boy is noticeably immature as far as acting goes. The F. P. appear to have rushed him into stardom several months before he was ready for it. A course of playing bits that would have given him the experience at least in some measure that he obviously lacks would have helped a lot. That might not have been so practicable as it sounds inasmuch as the F. P. had to star young Fairbanks in order to secure the prestige and box office value attaining from his name.

He isn't a bad actor by any means for a juvenile, but film acting is a profession, trade or art, it has its tricks that must be learned and young Fairbanks acting schooling hasn't been intensive or extensive enough.

There is an obvious effort to give young Fairbanks some athletic stuff that will recall Douglas, Sr. This has the boy jumping from a roof, topping a high wall, etc., but the gymnastics are only incidental however. A swing on a rope at a goodly distance from the camera by Fairbanks, Jr., would have been much more effective if a couple of close-ups had been inserted. While the swing was undoubtedly done by the boy, the distance from the lens lent the impression of a double being used that close-ups would have disposed of.

There is no love interest. That isn't a good idea either. Even allowing the youth of the hero of the story there could be a calf-love affair with an ingenue of the same age or a heart interest theme could have been incorporated in some way that would not necessarily have the hero as one of the principals.

Of human interest there is little, most of the action running along in the same mechanical way as program pictures usually do.

Briefly the tale treats of a kid who fails in school and his dad sends him to Turkey to study history. While in the Orient the boy meets a reporter and the latter arranged a publicity stunt which focuses the spotlight on the professor who held such high ideals he wouldn't pass a millionaire's son because he had a father with barrels of coin.

The kid comes back from his sojourn in Turkey with a better knowledge of the world than a thousand schools could teach him, and that's about all the film provides.

The supporting cast is unusually good. Theodore Roberts as the father has little to do, but does it as competently as always. Harry Myers is the reporter and plays it properly. Noah Beery makes a dandy villian with a Turk make-up that could fool Kemel Pasha himself. The rest of the cast just come and go doing what they're told to do apparently and doing that satisfactorily.

"Stephen Steps Out" is pallid entertainment, especially for a first picture for a star. The "name" thing will figure as a good box office asset without question for this one. But the next one should be a great deal better. *Bell.*

WILD BILL HICKOK

William S. Hart production, Zukor presentation and Paramount picture. The story by Hart, Clifford Smith directing, with Dwight Warren and Arthur Reeves the photographers. Showing at the Rivoli, New York, Nov. 18. Running time, 77 mins.

Wild Bill Hickok .... William S. Hart
Calamity Jane .... Ethel Grey Terry
Elaine Hamilton .... Kathleen O'Connor
Jack McQueen .... James Farley
Bat Masterson .... Jack Gardner
Clayton Hamilton .... Carl Gerard

A corking vehicle for William S. Hart's re-entrance into screen prominence. Although another western, it has much to compensate that fact through its ability to sustain interest and suspense, while the action is abundant.

Perhaps the most enticing morsel is that the theme is based upon historical fact revolving around the title role, which carries a mark of respect wherever known and especially throughout the west.

For Hickok was nothing less than a fighting fool in his day, and Mr. Hart is convincing in his portrayal of the notorious character.

The picture may appear to be overly hectic to some in its action, and if so it's simply because the high spots of Hickok's gunfighting career have been presented within 77 minutes.

But it makes for likable entertainment. If there is any doubt as to the suspense it contains, particularly as regards the youngsters, it might be said that at one point Hart drew cries of warning from two children at the Rivoli Sunday afternoon when about to be unsuspectingly set upon. Unusual, at least, in a Broadway house.

Other than the gunplay the author-star has surrounded the recorded instances with a tellable story worthy of note if for nothing else than that it lacks the proverbial clinch or happy ending. The termination reveals Hickok leaving the town he has helped clean of its lawless element after denouncing women from his life because of the discovery the girl he wanted is already married.

The love interest has a double angle of Calamity Jane's affections towards Hickok and his longing for Elaine Hamilton.

The narrative has its initial locale in Washington immediately after the Civil War, but as soon switches to the west, where it permits footage for the scrap between Hickok and a gang of outlaws which is historically believed to have been the greatest solo gunfighting exploit known of.

Succeeding that comes a street fight upon the cleaning up of Dodge City.

It incidentally permits of some praiseworthy night stuff. After which is also flashed the killing of McQueen by Hickok.

As for authenticity, the picture must be allotted a major degree of reasonableness, for it is known Mr. Hart had the idea to characterize Hickok upon the screen for a long time previous to the actual "grinding," and to this end added procured data to personal knowledge, with the object being facts.

That Hart convinces in his interpretation should suffice as to the merit of his personal performance wherein there is ample opportunity for overacting which he neatly sidestepped. It's a straightforward playing, most appropriate for the occasion of his return following a lengthy absence from the screen. His support throughout is capable, with, perhaps, Ethel Grey Terry predominating above the rest as Calamity Jane.

The film is excellent as concerns the camera work, while credit is due Smith for his handling of the sequence of events. Scenically the illusions are mainly exteriors, nicely chosen. Of the more important historical characters included in the version are Lincoln, Sheridan, Custer and Bat Masterson.

And now to moralize. Even if you have got this far, you haven't got what it means for Bill Hart to return to the screen.

Bill Hart is a regular guy, on and off. He never has been a faker, on the stage or on the screen. He holds a nation-wide regard and respect among all theatrical folks because he is an actor, was an actor when on the stage, one of the best, playing red-blooded roles, and played them; he went into pictures and made a name second to none in all of picturedom for the work specialized in, and Bill Hart did it so well he has been fruitlessly copied by others.

Then he got immersed in the wave of newspaper-made muck in the picture business through some New England woman believing she could hold him up on the sort of claim certain newspapers were satisfied with for "scandal stuff." And Bill Hart, with all of his red blood, broke before that kind of stuff. He couldn't fight a woman, no matter what kind of a woman, and he went back to his California ranch, remaining there until the revulsion of conscience, even in a woman, finally brought out what Bill Hart didn't try to bring out, stamping that regular guy as o. k.

And he returned to the screen in this picture, "Wild Bill Hickok," a real old tale of the real old west, so real it brings in a great western character even if little known to the now effete east, Bat Masterson, who lately died, as have nearly all of the great men of the old great west.

This is the sort of story Young America wants, that Young America should watch. It sets them tingling; it lets them know there were great men of the west in the days when the west had to have great men, and it is brought out by a great actor, on the stage or on the screen, William S. Hart, an unmeasurable credit to the screen because he is an actor, an actor who has done much for the screen, because William S. Hart was among the very first who proved to the whole American public that the screen did hold an actor who didn't have to be instructed how to register anything. Hart registered as an actor because he is an actor and an artist.

And that is why Bill Hart can and does make "Wild Bill Hickok" a real picture and that is why Bill Hart became the idol of the picture public.

Whether it is a western or anything else, the screen best hold on to all of the Bill Harts; they are as few as were the Wild Bill Hickoks of the way back west. *Skig.*

MAYTIME

Newark, N. J., Nov. 21.

Preferred Picture, presented by B. P. Schulberg, adapted from the musical comedy of the same name by Rida Johnson Young. Directed by Gasnier. At the Newark, Newark, N. J., Nov. 16. Running time, 70 minutes.

Ottilie Van Zandt .... Ethel Shannon
Richard Wayne .... Harrison Ford
Matthew .... William Norris
Alice Tremaine .... Clara Bow
Claude Van Zandt ...... Wallace MacDonald
Col. Van Zandt .... Josef Swickard
Mathilda .... Martha Mattox
Ermintrude .... Betty Francisco
Monte Mitchell .... Robert McKim

Evidently the producers decided to jazz up the famous musical comedy and concocted an incongruous mixture aimed to please every one which will succeed in pleasing no one. The first two-thirds is a simple story of disappointed love, rather thin but sentimentally appealing, while the last consists chiefly of the familiar wild party of the fast Bohemian set of New York with a wrestling scene thrown in.

Those to whom the latter still appeals will be bored by the original romance, while the extraneous rough stuff in the finish utterly spoils the picture for those who like sugar on their stories.

The well-known theme tells how

patrician Ottilie Van Zandt, of old New York, loves her gardener's son, Richard Wayne, but, separated from him by parental authority, finally marries her cousin Claude. Richard gains his fortune and returns just in time to find Ottilie wed. Later, to avoid scandal when Claude finds Ottilie in his arms, he announces his engagement to his devoted friend, Alice Tremaine.

Many years elapse and we find Ottilie and Richard with grandchildren. As she has lost her money, Richard buys her house in for her and they again say farewell. Again the time shifts to modern days and the grandchildren, Richard and Ottilie, are now in love, or at least Ottilie is. Richard is a scapegrace, a John and a liar. He attends a wild party of chorus girls and millionaires, while Ottilie is lured by a married man to his apartment through her love for his little daughter.

There ensues a catch-as-catch-can affair until the party which is going on overhead bursts in and Richard finds Ottilie. Not being believed, she dashes home in a very unreal storm, is struck by a falling tree and rescued by Richard. Next morning, reconciled, they find at the foot of the mementoes of their grandparents' love. It is manifest that Ottilie is stung with Richard, but it is a motion picture idea of a happy ending.

The picture, aside from the destructive fault mentioned, is fairly well done, but disappointing, as it could easily be so much better. The atmosphere of old New York is not well planted, much seems unreal, and the comedy of the first part is cheap. The cast is adequate, but neither has nor makes any opportunities to distinguish itself.

Color photography at the end is used to advantage.

The song "Sweetheart" is, of course, strongly played up in the picture and the accompaniment. The title will draw, and so would the original story if it had not been rewritten according to Hollywood taste.

HELL'S HOLE

William Fox production, starring Chas. Jones. Directed by Emmett J. Flynn. Story by George Scarborough. Western melodrama. At Loew's New York, Nov. 15. Running time, 70 minutes.

Ted Musgrave .... Charles Jones
Del Hawkins .... Maurice Flynn
Pablo .... Eugene Pailette
Conductor .... George Siegmann
Dorothy Owen .... Ruth Clifford

One of the usual run of westerns, with a train robbery, barroom battle, gun fighting, cowboys and similar familiars.

A dream gag tacked on the finish gives the impression it was placed there after the picture was finished to square the otherwise commonplace incidents preceding the snapper.

Chas. Jones does a cowboy role through part of the film, but for considerable of the action is forced to discard the plainsman's uniform because of the exigencies of the story.

There is a lack of dramatic suspense, and the general character of the story unreeled is ordinary. Jones as the hero and Maurice Flynn, the heavy, both play with an experienced technic. The leading woman's role by Ruth Clifford is similarly handled.

The action calls for exaggerated melodrama, and while the picture will have an appeal to the kids, who always were and always will be strong for westerns, it's pretty mild entertainment for adult intelligence.

An avalanche which entombs the three principals and another scene that has Jones making a getaway through a raging whirlpool on horseback are well produced. Photographically it averages with other westerns Jones has played in from time to time.

A bit done by some one not decipherable from the program in a prison scene is a first-rate piece of acting. This is the scene that has Jones presenting a prisoner with a Christmas gift.

The film makes a regulation one for the cheaper houses where program stuff is needed daily. *Bell.*

THE WHITE TIGER

Universal crook drama featuring Priscilla Dean. Story and direction by Tod Browning. Production time, 70 minutes. At the Broadway, New York, Nov. 20.

Universal just missed a one-hundred percenter in this production. They have a story packed with action, a high-grade production and excellent playing by several members of the cast, notably Wallace Beery, who does the heavy.

Heavy, florid titles make the picture drag.

The first good point is the well-wrought suspense of the interesting story, a crook drama of highly colored incident, and a well-built and effective finale which carries an especially strong punch.

Miss Dean scarcely comes up to the possibilities of the leading role, which calls for an actress of vigor and force rather than for one of her exquisite but aloof beauty. Also the costumer has handed her several costumes in strange taste. In one incident she walks down a noble staircase, dressed more like a "Follies" principal than a clever woman crook.

But the story holds through its length, long as it is. It starts with some shots in the London underworld, where one Hawkes betrays Donovan, another crook, to Scotland Yard. Donovan's two children are parted. Mary is carried off by Hawkes, who plans to train her to steal. Frank escapes and grows up in his own line of crime, but with a passion of vengeance against the man who killed his father. The girl in Hawkes' custody does not know his part in the treachery, but yearns to learn who killed the old man, upon whom she plans blood thirsty tortures.

Years later Frank is working the mechanical chess player in a Paris museum as a means of plying his pickpocket trade. Thither come Mary and Hawkes, also pickpockets.

The young people become friends, although they do not know their relation, nor the identity of Hawkes. Hawkes conceives the idea of taking the mechanical chess man to New York, framing to get into society there and make a big killing.

They rent a Fifth avenue mansion, where they meet a Mr. Leonard, who helps them into the best houses. Leonard's status is a mystery. From his actions, he might either be a Raffles or an aristocrat. The big job is pulled in the Bishop's home, and all three escape to Leonard's camp in the mountains.

The situation has all the time been growing more tense. Here it mounts to impressive heights. The three crooks become suspicious of each other until they become almost insane with distrust. Each thinks the others are trying to poison the food. But none can get away alone. The situation is complicated by the sudden appearance in evening clothes of Leonard, who advises that they give him the jewels for return to the owners.

He is accused of being a super-crook who is trying a double cross. Frank attacks Hawkes, having known all along that he is Donovan's betrayer, and is wounded, while Hawkes is driven raving into the mountains. Leonard and Mary then decide to make restitution. They are just bending over the hiding place of the loot when the police enter and are about to seize them, when a quick finish discloses that Leonard is really a man of rank. He dismisses the police with the explanation that the whole thing was a police experiment and the story closes with the boy restored, Leonard and the girl with a wedding in prospect and everything jake.

Good popular melodrama and promising box office feature. *Rush.*

TOILERS OF THE SEA

Released by the Community International Corporation and directed and supervised by R. William Neill. Distributed by Selznick. Suggested by the novel of Victor Hugo. Photography by Carl and G. Ventiniglia. At the Stanley, New York, Nov. 19. Runs 65 minutes.

The Priest .... Lucius Henderson
Helene .... Lucy Fox
Captain Andre .... Dell Cawley
Sandro .... Holmes E. Herbert

Although not as widely read as "Les Miserables" and "Notre Dame," "Toilers of the Sea" is one of the most striking and intelligent of the Hugo novels. But, tending as it does toward the descriptive and analytical, it is not as screenable as the other stories. R. William Neill has performed a moderately capable task considering the limitations and obstacles.

These limitations included the natural failure of the plot to measure up as either a particularly original or absorbing scenario, a cast of **newcomers with the only "name," the leading woman, badly miscast, and all the other difficulties attending the launching of a film by a heretofore unknown company. Neill went to Europe and apparently took along four American actors. The rest of the players and all the supers appear to be either Italians or Sicilians.**

The original Hugo story is but slightly adhered to, necessary perhaps to some extent, but not as much as here. Probably that is why the billing announces "suggested" by the novel. Neill has emphasized the love interest and entirely disregarded certain incidents, readable, but apt to prove ineffective on the screen. He has endeavored faithfully to reproduce the bits of local color and atmosphere, but has not been entirely successful. One reason is because Lucy Fox, who plays the heroine, is more the wholesome, robust Yankee matron than the delicate, romantic Helene of the story.

Photography bears a particularly important part in the production. The sea pictures are artistically focused, but not always as clear as they should be. There are some remarkable shots of a live volcano, where two men fight to a finish in a stream of burning lava. These scenes are the highlights of the film. The struggle is waged in the very path of the devouring flame and appears to be realistic.

Holmes E. Herbert, an ideal compound of the film Hercules and Apollo, plays the leading role in a manner that bespeaks a bright future for him in the school of rugged, virile heroes. The heavy, Captain Andre, is a departure from the ordinary as acted by Dell Cawley, who, with glasses and learned expression, is a scholarly sea captain. The Europeans in the cast over-act even more vociferously than in the recent German film importations.

Without the name Hugo, "Toilers of the Sea" wouldn't cause much furor around the box offices, but, particularly because of the success of the "Hunchback" film, it should be moderately successful in drawing them, if not in thrilling them.

IN SEARCH OF A THRILL

Metro picture, featuring Viola Dana from a story by Kate Jordan and Oscar Apfel, the director. Half of a double feature program at Loew's New York, Nov. 20. Running time, fifty-eight minutes.

Another inconsequential vehicle for Viola Dana, who never seems to get a "break" from those who are allotted the task of choosing her stories. If she's doing her own picking there's no one else to blame, but it's hardly plausible that anyone would have picked this narrative by choice in which to flaunt merrily forth. It screens as nothing above the average for intermediate houses, means nothing to Miss Dana and as little to Metro.

The tale relates how a young heiress investigates Paris in search of excitement. Bored with suitors, she again crosses the path of an author whom five years previously she would have married had he spoken. But being a man of principle his poverty, at that time, prevented the declaration. The girl being bequeathed a fortune further complicates matters so that when they meet within the Parisian atmosphere she is a true daughter of the rich while he also has prospered, but continues to be a most serious minded gentleman.

Spurning the frivolities of the girl's social set, including herself, the girl goes out after the writer by assuming the costume of an Apache and breaks into his home. Discovered and caught in the house by the author, himself, it leads to a visit to the slums, together, where he is in search of the atmosphere for his next book. The girl realizes the sham of her former mode of existence and the last moments fail to deviate from the convential terminations.

The picture is obvious at all times, backed by naught of the unusual either as to acting or production. A cabaret scene revealed Miss Dana in a most untasteful black evening gown, enhanced by white stockings, made to order for her leaving a table to dance with an entertainer that was beyond the bounds of all probability.

Included in the cast are Rosemary Theby, Warren Baxter, Robert Schable, Mabel Van Buren and Templar Saxe, all of whom turned in but mediocre support.

The film will neither do Miss Dana or Metro any good. *Skig.*

APRIL SHOWERS

B. P. Schulberg production, distributed by Preferred. Directed by Tom Forman and photographed by Harry Perry. Story and continuity by Hope Loring and Duryea Lighton. At Circle, New York, Nov. 20 as half double bill with "The Eternal Struggle." Runs 67 minutes.

Danny O'Rourke .... Kenneth Harlan
Maggie Muldoon .... Colleen Moore
Miriam Welton .... Ruth Clifford
Shannon O'Rourke .... Priscilla Bonner
Mother O'Rourke .... Myrtle Vane
Matt Gallagher .... James Corrigan

The film, "April Showers," bids fair to strike as responsive a chord of popular appeal as did the song of that name a few years ago. Every essential of the ideal Irish love story is to be found, and the picture may be ranked as one of the season's best light screen attractions.

Tom Forman, always one of the most human of directors, has performed his task splendidly, although it must be said that he had superlative material with which to work. The story is sure-fire all the way, the production costly and the cast almost perfect. Forman has not wrung his pathos dry, but puts it across with a wealth of simplicity and comedy relief that make it not the ordinary screen pathos, but genuine poignant human interest.

The action transpires in "Dugan's Alley," where "Big Tim" O'Rourke, fighting Irish cop and idol of the East Side, has given his life in performance of his duty. His son, Danny, aspires to his place on the force and is backed by the whole neighborhood, particularly Police Lieutenant Muldoon and his daughter, Maggie, who live next door. Danny and Maggie are typical Irish sweethearts, by which is meant they love to scrap, make up and then scrap some more.

But "April Showers" soon cloud the sky. Danny fails in his examinations and, worse than that, is almost vamped by the wealthy heiress who is doing settlement work. Then comes the worst crash. Danny's little sister, Shannon, frantic for some pretty clothes and goaded on by "Flash" Irwin (the kind O'Henry used to write about), has been shoplifting. Danny must replace the losses, and he is forced to become a prizefighter. Finally his fling at the champion comes. He learns the fight is crooked and that he is framed to win. He announces this to the fans, but the judges decide to let the fight go on and prove itself. The champion, incensed, realizes he must not stall now, and after a fierce struggle knocks Danny for the fatal count.

Danny is through as a boxer, but he wins his appointment to the force and wins Maggie besides. From a "flash" standpoint, there are several highlights to the picture. One is a cabaret scene with an underwater background. In this subterranean set mermaids, divers and large fish are seen swimming and swaying to the strains of a naval orchestra. Another incident is the dance at the settlement home. Forman has craftily introduced some of the never-failing bits of hoke attendant to a group of hoi polloi attempting to "put on the Ritz."

Besides, there are the fight scenes, full of action and not technical enough to bore the women and those not interested in boxing. But the real worth of the film comes in the simpler moments. One of these is when Danny comes home after finding he has failed in his examinations. Maggie is waiting for him in the rain on the corner and he hasn't the heart to tell her the bad news. He goes home to his expectant old mother, and there a genuinely touching scene takes place.

In a lighter vein we have the scene at the very end where Maggie comes to the hospital in which Dannie is recuperating after his greatest and last fight. She shows him an oil painting and says it is the man she is to marry. She has been studying correspondence school painting and working on this "portrait" during the times she has not been "mad" at her Danny. He looks at it and wants to know who it is, after which she becomes enraged all over again and asks him why he fails to recognize his own "bogtrottin' Irish mug."

Colleen Moore does the best work of her career as Maggie. There is no one on the screen who pouts as prettily as she does and very few who act in general as well. Kenneth Harlan is very likable and sincere as Danny and the balance are entirely admirable in their respective roles.

While the story is perhaps trite and adds nothing of intrinsic value to the screen, the film should be a winner anywhere. Probably one reason it is so successful is that almost everyone connected with it except Messrs. Schulberg and Lichtman are Irish.

M'LORD OF THE WHITE ROAD

London, Nov. 6.

This latest Granger-Davidson picture is one of the best the firm has done. It is mainly Victor McLaglen, but McLaglen without a big fist fight. Fights he has in plenty, but they are with foils, and only once or twice does he show his capacity for handing out a straight hard punch.

The story is a good one and is well told, the continuity being excellent. Adapted from a novel by Cedric D. Fraser, it is laid in the Regency period, when men drank and rode hard and had little respect for women or for life.

Especially good is the production work scenically. The interiors are dignified and beautiful, while the exteriors contain some of the most beautiful shots of old English homes and scenery we have ever seen.

This picture carries atmosphere and a sense of the open road.

In the dual role of Lord Anderley and Shale, McLaglen gives a fine show. Fred Wright is excellent as Cherryblossom, and infuses certain comedy without being eccentric. Although capitally played, the other male parts do not count for much. Marjorie Hume is good as the Lady Gloria. Leslie Eveleigh's photography is very good. There is little doubt but that this picture will prove an excellent box-office attraction.

Gore.

TO THE LADIES

Farce-comedy. A James Cruze production, presented by Jesse L. Lasky. George S. Kaufman and Marc Connelly wrote the original, which as a stage play had a moderately successful run on Broadway last season. Walter Woods adapted it for the screen. At the Rivoli, New York, Sunday, Nov. 25. Running time, 70 minutes.

Leonard Beebe	Edward Horton
John Kincaid	Theodore Roberts
Elsie Beebe	Helen Jerome Eddy
Mrs. Kincaid	Louise Dresser
Chester Mullin	Z. Wall Covington
Mary Mullin	Patricia Palmer
Tom Baker	Arthur Hoyt
Bob Cutter	Jack Gardner

This is a good picture, but it could have been a better one if the subject matter had been treated strictly as satire instead of frequently falling into caricature, and pretty broad caricature at that.

Its inclination toward caricature was also a fault of the stage play. This broadening of effects in the picture may be due to the scenarist, the producer, the actors or orders to hoke it up may have been issued by those higher up than any of the factors mentioned. At any rate, it's there, and what could have been one of the finest examples of satire the screen has ever had becomes an exaggerated cartoon in far too many instances.

Possibly some one was afraid the grade of picture audience intelligence that revels in train wrecks, mob scenes and so-called "punches" wouldn't get "To the Ladies" unless it was clowned up a bit, and it's more than likely some one was right. For program pictures must be easy to understand, apparently, and it's too much of a task to lift the foreheads up to any appreciable degree; probably it's just as well not to be a missionary and to follow the herd by playing down to the narrow foreheads.

The film holds two separate and distinct themes—one that treats of the playing of office politics as it goes on daily, weekly and yearly in every mercantile organization throughout the civilized world, and the other which shows how the wives of the average employes in a business concern superintend, manage and generally direct the activities of their husbands. In "To the Ladies" the wife of the boss himself is always a step behind her husband and, paradoxically, a step ahead of him in his conduct of the business as far as his employes are concerned.

For one thing, the picture mercilessly shows up and pitilessly lampoons the bootlicker, sycophant and petty conniver who tries to secure commercial advancement by obviously currying favor with an employer. All of the cheap little tricks known to the art of jockeying for promotion and power are nicely strung together and made use of in the relating of the story in "To the Ladies."

The office sneak and tattler, the heavy guy who forces himself on the boss whether he's welcome or not—and it's mostly not in the picture—and the timid, recently married man who suffers from an inferiority complex as big as North America are all represented in character. And the characters are faithfully drawn as far as external characteristics are concerned, but overplayed generally and unnecessarily exaggerated.

An instance of this was in Edward Horton's playing of the banquet scene, one of the best scenes in the stage play and an excellent comedy scene in the picture. Horton rather than suggesting timidity and stage fright appears like a man who is suffering from a sudden attack of dementia.

Other scenes are similarly overdone. As a farce "To the Ladies" easily qualifies as excellent entertainment for the average picture fan. There's laughs in plenty and a story that rolls along with a tight continuity that never sags or breaks for a second.

With the story concerning the lives of every-day folk and marked with incidents that every one is familiar with, "To the Ladies" should find no difficulty in thoroughly amusing as a program feature. That it could have been a crackerjack comedy instead of a farce probably makes no particular difference.

Among those who do excellent work are Theodore Roberts, Helen Jerome Eddy, Louise Dresser, Jack Gardner, Z. Wall Covington and Arthur Hoyt.

Bell.

LIGHT THAT FAILED

Jesse L. Lasky presents a George Melford Production (Paramount-Famous Players) feature, adapted from Rudyard Kipling's novel of the same name, by F. McGrew Willis and Jack Cunningham. Projection time, 72 minutes. At the Rialto, New York, Oct. 25.

Bessie Broke	Jacqueline Logan
Dick Heldar	Percy Marmont
Torpenhow	David Torrence
Maisie Wells	Sigrid Holmquist
Madame Binat	Mabel Van Buren
Binat	Luke Cosgrave
Donna Lane	Peggy Schaffer
Young Dick	Winston Miller
Young Maisie	Mary Jane Irving

Here is a picture done in good technical style, technical as regards settings and backgrounds, and with a good deal of interesting detail. But the whole effect is spoiled by serious errors in casting, by the forcing of "the happy ending" and by certain unwarranted liberties the adapters have taken with the original.

The picture has been done previously with the Kipling original finale (the death of Dick at the front), and was well received; but in the present case the theory appears to be that film fans haven't sufficient intelligence to accept that idea. If any audience is simple enough to be satisfied with an ending that leaves the Kipling hero to a life of helplessness yoked to the Mazie Wells created by Sigrid Holmquist in this case and then call it a "happy ending," why pick on this particular novel when the world is deluged with ordinary fiction that the screen is perfectly welcome to cheapen and abuse?

The casting stops the story cold. Jacqueline Logan is made to play Bessie Broke, the drab rescued from the streets by the war correspondent and done up as a combination Kiki and Sadie Thompson from "Rain." The result is as far from the author's intention as they could possibly get. One would suspect that the adapters had seen the two plays and decided that since they have the public stamp of approval they couldn't be misplaced in any screen story. If "The Merry Widow" had been a current reigning success they would probably have dressed Bessie up in a picture hat and made her waltz through the picture.

So they make Bessie a creature of fire and sparkle, while Mazie is a lukewarm puppet without vigor or character. They manage to make a dignified figure out of the tragic Dick (in the distinguished person of Percy Marmont), but the best they could do for the upstanding Torpenhow was to put a stagey actor in the part.

The whole picture is a series of annoyances. Why should the adapters send Bessie to France to bring Mazie home when Kipling had it done by Torpenhow (and made mighty good reading out of the incident)? Why not have gotten some picturesque atmosphere out of Madame Binat? The scenes of desert fighting in the early part of the story are eminently fakey and unconvincing, although they did cut in a section showing London scenes that were genuine, although the principals were not concerned.

Probably Kipling is beyond the reach of satisfactory screening. Certainly the staging of "The Light That Failed" was an unhappy experience for the Kipling fans. When somebody tried to screen "Fisher's Boarding House" they made Ann of Austria a saintly madonna. Why can't they either do Kipling right or leave him alone? *Rush.*

LONG LIVE THE KING

Baltimore, Nov. 28.

The chief defect of the Jackie Coogan adaptation of Mary Rinehart's novel, "Long Live the King," is its length—an hour and 45 minutes. The interest doesn't hold that length of time; even Jackie's admirers yawning and and then during the running.

But at that, it's a good picture, though not up to the standard set by "Daddy" and "Circus Days."

Jackie plays little Prince Otto, grandson of the King of Livonia, whose days are to be few on earth. Prince Otto is rather bored with grand opera and the other trimmings that go along with the job of being crown prince, so he yearns for freedom.

Managing to evade his guardians, Otto toddles out into the great, throbbing world. Here he falls into a democratic young American who takes him for a roller coaster ride. When young Otto returns he finds the royal castle in a turmoil over his disappearance, and thereafter he is more closely watched than ever.

Comes his birthday. Again he slips out from under the watchful eyes of his guardians. There is a big scene of a street carnival into which Jackie precipitates himself in characteristic manner, and, meeting his American friend, goes with him to his birthday party.

At the moment of drinking the king's health the bells toll forth the announcement of the old monarch's death. Otto rushes off to the castle but on the way is captured by a tribe of anarchists.

Ensue complications. Prince Otto escapes their clutches with almost the same ease he got away from his guardians and arrives at the conventional balcony in ample time to win the plaudits of his multitudes—a most effective scene.

Coogan carries off the honors with the savoir faire of a veteran. His facial by-play is often remarkable. Something, too, should be said for the supporting cast. There were some important names in it, and their work was most effective. Included were Rosemary Theby as the Countess Olga, and Ruth Renick and Princess Renick, whose affairs supplied the heart interest for the film, and Alan Hale and Alan Forest.

Coogan was supplied with the most magnificent settings he has ever had in any of his pictures. Metro claims to have spent $600,000 in the making, but it was spent so well from a photographic standpoint that the claim could have been boosted to a million.

A whole European court has been constructed, and the atmosphere is convincing; in addition there are spectacular high spots that add to the production's impressiveness. The carnival scenes are fine and full of color, and the scenes in the castle, with the high vaulted rooms and effective lighting, are among the most superb settings we have seen in a long time. *Cooling.*

THIS FREEDOM

From the novel of the same name by A. S. M. Hutchinson, directed by Denison Clift, and featuring Fay Compton. A Fox picture opening at the Central, New York, under a "continuous" policy Nov. 26. Running time, 83 minutes.

The Rev. Harold Aubyne .... Fewlass Llewellyn
Mrs. Aubyn .... Adeline Hayden-Coffin
Rosalie, their daughter, at 6 .. Bunty Fosse
Rosalie, 17 to 40 .... Fay Compton
Hilda } Rosalie's sisters { Joan Maude
Flora } Rosalie's sisters { Faith Garden
Anna } Her brothers ... { Iris Delaney
Harold } Her brothers ... { Percy Field
Robert } Her brothers ... { Mickey Brantford
Gertrude, the maid .... Gladys Hamer
Aunt Belle .... Gladys Hamilton
Uncle Pyke .... Charles Vane
Laetitia, their daughter .... Julie Hartley-Milburn
Miss Keggs ("Keggo") .... Athene Seyler
Harry Occleve, Rosalie's husband .... Clive Brook
Mr. Sturgiss (of Field & Co.) .... Myddleton Evans
Mr. Field .... Robert English
Huggo, at 8 } Rosalie's children. { Maurice Hopkins
Huggo, at 22 } Rosalie's children. { John Stuart
Doda, at 6 } Rosalie's children. { Betty Gardner
Doda, at 20 } Rosalie's children. { Nancye Kenyon
Benji, at 3 } Rosalie's children. { Tony Laing
Benji, at 17 } Rosalie's children. { Albert Brantford

Mayhaps a corking novel, but not overly impressive as screen material. In book form the story caused diversified comment. Seemingly, much of the percentage of its sale can be blamed upon "If Winter Comes," which preceded from the same author.

The simile may prove to be true in reference to the screen versions of both novels as regards the box office, but "This Freedom" carries a theme that has often seen projection within the confines of the intermediate houses and it is not above indulging in dramatics of the type that are now almost obselete among the cheaper productions.

Added to which there is a decisive incline toward tediousness which is fatal and should undergo correction, by deletion, when the picture reaches the regular houses.

Understood to have been "shot" in England, and comprising an all-English cast, Fay Compton, in the role around which the entire story revolves, by far predominates over and above any other supporting member. Miss Compton will hardly startle the average American audience with her Rosalie, but it suffices here.

Whether the filming closely adheres to the original script or not cannot be stated, but from general hearsay it would seem the story has lost some of its value in the transmission to the screen. Certain it is that there is a dire lack of action which the narrative is incapable of overcoming through interest, with the permittance of a retarded tempo in the telling emphasizing the situation.

Briefly, the story tells of a woman who devotes her life to a business career, thereby utterly neglecting her home life, which culminates in the death of the daughter and the sending to prison of one of the sons. Betwixt and between is placed the home atmosphere, which is responsible for Rosalie's determination to live her own life, the manner in which she is regarded by her children during the time they inhabit their playroom and the aftermath of Rosalie being held responsible for all the misfortune and her realization of the truth of the accusation.

The photography and production are appropriate, with but elimination necessary to make it an average feature on the strength of the book sale. *Skig.*

THE DAY OF FAITH

Goldwyn presentation. Tod Browning production, and adapted from Arthur Somers Roche's story by June Mathis and Katherine Kavanaugh. At the Capitol, New York, Nov. 25. Running time, 75 minutes.

Jane Maynard .... Eleanor Boardman
Michael Anstell .... Tyrone Power
Tom Barnett .... Raymond Griffith
John Anstell .... Wallace MacDonald
Montreal Sammy .... Ford Sterling
Yegg Darby .... Charles Conklin
Granny Maynard .... Ruby Lafayette
Red Johnson's Child .... Jane Mercer
Uncle Mortimer .... Edward Martindel
Bland Hendricks .... Winter Hall
Simmons .... Emmett King
Red Johnson .... Jack Curtis
Marley Maynard .... Frederick Vroom
Isaac .... John Curry
Samuel Jackson .... Henry Hebert
Kelly .... Myles McCarthy
Morris .... Robert Dudley

A melodramatic story based upon the psychology that faith will cure anything, superbly directed and unusually cast. The story in the screen transition covers too much territory and becomes far fetched. It is saved from mediocrity by the direction and cast.

"My Neighbor is Perfect" is the slogan adopted by Bland Hendricks, a small town philanthropist. He befriends a wandering yegg and saves him from arrest. The yegg commits a burglary and is indirectly responsible for the death from heart failure of the invalid house owner.

The dead man's daughter swears revenge. A mob attacks the philanthropist and he dies after the manhandling. The girl could have saved him, but doesn't. She repents and starts a mission in New York, using the slogan.

Millionaire's son falls in love with her, but his cynical father thinks her an adventuress and determines to ridicule her out of town by using his own newspaper. The cynical star reporter succumbs to her charms and is cured of lameness when he attempts to save another lame youngster from a fall.

The rich man determines to use the faith cure to create good will for himself and his own nefarious schemes. He promises to establish missions all over the world. He hires "fakers" and "dummy throwers" to feign miraculous cures, but all attempts to scoff are defeated. His own son is finally killed by a mob led by his private secretary, a son of one of his ruined victims. The picture terminates with the girl marrying the cynical reporter and the financial giant converted to the slogan, "My Neighbor Is Perfect."

The picture drags immeasurably in spots, but is exceptionally well acted. Eleanor Boardman in the principal role was excellent. Her emotional work was convincing and flawless. Ford Sterling turned in an excellent bit of character work as "Montreal Sammy." Tyrone Power as the financial wiz was well cast and convincing.

Despite its lapses this latest Goldwyn will interest the lovers of sentiment and thrills, for it embodies enough of each to make it safe from a box office angle. *Con.*

TIGER ROSE

Baltimore, Nov. 28.

Warner Brothers-Belasco production starring Lenore Ulric. Screen adaptation of the Willard Mack-David Belasco play by Edmund Goulding and Millard Webb; director, Sidney Franklin. Running time, 90 minutes.

Rose Bocion (Tiger Rose) ...... Lenore Ulric
Michael Devlin .... Forrest Stanley
Father Tibault .... Joseph Dowling
Pierre .... Andre DeBeranger
Dr. Cusick .... Sam De Grasse
Bruce Norton .... Theodore Von Eltz
Hector McCollins .... Claude Gillingwater

Lenore Ulric has created a living, breathing, character—screen person—in "Tiger Rose." Her performance is as individual and convincing as her part in "Kiki." The play loses little in translation for the screen; in many places it may be said to have gained.

The play has considerable of the much overworked Northwest Mounted Police hero: in it, but the threads are so deftly twisted that this becomes apparent only upon cold appraisal. It is seldom that one gets the opportunity to view a film in which the pictorial possibilities have been made so much of.

There are some extraordinarily tense moments and spectacular appearing stunts in the film. Attention is gained almost at the outset by a leap that Devlin, or his double, does. It is a jump from a high, over-hanging bank into swift waters that carry both the policeman and the girl on the raft perilously close to rapids. Faultlessly photographed.

The hand of Belasco is apparent in the settings. The interiors had the Belasco solidity; the clock kept time; the trapdoor to the cellar had hinges, but Miss Ulric wasn't as wet as she could have been when coming out of the water.

Something should be said, too, in credit to the cast. All of the major roles were capably acted. Forrest Stanley was a most engaging young Irishman, member of the Northwest Mounted; Theodore Von Eltz made a most acceptable hero, even though he did forget that his arm was presumably wounded. Claude Gillingwater, with the flowing beard, was convincing enough as Hector McCollins, the foster father of Tiger Rose. *Cooling.*

ST. ELMO

Fox production directed by Jerome Storm. Taken from the novel by Augusta Evans. Scenario by Jules Furthman, and photography by Joe August. At Loew's New York, Nov. 22. Running time, about 80 minutes.

St. Elmo Thornton .... John Gilbert
Agnes Hunt .... Barbara La Marr
Edna Earle .... Bessie Love
Murray Hammond .... Warner Baxter
Alan Hammond .... Nigel De Brulier
Mrs. Thornton .... Lydia Knott

Overflowing with cheap heroics of the Bertha M. Clay-Laura Jean Libbey style is this screen adaptation of Augusta Evans' once famous story. The sentimental reading public took to it as they have since to "Three Weeks" and "The Sheik."

It was then produced in play form and again achieved popular success, although panned by the critics. After this it was released for stock and except for "Uncle Tom's Cabin" there has been no more consistently successful stock play in the last generation.

Jerome Storm received the directing assignment from Fox. Some years ago one of the smaller companies produced a film adaptation of the same story, but in those days the industry was in its infancy, and the picture passed out almost unnoticed.

It seems Storm set about producing this new version with the wrong idea in mind. Instead of the character of St. Elmo (who is the hero and not the name of a hotel) Storm left the tawdry, unnatural figure of the novel strutting around in riding clothes with a sneer on his coldly handsome countenance. The plot is meagre, and there was a need to drag out the incidents for more than an hour and a quarter. Storm certainly allowed it to drag unmercifully. No comedy relief, and for the last half hour the action centers around only two characters, St. Elmo and Edna, the girl.

John Gilbert does as well with the impossible leading role as anyone else might, but that only means his performance was sincere and spirited though artificial and unconvincing. Miss Love has her moments of poignant charm and Barbara La Marr, Warner Baxter and the others do capable work. Fox has not held on expense, as both interiors and outdoor shots display lavish care.

With the combination of an extremely well known title and a cast with a strong draw, the picture may be a ready-made box office winner. But the discriminating will pan it and the average film-goer will feel not a little envy for his soundly sleeping neighbors in the audience.

THUNDERING DAWN

Universal production, directed by Harry Garson. Written by John Blackwood and adapted by Raymond Schrock. Scenario by Lenore Coffey and John Goodrich. At the New York Nov. 26. Runs about 70 minutes.

Phoebe Standish .... Georgia Woodthorpe
Mary Rogers .... Anna Q. Nilsson
John Standish .... Winter Hall
Jack Standish .... J. Warren Kerrigan
Morgan Sprott .... Charles Clary
Gordon von Brock .... Tom Santschi

Michael Carmichael..........Edward Burns
The Professor...............Richard Kean
Lullaby Lou...............Winifred Bryson

"Thundering Dawn" suffers from the plaint of so many of our program pictures—sameness; sameness not only in story, but in directorial touch, in Thespian work and in the all-important bits that lend color and individuality to a film.

It is the conventional South Sea formula, with the raging elements used to contrast the storm going on within the soul of the derelict hero.

South Sea tales are naturally colorful and can stand a good deal of hard usage. For that reason, although the present picture hardly differs from a hundred of its predecessors, it holds consistent absorption and a climax of dramatic intensity.

The action takes place in Java, and Universal has provided settings that, while not always realistic, lend the satisfactory atmosphere of palms, indolent South Sea natives and torpid, sun-scorched climate.

The plot is subsidiary to the physical and technical side of the film.

J. Warren Kerrigan is manly enough as the unfortunate hero, but in the more violent scenes overacts badly. This fault is noticeable in the majority of the members of the cast. Anna Q. Nilsson is her usual refreshing self. Winifred Bryson is one of the newer school of vamps. Could Miss Bryson act as well as she looks she would give the Misses Naldi, La Marr et al. a real run.

Harry Garson directed and daubed on the local color too thickly in places. Two or three of the characters introduced in the South Sea "honky-tonk" scenes are impossible.

THE VIRGINIAN

Preferred Pictures production adapted from the story by Owen Wister. Script by Hope Loring and Louis S. Lighton. Directed by Tom Forman. Shown at the Broadway, (N. Y.) week Nov. 20, 1923. Running time 73 minutes.
Virginian................Kenneth Harlan
Molly Woods.............Florence Vidor
Trampas..................Russell Simpson
Steve.......................Pat O'Malley
Shorty...................Raymond Hatton

This production of the famous far west story written by Owen Wister and afterwards adapted for the stage by Kirke La Shelle, despite there was a tremendous financial outlay in making it, ranks as just above the average western. There isn't a thing about the picture that is going to set the world afire, and nothing about it that is going to make the public break down the doors to any theatre where it is showing. In other words, it is a fairly well acted western, with the usual riding junk cut out of it.

Photographically it is a work of art. It is the photography that is the outstanding feature of the production. Other than that there is nothing that can be designated as particular cause to enthuse.

The story is fair enough in its way. The direction fairly human, the continuity a little choppy at times, the portrayal of the roles by the company not outstanding. The casting of the picture possibly was something of the reason for it failing to get over with a wallop. There are names enough in the cast, names that have screen value, but not the right names for this picture.

Kenneth Harlan is a mighty matter of fact Virginian; Florence Vidor not particularly impressive as Molly Woods and far from sympathetic. The Trampas of Russell Simpson made one want to see Bill Hart in the role again, and all of the cowboy bar-room comedy stuff was lost in the shuffle. As a big western, better than the regular state rights westerns, yes, but as a special it doesn't rank. *Fred.*

YESTERDAY'S WIFE

C. B. C. picture featuring Irene Rich and Eileen Percy. Adapted from a story by Evelyn Campbell with Ed Le Saint directing. Cast includes Lottie Williams, Lewis Dayton, Philo McCullough and William Scott. Half of a double feature program at Loew's New York, Nov. 23. Running time, 74 minutes.

A fair enough intermediate feature that would have enhanced its value by the elimination of some 15 minutes. As it stands the picture is a comedy drama that should fulfill its obligation in a middle class house. The work of the two predominating women is adequate, as might with a "break" be said of the remainder of the cast. Regarding production, the film, at one or two points, hints at being pretentious without ever quite reaching that classification.

The story is that of a married couple who are divorced, with the woman becoming a paid companion to a rich and scheming dowager, while the man again undertakes matrimony, this time selecting his telephone operator. Under those circumstances the two meet, which, between the muddling dowager and the flippant but former switchboard miss, leads to various stereotyped mixups. It culminates in the death of the second wife, through a boat accident, and the remarriage of the original duo.

Splitting a double feature at the New York the picture gave evidence of witnessing, albeit, at various intervals, the tale has a tendency to become lax and drags unnecessarily. *Skig.*

"Sir Loin" Shown in Chicago May Interest Cattlemen —Defects Easily Seen With Likelihood No Professional Players in Cast

Chicago, Dec. 5.

Propaganda film put out by the United States Department of Agriculture in three reels, shown for the first time publicly at the Live Stock show in Chicago. The names of the members of the cast are not given. It is not likely that any of the players are professionals or that the film was constructed under professional supervision. The film is described as "a story of beef from the plains to the plates."

"Sir-Loin," the star of a new propaganda film, described as "of T-Bone Ranch," is a prize bull. The propaganda of the film may be an urge to cattle raisers to provide themselves with a prize "Sir Loin," or it may be that the aim of the picture is to induce girls from the city to go to the country.

It is a photoplay which will interest cattlemen and appeal to all those who are interested in either the great west or cattle raising.

The story concerns a young man Robert West, shown at his home in the great west and on a trip to the city, and his final arrival there and his meeting with Virginia Lee, a city girl, who had been born in the cattle country. Then it carries West back to a lonely position on the plains, where he dreams of the girl. The next step is to show her succeed in getting a position as school teacher. After she has been at this work for a time she attends a rodeo and the star of the afternoon is Mr. West. They meet. She visits at his ranch and is entertained by his mother. He shows her around.

The cattle scenes and the ranch scenes where plans are laid to reap hay to feed the cattle during the winter are interesting. The love touch is not overdone, and there is just enough of the joint attraction of the pair for those who see the picture to know that it is "true love."

Without making any inquiries regarding the picture it is a safe bet to say that it was assembled with some difficulty, for there are so many noticeable defects that if the picture was forced to stand for President Coolidge's best, there would be a chance of Henry Ford being drafted for President.

The cattle are without horns in one scene and with long horns in the next. The cattle run on hills without trees in one scene, and there are trees all about in the next. From a single location Mr. West and Miss Lee look around at mountains on one side and a seemingly never-ending plain on the other side. The girl is riding in knickerbockers, gets off her horse and is in skirts.

The rodeo scene displays some splendid riding, and the scene where the ranchman takes his aunt living in the city through a meat market in order to show her how to buy choice meat is not uninteresting to the layman. The hard work the city folks have in cutting their meat at the dinner table is overdone.

The fact that the principals dine on "ranch-killed" meat when out west seems to be a slap at the packing concerns.

RENO

San Francisco, Dec. 5.

"Reno" is Goldwyn propaganda against the conflicting divorce laws of the United States. When you are divorced in Nevada it doesn't mean anything in some other state, or vice versa. The film was given its premiere at the California here Saturday.

While it is a good picture it loses some of its effectiveness because of the supposedly funny subtitles—written with an idea of convulsing the audience and furnishing most of the comic relief. These titles are nothing more than adequate.

The film has a punch which is a knockout in two ways: The start of the thriller business is in an automobile chase through Yellowstone park, and has its climax in a fight which is staged high on a cliff above one of the big geysers. With the geyser spouting and the fight on it makes great entertainment.

The story tells of Roy Tappam (Lew Cody), a much-married man, who is introduced in Reno as he is about to take on the shackles of matrimony for the third time. The deserted second wife (Helene Chadwick) is pictured in Atlantic City, almost penniless, with her two children. A former suitor who is very wealthy appears and renews his suit, and is accepted, but a lawyer friend warns them not to live together, as she (second wife) is still Mrs. Tappam except in Nevada.

The two couples are used as pawns in Rupert Hughes' game of showing the status of each in various states, and as the action shifts this is accomplished.

The story is good but ends abruptly, losing a little effectiveness. *Rivers.*

TIGER ROSE

Sidney Franklin Production presented by the Warner Bros. and David Belasco, starring Lenore Ulric, from the play by Willard Mack and David Belasco, adapted by Edmund Goulding. Shown at the Rivoli, New York, week Dec. 2. Running time, 77 minutes.
Rose Bocion.....................Lenore Ulric
Michael Devlin............Forrest Stanley
Father Thibault............Joseph Dowling
Pierre...................Andre De Beranger
Dr. Cusick...............Sam De Grasse
Bruce Norton............Theodore Von Eltz
Hector MacCollins......Claude Gillingwater

Northwest mounted picture that made its bid for fame as a play. The star of the screen version is the same that carried the play to popularity.

Otherwise it is just another northwest mounted, just the same in type as a hundred or more others that have gone before it, and were it not that Lenore Ulric gives a really remarkable screen performance (so different from the one that she gave when she made her film debut some years ago) the picture would have nothing particularly to recommend it. But the combination of Lenore Ulric and "Tiger Rose" should draw fair patronage.

The picture is one of the series of Belasco productions the Warner Bros. are presenting. At the Rivoli Sunday night it pulled terrific business, but Monday night the business was far from capacity at both night shows. That was on Broadway. In the towns where they have not seen Miss Ulric but have heard of her as a Belasco star she should be a real box office magnet.

The production is picturesque, the locations outdoors are beautiful scenically, but scenery won't bring them to the box office. In suspense the picture has a couple of thrilling moments that were cleverly handled by the director, Sidney Franklyn.

In the cast Forrest Stanley plays the role that was originated by Willard Mack, and he gives a corking performance of the Northwest Mounted cop. Theodore Von Eltz plays opposite the star and registers emphatically as the lover, while Joseph Dowling and Sam De Grasse, both veterans of many a hard-fought screen battle, deliver in their accustomed manner, as does also Claude Gillingwater.

"Tiger Rose" with a strong accent on Lenore Ulric and the Belasco connection will get money, not to the extent of breaking records, but it will roll up a nice comfortable average gross for the majority of houses that play it. *Fred.*

LONG LIVE THE KING

Metro picture starring Jackie Coogan. Adapted by C. Gardner Sullivan from the original story of Mary Roberts Rinehart, with Victor Schertzinger director. Showing at the Rialto, New York, week of Dec. 2. Running time, 96 minutes.

Crown Prince Otto	Jackie Coogan
Countess Olga	Rosemary Theby
Princess Hedwig	Ruth Renick
Archduchess Annunciata	Vera Lewis
King Karl	Alan Dale
Nikky	Alan Forrest
The Chancellor	Walt Whitman
The King	Robert Brower
Bobby	Raymond Lee
Old Adelbert	Monti Collins
Black Humbert	Sam Appel
Herman Spier	Larry Fisher
Bobby's Father	Alan Sears

Shaping up as one of the best efforts Jackie Coogan has given to the screen, and but for a few lax moments, due to superfluous footage, entertainment of the best, with young Coogan showing to superlative advantage.

"Long Live the King" will likely be ranked alongside of his "Oliver Twist." For individual effort on the part of the child star and the film's actual ability to please, mayhap it will top the Dickens picturization.

The film has about all the requirements with the one fault of an overly played-up atmosphere effect that, placed late, was unnecessary. Otherwise it's a corking effort on the part of the producing company, star, cast, camera men and director.

The screening appears to have adhered more or less faithfully to the novel, although the usual licenses have been taken to permit some additional mannerisms by Jackie.

Located in one of those musical comedy countries, the tale relates of a plot to overthrow the ruling dynasty to which Crown Prince Otto (Coogan) is the heir apparent upon the death of his grandfather.

Meanwhile the story mainly concerns itself with the trials and tribulations of the Crown Prince, who is subjected to an overbearing aunt and never can get away long enough to enjoy himself.

The climax revolves around the kidnapping of the youngster upon the day the country is celebrating his birthday, the cause for a realistic fight by the Prince's personal aide. It precedes the rescue and the dash to the palace in time for the child ruler to make his appearance on the balcony. For the death of the king is signalized in the midst of the festivities.

Of the cast Alan Forrest, in the "pie" role of the youngster's personal attendant, inclines to stand out, although the support accorded by the large personnel is at all times capable, if not more. Scenically the picture has been outfitted with a production that reveals some massive interiors, while the exterior flashes of the palace and carnival will undoubtedly attract attention.

Granted that at intervals the individual efforts and given action to the child star closely resemble outright "hoke," the bits, nevertheless, register for their full worth, and through the child's appeal are forgivable.

The picture unquestionably is a credit to Metro, Coogan, Sullivan and Schertzinger, and should go a long way in sustaining this youngster's drawing power in any film theatre in any country. *Skig.*

ANNA CHRISTIE

Thomas H. Ince production, from the play by Eugene O'Neil. Adapted by Bradley King; directed by John Griffith Wray. Special showing for National Board of Review, Town Hall, Nov. 28, 1923. Running time, 87 minutes.

Anna Christie	Blanche Sweet
Chris	George Marion
Matt Burke	William Russell
Marthy	Eugene Besserer

"Anna Christie" had the honor of being the first picture of the season of 1923-4 chosen for a special showing before the National Board of Review, which makes a specialty of picking the exceptional photoplays of the year for special performances for their membership.

"Anna Christie" proved itself worthy of the honor. It is a picture that is interesting. It is a picture that is as different to the regular runs of screen productions as the Eugene O'Neil plays are to the majority of hits and near-hits that come to the spoken stage; but, still, there is going to be a question whether or not it is going to pull money to the picture theatre box offices the country over. The reason for this is that Eugene O'Neil and his "Anna Christie" is not known to every exhibitor and picture fan of the country as the author and his play are known in New York, and it is going to be up to the exhibitor to go out and sell his public the idea that this is something different. If he can do that, then the picture will get money.

It is going to be interesting to watch the progress of this picture as it plays around the country, for it is going to be a criterion to go by.

At first glance "Anna Christie" doesn't look like a picture that is going to burn up Broadway, but it is a picture that will do business on Broadway as well as anywhere else. It seems like a picture that will build in business after the first day in the other places away from Broadway, for it is a picture that must compel word-of-mouth advertising.

There is one mistake John Griffith Wray made in the direction. In the usual picture fashion he tried to force his leading woman to overshadow the character role. Blanche Sweet wasn't the "Anna Christie" Pauline Lord was on the spoken stage, but George Marion was Chris, and as such he so far overshadowed the leading woman the director was undoubtedly forced to take the extremes he did to keep her in the eye of the audience. But that was not good direction.

William Russell made Matt Burke a convincing sort of a brute Irish coal passer on a steam tramp and put over his role with a wallop, and likewise did Eugene Besserer handle Marthy, so that in all Miss Sweet was the only weak spot of the cast of four.

The Pennsylvania Board is said to have ordered 28 cuts in the picture as it was shown at the Town Hall, New York. If that is the case there is a great argument against censorship in this picture.

The story as originally played on the stage was infinitely added to by the prefacing that the adaptor did in making the screen version, which in other respects sticks faithfully to the play. *Fred.*

PALACE OF THE KING

Goldwyn Production, directed by Emmett Flynn, written for the screen by June Mathis from the story by F. Marion Crawford. Shown at the Capitol, New York, week Dec. 2, 1923. Running time, 78 minutes.

Dolores Mendoza	Blanche Sweet
Don John	Edmund Lowe
Mendoza	Hobart Bosworth
Inez Mendoza	Pauline Starke
King Philip II	Sam de Grasse
Perez	William V. Mong
Princess Eboli	Aileen Pringle
Adonis	Lucien Littlefield
Gomez	Charles Clary
Alphonso	Harvey Clarke
Eudaldo	Tom Bates
Chamberlain	D. N. Clugston
The Guard	Charles Gorham
Captain of Guard	Jack Pitcairn
Guard	David Kirby
The Queen	Ena Gregory
Gaston	Bruce Sterling
Aide to Don John	Charles Newton

Another costume drama, one that has not an exceptional feature about it other than the cast. It is a screen vizualization of the story by F. Marion Crawford, adapted by June Mathis and directed by Emmett Flynn. The cast abounds with names, but in this late day after the market has been flooded with costume plays, exceptionally well done as to the matter of direction and thrills, this one seems rather tame and the cast not enough to put it over as a box office winner for the price that the exhibitor will be asked to pay for the picture.

"In the Palace of the King" looks to have had lots of money spent on it, but it is doubtful if it will ever step out of the red into the black as far as getting it back is concerned.

The story is another one of those romances laid in the royal court of Spain. This time during the reign of King Philip II, who was a murderer and a religious fanatic. His brother Don John of Austria is the hero, and the heroine Dolores Mendoza. These three roles are played by Sam De Grasse, Edmund Lowe and Blanche Sweet, respectively.

Don John is the warrior of the family and has been successful in a number of campaigns in behalf of Spain, thus having grown into tremendous popularity with his troops and likewise the people of the country. The King fears this popularity and sends his brother against the Moors in a religious war. Though on the verge of defeat because of the lack of co-operation at home, Don John finally turns the campaign into a triumph by utilizing the original K. K. K. method of driving the Moors in panic and chasing a lot of cooch dancers out of the tents in their encampment through lighting a fiery cross on the mountains opposite their stronghold.

He comes back to Spain, is supposedly killed by his jealous brother, but returns to life in time for a final clinch in the arms of his beloved after they both have gone through a series of complications that threatened to wreck their chances of happiness.

There are the usual tin hats of the usual costume play all over the place. There is the usual mob stuff with the soldiers storming the palace when they hear that their leader has been murdered. And likewise there is the usually scheming plotters who try to spill the beans whenever anyone is seemingly gaining favor with the King.

As the plotters William V. Mong and Aileen Pringle scored. The former with a clever performance and the latter because she looked like a million dollars. Edmund Lowe is getting to look more and more like John Barrymore on the screen every day. Incidentally he proved to be an acceptable lover in this case. Blanche Sweet played the heroine in most approved movie fashion, while Pauline Starke as her blind sister registered nicely in that role.

Emmett Flynn's direction was all that could be asked, but he did not drive home a single wallop. At times the action was decidedly draggy. The lightings and photography were pleasing, especially a few soft focus shots that were early in the picture. *Fred.*

THE NEAR LADY

Universal comedy, featuring Gladys Walton, from a story by F. R. Adams, with Herbert Blache directing. Cast includes Harry Mann, Kate Price, Florence Drew, Jerry Gendron, Otis Harlan, Emmett King and Harriet Floyd. Splitting a double feature one-day program at Loew's New York, Dec. 4. Running time, 58 mins.

An intermediate comedy that should satisfy in the middle class houses. The story is along a well-worn path, made so by poor families suddenly becoming rich and society representatives financially against the wall, with a daughter and son, respectively, the obvious means to a proverbial situation. It routines spasmodically for laughter, having a punch outburst at the extreme finish and in the form of a sub-title.

Miss Walton is the manicurist suddenly buried under an avalanche of coin who, through circumstances, becomes engaged to the social son, eventually "goes" for him, as he does for her, and the ceremony concludes.

Meanwhile is revealed the conventional "hoke" regarding the Schultz contingent attempting to live up to their wealth while the Van Bibbers tolerate the acquaintanceship in lieu of the money angle.

The work of Miss Walton befits, with Jerry Gendron doing nicely as the opposite half of the love-interest ingredient. Other than that, Florence Drew and Kate Price, as members of the Schultz regime, made their donations stand out for full value, while the former is allotted the laugh solo closing out at the termination of the film.

The picture pleased a Tuesday night audience on the Roof, having no minor portion of its entertainment qualities attributed to the titling, which provoked interspersed snickers throughout. *Skig.*

WHERE IS THIS WEST?

Universal release, from the story of George Hull, featuring Jack Hoxie, with George Marshall directing. At the Arena, New York, Nov. 30. Running time, 48 minutes.

Another of "U's" proverbial odes to the wide open spaces, revealing Hoxie in his oft-played role and containing little of specific interest other than that the cast includes Mary Philbin. It may be that this picture was made previous to "Merry Go Round," but if not, Universal seems to be wasting valuable talent and box office percentage in burying this young woman under such an intermediate release as this.

Following her performance in the "Merry" feature, Miss Philbin is deserving of better opportunities than this, and mayhap that should go for Hoxie as well.

Whether he can do anything before a camera sans boots, horses and guns remains in the air, but that he has hopes of getting away from the hectic action is hinted at in some press matter launched to the effect that Hoxie is desirous of "doing" Shakespeare.

Away from the propaganda, this particular Hoxie film resolves itself into just another Western that is meaningless, runs off the proverbial routine, but includes enough action to probably make it satisfactory before the audiences who inhabit the lower middle-class houses.

The story tells of a milkman and a waitress jointly inheriting a ranch as the basis for the Western migration, at which place the foreman takes it upon himself to scare the Easterners out of their intention to stick.

Included in the film is a badly pictured fake of a "stunt" that is so obvious as to make it well nigh an affront to an audience's intelligence. It shows Hoxie jumping a horse over a flat car of a freight train while the cars are in motion, and is such a mediocre attempt of double exposure as to fool no one.

Besides Hoxie and Miss Philbin, others in the cast are Sid Jordan, Bob McKenzie and Joseph Girard. All donate performances that suffice for the purpose in this more or less comedy that has the dominating figure, Hoxie, working on the level, or "straight," throughout.

The picture will likely satisfy in those houses where the patrons delight in applauding heroes rushing to the rescue of their damsels, but it's simply a matter of watching a succession of events that any one who sees pictures intermittently knows what is coming 500 feet ahead. *Skig.*

LADY HAMILTON

Sterling Production release by Hodkinson, starring Liane Haid. Shown at the Stanley, New York, Dec. 4. Running time 95 minutes.

This isn't a new picture. It must have been hanging around New York for some little time. Just how long the Hodkinson organization has been handling it is in doubt, but it is a picture. It is one of those that the smaller exhibitor can get for a price and, if he is smart, build it into a corking box-office card.

It all depends on the exhibitor and how he handles his house and advertising matter. The title "Lady Hamilton" means nothing. Liane Haid, who is starred, likewise is nil as far as advertising value is concerned, but the picture itself is one of those that is there.

It is just another of those big German affairs that were made during the war. It is the "inside stuff" on history of old England. The Germans were using the early history of all of the nations opposed to them in war to disclose the illicit love affairs of the great heroic characters their enemies worshipped.

Had this picture been properly handled it would have topped "Passion" at its best, for this is an interesting story of the manner in which a little greengrocer's daughter, through love affairs, finally achieved the station of Lady Hamilton, and her affair later with Lord Nelson, by whom she had a child just prior to her husband's death.

And, oh boy, the manner in which it is done! Even in the American censored version there is enough to slip the thrills over the plate when it comes to the undraped, and one can well imagine what it must have been as shown in Germany.

Any live exhibitor can take this in any town where it hasn't been played and work up interest in it if he goes after it right and put it over for a box-office winner. Don't try to get by with it by just sticking a three-sheet out in front, but shoot the works in an advertising way and make 'em believe it. In college and school towns it should be pie for the rousing of the history sharks at the local institution. Incidentally there is in addition enough pictorial stuff, intrigue and romance to the picture to make it mighty interesting to the average picture house audience. There are laughs, too, and acting such as only the Germans manage to get over on the screen when it comes to characterization.

Incidentally this Liane Haid, who is starred, appears to be a better screen bet than Pola Negri ever could have been from the first flash that we got in this country of Negri in "Passion." Miss Haid is "there" and should be brought across, and then sent across. *Fred.*

PASSIONATE FRIENDS

Taken from the novel by H. G. Wells and presented by George H. Davis of the C. B. C. Film Sales Corp. Directed by Maurice Elvey. At the Stanley Nov. 28. Running time, 70 minutes.

H. G. Wells, like most of the other great contemporaneous novelists, has written several books that seem more eloquent of his pocketbook than of his brain and soul. The person unfamiliar with the book who sees this picture will feel sure that it is adapted from one of the "potboilers." But Wells' numerous admirers claim "Passionate Friends" to be one of the most searching and intelligently written of his books.

Therefore, the deplorable part of the film is not that it is adapted from the Wells novel, but that it is so miserably adapted, and that H. G.

himself, according to an announcement, assisted with the direction. The plot as expounded in the picture holds considerable absorption and much of the delicacy of touch characterizing the British writer's work.

It is a story of a man's love for two women. The remarkable part of it is that both loves are defended and justified. The hero, jilted by the girl he adores, marries another, who has long cherished him. He never loses the love for the first woman, but with the passing years becomes more and more devoted to the little wife who, realizing his heart is divided, has been so tolerant. The husband of the other woman is jealous and suspicious and, believing there is cause for divorce, threatens to sue his wife, mentioning the hero as corespondent. The disillusioned woman, although entirely innocent, resolves to save the man she loves and the wife he is learning to care for. When all else fails she shoots herself. Her memory is cherished by the man who has always loved her and who now has learned to worship his own wife as well.

The cast is not billed, and it is just as well, because nothing favorable might be said about any member of it. The actors are all British, as is the direction and the locale in which the film was shot. Aside from the original story, only some of the photography and a striking fight scene in a typical London club stand out as better than mediocre. One of the worst faults of the picture from the viewpoint of the average American audience is that there is not one really pretty woman in it, a most unpardonable sin to a nation that exalts beauty contests at $5.50 a throw.

The film can only play the cheapest houses, and as the name Wells means considerably less there than in the more highbrow places, it seems to be S. O. L. all around.

THE EXILES

Fox Film production. John Gilbert featured. At Loew's New York Nov. 30. Running time, 75 minutes.

"The Exiles" is a gripping tale of a woman wrongly convicted of a murder on circumstantial evidence, for about four-fifths of the way. There is a compactness and coherence in the telling of this part of the story that keeps the eyes of the spectator glued right on the silver sheet without a distracting incident to cause interest to waver even slightly, and the same goes for the portion devoted to the district attorney's search for the persecuted girl even for considerable footage after he finds her in Algiers.

But when the battle arrives between the conscience-stricken prosecutor and the villain, the tale grows verbose and prosy, the action slowing down to a funereal pace. The fight itself is too broken up—lasts too long and covers too much territory, leaving the last "act" a tedious ordeal.

Care in putting on the court-room stuff reflects credit on the director and the atmosphere of the Algerian scenes is also authentically suggested.

John Gilbert makes a capable acting leading man of the matinee idol heroic type, and the part of the girl is also finely handled. All of the acting, in fact, is very good.

If the last part had held up as well as the first four-fifths, "The Exiles" would have been a much better picture than it is. As it stands, it qualifies as part of a double-feature bill satisfactorily for houses like Loew's New York. *Bell.*

PRINCE CHARLIE

London, Nov. 20.

The love story of Charles Stuart and Flora MacDonald is one of the

most beautiful in history, and the period in which they lived one of the most romantic. In making this latest Gaumont feature, C. C. Calvert has appeared to avoid these essential facts. There is not one thrill or heart-throb in the picture. It is colorless and insincere. The story as filmed is but a setting for many beautiful Highland scenes. Beautifully photographed, these charm the eye—and that is all there is to this story of '45. One of the most notable defects in the production rests in the pursuit and frequent escapes of the Young Pretender. Watching these, one gets the idea that Cumberland's men went out deliberately to allow him to escape.

The story keeps fairly close to history. Charles Stuart lands and is immediately surrounded by his faithful adherents. Edinburgh falls to him and at a state ball he meets Flora MacDonald. It is a case of love at first sight and she becomes his chief recruiting officer—a kiss goes with each white cockade. Then comes defeat, and with Charles a fugitive she still remains true and eventually helps him to make good his escape.

History records that the love between these two was of a virgin purity. The picture makes it a placid sort of affair, and without historical knowledge and the subtitles anyone would be excused for imagining there was no love as woman knows it for a man, but simply a staunch loyalty of a subject for a prince.

The playing cast is a good one. From a point of view of sheer good acting, A. B. Imeson leads with a fine but unfortunately very small character study of the Duke of Cumberland. He looks a soldier and a prince and more of him would have put some ginger into the picture. Hugh Miller gives a very good study of the treacherous Robert Fraser and Benson Klieve is capital as his hireling, Donald MacPherson. A capital little character study comes from Bromley Devonport as the English general, Sir John Cope. The present call for big names led to the engaging of Ivor Novello and Gladys Cooper for the leading parts. Novello turns out better than we expected, but has little of the soldier of fortune about him, while Gladys Cooper's performance of Flora MacDonald is chiefly an exposition of the physical beauty of the player. Their love-making they keep carefully to themselves and what the screen shows of it might be the timid adoration of any love-sick couple surrounded by none too sympathetic relatives. *Gore.*

THE SATIN GIRL

Ben Wilson production. Distributed by Ascher-Grand. Mabel Forrest, Marc McDermott and Norman Kerry featured. Directed by Arthur Rosson. "Mystery melodrama. At Loew's New York Nov. 30. Running time, 75 minutes.

Excellent program picture, with action that swings along at a fast, smooth gait, holding every minute the interesting mystery story is unfolding. The central female role is a sort of girl "Raffles"—full of ingenuous charm—and larceny.

The girl is induced to steal by a master-mind type of crook, an old fellow who wields a hypnotic influence over her. That recalls "Trilby," with the difference in Svengali's mesmeristic powers making Trilby sing instead of glomming everything in sight.

The master mind, it seems, is a sort of philanthropic thief, having the girl "Raffles" bring in the loot to secure funds which the master mind turns over to the poor.

A detective on the trail of the "The Satin Girl," so named because she always wears satin, furnishes a sharp conflict that keeps the plot sizzling from barrier to judges' stand.

Heart interest is provided through a doctor who, although suspecting

the "Satin Girl" not to be on the up-and-up, loves her just the same.

Sliding cellar doors, dark, mysterious underground chambers, stealthy footsteps, shadowy goings and comings and all the rest of the mystery technic have been deftly interwoven in the yarn. And yarn it is—for just as the spectator is about to decide the tale is a bit theatrical a flash shows the heroine reading it out of a book. It never happened, but it makes a very good story, anyway.

The book-reading thing is a second cousin to the dream idea, which has been worked considerably in pictures; but this is once where it doesn't appear to be dragged in as a squarer, as it happens along in an easy, logical way that convinces.

Scenes at a society function are properly staged. It really looks like a society racket, instead of a Saturday night rumpus of the Boiler Makers' Union in the local town hall.

Mabel Forrest can act, and does so with skill and intelligence. Then there's Marc McDermott, a character actor who classes with the very best of the screen's handful of good ones. Norman Kerry gives a dignified portrayal of the M.D., and the contributory parts are unusually well played.

This film was part of a double feature bill at Loew's New York, but it's strong enough to hold upon its own in the average type of house. *Bell.*

SLAVE OF DESIRE

Gilbert E. Gable presents melodramatic fantasy based on "The Magic Skin" by Honore de Balzac. Goldwyn distributes. George D. Baker directed and Charles Whittaker wrote the scenario. At Capitol, New York, Dec. 9. Running time 85 minutes.

Raphael Valentin............George Walsh
Pauline Gaudin....................Bessie Love
Countess Fedora..................Carmel Myers
Rastignac ....Wally Van
Antiquarian ....Edward Connelly
Mrs. Gaudin........................Eulalie Jensen
Mr Gaudin.........................Herbert Prior
Champrose ....William Orlamond
Tallifer ....Nicholas de Ruiz
The General...........Wm. von Hardenburg
Emile ....Harmon McGregor
The Duke.........................George Periolat
Finot ....Harry Lorraine
Major Domo....................Calvert Carter

An excellent entertainment different in many respects from the usual run of picture plays. The changing of the name of Balzac's classic "The Magic Skin" to "Slave of Desire" was a concession of course to the supposed liking of the rank and file picture fans for flashy titles. The adaptation gives the story as picturized a wealth of action with a quickly changing sequence of interesting episodes all compactly welded together in a manner that grips from leader to trailer.

The moral of the tale is that selfishness doesn't pay—a theme used quite frequently in literature and pictures, and while it contains a moral the film is not preachy or heavy in its promulgation of its object lesson.

In the screen version the director has modernized the fantastic story of the youth who possessed the magic skin which shrunk following the fulfillment of each succeeding wish with death looming as the ultimate outcome of his desires.

Inasmuch as this one made such a fine picture it would seem the classics of literature must hold a number of other stories that have not yet been done in films that would make equally good ones.

The cast is unusually good, George Walsh giving an interpretation of the principal male role that is convincingly sincere. Carmel Myers' vamp is also an outstanding characterization. Bessie Love has an ingenue part that she does perfectly and Wally Van gives the tale a touch of comedy relief with a finely balanced portrayal. The whole cast has been selected with intelligence and even the smallest parts are well played.

Scenically the film is much above the common place, the scenes in Paris in the attic home of the struggling poet in the first part of the picture being remarkably fine examples of photographic composition. Later in the scenes calling for interiors showing the home of the luxuriously housed Countess Fedora the back grounds are conspicuous for the sort of appointments a woman of the vampish noblewoman's wealth might be expected to boast of.

There's plenty of exciting melodrama notwithstanding the fact of the picture's high brow antecedents and it's all handled with an efficient directorial method that makes it click.

The antique shop scenes hold an element of mystery that adds charm to the unfolding of the story, and the introduction of the supernatural is adeptly manipulated.

It is a question whether the allegory that runs through the picture will be penetrated readily by the average picture patron but even if it isn't it should not materially affect their enjoyment of the film.

That's a danger perhaps the producer of the film will have to reckon with—the average picture fans are so used to trash and junk it is difficult to interest them in anything that even slightly borders on the highbrow. Gilbert E. Gable who presents the film deserves credit for getting out of the beaten path at any rate.

Bell.

DANGEROUS MAID

Constance Talmadge starred. Joseph M. Schenck presented First National release, directed by Victor Heerman. C. Gardner Sullivan's continuity from novel by Beth Ellis, "Barbara Winslow—Rebel." At Rivoli, New York, week Dec. 9. Runs 71 minutes.

Barbara Winslow......Constance Talmadge
Capt. Miles Prothero.......Conway Tearle
Col. Percy Kirk..........Morgan Wallace
Sir Peter Dare............Charles Gerrard
Cecelie Winslow.............Marjorie Daw
Jane, the cook..................Kate Price
Simon, the peddler..........Tully Marshall
Corporal Crutch..............Lou Morrison
Private Stitch...............Philip Dunham
Judge George Jeffreys.........Otto Matiesen
Jewars, Jeffreys' secretary..Wilson Hummel
John Standish Lane.......Thomas Ricketts
Prudence Lane.....................Ann May
Rupert Winslow..................Ray Hallor
Farmer.....................Lincoln Plummer

Another costume film entry, and not particularly auspicious compared to pictures of this sort seen before. Comparing the star to her preceding "Dulcy" production, this newest one suffers also. Not that it isn't a satisfactory enough film feature. In both precedents it is merely an instance of having established so high a standard it is not attainable by every production.

The period is 1685; the locale English, at the time when the young Duke of Monmouth was being fostered as a regal aspirant against the present ruler. Barbara Winslow and all the other Winslow descendants seem to favor the revolutionary cause. This centres attention on Barbara (Constance Talmadge) by certain officers of the King's regiment. The pitting of opposing forces against the heroine is always the centre of attraction, so much so that the general idea as to what it's all about is almost lost sight of completely were it not for an ever-remindful title.

Col. Percy Kirk (Morgan Wallace) is an unscrupulous, mercenary official who interprets his duties to include general welfare of all young damsels. Captain Miles Prothero (Conway Tearle), also a king's officer, is one of the few honest officers in the service. The captain's befriending of the Winslows leads him to arrest and reduction of rank, with the sentence imposed by the treacherous Judge Jeffreys of shooting at sunrise. Barbara Winslow is also meted out a three years' prison sentence plus a monthly dose of public whipping.

The outwitting of the tyrants by the important rebellious faction is interestingly portrayed. The star is constantly to the fore in a most appealing fashion. This creates an opportunity for the familiar Talmadge qualities, embracing hoydenish naivette and fearlessness. The fans, particularly the women, revel in this sort of thing, so much so that they seem to expect it with every Talmadge release.

The film, despite its costume idea, does not represent a particularly heavy production outlay. The action is centred and employs several interiors, sturdy looking and formidable, but chiefly studio stuff.

The Victor Heerman direction is satisfactory, and the continuity by Sullivan is on a par with this veteran scenarist's past performances. The cast is consistently good, Miss Talmadge and Tearle standing out, with the subordinate characters supporting faithfully. Morgan Wallace was perfect as the heavy, and Tully Marshall, in a character bit, clicked.

Charles Gerrard's conception of Sir Peter Dare, the former fiance of Barbara Winslow, could have made his contribution more legitimate in order to match up with his description of being the heroine's erstwhile betrothed. As it is, he delivered more on the order of a travesty character.

Abel.

OUR HOSPITALITY

Metro comedy. Story and title by Jean Havez, Joe Mitchell and Clyde Bruckman. Directed by Buster Keaton and Jack Blystone. Featuring Buster Keaton. Running time, 75 minutes. At Rialto, New York, Dec. 9.

William McKay.............Buster Keaton
Virginia Canfield..Natalie Talmadge Keaton
The Baby..................Buster Keaton, Jr.
Lem Doolittle................Joseph Keaton
Aunt Mary.....................Kitty Bradbury
Joseph Canfield..............Joseph Roberts
James Canfield............Leonard Clapham
Clayton Canfield.............Ralph Bushman
Lee Canfield....................Craig Ward
John McKay....................Edward Coxen
Mrs. McKay......................Jean Dumas
Rev. Benj. Dorsey.............Monte Collins
Sam Gardner...................James Duffy

This is an unusual comedy picture and probably the best thing Buster Keaton has been identified with. The picture is a novelty melange of dramatics, low comedy, laughs and thrills.

Jean Havez has built up a comedy masterpiece about as serious a subject as a feud. The feud between the McKays and Canfields starts dramatically in a prolog showing the double shooting of a McKay and a Canfield.

The McKay baby is taken North by the widow to remove him from the environment. He grows to manhood in the Northern home of his aunt, but is summoned back to his old home to claim an inheritance.

This brings the story up to 1830 and allows for a trip on a railroad train of that period that will go down in screen annals as a comedy classic. The journey of the hump-backed primitive carrier was a series of yells. A donkey blocked progress at one spot and refused to move. The engineer and conductor refused to be daunted and pulled the tracks away from him, then ran the train around the animal.

William McKay (Buster Keaton) meets Virginia Canfield (Natalie Talmadge Keaton) on the train. Unknown to each other, the girl invites him to her house for dinner. Her two brothers and father have sworn to kill him, but their code will not allow them to kill him in the house.

The boy discovers the state of affairs. The situation as handled is very funny. Keaton pops in and out of doors, but foils all attempts to coax him out into no man's land.

He finally escapes disguised as a woman. They pursue him. He takes to the hump-backed train again, which is wrecked. Thrills galore are mixed in his journey down a rapids to a dangerous falls. The girl has followed him. His rescue of the girl as she is going over the falls is as thrilling as the star catch of any casting act. If she is doubled, the substitution is beyond detection. This saves the day, buries the feud and marries off the children.

The picture is splendidly cast, flawlessly directed and intelligently photographed. The usual low comedy and slapstick allotted to Buster have been modified and woven into a consistent story that is as funny as it is entertaining. It marks a step forward in the production of picture comedies and may be the beginning of the end of the comedy picture without a plot or story that degenerates into a series of "gags."

"Our Hospitality" classes as one of the best comedies ever produced for the screen and will set a new fashion in picture comedy conception.

It's write your own ticket for the exhibitor; it can't miss anywhere.

Con.

SIX CYLINDER LOVE

William Fox production, starring Ernest Truex. Adapted from the play by William Anthony McGuire by Carl Stearns Clancy. Directed by Elmer Clifton. Special showing at Central, New York, Dec. 7. Running time, 76 minutes.

Gilbert Sterling ....Ernest Truex
Marilyn Sterling..........Florence Eldridge
Richard Burton....................Donald Meek
Geraldine Burton....................Maude Hill
Phyliss Burton..............Anne McKittrick
Marguerite Rogers...........Marjorie Milton
Bertram Rogers.............Thomas Mitchell
William Donroy....................Ralph Sipperly
George Stapleton...........Berton Churchill
Harold Winston....................Harold Mann
Tom Johnson........................Frank Tweed
Mary ....Grace Gordon

All of the laugh wallops present in the stage play of "Six Cylinder Love" are not present in the film version, but still it proves mighty good screen entertainment. Ernest Truex, the principal player of the spoken version, and a great many members of the cast of the original are present in the screen production. There is just enough combination of comedy and drama in the McGuire story to make a mighty interesting picture. The exhibitor can go out and practically say here is the time that the smaller towns are getting "the original company" of a stage success transferred to the screen.

The story of how the ownership of an expensive automobile wrecked the happiness of two families in turn and how finally when they were both broke and starting afresh in new fields the janitor of the apartment where they are living comes along and takes the car off their hands.

In the play itself Ralph Sipperly was the auto salesman and got a lot of laughs that he does not get on the screen. His delivery being lost made all the difference in the world, but he did manage to get the punch over with "That's a good car, too."

Florence Eldridge plays opposite Truex as his lead and Donald Meek is in the role that he had in the play. Meek makes a work of art of his characterization.

"Six Cylinder Love" looks like it is first run material for any of the better houses.

Fred.

KING'S CREEK LAW

Produced by William Steiner and released by the Photo Drama Co. Directed by and featuring Leo D. Maloney. Story and adaptation by Frances and Ford Beebe. At Stanley, New York, one day.

Tom Hardy.....................Leo Maloney
The Sheriff.................Horace Carpenter
James Lawton....................Frank Ellis
Saul Jameson...................Milton Brown
Kirk Jameson........................Chet Ryan
Milly Jameson..................Josephine Hill

It takes a mighty good Western to get across nowadays, and that lets this one out as far as the box office goes. The kids still like the cowboy and Injun stuff, and the majority of growth-ups still fall for films of the heavy dramatic "Squawman" and "Heart of Wetona" type or the light, speedy Tom Mix and Hoot Gibson specials. But "King's Creek Law" has neither Indians, dramatic intensity nor rip-snortin' humor.

Nevertheless, the plot, although basically trite, carries a novel twist or two. Leo Maloney plays a Texas Ranger. He is sent to the small and hard-boiled town of King City to trail down a murderer. He comes into contact with Saul Jameson, an old Confederate, who has moved west and has never surrendered to Union law. Old Jameson calls himself the law on King's Creek and conducts his own trials, without brooking interference from Federal officers.

The old man's beloved son, Kirk, becomes involved in the murder case, and his father decides to try him without tempering paternal affection with his idea of right. Maloney comes to the rescue with all sorts of physical and mental strategy. After many incidents have passed their frenzied way, he clears the son, captures the real murderer, convinces old man Jameson that the U. S. law isn't so bad after all, and to top it all, wins for himself Milly, the old boy's bouncing daughter.

Maloney gives a rather capable performance in the "pie" role of the hero, although he is essentially a man's man, and in the love scenes his work falls flat. Of the others, Horace Carpenter is best as a grizzled sheriff. Frank Ellis is a theatrical and affected heavy, and Milton Brown lets a good part go to waste as the old "rebel." Josephine Hill is the girl, and although she is probably representative of many of the rougher class of western women, her characterization is a trifle too common and crude to qualify her as a candidate for future screen honors as a much-adored heroine.

It is doubtful if there ever has been a film in which so much trick stuff with pistols is seen. It's a case of "now you have it and now you haven't" right along. The villain digs his gun into the hero's ribs, the latter kicks it away, and then another bad man crops up from behind and the battle of the gats is waged all over again.

If this were any other sort of picture and had as good a plot it might stand a chance. But the fact that the market is overflowing with Westerns kills "King's Creek Law" for the box office.

LET'S GO

Truart production, starring Richard Talmadge. Story and script by Keene Thompson, directed by William K. Howard. Titles by Ralph Spence. At Loew's New York, N. Y., double feature bill, Dec. 7, 1923. Running time, 61 minutes.

Barry Macklin............Richard Talmadge
Lucy Frazer....................Eileen Percy
Jack Frazer...................George Nichols
Ezra Sprowl...................Tully Marshall
Milo Sprowl....................Bruce Gordon
Ollie Banks.......................Al Fremont
"Dip" McGurk................Matthew Betz
Luke Hazey..........................Lou King
Mrs. Hazey....................Aggie Herring
Andrew J. Macklin.........John Steppling

This is the first of the series of Richard Talmadge pictures that Truart is to have. It goes without saying that in almost every respect this one is far better than the Richard Talmadge features that have gone before. Yet this is just a good average program picture for the popular houses, where the grind is the business done.

The biggest wallop is the titles, the work of Ralph Spence. To a wise audience there are a lot of laughs in the Spence stuff.

Talmadge isn't particularly different in this picture than he was in his earlier features. It is a case of build the story to order for him, so that he has opportunity to pull his usual leaps and other acrobatic stuff.

The star is the son of the head of a cement corporation. They have a contract to furnish paving material to a small town, but the mayor fails to kick in with the dough for the material. The cement head believes that his son isn't worth while having around the office, and tells him that were he any good at all he would have handled this small-town job. The boy then starts out to make it, but he is being watched for at the office by a couple of cops for speed, and the usual chase stuff starts. From then on it's all speed through the entire picture.

Eileen Percy, opposite Talmadge, hasn't much to do. Tully Marshall and a couple of other good names are worth while from a selling standpoint. Matthew Betz, in a character bit, stands out like a million dollars and pulls laughs every time on. *Fred.*

DOES IT PAY?

William Fox picture, starring Hope Hampton. Showing at Loew's Circle one day, Dec. 6. Running time, 81 minutes.

The regulation vamp routine, with Miss Hampton cast as the demure young miss who breaks up a home. It takes too long in the telling, besides is not convincing at any point, and leaves little for the star to do but parade before the camera. In those neighborhoods where they care for the ruthless women themes this film may have a chance, but it's strictly within the confines of the trashy melodrama class and not advantageously presented, directed, edited nor photographed.

One or two lavish interiors may make it more appetizing to certain audiences, but are not equal to pulling the script or playing out of the hole it soon slides into after the start. A minor number of color "shots" of the star were extremely mediocre, and if a color process was used, the results are but the more deplorable.

The tale strings along to tell of the father of two grown children being lured away from his home by a coin-grabbing damsel whom he later discovers has a liver, which ends that episode. It causes him to go out of his head. The return comes a year later, when physicians bring him to his former domicile in an attempt to restore his memory.

There was little that the cast could do to aid the theme, and they failed to do that. Various members give evidence of having struggled to overcome the dramatics, but the burden was too great. The playing of Miss Hampton will cause no special interest, for she does nothing.

"Does It Pay?" can hardly be termed a credit to any one. *Skig.*

BILL

Red Seal feature produced by Legrand Films. From a story by Anatole France. Presented by Edwin Miles Fadman. Edited by Hugo Riesenfeld. Starring Maurice De Faraudy. At the New York Dec. 11 as half a double bill. Running time 50 minutes.

Practically unheralded and with the billing announcing it only as a five-reel novelty film, this French picture crept quietly into one of the daily change houses Tuesday and proved itself nothing less than a screen masterpiece. The title role is taken by Maurice De Faraudy in a style that it is safe to say tops any bit of character acting that has heretofore enriched the films.

The story was suggested by Anatole France's "Crainquebille" ("The Majesty of Justice"), one of the greatest of this master's works. Edwin Miles Fadman presents it, but it is Hugo Riesenfeld, credited with having brought it over here and edited it, who deserves unstinted praise for his daring and sagacity.

Artistically "Bill" is a complete success, and commercially, while its beauty of characterization and dramatic artistry are probably above the head of the average filmgoer, it cannot fail to deliver, as it has the unmistakable air of greatness—neither lacking in interest nor too highbrow in treatment.

A foreword states in all frankness no love interest or mechanical thrills are to be expected. The audience is informed the film is to be a departure from the usual and will only strive to show a few simple episodes of ordinary life.

Bill is a pushcart peddler of Paris, a lowly and yet lovable character without a touch of maudlin sentiment. As played by M. De Faraudy (according to the billing one of France's most eminent actors), the peddler is a shabby, bedraggled old duffer, looking somewhat the way Marshal Foch would were he of the peasantry. Bill has been selling his vegetables in the same neighborhood for over 40 years and has built up quite a clientele among the housewives.

One day, through no fault of his own, Bill becomes involved in an altercation with a self-important gendarme. Before knowing what it is all about he is under arrest for insulting an officer of the law. There follows a mockery of a trial. Bill is sentenced to two weeks in jail and a fine of 50 francs. He serves his term without grumbling, rather enjoying the novelty of a soft bed and running hot and cold water. His only worry is what has happened to his pushcart.

When released Bill goes joyously back to work, only to find he is now considered a jailbird and has lost all his former customers. Discouraged and disheartened, he begins to drink heavily, is evicted from his garret and becomes a human derelict.

How France's story ends is not known by this reviewer, but it is doubtful if it is as unsatisfactory a happy finish as in the picture. Just as Bill is about to end it all in the Seine, a newsboy whom he had befriended restrains him and brings him to a rude shelter.

As he eats, drinks and warms himself Bill turns philosophically to the gamin and tells him that, though it makes no difference to the republic, he has saved a human life. The film ends here.

There are many laughs and these are the moments which will be most enjoyed by those not overburdened with literary appreciation. Similarly they will be touched with sympathy for the old peddler when he is buffeted by adverse fates. But only those conversant with France's sublime gift of satire will discover in the film a remarkably penetrating attack on not only the French courts but the entire system of social justice as it now exists throughout the world.

The court scene is one of the finest ever filmed. Once when the only witness for the defense is presenting his inadequate testimony the whole court drifts to slumber and even the head of the marble statue of justice (by a clever trick of photography) nods on its shoulders.

You see the court proceedings as they are visualized in the confused mind of the prisoner and later the distorted version of it dreamed by him in prison. It is all much more effectively done than attempted last year in Elmer Rice's "Adding Machine."

Bill is the only character of importance, but the newsboy, customers, court attendants and others are splendidly played. The Parisian atmosphere is perfect, with the local color never daubed on too thickly.

Riesenfeld did a good, sensible job in not aiming for the highbrows and translating the titles into colloquial English.

The entire film is art with a capital A. If the various "better film" associations fail to include this one in their selected lists for the year, there is no such thing as art in American filmdom.

SHEPHERD KING

A J. Gordon Edwards production presented by William Fox. Based on play of same title by Wright Lorimer and Arnold Reeves. Adapted by Virginia Tracey. Opened at Central, New York, for a run Dec. 10, 1923 Running time, 96 minutes.

Michal........................Violet Mersereau
Merab..................................Edy Darclea
Adora.....................Virginia Lucchetti
David...........................Nerio Bernardi
Saul................................Guido Trento
Jonathan...................Ferruccio Biancini
Doeg......................Alessandro Salvini
Adriel.........................Mariano Bottino
Goliath.......................Samuel Balestra
Samuel.....................Adriano Bocanera
Ozem..................................Enzo Di Felice
Abimelech..................Eduardo Balsamo
Omah.....................Amerigo di Giorgio
Egyptian Prisoner.......Gordon McEdward

William Fox beat the rest of the field to the barrier by being the first on Broadway with a feature film based on a biblical subject, through opening the screen version of "The Shepherd King" at the Central Monday for a run. The opening was the usual $5.50 invitational affair, usual for all of the Fox film premieres at this house, with the grind policy from 1 to 11 p. m. becoming effective Tuesday.

The Monday night audience, however, refused to enthuse over the screen version of the play that proved so popular on the spoken stage when presented by Wright Lorimer, who was its star and co-author with Arnold Reeves. There was a brief bit of applause with the flashing of the name of the director at the beginning. That was the only outburst of the evening.

As a play "The Shepherd King" might have had an appeal, but as a picture it is nothing but a series of quotations from the Old Testament. A "quotation" title, a camera shot, then another "quotation," until it seemed that the feature was about 50 per cent. title and about just as entertaining as sitting down and reading the Bible would be. One doesn't read the Bible for entertainment, nor seemingly did the Monday night audience want to read the Bible via the screen route under the guise of entertainment.

J. Gordon Edwards did not turn out a picture that the public is going to rave about. Mr. Edwards may have turned out a better picture than was shown at the Central; seemingly he must have, for the manner in which the flashes are cut shows that there must have been something to them, but they were snapped too tight in the cutting in order to get as much of the Bible as possible into the titles that the picture suffered.

The program informed the audience that the picture was made in New York city, Egypt and Palestine, and that the picture was shot "in the actual locations described in Biblical lore." The cast must have been recruited abroad, for the only name in it that rings at all familiar to American ears is that of Violet Mersereau. She plays the younger daughter of King Saul and acquits herself fairly well. Edy Darclea has the role of the elder daughter, and Virginia Lucchetti that of the bondgirl. This latter girl looks like a comer, and if she is brought to this country should make a place for herself on the screen.

Nerio Bernardi was the David of the screen production. He was over-madeup and prone to overact, the latter fact also being quite true of the majority of the members of the cast.

The Fox people will undoubtedly go out after this production and herald it one of the biggest screen offerings of the year, but it is hardly that, and the chances are that the majority of screen audiences seeing the picture will be disappointed. The first half hour of it is frightfully draggy and decidedly tiresome, and it is not until after David slays the lion and saves the life of Michal that anything at all happens.

It is to be hoped that as long as this picture is but the forerunner of the Biblical features to come those that come along later will be somewhat more interesting than this one proved to be. *Fred.*

LUCRETIA LOMBARD

or

(Flaming Passion)

Harry Rapf production presented by Warner Bros. Adapted from the novel by Kathleen Norris. Directed by Jack Conway. Monte Blue and Irene Rich featured. Shown at the Strand, New York, week Dec. 16. Running 72 minutes.

Lucretia Lombard................Irene Rich
Stephen Winship....................Monte Blue
Sir Allen Lombard........Marc MacDermott
(Mary Warren) Mimi........Norma Shearer
Judge Winship..............Alec B. Francis
Fred Winship.......................John Roche
Mrs. Winship..............Lucy Beaumont
Sandy.........................Otto Hoffman

Finally the Warner Bros. have come down the line with an attraction that is certain to be a box office hit There is nothing that can stop it with the possible exception of the title. For that reason the distributors are giving the exhibitor his choice of either one of two, "Lucretia Lombard," which was the title of the original, or the picture title, "Flaming Passion." At the Strand they used the first of these, possibly because they feared that the latter had too much similarity to "Flaming Youth," which was the attraction at the house only a week ago. On the screen the picture shows up like a million dollars, and it should in a great measure develop box office strength that should only be second to "Flaming Youth."

It's a whale of a picture that has everything. There is youth, mystery, love interest, sustained suspense, a combination forest fire and flood and wild animal thrills.

It's a tale of a woman who, dazzled by a title and fortune, marries a man much older than herself. After a few years, broken down by his early dissipation, he is the victim of drugs confined to an invalid's chair. The wife remains loyal and attends him. With all the craftiness of a drug addict the husband switches the covers of aspirin and drug containers, so that when he asks his wife for a double aspirin dose she gives him a double dose of dope, which kills him.

Her only friends in the town are the Winships, the father being a pastor, one son the district attorney and the other a starter in the lounge lizard race. There also is a young girl, ward of the pastor, who is very much in love with the elder of the two boys. The younger has been dancing attendance on the wife of the invalid husband, so when she calls for his assistance in the death matter he carries his elder brother along. This is the beginning and the ending of the story. The elder brother has just become engaged to the ward, but when he walks in on the freshly made widow all bets are off, and he falls like a ton of coal.

Later, at the country place of the Winships, the love between the district attorney and the widow attains such proportions that he is about to inform his fiancee that he does not love her when circumstances occur which force him to marry her to please his father, who has been accidentally wounded and near death. Then the widow returns to the scene and discovers what has taken place. The wounded pastor is to be removed to a hospital and the son and mother are to accompany him, leaving the two women in the mountain lodge alone. That is something of a situation; the one that he did not love and married and the one that he loved but didn't marry. They remain overnight, and during that time a forest fire starts, the hero returning in time to help the women escape, with the wife conveniently dying on the bank of a river after she has been rescued.

The cast is corking, Monte Blue appearing to greater advantage than he has in most of his recent pictures. Irene Rich gives her usual finished performance and handles three or four of the bigger scenes exceptionally well. The find of the cast is Norma Shearer. She plays a flapper type and then develops a dramatic strain that is above the ordinary. The girl is there in looks as well and screens in an attractive manner.

Conway's direction carries the story along in great shape, sustaining the suspense right to the final minute of the picture. His handling of the fire scenes was also clever. The rushing of the pack of wolves into the mountain home to escape the fire was realistic. *Fred.*

MAN FROM BRODNEY

Albert E. Smith presentation released through Vitagraph. Story by George Barr McCutcheon. Directed by David Smith. Running time, 75 minutes. Reviewed at Rialto, New York, Dec. 16.

Hollingsworth Chase...J. Warren Kerrigan
Princess Genevra..............Alice Calhoun
Lady Deppingham..........Wanda Hawley
Mrs. Brown.....................Miss Du Pont
Robert Browne................Pat O'Malley
Neenah.......................Kathleen Key
Rasnea.........................Bertram Grassby

A highly romantic meller feature with J. Warren Kerrigan doing the heroics in a fat role. The story includes all of the prop hokum, including a heroine princess who renounces a throne to marry the dashing hero; a tropical island, big fight scene when the natives stage an uprising; U. S. destroyer to the rescue and the valiant blue jackets arriving just in the nick of time to rescue the "whites," who are making a gallant stand in a house on the Island of Japac.

The tale concerns the inheritance of the island from two partners by the son of one and daughter of the other. The inheritance has a string to it. They must marry each other or the property reverts to the islanders after six months. This forms the background upon which the author has hung his highly sensational melodrama.

Rasnea (Bertram Grassby), a scheming native ruler, retains Brodney & Co., English lawyers, to look after the islanders' rights. The lawyers send Hollingsworth Chase (J. Warren Kerrigan) to represent them on the island, with instructions that no violence is to be permitted from the natives.

Chase is soon enmeshed in intrigues. Rasnea inflames the natives against him by telling them he is a traitor and friendly to the white heirs. The heirs arrive without much hope of qualifying for their inheritance, as the son, Robert Browne (Pat O'Malley), is married and brings his wife (Miss Du Pont) with him. The girl, Lady Deppingham (Wanda Hawley), is an adventuress. She beguiles Browne into a love affair.

The situation is further complicated by the arrival of Princess Genevra (Alice Calhoun) to visit Lady Deppingham. Chase and the Princess had met before and were in the first stages of a love affair. His efforts to protect the whites from violence are redoubled.

He finally thwarts Rasnea's plottings through information given him by two friendly natives, one a sister of Rasnea's wife. The uprising and attack are dramatically staged. Chase rescues Lady Deppingham and Browne from kidnapers, then leads the defense of the mansion where the heirs and party are housed.

The attack provides several thrills with the natives swarming all over the front of the house, taking realistic tumbles when beaten back by gun butts, etc. The regular steamer fails to land when natives feign plague by lying on the dock, but the steamer radios a destroyer about the uprising. The destroyer arrives with a bone in her mouth and sends a landing party of "gobs" ashore. The sailors and a shell from one of her guns quickly extricate the inhabitants and the author from the maze of trouble into which they have all wandered.

It's melodramatic hokum of imperial vintage, well cast and splendidly directed. *Con.*

CALL OF THE CANYON

Paramount picture adapted from the original of Zane Grey by Doris Schroeder and Edfrid Bingham. Directed by Victor Fleming and photographed by James Howe. At the Rivoli, New York, week of Dec. 16. Running time, 71 mins.

Glenn Kilbourne...............Richard Dix
Carley Burch.....................Lois Wilson
Flo Hutter.....................Marjorie Daw
Haze Ruff.........................Noah Beery
Larry Morrison.............Ricardo Cortez
Tom Hutter.....................Fred Huntley
Mrs. Hutter..................Lillian Leighton
Aunt Mary......................Helen Dunbar

Another edition of this Paramount unit's conception of how Zane Grey's originals should be transplanted to the screen and revealing workmanship from all angles. If nothing else this detachment is making a name for itself in turning out beauteous westerns as the picturesque exteriors of "To the Last Man" are paralleled in this effort. It about marks the first time that the author has ever received a real "break" from the film manufacturers so far as actual production is concerned.

Minus the swift and dramatic action that the "Last Man" enfolded Fleming has turned out a coherence of celluloid narration that plays itself along easily, not without comedy values and picturesquely cameraed.

Richard Dix, Lois Wilson, Marjorie Daw and Noah Beery make up the featured members of the cast all of whom combine for an adequate presentation of the characters portrayed.

It's the second start for the Dix-Wilson duo in the Grey repertoire and it looks as if the couple, and this particular unit, can take the writings of Grey in their entirety and cash in on them. Certainly the screen material is there.

The story tells of Glenn Kilbourne (Mr. Dix) ordered to Arizona after his return from overseas where he takes up sheep ranching. The girl (Lois Wilson) eventually follows him to be in turn trailed by a wealthy eastern suitor who loads a private car with members of the social strata, from which the young woman has strayed, to make the trip. A brief stay convinces the luxury loving miss that the wide open spaces are no place for her. She leaves her fiance under the supposition if he cares enough he'll come back, now that his lungs are cured.

The open country has secured a hold on the boy. It eventually develops that talk among the villagers forces him, more or less willingly, into marriage with the daughter of a neighbor who previously nursed him when he arrived. On the day of wedding the former fiance again comes to the canyon where she is on time for the ceremony but is spied by the bride-to-be who leaves the altar flat to give up the groom to his first love.

Throughout is inserted the carryings on of the wild eastern crowd, for which Fleming has a house party that includes a marathon dancing contest for many a laugh, a sand storm and the inevitable attack upon the girl, leading up to an active scrap between Dix and Beery.

The tale many appear to become somewhat wabbly as it nears its conclusion but the picturizing on a whole will sustain it. Whether or not the entire theme has been done many times previously the cast, direction and photography prove a sum total to make it entertaining and worthy to lead a first run program. ***Skig.***

THE ACQUITTAL

Universal-Jewel adaptation from play of same name by Rita Weiman. Directed by Clarence Brown. Cast includes Claire Windsor, Norman Kerry, Richard Travers, Barbara Bedford, Emmett King. At the Cameo, New York, week of Dec. 9. Running time, 69 minutes.

If nothing else, this picture will about hang up a record for cutbacks. It's practically comprised of nothing else with the initial 45 minutes solely devoted to this form of script construction.

It totals an unreasonableness difficult to surmount, enhanced by overly stressed dramatic sub-titles which give the film a decided lurid atmosphere that belies the splendid production U has backed the effort with.

It impresses as a celluloid work that will please in those houses where they are partial to "swell" dramas while the manner in which the theme has been treated projects as not the best in cinema entertainment.

The constant cut-backs are responsible for more or less confusion. Before the climax is reached much of the interest is sacrificed, due to this reason.

A borrowed Goldwyn cast (for which due title credit is given) portrays the enactment of the story to mediocre results. That may have been gained through Clarence Brown, the director, seemingly having been lenient with the players, who, at times, are prone to exaggerate the action to the point of heroics. Appearance is about the only attributive quality the picture has, due to a splendid series of interior settings, a neatly attired cast and adequate photography.

Adapted from the play, the tale is a mystery-drama concerning the murder of the father of two adopted sons, between whom there is the girl, with one accused of the deed while the other aids in the prosecution. The actual culprit is favorably concealed until near the conclusion, although it's some time before that when interest gives indications of lagging.

The women are secondary to their masculine co-operators in the playing, with the sub-titles especially harmful. None of the personnel is distinctive in individual effort, with each having many times turned in superior performances than here.

It is a story superfluously imbedded with the ultra-mystery that evidently necessitates much too many cut-backs, but having more than adequate mounting, may fulfill the assignment upon intermediate programs. ***Skig.***

DANGEROUS HOUR

A Johnnie Walker production starring Eddie Polo. Story by Rena Parker. Directed by William H. Curran. Shown as feature at the Stanley, New York, December 12. Running time, 40 minutes.

Jim Crawley.......................Jack Carlisle
"Dad" Carson.........George A. Williams
Anita Carson............Catherine Bennett
Eddie Polo, daredevil screen star..Eddie Polo

Those who have followed the daredevil antics of Eddie Polo in his previous serial contributions may find something in this latest Polo special, but those who have not will wonder what it is all about.

It is a sort of picture within a picture idea projected with the melodramatic complications of a mining town in Arizona, where the scenarist would have one believe that the only excitement the town ever enjoys is the blowing of a siren when some part of the decrepit mine caves in.

Jim Crawley, a fitting name for a villainous gent, controls the mine, and, according to the story, would rather have his workers perish than repair the mine. He may have had some sort of a tie-up with a local undertaker.

Jim is a robust, overfed type that dominates over his hirelings, who for the most part seem to be in the

last stages of some terrible malady. They seemed too weak to fight back.

Into this turbulent community, where wives and children seem disappointed if the breadwinner returns home intact instead of on a stretcher, drops Eddie Polo, daredevil movie star, who is trying to locate his company on location.

Eddie really crashed through the Carson homestead after having lost control of the airplane he had been piloting. Even in Arizona, or this part of it, despite the emaciated condition of its people, they must have a picture house, for the girl heroine readily recognizes him.

Crawley also is so pleased to see him that he loans him a bucking broncho that's a man killer by way of accentuating his delight at meeting him. But, of course, our hero readily masters it.

The subsequent daredevil stunts win the admiration of the girl. These are the same stunts Eddie has been doing in the serials, the only difference being that they are now bunched into a 40-minute showing.

Eddie returns to the lot with the picture company and is about to act his leap for life. The siren blows at the mines. The extras run helter-skelter to find that the men have been entrapped in a faulty shaft and are facing a watery grave. Eddie hops out of the film and makes for the mine, dynamites the wall, frees the captives, chases the villain who has abducted the girl, subdues him and wins her for himself.

Aside from the hoke story, there is quite a little action and perhaps an overdose of melodrama. Polo does his stunts as well as ever, and since this seems to have been the main occasion for the picture its producers will undoubtedly be satisfied with it.

As for the spectators, it may go a long way in the smaller houses of the countryside or perhaps in some of the neighborhoods. But it's only chance will remain in the popularity of Polo.

THE GRAIL

William Fox picture, starring Dustin Farnum and directed by Colin Campbell. Joseph Brotherton, photographer. Cast includes James Gordon, Carl Stockdale, Alma Bennett, Peggy Shaw, Leon Bary and Frances Hatton. Showing at Loew's New York theatre as half of double feature program, Dec. 18. Running time, 62 mins.

"Fair to middlin'" would describe this Fox western, which has Dustin Farnum's name surmounting the title. For intermediate consumption the film will probably be found satisfactory, but it hardly rates above that classification. Void of script material which would make it unusual, the subject-matter has received the average degree of workmanship from the director, cast and cameraman to make it passable entertainment and nothing more.

What reference the title has to the tale may be guessed at, but as it suggests a religious theme it may not be without a certain plausibility, for the story concerns a Texas Ranger who impersonates a Bible seller in order to "get his man." During the course of events he brings faith to an unbelieving youngster, whom he ultimately arrests, despair to the girl who trusted him and instigates the wrath of an entire township because of his disguise.

Midway the Ranger reveals himself and his true purpose and starts to resurrect the destruction he has caused during the initial half of the footage. Jack Rollens, as the religiously fanatic youngster, forced to the mountains with his father as a result of a killing in a feud, made the role predominate for its full worth despite a tendency to over emphasize.

Farnum, as the Ranger, strutted through his conception with the stern face of the man of duty whilst taking deep breaths to signalize the more emotional moments—convincing to a more or less degree. Alma Bennett and Peggy Shaw comprise the predominating women in the cast for average results.

The picture is no better than its story and, as it includes the ruined girl and the skulking villain, responsible for the shooting attributed to the Ranger, all the necessary ingredients are well planted. It comes and goes in the natural course to be suspected, realized and condoned according to the tax at the box office. *Skig.*

ENEMIES OF CHILDREN

Mammoth Pictures Corp. release adapted and directed by Lillian Ducey from the novel "Youth Triumphant," and featuring Anna Q. Nilsson. Cast includes George Seigman, Claire McDowell, Lucy Beaumont, Joseph Dowling, Raymond Hatton, Ward Crane and Charles Wellesley. Showing at Loew's, New York, one day, Dec. 18. Running time, 72 minutes.

Obvious melodrama that could have sailed under a hundred different titles and meant as much. A street waif of questionable parentage through circumstances is taken into a wealthy home where she is adopted and cared for until her marriage, which follows the successful attempt to expose the mystery of her birth. The celluloid version is jumpy in the telling, besides demonstrating a lack of attention to detail to the extent it may be classified as but a mediocre feature.

The names in the cast should carry some weight, but the respective performances are short of fulfilling the expectation. Raymond Hatton as a physically deformed and cynical member of the wealthy family impresses as the most legitimate characterization, with the others doing what they have to, which may or may not be attributed to the direction.

Miss Nilsson entrances when the story takes a 10 or 15 years' hop forward to turn in an average piece of work for the special billing. George Seigman is just about in the film long enough to receive listing; killed off shortly after the launching. And at least one of the more prominent characters missed naming altogether during the titling, which also left room for much improvement.

If playing before an audience which is prone to kid dramatics "Enemies of Children" probably will prove the source of some entertainment, but for other assemblages it will more than likely remain as simply "another picture." *Skig.*

SUPREME TESTS

J. E. Bowen production releasing through Renown. The Cosmosart Studios credited as manufacturer, with the story and direction signed W. P. MacNamara. Features Johnny Harron and Gloria Grey. Splitting double bill at Loew's New York, Dec. 18.

Cast includes Minna Redman, Eugene Beaudino, Dorothy Reveir, Ernest Shields, Geraldine Powell and Gene Walsh. Running time, 70 mins.

What a ballad singer or piano player is to a "stew" in the early hours of the morning so this picture would be to an audience were the assemblage well under the influence.

All they needed at the New York Tuesday night was some one to hop up and holler, "Take it off, it's breaking my heart," and the situation would have been perfect.

Within the 70 minutes is revealed years of dramatics dating back to the time whenever "The Old Homestead" and such others were penned. It's so eloquent with its appeal to evolve a tearful emotion that if anyone ever takes it seriously it will mark their last entrance into a film emporium where they supposedly project entertainment. A slight twist in the trend of the titling and "Supreme Test" would make a satirical comedy on about every dramatic angle ever written. As it is, that supreme test thing goes both ways.

There are any number of detail deficiencies which have been grossly overlooked to additionally make this one of the worst films to be seen in New York this season. *Skig.*

BREAKING INTO SOCIETY

F. B. O. feature, produced, written and directed by Hunt Stromberg. Photographed by Irving Reis. Starring Bull Montana. At the Tivoli, New York, Dec. 12, as half the bill. Runs 68 minutes.

Tim O'Toole	Bull Montana
His Mother	Carrie Clark Ward
His Father	Kala Pasha
His Little Brother	Francis Treboal
His Dog	"Rags"
Yvonne	Florence Gilbert
The Pittsburgh Kid	Chuck Reisner
Sally of the Alley	Gertrude Short
The Barber	Leo White
The Chiropractor	"Tiny" Stanford
A Man of Wealth	Stanhope Wheatcroft

While it cannot be denied there are laughs in this film and in all probability it will be a financial winner, Hunt Stromberg who produced, directed and wrote it, will be the severe loser, as far as prestige goes. Besides being cheap and vulgar, it cannot fail to insult every Catholic of breeding and intelligence, who will see in it repellant burlesque.

The Irish family of the story are shown to be a poor lot living in Tin Can alley, Pittsburgh. They find themselves suddenly made wealthy from an oil investment, and move to Pasadena, attempting to step out in the social world.

The plot ends right there. From then on there are just various episodes of a revoltingly unmannerly family. The chief scene is a dinner party, and it is here the low comedy reaches even further depths.

Some of the incidents are funny and serve to prove that humor must not necessarily be unrefined. One shows a girl peeling an olive and eating the pit; another the fat father being vigorously massaged by a chiropractor, and, one of the best, the little brother roller skating all over the polished floors.

Bull Montana is featured, but is given little opportunity for any of his familiar "tough guy" bits. He is secondary to Carrie Clark Ward, who plays the mother and is the worst offender in the matter of nastiness. At one point she sticks a banana skin down her bodice and later takes it out squashed. She is constantly raising her skirts above her knees, showing not only the ugly, awning-striped stockings, but the supposedly intimate wearing apparel above.

The rest of the cast holds some fair names, with Kala Pasha and Gertrude Short doing as well as possible under the circumstances, but Chuck Reisner proving himself to be a better song writer than screen actor.

This film has a good deal more crying need for the censor's scissors than many of the sex pictures attacked constantly by the reformers.

BIG DAN

Fox production, directed by William A. Wellman. Story by Frederick and Fanny Hatton. Photographed by Joe August. Starring Charles Jones. At the Circle Dec. 11 as half double bill. Runs 58 minutes.

Betty Baker	Eileen O'Malley
Dan O'Hara	Charles Jones
Tom Walsh	Milt Collins
Kate Walsh	Lydia Y. Titus
Doc Snyder	Charles Coleman
Dora	Marion Nixon
Cyclone Morgan	Ben Hendricks, Jr.
Charles Burke	Harry Durkinson

While it is improbable Charles Jones will ever become a star of the first magnitude, he is steadily graduating from the ten-twenty-thirty class to that of fair, intermediate comedy dramas. "Big Dan" is his best picture to date, not only in general amusement, but for individual acting.

This does not mean the film is a topnotcher, as Jones and the Fox company still have a long, hard task before he is firmly established in the ranks of the more popular stars. But it is o. k. for the daily change houses, and is a long step in the right direction.

The story is credited to Frederick and Fanny Hatton. Those who are looking for the subtle, scintillating and often naughty wit of this pair will be disappointed. The Hattons were probably told by Fox to write a suitable scenario for Jones. Consequently they have thrown to the winds all their racy ideas and turned out a plot combining prize fighting, drunken parties, unseen villains, and a whole campful of cute kids.

A variation of the usual has Jones playing the champion's trainer instead of the leather pusher himself. When it comes to a showdown and genuine bare fist fight over the girl the trainer wins, but only after a bitter battle. The love affair is hindered by other complications, chief of which is that the hero is already married. But the wife conveniently passes out in an Arizona sanitarium.

The chief asset of the picture is its humor. Most of the laughs are caused by the antics of the children, with a darling little girl, Eileen O'Malley, the chief comedienne. William A. Wellman has given a sympathetic direction, and the camera work of Joe August has included some lovely exteriors.

The role of the fight trainer gives Jones a splendid chance to appear in the clothes he looks best in—sweaters, sport clothes and all sorts of athletic outfits. His physique is magnificent, and he measures up as one of the best looking men on the screen. He still takes himself a bit too seriously, however. Marion Nixon is the girl, pretty and appealing, except that she tries too obviously to appear sweet. The rest of the cast hold up.

LADY OF MONOSREAU

Klein Co. release, in the Miles' projection room Dec. 14. Running time, 78 mins.

Alleged to be a historical romance by Dumas an oddity has been included in the migration to the screen which permits of half of the story to be projected in natural colors, after which it reverts to the normal method. The coloring allows for various exterior shots that are pleasing, but it fails to lift this foreign-made picture above the resemblance of but a continual succession of "stills."

It looks to have been the fault of the direction, for the characters lend nothing to the effort other than to carry out what the subtitles herald. Hence the film relies upon its reading matter to tell practically everything, gives no credit to any manner of intelligence upon the part of an audience besides revealing an evident lack of confidence in the cast to carry across the desired interpretations. Over 90 titles are numbered within the full projection time of the six reels.

The picture is said to have been taken on the other side of the Atlantic and looks it. Certainly the cast present unfamiliar faces, with their work decidedly below the normal. The action is seemingly nothing more than a series of poses, carried along at such a retarded pace that during the initial half of coloring, the film closely resembles a scenic.

In script the tale revolves around the nobles of Henri the Third's court in France with a girl the cause of an intricate three-cornered male situation.

It is not a first, or even second grade picture from any angle, but seemingly gives conclusive evidence as to the reason for the popularity of American films in foreign lands. *Skig.*

ONE ARABIAN NIGHT

London, Dec. 6.

There are several "stars" in this new Stoll feature, but they are the producer, the scenic artists, carpenters and mechanicians. Several well-known players are also in the show, but they are subordinate to the technicians.

"One Arabian Night" is a film version of "Aladdin and the Wonderful Lamp." It is supposed to be a super-comedy featuring George Robey. He is there, all right; in fact, there is little else; but the comedy is elusive.

Robey is not a screen comedian. His methods and everything are unsuitable to such work. His impersonation of the widow might almost be anything except that we are told he is enacting the historic widow, Thankee. His performance is really the Robey we have known for many years, the big eyes, exaggerated eyebrows, plus a dame wig. The comedy element comes from the well-known raising of the eyebrows and contortions of the mouth, but to infuse greater humor into it he has a peculiar hopping walk accompanied by a pronounced hip wriggle. These things can scarcely be taken as wildly funny in these days of grace.

More than anything we miss the spoken word. Here there is no chance for the quaintly worded gag, the soupcon of suggestion. Even a few sub-titles containing words such as he invariably speaks during his act go for nothing. They are lifeless things, arousing only a giggling titter here and there. Robey is purely a vaudeville player, and only his great name as a comedian will draw the public to see his screen efforts.

The story sticks fairly closely to the recognized version of "Aladdin." We have Aladdin, the son of an impoverished widow; his meeting with the wicked uncle and journey to the treasure cave; the wrath of the uncle, who is really a bad magician, when Aladdin fails to return with the wonderful lamp; his escape from the cave and sudden rise to riches; his courtship and marriage to the Emperor's daughter; the magician's successful "new lamps for old" stunt, and translation of Aladdin's palace and its fair inmates to the heart of Africa; Aladdin's successful counter-stroke, his renewed happiness and the widow's marriage with the Emperor.

As a spectacle "One Arabian Night" is very good. The setting throughout is beautiful, but we could swap a lot of spectacle for a really hearty laugh.

The subsidiary players are very good. A. Saunders as the Emperor, Harry, Agar Lyons as his rascally adviser, Julie Kent as the Princess.

"SEVENTH SHERIFF"

Five-reeler featuring Richard Hatton and Neva Gerber. Produced by Wild West Productions, Inc. Released by Arrow Film Corporation. Written and directed by Richard Hatton. Shown as feature at Stanley, New York, Dec. 17. Running time, 60 minutes.

A mediocre Westerner with the youth and personality of its featured players the only saving grace. Has a plot as thin and disconcerting as a turkey revue. It will have to depend upon that portion of Young America that wallows in dime novels for any play.

It seemed a pity that Richard Hatton and Neva Gerber should draw down such a tame vehicle. They both show promise. If young Mr. Hatton cannot provide better star material than this he had better call in a regular scenarist.

If the chief motive in assembling this film was to display the riding and athletic prowess of young Hatton it succeeds to a degree. But it would take more than the Hatton stunts to elevate it above the category of mediocrity.

Its plot is a dyed-in-the-wool dime novel yarn about a Western town and a group of bad men that believe in changing sheriffs every month. Since the bad men are not part of the local political machines, they accomplish their purpose by snuffing them out. Six have gone over the route when young Jack Rockwell, Eastern tenderfoot and adventurer, happens along and becomes the seventh.

Right off the bat, to show what a tough customer he is, he masters the worst bucking broncho in the village and trims the town bully, despite the latter having it on him both in stature and muscular development. Mary Tweedy, orphan daughter of Jack's predecessor, enchanted by his bravado, instantly labels him her hero.

Everything goes well until he visits the local cemetery with Mary and peruses the headstones marking the graves of his six predecessors. He loses his nerve. He tries to make a getaway.

After passing through more vicissitudes than Pauline's perils, the lovers are restored to each other.

Hatton does as well as could be expected with the role of the youthful sheriff.

Miss Gerber has little else to do than look charming.

If this film is a sample of what is foisted upon the folks of the outlying districts as feature films, it is high time some one philanthropically inclined would form a Film Patrons' Protective League.

MIRACLE MAKERS

Arthur Beck production, starring Leah Baird. Directed by W. S. Van Dyck. Shown at Loew's New York, N. Y., Dec. 7, 1923, on double feature bill. Running time, 60 minutes.

Fred Norton.....................George Walsh
Mrs. Emma Norton..............Edith Yorke
Capt. Joe Mansfield........George Nichols
Mrs. Martha Mansfield.....Edythe Chapman
The Boy.........Master "Dickie" Hendrick
Bill Bruce....................Mitchell Lewis
Doris Mansfield....................Leah Baird

A wild melodrama written by the star of the picture. It is just another example of the old "shoemaker stick to your last" adage. Leah Baird should hold to acting and leave the story writing to others. As a picture it is one of those average program pictures turned out for the smaller houses. As such it qualifies, but that is about all.

The story is laid in a small coast town, with smuggling, Chinese dens, kidnappings and all the usual rough stuff that goes with it. Miss Baird is a small town girl who secrets herself on her father's boat which has been chartered by the heavy for the purpose of smuggling a number of Chinese into the country. The aerial coast patrol spots the boat and the heavy wants to get rid of the evidence by dropping the Chinks overboard. The girl prevents this, and as the air man is her sweetheart she shows herself on deck and he doesn't suspect the schooner. Then the heavy lands his Chinks, kidnaps the girl and marries her. The same night she escapes from the den and her husband is arrested in a raid and sent to jail.

The girl's father is the only one knowing what has happened to his daughter, and the two decide to keep the secret. A few months later it develops that she is about to become a mother and her own mother accuses the aerial coast guard of having ruined the girl.

Then a period of time later the child's dad is turned out of jail and goes back to the little town to claim his wife, only to conveniently fall down a well and die, after acknowledging his wife and child, so as to clear up the situation for the real lover and the girl.

George Walsh plays the lead opposite the star, while Mitchell Lewis is the heavy. The picture is rather badly done as to continuity and the direction leaves a lot to be desired.

Fred.

TEN COMMANDMENTS

Presented by Adolph Zukor and Jesse L. Lasky (Famous Players); produced by Cecil B. DeMille, with story by Jeanie Macpherson. Full evening at $2 top, opening at Cohan, New York, Dec. 22.

CAST OF PART ONE
Moses, the Lawgiver......Theodore Roberts
Rameses, the Magnificent..Charles de Roche
Miriam, the Sister of Moses...Estelle Taylor
The Wife of Pharaoh..........Julia Faye
The Son of Pharaoh.........Terrence Moore
Aaron, Brother of Moses........James Neill
Dathan, the Discontented.....Lawson Butt
The Taskmaster........Clarence Burton
The Bronze Man............Noble Johnson

CAST OF PART TWO
Mrs. Martha McTavish....Edythe Chapman
John McTavish, her Son......Richard Dix
Dan McTavish, her Son......Rod La Rocque
Mary Leigh.....................Leatrice Joy
Sally Lung, an Eurasian.........Nita Naldi
Redding, an Inspector......Robert Edeson
The Doctor ....Charles Ogle
The Outcast ....Agnes Ayres

Paul Iribe, art director; Bert Glennon, Peverell Marley, Archibald Stout, photographers; J. F. Westerberg, technical director; Anne Bauchens, cutter; Cullen Tate, assistant director.

For picture houses "The Ten Commandments" will mob the box offices. No picturegoer will be able to resist seeing it. That is at picture houses and picture house prices.

The opening Biblical scenes of "The Ten Commandments" are irresistible in their assembly, breadth, color and direction; they are enormous and just as attractive.

Mr. DeMille has put in a thrill here with the pictured opening of the Red Sea for Moses to pass through with the Children of Isreal. It's a big way DeMille did that in this picture of a big idea, whether DeMille's, Macpherson's, Zukor's, Lasky's or whoever's idea it may have been.

It sounds presumptuous for a small reporter to suggest to big picture producers, but the glaring hole in this picture seems to be that with the ending of the 35-minute period or so the Biblical scenes are shown in the first part they end there. After that it is modern ordinary story with hoke and pictures (white and black). Were there some manner found to cut back to those enormous scenes in colors, even if blankly at the finish, it would give the audience another look at what they really want to see in this picture, and then at $2 to $1.65 "The Ten Commandments" would be worth it.

It may be said, however, that Mr. DeMille's picturization of the legends of the Bible is worth any price any one can afford to pay to see it.

Moses leading his people from Egypt, from the dreaded Pharaoh, and living the pictured legend, with Pharaoh and his horde chasing them in chariots, with Moses calling upon the Lord to preserve them, which the Lord did by opening up the Red Sea, through which the Jews passed in safety whilst Pharaoh and his mob when following were engulfed as the waters closed over them—it's big, bigger than it may be described and just as big in the way DeMille did it.

This section is in colors, and there are other big scenes besides that one. They are immense and stupendous, so big the modern tale by Miss Macpherson after that seems puny.

A simile might be to start your car in high, take it out of gear and allow it to run down. That's "The Ten Commandments."

The story is with the moral of obeying the Commandments, a preachment in its objective, besides as a base for the Biblical reproductions, but it's still a picture story of two sons, one his mother's boy and the other a harum-scarum atheist. Cheating as a contractor, the atheist's defects in building material result in the collapse of a partly built church's wall, with the mother killed by the falling debris.

In this scene some of the Harold Lloyd building stuff is introduced and other hoke, while the scene of the wife hiding her husband under the pillow as the officers enter to search it is from Du Barry.

Yet all of this could be gone

through without the tiring effect it now has if one or more of the big scenes were cut back to now and then if only for a glimpse. The anticipation for more repetitions would keep the interest keenly alive.

It's a great picture for the Jews. It shows the Bible made them the Chosen People, and also (on the statement of a Catholic) it will be as well liked by the Catholics for its Catholicity.

Its morals are pointed and there's naught a word against it as a picture house picture the way it is, the biggest picture house picture ever made. It seems doubtful, however, if the current manner of running will run it into runs at $2.

The best performance is given by Rod La Roque as the atheist son, Dan McTavish. Mr. La Roque really didn't get properly started until called upon for plenty of emotion toward the finish. Previously he had been only distinguished by his patent leather hair comb. Theodore Roberts as Moses was but required to stride majestically, something he can do perhaps a little better than any one else, while Charles De Roche as Rameses (Pharaoh) always appeared in a genteel, thoughtful mood as though wondering what it was all about.

The women did no better. Leatrice Joy wore a hat that may have been of the period of Moses; anyway it was an awful hat, and her acting was strong enough to make you forget it, while Nita Naldi vamped along without especial notice as Sally Lung, a Mongolian. The playing as a whole is very theatric.

Then again it may have been the magnificence of the big scenes that dwarfed all else, acting and people, with Mr. DeMille having swallowed up his picture and people with the immensity of some of it, exactly as he made the Red Sea swallow up the greater host. *Sime.*

BOY OF MINE

J. K. McDonald presentation, releasing through First National. Story by Booth Tarkington, with William Beaudine the director. Features Ben Alexander, Henry B. Walthall, Irene Rich and Rockliffe Fellowes. Showing at the Strand, New York, week of Dec. 23. Running time, 76 mins.

Bill Latimer..............Ben Alexander
Dr. Robert Mason........Rockliffe Fellowes
William Latimer.........Henry B. Walthall
Ruth Laurence.....................Irene Rich
Mrs. Pettis......................Dot Farley
Junior Pettis...............Lawrence Licalzi

Leading the Christmas week program at the Strand this latest is a narration by Booth Tarkington, screening as an enjoyable interlude for film patrons. It is another ode to youth by the author and given an excellence of direction convincingly carried out by splendid performances of the cast. It sums up as a suitable feature with which to head the holiday schedule.

The picture, figuratively, belongs to Ben Alexander, who has turned in a corking piece of work that reflects a quality of direction not to be denied. Besides which the production has been well mounted, supplemented by photography of the best and includes a minor number of exterior location insertions noticeable for their scenic qualifications.

Perhaps pointing a moral to strict fathers, the story tells of a misunderstanding parent who finally disrupts his home because of expectations that would have his 10-year-old son conduct himself along a path knowing little or no leniency.

It culminates in the mother leaving the big house, with her son, for a small cottage on the other side of town, where they reside until the father realizes the fallacy of his attitude toward the boy, and a reunion is accomplished.

The story presents numerous opportunities which invite the stressing of dramatics and an exaggeration of the tearful possibilities, but these have been neatly dodged to allow for the pathos to not overly predominate, while the antics of the youngster provide the comedy values.

The whole is well put together, making for a tellable story, excellently played and presented.

Henry Walthall, as the father, gives a dignified and capable performance that meets all requirements with Irene Rich as the mother, delightful in her mannerisms. Rockliffe Fellowes enters late, but gives enough strength to his assignment to constitute a definite impression. *Skig.*

A LADY OF QUALITY

Universal production directed by Hobart Henley. Taken from the novel by Frances Hodgson Burnett. Starring Virginia Valli and featuring Milton Sills. Adapted by Marion Fairfax, assisted by Marion Ainslee and Arthur Ripley. Photographed by Charles Stumar. At the Cameo, New York, starting Dec. 23. Runs about 80 minutes.

Clorinda Wildairs..............Virginia Valli
Sir Geoffrey Wildairs....Lionel Barrymore
Lady Daphne Wildairs....Margaret Seddon
Clorinda, aged 6.........Peggy Cartwright
Gerald Mertoun, Duke of Osmonde....
..............................Milton Sills
Dame Passett...............Florende Gibson
Mistress Wimpole........Dorothea Wolbert
Sir Christopher Crowell.........Bert Roach
Sir John Oxen.......................Earl Foxe
Sir Phumphrey Ware.............Leo White
Lord Porkfish...........George B. Williams
Pollard (Tavern Keeper).....Willard Louis
Annie Wildairs..............Patterson Dial
Annie, aged 8...........Yvonne Armstrong
Groom...............................Bob Mack

The curse of a great many of our feature films rests heavily upon "A Lady of Quality"—the curse of dragged out scenes and unending sequences in the latter half of the film. This leads to restlessness and discontent on the part of the audience overbalancing the effect of splendiferous spectacles and the lavish expertness of the whole.

Universal has gone about this picture with great earnestness and care. In the selection of Hobart Henley as director and Virginia Valli as star keen judgment was shown.

But a costume film such as this should be brimful of fiery action and romance to the very finish. That is where "A Lady of Quality" falls down. The original story by Frances Hodgson Burnett, creator of "Fauntleroy," may not have petered out toward the finish as the screen adaptation does, or perhaps the let-down was not as noticeable in book form.

The period is Queen Anne's reign in England, the end of the seventeenth century, and the time when British nobility consited largely of blustering blades and fastidious fops. Sir Geoffrey Wildairs has brought up his daughter, Clo, to suit his own ideas, and consequently she is a hoydenish tomboy, equally facile with the sword the horse and the swear word.

Enter Sir John Oxen, dashing and rakish officer of cavalry. Clo soon begins to realize she is feminine after all. Between Sir John's ardent wooing and the glorious moonlit splendor of love-laden nights she acts very much the same as any other girl would under the circumstances.

Miss Valli, in her first starring role, has a fat part and does remarkably well. Milton Sills as Osmonde has but a bit to play and seems to be miscast, winning snickers from the audience because of his rather ludicrous appearance in white knickers and hose, plumed hat, long hair and the other requisites of the dress of the period. A child, Peggy Cartwright, makes the character of Clo as a girl of six a living, pulsating little minx, and the rest of the cast, including Earle Foxe as the despicable Don Juan, give adequate if not notable performances.

Henley has directed with skill and Universal has provided him with a bix expense quota to draw on. The scenes where the victorious British army marches triumphantly past Queene Anne and the frenzied populace are particularly colorful. The castle interiors and the woodland exteriors, especially those used in the hunting and love scenes, are thoroughly beautiful, and in the hands of Charles Stumar develop into some of the best photographic shots of the year.

"A Lady of Quality" appears to be good for moderately successful runs at the l[illegible] important first run houses and the better neighborhood theatres. The last half of it may bore many, but on the whole it should make an impression and win new friends for Universal.

BIG BROTHER

Paramount-Allan Dwan production of Rex Beach's story, written for the screen by Paul Sloane. Cast includes Tom Moore, Edith Roberts, Raymond Hatton, Mickey Bennett, Joe King, Charles Henderson, Paul Panser, Neill Kelly, William Black, Martin Faust, Milton Herman, Florence Ashbrood and Yvonne Hughes. Running time, 75 minutes. At Rivoli, New York, week Dec. 23.

One of the best underworlds ever screened, due to the excellent cast, faultless direction and superb subtitling. The author of the sub-titles really runs away with the picture. Written in current topical slang, they are gems and add comedy relief just where needed.

The story is draped around the Big Brother movement sponsored by prominent criminologists and humanitarians. Jimmy Donovan (Tom Moore), gang leader from the car barn district, endeavors to father the kid brother of Big Ben Murray (Joe King).

Ben is croaked in a gang battle. Donovan grows to love the kid and is drifting away from the gang when the juvenile court decides he is no fit guardian, placing the boy in an orphanage.

Donovan runs wild after that, but is finally rejuvenated by the court's promise the kid will be returned when he (Donovan) proves he has the proper qualifications for a Big Brother and will set the boy a good example.

The scene in the juvenile court is a bear. Midge Murray (Mickey Bennett), the kid, is haled before the court. Thinking to impress, he tells the judge what a tough egg his adopted father and hero is. The sub-titles, representing the kid's conception of his gangster-hero, are comedy wows. The work of the youngster is also high class and will probably elevate him. He was the perfect type of a sophisticated child of the streets. His playing of the character and pantomime was unusual. The boy is a distinct "type" and could be featured in "tough kid" parts as long as the stories last.

Tom Moore, as the gangster who mends his ways to qualify as an example for the boy, is happily cast in a fat role that he milks expertly. Moore looked and acted the well-dressed gangster of real life, not the poorly clad idea of the average writer.

The photography and direction are high class all through the picture. A gang fight which started at the annual ball of the Pastime A. C. was another triumph of direction and technique. One little detail will suffice to illustrate the knowledge of gangdom by the author and director. The leader of the rival gang arrives with his "moll." He wanders inside and is promptly "fanned" for his "rod" by the two bouncers. He is "clean," for he had previously slipped the gat to the dame. She had it planted conveniently in her handbag. Even in gangdom it is unethical to search a lady.

A stick-up by four auto bandits was just as intelligently handled. The much-abused "cokie" was rejuvenated by the character work of Raymond Hatton. His dope fiend is a sterling bit of character acting and another of the many details that make this picture stand out among underworld shots like the Woolworth building in a Los Angeles suburb.

It is a realistic melodramatic triumph and a really great picture. *Con.*

STEADFAST HEART

Distinctive Production, adapted from the story of Clarence Budington Kell and by Philip Lonergan. Directed by Sheridan Hall. Shown at the Capitol, New York, week Dec. 23. Running time, 75 minutes.

Lydia Canfield...........Marguerite Courtot
Lydia Canfield at 8 years..Mariam Battista
Angus Burke....................Joseph Striker
Angus Burke as boy.........Joseph Depew
Mal Crane........................Hugh Huntley
Mal Crane as boy..............Jerry Devine
Crane.......................William B. Mack
Bishwang.......................Sherry Tansey
Mrs. Burke.........................Mary Alden
David Wilkins................Mario Majeroni
Titus Burke.......................Walter Louis

This is a rather draggy affair that starts depressingly and later lightens up. As a picture it doesn't appear on the surface to have any particular strong box office appeal. It is just one of the average run of program pictures.

There is one thing about the production, it has some half dozen names that might attract patronage. [illegible] Marguerite Courtot, who [illegible] reappearance after an absence [illegible] some length; Miriam Battista, William B. Mack, Mary Alden and Mario Majeroni. Incidentally, there are a couple of kid actors in Joseph Depew and Jerry Devine who make a decided bid for fame in the production.

The story is one of small town intolerance. The hero is a youngster with low-browed parents who live in a shack on the outskirts of the town. The father commits a robbery and makes his getaway. The mother, half-crazed from a beating, believes that the posse searching for her husband are really bandits and she instructs the lad to fire through the door when she gives the word. The boy does and kills the sheriff. He is tried for murder and acquitted, whereupon the editor of the local paper adopts him, starting to educate and raise him.

The other youngsters of the town, however, will have nothing to do with the boy. One in particular, the son of the district attorney who tried to have the boy convicted, takes every opportunity to call him "**murderer and jailbird." The boy is finally sent away to school by his foster father, and after 12 years returns to the town.**

The district attorney and his son are mixed up in a shady oil proposition scheme, and the local paper gets after them. The boy is the editor and he takes his stand to maintain it.

Finally he is made assistant manager of the bank. When the district attorney, driven to desperation through failure of the oil scheme to pan out, tries to decamp with the funds that the natives have invested. it is the boy that they have all cast out who goes after him and recovers the coin.

That makes him the hero, and the girl who was engaged to the district attorney's son breaks off the match, with the final fade-out finding her in the hero's arms.

The story drags along at a slow pace and at times becomes tiresome. The direction of Sherfdan Hall, while satisfactory from a perfunctory viewpoint, does not give the picture a wallop at any point that would register particularly with an audience.

Of the cast Mary Alden in a character role for a brief time at the opening of the story registers strongly. Marguerite Courtot as the heroine is conventional, but Miriam Battista, who plays the same character as a little girl, gets her work over with a bang. That is also true of the two youngsters, Joseph Depew and Jerry Devine. William B. Mack is the heavy and scores.

There is some fairly good photography in spots, and a couple of street fights between the kids register for comedy. *Fred.*

ENGLISH PROGRAM

Edward L. Klein Co., importers and exporters, screen a six-reel mixed program in the Miles projection room, late last week, giving six reels in a variety of one- and two-reelers, all British. Two of the single reelers are educationals. A two-reel dramatic, "The Reverse of the Medal," follows, and the finale is a two-reel comedy, "The Man Who Liked Lemons." The only star is Clive Brook, playing the lead in "The Reverse of the Medal."

It is not news that the English producers have made long steps forward in their production methods and the quality of output. But it seems they are no nearer the American. This group suggests some of the reasons why the English don't break in, although it does make it appear that they are doing extremely well with one-reel non-theatrical subjects.

The two educationals shown here are of high quality, scenically, and might make capital material for the surrounding bill of an American program. For American purposes they get away from time-worn ideas, have scenic beauty and illuminating titles.

They are part of a series called "Secrets of Nature." One gives the life history of the mayfly and the other deals with a small fish called the "stickleback." This doesn't sound nearly as thrilling as it is on the screen. The fish picture was taken in a glass aquarium tank and shows the stickleback mating caveman fashion, the male guarding the eggs and young until they are able to care for themselves. This process involves underwater battles with many queer creatures and other incidents of interest. The mayfly reel is just as interesting. Both were edited and titled by an officer of the British historical museum.

"The Reverse of the Medal" is a war drama, done in the typical British style, with particular emphasis on repression in acting and titling. It packs a whole six-reeler into two reels and has a good deal of merit. It is doubtful if the American fans will accept such a drama. We are accustomed to somewhat florid acting on this side, and particularly picture audiences like the "punch" in visible and concrete form, rather than by the indirect form of suggestion.

When the British general (it's a war picture) sends his own son to death behind the enemy's lines, he is expected by the Americans to show some emotion. The typical British action is to suggest the man's emotion by his stoical impassiveness. British audiences understand the man is concealing his emotions, but Americans probably would regard his actions as expressing phlegmatic indifference or at least heartlessness.

The series ends with a two-reel comedy, "The Man Who Liked Lomens," which is the least promising of the lot. America is pre-eminent in the comedy subject and has developed it 'way beyond the foreign makers. This one is slow in action, has no "stunts," no surprises, and seems to make an effort to follow the Chaplin design, without success. It deals with a comedian (somewhere between Lloyd Hamilton and Chaplin in style) who is thrown out of his lodgings for non-payment of rent. He loves lemons and in trying to steal one is about to be arrested. He escapes. A burglar seizes the sap and makes him his assistant in a "job." They are robbing a flat, after sandbagging the occupant, when the coin gas meter goes out. The simp is sent out to get two shillings change for a two-shilling piece, and he spends the whole coin for lemons, leaving the burglar to be seized.

There may be a British national wheeze about lemon eaters, but this reporter was too thick to get its humor. *Rush.*

THE RED WARNING

Universal, starring Jack Hoxie. Story, continuity and titles by Isadore Bernstein, direction by Robert North Bradbury. Shown at the Stanley, N. Y., Dec. 25, 1923.

Thos. Jeffries....................Fred Kohler
Frank Ainslee....................William Welsh
George Ainslee....................George Welsh
Louise Ainslee....................Elinor Fields
Harry Williams....Ralph F. MacCollougher
Philip Haver....................Jack Hoxie
Toby Jones....................Frank Rice

Fairly good western thriller of the cheaper program type turned out by Universal. In the houses where they like the western stuff of the rough-and-ready variety this one will please tho fans. There are a couple of touches suggesting local K. K. K. stuff, and should make it liked in the communities where that organization has a strong hold. In spots the photography and tinting are bad, and that hurts.

Jack Hoxie, the star, is set down in a small western town near the border that is being overrun by cattle thieves. He is the one to organize the natives into a vigilance committee, and brings about a roundup of the crooks.

The story is the old-time formula with the rancher having a pretty daughter and the heavy holding a note for the homestead. "Give me the girl and call it square" is the plot. When dad won't give up the girl and can't pay the note he goes into the desert and looks for the lost mine.

The heavy follows him and knocks him off, but before passing out he is found by two strangers, who get his story and go back to the little town to look after his daughter.

In the finish the desert hero wins the girl after he wipes out the band of rustlers, and finds the mine her dad lost his life in the search of.

There is a little too much of the riding footage to make the story a real fast one. But in the main it will hold interest in the daily change grind houses.

Fred Kohler handles the heavy role nicely and Elinor Fields as the ingenue lead does all that could be asked in a particularly strong part. In Frank Rice, U looks to have a character player they might build up along the lines of that of Ernest Torrence in "The Covered Wagon." He furnishes a comedy relief for the yarn. *Fred.*

A PRINCE OF A KING

A five-reeler produced by A. G. Stegmuller. Story by Alice Farwell Brown. Directed by Albert Austin. Featuring Dinky Dean. Released by Selznick Distributing Corporation. Shown on double feature bill at Loew's New York, Dec. 21. Running time, 60 minutes.

Dinky Dean is the youngster who appeared with Chaplin in "The Pilgrim." At the time the kid was heralded as another Jackie Coogan.

This producer evidently considers Dinky of stellar material, yet he has camouflaged him with a costume play that is a cross between melodrama and a comic opera. He has surrounded him with an adequate supporting cast, including Virginia Pearson and Sheldon Lewis.

The story revolves around a babe, heir to the throne in one of those mythical kingdoms. The babe is born on the eve of the king's death. Roberto, a cousin, next in line for the crown, commissions a hireling to steal the royal baby and make away with it, so that he can rule the kingdom. The henchman weakens and instead deposits the babe in the donkey cart of a troupe of strolling acrobats.

The latter bring him up. At the age of four he is taught all of their stunts and is their chief performer.

Little Crigi is the idol of everybody. When he performs the takings are of generous proportions. But he is beaten and maltreated by the acrobats and makes his escape. After numerous hair-raising vicissitudes he is restored to his queen mother and ascends the throne.

Prior to the climax the youngster has made his way to the castle in an attempt to flee the tyrannical acrobats. Roberto, who now occupies the thro e, sends for the acrobats and is about to give him back when the queen convinces the guards he is their rightful king. When the kid ascends the throne he asks if any command will be granted that he may wish. When told it would, he exclaims, "Then throw out those acrobats!" which provides the comedy punch finish.

Dinky Dean is undoubtedly a clever youngster and demonstrates it, especially in the early reels, when he does some clever acrobatic stunts. True enough, he has not that seeming sophistry of young Coogan, but this will probably come in time. His pranks were spontaneous and natural.

Miss Pearson gave a likeable delineation of the queen-mother. Sheldon Lewis did well as the giant acrobat. Sam De Grasse gave a villainous portrayal of the Black King.

Although having nothing to differentiate it from the rank and file costume play, this film will undoubtly appeal to a kid element because of its youthful star. It's best break will be on double feature bills or may do as a feature in the small neighborhood houses.

PREPARED TO DIE

Johnnie Walker production, starring Eddie Polo. Story by Keene Thompson, directed by Wm. Hughes Curran. Shown at the Stanley, N. Y., Dec. 23, 1923. Running time, 56 minutes.

Vivienne Van de Vere........Edna Gregory
John Pend eton Smythe.........Eddie Polo
Storekeeper......................John McElhern

Eddie Polo as a society dub with a monocle! That's the plot of this feature, at least that is about all that stands out in the production. The low down on the picture is that where it should be funny it is sad and where it should be taken seriously it is funny. On the whole, it is mighty poor screen entertainment except for the houses where they don't care what they see as long as it is something that moves on the screen. Otherwise this is one of those things that the average exhibitor wants to lay off of.

Possibly there was a story at the time that Keene Thompson turned in a script, but by the time that it reached the screen the story must have been dropped in some out-of-the-way corner in the studio. At any rate the tale ambles along without any attempt being made to plant a reason for anything that happens in the later episodes.

It is the yarn of a society dub having been jilted decides to commit suicide. He has a horror of bumping himself off, so he takes a friend's advice and hies himself to the Kentucky mountains, where there is supposed to be a feud killing every minute. When he gets there he finds the town fast asleep, and after he wakes it up sufficiently to register at the little one-horse hotel he starts out to have himself killed. His attemps, however, are taken for bravery, and he wins the admiration of the storekeeper's daughter. Later, when he decides that he wants to live again, he loses the girl through his backing down when one of the roughnecks tries to run him out of town. But his fighting spirit is roused with the loss of the girl, and he does put up a battle. That is the only thing about the picture that has any action.

Polo simply will not do when he tries these dressed-up parts, and seemingly, judging from the technique he disyplayed in this picture, the art of acting before the camera seems to have escaped him entirely. *Fred.*

BROADWAY BROKE

Murray Garson presents this film version of Earl Derr Biggers' story, originally published in the "Saturday Evening Post," featuring Mary Carr. Directed by J. Searle Dawley. Scenario by John Lynch. Distributed by the Selznick organization chain. Projection time, 80 minutes. At Loew's, New York, Dec. 22.

"Broadway Broke" may have made a good enough story. If Earl Derr Biggers wrote it and the "Satevepost" published it it is a reasonable presumption that it was. But it makes a pretty tiresome picture.

A writer in the medium of print could have built up the atmosphere of the 70's and a picture of other times gracefully softened by imagery and grace. The literal screen fails to do this, and the only possible charm of the picture is its spirit.

It has practically no action and never should have been adapted to the picture medium. Made into a film that runs for nearly an hour and a half, it is deadly.

The first reel or more are devoted to incidents backstage and out front at a premiere at Daly's theatre half a century or so ago. Actors impersonate General Grant, Mark Twain and P. T. Barnum, as first nighters, a matter of momentary interest.

All this to establish the triumphs of Nellie Gwynn (Mary Carr) as the Daly star. Mrs. Carr doesn't make the youthful actress by a wide margin, but there is a certain interest in this dip into old times, for adults.

The story jumps to the present day when the former toast of the town has fallen upon hard days of poverty, due to a selfish daughter married to a vaudeville performer, who has spent all her money. Her only comfort is a sweet granddaughter.

The vaudevillian is the heavy. He has committed forgery and is being pressed to make good his thefts. To do so he sells his trick dog, pet of the family, to a vivisectionist.

Grandma brings about a happy ending in about half a reel by selling the picture rights to a play written by her dead husband and signing to play in it at $500 a week.

There is nothing the matter with the material for a light, short, sentimental picture, but spread out into a crudely produced, sloppy, sentimental seven-reeler or more, it becomes soporific.

An exceedingly unattractive prospect. *Rush.*

SALLY BISHOP

London, Dec. 16.

This adaptation from the novel by E. Temple Thurston is a pleasing if not enthralling presentation to be added to the list of Stoll Picture Productions. The story has nothing in it of any particular novelty and does not provide a very substantial vehicle for Marie Doro and Henry, in the leading roles, to ride to any great heights. Yet it cannot be said that they make the most of the opportunities they do have, and the tone of the whole picture is just ordinary.

As is often the case when a novel is adapted for the screen, the action is apt to be disjointed, and the picture loses much through a none too careful linking up, which mars the continuity considerably. This is more noticeable in the early stages of the film.

It is the old story of the man of the world on pleasure bent, whose fancy is attracted by a pretty face and who responds to the instincts of the chase. John Thraill is a barrister, and after a chance encounter with a little typist he is interested enough to follow her, and after one or two meetings and a visit to his chambers he realizes her purity and warns her for her own sake he must not see her again, as they might get to care for each other, and he is not a marrying man.

Discontented with the tawdry atmosphere of her cheap boarding house and desperately in love, Sally finally becomes his mistress, and for three years all goes well. Her girl friend tells her, however, that if by that time he has not suggested marriage to her he will probably want to marry someone else, and her first intimation of this will be if he makes her a settlement. This, in fact, does happen, and is the beginning of the end.

Marie Doro is a pathetic and realistic figure as the romantic girl brought up in a country vicarage and plunged into the maelstrom of life in a bustling city. Henry Ainley does not fit into his character of the lover quite so neatly, but, then, his forte is the spoken stage, and he never seems quite at ease without the help of his voice.

The other parts were quite well played, the best performance being that of Florence Turner as the far-seeing, faithful boarding house friend of Sally.

1924

BLACK OXEN

San Francisco, Jan. 2.

First National production, made from Gertrude Atherton's novel of the same title. Directed by Frank Lloyd. Starring Corinne Griffith, with Conway Tearle featured. Presented at the Warfield, San Francisco, Dec. 29.

This Frank Lloyd film of Gertrude Atherton's novel is entertaining, with the story consistently told and the acting splendid. The only fault seems to be a disappointing ending. The audience, in its heart, wants to see the hero, Clavering, marry the rejuvenated Mary Ogden, even though the mind knows that her final refusal is the logical, sensible action.

It is here that Lloyd reveals the false note by closing the story with the intimation that Clavering will wed a horrid little flapper, adorably played by Mary Bow.

The story concerns Mary Ogden (Corinne Griffith), who, as a girl married an Austrian nobleman. After the war, when a woman of 60, she submitted to a rejuvenation operation and had her youth restored. She comes to America a beautiful young woman, and here meets Clavering (Conway Teare), a young critic and playwright. Mary seeks to hide her identity. Her girlhood friends, now grandmothers, marvel at the resemblance between the mysterious young foreigner and the Mary Ogden they knew as a girl.

Mary and Clavering fall in love, whereupon she confesses to him in a letter the truth of her life and at the same time tells the truth to the women who were her girlhood friends. But Clavering will have her in spite of all.

An Austrian count whom Mary loved abroad arrives, finds her out, and makes her see the folly of her romance with Clavering. She leaves Clavering and goes abroad with the Austrian. The end of the picture shows Clavering trying to reconcile himself with the flapper.

Corinne Griffith plays Mary convincingly and appealingly. Conway Tearle is thoroughly satisfying as Clavering. The rest of the cast and the settings are excellent. The direction is praiseworthy.

San Francisco is Miss Atherton's home town, and the town is for her.

Rivers.

THE RENDEZVOUS

Goldwyn-Cosmopolitan picture, both presented and directed by Marshall Neilan from the story of Madeleine Ruthven. Photography credited to David Keson. Showing at the Capitol, New York, week of Dec. 30. Running time, 79 mins.

Walter Stanford	Conrad Nagel
Vera	Lucille Ricksen
Prince Sergei Tamiroff	Richard Travers
Varvara Korenieva	Kathleen Key
Vassily Leonidoff	Emmett Corrigan
Juan Godunoff	Elmo Lincoln
Winkie Harrington	Sydney Chaplin
Mrs. Stanford	Kate Lester
Nichi Wandor	Cecil Holland
Samuel Klein	Lucien Littlefield
Nini Mushkuin	Eugenie Besserer
Czar	R. O. Pennell

An oft-repeated story, this, but changing the locale to Siberia serves to disguise it a bit, while the creditable direction and work of the cast is sufficient to make the picture suitable for the first-run houses. The film is noteworthy for the individual performance of Elmo Lincoln, who, cast as a renegade and uneducated Cossack become powerful with the advent of the Russian revolution, is the "heavy" of the script, and realizes upon the role to far overshadow any other quality that the presentation contains.

Neilan has done nicely in handling this somewhat aged theme in that he has carried the suspense along for a fulfillment of purpose while also inserting a comedy balance in the person of Syd Chaplin, whose characterization of a British "Tommy" and the "business" assigned places the role only secondary to Lincoln.

Lucille Ricksen, leading the feminine contingent, is alleged to have been around the studios for some time, but it looks as if this vehicle can be designated as her first instance of an emphatic bid for attention, and it should lead to further prominence. Conrad Nagel is the other "name," although his assignment is without difficulties for him.

The story is that of an orphaned girl, in reality a Russian princess, whose parents have been lost to her, while her identity must be kept a secret due to the establishment of a republic. Reared in Siberia she establishes a growing friendship with an American lieutenant who promises to return. During his absence Godunoff, governing the province, forces the girl into a matrimonial ceremony through the threat of death to her guardian, but at which time she faints, so that the marriage is uncompleted.

The Cossack's fall from power turns him into an outlaw during which time he continues to pursue the girl, and in one instance beats her to the extent of inflicting absolute deafness.

The title refers to a shrine beyond the village the girl's father had constructed upon the death of her mother, and at which place she and the lieutenant constantly meet. The return of the American youth with his mother signalizes the approaching finish, although before the end is reached the girl, in making her final pilgrimage to the shrine, locks the massive door, unknowingly imprisoning Godunoff, who has been lying in wait, and his cries go unheeded because of the deafness he has caused.

It is a credit to Neilan that he has been able to hold the story together for an interesting sequence of events, albeit a share of the praise should also be tendered Lincoln, who comes mighty close to "making" the picture. Scenically the locale is mostly within the village, although the opening includes a few flashes of the royal palace as well as an insert or two of the Czar.

The picture is not the best thing the director has ever done, nor is it the worst, but it can lead the better programs to satisfaction, and it may be said Neilan might have spared the American flag insert at the conclusion, for it was totally unnecessary.

Skig.

HER TEMPORARY HUSBAND

Associated First National Production with Sidney Chaplin, Owen Moore and Sylvia Breamer featured. Written by Edward Paulton. Directed by John F. McDermott. Shown at the Strand, N. Y., week Dec. 30, 1923. Running time 68 minutes.

Thomas Burton	Owen Moore
Judd	Sidney Chaplin
Blanche Ingram	Sylvia Breamer
John Ingram	Tully Marshall
Clarence Topping	Charles Gerard
Conrad Jasper	George Cooper
Hector	Chuck Reisner

One of those comedy pictures that come along just about only so often. It isn't a whale of a comedy and it hasn't any particular box-office appeal in the names that it carries, but it is a picture that is going to make the average picture house audience laugh and laugh a lot. This is due as much to the clever titling as it is to the action of the picture. As a matter of fact that title-writing stuff shows Edward Paulton, for he built his title gags as he would dialog in a play and it landed.

There is one thing about the picture decidedly in its favor and that is that it offers a break in the type of near society stuff that the majority of first-run features have been of in the most recent past.

The story of "Her Temporary Husband" is somewhat along the lines of "The Three Twins," at least there are three characters who all look alike, one in the original and two others who don false wigs and whiskers to resemble him. It deals with a young woman whose dead aunt has left her a fortune with the proviso that she marries within 24 hours after the will is read to her and to a man who will have sufficient money to banish any suggestion of his being a fortune hunter. A suitor for the girl's hand has been counting on this fortune and he is much put out but suggests that some wealthy man at death's door might be secured to undertake the role of bridegroom and then conveniently pass out of the picture.

This would have all been well enough hadn't the hero of the tale stepped in at about this stage of the game and decided to marry the girl. He is at the private sanitarium when the girl and her advisor arrive and hears the marriage being arranged. Then he gets a flash at the groom-to-be and sends his valet for a wig and whiskers to match them up. Once these are secured, it is he instead of the dying man that is married to the girl, and the balance of the story is pure in- and outdoor farce. The one outstanding bit of comedy is just the in and out of door stuff, showing three conspirators chasing three different men all looking alike through a series of rooms. The shot was a little long for the audience to get the full benefit of this and had it been done down a little closer it would have been a wow.

Sidney Chaplin puts over a very agreeable and humorous characterization as the valet of the hero, who is Owen Moore. Miss Breamer as the ingenue lead manages to score moderately. Chuck Reisner was a laugh as a tough customer.

Fred.

BLACK OXEN

Frank Lloyd production, starring Corinne Griffith and Conway Tearle. Adaptation of the novel by Gertrude Atherton, directed by Frank Lloyd. Released by First National. At Strand New York, week of Jan. 6. Running time, 90 minutes.

Madame Zatianny (also Mary Ogden)	Corinne Griffith
Lee Clavering	Conway Tearle
Charles Dinwiddie	Thomas Ricketts
Judge Gavin Trent	Thomas S. Guise
Janet Oglethorpe	Clara Bow
Jane Oglethorpe	Kate Lester
James Oglethorpe	Harry Mestayer
Donnie Ferris	Lincoln Stedman
Agnes Trevor	Claire MacDowell
Flappers:	Ione Atkinson, Mila Constantin and Hortense O'Brien.
Prince Hohenbauer	Alan Hale

In transforming this popular novel into a screen play those concerned will have to depend largely upon the readers of the book for any measure of success it may achieve. While it may have had value as literature, there is nothing outstanding to recommend it for screen entertainment save the attempted new angle on sex stuff that makes its 60-year-old heroine, promiscuous in her youthful love affairs, repent in a rejuvenated youth that is effected through a scientific phenomenon.

Some may argue that the unique thesis of the novel was in itself sufficient to warrant its conversion. But from a reviewer's angle it is probably much better reading than as screen entertainment.

Yeat's quotation, "The years, like great black oxen, tread the world, and God, the Herdsman, goads them on behind," undoubtedly provided the inspiration for the novel. The popular vogue of the latter also may have had something to do with its screening.

The novel has been more or less adhered to in the screen version, perhaps, if anything, playing the sex angle up for a more potent wallop.

At a fashionable theatrical premiere the cynosure of eyes are diverted from the stage toward a young woman of the audience. Many see in her a social favorite of yesteryear—Mary Ogden. "Preposterous," the dowagers exclaim, for Mary married into nobility 30 years before and was last seen abroad as a feeble woman of 60.

Some who had not known her affairs as well as others had speculated that the resemblance was so perfect that she must be Mary's daughter, while those in the know laughed and whispered that Zatianny's had no offspring. But even this did not assure the wiseacres that the girl was not Mary's daughter. Even when the Dowager bearded the girl in the Ogden mansion the latter all but verified the suspicions, and right here every one was predicting the yarn to take a "love child" angle.

But gossip did not stifle Lee Clavering's determination to meet her. Clavering, playwright and critic, was intrigued, if anything. Fate did the rest. Although a confirmed bachelor, he had yielded readily to the charm of the girl, and when others were paying her court forged to the front with a proposal of marriage.

This precipitated the revelation that the girl was Mary Ogden herself, acknowledgedly past 60, but rejuvenated to the youthfulness of a girl in her 20's. It had been accomplished primarily that renewed strength might permit her to return to America to dispose of her holdings so that she could assist in the restoration of her war-ridden country, Austria.

Her friends would not believe this. They saw in her purpose another desire again to tread the path of promiscuity, and hated her for it.

These suggestions held little weight with Clavering, who, through his unselfish love for her, had affected another phenomenon, that of making her heart young as well as her body.

Corinne Griffith gave a likeable portrait of the dual role, excelling.

of course, as the youthful Mary. Conway Tearle had a typical Tearle role in Clavering. Clara Bow contributed a flapper type that relieved the tensity of the dramatic moments and served as refreshing comedy relief.

Whatever chance the film has aside from its competent cast and some splendid acting, must come from its sex stuff. It's a 50-50 break they'll eat it up if it isn't over their heads.

PURE GRIT

Universal production, directed by Nat Ross and starring Roy Stewart. From a story by William McLeod Raine. At the New York Dec. 28 as half the bill. Running time, 53 mins.

Bob Evans....................Roy Stewart
Stella Bolling..............Esther Ralston
Jim Kemp......................Jere Austin
Frank Bolling..................Jack Mower
Buddy Clark...................Verne Winter

Universal may be putting out all sorts of "super-jewel" big films, but that they are still producing "junk" is amply demonstrated by "Pure Grit." It is a western, but as far as atmosphere goes it might just as well have taken place in any other locale. That William McLeod Raine is credited with the story is surprising, as he has been a consistent writer of strong adventure tales.

This time he has not only turned out a stereotyped, insipid plot, but one which violates one of the most important laws of filmdom—the insertion of a genuine punch or twist at the point where a climax is expected. There is the purely mechanical thrill of the fire in the shack in which the girl is fighting off the lusting villain. This has been better done so many times it will hardly create a stir.

The work of two helps a lot to keep "Pure Grit" from becoming the prize film annoyance. They are Verne Winter, a youngster who outfreckles Wesley Barry, and Esther Ralston, the school marm heroine. Young Winter is amusing as the village "tough kid" who chews tobacco, smokes on the sly and finally tracks down the villain after much detective work. Miss Ralston puts life and charm into an almost impossible role.

Roy Stewart is his usual placid self, impressing as a particularly colorless specimen of Texas ranger.

The film must have been dirt cheap for Universal to produce. The cast holds but five, and the only extras introduced are the children used for a schoolroom scene, that, like everything else, missed fire completely. It may bring in a little money at the cheapest houses because of the title and the Stewart name, but it never should have been flashed at an important house like the New York.

RENO

Goldwyn-Cosmopolitan picture written and directed by Rupert Hughes with J. J. Mescall the photographer. At the Capitol, New York, week Jan. 6. Running time, 74 mins.

Mrs. Emily Dysart Tappan, Helene Chadwick
Guy Tappan....................Lew Cody
Walter Heath................George Walsh
Mrs. Dora Carson Tappan...Carmel Myers
Mrs. Kate Norton Tappan..Hedda Hooper
Miss Alida Tappan.............Dale Fuller
Yvette .... Kathleen Key
Jerry Dysart....................Rush Hughes
Marjory Towne............Marjorie Bonner
Henry Nish..............William Orlamond
Judge Norton............Howard Truesdale
Paul Tappan..............Robert de Vilbiss
Ivy Tappan................Virginia Loomis
Arthur Clayton..............Richard Wayne
Justice of Peace..............Hughie Mack
Hal Carson....................Boyce Combe
McRae, the detective..........Victor Potel
Lemile Hake..................Percy Hemus
Mattie Hake..........Maxine Elliott Hicks
Tod Hake......................Billy Eugene
Mrs. Tod Hake..............Adele Watson
Mrs. Towne..................Evelyn Sherman
Hod Stoat........................Jack Curtis
Mrs. Hod Stoat...............Pattison Dial

Not the best piece of work this author-director has ever given to the screen and neither above nor below the average trend of prerelease features this house is accustomed to.

It amounts to little more than a lecture on this country's mixed divorce laws with the ludicrous angles attached through the many variations of the codes as upheld by the 48 states.

The picture is replete with statistics concerning annulments besides there being many an incident included only for the purpose of bringing out some special point as regards a court's decision. On the other hand the film should prove acceptable as a program leader for the larger houses on the strength of the cast names, production, title and divorce angle. The actual narrative is its most vulnerable point.

Not without many a comedy insertion the story attempts to follow the love affairs of Guy Tappan at one time confronted by a trio of Mrs. Tappans who are, or are not, his lawful wives according to the states wherein they may reside. Another annexation to the story is pinned to the two Tappan children. Over them is a continuous struggle due to the father's wealhty aunt who will not reimburse the financially embarrassed parent unless he procures the custody of his offsprings.

Then there is the second wife and mother of the children, her hectice maneuvers, chasing about the country, and mental anguish given to the cause of finding and holding on to her boy and girl, while the former lover is also at her elbow to assist, also willing to accept she and the children.

The tale covers much territory before the sequence of events concludes but will mostly interest in the passages confined to the Yellowstone park area wherein is displayed some beautiful exteriors and the "kick" of the action through a fight between the versatile Tappan and his second wife's champion. It results in the former's falling into the mouth of a geyser which begins to erupt, tossing and suspending his body in midair to culminate in his death.

The playing of the extended cast and direction is equal to calling forth all the possibilities of the tale while the feminine contingent must concede Helene Chadwick as their most prominent. Lew Cody is the amourous gentleman, thrice married, but actually has little to do other than to appear as a figurehead upon which the continuity must rest, while George Walsh, as the faithful suitor, impresses as being both off in appearance (possibly due to a faulty facial makeup) and performance.

Beyond that duo comes to light a corking donation in Rush Hughes, who, assigned as the brother of the second wife and in the midst of an affair of his own, assuredly equals any other member of the male end on strength of work. A whale of an appearance, supplemented by personality, young Hughes proves of sufficient background to step forth and emphatically cash in on this performance, following the possibilities first gleaned in a Lila Lee picture of the past. That is if real estate doesn't prove too great an attraction and "Roswell" can overcome a certain idea of service with a flourish.

As a whole "Reno" will be found fairly entertaining although it's not the best in pictures, but it serves the intended purpose of revealing the crudities of America's divorce laws, while it has been given an appropriate production and reveals excellent photography on the part of Johnnie Mescall.

In truth, though, "Reno" must depend upon its divorce argument for any draw. Peculiarly too with "Reno" opening Sunday at the Capitol, on Monday "The Pictorial Review" spread a page advertisement throughout the New York dailies, calling attention to its devotion to the many-sided divorce laws of the country and also to its 2,500,000 alleged circulation, mostly among women.

The paper said in its copy it felt as divorce was a distracting subject with women, it had to give attention to it and had been doing so for two years.

If there had been a tie-up by Goldwyn and "Reno" with the "Pictorial Review" it could not have broken better, so if the weekly sends its advertsiing campaign broadcast it should be of similar advantage. *Skig.*

GREAT WHITE WAY

Cosmopolitan production, directed by E. Mason Hooper. Full evening's entertainment at $1.50 top, opening Cosmopolitan, New York, Jan. 3 for run.

Mabel Vandergrift...........Anita Stewart
Jack Murray................T. Roy Barnes
Joe Cain........................Oscar Shaw
Duke Sullivan....................Tom Lewis
City Editor..................Harry Watson
Stubbs ....Olin Howland
Adolph Lutz..................Dore Dav'dson
Brock Morton.......................Hal Forde
Mr. Cain......................Stanley Forde
Arthur Brisbane...........Arthur Brisbane
Tex Rickard......................Tex Rickard
Ned Wayburn.................Ned Wayburn
Irvin S. Cobb.................Irvin S. Cobb
H. C. Witwer..................H. C. Witwer
Harry Hershfield..........Harry Hershfield
Damon Runyon.............Damon Runyon
Bugs Baer.........................."Bugs" Baer
George McManus..........George McManus
Nell Brinkley.................Nell Brinkley
Hal Coffman....................Hal Coffman
J. W. McGurk.................J. W. McGurk
Winsor McCay..............Winsor McCay
Billy De Beck.................Billy De Beck
Fay King............................Fay King
Earle Sande......................Earle Sande
Kid Broad.........................Kid Broad
Jimmy Stone....................Pete Hartley
Referee ....Johnny Gallagher
Cain's Second............Johnny Hennessey
Stone's Second.....................Billy Gould
McIntyre ....Frank Wonderley
Announcer ....Joe Humphries
Smoke ....Jerry Peterson
And the entire Ziegfeld "Follies" Chorus
Asst. Director.........Edward J. Babbille
Photography by Harold Wenstrom and Henry Cronjager

A glance at the cast above and you get the idea of this picture. It seems to have been made with a view of the glorification of prizefighters and Hearst newspapers. About the only syndicated light Hearst can't contract-claim is Irvin S. Cobb. At that, though, Cobb might be willin'.

On the screen you see the New York "American," and on the program it's mentioned the press room scene is from the Los Angeles "Examiner."

The newspaper men appeared human in the picture. They were all there in person excepting Arthur Brisbane. The Brisbane actor looked so faithfully Brisbane that if Brisbane has charge accounts, he's taking a chance.

Most all of the writing guys got applause from a first night audience that knew most by sight. Harry Hershfield was the busiest on the screen, and Damon Runyon the most retiring, while Bugs Baer got the most applause.

Some of the captions drew laughs. Who wrote the others no one around knew or would tell. Maybe Hearst himself, William R. It's his picture, so no one could stop him; but if he did, William need never expect to be syndicated himself as a funny feller.

Fine chance, too, in this picture for captions, all the way through it. It's that kind of a picture. Taken from the Witwer short story of "Cain and Mabel," the film-expanded adaptation is the excuse for ringing in all that's best or worst around Times square, its people and sports.

The sporting end is what gives the film a punch. It's of a prize fight for the welterweight championship with the ring in the Yankee Stadium and the mob which packed the Stadium for the Firpo-Willard fight. Neatly inserted, the ring proper scenes are of a corking battle between Oscar Shaw as Joe Cain and Pete Hartley, the pugilist, as Jimmy Stone, the English champion.

One of the causes for this stirring ring battle is that in rehearsal Shaw really knocked out Hartley, and Hartley, for evens, did the same thing to Shaw in the next round. Those rounds were substituted for the fight, but only one knockout naturally may be shown. The fight, however, will catch the crowd, whether of women, boys or men. It runs one round too short. Cain came back too fast after Mabel spoke to him in his corner.

Another well-pieced exhibit is a steeplechase at Belmont racetrack, with the picture given an awful wallop here through the clumsy manner the race was "jobbed."

A real mob scene was a dance hall fire with about 100 extras engaged that brought a crowd of 15,000 to watch it.

Plenty of action all the way, but the two parts were unevenly balanced. It was the second half that suffered with the scheme seeming to be to get to the fight and through with it.

As a round New York picture with Times square the stopping place this should be a box office card for any town away from New York, the farther away the better, and in the picture houses a wow. Announced to have cost a million or so, you can't see anywhere near that money.

Anita Stewart is the heroine, who is the star dancer of a new musical show, with the chorus girls doing their drilling, some in tights. That won't keep any of the men away from the theatre either, especially when hearing they are the Ziegfeld "Follies" girls of last summer. These scenes were taken in the Dresden theatre on top of the Amsterdam theatre, with Ned Wayburn the drill master.

Miss Stewart gave a first-class performance. Shaw did right well too as Cain, although the star of the acting cast is Dore Davidson as Adolph Lutz (Blum on the caption), the theatre manager. T. Roy Barnes was a press agent, of the usual, and Harry Watson played one of the Hearst city editors, doing his vaudeville telephone bit as a part of it.

Some of the all-ink cast were at the premiere to watch themselves and get a line on the public applause pulse. They were very modest going out, didn't ask anyone how they looked in the picture, nor did they say the director had crossed them. *Sime.*

PLEASURE MAD

A Reginald Barker production, presented by Louis B. Mayer. Adapted from Blanche Upright's novel, "The Valley of Content" by A. P. Younger, directed by Reginald Barker. Shown at the Rivoli, New York, week Jan. 6. Running time, 86 minutes. Released by Metro.

Hugh Benton ....Huntley Gordon
Marjorie Benton.......................Mary Alden
Elinor Benton...................Norma Shearer
Howard Benton ....William Collier, Jr.
Geraldine De Lacey.........Winifred Bryson
Templeton Druid....................Ward Crane
John Hammond..........Frederick Truesdell
Hulda ....Joan Standing

"Pleasure Mad," adapted from from "The Valley of Content," is just another modern version of "The Governor's Lady." Like all of the jazz-mad society melodramas of this type it runs along in a groove that has nothing in it that is new either as to story or direction. In fact it is just another one of the society mellers that can be matched up with several score that have hit the screen within the last few years. There is nothing to the picture that stands out except the performance of Mary Alden as the wife and mother who stood still when wealth came and her husband and family outstepped her. Mary Alden will carry the picture in the neighborhood houses and in the smaller communities, but in the big prerelease theatres there is nothing in it that will give the audiences a thrill, for they have seen it all in just the same way time and time again.

It is a tale of a family living in

the suburbs, the husband hustling to catch the 7:53 every morning and the wife working like a fool to scrimp and save. Finally the husband has an invention accepted by a big railroad and their fortune is made. From then on it is Fifth avenue for them. A mansion, servants, lots of spending money for the kids and life is just a merry round of pleasure. The husband with nothing on his mind except leisure falls for the heavy vamp in the scheme of things and the daughter is copped by the heavy. When the father decides that **he and the wife must live apart so that he can devote more time to the vamp who is playing him for a sap-o-dill, it is the son that decides to stick to mother's side while the daughter goes with dad.** On the night that this particular scheme is thrashed out in the home the vamp takes the father to a party, and while there he becomes aware that his daughter is in a private room with the heavy, with the result that he smashes down the doors and gets his man. Disgusted with the general scheme of things in the free and easy life, he welcomes the arrival of the little humdrum wife, and the whole family go back to the little suburban town where things are not as gay as in New York and everything is lovely again.

It is the same old hoke, dished up in the same old way.

Mary Alden, however, as the mother manages to walk away with that role and gather all the sympathy that there is in the story. Huntley Gordon as the husband gives a very convincing performance and registers well. Willie Collier, Jr., as the son scores as a youthful souse and wild kid, but little Norma Shearer manages to put over another wallop for herself in this picture that shows that she can troup. She sure looks like a real find. Winifred Bryson as the vamp was "there" with all the Thedaish stuff while Ward Crane was the heavy that got walloped behind closed doors. Frederick Truesdale had a minor role.

In direction there are a couple of things that manage to land. For instance, the idea of grouping a crowd outside of a closed door and letting imagination of what is occurring beyond get over in this manner. Likewise the car and taxi-cab bit also held a little punch. The comedy relief throughout the picture was distinctly forced.

Fred.

THUNDERGATE

First National picture adapted from a novel of Sydney Small's. Directed by Joseph De Grasse and featuring Owen Moore. Others in the cast, Edwin Pilton, Sylvia Breamer, Robert McKim, Richard Cummings, Tully Marshall, Virginia Brown Faire and William Dyer. Photographed by S. E. Landis and Robert De Grasse. At New York theatre, one day (Jan. 5). Running time, 82 minutes.

About capable as a middle class feature and mayhap a possibility for the larger houses, but it hardly looks as if it could satisfy in the latter theatres. The story is based upon a dual appearance with Moore in both roles and localed in China.

The lineup of the cast, due to some of the names included, may attract attention, but the script doesn't stand up on the screen, and other than being an average "movie" can make no assertive claims.

The production is suitable for the needs involved, although embracing a few faked exterior backgrounds while the players register for mediocre performances, outside of Richard Cummings, who, as an old sea dog, makes the characterization stand out and cash in for comedy.

Moore plays the American engineer sent to China to construct a railroad. He is framed and disgraced, but proves his alibi, also exposing those responsible. His other role is that of the heir to Thundergate, headquarters for the deposed Chinese royalist whose weakness for women leads to his death sentence and the substitution of the American in his place. The minor amount of double photography footage is aptly taken care of minus any attempt to make it particularly intricate.

Deletion would undoubtedly help to speed up the action which continuously threatens to bore and actually accomplishes just that in more than one instance. It will mean little to the producers or Moore as concerns prestige, while to term it anything more than "just a picture" would be an exaggeration.

Skig.

DEFYING DESTINY

Independent six-reeler from the story of Grace Sanderson Michie. Produced by Rellimo Film Syndicate. Directed by Louis W. Chaudet. Distributed by Selznick. Featuring Monte Blue and Irene Rich. Shown on double feature bill at Loew's New York, New York, Jan. 4. Running time, 72 minutes.

This feature looks like sure pop for the neighborhoods, and may also find its way into some of the better class picture palaces. Plenty of action, a well-balanced cast and adequate direction are a triumvirate of factors that should assure its popularity with the fans.

Although the story proper may not be sensationally original, its treatment is that in spots. It is fulsome, interesting and seldom slops over, if at all. Without going in for anything spectacular, it strikes a human note principally because of the simplicity of the story, and secondly because of the human portrayals of its characters by what is probably the nearest to an all-star cast that has yet been achieved by an independent producer.

The early reels are given over to a prologue in which Beth Alden, daughter of the town's most affluent citizen, and Jack Fenton, son of a middle-class family, are thrown together in a hay ride. A storm rages and the girl spends the night at the Fentons'. Lightning strikes and the house is set afire during the night. The boy rescues Beth, but **is badly scarred in the fire. His parents perish.**

Out of gratitude Beth's father gives him a position in the bank. The young folks are seen much in each other's company despite the fact that the father has practically betrothed his daughter to his partner. It is evident that the girl really loves her rescuer, but the hard-fisted money men, who have used their affluence successfully in turning the business world upside down, attempte to upset destiny.

The funds are short at the bank and young Fenton, who has been living beyond his means, is apprehended as the embezzler. Despite being cleared in a court trial, he is licked through public opinion. Fate sends him to the city, where he is trapped in another fire and rushed to a hospital. A noted surgeon bargains with him to undergo an experiment that will remove the scars. The boy is desperate, doesn't care what becomes of him and submits. It is successful. He returns home to have his hour of revenge, but is finally frustrated through the love of the girl.

Monte Blue gives a likeable delineation of young Fenton. In fact, the role gives him the best opportunity he has had in some time. Irene Rich easily shares honors with Monte as Beth, managing to get in some very acceptable emotional acting and later shading it with that of a lighter variety. Jackie Saunders gives a faithful delineation of an extravagant butterfly wife, while Tully Marshall is superb in the minor role of the surgeon. Practically every one in the cast does well in their respective roles.

The fire scene of the early reels is particularly well staged and provides a thrill punch. Those who enjoy a dash of melodrama with their love stories should undoubtedly find this admixture to their liking.

BLOW YOUR OWN HORN

R-C release from the authorship of Owen Davis and directed by L. W. Horne with Joseph Dubray at the camera. At the Stanley, New York, one day (Jan. 5). Running time, 73 minutes.

An intermediate program leader depending upon two male characters to carry it through, with little or no assistance from the remaining members.

Unfolding no claim for special merit, the picture soon resolves itself into a straightaway tale of a returned soldier actually forcing the preachings of a self-made millionaire back at him while grabbing himself the daughter and plenty of coin besides.

Warner Baxter is the returned service man and Ralph Lewis the financier. Each is responsible for whatever attractiveness the film contains.

The tale does not impress as having received an over-abundance of attention for screen presentation and projects for the logical results. There is nothing in the production to make it especially stand out, although an attempt at a thrill has been included in the happening of a cut wire crossing and electrifying a cabin where the "invention of the age" is contained as well as the millionaire's daughter and her supposed fiance. The rescue and success of the invention send the preceding events into the usual ending.

Besides the two principal players the cast includes Derelys Perdue Ernest Ward, Eugenie Forde, Eugene Acker and Johnnie Fox, Jr., who as the kid brother of the soldier gives the young, sissified heir of the estate, wherein most of the action takes place, many trials and tribulations for laugh inserts.

For the lesser houses this vehicle will probably suffice, but it is more than doubtful if it can stand up in more exclusive surroundings.

Skig.

THROUGH THE DARK

A Cosmopolitan production based on the Jack Boyle story "The Daughter of Mother McGinn" one of the Boston Blackie series. Adapted by Frances Marion, directed by George Hill. Colleen Moore featured. Shown at the Cameo, New York, week of Jan. 6. Running time, 87 minutes. Released through Goldwyn-Cosmopolitan.

Mary McGinn	Colleen Moore
Boston Blackie	Forrest Stanley
Mother McGinn	Margaret Seddon
Warden	Hobart Bosworth
Travel	George Cooper
"The Glad Rags Kid"	Eddie Phillips
Detective O'Leary	Wade Boteler
Sandy	Tom Bates
Ethel Grayson	Carmelita Geraghty

Here is a wow of a crook thriller. If the average audiences like this sort of stuff, and they pretty generally do, this one is going to pull real business at the box office. The picture carries all that any average picture audience could ask for. There is a whale of a love story, any quantity of suspense which runs right up to the final shot in the last reel and there are thrills galore to the picture. Withal there is nothing in the crook stuff that any of the censors could take offense at for the story is told in screen form with a moral. That moral being that no matter how bad you have been it is never too late to choose the straight and narrow and live down your past likewise that "the wages of sin is death." But boy, they certainly do tell it in a manner that carries a punch.

As to the yarn itself, Mother McGinn runs a refuge for the bad boys of 'Frisco, always preaching to **them that they had better turn over a new leaf. Her husband was one of the "boys" and finished his life** in State's prison. Her daughter, Mary, is a pupil in a fashionable girl's school, and has no inkling as to the true history of her parentage, but when an escaped convict runs across her path and saves her from injury by stopping her runaway horse she helps him to make good his escape. He is Boston Blackie. The cops on his trail inform the school faculty of the true story of Mary's father and she is turned out, to go back to her mother's home and there finds the man that she helped.

He is for playing one last job to get "getaway dough" with which to take Mary to another locality and begin life over again. Mary is against this and seeks to have him return to jail serve his bit and come to her a free man, unsought by the authorities so that they might start their lives togeher without fear of capture hanging over them.

Finally she accomplishes her purpose but not until Blackie has been mixed up in another jam. In the end however he is going back to the "big house" with the promise that he will be out on parole in a short time.

Colleen Moore, who created such a sensation in "Flaming Youth" is featured at the head of the cast in this picture as Mary, with Forrest Stanley playing opposite her as Blackie. Margaret Seddon scores as Mother McGinn while there is a real comedy wallop to the performance contributed by George Cooper as the superstitious crook. Eddie Phillips plays the heavy while Hobart Bosworth is the warden, giving the role an air of conviction.

Its a picture that will pull 'em, interest 'em and send 'em out boosting.

Fred.

VERLORENE SCHUH

(Cinderella)

Berlin, Dec. 25.

This film, which is a filmization of the fairy tale, "Cinderella," has been received by the German press with an ecstasy of delight which is really quite extraordinary, particularly as any German film man will admit to you at once that, considering the amount of money spent on it, it is a tremendous disappointment.

Berger, the director, also responsible for the scenario, has combined the French and German versions. He has in it as one of his leading figures the good fairy of the French version, called the Patin. A new point is brought in when at the ball the clock strikes 12 before Cinderella can get out of the palace, and she is changed back to her old drab clothes. The prince, then coming upon her, does not recognize her without her finery—a good situation well handled.

Berger in his direction undoubtedly had the idea of humanizing the story and making the characters live, but unfortunately instead of doing that, he has merely made it a conventional, mediocre film story, just plain, ordinary naturalism, without the slightest touch of fantasy or style.

The trouble with Berger remains as with his last film, "A Glass of Water," which seemed so promising—namely, a lack of real feeling for what the camera can do as opposed to the stage. He often gets quite a charming mood into his picture, but the inspiration which comes to a first-rate director like Griffith or Lubitsch is never present in his work. One feels always the stage director.

Helga Thomas as the heroine looks charming and does not act badly, her chief fault being a lack of animation. The best performance was by Hermann Thiemig as the funny young baron. The rest of the cast included many well-known names—Paul Hartmann as the prince. Frida Richard as the fairy.

Max Gulstorff as Cinderella's father, Lucie Hofflich as the bad stepmother and Maddy Christians and Olga Tshechowa as her daughters.

The film will do nicely for children, but it seems very unlikely, no matter how much the Ufa releasing organization pushes it, to ever return the money sunk in it. *Trask.*

THE HUMMING BIRD

Sidney Olcott production. Presented by Adolph Zukor and Jesse L. Lasky. From the play by Maude Fulton, adapted by Forrest Halsey. Directed by Sidney Olcott. At the Rivoli, New York, week Jan. 13. Running time, 76 minutes.

Toinette	Gloria Swanson
Randall Carey	Edward Burns
"Papa" Jacques	William Ricciardi
Charlot	Cesare Gravina
La Roche	Mario Majeroni
The Owl	Mme. d'Ambricourt
Henrietta Rutherford	Helen Lindroth
Bouchet	Rafael Bongini
Beatrice	Regina Quinn
Bosque	Aurelio Coccia
Zi-Zi	Jacques d'Auray

A picture you won't be able to get away from. It is the best thing Gloria Swanson has done up to date, and the best part of it is that in this production she puts over a role without a lot of clothes. Just Gloria Swanson, and Sidney Olcott has made her act. Together with that, it has a great story for pictures. True, there is all the old patriotic hoak and George M. Cohan that one could want, but that is the stuff that sells to the public, and this one is good enough to have gone into the Criterion, New York, and run at least 10 to 12 weeks to real money.

Gloria Swanson as an Apache, sometimes as a pickpocket along the boulevards of Paris disguised as a youth in a group of strolling musicians, and again as one of those wriggly dancers that just naturally trip off to the strains of "The Tales of Hoffman," but a Gloria Swanson such as you have never seen before and an actress in this picture that will make your audiences love her.

The story relates of her falling in love with a newspaper man in Paris before the war. When the big smash comes in 1914 they have been parted, and she sees him marching off to fight for France, although he is an American. It again renews her love.

Later, when she recruits all of the wolves of Montmartre, as the crooks and thugs were known, and in her boy's clothes marches at their head until they come up to front lines, where she is discovered and sent back, there is a real thrill.

Again, with the arrival of the first American troops there is another punch, and, finally, when the endless thousands seem to be streaming through Paris on their way to stop the German push, there is a real kick, especially as the little heroine of the tale is watching them from her cell window.

Yes, it is a war picture, as you must gather from this. But it is first a crook love story and secondly a war yarn. It is one audiences will want, even though for the greater part war stories are supposed to be a dead issue. This one has some touches of trench stuff in it that were done in the studio, but they are so blended into some of the genuine action of government pictures that that in itself is a work of art.

Then for the handling of the whole picture by Olcott. He has turned a real box-office attraction into the theatres and in a great manner. The earlier touches of detail in his boulevard cafe scene are fine. Later his dive stuff is likewise good, and through the picture Olcott has a touch here and there that is going to get anyone, and, what is more, he has rescued Gloria Swanson from a clothes horse.

It's a picture that is sure fire and bound to pull money.

Supporting is Edward Burns, who proved an acceptable lead. The French characters, played by real types, were splendid, especially the "Papa" Jacques of William Ricciardi and the characterization offered by Mme. d'Ambricourt.

Fred.

NAME THE MAN

Victor Seastrom production presented by Goldwyn. From the Hall Caine novel, adapted by Paul Bern. Directed by Victor Seastrom. Shown at the Capitol for trade Jan. 15. Running time 84 minutes.

Bessie Collister	Mae Busch
Victor Stowell	Conrad Nagel
Douglas Stowell	Hobart Bosworth
Alick Gell	Creighton Hale
Fennella Stanley	Patsy Ruth Miller
Dan Collister	De Witt Jennings
Lisa Collister	Evelyn Selbie
Sir John Stanley	Winter Hall

Almost safe to predict this early in 1924 that when the year ends this picture is going to be marked up among the screen achievements of the period. It is a gripping story, handled flawlessly by Victor Seastrom, the Scandinavian director, and is his first production made in this country. There is a strong cast that should sell it anywhere, and coupled with the name of Hall Caine the indications are that it is a box-office knockout.

The Hall Caine story is well known. It has been run as a serial in a popular fiction magazine and published in book form. The screen version is so well handled it is certain to impress audiences; all needed now is an advertising wallop to sell it to the public.

Mae Busch has a role of much sympathy and puts over a fine performance. Conrad Nagel also delivers, while De Witt Jennings makes a work of art of a character here, as the father of the girl. Patsy Ruth Miller and Creighton Hale in secondary roles also score.

However much depends on the story, and the cast, it is the direction that is going to go a long way toward carrying it to success. It is another proof that the foreign directors when given American casts and American co-operation in production can come pretty near topping all of the regular run of American directors with the exception of a few in the matter of detail. Victor Seastrom in making this picture handled it so that not a single little touch seemed out of place. More than that, he seemingly endowed his players with inspiration that made them go out and extend themselves beyond their usual limitations before the camera. With it all he has held to an intensely human note throughout the entire production. He starts building his story right from the first, and while there is but one big moment that gives the audience a real thrill that runs down the spine, the suspense is so well sustained that there can be none to find fault with it.

Audiences will love it, especially the women. It is one of those 'mother out of wedlock' affairs that the women will cry their eyes out for the heroine, and an audience of crying women is sure fire to the box office. *Fred.*

HALF DOLLAR BILL

Max Graf Production released by Metro. Directed by W. S. Van Dyke. All star cast. Shown at Loew's New York, New York, double feature bill Jan. 15. Running time 74 minutes.

Capt. Duncan McTeague	Wm. P. Carlton
Mrs. Webber	Anna Q. Nilsson
Martin Webber	Geo. MacQuarrie
Papeete Joe	Mitchell Lewis
Noodles	Raymond Hatton
Judge Norton	Alec B. Francis
Half Dollar Bill	Frankie Darrow

Mighty good little program picture with a little kid actor, Frankie Darrow, walking away with all the honors as against the more seasoned players. Max Graf has a find in this youngster. It isn't one of those special things, but just a good program picture that will suffice in the average neighborhood houses.

The direction by W. S. Van Dyke seems a little stilted at times, as though he were just following the written directions of the continuity writer, at least from the players it did not seem as though they were getting very much from their director. The photography, however, is good and there is some real good sea stuff on board a three-masted sailing vessel.

The story opens in a little seaport town near a big city. Capt. Mc-Teague and Noodles, cook aboard his ship, are to set sail the next morning. They are spending their last night ashore in the Captain's quarters. On their way there they discover a foundling in a box on the steps of a deserted house, and attached to his clothing is one half of a dollar bill. The mother has written a note that she hopes she will be able to return in time to claim her child, and she has kept the other half of her last dollar for identification purposes.

After four years at sea the little child has grown into a sturdy youngster and the Captain has practically adopted him. On his return to the home port the youngster stops a woman from jumping from the dock, and naturally it later develops she is the mother. The father is also on the job in the person of one of the heavies. To get square with the Captain he decides to take the child away from the mother and the sailing master, who has given her a home, with the result he is killed.

It is the kid, however, in his work on shipboard together with a couple of Boston terriers that are in the picture that carry the heart interest.

Miss Nilsson did not look her best. Wm. P. Carlton gave a good performance and Raymond Hatton as a pegleg cook was corking comedy relief. MacQuarrie and Mitchell Lewis as the heavies, the former as the boy's father, delivered nicely.

Fred.

SOUTH SEA LOVE

Fox production starring Shirley Mason. Story by Frederick and Fanny Hatton. Directed by David Solomon. At Circle Jan. 8 as half bill. Running time 43 minutes.

Dolores Medina	Shirley Mason
Gerald Wilton	J. Frank Glendon
Manuel Salarno	Francis McDonald
Maria	Lillian Nicholson
Captain Medina	Charles A. Sellon
Inn Keeper	Fred Lancaster
Stubbs	Robert Conville

If the Hattons keep on writing much more of this low-caliber film material they are going to obliterate the memory of "Upstairs and Down," "Lombardi, Ltd.," and other legitimate successes which established them.

"South Sea Love" is a pot-boiler. Its commercial possibilities are almost negligible.

In spite of several fine bits of photography, color is lacking. Its absence is a death blow to any picture which attempts to deal with the South Sea Isles.

Director David Solomon hardly seems to have been the man for this job and with one or two exceptions the players give distinctly mediocre performances.

There is one bit implying the Hattons almost lifted themselves from the rut. This occurs when the girl gets into the usual struggle for her honor with the villian. Instead of battling him at first she starts to laugh him out of it and nearly succeeds. That would have been a great twist but before she succeeds completely he changes his mind and the unfailing wrestling match and chase scene follows. A fair climax is worked up when Miss Mason saves her lover from being horsewhipped but the effect is nullified by Glendon's unconvincing acting.

After all the most favorable thing to be said about "South Sea Love" is that it runs for less than three quarters of an hour, making it useful in support.

TIMES HAVE CHANGED

Fox production starring William Russell. Story by Elmer Davis. Scenario by Jack Strumwasser. Directed by James Flood. At the New York, Dec. 11, as half bill. Runs 62 minutes.

Mark O'Rell	William Russell
Marjorie	Mabel Julienne Scott
Al Keeley	Charles West
Aunt Cordelia	Martha Maddox

Uncle Hinton..............Edwin B. Tilton
Cousin Felix.............George Atkinson
Irene Laird.................Allene Ray
Jim Feener................Dick La Reno
Gabe Gooch...............Gus Leonard
Dirty Dan ....Jack Curtis

William Russell is no longer appearing in those constantly-battling and overflowing with melodramatic heroic parts with which he served his apprenticeship under the Fox banner. Recently he has been doing roles more in the society and drawing room style. The change is emphatically for the better as Russell has become a good enough actor to retain all of his former virility and essentially masculine appeal even when dolled up in evening dress.

In "Times Have Changed" he has been given a vehicle that because of considerable individuality in treatment and theme as well as care in casting and direction is well above the average run of program films. The story, credited to Elmer Davis, becomes too involved at one or two spots, but it is fresh and diversified enough in its appeal to please almost anyone.

Mark O'Rell (Mr. Russell), ex-army captain and hero of Chateau Thierry, on returning to this country marries Marjorie Redman, youngest of a distinguished family dating to the Mayflower. He finds himself tied to the apron strings not of his pretty wife but of her diabolically prim Aunt Cordelia. The latter chases him to the city in search of a crazy quilt greatly valued by her as a relic under which 10 generations of the family breathed their last, and carelessly lent by him to a friend.

Meanwhile he quite innocently is the victim of slander concerning himself and the deadliest flapper in the high school over which he reigns as principal. When she unknowingly leaves for the city on the same train things begin to look black. Further complications follow as a result of a pair of crooks using the quilt as a hiding place for stolen diamonds. There are fights and chases and more scandal.

Russell is given uncommonly good support. Mabel Julienne Scott is reserved and sweet as the wife and Martha Maddox sufficiently austere as the aunt. The flapper is played by Allene Ray who brings a new face and a very pretty one to the films. Miss Ray overdoes her gum-chewing and other flapperish bits, but promises to be very appealing in a more sympathetic part.

The individual honors go to the writer of the subtitles, unnamed but apparently a witty and clever person. For instance when the aunt is convinced of the hero's faithlessness she wrings her hands and wails, "Oh! I wish the Pilgrims had never landed," and at another time when one of the cynical male friends refers to the "female of the speeches."

While the film is generally enjoyable there are a few items on the wrong side. Practically no pictorial beauty in the exteriors or interiors. Again, the family of supposed aristocrats rather like "boarding-house swells."

STING OF SCORPION

Arrow Pictures release. Starring Edmund Cobb (Two-Fisted Ed). Directed by Ashton Dearholt. At Stanley, New York, Jan. 9, day only.

The first of a series of Westerns starring Edmund Cobb (Two-Fisted Ed). The star is surrounded by an ordinary cast and saddled with a cheap, melodramatic story, with which he does as well as expected.

As a Western cowboy in love with the school-marm he has an opportunity to display horsemanship and a certain athletic ability which is never unusual or above the average displayed by the innumerable Westerns.

The story embraces the efforts of a Western dance hall proprietor and

gambler to win the girl. He frames a robbery on the cowboy and kidnaps Cheeko, an Indian suspected of having a hidden gold mine up his sleeve somewhere. The cowboy escapes by tricking the bad man, rescues Cheeko, who is bound and gagged, and stages a battle in Cheeko's cabin which winds up the career of the villain, etc.

It is the usual melodramatic hokum, with nothing to distinguish it from hundreds of others just as bad. Cobb will never startle with his histrionic ability and will find tough sledding following the pioneers in Western characterizations, who have about used up the bag of tricks.

The girl lead ditto.

The bad man turned in a stagey, stilted, unconvincing old school villain conception that was about on a par with the entire production. The jail escape and the fight in the cabin were the high lights.

Plenty of chase stuff to supply action.

Joseph Girard, Helene Rosson, Arthur Morrison and Henry Dunkinson were the support.

It's an ordinary program feature for the second-class picture houses, and probably aimed at that target.
Con.

THE THRILL CHASER

Universal, starring Hoot Gibson. Story by Raymond L. Schrock and Edward Sedgewick. Continuity by E. Richard Schayer. Directed by Edward Sedgewick. Shown at the Stanley, New York, Jan. 11, 1924. Running time, 58 minutes.
Omar K. Jenkins..............Hoot Gibson
Olala Ussan...................Billie Dove
Sheik Ussan....................James Neill
Prince Ahmed........William E. Lawrence
Lem Bixley....................Rob Reeves
Abdul Bey....................Lloyd Whitlock

If Universal wants to make Hoot Gibson really popular it should continue him in stories of this type. This is the best Gibson that has shown in a long, long while. It is broad burlesque of the picture making, the bunk meller stuff fed to the average screen fan as so much pap, and it has about a laugh a minute.

Hoot starts as a cowboy, becomes a screen actor double, working for the handsome cake-eater type of leading man who is afraid that he is going to have his pan slammed, and finally takes to doubling for an Arabian prince, who got the idea from the movies that it would be a good plan for him to have a double in his native country to take all of the slams and let him have all of the glory.

In the finish Hoot is just about licked, but the girl decides that to the real worker belong the spoils, and she elopes with him.

There is a lot of good fast hoak that audiences in the smaller houses are going to be strong for, and the picture will at a price give satisfaction.
Fred.

THE SOCIAL CODE

Metro release starring Viola Dana. Directed by Oscar Apfel and photographed by John Arnold. Cast: Huntley Gordon, Edna Flugrath, Malcolm MacGregor and Cyril Chadwick. At the Tivoli, New York, one day, Jan. 14. Running time, 47 minutes.

The proverbial vehicle for Viola Dana. It may possibly stand up as one portion of a double feature program, but lacks the strength to wander on its own. And that only within the intermediate houses.

It stars that oft-starred young woman, supplies a role which she has many times portrayed and sums as a haphazard effort that seems incapable of being received in any other way but indifferently.

The story leaves a few loopholes as regards its plausibility while telling of a sub-deb flapper who comes to the rescue of her beloved when he stands trial for murder, but refuses to alibi himself rather than

bring in a woman's name. The film is far from well padded out and fails to sustain what slight degree of interest the story may contain.

It's a simple matter for the cast to play it, for there's little opportunity afforded the players; besides, it is doubtful if an all-star line-up could make a go of this edition.

"The Social Code" is just such a release, meaningless to Miss Dana and worse to Metro. *Skig.*

THE EXTRA GIRL

Presented by Mack Sennett, with Mabel Normand starred. Story by Mack Sennett. Directed by F. Richard Jones. Shown for a run at the Central, New York, Jan. 20. Running time, 76 minutes. Released through Associated Exhibitors.
Pa Graham.................George Nichols
Ma Graham..............Anna Hernandez
Sue Graham..............Mabel Normand
Dave Giddings................Ralph Graves
Aaron Applejohn..............Vernon Dent
T. Philip Hackett........Ramsey Wallace
The Actor..............William Desmond
Belle Brown..............Charlotte Mineau
The Director.................Carl Stockdale
Studio Manager.................Eric Mayne
Serial Director..........Charles K. French
The Actress....................Elsie Tarron
Teddy........................By Himself

Mabel Normand came to town last Sunday at the Central on the screen in the form of "The Extra Girl." The picture is just another one of the comedy melodramatic type of things that Miss Normand has been appearing in recently. Had it preceded "Hollywood" and "Souls for Sale" it would have been a knockout, but coming as it does after those two "inside stuff" pictures, it doesn't deliver any particular kick. It is a good program feature, and in towns where the exhibitor feels he can get away with it the morbid interest in the star at this time may draw some money.

The story of "The Extra Girl" is by Mack Sennett and the direction by F. Richard Jones. As a matter of fact, the only credit overlooked on the screen titles is that the "stock is by Eastman."

Miss Normand has the role of a "female Merton." Back in the old home town in Illinois she is in love with a garage mechanic, while her dad wants her to marry the owner of the drug store. Mabel won't have any of the pill pounder, and on the wedding day runs away to Hollywood, with transportation and funds provided through her winning a beauty contest.

That beauty contest thing was a frame, though, for a jealous grass widow back in the home town who wanted to cop the auto surgeon switched the pictures in the envelope that went to the contest editor. So when Mabel gets on the Sennett lot she is given a job as an assistant in the wardrobe department.

That doesn't feaze her. She writes home of the glories of "the land of sunshine and flowers" and has dad and mother join her. They bring $15,000 with them. One of Mabel's obliging friends on the Coast invests it for them, telling them the next day that the company has gone to the wall and there is nothing left for them to do but go back home.

Right here Mabel comes to the fore and tracks the villain to his room and with her little revolver sticks him up to get the coin back, but he is getting the best of the situation when in bursts the little auto guy, who has been working props around the studio to be near Mabel. Between them they get the coin back.

The picture has a lot of hoke that will get laughs, and Mabel's camera test is one of these that is certain to get over.

The supporting cast has George Nichols and Anna Hernandez playing the Pa and Ma, while Ralph Graves is the hero and Ramsey Wallace the heavy.

Mabel has one bit, that of leading a lion around the studio, that is certain to give the audiences a thrill. The only question in the exhibitor's mind should be, Can he or can he not get away with showing a Mabel Normand at this time? If his public will stand for her—and for the greater part there is no reason why they shouldn't (at least until the trial of the shooting chauffeur proves different)—he will undoubtedly get some coin with "The Extra Girl." *Fred.*

ABRAHAM LINCOLN

Programmed as "Al and Ray Rockett present their picturization of the dramatic life of Abraham Lincoln." Story by Frances Marion; directed by Phil Rosen; produced by the Rockett-Lincoln Film Co. Opened at the Gaiety, New York, for a run Jan. 21, 1924. Running time, 124 minutes.

KENTUCKY AND INDIANA PERIOD

Sarah Lincoln................Fay McKenzie
Thomas Lincoln, father...Wescott B. Clark
Nancy Hanks Lincoln, mother...Irene Hunt
Isom Enlow, neighbor......Charles French
Mr. Gollaher, neighbor.......Calvert Carter
Mrs. Gollaher, neighbor........Madge Hunt
Austin Gollaher, boy chum....Raymond Lee
Sarah Lincoln (10 years old)..Ida McKenzie
Abraham Lincoln (7 years old)..Danny Hoy

THE NEW SALEM PERIOD

Abraham Lincoln, as a young man..........................George A. Billings
Anne Rutledge, first sweetheart..................................Ruth Clifford
John McNeil...................Eddie Burns
Jack Armstrong, leader of Clary Grove Gang.....................Pat Hartigan
Denton Offut, employer of Lincoln...............................Otis Harlan
Mr. and Mrs. James Rutledge, parents of Anne....Jules Hanft and Julia Hesse
Sally, country girl..........Louise Fazendo
A country politician.........Robert Boulder
Stephen A. Douglas, afterward U. S. Senator..............William Humphrey
Dr. Allen................William McIlhwain
Auctioneer at New Orleans Slave Market........................Fred Kohler
Southern planters.......... { Bob Milasch / George Reehms

THE SPRINGFIELD PERIOD

Abraham Lincoln........George A. Billings
Mary Todd, afterward Mrs. Lincoln................................Nell Craig
Mary Todd's sister, Mrs. Ninian Edwards..................Genevieve Blinn
Willie and Tad Lincoln, sons of Abraham and Mrs. Lincoln.......................Mickey Moore and Newton Hall
Richard J. Oglesby, afterward Governor, ...Francis Powers

THE WASHINGTON PERIOD

Abraham Lincoln, President................................George A. Billings
Mrs. Abraham Lincoln..........Nell Craig
John Hay, Secretary to President.............................Homer Willits
Tom, colored servant.......Jim Blackwell
William Scott, a Union soldier...............................Eddie Southerland
Scott's mother...........Frances Raymond
Union sentry................Jack Rollings
Corporal of Guard.....William MacCormack
Bixby, Union soldier........Frank Newburg
John Wilkes Booth..........William Moran
Chairman of Delegation......John Steppling
A Dancer..................Wanda Grazer
General U. S. Grant..........Walter Rogers
General George Meade.........Alfred Allen
General Robert E. Lee, C. S. A..............................James Welch
Major, afterward General Anderson...............................Miles McCarthy
Colonel Rathbone.............Earl Schenck
Miss Harris..................Dolly McLean
Mrs. Surratt.............Cordelia Callahan
A stable boy..................Dallas Hope
A bartender..................Dick Johnson
Ned Spangler.....................Jack Winn
Actor at Ford's...........Lawrence Grant
Actresses at Ford's.... { Ivy Livingston / Kathleen Chambers
Stage hand at Ford's....Harry Rattenbury
Allan Pinkerton, Chief of Secret Service.....................W. L. McPheeters

PRESIDENT LINCOLN'S CABINET

William H. Seward, Secretary of State, ...Willis Marks
Simon Cameron, Secretary of War..Joel Day
Edwin M. Stanton, Secretary of War.. ....Nick Cogley
Salmon P. Chase, Secretary of Treasury......................Charles Smiley
Hugh McCulloch, Secretary of Treasury. ....C. A. Smiley
Gideon Welles, Secretary of Navy...... ....R. G. Dixon
Caleb B. Smith, Secretary of Interior.. ....Harry Kelsey
Montgomery Blair, Postmaster-General.. ....Joseph Mills
Edward Bates, Attorney-General....... ....Fred Manly
James Speed, Attorney-General........ ....Van Hardenburg
William Dennison, Postmaster-General.. ....R. J. Duston

This picture will go down into history with the great books that have been written on Abraham Lincoln. What it will do on the screen as entertainment for the masses is problematical. It can be made the picture of the year, but it will cost tremendous money in a skillfully directed advertising campaign to put it over.

One cannot come into New York into a theatre devoted solely to legitimate stage attractions and expect overnight to bring the whole countryside to one's doors with staid and dignified advertising methods. At least not for a picture unless it be the biggest picture in the annals of the industry to date, and the "Life of Abraham Lincoln" as presented by Al and Ray Rockett does not quite qualify as the greatest picture ever.

Historically it is gigantic. There its greatest value lies. It is at once impressive and interesting, and the great reverence and respect which every true American holds for the martyred President should make it an outstanding screen achievement. There is however nothing inspiring or exalting about the picture.

It holds its audience after about the third reel in a grip that brings a sob to the throat, a sob that remains there through the picture to the very end. But when it is all over there is no great big moment, not a single great climax striven for and arrived at, that the audience will carry away to cause them to talk about the picture.

True the pictures aims at Americanization, a greater understanding on the part of the masses of the tremendous burden that Lincoln had to bear during the great crisis of the Civil War, but right here and now let it be said to those that are planning a road tour for the picture that they will never be able to get that portion of the country lying south of the Mason and Dixon line to accept it as entertainment.

There is a fact pointed out in picturedom that the three outstanding film successes to date have been those that have dealt with the historical periods of the country's history. "The Birth of a Nation," the first of the super-specials, had the period of the reconstruction in the south after the war; "The Covered Wagon" deals with the winning of the great west, and the third big money maker while not historical in fact was so typical of the hard rock-ribbed unforgiving conscience of the New England Yankee that "Way Down East" was considered a historical picture of New England life. Three sections of the country were touched on in this trio of films and it was believed that the next big picture that came along would naturally be one that was based on the man that gave his all, even unto his life, to holding these United States in union.

That is the story that the Rocketts have tried to put into Abraham Lincoln, but they have failed to put it before an audience in a manner that makes one want to get up out of one's chair at the theatre and go forth resolved to be a better American. It does make you proud you are an American in the same light that Lincoln was one, but it also makes you think that this country that should be made one of liberty in fact isn't at this particular time just what Lincoln would have wanted it to be.

Historically and pictorially there isn't anything that could be asked for.

Lincoln is depicted from the night that he made his advent in the world in a little cabin in the Kentucky wilderness during a frightful blizzard to that fateful night when he passed from this world and "belonged to the ages," after having been shot while at Ford's theatre, Washington.

The period of his life as a boy in Kentucky, followed by that as a young man in Indiana, his working as a rail-splitter and a Mississippi freighter, until chance brings him to Illinois and his first love affair with Anne Rutledge at New Salem, where he worked as a clerk in a store to be near her, his first great sorrow in her death before they were married, are all graphically pictured.

The following events of his life from the time that he went to Springfield, Ill., and his subsequent meeting with Mary Todd are splendidly set forth. The Todd incident as filmed however makes one wonder whether or not Lincoln was as much responsible for his finally occupying the White House as his wife may have been, for Mary had set her heart on marrying a man that was to become President of the U. S. and she passed up Stephen A. Douglass, whose prospects were much brighter at that particular time, to marry Lincoln.

During the period of his Presidency and the Civil War the political as well as the field of battle strife are set forth. Battle scenes follow one another, and the highest point that the picture touches is where the men of the north come marching into Washington from the east and the west in response to his call for 300,000 volunteers to put down the rebellion.

It is history, wonderful, vivid and colorful, and it is possible there is just enough Americanism in all of us to give it the box office response that it deserves, if the picture gets that then it will run on Broadway for more than a year, but in the same breath it is doubtful if our public is ready to accept history as entertainment, when it is naught but history which they have read.

In the selection of George Billings as Lincoln the Rocketts dug up a find. If the story that is told is true, that he had never played a single role on either stage or screen prior to his advent in this picture, it is all the more remarkable that they selected him, but Billings is a born actor, at least he was in the role of Lincoln.

Ruth Clifford played Anne Rutledge in the early portion of Lincoln's life and prove sweet, charming and delightful. Nell Craig was the Mary Todd, afterward Mrs. Lincoln, carrying it off convincingly.

From the program of characters at the head of this review it can readily be judged the number of persons who played roles both of major and minor importance, and in addition to these were thousands in the mob and battle scenes. The latter scenes were particularly well directed, but strange to say not a single bit of the action was the recipient of applause.

The written titles with excerpts from Lincoln's speeches won the heartiest hands from the audience on the opening night; likewise at the same time of all the national airs that were played "Dixie" was the one that received an ovation.

Fred.

THE ETERNAL CITY

Modern adaptation of Sir Hall Caine's novel of the same name, first screened by Famous Players-Lasky in 1915, with Pauline Frederick as Roma, the heroine. The new filming is sponsored by Samuel Goldwyn and released through First National. The scenario is Ouida Bergere's, and the production is by George Fitzmaurice. Projection time, 81 minutes; at the New York Strand, Jan. 20. Only the principal characters are listed among the dozen or so.

Donna Roma.............Barbara La Marr
Baron Bonelli............Lionel Barrymore
David Rossi........................Bert Lytell
Bruno ....Richard Bennett
Minghelli ....Montagu Love

"Samuel Goldwyn (who desires to have it known that he is 'not now connected with Goldwyn Pictures'), presents" this news-topical version of the famous Hall Caine novel. There is the bare thread of the Caine story, but the surrounding atmosphere is absent. The same picture as it was made by Famous Players was a faithful reproduction of the love story. Goldwyn's opus aims more to tie up present day interest in the political upheaval of Italy than to develop the human interest of the story itself.

There are long passages dealing with the intrigues of the Reds, the patriotic fervor of the black shirted Fascisti, and the arch revolutionist Bonelli. Of the religious pageantry which made the big feature of the first "Eternal City," there is not a vestige.

The production, which was made in Rome, is in reality a record of Italian politics since the war. David, the hero, is a lieutenant of Mussolini, while Bonelli is here the arch conspirator who seeks a dictatorship over the country through his secret backing of the native Bolshevists.

Perhaps there is no good reason why the original should not be revamped, but this method of revision gives to the story a special interest only to the Italian colony. Whether the rest of the United States will manifest enthusiasm over the alien political situation is something else again.

About two years ago the Goldwyn Company imported "Theodora," screen version of the Sardou melodrama, made in Italy. The Astor, New York, played for a few weeks, but when the production—one of undeniable beauty and force—got into the other big cities of the country it drew the Italian population and then blew up. Pittsburgh, for instance, played capacity two weeks and two of slim takings, closing suddenly at the end of the fourth, principally, so it was believed at the time, because the Italian population was about used up.

"The Eternal City" started last Sunday night at the Strand with a turnaway. At 9.40 (after the last show had begun) the lobby was filled with waiting people and there was a line from the boxoffice down nearly to 46th street. The capacity audience was obviously Latin. The 7.30 house received the picture quietly up to the introduction of poses of the real Mussolini. Then it burst into a demonstration.

So deliberate has been the intent of the present producers to give the picture historic rather than romantic coloring, that the lovers are rather an anti-climax, the real finish and high light of the picture being a view of Mussolini (present premier of Italy) standing on the balcony of the royal palace beside the king and reviewing the entrance of his troops into the city. This is a fine spectacle, but it kills off Sir Hall Caine's story, and it is rumored that Sir Hall was much put out about it all while the picture was in the making in Rome.

If the picture gets anywhere it will be due to some of the smashing bits of mob effects and to the assemblage of stars. But the work of the novelist certainly has been dealt with violently.

The scenic features, particularly the noble Roman palaces, woodlands and scenic shots, are splendid and the acting is fine. There are a number of effective shots of the Fascisti assembled in the ancient Roman Coliseum, but the melodrama involved in the trapping of the hero in Roma's house is rather rough stuff.

The point is that what was designed as a love story with emotional appeal, atmosphere of rich ecclesiastical pomp, and glowing romance has been turned into a rough and tumble "move" excellent of its type, but far from the spirit of Hall Caine's "The Eternal City."

Rush.

HERITAGE OF THE DESERT

Irvin Willat production of the Zane Grey story adapted by Al. Levino and presented by Jesse Lasky. Bebe Daniels, Ernest Torrence, Noah Beery and Lloyd Hughes featured. Shown at the Rialto, New York, week Jan. 20. Running time 70 minutes.

Mescal.......................Bebe Daniels
August Naab.............Ernest Torrence
Holderness..................Noah Beery
Jack Hare..................Lloyd Hughes
Mrs. Naab.................Anne Schaefer
Snap Naab...................James Mason
Dene.....................Richard R. Neill
Dave Naab..............Leonard Clapham

The pictorial aspect of this picture is the best feature about it. It is partially shot in Technicolor, and those portions of it that are prove a novelty and a thing of beauty. Otherwise it is a good western, but not as it has been stated a rival of "The Covered Wagon," even though it is also a Paramount picture. As a program feature it will get by nicely, but one need not ex-

pect to break any box office records with it.

It is a tale of the salvaging of the desert lands lying between the Mississippi and the Pacific Coast and it deals with the adventures of the pioneers who went into that part of the world to blaze the trail for the hosts that have come following after. Historical possibly to a certain extent, but not containing nearly the dramatic interest that there was in the Emerson Hough story of the "Wagon" pioneers.

There is a clash between the lawless and the law abiding that forms the background of the tale and little Bebe Daniels is the heroine of the situation. As Mescal she is decidedly a pretty picture, but that is about all. She has little or no chance to do anything worth while. Ernest Torrence carries the principal role. As the leader of the little law abiding colony, who has two sons, a good boy and a bad one, he walks away with about everything that there is to the picture, but that is much. His character is that of August Naab.

Naab turns down Holderness (Beery), who is trying to secure all the water rights in the country and that starts a feud, which finally ends up in the death of Naab's worthless son, the burning of the town in which the lawless gang hold forth, and the happy finish for little Mescal, who was to have married the dead son, and the stranger who Naab picked up on the desert and whom he now believes was sent to him to take the place of the dead boy.

Willat has directed the story nicely, but has failed to get any real character into the role portrayed by his cast. Pretty shots there are galore in the feature, but they do not make a box office attraction, which is exactly what this picture falls short of being. *Fred.*

DARLING OF NEW YORK

Universal-Jewel picture directed by King Baggot and featuring Baby Peggy. Others: Gladys Brockwell, Sheldon Lewis, Carl Stockdale, Max Davidson. Showing at Keith's 81st Street, New York, week of Jan. 14. Running time, 60 minutes.

Baby Peggy's first feature of extended footage, and agreeable so far as she, personally, is concerned, but nothing to otherwise issue exceptional comment. For those particularly addicted to the charms of this child the picture will appeal, and at the least it should increase her following, but it is in the script that the film reveals its most flagrant weakness.

The mediocre theme is adequately directed and played for the possibilities contained, being a comedy-drama of the tenement district in New York, which has the diminutive star the center of a gang of diamond smugglers, two of whom determine on adhering to the straight and narrow as a result of her association and provide the means of her reaching a millionaire grandfather.

Due to the locale of the story, there is no necessity for an augmented production with many of the exteriors appearing as studio stuff, although one or two are neatly faked even unto the prop elevated trains which pass back and forth.

As to the narrative, it gets under way in Italy, where the child's mother dies, leaving a note to the infant's grandfather in America. A feminine companion, chaperoning the sea voyage, loses her money and misses the boat, which allows for a diamond smuggler (Sheldon Lewis) to adopt the child on the crossing, who incidentally hides the stones within her rag doll.

America, with the proverbial flashes of Liberty as the boat comes up the bay and the hurrah subtitles, soon develops into a hectic existence so far as the youngster is concerned. A disgruntled member of the gang steals and deposits her in an ash can which causes much excitement among the lawless members when they learn the diamonds still repose on the inside of the doll.

From the ash can continues a series of wanderings, with a comedy interlude of being taken in by a Jewish family, culminating in the finding of the child by Kitty (Gladys Brockwell), feminine gangster, who hides the wandering waif in her room. Follows an immediate police raid with a fire starting during the scuffle that provides Kitty with the opportunity to dash back into the flaming structure, grab the youngster and make a three-story leap into a net. The final episode, at the grandfather's estate, is placed close behind.

Baggot appears to have done very well with the featured infant, giving full play to the child's facial expressions for utmost value. The supporting members contribute average performances to the point where the only doubt comes in the picture's ability to satisfy in the more imposing film theatres. It looks like a good bet for any other class of house. *Skig.*

THE LULLABY

Chester Bennett feature with Jane Novak starred. Distributed by F. B. O. Story by Lillian Darcy, adaptation by Hope Loring nd Louis D. Lighton, direction by Chester Bennett. Jack McKenzie, photographer. Projection time 72 minutes. At the Cameo, New York, Jan. 19. In defense of the title it is said Bennett informed Charles Dillingham he had the picture ready for filming when the stage "Lullaby" was first announced.

Felipa	Jane Novak
Antoinette	Jane Novak
Tony	Robert Anderson
Pietro	Fred Malestesta
Baby Antoinette	Dorothy Marion Mack
Mrs. Marvin	Marguerite Snow
Thomas Elliott	Otis Harlan
Thomas, Jr.	Peter Burke
Mary	Lydia Yeamans Titus
Elliott, Jr. (at 6)	Pat Moore
Elliott, Jr. (at 8)	Mickey Moore

Several exhibitors of the New York Chamber of Commerce have declined to play the picture on the score that the title would confuse the public with the idea it was taken from the Edward Knoblock-Charles Dillingham drama of the same title, in which Florence Reed starred at the Knickerbocker up to last week.

That probably would happen, although the two stories have nothing in common except that both touch upon the theme of mother love. The stage play deals with a woman who is innocently driven to a life of shame by crushing force of circumstance. The action takes place in France and (except that the realism of the play is objectionable) the technical construction is flawless and convincing.

The unplausible picture has to do with a newly married couple of Italian immigrants to New York. The bride is about to become a mother when she is besieged by her husband's best friend. The husband witnesses the man's brutal attack upon his wife. A fight ensues and the friend is shot down, really in defense of the woman's honor.

It is rather startling about 300 feet later to find both husband and wife railroaded to jail by an especially kindly judge, the husband convicted of murder in the first degree and presently hanged, and the wife sentenced to imprisonment for 20 years.

The producers must have realized the weakness of this passage, for they practically leaped the gap between the justified killing and the execution, with no longer a pause over the legal details than they could help. This episode robbed the picture of much of its effect.

It created in the spectator's mind the impression that it was only a trumped up story and put a severe dent in the illusion. That same poor illusion got some more swift kicks. When the mother came out of jail she was a wan, worn spectre. It didn't seem possible it was the same person, and probably wasn't, although Miss Novak was programmed for both parts.

A baby is born in prison and at three years of age transferred to an orphanage by order of the governor (the judge who sentenced the pair had by now became the governor), and the same governor adopted the child, knowing all the time who she was. Anyway daughter is about to have her coming out party some 17 years later, on the same day the mother is discharged from prison. It follows as night and day that mother breaks in on daughter's gay party, thus making way for more or less happy finale.

As appears from the narrative the story is full of illogical episodes, but none more violent to the conventions than the picking of the blonde and blue-eyed Jane Novak as an Italian bride. You'd as soon expect a red-headed Indian.

The picture is full of heavy, sombre emotional scenes, such as the separation of husband and wife, parting of mother and babe, and the hanging, indicated by the close-up of a swinging rope, and the prison scenes. The picture has some strong acting passages, but it is too plausible to hold together.

The production is especially good as to its scenic backgrounds and photography, but what's the use of right details and wrong essentials? *Rush.*

FASHION ROW

Tiffany Production releasing through Metro, presented by R. Z. Leonard and starring Mae Murray. Written by Sada Cowan and Howard Higgin with Oliver T. Marsh the photographer. Directed by Robert Leonard. Showing at the Capitol, New York, week of Jan. 27. Running time, 70 minutes.

Olga Farinova Rita, her younger sister	} Mae Murray
James Morton	Earle Foxe
Eric Van Corland	Freeman Wood
Mrs. Van Corland	Mathilde Brundage
Kaminoff	Elmo Lincoln
Papa Levitzky	Sidney Franklin
Mama Levitzky	Madame Rosanova
A Press Agent	Craig Biddle

A dual role for Mae Murray in this, her latest, backed by the usual augmented settings associated with her productions, a splendid supporting male detachment and excellent photography. A rather threadbare tale and an impersonation of one of the roles by the star that is not overly convincing about rounds out the other potentialities of the picture which under projection and as a unit screens as an entertaining interlude that should be found especially delectable to the Murray fans and satisfying to those not so highly prejudiced.

The story allows much leeway for the eccentric mannerisms of the star as a Russian actress but it is in her conception of the younger innocent and immigrant sister where Miss Murray secures her best results although the former role is the outstanding figure of the picture. A tendency to become somewhat theatric takes the edge off the stage performance and making it appear artificial while on the other hand the role of the retiring youngster is toned down and made to seem genuine by contrast which may, or may not, have been the purpose of the director.

Earle Foxe, Freeman Wood and Elmo Lincoln supply invaluable assistance with respective performances that can rank with the best among the regular program releases. It's a corking piece of work by Foxe in a somewhat secondary part which he makes assume first string importance. Wood is a compliment to whoever did the casting and Lincoln has turned in another of his Russian "heavies" of superior force. In fact the cast just about makes the picture in overcoming whatever tendencies the story may have to sideslip.

What might have been deemed an unsatisfactory ending, by the average picture goer, in the death of Olga, the actress, is more or less offset by the adoption of the sister and her ultimate marriage. It's not a bad twist at that to a cut and dried tale.

It relates of two Russian sisters, of the peasantry, whom a whip wielding father persecutes until the eldest runs away to this country where she becomes a famed stage celebrity and the proverbial "toast of New York." Eventually marrying into an aristocratic family and "squaring" it with the mother by an assertion of royalty parentage matters progress smoothly until the little sister comes up the bay on a ship which also carries a former Cossack who is in quest of Olga, the now Mrs. Van Corland, for the purpose of revenge.

Luring the star to an east side dwelling on the pretense of her sister's illness Kaminoff (Mr. Lincoln) reveals his identity through a scar the girl previously inflicted upon his face and attacks her but young Morton (Mr. Foxe), friend of the husband who has followed breaks in the door and there ensues as sweet and realistic a battle as has been around for some time. It concludes in Kaminoff shooting Olga who is in turn shot by the police.

Leonard has moved the action along at a fair pace in front of massive interior sets and the insertion of a Russian lawn party. The construction of events working up to the battle and climax of Olga is also a nice bit of staging.

The title amounts to nothing more than having been selected for its selling value although the inference made is to a promenade in a fashionable hotel where gather the social mighty.

The picture is equal to heading any film house program, should be just about "pie" for the Murray enthusiasts and may increase that enrollment. *Skig.*

FLAMING BARRIERS

Paramount-Geo. Melford production presented by Adolph Zukor and Jesse Lasky. Story by Byron Morgan adapted by Hervey Thew and directed by George Melford. Shown at the Rialto, N. Y., week Jan. 27, 1924. Running time, 65 minutes.

Jerry Malone	Jacqueline Logan
Sam Barton	Antonio Moreno
Henry Van Sickle	Walter Hiers
Patrick Malone	Charles Ogle
Joseph Pickens	Robert McKim
Bill O'Halloran	Luke Cosgrove
Mayor Steers	Warren Rogers

Here you are, a first-class rural melodrama, with all the earmarks of an "Easy Dawson" story that Hitchy played years and years ago. But it is the kind of hoak that the audience will go to see, and like, although there isn't any great chance that they will get absolutely crazy about it. But the picture has got the punch in the matter of cast, for Jacqueline Logan, Antonio Moreno and Walter Heirs are featured. The picture was directed by George Melford.

The small-town stuff is all that there is to the picture. Jacqueline Logan slipped the audience a few thrills as the driver of a motor fire truck and an aeroplane. She is the daughter of the builder of the auto-truck fire apparatus, and the heavy of the piece, played by Robert McKim, holds her father's notes on the factory and wants to win the girl.

Associated with him in the East is a financing company that has discounted the notes, and he advises them that they had best protect their interests by sending on a representative. The president's son (Moreno) is assigned to the job, and he manages to fall in love with the inventor's daughter, and from then on devotes all his time to foiling the villain and trying to get a showing for the motor truck for the visiting fire chiefs of the State. He almost succeeds by having a barn in the outskirts of the town set ablaze on the eventful day, but the fire truck is pinched for speeding to the fire.

Later, when the chiefs are being entertained at the heavy's mountain camp, a forest fire starts, and it is the truck that comes to the rescue of them all through playing its streams on the only bridge that leads to safety and permitting them to escape.

Miss Logan certainly appeared to advantage in the feature, while Moreno was a forceful hero. Heirs, as an efficiency expert, worked hard for laughs, and got a great many of them. *Fred.*

PIED PIPER MALONE

Paramount presented by Adolph Zukor and Jesse Lasky. Original story by Booth Tarkington adapted by Tom Geraghty. Directed by Alfred E. Green. Thos. Meighan star. Shown at Rivoli, N. Y., week Jan. 27, 1924. Running time 77 minutes.

Jack Malone	Thomas Meighan
Patty Thomas	Lois Wilson
Mother Malone	Emma Dunn
Jas. P. Malone	Charles Stevenson
Capt. Clarke	George Fawcett
Chas. Crosby, Jr.	Cyril Ring
Chas. Crosby, Sr.	Claude Brook
Mr. Thomas	Joe Burke
Betty Malone	Peaches Jackson
Louie, the barber	Charles Winninger
Photographer	Hugh Cameron
Housekeeper	Dorothy Walters
The Malone Sisters	Pearl Sindelar Marie Schaefer Elizabeth Henry Jean Armour Blanche Standing Mollie Ring
The M[illegible] Brothers	Charles Mussett Walter Downing Harry Mayo Lawrence Barnes David Wall Ed. Williams

Despite Sunday was almost a zero day along Broadway the Rivoli with Thomas Meighan in his latest "Pied Piper Malone" had capacity business and a corking line for the supper show. That is a test as to a star's draw.

"Pied Piper Malone" written directly for the screen by Booth Tarkington and adapted by Tom Geraghty, is one of the best of the most recent Meighan starring productions. It is a decidedly human story with the love interest paramount. While there is no great big thrill that stands out other than the sinking of a steamer in a typhoon in the China Seas, it is a picture that will hold the interest.

It has a cast that handles its assignments in most workmanlike manner. Lois Wilson opposite Meighan was a delight, while Emma Dunn as his mother was the true artist she always is.

The kiddie element is going to make it a particularly good card for afternoons for the smaller exhibitors when they get the picture. It is an angle that they can develop.

The story is a small town tale. Jack Malone (Meighan) is the 13th child of the Malone family, he has six brothers and six sisters all his senior. The boys have all settled down to staple business pursuits; they seemed to have gobbled everything in town so it left Jack nothing else to do except go to sea. He has been on a two years' cruise and returns in time for the Golden Wedding Anniversary of his parents, but before going to sea again he wins the promise of Patty Thomas that while he is away there will be no one else in her life.

On this trip he is the first officer under Capt. Clarke (Geo. Fawcett) while his rival Charles Crosby is second officer. The ship is struck by a typhoon in the China Sea and founders. Young Crosby getting home first tells that the captain and first officer were both drunk on the trip and that while he did all that he could to save the vessel, they overruled him.

Then it is up to the captain and his young first officer to vindicate themselves which they eventually do, and Jack wins the girl.

The picture is ably directed and there is considerable amount of comedy as well as real drama in the story, which is a 100 per cent clean tale, no sexy stuff at all, but still a picture that is sure to get the crowds. *Fred.*

PAINTED PEOPLE

First National picture starring Colleen Moore. Adapted from Richard Connell's "The Swamp Angel" and directed by Clarence Badger. At Strand, New York, week, Jan. 27. Running time, 70 mins.

Ellie Byrne	Colleen Moore
Don Lane	Ben Lyon
Stephanie Parrish	Charlotte Merriam
Preston Dutton	Joseph Striker
Tom Byrne	Charles Murray
Fred Lane	Russell Simpson
Mrs. Byrne	Mary Alden
Mrs. Lane	Mary Carr
Henry Parrish	Sam de Grasse
Mrs. Dutton	June Elvidge
Leslie Carter	Anna Q. Nilsson
Ed. Decker	Bull Montana

Colleen Moore starred and billed as "The Flaming Youth Girl!" in this follow-up feature appears as a "catch" title to secure the kickback on the impression "Youth" made.

As a picture "Painted People" needs the billing and title. It is an in and out comedy-drama that must chiefly rely on the star and Ben Lyon to score. The story has gone up against screen audiences many times and its treatment in this instance is of insufficient substance to especially make it stand out from its predecessors.

A liberal sprinkling of "names" throughout the cast will undoubtedly help at the gate. It's a fair series of performances the contributing members have turned in but as a whole it's a lightweight release little more than mildly pleasing.

The title remains something of an obscurity in that it is used to refer to both the social elite of a small town and those connected with the professional stage; more or less meaningless when connected with the story, hence the inference that it was but employed to impress as having some relation with the type of narrative "Youth" revealed.

The production is minus a much needed punch in telling of a boy and girl of the laboring class who foster their adolescent affections upon their counterparts of the upper regime and are made to feel ludicrous when invited to a birthday party of the town leader's daughter.

The youth leaves his birthplace to make good as a writer, and the girl, through circumstances, secures an opportunity on the stage which permits of a three-year lapse, denoting the boy as a failure and the girl, a successful actress.

They meet and collaborate on a new play which eventually receives its initial tryout in their home town. Both see their former idols again at which time the girl discovers her hero is but looking for a meal ticket and refuses him. Retaliating, he casts a slur upon her name before a gathering. In comes the newborn playwright messing the guilded youth about until an apology is forthcoming with the finale having the two former social outcasts realizing their love for each other.

Miss Moore gives a neat performance of the tomboyish girl who carves out a stage career for herself while Ben Lyon gathers strength as the story advances, to mark him as a juvenile who should be consistently heard from.

Needless of a lavish production outlay there is little included in settings to be of more than passing interest.

The direction as handled by Badger seems to have emphasized the comedy values to the detriment of the theme and to the extent that the film's main bid for approval will rest with the spirit in which the two leading characters are accepted and the laughs the situations are able to secure. *Skig.*

THE HEART BANDIT

Metro production starring Viola Dana and directed by Oscar Apfel. From the story, "Angel Face Molly," by Frank Kennedy Myton. Adaptation and continuity by Tom J. Hopkins. Photographed by John Arnold. Half the bill at the New York, Jan. 25. Runs 57 minutes.

Molly O'Hara	Viola Dana
John Rand	Milton Sills
Mrs. Rand	Gertrude Claire
"Spike" Malone	Wallace McDonald
Ramon Cordova	Bertram Grassby
Pat O'Connell	De Witt Jennings
Jenks	Nelson McDowell
Monk Hinman	Mathew Betts
Silas Wetherbee	Edward Wade

The deterioration in Miss Dana's pictures goes on and on and the legions who once hailed her as the screen's best ingenue comedienne are transferring their devotion to Colleen Moore and others of the newer school. The unfortunate part of it seems to be that Miss Dana herself is as pert and piquant as ever, but the vehicles given her recently have been almost without exception weak enough to overbalance the charm of any star.

In "The Heart Bandit" she has been provided with an excellent supporting cast, adequate direction and mechanical effectiveness, but a trite and totally unimportant story. That her work redeems it and makes it a fairly entertaining program only goes to prove how quickly she would recover her lost prestige with a story holding real heart interest and appeal such as might be provided by Mary Roberts Rinehart, Marshall Neilan, Rupert Hughes, or even Scott Fitzgerald, who turned out some of her earliest and best scenarios.

"The Heart Bandit" has Miss Dana cast as a hard-boiled little gyp artist who suddenly finds herself adopted by a sweet little old lady of the kind only found in books. The old, old gag of having the heroine reform, but then to crack one more safe in order to save the erring hero, is utilized with all the other ancient bits.

But to her credit let be said that Miss Dana affects the change from the little Bowery tough to the "perfect young lady" gradually. This makes her speedy marriage to the millionaire hero and her acceptance by his family seem the more ludicrous, but at least it is true to life.

Those scenes in which she shoots crap with the servants and swaggers around the magnificent estate with a regular "Tenth avenoo" air are good for laughs and the chief assets of the picture. For the rest it is overflowing with sentimentality that becomes sickening after a while. The story is helped by capable acting by all the cast, with Milton Sills his usual strong self as the Wall Street hero and Gertrude Claire making the old lady as convincing as possible.

The others include Wallace McDonald, Bertram Grassby and De Witt Jennings, the last again flashing his badge and cigar as the inevitable "bull."

Pretty good entertainment, for none of Miss Dana's films can be any less. But not what it should be, and neither has any of her other recent ones been, except, possibly, "Rouged Lips" last summer.

JUDGMENT OF THE STORM

Palmer Production written by Ethel Styles Middleton and directed by Del Andrews. Photographed by Henry Sharp and Max Du Pont. At the New York, one day, Jan. 19. Running time 77 minutes.

Mrs. Heath	Claire McDowell
Mary Heath	Lucille Rickson
Bob Heath	George Hackathorne
Dave Heath	Bruce Gordon
John Trevor	Lloyd Hughes
Helene Trevor	Myrtle Stedman
Martin Freeland	Philo McCullough

"Judgment of the Storm" if exploited properly should have no trouble cashing in. It is a Palmer Production produced by the Palmer Photoplay Corp., made up of former newspaper men, evidently with plenty of money and who threaten to be heard from if they keep up the same pace.

The story is a first effort, written by Ethel Styles Middleton, described in the billing as a simple, and domestic housewife of Pittsburgh. From the workmanlike construction of the story and the many old but always effective and clever tricks of the trade utilized, it seems likely that the "housewife" business is merely bait, or possibly that some experienced, crafty rewrite man fixed the plot up to suit himself.

It is a story that in spite of a few glaring inconsistencies and a tendency to become a bit too realistically stark at times, holds. The Heaths are a family living a happy but impoverished existence on the outskirts of a small upstate college town. The older son, Dave, supports the widowed mother, baby twins, the pampered younger brother and the daughter, Mary, who has come to love a student at the college, John Trevor.

The latter believes his mother to be in Europe but she is in reality running an exclusive gambling house in order to give her son an education and the luxuries that go with it.

It is in this gambling joint that Dave Heath, John's best friend in addition to being the brother of the girl, meets tragic death, when as a sightseer he is struck by a bullet meant for another man.

Here the first big dramatic moment occurs when John seeing

his pal lifeless on the floor pours invectives upon the "swine who run such places" only to learn a second later the owner is his mother.

Broken-hearted he leaves home and offers his life to the Heaths as recompense for the loss of Dave. Bob, the weakling younger brother, has had to run the farm since the death, much to his abhorrence, and he persuades his mother to take John as the "hired man" but at no wages and socially only a slave.

But Mary remains true to her love and Trevor's chance to risk his life in return for Dave's finally comes when the baby twins are lost in a driving blizzard. He finds them being warmed under the coat of his mother who has come after her boy and, also lost in the snow, discovered the children.

There follows another big scene, possibly unreal but extraordinarily gripping. John's mother, dying from exposure and realizing he cannot save all, commands him to take the twins and return them to the home so recently saddened because of her. He obeys but returns in time to rescue her too and the story ends in a halo of sunshine.

The snow scenes are the equal of any winter stuff including the famous ice scenes in "Way Down East." The photography and directing by Del Andrews are also far above standard.

An excellent all-around cast is an invaluable aid to the film. No one should really be singled out for special honors unless it be George Hackathorne, giving one more of his splendid characterizations of a weak-willed but not wholly bad youth. The rest including Myrtle Stedman and Claire McDowell as the respective mothers of the boy and girl, Lucille Rickson and Lloyd Hughes as the couple, and Philo McCullough as the heavy, are all more than adequate.

The picture is better than the majority of those shown in first run houses. With a few changes in the titling and the matter of more comedy relief, it might have been an outstanding film. As it is it should clean up in the program houses with a vengeance.

TRAIL OF THE LAW

Produced and directed by Oscar Apfel. Distributed by Producers' Security Corp. Half the bill at the New York, Jan. 25. Running time, 64 minutes.

Pictorial excellency, adequate direction, good acting and a story very thin, about sums up "Trail of the Law," an Oscar Apfel feature, good enough for the minor half of the average double bill. It features Norma Shearer, undoubtedly a comer, and Wilfred Lytell, announced as due to arrive for some time, but who never seems to be able to overtake his older brother.

The story is set in the Maine woods, all the action centering around two cabins bordering on a pretty lake. Apfel heretofore has been known for his sea pictures, but here he demonstrates that, pictorially at least, he can extract a great deal of beauty from the old New England state.

The charm in the exteriors is their great simplicity, with the majestic mountains and peaceful lakes shot from the best possible vantage points.

Miss Shearer is cast as a girl who, because of the dangerous community, masquerades as a boy during the day, only to become herself again when safely ensconced in her own home at night. Years before, her mother had been murdered by a renegade, and her father has sworn to get the villian. It develops that a nasty neighbor is the party wanted. The father gives him what's coming to him and is only prevented from homicide by Lytell, as the young man from the city who has fallen in love with the daughter while she was still a boy.

That's all there is to the plot, and it can be seen that the brain is not seriously taxed keeping up with it. Miss Shearer is cute and appealing, even in trousers and cap, but the usual imagination is needed to conceive her palming herself off as a boy. Lytell is O.K. except for a little stiffness, and the rest are up to the mark.

Apfel, who also was the director of the other picture at the house when "Trail of the Law" was reviewed, inserted a few touches here and there that help to keep an audience interested in a tepid story.

THE WAY OF A MAN

Pathe release from an Emerson Hough story, directed by G. B. Seitz. Cast includes Ellene Ray, Harold Miller, Bud Osborne, Kathryn Appleton, Carl Silveras and Lillian Adrian. Showing at Loew's, New York, as half of double feature program, Jan. 29. Running time, 76 mins.

A western of pioneer days on the frontier, with the wagon trains, Indian attacks and costumed characters. Rather hectic and haphazard in its dramatics, the picture simply amounts to a series of difficult circumstances for the hero, with the proof of the pudding being the fact that it must needs be included on a two-featured program to stand up. Neither does the abundant amount of footage help, for there are numerable instances where the picture could take cutting.

There is no lack of action, as the screening is well filled with hand-to-hand fights, shooting and riding, but the continuity gives the full impression an implausible sequence that is hard to digest. Where audiences are not so much concerned with the actual story as with the activities of the characters this picture should pass muster on the trials and tribulations fronting the youth who journeys west from Virginia in quest of a property deed stolen from his murdered father. A love theme is carried along that provides Ellene Ray with consistent opportunities to predominate, which she does at intervals. For the cast as a whole the term "uneven" describes adequately.

The story would seem to have been one of Hough's earliest, and certainly has not bee nexceptionally well treated in the filming. It consummates high melodrama throughout with Bud Osborne in the most emphatic role of the script in depicting the youthful "heavy," who is fearless, possesses a certain sense of humor that never lets him take his various foreboding situations too certainly has not been exceptionally as a ladies man. It's a corking character that Osborne plays well enough to make it stand out above the other portrayals, but could have been built up even stronger.

Seitz, who directed, looks to have sacrificed smooth continuity for the insertion of all possible action, and although the amount of the latter ingredient revealed serves to keep the screen very much populated, the story must correspondingly suffer. It appears to be a surety for the neighborhood theatres, and especially where there is a strong youthful clientele, for kids should eat this pioneer stuff up, but the audience at the New York simply reclined, took it all good naturedly and was satisfied to let it go at that. *Skig.*

HIS MYSTERY GIRL

Universal picture, featuring Herbert Rawlinson. Directed by R. F. Hill. Showing at Loew's, New York, Jan. 29. Running time, 54 mins.

Half of a double header and a comedy which Rawlinson plays nicely with little or no support from the other members. It's strictly a lightweight theme that moves fast, after once started, and has that attribute as its principal bid.

The story concerns two brothers who have been left a healthy inheritance, with Ralph McCullough cast as the gay life adherent and Rawlinson portraying the woman-hating member of the family. A melodramatic frame-up serves to bring the retiring individual to the fore with the finish of the plot having the involved young man marrying the heroine of the trumped-up tragics.

Other than Rawlinson there is little assistance derived as far as the players are concerned, with the picture resting upon its action and the featured member for approval.

As a contrast, this film will probably suffice on a double feature basis and in the smaller or neighborhood houses may satisfy as a solo, but it is strictly a secondary release that shows off Rawlinson favorably and no more. *Skig.*

LOVING LIES

Thomas Buchanan production presented by Associated Authors. Adapted from the Peter B. Kyne story, "The Harbor Bar," directed by W. S. Van Dyke. Shown on double feature bill, Loew's New York, N. Y., Jan. 22, 1924. Running time, 69 minutes. Released through Allied Producers and Distributors.

Capt. Dan.......................Monte Blue
His Wife......................Evelyn Brent

A melodrama that is a fair type of program feature. It has Monte Blue and Evelyn Brent featured at the head of a cast including Joan Lowell, Charles Gerrard, and Ralph Faulkner. The story is the Peter B. Kyne tale, "The Harbor Bar," adapted by Thompson Buchanan and directed by W. S. Van Dyke.

It is a North Pacific coast tale with the hero the captain of a tugboat in the employ of a lumber company. He marries the village belle, who has a great fear that her husband is going to lose his life in his calling. To allay those fears the husband resorts to lying whenever he has a particularly difficult piece of work to perform. On the night that an addition is expected in the family the husband, after promising to remain at home, is called to duty to save a steamer that is lying outside the harbor bar in danger. He performs his task, only to discover on his return his wife has almost died and that the expected child had died.

From that point on the wife becomes moody and suspicious of her husband, for, in a little neighboring town, one of the village girls who was to have married the mate of the tug commanded by Captain Dan, has taken up her home to hide her shame, for the mate was drowned on the day prior to their marriage date. For the sake of his old shipmate the captain assists the girl and her child. His wife believes that there is an affair between them. She prepares to leave her husband.

The day that she decides to run off, the girl in the neighboring town is killed through trying to board the captain's boat, but before passing away entrusts her child to his care. On his return home he finds his wife gone. Then comes another call to rescue a ship in trouble at sea and the captain goes to the task, and saves but his wife from the wreck. The finish finds husband and wife reconciled over the fact that there is a child in their home, even though it is that of another.

It is a depressing sort of a story, with the thrills provided by a series of shipwrecks and deaths. Pictorially it is rather well done, but the direction is decidedly draggy at times. *Fred.*

WINGS OF THE TURF

A George Clarke production presented by Wm. G. Smith. Starring Ivy Duke, directed by Guy Newell. An English production released in America through Fidelity Pictures Co. Shown at the Stanley, N. Y., Jan. 24, 1924. Running time, 64 minutes.

"Old Mat" Woodburn..................
A. Bromley Davenport
"Monkey" Brand..........John Alexander
Richard Cornwall..............Guy Newell
"Boy" Woodburn..................Ivy Duke
Ma Woodburn..................Mary Rorke
Rogers Jaggers............Cameron Clarke

This is one of those English melodramatic affairs, with the race course as the background. Like most English productions, it does not try to hold particularly to continuity as far as the story is concerned. The idea is to get to the thrill stuff, in this case the Polefox National Steeplechase, and build a reason for the race around it. It is one of those things that has a little of "The Whip" and a touch of "In Old Kentucky" in it, with the steeplechase relied on to get it over.

As far as the average motion picture house is concerned, where there is a daily change policy, this one will fit in on double feature bills as the weaker sister. Outside of that there is hardly any chance for it.

Ivy Duke carries off all of the honors. She reminds of Billie Burke on the screen, and in addition to looking rather pretty, manages to get over her role, which is an appealing one, rather well. Guy Newell, as her leading man and director, ought to confine himself to one or the other; in this particular case he didn't appear to cut very much ice in either capacity.

The balance of the company was fair.

One thing that the picture showed was that they still have a lot to learn on the other side about lighting a production.

Fred.

CAUSE FOR DIVORCE

Hugh Dierker production directed by Hugh Dierker from the story by Thelma Loimer. Released by Selznick. At Loew's New York, double feature bill, Jan. 18. Running time 78 minutes.

Tom Parker................David Butler
Mrs. Parker..............Fritzi Brunette

This is a very much jumbled and decidedly puzzling sort of a screen presentation of a theme that might have been worked out to much better advantage. The title is one that would appear sure fire for the smaller neighborhood houses, but the story doesn't stand up to it. The general idea is that there are two sides to every question and that the woman who doesn't go through with the husband is a slacker and a coward.

Maybe that will get them and maybe it won't, but the picture is hardly worth spending an hour and a quarter of one's time on to find out what it is all about. There are three different sets of characters to the story and they both wind through interminable episodes in the picture until finally they are brought together in the final couple of scenes of the story showing that there was really an earlier linking up of their lives.

The story deals with a young student of agriculture whose wife wants to live in the city, although all that he is fitted for is life on the farm. It takes five years for [illegible] finally the boy decides to go to ranching and his wife leaves him only to return later to her husband.

At the same time in society life there is a couple, the girl the daughter of a man who tried to break up the poor young couple. Her husband is neglecting her because of his work and finally she decides to run off with a supposed count. An automobile smash and her rescue by the farmer's wife prevents the elopement and there is also a happy ending of the story as far as the rich couple are concerned.

Despite a prolog tries to convince that there are two sides to every question, for the picture it appears that there is but one; the woman is to blame.

There are a couple of shots of spectacular scenes dragged in in an effort to make it spectacular. They don't help the picture any, rather tend to make it all the more draggy.

This is a good one to lay off of unless the price tag on it to insure you making money, no matter how bad the business might be. *Fred.*

THE WHITE PANTHER

Phil Goldstone production starring Rex (Snowy) Baker. Released in the Independent market. Shown at Loew's New York, N. Y., on double-feature bill Jan. 22, 1924. Running time, 54 minutes.

Shere Ali	Frank Whitson
Sir Arthur Fallington	W. H. Bainbridge
Major Bruce Wainwright	
	Rex (Snowy) Baker

Another of the Snowy Baker series which Phil Goldstone is marketing that are made-to-order story stuff to let the Australian film star display his prowess on horseback, with the sword and as a rough-and-tumble fighter.

The star displays a generous line for the edification of the screen fans in a story the scene of which is laid in India. There is some battle stuff toward the end of the feature so absurdly handled that the audience at the New York Roof gave it the razz Tuesday night.

As a picture feature this one is designed for the smaller neighborhood houses, where it will just about get by.

Baker is the commander of the British garrison at Shadkar, at the entrance to Khyber Pass. One of the officers of the command dishonors the daughter of the chieftain of the hillmen, and in retaliation the chief orders the daughter of the governor be seized for him. This gives Baker his chance to bring about her rescue single handed.

As a Snowy Baker thriller where the audiences don't care particularly what they get as screen fare it will do, but not where the fans are in the least particular.

Fred.

NO MORE WOMEN

Associated Authors present this Elmer Harris production directed by Lloyd Ingram. Released through Allied Distributors. Shown at Stanley, New York, Jan. 18. Running time 68 minutes.

Peter Maddox	Matt Moore
Daisy Crenshaw	Kathleen Clifford
Randolph Parker	Stanhope Wheatcroft
Peggy Van Dyke	Madge Bellamy
Tex	George Cooper
Beef Hogan	Clarence Burston

Fairly entertaining little program feature that is going to please the average audience in the daily change houses. Nothing stronger than that in story, but in photography it is one of the clearest shot pictures seen in several weeks. Lloyd Ingram directed the production from the story by Elmer Harris. Madge Bellamy is starred, while the cast has a couple of additional names that may mean something.

The story is one of the old, old theme of woman selecting, chasing and capturing the man she wants. Miss Bellamy is the grand-daughter of an oil millionaire. Deciding to find out how the other half of the world lives she takes a job hash slinging. There she meets a young man who stakes her to a dime and she falls in love with him. Later she discovers that he is in her grandfather's employ and lays plans to capture him, finally succeeding.

It is comedy drama certain to make an appeal in the neighborhood houses if nowhere else.

Miss Bellamy looks pretty and displays the fact that she can handle comedy on the screen. Matt Moore does fairly well as the hero. Little Kathleen Clifford as a vamp that first loves and then throws the hero over was striking in the little she had. The rest of the cast adequate. *Fred.*

CROSSING THE SAHARA

London, Jan. 22.

Hero worship is a strange thing The most idolized man in London today is Ivor Novello, whose exploits consist of looking well in a uniform, composing indifferent music and acting incompetently.

On the other hand, a modest, unassuming Scot who has crossed the Sahara on a journey from Lagos to Algiers is arousing so little enthusiasm that the film of his travels, now being shown at the Palace, looks like becoming a frost.

It is booked for no longer than a month, when the cinema version of "Anna Christie" will take its place, but there may not be enough people to know a hero when they see one to keep the show going even for that brief time.

Such disturbing signs as an audience dwindling during the performance are possibly due to the railway strike.

Angus Buchanan may have a thin personality, besides a mild voice, a stoop, not over-much stature and an inexpressive face, but he did explore the desert, and "Crossing the Great Sahara" is as convincing a record as anybody could wish. Cinema experts may suggest more rigorous cutting and the public may prefer stories to glimpses of an utterly strange land.

The opening scenes are rushed through. There is a glimpse of embarkation at Liverpool, another of Lagos and others of the outskirts of civilization, until Kano, an earth city possessing a unique architectural beauty is reached. Here there are several industries and a European bank, but onward the vegetation rapidly thins.

Just enough is shown of the preparations—buying camels and hiring camelmen—for the 16 months' journey over 3,500 miles of rock and sand. Then Buchanan develops his main theme, which is that the Sahara represents, not a quiescent state of desolation, but a rapid, inexorable decay of man, beast, vegetation and even of inorganic structures.

On the fringes of the desert the herdsmen feed their lean cattle on branches of trees because other fodder runs short at certain seasons. When the caravan leaves even the trees behind the sight of one withering thorn bush alone breaks the monotony of the vistas of sand. In the mountainous regions there are strange walled cities and villages of huts made of palm leaves, but everywhere there are signs that where hundreds now live there were once thousands.

There is a foreboding air of doom in all the picturesque walled cities, but the threat can be more sinister even than that. A village built next to a grove of date palms is shown, together with moving dunes of sand which are enveloping and submerging it.

To take the golden but uncharted road to the strange cities built of hardened salt in the very heart of the desert Buchanan joined the great salt caravan. His pictures show the trackless wastes where thousands of camels are launched to buy salt from the mysterious inhabitants of Fachi and Bilma, and they show the extraordinary face of the eagle-eyed guide, who must have inherited his job from the guides of days long past when the desert had accomplished less of its work of destruction.

By the time Buchanan, leaving the salt merchants at Bilma and traveling north alone, has come through shifting sands to Tonggourt, with its incongruously conventional railway station 400 miles south of Algiers every spectator capable of sympathetic emotion breathed a sigh of relief as profound as at the denouement of the most enthralling drama.

If hero worship (of the right kind) is not dead, Captain Buchanan's film would be the rage.

But veneration seems not to be the strong point of the present generation. *Jolo.*

WHEN A MAN'S A MAN

First National release presented by Sol Lesser. Adapted from the Harold Bell Wright story of the same title. Directed by Edward F. Cline. Shown at the Cameo, New York, for two weeks beginning Feb. 3. Running time, 74 minutes.

Lawrence Knight "Patches"	John Bowers
Helen Wakefield	Marguerite De La Motte
Phil Acton	Robert W. Frazer
Kitty Reid	June Marlowe
The Dean	Forrest Robinson
Stella	Elizabeth Rhodes
Nick Cambert	Fred Stanton
Yavapai Joe	George Hackathorne
Stanley Manning	Edward Hearne
Little Billy	Johnny Fox, Jr.
Professor Parkhill	Arthur Hoyt
Curley Elson	Ray Thompson
Jim Reid	Charles Mailes

A Western a bit different. It is a combination society and Western, with the latter element balancing the former.

But, all in all, it is a Western not unusual or extraordinary, but a fairly good program picture suitable for the average houses, without making any pretensions toward having the right to pre-release runs.

Despite the fact that Harold Bell Wright's story was a best seller, the fact remains that on the screen his tale of the tenderfoot who goes West, leaving his millions and life of ease behind him, to make a man of himself, is pretty much like a hundred other tales screened in the past.

As such it will have to be sold to the picture exhibitor and the public.

The early society element takes very little footage. It merely plants the reason for the young millionaire going West. Once in Arizona he gets a flash at a rodeo (the Prescott, Ariz., pioneer days being cut into the picture for some good shots), and decides that is the life for him.

He does eventually make a cowboy of himself, but not before he is accused of being a cattle thief and saved from a "Judge Lynch" party and a few other little things of that ilk.

Although there is sufficient love interest, the hero fades out of the final shot without any heroine to clasp in his arms. His cowboy pal gets one girl, and the girl "back East," who woke him up to the fact that he was wasting his life, comes to the West with her hubby on a honeymoon trip. But she looks as though she were sorry she married without first having gotten a line on what her former admirer made of himself.

The cast has John Bowers as the hero, delivering a very impressionable characterization. June Marlowe has the "fat" role among the women and did well with it, while Marguerite De La Motte is the society girl. Robert W. Frazer as the cowboy in the secondary lead put over his role with a wallop. George Hackathorne had a minor part, but made it stand up.

Eddie Cline, who handled the direction, turned out a workmanlike picture without any particular thrills, but telling the story in a straightforward manner and not dragging the action at any time. The picture should get money in the average run of houses. *Fred.*

MARRIAGE CIRCLE

Latest Ernst Lubitsch production, presented by the Warner Bros. All-star cast, with Florence Vidor, Monte Blue, Marie Prevost, Adolphe Menjou, Harry Myers and

Creighton Hale. Shown at the Strand, New York, week of Feb. 3, 1924. Running time, 83 minutes.

Charlotte Braun	Florence Vidor
Dr. Franz Braun	Monte Blue
Mizzi Stock	Marie Prevost
Dr. Gustave Mueller	Creighton Hale
Prof. Josef Stock	Adolphe Menjou
The Detective	Harry Myers

This picture marks an epoch in film direction. It is possibly the first time any director has had the nerve to put a farce comedy on the screen, play it legitimately and get laughs.

Almost any director would have resorted to the obvious hokum to get this one over. "Jazzing it up" would have been the thing that most would have tried and ruined a fine piece of work.

This picture is there. It has laughs and it has sex. This is a combination that can't be beaten at the box office. It may not get over with a bang the first day played, but it is one that they are going out to talk about and the business is bound to build. Not only that, but it's a picture that certainly gives Marie Prevost the chance of her life, and she assuredly makes the most of it, walking away with all the honors, although Monte Blue and Adolphe Menjou also registered with distinct force.

The detail in direction has a whole lot to do with the manner in which this trio impress the audience. The picture is played at a slow tempo. There is not the slightest suggestion of trying to force action or rush things for laughs; the situations occur naturally, are worked out logically and therefore all the more laughter-provoking to the audience.

It is the story of a wife who fears her husband is interested in another woman, so she makes the greatest effort to throw her husband and her greatest woman friend together.

In reality it is this same woman who has designs on the husband, who is a doctor specializing in nervous disorders. She arranges on two different occasions to have the doctor in her apartment alone, and although she employs every known female blandishment to make him fall, he resists her.

Finally her husband (yes, she is married) decides the wife has supplied him with sufficient evidence to have him get leave of her, something he has sought for years, and after the detective has turned in his report of the doctor's visit he calls on him the next morning and thanks him for the assistance he has given in bringing about the desired result.

It is corking farce comedy, decidedly Continental in flavor, and, while risque, there is nothing about it to offend audiences. The punch is "there" without the awful groggy effect that comes after it.

Florence Vidor as the wife handles herself admirably, but Miss Prevost so far overshadows there is no question as to whom the picture belongs.

Her husband, as played by Menjou, is a work of art. Repressed in style is his work, but with a touch of the finer little things, such as an arched eyebrow, a smile or a wink that mean volumes. Creighton Hale does fairly well as the doctor's associate, who, while in love with the wife, finally contents himself with the cast-off flapper wife who was the cause of all the trouble.

This is a picture that no one can go wrong with. *Fred.*

STRANGER OF NORTH

J. W. Noble production, both written and directed by him and carrying a Maritime Studios caption. Ned Van Buren the photographer. Showing at Loew's, New York, as half of a daily double feature program, Feb. 1. Running time, 62 minutes.

Located in the Nova Scotia region, with the lumber industry as its basic theme to provide an average secondary and indifferent feature.

Noble receives triple credit in that it is his production as well as having been both written and directed by him. The film assumes no relative importance at any time, is mediocrely played by a fair to middlin' cast and will probably fulfill its purpose best within those lesser houses where the sense of discrimination is not acutely developed. In this Broadway house the picture gave evidence of having made little impression either way.

Richard Travers and Ruth Dwyer are featured with others—Charles Graham, James McDuff, P. C. Hartigan, Louis Dean and De Sacia Morres.

The tale relates of an elderly Scot whose regional supremacy in lumber is threatened by a rival faction that is not above underhand methods. Into the situation stalks a youth from the native heath, the son of a friend, who has not been able to adjust himself to interior duties since the war. The elderly man's daughter, to whom he allows no man to speak, carries the inevitable love interest.

A walkout of the lumberjacks provides the native son with his chance and he makes good through going to a nearby military camp to surprisingly discover untold numbers of his former front line companions. Just how the boys are permitted to doff their uniforms and go a. w. l. to break the strike is never clearly explained, but they do, hence the fight and the girl are won.

Travers screens as a colorless leader whose total performance is just as shy of shading. Miss Dyer as the unsophisticated daughter provides the usual celluloid conception of the type, giving the role but a meagre amount of value, while Charles Graham's narrow-minded father was too greatly exaggerated to be convincing. *Skig.*

MARRY IN HASTE

Phil Goldstone production, directed by Duke Worne, with Jean Duvane, author. Features William Fairbanks and Dorothy Revier. At Loew's, New York, as half of daily double feature program, Feb. 1. Running time, 54 minutes.

The matrimonial difficulties of a couple who must needs settle down in a miniature ranch house after an acquaintance of but a week that concludes in the youth persuading the girl to give up her career as an artist.

The hitch comes when the husband's indulgent father places the ban on bringing the girl into the homestead.

The smaller living quarters, and a picture prone to follow proverbial lines too closely for the lifting of it beyond an intermediate classification.

The principal bid for attention comes with the husband entering the ring to stay three rounds with a barnstorming world's champ to glean the advertised $1,000 without knocking out the title holder. That either is or is not a commendable twist, according to the way you look at it.

In production the film contains little, as it is almost entirely located around the modest dwelling. Fairbanks and Miss Revier are adequate in their respective performances for a favorable combine that should do proportionately better if the material is forthcoming.

Others in the cast are Alfred Hollingsworth, Gladden James, William Dyer and Al Kaufman, the former heavyweight boxing artist, all of whom may be said to be doing just "bits."

The picture needs an additional feature to assist in the larger houses, but may possibly satisfy on its own within reduced dimensions. *Skig.*

THE STRANGER

Adolph Zukor and Jesse L. Lasky present the Joseph Henabery production based on John Galsworthy's story "The First and the Last." Featured in the cast are Betty Compson, Richard Dix, Lewis Stone and Tully Marshall. Adaptation by Edfrid Bingham.

Peggy Bowlin	Betty Compson
Larry Darrant	Richard Dix
Keith Darrant	Lewis Stone
The Stranger	Tully Marshall
Walenn	Robert Schable
Maizie Darrant	Mary Jane Irving
Jackal	Frank Nelson
Landlady	Marion Skinner

A fine, dignified screen production of a high, spiritual work. The cast itself will sell the picture to the public and the public will like it for its high standard of literary excellence, if you can speak of the literary worth of a film. At any rate the picture does get across something of the strength of the original.

Galsworthy once more is riding his special hobby of social equality—the proposition that position of eminence or social inferiority has no relation to nobility of character.

For purposes of his argument he takes a girl driven unwillingly into the streets, the humble porter of a "pub" and two brothers, one a ne'er-do-well, the other an eminent lawyer and politician. The ne'er-do-well falls in love with the unhappy girl and in defending her against a former master, kills the other man.

The humble porter (splendidly played by Marshall) takes the guilt upon himself and is prepared to go to his hanging without a word, in order that the young people who had been kind to him might be free to work out their romance. The ambitious brother struggles to keep his brother out of the affair, lest he be brought into it and his ambition thwarted. The girl merely is sorrowfully passive.

The treatment of the subject is broad and impressive, truly Galsworthy in its handling. There are broad effects, both of settings and lighting. The characterizations are well are managed with a certain unostentatious naturalness.

The action during a rainy night in London has some street scenes that somehow do not carry conviction, but the interiors, whether of the humble rooming house or the fine residence always look real.

Probably the element that will react against the picture in the public mind is its utter absence of comedy.

Much of the subject matter is overcast with gloom, although the production method saves these scenes from sordid aspect. Even the hanging scene which stops just short of the actual drop of the trap is saved from a natural atmosphere of shudders by the pomp of the ceremonies and the breadth of grouping in the prison setting.

Besides, the suspense of the whole story is so well sustained that one never loses interest. *Rush.*

COLLEEN BAWN

London, Jan. 29.

In making this picture Will Kellino had three versions of a famous story to choose from; Boucicault's drama "The Colleen Bawn" itself, Griffin's novel "The Collegians," and the legend of Hardess Cregan, his foster brother Danny Mann, and the two Colleens Bawn (the dark) and Rhu (the light) In using all three he has achieved another signal success for the Stoll Film Co.

He has here and there taken liberties with his material, for instance he has deleted the priest without which no Irish drama is complete and who is more than usually important in this romance, and he has cut out Anne Chute's lover, Kyrle Daly, completely, giving us in his stead three asinine suitors who have little to do with the story, while Anne Chute herself is only a mouthful of a part.

The photography by William Shenton is consistently beautiful and the exterior locations have never been surpassed in any picture.

The version tells how Hardress Cregan sees and falls in love with Eily O'Connor (the Colleen Bawn). Aided by the half-witted Danny Mann, his foster-brother, he tries to seduce her and fails. Then he obtains her by a secret marriage. This is discovered by Myles-na-Copaleen who is just about to murder the betrayer when Eily shrieks out her secret.

Hardress tires of his secret wife and falls in love with Anne Chute (the Colleen Rhu) who is of his own social class. Eily is in the way and at Hardress's instigation Danny tries to murder her by drowning. She is saved by Myles who nurses her in secret until Hardress' wedding night. Then he is confronted with his victim and accomplice and shot by the latter. Afterwards Eily finds happiness with the faithful lover.

Kellino's direction throughout is very good.

The cast could not have been better chosen. Colette Brettel gives a magnificent performance of the love-sick but innocent Colleen. Gladys Jennings, although badly treated as Anne Chute, maintains her position as one of Britain's best screen actresses. Henry Victor is notable as Hardress, Stewart Rome is excellent as Myles, and Clive Currie gives a fine performance as Danny. Marie Ault, Aubrey Fitzgerald, Dave O'Toole, and Marguerite Leigh all give good shows in smaller parts. This is a feature over which everybody concerned can be congratulated. *Gore.*

THE YANKEE CONSUL

Douglas MacLean starring production based on the musical comedy of the same title, adapted for the screen by Raymond Griffith and Lewis Milestone, script by Raymond Cannon. Directed by James W. Horne. Presented by Associated Exhibitors at the Central, New York, for two weeks, beginning Feb. 10. Running time, 68 minutes.

Dudley Ainsworth........Douglas MacLean
Margarita..............Patsy Ruth Miller
Jack Morrell.............Arthur Stuart Hull
Leopoldo..............Stanhope Wheatcroft
Donna Teresa..................Eulalie Jensen
Don Rafael Deschado.........George Periolat
John J. Doyle.......................Fred Kelsey
Admiral Rutledge, U. S. N.......Eric Mayne
Duncan............................L. C. Shumway
Servant.................................Bert Hadley

Here is an out and out laugh producer. A picture that pulls those oft sought for and seldom achieved laughs that are known to start somewhere near the solar plexus and end with a loud guffaw. This picture has them all the way from beginning to end, but not as most pictures achieve them—by titles—but from action. It is motion picture comedy pure and simple, no attempt to go after the fine points, but just broad wholesome humor that is pretty sure to please any sort of an audience anywhere.

In "The Yankee Consul" Douglas MacLean, the star, comes pretty nearly being as screamingly funny as he was in "The Hottentot," and that is saying a lot. Incidentally, in presenting this screen version of a musical comedy MacLean is opening a new field for the picture producers. There must be hundreds of comic librettos that are adaptable to the screen that if as well handled as this one will make mighty good entertainment in film form. This is.

Of course the title role as played by Raymond Hitchcock and as played by Douglas MacLean are two entirely different characters. MacLean is the young millionaire in whose family no one has worked for seven generations. He is on the verge of a nervous breakdown from doing nothing when a friend makes a bet that should he take a job he would have a new interest in life after a month.

The bet is taken and then things begin moving so fast in melodramatic form with MacLean as the comedy foil that laugh after laugh rolls aong. In the finish it is disclosed that all the melodrama was the result of a frame-up to provide the "new interest in life" in the form of Patsy Ruth Miller as Margarita. It works out nicely.

In addition to the laughs there also are innumerable thrills, and for a knockout that ride down the winding paths of a mountain (it looks like Griffith park) can't be beat. The car has no breaks, a fact which is planted before the comedian gets into it to start a stern chase of another auto, but MacLean doesn't know it and his ride is a howl from start to finish.

The cast supporting the star is a corking one and the direction carries the story along in great shape without a single dull moment.

It is a picture that no one can go wrong on. *Fred.*

DADDIES

Warner Bros. production of the David Belasco play, "Daddies," by John L. Hobble, adapted by Julian Josephson. Directed by William A. Seiter. Shown at the Strand, New York, week of Feb. 10. Running time, 74 minutes.

Ruth Atkins..............................Mae Marsh
Robert Audrey.......................Harry Myers
James Crockett.........Claude Gillingwater
William Rivers..................Crauford Kent
Bobette Audrey...................Claire Adams
Henry Allen..........................Willard Louis
Nicholson Walters................Boyce Combe
Mrs. Audrey...............Georgia Woodthorpe
Parker...............................Otto Hoffman
Lorrie........................Muriel Frances Dana
"The Triplets"
......De Briane Twins and King Evers
Katie..........................Milly Davenport

This is a fairly amusing screen entertainment, but not one that will prove an extraordinary box office winner. It will pull the average business to the average houses. There is one disappointment, and that is Mae Marsh in the leading role. Miss Marsh neither looks nor acts the character of the little English orphan who wins the heart of her adopted father. The others in the cast are all satisfactory, especially Harry Myers and Claude Gillingwater, and above all, the juvenile members of the company.

The story is that of the adopting of war babies and the wreck that one lone woman can make of a batchelor club, the woman in the case being the mother of one of the members whose belief that every man's debt to society is to marry and raise a family. Thus she arranges to have the four remaining members of the club, including her son, all agree to adopt a war orphan, with the result that, being fathers, they all finally decide that their children must have mothers.

Amusing enough, to be sure, but not with sufficient punch to make picture fans break down theatre doors to see it.

Harry Myers plays the son of the mother who wants to see her boy married, and Miss Marsh is the little war orphan that is picked out for him. He seconds the selection after viewing a photograph of the girl at the age of six and imagines that will be her age when she arrives, but instead it is a full-grown young lady. Another of the quartet gets triplets as his share of the bargain, while the old grouch at the head of the club who insists on having a boy gets a girl. This girl role, played by Muriel Frances Dana, is one of the works of art of the production.

There are a lot of good comedy situations and any number of laughs of light timber in the picture, but it isn't one of those comedies that could be described as a "wow." *Fred.*

MY MAN

Vitagraph feature, presented by Albert E. Smith, scenario by George Randolf Chester. Running time, 75 minutes. Reviewed at Rialto, New York, Feb. 10.

Molly Marley ....Patsy Ruth Miller
Sledge ....Dustin Farnum
Dicky Reynolds.....................Niles Welch
Fern Burbank...................Margaret Landis
Bert Glider.........................George Webb
Henry Peters.....................William Norris
Mrs. Peters..............................Edith Yorke
Jessie Peters......................Violet Palmer
Christopher Marley..........Sidney de Grey

The title is worth something at the box office due to the song hit. However, the picture in no way resembles the song theme. The picture is a hackneyed familiar, not particularly well cast, with Patsy Ruth Miller running away with whatever honors there were.

The strong political boss in love with the daughter of a rich man who doesn't love him is the flimsy rack on which the scenario is hung. The politician will brook no interference and breaks everyone who stands between him and the girl, including her own father and a lounge lizard who is after her money.

Much inconsequential kickless footage is exhausted trying to string this situation out to feature proportions, with the usual result. The picture is dull and dreary, in spots unconvincing and unentertaining.

Dustin Farnum as Sledge the politician plays in the stereotyped manner, smoking innumerable cigars, which seemingly are indispensable to a certain type of picture actor when cast as a business man, politician or detective. Tom McQuire claims the distinction of being the only human who ever played a dick without a nickel owl stuck between his teeth.

Sledge eventually wins the girl by showing up her gold digging suitor and after wrecking her father financially in a traction deal, he squares everything in time for the happy clinch and fade out.

The picture is the weakest sort of program addition. In the average picture house sans the elaborate presentation given at the Rialto, it will have less chance. The production deserved a better story. *Con.*

THE NEXT CORNER

Sam Wood production for Famous Players-Lasky, with a multiple star cast. Done from the book and play by Kate Jordan and adapted to the screen by Monte M. Katterjohn. Projection time, 61 minutes. At the Rivoli Feb. 10. Previously announced as "Nearly a Sinner."

Robert Maury................Conway Tearle
Elsie Maury..............Dorothy Mackaill
Juan Serafin.........................Lon Chaney
Don Arturo...................Ricardo Cortez
Nina Race, Elsie's mother...Louise Dresser
Countess Longueval........Remea Radzina
Paula Vrian...............Dorothy Cumming
Julie, Elsie's maid....Mrs. Bertha Feducha
The Stranger..................Bernard Seigle

All the surface elements of a fine picture are here assembled. Still, the production isn't worth the trouble, for the reason it has a silly story. It's all about a fool woman (played by Miss Mackaill) who is carried away by an infatuation for a he-vamp and then hadn't either the nerve to go through with it or to quiet her own sentimental conscience. In short, the sort of a conventional figure that lives only in books and movies.

This screen manniquin does emotional back somersaults at any excuse. Her husband (played by Conway Tearle in his usually smooth fashion) is quite contented to take her on faith, even after the hysterical episode with the dark and sinister homebreaker, but she persists in being comfortably tragic. The husband didn't call for much more sympathy than his wife. So careless a mate invited domestic disaster. The only detail of her conduct that aroused his objections was that she made up her face and smoked cigarettes. He seemed quite satisfied with her friends, who were obvious loose livers.

It is a pity this sort of fictional slush has injured a picture into which must have gone a vast amount of artistic effort. The scenic settings are magnificent, particularly those dealing with a storm in the mountains and gorgeous surroundings for social fetes in Paris. Some startlingly bizarre effects were secured in the interiors, while splendid dignity was expressed in other inside shots, such as Don Arturo's castle.

But when all is said and done the immediate appeal of the picture is in the women's fashions it discloses. Variety's expert, who sometimes can be lured to the pictures on off evenings, makes the declaration that some of the dresses shown in the pocture haven't yet got aboard ship at Havre. She (the fashion expert) said the film release has "beaten the New York market" on more than one "number."

The frocks are startling. One is so tight it has to be laced from hem to high neckband like a high hunting boot. Any woman has to be of severest Gothic lines to play such a dress and avoid making a scene. The prevailing note seems to be straight lines, stretched surfaces from east to west both fore and aft, and if you go into the subject any further you run into words and lines that a strictly family paper can't print. But this much one can declare—the new styles are going to put the girls on their honor as to their figures and diet and wreck Lane Bryant.

Lon Chaney has a weak part and gets into the fore only now and then in subordinate situations where he has little to build on, and another rather trifling role is dealt to Louise Dresser, who had only a couple of scenes that might as well have been played by an unknown grande dame.

Bernard Seigle, hitherto of no great prominence, has one impressive bit as an avenging Spanish father. He has a strong, rugged face and a stately presence, a capital type for roles of this sort. *Rush.*

SPORTING YOUTH

Chicago, Feb. 13.

Universal-Jewel starring Reginald Denny in Byron Morgan's story. Directed by Harry Pollard, with Clyde De Vinna the photographer. Cast includes Henry Burrows, Frederick Vroom, Laura La Plante, Lucille Ward and Hallam Cooley. At Randolph, Chicago, week of Feb. 11. Running time, 76 minutes.

Denny's second attempt since leaving the Witwer "Leather Pushers" series, also turned out by U, and playing under the guidance of the same director, Pollard. According to all reports, U is out to plug Denny into the place left vacant by Wally Reid, having bought a number of Morgan's stories for future production, who had many of his scripts adapted to Reid.

This particular narrative appeared in the "Saturday Evening Post," and outside of what kick the automobile race supplies the detachment assigned to making the screen version seems to have done little with it.

Denny is not particularly colorful as the chauffeur become an improvised race driver, and the combined efforts of the various contributing personnel gives reason to believe that there is much ground to be covered before Denny can equal the better Reid releases of the type.

The story projects as being unduly lengthy in reaching a specific point, and it is not until the action swings on to the track that any material happening takes place. The race, as well, appears to have been prolonged to past the breaking point, with more than one chance that some of the contest "shots" are repeated in quick snatches.

Two accidents have been inserted for the usual thrills. One has a machine taking a dive off a cliff, while the later incident provides the actual wallop of the picture in a wild car climbing a bank, tearing through a fence and somersaulting into a crowd of spectators. It's a long-distance glimpse of the smashup that at least constitutes a corking fake, while looking real enough to perhaps have been lifted from an actual race film.

The story is along light comedy lines, of a speed bug chauffeur who is sent on to California ahead of his employer with a mistaken identity alibi for the plausibility of driving the boss' raceabout to cop the $10,000 and the daughter of the maker of the car. They don't explain why the employer, detesting the high spots, possesses a roadster (and, incidentally, a machine that has been in other pictures besides this one).

Laura La Plante, opposite Denny, lends a nice appearance to the vehicle, but has little to do other than cheer the victor on. The remaining cast donations are negligible, with the production not screening as having caused an unduly heavy outlay of lucre beyond the four-wheel vehicles. The camera work has caught the race stuff for adequate presentation, but as a whole the picture lacks the necessary quality to make it outstanding in the larger houses, and more so is that true when the object in view is considered. *Skig.*

"WHISPERED NAME"

A Universal production directed by King Baggott. Adapted from the play, "The Co-respondent," by Rita Weiman and Alice Leal Pollock. At the New York Feb. 8 as half the bill. Runs about 65 minutes. Cast includes Ruth Clifford, Niles Welch, Jane Starr, Buddy Messinger, Carl Stockdale, William Lawrence, Hayden Stevenson,

Mary Mersch, John Merkyl and Charles Clary.

With the right kind of treatment "The Whispered Name" might have turned out to be rather a first-rate newspaper story, as the plot itself holds such potentialities. But Universal has provided a mediocre cast, old style direction, miserable photography and general, all-around atmosphere that detract severely from the story.

The characters move through the scenes in jerky, clumsy sequences and poses, and when the big climacteric moment arrived the director lost a splendid opportunity for the dramatic smash that should have crowned the situation.

However, the director was handicapped by a cast of players at best so-so and at worst poor enough.

Ruth Clifford and Niles Welch are the leads. Miss Clifford is pleasantly capable-looking as a young woman reporter, but too much rouge on her lips hurts her full-face shots. Welch is the leading man who, when he played opposite Elaine Hammerstein and Norma Talmadge some years ago, was heralded as having a great future.

Of the others, Charles Clary and Hayden Stevenson are the best, while, conversely, Mary Mersch and John Merkyl are not. They gave the film some very amateurish scenes. Almost as bad as their action is the photography.

Coming to the praiseworthy part, the plot, it is a typical newspaper and blackmail story, but with a few novel twists and kicks. The big idea is introduced when Anne Grey (Miss Clifford) is sent to interview a woman suing her husband for divorce, with Anne herself, innocently and unknowingly, mentioned as the co-respondent. Welch is the editor of the paper which employs Anne, and as he has lost his heart to her, he, too, is dragged into the mess.

The expose of a band of blackmailers clears the atmosphere.

"The Whispered Name" will serve as just about average fare for the intermediate houses. Whatever credit goes with this belongs to Misses Weiman and Pollock, who wrote the play from which it was adapted.

THE LOVE BANDIT

Charles E. Blaney production released by Vitagraph. From the play of the same title. Directed by Dell Henderson; stars Doris Kenyon. Shown at the Stanley, N. Y., Feb. 12, 1924. Running time, 73 minutes.

Jim Blazes................Victor Sutherland
Henri Baribeau..................Jules Cowles
Buck Ramsdell............Christian Frank
Maggie McGuiry..........Dorothy Walters
French Annie..................Miss Valentine
Madge Dempsey.................Cecil Spooner
Amy Van Clayton..............Doris Kenyon
Fred Van Clayton............Gardner James
John Lawson....................Walter Jones
Snapper Rollins...........Edward Boulden

This is a real cheap melodramatic thriller that has all the old tricks of the ten-twent-thirt shows of the days of old. In this particular picture it is played just as they did in the stage productions in the combination houses at popular prices, one of those companies to which a two-night stand was an event, and a chance to take a bath.

There is one real picture player, Doris Kenyon. It was a mistake to put her in this picture, as she shows up everyone else in the cast.

"The Love Bandit" is without doubt the most overacted picture in many moons. So exaggerated are the attempts to get over the real heavy stuff that instead of impressing an audience they bring roars of laughter. The picture, however, is intended as a serious effort, which makes the entire affair a rather sad one. Had the picture been kidded through titling it might have made a good comedy.

Dell Henderson, who directed, has made a reputation for himself as a fairly consistent director, so it seems hardly fair to charge the overacting and exaggerated antics of the players to him. Seemingly there must have been someone else connected with the production who took a hand in guiding the players as to what they had to put into their action to get it over.

The story is a lumber camp-society tale. There is a reason for a battle betwen the lumberjacks of both camps. That battle with about 24 men in it is a laugh in itself.

The picture didn't cost an awful lot to make, and if bought at a price it'll get by in the cheap admission houses. *Fred.*

THE NEW ENGLANDER

Equity Plays, Inc., Harry O. Stubbs, managing director, presents this four-act play by Abby Merchant. Staged by Henry Stillman and Gilbert Emery. Settings by Woodman Thompson. Opened at the Equity 48th St., Feb. 7.

Mrs. Ellery................Katherine Emmet
Helen Estabrook..................Louise Huff
Robert Keene.................Gilbert Emery
Annie Bennett..............Helen Strickland
Seth Ellery ....Alan Birmingham
James McCall..................Arthur Shaw

The program denotes this as "A study of New England character," which intention of the author was not gotten over with any degree of impressiveness approaching that of "Icebound," for instance.

Built along the familiar mother's sacrifice and errant son's misunderstanding, it contains a few interesting highlights here and there, but the sum total is not exceptionally brilliant. The idea revolves about the stoic Spartan will of a New England mother (the action is laid in a suburb of Boston), who relegates her mother love and forgiveness and urges the prosecution for larceny of her only son, an idea that lacks the homely attribute necessary to wallop the point across as poignantly and impressively as it might have been under other circumstances.

What recommended it chiefly, probably, was its economical production. The four acts are laid in one interior and require only six characters.

It permits for a number of histrionic highlights by the cast which does much make the evening passably interesting. Alan Birmingham as the son had the difficult role, but managed fairly well. Louise Huff, from pictures, accepted a couple of emotional opportunities interestingly and disproves part of what they say about movie people proving flops on the stage. Katherine Emmet as the mother was "sweetly" cast and an entirely sympathetic character. Arthur Shaw in a slangy role also was interesting.

The "unhappy" ending with the suicide by the mother is not likely to prolong its stay much beyond the regular subscription season allotted to each Equity offering. This makes the third production, with two more to go this season, exclusive of an all-star revival. *Abel.*

YOLANDA

Cosmopolitan special production starring Marion Davies. Opened at Cosmopolitan Feb. 19, to $1.50 top, running in two parts. Adapted from book by the late Charles Major, by Luther Reed. Settings by Joseph Urban. Photography by Ira H. Morgan and George Barnes. Directed by Robert G. Vignola.

Princess Mary of Burgundy (Yolanda)
Marion Davies
Charles the Bold, Duke of Burgundy
Lyn Harding
King Louis XI...............Holbrook Blinn
Bishop La Balue..........Maclyn Arbuckle
The Dauphin, Charles, Duke of Paris
Johnny Dooley
Maximilian of Styria.........Ralph Graves
Campo-Basso ....Ian MacLaren
Olivier de Daim.....Gustav von Seyffertitz
Queen Margaret..Theresa Maxwell Conover
Count Jules d'Hymbercourt.Paul McAllister
Innkeeper..........................Leon Errol
Antoinette Castleman.........Mary Kennedy
Castleman ....Thomas Findlay
Count Calli.........................Martin Faust
Lord Bishop...............Arthur Donaldson
Sir Karl de Pitti.............Roy Applegate

Billed now as "Queen of the Screen," Marion Davies has adopted the title given to her in a recent voting contest that will keep her stepping to hold it up on every end, for "The Queen of the Screen" appears to take in everything, from acting to looks.

In "Yolanda" Miss Davies has both, although her looks are not steady, due to either photography or lighting, but her natural beauty cannot be denied, so that is the least to worry her.

In acting, however, of the title role, Miss Davies well upholds the reputation as a screen artist she has intelligently, studiously and conscientiously erected for herself, with the public and in the picture business. But it's straightaway acting here, possibly the most difficult before the camera, for pantomimists who are, are rare.

Those who have watched the Marion Davies pictures continuously will miss that elf-like, cheery, charming cuteness or roguishness no one else on the screen can give to a light character or a shaded one as well as Marion Davies, not even Pickford.

But there's romance in "Yolanda," oodles of it, and romance goes with Marion's youth. It's the Major story of centuries ago, of the Princess of Burgundy who met her Prince of Styria, without either aware of the identity of the other, although betrothed in the kingly manner of those days (1490); how they were revealed to one another, although Princess Mary first and accidentally learned who her admirer was. Truth to tell, the Prince as played by Ralph Graves wasn't the Prince of action of Princess Mary's dreams, if one would gauge that by Princess Mary's performance. Miss Davies played it and Mr. Graves tried to act it.

The Queen Margaret of Theresa Maxwell Conover wasn't a bad piece of execution by any means, saying Miss Conover had strictly followed direction, although the masterful performance was Holbrook Blinn's as King Louis XI.

Blinn gave his character a Napoleonic touch in carriage and looks, almost in dress—it couldn't be missed, though not essayed in that direction.

Another performer is Lyn Harding, English, as the Duke of Burgundy, who made you feel the state did come first with him.

Leon Errol gave a laugh to his innkeeper role and Johnny Dooley as a foolish Prince gave two or three laughs, each time he did a fall, while looking every bit as idiotic as he was supposed to be.

The settings are massive; there are large mobs nicely directed and a battle with battle-axes of more or less thrill, depending upon how one might visualize what axemen would really do if allowed to chop at will.

The captions were always severe, often too much so, and one particularly in poor taste for modern consumption—where it spoke of "the smell of dead traitors."

A slight dragginess frequently made itself manifest, more so in the first part. There is no real kick at any time, but the romantically inclined will find all they want of that heart-stirrer; it's there all of the time, even though the picture could have ended with the conclusion of the first part—that was the story.

Following "Knighthood," the pedestal of her picture reputation, Miss Davies here presents another film tale not altogether apart from it in general outline and but a short distance away. That may have been the single error, for it cannot be forgotten so soon what "Knighthood" was and held. The kneeling scene by Miss Davies found its quiet echo in "Yolanda," as the almost similar scene had brought forth an applause explosion in "Knighthood." That may be dovetailed into the remainder for audience-effect.

"Yolanda" is a picture for picture fans, and looks the $650,000 it is said to have cost.

Cosmopolitan isn't economical in picture production.

Sime.

THE MAN LIFE PASSED BY

Metro production written and directed by Victor Schertzinger. Featuring Jane and Eva Novak, Hobart Bosworth, Cullen Landis and Percy Marmont. Shown at Loew's State, New York, Feb. 18-20. Running time, 72 minutes.

Hope Moore.........................Jane Novak
Joy Moore............................Eva Novak
John Corbin..................Percy Marmont
Harold Trevis....................Cullen Landis
"Iron Man" Moore........Hobart Bosworth
Mrs. Corbin........................Lydia Knott
Paula........................Gertrude Short
Jerry......................Walter Steadman

Here is an attempt at something that doesn't materialize. It starts off with a rush, looks as though it was really going to be something pretentious and worth while as a picture and then goes off into a long rambling affair that gets nowhere. It is just another case where the shoemaker should have stuck to his last.

Victor Schertzinger is a pretty good director, but he should stick to direction and let the writing end remain in hands more suited to the task, if "The Man Life Passed By" on the screen is as he wrote it. A writer might have whipped the tale into shape and worked out a continuity that would have meant something.

The cast has both Jane and Eva Novak as well as Hobart Bosworth, Cullen Landis and Percy Marmont featured. Each member of this quintet turns out an intelligible characterization of the role assigned to them, but they are not sufficient to speed up the ever lagging interest in a slow moving tale that jumps from one sequence to another and then doesn't seem to hook them up again.

As a flash for the neighborhood houses this picture will get by. This is particularly true in the daily change houses, but don't build too strongly on it.

It is a tale of a disappointed inventor and an unscrupulous ironmaster who steals his patents and compels him to seek life in the gutter. Broken in health and spirit, the inventor finally decides to kill the ironmaster, but is deterred in his desire by the beautiful girl mission worker in the slums. Later when the inventor has his chance to wreak his vengeance on a daughter of the iron king his hand is stayed by her resemblance to the mission woman who had faith in him, and it is finally disclosed that the women are sisters and there is a final happy ending all around.

In sets the picture is excellent. Some slum stuff is particularly well done. About 15 minutes could be cut from the film to advantage.

Fred.

TWENTY-ONE

Inspiration Pictures presents. John S. Robertson production. First National, distributor. Scenario by Josephine Lovett. Romance, with undertones of problem play and overtones of melodrama. At Rialto, New York, week Feb. 17. Running time, 75 minutes.

Julian McCullough.....Richard Barthelmess
Mr. McCullough...................Joe King
Mrs. McCullough.........Dorothy Cumming
Lynnie Willis.............Dorothy Mackaill
Paula..........................Elsie Lawson
Peter Straskl...............Bradley Barker
Mr. Willis................Ivan Simpson
Mrs. Willis.........Nellie Parker Spaulding
Mrs. Jordan.....................Helen Tracy
Julian McCullough, age seven.........
..................................Howard Merrill

"Twenty-One," which stars Richard Barthelmess, was scheduled for the Strand originally, but according to the "Times Square Daily," the Strand turned thumbs down on it. If the "T. S. Daily" knows what it's talking about, the Rialto, which is controlled by Famous Players, was a second choice.

And it looks as if the Strand pulled a boner and the Rialto got a break thereby—for "Twenty-One" is a good picture. It kept 'em waiting in line at the Rialto Sunday.

The time-worn Cinderella theme is dragged out of the camphor as the basic idea, but this is a Cinderella with trimmings—sex stuff, and the kind that is as full of pep as the w. k. Isle of Jamaica.

The familiar situation of a rich man's son in love with a poor man's daughter isn't exactly novel—especially when the couple traverse obstacle-strewn pathways to a happy climax. It's treated so well, though, and the action is so interestingly spun the yarn makes unusually good entertainment.

A conflict between the wealthy parents of the hero over the up-bringing of their only child leaves the boy in charge of his mother from the time he is 8 until he's 20. The mother is daffy on bizarre society fads and follies. The picture has the young fellow in an unhealthy environment of aesthetic dancers, etc., with the sort of "culture" surrounding him suggesting his mother's influence would tend to make him the antithesis of the manly chap his father wants him to be.

At the opening the boy, then eight, is boxing with his father, and the impression clearly conveyed is that the kid is a normal, manly youngster. That he remains manly throughout the story is no fault of the mother, for with her approval the youth, now 20, is seen prancing around the lawn in the measures of a Grecian dance.

He's made up as a Faun for this, with the scanty clothes and horns that go with the character—but obviously to his intense disgust. A character of a male dancing teacher with the business of the part having the role marked with unmistakably effeminate mannerisms completes the Grecian dancing picture.

This is a psycho-analytical touch inserted probably to show the bad influence the mother might have had on the youth's character development had he not been strong enough to overcome it.

A love affair crops up and the rich youth breaks the shackles that has kept him tied to his mother's apron strings. This proceeds with the usual obstacles that present themselves when a wealthy young fellow falls for a penniless girl.

A scene that has the young couple marooned on the road with a broken-down auto and finds them seeking refuge in a hotel—registered as sister and brother was conspicuous for some hectic petting in the auto, and looked at first as if the hotel scene was to hold dynamite. That brother and sister thing switched matters, however, at a crucial point.

A couple of good fights are contained in the action—one at a Slav picnic, with gunplay, and another in a garage which is the hiding place for a flock of stolen autos. The villain incidentally is an auto thief.

The father of the girl, hearing of the hotel episode, demands of the father of the boy the latter marry the girl. The rich man spurns the proposal and effects a proposition to buy off the father of the gal. The boy is handed a severe beating by his father and leaves home to make his way in the world.

He gets a job as a taxi-chauffeur and the development of the plot has him catching up with the villain and landing the whole crew of auto thieves in the jug—at the same time saving his old man from the clutches of the guerillas.

The production has been lavishly staged scenically and the director has turned out a compact story with continuity that holds consistently from leader to fade-out.

Barthelmess plays the rich youth with a complete understanding, and it's a decidedly difficult role that calls for the most intelligent shading and high-lighting.

The girl is Dorothy Mackaill, and she makes the part live. A certain wistfulness that adds to her charm is an outstanding feature.

The heavy is well done by Bradley Barker, and Joe King does the father of the boy with definite authority. Ivan Simpson contributes an excellent character study as the girl's father. The contributory parts are all played with equal artistry.

A play, "Go West, Young Man," produced several weeks ago, had a somewhat similar theme as regards the central character of the boy.

"Twenty-One" has all the characteristics of a good commercial picture.   *Bell.*

MAN FROM WYOMING

Universal production written by William McLeod Raine, directed by Robert North Bradbury and starring Jack Hoxie. Cast includes Lillian Rich, William Welch and Clayde Payton. At Stanley, New York, Feb. 15, one day. Runs about an hour.

The plains of Wyoming in all their rugged glory are the background for this latest Western which turns out to be a more effective program picture than might be expected. William McLeod Raine's novel, "Wyoming," serves as foundation for the story. It is stereotyped and built along formula but interesting.

Those who like the real violent stuff in fight scenes are sure to find their spines tingling with excitement in the last few minutes. It is not the struggle of the hero and villian alone that brings thrills but the stirring events leading up to and surrounding their scrap.

The hero (Jack Hoxie) has been railroaded to prison and in return for help in making his escape is being forced to herd the sheep of the villian on a cattle ranch belonging to the Wyoming governor's daughter. Determining to squash the sheepman she comes to the ranch only to fall in love with him instead.

The last few minutes are crammed full of ridiculous but at the same time gripping action. The comedy end is adequately held up by colored chef, Chinese waiter and a whole ranchful of the films' idea of the perfect comic cowboy.

Hoxie rides a horse as perhaps no one else in pictures can, also appears to be handy with his fists, and acts in general with considerable manliness and force. Lillian Rich is a charming heroine and if she does smile too much it is almost permissible in her case. The rest of the cast and the direction are adequate and the photography is uniformly exceptional.

The film is a bit slow in getting started but once underway they will like it in the neighborhood houses.

IN THE WEST

Western melodrama starring Richard Hatton and Neva Gerber. Distributed by Arrow Film Corporation. At Stanley, New York, Feb. 19. Running time, 70 minutes.

This is a western of the old-fashioned type—so bad it's funny. Many a travesty melodrama that announced itself as travesty lacked the burlesque elements of what is here set forth seriously.

There's a public for pictures like this just as there always has been since the days when the General Film Co. handled junk like it wholesale.

A young fellow (Richard Hatton) is a cowboy. He makes a visit east and falls in love with the heroine, played by Neva Gerber. The heavy is cowboy's rival and heavy cops the gal because cowboy is a thick lug when it comes to parlor manners.

A change of locale in the action finds hero and villain out west prospecting for gold. Heavy frames hero—but hero turns tables and shows up heavy for cur that he is. Heavy incidentally carries prize leer on his pan through picture—heroine is unsophisticated—and hero composite of all the good points a man can possess.

Finish is a darb. The hero and heroine both tumble into same pool of water—over a cliff and minister happens to fall over same cliff. That's coincidence. Minister marries 'em on the spot.

There's been many a banal western but for all round puerility this one cops the highest honors. Looking cheaply made it can probably be rented at a figure that makes it a bargain for the cheap houses.
                                                      Bell.

SOUTHERN LOVE

London, Feb. 4.

Before an audience numbering close on 10,000 this new Graham Wilcox picture featuring Betty Blythe was screened at the Albert Hall, Jan. 29. The entire building had been turned into a bullring and draped with the Spanish national colors while the screen was a special made one, 60 feet wide and raised high before the great organ. A specially written and arranged prolog was sung by Herbert Langley, Frank Mullings and Edna Thornton of the British National Orchestra under the baton of Albert Cazabon.

The film, directed by Herbert Wilcox, has not the extravagant beauty of the same producer's "Chu Chun Chow"; the story gives no opportunity for this, but it is exceedingly well done.

The story is a strong melodramatic one in which a beautiful woman and three lovers form the basis of the plot—a primitive brute, an aristocratic libertine and a pure and chivalrous young English artist.

It is to be noted that all English artists are pure in pictures; they also appear to be somewhat devoid of red blood and backbone.

The story is well told with a smooth continuity its only fault being the finish when to get the requisite happy ending the hero has to rescue the heroine from a prison van and convey her safely over the frontier while chased by gendarmerie. This chase was the weak thing in the picture and the gendarmes appeared not to care a rap whether they captured their prisoner or not.

The settings are very good, some beautiful, and those calling for "crowds" have been adroitly handled.

The two dances provided for Miss Blythe as the heroine, are excellently executed and brought genuine applause. The story tells how Dolores, daughter of a traveling showman, is beloved by the brutal Pedro whose glorious voice keeps the gaff together. She hates him but her father insists on their bethrothal.

About this time she meets the young artist, Tennant, and it is a case of love at first sight. Then the licentious Count de Silva sees her and although married to a beautiful young wife, he is immediately overwhelmed with passion for the dancing beauty. He offers to make her the greatest dancer in Spain an offer which Dolores, knowing something of counts and their habits, rejects. Later after Pedro has broken into her living van she decides to run away from the show and accept the count's offer.

Throughout the acting was excellent and has rarely been bettered on the screen. Miss Blythe forgetting her statuesque beauty made Dolores a woman of flesh and blood, spiteful, pathetic, but always truly loving the right man. Herbert Langley was excellent as Pedro. A notable thing in the production was that the last half of the film was practically devoid of sub-titles. Herbert Wilcox can say this work was the most beautiful British picture yet produced.   *Gore.*

AMERICA

D. W. Griffith presentation signalized as Series One and carrying a secondary title of "The Sacrifice for Freedom." Story and titling by Robert W. Chambers with the historical arrangement credited to John L. E. Pell. Griffith the director with Herbert Sutch named as assistant. Camera men, G. W. Bitzer, Hendrick Sartov, Marcel Le Picard and H. S. Sintzenich. Opening at the 44th Street, New York, Feb. 21, for run at $1.65 top. Running time, 164 mins.

Nathan Holden.............Neil Hamilton
Justice Montague..........Erville Alderson
Nancy Montague...........Carol Dempster
Charles Montague..........Charles E. Mack
George Washington.........Arthur Dewey
Capt. Walter Butler.....Lionel Barrymore
Samuel Adams....................Lee Beggs
John Hancock...............John Dunton
William Pitt...............Charles Bennett
Thomas Jefferson..............Frank Walsh
Patrick Henry.......Frank McGlynn, Jr.
Paul Revere...................Harry O'Neill
Capt. Hare.................Louis Wolheim
Edmund Burke......................W. Rising

Another outstanding achievement for Griffith which can't miss on its historical interest alone. The production is paramount as a box-office attraction and as a picture unquestionably ranks with the best that this director has given to the screen.

It marks an auspicious inaugural for the releases which are to follow, as indicated by the "Series One" designation, and looks sufficiently good to remain at the 44th Street indefinitely.

The main fault is in the length, with it reported the picture was in 16 reel before opening. An exact splitting of the two halves, in which the performance is divided, would reveal the initial portion consuming 92 minutes with the following stanza running 72. Much deletion may be done before the picture is fully set.

The major bid for enthusiasm is within the first half which mainly deals with the historic aspects and reaches the crest in the Paul Revere ride thence culminating in the reason for double headers on the Fourth of July.

That ride, due to the way Griffith has presented it, assumes the proportions of about as thrilling a picturization as the art of cinema making has yet reached, minus the aid of mob stuff. Placed midway in the first period it registers as the height to which the production soars. Previously it builds up coherently and with that certain touch for sustaining such a situation for which the director is so noted.

It is in the latter stages of this opening half, where the story commences to gain ascendancy, that it becomes lethargic, for no narrative is of that power to supercede the projecting of the happenings relative to the birth of the country.

In other words the conflicts at Lexington and Concord and the spreading of the alarm by Paul Revere contain too vital and intense interest for the script to follow, although Griffith has injected another solo gallop in the second half besides a dash of a body of horsemen on a rescue mission. Also, it's too well known what Griffith can do with numbers on horseback to need any comment.

Following the interval the remainder is mostly taken up with the carrying of the romance to a conclusion while constituting a secondary consideration. It includes the devastation wrought by the Indian forces who combined with the British during the strife with the story's punch revealing itself in an attack upon a small fort wherein are the heroine and her father—ultimately rescued along with the remainder of the refugees.

What amounts to practically an epilog is the inaugural ceremony of Washington for which the National anthem is played and upon which the pictures closes out.

The film is reported to have totaled in the neighborhood of $950,000. Certainly the screening says there was no effort to cheat.

Photographically it is superb even if the identical types of double exposure backgrounds for a magnitudinous impression that Griffith invoked in the "Nation" are again utilized. But it's good faking at the least.

Carol Dempster is the only girl of prominence and her performance should hereafter place her beyond doubt. The entire cast, listing 33 on the program, meet the requirements that such a picture demands with Neil Hamilton, Erville Alderson, Charles E. Mack, Arthur Dewey, Lionel Barrymore, as the "heavy" and Miss Dempster outstanding.

"America" is "in" as it stands and when the needed cutting is accomplished, it should closely approximate being airtight.

Not only that but it signifies another epic for Griffith who has lost nothing in the interim since his last big special. That the "Nation," now nine years old, recently did $55,000 in a week at the Auditorium, Chicago, is proof enough of the workmanship and qualifications that "America" must contain, for it's from the hands of the same director who can still be given an "edge" on any basis of comparison. *Skig.*

THE SONG OF LOVE

First National attraction, starring Norma Talmadge. Presented by Joseph M. Schenck. Adapted from the Margaret Peterson novel, "Dust of Desire," by Frances Marion, who co-directed with Chester Franklin. Shown at the Rivoli, N. Y., week Feb. 24, 1924. Running time, 79 minutes.

Noorma-hal..............Norma Talmadge
Ramon Valverde...........Joseph Schildkraut
Ramlika...........Arthur Edmund Carewe
Dick Jones...................Laurence Wheat
Maureen Desmard..............Maude Wayne
Commissionaire Desmard.......Earl Schenck
Chandra-lal....................Hector V. Sarno
Chamba...........................Albert Prisco
Captain Fregonne...............Mario Carillo
Dr. Humbert......................James Cooley

If you never got a real chance to see a lot of Norma Talmadge, this picture certainly gives it to you. Possibly Miss Talmadge is desirous of detracting attention from the rather tired look she is carrying about her eyes, so is exposing other of her charms. As the Arabian dancing girl she certainly does face the camera in a state of undress.

Outside of Miss Talmadge there isn't an awful lot to "The Song of Love." It is another of those desert stories, the same type more or less that went out of fashion a little over a year ago as far as the big first-run houses were concerned, at any rate! There is a lot of sand, some of the sheik stuff, some hard riding and gunplay, and above all Norma slips through a dance.

The scene is in Algeria, where a bold, bad chieftain of a desert tribe desires to be king of North Africa and to drive the unbelieving French from the territory. This role is played by Arthur Edmund Carewe, who presented a real heavy. Norma is a dancing girl in a native gaming house, and the chieftain desires to make her his queen when victory finally rests with his cause.

The French send for one of their secret service men to get the detail of the plot, and when he arrives in native disguise and enters the gaming house he wins the heart of the dancer. In the end she saves his life, and it all ends happily when the fanatic is killed and the girl saved from self-destruction, so that she can rest in the hero's arms.

The hero is played by Joseph Schildkraut, who makes a rather colorless job of it. Schildkraut won't do for pictures unless he gets roles different than the one here.

With Norma Talmadge as the star this is a picture you can play if they will stand for all that Norma shows—and they will. Without Norma it wouldn't be. *Fred.*

VIOLETTES IMPERIALES

Presented by Charles B. Cochrane at the Playhouse, New York, Feb. 24, to introduce Raquel Meller, Spanish stage star. Authorship and direction by Henry Rousell. Running time, 78 minutes.

Violetta.......................Raquel Meller
Hubert............................Andre Roanne
Eugenie de Montijo......Suzanne Bianchetti
Manuel.............................Sans Juana

Raquel Meller is to invade this shore and appear in the spoken drama. That is to be in the fall, and her season is to be under the direction of the Selwyns and Charles B. Cochrane, the London producer.

They believed as long as the Spanish star had made a picture abroad it might be a good idea to give us an idea of what she looked like and what she could do in acting.

It was a good idea, for Raquel Meller impressed. She is good to look upon, can act, has eyes that Pola Negri must envy, and at times looks like Mary Pickford in "Rosita," while at others she resembles Gloria Swanson to a certain extent. Her worst feature as far as the screen is concerned is her mouth. So much for the star.

"Violettes Imperiales" is the title of the picture in which she was shown. She financed its making personally. It is a story of the 19th century during the reign of Napoleon III of France. Historic and romantic, yes, but that is about all. For America the picture doesn't mean a thing.

Raquel Meller sold the world's rights to the picture immediately after the first showing abroad. Senorita Meller is to be congratulated on getting her money out of it. If it had been brought to this country under ordinary circumstances it would have been battered about from pillar to post, and the chances are that no one would have ever seen or heard of it.

Lighting and direction are both faulty, and the story, as edited and titled for America by Anita Loos and her husband, John Emerson, is extremely uneven, as was also the projection on the occasion of the special showing. *Fred.*

ROULETTE

S. E. V. Taylor production released by Selznick. All-star cast. Story by William McHarg, adapted by Lewis Allen Brown. Directed by S. E. V. Taylor. Shown at Loew's New York, N. Y., Feb. 25, 1924. Running time, 67 minutes.

Dan Carrington..............Montague Love
John Tralee....................Norman Trevor
Ben Corcoran................Maurice Costello
Lois Carrington.................Edith Roberts
Mrs. Harris.............................Mary Carr
Mrs. C. Marineaux...........Effie Shannon
Peter Marineaux..............Walter Booth
Mrs. Smith-Jones...............Flora Finch
Rita...................Dagmar Gowdowsky
Jimmy Moore........................Henry Hull

The list of names in the cast is the most imposing thing about it. The picture is just an average second grade program picture. It is a society melodrama with a gaming house angle, with the author drawing a parallel between the chance one takes in gambling and the gamble that every woman takes in life when she picks a husband.

In sets the picture is rather a good flash, but the action is so slow that at times the picture becomes fairly tiresome.

Edith Roberts plays the lead, that's all. She plays it in front of the camera with about as much effort as she would expend on drinking a cup of coffee. In her earlier scenes she is far from looking or acting the part at all. The leading man, Walter Booth, is even worse than the girl, so the least said about him the better.

Norman Trevor plays the heavy and he does endow the character with a sense of understanding, while Maurice Costello also scores. The others in the cast are practically playing minor bits. *Fred.*

3 O'CLOCK IN THE MORNING

C. C. Burr presentation, starring Constance Binney. Directed by Kenneth Webb, with Jack Brown and William McCoy the photographers. Cast, Richard Thorpe, William Bailey, Edmund Breese, Mary Carr and Edna Olive. Splitting double feature program at Loew's New York, Feb. 26. Running time, 76 mins.

Far too long, this one might have proved up in much better shape had discriminate cutting attended. Not sufficiently strong to stand by itself, the footage is overboard to make it fit a double feature program, and by itself would be tedious. Neither Constance Binney nor her support can lift the picture above that fault.

Miss Binney has made better pictures, and while her modern, headstrong girl it sufficiently strong, it nevertheless is strung out to such lengths as to make it a matter of indifference to an audience just what the conclusion will be. Richard Thorpe, opposite the star, about equals any other individual performance of the cast, giving evidence that he could have handled more than he was given.

An instance of the padding lies in the opening, where a Saturday night party of the girl's "crowd" is strung out for over 20 minutes before the story starts moving. The entire action is filled with unnecessary incidentals.

In telling of the high-living miss, who leaves home because of disapproving parents, the terrapin covered mostly centers upon the conventual celluloid cabaret where she is a dancing feature and the "heavy" secretly is donating the weekly salary.

It gives Miss Binney the opportunity to dance, which screens none too well, and keeps the scheming "money man" in evening clothes throughout the entire picture. The running down of a child by an automobile in which she is riding, her family having to sell the estate and the revelation of where the weekly check has been coming from throws the girl back into the arms of the family and sends her to the wharf to stop her former fiance from sailing.

A ludicrous finish has the boy spying the girl on the dock through binoculars and diving overboard to a swimming return.

The cafe scenes are just those and no more, with Miss Binney's best bet, in this particular release, her appearance.

The film is just about suited to the middle-class theatres, and it's an even split as to how much good either the Broadway musical in which the star is currently appearing or the picture will aid each other so long as the film lingers around New York. *Skig.*

NO MOTHER TO GUIDE HER

William Fox production, starring Genevieve Tobin. From the play by Lillian Mortimer, adapted by Michael O'Connor. Directed by Charles Horan. Shown at Loew's New York Feb. 21. Running time, 92 minutes.

Charles Pearson..........John Webb Dillion
His Wife.......................Lolita Robertson
Kathleen, their daughter.Katherine Downer
Kathleen, grown up.........Dolores Rousse
Jim Boyd......................Frank Wunderlee
His Wife..............................Maude Hill
Mary, his daughter...........Ruth Sullivan
Mary, grown up............Genevieve Tobin
The Grandfather..................J. D. Walsh
James Walling..............Jack Richardson
Donald, his son..................George Dewey
Donald, grown up...............Jack McLean
Walling's sister......................Lillian Lee
Widow Mills...............Marion Stevenson
Billy, her son....................William Quinn
Billy, grown up.................Irving Hartley

A bad boy.

It's miles too long and decidedly too much time was devoted to planting in the early section of the story. The title is about the best thing.

That should get some money at the box office in the cheaper neighborhoods. The picture is a slow moving and altogether tiresome affair. Genevieve Tobin, starred, shows nothing extraordinary before the camera that entitles her to stardom, and the balance of the cast is decidedly mediocre.

The tale is one of three families, all in the same town. The early life of the children is shown, and here is where the great waste of footage and time comes in. Two of the children are born in homes of wealth, the third is a child of a brutal father and without a mother. Of course, she grows into the wonderful self-sacrificing woman who has the principal role of the picture, and although she is under a cloud for a time, and the tongues of the scandal mongers of the town wag because of her, she comes in for a coat of whitewash in the end and manages to marry the town green grocer who loved her from the time that she was a little girl.

If there is anything else in sight with which to fill a date, the exhibitor might just as well pass this one up.

Fred.

DAMAGED HEARTS

Pilgrim Production, directed by T. Hays Hunter. All-star cast. Story by Basil King, adapted by Barbara Kent. Running time, 0̃5 minutes.

Mother	Mary Carr
David (boy)	Jerry Devine
The Girl	Helen Rowland
Sandy	Tyrone Power
Cecilia Stevens	Jean Armour
Hugh Winfield	Thomas Gillen
Innkeeper	Edmund Breese
His Wife	Effie Shannon
David (man)	Eugene Strong
Mrs. Langham	Florence Billings
Edwina Winfield	Sara Mullen
The Cripple	Charles Deforrest

A good melodrama of the program type. It is well directed and tells its story with lots of action. The scenes are in the Everglades of Florida, a picturesque background. The photography is good and there are any number of pretty shots.

In one scene of some underwater stuff the principals are placed in the three elements—water, land and air. The hero is under water in a diver's outfit, the heroine on the ground and the heavy in an airplane above. It is a good idea rather well worked out. The interest is sustained throughout.

For the medium-priced houses where there is a daily change of program the picture is above the average run of product that these houses have been getting.

The story is of a boy and girl, orphans. The boy is taken by a poor woman of the Everglades and the girl adopted by a wealthy one. The latter child dies through neglect. The boy grows to manhood, a rather rough character and outlaw.

Years have passed since the death of his mother and the separation from his sister, but he has sworn vengeance on those causing her death. When his opportunity comes and he makes off with the wife of the man who as a boy was partially responsible, instead of making good his oath he falls in love with the woman, and when the husband, playing the heavy, is killed, the road is left clear.

There are about a half-dozen names in the cast that can be played up.

Fred.

WATERFRONT WOLVES

Gerson Corp. presentation, starring Ora Carew. Written and directed by Tom Gibson. Cast includes Jay Morley, Hal Stephens and Dick La Reno. Showing on double-feature program at Loew's New theatre Feb. 26. Running time, 63 minutes.

A haphazardly put together picture possessing a story of little consequence, with the subtitles eliminating what small chance the tale ever had. Tuesday night the audience began kidding the film when it was half completed, from which time on the sarcasm came consistently. Placing Destiny and its mysterious weavings above the actual plot made much of the titling seem almost maudlin, with the dramatics already laid on heavy enough.

Starring Ora Carew above the title provided reason to give this girl an abundance of footage and a neat appearance, with the promise she might accomplish something if given a reasonable vehicle.

The tale leaves much that must be taken for granted in plausibility, telling of the theft of the Morgan pearls in China which are smuggled into this country.

The girl's father is the culprit, and her efforts to return the jewels consume a majority of the running time.

The invaluable assistance of an all-seeing and knowing Chinaman, whose life was once saved by the girl's mother, provides the "out" when the police close in, and a hectic few moments aboard a schooner, between the hero and father over the pearls, provide what action there is.

Also is an indifferent attempt at comedy.

The cast gives nothing to the release to lift it up, and it simply remains a program leader for the lesser houses without rating the double-feature designation.

Skig.

SODOM AND GOMORRAH

London, Feb. 19.

It was, we are told, to draw an analogy between modern Vienna and ancient Sodom that Michael Kertesz's film called "Sodom and Gomorrah" was produced in Austria. It is declared to be Catholic propaganda.

The trouble is, however, that though we are given a fair idea of the punishment of sin, the quality of sin is left a doubtful point. There is one moment where we are given to think that Sodom's chief offence is due to Lot's wife, who is inclined to get gay with her own husband.

This line of argument makes a strong appeal to married men. They watch Lot struggling to save his wife from the fire and brimstone in terrible suspense. In spite of the angel's disapproval and the fiery torments Lot succeeds in bringing her to safety. Then she looks back, and when she turns into a pillar of salt relief of the married men finds expression in a burst of applause.

The principal part is taken by Lucy Doraine, who plays both Lot's wife and a modern seductress.

The story is told according to Griffiths' principle in "Intolerance," modern and ancient scenes alternating. But this time the method is still further involved. Quite a large portion of the modern story is merely a dream of the seductress.

Unlike Lot's wife, she repents. Instead of being turned into a pillar of salt she becomes an extraordinary figure of remorse expressed in grimaces which cause the unkindly to titter.

The spectacular scenes are arranged on a lavish scale, and the temple scenes are impressive; but the handling of the crowds is more remarkable for discipline than verisimilitude.

THY NAME IS WOMAN

Fred Niblo production presented by Louis B. Mayer. From the play by Benjamin Glazer and Karl Schoenherr, adapted by Bess Meredyth. Ramon Novarro and Barbara La Marr featured. Shown at the Lyric, N. Y., for a run March 3, 1924. Running time, 102 minutes.

Pedro the Fox	William V. Mong
Guerita, his wife	Barbara La Marr
Juan Ricardo	Ramon Novarro
Capt. de Castelar	Wallace MacDonald
The Commandante	Robert Edeson
Juan's Mother	Claire MacDowell
Dolores	Edith Roberts

"Thy Name Is Woman," heralded as one of the big pictures, was presented by Louis B. Mayer at the Lyric Monday night. It did not prove to be a special in the sense of the word as applied to picture productions in these days. It is a program picture and it is doubtful if it will pay for itself during the Lyric run.

It is rather a mystifying thing, this Lyric run for the picture. The production, it is understood, has been sold to the exhibitors with the regular Metro program. In that case the legitimate house run is for the purpose of giving the exhibitors a little the best of it, for they will reap the benefit of the advertising the picture will get from a Broadway engagement.

The story is a tragedy and film fans do not particularly care for this type of tale. The happy ending is something that they must have in their film fare, and without it they aren't happy.

The scene is in the mountains of Spain and the tale concerns a head of a band of smugglers, his beautiful wife and one of the troops who is sent out to make love to the youthful wife in the hope that she may betray her elderly husband, who at the end of the picture stabs her to death when she would elope with the trooper. He in turn falls dead over her body, while the guard arrives to arrest the soldier for having proved a traitor through his love for the woman. The trooper is saved from punishment through the daughter of his commanding officer pleading for him.

There are portions of the second half where the sex stuff is permitted to run wild in the scenes between the trooper and the smuggler's wife. This may possibly prove the one box office asset, but that may not get by all censor boards.

Ramon Novarro plays the soldier lead, while Barbara La Marr is the wife. The two handle themselves fairly well, but the honors for acting go to William V. Mong. His elderly but still crafty Spaniard is a work of art.

The piece is a short-cast and in addition to the above trio has only Robert Edeson, Wallace MacDonald, Claire MacDowell and Edith Roberts. The latter has the ingenue lead.

It is not an expensive picture as far as sets are concerned, for there are but a few scenes shot other than in the hut of the smuggler. A street scene early in the picture was colorful and well handled and some of the exterior shots were decidedly pretty.

Fred.

ICEBOUND

William De Mille production. Presented by Adolph Zukor and Jesse L. Lasky. Richard Dix and Lois Wilson featured. From the Owen Davis play of the same title, adapted by Clara Beranger. Shown at the Rivoli, N. Y., week of March 2. Running time, 69 mins.

Jane Crosby	Lois Wilson
Ben Jordan	Richard Dix
Emma Jordan	Helen Dubois
Hannah	Edna May Oliver
Nettie Moore	Vera Reynolds
Sadie Fellows	Mary Foy
Orin Fellows	Joseph Depew
Ella Jordan	Ethel Wales
Mrs. Jordan	Alice Chapin
Henry Jordan	John Daly Murphy
Judge Bradford	Frank Shannon

"Icebound," the Owen Davis play that won the Pulitzer price, was more or less of a freak at the box office as a play. It just didn't quite hit right. The picture seemingly is going to repeat the history of the play. It is good entertainment, well played, but doesn't seem to have the box-office draft. Last Sunday at the Rivoli both performances, during the afternoon, found the attendance way below the usual quota that the house draws.

Davis' story has been transferred to the screen with an exact nicety that should make it appeal pretty generally, but there isn't anything in the story that is going to pull the young fans, although Richard Dix, on the strength of his work in "The Ten Commandments," is drawing a considerable following in New York, and Lois Wilson, as the heroine of "The Covered Wagon," is also in the public eye.

It may be that the cold chill the title suggests is to blame for keeping the public away, or it may be the "prize play" idea which leads the picture fans to immediately dub it "highbrow." Either way, they don't go to see it.

William De Mille has done the picture nicely in the matter of direction, and some of the lightings are particularly good. The cast, which is principally "types," is well selected, and both John Daly Murphy and Edna May Oliver scored heavily in character roles, especially Miss Oliver, who walked away with all the comedy there is in this rather dreary picture.

Fred.

WILD ORANGES

Goldwyn picture adapted and directed by King Vidor from the Joseph Hergesheimer novel. Photographed by John W. Boyle. Showing at the Capitol, New York, week of March 2. Running time, 66 mins.

John Woolfolk	Frank Mayo
Millie Stope	Virginia Valli
Poul Halverd	Ford Sterling
Litchfield Stope	Nigelde Bruillier
Nicholas	Charles A. Post

A corking demonstration in just what may be done with a small cast and a story of no unusual proportions. It's a suitable first-run for which most of the credit must go to the director, King Vidor, although he has been ably assisted by a well selected cast who have evidently followed instructions religiously and with no little skill.

The film looks to be one of those producer's delights in that it constituted a "nickel" production, but that's the least of it so far as the entertainment value is concerned. Localed along the Georgia coast, the action taking place within a barren inlet, the tale necessitates but a quartet of characters for sustenance, while six total the entire personnel screened.

Prudently cut, the presentation has been deleted of all immaterial footage to the point where this release might be a lesson in that particular department. It consumes but 66 minutes in the telling, wastes nothing, and has been aptly titled throughout. Nothing great about it, but just a well-handled bit of producing that will interest an audience and should impress for remembrance.

The story is that of a young bridegroom, John Woolfolk, who becomes a wanderer after his wife has been thrown and killed from a runaway carriage. Turning to the sea aboard a small sloop, with a male cook as his only companion, the couple some three years later enter an inlet in search of water, where they find a run-down house, of some proportions, in which live an elderly man, his granddaughter, and a gigantic half-wit wanted by the courts for murder.

The visit is an adventure to the girl, who suffers from an inherited mental twist of fear. Fighting against the attachment, Woolfolk suddenly sets sail, covering but a short distance when he puts about to return for the girl. A plan to take both she and the grandfather away is discovered by the maniac, which leads to a fight that is splendidly pictured, vitally realistic, and is about sufficient to put the picture across by itself. The elder parent is done away with through a blow from the maniac, who, in turn, succumbs to the attack of a dog which has broken its leash.

Charles A. Post, as the mentally deficient monster, comes very close to running away with the picture, while Ford Sterling, as usual, fulfilled his obligations. Virginia Valli convinces and Frank Mayo has turned in a more than creditable performance.

But the major share of credit must go to Vidor, who has done so well with a script which might so easily have been grossly exaggerated.

The photography meets all requirements to round out "Wild ranges" as a convincing argument against those who believe there is little or no merit connected with the art of celluloid story telling, and it certainly has been well made.
Skig.

DAUHTERS OF TODAY

Selznick Distributing Corp. offers this special, directed and produced by Rollin S. Sturgeon; running time, 72 mins.; cast, Patsy Ruth Miller, Ralph Graves, Edna Murphy, Edward Hearn, Philo McCullough, George Nichols, Gertrude Claire, Truman Vandyke, Dorothy Wood, Phillips Smalley, Zasu Pitts, H. J. Hobert, Fontaine La Rue, Marjorie Bonner.

A perfect example of venal picture-making with one eye on the box office and the other on the censor, with never a flicker of professional honor or artistic conscience. Strictly a combination of surefire sex hoke under camouflage of "teaching a lesson," ranging all the way from "The Little Girl Next Door" to "Flaming Youth."

The likelihood that any of it was lifted from the film version of the latter, the recent classic in such themes, is remote, since this one seems to have been on the shelf or marking time for many moons. Its feminine fashions are out of date and it still regards the "shimmy" as the last breath in naughty manifestations.

The book of "Flaming Youth," however, was for sale two years ago, and from it, undoubtedly, was filched the midnight bathing scene. The strip-poker bit was as certainly lifted from "The Demi Virgin." The rest of it was pieced together from "Way Down East," "The Bat," and other cinches. Wherever anything that had appeal appeared it was utilized, all into one melange of sex-mystery - sympathy - triangle chop suey.

The territory covers from the farmer father and mother playing at the bedside in the backwoods to the girl fleeing in overalls from the home of the lecherous young millionaire, who has "plied" her with moonshine and is mysteriously shot by an unseen hand while strugglind with the little wayward but still pure girl for her "honor.", She eventually marries her rube sweetheart after her mother has come to the garish New York apartment and found an absurdly overdone drunken revel of college-boys and college flappers in progress there.

At no time does the story carry conviction for a foot. The schoolgirls look like burleque chorus ponies, the college youth like race track touts, the rich co-ed's apartment like the love-nest of a Times square gold-digger, and the roadhouse where the gang puts up over 'night like "Papa Joe's" opium den in "Out of the Seven Seas." Every effect is smeared on. A group of church-goers returning from prayer meeting in a suburb, who surprise the moonlight bathers, look like a mob scene from a Keystone. Zasu Pitts, as an old maid comic, looks and acts like Harold Lloyd, even to bunk falls.

The "solution" of the crime, after the detectives work and details have

---

run for hundreds of supposed stirring, and surely extensive details, comes a phone conversation with no reason ever offered why the young millionaire's maid should have shot him just when she did, or at any other time; perhaps a censor cut out that portion; other connecting links are missing and the same reason may be at the bottom of the generally disjointed progress and so many angles left to conjecture.

It is quite likely that "Daughters of Today" will be a money-grabber for those who have no pride in their business and no respect for the opinion of sane people. Nobody will be fooled much by the "moral" of it; that gag is about exploded, anyway.

The production is nothing to rave about. It is a misfit for this film at best, and the whole thing gives one the impression of having been written and shot in a hurry to use some standing sets before striking to make room for a real picture. The photography is ordinary. The direction is uninspired, and the acting without a single high spot, even from Patsy Ruth Miller, who seems to take second place in the story to Edna Murphy, daughter of the sanctimonious farmer couple.

The best that can be said of "Daughters of Today" is that it may appeal to waitresses, teamsters, and others who still believe a "flapper" is a sort of precocious demi-monde, and a college boy is a flask-toting demon of depravity in embryo, and that the future is going to the bow-wows in the hands of a youth that is untrammeled, immoral, and wanton because of one of two reasons: that parents are too strict, or that they aren't strict enough. In "Daughters of Today" you can take your choice; it gives both reasons.
Lait.

GRIT

A Film Guild production starring Glenn Hunter, released by Hodkinson. Story by F. Scott Fitzgerald, script by Ashmore Creelman, directed by Frank Tuttle. Shown at Loew's New York, N. Y., double feature bill, Feb. 29. Running time, 62 mins.
"Kid" Hart....................Glenn Hunter
Annie Hart............Kelenka Adamowska
"Houdini" Hart.............Roland Young
Mr. Smith.................Osgood Perkins
Flashy Joe............Townsend Martin
Orchid McGonigle.............Clara Bow
Pop Finkel...............Dore Davidson
Bennie Finkel.............Martin Broder
Tony O'Cohen.,...........Joseph Depew

This is an east side gangster melodrama, full of types and crook stuff. Only fairly well produced, not particularly well directed or edited, with the street sets looking just what they are, studio stuff. However, Glenn Hunter and little Clara Bow make the picture stand up. For the neighborhood type of houses and in the bigger ones where they are in the habit of playing double feature bills it will get by nicely.

Its running time is just a little more than an hour and into this a gangster shooting, a couple of burglaries, a Chinese den with trapdoors and all the usual den hoke, including a corking fight, are jammed. There is action and lots of it.

The scene of the story is laid in Hester street, and in the parts of the country where they don't know New York the fact that one can see the tugs on the East River will be all right, but watch 'em on the lower east side. They'll tell you 'tain't so.

Roland Young has a little bit in the picture, that of "Houdini" Hart, a wire and pick guy on locks, who is trying to turn as square as he possibly can by opening a gin mill, because his wife is about to have a baby. The gang won't stand for it and they bump him off the night that he opens his saloon, which is likewise the night that the "Kid" is born, his mother dying from the shock of the father's death in a shooting scrape. The youngster is

---

painted as a child of fear and at the age of 15 is shown as such, an abject slave in the gang, the head of which is the man who shot his father to death. But there is a girl in the gang, a gamin of the street, who is finally sent to the reformatory for two years. On her release she determines to go straight, a young lady by this time, but the boy warns her that the fate of those who would break from the gang is that which was meted out to his dad. She, in love with the boy, determines to bring out his heritage of manhood and finally succeeds in doing so by taunting him to a degree that he voluntarily submits to a beating at the hands of a bully to discover that it "doesn't hurt to be hurt." That steels him for his final task, the killing of the gangster leader, the beating off of his mob and his final winning of the girl.

There are sidelights that tend to humor, but the Film Guild wants to watch carefully in its future productions that it doesn't overstep the mark of religious ridicule and bear in mind that all creeds attend picture shows, and in certain districts the patronage of a house may be decidedly all of one particular creed. That house may not play their picture and a rental lost is a thing gone forever, like an unsold theatre ticket. Too much "Algonquin round table cleverness" might be their undoing, which would be a pity.

As to the cast, Glenn Hunter gives an interpretation of the "fright child' 'tha' is a work of art, but it is Clara Bow that lingers in the eye after the picture has gone. The others, except for a little overacting, are passable.

Direction at times overdone, lighting bad, and sets—well, just sets.
Fred.

BAG AND BAGGAGE

Produced, directed and co-authored by Finis Fox. Scenario by Lois Zellner. Photography by Hal Mohr. Distributed by Selznick. At the Stanley, Feb. 27. Running time, 75 mins.
Paul Anthony..................Paul Weigal
Hope...........................Gloria Grey
Mrs. Cooper...............Adele Farrington
Lolo....................Carmelita Geraghty
Hal Tracy.....................John Roche
Jathrow Billings...........Arthur S. Hull
House detective...........Harry Dunkinson
Police inspector..............Fred Kelsey

Finis Fox has accounted for some very passable scenarios for the films heretofore, but in trying to do everything for this picture he has made something of a mess of it. Here, his story is not only ridiculous but is imbecilic enough to make one chafe to deliver a solid wallop to the dimpled jaw of the precocious little heroine.

This heroine is the sweetest and most stupid girl that ever bored an audience. We see her just 17, the daughter of a sentimental old music teacher. Her name is Hope, which might be taken ironically. She has a dog named Harmony and a "city feller," tall, handsome and rich, named Hal Tracy. Hope has only met him twice, but she's dead in love already. So when the "richest bachelor in New York" goes back to the city, for some reason or other, she decides to trail and land him.

With $50 in her pocket and wearing her mother's hoopskirt, she goes to the best hotel in town, takes in all the sights, including a so-called "orgy of pleasure" at the "Grotto Gardens" that might easily be delightful burlesque if meant that way, and then learns her suite is 50 bucks a day. She decides to beat her bill. In running away she is accused of stealing about $1,000,000 worth of gems. That brings the police court and more nonsense into the story. Gloria Grey is hopelessly incompetent to secure anything from her

---

role, ridiculous though it be. Carmelita Geraghty is considerably better as a ritzy relative and the rest of the cast is fair, with Arthur Hull taking the honors. The direction and photography are mediocre and the continuity poor, although all are doubtless handicapped by the exceedingly puerile plot.

If this one makes any money, anything should get by.

HAPPINESS

Metro picture starring Laurette Taylor. From the play by J. Hartley Manners, who prepared the screen version. Directed by King Vidor. Shown at the Rialto, New York, week March 9. Running time 76 minutes.

Jenny Wreary	Laurette Taylor
Fermoy MacDonough	Pat O'Malley
Mrs. Chrystal Pole	Hedda Hopper
Philip Chandos	Cyril Chadwick
Mrs. Wreary	Edith Yorke
Sallie Perkins	Patterson Dial
Jenny, a waif	Joan Standing
Mr. Rosselstein	Laurence Grant
Head Saleslady	Charlotta Minneau

Laurette Taylor has returned to the screen in a Metro production of "Happiness," a play in which she originally appeared on the spoken stage. Seemingly Miss Taylor is not going to permit anyone but herself to be seen in the screen versions of any of the play she has been in on the stage.

There are half a dozen actresses of the screen who would have been far more desirable in the role of Jenny Wreary than Miss Taylor. Miss Taylor seems a little too mature to take an errand girl on the screen. In trying to get over the impression she is a youngster, it forced kittenish stuff that didn't register.

The picture was partially shot in New York and on the coast. Any time a director thinks he can get away with those studio street scenes and match 'em with the real thing he is mistaken. In this picture the couple of studio streets used stand out like a sore thumb.

"Happiness" was a comedy drama with a message. As a picture it is neither comedy nor drama, and all the forced bits trying for comedy fall flat. Possibly that is the fault of Mr. Manners' adaptation of his play, for he may have held too closely to his stage version.

One good bit of matching in the film—a camera was placed in a machance in New York and driven down Sixth avenue, then the inside of the machine was shot at the studio with Miss Taylor, Hedda Hopper and Edith Yorke in the seat. The chauffeur who drove was a darb and must have graduated from a taxi.

Pat O'Malley plays the lead opposite Miss Taylor and endows it with an infinite touch making it stand out. Hedda Hopper as the society widow was also likable, while Cyril Chadwick was just himself.

There is a lot of fashion stuff and models parading gowns. This passed out of feature making years ago.

King Vidor in directing overlooked many little touches of detail; one particularly was the death scene of the mother. She was still breathing after supposed to have passed out.

Just a program picture is about all that can be said for it. *Fred.*

A SOCIETY SCANDAL

Adolph Zukor and Jesse Lasky present Gloria Swanson in an Allan Dwan production distributed by Famous Players-Lasky. Society comedy-drama based on play by Alfred Sutro called "The Laughing Lady," in which Ethel Barrymore starred at Longacre last season. Play ran for about three months with average success. Forrest Halsey did screen version. At Rivoli week March 9. Running time 80 minutes.

Marjorie Colbert	Gloria Swanson
Daniel Farr	Rod La Rocque
Harrison Peters	Ricardo Cortez
Hector Colbert	Allan Simpson
Mrs. Maturin Colbert	Mrs. Ida Waterman
Mrs. Hamilton Peanfield	
	Mrs. Thelma Converse
Mr. Schuyler Burr	Fraser Coalter
Mrs. Burr	Catherine Proctor
Mr. Hamilton Peanfield	Wilfred Donovan
Patricia De Voe	Yvonne Hughes
Friends of Marjorie: Catherine Coleburn, Marie Shelton, Dorothy Stokes, Cornelius Keefe

"A Society Scandal" should catch a lot of patronage from the rank and file picture fans. The title and subject matter will insure that, for the story is about the doings of society folk.

The picture on its merits classes as pretty good. There are portions that reach heights of excellence, and there's a lot decidedly ordinary. A little bit better than the average program feature about sizes it up.

The society atmosphere is consistently preserved. When the upper crusters are shown in action they look the part instead of appearing superficial and actory.

In settings the backgrounds harmonize properly with the high hat atmosphere.

There's comedy relief sprinkled through the exposition of the plot that arises naturally from the story itself. That helps to make the depiction of it interesting and entertaining, and the fact of the laughs not being dragged in by the heels keeps the action going at a swift tempo.

The titles are on the whole old-fashioned in construction. One, for instance, in cold blood and not in any manner facetiously reads: "In the great open spaces where men are men." This is descriptive of a camp location one of the characters has in the mountains.

In detail the director did very well with one exception, but he flopped badly on that one. This was the incidental business of a newspaper reporter.

Working for one of the big dailies, the reporter rushes in to the city room just before press time with a front page story. The general public will never know the difference, but that reporter certainly wasted a lot of time by not grabbing a phone in the usual way of "leg-men" on daily newspapers and phoning in his stuff to a re-write man.

An interfering mother-in-law, silly young wife, sap husband, a lawyer who secures a divorce for the sap husband and later falls in love with the sap husband's wife, and a boy friend of the wife are the principals around whom the tale revolves.

Gloria Swanson is the wife. She plays intelligently and with a likable repression. Husband is done competently by Allan Simpson, and Rod La Rocque plays the lawyer with a society polish that won't rub off. The wife's boy friend is capably done by Ricardo Cortez. Wilfred Donovan, aside from the business of the reporter's part, a directorial fault, makes the bit convincing as to characterization.

The title itself, "A Society Scandal," notwithstanding there isn't much that's more than very mildly scandalous in the story, should go a long way toward coaxing the customers up to the box office. *Bell.*

FLOWING GOLD

Melodrama presented by Richard Walton Tully, directed by Joseph De-Grasse, from the novel by Rex Beach. Distributed by First National. At Strand, New York, week of March 9. Running time 75 minutes.

Allegheny Briskow	Anna Q. Nilsson
Calvin Gray	Milton Sills
Barbara Parker	Alice Calhoun
Henry Nelson	Craufurd Kent
Buddy Briskow	John Roche
The Suicide Blonde	Cissie Fitzgerald
Ma Briskow	Josephine Crowell
Pa Briskow	Bert Woodruff
Tom Parker	Charles Sellon

Red-blooded feature which covers a whole lot of territory but has caught the atmosphere of a boom oil community; is full of local color, and while the story is stretched a bit to include several sensational melodramatic punches it is fairly credulous, due to the excellent direction, splendid cast, convincing work of Milton Sills and the speed with which the action moves along.

The story concerns the sudden enrichment of the Briskows by the bringing in of an oil well on the old farm. Calvin Gray (Mr. Sills), penniless adventurer, living on his wits, arrives in Dallas. He bluffs his way to wealth and the favor of the Briskows. He is a sort of social mentor and advisor to the nouve rich family, saving the son from marriage to a designing courtesan, The Suicide Blonde (Cissie Fitzgerald).

The daughter of the Briskows (Anna Q. Nilsson) is secretly in love with Gray but believes he loves Barbara Parker (Alice Calhoun), the sheriff's daughter. Henry Nelson (Craufurd Kent) is the heavy. He was Gray's superior officer in the United States Army, the latter being court-martialed out of the A. E. F. due to perjured testimony of Nelson.

Gray with the assistance of Briskow gains control of Nelson's bank and forces Nelson to sign a confession exonerating Gray from the army scandal.

Gray had previously defeated Nelson's attempt to brand him as a thief by accepting a mission from a local jeweler to sell the Briskow jewelry. He outwits a couple of crooks who hold him up by squirting tear gas in the hi-jacker's eyes.

A burning oil well and a cloudburst are a few of the mellow thrills provided, coming along near the end of the picture and leaving the hero and heroine atop a floating cottage. She rescues him by diving into the stream which is aflame with blazing oil.

The story is frankly hokum melodrama, but so well done it will interest the most hardened and blase picture fan. It is in treatment that the picture gets away from the obvious. It moves with a speed that defies vivisection of the story and is an interesting panorama, coated with the glamour of oil and sudden riches, a universally appealing topic to the present generation who arrived too late for active participation in the gold rush.

It's interesting for any program. *Con.*

MRS. DANE'S CONFESSION

Independent English film, with no information given as to direction, cast or distribution. Featuring Count Salm. At the Tivoli, March 5, as half the bill. Runs about 50 minutes.

"Mrs. Dane's Confession" was evidently made three or four years ago. Probably it would never have seen the light, had it not been for the marital adventures of Count Salm, who appears in it. As it stands, the screen owes very little to the husband of Millicent Rogers, as this English production must be numbered among the several far down in the negative class.

No announcements as to direction or cast are made, but anyone having read the papers about a month ago cannot fail to recognize the amorous count as the heavy. Strangely enough, this suave if somewhat greasy nobleman is not a poor enough actor to earn a genuine roasting.

Cast as the most despicable of movie villains, he does manage to shove a bit of ability into the work here and there.

The film is poor in comparison to the count's work, which means it's pretty bad.

The story is the old one about the woman who marries the wrong man, learns he's a brute, divorces him, marries the right, and then is hounded by number one until she shoots him. But she didn't shoot him in the first reel.

THE WANTERS

Louis B. Mayer presentation and a J. M. Stahl production, also directed by the latter. Releasing through First National. From the story by Leila Wells, with E. G. Palmer the photographer. Showing at Loew's New York theatre, March 5. Running time, 76 mins.

Marie Prevost heads an extensive cast, who, for the most part, are given minor bits to while away the time within this tale of a servant maid's desire for the advantages of her mistress. It is an average feature.

Miss Prevost, as the maid, does nicely and, at least, has eliminated the habit of talking from a corner of her mouth, if nothing else. The names, flashed en masse at the beginning, make it impossible to grasp who the individuals are, but the boy opposite Miss Prevost is deserving of mention for a reserved and dignified performance in tune with the cause.

The production, interior setting, and so forth, should prove of enough quality to make the picture a suitable program leader within the intermediate houses, despite the patrons will find they've gone up against the same type of story many times previously. Stahl has carried the theme along evenly, though certain deletion might help, as it threatens to hit an upgrade more than once.

The marriage of the maid to the son of the house, ultra wealthy and among the social elite, lays out the usual plan of continuity under those conditions with such a snatch of the inside love intrigues of the "400" inserted for what might be termed "sex stuff." The usual embarrassing situations are in the prescribed manner, ultimately pathfinding the way to the proverbial reunion at the finish.

A few comedy inserts early in the picture reveal Miss Prevost at her best, although her performance on the whole is adequate to the occasion. *Skig.*

THE LONE WAGON

Sanford production, written and directed by Frank S. Mattison. Photography by Elmer C. Dyer. Featuring Matty Mattison. Cast includes Vivian Rich, Lafayette McKee, Earl Metcalf, Gene Crosby. At Loew's, New York, March 4. Runs 65 mins.

Nearly a year ago "The Covered Wagon" opened at the Criterion and proved to be a screen epic of pioneer days. Since then there have been several imitations, good and bad. Now comes "The Lone Wagon," but no one need worry, as this new picture should make little or no impression on the screen world.

Not since the days of the second-rate serials has such stuff been flashed in a Broadway picture theatre. A synopsis of the plot would be next to impossible, as it is a most disconnected mess of nonsense.

The "Lone Wagon" seems to be one of a train bound for the west just after the Civil War. The story concerns itself chiefly with an attack by Indians and the supposedly intrepid and heroic defense by the pioneers. Love interest is dragged in, but it never seems to interfere to any great extent with the redskins and their ways. The hero is a Mexican who wins the girl in the end, despite her family's objections to him as a "foreigner." The reason he finally gets her is because all her folks have been slaughtered and there's no one left to squawk.

Matty Mattison is the featured name, and he might be worse. Vivian Rich is the girl and the rest are unfamiliar names except for Earl Metcalf, passe heavy, seen in a minor role.

The photography is good in spots, but there is too much shrubbery and not enough of the open spaces and prairies that lend color to outof-door shots. The fight scenes are amateurish.

NORTH OF HUDSON BAY

A Fox production starring Tom Mix. Directed by John Ford. Photography by Dan Clark. At the Circle March 6. Runs 55 minutes.

Widow Dane....................Jennie Lee
Michael Dane....................Tom Mix
McDonald ....Frank Campeau
Clough ....Frank Leigh
Loupe ....Frank Kohler
Peter Dane...................Eugene Palette
Jean ....Kathleene Kay
Guise ....Al Fremont

Tom Mix seems to have taken William Farnum's place as the leader of the neighborhood school of male stars. All his pitures are formula made, but it is a formula that has been soundly tested.

In "North of Hudson Bay" there is one departure. The locale is the Far North instead of the Western prairies usually serving as a background for Mix's reckless heroism. It is a change that the disciples of Mix will welcome, particularly as all the accustomed virility and "devil-may-care" characteristics are enhanced by the romantic backgrounds of snow and ice.

An alleged law of the North that may be new to picture patrons serves as the basis for the story. It tells how any one convicted of a murder is sent on the "death trail." This means he is forced to walk through the frozen wilderness guarded by a group of followers until death by cold, famine or wolves overtakes him. The watchers may eat and warm themselves as often as they like, but the victim must never halt for food or shelter. Furthermore, any one caught feeding him is given the same penalty.

It is because of aiding the man supposed to have killed his brother that Mix is sentenced to the horrible punishment. How he escapes leads to the thrills that come with a magnificent rush at the end of the film. First there is a startling bare-handed battle with a pack of wolves. Hand-to-hand encounters with the villains on the snow-covered ground follow this, and finally the escape from madly whirling canoes being dashed down frenzied rapids and whirlpools. These last shots, taken mostly from above for a blood-curdling effect, are as exciting in their way as anything heretofore screened.

It is these thrills that will sell the picture. The bits of humor are not up to the Mix standard, although one or two little incidents are good for chuckles. John Ford has directed efficiently, and Dan Clark made good use of his splendid opportunities for photographic splendor.

A new leading woman, Kathleene Kay, is pretty, and makes an insipid part stand out. Frank Campeau is his usual insidious villain, and Jennie Lee adds a fine bit as the hero's mother.

DISCONTENTED HUSBANDS

A Columbia Production distributed by C. B. C. Film Sales Co. Story by Evelyn Campbell. Directed by Edward J. LeSaint. Featuring James Kirkwood. At the New York, March 4. Running time, 70 mins.

Michael Fraser ....James Kirkwood
Marguerite Fraser ....Cleo Madison
Catherine Fraser ......Carmelita Geraghty
Dick Everton....................Arthur Rankin
Jack Ballard ....Vernon Steele
Emily Ballard ....Grace Darmond
Betty Ballard...............Muriel McCormac

"Discontented Husbands" is a conspicuous example of the fact that not infrequently in pictures "the cast's the thing." In it a familiar lineup of regulars, led by the dependable James Kirkwood, lift a trite story and not overly pretentious production above mediocrity. Because of it's "name" draw it should do business in the average house and the patrons will probably be sufficiently impressed by the work of the players to counteract the effects of an insipid plot.

All the credit does not go to the cast however as Edward J LeSaint has directed with skill and discretion. Photography and continuity also measure up as acceptable. The film could not have entailed much expense. The entire action, with the execption of some speeding auto shots and a scene at a hunting lodge, takes place at the homes of the two families around whom the marriage tangle centers.

The triangle here has been doubled and we have the "eternal sextette." Michael Fraser and Emily Ballard, married but not to each other, have fallen in love, he, because he feels his wife has refused to grow rich with him from the days of their poverty, and she, because she is dissatisfied with her husband's vain efforts to become wealthy.

But Ballard conceives the idea of checking the guilty love by planning a sham elopement with Fraser's adolescent daughter. When it strikes home naturally Fraser sees things in a different light and he is only too willing to give Emily back to her husband, return himself to his old-fashioned wife and hand his young daughter over to the faithful and worried stripling, who adores her.

Kirkwood literally "makes" the role of the erring, nouveau-riche husband whose wife insists on calling him "Mike." Cleo Madison is capable as his wife, and Grace Darmond makes the "other woman" a creature of charm and allure. Carmelita Geraghty, steadily coming to the fore, is sweet as the daughter and the others add praiseworthy bits.

The film proves that a good cast is often more than half the battle.

CRICKET ON HEARTH

Paul Gerson Production, directed by Lorimer Johnston. Adapated by Caroline Cooke from the novel by Charles Dickens. At the Tivoli (one day), March 8. Runs about 65 minutes.

John Peerybingle...............Paul Gerson
Dot Marley..........Virginia Browne Faire
Caleb Plummer...............Josef Swickard
Bertha Plummer...........Fritzie Ridgeway
Edward Plummer......................Paul Moore
Josiah Tackleton..........Lorimer Johnston
May Fielding...............Margaret Landis
Tilly Slowboy...................Joan Standing

Pleasantly mild, about sums up "The Cricket on the Hearth," the screen adaptation of the Dickens novel. A simple, old-fashioned story is told with none of the tricks of of "modern screen advancement" that would in this case prove detrimental. Probably the pace is too leisurely to suit everyone, but for the main the film has accomplished its mission.

Its chief merit lies in its faithful absorption of much of the quiet charm characterizing Dickens. Only in one respect does it fall down in this. It's characteristic humor is not played up. Tilly Slowboy, the maid-of-all-work, is the only character illustrating the droll types of Dickens to be introduced, and she is not so crafty as she might be.

Both Paul Gerson, the producer, and Lorimer Johnston, director, appear in important roles. Johnston is particularly effective as a snuff-sniffing heavy with a petrified heart. The role of the old toymaker, played in the stage version by Joseph Jefferson, is handled sincerely if not brilliantly by Josef Swickard. Three pretty women—Virginia Browne Faire, Fritzie Ridgeway and Margaret Landis—provide an unusual assortment of feminine pulchritude for one picture.

Miss Ridgeway (currently in vaudeville at the Palace, New York) plays the blind girl around whom the story centers. Fortunately, she is not guilty of super-sentimentalizing the role, as so often has happened with others of the rather weepy Dickens characters.

The settings are restful and expressive of mid-Victorian England, with all its quiet beauty. All in all, the picture should prove gratifying to the majority of Dickens' disciples, but film fans seeking thrills may keep away.

LOVE'S WHIRLPOOL

Regal Pictures, Inc., presentation releasing through Hodkinson. Features Lila Lee, James Kirkwood and Madge Bellamy. Story by Martha Lord and directed by Bruce Mitchell. Showing at the Cameo, New York, week of March 9. Running time, 67 minutes.

Marking the first of a series of Hodkinson pictures which are to be shown at this house under an eight weeks' rental by the releasing organization, the getaway film projected Sunday to more or less satisfaction.

It's a crook story, delving into spiritualism before it concludes to the point where it may antagonize believers and amounts to something of an expose on the inside and technical workings of fake mediums. Either way, the revealing of the manner in which the illusions, voice transmission and advance information are "staged" about marks the most interesting passage of the picture.

Otherwise it is a crook story concerning a gang leader determined to retaliate against a bank president who has sent the kid brother away for 15 years. A fire at sea, the rescue of the financier's daughter and the spiritual idea succeed each other as a means of vengeance abruptly halted by the underworld sweetheart taking a turn to the right, giving back the daughter because she loves he who would have his pound of flesh and would save him from himself.

Along the way there comes the planned escape of the youngster from prison, shot during the attempt, and the sinking of the ship with the latter, the thrill insert, moderately presented. Why directors insist on making fugitives silhouette themselves against a skyline might constitute a particular point the boys with the megaphones should look into for a change. It's been going on for years and years.

Bruce Mitchell, directing, has modeled an even sequence which could assimilate a certain amount of deletion for better effect. Otherwise it's a smooth presentation. The narrative about constitutes as weak an ingredient as the film possesses, although the principal players may offset that angle with their 'fan" following. Each performs to balance the script, with Kirkwood portraying the crook, Miss Lee the gang member who reforms, and Miss Bellamy as the daughter suffering from loss of memory as a result of the marine disaster. Robert Agnew drifts in and out, cast as the kid brother.

Others include Edward Maitland, Margaret Livingston, Clarence Geldert and Joe Mills.

The appropriateness of the title is open to question, as it seems as if a more definite designation could have been selected—probably to advantage. However, the combined efforts of the trio of featured players, the production and the story should meet the involved requirements in the houses for which the picture is evidently aimed. *Skig.*

I WILL REPAY

London, March 1.

The most recent Ideal picture can scarcely be called an all-British feature. It has an American producer, Henry Kolker, an English leading man long since made into an American star, Holmes Herbert, Pedro de Corboda, an American, playing the second male part, a few French actresses and an assortment of other players. Though the chief supporting parts are played by British artists.

Baroness Orczy's story is eminently fitted for the screen. It has romance, passion, and above all, swift movement. From the producer's angle it offers unlimited opportunities for spectacle and beautiful settings, while the players have parts which, if a little highly colored, are exceptional roles for the display of their art. Everybody connected with this production has seized upon all the available opportunity and the result is a feature pregnant with excitement and suspense. The six reels form capital entertainment.

The story opens with the killing in a duel of the Viconte de Marney by Deroulede, the lawyer. The latter had spoken slightingly of a woman's name and the result was the death of the man who upheld her honor. Desperate in his grief the old Duc de Marney compels his daughter, Juliette, to swear to avenge her brother's death.

Years pass, bringing the characters to the dark days of the revolution, with Deroulede as the idol of the people. One day Juliette is attacked by the crowd but rescued and taken to safety by Deroulede himself. Presently she learns with horror who her protector is but time has dimmed the power of her oath and hatred turns to love. Into the terror comes Sir Percy Blakeney, "the Scarlet Pimpernel," whose mission it is to rescue aristocrats doomed to the guillotine. There is a price on his head. Deroulede is his friend and so Sir Percy seeks his aid in rescuing Marie Antoinette. Deroulede consents but their conversation is overheard by Juliette. Immediately a struggle between what she considers her duty and her love begins and the former wins.

An anonymous note puts Deroulede in the power of his enemies. The soldiery arrive to arrest him and Juliette immediately realizes that her love is strongest. She manages to destroy incriminating documents but the authorship of the note is detected. In the end she is arrested herself. At her trial Deroulede takes his stand by the woman he loves and openly declares his guilt although Juliette adheres to her story—that the burned papers were love letters. The judge's decision hangs in the balance but the mob suddenly finds an unexpected leader and the lovers are both condemned to death. An escort arrives to take them to prison. Its leader is the Pimpernel and while the crowd fights among themselves he leads the lovers to freedom.

Scenically the production is very good. The interiors, made at the Boreham Wood studios, are as good as any we have seen from a British studio and the exteriors, made in France, are most picturesque. Throughout the production a great deal of attention has been paid to detail and the crowds have been exceptionally well managed. In the leading role of the "Scarlet Pimpernel" Holmes Herbert is excellent. He has acquired the Fred Terry atmosphere which, coupled with histrionic ability and some athletic power, enables him to put over a memorable performance. Another good portrayal comes from Pedro de Corboda as Deroulede. Flora le Breton is good as Juliette de Marney, although the part calls for a daintiness and sympathy rather than for any strong dramatic power. The rest of a long cast is admirably carried on the shoulders of the recruited "allies."

It is a pity this picture was not available for the British Film Week which has just passed in anything but a blaze of glory. *Gore.*

THE MAN WITHOUT DESIRE

London, Feb. 20.

Handled by the Swedish-Biograph and Seastrom this, the first of the Atlas-Biocraft pictures and the first British feature to be shown at the Tivoli, should have been a work of genius. As it is, it is one of the most interesting pictures ever made in this country. Adrien Brunel, the producer, had a difficult subject. A morbid story, devoid of light and shade, a story sometimes so slow in its movement that it becomes almost soporific, but saved by its sincerity and the enthusiasm of all concerned. Few more morbid stories have ever been told on the screen, and what might in other hands have become a weird melodrama appears as a complex creation of love and passion which would have delighted the heart of Oscar Wilde.

Vittoria, a noble of old Venice, is enamoured of Leonora, the wife of another noble, who neglects her and spends his time with notorious courtesans. Eventually Leonora yields to Vittoria's entreaties, is discovered and compelled to drink poisoned wine. Mad with grief Vittorio rushes to an English doctor, one Mawdesley, a believer in suspended animation, and allows himself to be hypnotized and placed in a tomb. Centuries elapse, and a distinguished scientist called Mawdesley gets a letter from a banker asking him to call. He does so and discovers that a large sum of money was placed in the bank hundreds of years ago together with a letter. The interest had to grow until a certain date, and then a letter had to be opened in the presence of witnesses. The letter contained the story of Vittorio's wooing of Leonora. The party proceeded to Venice and found the long-forgotten tomb. Vittorio lived, and in the temporary absence of Mawdesley and his assistants went to Leonora's old palace, creating a good deal of excitement on the way. There he met the counterpart of the long dead Leonora; in fact, his love's descendant. History repeated itself, but Vittorio had no passion. At last, after a row with Leonora who demanded passion above all things, he took poison. At his last breath the old passion for the old Leonora asserted itself, but in the middle of their first clinging kiss Vittorio dies.

The production work in many places is beautiful, especially in the real and reconstructed scenes of old Venice. Detail has not worried Brunel too much in many places, but he has been very careful in the scene where the body of Vittorio is disentombed.

Ivor Novello is not too satisfactory as Vittorio. He is overty "pretty" and his gestures at times remind one of a highly hysterical girl, but there is no doubt that he will be the picture's great attraction. Nina Vanna shows great promise as Leonora and also a remarkable immaturity. In time she will probably become quite a good actress, but at the moment she has a mistaken idea that a heaving bosom means genuine emotion. The rest of the cast, an exceedingly small one, do well. The "presentation" of Nina Vanna before the picture to tell how good England had been to her and to explain that she was not quite a "star" was a bit of crude showmanship which received little encouragement. The picture was well received by a poor house.

Gore.

THE TURNING POINT

London, Feb. 20.

Carrying the Censor's "A" certificate, which means it has only been passed for adult exhibition, this last Italian picture to be shown here is exceptionally strong even for a producing firm which has the reputation of calling a spade a spade. Many of the incidents are so Continental only the intense sincerity of the acting makes them plausible. The story is one of fever heat emotion, but the playing itself is never overdone.

Ten years before the story opened Monica Felt nursed the man she married back to health. Marriage swiftly brought disillusion. The lover was lost in the ambitious soldier whose thoughts were forever of his country and its army. Beautiful and neglected, she attracted other men, among them Beaurcourt, a rising politician. Bourcourt made no secret of his passion, but she remained indifferent. Meanwhile Felt, who still loved her but hid it under a veil of regimental discipline, had fallen into the hands of money-lenders in order to surround her with beautiful things. One night in a wave of passion he tried to enter her room, but was ordered out. Maddened, he used his brutal strength, bringing on an open rupture.

Things got worse, until one day a chance acquaintance, "a mystery man" named Glogau, offered to buy up all his I O U's, thereby becoming his only creditor. Felt gladly consented. Later with his wife he went on a visit to an old castle. Beaurcourt followed, so did Glogau. Violent scenes between husband and wife led to her making an appointment with Beaurcourt an hour after midnight in the room. Felt also had an appointment with Glogau. The wife waited for her lover, then suddenly Felt staggered in and begged to be allowed to remain. A furious scene led to the confession that Glogau had turned out to be a spy, and the husband had murdered him. Immediately all the woman's love returned. She helped him to get the body into its own room and comforted him throughout the night, having locked her door once more against the lover. With morning came the discovery of Glogau's body, swiftly followed by Beaurcourt's appointment to be Minister of Justice. In this capacity he learned the truth, quashed the trial on his own responsibility and gave up his love affair. The picture closes with the wife kneeling at Beaurcourt's feet and apologizing because she had refused to be seduced by him.

The production work is excellent and worked out to the merest detail. Scenically, the feature is excellent, but almost severe in the simplicity of some of the larger sets. Soane Galleone plays Monica Felt. She is not only a strikingly beautiful woman, but a tragic actress of great power. No other player's name is mentioned, but all the roles are well portrayed. As usual, incidental comedy is introduced, but remains pretty well under control.

LILIES OF THE FIELD

Associated First National Pictures feature, starring Corinne Griffith, from the stage play by William Hurlbut. Directed by John Francis Dillon. Scenario by Adelaide Heilbron. Supporting cast: Conway Tearle, Alma Bennett, Sylvia Breamer, Myrtle Stedman, Craufurd Kent, Charlie Murray, Phyllis Haver, Cissy Fitzgerald, Edith Ransom, Charles Gerrard, Dorothy Brock, Mammy Peters. Running time, at Mark-Strand Theatre, 85 minutes.

A flash at the names above this paragraph will give sufficient reasons why "Lilies of the Field" couldn't be a bad picture, and it will leave as sure a wonder regarding why it didn't come forth a great one.

To begin with, the original play was a second-rater, and, to end with, the scenario and direction of the film are soppy, soggy and uninspired. The photography is uncannily fine. This reviewer has never seen better camera work in any feature made up of interiors. And the production is prodigal as to sets, clothes, props—and wildly so as to cast, it would seem. Yet "Lilies of the Field" is effective only in one certain talking point, and that is—

Corinne Griffith!

If the direction helped her any and the story gave her any chances, she owes a debt to the lighting of the close-ups, which is marvelous, and to a chance for a background of easy women, against whom she shines, indeed, like a lily in the field of wantons. For the rest, she owes her author, scenario writer and director a lot of agony, action torn up by multitudinous and voluminous titles without kick or giggle, or even progress, a hundred scenes where she has to kiss photographs of her baby (the lovely little Dorothy Brock, who will get somewhere some day), and plenty of actionless acting.

Miss Griffith is glorious. Not only is she seemingly more beautiful than ever before in all her beautiful young career, but her eyes, her lips, her features—all seem to vibrate and live with a new something. If Dillon extracted that from Miss Griffith, then he may be forgiven his misdemeanors of commission and omission.

He may also be thank for his excellent taste in truly tony interiors, not showy or flashy, but rich and aristocratic.

But he might have dodged the plethora of unimportant titling at the start, the frequent and dramatically shabby use of telegrams that don't hold water, just to get melodrama and tears in between the receipt of one phony and its cancellation soon afterward by another just as preposterous; and he might have put less strain on the bathos with the baby's picture and the young bereft mother giving a birthday party to its teddy bear on a stormy birthday night.

That's the main trouble. One never for a moment, except when looking straight into those mesmerizing or heart-breaking eyes of Corinne Griffith, is unconscious of the rasping disillusionment that it is a movie—not even a motion picture drama, just a movie. One must now and then talk up and proclaim this fine or that neat or the other beautiful; but one is never immersed, except in Miss Griffith.

"Lilies of the Field" will be a strong box-office card on its title (a great film buy) and its list of standard and favorite names. But it will not repeat and it will not build up, propably.

Lait.

FIGHTING COWARD

James Cruze production releasing througgh Paramount. Adapted from Booth Tarkington's play, "Magnolia" by Walter Woods. Directed by Cruze with Karl Brown, photographer. At the Rivoli, New York, week March 16. Running time, 66 mins.

Gen. Orlando Jackson	Ernest Torrence
Lucy	Mary Astor
Blackie	Noah Beery
Tom Rumford	Cullen Landis
Elvira	Phyllis Haver
Major Patterson	G. Raymond Nye
Joe Patterson	Richard Neal
Mexico (Octaroon)	Carmen Phillips
General Rumford	Bruce Covington
Mrs. Rumford	Helen Dunbar
Rumbo	Frank Jonasson

James Cruze has taken this "flop" stage show and made it into one of the best program features "the street" has held this season. It's a sure thing that if the play had held the entertaining qualities the picture unfolds it would have been running yet. The play lingered but a month and a half.

The film projects as a satirical comedy of the old south when "honah" among gentlemen was supreme and the least infringement upon the esprit de corps was sufficient to instigate an immediate duel. The manner in which it has been treated, for screen presentation is a credit to all concerned.

The picture burlesques the south's former idiosyncrasies without becoming grotesque and not so obvious as to give an audience no credit for intelligence. The "kidding," for that is what it amounts to, is carried right into the titling and is backed by an abundance of atmosphere that has been more than averagely photographed.

Not the least of this picture's attributive qualities is the cast within which both Ernest Torrence and Cullen Landis stand out through superlative performances. Including everything that Torrence has ever done his role in this instance can rank with any previous effort including all the "specials." The entire list of players is airtight with the single exception of Phyllis Haver, who seems miscast.

The women are secondary to the men although Mary Astor is a joy to behold while G. Raymond Nye supplies a corking "heavy," Bruce Covington is superb in the early portions, Frank Jonasson makes a slave role connect for full value and Noah Beery convinces as a "notorious killah."

The story concerns the Rumford family whose son Tom, returns from the north with no passion for mint juleps or duelling, much to the disgust of his father.

A flagrant seri of insults, passed unheeded by the boy, proves the last straw to his parent, who disowns him on the spot with full approval from the entire household, outside of Lucy, a ward of the Rumfords, who loves Tom for his butterfly chasing and his correspondingly meek mannerisms.

Wandering into a gambling house the youth is dumbfounded by witnessing a shooting affray, but is befriended by General Orlando Jackson, owner of the establishment, who in turn is submissive to Blackie, a gambler and killer, desiring ownership of the place in lieu of his winning that Jackson can't meet.

Before quitting the gaming house the boy throws all discretion aside and embarks upon his career through retaliating to Blackie's insults by crowning him with a chair and establishing his reputation under the guidance of Jackson who, for the next three years, precedes him with advance matter of just how "bad" he is and instilling the "notorious" atmosphere which results in no one daring to start anything.

It's a great racket for the two men with the boy's quickness of hand, a development of the butterfly snatching, making him not without reason to be feared.

The psychology of the situation is based upon Jackson's philosophy that a small man must develop a reputation to stand a chance and gossip will take care of the remaining particulars.

A breakdown of a river sternwheeler at Magnolia gives Tom a chance to visit his home which has decayed under the guidance of his former nemesis in the person of

Major Patterson, since married to the elder ward of the Rumfords. Wearing a mask the resultant events within the old homestead are highly retributive until Lucy discovers the imposter is Tom and he then must assert himself in his own right, which he does.

The finish has the self-made desperado again chasing butterflies with the surrounding male community members also indulging in the pastime as a source of physical training and a means of developing a defense, or a reputation.

The picture is full of action, situations and comedy bits that are sure laugh getters, is backed by every need in production besides possessing that splendid cast.

It has everything and amounts to nothing less than another achievement for Cruze.

To say they proverbially "ate it up" at the Rivoli Sunday is but the half of it.

Skig.

THE HOOSIER SCHOOLMASTER

Whitman Bennett production released by Hodkinson. Story by Edward Eggleston. Shown at the Cameo, New York, week March 16, 1924. Running time, 63 minutes.

Ralph Hartsook.....Henry Hull
Hannah Thompson.....Jane Thomas
Dr. Small.....Frank Dane
Old Mis' Means.....Mary Foy
Old Jack Means.....Walter Palm
Bud Means.....Nat Pendleton
Mirandy Means.....Dorothy Allen
Bill Means.....O. W. Hall
Squire Hawkins.....George Pelzer
Pete Jones.....Arthur Ludwig
John Parson.....Frank Andrews
Walter Johnson.....Harold McArthur
Shocky Thompson.....Tom Brown
Dutchy Snyder.....Adolf Link
Prosecuting Attorney Bronson.Jerry Sinclair
Nancy Sawyer.....Dorothy Walters
Jeems Phillips.....Dick Lee

An ante-bellum period story that makes a fair program production. The picture isn't one that under ordinary circumstances would come in for a full week's run in any house in New York, but the Hodkinson people have the Cameo under lease for eight weeks to show their product, and this is the second of their productions to be presented there.

For the average daily change of program house the feature will hold its own and prove good entertainment. Henry Hull and Jane Thomas are the two featured members. Hull incidentally shows up in this picture as considerable of a comer as a film juvenile.

The story is a rural one of the period gefore the Civil War in Indiana. Hull has the title role. It is one of those stories that combines all the regular sure-fire elements, of the brow-beaten "bound girl," the band of night riders, terrorizing the countryside, and a cla h between the head of the band who poses as a respectable physician in the day time and leads his gang at night.

The schoolmaster is accused of the robberies and the gang arouse the countryside for a lynching party. It looks bad for the school teacher up to the time that one of the gang confesses.

As far as the production is concerned it is nothing to rave over. There is an unusual amount of heavy-tinted stuff for night scenes. This tinting is so heavy it is hard at times to follow the action. In the future prints care should be taken to lighten up the tinted portions. *Fred.*

THE DARING YEARS

Produced, written and supervised by Daniel Carson Goodman, featuring Mildred Harris. Directed by Kenneth Webb, with J. O. Taylor photographer. Cast includes Charles Emmett Mack, Mary Carr, Clara Bow, Tyrone Power, Jack Richardson, Joe King, Skeets Gallagher and Sam Sidman. At the Stanley, New York, one day, March 14. Running time 79 mins.

An attraction for the intermediate theatres that between Mildred Harris's appearance and the work of Charles Emmett Mack (loaned for this picture by D. W. Griffith) should satisfy the box office donaters. Substantial cutting would have enhanced the film's general value, while a tendency to become philosophical in the titling, both at the start and finish, seemed unnecessary.

Webb has carried the story on an even plane to the conclusion, while inserting a few trite flashes of Miss Harris in her bath and some "takes" of chorus girls flitting around their dressing room lightly clothed should attract attention. Probably more so in some states than others.

Beyond the prolonging of the footage and, mayhap, the theatrical license to stage a collegiate freshman-sophomore battle in an exclusive cabaret, Webb has fulfilled his mission capably.

The theme tells of an only and idolized son of a widow becoming smitten with a cabaret girl who ultimately is responsible for sending him to "the chair," from which he is rescued in the proverbial "nick" to return home to his mother and sweetheart.

Miss Harris, as the selfish stage representative, does a thankless role nicely, while young Mack stands alone for personal honors. This effort (besides his performance in "America") gives every evidence the boy is on the way, and he impresses as being not unlike Barthelmess, which is, undoubtedly, not an original discovery.

Others to stand out were "Skeets" Gallagher and Mary Carr.

The lighting, at various times, is prone to reveal defects.

A prize fight scene and the automobile chase to secure the governor's pardon provide the high action.

Skig.

FOOL'S AWAKENING

Metro production, directed by Harold Shaw. Adapted by Tom J. Hopkins. Photographed by George Rizard and Albert Ziegler. Cast includes Enid Bennett, Harrison Ford, Alec Francis, Mary Carr, Harry Northrup, Arline Pretty, D. O. Hatwell, Lionel Belmore, John Sainpolis, Edward Connelly, Lorimer Johnston. At the New York one day March 14 as half double bill. Running time, 73 minutes.

"The Fool's Awakening" is a film adaptation of "The Tale of Triona," one of the lesser known novels of William J. Locke, British author, who has given the screen some of its most successful stories. Here again it is his plot that is a big feature, although honors are shared with Harold Shaw, the director, and a cast that is a perfect constellation of minor stars.

The product is a good picture, one that with a few changes and the right kind of publicity might have been included in the realms of the first runs. Metro has spared no expense in putting it over, as the appearance of several prominent character actors in mere bits indicates.

Enid Bennett is the "name," but her part is subservient to that played by Harrison Ford. This young actor, hitherto seldom reaching beyond the leading man stage, has been handed a role that calls for all kinds of histrionic tricks. He gets away with it mighty well, but not well enough to drown out the potentialities of the role as it might have been played by one or two others.

He is a discharged British soldier with a gift for writing fiction, but at the start of the story with no better position than that of a taxicab driver. He has come into the possession of a remarkable little diary of a Russian secret service man's adventures during the revolution.

A stranger in London, with his mother ill at home in Wales and depending on him for money, and knowing that Russian to be dead, he decides to pose as the man to whom the adventures happened and publish them in autobiographical form.

Fame and riches crowd upon him, but his conscience is never easy. It becomes worse when he marries, and fears his wife loves him only as the Russian hero and writer he poses to be. But she proves her love when he is discovered and shamed in the eyes of the world.

Several side plots, most of more than average interest, are introduced. This gives room for fine bits of character work by such favorites as Alec Francis, Mary Carr, John Sainpolis, Harry Northrup, Lionel Belmore, Edward Connelly and others. Miss Bennett is, as always, beautiful, but in her acting is handicapped by the role, that of a rather silly, frivolous little thing.

The atmosphere is O. K. without being too British. This is fortunate, as the superabundance of such local color often grates on the average American mind. George Rizard and Albert Ziegler have utilized the photographic art in its highest sense, and the mechanical details are all perfect.

DRUMS OF JEOPARDY

Truart feature from the book of same title by Harold McGrath, presented by M. H. Hoffman, directed by Roland G. Edwards, featuring Wallace Beery, Elaine Hammerstein and Jack Mulhall. Distributed by Truart Film Corp. Reviewed at Loew's New York, March 11. Running time, 60 minutes.

Kitty Buelll.....Elaine Hammerstein
John Haykslev.....Jack Mulhall
Cutty.....David Torrence
Karlov.....Wallace Beery
Olga.....Maude George
Banker Buell.....Eric Mayne

This Harold McGrath story ran in the "Saturday Evening Post" serially and later was novelized. This will give the picture a certain box-office value, but to those who have read the story in book form it will prove a distinct disappointment.

The highly sensational and romantic tale which McGrath wove around the two emeralds, "Drums of Jeopardy," loses much of its fictional conviction when transformed to the screen.

The picture version closely follows the original story, but the cast, with the exception of Elaine Hammerstein and Wallace Beery, are more or less colorless. Jack Mulhall as Hawksley, the American who escapes from Russia after stealing the jewels from the Soviets, is badly miscast. He misses the virility needed by a wide margin and isn't even convincing in the lighter passages. His chief contribution is his ability to wear clothes.

Wallace Beery's Karlov carries conviction and Maude George's Olga also deserves brackets. Miss George contributed much needed atmosphere, acting and looking the Russian vamp in league with the agents of the Soviets, sent to recover the jewels.

One set representing a dungeon ruined the realistic possibilities early. It was one of those paper affairs with doors that roll back at the touch of a button and supposed to be hewn out of solid rock.

It's a romantic bunch of hokum as a feature, but should have some box-office value on the prestige of the author and the "Post." *Con.*

CONDUCTOR 1492

Warner Bros. production starring Johnny Hines. Story by Johnnie Hines. Directed by Charles Hines and Frank Griffin. Shown at Loew's Circle, New York, double feature bill, March 13. Running time, 80 minutes.

Conductor 1492.....Johnny Hines
Noretta Connelly.....Doris May
Mike O'Toole.....Dan Mason
Edna Brown.....Ruth Renick
Richard Langford.....Robert Cain
Denman Connelly.....Fred Esmelton
Robby Connelly.....Byron Sage
James Stoddard.....Michael Dark

A whale of a comedy of real laughs. Full of hoak of the real old-fashioned sort, a couple of thrills, a melodramatic love story of a poor Irish conductor's rise to the place where he wins the hand of the daughter of the owner of the street railway line, but handled in a fast manner that makes the picture good enough for any first run house.

It is a gag picture from beginning to end, and the audience not only howled with laughter but applauded it, something unusual at Loew's Circle in New York.

Johnny Hines is starred and he has Doris May playing opposite him. The two make a likable pair on the screen. It is Hines' hoak stuff that gets the laughs. He is a young Irishman who comes to this country and gets a job as a street car conductor. He manages to save the life of the young son of the president of the road, foil the villains who are trying to grab the outstanding two shares of stock that would break the tie in the board of directors, and in the end the president's daughter says she'll marry him.

But it is Johnny Hines in a boarding house waiting in line to get a regular Saturday night bath, Johnny Hines gagging with a cigar lighting bit. Johnny at a roller rink and a few other gags of that sort that put the picture over.

What a wonderful memory that Johnny must have to remember all of the gags that he pulls. He must have seen every burlesque show and vaudeville bill since the year one. He is pulling stuff that they would be afraid to show on the smallest small time today, but he makes 'em laugh with it, and that is the answer.

For thrills there are three stunts. The saving of the kid from the middle of the car tracks by hanging from the front of the trolley; an automobile chase with a miniature machine against a Mercer roadster; and a fire. Hines works in all three and does nobly. Doris May looks good and handles herself nicely. The others of the cast manage to fill the atmosphere nicely.

If you want laughs, play this one.

Fred.

NOT A DRUM WAS HEARD

Fox production, starring Charles Jones. Story by Ben Ames Williams. Directed by William Wellman. At the New York (one day), March 14, half double bill. Runs about 60 minutes.

Jack Mills.....Charles Jones
Joan Ross.....Betty Bouton
Banker Rand.....Frank Campeau
James Ross.....Rhody Hathaway
Sheriff.....Al Fremont
Bud Loupel.....William Scott
Jack Loupel.....Micky McBain

Probably best release Charles Jones has had to date. Not only has his acting taken a long leap in the right direction, but he has been backgrounded with a story and direction much superior to the usual Fox western stuff.

Ben Ames Williams is responsible for the story. He has turned out a plot with several twists and effective situations. In the first place, the central idea is not love, but friendship, something done before but can always stand repetition when strongly put over.

Damon and Pythias are two western boys who have stuck together through dozens of scrapes and adventures of all kinds. Jack (Charles Jones) is of the rough-and-ready school and Bud (William Scott), a college product, mild and well contrasted. Along comes Jean, home from finishing school, and both boys fall simultaneously. Bud is the lucky one, and Jack, a victim of conflicting emotions, returns to the plains with a parting entreaty that his pal name the first one after him.

Years pass, and Bud has hit the financial rocks. Stealing and then a murder in self defense follow. Jack tries to shield his friend, but vainly as the devotion is as firm on Bud's side as on his own. Before the law can decide which one is guilty death overtakes the young husband. The finish has Jack taking his pal's place and becoming a father to the youngster named after him.

The picture starts out as a rollicking story of the west, but soon changes and becomes very tragic, perhaps a bit unnecessarily so.

William Wellman directs with skill for the most part, but badly muffs his big opportunity in the climactic courtroom scene. A smashing big dose of the right kind of heart interest stuff here would have put the film on ice, but unfortunately all there is is a bit of slobbering pathos.

Jones is gradually overcoming his troublesome handicap of being too serious and restrained at all times. Scott, in the fat role of the erring but regular pal, takes the acting laurels. Betty Bouton is a charming heroine, and Frank Campeau sufficiently nasty as the man who pursues her.

The name, happily borrowed from the poem, "The Burial of Sir John Moore," is an appealing one, and those attracted by it will see something superior in the line of westerns.

THE BLIZZARD

William Fox release. From the novel by Dr. Selma Largerlof. Directed by Mauritz Stiller At Loew's New York, March 13. Running time, 78 minutes.

This picture bears all of the earmarks of Swedish make. None of the members are known over here. The picture, had it been properly edited and titled, might have been worked into something. As it stands it is just a film.

The only redeeming feature is that there is some rather good snow stuff and herds of reindeer.

The story is one of those more or less morbid and weird tales that the average Scandinavian is fond of, but in this country it won't do.

The story tells of a youth who in his infancy is told by his nurse of how the foundation of the family fortune was laid. His grandfather was a country peddler and in his travels went into the far north country and saw herds of reindeer running wild. He moved a herd into the southern country where he disposed of them for a fortune and bought a fine home. The grandad was also a fiddler and the grandson inherited his love for music, but the boy's mother won't let him indulge it, for music has brought naught but unhappiness to the family.

Finally the boy is attracted by the playing of a girl with a mountebank troupe. He takes the violin from her and plays it. The mother breaks the instrument and drives the son from home. He also goes north, determined to repeat the grandad's feat and win a fortune.

With his violin he secures enough money to gather a herd of reindeer and starts south with them. On the way a blizzard overtakes them and the animals, sensing that a continued snow means starvation for them, stampede, the bell deer dragging the boy over miles of snow until he finally is thrown unconscious into a snow bank where he is found hours later by his comrades of the deer drive. He is stark mad and after a period in an asylum is shipped to his home.

Here every effort is made to return his mind to functioning but it is unsuccessful until finally the vagabond girl of the troupe decides to try the violin again.

At the moment when the home is to be sold the boy's memory returns. He discovers there is copper ore on the estate and the family fortunes are rehabilitated.

The direction is spotty, and the usual overacting of the average foreign pictures also present. *Fred.*

MILE A MINUTE MORGAN

Lumber camp story, featuring Matty Mattison and Vivian Rich. Released by Sanford Productions. Loew's New York, one day, March 11. Running time, 55 minutes.

As stupidly and cheaply made a picture as has appeared since the days of the old hokum serials. The story is full of inconsistencies and the direction poor. Add to this a mediocre cast and the cheapest kind of a production.

The story concerns the black sheep son of a wealthy lumber man. The son and his pal after going broke return to California from Monte Carlo. The boat used in this shot couldn't cross the Pacific by parcel post.

The son (Matty Mattison) is stowed away in a rowboat aboard the ship. He has a black bag with him, and the old mixup in bags is worked in. The pair escape from the ship in a ridiculous manner and journey to dad's lumber camp, where they secure employment as lumber jacks.

Son's pal through boasting inveigles him into a prize fight with the lumber camp champion. The hero kayos the champ and wins the girl. His boxing would be a correct imitation of your Aunt Ella doing her daily dozen. The other pug is a professional with cauliflowered ears, and couldn't lose to our hero unless the latter stabbed him. However, he is knocked out.

Another "thrill" was the ensuing fight between son and villain. The latter jumped out of the ring on a tip the villain was ducking with the stakes, but he paused long enough to change his clothes for the next fight, which occurs on rocky ground, giving one the impression he knew in advance just where he would nail the departing one.

Real lumberjacks cutting down trees are spliced into the incoherent tale and is the only legitimate atmosphere the picture manages to work up. The cast is uniformly bad, the direction hopeless.

It's one of those pictures that men forget. It will be kidded by any intelligent audience, as it was at this house. *Con.*

RIDE FOR YOUR LIFE

Universal, starring Hoot Gibson. Directed by Edward Sedgewick. Shown at the Stanley, New York, March 17, 1924. Running time, 77 minutes.

Bud Watkins..................Hoot Gibson
Betsy Burke............Laura La Plante
"Gentleman Jim" Slade......Robert McKim

Just one of the usual type of wild and wooly westerns that Hoot Gibson is presented in from time to time. Every once in a while Eddie Sedgewick is let alone and permitted to furnish a story for the star and then something comes along that takes Gibson out of the ordinary stereotyped run of westerns and he appears to advantage. About then the studio staff gets busy again and he is shot right back to where he started. This picture is one of the examples. It is just hoke stuff, served in pictures ever since the day of outdoor production.

Gibson has a chance to ride and do a little shooting as well as a little love-making, and that about lets it out. He is the dreaming cowboy, in love with the daughter of the sheriff. This same girl is loved by the heavy, the bad man who runs the combination dance hall and gambling house of the rough mining camp.

Laura La Plante makes an acceptable heroine, and McKim is the heavy to perfection.

Just an average hot and cold western that will do for the nickel houses. *Fred.*

THIEF OF BAGDAD

Douglas Fairbanks production with Fairbanks .tarred; written by Elton Thomas; directed by Raoul Walsh; scenario, Lotta Woods; Arthur Edeson, photographer; Dr. Arthur Woods, research director, with Edward Knoblock consultant; William Cameron Menzies, art director. Special presentation opened March 18 at the Liberty, New York. Twice daily at $2.20 top.

The Thief of Bagdad...Douglas Fairbanks
His Evil Associate..........Snitz Edwards
The Holy Man..............Charles Belcher
The Princess..............Julanne Johnston
The Mongol Slave........Anna May Wong
The Slave of the Lute.....Winter-Blossom
The Slave of the Sand Board.....Etta Lee
The Caliph...................Brandon Hurst
His Soothsayer..............Tote Du Crow
The Mongol Prince......................So-Jin
His Counselor.....................K. Nambu
His Court Magician...Sadakichi Hartmann
The Indian Prince.........Noble Johnson
The Persian Prince............M. Comont
His Awaker...............Charles Stevens
The Sworder.......................Sam Baker
The Eunuchs............Jess Weldon / Scott Mattraw / Charles Sylvester

Douglas Fairbanks would have his public believe "The Thief of Bagdad" is the kind of picture he has always wanted to do—its flights of fancy, illusions of the magical "Arabian Nights" upon which the story is founded, the dreams that were his as a boy. Perhaps there is more to that than the publicity department's weaving of matter.

But Doug has come forth with an absorbing interesting picture, totally different than any of its predecessors. Never once does the present day commonplace intrude, nor the dramatics of countless pictures that have gone before. "The Thief of Bagdad" is not so much a story as it is a presentation of mystical events. It is laid in the mystic regions that lie eastward of the Suez.

Nearly all of it is fairy-tale like or phantasy, and so well is it done that the picture carries its audience along in the spirit of the depiction. "The Arabian Nights" are classic stories in book form. "The Thief of Bagdad" is a classic in pictures.

The wealth of magic that is applicable to pictures has finally been adapted by Fairbanks. Why someone else did not think of it before is one of the things that lend to motion pictures that unknown quantity—what they will develop. Doubtless others have prognosticated the production of a work of such caliber upon realizing the maze of detail, effort and executive brilliance.

The solving of the problem of how to picturize the castles and bizarre effects of the far east was worked out by a corps of glass blowers. Those men evolved airy castles high upon the mount and they wove gorgeous effects that the camera portrays as real.

There is a magic rope thrown into the air up which the Thief climbs high walls. There is a magic carpet upon which he sails with his princess away into the land of happiness. There is a magic chest which the favored one retrieved after heroic struggles through the valley of fire, the vale of dragons, even to the depths of the seas. It is the thief, now a prince who returns at the coming of the seventh moon to win his princess against the wiles of Oriental potentates seeking her hand. He wraps her in his invisible cloak and whisks her away.

The incident of the chest is one of many surprises and its useage near the close is something of a parallel to the army on motorcycles that gave the punch to "A Connecticut Yankee at the Court of St. James." Returning to the castle, the new silken-clad hero finds it overrun with soldiers of the powerful Mongol Prince. He rides about scattering sands from the chest and instantly a vast army springs from the ground to march forward and regain the castle.

The story starts with a scene in Bagdad, where the Thief, customarily stripped to the waist, purloins a magic rope. With it he scales the castle walls and is about to make off with the casket of priceless jewels when he looks upon the princess, glorious in her luxurious couch. It is her beauty that changes him from a laggard and he goes forth to win a long battle for the right to possess her.

There is a profusion of fine long shots and the maze of strange settings are great aids in keeping interest evenly balanced through the showing. Many of the scenes are tinted, designed to picture the spirit of the incident or event. So entirely different is "Bagdad" that it might have been shot in the lands it is supposed to picture. That it is authentic is not questioned, for clever people have aided in its making and persons who have visited some of the far away regions agree the picture is beyond criticism in that respect.

Fairbanks as the Thief gives a corking performance. Not so much of the athletic stunts of his earlier pictures are resorted to. He makes his hero more the dream lover of the story. Snitz Edwards as his associate in the evil days is one of the outstanding figures.

The cast has been brightly selected, as, for instance, players of Oriental extraction are used for such characters. At the head of those players and indeed second to Fairbanks is So-Jim in the role of the Mongol Prince, a really fine characterization. Anna May Wong as the little slave girl who is a spy for the Mongol Prince, proved herself a fine actress. Julanne Johnston as the princess is languorous, being more decorative than inspiring.

The premiere of "The Thief of Bagdad" was made sensational by the crush of picture fans who massed about the theatre entrance. Doug and Mary Pickford entered the lobby football fashion, a group of policemen forcing a passage. When the showing was over at nearly 11:30 the same crowd was outside, but kept in better order.

Morris Gest was the selection of Fairbanks to sponsor the film, Gest and his partner, F. Ray Comstock "having the honor to present." Perhaps some of Gest's ideas are the result of the Oriental atmosphere in the lobby, where Hindoo singers and musicians provide atmosphere and incense perfumes the air. Gest's bit is said to be a percentage arrangement whereby he receives about $3,000 weekly.

"The Thief of Bagdad" is the finished product of trick photography, a magical tale brilliantly picturized. A store adjoining the theatre has been hastily established by ticket speculators, a sure sign of a big demand. A clever sign showing Doug and his princess in midair upon the magic carpet attracts attention to the theatre, which should long hold the picture, incidentally a bear of a matinee card because of the kid draw

Ibee.

SECRETS

Joseph M. Schenck production, starring Norma Talmadge. Adapted by Frances Marion from the play by Rudolph Besier and May Edgington. Directed by Frank Borzage. Shown at the Astor theatre, N. Y., March 24, 1924, for a run. Running time, 91 minutes.

1923

Mary Carlton..............Norma Talmadge
John Carlton.................Eugene O'Brien
Dr. Arbuthnot......................Winter Hall
Robert Carlton.................Frank Elliott
John Carlton, Jr...............George Cowl
Audrey Carlton..........Clarissa Selwynne
Lady Lessington..............Florence Wix

1865

Mary Marlowe..............Norma Talmadge
John Carlton.................Eugene O'Brien
Susan..........................Patterson Dial
Mrs. Marlowe..................Emily Fitzroy
Elizabeth Channing.........Claire McDowell
William Marlowe............George Nichols

1870

Mary Carlton..............Norma Talmadge
John Carlton.................Eugene O'Brien
Bob.............................Harvey Clark
Dr. McGovern..................Charles Ogle

1888

Mary Carlton..............Norma Talmadge
John Carlton.................Eugene O'Brien
John Carlton, Jr.............Francis Feeney
Blanche Carlton......................Alice Day
Robert Carlton.................Winston Miller

Audrey Carlton....................May Giraci
Mrs. Mainwright...............Gertrude Astor

1923

(Characters same as in first episode)

Norma Talmadge is here in the greatest role she has ever been seen in on the screen. As Mary Carlton in "Secrets" she is shown first as a woman past 70, and then, as the action turns back, she is successively in girlhood, young wifehood, a middle-aged mother and then, finally, again as the aged but still loving and beloved wife.

It is a picture that is going to be a tremendous drawing card with women of all ages from the flappers to the grandmothers, and they are all going to love it.

On the screen "Secrets" is a far better entertainment than it was on the spoken stage. Its punches are driven home with greater effect than they were in the spoken play, and the interpretation Miss Talmadge gives of the wife who never wavered, but remained firm in the belief that her husband still loved her best of all, even at the times that she knew he was unfaithful, is something that will go down in film history. It is a work of art, deftly handled with a divine touch that makes it stand out as one of the greatest screen characterizations in years.

In the play the story was told in a straightforward manner, beginning with the early love story and the development of the theme from that point on. In the screen version there is a switch.

Frances Marion, who adapted the play, opens it with several scenes of the modern episode, after which she utilizes the dream idea for the showing of the preceding episodes in the life of the central characters. It is cleverly handled through the medium of the diary of the wife. Thus a lot of footage was avoided and the story runs along entertainingly to hold the interest.

The direction of Frank Borzage must be credited with a great part in the success that the picture is certain to have. He has taken Miss Talmadge and handled her in a manner that makes her reveal artistry such as she never displayed heretofore. Her make-up is a fine piece of work, and at times extends even to her hands. There is one scene for which Borzage must receive untold credit—the one following the siege on the ranch, when victory has perched on the side of the Carltons.

Mary Carlton's husband has gone forth to greet the rescuers, but she turns toward another room where her first-born lies dead. It is such a tremendous change of pace that it stands out like a Rolls-Royce in a showroom full of Cadillacs.

In casting Eugene O'Brien for the lead opposite Miss Talmadge, Joe Schenck made doubly sure of the selling value of the picture. Miss Talmadge and O'Brien as star and leading man built up a screen reputation in a series of pictures five years ago that helped a great deal toward Miss Talmadge's popularity. In "Secrets" O'Brien plays opposite her with the same verve he displayed in the earlier pictures, and the combination of the two is going to be one of the things the fans won't be able to resist.

The balance of the cast is more than adequate; it is splendid. In the second episode of the picture each and every member of the cast, in addition to the two leading players, scores. Patterson Dial as a slavey particularly stands out, while Emily Fitzroy as the mother, Claire McDowell as the aunt and George Nichols as the father are all splendid.

In one of the later episodes Gertrude Astor creates a decided impression.

With all of the telling of the tremendous love tale of Mary and John there is still lots of room for comedy, and not an opportunity has been overlooked to provide a laugh, while in the scene of the western ranch there is enough thrill in the gun fight to satisfy the most rabid wild and woolly fan of pintures.

The sets are colorful and the lightings in the second episode veritable works of art.

There is one question that remains, and that is whether or not this picture is of the required length to furnish a full evening's entertainment in a legitimate house at $1.65 top. It runs only an hour and 34 minutes, and that does not seem to be quite sufficient at that price, no matter how good the picture.

But this much is certain, the picture is going to be one of the biggest box-office knockouts of the year in the regular picture houses.

Fred.

SINGER JIM McKEE

Paramount picture starring William S. Hart. Story By Hart; adapted by J. G. Hawks. Clifford S. Smith, the director. Showing at the Rialto, New York, week of March 23. Running time, 75 minutes.

"Singer" Jim McKee.....William S. Hart
Mary Holden.................Phyllis Haver
Buck Holden..................Gordon Russell
Dan Gleason...................Bert Sprotte
Betty Gleason...................Ruth Miller
Hamlin Glass, Jr.............Edward Coxen
Hamlin Glass..................William Dyer
"Brute" Bernstein.......George Elegmann
Mary Holden, as a baby......Baby Turner

Showing at this house following a four weeks' postponement and marking the vehicle which brought to a head the controversy between Hart and F.-P.-L. The film was originally booked into this theatre about a month ago, but was withdrawn after the announced billing had gone out. No logical reason was given for the sidetracking, with the distributing organization inclined to be reticent in the matter, but leaving the impression the delay was caused by the business "A Song of Love" had done at the Rivoli, which warranted that picture's forcing out "McKee" at the Rialto the succeeding week.

The manner in which his picture was handled brought W. S. Hart to New York, where he now is, with a settlement between the star and Famous due to be reached this week.

"McKee," as a picture, starts out with a rush, but suffers a loss of speed along midway. Nevertheless, it should appeal to Hart's personal following.

What the others, not addicted to Hart or his particular style of screen work, will think of the release is questionable, although no one who views it will be able to resist a fall over a dirt cliff which Hart and his "paint" pony take. It marks as great a stunt of this kind as has been screened. Both horse and rider look to descend some 25 feet in a sheer drop before they again come in contact with the ground, followed by the resultant rolling. It is a distinct thrill.

Productionally, the picture is notable for its photography, which includes a full moon in a few exterior shots that is the most realistic depiction of that sphere yet seen while the scenic qualifications maintain the usual picturesque standards always associated with Hart's release.

Somewhat unfortunate for the general regard is the casting of Phyllis Haver. Screening as being limited to but one expression, she not only fails to convince but is especially colorless here. Ruth Miller is the only other woman in the cast in a secondary assignment. The star's most notable support comes from Gordon Russell and Bert Sprotte, who fulfill all obligations.

The narrative is named after a peculiar characteristic of the man, McKee, who must needs sing when experiencing emotion. A holdup and the fatal shooting of McKee's partner leaves the songster with his companion's child on his hands, for whom he effects an escape. Jumping 15 years, the story resumes in a mining town, where the child, now a young woman, becomes attached to a bank president's son, who invites her to a ball, and there deserts her because of her inferior appearance.

McKee, a window witness to the incident, goes back to "the road," holds up a bus to turn the money over to his ward as an inheritance. Caught, accused of having shot her father, revealed as not her uncle, as the girl supposed, and sent to prison, the reunion remains incomplete until after the sentence has been served. Riding through the woods the girl hears McKee's song being mimicked by a parrot, which he has picked up, and it leads her to him.

It is understood that Famous "squawked" on Hart's previous picture, "Wild Bill Hickok," claiming it to be not modern enough (whatever that might mean), and of just what effect that had on the making of this newest release probably Hart is the best judge.

There was some trouble over "McKee" a few days previous to the Los Angeles showing, and it is certain that the star has not been before a camera since its completion—but where they like Hart they'll like "McKee." *Skig.*

THE DAWN OF A TOMORROW

George Melford Production, presented by Adolph Zukor and Jesse Lasky. Jacqueline Logan, David Torrence and Raymond Griffith featured. From the novel and play by Frances Hodgson Burnett, adapted by Harvey Thew. Shown at the Rivoli, N. Y., week March 23, 1924. Running time, 72 minutes.

Glad ....Jacqueline Logan
The Dandy ....Raymond Griffith
Sir Oliver Holt...............David Torrence
Arthur Holt ....Roland Bottomley
Nod ....Harris Gordon
Black ....Guy Oliver
Ginney ....Tempe Piggot
Bet ....Mabel Van Buren
Madge ....Marguerite Clayton
Polly ....Alma Bennett
Barney ....Warren Rodgers

As a play on the spoken stage "The Dawn of a Tomorrow" was interesting. As a motion picture it it likewise good entertainment, but that is about all.

It is a slum story with a crook element, a love story that carries through and an element of surprise in it that is satisfying to the greater part of the film fans. It isn't, however, a picture that stands out as an extraordinary one as far as the Famous Players are concerned. With the majority of other producing organizations it would be remarked on as "great."

The trouble is that the majority of film followers have gotten to expect nothing but the best in Famous product and from the directors that that organization has raised to the degree where they have the pictures that they make as a production bearing their name specials are expected. When they don't materialize it's a disappointment.

However, in "The Dawn of a Tomorrow" George Melford has developed an actress in Jacqueline Logan. As Glad in this production she shows flashes of ability unsuspected in her heretofore. In the cast also Raymond Griffith gives a corking performance as Dandy and David Torrence as Sir Oliver Holt proves himself an extremely likable old man.

The story is laid in the London slums, with Glad and the Dandy sweethearts. The Dandy is a crook, and every one of the wretched creatures who live in the slum district believes that their only chance in life is to prey on the better classes. The Dandy is implicated by another crook in a shooting, but it is the kindly old Sir Oliver, who the Dandy believes to be a crook, finally proves his alibi, and a regeneration of Dandy is brought about through the efforts of Glad.

It is a slim waisted yarn, but it suffices to hang a picture on it. In the regular run of houses it will get the average business. *Fred.*

UNKNOWN PURPLE

Carlos production releasing through Truart. Adapted from stage play of the same name. Supervised and directed by Roland West with Oliver Marsh the photographer. Showing at the Capitol, New York, week of March 23. Running time, 79 mins.

Peter Marchmont........Henry B. Walthall
Jewell Marchmont...............Alice Lake
James Dawson..............Stuart Holmes
Ruth Marsh................Helen Ferguson
Bobbie ....Frankie Lee
Mrs. Freddie Goodlittle..Ethel Grey Terry
Leslie Bradbury...........James Morrison
Freddie Goodlittle...........Johnny Arthur
George Allison..............Richard Wayne
Hawkins ....Brinsley Shaw
Burton ....Mike Donlin

Roland West has taken his stage play, which he wrote in conjunction with Carlyle Moore, and given it able screen presentation. It is an exceptionally well-made picture—among the best of its type—a mystery.

Well dressed with extensive if not lavish interiors, and an assembled cast that plays the theme for its full worth, it is a release that impresses through that certain touch of class.

More than the usual credit should go to Oliver Marsh, who has handled the intricate lightings most aptly and given them excellent presentation through his photography. The tinting is an important ingredient to the story, and at this house the purple glow was carried outside of the screen itself by the rising of that color through border lights. The instance aided, but slightly draws attention away from the picture.

Henry Walthall, as the central figure, gives a performance of decisiveness that marks this as one of his best program contributions. The entire cast is invaluable in the manner in which they have evidently followed instructions. West is not new to the camera, but this release certainly marks him as particularly equal to the responsibility.

The picture has been nicely carried out, supplying all the elements of suspense, with Johnny Arthur relieving the tension through comedy upon which he has fluently realized.

Alice Lake stands out among the women for her efforts, while each of the men click.

The story carries a revengeful theme that has the innocent victim returning from prison to relentlessly hound the man who has stolen his wife and worldly goods. The pursuit is made the more baffling through a secret color process productive of a ray of light which makes the person within the glow invisible.

This screen version of the play is a sure program leader for any of the better houses, and even if the clientele doesn't particularly care for the mystery angle in their celluloid menu, the class the film possesses should hold it up.

Skig.

HIS DARKER SELF

Albert Gray Production released through Hodkinson. Starring Lloyd Hamilton in blackface. Directed by Jack Noble. Shown at the Cameo, New York, week March 23, 1924. Running time 51 minutes.

"His Darker Self" is the picture in which it was originally intended that Al Jolson, the famous blackface delineator of the stage, should appear under the direction of D. W. Griffith. When Jolson walked out, Lloyd Hamilton was secured from the Educational people for the picture and Jack Noble engaged to direct it. The picture completed proves itself to have a number of laughs from beginning to end, with Hamilton working both in white and blackface in it. It isn't exactly what one would term a comedy wow, but it is a good laughing picture.

Utilized as the principal laugh producer on an all-comedy bill, as it is at the Cameo this week, it manages to add a kick to the proceedings.

Hamilton plays the role of a fiction writer with a longing to become a crime detector, and achieves his ambition when an old colored servant is accused of a murder which in reality was the work of the leader of a gang of colored bootleggers. Hamilton disguises himself in cork to visit the colored cabaret where the bootleg mob hold forth, and his adventures there with the crowd of shimmy shakers and mean steppers are highly amusing. There is also a bit in a summer amusement park devoted solely to negroes that is also replete with laughs.

For thrills there is a lively motor boat chase and a knife throwing contest.

As a whole it can be passed as a decidedly different comedy production done in color, mostly black with a touch of high yaller.

Fred.

GEORGE WASHINGTON, JR.

Warner Brothers production adapted from the musical comedy by George M. Cohan. Starring Wesley Barry. Cast includes Gertrude Olmstead, Otis Harlan, Charles Conklin, Leon Barry and William Courtright. At the Circle, one day, March 18, as half the bill. Runs 60 minutes.

"George Washington, Jr.," was suggested, probably remotely so, by George Cohan's musical comedy of that name some years back. As incidental to Wesley Barry's befreckled mannerisms it serves its purpose, although taken by itself it is a cross between crude farce and cruder melodrama.

Wesley is no longer the little towheaded runt who charmed folks a few years ago. He 's nearly mansize now with long trousers and the beginnings of a beard crowding out his freckles. He is cast as an adolescent youngster who believes in truth above all things and sticks to his Washington-like theories through all obstacles.

This leads to complications of all sorts and not a little fun, although the picture never reaches the humorous heights that one anticipates. The young star does not seem to have enough opportunity to exhibit the facial expressions and other tricks of the trade that made him famous. Instead he indulges in a rough-and-ready with a gang of villains, further proof that maturity is creeping upon him. The fight scenes are well staged and a good portion of the laugh in the picture comes at this point.

Barry is the "little Mr. Fixit," straightening out everyone's trouble with a good deal of zest. His father, the senator, is forcing his young niece to marry the foreign nobleman. Wesley traces down the unwelcome suitor as a bogus count and famous international crook and turns the girl over to his pal, the boy who loves her.

The senator has been flirting with disgrace through his connection with the villain and only his young son's first lie clears the atmosphere. Wesley goes to the painting of his idol to crave forgiveness and the eye of the father of his country closes in an undeniable wink.

The trite story is improved by a capable cast. Gertrude Olmstead is disturbingly pretty as the girl and William Courtright makes the gruff old senator likable. Charles Conklin is cast as a colored servant, coming in for laughs with ghosts and other frights similar to those experienced by the negro servant in Griffith's "One Exciting Night."

Barry is at the awkward age now, too young for such roles as "Seventeen" or other Tarkington types and too old for the kid parts of the past. It must be difficult to secure the right kind of pictures for him. Considering this, "George Washington, Jr.," is an acceptable proposition for the box office of the average theatre, although its rating on any other score is not particularly high

DANGEROUS TRAILS

Rocky Mountain production presented by Morris R. Schlank. Directed by Alvin J. Meitz. Cast includes Tully Marshall, Irene Rich, Noah Beery, Jack Curtis and Jane Talent. At the New York one day, March 18, as half the bill. Runs about 65 minutes.

The one thing about "Dangerous Trails" that will linger in the minds of filmgoers a few hours after seeing it is the messy job made of the titling. Awkward, ungrammatical, stupid and entirely lacking in the knowledge of punctuation or clear construction, it would be enough to sink an otherwise shining production.

In this case, however, it cannot do much harm, as the film is bad enough. It is a tale of the Northwest Mounted Police, with a flavor of Chinese dope traffic included. The mixture as handled here is indigestible. Neither the heroics of the great Northwest nor the weird and supposedly exotic villainy of the Orientals ring true.

Bad continuity and insipid acting do not help. The story is disconnected and hard to follow.

Tully Marshall, in a right role one of the best of the screen's character men, is seen as a colorless old villain, not wicked enough to be genuinely interesting. Irene Rich is most unfortunately cast as the heroine. Miss Rich, who has heretofore been advantageously seen as restrained and quietly reserved women, is completely at a loss as a wild and almost hoydenish dancehall singer. Noah Beery, the only other familiar player, has practically nothing to do.

The producers evidently did not have to dig very deeply to meet the outlay. The dance hall scenes, employing a considerable number of extras, were the only ones that could have cost. Views of the dope dive, which might have held a kick, are held down to lily white mildness, either through fear of the censor or lack of enough box office spirit to put them across.

If the picture held one big smashing fight scene or thrill, one might excuse all the tedious moments leading up to it. But it peters out as it starts.

Finally the unpardonable sin is that the photography, instead of having a few shots of snow covered splendor such as almost every Northern picture boasts, is as drab and undistinguished as the picture otherwise.

SHADOW OF DESERT

Fox production from the story by E. M. Hull. Directed by George Archainbaud and photographed by Jules Cronjager. At the New York, March 20, one day. Runs 67 minutes.

Barry Craven	Frank Mayo
Gillian Locke	Mildred Harris
Said	Norman Kerry
Kunwar	Bertram Grassby
Lolaire	Evelyn Brent
Aunt Caroline	Edythe Chapman
John Locke	Josef Swickard
Peters	Lorimer Johnston

About three years ago a book by an unknown author appeared and proceeded to make flapper history in record style. It sold over a million copies, nearly as many in song adaptation and finally in picture form firmly established Rodolph Valentino, started a craze for things Arabian and coined a word for all particularly amorous and lady-killing young men, "sheik."

In "Shadow of the Desert" Miss Hull has tried again not at all disastrously but with a success that comparatively stands pigmy.

The chief appeal to this second attempt is that it is just about as trashy as "The Sheik" and should consequently prove equally entertaining to the millions who eat that kind of stuff raw.

Three years ago that might have held good, but since there have been so many imitations, the novelty has worn off and it will only be received as another of its kind although a rather interesting one.

Fox went after the film seriously and provided a big-time cast, direction, atmosphere and expense limitations for it. George Archainbaud has directed with one eye on artistic detail, but the other, probably his right, even more firmly focused on the box office. As a result there is an abundance of sizzling, sexy stuff that will cause laughs from those who see the hokum in it and talk and gasps from others.

Nothing very risque is flashed, but a few honeymoon tidbits and "pash" embraces that should give the followers of Miss Hull their biggest thrill since reading that one memorable consummation chapter in "The Sheik."

The sheik here is really secondary to two other characters in the story, the girl and a decadent British Earl who has married a native woman and found that to be only the beginning of his trouble.

Not Arabia but India is the locale this time, with some interesting and probably interpolated shots of the native water festivals adding local color.

Norman Kerry is the Oxford-bred sheik who only gets real sheikish upon one occasion when alone with the girl in the desert. Kerry makes a handsome oriental, but his admirers are sure to prefer him in such roles as the Austrian officer in "The Merry Go Round."

Mildred Harris again demonstrates she is at least learning to act as the heroine and Frank Mayo struggles manfully with the difficult role of the unfortunate hero.

The honors go to Evelyn Brent, the young woman of exotic dark beauty recently regarded as a comer but halted in her arrival by an unfortunate mixup as Doug Fairbank's leading woman. She plays the native wife and is seen for only about 20 minutes but makes a distinct impression during that time. The rest of the cast contains familiar names and lives up to its reputation.

At the first-run houses they'd label this one bunk, but if they play up the "sheik" thing properly elsewhere, the box office returns should justify its selection.

HOODMAN BLIND

Fox picture and John Ford production, adapted from stage play of H. A. Jones and Wilson Bartlett. Cast includes Marc McDermott, Frank Campeau, Gladys Hulette, David Butler and Edward Gribbon. Showing at Loew's, New York, March 19. Running time, 66 mins.

Just a picture along the "as ye sow" theme which may mean something to Gladys Hulette for her dual portrayal but otherwise has little to recommend it as above the average.

Localed in the village of Freeport, some 25 years ago, the story takes off with a father of wanderlust tendencies walking out on his wife and child to jaunt westward, accompanied by another woman whom he deserts with another daughter to make his way to South Africa, where he finds wealth. Thence the major portion of the footage takes up the Freeport situation of the first child's married life to a man of the seas and the drifting into the village of the second daughter who has become a girl of the streets.

The double crossing of the father's male friend, by holding out the money he sends to his child is revealed in time along with the return from Africa and the family reunion other than the father's two loves who have died.

Miss Hulette is cast as each of the sisters, handling both capably although not called upon for undue effort. The photography, in the instance of double exposure "shots," is neatly done, but undertakes nothing of the exceptional. The girl lends a sweet appearance to the screen and gives indications of being equal to a more demanding vehicle.

Frank Campeau walked through his "heavy" role for an average performance, while McDermott consumes the least footage of any member of the cast. David Butler and Edward Gribbon, late in the picture, stage a beach fight that convinces, while a small schooner on the rocks in a storm and the resultant rescues supply the climax, during which some of the incidents seem more than necessarily stretched.

The titling names no director, but whoever supervised copped at least one bit from a Neilan picture of many months ago and was careless as to the night street lightings during the storm. Lightning flashes are not in the habit of making themselves known through beams of light projecting from but one side of a thoroughfare.

The film stood by itself at the New York as a program leader and should be capable of holding its own if not biting off more than it can chew as regards houses to be played.

Skig.

AFTER THE BALL

Adapted from the song of the same title with the screen story also authored by the composer, Charles K. Harris. Dallas Fitzgerald directed.

Cast includes Gaston Glass, Edna Murphy, Thomas Guise, Miriam Cooper, Hugh Thompson, Robert Fraser and Edward Gribbon. Showing at the Stanley, New York, March 19. Running time, 80 minutes.

Known as one of this country's greatest ballads, it marks the screen version of the song for which the writer authored and titled, according to a slide.

The songwriter included a chorus of the lyrics into one title. Top that, and after 35 or 40 years. It's about the same psychology that led the publishers into the radio thing.

The picture is one of those bewailing editions that ridicules the younger generation, includes prison angles and goes on unendingly. At least 30 minutes could come out.

The film projects in the same tempo that the song stipulated and is easily a tear-rending ballad of the screen.

Though the somewhat imposing personalities in the cast may be of aid in holding it up, Gaston Glass and Miriam Cooper are a combine anything but hard to look at, while their merit has long been established.

Another distinct figure is that of Thomas Guise, who is passive in a stern parental role. Others register adequately though the outstanding fault is the overly dramatic theme.

Director Fitzgerald looks to have done little with the manner in which the script is played other than to have religiously followed the scenario. Whoever was assigned to the cutting seems to have had a consistent prejudice against anything resembling scissors. Either way the result is nothing less than inexcusable in this respect.

How closely the picture follows the song must be left to those who can accurately recall the lyrics, but for the uninformed it illusions as both a loose and free translation. Beginning with a wayward son of a rich father whose philanderings are consistently "squared" by a loving sister, the ultimate command to vacate comes when the youth marries a girl of the stage.

Circumstantial evidence, later, throws the boy in prison and reports his death. An escape from the penitentiary is managed and the return to Los Angeles made via freight conveyances where reunion eventually takes place between his wife, child, sister and parent. It might be interesting to number the succession of sub titles that are inserted during the telling.

Woefully careless in detail, an instance of which is the picturizing of the 20th Century, comprised of four cars and a smaller type engine, but make the script unconvincing to the point where it is beyond the realm of the first-class auditoriums, and can only hope to entertain in the less imposing houses. *Skig.*

FLOODGATES

Lowell Films, Inc., Production, featuring John Lowell. Released in the state rights market. Directed by George Irving. Shown in projection room March 21, 1924. Running time 70 minutes.

Dave Trask..........................John Lowell
His sister, Ruth Trask..Evangeline Russell
His wife, Alice.....................Jane Thomas
His little daughter, Peggy.........Ivy Ward
Lemuel Bassett.............William Calhoun
His nephew, Tom Bassett
F. Serrano Keating
Leslie Morton, Bassett's secretary
William Cavanaugh
Jeff Sumner...............Frank Montgomery
His wife.....................Mrs. Montgomery
"Sliver" Ohlman..............J. Nelson Bradt
His mother.........................Anne Brody
Dr. Jan Vedos.....................Homer Lind
A specialist..........................Fred Tiden
"Lovely" Regan...............Arthur Ludwig
"Goofy" Ladue..................."Hap" Hadley

"Floodgates," from the story by L. Case Russell, produced by the Lowell Films, Inc., featuring John Lowell, proves itself to be a state rights production that is decidedly above the average. It is a melodrama pure and simple, with the scenes laid in a rural community. There is thrill and punch to the story, a couple of corking fights and the action at all times moves along at a fast pace. The big wallop of the picture is the blowing up of a dam, opening the floodgates of a pent-up lake that carries away everything before it, including the house of the heavy who has been trimming all the landholders.

John Lowell plays the role of the poor but honest foreman of the lumber mill whose power with the others living in the neighborhood is so great that the heavy uses him to bring about his desires in the matter of taking over their land holdings. Lowell believes that he is acting for the best but finally when the real object of the land grabbing is shown he starts after the heavy and forces him to disgorge.

There is a great kick to the scenes where the tons of water are rushing down on the house of the heavy at the time when the child of the hero is there after having just undergone an operation at the hands of one of the world's noted surgeons, being restored the use of her limbs after she had been crippled by an automobile accident in which the car was driven by the nephew of the heavy, the nephew atoning for his fast driving by getting hold of the doctor to perform the operation, although he had to kidnap him.

The cast is above the average seen in this type of picture. The juvenile love story is carried along nicely by Evangeline Russell and F. Serrano Keating. Jane Thomas plays a corking lead opposite the featured member of the cast.

It is a mighty good average feature for almost any one of the average houses to play. *Fred.*

THE NIGHT MESSAGE

Universal picture written and directed by P. P. Sheehan and photographed by Jackson Rose. Cast includes Howard Truesdale, Robert Gorman, Edgar Kennedy, Charles Cruze and Gladys Hulette. At the Stanley, New York, one day, March 22. Running time, 55 minutes.

One of U's usual feud definitions regularly turned out. The entire vehicle is cut and dried, with its main attractiveness within the 55 minutes it has been held.

P. P. Sheehan has turned out much repeated tale of the hill people, holding insufficient material to make it register either way. The production is of the type generally given to these scripts and fails to vary above the usual trend. The cast plays the story adequately, in which Edgar Kennedy supplies the outstanding dramatics.

The picture should have a better chance of being approved if included on a double feature program, for it is much too much of a lightweight to stand by itself except in those houses which pick 'em out of the hat. *Skig.*

EYES OF THE FOREST

Fox picture, starring Tom Mix. Story by Shannon Fife, with Lambert Hillyer directing and Daniel Clark at camera. Cast includes Buster Gardner, Ed Wallock, Tom Lingham, Sidney Jordan, Pauline Starke and J. P. Lockney. Showing at the Loew's New York Theatre, New York, as half of double feature program, one day, March 21. Running time, 62 minutes.

Will probably please the most addicted of the Mix fans, but isn't especially meritorious as regards the actual script.

An aeroplane bit in which a pickup from a galloping horse is made and the following drop to the ground from the machine as it sails but a few feet from the ground are the highlights of the picture.

Otherwise it has Mix as a government flyer patrolling the large forests in search of lumber pirates.

The meeting of the girl, wrongly accused of the murder of her stepfather, and the expose of the villainous gang, are incidents filmed along lines which have long been followed.

Mix, personally, takes to the uniform portrayal well enough, though a haircut might have made the character more convincing. Beyond that the script calls for no exaggerated exertion upon his part, with it probably having been deemed the air stuff would get the release across.

The cast carries the theme along without difficulty, holding the usual contingent of "heavies" the star always must overcome before the finish.

Pauline Starke but walks through a mediocre role to which she is superior. No other women in the line-up.

The photography is of particular note through the nicety in which the altitude shots were taken, especially in the stunt instances.

Splitting billing with Cosmopolitan's "Unseeing Eyes," the Roof audience evidenced an interest in the Mix activities to the extent which would typify this film as a sure thing in the less demanding picture emporiums. *Skig.*

BEAU BRUMMEL

Warner Bros. production presented by arrangement with Mrs. Richard Mansfield, starring John Barrymore. Based on the play by Clyde Fitch, adapted by Dorothy Farnum. Directed by Harry Beaumont. Shown at the Strand, N. Y., week March 30, 1924. Running time, 120 minutes.

George Bryan Brummel....John Barrymore
Lady Margery Alvanley........Mary Astor
George, Prince of Wales.....Willard Louis
Frederica Charlotte, Duchess of York..
Irene Rich
Mortimer.......................Alec B. Francis
Lady Hester Stanhope........Carmel Myers
Lord Alvanley..........William Humphreys
Lord Stanhope.............Richard Tucker
Lord Byron..................Andre Beranger
Lady Manly..................Claire de Lorez
Lord Manly....................Michael Dark
Desmond Wertham............Templar Saxe
Mrs. Wertham..............Clarissa Seywynne
Snodgrass, an English Inn Keeper......
James A. Marcus
Mrs. Snodgrass....................Betty Brice
Mr. Abrahams..............Roland Rushton
"Poodle" Byng..........John J. Richardson

The combination of one of the most popular actors of the American stage, John Barrymore, in the role most celebrated of the repertoire of the greatest and most famous actor of America in the last score of years, is a combination sure of money on Broadway.

That is exactly what "Beau Brummel" is doing at the Strand this week. It is playing to capacity.

It may be another story as far as the smaller towns of the country are concerned. That is something that will only be worked out with the playing of the picture.

But the picture will go into the pre-release houses and mop up. In the smaller towns as a road show, providing that it has the proper advance work and not merely motion picture exploitation, it will get money, but they will have to play up the Richard Mansfield end as well as the Barrymore. The latter's possibility of succeeding to the crown of dead master might be another angle as well as the romances that are part of "Beau Brummel" story.

From the average exhibitor's standpoint the thing to consider about this picture is that it is another of the long run of costume screen plays. Another point is that it was the greatest box office attraction of the repertoire of the late Richard Mansfield; that it has John Barrymore at the head of a cast that holds some strong picture names, and, finally, that its story is told fairly interestingly on the screen.

The direction is not what it might have been, and the casting was also somewhat faulty. Irene Rich as the Duchess of York would have undoubtedly made a much better Lady Margery than Mary Astor, who played it. Although Miss Astor was seen to advantage from the standpoint of beauty, she did not display any great histrionic ability.

Willard Louis as George, Prince of Wales, was one of the real outstanding figures. He walked away with practically every scene in which he appeared. The part, during the moments that it called for coappearance with the title role, far overshadowed it. Here is a real find in the person of a new fat man of the films.

Carmel Myers as a vamp was a vamp of today rather than one of the period in which the action is laid. Alec B. Francis as the servant to Beau Brummel made a work of art of his role.

Then as to Barrymore, there were flashes in his characterization of the London dandy that were inspired, and there were other moments when he did not seem to get over with the audience at all. This might have been as much the fault of direction as it was of acting. There could have been more intimate shots shown, instead of the constant use of the three-quarter and the long shot.

The picture originally was in 14 reels, then cut to 12. At the Strand it is about 10 and takes two hours to show. As a result the Strand is only giving a news reel and overture with it. Sunday was a big day but not a record-breaker, because of the length of the feature. There is some talk of cutting the feature to eight reels, but it is believed that Barrymore protested so strenuously before sailing that this will not be done.

"Beau Brummel" is a good picture, for it combines a good play and a star who is worth while. It is simply a question of whether the costume play is a thing of the past and if there is sufficient interest in this stage star in the smaller towns to attract sufficient to make it worth while to play the picture on a basis that will make a profit at the rental that the distributors must be asking for it. *Fred.*

THREE WEEKS

Goldwyn production, directed by Alan Crosland from Carey Wilson's adaptation of Elinor Glyn's novel, continuity by June Mathis; principals, Conrad Nagle, Aileen Pringle, John Sainpolis, Helen Dunbar, Stuart Holmes, Mitchell Lewis, Robert Cain, Nigel de Bullier, Dale Fuller, Alan Crosland, Jr.; seen at the Capitol, New York.

"Three Weeks" was done some 10 years ago and wasn't much shucks then, as a state rights proposition, shabbily produced. The Goldwyn version is far different—in many ways. The censors were hot on the original film, screaming about the long kisses and other scenes then regarded raw. They couldn't have the heart to cut a foot of this picture, however.

It is a mild, almost milksop "Three Weeks," toned down in its sex kick by both Crosland and Miss Pringle. She plays the queen more royal than romantic. While the story carries out the well-known plot without dodging its responsibilities, it never rises at any time to a single moment of supreme passion.

The patrons with Freudian complexes who come in for a tingle, attracted by the title, may have a bleat. They will find their tiger-rug scene, which gave the flappers of the last generation sleepless nights, compressed into a somewhat dignified few seconds. But it is a beautiful rug!

That about tells the whole story. Everything about "Three Weeks" is beautiful and lovely. The sets, the clothes, the lightings—up to the finest in motion picture production, always. Interiors of the palace and the Swiss hotel are magnificent. The coronation of the royal love-child is impressive and gorgeous at the end.

But "Three Weeks" doesn't raise the temperature, as might be expected. So much sympathy is gotten for the queen by the very villainous behavior of the king-husband, as played with terrific power by John Sainpolis, that her romance becomes a protest rather than an urge; a methodical venture rather than a fervid adventure; a designed plan to get an heir who will have a decent strain of manhood for her country rather than an impulsive clicking of two wounded, wild, love-hungry young hearts.

That appeal was the making of the book and was in Miss Glyn's mind when she wrote it. The plot, without it, isn't beyond the commonplace in romance of royalty amidst high-power surroundings.

It is not fair to indicate that the spirit of the book is lost in this showing. But it isn't concentrated or climaxed at any time into one big, preponderant moment, either. One who sees this film may know what Miss Glyn meant but may not quite feel what she meant.

As a picture worth seeing this is undoubtedly in the front rank. What it misses is entirely psychological. Regular filmgoers will admire and praise it, and it is a credit to everyone associated from artistic standpoints and demonstrations of screen art. If it were just an unknown story it would still stand up; but the great furore caused by the girl-thrilling classic laid down an obligation which is not quite met by the respectable, legitimate progress of the scenario.

Should be a strong release everywhere on the title-draw and the standard names, and will please if not electrify those whom it lures in with pulses palpitating as they buy the tickets.

Lait.

WOMAN TO WOMAN

Selznick picture and a Graham Cutts production presented by Balcon, Freeman and Saville. Adapted from the play by Michael Morton and starring Betty Compson. At the Rivoli, New York, week March 30. Running time, 73 mins.

Deloryse ....Betty Compson
David Compton................Clive Brook
Mrs. Anson Pond..........Josephine Earle
Henriette ....Mrrie Ault
Little Davy.....................M. Peter

One of Betty Compson's English made features that has been playing out of town for a few weeks but marks this as its premier in New York and nothing either the British manufacturers nor Miss Compson need be ashamed of.

The picture will certainly do the star no harm, for with one exception it shows her to advantage throughout besides being excellently produced.

Technically, a certain portion of American consumers may find fault with the number of closeups, the tinting of a cabaret scene and a more or less amount of wasted footage, but as a whole it is not any more guilty of the usual sequence of deficiencies than is included in the average features produced and made within our home territory.

Besides which it has a story to tell, tells it and closes out upon the death of the heroine, leaving her child in the hands of its father and his wife.

No director is named either on the program or by caption which makes it no more than probable that the Graham Cutts Production introduction is the tipoff at to Cutts being the individual responsible. It's a workmanlike piece of production, who ever did it, and rates above some of the vehicles Miss Compson has done on this side. That it should increase this girl's following seems a surety and the drawing power of her name may show an inkling in that at seven o'clock, on a mild Sunday evening, the box office line was stretching beyond the 49th street corner, which isn't bad even allowing for the tremendous business the "street" theatres do on a Sabbath night.

The star receives excellent support in the persons of Clive Brook and Marie Ault, although the entire cast more than equals the individual responsibilities. The narrative covers the war period and is located in both Paris and London. It tells of a dancer in a Montmartre cabaret meeting an English officer while he is on leave, which soon develops into a love affair. On the eve of their marriage he is summoned to rejoin his unit and a loss of memory results from shellshock.

A five years' lapse reveals the girl as the current rage of London and the former officer, now a sedate and well provided for business man, with a wife who denies him children Persuaded to witness a performance and see for himself this sensation which has tuxedos and top hats (very natty, too) clamoring at the stage door, his initial glance from a stage box is sufficient to restore his memory and the arrangement of a meeting.

Uninformed as to his marriage, through his change of title, Deloryse brings to him his son. It complicates matters until the wife personally intercedes the night the trio are to make for Paris on the ground that she will take the child into her

home as an adopted son and in that way give him his rightful birthright.

The two women, previously acquainted to the point where Deloryse is to dance at a ball given by the wife, reach an understanding with the dancer agreeing to perform at the social event, knowing it will probably kill her because of a weak heart, against which she has previously been warned. And such is the end.

Miss Compson is viewed at various stages of undress other than in costuming, at which time she is burdened with little, but her actual work compensates other than when she dances, for it must be said the star is not fluently addicted to the art of high kicks nor "shiver" dancing.

The production includes an insert of a stage setting (evidently from the "Brighter London" show at the Hippodrome, London, that for eccentric and flash costuming will make the wise boys over here look the second time, while a majority of the interiors are lavish and are made to impress for full value through photography which takes advantage of the opportunity. A sense of lighting, especially upon the instance of a bedroom set, that can stand with the best is also noteworthy.

After viewing this picture there seems no evident reason for the continual antipathy expressed towards British-made films, as this assuredly must be an example of the better grade of work over there. It is unquestionably equal to a vast majority of the releases viewed in the first run houses over here and vastly superior to those witnessed in our daily change theatres.

What about it, Joe? *Sklg.*

SOCIETY SENSATION

Reissued by Universal as a "Universal Special." Story by Perley Poore Sheehan; directed by Paul Powell. Shown at Loew's New York, N. Y., March 31, 1924, on double feature bill. Running time 27 minutes.

Capt. H. H. Fairfax..........Alfred Allen
Margaret Fairfax............Carmel Myers
Just Mary.......................ZaZu Pitts
Richard Bradley........Rodolph Valentino

Monday night at Loew's New York Roof when this picture was shown as one half of the double feature bill the audience gave it and Rodolph Valentino the "razz" good and proper. It was a wise crackin' crowd of Broadway hangers-on that viewed the picture, the usual audience that the roof gets, and while they could not appreciate the fact that here was something Universal was putting over on them by issuing it in the guise of a "Universal Special" and playing it up with a lot of new paper which had Valentino starred top up with Carmel Myers and which also had some of his recent pictures slapped all over it, they could appreciate the crudity of the picture itself. Tha was what they razzed more than the star.

This is one of the things in picture business that the exhibitor has in his power to stop. All he has to do is to fail to book a picture of this sort and the distributor-producer will soon stop digging into his cut out to frame a picture just to be able to use a star's name. In the long run the exhibitor is the loser. Imagine a "special" that runs 27 minutes and you have the idea of how much of a special this is.

It is so old that the year of copyright is even left off of the leader. That in itself tells a story.

Valentino plays the lead opposite Carmel Myers, who is in reality the star. She is the daughter of a fishing boat captain who has claim to an English title. Because of this, one of the new rich decides to entertain the daughter and launch her as a summer sensation as a duchess. Her first appearance on the beach and she rescues the son of the real society leader of the resort from

drowning. The audience thought it was all in fun after the phoney fight stuff and the picture never had a chance with them.

Universal is a member of the M. P. Producers and Distributors of America. That organization has a code of ethics for its members, whether universal knows it or not.

Fred.

VIRTUOUS LIARS

Whitman-Bennett production. Story by E. C. Holland. Adapted by Eve Stuyvesant. Directed by Whitman Bennett. Shown at the Rialto, New York, week March 30. Running time, 60 minutes.

Norman Wright..............David Powell
Josiah Wright...........Maurice Costello
Edith Banton...................Edith Allen
Jack Banton..................Ralph Kellard
Julia Livingston........Naomi Childers
Livingston..................Burr McIntosh
Juanita.................Dagmar Godowsky

Possibly it was the title that might have been the one thing that swayed those booking the Rialto in favor of the picture, but even though it has one of those titles designed especially for the box office it is far from being a picture that measures up to the pre-release full-week-run standard. It is "just a feature." One of those for the average house where there is a daily change policy.

The story has nothing imposing in thought or action. The picture holds nothing extraordinary in the way of production or cast and the direction is the average.

True, David Powell heads the cast. He is a good leading man, and good in this picture. The picture also brings back Maurice Costello, and he gives a polished performance, looking well as an elderly man of wealth. Edith Allen, who plays the lead, is fairly average. Naomi Childers does nothing and doesn't mean anything. Burr McIntosh has a bit that amounts to nothing, and Dagmar Godowsky is shot after three scenes.

One can't hand Mr. Bennett anything on this production other than he was lucky in getting it on Broadway for a week.

Fred.

GENTLE JULIA

William Fox production, starring Bessie Love. Story by Booth Tarkington. Adapted by Donald Lee. Directed by Rowland V. Lee. Shown at Loew's New York, N. Y., March 31, on double feature bill. Running time, 67 minutes.

Julia......................Bessie Love
Noble Dill...............Harold Goodwin
Randolph Crum............Frank Elliott
John Atwater...........Charles K. French
George Atwater..............Clyde Benson
Uncle Joe Atwater......Harry Dunkinson
Newland Sanders........Jack Rollins
Mrs. Joe Atwater.........Frances Gaunt
George Plum....................Bill Irving
Mrs. Geo. Atwater.........Agnes Aker
Herbert Atwater...........William Lester
Mrs. Herbert Atwater......Gypsy Norman
Florence Atwater..........Mary Arthur
Herbert Atwater, Jr........Richard Billings

Nothing particularly stirring about this Booth Tarkington tale as revealed on the screen, although the story at times shows great humorous possibilities. These possibilities were not taken advantage of either by adapter or director. As a feature picture this one is just about capable of holding down one-half of a double-feature bill in the larger daily change houses. In some of the smaller houses that are also daily change it may also get by.

Bessie Love is at the head of a lengthy but more or less unimportant cast. The greater part of the picture was shot out of doors on exterior locations, so the picture wasn't an expensive one to make.

The story is that of a girl who is the queen bee in her own little home town and believes, because of this, she'll be just as great a favorite in a big town. Reaching Chicago, she discovers herself overshadowed. It is a tale of calf romance and juvenile pranks along the usual Tarkington lines, with the juvenile portion of the story running far in advance of the other.

Little Mary Arthur runs away with the honors as the little niece of the Gentle Julia.

Fred.

NORTH OF NEVADA

Monogram production presented by Harry J. Brown. Featuring Fred Thompson and directed by Albert Rogell. At the Circle as half the bill one day March 25. Runs 62 minutes. Distributed by F. B. O.

In spite of the "north" in its title, "North of Nevada" is a pure and simple western, pure in the sense that all these out-of-doors pictures are and simple because there is not enough gray stuff behind it to lift it to any higher level. The curse of 90 per cent of all westerns drains all the interest.

The strugle is purely physical, consisting of chases, fights, abductions and finally the triumph by force of the hero over the villain. The upright young foreman of the ranch is kept busy defending the new owner, the girl in the case, from the machinations of a band of villains who seek to swindle her of her property.

Affairs are complicated by the weakness of her brother, a semi-comic city knave who constantly plays into the hands of her adversaries.

Fred Thompson, the star, is handsome and earnest in his work and promises in time to join the large school of male leads already turning out a steady stream of westerns. A white horse, called "Silver King," is important. That he is a worthy rival for Tom Mix's "Tony" is evidenced by the laughs he won when showing his jealousy of the girl who is stealing the affections of his master. The rest of the cast, containing only one familiar name, Josef Swickard, is adequate, as is the direction.

In spite of a few attractive comedy bits and freedom from any outstanding deficiencies except the lack of novelty, "North of Nevada" hardly rated its showing at a fairly important Loew house in New York. In general it seems headed for the smallest houses.

GIRL SHY

Harold Lloyd production, released by Pathe. Story by Sam Taylor, assisted by Tommy Gray, Tim Whelen and Ted Wilde. Direction by Fred Newmeyer and Sam Taylor. Trade showing, New York Roof, March 28, 1924. Running 82 minutes.

Poor Boy..................Harold Lloyd
Rich Girl.................Jobyna Ralston
Poor Man.................Richard Daniels
Rich Man.................Carlton Griffith

Harold Lloyd's latest may well be called his best. There is so much action jammed into this picture that when it once gets under way one forgets the opening is rather slow. The last two reels move along so fast, with so many thrills, that the average audience is going to stand up and howl.

It's a wow of a comedy picture!

The story is by Sam Taylor, Tommy Gray, Tim Whelen and Ted Wilde. Taylor, together with Fred Newmeyer, directed.

Lloyd is a small-town tailor's apprentice, frightfully girl shy and prone to stuttering. In secret, however, he fancies himself as an author and feels the urge to write a book on girls and women, with himself figuring as the heroic character in a series of romances that are 16 in number.

The early part shows Lloyd laboring at night over a typewriter in an attic on his masterpiece; flashes of the script being shown, with Lloyd handling a vamp and another showing him pulling caveman stuff with a flapper.

It is this script that brings him in contact with the rich girl. He is on his way to the city with the script when he meets her on the train. There is a lot of good laugh stuff in the train scene, the first wow coming when he rescues the toy dog belonging to the heiress. The hiding of the dog to get past the conductor and the subsequent complications are also good for laughs.

The biggest of the picture, however, is the chase stuff that runs through both of the final reels. It starts off with Lloyd becoming aware his book has been accepted and he is in receipt of $3,000 advance royalties, this followed by the discovery of the fact that "the girl" is going to be married to his rival, who already has a wife, starts him off hotfoot for the scene of the wedding. What he goes through to get there is beyond the mere power of a typewriter to describe. It is a chase that caps anything else that has ever been done on the screen. In his race for the scene of the wedding the comedian uses automobile, motorcycles, horses, a trolley car, and the manner in which they are employed will bring howl after howl from picture fans.

Playing the lead opposite Lloyd is Jobyna Ralston, who proves herself considerable of an actress in addition to being decidedly pretty. The heavy is Carlton Griffith. No one in the cast other than four characters are mentioned, and, as a matter of fact, no one except Lloyd and the girl remain in one's memory.

The chances are that with "Girl Shy," Lloyd is going to run up a bigger sales gross than he has had with any of his previous productions. *Fred.*

FOOLS' HIGHWAY

Universal-Jewel starring Mary Philbin. Cast includes Charlie Murray, Lincoln Plummer, Buster Collier, Pat O'Malley and Max Davidson. Directed by Irving Cummings. Showing at Loew's New York as half of double feature program, March 28, one day. Running time, 77 mins.

Mary Philbin's name above that of the picture and an underline giving due credit for her performance in "Merry-Go-Round." Splitting honors with another feature, this Universal release looked to be the most capable of maintaining a solitary standard.

The story is that of New York's Bowery in the late 90's, accompanied by appropriate costuming and ward politics with the boss' cleanup youth eventually reforming and joining "the force" through the efforts of the girl.

The film projects two worthy performances contributed by Miss Philbin and Pat O'Malley. Others make their presence known through respective bits which Cummings, directing, has inserted for comedy. Incidentally, the director has sustained the script to round out a pleasing story that is, perhaps, slightly too lengthy.

The atmosphere of the sets includes the old miniature steam engines at one time used by the elevated trains and is replete with other instances of a like nature comprising one of the most attractive appeals the picture contains.

The fighting, gang stuff and snatches of comedy are well enough pictured to make this film an easy bill leader in the upper middle houses, besides which the name of Miss Philbin should help. *Skig.*

AVERAGE WOMAN

C. C. Burr picture adapted from the story of Dorothy De Jagers and directed by William Cabanne. Cast includes Pauline Garon, David Powell, Burr McIntosh and Harrison Ford. Showing as half of double feature program at Loew's New York, March 28, one day. Running time, 64 mins.

An in and out picture which doesn't hold water and neither does it spin. The cast names may prove of assistance, but the actual tale is too thin to prove other than a weakling in evidencing why modern girls are equal, or better, than their ancestors.

A newspaper reporter digging data on a special story of the average woman encounters the girl in a library and proceeds to follow her for material. Wise to the trailing the girl has a policeman grab the youth and turn him over to her father, an official, whom she warns to punish the boy by making him report to her once a week.

Opposite is the other suitor, secret owner of the city's worst cabaret, who ultimately secures what he thinks is an inside story on the girl's family. The usual private dining room, the raid and rescue of the daughter follow.

Burr McIntosh, as the father, does about as well as anyone, while Powell and Harrison do little but walk through their parts. Miss Garon is Miss Garon. If you like her—that's that.

Nothing outstanding in the production beyond the interiors which are tasteful and suitable to the purpose. About rightly placed when having another feature alongside on the same program. *Skig.*

TRY AND GET IT

S. V. Grand presentation, releasing through Hodkinson and adapted from the story of E. P. Lyle. Stars Bryant Washburn, with Cullen Tate directing. C. I. McDonnell, the photographer. Cast includes Joseph Kilgour, E. E. Horton, Lionel Belmore, Carl Stockdale and Billie Dove. Showing at the Cameo week of March 30. Running time, 59 minutes.

A breezy, light comedy, neatly presented, with which Lionel Belmore has not a little to do for its entertaining qualities. Despite the starring of Washburn, it is Belmore who stands out in bold relief, and a corking performance he has turned in. Otherwise, the film consummates a well-executed assemblage of units making for a flitting program leader that will amuse.

Tate has evidently cashed in on every angle, securing a uniform all-around portrayal from the cast, in which Washburn is cushioned so that he has but little to do other than permit the continuity of the tale to carry him along. The titling flashes as having been carelessly cut and constructed in various instances, but on the other hand balances the discrepancy through comedy verbalizing that injects a lilt.

The story has to do with a grudge debt between two men, which the youthful bill collector (Washburn) must secure in order to hold his job. The debtor (Belmore) is a cement manufacturer, forced to handle the financial end of his daughter's modiste shop. The overcoming of the obstacles in securing payment, with the girl (Billie Dove) thrown in at the finish, consumes all of the running time.

The fashion shop is an excuse for a brief parade of clothes, as well as constituting a neatly designed background in the way of an interior set. The film upholds a certain standard of appearance throughout, before which the action carries along without becoming tedious.

Washburn means little, as his portrayal could have been equally handled by many of less importance, but it may be of note that considering he was being starred he would permit himself to be so directed. It's a credit to him if he did, for the lessening of the usual predominance is more than of inconsequential assistance.

E. E. Horton lends able support, while Miss Dove is also par with a passive role; but it is Belmore as the grouch debtor, the comedy bits and the titling which make this a well conceived release, equal to the assignment of program leading where this type of picture is desired. *Skig.*

BY DIVINE RIGHT

A Harry Ascher production, featuring Elliott Dexter and Mildred Harris. Story by Adam Hull Shirk. Directed by R. William Neill. Shown at the Stanley, N. Y., March 28, 1924. Running time, 78 minutes. Released by F. B. O.

The Boss	Anders Randolph
The Prince	Elliott Dexter
The Girl	Mildred Harris
The Hireling	Sidney Bracey
Detective	De Witt Jennings
The Child	Jeanne Carpenter
The Wife	Grace Carlyle

Adam Hull Shirk in authoring this feature, tried for a Christian Science propaganda tale that might be likened to "The Miracle Man," but he failed in the job that he set for himself. He turned out a story that has an idea, but hasn't a punch to get it over. The result is that on the screen the production proves to be draggy and wearisome. The fact that Elliott Dexter and Mildred Harris are co-featured in the picture may mean a little at the box office, but the chances are that the average fan will be disappointed in the picture even in the smaller houses.

The story is one of a clash between political power as typified by the political boss of a big city and that of the Supreme Being through the head of a slum mission. The political boss is out to get a certain girl who seeks the protection of the mission. The boss then puts his gang on the job, the mission is fired and the preacher charged with having set the blaze, with the result that he is sent to jail for seven years. On his way to prison the train is wrecked and he escapes. Later, changed in appearance, he seeks employment in the home of the boss as his social secretary.

When the little daughter of the boss is pronounced a cripple for life by doctors the secretary takes hold and through prayer restores her to health overnight.

At the same time he effects a reconciliation between the boss and his wife, and there is a happy ending all around.

Mildred Harris as the girl has been "carrying on" in the mission during the absence of the preacher, she remaining firm in "the faith" that he is alive and will return.

For a thrill the picture has the train wreck, which is well worked up to the point where the actual occurs; then the pieced-in bit of a smash fails to slip over the kick. *Fred.*

THE BREAKING POINT

Herbert Brenon production and Paramount picture. Adapted from the novel and play of same name by Mary Roberts Rinehart. Directed by Brenon, with Julie Hearne and Edfrid Bingham the adapters. James Howe the photographer. Showing at the Rivoli, New York, week April 6. Running time, 70 minutes.

Beverly Carlysle	Nita Naldi
Elizabeth Wheeler	Patsy Ruth Miller
Dr. David Livingstone	George Fawcett
Judson Clark	Matt Moore
William Lucas	John Merkel
Fred Gregory	Theodore Van Eltz
Lucy Livingstone	Edythe Chapman
Louis Bassett	Cyril Ring
Sheriff Wilkins	W. B. Clarke
Joe	Edward Kipling
Donaldson	Milt Brown
Harrison Wheeler	Charles A. Stevenson
Minnie	Nalda Faro

The novel was a best seller, the play failed to cause a stir, but the picture should split the difference, with the odds favoring a like reception for the film as was given the book. It's good screen entertainment and especially favorable to this member of the Moore family, Matt.

The actual story is above the average celluloid menu and, portrayed by a smooth working cast, working under sane supervision, the total result of this intricate theme is satisfying.

In print, the narrative read as having great picture possibilities, and, while the camera product may not quite reach the classification of "great," it's well on the safe side to easily assume the burden of program leadership in the larger houses.

Moore, Fawcett and the Misses Naldi and Miller are featured of the cast, all of whom register convincingly, especially Moore, who gives a well-balanced portrayal of the principal figure sustaining a dual personality caused by a loss of memory.

The amnesia affliction is the basis of the script, which might have become unwieldly and knotted in less effective hands. Brenon has straightened it out, made it tellable and interesting, deserving much credit for the effort.

The production meets all obligations, with a few of the interiors particularly pretentious. The exterior schedule includes a raging blizzard that has been neatly photographed. Otherwise the locations include New York, a suburb and a western village.

Besides the prominently named players, Cyril Ring, as a reporter, and W. B. Clark, doing a sheriff, were capable of making their presence felt, with the former assuming a role of equal importance to any except that of Moore. A nice bit of work, too.

This film edition of the Rinehart story is a first-class product, there is no doubt of that, and besides pleasing those who read the book, it should prove something of a surprise to that consignment who witnessed the work in play form. *Skig.*

WHICH SHALL IT BE?

Renaud Hoffman production, based on the poem, "Not One to Spare," by Mrs. E. L. Beers, adapted and directed by Renaud Hoffman. Distributed by Hodkinson. Shown at the Cameo, New York, week April 6, 1924. Running time, 52 minutes.

John Moore	Willis Marks
Mrs. Moore	Ethel Wales
Robert Moore	David Torrence
Music Master	Paul Weigel
The Children	Mary McLane, Billy Bondwin, Newton Hause, Miriam Ballah, Dick Winslow, Buck Black, Thayer Strain

One of those tear-compelling little pictures that is going to be a money maker for producer, distributor and the exhibitor. It is a little picture that didn't cost a million dollars to produce, so the chances are that the exhibitor can get it at a fair price and sell it to his public. His public are going to love it. It is another one of those "Over the Hill" things, full of weeps, and that seems to be what the picture public wants.

The story is based on the little poem, "Not One to Spare," which has been published in the Fourth Readers in the public schools for about 25 years. It is told in a simple, straightforward manner without frills.

There are moments in the early section when it is a little draggy, but down to the real kick it gets over with a wallop.

The kick is in the trial of the mother and father in selecting a child to give to the father's brother in adoption, with the eldest daughter the final choice. Her leaving the home is another wallop, but when at the last minute the father changes his mind and she is returned there is the usual happy conclusion.

The picture is well directed and has a cast in which names do not stand out, but in which there is 100 per cent. playing value. The mother role, played by Ethel Wales, rings true, and of the children the two little girls, Mary McLane and Miriam Ballah, both deserve unstinted praise, especially the younger of the two, for there is a little artist if there ever was one. Of the boys the youngster who enacts the wayward son is also an understanding little figure in the cast.

You can't go wrong playing this one, for it is certain to hit 100 per cent. for the women. Tell them to bring extra handkerchiefs. *Fred.*

MORAL SINNERS

Paramount film, adapted by J. Clarkson Miller, directed by Ralph Ince, from story by C. M. S. McClellan; seen at the Rialto.

CAST
Leah Kleschna...........Dorothy Dalton
Paul Sylvain...............James Rennie
Anton Kleschna.........Alphonz Ethier
Schram.................Frederick Lewis
Raoul....................W. I. Percival
Gen. Berton.............Paul McAllister
Claire Berton............Florence Fair

A very exciting and excellently filmed free-hand version of "Leah Kleschna," the McClellan play in which Mrs. Fiske starred and George Arliss first won fame (as Raoul), back in 1905, with Dorothy Dalton, after a seemingly long absence from the Broadway screen, starred in the Fiske role of Leah, the pretty crook-daughter of a "master-mind" Paris thief.

Miss Dalton looks somewhat thinned down, almost peaked, but very engaging. In the later scenes, especially the meeting with the criminologist who falls in love with her, she is powerful. Rennie, in that part, plays excellently and with pronounced plausibility.

Some liberties have been taken with the story, such as a fire in the first reel, in which Rennie rescues Miss Dalton, but the script has not been manhandled ruthlessly. The entire sense of the famous yarn is preserved and expressed, and a strong story it always was.

The settings and lightings are of modern standards, and the Ince direction is sane, straightforward, and not too cluttered with comings and goings for the purpose of filling out a feature-length footage. Incident is thinly spread, however, over the first couple of thousand feet, even with the fire and a carnival, etc., thrown in.

The title seems rather heavy and old-fashioned, seemingly meant to synchronize with the star rather than the picture, because of some sex stories she has done in the past. There is little of what is commonly regarded "moral sin" in this picture, though Raoul is an all-around scapegrace, of course.

"Mortal Sinners" might be even more attractive with a title less alarming to parents of young daughters. However, that old question has never been decided—do scarlet promises bring 'em in or scare 'em off?

This feature will do handsomely everywhere without creating any sweeping sensation. It will offend no one, and will please the adult seekers of a grown-up story, even if a little passe, and the youngsters who fall for pretty girl crooks, "master" thieves who live double lives, rich men's drunken young villain sons, and touches of all-wool melodrama with a solid love theme. *Lait.*

A BOY OF FLANDERS

Metro picture starring Jackie Coogan. Adapted from Ouida's "A Dog of Flanders." Directed by Victor Schertzinger. Showing at the Rialto, New York, week of April 13. Running time, 72 mins.
Jan Van Dullen............Josef Swickard
Jehan Daas...............Nigel de Brulier
Baas Cogez..............Lionel Belmore
Marie Cogez.................Nell Craig
Alois Cogez..............Jean Carpenter
Baas Verhaecht (Landlord)..Russel Powell
Dumpert Schimmelpennick..Aime Charland
Vrow Schimmelpennick....Eugenie Tuttle
Petrasche..................."Teddy"
Nello....................Jackie Coogan

Just an in-and-out feature which gives the child star ample opportunity to glimmer, but lacks sufficient body in the script to make it get anywhere.

The story soon resolves itself into a pretty much revamped tale of the persecuted youngster who finally wins a prize for drawing and a home, after his grandfather has died and he has become the persecuted youngster of the village.

Located near Antwerp, the costuming runs to the Dutch mode of dress, making a neat effect for Jackie, whose best scene comes with the holding of a children's party for which he must do a female impersonation to gain the entrance.

Jack Coogan, Sr., is programed as having personally supervised the directing of Victor Schertzinger, although neither seems to have done much with the material. It may not be entirely their fault, for the story, in celluloid form, simply isn't there.

An extended cast routines easily, although somewhat overshadowed by the dog, "Teddy," seen previously in numerous comedy "shorts." The adaptation practically gives equal prominence to the canine with young Coogan, and it shows in the screening.

The picture is in no way to be compared with Coogan's "King," for it barely meets this child's requirements and is too shy of comedy to make it of interest to the average patron.

Settings and photography total a worthy appearance, but are unable to meet the full obligation. A balmy Sunday afternoon was hardly conducive to theatregoing, hence the Rialto held less than half a house at the Sabbath first show.

The picture won't do the younger Coogan any harm, but it is equally true that it will do no good, making it a certainty his next release will have to pick up considerably. *Skig.*

NELLIE, BEAUTIFUL CLOAK MODEL

Goldwyn production from the play by Owen Davis. Directed by Emmett Flynn. At the Capitol, New York, week of April 13. Running time, 69 minutes.
Nellie.....................Claire Windsor
(At 5 years old)........Betsy Ann Hisle
Jack Carroll..............Edmund Lowe
Polly Joy.................Mae Busch
Shorty Burchell.........Raymond Griffith
Walter Peck................Lew Cody
Thomas Lipton..........}
Robert Horton..........} Hobart Bosworth
Nita...................Lilyan Tashman
Mrs. Horton............Dorothy Cummings
Blizzard Dugan...........Will Walling
Miss Drake...............Mayme Kelso
Mosely.................William Orlamond
Gangster.................Arthur Houseman
Gangster...................David Kirby

Here is a picture that is going to take the majority of the old-timers who see it right back to the old days of the ten-twent-thirt mellers, for that is exactly what Goldwyns have turned out in "Nellie, the Beautiful Cloak Model." They haven't done anything that A. H. Woods didn't do in the original production in the days of the Stair & Havlin circuit. They have got it all in this picture; but in these days it certainly does look like crude stuff.

There are any number of names on the leader credited with having something or another to do with the adaptation or the scenario. They didn't supply a single thought to the picture that was not present in the original script. But the fact remains "Nellie" is just a hoak meller that

gets a laugh where it should get over its big punch.

In a couple of scenes there are a few thrills—just the same sort of a thrill as one would get in a roller coaster—but they are too oft repeated to have sustained punch.

The cast is the one thing that may be counted on to pull at the box office because of the "names" that there are in it. First, there is Claire Windsor, then Mae Busch, Edmund Lowe, Lilyan Tashman, Hobart Bosworth, Lew Cody, Raymond Griffith, Mayme Kelso and Will Walling.

As for the draw of the title, "Nellie, the Beautiful Cloak Model," that is something that remains to be seen. The picture itself isn't pre-release run material.

When Nellie grows into a beautiful girl and becomes a cloak model she falls right into the shop that is run by her own mother's nephew, who is now the heir to the oil millions, too much coincidence even for pictures.

In showing the tribulations that Nellie goes through is the scene of Nell unconscious on the "L" tracks, right in the path of a speeding express train, with the motorman dropping dead without notice. But a plumber with a monkey wrench was on the train, and the speeding express stopped right at Nellie's head. That wowed 'em Sunday afternoon.

Claire Windsor makes an entirely acceptable Nellie, but Mae Busch walks away with all of the scenes she is in, carrying the comedy relief, and, paired with Raymond Griffith, it is a corking combination. Cody as the heavy is right at home, while Lilyan Tashman does a loose lady vamp in a manner that registers as to the manner born. Hobart Bosworth in a double role gives one of the best performances he has shown in some time, while Edmund Lowe is a more or less wishy-washy hero.

It looks as though, after the picture was finished, the producers got somewhat afraid of it, for they tagged a bit on it to make it appear as if the entire action witnessed was in reality a 'meller" in one of the old-time houses, with the cast walking across the stage at the conclusion of the play to the usual accompaniment of cheers and hisses from the audience. That, to a certain extent, took the curse off the impossibilities. *Fred.*

CONFIDENCE MAN

Paramount release, Zukor-Lasky presentation, from story by Laurie York Erskine and Robert H. Davis. Directed by Victor Heerman. Adapted by Paul Sloane. Titles by George Ade. Seen at the Rivoli.
Dan Corvan...............Thomas Meighan
Margaret Leland...........Virginia Valli
Larry Maddox..........Laurence Wheat
Godfrey Querrit........Charles Dow Clark
Mrs. Bland...............Helen Lindroth
Jimmie Bland............Jimmie Lapsley
Mrs. X................Margaret Seddon
Wade....................George Nash
Mrs. O'Brien...........Dorothy Walters
The Minister.............David Higgins

A spiritless, tired sort of shamefaced imitation of "Get-Rich-Quick Wallingford," lacking in humor, action, romance or thrills of any sort, and dependent entirely on Tom Meighan's popularity, won in happier efforts, for its potentialities as a Paramount program release.

If any striking evidence of the economy policy of big film producers was required, here it is. Though the cast is a distinguished one and the star one of the surefires of the screen, the rest of the whole venture is bushleague.

It is a jitney story of a "master" stock swindler who hires a Wallingford in the person of Meighan and his side-kick, a near "Blackie" in the colorless and never amusing "comedy relief" character tossed to Lawrence Wheat, to go to a hick town and shake the local miser-millionaire for a chunk.

They invade the burg and go through numerous unimportant doings, by which time we have become acquainted with the heroine, this time the village Sunday School teacher instead of the steno, played by Virginia Valli, who drips honey until one is overfed with the sweet stuff. Of course, Meighan falls for her and she for him.

He rescues the old people in the leaky home for the aged and takes them to his hired house, somewhat a la "Dear Me." One of the old ladies, about to die, trusts him and touches his heart, whereupon he suddenly turns straight, smashes a mirror with a reflection of himself, abruptly decides to marry the queen bee, and then "The End" in nice scrolled letters.

Wheat as a comedian shakes his head at the climax of each bit to punctuate that it's through and to cue a laugh, but the laughs missed, all except a few on Ade's titles and a scene or two with whiskered old men.

Meighan got most of the comedy, himself. The love story was brutally difficult to sustain, since it was a picayunish conception and never carried conviction except that it was a good-looking boy and a pretty girl.

As a production it is negligible and has no sets or scenes of even memorandum value. The lighting and camera work are good but ordinary. The whole thing lacks material for the eye, the heart and the brain.

This film means nothing at all.
Lait.

THE ENCHANTED COTTAGE

Inspiration production released by First National. Richard Barthelmess starred. Adapted by Joseph Lovett from the play by Sir Arthur Wing Pinero. Directed by John S. Robertson. Shown at the Strand, New York, week April 13. Running time, 82 minutes.
Oliver Bashforth.......Richard Barthelmess
Mrs. Smallwood, his mother..Ida Waterman
Rupert Smallwood, his stepfather.......
............................Alfred Hickman
Ethel Bashforth, his sister...Florence Short
Beatrice Vaughn, boyhood sweetheart...
............................Marion Coakley
Maj. M. Hillgrove, D. S. O., M. C......
............................Holmes E. Herbert
Laura Pennington.............May McAvoy
Mrs. Minnett..................Ethel Wright

This picture is too far advanced and too artistic for the screen. It is one of those things certain to be above the heads of all but a few of the regulars at picture theatres. It is at once an artistic success that seemingly is doomed to be more or less of a disappointment at the box office. It is a picture that interests to a certain extent, but in its handling the general idea of the fantasy isn't driven home sufficiently early in the story to make it possible for the average film fan to grasp it.

Richard Barthelmess, the star; May McAvoy, in his support, and John S. Robertson, who directed, combined to make the picture somewhat different. They succeeded, and the result is about as artistic a production as has been shown in some time. In lightings, sets and action the story is perfectly handled.

Its theme is English, and that in a great measure may account for a slight miss here and there in its failure to get over and register with the average American. But it is a picture that has been cleverly done, and while in great measure it will get terrific praise from the average daily paper critic, it does not appear as though the box office strength is present.

Richard Barthelmess plays the war cripple whose life has been ruined, and the performance he gives is decidedly clever; but despite this, the picture in reality belongs to Miss McAvoy, who practically walks away with the production as the ugly duckling.

Holmes E. Herbert as a blind major also carries a great portion of the picture along. Others in the cast do not particularly amount to anything, except that Florence Short rather overplays the masculine sister of the cripple.
Fred.

A WOMAN'S SECRET

Allied Producers and Distributors Corporation production. Directed by Graham Wilcox and starring Mae Marsh. At the Stanley, New York, April 1. Runs 85 minutes.
Dorothy Forbes.................Mae Marsh
John Forbes.................Allen Aynesworth
Sir Richard Hawke...........Aubrey Smith
Dorothy's Aunt................Eva Moore
Henry Watson...........Herbert Langley
Kate Watson.................Hilda Bayley
Arthur Watson.............George K. Arthur

There is a dour, dank, dark-brown taste in one's mouth after sitting through 85 minutes of "A Woman's Secret." A happy ending cannot obliterate the memory of an exceedingly sombre, not to say disagreeable, theme. There are, however, several things to be praised in this British production.

The author is not credited in the billing, but he has provided a story of undeniable power. Dorothy Forbes, a girl of good family, is forcibly seduced by Henry Watson, her father's chauffeur, with whom she has had an incipient love affair. A child is born, but Dorothy's aunt forces her to give it up without anyone hearing of the scandal. The baby is intrusted to the care of Watson's wife, who almost glorifies in being the butt of her husband's brutality. Dorothy still conscience-stricken about her babe, meanwhile marries Richard Hawke, a prominent barrister, whose stringent methods with criminals has earned him the sobriquet of "Hawke the Hangman."

Watson has been going from bad to worse and one night in a drunken fury he savagely murders the child that has been given to his wife's charge, unaware that it is his own flesh and blood. The evidence is only circumstantial and Hawke is chosen to prosecute him. There follow some genuinely stirring trial scenes, shot, according to an announcement, in the original Old Bailey Court in London.

Dorothy finally confesses to her husband that she was the mother of the slain baby. Hawke realizes that a complete disclosure of the facts is necessary to bring justice upon the head of the brutal Watson. In a finely executed scene he gives up his profession as barrister and his claim to a promised title, but succeeds in getting the death sentence across. As the picture ends he is shown with Dorothy and their own child happy and care-free in a tiny rustic cottage.

The several strong situations are aided by a competent cast headed by Mae Marsh. Her part here is no simple ingenue. She is again forward with that exquisite shading and delicacy that distinguished her work in the old days under Griffith. Aubrey Smith, legitimate actor, is refreshingly different as the middle-aged hero barrister, lending a world of dignified restraint to the role. The rest, apparently all English, are generally good except for the villain, who stresses too heavily the dime novel stuff.

The direction sags at times, the subtitles are awkward and unconvincing and the photography ordinary. The chief faults, however, are the length and the total lack of any comedy touches. Perhaps the realistically stark flavor of it is to the British taste, but it is doubtful if there are many Americans who will be able to stomach it with more than a temperate interest in the workings of the story.

THE DANCING CHEAT

Universal production, directed by Irving Cummings. From the story, "Clay of Calina," by Calvin Johnston. Featuring Herbert Rawlinson and Alice Lake. At the New York (one day) April 1 as half the bill. Runs 55 minutes.
Brownlow Clay.........Herbert Rawlinson
Poppy ....Alice Lake
Bobby Norton..............Robert Walker
Moss ....Jim Blackwell
Eddie Kane...............Edwin J. Brady
Moron Mike..............Harmon McGregor

The supposition that all "Saturday Evening Post" stories make excellent pictures is given a jolt in "The Dancing Cheat." It is a film distinguished most, if any, by some rather extraordinary acting by Alice Lake. Miss Lake, at one time a star, drifted out of the picture and the pictures, but this production should go a long way to re-establish her as a most capable actress for the right role.

The "Post" story, "Clay of Calina," by Calvin Johnston, considered one of the most reliable of the magazine's regular fiction contributors, is the basis. One need go no farther to find out why the film is mediocre stuff, as the weakness lies in the ordinary story.

Irving Cummings, who bids fair to achieve more success as a director than an actor, has handled the reins **with fair skill and Miss Lake's associates, including the star, Herbert Rawlinson, give meritorious performances.**

The story features the old "badger game," with Miss Lake as an unwilling participant, as the victim is the man she loves. He is perfectly able to take care of himself, however, and not only frustrates the villain's plans, but refuses to have anything to do with the girl until the final clinch.

The atmosphere is a combination of semi-tropical and Spanish, neither played up to the picturesque possibilities. A gambling house and dance hall relieve the monotony slightly. The comedy relief is pitifully inadequate, the only laugh coming when the old darkie butler hides his African golf set in the safe.

Miss Lake's part is another of those "beloved demi-monde," so popular lately and she imbues the impossible woman with a charm that almost makes her seem real. Rawlinson is as well groomed as ever. He is, however, gradually joining that school of super-restrained film actors led by Conway Tearle and H. B. Warner. Except for Harmon McGregor, who seems to think all a moron does is wear an idiotic smile, the others are acceptable.

THE GALLOPING AGE

Universal production starring Jack Hoxie. Story by Jacques Jaccard. Scenario by Isadore Bernstein. Directed by Robert N. Bradbury. Photography by Merritt Gerstad. 60 minutes.
Jim Jordan.....................Jack Hoxie
Anne Morse.............Margaret Morris
David Kincaid..............Robert McKim
Zack Williams...............Frank Rice
Louise Williams.............Julia Brown
Susie Williams..........Dorothea Wolbert
Fred..........................Fred Humes

As explained in the "Times Square Daily," "The Galloping Ace" in general theme and treatment was almost the exact counterpart of a film reviewed the name night in a different theatre. This is not to be attributed to coincidence or plagiarism but rather that both are particularly ordinary examples of the poor done-to-death western school.

The basic ideas on which such films are built are easily discerned. It seems as though director, author, continuity man and general staff all strive to stick as closely as possible to a given formula.

This may impressionistically be described as follows: Hero—handsome, hard-riding and says, "I reckon, ma'am"; heroine—pretty, winsome and romantic but entirely without initiative; villain—first of all bewhiskered, desiring the girl almost as much as her property, and having his gang of hard-boiled cronies and hangers-on to back him up.

Bad boy says, "I want that mine" (or ranch or oil well or whatever it happens to be). Hero responds, "Try and get it." He does, and is not finally foiled until miles of western prairie have been chased over and death struggles have been waged on half the cliffs the other side of the Mississippi. In these fights the hero always get knocked down first and is in danger of losing both his life and his girl, but in the end he comes back with a rush and finally rides off in glory on his noble white steed.

The comedy relief is also as stereotyped as a chemical formula. There must be one old, eccentric cowboy, friendly to the hero, whose chief task consists of tiptoeing away with a sly expression when the lovers bounce into each other's arms at the finish. There is usually a kid present to promote the more innocuous sort of laughter, and more often than not a comic character woman.

"Galloping Ace" meets practically all these standard requirements. In one or two respects there is some slight variation. The best is when the hero dynamites a field to keep his adversaries out, a comparatively new idea.

Jack Hoxie, formerly a circus rider and now a western regular, proves himself primarily to be a star on the back of his fine white horse. The only other definite impression one gets is the devout wish that he would blow himself to a haircut. Margaret Morris makes the girl's role as colorful as possible, and Robert McKim adds one more pursuer to his long list.

There must be a strong market for westerns or producers would not keep turning them out by the gross at all seasons of the year. This picture is about as good as the average, but what a pitifully low average it is!

THE NIGHT HAWK

Hunt Stromberg production, starring Harry Carey and releasing through Hodkinson. Adapted from a magazine story of C. O. Raht. Directed by Stuart Paton. Showing at Loew's New York Theatre, New York, as half of double-feature program (one day), April 4. Running time, 59 mins.

Simply one of those pictures there is little or no excuse for. The cast is named in a group title at the beginning, and it's just as well the personal designations are missed, for none deserve mention and the players should be just as well satisfied after viewing the total result.

A reasonless theme that plays as hoke melodrama, having Carey the power behind a gang of crooks who makes his way west to kill a sheriff because the son of a cattle rustler has saved his life. He must do away with the gun fightin' law upholder in order to square the obligation with the beef boss' son.

That is, until he flashes the daughter, when all bets are off.

Many of the incidents are nothing less than ridiculous, besides Carey walking through the scenario with his hand in his shirt as a continual threat against all mankind that he's liable to "draw" at any time.

Outside of that there's the usual wild riding and hectic shooting, when the scene shifts to God's country, but no one cares what happens by that time.

The picture is strictly for the smaller of the small houses, where the clientele's idea of the west is Elizabeth, N. J., as the film is so asinine it's to wonder how it became a release under the Hodkinson mark.
Skig.

MILE-A-MINUTE ROMEO

Fox production, starring Tom Mix. Adapted from "The Gun Gentleman," by Max Brand. Directed by Lambert Hillyer. Scenario by Robert N. Lee. Runs about stad. Runs 57 minutes.
Lucky Bill.......................Tom Mix
Molly........................Betty Jewel
Landry....................J. Gordon Russell
Morgan.......................James Mason

Sheriff......Duke Lee
Coroner......James Quinn

The billing for "Mile-a-Minute Romeo" heralds that Tom Mix "rides like a Comanche Indian, shoots for honor and loves like a Romeo." With a few modifications that just about describes the picture. As such it is similar to the many others turned out in past months by this popular star.

The Mix films always avoid falling directly into the "ordinary Western" category. Either the has a few twists out of the ordinary, the comedy situations are really relieving or the general atmosphere is more in keeping with a comparatively better grade picture. Besides, Tom himself, although hardly of the "Romeo" type, is usually a distinctive actor, sometimes almost suggesting Will Rogers in his dryly humorous mannerisms.

"Mile-a-Minute Romeo" has three instead of the usual two men in love with the same girl. At first Mix is John Alden, who speaks and acts for his friend, but when he finds the latter has been tricking him he decides to land her himself. And he does with no further trouble than to show his rivals where to get off.

A good touch is inserted when Mix stops on his way back to the girl to get a justice of the peace. He picks the meanest one in the State and is forced to use strenuous means to get the scoundrel to accompany him. At the point of a pistol the justice is forced to allow himself to be tied to a little buggy, which, in turn, is attached to Mix's horse. The ride that follows is vastly amusing, with the buggy being dragged through swamps and marshes, over bumps and around sharp corners, until finally the wheels come off. Even then the anxious bridegroom does not let up, and when the justice finally arrives, most of his defiant spirit has vanished into thin air.

Mix demonstrates some of his best horsemanship. At one time he effects an escape from a surrounded spot by galloping through the hostile forces suspended on the side of his horse, with a dozen other horses circling around him, so that he is completely out of sight. A fall, in which both he and "Tony," the steed that is now billed in all his pictures, roll over an embankment, approached the sensational.

If there is any serious fault to be found it is that Lucky Pill (Mr. Mix) is entirely too illiterate and coarse-grained a man for a girl as refined and delicate as the heroine to fall for. His speech, as given in the subtitles, is the final word in rough Western lingo, such a specimen as "This gat is gonna render you defunct," being comparatively genteel.

Betty Jewel is Mix's leading lady and very acceptable. The others are the same, as is the direction and photography. Mix devotees should welcome this as one more in the long series, and even those who ordinarily dislike Westerns won't be particularly incensed by it.

CROSSED TRAILS

Jesse J. Goldburg production released by Independent Pictures Corp. Story by James Ormont. Directed by J. P. McGowan. At Loew's New York, N. Y., April 8 as half the bill. Runs 54 minutes.

The Hero......Franklyn Farnum
J. M. Anders......William Buehler
George Moran......V. L. Barnes
Buck Sloman......Mack Wright
Mary......Alyce Mills

"Crossed Trails," in spite of the work of its likable star, Franklyn Farnum, is a picture that measures up as something less than mediocre. Farnum, acting without all the heroics of the majority of the Western school of heroes, is refreshing with his straightforward portrayal, and when he fights he looks as though he's going to it in earnest.

But this vehicle is pitifully weak. Farnum plays an agent for a stage coach company, whose task it is to straighten out matters along the route in a hard-boiled section of the West. He is forced to wipe out a band of crooks, and even persecute the father of the girl in order to carry out his duty. After two murders and innumerable chases and scuffles, he not only gets the girl but is reunited with his mother, thought dead.

The meager plot covers practically all the side details of the picture. The runaway and halting of the stage coach is very crudely done, as is a leap on horseback into a river and a resultant struggle in the water.

The film makes no effort at comedy, but it is a question whether none at all is not better than the brand usually attempted in pictures of this sort. Besides Farnum, as the hero, there is one outstanding villain. The rest of the male characters are colorless. So much so in fact, that any audience will have trouble differentiating between three or four of them all playing parts in the action. This lack of character types is perhaps the picture's most serious fault.

Even the photography cannot be pointed out as impressive. A weak sister, this, and one that will handicap a program.

THE MARTYR SEX

Produced by Phil Goldstone. Scenario by Jefferson Moffett. Directed by Duke Worne. Story by Leete Renick Browne. Photographed by Roland Price. At the New York (one day) April 8 as half the bill. Runs about an hour.

Horseshoe Sam......William Dyer
Dr. Ross Wayne......William Fairbanks
Branch Paxton......Les Bates
His wife......Billie Bennett
Beulah Paxton......Dorothy Revier
Lem Paxton......Pat Harmon
Ed Carter......Frank Hagney

Stories of the squatters of Kentucky, Tennessee and the Carolinas have been among the most important contributions to the American drama recently. There have been "Sun-up" and "Hell-bent for Heaven" on the stage and "Driven" and "Tolerable David" on the screen, as well as several others equally meritorious.

These people are interesting because, despite all their uncouth and ignorant ways, they are romantic and different, particularly to those who have never had any dealings with them.

"The Martyr Sex" takes advantage of that and measures up as well above the average program film drab in entertainment.

Dr. Wayne (William Fairbanks), a young doctor, is called to an outlying cabin in the Southern hills to treat a squatter, wounded in a feud fight. This is Branch Paxton. With his son, Lem, he is continually abusing the mother and daughter, Beulah, of the family. When the doctor arrives, he finds Paxton in a bad way and is forced to amputate an arm to have his life. At the same time he warns the family the daughter must be given rest and quiet if she is to live.

Paxton, on recovering, swears vengeance on the doctor, believing in his ignorance and hate, that the latter amputated the member out of sheer malice. When thhe doctor calls again on the old man, his son and Ed Carter, a renegade friend with an eye on the girl, decide to "get" him.

There follows an outstanding incident when the doctor escapes with the girl to a shack in the woods. Immediate blood transfusion is all that can save her by that time, and Wayne prepares to operate on himself. Just then the three squatters attack the cabin.

The doctor tricks Lem into the cabin and forcibly performs the transfusion operation upon him. The others force an entrance before the work is completed, but are kept from interrupting by the splendid force and fearlessness of the doctor's will.

From then on things clear up and the ending is very happy, too much so in fact, as to appear to be synthetically injected hokum.

Fairbanks gives a sterling performance as the doctor, while a newcomer, Dorothy Revier, displays a strikingly picturesque beauty and some ability. Others are good and the direction of Duke Worne most praiseworthy.

A program leader for the average house and an oasis in these days of dry productions.

GAMBLING WIVES

Arrow production. Directed by Dell Henderson. Supervised by Ben Wilson. Written by Ashley T. Locke and adapted by Leota Morgan. Featuring Marjorie Daw. At the New York (one day), April 3. Runs 77 minutes.

Ann Forest......Marjorie Daw
The baby......Dorothy Brock
Vincent Forest......Edward Earle
Reggie Travers......Lee Moran
Sylvia Baldwin......Betty Francisco
Polly Barker......Florence Lawrence
Duke Baldwin......Joe Girard
Van Merton......Ward Crane
Madame Zoe......Hedda Hopper

"Gambling Wives" is nothing more or less than a fairly interesting but too drawn out rehash of the subject modern novelists, playwrights and picture producers seem to have chosen as their favorite theme. Once more is a young couple buffeting the storms of matrimony, almost crashing on the rocks of scandal and divorce, and finally extricating themselves just in time to live as happily ever after.

It has become a pet theory of many of the modern school of writers that the years between the first anniversary of marriage and the tin wedding are inevitably fraught with some domestic rash that almost disrupts the entire home.

"Gambling Wives" comes under the series of stories headed by "Lawful Larceny," to which its bears quite a resemblance, lacking only the big final kick of the Shipman piece.

Hubby has become bored with his wife and baby, and seeks diversion while the better half waits at home, thinking he's working. But his liking for cards soon changes to a more dangerous affection for Madame Zoe, owner of the palatial gambling house. She's the kind that he should forget only playing him to get her blase sweetie, Van Merton, ardently jealous.

Little wife finally learns the truth and like all good movie heroines decides to trim her bad husband at his own game. She sets her hooks for Van Merton, and by means of the "sweet and simple" stuff wins his devoted attention.

Things look blacker than usual for this sort of picture, and it is not until the jealous Madame Zoe dispatches Van Merton to southern regions with a dagger that the domestic clouds vanish.

In its important points the plot, as may be seen, is far from original. Dell Henderson has inserted some clever bits into the direction, however, and the cast holds a handful of prominent people. Marjorie Daw as the wife manages to look sweet, demure and wistful and at times almost worried and undecided. But in her general acting she is an expressionless as ever. Edward Earle too is colorless as the husband. Ward Crane is the suave knave who will haunt the dreams of flappers and Hedda Hopper (now through with De Wolf and going seriously in for the vamp stuff) may have the same effect on the masculine.

A bathing pool scene with one-piece beauties disporting in and out of the water is a boxoffice point to be recorded although the feature picture of this type that does not have one is rare indeed. The long running time of 77 minutes is caused chiefly by an extraordinarily slow introduction with more than a quarter of an hour consumed before the characters are firmly planted.

In the average house they will consider this film just one more screen dissertation on early conjugal difficulties, but since that has always been a popular subject and the picture is moderately well presented, it should bring in its quota of money to Arrow.

STORM DAUGHTER

Universal Jewel production starring Priscilla Dean. Directed by George Archainbaud and photographed by Jules Cronjager. Story by Leet Renick Brown. Cast includes Tom Santschi, William B. Davidson, J. Farrell McDonald, Bert Roach and Alfred Fisher. Runs about 70 minutes.

"The Storm Daughter" should go far in establishing George Archainbaud as a director of sea pictures, as it is a conspicuously good film of that type. Archainbaud heretofore has done little exceptional, but in this case he has turned out a picture that ranks as one of the most absorbing program productions seen in months.

The director had to work with a conventional though somewhat gripping plot but was fortunate in gathering around him an extraordinarily good company of screen troupers.

Priscilla Dean, the only woman, and apparently in but two costumes throughout, a plain fisherwoman's black dress and a considerably more colorful Chinese outfit, has found a role that suits her rather tempestuous thespian qualities ideally. Yet her work is overshadowed by that of Tom Santschi as the brutal sea captain whose regeneration forms the basis of the story. His is a splendid performance throughout in a part that until the very end is extremely unsympathetic.

No little portion of the success of the picture is attributable to the work of the various members of the crew of the schooner upon which practically all the action takes place. All of the romantic types are included—the rough and ready Irish mate with a heart of gold, the simple and devout Swedish "squarehead," the decadent British gentleman, and, even for comedy purposes only, the little Hebrew who pays the "Irisher" five dollars he owes him when assured the vessel is sinking. All these types are exaggerated and a long way removed from the artistically drawn men of the sea of such masters as Conrad, Masefield and Eugene O'Neill. But for this type of picture they are almost perfect, supplying a series of diversified incidents crammed with heart interest.

There are also some striking scenes in a waterfront dive, with the bar women and the habitues all impressing as most colorful types. The storm scenes, forming the physical climax of the picture, are apparently real and to a certain extent thrilling, but it would have been better had the action been more discernible.

Rescues, struggles and deaths all going on in the rain and darkness but the infrequent flashes of lightning do not permit anyone to recognize those carrying on the action. It is not until the next morning that it becomes evident that all but the captain and the girl are drowned.

As the picture ends she forgives all his abuse and brutality and agrees to help him start all over again with love in his heart instead of hate.

Only the ultra-ultra houses are too good for this one. In most other theatres they'll like it immensely.

PAYING THE LIMIT

Gerson production, featuring Ora Carew. Written and directed by Tom Gibson. At the Stanley one day, April 7. Runs 57 minutes.

The Girl ....Ora Carew
Joan Lowden ....Helen Nowell
Thunder Lowden ....Eddy O'Brien
Jerry Davis.............Arthur Wellington
Tom Dover ....Jay Morley
Ole ....Stanley Standford
Baptiste Tudor ....Dick Stevens

In a season of particularly vapid program pictures "Paying the Limit" has the dubious distinction of being one of the worst. There is no redeeming feature, unless it be the rather appealing work of the featured player, Ora Carew. Miss Carew at one time knocked on the gates of stardom and, although her work would hardly justify her entrance into the ranks of the big luminaries, she makes a very satisfactory leading woman. She has beauty, which in this sort of film, is about half of what is needed, and some little emotional ability besides.

Otherwise one may search in vain for a bright spot. The story is of a girl "Raffles" finally caught and sent to jail, with the picture opening on her release from the penal institution with the determination to go straight.

A few of the inconsistencies had even the far-from-discriminating audience at the Stanley laughing. "Paying the Limit" seems to be headed only for the smallest and even the film-goers in those theatres are likely to leave grumbling.

THE WOLF MAN

William Fox production starring John Gilbert. Story by Frederick and Fanny Hatton. Directed by Edmund Mortimer. Shown at Loew's New York, N. Y., on double feature bill April 11, 1924. Running time, 55 minutes.

Gerald Stanley.?..............John Gilbert
Elizabeth Gordon.........Elizabeth Shearer
Beatrice Joyce................Alma Frances
Phil Joyce ....Max Montisole
Sir Reginald Stackpoole......Edgar Norton

Just a little program production that seems to start off as though it was going to be a real tale, but does a flop before the finish and ends rather abruptly. Judging from the characters programmed by the regular press sheet and those shown in the picture, the tale must have been changed materially from the original and revamped after the picture was made. For the small houses where there is a daily change this will do well enough on double feature programs and satisfy on the strength of its whale of a fight.

It is a tale of a young Englishman who gets real rough when in liquor, and every time he places his monocle in his eye it's a sign of trouble. He gets stewed at his farewell dinner. The boys are sending him off royally, for he is to be married, and he has a fight with the brother of his intended. On the way home the two quarrel again. The finish is that the brother is found dead the next morning on the street in front of the house of the bad boy.

He goes to Canada, becoming a lumberjack, but stays off "the stuff" until he hears from London the girl of his dreams has married his brother. That starts him. He kidnaps a girl and makes off with her. Finally he is run down, and about to be lynched, when the girl intercedes and saves him. There the picture ends.

Fred.

Foreign Films

THE NIBELUNGEN

Berlin, March 20.

The first part of this two-sectioned film, centered about the Nibelungen legends, appeared at the Ufa Palast am Zoo under the title of "Siegfried," and was received with respect if not with acclaim. This film, which came out through the Decla Bioscop, and was directed by Fritz Lang, is the result of almost two years' work.

Perhaps its chief clair to fame lies in the fact that not a single scene in the whole 16 reels was taken outdoors; but all exteriors were built and photographed in a studio. The film will undoubtedly do a good business in Germany, as these stories about which it turns are part of the life of every German; but even the Germans had to admit that, as a whole, they found it rather boresome. For an American public it seems very problematical entertainment.

The story of the Nibelungen is known to all Americans who have attended the Ring operas by Wagner, but the present version is somewhat different, leaning more heavily on the original folk tales.

Siegfried, the son of King Siegmund of the Netherlands, has gone to learn to make weapons with Mime, a dwarf, who lived in the woods. There he forges a sword and sets out to win Kriemhild of Burgund, of whose beauty he has heard tell. On the way he kills a dragon, in whose blood he bathes himself, thus making himself unwoundable, except on his shoulder, where during the bath a leaf has fallen. Siegfried arrives at Worms, on the Rhine, where Kriemhild lives with her brother, King Gunther, and asks for her hand. Gunther, advised by his chief warrior, Hagen, agrees to grant the request if Siegfried will help him win Queen Brunhilde of Isenland, who can only be won by the most powerful hero.

They set out together, and Gunther, with the aid of Siegfried, wins the queen as his bride. This latter feat he accomplishes by putting on the tarncap, which makes him invisible, and thus he is able, unseen, to help Gunther perform the various feats of strength which give him the right to take Brunhilde away as his bride. (This tarncap he has won from the dwarf Alberich, along with a lot of gold, during one of his adventures.)

The cast, as a whole, was composed of little known and inexpensive actors, but they all did competently, and in some cases exceptionally. Especially to be mentioned are the King Gunther of Theodor Loos, the Hagen of Hans Schlettow, and the Brunhilde of Hanna Ralph. Paul Richter fulfilled at least the physical requirements of his part as Siegfried. The star is unquestionably Otto Hunte, who designed the scenery, and was brilliantly supported by the photography of Karl Hoffmann. Practically all the sets are successful, while many, particularly the exteriors, seem to strike an entirely new mood in tone and atmosphere.

Fritz Lang's direction is consistent, and achieves plasticity, dignity, and very nearly power—very nearly because, sadly enough, the film lacks a final kick. It just does not quite get there, and we feel this is due to the fact that the director and scenario writer, Thea von Harbou, were just a little afraid of their subject, treated it with respect where they should have gotten enthusiastic about it.

It left the German audience cold; will leave all audiences cold; that is the final analysis.

Owing to the Ufa's power as a releasing organization in Germany, it will be shown everywhere here and will undoubtedly do good business. There seems, however, little chance of it ever returning the money spent on its production.

Trask.

CARLOS AND ELISABETH

Berlin, March 20.

This latest production of Richard Oswald, at his own film theatre at the Kantstrasse, showed tremendous advances in the scenic investiture, the costumes, and the photography; but Mr. Oswald has made no advances as a director of acting, and as he was not successful in choosing the right types (in which case they would have played the parts for him) the film does not convince except in very rare moments.

The story is claimed to be taken from Spanish history, but is really nothing more than a free version of Schiller's "Don Carlos." It relates the story of Carlos, the crown prince of Spain, who loves Elisabeth Valois.

Of the whole cast, only one figure was really successful, that of Aud Egede Nissen as Eboli; Eugen Kloepfer lacked entirely the distinction necessary for Philip; and Conrad Veidt as Carlos was bad.

A hurrah must be given for the photography of Sparkuhl and Hasselmann, and most of all for the scenery and costumes of O. F. Werndorff.

For an American public the film has little appeal, but American directors and designers should not miss an opportunity to take a look at it.

Trask.

HELENA

Berlin, March 24.

"Helena," a classical spectacular film in two five-reel sections, has appeared here at the Mozart Saal. It is the production of the Emelka Co. of Munich, with the direction by Manfred Noa.

It tells the story of the fall of Troy as related in Homer's Illiad.

The film is lacking in novelty of conception. One not knowing its origin, would believe that it had been made in Italy 10 years ago.

There was the usual rushing about of great masses of costumed supers, but nobody seemed to know why, or to care much, for that matter.

The only interesting performance was that of Achilles by the strong man, Carlo Aldini. He was the only one of the whole cast who had anything Greek about him. When he picked up a couple of extras and threw them over the fence his actions carried more than superficial conviction.

Trask.

THE GREAT WELL

London, April 6.

Stage plays do not always benefit in screen adaptation, but this picturization of Alfred Sutro's work, produced by Matheson Lang at the New in 1922, is an exception. It is better as a film than it was as a play.

The producer, Henry Kolker, and the scenarist, Louis Stevens, are directly responsible. They have handled a mediocre "triangle" story with great skill and the result is a gripping drama. At first the action is slow and dragging, but it is carefully worked up, incident piled upon incident, until at the end the picture is holding its audience.

The one defect the feature has is in its women. Seena Owen is cold, hard, unsympathetic. Her Camilla is about the last woman breathing that men would give their hearts to and risk honor for, while Joan Morgan is utterly negligible.

The story tells how Pater Starling, a wealthy oil magnate, married Camilla, who is really in love with his pal, Darenth. Darenth is a cad, although a brave man, and Starling's strict attention to business leaves Camilla much in his company.

Comes a change in the Starling fortunes, the "Great Well" gives out and ruin faces the company. In touch with shady stock brokers, Darenth persuades Camilla to tell him the contents of the cable her husband has received. He sells the information.

The shares drop lower and lower, panic seizes the shareholders, but at the last moment Starling receives news which saves the situation. He forces the truth from a scoundrelly stock broker and returns home to have it out with his wife. She admits her treachery, but denies Darenth is her lover.

Darenth turns up and supports her word. Starling is about to strangle him when he remembers how Darenth saved him in France. Darenth, still plucky, clears the way by shooting himself, but only succeeds in putting his friend in the dock at the Old Bailey on a charge of murder. All the evidence is against Starling, but Camilla swears Darenth was her lover and the "unwritten law" does the rest. Husband and wife eventually come together again.

The production is exceptionally good. Kolker has seized every opportunity given him by the story and has created others. His Old Bailey scenes are the best and most realistic of the English screen, and the most minute detail has been carefully noted. The Stock Exchange scenes are also very good. Throughout the picture shows proof of a remarkable attention to the little things which, built up, make the big ones. The photography and lighting are alike excellent.

All the male characters are well played. Thurston Hall is very sound and convincing as Starling, as is Lawford Davidson as Darenth. These two players practically control the action of the picture.

Gore.

OLD BILL THROUGH THE AGES

London, April 2.

The synopsis of this new Ideal film explains the feature is just burlesque—"English history seen through the distorting mirror of Captain Bairnsfather's inimitable humor."

Bairnsfather has provided a story which might have been fine burlesque, but which, under the control of its filmic producer, has become only too often little more than crude slap-stick.

Thomas Bentley, the producer, has had the opportunities of a lifetime, but has not always lived up to them. Once, at least, he becomes almost blasphemous. This in the "Lest We Forget" scene, with its Cenotaph effect, immediately followed by the hero's mournful mention of the famous "plum and apple."

Bairnsfather has provided opportunities without number in this too lengthy feature (7,800 feet), and there is but little doubt that when cut it will provide unlimited hilarity.

"Old Bill' is in the days of William the Conqueror, as one of King John's barons at the signing of Magna Charta; as a cavalier of the days of Charles; as an Elizabethan courtier, until, in this year of grace and thirst, we find hi man American bootlegger.

All the episodes are well devised, and the costuming is excellent, save where the costumes of long ago are made to mingle with those of today—to win a laugh.

Throughout the settings and photography are far above the average.

Syd Walker is really good as Old Bill, and is ably supported by Arthur Cleve as Bert and Jack Denton as Alf. Bruce Bairnsfather is a British officer, "himself." A host of other parts are all well played.

Excellent laughing stuff as it is, in places the chief attraction will be the name of the famous hero, Old Bill, a name that will probably live long after some of the late war's living heroes are forgotten.

Gore.

EUGENE ARAM

London, March 25.

Lord Lytton is primarily to blame for this. Had he not seen in the story of a Yorkshire murderer's tragedy the material for a novel, which in due course became a play, we should never have had this latest Granger - Davidson attempt to brighten Wardour street.

It would appear at the outset the producer called his company together and said although the corpse was still warm the funeral was the great thing, more he impressed this attitude upon them until they became absorbed in it.

The result is a picture of almost undiluted morbidity and the mourners enter so thoroughly into the spirit of the tragedy, are so monotonous, stagey and insincere the thing soon loses grip and never regains it.

The Almighty, who provided the exteriors, and the cameraman are the only things which give this screen "Eugene Aram" a fighting chance for popularity.

The story, a combination of history and fiction in which Aram is made a heroic figure, is well told as far as continuity goes. It keeps strictly to legend and is provided with the conventional happy ending by the simply process of having another set of lovers, the leading character having previously been hanged.

The cast is good, although Arthur Wontner is not an ideal Aram. To be a West End legitimate leading man is one thing, to get it over on the silent screen is another. Walter Tennyson is unsatisfactory as Walter Lester.

Really sound performances come from Bromley Devonport, Lionel D'Aragon, James Carew and C. V. France, while Barbara Hoffe and Mary Odette are excellent in the feminine roles. The dressing is good. *Gore.*

HURRICAINE HUTCH :

London, March 21.

The explanation of this new Ideal feature starring the American "stunt" artist Hurricane Hutch, is in the title. The whole thing is crude melodrama and merely an excuse for exploiting the player and his acrobatics. Some of the stunts will thrill the pit and gallery while providing mirth for the more intelligent section of the house. Some come perilously near burlesque.

The story: After many years Frank Mitchell is about to return home. This annoys his wicked cousin who has hoped to usurp his place and the annoyance grows when old Mitchell leaves everything to Frank on condition he marries Nancy Norris.

While on the vayage Frank and his faithful friend are shipwrecked and Frank is left for dead.

Here is Hutch's chance to get busy with the raw meat. He impersonates Frank. Meanwhile the wicked cousin has imprisoned Mitchell in the "old mill" until he gives him power of attorney over the estate.

Hutch arrives and falls in love with Nancy. He suspects the plotters, they suspect him, and try to murder him but are easily foiled. Frank arrives and poses as Hutch's secretary. Hutch goes to the mill at night and promptly falls into the trap laid by the conspirators who lure Nancy away and compel the old man to sign documents. Frank rescues Hutch and the two pursue the villain to London.

This is what we have been waiting for. Hutch chases locomotives, falls from them, has a fight, gets a car and again goes in pursuit of the train, falls from a bridge, prevents a collision and does all sorts of things while the watcher almost forgets what the story is about.

In the end Nancy tells Frank it is Hutch she loves and the grateful old man makes their love possible by settling a handsome income of the train-chaser.

Railway scenes are rare in British pictures and the ones in these adventures are excellently done. The exterior work is good, some of it even beautiful. Hutchison's British company gives capital support, the players being Malcolm Tod, Warwick Ward, Lionelle Howard, Bob Vallis and Edith Thornston.

At times they appear to be more humor in some of the situations than necessary and fail to get the sincerity which helps to get features of this class over. *Gore.*

TRIUMPH

Paramount picture and a Cecil B. De Mille production. Features Leatrice Joy and Rod La Rocque. Directed by De Mille. Adapted from the magazine story of May Edginton. Showing at the Rivoli, New York, week of April 20. Running time, 88 minutes.

Ann Land	Leatrice Joy
King Garnet	Rod La Rocque
William Silver	Victor Varconi
James Martin	Charles Ogle
Varinoff	Theodore Kosloff
Samuel Overton	Robert Edeson
Countess Rika	Julia Faye
David Garnet	George Fawcett
Torrini	Spottiswoode Aitken
A factory girl	Zasu Pitts
A tramp	Raymond Hatton
The flower girl	Alma Bennett
A painter	Jimmie Adams

A corking re'ease that will stand up upon the work of the players, but a credit to the entire personnel concerned in the making.

Two minutes shy of an hour and a half in running time the feature could undoubtedly assume deletion without a harmful effect although De Mille has so routined the continuity that the story never becomes an out-and-out burden. It is in a minor number of prolonged closeups and in the repetition of a few stereotyped bits that the scissors might have been manipulated to advantage.

Productionally, the film conforms to the De Mille tradition in that the settings are more likely to be overdressed than sparce as to impression. The camera man, unmentioned, is also entitled to a bow for an excellent piece of work which includes a couple of new angles that are certain to receive impersonation by many.

Of the cast there are three distinct standpoints, Miss Joy La Rocque and Varconi, with the men overshadowing the girl on actual performance. The trio comprise the proverbial "blanket finish" as to effort, and if the definition is to become additionally stringent laurel wreaths may be addressed, sealed, signed and delivered to La Rocque. It's his picture.

The name of Varconi sounds new and should he be a recent acquisition to the studios this particular donation will establish him, and it marks something else for many of the Coast male celluloid contingent to worry about. Cast as an intermediate anarchist, with a chance to "dog it" as regards wearing apparel, Varconi struts through this theme to make it look a made-to-order role.

La Rocque is all over the screen as a wealthy spendthrift, a park bum, and finally as a normal example of American citizenship. This juvenile is building up a following for himself through successive and creditable performances, giving indications of reaching that strength where the name solos in front of the theatre. La Rocque may ruin a few masculine and egotistical personal opinions in a witnessing audience on the subject of appearance, but the girls gasp, and where they go the boys generally go, too, and like it, making it suitable for La Rocque, who must know Jack Buchanan.

There's nothing exceptional in the story other than the action is well sprinkled with laughs in telling of a tin manufacturer who dies and leaves a will stating that if his son doesn't settle down within two years the source of income, the factory, shall pass to the manager of the plant, unknowingly from every angle, also a son of the old codger by a secret marriage.

Little ambition to work and plenty of currency does away with any intention of labor on the part of King (La Rocque), with the business subsequently falling into his stepbrother's hands. Both having been, and being, in love with the forewoman (Miss Joy), who has operatic inclinations, the financial situation is reversed at the expiration of the time limit. Follows the girl's theatrical success abroad, after which smoke from a fire stifles her voice forever whence she returns home, under a promise to marry the former manager, but still in love with the previous president, who is now but an employee in the same factory.

Mismanagement of funds and impassioned declarations have the trio within the main office, where takes place the switch to the original status and the betrothal of King and the girl, with the stepbrother sworn to work in close harmony ever after.

DeMille couldn't resist philosophizing in the sub-titles, and if there's a moral in the picture it's well buried under the entertaining qualities revealed. Which may not speak so well for the film's uplift movement, but is certain to be remunerative.

The release has only the two weaknesses of duration and a slowing up of the script pace at the finish. However, it would still be above par with a conglomeration of other faults simply on the strength of the cast. *Skig.*

WORLD STRUGGLE FOR OIL

Semi-educational picture, produced by the Bureau of Mines of the United States Department of the Interior in co-operation with the Harry S. Sinclair Oil Corporation. Presented by H. E. Butler. Shown at the Cameo, New York, week of April 20, 1924. Running time, 48 minutes.

The picture causing considerable hubbub about for several weeks. When first offered to theatres along Broadway, there was accompanying the proposal to spend $5,000 in advertising the picture to the public.

The picture is to a great extent an educational, but at this time, when there is so widespread a general interest on the part of the public in the oil situation and the oil lands, it is worth while. The Teapot Dome oil land scandal, together with the inquiry in Washington, has whetted public interest in just the situation that this picture shows the complete detail of.

At present the picture seems a little too long. If there were about 18 minutes cut from it, it would be available to a greater extent. It isn't a picture that one can play to the exclusion of their regular feature, but, in conjunction with it, the oil film should prove a box-office help.

It is in reality a history of oil from the Biblical days to the present. The beginning shows the instructions to Noah to fill the chinks of the Ark with pitch, and from that point down the ages of history the part that oil has played to the beginning of the automobile days, the great amount used and the tremendous part played by oil-driven vehicles in the World War, the driving of the transatlantic ships, and now the home usages of oil for light and heat.

In showing the various oil fields and the pipe lines now down and those proposed in this country, there is a dotted line in one of the maps that shows a pipe line to be laid from Teapot Dome to St. Louis.

There is a lot of statistical matter shown in the picture as to consumption of oil in various parts of the world that could be easily eliminated. *Fred.*

SECOND YOUTH

Distinctive Production. Released by Goldwyn. Adapted from the novel by Allan Updegraff by John Lynch. Directed by Albert Parker. At the Cameo, New York, week April 20, together with "World Struggle for Oil." Running time, 63 minutes.

Mr. Francis	Alfred Lunt
Anne Winton	Mimi Palmeri

Mrs. Benson...............Jobyna Howland
McNab......................Walter Catlett
Whigam...................Herbert Corthell
Rose Bauman..............Lynn Fontaine
Phoebe.....................Winifred Allen
Mr. Remick................Lumsden Hare
Helen Remick...............Faire Binney

Fairly amusing little program feature that just falls short of being a comedy wow. With the cast it should have been one of the pictures of the year had the story and the direction reached the strength of the names, but as it fails in this respect, credit must be given to the players for having pulled the picture through.

Originally the story by Allan Updegraff must have had a lot of laughs which neither the script writer nor the director could kill. They do crop out here and there in the action.

The tale is one of a retiring silk salesman in a department store, who is much pursued by women, from the landlady of his boarding house right along the line to the steno in the buyer's office, and the heiress bent on a lark who flirts with him over the counter and finally falls 'for him at the end of the picture. But not until he is entangled with the boarding house mistress who holds him up for $500 for her shattered heart, the steno, who finally decides to marry a plumber from the Bronx, and the boss' daughter who thought he didn't look so bad after all.

Alfred Lunt plays the bashful salesman and gives him a doleful professional pallbearer appearance in the early part that brings laughs.

Jobyna Howland as the boarding house woman looks wonderful on the screen and puts over a majority of the laughs in this character. Herbert Corthell working with her at times is a splendid foil.

Mimi Palmeri looks decidedly pretty and has improved somewhat in acting since her first picture. Her vamping bit got over very nicely and she looks to be right in line for one of those flighty flapper roles if she is properly handled. One of those and she'll be assured as a box office draw. Lynn Fontaine, Winifred Allen and Faire Binney all contribute in looks and small bits in the picture.

The photography and lighting are far from good,and the tinting of the print at the Cameo almost ruins the picture entirely.

YANKEE MADNESS

Produced, written and directed by Charles R. Seeling. Photographed by Pliny Goodfriend. Released by F. B. O. At the New York, April 15. Runs 64 minutes.
Robert Morton...,............Arthur Millett
Cicero......................Tom Wilson
Richard Morton............George Larkin
Dolores.....................Billie Dove
Rodolpho....................Earl Schenck
Teresa......................Ollie Kirby
Esteban...................Manuel Camere
Pablo Delgado...............Walter Long

It seems that directors do not often make writers and that producers seldom make either. Charles R. Seeling has tried to be all three with the usual results. He is most successful on the producing end, as he has turned out a film that has considerable box office lure if exploited properly in the cheaper houses.

His story is emaciated and his direction so amateurish that even a cast of moderately well-known players cannot make it seem logical or effective. It is another of the musical comedy revolution plots. Its chief fault is that it lacks the subtle irony and humor of others that preceded it.

"Yankee Madness" has one or two of these spots, principally when Walter Long, as the native "bad man," becomes inebriated and starts to raise local cain. Long has hardly more than a bit, but his work dominates the picture. Tom Wilson has the other comedy role, but he fails

to win many laughs with his "scared darky" mannerisms, which are always the same.

George Larkin and Billie Dove are the leads. The girl is sweet in an unimportant part. Larkin, once famed as a king of serials and stunt pictures, shows nothing strenuous except the numerous fights with the villains. Otherwise he does not measure up as a particularly happy choice for a hero, displaying some atrocious taste in sartorial matters and very little emotional ability.

Shots of a fiesta and a cabaret scene, with Larkin doing a tango, add some slight interest. The work of the extra men and women throughout is noticeably bad.

However, they've picked a commercial title and some fair "names," and the picture may rake in a little money.

ARIZONA EXPRESS

Fox production, directed by Thomas Buckingham and written by Lincoln J. Carter. Cast includes Pauline Starke, Evelyn Brent, David Butler, Anne Cornwall, Francis McDonald and Harold Goodwin. At Loew's New York, April 17. Runs 76 minutes.

Chalk one up for Fox. "The Arizona Express" is pointed directly at the box office and its aim is sure. Furthermore, in spite of an excess of physical thrills in the last reel, it is a neat job throughout, and in spite of its 76 minutes it never drags. In fact, there are moments when the picture "gets" one, even though the obvious intention was to turn out a good action film.

Right at the start things look interesting. David Butler, cast as a romantic young mail clerk on the Arizona express, is seen getting his daily quota of sentiment by whiffing the perfumed letters in the mail he is assorting. His chance for adventure comes when he has the opportunity to help a girl, such as he has dreamed about (Pauline Starke), establish the innocence of her doomed brother. The latter has been "railroaded" to prison after an unfortunate affair with a dancer in which his uncle has been murdered, in reality by the heavy, but according to circumstantial evidence by the boy himself.

The story is not the outstanding quality of the picture, but rather it is the masterful handling of most of the various incidents. There is a scene in which an entire prison springs into revolt after cunningly laid plans. They drive a stone train through the jail wall to form an exit.

Another scene carrying a tremendous kick is a death struggle between the villain and the heavy in the girl's room. The lights are all out and the battle is illuminated only by intermittent flashes of lightning. That in itself is nothing new, but the fierceness with which the fight is waged and the striking pictorial values are corking.

During the last few moments the film deteriorates into a savage series of one scrap after another. However, that won't hurt the box offi appreciably, particularly since everything from a complete train to an auto load of humans plunges sensationally over a precipice.

The entire picture is a credit to Thomas Buckingham, the director. Even at the end when the old, hackneyed situation of staying the electrocution of the boy at the last minute comes up, he shows artistry and originality.

Butler and Miss Starke both do well, but they must surrender honors to Harold Goodwin as the brother and Evelyn Brent as the dancer, two remarkably good performances. The balance of the cast, continuity and photography, are all splendid.

The name "Arizona Express" is an unfortunate selection, sounding like a "western," and the picture is far removed from the average of that category.

FALL OF AN EMPRESS

London, April 10.
The censor having discovered suggestion, or something of the sort, in the title, "Messalina," the latest big Italian film to be shown here, is known as "The Fall of an Empress." It is a big film, much too big in every way. Its very vastness is wearying, and its length well nigh unbearable.

For three hours the audience was compelled to watch Messalina's love affairs, the love affairs of an Egyptian princess with a cultivated taste for sadism and the pure love of two slaves. The male slave was really the cause of the trouble. Messalina wanted him, so did the Princess Mirit. He smirked at both like a Wardour street shop assistant, but announced his purity when the ladies proposed getting to cues. In the end he was discovered to be a Persian prince, and all the amorous wenches having been wiped out, true love got its film reward.

The story is badly told. Scenically the picture is fine, and no more beautiful settings have ever been seen. Crowds running into thousands fill the reelage and speedily lose their interest, although their direction is brilliant. The acting is not good. Messalina is portrayed by the Countess Lina de Liguoro, the Egyptian princess by Gianni Terribilli Gonzales, and the slave girl by Lucia Zanussi. All three women depend on the exposure of their physical charms more than on histrionic art. The men are almost all bad. Despite the badness of the story and the poor acting there is little doubt but that this picture, with its magnificent spectacular production, will prove an exceptionally good showman's proposition.

Gore.

THROUGH THE SHADOWS

London, April 11.
It would appear that Italy is out to show she can beat Sweden in sordidness and morbidity. "Through the Shadows" has every feature, yet made, beaten in long drawn out wretchedness and under world realism. Throughout its entire footage there is not a single spot of sunshine, not a ray of relief, and the finale brings no reprieve. All is black horror and nastiness and there is no promise of happiness to come. In this, at least, the producer, Carmine Gallone, has had the courage of his convictions. Despite his sordidness he never goes out to create a suggestive situation, and there is no bit of business in the feature at which the most prudish could take offense. He has taken dirt and shown it as dirt, not as a chocolate-coated confection smothered in cheap scent, paint and powder.

Bijou runs away from a circus to escape the attentions of its proprietor. She finds shelter in a wretched cafe, and is protected by the owner. In the place is a half-starved violinist, and the two fall in love. Another customer is a drunken haridan, always searching for her lost daughter, and known to all the slum dwellers as "Mother." Bijou is kind to the old woman and wins her affection. After a while the proprietor shows his hand, and poor Bijou has again to run away. She is joined by the expelled violinist, and the two seek a wretched shelter. Here they are found by the old hag, who realizes Bijou is ill and bears her away to her own filthy cellar. There birthmarks prove she is the lost daughter, but the old woman remains silent. The boy gets a job humping coal, and so manages to keep life in his sweetheart. Anon, the rascally cafe proprietor finds out the party's hiding place, decoys the old woman and the boy away, and makes up his mind to assault the sick girl. She is saved by the old

woman, who in protecting her falls and hurts her head. Dying, she tells the girl everything, and there the tragedy ends abruptly.

Carmine Gallone has done his work well. His production is a cheap one, but with a little light and shade he might have turned out a great picture. His studied morbidness prevents this achievement.

Throughout, the acting is far and away above the average, and due to this the picture is worth seeing. Soava Gallone is excellent as the girl. No other names are given, but the players are remarkably good. As a popular attraction, "Through the Shadows" is well nigh hopeless; as an example of how near genius may be approached and just avoided, it is remarkable.

Gore.

BLUFF

A Sam Wood Production presented by Adolph Zukor and Jesse L. Lasky. From the story by Rita Weiman and Josephine L. Quirk, adapted by Willis Goldbeck. Featuring Agnes Ayres and Antonio Moreno. Shown at the Rialto, New York, week April 27, 1924. Running time 57 minutes.

Betty Hallowell	Agnes Ayres
Robert Fitzmaurice	Antonio Moreno
Norton Conroy	E. H. Calvert
Waldo Blakely	Clarence Burton
Mr. Kitchell	Fred Butler
Dr. Curtiss	Jack Gardner
Fifino	Pauline Parquette
Jack Hallowell	Roscoe Karns
Algy Henderson	Arthur Hoyt

"Bluff" is one of those typical "Saturday Evening Post" light fiction tales that reads great but picturizes without a kick, at least as far as the flapper and high school sheik element is concerned. As entertainment it is below the average as a program picture.

Agnes Ayres and Antonio Moreno are featured at the head of a cast that is light, and neither has anything in particular to do.

This picture is hardly one that can be counted on to get any money for the exhibitor.

The story deals with the power of "Bluff" in New York. The heroine is a dress designer who has struggled to make an impression on the Fifth Avenue clothes creators, but has failed. She has a brother who is a cripple as a result of having been run down by the machine of a political boss whom she is trying to support while the two are pressing an action for damages.

Then at the moment when things seem to be breaking bad the girl gets an inspiration from a daily newspaper story in which the disappearance of a famous European leader of fashion who designs her own gowns, is the leading yarn. The picture of the missing woman shows a startling resemblance to the little designer and she decides on a "bluff" that may put over. She takes a suite in a fashionable hotel, buys some startling gown creations and sends for all of the leading dressmakers in town. She is registered under her first name, but because of the resemblance to the fashion leader they take it for granted that it is a subterfuge that she is employing to remain among the missing and finally she closes a contract.

At that moment the police step in. The political leader has had his henchmen among the cops working and they decide that they are going to put the works to the girl. Either she is the missing woman, who by this time is also wanted for having misappropriated funds from the British Red Cross, or if she isn't she has posed as her and obtained a contract and money under false pretenses.

That is the time for the hero to make good and he does that little thing. He is a lawyer, loves the girl and manages to pull another bluff that gets a settlement of $20,000 for the girl's brother and then comes the usualy happy ending.

Light waisted stuff at the best and not handled particularly well in a pictorial way.   *Fred.*

CHASTITY

First National Production, directed by Victor Schertzinger. Story by Ernest Pascal. Edited by Eve Unsell. Featuring Katherine McDonald. At the New York, April 27. Runs 72 minutes.

Norma O'Neill	Katherine McDonald
Nat Mason	J. Gunnis Davis
Sam Wolfe	J. Gordon Russell
Darcy Roche	Huntley Gordon
Fergus Arlington	Frederick Truesdale
Mrs. Harris	Edythe Chapman

Those few film fans who believe posing to be the great art of pictures should revel in First National's "Chastity." The ordinary person, however, who demands some action even in "society" pictures, will label it the most boring production of the year. Certainly a more snail-paced film would be difficult to discover.

Katherine McDonald, in spite of her beauty, cannot pose and stall and drag her way through six long reels. Miss McDonald possesses the minimum amount of that quality called by the fan magazines "sex appeal." Consequently she is largely at a loss in the role she essays to portray in this picture.

She is first seen as an ambitious and thoroughly virtuous young actress who sets out to prove to the world (Barbara La Marr to the contrary) a really great artiste can play the famous roles of wicked women of the drama without becoming a siren herself.

The biggest inconsistency in a story of inconsistencies comes right here. Although she does not in reality become an evil woman, she purposely achieves notoriety and scandal for herself by posing as the **most sophisticated and loose-living woman imaginable.**

The lack of reluctance shown by her uncle, the best friend of her dead father, in accepting her proposition to pose as the man who is keeping her and backing her theatrical ventures, is not only incredulous, but laughable.

If Ernest Pascal was endeavoring to prove that a woman can be good in the eyes of the world and still achieve great dramatic success, he has begged the question entirely and only demonstrated that she can bluff her way into a lot of notoriety without paying the price. There will be many who will decry him even on that supposition.

Victor Schertzinger, who still has to direct a film one-tenth as fine in its line as his song, "Marcheta," has gone back to a lower level than that on which he started some years ago. It is true, however, that he had almost worthless materials on which to work, and some of his recent films, particularly the Coogan productions, show him to be rapidly coming up.

More miscast than Miss McDonald is Huntley Gordon, one of the most virile types in filmdom, playing Darcy Roche, a theatrical producer as sickeningly insipid as his name. Those scenes in which he and the star endeavor to thresh out matters toward the end seem unending and unbearable. Frederick Truesdale, old legit actor, takes all the honors in the impossible role of the uncle-protector.

If there is anything to praise in the picture it is the production itself — up to the First National standard in every detail. There are some striking cabaret shots, and the only bit of physical action, an auto plunging over the Palisades, is well done.

While Katherine McDonald fans have grown accustomed to quiet pictures, this one will put them to sleep.

CUPID'S FIREMAN

Fox production, directed by William Wellman. From the story "Andy McGee's Chorus Girl, by Richard Harding Davis. At Loew's New York, April 22, as half the bill. Runs 57 mins.

Andy McGee	Charles Jones
Agnes Evans	Marion Nixon
Bill	Brooks Benedict
Elizabeth Stevens	Eileen O'Malley
Chief	Al Fremont
Turner	Charles McHugh
Molly Turner	Mary Warner

It seems that every picture of Charles Jones' becomes better, and Cupid's Fireman" is no exception. Considering that it sports the name of Richard Harding Davis as author, it is just a bit disappointing. It starts out with a rush of human interest, but fails to live up to the early promise.

The Davis story is admirably suited to film purposes. McGee is a lad whose ambition is to join the "smoke eaters" and succeed in the path of his father, who died in his boots. The opportunity presents itself, and while doing theatre duty Andy meets Agnes, a specialty dancer. Cupid succeeds the love of smoke in his heart, but disillusion and pain follow when he finds the girl is married to a worthless drunkard.

The climax comes when Andy, after rescuing the girl at a fire in her house, must face the decision of going back after the husband, crazed by booze and responsible for his wife's peril. Duty wins, but the villain is put out of the way by the flames in spite of McGee's heroism.

It is at this potential moment that Wellman falls down in his direction. The wallop is not there. The fire scenes are well put on but show nothing new or sensational. Some earlier shots of the firemen practicing rope-climbing and net jumping pack just as much of a thrill and hold more interest.

Jones' role is hand-tailored and he should double his devotees through his work. Eileen O'Malley rates a special paragraph for herself. Not through any stretch of the imagination might she be called a pretty child, but when it comes to acting she is on a par with the other prodigies. She dances, cries, laughs, pouts and just acts natural, all with a charming appeal.

Marion Nixon strengthens her hold as Jones' leading woman and the balance of the cast do distinctive work. The film is far superior to the former westerns of "Buck" Jones.

THREE DAYS TO LIVE

Gerson picture production, written and directed by Tom Gibson. Starring Ora Carewe. At the Stanley, New York, April 22. Runs 54 mins.

Grace Harmon	Ora Carewe
Bob Raymond	Jay Morley
Wolf Raymond	Dick La Reno
Rajah	Hal Stevens
Hadj	Helen Lowell
Hakim	James Lono

"Three Days to Live" is a slight improvement over a film put out by and with the same people that played the Stanley a few weeks ago. But in spite of the improvement, "Three Days" is many miles from being even a fair picture.

Once again the work of Ora Carewe features the production. Jay Morley, who seems to be her permanent leading man and who is co-featured in the billing, hardly justifies the honor. He is awkward, generally unromantic in the love scenes and unimpressive, despite his huge bulk, in the all-important fight bits. The balance of the cast are less than ordinary, the work of Hal Stevens, the "heavy," being particularly exaggerated and amateurish.

The film gets its title from a warning sent out by the villainous Rajah to three men who had forced him, literally, to kiss the dust after attacking a slave in his native kingdom. He has come to America bent on revenge and before the picture ends he succeeds in doing away with two of them, one the father of the hero. The third, the girl's daddy, also receives the dreaded warning that his days are numbered to three and when the heroine endeavors to save him she herself falls into the oriental's trap.

The usual hoke follows: The near-sheik hisses, "You forget, my proud beauty, that I am master here," and the dauntless little lady responds, "Do what you will with me, but spare his life." The fight that follows when the hero arrives is lukewarm.

The Gerson company would seem to be wasting the efforts of Miss Carewe in mediocre vehicles.

WHEN ODDS ARE EVEN

Fox production starring William Russell. Written by Dorothy Yost and directed by James Flood. At the Circle, April 24, as half the bill. Runs 55 mins.

"When Odds Are Even" is considerably below the William Russell standard, but because of the star's personal magnetism, and some fair maritime atmosphere, it should serve as an adequate program attraction.

For awhile it looks as though some of the colorful atmosphere of the South Sea Isles is included. The action takes place, largely, at the romantically named Port o' Hope, on the island of Pago Tai. Very little local color is flashed. Instead there is a conventional story of two men, rivals for a girl and for the possession of a native mine. When the picture opens the girl is already engaged to the scoundrel. The usual misunderstanding follows, with the hero believing that the girl is framing him.

Russell is likable, although there is little opportunity for anything but physical stuff on his part. He fights a barroom full of ruffians for 10 minutes and the next day appears with a neat bit of court paster over one eye. The balance of the cast holds generally unfamiliar names and performs mediocrely.

Some of the sea shots raise the photography to a picturesque level not reached by the direction and the story. In general, it is a sorry effort and one that neither Russell or Fox can well afford to boast about.

Dorothy Vernon of Haddon Hall

A Mary Pickford Production made for the United Artists Corp. Adapted for the screen by Waldemar Young from the novel by Charles Major. Directed by Marshall Neilan. Opened at the Criterion theatre, New York, May 5, for a run. Running time, 106 minutes.

Dorothy Vernon..............Mary Pickford
Sir George Vernon..........Anders Randolf
Sir Malcolm Vernon......Marc MacDermott
Lady Vernon..................Mme. Daumery
Sir John Manners..............Allan Forrest
Earl of Rutland...............Wilfred Lucas
Queen Elizabeth ....Clare Eames
Mary Queen of Scots.........Estelle Taylor
Earl of Leicester...........Courtenay Foote
Dawson ....Colin Kenny
Jennie Faxton......Lottie Pickford Forrest

Mary Pickford as "Dorothy Vernon of Haddon Hall" made her bow at the Criterion Monday night. It isn't the best or the greatest picture that Miss Pickford has been seen in, but it is mighty good screen entertainment.

The Pickford film is intended to run on Broadway for a long time, according to those that are sponsoring its presentation, otherwise it would be hard to conceive their spending the money they did to transform the front of the theatre into a replica of the original Haddon Hall. This was done at a cost of $21,000, the work being of plaster with a coating of paint to give it the appearance of age. With it there is a corking electrical display that is mighty good advertising. That the men doing the work labored three days and nights while all passersby on the street stood and watched was alone worth the money that the job cost. Imagine the nationwide effect of the advertising during the next few weeks, when the Democratic Convention crowds come flocking to New York.

Just whether the picture will stand up as a $1.50 attraction is a question. As a road show proposition the picture doesn't seem to carry the punch necessary to put it over. Coming to the Criterion, it naturally courts comparison with "The Covered Wagon," which left that house Saturday after running 60 weeks. If "Dorothy Vernon of Haddon Hall" runs there for 12 or 15 weeks to the business "The Wagon" did on its first year's average it will be doing tremendously. The best that can be hoped for the production would be 20 weeks, and that would give it an extraordinary run.

However, as a production for the regular pre-release picture houses at regular picture prices it would be a knockout and a record breaker. In the first place the picture isn't too long, running just about an hour and three-quarters and having "the only Mary" as star would be certain to send it along with a wallop.

Mary Pickford is everything that she ever was in this picture—winsome, temperamental, a comedian and withal a loveable heroine. In fact, she is the picture even though surrounded by a really good cast, with care taken not to make the same mistake as was made in "Rosita," when a supporting player walked away with the picture from the star.

Those supporting Miss Pickford include a number of players of screen prominence, notably Anders Randolph, Marc MacDermott, Allan Forrest, Wilfred Lucas, the star's sister, Lottie Pickford Forrest, and Estelle Taylor. There is also Clare Eames, who, as Queen Elizabeth, gives a performance second to none in the picture. She was remarkable as the "Virgin Queen."

The story has Miss Pickford in the role of the wilful heir to Haddon Hall who as a child is bethothed to Sir John Manners, the heir of the Earl of Rutland, whose estates adjoin those of the Vernons. She is to be married on her 18th birthday, but prior to that time her father breaks off the betrothal to the heir of Rutland because his father has kept him too long in France, and the boy was one of those who accompanied Mary Queen of Scots from France.

The first section has the story to the point Dorothy refuses to accept her father's command that she wed her cousin, Sir Malcolm Vernon of Scotland, because she has seen Sir John, her former bethothed, and prefers him.

The first part of the picture is filled with sword play thrills and a lot of big sets.

In the second half is a thrill that outthrills even the Griffith ride of Paul Revere in "America." It is where Dorothy supposedly rides to the rescue of her lover whom she has betrayed to the Queen because she believes he and Mary of Scots are in love. That ride is a cuckoo, over hill and dale, along a castle wall and finally a terrific jump where the wall is broken down, and finally some cross country jump stuff that should pull the audience from their seats, and it would have had not they possibly seen a few "westerns" and the Paul Revere ride. Nevertheless, it is great screen stuff, especially as half of the audience won't be wise to doubling.

Finally there is the rescue of the Queen from those who would assassinate her and a comedy finish with Dorothy riding off with the hero.

Picturesque, yes; entertaining likewise, but as a road show a question. At regular houses with regular picture audiences there wouldn't be a thing that could stop it.

Fred.

MEN

Dimitri Buchowetzki production, starring Pola Negri, presented by Adolph Zukor and Jesse L. Lasky. Story and direction by Dimitri Buchowetzki. Script by Paul Bern. Shown at the Rialto, New York, week May 4. Running time, 68 minutes.

Cleo..Pola Negri
Georges Kleber.............Robert W. Frazer
Henri Duval.....................Robert Edeson
Cleo's Father..................Joseph Swickard
Francois..............................Monti Collins
The Stranger.......................Gino Corrado
The Baron.........................Edgar Norton

Pola Negri is the star, with three members featured. The trio are Robert W. Fraser, Robert Edeson and Joseph Swickard. What reason there was for the featuring is a question, for Pola Negri in her last couple of pictures has shown herself to be one of the real drawing cards of those working under the Paramount banner.

In addition, this picture, according to the advance tip-off, was supposed to have been one of the best that she has done. That cannot truthfully be said, but it is a picture the fans are going to flock to see and like immensely.

That makes it box-office sure-fire.

It is the first production that Dimitri Buchowetzki has done in this country. However, it is not the first that he has directed the temperamental Pola in, for it was he who first brought her to notice through pictures he made with her in Poland. Later she went to Berlin and from that city of kulture came to this country.

The story gives Miss Negri an opportunity to appear in clothes that are splendid, after she has first been seen as a little waitress in a small seaport restaurant. Nothing new about the general Cinderella idea except that Pola goes to Paris believing that she is to be taken to a dancing instructor by an old friend of the family's, while in reality he has made a deal with the procurer of a wealthy nobleman to deliver her in the city.

So Pola is trapped, turned out of doors or escapes the next morning, and finally finds herself in a cheap restaurant again, this time in Paris, but only for sufficient length of time to order a cup of coffe, smash a milk bottle over the head of a young man in evening clothes who wants to make friends with her, and finally to glance into the face of the friend of her father's who betrayed her into the hands of the procurer and read the true story there.

Her transition to the heights as the queen of night life in the city, that is built on night life is not disclosed, but when she is next seen she has achieved the heights. Gowns, jewels and admirers are all hers, the former coming from the latter, for wohm she cares not at all, and to make it all the more difficult the author-director tries to give the impression that Pola isn't returning anything for all she gets. The scene in which this thought is driven home is that where the wealth of the nation stands ready to bid as high as $200,000 for Pola's company. Some bid, even on Broadway!

In the end she finally falls in love with a penniless clerk of a banker; in fact, the one who is her protector, at least in a financial sense. To save the boy who has stolen to appease her whims she finally consents to accept the attentions of the $200,000 bidder. But he, big-hearted banker that he is, will have none of that. He leaves the lovers to themselves.

'Tis a pretty tale; but there is more in the telling than the mere language. It is in the direction of Buchowetzki and the acting of Pola that make it. Atmasphere! There's tons of it all over the place. Sets that are extremely flashy and a carnival scene that carries a real punch and carnival touch.

There is a lot of little stuff the director is responsible for that is the extreme in the art of motion picture making, and if Famous Players holds on to Buchowetzki they are going to find a distinct acqfiistion to their directorial staff.

Fred.

THE LONE WOLF

John McKeon presentation of S. E. V. Taylor production, adapted from a story by Louis Joseph Vance, released through Associated Exhibitors; running time, 68 mins.; seen at the Rivoli.

Lucy Shannon ....Dorothy Dalton
Michael Lanyard ....Jack Holt
Wm. Burroughs ....Wilton Lackaye
Bannon ....Tyrone Power
Clare Henshaw...........Charlotte Walker
Annette Dupre ....Lucy Fox
Popinot ....Edouard Durand
Solon ....Robert T. Haines
Wertheimer ......Gustave Von Seyffertitz
Eckstrom ....Alphonse Ethier
Ambassador ....William Tooker
Count de Morbihan........Paul McAllister

This is a very phoney, though often extremely enjoyable feature, held up by its unusually notable and effective cast, weighed down by fake effects, and a story as incredible as any episode in "Perils of Pauline."

The company is a powerful ensemble on paper and on celluloid. Dorothy Dalton, looking trim and wistfully lovely, gives a verisimilitude to the yarn, because the love story is otherwise without any foundation except that which the eye perceives, that any one could fall in love with her on sight without any scenario assistance. Jack Holt, as a master-mind-crook-hero, is nothing to go wild over.

The rest of the characters are cast with astute and extravagant judgment, and, though they all overact because the story is such that it has to be played with whitebrush brushes and axes, these sterling actors save it almost always from being entirely ridiculous. As it was, the Rivoli audience several times snickered out of turn at the inconsistencies and the overdrawn and yellow melodrama, especially the strain for lurid mechanical effects.

All sorts of visual props are employed, such as "the papers" hidden in a deck of cards, they being the secret plans of the United States to destroy an enemy in war; an airplane chase at the finish which is as palpably counterfeit as a clothing dummy; gunplay, taxi chases, dozens of telephones, smashed skylights, no end of taxis, code message, trap doors, secret passages, etc., ad lib.

The story is a wild melange of stock thrills, with the heroine turning out to be in the secret service all the time, the hero turning square after he baffled both police and arch-criminals for no known reason, since he is such a fine and simple chap. The "pack," the crime-trust of Paris, are a villainous lot, who have a most uncanny way of being everywhere, and, of course, getting nowhere, since they are "on the other side."

"The Lone Wolf" (a non-descriptive title evidently synthetic for box-office appeal irrespective of the material, being the nickname of the hero in the underworld) is a fair program picture and will get by with simple-minded folks who react to mechanical kicks and still believe sub-titles no matter what they say. Also, Miss Dalton will give it a rating.

Lait.

THE REJECTED WOMAN

Distinctive Production released by Goldwyn-Cosmopolitan. Story by John Lynch; directed by Albert Parker. Shown at the Capitol, New York, week May 4. Running time 85 minutes.

Diane Du Prez...............Alma Rubens
John Leslie....................Conrad Nagel
James Dunbar..........Wyndham Standing
Samuel Du Prez........George MacQuarrie
Jean Gagnon...................Bela Lugosi
Craig Burnett..............Antonio D'Algy
Lucille Van Tuyle.........Leonora Hughes
Madame Rosa..............Mme. La Violette
Peter Leslie......................Aubrey Smith
Leyton Carter..................Fred Burton

The best box office angle is in the title. That might mean something. The story itself is a combination northwest snow picture with a society angle. Alma Rubens plays the lead with her principal support Conrad Nagel and Wyndham Standing, the former as the lead and the latter the heavy.

It is in the snow country that the story opens with Miss Rubens as the daughter of the trading post keeper. Their domain is invaded in midwinter by aeroplane by a society man from New York who is looking for adventure. He gets it by remaining overnight in a cabin high in the hills with the girl when both are caught in a snow storm. After that there is nothing left for the boy to do except to say he'll remember her. She thinks that means marriage and finally follows him to New York, only to discover she is not as attractive in her shabby north country clothes as the natives.

At that point the heavy steps in. He has been the boy's father's general manager and hates the boy. He knows the contents of the father's will to the effect that in the event that the boy marry without the consent of the trustees of the estate he is to lose everything. He sends the little girl abroad and pays for her education for a year and when returning she steps right into society and cops the youth. After the marriage the heavy springs his ace and the two are parted after one night of wedded life.

Then it's a case of back to the snow country for the girl, and the heavy and the husband have to follow her in time for the big hand-to-hand contest. They stage it with all the frills; this includes the hurling of lighted lamps, which, strangely enough, in this instance does not mean the igniting and burning of the building, shots in the dark and all that sort of thing, finishing with the conventional close-up clinch.

As a hokum production in the cheaper grade of house it will serve well enough, but as a pre-release in a Main Stem house it runs for Sweeney.

Fred.

THE CHECHAHCOS

Capt. Austin E. Lathrop presents this Associated Exhibitors' picture released through Pathe Exchange. Directed and written by Lewis H. Moomaw.

"Horseshoe" Riley...........William Dills
Bob Dexter............Albert van Antwerp

Mrs. Stanlaw....................Eva Gordon
Prof. Stanlaw................Howard Webster
Richard "Cold" Steele.........Alexis B. Luce
Baby Stanlaw..................Baby Margie
Ruth Stanlaw..............Gladys Johnston
Pierre........................Guerney Hays
Engineer...........................H. Miles

"Chechahcos" (pronounced chee-chaw-koz) is the Indian word used to designate the tenderfeet or newcomers to the Alaskan country to distinguish them from "sourdoughs," or old-timers. This film of the frozen north" is distinguished by the fact it was produced and filmed wholly in Alaska.

It's a tale of the frigid country during the gold rush days. It includes plenty of ice and snow stuff that should make it likely for summer bookings. As a story it's pretty familiar stuff and includes all the old hoke. The simplicity of its recounting is none the less impressive.

The yarn starts with the separation of a young mother from her baby daughter as a result of shipwreck, having accompanied her college professor-husband to Alaska. Circumstances make her easy prey for the attentions of a professional gambler.

The girl grows up and is wooed by the young engineer, who, through the interest of a kindly "sourdough" of original "woman-hating" tendencies, prospers and sees that the girl has the best of attention.

The mother, despite her tainted existence the past 12 or 15 years, is sympathetically portrayed. The inevitable meeting and the dramatic pursuit to bring the villain to justice are the punches of the basically trite plot.

The scenery is the big thing. It is quite interesting despite overdoing. As the film ran 90 minutes at the special showing at the Ritz-Carlton hotel, New York, May 1, that speaks considerable for how much can be dispensed with.

Baby Margie of the cast, a winsome youngster, distinguished herself. Gladys Johnston, personating Ruth Stanlaw grown up, suggested brilliant possibilities as a screen personality. Her girlish charm typifies the adolescent period outwardly better than Marguerite Clark ever did, or anybody today. But she spoiled it with one attempt at an elemental "registering" of the sorrowing emotion. For sweet-and-pretty parts that do not call for any histrionics, she is a corking type for the screen.

The film at the special showing was introduced by a photoplay record of the late President Harding's visit to Alaska, showing the "Chechahcos" company intimately on location.

The film producers probably cogitated considerably on the retention of this unique title. Its value commercially is still open to discussion in view of its difficult pronunciation, but it may be the unique title will prove a distinguishing mark.

It's a satisfactory program feature for the daily change houses.

Abel.

THE WHITE SIN

Palmer Photoplay Corporation presents this dramatic feature. Adaptation by Harold Shumate, scenario by De Andres and Julian La Mothe, directed by William A. Seiter. Running time, 65 minutes. Reviewed at Stanley, New York, April 30.

Hattie Lou Harkness.......Madge Bellamy
Grant Van Gore..............John Bowers
Grace Van Gore.......Francelia Billington
Spencer Van Gore...............Hal Cooley
Peter Van Gore..............Jas. Corrigan
Travers Dale....................Billy Bevan
Grace's Aunt..............Norris Johnson
Aunt Cynthia.....................Ethel Wales
Judge Langley....................Otis Harlan
Mrs. Van Gore..................Myrtle Vare
The Doctor....................Arthur Millette
Yacht Captain................James Gordon

Madge Bellamy does splendid work in this feature in a role calling for constant emotional pyrotechnics and considerable versatility.

The story is swift moving, dramatic and convincing except in one or two spots. The author found it necessary to work in a fire and rescue to plant his hero and heroine for the final embrace.

Hal Cooley also was saddled with a villianous role that doesn't ring true at times. As a young rake intent upon the ruin of Hattie Lou Harkness, his sister's maid, he plans a mock marriage aboard the Van Gore yacht but is crossed by the captain who performs the ceremony outside the three-mile limit, making it legal.

The next day the girl discovers the supposed hoax and leaves the yacht. After her baby is born she decides to deceive Van Gore's parents by posing as his wife. This decision follows her discovery of a month old newspaper recounting the wreck of the yacht with all aboard reported lost.

The parents of Van Gore take her in, treat her kindly and give her a home. The eldest son falls in love with his brother's widow. The situation becomes complicated when a wire announces the return of the yachting party after a rescue from a south sea island.

The girl decides to throw herself on the mercy of Spencer. She is successful when his sister reveals the true marriage. Spencer attempts to attack her but is prevented by his sister who locks the girl in her room.

The house catches on fire with the girl and baby trapped in the burning building. Grant Van Gore attempts a rescue but is overcome by smoke outside of the locked door. The brother after appearing a craven is goaded into rescuing his brother's wife and baby by his sister's taunts. After carrying out his brother he returns and is burned alive. Meanwhile the girl has lowered the baby out of a window wrapped in bed clothes, following herself a moment later.

The cast is a strong one and the picture barring the one or two far fetched moments, a good entertaining feature with Miss Bellamy's emoting making it worth while all the while.

Con.

JUST OFF BROADWAY

Fox production, directed by Edward Mortimer and featuring John Gilbert. Name of author not given. At the Circle, New York, May 1, as half the bill. Runs about an hour.

Stephen Moore.................John Gilbert
Jean Lawrence................Marion Nixon
Nan Norton.....................Trilby Clark
Florelle.....................Pierre Glendon
Comfort...................Ben Hendricks

Starting as a drama of the Paris underworld, "Just Off Broadway" quickly shifts to a crisp and entertaining light comedy of New York's crook coterie. The film presents a rather complicated plot, but one that gives ample opportunity for interesting incident and flashy action.

It is in the lighter moments that the picture is at its best. An attempt to present a cold synopsis of the plot would resemble a cross-section of the Einstein theory, introducing, as it does, aphasia, mistaken identity, counterfeiting, detectives galore and even more crooks.

It will suffice to tell that John Gilbert is cast as a millionaire amateur detective who makes use of a nasty crack on the head to feign loss of memory and land a gang of counterfeiters, and incidentally the innocent little girl who has become tangled up with them.

This results in several clever farcical situations and more follow when the hero leads the gang into a robbery of his own home and astonishes them with his apparent knowledge of the safe, the jewels and the layout of the whole apartment. The girl becomes convinced to her sorrow that her man is a thief as well as a counterfeiter and it is not until the very end that the mystery is unravelled.

There will be some difference of opinion as to the wisdom of having the audience know right along the identity of the hero. However, the picture is essentially a comedy and not a mystery. There is not one real guffaw throughout but about a snicker a minute which serves just as well.

Gilbert who heretofore has been seen usually in heavy roles proves an adept farceur and puts a good deal of character into his rather light-waisted role. Marion Nixon shares honors with him with practically all the dramatic burden of the film on her shoulders. Ben Hendricks, Jr., is amusing as a "lovable crook" and the balance do very acceptable work.

A neat little program feature which should mean box office coin since no one should find serious fault with it save possible for the entire absence of logic.

WANTED BY THE LAW

Sunset Productions picture releasing through the Aywon Film Corp., starring J. B. Warner. Story and direction credited to R. N. Bradbury. Showing at Loew's New York as one half of double bill, May 2. Running time, 57 minutes.

An ordinary western having little to redeem it. A much hackneyed story of the oldest son assuming the blame of a shooting to save his kid brother. It fails to arouse more than meagre interest and the cast shows nothing to stand out above the picture.

Warner walks through the leading role for but an indifferent performance while the sequence of events is not such as to make the action overcome the remaining deficiencies.

Dorothy Woods plays opposite Warner for a colorless performance.

The picture is inadequate for the larger houses but will probably suffice in the miniature neighborhood auditoriums.

Skig.

GALLOPING GALLAGHER

Monogram production, directed by Albert Rogell and starring Fred Thompson. Written by Marion Jackson and photographed by Ross Fisher. Released by F. B. O. At the New York, April 29, as half double bill. Runs 55 minutes.

Bill Gallagher..............Fred Thompson
Evelyn Churchill..............Hazel Keener
Joe Burke....................Frank Hagney
Leon Berry................Nelson McDowell
Tub....................."Shorty" Hendricks
Slim..........................Andy Morris

"Galloping Gallagher" is fortunate in possessing the prime requisite of a Western picture—breeziness. It is this wholesome quality of not taking itself too seriously that makes the film entertaining.

The star's acting is refreshingly free from restraint and the photography conspicuously artistic. There are a good many laughs and one or two thrills contributed chiefly by the fine, white horse playing an important role.

Those are the good points and strong enough to overbalance the weak sisters; a trite, spineless plot, different only in that it is more illogical and far-fetched than the average; a cast that, aside from the star and his leading woman, does insipid work, and a general atmosphere suggesting the producers were only endeavoring to turn out a fair program attraction rather than a really good Western.

The hero in this case is a wandering Western adventurer who, happening upon a tiny town of the prairies just in time to beat up a gang of marauding robbers, is picked for the super-hazardous job of sheriff of the burg. Events follow the formula closely, with the usual villainous bank president, directing the raiders from the inside, and the new sheriff being warned that his term of office will be just a week unless he comes over to their side. A touch of novelty has the heroine as an evangelist parson, who sets out to convert the town and is aided to a great extent by the hero's guns in her reforming crusade.

Fred Thompson has a role just fitted to his rather rollicking talents. He is perhaps the handsomest of the Western regulars now that "Buck" Jones has graduated into the "Charles" and society class. His appearance and smile should win him many feminine admirers, and the horsemanship and athletic stunts of daring will please the majority of his own sex. "Silver King," his horse, is galloping nearer Mix's "Tony" with every new picture.

The comedy is supplied by the antics of an undertaker whose joy reaches its greatest heights when the shooting is thickest. He has plenty of opportunity for glorious expectations, as it's just a case of one battle after another.

So hot, in fact, were some of the fights, and so narrow the escapes, that the audience laughed louder and longer at them than at the optimistic undertaker.

CLAUDE DUVAL

London, April 26.

Recently there has been a boom in canonized ruffians invested with a halo of romance. "Dick Turpin," foulest of all petty sneak thieves, started it and has now been followed by the Gaumont "Claude Duval."

For the exaltation of Turpin there was little excuse except that his filmic heroism was a sure thing to keep children from spending their Saturday pennies anywhere else but at the kinema.

Duval is a bird of somewhat different color. Highwayman and common thief though he was he had been a gallant soldier although a mercenary one and it was the injustice of the King for whom he had fought which drove him to outlawry.

Turpin's alleged bravery was "penny plain, tuppence colored"; Duval's career possesses an element of romance and gallantry which shines out from a somewhat blackguardly and uncouth age.

George Cooper has taken full advantage of the mythical gallantry of his hero and has turned out a workman-like picture but his footage is ridiculous for such a feature. It takes a really great super feature to live for nine reels when it goes to the general public and it is that public which "Claude Duval's" success must depend upon. Cut out three reels and you have a picture possessing every possibility of a transitory popular success.

Throughout, Cooper's productive work is excellent; he has staged many fine scenes, those of the revels at the inn being exceptionally good. Here he shows something approaching genius and in these scenes his small part players, seen only in flashes provide some of the best genuine acting of the show. He has asked these un-named players to make bricks without straw and they have responded nobly.

Nigel Barrie is badly cast as Claude Duval. Never once does he get the atmosphere or give the faintest impression of the dashing outlaw. His gallantry does not ring true nor his horsemanship appear genuine. Fay Compton gives an exceptionally good performance of her Grace, the Duchess of Brentleigh. Hugh Miller is very good as the villainous Lord Malyn, as is A. B. Imeson as Chesterton. Betty Faire is good as Anne as is Dorlenea Shirley as Moll.

As is usual in such pictures much of the best acting is in the small unnamed roles.

Gore.

HENRY, KING OF NAVARRE

London, April 1.

The Stoll Film Co. has chosen one of the most intriguing and thrilling periods in French history and have managed to make a picture ("personal direction: Maurice Elvey") of extreme thinness. Technically perfect, the feature lacks sincerity and punch. It is stagey and throughout carries an atmosphere of unreality.

The watcher cannot imagine people are really fighting, drinking, loving. Everything they do is obviously under "personal direction." Even the rapier blades have to yield to it.

The whole thing is like a beautiful statue, cold, perfect, but without a soul.

The story tells of the best known period of the fight between Catholics and Huguenots. Henry of Navarre called to Paris to the deathbed of his mother is warned of the plot against him, a point in which is his marriage with Marguerite de Valois. He pretends to be a fool and the conspirators are taken in. On his wedding eve he drinks heavily, rather pretends to, leaving the way to the bridal chamber open to the Duke de Guise who speedily takes advantage of it only to be turned down by Marguerite. Then comes the eve of St. Bartholomew and its massacre, Henry seeking sanctuary in his wife's chamber. De Guise is defeated and the wounded Henry seeks shelter in his wife's arms. Marguerite has now learned to love him but the way she grabbed hold of his much wounded body gave every sign of her speedily becoming a widow.

Scenically there is much which is beautiful but an attempt to copy German methods of lighting is by no means wholly successful. The staging seems as unreal as the rest.

These beautiful settings are on the line of the kiosks and pavilions of an exhibition.

Humberstone Wright takes the palm for his performance of Charles I. It is fine character work in an extremely difficult part which might easily have been made ludicrous. Even in his most crazy moments Wright clings to a vestige of kingly dign'ty. The Duke de Guise is well played by Henry Victor. Matheson Lang has a great part in Henry, but never manages to make it gripping. Gladys Jennings is as beautiful as ever as Marguerite but has no material. Stella St. Audrie gives a fine character study as Catharine de Medici and Madame D'Esterre is responsible for the finest bit of acting in the film during the few minutes she is seen as Henry's dying mother.

Gore.

NATURE'S FAIRYLAND

London, April 20.

As an example of beautiful photography, divine patience and love of nature this feature is remarkable. As a showman's proposition it has scarcely any drawing power. Richard Kearton, brother of Cherry Kearton, who is responsibe for the pictures, is without an idea of showmanship. However, he is a great photographer and a great naturalist.

The series is all-embracing. Nothing has come amiss to him, from ants to snakes. All his stuff is beautiful and a monument to his patience. His colored "stills"are miles ahead of most of the public sees, but there is absolutely no showman's pull in the feature.

Gore.

WHY MEN LEAVE HOME

Associated First National feature, directed and produced by John M. Stahl, from the play by Avery Hopwood, adapted for screen by A. P. Young.

John Emerson....................Lewis Stone
Irene....................Helene Chadwick
Grandma....................Mary Carr
Grandpa....................William V. Mong
Jean Ralston....................Alma Bennett
Nina....................Hedda Hopper
Sam Neilson....................Sidney Bracy

"Why Men Leave Home" was one of those instances of picking up an old gag for a title, writing a bad play around it, selling it for a small fortune to the movies on the title, which never belonged to the play, in the first place, and selling nothing but the title.

This was a sad comedy as originally written by Avery Hopwood and presented for a flop at the Morosco. Hopwood will probably scream in agony and indignation when he sees the "adaptation," which is far afield from his play, and a whole lot better off that it is. A. P. Young has handled the text ruthlessly, but he has done the script a lot of good. This is rare, but this time it is true.

The story isn't really a story even now, but it has the rudiments of one, being wholesome, intimate and human. It handles the natural declension of the honeymoon as a preordained consequence rather than as a crime, a vice or a villainy. It divides equally between the man and the woman the responsibility, and could as well be called, "Why Women Leave Home," which wouldn't have cost a dime and would be just as good inside, if not as inviting in the billing.

Lewis Stone plays the groom and Helene Chadwick his bride, and very nice for the part they are, though Stone gets little chance to be romantic, even at the start, which may disappoint the young girls who sigh over his greyed temples and playing of lover parts. Miss Chadwick is a delight, playing with plausibility, simplicity and an endearing amiability of manner even when wrong in the story.

Of course, the subterfuges are pretty flimsy, such as having her leave him and divorce him because he smells of another woman's perfume, and admits he kissed a bimbo away from home while the Mrs. was gallivanting at a vacation resort. But that doesn't matter much. Also the gag of quarantining him with his ex-wife before he can honeymoon with the vamp he married after the divorce is also feeble.

But the twist after that is a wrench—and doesn't come from the play, either: his ex-wife, thus thrown in with him, and now the third party in a triangle, decides she'd rather be the "other" woman than the wife; and that's pretty sound stuff, and is something to take out of the theatre and think about.

Alma Bennett plays exactly the same little teasing demi-virgin here that she does in "Lilies of the Fields," also opposite Stone, which robs it of much effectiveness with one who has seen both films with a short lapse between. But she does very nicely and certainly is the type.

One bit of comedy which may be criticized as in poor taste did not offend the sensibilities of this patron, though as a rule he despises jokes about childbirth.

On the evening of the first anniversary, the bored husband who wants to nod over his paper, is dragged to the movies and squawks out. He sneaks up to bed and finds a baby sock knitted in his wife's work basket. He at once rushes down; she is moving a chair. He protests—there is a yell in front at that. She looks at some ivory monkeys, he takes them away and hides them behind his back—another and bigger wow. Then the colored maid reveals she is knitting the sock for her sister's baby.

Since the baby subject is never again mentioned, and since the whole thing is played and directed so humanly, it should not start up a grouch, though people have a tendency to be artificially and hypocritically thin-skinned over such "sacred" subjects used for laughs.

"Why Men Leave Home" is an all-right film, though it will never be a sensational draw because it lacks strident or glaring elements, and is not quite clever or classy enough to be a punch without them. But it will leave a pleasant taste and will bring in, wherever it stays long enough, people who aren't regular film fans and don't want to just see the same old slick-haired sheiks and bob-haired babies, but who will come out if they hear there is a film around that makes sense and doesn't challenge belief too hard.

Technically, this feature is finely directed and ably lighted, set and shot. It is a credit to Stahl and to Young.

Lait.

BETWEEN FRIENDS

J. Stuart Blackton production released by Vitagraph. Presented by A. E. Smith. Story by Robert W. Chambers. Shown at the Rivoli, New York, week May 11, 1924. Running time 71 minutes.

David Drene....................Lou Tellegen
Jessica Drene....................Anna Q. Nilsson
Jack Greylock....................Norman Kerry
Cecile White....................Alice Calhoun
Quair....................Stuart Holmes
Guilder....................Henry Barrows

"Between Friends" is a remake. Originally it was turned out by Vitagraph with Alice Joyce in the cast. In the present cast there are four players whose names have some value at the box office. They are Lou Tellegen, Anna Q. Nilsson, Norman Kerry and Alice Calhoun, but this quartet has to flounder around with a triangle tale that has nothing particularly new to offer to an audience, and the picture so far as direction is concerned is about as old fashioned as it could possibly be. From a box-office standpoint it is a production of ordinary program caliber that will serve in the daily change houses, but that is about all.

The Robert W. Chambers tale deals with the best friend who steals the wife, but manages to cover up his tracks so that the husband does not suspect.

After the woman commits suicide the doubl crosser returns home, with the husband still unsuspecting, and the friendship continues.

In later years, however, when the friend is in love with one of the husband's models, the fact is disclosed that the wife stealing was his friend's work and he plans a complete revenge. In the end, however, it works out evenly and all is forgiven and there is a happy ending with the artist marrying the model.

Tellegen mugs all over the place and his close-ups, which are almost continuous, become tiresome. Miss Calhoun as the model handles herself very well, but the best work of the picture is done by Kerry and Miss Nilsson in the earlier scenes.

Fred.

KING OF WILD HORSES

Western melodrama produced by Hal Roach and directed by Fred Jackman. Distributed by Pathé. Shown at Loew's Circle May 7. Running time, 56 minutes.

Figured in the light of drama "King of the Wild Horses" is apple sauce. But as a commercial proposition it shapes up like a million dollars. Especially for the unlimited number of neighborhood houses where they're not so apt to be captious about drama, but strong for thrills and action. And "King of the Wild Horses" has both in extravagant abundance.

A black horse of unusual intelligence is the actual star of the picture and he's some actor. A loosely strung together melodramatic story serves as a background for the horse's histrionic efforts, but the equine actor leaves the human actors out in the cold when it comes to holding the spectators' interest.

This is through no fault of the players appearing in the picture. They are all excellent. It's the exaggerated melodramatics they necessarily have to perpetrate because of the exigencies of the ultra-conventional "plot."

There are numerous scenes showing the "King" and his herd of wild horses roaming their native haunts and they're all engrossingly entertaining. These scenes have been beautifully photographed and possess high class educational values. The parts of the film devoted to the life of the wild herd and the thrill stuff of the "King" are sufficiently strong to put the picture over anywhere regardless of the human sections.

A leap across a chasm that looks bottomless and appears to be more than 15 feet wide by the "King," riderless first, and later with the hero on his back, constitute a couple of startlers of the type the picture fans go daffy over. At another point in the picture the horse leaps into a whirlpool from a dizzy height and rescues the hero from drowning.

A stick-up in approved western fashion, a chase by a posse, a gruelling battle between hero and heavy and the bull-dogging of steers are "punches" building up the part of the film played by the human actors, and they're all full of action.

At Loew's Circle the "King of Wild Horses" was half of a double feature bill, but that doesn't mean it could not carry a show singly with flying colors in a first-run house, for, despite its commonplace story, it's "different."

The Circle audience voted it a wow.

Bell.

AFTER A MILLION

Anthony J. Xydias presentation released through Sunset Productions. Melodramatic story featuring Kenneth McDonald. Director Jack Nelson. Caught at New York, May 6, half of double feature bill. Runs 55 minutes.

This meller is aimed at state rights and independent feature programs but qualifies as an ordinary program addition for the ordinary picture houses.

The story is one of intrigue and concerns the adventures of Gregory Maxim (Kenneth McGowan) to fulfill the requirements stipulated in the will of Count Orloff, a Russian noble and exile.

The usual efforts to prevent the consummation of Maxim and Princess Olga (Ruth Dwyer), as stipulated in the will, are the basis of the plot, which includes all of the usual clap-trap such as the villainous scheming of Ivan Senine (Alphonse Matell), surrounded by a gang of Bolsheviks.

The story allows McGowan to display his fistic prowess in a fight with the gang, his ability as a chauffeur in a thrilling chase in an automobile with a chasm jump worked in realistically—the only thrill in the picture, etc.

The supporting cast includes Joe Girard, Hal Craig, J. Hunt, Stanley Bingham and Ada Bell, all of whom do as well as could be expected with the highly incredulous story, reminiscent at all times of the novels of E. Phillips Oppenheim, although no one is program-credited.

"After a Million" qualifies as a fair feature for the ordinary programs. Its biggest asset is action and pep, but to achieve these the unknown author has sacrificed all semblance of credulity.

Con.

GIRL OF LIMBERLOST

A James Leo Meehan production of the Gene Straton Porter novel. Distributed by Film Booking Office. Shown at Loew's New York, N. Y., May 12, 1924. Running time, 70 minutes.

Very fair program feature. Interesting story that runs along in fairly entertaining fashion. There are spots where it is draggy and there are other moments when the yarn is decidedly gripping. Still, there is something of a punch lacking to send it over in the smash class.

The photography and direction are consistently good and the cast, while holding no names that will set the world afire, is of a calibre that will answer with the bigger part of the fans on their acting ability alone.

One thing always certain with a Gene Straton Porter story and that is that there are enough readers of her books in almost every community to make it worth while for the exhibitor to run a picturization of one of her novels.

This one should not be any exception. *Fred.*

THE SWORD OF VALOR

Phil Goldstone presentation featuring Rex (Snowy) Baker and Dorothy Revier, directed by Duke Worne, scenario by Jefferson Moffit, photographed by Roland Price. Cast: Rex (Snowy) Baker, Dorothy Revier, Percy Challenger, Eloise Hess, Stella D'Lanti, Otto Lederer, Fred Kavena, Eloise Hess, Edward Cecil. At the New York, May 6, as half double bill. Runs 55 minutes.

A romantic drama of Spain centered upon the athletic prowess of Rex (Snowy) Baker, an adept horseman and swordsman albeit not quite the type the matinee girls associate with a picture leading man. Baker is a well proportioned chap with a deeply lined face and a physiognomy that doesn't quite make the grade when compared with the "beauties" generally associated with male screen pulchritude.

Dorothy Revier as Ynez, the Spanish cause of all the trouble, amply repays and gives a legitimate motive for all the hullabaloo created by the rival lovers. No sweeter vision than Miss Revier in a one-piece bathing suit had flashed across the screen since Mack Sennett quit thrilling the fishes. The girl can act, too, and 's well in her stride toward stardom. She is a beauty and an actress—an unbeatable combination.

The story concerns the fair Ynez, the daughter of a Spanish Don living quietly in the ancient hacienda. Her father, Don Guzman de Ruis y Montejo (Otto Lederer), determines upon a rich marriage for the girl.

A chance meeting with an American, Captain Crooks, develops into love at first sight. Papa, not knowing, takes his daughter to the Riviera, where Ismid Matrouli (Edwin Cecil), a Levantine of mongrel origin, but wealthy, falls in love and asks dad for her hand.

The captain appears upon the scene in time to rescue Ynez from a watery death. Most of her costumes feature bare legs and shoulders. Matrouli sicks a professional swordsman on the cap, but the latter socks him in the jaw instead of arranging a duel.

All hands back at the old home with Matrouli pressing things and the cap showing up again, to be shortly followed by the big league swordsman. The inevitable duel follows, both men showing a marvelous knowledge of the art.

A gypsy lover of Ynez takes a pot shot at the cap during the duel, but hits his opponent. The latter then kidnaps Ynez and carries her away to a mountain stronghold, where the captain corners him and overpowers him in a realistic battle atop the rocks.

The picture is melodramatic hokum, but has a state rights chance, due to the excellent work of the star, who should build up a notable screen following in a short time. She looks like one of the finds of the season. *Con.*

LADIES TO BOARD

Fox picture starring Tom Mix. Story by W. D. Pelley, with Jack Blystone directing. Cast includes Gilbert Holmes, Gertrude Olmstead, Fay Holderness, Gertrude Claire and Philo McCullough. Showing at Loew's New York Theatre, May 8. Running time, 80 minutes.

Below the average of the usual Mix release, principally, because of an indifferent story and the lengths to which the director has carried it. The theme is a cinch for Mix who, in comparison to other screen exploits, does nothing more than walk through.

Containing an element of sob stuff, through an aged mother being neglected by an only son, the director has overly stressed the pathos out of all proportion. It is the principal reason for the film running eighty minutes, far too long for its type, and would project better nearer sixty.

The story is based upon a cowboy who inherits an old ladies' home through having saved the former feminine owner from a smash in a runaway automobile. The situations, continuity and general sequence are easily discernible with the flashing of the neglected inmate and the young nurse.

The picture includes an amount of comedy which serves to save it from being an absolute bust, for which the title writing is of more than passing assistance.

The cast gives intermediate performances other than Gertrude Claire, who makes the mother role click for its full worth and is hardly responsible for the amount of footage allotted. Otherwise the various portrayals call for nothing beyond the usual routine.

As a picture, "Ladies to Board" will probably please the Mix fans. It is unquestionably best suited to the worn trail that other Mix films have blazed, although this one will leave no definite insignia to mark its passing. *Skig.*

THE FIRE PATROL

Hunt Stromberg production, released in the independent market by the Chadwick Pictures Corp. Adapted from the play by Harkins and Barber. Running time, 63 minutes.

Mary Ferguson	Anna Q. Nilsson
Capt. John Ferguson	William Jeffries
Colin Ferguson	Dicky Brandon
"Butch" Anderson	Jacky Richardson
Molly Thatcher	Madge Bellamy
Emma Thatcher	Helen Jerome Eddy
Capt. John Ferguson	Spottiswoode Aiken
Colin Ferguson	Johnny Harron
"Butch" Anderson	Jack Richardson
Alice Masters	Gale Henry
The Village Belle	Frances Ross
Members of the fire patrol	Charles Murray, Heinie Conklin, Bull Montana, Hank Mann, Billy Franey.

An independent picture certain to be a box-office winner. It is so far ahead of the average independently made picture it stands out like a rose in a garden of weeds.

It has everything a picture should have to appeal to the masses. The title, however, is somewhat misleading, and the average exhibitor may expect a picture of a fire department nature. It isn't that; it's a sea picture, with the fire patrol in reality a coast guard patrol that fights fires at sea. This isn't apparent in the picture until more than half way, because there is some expectancy previously as to where the fire patrol part of the title comes in.

Its cast fairly bristles with names that mean something. The only weak member is Johnny Harmon as the hero loved by two sisters, and who in turn loves the younger of the two, although he lets himself be vamped by the older.

That vamping bit is going to be a wow in the smaller towns, for here is a homely, small-town girl who goes out and grabs off the man that she wants, with the aid of a nightgown and some perfume. How even a small-town guy could fall for that stuff after one flash at the two girls is a wonder. In the end the vamping sister is shot during the course of a fight in her home, and that leaves the way clear for the finish.

The story is told in a prolog and a period 18 years later. Remarkable sea stuff, with storms that sweep over everything in sight.

Stromberg has handled his picture very well, indeed. There are just a couple of spots where he has permitted his subject to get away from him, but the lapses are so slight they are easily remedied by a little cutting.

This is a picture certain to clean up almost anywhere, and it is a lot of real thrill stuff and a corking fight scene that is going to score. *Fred.*

WHEN A GIRL LOVES

Victor Hugo-Halperin Production, released by Associated Exhibitors. Written, directed and produced by V. H. Halperin. At Loew's Circle, New York, on double feature bill May 19. Running time 62 minutes.

Sasha Boroff	Agnes Ayres
Count Michael	Percy Marmont
Dr. Godfrey Luke	Robert McKim
Helen	Kathlyn Williams
The Czarina	Mary Alden
Rogojin	George Siegmann
Grishka	John George

The least that one can say about this picture is that it covers a lot of territory. It opens in Russia and winds up in New York. The story is a fairly interesting one, with the ending left somewhat in doubt.

There is a very strong cast of names that should make it stand up almost anywhere in the houses that change daily or split their week up. It mustn't be taken by that comment

that it is a picture that will stand up in a pre-release run house, but in all it is a mighty good average program film that should draw some money.

In the beginning is some rather good Russian stuff showing the revolutionary period. That makes for the swinging of the action of the tale to America.

Sasha Boroff (Agnes Ayres) is beloved by Count Michael, when the revolution comes along and changes all their plans. A coachman (George Seigmann), who has become a power in the new regime, orders the hero shot, so that he can possess himself of the girl. But the hero escapes and the girl finally comes to America, studies nursing and marries a wealthy doctor. The Count also comes to America, achieves success on the operatic stage, and marries, having heard that his sweetheart of Russia had died. Later they all meet, and the doctor becomes infatuated with the singer's wife and is finally caught in a roadhouse raid with her.

The singer, on learning of the true state of affairs, proposes a duel, and, as the doctor fires, his wife walks into the scene, receiving the bullet in her shoulder, while the singer swoons from the shock.

The doctor's wife leaves him and goes with the singer in an effort to nurse him back to health, but is unsuccessful, and, as a last resort, promises to return to her husband if he will save her beloved one's life.

An invention of a cripple, who loves the girl and who saved her from the clutches of the coachman back in Russia, is utilized at the last minute to save the life of the singer, and thus makes it possible for the doctor's wife to disregard her promise to her husband.

The picture is fairly well handled for the grim sort of drama it is, and Miss Ayres and Kathlyn Williams give good accounts of themselves in their respective roles. Percy Marmont and Robert McKim share the honors among the men. *Fred.*

Kean—The Madness of Genius

London, May 10.

Madness predominates in this picture which has just opened for a season at the tiny Embassy. Here and there, however, there are flashes of genius to indicate what might have been.

The story takes that period of Kean's life, 1787-1833, when at the zenith of his power he fell into depths from which he never rose. This the romancist would have the public believe was not the inevitable result of his drink-sodden debauchery, but the effect of his love for a woman, the wife of another man.

As a matter of film-fact, it is proved the direct cause of his final crash was the bad habit of making uncalled for speeches from the stage, a breach of professional etiquette apparently in evidence about the year 1833 as it is today.

The film story is somewhat a thing of shreds and patches. The opening is monotonous and long drawn out, while the attempt to liven it up with some knock-about buffoonry injures the dignity of the players and their theme. It is not until the second half is reached that we see much of the touch of genius; then the thing becomes human and begins to grip. It begins to possess scenes of power: Kean's drink-haunted memory of the insult offered his flowers, his broken-hearted, although drunken, attempt to gain redress, his wild denunciation of the Prince of Wales from the stage of Drury Lane, and best of all, the tiny episode in which the old prompter announces the great actor's collapse. Excellent, also, are the death scenes, although a little too long drawn out. These do much to eliminate the memory of the tedious opening scenes, the artificial and unconvincing scenes in the Coal Hole, and the bad acting of the English members of the cast.

What "Kean" wants is more suggestion and less attempted realism in its scenes of foulness, and a convincing love interest. Both the female roles are weak and subservient entirely to Kean, whereas both should have been used to build up and give sincerity to the main character. As it is, they are vague things floating in the background of an almost monolog.

At the zenith of his power, Kean attracts the attention of two women, the Countess de Keofeld, wife of an Ambassador, and Anna Danby, an orphaned heiress. He conceives a strong passion for the Countess, but the realization of her superior social station keeps him from any declaration of his passion. It, however, combined with the attention of his creditors, drives him to further excess, in which he is joined by his faithful friend, Solomon, the Drury Lane prompter. So things go on until one day Anna, fleeing from the persistence of an uncouth lover, comes to him and begs him to put her on the stage. She is seen to enter his house by this lover, Lord Melville, who swears to ruin not only Kean's character, but the girl's, at the Countess' reception. He is, however, frustrated by Kean who produces Anna's note asking for an interview. On the back of this note is one from himself, however, pleading for a secret appointment in his dressing-room.

That night Kean again holds high revel in the midst of which he sends Solomon with a bunch of roses to the Countess. The prompter arrives at the moment the woman is departing with the Prince to some fete. The roses are trampled underfoot, Solomon is insulted, and returns with his story. The insults combined with the rum punch produce a sort of delirium tremens in which the actor visualizes the scenes of the reception of his gift. Madly he rushes to demand satisfaction, only to be himself spurned. Comes the night of his performance of Hamlet and the Countess keeps her appointment. Anger vanishes and Kean is on the point of clasping her in his arms when they are interrupted by the arrival of the Prince and the Count. Hastily he hustles the woman away, but she leaves evidence which tells the Count of her proposed infidelity.

Angered by the presence of the Prince in the Countess' box and his air of possession, Kean breaks down in his performance and furiously denounces his royal patron. He collapses and the curtain falls on "the Sun of England" for the last time.

As he is dying the Countess comes to him and begs him to live for her, but she comes too late. It might be mentioned that Anna, learning of the hopelessness of her own passion, has already committed suicide. The "back-stage" scenes are excellent, but the greater number of the exteriors are very un-English. Every now and again detail has been neglected. For instance, Romeo drinks his potion out of what appears to be a modern small whisky glass, while a hansom cab is seen in one scene. The Regency period had no more knowledge of the hansom than had the Victorian era of the taxi.

Kenelm Foss as Lord Melville, and Mary Odette as Anna Danby, have little to do, but what they have to do forms the histrionic plot on the show. Mary Odette is peculiarly unconvincing and is losing the girlish prettiness which was her great charm. The show of the picture comes from Nicholas Koline as Solomon. This is a finely sincere performance which even manages to retain some vestiges of dignity amid the absurd buffoonry which the producer evidently looks upon as comic relief. Ivan Mosjoukine is excellent as Kean, but his earlier scenes suffer, like Koline's, from the producer's perverted sense of humor. Otto Detlefsen and G. Deneubourg are alike capital as the Prince of Wales and a host of minor parts are all well played.

Nathalie Lissenko is good as the Countess, while managing to evade any evidence of growth of passion. An interesting production which, with just a little trouble, might have been a great picture.

Gore.

THE COVERED TRAIL

Sunset Productions western, featuring J. B. Warner. Directed by Jack Nelson. Running time 55 minutes. Reviewed as half of double feature bill at Loew's, New York, May 16.

Ordinary western feature, the story sticking to conventional situations, featuring J. B. Warner, a tall, slim, hard-riding cowpuncher who has been saddled with a stereotyped role.

The story concerns the cattle country and centers around Bill Keats (J. B. Warner). Keats in an effort to save his wayward weakling brother from the influence of a gang of rustlers and bad men, is compromised and suspected as one of the gang. He is captured by the vigilantes and about to be hung, when the local sheriff (Robert McKenzie) liberates him through a ruse.

Keats is recaptured and lodged in the local jail, but escapes just in time to foil a lynching party, and to interrupt a robbery of the Wells Fargo office by the local gang. He and the sheriff capture the band. Subsequently, a confession from the dying brother, who has been shot by one of his old gang, exonerates Keats.

Ruth Dwyer adds the love interest as the heroine, playing the role acceptably and exhibiting horsemanship on one or two occasions. The picture is fairly well cast, being an economical western production that will pass with "western fans" through Warner's stunts and the numerous "chases" spliced into the yarn.

The sheriff as comedy relief didn't make the grade at all.

Con.

The Wanderer of the Wasteland

First complete production in natural colors by the Technicolor process. Made by Famous Players-Lasky from the Zane Grey story, directed by Irvin Willat. Special showing at the Rivoli May 19. Running time 73 minutes.

Guerd Larey....................James Mason
Jack Collishaw....................Richard Neill
Adam Larey....................Jack Holt
Roderick Vierey....................George Irving
Mrs. Vierey....................Kathlyn Williams
Ruth Vierey.................... Billie Dove
Dismuke.................... Noah Beery

To those who saw "The Ten Commandments," there was something of great promise in the natural color photography utilized in the forepart of that production. When seeing "The Wanderer of the Wasteland," an Irvin Willat directed production of the Zane Grey story of the same title they are going to forget the Biblical picture coloring and start raving about this production. It is a work of art. That is the only expression to describe it.

There have been color processes before, but none has given the screen anything of the perfect tones that are here. There are shots that one would swear were by Remington done in colors.

This picture for the first time around is going to be the talk of the screen fans who will flock to see it. There is a question, however, as to the matter of cost of prints on pictures made by this process. It is stated the color stuff costs about 24 cents a foot as against the three and a half to four-cent charge for the ordinary black and white.

That means a considerable outlay, so it is safe to say that the color pictures are not going to revolutionize the picture industry over night, but if they can ever get the color process down to a point where the cost will be anything within approach of the regular black and white price, watch out.

It is the biggest step in picture since the close-up was first used. As an instance it need only be figured that an average 5,000-foot length film production would cost about $200 for a positive print or about $10,000 for 50 prints, but in color a positive print would cost $1,200, and 50 prints, $60,000, considerable of an item that the producer would naturally have to look to the exhibitor for.

In putting on "The Wanderer of the Wasteland," Famous Players-Lasky got the jump on all of the other producers and the amount of newspaper space the first picture will get the country over should more than pay them for the added cost of the prints.

The story is laid on the great desert in the Southwest, including Death Valley in California back in the early '70's, when the gold rush was on. The country with its colors and the picturesque attire of the day and location lend themselves admirably to the color process.

What the directors will have to watch when they start shooting in color is the value of the lights, shades and shadows. It will mean that the director will have to have a sense of color value almost as much as the artist who paints.

Irvin Willat seems to have had this in the production just completed. He makes the most of his colors. If there are moments in the script where he has run to a little too much footage on the close-ups of Billie Dove, he should be forgiven for she certainly is beautiful to look at in color.

The story is one of the mining country with the usual attendant dance and gambling halls and bars, the rough characters, and the good brother and the weakling. The latter loses his all over the gaming table and tries to steal his brother's share of an inheritance to square his debts. He is caught in the act and while the two brothers battle for the possession of a revolver the latter explodes and the weakling falls to the ground, wounded. The other believing that he is branded with the mark of Cain, becomes a desert wanderer. In time it is disclosed his brother was only slightly wounded and he is free to return to the haunts of civilization and to the girl.

Miss Dove plays the girl, while Jack Holt is the wanderer. Both are admirable types for work in front of a color camera, and Noah Beery as an old prospector is a veritable wow.

In directing Willat has handled a couple of scenes that provide real thrills. The one showing a rattler striking at the hero gave the audience a shudder and there is a rough and tumble fight, a whale for action. Another thrill is provided by an avalanche of rock coming down the side of a hill and burying an insane wanderer.

It is the color stuff itself, however, that is going to make this picture easily the most talked of production of the year on the screen. From a box office standpoint it is certain to be a mop up.

Fred.

B'WAY AFTER DARK

Harry Rapf production, presented by the Warner Bros. Founded on the play by Owen Davis. Directed by Monta Bell. Shown at the Rivoli, New York, week May 18. Running time, 75 minutes.

Ralph Norton....................Adolpe Menjou
Rose Dulane....................Norma Shearer
Helen Tremaine....................Anna Q. Nilsson
Jack Devlin....................Edward Burns
Lenore Vance....................Carmel Myers
Mrs. Smith (landlady)....................Vera Lewis
"Slim" Scott....................Willard Louis
Carl Fisher....................Mervyn Le Roy
Ed Fisher....................Jimmy Quinn
The Old Actor....................Edgar Norton
Vera....................Gladys Tennyson
The Chorus Girl....................Ethel Miller
Norton's Valet....................Otto Hoffman
Tom Dvery....................Lew Hervey
George Vance....................Michael Dark

This picture looks likely to mop up in the picture houses outside of New York. It is essentially a box office attraction. The title seems sure-fire for out of town and the smaller the town the bigger the picture should go. It is a hokum tale, done with a lot of dash and pep.

One of the wallops in the fore part is the Actors' Equity Ball at the Astor Hotel last winter. This permits of the introduction of brief shots of any number of stage and screen celebrities and the exhibitors can utilize a list of names that will make the picture look as though it was a million dollar production; Mary Eaton, Raymond Hitchcock, Florence Reed, Florence Moore, Irene Castle, Fred Stone and his daughter Dorothy, Ann Pennington and Elsie Ferguson are a few of those who appear.

The story is good old-fashioned melodrama with the hero, Adolphe Menjou, playing a wealthy society idler who plays Broadway with the social circus set, tiring of the sham and bunk of the whole scheme of existence. He finally decides to lose himself right in the big town by dropping out of sight and goes to live in an actors' boarding house off Times square.

Here he meets and falls in love with a girl, formerly the cashier in a quick lunch room but sent away for having tapped the till to get the money to send her sick mother to the country. She has practically paid the money back when a slick plain clothes Dick gets her. She is out after having done her bit and is working as the maid in the boarding house.

There are many little local touches in the actors' home that Rapf must have a lot of fun in handling. The hick vaudeville team and playing up of the Shubert name in a couple of titles were all good for laughs.

The story progresses so that the wealthy hide away finally places the former slavey in society as his ward and in the end marries her.

It is just another version of the oft told Cinderella, but the Broadway angle to this one together with the shots of the Main Stem of Gothamtown have been skillfully blended and seem certain to make this a strictly money getter.

Fred.

THE GOLDFISH

Joseph M. Schenck presentation, starring Constance Talmadge. Adapted from the stage play of Gladys Unger by C. Gardner Sullivan. Directed by Jerome Storm and releasing through First National. Showing at the Rialto, New York, week of May 18. Running time, 78 minutes.

Jennie Wetherby....................Constance Talmadge
Jimmie Wetherby....................Jack Mulhall
Duke of Middlesex....................Frank Elliott
Herman Krauss....................Jean Hersholt
Amelia Pugsley....................ZaSu Pitts
Count Nevaki....................Edward Connelly
J. Hamilton Powers....................William Conklin
Casmir....................Leo White

A neat vehicle for this Talmadge family member that should be of no little assistance in strengthening her following and perhaps sowing in fields yet untouched. The picture is a light comedy, abundant in its "hoke" and laughably subtitled, with the excerpts sounding as being lifted verbatim from the dramatic presentation.

Originally played by Marjorie Rambeau on the stage, the story has been well constructed for the silent brand of entertainment in which Miss Talmadge is ably assisted by a well-suited cast.

The feature suffers from the proverbial ailment of longevity and could easily stand some discreet cutting to eliminate time consumption, but on the whole it is lightweight entertainment that rollicks its way along and is harmless.

The suitability of the title will undoubtedly be debated by picture men for box office value, but the calling refers to a "gag" upon which the theme is based and is the term used for the agreement existing between the newly wedded couple that when one tires of the other there will be no fireworks, but simply the presentation of a goldfish in a bowl, and the addressee will thereby know it's all over. In other words, it's "air," alias "goldfish."

The youthful couple cash in upon their agreement at the same time, which is the start of two more marriages for the girl before culminating in the final return to her first husband. Meanwhile is the struggle to become a "lady," she having been previously addicted to the flash clothing and gum chewing type.

Jack Mulhall, as the fiery tempered first husband, turns in corking support for the star, as may equally be said of Jean Hersholt and ZaSu Pitts, although the latter is giving a characterization of the underling with which she has too long ben affiliated and which will undoubtedly prove an impediment should she ever undertake to break away from that figure.

Full of low comedy situations, it is nevertheless true that they do laugh at it, and that comes close enough to covering everything, and it marks a First National picture in an F. P.-L. house, if that means anything.

A burlesque and imaginary "Faust" bit receives its quota of projection time while the action also delves into the uses to which the girl puts a pair of opera glasses and feathered fan when rehearsing for her attendance at the opera.

Miss Talmadge plays it breezily and with a sense of values that is assuredly an asset to her, albeit it's more than likely a great deal of the credit might be wafted towards Storm's territory without it being very far out of the way. Between the two, the star and the director, if this is a concrete example of what they can accomplish, the duo should trail together—for this picture will enhance reputations both wave

Skig.

THE LOVE MASTER

Laurence Trimble and Jane Murfin production written and directed by Trimble, starring Strongheart, the police dog star. A First National release shown at the Capitol, New York, week May 18. Running time 70 minutes.

Strongheart	By Himself
The Fawn	Lady Julie
Sallie	Lillian Rich
David	Harold Austin
Alec McLeod	Hal Wilson
Andrew Thomas Francis, Joseph Mulligan	Walter Perry
"Smilin' Jean" LeRoy	John J. Richardson
The Ghost	Joseph Barrell
Sweet Adeline Quartet	Timber Wolves

About the weakest of the series of pictures in which Strongheart has been presented. At the best it is a wishy-washy sort of a story loosely hinged together and which relies on a dog-sled race for its big thrill. That race is too long drawn out and doesn't carry sufficient suspense to make it interesting.

Outside of the dogs, there is little to the picture. Clever titling has been resorted to, and this brings a laugh here and there. There is a fight toward the end of the story between the hero and the heavy, about as good as anything in the rough and tumble line screened in a long time.

The picture, however, is pretty poor entertainment. It will only be acceptable in the pre-release runs, where the dog makes a personal appearance with the picture, as at the Capitol this week. The dog is introduced by Larry Trimble's brother, who briefly relates he is a German shepherd dog that has had police training, and this makes it possible for him to do the work that he does in the picture. The audience gives the dog a hand as he stands on his hind legs with his head on his master's shoulder as the picture fades into the tune of "He's My Pal."

The story is laid in the snow country, with a writer of animal stories played by Harold Austin as the hero. Lillian Rich plays the heroine and the heavy is John J. Richardson. There aren't any names in the cast of humans in support of the dog star that mean anything to the box office.

The hero is the supposed owner of the dog, and is hiding in the north country to escape the law, he believing that he has killed the man mistreating the animal. The dog seeks out a female police dog which has been running with a wolf pack. The two, together with a cast-off husky, make up the sled team that brings victory to the hero in the race and make it possible for him to win the purse with which he intends to return to his home and defend himself in the courts. At the last minute, however, his relatives show up and inform him that he wasn't guilty of any crime, and he is enabled to speak to the girl he loves and who helped him win the race.

The story is secondary to the work of the dogs. It is the romance of the big police dog and his light fawn running mate that holds more interest than the affairs of the humans. There is a litter of police pups in the final shots that bring "ohs" and "ahs" from the audience when the mother and father of them stand in the improvised kennel and watch their master with his lady love.

Unless they get better material for Strongheart the day of the dog star in pictures is going to be a short one in the future. *Fred.*

DANGEROUS BLONDE

Universal production, featuring Laura La Plante. Story by Hurlbutt Footner. Directed by Robert F. Hill. At the New York May 13 as half the bill. Runs 55 minutes.

Franklin Faraday	Arthur Hoyt
Mrs. Faraday	Margaret Campbell
Diana	Laura La Plante
Roy Randall	Edward Hearne
Marie Fontaine	Eve Southern
Gerald Skinner	Jhilo McCullough
Henry	Rolfe Sedan

"The Dangerous Blonde" impresses chiefly as a good two-reel comedy gone to waste. With about four reels of the present padding eliminated and more slapstick added, it would have been of the merriest of the Keystone-Sunshine-Roach school. Now it is a picture for the none-too-exacting program houses with a fair share of laughs and the enticing pulchritude of Laura La Plante yanking it out of the mediocre class.

Miss La Plante is the fair cheerleader in an upstate college, giving opportunity for some of the usual rah-rah stuff. Some day some intelligent, observant, university-trained director is going to put out a picture showing our American colleges as they really are.

The average movie fan will probably be disappointed at not seeing all the "kid" antics he has been led to expect, but thousands of college alumni throughout the country will bless it as the first adequate portrayal of undergraduate life ever flashed on the screen.

The story shifts to the discomfort of the heroine's father, who has become involved in an affair with a siren, and ends with the daughter coming to the rescue in time to avoid a scandal. There is a raid on a "wet" cabaret and a dozen assorted fights and misunderstandings.

The whole film is as dragged out as though a steam roller had flattened it. The laughs come chiefly with the titles, but they, too, become monotonous and similar in tone before the finish. For instance, when the hero is introduced as "the greatest full back since Kitty Gordon" there is quite a howl, but when a few minutes later we are told that the game is to be the greatest "since Victor Hugo tackled the Hunchback of Notre Dame"—not a snicker.

Miss La Plante acts nicely, but not as well as she looks; however, hardly necessary in this picture. Support, direction and photography, ordinary.

A MAN'S MATE

Fox production, featuring John Gilbert. Story and scenario by Charles Kenyon. Directed by Edmund Mortimer. At the New York May 13 as half the bill. Runs about hour.

Paul	John Gilbert
Julie	Renee Adoree
Lion	Noble Johnson
Bonard	Wilfred North
Father Pierre	Thomas Mills
Veraign	James Neill
Lynx	John Giddings
Sybil	Patterson Dial

Fox dived right into the vogue for Apache pictures and turned out one that measures up as satisfactory for the intermediate film houses.

In Renee Adoree a surprisingly charming leading woman has been secured. This young actress, heretofore waging an unsuccessful battle with wishy-washy roles, displays real talent as one of those Parisian gamines.

Otherwise the picture just gets by. It slows up perceptibly near the middle, when the scene shifts from Parisian cellars to the tranquil expanses of Normandy, but revives with the ultimate return to the Apache dives.

John Gilbert appears to be miscast. He has been seen to more advantage in lighter roles.

The picture is Miss Adoree's and Fox should play it up for the neighborhood houses by boosting her.

CYTHEREA

Sam Goldwyn presentation and George Fitzmaurice production. Adapted from Joseph Hergesheimer's novel of the same name by Frances Marion. Releasing through First National. Showing at the Strand, New York, week of May 25. Running time, 79 minutes.

Lee Randon	Lewis Stone
Savina Grove	Alma Rubens
Peyton Morris	Norman Kerry
Fannie Randon	Irene Rich
Annette Sherwin	Constance Bennett
William Grove	Charles Wellesly
Claire Morris	Betty Bouton
Gregory Randon	Mickey Moore
Helen Randon	Peaches Jackson
Daniel Randon	Brandon Hurst

With much of the spice the novel contained deleted, "Cytherea" closely resembles the long run of domestic problems the screen has been addicted to. However, the production, direction and cast are ample reason for its being termed suitable for the major film houses.

Two dream passages are woven in natural color photography and were picturesque enough to cause a murmur of comment. This particular insertion may have a tendency to take the edge away from Famous Players' "Wanderer of the Wasteland," completely done in colors but has yet to hit "the street." The "Cytherea" conception of the idea is a distinct asset to the picture.

The picture will probably resolve itself into another example of the novel selling the celluloid edition with the readers of the book being the only ones capable of filling in the "naughty" ingredient. As it stands it about classifies itself as the proverbial matrimony situation of a man with a wife and two children become obscessed with romance and migrating from the homestead accompanied by the woman only to find that conventions are too binding which concludes in his return to the family.

The story serves to take the locale to Cuba for which Fitzmaurice has provided convincing exteriors. The sets, especially the interiors, draw attention while the color episodes augment this department.

Lewis Stone, Alma Rubens, Norman Kerry, Irene Rich and Constance Bennett receive feature program mention. Stone gives a corking portrayal as the wandering husband while Miss Richc leads the feminine detachment through her playing of the wife. Kerry is cast in a secondary role and Miss Rubens, although placed as the woman in the case, is subordinated to her contemporary. Both fulfill their respective obligations. Constance Bennett (daughter of Richard Bennett and known as "Connie" among New York's younger tea-dancing set where she flourished not long ago), does adequately with the much abused "flapper" characterization. New to pictures she is, nevertheless, included among the featured members.

The photographer, unmentioned, has provided an example of his work that may stand with the best and is of more than passing assistance. Fitzmaurice has carried the narrative along for interest albeit there always seems the promise of a "kick" in the offing which never assumes a positive form. Hence the picture is simply an average story well told, superbly produced, adequately acted and has the book sale to materially aid at the boxoffice.

Skig.

CODE OF THE SEA

A Paramount Production presented by Adolph Zukor and Jesse L. Lasky. Adapted by Bertram Millhauser from the story by Byron Morgan and directed by Victor Fleming. Rod LaRocque and Jacqueline Logan featured. Running time 61 minutes.

Bruce McDow	Rod LaRocque
Jenny Hayden	Jacqueline Logan
Captain Hayden	George Fawcett
Ewart Radcliff	Maurice Flynn
Captain Jonas	Luke Cosgrave
Mrs. McDow	Lillian Leighton
John Swayne	Sam Appell

The usually strong and pleasant theme of the boy who lived down his father's misdeeds and by so doing won his lady fair is the backbone of "Code of the Sea." With the ocean as the locale for a series of stormy episodes, the whole picture frames up as an attractive program thriller of little more than average merit.

LaRocque is cast as the son of a lightship captain who once hauled anchor and left his station during a terrific storm. The boy in time succeeds to his father's position as captain of the ship, but there is always the memory of his father's violation of the "code of the sea," which is strictly honorable and hazardous and permits of none but the truest and bravest becoming its true exponents, according to the picture and general tradition.

Tradition is right in that respect. The son is in love with Jenny Hayden, the daughter of the captain of a big liner. Her father shares the contempt of the rest for the son, who is believed to have orangeade in his veins and the same yellow streak which marked his father. But the daughter loves him. One night, in a terrific storm, she is near death when a yacht upon which she is a guest crashes on a reef and begins to break up.

Simultaneously the huge ocean liner on which her father is captain loses its port propeller as it nears the same reef, while the lightship with its two lamps stands as the solitary warning signal. The son, in love with the daughter, and at the same time realizing the necessity of keeping the ship at its station, lowers the ship's yawl from the davits and points toward the yacht. He doesn't make it; the boat shipping so much water that the engine is stopped.

But he dives over and a few crawls takes him to the doomed vessel's side.

Meanwhile a life saving crew ashore are trying to get a breeches buoy line to the yacht, but their cannon is unable to propel the long throw of rope. But with the son in the water they shoot a spring line across him and he swims with it to the yacht.

Result, the girl is saved and the big vessel also gets in okay, as the lightship didn't desert her post.

In the yacht rescue, however, the boy is the last one to leave the ship and the breeches buoy line slips from him. Next morning it is believed that he is lost. He is found clinging to a small mast, and a clinch finish follows.

The story itself allows for great photography and the ship models necessarily used in several shots are strikingly good replicas. The thrill scenes are developed nearly to their utmost, and while the story isn't given particularly inspired direction, its continuity is good and the cast competent, with LaRocque giving the best performance and Fawcett handing in a typical gruff sea captain performance.

The lighting on the splendid storm scenes is at all times good and if anything is wrong with the film it is that several anti-climaxes crop up ahead of the last big punch.

For the great mass of picturegoers this picture will be acceptable in that it furnishes good average entertainment which combines thrills and the stuff known as heart interest.

Sisk.

SHERLOCK JR.

A Joseph M. Schenck production released by Metro. Story by Jean Havez, Joseph Mitchell and Clyde Bruckmann. Directed by Buster Keaton. Shown at the Rialto, New York, week May 25, 1924. Running time 48 minutes.

The cast includes Katheryn McGuire, Ward Crane, Joseph Keaton, Jane Connelly, Erwin Connelly, Ford West, George Davis, John Patrick, Ruth Holley and Horace Morgan.

This Buster Keaton feature length comedy is about as unfunny as a hospital operating room. It is far and away about the most laughter lacking picture that "Dead Pan" Buster has turned out in a long, long while. The running time of the picture also is such that it is far better suited to run at the finish of a program in which there is a good strong feature. That is about the only way that this picture will turn any money back to the exhibitors who play it. Although it is on Broadway this week in a pre-release house, the Rialto, is no reason that the average exhibitor has to believe that it is worthy of having that honor. In other words, it's a flop, and the week's box office receipts at the Rialto will undoubtedly prove that to be the case.

The picture has about all the old hoke that there is in the world in it. That ranges from a piece of business with a piece of flypaper to a money changing bit and, for added good measure, a chase. There are, in fact, two chases; that means that another one was thrown in for good measure, but neither of these chases can for a single second hold a candle to the chase that Harold Lloyd staged in his last picture and in comparison there appear actually child's play.

There is one piece of business, however, that is well worked out and that is worthy of comment. It is the bit where Buster as a motion picture machine operator in a dream scene walks out of the booth and into the action that is taking place on the screen of the picture that he is projecting. That is clever. The rest is bunk.

The chances are that this picture will turn about the lowest gross of any of the Keaton's that Metro has thus far handled. *Fred.*

MLLE. MIDNIGHT

Robert Z. Leonard feature, starring Mae Murray; story by John Russell and Carl Harbaugh; supporting cast, Monte Blue, Robert McKim, Robert Edeson, N. de Ruiz, Nigel de Brulier, Johnny Arthur, Otis Harlan, Evelyn Selbie, Nellie Comont, John Sainpolis, Paul Weigel, Clarissa Selwynne, Earl Schenck, J. F. MacDonald; Tiffany production, Metro release; seen at the Capitol.

Miss Murray, like all other notables marked by some famous and familiar personal characteristic, has an urge to see what would happen without it; therefore she plays a black-wig part, hiding her blonde locks. But she is still a dancer, frankly one in the prolog and suddenly one in the main portion, later as the Spanish daughter of the French mother.

It is a harum-scarum yarn, with melodrama shrieking and unashamed. There is an attempt at the intangible, also, with the girl haunted by the dancing spirit of her mother, which comes to her at midnight nightly, causing her to be plotted against as a maniac by the dirty greasers who want to steal her fortune and overthrow the Mexican government; and they would but for the ever handy "American," this time in the colorless person of Monte Blue.

Leonard has woven in big scenes galore, interior and exterior, and makes the otherwise meaningless presentation possibilities at least up to usual grade by overstaging them.

The photography is indescribably fine and the lightings in the close-ups are a study in perfection. Miss Murray stands them as perfectly, too.

A mushy love story, never sufficiently stabilized or substantiated, is a loose string in the bow, and will take away from the box office value of a feature which otherwise has considerable merit. Miss Murray's story-picker needs advice of counsel, anyway, revealing a penchant for trash of a brand which the better pictures have long since passed up.

But the handling of the star is mighty in the face of the pointless and punchless plot. And the support is strong, especially in the work of Johnny Arthur, erstwhile of the legit, who comes through with surprising vigor and effectiveness. Blue is tepid. Edeson as a heavy is heavy enough. De Ruiz is a perfect type as a Spanish "dirty dog."

The film reeks with old subterfuges, roaring coincidences, broad methods and unsubtle story-telling, with the titles long and flat and wearisome and the continuity jumpy and distracted.

This so disorganizes the interest that what might otherwise be a presentable entertainment on the strength of Miss Murray's splendid appeal and sterling work, the proportions of the production, the superfine photography and the action in ensemble scenes, is tortured along until what slight heart interest might be engendered is diluted and distorted.

Not a first-class Mae Murray film, though it will do to non-critical audiences as fair blood-and-thunder stuff. The likelihood of a strong gross at the Capitol is slim. *Lait.*

THE WOMAN ON JURY

An Associated First National production from the play of the same title by Bernard K. Burns, directed by Harry O. Hoyt. Shown at the Strand, New York, week of May 18, 1924. Running time, 73 minutes.

Betty Brown	Sylvia Breamer
Fred Masters	Frank Mayo
George Wayne / George Montgomery	Lew Cody
Grace Pierce	Bessie Love
Mrs. Pierce	Mary Carr
Judge Davis	Hobart Bosworth
Marion Masters	Myrtle Stedman
Prosecuting Attorney	Henry B. Walthall
Defense Attorney	Roy Stewart
Juryman	Jean Hersholt
Juryman	Ford Sterling
Juryman	Arthur Lubin
Juryman	Stanton Heck
Juryman	Fred Warren
Juryman	J. Edward Davis
Juryman	Arthur S. Hull
Juryman	Kewpee King
Juryman	Leo White

There is something of a question as the appeal that this picture will have on audiences generally. Ordinarily it should be touted as a sure-fire money-getter, but the question enters whether or not the sordidness of the story is a little too much for the average audience to bear. As a picture it is well done, and even to a person knowing the story in full there is a certain intensity of suspense that grips. That is all in its favor, as seemingly the general theme, which is decidedly sexy, should also be from a picture house standpoint, but it seems that audiences are not going particularly wild over the sex stuff as shown in this production at present, and that means that, while "The Woman on the Jury" is a darn good picture, it is not going to be out of the ordinary as a money-getter at the box office.

In the matter of cast there is a number of names that stand out as drawing cards; in fact, every one that is in one of the major roles is a name that is known to the picture fans. For instance, the line-up is Sylvia Breamer, Frank Mayo, Lew Cody, Bessie Love, Mary Carr, Hobart Bosworth, Myrtle B. Steadman, Henry Walthall and Roy Stewart.

That would usually sound like something, but the trouble is also disclosed to a certain extent thereby and it is simply this: Neither Sylvia Breamer as the wronged woman No. 1 nor Bessie Love as the wronged No. 2 can get any sympathy from the audience, whether it is their personal lack of appeal or the fact that the roles of the wronged women in this particular case do not tend to attract sympathy is a question, but it pretty much appears as though it were due to a combination of the two.

Frank Mayo makes an acceptable hero, and Lew Cody as the heavy is all that could be asked for. That about passes up the major portion of the cast. The next step is the jury. That in itself is a cast, with Ford Sterling, Jean Hersholt and others of like calibre included in it.

The principal action of the feature takes place in the jury room and the audience is in on the punch all the while. They know that the woman on trial and the woman on the jury have both been wronged by the same man, and likewise that the jurywoman is sooner or later going to spill her story, but still this scene is the woman that holds all the interest. It is cleverly handled and does not tire, as it easily might have, but the comedy relief that is furnished by Ford Sterling as a juryman manages to pull it through at any minute when it would seem that there was too much drama.

As a picture it will entertain, but as a money-drawing attraction it will have to be placed in the class of regular program features that are not out of the ordinary in box office value. *Fred.*

DARING YOUTH

B. F. Zeidman production featuring Bebe Daniels. Distributed by Principal Pictures Corp. Scenario by Dorothy Farnum. Directed by William Beaudine. At the New York, May 22. Runs 70 minutes.

Alexander Allen	George Parcec
Mrs. Allen	Lillian Langdon
Alita Allen	Bebe Daniels
Arthur James	Lee Moran
John Campbell	Norman Kerry
Winston Howell	Arthur Hoyt

A preliminary announcement offers the information "Daring Youth" was suggested by "Taming of the Shrew," the biggest laugh in this moderately entertaining picture. Any resemblance is as puzzling as Mah Jongg to a beginner, except that at the very finish a young husband, finally exasperated at his wife's giddiness, lays the law down in no uncertain fashion and completely tames her. But there is nothing shrewdish about her.

However, the film is good stuff for the better program houses. Its sexy name is of the character currently in vogue; the cast is there, and the story gives a comparatively new twist to the old happy marriage problem.

It uses as its theme Fannie Hurst's now famous mode of living with her husband; only two breakfasts a week together and freedom at all times.

The picture might have been called "Part-time Husbands."

Alita Allen has married John Campbell upon condition she enjoy her own idea of independence after the wedding and certain days a week "off" to do as she pleases. After a few weeks of this irregularity, it begins to pall upon her. She yearns for her husband's undivided attention. He is determined to cure her by tolerating like a lamb her petty indiscretions.

This in turn infuriates the little wife. She is about to elope with a boob-admirer when hubby steps in, cleans up the rival, and tells his overjoyed spouse where she will get off thereafter.

Bebe Daniels is as provocatively alluring as ever, and has one scene in her ever-ready night-gown (her pictures without it are as rare as Gloria Swanson's without a neglige) Norman Kerry wears nearly as many good-looking clothes as the star. He extracts a good deal of manliness and vigor as the husband Lee Moran, as the illegit triangler, is foolish enough to keep the picture from ever becoming serious.

William Beaudine has directed with snap and discretion, although he permits several instances of super-exaggeration. At the beginning the hero sends the girl huge boxes of flowers at five, seven and eight p. m., and then drags around an even bigger one when he calls at 8.30. That could happen only in Hollywood.

While not an expenesive film to produce the picture has been lavishlq set and the settings, costumer and artistic details are of the best

HIGH SPEED

Universal production featuring Herbert Rawlinson. Directed by Herbert Blache and written by Fred Jackson. Cast includes Carmelita Geraghty, Otto Hoffman, Bert Roach, Jules Cowel. At the New York, May 29. Runs about 65 minutes.

"High Speed" is speedy only in that it works about a dozen assorted different kinds of action into one hour of film. The result is a disconnected, jibbery-jabby hash, which, while not exactly irksome, certainly goes into the eyes, and through the head, coming out behind the drowsy ears and leaving no impression whatsoever.

That may be putting it a little strongly, as no film in which Carmelita Geraghty is displayed can leave one entirely unmoved. Besides beauty of the first order, Miss Geraghty has talent that crops out more in every picture. She is the perfect type for the better-class flapper with precocious, but still charmingly reserved ways.

The picture also has Otto Hoffman as one of the cranky old codgers he plays so well. That about ends its strong points. Herbert Rawlinson, a good actor when he has the right role, flounders around in a farcical part with nothing more than his winning smile as a seller. His pictures are usually lightwaisted, but this one has no substance at all.

At the start he is an amateur boxer who thrashes the ringer matched against him by a jealous suitor for the girl in the case and the latter's grouchy pa. Having won this battle, he proceeds to elope. When it comes to being married the couple are the victims of a fake ceremony performed by a crook posing as the parson.

This leads to a violent chase to catch the couple. Everyone is arrested for speeding and there is a general mix-up in court.

Finally Rawlinson and the new wife get to a hotel and there follows some glandless bedroom stuff. Just when things begin to look promising (for the audience as well as the groom) fire breaks out and there are another handful of complications.

The story in the telling presents comic possibilities, but they are allowed to float away with the stream for the most part. Universal, Herbert Blache, who directed, Rawlinson and everyone else can do better.

This one is only for the not-too-discriminating program houses.

GREAT PRINCE SHAN

London, May 18.

Stoll production based on the story of Phillip Oppenheim. Private view at the London Coliseum. Star: Sessue Hayakawa.

Though heralded as a special effort, "The Great Prince Shan" is chiefly notable for exhibiting the inherent absurdity in the story-telling methods of Phillips Oppenheim.

There is a great deal of smoke and very little fire. From start to finish, the story consists of threats, threats, threats and next to none put into execution.

A set of most undistinguished cabinet ministers—this effect may have been intended, but is unsuccessful—are lunching to celebrate their 10 years of office. They have created a trade boom. They have also abolished the army.

A protest is made by a former foreign secretary that the country is in danger. Glimpses are given of a Teuton calling on the "colossus of Asia"—Prince Shan—and also of a dummy fortress being irrelevantly blown up.

The ex-foreign secretary dies in mysterious circumstances just as he has obtained possession of an important document. His son and his niece, with the aid of American diplomats (also remarkable for their undistinguished appearance) carry on his mission in life. She, Lady Maggie, makes ardent love to Shan. A jealous Japanese dancing girl lays a trap, by giving Lady Maggie the Shan's keys. He catches her red-handed with his papers. She is about to pay some sort of penalty. But he lets her go free.

After this the film shows the comic downfall of the Teuton conspirator and the agonized parting of the Shan and Lady Maggie, who are in love, but decide to make a sacrifice which will live after them —how—we are not told.

To make matters worse, the captions were remarkable for their banality. "You have a nice villa," was one.

THE PIRATE

London, May 16.

A good deal of novelty and also a little inconsistency prevailes in this fullblooded picture of a corsair's wooing. It is full of rapine, murder and sudden death, yet withal, probably as a sop to film convention, its hero is allowed to forsake his wickedness and break down from sheer happiness through the knowledge that as a husband and father he is far happier than as the pirate.

The story tells how Fiamma, the village beauty, is posted to watch for any sign of the arrival of piratical craft. Should they come, she is to light a beacon. The pirates arrive, but, upon meeting the chief, she neglects to light the fire. Her sister-in-law, however, sees them and rings the church bell. Later, Fiamma remembers her duty and lights the fire. A fight occurs and the chief is captured. Something has upset Fiamma and her love turns to hatred, so she demands his death. However, he is only imprisoned. He is warned by his men of approaching rescue, but Fiamma goes to his cell determined to execute him personally. The chief's love has only grown stronger, and he is quite ready to die, now he knows Fiamma hates him. Fiamma does not proceed with the execution. In the morning she tells her brother of the proposed escape, only to immediately warn the pirate of what she has done. The pirate escapes. The truth about what happened at the beacon now leaks out and Fiamma is turned out into the world.

Meanwhile, the pirate is having his own troubles with his crew, which ends in his leaving the ship. Late, he meets Fiamma's brother and a terrific fight occurs, with the birate victorious. Fiamma and her child arrive, all is forgiven and the couple settle down to a life of humdrum virtue.

Much of the picture is damaged by the so-called artistic blurred photography which is used in the fights and crowd scenes. There is far too much of it. There are some really beautiful shots of the fleet putting out to sea and of the pirate craft. Much of the acting is impoverished, but Amleto Novelli, who died a little while ago, gives an excellent performance in the title role, being well supported by Edy Darclea.

Despite its oddities, this is an excellent all round Italian feature made by Augusto Genina and handled here by Pathe, who is dealing heavily in such subjects at the moment.

Gore.

MIAMI

Alan Crosland production produced by the Tilford Cinema Corporation and releasing through Hodkinson, starring Betty Compson. Crosland directing; story by John Lynch, and Dal Clawson, camera man. Showing at the Rivoli, New York, week of June 1. Running time, 74 minutes.

Joan Bruce	Betty Compson
Ranson Tate	Lawford Davidson
Mary Tate	Hedda Hopper
David Forbes	J. Barney Sherry
Veronica Forbes	Lucy Fox
Grant North	Benjamin F. Finney, Jr.

Originally slated for fall release, this feature was set weeks ahead when Hodkinson decided to bolster its hot weather program. It screens as a neat presentation especially suitable to the summer months.

Possibly a lightweight as to the story told being another transgression against the idle rich and their manner of killing time, the various phases of water sports included should make this a cooling interlude for a hot evening.

A high thermometer will benefit the actual viewing of the film, for the action lists motor boating, yachting, swimming, aquaplaning, bootlegging and seaplanes as insertions. Besides which the theme reveals a tendency to sustain a sex angle.

Crosland has told what he has to tell in a brisk manner without resorting to superfluous padding, and while the script fails to call forth undue effort upon the part of the cast the water activities and general breeziness are sufficient to keep the picture's head up. Lavish interiors have been interwoven to total the entire production as being distinctly in the better class as regards that particular department.

Giving Betty Compson the role of a fast living miss who finally succumbs to the serious minded construction engineer, the theme marks the end of her consistent pursuit of "thrills" until she is induced to board the "heavy's" yacht under the pretense a party is going on.

Whether anything happens on board the boat is guesswork so far as the picture is concerned, but the return of the fiance gives the villain sufficient hold upon the girl to make her break the engagement and resume her wayward career albeit she is still in love with her bridge builder.

The resumption of her hectic routine is marked by her mounting a diving platform, disrobing and plunging into the pool very negligee.

The girl's guardian, also fond of the boy, finally induces the youth to see the girl once more before he leaves, which brings about the chase to an isolated island where the heavy has taken the girl. Meanwhile his wife has phoned the coast guards telling of big liquor haul is expected that night and a rocket is to be the tip-off signal. The resultant "jam" when the girl touches off the flare, the fight, roundup of the bootleggers and the rescue done in order actively camerased.

Miss Compson as Joan Bruce gives a presentable performance, although not called upon for anything that might be termed exacting. The same holds true of the remainder of the players.

What chance the picture has to stand remains as to whether it can surmount the recent avalanche of films of the same type with their wild parties, etc.

The sport ingredient should be sufficient to sustain this release, as the outdoor angle is refreshing throughout and a body of water in the summer is never hard to look at—even if it is on a screen.

Skig.

WOMEN WHO GIVE

Reginald Barker production, presented by Louis B. Mayer, released by Metro. From "Cape Cod Folks," by Sarah P. McLean. Shown at the Capitol, N. Y., week June 1. Running time, 70 minutes.

Emily Swift	Barbara Bedford
Jonathan Swift	Frank Keenan
Becky Keeler	Renee Adoree
Captain Joe Cradlebow	Robert Frazer
Captain Bijonah Keeler	Joseph Dowling
Ma Keeler	Margaret Seddon
Sophie Higginbottom	Joan Standing
Ephraim Doolittle	Victor Potel
Noah Swift	Eddie Phillips
Ezra Keeler	William Eugene

Here is an instance of just how far the picture producers will go to get a title for a picture that they believe will mean something at the box office. Thus "Cape Cod Folks" becomes "Women Who Give" on the screen.

The idea is that the women of the New England neck whose husbands and sons follow the sea for their livelihood are supposed to give their all to the sea. Other than that it is just a melodramatic tale of the cod fishing industry along stereotyped lines, even to the ruined "gel," whose man comes back to marry her despite parental opposition.

It isn't by far the average type expected in a Broadway house as a pre-release attraction, but the summertime is here and the chances are there are some that will come along worse than this one, which has at least as a saving grace some fairly good sea stuff that provides thrills here and there.

The story is laid in a New England fishing village where the whole industry is codfish. If you live there you either go down to the sea in ships and fish for cod, or if you remain at home you pack it and send it out to a waiting public that gathers every Friday in the Childs feederies all over the country for their codfish balls.

The packer and shipper of this particular village has amassed a fortune and he has tried to get the cod smell away from his son and daughter by educating them in select schools "down Boston way," hoping that then when they came back they would be ready to settle down and marry some real people and not mix with the village folk. He loses his guess, for his daughter falls for a fishing schooner captain and the son for the daughter of the old lighthouse keeper.

That served the old packer right, for he wanted to cut the price of cod to the fishermen, and just for that they went right out to sea where the swordfish were and didn't catch any cod at all, but it gave the chance to piece in a lot of swordfish stuff.

Barbara Bedford looks like a million dollars with her bobbed hair. Whether wet or dry it still looks good, and in this picture they show her with her hair wet when she comes out of the sea. That in itself is a novelty.

Frank Keenan plays the stern old packer and puts the role over with a punch. Robert Frazer is the lead and does well enough, while Renee Adoree is the "ruined gel" who wins out in the end.

Fred.

MARRIAGE CHEAT

Thos. H. Ince Production released by First National. Story by Frank R. Adams, adapted by C. Gardner Sullivan. Directed by John Griffith Wray. Shown at the Strand, New York, week June 1, 1924. Running time, 70 minute.s

Helen Canfield	Leatrice Joy
Paul Mayne	Percy Marmont
Bob Canfield	Adolph Menjou
Rosie	Laska Winter

Thomas H. Ince seems to have beaten the "White Cargo"-"Rain" type of play to the punch as far as the screen is concerned, although there is no similarity in the story that could be linked to either of the plays other than he has a clergyman, a native vamp and a white woman in his production. It is a South Sea Isle tale that carries a lot of punch, some great sea stuff and is fairly interesting and should prove a money getter at the box office.

There is one thing, and that is the story is easy to follow, as there are but four principal characters, all featured—Leatrice Joy, Percy Marmont, Adolph Menjou and Laska Winter. That last named should be remembered, as she is the outstanding hit, playing a native vamp. How anyone could withstand that gal when she starts to strut her stuff! But the missionary in this story gets away with it.

It is a tale of a South Sea missionary station where the good-looking native girl, who is half white, has her eye on the preacher as her own. He manages to stand her off until one of the native canoes brings in a white woman who has been picked up at sea. She was one of a yachting party, and her husband loaded the boat with a sporty set, to escape whom she took the jump, expecting death, but instead landing on the native isle.

Shortly after her arrival she becomes a mother. The minister has fallen in love with her, and later, when her husband arrives on the scene, he tries to save her from returning. As the matter finally works out the yacht is wrecked in the little harbor and the husband loses his life, so the coast is clear for the two lovers, and the native vamp is cheated out of her man.

The picture is decidedly well done, especially the vamping stuff. The scenes on the yacht, with a wild party in progress, also fit in nicely. It is a peppy picture for the summer.

Fred.

MAYTIME

Louis A. Gasnier Production, presented by B. P. Schulberg. Adapted from the operetta of the same title by Olga Printzlau. Shown at the Rialto, N. Y., week June 1, 1924. Released by Preferred Pictures. Running time, 79 minutes.

Ottilie Van Zandt..............Ethel Shannon
Richard Wayne ....Harrison Ford
Matthew ....William Norris
Alice Tremaine.....................Clara Bow
Claude Van Zandt......Wallace MacDonald
Col. Van Zandt..............Josef Swickard
Mathilda ....Martha Mattox
Ermintrude ....Betty Francisco
Monte Mitchell ....Robert McKim

Preferred Pictures made a screen version of the Rida Johnson Young operetta "Maytime," and while it has been generally shown around the country the feature did not get a date for a Broadway showing in New York until this week, when it came into the Rialto. It is a decidedly sweet love story made likable to those that saw the stage presentation through the fact that the same musical score is used and as a picture well done from the standpoint of direction and production, but it does not seem to have any particular box office wallop.

Possibly the lack of box office interest is that "Maytime" as far as the stage is concerned is a thing of the past. Titles of operettas are all too easily forgotten on Broadway after a couple of seasons have passed. That, however, isn't true of the road, and there must be spots around the country where the lilting airs of the piece are still lingering. On the Main Stem, however, it does not look as though the picture is going to get very much of a return at the box office. Monday night at the Rialto there were about 500 people in for the early evening show and about 200 less than that for the last show of the night.

In transferring the story to the screen Olga Printzlau did a very good piece of work. She retained everything that there was in the original and then added a modern twist to the finish with all of the chorus girl stuff and a wild party. However, none of the comedy that there was in the play was present on the screen.

In the matter of direction Gasnier handled the picture perfectly, and there is a little touch of color photography at the finish of the production that gives the ending an added thrill. There is also some very good storm stuff toward the end, especially a lightning flash that knocks down the tree in the old garden about which the story revolves.

Ethel Shannon plays the lead, with Harrison Ford opposite her, the two running through the three generations of the story. Had the picture beaten "Secrets" to Broadway then Miss Shannon's performance would have been remarked as one of the outstanding pieces of work of the season as against Norma Talmadge's showing of the successive ages of a woman. William Norris is in the screen production in his original role, while Robert McKim plays a heavy in the later scenes that have been added.

As a feature "Maytime" ranks as about as good as anything that Preferred have turned out. It does not, however, appear to be a picture that is destined to break any box-office records.

Fred.

PAL O' MINE

C-B-C Production from story by Edith Kennedy, featuring Irene Rich and Pauline Garon. The cast also includes Joseph Swickard, Willard Louis, Al. Roscoe and Jean Debriac. Directed by Ed. J. Le Saint. Shown at the Circle; June 2, as half double bill.

Nothing new to the theme dragged out in this independent program production, although Director Le Saint has done his best to make several big climaxes save the picture from dropping below presentation par. That Irene Rich and Pauline Garon share the feature lines may help the box office, but their work isn't sufficient to make the picture stand out.

There are several scenes noteworthy as far as sustaining the melodramatic action, yet as a whole it drags interminably.

The picture tells of the formation of an opera company by a famous impresario who in his desire to engage a prima donna has a terrible time with applicants until Julia Montefort appears.

Some things pretty far fetched and streaks of attempted comedy fail to give picture proper stimulus.

Of the acting Miss Rich is head and shoulders above the rest, although Willard Louis' character was effectively done, and Debriac made his maniacal scenes as thrilling as possible.

Production appears to be held down in heavy settings, and at times the "shots" were inexpensive.

"Pal o' Mine" is passable even in the neighborhood where there is a constant run of a better grade of cinema entertainment. It's main draw are the two women.

FAIR WEEK

Presented by Jesse Lasky-Famous Players as a Paramount Picture. Walter Hiers starred. Directed by Rob Wagner. In Hiers' support appear J. Farrell McDonald, Constance Wilson, Robert Mack, Mary Jane Irving, Earl Metcalfe, Carmen Phillips and Knute Erickson. Shown at the Circle, June 2, as half double bill.

"Fair Week" is a story of a rural country, with Walter Hiers as Tod Swasey, the hotel runner, the hotel clerk and the handy man around the Coliseum Hotel.

The action is supposed to take place in Rome, Mo. The F-P money bags were pretty well unloosened; several scenes cost money.

It appears as though most of the money was expended on "extras," as the fair grounds scenes called for a lot of people. The Rome Tri-County Fair is well staged, with the meller idea of the story pretty well connected for the most part.

To Rome comes a trio of fast workers, one in particular being a reformed gambler, now known as Soapy Smith the fighting evangelist from Topeka. Soapy is there to take the town while Mlle. Le Grand was doing her balloon ascension and parachute drop. The other man was the balloon lady's manager.

It happens that four years before a circus had come through that section and a little girl was left behind. She just grew up as Sally Jo, and she and Tod were great friends.

In a succession of comedy chases, with Tod after Soapy, the blowoff comes in a church belfry, where the two have a fight, with the fat boy the victor. The money is saved, and Ollie finds what a merry chump she has been and Tod is the big hero after all.

Some of the best comedy moments are in the church fight, the recovery of the scattered money as it is kicked through the loft down among the excited townspeople below. There is chance for fun-making here, which Wagner works up for all there is in it.

"Fair Week" seems cut and dried for the countryside, with the Paramount bookers not having to worry whether the big cities like it, for its small-town atmosphere and its melodramatic continuity are sufficient for the small town.

FIGHTING AMERICAN

Universal production, directed by Tom Forman. Story by William Elwell Oliver and adapted by Raymond L. Schrock. Scenario by Harvey Gates. Photography by Harry Perry. At the 81st Street week May 26. Runs about 65 minutes.

Bill Pendleton ....Pat O'Malley
Mary O'Mallory.................Mary Astor
Danny Daynes ....Raymond Hatton
Fu Shing........................Warner Oland
Quig Morley....................Edwin J. Brady
W. F. Pendleton...............Taylor Carroll
W. A. Pendleton............Clarence Geldert
O'Mallory ....Alfred Fisher

A preliminary announcement above Carl Laemmle's name speaks for itself, although there may be some difference of opinion as to whether it is an explanation or an apology. It reads: "This picture is guaranteed not to make you think. Please do not take it seriously. It is intended only as a masterpiece of nonsense—just to entertain you, nothing more. If it succeeds in this it has accomplished its mission."

The "masterpiece" is throwing the flowers too freely. Still, "The Fighting American" is not a bad affair. It is hoke first, but hoke with a kick, laugh and action. The story won for William Elwell Oliver Universal's Intercollegiate Scenario Contest. It starts in a more or less serious vein, ending, however, in broad burlesque.

It follows the adventures of an All-American fullback (why is it always a fullback in the films?.. He gives more time and energy to aeroplanes and monkey business than to his studies and behavior, and consequently gets the gate at college and at home.

Landing in China, he is just in time to smear a young revolution and find the girl he had insulted in college busy converting the heathen as the daughter of an American missionary.

One or two twists are the highlights of an otherwise conventional plot, with China the locale instead of the usual Central American dive. The best comes when the girl is attacked by the heavy, incidentally the Chinese general behind the uprising. He forced her to his tent, and the last we see of them he is pawing her dress with lustful hands just where the frat pin of our hero nestles next to her heart.

There follows 10 minutes involving the hero and his efforts to break through the lines to the rescue of his beloved. Finally he reaches the entrance of the tent and the audience receives a thrill wondering what will be disclosed when he steps inside. He rushes through the flap, and there sits the Chink sheik playing the piano while, perfectly at her ease, the girl watches him smilingly from another corner of the tent. The explanation comes when it is found the villain has happened to notice the pin and found himself to be a fraternity brother of the hero. (You've got to let loose a snicker at that one.)

Another twist has Raymond Hatton, the common garden species of bum in the United States, developing into a military dignitary of China, second only to the President. Mr. Hatton is the best of a competent cast, which included Pat O'Malley and Mary Astor as the youngsters and Warner Oland as the heavy.

The rah-rah stuff at the beginning is perhaps more exaggerated than usual. There are some flashy and daring aeroplane shots and the horsemanship in the Chinese fight scenes is extremely fine.

Tom Forman and Harry Perry share as director and camera man.

Universal has spent money on the production and it will have to do business to make any money. This it should have no difficulty in accomplishing in the better program houses, although for the 81st Street, which ordinarily flashes only first-run attractions, it was a trifle below standard.

THE SIGNAL TOWER

London, May 27.

Put on for a season at the Rialto, May 26, James W. Bryson claims this to be the world's premiere of the new Universal picture directed by Clarence Brown. The picture is a particularly fine example of the American genius for taking an ordinary story, with scarcely a new angle in its "triangle" theme, and building the thin fabric without losing interest until a crashing sensation sends the audience out to talk of the new kinematographic wonder.

The few final feet kill the ordinary preceding reels, leaving only a dim memory which is utterly subservient to the closing thrill.

Again, the author has made romance out of the somewhat sombre lives of what, in this country, is somewhat snobbishly called the working class. Except for their surroundings, his characters might be moving in any walk of life, and it is this realization of the truth of Kipling's line about "Biddy O'Grady and the colonel's lady" that has given the American film such a big popular pull here.

An English producer would be almost shocked if asked to find romance in the life of a traction engine driver or a small business man. His views are narrow and he can only find beauty or heroism in the higher ranks of life; to him, all else is squalor and brutality, although useful at times in his search for light and shade. If he touches the lower strata, it is invariably to make a burlesque enlivened by an attempt at heart interest.

The picture tells the story of a railway signalman, his wife, little son and a blackguard. The latter, not the wealthy man from the city who chances to meet the wife and attempts to lure her away, is another signalman.

The production work is very fine throughout. The storm scenes are apparently those of a terrific tornado and are most realistic, while the final sensation has rarely, if ever, been equalled. The photography is of beautiful quality.

Acting honors go to Wallace Beery for a remarkably fine study of Joe Standish. He never exaggerates and his villainy is subtly suggested. When the final scenes come he presents a remarkable study of bestial passion. Rockcliffe Fellows is by no means as good in portraying Dave Taylor. His performance has the appearance of being machine made; his emotion, a thing of glycerin and water. Virginia Valli is excellent as Sally and plays with sincerity. A clever child study comes from Frankie Darro. These four players have the weight on their shoulders.

There can be no doubt but that this picture is a certain winner.

Gore.

HOW TO EDUCATE A WIFE

Baltimore, June 3.
Warner Brothers' production. Story by Elinor Glyn. Cast including Marie Prevost, Monte Blue, Claude Gillingwater, Vera Lewis, Betty Francisco, Creighton Hale. Edward Earle and Nellie Bly Baker.

The Glyn fans are handed a surprise in this Glyn picture. Its morals are decidedly middle class. One of the minor women does desert her husband for a home-breaker, but the incident isn't followed up. The nearest approach to naughtiness is a close-up showing the leading male and female embracing in neglige. But they're married.

Here, in brief, is a rather diverting comedy of suburbia, telling an amusing if not particularly exciting story of an ex-manicurist and a struggling insurance agent who fail to weather the first year of matrimony.

Monte Blue, as the husband, is short on cash and not especially long on ideas. A prosperous friend (Creighton Hale) tells him he should instruct his wife to attract trade, cites his own wife as an example, and quotes from "Prudence Prue's" newspaper department, "How to Educate a Wife," to back up his argument.

When Marie Prevost, as the wife, tries out the theory by keeping a luncheon engagement with the very man (Claude Gillingwater), who, incognito, writes the "Prudence Prue" copy, Monte makes the air blue and they separate. After a series of fairly amusing incidents a la "The First Year," mamma loves papa once more.

The characters, somewhat suggestive of a Norris novel, are rather good; but the story is loosely hung together, of varying mood and not wholly original. Blue, Prevost and Gillingwater are in character.

The film may have an asset in the title, which, coupled with Glyn's name, should prove a draw. The followers of the sexy scenario, however, will not find what they are looking for.

AN ALCOHOLIDAY

London, May 26.
Probably in the prehistoric days of kinematography someone may have made a worse picture. Also some genius for vulgarity may have dug deeper into the world's sewage, but it is doubtful.

This remarkable product, "An Alcoholiday: The Story of a Thirst," featuring Picard, the "Gentleman Tramp," is of doubtful origin. Continental it certainly is, and it is probably French; in fact, it is fairly certain that it is.

The firm who, from some mistaken idea of what the public wants, is handling it here, is Globe Films, a firm who apparently buy the cheapest junk they can find in the fond hope of finding some gutter market for it.

As the title hints, it deals with drink, drink, and nothing but drink. There is no humor, although it was doubtless made under the impression the spectacle of unclean men foully intoxicated and generally bestial and enormously breasted women, also drunk, would prove a spectacle of international joy.

What story there is in this five reels of putrefying tripe tells how one Picard, in a moment of greater than usual alcoholic excess, collapses and is taken into a hospital.

He wakes to think there is another war on.

His daughter, a chorus girl, is married to a nobleman who cannot pay his servants and who is in general financial difficulties. To cover these he insures his life heavily and a bogus doctor is employed to find a patient who will die quickly. This man engages a terrible nurse who has a gag line, "when I was in the trenches," to look after the pseudo count who is, of course, the alcoholic Picard. They remove Picard to the count's country villa and proceed to fill him up with liquor of every sort. Instead of dying he only gets stronger.

In the end the count is shot by the drunken nurse, the chorus girl gets the insurance money, and Picard returns to his old haunts with enough money to remain drunk until the end.

The whole thing is rubbish and utterly devoid of humor. It might with great luck, suit a penny show. No producer is named and no actor beyond Picard who, to give him his due, might, with a proper story and direction, become a passable comedian. *Gore.*

THE SEA HAWK

First National Pictures, Inc., present "The Sea Hawk," from the story of the same title by Rafel Sabatini, adapted by J. G. Hawks and directed by Frank Lloyd. Opened at the Astor theatre, New York, on June 2, 1924, for a run. Running time, 129 minutes.

Sir Oliver Tressillian	Milton Sills
Sakr-el-Bahr, the Sea Hawk	Milton Sills
Rosamund Godolphin, his fiancee	
	Enid Bennett
Master Lionel Tressillian	Lloyd Hughes
Master Peter Godolphin	Wallace MacDonald
Sir John Killigrew	Marc MacDermott
Jasper Leigh, a freebooter	Wallace Beery
Asad-ed-Din, basha of Algiers	
	Frank Currier
Fenzileh, his wife	Mme. Medea Radzina
Marzak, her son	William Collier, Jr.
Justice Baine	Lionel Belmore
Ali, Asad's lieutenant	Fred de Silva
Tsamanni, Asad's personal aide	
	Hector V. Sarno
Yusuf, a Moorish leader, Spanish prisoner	Albert Prisco
Spanish Commander	George E. Romain
Infanta of Spain	Christine Montt
Ayoub, Fenzileh's eunuch	Robert Bolder
Andalusian slave girl	Kathleen Key
The siren	Claire DuBrey
Inn Keeper	Louis Morrison
Inn Keeper's wife	Kate Price
Captain of Asad's guards	Al Jennings
Nick, Oliver's personal servant	
	Bert Woodruff
Oliver's young son	Walter Wilkinson
Sir Walter	Andrew Johnston
Bishop	Henry Barrows
Chief Justice of England	Edwards Davis
Boatswain	Robert Spencer
Turkish merchant	Theodore Lorch
Spanish slave girl	Nancy Zann

Just about every so often a picture comes along that has a real kick in it, a kick that makes a couple of hours of time pass while you are viewing the picture at a speed that makes it seem less than the usual 70 minutes it takes to see the average production. That speaks for entertainment value, and this picture has no end of that. It is just as thrilling and gripping as reading one of Sabatini's books, for all of the punch of that author's writings have been brought to the screen in this.

From a money standpoint it is going to stay at the Astor just as long as the First National people want to keep it there, and if they can get away with road-showing it over their franchise holders, they are pretty certain to clean up at the box office in the legitimate theatres.

There isn't a thing lacking in this picture that any picture fan could want. That is a lot to say about a costume picture, but, nevertheless, this one is 100 per cent.

There's action aplenty. It starts in the first reel and holds true to the last minute. Milton Sills, who is featured together with Enid Bennett, comes into his own in this production, and Miss Bennett also scores tremendously. One must, however, not overlook Wallace Beery, a low comedy ruffian, who wades right through the story and makes the fans out front love him to death.

So much for the players. If the performances on the part of the three mentioned are going to mean great things for them in pictures for the future, that doesn't hold a candle to what it must mean for Frank Lloyd, who directed. From this time on he is to be considered with the best that wield a megaphone. Mr. Lloyd turned out a picture that is a picture, and if he can repeat he's worth anything he asks.

According to report, "The Sea Hawk" cost around $800,000. The properties used alone cost $135,000. The picture looks it, but First National can start right in counting now, for that money is all in the bank, with a lot more if they handle the picture right.

The opening scenes in England are delightfully handled. It is in the days when a glittering sword was the readiest answer to the slightest insult. Here are two brothers, the eldest in love with the daughter of a neighboring house. The younger slays the girl's brother. When he fears the defense of the elder, who has been accused of the crime, will be the cause of his being found out, he plans to have him abducted and sold into slavery to the Moors. His abduction leads to the report of his fleeing the country, and it is taken as proof of his guilt.

All this is told to hold the interest, and then the real kick starts.

That kick lies in the sea stuff. The abductor (Mr. Beery) decides to loose his captive if the latter will pay for it. They reach a bargain as they are overtaken by a Spanish galley which takes them a prize. Sir Oliver (Mr. Sills) the hero of the tale, is chained to the oars of the Spanish ship. His rescue is brought about when the Spaniard in turn is taken captive by the Moors, Sir Oliver's companion oarsman having been the nephew of the Moorish commander.

This gives two seafights in the first part. The first just enough to whet the appetite, and the second a really fine bit of staging.

As the two ships come together the giant sweeps the slaves man are snapped off, the ships are grappled to each other, and the men of arms come swinging across the deck to do battle and at the same time the two slaves loose their irons and make their escape to the Moor. But a lone marksman on the Spaniard, who escaped the conflict, takes aim and kills the escaped Moor slave, to pay for it with his own life at the hands of Sir Oliver.

His experience at the hands of the Spaniards has made him only too willing to foreswear Christianity and turn to the faith of the Moors, which he does. In three years he has become their greatest warrior, making constant war on the ships of Spain and capturing prize after prize until his name is one feared in all the world of shipping.

The second part opens with his going to sea in command of his galley. The first prize he takes is the Spaniard that originally was the English ship from which he had been taken. Here he discovers his abductor of three years before, still held prisoner. He releases him and promises him freedom if he will command the prize and take her back to England as though nothing had happened and bear a message to the fair Lady Rosamund (Miss Bennett) which will prove his innocence.

When receiving the message she spurns it and the released sea captain has to return to his rescuer with the information the brother who caused his abduction was on in favor with the lady and about to marry her.

On the wedding night the Sea Hawk walks in and carries off both his brother and the latter's bride-to-be, taking them as slaves to Algiers, where, under the law, they are both sold at public auction together with other slaves captured.

The Sea Hawk buys them both in but not before the girl has taken the eye and fancy of the ruler, Asad-ed-Din, who wants her, and who goes to the house of his commander and demands her. This scene is exceptionally well handled, and the manner in which the Sea Hawk saves the girl is well worth while.

Again ordered to sea he smuggles his wife aboard, but as about to sail he is relieved of command by the ruler himself, who comes aboard with his son. Their ship is cornered by an English man-of-war in command of the guardian of the girl, leaving the hero betwixt the deep sea and the devil. To save the girl he will have to give himself up, whereas if he remains on board the Moorish he feels she will suffer at the hands of his ruler, so he decides to save the girl, with a final kick coming just as he is about to be hung, when his brother confesses on his death bed.

That is the story, but its handling is a work of art that will go down in screen history as a really great picture. *Fred.*

Shooting of Dan McGrew

S-L Special, directed by Clarence Badger and released by Metro. From the Robert W. Service poem. Shown at the Capitol, N. Y., June 8, 1924. Barbara LaMarr, Lew Cody and Mae Busch featured. Running time, 72 minutes.

The Lady Known as Lou	Barbara La Marr
Dangerous Dan McGrew	Lew Cody
Flo Dupont	Mae Busch
Jim, Lou's Husband	Percy Marmont
Isador Burke	Max Ascher
The Ragtime Kid	Fred Warren
Jake Hubbel	George Siegmann
Sea Captain	Nelson McDowell
Beach Comber	Bert Sprotte
An Actor	Harry Lorraine
Miguel	Eagle Eye
Mme. Renault	Millie Davenport
A Dancer	Ina Anson
The Purser	William Eugene
Little Jim	Phillipe de Lacy

Metro for the second time in 10 years is releasing a picture entitled "The Shooting of Dan McGrew." The first production was made by Popular Plays and Players and stuck pretty much to the original poem. The present picture is a Sawyer & Lubin production directed by Clarence Badger, which has been considerably embellished as to the original story. The picture while not a tremendous feature is one that on the title alone should get money.

The trio that carry the important roles are Barbara LaMarr, "the lady known as Lou," while that snakey screen villain, Lew Cody, is "Dangerous Dan." The work of carrying out the role of "the stranger" is entrusted to Percy Marmont.

Practically two-thirds of the story as shown on the screen is laid in an atmosphere entirely foreign to the original poem. "Dangerous Dan" in this portion is a card sharp in the South Seas, while Lou and her husband are members of a small musical comedy company touring the islands. Dan steals the girl, brings her to New York, makes a cabaret star of her and finally drifts to the far north with her. Years later the husband walks in on them, and from that moment the poem as it related the tale of the shooting is followed.

Mr. Badger has directed the picture with an eye to flash stuff. The role of Lou by Barbara LaMarr is not what one would term an inspired performance. She failed entirely to get the character over as the author wrote her. The happy ending when the stranger shoots and kills Dangerous Dan and he himself escapes with only a slight graze changed the tale around altogether.

In the flash stuff there was an elaborate cabaret scene on Broadway with a spectacular fire, and some really good dance hall shots in the Yukon country. There was a tendency to drag the picture in several scenes and that slowed the action. Cody was all that could be asked for and Marmont handled the heroics decidedly well. *Fred.*

BEDROOM WINDOW

William De Mille Production, presented by Adolph Zukor and Jesse L. Lasky. Story and screen play by Clara Beranger. Shown at the Rivoli, N. Y., week June 8, 1924. Running time 70 minutes.

Ruth Martin	May McAvoy
Frank Armstrong	Malcolm MacGregor
Robert Delano	Ricardo Cortez
Frederick Hall	Robert Edeson
Silas Tucker	George Fawcett
Matilda Jones, alias Rufus Rome	Ethel Wales
Butler	Charles Ogle
Sonya Malisoff	Medea Radzina
Detective	Guy Oliver
Mammy	Lillian Leighton
Gun Salesman	George Calliga

A real mystery play on the screen. A mystery play where the audience isn't in on the secret, but has the fun of doping it all out for themselves.

It is one of those pictures that your audiences won't particularly enjoy if they come in at the tail end, get the secret of the mystery and then have to sit through the fore-part. But to those sitting down from the start it is a wow. Incidentally the program at the Rivoli asks those who see it all not to divulge the mystery to those that have not seen it.

It is a gripping little screen entertainment, which, while it may not get a world of money at the box office, will prove satisfying entertainment.

In cast it stands up fairly well, with six of the company featured—May McAvoy, Malcolm MacGregor, Ricardo Cortez, Robert Edeson, George Fawcett and Ethel Wales. The latter runs away with the picture as a detective story writer who solves a mystery of her brother-in-law's death in her own way, incidentally clearing a young man who is the suitor for her niece's hand and also finding out a lot of dirt about her brother-in-law and a Russian dame.

Miss McAvoy and Mr. MacGregor furnish the love interest to the story while Ethel Wales and George Fawcett contribute a comedy element that gets over.

The action is well handled and moves along at a fast pace.

It is an ideal summertime picture that doesn't give the audience too much to think about but still entertains them immensely. *Fred.*

$20 A WEEK

Distinctive Pictures, Inc., production released by Selznick, and starring George Arliss. Adapted by Forrest Halsey from Edgar Franklin's novel, "The Adopted Father." Directed by Harmon Weight. Photographed by Harry A. Fishbeck. At the Strand week of June 8. Runs about 68 minutes.

John Reeves	George Arliss
William Hart	Taylor Holmes
Muriel Hart	Edith Roberts
Chester Reeves	Ronald Coleman
Little Arthur	Joseph Donahue
James Pettison	Ivan Simpson
Henry Sloane	Walter Howe
George Blair	Redfield Clarke

Not even the suave dramatic artistry of George Arliss saves "$20 a Week" from being an exceedingly tedious picture. In "$20 a Week" Arliss has a role no one could make convincing. He is given no opportunity for any of the whimsicality or crafty mannerisms that have distinguished him, but is cast as a cut and dried old fellow with little to recommend him but a sound business head.

At that Arliss does everything that is humanly possible with the part, and were it not for his work the film might have been rated as so much wasted celluloid.

The plot is fundamentally unsound. It starts with one of those ridiculous wagers wherein an old clubman as rich as Croesus, or nearly so, starts out to show his shiftless son that he (the old boy) can live on $20 a week.

This is almost immediately lost sight of, and the story switches to the tribulations of a brother and sister (Taylor Holmes and Edith Roberts), children of the old man's former business partner. She has adopted a precocious brat from the orphanage, and her brother, to repay her for the nuisance, decides to adopt the old man working in his office unrecognized, as an official father.

Arliss proceeds to straighten out the tangled business affairs of the household before revealing his identity. This is accomplished with a minimum of inventiveness and a maximum of footage. Finally his son and his adopted daughter decide to hit it off, and after another quarter of an hour's complications the audience is allowed to seek the air.

Mr. Holmes has the comedy assignment as the girl's brother, and that this usually capable comedian does not get more than three snickers throughout demonstrates just how dull the plot is. He is assisted in his would-be-side-splitting moments by a new child, Joe Donahue of Brooklyn, heralded in the press sheets as a butcher's son, and apparently destined to grow up in the atmosphere of meat rather than Kleig lights. This youngster pulls everyone's tie and shows the proverbial cute little bare back in a shower bath scene, but, on the whole, Master Coogan has less than ever to worry about.

Miss Roberts, wearing her hair differently, is prettier than ever, and Ivan Simpson is his usual capable heavy. The unimportant role of the hero is well handled by Ronald Coleman.

The film might best be described as "talky," even though it is of the silent drama. Only at the end, a stockholders' meeting, is there any real action.

Just how the Strand came to book it in spite of the Arliss name is not clear. In the program houses it should draw moderate business, but it will disappoint.

THE RECKLESS AGE

Universal-Jewell production, starring Reginald Denny. Adapted from a Saturday Evening Post story by E. D. Bigger and directed by Harry Pollard, with William Fildew the photographer. Showing at the Rialto, New York, week of June 8. Running time, 79 minutes.

Dick Minot	Reginald Denny
Cynthia Meyrick	Ruth Dwyer
Henry Trimmer	Hayden Stevenson
Lord Harrowby	William Austin
Mrs. Meyrick	May Wallace
Spencer Meyrick	John Steppling
Martin Well	Tom McGuire
George Jenkins	Frank Leigh
Manuel Gonzale	Fred Malatesta
Minot's Chum	Gino Carrado

Universal's follow-up on "Sporting Youth" and working the continuation of the Reginald Denny series may fill the void in light comedy portrayals left by Wallace Reid. The film is inconsequential film material but favorable to the star because of his performance which will satisfy his personal following and should place other spectators in a receptive frame of mind for future efforts.

Not given over to any great degree of action this release mainly relies upon the script, inserted "gags" and individual contributions by the players to get it across.

The story is in a thin vein, insufficient to stand by itself, hence the main burden rests upon Denny's shoulders and his supporting cast.

The picture is unquestionably meagre material for first run house consumption but marks a legitimate performance by Denny that should do him the world of good.

The narrative evolves from an English nobleman insuring himself against the possible failure of his marriage to an American heiress. Denny is the company's representative to see that the marriage goes through, but he falls in love with the girl instead.

The appearance of a bogus titled gentleman assuming the same nom de plume as the bridegroom to be makes for complications, with Denny the one who must straighten out all angles to save his company the $100,000 the policy calls for.

The turning over of the policy by the Count as collateral upon a $5,000 loan leads to a scandal sheet getting hold of the story whence the situation becomes known to the girl and her father, with the latter forced to buy the paper to suppress the issue. The terms of the policy are violated by the loan transaction which makes it clear sailing for Denny to win the girl without involving his company.

Located principally within a hotel there has been little need for more than normal expenditure in settings while the only chance Denny has to cut loose with his boxing comes in a rough and tumble scrap that takes place within the "yellow" paper's offices. Two comedy jaunts over rough roads in the same small car by Denny and the girl are relied upon as the principal laugh obtainers.

Ruth Dwyer does acceptably opposite Denny, with William Austin also turning in a capable bridegroom, Lord Harrowby.

A half-filled house Sunday afternoon seemed to adhere to a neutral morale in regarding the film as a whole, but if nothing else it brings forth that Denny can accomplish other things before the camera besides a battle within a ring and driving automobiles. *Skig.*

IN FAST COMPANY

Carlos Production, starring Richard Talmadge. Released via Truart (M. H. Hoffman's company). Cast includes Mildred Harris, Sheldon Lewis, Mark Fenton, Charles Clary, Snitz Edwards, Jack Herrick and Douglas Gerrard. Directed by James W. Horne. Shown as half of double bill at New York, June 6. Running time, 65 minutes.

Some wise picking in Jim Horne to direct Dick Talmadge in this newest of the Richard Talmadge series. Knowing Horne's proclivities for comedy flights, it was only natural to assume he'd put Talmadge through some zip paces.

Talmadge is improving. He is in more notable screen company. His leading lady is Mildred Harris. Sheldon Lewis is the main villain, and as the plot calls for a lot of rapid fire stuff, the answer, with Horne directing, is some lively animation.

One of the best props is the start with the wild college party, worked up well. The second part moves through an auto chase and prize fight, with the fight outclassing the other, overdone and widely exaggerated, especially the rough-and-tumble hurrah in the bungalow.

Talmadge brings back the halcyon days of Fairbanks when he doubled for Doug in his dare-devil work. Dick stages some thrilling stuff, the kind that used to knock 'em in all the program houses. They are spending real money on Talmadge. He has a good director in this story, and this story as a whole holds up well.

"In Fast Company" should make some money if handled right.

WANDERING HUSBAND

Regal production, released by Hodkinson, starring James Kirkwood and Lila Lee. Story by C. Gardner Sullivan. Directed by William Beaudine. Photographed by Ray June. At the New York, June 6. Runs 70 minutes.

Mrs. Moreland	Lila Lee
George Moreland	James Kirkwood
Pearl Foster	Marguerite Livingston

The latest addition to the dozens of different kinds of "husbands" and "wives" of pictures is C. Gardner Sullivan's contribution here, with the same old backbone, but a couple of incidental twists and novel situations.

The chief reason for its being more than an ordinary program attraction is the extremely human work of the principals, Lila Lee and James Kirkwood.

It is seldom that a plot sticks so closely to the three central characters of the triangle. They are the only ones introduced by name, and except for the baby daughter, her little friend "Fatty" and a nondescript gentleman used for a few minutes by the wife for the purposes of promoting jealousy, there is no one else occupying attention.

George Moreland (Mr. Kirkwood) can be described as nothing more than a fool. He has a charming little wife (Lila Lee).

"The other woman" (Marguerite Livingston) is the silliest, most childish and aggravating flapper ever annoying an audience.

But, according to this story, Barnum was right. Wifie tries every possible expedient and trick, but not until the end does she land the right one. She takes a leaky motor boat and husband and his inamorata for a ride. Some distance out they realize they're sinking. Moreland has to make his choice of which one to aid ashore. Without hesitation, he selects his spouse, leaving a disconsolate and hysterically frightened vamp to be picked up just in time by a boat previously arranged for by the solicitous wife.

Kirkwood shows unsuspected ability as a farceur and he is an ideal choice as the poor simp. Miss Lee is delightful even in those serious moments when the film sags dangerously. Miss Livingston does as well as might be expected with a role never sympathetic and always preposterously unreal. Two cute children add to the comedy value.

Hodkinson may have intended "Wandering Husbands" for the first-run houses. As far as picking a cast, inserting comic bits and setting the production, they were on the right track, but the very triteness of the story and the way it is generally handled limits it to the minor league circuits.

DEFYING THE LAW

William B. Brush production distributed by Gotham Productions. Story by John T. Prince and Bertram Bracken and directed by the latter. At New York June 3 as half the bill. Runs 55 minutes.

Pietro Savori	Lew Cody
Lucia Brescia	Renee Adoree
Michael Brescia	Josef Swickard
Francisco	Charles (Buddy) Post
Guido Savori	Naldo Morelli
Luigi Bevani	Dick Sutherland
Dr. Chong Foo	James B. Leong
Maria Baretto	Evelyn Adamson
Sylvia Baretto	Kathleen Chambers
Alicia Bevani	Marguerite Kosik

A glance at the list might indicate the locale is Corsica, Sicily or Italy, in spite of the alien name fourth from the bottom. But "Defying the Law" takes place on the waterfront of San Francisco. The color is Neapolitan throughout, even the important bits embracing the Chinese villain failing to wipe out the ripe, full and pleasantly novel flavor of the Mediterranean.

It is this same flavor of adventure and picturesque romance that, augmented by artistic direction and photography and a cast of first-run caliber, serves to make the picture a good one for the daily change houses. The rather trite story has been embellished with a dozen different twists and several striking dramatic situations.

Instead of the usual hero-villain conflict for the girl, there are four men involved in the struggle for her love. One, a crafty Chinese doctor, strives to gain it by unscrupulous strategy. Another, a bully of the Frisco wharves, uses only brute force in an attempt to gain his ends. The third, the central character, a young artist (Lew Cody), tries to win her first by gentleness and then, seeing she loves another, by evil plotting, but in the end repents just in time to save the man she really cares for. The latter, of course, is the fourth, an Italian fisherman who contributes nothing to the struggle but his devotion. The loose and unconvincing manner in which this character, the hero, is drawn is one of the chief faults of the picture.

The competent cast greatly aided Bertram Bracken in direction. Renee Adoree, whose last few pictures have demonstrated her to have the goods, after all, once again surprises with her simple and yet appealing Italian immigrant. Lew Cody as the weak-willed artist has another of his lovable villain parts, and he is his usual suave self. A newcomer from Italy, Naldo Morelli, debuts as impressively as possible as the namby-pamby hero. The others include Josef Swickard, Buddy Post and Dick Sutherland, the last finally given an opportunity to prove he can play comedy parts with his horrible face as well as human monsters.

The photographer, who is not mentioned, deserves a word for his artistic shots. Whoever named the picture picked a title unsuitable and far from striking.

The names in the cast should boost attendance in the program houses and, once inside, they are sure to enjoy the picture.

VAGABOND TRAIL

Fox production directed by William A. Wellman and starring Charles Jones. Story by George Owen Baxter, and photography by Joseph August. At Loew's Circle, New York, June 5, as half the bill. Runs 52 minutes.

Aces	Charles Coleman
Deuces	George Reed
Donnegan	Charles Jones
Louise	Marion Nixon
Her Father	Harry Lonsdale
Nick	L. C. Shumway

"The Vagabond Trail" is a step back to the days not so long ago when the star was known as "Buck" rather than "Charles" Jones. For some months the pictures with this actor were constantly getting better and better, due chiefly to the fact that Fox was giving him distinctive roles and human interest stories with the lighter, rather than the dramatic side, emphasized. But this current feature is a return to typical, heavy western formula stuff, and consequently a severe disappointment. At that it can hardly be rated as a complete failure, comparing favorably, as it does, with the majority of films of its type.

The first five minutes promise some interesting developments that never, unfortunately, pan out. The story opens with a gang of tramps of which Jones, as Donnegan, is a charter member. Had the writer kept his hero true to the ideals of trampdom, he might have achieved an O'Henry-like quality to the story. Instead, Donnegan soon proves to be a thorough gentleman in disguise; a gallant crusader who goes a million miles out of his way to try and reform the villian whom the girl in the case imagines she loves.

Finally credulity bursts its bonds when after Donnegan has refused to inflict bodily harm on the girl's wicked fiance and is in turn shot himself it develops that the villian who almost ki'led him is his long-lost brother, Red. It has been the search for the latter that has led Donnegan to his hobo wandering. At the end of the picture it is made clear that his knight of the road days are over and from then on the only tramping he will do will be with his and the girl's baby on the floor at night.

There are the perennial western saloon and gambling bits and the death struggle on the edge of a cliff. Marion Nixon as the girl has nothing to do but strum a guitar when she's happy and look slightly worried when things go wrong. The balance of the cast, composed chiefly of assorted villians, is as conventional as the film itself.

It seems a pity that this slip-up should have been made as it cannot help but dim the lustre of the Jones whose radiance was becoming brighter in the program houses.

Venus of the South Seas

Lee-Bradford presents Annette Kellerman in "Venus of the South Seas." Shown as part of double bill at New York Roof, June 6. Running time, 45 minutes.

The strength depends entirely upon the aquatic Annette Kellerman and some beautiful water scenes. There is a story about Miss Kellerman as Shonda being marooned upon a far away island in the South Sea with her daddy, and how she meets a nice looking boy who falls in love with her.

There are some "close ups" of Miss Kellerman in the water, which are based upon a legendary tale which Miss Kellerman is supposed to tell a group of native children. Quite a melodramatic theme but secondary to the Kellerman diving and swimming stunts.

The picture will prove of greater interest in the neighborhoods.

INFATUATION

Films Albatros presentation, released through Pinnacle Productions, Ltd. Directed by Ivan Mosjoukine.

London, May 30.

The version released at the Embassy, Holborn, of "Infatuation, or the Lure of Paris," seems to have been deprived of some of the kidding necessary to make the story coherent.

It is said that in Paris the leading characters were a rich husband, his wife and the detective, called in to cure her of her infatuation for city life, which she loves.

In London, the husband becomes a guardian and the wife his ward. The scene where he goes to the detective agency is wildly farcical, but his efforts to keep the girl's love are tragic.

Even in this divided state, however, the film has called forth warm praise in many quarters.

That Dirty Dog Morris

London, May 30.

Films Albatross presentation, released through Pinnacle Productions, Ltd. Story by Guy de Maupassant, freely adapted and brought up to date by N. Rimsky and V. Tourjansky. Staged by M. V. Tourjansky.

What looks uncommonly like a new type of comic film had rather a mixed reception when presented at the Embassy, Holborn. Audiences accustomed to humor, either knockabout or sentimental, may not wake up quickly to the joys of "That Dirty Dog, Morris"; but if adequately boomed as a psychological joke, so as to warn people not to come with cut-and-dried notions concerning what a comic film should and should not be, the mental processes of the poor fool named in the title would keep a better class audience laughing constantly.

M. N. Rimsky, who plays Morris, has his own type of clowning. At first sight, this bald, fox-faced actor seems too ordinary to possess many mirthful possibilities. But, while he drinks glass after glass in order to gain enough courage to approach the lady who is ogling him, his silly smile makes you realize what he is up to. His method is to reveal the comic side of the ordinary man who is not cut out to do big things but cannot see why. When he sees more fortunate people calmly helping themselves to forbidden fruit, he wants to do likewise.

Morris misses his chances at the party because he overdoes the "Dutch courage" and sees six ladies in the chair where the alluring one sat. The next morning he feels sorry for himself.

In the train he gazes longingly at a pretty girl, Henriette, who shares the compartment. Morris lounges disconsolately in the corridor. In another compartment he sees a young man ardently kissing a girl. Morris gets an idea. When he returns to his own compartment the humming of the wheels suggests the strumming of the banjo the night before and the girl before him suggests the lady of the party.

Morris springs upon her. The police are called.

To prevent further trouble, Morris calls on his friend, the editor of the local paper, who happens to be a friend of Henriette. Somehow or other, the peace-making efforts bring the editor and Henriette very close together.

Morris cannot understand why the editor can kiss the girl without fear of consequences. If he got into trouble because of his lovemaking, why should his friend escape scot-free? He follows them into the moonlight and even tracks them to the door of the girl's bedroom. But when he finds there is to be a marriage he feels satisfied—especially as it means a reprieve for himself.

The acting is high spirited throughout. Deise Legeay is Henriette.

SACRIFICE

London, May 27.

Some people attempt to win fame by giving of the best which can be obtained, others appear to wish for some notoriety by giving of the worst. Judging by the class of picture Globe is acquiring from the continent, the firm is hopeful of finding a high place in the latter category. Its supply of poor and bad pictures is apparently unlimited and this French (?) subject is among its worst. The story is poor and of threadbare theme, and is so badly told that toward the end the whole thing becomes a jumble.

Dorothy, a beautiful student, and the Count Roger de Sangro become enamored and marry. The Count is promptly disinherited. A year later Dorothy hears a scream from their bedroom and finds the Count has died suddenly.

Later Dorothy becomes a mother and her late husband's people persuade her to give up the child and not to attempt to see it until it is 18. Eighteen years later Dorothy is on the point of becoming a famous singer, when she is told her child is dead. Not believing this, she throws up her career and becomes companion to the Countess's child, Mara, aged 18.

The Countess in this case is the dowager, Dorothy apparently never having touched the title. Mara is engaged to the young Count, her cousin, and desires the marriage only because it will give her her freedom. There is a constant conflict of wills between Dorothy and this girl, but Dorothy wins.

The young Count arrives upon the scene and the likeness is so great to the dead Count that Dorothy promptly falls in love with him. By now everyone is certain the shrewish girl cannot possibly be Dorothy's child.

Can that child really have been a boy and his mother has unwittingly fallen in love with him? Suspense is soon ended by the fact being broken that the young count has fallen in love with a mysterious, pure and beautiful young girl adopted in babyhood by a grocer. Learning this, Dorothy smothers her love and swiftly finds this flower to be her che-ild. Mara marries the Count.

Dorothy keeps the secret of the pure one's parentage and, chucking up her job, acts as a go-between between her daughter and the other girl's husband. Presumably a strictly Continental idea of a mother's duty.

Mara hears of this liaison in good time and decides to divorce the Count. Everybody is pleased, but unfortunately Mara catches her husband with Dorothy and declares the divorce off. Dorothy then proves she'll gain nothing by the divorce or by shooting herself, and the audience is left in the belief somehow or another the matter will be smoothed out.

The production is uniformly bad; so is the acting, although the "star," with very stern production methods, might give a reasonably fair performance of some secondary part. The only novelty in the whole feature is that 18 years of sorrow, sacrifice, and all the rest of it makes no difference in the ages of the characters, nor apparently did they purchase any new clothes in that period. *tGorc.*

TIGER LOVE

Zukor-Lasky presentation, produced and directed by George Melford; adapted by Julie Herne from "El Gato Montes," by Manuel Penella; screen play by Howard Hawke; seen at Rivoli.

The Wildcat	Antonio Moreno
Marcheta	Estelle Taylor
El Pezino	G. Raymond Nye
Ramon	Manuel Camere
Victoriano	Edgar Norton
Miguel	David Torrence
Hunchback	Snitz Edwards
Father Zaspard	Monti Collins

This is a neat, appealing feature, notable for lovely work by the lovely Estelle Taylor, upstanding, oldstyle heroics and good love-making by Moreno, fine photography and good settings that give a complete and satisfactory atmosphere of Spanish locale, indoors and cut.

The story is no wildfire and the title is a misnomer. There is nothing tigerish about the love, and every situatio is an old one, though the whole makes up a running affair that sustains interest and keeps surprise alive at least as to which standard trick will come next.

Moreno plays a gypsy mountain bandit who is kind to the poor and hard on the rich, etc., as always. His hoodlums hold up the beautiful signorita whose father is to be dispossessed unless she gives her hand to the effeminate nephew of the grabdee, etc., as always.

The Wildcat rescues her from his men and escorts her safely home, and is lovesick and sad until he hears there is to be a fashionable wedding, and starts out to steal the girl. She loves him but deceives him as to her sentiments, being a proud beauty, etc., as always. He kidnaps her and the groom at the wedding-to-be, takes them to his lair, makes a boob out of the groom, etc., as always.

His devoted hunchback then reveals that the Wildcat is the mayor's own son and identifies him by a locket, etc., as always; and he marries the girl, etc., as always.

The professional touch throughout is excellent. The lightings are great and one rain scene is splendid. The interiors are in the atmosphere for all scenes, poor or magnificent, and the dressing and surroundings are in keeping.

Miss Taylor is gorgeous, both to look at and to watch. Her make-up could stand shading down, as her eyelids and lips are overtoned, and in the closeups this is quite apparent. Moreno makes a fine figure of a bandit, a lover and a hero, and, except where the plot shrieks for it, does not overact.

A pleasing, interesting and not brain-wracking feature, which will get by nicely everywhere without leaving much to be remembered except the haunting beatitude of Estelle Taylor. *Lait.*

LISTEN LESTER

Sacramento Pictures Corp. presentation releasing through Principal Pictures. Adapted from the play of the same name and directed by W. A. Seiter, with John Stumar the photographer. Cast includes Harry Myers, Louise Fazenda, Alec Francis, Eva Novak, George O'Hara, Lee Moran, Dot Farley and Eugenia Gilbert. Showing at Proctor's 23d Street theatre, June 11. Running time, 64 minutes.

Played as a farce this picture relies upon its situations to push the comedy across, with the story revolving around the pursuit of a package of love letters.

Alec Francis and Louise Fazenda are the principals, sustaining the film for its light entertainment value, with the remaining players contributing but secondary insertions.

Seiter has done averagely in directing as concerns the action. Although the picture will undoubtedly amuse in the intermediate houses, it

never threatens as uproarious, and aligns itself under the definition of being somewhat far-fatched.

It tells of an aged widower, possessing a grown-up daughter, and has a particular weakness for women. Consistently stalked by a feminine member, who holds the "breach of promise" epistles, the effort to get back the letters consumes a vast majority of the action, supposedly taking place in Florida.

The daughter meets her future life partner while at the resort and the girls finally fix it to be kidnapped as a means of aiding their cause. The kick of the story is evidently aimed to evolve when one of the men, not "in" on the abducting, attacks the daughter, which paves the way for a rough and tumble scrap. The finish has the father resigned to being the husband of his pursuer while the daughter is also set with her objective.

Alec Francis does adequately as the damsel chasing father to the point where he must be given first rating. Miss Fazenda, for honors, is close behind, while Harry Myers, in not holding an especially active role, registers proportionately. The remaining members are passive in their direct bearing upon the case. *Skig.*

SURGING SEAS

William Steiner production starring Charles Hutchinson and distributed by New-Cal Film Co. Directed by James Chapin. Story and scenario by J. F. Natteford. At the New York, June 10, as half the bill. Runs 52 minutes.

Bob Sinclair	Charles Hutchinson
Edith Stafford	Edith Thornton
Charles Stafford	George Hackathorne
Lionel Sinclair	David Torrence
Edwin Sinclair	Earl Metcalf
Capt. Regan	Charles Force
Hansen	Pat Harmon

Charles Hutchinson is starred, and it should just about measure up to the standards expected by those who followed "Hurricane Hutch" through his short reels of peril and miraculous escapes. As a film for the better program houses it fails to connect.

The title "Surging Seas" is ridiculous, as there is a minimum of maritime atmosphere to the story. Nine-tenths of it takes place on dry land, and the few moments on the water concern themselves with the land-lubbers on board rather than the sailors or the ocean.

The plot is a variation of the grizzled vet about two brothers, good and bad, with Abel blamed for Cain's misdeeds. They include a near-murder of their father as well as a robbery and several misdemeanors.

There is the girl-ward who sticks to the accused hero through thick and thin, and her weakling brother, against his will, forced to aid the machinations of the villain.

The feature as far as its class of screen fans will enjoy it, is the assortment of stunts and daredevil escapes performed by Hutchinson. The usual rope-swinging, mast-climbing, diving and jumping are in it, but one of the tricks looks new and is a thrill promoter. This occurs when Hutch, chased over half the city, comes to the railroad tracks as a fast-moving freight is passing and rolls under the car, avoiding the onrushing wheels and escaping his pursuers.

David Torrence and George Hackathorne, both good character actors, have parts that don't overtax them, but they lend name value. Edith Thornton is a sweet-looking heroine and Earl Metcalf a satisfactory heavy. Hutchinson's acting is better than one might expect from a man who is as apt at purely physical achievements as he is.

THE GUILTY ONE

Joseph Henabery Production presented by Adolph Zukor and Jesse L. Lasky. Agnes Ayres featured. From the play by

Michael Morton and Peter Traill, adapted by Anthony Coldewey. Shown at the Rialto, New York, week June 15, 1924. Running time, 58 minutes.

Irene Short	Agnes Ayres
Donald Short	Edward Burns
Philip Dupre	Stanley Taylor
Seaton Davies	Crauford Kent
H. Beverly Graves	Cyril Ring
Sam Maynard	Thomas R. Mills
Bess Maynard	Catherine Wallace
Captain of Detectives	George Seigman
Detective	Clarence Burton
Anne, maid	Dorothea Wolbert

Agnes Ayres never appeared to greater advantage than in "The Guilty One."

The picture, however, does not make for good hot weather entertainment. During the regular season it would have ranked as a fairly average program release. It is a good mystery story well handled.

Supporting Miss Ayres are Edward Burns, Stanley Taylor, Crauford Kent, Cyril Ring and George Seigman. Ring is the heavy and handles the role fairly well.

The story is based on the Elwell mystery in New York, but somewhat different from the play. In its screen form it is the story of the young wife of an equally young and ambitious architect who permits herself to run away with the idea that she can assist her husband in his ambitions through associating with a fast society mob.

As a result she is blazoned forth in the gossip sheets in an unfavorably light through the efforts of the owner of the sheet to shake down the man-about-town with whom the wife is most frequently seen.

The result is that the man-about-town is murdered and suspicion is directed at both the wife's brother and the husband, and the latter is finally charged with the crime, with the wife coming to the fore at the last minute with the solution which causes the arrest and the confession of the blackmailing editor.

The story holds no great punch at any time other than the remarkable beauty of Miss Ayres in the role of the wife. None of the supporting cast stand out to any great advantage. *Fred.*

THE WHITE MOTH

Maurice Tourneur Production presented by M. C. Levee, released by First National, featuring Barbara La Marr and Conway Tearle. Story by Izola Forrester, adapted by Albert Shelby Levino, directed by Tourneur. Shown at the Strand, New York, week June 15, 1924. Running time 73 minutes.

The White Moth	Barbara La Marr
Robert Vantine	Conway Tearle
Gonzalo Montrez	Charles de Roche
Douglas Vantine	Ben Lyon
Gwen	Edna Murphy
Ninon	Josie Sedgwick
Mrs. Delancey	Kathleen Kirkham
Tothnes	William Orlamond

Barbara La Marr, the great undressed, would be accurate billing for Barb, the vamp, in this picture. Maurice Tourneur has gone just about as far as the law will allow in undraping the physical allurement of Barbara, but by the same token he has not made her display any great histrionic ability.

He has turned out a picture, though, that will get money. It reeks with sex, bedrooms and pash, and that after all is the stuff the flapper and cakie get the thrill out of these days. The story is stereotyped, a tale used time and again. A heavy vamp doing a vaudeville act snares the younger of two brothers. The youth is engaged to a girl in his own set, but he is passing her up for the vamp when the older brother throws himself into the breach and kids himself he is sacrificing himself in marrying the vamp to save the youngster.

Instead, he is in love with the girl and can't keep away from her. One would think that when he arrived back on the job things would be rosy, but instead he walks into a new complication that arouses his jealousy and then a shooting affray, that has been dragged in by the heels. The picture would have been just as well off without it.

There is the usual happy ending, although in this particular instance Barbara is all dolled up for the hay and when hubby doesn't come to her room as quickly as she would like him to, she simply scales a pillow at his head and then the lights go out. Tourneur in his direction slipped everything he could into the sex end. It will get money, and lots of it, if the audiences want a smear of sex. *Fred.*

TRUE AS STEEL

Goldwyn picture, written and directed by Rupert Hughes. Presented at the Capitol, New York, week June 15, 1924. Running time, 63 minutes.

Mrs. Eva Boutelle	Aileen Pringle
Frank Parry	Huntley Gordon
Mrs. Mary Parry	Cleo Madison
Ethel Parry	Eleanor Boardman
Harry Boutelle	Norman Kerry
Gilbert Morse	William Haines
Miss Leeds	Louise Fazenda
Miss Laird	Jean Haskell
Jake Leighton	Louis Paine
Commodore Fairfield	William H. Crane
Mr. Foote	Lucien Littlefield
Mr. Townsend	William Orlamond
Great-Grandfather	Raymond Hatton

Every once in a while Rupert Hughes comes along with a screen wallop. Here it is a corking story from a short tale in a magazine from his pen.

The trouble is that this particular picture is getting the worst of it as far as the weather break goes this week at the Capitol.

Sunday and Monday business was off, and the chances are that the box-office statement at the end of the week won't show the real box-office value of the picture.

It's there, however. It's sexy and very much so, but cannot give the slightest offense and withal teaches a moral to married men and women.

Styled as "a drama of home and business," it is just that. The story is that of a mid-west business man, married and with a grown daughter, who comes to New York to place a big order with the main office of a large mill. The general manager of the mill is a latter-day type of business woman. She is a clever executive and gets $50,000 a year for her services. She, too, is married, with husband who is rather of the sheiky type and a dub at business.

It was because of his failure in business that she tried it.

Her husband, it happens, is conveniently out of town when the man from the west arrives. The two are attracted to each other. Possibly it was through admiration of the business quality that one found in the other, or maybe something else.

At any rate, he fell, did this man from the west, and likewise she slipped a little bit herself, catching herself just in time as she was going over the edge.

While the two talked it over in her private office her hubby was pacing the outer office, having come back from his trip. But in the end there is no harm done, and two rather mature people have had a slight touch of romance that they will carry along in their lives as a red light signal the next time temptation crops up.

Hughes splits the blame 50-50—just about where it belonged.

Aileen Pringle plays the business woman, while Huntley Gordon is the man. These two, with the aid of Cleo Madison, carry the brunt. Incidentally Miss Madison gives a performance that is corking. One can hardly see how a girl so young manages to get over a middle-aged wife n the screen so convincingly, but she does it, and how! Eleanor Boardman plays the flapper daughter, while Norman Kerry is the sheik hubby. In addition the cast carries the names of William H. Crane, William Haines and Louise Fazenda, which gives the exhibitor something to go out and advertise.

Rupert Hughes as director made the most of Rupert Hughes the author, as far as the story went. There are, besides, subtle touches in the direction that carry an undercurrent of humor quite welcome. *Fred.*

Down by the Rio Grande

Philip Goldstone's presentation, featuring William Fairbanks and Dorothy Revier. Alvin J. Neitz directed. Others in the cast include: Andrew Waldron, Olive Trevor and Jack Richardson. Showing at Loew's New York as half of double bill June 13. Running time, 55 minutes.

Just one of those things, and full to the brim with maudlin sub-titles, of which the first is the tip-off as to the merits of the picture, with the following footage living up to the expectations invoked by the initial wording. The story is negligible, neither Fairbanks nor Miss Revier mean anything, and the interest aroused took form in a general restlessness throughout the audience, which only relaxed when the finish had been reached.

Supposedly adapted from a magazine story, the title insertions read as having been elaborated upon, and the attempt at beauteous wording and flowery descriptive matter was met with snickers while coming under the heading of "sickening sweet."

The film is almost entirely actionless, with much of the footage given over to Fairbanks at a stand still, and gazing either out a window or into the great spaces. Miss Revier is also donated a superfluous amount of close-ups, and the fact that she adheres to one costume throughout most of the depiction marks another liability.

Neitz, in directing, has done little or nothing with the scrips in telling of a Spanish family who own an extensive ranch, with the deed to the property ultimately finding its way to the rightful owner, the unspoken-of relative (Fairbanks), after a villainous cousin has possessed the papers and stated marriage to the daughter as the price of his silence. Galloping along and picking the girl off the running board of an automobile and a jump into the swirling waters of the Rio Grande, with the takeoff as much as is depicted, conform the limits to which Fairbanks goes concerning active participation.

The picture is strictly for the smallest of the small houses, and there is doubt if it can satisfy even there. Otherwise it constitutes a complete "bust." *Skig.*

PERFECT FLAPPER

First National picture starring Colleen Moore. Adapted from a story by Jessie Henderson with John Francis Dillon the director. Showing at the Strand, New York, week of June 22. Running time, 72 mins.

Tommie Lou Pember	Colleen Moore
Dick Trayle	Sydney Chaplin
Gertrude Trayle	Phyllis Haver
Aunt Sarah	Lydie Knott
Reed Andrews	Frank Mayo
Joshua Pember	Charles Wellesley

Another depiction of the feminine lightweights by Miss Moore in which she gives a corking performance and the picture, as a whole, is major entertainment for the upper class houses, especially during the heat.

Going to great lengths for comedy in some instances, far-fetched and not any too plausible in the body of the story, the picture, despite this, keeps its head up because of the star, a speedily tempoed action and the capable support.

The scenario has been constructed to point a moral in the latter stages of the film's footage whence comes an argument between the girl and her serious-minded lover spaced by lengthy subtitles which hashes over the general situation of the plight of the modern girl. While it may "square" the character on the screen the title debate simply flashes as so much reading matter, will hardly cause concentration from the parents and is sure to sponsor an outburst of bright and witty sayings from the youths with their girl friends in the audience. It could have been advantageously eliminated, and at least scissored, for there's little use attempting to make an audience think while viewing a vehicle of this type.

The story opens with the prim and proper costume coming out party of Tommie Lou (Miss Moore) which remains a lifeless affair until the boys present make merry with the grape juice punch. Realizing herself as just a nice girl from a good family Tommie goes into tears and is soothed through consecutive glasses of the gingered refreshment served by her older sister's husband (Chaplin), also known as inoffensive, harmless and safe.

Resulting in a "stew" duet the couple, in full Romeo and Juliet regalia, drive to a roadhouse where they run into numerous acquaintances and a balcony scene is flashlighted by a newspaper cameraman. It brings a split between the husband and wife (Phyllis Haver) with the institution of a divorce action.

The lawyer (Frank Mayo) is the cousin of the wife, friendly with the husband and they finally figure the only way to smooth the rumpled waters is by Tommie Lou and Andrews, the plaintiff's representative, to stage a love affair. The assumed "crush" is on the level with the girl and the legal aspirant eventually gives in, too, which assures the usual cut and dried finish.

Backed by a couple of augmented settings Dillon has carried the theme along at a fast pace albeit the girl climbing a Fifth avenue traffic tower in order to ask the policeman in charge for a match seemed a more than necessary bit while, on the other hand the culmination of the coming out party which had more waiters than guests present with the recipients of the invitations deciding to wait upon the waiters proved a touch that will draw attention.

Miss Moore, currently identified with this type of portrayal, has contributed a neat performace that will enhance her standing as a flapper although there is the danger she may not be able to stand from under when this seige against modern youth quiets down.

Syd Chaplin is both prominent and efficient enough to tally a close second while Mayo, Miss Haver and the remaining members of the cast register as colorless in comparison to the first named pair.

It totals a neat presentation that will assertively entertain although Dillon has "lifted" a standing vaudeville gag for one bit of business and filmdom continues to think all the young bunch do is drink and dance. But where they eat this sort of thing up, the picture can't miss. *Skig.*

REVELATION

Metro picture, released by Metro-Goldwyn. From the novel, "The Rosebush of a Thousand Years," by Mabel Wagnall. Adapted and directed by George D. Baker. Shown at the Capitol, N. Y., June 22, 1924. Running time, 75 minutes.

Joline Hofer	Viola Dana
Paul Granville	Monte Blue
Mlle. Brevoort	Marjorie Daw
Count de Roche	Lew Cody
The Prior	Frank Currier
Augustin	Edward Connelly
Madonna	Kathleen Key
Mme. Hofer	Ethel Wales
Hofer	George Siegmann
Du Clos	Otto Matiesen
Jean Hofer	Bruce Guerin

Slow and draggy in spots and overacted in others is the way one must sum up this picture. It, however, has a cast that should mean a lot to the box office in the average house. In it are included Viola Dana, Monte Blue, Marjorie Daw, Lew Cody and others almost as prominent on the screen. The picture, however, is not exactly one that can be tabbed as a real attraction for the bigger and the better class of pre-release theatres. In the regular run of houses it should get by to average business.

The story is of the poor, ruined girl, who goes to the big city after she has been turned away from her father's door because she had a baby out of regular season. In Paris she becomes the favorite dancer in a Montmarte cabaret and, finally, to help a poor artist, offers to pose for him. Through his picture, which she is the inspiration, he rises to fame and fortune, but he wants to turn her off when he is commissioned to paint a Madonna. In the end, however, she convinces him, through chasing all the models who apply for the job and, as the painting is to be done in the monastary about which the legend is woven, she comes under the spell of religion and decides to return to the simple life.

Redeeming her offspring from a convent she goes to a small town and starts to earn her living, but in a short time the artist drives into town with a big car to take her in his arms for the final closeup.

There isn't much to it, but Viola Dana will get some laughs with her hoydenish antics at times. In the main the picture seems rather poor hop. *Fred.*

UNGUARDED WOMEN

Paramount production made by Alan Crosland from the Saturday Evening Post story, "Face," by Lucy Stone Terrill. Screen play by James Creelman. Bebe Daniels, Mary Astor and Richard Dix featured. Reviewed at the Rialto, New York, June 22.

Breta Banning	Bebe Daniels
Douglas Albright	Richard Dix
Helen Castle	Mary Astor
Larry Trent	Walter McGrail
George Castle	Frank Losee
Aunt Louise	Helen Lindroth
Sing Woo	Harry Mestayer
James Craig	Donald Hall
Capt. Robert Banning	Joe King

"Unguarded Women" is a screen rarity in that its story is really strong enough for feature length and that in every inch of it interest is sustained without the introduction of artificial thrill methods. Being a drama of intense love, it would have been easy to have introduced a note of objectionable sexiness. This has not been done. The result is that the screen version of "Face" is a fine photoplay from its purely artistic aspect and good in the sense that the names of its players, particularly Daniels and Dix, have a box office draught.

The story centers on Breta Banning (Miss Daniels), the widow of Capt. Robert Banning, killed in the World War. In China she is leading a wild and fast life—so swift a pace that to the conservative members of the foreign colony she has lost "face" or standing.

To China comes the hero, Douglas Albright (Mr. Dix), who was the best friend of Banning. Because he had wronged Banning and had since felt remorse, he obligated himself to work out the regeneration and salvation of the soldier's widow. There was but one way—he must marry her, and this he proposed to do, even at the cost of sacrifiicing his own sweetheart, played by Mary Astor.

The regeneration is worked out. The Banning woman experiences a change of heart, but when she learns that Albright is sacrificing his love affair to marry her from a sense of self-imposed duty, she commits suicide.

Such a story has its strong points. There is a grain of melodrama mixed in the plot, but its playing here by Dix and Miss Astor lend a sincerity to the picture as a whole that saves it.

Miss Daniels, as the woman who cut up high jinks, neither impresses one way or the other. Her performance is one of those hackneyed things that featured players turn out once in a while. Her appearance beside that of Miss Astor places her at a disadvantage, for her heavy makeup, accented on the lips and eyes, was decidedly unattractive, while Miss Astor, frail, slender and possessed of a patrician beauty, walked rings around the other woman as far as the performance went.

Dix gave a clean-cut and convincing portrayal. Harry Mestayer as his chink secretary did good character work and the dependable Frank Losee had a small father role.

"Unguarded Women" is strong in plot and suspense and at least two of its featured players turn in 100 per cent performances. Whatever may be its drawing power, it is certain to entertain once they get in. There is reason to believe that a picture like this, which really possesses merit, will make them talk about it in the larger places.

Sisk.

CHANGING HUSBANDS

Paramount, presented by Adolph Zukor and Jesse L. Lasky. From the story "Roles," by Elizabeth Alexander, adapted by Sada Cowen and Howard Higgen. Directed by Frank Urson and Paul Irbe. Shown at the Rivoli, N. Y., week June 22, 1924. Running time, 76 minutes.

Gwynne Evans....................Leatrice Joy
Eva Graham....................Leatrice Joy
Oliver Evans....................Victor Varconi
Bob Hamilton....................Raymond Griffith
Mitzi....................Julia Faye
Delia....................Za Su Pitts
Mrs Evans, Sr....................Helen Dunbar
Conrad Bardshaw....................William Boyd

"Changing Husbands" in printed form in "The Saturday Evening Post" was a much better story than it is a picture. The adapting may partially be responsible or possibly the direction. However, one or the other permitted a lot of hoak comedy to slip into the story and killed all the real suspense element.

In its present form "Changing Husbands" has in its title its greatest recommendation for the box office. As entertainment for the hot weather it is not of extraordinary value, although Leatrice Joy does give a fairly convincing performance in a double role.

The story is that of a startling resemblance two women bear for each other, one a mediocre and the other a society butterfly with a longing for the stage. They meet by chance and change their respective places in life.

This would have all been very well if the society woman did not have a husband, or the actress a young man who wanted to marry her. Each of the men, however, was looking for exactly the other type of girl and in the end a Reno trip is the idea all around to make everybody happy.

There is little pep to the story now. As written, it read interestingly, but that hardly can be said for the screen version.

The directors of the picture, Frank Urson and Paul Irbe, have recently been elevated to the post of directors, and this is their first effort. Possibly they will improve with time, at least that is to be wished for.

Fred.

6TH COMMANDMENT

William Christy Cabanne presentation, also directed by him, for Associated Exhibitors. Cast includes William Faversham, Charlotte Walker, John Bohn, Kathleen Martyn, J. Neil Hamilton, Coit Albertson, Sara Wood, Consula Flowerton and Charles E. Mack. Showing at Loew's New York, June 23. Running time, 65 minutes.

"Thou Shalt Not Kill" is the Sixth Commandment. May as well fix that, right away.

Otherwise the film screens as an intermediate feature that may satisfy in the middle class theatres, but of its being below first line quality there can be no question.

Faversham means little to the film other than the use of his name while superfluous footage, sets that smack too much of the studio and a dearth of action comprise a list of drawbacks that prove too great a handicap.

Revolving around the specified non combatant rule the tale commences with a child love affair, carries through the war, the hero's blindness and the regaining of his sight, a murder, trial and the preverbial straightened out finale.

John Bohn is given the principal allotment of responsibility and does acceptably with it, but can't uphold all the other discrepancies. Kathleen Martyn, former "Follies" girl, is meaningless playing opposite to him and the most meritorius assistance comes from the male contingent in the persons of Faversham, Hamilton and Mack. The entire feminine complement illusions as being entirely negative.

A costume ball and a snatch of war stuff are the flash insertions. As concerns the sets the repeated use of one interior was obvious as to flagrantly hint at a substantial effort to conserve the overhead. The theme, itself, does not convince and registers as being particularly vulnerable in its excuse to make a dastardly villain out of Coit Albertson when he shoots and kills the supposed fiance so that he may get the girl while she, in turn, is in love with another man.

Away to a slow start the sequence never seems to pick up any speed and closely approximates tediousness before closing out. At best it is but a leader for the average programs.

Skig.

TRAFFIC IN HEARTS

C. B. C. production featuring Robert Frazer and Mildred Harris, including Charles Wellesley, Edwin Tilton, John Herdman, Betty Morrisey, Dan Marion, Thomas O'Brien, Fred Kelsey and Arthur Rankin. Story by Dorothy Yost. Directed by Scott Dunlap. Half of bill at Loew's New York, June 20. Run 67 mins.

"Traffic in Hearts" falls in the category of those films that endeavor, none too successfully, to mix politics and sentiment. The story is as insignificent as the name and were it not for a few bits of excellent direction, and the all-around fine work of a good cast, the film would hardly have been worth shooting. However, its few good points are strong enough to qualify it for the program houses as an average feature.

It is the type of picture of which it is often said the moral tone is extremely high. The hero is a clean, young, political reformer, out to build modern tenements for the poor and to crush the crooked ring of grafters. The "power" behind this latter group has to be the father of the girl in the case.

One scene, in which a gang of rowdies raid a prayer meeting, is particularly well done, the fervor with which an old Irish cop vows to stick by the hero alone being enough to reach a responsive chord in the ordinary picturegoer.

The chief weakness of the film is that the other bits of action, pathos and humor, fall flat. Most of them center around the affection of the hero for "Shrimp," a kid of the streets.

Robert Frazer plays the lead about as well as anyone could. This young actor brings a most likable personality to the screen and with his appearance and thespian ability as added features there should be little to stop him. Mildred Harris does well in the small role of the heroine. Dan Marion is an appealing child and the others are well-chosen.

HIS FORGOTTEN WIFE

A Palmer Photoplays production made from a prize-winning story by Will Lambert and distributed by F. B. O. Scenario by Lambert and Del Andrews, directed by William A. Seiter, and photographed by Max Dupont. Madge Bellamy starred, and Warner Baxter featured. At Loew's New York, June 19. Running time, 73 mins.

"His Forgotten Wife" is another one of those amnesia and long arm of coincidence pictures, filled with the ancient hokum of the film business, to wit, two women after one man, automobile chases, the daring of the good woman to help the man she loves, the old family lawyer, and numerous clinch scenes.

Nevertheless, it is fairly interesting, with its place surely lying in the smaller film houses.

The opening scenes are during the World War in France. A soldier, badly wounded, has forgotten his name. He and his nurse are in love. They marry, and returning to America find jobs scarce. Forced to become domestics, they apply for a post at a Long Island country home. Accepted, it is revealed that the man, now a butler, is is reality the former owner of the place, who willed the estate and his money to his fiance. The fiance is unscrupulous, and when she sees that his love isn't for her any longer, skips with negotiable bonds. The wife and former nurse hops a taxi and pulls a stick-up on a country road, getting the dough back. Preceding this there is much chase stuff, and when a ball is given to celebrate the man's return to his estates, and the fiance finds that he intends to stick to wifey, she reveals wifey as the hold-up woman. More chase stuff with a happy ending tacked onto it. Through this all the old family lawyer acts as a protector against the unscrupulous fiance.

The chase scenes are the only exciting portions of the film, as the war shots are obviously taken from other sources. The production doesn't indicate lavish expenditure of money, but is never slip-shod.

Madge Bellamy, as the girl beloved, is fair enough, and Warner Baxter, as the man, gives a prosaic performance. There are no other names in the cast, and this, coupled with the air of production economy as well as the hackneyed story, unfits it for the bigger houses, but makes it suitable for the places where the family gathers.

It is one of the series of yarns produced by the Palmer Photoplay School as an inducement to show those who take their scenario courses that there is a production chance for the work they turn out after paying to learn how it is done.

Sisk.

THE SPITFIRE

Murray W. Garrson presentation adapted from the novel "Plaster Saints" by Frederick Arnold Kummer released through Pathe Exchange. Direction William Christy Cabanne. At Loew's New York, as half of double feature bill June 19. Running time, 65 mins.

Jean Bronson....................Betty Blythe
Marcia Walsh....................Pauline Garon
Joshua Carrington....................Burr McIntosh
Horace Fleming....................Lowell Sherman
Oliver Blair....................Robert Warwick
Douglas Kenyon....................Elliott Dexter

"The Spitfire" has an all star cast and a corking story. A sure fire combination. Douglas Kenyon (Elliott Dexter) is placed in an embarrasing position when he awakens after a heavy night and discovers a chorus girl Marcia Walsh (Pauline Garon) in his apartment. He had won the right to escort her in a poker game the night before and fell asleep on his couch while she occupied his bedroom properly chaperoned by his eminently respectable housekeeper.

Kenyon's fiancee Jean Bronson (Betty Blythe) grand daughter of millionaire Joshia Carrington (Burr McIntosh) hears of the affair but refuses to condemn her sweetheart unheard. Carrington has Kenyon fired from his band and the latter goes to work for Blair (Robert Warwick) a philanthropist who gave the party. Blair has evidence of Carrington's unscrupulous business methods.

Jean leaves home out of loyalty to Kenyon and secures a position in a revue. Horace Fleming (Lowell Sherman) the producer falls in love with her and tries to inveigle her into an affair. He is prevented by Kenyon and a dramatic fight between the two on a roof top is one of the thrills. The picture ends conventionally when Blair presents his evidence to Carrington without any strings attached after trying to make a deal concerning the future happiness of the lovers.

All of the "names" have been splendidly cast. Pauline Garon is lovable and unconventional as the chorine. Betty Blythe is a beautiful heroine and Lowell Sherman a suave modern young man out for no good. Warwick has a fat role as the dignified philanthropist the victim of an unhappy love that ended with death and McIntosh as the straight laced old hypocrite is immense.

It is a story that lends itself to screen adaptation and with such a list of names certainly should draw.

Con.

CIRCUS COWBOY

William Fox production featuring Charley Jones in a combination western and circus picture. Direction of William Wellman from story of Louis Sherwin, scenario by Doty Hobart. Running time 65 mins. At Loew's, New York, June 19. Half of double feature bill.

Once in a while along comes a picture full of melodrama with high strung and far fetched situations which, nevertheless, gets over through the excellent direction and strength of the story. This is one of those rarities.

Charley Jones is the star and is given a role that could easily become ludicrous if Jones tried to overact. He wisely refrains and turns in a convincing performance.

Marion Nixon, as the ingenue lead, also does sterling work. One of Jones stunts is a hand over hand climb across a canyon. The rope is shot in half from below making a thrilling bit.

The story opens in western fashion with Jones in love with one of the village belles. He is called away and during the interim the girl marries the town rich man and grouch. He is insanely jealous of Jones. The latter returns and is seen by his former sweetheart. She confesses her love for him but he resents her advances. Her stepson overhears and tries to blackmail her. Jones appearing in time to throw the youth through a window. He has been followed to the house by the old man who shoots his own son as he is climbing back through the window under the impression it is Jones.

Jones is suspected of the crime and leaves with a posse in pursuit. He is aided by the girl who is going to join a circus and tells him to do likewise.

The circus scenes are interesting with Jones doing a legitimate rope and bronk turn. A rescue of the girl, who is wire walker, is realistically handled. An animal trainer enamored of the girl cuts the rope that holds her apparatus but Jones seeing it rides underneath on his horse and catches her in his arms.

The picture eventually works out its own salvation and is an interesting program addition for the neighborhood houses. *Con.*

RIDGEWAY OF MONTANA

A Universal Western Series, starring Hoxie and including the Universal Riders. Directed by Clifford Smith. At the Stanley, New York, June 20. Running time, 53 mins.

Like all other Jack Hoxie films, this one is no exception in that its lays its stress upon the great outdoors and its men, but a different step and a not unattractive one is taken when the modern flapper theme is brought into conflict with the supposedly woman hating qualities of the cowboy hero.

Hoxie, as the leader of the ranch, is after a band of cattle rustlers. He loses the leader and in the meantime, to avoid losses by the outlaws, goes away to sell his stock. He meets a modern flapper who sets out to make a sap of him because he didn't fall hard enough for her. She doesn't succeed at her home, where he is a guest, and so follows him to the ranch, finally locating him in his hunting lodge in the mountains. Arriving there, a snowstorm forces her to remain overnight. He considers her compromised, has incidentally fallen in love with her and so makes her marry him.

Against this she rebels but the rescue provides the clinch finish and closes a picture that is economically produced and suitable for the small houses for which it was undoubtedly designed.

Hoxie is as usual in this picture while the heroine whose name isn't given, proves herself a corking flapper.

The others in the cast are okay and the outdoor shots fill the eye at times particularly some snow scenes on the mountainside. *Sisk.*

CIRCUSMANIA

London, June 12.

Shown privately in London at the Scala, "Circusmania" is an Anglo-Austrian production starring Max Linder, made by Granger-Vita and is without doubt one of the best comedies ever screened.

Opening inauspiciously with the Continental idea that alcoholism is the alpha and omega of humor it soon becomes genuinely funny and runs at such a speed its length appears to be little more than the average two-reeler whereas it runs into the six reel category.

The chief blot on the presentation, but one which had nothing to do with the picture, was the Scala orchestra. Good in itself this collection of musicians and their conductor let the picture down badly by ignoring anything so common as "big top" music and playing soft and subtle waltz refrains. Even when the old roll was required to help out a stunt acrobatic trick the drummer did his job as though ashamed of being concerned with a picture much less one dealing with such inferior things as tan, orange peel, and the odor of animals. Provincial and other exhibitors will, however, speedily rectify this.

The circus scenes are very good, while all the other scenic work is admirable.

The story tells how the Count Max de Pompadour, a drunken and worthless young fool, is offered marriage or disownment by his guardian. He has three choices of a bride and desires to marry the one whose photograph he hits first with a revolver bullet. He misses all three but frightens a pretty girl into a fainting fit. She makes an appointment to meet him at the Cirque Buffalo the following night. He goes with his uncle, looks in vain for her in the auditorium and eventually finds she is a trapeze artist. His ardor is increased but receives a severe shock when her burly father says she can only marry "in the profession." The girl gives him a book "How to Become an Acrobat," but his studies prove disastrous. He assays to become a flea-tamer with even more disastrous results and loses his troupe. His future father-in-law, however, provides him with lions. Things are awkward but a friendly clown agrees to see him through. His rival foils this attempt and things get worse but ultimately he wins the day and the girl.

Max Linder makes a great comeback as de Pompadour. He never clowns and much of his business is delightfully original. Moreover he never shows a trace of vulgarity or suggestiveness once he has got over his opening drunken scenes and even into these he manages to get some novel work. No support is named but it is consistently good and his leading lady is not only a beautiful woman but a fine feeder.

Feeding is the key-note of this picture but so skilfully is it done nobody not conversant with the art will realize Linder practically plays the thing himself with every other character merely forming part of a perfect frame. *Gore.*

THE VAST SUDAN

London, June 12.

However good or interesting a travel picture may be someone with a gorgeous idea of his own eloquence, and a carelessness for other peoples, time, will try to kill it. This was again the case when Major Radclyffe Dugmore's new Sudanese picture was shown for the first time at the Polytechnic. Highly intellectual though the introductory speech may have been, most of the audience heard little of it beyond frequent allusions to the "Su-daarn" and "Mee-jor Dugmore" and everyone was heartily glad when an apparent shortness of breath brought the oration to a close and allowed the cameraman to get on with his job.

Dugmore's new contribution to travel kinematography is excellent. His picture lecture takes the watcher over much unknown ground and gives a wonderful insight into strange tribes and tribal customs. Some of his finest stuff consists of the "shots" of the building of a railway as the train passes over it, of the building against time of a huge dam on the Nile, and of the Camel Corps. Other vastly interesting pictures show herds of elephants, crowds of anything but beautiful women, a sham fight by the Camel Corps, a fight by natives, dances, etc.

Throughout, the photography is beautiful and although the picture is one of exploration and travel it is obvious the cameraman has in many cases contrived to link up his love for the purely educational with a sense of the really artistic. *Gore.*

THE CONSPIRATORS

London, June 4.

Another product of the Stoll film factory. Made by Sinclair Hill from the story by E. Phillips Oppenheim, the feature is melodrama with a touch of mystery. Although the scenario is somewhat weak, the story is interesting and keeps its audience guessing.

There are far too many subtitles between "close ups" and the drawing of the various characters is not too convincing. The staging is good and the photography excellent.

The Queen of Mexonia has had an intrigue with a young Englishman, FitzMaurice, who dies. The indiscretion was really the outcome of her husbnd's brutality and unfaithfulness. Her letters to the Englishman fall into the hands of a blackmailer, Barnes, who proceeds to make hay while the sun shines. Her great friend, Louise, sister of the dead man, determines to obtain the letters, and plans to burglarize the blackmailer's flat.

Instead, she breaks into another apartment occupied by a man, Wrayson. To him she tells her story and he admits her to the Barnes flat and keeps watch while she searches it. Wrayson is called away and when he returns Louise has vanished. A little later the dead body of the blackmailer is found. Wrayson suspects Louise and the dead man's brother suspects Wrayson. The letters cannot be found, but when the murdered man's widow arrives it is discovered they are in her possession. She offers them in return for the name of the murderer. In the middle of an angry discussion a man staggers in and tells how he committed the crime. The Queen's letters are returned and Louise and Wrayson provide the orthodox finale.

The acting is inclined to be stagey. Moore Marriott is excellent as the blackmailer, and his brother, David Hawthorne, is inclined to pose as Wrayson. Fred Rains has much too small a part as Benson. Betty Faire relies more on beauty than on histrionic art as Louise, and several smaller parts are adequately filled.

The feature will doubtless prove a useful unit in the Stoll program. *Gore.*

THOSE WHO DANCE

Thomas H. Ince presentation, releasing through First National. Story by George K. Turner, with Lambert Hillyer directing. Cast features Blanche Sweet, Bessie Love, Warner Baxter and Robert Agnew. Showing at the Strand, New York, week of June 29. Running time, 76 minutes.

Something of an augmented program at the Strand this week and the special souvenir Convention program must have proved a taxing problem, for the scheduling of the feature had little in common with the actual film, so far as designating the characters was concerned.

This particular vehicle is devoted to bootlegging, but may have a little trouble in getting by the state censor boards because of the manner in which the stuff is made, which may be something of an expose, although seemingly exaggerated. The story's inclination is to evolve a lesson on the folly of imbibing in booze of native manufacture under imported labels. As a program leader the picture assuredly has pace, and with the interest the subject will universally draw, it should prove entertaining.

The title was derived from a subtitle quotation and is obviously misleading. That the bootlegging industry should have been inferred in the title is apparent within the first half reel, but the inclination to dodge issues with the various state scissoring detachments may have had some influence.

With no necessity for resplendent settings and localed in a higher or lower underworld atmosphere, the action mostly takes place within apartments and flats, with the climax placed inside of a neighborhood dance hall.

The getaway is one more of the wild youth drinking parties that leads to an innocent girl being killed when her drunken companion goes blind while driving her home and the car plunges over an embankment.

During the illusioning of the party is shown the "still," the bootlegger picking up the booze and delivering to the back door. The older brother of the girl, following her death on the operating table, vows vengeance on all rum-runners and immediately joins the prohibition forces.

On the other side of the scenario is a kid brother (Robert Agnew) who acts as a truck driver for the gang and whose scatheless sister (Miss Sweet) journeys from the small town to take him home. Having once run past a police blockade with a "load," the youngster tries it again when accompanied by "Red" Carney (presumably Mathew Betz), leader of the gang, who shoots and kills one of the prohibition men and frames with his fixed agent on the squad to "plant" the gun on the youth.

"Framed" and slated for the electric chair, the sister forces the truth from Carney's wife (Bessie Love) and goes to headquarters, where she makes a tieup with the brother (Warner Baxter), who would himself extinguish bootlegging because of his sister.

Mathew Betz, as "Red" Carney, if it is he (for neither the program nor the film substantiates the conclusion), gives a corking performance that stamps him for predominating honors. Both Miss Sweet and Miss Love have adequately taken care of their respective assignments, while Warner Baxter and Bob Agnew meet responsibilities. Frank Campeau, unmentioned in any manner, supplies his usual and reliable vallainy.

Hillyer has turned out a creditable piece of work, and various touches are certain to attract particular notice. Notably, a youthful couple getting booze at a soda fountain and the picturing of Kane and Rose Carney in bed together, as propaganda for the gang leader to assimilate. Just how often that last scene will get by is, of course, questionable.

Other than these insertions, the director has happily dodged the dramatics which could have easily been included, and beyond the constant pulling of a gun on the least pretext by Carney, the picture is pleasingly void of overly emphasized conduct.

The bootlegging thing being a timely subject for some years now, with present conditions still attentive to the general liquor situation, points that there is no reason why this story, and the playing of it, should fail to click.

It is deplorable that the title is misleading, but, even aside from that, the film gives evidence of being able to make an audience talk about it, and that's the best "plug" yet devised. *Skig.*

RECOIL

J. Parker Read, Jr., production of the Rex Beach story. Produced by Cosmopolitan-Goldwyn and distributed by Metro-Goldwyn. Directed by T. Hayes Hunter. Screen story by Gerald C. Duffy. Reviewed at the Capitol, New York, June 29. Running time, 65 minutes.

Gordon Kent	Mahlon Hamilton
Norma Selbee	Betty Blythe
Laurence Regan, Marchmont	Clive Brook
William Sothern	Fred Paul
Jim Selbee	Ernest Hilliard

Notwithstanding the good start Rex Beach gave this picture by furnishing its producer with a corking story and not forgetting the excellent touches in the direction of T. Hayes Hunter, "Recoil" cannot claim rank as a money-getter.

The first and most important of the reasons is that the Betty Blythe and Mahlon Hamilton names possess no great box office draught, and the second is that the picture itself isn't quite "there."

One is inclined to blame this on the cast more than upon any one else. Neither Miss Blythe nor Mr. Hamilton, the featured people, do any histrionic pyrotecnnics worthy of note, and the fact that it is a short cast piece, with the smaller roles filled out by comparatively unknown actors, works to a disadvantage.

Basically "Recoil" preaches the theme that when wronged people wreak vengeance they become wrongdoers themselves.

Kent, the hero, has spent 20 years getting rich in South America. Having gotten the money, he wants to live and spend it in the atmosphere where pink cheeks and white shoulders are plentiful.

So he hikes to Deauville. There he meets Norma Selbee, a poor girl, who worms her way to the point where she can join his party in the gambling Casino. Two days of acquaintanceship and he proposes.

One-half a reel and they're married. In about another reel they're splitting up and Norma is running off with Laurence Marchmont, a guy who isn't good at handling men, but who can get by with the dames.

The husband, finding out through his friend Sothern, who is a detective, that Norma is the wife of a New York crook and that in marrying him she has committed bigamy, and that Marchmont is a jewel thief, determines to put the screws on both of them. To do this he tells them that unless they continue living together he'll give them up to the cops. Wherever they go they are shadowed until life becomes a specter of unpleasantness.

In the wind-up they all meet in New York, the woman's husband is killed and Marchmont implicated in the crime, thus clearing the way for the two sweethearts, who by this time have found they are really in love. Then they hike it back to South America.

There is a decided punch to the story, but its screen continuity arrangement disregards that fact. In addition, the camera work isn't notable. The sets are tasteful, but didn't cost a million. Some of the scenes are taken in Deauville, but aren't great, at that.

The direction is okay. Mr. Hunter has handled every individual scene well, making it seem a tough break for him that his material wasn't first rate. The subtitles are funny in spots, but run too much to epigrams in others. All around they are much better than the pictures, albeit there are too many subtitles.

"Recoil" is satisfactory for the daily change houses, but as first run film fare it leaves much to be desired. *Sisk.*

WINNING HIS WAY

("Fight and Win" Series)

First episode of Jack Dempsey serial. Universal production and release; seen at Rialto theatre, length about 2,500 feet.

On a bill with a full-length feature, this first chapter of the Universal serial starring Champion Jack Dempsey seemed to have advance interest, but proved rather flat.

The outstanding novelty is Dempsey himself, prettied up with a puttied and blended nose, so that he looks nothing like the familiar heavyweight idol or anybody else. To anyone with a memory for faces, and almost every one has a set mental image of such a celebrity, the effect is garish. It is Dempsey, and yet it isn't—and it doesn't miss much of seeming to be a wax figure, animated.

This is a serious blunder. If the purpose was to camouflage the somewhat distorted nose caused by punches early in his career in order to make Dempsey look like a matinee idol to the ladies, it misses. He now loses his own personality and what charm goes with it, and takes on no synthetic good looks, for the nose isn't even a good bit of modeling. It is snubby, stubby and palpably phoney. And because Dempsey's features are so well known the change is conspicuous and distracting.

Dempsey doesn't appear in the best-looking physical condition, either. There have been dozens of regular movie stars who played fighters and looked the part much better than this greatest of all fighters. In the ring he has always appeared browned, fine-drawn and like a tiger. In this film he is white, flabby and, somehow, so self-conscious of the camera that he looks like a dub actor who never raised his hands trying to do his best in a miscast pug role.

In truth, he looks better and registers better in street clothes and in a scene where he is a laborer in a steel works at night, a genuine and impressive bit all around.

The story is cheesy.

"Our hero" is hired as a "set-up" for the heavyweight champion, who is a dissipated rounder, by some crooked promoters, and he is "framed" to go in without training. He takes the fight only because his poor old ma is sick and the big-hearted lad needs the money to send her to the country. He saves the villain's kid from being killed by a train and the double-cross is turned, so that Jack gets training and comes into the ring all fit.

Now comes the fight—a two-round affair. Dempsey, not looking himself at all, goes after his man. The milling is so fast and indistinct that it lacks all thrill. One would think that at least in this part a Dempsey film would be great, but here it is at its worst, in direction and conception.

It is usual for the hero to win. Sometimes, to make it plausible, the dirty dog gets in a few licks, too. If there is one screen actor who might be allowed to win quick, snappy and decisive, it is Dempsey, who has done just that to the whole heavyweight field. Instead, he is knocked down twice and the bell saved him while he is unconscious. Later he puts out his man with one punch. He exhibits no ring tricks, no punches that make one gasp, and the fight is not spectacular; not even interesting, which seems incredible for a Dempsey film.

Anyway, he wins the heavyweight championship, and that is the end. It is worth speculating over where the serial will go from there, as it looks as if the climax has been blown in the first episode.

There is no love story at all in his chapter. Carmelita Geraghty, the young leading woman, appears only for a flash as a waitress in the boarding house.

The titles have some catchy phrases, but the story is painfully dime-novel. Dempsey, bereft of his individuality, a disappointment in physical looks, too, neither a film fighter nor a film actor, will not build up as the series unfolds. He will have to get by entirely as a freak novelty.

As such the serial may get a wide play. But that is the only angle from which it can, as judged by the initial release.

Dempsey is said to be getting a million dollars for his work. If so, of all his push-overs, that is the cat's cream. He probably raised the price after he looked at himself in a mirror with that nose. *Lait.*

CODE OF WILDERNESS

Albert E. Smith presentation, Vitagraph Picture, directed by David Smith; story by Charles Alden Seltzer; seen at Rialto.

Rex Randerson	John Bowers
Willard Masten	Alan Hale
Ruth Harkness	Alice Calhoun
Uncle Jephon	Otis Harlan
Hagar	Charlotte Merriam
Aunt Martha	Kitty Bradbury

This is a regulation western, with the conventional ingredients. It impresses one as having been made about five years ago, for it is of that vintage.

Just a hard-riding ranch affair, with an eastern girl inheriting the place and finding a handsome cowboy running it. Otis Harlan plays her uncle and injects some fat tenderfoot comedy, otherwise it is quite without individuality or highlights except that John Bowers is an exceptionally handsome and presentable fellow and player and invites interested observation.

With the girl comes Alan Hale as her fiance, a deep-dyed wretch who betrays a mountain girl and plots to have the hero murdered. He doesn't get away with it because of some fast hip-shooting.

That's about all there is to it. Almost all the action is outdoors and there is no production attempt. Charlotte Merriam as the wild young thing has some worthy moments, but her pathos is sometimes very glycerine.

A program item that neither helps nor hurts. *Lait.*

40-HORSE HAWKINS

Universal production, starring Hoot Gibson. Written by R. L. Schrock and Edward Sedgwick and directed by the latter. At the Stanley, New York, one day (June 27). Runs 76 minutes.

Bud Hawkins	Hoot Gibson
Mary Darling	Annie Cornwall
Rudolph Catalina	Richard Tucker
Helen Holmes	Helen Holmes
Johnny	Jack Edwards
Sheriff	Ed Burns
Stage Manager	Edward Sedgwick

Some time ago Universal discovered (or thought it did) that Hoot Gibson could give a fair performance as a boob. Since then it has added a slightly nutty flavor to each of his roles; but, for the first time, in "Forty-Horse Hawkins" he has the role of an absolute dope to play.

The result is far from gratifying. One doesn't realize how comparatively good were Gibson's much-abused straight westerns until he is forced to sit through this drivel. There is no need going into the dozens of discrepancies and inconsistencies of the plot. If being preposterous were the only thing wrong with the firm, it would not be so bad; but when the episodic incidents have all been seen before and better done, there is no excuse.

Gibson is the man-of-all trades in a small western town. The ancient gag of having him use a different hat for each of his jobs—expressman, porter, waiter, fireman, policeman, et al.—is utilized. The heroine is the leading woman of a one-night-stand theatrical company that hits the village. The performance, with all the old bits of burlesque, paper snow, non-working curtains, hissing the villain, and so on, takes nearly half an hour's running time.

Not content with that, we have to follow the bumpkin to the city where he has gone in search of the girl, there follows another long-drawn-out performance, with the heroine now a Broadway star, her hick lover a super, with neither cognizant of the other's presence in the company.

How much padding it takes to fill out this less-than-meagre plot may only be imagined. A few laughs have found their way into the footage, attributable for the most part to Gibson's clumsy mannerisms. In fact, he struggles manfully with the puerile script, but only to fair success. A bright spot is the refreshing prettiness and appeal of Anne Cornwall as the actress, while Richard Tucker gets something out of the heavy.

"Forty-Horse Hawkins" is one of the poorest Universals seen in many a day. It is suitable only for the Gibson clientele, and even they will have to be tolerant this time.

LOVE'S INFLUENCE

London, June 18.

Amid an outcry against sex films, films whose chief claim to popularity is nastiness or the undressing of women, we have a film of our own which is eminently pure. Under no circumstances would it lead maiden or callow youth from the very straight path nor would it excite any old gentleman to forget his good manners and go astray in Piccadilly. Any more wishy-washy picture than this "Love's Influence" shown by Unity Films has never been seen. It's chief charm is that any audience witnessing it can sleep without hindrance; even the orchestra comes under the influence of this masterpiece.

The story is of an originality that was old in drama 100 years ago. To her stern parent comes the daughter who left home for the man she loved. The stern parent continues stern and refuses to harbor her. She tells him her husband is dead and she is in a certain condition. The old man is adamant and she goes to an old servant, where her child is born. After the fashion of village maidens who leave home, having given birth to her offspring, she dies. The years roll by until 18 are told and we find the child as a village bad lad. He plays about in the clothes of a youngster who has just been breeched; his bad habits are those of a naughty child. Then love's influence takes a hand in the game. He meets the village parson's peculiarly immature daughter and "the dawn of love" rises with appalling swiftness. These two poor fools walk about village streets hand in hand, and do little else.

Anyhow, love's influence continues and he gets a job in a printer's office. Doing well, the boy gets a job in a Fleet street office. Within 100 feet of film he has a wrist watch, fashionable clothes, and seems to be running the show.

Then he comes into a fortune and goes wild. He takes women out, and this is a strong thing in the favor of this picture. It is intense prohibitionist propaganda.

The end of the picture is up to the usual sample of conventional endings.

The feature is a poor story, badly produced. George K. Arthur as the "hero" shows no dramatic ability and his expressions are for the most part purely facial contortions. Flora le Breton as the girl is nothing more or less than a mechanical doll. Several small parts are well played. The whole thing is hopeless.

Gore.

CAPT. JANUARY

Sol Lesser presentation, a Principal Pictures Master Production and starring Baby Peggy. Adapted from the story of Laura E. Richards and directed by Edward F. Cline. Showing at the Strand, New York, week of July 6. Running time. 69 mins.

Captain January	Baby Peggy
Jeremiah Judkins	Hobart Bosworth
Isabelle Morton	Irene Rich
George Maxwell	Harry T. Morey
Bob Pete	Lincoln Stedman
Herbert Morton	John Merkyl
John Elliott	Emmett King
Lucy Tripp	Barbara Tennant

Both a sweet and weak feature, containing a minimum of entertainment while revealing nothing beyond the "cute" and "adorable" mannerisms of the child star, Baby Peggy, and a legitimate performance by Hobart Bosworth. Its inactivity is fatal.

There can be no question about this picture, as it includes no artistic passages which might be an argument to offset the inertia, while a majority of the footage is simply a series of inserts of the love between an aged lighthouse keeper and his ward. Those passages conform pretty much to the sequence film workers have ever followed. Although Baby Peggy may be rated at the head of the present juvenile contingent, the hashing over of this much-abused "great love" palls when the actual story gives it no interest as a background.

The names of Irene Rich, Harry Morey, Lincoln Stedman and Emmett King are meaningless other than as billing. Any number of screen players could have done as well in the roles which call for no effort. Productionally, the theme is not too demanding and the producers were evidently satisfied on that basis.

The story is of the keeper of the beacon finding a babe roped to a spar which has floated in from a wreck. Unmarried and bringing up the child for five years fostered the biggest thing in his life with an enemy (reason ungiven) in the small Maine village attempting to have the youngster taken from him.

Eventually a yacht comes along and goes on the reef because the elderly guardian has overslept. There is no danger, but the owner and his wife come ashore to discover the child is the daughter of the wife's sister, who was drowned. The separation of the old man and the baby is subsequently pictured, as is their reunion.

It's sweet, sickeningly sweet, and will be meaningless, perhaps harmful, to Baby Peggy at the box office. The total result can hardly be placed at the feet of any of the unit; it is just an instance of where the story could have been better left undone.

The only certainty is the next Baby Peggy film will have to contain considerably more body to it than this one for "Captain January," but paves the way for a comeback. *Skig.*

BETWEEN WORLDS

Artclass Production presented by Weiss Bros. Written and directed by Fritz Lang. Titles by Katherine Hilliker and H. H. Caldwell. Shown at the Capitol, New York, week July 6. Running time 67 mins.

The Lovers {	Lil Dagover
	Walter Janssen
The Stranger	Bernard Goetzke
Monna Fiametta	Lil Dagover
Giovani Francesco	Walter Janssen
Messer Girolamo	Rudolf Kleine-Rogge
The Moor	Lewis Brody
The Viceroy	Karl Huszar
The Magician, Ahi	Paul Biensfeld
Tiao Tsien	Lil Dagover
Liang	Water Janssen
The Archer	Bernhard Goetzke
The Caliph	Edward von Winterstein
Zobeide	Lil Dagover
The Frank	Walter Janssen
El Mot, the gardener	Bernhard Goetzke
The Apothecary	Karl Platen

Weiss Bros. are the sponsors for the German-made fantasy at the Capitol this week entitled "Between World." It is a production that has been in this country for almost two years. Originally it was the hope of those who held the picture they would be able to road show it, but that it is rather gruesome in theme discouraged this. Countless people in the trade have seen it in New York and when Douglas Fairbanks came along with "The Thief of Bagdad" also a fantastic tale with some magical stunts for appeal it was believed that there is some chance for this picture.

This would hardly seem to be the right answer, judging from the manner in which it appealed at the Capitol Sunday. There is practically nothing to the picture outside of the photography that will appeal.

The story is of reincarnation. A pair of lovers have had a series of unhappy love affairs through the centuries as the love of the woman was a highly selfish one.

The story opens in a small German town where a mysterious stranger arrives and takes the lover of the girl from her. The girl starts out to seek him and falls exhausted by the side of the grave yard wall.

Then the story becomes a dream in which it is disclosed the girl and boy had been lovers in the distant past, first as Chinese, then as East Indians and also Venetians. All the affairs ended disastrously for both.

In the finish it is disclosed to the girl the only way her lover can be returned to her is through the medium of her making a sacrifice. She does and there is the usual happy ending. Trick photography and double exposure stuff runs all through the picture.

The leading roles are played by Lil Dagover and Walter Janssen, while The Stranger is played by Bernard Goetzke who goes right out after the record as the champion "dead pan" actor of the screen. *Fred.*

MONTMARTRE

German-made production released by Paramount. Starring Pola Negri. Other players in the cast not announced. From the play, "The Flame," by John Mueller. Directed by Ernst Lubitsch. Edited and titled by Hector Turnbull. At Loew's New York, one day, July 1, as half bill. Runs 84 minutes.

"Montmartre" will disappoint those filmgoers who demand complex sex stuff and lavish settings and clothes in heavy portions. Perhaps the lack played no little part in preventing it from obtaining a first run in New York and several other important cities.

But no picture directed by Ernst Lubitsch and giving Pola Negri an opportunity can be wholly negligible. "Montmartre," in spite of its several deficiencies, measurees up as better audience stuff than 60 per cent of the films that play the best houses.

Shot in Germany, it exhibits all the crude and stilted characteristics (to American eyes at least) that have featured these foreign films. But, like "Passion," there are moments of dramatic intensity, bits of comic by-play and other directorial touches that come like a rush of fresh air after the conventional Hollywood-made pictures.

Miss Negri is cast neither as her usual virago, trollop or vampire, but, probably for the first time, as a much-wronged and womanly sweet girl. True, she is a Parisian grisette at the time (60 years ago). But aside from a tendency to have a little fling or two now and then she is as pure in heart as any of our virginal American heroines.

That Miss Negri is able to make this weak and rather vacillating character one of pulsating flesh and blood is another convincing proof she belongs in the very top rank of our screen emotionalists. The mergre plot concerns her marriage to a man above her social station. There is a conniving cousin who desires the girl and contrives to keep the wounds of the unhappy marriage open in the hope he may be benefited. In the end the tangle is straightened out by the same factor that has solved so many dramatic difficulties, the knowledge the family census will soon be raised from two to three.

With that story and the running time almost an hour and a half, the film is bound to drag in spots. Lubitsch, however, has directed so well the wearisome moments are few and far between. A more pressing obstacle in his path was the cheapness of sets and costumes, more meagre in richness and beauty than those used in the tawdriest American comedy.

The supporting cast, none by name, will probably be considered mawkish, not to say comical, over here. But although the work is unnatural and uncouth in many respects, it is superior to that seen in most of the foreign pictures since "Passion."

There is a minimum of sex appeal, with Miss Negri showing nothing in the way of undress to compare with her revelations in "Men" and other more recent films. The title "Montmartre" is entirely misleading, for instead of the colorful, bright story one is led to expect, the picture is sombre and almost drab in its general tone.

"Montmartre" got off to a bad start with poor notices, and Paramount has done little for it since. It is no knockout, but neither Miss Negri's nor Lubitsch's reputation will be damaged by it. In fact, in some locales it is liable to draw raves.

As a commercial proposition it is average program stuff.

WOMAN WHO SINNED

Produced, written and directed by Finis Fox. Released by F. B. O. Photographed by Hal Mohr and Jean Smith. Featuring Mae Busch. At the New York one day, July 5. Runs about 75 mins.

Wall Street Broker	Morgan Wallace
His Wife	Irene Rich
Minister	Lucien Littlefield
His Wife	Mae Busch
Their Son	Dicky Brandon
Burlesque Queen	Cissy Fitzgerald
Young Evangelist	Rex Lease

While no denying Finis Fox has a gifted sense of dramatic screen values, in this picture, at least, he has turned it in the wrong direction. "Woman Who Sinned" is a bungling piece of bathos. Unless it brings in large monetary returns (extremely doubtful), there was little or no reason for shooting it.

Most of the action transpires a score of years ago but seems to hark even further back to the days when stories of this type were in vogue. There is more than one moment when it suggests a screen version of "The Fatal Wedding" if such were to be filmed with all the dastardly machinations, long-suffering abuse and mock heroics.

If Fox had directed his picture in somewhat lighter vein some of these supposedly tragic incidents might have been laughable. There is now a paucity of laughs and lighter moments that makes the slow-moving dramatic action all the more monotonous.

The plot concerns two contrasted couples, one, a viper of a Wall Street broker and his poor neglected, love-hungry wife; the other a placid New England minister and his contented although romantic spouse.

The city Lothario sails to the small town on his majestic yacht and awakens an interest in the preacher's wife by playing up to her little boy. He inveigles her aboard the boat and by force and trickery does more than his share of the shining. She is conscience stricken and afraid to face her husband and child. Her revenge is obtained when she aids in sending the scoundrel to prison for gypping the government.

Years pass. She has become as cold and calculating as any Broadway gold digger. But her reformation is accomplished by a young evangelist. He, much to her surprise (if not the audience's) turns out to be the son left years before. Meanwhile the other wife freed from an asylum to which she had been railroaded does away with the villain, and everything is Jake.

This is not enhanced in value by a good many inconsistencies and other errors in production. The women wear the outfits of 1904, but the men are dressed in most up-to-date fashion. The cast gets a minimum out of its chances, with Mae Busch beyond her depth in the preposterous role of the heroine. Morgan Wallace is a Keystone comedy villain and Irene Rich has only a bit.

The best commercial thing about the picture is the name, sexy and arresting enough to draw attention from the masses. Unquestionably there are those who will swallow this sort of stuff, as it always has been swallowed and always will be, but it does not seem probable that enough will like it to make it a good-sized financial success.

Even if it makes a million it still deserves the rating of one of the poorest pictures of the year, at least so far.

WESTERN LUCK

Fox picture starring Charles Jones. Directed by G. Beranger with R. N. Lee the author. Showing at Loew's Circle as half of double bill July 3. Running time, 53 mins.

A conventional and mild Western, not pausing to unfold any unusual angles to make it stand out from numberless others of the kind. Charles Jones, starred, is apparently suited to this type of vehicle, and hints that he would be seen to better advantage were the story to assume reasonableness and should it make definite thespian demands. As it is, he does little but ride, scrap and wriggle out of eighteen different "tight corners."

Projecting mostly Western exteriors and indifferent studio sets, the action leaps from Wyoming to New York and back again. Getting a 25-year start on the main theme, the narrative opens with two baby brothers separated in the midst of a prairie tent village fire, the mother dying, and the lost new-born babe rescued by a rancher. The quarter of a century jump reveals the father with an office in Wall Street, his son a saturized villain, and the rancher in danger of losing his home through the father's Western representative hold on the lease to the property. The lost boy is now the ward of and in love with his rescuer's daughter.

Oil on the land makes it more difficult for the unknowing family to secure leniency from him, who also covets the daughter, hence the way is paved for the inevitable sequence of events, and the picture doesn't disappoint in this respect.

Comedy is supplied by the friend of the cowboy.

Averagely produced, cameraed and presented, the film may find itself capable of remaining upright if bolstered by a companion feature on the program, but can only hope to solo where the seating capacities are limited and where there are no marquees.

In the cast, besides Jones, are J. F. Macdonald, Beatrice Burnham, Thomas Lingham, Bruce Gordon and Patrick Hardigan.

Skig.

WHO'S CHEATING?

Lee-Bradford present "Who's Cheating?" Story by Dorothy Chappell. Directed by Joseph Levering. Cast includes Montague Love, Marie Burke, Ralph Kellerd, Zena Keefe, William H. Tooker, Frank Montgomery, Ed. Rosemon, Dorothy Chappell and Marcia Harris. At the Stanley, New York (one day), July 7.

"Who's Cheating?" sounds spicy enough these flapperish days, but it is nothing of the sort. Just a love story of the mines, with melodramatic climaxes.

At first it looked as though the story was going to pan out unusually interesting, and bade fair to give Miss Keefe and Mr. Love plenty to do, yet they were cut out of the picture very early.

The announcement of "credits" has the story by Miss Chappell and she also has the leading feminine role, which may have accounted for slashing Miss Keefe out in the early rounds.

Miss Keefe played Myrtle Meers, who became engaged to Larry Fields (Mr. Kellerd). When he failed to run and dive into the lake and save a man who had fallen from a boat, another person effecting the rescue, she returned his ring. That was the last seen of Miss Keefe, for the picture switched to the coal mines of Pennsylvania, where our hero went to make a man of himself.

At the mines he meets June Waugh (Miss Chappell) and she falls in love with him and later saves his life. Several thrills, although the dumping car climax was more effective than the one where the man and woman come out of the mine, which has been blown up. There is a lot of high and low villainy afoot with the usual hand of retribution.

Love played the hero's father, and got in some effective work, while in sight. Miss Keefe was splendid during the short time in view. Miss Chappell worked hard to meet all requirements of her own picture heroine.

According to a date on a letter, the picture was made in 1923.

THE HEART BUSTER

Fox presents Tom Mix in "The Heart Buster." Story by George Scarborough. Scenario by John Stone. Directed by Jack Conway. Cast includes Esther Ralston and Frank Currier. At the New York (one day), July 7.

A wishy-washy romance that reminds one of the old days. Tom Mix appears in his newest film, "The Heart Buster," a George Scarborough story. In this Mix production there is nothing new, novel or exceptional.

Jack Conway directed and tried to do the best he could out of a story that is about the "weakest sister" on the Mix reel family roster.

Mix rides his usual way and the whiz-bang entry he made at the start gave the picture a flying start. Then it did a highland fling backward, and heroic efforts were made in a comic way to save the story from falling from grace altogether.

There are some entertaining "shots" and Mix's horse does some marvelous hurdling, yet the love story could not keep up with his high jumping.

It's a Western, with the heroine to marry the villain if the daredevilish hero, "Split-Second" Tom Walton doesn't prove to the girl that her "intended" is "bad folks." But Tod, played by Mix, accomplishes the "impossible" and brings the rascally "heavy" to justice.

Mix is the same, but appears to have a new outfit. His sombrero is as shiny as a plug hat and gloves which he never removed. As a Jim Dandy cowboy or riding fool of the Western prairies, Mix is there.

In "The Heart Buster," the Mix devotees will find entertainment perhaps, but not as doublebarreled and triphammered as other Mix subjects. The story misses.

THE VALLEY OF HATE

Russel Productions presentation, featuring Helen Ferguson, Raymond McKee and Earle Metcalf. Supporting cast: Wilfred Lucas, Helen Lynch, Frank Whitson and Ralph Yearsly. Story by Harry Farnsworth MacPherson, continuity by Geo. Hively, directed by Russell Allen, photography by Ernest Miller. At Loew's Circle, New York, June 24. Running time, 65 minutes.

Very ordinary feature, due to the hoke story. The plot is as familiar as poverty. The locale of the story is South Carolina, written around the love affair of a wealthy young man who enters the valley to inspect some property he has inherited.

The old, old one of having him suspected as a possible revenue officer by the moonshining natives gets it as the plot. He is loved by the ward of the eldest moonshiner, who has been bethothed against her will to one of "pap's" cronies.

A long drawn-out fist fight between the rivals was sadly overdone. The most realistic touch was a conflagration and a gun battle between the moonshiners and a couple of revenue officers.

The high light is the photography, the footage containing some excellent outdoor shots. It is an economical production all the way through, the interior shots consisting of a mountaineer's cabin and the barn. The cast is adequate, Raymond McKee working hard but ineffectually as the hero of the hackneyed tale.

The picture is for the smaller of the small houses, although it might pass as half of a double feature in houses where they are not over discriminating.

Con.

THE ARAB

Jamil	Ramon Navarro
Mary Hilbert	Alice Terry
Dr. Hilbert	Gerald Robertshaw
Governor	Mexudian
Hossein	Count de Limur
Abdullah	Adelqui Miller
Iphraim	Paul Vermoyal

This is the finest sheik film of them all. Perhaps it will not be the synthetic money hit that the Hull picture was, which made Valentino and a dull book, which was a mid-Victorian fake that swept the nation's chambermaids off their seats. But "The Arab" is a compliment to the screen, a verification of the sterling repute of Rex Ingram, and, withal, a sure financial hit.

Years ago this play, by Edgar Selwyn, was done with Robert Edeson and the then budding Mary Ryan. It is screened with Ramon Navarro and Alice Terry, quite worthy successors to the legitimate creators.

As a sheik (it is spelled "cheik" here) Navarro is the acme. Surrounded as he is by genuine men of the desert, for the scenes were shot in Algiers and the mobs are all natural natives in the natural environments, he seems as bona fide as the Arabs themselves.

Miss Terry as the wistful, frightened, assailed little Christian whose winsomeness and piety, even though it is foreign and even hostile to all that this thieving, concubinous rogue stands for, makes the presentation plausible, romantic and attractive.

The "happy ending" is wisely left "open"—it is asking too much for her to dismiss the handsome, nable Moslem who has saved her and her whole white family and flock, given up his indigenous rascalities for her and fallen in love with her; yet he is "tan," by birth and by tradition, and she is white—oh, so white.

Therefore there is an implied promise—of a future. Which is very savory and satisfactory.

The magnificence of the ensembles and the selection of backgrounds set "The Arab" out in the class of artistic masterpieces.

Ingram not only knows how to exact emotion from players, how to cast and how to sustain and progress a human story, but he has an artist's rare faculty for making a single tree throw into perspective on a screen a vastness and grandeur supplied by the imagination and memory.

Throughout the unfolding of this picture there is a complete illusion of being there with the events. "The Arab" gives the truest impression of the great desert that this reviewer has ever enjoyed, even when in the desert himself, for Ingram is a better picker than this reviewer and a more inspired translator of symbolisms into concrete picturization.

Though this is in a measure a "sex" picture, it may be recommended to high school classes. And it may be recommended to post graduate students in constructing, developing and presenting worthwhile material for the screen.

A certain money-maker and at the same time an uplift and advancement for the industry, this almost perfect combination of drama, scenery, atmosphere, high art photography, human interest and poise is probably the grade A release of the year.

Lait.

BABBITT

Warner Bros. production from the novel by Sinclair Lewis, directed by Harry Beaumont. Shown at the Rivoli, week July 13. Running time 74 minutes.

George F. Babbitt	Willard Louis
Mrs. Myra Babbitt	Mary Alden
Tanis Judique	Carmel Myers
Theodore Roosevelt Babbitt	Raymond McKee
Verona Babbitt	Maxine Elliott Hicks
Tina Babbitt	Virginia Loomis
Paul Reisling	Robert Randell
Mrs. Zilla Reisling	Clssy Fitzgerald
Eunice Littlefield	Gertrude Olmstead
Edward Littlefield	Lucien Littlefield

Tillie, the maid................Dale Fuller
Miss McGoun, Babbitt's stenographer
Kathleen Myers
Michael Dark..................Chum Frinck
Virgil Gunch................Chas. McHugh
Mrs. Littlefield..................Frona Hale

Another "Main Street" novel brought to the screen by the Warners. "Babbitt" is by the author of "Main Street," and it deals with the old, old adage of "there's no fool like an old fool."

The picture should get some money on the strength of the sale of the book and that the Warners have given it an all-around good cast, though there isn't a single outstanding name in it. Three are featured, Willard Louis, Mary Alden and Carmel Myers. They are capable enough as players but do not particularly mean anything at the box office, so the story will have to be the main reliance.

The plot takes the time-worn tale of the middle-aged fairly successful business man, tired of home surroundings and the wife who has reared his three children. He is ripe for the first vamp who makes up her mind to ensnare him. Miss Myers is this particular vamp. She walks into the real estate office that Willard Louis, as Babbitt, is conducting in search of a studio apartment. Babbitt is right on the job and takes care of her wants personally. He even goes further than that when she is short and slips her a couple of hundred.

The game grows swifter and he suggests to the wife "she take a little trip." While she's away the vamp brings her heavy artillery to bear and suggests they both start life anew together. When the son of Babbitt interposes, the vamp is right on deck with the plea she is in love with his father, but the boy finally persuades his dad to give up the trip and return home.

It is all told in a human vein with an eye on the main chance for laughs, and the latter are plentiful.

Louis gives a corking performance of the "sap" who falls for the goo-goo lamp stuff. He is one of those eggs all puffed up with his own importance. Miss Myers rather overdoes the vamp stuff at times and might profit by watching some of the real girls working in life if she intends to follow the line laid out for her in this picture. Miss Alden as the mother has the sympathetic role.

One does not, however, want to overlook Raymond McKee as the juvenile. He pulls a couple of moments of acting out of the role.

For fair sized town the local exhibitor might pull, "How many Babbitts in this town?" and start a guessing contest. *Fred.*

FOR SALE

First National Production made from a story by Earl Hudson. Claire Windsor, Adolphe Menjou, Robert Ellis, Mary Carr and Tully Marshall featured. Directed by George Archainbaud. Running time, 83 minutes. Reviewed at the Strand, New York, July 13.

Eleanor Bates..............Claire Windsor
Joseph Hudley.............Adolphe Menjou
Allan Penfield..................Robert Ellis
Mrs. Harrison Bates...............Mary Carr
Harrison Bates..............Tully Marshall
Cabot Stanton..................John Patrick
The Butler........................Finch Smiles
Parisian Dance Hall Girl..Marga La Rubia

Once upon a time the "Song of Songs" belonged to Solomon. Then Suderman took it for his own, and finally our Ned Sheldon perched on it. The same goes for "The Bartered Bride" as a story. It has been used for time immemorial as one of the dramatic standbys. DeFlers and other French dramatists, notably the younger Dumas, have used the theme of a marriage of convenience often. It was old when Shakespeare began writing, yet he used it. John Dryden found it didn't put a crimp in his snappy stories, and even during the period of Sir Walter Scott it was one of the old reliables.

Earl Hudson, a more or less unfamiliar writer of this day and generation but very well known generally in picture circles, has probably figured that where it served the old boys it would probably serve him. Accordingly, in "For Sale" he has whooped it up in exactly the same way of unknown hundreds before him, and in an attempt to give the story a twist of originality he has thrown in the Montmartre section of Paris as the story books show it.

The whole result is that the picture is as colorless and obvious as a piece of glass.

Eleanor Bates is a daughter of society people. By her parents she is regarded as the niftiest thing around, and two men regard her the same way. Allan Penfield is not rich. Cabot Stanton has dimples, vaselined hair and a flock of dough. Because the family fortunes are in a tough way, she is literally "sold" to Stanton.

So the poor young man hops to Paris and begins staging a booze marathon of several weeks' duration. After Stanton has been killed in an automobile accident and Eleanor is in Paris (weeks later, with her parents and new suitor, Joseph Hudley, who has her father by the ears), Penfield is found in an apache dive up to his neck in liquor.

Again the family is hald up, and once more Eleanor is to be "sold" to Hudley. In appearance he is the typical roue. At their engagement dinner Hudley has arranged for Eleanor, Penfield shows up, a reformed booze fighter, and anxious to win back the girl. When she attempts to kill herself by drinking poison to escape the Hudley marriage, Penfield slaps the glass from her hand, and when Hudley sees Eleanor really hates him, he turns out to be a melodramatic good fellow, forgives the father for being brooked with a lot of his money and gives the girl to the man she loves.

Which makes the story applesauce.

Menjou, as Hudley, is the sole capable member of the cast. Tully Marshall and Mary Carr are woefully miscast, Marshall looking totally unlike a society father. Khaki becomes him better than broadcloth. Claire Windsor is a negligible leading women, and the direction by George Archainbaud contains so many lamentable errors of good taste that they do not bear recounting.

In addition, a shot of some Park avenue homes by night shows them to be lighted scenery, while in one of the interior views a heavy sunbeam is shining on drapery near the ceiling. It has often been suggested that sunbeams can't crawl through ceilings.

The subtitles are weak.

"For Sale" is a very light first-run picture, as to drawing or entertainment qualities. *Sisk.*

BROADWAY OR BUST

Universal production, starring Hoot Gibson. Written by Edward Sedgewick and Raymond Schrock, script by Dorothy Yost. Directed by Edward Sedgewick. Shown at Loew's Circle on double-feature bill with reissue of "Blood and Sand," July 14, 1924. Running time, 63 minutes.

Dave Hollis...........................Hoot Gibson
Virginia Redding.....................Ruth Dwyer
Jeff Peters..............................King Zany
Mrs. Dean-Smythe...............Gertrude Astor
Freddie..................Stanhope Wheatcroft
Count Dardanella........:.....Fred Malastesta

Here is a wow of a hoke comedy. It's made to order for summer audiences, and in the bigger neighborhood houses it cannot fail to please the audiences on double bills, such as it played at the Circle.

Eddie Sedgewick, who wrote and directed the picture, hasn't overlooked a bet to get laughs. He resorted to everything that was in the first Joe Miller book published. It's all in this picture from the "grape fruit juice in the eye" to the old gag of trying to blow out the electric light. He couldn't go back any farther than that. But how the audience loves it!

"Broadway or Bust" is just a story of a cowboy turned down by his girl because she has inherited $200,000 and gone to New York. He sells his ranch for a million, and follows her, busting right into society and saving her from the villain in the last couple of hundred feet of Eastman stock.

But that doesn't tell the yarn. The first couple of reels are the usual hoke western stuff that has been shot a hundred times. The old dance at the ranch house and the rivalry between the city slicker and the cowboy sweetie.

The big-town stuff is where the wallop comes in. The cowboy, after selling his ranch with its radium deposits, starts for the big town, taking his ranch man-of-all-work and their horses. When they reach the Fritz Hotel in the big town they insist on a suite for their horses as well as one for themselves, and the enterprising press agent of the hotel convinces the management it'll be good stuff for the papers.

The idea is so good that the society queens start flocking around the millionaire cowboys, and they are invited out to the self same country home that the ranch sweetie is stopping at. All this stuff is just one laugh after another, but there is a little touch of the seasickness stuff on a yachting party that is a little overdone.

Hoot Gibson slips over the cowboy stuff, with King Zany as his companion with a kick. The girl, Ruth Dwyer, is colorless. Gertrude Astor as the society queen was "there" 40 ways. Fred Malastesta as the heavy just about got by. Outside of Gibson there wasn't anything to the cast, but the hoke story and the direction got it over. *Fred.*

DARK STAIRWAYS

Universal production from story by Marion Orth, with scenario by L. J. Rigby. Herbert Rawlinson featured. Directed by Robert F. Hill and reviewed at Loew's New York July 14 (one day). Running time, 68 minutes.

This is one of Universal's less important releases, from the appearance of the paper prepared for it and other tokens, yet as a program feature for the neighborhood and daily change houses it serves its purpose by being good entertainment. Whether the Rawlinson name is a potent money draw in this type of film (crook stuff) is problematical.

Briefly, the story tells of a bank cashier falsely convicted of the theft of a $100,000 necklace. In prison the lesser crooks respect him for daring to pull such a big job. Though innocent in reality, he escapes with an Irish thug so that he will have the opportunity to clear his name. A dirigible hovers over the prison and takes them away—a highly improbable thing—and, once out, he finds the real thief and clears himself, working around to a happy ending with the girl who stuck by him when the riot was on.

Ruth Dwyer is the nice-looking girl. The crook stuff is all done as the magazines write it, but as the film makes no pretense of being anything else than pure fiction, no fault can be found with it. It is adequately staged, well directed, and although Rawlinson is the only name of note in the picture, the others are sufficient unto the tasks assigned them.

"Dark Stairways" is a good average second-string release. *Sisk.*

YANKEE SPEED

Sunset Production, presented by Anthony J. Xidias. Written and directed by Robert North Bradbury. Featuring Kenneth McDonald. Cast includes Jay Hunt, Richard Levis, Milton Tabney, John Henry, Viola Yorba and Virginia Ainsworth. At the Circle, New York, one day (July 10), as half the bill. Runs about an hour.

A typical moment in "Yankee Speed" comes when the villain, after glancing carefully around the empty room, hisses to the villainess, "Are we alone?" There follows the careful plotting of a scheme to steal the hidden plans, get the money, fool the heroine and split the proceeds.

When it is added that the locale is the border line of Arizona and Texas, the girl in the case a Spanish-type beauty, and the hero an American roof-climbing athlete, there remains little else to tell. It is similar to 100 that have gone before it, a bit weaker in continuity and plot construction, perhaps, but with some effective local color and striking photography.

McDonald, a comparative newcomer, is the Yankee knick-of-time boy. He is tall and good-looking and vaults fences gracefully, but his facial acting as yet is below par, and his acrobatics and fighting lack the snap by some of our other film-supermen. Opposite Viola Yorba gives a fair performance that will improve when she learns how to put more animation into it. The balance of the cast is none too impressive, with the villain a particularly vapid specimen of the bewhiskered, nasty-minded variety.

The film has the usual quota of chases and fights, with the brawn of one Americano superior to that of an army of gringos. Some shots in the Mexican cafe containing excellent Spanish dancers lend much color. The exteriors are lovely and photographed with taste and skill.

"Yankee Speed" is an average film of its type.

THE BATTLING FOOL

Perfection feature releasing through C. B. C. Directed by W. S. Van Dyke and featuring William Fairbanks and Eva Novak. Showing at Loew's New York, July 12. Running time, 57 minutes.

Fairbanks' boxing and ably taking care of the portrayal, while backed by a rural story that's been blocked out many times before. However, the ring action overcomes the weakness of the narrative and besides giving Fairbanks a better vehicle than he has had in some time, the picture screens as a certain entertainer for the middle class houses.

Van Dyke has capably handled the fight stuff, which takes in the start of the minister's son'ring career by staying three rounds with a barnstorming champ, and finishes with the winning of the championship. In between is spaced the daughter of the village mayor who is partial to the fighting youth with the two parents being aspiring reformers.

Miss Novak has little to do, but Fairbanks breezes through the script neatly and at least is constantly moving around, which is something many of his previous films have lacked. The story overly stretches itself at times to make it strictly a moving picture tale, and accordingly loses caste.

A local poolroom proprietor teaches the son to box whence the father ousts the youth from the homestead and he goes to the city. Meanwhile the daughter has become crippled through being trampled upon in the aftermath of the three-round stay in the town hall, for which her father will do nothing, as he believes it a form of retribution for her having attended the affair disguised as a boy.

Six hours before the battle for the belt the boy hears of the girl's condition, hops into a machine and tears to the village and brings her back where she can obtain medical attention. Placed within his apartment, phone receiver at her ear during the fight, her welfare becomes further impaired through fire breaking out from which she must needs be rescued by the new champ, still in his ring togs and a bathrobe.

It's necessarily the flight stuff that must carry the picture, and being handled sufficiently well to make it interesting, "squares" many of the other faults.

Other cast members are unnamed The titling of the picture runs true to form in that it follows the usual tendency of this class of release to become obstructed with flowery phrases. *Skig.*

TUCKER'S TOP HAND

Neal Hart starring vehicle presented by William Steiner and distributed through New Cal Film Corporation, 220 West 42nd street, New York. Directed by Hart. At the Stanley, New York, July 11 (one day).

This looks like the most inexpensive film that has struck the screen in several years. It is a western picture of the most ordinary and obvious type and reminds one of a reversion to the old Kalem-Essanay-Lubin days rather than the Metro-Famous-First National period.

An invalid ranch owner signs a note on money borrowed from a couple of crooked western moneylenders. Their object was to foreclose on his ranch and thereby get not only their principal but a good piece of property besides. Hart, in the role of the top hand of the ranch, "outs the villains and wins the hand of the girl who was brought out to nurse the old invalid.

Stretched over five reels, this is gauze-like film fare, gauze-like without having any light touches, for all the humor is forced, some of it in bad taste and never funny. The star, Hart, is not comparable with the other present-day Western character delineators and his support holds more unfamiliar names than a casualty list of the Finnish army.

As it didn't cost much it can't lose much. but it's a pipe that the film will not draw to any extent and will not entertain even the average daily change house audience. Those audiences are used to much better fare than this and it cannot be recommended for any program. *Sisk.*

ROMANCE RANCH

Fox picture, starring John Gilbert and directed by H. M. Mitchell. Cast includes Bernard Siegel, Evelyn Selbie, Frank Beal, John Miljan and Virginia Brown Fair. Showing at Loew's New York, July 9.

The only angle on this picture, other than its being a casual western of the well-known type, is the similarity in theme to the Goldstone film, "Down by the Rio Grande," which was reviewed by Variety recently. The stories are practically identical, with hardly a variation revealing itself. As the "Rio Grande" was nothing to go into hysterics about, and as this release will not upset anyone, the harm done seems negligible, unless an exhibitor were to play the two films successively. At the New York they were spaced by about three weeks.

Mitchell has done little to bring his subject up to normal, and Gilbert is a passive personality in this instance, who fails to demand definite consideration. The remainder of the cast play methodically to round out a second division feature.

Starting by depicting a pony express rider being killed and his mail bag found some 50 years later, the general situation of the oppressed Spaniard who despises his brother is well under way. The delayed postage brings the letter in which the father's forgiveness is found, along with his acquiescence that the rancho belong to the son, now old and just about able to manage an existence.

The young grandson must needs regain the property for his relative, with the complications setting in through the dastardly brother's beautiful daughter. That's the layout, of which there is no more, no less.

Neither Neitz, who directed the Goldstone edition of this scenario, or Mitchell, supervising for Fox, have much to brag about, albeit it is also more than likely that the limitations of the story were sufficient to forcibly crimp any superlative ideas.

The two pictures are so closely allied in their respective situations and action that these twins smack of a possible story.

Otherwise the same goes for this picture as the other. Both are mediocre screen entertainment. *Skig.*

SIDE SHOW OF LIFE

Famous Players' picture and a Herbert Brenon production releasing through Paramount. Adapted from the novel, "The Mountebank," by W. J. Locke, and the play by Ernest Denny. Features Ernest Torrence and Anna Q. Nilsson, with Brenon directing. James Howe, photographer. At the Rivoli, New York, week of July 20. Running time, 83 minutes.

Andrew Lackaday..........Ernest Torrence
Lady Auriol Dayne.........Anna Q. Nilsson
Elodie....................Louise Lagrange
Horatio Bakkus..............Maurice Cannon
Charles Verity-Stewart.......Neil Hamilton
Mignon....................William Ricciardi
Ernestine.......................Mrs. Pozzi
Sir Julius Verity-Stewart..Lawrence D'Orsay
Lady Verity-Stewart..........Effie Shannon
Evadne......................Katherine Lee

Strictly a first-class presentation, with Herbert Brenon having treated his subject superbly. The work of Ernest Torrence is outstanding, and not alone through his being listed as the character which carries the love interest in the sequence for what may constitute his first screen "affair."

The supporting cast gives a corking performance, amplified by the work of Louise Lagrange as a French music hall girl, who overshadows everyone but Torrence. The featuring of Miss Nilsson simply means a name outside the theatre.

Brenon has made the entire picture so human that the time the picture consumes, almost an hour and a half, is not only necessary but justified.

Starting with Torrence as Lackaday, a clown in a French circus, the picture opens with the tent show blowing up. Trudging away his partner, a dog, is killed by an automobile in which rides Lady Auriol Dayne, serving to introduce the clown's etherized castles. Meeting Elodie, the music hall girl, who is in similar circumstances, the two form a partnership in an act that is a small time success but which the war interrupts.

Lackaday, a pronounced militarist, enlists with the English, rises to the rank of colonel, and saves a young captain. The leave of absence, which he spends at the latter's home, reintroduces Lady Dayne. Then follows the information he has been promoted to a Brigadier General.

About to answer a toast on his advancement he is cut short by the announcement of the Armistice and sees himself, again, as the clown, for it is the only profession he knows.

Going back to France, rejoining Elodie and whipping their former act into shape ends in disaster at the opening performance, when Lackaday discovers he can no longer entertain, but goes on with the act despite the booing and catcalls.

Elodie rushes to the dressing room to return with a Legion of Honor Cross and the announcement of the rank held by the clown in the army. It brings cheers and an apology from the broken artist, who realizes his days as a performer are over.

Lady Dayne, having followed Lackaday to France, is in the audience at the time. A meeting in his dressing room is evidently the climax of that affair until he boards a boat for Australia to accept an offer, the outcome of a service comradeship, and the titled miss has her deck chair placed beside him.

Torrence is the clown for its full worth, while Brenon's handling of the scenes of the announcement of the Armistice at the dinner table and failure of the act upon its reopening are scenes that grip and hold to give the picture two high spots.

Miss Lagrange has been perfectly cast as the temperamental French girl, deserted by her husband and in love with the clown. Their retaliations are purely platonic. Her work is in a prominent role upon which she has capitalized to run second only to Torrence.

Meeting all needs as to production, the photography reveals the settings to full advantage, including the brief footage given over to the warfare, which may wean away from orthodox military strategy, but is just as effective.

It's a picture in every sense of the word that, with elaboration, might have come very close to being a special. It is also an example of what may happen when a sound (and clean) story is told by a director who knows what he is doing and has a cast of capable players with which to work. *Skig.*

THE SIGNAL TOWER

Universal-Jewel. From the story by Wadsworth Camp, adapted by James O. Spearing, directed by Clarence L. Brown. Shown at the Strand, N. Y., week July 20, 1924. Running time 65 minutes.
Sally Taylor..................Virginia Valli
Dave Taylor............Rickliffe Fellowes
Joe Standish................Wallace Beery
Sonny Taylor...............Frankie Darro
Old Bill.................James O. Barrows
Pete.............J. Farrell MacDonald
Gertie...........................Dot Farley
The Dog..........................."Jitney"

An old fashioned meller. The story in screen form depends on the derailing of a runaway freight train to save the "Limited" from a smash-up, this action taking place while the wife of the tower dispatcher is struggling to fight off the heavy who is chasing her from room to room and breaking down a few doors to get at her.

It is not a picture that is really material for the bigger pre-release houses, but in the regular run of theatres in neighborhoods where there is either a daily or semi-weekly change should prove fair entertainment, although its box office value is going to be a matter of question. It does not appear at this time that it would prove anything out of the ordinary as a drawing card.

The picture is from the story by Wadsworth Camp, adapted by James O. Spearing and directed by Clarence L. Brown. The trio of principal players are Virginia Valli, Wallace Beery and Rockliffe Fellowes. In the order named they are the heroine, heavy and hero. Beery gives a very well thought out performance.

The leads are also well handled. In the supporting cast Frankie Darro, a kiddie player, lends atmosphere while Dot Farley as a "man-made" relative of the wife also added a touch of color to the company.

In the matter of cost the picture is not one of those on which U. has spent a lot of money. The production runs largely to exteriors and what interiors there are did not cost a great deal.

The story is simple; the tale of a tower train dispatcher who lives at a water tank. He has built a home for himself, his wife and child and to pay this off he is in the habit of taking his relief dispatcher to live at his home and pay board.

This is all very well until the "railroad sheik" comes on the scene. This is the heavy, played by Beery, who shows up dolled in the latest in "cake eater clothes" and patent leather shoes. The wife's relative falls for him hook, line and sinker, but the he-vamp won't have any part of the game with her, starting out to cop the wife, the interest culminating in the scene where the husband derails the runaway freight train to save the Limited although he is aware his wife is struggling for her honor a couple of hundred feet away.

The railroad stuff is well handled and the derailing with a flock of freights going over an embankment just as the Limited comes to a stop within a few feet of the scene, is a thriller. *Fred.*

BREAD

Metro-Goldwyn adapted from the novel by Charles G. Norris. Directed by Victor Schertzinger. Script by Lenore Coffey and Albert Lewyn. Shown at the Capitol, N. Y., week July 20, 1924. Running time 72 minutes.

Jeanette Sturgis................Mae Busch
Martin Devlin..................Robert Frazer
Alice Sturgis..................Wanda Hawley
Roy Beardsley..................Pat O'Malley
Mr. Corey.....................Hobart Bosworth
Mrs. Sturgis..................Eugenie Besserer
Mrs. Corey....................Myrtle Stedman
Gerald Kenyon..................Ward Crane
Ralph Beardsley...............Raymond Lee

"Bread" is a rather doughy mass, so sticky it gets in its own way and gums the works to such an extent that the picture is a draggy tale without a particular wallop.

The Charles G. Norris novel in type must have made much better reading than it does a picture. The film story is headed somewhere, but no one seems able to figure out where. That must have been the fault of the adaptation or the direction. Possibly the editing had something to do with it for there were stills of scenes that failed to show in the picture exhibited. The title doesn't seem to have any particular box office value other than that the book was a best seller.

In the matter of cast the strong sales point of the picture to the public shows. The names that should be worth something at the box office are Mae Busch, Robert Frazer, Wanda Hawley, Pat O'Malley, Hobart Bosworth and Myrtle Steadman.

The Capitol presentation, prefaced with a male quartet chanting a portion of the Lord's Prayer ending with "Give us this day our daily bread," at which the picture starts, was quite the best thing about the entertainment.

It is a tale of a girl that chooses a business career finally giving it up for marriage, which does not turn out any too successfully, whereupon she returns to business. After three years of separation she decides that both she and her husband were about equally to blame for the mess they have made of their lives and a reconciliation is brought about.

The moral of the tale is that a woman who once has made her own living is very apt to be too independent to make a good wife. At least that is about as near as anyone can come to digging a moral out of it.

Miss Busch is the business wife who prefers her own way in most everything, handling the role exceptionally well and gives further proof that she is coming along as an actress. Robert Frazer opposite delivers as well as could be expected. Wanda Hawley and Pat O'Malley should have been directed for greater comedy effect. It isn't until the final couple of shots the laughs that are in the characters are brought out. The support to this quartet of leading characters is uniformly good.

Fred.

LURE OF THE YUKON

Lee-Bradford Corporation presentation of Alaskan drama. Direction, story and production by Norman Dawn. Half of one-day double feature bill at Loew's New York, July 15. Running time, 55 minutes.

Sue McCraig................Eva Novak
"Sourdough" McCraig,
Spottiswoode Aitken
Bob Force..............Kent Sanderson
Kuyak....................Arthur Jasmine
Dan Baird............Howard Webster
Ruth Baird...........Katherine Dawn
Black Otter................Eagle Eye

A cheap hokum melodramatic picture with amateurish direction and a cast that is 80 per cent. ludicrous. The director has attempted to inject all of the standard hoke thrills around a "gold rush" tale of Alaska. He has only succeeded in making the picture interesting where he is aided and abetted by nature and the great oudoors.

Whatever interest attaches will come from its locale, Alaskan. The herds of reindeer, snow scenes and malamutes were the real thing and provided a background muffed entirely and made silly by artists and director.

An attempt at a thrilling fight between the hero, Kent Sanderson, and three Eskimos was the most amateurish thing seen on the screen in many a day. Sanderson was mis-spotted all through the picture and failed to convince.

Arthur Jasmine's conception of an Eskimo was almost as bad. He succeeded in projecting the illusion of a half-witted male, nothing else. Eva Novak as Sue McCraig, the center of the story, was blondly beautiful, wore good looking fur costumes and struck the most sincere note.

The George Madden photography was excellent, and coupled with the splendid outdoor scenery, saved the picture from utter mediocrity. An old river steam or stern wheeler was another realistic touch.

The story concerns Sue and her father and the efforts of a villainous neighbor reindeer rancher to get the girl by playing upon her father's weakness for moonshine and his need of financial help to winter his herd.

A gold strike is announced with all hands hitting the trail. Sue's father dies and a duel of wits ensues between the villain and hero for her, with odds on the villain, due to Sue's stupidity in not being able to recognize the sterling qualities of her hero, until the director had mushed his extras all over the North for a few thousand feet.

The customary "thrills" of blizzard, avalanche, etc., were worked in before the usual clinch and the discovery of gold by the hero. The director's idea of a situation between the principals (after a caption had stated that it was away below zero) was to have every one stand around talking with their hats off as though at the indoor pool at Miami.

Just another waste of footage, except for the natural scenes, not helped much by the human accessories.

Con.

BEHIND THE CURTAIN

Universal production directed by Chester Franklin. Written by William J. Flynn and adapted by Emil Forest and Harvey Gates. At the Circle one day (July 15) as half double bill. Runs about 55 minutes.

Sylvia Bailey...........Lucille Ricksen
Hugh Belmont...........Johnny Harron
Laura Bailey..........Winifred Bryson
George Belmont...........Charles Clary
Prof. Gregorious...........Eric Mayne
"Slug" Gorman...........George Cooper
District Attorney.......Clarence Geldert

With William J. Flynn, who should know something about murder mysteries, as author and two rather well-known adapters on the scenario, it seems strange Universal should have turned out such a muddled affair as "Behind the Curtain," ranking as the season's most slovenly constucted photoplay. Even a good cast fails to put it across as a mystery, melodrama, love story, expose of spiritualism or average entertainment.

It starts out as a mild and mushy romance with a couple of eloping prep school kids as the central figures. For nearly a reel you watch them playfully chase each other around the meadows and coyly arrange the forbidden elopement. This, senseless and kickless though it be, is the pleasantest part, chiefly because of the charming photographic shots.

Suddenly the plot swerves to a different track and the young couple after that are merely incidental; into the paths of spiritualism introduced by the villain of a clairvoyant. This charlatan's methods of bringing back the dead are demonstrated but not explained, except to say that he has an able assistant with a collection of wigs and costumes.

Another change of plot introduces a second love affair (intimated this one is not so innocent), with its principals the boy's father and the girl's older sister. The old boy is popped off and his sweetie, with whom he has become estranged because of the elopement of his son and her sister, is held for the murder. Considerable more spiritualistic nonsense. Finally the clairvoyant is proven the killer.

For a few moments the spiritualistic bits are attention compelling, but for the most part the action drags and the supposed thrills will give no one the heebie jeebies. Lucille Ricksen is her usual superlatively sweet self, quite enough to win her a raft of new admirers. The balance does well, with George Cooper giving another convincing performance as a gangster.

To enumerate the gaps in continuity and the absurdities of various of the incidents would entail columns of copy. Acknowledging the weakness of Detective Flynn's original story, there remains no excuse for the inexpert treatment given the film by the experienced Universal's staff.

This one is only for the cheaper houses and the cheaper houses had better accept it only on double feature days, or because this is the summer time.

LOVE OF WOMEN

H. Clay Miner Production distributed by Selznick. Directed by Whitman Bennett. Written by E. C. Holland and photographed by Edward C. Paul. Featuring Helene Chadwick. At the Circle one day (July 15) as half double bill. Runs about 65 minutes.

Cynthia Redfield......Helene Chadwick
Bronson Gibbs..........Montague Love
Mr. Redfield...........Maurice Costello
Veerah Vale...............Mary Thurman
Ernest Herrick.......Lawford Davidson
Eugenie Redfield........Marie Shotwell
Frankie.................Frankie Evans

It seems the only new angle that might be obtained on the divorce situation from the standpoint of the films would have to come from a story of a childless couple. Always it is the "little child" that yanks them together after the marital ship is on the rocks. "Love of Women" is no exception. In story it is a carbon copy school, but direction and capable acting make it a better-than-average.

Its sermon intends to show that couples who really love are often drawn apart by outside pressure or temporary misunderstandings, and that divorce in such a case will only ruin both. Thus our hero and his wife, after having eloped some years before against the wishes of the bride's selfish mother, find themselves buffeting the opposition of a family trying to cause a conjugal rumpus.

The young husband has an insincere affair with a Greenwich Village Circe, and, although cured in no time, his wife is influenced to divorce him in spite of her love and forgiveness. There follows the serious accident to their baby right on the day the final decree is to become valid. The usual hoke at the kid's bedside, but well done, and its pathos should sofen any audience.

In fact, Whitman Bennett has directed the entire picture with a great deal of promise. At times he tries for some certain effects and misses, but his more serious bits disclose a fine sense of screen values. In this he is aided by the sympathetic work of Helene Chadwick and Lawford Davidson as the young couple. Montague Love is an ineresting villain in that he is not too heavy, and Maurice Costello adds name value in a minor role. Mary Thurman is the vamp, overacting just a bit.

The Greenwich Village scenes are snappy. One bit in which the hero takes off the wild lady's stocking is going to make the straight-laced sit up. The film is nicely set and the photography excellent.

With Miss Chadwick's name and a good audience picture to back it, "Love of Women" should bring money to the Selznick coffers.

DAUGHTERS OF PLEASURE

B. F. Zeidman-Principal production, directed by William Beaudine. Story written by Caleb Proctor and adapted by Eve Unsell. At the New York, one day (July 17), as half of the bill. Runs about 70 minutes.

Marjory Hadley.............Marie Prevost
Mark Hadley................Wilfred Lucas
Mrs. Hadley...............Edyth Chapman
Lilla Millas.......................Clara Bow
Kont Merrill......................Monte Blue

"Daughters of Pleasure" is rather more than moderately strong program entertainment. Its story, that of a nouveau riche family hitting the shoot-the-chutes with a vengeance and just pulling in the reins before the final splash, has been told before. But William Beaudine has outdone himself in direction and a cast of screen notables lends invaluable aid.

If the film had lived up to its early promise it might have qualified for the first-run houses. But after the story has reached a certain point, there is a definite lack of fresh inspiration and from then on it is just a commonplace readjustment.

There are several laughs, chiefly at the efforts of the old boy to fit his number 48 self into a perfect 36 corset and his subsequent attempts to buffalo the family. Wilfred Lucas plays this role with a deft comic touch. Marie Prevost rivals Miss Bow in provocativeness, and in the matter of tantalizing lips she need give ground to no one. Edyth Chapman and Monte Blue round out the cast, the latter rather out of his element as the chippy-chasing young rounder.

With these names and with a story as sexy as the title, "Daughters of Pleasure" should be a box office beauty for the average house.

YOUNG IDEAS

Universal, star ig Laura La Plante. Story by Sophie Kerr; script by Hugh Hoffman. Directed by Robert F. Hill. At Loew's Circle, New York, on double feature bill with "Peter the Great," July 17. Running time, 52 minutes.

Octavia Lowden..............Laura LaPlante
Pritchett Spence.............T. Roy Barnes
Eloise Lowden...............Lucille Ricksen
Uncle Eph.................James O. Barrows
Aunt Minnie..........Lydia Yeamans Titus
Grandma.........................Jennie Lee
Bertie Loomis....................Rolfe Sedan
Bob Lowden..................Buddy Messinger

A short-length feature of the farce comedy order, but played along hoke comedy lines. There must have been a whole lot more to the story than appeared on the screen, but it is a fair hot weather laugh getter, especially if played in a neighborhood-house on a double feature bill as utilized at the Circle. Does not mean anything by itself except in the smaller houses. Names in cast mean nothing also.

The story is that of a girl devoted to her family, with the result that her aunt and uncle, brother and sister, stay at home and take it easy while she acts as the bread winner, and on Sundays denies herself the simple pleasures that might be at her command so that she can nurse and cook meals.

Her employer, in love with her, conspires with the family physician to break up the slavery of the girl. They plant her in a house that is quarantined for supposed smallpox. The result is that the family leeches have to go to work or starve. They all get jobs, after which the original bread winner is returned home and in a willing mood to hear the proposal of the leading man.

The picture isn't one that anyone will rave about, but it does contain a few laughs. *Fred.*

FOREIGN REVIEWS

ONE NIGHT

London, July 14.

A new Granger-Vita production which will not help the firm, the producer, or anybody else to fame or fortune. The story is typically Continental and follows slavishly the new fashion of "framing" a dramatic plot to win the hero from depression, self-destruction or an unfortunate love affair.

These "mysterious" plots are the direct descendants of the old "dream," formerly used when the enterprising producer and author had gotten their characters into such a tangle that no other means beyond the awakening of the lead could bring the story to a successful ending.

"One Night," a title which gives a suggestion the picture fails to carry out, is a particularly poor example. Lord Henry Derleigh has done everything man can do and is bored stiff, stiff to the point of wondering if death holds any adventure. His uncle, Lord Sorel (this story runs among the aristocracy) is disgruntled at Henry's goings on and says so. Henry is not impressed and offers a reward of $500,000 to anyone who can bring about his death by novel and adventurous methods.

A stranger comes along and introduces himself as John Wirth. He is a sardonic individual, and everybody begins to be hopeful as to the novel means to be employed for Henry's finale. True enough, Wirth has a scheme and promises the adventurer all he asks.

Some nights later Henry is compelled to seek shelter at an inn, a sinister inn, where anything could happen. He sleeps and in his sleep changes to a noble of hundreds of years ago. He meets an old hag who implores him to lead her to the Fountain of Youth. This Henry, always chivalrous, does.

The hag drinks and immediately becomes a beauteous maiden while other diaphanously-clad maidens skip about around them. Henry falls in love, but before he can get far with it rough soldiers seize and cast him into a dungeon. From thence he goes to be burned alive at the stake. As the flames lick around him he awakes to find himself miles from anywhere on a desolate moor. He has still, however, a ring the maiden gave him.

Days later he sees an advertisement for the ring and goes to make inquiries. He finds the maiden playing a piano and promptly declares his passion. The maiden, full of maidenly indignation, turns him down. Then Wirth and Lord Sorel arrive, and the explanation is that the whole thing has been a film stunt with the doped Henry as leading man. The maiden is the one his aristocratic relatives have long wished him to marry.

The production work is good but the story impossible. Jean Angelo plays the young lord and Vilma Blanchard the girl. The most interesting thing is that it gives away the identity of the girl in the Max Linder comedy, "Circusmania," the part having been played by Blanchard. *Gore.*

SEN YAN'S DEVOTION

London, July 14.

It is unfortunate a better story could not have been found for this second Stoll picture, featuring Sessue Hayakawa and Tsuru Aoki, and

produced by A. E. Coleby, who is also responsible for the story.

As an author Coleby gives his star but little chance. His work is crude melodrama with well-worn situations, such as the extermination of the master villain, who is crushed to death by a many-armed, fire-breathing idol. As a producer he achieved the customary scenic success of the Stoll studios but has shirked important detail.

A noticeable thing is that while the Oriental hero and heroine walk like normal human beings the Chinese villain, played by an Englishman, shuffles about after the fashion invented by the late George Edwardes for his musical comedy geishas. The climax is also typical of transpontine drama, for the elderly English friend of the Orient whisks off beard and moustache and stands revealed as the Chinese hero.

Coleby's story is one of political intrigue. The Prince of Kloto is dying and the heir is a small boy, his son. The succession depends upon the production of documents which for countless ages have been guarded by a sacred idol. The opposition goes out to get the documents with the aid of the musical comedy gentleman Wun Li, and an individual known as Lutan Singh. On the young heir's side are San Yan, his wife, and a mysterious Englishman, Mr. Oliphant. Adventures are many and include the crushing to death by the angry fire god of the ruffianly Lutan Singh. In due course the prince dies, but Oliphant has the papers all right and produces them at the right moment. He then tears off his hirsute adornments, revealing that Oliphant, the Englishman, is really Sen Yan in disguise.

Hayakawa gives an excellent performance in his dual role, particularly in his disguise as the Englishman. This make-up is really a fine achievement for one with so determinedly marked Oriental features. Tsuru Aoki is capital as the wife, and the picture would have been greatly improved had she had more to do. Nicholas Bates is ineffective as Wun Li, but the fault is more the producer's. Harry Agar Lyons, Tom Coventry, and Jeff Barlow are each good in smaller parts.

The pulling powers of this picture will have to rely entirely on the name of the star. *Gore.*

THE GAME OF LIFE

London, June 24.

"The Game of Life" is the last word in morbidity and sleep compelling length. It seems interminable, and just when the worst seems over it switches to some other phase. The producer takes every shade of sentiment, genuine or mock, and flogs it to a jelly. He piles on "sob stuff," and the greater portion of his comedy is banal.

He has left nothing undone which can be done in his "dramatic spectacle," and as a result has achieved a masterpiece of consolidated boredom.

Even without the boring length (about 10 reels) the story is hard to follow. It deals with three sets of people in different walks of life, the Travers, the Fletchers and the Gobbles, and their lives from youth to old age are an amazing and bewildering hotch-potch of events. Its action is so tedious and involved that it is impossible to detail it except at great length.

The actual production is patchy. The many fine spectacular scenes include Derby Day in the early Victorian era; a music hall of the same period, with reproductions of the acts; the charge of the Light Brigade at Balaclava, an exceptionally fine scene; and Queen Victoria's Coronation and Jubilee procession. Sensationalism is represented by an escape from a burning prison. The scenes around this are absurd, al-

though possessing a certain amount of dramatic value. Bad also are the various newspaper insets.

The cast is long and good, including Isobel Elsom as a blind girl; Lillian Hall Davies as a girl who goes blind; James Lindsay as the villain who is blinded; Tom Reynolds, Dorothy Minto, Campbell Gullan, Allan Aynesworth, Wyndham Guise, many other players, and some thousands of supers. *Gore.*

MANHANDLED

An Allan Dwan production presented by Zukor and Lasky, starring Gloria Swanson. Story by Arthur Stringer, adapted by Frank W. Tuttle, directed by Allan Dwan. Shown at the Rivoli, New York, week July 27, 1924. Running time, 77 minutes.

Tessie McGuire	Gloria Swanson
Johnny Hogan	Tom Moore
Riccardi	Frank Morgan
Pinkie	Lilyan Tashman
Paul Garretson	Paul McAllister
Brandt, the sculptor	Ian Keith
The Salesman	Frank Allworth
Boarding House Keeper	Carrie Scott
"Chip" Thorndyke	Arthur Housman

In this picture rides the distinctive proof that the business end that has to do with the selling of films knows what is needed in a picture to pull money at the box office. "Manhandled" is a picture the story of which originated in the brain of S. R. Kent, general sales manager of Paramount; therefore, like most stories that are finally filmed, this particular tale started from the other end. It was first conceived as a picture story, turned over to Arthur Stringer to write, and when completed, sold to "The Sat. Eve. Post." By the time it appeared, however, the picture was almost completed.

It is essentially a box office attraction from beginning to end. Likewise it is true that it is based on the old reliable "Cinderella" theme; but that always makes money, especially if there is sufficient sex appeal. This picture has nothing more or less than a series of episodes of a girl with various men, showing her playing with fire and finally escaping being scorched to go safely to her lover's arms, who practically overnight has become a millionaire through selling an automobile invention.

It is of a typical hick salesgirl in the basement of a department store, one of those tough, gum-chewing slang slingers. She manages to climb out of the cellar into the Bohemian set through the fact that an author who wishes to make an experiment pulls her out of the place and introduces her to artists, sculptors and a gown creator. Each warns her against the other, and all three are trying personally. Finally the son of the owner of the department store in which she was employed tried to put it over on her, but she escaped, only to walk into her furnished-room house and find that her sweetheart, who had been out of town, has returned. Noting the finery she accumulated in his absence, he is fearful that the worst has happened. Of course, this little complication is straightened out.

Gloria Swanson again reveals unsuspected qualities as an actress. In a way this picture is as much of a revelation as to her personal achievements as was "The Humming Bird." This picture doesn't carry the wallop that one did, but it is sure fire for the box office. Tom Moore plays the young mechanic hero and handles it very well. Frank Morgan, Ian Keith, Paul McAllister, Arthur Housman and Lilyan Tashman are also in the cast. Ann Pennington is also in a brief scene.

In the direction Allan Dwan has shown some clever work. His subway rush hour scene is true to life and yet one of the funniest that has been screened of the underground. The studio parties also had touches of comedy here and there that were enjoyable.

Incidentally, the sub-titling is a work of art. *Fred.*

TESS OF THE D'URBERVILLES

Marshall Neilan production presented by Louis B. Mayer and distributed through Metro-Goldwyn. Adapted from novel by Thomas Hardy by Dorothy Farnum, and featuring Blanche Sweet, Conrad Nagel, Stuart Holmes and George Fawcett. At the Capitol, New York, July 27. Running time, 88 minutes.

Tess Durbyfield	Blanche Sweet
Alex Stoke	Stuart Holmes

Angel Clare..................Conrad Nagel
The Priest..................Joseph Dowling

"Tess of the D'Urbervilles" isn't a complex Hardy story. It is, in its elementals, the narrative of a pure woman who was besmirched by an aristocrat, and of the effect which this forced sin had upon her life.

Tess, as Thos. Hardy unveiled her, was a girl-woman, beautiful and pure, the daughter of the town drunkard and the descendant of an aristocratic family. Tess, as Blanche Sweet plays her, is exactly that, half woman and half girl, but the play itself, in the Mayer presentation and in the Neilan direction, becomes a sex melodrama with its one redeeming feature in the courage of Neilan in sticking to the tragic ending. Aside from that, the picturized version of one of the world's famous novels and one of the stage's famous plays is disappointing and altered to conform to present-day picture demands.

It should have made an excellent movie. The story is there, the atmosphere is ideal for settings, and the role for a dramatic actress has never been surpassed.

But here it is only fair. Miss Sweet, despite her amazingly youthful appearance (and she is beautiful for every inch of the film) never measures up to the emotional possibilities. The famed and traditional atmosphere of the Wessex country has been superficially treated with a native folk dance, a few castle shots, etc., sufficing.

The people are all people of the present day. While there is an excuse for this in that true basic drama is applicable at any age, much more respect should have been given to the tradition which Hardy wove about his native Wessex and Dorsetshire land. That is a mistake to those knowing the book and play. It also disappoints those who don't know it, for the tragic ending isn't conducive to the gathering of fan applause. That was an obstacle in the way of filming "Tess." No one would have dared do it without the hanging of the heroine. With the hanging of the lady it isn't pleasant.

As it is it cannot be regarded as a potential money draw for the box office. Money has been spent on it; time also has been lavished. But the intent is wrong, for "Tess of the D'Urbervilles" isn't a story that can be faithfully filmed in a land where movie censors are appointed just because they happen to belong to a political party and where they regard themselves as custodians of public morals. Because the seduction of Tess is necessary to the plot (and it is barely hinted at in this picture) and because her subsequent life is badly interpreted, the picture must be stamped as an artistic failure and it is forecast that it will not be a box office sensation.

Sisk.

SINGLE WIVES

First National production starring Corinne Griffith. Story by Earl Hudson and direction by George Archainbaud. At the Strand, New York, week of July 27. Runs 85 minutes.

Betty Jordan..................Corinne Griffith
Perry Jordan..................Milton Sills
Dorothy Van Clark......Kathryn Williams
Marion Eldridge..............Phyllis Haver
Tom Van Clark.............Phillips Smalley
Dr. Walter Lane..................Jere Austin
Martin Prayle..................Lou Tellegen
Franklin Dexter.........Henry B. Walthall
Billy Eldridge..................John Patrick

During the past year the films have provided us with restless, daytime, flapper, foolish, virtuous, flaming and perhaps a dozen other varieties of wives, as well as an equal assortment of husbands. Now comes "Single Wives." Its chief difference from the majority lies only in the first word of the title.

Because not even a cast studded with important names and a monetary output by First National that resulted in a lavish and splendiferous production can blot out the weakness of an insipid, hackneyed story, indifferently filmed in everything but beauty of settings and costumes.

The picture has given another opportunity to the lovely Corinne Griffith and she makes enough of it to gratify her most exacting admirers.

For more than half of its overlong running time (85 minutes), "Single Wives" plants its moss-covered plot of the bride of a year whose husband is giving to his business the attention he should be showering upon her. Lou Tellegen is the third angle who tries to take advantage of this, although to his credit he is always more the gentlemanly, ardent lover than the conniving seducer.

The twist that follows should be responsible for whatever limited popularity the film enjoys, because it has not been seen as often as the developments that usually take place in a similar situation. The young wife's mother (Kathryn Williams) has been neglected by her husband, too, and after years of struggling against loneliness has sought solace with a lover. The daughter discovers this when in a rather sordid incident the elder woman is taken ill in a hotel to which she has gone with her inamorata.

The bride realizes that she too will be driven to similar extremes some day, and to save herself asks her husband to divorce her, insinuating she loves the other man.

At this point nearly 80 minutes of footage have been absorbed. The director and author must have then decided to untangle the mess without further ado. So the young husband, just as he is about to leave his wife, is banged up in an auto accident, very crudely filmed, incidentally. Her devotion and sympathy settle their problem in about two minutes and the picture ends leaving the miserable affair of the older "single wife" suspended.

That's only one of several oversights and inconsistencies, chief of which are a ridiculous side plot concerning the heroine's younger sister and an incident in which a $100,000 string of pearls is allowed to break and play marbles all over the floor.

There are a few praiseworthy bits to be found in the production, principally the photography, luxurious sets and gowns, and a good part of the acting. Miss Griffith is generally gorgeous and handsomely dressed and her thespian work convincing, although she still seems to retain some of the uncalled for reserve and repression so becoming in "Black Oxen."

Milton Sills is the young husband, doing wonders with a most thankless role in which he sulks the first part and weeps all over himself later. Kathryn Williams is charming, as always, and even Mr. Tellegen is less theatric than usual. Henry Walthall does little with the unimpressive role of the mother's lover.

A dearth of humorous relief won't help matters, and the box office won't be aided by any extreme sex or undress stuff. The stars in the cast should help it commercially, but the general verdict will label it dreary, cheerless and unexciting.

THE SAWDUST TRAIL

Universal production, starring Hoot Gibson. Story by W. D. Pelley. Direction, Edward Sedgwick. Photography, Virgil Miller. At Loew's Circle, New York, July 24, as half the bill. Cast includes Josie Sedgwick, David Torrence, Charles French, Pat Harmon and G. Raymond Nye.

The happiest of mediums has been struck wth "Sawdust Trail," which combines just enough western thrills and eastern farce comedy to make it one of the most rip-snorting little program pictures of the season. As has been the case with Mix, Jones and one or two others of the same school, Hoot Gibson has been trying to get away from the conventional western stuff. This has led him into playing ridiculous boob roles in equally silly pictures, and the results have not been gratifying.

However, in "Sawdust Trail" he has walloped the right combination on the button. Credit must go to William Dudley Pelley for the story, and to Edward Sedgwick for a tidy bit of direction. The locale is an eastern college town, but the western atmosphere is introduced when a circus and rodeo arrive.

Gibson is a young collegian, really a specimen of health and pluck, but pretends to be an ailing nincompoop. Consequently his father (David Torrence) gets him a job with the circus where, it is hoped, a man will be made of him.

The sawdust people take Hoot for an impossible sissy, and in order to prove his grit he sets out to tame the wildest thing in camp, a broncho-busting, man-hating young lady. She makes everyone step, and the few bold ones who have attempted to josh or court her have been dragged around the grounds by her on the wrong side of a lassoo or otherwise badly banged up. But Hoot goes right after her, gives her a pair of boxing gloves for a birthday present, pulls the chair from under her just as she is about to sit down, and generally torments her until she learns to love him.

The taming holds dozens of incidental laughs. The circus atmosphere is there at all times, with some of the attending characters vastly amusing. Some excellent bronk riding is included, although it is unfortunate that a few shots of the actual circus were not taken. At the finish there is a mad auto chase, the photography doing credit to the work of Virgil Miller.

Gibson is at his best as the college boy because he doesn't overdo the "simp" stuff. Josie Sedgwick is sufficiently formidable and attractive as the heroine, and the others give excellent performances.

This is a dandy little film of its type, and it should be a red-hot hit for Gibson.

MAN WHO FIGHTS ALONE

Zukor-Lasky presentation, starring William Farnum. Lois Wilson and Edward Horton featured. Wallace Worsley production, authored by William Blacke and James Hamilton. At the Rialto, New York, week July 27. Running time, 68 minutes.

John Marble..................William Farnum
Marion..........................Lois Wilson
Bob Alten..................Edward Horton
Meggs..........................Lionel Belmore
Mike O'Hara..................Barlowe Borland
Dr. Raymond..................George Irving
Dorothy..........................Dawn O'Day
Aunt Louise..................Rose Tapley
Struthers..................Frank Farrington

Nothing out of the ordinary in this release, and William Farnum curtailed in his activities through playing a cripple during most of the footage. Void of novelty, the story places its ability to please and hold interest upon the shoulders of the featured trio, who rise sufficiently to the occasion.

Picturesquely the film contains a minor number of "shots" that especially appease the eye, while the settings, in interiors, have also been nicely appropriated.

The story is of a clean triangle, which has two pals in love with the same girl. Farnum as Marble, the unsuspecting one, wins out whence the sequence jumps to his continuance at work, bringing about a breakdown and paralysis of the legs brought on by nervousness during the birth of his daughter.

Forming a partnership with his lifelong friend, Alten, causes the latter's constant presence in the household, which causes the suspicion his wife and partner are in love with each other. Follows the extremes a mentally depraved mind will go to, with the husband's suicide prevented by the timely entrance of his little daughter. The climax is reached when the cripple arises from his chair and walks to warn his wife and child who, from opposite sides, approach a bridge he knows to be on the verge of collapse.

Miss Wilson as usual, gives a neat characterization as the wife in her unassuming manner, while Horton provides an adequate foil to round out the three-cornered affair. Farnum is actively restrained by his role, but, at that, registers as a stationery pantomimist to a greater degree than might ordinarily be supposed. Other contributing players are but secondary.

The picture is away from the general trend of the Farnum releases. For that reason it may lay claim to be a novelty, but otherwise there is nothing to make it stand out from many of the type, despite the possible exception of the tasteful backgrounds.

Lightings on the facial make-up of the cast are prone to become glaring at intervals. The director might have spared a few of the bits in connection with the expected family arrival that seemed something more than necessary, but he didn't.

Skig.

WESTERN VENGEANCE

Jesse Goldberg production starring Franklyn Farnum, at Loew's New York, July 25, on double feature bill. Running time, 58 minutes.

Jack Caldwell..............Franklyn Farnum
Sontag..............................Jim Curley
Helen..........................Doreen Turner
Luke Mosley..................Martin Turner
Dick Sterling..............Mack B. Wright
Ann Sterling..................Marie Walcamp

After looking at this picture the thought occurs that if someone doesn't cable Marcus Loew to come back home and exercise a supervision over the pictures that are being booked in his houses he will wake up some morning among the ruins of a lot of spaghetti in that dear old Rome and discover that he hasn't got any more circuit back in America.

"Western Vengeance" is a bad picture, no matter from what angle it is viewed. The story is bad, the continuity worse, the direction terrible, and the acting awful.

The spectacle of Franklyn Farnum cavorting about and trying to look and play the dashing youthful juvenile is enough to make a horse laugh. Poor Marie Walcamp, one had to feel sorry for her on finding her in the company she was in. The only thing in the picture was a Boston terrier. He did the best he could but couldn't save the picture alone.

Fred.

ALONG CAME RUTH

Metro-Goldwyn picture, starring Viola Dana. Adapted from the play by F. Fonson and Wicheler and directed by Edward F. Cline. At Loew's New York, July 26. Running time, 68 mins.

CAST

Ruth Ambrose..........................Viola Dana
Plinty Bangs..........................Walter Heirs
Israel Hubbard..................Tully Marshall
Allen Hubbard..................Raymond McKee
Captain Bradford..........DeWitt Jennings
Widow Burnham..........Adele Farrington
Annabelle Burnham..........Brenda Lane

This is a slim-waisted little film of the inexpensive type, but pleasant and satisfactory entertainment. Framed for the daily change houses, it is okeh there and actually is a lot more fun than some of the lemon specials that have appeared in the past few months.

Dana plays the city girl who comes to the country because she can't get a job at interior decorating in the city. Action is the name of the town where she stops. Captain Bradford owns a dusty old store there and the town also holds a swain, Allen Hubbard, played by Raymond McKee.

When Viola sets the dusty old store going again and spreads a little sunshine the swain decides she'd make a good wife, and the Captain gets conventional and gives them his blessing.

As a plot it is as thin as Coney Island's cotton candy. But, like the same candy, it is sweet and sugary and will please 99 out of 100 attendants at the neighborhood houses. Viola Dana will rebuild, to a large extent, her following with a few of this type. *Sisk.*

LOVE AND·GLORY

Universal-Jewel production, directed by Rupert Julian. From the story, "We Are French," by Perley Poore Sheehan and Robert H. Davis. Supervised by Raymond L. Schrock. Photographed by Gilbert Warrenton. At Lyric, New York, starting Aug. 4. Runs 78 minutes.

Pierre Dupont, the village smithy....	Charles De Roche
Anatole Picard.........	Wallace MacDonald
Gabrielle, his sister.........	Madge Bellamy
Emile Ponpaneau, Mayor of Mirabel...	Ford Sterling
Jules Mallcorne............	Gibson Gowland
Little Marie..............	Priscilla Moran
The Imp...........	Charles D. Ravenne
Fleurus Dissard..............	Andre Lancy

"Love and Glory" came to the Lyric Monday night for a limited run to fill in the time before Fox takes over the house Sept. 1. Universal-Jewel will be fortunate in staying its allotted time. The picture rates as a disappointment.

Universal calls attention to Rupert Julian, whose direction was also responsible for one of the finest photoplays of the decade, "The Merry-Go-Round." This is, perhaps unfortunate, as by means of contrast it brings more forcibly to mind how unconvincing "Love and Glory" is.

Here Julian did not have a Philbin, a Kerry, a Hackathorne and a Seigman to work with, and even should he have had he would have had nothing but insipid roles to offer them.

The film is French in tone, but it never strikes the clear note of patriotic fervor reached in "Scaramouche" or "The Four Horsemen." Julian has endeavored too obviously and painstakingly to intertwine his humor and pathos in the best cinema fashion, and as a result the film neither sounds any great emotional depths or tickles the risibles to any marked degree.

The action transpires in France in the late 60's, at the time when war in Algeria was imminent. The central characters are Gabrielle (Madge Bellamy) and the two men who worship her, Anatole, her brother (Wallace MacDonald), and Pierre, the village smithy (Charles De Roche), whose love is not at all so fraternal. From the peace and happiness of the little village the men are sent to the sands of Algeria, and soon false word comes to the girl of their death. They return to the town and find she has been abducted by the heavy.

A long search follows, so long in fact that the caption suddenly announces a mere 50 years have passed. Rip Van Winkle stuff for the films is ruinous.

The two old vets have stuck together, and when Anatole is called to Paris to receive a much belated decoration for his bravery a half century before, both, like the old morons they are, decide to hike the 100 miles to the capital.

As a result Anatole passes out on the trip and Pierre goes on alone to accept the medal on behalf of his old pal. Finally, in a scene that was doubtless intended to be extremely affecting, but that is merely annoying, the French President brings forth the long-lost Gabrielle and the film ends with a lot more would-be sentimental hokum over the dead body of the old friend and brother.

Pretty poor stuff, all of this, and most of the other by-play, comic and sad is no better.

The picture has some colorful military scenes and the fighting in the Algerian deserts is effectively, if not stupendously, staged.

The best bit of popular stuff comes when Anatole, captured by the Arabs and ordered to blow the French retreat on his bugle, sounds the charge. That's a good deal like Service's poem telling how "Jean Duprez reached out and shot—the Prussian major dead" and packs about the same wallop to the average mind and heart.

Miss Bellamy would get by if all she had to do would be look pretty, but her role calls for considerably more. As the old lady toward the end she seems to think that age was best expressed by a movement of hands, head and limbs most closely suggesting the famed St. Vitus shimmy. Charles De Roche is particularly expressionless, but his massive physique and virility should win him a few more feminine devotees.

The best performance is given by Wallace MacDonald, never a particularly impressive actor, but doing satisfactorily as the brother. The selection of Ford Sterling to play a comic French mayor was particularly unhappy. All of his Dutch mannerisms and Keystone comedy antics, including the reception of a decayed piece of fruit in his eye, add a vulgar taste to an otherwise genteel, if nothing else, picture.

"Love and Glory" may do some little business the first week or two because of Universal's rather expensive advertising campaign behind it. But as a "special" it's a flop and doesn't rate as a good picture for the program houses.

BEING RESPECTABLE

Warner Brothers' production of the Grace H. Flandrau story. Scenarist and technical staff not listed on Strand Theatre print or program. Directed by Phil Rosen, with Monte Blue, Marie Prevost, Irene Rich and Louise Fazenda featured. At the Strand, New York, week Aug. 3. Running time, 70 minutes.

Valeria Winship..............	Marie Prevost
Charles Carpenter...............	Monte Blue
Deborah Carpenter.........	Louise Fazenda
Suzanne Schuyler................	Irene Rich
Stephen O'Connell......	Theodore Von Eltz
Darius Carpenter............	Frank Currier
Louise Carpenter............	Eulalie Jensen
Mrs. Winship..................	Lila Leslie

That there is no visible kick to "Being Respectable," but that there is an unseen wallop for a great many, will not help this picture much at the box office unless it is strongly promoted by the exhibitors. It's one of those "What Would You Have Done?" affairs, and here there is a logical as well as sexy reason for it.

Probably the Warner Brothers' press department already has taken up this item, and it should hold up. While this is a picture that only in part appeals to the flapper trade, if the proper query is put before the public, all will become interested in the fourth angle to the triangle.

The picture runs as though the director had one eye on the set and the other on the censor. Everything is squared before or immediately after. Just a little too much so, perhaps, for the best benefit of the Warners.

Had the feature picture held itself up for the element instead of the mob, the kind of a picture this one is, acknowledging its weakness of action, would have been an "up-lift" among the higher grade. As it is now the picture fans will say it is inconsistent, incongruous and improbable, albeit at the same time they will be irresistibly drawn toward the story with its crudities (to save footage) always apparent, for the tale is of love.

The query that should be propounded is whether a man as weak as Charles Carpenter proved to be when he permitted his father to force him into an engagement with an unloved, could have withstood through exerting a will power he seemingly did not possess, the desire to run away with his beloved, after four years of a loveless marriage on his part.

But the loveless marriage brought a child, and "a little child shall lead them" again came to the rescue. That was a semi-natural result and should have been the big scene, but it wasn't. The big scene was when Suzanne Carpenter (Schuyler) slapped her husband's face—that was a big scene! But only when mentally visualized, because the director muffed it a mile. He had a real scene in hand there, but it passed off mildly, even to the working up of it.

Centering the action is the father of Charles, a dominant parent who wanted to steer the marriage of his son, to prevent his marriage to a vamp, but why and how Marie Prevost as Valeria Winship was a vamp isn't made known, and if a vamp, what had she been doing during those four years? One of the many unexplained points.

Anyway, all of the ifs aren't so material—there the picture is, not a bad twist at all to a hammered subject, and enough there to make the box office drag 'em if tackled in the right way.

Production o. k. and no criticism on direction through the story, which is not boisterous.

And as for acting, Irene Rich takes everything away so thoroughly and convincingly everyone else excepting Louise Fazenda is too mild to be noticed, including Monte Blue. Miss Fazenda is doing a straight role in a love aside that is also ended with an inconsistency.

The exhibitor may say to anyone of a married couple or both: "Find the wallop in 'Being Respectable,' for it's there for married people."

And just to add, "Being Respectable" is a mighty poor title for this feature. *Sime.*

THE GAIETY GIRL

Universal-Jewel production starring Mary Philbin. Story from the novel, "The Inheritors," by I. A. R. Wylie. Adapted by Bernard McConville. Directed by King Baggot. Photographed by Charles Stumar. At the New York one day (July 31). Runs about 70 minutes.

Irene Tudor..................	Mary Philbin
William Tudor........	Joseph Dowling
Owen Tudor St. John......	William Haines
Pansy.....................	Grace Darmond
Evan Evans.................	Otto Hoffman
Juckins................	James O. Barrows
John Kershaw...........	De Witt Jennings
Kit Kershaw..............	Freeman S. Wood

The most promising of the younger screen actresses, Mary Philbin, has in "The Gaiety Girl" a vehicle that while vastly more entertaining and artistically produced than the average release, is not up to her seemingly unlimited thespian powers.

When Miss Philbin first startled the cinema world as the little Austrian girl in "The Merry-Go-Round," the verdict was "Great, but she can only get away with a certain kind of roles." She followed with "Fool's Highway," as a little Bowery girl, giving another splendid performance in a role largely different although still of the humble class. Now to cinch her versatility she appears in "Gaiety Girl" as a little British blueblood. The part does not give the opportunity for character work as did her earlier ones, but she gets every possible ounce of sympathetic appeal and emotion out of it.

Since Mae Marsh was at her height there has been no one on the screen with Miss Philbin's poignant wistfulness. She is not strictly a beauty physically, but it is to be doubted if as lovely a figure has ever been seen as she presents as the bride in the closing moments of this film. Her wedding dress puts masculine powers of description to route, but it is ideal, whether satin or silk, ruffled or straight, and trimmed with Irish lace or plain cheesecloth.

But Universal has not done right by our new Mary this trip. King Baggot directed with a good deal of skill and the production is nicely set, but the story is trite and the whole presentation, in spite of many careful efforts at atmosphere and color, does not register as should a big Jewel special.

The plot in half a nutshell concerns the little British aristocrat who is tricked into marrying the heavy when she is told that her real sweetie was killed in Africa. Her grandfather is dying in poverty and she hopes to brighten his last days by marrying wealth. The ceremony takes place. On the wedding night the bridegroom proceeds to get lit up and too arduous. But lovey comes back from the Congo just in time to see a chandelier obligingly fall on the drunken husband. That leaves the bride free to grab her true love and the audience its hats.

The clash between the bluebloods and the red has its moments of interest. The title "Gaiety Girl" is derived from those scenes taking place at the gay London theatre at which the aristocratic little lady dances nightly. These episodes are the most disappointing in the picture. While it is true the British girls may not be as worth glorifying as their American sisters, there was no reason for Universal to pick such a frowzy and aged looking crew as represents the premiere British chorus here (page M. Charlot).

William Haines as the hero, Freeman Wood as the heavy and Grace Darmond as a showgirl give good performances, as do the several character actors. De Witt Jennings will amaze the fans by proving he can play other roles than those of detectives and police inspectors. The photography is picturesque with fine shots of the British castle included.

"Gaiety Girl" is no epic, but, chiefly because of the charm of the star, ranks as a good picture and should do well from a box office point of view.

WHY GET MARRIED

An independent, starring Andree Lafayette. Shown at the Stanley, N. Y., Aug. 1, 1924. Running time, 59 minutes.
Janet Carroll................Helen Ferguson
Jim Allen...................James Constant
Marcia Wainwright.......Andree Lafayette
Jack Wainwright..............Jack Perrin
John Strong...............Edwin B. Tilton
Rodney Strong...........Bernard Randolph

This is a business drama of the stereotyped program quality that qualifies the picture to play the smaller daily change houses, but that is about all. The production can also get by as the weak sister on double program bills in the better houses.

The story is that of a man and woman who both continue in business though married. The woman achieves success while the husband at first achieves nothing but failure. This brings discord, and the pair are almost on the verge of parting when an incident in life brings them together again. The wife comes to the realization that her place to achieve happiness is in the home.

Running parallel with their story is that of another young couple where the wife undertakes the home duties and the husband becomes the sole breadwinner, finally climbing to the top of the ladder of success.

The continuity as screened is poor, and one has constantly to keep one's thought jumping from one theme to another in an effort to hold the thread of the tale.

In production the picture is cheaply done and the glaring faults that stand out are the use of painted back drops to represent building tops and the sets that are stock all the way through.

The direction is nothing extraordinary to speak of and the photography is passable.

There are several scenes where an attempt has been made to achieve bigness, notably a cabaret shot, but the only effect obtained is to show that every effort was being made to hold down the cost of the picture.

Andree Lafayette at moments is really pleasing in the picture, but she is not the type that permits of close-ups, and the director should have passed up every one of these shots. There are deep shadows and lines about her eyes that show up too strongly in the near shots. Of the supporting cast James Constant and Ed Tilton stand out as the near-

est approach to players. Bernard Randolph as the heavy overacted his scenes horribly and almost made a comedy of what is intended to be a drama.   *Fred.*

THE BACK TRAIL

Universal production, starring Jack Hoxie. Written by Walter J. Coburn. Scenario by Isadore Bernstein. Directed by Clifford Smith. At the New York one day (July 29) as half the bill. Runs 61 minutes.
Jeff Prouty..................Jack Hoxie
A Tramp.....................Alton Stone
Ardis Andrews.........Eugenia Gilbert
Harry King...............Claude Payton
Jim Lawton.................Billy Lester
Judge Talent............William McCall
Shorty...................Buck Connors
Curry......................Pat Harmon

Exceptional photography and horsemanship are the two things one expects to find in every Western, no matter how puerile the story, amateurish the actors or inexpert the direction. In "The Back Trail," Jack Hoxie's latest Universal, the expectation regarding the camera work and the equestrian prowess will be more than fulfilled. Outside of that there is little favorable to be said of the production; just one more in the long string of mediocre Westerns.

The photography particularly is glorious. Ironically enough, the man at the camera is not credited in the billing or preliminary announcement. But to him and to Clifford Smith, directing, must go credit for some of the finest shots of the Rocky Mountain country ever seen. At all times are the figures of the story backgrounded against scenes expressive of nature's grandeur at its best.

The horsemanship of Hoxie and his company of cowboys, hustlers and cow punchers is also above par. If there is one thing that Hoxie can do well, it is to ride that white steed of his.

The latter starts in a bit more interestingly than usual, with Hoxie a shell-shocked veteran who has lost his memory. A blackmailer pins a series of past crimes on him, and the heroine sets about reforming him, only to learn that he wasn't responsible for all the misdeeds, after all.

The story soon deteriorates into the usual series of chases, scraps, kidnappings and rescues, with the villain and his gang bent on stealing the heroine's property and her big boy challenging them to try it. Hoxie is O. K., but Universal would act wisely if they left him as a rough-and-ready cowboy rider rather than attempt to make a matinee idol out of him. As it is, they jammed the action by inserting far too many close-ups of him.

The leading woman is a newcomer, Eugenia Gilbert, and her beauty and appeal should be added to the photography and horsemanship as the only outstanding bits of a conventional film.

CALL OF THE MATE

Phil Goldstone production, featuring William Fairbanks. Directed by Alvin J. Neitz and photographed by Roland Price. Written and adapted by Jules Furthman. At the New York one day (July 29) as half the bill. Runs 55 minutes. Cast includes Dorothy Revier, Milton Ross, Billie Bennett, Earl Close, Neil Keller, Stanley Bingham, Marguerite Neitz.

"Call of the Mate" has more substance to its plot than the average Western film and it ranks as considerably better than most of the pictures recently produced by Phil Goldstone.

It derives its name, peculiarly enough, from a little whistle indulged in by the hero when he feels like mastering beasts or women. He has learned this potent musical

symbol in a circus, and whenever the heroine or the wild hogs of the story gets a trifle zippy he crushes them with his melodic power.

The rest of the story is perhaps as unbelievable but not as ridiculous. There are the girl's cranky father and sullen brothers, the villainous gambler and the wronged dance-hall gal with her fatherless child. They call her "Frivolous Sal," and the press matter claims that she loves the hero with a love of a bad woman for a good man.

So when the gambler takes a shot at him she steps in the way and gets more than her share of lead. As she is dying she begs the hero to marry her before the end and give her little girl a father to take care of her. Since she has saved his life, he cannot refuse, whereupon the naughty lady turns right around and gets well.

The unwilling husband is in a fine fix. He cannot exactly hope that she will die, and yet he knows that love in the form of his real sweetheart is waiting for him elsewhere. But his wife is conveniently murdered, and although the blame is first pinned on him, they finally get the real culprit, the gambler, and everything is serene.

The lighter moments of the plot come with the efforts of the hero to tame the girl, a self-willed little vixen who is extremely handy with her riding whip. After he lands her he's up against her family, and this too, takes more than the whistle.

The photography, particularly in the exteriors, is eye-gratifying, and the direction and continuity satisfactory. William Fairbanks makes a neat job of the lead role. He suffers, however, from the plaint bothering almost all the Western boys except Mix and Gibson—an overdose of seriousness and too few lighter moods. Dorothy Revier is sufficiently charming and the balance do good work.

Those patrons of the cheaper houses who like Westerns (and apparently they are more than legion) will consider this one "grand and glorious romance" of its kind. In general it measures up as a pretty fair effort.

FIGHTING FOR JUSTICE

J. Joseph Sameth production, distributed through Madoc Sales Corp., and starring Art Acord. Directed by Walter de Courcey. Scenario by J. Anthony Roach. At the Stanley, New York, July 31, one day. Running time, 65 minutes.
Sam Culvert..................Paul Weigel
Shirley Payton.............Vane Truant
Bullets Bernard.............Art Acord

Another inexpensive western made from Form 34 of the Scenarists' Union. While the story is so much tripe, it has been strung together with such good and swiftly moving continuity the film takes on an undeserved interest.

Bullets Bernard is the hero. Shirley Payton is the heroine. Paul Weigel is the Big Hearted Jake. Two villains figure, plus a judge and prop sheriff.

A few hills, pine board huts and horses, plus shooting, make up the picture.

The hero is wrongly accused of a hold-up. The heroine still loves him. Big Hearted Jake, who has fallen from grace to booze, meets him when they're both put in the same jail cell. As Jake was once a lawyer, he offers to plea his friend's case. He advises him to skip—and Bullets does so just in time to catch one of the villains running off with his girl. He lassoes the villain, brings him to court and then shows the opposition lawyer up to be a scoundrel.

Stirred well and strained into the fifth reel, this resulted in a clinch fadeout followed by one of those "several years later" subtitles and a kid wearing his old man's felt.

Acord does little fancy riding and little acting, but his part is ingra-

tiating. Vane Truant, the girl, is as stolid a leading lady as could be used with safety. Paul Weigel's character work as Culvert is the outstanding thing of the picture.

It's okeh for the small houses where audiences aren't too particular.   *Sisk.*

MONSIEUR BEAUCAIRE

Zukor-Lasky presentation. Paramount picture and Sidney Olcott production starring Rudolph Valentino. Adapted from the novel and play by Booth Tarkington. Screen play by Forrest Halsey, with Harry Fischbeck the photographer. Cast features Bebe Daniels, Lois Wilson, Doris Kenyon and Lowell Sherman. Showing at the Strand, New York, week of Aug. 10. Running time, 100 minutes.

Duke de Charres (Monsieur Beaucaire)	Rudolph Valentino
Princess Henriette	Bebe Daniels
Queen Marie of France	Lois Wilson
Lady Mary	Doris Kenyon
King Louis XV of France	Lowell Sherman
Madame Pompadour	Paulette du Val
Richelieu	John Davidson
Miropoix	Oswald York
Duchess de Montmorency	Flora Finch
Francois	Lewis Waller
Duke of Winterset	Ian MacLaren
Badger	Frank Shannon
Molyneux	Templar Powell
Beau Nash	H. Cooper Cliffe
Lord Chesterfield	Downing Clarke
Voltaire	Harry Lee
Colombine	Florence O'Denishawn

Valentino's return to the screen and Famous Players is signalized at a First National house in what is unquestionably a "money" picture.

For those who may think this film star has lost his drawing power, the numbers which gave the Strand a capacity house at both midafternoon performances Sunday and were behind stretched guidons going into the third showing were in distinct contrast to such a contention.

And this in the midst of weather that made the theatre well nigh insufferable. Gauged upon the Sabbath projection and the applause receptions which greeted both the picture's conclusion and Valentino's initial entrance, the film looks like a certain holdover from a box-office basis.

What may surprise is the wholesale relegating of practically the entire cast to the background, so that this feature amounts to nothing less than 100 minutes of Valentino. It's a "pie" role for the star, upon which he cashes in to the fullest extent.

To say that the story carries him would be an injustice, for Valentino has contributed as neat a piece of work as he has ever done before the camera. While the vehicle offers him in a part distinctly characteristic of his screen reputation, it must needs be said that he has, nevertheless, gone out and enhanced that impression.

On the other hand, the one passage that grates and places the returned actor's morale under the supposition that posing before the lens is not without a certain fascination is prominent in that amount of footage given over to his being bare above the waist and going so far as to register tediousness by means of stretching, and thereby giving the populace an informative view of his muscular development. Something like five minutes is consumed in this one episode, with it only remaining for Valentino to have turned his back and folded his arms to make the illusion of a strength act complete. The entire scene might be termed superfluous.

Olcott, in directing, has had difficulty in revealing all the points of the Beaucaire character in order to show that, besides being a consistent, haphazard and successful lover, he is not entirely an indoor man, but has a craving for athletics and possesses a mellow heart. The definition of these personal assets are too obviously, and somewhat awkwardly, introduced to make for complete coherence in the continuity, but they about total the faults of the picture which would probably get over upon the magnitude of the sets and costuming even though played by a lesser "name." With Valentino out front it simply becomes that much more valuable.

Lois Wilson is given such a negligible role as to be purely of value through her name, while Bebe Daniels, opposite Valentino, is deleted from much of the central portion, with Doris Kenyon taking up the feminine cause to the extent of making herself the outstanding woman in the production.

Lowell Sherman is also an early luminary who soon joins the list of eliminations, but makes it worth while and is principally responsible for the picture's initial momentum.

The story is that of the Duke de Charres (Valentino), who is the pride of the king's court, but suddenly disappears under the caustic glances and remarks of the ruler's young cousin, the Princess Henriette (Miss Daniels). To England, he installs himself as a barber under the nom de plume of "Monsieur Beaucaire," where he pays court to another fair **damsel (Miss Kenyon), who refuses him when he is exposed as but a barber, and to whom he fails to reveal his true identity. Ultimate justification comes before an assemblage, whence the Duke determines to return to France and there find if the maiden who shamed him into leaving can forgive.**

In settings, costumes and numbers the picture screams money, and it seems assured that it will come back through rentals. It's as choice a bit of picking as could have been done in the selecting of a piece for Valentino's screen return. The women will "go" for this one by the thousands. The girls made up three-quarters of a sweltering house when this feature was reviewed.

Skig.

JANICE MEREDITH

Cosmopolitan production starring Marion Davies. Adapted from the old novel by Paul Leicester Ford. Scenario by Lilly Hayward. Directed by E. Mason Hopper. Settings by Josef Urban and musical score by Deems Taylor. Reviewed at the Cosmopolitan, New York, Aug. 8. Running time, 153 mins.

Janice Meredith	Marion Davies
Charles Fownes	Harrison Ford
Squire Meredith	Maclyn Arbuckle
Squire Hennion	Spencer Charters
Philemon Hennion	Olin Howland
Lord Howe	George Nash
George Washington	Joseph Kilgour

And many others, including impersonations of Major Pitcairn, Benjamin Franklin, Patrick Henry, Paul Revere, Alexander Hamilton, Louis the VI. of FrFance, Marie Antoinette, Marquis de Lafayette, and other minor characters used in the development of the story.

This latest Cosmopolitan starring vehicle for Marion Davies was aimed for road showing and, while it is a great program picture, its two themes necessitate a jerky and ofttimes illogical scenario. On this count and its consequences the film drops from the $2 class to the 50-75 cent group.

It is a good picture. Money has been spent without stint in some of the scenes, whereas in others a plainly painted backdrop looms up to spoil an otherwise perfect illusion. There are brief shots of brilliant court balls, good battle scenes, houses tumbling to destruction during Revolutionary encounters, great armies marching and then the great and undeniable punch of the picture—Washington crossing the Delaware.

That was wonderful stuff and drew the only applause of the picture from a Friday night audience unaffected by first night enthusiasm.

The story tells of Janice Meredith; of her love for a bond servant, Jack Brereton, later found to be a British Lord, and who joined the Revolutionary cause as an aide to General Washington. Janice saves Jack and Jack saves Janice before it is all over. Their careers are joined so closely with the war that it would seem that Washington, Janice and Jack saved the country.

Neither the love nor the Revolutionary theme predominates. The story jumps from one to the other and invents excuses to move Janice from Jersey to Boston—and Jack follows. From Boston to Philadelphia —and Jack follows. And then from **Philly to Yorktown, Va., where again Jack follows, and eventually takes his lady fair—by this time won for a bride—to Mount Vernon, where on the lawn (and in colors) they drink a toast to Washington, who Janice pronounces the Father of His Country.**

The historical items included are, summarized:

The ride of Paul Revere, well done, but not up to the same episode in Griffith's "America."

The Boston Tea Party-short and snappy.

The speech of Patrick Henry before the House of Burgesses, Virginia.

Washington Crossing the Delaware—a real kick.

The Hessians feasting before the battle of Trenton—forced.

The winter at Valley Forge; also inferior to the Griffith version of the same event.

The batle of Yorktown and the surrender of Cornwallis—impressive in a stagey way.

The other scenes of the picture, and there are many, are concerned with the love story.

Harrison Ford is the hero and Marion Davies the film heroine of the Ford best seller of its day—both sufficiently young to be true to type. In the supporting cast comes a great string of legit actors: W. C. Fields, the momentary hit of the film as a British sergeant with humorous proclivities; May Vokes, a tipsy maid; Helen Lee Worthing, one of Zieggy's beauties, as the elegant Mrs. Loring, an old flame of the hero; Spencer Charters, excellent in a small character bit; Olin Howland, whose humor is of the "simp" variety; George Nash, excellent as the villain; Joseph Kilgour, superb as General Washington; Macyln Arbuckle, fine as the father of Janice; Lee Beggs, who looked as much like Benjamin Franklin as he does like Abraham Lincoln, and George Seigman, as a Hessian officer, okay in the part.

With this talent, the picture cost money—more than $1,500,000 is the claim. Its setting and treatment with regard to historic detail and gorgeousness makes that even more apparent. On that score there is nothing wrong.

But 153 minutes is too long for a story that could be cut in many spots to avoid repetition. The film suffers by this and by a superfluity of flat subtitles. It is aided, however, by the best musical score ever written for a movie, and to Deems Taylor, music critic of the "World," goes the palm. One or two of his strains have a great audience appeal and carry the picture over a few rough spots. With all the rah-rah patriotic stuff, the score never gets stricken with the "Star Spangled Banner" fever.

Another thing in its favor is the presentation, this consisting of a magnificently set stage, the representation of a ballroom used in one of the scenes. Then Eddie Mochary, manager of the Cosmopolitan, has put 12 ushers, all beauties, in silk Colonial gowns, and has trained them to be the most unobtrusive set in town.

These things all favor the picture in its present home and a respectable run can be looked for, on the strength of the Hearst paper advertising and the draw of the star, but Miss Davies' personal success in this is surpassed by both "Little Old New York" and "Knighthood."

On it merits "Janice Meredith" is a whale of a program picture because of its scenic magnificence, but its scenario incongruities and inferior handling of some historic episodes keep it out of the $2 class. Compared to "America," which got just about an even break as a road show, "Janice" is inferior, which comparison seems fair and conclusive as far as its $2 box office draw out of town is concerned.

Sisk.

WINE OF YOUTH

A Louis B. Mayer Production of the Rachel Crothers' stage play, "Mary the Third." Directed by King Vidor. Scenario by Carey Wilson. Distributed through Metro-Goldwyn. Reviewed at the Capitol, New York, August 10. Running time, 70 minutes.

THE CAST:

(Episode of 1870)

Mary	Eleanor Boardman
Clinton	James Morrison
William	Johnnie Walker

(Episode of 1879)

Mary	Eleanor Boardman
Robert	Niles Welch
Richard	Creighton Hale

(The Modern Story)

Mary	Eleanor Boardman
Lynn	Ben Lyon
Hal	William Haines
Max	William Collier, Jr.
Tish	Pauline Garon
Mother	Eulalie Jensen
Father	E. J. Ratcliffe
Granny	Gertrude Claire
Bobby	Robert Agnew

There is reason enough for the picturization of Miss Crothers' "Mary the Third" play. Aside from the literary and dramatic values which stamped it as one of the artistic successes of the season of 1923-1924, it holds a strong story with several definite punches and, moreover, offers several legitimate excuses to show a few flapper and sheik petting parties and gin contests in full swing.

Accordingly, King Vidor and his excellent cast, with the exception of Robert Agnew and Ben Lyon, both of whom are colorless juveniles, have made a first rate picture that is at once serious, sardonic, humorous and instructive in more than a subtle way.

Marriage, its success and failure, is the theme. Marriage has been the theme of more than one play from the same Crothers' typewriter, and she also has been one of the leaders in the hue and cry against our apparently decadent youth. However, in "Mary the Third," she preaches her pet topic forcibly and momentarily impresses audiences with logic that is later seen as false.

The production is excellent. Eleanor Boardman as Mary the Third is ideally cast, while Eulalie Jensen as the mother and Gertrude Claire as Granny do outstanding work. Pauline Garon is the most attractive of the younger set in the picture, and contrasts pleasantly to the more quiet Mary. The men in the film aren't so good, being, except for the old boy, of vaseline variety—who'd rather sheik than work their way through the world. In the prolog several well known **people appear momentarily and except for the few brief excursions taken by the director into the land of flapper's folly, the continuity and scenario stick to the original with amazing and commendable fidelity.**

"Wine of Youth" is an okeh film for any type of theatre. Its moral tone is above reproach, its treatment is good, and while the whole thing is, in a sense, a Crothers' preachment, it is intelligently handled and made interesting. A little cutting would help and will probably be given the reel. But it needs exploitation stuff that'll get an audience in. There are really no big name draws in the cast and as the play itself was never a commercial success, the success or failure of the film as a money card lies largely with the exhibitor. It is certain to please, however, once the crowd is in.

Sisk.

AGAINST ALL ODDS

Fox production starring Charles Jones. From the story "Cuttle's Hired Man" by Max Brand. Directed by Edmund Mortimer. Photographed by Joe Brotherton. At Loew's, New York, Aug. 8, as half the bill. Runs 57 mins.

Chick Newton	Charles Jones
Judy Malone	Dolores Rousse
Jim Sawyer	Ben Hendricks, Jr.
Bill Warner	William Scott
Olivetta	Thais Valdemar
Tom Cuttle	William Bailey
Lewis	Bernard Siegel

"Against All Odds" is heavier and rather more complex than the average western picture, and except for the work of its star it is hardly any more worth while. They've got Jones back at the prairie stuff again, but with his return to westerns he goes back to conventional film stuff and departs from the promising sparks of originality exhibited in those films in which he played fireman, circus rider, tramp or some other individualistic type.

The present feature is, if anything, poorer than the majority of Jones' earlier westerns. In the first place the story is entirely too complicated. Instead of the usual gang of villains lined up against the hero there are half a dozen assorted scoundrels fighting each other.

The central plot deals with Jones' efforts to save the life of a pal accused of murder. "Buck" is convinced the alleged slayer is innocent and it finally becomes necessary for him to resort to force to rescue his pal from the deputies on the way to the execution. He then dives into the mystery and finally untangles it when he discovers the supposed victim had never been harmed at all, but was merely laying low because of blackmail.

The action carries Jones into a haunted house with the usual movie scare-providers all present. For an actor who is pre-eminently a battler and "hoss" buster he shows considerable talent as a comedian. At other moments he puts all he has into his work and his all-around performance, including some thrilling jumps from train to horse and vice versa, is again the feature of the picture. Dolores Rousse is rather an insipid heroine, possibly because the love interest is never emphasized to any appreciable degree. William Scott gives a particularly sincere bit and the balance are more than acceptable.

Photography is outstanding, but the continuity shows glaring deficiencies. This film is not a particularly good release for Jones, but his worst is pretty sure to be better than most of the western boys' best and it should please a majority of his disciples.

EMPTY HANDS

Victor Fleming production featuring Jack Holt and Norma Shearer. Adapted from the novel by Arthur Stringer by Carey Wilson. A Paramount picture, reviewed at the Rivoli, New York, August 17. Running time, 80 minutes.

Jack Grimshaw.................Jack Holt
Claire Endicott...........Norma Shearer
Robert Endicott..........Charles Clary
Milt Bisnet....................Ward Crane
Indian Guide............Charles Stevens

It was more than five years ago Cecil B. DeMille produced "Male and Female," in its day a sensational artistic and commercial triumph. The old Barrie story, which was woven through his "Admirable Crichton" play before being taken into the movies again forms the backbone of this firm play—"Empty Hands."

But "Empty Hands," being a latter-day production, combines a portion of the Barrie scheme (desert island stuff with a man and a woman) and also works into its first part a luxuriancy of shots displaying the post-flapper period amusements and escapades, all to show how Claire Endicott has deteriorated from the girl her father would have her be.

Claire kisses the gentlemen publicly, she smokes, wears one-piece bathing suits and is generally scandalous.

When with her father to visit some Canadian holdings she is thrown with his chief engineer, played by Jack Holt, and this reman is rather contemptuous of her ways. But when she is swept down the rapids in a canoe he goes after her and, while he effects a rescue, they are landed in unexplored country—far from human help.

And like the lady in "Male and Female," Claire can't do a thing, so the man does it all. He brings down game, builds a hut, makes cooking utensils, extracts fire from sticks and shows her that while she may be ace high on Broadway she is a deuce in the wilds.

Her regeneration is here worked out and when the sex impulse becomes great in both of them, the girl has become sufficiently strong to resist it—and the same goes for the man. A love is born where once was contempt and when an aeroplane rescue is worked both are transplanted to civilization.

Here the second big part of the story comes. Because of her previous escapades Claire is named in a divorce suit. The gossip sheets take it up and insinuate that by marrying the he-man engineer she will save her reputation. Because she loves him, she is unwilling to hurt his chances and so sends him away. But he sees through it and, admiring her for having developed into a thoroughbred, gives her a wow of a hug and a three-star-plus kiss.

It's a corking story, excellently directed, filled with matchless exterior shots and, despite the centralized love interest and the exclusion of every other theme, interest of a high order is maintained.

The film isn't expensive in the making and has Holt as its chief draw. Carefully planted details clarify the disagreeable sex air that might easily have hung about.

All in all, "Empty Hands," while it has been more or less unheralded, can take its place as a first-rate first run and in addition it can almost be guaranteed to suit ninety-nine out of one hundred average audiences.   *Sisk.*

THE 40TH DOOR

Pathe picture with Allene Ray featured. From the book by Harry Hasting Bradley. Produced by C. W. Patton. Directed by George B. Seitz. Seen at the New York Aug. 14.

In "The 40th Door" the sands of the desert never have a chance to grow cold. George B. Seitz, long accustomed to a kaleidoscopic change of scenes for any script he happens to be working with and particularly one like "The 40th Door," which reminds of the days of the Pathe serials that had Pearl White escaping pitfalls.

Once Seitz unleashed some of his swarthy-faced types of Oriental "sheiks" and had his villains dashing madly across deserts with the lives of both the hero and the heroine at stake, one forgot that there was a story and awaited for the grand finale which seemed interminably long in the windup.

There are long underground avenues, trick doors, trap doors and many ways of the unwily villuns to torture the innocent ones continually running the gamut of danger.

Allene Ray is featured. She is the daughter of a desert merchant. It isn't so sweet and nice for an audience to watch a Christian make violent love to a Mohammedan girl on short notice, so the secret comes out that a young explorer and scientific research expert in his work of opening King Tut's grave or one of the king's buddies discovers that the girl is French and that under no consideration should she wed the ruler of a harem.

Through thousands of celluloid feet, so it seemed, villainy appeared to have the upper hand, but just as the desert villain mustered up his Oriental sand marines the hero got the British army to stand them off.

The picture jumps around like butterflies; the continuity does fancy hurdling and the actors swarm in and out of camera focus.

Miss Ray does her best to make the principal feminine role stand out but the romance is a little too much for her, although the scenario made it easy for her to accomplish the impossible.

Pathe has a picture here which bears all the earmarks of one of the numerous serial specie, a "serial" in one volume.

Little to recommend it but an audience with nothing on its mind and nowhere to go may like trying to figure it out.   *Mark.*

FOOLS IN THE DARK

F. B. O. production of a story by Bertram Millhauser. Directed by Al Santell and featuring Matt Moore and Patsy Ruth Miller. Reviewed at the Cameo, New York, Aug. 17. Running time, 95 minutes.

Ruth Rand............Patsy Ruth Miller
Percy Schwartz...............Matt Moore
Kotah......................Bert Grasby
Dr. Rand................Charles Belcher
Diploma.....................Tom Wilson

Corking mystery comedy, ranking in entertainment value with Griffith's "One Exciting Night." Based on an uncle's desire to test the courage of a suitor for the hand of his niece, the man is put through his paces in a house apparently haunted.

It is all doughty stuff, well played and directed, having, moreover, the advantage of excellent continuity. Matt Moore and Bert Grasby are the outstanding cast figures, while Tom Wilson, in a portly negro role, contributes comedy relief that is as good as it is old—based on a negro's reactions to a haunted house.

The film doesn't size up as having cost a great deal to make, but for all that it is first-rate entertainment. While it isn't one of those things calculated to do much drawing for the exhibitor, it will give satisfaction all around. Even with its lengthiness, there are no smeared-over stretches where entertainment ceases and boredom begins—it's okeh throughout.   *Sisk.*

BETWEEN TWO HUSBANDS

Great Western Productions release starring Arline Pretty. Directed by Jean Gabriel. At the Stanley, New York, Aug. 8. Running time, 52 mins.

A commonplace effort taking itself most seriously and concerning the country maid betrayed by the wayward son and left stranded in the big city. The wayward's brother, a minister, marries the girl to give her child a name, while his villainous twin stumbles downstairs and kills himself during an attempt to abduct the infant.

Very sparse as to background, Gabriel, who directed, also takes the dual role of the twin brothers, and colorlessly. Opposite him Arline Pretty gives evidence of deserving a better fate than this conglomoration of sob footage, but could do little to help the descendance to strictly cheap screen entertainment.

That the film is very much concerned with itself is witnessed through the subtitles which tag New York as the "flame around which many moths are burned," succeeded by the inevitable flash at the city's skyline from the bay. Other wordings are in a similar vein to register the picture as being embodied upon a 1905 chassis.

None of the interiors is imposing, besides which there isn't a "flash" insert included at any time. The entire action is given over to the star and Gabriel with the latter unable to register as convincing.

Every reason is given to believe this a "shoestring" production that, outside of Miss Pretty, contains no cast talent and is too burdened with tear "hoke" to ever raise it above the most indifferent of the smaller houses.   *Skig.*

RACING FOR LIFE

Perfection production, distributed by Commonwealth. Directed by Henry McRae. Photography by Allan Thompson. Featuring William Fairbanks and Eva Novak. At Loew's New York, Aug. 8, as half the bill. Runs 60 mins. Cast includes Philo McCullough, Lydia Knott, Wilfred Lucas and Edwin B. Tilton.

Those who do not delve too deeply into the inconsistencies and impossibilities of their film features should like "Racing for Life" moderately well. An acid-penned critic would have no trouble pulling the picture apart foot by foot, as it is inexpertly thrown together.

However, the net result is mildly entertaining. The subject carries a popular appeal and a first-rate cast to put it across.

The plot suggests the auto racing films of Wallace Reid. There's the speed devil who is forced to promise his mother he will never race again because any shock to her weak heart would kill her. And there's the father of the girl in the case, an auto manufacturer, who has wagered practically his business on the outcome of the big race.

The climactic twist is really a punchy one. The hero's brother, general manager for the automobile concern, has been gypping the firm and caught with the goods. The hero, realizing that such a disclosure would be equally as disastrous to his mother, promises to drive his future father-in-law's car on provision they refrain from turning his brother over to the authorities.

He is kidnapped by a rival firm just before the race and has all sorts of battles and chases before he reaches the track and starts the race a lap after the field. It is needless to say that he wins, saving the manufacturer's dough and his mother's life. It is during the race scenes that the biggest disappointment comes. These shots are actually of a genuine auto race, as Ralph Di Palma is shown among the contestants. But the car of the hero and his spurt from last to first with a wonderful last-lap finish, although described in the sub-titles, cannot be identified. The struggle between the cars, never particularly well filmed, is merely impersonal, and does not introduce that sense of satisfaction one should experience at seeing the hero's car shoot ahead of its rivals.

Far better is the love interest which is nicely sustained and heightened by several comic bits.

For instance, the girl always comes upon the hero when his face and hands are grimy with car soot, and she nicknames him "Dirty Face." Eva Novak plays this part with an abundance of girlish freshness and charm.

William Fairbanks, who seems to have graduated from the Western school and who has been getting a great break in the Broadway daily change houses recently, gives another clean and manly portrayal. For this type of picture he's about as good as they come. The rest of the cast, holding three or four fair "names," is also effective.

Had the racing scenes been real thrillers, this would have been a mighty neat little program picture. As it is, it lacks a real kick, but is satisfactory intermediate film fare.

OTHER KIND OF LOVE

Phil Goldstone production, directed by Duke Worne. Photographed by Roland Price. Story and scenario by Jefferson Moffatt. At the Stanley, New York, Aug. 5. Runs about 60 minutes.

Adam Benton	William Fairbanks
Elsie Brent	Dorothy Revier
Mary Benton	Edith Yorke
George Benton	Robert Keith
The Chorus Girl	Rhea Mitchell

"The Other Kind of Love" brings up the old Cain and Abel theme, yet it is interesting.

In this unpretentious but rather neatly done little film, Adam Benton (William Fairbanks) is the righteous brother and George (Robert Keith) is the other, who, in spite of college training, is a cur at heart. In their relations with the girl (Dorothy Revier) is exemplified the difference between the two kinds of love, evidently intended to be (with apologies to Elsie Ferguson) sacred and profane.

Because of his polish and exterior educaiton it is the weakling brother who dazzles the heroine and succeeds in leading her to the parson. But just when the honeymoon is officially to begin she realizes her mistake and fights for her virtue.

Meanwhile no less a person than the wicked brother's deserted wife comes looking for him, and after she convinces the hero he resolves to save the girl he loves. He arrives at the little honeymoon retreat in time for a big battle with his passion-crazed younger brother. It is not until the latter has almost killed the hero that he realizes how Cain-like he has become. In a frenzy he hurls himself towards a cliff, but is saved from a hazardous ledge by his brother, who realizes that blood is pretty thick after all.

George reforms and is nursed back to life by his real wife, while the same office is performed for his big brother by the heroine.

The acting is a big aid, with Fairbanks doing exceptionally well as the long-suffering older brother. Robert Keith is wise in never totally losing sight of the heavy's better nature and Dorothy Revier, whose name is given precedence over Fairbanks' in the billing, is an appealing heroine. Photography and direction are satisfactory.

While far from being a K. O., the picture is surely O. K. for the ordinary run of houses.

TIGER THOMPSON

Harry Carey starred. Produced by Hunt Stromberg. Released by Hodkinson. Story and scenario by Buckleigh Fritz Oxford. Edited by Harry Marker. Photographed by Henry Sharp. Directed by E. Reeves Eason. Players include Marguerite Clayton, John Dillon, Jack Richardson and George King.

Harry Carey, after his long Universal service, severed connections with the U. Then came a new line of productions with Carey as the star and Hunt Stromberg as "personal supervisor." In "Tiger Thompson" Carey is again in his familiar western character.

The story is of the plains, with bandits, hero and heroine and a little kitten that does some superb work in helping Carey work up a number of comedy "bits" that are necessary in "westerns." There is also a Chinaman who injects several laughs with his efforts to ride a mule that balks in midstream.

A girl's daddy is a train robber. He and his gang hold up a fast mail, but the sheriff rounds them up and the leader is shot and wounded, the injuries proving fatal after the bandit has reached the shanty of Tiger Thompson, the star role played by Carey.

The dying bandit gives Thompson instructions to find his ranch and tell his daughter, Billy Brandon, that he wants loot returned and that Thompson should look after her.

At the ranch there are two heavies, and judging from the trouble they make for Thompson, one was plenty.

In some fast and exciting scenes the efforts of the bad men to get the map showing where the dead bandit has secreted a fortune in loot and jewels which Thompson plans to return to their owners cause no end of excitement, the kind of western entertainment that audiences delight in when properly handled.

"Tiger Thompson" has real atmosphere. Carey sticks to his knitting and makes a manly, scrapping two-fisted hero of Tiger Thompson.

The continuity as a whole is about the best that Carey has yet stepped in and the picture will give satisfaction anywhere. There are some corking "exteriors," the rescue of the girl after a fall over a cliff is capitally enacted.

As one of the late films of the wide open spaces, this one fills the bill.

Mark.

RAINBOW RANGERS

Goodman-Sheldon production presented by William Steiner. Starring Pete Morrison. At the Circle, New York, Aug. 14, as half the bill. Runs about 60 minutes.

Buck Adams	Pete Morrison
Rose Warner	Peggy Montgomery
Manuel Lopez	Lew Meehan
Anteater Jake	Eddie Dennis
Deacon Slim	Nelson McDowell
English Charlie	Milburn Morante
Barbecue Sam	Martin Turner
Luke Warner	L. S. McKee
Frank Owens	Victor Allan
Tillie	Rae Hampton

Described in the billing as a "western comedy drama of courageous deeds and laughable doings," "Rainbow Rangers" is obviously aimed at the film houses of the lower hoi polloi. As such it hits the mark. As a split-bill vehicle for one of the metropolitan Loew theatres it is another story, but at that, the picture is no poorer than a majority of westerns of its type.

Outside of the comic attempts, the picture has some good exterior photographic shots, some daring horsemanship, a harmless little love story, three or four scraps and a general plot even more trite than usual.

A newcomer, Peggy Montgomery, dominates the picture in the ordinary role of the heroine with her beauty and ability. It won't be long before she graduates to a more fertile field.

HUTCH OF THE U. S. A.

William Steiner production starring Charles Hutchison. Directed by James Chapin. Story and scenario by J. S. Natteford. At Loew's, New York, Aug. 5, as half the bill. Runs 55 minutes.

Hutch	Charles Hutchison
Marquita	Edith Thornton
Moreno	Frank Leigh
Ruiz	Jack Mathius
Saturday	Ernest Adams

A typical program film concerning South American revolutions and somewhat better than Hutchison's last feature, although it lacks the "names" of the previous release. However, its cast is adequate and from the popular point of view it has several distinctive features.

The sets and photography are spectacular, some of the shots being far above the average. The fight scenes are extravagantly and furiously staged and there is some welcome comedy relief, contributed chiefly by Ernest Adams. "Hutch" again shows his undoubted athletic prowess and plenty of hazardous-looking stunts. His acting, too, is rather good, and in Edith Thornton he has a pretty and talented leading woman.

The worst thing that may be said about the picture is that it's absolutely stereotyped. The neighborhood audiences don't seem to mind that as long as they get their gentle thrill, and the film should make money.

MADAME GUILLOTINE

London, July 31.

Shown by Western Import and starring Lyda Borelli, this latest Italian picture possesses one of the poorest stories ever seen in a feature, with the French Revolution as a framework. Italian films are apparently of two classes—those that go in for story and acting and those that let everything else go in favor of spectacle.

"Madame Guillotine" belongs to the latter category. Spectacle and huge crowds are there, but the story is an ill-constructed thing of shreds and patches, while the acting is poor and utterly unconvincing.

Robespierre as usual is the monster of the story, which tells how one Therese, Marquise de Fontenoy, insults a poor journalist and critic. The Revolution breaks out and the once scorned scribe becomes one of Robespierre's right-hand men.

Meanwhile, the Marquise has divorced her philandering husband and raised a Royalist spy to the position of her lover. The journalist meets her again and begins to get his own back while declaring his passion for the haughty beauty.

To save her lover she becomes of the people. Eventually she is caught harboring the spy, and the whole bunch are condemned to the guillotine. Before sentence can be carried out, however, Robespierre falls from power and perishes. The lovers are reunited and the journalist probably returns to worrying editors.

Much of the scenery is very beautiful and the crowds are splendidly handled. These things, however, do not make a picture.

Described as the "great emotional actress," Lyda Borelli immediately proves she is nothing of the sort. She is heavy and her emotion is insincere. Never for a moment does she convey the impression that Therese is a great lady of the Revolutionary period; instead, she might be a cook masquerading in her mistress' clothes. Fabiani is good as Robespierre, but the rest of the cast is "penny plain and tuppeny colored." Stage managers, carpenters and property men are the real "stars" of this production.

Gore.

LILY OF THE DUST

Paramount production, adapted from the novel, "The Song of Songs," by Hermann Sudermann and the play by Edward Sheldon. Adapted for the screen by Paul Bern and photographed by Alyn Wyckoff. Reviewed at the Rivoli, New York, Aug. 25. Running time, 83 minutes.

Lily	Pola Negri
Lieutenant Prell	Ben Lyon
Colonel Mertzbach	Noah Beery
Richard Dehnecke	Raymond Griffith
The Uncle	William J. Kelly
Julia	Jeanette Daudet

Considering the moves which Will Hays and his associates are making to clean up the screen, it was surprising that Famous Players should have even considered the making of a film version of "The Song of Songs," which has, so Walter Pritchard Eaton says, belonged at various times to Solomon, Sudermann and Sheldon.

The story itself, written by Sudermann and in its original, was the episodic history of a woman's downfall, with each step to the conclusion definitely explained and logically presented. It wasn't a pleasant story—nor was it unpleasant—for Sudermann possessed enough sophistication to know that somewhere in the world there must be people who didn't believe in the stork legend nor in the fallacy that a Republican administration is good for business.

Consequently, when he chose Lily as the protagonist of his theme, he wrote of her with a certain vigorous sympathy, making her path from that of an innocent girl to the mistress of an artist plain but plausible. One of the characters which he used but momentarily was a Lieutenant Prell, whose little love affair, according to Sudermann, taught Lily what lust meant.

That was Sudermann's idea.

Ned Sheldon stuck fairly well to it and wrote such a play that it immediately became and still remains famous.

But Paul Bern and Dimitri Buchowetski, in charge of this production for Paramount, have produced an abortive effort which has as its main theme the true love (never mentioned by Sudermann) of Lily and the lieutenant.

She marries a colonel. They divorce. An artist befriends her. She becomes his mistress. Back into her life comes the young lieutenant. When he takes her before his uncle to get her okehed as a possible wife, Lily becomes drunk and also is interrupted by Bohemian friends who rush in.

So circumstances take her from a pure love (in the movie version) and force her to wear the rouge, earrings and bracelets of a mistress.

The moral of it all, according, once more, to this peculiar movie version, is that all women seek love; some few find the real thing and others are forced to seek satisfaction in compromise.

Negri is not at her best. Ben Lyon is the young lieutenant and does nothing to get enthusiastic over. Noah Beery gave a masterly performance as a Prussian colonel. The others were adequate.

The production is fine. Expensive and genuine, the settings are at times dazzling, but the heart of the story isn't there, and many bits of detail, wholly justified in themselves, string this picture out to an almost interminable length, making it tiresome. The principal fault is that a famous story has been maltreated beyond recognition to make a movie holiday, and the result is so mediocre that an audience will probably not break their necks to see the work.

"The Song of Songs" still belongs to Sudermann. Buchowetski, with the aid of the most eloquent means of expression in the world, has failed to take upon himself any portion of the German novelist's credit.

Sisk.

MESSALINA

Presented and directed by Enrico Gauzzoni, who also wrote the story and scenario. Released by F. B. O. Photographed by Alfredo Lunci. At the Cameo, starting Aug. 24, indefinitely. Runs about 85 minutes.

Messalina	Rina de Liguoro
Princess Mirit	Giovanna Terribili
Ela	Lucia Zamissi
Ennio	Gino Talamo
Apolonius	Gildo Bocci
Marcus	Alfredo de Folice
Narcissus	Aristide Garbini
Caius	Mario Cusmic
Tigris	Adolfo Trouche
Claudius the Emperor	Augusto Mastripietri

One carries away from "Messalina" a strange mixture of awe at scenes and settings of beauty and grandeur, and ridicule at human faces and forms of ungainliness and cumbersome unattractiveness. This comparison of worth and girth strikes the two extremes of the Italian film, which is a balanced combination of good and bad screen accomplishments.

Enrico Gauzzoni, responsible for "Quo Vadis" and "Julius Caesar" some years ago, has written, directed and produced "Messalina." The advance in film technique does not permit comparisons, but it is safe to prophesy that the present picture will not arouse the enthusiasm that did Gauzzoni's earlier productions, particularly the one dealing with the Fall of Pompeii. "Messalina" is primarily a spectacle; but even in that field it is not to be mentioned at the same time as other recent stupendous American films.

It is claimed that 10,000 extras took part in the huge mob scenes and that more than $2,000,000 was the cost of production. If the first statement is true, the eyes deceive badly, as there does not appear to be more than 500 to 1,000 people in view at any one shot. As for the cost, it must be remembered the Italian lira was inflated, too, although not in proportion to the German mark, and perhaps the publicity man made good use of this.

Not that it is a cheap production in any sense. The mob scenes are spectacular in a way, but it is in the reproduction of the old Roman settings that the financial tax must have been heaviest. Augmented by fine photography, the views of the forum, palaces and public buildings, with splendid attention to detail being evident and the highest artistic taste prevailing, are the highlights of the picture, and worth going to see in themselves.

The picture starts in as though it were trying to eclipse the sex stuff in our modern "Flaming Flapper" films. The title itself brings to mind hazy suggestions of a vamp ne plus ultra; the most profligate of the naughty Roman empresses and a character sufficiently wicked to cause the yellow newspapers to refer to our present humdingers as "modern Messalinas."

A Roman orgy or two gives promise of some extreme sex stuff, but the film has evidently been cut right at the most characteristically Italian places, and after the first 20 minutes the pace is as voluptuous as a Baby Peggy special. It might be said, however, that brassieres, or whatever the Roman ladies wore in place of them, are nearly as much out of evidence as at Times square on a hot July afternoon.

Messalina herself is let down easily as far as viciousness goes. She is not nearly so wicked as the chubby Princess Mirit, her rival for the affections of Ennio, the sheik-like Persian slave, who hacks Roman chariots on the side and has every woman in the cast cuckoo about him.

This is Messalina's first pure love, and in trying to win his heart she brings about her own ruination.

The story is extremely disconnected and hard to follow. A multitude of flowery, stilted titles do not help much. These captions sound as though they were often literally translated from the Latin. However, the job of trying to make the various mix-ups clear must have been more than man-sized, and it is doubtful if any explanatory matter would have served much better.

The role of Messalina is played by Countess Rina de Liguoro. She plays the part with an admirable mixture of majestic poise and passionate lust, but, like most of the other foreigners, overacts badly, as far as American standards go. Her face is handsome, but her figure might lead one to paraphrase facetiously:

"Rina plays the queen called Messalina—
What a shame she's not a little leaner!"

She's not the only hefty one, however, as the only slim woman in the cast is Lucia Zamissi, who makes up for it by poor acting. All the men are either bulky or insipid. The clumsy figures are shown off particularly by the Roman togas worn. Messalina's rival, the Princess Mirit, is very badly done by Giovanna Terribili, which proves that Shakespeare may have been wrong after all in "Romeo and Juliet."

There are some interesting shots of the Roman circus in the Forum, with foot-runners, wrestlers, gladiators and finally charioteers doing their stuff. There are other absorbing moments, although the story does tend to drag toward the finish.

"Messalina" should have a big week at the Cameo, as patriotic Italians and many spectacle lovers will flock to see it. Business may hold up for some weeks more, but the chances for a long run are doubtful. With F. B. O. exploiting it heavily, and the name in itself a draw, it should do business when released around the country; but, as has been said, it is far from being a natural sensation.

UNSEEN HANDS

Presented by W. G. Graves, featuring Wallace Beery. Directed by Jacques Jaccard. Released by Associated Exhibitors. At Loew's Circle, New York, double feature bill Aug. 25. Running time, 60 mins.

Joseph Le Quintrec	Joseph Dowling
Jean Scholast	Wallace Beery
Mme. Le Quintrec	Fontaine La Rue
Armand Le Quintrec	Jack Collins
Matoaka	Cleo Madison
Wapita	Jim Corey
Nola	Jamie Grey

This looks like one of those things that happens in pictures and when all over no one knows why it was done. At least that is the impression obtained from looking at this picture on the screen. It is just so much good raw stock wasted. One would hardly expect anyone to go out satisfied with the entertainment after they had spent good money to see this picture. It's slow and tiresome stuff.

There is no head or tale to the story, except that it was constructed to give Wallace Beery something to do. He doesn't need this sort of tale for that purpose; he is too good in his own line without slipping in one of these things on him.

After seeing Beery in "The Sea Hawk" and then viewing him in this picture it is hard to believe that it is the same person. But Beery is in the picture. He starts out as a tramp in France, works his way into a family that owns a coal mine, sees that the husband dies, marries the widow and makes off with the family fortune, only to be followed to America by the son of the family, who corners him in Arizona, and there the story finishes.

Jacques Jaccard, who directed, has dragged the action so that it induces sleep. The casting is also below par. How anyone could place Fontaine La Rue in the role of the wife and mother, with a son who looks older than she does, is inconceivable. Cleo Madison, doing an Indian squaw, managed to give one of the best performances of the picture. Jamie Grey as her daughter was decidedly miscast.

It's a good one for the average exhibitor to pass up. *Fred.*

BORDER WOMEN

Phil Goldstone production starring William Fairbanks. Written by Keene Thompson; directed by Alvin G. Nietz. At Loew's Circle, double feature bill, Aug. 25. Running time 44 min.

Big Boy Merritt	William Fairbanks
May Prentiss	Dorothy Reviere
Gentleman Jack	Jack Richardson
Cocas Kid	Chet Ryan
McGiffigan	William Franey

This is a somewhat better picture than the average run of Westerns that the Goldstone people have been turning out with Fairbanks as the star. Possibly it is better because there isn't so much of it, the running time of 44 minutes being just about all that the story could stand in footage without excessive padding. As for anything else about it, calling it a Western about sums it up.

It is the story of a Texas ranger who is the hero, a girl whose brother is mixed up with a lot of roughneck crooks and who finally gets into a jam and is bumped off, although his last request to the ranger is to save his sister from the gang. The ranger does that little thing and saves her so well he marries her.

There is a lot of riding stuff, some shooting, a couple of good fights and in all it moves along fairly fast on the screen.

If they like Westerns this one can be slipped into a double feature bill and it will get by nicely with able support.

William Fairbanks is beginning to show something of a finish to his work and it would not be at all surprising if he managed to get away from the rough and tumble western stuff and do better things. In his support there is on one that stands out.

Fred.

FLYING FISTS

First three of a series of six two-reelers featuring Benny Leonard, lightweight champion. Scenarios by Sam Hellman. Direction Larry Windom. Reviewed pre-release showing Aug. 21. Running time, each episode, 25 minutes.

Benny Lane	Benny Leonard
Eli Graham	Frank Evans
"The Girl"	Diana Allen
Manager	Frank Allsworth
Trainer	Tammany Young
"Cream Cheese"	Billy Mitchell
The Vamp	Helen Feldman

The first three two-reelers of the series of six featuring Benny Leonard, world's lightweight champion, are fast, peppy pictures with all the necessary ingredients to make for success at the box office.

Leonard, in addition to his ring prestige, has unusual ability in pantomime. His stage experience has given him a confidence reflected upon the screen. The champ even essays melodramatics and gets away with it.

Sam Hellman has equipped him with good stories and supplied some corking slang titles. The other comedy relief is furnished by Tammy Young, world's famous gate crasher, and Billy Mitchell, a colored youth, who never fails to pull laughs. As Benny's trainer the colored boy is a howl and something new in pictures, where the usual procedure in the past has ben to cast a white comic and black him up if playing a colored role.

The Hellman stories are strictly for popular consumption and contain all the hoke situations of the prize ring. There is a young, sweet girl who loves Benny and a villainous rival. A crooked manager of a rival fighter who knows all the tricks from corking the scales to dropping the lights on a fighter's dome, also tries to gum things up for the champ, but in vain.

Leonard as a hard-working booker, who is trying to earn enough money to send his crippled brother to medical college, turns to the ring after he has been fired from his job following a bout. One funny situation had the two pugs battling when the building catches on fire. The fighters are so intent upon the work at hand they continue to fight amid the smoke and flames. Leonard knocks his opponent out and carries him to the sidewalk. Hunting up the referee he makes him count the unconscious fighter out.

The first three subjects contain a boxing bout in each with Leonard as a principal. Leonard's camera boxing is realistic, although some of his roundhouse uppercuts—which would have broken his wrists if they were used in a real contest—look ridiculous to the dyed-in-the-wool fight fans.

Benny wears clothes, appearing in tuxedo, business attire, golf suit, etc., and carrying his wardrobe as nonchalantly as any of the leading men.

Diana Allen, programmed as of "Follies" fame, is a cute blonde ingenue who appeals. As the daughter of the grouch employer of Benny who is an under-cover fight fanatic, she shows all over the picture.

A rough battle in a roadhouse gives Benny an opportunity to show his skill in a rough and tumble. He swings his famous right to good effect, winding up the battle by leaping on one of the guerilla's necks from a breakaway balcony.

The two-reelers are titled Bout One, "Breaking In"; Bout Two, "Hitting Hard"; Bout Three, "Soft Muscles," etc. The first three are by far the best things attempted by any of the actor-pugilists and are made doubly entertaining by the presence of Leonard and his intelligent work before the one-eyed monster.

They ought to be a corking box office bet. *Con.*

THE IRON HORSE

John Ford production presented by William Fox. Story by Charles Kenyon and John Russell. Directed by John Ford. Presented at the Lyric, New York, August 28, 1924. Running time, 130 minutes.

Davy Brandon, age 10......Winston Miller
Miriam Marsh, age 8.....Peggy Cartwright
Abraham Lincoln....Charles Edward Bull
Dave Brandon, Sr..........James Gordon
Thomas Marsh................Will Walling

Davy Brandon..............George O'Brien
Miriam Marsh...............Madge Bellamy
Abraham Lincoln.....Charles Edward Bull
Thomas Marsh..................Will Walling
Deroux.........................Fred Kohler
Peter Jesson...............Cyril Chadwick
Ruby..........................Gladys Hulette
Judge Haller..................James Marcus
Sergeant Slattery...........Francis Powers
Corporal Casey........J. Farrell MacDonald
Private Schultz..................James Welch
Tony...........................Colin Chase
Dinny...........................Jack O'Brien
Gen. Grenville M. Dodge....Walter Rogers
Col. Cody (Buffalo Bill)....George Wagner
Wild Bill Hickok...............John Padjan
Major North..............Charles O'Malley
Collis P. Huntington.......Charles Newton
Charles Crocker..............Delbert Mann
Gov. Leland Stanford..........John Padjan
Thomas C. Durant..........Jack Ganzhorn
Cheyenne Chief..............Chief Big Tree
Sioux Chief............Chief White Spear
Polka Dot...................Frances Teaguue
John Hay...........Stanhope Wheatcroft
Old Chinaman..................Edward Piel
And a regiment of United States troops and cavalry; 3,000 railway workmen; 1,000 Chinese laborers; 800 Pawnee, Sioux and Cheyenne Indians; 2,800 horses; 1,300 buffalo; 10,000 Texas steers.

William Fox presented his super-Western, "The Iron Horse," at the Lyric last Thursday night. The production is intended as a special, to be road-showed and not reach the motion picture theatres until next year. That is, at least, the present plan of the Fox executives. They are of the belief that they have a world-beater in this picturization of an epoch in American history which in historical value ranks on a plane with "The Covered Wagon," for "The Iron Horse" is the story of the winning of the great West through the medium of the linking of the Atlantic and Pacific coasts by rail.

"The Iron Horse" as a picture entertainment holds all the elements that make for a box-office success. It contains a powerful theme of historical value as the basis around which a romance has been woven that ties the leading characters to the history of the building of the first transcontinental railway. There are comedy, tragedy and a love theme, Indians and soldiers, the hordes of the construction gangs, the camp followers, both men and women, gamblers and dance hall girls, shooting and riding, a tremendous cattle drive, the fording of a river by the herd of beeves that brought applause of the caliber that was tendered to the wagon train fording of the river in "The Covered Wagon."

While this picture deals with the West almost a score of years after the period depicted in "The Covered Wagon," following the Civil War, there is of necessity immediate comparison made between the two productions, for they both deal with empire building. It must be said that "The Covered Wagon" seemed to sound a truer note than does "The Iron Horse," but still the latter has almost as many great moments as did the former, and the score that was supplied for the picture by Erno Rapee added considerably to the thrill moments.

John Ford, who directed, put his story over on the screen with a lot of punch. His handling of the trio of ex-soldiers of the Civil War who as the three musketeers of America battled through the building of the great Union Pacific railroad is exceedingly clever. They lend the touch of comedy in this picture much the same as did Ernest Torrence and Tully Marshall in "The Covered Wagon." Francis Powers, J. Farrell MacDonald and James Welch enact the roles and Ford touched them with just a bit of pathos in the end that made them stand out as real humans and not as out-and-out buffoons just created for a laugh.

The love interest is carried on by George O'Brien and Madge Bellamy as Davy Brandon and Miriam Marsh, with Fred Kohler and Cyril Chadwick as Deroux and Peter Jesson, the heavies. O'Brien gave a corking performance as the youthful scout and lover and Miss Bellamy shone as his beloved. Kohler's characterization of Deroux was a piece of classic work.

But it isn't the roles that make this a great big picture; it is the combination of the playing, the direction and the general theme, together with its big scenes including the Indian fights and the hauling of the locomotive over the mountains, the battle scene in which the women of the dance halls kneel side by side with the men and fire shot for shot with them at the riding savages, that bring "The Iron Horse" into the classification of 'great' in motion pictures.

One can rest assured that the picture is going to make a lot of money for William Fox. In exploitation it has been given one of the best directed and most intensive campaigns that has been seen in New York for a screen production in almost a year. Incidentally, the lobby of the Lyric theatre was so redecorated one did not recognize the old house. All of that dreary and cold feeling was utterly removed through the very effective use of hundred of yards of silk in a combination of blue and gray.

"The Iron Horse" is a picture packed with action, a laugh and a tear together with a real heart throb and thrills—that is what makes the money jingle in the box office.

Fred.

THE MAN WHO CAME BACK

A William Fox production, adapted from the Jules Eckert Goodman play by Edmund Goulding. Features George O'Brien and Dorothy Mackaill. Directed by Emmett Flynn. Opened at the Central Theatre, New York, for a run Aug. 31, 1924. Running time, 104 minutes.

Henry Potter..............George O'Brien
Marcelle.................Dorothy Mackaill
Captain Trevelan.........Cyril Chadwick
Thomas Potter...............Ralph Lewis
Aunt Isabel................Emily Fitzroy
Charles Reisling...........Harvey Clark
Sam Shu Sin.................Edward Piel
Gibson.........................David Kirby
Captain Gallon............James Gordon
Henry Potter (at the age of four). Walter Wilkinson
Henty Potter (at the age of twelve) Brother Miller

This is the second feature of the William Fox 1924-25 product to be revealed within the last few days. Last Thursday night "The Iron Horse" opened at the Lyric as a legitimate attraction. On Sunday at the Central this feature was presented at a grind policy, with 99 cents the top admission. From indications, this picture is going to prove to be one of the big money-makers of the year—not as a special, but as a corking good box office bet.

It is interesting, although there are a couple of spots where the picture could stand a little cutting. One of these is the long series of close-ups of Dorothy Mackaill shown on her first appearance in the story; the other is the whipping scene toward the end.

In the first place, as regards Miss Mackaill, no one should ever shoot a close-up of her showing her full face. Profile views of her are good, but the others show her nose at a disadvantage. George O'Brien, who is co-featured, will register strongly on the strength of his work in this film, and it is a safe bet that he is going to be a favorite with women fans. This boy is there. He has looks, can troupe, and sells his winning personality for all it's worth.

The story is long on possibilities of tie-ups with the church element. It is a preachment against the use of liquor and narcotics, and as a screen entertainment closely follows the play, which was a tremendous box office hit when originally produced.

The supporting cast is good, and in the main Emmett Flynn has kept his action moving along at a fast pace. The action takes place in New York, San Francisco, Shanghai and Hawaii. The story is told in mileage, first the jump from New York to Frisco, next to China and then the road back, until finally the regenerated couple come back into the home of the boy's father in New York. The interest mainly is held in the two principal characters, but while the supporting players try to get over, **there is a lot in their roles lost on the screen.**

But the picture itself is sure-fire at the box office, and it should not only make money for Fox, but for exhibitors. The chances are that the Broadway run will be limited, as Fox has taken the Central to give all of the better pictures of this year's program a Broadway showing; otherwise it would be fairly safe to say that "The Man Who Came Back" could get money here for 10 weeks.

Fred.

THE FEMALE

Sam Wood production for Famous Players-Lasky. Adapted from the Cynthia Stockley story, "Dalla, the Lion Cub," and made into a screen play by Agnes Christine Johnson. Betty Compson starred. At the Rivoli, New York, week Aug. 31. Running time, about 75 minutes.

Dalla........................Betty Compson
Col. Valentia.................Warner Baxter
Barend de Beer..................Noah Beery
Clodah Harrison.........Dorothy Cumming
Clon Biron....................Freeman Wood

After seeing "Lily of the Dust" and its highly sexful theme and now viewing "The Female" and its insidicus suggestiveness, the question arises whether Will Hays merely read the titles on Paramount's "famous forty" or whether he actually viewed the pictures. If he saw the films and really meant what he said about suggestiveness on the screen, then the color in the lumber is apparent, but for him to lay a ban on a serious problem play like "Tarnish" and to permit such flabby pieces of pernicious trash as the two named above to slip through is beyond all manner of reasoning. Unless of course he knew of "Tarnish" and not of the others.

"The Female" tells the highly improbable story of a semi-wild girl of Africa who sells her body and soul (possession to be given at the end of three years) to an old Boer of wealth. In reality she loves a Col. Valentia and is also sought after by Clon Biron, a waxed-mustached nincompoop. Time after time the old husband walks into her bedroom—and she draws the curtain. Once he grabs her and tries to take her in his arms—and she threatens to jump off a balcony. Another time she returns from England about two months before the three-year term is up, and when the old boy asks if she now intends to live with him as wife, she tells him that there are yet so many days, hours and minutes before he gets her.

And then, on the night before the husband comes into possession of his beautiful chattel, he is conveniently killed during a lion hunt in the jungle. Result—Col. Valentia gets the girl and her wish about the moon for a light, the sky for a roof and the earth for a bed—and alone with the man she loves—comes true. Showing that true love comes to the patient and that virtue is rewarded, etc, quot erat demonstrandum.

Miss Compson is the girl and she opens her act in half-length dresses. Jumping into the big sets she dons a few tight waisted and figure revealing gowns. Near the finale a pair of riding breeches encompass her and one long scene is devoted to Valentia's fondling of her leg after she had sprained an ankle. Warner Baxter is the Valentia and with Noah Beery as the rather pathetic old Boer is the best thing in the whole piece.

Miss Compson is never called upon to do any acting and her nickname of "the lion cub," through her wild early life on the veldt, seems more phoney than real. She never looks the role, resembling instead an Alfred Cheney Johnson portrait makeup rather than a real wild kid.

The general moral tone of this piece unfits it for family audiences and the long stretches that hold tiring qualities will not help it along with the first runs. In truth, it is not first-run fodder. The mechanical end is perfectly handled, as in all F. P. product, but the mental end of this one went wrong.

On entertainment values of this picture itself, it looks like the "famous forty" is reduced to 39.

Sisk.

ROBINSON CRUSOE, JR.

Metro-Goldwyn picture starring Jackie Coogan. Adapted from a story by Willard Mack. Directed by Edward Cline and supervised by Jack Coogan, Sr. At the Capitol, New York, week Aug. 31. Running time, 65 minutes.

Captain McDavitt.............Will Walling
Captain Dynes................Tom Santschi
Miramba.......................Noble Johnson
Ugandi ....Tote Ducrow
Adolphe Schmidt...............Bert Sprotte
Gretta Schmidt..................Gloria Grey
Mickey Hogan................Jackie Coogan

Since the flop of "A Boy of Flanders," some doubt had been expressed as to whether young Coogan's life as a b. o. attraction was over, but with the showing of "Little Robinson Crusoe" it is a safe bet that as long as the kid keeps small and is fed a few more stories like this he'll be as good as he was at the start.

This one is wild, improbable, heroic and melodramatic and with Coogan as Mickey Hogan, the son of a scrapping Irish policeman, everything fits together in the end just as nicely as it used to in the **Rover Boy books and the days of Frank Merriwell.**

Mickey, an orphan, is to be shipped to Australia from Frisco, so that a wealthy aunt may take care of him. On the way across a typhoon hits the tramper on which he is sailing and he, of all the crew, survives. On a raft and with a black cat he sails into an inlet of a tropic island. After being ashore for two minutes he is pounced upon by cannibals. But because he fights back and doesn't seem afraid, they make him their god of war.

Shortly afterward these cannibals catch two good specimens of white men and are preparing a barbecue with the gang invited. Young Hogan, with one fell swoop of his heroic tendencies, saves the white men, keeps a buck cannibal from attacking the daughter of one, and finally, by finding a radio set, shoots out the S O S to a U. S. destroyer. This ship does a georgemcohan with its flag for the sake of the cameraman and applause, turns around and heads for the island, arriving just in time to rescue everyone from the dusky epicureans.

Back the scene goes to Frisco. Word of the story has been wirelessed ahead. When Mickey arrives, a uniform is dropped aboard the destroyer from an aeroplane and he climbs up the dock as a cop in miniature. He is received by the force and put back once more under the guiding wing of his friend, Captain McDavitt.

That's all of the story, but the action moves with the rapidity of a gold digger and interest never lags. The island settings, moreover, are interesting, while Coogan himself turns in a corking performance filled with laughs and tears for the audience.

At the Capitol Sunday it was

eaten up by an audience sweltering with the heat. Because it is such genuine and clean entertainment, there is every reason to believe it will get a good reception all over the country. Its showing at the Capitol this week need not be taken too much to heart, as any picture would be affected by this torrid weather, but on a normal week it will do business. *Sisk.*

FLIRTING WITH LOVE

First National release, presented by the First National Pictures, Inc. From the story by Leroy Scott, directed by John Francis Dillon. Colleen Moore and Conway Tearle featured. Running time, 73 minutes. Shown at the Strand, N. Y., week Aug. 31, 1924.

Gilda Lamont	Colleen Moore
Wade Cameron	Conway Tearle
Estelle Van Arden	Winifred Bryson
Mrs. Cameron	Frances Raymond
Dickie Harrison	John Patrick
Franklyn Stone	Alan Roscoe
John Williams	William Gould
Henderson	Marga La Rubia

Just a light-waisted story and picture production about on a par with the average run of the Universal program productions, so hardly worthy of a pre-release showing. If the picture had not Colleen Moore and Conway Tearle it would not be worthy of playing the better houses at all.

In this story the heroine is a temperamental actress, risen from a buttonhole maker in a shirtwaist factory to the heights of stardom, but who has had four flops in a row. Her final play, decidedly risque, is closed on its second night by the police through the activity of a reformer.

The story in reality deals with the actress' plan for revenge on the reformer, but its final development is that she confesses her love for him.

Tearle plays the reformer. Alan Roscue as the theatrical manager gives a corking performance. There are times when he even seems to overshadow the male lead. They are both of the same type and Roscoe is a capable actor. John Patrick plays the bubbling press agent convincingly. William Gould stands out as a distinctive type.

With the Moore-Tearle names in connection with it the picture may attract some money. On Sunday night, the hottest of the year, it filled the Strand for the lae show. *Fred.*

DARING CHANCES

Universal Production, starring Jack Hoxie. Half of a double feature bill at Loew's, New York, Aug. 26. Running time 40 mins.

A fair program addition featuring Jack Hoxie, who has become identified with Westerns. Hoxie is a well-built, hard-riding, athletic leading man and in this picture is given many opportunities.

The story is far-fetched and the dramatics as overdone as in the usual picture of this type, but Hoxie gives a semblance of credulity by his excellent work.

As an entry in the big rodeo steeplechase, Hoxie has many adventures in outwitting the schemes of his saloonkeeper brother-in-law and Sampson Burke, a crooked gent, who has the race sewed up.

Hoxie's sister dies and Jack kidnaps her little daughter to remove her from evil influence. While escaping he is wounded and is succored by Agnes Rushton, a rural school teacher with whom he falls in love. Burke also loves the girl and tries to prevent Hoxie from riding in the big race by having him arrested for abduction on the day of the rodeo.

Hoxie persuades the sheriff to trust him and is released in time to start in the race, which he wins despite the efforts of the bribed cowpunchers to rough him. During the race Slavin steals the child and robs the gate. Hoxie leads a posse in pursuit. Slavin is overtaken by Hoxie, who snatches the child from his arms on the edge of a cliff, over which Slavin's horse plunges, to allow the principals to unite for the inevitable clinch and close-up. A fair picture for the easily pleased. *Con.*

YOUTH FOR SALE

C. C. Burr Production. Story by Raymond S. Harris, directed by Wm. Christy Cabanne. At the Broadway week Sept. 1, 1924. Running time, 72 minutes.

Mrs. Malloy	Alice Chapin
Molly Malloy	May Allison
Bill Brophy	Tom Blake
Connie Sutton	Sigrid Holmquist
Pansy Mears	Dorothy Allen
George Archibald	Charles Beyer
Tom Powers	Emmett Mack
Monty Breck	Richard Bennett
Edward Higgins	Harold Foshay

There is nothing about this picture that takes it out of the run of the ordinary. It is an independent production and therefore is entitled for a little more credit than if made by one of the big organizations. For a big organization it would be ordinary, but for an independent it is above the average. There are three names in the cast that can be played up—May Allison, Richard Bennett and Sigrid Holmquist. Rented at a price, the picture will get a little money in the smaller houses, for the title has a box office value in the neighborhood theatres, and this coupled with the three names mentioned should draw.

The production was made and is released by C. C. Burr, directed by Christy Cabanne, which means that it was turned out in a hurry and at a cost that was quite within reason.

Raymond Harris, who turned out the story, furnished a script that is quite stereotyped as to plot. It is the old, old story of chorus girls and jazzy parties. There are two girls, both working in a department store, and both live in the same boarding house, which is conducted by one of the girls. It is the other girl that first gets a job in the chorus, and to convince her friend that "that is the life" she invites her to a party where the girl friend takes a drink of hootch and goes blind. Then it is up to the chorus girl to marry the wealthy old John in order to get money enough to cure the blind girl. This brings about a happy ending all around.

Not much of a story and not much of a picture as far as pictures go in this day of big ones, but a production that will get by in the smaller houses.

May Allison handles what she has to do rather well, although she has pretty much lost her youthful freshness. Sigrid Holmquist walks away with the honors of the picture easily, while among the men there is no one except Richard Bennett who stands out. Emmett Mack, who plays the juvenile lead in the picture, seems entirely miscast. *Fred.*

PAYING THE LIMIT

Gerson Pictures Corporation Production, written and directed by Tom Gibson. Featuring Ora Carew. At Loew's, New York, Aug. 26, as half of double bill. Running time, 50 minutes.

The Girl	Ora Carew
The Man	Jay Morley
Lowden	Eddie O'Brien
May	Helen Howell
Davis	George Wellington
Boden	Dick La Reno
Ole Swanson	Stanley Sanford
Jean	Hal Stephens

Another hokey pokey picture with a rambling plot technically all wrong and for the peasants strictly. The story concerns the efforts of an ex-convict (Ora Carew) to live down her past. She becomes a domestic in a wealthy lumberman's house. There is a theft by the lover-crook of the daughter of the house. Her past is disclosed and she is suspected. She follows and exposes the real culprits, saving the daughter just in time from marriage with the crook.

A fight in an automobile between the escaping crook (George Wellington) and the hero (Jay Morley) was as ridiculous a piece of far-fetched melodramatic thrill hokum as the screen has reflected in some time. Both of the combatants are struggling furiously all over the open touring car, neither making any attempt to handle the steering wheel, yet the car takes curves and winds in and out of a forest road as smoothly as though Barney Oldfield were aboard.

The work of Ora Carew was good in a trying role, and Jay Morley was a virile and likeable leading man. The cast as a whole is fairly adequate, but the picture is as artificial and kickless as near beer. *Con.*

THE KELLY GANG

London, Aug. 20.

The British Board of Film Censors is supposed to be strongly against films dealing with the lives of famous criminals. Having created a precedent by licensing "The Man They Couldn't Hang," an absolute trite production, they recently declared under no consideration would they license another "real life" crime film. This is probably why "The Kelly Gang" carries no certificate. Its owners, "United Films and Theatres, Ltd. (Australia)," need have no fear. They have a fine showman's proposition, and as the picture is intended as a road show they will probably get away from the censorial authority, although managers of popular kinemas will doubtless fight to book it.

Made by Harry Southwell for the Australian Players, the picture is said to be founded on fact and taken on the exact locations. This "publicity" stunt we need not quibble at, but Southwell can be congratulated upon turning out a fine dramatic story and carefully refraining from any temptation to sensationalism for sensationalism's sake. He has handled his story admirably, and while extenuating nothing by the introduction of love affairs or the canonization of his bushranger heroes he manages to win the sympathy of his audience for the Kellys in their long fight with the police. His production work is remarkably good and the many really beautiful scenes and "shots" he uses have rarely been equaled. The riding in the feature is also superb. The interior settings are poor and unrealistic, but the burning of the inn at Glenrowan is a fine example of actually doing things without the aid of "close up" models or fake. The fight actually rages round the burning inn, and several quite ordinary "shots" leave no doubt as to the genuineness of the conflagration.

The story of the Ned Kelly gang is history, and whoever adapted it for the screen has kept close to the known facts. There is the threatened arrest of one of the boys for horse-stealing, his flight with the elder brother, Ned, to the mountains, and their joining up with the already outlawed Byrne and Hart. The rest of the feature shows the heroism of their womenfolk, the cowardliness of a common informer, the pluck of both police and outlaws, and Ned Kelly's final stand in the armor he had made out of plowshares and the like. At the end, probably to put a little oil over on the censorship, Southwell tries to kill his picture by the insertion of two trite and tawdry sub-titles pointing a moral lesson. These are easily removed, but their introduction sends an audience out dissatisfied. He might just as well have written in a scene in which a policeman gave the outlaws a free pardon and so paved the way to Ned Kelly finding a golden-locked girl "in the summertime."

The acting, principally of the type order, is exceptionally good. Every man, woman and child in the picture is perfectly natural and sincere. Doubtless the high-brow and the captious critics will damn the feature whole-heartedly, but their anger will not affect the "hold up" at the box office. *Gore.*

PIXIE AT THE WHEEL

London, Aug. 20.

Controlled by the Phillips Film Company, produced by Lee Morrison, and featuring Peggy Worth, this series of six two reelers are up to the average of their class. As the title denotes, motoring provides the basis of the stories which, however, do not rely solely upon motoring stunts for effectiveness. The stories are all capital and the continuity is fair, although a little judicious cutting would be a great improvement. The direction is, on the whole, good and care has been taken to give a big diversity of scene. The producer goes astray, however, when he allows a speedometer to register a mile a minute and shows the car traveling at half the speed or less. This, however, is probably filmic license.

The stories tell of the adventures of Pixie O'Hara an American girl racing motorist who, through financial reverses, has been compelled to become a journalist. As a newcomer to journalism she is naturally assigned to interview the Prime Minister who is, however, out of town. Being a "special" on an important paper she is beaten by this information and is ruminating on the general rottenness of things when she meets Charles Egbert Cromwell, a nephew of a Bishop, whose natural aptitude for "speeding" has been hampered by having his license taken away for 12 months and a $250 fine. They become acquainted through Charles' car and he suggests she drive him back to town. She agrees.

On their way they see an aeroplane descend and to Pixie's surprise the passenger is the Prime Minister. She remembers her job as a journalist and makes him consent her paper shall have the exclusive story of the negotiations he is carrying through. Then she drives him to the Foreign Office.

True to the word of a Prime Minister (no P. M. ever makes promises he cannot or won't fulfill) he gives her the story and she tears off to her paper. Arriving at the office she leaves Charles outside while she gets on with her job. Finishing she finds Charles has gone but has left a note giving her the use of the car for the 12 months he is barred from using it. With the aid of the car Pixie achieves wonderful feats for her paper while the dawn of true love takes its usual screen course.

Much of the attractiveness of this series will be found to exist in the beautiful scenery used up in the adventures. The camera work is very good.

Peggy Worth is quite acceptable as Pixie and without reaching stellar distinction puts the part over well. Walter Tennyson is excellent, in fact better than he has ever been before, and a number of subsidiary parts are well played.

These two-reelers will prove a more than usually useful "fill-up." They possess a novelty and freshness usually absent from features of their length, the majority of which are crude melodrama or rubbishly slap-stick. *Gore.*

MERTON OF MOVIES

Famous Players-Lasky production, made from the story by Harry Leon Wilson and the George S. Kaufman-Marc Connelly play. Directed by James Cruze and adapted by Walter Woods. Glenn Hunter starred and Viola Dana featured. Reviewed at the Rivoli, New York, week of Sept. 7. Running time, 80 minutes.

Merton Gill	Glenn Hunter
Sally Montague	Viola Dana
Jeff Baird	DeWitt Jennings
Harold Parmalee	Elliott Roth
Gashwiler	Charles Sellon
Mr. Montague	Charles Ogle
Mrs. Montague	Ethel Wales

Aside from the fact that "Merton of the Movies" represents the astounding spectacle of the movie industry making fun of itself, it also represents the greatest piece of film to come from the F.-P. studios since "The Ten Commandments." Which means that "Merton of the Movies" has been turned into a photoplay that is as far above the rank and file of the features as New York City is beyond Kalamazoo. That goes from the artistic and commercial angle, for this one has been so well done, thanks to James Cruze and Glenn Hunter and everyone else connected with it, that the laughs roll along with the ease of a waterfall and with the staccato frequency of machine gun fire.

That's what "Merton" is, a great laugh film. Moreover, it is intelligent, a shaft of satire that will appeal to the most discriminating audiences and at the same time amuse any bunch of mugs in the world. It is built for everyone, will suit all audiences.

The story of "Merton" is familiar. First, Harry Leon Wilson wrote it for the Saturday Evening Post, and a few weeks later it was hailed the country over as being a fine piece of literature in that it so accurately and appealingly expressed the symbolic youth of this land and his leading man aspirations. The idolatrous worship in which some of the worthless picture stars are and were held is amusingly set forth.

Then came the George Tyler production of the adaptation by George Kaufman and Marc Connelly. In this Glenn Hunter and Florence Nash played the leads and were backed by a remarkable production.

Now the picture. Hunter is again the lead in the role he so perfectly fits, playing once more the movie-sick youth, the boy who wanted to improve pictures by acting in them himself. The tremendously appealing love story of the halfway hard-boiled and halfway sentimental Montague Girl carries most of the way. With Viola Dana handling the Florence Nash role it is in competent hands, but then Viola isn't a Florence Nash by many miles. But for that she is satisfactory, and when Hunter flashes the most compelling line of pathos and hick comedy that the screen has caught in months it makes for an almost fool-proof combination.

Backed by a perfect cast that includes Ethel Wales, Charles Ogle, DeWitt Jennings and Elliott Roth, the leading players get rare support. The scenario, too, has been carefully prepared, and although there are omissions of stage play incidents, the whole thing runs along with greased lightning continuity and spring water clarity.

The direction is great—the photography up to par and made on the Lasky lot, with many familiar Vine street scenes occurring throughout. The mistake of introducing Hollywood celebrities was not made, and the story itself, instead of the deviations, is the main thing.

"Merton of the Movies" looks like a box office cinch. It is good for two weeks at least on Broadway in the regular houses. Last Sunday night it filled the Rivoli to overflowing with people and laughs. With decent weather breaks and intelligent publicity it should do the same elsewhere. No matter about the strength of one or two of the other "famous forty" gang, mark it down that this one is "there" in a dozen different ways and can be safely played to the limit.

It seems as near the ideal program picture as the United States has yet seen. *Sisk.*

HOT WATER

Harold Lloyd production releasing through Pathe and starring Harold Lloyd. Directed by Sam Taylor and Fred Newmeyer with Walter Lundin, photographer. Cast includes Jobyna Ralston, Josephine Crowel and Charles Stevenson. Running time, 57 minutes.

Lloyd's latest is strictly a gag picture that starts out like a whirlwind, drifts into a calm and then comes back to a yell finish through "scare stuff." At a hide-away showing there was no questioning the final result. They laughed plenty, often and loud.

The current vehicle being so obviously a series of gags is said to have resulted from "Girl Shy," Lloyd's preceding effort, being overboard with story and as a result of the intermediate house exhibitors crying about the time consumed by around 8,000 feet that film contained.

The theatre group want Lloyd, but evidently not in eight reels, for it cuts into the programs too much. That being the general consensus of opinion, with the releasing organization acquiescing as well, the idea crystallized with the studio unit, and "Hot Water" is the outcome. The film is now down to around 5,000 feet, with it not being impossible that more footage will feel the scissors. The middle passages look particularly susceptible to chopping.

Lloyd is doing a domestic story and characterizes a newlywed husband who goes up against the shopping thing, traffic regulations with his new car, and the mother-in-law. Those three episodes mark the basic gags from which any number of "bits" emulate. Much of the picture's initial velocity is gained by the first four or five subtitles. The comedy wording gave it a distinct break from the brarier at this particular showing and will undoubtedly repeat wherever shown.

However, the titling is not consistent. When the action begins to weaken the inserts fluctuate right with it, thereby leaving it to the sleep-walking mother-in-law, whom Lloyd believes he has murdered with an overdose of chloroform, to raise the continuity for equality with the early moments. The scare thing has been adroitly handled to the point where the audience actually screams.

There's many an awakened snatch of business during the street car ride with Lloyd burdened under bundles, added to which is a turkey he has won at a raffle. The traffic congestion difficulties of the new car has its points, but reveals the greatest weakness, although overshadowed by the thrill conclusion which is sufficient to top the picture off and about make 'em forget everything but the start and finish.

Lloyd parallels his work in previous efforts here, and certainly will not suffer from the picture. The release is clean, wholesome and fast moving, with the comedian out front all the way, which is the sort of entertainment he has identified himself with and which is not in danger of deteriorating from this effort.

Next to Lloyd comes Josephine Crowel as the mother-in-law, who has turned in an excellent performance. Good enough, in spots, to hint at taking a scene or two away from the star. Miss Ralston continues to be a soothing illusion besides deftly handling a minor assignment.

With the abundance of gag stuff in the film those in command of the continuity are deserving of more than usual credit for holding the sequence together, and that the projection is as smooth as shown points to valiant service on someone's part.

There was a rumor along Broadway that the "sneak" showing was for the purpose of determining whether the plan to sell "Girl Shy" and "Hot Water" to the exhibitors on a successive day's basis would be feasible, but this piec of news remains without verification. As "Hot Water" stands it couldn't follow "Girl Shy" within two weeks at the same house, leave alone one day, but a deferential and diplomatic spacing should see this latest Lloyd release roll up plenty of points while it is said to be paving the way for a collegiate theme which will be the star's next production, also understood to be slated for around the five-reel mark. *Skig.*

CAPTAIN BLOOD

Vitagraph picture, presented by Albert E. Smith and a David Smith production. Adapted from the novel of the same name by Rafael Sabatini. Directed by David Smith and photographed by Steve Smith, Jr. Music score credited to J. C. Bradford. Opened at the Astor theatre, New York, Sept. 8. Running time, 118 mins.

Captain Blood	J. Warren Kerrigan
Arabella Bishop	Jean Paige
Mary Trail	Charlotte Merriam
Jeremy Pitt	James Morrison
Lord Julian Wade	Allan Forrest
Don Diego	Bertram Grassby
Corliss	Otis Harlan
Colonel Bishop	Wilfrid North

Believed by many to be the most adaptable for the screen of all Sabatini's historical romances, Vitagraph has taken "Captain Blood" and given it about everything but a competent cast. The picture meets the requirements of production, but the weakness displayed in the cast may keep it from being ranked with its predecessors, although there is little doubt the film will be distinctly first-rate fare when released to the regular program houses. If they intend to road-show it around the country, that's something else again.

No names other than J. Warren Kerrigan will raise the eyebrows of the skeptics, while the viewing of the actual work of the players will confirm that lifting. It is more than regrettable that the acting personnel fails to equal the staging, as Vitagraph would then have had something of which it might well feel proud. As currently screened, whatever success the picture meets with will be in spite of the cast, and its bid for outstanding rank among the remaining specials of the season must of necessity correspondingly suffer.

Only two women are listed, and each gives a meaningless and listless performance. Kerrigan plays the title role well enough without rising to any heights, while James Morrison, generally submerged, manages to break through long enough to make himself known. There the individual scoring terminates. Wilfrid North as an island governor, the logical villain, was decidedly mediocre in his interpretation, with Bertram Grassby giving him a corking race.

Minus any love interest the first half of the picture carries itself along at a satisfying gait, probably due to the fact that during this portion the continuity follows the novel rather rigidly. In the second half comes the omissions from the story, the bringing into prominence of the love theme and the kick of the presentation in the naval battle of three or four frigates.

Well staged and pictured, the aquatic warfare is eye-filling and registers for its full worth. Other instances of the old sailing vessels navigating carry a decided smack of miniatures and slow photography. The water combat is the high point of the presentation, culminating in the blowing up of two of the ships, although it doesn't quite suffice to lift the second half entirely above the morale provoked by the preceding slow moving footage.

A brief of the story would tell of Peter Blood, physician, through circumstances being shipped to the island of Barbados as a slave, where his medical skill takes him from the fields to make him the governor's doctor. A raid upon the island by a Spanish vessel gives Blood and his fellow captives a chance to escape by taking over the vessel when the Spaniards come ashore to celebrate the surrender. Forced to plunder other ships on the high seas and unable to return to England during the reign of James II, Blood soon procures himself a resounding reputation for ruthlessness.

His career as a fearless navigator ends with the overthrow of James and the placing on the throne of William III, of which Blood learns when he rescues the new governor of England's outlying possessions from a burning ship. Offered the post of overseer of the island of Barbados, Blood accepts, gives up his wanderings, and returns to a life on the soil accompanied by Arabella Bishop, the villain's niece.

David Smith has done exceptionally well with the battle scenes and the hand-to-hand fighting on board the ships. As soon as the story gets out on the water it remains continuously picturesque and has little difficulty in holding interest and imagination.

The outstanding fault is unquestionably the cast and that the other counterparts of the production can equalize that handicap speaks much for the excellence of the picturization as a whole.

"Captain Blood" is a certainty as a super-program insertion and can stand a certain amount of special housing. *Skig.*

SINNERS IN HEAVEN

Alan Crosland production, presented by Adolph Zukor and Jesse Lasky. From the novel by Clive Arden; adapted by James Creelman. Directed by Alan Crosland, featuring Richard Dix and Bebe Daniels. Shown at the Strand, New York, week of Sept. 7. Running time, 75 minutes.

Barbara Stockley	Bebe Daniels
Alan Croft	Richard Dix
Hugh Rochedale	Holmes Herbert
Mrs. Madge Fields	Florence Billings
Native Girl	Betty Hilburn
Native Chief	Montagu Love
Mrs. Stockley	Effie Shannon
Barbara's Aunt	Marie Harris

Here is a chance to get a great eyeful of Bebe Daniels when that gal steps out to take a bath in a tropical pool on the South Sea island where she and Richard Dix are marooned when their plane is destroyed. Bebe is rather generous in her display of nakedness when she swims about the pool, and some of the small town boys will get a real thrill out of this. In the end the "wise ones" may note that she wears a bathing suit of white, but still the "kick" is there. Not only does this feature bespeak of box office possibilities, but there is a lot of sex kick to the picture that will get it over. Judging from its reception at the Strand on Sunday, the house should be in for a decidedly profitable week.

In addition to the sex stuff there are a couple of corking thrills, not the least of which is the nose dive the plane takes into the ocean. This is most cleverly handled. Then there are a couple of fights with the black savages and a corking bit of night photography for a sacrifice scene.

"Sinners in Heaven" is the story of a young woman who with a chaperon, accompanies an English aviator on what is hoped will be a world's trip, laying out an aerial mail route for the British Government. When the plane is wrecked the girl and the aviator are the sole survivors. They fight off the savages, and finally convince them that they are Gods, although in the finish a native woman whom the aviator scorns explodes the God idea, and just as the rescuers arrive in another plane the two are attacked. They also fight off the natives, but when the two rescuers take the girl and make a getaway the aviator was wounded by an arrow and left to his fate. Later he turns up in England, having been nursed back to health by the native woman and making his escape when a trading boat stops at the island.

Of course his arrival is just in time to bring about a happy ending for the girl on her return has confessed that she and the aviator were wed by their own ceremony while on the island, but the folks back home can't grant this was on the level and she is shunned.

Both Dix and Miss Daniels register heavily in the picture. Dix, from the manner in which the women fans are beginning to rave over him, looks as though he is ripe for starring honors. Betty Hilburn as a native girl also looked mighty good with the dark make-up. Effie Shannon and Maria Harris both play character roles and get them over, the latter particularly so with a grouchy old girl.

"Sinners in Heaven" seems to be a sexy box office bet. *Fred.*

OPEN ALL NIGHT

Paramount picture presented by Adolph Zukor and Jesse L. Lasky. Suggested by the stories of Paul Morand; adapted by Willis Goldbeck. Directed by Paul Bern, with Viola Dana, Jetta Goudal, Adolphe Menjou and Raymond Griffith featured. Shown at the Rialto, New York, week of Sept. 7, 1924. Running time, 63 minutes.
Therese Duverne..............Viola Dana
Lea........................Jetta Goudal
Edmond Duverne..........Adolphe Menjou
Igor....................Raymond Griffith
Petit Mathieu............Maurice B. Flynn
Isabelle Fevre................Gale Henry
Von De Hoven.............Jack Giddings
Bibendum..................Charles Puffy

Rather unusual picture, and on the surface suggest: real box office returns. "Open All Night" does not refer to a drug store or a Child's restaurant. It is simply a comedy of the happenings of one night in Paris, with a husband and wife the principal characters.

The greatest part of the action takes place at a six-day bicycle race, and there is an untold amount of comedy that pulls laughter. There is a possibility that for some localities the picture will be a little too sophisticated and offend certain audiences, but on the whole it looks as though it will prove a money bet for exhibitors.

The husband believes a wife can only love and respect her husband providing he is most considerate of her every whim. The wife, on the other hand, is craving the attentions of the cave man type.

On the evening the action occurs a woman friend takes the wife to the bike race and introduces her to the champion bike pedaler of France, a real he-man, one of those guys who treats 'em rough and tells 'em nothin'.

As the evening progresses the husband, also on a spree, meets the sweetheart of the bike rider in a cafe and goes with her to see the finish of the big race, only to find his wife waiting hand and foot on the husky pedaling champ. In the finish the husband changes his theory regarding women and shakes his better half up considerably, thereby winning her, for he has asserted himself as master.

Viola Dana plays the adventure-questing wife, and Adolphe Menjou the husband, he handling the role with delightful finesse and getting it over with a wallop. Raymond Griffith is the comedy foil and scores laugh after laugh with his souse. Gale Henry, who works opposite him, delivers a neat piece of character work, but the honors of the picture must go to Jetta Goudal. That girl just about walks away with all that there is to be had as the grisette-sweetheart of the bike

rider. Lefty Flynn plays the pedaling Frenchman and slips it over.

The six-day bike race scenes are the best bits. The riders are introduced as to their nationality or as from the cities they hail from. The "New York boy" who wins the race is a kid with a great hook that shows he came from the Ghetto district of the big town. His introduction is a laugh.

Paul Bern, who directed, carried the story along at a nice, even pace, and dug up a few of the old boys in the gag department for Griffith to get laughs with.

Griffith looks as though he was on his way to be the American Max Linder. Without doubt, his handling of this role is going to put him in line for some great comedy parts. *Fred.*

SINNERS IN SILK

Hobart Henley production for Metro-Goldwyn. Story by Benjamin Glazer. Shown at the Capitol, New York, week of Sept. 7. Running time, 68 minutes.
Arthur Merrill..........Adolphe Menjou
Penelope Stevens........Eleanor Boardman
Brock Farley................Conrad Nagel
Dr. Eustace................Jean Hersholt
Bates...................Edward Connelly
Bowers.......................John Patrick
Mrs. Stevens.............Hedda Hopper
Inez......................Miss Du Pont
Flapper..............Virginia Lee Corbin
Ted.......................Bradley Ward
Rita.....................Dorothy Dwan
Sir Donal Ramsey.........Frank Elliott
Mimi......................Ann Luther
Estelle..................Peggy Elinor
Cherie..................Eugenie Gilbert
Peggy....................Mary Aitken
Carmelita................Estelle Clark

"Sinners in Silk" are the New York bed-haters and check amplifiers who "sit in" and make merry at the instance of almost any one who will award them gratuitous provender, according to Benjamin Glazer, author of this celluloidic imprint, which features Adolphe Menjou and Eleanor Boardman.

Menjou is the same suave, ash-flicking, shoulder-shrugging, mustache-curling fellow in this picture which he dominates indubitably. For a few hundred feet he is made to appear old, but a scientist turns back 30 years from his span quickly, and he again becomes Menjou of the movies, a particularly well-established entity these hectic days.

"Sinners in Silk," as far as the story goes, could be written on one cuff. Arthur Merrill (Mr. Menjou) has lived well, but not wisely. A scientist (Jean Hersholt) insists he can make him young again. Merrill welcomes returning youth, as he achieves a fascination for Penelope Stevens (Miss Boardman). He attempts to win her just when she becomes enamoured of Brock Farley (Conrad Nagel), from Ohio. Merrill realizes his suit is without avail first, and later discovers Farley is his own son.

It's an old, old theme, done countless times before and ever so much better. The end comes rather quickly in a sudden, jerky manner that militates against a smooth denouement, one of the prime requisites of picture making.

The film seems to have lost something in the cutting room. That is quite evident in the rather abrupt switches, apparent several times in the running.

Miss Boardman plays naturally, lending a personality befitting the story. She disclosed a bit of surprisingly good acting in the one fairly big scene in the picture. Conrad Nagel has a light role as an upstanding young man who wooes and eventually wins the heroine, but the part seemed like a holiday for him, as it required but slight effort. There's very little to "Sinners in Silk." It's mostly interior studio stuff, and it did not cost a deal.

It's a program release, purely. "Sinners in Silk" looks like a good title gone wrong, but the title at the same time may help to get them in. *O. M. Samuel.*

POISON

William Steiner production, starring Charles Hutchinson. Shown at Loew's Circle, double feature bill, Sept. 4, 1924. Running time, 55 minutes.
Joe Tracey................Frank Hagney
Police Chief O'Brien, S. F........Himself
Bob Marsdon............Charles Hutchinson
Doris Townsend..........Edith Thornton
Roger Harvey..................John Henry
Grace Elliston............Ethel Stairt
Gale Preston.................Otto Lederer
Gordon......................Jack Mathis

This is a bootleg story, one of those screen tales that is built so as to give the star every chance possible to mix in up in a half dozen fights, pull a lot of athletic stuff, and finally wind up with the heroine of the story clasped in his arms. As that, it serves for a filler-in on a double-feature bill. There isn't anything about the picture that is going to send the audience out and make them shill in others.

At the Circle the opening shot, which shows a whiskey bottle labeled "poison" got a hearty applause.

Hutchison plays the role of a young San Francisco society man whose hobby is doing detective work. Chief of Police Dan O'Brien of San Francisco, who appears in the picture for a brief shot, enlists the aid of the hero to help run down a bunch of bootleggers who are flooding the city with bad booze.

Hutch goes out to do the little job, and he manages to have half a dozen narrow escapes, exposes the fact that some of the smart set are mixed in with the bootleggers, and finally rounds up the entire gang and turns them over to the cops.

Of course the heavy is his rival for the hand of the girl and mixed up with the liquor ring; likewise, one of the roughnecks of the booze mob is also after the girl, which shows that she was popular in all walks of life.

Incidentally, the picture plays up that 100 per cent. American thing, so the boys of the Klan should want to see it anyhow, even if nobody else does.

In directorial detail there are the usual slips. The hero on two occasions manages to take a dive into the ocean, and both times after he has emerged he is shown in a shot immediately afterward completely dry. Even though it is hot in sunny Southern California, it isn't quite hot enough for that to happen.

But for a cheap picture one has to admit that "Poison" is crammed full of action and just the type for the cheap houses.

No one in the cast stands out very much, but there is a little character bit that is played by Jack Mathia (incidentally, Jack Mathia, if he isn't J. Herbert Frank under a phoney name, is a ringer for J. Herbert) that stands out.

Fred.

HER OWN FREE WILL

Eastern Productions, Inc., picture, distributed through Producers' Distributing Corporation (Hodkinson). Adapted to the screen by Gerald C. Duffy from the Ethel M. Dell story. Directed by Paul Scardon, and starring Helene Chadwick. At Loew's New York Sept. 5, as half of double bill. Running time, 68 minutes.

This is one of the new Chadwick films, one of a series highly touted by the Producers' Distributing Corporation, but for all its touting and everything else, it is nothing more or less than the century-old yarn of the girl who sold herself into marriage to help papa.

It is produced with a cast of little distinction and with no twists to lend class.

Chadwick plays the wilful daughter of an old patrician. She has two sweethearts, one a college boy and the other a man of about 30, wealthy and very fond of her. The college boy has her heart. When she finds her father hard up she marries the rich man. After the wedding she gets a telegram from the college boy, signed "Your loving."

After that it's write your own ticket on parchment and no prizes offered for the solution.

The cast includes Violet Merserau, a former star, in a subordinate role; Holmes Herbert as the man she married, and Allan Simpson as the college boy. Neither Miss Chadwick nor her associates do anything to justify the moderate expenditure on the piece so that as half of a New York double bill it was just about traveling in its future company. For an ordinary program picture it is below par and as entertainment nil. It might do to keep a country town house open on a rainy night if it could be bought cheaply enough. *Sisk.*

THE ALASKAN

Herbert Brenon production, presented by Adolph Zukor and Jesse L. Lasky. From the James Oliver Curwood story; adapted by Willis Goldbeck; directed by Herbert Brenon, starring Thomas Meighan. Shown at the Rivoli week of Sept. 14, 1924. Running time, 75 minutes.

Alan Holt	Thomas Meighan
Mary Standish	Estelle Taylor
Rosaland	John Sainpolis
Stampede Smith	Frank Campeau
Keok	Anna May Wong
John Graham	Alphonz Ethier
Tautuk	Maurice Cannon
The Lawyer	Charles Ogle

Picture should more than satisfy the Thomas Meighan host of fans clamoring for his return to a real "he man" story. It's a whale of a tale for action, mystery and an over-mastering love, crammed full of pep and go, and it runs along in a manner that will hold the interest right from the start and maintain it to the last fade-out. The cast is great, the photography beautiful, direction corking, and above all, the star marks his return by giving a great performance.

"The Alaskan" is a James Oliver Curwood tale with the Northwest Mounted Police absent. That in itself is a novelty. It is a story of the making of Alaska and the attempts of big business interests to oust the pioneers who made the settlement of the country possible and their final defeat.

Running through it is a vein of mystery surrounding the heroine that isn't cleared up until about three-quarters way. This naturally holds the interest of the audience. Meighan as the young Alaskan, who, after the death of his father through the fault of the representatives of the big business interests, tries single-handed to defeat them before the Senate investigating committee, and later almost single-handed holds off the hordes of roughnecks in a great gun battle that finally works down to a hand-to-hand battle between the hero and the heavy that rivals the greatest of all hand-to-hand fights that the screen has ever seen.

Of course the heavy and his gang are licked and the former killed, which clears the way for his widow and the hero to be clinched for the happy ending.

Estelle Taylor plays opposite Meighan and handled the early part of it in great shape. It is only in the heavy love scenes she becomes a little too mushy. Incidentally, here is a chance to play up the girl engaged to Jack Dempsey.

Frank Campeau as a rough and ready shootin' fool, foreman of the hero's outfit, puts over a characterization that ranks with that Torrence and Tully did in "The Covered Wagon." Anna May Wong as an Indian girl scored nicely.

Herbert Brenon plays a bit in the picture. On board the steamer bound for Alaska he is one of the officers aboard ship and looks snappy in a uniform.

The natural scenic beauty of some of the shots is so great as to almost appear faked.

The picture looks like it is going to be the biggest money-getter of the last four or five pictures that have starred Meighan. *Fred.*

THE CLEAN HEART

J. Stuart Blackton production, presented by Albert E. Smith; released by Vitagraph. From the story by A. S. M. Hutchinson. Shown at the Rialto, New York, week of Sept. 15, 1924. Running time, 86 minutes.

Philip Wriford	Percy Marmont
Puddlebox	Otis Harlan
Essie Bickers	Marguerite de la Motte

There is something about the English story of this particular type that does not lend itself particularly well to picturization. In the printed form the story may hold all the elements necessary to sustained interest, but on the screen becomes draggy and uninteresting. That is what this study in a mild form of insanity by A. S. M. Hutchinson is. The general American picture-going public is not at this time ready for studies in psychology.

The tale is of a noted author of a number of novels who tires of the material in life and takes to the road in search of the elusive perfect happiness. He meets with a wanderer. They are engulfed in the rising tide along the ocean and the fellow wanderer sacrifices himself so that the younger man may live.

This sacrifice, together with the horror attending the situation, results in a mild form of insanity with the writer. On his recovery in a hospital a nurse in training takes him to the home of her parents. Finally, as his further recovery comes about, the author proposes to the girl that she go away with him. But the girl, a foolish little thing with a foolish little giggle, who is always saying "Let's have a laugh," refuses.

Through circumstances she runs forth into the storm and topples over the edge of a cliff into a bay many feet below. Before falling she stopped long enough to ask if the author really loves her. This scene held the one real kick, and that was spoiled by the silly question. She is rescued, but how it happened isn't part of the picture story, and the writer after having wandered away returns after a year to find the girl a cripple and proposes to marry her.

As a study of mind and character the theme may be all there, but as a picture there is nothing to rave about. The best definition is that it is about on a par with the average program picture that might have been turned out by an English producing company.

Percy Marmont, who played the principal role in "If Winter Comes," by the same author, as the writer in this story has the principal role. His more or less whimsical appearance seems to fit particularly well to the heroes Mr. Hutchinson pens. Marguerite de la Motte did fairly well as the nurse, although appearing a trifle too mature for a giddy young thing. Otis Harlan seemed the best cast. *Fred.*

WINE

Universal-Jewel release, adapted from a "Saturday Evening Post" story by William X. MacHarg. Directed by L. J. Gasnier, and featuring Clara Bow. Cast includes Myrtle Stedman, Huntley Gordon, Robert Agnew, Walter Long and Forrest Stanley. Showing at Moss' Broadway, New York, Sept. 15. Running time, 68 mins.

A jazz age theme preceded by a discourse signed with Carl Laemmle's name as to just what Universal's president thinks of bootleggers. The basic idea of the picture has had countless retakes under as many titles, but the outlay of names and the work of the cast gives the film reasonable plausibility for standing as a program leader.

Clara Bow does the giddy flapper who has her head turned by the ball which premiers her social career. Huntley Gordon is the father become bankrupt on the night of his daughter's large evening, and Myrtle Stedman is the fixing mother who induces her husband to lend his name to a prominent bootlegger and pursuant enterprises in order not to disturb the daughter. Walter Long, as always, is capable, but the story gives him an entrance into the elite circle as a fake count, and while it doesn't necessarily hurt Long, it doesn't do the tale any good. Other characters list Robert Agnew as the young blood attempting to lead the deb astray, while Forrest Stanley is the friend of the family and the ultimate winner of the girl.

The kick evidently was aimed to consummate in the aquatic cabaret on the 12-mile booze limit line. It's a disappointment from any angle. Approach night "shots" only show skyrockets going up from the ship, there's not one good flash at the floating emporium, and the interiors are distinctly average scenes, topped by hundreds of others of that ilk.

Gasnier, for the most part, has kept his players away from becoming overly dramatic, although the story is such as to make this practically impossible at times. Following the financial failure of the father and affiliating himself with the rum runner comes the ultimate temporary blindness of the mother from imbibing in the "hooch," the wayward path the daughter is threatening to succumb to through parental absence and her eventual betrothal to the family friend who has the means to see the entire household over the breach.

Miss Bow is an acceptable giddy young thing, going to the extreme of three different coiffeurs to make it more realistic, while Mr. Gordon and Miss Stedman are outstanding as the parents.

Productionally the home interiors are solid and in good taste, but the roadhouse and boat cafe leave much to be desired.

The film has not body enough to make it a convincing epic in the better houses, although intermediate audiences will undoubtedly go for it, whether they believe it or not. *Skig.*

ANOTHER SCANDAL

Continuation and sequel to the play "Scandal," by the same author, Cosmo Hamilton. Produced by the Tilford Cinema Corp. and distributed through Producers' Distributing Corp. (Hodkinson). Directed by E. H. Griffith and screen play by G. Marion Burton. At Loew's Circle, Sept. 15, as one-half double bill. Running time, 65 minutes.

Beatrice Vanderdyke	Lois Wilson
Pelham Franklin	Holmes Herbert
Mrs. Beamish	Flora Le Breton
Cousin Elizabeth	Hedda Hopper
Mally	Ralph Bunker
Brownie	Zeffie Tilbury

Here's a good one.

"Scandal" as a play achieved more than the usual hit success on the speaking stage. It was a spicy story, well told. During the first few moments of this film, the gist of the former play was introduced swiftly, neatly and sensibly. It planted the idea of how Beatrice Vanderdyke, the one-time typical flapper, had practically ensnared Pelham Franklin, then a 35-year-old bachelor—but handsome, healthy and wealthy.

That done, the new story begins. Pelham and Bee have been married. A child is on the way. Pelham worries and his friend, Mally (introduced for comedy purposes as the man who knew about women), tells him that his wife would really rather not have him around when the child is born.

A yachting party, which includes the angling Mrs. Beamish, Cousin Elizabeth (a schemer), Mally and Pelham, is arranged, and during the course of the trip Mrs. Beamish tries every method — or nearly every—known to woman to "get" the man she wants. In her one-piece bathing-suit drowning effort she gave a neat flash that the censors in Maryland, Ohio, Pennsylvania and all the other "moral" states will cut out, but which will at least give the censors a thrill.

Back with his wife, the child born, Pelham is at her feet with his love, solicitous, kind, child-like in his complete adoration. This gets on the wife's nerves, for she would rather be commanded than command; so the rest of the film resolves itself into her efforts to stir up his jealousy and thereby awaken the old lover in him.

Lois Wilson, topping a good cast, is ideal in the role. Her slender figure, and almost total lack of sex appeal tames down what might have been a very suggestive role, while Holmes Herbert as her husband is corking—and mightily suggestive of Elliot Dexter in the days when the latter was working big pictures instead of vaudeville. Of the others, Flora Le Breton as Mrs. Beamish stood out.

E. H. Griffith has done a good directorial job and the mechanical details, such as the reflection of water in the rooms aboard the yacht, are well handled. Big shots of handsome Florida homes (piece located there) lend a massive touch that didn't cost the producers much, while the typical high life trappings give the film a glitter which is agreeable. All the sets are well done and some little money has apparently been spent.

While "Another Scandal" isn't exactly first-run material, due to the lack of real big names, it is entertainment and entirely suitable for the second-string houses. Its placing at Loew's Circle as half of a double bill is an injustice to the quality of the film, for it is in reality better than some of the recent Broadway week-runs.

It is a moot question whether Lois Wilson will draw money on her own; but that aside, for a house with an established clientele, the picture is there. *Sisk.*

PASSION'S PATHWAY

Lee-Bradford Corp. picture, starring Estelle Taylor. Cast includes Jean Perry, Tully Marshall, Ben Daly, Snitz Edwards, Wilfred Lucas and Fed De Silva. At Loew's Circle, New York, as half of double daily bill. Running time, 63 minutes.

What connection the title has with the picture remains entirely obscured, and the same might as well be said of the billing for Miss Taylor, other than the recent publicity attendant upon her reported future marriage to Jack Dempsey. Miss Taylor does nothing to warrant the concession and the labeling is simply one of those "catch" namings.

The film is another example of a timid director afraid to let an audience take something for granted. Explanatory sub-titles and superfluous bits, emphasized at each and every "sob" opportunity, were just so much padding and meaningless. It took the running time to over an hour when the entire matter could have been cleaned up much earlier.

A villainous assistant superintendent craves the stenographer, who marries the superintendent. When the latter leaves to straighten out the firm's mines in Mexico the assistant frames the books and the superintendent gets notice he's fired, after having saved his boss' son in a fracas with bandits.

Tully Marshall does a bit as a butler very good. Jean Perry plays the hard luck super averagely, while there probably aren't more than a thousand girls around who would have done as well as Miss Taylor as the stenographer-wife.

Whoever directed evidently had in mind the intermediate house clientele, as the entire construction of the film points that way.

It's a strictly second-class release fitted for the lesser house and in need of assistance from a co-operating feature on the same bill. *Skig.*

DARING LOVE

M. H. Hoffman presentation, releasing through Truart Film Corp. Starring Elaine Hammerstein and adapted from Albert Payson Terhune's story, "Driftwood." Cast includes Huntley Gordon and Walter Long. At Loew's Circle, New York, half double bill, Sept. 11. Running time, 57 minutes.

Elaine Hammerstein doing a dance hall girl in an inconsequential story, unwinding itself as average entertainment and scheduled to find its plane in the middle class houses.

The story is a switch-back from a discussion between three men with the tale revealing it is the story of the state governor, the dance hall girl and the relator of the narrative.

Photographed and titled in broad strokes, with the audience given no credit for being able to perceive the obvious, it tells of a brilliant lawyer addicted to liquor who swears off, but goes back when discovering his wife in the arms of the family friend. Hitting the byways, the lawyer, John Stedman (Huntley Gordon), induces Bobo (Miss Hammerstein) to take him to her apartment, where his wife's detectives, of whom he is aware, come in and secure the necessary evidence for a divorce. The frame provokes an outcry from the innocent girl, but Stedman folds up with illness and is nursed back to health by her.

The war, the report of Stedman's death and the wife's attempt to induce him to return to her when he comes back as a captain consume the remaining footage in a perfectly plain screen tale not overly creditable to Miss Hammerstein, Mr. Gordon or Mr. Long.

The latter is the uncouth district politician and proprietor of the dance hall in the switch-back, also the Senator at the Inaugural Ball who tells the story.

The information of it being adapted from a Terhune tale promised something, but the picturization failed beyond an average well-worn theme.

Nothing in the production to cause comment. The war is implied through the wearing of uniforms. Loew's Circle seems to have gauged the value when placing it alongside of another feature the same day.
Skig.

RIDERS OF MYSTERY

Western five-reeler, produced by J. J. Goldberg and distributed by Independent Pictures Corp. Bill Cody starred and Peggy O'Dare featured. Direction by Robert North Baker. At Loew's Baker for a double bill Sept. 15. Running time, 68 minutes.

As a rule, most of the cheap westerns are interesting because they follow a set formula of well-developed thrills and the old heart-interest stuff between the new hand and the boss's daughter. But this one, even with those attributes, doesn't hold interest, and one glaring directorial mistake brought howls of laughter at the Circle—laughter that will be repeated wherever the film is shown.

The reference is to a plunge over a cliff by a carriage. A faraway shot shows an empty carriage going over the embankment in water many feet below. The next shot, a close-up of the carriage crushed on rocks, reveals a man swimming away. This is ridiculous from two angles, the first being that ordinary common sense would demand a dummy in place of the man as the fall was made; and the second, that a man could swim after dropping a hundred feet or more to kiss a rock in the face.

Bill Cody, a phoney name like the rest of the $200 weekly western heroes of the cheap films, isn't as good as the multitude of young men who are doing his same stuff. For some of his rides the projection is plainly accelerated, and he really does nothing that would entitle him to starring honors. Peggy O'Dare, playing opposite, is a poor heroine, having snatched too much rouge and too much Ziegfeldian coquettishness for a ranch girl. The others are typical western characters, neither good nor bad.

The story concerns a man of mystery who has been raising a rumpus and of his capture by the hero and the sheriff. Thin stuff in itself, and

thinner still when spread over multiple reels.

"Riders of Mystery" is a cheap picture all through. *Bisk.*

COYOTE FANGS

A western production by J. Joseph Sameth starring Jack Perrin. Directed by Harry Welt and distributed by Madoc Productions, Inc. At Loew's New York, Sept. 5, as half of double bill. Running time, 61 minutes.

This is another of the flood of cheap westerns on the market at present and as satisfactory as most of them. Following the machine-made plot, which includes the girl, the cowboy, wronged but vindicated, a sheriff's posse and a villain, this one fills the footage with no little action and one or two riding thrills.

Jack Perrin, the star, is a likable screen cowboy. He is large, stalwart and handsome. Moreover, he doesn't try to hog the camera. Therefore, in such a production as this he fills the bill. In the smaller neighborhood houses the film is okeh, and as that is the only place the makers have in mind during the production period, nobody has a kick.

None of these westerns has any pretensions. They are made with cheap stars, cheap cast, cheap scenery, and look it. Their mainstay is the atmosphere of the west, which is apparently just as surefire today as when Essanay, Kalem-Selig and Vitagraph did little else beside manufacture pictures of the plains. *Bisk.*

THE FAMILY SECRET

Universal-Jewel, starring Baby Peggy, directed by William Seiter. From the play by Augustus Thomas entitled "The Burglar," based on the Frances Hodgdon Burnett story, "Edith's Burglar." At Loew's Circle, New York, on double-feature bill Sept. 4, 1924. Running time, 65 minutes.
Edith.........................Baby Peggy
Her Mother.................Gladys Huelette
Her Father...................Edward Earle

This selection of a real story with a real child's part for a Baby Peggy vehicle reflects credit on the production department of U. It is a corking story that has a lot of interest and gives the little baby star a chance to deliver legitimately. If a kid picture with a real story can get over anywhere then this one is set about right for any audience.

Edward Earle and Gladys Huelette support the youthful star. Both manage to give interesting and sustained characterizations of the roles assigned them. Earle is particularly good as the penniless youngster who married the daughter of the millionaire only to be railroaded up the river for attempted burglary when he broke into his father-in-law's home to see his wife and child. Gladys Huelette in several scenes showed a flash of the ability that made her a favorite in other days.

In this day pictures starring youthful finds are not the rage that they were a couple of years ago, and because of this a lot of the exhibitors have been laying off of them; but here is one that you need not be afraid of. It will interest, entertain and get some money.

William Seiter handled the little star skillfully and got everything out of her that could be worked into the picture. His handling of a couple of human interest bits with a dog was exceedingly well done. The comedy stuff of the fleas at the spinster tea fight and the bath stuff got over to good laugh producing result.

The story holds up well and the action moves along nicely. *Fred.*

FOREIGN REVIEWS

DECAMERON NIGHTS

London, Sept. 2.

"Decameron Nights" is adapted from the Robert McLaughlin and Boyle Lawrence Drury Lane drama, and premiered at the Lane last night. The picture was made in Germany wish a cast including many of the foremost Teutonic players and with the entire resources of Germany's biggest studio at the disposal of the director, Herbert Wilcox. The studio used was the same which saw the production of "The Nibelungs," and the present picture is not far beyond the former in scenic beauty.

Some of the shots are remarkable. The Venetian scenes, the market place, the Soldan's court—these sets have never been bettered in any picture. Every set, small or large, has been built with a massive dignity. Exterior locations are few and ordinary.

A great feature is the mob work of the dense and excited crowds. Wilcox has handled some of the "near-the-knuckle" scenes with great care and tact, including the telling of the nightingale's story, the penance (particularly good is the eclipse in this scene) and the rape of the talisman and search for the mole on the heroine's body.

The scenario sticks faithfully to the double-barreled story of the Drury Lane play.

Torello and Ricciardo leave their vastly different wives, Violente, the free lover, and Teodora, the pure pride of Venice, to join in a crusade against the Saracen. Meanwhile the Soldan and the Algarve have patched up their quarrels, and Saladin, the Soldan's son, is sent to woo the Algarve's daughter, Perdita. He is compelled to seek shelter in a monastery, where the Crusaders have also taken cover from a terrific storm. A ship is wrecked and a beautiful maiden, Perdita, is rescued. She has lost her memory and is sent by Torello to Venice under the care of the licentious libertine Ricciardo. This worthy plots not only her ruin, but that of the lady Teodora, while Saladin falls in love with her, not knowing her real identity. By a trick Ricciardo steals the talisman from Teodora and searches for the mole on her body, "the whereabouts of which only her husband knows." This is seen by Torello, now a prisoner in Saracen hands, in a magic crystal, and, thinking his wife guilty of unfaithfulness, sends a message to the Doge demanding justice. The Doge finds Teodora guilty, and orders her to stand naked before the populace at the Feast of Purity. An eclipse of the sun, however, saves the situation, and her innocence is taken as proved.

Meanwhile Saladin has rescued the beautiful Perdita from Ricciardo and taken her to the Soldan, who is furious and has the lovers cast into a dungeon. Perdita is recognized by two of the Algarve's retinue, but the monarch arrives only to find Saladin and Perdita dead. The picture closes on the Algarve furious, once more declaring war on the Soldan.

The subtitling by Frank Tilley is excellent, and, as far as acting goes, the few English and American members of the cast are easily outclassed by the Germans.

Lionel Barrymore is excellent if somewhat colorless as Saladin, and Ivy Duke is without life as Perdita. She merely walks through, without feeling or expression, and is apparently content to pose with an artificial beauty which by no means fits the drama of the part. Xenia Desni gives a fine performance of the Lady Teodora, and, although not "starred," she carries the weight of the production from the feminine point on her shoulders. In the smaller part of the Lady Violente,

nna Ralph is very good. The Soldan of Werner Krauss is a masterpiece of cleverly conceived characterization. Randle Ayrton gives a fine performance as Ricciardo, which, in its way, is as powerful and convincing as that of Krauss. Bernhard Goetzke is excellent as Torello, and all the other members of the cast play with an ability far above the average.

Herbert Wilcox can safely claim to have made the first big British super. *Gore.*

FEET OF CLAY

Cecil B. De Mille Production presented by Adolph Zukor and Jesse L. Lasky. Adapted by Beulah Marie Dix and Bertram Millhauser from Margaretta Tuttle's novel. Shown at the Rivoli, New York, week Sept. 21. Running time, 90 minutes.

Amy Loring................Vera Reynolds
Kerry Harlan...............Rod La Rocque
The Bookkeeper.............Victor Varconi
Tony Channing..............Ricardo Cortez
Bertha Lansell..................Julia Faye
Bendick...................Theodore Kosloff
Dr. Fergus Lansell..........Robert Edeson

A whale of an audience picture that will top money anywhere. It has a couple of thrills that are real thrills, and with it a society atmosphere with a full portion of sex stuff that will get over in great shape. Incidentally Cecil De Mille hasn't a bath tub in this one, but has a wonderful jazz band dance scene that should be looked at by all of the big band leaders to catch the idea of the novelty. They could use it sometime or another in the event they managed to land a big restaurant for an extended engagement.

The story is simple enough, but it is made into something really worth while through screen treatment.

Kerry Harlon, though poor, moves in society circles because of the "first families." He is in love with the step-sister of the wife of a noted surgeon, who in turn is very much in love with the young man. The characters are at Catalina Island, having cruised there in the yacht of the surgeon. Here Kerry and Amy Loring, the step-sister, are paired off as partners in a surf-board race. During the race the speed boat Kerry is driving catches fire and blows up. Kerry had jumped and made his way to Amy's surf board when the dorsal fin of a shark is seen. Kerry, to protect the girl, goes overboard and gives battle to the sea-tiger. Succeeding in beating it off he is bitten in the foot.

The pair are married on the return trip to New York, and their first appearance is at a formal dance party the surgeon's wife gives. Kerry is warned not to dance a single step for fear he might cause additional injury to his foot. In consequence he relinquishes his wife for the first dance to his former rival for her hand. This is an opportunity the still enamoured wife of the surgeon cannot overlook and she takes advantage by sowing seeds of jealousy, with the result the husband takes to the dance floor with his wife. After a few steps his foot gives way under him and he collapses.

"One year without putting that foot on the ground" is the verdict of the doctor and the wife, then shoulders the burden of providing for the family by accepting the proffer of a position as mannequin with the most fashionable of New York's male modistes.

That is the opportunity the surgeon's wife has looked for. While her stepsister is earning money to cover the expense of the home she lays siege to the heart of the husband, calling with lunches and reading him poems of passion. Her husband becomes aware of the visits and forbids her going to the house. She disobeys, only to be caught, another thrill, with the wife standing on a narrow coping outside of a window while her husband searches the apartment for her. She finally falls to the courtyard below and is killed.

A decided scandal is raked up by the paper. That evening the wife of Kerry, learning the story, comes to the house determined to leave her husband. It gives way to a suicide pact on the part of the two. At this point a sequence of the Beulah Marie Dix play, "Beyond the Border," is utilized effectively. For a finish there is a happy ending which must be seen to be appreciated.

The cast is a splendid one. Rod LaRocque makes a corking hero, while Ricardo Cortez as the rival for the girl appears to distinct advantage. Cortez is improving as he goes along in pictures. Vera Reynolds plays the little heroine and Julia Faye is the blonde vampish wife of the surgeon. Theodore Kosloff handles the "male modiste" cleverly, but the star characterization is by Robert Edeson as the surgeon. His was a work of art.

In setting the picture is splendidly done. It is certain to get record box office returns, although it does seem that "Lost Souls" might have been a better title than "Feet of Clay."

Fred.

NEVER SAY DIE

Douglas MacLean Production released through Associated Exhibitors. Founded on the William Collier play of same title. At Loew's Lincoln Square Sept. 22-24. Running time 59 minutes.

Jack Woodbury...........Douglas MacLean
Violet Stevenson..............Lillian Rich
La Cigale...................Helen Ferguson
Hector Waters................Hallam Cooley
Griggs.....................Lucien Littlefield
"Gun" Murray..................Tom O'Brien

The Pathe organization may be cornering the laugh market in feature films. With Harold Lloyd and Douglas MacLean they have a couple of male stars that make the public laugh. Especially is this so in MacLean's latest, "Never Say Die," which packs a laugh wallop from beginning to end and is better than his "Yankee Consul" was.

Right now to sum up between MacLean's "Never Say Die" and Lloyd's "In Hot Water," the latest feature by that comedian, the MacLean picture must be judged the better of the two by hundreds of laughs.

And MacLean goes in for the thrill stuff. There is a sequence in the picture with MacLean walking onto a window ledge outside of a doctor's office with his eyes blindfolded, more of a thrill than if Lloyd had done it. One expects it from Lloyd, but coming from MacLean it was such a surprise there was 100 per cent added to the thrill.

The story is that of a wealthy young man who walks into the office of a group of doctors. They mistake him for an expected patient and go over his person thoroughly. Through a series of comedy events they pronounce that he has but three months to live.

It is during this examination one gets the thrill with the comedian walking out of the office onto the window ledge, and this scene is a wow of laughter.

To do the right thing MacLean decides he will marry the fiance of his artist friend so that at the time of his death he will be enabled to bequeath them his fortune. This step is taken because his uncle's will provided that on the death of the young heir the money must go to someone in the family. As there is no family, one must be provided.

After the three months and death still sidestepping, husband and wife meet for the first time since the wedding ceremony. Both have come to the conclusion they are really in love with each other. Despite the attempts of the former fiance of the wife, those of a gunman to bump off the hero, and an amusing situation through the introduction of a professional co-respondent, the pair make their escape from the city on a steamer for a long-delayed honeymoon.

In addition to the window ledge stunt there is a screaming chase scene with MacLean seated in n old-fashioned cab. It first loses its driver and later the horse, but goes careening madly on its way down hill, past autos and trolley cars, escaping trees by fractions of an inch, with the hero for the greater part of the time sitting serenely inside, unaware. This is another succession of heavy laughs. The finish with MacLean hoisted on board the steamer in an auto to escape the gunman makes a fitting climax to the series of laughable mishaps that have preceded it.

The titling is almost as clever as the action, with the result a 100 per cent laugh producer that abounds in thrills.

It is well cast and well played. MacLean on the strength of it takes his place side by side with Lloyd when it comes to real story and laughs combined in one picture.

Fred.

FIGHTERS' PARADISE

Phil Goldstone production (independent), featuring Rex (Snowy) Baker. Story by J. F. Natteford. Directed by Alvin J. Neitz. Cast includes Andrew Waldron, Dick Sutherland, Jack Curtis, Harry Burns, Kenneth Benedict, Margaret Landis. At Tivoli, New York, Sept. 19.

Lamentable fact in the presentation of many independent productions that the title-writing is for the most part abominable. In "Fighters' Paradise" Phil Goldstone has made a determined effort to improve his captions and the improvement is commendable. The title writer as a whole steamed up the "wording" to laughing results.

Not much to the story, as it travels a path worn down by such picture visualizations of the hero having a dream and seeing himself accomplish what he considered "the impossible" to receiving a sock on the head that made him just the reverse of what is in fighting spirit.

Snowy Baker has the pat part of the young man who looks like Cyclone Carter, a famous pug, who at heart is a coward. The girls all admire Baker, who, as the soda water slinger in the small town, is pointed out as the real fighting champ.

The heroine is played by Margaret Landis, who goes through some extenuating scenes with Baker, a wild, exciting ride in an auto and a plunge down an embankment with the car burning up being one of the features.

The fight was well staged and full of excitement. At the Tivoli it had the boys rooting involuntarily for the favorite.

Not a great picture, nor a bad one. Will fill in acceptably where the 2-in-1-day policy prevails. As an independent it should keep working.

Mark.

IT IS THE LAW

Fox picture adapted from the play by E. L. Rice. Directed by J. Gordon Edwards. Cast includes Arthur Hohl, Herbert Heyes, Mimi Palmeri. At Loew's New York theatre Sept. 18. Running time, 86 minutes.

Too much footage with no apparent necessity for consuming close to an hour and a half in the telling. Other than that the adaptation of this play, which premiered on Broadway in December, 1922, shapes itself as interesting screen entertainment, has received able treatment and as regards the cast sums up as a one man picture.

Arthur Hohl, assuming a dual role, runs away with the individual honors. That is not illogical, inasmuch as he is duplicating his performance in the legitimate presentation. Hohl does three distinct characters before the film terminates—the rejected and vehement lover, his double, whom he discovers in the person of a street bum and a dope fiend, and the suave proprietor of an exclusive gaming establishment. It marks plenty of work for Hohl, and outside the corresponding amount of footage given him his performance is such as to practically bury the accompanying players.

The celluloid version is fairly strict in adhering to the story as told upon the stage, although J. Gordon Edwards, in directing, has seemingly taken every advantage to pad out the action.

The story is based upon the theory that no man can be prosecuted twice for the same crime. Albert Woodruff and Justin Victor are in love with the one girl, Ruth Allen. The girl chooses Victor, and Woodruff, jealous, goes completely out of his head when a family friend picks up a pair of tongs from the fireplace. Victor explains that Woodruff carries a life scar from such an implement, but it doesn't stop the latter from swearing vengeance upon his life-long friend, who is to be the future husband.

The night of the wedding, and after the ceremony, Woodruff induces his double, the street derelict, to come to his apartment and threatens the bride over the phone with blackmail as a ruse to draw the bridegroom to his abode. When he sees Victor arrive downstairs Woodruff takes the receiver off the phone, cries for help, shoots his twin likeness and escapes, leaving Victor to be compromised and sentenced to life imprisonment.

A five years' lapse brings Woodruff back to this country with a monocle and a beard to again pursue his former love. A Scotland Yard man has been following the trail of "Sniffer" Evans, the double killed by Woodruff and wanted in England, but when Woodruff is accused of being Evans the difference in finger prints destroys the contention.

The girl finally discovers the true identity of Woodruff when she picks up a pair of tongs and he becomes maddened by the sight. Rushing to her guardian, now Governor of the State, she secures her husband's release. He immediately walks into the gaming rooms and shoots Woodruff.

The court room scene, wherein Victor tells his story and asserts he will leave a free man because of the clause in the law code which stipulates there can be no second prosecution for the same crime gives reason for the title and the happy ending.

The picture is so constructed as to be a straightaway story, whereas the play had "switchback" construction and the continued life of Woodruff to save the persecuted Victor from stained hands. The interiors have been well selected and the double photography is noteworthy.

Had the film been held down to around one hour it would have been a corking presentation, but as it is it just misses being in that classification. The story, alone, is sufficient to stand by itself, especially when compared to other scripts that reach film production, and the work of Hohl is so much velvet.

However, "It Is the Law" looks like a capable program leader for the better class houses, with but its one glaring fault, length.

Skig.

CONDEMNED

One of those "more sinned against than usual" themes, with nothing to lift it above the obvious melodramatics, makes this picture steer a direct course for the lesser houses.

Those witnessing must take plenty for granted, as the tale has more than a few improbabilities and the harassed heroine runs the gamut of a small town's narrow-mindedness without missing a thing. And it's all because the girl sneaks her dog on a train under wraps as a baby, and kidnapers mistakenly exchange bundles, which leaves the girl to enter the village with an infant and a long explanation.

She can't "square" the mite; her aunt is entirely skeptical, and when the youthful president of the village's anti-vice society moves his sleeping quarters to the garage and the girl takes refuge in his house, as her only means of abode, the town inhabitants instigate a tar and feather party.

The picture has been plentifully padded, and when everything else fails superfluous sub-titles make the extra footage. The cast parallels the scenario in leaving vast stretches of indifferent projection, and the film is such as to make it a practical necessity for another feature to be included upon any program where a theatre has any sort of a reputation. *Skig.*

LAST OF THE DUANES

Fox production, starring Tom Mix. From the book by Zane Grey. Directed by Lynn Reynolds. Scenario by Edward J. Montagne. At the New York one day (Sept. 15). Runs about 75 minutes.

Duck Duane....................Tom Mix
Jenny....................Marian Nixon
Cal Bain....................Brindsley Shaw
Euchre....................Frank Nelson
Mother....................Lucy Beaumont
Jenny's father....................Harry Lonsdale

One of the better Tom Mix features and consequently a good western. The combination of the star and Zane Grey, with the capable Lynn Reynolds directing and a hand-picked cast, is supremely happy for this type of film. Those who like westerns (and who can begin to count them) will rave, and the comparatively few who don't will feel a lot more kindly toward them.

Young Duane is the son of a fiery old battler murdered in his tracks after having carved eight niches on his gun in memory of those who tried to mix things up with him. The son inherits his old man's marvelous mastery of firearms but not the battle instinct and the lust to kill anyone who crosses his path.

Duane tries his hardest to be a coward and dodge all fights, but he is finally forced to defend himself and murder a scoundrel who would have plugged him first.

There is strong continuity between the various episodes, in which Mix is given opportunity to exhibit how much he can accomplish with his horse, Tony.

The western scenery is magnificent, and the camera man shot it from the best possible points of vantage. The whole production indicates an attentive care in supervision lacking in 95 per cent of program features. "Last of the Duanes," while it must be placed in the latter category, ranks at the top, and once again Mix has firmly planted his spurs in the steed of popularity.

PRIDE OF SUNSHINE ALLEY

I. J. Bud Barsky production, starring Kenneth McDonald. Story by Samuel M. Pyke. Directed by Wm. James Craft. Shown at Loew's New York, double-feature bill Sept. 19. Running time 57 minutes.

One of those dear old "sidewalks of New York," with its scenes of action on the lower east side, with the hero a young Irishman, appointed to the police force. It's not a world-beater, but will serve in the daily change houses and will get by on the strength of a couple of good fast rough-and-tumble fights.

The story is just a little romance, with the copper stuck on one of the girls of the neighborhood. She is the sole support of an invalid mother, and her brother is a worthless kid who hangs out in the pool parlor run by the ward heeler in love with the girl.

McDonald seems to be a rather likeable type of a young lead for the screen, with personality, who shows up much better in a profile shot than when photographed full on. Violet Schram plays opposite, and handled it rather nicely.

The picture wasn't an expensive one to make. While there are some technical faults here and there, it will do for the cheap houses.

Fred.

DANTE'S INFERNO

Presented by William Fox; directed by A. Henry Otto. Modern story by Cyrus Wood, adapted by Edmund Goulding. Based on Dante's famous poem. Shown at the Central, New York, for a run beginning Sept. 29. Running time 63 minutes.

Dante....................Lawson Butt
Virgil....................Howard Gaye
Mortimer Judd, millionaire....Ralph Lewis
Marjorie Vernon, nurse.....Pauline Starke
Eugene Craig, the victim...Josef Swickard
Mildred Craig, his daughter....Gloria Grey
Ernest Judd, the son..........William Scott
The Fiend....................Robert Klein
Mrs. Judd....................Winifred Landis
The Doctor....................Lorimer Johnston
The Secretary....................Lon Poff
The Butler....................Bud Jamison

According to the title leader to this production, it is presented as "an achievement" by William Fox; likewise it is presented "reverently." The latter should take the curse off the nude stuff in the picture.

There was a little jam with the censor board before it got by in New York, but when the producers finally convinced the board the men and women who had every appearance of being naked in Hades really wore union suits the picture got by.

It is a preachment to be sure, but the audiences are going to be fooled by that nude stuff. If the dames and guys who usually ride down in the subway early in the morning reading the "Daily Dirt" while chewing gum on their way to the office ever get wise to the undressiness of this picture, the Central is going to do a turnaway. It wouldn't be a bit surprising if the picture stayed longer than the time allotted according to its present schedule.

It's the naked stuff only that is going to make the picture. At the same time there isn't anything vulgar, salacious or suggestive about it, but it certainly does lend itself to a flash on nudity.

The picture proves again that if given a subject where he is able to run wild with an idea, Henry Otto can direct a picture that will have box office appeal and still get away from the censorship angle.

The modern story is by far the weakest portion. However, it is as good an excuse as any for the ringing in of a visualization of Dante's "Inferno" on the screen. It is a dream idea.

That modern portion bespeaks of a modern money-grabber, grown hard in his pursuit of wealth. He has practically brought about the ruin of his neighbor and the latter, in the last minute before he decides to end it all, sends a copy of the "Inferno" to his financial enemy and on the fly-leaf inscribes a curse. As the recipient reads the opening passages the screen shows a visualization of the "Inferno." Evidently the illustrations of Gustave Dore have been faithfully followed. Everything that Dore had in his half life-sized oils of Dante's descriptions except the "scandalmongers" in ice and the disembowelment of murderers is shown. The naked spirits of the harlots, the deceivers, the transgressors of every type and nature are in the scenes of Hell.

There are a couple of short flashes where there is a close-up of a nude figure. This leads to the belief that when the scenes in which there are 500 or more seemingly nude figures in the longer shots they must have been just as were the close-ups. It is a great audience angle.

In the end of the modern story is a happy ending. When the money-grabber has the dream that the reading of the book has brought, he realizes the eror of his ways and has an according change of heart.

The trouble is that the general idea in regard to the picture has been an educational one so far as the public is concerned. This in reality is a subject that tends to put the fear of God into the hearts of the transgressor, providing they take time enough to think while trying to get a flash of the undressed mob as to what is really being set forth before them. The exhibitor is fully justified in asking the message of the picture to be broadcast to the multitudes from the pulpits for the visualization of Hell as it is set forth in this picture. Punishments meted out are far more forceful than any that may be set forth by rabbi, priest or minister, for the fire and brimstone are right there.

In the cast of the modern story no one stands out particularly. Ralph Lewis is the money-grabber and does fairly well; also Josef Swickard in his role. The juvenile lead is rather weak and Pauline Starke and Gloria Grey do nothing that distinguishes them. *Fred.*

THE RED LILY

Metro-Goldwyn production from original story by Fred Niblo. Adapted to screen by Bess Meredyth and directed by Niblo. Ramon Novarro starred. Reviewed at Capitol, New York, Sept. 28. Running time, 65 minutes.

Marise LaNous....................Enid Bennett
Jean Leonnec....................Ramon Novarro
Bobo....................Wallace Beery
Hugo Leonnec....................Frank Currier
Nana....................Rosemary Theby
D'Agut....................Mitchell Lewis
Mama Bouchard....................Emily Fitzroy
Papa Bouchard....................George Periolat
Mme. Poussot....................Milly Davenport
The Toad....................Dick Sutherland
Le Turc....................Gibson Gouland
Concierge....................George Nichols

With its locale in the Apache sections of Montmartre, its hero and heroine both prime specimens of degraded humanity, 'The Red Lily" isn't a pleasant picture. In addition to being unpleasant, condemnatory at the start, the plot is weak and hackneyed.

In a French village the daughter of the cobbler and the son of the mayor are in love. The mayor objects and when the girl's people die she is sent away to earn her living, turning up in the big city, as does the boy—his occupation now a thief and her time mostly taken up in protecting her virtue.

After many vicissitudes, the boy is sought by the police and is saved by the girl, who lets him escape into a sewer while she is on the receiving end of a bullet meant for him. In the hospital he visits her and decides to reform—as the Gendarme Brothers, a standard French melodramatic two-act, place their hands on his shoulders and take him away.

The ending, however, is happy, with the pair riding along a country road—away from the influences of a city that "ruined them."

Novarro's acting is almost negligible. Miss Bennett has never done better, and with her beauty discarded, as it is in many of the scenes, surprised the talent. Wallace Beery has a roughneck part that is about fair. The others of a long and competent cast did well and the settings in the underground dives were heavy and impressive—that going for a sewer interior.

But the story itself is so weak and unattractive that good acting couldn't have made it entertaining.

This is one that may get a little money at the Capitol, having made a tremendous start Sunday with that house packed most of the day and night, but after its Broadway run is over and the word gets around, it doesn't look like an especially good bet if the price is high—and it is. *Sisk.*

CITY THAT NEVER SLEEPS

James Cruze production, presented by Adolph Zukor and Jesse L. Lasky. Adapted by Walter Woods and Anthony Coldeway from the Leroy Scott story, "Mother O'Day." Directed by James Cruze. Shown at the Rialto, New York, week of Sept. 28. Running time, 67 minutes.

Mother O'Day....................Louise Dresser
Mark Roth....................Ricardo Cortez
Mrs. Kendall....................Kathlyn Williams
Molly Kendall....................Virginia Lee Corbin
Cliff Kelley....................Pierre Gendron
Mike....................James Farley
Tim O'Day....................Ben Hendricks
Baby Molly....................Vondell Darr

This Leroy Scott story makes medium good screen fare. It won't set the world afire, but the name of James Cruze hooked up with it as the director should have some pulling quality at the box office. The tale has society and the slums mixed in; likewise, it is an attack on the type of hypocrite of social standing who, since the advent of prohibition, has made a private barroom of his home, though attacking the selling of liquor in public.

The story is admirably cast. Right at this time it must be said that Virginia Lee Corbin as the flapper makes a spot for herself in the picture world.

Little Molly O'Day is born in the saloon of her dad in a slum section. She is the heroine. Her father is shot in a barroom brawl before her eyes, and her mother decides the baby girl shall not be brought up in the saloon atmosphere. She continues to conduct the saloon, but sends her daughter into the home of a socially prominent but penniless widow, who rears the child as her niece for $20,000 a year.

With the child grown to flapperhood, prohibition comes along. Mother O'Day instead of still conducting a saloon converts her place into a swell cabaret and gets stiff prices. The best people patronize the resort. As she notes the flappers of about her own daughter's age getting tipsy she is thankful her girl is in safe hands, or at least she so believes. It is inevitable the girl should come to the place and in company with a greaseball who is on the fortune hunting trail. He announces his engagement to Mother O'Day, and she turns the girl from the place, at the same time resolving to save the girl if possible from the man.

In the end the mother is successful, but at the cost of revealing to the girl the history of her parentage. When the police start to take her fiance he pulls a gun and starts shooting, which immediately recalls to the girl's mind the picture of her father's death.

The direction is flawless and the story is carried along in a most interesting manner. The old New York scenes with the free and easy barroom and the atmospheric surroundings are exceedingly well worked out.

Louise Dresser handles the role of Mother O'Day, giving it all that could have been placed into the characterization by any one. Her transformation from the saloon-keeping widow to the stylish hostess of an all-night cabaret shows how capable an actress she is. Kathlyn Williams as the penniless society widow also handled a character role cleverly. Ricardo Cortez must have felt right at home in the heavy role, for it must have recalled his Broadway days to him. Pierre Grendon as the juvenile lead was the one faulty spot. He wasn't weighty enough for it.

"The City That Never Sleeps" may not be a world beater at the box office, but it is a picture the fans are going to enjoy. It also speaks the truth about the evils of prohibition, not only to the flappers, but to thousands upon thousands of the youth, boys and girls, of this country. The inside of that could not be told on the screen nor anywhere else, but it is known and may have been Dr. Murray Butler's best and most excellent reason why he decries the hypocrisy of prohibition.

Fred.

BARBARA FRIETCHIE

Thos. H. Ince Production featuring Florence Vidor and Edmund Lowe. Adapted from the Clyde Fitch play by Lambert Hillyer and Agnes Christine Johnson. Directed by Lambert Hilyer. Released by Producers' Distributing Corp. Shown as initial attraction at Piccadilly, New York, opening Sept. 26. Running time, 80 minutes.

Barbara Frietchie..........Florence Vidor
Captain Trumbull..........Edmund Lowe
Colonel Frietchie............Emmett King
Jack Negly...................Joe Bennett
Arthur Frietchie..........Charles Delaney
Colonel Negly...............Louis Fitzroy
Sue Royce.................Gertrude Short
Manning Lou...............Mattie Peters
Fred Gelwex................Slim Hamilton

"Barbara Frietchie," adapted by Clyde Fitch and presented on the screen as a Thos. H. Ince production, proves a real old-fashioned Civil War melodrama that has had a modern angle in the form of a short epilog, far from helping the play along.

The Fitch play was based on the poem, and the author took a number of liberties with the poem to give the piece love interest. Barbara became the young and beautiful daughter of a fiery old Southern Colonel, her brother a cadet at West Point. He brings his classmate with him when the two graduate, arriving at the Frietchie Maryland home on the day that war is declared between the North and the South.

Florence Vidor is the charming Barbara and she gives a truly fine performance. Playing opposite is Edmund Lowe as the Union officer who loves and is loved by the Southern girl. His performance places him with the foremost of the leading men of the screen.

On the night of the declaration of war, following hard on the heels of a declaration of 'ove between Barbara and Captain Trumbull, the latter leaves to return North to join the Union forces and Barbara says she never wishes to sse him again.

During the war he returns to the town at the head of the victorious Union troops, and saves the brother of the girl he loves (who was his West Point classmate) from capture as a spy.

Barbara then promises to marry him the next day in Hagerstown, despite her father's objections. When the marriage is to take place the Conferedates attack and the Union forces have to fall back. The Captain is wounded and brought to the Frietchie home in Frederickstown. The morning following Barbara, believing he has died, places the Union standard at half mast before her house just as the Confederate army comes marching through with General "Stonewall" Jackson at its head. Here is enacted the famous stanza of the poem and it is the one thrill in the picture—one that brings a sob.

As Barbara stands beside the flag in her grief a crazed rejected suitor of the girl disobeys the General's orders and fires, wounding her in the shoulder and she returns to the bedside of her dead. This is where the picture should end, but instead there is another sequence tacked on in which the Captain returns to life and after the war is over there is a double wedding.

Then 1917 with the grandson of Barbara and the Captain going forth "to make the world safe for Democracy." While it is a pretty bit, it doesn't seem to fit.

The picture is about 20 minutes too long at present and could easily be cut that much.

Lambert Hillyer has handled the direction very well and has some real thrilling battle scenes. There is one, the attack on the Confederate guns just prior to the wounding of the hero, that is corking stuff.

Joe Bennett plays the heavy and delivers a characterization that is really a work of art. His work in the scene in the Fritchie home after he has entered the Confederate army is a wow.

Fred.

IN HOLLYWOOD

Samuel Goldwyn presentation and a First National picture. Taken from the play, "Business Before Pleasure," by Montague Glass and Jules E. Goodman. Adapted by Frances Marion. Al Green, the director; Harry Hallenberg, photographer, and titles by Montague Glass. Cast features Alexander Carr, George Sidney, Vera Gordon and Betty Blythe. At the Strand, New York, week of Sept. 28. Running time, 72 minutes.

Alexander Carr........Mawruss Perlmutter
George Sidney..................Abe Potash
Vera Gordon..................Rosie Potash
Betty Blythe..................Rita Sismondi
Belle Bennett.............Mrs. Perlmutter
Anders Randolph................Blanchard
Peggy Shaw....................Irma Potash
Charles Meridith...........Sam Pemberton

A laugh-getting picture that starts like a whirlwind in provoking salvos for about the first 1,000 feet, then slows down and holds a normal pace until the climax. It's a good picture and can easily front any program house.

George Sidney, replacing the late lamented Barney Bernard, is an able choice. While perhaps missing the degree of pathos in his work Bernard gave out, nevertheless he gives a performance that is an assured fulfillment of the assignment. Carr has lost nothing during the interim since the last "Potash and Perlmutter" release.

The feature is abundant in titles, many reading as having been lifted intact from the play, and there is a snicker in all of them. Others often top the action for securing results, but most of the outstanding wordings are spotted up front and the pace is too fast to be consecutively equaled for 72 minutes. It looks to be a workmanlike piece upon the director's part. Green has carried the story along by steps which give no hint of stalling, and only at one point, in the later moments, has a tendency to lose its smoothness.

Something of a surprise may be the inclusion of the two Talmadge girls, Constance and Norma, who occupy the screen separately for brief bits. Both are applicants for the vampire role for which the heads of the concern have advertised. Each is a comedy scene.

A summary of the story would list the theme as telling of the trials and tribulations of the two P's invading the picture field from the producin gend. Including their families in the different casts, the troubles become plentiful, and when the vamp arrives the respective home camps of the men become tempestuous.

Everything and everybody is subjected to a certain amount of shading through Carr and Sidney, either together or singly, being constantly before the camera. Vera Gordon moderately plays Mrs. Potash and is not given overly prominent footage, while about the only other two principals to stand out are Betty Blythe as the vamp and Anders Randolph portraying the heavy.

Different instances glean of some one having delved back a few years for "business" episodes, but as a whole the picture is responsible for quite an amount of originality, and where there is any cause to fear weakness the sub-titles generally bolster.

It brought constant responses from a well-filled matinee audience at the Strand Sunday. It doesn't seem possible that any one, whether they get any laughs out of the film or not, can deny that this current depiction of Potash and Perlmutter has its points.

Skig.

THREE WOMEN

Ernst Lubitsch Production presented by the Warner Bros. Directed by Ernst Lubitsch, featuring May McAvoy, Pauline Frederick, Marie Prevost and Lew Cody. Shown at the Strand, N. Y., week Oct. 5, 1924. Running time, 82 mins.

Jeanne Wilton.................May McAvoy
Mabel Wilton, her mother.Pauline Frederick
Harriett.......................Marie Prevost
George Lamont....................Lew Cody
John W. Howard.............Willard Louis
Fred Colman................Pierre Gendron
His Mother......................Mary Carr
Fred's friend..............Raymond McKeee

"Three Women" is an exposition of as pretty a piece of direction as has been seen on the screen in some time. For this Ernst Lubitsch is to be credited. With it all there is a story that will get to audiences, women especially, for it is a type of society drama that they all like in the picture houses. This, in addition to a quartet of names that mean a lot at the box office, makes this a sure-fire production to pull money.

There is one thing that audiences wont want until they have seen the picture, for Pauline Frederick is not yet of the age where she is to be relegated to "mother roles." In this picture she plays a mother to an 18-year-old daughter. However, the manner in which the story is handled and the characterization that Miss Frederick gives makes her just as charming as in the days when she served tea in her dressing-room at the old Savoy theatre on West 34th street. Pauline Frederick playing mother to Mac McAvoy is something of a shock at first glance, but not so great after one has seen the picture.

The heavy is handled by Lew Cody, who appears as a penniless Don Juan and lays siege to the heart of the $3,000,000 widow, Pauline Frederick. She is strikingly bedecked in jewels, and Cody, with his creditors hounding him, steps right into the picture, and before long manages to lay a touch for $100,000, which is pretty heavy lover stuff, even with a $3,000,000 widow. He is not aware that she has a daughter until the night he makes the heavy touch. The young girl has returned from school unawares and stepped right into her mother's romance. When Cody hears that the daughter is to receive half of the family fortune on her marriage he lays plans to win her; in fact, he compromises her, which makes the marriage a necessity. As soon as the ceremony is set he starts playing around on the outside and sets up a second establishment, which is where the third woman comes in. She is Marie Prevost; but her's is little better than a bit in the picture.

In the finish it is the wife's mother that comes into the breach to save her daughter's happiness, and when her former lover attacks her she shoots him down, finally being acquitted for the crime. This leaves the daughter free to revive a school-time romance and bring about a happy ending.

In flavor the story is decidedly European, although its scenes are laid principally in New York, with a few early shots in Berkeley, Calif.

Lubitsch does not resort to but one written title to convey the entire story of the young daughter's downfall in the entire sequence. That is direction. Everything is suggetsion in facial expression, without a single scene that anyone, censor or otherwise, could find fault with.

Cody in his role is magnificent, but it is to Pauline Frederick that the honors for the best performance in the picture must be handed. She walked away with every scene she was on in, no matter who was playing opposite. May McAvoy displayed decided talent as the daughter, but she could not for a moment compete with the more experienced actress. Willard Louis, in a comedy role, handled himself competently, while Mary Carr also filled in aptly in several scenes. Raymond McKee and Pierre Grendon are also in the cast, completing a list of names that might well be designated as "All Star."

The sets and the lightings are as near perfect as have been seen in some time, and the story is carried along so smoothly that there is not a draggy spot in the picture.

This one will get money.

Fred.

HIS HOUR

Louis B. Mayer production of the Elinor Glyn story. Scenario by Elinor Glyn and direction by King Vidor. At the Capitol, New York, Oct. 5. Distributed through Metro-Goldwyn. Running time, 65 mins.

Tamara Loraine.............Aileen Pringle
Prince Gritzko..................John Gilbert
Princess Ardacheff...........Emily Fitzroy
Count Boris................Bertram Grassby

Whatever may be the merits of Elinor Glyn's writings, and a world of literary gentlemen have decreed that she is as negligible as last year's snow, it is a cinch the lady has a box-office potency. In her films for Metro she is generally accredited with turning out money-makers, and in "His Hour" she has repeated.

The sex stuff, as sensational as the screen and the censors allow, is her main prop. In New York, California, Chicago and free-thinking centers she is all to the mustard as far as delivering that sensation goes; but down in Maryland, out in Ohio, over in Pennsylvania and a few other centers where Democrats, Republicans and Methodists control the censor board her films lose their kick.

In the latest tome of gushing, passionate screen writing Elinor has worked a gentle-born Englishwoman against a stubborn and half-barbarian Russian prince. The prince wants the woman. The woman doesn't want the prince. He is persistent. In St. Petersburg he tricks her to his home. She faints. Upon awakening she finds her waist torn open (the prince had done that to see whether her heart was beating and also because it furnished the dirt punch of the film) and the woman assumed immediately that she had been violated. Thereupon she married the prince, only to find out later that he loved her and that when "his hour" arrived he had let it slide.

John Gilbert is the prince and Aileen Pringle the woman. Bertram Grassby as Count Boris, who also loved the woman, turns in a far better performance than either of the two principals, while many of the minor characters do outstanding work. Gilbert is very actory in his role. Miss Pringle stands still, emoting silently and stoically. The others are sufficient unto their parts.

The settings are very handsome and in gaudy movie taste. The same goes for the costumes and certain winter exteriors in St. Petersburg. The continuity of the film is monotonous and the direction not particularly inspired.

"His Hour" is not a great picture, but on the strength of its paper-back sensationalism and its expensive production it should stand up financially well in the towns where censorship isn't prevalent, and should do moderately in the places where the shears get exercise.

At the Capitol Sunday it drew tremendous audiences that stretched down the street and around the corner for the first night performance. Its start-off should be indicative of what it will do in oher big centers.

Sisk.

HER LOVE STORY

Alan Dwan Production presented by Adolph Zukor and Jesse L. Lasky. From the story by Mary Roberts Rinehart, adapted by Frank Tuttle, directed by Alan Dwan. Starring Gloria Swanson. Shown at the Rivoli, N. Y., week of Oct. 5, 1924. Running time, 74 minutes.

Princess Marie..............Gloria Swanson
Capt. Rudi........................Ian Keith
Archduke.....................George Fawcett
The King.......................Echlin Gayer
Prime Minister...............Mario Majeroni
Archduke's Adviser..........Sidney Herbert
Court Physician.................Donald Hall
Lady-in-Waiting....Baroness de Hedemann
Clothilde, maid.................Jane Auburn

The Boy....................................Bert Wales
Minister of War............Gen. Lodijensky

Here is a picture who's popularity will depend on the fact of whether the cycle in fiction likes has swung fully around to the point where the public is ready to accept a yarn of the Graustark type again. It seems hardly probable that Broadway will want it or that the Main Street folks will go wild about it.

There is one thing, however, in the picture's favor, and that is the coupling of the name Gloria Swanson with the title of the picture, "Her Love Story." That combination may do the trick, but it is a certainty this picture will not get the money that the last two or three Swansons took in the big houses in the key cities. In the smaller towns it may do even better than some of the former releases, but not at the Rivoli or the houses of that caliber.

The story, in brief, is that of the young and beautiful daughter of the Archduke of a small Balkan principality who, although in love with the Captain of the Guards in her father's palace, is betrothed to the ruler of a neighboring kingdom. But before this takes place she marries the young captain in a Gypsy camp by Gypsy ceremony, and the night of the ceremony he manages to slip into her chamber. The next day he is thrown in jail and the princess is married off with royal pomp to the king, whereupon the captain is exiled.

Sometime later a child is born. It is a boy and hailed throughout the kingdom as the heir to the throne. Then the queen mother declares to the king that it is not his son, a fact that he is fully aware of because of the premature birth, and in his wrath he orders the queen confined in a convent as insane, but retains the young prince because he fears for the continuance of his reign should the public become aware of the true situation.

A faithful maid of the queen sends letters broadcast to the captain who has fled the country believing the message that he received from the archduke to the effect that his daughter had consented to marry the king and that she hoped that he would not pursue his friendship for her in the future. One of these letters finally reach him after about five years, and he learns the true state of affairs and hurries back to his native land and rescues the queen from her imprisonment and later helps her to secure possession of her son, he still believing that it is the child of the king. It is not until the latter's death that he is brought to the realization that it is his own child and that the queen mother has remained faithful to her gypsy marriage vows.

Alan Dwan has not attacked the story from the point of greatest vantage, and his direction cannot be said to have brought it out to its fullest extent but as a program picture it will pass.

Gloria Swanson is delightful as the young princess and magnificent as the queen. The one scene alone, where she is being torn from the cradle of her son, is worth sitting through the picture. Ian Keith, who plays opposite her, manages well enough as the captain, but he failed to impress greatly. George Fawcett, superb actor that he is, manages to create a certain atmosphere about the archduke that is along the lines of his usual well-developed work. The balance of the cast carried along their roles in a satisfactory manner. *Fred.*

Story Without a Name

Paramount picture written by Arthur Stringer and directed by Irvin Willat. Adapted by Victor Irvin. Agnes Ayres and Antonio Moreno featured. At the Rialto, New York, Oct. 5. Running time, 74 mins.
Mary Walsworth.............Agnes Ayres
Alan Holt.................Antonio Moreno
Drakma ....Tyrone Power
Kurder ....Louis Wolheim
Claire ....Dagmar Godowsky
Don Powell ....Jack Bohn
The Cripple ....Maurice Costello

Whatever the gag may be in releasing this member of the "Famous Forty" under its present title is unknown, but where one expects to see something serious enough to provoke discussion over its titular appellation, one finds a melodramatic thriller that makes the independents look sick. Not that it is so good, but so melodramatic and blatant in its hoke heroics.

The plot tells of an inventor with a radio death ray, the same sort of stuff which recently received much publicity in the dailies. He loves a lady. The head of a bootlegging mob off the Bahamas wants his radio death ray. The gang leader captures the man and his lady fair. Marooned on a coral island, the hero rigs up a sending station and shoots his message for help just at the time the President is about to broadcast his speech. The air being clear, everyone hears his help cry and immedately the Navy effects a rescue.

It is all very childish and obvious. It is, however, exceptionally well produced, without being well acted, save for Louis Wolheim's part.

Some of the sea shots are great, although miniatures of vessels are used. The action stuff, too, is smeared on heavy.

Because it is so very melodramatic the impression is given that the big cities won't take so kindly to it, but in the wheat and corn belts they will probably sit in open mouthed amazement and applaud at the proper time.

"The Story Without a Name" has its place in the movie sphere but that place isn't in the expensive "Famous Forty" list, nor in a first run theatre.

This one was strictly built for the sticks. *Sisk.*

THE WARRENS OF VIRGINIA

William Fox Production, based on the play by William C. DeMille, originally produced by David Belasco. Directed by Elmer Clifton. Shown at Loew's New York, N. Y., Oct. Running time, 78 minutes. Only male members of cast named.

Fox production in the making of which Martha Mansfield lost her life. That is the reason for the failure to mention any of the women of the picture in the title leader. Only the men are mentioned, and of the lot there is but one who stands out, the hero played by Wilfred Lytell opposite Miss Mansfield in the role of Lieut. Burton. Miss Mansfield had the role of the daughter of the Warrens.

There is an effort made to make the picture stand on the fact that it features the characters of General U. S. Grant and General Robert E. Lee in the advertising, but in reality they are decidedly subsidiary characters to the hero and heroine, who carry the real story.

At the New York Monday night the picture seemingly did not pull particularly at the box office. The plain title of "The Warrens of Virginia" without the names of any star displayed in front of the house did not seem to attract.

There is also failure to credit Elmer Clifton as director on the leader, not that credit would have meant anything to him, for it is hard to believe that the same man who turned out "Down to the Sea in Ships" is responsible for this one. The "Warrens" is just another Civil War drama.

The time of the story is laid almost at the close of the Civil War when the fighting just prior to Lee's surrender was waged about the home of the Warrens in Virginia.

It is a tale of a Southern girl and a Northern officer, with the pair torn between love and duty. The same old story and handled pretty much in the same old way.

Had Martha Mansfield lived she gave promise in this picture of being a screen actress of some ability, a good ingenue lead for program productions.

Otherwise the best that can be said for "The Warrens of Virginia" is that it is good enough to stand up on double feature bills. *Fred.*

LIFE'S GREATEST GAME

Emory Johnson production, released by FBO. Story and direction by Emory Johnson. Featuring Johnnie Walker. Shown at the Cameo, New York, for two weeks, at the Cameo, New York, week Sept. 28. Running time, 82 minutes.
Jack Donovan..................Tom Santschi
His Wife.......................Jane Thomas
Mike Moran......................Dave Kirby

Decidedly wearying picture. It is much too long and could stand cutting. Whatever the reason for a Broadway showing is, it doesn't appear on the screen. It seemingly must be that FBO feels it needs the Broadway run to the credit of the picture to enable them to jack up the prices on the exhibitors. The picture itself does not qualify for an extraordinary rental.

There are really two distinct epochs told. The first is of the period when baseball players wore mustaches and sideburns and the latter of present day baseball.

Jack Donovan is the star pitcher of the old Chicago club. A gambler who could not get him to throw the deciding game of a crucial series which decided the pennant, frames the pitcher to make him believe his wife has been faithless and that the child he has believed his own is not. When the player discovers the truth his wife and the child have sailed for Europe but missed the boat.

The steamer is wrecked and his family are reported among the missing. Later when they have been rescued he fails to note it in the papers. Years after when his son has grown to young manhood and has pitched a college game a scout of the big league team the father is managing picks up the boy. The latter on meeting his father keeps his true identity hidden and finally at the precise minute of the crucial game for the world's championship between the Giants and the Yanks, the kid, though a rookie, is put in the box and saves the day by pitching a flawless inning, adding a heavy clout to cinch the world's championship, practically single handed.

For around the country the picture is a good bet during the world series time. Other than that it is a picture for the house where the regular policy is a daily change.

Johnnie Walker does fairly well with a role that has no particular punch. Tom Santschi in reality is the star. Balance of the cast fair.

For the baseball shots of the big series those taken by news reels have been pieced, in which the shots with the principals of the picture's cast. The matching is not very well done.

Twenty minutes cut out and it would be a far better feature. *Fred.*

FIGHTING FURY

Universal five-reeler of Jack Hoxie western series. At the Stanley, New York, Oct. 3. Running time, 58 mins.

Better than the average can be credited to this one of the seemingly unlimited western series flooding the cheaper screen throughout the country.

Hoxie is cast as a Mexican with a grudge against the crooked owner of a ranch. Securing employment on the ranch, which devotes its activities more to cattle rustling than to cattle raising, Hoxie and a companion eventually round up the entire gang of thieves and give them bitter medicine.

It has fast riding, magnificent scenery and a good all-round cast boasting no "names." Its production apparently hasn't entailed any great expense, but it hasn't the appearance of being so blatantly cheap as some of the others on exhibition.

As a program for the cheaper and smaller houses catering to a more or less male audience it is a good bet. *Sisk.*

DYNAMITE DAN

Anthony J. Xidias presents. Sunset Production featuring Kenneth MacDonald. Written and directed by Bruce Mitchell. Photographed by Bert Longnecker. Distributed by Aywon Film Co. At Loew's New York as half the bill Oct. 3. Runs about 55 mins.
Dan..............................Kenneth MacDonald
Boss...................................Frank Rice
Tony..................................Boris Karcia
Sherlock Jones......................Eddie Harris
Helen..................................Diana Alden
Brute Lacy...........................Harry Woods
Manager...........................Jack Richardson

This one is so bad you can't get het up about it; you've got to laugh at its weaknesses and accept its ridiculousness with as much good humor as possible. There are moments when it seems certain that Bruce Mitchell was having a little fun at the expense of a gullible public, because it is almost impossible that a director should offer to adult picturegoers such asinine material as "Dynamite Dan" holds.

Never in the wildest dreams of Alger, Henty, Barbour and the gentlemen who wrote the classic "Rover Boys" and "Frank Merriwell" series was there pictured such a hero as Kenneth MacDonald portrays in this film. He is first shown as a day laborer wheeling a load of bricks while dressed in spotless white flannels, sport shirt and hair slicked back.

The gallant hod carrier's "steady" is the belle of the neighboring exclusive finishing school. His opportunity to shine comes when he finds the heavyweight champ and his manager insulting the girl and her friend. One little left hook to the jaw drops the champ for the count, and the manager doesn't require half that much. So Kenneth becomes a pug, and, after winning some 21 fights in the first round or thereabouts, he tools off the champ again, this time in the title battle, at which there must be 100 people present.

There is some poisonous near-comedy attempted by an amateur detective nuisance and some shots in the gymnasium of the girls' school that, looked at from one point of view—the essentially masculine one—are the only invigorating moments of the picture. MacDonald, unfortunately, is no better an actor than a boxer, and in the latter category he makes Firpo look like Pavlova. The rest of the cast is not much better, although Diana Alden has her moments of charm.

A college audience would have a great time at "Dynamite Dan." But for a metropolitan downtown theatre it is an atrocity.

FIND YOUR MAN

Warner Brothers' picture, starring Rin Tin Tin and releasing through Apollo Exchange. Directed by Mal St. Clair. Cast includes Eric St. Clair, June Marlow, Charles Mails and Pat Hartigan. Showing at Moss' Broadway, New York, Sept. 22. Running time, 68 minutes.

Everything framed to bring the dog, Rin Tin Tin, to the front, and an interesting feature from the canine angle. The animal's main forte would seem to be jumping, and a couple he cuts loose are corkers, as is also the leap up a chimney which runs from the ground.

Starting on the other side during the war, it shows the dog in the Red

Cross service, after which the locale takes a leap to his adopter, back home and broke, finally locating his fiance in a lumber camp in the north woods.

The villain, court trial for a murder and the happy ending follow in sequence, with the dog pulling the characters out of every jam the scenario places them in.

Given to unnecessary footage, in various passages, registers as the picture's principal obstruction, with the story necessarily curtailed by the limitations of its star. Productionally the film calls for no extensive interior work, with a majority of the shots being in the open, supplemented by cabin scenes.

Pat Hartigan gives a neat performance as the lumber thief, overshadowing both Eric St. Clair and June Marlow, who hold the love interest, although both of the latter meet requirements.

Mal St. Clair, directing, has balanced nicely, without making the feats of Rin Tin Tin too impossible, and has slipped in a few instances of comedy distinctly valuable and nicely spotted.

The picture looks to have every chance to get by on the strength of the dog, which is certainly both a beautiful and well-trained animal.

Skig.

GIRL IN LIMOUSINE

I. N. Chadwick production starring Larry Semon. From the play by Avery Hopwood and Wilson Collison. Directed by Noel Mason Smith; supervised by Larry Semon. First National release. At Loew's New York as half the bill Oct. 3. Runs about 70 mins.

Betty	Claire Adams
Freddie	Oliver N. Hardie
Tony	Larry Semon
Riggs	Charles Murray
Bernice	Florence Gilbert

Larry Semon's first feature-length comedy is a disappointment. As farce it misses almost completely and as slap-stick it is far too long. There are laughs, but in all the five reels there are not as many real guffaws as there have been in several of the Semon short comedies.

Semon probably will never be a genuine farceur. He is a particularly bad choice, and, since the direction and the rest of the cast are couched in similar broad pie-throwing terms, the stage hit of Avery Hopwood and Wilson Collison loses almost all the farcical lustre it possessed when produced as a play five years ago.

Opportunity after opportunity has been muffed. All side plots of the original story have been dropped, the picture concerning itself with the adventures of Tony when dumped unaware into the room in which the girl he didn't marry but wanted to is sleeping. There are some good bits, but even in these the laughs come more from such incidents as Semon bumping himself headlong into a deceptive mirror than the cleverly thought-out by-play seen in first-rate long comedies.

There can be no complaint on the score of action, as the film is brimful with it, although it does drag interminably toward the finish. The fight scenes are jammed with motion, and in the end a chase with autos, trains and motorcycles is well pictured.

Semon is hard to take seriously in the quieter passages of the films. He is never more than a clown, lacking wistful poignancy when things go wrong. Charlie Murray has practically nothing to do; Claire Adams is restful on the optic nerves, and the balance of the cast satisfactory.

"The Girl in the Limousine" will do for the average program house, but is not a first-run feature by any stretch of the imagination. What Semon needs for a long picture is pure rough-house stuff with a barrel of new ideas.

THAT FRENCH LADY

William Fox production starring Shirley Mason. Adapted from the William J. Hurlburt play, "The Strange Woman," by Charles Kenyon. Directed by Edmund Mortimer. Shown at Loew's Circle, New York, double feature bill, Sept. 18. Running time, 57 minutes.

Inez De Pierrefond	Shirley Mason
John Hemingway	Theodore Von Eltz
Charles Abbey	Harold Goodwin
Uncle Walter	Charles Coleman

The play on which this picture is based could easily have been adapted in a manner that would have made this picture a very rough affair. As it stands it is simply a harmless little feature, entertaining in spots and laughable at times. It is a tale of small town hypocrisy in the United States, with some of the action laid in Paris.

A small town American boy goes abroad to study and meets a youthful widow whose first marriage has given her a set purpose in life, that of saving other women from a fate similar to hers, and she writes a book on the subject.

Observation has brought her to the decision that free love is the best way. She and the boy fall in love, and three years later, when he is returning home, he asks her to accompany him as his wife. This she refuses to do. She is willing to make the trip with him and live with him, but the marriage part is out.

She does come to America, and when the two arrive at the small town that the boy hails from the tongues start wagging, especially when one of the women secures a copy of the book written in Paris.

In the end the usual wedding bells.

The development in the earlier reels is rather slow, but the small town stuff has a kick through a number of character types.

Shirley Mason makes a happy lead, but Theodore Von Eltz at times seems a little aged for the part. This may have been due to the lighting as much as anything else, as Miss Mason also seemed to suffer from the same thing. The balance of the cast is adequate.

Fair little feature of the cheaper grade.

Fred.

A BRIDE FOR A KNIGHT

Produced by the Syracuse Pictures Corp. Featuring Henry Hull and Mary Thurman. Dialog and titles by Jos. W. Farnham. Shown at the Stanley, N. Y., Oct. 6. Running time, 59 minutes.

Jimmy Poe	Henry Hull
Jean Hawthorne	Mary Thurman
Aunt Octovia	Marcia Harris
Uncle Frank	Wm. H. Tooker

A picture that started with an idea but ended in a tragedy. Of 33 people present on the lower floor of the Stanley Monday night six men and one women were asleep. In the 33 the reviewer is counted and he had to remain awake.

The idea is that a weak farce comedy was taken and pepped up with a new title scheme. It was the plan of putting the story up to the audience. The producers confessed that they had the actors, the studio and the money, but they didn't have a story, so it was up to the audience to go out with them and look for one.

That was a pretty good introduction, but that is about as far as it went. From that point on the titles were of the question and answer sort. "Well, what will we do now?" "What about going to the park and looking for a plot there even though it would be easier to find one in a cemetery." That was the idea all the way through, just cheap punning.

The story has a young short story writer as the hero and a girl who is interested in art as the heroine. They are engaged, but she finds him chatting with another girl at a studio party, and breaks the engagement. The boy's aunt, who is wealthy, wants to see the match carried out, so she sends the boy notification that if he is married to the girl by midnight of the following night all will be well and he will get $50,000.

The boy gets mixed up with a flock of crooks and finally a couple of detectives, but in the end all is straightened out there is a fairly good final shot to the picture.

Henry Hull rather overacted as the young writer and Mary Thurman seemed a little too mature for the giddy young thing. At that she looked pretty good in the bedroom scenes.

The picture is distinctly a commercial product. Made for a little nickel and supposed sold to the exhibitors on the same basis, that is about all it is worth.

Fred.

LOOPED FOR LIFE

J. Joseph Saneth production, released by Madoc Sales Co., starring Art Acord, directed by Park B. Frame and photographed by Chuck Welty. At the Stanley one day (Sept. 15). Runs 50 minutes.

Buck Dwan	Art Acord
Jack Hawkesby	Jack Richardson
Mary Baker	Marcella Pershing
Sheriff	Charles Adler

"Looped for Life" must be labelled a bad boy, even considering it comes in the category of those cheaper westerns whose entertainment average is not very high. Besides its short running time, the only favorable things that might be said of it are that it has a fair share of western small-town atmosphere and the exterior photographic shots are nearly up to the standard in beauty and scope.

There has seldom been a film with so pitiful a share of continuity, such inexpert direction and so tottering a plot.

For some reason, the heavy is first introduced as a lifelong friend of the hero, a most likable fellow, whose surprising descent to villainy is caused over-night by one pang of jealousy and one pint of Scotch. All the way through, one expects him either to reform or die penitent, but the film ends suddenly after the hero's last hair-breadth escape, giving one more reason for the audience's apparent dissatisfaction with the scenario.

Art Acord is given opportunity for broncho taming, lariat swinging, hard riding and other characteristic western amusements, at all of which he is sufficiently adept. His acting, however, cannot be compared to certain others of the western stars, although he does stand above the rest of the company as John Barrymore would in a coffee-and-cake vaudeville show.

"Looped for Life" is for the sticks.

DANGEROUS COWARD

Andrew Callaghan production starring Fred Thompson. Story by Marion Jackson, directed by Albert Rogell. Loew's Circle, New York, double feature bill, Sept. 18, one day. Running time, 53 minutes.

Wildcat Rea	Frank Hagney
Conchita	Lillian Adrain
The Weazel	Jim Corey
David McGinn	Andrew Arbuckle
May McGinn	Hazel Keener
Red O'Hara	David Kirby
Battling Benson	Al Kaufman
Bob Treat	Fred Thomson
Silver King	Himself

One of the best of this particular type of Western that has come along in some time. The picture was originally scheduled for release some months ago, but it only came to Broadway during the last few weeks. It has everything the crowd can ask for. It is a story with a prize fight angle, full of thrills, a couple of corking chases, a little love theme nicely done, and in all very satisfactory entertainment for the screen.

Fred Thomson is coming along, and if they continue to handle him as they have in this picture and supply him with as good story material this boy is going to be one of the prime box office favorites for the popular-priced houses where they eat up this Western stuff.

Hazel Keener, playing opposite, is decidedly clever. She is the personification of naturalness and never overacts.

The direction must also come in for commendation. Albert Rogell has done some corking work. His catching of close-up shots around the ringside in the prize fight scenes and the shots of the fighters from overhead were corking. The action moves along without stalling, and there is a lot of welcome comedy relief.

Thomson is a prize ring favorite who was on his way to a championship when he quit and went to cow-herding. The reason for leaving the ring was he was under the impression in a fight he had crippled his opponent for life. It later developed the opponent was only posing so that he might pick up an easy existence at the expense of the better fighter.

The action takes place in a small Western town where the pooh-bah is the former heavyweight champ. He runs the works, a dance and gambling hall, and on the side promotes sporting events, the program being one week a rodeo and the next a prize fight. The young fighter becomes a favorite and champion in the cowboy sports, but will not go into the ring. Finally his old manager drifts into the town and recognizes him, with the result that he finally does go into the ring to save the boys of the town from a trimming the heavyweight has engineered to make a money clean-up and a getaway. He is the winner, and then he has to chase the departing pooh-bah to get the coin he is making away with.

There are some tense minutes in the fight scenes, and the excitement is held high with the audience. There are some real thrills in the chase, with a Ford careening along a road at the edge of a cliff with a fight going on in the car. All good stuff.

"The Dangerous Coward" is a picture that can go into any of the neighborhood houses and get by.

Fred.

THE NAVIGATOR

Metro-Goldwyn picture and a Joseph M. Schenck presentation. Starring Buster Keaton. Story by Jean Havez, Clyde Bruckman and Joe Mitchell. Directed by Donald Crisp and Buster Keaton. Cast includes Kathryn McGuire, Frederick Vroom, Noble Johnson, Clarence Burton and H. M. Clugston. At the Capitol, New York, week of Oct. 12. Running time, 60 mins.

Keaton's latest and extended comedy is spotty. That is to say it's both commonplace and novel, with the latter achievement sufficient to make the picture a laugh getter and an established program leader. Columbus Day at the Capitol saw a house jammed to the doors. Though the laughs came late in the footage they were there nevertheless, with the audience giving every indication of being well satisfied.

The film is novel in that it has Keaton in a deep sea diving outfit with the camera catching him under water for comedy insertions. There's a possibility of doubling during some of the action, but close-ups are registered under water that reveal Keaton, personally, behind the glass within the helmet. There's an abundance of funny business in connection with Keaton's going overboard to fix a propeller shaft and a thrill has been inserted through the comedian getting mixed up with a devil fish. That passage is cut to the mere facts, with the supposed struggle blinded by a rock, but an effective insertion. Another outstanding submerged laugh provoker is in Keaton's being attacked by a sword fish which he catches in his hands and uses to duel with a second fish of a like specie. That one drew plenty from the witnessing throng.

The actual story carries little weight. It has Keaton as a wealthy young man being matrimonially rejected by the girl. Having secured passage to Hawaii he unknowingly boards a deserted steamship selected to be destroyed by foreign and warring factions. The girl's father, owner of the vessel, visits the dock, is set upon by the rogues who are bent on casting the liner adrift, and when the girl goes to her parent's rescue she is also caught on board with no chance of a return to land.

That about sums up the script layout, whence follows the much-abused improvising of eating utensils and the final grounding of the vessel off a cannibal island. The rescue is accomplished through Keaton and the girl attempting to drown together, going under but coming up on top of a rising submarine.

The entire action practically takes place on the deserted ship, with the girl (Kathryn McGuire) and Keaton the only figures. The remainder of the players are simply used to get the story under way and to effect a suitable conclusion.

A deft title writer would have been invaluable during the first reel, as the feature undoubtedly is slow in getting away. But at least it builds as it runs, with the genuine howls coming in the scare stuff inserted during the action aboard ship. Incidentally, it begins to look as if film audiences were in for an epidemic of scare stuff, as with the advent of the major comedy units becoming disciples of this type of entertainment it can be imagined what the smaller companies will turn out in following the lead.

However, there's an abundance of amusement contained in this latest Keaton release, and while Keaton, himself, has done better work in previous efforts, the gag bits will uphold the picture beyond a flop classification. Besides which the novelty of the under-water stuff is a sure attention bringer, if nothing else. ***Skig.***

TARNISH

Gilbert Emery play picturized by Samuel Goldwyn. Adapted by Frances Marion and directed by George Fitzmaurice. Mae McAvoy, Marie Prevost, Ronald Colman and Albert Gran featured. At the Strand, New York, week Oct. 12. Running time, 73 mins.

Letitia (Tishy) Tevis	May McAvoy
Emmett Carr	Ronald Colman
Nettie Dark	Marie Prevost
Adolph Tevis	Albert Gran
Mrs. Tevis	Mrs. Russ Whytall
Aggie	Priscilla Bonner
Mrs. Stutt	Kay Deslys
Mrs. Healy	Lydia Titus

"Tarnish" was bought by Samuel Goldwyn at a price reported as $75,000. Then Will Hays said that it shouldn't be produced, that its theme wasn't entirely suitable for the screen. During the interim, however, Paramount and Metro cut loose with some pretty sexy stuff that Hays didn't forbid, so "Tarnish" naturally wasn't banned, nor did anyone expect that it would be, despite the Hays pronunciamento.

Some folks recently hailed the picture as a masterpiece. Taking their cue from the fact that the play itself was one of the finest written in the last decade, they touted the film as being even better.

They're wrong, for as far as commercial and artistic values are concerned, "Tarnish" is just a good picture of average quality and not nearly so effective on the screen as on the stage.

The story concerns Tishy Tevis, the daughter of Adolph and Mrs. Tevis. She shoulders responsibilities of a family once rich but now poor and proud. The father, always a rake and a blow-hard, is a spendthrift. Any manicurist with a good line can "take" the old boy for his roll. The climax of the film comes when Tishy goes to recover $500 **which a shady lady (Nettie Dark) had taken from the father. In Nettie's apartment Tishy finds her sweetheart, Emmett Carr. Disheartened, disillusioned and crushed, Tishy tells Emmett never to see her again.**

Emmett, however, had behaved himself since going with Tishy. He had explained to her that before meeting her he had done things of which he was now ashamed—that he was perhaps tarnished. And Tishy, loving him, told him that tarnish could be cleaned. His visit to Nettie's apartment was a frame, he having been lured there on the pretext that Nettie was ill and desperate.

So, enraged and stubborn enough to persist in winning Tishy, he forces Nettie to go with him to her apartment, late at night, and tell the truth. They go, and explain. Tishy is adamant. So Emmett, bowed and repentant, leaves her front door and sits on the steps, crying. Up walks old Mrs. Healy, Tishy's girlhood nurse, and sensing the trouble and talks to Tishy, which brings about a happy ending.

The principal situation in this play is novel and strong, the idea of having a girl's father and sweetheart both mixed up with the same woman.

The action of the play is on a New Year's Eve. Because of this, **Fitzmaurice, the director, has made much of the alternating and contrasting joy and sorrow in Tishy's heart. The frolicking crowds are shown often and with good effect.** Another addition to the play is what corresponds to a brief prologue when three 1890 flappers predict the ultimate end of Mr. Tevis, for then he was a gay dog.

May McAvoy has the Tishy role, and despite her pretty face, she doesn't nearly plumb those emotional depths requisite to an adequate portrayal. On the other hand, Marie Prevost as the manicurist is excellent, and Ronald Colman, as Emmett Carr, is the best thing in the film. Albert Gran and Mrs. Russ Whytall have the roles which they played on the stage. The rest of the cast is quite competent. The direction is fair enough, but the terrific punch expected when Nettie and Tishy meet (and on the stage it was a smash) is absent. In fact, what should have been an inspired production seems strangely uninspired and workmanlike.

"Tarnish" didn't pack the Strand Sunday afternoon, even with a fine surrounding program. It is forecast that it's week's business will be good but not smashing, and that throughout the country, where the play has not yet been seen, the interest in it will be no greater than **the interest in the ordinary first-run special.**

Despite what the Hays' announcement might have inferred, there is no suggestion of vulgarity in the film except a bathroom scene with a woman in the tub, the director's addition to the script. Everything in the picture, while concerned with sex to a certain extent, is life-like, natural and vital to the carrying out of an intensely strong story.

That story, however, stood up better when supported with Emery's magnificent dialogue than with Sam Goldwyn's flicker cast. ***Sisk.***

ROARING RAILS

Hunt Stromberg production starring Harry Carey, distributed through Producers Distributing Corporation. Story and scenario by Stromberg and Doris Dorn; directed by Tom Forman; photographed by Sol Polito. At Cameo, New York, week Oct. 12. Running time, about 60 minutes.

Big Bill Benson	Harry Carey
Little Bill	Frankie Darro
Nora Burke	Edith Roberts
Malcolm Gregory	Wallace MacDonald
Red Burley	Frank Hagney

A substantial release feature of the melodramatic and romantic type. It holds one or two new twists to an not unfamiliar tale otherwise.

Starts with a shot of the A. E. F. at Chateau Thierry, but just a few flashes to plant the tale. Thereafter **it shifts over here, to the west in the days when the railroads were making their slow but certain way to the Pacific Coast.**

On the melodramatic side is action, plenty of it, besides a railroad head-on collision, and explosions, while for romance is the mutual love of the former A. E. F. soldier and the little French boy he promised a dying mother in France he would care for, though mother and son were strangers to him.

One twist is where the A. E. F. agreed to give up his life to save the sight of the boy blinded in the explosion. Another is where he believed his love for the foster-son was stronger than that for the girl who confessed to him in his prison cell she loved him.

Picture license has been allowed for. That enters under the heading of faith. Some of the most striking bits are somewhat vague in completion of detail, suggesting inserts in two or three spots, while at other times there is too much detail, but this does not necessarily count against the direction. That direction is smooth and stirring, for a fist fight here is but an incident.

One of the best scenes should be hugged to death by all railroad men. It is the bit where Bill Benson (Mr. Carey) while driving the engine in **its** cab and to rescue his little lad **who** had near-fallen out over the **side** after hiding in the tool box, **necessarily** overlooked a danger signal set against the next block. His **train** ran into a free engine, both **head**-oning in the centre of a bridge **over** a deep ravine. That bit is a convincer for the "human element" that is and always has been as it must be, considered with all of the safety appliance devices of the universe on the railroads.

From there, Bill became a bum, riding the rods and taking the boy with him. This little boy (Frankie Darro) is not only a likeable kid in the picture but he was consummately coached. To see him cry when his "Pop" was about to send him away to board was well worth watching.

Then, again, at the bridge explosion, to prevent the execution of a **contract, with plenty of villainy around, the boy was blinded, needing money for an operation Bill could not afford nor borrow. Bill agreed to confess he was a murderer to save the son of a railroad president if the son would agree to see that Little Bill got the operation necessary to save his eyesight.**

That's when Nora Burke (Miss Roberts) commenced to loom up. It made the other love angle.

And still later, another twist, when Bill, an escaped murderer (by Nora's aid) drove the first engine through a burning forest, not to protect the contract of the millionaires as they thought, but to rescue his little boy from a cabin in the midst of the fire.

That got Bill freedom and a regular job driving the Limited on the new road.

This production is rather expensive looking for its kind. Despite inserts for anything else it does look money for extras and scenes, although the entire picture is mostly out of doors. It's rather unique in that respect.

"Roaring Rails" is an unsexed romance of thrills that leaves a yearning for the heroic instead of whatever the sex pictures may leave.

It will stand up as a regular release—it's one of those reliables—the best kind of pictures ever made for program service. ***Sime.***

DANGEROUS MONEY

Presented by Adolph Zukor and Jesse L. Lasky, starring Bebe Daniels. Based on Robert Herrick's novel, "Clark's Field." Adapted by Julia Herne. Directed by Frank Tuttle. Shown at the Rivoli, New York, week Oct. 12. Running time, 71 mins.

Adele Clark	Bebe Daniels
Tim Sullivan	Tom Moore
Prince Arnolfo de Pescia	William Powell
Signorina Vitale	Dolores Cassinelli
"Auntie" Clark	Mary Foy
Sheamus Sullivan	Edward O'Connor
Judge Daniel Orcutt	Peter Lang
O'Hara	Charles Slattery

This is the first Bebe Daniels starring vehicle for Famous Players. It proves a fairly entertaining comedy-drama but not a picture that is going to pull heavily at the box office. It will do business, but it won't break records.

Miss Daniels, however, manages to give a decidedly good performance of the little girl who virtually rises, Cinderella like, from the garden of weeds under the Queensboro Bridge to the heights of society and marries a financially inclined Italian prince. Later she regrets the step and turns back to her sweetheart of the days of poverty.

Frank Tuttle, directing, has managed to give the film several very human touches, but the picture is lacking in a big kick. A hotel fire scene is utilized at the end in order to clear the situation and take the husband out of the picture. That is the nearest approach to a thrill.

Tom Moore plays the heroic role opposite the star, first as a deckhand on a scow and later as the foreman of the construction gang on Clark's field. William Powell enacts the heavy in the role of an Italian prince, while Delores Casinelli, as the head of a fashionable school for girls, acts the matchmaker.

In the story there is one of those famous lost wills which, when it crops up, gives the fortune to the scow deckhand and reduces the heroine to poverty again. The moral is aptly disclosed in one of the early scenes of the picture, when the hero of the tale tosses a dime to two youngsters who are peaceably sharing a bottle of pop. With the advent of the dime they both start fighting for it, and in the tussle the dime slips through a crack in the dock, the half-filled bottle of pop is overturned and at the finish the youths are bad friends. That's what the question of money will do. In the case of the heroine and hero it is a fortune that reacts similarly, but matters are so swung about that there is the usual happy conclusion.

"Dangerous Money" will please, but it won't pull beyond 75 per cent of the average business.

Fred.

WELCOME STRANGER

An Edward Belasco Production. Adapted from the Aaron Hoffman play of the same title by James Young and Willard Mack. Directed by James Young. Released by Producers Distributing Corp. Shown at Piccadilly, New York, week Oct. 11. Running time, 85 mins.

Isadore Solomon............Dore Davidson
Mary Clark..................Florence Vidor
Essie Solomon........Virginia Brown Faire
Icabod Whitson.................Noah Beery
Ned Tyler......................Lloyd Hughes
Eb Hooker....................Robert Edeson
Clem Beemis..................Wm. V. Mong
Seth Trimble.......................Otis Harlan
Gideon Tyler....................Fred J. Butler
Detective..........................Pat Hartigan

Aaron Hoffman's play, "Welcome Stranger," makes a corking human interest drama on the screen, and it should prove satisfactory entertainment to the majority of the audiences. There is practically an all-star cast in the picture, with Florence Vidor, Dore Davidson, Virginia Brown Faire, Robert Edeson, Noah Beery and William V. Mong among the players.

Strange to say, in the picture version it is not Dore Davidson, in the George Sidney role, that walks away with the honors of the picture, but William V. Mong, as Clem Beemis, the small town electrical shark, who gathers the honors for giving the outstanding performance of the production. Davidson tried too hard to vaudeville the role of Isadore Solomon, utilizing gestures overtime in an effort to play for laughs, which he did not get.

The screen version fully follows the play. It is the tale of a hide-bound New England town where Jews are taboo and where one, through his sticktoitiveness, manages not only to overcome the prejudice but becomes the hero of the town through giving it electric lights and trolley cars.

Florence Vidor plays the role of Mary Clark, the runaway steno from Manchester, while Lloyd Hughes is opposite as the banker's son who casts his lot with the invader and becomes a partner in the power company. Virginia Brown Faire is Essie, daughter of Solomon.

In handling the direction of the production James Young has carried the story along cleverly, and although it runs almost an hour and a half there is not a dull spot in the picture.

Mixed with the drama there is sufficient comedy to bring laughs and the titles, which must have been the dialog of Hoffman, brought howl after howl from the audience at the Piccadilly.

"Welcome Stranger" is a good commercial picture and should show up well at the gate. *Fred.*

THE TRUTH ABOUT WOMEN

Burton King production, made by Banner Productions. Story not credited. Directed by Burton King. Show at Loew's New York, New York, Oct. 10, on double feature bill. Running time, 65 minutes.

Howard Bronson..................David Powell
Knobbs..............................Charles Craig
Warren Carr.....................Lowell Sherman
Nona Boyd.......................Mary Thurman
Hilda Hammond.........Hope Hampton
Blossom...............................Dainty Lea

Martin Beck and Charles Dillingham can get a good line on Hope Hampton's dancing ability if they look at this picture. After seeing her here, let's hope she isn't going to dance in the stage "Madam Pompadour." Outside of that Miss Hampton does not seem qualified to carry the heroine's role in the picture, the production would almost have been worthy of a pre-release run in one of the big Broadway houses. The roles by Mary Thurman, David Powell and Lowell Sherman are splendidly taken. Miss Thurman puts it so far over Miss Hampton it would seem the latter screen celebrity would never want to have Miss Thurman work opposite her again in any picture.

"The Truth About Women" is that no matter how much one thinks they know about them, they really don't. The plot would have made a corking play, in fact, possibly a better play than picture.

It has four characters almost throughout. There is the novelist, a bachelor, who is writing "The Truth About Women (Mr. Powell). Lowell Sherman is the artist illustrator of the novels. His wife is a former vaudeville dancing star (Miss Hampton), and Mary Thurman is the artist model vamp who wins the artist from his wife.

The story is almost all told in that. The author cannot continue with his novel, and walks into a situation in the artist's home. The artist and his model have come to the wife to explain their infatuation and ask for a divorce. This is finally granted.

Then the author walks into the picture again, when the baby given into the custody of the wife dies. He takes her to his home, and a romance starts.

The only flaw in the amber is that the author still believes the divorced wife is in love with her former husband. He plans a reconstruction of the situation whereby the model-vamp wins the husband away. The scheme works, but in the end the first wife says nothing doing, and turns to the author-hero of the story for the final fade-out.

The men were great and the handling of a comedy role by Charles Craig was a skillful bit of work.

Burton King, with his direction, carried the story along in fine style. *Fred.*

VANITY'S PRICE

Gothic Production picture releasing through F. B. O. Story by Paul Bern and R. W. Neill, the director. Photography by Hal Mohr. Features Anna Q. Nilsson. Cast includes Stuart Holmes, Robert Boldra, Cissy Fitzgerald, Wyndham Standing, Arthur Rankin and Lucille Ricksen. Showing at the Cameo, New York, week of Oct. 5. Running time, 63 mins.

A likeable screen yarn, somewhat overdressed, perhaps, but nevertheless an interest sustainer and superior to many of the features that have edged their way into the major first-run houses.

Judicious picking by the casting director is an outstanding note, while Neill has slipped in a few novel touches that will surely be repeated by others who serve the silent art in like capacity. The error is in the settings, which illusion as being too gaudy to be reasonable. Such furnishings may awe the intermediate theatre clientele, but it is hardly to be supposed that the magnitudinous display was ever concocted in the most regal of genuine homes. And even that the interiors are supposedly the abode of vanity fanatic of the stage fails to offset the trappings.

Nevertheless it's a good picture, well able to lead a program and is a "break" for Anna Q. Nilsson, who is not always cast so happily as in this vehicle.

Portraying a dramatic celebrity with a 19-year-old son who refuses to quit simply because she is vain, Miss Nilsson does yeoman service as Vanna de Maurier. The story carries along pleasingly but without specific incidents until Vanna's second husband (Stuart Holmes) pays his respects socially and launches a bestial attack. The shock terminates the active career of Vanna, who is warned by medical advisers. Restless under the restrain, Vanna turns herself over to magical physicians in Vienna, who restore her youth, and she returns to this country for further glory.

The homecoming is not all it should be, in that her second husband has forced her son's sweetheart to flee to the river following another of his assaults, and the boy threatens to leave his mother unless she deletes this man from her life. A meeting between the separated couple in the wife's lavish home culminates in her beating him with a cane and the son taking up the strife upon his entrance and being rendered unconscious. One step farther has the honest but moderately wealthy playwright (Wynham Standing), who has been pleading with Vanna for years to wed, calling upon the husband and administering a neat and tidy beating.

The outgrowth of the mixups is the realization by Vanna of what price glory, hence she marries the playwright, and the son takes unto himself the girl his stepfather had designs upon.

Neill's best example of interpretation is marked during the struggle between Vanna and her husband at the time the son enters the combat, when she turns her back squarely into the camera, and, upon moving away, the boy is seen to be lying prone. Well spotted and excellently handled, the incident was most effective.

Miss Nilsson never looked better in her life than in this picture, and equals the physical qualifications with her work. Holmes makes a superlative villain, and Standing is a logical, ultimate husband. Cissy Fitzgerald is allowed sufficient footage to insert comedy, while Arthur Rankin and Lucille Ricksen nicely qualify as the youngsters.

The film will undoubtedly suggest another past celluloid release in its theme of a rejuvenated woman, and may recall instances of another film in some of the bits of business given Holmes as the nonchalant femininity pursuer, but it entertains and will hold intact those who have witnessed enough of the sequence to gather the trend of the tale.

Skig.

YOUTH FOR SALE

C. C. Burr production. Scenario and titles by Raymond S. Harris. Adapted from Izola Forrester's magazine story. Directed by W. C. Cabanne. Running time, 60 mins. At Loew's New York Oct. 7 as half of double bill.

Molly Malone.........................May Allison
Connie Sutton...............Sigrid Homquist
Montgomery Breck..........Richard Bennett
Tom Towers.................Charles E. Mack

Another picture purporting to show the pitfalls and snares that are in the path of young girls. The story concerns Molly Malone (May Allison) and Connie Sutton (Sigfrid Holmquist), two department store employes.

Connie is suspected of theft at the store. She has previously shown some talent as a dancer. She leaves the store after she is exonerated and enters the chorus of a local musical show. She is vamped by Montgomery Breck (Richard Bennett), a rich rounder and the "angel" for the troupe. Breck promises her the usual costly gifts and rushes her around to cabarets, etc.

Tom Towers (Charles E. Mack), Molly's fiance, is the stage electrician at Connie's theatre. Connie's tales of the alluring life back of the foots, influence Molly to accept an invitation to one of Breck's dinners. She drinks wood alcohol proferred by one of the drunken guests and is stricken blind.

Connie promises to marry Breck if he will finance Molly's trip to a specialist in Vienna. Molly hears of it and determines to prevent the wedding. She leaves the house feeling her way to a taxi and arrives at Breck's apartment. Breck refuses to wilt and she threatens him with a revolver. As he manoeuvres to get behind her sightless eyes Tom arrives and in the battle which follows knocks Breck unconscious.

Connie has been locked in a closet, and when released insists she is ready to go through with the marriage if it is necessary to save Molly's sight. Tom tells her he and Molly are to be married and will go to Vienna on their honeymoon.

The picture is far-fetched, but interesting, due to the excellent cast. Sigfrid Holmquist was alluring and convincing as the bobbed-haired blonde flapper of easy conscience, and May Allison gave a splendid portrayal of the better balanced Molly. Charles E. Mack showed up nicely in the role of Tom, while Richard Bennett did the best he could with a heavily censored "rake" role.

The photography and direction are adequate and the picture is given a generous production. It's good hokum melodrama in a popular vein and should have a fair appeal at the box office through the subject and the "names" in the cast.

Con.

AMERICAN MANNERS

Richard Talmadge Production featuring Richard Talmadge. Screen adaptation by F. H. Clark. Directed by James W. Horne. Running time, 63 mins. At Loew's New York Oct. 7 as half of double bill.

Roy Thomas..............Richard Talmadge
Dan Thomas...........................Marc Fenton
Clyde Harvey.....................Lee Shumway
Gloria Winthrope.................Helen Lynch
Conway..............................Arthur Melette
Jonas Winthrope...............William Turner
Mike Barclay..........................Pat Harmon

This is purely a stunt picture, with Talmadge in his usual athletic role. It is draped around the story of Roy Thomas, an American boy, educated abroad, who returns to help his father, Dan Thomas (Marc Fenton), a shipping magnate.

Young Thomas is instrumental in the uncovering of a smuggling ring on the ship of Jonas Winthrope (William Turner), thereby saving his father who was suspected of implicity by the government and, at the same time, copping Winthrope's daughter.

The story carries the usual villain who is after Gloria, and who turns out to be the brains of the ring. A comedy detective fails to comede. The action mostly transpires aboard the ship, where Talmadge is sorely beset by the villanous crew who suspect him. He battles the entire crew and, of course, vanquishes odds that would cause Dempsey to run for his life. This portion of the picture descends to farce comedy, but is intended seriously.

Talmadge, as an American returning in French get up and assuming the mannerisms of a musical comedy Frenchman to have some fun with his family, is mildly amusing. He isn't an actor depending upon his athletics to get him over.

The thrill of the picture was a dive from a mast into water. A water chase is in the routine when the ship gets under way acting upon orders of the rascally captain. The picture has many technical faults, such as wild fighting along the decks with a tug standing by nonchalantly, and a ship underway with an unruffled prow.

The work of the supporting cast, artistically was far above Talmadge's conception of the role, but it was next to impossible for the cast to put the picture over as a serious effort due to the low comedy injected in the "fights," which have about outlived their usefullness as screen "thrills."

Just another program addition for the smaller houses.

Con.

WHAT SHALL I DO?

Hodkinson production, starring Dorothy Mackaill. Written, supervised and edited by Frank Woods. Directed by John G. Adolphi. Photograpghed by Joseph Walker. At the Arena Oct. 9. Runs about hour.

Jeanie Andrews..........Dorothy Mackaill
Jack Nelson..................John Harron
Mrs. MacLean..............Louise Dresser
Henry MacLean..........William V. Mong
Dolly MacLean............Betty Morrissey
Mary Conway....................Ann May
Tom Conway............Ralph McCullough

Dear old amnesia or aphasia, or whatever it is they call it when some one gets a sack on the crown and forgets what has happened, comes galloping to the rescue of the plot in "What Shall I Do?" No matter how many times they use it, it always seems to be effective and to lend suspense to plots that would otherwise totter to the floor of the projection booth.

Even though the absorption may have been synthetically injected by the use of the old aphasia idea, 'What's Shall I Do?" must be praised as considerably above the average program picture in interest. It has, besides, in Dorothy Mackaill one of the most swiftly and surely ascending luminaries of filmdom and a supporting cast of comparable merit.

The direction has handled a rather heavy and sob-laden story without too much maudlin slush and hysterics, with the whole production nicely set.

The inquiry in the title expresses the plaint of a young wife, deserted with a tiny baby on her hands and no job in sight. But the husband's act has been unintentional, as he has been caressed by a truck and had the memory knocked clear out of him. Since he had married secretly and his parents were not aware of the fact, the little wife is certainly up against it. But just when things are most firmly at sixes and sevens the old gang from the lunchroom she knew in her days as waitress before she married decides to go out and force the young husband to recognize his family. It does not even become necessary for them to bounce him on the head again, as his memory is awakened by the sight of familiar objects in the little home.

Miss Mackaill is as appealing and talented in he racting as she is delicate and blessed in beauty. John Harron is a convincing hero, Louise Dresser most charming as his understanding mother, and all the rest good in their roles. The comedy of the lunchroom gang is a feature, and in this Tom O'Brien again demonstrates he is one of the best toughs on the screen.

Hodkinson has spent considerable money advertising "What Shall I Do?" It should more than reimburse them, as it is excellent entertainment for the neighborhood houses.

THE ROSE OF PARIS

A Universal-Jewel. Story by Delly. Adapted by Melville Brown and Edward T. Lowe. Directed by Irving Cummings. Starring Mary Philbin. Shown at Loew's Circle, N. Y., on double-feature bill Oct. 1. Running time, 73 mins.

Mitsi........................Mary Philbin
Christian......................Robert Cain
Andre du Vallois...............John Sainpolis
Mme. Bolomoff.....................Rose Dione
Florine du Vallois..........Dorothy Revier
Paul Maran......................Gino Corrado
Yvett........................Doreen Turner
Jules......................Edwin T. Brady
Victor...................Charles H. Puffy
Mother Superior............Carrie Daumery
George Der Vroo.............Frank Currier

This is just a program production of the Cinderella type. It is fairly well directed, although the story story seemed to be a little too involved by the number of characters. The greatest appeal to the exhibitor is the name of the star, Mary Philbin, on the strength of the showing in past pictures. The picture will get by with the audiences in the average daily change and smaller neighborhood houses.

The star has the role of a young orphan reared in a convent. Her mother has been disowned by her grandfather after a marriage to which he objected. On his deathbed he asks an acquaintance to seek the daughter and give her his forgiveness. The friend carries his search to a cafe in Paris, and there discovers that the mother has died but that a daughter was born and left by her in the hands of the Sisters. The cafe keeper proposes to bring the daughter to the cafe for the searches, and imposes on the Mother Superior a tale that secures the release of the girl. The latter, however, discovers that she has fallen into the hands of those who would do her harm, and she escapes them.

On the road from Paris the youngster is given a lift by a man whom she recognizes as one who adopted a child from the convent she was at, and in the end she marries him after she has been given shelter in his home.

Mary Philbin handles the role rather nicely, although it is not a characterization such as she gave in "The Merry-Go-Round." Robert Cain, handling the role of the hero, does not seem to ring true. Possibly the fault lies in the fact that he is frequently seen in heavy roles and it is hard to reconcile him as a hero. The balance of the cast was adequate.

In direction Irving Cummings has done about all that could be expected with the script material in hand.

Fred.

WESTERN WALLOP

Universal, starring Jack Hoxie. Story by Adolph Bannauer, originally entitled "On Parole," adapted by Isadore Bernstein. Directed by Clifford Smith. Shown at Loew's New York, New York, on double feature bill Oct. 10. Running time, 65 minutes.

Bart Tullison..................Jack Hoxie
Anita Stillwell.............Margaret Landis
Jefferson Bradshaw...James Gordon Russell
Sheriff Malloy.............Charles Brinley
Pedro.........................Duke R. Lee

The title is as weak as the weakest feature in the picture. "On Parole," the original title, would have been far better. It is a typical western, with the usual chase, the free-for-all-fight and the love-story background. The best is a tumble from a horse that the star takes, which must have been caught by a lucky camera shot.

In the houses where they like western stuff this one will get by; in the other houses it had better be bolstered up by a good strong additional feature.

It is a draggy visualization of what might have been a good story. The hero is a former convict on parole who cannot cross the state line under the rules that gave him his freedom. Because of this he is dubbed a coward when he won't take up the trail into a neighboring state after cattle rustlers. Later the same fact is used by the heavy to bring the sheriff down on the trail of his rival.

Jack Hoxie serves well enough as the hero, and the heavy of James Gordon Russell is also satisfactory. Margaret Landis plays opposite the star, but does not give promise of ever climbing the ladder of fame in front of the camera.

Like most all westerns, this one is principally an outdoor picture, so the cost didn't mount up.

Fred.

THIS WOMAN

Warner Brothers' picture. Adapted from the novel by Howard Rockey. Phil Rosen director and Lÿman Broening photographer. Stars Irene Rich. At the Piccadilly, New York, week of Oct. 18. Running time, 72 mins.

Carol Drayton..................Irene Rich
Whitney Duane ....Ricardo Cortez
Rose ....Louise Fazenda
Gordon Duane ....Frank Elliott
Bobby Bleecker ....Creighton Hale
Stratini ....Marc McDermott
Mrs. Sturdevant...........Helen Dunbar
Aline Sturdevant ....Clara Bow
Judson ....Otto Hoffman

Satisfying program leader, albeit a conventional tale, and showing Irene Rich to the fullest advantage. It is emphatically Miss Rich's picture, although better than average support is forthcoming from Marc McDermott, while Creighton Hale is active enough to stand out.

Rosen, directing, has blended the sequence together to make an interesting story besides holding the players from becoming too assertive and overacting. McDermott's performance reveals a tendency to stretch a point here and there, but the total impression is sufficiently meritorious to offset that leaning.

The script tells of Carol Drayton, a vocal student, interrupted in an attempt upon her own life by gas through a fire starting in the next room. Extinguishing the flames leads to the other feminine boarder discovering the financial and moral condition of the songstress. That leads to both and to a cheap cabaret, which is raided.

A well-to-do transient is at the table with the girls at the time of the uniform avalanche, whereupon he lies himself clear, but his tale sends Carol (Miss Rich) up for 30 days. Released and wandering, the girl walks into a crying stew serenading his sweetheart with an organ grinder. In dire need of money, she offers to sing accompanied by the organ. On the inside of the house is the master music teacher. One earful and Carol is welcomed, with all arrangements made for her to seriously take up her work.

The usual love affair with a socialite follows, who is too inquisitive when the kickback of the prison term eventually becomes known, so it's "air" for him, and the girl turns to her music teacher as her future husband.

Productionally the picture has been tastefully staged as to settings while the photography is an enhancement. However, it is the work of Miss Rich and Rosen's ability to keep the continuity at a sustained pitch that makes this feature well able to step out and remain upright by itself.

Louise Fazenda drifts in and out but not before turning in a serviceable contribution early in the footage. Clara Bow is given little to do, while Frank Elliott, as the half villainous villain, breezed through without leaving a mark. The one blemish in the cast is Ricardo Cortez, who projected as being both colorless and meaningless despite a sizeable assignment before the lens.

Skig.

THE BORDER LEGION

Picturization of the Zane Grey novel. Produced by Famous Players-Lasky. Screen play by George Hull and direction by William K. Howard. Antonio Moreno and Helene Chadwick featured. At the Rialto, New York, week Oct. 19. Running time, 68 mins.

Jim Cleve.....................Antonio Moreno
Joan Randle...............Helene Chadwick
Kells ....Rockliffe Fellowes
Gulden ....Gibson Gowland
Harvey Roberts................Charles Ogle
Pearce ....James Corye
Blicky ....Edward Gribbon
Bill Randle....................Luke Cosgrave

An out and out western produced with a great deal of care and with a good cast, made from one of the most famous Grey novels and yet it doesn't sum up as anything great. The reason for that may be the age of the plot, for from the beginning to the end there is never a doubt as to its outcome.

Joan Randle loves Jim Cleve, a good-for-nothing. When Jim loses his job minding cattle and declares he'll join the Border Legion, a notorious outlaw band, the girl is worried. She is captured by the leader of the band, a roughneck at heart but a fellow with a streak of humanity in his makeup. So Jim joins the Legion. When Gulden, a renegade and cruel member, goes after the girl, Kells, who really wants her himself, is so struck by the girl's devotion to Jim and also by her sterling qualities that he does a little quick trigger work to stop the bad boys from getting the nice girl.

That is the windup.

Fellowes is the only member of the cast to shine by his work. Members of the Lasky stock are used and fill in minor roles superlatively, but the principal parts, with the exception noted, are done pretty much in a so-so way. Photography is excellent.

"The Border Legion" is weak first run material but a fair program picture on the strength of its treatment. As a member of the "famous forty," however, it might be said that it was let in on a guest card.

Sisk.

THE SILENT WATCHER

Frank Lloyd Production, released by First National, featuring Glenn Hunter and Bessie Love. Adapted for the screen by J. G. Hawks from the Mary Roberts Rinehart story, "The Altar on the Hill." Shown at the Strand, New York, week Oct. 19. Running time, 78 minutes.

Joe Roberts..................Glenn Hunter
Mary, his wife..................Bessie Love
John Steele, "The Chief"..Hobart Bosworth
Mrs. Steele....................Gertrude Astor
Jim Tufts, stage doorman..George Nicholls
Mrs. Tufts......................Aggie Herring
Barnes, Steele's campaign manager.....
Lionel Belmore
Stuart, the detective.......DeWitt Jennings
Lily Elliott, the soubret.......Alma Bennett
Harrold, the reporter........Brandon Hurst

Combination of society and middle-class life, the stage, politics and police, a story but mildly interesting at times, yet at others gripping because of the performance of Glenn Hunter and the able direction of Frank Lloyd. The title is one that seemingly won't mean anything at the box office, yet the picture should do about the average business for any house. A delightful vein of comedy runs through the story.

"The Silent Watcher" is the Unknown Soldier who lies in Arlington. That he gave his all for the country is the example the lawmakers in Washington should have in mind and give to their task of preserving the country their best in effort, mind and life. That is all very well for picture sentiment, but it doesn't hit so hard in Washington, nor does the title suggest the public will beat down the doors of the theatre to see it.

The title is derived from an incident in the story. The real underlying theme is loyalty. It is the loyalty of the secretary of a noted attorney who is running for the Senate that keeps the name and reputation of his employer unsullied in the midst of the campaign when his political enemies would involve him in a huge scandal through the suicide of a musical comedy star whom the lawyer had been maintaining in a separate establishment which was in his secretary's name. The jam that the little secretary gets in with his wife over the affair almost ends in the wrecking of their happiness, but it is straightened out.

Bessie Love, playing opposite Hunter, gives a corking performance as the home-loving but slightly suspicious wife of the little secretary—Hunter's role. He is doing pretty much the best work of his screen career in it. Simplicity in action gets his point over every time. Hobart Bosworth as the attorney played in forceful manner. De Witt Jennings did his usual chief of detectives that made one thing of "Within the Law." Alma Bennett as the Broadway stage siren planted the role skillfully. In a bit of natural color photography for a stage scene she looked like a million dollars.

That little touch of natural color stuff was a real idea. It gave the stage stuff in the picture a new angle. *Fred.*

THE SPEED SPOOK

Johnny Hines starred, with production presented by C. C. Burr. Charles Hines directed. No players programmed. At Cameo, New York, week Oct. 19. Runs about 75 minutes.

Excellent ballyhoo (street) for this used at Cameo, and should be good anywhere. Likely no municipal permit necessary. Ballyhoo based upon title and principal subject of story, an auto without a driver in sight. The driver is really under the high-built hood, made high for that purpose. In the picture the car is of the racing type. The picture's management may provide this ballyhoo. In New York some weeks ago, as an advance exploitation, the sight of an auto running about the streets with apparently no driver got some newspaper comment, although on that ballyhoo car were the names of Hines and the picture.

It will provoke comment, and the smaller the town the better.

Designed as a comedy for Johnny Hines, "The Speed Spook" is more of a melodrama with comedy; with too much story and all of the story flimsy. In its main plea as a novelty picture through a driverless auto and fast driving, it can be depended upon as a release with laughs and some interest. But it is not a big program picture in either of its ends.

Hines as an auto racing driver returns to his home town as a popular hero. While there he runs into a spirited local election for sheriff. One of the nominees is the father of his girl, and the girl has opened an auto sales agency, running $14,000 behind before Hines gets in. He decides to take the girl's place out of the red and see that her father wins, which he does, and probably married the girl in the footage that didn't show.

Running 75 minutes, the picture would be improved by taking out 15 minutes. That's a long stretch to suggest out after the final cutting, but it can be done here, for there is too much story, so much so and of such a light texture that plenty of it out will leave the main thread down to cases. The eliminations would also draw the laughs closer together. There are two or three real laughs here, but widely apart.

In the effort for laughs and also melodramatic points, there is a laboriousness that cannot be missed. It might be overcome by the cutting, at least to an extent.

It seems as though Hines is trying to be more of an actor than a comedian and the story is more melodramatic than funny. In fact, there are too much melodramatics and not enough laughs.

In the driverless auto the film has a safety, for that is novel, while there is some speed driving that must have been done by a pro. The racer is of the old type and looks like a Benz 6. It reveals to the auditors how a driverless auto may be manipulated.

In direction are several holes, mostly minor and of detail, but evidencing unthinking while the making was in progress.

If this is the style of story Hines must have, it wouldn't be a bad idea to gag it up more, and also if Hines must be melodramatized, make him burlesque it.

Why try to spoil a possible comedian by making him an impossible actor?

This "Speed Spook" on its novelty end and the few good laughs it does hold can stand up in an average way where Hines has been previously liked. If the ballyhoo plan is adopted as mentioned at the head of this story, the drawing power of the picture should be immensely increased. It's no word-of-mouth advertiser though as just a film.

Sime.

CORNERED

Dodson Mitchell-Zelda Sears play picturized by Warner Brothers. Distributed by Dependable Exchange. Directed by William Beaudine, with Marie Prevost starred. Cast also includes Rockcliffe Fellowes, John Roche, Cissy Fitgerald and Raymond Hatton. At Loew's, New York, Oct. 15. Running time, 70 minutes.

Another one of the big releases to get its first run in the New York. Accuracy compels the statement this one of the Warners' product is superior to "Being Respectable," given a week at the Strand last summer. However, the flood of big pictures probably made the pop house showing a necessity. Whatever its New York start, "Cornered" is a good film, fit for almost all of the houses. The average high-class neighborhood house will like it, and that also goes for the cheaper places that insist on thrills.

"Cornered" has those audience thrills. It also has suspense and a good plot which concerns the resemblance of a girl in the Hell's Kitchen section to a girl who lives up where Swells are Swells and the maids speak French. Crook stuff forms the basis. Several crooks plan a robbery by having the Hell's Kitchen lady impersonate the other in her own home. The girl is caught and a locket around her neck, left by her dead mother, makes a revelation or so.

Madge Kennedy played the dual role when the piece was at the Astor, New York, several seasons ago. As a piece of stage property it was also played on tour.

It was written by folks who knew the value of hoke, and knowing it, smeared that old salve on thick. The picture people have done the same, and in Marie Prevost they cast a girl able to handle the dual role stuff with ease. Supporting her is a good cast, with Rockcliffe Fellowes and Raymond Hatton (again playing a snow bird) standing out. The direction by Beaudine is excellent, and all the sets faithful and adequate. If a flaw is to be found it is the large number of subtitles necessary to explain the conversation. Rapid development requires the subtitles, but even though necessary, they are overabundant.

All in all, "Cornered," one of the in-between films as regards expense in the making, should be able to command a wide showing and please the average movie goer. Captions critics may not like it so much—it is the sort of a film they wouldn't, but they're usually the pass holders and don't matter. *Sisk.*

GREAT DIAMOND MYSTERY

Fox production starring Shirley Mason. Directed by Shannon Fife, written by Denison Clift, and adapted by Thomas Dixon, Jr. At the New York one day (Oct. 17), as half the bill. Runs about an hour.

Ruth Winton	Shirley Mason
Murdock	Harry von Meter
Peter Standish	Hardee Kirkland
Perry Standish	Buster Collier
Diana	Mary Mayo
Phyllis	Jacqueline Saunders
Mallison	Philo McCullough

"The Great Diamond Mystery" measures up as a lightweight. It concerns its simple little self with diamonds, murders, suspicious-looking butlers, plenty of cops, and a number of young men with vari-shaped mustaches who make unscrupulous love to the little heroine.

When the hero is found to be innocent on the eve of his execution, the director did not have him saved just as he sat down on the well-known chair but had the governor called in plenty of time and the prison notified even before the chaplain came in to apply the usual comfort applesauce.

Shirley Mason has a better role than usual. Buster Collier is likeable as the falsely accused hero, and Philo McCullough as the villain is as oily as tea pot dome. The others are satisfactory, with that going also for direction, photography, continuity, and general production.

The mystery element is decidedly weak, however.

THE VIRGIN

Phil Goldstone Production from the Spanish ballad, "The Virgin of San Blas," by Julio Sabello. Translated and adapted by J. F. Natteford. Directed by Alvin J. Neitz. Running time, 65 mins. Reviewed at Loew's New York, Oct. 15. Half of double feature bill.

David Kent	Kenneth Harlan
Maria Valdez	Dorothy Revier
Ricardo Ruiz	Sam de Grasse
His Valet	Frank Lacteen
The Widow Montez	Rosa Rosanova
Rosa, her daughter	Alice Lake
Sam Hawkins	Walter Hiers
The Duenna	Nell Clarke Keller
The Maid	Lois Scott
Major Domo	J. P. Lockney

Splendidly cast picture of Latin love and intrigue made unusual by the splendid acting and appealing beauty of Dorothy Revier, sympathetically cast as Maria Valdez, "The Virgin of San Blas." Miss Revier was exquisite and convincing. It was she who gave the story the semblance of credulity, for she was in truth the type for which men battle to possess.

The story has atmosphere in the Spanish town of San Blas. Maria Valdez is known as "The Virgin of San Blas" through her many charities and exceptional beauty. David Kent (Kenneth Harlan), an American, is investigating the death of his father in San Blas years before.

He falls in love with Maria but doesn't know she returns his affection until he comes to bid her adieu. Ricardo Ruiz (Sam de Grasse) duellist and rake, thinks to retrieve his damaged fortune by a marriage with Maria. He is enraged when perceiving her love for the American, following her refusal to marry him. He bribes the Widow Montez (Rosa Rosanova), an innkeeper, to aid him. The Widow, on the night Maria is giving a siesta in honor of her approaching marriage, informs the bride-to-be her father was killed by the senior Kent. Ruiz has manufactured the tale which later turns out to be true.

Maria learns the truth. Torn between love and the Latin desire for revenge, she decides to punish Kent and marries Ruiz with the understanding the marriage is in name only. Kent comes to learn the truth and Maria is weakening in his arms when Ruiz discovers them. Ruiz decides to break the pact with his wife and hides in her room. He attacks, but her duenna enters in time. Ruiz then lures Kent to Maria's home by a message, and finding him with his wife insists upon satisfaction.

Locking the women in a room he insults Kent and then hands him a sword. Ruiz is an expert duellist, but to avoid any chance for a slip he has his valet posted on a balcony with instructions to shoot Kent if he is gaining an advantage. The duel begins and Kent, badly outskilled, is being slowly lured on to certain death when he dashes out the candles. The duel continues in the gloom and the valet fires, killing Ruiz.

The work of the cast is above the average. Walter Hiers as an American drummer of chewing gum is the comedy relief and gets a few laughs, but the appeal is Dorothy Revier, a girl who seems destined for screen stardom within a very short time.

She's an eye-bath and can act, a sure-fire combo. *Con.*

A FIGHTING HEART

Produced by the Hercules Film Productions. Story and direction by Jack Nelson. Starring Frank Merrill. Shown at the Stanley, N. Y., Oct. 17, 1924. Running time, 64 minutes.

Jack Melford	Frank Merrill
Rae Davis	Margaret Landis
"Cloudy" Day	Milford Morante
Julia Cunningham	May Sherman
Dr. Logan	Otto Lederer
Dr. Delhi	Alphonse Martell
Blanche Renault	Kathleen Calhoun

Just one of those hokum stories written especially to fit the star's ability to do some hurdling. In this case it seems that the picture producers have picked a boy with a name that is about as near that of Frank Merriwell as possible. Only in this case it isn't a boy, but a man full grown and middle-aged. The picture is of the type that is utilized to fill in the cheap admission-priced daily change houses between a couple of fairly good pictures to cut the expense on the three days, two good ones and one not so good, and this picture is the one that fits the latter designation.

There isn't a single thing about the picture that would tend to bring money to the box office even in the smaller houses.

Merrill as Jack Melford is the prize hurdler at a small college. He wins a race and immediately afterward is informed that his father is near death. He arrives home to find that his dad has died and left the boy penniless through having willed everything to a Dr. Delhi, a foreign specialist who treated him.

By coincidence the same Dr. Delhi shows up in the home of the boy's sweetheart, where he is treating the girl's aunt, with whom she lives. The girl and her younger brother are orphans and the doctor has prevailed on the aunt through hypnotic suggestion to turn the girl out of the house. It is up to the hero to expose the doctor and round up the crooks who are associated with him and save the day for the aunt and his girl.

Nobody stands out. There is a woman lead who doesn't impress and a vamp that is everything but. Just five spools. *Fred.*

MAN FROM GOD'S COUNTRY

Renown (Phil Goldstone) production, written by George C. Hill. Photographed by Roland Price, and directed by Alvin J. Seitz. At the New York one day (Oct. 17), as half the bill. Runs about 55 minutes.

Carmencita	Dorothy Revier
Pete Hurly	Lew Meehan
Bill Holliday	William Fairbanks
Don Manuel	Milton Ross
Romero	Carl Silvera
Judge Packard	Andrew Waldron

"The Man from God's Country" is as familiar to those acquainted with western pictures of its type as the formula. There is only one real departure and it was inserted to bolster up the romantic appeal. This has the two suitors for the heroine's hand, a Mexican and a Yankee rover, fast friends instead of hostile rivals, with the Mexican gracefully making his exit when he realizes he has been fairly licked in the great pastime of two fellows and a girl.

Otherwise the production is entirely conventional, with an American foreman brutally filling the role of the villain usually given to the Mexican suitor.

Some beautiful photography, considerable gun play and several daring and colorful bits of horsemanship. In this case it is the girl who gets shot and the hero who first receives the blame and almost gets the lynching because of her mishap.

William Fairbanks plays in his usual virile manner a role that requires little but passive strength and to ride a horse. The pulchritudinous

Dorothy Revier rather overacts the Spanish charmer, and the rest of the cast averages up as considerably less than fair.

The dearth of good acting is balanced by direction above the ordinary, everything combining it to make it an average western for the program houses.

THE TENTH WOMAN

Warner Brothers' presentation, releasing through First National. Features Beverly Bayne, June Marlowe and John Roche. Others in the cast, Raymond McKee, Alec B. Francis and Charles Post. Adapted from the novel of the same name by Harriet Comstock. Directed by James Flood, with J. J. Mescall photographing. At Loew's New York, New York, Oct. 2. Running time, about 65 minutes.

A likely feature that shows the three principals, Beverly Bayne, June Marlowe and John Roche to advantage. Totaled up it amounts to a lightweight comedy drama that remains horizontal principally because of these players.

Some of the billing matter has June Marlowe's name over the title of the picture balanced by other displays revealing Miss Bayne and Mr. Roche in large type, but beneath the name of the film. Anyway, the trio have no competition during the time the screening is actually taking place, and the advertising matter doesn't propound a great question so long as all receive mention.

The story continuously see-saws between the east and the west, telling of young Campton, owner of a ranch, rescuing a rejected girl (Miss Bayne) from the act of suicide. A jump to Boston shows June Marlowe as a hectic young lady, Rose-Ann, about to become the wife of a timid youth, supervised by family tradition that deviates not from a narrow path. A former admirer of Compton, the complications arise when that lad arrives in Massachusetts after the ceremony and the girl he has left at the ranch comes across a picture of the now wedded Rose-Ann.

The conservative husband (Raymond McKee) finally drives his bride out of the house with his bickerings, and she goes straight to Compton's ranch so fast she beats the owner there. Hence, the two women spend many ruffled hours until Compton returns. Situations point to the rancher preferring the visiting eastern lass, and the girl who has installed herself as house keeper packs her bag and starts away for places unknown. Compton discovers the departure and give mad chase, which leads into a runway and rather a far-fetched rescue, during which the "doubling" is somewhat obvious. The usual clinch finish is provided.

Flood, who directed, has inserted a number of comedy instances, and has made an attempt at showing wild life by means of a midnight swimming party. It suffers through pictures of recent months, narrating that all aquatic sports of the young set never get under way until the middle of the night, and this is a tame affair, compared to some that Broadway screens have held. Otherwise, the continuity never reveals what brought on the attempt at suicide, nor is shown the reason for the later threats to the girl of exposure proffered by a rejected ranch foreman.

Miss Bayne gives a praiseworthy performance which carries the right amount of sedateness to balance the giddiness contained in Miss Marlowe's role. The latter also deserves much commendation, and if she can sustain the pace hit in this vehicle the future should be very bright from her viewpoint. Roche makes an adequate exponent of the outdoors, although Charles Post is buried in the role of the ranch foreman. Raymond McKee does nicely with the interpretation of the backward husband.

It's a fair enough feature for the better houses, and marks the return of Miss Bayne to filmdom after a long absence to the extent of her ability and appearance are a welcome recurrence. *Skig.*

MEASURE OF A MAN

Universal. Story by Norman Duncan, adapted by Isadore Bernstein. Continuity by Wyndham Gittens. Direction by Arthur Rosso. Running time, 65 mins. At Loew's, New York, Oct. 14, half of double feature program.

John Fairmeadow	William Desmond
"Pale" Peter	Francis Ford
Clare	Marian Sais
Billy, the Beast	William J. Dyer
Donald	Bobbie Gordon
Charley	Harry Tenbrook
Jennie Hitch	Zala Davis
Tom Hitch	William Turner
Pattie Batch	Mary McAllister

A hokum western with all of the standardized props, the story or treatment offering nothing new and built on a theme that has formed the background for westerns since the invention of pictures.

A Bowery bum, a derelict (William Desmond), turns up in Swamps End, a tough logging camp. Desmond has been regenerated. He is known in the camp as The Parson.

He saves a few drunkards after besting half a dozen of the sawdust champs and runs through the usual gamut. There is a wayward son sent back to his mother through the Parson's efforts; an orphan girl, whom the parson loves, and the efforts of the saloon keeper and gambler to run the Parson out of town, all winding up with the Parson sitting on the world and the tough boys taking their nourishment from pop bottles through straws after the saloon folded up.

The picture is just another one of those things that makes a layman wonder.

The story allows for plenty of outdoor scenes, a couple of interiors representing about all of the production expense represented. This wouldn't be cause for criticism if the story and direction were above the most ordinary. *Con.*

FOR WOMAN'S FAVOR

Lund Productions. Directed by Oscar Lund. Story adapted from "The Falcon." Reviewed at Loew's New York Sept. 16, one day only, half of double feature bill. Running time 60 mins.

The Man	Elliott Dexter
The Girl	Seena Owen
The Shark	Wilton Lackaye
The Lamb	Irma Harrison
The Fool	Henry Hull
The Wolf	Paul McAllister
The Brother	Arthur Donaldson
The Lover	Henry Hull

This picture, heavy with names and featuring a "cut back idea" with Boccaccio's "The Falcon" used as an antithesis in natural colors, doesn't kick like it should or live up to its program promises, mainly on account of the crudely melodramatic prelude used to hang "The Falcon" upon.

The black and white portions of the story concern Howard Fiske (Elliott Dexter). His sweetheart, June Paige (Seena Owen), is about to marry a millionaire for his money. She is being forced into the marriage by her scheming parents. Braken (Wilton Lackaye), a villainous friend of Fiske, is hounding him for money and demands he blackmail June Paige by selling her old undated love letters to Fiske. Braken lures June to Fiske's house, promising her the letters upon payment of $10,000.

Fiske picks up a copy of "The Falcon" and begins to read the "cut back," showing the immortal story of Boccaccio, with Henry Hull as the lover. It is a splendidly mounted and beautiful piece of photography, the sacrifice by the lover of his dearest treasure to satisfy the desire of his lady-love.

After completing the book June comes and asks for her letters. He is about to give them to her when Braken appears and demands $10,000. Seeing that June has agreed to a bargain with Braken, Fiske relieves her of fear and anxiety by throwing the letters into a fireplace. June, realizing the depth of his love, suddenly sees things in their true light and paralleling the words of the girl in "The Falcon," gives herself to Fiske, saying, "You have always possessed me with your love."

The picture is splendidly cast and the photography excellent. During the period of "The Falcon" the natural coloring allows the costuming to be kaleidoscopic.

The weakness lies in the abrupt transition back to this prosaic, humdrum present. It's an entertaining picture, for all of that. *Con.*

LONDON FILM REVIEWS

11TH COMMANDMENT

London, Sept. 26.

Made by George Cooper for the Gaumont company and given a premiere at the Palace "The Eleventh Commandment" is a good example of the "problem" play treated with decorum. The story has been adapted from a stage play by Brandon Fleming which ran at the Royalty without creating any great success. The story is essentially British and free from nastiness. Cooper has taken great pains with his production and has done admirably.

Sir Noel Barchester is wrapped up in the spotless honor of his house so that when his eldest daughter falls in love with a young man she has given a motor-lift when he was in an intoxicated condition, he is furious. She goes on the stage and is practically disowned. His youngest daughter is the apple of his eye and he looks forward to her marriage with a man after his own heart. On the eve of the wedding appears a blackmailer. This man announces he is the brother of an artist with whom the youngest daughter has carried on an intrigue. The girl denies this, but the man produces letters proving his story. When it comes to sacrifice, Barchester believes in doing it right and sends for the girl's fiancee in order to exploit her shame. Meanwhile, the girl has persuaded her actress sister to take the blame. This she tries to do, but a little cross-examining on the part of the bad young man, whom love has turned good, knocks the bottom out of her story. The girl has broken the eleventh commandment in being found out and the "good young man" crawls away, leaving her to fight it out alone. The actress and her lover are apparently restored to favor and have the customary final "close-up."

The acting on the part of several stage favorites is excellent. Fay Compton has a hard part as the actress-sister and triumphs. Lillian Hall Davis is very good as the erring sister. Jack Hobbs, Charley Quartermaine, Stewart Rome and Dawson Millward all do well. Louise Hampton is something of an enigma as Lady Barchester. It is impossible to tell whether she is utterly broken down with grief or merely suffering from the primary stages of some peculiar form of facial paralysis. *Gore.*

MANHATTAN

Famous Players-Lasky production based on "The Definite Object," by Jeffery Farnol. Adapted by Paul Sloane and Frank W. Tuttle. Directed by R. H. Burnside. Starring Richard Dix. Presented at the Rivoli, New York, week of Oct. 26. Running time, 70 minutes.

Peter Minuit	Richard Dix
Mary	Jacqueline Logan
Spike	Gregory Kelly
Bud McGinnis	George Seigman
Joe Madden	Gunboat Smith
Brimerton	Oscar Figman
Mrs. Trapes	Edna Mae Oliver
Housekeeper	Alice Chapin

The exhibitors of the country, the Famous Players-Lasky Corp. and the film industry generally can hail Richard Dix as one of the real new stars of the picture field, and at the same time they can pass a couple of hails to R. H. Burnside, veteran stage director of both musical comedies and dramatic offerings, who makes his debut as a director with this presentation. The combination of Dix and Burnside proves a happy one.

"Manhattan" as a picture is going to start Dix off with a bang. He has youth, looks, personality, and above all, he can troupe. Together with this he puts over a fight in this picture that is going to go down as one of the greatest. The fight in "Manhattan" is an out-and-out wow from any angle.

After the screening of the final show at the Rivoli Sunday night there was frequent comment among the women folk of the audience as they were leaving the theatre which was absolute proof that Dix had struck their fancy and that he was going to be one of their favorites.

"Manhattan" is a story of New York, Fifth avenue and Hell's Kitchen. The opening scenes show Dix in the role of Peter Minuit, the last of the Minuits, whose great-great-great-great - great - granddad was the guy that slipped the Chief of the Manhattans $24, a bottle of rum and a couple of blankets for all of Manhattan Island. The present Peter is a rumbound and a social butterfly, with nothing to do except spend money. His introduction to the audience is tumbling out of bed fully clad in evening clothes with his shirt front decorated with postage stamps and a special delivery which shows how he was shipped home the night before. Peter, however, is tired of it all and wants romance and adventure.

The evening papers suggest Hell's Kitchen, where there is a gang feud on, but when he hits the Kitchen what he can see on the surface is all applesauce. Back home again, he sticks up a safe-cracker who has entered his home. The safe-cracker takes him for a fellow crook and Peter goes back to Hell's Kitchen with him, there to meet the safe-cracker's sister, with whom he falls in love. Of course, there is a heavy in the story. He is the district leader, who has all of the youths of the neighborhood working for him on crooked deals in return for the protection he gives them. He is also in love with the girl, and that is where the trouble starts.

At the finish Peter finally has to go to the leader's pool shooting joint, lick the leader and a mob of his men while saving and winning the girl.

The story, thoroughly melodramatic, is relieved with a corking comedy vein. The comedy is likewise present in the titles. Providing Famous keeps up the pace as to story and direction with Dix, there is nothing that is going to stop him from soon hitting the top as a box office attraction.

Supporting Dix is Jacqueline Logan as the girl, she handling her role decidedly well. George Seigman plays the heavy, and was on the receiving end in the battle with Dix. Gregory Kelly in a character role, that of the young safe-cracker, managed to be most convincing as a weak-chinned boy that is forced to do the bidding of others. Edna Mae Oliver as a tenement character managed to score.

"Manhattan" will get dough and entertain anywhere. *Fred.*

MADONNA OF THE STREETS

Edwin Carewe production released by First National. Adapted from the W. B. Maxwell novel, "The Ragged Messenger." Directed by Edwin Carewe. Featuring Mme. Nazimova and Milton Sills. Shown at the Piccadilly, New York, two weeks, beginning Oct. 25. Running time, 87 minutes.

Mary Carlson / Mary Ainsleigh	Nazimova
John Morton	Milton Sills
Lord Patrington	Claude Gillingwater
Dr. Colbeck	Courtenay Foote
"Bull" Brockins	Tom Kennedy
"Slippery" Eddie Foster	John T. Murray
Lady Sarah Joyce	Vivien Oakland
Howard Bowman	Harold Goodwin
Mrs. Elyard	Rosa Gore
Judy Smythe	May Beth Carr
Nathan Norris	Herbert Prior

First of the First Nationals at the Piccadilly. Reason for Piccadilly getting the production is said to be because the Strand is over-booked and couldn't give more than a single week, while at the Piccadilly it goes in for two weeks, with the house guaranteeing First National $10,000 for its end on a percentage basis of 17½ per cent. of the gross for the two weeks. The distributors in turn agree to spend that amount in daily newspaper advertising for the picture.

Although Nazimova and Milton Sills are featured in the picture, at the Piccadilly, they are starred in the lights. It appears as though the combination of the two names, together with the title, should be effective.

The picture is not particularly a wallop. It is interesting to a degree, but perhaps a little too long. There is also a chance the ending could have been more effective if the heroine had been permitted to die, although that would have killed the possibility of the "miracle" ending.

W. B. Maxwell's story has its scenes laid in the Limehouse district of London, except for a few scenes in a fashionable church and some shots in the apartment of a detained woman in New York.

Sills is the pastor of fashionable St. Andrew's, London. His uncle in New York is maintaining an apartment for Mary Carlson (Mme. Nazimova). The uncle dies and his will cuts off the woman, giving his estate of $5,000,000 to the rector of St. Andrew's. Whereupon the woman decides she will beat the news abroad and vamp the preacher if she can.

As John Morton is preaching on the streets of Limehouse the girl comes upon him. Her story leads both into the Mission, where he finally falls for her wiles and marries her. She is his wife when he receives news of his good fortune, but instead of living in luxury the minister decides to devote his fortune to charitable works.

This enrages the wife. Later when it is disclosed she had been the pastor's uncle's mistress he drives her away, only to follow and search for her through endless months. Finally she reappears at the Mission he has built for fallen women. She is ill and the doctors say naught can save her life. They predict a swift end, but the prayers of her husband seemingly are heard and answered, for she apparently returns from the dead.

In direction and lighting the picture is almost perfect. The support is also strong, with the surprise performance contributed by the former musical comedy comedian, John T. Murray, in a cockney comedy character. He and Tom Kennedy working together score laugh after laugh.

Nazimova looks a little tired under the camera's searching lens.

Vivien Oakland in a small role was exceedingly pretty and handled herself decidedly to advantage. *Fred.*

THE BANDOLERO

Metro-Goldwyn feature adapted from novel of same title, featuring Pedro De Cordoba, Renee Adoree and Rita Rossi, directed by Tom Terriss. At Cameo, New York, week Oct. 26. Running time, 80 minutes.

Dorando (Bandolero)	Pedro De Cordoba
Petra (His Daughter)	Renee Adoree
Marques de la Torre	Gustav Von Seyffertitz
Ramor (His Son)	Manuel Granado
Padre Dominguez	Gordon Begg
Concha	Rita Rossi
Juan	Arthur Donaldson
Maria	Maria Valray
El Tuerte	Jose Rueda

This feature was partially made in Spain and destined as a Metro-Goldwyn special. Second thought upon the producer's part releases it as a program picture, and as such can hold its own with most of them.

Sunny Spain provides an adequate framework for this melodrama of hatred, romance and the bull ring, with the latter providing a genuine thriller by depicting a bull fight in action. The story is engrossing and has a sufficient number of twists to keep the auditor guessing. Also a love interest carries along.

Dorando, former soldier, adopts banditry to visit vengeance upon the Marquis, one of whose guard killed his beautiful wife when Dorando surprised his superior in an attempted attack upon her.

Not unlike Jesse James, Dorando pilfers only from the rich and tosses the proceeds to the poor, save what he is compelled to share with his comrades.

The bandit band storms the palace and makes off with the Marquis' son, Ramon, who is held by the band until grown up. An early attachment has sprung up between Ramon and Petra, the bandit's daughter. Unsuccessful in curbing its progress and unable to tell his daughter his true identity, he swears to kill Ramon. Concha, another charmer, would welcome Ramon's attentions, but he has eyes for none than Petra. When the latter is influenced to renounce him he makes way to the city and wins fame as Caneroa, matador idol.

Concha, who has also followed, wins fame as a dancer and also the attention of the Marquis. Concha, jealous because of her rebuffs from Ramon, intrigues the Marquis to order the matador to enter conflict before he has tired the bull, with a view to sending him to his death. Ramon is injured and taken to the chapel.

The Marquis finally is advised of the young man's identity and crumbles at his bedside. Dorando also relents, leaving Petra to nurse him back to health.

Pedro De Cordoba contributes an excellent performance of the vengeful bandit. Rita Rossi brings the requisite fire to the role of Concha, while Renee Adoree is at all times charming as the unsophisticated Petra. Manuel Granado looked and acted well the part of Ramon.

The production at all times reflected adequate direction, with several episodes in particular exceptionally well handled. *Edba.*

MINE WITH THE IRON DOOR

San Francisco, Oct. 22.

Sol Lesser has given the screen another of Harold Bell Wright's novels in "The Mine with the Iron Door," which had its world premiere here at Loew's Warfield last week. The poorest thing about the feature is the title, which at first glance suggest a "western." On the other hand, it will be offset by a direct appeal to the followers of Harold Bell Wright who are legion.

"The Mine with the Iron Door" is not a "western" in the sense of the term as used in the film world. True, its story is of the west and told by western characters, but the plot has dignity, drama, romantic interest and a definite appeal. When melodrama enters the story it is true melodrama and grips because it carries the suggestion of reality. One of the outstanding beauties of the picture is the photography. The location picker deserves a line all by himself. They are truly works of art and a delight to the eye. The cast also is well chosen and includes some names that are of meaning to the picture followers. The players are Pat O'Malley, Dorothy Mackaill, Raymond Hatton, Charles Murray, Bert Woodruff, Mitchell Lewis, Creighton Hale, Mary Carr and Willie Collier, Jr.

The story opens in the desert showing two old prospectors. Out of water they come upon a cabin and seek to replenish their supply. At the cabin and in the custody of an old Indian woman they discover a white child. Previously we have seen a villainous character, Sonora Jack, leave after admonishing the woman to take good care of the youngster as some day she would bring much gold. The prospectors take this child by force because it is white and proceed to raise it as their own. Due to the child, they decide to quit their meanderings and settle down. The girl grows to womanhood. She is taught the rudiments of an education by a young physician neighbor, out there because of his health and known as "Saint Jimmy."

About this time is made known that a legend persists in the Arizona country of the existence of a mine with an iron door which had been the property of padres. Into this situation comes the hero, who says he is a prospector. He meets the girl. Later it is discovered, this youth is a fugitive convict. Meanwhile, the old prospectors inject much comedy through their desire, but lack of courage, to tell the girl her real origin. A renegade, who would marry her, when spurned finally tells her, and the girl feels her humiliation so keenly she attempts to go away. She is caught in the path of a terrific storm and saved from death by an educated Indian who has left the white man's school and gone back to the land of his people. This Indian cherishes a latent hatred of the whites. He brings the girl back. Later he learns the identity of the convict-prospector and threatens to turn him over to the sheriff unless the white man comes with him. He compels the white man to share his cabin in the hills and there search for gold, and finds satisfaction in watching his suffering. Eventually Sonora Jack and his gang get information that leads them to believe the Indian knows the secret of the lost mine. They capture him and try to force him to divulge, resorting to torture.

The Indian knows the location, as he has led his captive blindfolded into the mine, laughed at him and then led him back again.

The young convict-prospector is instrumental in saving the Indian, much to the latter's surprise. In gratitude the Indian takes the white man back to the mine and permits him to gather all the gold he can carry away.

In the meantime, Sonora Jack and his gang learn of the white girl's identity and come to recapture her. In the fight that ensues one of her prospector protectors is killed and the other badly wounded. The outlaws are traced by the Indian and the young convict-prospector. The Indian stages a sensational knife fight with Sonora Jack and slays him, the youth eventually is cleared of the crime for which he was sent to prison and the lovers are brought together.

This may sound melodramatic, but in the telling there is much skill of direction and artistry in the unfolding. *Rivers.*

STEPPING LIVELY

Carlos Productions, featuring Richard Talmadge. Distributed by Renown Pictures, Inc. Screen adaptation by Frank Howard Clark. Directed by James W. Horne. Running time, 60 mins. Reviewed Oct. 21 at Loew's New York, as half of double feature bill.

Dave Allen	Richard Telmadge
Evelyn Pendroy	Mildred Harris
James Pendroy	Norval McGregor
Robbins	Brinsley Shaw
Artemus Doolittle	Fred Kelsey
Josef Le Baron	Mario Carillo
Black Mike	William Clifford
Dan Carter	John W. Dillon
Chicago Red	Victor Mezetti

Another "chase" picture for Richard Talmadge, the author being hampered by Talmadge's lack of dramatic ability and hence restricted to a story which will allow Telmadge to show his bag of athletic stunts, which don't vary a hair's breadth in any of his pictures.

There is the same old scaling of fences, jumping onto a moving train, diving into water, etc., with which this motion picture "whatizit" has been sold, and at a profit, according to report, in the houses playing the cheapest kind of hokum pictures.

"Stepping Lively" has a bit more story then the usual "Talmadge" and a very fair cast, headed by Mildred Harris, who does what she can with a watery role. Talmadge as secretary to a bank president is kept busy foiling Josef Le Baron (Mario Carillo), a scheming crook posing as a nobleman. Le Baron is a suitor for the banker's daughter and robs the old man of a flock of bonds by "crowning" him as he is putting them in the safe.

Dave Allen (Talmadge) enlists the aid of Black Mike, an underworld character, and by posing as a gorilla gets Mike's gang to aid him. The director's conception of the costuming of a modern gunman would make the late Chuck Connors shed tears of envy.

The gang find Richard has given them the works and isn't a paid-up member of, the "cannons" union which starts one of those screen battles in which the hero nonchalantly disposes of two, maybe three, dozen of the toughest looking eggs the assistant casting director can hire for three bucks a day.

After the inevitable chase the crook is apprehended and the lovers given the blessing.

The picture is supposed to be a mystery drama, the mystery coming from the introduction of a character, a butler, who has done a stretch. The butler's function is to act as guilty as possible to distract the attention of those who haven't figured out the finish and gone home. The butler cops some jewels, adding to the general impression he is a bad boy, but this is found not to be the case at all, for the solution tells us the butler did it to protect them from Black Mike's gang and the other "collectors" with which the picture swarmed.

The story is about as original as a pancake recipe and less interesting, but it's quite a stunt to parlay an "athlete" of Talmadge's ability into a lead for six releases yearly anywhere. *Con.*

NOT BUILT FOR RUNNIN'

Lee Maloney has a new sounding name as a Western thrilling picture star. It's here in "Not Built for Runnin'," caught at Loew's New

York as its single day's single feature.

A rich ranchman persecutes the girl. She owns the neighboring ranch. In this part of the West they are not neighborly, so the rich guy has never seen her. You may guess for yourself she's a good-looking gal, and that lets you in for a guess that's why the rich ranchman never did see her before he started persecuting was just a whim of the scenario writer, to make it easier for Leo Maloney.

Yes, you're right, Leo is the fighting, fearless hero. He wanders in just at the right moment, stands off the wealthy villain and between fights makes love to the girl.

That's not new stuff in westerns, but this is not a picture for deep thought.

After Leo runs amuck with his love-sobbing stuff, he reveals that his sweetie ranch owner is the daughter of the fellow next door who had escaped somehow, getting a flash at her. Why one ranch should make a girl poorer and the one next step over should make a man richer is another important point hedl out on the film analyzers.

When Leo pulled the daughter thing the ranch magnate wanted to make retribution, but it's a new word in westerns, and his daughter walked out on him, perhaps over to her own ranch.

The net result is that though a prosecutor in the first reel and wealthy, the cattleman slinks out of the picture when daughtie turns him down in the final stanza. One could infer that he slunk away to buy another ranch, but not his daughter's.

It still called for another hundred feet to get to the clinch of Leo and his discovery.

There are thrills here, and it looks like an evening's fun besides minus the thought, deep or otherwise. And the fun is not in a kidding way. A lot of people are going to call this one a real western thriller.

GARDEN OF WEEDS

Paramount picture, James Cruze production. Starring Betty Compson. Adapted from the stage play of the same name by Walter Woods and Anthony Coldeway. Directed by Cruze, with Karl Brown photographer. Showing at Rivoli, New York, week of Nov. 2. Running time, 67 mins.

Dorothy ....Betty Compson
Flagg ....Rockliffe Fellowes
Douglas Crawford ....Warner Baxter
Paulson ....Charles Ogle
Jack Lane ....King Zany
Archie ....William Austin
Old Maid ....Lucille Thorndyke
Theatre Manager ....William Turner
Nick ....Toyo Fujita
Hazel ....Lilyan Tashman
Nat Barlow ....Al St. John

A neat bit of drama with a sex angle which James Cruze has held together for interest until the climax. The picture should both draw and hold the Compson following, while others outside that contingent will be satisfied with it as a whole. It pleased a sabbath matinee gathering at the Rivoli.

The story is not too plausible and a certain stretching of the imagination is essential. The somewhat far-fetched characteristics in the composition may be qualified as "theatrical license," and under that circumstance sympathetic disciples of Miss Compson will undoubtedly okeh the script. Disinterested individuals will probably scoff, but there can be no denying the picture has been well made.

The film carries a distinct resemblance to former vehicles of the star in that the opening "shot" of Miss Compson has nothing between her and the lense except a bathtub and a cloud of soapsuds. Despite that she has been probably on the screen asked out of more boarding houses than any other film luminary, Miss Compson is again a victim of similar circumstances with the continuity ultimately revealing her as a ruined theatrical understudy registering a complete comeback under the guidance of a husband who's mind is broad as the Famous Players' lot.

That the wealthy bridegroom knows the complete story of his wife's degradation and feigns sleep at the time she acquires enough courage to tell him is ultimately unfolded. The threatening situations the bride has to face upon the return from the honeymoon are also pictured, as is the final struggle between the husband and the oppressing former provider.

It may read as a stereotyped theme, especially in connection with Miss Compson, and such being the case the more credit is due Cruze for handling it in such a manner as to make the silent version of the play stand up. The director has obtained an assembled total that runs itself off without a tremor, and it is principally because of his conception, worked out by a competent cast, that the picture surmounts the handicap of similarity regarding the star. However, the story does call for indulgence from those who rigidly take their stage or screen writing seriously.

This latest Compson edition is an evening dress affair, balanced by the boarding house opening with Al St. John doing a vaudeville performer "making a play" for the girl and responsible for her ejection through forcing his way into her room. Later the action switches to an estate where Flagg (Rockliffe Fellowes) keeps his outfit of "steerers," of both sexes, whom he uses to trim his selected "money men." It's this "confidence" gang and Flagg that Dorothy (Miss Compson) joins when she is in the dregs and later breaks away from to marry Crawford (Warner Baxter), a prospective victim.

Mr. Fellowes makes a convincing obstacle to the happy ending and runs a close second to the feminine lead for honors. Mr. Baxter secures his majority of footage toward the latter reels, and although equaling demands they are not such as to call for exceptional playing. Charles Ogle does little more than a bit, albeit included in the underline billing along with Fellowes and Baxter as features of the cast.

Miss Compson gives a creditable performance while flashing a few gowns that should bring attention from the women. Roles of this type have about become second nature to this girl. While her successive characterizations may vary as to merit, it is interesting to note the treatment accorded under the different directors.

Settings, interiors and exteriors, inclusive of a swimming pool passage, are eye filling and displayed by excellent photography. *Skig.*

THE ONLY WOMAN

A Norma Talmadge production presented by Joseph M. Schenck. Distributed by First National. Story by C. Gardner Sullivan, directed by Sidney Olcott. Shown at the Capitol, New York, week Nov. 2. Running time, 68 minutes.

Helen Brinsley ....Norma Talmadge
Rex Herrington ....Eugene O'Brien
"Fighting Jerry" Herrington, Rex's father ....Edward Davis
William Brinsley ....Winter Hall
Ole Hanson ....Matthew Betz
Rodney Blake ....E. H. Calvert
Bingo ....Stella di Lanti
Yacht Captain ....Murdock MacQuarrie
Minister ....Rev. Neal Dodd
First Officer ....Brooks Benedict
Steward ....Charles O'Malley

If it wasn't for Norma Talmadge being the star of this production and if it hardn't been directed by Sidney Olcott, "The Only Woman" would be a typical small timer. The story by C. Gardner Sullivan is one especially written for the screen. It is an old told tale, oft told in the movies and minus a single new angle. When it starts one knows immediately the finish. With Norma Talmadge the picture will get some money at the box office, but it is certain that Miss Talmadge can't go along with pictures of this sort and hold her place.

The plot concerns the daughter of a man who has utilized a trust fund for his personal speculations and the son of a wealthy banker who is a stew. The banker is aware of the speculations of the father of the girl and proposes that the daughter marry his son, make a man of him, or he will expose the breach of trust. The girl to save her father, consents to the arrangement, and after a time succeeds in making a man of the boy falling in love with him during the process of his regeneration.

The picture must have cost something fancy to make because of the sea stuff it carries. Olcott has handled his share of the work wonderfully well, carrying the story along in great shape and not permitting it to lag at any stage. He might have done a whole lot worse with the material in hand.

Eugene O'Brien plays the lead opposite the star and does fairly well in the role of the rich man's sodden son. Edward Davis plays the banker and looks the role from the ground up. A heavy bit is contributed by Mathew Betz, who looks good for a No. 2 Wolheim in a second company of "What Price Glory." Betz is there in what he does in this picture. The others of the cast with the exception of Winter Hall, do not matter much. They fill the picture and that lets them out. *Fred.*

WORLDLY GOODS

Presented by Adolph Zukor and Jesse L. Lasky, starring Agnes Ayres. Adapted from the Sophie Kerr novel by A. P. Younger. Directed by Paul Bern. Shown at the Rialto, New York, week Nov. 2, 1924. Running time 61 minutes.

Eleanor Lawson ....Agnes Ayres
Fred Hopper ....Pat O'Malley
Clifford Ramsay ....Victor Varconi
Mrs. Lawson ....Edythe Chapman
Mr. Lawson ....Bert Woodruff
Letitia Calhoun ....Maude George
Vivian Steel ....Cecile Evans
Sol Sahipik ....Otto Lederer

A rather entertaining story that makes very neat program material. The picture isn't one that is going to get any great big box-office return, but it will get by with the majority of fans. There is one thing about the tale—although Agnes Ayres is starred, it was the male role that was really the starring part. In making the adaptation that role should have been played up stronger. It is in a sense one of those "show off" propositions and it could have been worked up into something worth while.

"Worldly Goods" is a story of the four-flushing type of young smart aleck who is going to set the world afire. He marries a girl who is employed as the secretary to the head of a big department store, takes her out of her job and then during the first year of their life leads her a miserable existence. He is conning his way through life by running up bills, handing out checks that he knows are wothless, but won't look for a job as he is too filled with big ideas and an exaggerated sense of his own importance. He does not come to a realization of what is what until his wife, who has taken a job in a smart modiste shop, decides that she will leave him flat and obtain a divorce. She comes to this frame of mind after she has caught him in a lie regarding another woman. However, it is through this "other woman" that the husband gets a stake which enables him to put over a deal which gets a profit of $70,000. He then meets his wife in a lawyer's office where she has gone to start her divorce action, and with the check for his deal in his hand he starts in to four-flush all over again.

It is a simple little tale well played and fairly well directed by Paul Bern. Agnes Ayres as the wife manages to make her role convincing, but Pat O'Malley has the fat role as the husband. Maude George does the heavy vamp stuff and puts it over in great shape. Edythe Chapman and Bert Woodruff in a couple of character roles are convincing. *Fred.*

THE BATTLING ORIOLES

Hal Roach production distributed through Pathe. Story by Roach; direction by Ted Wilde and Fred Guiol. Glenn Tyron featured. At Cameo, New York, week Nov. 2. Running time, about 65 minutes.

Tommy Roosevelt Tucker ....Glenn Tyron
Hope Stanton ....Blanche Mehaffey
Cappy Wolfe ....John T. Prince
Sid Stanton ....Noah Young
"Jimmy the Mouse" ....Sam Lufkin
Inspector Joslin ....Robert Page

This five-reeler from Hal Roach's plant is a slam-bang slapstick farce furnished with a good story, a capable light comedian and support and general detail that is of a quality to make all the directorial efforts successful.

The Battling Orioles are the members of the famous old baseball team (mention was neglected that Muggsy McGraw and Uncle Wilbert Robinson had played on original), who have grown old and are, at the time the picture begins, in their dotage. On the scene comes little Tommy Tucker, son of one of their number. Tommy, through the medium of fighting to save the girl he loves, brings back the fighting spirit of the old boys and at the same time he gets the gal before her villainous uncle can make a crook of her.

Of such dramatic cloth is "The Battling Orioles" cut. Glenn Tyron, as Tommy, is a corking little comedian whose bag of tricks is seemingly inexhaustible. Maybe Pathe means to use him as a No. 2 Harold Lloyd, and if they do they're not far wrong, for their separate lines bear resemblance.

Blance Mehaffey as the girl hasn't much to do. The old men are corking types and good for laughs. The fight scenes in a tough saloon are hilariuos at times and never uninteresting. "Our Gang" is brought in for a flash near the front.

"The Battling Orioles" probably hasn't a great deal of drawing power and it isn't such a smash its word-of-mouth advertising will help business, but as a change of program pace it is eminently satisfactory and probably the forerunner of better things, at least from Tyron.

Sisk.

MEDDLING WOMEN

A seven reeler, starring Lionel Barrymore. Written and directed by Ivan Abramson. Produced by Chadwick and released through Commonwealth. Shown at Loew's New York on double bill Friday, Oct. 31. Running hime, 80 minutes.

Edwin Ainsworth } ......Lionel Barrymore
John Wells }
Grace Ainsworth..........Sigrid Holmquist
Madeline.................Dagmar Godowsky
Harold Chase..............Hugh Thompson
Mrs. Ainsworth.................Ida Darling
Claudia Browne.............Alice Hegeman
Vincente...................Antonio d'Alagy
Dr. Giani.................William Bechtel

Lionel Barrymore inherits another dual role in this modern melodrama, which is a celluloid preachment against feminine interference and a splendid object lesson for the gossipy sex, regardless of whether the busybodies are relations or just friends. In this instance it is the mother of a successful playwright who has meddled in the marital affairs of Edwin and Grace Ainsworth until she has accomplished her purpose—that of dividing the couple and seding her son into the clutches of a cabaret gold digger. In a drunken brawl Ainston is beaten by the dancing partner-admirer of the girl and suffers temporary loss of memory through the shock.

Simultaneously John Wells, a rum runner, has succumbed to "poisoned hootch." The gang, wishing to avoid police scrutiny, recognize a remarkable resemblance between the stupified Ainsworth and the deceased, and arrange to have it appear that Ainsworth had committed suicide by placing the latter's credentials in the dead man's pocket and tossing him overboard and also making Ainsworth believe that he is Wells, the bootlegger. Ainsworth's wife and mother have identified and buried the wrong body. The wife remarries the opera impresario, whose proffered chance to resume her career had started the couple on the rocks through the meddling of Ainsworth's mother and Grace's aunt. Their imaginations conjured and convinced Ainsworth that his wife no longer loved him but was really in love with Chase. A fight among the bootleggers and a pistol shot restores Ainsworth's memory, and he reaches home in time to witness the marriage ceremony. He is later shot by the cabaret girl, which would have provided a typical Eugene O'Neill finish had not the following closeup revealed Ainston reading it all from a script and eventually convincing the meddlesome mother and aunt what could happen through their meddling.

Lionel Barrymore is capital in both roles, possibly contributing his best acting in the episodes where he believes he is Wells, the bootlegger. Sigrid Holmquist and Dagmar Godowsky also contribute some excellent acting in their respective roles.

The story is interesting and well acted from all angles. It should easily be a demand as a program release.

Edba.

THE TORRENT

Adapted from a Langdon McCormack story by A. P. Younger. Produced by Phil Goldstone and released by Renown Pictures. Directed by William K. Howard and A. P. Younger. Presented on double feature bill at Loew's New York, Oct. 31. Running time, 70 minutes.

Hale Garrison..........William Fairbanks
Gloria Manners................Ora Carew
Ernest Leeds.................Frank Elliott
The Cast-Off...............Gertrude Astor
The Bachelor..............Joseph Kilgour
His Friend.................June Elvidge
Dancing Girl............Fontaine La Rue
Butler......................Ashley Cooper
Detective....................Robert McKim
Captain.....................Charles French

Another psychological study of the emotions seething within humans, such as in the author's previous work, "The Storm." For a dash of modernity he takes a fling at this reckless age and more reckless sex who, according to the author, float through life on a torrent of high living.

Gloria Manners is typical of the type she would simulate, a young woman, slightly beyond her flapper years, but still retaining a jazz appetite and coquetry.

Engaged to a wealthy suitor she encourages another, a serious-minded chap, during an ocean voyage home, only to cast him off before the ship docks.

However, they had gone through a mock marriage, which they later find was legal because of having been performed on high seas by the captain.

Gloria has no intention of allowing it to interfere with previous plans. Her suitor meets her but the man she has tricked determines to teach her a lesson. He whisks her off to his country lodge and keeps her there, figuring he can eventually bring her to her senses. Her friends pursue, and when unable to regain her, hire a thug to toss her captor off a cliff and make off with her in an auto.

The man is swept by the current and is about to be carried over the falls when rescued by an Indian guide. An auto accident to the girl throws them together. When he is about to acknowledge he has failed, she surrenders.

The story is interesting and unraveled to retain suspense. Several of its scenes provide genuine thrills, particularly a spirited fight abroad the liner between Hale Garrison (William Fairbanks) and a drink-crazed stoker. It is remarkably well done, also the subsequent struggle of Garrison in the watery torrent.

Mr. Fairbanks handles his role with a naturalness and sincerity that makes his work outstanding. Ora Carew is charming as the headstrong Miss Manners. The other roles are in the hands of screen names which gives the idea that Goldstone had attempted to exploit the cast as heavily as the author.

A good program picture. Has thrills, love interest and a sufficient tinge of the sexy stuff for appeal.

Edba.

THE DESERT OUTLAW

Fox production, starring Charles "Buck" Jones. Directed by Edmund Mortimer. At the Stanley one day (Oct. 29, 1924). Cast includes Evelyn Brent, De Witt Jennings, William Haynes, Robert Klein, Claude Payton. Runs about 65 minutes.

This is one of the Jones pictures in which the Fox star is decidedly more "Buck" than Charles. Although draggy at the start, it eventually develops into western considerably more jammed with action toward the finish than the majority of its school, but it is a western, first, last and always, bound by all

the traditions of that category of program picture and never giving Jones a chance at real human interest stuff.

However, there is more soul to "Desert Outlaw" than is usually the case. Here is a hero who when he thinks the girl has tricked him resolves to punish her. But he is stopped by the appeal in her eyes and the knowledge that his love is stronger than his lust.

The girl is played by Evelyn Brent, who is given no opportunity to wear colorful clothes but who is startlingly attractive even in shirtwaist and skirt. Jones' placid mannerisms stand out even more strongly against her fiery work, but he is, as always, likeable and appealing in the role. De Witt Jennings heads the assorted heavies in the cast, which is more than satisfactory.

While it has become bromidic to praise the photography in western films, this must be mentioned as the height of artistic and creative camera work from the opening caption to the final fade-out. The riding scenes are well directed, and there is a stirring under water fight near the end that gets away from the usual cliff-edge stuff.

Though the story itself and the general atmosphere are no advance over the better-class westerns aimed at the program houses, "Desert Outlaw" is above the average in other details and should rate as a good effort of its kind.

LOVER OF CAMILLE

Presented by the Warner Bros. Screen version of Sacha Guitry's play produced by David Belasco under the title of "Deburau." Directed by Harry Beaumont. At the Piccadilly theatre, New York, week Nov. 8. Running time 76 minutes.

Jean Gaspard Deburau..........Monte Blue
Marie Duplessis.............Marie Prevost
Robillard ....Willard Louis
Charles Deburau (at age of 10)
                          Terrence "Pat" Morre
Charles Deburau (at age of 17)
                          Pierre Gendron
Madame Deburau................Rose Dione
Madame Rabouir..........Rosa Rosanova
Madame Rabard.............Trilby Clark
Bertrand ....Brandon Hurst
The Unknown Lady........Winifred Bryon
The Charwoman...........Rosita Marstini

In the changing of the title of "Deburau" to "The Lover of Camille" for the screen the Warner Bros. likewise took the liberty of modernizing the story. That made for far better screen material. The average picture audiences does not care for the costume type of play, especially of the 1840 period. Jean Gaspard Deburau, clown of the French stage, is a very dapper Deburau in very modern attire off; likewise is Marie Prevost, a very modern lady "who takes her men where she finds them and leaves them where they fall."

Undoubtedly "The Lover of Camille" is going to prove more attractive at the box office away from Broadway than the title "Deburau" would have been, and by the same token the modernized screen version of the play will be far more entertaining to picture house audiences than strict adaptation of the play would have been.

In the play Camille was but a minor incident—on the screen she is everything to the story. She meets Deburau at the height of his career. Flirts with him during a performance and he takes her home. That is the beginning and the end right there, for Camille is one of those girls who sees and wants. When she sees someone else it is the same story all over again. In this case the second man comes into her life shortly after. That breaks up Deburau and he is through with the stage from then on, until at a time in his life years later when Camille reappears, only to die in his arms. He returns to the theatre, but his reappearance is an utter failure and it is his son who takes his place in the hearts of those who loved the art of the father.

The picture is entertaining and the work of Monte Blue and Marie Prevost is decidedly clever. Possibly Miss Prevost has a shade the best of it but that cannot detract from the really good performance Blue gives as the clown. Willard Louis, who is rapidly proving himself in various roles in the Warner productions, against stands out in this. There is hardly anyone else of the cast that matters, except for Rose Dione as Madame Deburau.

What the exhibitor will have to watch out for in playing either this picture or "He Who Gets Slapped" is that he does not want to play the two too close together, as the principal characters in each are clowns, working in white face.

Fred.

HE WHO GETS SLAPPED

Victor Seastrom production presented by Louis B. Mayer, released by Metro-Goldwyn. Adapted from the Leonid Andreyev play by Carey Wilson and Victor Seastrom. Shown at the Capitol, New York, week Nov. 9, 1924. Fifth anniversary of house opening. Running time, 71 minutes.

"He Who Gets Slapped".......Lon Chaney
Consuelo.....................Norma Shearer
Bezano........................John Gilbert
Count Mancini.................Tully Marshall
Baron Regnard............Marc McDermott
Tricaud......................Ford Sterling
Clown........................Clyde Cook
Briquet....................Harvey Clarke
Zinida.......................Paulette Duval
His Wife.....................Ruth King

Clown..........................Brandon Hurst
Clown..........................George Davis

While this picture may not quite live up to the claim made of "the perfect motion picture," it is nevertheless a mighty fine screen entertainment, capably acted, almost flawlessly directed and photographed with a fine sense of fitness. As to the title "He Who Gets Slapped" might mean anything. It's worth at the box office away from the Main Street is problematical. But what it is that is going to bring them to the box office, once inside they are going to be satisfied with the entertainment.

Lon Chaney as "He" stands out as possibly the greatest character actor of the screen. In this role he displays an understanding of character beyond anything that he has done heretofore. Those who have seen him in "The Hunchback" will want to see him in this, and they are going to be agreeably surprised at his work. For once Chaney is not called upon to contort his being into a disagreeable posture to achieve interest.

Norma Shearer as the little circus rider about whom the love interest revolves is charming and delightful. At the same time she lends the needed touch of youth to the cast. John Gilbert, who plays opposite, is fully adequate as the young lover.

The support that Chaney receives from Tully Marshall and Marc McDermott, the former as the father of the girl and the latter as the Baron Regnard is 100 per cent. Tully Marshall scores for comedy, while McDermott handles the heavy superbly.

The picture itself is well done from every angle. The scenes in the Paris Circus where "He" is the star clown after his painful experience in life while he was a scientist and the theft of his brain work and wife as well, are shot in a manner that gives the audience everything. Instead of looking at a picture one feels that they are part of the audience watching the clown. The final scenes of the picture, with the lion loosed by the clown to save the young rider from marriage to the heavy, are so worked out that the audience gets everything by suggestion.

At the Capitol on Sunday it looked as though that house was going to break all records, for the business was terrific all day, even the supper show being played to a house jammed with standees. *Fred.*

GREATEST LOVE OF ALL

Screen play written, directed and starred in by George Beban, who also appears in person in a scene that fits into the photoplay. General release to be announced. Shown at the Rivoli, New York, week Nov. 9, 1924. Running time, 82 minutes.

District Attorney Kelland....J. W. Johnston
Mrs. Godfrey Kelland..........Wanda Lyon
Their Daughter..................Baby Evelyn
Marie Simpkins, the maid..........
Nettie Belle Darby
The Cobbler....................O. Zangrilli
His Daughter Trina..........Mary Skurkoy
Joe the Iceman..................George Beban
His "sweetheart"..........Marie di Benedetta
The Presiding Judge..........William Howatt
The Attorney for the Defense..........
John K. Newman
Court Officer..................Robert M. Doll
The Interpreter..............George Humbert

"George Beban on the stage and screen" is the manner in which the attraction at the Rivoli is announced this week. That is just what it is. George Beban is the author of "The Greatest Love of All." He directed the picture, stars in it, and George Beban makes a personal appearance in conjunction. In that he is doing exactly what he did with "The Sign of the Rose."

At a certain point in the screen story the action fades from the screen to the stage proper and Beban, supported by a company of nine acting players and a number of stuges who fill the picture acting as a jury, enacts a trial scene.

It all is pure hokum melodrama but the kind that the majority of picture audiences like. Possibly not the wise Broadway audiences, but those attending the bigger picture theatres in other towns will eat it up. Beban plays that trial scene for all that it is worth, getting as much comedy out of it as is possible, and resorting to everything except the bladder and the slapstick to get it. It isn't possible that even the most indulgent judge sitting in a criminal court would permit of any witness taking the liberties that Beban did in the court room and get away with. But Beban did it, and even the Sunday night audience at the Rivoli laughed and laughed a lot. That is the answer.

At present there is 23 minutes of speaking action in the 82 minutes that the presentation of "The Greatest Love of All" consumes. The trial scene on the screen undoubtedly would be much shorter than that, so that the picture without Beban in person might possibly run about 70 minutes at the most.

Beban is again in his character of an Italian immigrant. He is Joe, the iceman, of the lower East Side, in love with the daughter of the cobbler next door. After a couple of years in this country he has accumulated wealth enough to bring his mother from Italy, and the old lady in her desire to help her son toward his ambition, a farm in the country, conspires with his sweetheart to take in washing. This is the cause of all their trouble, for in accepting the laundry work of the family of the district attorney a bracelet of his wife is placed in with the soiled clothes. Joe's mother is accused of the theft and arrested, tried and sentenced to three years.

Through all of this there is an undercurrent of underworld stuff that builds circumstantial evidence. A gang finds Joe ready and willing to assist them in a plan to be revenged on the district attorney. A golf ball is filled with nitro-glycerine and Joe is given the task of planting it on the links when the district attorney is out shooting golf, but at the crucial moment the district attorney's wife and Trina, Joe's sweetheart, appear. Joe, believing that his girl's life is in danger if the D. A. should decide to hit the ball first and talk afterward, jumps in between. Then the mother is cleared through the discovery that the district attorney's little daughter liked to take her mother's bright jewels and throw them into the basket for soiled clothes.

Beban is George Beban all over the place. His supporting cast is fairly good on the screen, but as much cannot be said for the stage other than the ladies playing the mother and his sweetheart.

Beban "on the stage and screen" will get money into the box office, and the picture, when finally released as a straight picture proposition, must be judged as a grade above the average independent-made production. *Fred.*

THE BELOVED BRUTE

Albert E. Smith picture releasing through Vitagraph. J. Stuart Blackton production and directed by Blackton. Features Marguerite de la Motte and Victor McLaglen. Story by Kenneth Perkins. Showing at the Rialto, New York, week of Nov. 9. Running time, 68 minutes.

Jacinta..................Marguerite de la Motte
Charles Hinges................Victor McLaglen
David Hinges..................William Russell
Augustina...........................Mary Alden
China Jones......................Stuart Holmes
Phil Benson....................Frank Brownlee
Fat Milligan.....................Wilfrid North
Swink Tuckson....................Ernie Adams
Peter Hinges.......................D. D. McLean
Sheriff Swanson................William Moran
Pez Reverly.....................George Ingleton
Hump Domingo.......................Jess Herring

Sufficiently sparkling with action to overcome the much maligned and conventional finish generally connected with "westerns." For a major portion of the footage the script gets somewhat, and creditably, away from the average scenario construction of the open country as uniformly screened. At that, the picture well rates the qualification of a program leader if for nothing else than the activity it contains.

Reverting to a lynching bee, in which the long separated brothers are to be hung, and eventually stopped by the girl heading a rescue party, tends to instigate a decided let-down following the previous happenings. It's regrettable and possibly excuseable. You can't expect everything in a "western," but it is also true that Blackton has just missed turning out a leader among releases of the type due to the dive the story takes as it nears its conclusion.

Scenically, photographically and directorially the film plays easily and with the assurance those in charge must have had during the making. A competent cast, including "bit" players, makes the script stand up for reality, and other than Miss de la Motte's inclination to overact, is much above the average personnel generally entrusted with the boots and saddles scenarios.

The yarn is spun of Charley Hinges, a two-handed fighter who has never known defeat, and believes himself unbeatable. Chafing under the prophecy of his dying father that his younger brother will prove his nemesis and that he is just a fighter without a soul, he awaits the eventual meeting and passes the time by cleaning out a dance hall, bare-handed, in the service of a girl about to become the property of the establishment's owner. He leaves with the girl and her feminine companion.

A desert voyage ultimately sees the trio trading in their horses for a dilapidated circus wagon and a team. In need of money, they placard the wagon with signs advising the girl is Egypt's greatest dancer, her elder companion becomes a seventh daughter of a seventh daughter, and the man's objective is a strength act and an open challenge to a wrestling match.

Coming into a town, the challenge is accepted by the villagers on behalf of one whom they believe physically supreme. Ignorant of the fact that the trouping wrestler is his brother, David Hinges accepts on behalf of his friends and triumphs. Believing that the girl doesn't love him, but only admires his strength, and as he has been beaten, the brute turns on her and orders her to join his conqueror, whose identity he knows.

The shooting of the former dance hall proprietor by the girl's companion compromises both she and David. The latter is about to be hung when Charley dashes up to declare he did the shooting. The girl figures out the responsible party, dashes back to obtain a confession and returns with the rescue party. Acknowledging her love for the defeated unbeliever concludes the narrative with the handclasp of the two brothers.

Victor McLaglen as "the brute" has completed a sterling performance. His work as a Thespian almost approximates the merits of his physical efforts and the witnessing of this picture will attest to his ability as a battler. Stuart Holmes made the scheming proprietor role stand up for all it was worth, as did Mary Alden with her assignment. The caricature of Miss de la Motte is unstable and might be termed "spotty." George Ingleton made but a snatch of footage memorable, which, as previously mentioned, is also true of other players in minor roles.

A scrap at the opening sends the picture away to a flying start, while further action is provided through the dance hall warfare and the match between the brothers. The passage wherein the lynch thing is reverted to marks the point where the picture falls down, but even so it's a two-fisted release that will entertain in the larger houses and is good enough to draw repeats in the lesser class theatres. *Skig.*

THE OFFENDER

Margery Wilson Production released independently. On double feature bill at Arena, New York, Nov. 6, 1924. Running time, 63 minutes.

The title "The Offender" starts one wondering who. It must be Margery Wilson. She is the star of the feature and the picture is labeled "A Margery Wilson Production." Margery might be far better thought of if she left her name off of it.

The Arena is one of those 700-seat houses on Eighth avenue below 42d street. It gets a straight 25-cent admission at night, and last Thursday night seemed to have capacity with a double feature bill. This, however, cannot be credited to the Margery Wilson feature. "The Spitfire," playing with it, had the names of Betty Blythe, Elliott Dexter, Robert Warwick, Pauline Garron, Burr McIntosh and Lowell Sherman.

The Margery Wilson production is one of those independents shot around New York during the summer, maybe last summer or the one before, with a company that does not seem to have any more than five professional players in the cast. The others looked like local pickups, and acted like it. The chances are that the five reels must have been shot at the rate of about $1,000 a reel.

The story is weird. It has burglary, kidnapping, a couple of fights, murder, and a chase. Margery is the much abused heroine.

Story horrible, direction terrible, acting awful. *Fred.*

THE SUNSET TRAIL

A Universal Western starring William Desmond. Shown at the Stanley, New York, Oct. 30. Running time, 62 minutes.

Just one of those "westerns," cheaply made from a matter-of-fact story. There is nothing novel, nothing new, nothing thrilling. Therefore, it is a picture that will sneak by in the cheaper priced admission houses where the audiences don't expect too much.

The pathetic part of it all is that one should see a player of the former popularity of William Desmond in a picture of this caliber. True, Demond has put on weight, and is pouchy, but at that he is worthy of something better.

The tale concerns one "Happy Hobo" played by Desmond. He was formerly a sheriff in a small border town and was accused of having turned off the bank, so took the trail as a wanderer. Of course he wasn't guilty, and that is all cleared up in the end. In the course of his wanderings, however, he runs across a girl. She is riding on a train while he is tramping the tracks. When the train stops and he comes up to it, she, attracted by his happy smile despite his more or less unkempt appearance, drops a rose from her coat for him.

Later he runs across a desert wanderer who has been on the hunt for gold and has found it, but just as he reaches the railroad track passes away. In his pocket there is a picture of the girl of the rose, which is just a little motion picture license, and naturally the hobo is accused of having caused the man's death, but later cleared. Then he goes forth to find the girl—which he does.

Exhibitors can safely pass this one up with the assurance that their public will never come to the door clamoring for it. If it can be bought for a little nickel, and there is a hole in a double feature program, then it can be used. *Fred.*

EAST OF BROADWAY

Associated Exhibitors, distributed through Pathe. Directed by William K. Howard. Owen Moore and Mary Carr featured. At Cameo, New York, week Nov. 9. Runs about 60 minutes.

It's a pity to have wasted an excellent title like this. For "East of Broadway" has nothing but its title. Not one thing of general appeal. Any appeal it develops will be in those neighborhoods where there may be some interest in the tribulations of a young man who wants to be a cop.

As for the east side of New York, intended from the title, there only remains the opportunity to play the old, familiar and popular melodies identified with that section. It may help some, but it won't be enough.

Other than Owen Moore and the player of the Gaffney (policeman) character, the acting is no better than the story, mostly through the scenario not affording chances. Even Mary Carr as a boarding-house keeper has nothing to do anything with. Marguerite de la Motte plays a simple orphan and rather repels than draws through her wishy-washy conception. Moore has a couple of fights and his expression is really fine. He suited the role and helped it, but unfortunately it happens to be a role that the best made of it leaves naught.

The great East Side, with material enough to furnish themes for a thousand pictures and enough background to have made this an actual seeing-New York affair, is left wholly alone, to simmer down to the interior of the boarding-house.

In story the film is never holding. There is no story. It's more like a motley collection of incidents. Nor did the direction lend assistance.

It's a tale that seemed to start two ways—to mark the progress of an applicant for police service and to bring in the East Side. After watching it about 20 minutes, one commences to ask, "What's the idea?" Moore as the recruit fails on his civil service examination, for as much reason in logic as there is reasonable logic in any other point the film goes after. Following rejection, he secures permission for a had shot Gaffney. That put him captures two burglars, one of whom final police tour, during which he into the hospital and also on the force.

As an East Side picture "East of Broadway" muffs it by miles. And as any other kind of a picture, neither is it there.

A real good title gone wrong. *Sime.*

LEND ME YOUR HUSBAND

Charles C. Burr production directed by William Christy Cabanne. Story by Marguerite Gove, scenario by Raymond S. Harris, and photography by Jack Brown and Neil Sullivan. At the Stanley, one day (Nov. 1, 1924). Runs about 75 minutes.

Aline Stockton..................Doris Kenyon
Henry Seton....................David Powell
Mrs. Seton.................Dolores Cassinelli
Burrows Stockton..........J. Barney Sherry
Jennie McDonald..........Violet Mersereau
Fergur McDonald.............Burr McIntosh
Robert Towers.................Connie Keefe
Count Ferrari.................Colt Albertson
Countess Ferrari..............Helene D'Algy

With a commercial title, a cast studded with box office names, and a host of opportunities for clever exploitation angles, "Lend Me Your Husband" stands as a very good bet for the better program houses. In addition to drawing the patrons it should hold them moderately absorbed and pleased, as it tells a fairly conceivable, dramatic and coherent story in a straightforward fashion. The running time, unfortunately, is a bit long for this type film.

The plot veers considerably from the ordinary, inasmuch as the central theme is not love, but the friendship between the girls of different social stations. Of course, romantic interest plays an important part, but the picture begins and practically ends, except for the final clinch, with the mutual devotion of these two motherless young women. When one, a gardener's daughter, foolishly permits herself to become mixed up in a compromising situation with the town rounder, the other, a slightly giddy and flirtatious heiress, loses no time in sacrificing her reputation and her own man, in saving her buddy's reputation.

It is this second girl, the wealthy one, who has been in the habit of borrowing other women's husbands, though for no other purposes than those of the dance or the mild flirtation. However, when the picture ends we are led to assume that she has been cured of her borrowing ways, and her little friend has also learned her lesson. As the villain has received his wallop on the button by this time, everything is squared and love at last takes precedence over friendship.

Doris Kenyon and David Powell are the featured names. Powell plays a heavy, who is heavy throughout, with not even a Menjou-like touch of goodness at the finish to mar his perfect villainy. He leaves the heroics to Connie Keefe, a newcomer, who is handsome enough and shows promise as an actor. Violet Merserau returns to the screen after some years as the poor girl, and Burr McIntosh and J. Barney Sherry are included in the balance of the strong cast.

The film has been lavishly set and the scenes on board a transatlantic line and at a big country club dance are particularly expensive looking. If any fault is to be found it is the almost total absence of comic relief.

TURNED UP

William Steiner Production, featuring Charles Hutchinson. Distributed by Hurricane Film Corp. Running time, 55 mins. Reviewed at Loew's New York, Oct. 28. Half of double bill.

Bruce Pomroy ....Charles Hutchinson
Betty Browne............Mary Beth Milford
Paul Gilmore ....Crauford Kent
John Creighton.................Otto Lederer
Lola ....Betty Morrisey
Joe Turner ....Charles Cruz
Tom Martin ....Charles Force
Ed Carter ....Leroy Mason

Another "thrillingly melodramatic" attempt with too many thrills and too much hokum dramatics to allow for credulity or realism. However, the picture has much to recommend it, thanks to the excellent cast and the good work of Charles Hutchinson, who seems to be one of the few athletic artists who can act.

Hutchinson as Bruce Pomroy, a bank cashier, has for an employer and rival Paul Gilmore (Crauford Kent). Kent is using the bank as a clearing house for stolen bonds. Pomroy and Gilmore were classmates. Both love Betty Browne (Mary Beth Milford). Hutchinson frames Pomroy through Joe Turner (Charles Cruz), the teller. He steals $5,000 from Pomroy's money. The shortage is reported and Gilmore offers to cover it up with his own money. Pomroy refuses. The directors are notified and vote with Gilmore to arrest Pomroy. He eludes the police, and after a "chase" jumps off a roof into the office of the gang of bond thieves who are working with Gilmore.

The master mind of the crooks hides Pomroy and then proposes he join the gang. He appears to do so, and remains at their headquarters, a suburban mansion. He places a dummy in his bed and escapes to warn Betty of Gilmore. The robbery is successful, Pomroy making a giant swing over and back to the office building to be robbed.

The picture ends in a wild battle in and around an abandoned mill where the gang congregate, with Pomroy and Gilmore tumbling over a precipice in their struggle. The denouement develops that Pomroy is working with a couple of Department of Justice detectives after men higher up in the bond thefts.

The direction is the weakest part of the picture and is responsible for the unconvincing portions. The technical errors are many and glaring. The "surprise" expected when Pomroy is revealed as working with the detectives doesn't materialize, due to faulty continuity, and several other portions are equally as vague. This makes for a very ordinary picture, with the usual strained attempts to inject thrills for which the story has been sacrificed. The work of the cast is splendid but powerless against the faults of the director and the spotty continuity. *Con.*

Napoleon and Josephine

Foreign-made production. No director or players named. Shown at the Stanley, N. Y., Oct. 20. Running time, 63 mins.

This is another of those "French Revolution pictures," as the exhibitors are terming all of the costume stuff. This one is simply a straightforward picturization of the rise and fall of the Corsican who became the Emperor of France. The Empress Josephine and later the Empress Marie-Louise are the two leading characters, together with that of Napoleon. There possibly is an audience for this type of picture, but it seems that they would be rather hard to find among the average run of picture fans that attend the cheaper priced admission houses. Yet there is nothing about this picture that would make it worthy to play any of the better houses.

History is the base of the story. It takes Napoleon through to Moscow and later Waterloo. The battle scenes in the latter event are only fair.

The film is cheaply produced and in spots the tinting is decidedly bad. *Fred.*

THE LOST TRIBE

Distributed by Aywon Film Corp. An educational feature credited to Capt. Frank Hurley. Showing at Loew's New York as half the bill, Oct. 24. Running time, over 60 mins.

An interesting educational program addition that might enhance its value with deletion. The film is dedicated to Sir Ernest Shackleton by Capt. Frank Hurley and is the depiction of the latter's exploration of remote regions in New Guinea.

The picture is given novelty through the invading party having imported two sea planes from which many "shots" have been obtained. Otherwise the action does not deviate from others of the type in showing the native dances, made of living and "types."

The film claims to reveal the discovery of one of the Lost Tribes of Israel and asserts that it is the first time white men have invaded this New Guinea sector.

The titling is out of proportion to the photography in referring to threatening "head hunters" and the natives working themselves into a frenzy, as throughout the action the subjects appear extremely calm and docile. The danger is not apparent on the screen and might just as well have been eliminated from the wording, for under the circumstances it fails to ring true.

However, the showing of stuffed skulls and other somewhat gruesome details attain interest, while the aeroplanes comprise a new twist for this sort of camera work that should make the picture playable with judicious placing.

There is little or no comedy attempted to ginger the continuity, hence it remains a straightaway telling of the Hurley expedition that is well told, photographically speaking. *Skig.*

LONDON FILM REVIEWS

ZEEBRUGE

London, Oct. 27.

The success of the War Office supervised film, "Armageddon," caused a cert in liveliness at the Admiralty, with the result the Sea Lords decided to have their own film. The picture, just shown here, is in the hands of New Era Films, and the actual production work has been done by Bruce Wolfe and A. V. Bramble. Bramble was the man responsible for the "Armageddon" production and has the distinction of being closely related to several of the officers taking part in the attack on the Mole at Zeebruge.

In the present case his work is every bit as good as in the former picture, particularly in the V. C., scenes which have been reconstructed with remarkable care and an entire absence of histrionics. The famous signal to those who were about to make the attack and reminding them it was the eve of St. George's day brought their reply to the effect "they'd give the dragon's tail a damned good twisting," and supplies a keynote to the feature, which is not devoid of a dry humor even in its most thrilling moments.

Among the V. C. episodes is the story of how Sergeant Finch was in the fighting—top of the "Vindictive" when it was shattered by a shell. He crawled out of the wreckage and went on working his gun alone. The actual gun was shown to the audience. Another episode shows Lieutenant Deane rescuing over 100 men in a launch built to take 40. The Victoria Crosses given for this action were voted by the men.

Many of the actual officers and others taking part in the fight were present at the Marble Arch Pavilion, where the premiere took place. *Gore.*

WHAT THE BUTLER SAW

London, Oct. 27.

Made by George Dewhurst with American stars and handled by the Gaumont Co., this feature is a really excellent example of a stage farce transferred to the screen. Dewhurst has adhered faithfully to the play by Fred Mouillott and Judge Parry. His production work is exceedingly good, and several situations which might have been vulgar and suggestive have been skilfully handled. There is nothing to offend the most fastidious.

A young taxi driver suddenly comes into a fortune and goes to the ancestral home, taking with him the memory of a girl he has met casually and his "runner." The latter becomes the butler and the good fairy, or evil genius, according to individual fancy. Money is lacking, and the two of them quickly turn the old home into one full of ailing and paying guests. Among them is the ex-taximan's dream girl, only she turns out to be a married woman who has come down to give her husband, somewhat of a gay Lothario, a surprise. He is making love to every woman in the place, and the surprise is very complete. Then the hero's maiden aunt arrives and brings her parrot with her.

Events move rapidly. The young couple wish to spend the night together, but at the last moment the maiden aunt changes her bedroom for that of the girl. The husband enters, having had some difficulty in getting rid of his fellow guests, only to be severely bitten by the parrot. Every man in the place is blamed and everybody is watching for a parrot-bitten individual, while the young husband in one way and another manages to get every male guest bitten. In the end the butler is blamed and happiness restored to everyone.

The acting on all sides is far above the average, and a finer allround cast has rarely been seen in a British picture. Chief honors among the women must go to Pauline Garon for a really clever performance of the aunt's companion. She has the light touch necessary for such airy comedy. Irene Rich is good as the young wife. Guy Newall, as the husband, and Bromley Devenport do fine work. As the butler John MacAndrews is capital. A. B. Imeson is excellent as the ex-taximan. Many small parts are well played. The production is also very good.

Gore.

HINTS ON HORSEMANSHIP

London, Nov. 1.

Made by Geoffrey Benstead, an ex-officer of Hussars and one time show rider for the army, these one-reel interest and educational films are capital. In reality a sort of film lecture on "how, and how not, to do it." The pictures are full of interest and sage advice.

Benstead, however, refrains from wearying his watchers with too much instruction. Supporting the directly educational matter are many fine scenes of racing, hunting, driving, etc. The army bears its share of the work and the cavalry school scenes are excellent. One section is devoted to the Italian army, and here the watcher gets a fine idea of the Italian military school of Polpirro. A "cut" from a Red Indian drama has no bearing on the subject and should be removed immediately.

These features will, without doubt, be popular. *Gore.*

SIREN OF SEVILLE

A Producers' Distributing Corp. release starring Priscilla Dean. Story by H. H. Van Loan. Directed by Jerome Storm. At the Piccadilly, New York, week of Nov. 15. Running time 71 mins.

Dolores........................Priscilla Dean
Gallito........................Allan Forrest
Cavallo........................Stuart Holmes
Ardita........................Claire Delorez
Palomino........................Bert Woodruff
Pedro........................Mathew Betz

This picture marks the return of Priscilla Dean to the screen after an absence of about a year. It is a corking picture for almost any audience and a production that certainly should have a tremendous vogue in the Latin-American countries as well as in Spain. It is a Spanish tale of the bull ring, interwoven with colorful romance and the love of a toreador for a dancing girl. The picture is well done with the bull fighting scenes so skillfully blended into the story that one would actually think that they were taken especially for the picture. If one hadn't seen the Fox educational on bull fighting and recognized the same scenes it would hardly have been suspected that the bull fight stuff in this picture wasn't on the up and up.

The cast headed by Miss Dean is a most adequate one and Claire Delorez proves herself to be a find of th vamp type of actresses. Stuart Holmes plays the heavy with his usual craftiness and Allan Forest is a most acceptable hero.

Miss Dean gives a really good performance in the role of the little peasant girl who comes to Seville with the determination to make her beloved Gallito one of the bull slaying heroes of Spain. She succeeds but at the price of his affection, for as soon as he is crowned in the bull ring the heavy vamp grabs him off.

Then comes a counter plot when the President of the Arena tries to grab off the peasant girl, finally making up his mind to drug the bull fighter before he goes into the ring, feeling that with the hero out of the way the girl will be his. He fails to count on her loyalty for she becomes aware of the plot and battles her way out of the home of the vamp and drives to the bull ring to enter just in time to dash into the arena and slay an infuriated bull just as he is about to finish her lover. Then there comes the happy ending.

The picture is full of pep and runs along without any slow moments in the story.

Fred.

MARRIED FLIRTS

A Robert Vignola Production, released by Metro-Goldwyn. From the Louis Joseph Vance novel, "Mrs. Paramor," adapted by Julia Crawford Ivers. At the Rialto, N. Y., week Nov. 16. Running time, 71 mins.

"Mrs. Paramor" ....Pauline Frederick
Perley Rex........................Conrad Nagel
Jill Wetherell........................Mae Busch
Pendelton Wayne..............Huntley Gordon
Evelyn Dracup ....Patterson Dial
Pater Granville ....Paul Nicholson
Mrs. Callender................Alice Hollister

A fairly interesting society drama in which there are two star roles for women. These characters are played by Pauline Frederick and Mae Busch, who just about divide the acting honors 50-50. The two principal male roles are played by Conrad Nagel and Huntley Gordon. Robert Vignola, who directed, has turned out a consistent film version of the novel that runs along in a manner which holds attention. The picture is not a world beater from the box-office standpoint, but it is a good picture of the usual program type.

It is the story of a youthful vamp who sets out to get a husband. Anybody's husband will do providing she can't snare an unattached male. She manages to vamp the husband of a novelist, and one evening at an exclusive country club the wife comes upon her husband and the young vamp in each other's arms. There is the usual scene between husband and wife and the latter goes her way alone. Atop of this scene one of the younger men who has witnessed the embrace between the girl and the older man appears on the scene and also proposes and is accepted, the girl giving the older man "air." But the damage has been done as far as his wife is concerned and she leaves him. Then, after a period of time, she attains fame as a writer, and while abroad runs into the girl who broke up her happiness and the latter's husband at a French resort. They are to return to America and she makes it a point to take the same steamer. She has mapped out a plan of revenge on the younger woman and she proceeds to vamp the young husband. She succeeds so well it is but a short time after they are back in the United States that the scene between the two women is repeated, except for the fact conditions are reversed. The young woman pleads for her husband and married happiness, with the older woman relenting and calling all bets off. In the end she forgives her husband and the two start on a second honeymoon.

Pauline Frederick makes the role of the novelist a work of art. She looked stunning in the latter scenes of the picture and scored heavily. Mae Busch had to overcome a role that contained no sympathy and she did that. Her task to win her audience was twice as difficult as that of Miss Frederick, but she managed to land 100 per cent.

The picture is not an expensive one and there is nothing unusual in settings or direction that is going to make the public want to rush to see it. *Fred.*

THE FAST SET

Paramount picture and a William De Mille production, directed by De Mille. Adapted from the play, "Spring Cleaning," by Frederick Lonsdale. Clara Beranger, adapter, and L. Guy Wilky, photographer. Features Betty Compson, Adolphe Menjou. Elliott Dexter and ZaSu Pitts; Showing at the Strand, New York, week of Nov. 16. Running time, 73 minutes.

Margaret Sones..............Betty Compson
Ernest Steele..............Adolphe Menjou
Richard Sones..............Elliott Dexter
Mona........................ZaSu Pitts
Little Margaret Sones.........Dawn O'Day
Jane Walton..............Grace Carlysle
Fay Collen..............Claire Adams
Connie Gallies..............Rosalind Byrne
Archie Wells..............Edgar Norton
Billy Sommers..............Louis Natheaux
Walters ....Eugenio de Liguoro
Simpson ....Fred Walton

Another legit vehicle that has had its title changed for screen consumption, but following the original script somewhat rigidly. Strictly parlor comedy, given to sumptuous settings and evening clothes, the smart repartee which the play unfolded is naturally in the sub-titles and the presentation shapes a suitable program feature without revealing any definite kick.

Incidentally, the picture is the first of two Paramount releases due at this First National House during November, as the new Valentino film is scheduled here next week.

Somewhat restricted as to action, the sequence is all story, with the roles being-set-ups for such experienced social portrayers as Miss Compson, Mr. Menjou and Mr. Dexter. The trio simply walk from room to room and let the narrative take its course, hence it's practically a director's picture, and De Mille has handled the subject in a logical and entertaining manner.

Located entirely indoors, the sets are on a par with all previous De Mille conceptions and have been excellently photographed by Wilky. The director has made one or two attempts to get away from the conventional in various bits, and while commendable the efforts are hardly significant to draw more than passing attention.

The comedy is decidedly in the titles, although some credit is due the players for making the interest hold at an even level. The role of the street walker, as done by ZaSu Pitts, revealed an identical make-up to Estelle Winwood's "Mona" at the Eltinge. While overly emphasizing a lounging gait, Miss Pitts, nevertheless, made the depiction broad enough so that it can't miss.

The tale is a family affair having to do with Mrs. Sones (Miss Compson), who becomes weary of her husband's (Mr. Dexter) literary friends and associates herself with a fast-moving set prone to moral laxity. Mr. Sones' unknowing neglect makes way for Ernest Steele (Mr. Menjou) to carry on a flirtation with the wife, which ultimately divulges to Sones the situation in his home.

The zenith of the film, as also in the play, is the scene in which Sones introduces the woman of the streets to his wife's guests at a dinner party and sits her at the table. The line of the husband's concerning "I never heard of an amateur billiard player refusing to play with a professional" is retained at the time the guests arise from the repast, but "Mona's" opening shot has been deleted. The added climax is with Sones and Steele sharing a drink together and discussing the best means for the former to win back his wife. The clinch finale concludes.

Menjou is his usual suave connoisseur of femininity, ably abetted by Dexter as the blundering husband fighting to retain his wife's affections. There's little for Miss Compson to do other than to flash clothes. The rest of the players simply round out the character assignments without definite individual designation as to the respective types they represent. Something that De Mille has passed up in favor of unnecessarily inserting the child daughter of the Sones. It would have made the picture stronger had the "types" been accentuated and the infant left out.

Sumptuously presented, both the story and the cast carry sufficient class to make the film able to keep its head above water in the major houses, while the intermediate theatre patrons should enjoy the material ingredients if nothing else.

Skig.

FORBIDDEN PARADISE

A picturization of "The Czarina," a play by Lajos Biro and Melchior Lengyel, with Pola Negri starred. Direction of Ernst Lubitsch. Screen play by Agnes Christine and Hans Kraly. Produced by Famous Players-Lasky. At the Rivoli, New York, Nov. 16. Running time, about 80 mins.

Queen Catherine..................Pola Negri
Alexei........................Rod La Rocque
Chancellor ....Adolphe Menjou
Anna ....Pauline Starke
French Ambassador ....Fred Malatesta

When "The Czarina" was produced as a stage play by Gilbert Miller about five years ago, it was a success for both the producer and the star, Doris Keane, and the picture version, "Forbidden Paradise" looks like the same thing. If ever a star did good work, Pola Negri does it here; if ever a film company threw in the hot love scenes, Famous has; if ever a director used his head and artistic sense, Lubitsch did. "Forbidden Paradise" represents the union of a good story, expensive scenery, a perfect cast and direction of the highest order. And in addition to rating as an artistic ace, it is a money bet, for the love of interest is plenty and heavy, yet always relieved by some cynical bit of comedy, for which Menjou is usually responsible.

In the play itself, Catherine the Great of Russia was the central figure. The period was of her day. In the film Queen Catherine of an unnamed kingdom is the central figure and the time is of today. That change in period worked no wrong in this case, as no mention was made of the "Little Mother of All the Russias," and many bits of comedy were worked in which could never have been placed in a costume picture of several hundred years back.

Queen Catherine likes men. New ones are preferred, so when a dashing young army officer (Rod La Rocque) comes in one day to warn her of an impending revolution, she waves the French Ambassador aside without meeting him and sets out to win the young officer. But his sweetheart is the queen's lady-in-waiting and complications ensue. The officer falls from grace, and, becoming angry, starts a revolution of his own. For a few brief moments he has the queen in his power. But the tide turns and he is sentenced to die. The queen, however, relents, allows him to unite with his sweetheart, while she, as full of anticipation as usual, gaily calls out that the French Ambassador, who has been kept waiting all these weeks, be shown in. When he emerges a few hours later, on his breast is the crest of the royal order, a mark of especial favor. So he and the queen's chancellor, both winking, shake hands, and the picture is through.

It is a happy combination of love, romance and comedy. More than that, it is never maudlin, seldom too melodramatic to be plausible, and always funny enough to get deep-rooted laughs and many a subtle chuckle. The scenario is almost air-tight, each scene being fitted beautifully into what has gone before, and each benefitting from the whimsical touch of Lubitsch, who assuredly rates as among the Big Three of directors.

The picture cost a great deal. Several palace scenes are massive, while the interiors are all in perfect and expensive taste. The gowns worn by Negri are kayos, while her new bobbed hair should get feminine attention. La Rocque, too, is a good card for the women, and the hot love scenes of the queen and the officer should satisfy audiences who want a dash of paprika with their chicken. Menjou, needless to say, carried off a suave role high on a silver plate, while the others of the cast were good enough.

"Forbidden Paradise" may need a little exploitation to convince the public it really is a corker, for some of the Negri product recently hasn't been so good. But once the word gets around, it looks as though this one should do a mop. At the Rivoli last Sunday the house was S. R. O. from 2 o'clock on, and that went for the supper show.

"Forbidden Paradise" looks like one of the few famous members of the "famous 40," and there's not a picture house in America too good to play it, nor one with such a dumb audience that it couldn't be understood. In other words, this one is a combination of popular appeal with intelligence, and the result is pretty fine. *Sisk.*

K—THE UNKNOWN

Universal-Jewell starring Virginia Valli and featuring Percy Marmont. Adapted from the story of same title by Mary Roberts Rinehart. Directed by Harry Pollard. At the Cameo, New York, week of Nov. 15. Running time, 80 mins.

Sidney Page................Virginia Valli
"K" Le Moyne............Percy Marmont
Carlotta Harrison........Margarita Fisher
George "Slim" Benson.....Francis Feeney
Dr. Max Wilson............John Roche
Joe Drummond.............Maurice Ryan
Aunt Harriet Kennedy........Myrtle Vane
Dr. Ed Wilson.........William A. Carroll

Nothing extraordinary about this latest Mary Roberts Rinehart opus yet it displays certain qualities, particularly an absorbing love interest, that should make it likable as a general program release.

In spinning the yarn the authoress has provided a complex of puppy love and hospital intrigue that carries along at an even pace to the usual happy culmination. She has set her characters in one of those mythical small towns where love smites the youth at an early age and it is ever open season for gossips and scandalmongers.

Into this placid center comes K. Le Moyne, a man of mystery to those unable to pry into his affairs. His taking up lodgings at the home of Sidney Paige, village belle, also complicates matters, inasmuch as two younger swains have previously been in hot pursuit. Sidney has long had a yen for nursing and when the appointment at the local hospital comes is extremely happy. Simultaneously Dr. Max Wilson, world-famous surgeon and "lady killer," has been appointed head of the institution. Although owing his rapid rise partially to his assistant, Carlotta Harrison, he loses no time in making a play for the heart of Sidney, eventually extracting a promise of marriage.

The broadcasting of the coming marriage causes Carlotta to give one of Sidney's patients an overdose of medicine, thereby causing Sidney to be dismissed for negligence. Joe Drummond, a discarded suitor, vows that unless Wilson plays fair with Sidney he will make him answer for it.

A clandestine meeting between Max and Carlotta, intended to be the finale of their affair, is climaxed by Joe figuring that it is Sidney the physician has taken to an ill-famed roadhouse and shooting him. Back at the hospital the other doctors refuse to operate, claiming that the only operation that might pull him through would be the Edwardes method, and that Max was the only one who could perform such an operation aside from its originator, Dr. Edwardes, now dead.

The surprise punch is planted when Carlotta hunts up Le Moyne, in reality Dr. Edwardes, and cajoles him into performing the operation, which is successful. While in the operating room a detective appears with a warrant for Edwardes' arrest on a charge of manslaughter based upon supposed negligence in a previous operation. Carlotta, grateful to Edwardes for having saved the man she loves, confesses it was she who resorted to intrigue to disqualify Edwardes so that Wilson, his assistant, would enjoy the fame and wealth instead. Sidney has been awakened to Wilson's inconstancy, breaks their engagement and marries Edwardes.

Virginia Valli gives one of her best performances as Sidney, registering remarkably well in her emotional scenes and contrasting others with a delightful piquancy. Percy Marmont also is superb as Edwardes, the man of mystery. Margarita Fisher and John Roche contributed commendable portrayals. *Edba.*

LOVERS' LANE

Warner Bros. production, the author of which was the late Clyde Fitch, adapted by Dorothy Farnum. Directed by Phil Rosen. At Loew's New York, New York, Nov. 14, on double feature bill with "That Wild West." Running time, 53 minutes.

Dr. Tom Singleton.............Robert Ellis
Mary Larkin..........Gertrude Olmstead
Simplicity...........Maxine Elliott Hicks
Aunt Mattie................Kate Torncray
Rev. Dr. Singleton........Norval MacGregor
Herbert Williams..........Crauford Kent
Uncle Billy...................Charles Sellon
Millessia.....................Ethel Wales
Dr. Stone...........George Periolat
Mrs. Stone.................Dorothy Vernon
Mrs. Williams...............Frances Dale
Jimmy...........................Bruce Geurin
Miss Mealy...................Aileen Manney

This looks like it was a secondary line production as far as the Warner Bros.' product is concerned. At that it is a picture that is strong enough to stand up on its own on the ordinary bill run in the average neighborhood house. It will be liked in the small towns. Teaches a moral there is always a happy ending for those that have faith enough to believe that there is happiness for all in the world.

It is a small-town story, with the hero a youthful doctor who turns down the wealthy local belle because he wants to remain in the home town and do his bit for the people there. She has money and wants him to step out. When he refuses she breaks off their engagement. In the end she turned back to him.

Robert Ellis and Gertrude Olmstead carry the principal roles, and do very well. The balance of the cast has been picked for types, and they are that, together with quite some acting ability.

The direction has some very human touches in it, and the story does get over to the audience.

It isn't a picture that the Warners could carry along with their first-line productions, but one that the average small-town exhibitor with a daily change can slip over on his audiences without fear that they are going to pan him for it. *Fred.*

A SAINTED DEVIL

Paramount production starring Rudolph Valentino. Story adapted from Rex Beach's "Rope's End" by Forrest Halsey. Directed by Joseph Henaberry and Nita Naldi, Helen D'Algy and Dagmar Godowsky featured. At the Strand, New York, week of Nov. 23. Running time, 83 mins.

Don Alonzo Castro......Rudolph Valentino
Carlotta....................Nita Naldi
Julietta...............Helen D'Algy
Dona Florencia..........Dagmar Godowsky
Casimiro...............Jean del Val
El Tigre...........George Seigman
Estella....................Louise Lagrange

Since Valentino's "Monsieur Beaucaire" film is said to have done a flop outside of the big towns there is some speculation over "A Sainted Devil," which isn't as good a proposition as the first film upon the Mineralava ballyhoo's return to the screen. "Beaucaire" had the advantage in that it was the artistic type of production to draw good notices from the dailies, but unless Rudy makes a swing over the country and feeds the newspaper boys and girls like he did in New York it doesn't look like he'll get much of a newspaper break. The women reviewers in New York—and they predominate—always give him a break here, be the film good or bad.

"A Sainted Devil" tells the story of Don Alonzo Castro, scion of a Spanish family in South America. In his youth he falls in love with a luscious lump of what he believes to be pure femininity, but one night, when he sees her in the arms of El Tigre, an ogreish sort of a fellow, Alonzo becomes peeved, disillusioned and blase, all in a few minutes. In reality another woman was wearing her mantilla and comb, thereby creating one of those mistaken identity situations to provide suspense.

The picture is not notably produced, although it is evident a flock of money has been spent. The Henaberry direction is undistinguished and featured principally by the number of soft focus closeups which he gives the star, closeups which give full face, profile, ear, eye, nose and throat views of Rudy, which may be what the women want. The combination, too, of the two exotics, Nita Naldi and Dagmar Godowsky, may help the film, but of the two, Nita is the only one who shows any knowledge of acting. Dagmar is just a subtraction mark when it comes to acting, so to make up the "diff" she wears some weird-looking vamp property costumes.

All in all, "A Sainted Devil" is more of a personal Valentino vehicle than a regulation picture. Its exhibition value and the price the first run exhibitors have to pay is going to have a lot to do with its money-making potentialities as far as the exhibitor is concerned.

Its opening at the Strand was tremendous. From the opening to the closing standing room only and none to spare of that was the rule. Monday the house wasn't nearly filled when the second performance began, but was filled rapidly. That it will stay two weeks at the Strand is certain, but the Strand isn't the only house in America, and the first run houses aren't the only ones to be considered.

Maybe it'll satisfy the Valentino rooters. Most of them are women, and this is a woman's film. *Sisk.*

WAGES OF VIRTUE

Zukor-Lasky presentation, an Allan Dwan production, directed by Dwan, starring Gloria Swanson and releasing through Paramount. Original story by Percival Wren with Forrest Halsey the adapter. Showing at the Rivoli, New York, week Nov. 23. Running time, 70 mins.

Carmelita..............Gloria Swanson
Marvin...................Ben Lyon
(Courtesy of First National)

John Boule....................Norman Trevor
Luigi.............................Ivan Linow
Guiseppe.......................Armand Cortez
Madame La Cantiniere,
Adrienne d'Ambricourt
Sergeant Le Gros..............Paul Panzer
Le Bro-way......................Joe Moore

Sufficiently romantic to appease those addicted to this sort of screen fare, but too theatrical to convince. That qualification also includes the cast, with two exceptions, Norman Trevor and Ivan Linow. The picture totals as indifferent.

The padding allotted Miss Swanson and Ben Lyon, wherein they playfully vie with each other, closely resembles a contest as to which one is the more cute and is obviously the fault of the director. Neither approach the quality of work they are capable of, and by no means can this film be included among the best in which Miss Swanson's name has superceded the title.

Norman Trevor and Ivan Linow actually give the only legitimate performances included in the filming, with Trevor particularly standing in relief, although a secondary figure in the script. Linow, believed to have been a former professional wrestler, somewhat surprises with the authenticity of his "heavy" characterization. In more than one instance he upholds the story, from a spectator's viewpoint, where otherwise a general cave-in is threatened. The same may be said of Trevor, hence the deduction is that the saving grace of this release tabulates as these two men.

Based upon that unit in the French army as the "Foreign Legion," the story centers on a young American who has joined in search of adventure, and a girl going through a "mother" of the regiment" routine while minding a cafe.

Film actresses who have played this identical role are countless. Miss Swanson offers nothing in the portrayal to register superiority over the previous definitions. The same is true of Mr. Lyon, although responsibility hardly rests upon either of their shoulders. Others in the cast play acceptably, albeit the ability of Mr. Trevor to make what practically amounts to a minor assignment predominate must take its place as the foremost item among the personnel.

Productionally, the film is substantially set and the photography is certainly adequate. It is in the 76 minutes the main fault will be found, for the story could have been screened to as much advantage, maybe more, in an hour.

The release will please the ardent screen-goer, but it also is an example of that type of film which the anti-picture exponent ridicules, and not without cause. The term, "just a picture," covers everything.

Skig.

THE SILENT ACCUSER

A Louis B. Mayer Production released by Metro-Goldwyn. Story by Jack Boyle, directed by Chester M. Franklin, shown at the Capitol, N. Y., week Nov. 23, 1924. Running time 69 minutes.

Barbara Jane...........Eleanor Boardman
Jack.......................Raymond McKee
Phil...........................Earl Metcalfe
Grandfather.....................Paul Weigel
The Painted Lady..........Edna Tichenor
Peter the Great......................Himself

Metro-Goldwyn must have used considerable pressure on the management of the Capitol to put this picture into the house. The production is far from the caliber of picture usually shown in any of the big four Broadway picture houses. The film must surely have been turned out for a little nickel and looks it. Louis Mayer may think that in Peter the Great he has a great police dog find and one that will overshadow Strongheart on the screen. That may be possible but he had better use his dog star in pictures that have a little more weight than this one. It isn't only weak as to story, but it is poorly directed, wretchedly edited and badly titled.

In addition to the dog star there are but three characters that amount to anything. They are played by Eleanor Boardman, Raymond McKee and Earl Metcalfe. It is upon Metcalfe the heavy role falls.

Both men are in love with the girl. She favors Jack but grandfather objects to her marriage, so she and Jack plan to elope. The "heavy" is boarding at the girl's home and he walks into her room as she is packing to go away. He seizes her and she faints just as grandfather appears and the "heavy" knocks him down a flight of stairs, causing the old man's death. The hero walks in at this point, is accused of the crime, arrested and sent to jail. From this climax the picture is devoted to prison scenes with the dog star following his master to jail and aiding in his escape. Later the dog and his master, assisted by the girl, manage to corner the "heavy" and exact a confession from him. The lovers are seen in the usual clinch at the final fade-out.

"The Silent Accuser" is the bunk as a picture for first-run houses and is worthy only of playing the daily change houses of the cheaper variety. The exhibitors don't want to be bunked by the fact that the Metro-Goldwyn were able to compel a Broadway showing for the picture in the house they control.

Fred.

PRICE OF A PARTY

Howard Estabrook presents with Hope Hampton, Harrison Ford and Mary Astor featured at the Cameo, New York (by the house and in the lights), although Miss Astor is not featured by the producer on the billing. It's an adapted magazine story for the screen by Charles Forrest Roebuck, directed by Charles Giblyn. Assistant director and editor, Bert F. Siebel. Photographer, John F. Seith. Opened at Cameo Nov. 23. Running time, 55 minutes.

Grace Barrow.................Hope Hampton
Robert Casson ....Harrison Ford
Kenneth Bellwood....Arthur Edmond Carew
Alice Barrows ....Mary Astor
Evelyn Dolores.........Dagmar Godowsky
Stephen Darrell....................Fred Hadley
Evelyn's Maid................Edna Richmond
Hall Boy ....Donald Lashey
Officer ....Edward Lawrence

Not a big picture, but mildly interesting story that should have some appeal to the flapperish element in its romance and melodrama. In subject matter it is threadbare, that of innocent girls and wise New Yorkers, but the magazine author, William MacHarg, gave this tale a couple of twists that will be a bit deep for logical reasoning to the countrified observer. Mr. MacHarg, however, wrote a mighty wise story in this one. It reads with more force likely than it plays. That is not against the players, since they can't do much with the mushy version for the screen.

In the countryside where this will go best, it should do if played up, but only in an ordinary way, as it can't stand too much booming. The best plug for publicity is that Hope Hampton is in it, the same Hope Hampton who became the center of a violent controversy whether she was suitable for the title role of "Madame Pompadour" on Broadway, her stage debut, and the result—she didn't debut but may yet. Current report is Miss Hampton may alternate with Wilda Bennett in that musical at the new Beck theatre.

Miss Hampton doesn't distinguish herself here. She glides through unemotionally, and there doesn't seem much else for her to do. Harrison Ford can do little else in his heroic part, that isn't heroic at all. If there is one of the cast who makes his character stand up and out for strength it is Arthur Edmond Carew as the semi-heavy. Dagmar Godowsky looks "fierce," and that's about all Dagmar was called upon for.

It's the tale of a pure but broke cabaret dancer who got a job just in time to send her mother to a hospital. The job was to vamp a visitor to New York and hold him beyond a time limit for business reasons only. To enable the dancer to do that she was given an apartment by the plotters. The plotter who turned over his apartment at the same time had to turn out his mistress from it. In the end the mistress shot the plotter and the near-hero married the pure but broken dancer—still pure and still broke. The dancer's sister enters as a side line for cause for the murder.

There are some cabaret scenes, ordinary, and Miss Hampton did some light stepping during them. Nothing on high in production or scenes, but still with that verging sex subject always to the fore there is enough curiosity to find out what may happen.

The picture's weakest point is that no one secures sympathy at the outset.

Good enough, however, all over with the cast besides to figure out, but don't gamble for big money—this isn't a big money picture.

Sime.

BREATH OF SCANDAL

B. P. Schulberg production directed by Gasnier. Cast includes Patsy Ruth Miller, Jack Mulhall, Lou-Tellegen, Forrest Stanley, Myrtle Stedman, Betty Blythe, Frank Leigh, Charles Clary and Phylis Haver. Showing at Moss' Broadway, New York, November 24. Running time, 73 mins.

Conventional screen menu and in more ways than one following in the path of a well-worn trail. However, the subject has been both dressed up and given an imposing production while the names in the cast should mean something for selling value. In other words, a picture particularly adapted to the intermediate houses.

The players do much to sustain the script, and in this respect Patsy Ruth Miller and Lou-Tellegen are outstanding. The latter gives a quiet and restrained performance that constantly registers, while Miss Miller upholds a well-established reputation in an "unsophisticated" role.

Asking the question whether the modern girl actually knows more than her grandmother did at the same age, the picture concludes without reaching a decision, but meanwhile spins the tale of the daughter of the house struggling to keep knowledge of her father's "affair" away from her mother.

Where the script takes its principal nose dive is in narrating the daughter's becoming a manicurist as a means of self-support and accompanying "the worst man in town" to a dance hall where the father and the young attorney discover her in a private dining room.

Miss Blythe leans toward dramatics to give an exaggerated performance, although marking about the only false note in an otherwise suitable cast. Frank Leigh is obviously the "heavy" from the initial flash, on makeup alone, while Miss Stedman and Phylis Haver flit in and out with little territory to cover.

The film reveals some splendid interiors, perhaps overly dressed in some instances, and should fulfill obligations if the stipulation is kept within reasonable bounds.

Skig.

THE DARK SWAN

A Warner Bros. Production, starring Monte Blue, Marie Prevost and Helene Chadwick. From the novel by Ernest Pascal, directed by Millard Webb. Shown at the Piccadilly, N. Y., week Nov. 22, 1924. Running time 67 minutes.

Eve Quinn......................Marie Prevost
Lewis Dike......................Monte Blue
Cornelia Quinn...........Helene Chadwick
Wilfred Meadows.............John Patrick
Sybil Johnson.............Lilyan Tashman
Mrs. Quinn.........................Vera Lewis
Tim Fontanelle..............Carlton Miller
Mary Robinson.............Mary McLaren
Clifford Raynes.............Arthur Rankin

This is a slow moving, rather cumbersome story that drags for more than an hour without getting anywhere. The story is one that it is going to be mighty hard to sell to small town audiences. It may get by in the bigger towns but it will not make any great impression at the box office despite a trio of stars in the picture.

"The Dark Swan" is one of those ugly duckling tales. There are a couple of foster-sisters, the oldest devoting herself to business and sacrificing herself so the butterfly of the family might have all of the luxuries. Finally the ugly duckling falls in love but the good looking young sister steals her beau and marries him, only to start playing around with a heavy lover almost immediately after the ceremony. The husband becomes disillusioned and parts from the butterfly wife, turning again to the ugly duckling whom he deserted for the giddy young beauty.

The story is related in a very much jumbled manner on the screen and the trend of the tale is at times exceedingly hard to follow. The titling is so bad in spots that it is almost laughable.

Monte Blue gives a neat enough performance of the role that means very little. Marie Prevost has the decidedly unsympathetic role of the flapper vamp, while Helene Chadwick is fine as the self-sacrificing sister. The others do not stand out particularly at any time.

No audience will rave over this one.

Fred.

GIRLS MEN FORGET

Maurice Campbell production from the American Magazine story "The Girl Who Was the Life of the Party," by Fannie Kilbourne. Directed by Maurice Campbell. Distributed by Principal. Half the bill at Loew's Circle, N. Y., Nov. 17. Runs short of an hour.

Kitty Shayne..............Patsy Ruth Miller
Jimmie Masson.......................Alan Hale
Russell Baldwin...........Johnnie Walker
Michael Shayne ....Wilfred Lucas
Aunt Clara...................Carrie Clark Ward
Ruby Thomas....................Shannon Day
Mrs. Baldwin..............Frances Raymond

So ridiculous it can't displease, but because of the spineless thesis it won't make very much of an impression anywhere. It has a share of mild amusement and those few laughs provided are all that saves it from being an almost worthless affair.

Fannie Kilbourne has written some clever stories but if this one did not suffer too much in the voyage from magazine to screen it can hardly be described by that adjective.

ISN'T LIFE WONDERFUL?

D. W. Griffith Production released by United Artists. Story by Major Goeffrey Moss. Directed by D. W. Griffith. Carol Dempster and Neil Hamilton featured. At the Rivoli, New York, week of Nov. 30. Running time, 90 minutes.

Inga .... Carol Dempster
Hans, son of the professor... Neil Hamilton
Grandmother .... Helen Lowell
The Professor .... Erville Alderson
The Brother.................. Frank Puglia
The Aunt..................... Marcia Harris
Strolling players............ Lupino Lane
The Hungry Workers.......... Paul Rhekopf
Count von Schact

D. W. Griffith again comes to the fore with the unusual on the screen, in "Isn't Life Wonderful' 'at the Rivoli this week. Just as his "Broken Blossoms" was a departure from the usual picture fare, so also is this present film.

It is a picture that has something more behind it than the mere idea of entertainment. It should to an extent give the American public an insight into the lives of the simpler German folk and their sufferings as a result of the great war's aftermath.

Whether or not the picture will be a box office success is another question. Off hand it seems doubtful if the story will have sufficient appeal to make it a record breaking money venture.

The story is too realistic. It is a page torn from life. Those who rave about "the finer things in pictures" may not come to the box office in sufficient numbers to offset the out and out fans who will stay away. After all the latter are the ones to be catered to. Fans like naught but the sweetened pap fed to them day after day on the screens of the country.

One point about this story should be pointed out immediately before some rabid anti-German jumps to the fore, proclaiming it another example of German propaganda. That is the fact that Major Goeffrey Moss, the author, is of the British army. In itself that should be sufficient to still those who might shout "propaganda."

This is the picture that Griffith shot partly in Germany and partly in this country. Griffith's handling of the theme is little short of wonderful. His composition in mass scenes as well in those with but few characters is in line with the best he has ever done. The photography at times shows some remarkable shots. There is one thing about this work of the master director and that is that he has held to his idea that a story can be told with but few principals; also that he has kept his love theme in the foreground.

It is of the privations and struggles of a German family following the war and the collapse of the German exchange. A tale at once gripping and interesting though heart rending and depressing.

A German professor is impoverished. He and his family have been driven from their home. They are in Berlin. One son is studying and working as a waiter in a night club, the other laboring in the shipyards until his strength, weakened through the war, fails him.

The entire family is living in two rooms, eating a potato each a day.

Their final working out of an idea with the one son cultivating a potato patch, his building of a one-room house on alotted ground so that he may marry and finally, when the crop is harvested by himself and his bride-to-be so that the family may have enough to live on and the two youngsters can marry, they are set upon by robbers on their way home with their cart of food and stripped of it all.

And in the finish it's the girl that says, "I still have you, so isn't life wonderful."

Carol Dempster and Neil Hamilton are featured as the lovers. Miss Dempster does work of which she may well be proud. As for Hamilton his characterization ranks with anything that he has done in this particular line.

The support has Helen Lowell and Marcia Harris in two character roles, both women scoring terrifically. Erville Alderson as the aged professor likewise delivers a characterization that is a gem.

But to Lupino Lane must go the honors for several laugh bits. He virtually makes his feet and legs do comic grimaces before the camera and the audiences will just howl at his work.

As a screen work of art "Isn't Life Wonderful" must be rated with the best. As a box office attratcion it is possible Griffith's name coupled with the two featured players may overcome any hesitancy audiences may have when it comes to paying at the window. *Fred.*

SUNDOWN

First National Pictures, Inc., production. From the story by Earl J. Hudson, directed by Larry Trimble and Harry Hoyt. Presented at the Piccadilly theatre, New York, week Nov. 29. Running time, 73 minutes.

Ellen Crawley.................. Bessie Love
Hugh Brent..................... Roy Stewart
John Brent.................. Hobart Bosworth
Mr. Crawley.................. Arthur Murray
Pat Meech.................... Charlie Murray
John Burke....................... Jere Austin
Joe Patton................ Charles E. Crockett
President Roosevelt.......... E. J. Radcliffe
Mrs. Brent................ Margaret McWade

One weeps to think what a chance was left to run wild here. This might have been as great a picture as "The Covered Wagon," for seemingly the material to work from was there; but it isn't a "Covered Wagon" by a long shot. It isn't even anything beyond what would ordinarily be termed a "western." There was entirely too much cattle stuff and not enough story to the picture. Whoever was responsible for the crowding in of all of the cattle stuff and letting the story take care of itself should be taken to task for it.

If it is true that all the time and money that they say were expended on this picture, then some one must have gone crazy in the making of it.

It is known that First National had counted on this to be a super-special and that they finally cooled down, regarding it simply as one of the regular releases; but it is less than that. It could'nt even break into the Strand, New York, the regular First National house, and was switched to the Piccadilly, Lee Ochs arranging for the booking of it at a time when he did not know where to turn for product. If Ochs had been situated then as he is today regarding pictures, it does not seem likely he would have booked it.

"Sundown," judging from the foreword, offered as great an opportunity for graphic filming of the passing of the great west as did the winning of the west. But it was "muffed" in the making. There was right at hand the material with which to construct a story of tremendous patriotic value, into which could have been woven all of the hardships and heartbreaks that the pioneers suffered, blazing the trail, only eventually to go down before the conflagration that they themselves started, and forced in time by this self-same civilization not only out of their own homes and grazing lands, but actually out of their own country into a foreign land—Mexico. But, pioneers to the last, they take their medicine and go forth under a new flag to conquer new wilds that the United States, which they loved and made, may continue in its greatness with its millions fed by the beef that they provide.

They give you the beef on the screen, but overlook the romance entirely. There is a love theme running through the tale, but it never means anything much. Bessie Love is the little heroine, who, with her timid bookkeeping father and a little brother and sister, have come out of the east to "take up" a quarter section. It is the inroads that these homesteaders are making that is driving the cattle people out of their own country. On the train the little eastern group run into the son of the spokesmen of the cattlemen. He is on his way back home with his father from a conference in Washington. There is nothing for the government to do but to compel the cattlemen to move their herds, and the best that they can expect is to be granted grazing lands in Mexico if they will go there. The Foreign Office has obtained this concession for them.

Later, when the cattlemen have decided to move and start their tremendous herds south to cross the line, the cattle stampede and wreck the little homestead that the same little group of the train have set up. There is nothing left but to take them along, and this is done. Finally, when the line is reached, the hero bids the heroine good-bye, with the declaration of his love and the promise to come back and claim her when he makes a home for her in the new country.

On the screen the telling of the tale is just as matter of fact as above.

There are some corking photographic shots, likewise a stampede of cattle and a prairie fire to add thrills, but that has all been seen before.

Hobart Bosworth as the leader of the cattlemen is the outstanding figure of the cast. He stands head and shoulders above everyone else. While Bessie Love is charming enough, she has nothing to do and what little she does do is unconvincing. Roy Stewart as the hero doesn't mean a thing.

Charlie Murray (yes, of the Keystone days!) plays a comedy character, and does it fairly well, without any particular opportunity to distinguish himself. Charles B. Crockett also contributes a character bit.

"Sundown" is a great opportunity lost. *Fred.*

THE ROUGHNECK

William Fox Production, starring George O'Brien. Story by Robert W. Service, adapted by Charles Kenyon. Directed by John Conway. Presented at the Central, New York, for run, beginning Dec. 1, 1924. Running time, 87 minutes.

Jerry Delaney .... George O'Brien
Felicity Arden .... Billie Dove
"Mad" McCara............... Harry T. Morey
Ann Delaney.................. Cleo Madison
Sam Meldon .... Charles A. Sel'on
Zelie .... Anne Cornwall
Fight Manager .... Harvey Clark

This is a corking box office picture of the program variety. The Fox forces, however, need not expect that this picture will duplicate the tremendous business at the Central which "Dante's Inferno" did. This picture will run for a couple or three weeks at the Central to fair business, but around the country the exhibitors can count on it getting money for them in the short runs.

It is a combination San Francisco and South Sea island tale that carries a couple of fight wallops and likewise a flash of the undressed stuff among the island maidens. All great for the box office. The story is slow at times and in its present shape the picture is somewhat long for the average house. It could easily stand 12 to 15 minutes of pruning.

The Service tale is of a young widow with a three-year-old son, the widow being taken to sea aboard a ship bound for the South Sea Islands by a skipper who has promised to marry her. She tried to take the youngster with her, but the skipper sees the babe is left behind.

The woman is later cast aside by the ship master. About this time the son has grown to man's estate, and through a series of circumstances he finally winds up on the same island where his mother is. Also he crossed the path of her seducer.

The picture has a rather thrilling underwater fight with sharks and a wow of a battle between Harry T. Morey, the heavy, and George O'Brien, the hero, in which the latter pulls the only new thing that has been seen in a screen scrap in a long while. Early in the fight his arm is injured and he fights through to the finish with one hand. It is effective.

The water stuff and the shots of the native girls scantily clad for the surf are all there.

Billie Dove looks pretty and gets away with her role in fairly good shape, although nothing taxing her is required. She did not get over as well as she might have in the scene with the villain in his quarters. Cleo Madison is seemingly going to continue to be cast for mothers, simply because she does them so well despite her still apparent youthfulness. Harvey Clark furnishes the comedy relief for the story and clicks especially in his scenes on the island with the fat native wife.

"The Roughneck" is not as rough as the title sounds, but a good box office picture for the houses that change during a week. *Fred.*

HOUSE OF YOUTH

Ralph Ince Production, presented by Regal Pictures, Inc. Features Jacqueline Logan. Based on the Maude Radford Warren novel. Adapted by C. Gardner Sullivan. Released by Producers Distributing Corp. At Loew's New York Nov. 25, half of double-feature bill. Running time, 65 mins.

Corinna Endicott.......... Jacqueline Logan
Spike Blaine............ Malcolm MacGregor
Rhodes Winston................ Vernon Steele
Amy Marsden...................... Gloria Grey
Mitch Hardy.................. Richard Travers
Linda Richards................. Lucila Mendez
Cornelius Endicott...... Edwin Booth Tilton
Aunt Maggie Endicott...... Aileen Manning
A Butler.......................... Hugh Metcalf
Mrs. Mitch Hardy......... Barbara Tennant

A real modern story treating with the "terrific pace" of the younger generation. The escapades of the youngsters in this picture are a trifle far-fetched but plausible. The story has Jacqueline Logan in a role that gives her all kinds of scope for her girlish charm and ability. As Corinna Endicott she is one of the leading lights of a fast younger set, given to staging wild parties at roadhouses and much burning of the midnight oil.

Her alcoholic and platonic companion is Spike Blaine (Malcolm MacGregor). She and Spike make an entrance at one roadhouse dance by driving Spike's roadster through the side of the building onto the dance floor.

Rhodes Winston (Vernon Steele), back from France, falls in love with Corinna. He condemns the life she is leading, and she determines to tone down. She is enticed back to a roadhouse and compromised by a married cad whom she despises. The place is raided as she struggles with him, and the newspapers feature the story. Winston breaks off their engagement, but Spike calls at the house to propose. She refuses, thinking it is pity on his part prompting the offer.

Concluding to live down the scandal, Corinna starts a Fresh Air Farm for kiddies. Spike is her chief lieutenant, and she realizes she loves him.

Rhodes returns from Europe, seeks her out and confesses his love. He tells Corinna he needs her for inspiration in his literary efforts. She is forced to choose between he and Spike, and chooses the latter.

The story runs along smoothly and is interesting at all times. The direction by Ralph Ince is high class, assisted by a splendid cast. Miss Logan is girlish, appealing and convincing. Mr. MacGregor was a likeable Spike, and Mr. Steele splendid as the selfish writer who lost the girl because he lacked the courage to face the scandal following the police court incident. The balance of the cast averaged up well.

Strong program feature for the intermediate houses. *Con.*

MIDNIGHT EXPRESS

Geo. W. Hill Production presented by Columbia Pictures. Features Elaine Hammerstein. Adapted and directed by Geo. W. Hill. Shown at the Broadway, N. Y., week Nov. 17, 1924. Running time, 60 minutes.

Mary Travers.............Elaine Hammerstein
Jack Oakes....................William Haines
John Oakes....................George Nichols
Joseph Davies....................Lloyd Whitlock
James Travers..........Edwin Booth Tilton
Silent Bill Brachley..............Pat Harmon
Arthur Bleyden..............Bertram Grassby

Here is a wow of a railroad meller adapted from the old popular-priced stage thriller of the same title. It is the C. B. C. picture in the independent market, and good enough to get a Broadway showing for a week on its merits in a combination vaudeville and picture house. In the regular daily change houses it should do a corking business; in the houses where it is usual for a double feature to be run this one can be relied to supply the main strength of the program. It will in most cases stand by itself.

Elaine Hammerstein, featured, is supported by a corking cast, the outstanding member being William Haines, in whom the C. B. C. have a bet if they can hold him. He looks to have everything a leading man for the screen should have and, opposite Miss Hammerstein, he appears to good advantage. He and Pat Harmon (the heavy) put up as exciting a fight as has been witnessed in a long time. Edward Booth Tilton and George Nichols are also both to be commended on their performances.

The picture is the purest form of melodrama. Jack Oakes, son of a railroad president, is a pretty wild boy running wild in San Francisco, mixing both wild women and bad booze. His dad finally gets wild and turns the boy loose. The latter, however, believes that he can make good on his own, so he goes to Los Angeles and starts in the railroad shops there as a laborer. He becomes a fireman and, in turn, is given a switch engine to run. This proves his second undoing, for he runs over his helper on the engine. Though he is not to blame, he is unnerved and asks for another assignment. Placed as a night operator in a small station half-way up a mountain grade, he finally saves the midnight express from a runaway freight. His heroic work also saves from injury his father as well as the girl he loves, both passengers on the train.

Elaine Hammerstein plays the girl, and, although featured, really has the secondary character, for it is the boy who stands out all the way.

Through the story is Harmon, a desperate character, being sent away for life. He escapes from the train, is caught through the efforts of Jack, again escapes from prison and shows up at the little mountainside station in time to battle with the operator while a runaway string of freight cars is running down the mountainside head-on toward the express. Much suspense in this sequence.

The picture could stand a little better editing and titling, some small details being overlooked in hooking the story together; but on the whole a most satisfying production to the average run of film fans. *Fred.*

TROUPING WITH ELLEN

Producers Distributing Corp. production. From Earl Derr Biggers' Saturday Evening Post Story. Scenario by Gerald C. Duffy. Photographed by J. Roy Hunt. Directed by T. Hayes Hunter. At the New York one day (Nov. 21) as half the bill. Rus about 70 minutes.

Ellen....................Helene Chadwick
Lil....................Mary Thurman
Andy....................Gaston Glass
Tony....................Basil Rathbone
Manager....................Riley Hatch
Mabel....................Zena Keefe
Mrs. Llewellyn....................Kate Banke
Mr. Llewellyn....................Tyrone Power
Dave....................John Tansey
Dan....................Charles McDonald
Jack....................Ernest Hillard
Mrs. Wintership....................Jane Jennings
Grandmother....................Esther Banks

The chief reason for this being a particularly good little program picture is the very human story provided by Earl Derr Biggers. This fiction writer has turned out one of those back-stage bits that seem to be perennially popular with all classes. T. Hayes Hunter directed with skill and discretion, and a cast really notable makes the action vital.

Biggers has used the Cinderella theme but inserted a twist decidedly unique. Here the poor little heroine finds her dreams come true and herself safely ensconced in the palatial home of her fairy prince. But instead of being contented and happy, Cinderella finds things unutterably dull in the home of wealth and longs for the days that were not quite so pa'my.

This is Ellen, who has been just about the most refined little chorus girl ever introduced to the screen. Her sweetie when the picture starts is Andy, an orchestra leader, but she fears he is ambitionless and refuses to encourage him. Tony, a gentlemanly but uninteresting Bostonese aristocrat, is introduced to Ellen and falls as heavily as his dignity will permit. When she catches pneumonia on an auto ride with him he feels responsible and has his mother invite her to their magnificent estate to recuperate.

But Ellen, although she realizes that all this grandeur might become hers by merely saying "yes," longs for her Andy and goes back to find him a luminary of Tin Pan Alley, fired by her desertion to real ambition. Thus Cinderella returns not to the step-sisters and life of drudgery but to marriage with a song-writer.

The film is enlivened with several delightful atmospheric bits. One occurs at the beginning when Ellen, successful chorus girl, returns to her humble home for the first time in two years. Another more amusing interlude is in the aristocratic home where the hit honors are gathered by Esther Banks as the grandmother who had married into the ritzy family 60 years before but still retains her sense of humor.

The cast is dotted with prominent names. Helene Chadwick plays Ellen with a touch of gentility that does credit to Miss Chadwick if not to her portrayal. Gaston Glass is appealing as the poor chap, while his wealthy rival is well played by Basil Rathbone, better known to the legitimate stage. Such established favorites as Riley Hatch, Zena Keefe, Mary Thurman and Tyrone Power have little more than bits.

"Trouping with Ellen" is a picture without a villain and also without any heavy tiresome plotting. Nicely set and produced with an all-around touch of class, it measures up as a sure for almost any theatre.

THE LEGEND OF HOLLYWOOD

Producers Distributing Corp., presented by Charles R. Rogers. Originally written by Frederick Arnold Kummer and retold in a magazine story by Frank Condon. Directed by Renaud Hoffman. Photography by Karl Struss. At the New York one day , Nov. 28, as half the bill. Runs about an hour.

John Smith....................Percy Marmont
Mary Brown....................Zasu Pitts
Mrs. Rooney....................Alice Davenport
Blondie....................Dorothy Dorr

This would have made a fine little two-reel feature but as a full-length film it takes the prize for lack of action as an offset however is the title. The characters moon and mope around through five or six long reels, spoiling the effect of a story that, although slight, holds not a little intrinsic merit. A foreword discusses this plot stating that it was written some years ago and revamped for a fan magazine story. Attention is called to the unique idea but this is not so apparent although the film is presented in novel fashion.

John Smith has come to Hollywood to write a scenario that will not only start him on the road to fame but will revolutionize the whole film industry. He has the talent but cannot get the proper entree and start. Finally down on his luck and mentally whipped he is told by his landlady that in seven days he must get out.

Filling seven glasses with wine he puts poison into one and spins them around so that he cannot distinguish. Deciding to drink one a day until his week is up, he gambles with fate.

The seventh day arrives and there is only one glass left. As he drains it a letter comes accepting his script, offering a contract and enclosing a substantial advance. In misery he sinks into unconsciousness, only to learn a bit later a maid had spilled the poisoned liquor previously and replaced it. He had fainted from shock.

As a counter-plot there is a story of a little ugly duckling girl who has been joshed by her friends that she should go into pictures. Taking them seriously, she has come to Hollywood. Disappointments follow but in the end the writer realizes here is a jewel beneath her plainess and romance appears.

The Hollywood scenes are colorful and probably true atmospherically. Karl Struss has performed a most artistic camera job and Renaud Hoffman, except where he lets the picture drag unmercifully, a good directorial piece of work.

Percy Marmont, who suffers more than anyone in films, is miserable as ever but effective. The policy of having a heroine almost to be described as homely is courageous but as played by the talented Zasu Pitts, the character is vastly appealing.

"The Legend of Hollywood" has more substance to it than the average picture for the neighborhood theatres, but it has been spread to thinly over too much territory.

WARNING SHADOWS

London, Nov. 20.

German production at the Tivoli, London, Nov. 17. No details given on program, neither producer nor cast beink named. Inquiry elicited the information it was originaly called "Shadows," but it was necessary to alter the title because it was used for a Lon Chaney feature. The leading actor is Fritz Kartner.

Whether or not "Warning Shadows" arouses intense admiration or intense dislike, there is no half-way attitude; no one will deny that it is unlike any other film ever shown. Its appeal is uncompromisingly high-brow. If advertised as a show for those who have the taste of connoisseurs it could be screened in New York with every chance of success.

"This drama," say the program which is so silent regarding facts, "is wholly dependent upon the mental co-operation of the spectator. You are asked to replace the sub-title, which is entirely absent, out of your own imagination." The plot is not so difficult as that; it is, in fact, simple enough to do without captions.

The scene is a manor overlooking the market place in a small German town. But no particular period is indicated, as the costumes, faintly suggestive of the Empire period, are the design of fancy. There is a husband whose massive features make one think of Beethoven. There are three cavaliers who call to pay their respects to his wife and, while doing so, amuse themselves by making their shadows kiss and caress her shadow on the blind. The husband, seeing these amorous silhouettes, is consumed with jealousy.

At dinner, noticing the love-lorn glances his wife and a youth are exchanging, he is enraged still further. A glass is shattered in his hand. The servants are called to take away the wine-stained cloth. They do not answer the bell, and their master goes to fetch them. He finds them in the hall entranced by the shadowgraph performance of a wandering showman. The husband has the entertainment brought to the dining-room, and the guests take amusement in a story of a mandarin's jealousy acted by the shadows of cardboard figures on the screen. In the midst of the drama the showman reverses all the shadows in the room so that the diners sit watching their silhouettes. The wife goes to her chamber, the youth follows, the husband sees them kiss. Maddened by jealousy, he binds si wife, places her on the table and forces the three cavaliers to advance upon her with leveled swords until the points pierce her breast. At the youth's instigation they then turn their swords upon the husband and drive him through a window. He falls upon the cobbles of the market-place, dead. The shadows in the room reverse themselves again. The husband, the wife, the youth and the three cavaliers awake to find themselves still sitting at table. The husband and wife cling to each other while the guests depart. The showman leaves with a great jewel to mark the hosts's gratitude. Lastly, the servants who have also been laid under the trance, awake. The dawn breaks and the market stirs with life.

This magical and magnificent film ends with quiet, homely touches to assure us that the world is sane when not colored by the emotions of the spectators.

Throughout, the perfection of details shows the hand of a master. The photography, too, is excellent. Yet "Warning Shadows," it is said, has had to wait two years before being exhibited in London. How long will it have to wait before it will be ready for exhibition to the average picture patron? *Jolo.*

GREED

Metro-Goldwyn production presented by Louis B. Mayer. From the novel "McTeague" by Frank Norris. Adapted by June Mathis and Eric von Stroheim. Directed by von Stroheim. Presented at the Cosmopolitan theatre, New York, fro run starting Dec. 4. Running time, 114 minutes.

McTeague.....................Gibson Gowland
Trina...........................Zasu Pitts
Marcus Schouler............Jean Hersholt
Mr. Sieppe...............Chester Conklin
Mrs. Sieppe..................Sylvia Ashton
August Sieppe................Austin Jewel
Sieppe Twins................{ Otto Gottel
                            { Oscar Gottel
Maria.........................Dale Fuller
Mr. Heise...................Hughie Mack
Selina......................Joan Standing

"Greed," the screen adaptation of the Frank Norris story, "McTeague," opened at the Cosmopolitan last Thursday night for a run. Metro-Goldwyn presented the picture with Louis B. Mayer acting as sponsor for the production.

It was directed by Eric von Stroheim, and the possibilities are that the director himself selected the story. Nothing more morbid and senseless from a commercial picture standpoint, has been seen on the screen in a long long time than this picture. Long awaited, von Stroheim having utilized two years and over $700,000 of Goldwyn and possibly some Metro money in its making. It came as a distinct shock to those viewing it.

Never has there been a more out-and-out box office flop shown on the screen than this picture. Even D. W. Griffith's rather depressing "Isn't Life Wonderful?" is a howling comedy success when compared to "Greed." Metro-Goldwyn will never get the money that was put in this picture out of it, and the exhibitors that play it will have a heck of a time to get back via the box office route what they pay out in rentals for the picture.

On this picture von Stroheim shot 130 reels of stuff in the two years. He finally cut it to 26 reels and told the Metro-Goldwyn executives that was the best he could do. It was then taken into hand and cut to 10 reels, and as such registered a decisive and distinct flop at the Cosmopolitan Thursday night.

It is a cinch that there isn't going to be a mob clamoring at the door of the Cosmopolitan comprising mothers and fathers who are taking their children to the theatre to give them a good time. After all, the province of the theatre is to provide amusement and entertainment, but "Greed" provides neither.

True, there may be a moral, but it applies to wives only, to the effect wives should not be miserly, greedy, or money-crazed, and with it consequently intolerant of a husband's welfare.

That is another count against it, that the women won't like it. Imagine any girl keeping company with a young fellow urging him to take her to see "Greed" when she knows the night that he sits through it he is going to sour on every thought that has to do with marriage!

As for the men? Well, take this reviewer as an average human, possibly a little more hard-boiled than the average man that one would meet in the average small city. He had to violate the Volstead act to the extent of three shots before starting this story.

From the artistic angle, there is no question but that at directing von Stroheim is a wizard as to detail. His little intimate touches are little short of remarkable, but what of it if the story in which they are employed is such that it offends rather than entertains?

McTeague, a worker in a gold mine, serves an apprenticeship with an itinerant dentist and in years after sets up an office in Market street, San Francisco. A chum brings in his cousin as a patient. The chum is in love with the girl. McTeague also falls in love with her, and the chum finally steps down in Mac's favor.

But before Mac and she are married the girl wins a $5,000 lottery prize and the chum curses himself for a fool, but Trina, the girl, starts on a career of money hoarding.

Several years afterward the chum, still revengeful because of his failure to share in the spoils, tips off the Dentists' Society that Mac is practicing without a license. Mac then drifts from bad to worse. With a few drinks of whiskey under his belt he walks out on the money-grabbing wife.

Months later he runs across her. She is working as a scrubwoman. He tries to compel her to give him money, later murdering her to secure it.

After the crime Mac makes his way to the desert, in the direction of Death Valley. A posse starts after him from a small New Mexico town. In it is the former chum, still actuated by his greed for the $5,000.

The posse gives up the chase, but the chum insists he be permitted to follow the trail. This he does, meets his man, the two come to blows in the midst of the desert, and in the fight the chum, before he is killed, snaps handcuffs on Mac's arm.

Mac kills him, only to find that he is now manacled to a dead man, 100 miles from water. In the fadeout is the quick lying down beside the dead to await the fate that is before him.

Wow! Imagine that for a finish! There is this about the picture, however: It brings to light three great character performances by Gibson Gowland as McTeague, Jean Hersholt as the chum, and Zasu Pitts as the wife. Those three players as types are made for all time as far as the screen is concerned. Each individually scored a tremendous personal success. Chester Conklin was another who registered with a performance that is marked, although it is noticeable the part that the von Stroheim direction played in it.

But "Greed" will never get a cent at the box office commensurate with the time and money put into the picture. *Fred.*

There should be this much stated as an offset for von Stroheim, if he wants it—that von Stroheim stopped cutting at 26 reels. It was at that time almost decided by the Metro people to play the picture in two showings of 12 or 13 reels each. Later the conclusion was reached that plan was commercially wrong, and more cutting was ordered, but von Stroheim did not further cut himself.

In cutting from 130 to 26 reels von Stroheim, who must have lived the story to have gone that far in the first process, knew the picture so intimately that if he stopped at 26 reels "Greed" might have been "Greed" in 26. To have cut to 10 reels must have deleted a large quantity of film von Stroheim thought necessary, and von Stroheim was the director.

On the trade side no one can know just what was cut out. They see only what was left in. Whose judgment is to be preferred, the director's or the cutter's?

If for commercial purposes a picture must be slashed to this great extent after a director had been permitted to go as far as he did in the taking of it, and the producer at one period seemed content with 26 reels, it does not sound quite fair to an able director such as von Stroheim is to throw the entire blame on him. The fault of von Stroheim stopped with making what he expected would be a special in 26 reels.

Reviewers can only comment upon what they see before them. To locate the exact trouble for a final trade decision on "Greed" the picture in 26 and in 10 reels should be first seen.

As another possibility—because no American picture was ever shown before in two sections of the length of 26 reels is no positive reason why it couldn't be done. Did Griffith in his Biograph days ever believe he would spend $1,000,000 in making a picture like "America?"

"Greed" may be the means of fixing responsibility for pictures. If it does that it will then have been worth all that has been spent upon it. It could result in the strictest maximum for investment and takes for any picture by any producer and for any director, giving both protection in that method, with the understanding that if the director assumes the story after reading it under the conditions imposed, he must stand or fall with what he makes.

***

THE LAST MAN

U. F. A. production. Story by Carl Mayer, directed by F. W. Murnau. Stars Emil Jannings. Shown privately at the Criterion theatre, New York, December 5, 1924. Running time, 68 minutes.

The Porter...................Emil Jannings
His Daughter..............Mary Delschaft
Her Bridegroom..............Kurt Hiller
His Aunt................Emelie Kurtz
Hotel Manager.........Hans Unterkircher

The special little program distributed at the Criterion theatre Friday night for the special 11.30 showing of "The Last Man" said:

"The story of our picture is this: 'Take a man's uniform away—what is left?' In his uniform he may be king, general, judge, policeman, with all the power of his position. Take away his uniform! What remains?

"'The Last Man' is a film without titles. Not for theoretical reasons. But for the sake of an art. Which is the best expression of this age. It is said that motion pictures cannot be supreme art because titles are used. And titles are but an expression of literature.

"Therefore, in 'The Last Man' an attempt has been made. To use the medium of pictures. To express action and thought. Without words. Without titles."

The foregoing must give some understanding that here was something quite revolutionary in pictures. Those who read the program sat awaiting the worst. They were agreeably fooled. The picture wasn't alone revolutionary, but it was a tremendous work of motion picture art, and if it is to be accepted as a criterion of what the U. F. A. is going to offer in this country, then by all means throw open the screen of the country to pictures of this type, wherever made.

This is a film that will go down in history as one of the big pictures of this decade. In it the U. F. A. must have $500,000 which can be gotten out of the American market.

A number of foreign directors have come to this country within the last few years and showed us something in the way of directing. But if F. W. Murnau ever starts directing in this country it would seem almost a certainty he would show us additional directorial feats, for his "The Last Man" gives every indication that he is a past master at the art of making pictures.

"The Last Man" is a story that is simplicity itself. Its principal characters are few. The lead, played by Emil Jannings, is that of a head porter in a Berlin hotel. In all the majesty of a gold-braided uniform he stands at the outer portal and directs the guests and the chauffeurs, the latter trembling at his majesty. There stands he in all the glory of his Emperor Franz Joseph mustache and sideburns. He is king, and as he stalks majestically homeward to the tenement court where he lives with his daughter, passers-by salute him with military precision. And at home, in the court and the building he is a personage of note and consequence.

But he is getting aged. On the night the opening scenes of the story take place it is raining and the old boy gets a little attack of rheumatism. The manager of the hotel is quick to notice the porter is not quite as spry as he should be, and decides that it would be best to give him an indoor job. He is assigned to the care of the men's room. Possibly the job was more remunerative, but the glory of his grand uniform was gone. He felt that keenly, and tried to hide it from his neighbors at home, even going to the extent of stealing the uniform coat nightly from the hotel office to march home in it. But he only did so for two evenings, after which his degradation is made public to the tenement through one of the women, a kinswoman by marriage, who came to offer him a hot lunch, still believing him the major domo of the hotel.

Then those who had bowed before him gave him the razz, and the old boy turned back to the lavatory to spend the night there, and to all intents and purposes to possibly end his days, a broken spirit, all because he was stripped of his gorgeous uniform coat.

But the author gives the story a twist. A Mexican millionaire comes along, goes into the lavatory and drops dead there in the arms of the former porter. He left a freak will, to the effect that all his tremendous wealth should go to the person in whose arms he died. Then we have the gloriously humorous picture of the ex-porter reveling in his wealth at the same hotel where he was once employed as a guest, and the consequent kow-towing of those who once scorned him.

It is an effective tale, most effectively told on the screen with an eye to detail little short of marvelous. Murnau, who handled the direction, has achieved some really remarkable touches. Words cannot do justice to what he has achieved on the screen and the picture must be seen to be appreciated. His scene showing the transition from night to morning, the opening of the windows to let a smoke-filled room air while a wedding party is in progress, his handling of the drunken dizziness on the part of his leading character and the latter's alcoholic dream are masterpieces of direction.

As for the photography! No word applies because none is sufficient to describe it.

Mr. Jannings as the porter presents a character study that is indeed a triumph. Nevermore should this actor ever permit the producers to cast him in costume pieces. Here he is startling in the tragic moments and in the comedy a positive delight.

The supporting cast really means nothing. They all do clever work, but are so far overshadowed by Jannings, the actor, and the character of the porter, that one hardly notices them.

This picture, on the strength of its humanness, its tremendous comedy kick at the finish and the art of the production itself, is going to prove a real clean-up at the box office. It is a production that will be made by word of mouth advertising, such as no other picture has received in years. *Fred.*

NORTH OF 36

Irvin Willat production released by Famous Players-Lasky. From the novel by Emerson Hough. Directed by Irvin Willat. Shown at the Rivoli, New York, week of Dec. 7, 1924. Running time, 78 minutes.

Dan McMasters..........................Jack Holt
Jim Nabours.....................Ernest Torrance
Taisie Lockhart.......................Lois Wilson
Sim Rudabough......................Noah Beery
Del Williams......................David Dunbar
Cinquo Centavos..................Stephen Carr
Mayor McCoyne.......................Guy Oliver
John Pattison.....................George Irving
Col. Griswold...................Clarence Geldert
Jackson..............................Bert Hadley
Hanson...........................Robert Kortman
Milly......................................Ella Miller

Without doubt almost as great a picture as "The Covered Wagon."

Had "North of 36" come along prior to the "Covered Wagon," it would be a case of the former overshadowing the latter, possibly with a great many film fans.

"North of 36" is another story of the making of the west, written by the late Emerson Hough, who wrote "The Covered Wagon." In it he has embodied as much of historic romance as there was in the tale of the great white wagon fleet that broke through to the Pacific in the days of the gold rush.

This story, however, deals with the breaking of the trail out of Texas north to the railroad with a herd of cattle, the first herd of beef to come out of the state after the Civil War. It is presented on the screen picturesquely and interestingly. The picture contains about the best cattle stampede that has been seen on the screen.

"North of 36" will get money in any type of house and interest and enthuse all types of audiences. This is one the exhibitor can't go wrong on. If he is located where they are strong for westerns he won't go wrong if promising a picture as great as "The Covered Wagon."

The cast of "North of 36" has two players who won fame in "The Covered Wagon." Lois Wilson and Ernest Torrance. In this instance Jack Holt plays opposite Miss Wilson (instead of J. Warren Kerrigan) and he makes a very pleasing character of the mysterious stranger that one minute seems linked with the forces opposing the girl, and the next seems to be fighting for her. Noah Beery has the heavy role. He is the land-grabbing crooked carpet-bagger who has been placed in the office of Secretary of State in Texas, and tries to control all the land script that he can lay his hands on, not stopping short of murder to achieve his ends.

Miss Wilson is the altogether charming Taisie Lockhart, sole survivor of the Lockhart family of Texas. She has a ranch and cattle, but that is all. Land poor and cattle poor, with no market for beef on the hoof.

Along comes McMasters with the story the railroad has been brought through to a town in Kansas where they are waiting for cattle to ship east. The little ranchwoman decides to drive her stock north, and the picturization deals with the hardships of the drive; combatting the forces trying to block her way at the behest of the crooked Sim Rudabaugh; the hostile Indians who do not want the whites to graze through their lands; fording of streams with the immense herd and the final triumphant close with the cattle brought to the market where they bring $20 a head, making Taisie Lockhart the richest woman in Texas.

At the same time is seen the passing of the heavy, who was handed over to the Indians for causing the death of two women members of the tribe, and the clearing of the character of McMasters, who Taisie loves, but whom she is afraid is in cahoots with her enemies.

The picture is finely directed and carries with it a thrill almost as great as that which there was in **"The Covered Wagon" when the long, white, covered chain of vehicles started on the move "Westward Ho!" It is American, and with all its seriousness has in it a vein of comedy that lightens the heavier moments.**

A whale of a picture that will clean up. *Fred.*

CIRCE

Mae Murray starring vehicle, produced by Tiffany Productions and released through Metro-Goldwyn. Story by Vicente Blasco Ibanez, and direction by Robert Z. Leonard. Reviewed at the Capitol Dec. 7. Running time, 75 minutes.

Circe, the Goddess...............Mae Murray
Cecilia Brunne.....................Mae Murray
Dr. Wesley Van Martyn...James Kirkwood
Archibald Crumm................Tom Ricketts
Ballard Barrett...............Charles Gerard
William Craig..................William Haines
Sister Agatha..................Lillian Langdon

This is the story especially written by Ibanez, the Spanish author, for Mae Murray. Its basis is the mythical Circe legend, that of the goddess who turned her sailor admirers into swine and was sought by every man save Ulysses. Therefore, as film material it provides one of those "I'm-sought-by-all-the-men" roles, and as its opposite one of those "no-woman-can-touch-me" parts.

So in the film one Cecilia Brunne is shown as the mistress of a Long Island place where the corks pop with steady precision and where the young, middle-aged and old-boy admirers gather to worship the much sought after woman.

The modern Circe eludes them all—all but the man who plays the "no-woman-can-touch-me" part, in this case a doctor. The doc doesn't have much shine for the Circe imitator and lets her know it. That makes her sorrowful, and because of the sorrow a series of flashbacks reveals the reason for the downfall of Cecilia from a girl in a convent to the mistress of a Long Island boozerie is because she has always fascinated men. At first her employers "got fresh" and then she later learned to capitalize the whole thing.

She did—and how?

But after a hectic crapshooting episode, in which her liquor impaired her ability to roll the "big Dicks from Boston" Cecilia lost her home, and when she refused to live with the man who won it, went back to the convent. Meantime, the doc begins to see some good in her, and finally locates the convent. Before he arrives, however, the girl has suffered fractured legs in an accident. Then the blow-off is when the doc gives her so much confidence she walks—on her weak legs—to his arms in time for a clinch finish.

It is all fair movie material, none too well developed. The wild party scenes are very much like others, and the bits wherein Mae gets hot feet and dances with a colored jazz band trumpeter are none too pleasant. Another bit shows Mae doing one of those cheesecloth dances in slow motion—with neither enough motion nor cheesecloth. At all times Mae tries emoting—and gets a hand on her dancing.

James Kirkwood in the doctor role has a stencil part, while the rest of the supporting cast are more or less in the background, all except a kid who plays a nance and grabs a few laughs on his own account.

This Murray film isn't up to her others, which isn't handing it a very big laurel. Where Mae is popular, maybe it's all right, and where they don't like her, nothing would do. As first run material it is elaborate enough, for money has been spent freely, but as for being a really distinctive picture, as it was heralded, that is the wrong dope. It is in reality a fair program picture, and none too big at that. *Sisk.*

HUSBANDS AND LOVERS

John M. Stahl Production presented by Louis B. Mayer. Released by First National. Story by John M. Stahl, adapted by A. P. Younger. Directed by Stahl. Features Lewis Stone, Florence Vidor and Lew Cody. Shown at the Strand, N. Y., week Dec. 7, 1924. Running time 81 minutes.

James Livingston ....Lewis Stone
Grace Livingston ....Florence Vidor
Rex Phillips ....Lew Cody
Marie ....Dale Fuller
Robert Stanton ....Winter Hall
Mrs. Stanton ....Edythe Yorke

Average domestic drama with the usual triangle situation. That is the basic plot, and John M. Stahl has padded out this trite idea to such an extent that it runs for an hour and 21 minutes without ever getting anywhere except in the last 20 minutes.

It has one hour devoted to planting a story that could have just as easily been set in 15 minutes of real action, handled by a director that had a real idea in his mind. The best thing is the title, "Husbands and Lovers," and the trio playing the principal roles. The title reads "Husbands and Lovers," while the story is simply that of a husband, a wife and a lover. Had Stahl run a parallel story with the one now in use and made use of the plural of his title, he might have had a real box office feature. Now, it just qualifies as an average program feature as far as the first runs are concerned. For the neighborhood houses and the average small town runs it will be a fairly good business getter.

The tale is that of a husband and wife who have arrived at that stage in married life where the wife, while waiting on the husband hand and foot, is neglectful of her own appearance. When her husband chides her, she goes to the other extreme and neglects her husband to teach him a lesson. At that stage her husband's "best friend" begins noticing the wife, because of her dolled up appearance, and finally he makes violent love to her, winning her away from the husband, at least to the extent of bringing about a separation, although the wife continues to love her husband. There is a divorce, and the wife is about to marry the lover when the ex-husband reappears, a reconciliation is effected, and the lover is left waiting at the church, while the former husband and wife elope to remarry.

Lewis Stone as the husband, Florence Vidor as the wife, and Lew Cody as the heavy are certainly a type trio for the roles.

Nothing startling with the picture, extremely draggy in part. *Fred.*

Christine of Hungry Heart

Thos. H. Ince Production released by First National. Story by Kathleen Norris. Directed by George Archainbaud. At Piccadilly theatre, New York, week beginning Dec. 6. Running time 75 minutes.

Christine Madison ....Florence Vidor
Stuart Knight ....Warner Baxter
Dr. Alan Monteagle ....Clive Brook
Ivan Vianney ....Ian Keith
Dan Madison ....Walter Hiers
Mrs. Michael Knight ......Lillian Lawrence
"Jeffy" ....Dorothy Brock

In "Christine of the Hungry Heart" the Thomas H. Ince plant turned out a very good audience picture. It is a good program feature appealing to a great extent to the women. There are a few spots that might slightly offend in the smaller towns, but, other than that, the picture is almost certain to give general satisfaction. It won't be a box office knockout, but it should do the average business almost anywhere. It is well played with Florence Vidor in the title role and a supporting cast decidedly capable. As Christine, Miss Vidor has a role that compels the sympathy although there is a moment or two in the latter part where she breaks it down through her elopement with an author. Warner Baxter plays the first husband, who is leading a gay life after his marriage; Clive Brook registers decidedly as the second husband, and Ian Keith is the lover.

Keith at times managed to look very well before the camera, but there were other shots in which he was very bad. Walter Hiers fitted in a laugh or two.

"Christine," as a picture, starts where most others end. It begins with a marriage ceremony. She marries young Stuart Knight. A year after their marriage, Knight is seen turning day into night with afternoon parties on board a yacht with girls and booze. He neglects his wife, and finally, when drunk and driving his car with a girl friend, runs into his wife's machine, smashing the two cars. Result, a divorce and the marriage of Christine to the doctor who attended her.

But after a couple of years, when her doctor-husband becomes immersed in his profession, Christine's heart still hungers, and she listens to the passionate love speeches of a poet-playwright and, taking her child with her, elopes with him to Brazil. Once there, the child is taken away from her by the American Consul on court orders from New York, and the babe is returned to its father. The mother, realizing that she has been foolish, leaves the lover and returns home. After a few years, during which she tries to atone for her foolishness, she and her husband are reconciled.

The story is told in a manner that holds the interest, and Miss Vidor puts a lot into the role of the heart-hungry young matron. *Fred.*

THE FOOLISH VIRGIN

Columbia Production, featuring Elaine Hammerstein. From the Thomas Dixon novel. Directed by George W. Hill. Released in the Independent market. Shown at the Broadway theatre, New York, week Nov. 8, 1924. Running time, 63 minutes.

Mary Adams..........Elaine Hammerstein
Jim Owens........................Robert Fraser
Nancy Owens................Gladys Brockwell
Elphan Owens....................Robert Fraser
Jane Sanderson..................Phyllis Haver
Charles Spencer..............Lloyd Whitlock
Mrs. Dawson..........................Irene Hunt
Dr. Dawson..................Howard Truesdell
Sam Allen.....................Jack Henderson
Chuck Brady.......................Roscoe Karns
Lawson Howard....................Oliver Cross
Dan O'Leary..........................Ed Borman
Little Boy....................."Spec" O'Donnell

"The Foolish Virgin" is a title for the box office; as a matter of fact, it is the outstanding thing of this picture. The story and the picture rank with the average of program features; nothing extra about it and, at the same time, nothing that is going to drive the audience out of the theatre. It has a good cast of names, with Elaine Hammerstein featured, and supported by Robert Fraser, who gives a corking performance.

A forest fire is a thrill-provider, it being the big punch of the picture.

Elaine Hammerstein plays the title role and is the school teacher who mixes in with the fast set through her cousin. She is resued from the clutches of a scheming lawyer by the hero, and finally marries him. They spend their honeymoon in the mountains of Carolina while the boy starts a search for his mother. The search successful, the mother a crazed woman, believes her boy to be her husband returning after years, and she stabs him. While he is recovering, the wife is ill at the house of a neighbor, refusing to see her husband, whom she believes is a thief.

Finally the husband dashes through miles of burning forest to rescue his wife and the child of the neighbor with whom she is living, and a reconciliation is effected.

For the average house this picture will do. It won't prove to be a box-office knockout, but it should please the average audience.

Fred.

BLACK LIGHTNING

Samuel Sax presents "Black Lightning," with Thunder (dog) featured, with Clara Bow the principal player. A Gotham Production, distributed by Lumas Film Corp. Story by Harry Davis, adapted by Dorothy Howell. Directed by James P. Hogan. Reviewed Dec. 8 at Loew's Circle as half double feature bill.

Martha Larned ....Clara Bow
Roy Chambers.....................Harold Austin
Ez Howard.........................Eddie Phillips
Jim Howard........................James Mason
Joe Larned.....................Joe Butterworth
Frank Larned..................James P. Hogan
Country Doctor....................Mark Fenton
City Doctor ....John Prince
Thunder, the dog..................By Himself

"Black Lightning" is an independent, produeed by Samuel Sax, who is still quite active in making melodramas, with James P. Hogan handling the megaphone. "Black Lightning" seems to be aimed at the neighborhoods where families know a lot about dogs and children.

There are some padded-out sections and some noticeable stretches of action that are unnatural, but the picture holds tension through "Thunder's" splendid work. Miss Bow's acting and the character of an illiterate, ragged, half-wit by Mr. Phillips.

Here is a rank melodramatic picture with the juvenile Harold Austin, bucking all kinds of risks in a strange country without once carrying a firearm or keeping a strong weapon of any kind handy at his elbow. There are two villains and they are villainously handlde by Mr. Phillips and Mr. Mason.

There is a "flash back" of a war scene, showing where Roy Chambers was saved by the brother of the mountain orphan, thanks to the conspicuous work of the police dog, then doing Red Cross service for the German army. Just how the dog got on this side wasn't denoted, yet the dog was there, and who should come along at a most opportune time—a time when the dog was tied and was being beaten by a couple of hoboes—but the boy who owed the animal an everlasting debt of gratitude.

Hogan has done real well with a story that flounders at times.

This picture should keep playing right along and encourage Mr. Sax to try for something a little better the next time.

Mark.

UNMARRIED WIVES

Gotham Production distributed by Lumas Film Corp. Written by Dorothy Howell, photographed by Jack MacKenzie and directed by James P. Hogan. At the New York one day, Nov. 28, as half the bill. Runs about 65 minutes.

Princess Sonya.....................Mildred Harris
Mrs. Gregory...............Galdys Brockwell
Tom Gregory.....................Lloyd Whitlock
Morris Sands..................Bernard Randall
Joe Dugan.......................George Cooper
Ma Casey ....Mrs. Davenport
Mrs. Lowell.......................Mabel Coleman

"Unmarried Wives" as a box office name may be effective but not nearly as much so as "Unmarried Mothers" has proven to be in the past. The lady thus parodoxically described in this picture is not the heroine but the neglected spouse of the stage-door hanger-on who finds the society of theatrical professionals more exciting than the company of his lawful leading woman.

The wife has a role subservient to that of the little stage star. The latter is Princess Sonya, Russian importation, but in real life Mame Casey whose introductory remark to her old Irish mother is "Hey! You wasn't raised in no barn."

She's not a bad kid by any means however and doesn't realize the married man "chasing" her means harm.

When the wife comes to her and registers a bit of sob stuff Mame gracefully agrees to tell him where to get off. Meantime the theatrical manager heavy decides that looking at his little Russian star in her abbreviated costumes is not quite enough to satisfy him. He forms an insidious plot to start in himself where the married man left off. Usual struggle for honor but the girl is finally saved by a fire and from the fire by the tough Irish press agent, who has always loved her.

With this well-trodden plot there is not much chance for the film to attain great heights but by dint of very fair treatment it is moderately entertaining. The back-stage scenes are interesting and there is a view of the performance (not the opening night) with the entire audience in full evening dress, following the best traditious of moviedom. The fire scenes are crammed with action and the fight bits lively enough.

Miss Harris wears gorgeous gowns and acts satisfactorily a preposterous role. Miss Brockwell is more at home in vamp parts than as the patient little wife she plays here. George Cooper, famed for his gangster characterizations, makes a novel hard-boiled hero and the rest are adequate.

"Unmarried Wives" misses chiefly because its back-stage stuff lacks the human interest appeal often found in such stories. In spite of its peculiar and rather cold set of characters ,it is nicely put on and can play the program houses without arousing unfavorable comment.

HONOR AMONG MEN

William Fox Production starring Edmund Lowe. Story adapted from Richard Harding Davis story, "The Kings Jackal." Directed by Denison Clift. Running time, 65 mins. Reviewed at Loew's, New York, Dec. 2, half of double feature program.

Prince Kaloney.....................Edmund Lowe
Patricia Carson.....................Claire Adams
King Louis.........................Sheldon Lewis
Countess Zara DeWinter......Diana Miller
Colonel Erhaupt....................Fred Becker
Baron Barrat........................Paul Weigel
Renauld ....Frank Leigh
Nichols ....Hector Sarno
Count DeWinter ....Fred Malatesta
Little Crown Prince......Walter Wilkinson

Edmund Loew's first starring vehicle is a highly romantic picture of court intrique. Lowe as Prince Kaloncy, the loyal subject and defender of the dethroned monarch, Louis IV King of Messina (Sheldon Lewis), gives an eminently satisfactory screen performance. He should have little or no trouble holding the pace set by the other Fox stars.

The story is dramatic, clean and well cast, throbbing along without dull spots. It could almost be classed as a male costume film, the court uniforms of the star and his support allowing for considerable flash.

The story starts at Monte Carlo where the King is living in state surrounded by a syncophantic gathering of the equivalent to the modern yes-man. His attentions to the Countess Zara (Diana Miller) provoke her husband. Kaloney, to save his King engages in a duel with the Count and is wounded.

The King and Zara frame a fake revolution. Kaloney thinking it genuine obtains the financial support of Patricia Carson (Claire Adams) an American. Kaloney falls in love with the girl. When the perfidy of the King is exposed by Renauld (Frank Leigh) it places Kaloney in a bad light.

The Countess DeWinter however exonerates him with a confession and Kaloney denouncing his King starts another revolution which places the little Crown Prince on the throne.

The picture has been given an excellent production and is strongly cast. Miss Adams is sympathetic and effective in the female lead and the balance of the cast well averaged.

The release is a very good program addition for the intermediate houses. Lowe should find no difficulty building up a strong following among the female fans. *Con.*

THE SMOKING TRAIL

D'Allesandro Production releasing through F. D. H. and starring Bill Patton. Cast includes William Bertram, Jack House, Tom Ross, Alma Rayford, Adrian Rayford and Maine Geary. At Stanley, New York, Dec. 5. Running time, 60 mins.

More hashing over of the West. Nothing to stand it in relief from hundreds of other releases of the type and but suitable to the middle class houses as a solo feature and possibly more adaptable to double bill showing.

The picture fails to impress in settings or by weight of numbers with an audience unlikely becoming too excited over witnessing the rustling of some 20 head of cattle. Cameraed in the open, most of the action is on horseback, with Patton as a Texas Ranger working under cover to wipe out what seem cut-rate rustlers. That the thieving takes place upon the ranch of the girl's father is but logical.

Whoever directed displays a hobby for sandhill tumbling descents.

Patton does moderately in the central role, being foiled by Alma Rayford, who conforms to the general character conceptions which dominate the picture.

It totals as a western void of any substance to raise its head above the mass. *Skig.*

RECKLESS SPEED

Hercules Productions, starring Frank Marrill. Story by William Wing. Directed by Wm. James Craft. Distributed by Bud Barsky. At Loew's New York Nov. 25. Half of double-feature program. Running time, 60 mins.

Speed Creswell.....................Frank Merrill
Vera Wray...................Virginia Warwick
Dad Creswell.............................Joe Girard
David Brierly.....................Geno Corrado
Creswell's valet.......................Ed O'Brien
Mr. Jackson...............................Slim Cole

Merrill is the newest of the athletic leads, and seems to have as many tricks as any. He is a clean-cut chap, and in this picture reminds of the earlier Fairbanks releases, both being prone to jump over a gate rather than walk through. The same applies to Merrill's entering of a motor. He leaps over the back onto the seat.

The story given him by William Wing has more body and consistency than the usual light vehicles allotted to this type of artist, due to the limitations of the stars. It deals with a father and son theme that calls for action at all times. Merrill does a hand-over-hand climb between two buildings that is realistic and thrilling and also stages a battle on a structure over an oil well that was well done.

In his fights he sticks to one punch—a right uppercut, with which he knocks his opponents bow-legged. A little variety of blows would help.

The story has to do with "Speed" Creswell (Mr. Merrill), sone of Magnus Creswell (oil man). Speed is averse to business and spends most of his time in the gymnasium. The father is a disciple of brain over brawn.

Creswell, Sr., owns an oil lease, in which he has invested his entire fortune. A competing company owns a lease on the same land, to take effect the moment Creswell's expires. A crooked foreman is conspiring with Brierly (Geno Corrado) to prevent the bringing in of the Creswell well.

Vera Wray (Virginia Warwick), a woman reporter, learns of the plot, but is discovered by the gang. Her screams bring "Speed," and a wild fight is staged. "Speed" realizes his father needs him. By a swing on a telegraph wire he lands in Brierly's office in time to prevent the father from transferring the property.

The story is highly melodramatic, but Merrill's athletics ande the excellent work of the cast will make it interesting for picture fans who like the athletic heroes. Merrill is a fair actor and a fine athlete. *Con.*

WOMEN FIRST

Produced by Perfection Pictures and distributed by C. B. C. Productions. Featuring Eva Novak and William Fairbanks. Directed by Reeves Eason. At the New York one day (Dec. 5) as half the bill. Runs about an hour. Cast—Eva Novak, William Fairbanks, Lloyd Whitlock, Lydia Knott, Meta Sterling, Max Asher, Bob Rhodes, Jack Richardson, Andy Waldron, Dan Crimmins, William Dyer, William Carroll.

The Eva Novak-William Fairbanks combinaion has turned out a series of rather neat little program pictures for C. B. C. with the latest, "Women First" proving to be about as good as any. Fairbanks seems to be as much in evidence in the cheaper houses this season as the more polished Messrs. Menjou, La Roque, Blue and Tearle combined are at the spiffier palaces of moviedom. In Miss Novak, sister of the equally prominent Jane, he has a leading woman of the wholesome and sturdy but sweet and demure type with a Colgate's Ribbon Dental Paste smile, a luscious little figure never extravagantly revealed, and not too much acting ability to make her appearance secondary.

The title "Women First" suggests a sea story but in reality the action has as little to do with the ocean as the name with the plot. Probably a bid at a box office lure the title even misses in that direction. It is nothing more or less than the usual tale of Kentucky racing with the heavies plotting to put the heroine's unbeatable thoroughbred out of condition before the race. The hero and his aides foil them in this but they do manage to get to the jockey and spoil his chance to ride.

If Johnnie Hines, Ernest Truex or Buster Collier were playing the lead it would have been a pipe for him to pinch hit for the jock, but Fairbanks' 180 pounds would break the morale if not the back of any nag. So it devolves upon little Miss Novak (who looks particularly cute in the cunning striped panties and rakish cap) to ride her own horse to triumph in the big derby.

A pleasant little love story is interwoven with the machinations of the villains and the various defensive methods devised by the hero for the horse's protection. But perhaps the film's strongest point for the neighborhood audiences is the liberal portion of laughs provided in the lighter moments. These are due chiefly to the work of Max Asher, playing a colored servant. Though not billed on the posters with the five or six members of the cast mentioned, he shuffles off with the honors of the picture. With Meta Sterling playing the "mammy" opposite him, he gets away with considerable stuff that will bring howls in the cheaper houses. It is barely possible however that certain sections o fthe south will object on the ground that the film shows the negroes taking too many liberties.

A fire scene is full of action and the racing bits genuinely exciting, although everyone knows just who is going to win.

COWBOY AND THE FLAPPER

Renown production presented by Phil Goldstone. Story by Jefferson Moffitt. Photographed by Roland Price. Directed by Alvin J. Neitz. At the Stanley one day (Dec. 3). Runs about 50 minutes.

Al Lyman...............Andrew Walton
Dan Patterson...........William Fairbanks
Colonel Allison............Milton Ross
Jack Harrison............Morgan Davis
Red Carson..............Jack Richardson
The girl.................Dorothy Revier

The Moffitt-Neitz-Price combination, responsible for many westerns, has added another to their string, and it ranks fairly well up in the list. The "flapper" angle as intimated in the title is applesauce, as the heroine is just a kidnapped, long-suffering little western girl home from the usual eastern finishing school, but not particularly flapperish nor unique. As played by Dorothy Revier this role is colorful, but it is because of the work of the actress and not the character.

The film devotes its first few moments to love interest, switches suddenly to the adventures of the sheriff hero in conquering a gang of outlaws single-handed, and then finally switches back to the romance a few feet from the final clinch. An unusual bit of action has the hero actually mishandling the girl, when, posing as a member of the gang of bad boys, it becomes necessary for him to assist in her abduction.

Consequently she hates him nearly as fiercely as the rest, but on learning that the rough stuff was necessary for her later escape she forgets about her mussed hair and black and blue spots.

William Fairbanks, playing the lead, outfairbanks his noted namesake in the matter of battling a baker's dozen of ruffians lonesome-handed. A few of the strategic tricks he uses at first will make the devotees of western pictures sit up and swallow them whole, but at the finish it develops into the usual "wallop-'em-all-in-their-turn" affair with each villain obligingly resting on his haunches until it is his turn to get up and get socked. Even more ridiculous is the scene that follows. The sheriff, victorious and a trifle tired, but with not a mark of combat on his physiognomy, fools around the scene of the recent battle with the girl while his late adversaries gradually recover consciousness.

Except for these ludicrous scenes, however, the story is fairly logical and the direction sound. Good work, too, is performed by the cast, containing, besides Fairbanks and Miss Revier, about the same line-up of troupers that has appeared in other Phil Goldstone westerns. The photography is picturesque and the riding scenes are up to the standard.

The apparently limited number of western film fans in the country should like "Cowboy and the Flapper" as a very passable production of its kind.

THAT WILD WEST

A Renown Picture presented by Phil Goldstone, starring William Fairbanks. Story by J. F. Natterford, directed by Alvin J. Neitz. Shown at Loew's, New York, New York, Nov. 14 on double feature bill with "Lover's Lane." Running time 53 minutes.

Independently made Western out of the Phil Goldstone bag of tricks that is about on a par with the usual westerns this organization turns out. If anything it may be a little better and for the houses where they like this stuff it will get over in fairly good shape. There are the usual fights, chases and gun play and love interest.

The story by J. F. Natterford, has a New York girl who owns an Arizona ranch as the heroine. She is at the home of her uncle and aunt on Fifth avenue when a telegram arrives saying her ranch foreman has run off and married the cook. She decides to go west and when on the ground starts re-

forming the cow hands with the result she finally falls in love with one. He in turn is accused of murder and robbery, but in the finish rescues the ranch owner from the hands of the real culprits and saves the day for her and himself both.

A comedy Sheriff is the one new feature in the picture. Andrew Waldron plays the role with as much understanding as if he were William Crane or Col. "Mike" Arbuckle.

Dorothy Revier rather overacts and seems miscast. William Fairbanks is all that could be asked in this sort of a role in this sort of a production, made under the circumstances that the majority of these westerns are.

There is an angle that should have been improved on and that is the direction. There are many minor faults that could have been easily remedied without adding a cent of additional cost to the picture. It was just a matter of detail.

Fred.

THE SNOB

Louis B. Mayer presentation releasing through Metro-Goldwyn. Based upon the novel by Helen R. Martin. Adapted and directed by Monta Bell. Features Norma Shearer and Conrad Nagel. At the Capitol, New York, week of Dec. 14. Running time, 68 minutes.

Eugene Curry............John Gilbert
Nancy Claxton...........Norma Shearer
Herrick Appleton........Conrad Nagel
Dorothy Rinshelmer......Phyllis Haver
Mrs. Leiter.............Hedda Hopper
Mrs. Curry..............Margaret Seddon
Lottie..................Aileen Manning
Florence................Hazel Kennedy

A corking program leader that has a tale to spin, and spins it minus any superfluous additions. It comprises a well-conceived example of screen construction and is a credit to Monta Bell.

Not given to pulse quickening nor calling for lavishness in settings, the film rests upon the story it has to tell and the manner in which it has been directed and played. Mr. Bell, in supervising the making, has given the narrative a vein of comedy that continuously registers, and undoubtedly is the means of lifting this issue above what might be a drab classification. That it would still be a good picture without the comedy is a distinctive asset, but that its entertainment value would appreciatively suffer were it eliminated is undeniable. Hence, the entire conception as screened assumes proportions to make it stand well above the ordinary trend of celluloid fairy tales, although there is no myth connected with this one.

Neither of the featured players is in the title role. "The Snob" is John Gilbert portraying Eugene Curry, a small town educator, whose success before women's clubs goes to his head and a social career becomes the ambition of his life. The story starts conventionally enough with a coming out party for Nancy Claxton (Miss Shearer), just returned from a convent, in the midst of which comes a telephone message that her father has been killed in a brawl over a woman. Stunned, after having been shielded all of her life, the girl runs away from the notoriety and her inheritance of millions, leaving behind but a note to Herrick Appleton (Mr. Nagel), an equally wealthy youngster, who has loved her since childhood.

A jump of three years changes the locale to a small Pennsylvania town, where Nancy is teaching school and is in love with Eugene, who is about to leave for a larger metropolis to become a faculty member of an institution.

Featuring Miss Shearer and Mr. Nagel, the underbilling should also carry the name of Mr. Gilbert, for, if not meaning anything to the box office, his performance is deserving. That doesn't mean that the featured members do not equal the heralding. On the contrary, Miss Shearer does especially well with her portrayal of the reserved heiress, adding to her appearance by a performance that bears out the contention this girl both is and has been continuously progressing.

Mr. Nagel's assignment is somewhat inactive and relegated more to the background than is usual for him, but that he makes the role stand out in full is the justification of the casting director. Gilbert's playing of the egotistic snob parallels anything in the film, and probably will receive a shade of favoritism through the prominence he is necessarily allotted. The supporting members are easily above reproach, and notable are Margaret Seddon as Eugene's mother and Phyllis Haver, who has turned in a genuine effort.

Bell has inserted his comedy principally through Eugene's relatives of the lower social strata, but has especially connected in the

manner in which he has handled Eugene's little niece (Florence Kennedy), the child of a stringent mother. The passages in which this youngster is put through her recitation paces are classics as to cutting, through the manner in which the sub-titles have been inserted, treatment and characterization. Another assertive quality is that this child is not of the usual "beautiful" screen type.

"The Snob" should click with the viewing, for it has the genuineness and sincerity that most releases lack, and has been superbly played, directed and photographed.

It's a first-rate picture. *Skig.*

THE TORNADO

Universal, presented by Carl Laemmle, starring House Peters. Adapted from the Lincoln J. Carter play. Directed by King Baggot. At the Piccadilly, New York, week Dec. 13. Running time, 65 minutes.

"Tornado"................House Peters
Ruth Travers............Ruth Clifford
Ross Travers............Richard Tucker
"Pewee".................Snitz Edwards
"Gorilla"...............Dick Sutherland
"Hurricane".............Jackie Morgan
Emily...................Kate Price
Molly Jones.............Charlotte Stevens
Pa Jones................Fred Gamble
Ma Jones................Caroline Irwin
"Drunk".................James Welsh

Real rugged melodrama, with a flock of real thrills in it. The picture is certain to get money in the average small town, although it does not measure up particularly to the standard for pre-release showings in the bigger houses such as the theatres in the Broadway district.

The big kick is a log jam, a tremendous storm scene and the carrying away of a railroad bridge by the logs coming down the river while a train is crossing the bridge. This is actually done (not with a model).

House Peters plays the lead. He is the boss of a western lumber camp, where he has buried himself because of a love affair in which his best friend stole his girl. In the camp he is known as "Tornado" with no reason given for it. The former friend and his wife come to the town and, unaware of the identity of Tornado look him up. The woman was of the opinion he was dead, her husband having told her he fell in France. She still loves him and goes to his cabin for an explanation. The husband on her return upbraids her for having done so, but the hero walks in time to save her from being roughly handled.

On the early train out of the camp the next morning the two depart. It is this train that is caught on the bridge. The husband is killed, and Tornado, who has been handling the log jam, rescues the wife.

The picture for the greater part leading up to the storm and log jam is rather slow in spots, but the last couple of reels hold a corking punch.

One thing King Baggot did in direction: He avoided any of those rough and tumble fist fights that usually go with logging camp stories. There are a couple of blows struck, but they come so fast and are over with so quickly they are not noticed.

Peters handles the heroic role very nicely, while Ruth Clifford plays opposite him. The heavy is Richard Tucker. Snitz Edwards contributes a comedy characterization that gets over nicely. There is a kid actor not given program credit, but who should have had it.

"The Tornado" will please mightily in the smaller towns and get money, too. *Fred.*

TONGUES OF FLAME

Paramount production starring Thomas Meighan. Adapted from the story by Peter Clark McFarlane by Townsend Martin. Directed by Joseph Henabery. At the Rivoli, New York, Dec. 14. Running time, 70 minutes.

Henry Harrington	Thomas Meighan
Lahleet	Bessie Love
Billie Boland	Eileen Percy
Boland	Berton Churchill
Scanlon	John Miltern
Hornblower	Leslie Stowe
Adam John	Nick Thompson
Clayton	Cyril Ring

Although this Tom Meighan release has it several ways over "The Alaskan," it is still far from holding the entertainment values of his older ones, "Back Home and Broke," for instance.

Here again he plays a straight heroic role adapted to any one of a thousand pictur_ leading men, while his other films were distinctive because of their humorous and human qualities. But, like "The Alaskan," this is the story of a real hero, and not a touch of humor is contained in the entire film.

In other words, there's nary a laugh.

Its plot is the rivalry between citizens of a town and the Indians who held a reservation across the river.

No one does any outstanding acting, unless it be Berton Churchill, who makes his screen debut (from the legit) in the father role. John Miltern is another legit player prominent, having a heavy part. Eileen Percy is the daughter, but means little. Bessie Love is competent as the Indian girl, and the tribe types are interesting.

Meighan has no acting to do; it is all cut and dried for him.

Production expense fairly heavy, with many mobs and much destruction. In sections it looks as if an entire city street—and an accurate one, too—has been built.

But, for all that "Tongues of Flame" is a mediocre picture, not up to the old Meighan standard. What he needs is another George Ade story and a real leading woman. This film will not create a sensation anywhere. It's one of those things that will get the Meighan fans at the outset, but won't create enough word-of-mouth talk to draw many others in.

Sisk.

Inez from Hollywood

First National release presented by Sam E. Rork, Inc. Featuring Anna Q. Nilsson, Lewis Stone and Mary Astor. From the Cosmopolitan story, "The Worst Woman in Hollywood," by Adela Rogers St. Johns. Adapted by J. G. Hawks. Directed by Alfred E. Green. At Strand, New York, week of Dec. 14. Running time, 74 minutes.

Inez Laranetta	Anna Q. Nilsson
Stewart Cuyler	Lewis Stone
Fay Bartholdi	Mary Astor
Pat Sommerfield	Laurance Wheat
Marie d'Albrecht	Rose Dione
The Old Sport	Snitz Edwards
Scoop Smith	Harry Depp
Freddie	Ray Hallor
Gardner	E. H. Calvert

This is neither here nor there when it comes to summing it up as a box office attraction. It is one of those pictures that just happens along and doesn't cause any particular stir in the pool of popularity.

When Adela Rogers St. John's story appeared in the "Cosmopolitan" it was a fairly interesting little tale, but hardly heavy enough to be strung out into a full length feature. It is a story that would have been told much better in two or three reels instead of six. Originally it was called "The Worst Woman in Hollywood," but it isn't the worst picture that has ever come from Hollywood, nor is it the best. It doesn't appear that "Inez" will break any box office records anywhere.

It is a story of a screen vamp who for professional reasons is dubbed "The Worst Woman in Hollywood." In reality she is a smart gold digger who is educating her little sister, and whose motto in life is that the man shall pay and pay and pay.

So far so good. The picture opens with Inez giving a pool party at her Hollywod home. An old boy with more money than brains throws a diamond bracelet into the pool and tells the girls to go after it. At that point the cops, who have been tipped off by the star's press agent, raid the place. That makes for a front page spread in the Los Angeles papers.

The next morning one of Inez's admirers warns her that some day she may regret the notoriety achieved and may have to pay a price for it that even her fame won't compensate her for. At the same time he informs her she is a cheat, and he suspects that there is another man in the case. Noting a letter on her table, he memorizes the address, and on his return to New York looks up the place. There he meets a demure little girl, with whom he falls in love. It is the sister of the famous vamp, although he doesn't know it, and no more does the younger girl suspect her sister is the notorious vamp of screen fame.

The guardian of the girl, however, shoots a wire to the west coast informing the star of her sister's flirtation, and the star comes east with a rush. She is determined to save her sister, no matter the cost, but when she learns that her former admirer's intentions toward the little girl are most honorable she consents to the marriage and effaces herself so that society won't know the little girl is the sister of "the worst woman."

Anna Q. Nilsson does fairly well with her role, although at times she looked not at all vampy. Mary Astor as the young star really walked away with the honors. Lewis Stone is the man in the case, while Larry Wheat also has a role, but of secondary importance.

There is some "inside stuff" regarding picturing and the films that won't get over particularly well with the fans.

Fred.

LAST MAN ON EARTH

William Fox production. Story by John D. Swain. Directed by J. G. Blystone. Shown at the Central, New York, beginning Dec. 12. Running time 63 minutes.

PROLOG

Hattie, age six	Jean Johnson
Elmer, age eight	Buck Black
Elmer's pal	Maurice Murphy
Hattie's father	William Steele
Hattie's mother	Jean Dumas
Elmer's father	Harry Dunkinson
Elmer's mother	Fay Holderness

THE PLAY

Elmer	Earle Foxe
Hattie	Derelys Perdue
Gertie	Grace Cunard
Frisco Kate	Gladys Tennyson
Red Sal	Maryon Aye
Doctor Prodwell	Clarissa Selwynne
Furlong, explorer	Pauline French
Paula Prodwell	Marie Astair

Here is an idea that could have been worked out to much greater advantage. Another $100,000 in production would have added a million in box office possibilities.

As it is it will be just a good average program feature with laughs for the average picture audience. The story had possibilities; what it really needed was a good idea man on the job to have realized them. Suppose there had been a shot of the main street of every main city in the country showing how it would look in the day when there were no men on earth? That would have put in a local touch for every one of the key cities.

As it is the picture will do nicely in the majority of houses. It is not, however, pre-release material for the big first-run houses.

The story is just a fantasy, cheaply worked out. The yarn is picturized with a prolog by kid actors. The story starts 20 years later.

At that time there is an epidemic called "masculitis" that sweeps the country attacking all males over 14 and killing them. There isn't a single man left. Women are running the country. They are the street sweepers, cops, chauffeurs, politicians and a woman sits in the Presidential chair. The House of Representatives has been done away with and there is only the Senate.

Suddenly a gang of women crooks in Chicago discover a man living as a hermit in a huge forest. They capture him and bring him to Washington, selling him to the government for $10,000,000. Comes the clash in the Senate as to who shall possess the man as a husband. The President as "the First Lady of the Land" believes she should get him, but a couple of senatoresses object. Finally it is decided that the members from California and Virginia shall fight it out with boxing gloves in the Senate chamber. Just as the member from California wins by a knockout in walks the old sweetheart of the man and he leaves them all flat for the girl of his childhood days.

A flock of comedy touches through out the picture. Earle Foxe, who plays "the last man," is given a little too much to mugging as the picture goes along. The girls really amount to very little except there are so many of them. In fact the picture is just a super-bathing girl comedy and would prove a great attraction for the average burlesque houses.

Fred.

THE EARLY BIRD

East Coast Film Productions, presented by C. C. Burr, with Johnny Hines starred. Story by Richard Friel, titles by Ralph Spence, directed by Charles Hines. Shown privately at the Hotel Astor, Dec. 12, 1924. Running time, 73 minutes.

Jimmy Burke	Johnny Hines
Jean Blair	Sigrid Holmquist
George Fairchild	Wyndham Standing
The Great La Tour	Edmund Breese
Miss Quincy	Flora Finch
Mrs. Havlland, Jean's aunt	Maud Turner Gordon

Johnny Hines is "in" again with another of the gag comedies sure fire for picture house audiences. It has laugh after laugh from beginning to end, with just enough of a story to carry the gags. Hines is as funny as usual and gets his milkman role over with pep. In addition to the gags there are lots of laughs in the Ralph Spence titles.

One thing about the picture: it is proof absolute that both Hines and Spence have very long memories. Nither one has overlooked anything in vaudeville or burlesque for a year that would make for a laugh.

The picture starts with a gag, with Hines delivering milk along his route. He has his horse and cart, and stops at a house where the milk is placed in the awning so it won't be stolen. In another place the bottle is fastened by lock and chain. Johnny is an independent milk dealer, and there is a trust. He organizes the independents to fight the trust, and finally wins the daughter of the head of the trust and combines the independents with it.

A recital of the story does not give an idea of the laughs crammed into the action. There is an average of a couple of laughs a minute and, in addition, is a touch of melodrama at the finish that gives a kick. They went back to "Blue Jeans" for the kick, showing the heroine being carried to certain death in an ice-chopping machine, only to be rescued at the crucial moment by the hero.

Sigrid Holmquist is the heroine. While not called on to do great acting, she makes a pretty picture opposite the comedian. Wyndham Standing is the heavy, without particularly distinguishing himself. Edmund Breese had a secondary role of a broken-down magician, getting it over for a few laughs here and there.

"The Early Bird" is a corking audience picture. It will make them laugh, no matter how tough an audience.

Fred.

DANGEROUS FLIRT

Gothic production of the Julie Herne novel. Distributed through F. B. O. Directed by Tod Browning. Evelyn Brent starred. At Loew's New York, Dec. 13, as half of double bill.

Priscilla Fairfax	Clarissa Selwyn
Sheila Fairfax	Evelyn Brent
Dick Morris	Edward Earle
Jose Gonzalez	Paul Gordon

An intentionally dirty picture with its basis placed upon the fear a young girl holds of her husband on their wedding night. Such stuff is for defter hands than Julie Herne and Tod Browning. From the story the director has fashioned a set of sequences that are as crude as they are distasteful. They leave the picture unsuited to family houses and the better theatres.

Sheila Fairfax is so innocent and her aunt, Priscilla, is such a stickler for modesty that when Sheila walks through the bedroom in her combo and little else (with no one but the aunt looking) the old lady gives her a sub-title lecture which has in it the choice philosophy that a girl who is immodest in her boudoir will be immodest outside.

Two men are after Sheila, one of them, Gonzalez, for reasons purely movie, and the other, Morris, because he loves her. Morries marries her when a scandal crops up and then the nuptial night stuff crops up—with the girl fully clothed yet crouching in horror at the knock of her husband at the door.

Miss Brent as the girl probably doesn't mean anything as a draw, although starred. The rest of the cast is fair, while the sets, etc., are cheap.

Sisk.

SO THIS IS MARRIAGE

Louis B. Mayer's presentation of the Hobart Henley production of Carey Wilson story. Directed by Hobart Henley. Distributed through Metro-Goldwyn. At the Capitol, New York, Dec. 21, 1924. Running time, 68 minutes.

Peter Marsh..................Conrad Nagel
Beth Marsh..............Eleanor Boardman
Daniel Rankin ....Lew Cody
Vera Kellogg..................Miss DuPont
Biblical Episode (B. C.)
King David...................Warner Oland
Bath Sheba...........Mabel Julienne Scott
Nathan ....Edward Connelly
Uria, the Hittite ....John Boles

Here's a great audience proposition in more ways than one. It is sexy enough in spots to tickle the bald-headed palates and it displays (merely as a matter of record is this stated) for the first time the undraped breast in the movies. Its depiction of young married life has its alternating happy and unhappy moments which should find ready recognition from married folks—and should get a snicker from those who aren't. The Biblical episode showing David and Bath Sheba, the woman he coveted after seeing her taking a bath in her back yard—long ago—is done in colors and mounted lavishly, comparing in spots to moments in the biggest of spectacles.

The story proper concerns a young couple whose married life is a series of quarrels, coming with unrelenting regularity upon the first of the month when the bills come in. But the pair loved each other and always made up—until a middle-aged chippie-chaser perched his eye on the young Mrs. and was partially successful in making her acquaintance. The husband at this became aroused and finally so angry the wife left to take refuge and comfort with the other man.

That man, however, made her an ambiguous offer that she retain her husband and come to see him once in a while on the side. He did this under the guise of offering her the Great Love, which ignored talk, etc. To this end he recounted to what lengths one possessed with the Great Love will go, and recounted the story of Bath Sheba, this running for over five minutes in two sections and making for a hit in the midst of a story strong in itself.

But the girl couldn't see it, and repented her little bit of wrong, so it was back to hubby and the child for her at the fadeout.

Henley's directorial touches in this film are corking and funny. To illustrate a gabby dame he flashes a windmill working at full speed and in another scene he gets a big laugh through use of Elinor Glyn's "His Hour" book (which may be a two-way plug, for Metro has the book in film form and current).

The sex stuff is here and plenty. A bacchanale is given for King David's benefit, and in this the breast is exposed. The shots of Bath Sheba show the lady with loose clothes that can't, in spots, be coaxed below her pretty knees, while many other gals hanging around are dressed skimpily enough.

These Biblical scenes, incidentally, look like many dollars, and the film as a whole is mounted very lavishly, as its protagonists are folks of high society who have marble bathrooms instead of tile. That's the real distinguishing mark—according to the movies.

Conrad Nagel and Eleanor Boardman and Lew Cody are the three principal characters, and they're okeh all the way through, with Miss Boardman and Nagel registering especially heavy at times. Miss Boardman, like Norma Shearer, seems to be bearing a heavy burden in the Metro shops these days, and is standing up under it with increasing impressiveness.

This film is frankly framed for the box office, but it is handled with a humorous nicety that lifts it from the run of married life pictures. This, combined with the spectacle stuff done in color, should put it over heavily, for it looks like one of the best picture bets Metro has yet put into the Capitol. *Sisk.*

ARGENTINE LOVE

Zukor-Lasky presentation and an Allan Dwan production directed by Dwan. Features Bebe Daniels and Ricardo Cortez. Adapted from the story of Vicente Ibanez by John Russell. At Rivoli, New York, week of Dec. 21. Running time, 63 mins.

Consuelo Garcia..............Bebe Daniels
Juan Martin..................Ricardo Cortez
Philip Sears...................James Rennie
Senator Cornejo............Mario Majeroni
Emanuel Garcia................Russ Whital
Mme. Garcia....................Alice Chapin
La Mosca........................Julia Hurley
Rafael Cornejo.............Mark Gonzales
Pedro...........................Aurelio Coccia

Decidedly a woman's picture with enough men strolling by the camera who look like Valentino to make it appear as a musical comedy production number dedicated to Rudolph. As a picture the settings are eye-filling and lavish with the ailments appearing the work of the leading cast members other than Bebe Daniels.

Allan Dwan, in directing, has taken close-up after close-up to the point where they become monotonous. The work of Cortez as the villain who finally gives his life for the girl as a saving grace is distinctly spotty. His performance is particularly impaired through the inadequacy to withstand the ordeal of the close shots in other than a detrimental manner. The same may be said of James Rennie, who consummates a passive and expressionless hero. On the other hand Miss Daniels has supplied an even performance supplemented by a well-groomed appearance. Others of the players lend able assistance minus predominance.

The story doesn't register as particularly strong. It tells of Juan Martin (Mr. Cortez), who awaits the homecoming of his betrothed, Consuelo (Miss Daniels). He is the refined "strong man" of the locality. The complications set in when Consuelo falls in love with an American engineer, Philip (Mr. Rennie), who is bridge-building in her native land.

The telling is smooth enough and the film is picturesque but it's far from being vital and the masculine viewpoint is almost certain indifference. It is seemingly one of those which will have a strong feminine appeal. The suave Cortez and expressionless Rennie are destined to figuratively roll off masculine patrons' knives. Hence the business the picture will get is reasonably sure of coming from the womenfolk.

Picturesque and almost approximating a costume episode, the similarity between the men, even including some of the extras, is a dull tone that encounters no relief.

That the film is equivalent to major house exhibiting is unquestioned but it hardly seems a "smash" unless the girls flock by the gate in droves, and they too will probably be disappointed after drawing their own conclusions as to the inference to be construed from the title. *Skig.*

LOVE'S WILDERNESS

First National picture made by Corinne Griffith's unit. Adapted by Eve Unsell from the novel "Wilderness" by Helen Klump. Directed by Robert Z. Leonard. At Strand, New York, Dec. 21. Running time, 70 minutes.

Linda-Lou Heath ....Corinne Griffith
David Tennant ....Holmes Herbert
Paul L'Estrange ....Ian Keith
Pierre Bazin.................Maurice Cannon
Matilda Heath..................Emily Fitzroy
Prudence Heath.............Ann Schaefer
Colonel Mosely.............Bruce Covington
The Governor...............David Torrence

This one is good all the way through except in spots which could stand heavy editing. A copy-reading fool with a pair of shears should be turned loose on it. Pared to about an hour and its action accelerated, many of the platitudinous sub-titles eliminated etc., it would be a good piece of film. As it stands now, the "too-long" plaint is the only one that can honestly be registered.

The beginning shows Linda-Lou Heath as a little southern beauty in one of those towns on the Mississippi where the flat bottomed steamers come down two or three times a week. David Tennant is a scientist, but a life long friend and when he prepared to leave for Africa, there to work for the French government, the just-grown-to-womanhood Linda Lou is mute to tell him she loves him.

So he sails and into town comes Paul L'Estrange, a bad boy. But Linda likes him and despite the protests of her maiden aunts, she marries him. They go to a farm in Canada upon which the uncle of L'Estrange has placed him. But he turns out to be a lemon and deserts her near the time of child-birth, so when he comes to in a hospital, she finds that her baby is dead and that her husband is also reported as drowned in an icy river. On her sick-bed, however, solace is found, for David turns up and they marry.

David then takes her back to the African Coast, where he is stationed on a prison island. There Paul turns up as a convict. He incites mutiny and panic follows. In a terrific jungle storm Linda-Lou, out looking to verify her suspicions that Paul is on the island, is caught. Paul saves her from death in a stream, which has as one of its inhabitants a pouchy looking crocodile. The windup is that David tells the governor of the island of Paul's heroism and clemency is promised, but eventually another prisoner kills him. So David and Linda-Lou are left happy.

All of this is somewhat involved and the story at the end too drawn out. Directness could certainly be achieved by cutting and then the yawns could stop during the last 15 minutes. Many in the Strand Sunday night became bored with the film for this reason.

Miss Griffith does corking work as the young girl, actually looking the part, and that's not a bad achievement for an actress who has been playing these heavily sexed ladies for many moons. Holmes Herbert as David is satisfactory, while Ian Keith, the legit actor, is at a disadvantage in the earlier shots. His makeup was bad and his face looked much heavier than it actually is. Nobody else in the cast mattered much, for this was nothing more or less than the old triangle proposition, with its right and obtuse angles and the intersection of the love affairs.

The southern atmosphere in the early part of the picture was good enough for picture purposes, but smeared it on a little thick. The Canadian snow scenes were wows and the jungle stuff was exceptionally well done.

"Love's Wilderness" should go well with the Griffith fans. It has her close-uped in every facial position imaginable but she bears it bravely. It is a carefully made film, averagely directed but its intense love interest can be depended upon to create interest. *Sisk.*

SANDRA

Presented by Sawyer-Lubin Productions. A First National release, co-starring Barbara La Marr and Bert Lytell. From the novel by Pearl Doles Bell. Directed by Arthur Sawyer. At the Piccadilly, New York, week Dec. 20. Running time, 78 minutes.

Sandra...................Barbara La Marr
David.................................Bert Lytell
Mate Stanley.................Leila Hyams
Bobby Stanley..........Augustin Sweeney
Eve Stanley......................Maude Bill
Peter Stanley...................Edgar Nelson
Stephen Winslow..............Leon Gordon
Rev. William James Hapgood.Leslie Austin
Francois Molyneaux.......Wallace Morgan
Henri La Flamme.Arthur Edmund Carewe
Mimi.........................Lillin Ten Eyck
La Flamme's Wife.........Helen Gardner

"Sandra" as a picture released by First National bears all the earmarks of a feature made with an economic perspective. There are a lot of little touches in the picture that are of the picture-making days of a decade ago, practices that today are not resorted to when one is making a picture for release by one of the bigger organizations. The coupling of Barbara La Marr and Bert Lytell as co-stars for the picture may, however, draw to a certain extent at the box office in certain localities. The picture, however, is far from the standard usually exacted by those managing the pre-release theatres.

The Saturday night audience at the Piccadilly, which jammed the house, laughed at two of Barbara's love-making scenes, both of which were enacted in exactly the same manner.

Miss La Marr incidentally seems to be putting on some extra weight which is particularly noticable when she presents a profile view of her figure. She also must have had a particularly well wearing evening gown for she wore the same gown in several scenes in various parts of the world, something that it seems certain is not in keeping with the character of adventuress of the type she was portraying. The gown was particularly noticeable because of its bird plumage trimming.

The story is that of a woman with a dual personality. One expressing itself in the desire for a home and husband, the other in a craving for adventuress excitement. The latter wins out for a while and under its spell she leaves her husband for a theatrical manager, but she evidently blows out on him although the picture never tells it and the next thing we know she's in Paris, flitting from there to one of the fashionable watering places of the Continent where she becomes the tool of a professional gambler. After that there is an affair with a banker which ends in his arrest and the disclosure that he has a wife, so there is nothing left for Sandra except to come home again. She does that, peeks in at the window of the old homestead, sees her husband with the neighbor's daughter and then walks off, but not before she has made up her mind to send her former husband a note. She intends committing suicide, but the husband finds her in time and there is a clinch for the ending.

Bert Lytell plays the husband and makes him a pretty weepy sort of a guy all through the picture. The heavy lovers are Leon Gordon, Wallace Morgan and Arthur Edmund Carewe. All three were about on a par without there being anything extraordinary in the characterizations presented by either one.

The first couple of reels of the picture moved along fairly well, although the photography was not particularly good. There was one well handled scene in a cabaret in New York, with a hint of color stuff either in tinting or in the original photography. The latter scenes supposedly having taken place abroad were not very good.

The action of the picture is particularly slow in spots because of the excess footage given Miss La Marr, who is shown walking, sitting, standing and with her back turned all in one weep scene. It was overdone, especially as it was resorted to several times in the picture.

In some of the big towns there may be a chance in the neighborhood houses but it doesn't appear to be a small town picture at all.

Fred.

THE EPIC OF EVEREST

London, Dec. 15.

Very few pictures have had the good and bad luck of this one on their first presentation to the public. Good, because the screening was in the presence of members of the Royal family, and a very distinguished array of arts, letters and **social lions; bad, because the elements conspired to fill the Scala, where the picture is running, with a thick fog which at times almost rendered the screen invisible. A previous run had, however, proved the beauty of the photography, the greater part of which was acquired through the medium of powerful telephoto lenses.**

There are no preliminaries to the picture which starts right off with the expedition in Thibet. Here a Llama warned Captain Noel, leader of the expedition, they would never reach their objective and disaster would overtake them, a prophecy which proved only too true when Mallory and Irvine died within a few hundred feet of the mountain top.

Among the Thibetan scenes are many of real value but it is not until the party approaches the mountain that the real beauty of the feature is apparent. Such scenery and awesome grandeur have never before been "shot" by a camerman. The loss of the two men is not used as a morbid adjunct to showmanship but the audience watches them climb away with their breathing apparatus and vanish round a corner, the last mortal eyes ever saw of them. Later the search parties are shown and the signal **that all hope had to be abandoned, the laying of six blankets in the form of a cross on a snowy slope. There is a remarkable grip in these final scenes.**

Prior to the screening General Sir Francis Younghusband, who 20 years ago led a military expedition into the heart of Thibet, introduced H. R. H. Prince Henry to the audience, who in his turn introduced the picture. An added attraction rests in the appearance of a party of Llamas who contributed strange music for about half an hour, after which the chief blessed the audience.

Made by Explorers, Ltd., this picture deserves success but it is doubtful whether the general public will realize and appreciate its value.

Gore.

PETER PAN

Herbert Brenon production presented by Adolph Zukor and Jesse L. Lasky. Adapted by Willis Goldbeck from J. M. Barrie's play, "Peter Pan." Directed by Herbert Brenon, assisted by Roy Pomeroy. At the Rialto and Rivoli theatres, week Dec. 28. Running time, 101 minutes.

Peter Pan	Betty Bronson
Captain Hook	Ernest Torrence
Mr. Darling	Cyril Chadwick
Tinker Bell	Virginia Brown Faire
Tiger Lily	Anna May Wong
Mrs. Darling	Esther Ralston
Nana (the dog)	George Ali
Wendy	Mary Brian
Michael	Philippe de Lacey
John	Jack Murphy

"Peter Pan" with his Pirates, Redskins, Never-Never-Land and all the other accessories that make up the dreams and ambitions of youth came to Broadway on Sunday at both the Rialto and Rivoli. Peter Pan, the boy that would never grow up, who ran away from home the day he was born; Peter Pan, the pirate killer; Peter Pan, who makes you clap your hands if you believe in fairies, proved one thing, if nothing else, that Betty Bronson is the find of years as far as pictures are concerned. It is to be hoped that Betty Bronson will be the Peter Pan to life and be just a "never grow up" of screendom, for she is a delight, a love and sure to be the idol of the children from 7 to 75 who will see her performance in this picture.

To Herbert Brenon must go a full share of credit for having turned out a picture that with its fantasy holds the attention. At the early performances at the Rivoli Sunday the children shrilled their delight over the adventures of the Band of Lost Children, and the older kiddies were just as spellbound by the suspense the director managed to weave into the fantastical tale of the noted English playwright.

But, above all, it is Betty Bronson who achieves the big things in the public eye as far as the picture is concerned. At times she reminds one of Marguerite Clark of the earlier days of screen history. She has that same dash of youthful verve; then in another moment will come the gentle hint that she is as Mary Pickford was, and a combination of those two means only millions at the box office in time, providing, of course, she is properly guided.

Then as Wendy, Mary Brian proves to be another youthful find for the screen. Sweet, demure and with a sort of a self-effacing manner she wins the hearts of those in front. Ernest Torrence as the famous Captain Hook, the pirate leader, is another delight and scores very neatly indeed.

The production is remarkable for its beauty, and in it was an opportunity for Brenon to work in his mermaids again. While shooting that scene his memories must have harked back to other days when he was with Fox. The scenes in Never-Never-Land and the home of the Lost Children underground were exceedingly well handled, but the real thrill came with the pirate ship and the battle on its deck, with the little youngsters worsting the pirate band.

"Peter Pan" is a picture that will go down the years as a delightful fantasy and crop up again and again as time rolls along, and with each return be welcomed with a new joy by a new band of children, who will join the ranks of the never-grow-ups.

On the first de luxe show on Sunday the Rivoli started to "stand 'em up" as early as three o'clock, and that, after all, is the sure sign whether or not the picture will get the money.

Fred.

CLASSMATES

Inspiration Pictures, Inc., presentation, starring Richard Barthelmess. A John Robertson production. Releasing through First National. Adapted from the stage play by Margaret Turnbull and William De Mille. At the Strand, New York, week of Dec. 28. Running time, 74 minutes.

Duncan Irving, Sr.	Claude Brooke
Duncan Irving, Jr.	Richard Barthelmess
Bert Stafford	Reginald Sheffield
Mrs. Stafford, his mother	Charlotte Walker
Sylvia Randolph, her niece	Madge Evans
Bobby Dumble	Beach Cooke
"Silent" Clay	James Bradbury, Jr.
Jones, a West Pointer	Antrim Short
Captain Lane (officer in charge)	Major Henry B. Lewis

It's hard to see how Richard Barthelmess can miss with this picture. There doesn't seem to be much doubt it's his best since "Tol'able David," and that's going back a few. The West Point angle alone is sufficient to have almost put any film across. With the addition of Barthelmess and the personal performance he gives they make this release a sure thing.

The story is secondary to the action at the academy, although it's a good tale and neatly told. Robertson has done exceedingly well in getting the general spirt of the cadet corps on the screen, and in lifting the jargon of the Pointers into the sub-titles has enhanced the value just that much more. To give an idea how far Robertson has gone in maintaining a faithful representation of the Point it is noteworthy that the few hotel scenes the script calls for look as if they had actually been taken in the lobby of the Hotel Astor, New York, which for years has been the metropolitan headquarters of the Pointers. The camera work has taken every advantage of the opportunity, having secured a few viewpoints the news weeklies have missed.

The comedy is given over to the titles during the time the script is localed up the Hudson and in the plebes running the gamut of the upper classmen.

It tells of young Duncan Irving (Mr. Barthelmess) entering the Point and in his third year expelled for striking a plebe, Bert Stafford (Reginald Sheffield), who is from the home town, a cousin of the girl (Madge Evans), and a snob. He goads young Irving into striking him and then feigns blindness to secure his own release.

After leaving the Point the story jumps to South America, where Irving searches for Stafford in order to clear his name before the girl and secure his reinstatement at the academy so he may graduate. The film climaxes with a military wedding party emerging from the chapel at West Point.

Barthelmess blends into the characterization as if it had been originally written for him. It's doubtful if any other male "name" in pictures could have done as well with the role, even though the picture would have carried almost any one. Miss Evans sweetly balances as the southern miss, while Mr. Sheffield succeeds in making himself a detestable cadet and a corking "villain." More and capable support is forthcoming from Beach Cooke and James Bradbury, Jr., as the particular classmate chums of Barthelmess.

It's a whale of a picture that has already run up sizable grosses out of town and will do as well wherever it plays unto foreign countries simply on the strength of the West Point thing, if nothing else. The "inside" flashes of the government institution are bound to entertain besides, which Robertson has creditably kept away from tinging the scenes and players with that distinct movie flavor which is a habit with most directors no matter what the location.

They liked it plenty at the Strand.

Skig.

THE DIXIE HANDICAP

Louis B. Mayer's presentation of Reginald Barker's pr ction, "The Dixie Handicap." Picturization of Gerald Beaumont's story "Dixie," which appeared in the Red Book magazine. Distributed through Metro-Goldwyn. At the Capitol, New York, Dec. 28, 1924. Running time, 68 minutes.

Virginia	Claire Windsor
Judge Roberts	Frank Keenan
Johnny Sheridan	Lloyd Hughes
Dexter	John Sainpolis
Noah	Otis Harlan
Bubbles	Joseph Morrison
The Major	Otto Hoffman
Mr. Bosworth	Edward Martindel
Mrs. Bosworth	Ruth King
A Tout	William Quirk
A Tout	James Quinn
Losing Jones	Loyal Underwood
Conductor	Bert Lindley
Sheriff	William Orlamond
Constable	Milton Ross
Milkman	J. P. Lockney

As the title implies, a race track story. Southern romance. Theme along the lines of the racing type presented on the screen in other seasons. The Mayer Barker combination has devoted a lot of attention the [illegible], although there is a fling at old melodrama when the juvenile hero (Lloyd Hughes) uncouples the car containing the horse from another car that is ablaze, the train running as this fire scene is pictured.

The comedy element comes from the darkies, with one character handsomely portrayed by Otis Harlan. It was a sort of race, too, between Frank Keenan as the old judge and Harlan as the old negro. Both corking characters and admirably conceived. The girl is Claire Windsor. Her scenes with her "daddy" were impressionably done.

An old judge, proud, owns a race horse. That his daughter does not have to wed a rich man she does not love just to save their home, he sells the horse and the girl goes to Europe. While there her sweetheart has the horse given him when it bowed a tendon and he brings it back to racing form and wins the big handicap.

Not a great story. The "exteriors" are in keeping with the story. The photography is A1. The story limps along, but the racing scenes are photographic classics.

Good for the neighborhoods.

Mark.

Lighthouse by the Sea

Warner Bros. production, featuring Rin-Tin-Tin, Louise Fazenda and William Collier, Jr. From the stage play by Owen Davis. Directed by Mal St. Clair. Shown at the Piccadilly, N. Y., week Dec. 27, 1924. Running time, sixty minutes.

Rin-Tin-Tin	Rin-Tin-Tin
Flora Gale	Louise Fazenda
Albert Dorn	William Collier, Jr.
Joe Daggett	Mathew Betz
Edward Canavan	Douglas Gerard
Caleb Gale	Charles Hill Mailes

Little different from the usual run of the stories in which the police dog stars have been appearing. It is a combination of a rum-running theme and the usual melodramatic heroics that go with the final victory of the virtuous and the clinching close-up that is likewise the usual finish. From a money standpoint it is hardly a picture that one would expect to stand up in a house of the type that is presenting prerelease showings with de luxe presentations, but in the average run of neighborhood houses it should get by in good shape and pull some money, for it has a couple of real thrills in it.

By the same token it is likewise full of little inaccuracies in direction that could have easily been eliminated. One is the spectacle of the hero of the story just rescued from the sea and so weak he cannot stand on his feet, yet he has sufficient strength to hold a Shepherd dog trying to attack. That the hero succeeds is a confession that the director, Mal St. Clair, never tried to hold one of those dogs when it was up and going. Another touch is bringing on an English bull to give battle to the shepherd. It's all right to build up your dumb hero by having him worst the heavies of the cast, but it is bad business to stage a dog fight in any picture and the chances are that in some localities it will mean that the A.S.P.C.A. will get after that sequence. Besides, nobody should pit an English bull against a shepherd at any time.

Then we have the spectacle of an aged lighthouse keeper, stone-blind from old age, which means that, if he is a day, he's eighty, yet he has a daughter who can't be any more than eighteen.

The story is on the coast of Maine where there is a light known as Seville Light. It is in charge of the aged and blind keeper, who has kept his affiication from the authorities so he may retain his position, and the light is tended by his daughter. Nearby is a village held by a crew of rum-runners and the revenue authorities are on the scene. A revenue cutter is in use and the light must be kept up at all costs so that the rum-runners cannot land their cargo in the darkness. About this time a boat containing a youth with his dog, the sole survivors of an emigrant ship, are cast ashore at the light and the girl rescues him only to have one of the heavies step in and start a battle in which the dog comes to the rescue.

From that time on the castaway becomes part of the lighthouse staff as assistant to the aged tender. Between the boy and the dog, the rum-runners are finally brought to bay, arrested and packed off, but not until the dog has had a hand in rescuing everyone of the virtuous members of the cast. He saves his master on three or four occasions; saves the girl, pulls the old man up when he is about to tumble over a cliff, and finally runs with a lighted bunch of flaming waste to relight the signal lamp put out of commission by the rum-runners. That last trick of getting the dog to carry fire must have been about the hardest feat he could have been made to accomplish. The dog is there and even the Broadway audiences go to applause when he is seen dashing along to the rescue.

Louise Fazenda and William Collier, Jr., do nothing unusual, and the balance of the cast is nothing to rave about. The scenes with young Collier besting the heavy are almost funny as it is dead open and shut little Collier could never have handled Betz any day. *Fred.*

THE TURMOIL

Universal-Jewel production directed by Hobart Henley. From the novel of the same name by Booth Tarkington. Cast features George Hackathorne and includes Eleanor Boardman, Emmett Corrigan, Eileen Percy, Pauline Garon, Edward Hearn, Kenneth Gibson, Theodore Von Eltz, Winter Hall and others. At the Stanley one day (Dec. 26). Runs about 70 minutes.

It is rather surprising that "The Turmoil," released nearly four months ago as a Universal-Jewel special, has been as little in evidence around the larger picture houses in New York city. Except for an engagement at a few of the neighborhood vaudeville houses about a month ago this reviewer had never seen it billed until at the Stanley.

Something must have been wrong with the exploitation or distribution somewhere because in spite of its slim exhibition showing around New York (whether this holds true out of town too can only be conjectured) "The Turmoil" is a film that any picture audience will enjoy. Taken from the Booth Tarkington novel and in general intelligently handled by the director, Hobart Henley, it tells a straightforward story in interesting fashion. Besides it is acted more than capably by a competent group of Universal troupers, whose more or less well-known names should be another argument for the box office.

The story, considered one of Tarkington's best, treats of family life in a typical manufacturing city. James Sheridan (Emmett Corrigan) has been the dominating figures in building up the town. A self-made man, his creed is work and his motto, where one blade of grass has grown heretofore, two must be made to appear. His two older sons, Roscoe and Jim (Edward Hearn and Theodore Von Eltz) have become imbued with his hard ideas on life, but the youngest, Bibbs (George Hackathorne), considered a weakling by the family, believes poetry and art are worthier things than smoke and steel.

Tragedy comes to the two older boys when Roscoe loses his wife to an idler who has more time to devote to her than he has, and Jim is killed in an accident in a dam made faulty by his desire to complete a job in record time. The little sister, too (Pauline Garon), has eloped with a ne'er-do-well and soon it dawns on the old man that there are bigger things in life than financial success and industrial progress. At the end when Bibbs finds his literary efforts crowned with success his father is only too ready to turn to him as the consolation of his declining years.

The scene in which the father learns the death of his favorite son, Jim, Jr., is as well handled as any bit of pathos in the films in months. The old man has entered the barber shop after a day in the country, unaware of the accident earlier in the afternoon. The manner in which he gradually becomes aware of the horrible news awaiting him is dramatic fare par excellence. One fault, however, either in direction or story, is leaving the tangled affairs of Roscoe and of the poor, misguided little sister in mid air as the picture ends.

Corrigan shares the acting honors with Hackathorne, who is featured. Eleanor Boardman is deliciously pretty as the girl forced to chose between Bibbs and Jim before the latter's death. All the others are acceptable, although Eileen Percy may make the role of Roscoe's wife a bit more disagreeable and unsympathetic than it was intended to be.

In the face of its meager dates in the metropolitan district it may be foolish to call "The Turmoil" good box office stuff. But when the final returns from all over the country are in its record should substantiate that belief. Whether it does or not, there's more meat to it than the majority of the films seen in the first-run houses.

WINNER TAKE ALL

Fox production, starring Charles (Buck) Jones. Story by Larry Evans. Scenario by Ewart Adamson. Directed by W. S. Van Dyke. Distributed by Fox. At the New York Dec. 26 (part of double feature bill).

Perry Blair	Buck Jones
Cecil Manners	Peggy Shaw
Jack Hamilton	Edward Hearn
Felicity Brown	Lilyan Tashman
Jim Devereaux	Wm. N. Bailey
Charles Dunham	Ben Deeley
Dynamite Galloway	Tom O'Brien

As usual, the camera finds Buck Jones a ridin' fool, but in this one much of his time is spent with the padded mitts. It is a story of the prize ring. Larry Evans wrote it for a magazine, and its main theme is wrapped up in boxing gloves.

Jones appears as Perry Blair, the shifty fighter, who refuses to stand for the crooked game of two unscrupulous promoters. There is a girl, a little lady of the city who thinks Perry means to take her west and not marry her. Perry means all that is sweet and honorable, but there is a slip between the parson, the license bureau and the girl's city domicile.

Buck has his eyes on a ranch, and the picture shifts so that Buck gets into his riding clothes of the wild west to do a little rough riding, not the kind Buck generally shows when chasing bandits or the bad men of the prairies and mining towns, but just a ride while the villain, none other than the big fight promoter, cast aside by Blair when he became famous as a fighter, was trying to force his attentions upon the heroine.

It all ends well with Buck as the ring fighter taking all, even the girl, away from Dunham. The success and strength of the picture rest solely on the big fight. It is finely photographed and splendidly staged, yet it is a question whether it means anything at the box office.

Buck makes a good fighter and goes through his stuff most satisfactorily. The girl is at the ringside, the villainous two ring sharks taking her west to see the fight and give her a vacation. She goes and has a seat that would make a vet sports writer turn green with envy.

Buck finally wins on a knockout when it had been noised around it was framed, the K. O. to come in the fifth round with Galloway laying down to Buck. It goes beyond the "framed" point, with the closing minutes arousing the most excitement.

The finale is tame, very tame for a Buck Jones windup. The whole picture has its emphasis on the fight. Hard to follow at times, but as a whole thrilling in a way if one can get a thrill that way.

It is a fair picture, as the fight causes the love interest to become a secondary if not a submerged consideration. When the fight is over the picture is over, although the scenarist has tried to make it further exciting by having Buck ride across the desert and get there in the nick of time.

uck is about the whole show, with Miss Tashman doing well with a thankless role and Miss Shaw working hard to please as the girl. ***Mark.***

THE BEAUTY PRIZE

Louis B. Mayer presentation releasing through Metro-Goldwyn and starring Viola Dana. Adapted from story by Nina Wilcox Putnam. Directed by Lloyd Ingraham. At Loew's New York theatre Dec. 27. Running time, 60 mins.

Nothing that will make the major releases tend to such laurels as they gain, but a good picture for Miss Dana and the intermediate houses, especially when considering usual scenario morsels passed out to this feminine light, with which she must struggle.

The picture makes a decided bid for comedy, particularly in the subtitling. While the wording may strike the minority as being hilarious, it befits the story, and for those not expecting too much it will suffice. Miss Dana frolics through the footage easily, passively abetted by Pat O'Malley and Eddie Phillips, who fail to dent as regards making an impression.

Dealing with the national beauty contest, annually held as a local plug for Atlantic City, the story has Miss Dana as a manicurist who takes over a client's Fifth avenue home for the summer in the role of caretaker. A wise kid salesman, of the dance floor type, inaugurates the bug for face and form honors which breaks off the engagement to the boy back home. The winning of the title means little to the girl upon discovering herself appointed press agent is after the cash prize, but things shape up when she is requested to broadcast over radio and puts in a call for the home town youth to come back.

Incidentally, that radiocasting bit is subject to legal action on the part of Sir Joseph Ginsburg, for Miss Dana etherizes her conversation in the same dress with which she wins the beauty title—a distinct lift from Sir Joseph's original conception of singing his fireman's ditty in a fire hat. That Miss Dana sends over station MTRO (the nearest the director could get to Metro) and Sir Joe goes out from the Loew State building smacks of a tie-up that should hop Ginzy into Variety's office with a healthy squawk.

Inserts of what appear to be last summer's genuine beauty contest on the boardwalk are used for atmosphere, while Miss Dana poses among a group of entrants, in bathing suits, who wouldn't draw a dime were they advertisements in the flesh for "Artists and Models." A couple of shots actually look as if Miss Dana and a few of the company had spent a brief period at the summer resort.

Anything resembling a lavish display or flash has been passed up, not too neatly, to make the film register as a not overly expensive piece of production. A bit of splurging and some attention given to the sub-titling might have pushed this release up a notch, but as it stands it's mainly indifferent fare that should find its level in the middle class theatres. *Skig.*

CHEAP KISSES

C. Gardner Sullivan presents "Cheap Kisses," featuring Lillian Rich and Cullen Landis. Made by the C. Gardner Sullivan Productions. Released by F. B. O. Directed by John Ince. Edited by Barbara Hunter. Shown at the Greeley Square, New Hunter.

Donald Dillingham	Cullen Landis
Kitty Dillingham	Vera Reynolds
George Westcott	Phillips Smalley
Jane Dillingham	Louise Dresser
Gustaf Borgstrom	Jean Hersholt
Maybelle Westcott	Bessie Eyton
Billy Kendall	Lincoln Stedman
Henry Dillingham	Sydney de Grey

Nothing to get excited over, although the title might lead some of the villagers to look for a modern story of spice and raciness. The story brings nothing new to the screen.

"Cheap Kisses" has a cast that looks like a master production, yet the cast as a whole flounders around with little to do. There are several redeeming features, but not sufficient to label this one as "near great." It misses because of the failure of the story to reach.

Lillian Rich is co-featured with Cullen Landis. She should have been starred, as Landis does nothing to warrant so much type being wasted. There are others in the cast just as important and with bigger names as far as some of the neighborhoods will be concerned.

Miss Rich has the looks, an ingratiating personality, and walks away with honors.

The story takes a pretty chorus girl and marries her to a rich man's son. They win the boy's folks over when they get in the good graces of a portrait painter, who is more at home drying dishes and playing woman's protector than daubing with the brush.

There are some fine scenes photographically and no doubt cost real money.

A few of the captions are bad boys, one in particular out of alignment.

"Cheap Kisses" has a notable cast to help it move along, and, above all things, the captivating, winsome Lillian Rich. No wonder Paramount grabbed her. *Mark.*

FLATTERY

Chadwick production written by H. H. Van Loan. Directed by Tom Forman and supervised by Norman Walker. Half the bill at Loew's Circle, New York, Nov. 17. Runs about 62 mins.
Reginald Mallory..............John Bowers
Sloane....................Lewis Morrison
Arthur Barrington..............Alan Hale
Betty Biddle......Marguerite De La Motte
Allene King..............Grace Darmond

In "Flattery" a more digestible mixture of politics and romance is to be found than usually the case in pictures of this description. H. H. Van Loan has written a story that has no startling twists, but has received expert treatment at the hands of Tom Forman, the director, and a particularly good cast.

The film's chief appeal to public interest lies in the fact that its hero is not the usual screen darling, but a vain and conceited ass who doesn't get wise to himself until the last few hundred feet. As the audience always knows this is coming, the role is never unsympathetic, and as played by John Bowers the character is a relief from the usual formula.

Reginald Mallory has been a victim of flattery all his life. As a baby he has been petted and pampered even more than the average infant, and as a small boy he is made the revered idol of a group of worshiping young satellites. Growing to manhood and on the threshold of a brilliant career as engineer, he is still too prone to lend a ready ear to those who wish to praise him. Because of this he is chosen to become city engineer by a crooked mayor and construction company official who see in his weakness a chance to put over some dirty work on the city.

By flattering young Mallory they manage to have their own way for a while. But finally he realizes their evil designs, and although it means incriminating himself because of his earlier negligence he supplies evidence that puts them behind the bars. Meanwhile his girl has effectually cured him of his flattery complex, and when at the end she calls him wonderful he almost refuses to listen to her.

There are several cabaret and private dance scenes that are well put on. A scuffle between Bowers and Alan Hale, the heavy, is of fiery quality, but the scenes in which the huge city hall topples to the ground, because of the rotten cement, are obviously faked.

"Flattery" measures up as a rather good program picture because the subject hinted at in the title plays an intrinsic part in the story and there has been capable handling.

MY HUSBAND'S WIVES

William Fox Production starring Shirley Mason. Script by Barbara La Marr. Directed by Maurice Elvey. At Loew's New York, New York, on double-feature bill with George Beban's "Greatest Love of All" Dec. 19. Running time, 58 minutes.
Vale Harvey ....Shirley Mason
William Harvey ....Bryant Washburn
Marie Wynn.,.............Evelyn Brendt
Madam Carregio...........Paulette Duval

Barbara La Marr wrote this story, possible from personal experience for it seems to be more than a coincidence that she should have applied the name of Marie Wynn to one of her characters and made that character a particularly catty one. Those who are more or less familiar with Miss La Marr's life history

know that a name very similar to that was very much in her life at one time. Possibly Miss La Marr intended "My Husband's Wives" to be played seriously, but if she intended it as comedy, then the director flopped in trying to get effect over on the screen, and it was the only treatment that the story should have had.

As a picture "My Husband's Wives" does not mean very much. It is a little picture and utilized as it was in the New York's double feature bill it sufficed. It isn't strong enough to stand itself in anything except the smallest houses.

The story is that of a girl who marries a divorced man but insists that he should not tell him anything about his first wife, mention her name or who she was at any time. After her honeymoon she invites a former school chum to visit her. The chum is the former wife and she arrives with malice aforethought, determined to win back her former husband if possible. In the end however the little wife proves too much for her. The idea could have been worked out as corking comedy material but as it now stands it isn't anything.

The three girls all do well enough, but Bryant Washburn as the husband should make it a point never to wear a moustache on the screen. The one he wore in this picture was terrible.

The picture looks as though it had been ground out just as one of the Fox program fillers and let go at that. *Fred.*

Comin' Thro' the Rye

Hepworth Production made in England. Shown to invited audience at Wurlitzer Hall Dec. 10. No distribution arranged. Running time 80 minutes.

Hepworth of England is responsible for this picture. The London notices in the daily press of that city were reproduced in part and handed to the American reviewers as they entered the hall. The English notices were laudatory in the extreme. After viewing the picture it must be stated that from the American viewpoint and the commercial end of the picture business the London reviewers must know even less than our own New York daily paper reviewers on the value of a picture, at least for the American market.

To quote the London "Daily News": "This picture . . . will appeal to Americans . . . just as their own 'The Covered Wagon' and 'Way Down East' appeal to us."

Possibly the person who arranged the folder may have taken some liberties with the exact review in the London paper; if they did not then it must be said that the London reviewer of the "Daily Mail" must be off his nut in his ideas as to what will appeal to America.

"Comin' Thro' the Rye" as a picture is just as much a picture as the average English production was back in 1912 when they were being distributed in this country through Mutual. They haven't advanced a bit. The handling of the story is wretched, the story itself being worse than that; the photography is bad and the cameraman certainly showed that it is easy to take a darn good-looking juvenile, as in the case of Ralph Forbes, and make him look his worst.

Atop of that the picture is a costume piece laid in the period of the early fifties, which is enough to condemn it in American eyes.

With the English clamoring to get into the American market it seems surprising that they would not educate themselves in the picture producing field and ascertain what is wanted. Certainly this example of

production is not what will sell on this side of the Atlantic.

The picture is draggy. It is shot principally in exterior scenes until it gives the impression English must live in their gardens. The photography is what might be termed foggy almost through the picture and the actors walk right up to the camera as in the old days and make faces at is, showing plainly they have too much make-up on. Especially true of the men.

The story concerns an ugly duckling of a family becoming betrothed to a man who was once tricked by a girl. The latter, however, has not given up hope of winning him and through her scheming the existant engagement is broken off and the hero and heroine parted. The schemer wins the hero and they live unhappily ever afterward. Finally the closing scene of the picture shows the heroine reading a letter that her beloved has died as a brave soldier on the field of action.

The story could just as well have been modernized. There was no reason to plant it back in the Victorian days, but for some reason or other the English producer preferred to keep it there.

As far as the American market is concerned it hasn't a chance. There is hardly a possibility it will even get by in the state rights field, out of which the Hepworths would have a hard time to get their money. *Fred.*

1925

SO BIG

First National production of the Edna Ferber novel, adapted and supervised by Earl Hudson and directed by Charles Brabin. Scenario by Adele Heilbrone. Colleen Moore starred. Reviewed at the Strand, New York, Jan. 4. Running time, 85 minutes.

Selina Peake................Colleen Moore
Simeon Peake............Joseph de Grasse
Pervus de Jong...............John Bowers
Dirk de Jong......................Ben Lyon
Klaas Poole.................Wallace Beery
Maartje Poole............Gladys Rockwell
Aug. Hempel.................Jean Hersholt
Julia Hempel............Charlotte Merriam
Widow Paarlenburg............Dot Farley
Jacob Hoogendunk............Ford Sterling
William Storm...............Henry Herbert
Paula Storm..............Rosemary Theby
Dallas.........................Phyllis Haver
Baby Dirk..................Dorothy Brock
Dirk (later)..............Frankie Darrow

To render a decision on such a picture as "So Big" is a terrible task. That it is one of the most artistic pictures ever produced is beyond question. That it is the medium wherein Colleen Moore exceeds the wildest expectations by her portrayal of an old woman is also indisputable.

That the famous Ferber novel has been handled intelligently and with a fine directorial sense is something else that can't start an argument, but whether it will draw money at the box office is doubtful.

Picture men concede that Colleen Moore is First National's best money bet now that Norma Talmadge has announced she will in the future release through United Artists. But whether Colleen's fans will stick to her in this radical derivation from the flapper roles is something else again.

The story of "So Big" is of a girl, a woman and a mother. It develops into a compelling and forceful portrayal of mother love and sacrifice. From the time Selina Peake was left fatherless and went to the Dutch rural region near Chicago to teach school (in 1888) to the period where she worked in the fields to help her new husband; from the time she wore her fingers to the bone to rear her son, Dirk; from the time she saved him from a scheming woman to carry him once more back to the influence of a mother is told graphically and with a driving force that compels admiration and attention.

The son whom Selina worked for when he was—*so big*, became the young genius in whom she gloried when he had become SO BIG. Then came the crisis. An older woman wanted him—and the mother fought. Tarnished fame would have been his lot and the mother knew it. Tarnished fame is a perilous perch. That his mother also knew. So in the end, after all her struggles, the grim, resolute, determined little woman, upon whose tiny shoulders had rested the cares of an Atlas, grasped the boy—the idol of her life—and held him.

She was happy and the worry of a mother over her son was worth the reward. That is the story of the picture.

Miss Moore plays Selina straight through. From the girl out of boarding school to the gray-haired mother is a long stretch, and putting the flapperish Colleen in such a role is daring. It took lots of nerve, but Miss Moore came through with an electric performance that grew in amperage as the age of her character increased. Beside being a delineator of flappers, she showed herself as a character actress of the highest quality. Her performance will stand out as one of the big things of 1925, no matter what comes after. It is THE big thing of her career. Whether it will advance her or be the means of her returning to the flapperish parts is something that only the box office can show.

Ben Lyon played the grown-up son badly. His performance was static and unimpressive. Wallace Beery as a Dutch farmer was great, and Gladys Brockwell as his weary wife also splendid. The others of **the long and imposing cast didn't falter for a moment and contributed to their utmost.**

Charles Brabin, in directing this work, with its infinite amount of the last century color and settings, did a job that will stand to his credit for a long time.

But the thing about "So Big" is the story itself and Colleen Moore. It is a long film, but interesting, sometimes in a morbid and sometimes in a comic manner, all the way. The fact, however, that the costumes are old-fashioned and that the popular star is taking a flyer in a new role may mitigate against financial success.

Its appeal certainly will be only to the better class audiences. In the small towns they may wonder what it is all about.

Sisk.

EAST OF SUEZ

Paramount Picture, starring Pola Negri. Edmund Lowe, Rockliffe Fellowes, Noah Beery featured. From the play by Somerset Maugham, adapted by Sada Cowan. Directed by Raoul Walsh. Shown at the Rivoli, New York, week Jan. 5, Running time, 76 minutes.

Daisy Forbes..................Pola Negri
George Conway...............Edmund Lowe
Harry Anderson..........Rockliffe Fellowes
British Consul..................Noah Beery
Lee Tai.........................Sojin Kamiyama
Amah. ....Mrs. Wing Wong
Sylvia Knox...............Florence Regnart
Harold Knox.................Charles Requa
Sidney Forbes..................E. H. Calvert

"East of Suez," the Somerset Maugham play that served Florence Reed so well on the stage, is a good vehicle for Pola Negri on the screen. As a matter of fact Miss Negri's performance is to be desired above that of Miss Reed, if anything. As a picture "East of Suez" won't break house records in the first-runs, but it will do better than the average program attractions. There is a glamor and lure about the title that will appeal, and the fact that it has almost an all-star cast should prove of value to the box office.

Miss Negri as Daisy Forbes, the half-caste, who, after being educated in England, returns to China to find herself socially beyond the pale because of the taint of yellow proves that she can troupe with a repression **and still get over all the fire of dramatic intensity. She is the girl that has all the advantages of a white civilization education, but still is part Chinese, as far as the picture is concerned.**

Edmund Lowe is getting to look more and more like one of the Barrymores every day, and in this picture in certain shots, if one did not have a program, they would say that it was John Barrymore at his best on the screen. The heavies, two of equal importance, are Rockliffe Fellowes and Noah Beery, with the greater burden of the work falling to Fellowes.

But for a wealthy Chinese there is nothing that can beat the characterization that is the work of Sojin. It is perfect. Here is an artist to the tip of the long nails that he affects in the picture.

The scenes are all in China, and there is action and lots of it. Murder, abduction, parted lovers and scheming Chinks worked up into a thriller that in the olden days would have been a ripsnorter meller for the pop-priced house; but, dressed up as it is in a society atmosphere, it is mighty good fare for the film fans.

There are a number of little comedy touches that have been added to the script that make it thoroughly enjoyable. The handling of the scene on shipboard, where all of the **men are anxious to dance with the girl returning to China, and the tricks resorted to by the various ship officers to cut out their fellows, are amusing.** There also is the touch of Pola jumping into the harbor at Shanghai, and when Pola comes out of the water she's really wet. Most stars are all dry when the next shot of them is taken.

Raoul Walsh has directed a picture that holds the attention from beginning to end with its suspense. In a scene where there are three glasses, one of which contains poison, the audience is kept guessing for a number of minutes as to which one of the trio really got the poisoned cup. That was a good piece of business.

The combination of Pola Negri, the title of the pictures and the strong supporting cast should mean money to almost any box office anywhere.

Fred.

Wife of the Centaur

Metro-Goldwyn picture, Louis B. Mayer presentation, and a King Vidor production. Directed by Vidor. Adapted from the novel of the same name by Cyril Hume. Photographer, John Arnold. Showing at the Capitol, New York, week of Jan. 4. Running time, 73 minutes.

Joan Converse..........Eleanor Boardman
Jeffrey Dwyer......................John Gilbert
Inez Martin.......................Aileen Pringle
Mrs. Converse......................Kate Lester
Edward Converse..........William Haines
Mattie.................................Kate Price
Hope Lorrimore.........Jacquelin Gadsdon
Mr. Lorrimore............Bruce Covington
Harry Todd...................Philo McCullough
Chuck........................Lincoln Stedman
Uncle Roger...............William Orlamond

A picture that will be both lauded to the skies and scorned. At least that's the impression practically a capacity matinee audience gave. One thing seems certain, in order to give the film its just due it must be witnessed from the start. To walk in on it will decrease its strength two-fold. It's one of those pictures.

For 73 minutes Sunday afternoon there wasn't a stir in this house, which seats 5,300, until Aileen Pringle, in a somewhat vampish role, threw on a transparent negligee. That drew a titter. The tenseness which those present manifested was an achievement few films in the Broadway program theatres have been able to accomplish.

For those who read the book the picture is a study in what a screen adaptation can do to a novel. Manifold liberties have been taken unto important situations being given. But it's all good "theatre," and as Vidor has applied to the screen the total result figures as a corking piece of work, ranging from the individual who picked the cast to the electrician who figured on the lights.

Majorly an "interior" episode, the settings are such to overcome this generally conceived handicap, while a skiing insertion, mayhaps lifted from a "short" on that sport, is a punch that gives the release that finishing zest which it needs to click as celluloid entertainment.

It marks another notch for John Gilbert, in the central role, following so close upon his work in "The Snob." It is bound to make his name impressive with Capitol patrons if with no one else. Incidentally, it is also the second time Gilbert has emerged from ordinary cast billing to rate feature naming. About one more picture like this and he's bound to get in.

Vidor's treatment of a house party, a cafe scene and a swimming party have caught the collegiate atmosphere (interspersed with comedy) to a greater extent than most of his contemporaries have ever done. But whatever Vidor lacks in not having followed the book too rigidly he has compensated for in the handling of his group scenes, splendid examples, and the manner in which he has carried the theme along for sustenance of interest.

Miss Boardman and John Gilbert run away with the film for honors. The performance of Miss Boardman is perfectly attuned, never presumes too much, and is played in a logical vein wholly in accord not only with the picture but the novel. If you care to include appearance, she is that much stronger. Aileen Pringle seemingly loses caste in but one scene, and that her most important one. Besides that her performance meets requirement, although marking the one questionable selection as a "type." Others in the cast are confined to secondary consideration through the footage assigned, but among them will be noted the late Kate Lester.

The picture is one that should cause talk, and it doesn't matter which way, for if there are arguments they'll troop through the gate. How pleased the author is with the screen adaptation is something else again, but it looks very much as if he'll have to be afraid they made a good picture from his novel.

Skig.

THE DANCERS

William Fox Production from the play by Gerald DuMaurier and Viola Tree. Adapted by Edmund Goulding. Directed by Emmett Flynn. Shown at the Central, N. Y., for a run, beginning Jan. 5, 1925. Running time, 74 minutes.

Tony ....George O'Brien
Maxine ....Alma Rubens
Una ....Madge Bellamy
Fothering ....Templar Saxe
Pringle ....Joan Standing
Mrs. Mayne ....Alice Hollister
Evan Caruthers ....Freeman Wood
The Argentine ....Walter McGrail
Ponfilo ....Noble Johnson
Captain Bassil ....Tippy Grey

Here is a picture pretty certain to be sure fire at the box office. It has the modern sexy wallop, which, while not offensively developed on the screen, is nevertheless 100 percent in the picture. That is going to mean a lot at the box office. There are certain little liberties that have been taken as far as the script of the play is concerned, but one can always leave it to Edmund Goulding to turn out a screen script that is going to show something that has box office punch when the picture is projected on the screen. The combination of Goulding's script together with Emmett Flynn's direction has brought about a real screen wallop.

One thing not to be overlooked, however, and that is the performance of two of the principal women. Madge Bellamy, first and foremost. In "The Dancers" she is giving a performance that is going to make her as far as the screen is concerned if anything ever will. And atop of that is the performance Alma Rubens gives as the little dancer of the Central American cafe. She is there 100 percent.

Of the men George O'Brien stands out like a house afire as the hero. But that doesn't detract from the performance Freeman Wood gives in the secondary role. For once in his life that boy seems to be sincere in what he is trying to portray on the screen and he gets it over. In the character roles Walter McGrail playing the Argentine looks and is the part. He is the nearest suggestion to a heavy that there is, and he puts on a make-up that is a corker. Temple Saxe as a barrister makes much of a fussy old man bit.

The story is based on the wild madness that has overcome the younger generation of the world since the war and the advent of jazz and the dance craze.

Back in London where Una is one of the dance-mad throng, penniless but still holding her own on the edge of society, she is stepping out nightly. In the Latin Americas there is a boy who has stepped out of England because he was penniless. He is running a bar, and in it he has a dancing girl. She is in love with him, but he is remaining true to the memory of a childhood sweetheart, who is the same Una that is stepping in London. She has almost forgotten the boy and the promises that they made each other in their early 'teens. Then comes the chance of the boy. He succeeds to a title and about $5,000,000 through the accidental death of two relatives. His first thought is of the girl back home. He cables, but the message is delivered a day too late by his lawyer. The night before the girl through a mad whirl of dancing has let herself slip and accepted the embraces of a dance companion. He is honorable enough and wants to marry her, but she refuses the morning after. Both are penniless, and it doesn't mean a thing. Then comes the return of the childhood chum. The marriage is all arranged for while he is en route and he walks in on his sweetheart of youthful days in her wedding gown. She, however, confesses before the ceremony, and just prior to the moment that he turns to forgive all she swallows an overdose of a narcoaic to which she is to a certain extent addicted and dies.

Then a year passes and the hero returns to his bar, and in the end there is just a repeat of a sequence that occurred early in the picture except that the situation is reversed. It makes for a snappy ending. The hero and the girl of the saloon are together, with her saying "Let's dance."

You can't go wrong on this one.

Fred.

TOMORROW'S LOVE

Paramount Production, starring Agnes Ayres. Based on story, "Interlocutory," by Charles Brackett. Adapted by Howard Higgin. Directed by Paul Bern. At Rialto, New York, week Jan. 4. Running time, 65 minutes.

Judith Stanley....................Agnes Ayres
Robert Stanley....................Pat O'Malley
Brown....................Raymond Hatton
Bess Carlysle....................Jane Winton
Grandmother....................Ruby Lafayette
Maid....................Dale Fuller

A snappy tale of romance, honeymooning, battling, divorce and reconciliation, treated in a manner rather amusing and flippant, with the result it is good entertainment. Not one of those pictures the audience will break down the doors to see, but it is going to satisfy. Should do an average business in the average houses along the line.

Agnes Ayres proves herself to be rather winsome and appealing in this production, and Pat O'Malley, opposite, registers as a perfect foil. There is a vamp, handled by Jane Winton pleasingly, although the hit honors for a character role must be tendered to Ruby Lafayette as the grandmother of the husband.

The story has a moral for young wives, at least. The moral, as far as the screen discloses it, is that all men, no matter how young or old, like to have some girl babying them. It is the grandmother that voices this, and atop of it the vamp proves it by almost stealing the husband away from the wife.

There are a couple of real thrills in the picture. One is a wild automobile ride taken by the wife, who has been abroad after having obtained her divorce. She is returning home on the day that the decree becomes final, and has been advised by her husband's grandmother that the vamp has things all fixed to marry the man immediately after midnight. Then she tries to get to the scene to prevent the ceremony, for she still loves her husband and believes he loves her. In getting across the country the machine hurdles an open draw bridge and finally beats out a freight train at a railroad crossing only at the last minute to have the machine overturn right in front of the house.

Paul Bern in directing has shown his association with the De Milles registered with him, for he goes after bathroom stuff on a couple of occasions, but at that Agnes Ayres has a very pretty back. *Fred.*

NARROW STREET

Warner Bros. production, starring Matt Moore and Dorothy Devore. Adapted from the novel by Edwin Bateman Morris; directed by William Beaudine. Shown at the Piccadilly, New York, week of Jan. 3. Running time, 75 minutes.

Doris....................Dorothy Devore
Simon Haldane....................Matt Moore
Ray Wyeth....................David Butler
Garvey....................Russell Simpson
Nell....................Gertrude Short
Aunt Albina....................Kate Toncray
Aunt Agnes....................Tempe Pigott
Edgar Deems....................George Pearce
Easter....................Madame Sultewan
Office Boy....................Joe Butterworth

Why the Warner Bros. co-star Matt Moore with Dorothy Devore is going to be the most interesting question. Matt Moore gives a performance that is a masterpiece of its kind, but Miss Devore is nothing more than an average ingenue lead, and seemingly it would have been better by far to just have had Moore as a star and let it go at that. There is no question but that "The Narrow Street" is an entertaining picture; it is all of that, due to Moore's performance and the titling. It is a story light in the way that "Satevepost" stories are, and that means that it will appeal thusly to the majority of the regular picture house fans.

Moore on the strength of his performance deserves to have someone take hold of him and build him into stardom in a series of stories in which he would be asked to deliver characterization of the same style that he has registered in this picture. Moore would develop into a box office bet undoubtedly on a par to what Charlie Ray was when he did those boob country town boys. Moore's is a boob type, but a city boob, and possibly that makes him more interesting to the average "city feller."

The picture isn't one that cost a million dollars to make—far from that—but it is the best picture Lee Ochs has had at the new Piccadilly since he opened the theatre from a light comedy entertainment standpoint. The audiences on the opening day liked it and laughed heartily.

The story is of a young fellow who is an office worker living alone in a whole house all by himself. He has two maiden aunts who live apart from him, but who every so often call on him and remind him that it is time to put on his heavy flannels, etc.

In the office he is the official gloom on whom everyone picks, especially the flip city salesman of the organization, incidentally the heavy in the story. Into the bashful one's peaceful domicile slips a load of dynamite in the form of a girl. She is being pursued, no one knows why, and seeks refuge in the boy's home. The two maiden aunts slip in after her, and she hides behind a curtain; then come the pursuers, who believe the protestations of the youth that there isn't a stranger in the house, and they depart, as do the aunts after making a couple of wise cracks. The girl retires on the couch after the boy has done likewise above stairs. In the morning he finds her.

That is about where the complications begin. The girl can't leave, so feigns she is ill, and he gets a doctor, a neighbor, who naturally takes it for granted the bashful youth has married and spreads the tidings. In the finish everything is straightened out by the youth fighting his way to the top of the office staff, winning the girl, who happens to be the daughter of the president of the corporation that he is working for.

Miss Devore just manages to get by. In certain shots she looks good, but in others not so good. The heavy, David Butler, looks like a bet for the future, only too many close-ups may spoil him, for he gets a bit posy now and then. A comedy bit played by Gertrude Short stood out like a house afire in the few scenes she had.

William Beaudine, who directed, slipped a couple of pieces of comedy business to Moore in the early scenes that were wows. *Fred.*

South of the Equator

Independent feature produced by I. J. Barsky, starring Kenneth McDonald. Written by Robert Dillon and directed by William James Craft. At the Stanley, New York, Jan. 5. Running time, 57 minutes.

This picture introduces a comparatively unknown stunt man, Kenneth McDonald, and it also shoves out a pretty bold lift on the old Doug Fairbanks Triangle feature, "The Americano." The story is one of those Richard Harding Davis propositions about a small and indefinite South American republic somewhat addicted to revolutions. When the old president is chucked from his roost, his lovely daughter hies herself to the Estados Unidos and gets some guns and much assistance from a handsome young American.

This young American takes along his colored pal for comic relief principally. Down in the old South American country they defeat the villuns, stage a phoney battle, wave a few flags, march through some pretty cheesy looking interiors and call it a day.

McDonald does most of the stunt work and puts on quite a few top-notch fights. He also does some general climbing that rings the bell, while the colored man doing the comedy stuff pulled some real comedy stuff and plenty of it. Some thrills, too, were thrown in during ship scenes.

"South of the Equator" is an okeh small time film. That's about all it sets out to be. For the solidity of the sets and the careful direction of the various types, it seems a shame the direction and titling were not better. The direction brings out little, while the titles are stilted, often misspelled and not so very expository. But even with these defects, McDonald pulls the film out of the rut due to his everlasting get-up-and-go spirit.

It's one of the shooting gallery specials and, provided the crowd isn't too wise, it'll be perfectly suitable.

Sisk.

AFTER DARK

William Steiner production starring Charles Hutchinson. Written by J. F. Natteford and directed by James Chapin. Reviewed Jan. 2 at Loew's New York Roof as half of double bill. Running time, 55 minutes.

This one of the Hutchinson series is a typical "stunt-man" release and, aimed as it is for the straight-shooting gallery trade, fulfills its destiny nicely.

Here Hutchinson is the dupe of a woman operating with crooks. After rescuing her from death, he enters a house to regain some love letters for her, she having tricked him with a story. The letters are in reality valuable bonds. Inside the house, he awakens the daughter, points a pistol at him, calls the cop, but before the copper arrives becomes interested in his story, and, to save him, declares they were married.

Then the family enters and more complications, but they take it nicely. The thieves, however, do secure the bonds, and Hutch, to make himself solid (by this time, all of 15 minutes, he has fallen in love with the girl), chases them, first in a wild auto race, then he grabs the stern line of a motor boat and is pulled for some distance. Then in the car again he heads off the boat by a short road and engages in a cliff fight which marks the near-finale. A clinch with the beautiful blonde is all that comes after.

Mary Beth Milford, who was, if memory isn't too much at fault, one of the chorines with the first of the "Music Box" series, plays the feminine lead, and does it well. At times the photography darkens the lower part of her face, but that can't be blamed on the gal. The settings, such as they are, are cheap and tawdry, especially a street exterior which is plainly painted canvas, and in flat tones, at that. A drawing room interior is also painted, and obviously so from the front.

But that doesn't matter much in a picture of this type. Figured as a cheap buy and as something for the mug audiences, it is okeh.

Sisk.

THE HURRICANE KID

Universal Western starring Hoot Gibson. From the story by Will Lambert, adapted by Richard E. Schyer. Directed by Edward Sedgewick. Shown at Loew's New York, N. Y., on double feature bill with "The Breath of Scandal," Dec. 30, 1924. Running time, 57 minutes.

The Hurricane Kid....................Hoot Gibson
Joan Langdon....................Marian Nixon
Lafe Baxter....................William Steele
Hezikia Potts....................Harry Todd
Col. Langdon....................Arthur Mackley
Joan's Friend....................Violet La Plante
Jed Hawks....................Fred Humes

One of those "back to the earth" westerns crammed full of action, bristling with pep and with a love story that goes along in a fairly consistent manner. The photography is particularly good, and Eddie Sedgewick has managed to get a flock of outdoor shots full of atmosphere. In the houses where they like westerns it is sure to hit 'em right. Hoot Gibson puts over a really convincing performance as the cowboy hero, principally because instead of handling himself seriously he gives it a flip touch, which is the idea that is also carried out in the titles, and that all makes for good entertainment.

The story is one of a cowboy who in addition to being a hand is a ladies' man. He has a collection of pictures of screen stars that would make the average fan look dizzy and a smooth but snappy manner of approach with the girls that has managed to get him by for a great many years. At the same time it has been his desire to capture a wild horse that has been the talk of the range. He starts after her but falls and breaks his arm, which fact gives him entrance into the home of the heroine.

Once there it is dead open and shut that he'll win her heart, lick the tough foreman who is trying to get the girl and a share of the ranch at the same time, and Hoot does exactly those little things. In the finish there is a horse race with the hero the winning jock. He rides the wild horse that he has managed to capture and her share of the victory is that she is turned loose again and returned to her mate. That is a human note that will be liked.

Marian Nixon is all that could be asked in the part opposite the hero. Fred Humes, playing the friend of the star, dressed and looked so much like him in shots that it seems that U. must be grooming another western star. *Fred.*

Reckless Romance

An Al Christie production released through Producers' Distributing Corporation. Adapted from the stage play, "What's Your Wife Doing?" by F. McGrew Willis and directed by Scott Sidney. Harry Myers, T. Roy Barnes, Wanda Hawley, Tully Marshall, Sylvia Breamer, Lincoln Plumer and Mitchell Lewis in the cast. Running time, 62 minutes. At Loew's New York Roof, Jan. 2, as half of a double bill.

This picture is made from Arthur Klein's one and only legit venture, "What's Your Wife Doing?", produced on Broadway last year. Emil Nyitry and Herbert Hall Winslow were the authors.

The picture version is good farce and excellently played in several instances, particularly by T. Roy Barnes, Lincoln Plumer and the actor playing the old man. Its plot concerns the efforts of a grandfather to have his grandson unmarried because he feared that the wrong kind of a wife had grabbed the boy. An inheritance was involved, so the boy, his wife and their best friend arrange to plant evidence so that a divorce can be secured until the inheritance thing has been straightened out. The idea is to have grandfather see the young wife hugging the other man in front of her husband and, pronto, the divorce.

But it doesn't work, for the other man's rich uncle from the west blows in and with all the good intention in the world secretes the girl, so that grandpa's every interruption is on a harmless scene. Laughs come when the other man's girl really comes in and sees the would-be-divorced woman going through the hugging scene again, under the impression granddad is looking.

It isn't very complicated and is well handled. These qualities, could with a tasteful and not skimpy production, should qualify it nicely for the middle class houses, for which "Reckless Romance" is undoubtedly aimed.

Sisk.

RAMSHACKLE HOUSE

Tilford Cinema Production, starring Betty Compson; scenario by Coolidge Streeter; adaptation from novel by Harmon Weight. Direction, Harmon Weight. Distributed by Prod. Distributing Corp.

Pen Broome	Betty Compson
Don Counsell	Robert Lowing
Ernest Riever	John Davidson
Pendleton Broome	Henry James
Keesing	William Black
Spike Talley	Duke Pelzer
Blanche Paglar	Josephine Norman

"Ramshackle House" is aimed as a thriller, but succeeds only in becoming highly dramatic hokum, due to the meller qualities of the story.

Don Counsell (Robert Lowing) is camping in Florida. He meets Pen Broome (Betty Compson). Pen is trying to keep up a rundown estate. Counsell has quarreled with his partner. The latter is murdered and Don suspected. He wants to give himself up, but Pen's father has aroused a mob by telling the camper's identity.

Ernest Rivier (John Davidson) offers a large reward for Don's capture. Rivier comes south with a detective to take charge of the case. Pen suspects him. Rivier is infatuated with Pen, and through her cleverness is exposed as the employer of the gunman who committed the murder. The motive is revenge. The story is unconvincing.

Miss Compson is not happily cast, while the performance of John Lowing as Counsell is a stereotyped exhibition. Ernest Rivier succeeds in being villainous in spots.

The outdoor shots of the land of flowers and the photography all through was one of the high lights of the picture, which doesn't seem destined to ge any unusual box-office play in the large or small cities.

"Ramshackle House" is just an average program feature for the second-run houses from every angle, including the cast.

Con.

THE FAST WORKER

Universal-Jewel Production, starring Reginald Denny and Laura La Plante. Scenario by Beatrice Van and Raymond L. Schrock, adapted from George Barr McCutcheon's "The Husbands of Edith." Running time, 70 mins.

Brock	Reginald Denny
Connie	Laura La Plante
Edith	Ethel Grey Terry
Toodles	Muriel Frances Dana
Freddie	Lee Moran
Roxbury	Richard Tucker
Mrs. Rodney	Margaret Campbell
"Kath" Rodney	Betty Morrissey
Nurse	Mildred Vincent
Mr. Rodney	John Steppling

This latest Universal co-starring Reginald Denny and Laura La Plante should send the couriers scurrying in all directions for athletic stories for Denny. Denny built up a following through his boxing and portrayals of clean-cut, out-of-door types, but since handed more or less straight comedies seems to be floundering around.

The latest picture doesn't compare with his previous two releases. It holds little or no athletics, and calls for a comedy technique which Denny does not possess.

The picture's weakness is squarely up to the producer. It doesn't fit the star. The story is a good one, but was wasted upon Denny.

As Terry Brock (Mr. Denny) he is persuaded by Roxbury Medcroft (Richard Tucker) to assume the latter's identity for business reasons and travel to the Coast, leaving Medcroft in New York. Brock accepts, but discovers he also has to pose as the husband of Edith, his friend's wife, and father to their small daughter. Her sister accmopanies them on the trip. Terry falls in love with her. Gossips at the hotel discover this, and the scandal following causes the hotel management to investigate. They discover Terry isn't Edith's husband.

Terry proposes to Connie (Miss La Plante) and she agrees to elope. A "chase" follows, two autos and truck trailing each other up and down hill for one of the best "thrills" seen on the screen in a long, long time.

The picture is summery and interesting, due to the corking cast, the outdoor scenes and the excellent story. Denny, however, as the ready-made husband, is most unconvincing and miscast.

It's just a program addition for other than the first run houses, and will prove disappointing to any rabid Denny fan.

Con.

NIGHT OF ROMANCE

First National release presented by Joseph M. Schenck. Starring Constance Talmadge. Story by Hans Kraly, directed by Sidney Franklin. Shown at the Capitol, N. Y., week Jan. 11.

Dorothy Adams	Constance Talmadge
Paul Menford	Ronald Colman
Joe Diamond	Jean Hersholt
Samuel G. Adams	Albert Gran
Prince George	Robert Rendel
Butler	Sidney Bracy

"Her Night of Romance" proves to be one of the most delightful of the comedy-drama type of pictures that Constance Talmadge has starred in in some time. The last series of this ingenue's pictures have more or less fallen down at the box office, but this one bids fair to again raise the status of Constance as a drawing card. It is a good story with just enough touch of sex to get it over. There are any number of amusing situations that get to the audience and there are plenty of laughs scattered through the picture.

Miss Talmadge has the role of a marriageable daughter of an American multi-millionaire who is being taken abroad for her health. The tip-off as to her beauty and wealth have preceded her. To counteract it she distorts her features when the ship news photographers corner her on landing in England. But as she leaves the ship she stumbles and falls into the arms of a young Englishman who is waiting to greet an English actress returning home from America.

A second meeting comes about when the young man goes to the compartment in the train to return the young lady's watch which caught in his clothes at the time of the accident. He is very much struck with the change in her appearance.

Then there is a third meeting, out of which the romance grows. The young man's uncle, a prominent specialist on nervous cases, is summoned to attend the young lady, but the nephew gets the message and poses as the doctor.

Meantime the girl's father arranges to purchasce Menford Manor, which is the young man's property. The transfer is made through the agent, and the girl goes to the house to be alone, following a letter she has received from Menford to the effect he has imposed on her. While she is alone in the manor house, His Lordship, who has imbibed rather freely to drown his sorrows over having to break off his friendship with the young American heiress, returns, not knowing that one of the new owners has taken possession. The two spend the night under the same roof after several amusing scenes.

In the morning, upon the arrival of a friend, His Lordship, to protect the girl, announces they have been married. With the arrival of the father matters are further complicated. The best scene is where the father, believing the young couple have been married and ignoring the statement from the supposed son-in-law to the contrary, pushes the latter into the girl's boudoir with a pleasant "good night, kids."

Miss Talmadge handles the role assigned to her exquisitely and Ronald Colman, opposite, is possibly the best leading man she has had in some time. He acts with an ease of manner, yet with an assurance that is compelling.

There is one thing, however, that might be desired in regard to this picture, and that would be to see the treatment that Lubitsch would have given this story in direction had he handled it. It is of the type built to order for him.

Fred.

IF I MARRY AGAIN

First National Production from story by Gilbert Frankau and directed by John Francis Dillon. Entire cast, with exception of little Dorothy Brock as baby, featured. At the Strand, New York, week Jan. 11. Running time, 80 minutes.

Jocelyn Margot	Doris Kenyon
Charlie Jordan	Lloyd Hughes
Jeffrey Wingate	Frank Mayo
John Jordan	Hobart Bosworth
Alicia Wingate	Anna Q. Nilsson
Madame Margot	Myrtle Stedman
Sonny	Dorothy Brock

Another story of the good daughter of the bad woman. As in the rest, she keeps good after the rich husband dies and she is left with the son to take care of. In this case the rich husband's father is apparently himself the son of Hard-Hearted Hannah, for it takes 78 minutes of the running time for him to see things the girl's way.

Charlie Jordan, son of the head of a famous mercantile firm, marries the daughter of a woman who presides over a famous establishment—Margot's. And to Barlacca they go, a place where rain and heat combine to make fever, and also came in handy because looking like some of the jungle sets in "Love's Wilderness," the recent Corinne Griffith First National release. And the interiors looked like revamped interiors from other First National pictures.

However, in this Barlacca country, young Jordan died and left his young wife with a son. When back, she and the elder Jordan don't get it off very well. On a dare she burlesqued the film of Jordan's, Limited, but reopening her mother's old place as Jordan's, Unlimited. This she doesn't keep up, for her conscience gets the better end of the situation. As old Jordan rushes in the door, furious, the young woman is forcing the guests out. So the old man forgives her, and his confidential business manager escorts her home—meant to mean that he'll marry her.

The idea of the title is that the young man and woman were very much in love because they shared each other's hopes and joys as well as sorrows and disappointments, and that this common interest had welded them. And the business manager, whose wife had died before they really understood ach other, was firm in his opinion that if he married again it would be a woman who would share his life.

Doris Kenyon is good as the woman, and the same goes for Lloyd Hughes as the young man. Hobart Bosworth is fine as the father, and Frank Mayo the best of all as the business manager. The whole thing is admirably cast and well directed, besides possessing good continuity. The general theme holds so many illogical propositions and situations that, on the whole, it doesn't assay much beyond a mediocre program feature.

The lighting is very bad, as First National's continued use of spotlights, shooting rays and uneven splotches of light on interiors becomes not only annoying, but hard on the eyes. Every law of natural lighting is violated as well as the lessons taught by the great electricians of the stage, who long ago abandoned the idea of making the sun shine on rainy days.

"If I Marry Again" is hardly big city stuff. In the medium-sized towns the cast and plot interest might carry it along to the in-between class. That's about the place.

Sisk.

LOCKED DOORS

William De Mille production, directed by De Mille and a Paramount picture. Written and adapted by Clara Beranger. Features Betty Compson, Theodore Roberts, Kathlyn Williams, Theodor von Eltz and Robert Edeson. Showing at the Rivoli, New York, week of Jan. 11. Running time, 69 mins.

Mary Carter	Betty Compson
Mr. Reid	Theodore Roberts
Laura Carter	Kathlyn Williams

John Talbot..............Theodor von Eltz
Norman Carter.............Robert Edeson
Mickey.;................Elmo Billings

An ordinary better house program leader that must draw through the appeal of the cast names. It's an indifferent story allowing little action. The claim to major house projection is in the tone of the production marked by substantial interiors, gowns, etc.

The picture will mean little to Miss Compson, who in this instance sustains her reputation of being allotted inconsistent scenarios. Others in the cast are not called upon for what might be termed difficult trouping, albeit it may signalize the return of Theodore Roberts to Broadway after a prolonged absence. This veteran player is in his proverbial role of a "father" with a hobby for solitaire and an inclination to cheat himself. That he plays it for full worth is, of course, understood.

The tale is one of those youth-age marriages with Miss Compson the bride of a year who admires and respects her much older husband (Mr. Edeson). A house party in the Sierras provides the chance meeting of the wife and John Talbot (Mr. von Eltz), after which the drive for interest is gone after through John being befriended by the husband and taken to his home. A night fire catches John in the wife's room, the husband making the discovery. But everything is strictly aboveboard and the finish has the head of the house assigning a willingness to give his wife her freedom.

It's principally parlor work with De Mille trying to get across the suppressed anguish of the two lovers. A somewhat mechanical interpretation by Mr. von Eltz failed to appreciably assist, while Miss Compson was negative in a character continuously calling for a dejected attitude. Mr. Edeson, as the husband, made the best legitimate impression.

The subtitling is notable for its briefness in wording although numbering the usual amount. De Mille's directing effort is adequate but strictly standard with no illuminating flashes to give it rating as a particular achievement.

As previously stated, an ordinary Class A house picture.   *Skig.*

THE PRICE SHE PAID

C. B. C. production, distributed by Commonwealth. From the novel by David Graham Phillips. Directed by Henry McRae. Photographed by Dewey Wrigley. Featuring Alma Rubens and Frank Mayo. At the Broadway, New York, week of Jan. 12. Runs about 70 mins.
Mildred Gower ....Alma Rubens
General Lemuel Siddell.....William Walsh
Mrs. Gower ....Eugenie Besserer
Stanley Baird ....Freeman Wood
Secretary ....Otto Hoffman
Donald Keith ....Frank Mayo
Jack Presscott ....Lloyd Whitlock
James Bechary..............Wilfred Lucas

Variety's files disclose a Selznick production reviewed early in 1917 under the identical title and taken from the same novel by David Graham Phillips. Clara Kimball Young was the star, David Powell the hero and Allan Hale and Snitz Edwards the heavies. Praising all except the latter, *Jolo* called the film well acted and interesting in nearly every detail.

Unless eight years has brought about too great an advance in general picture technic, some one might do well to bring the old film out to buck this present release. It couldn't be slower or more amateurishly acted and directed.

Possibly Mr. Phillips' plot, or at least some of its twists, appeared new in 1917. But since then this particular angle of the proverbial triangle has been used so frequently it is a wonder the reels do not creak as they run through the machine. It is the old one about the girl who marries the nasty and rich codger in order that her entirely selfish mamma may not have to lose the family mansion. Along comes the young doctor who accuses her of having sold herself. So she decides to keep herself a wife in name only, as the captions have it, and then when the old boy conveniently drowns at sea, she, with all his dough, can go pure to the arms of her hero. So she hasn't paid any price, but how about the price paid by the customers to see all this?

With moderately intelligent handling something can be done with even such a moth-eaten plot. The earlier Selznick production may have proven that. But this time Henry McRae has directed without any ingenuity whatsoever, and the cast does not hold up the lagging interest. Alma Rubens is insipid and Frank Mayo is hardly better. The few other "names" in the cast, such as Wilfred Lucas, Freeman Wood and Lloyd Whitlock, have only the smallest bits.

The very small column on the credit side might list Miss Rubens' gowns, some of the sets, a lavish wedding dinner scene and some sea shots on board an ocean liner and a private yacht. The situations in which the latter burns at sea and the attendant rescues are not particularly well handled. Throughout the film there are inconsistencies in story and continuity that at times are almost laughable, incidentally the only comic relief in the picture.

C. B. C. spent jack on "The Price She Paid" and probably intended it for more or less of a first-run affair. It misses that by a mile and only qualifies on the strength of the author's and cast's draw.

THUNDERING HOOFS

An F. B. O. at Loew's New York, with Fred Thompson as the dynamo that brings you to the edge of your seat and keeps you there. Unless set against Westerns, you'll get many times your money's worth in thrills, including a Mexican bull fight staged with a fidelity to the real thing that will make you want to go across the border and swap hisses and bravos with the natives.

Thompson in this latest exhibit directed with inspiration by Al Rogell, proves as he has before that he owes nothing to Douglas Fairbanks, Helen Holmes or the long trail of exciting realists who get their effects from slap-bang encounters with the real thing in flying leaps, astounding vaults and multiple other strong arm and leg stuff.

Marion Jackson has supplied a romantic background, frankly offered as a picaresque of the Southwest border of Mexico. It fulfills all promises. The romantic motivation gets its impetus through the presence in the Southwest of the play of an unknown outlaw who preys upon passing travelers. Comes to the states from over the border a governor of a Mexican province with his pretty daughter, carrying gold to buy carloads of horses for Mexican cavalry. The highway, through accomplices, holds up the caravan, and steals the gold, but the stage coach robbery proves a boomerang for its perpetrators and leader through its frustration by Thompson's lickety-split arrival.

A he-man wallop-for-wallop fist fight between the hero and the heavy precedes this incident, followed by a fine bit of fancy whereby Silver King, originally owned by the marauding highwayman, becomes the property of the hero, the steed itself, offered a choice of masters, stalking deliberately to Thompson, yet with exhibits of thought, or something like it, before it finally settles upon the preference. Packed fast on the heels of these several agitations is Thompson's chase after a runaway coach with the heroine within. The director, Thompson, Miss Jackson, credited with the continuity as well as the fiction, and several daring riders not listed in the cast, combine to get an effect here that has no superior in the way of equine pulse jumping danger, actual or fabricated.

As indicated, the cutting is craftsmanlike to the nth degree. The photography is faultless. One might wish for more of the bull fight. The picture is an all right buy.

THE GOLDEN BED

Paramount picture and Cecil B. DeMille production, directed by DeMille. Story based on a novel by Wallace Irwin. At the Rivoli, New York, week Jan. 18. Running time, 88 mins.
Flora Lee Peake...............Lillian Rich
Margaret Peake.............Vera Reynolds
Colonel Peake...............Henry Walthall
Admah Holtz.............Rod La Rocque
Marquis de San Pilar......Theodore Kosloff
Bunny ....Warner Baxter
Savarac ....Robert Cain
Mrs. Amos Thompson........Julia Faye
Amos Thompson ....Robert Edeson

Right in DeMille's corner, this bed thing, and for 88 minutes the reclining contrivance is anything but a fourposter. It's a story that has provided ample leeway for DeMille to indulge himself in his customary and ponderous interiors, although the script fails to carry weight, while only one player predominates, Rod La Rocque.

The bed and De Mille has fashioned looks more like one of those contraptions that used to arise from the Hippodrome tank. Other than that he has a wedding to stage and a gala social event in the way of a candy ball that is probably as lavish as anything of its kind ever screened. To that end the picture looks money. There can be no question on that point.

This is one of those films a minor house audience supposedly revels in. The script has the old Colonial mansion in hock to the furniture, with the beauteous and selfish daughter marrying foreign coin to save the estate. Her moral laxity leads her husband and an acquired admirer plunging to their death during a struggle. She returns to the home town, two down and looking for a next. The president of a young and promising candy concern is the follow up. She ruins him through extravagance. That her sister has helped build the business and is in love with the firm's leader is by the way.

Mishandling of the company's funds sends the president to do five years. His release is signalized by a sentimental return to the old mansion, which he restored to his wife at their marriage. It is now a boarding house. The wife has tumbled down the social scale, and preceding him to the room in which stands the golden bed by about five minutes, she dies there. Leaving the newly emerged inmate to return to the sister and embark upon a fresh start. That winds up.

Into this DeMille has woven what seems thousands of philosophic subtitles besides an interpretation of a myth, always an inevitable DeMille touch. All this goes on for just short of an hour and a half. It's far too long. Scissoring could reduce the footage 1,000 feet. DeMille must be given credit for that candy ball, both as to its dimensions and the manner in which it has been handled. Another outstanding item is the plunge the two men take. The fall into a deep crevice is pictured by the figures of the men tumbling over and over while continuously growing smaller. Obviously well done and effective.

Lillian Rich, as the destroying damsel, is overly mechanical, while Vera Reynolds supplies a fair enough ingenue. Such names as Walthall, Edeson and Kosloff are relatively confined to restricted footage, with Warner Baxter running second among the male contingent for space and workmanship. At the start of the story are pictured the three main characters as children, of whom Mary Jane Irving was the most legitimate in her efforts.   *Skig.*

FLAMING LOVE
(FRIVOLOUS SAL)

Released under both titles and using the first in New York. A J. K. McDonald production for First National. Story by J. K. McDonald, and direction by Victor

Schertzinger. At the Strand, New York, week of Jan. 18.

Roland Keene	Eugene O'Brien
Sal	Mae Busch
Benny Keene	Ben Alexander
Steve MacGregor	Tom Santschi
Red Osner	Mitchell Lewis
Chita	Mildred Harris

Just why First National should call this one "Flaming Love" isn't clear. "Frivolous Sal" is the title used on the out-of-town showings. Certainly it is the more appropriate, for there isn't a hint of any flaming love anywhere. What love there is can be classified under the stolid, domestic brand.

The story is commonplace and handled in a like manner by all of the cast except little Ben Alexander in a boy role. Roland Keene, an actor, is with a troupe in the west. On the day before returning to New York he meets Sally Flood, owner of a saloon and known as Frivolous Sal. He woos and wins her in an attractive love match, beating out Steve MacGregor, gold mine superintendent.

Their love is strained and Sal is made even more unhappy because her husband's little son won't accept her as his new mother. The climax comes when Keene, in weakness, helps the villain rob the safe holding some gold dust, and in a thrilling pursuit following the man doubling for Eugene O'Brien makes a marvelous leap over a deep canyon. MacGregor, following, attempted the same leap, but his horse missed footing in a remarkable sequence and fell to the bottom of the canyon, while MacGregor clung to tree trunks along the sides and pulled himself out.

The other big kick is a fight between Keene and Osner, the villain, after Keene has regretted his bad actions and is trying to replace the gold dust. Osner loses and falls hundreds of feet from a conveyance car spanning the valley. The fight, thrilling and well staged, was staged effectively in this tiny car.

These two punches are the only real things although a fairly good fight precedes. As may be guessed it is typical western dance hall stuff and cut from a skimpy piece of cloth. Mae Busch nominally heads the cast and her name flashed on a sub-title carried a "Courtesy of Metro-Goldwyn-Mayer" credit. Eugene O'Brien is the lead and Tom Santschi the friend of the wife. Mitchell Lewis as the villain is effective and Mildred Harris Chaplin returns to the screen wearing a black wig, making her almost unrecognizable.

"Flaming Love" doesn't look to have cost much. What interiors are used are cheap and rough and many exterior shots, some of them beautiful, are made. Except for its two punches, "Flaming Love" would be at home in the daily change class, and even with the big kicks there is a question as to whether it is legitimate first run material.

Sisk.

A LOST LADY

Warner Brothers' presentation with program billing starring Irene Rich. Adapted from the novel by Willa Cather and directed by Harry Beaumont. Showing at the Piccadilly, New York, week Jan. 17. Running time, 68 mins.

Marian Forrester	Irene Rich
Niel Herbert	Matt Moore
Constance Ogden	June Marlowe
Frank Ellinger	John Roche
Ivy Peters	Victor Potel
Captain Forrester	George Fawcett

A corking picture for Irene Rich from a personal angle but leaving a doubt as to its acceptance on the whole. The story is tagged by an indefinite ending, neither sorrowful nor joyous, to the extent of marking this vehicle as a hangfire release only memorable for the performance of Miss Rich.

Well produced and with ample assistance from George Fawcett, Miss Rich follows the trend of the times by growing older as the footage increases albeit stopping this side of a gray-haired wig. The character is that of a young girl married to an elderly railroad president who craves male companionship in proximity to her own years. Idolized by a village youth, she falls in love with a connoisseur of women of whose marriage she ultimately reads. Made a pauper by her husband giving away his wealth before dying, she refuses her youthful admirer when he proposes marriage, and the conclusion has her the wife of another elderly man and in South America, the boy being told of it by a friend.

The continuity is inconsistent, with the husband's sudden philanthropy a hazy impulse, besides which the sudden switch to South America is not completely explained. For that matter the story fails to convince, hence the picture must stand or fall upon the indulgence Miss Rich will demand. It is regrettable that such a personal performance as hers should be void of a parallel in script. Miss Rich is unquestionably superior to the story in this instance.

Mr. Fawcett, as the first husband, is as uniform as always, while Matt Moore averagely plays the idolizing country boy. June Marlowe is but briefly seen, with John Roche turning in a lukewarm "heavy."

Inconsistency is the outstanding fault but where Miss Rich is favored they'll like it, and when the verdict is thumbs down on the picture this girl is certain to impress and make them remember her.

Skig.

THE REDEEMING SIN

A Vitagraph production directed by J. Stuart Blackton and one of their specials for this year. Alla Nazimova featured with the front name left off both in house and reel billing. Lou Tellegen featured. Running time, 75 minutes. Reviewed at the Rialto, New York, Jan. 18.

Joan	Nazimova
Lupin	Lou Tellegen
Paul Dubois	Carl Miller
Papa Chuchu	Otis Harlan
Mere Michi	Rositta Marstini
Gaston	William Dunn
Marquise	Rose Tapley

Nazimova, now with Vitagraph, is cast as a gamin of the Montmartre section of Paris, a section where Apaches carry knives, wear velvet trousers and flowing neckties.

Her lover is Lupin, a tough guy. She is a dancer in the Blue Rabbit, a nondescript cafe. One night a society swell tumbles in with a group of his high-hat fellows, there to meet with a hefty rebuke at the hands and tongue of the girl, who resents the invasion on what she termed the privacy of her people.

But shortly after that the high-hat boy moves down with a sculptor friend to do some art work. There he again meets the girl. A friendship springs up. It is suddenly terminated when the gamin sees the young man, Paul Dubois, kissing another woman. The other woman was his sister but the kid didn't know that.

Back to her Apache gang she goes and spills the news that shortly in the Cathedral a new statue of the Madonna will be unveiled, and that famous jewels will be left on the statue as an offering. So the gang cops the jewels, after working their way through a picturesque sewer, but the girl finds out Paul was kissing his sister. She regrets her action, demanding that Lupin, her lover, replace them. He does, but is badly wounded while doing so by his own gang, who feel that he is deserting.

But the windup shows the high-hat boy arriving at the realization that burlap and silk don't mix.

The story, not so very original, is well produced and directed. Despite length it moves with commendable directness, for an excellent scenario has been provided. Nazimova is all over the picture in many closeups and Tellegen gets enough footage, while Carl Miller as the rich man is the other important member. The others are all capable, with a newcomer, Violet Virginia, showing promise.

Aside from its hackneyed story, the production would make it big town stuff, but as it is the smaller cities will be its most favorable screening places. It might be added that any disagreeable sex feature is missing.

Sisk.

The Deadwood Coach

Fox production starring Tom Mix. Directed by Lynn Reynolds. From Clarence E. Mulford's novel, "The Orphan." At Broadway, New York, week beginning Jan. 19. Runs about hour.

Tex	George Bancroft
John Gordon	Frank Coffin
Tad	Ernest Butterworth
Orphan	Tom Mix
Shields	De Witt Jennings
Helen	Doris May
Charlie	Lucian Littlefield

From the standpoint of view of scenic grandeur and the photographic ability to shoot it at the best possible vantage "The Deadwood Coach" probably surpasses any of the earlier films of Tom Mix, or, for that matter, of any of the numerous other western stars. For that reason alone the picture is worth seeing, as seldom, if ever, before has the beauty of the West been so artistically and graphically photographed.

For the rest, it is a typical Mix release, which means better in most details than the best his rivals can turn out. In this case the story has few twists and less logic, but, thanks chiefly to Director Lynn Reynolds, the action is never-ceasing and the running time seems much less than the actual hour.

Mix plays a character of the '70s and '80s known as Orphan. His parents have been brutally murdered years before by a bad man and his life is consecrated to plans for revenge. Because of this he is feared and hated, not only by his one enemy, but by most of the people around, who misunderstand his motives and accuse him of all the crimes committed in the county.

A kindly and understanding sheriff has kept Orphan from arrest, and when the heavies, led by the murderer of a dozen years before, decide to take the law into their own hands they find staunch opposition.

After several close escapes from lynching by everyone concerned law is restored and Orphan marries the sheriff's kid sister. Just as the ceremony is being performed an anti-climax comes when the original bad man holds everybody up and takes a free shot at the hero. This gives opportunity for the inevitable chase from cliff to cliff and crag to crag, ending when the villain conveniently slides off a particularly high one.

There are some ridiculous inconsistencies and errors sprinkled through the film that detract from the general value. At one time three men charge upon Mix and a helpless companion. He slides into a shallow creek and submerges completely, gun and all, only to rise a second later and pop all three off with a couple of shots from the dripping rifle. That's particularly bad when it is realized that in 1880 water-proof ammunition had never been heard of. A second later Mix is shown in a close-up as dry and well-groomed as though he hadn't been near the water for a week. (That, however, is far from rare in pictures, the actors apparently hating worse than anything to stay wet for any length of time.)

The comic interest is very well taken of by Lucien Littlefield as an original kind of cowboy boob. The rest of the cast is fair, with De Witt Jenning his usual capable self as the sheriff, but Dorie May a more or less vapid heroine. Tony enhances the gorgeous scenery, as only a steed of his beauty can, and the riding by everyone is fast and furious.

"The Deadwood Coach" is not Mix's best because of the rather hackneyed story and lack of attention to detail. But it ranks well up on his list. As a program attraction it's as safe as Liberty Bonds.

BUTTERFLY

Universal-Jewel production of the Kathleen Norris novel. Directed by Clarence Brown and scenario by Olga Printzlau. Laura La Plante featured. At Loew's New York Roof Jan. 15. Running time, 64 minutes.

Vi Vanderwort	Margaret Livingstone
Craig	Kenneth Harlan
Konrad Kronski	Norman Kerry
Butterfly	Laura Le Plante
Hilary	Ruth Clifford

Based not on a triangle proposition but upon a four-cornered love affair, this film is interesting pretty much all the way, not only on its actual plot merit, but because of cast and direction, unusually good for this type of film. "Butterfly" is built not for the first runs. There isn't a name in the cast that is admitted to hold real pulling power, but as a program proposition in the rank and file of film houses it is perfectly suitable.

The story concerns a famous violinist, beloved by two sisters. One of the sisters, Butterfly, is a flapperish sort, but married to Craig, a rich young man. The older sister is self-sacrificing and gives in to the kid on everything except on the love showdown.

With the two sisters in the musician's apartment at 2 a. m., the husband enters. Instead of the old scene, an all-around reconciliation is peacefully effected, with the flapperish kid set firmly on the right road.

Kerry plays the violinist well and that also goes for Harlan as the husband. Miss La Plante is the flapper wife, but the actual honors go to Miss Clifford as the older sister. To Clarence Brown as the director goes another palm. In face of what was evident production economy he has many deft and original touches and his comic relief was corking.

One particularly noticeable touch given by Brown was the insertion of a new closeup shot. Instead of shooting his star against the regulation black background, he used a lighter shade and to one side of his subject had a small vase. This touch in itself, relatively unimportant, gave composition to the picture. Admitted that that has always been done in stills, there is the argument as to whether it is permissible in motion pictures. However, Brown has done it, and well, too.

Sisk.

On the Stroke of Three

Associated Arts Productions-F. B. O. feature, starring Kenneth Harlan, Madge Bellamy, with Mary Carr among the principals. Story adapted from Henry Payson Dowst's romance, "The Man from Ashaluna," that appeared in the "Saturday Evening Post." Scenario by O. E. Goebel and Philip Lonergan. Directed by F. Harmon Weight. Shown as half of double bill at New York theatre Jan. 16. Runs more than 60 minutes.

Judson Forrest	Kenneth Harlan
Mary Jordan	Madge Bellamy
"Ma" Forrest	Mary Carr
Lafayette Jordan	Edwards Davis
Henry Mogridge	John Milgan
Jasper Saddler	Robert Dudley

Lillian Haskins................Lenore Matre
Austin Dudley.............Edward Phillips

The picture celluloids its way through devious and divers ways mysteries to perform, and in this feature a miracle is enacted.

Jud Forrest is going like the wind in an auto, with money in his pocket to meet the villain and prevent that bird from foreclosing on the little home he (Jud) and Ma Forrest love so well.

An accident happens. Some accident! That machine going 45, 60 or 80, shoots like a flash off the roadway and down an embankment, 40, 50, 60, maybe more, feet, demolishing the car and sending Jud to what seems certain death.

Now the clock is ticking the minutes and Jud has only a few to go when three bells will strike and Jud's home goes to the rich man, whose unscrupulous lawyer is moving anything to ruin Jud and get his land.

Jud lifts his head. There's a cut-off and the next thing the audience sees is Jud walking safe, sound and immaculate into the lawyer's—on the stroke of three.

How he recovered, washed up and covered the distance nobody knows, but there he is.

Otherwise a plain story.

A cast that reads like money on paper that should help sell the film. Miss Bellamy is a screen delight, winsomely sweet and attractive. Miss Carr is admirably cast as the mother.

There are some fine camera "shots" and the settings are adequate and convey impressions desired. The story forms the weakest part. Padded out at times, but showing class at others.

The cast may save the picture from the mothballs, yet credit must go to the director (Mr. Weight) for making as much as he did out of a story almost as ancient as the sun.

Mark.

THE LOSER'S END

William Steiner presents Leo Maloney in "The Loser's End," western melodrama, distributed by Productions, Inc., independent production. One-half of double bill at New York theatre, New York, Jan. 16. Running time, 56 minutes.

Captain Harris ....Roy Watson
Barney Morris.................Tom London
John Kincaid.....................Whitehorse
Lois Kincaid.................Josephine Hill
Bruce Mason...................Leo Maloney
Lucky Harnish...............Bud Osborne
Bullet (trained dog)............By himself

Another of the Leo Maloney series of westerns that William Steiner hands the screen, with only one woman in the cast. It's a little romance of the western prairies and hills that calls for gun play, physical contact, rough riding and mistaken identity, but mostly an outdoors story that didn't require the Bank of England to sponsor. It stars Maloney, who has the pat hero part and makes the most of it. Maloney is a ranch hand falsely accused of smuggling opium. While Maloney walks or rides or fights his way, he has several fistic encounters before the final embrace comes between Maloney and Miss Hill, the heroine.

It is not a great cast, but the characters are satisfactorily presented in a way that carries the story along.

For those that like the westerns with men fighting their way for the "purty gal"—and all gals are pretty to the rustling, riding cowboy heroes and villains—this picture is possible.

There are some bully scenes, but much of the film runs through footage that could ordinarily confine the entire story to two reels. Incidentally, credit must be given to the work of a trained dog called Bullet. This canine actor is an important part of the big scenes.

Mark.

HELEN'S BABIES

A Baby Peggy picture with the Sol Lesser tag. It's of the childish pranks one could expect or suspect, and some action. There's a laugh here and there.

A thrill is worked up in a single track railroad scene. Beyond that is very little.

The picture ran as though built to fit Peggy, which it may do, but not snugly.

An illogical story of a bachelor writing a book on order around how to bring up children. When left with the two little girls of his married sister, they run themselves and him in their childish way. For Baby Peggy admirers only, but for a matinee trade of children, better.

One half of a double bill at Loew's State, but the other picture, "Women and Gold," was by far the larger half. ***Sime.***

PELL ST. MYSTERY

Rayart production of story by Jeanne Poe and George Larkin. Directed by Joseph Franz and supervised by Robert J. Horner. George Larkin starred. At Stanley, New York, Jan. 19, one day. Running time, about 65 minutes.

The name is the tip-off for Chinatown stuff. Filled with glaring directorial errors and cheap sets, at the same time it is possessed of an undeniable and impressive audience punch. George Larkin is a police headquarters reporter, who comes to work in a pearl gray hat and a suit for which he walked up many flights. Hopped into a murder mystery in Chinatown. Despite its "Pell Street," the locale isn't New York's. He wins himself a blonde gal. After fighting and chasing a flock of thugs and Chinks, goes into a clinch.

Larkin is the only name, but others flashed are Florence Stone, Frank Whitson, Ollie Kirby and Jack Richardson, none of whom do more than sublimated suping. The Chinamen used are conventionally shifty and given to walking with crooked knees, but even at that they form the elementary interest of the plot.

For the cheap daily changes this one fills the bill. *Sisk.*

HEARTS OF OAK

Wm. Fox production, directed by John Ford. From the melodrama by James A. Herne. Scenario by Charles Kenyon. At Circle, New York, one day (Jan. 15). Runs about 63 minutes.

Terry ....Hobart Bosworth
Chrystal ....Pauline Starke
Ned ....Theodore Von Eltz
Owen ....James Gordon

"Hearts of Oak" convinces that the directorial genius flashed by John Ford in "The Iron Horse" was not an accident. Here Ford has not been dealing with the development of the west, but with the sea and its men, and yet his skill makes a living, gripping tale of a story almost ridiculously far-fetched. His work has been aided by a capital cast, headed by Hobart Bosworth in what is probably the finest portrayal of his many years in the films.

The sea plays importantly, but it is secondary to the three chief characters. Their temperaments have been molded by the constant contact with the ocean, but as far as the actual story goes they might have been people from another section of this or any other country.

James A. Herne has contrived a plot in which the nobility of sacrifice is stressed to the limit. As a result it becomes difficult at times to swallow the heroic hoke in its entirety. But the suspense is perpetuated and the pathos at the finale is certain to start fountains of tears.

Ned and Chrystal have been brought up and cared for by Terry, a veteran sea captain in a small New England maritime town. The girl has promised to wed Terry because of gratitude, but her heart yearns only for the younger man.

On the day before the wedding Terry learns of this, and tells Ned he will not stand in his way. Ned, joyous at the prospect of claiming the girl, is about to rush off to tell her the happy news when he notices the grief of the man who has been more than a father to him. Because of his love for Terry he in turn sacrefices himself, telling the older man it is he (Terry) that Chrystal has loved all along.

With this rather interesting situation for a start the picture goes on to show the wedding that makes one heart glad and two unhappy.

Two years after Ned is a derelict slave to drink on the waterfronts of Boston. He is about to sail for the Arctic regions on an unseaworthy ship that spells almost positive suicide for the human wrecks making up its crew. Terry, happy with his wife and baby, hears of this. After learning the former still loves Ned he forcibly prevents him from sailing and takes his place on the miserable craft.

Another jump of years finds Ned with a rescuing party discovering Terry, the last survivor of the frozen, ill-fated vessel, as his life is ebbing away. Terry's last wish is to hear his wife and baby say goodby and for this the radio is utilized. As Terry slowly passes out in the still, white North, the farewell messages of his loved ones at home are brought to his ears from the air.

It's hokum, but when the little daughter whispers "Goodby, Daddy, dear; I love you very much," in the microphone, and Bosworth is seen thousands of miles away doing a really remarkable piece of acting, it's a mighty hard-boiled egg that won't loosen up for a couple of sniffles. At the Circle they sobbed in unison, women, men, ushers and even assistant managers.

On the other hand, the film suffers from an almost total absence of comic relief. The sea shots both in the Arctic and in a wreck earlier in the film are particularly fine, as is the atmosphere in the sailors' dives around Boston.

Altogether, it's a bird of a program picture, and should please everybody unless the lights are switched on too quickly at the finish and some virile gentlemen are discovered with the tear works in full flow.

WOMEN AND GOLD

An independent with the Renown brand and Lumas distribution, featuring Sylvia Breamer and Frank Mayo. About 58 minutes.

A little too good is this meller to split a double bill at Loew's New York. Plenty of anguish and heavy heaves, with much registering, but withal there is action often and a gripping scene where the foster mother of a little boy must give him up to his own mother.

That little boy is a little dandy in this screening.

But on the other hand in the two or three fist fights it must have been understood that the principals hit each other under the shoulders. They aimed for there and made it. Neither one of the men is so terribly handsome he could not have taken a chance. Or perhaps the director stood in with them to nullify what should have been the action bits.

Sylvia Breamer rolled dem eyes of hers and emotionally, getting away quite nicely with one spasm, but when the eye rolling became universal, it could be gleamed that this was registering instead of acting. Frank Mayo had to go to jail and grew a nasty looking full beard before he escaped. Another prisoner, and in the same cell, waited awhile after Mayo got there before tipping off he had finished a dug-out to the outside world. It seemed they had a common bond of revenge. A Spaniard has copped the other fellow's daughter, and Mayo thought the same guy had grabbed his wife. But the wife was safe, although absent-minded for sometime. At the finish the Spaniard passed out almost on his wedding night, killed by a knife thrown by the other fellow. Up to that moment, though, it did look as though the heavy had the hero whipped in a fist fight.

Strong enough is "Women and Gold" for the one-dayers, all by itself.

The reason of the title is caption-explained as that men will disregard all laws for either. That caption forgot to add that gold is always pure. *Sime.*

PAINTED FLAPPER

Chadwick production released through Commonwealth on the state-right basis. Directed by John Gorman and featuring Kathlyn Williams, James Kirkwood, Crauford Kent, Claire Adams, Pauline Garon, Johnny Harron, Al Roscoe and Gerald Griffin. Reviewed as half of double bill at Loew's New York Roof. Running time, 69 minutes.

Probably the potency of the names in this one was figured on to sell it. They're good names, but the story itself is the same old society, crook and flapper hoke, without even a revision of the general working scheme of such stories. Moreover, there's nothing above the mediocre acting level in the whole works, so the names are drowned in a morass of muck.

James Kirkwood plays a husband who didn't get along with his wife. The split follows. Two beautiful daughters with sweethearts are left behind. When the hubby comes back the wifie is carrying on an affair with Egbert Van Alyn, a very smooth gent. The upshot of it all is that the Egbert guy is shown up as the master mind of a flock of crooks, while the daughters, who had erred slightly during the matrimonial bust, went back to their true sweeties while papa and mama pulled a coupla nifties on what was wrong with the modern generation.

The production end of this picture is well handled as regards sets, but the gowns worn by the women look like years gone by. That hurts, because women play a big part in this picture, as they do in most.

So mark "The Painted Flapper" down as an unexciting weak sister. *Sisk.*

Another Man's Wife

Regal Production released by Producers' Distributing Corp. Story by Elliott Clauson and Bruce Mitchell. Directed by Bruce Mitchell. James Kirkwood and Lila Lee co-starred. Running time 60 minutes.

John Brand..................James Kirkwood
Helen Brand............................Lila Lee
Capt. Wolf.....................Wallace Beery
Philip Cochran.....................Matt Moore

A good little commercial program picture that will do well enough in the daily change houses. At this time with James Kirkwood and Lila Lee still looked upon as newlyweds there may be sufficient interest on the part of the fans to pull fair business.

Nothing wonderful about the picture either as to story or manner in which it is enacted and the director has dragged in a couple of cabaret scenes by the heels just to make the picture look "big." The principal trouble with the tale is that it is draggy in the early portion with three cut-backs following one after the other, too much telling of what happened in the past and not enough action to tell what is happening in the present.

It is well cast as to the four principal roles with Wallace Beery and Matt Moore in support. All four deliver in their characterizations, Moore particularly getting over a couple of good comedy bits.

The story is a domestic drama of society flavor. The husband, immersed in his business, neglects his wife. She, to awaken him, decides to lead him to believe that she has eloped with another man. In reality she goes off by herself. The husband, believing the worst, goes on a bat and then follows the trail with the intention of killing his wife and the other man.

He never gets to it, however, for the simple reason that there is no other man and he sobers up before he actually meets his wife. The locale is laid on the west coast with San Francisco and a Mexican town as the scene of action.

In the latter there are a couple of fairly good bits, especially the one with Kirkwood shooting up the Mex dance place. There is a shipwreck scene well handled with the biggest part of the drama coming after the rescue of the principals by a barge loaded with rum in the hands of a roughneck crew. Of course the wife is the only woman on board, the husband is unaware of her presence, and the roughneck leader tries to assault her, then for the usual big fights between the husband and the heavy. Finally there is the U. S. navy, in the form of a submarine, to the rescue and everything ends happy.

For the ordinary house with the ordinary picture clientele this one will get by, although they won't rave over it. *Fred.*

OUTWITTED

Jesse J. Goldburg presentation featuring Helen Holmes and William Desmond. Direction J. P. McGowan. Distributed by Independent Pictures Corp. Running time, 65 minutes. Reviewed at Loew's, New York.

Tiger McGuire	J. P. McGowan
Lucy Carlisle	Grace Cunard
John Kinney	Alec Francis
Helen Kinney	Helen Holmes
Meg	Emily Fitzroy
Detective	William Desmond

This one looks like a composite of all the serial thrillers with which Helen Holmes used to be identified. The story is about as improbable a tale as has ever hit the screen and its wanderings defy concentration and analysis.

Tiger McGuire (J. P. McGown), a counterfeiter, escapes on his way to prison and joins his gang. They steal the plates of a new series of $10 bills. The balance of the footage consists of the agents of the Treasury Department trying to outwit McGuire.

All of the stock hokum and thrills are worked into the script at one time or another, among them being a fight on a burning ship, as ludicrous an incident as any brain ever conceived.

Miss Holmes, as in her serials, is doubled in the real tough stunts, and for the balance turns in a colorless, unsympathetic performance which adds little to the merit of the picture.

Desmond in the role of a Treasury agent who asks his chief for 48 hours to apprehend the criminal is just as unconvincing. Alec Francis, a veteran of the screen, is the one realistic touch as Secretary of the Treasury, and Emily Fitzroy does a good bit of character work as the old hag, Meg.

The story is laughable in its improbabilities and absurdly directed. Technical faulty details of direction, continuity and cutting are so numerous it is hard to believe they could all be included in one picture.

The picture is announced as the first of a series of eight society stunt melodramas. It appears to be a cheap imitation of the old two-reel thriller serials, strung out and padded to make up the full five reels. It's the cheapest kind of a meller for the non-discriminating houses. *Con.*

HER MAN

Philip Goldstone presentation releasing through Renown Pictures. Starring William Fairbanks. Cast includes Tom McGuire, James Pierce, Frank Whitson and Margaret Landis. Running time, about 60 minutes.

Every so often William Fairbanks threatens to break away from the tried and true western, but this one doesn't even resemble a threat. Whatever resemblance the film contains may only be counted by the uncountable feet of celluloid which have been dedicated to like subjects. Neither Fairbanks nor the cast maintain a sufficient average to hold it up.

A high hat debutante accompanies her father west where she is made the gearshift of a one-speed "big business" controversy. Friendly rivalry privileges the father's opponent to have her innocently abducted so he can wager on her return as to whether he will receive one or two million dollars for selling the power generating falls, which, incidentally, pour water much as inserts of Niagara are in the habit of doing.

Fairbanks is the outsider who breaks up the $1,000,000 gag by foiling 15 different men and eventually turns out to be an offspring of "big business" in that his papa is the biggest meat packer in the country, hence acceptable to the girl. It all ends at a masquerade in the girl's eastern home.

Miss Landis is a particularly colorless heroine with Fairbanks also guilty of an indifferent effort, though possibly excusable through the scenario. James Pierce and the star are responsible for the only live moments when hammer and tonging it over the girl and making it look on the level.

Most of the "big business" connected with the picture will remain in the sub-titules. *Skig.*

TRIGGER FINGERS

Jesse J. Goldburg production, released through F. B. O. Starring Bob Custer. Direction of "Breezy" Reeves Eason. Running time, 65 mins.

A new idea in westerns and one that properly handled should prove a great bet for the intermediate houses. This is the first of a series to be released by F. B. O. featuring the new western athletic lead, Bob Custer, in stories dealing with incidents in the life of a Texas ranger.

The strength lies in the scope for melodrama, horsemanship, etc. being a screen antithesis of the old dime novels when the James boys and other outlaw heroes thrilled the youth of the land.

Custer as the prize sleuth of his outfit is sent out on the trail of the Black Hawk, a desperado who has been terrorizing Texas. Disguising himself in the clothes of another outlaw whom he captures, "Trigger Fingers" (Custer) succeeds in locating the gang. He trails them to a country store, where the mine superintendent lives. The Hawk seals the lips of the super by some kind of hocus pocus, which immediately robs the story of all credulity.

The super had given the gang the wrong steer on a gold shipment. Custer is hiding in the store when Dr. Deering and his daughter enter to minister to the mutilated man. The doc leaves, claiming an operation is necessary, and he must get his instruments. The gang returns and Custer puts up a merry battle. He finally traps the Hawk, who, unmasked, proves to be the medico.

The action allows for thrilling horsemanship on Custer's part and also calls for several of those battles in which the hero disposes of more opponents than twin Jack Dempseys could handle in a week.

It's all right for picture producers to leave something to the imagination, but why ask an audience to think even a bandit parent would leave his only daughter alone with a reputed desperado while he went to join his own gang. Several other ocular boots are just as glaring.

Custer, however, is a find. He is a good-looking, clean-cut and intelligent youth. Proper stories will do things in his particular field. The Texas Ranger idea is a pip, but the development will make it or break it. The outdoor shots were scenically majestic. *Con.*

The Man Without a Heart

Banner production of the novel by Ruby M. Ayres. Directed by Burton King, with Jane Novak, Kenneth Harlan, Faire Binney and David Powell featured. Running time, 62 minutes.

A better than usual independent cast holds up the picture. The story concerns a matrimonial mixup in which one man tries to save a woman from a bad man and having saved her—takes a few wallops at the man himself.

Wild measures are taken, however, in this saving process. The man even goes so far as to kidnap the sister of the woman under consideration and make her live in the mountains with him.

Kenneth Harlan's role makes him a combination hero and heavy, with Jane Novak as the girl he's after. Faire Binney and David Powell are the other sweetheart combination, and Bradley King, the villain.

It's an inexpensive and fairly entertaining film, with its destiny lying in the smaller houses. Bought reasonably it fills the bill without providing much of a draw. *Sisk.*

THE LADY

First National picture sold on open market. Produced by Joseph M. Schenck and made from the play by Martin Brown. Directed by Frank Borzage and Norma Talmadge starred. At the Colony, New York, Jan. 25. Running time, 75 mins.

Polly Pearl	Norma Talmadge
Leonard St. Aubyns	Wallace McDonald
St. Aubyns, Sr.	Brandon Hurst
Tom Robinson	Alf Goulding
Fannie LeClair	Dorris Lloyd
Freckles	John Fox, Jr.
Mme. Adrienne Chatellier	Paulette Duval
A London Boy	Edwin Hubbell
Mme. Blanche	Emily Fitzroy
John Cairns	John Herdman
Mrs. Cairns	Margaret Seddon
Mr. Grave	Myles McCarthy
Leonard Cairns	George Hackathorne
Mr. Wendover	March McDermott
Blackie	Walter Long

A fine story, fine cast, with work by the star and director that is both intelligent and straightforward, combine to make "The Lady" take equal rank with the greatest Talmadge efforts.

B. S. Moss bought the picture up for its first-run New York rights, and is said to have guaranteed $25,000 for the privilege. From its start Sunday afternoon it looks as if he'll get out nicely.

"The Lady" is the Martin Brown play produced by Al Woods last year in Chicago and later brought to New York, where it played at the Empire. It's theme is a cut-back from the life of an English woman, Polly Pearl, running a French bar during the time she is a music hall performer, is wooed and won by a rich young dandy, whom she marries and for whom she bears a son. But the father cuts them off, passes out, and she is left alone with her son and no money. So it's any kind of a refuge for her, and she goes into a combination brothel and cabaret run by a Madame Blanche, who soon sympathizes and limits her work to singing for the customers. The wistful part of the story is this woman, down in the world, praying for great things of her son but principally asking that he be a gentleman, because she wanted so to be a lady.

The boy is taken to raise by a clergyman and his wife, when the father of her husband tries to take him from her, and five years of bitter poverty follow. But Madame Blanche dies and leaves her money to Polly Pearl. Polly goes to Marseilles and opens an English bar. Into her place come two British soldiers, one drunk and the other protecting him. The drunkard brings on a fight, and in a brawl both he and his little pal are shot. The drunkard is killed, but the little fellow is only knocked out temporarily. While he's out, Polly discovers he's her son, and when he comes to, tries to assume the blame. But the boy denies her that privilege because it would be ungentlemanly.

Then comes over a friend, who says he'll stick around until the boy is free, while Polly, in an ecstasy, tells him she's so pleased that her son is a gentleman. And the stranger tells Polly that the reason her son is a gentleman is because his mother was a lady.

There's the theme, played as a cut-back. Norma Talmadge is first the showgirl, then the cabaret entertainer, the old flower woman of the London street and, finally, as the proprietor of the bar. It is interesting every minute.

The production is elaborate and well handled, while Miss Talmadge does wonders with the title role. Of the cast, everyone in the long list performs well, and not a blunder is discernible.

From the exhibitor's angle there is this much—the picture itself is okay, and with the Talmadge draw "The Lady" is safe. *Sisk.*

DICK TURPIN

Tom Mix starring vehicle, produced by William Fox. Story by Charles Kenyon and Don Lee. Direction by J. G. Blystone. At the Piccadilly, New York, week of January 24. Running time, 70 mins.

Dick Turpin	Tom Mix
Alice Brookfield	Kathleen Myers
Lord Churlton	Philo McCullough
Squire Crabtree	James Marcus
Sally	Lucile Hutton
Tom King	Alan Hale
Bully Boy	Bull Montana
Bar Maid	Fay Holderness
Bristol Bully	Jack Herrick
Taylor	Fred Kohler

The trade story is that William Fox and $400,000 parted company in the making of this Mix picture. The film looks it.

It's the most elaborate release the western star has ever had and is revolutionary in that the old west is forgotten and Mix is cast in the role of the brave and chivalrous bandit, Dick Turpin, who, in English lore, was what might be termed a No. 2 company of Robin Hood. But this film is absolutely sterling and is pure entertainment for nine-tenths of the way. Its combination of laughs, thrills and love interest, combined with a suspense that is admirably maintained and executed, makes it the best Mix film to date and the logical vehicle for him to bow into the first-run houses.

The big first-runs have more or less ignored Mix heretofore. However, he has crept along from the star of ordinary westerns to the point where his boxoffice pull in state after state is greater than that of most of the other stars, many of them more widely advertised. Variety's story of his $2,000,000 and three-year contract with Fox is proof conclusive that he draws. But the first-runs have ignored him. Now they will have to watch him, for this picture is suitable for any house in America, bar none. It will be a queer audience not liking it and even if the story is laid in old England and in addition is a costume play, it is a tale that doesn't gasp for air after thirty minutes of running time has elapsed.

Briefly, Dick Turpin finds that Lady Alice Brookfield is being forced by her father to marry a Lord Churlton, a well-dressed bum. So Dick meets the lady, rescues her from the Lord, who would her husband be, eludes a flock of British soldiers, police, mobs, etc., rides his beautiful black horse over treacherous roads and high walls and winds up on the scaffold from which he fights his way in time to finally save Lady Alice from marrying Churlton.

Naturally, much skullduggery (that's what they called dirty work in those days), is unearthed and the interest part of the plot concerns Turpin's escapes and fights with the authorities and of his idolized position with the common people.

Mix is Turpin and as an actor he's on a par with a thousand others, but as a rider, fighter and general all around stunt man, he makes the others in the same business look foolish. His horse, too, is a tremendous asset to the film and the settings, of which there are many, are solid in spots and canvas curtains in others, albeit the curtain stuff is well handled and hardly noticeable.

The action in this picture should assure it of instantaneous success and, if the enjoyment of its premier Piccadilly audience is any criterion, both William Fox and the exhibitors will get plenty back when the returns are in.

"Dick Turpin" is one of the real entertaining films of the year. It's just dime novel hoke realistically treated, but the dime novel craze still has plenty of followers.

Sisk.

EXCUSE ME

Metro-Goldwyn picture presentd by Louis B. Mayer from Rupert Hughes' play of the same name. Directed by Alf Goulding. Showing at the Capitol, New York, week of Jan. 25. Running time, 57 mins.

Marjorie Newton	Norma Shearer
Harry Mallory	Conrad Nagel
Francine	Renee Adoree
Porter	Walter Hiers
Lieut. Shaw	John Boles
Jimmy Wellington	Bert Roach
Rev. Dr. Temple	William V. Mong
Mrs. Temple	Edith Yorke
Lieut. Hudon	Eugene Cameron
George Ketchem	Fred Kelsey
Rev. Job Wales	Paul Weigel
Mrs. Job Wales	Mae Wells

Probably the first picture adapted from one of his own works that Rupert Hughes hasn't personally directed. However, and undoubtedly under his supervision, Alf Goulding has turned out a rollicking farce that would have scaled the heights were it not for the insertion of a dime novel thrill passage.

For three-quarters of the way the picture is actually overboard with laughs with much of the credit due Conrad Nagel and Bert Roach. For those who doubt Nagel can play farce release is going to be a revelation.

The comedy is localed, principally, upon a train wherein a young naval officer and his would-be bride continuously try to find a minister to make the elopement according to Hoyle. They fail and the resultant situations pile up. The thrill is the chasing of the train by Nagel in an aeroplane to save the rail demon from plunging over a cliff where the bridge has burned away. The leap to the train and the dive of the engine is all pictured, but the fakes are obvious enough to offset any imaginative angle a well-wisher might care to imply. Besides which it deducts, drastically, from the farce ingredient.

Norma Shearer and Mr. Nagel are both featured in the billing with Roach gaining equal prominence, as regards comedy, through offering a whale of a "stew."

Running but 57 minutes, the picture teems with action, and it's a sure laugh-getter on any screen.

Skig.

THIEF IN PARADISE

Goldwyn presentation of George Fitzmaurice production, adapted by Frances Marion from Leonard Marrick's novel, "The Worldlings." Released by First National. Shown at Strand, New York, week of Jan. 25. Running time, 71 mins.

Helen Saville	Doris Kenyon
Maurice Blake	Ronald Colcman
Rosa Carmina	Aileen Pringle
Noel Jardine	Claude Gillingwater
Bishop Saville	Alec Francis
Ned Whalen	John Patrick
Phil Jardine	Charles Yourse
Maid	Etta Lee
Secretary	Lon Poff

Strictly box-office stuff and should hit that way. The standard ingredients, some of them palpably dragged in, but nevertheless valuable, make of this rather tall, and ofttimes inconsistent, tale an entertaining and thrilling film drama.

Starting in the hectic atmosphere of a derelicts' island off the China coast, with somewhat of a "Rain" and "White Cargo" flavor, it drifts to California, where the "hero," having stolen the papers of a missing prodigal, comes to claim the fortune as an impostor, accompanied by a sultry half-breed lady of no virtue, former mistress of the dead heir.

The thief falls in love with the daughter of the crusty father's crony, tries to shake off the vampy villainess for a long time without avail, marries, is threatened, confesses, shoots himself, is forgiven. Some of this portion is pretty sloppy, but it is great fare for the sentimental.

Doris Kenyon as the sweet ingenue is sweeter even than usual, and clicks. Aileen Pringle as the Oriental baby is never plausible and gives nothing to the product except hard work and gestures of the sort supposedly obsolete these many years in first-rate films.

But Claude Gillingwater as the grouchy but lovable old father hands forth a character portrayal such as has perhaps not been seen twice since Menjou in "A Woman of Paris." Tragedy, comedy, story-punch, flow from his gifted work. Ronald Coleman as the impostor does well enough, but fails to reach the heights.

With bathing girls and polo scenes and mansions and no end of sure-fire stuff ladled in, a wild, barbaric dance that is magnificently staged, and shifts from comedy to the depths and from drama to hokum, "A Thief in Paradise," running with its snappy title, should get the money.

Lait.

MISS BLUEBEARD

A Paramount picture starring Bebe Daniels and adapted from the Hopwood-Dregley farce, "Little Miss Bluebeard." Adapted to the screen by Townsend Martin and directed by Frank Tuttle. At the Rivoli, New York, week of Jan. 25. Running time, 65 mins.

Collette Girard	Bebe Daniels
Larry Charters	Robert Frazer
Bob Hawley	Kenneth McKenna
Hon. Bertie Bird	Raymond Griffith
Lulu	Martha Madison
Gloria Harding	Diana Kane
Colonel Harding	Lawrence D'Orsay
Eva	Florence Billings
Bounds	Ivan Simpson

On the stage "Little Miss Bluebeard" was a made-to-order vehicle for Irene Bordoni. In view of the fact, therefore, that the stage version was all Bordoni, it was apparent that, to suit this play to the screen, great alterations were necessary.

These alterations, let it be said, have been performed with much skill. Townsend Martin, a young Princeton man, has them to his credit. But the whole thing is hindered for no other reason than that it is a starring vehicle and that the star, Bebe Daniels, never suggests the flaring temperament associated with the Collette Girard role in the piece. Miss Girard, so the sub-titles tell us, is the temperamental French actress, a woman of fire and fury when cross; but the sub-titles alone suggest this. Miss Daniels contents herself with wearing feakish-looking clothes and becoming a veritable manikin.

With Miss Daniels out of the running only, it is natural that the honors go to someone else—Raymond Griffith. Griffith plays the sapheaded Bertie Bird, which was also the comedy hit role of the play, and with all the hoke in the world he carries it so far that the audience screams for 15 minutes solid in the mid-section of the film. That a star is present is remembered through Miss Daniels returning for more weary stretches of footage, but near the end a bedroom mixup brings a few more laughs.

The theme concerns the mistaken identity of a good-looking young man who is, by the error of a drunken French village mayor, married to the aforementioned Collette. But he had told her he was Larry Charters, a famous song writer, whereas Larry was his best friend and quite unwilling to get married. But Larry, seeing Collette, falls hard. The mix-up comes when Larry's other lady friends, all of whom he has been playing strong, fast and heavy, get sore and when they all start trooping into his apartment with Bertie Bird trying to sleep. Here Griffith wallops himself home many a comedy homerun, and if ever a member of the cast stole a picture from the star, he does it.

Robert Frazer and Kenneth McKenna do corking work, while a capable supporting cast, including the blonde little Martha Madison and the be-mustachioed Lawrence D'Orsay, is to be seen to advantage.

The settings are very fine and the direction good, although too many closeups are evidenced. Much care has been taken with all technical work, and good photography is apparent.

Had "Miss Bluebeard" held in its cast a competent comedienne it would undoubtedly have been a comedy wallop of the highest type. But as it stands "Miss Bluebeard" is an average program picture of the better type, and for nine-tenths of its entertainment this boy Griffith is responsible.

Sisk.

A MAN MUST LIVE

Paramount picture and Famous Players-Lasky presentation directed by Paul Sloane. Stars Richard Dix. Based on I. A. R. Wylie's story, "Jungle Law." At the Rialto, New York, week of Jan. 25.

Geoffrey Farnell	Richard Dix
Marguerite (Mops) Collins	Jacqueline Logan
Job Hardcastle	George Nash
Eleanor Ross-Fayne	Edna Murphy
Clive Ross-Fayne	Charles Byer
Mrs. Jaynes	Dorothy Walters
Cabaret Owner	William Ricciardi
Tod Cragg	Arthur Housman
Ross-Fayne	Lucius Henderson
Mrs. Ross-Fayne	Jane Jennings

Richard Dix is now a star in his own right. However, in "A Man Must Live" Dix works hard, but naturally there are comparisons and the procedure gives "Manhattan" the shade.

This vehicle is a combination of war, newspaper and good samaritan theme, with Dix playing the "regular guy" who befriends a young dancer who should have been food for a sob story for his (Dix) newspaper.

Dix, after returning from the war a captain, finds himself penniless and forced to work on a paper for sustenance. Just before he went abroad with a buddy, who was thought to have been killed but later turns up shell-shocked and selling dope, Dix was fighting a court case which meant $100,000 to him. This blew up when he rushed away to war.

Dix, as young Farnell, gets fired when he fails to handle a story assigned by the managing editor (George Nash), but recognizes a court prisoner as his buddy, Captain Clive Ross-Fayne. Here's a story. He finally sells it and then discovers that the young girl of his romance is none other than the beautiful sister of Captain Ross-Fayne.

Farnell tries to stop the story but sees it carried in the New York "Chronicle." The dancer that Farnell helps dies, and Clive's sister comes to upbraid him for being a cad. However, just before the climax, Farnell receives word his steel case has been settled and he is the victor with a check for $100,000. There's forgiveness by the girl and the big love embrace.

Much importance is attached to the newspaper climax, something that has been done before. Perhaps too much detail, mechanically, prevents grinding presses from telling the real story of their apparently ceaseless grind. Things almost unfold themselves without little effort on the part of the camera to tell the story in action.

Dix and Edna Murphy go in for considerable love making, there being several closeups. This girl appears to be doing the best work of her screen career.

Dix adds to his laurels but does not get his usual quick response. George Nash was superb as the managing editor as far as "acting" was concerned.

Credit must be given for the work of Jacqueline Logan as "Mops" Collins, the dancer. Charles Byer was acceptable and the minor roles were passable.

It is not a big story despite efforts of scenarist and director and cameraman to make it so. It is quite preachy and there are some celluloid stretches that only kill footage.

The picture depends upon the way Dix will be received. *Mark.*

FOLLY OF VANITY

William Fox production written by Charles Darnton, directed by both Henry Otto and Maurice Elvey. Betty Blythe featured. Reviewed Jan. 26 at the Central, New York. Running time, 65 mins.

(Modern Sequence)
Alice....................................Billie Dove
Robert..................................Jack Mulhall
Mrs. Ridgeway......................Betty Blythe
Ridgeway.............................John Sainpolis

(Neptune, etc., Sequence)
Neptune................................Bob Klein
The Witch.............................Lola Drovnar
The Siren.............................Edna Gregory
Alice....................................Billie Dove

This picture is a far-fetched excuse to do some more pandering, but it is true that while "Dante's Inferno" flaunted plenty of undraped femininity, it did with some intelligence. Here, however, the undraped opportunities were dragged in by the neck and staged with all the deftness of an amateur magician.

The story itself concerns a young husband and wife. A wealthy friend of the hubby throws a wild party. Here the young wife attends and the wealthy friend bestows on her a beautiful necklace. She accepts, temporarily, when told that if she'll wear it the pearls will regain their lustre. Then, for a not very logical reason, the hubby and wife begin sleeping in separate rooms (another deft touch indicating that they're at odds) and finally a big party is thrown aboard a yacht. Here the climax comes and the wife, dreaming that the acceptance of the necklace compromises her, imagines that the wealthy man is pursuing her. Then up she jumps in a thin nightie, runs up to a portion of the deck so that the moonlight can shine through the nightie, poses long enough, to give the infants a kick and then jumps overboard, going down to Neptune's realm.

The first part of the story Maurice Elvey directed. In the alleged fantasy, however, Henry Otto takes the reins and to show a carnival in the lower regions he throws a Pain's fireworks celebration; holds a diving contest; has a few of the not especially good-looking gals pose as if they were doing art studies for a mail order house, and then has a witch frame the good little girl so that she'll be hurled into the outer darkness.

Then she awakes and no prizes are offered here for the solution.

Although Betty Blythe is featured, she hasn't much to do, most of the action revolving around Sainpolis, Mulhall and Miss Dove. Granted that Miss Dove is physically quite alluring, this release isn't going to do her picture reputation a bit of good. Aside from that she performs creditably and the same goes to Mulhall. The principal ones at fault in this story are those who introduce its many moments of attempted salaciousness.

"Folly of Vanity" is undoubtedly aimed at the box office. The undressed ladies testify eloquently to that. But other undressed pictures have been aimed at the box office before without clicking, and there's no reason to believe that this one will be a sensation.

For a daily change, where the customers take their amusement without demanding intelligence of story or artistry in the direction, this one may suffice. *Bisk.*

THE FATAL MISTAKE

Perfection Pictures Production. Cast: William Fairbanks, Eva Novak, Wilfred Lucas, Dot Farley, Bruce Gordon, Harry McCoy, Paul Weigel, Frank Clark. Direc-

tion Scott Dunlap. At Loew's State, New York, Jan. 21. Half of double feature program. Running time, 65 mins.

More attempt at a story in this picture than in the usual "stunt" appearances of William Fairbanks. The tale is mediocre and lacks atmosphere. No one is credited with authorship which is just as well.

The story has to do with a cub reporter (Fairbanks) who is the office "Patsy." The cub is employed by the "Star" and his paper is getting the worst of it in a news duel with the "Herald."

The latest scoop concerns the Rigo diamonds. The star reporter is shot out on the story and the city editor turns deaf ears on the cub's plea to be allowed an opportunity to secure a photograph of Helen Van Dyke. Helen, it seems, has never been photographed. The author and direct neglect to tip us just why a society deb should be camera shy, but let it go. The cub decides to try it on his own and grabs a camera. He hides in a dog kennel on the estate and then climbs a trellis to get a flash at the girl posing in a wedding dress. The paper gets out an extra to flash the photo. Evidently no one on the "Star" had ever seen Helen, although she is quite prominent locally. However, let that go too.

The photo was one of the maid who was preening herself in her mistresses' dress. The cub loses his job. So does the maid. They meet. She is his long lost sweetheart from another town. He doesn't know it at the time, but you can bet he finds it out before the final clinch. Between them they manage to outwit the villians. She reminds him of a girl he loved long ago. He photographs pretty young, but probably has a poor memory.

Prince Rigo is giving a reception in honor of the Van Dykes. The star reporter has been invited. The cub decides to get the photo and peddle it to a rival sheet to get hunk on the musical comedy city editor who fired him. At the house he is unable to secure a photo, the police driving the camera hounds away. Our hero wanders around the grounds. Looking at the house he sees the maid with a man on the porch. Suddenly the lights in the house go out and cries of "thief" are heard. A man rushes out, picks the maid up in his arms and carries her to a car. The usual "chase" follows.

The police are in one car and the cub in the second. They fire at him thinking he's the thief. The bulls conveniently fade from the picture via the flat tire route but the **cub pulls up to the fleeing car and jumps into it from his own. He overcomes the man on the back seat and with the aid of the girl dittoes the driver.**

On the way back he learns she's the girl he used to love in Hensfoot Corners, now a special operator from the central police office. She has been working with the crooks in order to get them red handed.

The cub reports at the "Star" office, shakes the editor down for a raise, borrows three bucks and leaves to marry the girl. An artistic touch was the cub refusing to divulge the story until he got the three dollars and then telling the city editor he would phone it from the marriage license bureau in time for the early edition. It's too bad he phoned.

This one is strictly a "chaser." *Con*

LAUGHING AT DANGER

Richard Talmadge production released through Renown. Made by A. Carlos and directed by James W. Horne. Talmadge starred and Eva Novak and Bull Montana featured. At Loew's New York Roof. Running time, 63 minutes.

By the token that Richard Talmadge is established as a stunt star this is a melodramatic film filled, toward the latter part, with a succession of hair-raising stunts which immediately qualifies the picture for the small houses.

The melodramas of Talmadge are wild affairs; they lack the satire and the comedy which marked the old Fairbanks propositions, but as a pure and simple stunt man the screen has yet to see one who can draw rings around this boy. He leaps, rides, fights and drives a car like a flock of vase-lined comets, and with something big at stake, as here, the suspense and interest aroused is considerable.

Here the young man starts off as a lad discouraged in love. His father feels that the provision of excitement is the antidote. Excitement is provided—and routed. Then comes the real excitement with the boy believing it phoney and going through with it all just to humor dad. But some very vile conspirators are after a death ray invented by an inventor with a blonde daughter. They nearly blow up the Pacific fleet, but the kid steps in at the last minute and upsets both the bad men and their bad plans. And he marries the girl.

This stuff, punctuated as it is with honest-to-Henry fights—swift and exciting chases and some fair comedy, is just a set-up for the houses that don't play so heavy on anything except entertainment. Made primarily for the cheaper grade of picture-goers, it fills the bill like a sponge fills with water. *Sisk.*

LET WOMEN ALONE

Frank Woods' Production. Adapted by Frank Woods, from Viola Brothers Shore's story, "On the Shelf." Direction Paul Powell. Released by Producers Distributing Corp. At Loew's State, January 20. Half of double feature program. Running time, sixty-five minutes.
Tom Benham........................Pat O'Malley
Beth Wylie..........................Wanda Hawley
Cap Bulliwinkle....................Wallace Beery
Ma Benham...........................Ethel Wales
John Gordon.........................J. Farrell MacDonald
Jim Wylie.............................Harris Gordon
Jean Wylie...........................Betty Jane Snowden
Alec Morrison.......................Lee Willard
Isabel Morrison....................Marjorie Morton

A fast-moving melodrama with a couple of thrills, one a corking good free-for-all battle at sea on two fast-moving motor boats. The picture lacks comedy relief and the efforts of the adapter to make Tom Benham (Pat O'Malley) a breezy comedy insurance salesman almost destroy the credulity of the tale which, however, is convincing in most of its footage.

The story in the screen adaptation suffers but the excellent cast make it stand up well enough to satisfy the average second string picture house audience.

Beth Wylie (Wanda Hawley) supposes her villainous husband, Jim Wylie (Harris Gordon) dead. Wylie has planted the supposition to escape the police. In reality he is smuggling Chinese into the country. Meanwhile, Beth quarrels with her wealthy uncle, Commodore John Gordon (J. Farrell MacDonald) and refuses to live at his house. He opposes her opening a decorating shop. Beth meets Tom Benham when he apprehends a pickpocket who has copped her poke.

Tom's mother meets Beth when she finds Beth's lost child and takes her home. The old lady is tired of idleness and, when Beth mistakes her for a woman she has been expecting from an employment agency, she allows the deception to stand and takes the job.

Gordon calls to protest against Ma's financial aid to his niece but is routed by the old lady. Gordon denounces Tom when the latter tries to insure him and Tom announces his intention of marrying Beth. Gordon sets out to upset Beth's business and stop the marriage.

Wylie turns up and attempts to blackmail Gordon, but failing, kidnaps Beth. There is a nautical "chase" with the battle one of the high lights of the picture. Jim Wylie is drowned, clearing the way for the usual finish.

The picture is a good program addition for the intermediate houses. Wanda Hawley is beautiful and convincing and Pat O'Malley, barring the moments he was unsuccessfully attempting a T. Roy Barnes, got over. Wallace Beery had a small and profitless role, Harris Gordon copping the heavy honors as the scapegoat husband. The rest of the cast averaged strongly. *Con.*

RIDIN' MAD

Ben Wilson-Arrow Production, starring Yakima Canutt, world's champion cowboy. Story and direction by Jacques Jacard. Running time, 58 minutes.
Steve Carlson........................Yakima Canutt
Marion Putnam......................Lorraine Eason
Ruth Carlson.........................Helen Rosson

Second of series of State right Westerns starring Yakima Canutt, world's champion cowboy, who has won innumerable rodeo contests in various parts of the country, and who for several years was the champion of record for bronc riding and other events of a like nature.

As a western it is about on a par with the average State right picture of this kind. It has some corking riding scenes in it, both in the rodeo and in a couple of chases. There is a love story fairly well handled, and, while Canutt is at present a far better horseman than he is an actor, he certainly will improve in the latter. He has personality and is a real westerner, not a stage western, and looks it.

In the daily change houses, where they like westerns, they will like this, one for it is just like all of the rest as to story and the general handling in direction. There is a rather labored attempt to get over some comedy through the medium of a younger sister of the hero, but that is so palpably forced it seems painful, but in the small towns the audiences may like it.

Yakima plays a young cattleman, who, through drought and his cattle dying off is forced to go into the rodeo game to win some money. He rides into a town, where he has a fight with a bully, who is his most dangerous riding opponent. The latter tries by foul means to cause the hero to lose the contest, and is walloped in the jaw for his shady tricks.

After they have returned to their home town, the bully undertakes to ruin the victor, with the result a shooting duel takes place and the bully is killed. While the hero is hiding a couple of oil well promoters nearby become acquainted with a sister, and one of the men pays court to the older one, promising to marry her, which with him is all part of Form 34 in Rules of Romance. The boy, hearing of the true state of things, takes a chance and comes to protect his sister with the result he is arrested.

The two oil well promoters had previously operated in another part of the country and were the cause of the death of the father of the girl the hero is in love with. When she appears and recognizes one of the men, the hero makes an escape from jail, kills the bad boy and the other makes a confession that clears the hero of both crimes.

The story is rather crudely done on the screen. For some of the riding stuff the tipped camera is used, and that is so readily recognized by the audience it is laughed at. Those scenes could have just as well been cut, for there is enough real riding to put it over without resorting to the trick stuff.

Canutt handles himself real well, and is especially nifty with a couple of guns, so much so, that he can replace Bill Hart as the two-gun man. Lorraine Eason does well enough playing the lead opposite the cowboy star. *Fred.*

HUMAN DESIRES

London, Jan. 16.

A foreword in the synopsis states some people sneer at the alleged parsimony of British film producers and pretend we cannot compete with America because we do not spend enough money on our pictures.

This may or may not be so, but one thing certain is that the people who have invested money in this Anglia picture will deplore putting good money in it. Burton George, the producer, is said to have spent over $175,000 on the feature, and all he has achieved is a mass of extravagant scenery, a poor story and a good deal of mediocre acting. The picture is being handled by Gaumont. Boast is made of the settings. To achieve this George has taken pains to build gigantic and thoroughly artificial sets to frame a story which is about the last word in bloodless inanition.

Joan Thayer is a pure young English artist working in a vile French cabaret. She is fired because she will not encourage the place's patrons. She is chased home by a young officer, Pierre Brandon, and although she, in her innocence, takes care to leave her bedroom door invitingly open, he merely leaves a note saying he'll call again when she feels better.

When next we meet the couple they are close friends, but he unfortunately introduces her to a friend, a theatrical manager. In no time she is a star and the manager falls in love with and marries her. His old flame conspires to part them, and succeeds admirably, thereby paving the way for the usual ending.

The story is mawkish and without a single genuine note. The production work reflects great credit on the carpenters and scenic artists, to say nothing of the floor room at the Famous-Lasky studios (Islington). The cabaret scenes are good, but strictly conventional, but it is encouraging these days to learn that some theatrical managers do live in apartments about the size of Trafalgar Square. There are many good shots of Paris and the race-course crowds at Auteuil.

Marjorie Daw, specially imported from America to help the marketing of the picture, gives a true-to-type reading of the ordinary heroine, but is without sincerity, Juliette Compton is quite good as the theatrical manager's mistress, Clive Brook is wooden and immobile as the virtuous manager, and Warwick Ward does his best with Pierre.

"Human Desires" will create no sensation beyond grief at the enormous amount of money wasted. *Gore.*

Salvation Hunters

Josef Von Sternberg production released by Academy Pictures and distributed through United Artists. Written and directed by Von Sternberg. At the Strand, New York, week of Feb. 1. Running time, 63 mins.

The Boy..................George K. Arthur
The Girl..................Georgia Hale
The Child..................Bruce Guerin
The Man..................Otto Matiesen
The Woman..................Nellie Bly Baker
The Brute..................Olaf Hytten
The Gentleman..................Stuart Holmes

Word came a month or so ago from the west that "The Salvation Hunters" was the work of a new cinema genius, that it was a revolutionary picture, that its theme was original and the treatment masterful. On top of that Charlie Chaplin, Doug. Fairbanks and Mary Pickford endorsed it as being the ultra-ultra in picture production. Applesause.

"The Salvation Hunters" is nothing more nor less than another short cast picture to express an apparently Teutonic theory of fatalism. The derelicts of the world are the characters and a flock of freshman philosophy the theme. The idea of the whole thing is that, although we're born in the mud, we can lift ourselves by our own boot-straps until we see the sun. That's the alleged original idea. It would be taking up too much time to figure out the boys who've expressed it before, but they run all the way from Aristotle to Elbert Hubbard. The picture itself announces that it is photographing a "thought" and that heretofore the motion picture had refrained from so doing. That's all wrong. "So Big" was certainly nothing more than the photograph of a thought, and certainly the subtlety behind "Broken Blossoms" had something to do with thought. And there are other films, too—"Tol'able David," "Driven," etc. The boast made by Von Sternberg doesn't stand up.

The story concerns a young coward and his young wife. They start on a mud-scow, where he lives. The symbolic mud is everywhere and the ominous shadows of the dredge seem to haunt their lives. But the boy is a coward and the girl bitter toward life in general. Eventually, however, they pick up a little foundling and go to the city, where a procurer for a brothel gives them lodging in hopes of obtaining the girl. From then on a harlot figures in the cast, and she is exceptionally well played. The wind-up is that the procurer mistreats the kid one day and that the coward is spurred to action, something rare. He beats the other man and thereby begins to get his own measure. And so it ends.

The cast, with the one exception named, is poor and is continually being posed by the director to look straight at the camera. Little Bruce Guerin as the child is especially badly directed, while the others don't fare much better.

There's nothing lavish in this one, and although it isn't entirely a bad picture, it is uninteresting most of the way because of some glaring directorial faults and also because of the illogical story. That the general public will take to it is inconceivable, and despite the tremendous heralding given Von Sternberg on the Coast, it looks as if the old reliables were pretty safe with their reputations. *Sisk.*

CHEAPER TO MARRY

Robert Z. Leonard production, Louis B. Mayer presentation, Metro-Goldwyn release; from the stage play of Samuel Shipman; adapted by the Hattons; directed by Leonard. Running time, 74 mins. At the Capitol, New York, week of Feb. 10.

Dick..................Conrad Nagel
Jim Knight..................Lewis Stone
Evelyn..................Paulette Duval
Doris..................Marguerite de la Motte
Flora..................Louise Fazenda
Riddle..................Claude Gillingwater
Dal Whitney..................Richard Wayne

One glance through the cast above will show anyone who knows anything about films that this one couldn't be bad. Without any sky-written stars, that is about as workmanly and competent an outfit of screen players as could be assembled. And they carry the film like a mother carries twins, plenty to hold up, both arms busy, but in all one bang-up job.

Not that the story or scenario necessarily cries for help. It isn't a bad yarn, and is rather skillfully turned into film material. But on sheer narrative values it wouldn't class with the best and wouldn't "make" the Capitol. In its finished shape, it measures up fairly, and should do an average week.

Miss Fazenda's comedy, dragged in as "incidental" and played against the smooth and unctuous support of Gillingwater, is a delight. Stone is his ever suave self as a "heavy" who can hold sympathy. Nagel and Miss de la Motte have negative though busy roles and carry them without effort.

Paulette Duval flashes, perhaps, the most striking physique in the motion picture directory, a statuesque brunette with a figure which 20 years ago would have had Broadway at her feet and even now, in the flat-chested flapper generation, is a banquet for the eye.

With some typical Hollywood intrusions such as a reducing club and swimming pool for women, a Wall street panic scene and a dream of a cabaret effect, the story in the main is Shippy's. That is, after one has seen the play after one has seen the film, the mental reaction and the moral sustenance is about the same.

This feature has been intelligently, faithfully and lavishly done and will have good luck around the wheel of endeavor, though it will not rank with the year's leaders because it has no one outstanding, talkable punch with all its intrinsic and honest merit. *Lait.*

Capital Punishment

B. F. Schulberg production bearing Renown Productions label. Also bearing Preferred Pictures classification. Scenario by John Goodrich; directed by James P. Hogan. At B. S. Moss' Cameo theatre, New York, Feb. 1.

Della Tate..................Clara Bow
Danny O'Connor..................George Hackathorne
Gordon Harrington..................Elliott Dexter
Mona Caldwell..................Margaret Livingston
Harry Phillips..................Robert Ellis
Priest..................Alec B. Francis
Mrs. O'Connor..................Mary Carr
Mother of victim..................Edith Yorke
Officer Dugan..................Wade Boteler
Innocent Victim..................Eddie Phillips
The Governor..................Joseph Kilgour
Warden..................George Nichols
Doctor..................John Prince
Pawnbroker..................Fred Warren

Looks like a "break" for Ben Schulberg in New York with "Capital Punishment" at a time when Bernarr McFadden's daily tabloid, the "Graphic," is out with daily type shrapnel for the abolition of capital punishment in this state. Anyway right off the reel, the general theme of the Schulberg picture, which is out-and-out screen propaganda against the death of convicted men in the electric chair, grabbed a tie-up with the "Graphic."

It's a sordid picture at best, despite its try for comedy angles. Sordid through the fact that one boy is electrocuted in the prologue and another is about to be bumped off a la Edison by the state's official permission. This is not the first time that such a story has been screened.

"Capital Punishment" doesn't ring true and seems lost through depicting how easy a young man can be framed and sent to the chair.

It's the easiest thing in the world for a criminologist to bet $10,000 with a friend that he could have an innocent man convicted for murder by the friend agreeing to disappear and stay at least two weeks on the criminal expert's yacht. The expert then looked around and got a little Irishman, an erstwhile crook, who was trying to go straight, to go to jail and permit himself to be booked for murder, the price being the $10,000 that the expert was to win off his friend.

The friend of the criminologist goes out on the boat, stays a while, gets tired and desires to be back making love to the girl that is in love with the expert. This peculiar triangle smooths the way for the story to hit tragic channels later.

The expert has a fight with the friend and the result is the death of the latter, with the girl an eye-witness. As there's a man already charged with the "murder" the girl begs the expert to cover the real crime on him and then the plot thickens. The signed agreement is easily stolen from the boy's home.

There's an abundance of mawkish sentiment. It's just a picture, with a few efforts at "thrills," commonplace at best. The cast works heroically, with such players as Clara Bow, George Hackathore, Elliot Dexter, Mary Carr and Joseph Kilgour.

The main dependence for boxoffice play will be through the title, the picture's propaganda, and where tie-ups with newspapers cane be made. *Mark*

THE DEVIL'S CARGO

A Paramount Production directed by Victor Fleming and adapted by A. P. Younger from the play of Charles E. Whittaker. Pauline Starke, William Collier, Jr., Wallace Beery and Claire Adams featured. At the Rivoli, New York, week of Feb. 1. Running time, 75 minutes.

Ben..................Wallace Beery
Faro Sampson..................Pauline Starke
Martha Joyce..................Claire Adams
John Joyce..................William Collier, Jr.
Mate..................Raymond Hatton
Jerry Dugan..................George Cooper
Millie..................Dale Fuller
Jimmy..................."Speo" O'Donnell
"Square Deal" Sampson...Emmet C. King
Farewell..................John Webb Dillion
Briggs..................Louis H. King

This member of the second "40" group is a fairly forte melodrama with both action and a strong love interest. Moreover, it is a well produced film, capably directed and mounted with the usual Famous-Players attention to that kind of detail.

The story is of Sacramento in 1850, right after the gold rush. A young editor from the east settles there with his sister and meets the daughter of the gambling house-keeper. She's a corking little girl, but his reforming nature gets the better of him and he tries to reform her. His efforts stir up the town so that the Vigilantes are organized and the "questionable" characters whose only sins were that they drank too often and not so wisely, are driven from town. The bigots remained. They were loaded on a river boat, but near the Frisco landing, an explosion occurred and the ship was left without means of propulsion. Caught in the ebbing tide, it is carried to sea and a burly stoker, Ben, assumes charge of the boat, worrying the ladies and fighting with the men. But Ben, after making some fiendish attacks on both the hero's sister and sweetheart, is licked and the gang rescued for a happy finale.

Done in costume, the picture is splendidly handled. The love-making is strictly modern and that helps. Pauline Starke, as the saloon-keeper's daughter, gives a brilliant performance and so does Wallace Beery as the stoker. Claire Adams, as the sister of the reformer, is good but William Collier,

Jr., in the lead male role seemed colorless.

As it stands, it is doubtful whether "Devil's Cargo" has much drawing power, but aside from that, it is a good standard melodrama done much better than usual.

The performance of Pauline Starke, however, is the thing to talk about and if a few more films like this are given her, there seems but little doubt she will develop a following. *Sisk.*

FORTY WINKS

Screen adaptation of "Lord Chumley," by David Belasco and Henry C. De Mille; produced by Adolph Zukor and Jesse L. Lasky as a Paramount release with Viola Dana, Theodore Roberts and Raymond Griffith featured. Screen play by Bertram Milhauser. Directed by Frank Urson and Paul Iribe. At the Rialto, New York, week of Feb. 1. Running time, 68 mins.

Eleanor Butterworth............Viola Dana
Lord Chumley............Raymond Griffith
Adam Butterworth........Theodore Roberts
Gaspar Le Sage............Cyril Chadwick
Annabelle Wu............Anna May Wong
Lt. Gerald Hugh Butterworth.William Boyd

Corking melodramatic farce giving Raymond Griffith one of the best roles he has had in some time and the latter more than living up to expectation as the lovable, foppish Chumley.

Although the main plot has been culled from the stage success of past decades the scenarist has not lost the opportunity to inject modern touches at every opportunity. It is done with a deft hand that never once mars the primary foundation of the young Englishman who, through circumstance, has been suspected as the interloper and spy.

The plans are stolen early in the picture and the effort to regain them to save the youth from court martial provides impetus for the subsequent spinning out of a story that blends thrills with laughter and in which laughter dominates.

"Chumley" finally traces a clue to the apartment of "Annabelle Wu," who lifted the plans from young "Butterworth" at the behest of "Gaspar Le Sage," whose price for their return was the hand of "Eleanor Butterworth," already betrothed to "Chumley." The latter's stupid wise attitude fools everybody, even the lady who has the plans which eventually come into possession and are returned.

Griffith was capital throughout as "Chumley." Viola Dana was charming as "Eleanor Butterworth," although having few opportunities. Theodore Roberts was excellent as the elder "Butterworth, while Anna May Wong, Cyril Chadwick and William Boyd rounded out the cast of principals giving adequate delineations of their respective roles.

Although a surefire laugh-getter it is hardly strong enough to hold its own in cosmopolitan stands, but should be a "puller" in the smaller towns. *Edba.*

THE CHORUS LADY

Producers Distributing Corp. Production. From the play by James Forbes. Directed by Ralph Ince. Adapted by Bradley King. Featuring Margaret Livingston. Photographed by Glen Gano. At Loew's New York, Jan. 30, as half the bill. Runs about 65 minutes.

Patricia O'Brien ......Margaret Livingston
Dan Mallory ....Alan Roscoe
Nora O'Brien ....Virginia Lee Corbin
Mrs. Patrick O'Brien.......Lillian Elliott
Patrick O'Brien ....Lloyd Ingraham
Dick Crawford ....Philo McCullough
Miss Simpson....................Eve Southern
Duke ....Mervyn Leroy

"The Chorus Lady" is an adaptation of the Jimmie Forbes play which provided Rose Stahl with one of her greatest successes some years ago. It was produced once before as a picture, in 1915, by Lasky (Paramount). Cleo Ridgely was featured as Pat, with Margery Daw, Richard Grey and the late Wallace Reid, the latter just approaching his later tremendous popularity, supporting.

The present production must be ranked as one of the most poorly acted, insipidly directed and generally all-around exasperating films in some time. Possibly the situation of having an elder sister sacrifice her rep and her sweetie by allowing herself to be caught in a young roue's rooms, where she has gone to save her silly kid sister, was a new one when Forbes wrote it.

The story treated properly would have gone across, as it has a good share of human interest. But the slangy chorus girl line which was such a riot in the spoken version has not been modernized and introduced in the subtitles as it should have been. Nor are the back-stage shots as spicy and intimate as they might have been.

As it stands the only episode in the film that really proves enjoyable is the one in which Pat after saving her sister and losing her beau proceeds to wreck the heavy's gorgeous apartment. Walking up to him pleasantly enough she suddenly lands a full-swing wallop right square on his jaw and then follows by chucking every vase and ornament in the room at him and his frightened Jap butler.

Margaret Livingston in the title role seemed intermittently colorless and ridiculous. The remainder of the cast contains few names of any box office worth.

BROKEN LAWS

F. B. O. production starring Mrs. Wallace Reid. Written by Adela Rogers St. John. Directed by R. William Neil. Photographed by J. R. Diamond. Adapted by Bradley King and Marion Jackson. At Moss' Broadway, week beginning Feb. 2. Runs about 70 minutes.

Joan Allen..............Mrs. Wallace Reid
Ralph Allen...............Ramsey Wallace
Richard Heath..............Percy Marmont
Muriel Heath.........Jacqueline Saunders
Bobby Allen....................Arthur Rankin
Patsy Heath...........Virginia Lee Corbin
Bobby (child)......................Pat Moore
Patsy (child)......................Jane Wray

Pictures expounding a definite "moral" often defeat their own aims by overstepping the limits of propriety in illustrating too freely the very evils they are trying to remedy. "Broken Laws" doesn't, and it must be rated as a straight-from-the-shoulder, absorbing film, in which Mrs. Wallace Reid gives a most sincere performance.

R. William Neil's work with the megaphone accomplished the almost impossible; made a genuinely human and vital film of one that might easily have become a stereotyped sermon. And the remarkable part is that, although the picture is primarily entertainment, dramatic and comic, the lesson it has striven to teach is always discernible.

"Broken Laws" should obtain its greatest play in the smaller cities and towns, where the attention of women's clubs and church societies can be focused upon it. While it goes thoroughly into the alleged vices of the present-day genration, it does not make the mistake of laying the sex and booze angles on too heavily, thus avoiding any loopholes for criticism on the grounds of frankness.

Mrs. Reid plays an indulgent mother who has petted and cajoled her wayward son since childhood. At eighteen he's a scoffiaw of the worst type. A liquor party at a notorious roadhouse, followed by a wild flight in a sporty Stuts from a pursuing motor cop, leads to a collision with a wagon and the death of the particularly sweet old lady riding in it with her husband.

In the trial that follows, the mother realizes that she has been the real culprit because of her uncalled-for indulgence, and when the verdict of first-degree manslaughter is given she offers to go to prison for her boy. But this, of course, is impossible, and just when things look blackest she wakes up. It was all a dream and her son just a kid of seven or eight who needs a good tanning occasionally.

Percy Marmont lends his prolific thespian talents for just a few moments as the grieved father of the flapper. Arthur Rankin and Virginia Lee Corbin are convincing. Ramsey Wallace adds a distinctive bit as the boy's father. The film has been richly set and photographed with great skill.

HELEN OF TROY

London, Jan. 21.

There is a tradition here to the fact that should a picture be mediocre everybody concerned is starred, the name of the producing company is printed in large caps and everything possible is done to throw sand in the eyes of critics and exhibitors. But, on the other hand, should the feature be of sterling worth, although of foreign birth, then the system is "hush-bush," and all are robbed of their legitimate kudos. "Helen of Troy," shown at the Palace by Cosmograph, is one of the latter. Of mixed Italian and Teutonic origin, it is a brilliant production in every way.

As a spectacle carrying the imprint of truth and realism it would make D. W. Griffith sit up and consider his laurels, while the acting has never been bettered from the anonymous leads to the tiniest small part.

The story of fair Helen's rape by Paris to the fall of Troy is faithfully adhered to, and the greater part of the feature is devoted to the long-drawn-out fight betwen the Greeks and Trojans. Here and there the story may take original and unhistorical twists, such as the episode in which Menelaeus orders his queen, Helen, to expose herself to the common public before serving in the Temple of Adonis.

The majority of the settings are magnificent and the handling of vast crowds of soldiery is beyond all praise. The famous episode of the horse is fine.

The acting from first to last reaches a remarkably high standard, and it is to the disgrace of the renters that this should be allowed to go unknown when so much solid incompetence is extolled to the skies.

"Helen of Troy" is, however, very heavy stuff. There is no cessation for eight reels from the gigantic crowds and enormous settings.

Gore.

Two Little Vagabonds

London. Dec. 30.

Made by Louis Mercanton for Phocea (France) and handled here by the Gaumont Co., this film of Arthur Shirley and the late George R. Sims' melodrama, "The Two Little Vagabonds" opened for a run at the Empire Dec. 20. Ever since its original production at the Princess', in 1896, this melodrama has been one of the biggest draws both in London and the provinces and has had several West End revivals. As a picture it is likely to be as popular.

In adapting the story Louis Mercanton has adhered to the story and the main situations. True, his atmosphere is typically French, and his three hooligans, the Gaffer, Dido Bunce and the Coughdrop, are purely apache and have entirely dropped the characteristics which have endeared them to thousands of theatregoers. This, however, in no way injures the interest of the picture. Another production point which shows some negligence is that although the names of the characters as we know them are English, everything else is absolutely French.

Marion Thornton attempts to screen her sister from the results of a guilty intrigue, and as a result is blamed herself. Everything points to her guilt, and in his fury her husband gives their little boy, Gerald, to a traveling showman, the Gaffer. Years pass and we find Gerald, now known as Dick, a healthy lad, taking care of a consumptive youngster, Wally. Both boys are badly treated by the Gaffer and his hag of a wife. Meanwhile Marion has vainly tried to prove her innocence. Her one chance is to produce a packet of letters written by her sister, but these were stolen by a servant and given to Dido Bunce on the eve of the original catastrophe. The Gaffer tries to levy blackmail, and as a result the consumptive, Wally, is palmed off onto the Thorntons as their boy. He has every luxury, but the mother cannot kill the feeling in her heart that something is wrong.

When Dick arrives suspicion becomes certainty, and Thornton goes after the villains who have tricked him. This results in exciting rescues and other sensational events leading up to the death of the sick boy and the return of Dick to his reunited parents.

The production work and photography is excellent throughout. Mercanton has made the utmost of many beautiful interior and exterior settings and locations. The only English-speaking adult players are Marjorie Hume and Carlyle Blackwell; neither approach their French comrades in histrionic power. Lewis Shaw and Jean Forest are remarkably good as the boys, and a long cast, including Yvette Guilbert, is as near perfection as possible. This feature should be a success from every standpoint. *Gore.*

MOON OF ISRAEL

London, Dec. 15.

A curious situation has arisen in the pre-release presentation of "Moon of Israel" at the Pavilion. It is a Continental super film and released in this country under the Stoll Film Co. banner. As a production it enters into direct competition with "The Ten Commandments," the locale and many scenes bearing a close resemblance to the first half of the De Mille picture. It continues along those lines until "the big punch," which is the dividing of the Red Sea, permitting the Israelites to cross, later closing up and engulfing the Egyptians.

The present lease of the Pavilion is held by Famous Players, which recently showed its "Ten Commandments" picture at that house, and within a very few weeks later sublet the house for four weeks to the Stoll people for a picture that is so nearly identical in theme.

While the same background is employed in both pictures, "Moon of Israel" is based on Rider Haggard's novel of that name, which tells the beautiful love story of the son of Pharaoh for a Hebrew slave girl, in which he even goes so far as to forfeit the throne to which he is heir rather than persecute the Israelite slaves.

Adelqui Millar is the heir apparent with a fine sense of values and commanding dignity, but somehow leaves an unfavorable impression. The slave girl, by Maria Corda, is most effective. She is apparently a first-rate film artist, but both of them, as well as all the other players, suffer by comparison with the standard of film acting set by the American producers.

In direction and production "Moon

of Israel" is strong enough to enter into competition with the "Ten Commandments" anywhere in the world, even in the United States. Its success in America will depend to a large extent on how big and effective will be its publicity campaign, and if even so, it could still follow "Commandments." *Jolo.*

CRUISKEEN LAWN

London, 1 ec. 20.

This picture is not a joke. It is the first "all Irish" feature to be shown in London, and its producers evidently believe in it. It bears the official trade-mark of the Irish Republic and its registration number is 0829. Moreover, it is announced as "an Irish story acted and directed in Ireland by Irish people for the picturegoers of the world, a tonic for jaded patrons who are clamoring for something different in photoplays."

It is different from the majority of pictures seen within the last 10 years, in fact it could almost lower the existing record for the world's worst. It is bad, a thing of amateur experiment. The producer, his name appears to be Macdonagh, is responsible for everything, including the story. He probably "acts," but modesty compels him to refrain from acknowledging his guilt.

The leading people do not share the modesty of the producer-author. They are all poor and amateurish.

Even the chance to exploit the beautiful scenery of the Emerald Isle has been studiously avoided. *Gore.*

THE LOST WORLD

First National release, by arrangement with Watterson Rothacker. Directed by Harry O. Hoyt under the supervision of Earl Hudson. Adapted from Sir Arthur Conan Doyle's story by Marion Fairfax. Research and technical direction by Willie H. O'Brien. Photographed by Arthur Edeson. At the Astor theatre, N. Y., for a run beginning Feb. 8. Running time 104 mins.

Paula White	Bessie Love
Ed Malone	Lloyd Hughes
Sir John Roxton	Lewis Stone
Professor Challenger	Wallace Beery
Professor Summerlee	Arthur Hoyt
Mrs. Challenger	Margaret McWade
Austin, Challenger's Butler	Finch Smiles
Zambo	Jules Cowles
Apeman	Bull Montana
Colin McArdle	George Bunny
Major Hibbard	Charles Wellsley
Gladys Hungerford	Alma Bennett

Without doubt an unusual and interesting picture. A picture that will get a load of money at the boxoffice, create a tremendous amount of discussion and achieve about as much word of mouth advertising as anything has ever had in motion picture history. First National should clean up on this one, and Earl Hudson, who supervised the making, can be justly proud of what he has achieved.

Sir Arthur Conan Doyle's fantastical novel, "The Lost World," deals with a myth that there still exists in this world a plateau, somewhere in the unexplored wilds of South America, upon which the animals of prehistoric times still live. Animals which, as far as science could discover, had passed from the world some 10,000,000 years ago. This fantastical tale was made possible for the screen through the perfection of mechanical reproduction of the animals done in miniature and so superimposed on the actual scenes that were photographed that they appeared to be there full size.

The photography in itself is a work that must have taken a tremendous amount of energy and patience to achieve. But no matter what the cost, either in labor or money, the results fully justify the expenditure.

The story opens in London, where a scientist is being taken to task by his fellows because of their lack of faith in his reports of a trip into the unexplored portion of South America. He has presented these reports, and his fellows accused him of trying to perpetrate a fraud on them. He then offers to guide another expedition to the point where he made his discoveries, and the trip is financed by a newspaper.

The adventures of the quartet of men and the daughter of an explorer, who lost his life in the previous expedition, and the two servants that make up the party are both thrilling and amusing. But it is the remarkable antics of the mechanical figures, their struggle for existence, the protection of their young from the attacks of other tremendous beasts, which all figure in the tale, that make it stand out.

Finally, the return of the expedition is brought about after its members have managed to capture one of the great beasts, and they are about to bring the animal into London when it escapes and practically wrecks the entire city, spreading havoc and terror before it until finally it breaks through London Bridge and is last seen swimming down the Thames out into the open sea. In the latter scenes there are sufficient laughs to lift the audience from the slump that it falls into during the tremendous jungle scenes.

There is a love story that runs through the adventures, and in its enactment Bessie Love and Lloyd Hughes portray the principal roles. Miss Love particularly comes back into her own with a bang in this

picture and Lloyd does a really worth while piece of work as the juvenile lead. Lewis Stone and Wallace Beery bring to their respective roles the usual finished performances they are noted for, while Arthur Hoyt and Alma Bennett both give capable performances.

There is one shot in the picture showing Bessie Love beside a lighted candle in a cave that is as fine a piece of photographic art as has been seen in a long, long while.

"The Lost World" will get money in the special run houses, the first run theatres and all of those that play it subsequently, for it is a most unusual picture that has a most unusual appeal. *Fred.*

CHARLEY'S AUNT

A feature length Christie Comedy made in conjunction with the Ideal Films, Ltd., of London. From the stage farce by Brandon Thomas, adapted by F. McGrew Willis. Directed by Scott Sidney. Titled by Joseph Farnham and photographed by Gus Peterson and Paul Garnett. Distributed by Producers' Distributing Corp. At the B. S. Moss Colony for a run beginning Feb. 8. Running time, 75 mins.

Sir Fancourt Babberley, "Babbs"	Syd Chaplin
Ela Delahay	Ethel Shannon
Spettigue	James E. Page
Brassett, the Scout	Lucien Littlefield
Mr. Delahay	Alec B. Francis
Sir Francis Chesney	Phillips Smalley
Donna Lucia D'Alvardorez	Eulalie Jensen
Jack Chesney	David James
Charlie Wykeham	Jimmie Harrison
Amy	Mary Akin
Kitty	Priscilla Bonner

Here is a champ of champs as far as full length comedies are concerned. The old stage farce, "Charley's Aunt," has long since outlived its general popularity in America but is one of those plays that seem to be perennially popular with our English cousins. It makes a most laughable and intriguing picture and the general batter of discussion is as to why it has taken motion picture producers so long to discover it.

Incidentally, it gives Sydney Chaplin a straight comedy role that holds every sort of an opportunity. For good clean enactment of comedy and for real laugh purposes Syd Chaplin, who has always been designated as "Charlie Chaplin's brother," comes into his own and achieves a place for himself irrespective of his relationship in the world of the silent drama.

"Charley's Aunt," after the first part of the planting of the story, proves to be a succession of laughs from end to end. They are laughs that are achieved without "gagging" and from natural situations that are part of the farce itself. True, there are a couple of little gags injected but they play such a small part as to be negligible.

From the general acceptance by the public, as represented at the Colony at the first de luxe performance on Sunday, it would appear as though this picture was destined to break the house record, not only for receipts but for the length of run as well. The record now stands at three and a half weeks for "The Thief of Bagdad."

The story of the farce needs no extensive description. Suffice to say it is just the tale of three college boys who need an aunt to chaperon a party and impress one of the trio into service.

Syd Chaplin is in the role of the boy who enacts the eccentric old lady and he both scores in the characterization and in the "straight" role earlier in the picture. James E. Page who has played the role of Spettigue in the stage production more than 4,000 times just reveled in the part on the screen. He is set as far as the future is concerned when it comes to character playing. Ethel Shannon plays the ingenue

lead, opposite Chaplin, and does well with the little that falls to her lot. David James and Jimmie Harrison, as the two college chums, managed to extract all possibilities while Mary Akin and Priscilla Bonner, as the girl friends, were worth while. Alec B. Francis, Lucien Littlefield and Phillips Smalley all scored cleverly while Eulalie Jensen looked a million dollars as the dashing widow.

The action closely follows that of the play and because of that it is going to pull tremendously among the old timers who saw the original. In addition it is going to be tremendously amusing to those who not only never saw the play, but never heard of it.

This is Producers' Distributing Corporation's first shot at handling a picture for a tremendous gross but they need not fear for this one as it is certain to create a sales gross figure for them that they will have to shoot at for some time.

No exhibitor need worry about this one. It is going to get the money. *Fred.*

AS MAN DESIRES

A First National production from Gene Wright's novel, "Pandora La Croix." Milton Sills starred with Viola Dana, Ruth Clifford and Rosemary Theby featured. Directed by Irving Cummings. At the Strand, New York, week of Feb. 8. Running time, 81 mins.

Major John Craig	Milton Sills
Pandora La Croix	Viola Dana
Gloria Gordon	Ruth Clifford
Evelyn Beaudine	Rosemary Theby
Major Singh	Irving Cummings
Col. Carringford	Paul Nicholson
Gorilla Bagsley	Tom Kennedy
Toni	Hector Sarno
Major Gridley	Lou Payne
The Duchess	Anna May Walthal
Camille	Edneh Altemus
Watkins	Frank Leigh

This picture stands head and shoulders above the recent First National releases, for it has a definite and interesting story to tell, and tells it. Moreover, Sills and Miss Dana give fine performances. The production is also well done. Once or twice a painted backdrop on a natural scene was observed but it was a good backdrop, so the odds aren't heavy against it.

The plot concerns Major John Craig, connected with the British forces in India as a surgeon. He is engaged to marry Gloria Gordon, a girl of the army post, when shortly before the wedding his superior officer, a colonel, reveals that in the past he has had a hold on the girl and isn't figuring seriously on losing it. As the theme of the play is that any woman moulds her character to please that of the man she loves, the girl tells the colonel that so far as she's concerned he's demoted on her staff. But then her fiance walks in, smacks the colonel down and goes out. Immediately afterward, however, a native sergeant who has been beaten by the colonel whacks him several times with a candelabra and the rumor is immediately circulated that the major killed his superior.

Of course a flight is necessary. So to the South Seas he goes and becomes wealthy gathering pearls. Setting himself up as lord of an island, a native girl, Pan, attaches herself to him and, although in the past she has been a depraved little rat, she gets better and better until one day, through trickery, an agent is sent out, ostensibly to bring him back to justice. But the men who framed him are fooled, for the agent really came to say that he has been pardoned. That, however, is after the agent is suddenly stricken with appendicitis and a hurried operation performed. That incident was unnecessary and merely prolonged the running time. But the bad men come back, do a little shooting, and in this the native girl is killed, leaving the surgeon ready for his first love.

The story is full of interest and many of the water scenes beautiful. Added to the care taken in production details, the total of entertainment is high. And if Sills has any box-office pull it should be enhanced by such a vehicle.

The Dana support shouldn't hurt, either, so this one can be chalked up as an okay program proposition.

Sisk.

THE GREAT DIVIDE

Metro-Goldwyn-Mayer production of the William Vaughan Moody play. Adapted by Benjamin Glazer and directed by Reginald Barker. At the Capitol, New York, week of Feb. 8. Running time, 78 mins.

Ruth Jordan....................Alice Terry
Stephen Ghent..............Conway Tearle
"Dutch"......................Wallace Beery
Philip Jordan..............Huntly Gordon
Dr. Winthrop Newbury.......Allan Forrest

They've been heralding this one for a long time, probably figuring on the strength of its stage reputation, but the picture itself is a great disappointment. For as a variation of the "squaw man" idea it is mild in both theme and treatment and nobody does any acting, not even Wallace Beery. Henry Miller and Margaret Anglin played it at the old Bijou in New York and at that time it was one of the first short cast plays ever brought out in New York.

The plot concerns a beautiful girl left alone in her cabin over night. Three ruffians surprise her, but one of the crew, a gentleman, disposes of the other two after making the girl promise that she'll stick to him.

So she sticks, a child is eventually born and eventually she learns to love him. He had fallen in love with her on the spot. But her family, finding out the conditions under which she married him, gets a bit riled and they threaten to throw him out. This, however, amounts to little and the fadeout shows the one-time intruder accepted by the woman after he had magnanimously offered to skip, for her sake.

It is a western film and as such has some great pieces of scenery, but the only chunk of excitement is pulled when a bridge is washed away immediately after a daring rider has crossed it in the midst of a terrific storm.

The cast is good, with Alice Terry and Conway Tearle doing the best work. Wallace Beery is cast as one of the three attacking ruffians, but his work hasn't any comedy in it this time and it has been proven that the Beery forte is comedy. The others are sufficient unto their parts and that lets them out. There isn't any indication of great expenditure, although nothing is skimped.

The exhibitor playing this one will do well not to promise too much. It is actually nothing but an average program picture.

Sisk.

COMING THROUGH

Zukor-Lasky presentation, adapted by Paul Schofield from Jack Bethea's novel, "Bed Rock." Directed by Edward Sutherland, titles by Julian Johnson, released by Paramount. Running time, 66 mins. At Rivoli, New York, week of Feb. 8.

Tom Blackford...............Thomas Meighan
Alice Rand..........................Lila Lee
John Rand....................John Miltern
Joe Lawler...................Wallace Beery
Munds.......................Laurance Wheat
Shackleton..................Frank Campeau
Dr. Rawls....................Gus Weinberg

Whoever selects the stories for Tom Meighan, probably Meighan, should be called into a corner and told:

"There is no love interest in 'Coming Through,' and that is enough reason why Meighan shouldn't have come through in it."

He gets a chance to fight a roughneck villain all over some dirty mining machinery, and to wear a flannel shirt and high laced boots—and to hold his head in grief because his bride (Lila Lee) lives with him but "not as man and wife," a childish old subterfuge to keep suspense breathing.

He marries her in the first reel. Only a second of romancing is shown. Then he weds her suddenly because her rich father, his boss, wouldn't give him a raise. At least that is all the action reveals. When that is brought before the girl she logically believes it; so does the audience. It puts the beloved Tom in a most shabby light, and in that color he has to proceed through the whole picture.

Though he battles, puts a mining-camp saloon out of business, etc., and the technical elements are O. K., at no time is it made clear that this has anything to do with the "misunderstanding," except that he isn't exactly a "fortune hunter" and is willing to make his own way. That willingness is practically forced on him as the story is told.

Lila's role is negative. After wading through a few comings and goings of no dramatic or other consequence, she tells him solong and starts off with her father, to leave him behind. He fights his fight and wins, and returns to the desolate cottage, flings his hat off, and sits down to have a good, hard cry or something like it, when, lo! Lila.

She hasn't left him. Why she started if she didn't mean it, and why she didn't mean it if she started, is never explained. There is an abrupt clinch, with the supposition that thereafter they will "live as man and wife."

What this gets at the box offices it will have to get mainly on Meighan's name alone.

Lait.

Man Without a Country

William Fox production made from Edward Everett Hale's classic, "The Man Without a Country," and adapted to the screen by Robert N. Lee. Directed by Rowland V. Lee. At the Central, New York, Feb. 11.

Lieutenant Nolan..............Edward Hearn
Anne Bissell.................Pauline Starke
Mrs. Nolan..................Lucy Beaumont
Aaron Burr..................Richard Tucker
Lieut. Riddle..................Earle Metcalf
Lieut. Harper.................Edward Coxen
Major Bissell..................Wilfred Lucas
Col. Morgan.................Francis Powers
Peter..........................Harvey Clark
Capt. Shaw..................William Walling
Capt. Kearney..................Edward Piel
Admiral Decatur.........Edward Martindel
Capt. Danforth............William Conklin
President Jefferson.............Albert Hart
President Monroe.............Emmett King
President Lincoln...........George Billings
Mrs. Burke.....................Pauline Neff

In that long list of American historical pictures, and that list includes "The Birth of a Nation," "America," "The Covered Wagon," "The Iron Horse" and "Janice Meredith," none is so rich in the vivid portrayal of convincing patriotism as "The Man Without a Country." For this picture is as inspiring as any ever produced, its message is confined to no land or period, it neither preaches nor offers to teach, yet by its magnificently worked out story it delivers a crashing, thundering lesson that had its opening night audience working the handkerchiefs overtime. And any film that jumps from the screen into an audience is "there."

The theme, sad and pathetic, is forceful but different from the usual patriotic drama. There are but two efforts for a big mass thrill—and those efforts go across with a wow. The rest of the time is concerned with the story itself, and it's a great story. For a good many years it has been one of the classics of American literature. Primarily, because the theme was something surefire.

So is the production.

The story, which is probably familiar everywhere, bears this much retelling. Lieut. Nolan, a promising young officer in the American army, is attached to an army post on the frontier around 1800. Before him his father was in the army, so patriotism is rife in the family. Along comes Aaron Burr with his dream of a great western empire. He wins the lad to his cause, and when word comes from President Jefferson that Burr is to be apprehended, young Nolan is still firm in his belief that Burr is a great man and worth following. So the deluded youth, firm in a belief, is court-martialed and, after his jurors have returned, he is asked if he wishes to recant. Then he utters the words:

"Damn the United States. I hope that I may never hear of the United States again."

Then the sentence, he is sent aboard ship and word is given that he is never to hear the words "United States" again, nor is he to ever set foot in America. The long journey begins, a journey which carries him through the world and the administrations of 10 Presidents and during which time his faithful sweetheart, Anne Bissell, is untiring in her efforts to free him. But he is a man without a country, the government knows little of him.

Finally, however, Lieut. Nolan distinguishes himself in several heroisms at sea. In a fight with a pirate vessel he saves the day, and Miss Bissell, old and nearly dead, secures a pardon from Lincoln. Word of the pardon comes to Lieut. Nolan. He dies. On the end of a pier his waiting sweetheart also dies, but these deaths are gently done. After which comes the wallop. From the dead, gaunt spectre of a once promising man the figure of his youth arises, while down the cabin comes the spirit of his sweetheart in her youth. Around the shoulders of the lad she drapes the American flag and that is the finish. It signifies all anyone could want. It meant that at death Lieut. Nolan had absolved himself, that he had fought a hard fight and won.

Commercially, where "The Man Without a Country" has it over some of the others is that no conflicting nationalities are involved. There is no fighting with either the French or the British nations and the theme itself is as universal as music. Its one fault is that it starts slowly. Quite a few elisions could be made and some of the subtitles could come out. However, it is being shown in two sections, so a little padding was probably necessary.

The production looks like money in spots. The thing about it is that the theme has been rigidly adhered to, no cheap or sensational stuff is pulled nor is any effort made to drag in a detrimental scene. In the sea stuff a good storm is shown, the classic of the big cannon loose in a storm is also used, and in the sea fight between the U. S. ship and the pirate vessel good direction is apparent.

The cast is okay. Pauline Starke is probably the best name in the list and her performance of "Miss Bissell" is just as corking as that of Edward Hearn, a newcomer, who plays the "Nolan" role. Everybody else is up to scratch, but it is the tremendous theme itself and the innumerable opportunities it offers for tieups of the finest type which make it something out of the ordinary.

William Fox was born a Hungarian. He is now a naturalized American and has to his everlasting credit the distinction of having produced a dramatization of America's greatest patriotic classic. It is a production that in the picture houses, once pared and shortened, will stand up with the best of them.

Sisk.

QUO VADIS?

A Unione Cinematografica Italiana production presented by First National. From the novel and play by Henry Sienkiewicz; directed by Arturo Ambrosio, assisted by Gabriellino D'Annunzio and George Jacoby. At the Apollo theatre, New York, for a run Feb. 15. Running time, 102 mins.

Nero..........................Emil Jannings
Lygia.....................Lillian Hall Davis
Poppaca...................Elena Di Sangro
Domitilla............................Elga Brink
Eunice.....................Rina De Liguoro
Vinicius....................Alphons Fryland
Ursus....................Bruto Castellani
Cheilon Cheilondies..............Gino Viotti
Tigellinus........................R. Van Riel
Petronius.....................Andree Habay

The first of the screen productions of "Quo Vadis" that was made abroad came at a time when the entire film industry was still in its swaddling clothes, and because of this the picture was a distinct achievement. The present production, with Emil Jannings as the star, does not stand out as anything remarkable. The industry has gone forward tremendously since the first "Quo Vadis" was made, but in this present picture one does not find any great exposition of the advancement. "Quo Vadis," while a big picture in a way, is not one that is going to set the country afire, nor is it of the calibre to warrant it being set before the public as a road show. It will stand up in the exploitation runs well enough and in the regular run of motion picture theatres it should attract business, but it is not $2 road show material.

A great measure of the disappointment is undoubtedly due to the expectations that one had of the performance that Jannings was to give as Nero and the fact that this player did not give something away from the ordinary.

The big punches of the picture are all retained for the second half of the film. They are the burning of Rome and the slaughter of the Christians in the Circus. Here they are shown with the lions turned loose to tear them limb from limb; later others are shown lashed to the chariot wheels, and the final scene with the ever-charming Lygia lashed to the back of a maddened bull is rescued by the giant Ursus, whose tremendous strength turns the neck of the bull.

The entire forepart of the picture is given over to the planting of the story and the holding of Roman revels, in which old Nero proved that he was "just a good man," and although an Emperor, he was "just a man" when the Empress walked in on him at the time when he was trying to force his attention on Lygia.

There are any number of terrific mob "shots," but the best handled are the scenes in the Circus when the Christians are slaughtered. Here thousands upon thousands of men and women are shown reveling in the sport that the executions are affording them.

The chariot race scenes with seven cars drawn by four horses, each coming down the track on either side of the festooned pillars in the center of the circus, is a really imposing sight.

Andree Habay, who plays the role of Petronius, gives really the best performance of the picture, with Alphons Fryland as Vinicius a strong runner-up for honors. Lillian Hall Davis plays Lygia convincingly, and Elena Di Sangro as the Empress is a rather imposing figure. *Fred.*

NEW TOYS

Inspiration Pictures presentation, John Robertson production, First National release; adapted by Josephine Lovett from the play by M. H. Gropper and Oscar Hammerstein, II; titles by Agnes Smith. At Strand, N. Y., week of Feb. 15. Running time, 82 mins.

Will Webb............Richard Barthelmess
Mary Lane......................Mary Hay
Natalie Woods...........Katherine Wilson
Sam Clark................Francis Conlon
Tom Lawrence.............Clifton Webb
Mrs. Lane..............Bijou Fernandez
Manager..................Jules Jordan
Manager..............Jacob Kingsbury
Doorman..............Tammany Young
Baby........................Pat O'Connor

Here is an excellent example of how a bad play can make a good film. And still it leaves much to be desired. If anything is often at fault in "the movies" it is the scenario. In this instance the scenario is more than perfect, it is constructive, salutary. To one who suffered through the spoken play, this is palpable.

The next usual discrepancy is the direction. That, also, in this case is practically past reproach. The titles are unusually fine, funny and wise. What, then? The matrimonial complex.

Only "show business" is burdened with the responsibilities in artistic and professional manifestations of domestic relations. And those who know it best know that this is no frivolous or negligible element in the dramatic arts. In this connection it chances to be the domestic attachment of Richard Barthelmess.

Barthelmess is married to Mary Hay, a charming young woman, an artiste in her own right, a very sweet dancer, a Ziegfeld beauty.

But, Miss Hay does not screen, nor is she a screen actress, though some of the reigning comediennes might study her technique and learn from her some worth-while tricks of comedy business.

There is no doubt that, had Miss Hay been anyone other than Mrs. Barthelmess she would not have been cast for the feminine lead, featured, in "New Toys." And, since she has neither the experience nor many of the other faculties requisite for such a responsibility, she makes the otherwise past-par picture spotty, even though she does here and there contribute moments which

the most expert feminine stars of the celluloid, one or two excepted, would "muff."

Miss Hay's makeup is not for the Cooper-Hewitts, nor is her very saucy but not film-proof profile. Her principal assets, which made her famous on the Ziegfeld roof, get small chance to twinkle. Therefore, Barthelmess, who has not been anything but a "hug-the-girl-in-the-fade-out "hero" since "Broken Blossoms," is handicapped in probably the best work he ever did for the screen.

Clifton Webb, another newcomer, plays the role of an amateur director a la "nance," to the amusement of the audience but not to the advantage of the after-effect, as he takes from the excellent screen-story its plausibility, and from half of it its dramatic element of "danger"; for he is wooing the bride while the bridegroom's ex-fiancee is rushing him.

And how differently she does it. Her name is Katherine Wilson, to this reviewer thereunto unknown, but a bearcat. Miss Wilson plays it from the floor up, every fiber of her. She sustains the verisimilitude, and so does Barthelmess, while the other two, the opposite sides of the quadrangular figure, clown it, foozle it and bungle it, even though they do make for some occasional explosive laughs.

"New Toys" just misses being a great money picture and, considering that it cannot have cost much, it thus misses a great opportunity. It is far from a bad programmer at that. *Lait.*

THE MONSTER

A Roland West production released by Metro-Goldwyn. From the stage play by Crane Wilbur; directed by Roland West. Titles by C. Gardner Sullivan. At the Capitol, New York. week Feb. 15. Running time, 63 mins.

Dr. Ziska....................Lon Chaney
Betty Watson............Gertrude Olmsted
Watson's Head Clerk........Hellam Croley
Under Clerk.................Johnny Arthur
Constable..............Charles A. Sellon
Caliban....................Walter James
Daffy Dan..................Knute Erickson
Rigo......................George Austin
Luke Watson.............Edward McQuade
Mrs. Watson................Ethel Wales

"The Monster" was a corking stage thriller. As a picture it proves to be somewhat suspenseful, but it seemingly is played too fast to get the full effectiveness that there was in the play. It has a couple of good laughs in it and it gives Johnny Arthur an opportunity to shine almost as bright as Harry Myers did in "A Connecticut Yanke—" The picture as a whole, however, falls somewhat short of expectations, although it should prove a rather consistent money-maker of the program variety. The fact that it has Lon Chaney as the star should be of help to the box office.

One thing that Roland West must be given credit for was the selection of a cast to enact the characters of the piece. He has Knute Erickson doing the silly nut bit; Lon Chaney in the title role as Dr. Ziska; Walter James, who was in the original cast, as the silent slave, while Gertrude Olmsted and Johnny Arthur carry the love interest.

Lon Chaney does not make the crazed surgeon as terrifying a picture as he might have, and in that the film lets down to a certain extent.

The story tells of one of the inmates of a sanitarium taking over possession of the building and imprisoning the physician in charge in the cellar. Then the crazed surgeon, who is in command, evolves a scheme to entrap travelers so that he may obtain subjects on which to carry out his surgical experiments. The disappearance of a wealthy farmer on his way home brings the detective of the insurance company to the ground to solve the mystery,

while the hero, who has completed a correspondence school course in detecting, is also on the job. He stumbles into the building and arrives just before his sweetheart and his rival, who have been trapped by the crazed surgeon servants, arrive. Then come the complications. The three are prisoners and trying to escape. Finally the hero manages to entrap all of the crazed ones so that it is possible for him to summon help and rescue his girl, his rival and himself.

The picture ends rather abruptly with a fade-out of the hero and the girl in a motor car breaking all the speed records.

A slower tempo in the playing of the scenes in the sanitarium would have added much to the suspense qualities of the picture. *Fred.*

TOP OF THE WORLD

Paramount production of Ethel M. Dell's novel. Adapted to the screen by Jack Cunningham and directed by George Melford. Anna Q. Nilsson, James Kirkwood, Raymond Hatton and Sheldon Lewis featured. At the Rivoli, New York, Feb. 15. Running time, 72 mins.

Sylvia Ingleton..............Anna Q. Nilsson
Burk Ranger }
Guy Ranger }.............James Kirkwood
Capt. Preston................Raymond Hatton
Saul Kieff................Sheldon Lewis
Hans Schafen............Charles A. Post
Squire Ingleton..........Joseph Kilgour
Mrs. Ingleton.............Mary Mersch
Mary Ann..............Mabel Van Buren
Joe........................Frank Jonasson
Vreiboom..................Lorimer Jonston

This member of the second "Famous Forty" series is a good picture for any film house. It is good in spite of the terrible acting by one or two of the cast, for the story is well knit and strong, capable of withstanding the Thespian atrocities.

It is taken from one of Ethel Dell's "hot" yarns and put into a well-censored picture which has been given the usual F.-P. elaborate and careful production. Incidentally, it is easy to carp at Famous for some of their stories once in a while and for some of the women stars they exploit as being actresses, but nobody can honestly kick at the mechanical and setting details which mark all their pictures, for it is everywhere apparent that this firm knows and has the technical stuff down "pat."

"Top of the World" is a story of South Africa and of a woman who loved a drunkard. Drunkards, as a rule, are pretty terrible people, and the drunkard in this was worse than the rule. He chucked everything for booze, and his cousin, who resembled him greatly, married the gal who left her 'appy 'ome in Merrie Hengland to get away from a not-so-pleasant stepmother.

Then the drunk tried to straighten himself up, but it didn't work. Yet the girl, although married to the cousin, figured it as one of those married-in-name-only games, and really loved the stew. But when the drunk stole his brother's money and gambled it away, everybody got pretty peeved. Finally, however, came a corking good flood and the bad boy got drowned while the good little boy and the good little girl managed to live through it all and clinch for the finale.

The story has interesting ramifications and, due to the intelligent direction and splendid settings, both interior and exterior, the film took on values for which neither the book nor the scenario can claim credit.

To say much in praise of the acting would be inaccurate. Miss Nilsson really hasn't much else to do except look pretty. James Kirkwood, however, in a double role, is not so happily cast. His portrayal of the drunken brother was done with an abundance of exaggeration, while the sober guy could have passed for a Sunday school super-

intendent in any C. E. convention. Hatton's work consisted of a two-minute conventional bit, while Sheldon Lewis, in a villain role, did pretty much as he was told, and that's all.

From this it may be gathered that "The Top of the World" is hoke. It is precisely that. But it is well mounted and well handled hoke and, in other words, is buncombe stuff directed and mounted by people who have a fair idea of what the people want.

The picture may be safely figured as a program bet. It has several thrills and a flock of love making. *Sisk.*

THE PARASITE

A screen version of the Helen R. Martin novel, adapted by Eve Unsell. Produced by B. P. Schulberg for Preferred Pictures. Directed by Louis Gasnier, with Owen Moore and Madge Bellamy starred. At the Piccadilly, New York, week of Feb. 14. Running time, 70 mins.

Arthur Randall..............Owen Moore
Joan Laird.................Madge Bellamy
Laura....................Lilyan Tashman
Mrs. Laird..................Mary Carr
Dr. Brookes.............Bryant Washburn
Bobby.....................Bruce Guerin
Sally Van Bueren...........Dorothy Dwan

Schulberg has produced better pictures than this. "The Parasite" is a poor and badly directed mixture of good love and bad, hate and a would-be "thrill," which never materializes. At least two people are at fault, the scenarist and the director, Louis Gasnier, who has done hotchy-botch with several scenes. The scenarist has pushed out a script as full of holes as a sieve, which hasn't helped any.

The story briefly, is this. In high society, Arthur Randall and his wife have been divorced. The wife Laura, finds that hubby has become famous since she left him, so on the pretext of wanting their child back wifie makes a play, but loses out. When the child becomes ill Joan Laird, a good kid, but one burdened with a proud mother, helps Randall and the little boy becomes endeared to her and her to him. In that manner she and her mother become occupants of the Randall home, while the world looks on and calls them parasites. The ex-wife, however, still in an effort to get the child, writes a letter to Miss Laird concerning the divorce of her husband, and that letter throws the man in a bad light. Hence, when he proposes she turns him down.

Then Randall goes on a trip. While away the son is kidanpped from Joan. She starts in hot pursuit after Laura and Dr. Brookes, who took the boy from her. But they get bumped off in a tremendous auto accident, but the boy gets off okay. Rescuing him, Joan gets lost in the hills. For three days they are unable to move because she hurt her ankle, and the boy begins to cry for his cakes. Then the girl uses her nut, and cracks an empty whiskey bottle and cuts into her arm until the blood flows. With this blood she nourishes the boy, and so, when the rescuers do arrive, she is in pretty solid with Randall. Result: she gets herself a papa and little Bobby gets himself a new mamma.

Of the cast Owen Moore alone is capable. Miss Bellamy isn't as good as recently in "The Dancers," and much of her emoting seems artificial. Little Bruce Guerin once more proves himself a static and uninteresting child actor, who is either being constantly misdirected or who is without any real histrionic promise. Lilyan Tashman has a so-so part, to which she contributes so-so acting, while Mary Carr is once more in a mother part, badly handled in this instance. Dorothy Dwan, Larry Semon's new wife, is in a small part, and is as pretty as a certified check.

The bad direction, coupled with the weakness of the story, makes this one but a mediocre program bet. It's rather a shame, too, for the technical work and the settings are finely done.

Sisk.

CHU CHIN CHOW

Screen adaptation of the stage spectacle. Made in England by Graham Wilcox Productions, Ltd., and distributed here by Metro-Goldwyn. Story by Oscar Asche and Frederick Norton. Directed by N. G. Arnold. At the Piccadilly, New York. Running time, 65 mins.

Zahrat	Betty Blythe
About Hassan	Herbert Langley
Alcolom	Eva Moore
Kasim Baba	Randle Ayrton
Omar	Jameson Thomas
Ali Baba	Judd Green
The Cobbler	Jeff Barlow
Mukbill	Olaf Hytten
The Dancer	Dacia
Mububah	Dora Lewis

The tip-off was obvious on "Chu Chin Chow." It had to be a spectacle, and to maintain that reputation lavishness would be its primary requisite. As it is screening here "Chu Chin Chow" is a spectacle, crudely directed, with its cast made up of crepe-adorned characters whose comedy falls short and whose inability to express pathos is pathetic.

However, the direction is most at fault. The utter lack of suspense, the naivete with which certain important scenes are passed over and the bad handling of mobs combine to down whatever chances the film might have had on the strength of the stage production.

The story concerns Zahrat, a good-looking girl, who leaves most of her clothing home when she goes loving. Zahrat is to be married and, on her wedding day, Abou Hassan, the robber chief, comes with his thieves and takes her away. But an old man discovers the cave of the thieves, does himself an "Open Sesame" with the door and grabs a flock of dough and jewelry. Besides which he sees the girl, frees her and flees. Back home, he sets up a handsome shop with the money, but the robber, being smart and figuring out that the old man must have stolen it, frames it with his men for a good butcher party. Zahrat, however, is grateful, and nips his plan in the bud by pouring hot oil over the robbers as they lay concealed in large vessels. And so the robber chieftain is killed and the lovers united.

Treated by somebody with a sense of humor, it would have made a corking comedy or, treated masterfully, it would have been a fine spectacle; but the sense of illusion is missing. The staging is heavy-handed and the sense of a fairy story is never maintained.

"Chu Chin Chow" seems a muffed opportunity which will be handicapped by the advertising of its first audience.

Sisk.

EPIC MT. EVEREST

A film record of the Norton expedition to reach the top of Mount Everest, presented by J. G. Wainwright. Shown to the press Feb. 12 in New York. Running time, 81 mins.

This film of the heroic efforts made by a band of pioneers to reach the top of Mount Everest, the highest peak of all the Himalayas, the highest mountain range in the world, may have a unique and extraordinary value as a historic record and it might be successfully exploited as an educational picture possibly with a lecture, but in the commercial theatre it is without value whatsoever unless cut down to such length that will bring it into the classification of a "short."

The present running time of an hour and 21 minutes is far too long,

carrying the details of the expedition, the film becomes rather tiresome because of the fact that there has been no attempt in the editing of the picture to inject the personal element. Had this been done in the early part of the picture, and had the audience been enlightened as to some of the facts regarding the expedition in the lead title, they possibly might have had a greater interest in the events which followed.

As it is, the picture starts off with the information that Mount Everest is the one point in the world that still holds a lure for the explorer, because man has conquered all other points, the poles, the sea and the lands. This title is rather too lengthy, and, although the language is flowery, it will mean nothing to a picture audience. They want facts and they want personalities, and if there are any close-up shots of the members of the party they should, by all means, be used at the outset of the picture, especially pictures of Mallory and Irvine, who both lost their lives in the ascent.

Throughout the picture there are scenes that should be, and could readily be, shortened, and some that could be cut altogether. The one of the picking vermin from a child's head and eating it is outstanding.

Pictorially, the picture has some great shots, and undoubtedly the story of the climb told in a more brief form than at present would be interesting.

Fred.

THUNDERING HERD

Famous Players-Lasky production of Zane Grey's story. Directed by Irvin Willat. Reviewed at special showing at Rialto theatre, New York, Feb. 24. Running time, 70 minutes.

Here is the greatest western picture since "The Covered Wagon" and if anything it is as great, if not greater than that Western epic at least from the standpoint of thrills. For pure punch this production is pre-eminent. From a box office standpoint it should score terrifically. It is a picture that everyone in every audience that sees it is going to go out and boost.

The credit for the wallop goes to the director, Irvin Willat, who certainly has turned out a masterpiece of screen art in this production. It is a western that carries its thrilling punches done in snow. Willat's composition photographically is something that stands out tremendously. He has achieved groupings and scenes that rival the best that that great artist of the west Frederick Remington, has done. Willat qualifies as the Remington of the screen after this one.

Heading the cast are Jack Holt, Lois Wilson, Noah Beery and Raymond Hatton. This quartet stand out wonderfully well in their characterizations. Miss Wilson is coming along so strongly in pictures of this nature that it won't be long when the screen will have a woman western star and her name will be Lois Wilson. Jack Holt is doing some of the best work that he has ever done before the camera. Noah Beery is lighter in tone playing the heavy than usual and because of this creates a much better impression. Hatton with his suppressed comedy qualifies perfectly, but there is another member of the cast to whom all credit should be given, Eulalie Jensen. Miss Jensen enacts the role of a heavy that is willing to stick a knife or fire a shot into anyone that crosses her and the manner in which she registers it makes her stand out remarkably. The rather youthful Maxine Elliott Hicks with only a rather small bit handles it sufficiently well to warrant notice.

But it isn't the cast, the director, the story or the photography that makes "The Thundering Herd" a truly great picture. It is the thrills. They come along in the snow scenes and are without doubt the greatest punch wallops that have been seen on the screen in a long long while. So thrilling are the crashes of the wagons, the falling and kicking of the horses that women in the audience gasp as they come to pass.

The story of "The Thundering Herd" is that of the group of buffalo killers that invaded the territory which were the feeding grounds for the great herds of bison that formerly thundered over the plains. They were professional killers who were after the hides. They are first introduced at a small trading post where they are getting the wagon trains together for the final drive to the killing grounds. All sorts, from the killers who are professional huntsmen, the fortune seekers who have left their farms in Illinois and Indiana to gather wealth in buffalo hides (for hides brought $3 each in those days) and a good day's kill might mean 200 hides; to the fugitives from justice, some with a hangman's noose over their heads if they were ever caught and the stick-up boys who were also on the hide out.

In one group from Illinois are father and son, wife and daughter represented with an old buffalo hunter, his nephew, a pal and a younger man. In another there is a young girl, her step-father and a woman he married after the girl's mother's death together with three men of shady character.

It is with this set of principals that the story concerns itself. The

girl is anxious to get away from her evil companions. The young man with the other party falls in love with her but after saving her from the grasp of the dance hall proprietor of the trading post loses sight of her for her step-father starts off that same night. Later the two again meet with the result that they are once more parted through the step-father getting the drop on the youngster and then after tying his hands to the pommel of his saddle, starts his horse off and fires a shot into the hero.

But on the final day of the story things happen fast. The Indians aroused because they are starving as all of the buffalo have been driven off by the white hunters, rise and start on the war path. A messenger rides to all the little wagon trains and bids them to a rendezvous to make a stand against the savages. That message comes a little late to the train of the Illinois party, but soon enough to start the hero on the trail for the girl he loves.

Meantime in that camp a double murder has been committed by the woman of the leader, and he in turn kills her when she tries to stab him in a jealous rage, with he being ~~killed by the other remaining man~~ ~~in order to save the girl, her~~ ~~rescues in turn remaining behind~~ to fight off the Indians so that she can make her escape. With the savages on her trail she drives a four-horse outfit helter skelter across the snows, while the hero comes cutting across country to come to her rescue, but it is the thundering herd of bison started on a stampede south because of the snow that intervenes and cuts her off from the savages, so that the hero can just ride up in time to pull her to his horse from the path of the oncoming buffalo. That relates a few of the first thrills.

Then for the big stuff. A wagon train unable to reach the meeting place surrounded by galloping Indians and a fight for life, with the rescuers coming in wagons and a horseback over the ice and snow, with horses slipping and falling, wagons skidding in complete circles across a lake of ice and crashing into each other, horses falling into dead falls covered with snow and all the while the fight with the Indians going on. It is a wow of a rise to the rescue, one that has the audience right on edge and it finished with some of the best Indian battle stuff that has been shown in a long, long while.

In the finish the lovers are reunited and all ends happily with a corking silhouette of an Indian on his pony on a hill top watching the wagons wind away.

Then comes an inserted letter from the Department of the Interior informing the public that in reality there were no buffalo killed or any cruelty inflicted in the making of the picture, which was a mighty good idea for a lot of fanatics might have started letter writing to the papers and to Washington protesting against the inhumanity of man to dumb beasts in order to achieve a picture that has box office angles.

No matter what happens or where you are if you get a chance to grab "The Thundering Herd" do so and play it for all that it is worth, for it is certain to get the big money. There are few pictures I want to see twice but this is one of them.

Fred.

In a review of "Thundering Herd," Irvin Willat was erroneously credited with the direction instead of William K. Howard who directed the feature.

Miracle of the Wolves

Produced under the direction of the French Government. Retailing the early history of France. Directed by Raymond Bernard. Presented in New York under the auspices of a committee composed of Barron Collier, Rodman Wanamaker, William Wrigley, Jr., William Ziegler, Jr., Cornelius Vanderbilt, Jr., R. A. C. Smith, Myron T. Herrick and Gen. Coleman duPont. At the Criterion, New York, for a run beginning Feb. 23. Running time, 113 minutes.

Jeanne Fouquet	Yvonne Sergyl
Robert Cottereau	Romuald Joube
Louis XI	Charles Dullin
Charles the Bold	Vanni Marcoux
De Chateauneuf	Gaston Modor
Maitre Fouquet	Georges Maupin
Bische	Armand Bernard
Tristan l'Hermite	Phillipe Heriat

"The Miracle of the Wolves" heralded heavily as a super-special made in France was viewed for the first time at the Criterion Monday night by an audience that far from filled the little theatre even though the box office was announcing to late comers that the house was entirely sold out. It had many empty seats and those that viewed the picture failed to grow enthusiastic over it.

There was nothing to grow enthusiastic about. The big scene from which the production derives its name resolves itself into seven police dogs, well trained in protection and the fight they put up with the men was to all appearances a real one. Some of the shots were sufficient to make anyone versed with the tactics of these animals believe the wolves were tearing at the very vitals of the men. It was a good fight while it lasted and thrilling enough to please but it isn't enough to make the picture go over in America with anything like a bang.

There were some tremendous battle scenes when Charles the Bold and his army attacked the walled city, but there was nothing in all of this that transcended the tremendous walled battle scenes that Griffith gave in "Intolerence," nor was there anything in the entire picture that has not been seen done as well if not better in the past.

From a box office standpoint "The Miracle of the Wolves" will for a period of four weeks possibly do a good business at the Criterion but it is safe to predict that won't be turning away any business even for this limited period. If in for a run of longer duration than that it will not hold up. In the pre-release first runs it may do business in spots but in the regular run of picture theatres the exhibitors do not want to count on it bringing anything like real money. There is no one that the general run of fans in America are acquainted with in the cast, the title of the picture does not mean anything in particular, and the picture itself after all is another costume affair and that about sums it up.

It is a review of the history of France from 1461 on, following the period of 100 years of war the Kingdom went through. It picks up the history from the time that Louis XI was exiled by his father and was given refuge in Burgundy.

At the same time there is a love tale that runs through the picture. It concerns Jeanne Fouquet, goddaughter of Louis and Robert Cottereau, a follower of Charles the Bold. They remained parted through the entire story until the finish, after the retreat of Charles and his hosts, when they are together for a clinch at the final fadeout. The director has failed in keeping his love story in the foreground and while he undoubtedly has stuck to historical fact in the making of his picture, the love theme would have proved far more interesting to American audiences than the recital of the history of France.

The early part of the picture is a slow recital of events leading up to the time that Louis XI takes the throne after the death of his father. Then comes the initial attempt of the hosts of Burgundy to assert themselves and at the finish of the first half of the picture, there are some ancient battle scenes most cleverly handled. This takes up the final five minutes of the pre-intermission section after 45 minutes of slow moving planting.

The second section is almost all war culminating in the final big battle scenes before the walled city. This is by far the best that the picture affords.

The title is derived from the scene where Jeanne in order to save the life of her King at her fathr's urging carries a message to the stronghold of the Burgundy Princes and the camp of Charles where the King is being held prisoner. De Chatenunuef, a follower of Charles and desirous that his master shall become King of France, tries to stop the message. With some of his men he tracks down the girl through the snows, but the wolves appear just as he is about to seize her. After letting her pass, the wolves leap upon the men when they try to follow her. She makes good her escape and arrives in time to save the King's life.

Some of the detail in production is poorly handled especially the snow storm scenes which show an artificiality surprising at this late date in picture production.

In the cast of the French players there is no one that offers anything in particular any American producer would want with the possible exception of the leading lady, who while a little mature for ingenue leads in this country, might develop as a vamp type.

There is hardly a chance that "The Miracle of the Wolves" will get very far on this side of the Atlantic, although in Paris it was the first motion picture shown at the Grand Opera. *Fred*

LEARNING TO LOVE

Joseph M. Schenck presentation, First National release, starring Constance Talmadge, featuring Antonio Moreno. Story and screen version by John Emerson and Anita Loos. Directed by Sidney Franklin. Running time, 79 mins. At the Strand, New York, week of Feb. 22.

Patricia Stanhope	Constance Talmadge
Scott Warner	Antonio Moreno
Aunt Virginia	Emily Fitzroy
Tom Morton	Johnny Harron
Billy Carmichael	Ray Hallor
John the Barber	Alf Goulding
Prof. Bonnard	Wallace MacDonald
Aunt Penelope	Edythe Chapman
Count Coo-Coo	Byron Munson
Butler	Edgar Norton
Butler	Percy Williams

A typical Connie Talmadge feature, except that it is an original story instead of an adapted play. As a vehicle it is built to order, and Emerson and Loos, among the first and foremost artists at that specialty, are as screen-sure as usual in "Learning to Love," a good title, by the way, especially for this star.

The plot is a combination of stable values, and, in description, would not measure up as much of a story. But for picturization, and with Connie in view, it makes snappy and happy theatre material, which, after all, often brings home more bacon than sheer art.

It tells of a willful young heiress, just coming from finishing school, who is a natural-born "necker," "petter," kisser and trifler. She flits from man to man, and, as she is Connie Talmadge, she naturally leaves them all fighting mad, fuming and maudlin. This gets her good name talked about and printed about.

Of course, she meets the man she really loves—her guardian, played by Moreno. He is a sane gentleman, and is shocked and wounded by the frivolous behavior of his ward and the contempt she seems to have for her own reputation. He takes her overtures at him as merely another of her light-hearted jests. He is severe, cold and, at times, even harsh. The more does that make her want him. Finally he threatens that the next man she gets into a scandal with he will force her to marry. So she promptly, and almost villainously, gets herself into a scan- with him by sneaking into his apartment and spending the night there. When he frantically gets her an alibi to save the aftermath, she telephones the facts to a gossip sheet. He then gallantly marries her.

On the wedding night he upbraids her and walks out. She goes to Europe, heartsick, to get a Paris divorce. On the ship she meets an exfiance, who is drinking himself to death over her, and she again falls, promising to marry him when she is freed. But the husband comes to Paris, says he did it to "teach her a lesson," that he always loved her but had to make her see the light. They go to a cafe, and the desperate fiance is soused with a boulevard vamp.

The fadeout is different and smart. The lackey is seen, next morning, bringing back, polished, Moreno's manly shoes, and, beside them, Connie's dainty mules.

It isn't much of a "lesson," as the girl who makes all the mischief and virtually blackmails a man into marrying her gets the happiness she was after, while the men are left laid out in miserable heaps. But the screen isn't a sermon sheet, and, besides, Connie's mission is scarcely that of a moralizer.

The production is adequate, the direction is unusually intelligent, colorful and spirited and the acting is of the best camera grade. Moreno is not at his full advantage in a civilian-clothes part, but makes a strong figure as Miss Talmadge's lead in a role not up to some more important work he has done in the past. The cast is ideal in types, otherwise.

This picture should rank at the box office and in all other estimates of cinema values with Miss Talmadge's worth-while output.

Lait.

OH, DOCTOR!

Screen adaptation of the Harry Leon Wilson short story. Produced by Universal and directed by Harry Pollard. Reginald Denny starred, with Mary Astor featured. Reviewed at the Piccadilly, New York, week Feb. 23. Running time, 70 minutes.

Rufus Billops, Jr.	Reginald Denny
Dolores Hicks	Mary Astor
Mr. Clinch	Otis Harlan
Mr. McIntosh	William Mong
Mr. Peck	Tom Ricketts
Aunt Beulah	Lucille Ward
Buzz Titus	Mike Donlin
Osteopath	Blanche Payson

It was long ago, when Macauley wrote his famous essay on Samuel Johnson, that the word "hypochondriac" came into general use, for every schoolboy had to learn that long chapter which began: "In the years which followed, Johnson was an incurable hypochondriac." At that time they learned that the word referred to a person who looked continually on the gloomy side of things with even greater vigor than a pessimist. Librettists have used the pill-taking hypochondriac innumerable times, witness "Firefly" and the secretary character there. Jenkins. Then in the movies and on the stage it has been worked to death. Recently Harold Lloyd used it, but in "Oh, Doctor," Harry Leon Wilson and Reginald Denny have used it in a manner far superior to any of the others.

The plot of this picture concerns young Billops, a lad chronically ill and always expecting to die. In California, where he goes for his last days, a physician advises him to go to a sanitarium. Telling the medico he hasn't the money, Doc arranges with three old geezers to advance him $100,000 against $750,000 which he will inherit in three years. And the boy, not sure he will live three years, deeds over his inheritance to the old timers, who as comedy characters, are similar to the "Three Wise Fools" of recent stage fame.

But a pretty nurse comes on the scene, and with her love interest. So, to cure himself of fear, Billops successively tries auto racing, motorcycle riding and finally begins painting a flagpole hundreds of feet in the air. At these escapades the old men get frightened and are finally persuaded to tone down their contract a bit, so that at the termination of the three years they will receive but their principal and interest.

And the boy comes through it all, winning the girl and conquering himself of fear and a nance-like series of gestures that were good for howls whenever used.

The titles are corking. Asked whether he dove a racing car, the hero answered, "I drove my mother's electric as a boy." There are others like that, all wows when used with the action, which is mainly built on sure-fire situations splendidly staged and directed.

In Reginald Denny Universal has a star whose recent stuff has been riotously funny. It hasn't received much big-time showing, however, and maybe for that reason he isn't as famous as he should be. But in some houses he has, like Johnny Hines, built up a clientele which keeps grosses at a good level. But let this picture get any kind of distribution break—and some effective exploitation—and Denny's next will be looked forward to with real anticipation. Here his performance is always first rate. Aided as it is by one of the best farces ever transferred to the screen, it looks like a pipe to go out and clean up. Whether it will be held over at the Piccadilly is unknown, for that house is booked well ahead, but right now it is safe to hazard the prediction that the gross this week will be well over the average, and it is patent that in a new house grosses are dependent almost entirely upon the feature.

Mary Astor in support is a good-looking girl who does her acting chores well, while the three old fogies are played with much comedy gusto by fat Otis Harlan and the lean William Mong and Tom Ricketts. Much footage is given to these boys, and not an inch is wasted. They are all necessary to a plot which develops speedily and which is not impeded by an unnecessary center of the stage urge.

"Oh, Doctor" compares with the best in screen farces. It doesn't take a seer's mind to see that it is the type which gives satisfaction to both exhibitor and audience, for certainly it isn't under the heavy expense of salaries, etc., which weigh down the others. *Sisk.*

Salome of the Tenements

Sidney Olcott production. Presented by Adolph Zukor and Jesse L. Lasky. From the novel by Anzia Yezierska, adapted by Sonya Levien. Featuring Jetta Goudal, Godfrey Tearle and Jose Ruben. Shown at the Rialto, New York, week Feb. 22. Running time, 69 minutes.

Sonya Mendel	Jetta Goudal
John Manning	Godfrey Tearle
Jakey Solomon	Jose Ruben
Jacob Lipkin	Lazar Freed
Gittel Stein	Irma Lerner
Mrs. Peltz	Sonya Nodell
Banker Ben	Elihu Tenenholtz
Mrs. Solomon	Mrs. Weintraub

"Salome of the Tenements" is a disappointment as a picture and will be a disappointment at the box office for any one that expected big things of the production. It has all the earmarks of something that had been hashed and rehashed as to story in order to get something out of it that was to be had. Even the directorial genius of Sidney Olcott could not pull this one out of the fire, even though he tried hard with it. In addition he gave it a host of cleverly handled local color touches that under ordinary circumstances could have gone a long way toward making a picture look like a winner.

Another thing, the director must have been handicapped by the two leads that were given him to work with. Godfrey Tearle hasn't an inch of screen personality or presence, and Conway Tearle need never fear that the other member of his professional family is going to tread on his heels as far as the screen is concerned. As for Jetta Goudal, she simply does not hit in this characterization. That girl has a habit of showing the gums above her upper teeth when smiling that detracts from her appearance, and the effectiveness of her eyes is lost except in the close-up shots when she is holding a scene all to herself.

"Salome of the Tenements" has Jetta in the title role. She is so named by a co-worker, a woman, on the Jewish "Daily News," because Jetta as Sonya, a child of the Ghetto, is a head hunter and carries a string of male scalps on her belt.

In the finish she goes after John Manning a millionaire from the upper section of the city, who has endowed a settlement house on the east side and who takes a real active interest in the work, so much so that the grafter and the parasites fear his presence. The girl to make an appearance as far as her meager home is concerned plays right into the hands of this clique when she borrows sufficient money from a usurer to beautify the place against the call Manning is to pay her. To get $200 she signs a note for $1,500, payable when she marries the man in question.

In the finish the band tries to blackmail the husband, for she is successful and does marry him, threatening to reproduce the note in the papers and make him the laughing stock unless he backs down on the stand that he has taken against their activities. At this point the wife proves her love, because she is willing to sacrifice herself and go to prison rather than have her husband give up his life's work for her people in the Ghetto.

It is a mighty wishy-washy tale at its best. But in direction and atmosphere it is there. Sectionally it might get some money. Along the lower east side, for instance, it would clean up for the exhibitors, and possibly in the towns where there is a large Ghetto population it would duplicate, but it isn't strong enough to be counted as a big picture suitable for the pre-release runs in the bigger cities.

It is a program picture and just that. *Fred.*

Daddy's Gone A-Hunting

Frank Borzage production released by Metro-Goldwyn, featuring Alice Joyce and Percy Marmont. Adapted from the play of Zoe Akins. Shown at the Capitol, New York, week of Feb. 22. Running time, 67 minutes.

Julian.......................Percy Marmont
Edith...........................Alice Joyce
Janet......................Virginia Marshall
Olga..........................Helena D'Algy
Oscar..........................Ford Sterling
Greenough ....Holmes Herbert
Mrs. Greenough............Edythe Chapman
Colonel Orth.................James Barrows
Bensen.....................James Macelhern
Mrs. Wethers................Martha Mattox

In adapting "Daddy's Gone A-Hunting" for the screen a great deal of what was mighty good dialog in the play itself has been lost. It was the dialog that made this play possible, and there was seemingly nothing left but the basic drama when it got to the screen, and all of the lighter touches were missing. The result is a picture that gives you the weeps at the end, but which is a long, long while getting to the end, and in the meantime there is little or nothing doing.

The story is that of an artist who, after seven years of married life, decides that for real inspiration he will have to go abroad and study. He packs off and leaves his wife and child behind. The wife goes to business and supports herself and daughter while daddy is away. When he comes back he frankly confesses that he has undergone a change of ideas in regard to his wife and that he has been unfaithful. But they go on living under the same roof, the wife trying to win back his affection and he roistering with Bohemian companions. Finally the wife leaves him and goes to live with wealthy friends, taking along her daughter. After the separation the husband realizes he has finally discovered his real love only when he has lost it.

As a result of an accident the daughter dies, and this brings about a reconciliation, the wife spurning the love and affection of a wealthy man, the son of her benefactress, to return to the worthless husband after the death of the baby.

Alice Joyce gives a performance that has nothing particularly brilliant in it at any time. She plays the wife in an even tone that has no color or fire at any time, although there were a couple of opportunities where she should have flashed. Percy Marmont as the worthless husband does the best work. Little Virginia Marshall in the role of the daughter proved a pretty child that acted capably.

A fair program production that no one is going to go particularly wild about, at least from a box office standpoint. It is a little picture as far as productions that are usually shown at the Broadway pre-release houses are concerned. In all it is a film that has more or less of a depressing effect on the audience, judging from the manner in which it was accepted by the audience at the Capitol at the second afternoon performance Sunday. Incidentally, the Capitol's business for the matinee was considerably below the usual done there in some time, but Sunday was fine in weather for New York.

Fred.

THE SWAN

Famous Players-Lasky production of Ferenc Molnar's drama. Adapted to the screen by Dimitri Buchowetski and directed by him. Adolphe Menjou, Ricardo Cortez and Frances Howard featured. Reviewed at the Strand March 1. Running time, 65 minutes.

Princess Alexandra.........Frances Howard
Prince Albert..............Adolphe Menjou
Dr. Walter, the tutor.......Ricardo Cortez
Princess Beatrice...........Ida Waterman
Amphirosa...................Helen Windroth
Wanda von Gluck.....Helen Lee Worthing
George and Arsene, the young princes,
George Walcott
Father Hyacinth ....Michael Visaroff
Colonel Wunderlich.........Michael Vavitch
Lutzow......................Nicoli Sousannin
Princess Dominica............Clare Eames

This picture, made from one of the notable stage hits of last season, bears but little relation to the play, for the plot has been turned topsy-turvy, the symbolism of the play is forgotten in the rush to frame an exciting plot, dialogue is quoted which never existed and one of the film's leading characters, Wanda von Gluck, had no counterpart in the play.

Moreover, the leading male role, that of the Prince, has been changed here to fit Adolphe Menjou, so that instead of being the stolid fellow of Molnar's authorship, he is a booze-fighter and an all-around rake. Consequently, with these alterations, it is silly to compare the stage play with the picture, for the picture cannot even be called a filmization of the stage drama—it is something else again with a dash of the original plot.

In the film the Princess of a kingdom is reserved and haughty—and the picture for that reason calls her a swan. The Prince of another kingdom comes to her with the idea of marriage. Once arrived, he takes on rapidly with a lady in waiting, so the queen, worried because her daughter had failed to attract the prince, suggests to the daughter that she make him jealous by flirting with the tutor, a young man who is really in love with the princess.

So she does, and the tutor, in his madness, kisses her. That caused quite a rift, but as it happened during a terrible storm in which they were secluded in a lone cabin (something the play didn't mention) the consequences weren't so severe. The climax, however, arrives after the engagement of the prince and the princess has been announced. The tutor is invited on a drinking party with the prince. During the course of the party the prince makes a slurring remark about his betrothed. Instantly the tutor dashes his glass to the floor and in a short duel the prince is put out of business. Then his aid takes up the fight, and in a really exciting match (which wasn't in the play, but which is good) the two fight until the entire castle is aroused. When the young man is wounded the proud princess dashes from the crowd and tells them all that she loves him. By this time the prince has so recovered that he returns her promise and even the old folks are reconciled to the marriage.

In the play nothing of the sort happened—the princess married the prince and the tutor went his way.

"The Swan" has been staged with magnificent scenery which never for a moment becomes anything else than scenery. One garden set in particular is so strictly formal that all the illusion of a garden is lost. As for the other scenes, even their size and magnificence fail to achieve naturalness. The direction is good, but unsympathetic, while the acting is alternately good and bad. Menjou stands up, but Frances Howard and Ricardo are cast in extremely sympathetic parts, and through this ordeal Cortez best emerges. There are some names in the cast, but the abortive story so mixed the two plots that there was much unexplained.

Considered purely on its own merits as a picture and forgetting all about the play, "The Swan" seems like second-rate box office stuff. Its tranference to the screen was done expensively, but without understanding—such a contrast to the triumph achieved when "The Czarina" was made into "Forbidden Paradise" by Lubitsch, who knew his business well enough to retain the subtlety and sparkle of the piece and at the same time turn out a box office smash. Because it has been heralded so long and highly, "The Swan" is a double disappointment and will probably rank with the low gross films of the year. Certainly it has little besides Menjou now to attract. *Sisk.*

TOO MANY KISSES

Paramount picture, presented by Adolph Zukor and Jesse L. Lasky. Starring Richard Dix, with Frances Howard featured. From the story "A Maker of Gestures," by John Monk Saunders, adapted by Gerald Duffy, directed by Paul Sloane. Shown at the Rialto week March 1, 1925. Running time, 62 minutes.

Richard Gaylord, Jr.............Richard Dix
Yvonne Hurja ....Frances Howard
Julio ....William Powell
Gaylord, Sr..................Frank Currier
Mr. Simmons........................Joe Burke
Manuel Hurja.............Albert Tavernier
Miguel ....Arthur Ludwig
Flapper ....Alyce Mills
Pedro ....Paul Panzer
The Village Peter Pan......"Harpo" Marx

Here is a comedy drama that the average picture house audience is going to love. The flappers will go wild about Richard Dix, who in the work that he does in this production stands out as a sort of a combination Wallace Reid, Doug Fairbanks (in the days when he did things like "Manhattan Madness") and Tom Meighan. That is a pretty big order to slip into one human shell, but Dix seems to take to it, and the way he makes an audience laugh and thrill with him as the young American in Spain is a certain indication that he is one of the real coming box-office bets.

The picture has one thing audiences want, and that is laughs, in addition to a thrilling romantic love story.

A couple of typical New York flappers seated next to the reviewer went into raptures over the leading man, telling him when to wallop the heavy and when to kiss the girl. They counted the kisses in the picture, too, and they didn't think that there were too many, especially with Dix on one end.

It is the story of a young American abroad whose father has sent him traveling in the keeping of a companion because dad thinks the boy has had too great a romantic streak. All goes well for a couple of months until the pair reach a town in Spain, and there in a cafe the boy falls head over heels for a senorita who is virtually bethrothed to Julio, a Spanish captain, fire-eater and expert knife thrower. It is nip and tuck between the pair for the girl. She favors the young American, and finally he bests the heavy and his gang. There is a whale of a fight between Dix and William Powell, who plays the heavy, and there are any number of laughs lightening the battling aspect of the punch fest.

Frances Howard, who is Dix's leading woman, does nothing that would particularly entitle her to feature honors, but her name is played up under that of the star. She is, however, a mighty good leading woman when it comes down to expressing desire for a kiss, and for that alone deserves credit as far as this picture is concerned. Powell handles the heavy role with a nicety of touch that makes it stand out. Paul Panzer as one of his henchmen contributes a bit that registers. Incidentally "Harpo" Marx, of musical comedy fame (Marx Brothers), does a half-wit that makes him a screen possibility for comedies who will bear watching. *Fred.*

LADY OF THE NIGHT

Monta Bell production featuring Norma Shearer. Story by Adela Rogers St. John. Directed by Monta Bell. A Metro-Goldwyn release. At the Capitol week March 1. Running 58 minutes.

Molly / Florence	Norma Shearer
David	Malcolm McGregor
Oscar	George K. Arthur
Judge Banning	Fred Esmelton
Miss Carr	Dale Fuller
Chris	Lew Harvey
Gertie	Betty Morrissey

"Lady of the Night" would seem at off-hand an attempt to play on the title of the David Belasco show, "Ladies of the Evening." The chances are that thought was in someone's mind when the picture was titled. Be that as it may, that is about the only chance that the picture has of pulling any money at the box office.

In other words, the production is a cheater, one of those very cheaply made program pictures that they are trying to shove over the plate with the selling punch, "this played at the Capitol, New York, and if it's good enough for that house, it's good enough for you." The point is that the picture isn't good enough for the Capitol, and the box office receipts of that house for the current week will undoubtedly reflect that.

"Lady of the Night" is just an ordinary program picture only saved through the performance that Norma Shearer gives in the principal roles of a dual character.

One of the faults is that it has three reels of planting before there is action. Had possibly one reel been devoted to laying the plot, and the other four to the conflict between the two women for the love of the man, it would have made a better story. Also to the majority of the picture audiences it would have been a better ending if the tough girl had won the handsome hero instead of him falling for the wealthy deb.

The story starts with a prolog, showing a crook being sent away just after a girl baby has arrived at his home. At the same time, the judge who sentences him also has a girl baby. Some 18 years later the judge's daughter is shown graduating from a Select Girls' School, and at the same time the daughter of the crook is freed from a Reform School. Norma Shearer plays both roles. As the crook's daughter, she is a habitue of a cheap dance hall; as the judge's daughter she is a sheltered society deb.

Mollie, the dance hall girl, meets a young inventor who has perfected an appliance that will open any safe, and one of his cronies wants him to sell it to a safe-cracking mob, but Mollie prevails upon him to turn it over to the banking interests. There is a sub-title here that the banking fraternity may get after, it is, "Don't give it to the bankers, they'll rob you. Give it to the crooks, they'll treat you square." It was a great laugh to the Capitol audience.

Through the selling of the invention, the boy meets the daughter of the judge, who is the attorney for the banking interests, and she falls in love with him, while he is very much in love with her, and the dance hall girl eats her heart out silently, finally sacrificing her own love so that the boy may be happy.

Miss Shearer's work in the dual role is perfect, and incidentally there is a bit of double exposure work done in the automobile shots that is the best that there has been shown in the line of one character in a double role in a long time. Malcolm McGregor in the lead handles himself nicely, but in the cast there is a possibility as a film comedian that will bear watching; he is George K. Arthur, and if he is properly developed he will be one of the laugh makers of the future on the screen. Others in the cast just handled minor roles. *Fred.*

NEW LIVES FOR OLD

Famous Players-Lasky production starring Betty Compson. Adapted by Adelaide Heilbron. Directed by Clarence Badger. Shown at the Rivoli week of Feb. 22. Running time, 75 minutes.

Olympe	Betty Compson
Hugh Warren	Wallace MacDonald
De Montinrich	Theodore Kosloff
Pugin	Sheldon Lewis
Jean Bertaut	Jack Joyce
Widow Turrence	Margaret Sneddon
Senator Warren	Joseph Dowling
Mrs. Warren	Helen Dunbar
Berthe	Gale Henry
Nancy	Maravel Quivey
Cafe Manager	Ed. Faust

This seems rather a late date to bring along a war drama of this type to Broadway even in pictures. It is one of those stories that is at once conventional and stereotyped in plot and action. Just a cafe dancer who falls in love with an American officer in Paris. He doesn't know that she is the dancer. After he goes to the front she wants to do her bit and so becomes a member of the War Department's secret corps. Under orders she carries on an affair with a suspected Major, and finally traps him. The Department, unable to show its hand, lets the accusation stand in the general mind that she was the spy's accomplice. There being but one way out of the predicament, her death and burial are arranged for, in proxy, just at the announcement of the armistice. She returns to her little Normandie home, where her American sweetheart finds her and takes her back to the States as his bride.

At this point the spy who made his escape again turns up on the scene with a title and as a suitor for the hand of the sister of the officer to whom the dancer is married. When she, in order to save her sister-in-law, exposes him, she does so at a cost of her own exposure, but, although her husband's family turn from her, he remains loyal, his faith being rewarded by the arrival of the chief of the French Embassy, who clears up the situation and informs her in-laws that the French Government has been searching for the girl to decorate her for her war work.

Betty Compson as the heroine manages fairly well with a role that does not offer any real opportunities. Wallace MacDonald handles the hero rather nicely, but the outstanding hit is the performance that Jack Joyce, the one-legged dancer from vaudeville, gives as a French hero who has lost his leg in service. Joyce displayed a great deal of personality and seemed to get to the audience. Naturally, sympathy was with him and the role called for just that.

"New Lives for Old" does not look as though it was going to be a particularly strong box office card in the pre-release houses, but it is a program picture that will get by in the regular run of things in the subsequent runs. *Fred.*

THE RAG MAN

Metro-Goldwyn production, starring Jackie Coogan. Written by Willard Mack. Directed by Eddie Cline. Supervised by Jack Coogan, Sr. At the State, New York, week of February 23. Runs about 70 minutes.

Tim Kelly	Jackie Coogan
Max Ginsberg	Max Davidson
Mrs. Malloy	Lydia Yeamons Titus
Bernard	Robert Edeson
Kemper	William Conklin

"The Rag Man" is Coogan's final picture under his present contract with Metro-Goldwyn. In it Jackie again plays the ragged urchin seen in "The Kid" and several other Coogan films. The return to battered cap, sweater and long trousers shows that Jackie, naturally enough, has grown considerably since the days he first became the world's favorite youngster. He is still small enough to be entirely winsome and appealing, and there appears a new boyishness about him that ingratiates. His comic technique is surer than ever, but in the moments of pathos, a studied thespian attitude, clever enough in itself, has unfortunately taken the place of the wholly natural, unsophisticated charm.

Primarily a gag picture, "The Rag Man" has nevertheless a diverting story. The never-failing Irish-Jewish theme that has given the country its most sensational legit hit in years has been used here to its best advantage. Wisely enough, the author and director decided not to let too heavy a burden fall on Coogan's little shoulders and have given almost as important a role to Max Davidson.

Davidson, cast as Ginsberg, a junk man, takes care of Timothy Michael Patrick Aloysius Kelly after an orphanage burns down. The kindly old Hebrew proceeds to make a real "business man" out of little Tim, and the little fellow learns so quickly Ginsberg is forced to claim he couldn't be smarter if he were born in Moscow or named Levinsky. Tim buys more for four dollars than the junk cart will carry, talks with his hands, bargains and haggles and finally is the means of bringing to Ginsberg a fortune rightfully coming to him as royalty from a sewing machine patent stolen from him years before.

The finish is a wow. The two partners, now described as the "biggest dealers in antiques in the city," are shown at an ultra-fashionable golf club. Just as Timmy is driving someone at the next tee shouts "Fore" whereupon the little merchant responds "Not a cent more than 3.98" or something to that effect. They are then shown driving to the next hole in a stunning Rolls-Royce.

The film is crowded with similar gags, with perhaps the biggest laughs on the captions, not credited in the billing. Robert Edeson, Lydia Yeamons Titus and others in the cast are entirely capable.

PAMPERED YOUTH

Film adaptation of Booth Tarkington's Pulitzer prize novel, "The Magnificent Ambersons." Produced by Albert E. Smith. Directed by David Smith and released by Vitagraph. Running time, 67 mins.

George Minafer (as man)	Cullen Landis
George Minafer (as boy)	Ben Alexander
Eugene Morgan	Allan Forrest
Isabel Minafer	Alice Calhoun
Major Amberson	Emmett King
Wilbur Minafer	Wallace McDonald
Lucy Morgan	Charlotte Merriam
Fanny Minafer	Katheryn Adams
Mrs. Foster	Aggie Herring
George Amberson	William J. Irving

This production heralded by Vitagraph with much trumpet and fanfare missed by a wide margin living up to expectations. Reputed as having been adapted from a Booth Tarkington prize winning novel, the surmise is that it made better reading than film entertainment.

Although Tarkington may have written a faithful sketch of the proud Ambersons, much artificiality has crept into the film play. Most of the characters amble through more like automatons than characters of the flesh, and never once throughout its spinning does any of the touted cast skim the surface of a brilliant performance.

Just what recommended the story as a film subject, aside from the Pulitzer award and the reputation of its author, is a secret of the producers. Its story is the stereotyped yarn of southern pride and a wilful offspring of a loveless match who makes himself despicable from childhood only to grasp at the straw of redemption when fortune is swept from under him, and he is compelled to support himself and mother.

Cullen Landis gives a flat performance as the grown-up cad. Even in the pathetic moments he fails to be convincing. The part is not a world beater, but it seems more could have been done with it than Landis accomplishes. Alice Calhoun was charming as "Isabel Minafer," mother of the boy, while Allan Forrest, Emmett King and Charlotte Merriam gave creditable performances in their respective roles. From all angles a weak sister and especially for the Rialto. A great selling title, perhaps, but it has little chance of holding up unless booked on double feature bills. *Edba.*

I AM THE MAN

Chadwick Pictures Corp. release, directed by Ivan Abramson. Story by Ivan Abramson. Starring Lionel Barrymore. Shown at the Broadway, N. Y., week of March 2. Running time 56 mins.

James McQuade	Lionel Barrymore
Julia Calvert	Seena Owen
Daniel Harrington	Gaston Glass
Robert McQuade	M. J. Faust
Corinne Stratton	Flora Le Breton
George Lawson	James Keane
Billy Gray	Joseph Striker

This is a real domestic melodrama that they will like in the smaller towns and with the name of Lionel Barymore it should get some money at the box office. The trouble with the picture at the Broadway was that the operator rushed it through in less than an hour and had the action jumping all over the screen.

The story is a big city tale of politics and matrimonial intrigue. There are any number of minor directorial details that are at complete variance with what would actually happen in real life, but Abramson has a habit of making his characters naturally do a lot of things that wouldn't happen, and this picture is no exception to his proverbial rule.

Lionel Barrymore is in the role of the political power who ruins another politician so that he may obtain the hand of the latter's daughter. Seena Owen plays the daughter, looking slightly mature for a role of this type. However, later in the picture she qualifies when dramatic punch is needed. Flora Le Breton, as a young chorus girl, carries away the honors of the film. Gaston Glass plays the juvenile lead and manages to get by with it, although he has nothing too much to do, while the second heavy is in the hands of M. J. Faust, who registers well enough.

The McQuade brothers, James and Robert (Barrymore and Faust), have come to New York from the west, having changed their name to embark in politics, and James becomes a power. He wants to marry the daughter of John Calvert, but being rebuffed frames Calvert, and the latter is about to be sent to state's prison when James McQuade steps in and saves him with the understanding that Calvert's daughter is to become his wife. Sometime later McQuade becomes suspicious of his wife and a young lawyer whom he has named district attorney and sets his brother to spy on them. The brother has a soft spot for his sister-in-law and tries to make love to her. James finaly kills him for this and the crime is fastened on a young chorus girl who has been friendly with the brother and who is also a friend of the wife.

At the trial, when the girl confesses her real name and relates that her father deserted her mother when she was but a small child, James realizes that he is sending his own daughter to the chair, and after obtaining an adjournment of the trial makes a confession and commits suicide.

It is one of those pictures where a lot of unhappiness is cleared up through a couple of violent deaths and in some parts of the country they like that sort of stuff.

This picture was finished more than six months ago but at the time there was considerable controversy regarding it between I. E. Chadwick and Ivan Abramson, which may account for the length of time it has taken for it to obtain a showing on Broadway. Without Lionel Barrymore or a name of equal strength it would never have been shown on Broadway, as the story and direction hardly class it with the better program productions.

Fred.

FLYING HOOFS

Universal production, starring Jack Hoxie. Story by Clee Woods. From original story, "Beyond the Law." Directed by Clifford Smith. Reviewed at the Tivoli, New York, Feb. 25. Running time, 65 minutes.

Frank Moody	Jack Hoxie
Henry Moody	Bartlett Carre
Banker Connor	William Welsh
James Perdee	Gordon Russell
Emily Perdee	Charlotte Stevens
Mary Connor	Alys Murrell
The Raven	Duke R. Lee

'Tis verily the age of flying, thundering herds and hoofs on the screen these hectic days of "westerns." "Flying Hoofs" is a typical western, with Jack Hoxie, as the sheriff, who must ride a fast horse whenever his posse was called forth or whenever he went in pursuit of "The Raven," a bold, bad man, a man given to disguises and robbing folks who drew money from Connor's Cattlemen's Bank.

The story is one that jumps a few hurdles in so far as screen license is concerned. There's a reward by the western town's leading bank for the arrest and capture of The Raven, the outlaw, and Sheriff Moody (Hoxie) has sworn to get him, dead or alive. In the getting, however, strong suspicion and village gossip point the finger at the sheriff's tall brother, Henry Moody, who, to make the story more intricate, loves the banker's daughter, Mary, but hates the girl's father worse than pizen because he believes Connor gypped him and his brother out of their ranch. Now Henry makes no bones about his public sentiment regarding Connor and once came close to giving him a sock on the nose.

Hoxie has a sweetie, a peart, cute, little miss, Emily Perdee, who is simply bugs over the sheriff and has several effective little scenes where she tries to force him to acknowledge his affections. Of course, the sheriff is letter perfect when it comes to riding and gun-spitting, but at love he's in the wrong pew.

As the love affair between the sheriff's brother and the banker's daughter moves apace, it develops that the taller Moody is going to rob the bank after all. He does and is brought back to jail by his brother. Then comes the trial and Henry is sentenced to hang. How, when and where it all came about, nobody knows, and no caption was flashed to tell the screenlookers why the execution.

A tip comes that Henry is not The Raven, even the sheriff's girl and Henry declare that he (Henry) isn't. The sheriff then pulls a ruse as word has been sent Henry by The Raven that he will not hang. Henry, by-the-way, had hidden the bank's money and only he (Henry) knew where it was cached.

The sheriff is led to the gallows but along comes a rescuing party which winds up by the sheriff, handcuffing his main rescuer, The Raven, and, who is none other than the manager of the bank and the old enemy of the Moody boys.

Of course Henry is freed, the money's returned to the bank, Mary and Henry do the big embrace, and Emily finally gets Frank to declare his love, and everything ends happily, just as audiences have long been accustomed to seeing them when Jack Hoxie and the Universal ranchers start to ride with hoofs flying and guns ready for the draw.

Story misses. Hoxie sure looks an ideal sheriff whether riding or striding to and fro, and he's a type that fills a bill when there's physical encounters or gunplay to be considered.

There's a corking comedy bit, a bunch of cowhands or, rather, the sheriff's posse, who try to run an auto and it creates consternation when it runs wild. Well worked up.

Of the feminine contingent, Miss Stevens deserves special praise. She has everything in her favor and makes the best of it. *Mark.*

GIRL ON THE STAIRS

Peninsula Studios, Inc., production, starring Patsy Ruth Miller. Adapted from story by Winston Bouve. Directed by William Worthington. Released by Producers Distributing Corp. Running time, 60 mins.

Dora Sinclair	Patsy Ruth Miller
Agatha Sinclair	Frances Raymond
Joan Wakefield	Arline Pretty
Manuela Sarmento	Shannon Day
Frank Farrell	Niles Welch
Dick Wakefield	Freeman Wood
Jose Sarmento	Bertram Grassby
Wilbur	Michael Dark

An interesting murder mystery starring Patsy Ruth Miller. If one accepts the theory that the subconscious mind directs the activities of sleep walkers and that the somnambulists do not remember anything they do while in the coma, but if put to sleep by artificial means will reveal the promptings of the subconscious mind, the picture is credulous.

Whether one admits its plausibility or not, it is an engrossing picture, admirably cast and directed and sumptuously produced. Miss Miller is Dora Sinclair, the sleep-walking miss. She is cured of the habit by Dr. Bourget (Geo. Periolat) by the method referred to above.

Dora at school carries on a flirtation with Dick Wakefield (Freeman Wood) and writes him love letters. She is engaged to Frank Farrell (Niles Welch), a young attorney. Later she discovers Wakefield is married to one of her best friends. The Wakefields lease the place next to Dora's home.

Dora attends a "wild party" at the Wakefields and tries to recover her letters from the philanderer, who demanded a kiss for each letter. He struggles with her and is surprised by his wife, who leaves the house.

That night Wakefield is found murdered by his wife when she returns from her mother's. The maid declares she saw a ghost walk up the stairs. Dora's footprint is found on a knife in the room of Wakefield and his wife recalls she overheard her say to Wakefield, "You ought to be killed."

Dora is arrested and tried for the murder. Farrell defends her, but the case seems a perfect circumstantial one, when Farrell learns of Dora's early sleep walking affliction. Dr. Bourget is placed on the stand and allowed to place Dora under influence. She describes the murder, which was committed by Jose Sarmento (Bertram Grassby), a rich South American, whose wife was keeping an amour with Wakefield when the husband entered.

Sarmento and wife are in court and following the testimony, he confesses. Miss Miller is girlishly appealing and convincing throughout.

Niles Welch was splendid as her fiance and Freeman Wood was the husband who likes to play to the life. Arline Pretty had a negative role as his wife, but handled it satisfactorily. A corking good feature for the second run houses. *Con.*

SIGN OF THE CACTUS

Universal production, starring Jack Hoxie. Adapted by Isadore Bernstein from the story by Norma Wilde. Photographed by Harry Neumann. Directed by Clifford Smith. At Loew's New York, Feb. 20, as half the bill. Runs about an hour.

White Horse Cactus	Jack Hoxie
Belle	Helen Holmes
Henderton	J. Gordon Russel
Panhndle George	Francis Ford
Hayes	Joseph Swickard
Earl of Chico	Frank Newberg
Sheriff	Jack Pratt
Jack (boy)	Bobby Gordon
Belle (girl)	Muriel Frances Dana

Except for some exquisitely beautiful shots of Jack Hoxie riding through moonlit western valleys on a magnificent white horse there is little to "The Sign of the Cactus" that cannot be found in a thousand other program pictures of the same category. The story, dealing with a feud between western ranchers and a water company that attempts to take their land is totally trite and is unrelieved by several clumsy attempts to provide novel situations.

Hoxie is White Horse Cactus, so called because of his unlawful activities against the water company and for the benefit of the ranchers who are having their livelihood taken from them. His father had been killed defending his property years before, and White Horse is out on a rampage of revenge. The introduction of a gang of eastern gunmen, imported to do the water concern's dirty work, is a slight innovation from the usual western heavies. The love interest is taken care of by the daughter of the general manager of the water outfit, recognized by the hero through a scar dating from years before, when they had played together.

Hoxie saves her from drowning in a mildly staged bit, and finally gives up his revengeful pursuits to please her. The former rodeo rider has improved his general acting, but in the love scenes his work is unconvincing. Helen Holmes, veteran of many serial pictures, is not very prepossessing as the girl, but Francis Ford, another old-timer, takes the honors as an old shyster lawyer.

The photography is up to the usual standard, and some of the gunplay and chase bits hold a good share of action and excitement. But on the whole it's just one more western, and as such should satisfy the many lovers of this school of film.

IS LOVE EVERYTHING

Murray Garsson production distributed by Associated Exhibitors. Directed by W. Christy Cabanne,

Virginia Carter	Alma Rubens
Robert Whitney	Frank Mayo
Jordan Southwick	H. B. Warner
Boyd Carter	Walter McGrail
Edythe Stanley	Lilyan Tashman
Mrs. Carter	Marie Schaeffer
Mrs. Rowland	Irene Howley

"Is Love Everything" screens a combination of just plain applesauce.

At first the film gives promise of developing into a worthwhile study of the favorite old theme "two fellers and a goil." But once Virginia Carter (Almo Mayo) has made her choice and picked the man of wealth rather than the one she loves, it becomes a pitifully stereotyped story with the husband putting his wife to the test to see if she still cares for his rival. A wreck at sea gives the script opportunity to palm the husband off as drowned.

The Enoch Arden stuff culminates with the voluntary disappearance of the husband after he learns his wife can be happy only with her lover. That's a so-called twist that has been seen countless times. In this picture the handling does not lift it from the ordinary.

The wreck of the yacht show the heroine and her sweetie (not the lawful one) picked up by a rum runner. Hope runs high that the picture turns fo. the better. But action that follows, telling of mutiny, is slovenly and unconvincing. The director has done little here but turn on a terrific rain storm in which the asserted group of villains are hurled overboard. It is about the dullest collection of sea incidents seen in months.

In this stupid picture the distinguished legitimate actor, H. B. Warner, provides a spark of relief as the husband and overshadows by far the other principals, Miss Rubens and Frank Mayo. Walter McGrail contributes a fair bit as a comic heavy.

The scenes in handsome country estates and on the yacht bespeak costliness. Miss Rubens wears some beautiful gowns.

BATTLING MASON

A Hercules Film Production distributed by Bud Barsky. Frank Merrill starred with Billy Elmer, Dick Sutherland, Wilbur Morante and Eva Novak in the supporting cast. Written for the screen by W. E. Wing and directed by Jack Nelson and William James Craft. At Loew's, New York, Feb. 19.

This release, made by a minor independent company, is one of the best of its kind ever thrown on the market. Had it been written with a sense of humor it would be equal to the old Fairbanks Triangle brand, insofar as story goes, but as it stands, with its fights, thrills, stunts and love interest, it is fit to go on any second-run screen of the average caliber, and as a split feature with a vaudeville show "Battling Mason" is exactly the sort of stuff those patrons devour with relish.

The story concerns a young gentleman of the east who is hard with the fists. Out west he has a rich uncle who holds the money-bags and he doesn't want unk to know that he and the dukes get along well in a fight. But along comes a political press agent who runs him for office under a contract that he mustn't fight during the pre-election period. Uncle comes east during this time. There's also a girl, a blonde with a prize-fighting brother, so when the boy takes all kinds of insults without raising a hand the cry of "yellow" is raised.

But down in the gas house district the ruffians set upon him during a political speech. He has to run, due to the contract, but when they steal his girl he turns and shows them what hitting the floor feels like. And he wins the girl and the election and tickles uncle with his pugilistic ability.

Frank Merrill, who plays this role, isn't much of an actor. Probably experience is what he needs, but he has an arm on him like a telephone pole. He's good looking, too, and this film, contrary to most of the cheap thrillers, indicates some care of production and some expertness in the handling of the scenario. For entertainment it backs the sex dramas off the boards.

Eva Novak is the girl and good, while Billy Elmer, as her tough brother, is enough like a pug to get by with the role. The others in the cast don't mean a whole lot, but suffice.

It can be safely said that of all the minor independent releases of recent date this stands near the top of the list. And lest that "minor" be misleading, this one will entertain most audience which doesn't demand a star and a million dollars worth of scenery. And it beats some of those that are included in the blocks issued by the big producers. *Sisk.*

ℍE HAPPY ENDING

London, Feb. 13.

Founded on the successful play by Ian Hay, "The Happy Ending" provides entertainment which is typically British both in sentiment and setting. P. L. Mannock, responsible for the scenario, has handled his subject well and, despite the length (eight ·jels), has provided a story which is gripping.

This portion of the work is excellent, and once more George A. Cooper proves his right to stand at the head of British producers. His work is consistently good and, in using the Thames, old country gardens and few interiors, he has achieved a picture of artistic beauty.

Mrs. Craddock has brought her three children up to believe their father the whitest of men, who died a hero's death while rescuing a child from drowning. As a matter of fact Craddock was a cur of the first water, and soon proves it by turning up and blackmailing his unhappy wife. He seeks to lead the eldest boy astray, and almost succeeds. In the end, finding his course nearly sped, Craddock decides to go away, but before he can do so he loses his life in saving a child in almost identically the same way Mrs. Craddock has so often described to her children.

Fay Compton is excellent as Mrs. Craddock, and Jack Buchanan, departing momentarily from light comedy, shows he can do fine work by his performance of the blackguardly husband. Donald Searle gives a good performance as a boy friend of the family, and Jack Hobbs is well up as the eldest Craddock boy. *Gore.*

GOOSE HANGS HIGH

Zukor-Lasky presentation, James Cruze production, from the play by Lewis Beach, adapted by Walter Woods and Anthony Coldeway. Seen at Rivoli Theatre. Running time, 76 minutes.

Lois Ingals..............Constance Bennett
Eunice Ingals..............Myrtle Stedman
Bernard Ingals..............George Irvin▸
Dagmar Carroll..............Esther Ralston
Hugh Ingals...........William R. Otis, Jr.
Bradley Ingals.............Edward Peil, Jr.
Granny.....................Ge.trude Claire
Elliott Kimberly..........James A. Marcus
Rhoda......................Anne Schaefer
Noel Derby..............Z. Wall Covington
Mazie........................Cecile Evans

An extremely pleasant dish, this picture, typical of what the screen must have if it is to endure ad infinitum. An occasional wonder film, like an occasional wonder-play, can be expected at irregularly recurring intervals. But the daily fare must be like this feature—durable, wholesome, domestic, native, mingled comedy and drama, for that is life's way, and life's way is the theatre's best way except in those exceptional instances which punctuate the mimic world as they do the real.

This story, which made a palatable comedy in the spoken medium, surpasses itself in the silent translation. Intelligent direction—intelligent enough to stand on a simple narrative with its human elements of amusement and contact with our healthy emotions without straining for distracting spectacle and high-power movie effects—must be credited with gilding this goose and making it an appetizing and flavory goose instead of half peacock and part crow.

All that may sound figurative, but it means plainly that "The Goose Hangs High" is a swiftly running comedy-drama of middle-class small-town life, love of parents for modern children and affection of children for those parents despite their modernity.

That being the gospel of Beach's play originally, it remains undoctored in the Woods-Coldeway screen conception. The screen gives it more than it had, but the more is in the same vein, feels the same pulsations and preserves the same tempo and the same homely sentiments.

The casting is as sound. Myrtle Stedman, as the mother, gives the part mature beauty of features and of spiritual radiance; George Irving as the father plays it just as Norman Trevor did it (and probably is still doing it) on the stage; the children are far superior to those in the conversational presentation.

Constance Bennett, though her make-up seemed to make her skin too dark, does easily the most eloquent and promising work she has shown on the silver sheet, as the flapper daughter. William R. Otis, Jr., as the older son, is manly and deeply sympathetic. Eddie Peil, Jr., is a find as the adolescent boy.

But the tip-topper is in one Esther Ralston, to this reviewer hitherto unknown, in a bit as the older son's sweetheart. Miss Ralston is a new beauty of the screen, certain to make a high mark. Her features are girlish, patrician and instantaneously captivating. Men and women let their admiration spring forth audibly. She is a blonde and young. She can troupe, and, so far, abjured affectation. Only untoward circumstances can clamp limitations on her screen potentialities.

While "The Goose Hangs High" will perhaps not pile up anything approaching record grosses, it need not, for it piled up nothing terrifying in costs. As a program feature it will make good heartily everywhere, and as it goes it will drive a solid peg for the stability, respectability and durability of the screen as an institution in worth-while American life. *Lait.*

INTRODUCE ME

Associated Exhibitors picture, starring Douglas MacLean. Directed by George J. Crone, with Jack Mackenzie and Paul Perry photographers. Story by Raymond Cannon and Wade Botofer. At the Strand, New York, week of March 8. Running time, 78 mins.

Jimmy Clark.............Douglas MacLean
Algy Baker.......................Robert Ober
John Perry....................E. J. Ratcliffe
Betty Perry...................Anne Cornwall
J. K. Roberts..................Lee Shumway
Bruno..........................Wade Boteler

A neat comedy for Douglas MacLean, not entirely original but wrapping up enough laughs to send it through as solid entertainment.

The story is based upon mistaken identity for its situations, although this time the action revolves around a mountain climbing contest.

Principally located in Switzerland the film gets under way in Paris with much of the early merriment taking place in a railroad station. A desire to meet an American girl, touring with her father, supplies the reason for Jimmy Clark (Mr. MacLean) visiting the Alps and a porter's mistake tags him with the cognomen of J. K. Roberts, supposedly America's mountain climber. Roberts' eventual presence with the demand that Clark either denounce himself as an imposter or climb, leaves but the latter alternative because of the girl.

The troubles Clark has in reaching the peak are plenty and laughable. His method of descent is strictly a film "gag," in that he drops and starts rolling to accumulate himself as a mammoth snowball to ease the final crash.

Crone, in directing, has given the laughs consistency, with no great amount of footage spacing them. At times they come in bunches. MacLean breezes through for the role's full worth, registering many an item through pure "trouping." E. J. Ratcliffe about garners himself second honors as the girl's father, antagonized by Clark through innocently offered exploding cigars, while Robert Ober is well enough as Clark's touring companion who denies all knowledge of Clark after one look at the girl. Anne Cornwall is the only principal woman and adequate.

The high spots list the cigar fireworks, and the suspense attached as outstanding, while MacLean's flight from a bear along mountain ridges is also sufficient surefire hoke to sponsor a couple of thrills and give the latter stages of the film a wallop, the obvious intent.

MacLean has lost nothing of a winning personality, and that he is able to create a certain sense of pathos in his work is just that much more of a value, which should keep him with the leaders, if any at present, of the light comedian division. *Skig.*

THE DENIAL

Hobart Henley Production, released by Metro-Goldwyn. From the play, "The Square Peg," by Lewis Beach; adapted by Agnes Christine Johnson. At the Capitol, New York, week of March 8. Running time, 53 mins.

Mildred.......................Claire Windsor
Arthur............................Bert Roach
Lyman.......................William Haines
James.......................Edward Connelly
Dorothy.......................Lucille Ricksen
Bob..........................Robert Agnew
Rena..........................Emily Fitzroy
Effie.............................Vivia Ogden
Gene............................Billy Eugene
Rosie...........................Estelle Clark

Hobart Henley has turned out a good little human-interest picture in this production, based on the play that was entitled "The Square Peg," by Lewis Beach. There is no great box-office wallop, but the picture carries strong entertainment value in the theatre. There is one point in the story where a Sunday afternoon audience fairly howled, when Edward Connelly, in the character of the henpecked father and husband, turned and asserted himself just before committing suicide.

From the picture standpoint the story is just one of those tales that shows a slice of life in an American home where the mother is the dominating factor, the result being that her son turns out to be a burlesque show hound instead of attending temperance lectures, and 20 years ago that was some offense. The husband, to secure money to get the boy out of a scrape with a girl, taps the bank for $2,000, and, when found out, commits suicide. But not because he was to go to jail; the wife squared that. It is when he discovers that he can't get away from her even by going to prison that he decides he'd be better off dead. The daughter marries the man that her mother picks for her, and, although not in love with him, remains faithful and rears his child.

The story is told in retrospect. The opening scenes show the child of this marriage, a young deb who has been proposed to by a young army officer. The two appear and ask the mother's consent to their marriage, but the mother says that they are rather hasty, and forbids the ceremony. The girl then turns to her mother and remarks, "I wonder what you would have done if your mother had refused to let you marry the man you wanted?" This brings the story to a point more than 20 years before, when the true tale is told.

Claire Windsor does extremely well in the role of the mother, who turns back the picture of her life to the time when she was a girl and her mother forbade her marriage, her lover being killed with the Rough Riders and she marries a wealthy young man. William Haines plays the hero in the Spanish war sequence of the story, while Robert Agnew is the hero of the modern story. Lucille Ricksen is the younger girl. Edward Connelly as the father gives the performance of the cast, although Emily Fitzroy as the mother makes herself more forcibly felt.

As a good program picture this one will go along nicely and prove entertaining to most audiences. It may possibly be the cause of a revolt here and there by the husbands who have just the kind of a wife depicted in this story. *Fred.*

ON THIN ICE

A Warner Bros. production co-starring Tom Moore and Edith Roberts. Directed by Mal St. Clair. At the Piccadilly, New York, week of March 7. Running time, 59 mins.

Charles "Chuck" White.........Tom Moore
Rose Lore.....................Edith Roberts
Dapper Crawford...........William Russell
Dr. Paul Jackson........Theodore Von Eltz
Harrison Breen..............Wilfred North

This is a crook story of the type of program picture that will go fairly well in the neighborhood houses but it hardly seems strong enough to run in a pre-release theatre or where the house policy calls for a full week. The picture is one of those melodramatic tales of underworld life in which the heroine is a poor girl wrongfully accused and the hero a crook whose regeneration she brings about. Tom Moore and Edith Roberts have these two roles.

The plot gets under way with a street stick up; the crooks, being chased by the cops, throw their loot over a fence and it is picked up by the girl, who returns the bank's money bag intact. But when the bag is opened it is discovered that it contains cut newspaper and a lot of cast-iron washers, and the girl is accused of having opened the bag and taken the money. She is tried and found guilty of the theft and sent away for a short time, the detectives believing she is certain to go after the money when she is released.

At the same time the crooks who originally planned the crime figure the same thing and they have arranged a plant for her when she gets out. They manage to get her away from the detectives when she gets out of jail and two of them take her to a secluded farm where one is posing as her brother. She believes that he is the long lost relative that her father had spent years searching for before his death.

Both the supposed brother and the gang leader fall for her and when the latter is killed the real thief is disclosed in the person of the bank president. Thence the "brother" marries the girl, having revealed he is not related but was only posing to try to find if she had hidden the loot. There is a happy ending which shows the reformed crook in the role of a traffic copper. One of those "From Crook to Copper" tales but without a real punch to make it stand out at the box-office.

William Russell, in the supporting cast to Moore, and Miss Roberts give good performances, but it seems a little unusual to see a former leading man playing heavies, although Russell makes a good job of it. *Fred.*

Barriers Burned Away

Associated Exhibitors Release produced by Arthur F. Beck. Founded on the novel by the Rev. E. P. Roe and scenarized by Leah Baird. Directed by W. S. Van Dyke. At the Cameo, New York, week March 8. Running time, 68 minutes.

Christine Randolph............Mabel Ballin
Mark Randolph............Eric Mayne
Wayne Morgan............Frank Mayo
Molly Winthrop............Wanda Hawley
Gale Winthrop............Wally Van
Mildred McCormick............Arline Pretty
Earl of Tarsney............Lawson Butt
Hon. Bill Cronk............Tom Santschi
Howard Mellon............Harry T. Morey
Patrick Leary............J. P. Lockney
Mrs. Leary............Mrs. Charles G. Craig
Peg-Leg Sullivan............William V. Mong
Halsted Street Terror............Pat Harmon
Kitty............Frankie Mann

This is the film which has Chicago at the time of its fire as the subject. To the end of attaining accuracy, the titles announce that the Chicago Historical Society co-operated with the producers and that everything has its basis in fact. Nevertheless and notwithstanding, the important thing is that with a great street and lobby ballyhoo and plenty of advertising, it could not even do business on the home grounds.

And that's the answer to the film—it is one of the type that holds neither drawing nor entertaining powers and is therefore of little use to the average exhibitor. The Cameo is playing it on a guarantee—which explains everything.

The plot concerns Chicago of 1870. A love story runs through it. It seems that a famous painting was stolen from the Morgan family and that it finally was sold to an art dealer, Randolph, by the villain, Howard Mellon. Young Wayne Morgan, disguising himself as a porter, gets entree to the Randolph establishment and discovers the work of art. From then on the love affair with Randolph's daughter takes varying turns, for he denounces her copy of the thing as the work of an artist without a 'soul.'

In sequences which introduce the old Bismarck saloon and in one fight there, some interest is maintained. The flash of the widow Leary's cow doing the only back-kick in the world that ever rivaled George Cohan's also was historically engrossing — but not dramatically. The various Chicago characters introduced—Potter Palmer, the detective William Pinkerton, Marshall Field and the Halsted Street Terror, were all right but if they mean anything to the average audience in either Seattle or Miami it's doubtful.

The production is tawdry and not well made. No one in the cast, unless Eric Mayne and Tom Santschi be excepted, does anything above the ordinary in acting, while the direction and story are at fault in many places.

The whole thing lags badly, has split continuity which kills much of the interest and the fact that in Chicago it meant applesauce is proof that "Barriers Burned Away" is an ordinary film. Even Jack Lait wouldn't like it. *Sisk.*

Gerald Cranston's Lady

Fox Film Production made in England and based on the stage play of the same name. James Kirkwood featured. Reviewed at the Circle, New York, March 9. Running time, 64 minutes.

"Gerald Cranston's Lady" is an English-made film from the famous novel and play, with James Kirkwood in the leading male role. Distributed here by Fox, it shapes up as an above the average daily change feature, yet its Circle showing had it as half a double bill with the First National feature, "Idle Tongues." Both were good.

The story of the play concerns an ambitious man whose boyhood was spent in poverty but whose manhood was one of wealth—a wealth achieved by hard work. But with the wealth there was no social position, and in order to attain it Cranston marries a woman with that understanding. She is young and has borne a son by a former husband. When going to live with him, she reminds him often and emphatically that love isn't in their agreement. The son becomes firmly attached to the father.

Business reverses set in upon Cranston after he has been knighted and it seems that his enemies are about to get the best of him. In addition, the cousin of his wife plays the temptress and tries to make him fall. He doesn't, although for a time the wife figured that he had. The windup is that Gerald Cranston, poor and ill, finds that his reverses have brought him the love of a woman for whom he cared deeply.

This production is good scenically and is, for the most part, well acted by both Kirkwood and Alma Rubens. The direction has some excellent touches which amply compensates for the lost subtitles, while in other spots the subtitles fly thick and fast and the continuity becomes jerky in shifting from a few African sequences of unimportance to the English locale.

"Gerald Cranston's Lady" isn't an especially engrossing film, but its sex interest, clean for the greater part, and the finished production fit it for the daily changes neatly.

It has been playing in and around New York off and on for some weeks. *Sisk.*

"Gerald Cranston's Lady," a recent Fox release featuring James Kirkwood and Alma Reubens, was described recently in a Variety review as an English-made picture.

Winfield Sheehan, of the Fox organization, says that the firm appreciates the compliment, etc., but that the film was produced in Hollywood with an American director and an all-American cast.

IDLE TONGUES

First National Production, made by Thomas H. Ince. Made from the Joseph C. Lincoln novel, "Dr. Nye." Scenario by C. Gardner Sullivan and direction by Lambert Hillyer. Supervised by Ince. Reviewed as half of a double bill at the Circle, New York, March 9. Running time, 70 minutes.

Dr. Nye............Percy Marmont
Katherine Minot............Doris Kenyon
Judge Copeland............Claude Gillingwater
Faith Copeland............Lucille Ricksen
Cyrenus Stone............David Torrence
Tom Stone............Malcolm McGregor
Althea Bemis............Vivian Ogden
Miss Pepper............Ruby Lafayette
Peg-Leg Henry............Dan Mason

This was Tom Ince's last production, and, although released for two months, a review does not appear in Variety's files, hence this one.

Based on one of the recent Lincoln stories, "Dr. Nye," which was a continuation of his Cape Cod lore, its folks and ways, it turns into an interesting study of people with the hate of a small town vividly shown in the attempted persecution of a physician who went to jail to save his wife's name.

The story of Dr. Nye was that in marrying Judge Copeland's sister he was practically forced into it by her lies and ways. Katherine Minot was the woman he really loved. But his wife stole the church funds and, to save her, Dr. Nye did a five-year stretch.

Returning to town, he was bitterly denounced as a pariah by Judge Copeland, and, except for his friends Cyrenus Stone and Katherine Minot, he was out of contact with the villagers. He and an old salt, Henry Payson, lived together in a house near the sand dunes. Over the village came an epidemic of typhoid. Dr. Nye discovered that the town's water source, owned by Copeland, was responsible. When he arose in town meeting to tell this, Dr. Nye found the air charged with enmity toward him, and, at Copeland's word, the men jumped at him and rushed him off to the beach, where he was stoned. Small-town bigotry was exemplified here, and it was not until Nye, driven by desperation, told the story to Copeland.

Then the feud ended, Nye and Katherine married and Copeland's daughter married her young sweetheart—all because Dr. Nye had changed the parental attitude.

This film is beautifully cast and played. Though the sea atmosphere is but faintly suggested, a pleasant atmosphere hovers over the whole thing, and if the small-town types are heavily accentuated it is only for the purpose of bringing narrow-mindedness to life in a pictorial form.

Percy Marmont as the persecuted medico does excellently, while Doris Kenyon follows him closely. Claude Gillingwater as the stern judge is quite in the picture, and David Torrence as his enemy also. Dan Mason has a neat comedy hit and the others aren't three cents worth out of place. The settings are modest and good.

Because the direction is corking, the scenario well handled and the acting competent, this makes a satisfactory program film. Its sole fault lies in the plot, which leaves the typhoid angle up in the air. *Sisk.*

Youth and Adventure

Carlos Production starring Richard Talmadge. Distributed by Renown Pictures, Inc. Story by Frank Howard Clark. Directed by James W. Horne. Photography by William Marshall. At Loew's, New York, one day (March 7) as half the bill. Runs about an hour.

Reggie Dillingham............Richard Talmadge
Joe Potts............Pete Gordon
Clint Taggart............Joseph Girard
Mary Ryan............Margaret Landis
Red Mullin............Fred Kelsey
Phyllis............Katherine Lewis

In spite of all they say about Norma, Constance, Natalie and the Reverend De Witt Talmadge, Dick is really the high flyer of the genus homo bearing that good old Brooklyn name. Certainly there is no-one in pictures or out who jumps through as many windows, skylights and cubby holes, swings perilously from as many skyscrapers, ocean liners and high fences, and vaults, hurdles and aeronauts through as much space as this athletic young gentleman.

The foreword to "Youth and Adventure," his latest and ineptly named feature bears the information that all athletic stunts have been conceived and executed (possibly it said copyrighted, too) by the star. If trick escapes and feats of agility and strength are all that the public expects from Mr. Talmadge this film will certainly be considered one of his best. The trouble with his stunts, however, is that he injects into them hardly any of the humor that Fairbanks and one or two others put into them. Ease and grace he possesses in full shares but very little of that essential ability to get across the impression that his escapes and fistic triumphs are more in the spirit of fun than of dire necessity.

The present opus concerns Reggie Dillingham, as plutocratic and shiftless as his name, and his gradual regeneration into a three or four-fisted youth. The family lawyer has informed him that his fortune has melted in the stock market and it is up to him to get out and hustle. He battles politics, liquor rings, roughnecks, and finally wins his toughest fight, the love of the little lady who has spurned him at first.

The direction, supporting cast, photography, incidental comedy and romantic interest are all subservient to Talmadge's perpetual gymnastic and bombastic endeavors. If action were heart interest this baby would be "Humoresque," "Broken Blossoms," and "The Last Laugh" combined. But too much of it and too little of everything else palls.

Incidentally, this is said to be Talmadge's last picture for the independent state right's market. He begins soon on a contract with F. B. O., who have starting touting him already on the billboards and in the trade papers. They might do well in using "Youth and Adventure" as a model regarding athletic activity, but if they are wise they will lean more to the human side and less to the physical.

FLAMING FORTIES

Stellar Production, supervised by Hunt Stromberg. Distributed by Producers Distributing Corp. From the story "Tennessee's Pardner," by Bret Harte. Directed by Tom Forman. Harry Carey starred, with James Mason, William Bailey and Jacqueline Gadson in the cast. Runs about 55 mins.

The presence of the Bret Harte name on "The Flaming Forties" should have set it apart from the majority of western program pictures. "Tennessee's Pardner" is one of his better known stories, and in the reading contains a good deal of dramatic material. But somewhere along the line this Hunt Stromberg production. missed. Neither Tom Forman provided his customary bits of excellent human-interest stuff nor did Harvey Gates do his usual sterling hits in adapting it. Consequently it must be rated as just another ordinary western, with Harry Carey likable but not convincing in the chief role.

Carey plays a simple, hard-working farmer in those hectic days of the far west from which the film derives its title. This "rawbone," as he is described in the captions, has never seen a boat, owned a horse or loved a woman.

The latter accomplishment, however, becomes possible when a Tennessee belle comes west to look for her outlaw husband. The latter, Captain Jack Desparde, owes his life to Bill Jones (Carey), and the two have become "pardners" in the fullest sense of the word. When desperate Desparde is finally cornered, it is Bill who saves him from hanging, even though he realizes the girl can't be his with her husband alive. The angry mob decides to string Bill up instead of the Captain when the latter, spying this from the distant hills where he is hiding, decides it is his chance to do a sacrifice. Calling the gang's attention to himself, he leaps off a cliff on horseback. The animal emerges from the water unharmed, but all that is seen of the bold highwayman is a few bubbles. The gang decides that if the friendship was as glorified as all that they might as well let Bill go free to console the widow.

Jacqueline Gadson is pretty as the belle, and the balance of the short cast is adequate. The film abounds with gun and fist fights, near-hangings and the rest of the usual western routine.

Only those who fancy raw prairie melodrama will like this picture, but there are enough fans in that category to insure moderate box-office takings in most places.

THOSE WHO DARE

Creative production presented by Fred Kusse. Adapted from the story, "Trapped," by I. W. Irving. Directed by John B. O'Brien. Released by Renown. Running timee, 65 mins.

Captain Martin Manning......John Bowers
David Rollins..............Joseph Dowling
Mrs. Rollins..............Claire MacDowell
Cecilia Thorne............Martha Marshall
Harry Rollins...............Edward Burns
Marjorie...........Marguerite de la Motte
Capt. Thorne Wetherell.Spottiswood Aitken
Serpent Smith...............Sheldon Lewis
Panka......................Caesar Gravina

An unusual sea drama well done and full of action and thrills. The story is told in flashback style. Captain Martin Manning (John Bowers), an old captain, is ordered out of Mariners Harbor for mooring his schooner, "The Swallow," in the harbor. The order is based upon the sinister reputation of the ship and the belief a sunken ship belongs to the sea and shouldn't be raised.

Manning, in defense, tells the story of the ill-fated ship. Years ago to affect a drug cure for Harry Rollins (David Burns), son of David Rollins, wealthy ship builder, Manning took charge of a yachting cruise. In mid-ocean a signal of distress was flown. Manning investigated and discovered the old captain of the schooner seriously ill. His tomboy daughter and a villainous crew, under the leadership of Serpent Smith, a voodoo believer, were the occupants.

Manning obtained permission from the yacht owner to take charge of the schooner and took Harry with him, thereby cutting off his drug supply by separating him from his valet, who was secretly giving him the drug. The crew immediately became ugly, but the two youths assert themselves and with the aid of a loyal cook start the ship under full sail for Honolulu. Smith, the leader, poisons the old captain, leaving the girl an orphan. The crew, in a drunken orgy, overpower Harry and Manning and draw lots for the girl.

Smith loses and is chagrined. He tries to doublecross the winner, which precipitates a fight between he and his followers. The events which follow before the three make their escape and the schooner, without direction, flounders upon the rocks with all hands aboard lost, completes a highly interesting feature, intelligently directed and well cast.

The story lends itself admirably to transition to a motion picture, and despite its dramatic pyrotechnics is convincing and will appeal to lovers of a good marine yarn.

After hearing the story the inmates of Mariners Harbor vote to allow the "Swallow" a permanent anchorage. In gratitude for the saving of his son Rollins presents the schooner to Manning.

Bowers, in the dual role, was an upstanding figure. *Con.*

BLOOD AND STEEL

Renown production by Jesse J. Goldberg. Distributed by Independent Pictures Corp. Directed by J. P. McGowan. Written by George Plympton.

Palmer.......................Mack Wright
Jurgen....................Albert J. Smith
Vera......................Ruth Stonehouse
Grimshaw...................Robert Edeson
Helen Grimshaw..............Helen Holmes
Gordon Steele.............William Desmond
His Father...................Louis Fitzroy

A thrilling railroad insertion at the finish and a cast of considerable capability almost succeed in making up for this picture's deficiencies. There is lack of pictorial beauty, something even the cheapest of the westerns usually provides in great quantity. In "Blood and Steel," while it is a railroad story rather than a straight western, almost all opportunities to shoot the natural grandeur of the west have been neglected.

It is a film bringing little to the sense of beauty and sight save in the latter case the runaway locomotive near the finish. In plot the usual story has been utilized, that of the earnest young construction manager who completes the extension line on time despite all opposition.

The hero wins the general manager's daughter, who for various reasons had been led to believe him cruel, philandering and deceitful. The infrequent attempts at humorous relief fail to amuse very much, but some of the atmosphere around the railroad gang's hangout is well put on and the fight scenes are moderately exciting.

Robert Edeson and Ruth Stonehouse assist William Desmond in raising the acting average to respectable heights. Helen Holmes, playing opposite him, was disappointing. Albert Smith, as one of the heavies, gave a somewhat different characterization.

Man Who Played Square

William Fox production starring Buck Jones. Story by Wallace Cook. Direction Al Santell. Running time, 65 mins.

Matt Black.....................Buck Jones
Spofford...............Ben Hendricks, Jr.
Piggy..................David "Red" Kirby
The Cook......................Hank Mann
Spangler....................Howard Foster
Steve.......................William Scott
Bertie.......................Wanda Hawley

It looks more and more as though the Fox had the makings of another western "find" in Buck Jones. Jones' physiognomy would give rise to the suspicion he was at one time active as a boxer. He has the nose of a professional "pug." Otherwise he is a clean cut youth and a whale of an athlete.

His latest picture gives him ample scope for action and includes plenty of riding, also a couple of good fights, one strung out beyond credulity due to the contestants who start battling in a house and wind up a mile or so distant after fighting their way across the approach to a mine and then down onto and off a roof. In the fight both contestants take enough punches on the button to knock out all the pugs at McLevy's gym but it doesn't stop either of the boys from getting up and covering more territory.

The story has to do with Matt Blake (Buck Jones) who, in order to avenge his pal Steve (William Scott), takes a job in a mine run by Bertie Spofford, (Wanda Hawley). Steve's father had a half interest in the mine for grub staking Spofford but when Steve presented his claim he was horse whipped. He afterward is shot by Spofford but gets him too. Dying he sends for Matt and extracts a promise of vengeance.

Matt finds the Mexicans arraigned behind Spangler (Howard Foster). He lines up the loyal faction who stick with Bertie. Things come to a head when the Mexicans attack the office trying to get the gold stored there. A pitched battle ensues. Matt is shut in a cabin after his fight with Spangler but escapes by backing up to a wall and blowing to bits a rope tied to his wrists by firing the rifle with his toe. He then overpowers the guard and returns to Bertie's house.

Her suspicions, aroused against him by Spangler, are lulled when she discovers he has torn up Steve's claim and another document he found, proving the truth of Steve's father's claim of a half interest in the Gar Eagle mine.

Hank Mann, as the cook, holds up a comedy role and is splendid. His relating of an imaginary tale explaining how he won the Croix de Guerre is a comedy wow. Jones is convincing at all times and can act in addition to his athletic talents and superb horsemanship. Wanda Hawley is pretty, but light, and the rest of the cast is worthy.

The picture is a good program addition for the neighborhood film houses and averages up with the best of the westerns seen hereabouts this season. *Con.*

THE WHEEL

London, Feb. 20.

There is an idea deeply rooted in the minds of all producers, renters and exhibitors that to be a popular success, or a success of any sort, a picture must have a happy ending. This idea has all but ruined the new Abel Gance picture, "The Wheel," which has been made with a French cast supporting an English female "star." Throughout his long reelage Gance never loses his grip on his audience; all his tricks of suggestion are present, all the horror or joy he can get out of trivial things, then in his last few hundred feet he deliberately damns all he has done, ruins the quality of the characters he has created, and turns great art into mediocrity for the sake of a happy ending, which rings superbly false and is utterly futile.

After a terrible railway accident Sisif, the engine driver, adopts Norma, whose mother has been killed. He brings the child up as his own, side by side with his motherless boy, Eli. As the years roll on Eli becomes a violin maker, but the once jovial workman, Sisif, becomes a drunkard. He is, however, allowed to drive express trains, which perhaps provides a little "inside" stuff on the number of serious French railway accidents.

The truth is he has fallen in love with Norma, but, having brought her up as his child, does not dare tell the truth. Eli also loves her, but thinks it merely brotherly. The superintendent of the line, Hersan, wins Norma's hand by a trick. Shortly after her marriage Sisif is the victim of a bad accident and, his sight being impaired, is sent to drive an Alpine train. Norma follows, and Eli, having discovered the truth, sends her a declaration of love hidden in a violin. This Harsan finds. A furious quarrel between the two ends in Eli being hurled over a precipice and the shooting of Hersan. Norma is seen in a superb Alpine setting silhouetted against a cross erected where Eli met his death.

Here the picture should finish, but the "happy ending" has to be considered. Therefore we have Sisif, now totally blind and looking a centenarian, and Norma not a day older. It is a feast day, and all is rejoicing among the simple Swiss people. Norma drags Sisif around in an elephantine jig, denoting happiness, and we see the ruin of a fine picture.

Most of Gance's work is excellent, and his working out of the ever-turning wheels idea is very fine and imaginative. All his settings, mostly among locomotives and rest sheds, are very good, and his Alpine locations are remarkably beautiful. This picture is being handled by Springers, and, with the "happy ending" deleted ruthlessly, the firm will have one of the best pictures seen in many a day.

Ivy Close as the girl does her best work, and Severin Mars gives a fine character performance as Sisif. The support throughout is capital.

Gore.

TEETH

A Tom Mix production made by Fox and directed by J. G. Blystone. Running time, 65 mins.

This picture of the Fox-Mix series is below the general par of the others, for the reason that the supporting cast is ever and always pretty mediocre. Mix himself is as okeh as ever and gives the thrilling moments.

Notable, however, is the presence of a new dog actor, not of the police dog type, who co-operates with the horse, "Tony," for some great stuff. At times the subtitles make the intelligence of the dog ridiculous and they tend to stick in a few unintended laughs. So far the Mix popularity has been founded on the fact that most of his stories were straightaway Westerns, but this one makes even he look foolish as he talks to the dog, who obeys his every word.

it. *Sisk.*

March 18, 1925

SALLY

First National presentation. Colleen Moore starred; directed by Alfred Green, from the Ziegfeld musical show of same title, book by Guy Bolton, music by Jerome Kern; running time, 72 mins.; seen at Strand.

Sally.......................Colleen Moore
Blair Farquar.................Lloyd Hughes
Duke............................Leon Errol
Pops............................Dan Mason
Otis Hooper...............John T. Murray
Rosie Lafferty..................Eva Novak
Jimmy Spelvin...................Ray Hallor
Sascha........................Carlo Schipa
Mrs. Ten Brock...........Myrtle Stedman
Farquar.................Capt E. H. Calvert
Mme. Julie...................Louise Baudet

Rarely does a musical book, even a grand opera, make a good film. "Sally" makes a bearcat. Maybe some more of them would, too, if Alfred E. Green directed and Colleen Moore romped through them.

This Green has a human understanding which is colossal as applied to screen expression of a theme, a plot and a story. The program does not credit the scenario adapter, who may share some of the result, but there can be no doubting by an experienced observer of projected material that the director in this instance is the motivating influence. And in this instance he has done a super-job.

The story is well known. But few suspected its depths and breadths until it hit in its present form. Starting with "the alley," it works up a profound rapport with Sally which carries her through the high drama and low comedy episodes to follow, the two threads going along, intertwined at times and each alone at times, but never snapping and seldom straining.

Miss Moore reaches the high peak of her young career, an actress of versatility, charm, talent that knocks at the door of genius, and that greatest and rarest of inspirations — fidelity. With her face smeared with tomato as a foundling brat or covered with royal jewels and regal gowns as the spurious international vampire, she gives the verity of life, itself, to the famous native Cinderella.

It is dubious whether Marilynn Miller herself could have approached her in the role, despite Miss Miller is one of the most exquisitely pulchritudinous creations of the Almighty and Miss Moore, while pretty, is far from being a ravishing or intoxicating beauty. She is only a youngster, half matured.

As a comedienne, she threatens Mabel Normand, for she is funny with her eyes, her feet, her every gesture and glance; as an emotional actress she is easily of the grade of Mary Pickford's finest, even today; for almost incredible flexibility of artistic finesse and verisimilitude of nature she is far beyond either. Those who regard that verdict as hysterical may find it verified by seeing this child sustain a half-million-or-so-dollar production at the apex of Broadway, most of the time in the gingham rags of an asylum orphan, as a dishwasher, as a topsy in whiteface.

Leon Errol is an interesting experiment. Usually the application of stage "originals" to screen roles has not been crowned with orchids. In this case it was a dancing comic whose only camera experience had been lukewarmly rewarded some years back in a series of indifferent two-reel slapsticks.

Errol is famously limited, being funny from the knees down, principally. In the musical show his dancing got him by powerfully. Here he does none, as it was show dancing and not plot dancing. Miss Moore has to dance as did Miss Miller, but Errol doesn't have to dance as did Errol.

His falls and gutta-percha ankles get a big laugh the first time and some laughs all the time. Some other stumbling business is excellent. As a character comedian, however, the limber-footed Errol is no important contribution to the gallery of the screen's elect.

Where the production calls for splendor, "Sally" is just that word itself. Otherwise it is in the character of the story, as it should be, with no straining of the narrative to let in expensive displays just to show that the producers are well off.

It is a fine film, an exuberating and amusing and affecting and impressive film. Green and Miss Moore should be proud of it, and so should Bolton and everyone who had a finger in it. And it will make money as well as friends; that is as certain as human nature is natural and human, for it has all the components of healthy appeal.

Lait.

SEVEN CHANCES

Buster Keaton production released through Metro-Goldwyn-Mayer. Presented by Joseph M. Schenck and made from the Roi Cooper Megrue farce, dramatically produced by David Belasco. Screen version by Jean Havez, Clyde Bruckman and Joseph A. Mitchell. Reviewed at the Capitol, New York, week March 15. Running time, 57 minutes.

James Shannon...............Buster Keaton
His Partner...................T. Roy Barnes
The Lawyer....................Snitz Edwards
The Girl.........................Ruth Dwyer
Her Mother................Frankie Raymond
Hired Man......................Jules Cowles
The Clergyman..............Erwin Connelly

A chase, probably one of the best ever screened, is the big thing of Keaton's latest release. It may seem this chase stuff is as old as the first motion-picture comedy, but it is done here with a novelty touch which makes the picture stand up as something exceptional.

The plot concerns a man who must marry by 7 o'clock to inherit $7,000,000. His own girl turns him down when he pulls an awkward proposal. Then his partner walks with him into a hotel dining room. Asking him how many girls he knows, the comic says "seven." Thus the seven chances. But one by one they are crossed out and things look tough, until the partner causes the afternoon newspapers to print a phoney yarn stating that the first girl in town to arrive in the church by 5 o'clock wins the millionaire. From the far sections they come scurrying—and the church is mobbed. So is Shannon, when they get a flash at him. After escaping from them temporarily the hird man of his girl's family tells him that the girl has reconsidered and if he can get there by 7 o'clock, getting married will be a cinch.

But the outraged dames start a chase that carries far out into the country, through and in rivers, over hills and down them, until at last one dislodged boulder sends hundreds of other boulders chasing the fleeing bidegroom. This boulder stuff is magnificently done. Large ones are dodged, small ones scare him to death, but, with all his troubles, the fadeout happy ending gets around. It's papier mache, of course, but great.

Keaton works straight here, minus tramp clothes and low-comedy methods. Therefore he isn't so effective in the early part of the film. But once it all gets underway—and the plot is really developed with celerity—laugh follows laugh in rapid succession.

"Seven Chances" doesn't look like it cost a million to make. Nine-tenths of the scenes are exteriors, and the interiors aren't expensive looking. Keaton himself directed.

Where the comedian draws regularly this one will satisfy. Considered by itself, the film is first-run material.

Sisk.

Dressmaker from Paris

Zukor-Lasky presentation. Paul Bern production and direction. Story by Adelaide Heilbron and Howard Hawks. Screen play by Miss Heilbron. Paramount release. Running time, 77 mins. At Rivoli, New York, week of March 5.

Fifi..........................Leatrice Joy
Angus McGregor...........Ernest Torrence
Billy Brent....................Allan Forrest
Joan..........................Mildred Harris
Allan Stone.......................Larry Gray
Mayor.....................Charles Crockett
Daughter..................Rosemary Cooper
Jim.........................."Spec" O'Donnell
And 4 Beauty Models

A spotty picture, great in some respects and undergrade in others, but destined to draw.

The producer, Paul Bern, who right now is being nursed as a De Mille in the making by the Zukor-Lasky coterie, comes out with glory. What price the glory set them back may be answered by a considerable figure. The fashion show in "The Dressmaker from Paris" is as prodigal a scene of its type as the screen has ever revealed.

The cast is a costly and a large one, with a mob scene of hundreds and no end of locations, ranging from Paris (on the level) to Chicago, California, etc. A flock of models wear an orgie of furs, lingerie and gowns that must have cost the price of a studio.

With all that, this screening leaves much to be wished for, mostly in the story, which starts excellently and turns into rank poppycock with as thin and abrupt a "happy ending" as ever insulted an audience. Beginning with the war romance of a midinette and an American shavetail, it veers to a boob mid-west burg with small intrigues, hokum comedy and relief "business," makes an absurd foundation for the gigantic and gargantuan clothes-flash, turns to rank melodrama, peters out to a finish and fades away on "One-Year Later," with a cooing baby for "sympathy."

Leatrice Joy, a year back one of the most startlingly attractive personalities in films, has unfortunately grown fleshy, her face is lined and she seems to have prematurely returned to the camera after her recent domestic blessing—motherhood.

She cannot stand close-ups, or could not when they were shot for this feature. Miss Joy will doubtless be restored to her beatific freshness, probably by now has been. But she did this film too soon.

Torrence, out of the character or any other character, gets laughs as the rube Scotch keeper of a small-town store where the Paris dressmaker inappropriately comes to turn the place upside down and win back the lieut. who helped her in those days during the war, since which, in seven years, she has become the leading gownist of the world (it can't be done), and has been the subject of many similarly absurd inconsistencies, many much more raw.

However, the women will want to see those clothes and the men will eat up those models, one of whom, unprogramed, is as beautiful as anything that ever was projected. Especially with the Gimbel-Paris Fashion Parade at the Rivoli, the week should be a hummer.

Lait.

March 25, 1925

DECLASSE

First National production of the Zoe Akins stage play in which Ethel Barrymore starred. Corinne Griffith starred on screen and direction by Robert G. Vignola. Scenarist not credited on print reviewed at the Strand, New York, March 22. Running time, 83 minutes.

Lady Helen Haden.........Corinne Griffith
Ned Thayer...................Lloyd Hughes
Rudolph Solomon...............Clive Brook
Sir Bruce Haden.......Rockcliffe Fellowes
Mrs. Leslie...............Lilyan Tashman
Lady Wildering.............Hedda Hopper
Sir Emmett Wildering......Bertram Johns
Timmins........................Gale Henry
Mrs. Walton...............Louise Fazenda
Mr. Walton....................Eddie Lyons
Hotel Manager..............Mario Carrillo

"Delcasse" is first and foremost, another example of inexpert writing marring an expensive and otherwise good production. For, as it is done in the movies, "Declasse' is as heavy-footed as a thing can well be, while its acted version was at once fragile and powerful. What the Warners did to "Deburau" First National has done to "Declasse." "Deburau," which was cinematized as "Lover of Camille," was written by the younger Guitry with the express purpose in mind of showing Camille when she was not in the throes of t. b. The picture flopped when the Warners had the lady coughing all over the lot.

In "Declasse" Zoe Atkins used the dramatic experiment of having her opening scene one in which a tense situation was on as the curtain arose. And it was successful. Those who recall the stage version recall that at the play's opening Lady Haden was making her husband apologize to guests after he had accused them of cheating at cards.

In the film all this is preluded by 20 minutes of piffle. First, to impress the idea of Lady Helen's noble ancestry, we are given a cut-back to one of her feminine ancestors who was decapitated when she refused to dishonor herself. Then much unnecessary footage is wasted, and the plot doesn't begin to develop until Lady Haden's pure love with young Ned Thayer is revealed by his unscrupulous sister-in-law. Then her divorce, and subsequently that declasse position which was hers when society made her an outcast. Through all of this Rudolph Solomon, a wealthy man, has followed her, wishing to make her his own. But always she turned him down, and as she lived moderately with her pearls and jewels slipping away one by one, the spectre of tomorrow, tomorrow and tomorrow forced her to Solomon.

But then young Thayer came back after years of regeneration in South Africa, and although Lady Helen dashed from Solomon's house to purposely throw herself before a cab—Thayer saw that she didn't die, and the happy ending replaced the death in the legit. That's only fair enough, of course, but the scenario and casting here has made for a flock of jumbled characters who mean little. They are competent enough actors and actresses, with the exception of Lilyan Tashman, but the distorted scenario has overridden the atmosphere of real gentility which pervaded the piece and has flooded it with so many strictly movie ideas that it is ineffective. Regarding Miss Tashman, it may be said that she photographs badly and is out of place in the role of Mrs. Leslie.

Corinne Griffith is but fair. Certainly it was expected that she would be very dramatic in this piece, but such is not the case. Actually, the hit of the film was made by Louise Fazenda and Eddie Lyons, who as a pair of coffee and cakers walk on the set with Variety flashed prominently through several sequences.

Settings are good, but some painted on flats and look it, even though they're not photographed close. The direction is way under the Vignola standard and the film as a whole is not to be regarded as above the average in box office value. Where Miss Griffith is a draw it may get by—where she isn't it looks like Cupid has shot his arrows in vain.

Despite a long New York run and reputation in the legit, it but half filled the Strand at Sunday's first de luxe show. *Sisk.*

SACKCLOTH AND SCARLET

Henry King Production, presented by Robert Kane, released by Paramount. Featuring Alice Terry. Story by George Gibbs, adapted by Tom Geraghty, Jules Furthman and Julie Herne. At the Rivoli, N. Y., week March 24. Running time, 70 minutes.

Joan Freeman .... Alice Terry
Stephen Edwards .... Orville Caldwell
Polly Freeman .... Dorothy Sebastian
Etienne Fochard .... Otto Matiesen
Beatrice Selignac .... Kathleen Kirkham
Samuel Curtis .... John Miljan
Miss Curtis .... Clarissa Selwynne
Jack .... Jack Huff

"Sackcloth and Scarlet" sounds like a title that is going to mean real money at the box office. Those that read the novel, either in its serial form or as a book, will want to see how it was possible to get the punch across and still escape the censors. That is exactly what has been done in this case, even though it took three crackerjack script writers to do the trick. Henry King, in directing, handled the sex stuff so delicately that while the suggestion is all there there is nothing that offends.

Alice Terry is featured above the other members of the cast, but it is little Dorothy Sebastian, in the role of the erring sister, that takes the picture away from her in practically every scene that they have together. Miss Terry, however, looks radiantly beautiful and really carries the heavy portion of the story, characterizinz the role of the mature sister in a spiritual manner that registers splendidly.

Orville Caldwell, as the hero, rugged in appearance and fitting the type, did not quite measure up in the later scenes. Little Jackie Huff, as the youngster, was outstanding and showed careful direction.

"Sackcloth and Scarlet," as a story, tells of the wilful selfishness of a younger sister of a wealthy family. She wants to live and adventure in life and takes it upon herself to run off under an assumed name, vamp a guide who has taken her to the top of the mountain, and then, when it comes to paying for her misstep, she lets the burden fall on the shoulders of the older sister, who takes her child and rears him.

When the youngster is four or five years old the elder sister meets the same man. He, in the meantime, has risen politically and is in Washington. The two fall in love, but at this point the younger sister walks into the picture again. She has taken her inheritance and squandered it in riotous living and is ill. She turns to her older sister for assistance, and when the latter discovers that the man she loves is the one that is the father of the youngster she compels a marriage. Then in another year after the younger girl has died there is the suggestion of the happy ending, worked out without the all too obvious picture clinch.

There are spots in the picture where it is a little draggy, but in the main there is a wallop of sex in the feature that will make it stand up at the gate. *Fred.*

THE BRIDGE OF SIGHS

Phil Rosen production presented by the Warner Bros. Story by Charles K. Harris. Dorothy Mackaill, Creighton Hale, Alec B. Francis, Richard Tucker featured. Piccadilly, New York, week March 21. Running time, 71 minutes.

Linda Harper............ Dorothy Mackaill
Billy Craig.................. Creighton Hale
John Harper.................. Alec B. Francis
Glenn Hayden.............. Richard Tucker
William Craig.................. Ralph Lewis
Smithers....................... Clifford Saum
Mrs. William Craig......... Fanny Midgley
Mrs. Smithers.............. Aileen Manning

Phil Rosen, who directed this picture, made the production of "Abraham Lincoln." In this particular instance he has taken a story that in itself was evidently pretty weak material and developed it by his humanism of direction into a picture that is going to be well liked by audiences. He might have easily overshot the mark and jammed a lot of heroic melodrama stuff into it and killed what little chance the story afforded, but instead he shot a picture that will make good on the manner in which the characters are interpreted by a capable cast.

As might be judged from the title, "The Bridge of Sighs" is a story built on that famous structure that leads from the Tombs to the Criminal Court in New York.

For characters we have on one hand a wealthy man with an invalided wife and a grown son who is a pretty wild youngster; on the other a widower who works in the office of the young man's father, and a daughter. The wealthy man's son and the employe's daughter have to be brought together, and therefore we have a picture script. The manner of their meeting is neatly contrived and plausibly led up to by skillful direction, and from then on romance is let to take its course, although the young man steals a couple of thousands from his dad and the girl's father is accused of the crime, found guilty and convicted, is not permitted to wreck the love affair, for when the victim of circumstantial evidence is informed of the facts, he knowing his daughter loves the young man, refuses to continue his fight for justice, being satisfied with the pardon the Governor has signed. Therefore, in the end the two young people dash off for the marriage license bureau, but not until the little hero has planted a smacking right under the jaw of the towering heavy and sent him sprawling. That was to be expected, for what other reason is there for heaving a heavy in the picture unless to have the hero wallop him some time or another during the proceedings?

Dorothy Mackaill makes a very charming lead to Creighton Hale and gives the role everything that she has without ever emoting, and there were lots of spots where that could have been done all too easily. Hale is convincing enough as the hero, while Alec B. Francis as the father of the girl gave his usual finished performance.

"The Bridge of Sighs" is an altogether satisfying program picture that will stand up in the average neighborhood house and get some money. *Fred.*

PERCY

Thos. H. Ince presentation starring Charles Ray. Adapted from the novel, "The Desert Fiddler," and directed by R. William Neil. Showing at the Colony, New York, week of March 22. Running time, 59 mins.

Percival Rogeen.................. Don Marion
Mrs. Rogeen...................... Louise Dresser
Jasper Rogeen.................. Joseph Kilgour
Percival Rogeen (grown up)...... Chas. Ray
James.............................. Clyde McAtee
"Breezy" Barnes................ David Winter
Holy Joe......................... Charles Murray
Reedy Jenkins............... Victor McLaglen
Lolita, a dancehall senorita.... Betty Blythe
Imogene Chandler.......... Barbara Bedford

A picture mishandled and brutally treated, which leaves Charles Ray as far away from the objective of turning out a good film as he was before starting. Also there is the dubious aspect of a supporting player stepping in and running away with the personal equation.

Charles Murray, the same comedian of the old Keystone days, is the outstanding personage in a characterization of a versatile and gambling "sky pilot" that shames the remaining component parts of the release. The film looks to have been the victim of faulty cutting and direction, in that it jumps back and forth in a haphazard career to quell any interest in the story which comes disastrously close to rank melodrama. This is true to such an extent it is simply a question of watching Murray while sitting through the picture. If it weren't for Murray "Percy" would be minus a redeeming feature.

The fault is not Ray's. He does as best he can in defining a youth, who has been closely guarded by his mother, suddenly left in the middle of a desert to eke out an existence as best he can with nothing but his ability to play a violin. The sequence virtually bursts into each episode without semblance of blending.

After jumping out west the action includes the dancehall proprietor's hold over the ranchers by underhanded methods of curtailing the water supply, the appeal of the girl rancher in an executive position because of an invalid father, the proprietor's subsequent attack upon her, the rushing of troops to the dam and Ray coming out of the boiling pot a man.

It's almost enough to style the picture an epic in hoke, and is sufficiently bad to provoke surprise as to how it ever reached a release state in its present condition.

If nothing else, the picture can't do Ray any good. That's undeniable, and Ray, as concerns the screen public, is in no condition to fool around with indifferent or actually poor pictures.

As it stands, Percy" is a great picture for Murray. Other than that it's as close to a complete "bust" as any of the Broadway houses has held this season. *Skig.*

CONTRABAND

Paramount picture made from Clarence Buddington Kelland's novel and scenarized by Jack Cunningham. Directed by Alan Crosland, with Lois Wilson, Noah Beery, Raymond McKee and Raymond Hatton featured. At Rialto, New York, week March 23. Running time, about 70 minutes.

Carmel Lee.......................... Lois Wilson
Deputy Jenney...................... Noah Beery
Launcelot Bangs............ Raymond Hatton
Evan B. Pell................. Raymond McKee
Sheriff Churchill................ Charles Ogle
Tubal......................... Luke Cosgrave
Abner Fownes................. Edwards Davis
Simmy............................ Johnny Fox
George Bogardus................ Victor Potel
Jared Whitfield.............. Alphonse Ethier
Pee Wee Bangs............... Cesare Gracina
Mrs. Churchill............... Lillian Leighton

"Contraband" represents one of those funny movie things, as perfectly produced as pictures can be. The scenario is corking and airtight. The acting is thoroughly capable. But the thing as a whole is unreal, not very interesting and certainly not box-office fodder.

The story is by Clarence Buddington Kelland. His "Mark Tidd" stories formerly ran in the "American Boy" magazine and, as kid stories, they were suitable. Yet, even rating the movie intelligence as low as some producers claim, the story of "Contraband" is still childish. It is on the same general plan.

It concerns a small-town newspaper and the girl to whom it was left. She came to Gibeon, penniless, to take it over. There she found a gang of crooks bootlegging, even going so far as to kill off the sheriff to carry out their work.

But she, with help, finally rounds them up and brings the town's most respectable citizen in under his own colors—bootlegger.

In the plot is a foolish college professor who, upon being ejected from his lodging house for non-payment of dues, promptly established himself in a hay loft with a handle for light.

Also the illuminating spectacle of submitted photographs to the paper—so small the type was set by hand. (A paper setting by hand boasts no engraving devices.)

There is a good laugh, however, and that comes when printer's devil upsets a long galley of hand-set stuff. But maybe even that laugh is restricted to printers and others of the illuminati.

The acting is good always. The sets are beyond reproach and the printing office was a faithful reproduction of a small-town plant. It looks as if money had been spent on the film, but Kelland's story is so out of touch with modern fiction—his characters so unconvincing that the audience apparently took little interest in the proceedings.

As a member of the Famous Forty (second stanza), this looks like an ill sister. Principally because its title has little drawing power, the cast contains no pulling names and the story itself fails to satisfy. *Sisk.*

ENTICEMENT

First National picture and Thomas H. Ince production. Adapted from novel of same name by Clive Arden. Directed by George Archainbaud. Features Mary Astor, Ian Keith and Clive Brook. Louise Dresser also in the cast. Running time, 73 mins.

Somewhat of a sexy theme, with enough of the fire deleted to make it a disappointment for the expectant, but well enough as suitable screen fare for the better class houses.

Evidently "shot" in the Canadian northwest for its Switzerland scenes, probably Banff. It's a beauteous piece of photographic work for so long as the narrative clings to the "Alps" as a location. Many of the interiors are also handsomely dressed, hence the picture does not lack in appearance.

If the story has a tendency to drag, the scenics are sufficient to overcome the slow-moving narration during the midway passages. And then there is Mary Astor, her work and the personal illusion she presents, both worthy of high rating. As run off "Enticement" looks to be conscientious acting by Miss Astor that should definitely establish her in the minds of numerous film followers, especially of the male gender. Clive Brook has been more to advantage than he is seen here, while Ian Keith makes a suitable semi-heavy, delineates the hungry-hearted opera singer to convince, and makes an appropriate balance for Miss Astor's winsomeness.

If the players are satisfactory, not so the story. It makes merry with time and passes it off as many scenarios have done before it. Besides, it includes the situation of the young American girl shocking an old and aristocratic English family by her modern conception of propriety and morals. And she is so pure minded. That is, until the opera singer has occasion to take off her stocking in a lonely mountain hotel, whence follows the outburst, his overthrowing of discretion to the disillusionment of the girl and her ideal of a sexless friendship with the opera star, an outgrowth of war days.

The tale starts immediately after the war, jumps two years and into Switzerland, thence to Paris and on to London. The girl finally marries her former English admirer, but the complex is inserted when a busybody couple let loose the information they had previously seen the youthful now English wife with the singer amidst the Alps. To close everything out peacefully, and so that he may rid himself of a pestering but absent wife, the opera luminary conveniently takes it upon himself to walk in front of a bus.

A snow avalanche effect during the mountain sojourn is well done, evidently made magnitudinous through slow photography, and carries a certain degree of punch.

Louise Dresser is in and out with limited footage, but capably takes care of such responsibility as has been given her.

It's far from poor screen entertainment, with the playing of Miss Astor and Mr. Keith sufficient to belie such contention. The picturesqueness and snow-slide stuff will help, and the broad hint at the sex ingredient should restrain the number of walkouts.

At the very least it's a feather for Miss Astor. *Skig.*

BAD COMPANY

St. Regis picture, starring Madge Kennedy and Conway Tearle. From story by J. C. Brownell and directed by E. H. Griffith.

Gloria Waring	Madge Kennedy
Peter Ewing	Bigelow Cooper
James Hamilton	Conway Tearle
Teddy Lamont	Lucille Lee Stewart
Dick Reynolds	Charles Emmett Mack

An unimposing vehicle possessed of a few lavish interiors and showing Madge Kennedy to advantage. Hardly new to pictures, this girl has a chic appearance and continues to handle herself in a manner superior to more than one pantomiming actress flickering consistently on first-run screens.

Mr. Tearle is opposite in a lackadaisical performance he has surmounted many times. Lucille Lee Stewart has turned in a monotonously toned piece of work, while Charles Emmett Mack is virtually buried in an insipid role that must have rolled off his knife and means as much to him.

The story surrounds the stage, and in this respect includes the "Counting the Hours" number from Carroll's late "Vanities." This bit is given special program mention, as is the specifying of the entire chorus of the "Greenwich Village Follies," although just where the latter choprines enter is not clear or discernible, unless the "Follies" bunch hopped into the "Hours" number just for the picture, and that doesn't seem plausible.

Gloria Waring (Miss Kennedy) is a musical comedy star with a "John" brother (Mr. Mack), whom she must rescue from the arms of a coin-digging vamp (Miss Stewart), and to this end enters the house of James Hamilton (Mr. Tearle) to rob the safe of her father's will, so her brother can't get the inheritance. Hamilton traces the holdup miss through the cigaret containing pistol used, and it's a love match from the gun.

The prospective "jam" becomes apparent when Hamilton, in taking a hand in the rescue work, discovers that the kid brother's idol is a former flame of his own and he must denounce himself to save the youth.

The picture plays nicely minus a decisive punch, and should steer an easy course through the maze of middle-class houses. Miss Kennedy can hold it up with her "class," under that specification, while the aforementioned bedecked interiors are an appearance asset. Miss Kennedy inserts some mild comedy bits for registration points, and the continuity is at least smooth. Photographically the film is according to general requirements. *Skig.*

THE AIR MAIL

Irvin Willat Production. Presented by Adolph Zukor and Jesse L. Lasky. Story by Byron Morgan, adapted for the screen by James Shelly Hamilton. Featuring Warner Baxter, Billie Dove, Mary Brian and Douglas Fairbanks, Jr. Running time, 75 minutes.

Russ Kane	Warner Baxter
Alice Rendon	Billie Dove
Minnie Wade	Mary Brian
Sandy	Douglas Fairbanks, Jr.
Peter Rendon	George Irving
Jim Cronin	Richard Tucker
Bill Wade	Guy Oliver
Scotty	Lee Shumway
Rene Lenoir	Jack Bryon
Donald McKee	John Webb Dillion
Speck	Lloyd Whitlock

Out and out melodramatic thriller, constructed with a view to assisting the postal authorities to call attention to the air mail service, but nevertheless a picture that holds a lot of wallop for the audiences that want a hazard kick in the screen entertainment. This picture provides just that, and because of it "The Air Mail" is going to prove a whole lot more satisfactory to the smaller houses from a box-office standpoint. In the regular pre-release theatres it won't stand up quite as strong, but when it hits the houses that cater to the masses it is going to be sure fire.

There are a quartet of names featured at the head of the cast. They are Warner Baxter, Billie Dove, Mary Brian and Douglas Fairbanks, Jr. Misses Dove and Brian are the only two women in the cast, the balance being all men.

The picture shows the hardships of the men flying the mail planes through all sorts of weather. The air mail service slogan, "No rain nor snow nor wind nor night can stop the pilot in his flight," is played up heavily in several scenes

The hero, played by Baxter, joins the service with the idea of turning off the registered mail sack some time or another when it is heavily enough laden. Instead of this, however, the spirit of the service gets him, and his regeneration is brought about. Billie Dove is the girl of the story. She and her father are the occupants of a "ghost city," one of those places in the desert where a boom has collapsed and everyone has pulled up stakes. They and a lone Chinaman are the sole inhabitants of the little town. Forced down in the midst of a rainstorm, the pilot-hero meets the girl, and later, when she runs out of medicine for her father, she signals him in his daily flight, and he stops and promises to return the next day with a prescription filled for the old man. But on that trip he is attacked by two planes filled with aerial mail robbers, and they force him down just outside of the ghost city. Gun play and hand-to-hand combat follow, but the hero manages to win out in the end.

The open scenes give an idea of the territory covered by the mail fliers, the shots being taken from a plane. It is a good atmospheric touch.

Douglas Fairbanks, Jr., has the role of a youthful hanger-on about the mail air port, and scores in a comedy way. He does one bit in escaping from a trio of tough characters that suggests his dad in adeptness. Mary Brian plays opposite the young Fairbanks. *Fred.*

A CAFE IN CAIRO

Producers' Distributing Corporation picture, supervised by Hunt Stromberg and directed by Chet Withey. Priscilla Dean starred. Founded on the novel by Izola Forrester. Running time, 65 minutes.

Naida	Priscilla Dean
Barry Braxton	Robert Ellis
Jaradi	Carl Stockdale
Batooka	Evelyn Selbie
Kali	Harry Woods
Tom Hays	John Steppling
Rosamond	Carmen Phillips
Col. Alastair	Larry Steers
Evelyn	Ruth King

Priscilla Dean is being widely advertised as "Empress of the Elemental Emotions." To use some more alliteration, it can be explained that the difference between "Elemental Emotions" and "Primitive Passions" is nux vomica and void.

On the basis of this exploitation, her recent vehicles have been bizarre propositions showing her as the freak woman with a Great Love. This time she is a cafe dancer in Cairo, a white girl, the tool of unscrupulous Arabs. Taken by an Arab who witnessed the death of her father and mother, she is raised in his family, ignorant of her parentage. When the desert tribes start an uprising, a young diplomat is found to hold a paper greatly desired. And because Naida has wiles, she is sent to get the paper. She gets it—and love hits her a swift one, so she doesn't give the paper to the chieftains.

Thereupon her foster-father gets sore and attempts to force her to marry Kali, a sensuous member of the chief troupe. But she rebels and when sent to the Palace of Stars on the Nile where maidens about to be wed are sent for rest and meditation, she gets a message to him—and he busts in the sacred doors and does his stuff. But he is nicked by the villains and nearly drowned when the girl dives from a high tower and brings him to the surface. Then, rescued in a swift motor boat race, they sail away to get married.

Miss Dean plays the girl and does her work well. Robert Ellis as the hero is also good, while the various native types are chosen with discriminative care. So the cast is okay. The same thing goes for the production, solid and elaborate in spots, indicative of considerable care and money. But the scenario is weak and wobbly, and the story so shot full of inconsistencies that in toto it lines up as a fair out-of-town program picture unworthy of being branded as a "special" release.

It isn't big city first run stuff but falls in that group one peg below. With an air-tight scenario and a concentration of the numerous thrills depicted, this review would have read differently. *Sisk.*

SECRETS OF NIGHT

Universal production directed by Herbert Blache. From the play, "The Night Cap," by Guy Bolton and Max Marcin. Photographed by Gilbert Warrenton. Cast headed by James Kirkwood, Madge Bellemy, Zasu Pitts, Tom Wilson, Rosemary Theby and Otto Hoffman. At the Broadway, New York, week of March 23. Runs about 70 mins.

"Secrets of the Night" starts out to be heavy, involved melodrama, suddenly switches to mystery and ends in a ridiculously farcical vein. Perhaps that's one of the things that is the matter with it as a picture. None of its varying interests seems to get anywhere. It is an adaptation of the legitimate piece by Bolton and Marcin that under the title of "The Night Cap" enjoyed a fairly prosperous three months' run at the 39th Street some four years ago.

The stage version, if memory serves, had its comic situations subservient to the mystery and dramatic incidents, and the laughs, while there were quite a few, were merely incidental. The film makes the mistake of trying for comic business primarily and because it is lacking in speed, pep and a cast that fully understands farce playing, it fails to be a first-rate comedy. Naturally the dramatic and mysterious sides of the story cannot be expected to figure much, although at times there is some spooky atmosphere.

The plot treats of the murder of a wealthy banker and the rounding up of no less than a dozen persons upon whom suspicion equally seems to rest. This was an ingenious thought long before Barrie ever used it for his "Shall We Join the Ladies?" but the adapter and director have not worked it up to its possibilities. At the finish it develops, not much to the surprise of any one, that the murdered man is not dead at all, and the whole thing has been a hoax to put across a business deal. This does not explain the majority of the mysterious happenings that occurred earlier in the evening and that would be excusable under the law of dramatic license were the picture as a whole more enjoyable.

The few laughs in the film come chiefly from the antics of an old colored servant and a spinster maiden lady (played adequately by Tom Wilson and Zasu Pitts), who are frightened out of their wits. The rest of the cast, headed by James Kirkwood, Madge Bellamy and Rosemary Theby, seem unable as a unit to do anything with their impossible parts. The film has cost little aside from the "names," as the action is almost wholly within not overlavish interiors and there are no mechanical or scenic effects worth mentioning.

In the cheaper houses they may think some of the later scenes funny. That and the fact that most audiences, no matter how bored, will, for curiosity's sake, want to see how the mystery is explained, are about the only things that can be said for "Secrets of the Night."

THE COAST PATROL

Bud Barsky production, starring Kenneth MacDonald. Story by William E. Wing and direction by Barsky. Cast includes Claire de Lorez, Fay Wray, Spotiswoode Aitken and Geno Carrodo. Reviewed March 20 at the Stanley, New York. Running time, 65 minutes.

Barsky pulls a nifty in this one. He announces the production of "Bud" Barsky, the personal supervision of I. J. Barsky and the direction of Irving J. Barsky. The difference between I. J., Irving J. and "Bud" is the difference between Julian Eltinge and Bill Dalton.

Kenneth MacDonald seems to be the Barsky star. Why is something else again? As a rule, most of the independents like Barsky, Steiner, Carlos, and the rest have stunt men as their main bets. In this manner they are enabled to put out entertaining films at a slight cost. MacDonald, aside from being a powerful but awkward fighter, possesses little movie value. He acts as badly as most of the stunt men, but he hasn't the redeeming feature of their daring feats, while in appearance he is clean-cut looking without winning any prizes.

The story in which he is starred has him as a revenue agent after smugglers who have made their rendezvous on the Maine coast—one of those towns with the odor of fish scales at one end of the beach and the flash of headquarters uniforms at the other. And at the fish scale end of the beach is the protege of the old lighthouse keeper. The ringleader of the smugglers sets a trap for her and almost ruins her life in the good old way made famous by the 10-20-30 rep shows. With him is a vampy accomplice who eventually goes straight, while the revenuer gets the smugglers, the girl and the villain jumps overboard to save himself a worse death.

"The Coast Patrol" was plainly made for the shooting galleries. It is plainly a 15-cent admission film once it strikes its spots. As such it has a good production and a good story. The sub-titles are flagrantly melodramatic and the acting at times very hammish, but the story demanded that sort of stuff.

In general detail this film compares very favorably with the better independent releases. Some of the sets are good and indicate some expenditure on Barsky's part. But the mistake is in featuring MacDonald all over the picture, for as a star he doesn't measure up—even in an independent. Aside from that "The Coast Patrol" is competently cast and well acted. *Sisk.*

BRANDED A THIEF

Arrow Film starring Yakima Canutt. A Ben Wilson Production directed by Paul Hirsch. At Stanley, New York, March 19, one day. Running time, 58 minutes.

Jess Dean....................Yakima Canutt
Granddaddy Jim..........Judge Hamilton
"Horse" Williamson......Wilbur McGaugh
Jeanne........................Alys Murrell

Despite the first name, Yakima Canutt isn't a Jap star. He's the world's champ cowboy, according to his title billing. Apparently Arrow Film is entering him against the million and one lesser Tom Mixes who seem to have sprung up since the favorite western star's draw came to be recognized. Canutt is pretty much like the rest of them in build; he's tall, rangy and shuffling in his walk. His face is pleasant but his acting ability not so pronounced. As a rider and fighter, however, he holds his own beautifully. Therefore he probably qualifies for the cheap stuff in which he is being starred.

The story of this one concerns an old man, the owner of a productive gold mine. The hero is his friend while the villains are out to murder the old man and slip the blame on the hero.

When they see the old boy give Young Apollo some gold dust for the grand-daughter (and she's the love interest) they fire at the old man. Thinking they've killed him, into town they frame the youngster for the job. Things look tough until it is found the old man hasn't been killed.

The rest of the film shows the lone cowboy stalking and defending himself alternately against his three enemies.

For comedy, a six-year-old girl with the regulation cowboy lingo is used to good effect. The kid isn't programed, but she's a blonde with a pug nose and a possibility.

But one interior set was used. The rest was natural background with the locations good in spots and decidedly poor in others. Direction showed some lapses in allowing faraway shots, while in other instances the terrific fight stuff held a punch due to the piling of one climax on another.

"Branded a Thief" should sell cheaply because it has the dime cost mark written all over. Even though fair entertainment, it is far too weak to hold the bill by itself except in the smallest of houses and neighborhoods. Its spot is the shooting gallery, where, bought cheaply, it will suffice.

The thing to remember about all these minor westerns is that unheralded stars in makeshift plots possess no drawing power on their own. *Sisk.*

SOFT SHOES

Steller Productions, released through Producers Distributing Corporation. Underworld comedy drama starring Harry Carey. Directed by Lloyd Ingraham. Story by Hunt Stromberg and Harvey Gates. At Loew's New York, March 24. Half of double feature program one day. Running time, 65 mins.

Pat Halahan...........................Harry Carey
Faith O'Day...........................Lillian Rich
Dummy O'Day.........................Paul Weigel
Quig Mundy..........................Francis Ford
Bradley...............................Stanton Heck
Mrs. Bradley.....................Harriet Hammond
The Chicago Kid...................Jimmie Quinn
Yet Tzu...................................So-Jim
Mabel Packer......................Majel Coleman
Markham.............................John Steppling
Hank.......................................By Himself

Comedy dramatic picture with a fast-moving, well written story which just escapes farce classification. Harry Carey looks better here than in any of his recent releases. He is surrounded by an excellent cast and a leading woman, Lillian Rich, who should be heard from.

The story concerns the adventures of Pat Halahan (Mr. Carey), a small-town sheriff who goes to Frisco to spend a legacy. At a restaurant one night he is accused by a diner of flirting with his wife. Later that night Pat captures a pretty girl thief, Faith O'Day (Miss Rich) invading his apartment. He offers to return a brooch she has stolen elsewhere if she will turn straight. She agrees, and he enters the boudoir of the owner of the brooch, only to discover it is the woman of the cafe. Her husband detects him, but he escapes.

Returning to his hotel he and Faith explain they are married when house detectives and police break in. Faith escapes. Pat visits her at her home and meets Quig Mundy (Francis Ford), a gangster, who is after Faith. Pat impersonates the Chicago Kid, a crook, and appears to join the crooks. Secretly he has warned the police. The gansters discover his falseness when the Real Chi Kid breezes in.

They entice Pat to a cellar and proceed to beat him up. His allies, the police, arrive in time. Returning to the girl's home he saves her from Mundy, who has gone to square accounts with the stoolpigeoness. Mundy is bumped off by a mysterious Chink, who turns out to be a detective watching the gang.

The picture will entertain second-string house audiences. It's strongest assets are speed and excellent continuity, despite the adventurous detail crowded in.

Evidence of copious cutting are visible, with the footage whittled right down to the bone. *Con.*

BATTLING BUNYAN

Crown Productions, Inc., starring Wesley Barry in boxing comedy, from the "Saturday Evening Post" story by Raymond Leslie Goldman. Adapted by Jefferson Moffit. Directed by Paul Hurst. Released through Pathe. Running time, 65 mins.

Battling Bunyan............Wesley Barry
Peterson.....................Landers Stevens
Rudy..............................Pat Kemp
Molly Costigan..................Molly Malone
Johnny Prentiss...............Johnny Relasco
Reilly.............................Harry Mann
Jim Canby.....................Frank Campeau
Sailor Levinsky...............Frankie Fields
The Stranger...................Chester Conklin
The Referee......................Al Kaufman

This is a small town boxing story which will gain the grown-up Wesley Barry many picture friends. Barry has shot up over night into a tall, gangling youth, but he hasn't lost his freckles or his likable screen personality through adolescence.

His success in this picture may determine his future screen classification as a youthful, athletic lead who will appeal to the lovers of youth, particularly those fans not given to over-impartiality toward the cake-eater type of youth so numerous in motion pictures.

Barry is a wholesome looking type of kid, and though not the collar adv. type, arouses just as much sympathy and feminine admiration.

In this boxing comedy drama he is introduced as Battling Bunyan, a young mechanic in a small town garage. He is in love with Molly Costigan (Molly Malone) and has ambitions to purchase a partnership in the flivver hospital and marry Molly.

Johnny Prentiss, lightweight champion of the world, meets Molly while motoring through, and antagonizes Bunyan by his attentions. Prentiss promises Molly he will return, and when Bunyan calls him for undue familiarity he handles the apprentice roughly and drives off.

Bunyan's pugnacity attracts the attention of a local fight promoter, who puts him on at the local club, where he becomes a comedy card through his awkward and unorthodox methods of boxing. He wins consistently, however, and is fast approaching the goal he has set, the partnership in the garage, when Prentiss returns and renews his attentions to Molly.

Prentiss is asked to box for the local club, but stipulates he must be handed a set-up. Bunyan is picked, but refuses to frame anything. Bunyan demands $1,000 for the bout, and insists it be on the level. They compromise by giving him $200 a round.

Bunyan takes a terrible beating, but lasts four rounds, when the police stop the bout. Bunyan pleads to be allowed to finish, and begs the audience to keep on laughing for a couple of rounds more, but not to stop the bout. He collapses in the middle of the speech and is carried to his dressing room.

Molly seeks him and runs into Prentiss, who was dressed. The latter tries to force his attentions on her after his manager has locked them in the dressing rooms. She calls for help, and Bunyan staggers out. He and Prentiss mix it up behind locked doors, Bunyan succeeding in beating the champ in the rough and tumble rumpus.

The crowd break the doors down and Prentiss and his manager are given one hour to leave town. Bunyan wins Molly and the partnership, concluding a most entertaining picture capably directed.

The difference in weight between Barry and Johnny Relasco was noticeable, but partially disguised by the speed of the bout shots. This same element also effectually disguised Barry's mediocre boxing ability.

Molly Malone was sweet and appealing as the youthful heroine, and Harry Mann convincing in the impossible role of Reilly, the Hebrew manager of Prentiss. This character will not be conducive to endorsement from the boxing profession, for the manager has been villainously painted by the author, who has usurped the limits of license to incorporate a heavy into his story. Present-day fight managers and methods bear about the same resemblance to Reilly as Nome to Miami.

Picture fans will like this picture, and it can stand on its own in the second run houses as a feature. In first run houses it qualifies as a strong half-program feature. *Con.*

PORTS OF CALL

William Fox presentation starring Edmund Lowe. Directed by Denison Clift. Story by Garrett E. Fort. At Loew's, New York, March 24. Half of a double feature program. Running time about 70 mins.

Kirk Rainsford...............Edmund Lowe
Marjorie Vail...................Hazel Keener
Randolph Sherman.......William Davidson
Archer Rainsford..........William Conklin
Sly..................................Bobby Mack
Lillie.........................Lilyan Tashman
Mrs. Rainsford.................Alice Ward
Peggy........................Mary McLean

A highly dramatic and romantic story of prenatal influence, showing the transition of a moral and physical coward into a couragous, firebreathing hero through the influence of a woman.

Edmund Lowe makes a human being of Kirk Rainsford, the young clubman, who loses the girl he is engaged to by an exhibition of cowardness following which he is kicked out of his home by his father who is responsible for Kirk's weakness

The boy wanders to Ports of Call and meets Lillie (Lilyan Tashman), another outcast. He and the girl become friends. Leaving a gambling house with a heavy winning Kirk is set upon by highjackers and under the girl's stimulus puts up a courageous battle. He is stabbed during the mix up and nursed back to health by the girl.

The pair decide to seek employment and Kirk goes to Costa, who has promised to aid him. The long arm of coincidence is slightly fractured here. Costa is overseer on an estate recently purchased by the husband of the girl Kirk lost. Both are living at the place and Castro has planned to rouse the natives, abduct Marjorie, and acquire the place himself.

Kirk and Lillie inform the Sherman's of the plot with Kirk and Lillie aiding them when the uprising occurs. Sherman and Costa are killed in the battle and Kirk confirms his mastery of his former fear by taking a leading part in defeating the insurrection.

The story is interesting, and Lowe is happily cast in a sympathetic role. His recent elevation to stardom seems amply justified, for he compares favorably with any of the screen sheiks. Miss Tashman, in a "Rain" role, also shows to advantage. She is acquiring poise and seems more at ease in this picture than previously. As Loew's leading woman she helped make the story stand up.

The balance of the cast are well chosen, Hazel Keener playing intelligently as the girl who misjudged Kirk and Bobby Mack turning in a good bit of character portrayal as "Sly," a sort of a "Friday" for Loew.

The picture is a good program feature for the neighborhood houses and will stand up despite south sea and tropical scenarios have been as prevalent as flivvers in Detroit. *Con.*

RIDIN' THROUGH

Universal release starring William Desmond. Directed by Arthur Rosson, with story by Charles Logue. Cast includes Claude Payton and Ruth Stonehouse. Showing at Loew's New York as half double bill March 19.

Indifferent western with little to raise it above the mediocre.

Following the orthodox conception that has turned out 90 per cent of all westerns, this one tells of a gunman doing an about face through a mania to do good deeds, thereby getting into a "jam" with his best friends and his pal's wife and sister. The film includes the inevitable chase.

Desmond falls far short of being able to convince in his personal portrayal with the only legitimate performance coming from Ruth Stonehouse, opposite Desmond, as the sister.

Placed upon a double feature bill this picture threw the burden of responsibility upon the other half.

Skig.

THE WAY OF A GIRL

Metro-Goldwyn-Mayer picture and a Robert G. Vignola production, presented by Louis B. Mayer. Vignola the director; staged by Katherine N. Burt. Features Eleanor Boardman, Matt Moore, William Russell and Mathew Betz. At the Capitol, New York week of March 29. Running time, 62 mins.

Rosamond	Eleanor Boardman
George	Matt Moore
Brand	William Russell
Matt	Mathew Betz
Police Judge	Charles K. French
Prize Fighter	Jack Herrick
Traffic Cop	Leo Willis
Woman in Jail	Kate Price

Away from the ordinary and a well-made picture, but the question concerning its entertaining qualities must remain open because of the yarn it spins.

The script includes the personal angle of the scenario writer and the players figuring out the continuity. That provides ample leeway for what seems to be perfect double photography of Eleanor Boardman, in miniature, climbing all over a typewriter and taking the author to task for getting her in various "jams." These insertions are equal, if not better, to anything of the type which has been seen on a Broadway sheet.

But the picture's strength may be its weakness, for it is problematical as to the manner in which a film-going public will receive the excellently pictured crossfire between Miss Boardman and the author, breaking in as it does into the "tight" situations so as to disrupt any illusions the tale may have built up. Photographically and technically the film is a balm to those interested in trick camera work and leaves a mark which many a crank spinner will find it difficult to hit.

The opening is the scenario writer order to rehash his script by command of M.-G.-M. Looking over "stills," he picks Miss Boardman, who walks out of the "still" to discuss who will be her leading man. Following this the tale goes into a headstrong girl determined to retain her independence despite her engagement.

The players are actually subordinated to the camera work and the speed with which the action moves, making this release not so much a question of playing as of story with a rapid continuity. The "names" mean little other than as outside billing, although there is nothing resembling a poor performance.

"The Way of a Girl" should prove a barometer as to how familiar a film may become with an audience.

Skig.

MEN AND WOMEN

William deMille production, presented by Adolph Zukor and Jesse L. Lasky, featuring Richard Dix at the head of an all-star cast, including Neil Hamilton, Claire Adams and Robert Edeson. From the play by David Belasco and Henry C. De Mille. Adapted by Clara Beranger. Shown at the Rivoli, N. Y., week March 29, 1925. Running ime, 64 minutes.

Will Prescott	Richard Dix
Agnes Prescott	Claire Adams
Ned Seabury	Neil Hamilton
Marco Culman	Robert Edeson
Arnold Kirke	Henry Stephenson
Cousin Kate	Flora Finch

Looks to be one of the best box office bets William deMille has turned out in some time. It does prove that Richard Dix, featured over the rest of the all-star cast, is one of the most versatile of the men of the screen. With his performance in "Too Many Kisses" fresh in mind, those who see him in this will come to the realization that here is an actor and not just a type.

There are, however, a couple of mistakes in "Men and Women," but easily rectified, nothing more or less than titles. The first one is the one to the effect that here is a story

without a "hero or heroine." Picture house audiences want heroes and heroines. The others are two spoken titles in the latter part, spoken between the banker and the assistant cashier and overheard by the cashier. The first is the one in which the banker refuses to believe his cashier had sunk so low that he would have planned the theft to have the assistant sent to prison. That should be taken out, as well as the next spoken title.

Through it greater sympathy will be gained for the real thief where the public really want it, and incidentally make the effect of his receiving inspiration at the stained glass church window the more effective.

Of course, the fact that here is the Jewish banker's home with a glass window of the period of the New Testament is never brought out anywhere, although an attempt is made to do so. It doesn't register, simply because that the banker is a Jew, was never planted.

But the picture is a sob melodrama that will get to audiences 100 per cent. It has a universal appeal and will hit the society set as well as the masses, men and women alike. It isn't a picture that they are going to applaud, but it is one that is going to hold them by sustained action and trying to figure its outcome. The finish may come a little abruptly, but it is one of those things that the audience wants to happen, and whether it happens sooner or later doesn't seem to make material difference to them.

The story concerns four people— a banker (Robert Edeson), his cashier (Richard Dix), his wife (Claire Adams) and the assistant cashier (Neil Hamilton).

The cashier and his wife are happily married and living within their means; the assistant cashier loves his superior's wife. Unmarried and without responsibilities, he is in position to take a chance on the stock market, in which he makes a couple of winnings, the greater part of which he devotes to making gifts to the wife. Finally he frankly confesses to the cashier that he loves the latter's wife and intends winning her. The husband forbids him his home, but on the advice of his employer, who walks in on the scene between the two, says nothing to his wife about the matter.

The banker is aware that his young assistant cashier is dabbling in the stock market, so later, when $30,000 worth of bonds are missing, he naturally has his suspicions as to who committed the theft. He does not suspect the cashier, who has really committed the crime in order to vie with his rival for his own wife's affections. The cashier could have let the rival pay the penalty, as all the circumstantial evidence was against him, but instead he confesses and is taken to jail.

On the wife's plea that she is really in love with her husband and has come to see the error of her way the banker pockets the loss, refuses to prosecute and gives the couple another chance with the husband managing a coffee plantation that he has in South America.

The story is screened in such a manner that the audience at all times is in sympathy with the man who committed the theft, and their own solutions worked out as the story proceeds aids materially to the suspense element in the picture.

It will get money and entertain, and Dix himself is going to be the greatest surprise to all of them who have seen "Too Many Kisses."

Fred.

Wonders of the Wilds

Travel picture made by Burr Nickle, depicting his travels in many strange lands. Shown at the Broadway, New York, week March 30, 1925. Running time, 76 minutes.

The box office strength does not lie in the fact that it is a real pic-

ture for picture theatres. It is, rather a novelty that can be built up in picture houses, but appears to be a better attraction for the popular vaudeville which plays pictures and where it can be ballyhooed to a fare thee well. The average picture house man would look at the picture and say that it was just another travelog and let it go at that, but a smart showman might see the possibilities for unusual publicity and build up on the East Indian fire dance feature of the picture with a fire dance presentation that should send it over.

At the Broadway, New York, this week, Burr Nickle, the traveler who made the picture, is appearing in person in a nine-minute talk in advance of the film offering. He relates some of the hardships of the trip and gives the audience a general idea of what they are going to see. He is not the typical type of lecturer, but is more of a showman and makes a corking appearance on the stage, with a good address.

Then the picture itself runs 76 minutes. It starts with Mexico. From Mexico City a map shows the trip by burro up into the lands of the Yaqui Indians and back down the west coast over the snow-covered mountains to a sea coast town, where he met up with three friends from Los Angeles and started for several of the islands off the coast of Southern California. This sequence takes 22 minutes. The next 13 minutes are devoted to the islands, fishing, and a herd of sea elephants that make their home on one of the most inaccessible islands off the coast.

From this point returns to the coast of Mexico and starts for Yokohama, thence to Borneo.

The Borneo sequence runs 26 minutes and is by far the most interesting. It is full of thrills and interesting material, especially showing the tribes that are the lowest form of human life, living in the trees exactly as do the monkeys. Going on again by elephant-back to the interior of the jungle across a great stretch of the island until another stream is reached, which carries one out on the other side of the island. Finally an escape down the river.

The final sequence is the spectacular. An annual Hindoo worship fete in the great Mammam Temple at Singapore. Here Nickle has another achievement to his credit. He was the first white man permitted to enter the temple, and accomplished the unusual in photographing the religious rites, to which the native fanatics travel for days from all parts of India. It shows some 12,000 natives in the temple at the time of the rite. A huge blazing pyre of sacred wood is burned for a day, and at nightfall the red-hot coals are smoothed out and the religious fanatics walk across them, under the belief that if the gods have heard their prayers they will come through the fire unscathed. Mr. Nickle says that, strange though it may seem, some do come through without burns on their feet; others fall into the coals and have to be carried out.

It is a corking picture for houses where an occasional bid for the unusual can be made, and especially a picture that will appeal in communities where there are audiences of the higher type interested in travel and the unexplored parts of the world.

Fred.

SCHOOL FOR WIVES

Victor Hugo Halperin production distributed through Vitagraph. Story adapted by Halperin from the Leonard Merrick novel, "The House of Lynch." Directed by Halperin, with Conway Tearle featured above cast. Reviewed at the Rialto, New York, March 29. Running time, 70 minutes.

Richard Keith	Conway Tearle
Betty Lynch	Sigrid Holmquist
Lady Atherton	Peggy Kelly
Jordan B. Lynch	Arthur Donaldson
Howard Lynch	Allan Simpson
Dardy Waldehast	Jill Lynch
Ralph	Brian Dunlevy
Tomlinson	Dick Lee

Muggins	Dorothy Allen
Ronald Van Stuyvesant	Gerald Oliver Smith
Kitty Dawson	Emily Chichester
Mary Wilson	Alyce Mills

With such a title, a lurid sex proposition might have been expected, but instead an intelligent and entertaining picture made from a story which had to do with that purification of the soul which arises (in books and drama) from real love. The characters are an artist and a wealthy young girl. The girl loves the artist, but the artist refuses to marry her until she rejects her father's money, which the artist claims is tainted with the blood of worn down employes.

Finally, the girl agrees to marry the man and live on his income. A child is born, but in the passing months the irksome condition of genteel poverty wore down good resolutions and the girl returned to her father and his many millions.

Home again, she saw her father's heartlessness in another light, and decided that after all love in a cottage was better than unlimited wealth.

Such a story is full of symbolism and Halperin, hitherto an unimportant director, has treated all of his subject matter with such unfailing showmanship and intelligence he is now someone to notice. Only in spots does he get maudlin and, although his casting isn't all it should be, and the sets are plainly of that type used in cheaper productions, the general impression is that the story, backed by good scenario and direction, has made "School for Wives" a good film.

Its drawing powers are doubtful. Conway Tearle on his own may mean some boxoffice money, but the other names don't hold penny potentialities. With exploitation, however, or as a filler in an already-laid-out list of program features of the better type, this one should hold up. Heaven knows it has most of the Vitagraph output beaten a mile.

Sisk.

SMOULDERING FIRES

Universal-Jewel, starring Pauline Frederick and featuring Laura La Plante. Story by Sada Cowan and Howard Higgins. Directed by Clarence Brown. Shown at the Piccadilly, N. Y., week March 28, 1925. Running time 80 minutes.

June Vale	Pauline Frederick
Dorothy Vale	Laura La Plante
Robert Elliott	Malcolm McGregor
Scotty	Tully Marshall
Lucy	Wanda Hawley
Kate Brown	Helen Lynch
Muggsy	George Cooper

Maybe the authors of screen play didn't see "Three Women," which Ernst Lubitsch produced for the Warners, with Pauline Frederick, May McAvoy, Marie Prevost and Lew Cody in the cast. Either way they have turned out a story in which the central situation is so similar to the one in the previous picture it seems to be more than a mere coincidence, especially as Miss Frederick is in the cast.

"Smouldering Fires" is a decided step forward as far as the average run of Universal productions go. It is better in story, production, direction and, what is most remarkable, photography. As much cannot be said for the final editing, for there are three or four spots where it just jumps from one sequence to another without rhyme or reason.

From a boxoffice standpoint it looks as though here is a picture that will do far better than the average Universal-Jewel. It has two names in Pauline Frederick and Laura La Plante and is acted by a cast that seemingly knows what it is about, due to the direction of Clarence Brown, who, by this time, should rate the top grade among the U. directors.

A self-sacrificing love on the part of an older sister, who divorces her husband, years younger, in favor of her more youthful sister, is the theme. In the case of "Three Women" it was the mother who first won the man and then he managed to vamp the daughter also.

Miss Frederick gives a fine performance as in "Three Women." Miss La Plante scores, and in Malcolm McGregor U. has a leading juvenile it can build into starring material eventually. Tully Marshall gave his usual finished performance, while George Cooper was the comedy relief who landed his points.

Fred.

Confessions of a Queen

Metro-Goldwyn release, Victor Seastrom production, Louis B. Mayer presentation. Adapted from Alphonse Daudet's novel, "Kings in Exile." Running time, 64 mins.

Queen	Alice Terry
King	Lewis Stone
Prince Alexei	John Bowers
Eleanora	Eugenia Besserer
Sephora	Helena D'Algy
Prince Zara	Frankie Darro
Duke Rosen	Joseph Dowling
Lewin	Andre de Beranger
Revolutionist	Bert Sprotte
Officer	Wilbur Higbie
Valet	Otto Hoffman
Maid	Frances Hatton
Paris Valet	James McElbern

With the sort of a title which has long been in use as a catch-quarter device by sensational newspapers, one-night stand rep shows and program feature films, this high-grade presentation holds forth a promise which it never fulfills. The "confessions" part is justified by a preliminary shot of a diary and a finishing flash of the feminine hand writing "The End." Otherwise it is no confession, except perhaps a confession of weakness.

The story, as it plays, gives easy evidenced to experienced eyes of having been considerably chopped in the cutting. The finish is abrupt, the motive for the happy ending is nebulous and thin, and the narrative as a whole is disjointed and unimportant, nothing like the study of royalty in exile drawn by Daudet, the master, in his original story. Miss Johnston is far from a Daudet. The screen story is far from an adaptation, it is a corruption.

As a vehicle for Alice Terry and Lewis Stone, seemingly the two busiest players in the world, it is strictly along the archaic idea that the people will flock to see certain persons in "clothes."

The royalty thing, which once gave the public a kick, is also out of date, since kings and queens have been bandied about on the silver sheets with considerable abandon by now.

Therefore, if "Confessions of a Queen" is to stand on its own feet as a thriller, a sexer or a pleaser, it misses in each of the three respects and comes out, at best, as merely another picture for a producer to show big sets and for well-known and well-liked performers to flicker again through a series of projected vicissitudes.

The story is of the "married but platonic" family, the point being to get husband and wife "together" for a wind-up. This is done without any cogent reason except that the king agrees to abdicate, and the queen, who until then has stood pat for the crown, suddenly gets a yen for maternity and domesticity. A vamp twirls her futile eyes through the film in the person of Helen D'Algy, and, if she would intrigue a monarch, this king did well to resign.

Some outdoor and one indoor among the settings are magnificent. Stone at all times comports himself as befits. Miss Terry as a haughty regal bride is excellent, but in her softer moments is hard; she does not even look pretty at all times and does not seem to stand profiling as well as when her face was a whit rounder.

Despite a costly cast, a sumptuous production and all the usual trimmings, the result scarcely justifies the expense and effort. "Confessions of a Queen" will draw some on its far-fetched title, but does not come up to expectations.

Lait.

Waking Up the Town

Directed by James Cruze, from a story by Frank Condon. Jack Pickford starred. Running time, 62 mins. At Moss' Colony, week March 29. No producer or distributor mentioned.

Jack Joyce	Jack Pickford
Mrs. Joyce	Claire McDowell
Abner Hope	Alec B. Francis
Mary Ellen	Norma Shearer
Curt Horndyke	Herbert Pryor
Helen Horndyke	Ann May
Joe Lakin	George Dromgold

Somewhat off balance for the usually accepted box-office proportions. This starring vehicle for Jack Pickford is practically a screen "monolog," with even the love-interest played down, since it isn't a story much about two young people—almost entirely about one.

As a sort of village Edison, Jack invents all sorts of weird contraptions. He cherishes a big dream of turning the local waterfalls into a power source and making a metropolis of his burg. He gets his uncle, a nut who thinks the world is coming to an end, to sink his nest egg into the ventures.

The only novelty is that the great plan doesn't succeed. But a thin romance peters along, there is much light and likeable comedy, which rarely becomes slapstick, and some of the scenes in which the hero's partner figures as the foil for his humorous vagaries are rich in the meat of amusement.

With a high-grade director like Cruze there must be high spots, no matter how feeble the material. Toward the end there are some end-of-the-world bits (some looked as though filched from the newsreels) to express the boy's nightmare that the world is really being washed up.

In these and many other spots—rather scattered, though, and not strung together even by a thread of sex interest—the film is a corker.

Norma Shearer, beautiful as ever, has a surprisingly meager part as the hoyden daughter of the boy's business associate, and Alec B. Francis, as her father, scores personally.

So there is much that is pleasing, but in all "Waking Up the Town" can scarcely be rated as an important or outstanding contribution, the less so in view of the several impressive screen-world names attached to the various departments responsible.

Lait.

THE RECKLESS SEX

A Renown picture and Truart production presented by Phil Goldstone. Story by Travers Wells and direction by Alvin J. Nietz. At Loew's, New York, March 27, as half of a double bill. Running time, 65 minutes. Cast includes Madge Bellamy, William Collier, Jr.; Wyndham Standing, Wlter Long, Claire MacDowell, Johnnie Walker, Gertrude Astor, Alec B. Francis, Gladys Brockwell and David Torrence.

Rarely do they flash an independent film with such a list of sterling names. In this case, and it is a rarity, the story, names, acting, settings and direction, are of such quality that "The Reckless Sex" makes a program picture of infinitely higher calibre than is usually turned out by the independent producers.

The plot concerns a rich Bostonian whose son is sent to his New Mexico ranch to investigate charges that an employe is in league with conspirators who are smuggling guns into Mexico. Arriving at the station, a little lost actress from a straggling "Tom" show meets the hero. As she can't get a train for several days, she is taken to the hacienda until that time. A veritable hot-bed of seething plots is discovered and the young hero walks into a flock of trouble, routs the conspirators and falls in love with the little actress.

Considerable by-plot and humor is attached while there isn't a piece of poor acting anywhere in sight.

Johnnie Walker, Wyndham Standing, Madge Bellamy, Walter Long and young Willie Collier carry most of the plot all of which is enacted before suitable backgrounds. The continuity, too, is tight and some of the comedy stuff well inserted.

Where it is the custom to run independents, this one can be boosted a bit. If it's any indication of what Goldstone is doing regularly, it looks as if business isn't so tough.

It was noticed on the titles that this film was made in 1924, indicative of the trouble in getting a Broadway showing for an independent film.

Sisk.

THE NO GUN MAN

R-C picture made by Harry Garson and distributed through Film Booking Offices. Directed by Garson with Lefty Flynn starred. Cast also includes Gloria Grey, J. Gordon Russell and William Quinn. At the Stanley, New York, March 30 (one day).. Running time, 59 minutes.

About 10 years ago, the same Lefty Flynn, who stars in this picture was about the swellest end who ever appeared in collegiate football in the United States. He played for Yale and made a rep that has lasted for a good many years. Recently he was a member of the "Open All Night" cast for Famous Players, but in this, one of an F. B. O. series, he plays a semi-western role in which riding, acrobatics, fighting and general acting ability all count.

Flynn has a magnificent physique, a fine face and a good manner which set well with the audiences. In addition, he has been given here a story which is well enough produced and directed to qualify it nicely for the intermediate houses. The lack of a positive snap in certain swift scenes keeps "The No Gun Man" from getting higher rating, but as it stands, it is good.

The plot concerns a bank robbery which remained unsolved by the police. A member of the bank (Mr. Flynn) goes to a small western town and eventually rounds up a gang of desperate criminals and wins himself a swell looking blonde. The comedy relief is furnished by a fine negro actor—bulging eyes, protruding mouth and thick lips with slicked black hair finely set against a face of a thousand ebony dippings.

The production end of this is well handled and although it doesn't total a million dollars, it looks like "The Covered Wagon" would have looked in 1915 against some of the 10-cent western releases thrown periodically on the market by the smaller independents. Gloria Grey, as the leading woman, is pretty; J. Gordon Russell, a real vet whose screen career dates from the old Vitagraph, is a blacksmith here, while William Quinn nicely handles a villain part.

"The No Gun Man" is neat entertainment and although not first run stuff it reveals the best of all the independent stunt actors, a man who can do stunts and not look like the ice man. Lefty Flynn is a sure picture comer and with a good story and cast fit for the big films.

Sisk.

TAINTED MONEY

Perfection Pictures presentation featuring Eva Novak and Walliam Fairbanks. Directed by Henry McRae. Cast includes Carl Stockdale, Bruce Gordon, Edward Davis. Running time, 60 mins. Half of double program at Loew's New York, March 24.

This independent is a good program addition and will please lovers of the athletic type of leading man. William Fairbanks belongs to that school and averages up athletically with any of the second string action leads. He is fortunate in this picture in being surrounded by an excellent cast, with Eva Novak, a winsome and beautiful blonde, opposite.

The story is an interesting one and an effort to dodge the usual string of stunts, which usually satisfy as background for the athletic boys, is noticeable.

John J. Carlton, lumber magnate, is attempting to secure timber from his rival, Adams. Carlton has subsidized the Adams' manager, Marston, and holds a forged check over his head.

Carlton's son, a ne'er-do-well, is ordered from home by Carlton and while working as a taxi chauffeur saves the life of Adams' daughter. Marston has planned to marry the girl, but young Carlton (Fairbanks) is engaged by Adams as his chauffeur and proceeds to win her love.

The rest of the footage concerns itself with the plots and counter-plots and Carlton's effort to secure the timber by hook or crook. Young Carlton foils every move of the Carltons. Working under an assumed name, his identity isn't discovered until his rival, Marston finds a watch with his name inscribed in the case and two photos, of Carlton and his son.

Marston shows the watch to Adams, accusing young Carlton of secretly aiding his father. Carlton meanwhile had been trussed up in a shanty by two of Marston's henchmen. Marston also has the father captured, intending to dynamite the place and remove both enemies at the same time. The son liberates himself and pounces on Marston. One of those movie battles on the edge of a cliff follow, with the girl deciding the issue by appearing in time to knock Marston unconscious with a club. The direction is faulty here for the first time. In order to get the principals to the cliff edge, the director has them start their battle in the cabin and roll a considerable distance in an unnatural manner that spoils the realism of the bit.

Edward Davis as John Carlton leans a trifle to overplaying the unscrupulous business man. The best performance was turned in by Bruce Gordon in the heavy role of the scheming lumber foreman. Miss Novak's blonde beauty lends itself admirably to photography and her acting is at all times convincing. Fairbanks is an all around athlete and given the proper stories should continually add to his admirers, particularly of the male sex.

Con.

Barriers of the Law

J. P. MacGowan production, presented by Jesse Goldburg through Independent Pictures Corporation. William Desmond and Helen Holmes featured. Directed by J. P. MacGowan, with J. P. also in a leading role. At Loew's, New York, March 27, as half of a double bill. Running time, 62 minutes.

It's been a long time since Bill Desmond and Helen Holmes have had congenial roles such as the Triangle and Kalem companies, respectively, used to deal out. In the old days, when Triangle films were the class of the market, Desmond was a big star, while Miss Holmes has probably ridden enough rails in her old Kalem serials to double track the line from Weehawken to Santa Barbara. So it's nice to see them together in a good program picture. Neither seems to have slipped and both are good screen personalities.

The story in this instance is of the thrill order with the thrills held for the latter part of the running time. Briefly, a gang of bootleggers holds Rita Redding in their control. She really wants to go straight and when she tells the chief, he has her taken to a dive which he runs and there has her stripped and put in a kimona.

But the girl escapes and falls into the bedroom of the district attorney who has been hounding the bootleggers. Eventually they are married, then the bootleg crew tries to get at the d.a. by putting the routine to his wife. Together they fight it out, and the finale comes when he rescues her from a blazing freight car.

Aside from Desmond and Miss Holmes, the cast holds Mark Fenton and Marguerite Clayton, each a favorite a decade ago, or less. J. P. McGowan, producer and director acts a heavy role nicely and the cast, throughout, is capable. The sets are fair and the photography above par. As an independent program release it ranks above the average but its business powers will be dependent upon the pull of its featured players.

"Barriers of the Law" is good entertainment. *Bisk.*

A KISS IN THE DARK

Frank Tuttle production, presented by Adolph Zukor and Jesse L. Lasky. From the play "Aren't We All" by Frederick Lonsdale. Screen version by Townsend Martin. Featuring Adolphe Menjou, Aileen Pringle and Lillian Rich. At the Rialto, New York, week of April 5. Running time, 68 minutes.

Water Grenham	Adolphe Menjou
Janet Livingstone	Aileen Pringle
Betty King	Lillian Rich
Johnny King	Kenneth MacKenna
Dancer	Ann Pennington
Chorus Girl	Kitty Kelly

It's a pipe that if Freddie Lonsdale ever sees this picture he'll never recognize it as the brain child he turned out under the title of "Aren't We All." There's not a darn thing left of the play, at all. That's a funny idea in the first place, buying the rights to a play then having an entirely new story written and throwing away the original title. Why buy the play at all? It would be cheaper to have Townsand Martin write an original in the first place and stick a title on it.

Of course, they figured that "A Kiss in the Dark" would mean dough at the box office. Maybe it will and maybe it won't. There are a couple of rather sexy kicks in the picture and they may help, but the chances are that the picture will flop pretty much, except in th' houses where the business comes anyway. There surely is nothing about it, either title or otherwise, that is going to especially draw.

For screen purposes the Egypt of the play became Cuba; Lord Grenham, who was the old daddy, becomes the gay young philanderer at the hands of Adolphe Menjou. Aileen Pringle plays the girl he was seriously courting while Lillian Rich is the frolicsome young wife looking for an outside thrill and who gets it with his lordship, although it is simply an innocent flirtation, for she really loves her husband, after all.

Walter Grenham in this case is a wealthy young American who owns a sugar plantation in Cuba and winters regularly in Havana. He is a bachelor, has a wonderful house and a wonderful garden. It is this garden that seems to get to the girls and possibly takes the place of the British Museum of the play. At any rate, Walter seems to have a stock line for all of them, even when he forgets names and faces. That is to simply say that he will never forget that wonderful night in his garden. Seems like the girls, for the greater part, recall it pleasantly also.

The Kings are wintering in Cuba and Johnny seems to let Betty play around as she pleases, with the result that she and Walter start a young romance, but the day comes for the Kings to sail and on the same steamer Janet Livingstone is also departing. Suddenly Mrs. King recalls that she has forgotten her bag at the hotel and she and Walter dash off to get it with the result that she misses the steamer and has to remain over in Havana while hubby sails homeward. That is the night that "the kiss in the dark occurs." They are in Grenham's garden, next door the violins are playing and there is a moon. But that is all nothing more, just a kiss.

Then home, and hubby is caught embracing a chorus girl, or rather she is embracing him as wifey walks in. That switches things for a moment, but in the end it is all ironed out nicely.

Adolphe Menjou has not his usual appearance as he plays in this picture and does not quite snap his role over with the 'im it should have had, while Lillian Rich does well enough. Aileen Pringle failed to score at all. Ann Pennington, in a bit, did far better work that either of the featured women of the cast. *Fred.*

I WANT MY MAN

First National Production starring Milton Sills. Adapted from Struthers Burt's novel, "The Interpreter's House." Directed by Lambert Hillyer, and Doris Kenyon featured. Reviewed at the Strand, New York, April 5. Running time, 66 minutes.

Guilan Eyre	Milton Sills
Vida Eyre	Doris Kenyon
Lael Satori	May Allison
Drusilla	Phyllis Haver
Phillip	Paul Nicholson
Mrs. Eyre	Kate Bruce
Mrs. Satori	Theresa Maxwell Conover
Mr. Eyre	Louis Stern
French Doctor	Charles Lane
American Doctor	George W. Howard

Peculiar that First National, after making Milton Sills a star by virtue of the fine work which he has done so regularly in the years past, should exercise such slovenly care in selecting for him a genuine starring vehicle. For certainly, although he does good work in this film, Doris Kenyon really has the starring role and also wins for herself the leonine share of the w. k. laurels. And that being the case, it shouldn't be long before First National makes Miss Kenyon one of its stars, for recently she has been running along at a surprising rate and doing the best work of a career that has embraced many things in the movies—from serials to independents.

The plot of "I Want My Time" is centered around Guilian Eyre, a man blinded in the war who is nursed and married by Vida, who marries him because she loves him but who says, to explain it all, that she has also been left badly hurt by the war and that her face is a livid scar of injuries. But she hasn't—she's as beautiful as the cherry blossoms in Washington at springtime—so when it is found that Gilly will remain his sight, she leaves him because she knows another woman is after him. Her idea is to fight the other woman on equal terms and actually wins, on fair grounds, her own husband. So, back in the States, she becomes a nurse to her husband's mother, and the finale is that with business reverses the other girl decides to back out while Vida steps into the glory that should and is hers.

Sills plays the blind man and does his job well. But Miss Kenyon is really the star of the film, while May Allison, as the other woman, really means little.

The production is slip-shod and staged, while the direction isn't so much better. The time-honored F. N. lighting system is used, that system which throws spotlights all over rooms and which admits light from the ceilings where no sunbeam ever entered. Consequently, the photography isn't improved and the general effect of whatever money has been spent on production lowered.

The film scenario, however, is well knit together and the action not drawn out. The whole thing looks like a cheap film and sold cheaply enough. It may be a money-maker, but it isn't anything to crow over, just a factory-made product. As a program picture it is okeh, as a first run feature is resembles strongly the weak sister.

If the Sills-Kenyon clientele is strong in neighborhood or community, the film is satisfactory, for both the stars have their opportunities, but if they mean nothing as draws anywhere, then "I Want My Man" is so much footage and might just as well have been left undone. *Bisk.*

HEART OF A SIREN

First National release and Sawyer-Lubin production for Associated Pictures. Features Barbara La Marr and Conway Tearle. From the stage play "Hail and Farewell," with adaptation by Fred and Fannie Hatton. Directed by Phil Rosen. At the Colony, New York, week of April 5. Running time, about 60 mins.

Isabella Echevaria	Barbara La Marr
Gerald Rexford	Conway Tearle
John Strong	Harry Morey
Duchess of Chatham	Ida Darling
Lisette	Florence Auer
Maxim	Clifton Webb
Emelio	William Ricciardi

Nothing less than a ridiculous picture other than in production. Lavish sets and clothes, but the story, direction, subtitling and acting drew laughs from a Sunday matinee audience while this ultra-melodramatic and nonsensical tale was being unwound.

It doesn't seem possible that the Hattons, who have a reputation in the legitimate field as writers, could have turned over a scenario in the 10-20-30 manner in which this one reveals itself. The Hattons, primarily humorists, must have temporarily lost all sense of humor. And Rosen, directing, laid on the heavy emoting to the utmost extent with broad strokes that are as wide as the screen will permit.

Both the staging and clothes of Miss La Marr are sightly, although there are passages where this featured player is anything but heavily adorned. However, the raiment and scenery angles are only abetted by Clifton Webb, who gives the film its one genuine performance. Otherwise the footage is replet ewith closeup after closeup of Miss La Marr, and if the camera is not exhibiting this player from the shoulders up, it has been trained on her during a series of poses with heaving chest and alternating wide and narrow heavily beaded eye brims. Another monotonous item is the flagrant padding.

The story tells of the leading vamp of Paris who is pursued by an American millionaire, snubbed by an Englishman and who scorns a fellow Parisian into shooting himself. The Britisher (Conway Tearle) is eventually won over so that he breaks with his betrothed, but Isabelle, the all-devouring, relinquishes her claim upon appeal of his mother. To find whether he did go back or not would have interfered with a dinner date, much more important.

How Isabella is procuring the money to make the flash she does wherever her presence may be is never submitted. Other instances are equally as vague. Meanwhile the only relief from this asinine grind is Mr. Webb as Isabella's manager, and his performanc eis nearly spoiled by prolonged bits evidently aimed for comedy.

The pictur egives itself away in the title, "A Heart of a Siren." What that portends the actual seeing realizes. Rosen has lapsed seriously in this effort which is of the same kind that when they come from England the American picture people scoff at. If this example of American production ever reaches England they'll do plenty of laughing over there.

Either way this release marks the third bad picture in as many weeks for the Colony. Larry Seamon's "Wizard of Oz" next week. *Skig.*

MAN AND MAID

Elinor Glyn's production. Presented by Louis B. Mayer. Directed by Victor Schertzinger. Supervised by Elinor Glyn. Story, scenario and continuity by Elinor Glyn. At the Capitol, N. Y., week of April 5. Running time, 68 mins.

Sir Nicholas Thormonde	Lew Cody
Alathea Bulteel	Harriet Hammond
Suzette	Renee Adoree
Coralie	Paulette Duval
Burton	Alec Francis
Colonel George Harcourt	Crauford Kent
Maurice	David Mir
Hon. Bobby Bulteel	Gerald Grove
Lady Hilda Bulteel	Jacqueline Gadsden
Little Bobby	Winston Miller
Little Hilda	Jane Mercer
Atwood Chester	Irving Hartley
Odette	Dagmar Desmond
Alice	Leoni Lester

The only thing that Elinor Glyn missed doing in this picture was acting all of the parts and sitting in the box office to try to get the public to spend their dough to look at it. Had she done the latter there might be a chance for the picture, but if any exhibitor thinks he is going to get any dough with this one without Elinor making a personal appearance he is mistaken. As a picture "Man and Maid" is an out-and-out flop. In a foreword to the picture Ellie says: "Women always do one of three things to men—elevate men, degrade them, or bore them to death." If women in general do that, imagine what Ellie can do to mere motion picture men. From an audience standpoint in this case Ellie fails to either elevate or degrade, but she does bore.

Still and all the picture has its compensation, and that is that it gives Harriet Hammond a chance on the screen. If the authoress is responsible for the selection of this girl for the role that she plays, then she can be forgiven everything else. Harriet Hammond is easily the find of the last couple of years. Here is a blonde that has beauty and with it a personality that will get to anyone. Besides which she has acting ability that is going to carry her a long, long way. Metro-Goldwyn have something in this girl if they can hold on to her.

Then there is Lew Cody playing a hero role. Suffice to say he takes a stab at it and it's not so good. Renee Adoree as a French "hotsy-totsy" (exactly as the titles describe her) and Paulette Duval easily top Cody with the audience, so that the one outstanding male figure in the cast finished a bad forth to three women.

The story is laid in France in 1918. The hero is a wounded British officer, the heroine a steno for the American Red Cross, although she is English by birth and the daughter of a noble who has squandered his wealth by gambling. She and her family are living in an attic, while father, though in the British army, seems to have nothing to do except get in dutch in Parisian gambling hells. In the end the girl, who has been engaged by the hero as his secretary, listens to his proposal of marriage to save the dear old dad from being disgraced, providing, of course, that the husband-to-be will pay the debts. In the end, however, she discloses that she has married because she loves.

The picture is well directed, but as much cannot be said for the editing and titling. *Fred.*

THE CHARMER

Paramount Picture, produced and directed by Sidney Olcott. Pola Negri starred and story taken from Henry Baerlein's novel, "Mariposa." Adapted by Sada Cowan. Reviewed at the Rivoli, New York, April 5. Running time, 72 minutes.

Mariposa ....Pola Negri
Ralpe Bayne ....Wallace MacDonald
Dan Murray ....Robert Frazer
Mama ....Trixie Friganza
Senor Alessandro Sprotti.....Cesare Gravina
Bertha Sedgewick ....Gertrude Astor
Mr. Sedgewick ....Edwards Davis
Mrs. Bayne ....Mathilde Brundage

Although this picture is off Negri's hunting ground, insomuch as she does no vamping or sophisticated female stuff here, it demonstrates a versatility which extends to the playing of sweeter and more sympathetic roles—such as the Mariposa of the play, the role being that of a Spanish dancer transplanted to fame in America. And with fame came two men at her feet—one a chauffeur and the other his employer. She chose the chauffeur.

This film has much interest, is clean and funny whenever Trixie Friganza elects to be. More comedy than is usual in a film of this type, but it is all for the best. Sidney Olcott and Miss Cowan have shown sense in not taking it all so seriously. In production, usual Famous Players detail. Some of the sets here are large, but good and well handled, with a theatre interior, shot from the front and back stage, was exceptionally well done.

"The Charmer" is excellent first run material, will fit any program and give entertainment. Just because it has Negri in a different sort of a role—don't get frightened. Apparently the change is well advised. *Sisk.*

OLD SHOES

Los Angeles, March 29.

Knickerbocker Pictures presents Frederick Stowell's production "Old Shoes," featuring John Harron, Viola Daniels, Ethel Grey Terry, Zasu Pitts, Noah Beery and Russell Simpson. Story by Frederick Stowell. Running time, about 70 minutes. At California, Los Angeles, week of March 28.

"Old Shoes," to all appearances, is another attempt to duplicate Richard Barthelmess' "Tola'ble David." While telling a homely and, at times, poignant story, it falls considerably short of the Barthelmess epic.

The thing that stands out in this feature is the heart interest, sustained effectively and climaxed by two thrilling fist fights. The first takes place between the boy (Harron) and the smart-aleck village dude. The second, and more sensational of the two, is when Beery, as the heavy, gets a blacksnake whip and is about to administer a whipping to his wife, the boy's mother. The lad, meek mortal, turns upon his step-father and they rough-and-tumble it all over the place.

"Old Shoes" is a story of persecution. It unfolds the studied efforts of Beery to inflict pain and humiliation upon the woman who bears his name and her son. It appears that the mother, in her girlhood, had been the belle of the village and was courted by two brothers. The younger, Marcus, a mild-mannered youth, won.

The other brother never forgives the girl.

Years pass and Marcus dies. Then Mary, now a woman of middle age with a young son, consents to become the wife of her rejected former suitor, because she feels that her rejection ruined his life. She soon discovers that she still loves her dead husband and the brother also discovers it. He proceeds to inflict pain upon his wife and step-son whenever he can. He gloats over the fact that they believe him insane. The picture, from this point on, is merely a series of episodes exemplifying the forms of cruelty practised by the step-father.

The youth finally downs the stepparent in the final fight with a small statue. The step-father regains consciousness, however, and, taking a sabre, is about to wreak his revenge. He leaves his office but a horse gets in his way. He strikes the animal with the sabre and it becomes maddened and the heavy is trampled to death under its hoofs.

The title is obtained from the fact that the boy, all through the picture, wears a disreputable-looking pair of shoes and is always longing for new ones.

The direction is well done and the sets and cast are satisfactory. It should be a popular subject, especially in the smaller towns.

LIGHTNING ROMANCE

W. Ray Johnston presents this Harry J. Brown (Rayart) production. Starring Reed Howes. Directed by Albert Rogell. Story by Marion Jackson. Photographed by Ross Fisher. Runs about an hour.

Jack Wade.........................Reed Howes
Lila Grandon...................Ethel Shannon
Red Taylor.........................David Kirby
Arnold Stewart................Cuyler Supplee
Richard Wade...................Wilfred Lucas
Arizona Joe.....................Frank Hagney
Butler..........................H. C. Hallett
Rex..................................By Himself

"The youngest, handsomest, snappiest, peppiest fellow on the screen today" is the way Rayart is billing Reed Howes, the star of "Lightning Romance." By playing him up heavily as a stunt man who has, in addition to athletic ability, the youth, clean-cut appearance and sartorial fitness that seldom go with it in pictures, the film company may be on the right track.

Howes' face is familiar as one of the original "Arrow Collar" men. That in itself guarantees a certain amount of masculine comeliness, but it must be remembered that Leyendecker, the artist, gave pictorial values to the face that the screen fails to show up. Nevertheless, Howes is one of the best-looking men in the films.

"Lightning Romance," therefore, makes a feature of this male beauty, emphasizing the close-up and posing shots as have not even the Valentino films. The first few scenes, holding western atmosphere, do not show off the new sheik to best advantage, but the action soon switches to a social resort of Florida, and Reed blossoms out in sport clothes de luxe. The girls are bound to like him.

While his looks are of chief importance, Howes' acting is not at all bad, standing favorable comparison with the great majority of stunt stars. His athletic prowress, while he is graceful enough about it, seems to be but average, although he is apparently a powerful swimmer. One or two of the stunts, such as riding a motorcycle off a cliff into the water, didn't impress as being genuine in every detail.

The film is a very conventional one of its type, holding crude discrepancies in direction and continuity as well as plot. It tells of the son of a wealthy shipbuilder getting his fill of adventure by outwitting, more physically than mentally, his father's unscrupulous competitors. The balance of the cast is satisfactory and the photography ditto.

Rayart may have a good bet in young Howes. The wise exhibitor will tie up with Arrow Collars, Chesterfield Cigarettes and Stetson Hats, for all of which Howes has posed. It might be well to play up heavily certain statements made by the press sheet, namely, he is the third most photographed man in the world, and hopes to be the successor of Wallace Reid.

SUPER SPEED

Rayart film, made by Harry J. Brown. Directed by Albert Rogell, with Reed Howes, former Arrow Collar model, starred. Released independently by Rayart. At the Stanley, New York, April 2. Running time, 55 minutes.

Reed Howes, apparently, is in for a series of stunt films, and if they measure up to "Super Speed" they will fill the bill adequately for the middle-class houses or for the combination theatres of a lower grade. Howes himself never really impresses strongly as a stunt man, and as an actor he has his bad moments, and plenty of them; but he is good looking in a collegiate way and the clothes-wearing angle is stressed nicely in spots.

The story here concerns the rich hero who meets the rich girl, but she meets him in the guise of a milkman—just one of those things that Johnny Hines used to do a million times better in "The Early Bird." But having met the girl, he finds her daddy is being hounded by a gang of desperate villains, who hold notes over his head. Therefore the hero bests the villains by winning an auto race in a car manufactured by the girl's father, and the day is saved.

The story is what's wrong with the picture. The suspense never really amounts to a whoop. Melodrama it is, surely; but even melodrama mustn't always travel time-honored paths. Such Rover Boy stories will probably hurt the star, whose potentialities plainly lie in the small time of pictures. But with good stories, well developed and with a degree of plausibility, Howes would show to much better advantage. Here he is supported by a good cast, which includes Mildred Harris and Mitchell Lewis.

This production is well made technically, some of the photography being excellently handled and certain phases of the auto race, namely, when the villain makes his wheels interlock with those of the car of the hero in an effort to force him from the track, are done expertly. The stunt stuff consists of fights on the edges of roofs, climbs down drain pipes, prodigious leaps, and what-not—all somewhat unthrilling.

So analyzed, this Howes series has many merits and demerits, but no demerits which cannot be remedied. The star looks okay for the femme trade, but he won't make a hit with the men. His hair is combed too carefully. But let him get rumpled up and really be masculine instead of being actory-masculine, and it's a safe bet for the series and "Super Speed" in the market for which they were intended. As it is, this one didn't cost so much, so it can't lose much, and certainly should make something.

But there is no reason to bank on this "former Arrow Collar model" stuff for business. That face may be famous, but so was the face of Lotta Miles, the girl who posed for the Kelly-Springfield tire ads, and it isn't on record that she was responsible for the business of "I'll Say She Is" when she quit modeling and went into the show. *Sisk.*

THE NIGHT SHIP

Gortham production, presented by Samuel Sax. Released by Lumas Film Corp. Story and direction by Henry McCarthy. At Loew's, New York, N. Y., on double feature bill April 3. Running time, 64 min.

Martha Randall.......................Mary Carr
Capt. Jed Hobbs................Tom Santschi
Robert Randall................Robert Gordon
Elizabeth Hobbs..........Margaret Fielding
Jimson Weed.................Charles A. Sellon
Casidy.............................L. J. O'Connor
Pedro Lopez......................Julian Rivero

This is a melodramatic thriller that relies for its big punch on a burning schooner at sea. The playing up of the name of Mary Carr in the billing is more or less a trick to cash in on her name, for the chances are that she got little more than one day's work in the picture, as she is only in one sequence at the beginning of the story and conveniently dies off, mayhaps to save the salary. From a box office angle it looks like a story that will get by in the cheaper daily change houses. Four names are featured at the head of the picture—Mary Carr, Tom Santschi, Robert Gordon and Margaret Fielding.

Santschi plays the heavy and walks away with the acting honors. It is hard to look at Gordon and imagine him laying Santschi away with a punch, but he does it, not only once but on two occasions. Margaret Fielding hardly counts with what she has to do any more than Mary Carr does.

It is a story of a Maine sea coast village where Bob Randall has been the suitor for the hand of the heroine, but he goes to sea and isn't heard of for six years. When he returns he finds that his mother has died of a broken heart and that his sweetheart is the wife of the heavy. So that puts it up to the hero to get even with the villain, get him out of the way for keeps and marry his widow. That is exactly what occurs.

There is a gun running plot included and the villain is master of the schooner that is to take the guns to Central America. However, the hero stows away aboard the boat, with the aid of a cowboy pal ropes all the crew, and finally finishes it with a fight with the heavy. The latter to square matters sets the ship afire and perishes in the flames, although all the others escape to make a happy ending.

It's melodramatic hoak of the kind that they like in the store show joints. *Fred.*

THE MIRAGE

Producers Distributing Corporation presentation starring Clive Brook. Story adapted from Edgar Selwyn's stage play by G. Gardner Sullivan. Directed by George Archainbaud. Running time 65 minutes.
Irene Martin.................Florence Vidor
Henry Galt...................Clive Brook
Al Manning...................Alan Roscoe
Betty Bond...................Vola Vale
Mrs. Martin..................Myrtle Vane
Irene's Sister...............Charlotte Stevens

If this picturized version follows the stage story both the motion picture and stage tales prove Edgar Selwyn remembers the life of Diamond Jim Brady, the stage play of a decade ago "Today," and "The Chorus Lady."

"The Mirage" tells the story of a small town girl Irene Martin (Florence Vidor), who comes to New York for an operatic career and winds up in the chorus. She meets Henry Galt (Clive Brook) man about town. Galt does a Diamond Jim inasmuch as he hires chorus ladies to help him entertain prospective customers.

Irene doesn't know the routine and is insulted when she receives a $50 bill from Galt after a party. She dashes to Galt's office and "how dares him." Galt explains he hires her the same as a theatre hires actors.

Galt, realizing Irene is a good girl, falls in love with her. Her corn-fed sweetheart, meanwhile, has come to New York to do business with Galt. He learns Galt is in love with Irene and when she joins the party at Galt's invitation the corn-fed immediately figures she has gone to the bow-wows and breaks off their engagement. However, he tries to proposition her along non-matrimonial lines, but Galt wins out in time for the usual clinch.

The picture is well cast. Florence Vidor handles the virtuous chorus lady well, playing the role straight. The comedy burden is alloted to Vola Vale, who slings a mean shovel as an acquisitive gold-digging chorister. Vola's system was to show them a hock ticket as the tip-off on how the panic was on. Even the Mutual burlesque girls have discarded that one.

Clive Brook looked pale but interesting as the man about town. Clive, for several hundred feet, had all the earmarks of a villainous sheik, but he crossed the audience by turning out to be as thrill-less as a Sunday in Asbury Park.

"The Mirage" is okay as a feature for the second run houses, where the story probably won't be pegged as an assembled vehicle. *Con.*

ACROSS THE DEADLINE

William Steiner production, starring Leo Maloney. Story by Ford I. Beebe. Directed by Leo Maloney. At Loew's New York, N. Y., on double feature bill April 3. Runing time, 61 min.
Martin Revelle..............T. Lingham
Mrs. Revelle................Florence Lee
Rance Revelle...............Rulon Slaughter
Their Daughter..............Josephine Hill
Ben Larrago.................Bud Osborne
Shifty Sands................Pat Rooney
Clem Wainright..............Leo Maloney

Another of the Leo Maloney westerns, fast moving, although constructed along stereotyped lines. From a box office angle it is a picture that will fit in the daily change houses where a double bill is the occasional trick of the week.

It is a tale of a 30-year feud that has existed between the Revelles and the Wainwrights. The end comes with the love affair of the daughter of the Revelles and the last of the Wainwrights, played by Leo Maloney.

The action gets under way early in the picture and there is a fight before the first reel is ended. Later there is a lynching party following a holdup of the overland stage, a ride to the rescue on the part of the hero, a chase after the bandits and a thrill when the hero, who is unarmed, ropes them both. Also for the finish of a fadeout with the lovers clasped in each other's arms and the finish of the feud.

Maloney, despite a little hogging of the camera, does decidedly well considering that he played the lead as well as directing it. Josephine Hill, opposite him, had little to do and did that only passing well. Rulon Slaughter, juvenile brother of the heroine, looked to be the best actor in the cast. The kid was natural.

The riding stuff is about the best thing, although some of it was camera tricked. *Fred.*

AFRAID OF LOVE

London, March 16.

"Her own original story," by the Hon. Mrs. John Russell, "all gowns worn by Hon. Mrs. John Russell and models in mannequin parade by Christabel Russell, Ltd." (the Hon. Mrs. Russell), and the Hon. Mrs. John Russell very heavily starred. This all takes place in one film that is one of the worst ever seen.

Of course, there are other things as well. A cameraman, a stage director, a censor's certificate and several well-known actors who work heroically to try to make some sort of an entertainment of the neurotic "sex" balderdash, which is thrown forth by the crude sub-titling.

The "original" story tells of Rosamond Bond, who leads a lonely life with Anthony, her fast-living husband. They have one child' a boy. She meets an old lover. Meanwhile Anthony has seduced the daughter of a respectable middle-class family. This girl is rather undecided what to do next, but decides to become Bond's mistress. Rosamond accepts her old lover's backing and becomes a modiste. She gets on rapidly and her husband brings the other woman to one of her mannequin shows.

Five years elapse and Rosamond still prospers while the lover still pays the bills, only his love is of a pre-eminently pure description. Then comes Bond to claim his son. The youngster has a chat with his parent, without knowing who he is and informs him what a topping fellow his dead father was one of the best, his mother has taught him. Whereat Bond goes out of the boy's life unknown. (There is no acknowledgment to Ian Hay's "The Happy Ending.") Bond returns to London and shoots himself at the moment the girl he seduced arrives at his house. The lover marries Rosamond and everybody gets back to dressmaking.

Frankly, this conglomeration is nothing but an advertisement for the Hon. Mrs. John Russell's dressmaking establishment and a subtitle, immediately prior to a wearisome mannequin parade, is as impertinent an announcement as the screen has ever seen. Throughout the picture mannequin parades predominate, so that it is hardly more than a dress parade for 7,000 feet.

The lady may be an excellent modiste, but she should never be allowed to act. She wears many clothes, most of them without any respect for atmosphere.

Leslie Faber, Jameson Thomas, Moore Marriott, Micky Brantford and Juliette Compton tackled the fight gamely, but were hopelessly outclassed from the start.

No producer's name is mentioned and whoever is responsible should be grateful for the reticence so kindly shown. This "super" is being handled "for the world" by United Kingdom Photoplays and Frederick White of Manchester. The film must draw from public who want to see what the heroine of the notorious Russell case is like. *Gore.*

Riders of the Purple Sage

Fox production, with Tom Mix starred. Zane Grey story, adapted. Same story formerly done on screen by William Farnum. Fox version directed by Lynn Reynolds. At Piccadilly (independent), New York, week April 12.
Jim Lassiter.................Tom Mix
Mili Erne...................Beatrice Burnham
Frank Erne..................Arthur Morrison
Bess Erne, a child..........Seesel A. Johnson
Lew Walters—Judge Dyer...Warner Oland
Metzger....................Fred Kohler
Herd.......................Charles Newton
Slack......................Joe Ricksen
Jane Withersteen............Mabel Ballin
Richard Tull...............Charles LeMoyne
Bern Venters...............Harold Goodwin
Bess Erne..................Marion Nixon
Fay Larkin.................Dawn O'Day
Oldring....................Wilfred Lucas

The ambition of a boy and the heart of a girl! Between the two, how can Tom Mix miss?

Every boy wants to be a Tom Mix; every girl wants her boy to be a Tom Mix.

And not only to the youth does the heroic figure of Tom Mix appeal as the daring, riding, shooting, handsome Westerner, the living reminder of the days that never can fade out of American history, but it hits the grit and sympathy of the grownups—those who in their youth also wanted to be or have a Tom Mix.

That being so, and getting away from a regular review of this particular Zane Grey story (the first by the way, that put that great writer of the woods and wilds on the literary map), for a Tom Mix picture of any kind is only a reason for Tom Mix himself now that he is so firmly set in filmstardom, it may be worth more to get an outside observation on this same Tom Mix and his value to the picture industry, for he has an untold and uncounted value.

Tom Mix is an outdoor man—an athlete and one of those rare all-around everything of the open that bespeaks health, vigor and cleanliness—cleanliness of mind and body—that God-given opportunity to every boy and girl, with comparatively so few accepting their chance, and perhaps many unfortunately unable to take their chance through conditions.

If you would ask Will Hays today, tomorrow, yesterday, what is the foundation of the film business for all time, he will tell you cleanliness, for Mr. Hays doesn't decide by the box office.

Those independents who pick out salacious, lurid or suggestive titles and build a story around them—those organized picture producers and distributors who are willing to wreck the youth of the country for another $5 bill over the average of the gross—those directors who figure they can raise their salary if they can ruin the screen, and the others who want to commit ruin on the screen, all for money and all for themselves—even those with their millions invested—all of those may disregard cleanliness, and while they are disregarding it, their quoted stocks, their plants and especially their good will are not worth 10 cents on the dollar, book or phoney values.

Tom Mix is in very close touch with the future of the picture business, probably too close for the coin-getting traducers to see the angle, but it's there, and very simply there. For as the reformers are agitating against pictures and against the youth seeing them, so Tom Mix is working for pictures through drawing the same youth into the picture houses to see him in his magnificent toga, his phenomenal skill at drawing guns, his remarkable riding and his nonchalant bearing that makes no pretensions for acting, but still may be the best of acting—natural playing.

Which gets down to the point, to wit:

If Tom Mix can attract the boys and girls of America, not taking in the world, which he also does, is it correct to assume that those boys and girls, growing up and as admirers of Tom Mix, will continue to like pictures if they are as clean as those that Tom Mix gives to them?

All pictures cannot have a Tom Mix, but all pictures of romance may have clean romance, the kind of romance the youth should have in his or her mind and heart, not the vile vamps, the dirty dames, the rotten roues and the lustful villains to exite the imagination, or the pictures maybe of adventure or with any subject, but clean—have them clean, for if not, the very children of today, who, as they advance in maturity and observe the kind of licentious pictures now that so many producers are trying to sneak past the censors, those same children, as parents, will will that their children shall not go to the picture houses.

"Tony" may have its place as the adorable horse, but it's Tom Mix who makes the draw, and it's Tom Mix whom you can't forget in his cowboy regalia.

As a matter of review on this "Riders of the Purple Sage" it may be said that the Fox cutters don't seem to pay much attention to the Mix pictures, at least this one, and the director was most careless in ever so many spots. It is all right to understand Mix and know what his admirers want, but it is just as well to recollect that adults watch Mix pictures also, and it would be just as well if some of these directorial absurdities were omitted or made to blend. Mr. Mix himself might ask for a little more attention to detail.

As production "Riders" is a Mix picture, inexpensive to Fox, another thing about Mix. Among the leading film favorites and Fox's star bet, Tom Mix's pictures cost less than any other drawing picture possibly could. In the current film the chances are that Mix's dandy purple or black Western costume, with Stetson to match, probably cost more than any individual thing in the picture.

For the final show at the Piccadilly Sunday night they were still standing up. The Piccadilly (independent) was lucky to get this Mix and on Easter week. *Sime.*

PROUD FLESH

Louis B. Mayer presentation of a King Vidor production and a Metro-Goldwyn-Mayer release. Adapted from the novel of the same name by Lawrence Rising. Vidor the director. Features Eleanor Boardman, Pat O'Malley and Harrison Ford. At the Capitol, New York, week of April 12. Running time, 70 minutes.

Fernanda	Eleanor Boardman
Pat O'Malley	Pat O'Malley
Don Jaime	Harrison Ford
Mrs. McKee	Trixie Friganza
Mr. McKee	William J. Kelly
Vicente	Rosita Marstini
Wong	Sojin
Spanish Aunt	Evelyn Sherman
Spanish Uncle	George Nichols

A corking light comedy picture that should be the more approved as the admission scales tilt.

Vidor has turned out an excellent piece of work with this release which has Harrison Ford satirically playing the Valentino type of screen lover leaving ample room for much subtle humor and for which the director doesn't seem to have overlooked a bet. Some of the comedy touches are so lightly and finely drawn that it's doubtful if any audience habituating less than the middle class theatres will give this film its due, hence the statement that this celluloid concoction will be of more entertainment value in the better tone theatres.

Other than the picture itself a sidelight on this showing is the propaganda M.-G.-M. is cutting loose with in favor of Eleanor Boardman at the Capitol. This latest release closely approximates the sixth film in which Miss Boardman has held a role within the last 12 weeks at this house, marking a method of concentration upon one player that is bound to have an effect. Minus any trumpeting in the way of extra billing the system has been simply the constant showing of Miss Boardman on this theatre's screen and that the Capitol clientele has yet to tire of her is but the proof of the pudding in M.-G.-M.'s conception that it has a personality worth building up. As far as Broadway is concerned Miss Boardman is well on her way to becoming a "name" with that morale needing but one or two more good releases to crystallize.

This girl has proved, at least to Capitol audiences, that she has ability and there being little question of her meeting all requirements as to appearance, it is now purely a matter of suitably adapted pictures to fulfill the conception of Miss Boardman as a "name."

"Proud Flesh" marks a terrific boost for the personal stock of Harrison Ford, who actually outshines the other contributing members. As a "class" performance Ford's effort, herein projected, rivals the tone which Clive Brooke gave to "Declasse." Playing a self assured Spanish nobleman of many loves and who lets nothing disturb his mental composure, Ford fairly scintillates in portraying the role as mayhaps conceived by the director, Vidor. If the conception is Ford's personal idea there is that much more credit coming to him. Either way it's an achievement only seen on a screen every so often.

Opposite Mr. Ford is Pat O'Malley, cast as a money making contracting plumber, whose rough wooing eventually wins the girl in spite of herself. O'Malley is very much in the spirit of the thing to nicely balance the triangle of the three featured players. Trixie Friganza and William J. Kelly are more than adequate in their assistance while a Chinese servant bit was made to stand in relief by a cast member listed as Sojin.

The story starts in San Francisco with the birth of Fernanda (Miss Boardman) in the midst of the earthquake. The first switch is to Spain where the child, now a young woman, is being raised by Spanish relatives. Thence back to San Francisco where O'Malley meets Fernanda and where Don Jaime (Mr. Ford) precedes her. While the location remains in Spain the action concentrates on Don Jaime's serenading of Fernanda with the assistance of a troupe of acrobatic and singing servants with whom he has played about every balcony in that country. Jaime's finishing trick of clownmanship is to have his followers form a human pyramid which he mounts to converse with the object of all the attention. Thence to 'Frisco where a ball in honor of Fernandez allows for a tango by Jaime and the girl, with one of Vidor's sidelights being the fighting of the couple to get before the one mirror between bows.

The finish of the picture has Fernanda waving from a window to her Spanish cavalier who, when he realizes its "air" so far as he is concerned, pulls out an address book and waves his chauffeur on. The showing of the address selected, that of a cigar stand girl in a hotel, was the one grating note in the picture. The climax could just as well have been the thumbing of the feminine directory.

Vidor has injected any number of subtleties that more than lift this picture above the average, while the subtitles take a full quota by themselves. In a few instances, they are responsible for honest and spontaneous outbursts.

An excellent production forms the background, finely set off by the photography of John Arnold.

Summing up, "Proud Flesh" marks itself as one of the best of its type and if it doesn't get money there's no justice and if it fails to entertain it's simply ahead of its audience. *Skig.*

CODE OF THE WEST

Zukor-Lasky presentation of Zane Grey's story of same title; adapted by Lucien Hubbard, directed by William K. Howard; Paramous release; running time, 72 mins.; seen at Rivoli.

Cal Thurman	Owen Moore
Georgie May	Constance Bennett
Mary	Mabel Ballin
Henry Thurman	Charles Ogle
Bid Hatfield	David Butler
Enoch	George Bancroft
Mollie	Gertrude Short
Ma Thurman	Lillian Leighton
Tuck Merry	Edward Gribbon
Cal Bloom	Pat Hartigan
Bud	Frankie Lee

This is a fill-in, booked to run only five-sevenths of a week, with the $5.50 Gloria Swanson premiere dated for Friday. Otherwise its occupancy of such a house as the Rivoli would be scarcely credible. It is doubtful whether a weaker feature has ever played one of Broadway's top-hole houses.

Miscast, misdirected, misplaced, misplayed, mis-fire, it is a weird anachronism on the Main Street of filmdom in this year of its pride and might. Were it relieved of all its technical faults, it might be described as a typical outdoor Western of 1915, when hard riding on a screen astonished the natives in the store-theatres, and a city gal on a ranch was still a "twist."

One might believe that it was a discarded five-reeler of those days, gone wrong but forgiven long after the wound had healed, were it not for the presence of Constance Bennett, one of the newest of the cinema personalities, appearing in the leading feminine part. "Appearing" is right, too. To give this promising girl such a wishy-washy job in such an atmosphere at this stage of her upward career is no less than a sin.

Tom Moore, one of the veteran old-timers, can better withstand being tossed what would be a Bill Hart part, were it a part at all. Since when Moore became a cow-puncher, land-clearing pioneer, fire-fighting woodsman, girl-shy son of the soil, has been carefully withheld from advance publicity, which is perhaps just as well.

Moore neither looks, acts nor registers the type. What assets he has of physique, manner and individuality are swamped under the demands of the soggy book and the malapropos character. He is neither Moore nor Cal Thurman. Miss Bennett, appearing for a few feet as a big-town flapper, is herself; thereafter she is as out of her type element as the author intended, but she is also out of her acting element, which probably no one intended.

It is obvious that the riding and stunts performed are impossible for both Moore and Connie, and the doubling is palpable throughout. No point is made, either, of this tenderly-reared girl going up against the unwonted hardships, as is emphasized in the case of an incidental hobo who becomes acclimatized, whereas no explanation is attempted of this asphalt-reared hothouse chicken turning circus-equestrienne without notice.

The story is all but nil. What turns it has are, in the main, left raggedly open. The complications are specious and phoney, and the abrupt fade-out kiss clears up nothing.

One of the sons of a respectable rancher is sent to an Arizona town to meet his brother's fiancee's sister, a city skirt; she immediately flirts with everybody (so say the titles, though little evidence is shown), and the quiet cow-lad is in love and desperate. A hobo he has befriended advises him to caveman the frivolous babe; he forces a marriage on her, takes her to his cabin, lets her sleep alone. A forest fire (supposedly started by the hated rivals on the next ranch, but not so explained) gives many, many feet of riding-through-flames stuff, deadly with repetitions; afterward she comes to him and kisses him and it's all over.

If Zane Grey wrote the story that shows on the screen he should be severely talked to; if he didn't, whoever slaughtered his script should get the woodshed conference.

There isn't much lost in any event, as the picture cost next to nothing as such things go nowadays. *Lait.*

THE FOOL

Fox film production of Channing Pollock's stage play. Directed by Harry Millarde with scenario by Edmund Goulding. At the Central, New York, April 12, for a run. Running time, 112 mins. Twice daily policy at $2 top.

Daniel Gilchrist	Edmund Lowe
Jerry Goodkind	Raymond Bloomer
Stedtmann	Henry Sedley
Umanski	Paul Panzer
Hennig	A. J. Herbert
Goodkind	George Lessey
A Poor Man	Fred C. Jones
Mary Margaret	Anne Dale
Pearl Hennig	Mary Thurman
Clare Jewett	Brenda Bond

Fox paid a lot of money for "The Fool," and has spent a neat little sum in making it. Not any prodigious amount, but far more than is usually spent on the product issuing from the 55th street and Tenth avenue plant. As a result he has a good picture on his hands.

As it stood Sunday night at the Central "The Fool" was at least half an hour too long, too finely crowded with closeups and unnecessary titles and cluttered with a mass of detail. But Mr. Fox and Winfield Sheehan know that "The Fool" has some neat cutting coming its way. With that done, they have a picture which has many more possibilities than its New York showing may indicate.

"The Fool" is not primarily a New York special run picture. In the medium-sized cities and the small towns, especially the latter, where there are communities, churches and schools, this one should tie up so closely with people who never go to movies that business is almost assured. In some of the cities it is altogether more than likely that the reviewers will treat this one with scant courtesy. They will be bored to tears at the moralizing and preaching of Daniel Gilchrist, the minister who tried to live like Christ, and if they're witty enough they may make merry at the expense of the picture. But that won't stop it.

Ministers will probably preach about it, and there is no doubt that any school so requested will recommend it without reservation. And it will deserve it, for "The Fool" is as clean as a mountain lake, forceful in its religious lesson, and made of that stuff which gets ready audiences from the home folks. So, even if it doesn't become a Broadway smash the picture will go solid over the country at large. Its religious trend will offend no one, its symbolism will attract many, and with its story tightened (the cutting will do that automatically) the film will stand on its own feet as entertainment.

Edmund Lowe plays the Gilchrist role and plays it well. Next to him A. J. Herbert as the leader of a mob which mistook the motives of the minister stood out. Herbert is a corking legit actor whose picture work has been scarce, but here he reveals himself as a good bet. Anne Dale gives a touching performance of the little crippled girl, while Paul

Panzer, a real veteran, and Raymond Bloomer also stand out.

Exhibitors need only remember that "The Fool" was viciously panned as a stage play and that five legit companies of it went out an collected kal.

It is the sort of film that can be boosted among the irregular patrons, an audience picture out of the ordinary. All it needs is advance advertising carefully planted.

Sisk.

His Supreme Moment

A George Fitzmaurice production presented by Samuel Goldwyn, released by First National. Adapted by Frances Marion from May Edginton's novel, "World Without End." Featuring Blanche Sweet and Ronald Colman. Shown at the Strand, N. Y., week April 12, 1925. Running time, 75 minutes.

Carla King	Blanche Sweet
John Douglas	Ronald Colman
Sara Deeping	Jane Winton
Mrs. King	Belle Bennett
Harry Avon	Cyril Chadwick
Adrian	Ned Sparks
Mueva	Nick De Ruiz

Three color sequences, giving the audience an element of surprise and delivering a real kick. In addition to this it is safe to predict that wherever the picture is shown the women are going to go wild over the love making Ronald Colman does on the screen. He is out for the matinee idol honors and bids fair to receive them.

Opening with a color sequence of a scene in a Moorish harem with Blanche Sweet a blonde dancer of the harem, the audience gets the impression it is going to see another of those sheik tales. When the switch arrives that gives them the realization they were viewing a stage spectacle and were just as much a part of the audience as the one that flashes on the screen there is an element of genuine surprise.

With that the real story starts. It is a clash between the star o. the stage production and a wealthy society woman for the affection of a young mining engineer, he falling for the beautiful blonde stage star, and Miss Sweet certainly does look wonderfully well, almost startlingly so in the color shots. Then the society woman, through a friend, finances the young engineer to return to South America, figuring that it will be a case of out of sight out of mind as far as her stage rival is concerned. In this she is mistaken, however, for the girl of the stage goes with him, the two forming a pact to live together for a year to ascertain whether or not their love will be enduring, or if the lure of the stage will be too great for the woman.

It is a well done tale with the sex element played up about as strongly as possible, although in the color shots there are some studies of remarkable beauty. How they ever managed to get by with the censors on the Moorish bath scene is going to be a mystery that will remain dark forever. It is beautiful, true, but there are elements that will look on it in a decidedly different light. One girl never shows her face at all.

Blanche Sweet has done a comeback in this picture and seemingly the opportunity was all that she wanted. June Winton as the society woman heavy was somewhat stilted at times but gave the role about all that it required. Suffice to say she was clever enough actress to make the women dislike her. The others played little more than bits.

MADAME SANS GENE

Presented by Adolph Zukor and Jesse L. Lasky. Directed by Leonce Perrett. Adapted by Forrest Halsey from the play by Victorien Sardou and Emile Moreau. Shown at the Rivoli, N. Y., beginning April 17, 1925. Running ime, 111 minutes.

Catherine Hubscher (Mme. Sans-Gene)	Gloria Swanson
Napoleon	Emile Drain
La Rousotte	Madeleine Guitty
Lefebvre	Charles de Roche
Neipperg	Warrick Ward
Fouche	Henry Favieres
Caroline, Queen of Naples	Arlette Marchal
Eliza, Princess of Bacciochi	Renee Heribelle
Empress Marie Louise	Suzanne Bianchetti
Mme. de Bulow	Denise Lorys
Savary, Minister of Police	Jacques Marney

Were it not Gloria Swanson appears in the title role Famous Players would have nothing to brag about as far as motion picture entertainment is concerned in this particular case. But Gloria is in the picture and Gloria does make it possible for one to sit through the feature.

It is said that in the neighborhood of $700,000 was spent in the making of the screen version of "Madame Sans-Gene." That may or may not be true. If so, a lot of money was wasted. "Madame Sans-Gene" on the screen proves one thing: foreign directors handling a foreign subject get away from the angle of what is wanted in pictures for American distribution. And here the cast of foreign players surrounding Miss Swanson do not register with anything like the wallop they should have. As Napoleon, Emile Drain, a French player, does well enough, but Holbrook Blinn could have given him cards and spades putting that character over.

Of the others, Madeleine Guitty, a character woman, playing the overportly La Rousotte, is the only one registering effectively as far as the audiences are concerned.

But "Sans-Gene" is going to make money. The tremendous publicity and exploitation campaign put behind it and Miss Swanson will take care of that. Never has Broadway seen a splash such as was given to this star. Her name in the largest electric letters ever given to an individual on Broadway decorate the facade of the Rivoli; the house is shrouded in the tri-color of France and the Stars and Stripes, and all the other buildings on both sides of Broadway from 49th to 50th streets are similarly decorated, with the result one can hardly get standing room in the theatre since the doors were opened to the public at the regular admission scale of prices at 10:30 Saturday morning, following the $5 opening Gloria had Friday night, when she made a personal appearance and heard the crowds acclaim her loudly.

Outside of the theatre the police reserves from the West 30th and West 47th street police stations were trying to hold back the frantic mob of sightseers who were trying to glimpse the star and the other celebs attending the opening performance, so intent on rubbering they did not notice the dips working in the crowd, and many a one went home lighter in pocket because of the light-fingered gentry present.

The picture itself runs almost two hours—a little long. It is in 11 reels, but the chances are it will be chopped to about eight before generally released.

Screen and program credit is given to the Fine Arts Ministry of the French government, under whose supervision the picture was made; also attention is called to that government permitting the producers to use the palace of Fontainebleu, the palace of Compeigne and other historical scenes for the production.

In places the screen shots are superb, and some of the bigger scenes, with the revolutionaries attacking the palace and later scenes at the court of Emperor Napoleon, are splendid in their grandeur.

The titles carry the information as to the historic significance of each room in which the scene has been shot, in addition to the title descriptive of the action.

But, after all, the little exhibitor of an east side house, in referring to all costume pictures as a whole, said a mouthful when he remarked: "The French Revolution just raises hell at my box office."

"Sans-Gene" is the French Revolution; it is history, and one cannot go back of that. But without Gloria Swanson it would stand mighty little chance as a picture to attain box-office popularity.

Fred.

FREE AND EQUAL

Presented by the Frequal Co. Directed by William Neill. At the Astor theatre, N. Y., beginning April 19, 1925. Running time, 65 minutes.

Judge Lowell	Charles K. French
His Daughter	Gloria Hope
Her Fiance	Jack Curtis
Mrs. Lowell	Lydia Knott
The Creole	Jack Richardson
Prosecuting Attorney	Thomas J. Guise
The Colonel	J. J. Dowling

"Has Al Woods gone nutty?" was the question often asked Sunday night at the Astor after he had shown "Free and Equal" at that house. It is possible that Woods was playing a joke on all of New York and the newspaper crowd in particular by presenting the picture. If so it's a good joke, although an expensive one.

Woods has had "Free and Equal" in a vault for some eight or ten years. It was made by the late Thomas H. Ince shortly after "The Birth of a Nation." New York, however, never saw the picture. There were stories to the effect that it had been shown for about three days in Los Angeles and that the exhibitors there got together and called on the one showing the picture and informed him that it would be advisable for him to take it off or things might be made more or less uncomfortable for him. The picture was taken off.

But nothing like that is going to happen in New York. As a matter of fact there is nothing to cause any one any worry about this picture, least of all Will H. Hays, for all that is necessary is to ignore the picture and it will die; in fact, it gave its death rattle at the Astor Sunday night.

As an example of how pictures have improved in the last decade this production is a striking object lesson. It is horribly overacted, badly directed and just about everything that a picture should not be.

Woods' name is not used in connection with the presentation, but he was very much in evidence Sunday night and keeping a check on the box office, although it didn't look as though that would do him any good.

Prolog and epilog with the picture. The prolog runs about 15 minutes and has 11 people, all colored, in it. It is a levee scene, with five dancers and six singers, plantation melodies and some fast stepping for applause. Jack Richardson, who plays the Negro who poses as a white in the picture, appeared in person and plays the role of an educated Negro who is trying to exhort his fellows to make the most of their opportunities to assert themselves as the equals of the white mentally, socially and physically. At the close of the picture he is again in the epilog awakening from a dream which the picture is supposed to represent and says that Booker T. Washington is right—the Negro must stay in his place.

The picture in brief has as its theme the question of the equality of the races. Judge Lowell believes that he can solve the question by taking a mixed blood who looks like he were a white man into his home as his secretary and has him pose as a white. In the end the mixed blood commits a murder after having married the daughter of his benefactor secretly, the girl believing him to be white, and messed up the works generally.

There is no chance for the picture to get a nickel anywhere. It is not only old-fashioned, but so crudely done that the Sunday night audience laughed it practically out of the theatre. Any exhibitor who takes it after it has played Broadway will gain nothing but the ill will of his audience.

"Free and Equal" is just so much junk.

Fred.

RECOMPENSE

Warner Brothers' picture, directed by Harry Beaumont, featuring Marie Prevost and Monte Blue. Adapted from the novel of Robert Keable and sequel to this author's "Simon Called Peter." At the Piccadilly, New York, week April 18. Running time, about 72 mins.

Julie Gamelyn	Marie Prevost
Peter Graham	Monte Blue
Dr. Sampson	John Roche
Stenhouse	George Siegman
Moshesboe	Charles Stevens
Angelica	Virginia Brown Faire
Col. Donovan	William C. Davidson
African Dancing Girl	Etta Lee

This is the picturization of Robert Keable's follow up on his novel, "Simon Called Peter." The latter has not reached the screen.

"Recompense" is an average feature that may satisfy its readers, but isn't particularly interesting to those who missed the story in print.

It's war stuff, somewhat augmented by "lifts" from official or news reels. The tale jumps to South Africa and then to London. The film has a decided leaning toward the sex angle between the minister and the nurse, while an additional insertion is the reverend's former fiance as a woman of the streets who conveniently dies.

That the hectic affair of Julie (Miss Prevost) and Peter (Mr. Blue) is still in a turbulent state is revealed through the nurse twice dismissing her beloved before the last reel is unwound. The first time she gives up the ghost is the night of the Armistice in their room at a small inn, and the second requested withdrawal is staged in South Africa, giving the impression Julie dotes on waving her boy friend away to any location.

The South African episode allows for an active tussel between Peter and a slave driver (Mr. Siegman) which eventually leads to the former minister (he forsook the church to enlist) being shot, but saved through the efforts of a slave he has befriended and the arrival of Julie, who nurses him through the crisis.

In London Peter sets up a home for the wayward (much as Edmund Lowe is supervising in "The Fool" at the Central). Into it drops the former fiance and then Julie, who finally has concluded to marry Peter and be done with it, after having lived with him through two novels, a few thousand feet of film, and without the aid of a bathtub in this last instance.

The transplanting of this trailer of "Simon" to the screen presents itself as a series of happenings in the lives of Julie and Peter that to those who didn't meet this duo in type will be indifferent. It may be because "war stuff" is now passe as film fare or the fault of the director or the cast, but most likely it is right in the story. The tale doesn't seem especially vital and it's of little matter to a screen audience as to characters that can't attract sympathy.

Miss Prevost plays an appropriate Julie, a bit theatric for the type, perhaps, but on the whole okeh. Mr. Blue doesn't impress as a genuine deciple of the cloth albeit his switch to enlisted khaki enhanced his general performance. Mr. Siegman has turned in his usual par definition of a "heavy" in the brief time allotted, while Charles Stevens is particularly able as the befriended and appreciative slave.

There's nothing risque, and those who have any such expectations will be disappointed. "Recompense" is just average celluloid. *Skig.*

MY SON

Edwin Carewe Production released by First National. From the play by Martha Stanley, with Nazimova starred. Shown at the Strand, New York, week April 19, 1925. Running time, 78 minutes.

Ana Silva	Nazimova
Tony	Jack Pickford
Ellery Parker	Hobart Bosworth
Felipe Varas	Ian Keith
Rosa Pina	Mary Akin
Capt. Joe Bamby	Charles A. Murray
Betty Smith	Constance Bennett
Hattie Smith	Dot Farley

One of the best pictures First National has released in some time. It is a picture with a lot of punch, a lot of up to the minute jazz, and with a cast that gives the exhibitor about as corking a collection of names as any picture has had in a year. Nazimova is starred in the mother role, but it is Jack Pickford and Constance Bennett who carry away the honors. In addition Hobart Bosworth, Ian Keith, Charles Murray and Dot Farley contribute to the entertainment value.

"My Son" is a screen adaptation of the play with the same title current in New York. It is a story of life in a New England fishing village, stirred up by the return of one of the native daughters who married money and lived in New York. She brings her daughter, of the typical flapper type, and the manner in which Constance Bennett puts that role over on the screen is a wow.

Nazimova is the patient suffering mother of the boy Tony who is playing around with the flapper. Nazzy overacts at times, and her grimaces are not at all pleasant when shot in close-ups. Pickford gets away with the boy role in good shape.

The story has a moral and it is to the effect that present day mothers and fathers have but to assert themselves in the good old-fashioned way with a wallop to bring the younger element to a realization that they are still kids and not the rulers of the universe. That the public is in attune with this is showed when the flapper's mother takes her in hand and starts slapping her all over the place and they applaud heartily.

"My Son" is good screen entertainment and it is going to be just as welcome in the smaller towns as it will be in the larger pre-release houses. *Fred.*

TIDES OF PASSION

Vitagraph production starring Mae Marsh. Adapted to the screen from Basil King's novel, "In the Garden of Charity." Directed by J. Stuart Blackton. Reviewed at the Rialto, New York, April 19. Running time, 70 minutes.

Charity Byfleet	Mae Marsh
William Pennland	Ben Hendricks
Hagar	Laska Winter
Jonas	Earl Schenck
Alick	Ivor McFadden
Michael	Thomas Mills

This marks Mae Marsh's return to the screen and although it would be gratifying to record that this well liked and perienially youthful veteran had made a smash "comeback," it cannot be done in all truthfulness. For, despite a production remarkable in many respects, a bad continuity had wrecked its chances for real success.

The story is attractively laid on the bleak Nova Scotia coast. In this atmosphere lives Charity Byfleet, orphaned daughter of a sea-going family. She has two suitors, Jonas, a peddler, and the other William Penniand, soldier, whom she marries. After the marriage he leaves and goes to many lands—but doesn't come home until many years later and then stops on the way to get hooked up with Hagar Levanti, a hybrid Greek-Portuguese woman. By Hagar he has a child—and then dies, a victim of her relentless selfishness.

But Charity, hearing of it all, brings Hagar to live with her and until the pious villagers, hearing of Hagar's more or less doubtful reputation, decide to stone her, things go smoothly. Even then Charity defends her and in the end, Hagar and Charity are happily married once more.

Miss Marsh isn't given any sustained work. Most of the interest is centered on the other characters, particularly on Pennland and Hagar, well played by Ben Hendricks (the younger) and Laska Winter. Of Miss Marsh the shots are episodic and short, thereby lessening whatever effect one sustained charactization would have had on the picture. Miss Winter in the Hagar role, is really given quite a part, but it is introduced late in the picture—too late for it to assume its real importance.

"Tides of Passion" has been very well produced—probably better than anything recently from Vitagraph and its sea stuff is corking. But even the Mae Marsh name and the rep of the King novel will not lift it into the strict first run class—rather say that it is an average picture—not bad, but not so good, either. *Sisk.*

ADVENTURE

Victor Fleming production, presented by Adolph Zukor and Jesse L. Lasky. From the novel by Jack London adapted by A. P. Younger and L. G. Rigby. Featuring Tom Moore, Pauline Starke, Wallace Beery and Raymond Hatton. Shown at the Rialto, N. Y., week April 12, 1925. Running time 78 minutes.

David Sheldon	Tom Moore
Joan Lackland	Pauline Starke
Morgan	Wallace Beery
Baff	Raymond Hatton
Tudor	Walter McGrail
Noah Noa	Duke Kahanamoku
Adam	James Spencer
Googomy	Noble Johnson

"Adventure" is a very interesting picturization of one of Jack London's South Sea stories. It is a well-handled melodrama on the screen, full of action and sufficient suspense to make the average audience like it. It isn't from the box office viewpoint a picture that is going to smash records as a draw, but those who do come are going to be thoroughly satisfied with what they see. Incidentally the exhibitor has four names that he can advertise and that ought to help bring 'em in.

Starting with "blackwater fever" in the first reel the story swings along into a romance with the arrival of Joan Lackland, 18, white and able to take care of herself. In other words, a girl that wants to be a boy and has taken a small schooner and native crew to make a tour of the islands. When she arrives at one of the Solomon Islands she finds a lone Englishman there, the owner of a cocoanut plantation, who is on the verge of collapse from the fever, which has also laid low a number of his blacks, while the remainder are in open revolt against his rule. She nurses the Englishman back to health and he falls in love with her, but she has her doubts and makes him sign an agreement not to speak of his heart troubles for a period of six months.

Shortly thereafter she rescues him from a financial problem when a couple of shrewd island traders want to foreclose on the plantation. First she pays them and then, being a smart girl, wins it all back at poker and takes their schooner to boot. That makes her a partner in the plantation, so that when the heavy arrives, a gentleman adventurer, she is in a position to invite him ashore to stay, a situation and invitation that he takes full advantage of, and tries to make the girl, that leading to a row between the two white men and results in the shooting of the heavy.

While the Englishman goes for a doctor located on one of the other islands, the blacks rise through the urging of the two traders trimmed at poker and who are anxious to get their schooner back. When the Englishman returns he has his hands full. He meets the situation, however, and rescues the girl from the schooner on which the traders are carrying her off.

There are a couple of good fights, several thrills and a lot of love interest, all carried out in a natural manner and never too mushy.

Tom Moore as the young Englishman handles himself exceeding well, and Pauline Starke as the boy-girl has both a charming smile and a winning manner. Walter McGrail is the heavy, who does not try to overplay the role. The comedy traders are the work of Beery and Hatton, and they make both roles stand out.

Victor Fleming has directed the picture skilfully and held it down in footage so that it never drags. *Fred.*

THE WIZARD OF OZ

Chadwick Production starring Larry Semon. Adapted from the play of the same title which was Montgomery and Stone's first big hit. Directed by Larry Semon. Shown at the Colony, N. Y., week April 12, 1925. Running time, 66 minutes.

The Scarecrow	Larry Semon
Prince Kynd	Bryant Washburn
Dorothy	Dorothy Dwan
Countess Vishus	Virginia Pearson
The Wizard	Charlie Murray
The Tin Woodman	Oliver Hardy
The Prime Minister	Josef Swickard
Dorothy's Mother	Mary Carr
Rastus	G. Howe Black

Despite Larry Semon must have tried every conceivable manner possible to ruin this picture he has failed to do so and has probably turned out one of the best pictures of all times to take the kids to see. It is a kid picture out and out, and even though it may seem frightfully mixed up to them they certainly laugh themselves almost sick at it. That goes for a lot of kids, some of them four and some of them forty, but the younger were in the majority by far at the Colony Monday afternoon. They couldn't have remembered the play, and the chances are the folks didn't drag them to the theatre, but in addition to being a play "The Wiz" is an admirable fairy story that has sold in the millions and the kiddies may have obtained the urge to see the picture from that source.

But how this Larry Semon did manage to jam things up. He just wanted to show the folks that he could act and he was going to do a Warfield if it killed him. Well, it almost did. Not only he, but the picture as well, and the production would be a whole lot better off if they were to eliminate the scenes that had Larry as the old toy maker reading fairy stories to a little girl.

There are three separate sequences to the story in the manner that screen version handles the story. First there is the old toy maker theme; then the Court in the Land of Oz, and, finally, the farm out in Kansas where the missing heir to the throne has been left with a family on the farm.

The chances are that the picture would have been a better one had they just run the story in a straight sequence. But it certainly has been hoaked up with all the slapstick in the world for laughs, and it does get them, although there is a little too much of the repeat stuff, both in the packing case gag and the lion stuff. But the laughs are there, and in the small towns and smaller cities the picture should mop up.

There is a great chance to play up the names in the cast, for every one with the exception of the phoney name used for the colored boy, although he deserved better fate than to be christened G. Howe Black (for he was almost as funny as Semon) is a worth while player who has had outstanding roles in other film productions.

Bryant Washburn looks like a million dollars, and there doesn't seem a reason in the world why he should not stage a terrific screen comeback. Dorothy Dawn is pretty enough, and Virginia Pearson looks about as good as she did when she first started before the camera. Charlie Murray landed with his mugging to such an extent that the kids were howling at him, and Josef Swickard proved himself to still be the capable artist as in the past. Of course, nothing need be said regarding Mary Carr, for she is cast as a mother, and no one could ask for more.

"The Wizard of Oz" is a corking picture when it is considered that it was independently made, unusual in fact for something that is in that market, and outside of the prerelease runs the exhibitor can count pretty much on getting money with it, especially if the kids bring their elders in the towns where it plays the same as they do on Broadway. *Fred.*

CURLYTOP

Fox Film Production, adapted by Frederic and Fanny Hatton from the "Limehouse Tales" stories of Thomas Burke. Directed by Maurice Elvey. Reviewed at the Stanley, New York, April 20. Running time, 57 minutes. Cast includes Shirley Mason, starred; Warner Oland, Wallace MacDonald.

The Limehouse stories of Thomas Burke concern that section of London as integral and famous a part of the British capital as the Bowery was of New York. Its people are the cockneys and the Chinese, and "Curlytop" is no exception. One suspects that some liberties have been taken with the story as Burke wrote it, but as it stands it makes nice picture material, and in the hands of Director Elvey is finely handled.

Plot proper concerns Curlypop, a beautiful and innocent little waif of the Limehouse section. Orphaned, she lived alone, until one day Bill came into her life as the "steady." From then on it was peaches and cream until Bill's ex-sweetie butted in and clipped the curls from Curlytop. Ashamed, she disappeared, and finally took a job offered her by Dan, a Chinese, as waitress aboard his gambling barge. There Dan cornered her one night, but a jealous compatriot set the craft adrift, where a swift-moving liner struck it square amidships, crushing it like an eggshell. Curlytop was nearly drowned, but Bill, close on her trail, swam and rescued her, thereby bringing happiness to her and an end to the film.

Herein Miss Mason wears a blonde wig, which isn't so becoming, but, for all that, she does much really popular acting, while Wallace MacDonald is attractive as her sweetheart. Acting honors, however, go to Warner Oland as the Chinese, a part probably easy for him, but, nevertheless, the most impressive on the screen.

If anybody should ask about "Curlytop" you'd be safe in saying that, as a straight program picture for the daily changes, it is entirely up to scratch. *Sisk.*

THE SADDLE HAWK

Universal production starring Hoot Gibson. Story by Raymond L. Schrock and Edward Sedgwick. Directed by Edgar Sedgwick.

Ben Johnson	Hoot Gibson
Rena Newhall	Marian Nixon
Zach Marlin	G. Raymond Nye
Mercedes	Josie Sedgwick
Jim Newhall	Charles K. French
Vasquez	Tote Ducrow
Draw Collins	Fred Humes
Steve Kern	William Steele
Buck Brent	Frank Campeau

A fairly good western with Hoot Gibson back in the chaps and riding again after a brief sojourn in drawing room and parlor dramas. The story is along familiar lines, having to do with the feud of the sheep and cowmen.

Ben Johnson (Gibson) is working as a sheepherder, although he is a cowboy. He pines for the former atmosphere and duties and when his employer asks him to escort the daughter of a local cow magnate to her home he eagerly responds.

The girl is kidnapped by a bitter rival of her father's. Johnson rescues her after getting into the good graces of the villain. A chase, hard riding and shooting are blended into the usual western sequence.

Gibson's acting has improved and his registry of discontent with his lot as a sheepherder was much more convincing than some of his former emotional attempts. His riding remains high class and on a par with any of the western stars.

The picture, although offering nothing new in treatment or story, is an interesting western, and will please fans who crave this type of film nourishment.

Con.

SPEED

Banner production distributed by Dependable Picture Inc. From the "Saturday Evening Post" story by Grace Startwell Mason. Directed by Edward J. Le Saint. Ben Verschleiser production. At Loew's New York one day (April 17) as half the bill. Runs about 65 minutes.

Mary Whipple	Betty Blythe
Wiletta Whipple	Pauline Garon
Sam Whipple	William V. Mong
Dick Whipple	Arthur Rankin
Nat Armstrong	Alfred Allen
Nat Armstrong, Jr.	Robert Ellis
Jack Cartwright	Eddie Phillips
Senor Querino	Fred Becker
Senorita Querino	Duchess Stella di Lanti

"Speed" lives up to its title, inasmuch as it is a breezy, pleasant little program picture, although it does lag a bit just before the final mad auto chase. Its plot ranks as about number 1,492 of that popular modern series in which the struggle between the old and new generations is fought. Nevertheless, it holds some well-thought-out twists, a fair share of comedy and light romance and a sizzling thrill at the finish. In addition the cast is excellent and the direction, photography and adaptation all that any neighborhood picture require.

Grace Startwell Mason wrote the original story for the "Saturday Evening Post." Here, once again, is the familiar situation of the family of four, isolated because the over-stressed speed antics of the young son and daughter are totally incomprehensible to the old-fashioned parents. Scrapes and arguments come in torrents and there seems to be no happiness in sight until the mother conceives the idea of outspeeding the kids.

Consequently she and the old man put on the dog in true style and soon have the youngsters content to stay at home and take it easy by comparison. But pa and ma are not accustomed to the fast life and they become entangled with a couple of society crooks. That gives opportunity for the children to show what they are made of in going to the rescue and for the above-mentioned auto chase down the mountain with brakes running wild and thrills aplenty.

Pauline Garon heads the very competent cast. Miss Garon seems to be about as good an example of the pouting, ungovernable flapper as can be found. Why she didn't ride to the top some two or three years ago when the flapper wave first reached its crest is hard to understand. Betty Blythe appears as the mother, at first in unaccustomed ginghams, but then blossoming out as a stunning, if rather mature, lady of fashion. Robert Ellis is a likable hero, Eddie Phillips a slimy light heavy, and William V. Mong and Arthur Rankin very acceptable as father and son.

Banner's budget for "Speed" was undoubtedly a heavy one for an independent, as the film has the unmistakable air of money about it. They should get it back without trouble, however, as the picture is a good one in every detail, from Miss Garon's matchless ankles to the cleverly worded titles.

THE CROWDED HOUR

Zukor-Lasky presentation and a Paramount picture adapted from the stage play by Channing Pollock and Edgar Selwyn. Directed by E. Mason Hopper. At the Rialto, New York, week of April 26. Stars Bebe Daniels. Running time, 68 mins.

Peggy Laurence	Bebe Daniels
Billy Laidlaw	Kenneth Harlan
Matt Wilde	T. Roy Barnes
Bert Caswell	Frank Morgan
Grace Laidlaw	Helen Lee Worthing
Captain Soulier	Armand Cortez
Grandmere Buvasse	Alice Chapin
Operator	Werner Richmond

A war picture, but contrary to the impression that implies "The Crowded Hour," is close to the best vehicle Miss Daniels has had in many moons. The field stuff is almost entirely restricted to the fighting sector, although there are occasional glimpses of the boys marching down a U. S. street. Such battle activities as have been "shot" on this side are exceptionally well done, besides which the film has been neatly sliced for the slipping in of the news reel, and mayhaps, semi-official or official excerpts as gleaned by the war cameras.

The story starts before the war and concludes ahead of the armistice, leaving the principal within the grounds of a base hospital with Miss Daniels giving her lieutenant back to his wife, who has crossed as a Red Cross nurse.

Previously, Peggy (Miss Daniels) is in a tryout act at an amateur night with Matt (T. Roy Barnes) as her partner. A grand flop leaves Billy (Mr. Harlan) unconvinced, and he goes backstage to give Peg a card to a producer. Follows a triumphal stage career for the team and a growing friendship between the actress and Billy, with the latter continuously drawing further away from his wife. Peg follows Billy to France, and when it comes to a showdown phones through a message to save a battalion rather than call the station which will save him a perilous mission. An attempt to stop him en route ends in both Peg and Matt landing in a hospital, with Billy's wife becoming the nurse for Peg. Both believe William dead, and when he shows up Peg sends him back to his wife following the understanding the two girls have reached during the convalescence.

Miss Daniels is very much up to scratch in making her portrayal convince. Especially is this true during the hectic action. T. Roy Barnes plays the smalltime actor neatly, albeit, Hopper, the director, has allowed him to lay it on rather broad at times. Harlan secures much from his role of the more or less philandering husband, while Helen Lee Worthing gives a more than apt performance as the somewhat frigid wife who later relents. Her work in this picture will probably lead to much film activity by this former "Follies" girl. Others in the cast—and that actually includes all the names on the program—make themselves known in their respective roles.

The war stuff, as it has been conceived and presented in this picture, is alone sufficient to see the film through as first-class screen entertainment, while the performances of the players enhance that value.

In all, this is a war picture that's got some sense to it. *Skig.*

CHICKIE

First National release, directed by John Francis Dillon, from the newspaper serial by Elenore Meherin; seen at the Strand.

Chickie	Dorothy Mackaill
Harry Dunne	John Bowers
Jonathan	Hobart Bosworth
Jennie	Gladys Brockwell
Jake Munson	Paul Nicholson
Janina	Myrtle Steadman
Ila	Olive Tell
Bess	Lora Sonderson
Mrs. Dunne	Louise Mackintosh

"Chickie" was one of those circulation-making newspaper serials which come once in a generation—one of those oh-so-true stories of the struggles within the heart of a poor girl who wants on one hand to go straight, and on the other to have luxuries and "the life."

Elenor Meherin is a California newspaper woman who became rich and famous through it. The tale was so pulling and compelling that after it had been published serially the demands for back copies were so numerous and insistent several newspapers had to publish it in full as a pamphlet and sell it both by mail and on the stands.

As a picture it will indubitably inherit some of that drag. The picture is not quite as sure of it as was the serial, but it has some of the quality retained, and will be a cinch money-maker. Dillon has done a not-bad job on it, though he overreached himself in some of the majestic interiors and some of the low comedy (such as a rich young stew taking a shower bath partly dressed and smoking a cigar, etc.), so that the open-and-shut heart attack which the story made is somewhat confused and diluted.

Of course, the film has the advantages of the physical story—telling with a beautiful person like Miss Mackaill personating the lovelorn and doubt-torn Chickie. At the start the picture, dealing with the girl in her office-work stage, seems to promise a terrific study of such a girl's soul. Her girlish flirtation across the court with the young lawyer is perfect. Her first "party," among the moderns of the night-life, is well developed, also.

Later the story wanders some. However, we extract the plot as being the adventures of a poor and pretty working girl, fond of a promising but not prosperous law clerk, egged on by her mother to "do better"; she feels she would only be a ball and chain on the honest youth, and she lets herself be beckoned on by the rich roisterer, going through the gamut of petting parties, booze festivals, perils and latter-day Arabian nights. At last she cables her young hero, he comes, and they fade-out.

Some father and mother stuff, heavily stressed in the story, was not so walloping on the screen. Hobart Bosworth gives a study of the father, sure-fire for critical analysis, but not so pleasing for the audience "rooting" for the pretty, animate, sorely distressed and tempted girl. Miss Brockwell as the mother is grim and unpleasant, not in person, but in role. Miss Tell, as the "other woman," is over her head.

The film could still stand some ruthless cutting. But in its current shape may be rated as a box office attraction anyway. It has many elements, including the limitless drag of the story, the notable cast, the prodigal production and the happy work and personality of Miss Mackaill, who here scores easily the highest mark she has yet registered on the screen. The advertising that the title has enjoyed will put it over the top even if some of the assets remain unappreciated.

So here is what looks like a strong box-office feature. *Lait.*

RAFFLES

Universal-Jewel, produced and directed by King Baggott, starring House Peters. Adapted to the screen (for second time) by Harry Thew, from the novel by Ernest William Hornung. Reviewed at the Broadway, New York, April 27. Running time, 65 mins.

A. J. Raffles	House Peters
Bunny	Freeman Wood
Clarice Vidal	Hedda Hopper
Lord Amersteth	Winter Hall
Lady Amersteth	Kate Lester

Lady Gwendolyn..............Miss Dupont
Captain Bedford........Frederick Esmelton

It's a famous story, this legend of Raffles, the gentleman crook who stole from the rich and then returned their goods—in order to get contributions for the soldiers' fund. It has suspense, mystery, love interest and the excuse for a moderately lavish production. Because of this it is naturally good film program, with the merits out-numbering the faults.

There are but two faults—bad editing, which leaves a host of subtitles and close-ups in the picture, and the casting of Miss Dupont, saccharine and minus a front moniker, for the role of the heroine. House Peters and a great cast overcome these. And, yet, those little faults have kept "Raffles" from being a quality first run film, for the speed is retarded by the superfluous footage.

Mr. Peters is an ideal Raffles. He has a sense of humor. Hedda Hopper appears to advantage as a jealous woman; Winter Hall once more carries the mark which his name implies into the Lord Amersteth impersonation, in which he is ably backed by the late Kate Lester, who was tragically burned to death recently. Miss DuPont is colorless and blonde—not that the two go together—but she has both in plenty. Frederick Esmelton and Freeman Wood fill out the cast.

King Baggott's direction is always sure, while the sets are of big time quality. "Raffles" first run worth must be judged greatly on Peters' popularity with your patrons.

There may be a laugh at the beginning of this picture for the trade. Instead of the name of the film at screening, a full picture of Carl Laemmle, president of Universal, is shown, and that fades into "Carl Laemmle." Then comes the explanation to the world that Mr. Laemmle is president of Universal and then that Universal presents the picture. There are some more credits and once more "A Universal-Jewel Production made by Universal Pictures. Carl Laemmle, president." After that it sounds set that Laemmle has something to do with it. *Sisk.*

THE MAD DANCER

H. F. Jans production, starring Ann Pennington. From the "Young's Magazine" story by Louise Winter. Directed by Burton King. Photographed by Charles Davis. Scenario by William B. Laub. At Loew's New York one day (April 17) as half the show. Runs about 67 minutes.

Mimi ....Ann Pennington
Keith Arundel..............Johnnie Walker
Orchestra Leader............Vincent Lopez
The Princess................Nellie Savage
Serge Verlain...............Coite Albertson
Jean Gaboule...........Frank Montgomery
Robert Halleck.............John Woodford
Ada Halleck..................Recca Allen
John Arundel.................John Costello
John Halleck.............William Haddock

Ann Pennington's screen debut is inauspicious, not because her work is necessarily bad but the vehicle is a mediocre one in almost every detail. At the box office, however, "Penny's" name and knees may draw, and that the story is from "Young's Magazine," one of a newstand group of semi-blue publications that total a large circulation, shouldn't hurt the commercial possibilities.

This story, by Louise Winter, has Miss Pennington as a little Parisienne who poses in the absolute for a French sculptor in order to pay her rent. Later she comes to the United States, becomes a perfect little lady and heavily reciprocates Johnny Walker's show of affection. But the villainous sculptor, unable to forget what he has seen and modeled, has followed her and threatens to expose her as the model for his daring figure, "The Mad Dancer," unless she consents to marry him.

Here the plot none too deftly gives Ann ample opportunity to chisel the face of the statue into bits. Since the scene now is Washington and not Paris, no one cares to identify her otherwise as the model for the marble and everything is tranquil.

The little Ziegfeld star skips through her role with as much cuteness and charm as the average screen actress of such parts, but not, however, a very high average when it comes to general acting ability. However, for a dancer she does surprisingly well. Her sparkling eyes and the even more famous legs are shown to best advantage, and except during a few of the close-ups she makes an adorable little figure. Miss Pennington is given opportunity for two of her characteristic dances, first on the Paris streets and then in a Washington ballroom to the accompaniment of Vincent Lopez' Orchestra.

The film has been sluggishly directed and the supporting cast is particularly weak, although Johnny Walker will be as welcome as ever to those that like him. The photography is also below par, some colored shots of roses being pictorially atrocious. The picture evidently cost money, but the handling of the extras was poor enough to almost spoil the lavish scenes. Finally the titling is very trite and the scenario disjointed.

The clever exhibitor will play this one up with advertising of the "she-had-posed-as-the-half-naked-dancing-girl-frenzied-with-desire" school provided he can get away with it. The Pennington, Lopez, Young's and dance angles give all sorts of opportunities for tie-ups that should put this picture across, even though in itself it is hardly deserving of that. And also remembering Loew's put it on as a half of a double bill at the New York in Times Square, where Ann Pennington is best known.

CHAMPION OF LOST CAUSES

William Fox production, starring Edmund Lowe. Story by Max Brand, script by Thomas Dixon Jr., directed by Chester Bennett. Running time, 57 minutes.

Loring ....Edmund Lowe
Beatrice Charles..........Barbara Bedford
Zanten-Dick Sterling.......Walter McGrail

Corking mystery melodrama with a society element that is presented in compact story form on the screen with sustained suspense throughout. Edmund Lowe as the hero of the presentation manages to score rather nicely, and Barbara Bedford playing opposite him lands with both feet. For the sections where they like mystery meller this one is sure to please, as it is strictly an audience picture, and Lowe seems to be coming along as a favorite.

Lowe has the role of an author out looking for local color and he becomes involved in a murder mystery to solve which he risks his own life, clears the name of the father of the heroine, and wins her hand. The heavy plays a dual role, that of a gambling house keeper and likewise the rival suitor for the hand of the heroine.

The action is well sustained through the entire picture, and the audience gets a number of thrills from the situations. Especially the series of narrow escapes that the hero has after he has ordered himself put out of the way in order that he might track down the gang that he believes is responsible for the murder. The reason for the crime itself is very logically worked out, and there is a corking fight and thrill at the finale minute of the story.

It's a picture well worth while in most localities. *Fred.*

RECKLESS COURAGE

Buddy Roosevelt Production presented by Lester F. Scott, Jr. Story by Victor Roberts, directed by Tom Gibson, script by Betty Burbridge. Released by the Weiss Bros. Artclass Pictures Corp. Running time 52 minutes.

Bud Keenan.............Buddy Roosevelt
Jasper Bayne..................J. C. Fowler
Doris Bayne.................Helen Foster
Butler......................W. A. McIlwain
Jim Allen........................Jay Morley
"Scar" Dugan................Jack O'Brien
"Shorty" Baker.............N. E. Hendrix
"Chuck" Carson.......Merrill McCormick
"Slim" Parker..................Eddie Barry
Winona.........................Princess Noola

Fast moving picture with a flock of thrills for the cheaper class of houses. It is the first of the 1925-26 series of new Buddy Roosevelt westerns, and if the balance of the productions keep pace with this one it looks as though this cowboy hero of the screen is on the way to build himself considerable popularity in the smaller picture houses.

"Reckless Courage" has a crook plot. Doris Bayne is the daughter of a wealthy importer of diamonds and undertakes to make a delivery of precious stones for her father via aeroplane. She starts off and the butler in her home, who is in league with a band of crooks, tips off his leader that the stones are on their way. A second plane containing one of the crooks and a pilot start after the girl and the crook makes a leap from one plane to the other in midair. This will give the average film fan a great kick.

Of course the girl outwits him and throws the box with the jewels from the plane. It hits the cowboy hero on the nut as he is riding below and then things come down to earth. The girl, the crooks and the hero all chasing one another for the jewels. The gang have them one minute, the girl the next, the hero after that, and there is fight after fight, chase after chase, and action every minute of the film.

From a production standpoint the picture looks classy for this type of feature. While most of the scenes are outdoors there are a few interiors, and they are all elaborate, especially the home of the diamond merchant.

Roosevelt is a rather good-looking youngster who rides hard and doesn't seem afraid to mix it when the picture calls for a scrap. It looks as though he is a real bet for those houses where the westerns are popular fare with the fans. *Fred.*

THE LOST CHORD

Arrow Film Corporation presents dramatized story of Sir Arthur Sullivan's song, "The Lost Chord." Whitman Bennett production, directed by Wilfred Noy and made in Yonkers. Cast includes David Powell, Alice Lake, Dagmar Godowsky and Charles Mack. Reviewed at the Stanley, New York, April 17. Running time, 58 minutes.

An organist has lost his belovedest—she died. Later he thinks he has fallen in love with another girl, but she is young and he is old. A boy who has gone away from home really loves her, yet when he comes home he finds she is engaged to the older man. But the older man, seeing she loves the lad, leaves the way clear.

Groping once more, as he does throughout the picture, he plays over the keys of his organ in search of that "Lost Chord," but finally concluding that all the naturals or their combinations, or the sharps and flats in any combination can not bring that lost chord to his finger tips. So in the fade-out, the effective words of the accompanying poem say effectively that only in Heaven shall he hear that "Great Amen."

As a cheaper independent, this one holds a good cast and is marked by capable production and acting. In its own market and the middle-class houses it is a desirable film, but probably without drawing power of its own. Therefore, it is really a good "filler." *Sisk.*

THE BURNING TRAIL

Universal blue-streak western starring William Desmond. Story by Herbert Knibbs; script by Isadore Bernstein; directed by Arthur Rosson. Running time, 54 minutes.

"Smiling Bill" Flannigan...Wm. Desmond
"Texas".......................Albert J. Smith
Nell Loring......................Mary McIvor
"Black" Loring.................James Corey
John Corliss................Jack Dougherty
Tom Corliss..................Edmund Cobb

Just one of those westerns slapped out on the market to make it possible for the Eastman Co. to declare huge dividends because of the raw stock used. No reason for this picture, and it certainly doesn't do Bill Desmond any good.

It is understood William Desmond is a name that means something to exhibitors, and possibly still to the public, but it isn't going to mean anything to anybody in a short time with story material of this sort. Therefore the U. would just be killing an asset to their sales program. The picture will get by on double feature bills in the cheaper admission houses where the audiences don't care what they look at as long as there is something moving on the screen. At the New York Friday night of last week it was given the "ha, ha" in a couple of spots.

Desmond has the role of a New York pug who quits the ring because he knocked an opponent dead. He heads west and becomes a tramp. Why the idol of New York's boxing fans, as one of the titles describes him, should be dead broke immediately after the fatal fight is a mystery, but here he is a tramp working as a cook for a cattle outfit. In addition to this there is the regulation feud between the cattlemen and the sheep ranchers, the ex-pug working into the picture as the hero that assists in settling the fight between the two factions and bringing about a happy ending.

There is a flock of gun play and a lot of riding and all the usual frills that go with westerns, but the story and its enactment isn't anything that anybody would want to brag about. The best thing about the picture is the exterior mountain locations that were selected by the director as the background for the shooting. *Fred.*

STAR DUST TRAIL

William Fox production. Directed by Edmund Mortimer. Story by Frederick and Fanny Hatton. Running time 65 minutes. Loew's New York, April 14. Half of double feature one-day program.

Sylvia Joy.......................Shirley Mason
John Warding................Bryant Washburn
Horace Gibbs.................Thomas R. Mill
John Benton...................Richard Tucker
The Maid..........................Merta Sterling
Nan Hartley.....................Shannon Day

This picture just misses being good. The story is well written and the cast adequate with the exception of Bryant Washburn who turns in a non-registering conception that injures whatever sympathetic appeal his role ordinarily would have built up.

The direction is well enough, barring one fault; whenever the director wanted to register poverty or changed circumstances he did it through the medium of a rainstorm. Washburn was caught in enough rain to irrigate the Great American Desert and always in the best ten, twenty and thirty manner without a rain coat and the coat collar of his street suit turned up.

The story features Shirley Mason as Sylvia Joy, a cabaret dancer, loved by John Benton (Richard Tucker), millionaire patron of the night clubs and art. Sylvia marries John Warding (Mr. Washburn), an actor. The Wardings, living expensively, find John's salary of $350 weekly in a current show not enough. Sylvia offers to share the household expenses, but he refuses.

Sylvia, through Benton's financial help, is elevated to stardom. Warding is jealous of Benton, and it affects his stage work so much he loses his job. Overhearing gossip at his club, while still out of work, he decides to leave his wife until in a position to support her. He moves to a cheap theatrical boarding house. A girl he has befriended lives there. Benton finds them together in Warding's room and tells a scandalous tale to Sylvia.

Warding the same night, believing Sylvia in love with Benton, writes her a note releasing her from their marriage. On the way to post it he is struck by an automobile.

Nan Hartley (Shannon Day), the chorus girl acquaintance of Warding, hastens to his wife's home to tell her of the accident. She is admitted while a party is on celebrating Sylvia's triumph in her new starring vehicle. Benton is pressing his suit, and has almost received her consent when Nan enters.

Sylvia, prompted by Benton, accuses Nan of being in love with Warding. Nan readily admits it, but convinces Sylvia Warding has no thoughts except for her. Benton threatens to ruin Sylvia's career if she returns to Warding, but she defies him and rushes out to effect the reconciliation.

The story is interesting and the cast excellent. Richard Tucker was a most convincing middle-aged lover and Thomas Mill equally so in a moderate role. Miss Gay made the chorus girl really human and Miss Mason looked attractive as the cause of it all. Her work in the emotional scenes was first rate.

Con.

Wild Men and Beasts

San Francisco, April 23.

Back in 1921 Lou Hutt, one of the best news cameramen on the Pacific Coast, interested local capital in a jaunt into the jungles of Borneo for a series of pictures. Hutt, together with his wife and the members of his party, spent two years in the wilds of Borneo. Pictures finished, the cameraman and his negatives returned to San Francisco right on the heels of the Snow animal pictures, and the Hutt films lay in the vault. Last week Loew's Warfield brought them to light.

"Wild Men and Beasts of Borneo" is the title, and for straightaway action, good photography and interest the Hutt pictures are ahead of anything that has been seen here in five years.

The story starts with the sailing from the United States, the landing in Hong Kong, the start into the Federated Malay States and the meeting with the Sultan of Perak, this to lend the magic of the Far East and the gaiety of the Sultan's court, with its dancing girls. Then comes the trip up the river into the interior, scenes that are splendidly photographed and scenery that is seldom recorded on a screen.

As early as the finish of the second reel the action starts with the trailing and trapping of the elephants. A long-distance lens brings the herd of white elephants right up to the camera, and the trapping of the leader of the herd in the pit is made doubly interesting because the action is night photography.

Following this comes a four months' stay with the Pygmies condensed into two reels of dramatic interest as well as educational value. The photographers were given the assistance of British agents, and in this way secured scenes in the native villages that could never have been recorded otherwise.

The trapping of leopards and other animals of the jungle, the catching and caging of a 40-foot python, and close-ups of the jungle birds and monkeys follow. The latter contains a great deal of comedy.

"Wild Men and Beasts of Borneo" is the sort of screen entertainment that is worth while. It is a trifle over 5,000 feet in length and there isn't a drag nor a letting down of interest in all of the five reels. This picture is good for any house and any type of audience.

FRIENDLY ENEMIES

Starring Weber and Fields, directed by George Melford, produced by Edward Belasco Productions, distributed by Producers Distributing.
Adapted from the stage play of same title by Samuel Shipman and Aaron Hoffman. Corp. H. Sebastian presents. At Colony (Moss), New York, week May 3. Running time about 70 minutes.
Karl Pfeiffer..................Lew Fields
Henry Block....................Joe Weber
June Block..........Virginia Brown Faire
William Pfeiffer............Jack Mulhall
Hilda Schwartz......Lucille Lee Stewart
Miller (alias Walter Stuart).Stuart Holmes
Mrs. Marie Pfeiffer.......Eugene Besserer

"Friendly Enemies," through its dramatics, melodramatics and comedy standoffs, besides its stars, Weber and Fields, should class for anywhere. There may be said to be an overdose of heart interest in this picturized story, now that the war is over, but nevertheless the comedy of the action as well as in the captions is a perfect offset.

The captions are in the pigeon-English language of those famed comedians, Joe Weber and Lew Fields, but here Mr. Weber only assumes the laugh burden. His stage companion, Mr. Fields, does act in this film. In fact, this picture of the Shipman-Hoffman Broadway success, "Friendly Enemies," will become noted for the acting in it. While Mr. Fields easily leads and has some heavy emoting at times, not one member of the cast lags far behind, while Mr. Weber in his imitable Joeweber way, never muffs a laugh and often is in on the tears.

It's a good education at this date after hostilities. Its point as created by the authors was the German-Americans and their progeny. In its stage day the piece was a sensational success as a comedy-drama through its faithfulness to the then war condition. Now it may remain the same and in the film for all the foreign borns and their native children to take heed that when in America there is but one country—America.

Thus are the dramatics and the emotions played upon, strongly at times, as the Pfeiffers see their own son commissioned as a second lieutenant in the U. S. Army. He is engaged to June Block, daughter of Henry (Mr. Weber), who is an avowed partisan of the country he adopted, while his "friendly enemy," Karl Pfeiffer (Mr. Fields) is still with the Fatherland though a naturalized American.

Off young Pfeiffer goes, on a transport supposedly and which is blown up in New York Bay, through the machinations of the German Secret Service and with the assistance of a $10,000 check given Miller, the German agent, by the elder Pfeiffer with the hope it will aid in ending the war if the American troops may be stopped from going over. Young Pfeiffer missed the boat.

An explosion of the transport, though but suggested, with melodramatics involving the U. S. Secret Service and inserts of marching troops for thrills, while for emotion is the anguish of the elder Pfeiffer, the contrast of Mrs. Pfeiffer, who is in sympathy with her son's patriotism and the shrewdness of Henry Block, which leads him to cheat a bit on Pfeiffer when playing pinochle much as Weber and Fields do in their famous poker scene on the stage.

Perhaps just a bit overdrawn or drawn out in its pathos at times, still the script is holding for the elders and a thrill for the young, having everything from love to laughs.

It often has been said by show people that Lew Fields is a great actor aside from his comedy achievements. He is certainly a great actor in this picture.

"Friendly Enemies" was a stage hit and it should be a screen hit. So much may be said of Weber and Fields in any connection that it seems only a matter of proper publicity to put this picture over for

the limit, with the picture itself backing up all claims made.

"Friendly Enemies" is the first full five-reeler Weber and Fields have appeared in. They are looked upon as strictly comedians. Now that they have gotten away with this and to a superlative degree in work away from them as a team, why not put them out in a straightaway five-reel-all-comedy? *Sime.*

THE NIGHT CLUB

Paramount picture presented by Adolph Zukor and Jesse L. Lasky, featuring Raymond Griffith. Adapted from William de Mille's play, "After Five," by Walter Woods; script by Keene Thompson; directed by Frank Urson and Paul Iribe. At the Rialto, New York, week May 3, 1925. Running time 60 minutes.
Robert White............Raymond Griffith
Edith Henderson............Vera Reynolds
Diablo ....Wallace Beery
Carmen ....Louise Fazenda

Are pictures reverting to type that was the vogue about 15 years ago? That question might rightfully be asked after viewing "The Night Club," in which Famous Players - Lasky feature Raymond Griffith, which was directed by Frank Urson and Paul Iribe. Possibly the training the latter of the two directors had in France may account for a lot of the old stuff that there is in this picture, for a decade or so ago when they were making comedies, especially Pathe comedies in which Max Linder was the star, there seemingly was a slogan "When in doubt insert a chase." That is exactly what has happened in the case of "The Night Club." Looking at it one is more than reminded of Walter Hill's classic "Chaining the Canary Loose," which broke into print in December of 1909, for "The Night Club" is just as traditional a motion picture, done in just as traditional a manner as that was.

The only difference is that this picture with the title "The Night Club," having nothing to do with either the story or the picture, is in 5,000 feet of film instead of the 1,000 feet that they used in the dear old days agone.

Sure there is a reference to "The Night Club" in one title at the beginning of the picture, but that is all, there isn't any more. The first 1,000 feet of Eastman stock is used up in planting a plot with the hope and expectation that the next 4,000 feet will find something to harvest, but they might just as well have planted the seed in the ocean as in the plot.

Bob White (not the bird with the whistle, but a batch) falls from Grace or for Grace, one way or the other it matters not, except that he is at the altar and about to become a sacrifice to advance Matrimony, who has made a safety and reached first, but he's called "out" by the ump, who is the long lost holder of the previous engagement belt, and Grace walks. That looks like a promising beginning. Bob White—the batch, not the bird—is going to dash right out into the middle of gay old New York's night life, for isn't that the title of the picture "The Night Club"? Does he do that? Not on your last 100 feet. He goes home and fires his housekeeper because she's a woman.

Now for a little more planting. In comes the mysterious stranger and shrieks, "Ha, am I in time?" He has the old Unk's will in his hand, and Unk is going to give Bob—the whistle, not the bird — a million bucks—providing Bob isn't married and will dash right out to marry Edith Henderson. Edith Henderson is a little girl going to school somewhere, nobody seeming to know, but it is hoped that she wasn't taking a motion picture course in that new Paramount Screen Sirens School, bring your own lunch, and for which "the authorities have selected two excellent hotels where the students will be lodged, the girls at one, the boys at the other, well situated, being close together and within easy access," but she couldn't be because the director would have known where she was. And, besides, Bob—the bird, not the whistle—has also inherited Gerley, a valet, from Unk, so that squared it for the firing of the housekeeper.

Annyhoo, Bob the batch and Gerly (note: not "girly") start traveling cause Bob the Batch is through with women forever. Maybe 1,500 or 2,000 feet at this time.

For no good reason let's show up in Spain and have a bathing beach and a trick bath-house and a lot of Max (no, not Mack Sennett) bathing girls. All right, that's a good idea; we'll do that. So there we are in Spain with a bathing batch, no beach, a hotel and a lot of girls. We'll send Bob with his whistle into the hotel to find his valet and yell "Gerly" in one of the halls, and—you're right, that's exactly what happened—they all came out in the hall and Bob jumped out of a window. This is cue for the first "chase." Bob chases up the street and into a Spanish house, finds Diablo chasing Carmen all over the lot with a lot of knives and everyone else knocked cuckoo, but they never sees him and he never sees them, and just for that he wants to rent a room, but instead of that when Diablo finally sees Bob the Batch he wallops him and throws him over the bar against a lot of bottles. Then you say, "Ah, at last, a 'night club' in Spain," but you are all wrong again; it's a hotel for men only with lady guests, so that's out, and so is Bob.

Time for another chase, so it's a good idea to bring the heroine into the picture about this time and have her drive a wild automobile up the crooked street and chase Bob; that'll take another 200 feet. Finally when that piece of chase is over Bob decides that he likes the heroine and the heroine decides she likes Bob, and everything is all set, except one believes that she has to marry some guy for coin and the other believes he has got to marry some girl for ditto—and they both decide they won't, so there!

Then Bob suddenly discovers that "she's" the girl and she discovers that "he's" the man, and then she won't all over again. Bob decides that he'll have his whistle cut short so as to give her the dough and thus prove that he really loved her and didn't want to marry her to get the coin. That's a job, getting bumped off in a manner that will be satisfactory to Unk's will, even if you are willing to pay for a good job.

But then, still in Spain, have a bull fight to draw on, and a bull, little or big, is relished more or less by everybody in the picture business. So turn the bull loose.

Don't you remember that picture that Doug MacLean did, "The Yankee Souse," or something like that, when he had a runaway automobile go down a mountain? Well, let's run our automobile backwards and mebbe no one will notice it. That will use up all the footage to the limit of five reels and we can have Diablo chase him on a bicycle and then let the lovers clinch at the finish.

All right, let's shoot, and if we don't make a star out of Griffith with this sort of stuff, mebbe we can try something else.

That's exactly what you'll have to do, Mister Zukor and Mister Lasky, for you have got a bet in Griffith, but you'll have to give him something other than the material of this picture. And remember, don't try to make Griffith a Max Linder, for that is what he looks like and acts like in this "Day Stick" or whatever the name of it is.

There is one mighty good bet in the picture, Vera Reynolds. She can troup, and you had better give her a chance in the future. Maybe she will develop.

Oh, yes, the audience at the Rialto Sunday laughed a little, but they didn't laugh as they should have to put over this picture as a hit. The picture as it stands isn't going to advance the name of Raymond Griffith a single step as an asset to the exhibitor at the box office.

Fred.

ZANDER THE GREAT

Cosmopolitan production released through Metro-Goldwyn. Made from the stage play by Salisbury Field and adapted to the screen by Frances Marion. Marion Davies starred. Directed by George William Hill. Reviewed at the Capitol, New York, May 3. Running time, 74 minutes.

Mamie Smith..................Marion Davies
Juan Fernandez..............Holbrook Blinn
Dan Murchison................Harrison Ford
Good News.....................Harry Watson
Texas............................Harry Myers
Bart Black................George Seigmann
The Matron.....................Emily Fitzroy
The Sheriff...............Hobart Bosworth
Mr. Pepper......................Richard Carle
Mrs. Caldwell..................Hedda Hopper
Elmer Lovejoy..................Olin Howland
Zander.....................Master John Huff

Marion Davies once more, after spectacle films, has found a happy medium in comedy. Not since "Little Old New York" has she been cast so well. "Zander" can be welcomed as a good program comedy. For that's its classification. The picture is taken from the stage play, in which the Frohmans starred Alice Brady.

The story concerns an orphan girl, mistreated, but finally taken into the home of a Mrs. Caldwell, whose husband has deserted her and gone to Arizona. Mrs. Caldwell dies and leaves a young son, Alexander, whom Mamie calls Zander—the long name being too big for a tiny boy. It's off to Arizona in a Ford, and there she finds that the boy's father is dead, but runs into three other men, one the hero and the others characters. She reforms their stablishment, makes them quit bootlegging, and settles. In these latter sequences some extraneous but interesting fight and chase stuff is worked in advantageously.

Early in the film, as the pug-nosed orphan, Miss Davies does great work, but in the latter part is merely pretty. Her cast is fine, headed by Holbrook Blinn in a familiar Mexican role, Harry Watson in a comedy part, and numerous other sterling legit names in comparatively small roles. The whole thing is lavishly put on and fairly well directed. At the Capitol Sunday afternoon, before its first audience, it drew plenty of laughs and held the interest fairly well.

"Zander" can be counted on to hold up particularly well in the territory where the Hearst journals circulate, and in other cities on its own merit figures strongly as a program feature. It is clean, direct, thrilling, has plenty of love interest and the advantage of some nifty comedy.

Sisk.

SOUL FIRE

Presented by Inspiration Pictures, Inc., released by First National. Adapted from he play, "Great Music," by Josephine Lovett, directed by John S. Robertson. Starring Richard Barthelmess. At the Strand, N. Y., week May 3. Running time, 88 mins.

PROLOGUE

The Critics: Percy Ames and Charles Esdale
Howard Fane........................Lee Baker
Mrs. Howard Fane...........Effie Shannon
Conductor........................Carl Edouarde

ITALY

Eric Fane..............Richard Barthelmess
The Princess Rhea.......Carlotta Monterey
Howard Fane........................Lee Baker
Mrs. Howard Fane...........Effie Shannon
The Old Musician...............Gus Weinberg

PARIS

Eric Fane..............Richard Barthelmess
The Princess Rhea.......Carlotta Monterey
The Prima Donna.................Rita Rossi
The Orchestra Leader....Edward La Roche
The Dancer in the Music Hall.Ellalee Ruby
Fleurette, a manikin..........Aileen Berry

PORT SAID

Eric Fane..............Richard Barthelmess
San Francisco Sal...............Helen Ware
Herbert Jones, a sailor........Walter Long
Dancers........Leah La Roux and Zebaida

THE SOUTH SEAS

Eric Fane..............Richard Barthelmess
Teita..............................Bessie Love
Ruau.......................Harriet Sterling
Dr. Travers....................Arthur Metcalfe

Here is a corking box-office picture, screen entertainment that will get money almost anywhere with a star name to draw 'em in and something on the celluloid to entertain after they are in their seats. It doesn't matter that the star is overshadowed by Bessie Love, who only comes into the picture after about three reels of it have passed, for the audience is getting real entertainment out of the picture.

The role that Richard Barthelmess has—that, virtually, of a pander—is not one that will win any sympathy for him, albeit he plays it for its full worth.

The picture is built in a series of four sequences, each with its own love affair between "the kid" and some woman. There is an introductory prolog in which Carl Edouarde, musical director of the New York Strand, makes his debut as a screen artist. It is in a concert auditorium where the concerto from the pen of Eric Fane is to have its initial rendition. The various phases of the composition are supposed to interpret an episode in the life of the composer as he lived his earlier days in search of the indefinable something that would awaken his genius.

First he is shown in Italy, where he has been studying for a year and has failed to succeed. Refusing the aid of his father, who wants him to forsake music and enter the commercial field, the boy runs off to join a mistress in Paris. He lives with her for a time, but finally, when she comes to the realization that he is in reality an idealist and will not prostitute his gifts in the composition of popular music, she casts him off.

The second sequence is one that shows a soubret in a cabaret and a revue prima donna who are ready to fall if the composer will only say the word. But instead of turning to either of them he leaves Paris flat, and is next seen in the dive section of Port Said, where the madame of a girl-and-booze joint falls for him. And what a performance Helen Ware, as San Francisco Sal, gives in this episode! She just about walks away with everything that there is in the picture at this point. He flees that section of the world because he believes he has murdered a sailor in defense of Sal, and next shows up on a tramp steamer lying in a harbor in the South Seas. He makes his escape over the side of the boat and swims ashore, falling exhausted on the sands, to be found there the next morning by an orphaned half-breed girl. Her father was an Englishman and her mother a native. She has him brought to her hut and falls in love with him. It is the night before the native marriage ceremony is to be celebrated, when it is discovered that the girl has been infected with what is suppose to be leprosy. During the next reel there is sufficient suspense to hold the audience until it is discovered that it isn't the dread disease, and then for the happy ending.

At last the concert ends, and the most dreaded of all the metropolitan music critics turns to the parents of the composer and informs them that their son is a genius, and the final fadeout still shows the boy on the South Sea isle with the half-and-half girl. Whether he ever came back and whether he brought her with him are items that are left to the audience to interpret, as they please.

"Soul Fire" is a picure for the money. It is sexy, but not to the extent to arouse the censors.

In the first two sequences Carlotta Monterey plays the role of the Princess that is enamored of the musician. She looks the part and plays it remarkably well, but John Robinson should never have shot her profile. Helen Ware walks away with the third sequence, although Walter Long provides a very good heavy.

Then, in the final sequence, Bessie Love manages to take the picture entirely away from the star. She is a delight and looks like a million dollars.

Robertson direction carries the picture along in good shape. At this house, where the audience recognized Carl Edouarde, musical director, he was accorded a decided reception when appearing on the screen.

Fred.

FIFTH AVE. MODELS

Universal-Jewel starring Mary Philbin and Norman Kerry. Adapted from the novel "The Best in Life" by Muriel Hine with Svend Gade the director. Showing at the Piccadilly, New York, week of May 2. Running time, more than 60 mins.

Isobel .... Mary Philbin
Francis Doran .... Norman Kerry
Joseph Ludani .... Joseph Swickard
Abel Von Groot .... William Conklin
Mrs. Tory Serecold ..... Rosemary Theby
Mme. Suze .... Rose Dione

Confined to Greenwich Village and the art angle, at a time when the Village is well on its way to oblivion, this Universal-Jewel projects as a middle class feature of but average merit.

Mary Philbin is the daughter of a struggling artist who is sent to prison when accompanying two thieves into a mansion to point out a Rembrandt they are after. His fall is brought on by Isobel having been discharged from a modiste shop after a fight with one of the girls during which she ruins a gown and is notified she must make good or take a jail sentence.

The father gets the sentence and it is never explained who makes good the money for the dress. However and meanwhile, Isobel has secured a hearing from Doran, proprietor of an art gallery, where she has taken her father's pictures. The subtitle of Doran immediately asking Isobel to become his private secretary brought laughter and applause from a Saturday night audience due to the blunt manner in which it is introduced. Following that the audience obviously lost interest.

A number of the settings are **lavish and there is included a sunken ship cafe which includes the usual celluloid cabaret eccentricities.**

Miss Philbin and Mr. Kerry are superior to the picture but are so restricted by the script. Others in the cast fall short of making themselves significant.

The picture meant little to a Piccadilly audience and will hardly improve that rating except as the grade of houses it plays descends.

Skig.

Troubles of a Bride

William Fox Production. Directed by Thomas Buckingham, from story by John Stone. Robert Agnew, Alan Hale, Mildred June and Bruce Covington in cast. At the Stanley, New York, May 4. Running time, 58 mins.

This picture is the only one of its kind. Pipe its contents.

One nasty villain and assistant; one Southern colonel, daughter and fiance; one family fortune; seven wild rides on horseback; three wild chases in automobile; a wild train ride; the switchman bound; the burning coaches, and, finally, the derailment at the drawbridge just after the hero saves the heroine. It's all chase stuff.

However, the picture goes like this: A smooth crook, The Baron, gets into the home of a Southern colonel. He is after the family fortune and gets it, kidnapping at the same time the bride from her wedding. The entire guest list chases after in staid chaises, but with guns. However, his car wins, and if it hadn't crashed into a house it would have taken the villain to safety. But when he gets the girl in this house he locks all doors carefully and begins wearing his dirtiest look. He doesn't mean to do right by the gal, and she doesn't mean to be wronged if she can help it. So she gets her sweetie on the phone and tells him that things look pretty dark and would he please give a lift. He allows as how he would, grabs a horse which vaults nine fences, three hedges and a few mole hills and falling down several times in the process. But hero keeps on and arrives just in time. But villain knocks out the hero and sticks up a train, forcing it to move on. Running all the passengers into one car, he gets the gal in another, but this car catches fire. Then he, seeing that the hero is chasing him, hops off the train, gets on top of a 500-foot cliff and jumps down into the hero's buggy below. Then there's another fight and a long tumble down hill, which ruins the villain, but the hero, still undaunted, hops a spare engine and chases the burning cars, because his girl has long black hair, and he doesn't want it to get singed. He arrives in time. The next scene is a shady lawn, and hero and heroine are embracing.

Plenty of action and real thrill stuff. Acted by a good cast, which includes Agnew as the hero, Alan Dale as the villain and Mildred June as the girl, it bears up better than if others had handled. The action stuff is perfactly directed, and if somebody didn't get hurt in making this film, then there isn't a law of retribution.

"Troubles of a Bride" isn't sexy, as might be expected. It's almost an ideal proposition for the neighborhoods which draw on the working classes. And make as it is its makers didn't aim at anything else. That much they say in a foreword which explains that "Troubles of a Bride" is made solely for entertainment purposes and that if you don't like it you'd better hop. After watching that first chase nobody is going to hop, for the other chases follow rapidly. *Sisk.*

PORTS OF CALL

William Fox feature, starring Edmund Lowe. Produced and directed by Denison Clift. At the Stanley, New York, May 1. Running time, 61 minutes.

Domestic triangles, like others, have three sides. The acuteness of the angles depend largely upon the attractiveness of the men and women involved. And the sum of the angles of a triangle are together equal to two right angles—that means that two separate domestic affairs are straightened out.

In this picture the locale is on a far away island. On that island is The Man, The Woman and The Other Woman. The Woman has a husband, while The Other Woman has regenerated The Man. But the husband is a bad egg, and is inciting insurrection by his continued bad treatment of the natives. And the natives, getting a little bit sore at this, rush the joint one night and do some fancy shooting and flame spreading. They are dispersed, however, by a trick, and The Man, The Woman and The Other Woman are left to work out their own salvation. To kill this suspense The Other Woman wins.

It's well acted and produced. Edmund Lowe is a handsome fellow, and from the exploitation Fox is giving him is apparently holding up as a draw in the Fox product. That being the case, this vehicle is perfectly satisfactory, and even with a Lowe draw it qualifies as a program feature for the middle-grade houses. Some expense is evi-

denced and good direction is always in evidence. Besides, the subject matter is treated in a virile manner, and if anybody should ask you, virility in treating a domestic problem has the English drawing room way backed off the edge of the dock. *Sisk.*

PLAYING WITH SOULS

First National picture, made by Thomas H. Ince Corp. Directed by Ralph Ince and adapted to the screen by C. Gardner Sullivan. Jacqueline Logan, Mary Astor and Buster Collier featured. At B. S. Moss' Colony, April 30. Running time, 70 minutes.
Bricotte....................Jacqueline Logan
Margo............................Mary Astor
Amy Dale......................Belle Bennett
Matthew Dale, Sr..............Clive Brook
Matthew Dale, Jr. (aged 4).....Helen Page
Matthew Dale, Jr. (aged 20)..........
...................William Collier, Jr.
Louise.....................Jessie Arnold
Monsieur Jomier............Josef Swickard

Illegitimacy and its blight, treated in a sensible and effectively dramatic way, is the keynote of this picture. The plot concerns a man and woman, wealthy but unhappily married. Their son is neglected and, until he becomes mature, is by himself at a private school in France. There he is continually taunted by his companions because the parents never visit him, and the implication of the boys is that the youngster, Matthew Dale, Jr., is illegitimate. He begins to believe this himself.

So to Paris he goes, tells the banker through whom his checks come that he doesn't want them any more and that he is going to the dogs. Then the banker comes to Paris, meets his son without the boy knowing he is trotting around with his father. From cabaret to cabaret they go, with the boy, madly in love with a gold digger, while his true sweetheart waits for him back at the school. But he has told her that, unlti his legitimacy is established, he can never marry her.

The punch, however, comes when the boy's mother arrives in Paris, and, dolled up to the point of youthful 50, she flirts with her own son. Then the father comes, tells her what she has done. That leads to a happy all-around finish, with a wedding between the boy and his true sweetheart and a reconcilation between husband and wife.

This film is well made and well directed by Ralph Ince. Moreover, the cast is very capable, with Clive Brook, Buster Collier and Mary Astor taking the acting honors as father, son and sweetheart, respectively. Belle Bennett is the mother and does good character work. Joseph Swickard and Charles Mailes, both excellent character men, are seen to advantage, doing the reliable work which has enhanced their reputations. *Sisk.*

THE TRAIL RIDERS

Fox Film production, starring Buck Jones. Direction by W. S. Van Dyke. Running time, 57 minutes.
Tex Hartwell...................Buck Jones
Jim Mackey.................Carl Stockdale
Malcolm Duncan.........William Walling
Sally........................Nancy Deaver
Marie............................Lucy Fox

Buck Jones may never be awarded any horseshoes as the gayest of love-making Lotharios, but when it comes to riding and the physical rough stuff he's there. Buck is no novice in a western, and many of his stories have been duds as far as continuity is concerned; yet this one does pretty well in keeping the tension running dramatically high in its meller way.

There are some hectic moments in "Trail Riders," and Buck rises from the ashes of some tough breaks to prove that he's the squarest two-handed, gun-toting trail rider that bobs up in Elk county.

There are really two heroines, one played by Lucy Fox and the other

by Nancy Deaver. The lead, however, is Miss Fox, who also does some neat riding.

Buck Jones faces a mean guy in Jim Mackey, played well by Carl Stockdale, and this bird slams all kinds of trouble at Buck, who as Tex Hartwell is trying to prove to the leader of the trail riders that he is not in league with cattle rustlers.

The climax is the scene where Dell Winch rides into town to shoot Tex because Winch is fully convinced that Tex has double-crossed the riders by letting a herd of cattle cross Winch's deadline with infection.

A good picture of its type.

THE SHOCK PUNCH

Paramount Picture, starring Richard Dix. Adapted by Luther Reed from the play by John Monk Saunders and directed by Paul Sloane. Reviewed at the Rivoli, New York, May 10 week. Running time, 60 minutes.
Ranny Savage.................Richard Dix
Dorothy Clark............Frances Howard
Dan Savage...........Theodore Babcock
Jim Clark....................Percy Moore
Stanley Pierce............Charles Beyer
Terence O'Rourke..........Gunboat Smith
Mike......................Jack Scannell
Bill Mullarkey..............Walter Long
Italian Laborer.............Paul Panzer

The best picture Dix has yet made. It's filled with laughs and packed with thrills.

Sunday night it had the Rivoli audience in alternate spells of gasping and hysterics, and no matter what its narrative lapses may be, it has the ever-desirable laughs and the scarce punch. In other words, it is there with all its clothes on, looking like a million dollars.

Whether it will mop at the Rivoli this week isn't the question, for this week is admittedly off along the street, but it is first-rate film, and will give Dix the greatest boost he's yet had since attaining the star ladder.

The plot is not bothersome and concerns the son of a wealthy man who has pugilistic tendencies. His trainers discover he has that rarity, a shock punch. It is proven one night, when he engages tough Bull Mullarkey, at a riverter's ball. He knocks Mullarkey for a couple of goals and a field punt, and then chases after the sweet girl who didn't like to see him fight. She is the daughter of a wealthy contractor, whose current trouble is getting a huge structure completed on contract time. In this he is opposed by a plot among his laborers, one of whom is Bull Mullarkey.

So the hero becomes a laborer. His first job is to carry a keg of rivets up to the top floor of a 50-story building. In doing this he walks over the girders with nothing but space and other girders below. He slips many times, but always come up smiling and waving his hand up to his sweetheart. Finally, however, he overhears a plot to keep the last girder from going into place. As they are lifting it, he rides up and reaches the top a second before the cable snaps, as planned. But the girder by that time was safe, and it was his job to fight Mullarkey on the top floor. And then a whale of a fight, with the hero victorious.

This sky-scraper comedy stuff is dangerous comedy. It has plenty of thrills, and as Dix does them, they look more on the level than usual. His riding of the girder is accomplished by some excellent trick photography, but in all his other escapades, the sky line of New York is always visible, and not through trick photography.

Frances Howard plays the girl well, giving her best performance to date on the screen, while Walter Long gives another scowling villain performance as Mullarkey. Jack Scannell, from legit, is a miniature pug assistant to Gunboat Smith, and good. Everyone in the cast, as a matter of fact, is up to the acting scratch, while the production, continuity and direction is up to a high standard.

If Dix is a draw then this will give satisfaction, and in the towns where he isn't, it should be a tonic. It is just one of the real action picture of the year, with Dix going through stuff that would shame some of the other stunt men who think they're good. Dix is not only good at the stunts, but he can act and has a sense of humor. *Sisk.*

SPORTING VENUS

Metro-Goldwyn. Produced by Marshall Neilan and presented by Louis B. Mayer. Scenario by Frank Geraghty from story by Gerald Beaumont. Directed by Neilan, with Blenche Sweet, Ronald Colman and Lew Cody featured. At the Capitol, New York, May 11 week.

Lady Gwendolyn	Blanche Sweet
Donald MacAllan	Ronald Colman
Prince Marno	Lew Cody
Countess Von Alstyne	Josephine Crowell
Donald's Father	George Fawcett
Sir Alfred Grayle	Edward Martindel
Housekeeper	Kate Price
Marno's Valet	Hank Mann
Detective	Arthur Hoyt

Granted that the story of this film has one serious fault, it is nevertheless a good piece of film because of constant entertaining values. For those values Marshal Neilan as director is partly responsible but from the public's point of view the whole thing is wrapped up in Ronald Colman and Blanche Sweet who never looked better in a long screen career.

She's down to a jockey weight and is wearing some evening gowns that go a trifle below the temperate zone and yet do not offend. Moreover, they're creations.

In Scotland Lady Gwen Grayle is in love with Donald MacAllan, a commoner in the village of their castle. But she loves him and when the war comes, promises to wait. After two years he returns but in London is told by Prince Marno that Lady Gwen no longer loves him and is engaged to take a Prince's title.

That wallops Donald and when he meets Lady Gwen on his last night of leave, he is cold and she is at a loss to understand for Marno has lied. But later she accepts Marno to assuage part of the grief which ensued after Donald's coldness and afterward a wild life of parties, liquor, night clubs, etc. But the war is over and when her marriage to Marno is about to be consummated, her lawyers investigate him and find that he is a penniless bounder.

The flaw is that Marno, obviously a roue, should have been accepted by Lady Gwen without knowing him and that Donald should have let Gwen go without questioning her on the night of their meeting in London.

This film was made abroad, according to the dope, and though it isn't immediately apparent why this expense should have been incurred, it is probably because Metro intends to exploit it in England. The Scotch scenes are of rare beauty. One sea coast scene, supposedly off the coast of France, is as perfect as any painting could have been.

The cast is perfect with Miss Sweet and Colman taking the laurels. Cody plays a typical part with neat humor, while Hank Mann is a semi-nance valet for plenty of laughs. The others were unimportant, even George Fawcett being limited to a single scene.

Neilan's direction is straightforward for the most part, but toward the end he compares the tread of the heavy dowager to whom Marno is being wed with the oncoming ferocity of a tank. Some comedy is brought in this scene, all counterbalanced nicely by the sincerity of the wedding scene between Lady Gwen and Donald.

"The Sporting Venus" derives its title from the orgy of spending and sporting which Gwen does when she becomes heartbroken.

As a first run this one is okey on the names alone, as both mean something at the box office. The picture is entertaining and the production details very fine, something, incidentally, noticed in all the recent Metro output. *Sisk.*

THE TALKER

First National photoplay made by Sam Rork. Lewis Stone starred in story by Marion Fairfax. Anna Q. Nilsson, Shirley Mason, Tully Marshall and Ian Keith featured. Directed by Alfred E. Green and reviewed at the Strand, New York, May 10. Running time, 84 minutes.

Kate Lennox	Anna Q. Nilsson
Harry Lennox	Lewis S. Stone
Ruth Lennox	Shirley Mason
Ned Hollister	Ian Keith
Henry Fells	Tully Marshall
Mrs. Fells	Lydia Yeamans Titus
Maude Fells	Gertrude Short
Barbara Farley	Barbara Bedford
Lonnie Whinston	Harold Goodwin

Marion Fairfax, who wrote the story of this film, is the syndicate writer who advises on domestic troubles, and who, in a few paragraphs, prescribes for serious marital ailments. Therefore, this is a picture of domesticity in some of its unfavorable forms, and Kate and Harry Lennox are the principals. Kate and Harry have been married some time, but Kate tires of living in the suburbs. With her is Harry's kid sister, Ruth, and Kate's preachings of "living the way you want" finally touch the kid until she runs away with Ned Hollister, a rounder and roue. But she gets away from him and is given up for lost.

That causes a rift between the married pair until she finally comes back home as things are about to change, and here she reunites Harry and Kate and falls into the arms of her one-time sweetheart, Lonnie Whinston, whom she had refused long before.

Much of this slight plot is advanced through the old procedure of the garrulous child, in this instance Maude Fells of the Fells family next door. The child says things when she shouldn't, and being a close observer, sees things that look bad. Tully Marshall and Lydia Yeamans Titus provide the comedy interest as Mr. and Mrs. Fells, a scrapping old couple.

Much of the footage can be easily eliminated and half of the subtitles can be scrapped, for they are long and preachy as well as uselessly explanatory. It is mostly a Fairfax preachment of a familiar nature.

The cast is excellent and performs well throughout, with the exception of Harold Goodwin as the juvenile. He doesn't seem adapted to movies, and in one melo scene grew ten-twenty-thirt' in his actions. But everyone else is fine, with Stone and Shirley Mason getting the acting breaks. Miss Mason in the final sequences returns home after having worked for a long time in a factory, and as an emaciated girl is wonderfully made up. Her acting here is also above par. The direction is average, with nothing outstanding. One error in casting was putting Gertrude Short, a pudgy grownup, in the kid role, for which she is unsuited on but one score—size.

"The Talker" isn't up to First National's standard, and though the Fairfax exploitation may mean something in some communities, it will never be enough to put this one across. It is just an eight-reeler, and one which will, in its present state, tire audiences. *Sisk.*

THE CRACKERJACK

East Coast Films, Inc., production presented by C. C. Burr, starring Johnny Hines. Story by Dick Freil, script by Victor Grandin and Argyll Campbell, directed by Charles Hines. At special showing Hotel Plaza, May 8. Running time, 72 minutes.

Crackerjack Perkins	Johnny Hines
Rose Bannon	Sigrid Holmquist
Col. Perkins	J. Barney Sherry
Lopez	Bradley Barker
General Bannon	Henry West

This is the final production of the series of independently made and distributed pictures with Johnny Hines as the star to be presented by C. C. Burr prior to Hines switching his releases to the Associated First National. The four of this Hines series, all feature length comedies, have been good for laughs and the last one is no exception. Incidentally the First National theatre franchise holders have a chance for this picture from the independents at a price that will be undoubtedly under the exhibition value First National will put on the future Hines comedies and play it as a step toward building box office good will for a star that they are later going to present as a regular First National player.

"The Crackerjack" is built entirely for laughing purposes. There are laughs in the action and in the titles, were done by Johnny Kraft, and laughs are what picture house audiences want the most and get the least of.

The story is simplicity itself, but the manner in which it is produced and the gags that have been injected make the picture virtually a scream from beginning to end.

Hines plays a boy working his way through college. His uncle lives in the South and is paying for the boy's education, but the youngster is banking the dough and living on what he makes in a white front restaurant as cashier and chef. The financial strain on unk's bank roll for the education, coupled with his natural Southern indolence wrecks the pickle works, his sole source of income. Finally, he writes to the youngster that he better come home, for the works have gone to smash. While in the east, Johnny has become imbued with New York pep, and on his return begins to make the works hum. The money he has saved is put into an advertising campaign behind an innovation that he has conceived, stuffed pickles, and the brand is known "Perkins' Stuffed Pickles." Johnny starts out with a cart to handle the advertising and sales.

Near the border he hits into a small town and there discovers a girl whom he had seen in New York. Her father is running a large grocery store as a cover-up for his activities in starting a revolution in Esquasado, the neighboring republic. Here they have 50,000 rounds of ammunition hidden, but they cannot find a way to get them across the border. The stuffed pickle idea solves their problem, and they buy 5,000 jars, intending to remove the cheese stuffing and replace it with the cartridges. The girl, fearful of the consequences to her father in the event that he should engineer the revolution, pleads with the pickle salesman to do something to save the day. He promises, and wires the pickle factory to duplicate the order of stuffed pickles that he has already sent, but to stuff them with bullets of cheese. He then engineers a switch in the shipment, and we next find him in Esquasado, and the fun begins.

Suffice to say that Johnny thwarts the revolutionary party and wins the girl in the end. How he does it holds too many laughs and gags to be set forth, but one that is a wow is where a Central American vamp is putting on the business for him, believing him to be a general, and he does a bit of radio business that fits with the "Wait, I'll get India" story that has gone the rounds of the stag audiences. *Fred.*

UP THE LADDER

Universal Jewel, presented by Carl Laemmle, starring Virginia Valli. Adapted from the Owen Davis play; directed by Edward Sloman. Shown at the Piccadilly, New York, week May 9. Running time, 61 minutes.

Jane Cornwall	Virginia Valli
James Van Clinton	Forrest Stanley
Helene Newhall	Margaret Livingston
Robert Newhall	Holmes Herbert
Judge Seymour	George Fawcett
Peggy	Priscilla Moran
Dancer	Olive Ann Alcorn
Housekeeper	Lydia Yeaman Titus

Society drama with little different twist to vamping division. It is a married woman pal of the wife's that does the vamp stuff instead of a cabaret dancer or an actress. But then Owen Davis will have to be credited for that innovation, for that was what he held to in the play itself.

The picture does not seem quite strong enough to offer any opposition to the regular run of pre-release showing in the big six of Broadway, but in the average houses with a daily change of bill it will stand up as a fair program picture.

The story is there, but there isn't an outstanding personality in the cast. With a real cast this could have been made a real box office picture.

The story is that of a wealthy orphan in love with the boy next door ever since their pinafore days. He has frittered away his fortune trying to invent a tele-photo telephone. The family estate has been sold and he is up against it for more money just as he is on the verge of success. The girl, returning from a tour about the country, discovers her own fortune practically has been wiped out, but she orders her guardian to sell the home to get the money so that the boy can proceed with his work, insisting the guardian give him the money and go into partnership without divulging she made the sacrifice to finance him.

Success comes and it blinds the inventor to everything except his own part in evolving the invention. At the same time he falls for the vamping of a married friend of the wife's, showering her with jewels and forsaking his business. The inevitable happens, his own invention is his undoing. The wife calling on her friend to invite her to a party, sees her husband in her apartment and the next day there are considerable fireworks.

The husband is at the edge of a crash, the wife being able to save him if she will dispose of her half interest in the project, but to save her husband from his own success she decides to let him go to the wall, figuring that it will bring him to his senses. It does just that, for after a year's separation from his family, they are reunited, when she is again made a partner by the big corporation that has taken over the invention.

Virginia Valli does fairly, but not convincingly. George Fawcett as the guardian delivers as he always does. Outside of little Priscilla Moran, a child actress, there is no one in the cast that really amounts to anything in as much as this picture is concerned. William V. Mong does a bit and isn't even mentioned on the program. If it wasn't Mong it was a mighty good impersonation of him. *Fred.*

TOO MUCH YOUTH

Renown picture, produced by Gerson Pictures Corp. and presented by B. Berger. Directed by Duke Worne, with Richard Holt starred. At the Stanley, New York, May 7. Running time, 58 minutes.

George Crandall	Eric Mayne
Marguerite Crandall	Sylvia Breamer
Jimmy Kenton	Richard Holt
Mark Kenton	Charles K. French
Casey	Walter Leroy

Richard Holt is a new one and a greater puzzle than the rest of these independent male stars. Few of them have any advance reputation, but flash on the screen for a series of five or six films and then fade from view, not even showing as a minor character in larger productions later. So with Holt, for he isn't of the athletic sort, isn't as trim and lithe as those who feature their agility and has a face not destined to attract b[illegible] rea[illegible] its compelling features. He's a nice looking fellow, but [illegible]ere are plenty in show business who have the looks and who aren't stars.

The story in which he appears, on the other hand, is far superior to the usual run of independent script. It has a real comedy idea which would be, in the hands of Doug McLean or Lloyd, the cat's whimper. It is this: A deal is to be transacted, and a father takes his son's word that it will be closed before he goes to sleep. Thereupon he gags the man on the other end of the deal to delay it as long as possible.

All of that admits of funny business, but Holt plays it straight in an uninteresting manner, while his supporting cast, although excellent, isn't directed speedily. So what should have been a whiz bang picture is more or less of a leisurely proposition.

Because of the names in its cast and some thrill stuff, a forest fire toward the finish, the picture is fair program stuff. Its star and direction, however, preclude it from getting first-class rating. *Sisk.*

ARIZONA ROMEO

William Fox production, "An Arizona Romeo," starring Buck Jones. Directed by Edmund Mortimer. Story and scenario by Charles Kenyon. In the support of Jones appear Thomas Mills, Wayne Geary, Lucy Fox, Lydia Yeamans Titus. At Loew's Circle, New York. Running time, 57 mins.

There are some comedy scenes in this Fox production that will create laughter in any neighborhood.

At first one sits expectantly for Buck Jones to swing into the saddle, start his gat into action and make mincemeat of any of the cow rustlers that cross his path. Nothing doing. Buck eschews the wild west stuff with one exception, when he shows some gunplay and a fistic encounter with a couple of burly birds trying to get familiar with the heroine and her maid who at the time are manicures in a western ranch town barber shop.

Things get pretty lively when Buck, in love with the girl, tries to help her marry a young man from the east whom he believes is loved by Sylvia.

After all the story didn't matter when Buck was riding like mad to catch the eastern express and snatch the girl from the man she didn't love.

He made some Lochinvar ride.

It's a picture that for the most part gives satisfaction and one that has strong comedy relief to make it entertaining. *Mark.*

Daughters Who Pay

Banner Production, released in the Independent Market. Directed by George Terwilliger. Running time, 61 minutes.

Mary Smith / Sonia	Marguerite de la Motte
Richard	John Bowers
His Father	J. Barney Sherry

Combination Secret Service thriller with a little cabaret world, some Soviet propaganda, a touch of blood and thunder and a dash of romance. It is constructed not to leave anything out that might strike the fancy of the state right buyer. The result is a picture full of action and should please in the daily change houses. At the New York it played on a double feature bill with "The Prairie Wife," and the result was a turnaway necessitating an extra midnight performance. That cannot be credited to either of the pictures, however, but possibly to the "Daughters Pay" title besides names in the cast of each.

The "Daughters" title has nothing to do with the story. Some titles are better than others.

Marguerite de la Motte plays the Secret Service agent. Because of it she leads a double life. During the week she is a Russian dancer in a cafe and on Sunday goes home to her place in the suburbs. Out home is a brother who has been weak enough to trim the office he is working for for $10,000. Sis promises to fix it up a week later. Meantime she is aware that in the guise of "Sonia" the Russian dancer she has the son of her brother's boss pretty well vamped, so as the dancer she goes to the father and makes a deal—she will disillusion the son providing he will let the Smith boy off.

Later it all comes out in the wash, the Smith girl and Sonia are one, and besides working for the government. Her Russian is accounted for through the fact that "father was a Russian consul for eight years and I studied ballet dancing there," that would mean that she must be a Democrat, too, for judging from her age, etc., dad must have had his job during the Wilson administration.

Miss de la Motte makes her role halfway convincing. A pair of Harold Lloyd goggles serve to transform her from Sonia to Miss Smith, but no one in the picture seemed to get wise that it was one and the same person, at least not for a long time. John Bowers was outstanding as the lover, and Barney Sherry was all that could be asked as a stern father. There were a couple of Russian heavies that didn't amount to much. *Fred.*

THE PRAIRIE WIFE

Hugo Ballin Production, released by Metro-Goldwyn. Running time, 63 minutes.

Chaddie Green	Dorothy Devore
Duncan McKail	Herbert Rawlinson
Olie	Gibson Gowland

Decidedly different sort of a western. It isn't a western of the hills, but of the prairies. It really looks as though some one or another said, after viewing "Secrets," "Why wouldn't it be a good idea to take a modern society girl and set her down in the grain prairies of today with a husband and see how that would work out?" That's what they have done, and it has worked out into a fairly good feature as far as the daily change small houses are concerned.

Dorothy Devore gives promise, if she is properly handled and supplied with the right sort of material, of developing into a "Connie" Talmadge with a little more heart appeal than "Connie" has.

Miss Devore has the role of a society-bred girl who, while living abroad, is informed her fortune is wiped out and that she had best return home. Comng back on the steamer she meets an old flame. He is no better off financially, except that he owns vast acres of grain land in the northwest. They marry and start west, and the balance of the picture is a comedy drama of the next two or three years of their life, ending in happiness and wealth.

The sub-titles are done in the form of the girl's diary—another suggestion from "Secrets."

Direction and action fairly well handled and, for a cheap picture, it should more than get the production cost back and show a corking profit.

Herbert Rawlinson as the "heman of the wide open" does well, but Miss Devore is the picture. There are a couple of spots where the director reverted to the old-fashioned cut-backs to explain his action. Gibson Gowland as a mysterious character had the audience guessing, but the fears that they had for the woman in the story were never realized.

At one time there must have been much more story to "The Prairie Wife" than at present, but it is just as well that the cutter eliminated all the horse thief stuff and other action that would have detracted. *Fred.*

FORBIDDEN CARGO

Gothic Pictures presentation. Distributed by F. B. O., featuring Evelyn Brent. Story and scenario by Fred Kennedy Myton. Directed by Tom Buckingham. Running time, 60 mins.

Captain Joe	Evelyn Brent
Jerry Burke	Robert Ellis
Pietro Castellano	Boris Karloff

Ultra modern story dealing with the Bahamas and rum runners. The yarn is interesting, although farfetched. Evelyn Brent as the heroine and captain of a rum-running yacht, with a crew of cut throats, has a role which strains credulity, although her conception of Captain Joe is excellent.

As the daughter of an unjustly disgraced naval captain exiled to the Bahamas, she is determined to recover the money her father lost through the mistake of his country. The story opens with the yacht making one of its last few trips.

Jerry Burke (Robert Ellis) a secret service agent, who is lurking in the Bahamas, meets Captain Joe in a cafe frequented by the bootleggers and their light o' loves. Joe falls hard for him, but Pietro (Boris Karloff) her mate, discovers Burke's identity and they shangai him. Burke is made to do menial work aboard the yacht, with Captain Joe, a hard taskmaster.

The yacht is attacked by hi-jackers, and Captain Joe is shot in the arm. Burke saves her by stealing the hi-jackers' motor boat. The motor boat catches fire and the pair take to the water, landing on an island inhabited by a recluse. Joe induces him to seek her father, unknown to Burke.

While awaiting her answer she is awakened spiritually and physically by Burke and is in his arms when her crew arrive. They refuse to obey her and again capture Burke, taking him to the yacht, Pietro, who is in love with Joe, strings Burke up by his thumbs and locks Joe in a stateroom. She signals a passing destroyer by using a lantern through the porthole.

Pietro, rather than have the yacht captured, sets a time fuse which blows up the ship before he and his gang can escape. Joe batters down the door and releases Burke just before the explosion. They are saved and through the intervention of Burke's father, a senator, and a death-bed confession, Joe's father is forgiven and recognized by his government.

The picture is splendidly directed and intensely interesting, despite the highly dramatic sequence of events. The fight between hi-jackers and rum-runners has been cleverly staged and is a realistic bit. The author muffed a great chance to bear down heavier on the outwitting of the revenue officers, on of the high lights.

The inconsistencies are the girl of obvious refinement dominating a group of nautical vagabonds and her invalid father trusting her to the tender mercies of this gang, not to speak of the elements and revenue men. *Con.*

Playthings of Desire

H. F. Jans production starring Estelle Taylor. Written by J. Wesley Potnam, scenario by William B. Lamb and directed by Burton King Distributed by Renown Pictudes, Inc. Runs about 65 min.

Gloria Dawn	Estelle Taylor
Pierre du Charme	Mahlon Hamilton
Renee Grant	Dagmar Godowsky
Anne Cabbot	Mary Thurman
James Malvern	Lawford Davidson
Brom Jones	Walter Miller
Governor Cabbot	Edmund Breese
Wheeler Johnson	Bradley Barker
Gloria's Mother	Ida Pardee
Caretaker	Lee Beggs

In spite of an alluring title this picture holds only two points of interest for the average film fan. The first of these is the appearance of Estelle Taylor in what is probably her first starring vehicle since she became Mrs. Jack Dempsey. This may be dismissed by saying that Miss Taylor remains a very colorless and ordinary actress, but that statement doesn't go if Jack hears of it.

The second point is the similarity of certain bits of the story to the well-remembered Stillman divorce case. Even a Canadian Indian guide is introduced and the Flo Leeds angle as far as the husband goes is not neglected. But the wife is free from blame throughout, although her rounder husband, anxious to be free, tries to trick her and the handsome I. G. into giving him grounds for a divorce. The names and locales are carefully concealed and switched to make the plot safe from legal attack. Any one who has read the Stillman matter, however, will recognize certain of the details.

Otherwise the film is more or less of a mess. The plot is complicated, inasmuch as instead of the usual triangle there is a full-fledged sextette. Thus the wife has two men besides her husband in love with her and her spouse is carrying on much less platonic affairs with a pair of other women. There is a murder caused by the flighty sister of the governor, the last-minute snatching from the chair of an innocent man by the same governor, a rescue from the falls in the best hokum film style, etc.

The cast holds some names and presents good performances by Lawford Davidson, Edmund Breese and Mary Thurman. Dagmar Godowsky is less freakish than usual. The picture has been nicely set and Burton King has inserted a few deft directorial touches.

It would have been interesting to notice whether business at the Stanley on the day the film showed there would have been better had the billing read "Mrs. Jack Dempsey." It seems certain that that would have brought quite a few in out of curiosity, whereas the name Estelle Taylor means little commercially in itself. "Playthings" is a mediocre production and needs all the trick advertising the exhibitors can give it.

FIGHTING SHERIFF

Jesse J. Goldburg (Independent Pictures Corp.) production, starring Bill Cody. Directed by J. P. McGowan. Story by George W. Pyper. Photographed by Al Zeigler. Edited by Betty Davis Private screening May 11. Runs about 50 minutes.

Larry O'Donnell	Bill Cody
Madge Blair	Hazel Holt
Jeff Bains	Frank Ellis
G. Smiley	Walter Shumway

Extraordinary pictorial value features almost every foot of "The Fighting Sheriff." Otherwise it is just one more of the long, unending stream of conventional westerns. J. P. McGowan, the director, is known as an in-and-outer, and though his work has been ordinary in every other respect, he has registered an artistic triumph in choosing supremely beautiful locales for his action and in making that action, where it concerns horsemanship on the western prairies, worthy of the scenery. Al Ziegler, who photographed the picture, shares the honors for his clear, bright and delicately handled work with the camera.

But the film has its serious deficiencies. No comedy attempts at all are to be found, something that heretofore not even the crudest of westerns have neglected. In a way none at all is better than some of the humor found in this type of production, but if just a few bright bits had been inserted it might have been a different story. Except for the star, the cast is almost entirely without merit. Unfortunately, Hazel Holt's first appearance as a leading woman is liable to be her last, as she very definitely cannot act, and particularly because of the unbecoming way she fixes her hair, does not seem to have the beauty to make up for it.

Bill Cody is acceptable for what he is called upon to do. He is spry, graceful and an expert horseman and, except when the close-ups become too merciless, appears to be rather good looking. His small, wiry stature is a relief after the succession of great big husky western stars.

The story introduces our old friend aphasia, this time in a new setting, and providing the plucky sheriff with an excuse to get blamed for the gold robbery.

If the average western fan is observant enough to notice exceptionally fine scenic effects he may regard "The Fighting Sheriff" as slightly out of the ordinary. Otherwise he'll accept it for what it is—number four in the Bill Cody series, with Cody ranking at present about tenth in the ranks of the "Yes, ma'am, I reckon I am th' fightin' sheriff" stars.

BORDER INTRIGUE

Jesse J. Goldburg (Independent Pictures Corp.) production starring Franklyn Farnum. Directed by J. P. McGowan. Photographed by Walter Griffin. Story by James Ormont. Private screening May 11. Runs about 55 minutes.

Tom Lassen ....Franklyn Farnum
Dick Lassen ....Jack Vernon
Mrs. Lassen..............Mathilda Brundage
Edith Harding ....Dorothy Wood
Bull Harding ....Robert E. Cline
Juan Verdigo..............Mack V. Wright
Pedro Gonzales........"Slender" Whittaker
Rita ....Emily Barrie
"Tough" Tidings.............J. P. McGowan
"Tough's" Sister ....Dot Farley

The press sheet hails "Border Intrigue" as a new type of western with "the steady diet of gun play, murder and chases, to which the public has been fed for the post 10 years, altered by a great attention to the story and a portrayal of incidents that had some foundation in fact and a more detailed attention to the delineation of characters together with a great stress upon heart interest."

Perhaps Jesse Goldburg and his staff of assistants struggled along this line and if so let them be given credit, at least, for a worthy motive. But the fact remains that "Border Intrigue" is one of the poorest westerns of this season. Certainly J. P. McGowan, who turns out a good one every once in a while, never did a worse job of directing, and Franklyn Farnum, although he tries hard, has never been seen to less advantage.

No originality or ingenuity may be found in the film although it is complicated beyond measure. Woven into the story are two brothers, an American girl, several senoritas whose implied characters are nothing to boast of, and the usual assortment of villains from both sides of the border. The older brother resolves to show the younger how false the latter's Spanish sweetie is, flirts with her himself, loses his own girl and finally wins her back as has been done only several thousand times in various forms of fiction and the drama.

The Goldburg leading lady crop seems to be at low ebb this season as Dorothy Wood gives as colorless a performance as have several other heroines in pictures bearing the same name. McGowan takes a second flop in the chief comedy role. The rest of the cast averages up poorly, too, and even the settings and photography are far below standard.

In the projection room without any redeeming music this may have seemed particularly vapid and boring but even if it were shown at the Capitol with Whiteman's Band playing "Marcheta" in the pit, it would still be a "turk."

WILLIAM TELL

Foreign-made production, presented by Emil Harder, who adapted it from the Continental drama and opera of similar name. Edited and titled by Hoey Lawlor. At Cameo, New York, week May 17. Runs about 95 minutes.

"William Tell" on the screen is too heavily historical of ancient Switzerland for universal appeal to present-day American picture house audiences. If the legendary story, illustrated, of William Tell arching the apple on the head of his son is of value, this picture may have some draw on that account, but on that account only. It may find a play among studious adults, but for the common classes, taking in the flappers and the flippant kids who like their pictures the way they like them, "William Tell" won't start a whisper.

About all it can surely depend upon is a colony anywhere of the Swiss or those Continentals with sentimental leanings toward Switzerland.

And withal, a most interesting picture, well made, finely directed, extremely well cut (so well it could not much run below its present long running time of 95 minutes without the excellent continuity being spoiled) and with some thrills as well as spectacular sight scenes amidst the picturesque Alps and hills.

On a venture it might be said that this is a propaganda or subsidized picture for the Switzerland Government or sponsored or promoted by it. In that or surrounding European countries, "William Tell" would be a big special. It probably has played those countries. Over here it is merely historical film with interest centered through the William Tell story. It tells of Switzerland gaining her freedom in 1308, fine in history and fact, and fine for Switzerland, but dance and jazz mad Americans in 1925 are not patronizing picture houses to go back 600 years in the history of any country, not even their own (if America could go back that far).

For school children who know their history it might be of interest for them to see how the first of all republics gained its freedom from a tyrannical king and more tyrannical underlings. But if the history of the U. S. A. in pictures were impressed instead upon the school children of the U. S. A., it would be far more beneficial to future generations.

In an introductory on the sheet, signed by Emil Harder, who made and adapted the film, he concludes the preface by a statement that America is his home. Mr. Harder as an American made a fine picture abroad, but neither will help it here.

Not much doubt that the historical portion of the story is fairly authentic, with credit on the program for the courtesy of foreign nations especially Switzerland, in lending assistance in properties and otherwise, also that the scenes are originals, and they may be.

A love interest is nicely worked in with other romantic asides, but the thread bears so strongly on the the historic there is no counter effect of sufficient weight to balance. But to the interested the "William Tell" picture will hold until its finish. The apple-arrow shooting incident is well worked up and out, while the Tell character is commanding in stature besides an actor of the first grade.

There are other good actors in this picture play, men and women; many extras (armies) were employed, the picture cost some money to make and it has everything in its favor, excepting for America.

Its intense historical record of a great event for current times is of most moment to the country reaping the benefit 617 years ago—Switzerland.

Sime.

BLACK CYCLONE

Pathe film, produced by Hal Roach and starring Rex, the horse. Directed by Fred Jackman. At the Capitol, New York, May 18 week. Running time, 60 minutes.

The Horses	The People
Rex	Guinn Williams
Lady	Kathleen Collins
The Killer	Christian Frank

An astounding film is "Black Cyclone," and one sure to cause a raft of talk before it gets far. With horses playing the leading roles and sustaining the principal interest, this one is full of laughs, thrills, drama and suspense. They don't come much nearer to filling the entertainment order. It is the second in which Rex has appeared, the first being "King of the Wild Horses."

A colt left motherless is out in the Wild Lands. It grows up alone, takes care of itself, and finally becomes a broad-flanked, nimble-footed free-lance, roaming the prairies and fighting its way. Only The Killer, a vicious outlaw horse, is its master.

One day Rex goes courting, wins Lady for a mate, and the two ever afterward stick together through tough times. In a fight with The Killer, who is after the Lady, he is worsted, but continually think of some plan to win back the mate Then the sequence shifts.

A cowboy is courting his girl, and in the shadows lurks a rejected rival. Exit cowboy from the girl's home and the rival fires, but misses, getting stunned himself. But the cowboy, fearing the rival's gang, makes for the Wild Lands, and there lives a long time.

One day he starts to cross a stream and notices a horse imbedded and unable to get out. It is Rex, who has fallen into quicksand in an effort to save Lady. Struggling and struggling, he finally makes the horse kick enough to extricate itself. From then on it is Rex and the cowboy, although the horse doesn't know the feel of a saddle.

But into the desert comes the villain, and behind him the girl, to warn her lover. The villain, however, shoots at the cowboy and kills the horse, but around the bend comes Rex, still on the search for the man who freed him. Rex's mane the cowboy grabs, straddles the broad back and is borne with the velocity of a cannonball to the villain. And the cowboy stages a battle and wins.

Meantime Lady has escaped from The Killer and is being pursued by wolves. Finally Rex reaches her and fights them off, but as he does, The Killer arrives. Rex, however, is full of the enthusiasm of fight, having seen his master win, so he leaps on The Killer and paws him pretty badly. By that time Rex has his Lady, and the cowboy has his girl.

It's a happy ending that brought a storm of applause.

The way these horses perform is little short of miraculous. Every move is life-like, natural and registers. That goes for Rex, Lady and The Killer, the latter being an especially mean-looking rascal, while Lady is a fine light mare. The humans in it don't have much to do, but do it nicely.

"Black Cyclone" is a film to make movie history. Its achievements made in America are none the less important, for its vigorous and pulsing story, carried forward with directness and a minimum of footage, fairly shrieks aloud to those who ask for better films.

They couldn't be much better than this. For any first run, anywhere, it is fit provided intelligent, educational exploitation is used, and in the country towns it is a cinch setup.

Sisk.

MY WIFE AND I

Warner Bros.' production, starring Irene Rich. From the novel by Harriet Beecher Stowe. Directed by Millard Webb. At the Piccadilly, N. Y., week May 16. Running time, 77 minutes.

Mrs. Stuart Borden...............Irene Rich
Mr. Stuart Borden...........Huntley Gordon
Stuart Borden, Jr..................John Harron
Spencer Hobart......................John Roche
Aileen Alton...............Constance Bennett
Valet.................................Tom Ricketts
Estelle Loring..................Caire de Lorez

"My Wife and I" is a society drama, conventional. No great kick and, as far as its box-office potentialities are concerned, it does not rise above the category of "a program picture." For the average run of daily change houses it will get by.

This picture is a sterling example of how great a part adequate and skilled lighting plays in picture making. Whoever is responsible for the lighting and camera work just about botched this particular part as far as possible. They made Constance Bennett look hideous, and as for the shot with Irene Rich on the floor and partly in her husband's arms, that should never have gotten into the picture at all. The angle from which that was taken was all wrong, and the director should have remade the scene after seeing the "rushes."

The story concerns a family of three. Mother, father and son comprise the Borden menage. Father has accumulated a fortune and is a successful market operator. The son is about 23 and trying to spend as much of the family b. r. as possible on a dame, who, as soon as the boy's dad cuts off the allowance, gives the kid the air. But within a few weeks she meets the father of the youth while at luncheon in a smart cafe, and the old boy falls for the same girl. The girl plays dad exactly along the same line as she did the boy and gives the older man the same routine, and it works.

Along comes the 25th wedding anniversary of the Bordens. Just prior to its advent Mrs. Borden becomes aware of her husband's outside play pal, but hides the true state of her feelings. On the night of the anniversary the hubby remains at home, but his dame, who is having a birthday party the same night, is peeved. She jumps in her car and rides right over to his house, sending in for him. He comes out and gets into the car with her, allowing the car to remain on the driveway in front of the house. His wife, looking out, sees him.

Later the same night he leaves the house after he and his wife have decided to part, and goes to the apartment of the girl. His son, who has been aired, determines that he is going to "get" the man who cut him out, and walks into the apartment, fires a shot at the back of the man without knowing it is his father, but at that precise moment mother, who has followed them both, knocks his arm up, so there is no damage done.

The final view of the vamp is the cleverest of the whole picture, or would have been if a title had not been inserted. The shot shattered a mirror and, after locking Borden out of her bedroom, she takes a look at it and counts off seven on her fingers. That was enough for any audience, but the title man didn't think so, so he had to put it all in the title.

Fred.

WELCOME HOME

Famous Players picture made from the play "Minick," by George S. Kaufman and written by him from Edna Ferber's story. Adapted to the screen by Walter Woods and F. McGrew Willis. Directed by James Cruze.

Old Man Prouty..................Luke Cosgrave
Fred Prouty......................Warner Baxter
Nellie Prouty......................Lois Wilson
Jim Corey.......................Ben Hendricks
Lil Corey......................Margaret Morrie

Miss Pringle..............Josephine Crowell
Annie.....................Adele Watson

No doubt the idea in this film was for James Cruze to create another great "home" picture, as he did with "The Goose Hangs High." But the dramatic material of "The Goose" was infinitely greater than that of "Minick," proven by its reception in New York and on the road. In New York, also "Minick" owed the greater part of its success to the sterling performance of O. P. Heggie in the title role. In the films it has no such exponent, which leaves "Welcome Home" not a big first-run film.

The story is that Old Man Prouty comes to live with his married son and wife in their Chicago home. Being an old man he has a thousand and one set ways which worry and annoy the family, who try to be kind but who cannot help but allow their impatience to show. This the old man sees and deserts his family for a place in the old men's home, where he can be happy in his discussions of whether China should sign the Four-Power treaty or whether France can pay her debts.

It is easy to see then that the whole thing is a character study. Cosgrave is hampered at the start. He has a full white beard and bushy hair, so a comparatively small portion of his face shows. Therefore when his mouth drops to register disappointment, nobody can see it. If he smiles, that is also hard to discover underneath the beard. Cosgrave's work must all be explained in subtitles. He does excellently within the limitations prescribed, but insofar as the movie public is concerned it is a miscast role.

Lois Wilson has nothing to do, and Warner Baxter is also at a loss. No one else of importance is in the film, which has neither high point of drama nor comedy. There is a note of wistfulness, but wistfulness strung over 70 minutes is like a string of fudge stretched 70 feet. It doesn't hold together.

"Welcome Home" is okay for the daily changes if rushed in and out quick. It's well made and all that, but the story just isn't there for movies and the casting hasn't helped it any. Why it should ever have been figured as available for films is more or less problematical. Even by adapting it liberally, the main theme would have persisted and the attractiveness of that theme on the stage was 90 per cent due to Mr. Heggie, without whom the play wouldn't have gotten across in New York.   *Sisk.*

B'WAY BUTTERFLY

Labeled one of Warner Bros. "Classics." William Beaudine production. With introduction by O. O. McIntyre. Directed by William Beaudine. Running time, 1 hr. 12 mins.

Donald Steel..............Cullen Landis
Charles Gay ....Willard Lewis
Wilbur Crane...............John Roche
Stage Manager..............Wilfred Lucas
Cookie Dale...............Louise Fazenda
Thelma Perry..............Lillyan Tashman
Sally Brown...............Dorothy DeVore

"Broadway Butterfly" started out like it was going to be a whambang or a whizzling snorter, and then skidded off into commonplace celluloid. Quite a lavish display of film expenditure, and the way that stag party was staged recalled some of the vivid days of Cecil De Mille's mazuma fireworks in former Paramounts.

It's a stage story and, while showing little that has not been done one way or another in dramatics and comedies, it dovetails sufficient interest to give the picture cameras a lot of shots behind scenes and in the flats and studios where the chorus dames are pictured as spending their time when not strutting their pony stuff.

Looks like Warner Bros. will give the small towns something away rom the beaten path, for there are some lively scenes.

The story, after all, has a moral old as the hills—girls with stage aspirations had better watch out or the chorus will get 'em, and if the chorus does not some money-spending bird will.

The heroine was Dorothy Devore. Innocent, unsophisticated lambkin, she meandered into a Broadway chorus and got not one John but three, all wealthy and each dead set for her. Miss Devore as Sally Brown was in love with Donald Steel.

The fat part was carried and upheld by Miss Fazenda, who, as Cookie, was the life of every party (so a caption stated) and also the life of the film. Miss Devore was cute, pert and sweet in several of her short love scenes, and also handled her backstage debut nicely.

Of the men, John Roche had the hardest task of acting the role of a caddish gink who rented a cosy little Greenwich Village apartment which had two attractive single beds, and the heroine curled up in one as he entered later and proceeded to make himself at home.

Cullen Landis did a lot of posing and looked like he needed a 1925 haircut, but it didn't require much acting to carry him through. The women skated circles all around the men.

"Broadway Butterfly" advertises the "Follies," Times square and Greenwich Village and "Variety." This paper was there for a dash of atmosphere in typifying what kind of literature chorus girls read when sipping tea.

On the road and in the family neighborhoods where the old folks listen to the radio when not taking in the movies, the opinion they have of stage life will be further and more deeply confirmed. In other words, "show life ain't what it's cracked up to be."

It's a picture that mirrors a lot of true life and a lot that isn't true, yet that first part is A1 film stuff. Beyond that it simmers into the ordinary feature category.   *Mark.*

BAREE, SON OF KAZAN

Vitagraph Production, starring Anita Stewart. Adapted from James Oliver Curwood's story. At the Rialto, New York, week May 17. Running time, 78 Minutes.

Nepeese.......................Anita Stewart
Jim Carvel....................Donald Keith
Pierre........................Joe Rickson

Superfluous footage is a severe handicap. The padding, principally dedicated to the star, Anita Stewart, is all too obvious in a well-worn story that could just as well have been told under one hour. Hence, the conclusion that the picture is not strictly first class first-run fare, but average entertainment, minus high-lights.

As with most of the Curwood stories, the location is in the North Country where a half-breed trapper and his daughter (Miss Stewart) are the objects of designing schemes by the Factor of the trading post, who covets the girl.

Baree, the pup, is nursed back to health by the girl after having been caught in a trap, which leads to the dog's eventually bringing the lovers together, followed by his killing of the Factor. The dog in the picture is named "Wolf" and is given "war hero" billing.

A great deal of time is taken up in showing just how cute Miss Stewart is as a nymph of the big spaces, and it is here that the continuity becomes monotonous. The killing of the Factor by the dog is cameraed as happening inside a tent, and with the natural interest of the audience in the animal he is too much relegated to the background for the good of the film as a whole. A chase of a deer, or moose, by a pack of wolves is interesting, but the fact remains there isn't enough of the dog.

Miss Stewart does well enough as the heroine, while Jack Curtis is a passable and very bewhiskered villain. Donald Keith is briefly seen as the ultimate husband, while Joe Rickson passes out of the action at about half way.

The picture needs substantial cutting to build up the pace which it must have in lieu of a not overly strong story.   *Skig.*

Drusilla with a Million

Associated Arts Production, adapted from the novel by Elizabeth Cooper. Directed by F. Harmon Weight. Released by F. B. O. At the Capitol, New York, week May 24. Running time 66 minutes.

Drusilla Doane.................Mary Carr
Sally May Ferris..........Priscilla Bonner
Colin Arnold..............Kenneth Harlan
Elias Arnold...............Henry Barrows
John Thornton.........William Humphreys
Daphne Thornton..........Claire Du Brey

This picture would be a mop up in the picture houses, even the pre-release first runs, providing those exploiting it had had the vision to give it a forced Broadway showing and the same treatment William Fox gave his "Over the Hill," for if there ever was another "Over the Hill" from a box office angle this is the one. Like the Fox wonder it is just one of those accidents that happen, for the picture does not look as though it cost $100,000 to make, but it has all the old surefire heart throb and hoak stuff that gets to the average picture house audiences, and, after all, that is what counts.

"Drusilla" isn't a picture audiences are going to flock to see without a campaign behind it, but those seeing it are going to be mightily entertained. It will build up. If given a Broadway showing in a legitimate house the chances are that the first four weeks would have been played at a loss, but after that it would have built, and with six months on the street behind it (for it surely would have run that long) it would have been a mop in the regular film houses and the rentals that could have been gotten for it by the distributors would be double what they will get for it now.

No, it isn't a great story on the screen, not as great as the book was. The adaptation is responsible for that. It isn't exceptionally cast, except for Mary Carr, and its direction is faulty in spots, but despite all this it has the fundamental heart appeal, built to order for the masses, and when this is brought home to them they'll give up their money to see it.

Melodrama of the wildest sort, but Sunday afternoon the audience that jammed the big Capitol saw it and love it. They even went so far as to hiss the woman heavy, applauded the hero to the skies when he turned in time to save the heroine from jail and acted exactly as the audiences that crowded the American gallery deported themselves in the days of the old Stair and Havlin circuit.

In adapting the story a youthful love interest was added, but even though there are certain moments when the trials and tribulations of the hero and heroine overshadow Drusilla herself, it is Mary Carr who stands out for her performance as the only charity boarded in the old ladies' home, who suddenly inherits a million and starts to take in all the foundlings left on the doorsteps of her home in the fashionable section of the town, to the horror of the wealthy neighbors.

Of course, when the hero, who was the disinherited son and thus made it possible for Drusilla to get the million, and his wife are parted by the boy's former fiancee, and a baby is born, what is more natural than the wife should leave it on the doorsteps of Drusilla's house. She is pinched for it and taken to court. This is all part of a plot between the heavy and her father to show that the old lady is incompetent to administer the fortune left her.

Then the boy steps in, but the heavy succeeds through a ruse to get him out of the room when the heroine is on the stand and undergoes a terrific cross-examination, one as a matter of fact that could only take place before the camera, but this does the work and has the audience at a pitch that causes them to burn up. The finish finds husband and wife in each other's arms 'to the discomfort of the law-·r and his daughter.

It's a wow as far as the audience is concerned, and although it may not meet with the approval of the picture reviewers on the dailies, it is going to be a money-getter, nevertheless.

Miss Carr walks off with all the acting honors, with Kenneth Harlan second choice for the money. Priscilla Bonner fails to register in the early sequences, due to faulty direction, but makes good later on. The additional trio in the cast did nothing that particularly distinguished them, for their roles practically played themselves. *Fre:*

OLD HOME WEEK

Famous Players production, starring Thomas Meighan. Suggested by George Ade's story. Adapted by Thomas J. Geraghty. Directed by Victor Heerman. At the Rivoli, New York, week May 24. Running time, 75 minutes.

Tom Clark................Thomas Meighan
Ethel Harmon.....................Lila Lee
J. Edward Brice..........Lawrence Wheat
Marshall Coleman.......Charles Dow Clark
Townsend Barton.............Max Figman
Uncle Henry.................Charles Sellon
Mary Clark......................Zelma Tiden
Judge Harmon................Sidney Paxton
Jim Ferguson.................Joseph Smiley
Frikkle...........................Jack Terry
Otey Jinks......................Leslie Hunt
Mrs. Clark......................Isabel West
Congressman Brady...........Clayton Frye

At the Rivoli this week they are advertising in the lights that Tommy Meighan is appearing in "Old Home Week." The dignity of the formal Thomas is thereby shot all to pieces; but possibly it is a good idea, for Tommy's public always call him "Tommy," and he might just as well let it go at that. Incidentally Tommy is appearing in one of the best pictures he has done in some time, and it will take only a few like this to put him right back at the top of the film box-office attractions.

With Meighan it is a matter of stories, and this present one should about fill the bill, delighting the Meighan fans and possibly attracting a lot of new ones for him. It is a George Ade story, adapted by Tom Geraghty and directed by Victor Heerman. Geraghty developed a smooth-running continuity, with the comedy element very much in the foreground, but with sufficient element of suspense to hold the interest of the audience. Heerman did a workman-like job in turning out the picture.

It is a story of "Old Home Week" in Clarksburg. All the successful boys that went out in the world and made their mark are coming back to gloat over those that didn't have sense enough to leave the old homestead.

Four really successful ones return, but the fifth, Meighan, who also returns, is far from a business wizard. He is in the oil business, running a gas station on a road that is under repair and won't be opened for six months at least, but in the old home town they believe that he is the rival of Jawn D. himself, and they insist that he take over the management of an oil well being sunk outside the town by a couple of slick promoters.

They assigned their rights to him for 30 days before they find he hasn't enough dough to keep a peanut stand whistling. They want to hedge, but he has discovered the oil well is a phoney and with the aid of the driller who is on the job rigs up a water-pipe connection with the local waterworks, stages a "gusher" and the slick promoters buy out the stock held by the locals.

Love interest supplied by Lila Lee as the daughter of the town's wealthiest man, who thinks he's a flop; but when the boy trims the sharks he's all for him and consents to the young people doing the "happy ever after" embrace.

The combination of Meighan with Miss Lee featured and a good story should sho wthis picture somewhat above the average of the late Meighans for box-office qualities.

Fred.

JUST A WOMAN

First National picture, presented by M. C. Levee. Directed by Irving Cummings, featuring Conway Tearle, Claire Windsor and Percy Marmount. Adapted from the play by Eugene Walter. At the Strand, New York, week of May 24. Running time, 65 minutes.

June Holton...............Claire Windsor
Robert Holton.............Conway Tearle
Bobby, their son...........Dorothy Brock
George Rand...............Percy Marmont
Clarice Clement............Dorothy Revere
Oscar Dunn.................George Cooper

Intermediate silent entertainment revolving about the steel industry about describes this First National release. The story is without novelty, but the interest the players and production arouse give it enough class to send the film into first-run houses.

The three featured cast members —Miss Windsor, Mr. Tearle and Mr. Marmont — are of the working class. An invention of a new steel treatment process by the latter raises them to wealth through the business capabilities of the woman. Mr. Marmont is the friend of the family that comes near being disrupted when Holton (Mr. Tearle) falls for a home-town girl who has successfully made the theatrical grade, but turns gold digger upon the information of the Holton money. The feminine warfare for the husband, and the resultant divorce trial, which the husband abruptly ends by declaring he has done his wife a great injustice, consumes the major part of the footage.

Dorothy Revere plays the homewrecker, with George Cooper opposite as a small-time ventriloquist who flashes forth "Variety" upon various occasions.

A glimpse at the inside routine of a steel plant serves to establish the atmosphere, but after that the story keeps away from the furnaces. It hies itself to a directors' meeting, where the wife (Miss Windsor) issues her ultimatum concerning just what the company will have to do in order to gain the use of the revolutionizing process.

The sextet of players all connect in their roles, while the script goes out after something of a sex angle, through the wife being "framed" into a compromising bedroom scene so that the husband can commence his divorce suit.

This picture should take its place alongside the many program leaders which have gone before, neither above nor below that innumerable quota.

Skig.

ANY WOMAN

Henry King production presented by Robert Kane with Alice Terry featured. From the story by Arthur Somers Roche, adapted by Jules Furthman and Beatrice Van. Released by Paramount. At the Rialto, New York., Week May 24. Running time, 66 minutes.

Ellen Linden........................Alice Terry
Tom Galloway.....................Ernest Gillen
Mrs. Rand.....................Margarita Fischer
James Rand.......................Lawson Butt
Mrs. Galloway....................Aggie Herring
William Linden......................James Neil
Mrs. Phillips...................De Sacia Mooers
Egbert Phillips...................Henry Kolker
Alice Cartwright................George Periolat
Agnes Young.......................Lucille Hutton
Jones...................................Arthur Hoyt
Lord Brackenridge..............Malcolm Denny

Thoroughly synthetic screen entertainment. Utterly lacking in punch and kick and just winds its weary way through seeming endless reels of film without arriving anywhere. An attempt to lighten up the story with some fairly humorous titles by Randolph Bartlet is about the best that the picture offers. From a box office angle the picture means nothing at all.

Alice Terry, featured, just walks through with about as much expression as Mildred Harris would have given it.

The chances are that when Arthur Somers Roche looks the picture over he'll wonder where his story went to.

Miss Terry has the role of a young lady educated abroad returning to Los Angeles, only to discover that while away her father lost the family fortune and his health. She can't see it at first and seem inclined to want to take a fall out of father for being so inconsiderate.

In fact, the first couple of reels seem to be especially designed to work up an unsympathetic attitude on the part of the audience, as far as the featured lead is concerned. Finally she hunts a job to take care of father, eventually finding employment with a firm of promoting brokers, both partners and they try to make her. Neither succeeds. In the end she marries the hustling advertising agent of a new soft drink, who was attentive to her father during his illness. Incidentally she gets the brokerage firm to finance the soft drink proposition.

The soft drink wasn't the only thing soft about this picture.

Ernest Gillen plays opposite Miss Terry, doing fairly well. He is capable of development into a leading man. Henry Kolker and Lawson Butt are the partners with the "making" tendencies and endow the roles with about the only real acting in the picture.

"Any Woman" doesn't stack up.

Fred.

CRIMSON RUNNER

Hunt Stromberg production released through Producers' Distributing Corporation and starring Priscilla Dean. Story by Harvey Gates and direction by Tom Forman.

Bianca Schreber...............Priscilla Dean
Alfred Schreber...............Bernard Siegel
Von Krutz...........................Alan Hale
Count Meinhard von Bauer.....Ward Crane
Rudolph...............................James Neil
Semlin..............................Charles Mailes
Princess Cecile.................Ilsa de Lindt
Conrad the Black...............Mitchell Lewis
Bobo, the valet.................Taylor Holmes

Priscilla Dean is one of the screen's interesting personalities, come to think of it. Each of her pictures has her cast as an up and doing stunt woman, either in some exotic role of hoydenish nature or as the avenger of the weak. Yet Miss Dean does no stunts—her vigorous actions are suggested by the sub-titles and her great part of it consists in walking around the set in a confident and ingratiating manner. The whole thing can be summed up that as a stunt star Miss Dean is the phoney bologna, but as a star with a following and the ability to keep running in a fair line-up of film, she's there. For, although her stuff never hits a high level, it doesn't suffer the sags known to a few others.

This one has her as the Crimson Runner, the woman leader of an Apache band in Vienna whose life is devoted to robbing the rich to feed the poor. A female Robin Hood and she falls in love with an aristocrat, avenges the death of her father, pulls a few neat robberies and is finally vindicated and restored to respectability.

As a yarn it is strong stuff, for the continuity has action every minute, contrast between the rich and the poor, the love interest aroused between the love of a Princess for the man she marries and finally the unique personality which she becomes solely through the medium of the story. For "The Crimson Runner" is an interesting film filled with the hop, skip and jump of action and the kiss, clinch and hug of movie love.

Because of that, it is okay for most any screen, except the classy first runs where real quality is demanded.

Technically, these films leave flocks to be desired. The personal supervision of Hunt Stromberg doesn't mean anything, for all the sets are bad, obviously flimsy. In spots the society gatherings of Vienna's ultra folk look laughable, the types of women being cabarety to the extreme, while the men don't look much like noblemen. Ward Crane, a fine leading man, is the exception, while the others are obviously just actors playing noblemen. The Apache types, on the other hand, are authoritative, with Mitchell Lewis leading the crew. Taylor Holmes is also in the cast, playing a nance butler for laughs.

A second woman in the cast, Ilsa de Mindt is notable because she looks like a double of Dorothy Mackaill, and under the lid, anybody who resembles Miss Mackaill is there with the looks.

"The Crimson Runner" isn't a whale of a film, but as a program feature for the intermediate houses it is aces up on the story and action alone while in even the better type houses it is passable.

Probably Miss Dean isn't much a personal draw, certainly not in New York, but at a reasonable price and exploited, this one should stand up nicely.

Sisk.

PRICE OF PLEASURE

Universal. Adapted from the story "Clinging Fingers" by Elizabeth Holding and Marion Orth. Directed by Edward Sloman. At the Piccadilly, New York, week May 25. Running time, 70 minutes.

Linnie Randall.................Virginia Valli
Garry Schuyler.................Norman Kerry
Stella Kelly...................Louise Fazenda
Mrs. Schuyler.......................Kate Lester
John Osborne..................George Fawcett
Bill McGuffy......................T. Roy Barnes
Jenkins.......................James O. Barrows
Grace Schuyler..................Marie Astaire

Plenty of technical flaws in this film and once in a while the story goes a bit far-fetched, but it always holds up in the entertainment values. The main fault is that while the locale is New York, we get flashes of Owl drug stores, institutions of soda water and medicine peculiar to the coast. The taxis, too, aren't New York style and the street scenes don't look like they're near the Hudson.

The plot concerns that old Cinderella story of the girl who yearned for one good time. Working in the hardware section of a department store, the hero comes along and promises it, making a date for the evening. When evening arrives, instead of a fellow with a flivver, he shows up as an aristocrat in Tuxedo, boiled shirt, gloves and a fine limousine. She balks for a minute, but he takes her to his home and, as his mother and sister are away, lends her his sister's gowns.

For a week this continues, and the lady retains her chastity, but on the last night, as the clock strikes midnight, she hesitates about going, and they go into a clinch. The next scene is morning and they're coming back from the minister's.

He tells her that as mother and sister will be away a month, they'll spend the honeymoon in the maternal mansion. Mother and sister walk in unexpectedly and the girl, Linnie, is driven out. Then the son goes in pursuit. A violent rainstorm is on. Driving after her in his car, he skids and knocks her unconscious. She is taken to the hospital and given up for dead, while his brain snaps and he's sent away.

But she recovers, and many months later, she is a Broadway dance star in a "class" cabaret and caring for her child. Then the rich family put her through a series of frame-ups to get possession of the child, each of which fails, and the husband finally comes back and finds her.

In all this latter section Louise Fazenda and T. Roy Barnes figure as a comedy nurse maid and janitor, in an apartment house, getting plenty of laughs. Virginia Valli and Norman Kerry have the leading roles and both do well, particularly Miss Valli, who works quietly, but effectively. The late Kate Lester has the rich mother part, while George Fawcett plays a political scoundrel used in the frame-ups to secure the child.

A particularly good piece of direction is apparent where the nurse girl is chasing a woman who has abducted the baby. The scene is laid in two elevators, side by side, and the shots are made from the top, showing clearly the action of one machine in which the nurse takes the operator from his post and runs it herself.

"The Price of Pleasure" will hardly be a sensational drawing card except in certain localities, but as a program picture it can be recommended heartily.

And nine-tenths of the out-of-towners won't notice the anachronisms of the New York episode.

Sisk.

MY NEIGHBOR'S WIFE

Clifford S. Elfelt production. Story by James Oliver Curwood. All star cast. At Loew's New York, May 21. Running time, 76 minutes.

Jack Newberry............E. K. Lincoln
Florence Keaton............Helen Ferguson
Her Father............Edwards Davis
Alen Allwright............Herbert Rawlinson
Eric Von Greed............Wm. Russell
His Assistant............Wm. Bailey
Camerman............Chester Conklin
The Inventor............Tom Santschi
His Wife............Mildred Harris
Bertie............Douglas Gerard
Kathlyn Jordan............Margaret Loomis
Wm. Jordan............Ralph Faulkner
Wm. Jordan, Jr............Philip de Lacy

A wow for names. Those mentioned in the cast and more besides appear, names that mean a lot to the fans for the picture is one of motion picture life in Hollywood and those named are in the picture for several scenes, while the unnamed ones are in for brief shots. The picture was made so as to look from the names as though it cost a million, but in reality it is one of those independent special tricked into looking big.

The picture has everything except the kitchen stove. It appears as though a James Oliver Curwood short story was taken and placed in the middle of another story written to pad out the original. At that it is a picture that the daily change neighborhood houses can well afford to play, for the names should get them some money.

In the story E. K. Lincoln is a millionaire's son who is trying to pick up the picture game in Los. He is in love with a wealthy girl, but her father wants him to prove himself a business man. So the young man goes out and spends his last nickle on an option on a story. He has made up his mind to make a picture that will bring the film industry out of the infant class, but at the last moment the girl has to appeal to her father to save him from going broke. Father consents and advances $40,000 to make the picture (this one, however, doesn't appear to have cost that) and the boy goes ahead. The engaging of the director and the actors is planned as a satire on a certain extravagant foreign director. Finally, the picture is started and finished and then sold to a releasing company for a good profit.

Action, love and intrigue, together with a bit of burlesquing of the producing end of the industry, all done in good enough fashion to please the average neighborhood audiences.

Fred.

ON PROBATION

William Steiner production. Story by Jack Natteford. Features Edith Thornton. Direction Charles Hutchinson. Running time, 65 mins.

Bruce Winter............Robert Ellis
Judge Winter............Joseph Kilgour
Detective Reilly............Wilfred Lucas
Tom Kincade............Charles Cruz
Nan Miller............Helen Lynch
Dolores Coleman............Betty Francisco
Phil Coleman............Eddie Phillips
Ralph Norton............Lincoln Stedman
Mary Forrest............Edith Thornton

In many respects this story reminds of "Manslaughter." In both tales the heroine is a young girl going the modern jazzy pace and brought to her senses through an automobile accident. In "Manslaughter" the heroine received a jail sentence for killing a motorcycle cop, despite all her influential friends could do. In this picture the girl is placed on probation.

To receive the probation it is necessary for her to secure some one to sign a bond guaranteeing her future behavior. The judge stipulates his son, in love with Mary, cannot sign the bond. After canvassing her friends Mary has to come before the court for sentence without a guarantor. The judge, convinced she has learned a lesson, signs the bond himself.

Events leading up to her trial and conviction are handled convincingly with the exception of the framing of the girl by two of her friends. Dolores Coleman, in love with Mary's sweetheart, and Phil Coleman, in love with Mary, conspire to plant incriminating evidence in the wrecked car after the police have evidently been unsuccessful in pinning the reckless driving charge on her.

The scheming was unconvincing, far-fetched and spoiled an otherwise interesting story of modern life and environment.

Edith Thornton as Mary Forrest and Robert Ellis as Bruce Winter, her sweetheart, were excellent. Miss Thornton is a dark beauty who can act, and should have a bright future in pictures. She has youth and the other attributes for screen success.

The picture on the whole is a good average program bet for the second-run houses. It has been generously produced and well directed. Joseph Kilgour as Judge Winter and Wilfred Lucas as Detective Reilly also deserve brackets.

Con.

VIRTUE'S REVOLT

William Steiner Production, released in the independent market, starring Edith Thornton. Story and adaptation by Frederic Chapin. Shown at the Stanley, New York, May 21. Running time, 60 minutes.

Streisa Cane............Edith Thornton
Bertram Winthrope............Crauford Kent
Tom Powers............Charles Cruz
Ruth Cane............Betty Morrissey
Mrs. Cane............Florence Lee
Elton Marbridge............Edward Phillips
Steve Marbridge............Niles Welch
Prudence Marbridge............Doris Dare

Melodrama of the stage and society designed for the smaller houses where it will suffice to entertain. For the average type of small neighborhood house the picture should get a little money. It is better than the average of this type released usually in the independent field.

It has a couple of names, Niles Welchand Crauford Kent. These two players are so much better than the balance of the cast there is no comparison.

The story is trite and stereotyped. It is the tale of a struggling stock ingenue trying to break in on Broadway with the usual (motion picture) proposition of a manager offering to trade her a starring role—providing. That's old stuff and it doesn't go as far as the insiders know, but possibly for the houses where this picture plays it will be swallowed whole and thought great stuff. The girl gets the role honestly and is finally saved from what might have been an ugly situation in the apartment of the manager by the hero.

No credit given to the director, just as well for no one could give him any credit for the way he handled this one. The sets are good and there seems to be some "cut ins" that show a house packed with people viewing a theatrical performance. They are pretty well matched up.

Edith Thornton who plays the lead doesn't mean a thing to the box office or on the screen.

Fred.

Unrestrained Youth

Lee-Bradford production featuring Brandon Tynan. Directed by Joseph Levering. At the Stanley, New York, one day (May 25). About 75 minutes.

John Powers............Brandon Tynan
Jamie Powers............Gardner James
Mary Powers............Mildred Arden
Mrs. Powers, Sr............Blanche Davenport
Fred Whitney............John Hopkins
Arthur Blake............Deek Reynolds
Betty Brown............Alice Mann
Mrs. Brown............Helen Lindroth
Jerry Powers............C. H. Keefe
Stewart Ransom............Charles McDonald
Randolph Smith............Thomas Brooks

A few deft directorial touches lift this feature in spots to fair entertainment values. The story, sordid, grim and far from original, manages to be moderately gripping because of its tragic theme. The photography, particularly as to lighting and tinting, is a decade behind present-day standards.

The title is misleading, as none of the usual flapper age rebellion and hilarity enters into it. Two murders, an accidental death and still another one from a broken heart, as well as insanity, embezzlement, forgery, ice-water poisoning, fatal train smashes and 20-year prison stretches are the pleasant subjects dealt with.

John Powers' younger brother Jamie has been injured in early childhood so that his brain is impaired and the former holds himself responsible for the mishap. The boy whose venomous temper caused the misfortune is Fred Whitney, who grows to manhood still hating the Powers brothers. His chance comes to frame Jamie in an embezzlement scandal and John goes to prison to shield the youngster. The rest of the film stretches over a period of 20 years.

Mr. Tynan, an actor in pictures and out, is handicapped as a younger man by too many close-ups with poor make-up. The rest of the cast, almost entirely unfamiliar, is hardly satisfactory, except for Blanche Davenport, Deek Reynolds and C. H. Keefe.

The sombre and at times ugly subject matter does not speak well for the box office hopes and the title is clumsy as well. Tynan may draw in spots, but at the Stanley the billing was only "All-star cast."

THE MEDDLER

Universal western, starring William Desmond. Story by Miles Overholt, adapted by Isadore Bernstein. Directed by Arthur Rosson. Shown at Loew's, New York, May 22, on double feature bill with a Hoot Gibson western. Running time 58 minutes.

Richard Gilmore............William Desmond
Gloria Canfield............Dolores Rousay
Dorothy Parkhurst............Claire Anderson
Bud Myers............Albert J. Smith
Capt. Forsythe............Donald Hotswell
Secretary............George Grandee

Rather a wishy-washy Western tame from the beginning. While it gives William Desmond a chance to appear as a city feller and as a bold, bad stick-up guy of the wilds, there is little about the picture that is going to make audiences, except those frequenting the very cheapest admission houses.

Desmond plays a society chap who takes to the wilds and begins a sort of modern Robin Hood existence because he has been jilted. He carries a secretary, a sort of a Margarie guy, with him. There are all sorts of rewards offered for him in his guise as "The Meddler," which title is bestowed upon him after his first few hold-ups, but the sheriff never catches up with him.

As a result of his sticking-up of a stage coach he meets a girl of the plains whom he finally woos and weds.

A couple of good fights and some corking riding stuff, but the picture falls above anything other than a double feature bill.

Fred.

TEN YEARS

Gerson production distributed by Renown Productions, Inc., directed by Duke Worne, written by Arthur Hoerl and photographed by Rollia C. Price. Stars Richard Holt, with Hazel Keener, Joseph W. Girard and Vic Potel also in the cast. At the Stanley, New York (one day), May 19. Runs about 55 minutes.

Granting it is an independent film, produced with a minimum expense and aimed at the dullest class of picturegoers, "Ten Years" is inexcusably puerile and slovenly. Not in several years has such a bad job of continuity been seen, at times it seeming as though the filmage has been wrongly pieced together, so jerky and disconnected is the action.

The star is Richard Holt, a stunter, and one of the weakest of all his type. Particularly unconvincing as an actor, he has neither the grace, strength or agility to perform certain athletic feats that make the other stunt stars at least bearable.

However, it's not all Holt's fault, as the story, one of those things about a rich man's lounge lizard son, an actress and a fake abduction, about takes the cake for silliness and lack of coherence.

The photography is not as bad as the rest, which means the cast, direction, titles and general atmosphere. Such bits as "Are you an expert swimmer?" Yes, I rowed on the Yale crew" (an almost perfect example of what the student of logic calls *non sequitur*) are characteristic of the entire picture.

The Stanley audience looked bored most of the time and laughed once or twice in the wrong places. The film is many miles under even this house's cheap standard.

Foreign Films

THE BLACKGUARD

London, April 21.

With an Albert Hall premiere this eagerly looked for British picture turns out to be carrying the UFA brand mark. Its composition consists of a British producer, Graham Cutts; an American "star," Jane Novak; one English actor, Frank Stanmore, and a full German supporting cast.

The script is exceedingly sordid and typically Teutonic. Although carrying the British Board of Film Censors' "Universal" certificate, in places it is distinctly nasty without being daring. The producer who up to now has adhered to following the ordinary American feature productions has now gone over to the German idea of realism coupled with gigantic and, in some cases, almost unnatural settings. The result is that he has a picture which, whether it proves a showman's proposition or not, is miles above the average production.

The story tells how a ragged boy, Michael, has a passion for music. One day this is noticed by an artist who, struck with the boy's beauty, promises him a violin if he will sit for a picture. Later the artist engages a once famous violinist, Levenski, to teach the boy.

Michael grows to adolescence and one night is struck down by his drunken grandmother. In his insensibility he dreams he climbs a great stairway (a wonderful scene), at the top of which sits the God of Music, Maliol. The god promises him fame as a musician, but he must love nothing but his art. Awaking, Michael finds a sum of money dropped by a drunken customer of his grandmother's, and thinks it is a direct gift from the god to help him.

The years roll on, and in manhood he becomes irresistible to women. Princesses fall for him almost on introduction and a famous poetess shoots herself because he refuses her obvious desire to become his mistress. He, however, loves the princess, and when revolution breaks out in her country he discovers the revolutionaries' leader is his old music master and saves her. Later, when she is beggared, the two of them provide the orthodox finale.

The story is ordinary and in places banal. It is the production and the acting which carry the feature through. Cutts has so many brilliantly staged scenes, crowds, rioting, fashionable mobs in theatres, etc., that it is almost impossible to differentiate, and the general excellence of his work makes it the more remarkable that his imaginative scenes should be so weak.

During the picture there is an effect which has never been bettered. It occurs at the hero's big concert when the perfectly synchronized orchestral accompaniment of the violin on the screen is followed by the enthusiasm of the screen audience. As it applauded a wonderfully well placed claque carried on the applause, giving remarkable power to the scene.

The acting is excellent. Jane Novak, with the most difficult role, is capital as the Princess. Walter Rilla, who plays Michael in manhood, is very good, but he and every other member of the cast is overshadowed by Martin Hertzberg as the boy, Michael. Whatever be the future of this picture there can be no doubt as to its value as a proof of what international co-operation can do. Presented by Michael Balcon it is being handled by W. & F.

Gore.

Midsummernight's Dream

Berlin, April 22.

A film around this fantastic lyric comedy by Shakespeare would seem to be a most difficult and hazardous enterprise, but, on the whole, the attempt is successful under the direction of Hans Neumann. And not only an artistic but also a financial success as the Nollendorf Platz theatre has been doing turnaway business for the past six weeks.

The beginning of the picture is by far the best, since here the scenario writer, Hans Behrendt, does not have to hold to a stage plot but can invent situations suitable to the film. He does so and the battle scenes between the Greeks and the female Amazon soldiers are broad comedy. Later, the scenes of the fairies in the forest and the troupe of amateur actors fall down in comparison.

The big cast contains many expensive names but the best performances were not always given by the stars. Werner Krauss, as Bottom, was a good deal of a disappointment. Good work, however, was done by Ruth Weyher, Ernst Gronau, Valeska Gert and Hans Albers.

Almost the best part of the evening is the music arranged and composed for the film by Hans May and played by Eric Borchard's American jazz band, strengthened by a few string instruments. It marks a real advance in scores for accompanying comedy pictures. At one moment Wagner is being seriously interpreted and the next the latest from "Tin Pan Alley." Often the music secured an outright laugh and applause for itself alone. And how the boys did play it, the classical as well as the bluest of the blue. When they got hot they just tore the roof off the joint.

Trask.

Squire of Long Hadley

London, May 18.

The influence of H. C. Hoagland, the American chief of the Stoll Film Co., was very evident at the trade showing of the firm's latest picture at the Coliseum. Despite Sunday night there was no overcrowding in the audience and the screening started punctually. Both these things mark progress where British trade shows are concerned.

The present feature is frank melodrama, very well done, with plenty of comedy and sensational incident. An utter absence of tooth-grinding by the villain and saintliness by the hero. The production work has never been better in a British picture, and the big thrill, in which hero and heroine are practically under the wheels of an express train has never been excelled for realism. This scene should make "The Squire of Long Hadley" anywhere.

Sport has much to do with the story, and here again the work is far above the average, hunting and hunt cup races being cut into the story with fine effect and well done. All these sporting scenes, and there are many, could be used with great effect in any feature of English country life. The interiors are very good, with no relationship to the showrooms of furniture stories, and the exteriors are of genuine beauty without showing any signs of Christmas card artificiality.

The acting is generally very good. Brian Aherne, new Stoll star, is somewhat miscast as Jim. He has no ruggedness and is too youthful for the Marjorie of Marjorie Hume. She, while playing admirably without having any scene calling for histrionic power, is mature beside the gawkishness of her hero. G. H. Mulcaster gives a fine, restrained study of the villainous cousin. Eileen Dannis, as the betrayed girl, Lucy, does well. An exchange in the principal women roles would have been to the picture's advantage.

Gore.

THE DESERT FLOWER

First National production of Don Mullally's stage play of last season. Adapted to the screen by June Mathis and directed by Irving Cummings. Colleen Moore starred. At the Strand, New York, June 1 week. Running time, 70 minutes.

Maggie Fortune	Colleen Moore
Rance Conway	Lloyd Hughes
Mrs. McQuade	Kate Price
Jose Lee	Gene Corrado
Dizzy	Fred Warren
Mike Dyer	Frank Brownlee
Inga Hulverson	Isabelle Keith
Flozella	Ann May Walthal
Jack Royal	William Norton Bailey
Mr. McQuade	Monte Collins
Fay Knight	Edna Gregory

Al Woods opened this show in Baltimore last winter under the title of "Maggie." It was brutally panned. He brought it to New York, and under the title of "The Desert Flower" the reviewers here hammered it so hard that four weeks were enough.

Now it has come to town in film form, and the daily reviewers jumped it with decisive firmness. And yet Monday night's audience laughed its head off. There was plenty to laugh at, for Colleen Moore has here achieved probably her greatest personal triumph insomuch as she is 90 percent of the film. The rest is in interesting and humorous local color.

The story is that of an orphan girl in the west, living with a stepfather in a freight car (he is section boss on a railroad), tending her baby sister and running around like a wild arab. One day a young tramp, a boy whose proficiency at drinking was the result of honest practice, straightens up for a while, becomes interested in her and teaches her the rudimentary things of an education. But he gets fired and goes his way after promising the girl he will try to straighten himself out.

The girl, meantime, finds her stepfather has designs on her, so she packs out with the baby sister and goes to a nearby dance hall and there obtains work.

The young tramp comes back here to see her and he nearly made good, but after cleaning up money went on the loose again. Under protestation she grub-stakes him once more, and finally he wins out. The suspense and high point of the play is where the stepfather comes after her and where a Mexican friend shoots him sufficiently to make him drop. At that minute the sweetheart comes in and assumes the blame. The girl also assumes the blame before the sheriff, and while the informal query is still on the Mex who did the shooting walks in and gives himself up.

Then the sheriff, seeing how things stood, bit off a chaw of tobacco and said it looked to him like a clear case of suicide.

The finale is that the young tramp is revealed as the erring son of a railroad president, and so he marries the girl who brought him around and they start the trip back east in a private car.

It is apparent that the yarn is fanciful and far-fetched, but it is continually interesting because of Miss Moore, who gives an impish performance, always delightful. She handles the drama just as capably and has a thousand comedy tricks in her little bag. Kate Price as a fat Irish woman also gets a flock of laughs, while Lloyd Hughes makes an acceptable hero. Everybody else is capable and the direction has been well handled in this instance.

"The Desert Flower" is a good first-run picture. The heat is going to bump it in New York this week from the looks of the start-off, but its entertainment values and laughing qualities should guarantee it welcome reception by picture audiences. As a program feature for the daily changes and combination houses it fits like the paper on the wall.

Sisk.

LITTLE FRENCH GIRL

Famous Players production of Anne Douglas Sedgewick's novel of same name. Screen adaptation made by John Russell. Directed by Herbert Brenon, with Alice Joyce, Neil Hamilton, Esther Ralston and Mary Brian featured. At the Rivoli, New York, May 31 week. Running time, 75 minstes.

Mme. Vervier	Alice Joyce
Alix Vervier	Mary Brian
Giles Bradley	Neil Hamilton
Toppie Westmacott	Esther Ralston
Owen Bradley	Anthony Jowitt
Mother Bradley	Jane Jennings
Ruth Bradley	Mildred Ryan
Jerry Hamble	Maurice Cannon
Lady Mary Hamble	Maude Turner Gordon
Andre Valenbois	Paul Doucet
Mme. Dumont	Julia Hurley
DeMaubert	Mario Majeroni

The novel from which this film was made has had a wide sale and has also received much favorable discussion and criticism. Primarily it was a character study of a lovely little girl, Alix Vervier, and her mother, a lady whose loves were always gentlemen but not always wise.

The plot starts off with the war days, when Capt. Owen Bradley spent his leave in Paris with Mme. Vervier, and of how he loved her. His Anglo-Saxon ideals pictured love as something staple, true and fine, while Mme. Vervier and her French ideals pictured it as a transient pleasure, made for a few moments. Owen was killed in the war, and his brother Giles, holding the dying man in his arms, promised that Mme. Vervier's daughter, Alix, should have the careful upbringing in an English country home.

So Alix goes to England and lives, but meantime Giles, himself a fine young man of strict ideals, discovered Mme. Vervier's nature. Mme. Vervier was not an adventuress nor was she a vampire, but simply a beautiful woman with whom men fell in love and in whose nature was the desire to reciprocate their affection. She wanted Alix to be different and suggested that Giles marry her. It got to the point where Jerry Hamble, of a noble family, proposed and was accepted. Giles at that time had hopes of marrying Toppie Westmacott, daughter of a minister and beloved by his dead brother.

Giles' dream faded and Toppie found peace in a convent, while an old crone from France ruined the chances of Alix by telling inside stuff on her mother. Alix rejoined her mother, and it was sometime later in Venice that Giles knew he loved her.

The story is excellent and while not strictly faithful to the book, is fine movie material and at all times is well played by a finely balanced cast. Alice Joyce is particularly fine as Mme. Vervier, while Neil Hamilton and Paul Doucet turn in impersonations as the hero and parasite that are worthy of high ranking. Mary Brian is sweet and appealing as Alix. Brenon's direction is even and sure, while the technical work is as usual—unbeatable. Some of the exterior scenes are beautiful.

Although "The Little French Girl" is a good picture on its own, its worth to the exhibitor depends principally on the names in the cast, for no book yet has ever circulated this country to the extent of penetrating all of the country towns. It looks like the film will be an excellent program picture but may be a first run disappointment. Exploitation can help it, but it should not be of the sensational or sexy variety. This is a well considered picture and any advertising connected with it should be of the same type.   *Sisk.*

THE RAINBOW TRAIL

William Fox production starring Tom Mix and "Tony." From the Zane Grey story, directed by Lynn Reynolds. Shown at the Piccadilly, N. Y., week May 30, 1925. Running time, 57 minutes.

John Shefford	Tom Mix
Fay Larkin	Anne Cornwall
Jake Willets	George Bancroft
Joe Lake	Lucien Littlefield
Beasley Willets	Mark Hamilton
Bess Erne	Vivian Oakland
Nas Ta Bega	Steve Clemente
Venters	Tom Delmar
Shadd	Fred De Silva
Jane	Carol Halloway
Anne	Diana Miller

A wow of an action western that has Tom Mix doing all sorts of stunts to keep the audience on the edge of their seats. It is one of the best action westerns even this star has turned out. In this one Mix qualifies as a "ridin' fool" and in addition he slips over athletics containing any number of thrills. The story is not one of the best Zane Grey has turned out, but serves its purpose in giving the king of western stars a role that permits him to put Tony through a flock of steps for the benefit of his admirers.

Mix as John Shefford is trailing the west to seek an uncle, his wife and their ward, who have been lost for a number of years. He saves the squaw of an Indian from an attack by a half-breed and thus wins the gratitude of the brave. At the same time he hears the story of an attack on his uncle and the manner in which the latter frustrated a group of outlaws and in doing so blocked the only entrance to a valley hemming his family behind a wall of rock.

Mix in the role of rescuer braves an outlaw settlement, battles the chief to a finish, saves the girl, who is his uncle's ward grown to womanhood, and finally beats off the whole gang, rescuing both his aunt and uncle as well as the girl.

The picture starts with an Indian attack on the wagon of a lone prospector and his family, with Mix riding to their rescue and the routing of the redskins. From that point on there is no letup to the action, with Mix always in the forefront. Mix in addition to his riding, shooting and hand-to-hand battling, does some very strenuous rope climbing to get out of the valley where the outlaws have marooned him after he rescued his uncle and aunt. Hand over hand up a rope in the face of a cliff that seems to be a sheer drop of half a mile the cowboy athlete goes. At the top he wades into a bunch of outlaws and licks them all over again.

Lucien Littlefield as a pack herder got laughs with frequent comedy bits. Playing opposite Mix was Anne Cornwall, who did not seem to score particularly in this role.

It is a corking action western and it should get a lot of money with the Mix name.   *Fred.*

PARISIAN NIGHTS

F. B. O. release presented by Gothic Pictures. Original story by Emil Frost, adapted by Kennedy Myton, directed by Al Santell. Starring Elaine Hammerstein. At the Capitol, N. Y., May 31. Running time, 67 minutes.

Adele	Elaine Hammerstein
Jacques	Gaston Glass
Jean	Lou Tellegen
Fontaine	Wm. J. Kelly
Pierre	Boris Karloff
Marie	Renee Adoree

Must have been a powerful reason for this picture ever getting a Broadway pre-release run in the Capitol. Maybe the Capitol is hard put to find product that is worthy of showing in that house other than the pictures Metro-Goldwyn release, and the latter organization, it is said, is out of all product now. That may be the truth, for Vitagraph has a picture scheduled for the house next week.

But even at that there surely must have been some pictures floating around the independent market better than "Parisian Nights."

"Parisian Nights" is the kind of a picture that is played seriously and the audiences laugh at it. With it at the Capitol it will be interesting to watch just how far the receipts of that house flop for the current week. Seemingly it would be easy to predict that the house will have one of the worst weeks at the box office it has had in a long, long time.

"Parisian Nights" is just another one of those Paris underworld stories without any great thrill, a sustaining interest that will hold the audience. There are two rival gangs of apaches, a wealthy American girl who is the rage of the artistic set because of her ability in sculpture and as a hostess.

Naturally there are two gang leaders, one of whom is Lou Tellegen. He with a couple of companions enter the house of the American and rob her, the leader's two companions escape when the police come in and the American girl saves Tellegen from arrest by declaring he is her model. She fell and fell hard when he walked into the scene. She follows him to his retreat and finally beguiles him into posing for her. They fall in love with each other, but not until one of the girls of the dive decides the American can't have him because he's "her man," and pulls a double cross on her lover. In the end, however, the two are clinched for the final fade-out, watching the gangsters' retreat going up in flames after the chief of police has sent for a couple of .75 guns to knock the place to pieces. Pretty tough when the cops have to get the artillery out to clean up 10 crooks.

Elaine Hammerstein plays the young American. She walks through the role. Renee Adoree walked away with everything else in the way of honors in acting as the little tough underworld character. Gaston Glass was stabbed to death early in the picture, just as well.

"Parisian Nights" is an out and out meller intended to play to cheap audiences.   *Fred.*

IF MARRIAGE FAILS

F. B. O. production made and written by C. Gardner Sullivan. Directed by John Ince and featuring Jacqueline Logan and Clive Brook. At the Colony, New York, May 31 week. Running time, 70 minutes.

Nadia	Jacqueline Logan
Eleanor Woodbury	Belle Bennett
Joseph Woodbury	Clive Brook
Dr. Mallini	Jean Hersholt
Lisa	Mathilde Comont
Mrs. Loring	Cissy Fitzgerald

Another of that series of 12 which F. B. O. is entering as first-run opposition to the world. It doesn't nearly stand up.

The story is called by the press agent as a "tremendous drama," while in actuality it is hackneyed and so monorail in its plot that it is hard to believe that Gardner Sullivan, one of the best scenarists in pictures, would tag his name to it as author.

Eleanor Woodbury is a rich woman of the silly kind, while her husband, Joe, is a wealthy man of intelligence. They are as mismated as beer and champagne in the same glass, but are sticking it out for appearances. Into the life of Joe comes Nadia, a smart little Italian girl, who has rigged herself up a fortune telling place, and has worked the old hocus-pocus so well that society is at her feet. Without conflict, Woodbury's love develops for her, while the wife is resentful merely because of the hurt to her pride. The windup is that he arranges to divorce the wife and marry the other woman.

It is a stupid and unoriginal story, told and retold a thousand times, repeated in every legend of every land, but rehashed here without attractive trimmings.

Jacqueline Logan is the Italian girl, Clive Brook the husband, and Belle Bennett the wife. All give good performances. Although Miss Bennett has an extremely disagreeable role, her work stands out. A messy-looking blonde wig detracted. Miss Logan is nice to look at, but acts like she might be in the throes of a St. Vitus contest. Brooks, reliable, is suave and manly.

The production end is fairly well handled and there are some good comedy scenes. But notwithstanding the good cast, this film is apparently a cluck, for it doesn't entertain.

Beggar on Horseback

Famous Players production made from the play by George S. Kaufman and Marc Connelly. Adapted to the screen by Walter Wood and Anthony Coldeway. Directed by James Cruze. Opened at the Criterion, New York, June 5, at $1.65 top on twice daily basis. Running time, 90 minutes.

Neil McRae	Edward Everett Horton
Cynthia Mason	Esther Ralston
Frederick Cady	Erwin Connelly
Mrs. Frederick Cady	Ethel Wales
Gladys Cady	Gertrude Short
Homer Cady	James Mason
The Prince	Theodore Kosloff
The Princess	Betty Compson
Dr. Rice	Frederick Sullivan

"Beggar on Horseback" is a fine production made with much intelligence and insight, yet for all James Cruze's skill, all the work of a fine cast, the effect of fanciful settings and even the fame of the play, the picture is miles over the heads of picture audiences. So the forecast is that like "The Golem" and "The Last Laugh," both futuristic in their manner of treatment, "Beggar on Horseback" will prove a poor draw even for the first runs. That excepts, however, the cities wherein the play made a hit.

George Kaufman and Marc Connelly got their idea from a German play and developed it so that "Beggar on Horseback" is a satire at the standardized methods of business and the pettiness of some of our big business men. It derides their lack of the aesthetic, lack of taste and the importance they attach to money. In New York, where many of the aesthetic are able to get by on the post, it found big success, but out in the country at large, where the aesthetic pose doesn't mean anything, it didn't hold up.

Neil McRae is a composer, struggling to get along, and while he works on his symphony he orchestrates rag-time stuff for the Tin Pan Alley publishers. The girl across the hall, Cynthia Mason, shares his ambition to succeed, while his music pupil, Gladys Cady, is the daughter of a newly rich man whose idea of wealth is to show it off externally. The proposition is made to Neil by his friends that he marry Gladys and so live in luxury. Then he falls asleep and dreams. First he sees the Cady home, a terrific mansion with scores of butlers. He sees everything in an exaggerated form, for Mrs. Cady, partial to a rocking chair, is pictured as being strapped to one even when she walks, while the loud golf clothes of Mr. Cady become burlesque grotesqueries. His persistent habit of telephoning is enlarged to the point where he speaks into tremendous instruments. The Cady women are pictured with dollar-mark dresses, while their relatives are a hideous looking bunch. Between the musical soul of Neil and the vapid souls of the Cadys there is no bond, and after poking fun at the red tape of Cady's business, his board of directors, etc., Neil kills the family.

He is brought up for trial before a judge who smokes three-foot cigars and before a jury sombrely clad in undertaker's clothes. Asking that his case be taken to a higher court, the judge immediately applies the juice and his bench rises several feet for a laugh. The Cadys are present at his trial for accomplishing their deaths, and his defense is that they made him lose out on his symphony. Stating that he will play it, he finds it has been destroyed, so instead he plays a pantomime which he and Cynthia wrote, "A Kiss in Xanadu."

On the stage it was one of the loveliest things imaginable, but screened it is flat and without even the delicate punch which characterized Winthrop Ames' presentation. But Neil is convicted and forced to serve in Cady's factory, where he was jailed and made to write jazz songs perpetually. Here with other unfortunates he revolts and is being cut up by a thousand knives when he awakens and finds

Cynthia stroking his head. It was all a nightmare and ends happily.

Horton as McRae is fine; Miss Wales as Mrs. Cady ditto, while everyone else was ideally cast. The settings can't be given too much praise, for they are original and beautiful as well as inspiring at times. That same praise goes for all the technical work and the direction, in fact, for everything about the film but its general effect. For its great fault is that the mass of people will not appreciate it, and there's no reason why they should, for its theme is a vain sop to aesthetes and those who would be. They'll be interested in the big production and may be the exploitation which the film affords will draw some, but the absence of stars and Cruze's recent flop with "Welcome Home" will tend to diminish whatever potency his name might have had.

The exhibitor can rely on "Beggar on Horseback" as an elaborate and well made film, but he will know his clientele before playing it up heavily. For there will be spots where it may hit, but for every one where it hits there will be 20 where it won't.

It's a great artistic success and a commercial failure, from the present outlook and the discouraging New York start. *Sisk.*

THE WHITE MONKEY

First National presentation of the Galsworthy novel. Made by Sawyer-Lubin, with Barbara LaMarr starred and Thomas Holding featured. Directed by Phil Rosen. At the Colony June 8 week. Running time, 70 minutes.

Fleur Forsyte	Barbara LaMarr
Michael Mont	Thomas Holding
Wilfrid Desert	Henry Victor
Soames Forsyte	George Marion
Ethelbert Danby	Colin Campbell
Tony Bicket	Charles Emmett Mack
Victorine	Flora LeBreton
Bill Hawkes	Tamany Young

This picture version of the Galsworthy novel is faithful, concise and well knitted together. Phil Rosen's direction has shown itself in many nice touches. That the whole thing is a sensible discussion on right living without the phrase being used is patent, although the method of arguing this involves a trace of the sexy now and then. But there's nothing offensive and much commendable.

The story is of Fleur Forsyte, who marries Michael Mont. She is a frivolous woman who cavorts about with the men quite a bit more than her stolid husband likes to see. Her father, Soames Forsyte, doesn't care much for it, either. She becomes involved with a decadent artist, but finally patches things up and gets around to the happy ending.

Also in the plot is Tony Bicket, formerly of Mont's publishing house, but discharged. The fortitude of his wife in helping him through misfortune takes her to the artist, for whom she poses in the nude to earn money for their emigration to Australia. Tony gets het up when he finds out about it, but trusts his wife, and they, too, sail away happily. An excellent comedy role, Bill Hawkes, is embodied in the Bicket episodes.

Miss LaMarr is the Fleur of the film and for the LaMarr fans may be okeh. The individual hits are made principally by Tamany Young, who goes great in some comedy scenes, while George Marion, as Fleur's father, clicks. Flora LeBreton, as Tony's wife, looks as welcome as rain in the desert. These individual performances help the film tremendously.

"The White Monkey" as a book was a great seller, probably the biggest John Galsworthy has turned out. To the credit of the film makers it may be said that their scenario hasn't tried to improve on Galsworthy. The title, incidentally, comes from a painting wherein a monkey is disclosed squeezing the juice from an orange and scattering the rinds.

This one is all right on the strength of the book and the tone of the picture, for which Rosen's excellent direction is probably responsible. *Sisk.*

SILENT SANDERSON

Hunt Stromberg production released by Producers Distributing Corp., starring Harry Carey. Story by Kate Corbaley. Directed by Scott R. Dunlap. Photographed by Sol Polito. At the Cameo, New York, week June 7. Runs about 58 minutes.

Joel Parsons (Silent Sanderson)	Harry Carey
Judith Benson	Trilby Clark
Jim Downing	John Miljan
Silver Smith	Stanton Heck
Art Parsons	Gardner James
Single Tooth Wilson	Sheldon Lewis

About a year ago Harry Carey, whose days as a box-office factor were considered numbered by many, made a sensational come-back with "Tiger Thompson," and since then he has again become important among Western stars. So much so that when P. D. C. leased the little Cameo for 10 weeks his new production "Silent Sanderson" was chosen for the first week.

As a feature for a house usually regarded of strictly first-run caliber there may be some doubt as to the wisdom of the choice, particularly in New York City. But as a very superior Western film for the program houses "Silent Sanderson" is dead-on. The word "Western" is used advisedly, as more than half the action transpires in Alaska, with the remainder in Texas, and there is a minimum of riding, pistol shooting, cattle herding and other cowboy stuff. However, the story and atmosphere most nearly suggest that category of picture, and Carey himself can hardly be dissociated from the ranks of Western stars.

The story holds little that is original, but manages, in spite of its triteness, to get away from the conventional incidents of Western life as portrayed usually on the screen. The heroine, for instance, instead of being an angelic, saccharine little moron, as is customary, is a faithless, weak-willed but always interesting character. Mild sex stuff, in fact, plays more of a part in the plot than ordinarily in pictures of this sort, a circumstance that is rather more advantageous than otherwise.

The final scenes introduce an Alaskan blizzard with the hero performing the miracle of the wolves by getting away almost unharmed after having been attacked by a pack of them. These shots are adequately exciting, but the photography is not clear enough to provide room for guesses as to whether the savage beasts are really flesh and blood or merely mechanical contrivances. They look human, however.

For a Western, the entire film has been produced with a great deal of care and taste. The direction is always of high imaginative grade and the photography artistic and clear. Carey's performance is one of strength and sincerity, while the new leading woman, Trilby Clark; the heavy, John Miljan, and the balance of the cast are exceptionally capable. The one serious fault is the almost total absence of comic byplay.

The film will not set 42nd street afire, but it should gross far from the lowest week the Cameo has had and it more firmly than ever secures Carey's place with Hoot Gibson and Buck Jones on the rung that comes just below that occupied exclusively and majestically by the opulent Mr. Mix.

WILDFIRE

Distinctive Pictures Corp. production, bearing the Vitagraph trade-mark. Produced under personal supervision of Albert E. Smith. Aileen Pringle starred in this picture, shown as the feature at the Capitol, New York, week June 7.

Although all Vitagraph pictures have been taken over by Warner Bros., their name did not appear in any of the Capitol billing. The picture was adapted from story by George V. Hobart and George Broadhurst. Directed by T. Hayes Hunter. Reviewed at the Capitol June 8 week. Time of running, 55 minutes.

Claire Barrington	Aileen Pringle
Myrtle Barrington	Edna Murphy
Garrison	Holmes Herbert
Dr. Woodhurst	Edmund Breese
Marie	Mary Thurman
Ralph Woodhurst	Antrim Short
Matt Donovan	Tom Blake
John Duffy	Lawford Davidson
Bud	Will Archie
Hortense	Edna Morton
Chappie Raster	Arthur Bryson
Valet	Robert Billoups

The story of "Wildfire," made famous by the stage, has been done in pictures before and is about as familiar to the schoolboys as Paul Revere's historic ride. This Vita at best is a feature that cannot stand a run in the big cities, yet can go into the neighborhoods and give general satisfaction.

There are some noteworthy sections. Director Hunter at times did himself proud, but the story is also known to the news reels and lacks the big punch romantically.

The horse race was exceptionally well done. The picture sags off after the race and just about simmers down to the dull and commonplace finishes seen in some of the independents.

A modern touch was given the play by showing a brief overseas war scene. Some fine photography and some of the scenes between Blake and Miss Pringle were faultlessly cameraed. That stable fire scene took up more celluloid than anything else.

The Vita company went south for the picture and this helped in a great measure for some beautiful backgrounds. *Mark.*

EVE'S SECRET

Famous Players production, adapted from the play, "The Moonflower," which Zoe Akins adapted here from the original by Lajos Biro. Screen play by Adelaide Heilbron, and directed by Clarence Badger. Betty Compson and Jack Holt starred. At the Rialto, New York, week June 7. Running time, 72 minutes.

Eve	Betty Compson
Duke of Poltava	Jack Holt
Pierre	William Collier, Jr.
Duchess	Vera Lewis
Baron	Lionel Belmore
Prince Boris	Mario Carillo

Well-made picture is this and well cast. But its story is trivial. Except for the performances of its stars and Willie Collier, Jr., it holds little stuff calculated to intrigue any man's box office customers.

A peasant girl is noticed by a duke who has gotten tired of the women of his own set. He determines to marry her and sends her to Paris to learn duchessing. When she returns and they go, chaperoned and not married to a resort, she is so luscious looking all the men fall hard.

The Duke has a reputation as a hard guy, and one look from him sets them scattering. Into the resort comes Pierre, once a tailor in the peasant girl's town, but now wealthy because of breaking the roulette bank regularly. He of them all carries on a little affair with the girl, innocent, but enough to make the titled one sore. They pull a duel.

It turns out the Duke, because he really loves the girl, gets a break.

Just what "Eve's Secret" was is as deep a mystery as the disappearance of inch-thick veal cutlets from the restaurants.

Both Miss Compson and Mr. Holt turn in nice performances, while Willie Collier was an able second. The rest of the cast was somewhat below the standard, although the director did well with his material. The feature of this film is its fine exteriors, some of which are beautiful. So it looks like the location man is the real hero of it all.

For the daily change houses where the stars may get them in, "Eve's Secret" may be suitable, but in the first runs it is weak and undistinguished. *Sisk.*

I'LL SHOW YOU THE TOWN

A Universal-Jewel starring Reginald Denny. Story by Elmer Davis. Directed by Harry Pollard. Shown at the Strand, New York, week June 7, 1925. Running time, 78 minutes.

Alec Deupree	Reginald Denny
Hazel Deeming	Marion Nixon
Professor Carlyle McCabe	Edward Kimball
Fan Green	Lilyan Tashman
Martin Green	Hayden Stevenson
Agnes Clavenger	Cissy Fitzgerald
Lucille Pemberton	Margaret Livingston
Billie Bonner	Neely Edwards
Professor Goodhue	William A. Carroll
Aunt Sara	Martha Mattox
Edith Torey	Helen Greene
Frank Pemberton	Lionel Braham

This is the very first Universal picture of the regular program variety to play the Strand. Reginald Denny can possibly be credited with the bust-in for the U. people. The picture is a fairly good comedy, but it does not stand up as pre-release quality for a Broadway house, no matter what theatre it may be playing. If the Strand got the picture dirt cheap there may be a reason for it playing the production, but instead it is said that they came across with a good price for it to get it away from Lee Ochs and his independent house. There are some laughs in the picture, but they do not measure up as comedy wallops.

Reginald Denny rather overplays in the role of the hero and he is taking on weight at a rate that if it keeps up will soon make him a type right to succeed the departed Fatty Arbuckle. Harry Pollard, who directed, did not particularly distinguish himself in this picture, and resorted to a lot of in and out of door stuff that was very much to the two-reel comedy flavor.

Cissie Fitzgerald in the role of a rather frolicsome widow managed to put a kick into her scenes; there were also a couple of moments where Lil Tashman looked as though there would be a chance for her in comedy one of these days.

"I'll Show You the Town" isn't Main street material for the big cities.

Fred.

THE VERDICT

Truart production, made by Phil Goldstone and directed by Fred Windemere. All-star cast includes William Collier, Jr., Lou Tellegen, Gertrude Astor, Louise Lorraine, Charles Clary, Josef Swickard, Taylor Holmes, Elliott Dexter, Walter Long, George Fawcett and Gaston Glass. Reviewed at the Broadway, New York, June 8 week. Running time, 60 minutes.

"The Verdict" is one of the best made independent films ever put out in cast, production and direction, and it bears comparison with any of the program releases of the bigger companies. That's going strong, but perusal of those 10 big names up above verifies the statement. A look at the picture shows immediately that the production technically is good, while Fred Windemere's direction is big league. Phil Goldstone made the film, just as he has made hundreds of others for release on the state-right basis. It is said that in making his features he puts anywhere from $60,000 to $75,000 in the film. This one looks to cost all of that and, what's more, its old yarn of the wronged gal, the brave but framed sweetheart, the villain and the last-minute trial and reprieve is well handled.

The sweetheart, Carol (Astor), works as model in an establishment in which the junior partner (Lou Tellegen) likes his ladies pretty and young. Finding that she is to marry the young bookkeeper (Wm. Collier, Jr.), the partner frames him for a shortage in the accounts, and the girl, coaxed to save him, visits the partner's for dinner on the promise that she'll get the papers which hold the evidence against him. At the home he attacks her, but the butler pleads with him not to ruin her as he has others. At this the partner jumps on the butler and canes him, while the butler pulls a gun and does a killing. By this time the hero arrives, and he is picked by the police, shot through a trial and convicted. New evidence is discovered, and his lawyer (Dexter) convinces the judge (Fawcett) that his man is innocent. The butler then confesses and gets off on a self-defense plea.

From the story the exhibitor can decide whether it is suitable to his audiences. There is nothing offensive in "The Verdict," while every performance is good. Collier especially does well, and Tellegen has his best part in a long time. So there's lots of praise for this one, coming from the independents, who are berated as producing a stream of continuously cheap film. In direction, settings, etc., this one can stand with the rest of the current releases, and the story is developed so that it holds considerable power.

True, it's an old story, but it is well done, and Windemere, the director, has inserted enough touches to keep it away from the sordid and conventional.

All okey is the verdict.

Sisk.

Dangerous Innocence

Universal Production of Pamela Wynne's novel, "Ann's An Idiot." Directed by William A. Seiter, with Laura LaPlante and Eugene O'Brien starred. At the Piccadilly, New York, June 6. Running time, 70 mins.

Ann Church	Laura LaPlante
Anthony Seymour	Eugene O'Brien
James Gilchrist	Jean Hersholt
Captain Rome	Alfred Allen
Stewardess	Milla Davenport
Muriel Church	Hedda Hopper
John Church	William Humphrey
Aunt	Martha Mattox

The novel from which this was made, "Ann's An Idiot," achieved a fair sale last year, probably not strong enough to mean anything on the drawing power of this film, but it furnishes an "out" for publicity that the new title would never get. As it stands, "Dangerous Innocence" is a good film, well produced and cast, and interesting.

The plot concerns little Ann Church, who leaves England at 19 to return to her father in Bombay, where he is a Colonial official of the British Empire. On the way over she meets Major Anthony Seymour, of the British army, and falls in love with him. Ann at this time is an old fashioned girl with long hair, high shoes with low heels, middy blouses and big wide hats. The love affair makes her bob the hair and affect other alluring changes.

Through all of them she maintains a sweet innocence. One night, as their ship was going through the Red Sea and its terrifying heat, she left her stateroom in her negligee to sleep on deck, as others were doing. There she saw Major Seymour and stopped to adore him. The Major realized the gossip opportunity this gave, so he carried her back and deposited her in her stateroom. In doing this another man saw him and took the wrong angle.

The next day, the major proposed to her and she accepted. He didn't tell her that once he had been in love with her mother, so when they reached India that reached her ears. She was also told that the captain of the vessel forced Seymour to propose to her to save her reputation. These lies were cleared up for a happy ending.

Miss LaPlante does very excellent work, while Hedda Hopper, in a fat role, also shines. Eugene O'Brien, a steady feminine favorite, is good at all times, while the others threw in good performances.

Of greatest importance seemed the direction of Seiter. He has been making serials for many years and was recognized as probably the best in that line. Now, branching out and handling feature length films, he has ideas of his own that are new and hold water. This film certainly places him in the rank of the dependables who are not freakish, yet who can be noticed every once in a while inserting a novelty which tells.

For the first runs "Dangerous Innocence" qualifies. As a program picture it is thoroughly satisfactory. Matter of fact, its story is about the best Universal has screened in a long time, for, as a general thing, its scenario department seems to lean on the old hokum. This time things are changed a bit and "Ann's An Idiot" has made a good film.

Sisk.

DON Q, SON OF ZORRO

Douglas Fairbanks Production from the novel by K. and Hesketh Prichard entitled "Don Q's Love Story." Adapted by Jack Cunningham and directed by Donald Crisp. Photography by Henry Sharp. Shown at the Globe theatre, N. Y., for eight weeks beginning June 15, 1925. Running time, 110 minutes.

Dolores de Muro	Mary Astor
General de Muro	Jack McDonald
Don Sebastian	Donald Crisp
The Queen	Stella De Lanti
The Archduke	Warner Oland
Don Fabrique	Jean Hersholt
Colonel Matsedo	Albert MacQuarrie
Lola	Lottie Pickford Forrest
Robledo	Charles Stevens
Bernardo	Tote Du Crow
The Duenna	Martha Franklin
The Dancer	Juliette Belanger
Her Admirer	Roy Coulson
Ramon	Enrique Acosta
Don Cesar de Vera / Zorro, his father	Douglas Fairbanks

Douglas Fairbanks is back again, and back with a picture that is Doug at his best, the same old Doug that made "The Mark of Zorro" a real picture. This production, which is in a measure a sequel to that screen masterpiece, is without doubt one of the best that Doug has had in some time from an all around entertainment and picture house standpoint. It is a picture that has been designed for the Fairbanks fans, and as such it should get a world of money.

It isn't destined to hit the legitimate houses as a special attraction, but it is a picture for picture houses and picture audiences. From an out and out picture entertainment standpoint it is a better picture than "The Thief of Bagdad," not as spectacular as the latter by far and by many thousands of dollars, but it is Fairbanks as the public wants Fairbanks.

At the Globe Monday night, where the picture opened for an engagement of eight weeks, a prolog precedes it. It's atmospheric, and for its big punch has Fred Lindsay, the Australian stock whip manipulator, who proved to be a tremendous surprise to the first-night picture audience. His manipulation of the whips brought him round after round of applause, even though the effectiveness of his performance was marred by the limited stage space.

"Don Q" gives Fairbanks a chance to play a double role, as the youthful Don Q and as Zorro the father of the dashing young Californian who is completing his education in Spain. His adventures there form the basis of the picture. He becomes involved with royalty, is accused of the murder of a visiting archduke, feigns suicide, almost loses the girl, but in the end emerges triumphant.

The story is simple enough, but it is the manner that Fairbanks plays the dual roles that carries it to heights. His tricks with the stock whip, his duels with the heavy, his capturing of an escaped mad bull are such as to make the average fan wants to see the picture all over again. That is the real test and "Don Q" stands it 100 percent.

There are a few flash backs to "The Mark of Zorro" in this present picture, and to appreciate how much the public thought of Doug in that one needs but to listen to the applause greeting those scenes.

Mary Astor plays opposite the star. She appears to beautiful advantage in the little that she has to do, while Donald Crisp as the heavy scores, although the supporting cast honors of the picture must be divided between Jean Hersholt and Warner Oland. Hersholt gets rather the better of it. His role isn't as strong as the one he had in "Greed," but it shows him capable of intense characterization that registers heavily.

When "Don Q" hits the picture houses, which will be in September, it is certain to be a clean up for the exhibitors.

The direction is splendid and there isn't a lagging minute in the picture, even as it stands at present. The action is always fast and the suspense element is beautifully maintained throughout. The photography is excellent and there is some footage that appears to be hand colored in a manner that is most effective.

Fred.

SIEGE

Universal-Jewel production of the Samuel Hopkins Adams novel. Directed by Svend Gade as his first U release. Virginia Valli and Eugene O'Brien starred. Week of June 14 at the Capitol, New York. Running time, 70 minutes.

Fredericka	Virginia Valli
Aunt Augusta Ruyland	Mary Alden
Kennion Ruyland	Eugene O'Brien
Norval Ruyland	Marc McDermott
Dawley Cole	Harry Lorraine
Fredericka's Mother	Helen Dunbar

One of the year's most engrossing pictures.

Made from a fine novel, it has followed that script until a happy ending, for pictures necessitated a change—which hasn't done any harm. Moreover, Mary Alden as the central figure (Aunt Augusta) gives one of the season's great performances. She is backed by a fine cast and handled by a director, Svend Gade, who has apparently turned out the best serious effort (save "The Hunchback") ever made by Universal. This film may come as a surprise to the trade, for Universal's product in the past has hinted at nothing so fine as this.

"Siege" is the story of an aristocratic New England family, the Ruylands, owners of iron mills and lords of their town. At their head was Augusta Ruyland, a stern old woman, whose word was law and whose business tyranny was absolute. As a character she is fascinating (in the novel and the play), for occasional touches of tenderness bring her a degree of sympathy, while a look at some of the other Ruylands explained without subtitles to the audience why she (who looked like her brains were in good working order) had to control the family destinies.

The interest and conflict of the story is when Kennion Ruyland, who is to be her successor, brings his new wife to the family seat.

This new wife, reared in New York, knows nothing of the old traditions, and without being vicious, upsets them all. And Aunt Augusta, of that tribe which worships tradition, is hurt. Finding that Kennion intends clinging to his wife, they are both ordered out. When they leave, Norval Ruyland, one of the mills' biggest stockholders, commits suicide, for this mute, for such he was, found in Fredericka a bond of sympathy. So he left his holdings to her, and, coupled with those of her husband, they constituted the controlling interest of the mill.

At this Aunt Augusta didn't quiver. The old woman of iron leaped to her carriage and drove her horses into a runaway pace. When Kennion's wife stopped them after a hard chase the old woman recognized in her a member of the New Generation, a woman of courage and worthy of acceptance into the Ruyland clan.

Miss Alden isn't featured, but she deserves it, and more. Her performance in the old woman's role is superb and magnificent. Instead of doing a traditional "iron woman" act she responds to Gade's fine direction so that every action counts for lots. Gade has handled Miss Valli and Mr. O'Brien well, while many minor types are particularly well chosen.

"Siege" is first-rate first run material. Whether the lack of noted names will hold it back remains to be seen, but big names or not, this picture is "there."

Because the director, Svend Gade, is of the foreign lot, the exhibitor needn't fear a bunch of impressionistic stuff. What he does is straight-

forward and concise—and therein lies much of the film's power—it doesn't ramble into blank space.
Sisk.

THE MANICURE GIRL

Paramount Picture presented by Adolph Zukor and Jesse L. Lasky.—Story by Frederic and Fanny Hatton. Adapted by Townsend Martin, directed by Frank Tuttle. At Rivoli, New York, week June 14, 1925. Running time, 65 minutes.

Maria Maretti	Bebe Daniels
Antonio Luca	Edmund Burns
Flora	Dorothy Cumming
Jamee Morgan	Hale Hamilton
Mrs. Morgan	Charlotte Walker
Mother Luca	Ann Brody
Mrs. Wainwright	Marie Shotwell
Mrs. Root-Chiveley	Mary Foy

Nothing so "hotsy-totsy" about this picture, despite the fact that the title might suggest it. As a matter of fact the story is a rather trite one, and the picture on the whole one of the very best ads for "Able's Irish Rose" that has been screened in some time. There is one sequence that shows the front of the theatre where "Able" is playing and the electric sign advertising the show is in full view all through it.

"The Manicure Girl" is just one of those pictures that is going to come pretty near satisfying the fans in the neighborhood localities, but it isn't going to help Bebe Daniels on Broadway. What Bebe Daniels needs is comedy material, good comedy drama, and not the melodramatic fodder she has been forced to appear in. She can troup and looks good on the screen and all that she really needs is a real chance to show her stuff. Up to the present the F. P.-L. executives do not seem to have struck the medium in which she can best express herself.

Miss Daniels has the role of a little manicure girl in a smart hotel. She is in love with a little fellow from her own neighborhood and the two are engaged. But the "boy friend" is one of those guys who is just a mug and he becomes very suspicious when the little girl stays out a little late one night. The girl in the meantime, seeing her associates in the manicure shop operate and put the works on some of the daddies, believes that she is likewise entitled to the sables, motor cars and evening gowns and she starts out to get them, but she stops before her foot slips too far and she doesn't get round heels. Instead, she brings about a reconciliation between the estranged husband and wife, and also at the same time squares things with her "wop" boy friend so that everything ends happily.

In the writing of the tale that dear old friend of the screen, coincidence, is just about worked to death and the chances are that at least a two weeks' vacation was necessary after this one was shot.

It is really a shame that Bebe Daniels doesn't get a real chance to do something worth while on the screen, for she has it in her.

From a "commercial" standpoint the picture does not look as though the cost sheet registered very heavily and with Bebe at the head of the cast it looks strong enough to register a profit.
Fred.

THE TEASER

Universal, featuring Laura La Plante and Pat O'Malley. From the play by Adelaide Mathhews and Martha Stanley. Directed by William A. Seiter. At the Strand, New York, week of June 14. Runs 77 minutes.

Anne Barton	Laura La Plante
James McDonald	Pat O'Malley
Margaret Wyndham	Hedda Hopper
Roderick Caswell	Walter McGrail
Perry Grayle	Byron Munson
Lois Caswell	Vivian Oakland
Jeffry Loring	Wyndham Standing
Janet Comstock	Margaret Quimby
Jenkins	Frank Finch Smiles

The unimportant showing registered by "The Teaser" as a legitimate attraction four years ago will more than likely be repeated by it as a film. Certainly the story, from the standpoints of both technique and originality is one of the poorest ever turned out by the Misses Mathews and Stanley. That Universal has done as well by it as it has is surprising, because basically, he picture is only of the "daily change in program" variety.

The chief reasons for its becoming as good as intermediate grade entertainment are the worth of the cast and the direction. The latter, wielded by William Seiter, has inserted some subtle comedy touches and compact bits of action, but errs by allowing the picture to run some quarter of an hour over time. The result is dragginess throughout most of the second half of the film, relived only at the finish by the working out of the final farcial situation.

The rusty old Cinderella theme is dragged headlong into the story at the very outset when Anne Barton (Laura La Plante) is taken from behind a cigar counter in a hick Michigan town and transplanted into the high-hat home of the Park avenue aunt who has adopted her. Six months in a finishing school turns her not only into a heavy swell, but also into an outrageous flirt, a *ne plus ultra* specimen of the flapper and a general nuisance who might have been a literal bringing to life of the heroine in the novel, "Anne's an Idiot."

Of course, the poor unfortunate who finally gets her is the wise-cracking cigar salesman whom she first loved in Michigan. In those days he is to be seen taking her riding in a creaky Ford bearing appropriately enough the legend, "Capacity, One Sweet Mama." Later, however, realizing that his uncouth style will never fit, he breezes into the picture with a new set of manners and an equally new Mercer roadster, both looking very sporty for a salesman of bum cigars.

Pat O'Malley plays this role and, although never overworked, garners the film's honors with his neat comic methods. The constantly improving Miss La Plante looks as luscious as ever and while not yet an accomplished comedienne, does well enough with her silly role. Hedda Hopper's decorative charms are constantly in evidence, Walter McGrail is his usual breezy light heavy and the rest are always satisfactory.

The title seems to be hardly better for the box office than "The Talker," which took a severe header at the Strand about a month ago. While "The Teaser" may be a more diverting picture than that, it is at best conventional "movie" stuff and with a torrid week impending the business prospects are far from bright.

STEELE OF THE ROYAL MOUNTED

Vitagraph production written by James Oliver Curwood. Directed by David Smith. At Rialto week June 14. Runs about 58 minutes.

Philip Steele	Bert Lytell
Bucky Nome	Stuart Holmes
Isobel Becker	Charlotte Merriam
Mrs. Thorpe	Mabel Julienne Scott
Colonel Becker	Sydney DeGrey
Colonel McGregor	John Toughey

When the name James Oliver Curwood is noted as the author of a picture a high-class, artistic and philosophical film may not be looked for, but one expects at least the elements of suspense, adventure and romance to be present in strength. "Steele of the Royal Mounted" has none of these in even moderate quantities, and the Curwood fans are going to get the shocks of their expectant, young lives.

Consequently, in spite of some excellent pictorial photography and one or two of the attributes that go with a picture on which a moderately large amount of money has been spent, "Steele" hardly measures up as good neighborhood house material.

The story, which can be told in half the proverbial nut shell gives an idea of the stupid simplicity of the film. Steele has come to Canada and joined the "Mounties" because his girl had in a foolish prank introduced her father to him as her husband, thus destroying his faith in womankind. Bucky Nome, gambler, has become implicated in a murder, due to his affection for the society of married women, and it becomes Steele's duty to track him down. Following the Royal Mounted's now over-familiar creed of "Get your man," he finally lands the culprit, and then turns to the arms of the girl from the States who has taken all these years to right her little mistake.

The love interest is neglected for more than half the picture and no suspense as to the outcome is ever introduced. In other respects, too, the picture lacks unity and ingenuity. The supposed Alaska scenery is beautiful, but as the production was filmed in summer and snow is at a premium it is small comfort on a sweltering day.

Bert Lytell heads the cast in his usual studied manner, giving away the honors to Stuart Holmes, whose heavy is one of the picture's too few bright spots. Charlotte Merriam, on the contrary, is a thoroughly insipid heroine, and the balance of the players are none too strong.

The almost unbroken strings of Vitagraph flops on Broadway has a notable addition in this one.

After Business Hours

A society drama presented by Columbia Pictures. Starring Elaine Hammerstein and Lou Tellegen. Story by Ethel Watts Mumford. Directed by Mal St. Clair. At the Colony, New York, week June 15. Running time, 56 minutes.

June King	Elaine Hammerstein
John King	Lou Tellegen
Sylvia Vane	Phylis Haver
Richard Dowling	John Patrick
Mrs. Wentworth	Lillian Langdon
James Henricks	William Scott
Jerry Stanton	Lee Moran

First one of the Columbia productions that has hit a first run picture house in the Times square section. It is a society meller of the stereotyped sort that may fit well enough in some of the regular neighborhood theatres, but does not develop sufficient strength to qualify on Broadway. The picture for the smaller picture houses is exactly the type of fare that the average fan audience likes, and in the houses where there is a daily change of bill it can stand up as the stronger of the two pictures on a double feature bill.

The story is that of a newly married couple of wealth. The husband has given his wife charge accounts in all the exclusive shops and loves her dearly, but he has a theory that no woman is to be trusted with money and in the case of his wife he stints her in the matter of spending money with the result that she becomes involved in a series of complications because of his penury. In the end, when his wife has committed a crime to get ready cash and is about to be arrested, the husband comes to her rescue and saves her from that fate, likewise from falling for the villian, to whom he administers a beating, and the two decide to start their married life all over again on a new basis.

Elaine Hammerstein, as the heroine, develops little on the screen that makes her stand out and Lou Tellegen easily runs away with the picture. The heavy of John Patrick would easily qualify in a Christie Comedy, but it has no place in this picture. Patrick should be a find for some one making comedies, but as far as casting him in productions that are intended to have serious characterization finds him all wet.

Phylis Haver, in the role of the friend of the wife, a girl who is out leading the jazzy life, shows up in great style. Lee Moran in a souse bit, also registered nicely.
Fred.

LYING WIVES

Ivan Abramson production. Presented, written and directed by Ivan Abramson. Clara Kimball Young, Madge Kennedy and Richard Bennett starred. The Piccadilly, New York, June 13 week. Running time, 70 minutes.

Patricia Chase	Clara Kimball Young
Theodore Stanhope	Richard Bennett
Margery Burkley	Madge Kennedy
Elsie Chase	Edna Murphy
Wallace Graham	Niles Welch
Alvin Chase	J. Barney Sherry
Wallace Graham, Jr.	Buddy Harris
Betty Lee	Bee Jackson

Although Ivan Abramson has spent some money here and has assembled a good cast, the plot is illogical and old. It is the triangle story with an added angle for more interest. In this cast a middle-aged woman, Patricia Chase, is after Wallace Graham, who loves and has married Margery Burkley. The Chase woman fills the head of Graham with doubts of his wife and Theodore Stanhope, an elderly man and friend of the family. Finally, when Graham gets in a financial hole, the Chase woman says that he can use her securities to get out, and after he has used them she charges him with embezzlement, throws him in jail and then withdraws the charge—this being done to force the wife to Stanhope for aid. It works and Graham is on the verge of leaving with her when Stanhope declares he is the father of Graham's wife and that he did not reveal his identity because until recently a false murder charge had hung over him.

Richard Bennett and Madge Kennedy run away with the picture, and though Clara Kimball Young does excellent work as the other woman, it is such a disagreeable and distasteful role that it can hardly be counted upon to help her much in the come-back which she has been attempting recently. Niles Welch is the leading man and good, while Barney Sherry makes a reappearance on the screen after quite an absence.

From the plot of "Lying Wives" it is not difficult to imagine the picture and exhibitors know their own audiences' likes. The production is up to a high independent standard, and the cast "names" will probably count. While hardly suitable for first runs, it may do for the other theatres. It seems to be of that type which combination houses have been using plentifully.
Sisk.

STOP FLIRTING

Christie feature length comedy based on the musical comedy by Fred Jackson. Released through Producers' Distributing Corporation and directed by Scott Sidney. At the Cameo June 14, week. Running time, 65 minutes.

Perry Reynolds	John T. Murray
Vivian Marsden, his fiancee	Wanda Hawley
Geoffrey Dangerfield	Hallan Cooley
Marjorie Leeds	Ethel Shannon
Suzanne	Vera Steadman
Count Spinagio	Jimmie Adams
Butler	Jack Duffy
Teddy	Jimmie Harrison
Bobby Anderson, aviator	David James

First Christie long comedy since "Charley's Aunt," which was a whale. Comparatively, this is a minnow.

"Stop Flirting" is accredited to a musical comedy book. That is apparent by the skimpy plot and the reliance placed upon built-up structures. Moreover, it is easy to see that quite a few additions have been made to the original plot. But once the story has been developed, the whole thing turns into a rough-house that chases, fights, leaps, and some element of mystery.

At the start a girl is peeved as she thinks her husband is flirting, and to make him peeved she invites all the boy friends in. This gets him sore. A friend suggests he smuggle away in an airship going to Hawaii and then sneak out before it starts off. He doesn't, but is rescued by a fast motor boat. Back in the house, his wife still believes him in the plane. She later gets on, however, and lets them think they're fooling her.

About this point it is announced a man who thinks he is the Hunchback of Notre Dame has escaped from the booby hatch. Three other men dress like him and begin to frighten the guests. From then on it's the rough-house for a happy finish.

John T. Murray has the lead role and, although an excellent stage comedian, he falls down here. Wanda Hawley is pretty enough opposite, but the only one who draws laughs on his own is Jack Duffy in an old butler role.

"Stop Flirting" is well directed and the situation handled okeh, but the whole thing hardly impresses as anything more than a daily change proposition. *Sisk.*

THE PEAK OF FATE

Frank B. Rogers' presentation of a story of Alpine life. Edited and titled by Eugene Walter. At the Central theatre, New York, June 13, on run. Running time, 69 minutes.

A picture dsitinctly different, thrilling and compelling, keeping you on the edge of your seat for the hour and a little more that it runs. There is as much kick in the mountain-climbing stuff as one would get out of seeing Harold Lloyd doing his stunts atop of one of those tall buildings, and as much kick out of it as anything of that sort has been done in the way of providing thrills for picture house audiences. It is a mighty good picture for the warm weather season, as it combines the effect of tremendous mountains, their snow-capped peaks and a blizzard raging.

There are no actors, according to those connected with the picture, particularly Gene Walter; but, then, he was one of the world's best press agents before he became a dramatist. Mr. Walter took this picture when it was just 18,000 feet of scenic and put a story in it. There are eight people in the cast, of whom it is said that they are just people of the mountains. There is a mother, aged and wrinkled, of mountain stock, and her son, who is married to a woman from the lowlands who cannot appreciate the urge that there is inborn in these mountain folk to conquer the inaccessible mountain peaks. They have a son who as a little chap wants to follow in his dad's steps and be a climber. The father loses his life trying to climb the Devil's Needle, an unconquered height. Years afterward the boy flirts with a like fate, but to rescue his sweetheart, who has tried to climb to the top to preserve the local pride, because two men from a rival community are trying to win the honor of being the first to reach the crest.

The hairbreadth escapes the principals have in climbing the crags and the seemingly impassable sheer walls of the mountains make for thrill after thrill. The falls some of them must have taken would have been enough to shake the spirit of the most intrepid stunt man of the American picture field. It looks as though some of the drops

must have been from 400 to 600 feet, and even though the nets were used it was still something of a drop. One can almost imagine a director saying to one of these climbers: "Hey, youse'll have to take that flop again; we didn't git it the first time." And then what?

But the picture is so gripping in its thrilling qualities that even on a cool night it leaves one dripping with perspiration.

It is just one of those pictures that people will want to go and see because it holds the same qualities as a performance in a cage of wildcats does to those who like to get the wallop that there is in watching a trainer put them through their paces.

It's a picture that should get some real money because of its novelty and thrills. *Fred.*

THE SNOB BUSTER

Rayart (W. Ray Johnson) production starring Reed Howes. Produced by Harry J. Brown. Directed by Albert Rogell. Photographed by Ross G. Fisher. Story by Forrest Sheldon. At the New York one day (June 9) has half the bill. Runs about 58 minutes.

Theodore Prendergast........Reed Howes
John Prendergast...........Wilfred Lucas
Uncle Tobias..............George Tobias
Butch McGuire...............David Kirby
Molly McGuire..............Gloria Grey
Kid Lowry...................Ray Johnson
Schultz.....................Max Asher

Notwithstanding some rather serious discrepancies in continuity, editing and general production, "The Snob Buster" measures up as a surprisingly breezy little stunt film. In it Reed Howes, the genuine Arrow Collar specimen, shows an improvement, indicating that some day his acting may be compared to his good looks.

Credit for the swift action and more or less appealing heart interest in the film goes to the author and director. Not that any startling originality has crept into the story, but it is the sort of popular stuff that stands for a lot of repetition and abuse and the best points are deftly brought out.

The hero leaves for the war at the beginning of the film a snob through and through because of his ultra-plutocratic home environment. The big fight takes the cockiness out of him and when he returns, a buck private, he finds his former life unbearable. So he runs away, falls in with a gang of boxing club "lovable roughnecks" and then falls again, this time in love, with the dainty, little proprietress of a neighboring beanery. For her love and his own honor he battles the bully and champ of the outfit, finally emerging victorious after a cleverly staged though somewhat drawn out encounter.

Howes is not much of a boxer, but when stripped for action reveals a graceful physique and muscular development that are quite in line with his renowned profile. At the finish of the gruelling battle, which has led them to a roof-top after the impromptu bout at the club had been raided by cops, he is shown amorously caressing the girl, with his face free from discoloration or perspiration, every hair in place and his whole bearing as immaculate and neat as Tom Gibbons' was "shot" the other night.

Several other inconsistencies cannot help being noticed, while the titles make that frequent "your" for "you're" mistake and three or four more.

George Tobias and David Kirby provide some welcome comedy moments, while Ray Johnson makes the heavy more of a big bully than a real villain. Gloria Grey overdoes the sweet stuff a bit, but manages to be generally appealing, nevertheless The film has been nicely set and photographed, although some of the early interiors are ugly.

Altogether it is a better bet for

the exhibtors than "Lightning Romance," the collar Adonis' last production, and even that wasn't half bad as such films go.

Passionate Adventure

Distributed here by Lee-Bradford, but produced in England by Graham Cutts for A. C. and R. C. Bromhead. Scenario by Alfred Hitchcock and directed by Cutts. Marjorie Daw and Alice Joyce feature. At the New York, June 13. Running time, 68 minutes.

Vickey ....Marjorie Daw
Drusilla ....Alice Joyce
Adrian St. Clair.............Olive Brook
Harris ....Victor Mc. Laglen

This British film, distributed here by Lee-Bradford, is a serious sex play of high order in that its direction and action seem both concentrated on the story itself rather than on the proposition of emphasizing whatever of sex is contained therein. In brief, the proposition is that the sex-starved husband of an aristocratic family comes through the war to find that his wife is still cold to him. On a remarkable trip to the slums he finds a beautiful girl there. Protecting her, he is knocked out, but, taken to her flat unconscious, revives, and, in a struggle with her "man," a brute, kills him. That is all smoothed over and the girl serves as the medium for making the wife realize her shortcomings in their married state.

For a British production, this is up to the American standard of high-grade program releases. The direction is excellent, the continuity air-tight, and the acting up to scratch. Alice Joyce is the cold wife, Marjorie Daw makes an appealing slum girl, while Clive Brook gives his usual finished performance as the husband. There are several excellent minor characters, all well played, while the scenes of homecoming from the war, etc., bear pathos.

"The Passionate Adventure" isn't trashy, though the title may sound that way. That title is based on the saying of Oscar Wilde that passion is the only serious thing in life (a belief that got Wilde into plenty of trouble). It is a high-grade film for high-grade audiences, and the theme is inoffensively handled so that censorial trouble will hardly result. It was made during the recent stay of the Misses Daw and Joyce in Europe, before the time Mr. Brook became such a prominent figure on the American screen. *Sisk.*

THE BANDIT'S BABY

F. B. O. production starring Fred Thompson. Story by Leete Renick Brown. Directed by James P. Hogan. At Loew's New York one day (June 9) as half the bill. Runs about an hour.

Tom Bailey...............Fred Thompson
Esther Lacy..............Helen Foster
Mat Hartigan.............Harry Woods
Baby....................Mary Louise Miller
Sheriff.................Clarence Geldert
Bill Henry................David Kirby
Doctor...................C. W. Mack

Someone somewhere suggested that a better title for "The Bandit's Baby" would have been "The Son of a Gun-Man" or something to that effect. Be that as it may, the baby idea seems to be the right one to play up if F. B. O. hopes to attract a lot of women who never before have shown much interest in Westerns.

The film gets away from the old prairie formula pretty well in its comedy moments, although its dramatic theme follows closely the old idea of the hero unjustly accused of robbery and murder and then hounded until the last 100 feet by the scoundrel who really did the dirty work. Fortunately, the serious parts of the picture are not the all-important ones, and the humorous

moments are good enough to pull the production well up to a standard at least as high as any earlier Thompson releases.

The kid interest is vital throughout, with even the love theme subservient to the cowboy hero's affection for his girl's baby brother. This apparently is intentional, for even at the finish, when Thompson proposes, he says half seriously that it's because he can't live without the infant that he's asking its sister to marry him.

As so much hinges on the baby in question, it is a very fortunate thing the producers were able to secure a girl, Mary Louise Miller, evidently about two years old, for the part of the boy. She's a knock-out and tough old masculine film-goers as well as everyone in skirts will have to let loose at least one snicker at her antics.

Thompson has all sorts of opportunities, from judging a baby show to dragging the kid from in front of an on-rushing locomotive in the nick of time. His beautiful white horse, "Silver King," which like Mix's "Tony," has become a trademark, is again outstanding, and there are no fake mechnical tricks about his galloping and acting, either. The others in the cast (people, not horses) are satisfactory, the photography up to the high standards of better-class westerns and the direction all that is necessary.

The Adventurous Sex

Produced by Howard Estabrook for Associated Exhibitors release through Pathe. Story by Hamilton Mannin and directed by Charles Giblyn. Reviewed as half of a double bill at Loew's New York, June 12. Running time, 58 minutes.

The Girl.......................Clara Bow
Her Sweetheart........Herbert Rawlinson
The Adventurer..............Earl Williams
Her Father................Harry T. Morey
Her Mother.................Mabel Beck
The Grandmother............Flora Finch

Somehow, with Flora Finch, Earle Williams and Harry Morey, one is reminded of the Vitagraph days. At the same time, it is proven once more the changes time can make. For Flora Finch has now settled into a serious part and the one time partner of the late John Bunny doesn't even try for a laugh. Harry Morey isn't the Jack Holt type of hero, but is now playing father parts, while Earle Williams is the villain instead of the hero. Herbert Rawlinson, another veteran, but of the Universal forces then, is still the hero, while Clara Bow, a recent newcomer, is the heroine.

In theme "The Adventurous Sex" concerns a flapper whose semi-wild ways caused her to give her sweetheart the air, take up with another man, the villain, and finally get into a compromising situation with him. The situation, however, was blameless on her part, and when the villain felt that he had embarrassed her sufficiently by forcing himself into her hotel room and then calling in his friends, the hero arrives. Following this comes the punch of the picture, a series of scenes in which the girl hurls herself into the rapids of Niagara river with the hope of going to death over the falls. The hero jumps in after her and both seemed doomed when an aeroplane swoops down, drops a ladder to which they cling, flies over the falls and drops them in shallow and smooth water.

Faked, but interesting.

With a good cast, fair production, etc., but obviously skimped in parts, "The Adventurous Sex" falls into the middle class of pictures and looks best suited for the daily changes. *Sisk.*

ANYTHING ONCE

Produced by Jack Weinberg and released through Aywon Pictures on state right basis. From story by Nate H. Edward and directed by Justin H. McCloskey. Gladys Walton featured, and cast includes Harold Austin, Tully Marshall, Mathilde Brundage, Arko, the dog, and Francis McDonald. Reviewed at Loew's New York, June 12, as half of a double bill. Running time, 64 minutes.

This is a comedy drama of the cheaply produced type, yet its story carries it through satisfactorily.

A sailor fresh from the navy lands **without $2 in his pocket. Acquiring a suit of English cut and a turn-down hat such as the Prince of Wales wore, he was invited to the home of a man whose daughter was infatuated with a phoney Duke. And although introduced as a Prince, he lives that down, captures the Duke, who is a crook, and marries the girl. This plot, though simple, is gagged in many spots for laughs and other little incidents, chiefly to show the affection of the sailor for his dog, fill out the running time without the usual wearisome padding.**

Harold Austin, a new face, does excellently as the sailor. Gladys Walton, featured, is an acceptable sweetheart, while Tully Marshall plays a grouchy father role pretty much as only Tully Marshall can. The direction is up to standard and the sets good. Some of the exteriors were tastefully chosen.

Chiefly, however, because of its action, gags and novel love interest, "Anything Once" figures as an acceptable program feature for the smaller houses. *Sisk.*

THE CANVAS KISSER

B. Berger production released by Renown Productions, Inc. Starring Richard Holt and directed by Duke Worne. Story by Grover Jones. Photographed by Alfred Cosden. Cast includes Ruth Dwyer, Garry O'Dell and Cecil Edwards. At Loew's New York one day as half the bill. Runs about 58 minutes.

"The Canvas Kisser" while it does not rate as a good feature for even the "stunt" star class, is considerably better in every respect than the last of the Richard Holt seris, "Ten Days." Here at least is a stoy with a grain of heart interest, despite ridiculousness and direction and continuity that are passable, if not exactly worthy of praise.

In the work of the star, too, there seems to have been an improvement, but a mistake was made by casting him as a prize fighter. In the ring he appears fat, flabby and funny, with even less knowledge of boxing and fighting displayed than is apparent in the work of some of the gild-edged sheiks of higher celluloid prestige. Aside from this clumsy exhibition in the roped roped arena, Holt almost succeeds in making the young tough he is supposed to represent, a likable and appealing character.

The story concerns one of those fistic young gentlemen who have (supposedly) considerable fighting prowess, but who find making a living easier by betting on their opponets and then laying down. The exalting influence of the girl in the case in the case changes his viewpoint, and he becomes scrupluoisly correct, even promising her never to battle again. This results in the usual complications which are cleared up in a manne neither mroe interesting nor original than in countless other films.

An important switch for the better not yet mentioned in the presence of a new leading woman, Ruth Dwyer, whose charm is outstanding. The balance of the cast is not so bar either, although Garry O'Dell can do little with astupidity overdone comedy role. The fight scenes are ludicrous, but can scarcely be otherwise, with Holt as one of the contestants.

Whoever wrote the titles did a good job. Although the picture has an aroma of cheapness about it it is encouraging as a better effort than the last and should get by in the program houses. If the improvement keeps up Holt might really turn out a good one some day.

FLAMES OF DESIRE

Fox production from the novel "Strathmore," by Ouida. Directed by Denison Clift, who also wrote the scenario with F. G. Fogwell. At the Stanley, New York, one day. Runs about 65 minutes.

Daniel Strathmore......Wyndham Standing
Marion Vavasour..............Diana Miller
Dick Langton...............Richard Thorpe
Ferand Vavasour..............Frank Leigh
Lionel Caryll.............George K. Arthur
Viola Lee.....................Jackie Saunders
Lucille Errol.............Frances Beaumont
Secretary ....Hayford Hobbs
Clive Errol....................Charles Clary
Mrs. Courtney Ruhl........Eugenia Gilbert

The latest in the "worst woman of the world" series of films. Ouida wrote the original novel, "Strathmore." Although considered one of her best by those who have devied into her romantic pages it comes rather a long way short of making good picture material, even for those houses where intelligence isn't necessarily requisite.

The interests are too many and too loosely centered. The characters are either wicked or wishy?washy with the result that one feels only revulsion at the slimy courtesan of a heroine and ridicule for the vacillating weakling of a hero.

During the course of its action the story takes in several lavish looking scenes with one Spanish fiesta bit expertly filmed.

Diana Miller, a comparative newcomer who looks like a brunet, vampirish and slightly hard-boiled edition of Mildred Harris, plays the difficult, unsympathetic leading role with efficiency if not inspiration. Wyndham Standing and Charles Clary give their usual intelligent impersonations. The rest of the cast is well chosen, too, save for Frances Beaumont, whose ingenue is most insipid. George K. Arthur, Jackie Saunders and Frank Leigh, all more or less potent screen "names," have only bits. Denison Clift, directing, has inserted a few deft touches.

As a sexy proposition the film doesn't cut (or melt) much ice aside from the sizzling, but hackneyed title. Miss Miller wears two or three daring gowns and one sufficiently revealing night-gown, but lacks the much-abused stuff known as sex appeal to set them off in really spicy fashion.

SELL 'EM COWBOY

An Arrow production made by Ben Wilson. Dick Hatton starred with Yakima Canutt and Marilyn Mills featured. Reviewed at the Stanley, New York, June 11. Running time, 62 minutes.

Frank Mathewson, Jr.........Dick Hatton
Sheriff.......................Ed La Niece
Luke Strong.............Yakima Canutt
The Sweetheart in Arizona..Marilyn Mills
The Sweetheart in Chicago.Winona Wilkes

Of a different type than the usual western is this, in that the hero, instead of being planted first as an out and out cowboy, is shown as the would-be cowboy son of a Chicago saddle manufacturer. The saddle business, of course, depends largely on the western trade and the firm has been meeting some unexplained opposition, so the son goes to the cattle country in an effort to revive business.

Hopping from the train, he fixes himself out in cowboy garb and on his shirt are the intitials "T. P. O." which the natives believe stand for Texas Pete Owens, a noted desperado and hard boiled character. So at the crack of his whip they scatter—something quite mysterious, yet agreeable to the hero.

In Arizona, Luke Strong, a tough cowboy has been framed by opposition saddle manufacturers to keep other saddle men out of the territory, so it was apparent the Chicago salesman had been chased. The son conquers the difficulties, does some typical stunts and wins himself a girl.

Hatton in the lead is adequate, while the production and cast for a picture of this sort is up to standard. The story, too, is different so that "Sell 'Em Cowboy" seems an agreeable independent release of the western order. The exhibitor, of course, understands the usual run of these independent westerns and can take the above to indicate that this one is above the average. *Sisk.*

LONDON FILM REVIEWS

SATAN'S SISTER

London, May 25.

The spirit of Robert Louis Stevenson hovers insistently over this latest "all British" film, the story by Devere Stacpoole, production by George Pearson, which "W. & F." screened to a huge and enthusiastic house at the Alhambra on the evening of Empire Day, May 24. For once in a way the trade found it worth while to give up Sunday evening to business.

The story is a thoroughly good one of the South Seas—buccaneers, "port scourings," humorous villains, beauteous maidens disguised as insubordinate ship boys, and all the characters R. L. S. gloried in abound in this story, which forms the basis for one of the finest entertainments ever offered by a British producer to the cinema public. Its suspensive value is great—even the most seasoned viewer of pictures has no idea what will happen next, although the story never sidetracks and nothing is used for thé sake of creating mystery or suspense. Only once do author and producer get slightly off the rails, and that is when the heroine, an uncultured sea-gamin, pretends to be a "movie picture" producer in order to win the protection of a naval landing party and get away from an opposition piratical crew. The whole story is flavored with a touch of burlesque and is told without any killing or attempts to outrage the heroine, although good lusty oaths, such as "I'll have your blankety-blank liver," and much flourishing of knives permeate the atmosphere while a parrot swears lustily in the language of the Spanish Main whenever an opportunity is given. British producers who were present might well study the methods of George Pearson, who was also responsible for "Reveille."

Captain Tyler is skipper of the disreputable "Sarah Tyler"; his son Satan and his daughter Jude are the "crew." Jude has worn breeches all her life and has a profound dislike for women and their ways—rum and the language of the fo'castle are more to her liking. Old Tyler manages to steal the chart of a treasure island but dies at sea before he can lift the loot. Satan and Jude carry on. The existence of the treasure is, however, known to two opposing gangs of ruffians, one commanded by a humorously sinister ruffian, Cleary, the other, by a horrified individual, Cark. Satin gets busy with both sides and does a little private double crossing, with the result he takes both gangs into partnership and extracts $1,000 from each side as payment in advance. Meanwhile a young and wealthy Britisher has joined the "Sarah Tyler" and the "dawn of love" is seen in the offing. Satan's business-like methods quickly lead the party into trouble and he then explains he has another chart giving the correct position of the treasure which was moved to another island years before. The crew of the "Sarah" Tyler" slip out without lights under the shadow of night, leaving the other people to blow up the wreck which is discovered to be full of "skillingtons." Arriving at the other island Captain Satan discovers he, too, has been badly hurt, but the two other piratical craft have joined hands and it is then Jude adopts the "movie producer" stunt to get herself and party away. There is no treasure beyond the $2,000 lifted from the opposition by the business-like Satan, the adventure is over, but romance begins in real earnest when Jude decides to study feminine acts under the tutelage of the volunteer crew.

This rollicking story has been made in Jamaica with the result it is framed in glorious scenery, while the shipboard scenes are capital. Some good studio scenes, notably a piratical haunt devoted to liquor, love and knife-throwing, known as "The Doggery," are well staged and directed. The acting is far and away above the British film standard. Betty Balfour, who cannot get away quite from the tricks which marked her various "Squibbs" performances, is very good as the girl and is ably seconded by Guy Phillips as Satan. Frank Stanmore is very fine as the humorist villain Cleary, while Caleb Porter does excellent work as Cark. All the other "pirates" are well played, and particular care has been given to atmospheric make-up. James Carew has only a very small part as Captain Tyler but does well. The hero is played by, so it is whispered, a young gentleman brought for that purpose from his studies at Cambridge University. He is fair, but the film industry will not suffer if he remains at his studies. *Gore.*

SPORTING CHANCE

Tiffany Production starring Dorothy Phillips and Lou Tellegen. Story by Jack Boyle, directed by Oscar Apfel. Shown at the Colony, New York, week June 21, 1925. Running time, 64 minutes.

Darrell Thornton................Lou Tellegen
Patricia Winthrop..........Dorothy Phillips
Caleb Winthrop............George Fawcett
Robert Selby..............Theodore Von Eltz
Michael Collins..............Sheldon Lewis
Jockey......................Andrew Clark
Kentucky Boy................Kentucky Boy

Another horse race drama, except that instead of being set down in Dixie the action takes place in New York, and instead of a Kentucky Colonel facing ruin and the loss of the old plantation, in this case it is the girl's father who is up against it. She is saved from a nasty situation by a southern boy who owns Kentucky Boy, whom he has brought north to race. Other than that the plot is the self-same old timer.

One touch is different, the casting of Lou Tellegen to play the principal heavy. The return of Dorothy Phillips to the screen as the heroine is also a point in the picture's favor, as some of the old-time fans will want to look her over again.

The picture will do well enough in the neighborhoods, but while it is on the par with the greater amount of product that is being shown these days in the Broadway houses it is far from the standard those houses should hold to. There is one big thrill and that is the old reliable horse race scene.

Miss Phillips is the daughter of a wealthy promoter, about to go to prison because of financial straits. The girl has virtually engaged herself to the young Southern horse-owner when she learns that her father is in trouble and she breaks off her engagement and consents to marry the heavy to save her dad. The heavy, Lou Tellegen, has loaned the Southern horseman sufficient money to bring his stake horse north and then has attached the horse for the debt, it being his way of getting possession of the animal which he couldn't buy and eliminating it from the big race which he has one of his own horses entered At the last minute the girl and the owner overcome the villain and steal the horse from the under the sheriff's eyes, sneak him into the track drawing an ice cream wagon and win the race, the purse saving dad from jail and the winnings on the side making it possible for the young people to live happily.

The early portions of the picture are rather draggy but the action gets faster as the story rolls along and finally culminates in the race scene, which is a wow. *Fred.*

SMOOTH AS SATIN

Gothic Production, starring Evelyn Brent, directed by Ralph Ince, released by F.B.O. From the Bayard Veiller play, "The Chatterbox." Shown at the Capitol, New York, week June 21, 1925. Running time, 64 minutes.

Gertie Jones..................Evelyn Brent
Jimmy Hartigan..............Bruce Gordon
Kersey. ....Fred Kelsey
Bill Manson................Fred Esmelton
Mrs. Manson..............Mabel Van Buren
Henderson....................John Gough

For a cheap picture this one is at least entertaining. The story isn't a strong one and has a theme that has been done before, but it is very well directed and the interest is sustained principally through its handling, although toward the end it fades into the rather commonplace with a railroad wreck pulled in by main force to provide a big thrill.

It is a picture that should please the audiences in the average neighborhood houses, but it really hasn't a place in one of the first class pre-release run theatres unless they are pretty hard put to it for product. There is one thing and that is that the name of the star won't mean a thing at the box office on Broadway, and the chances are that the week's business at the Capitol will hardly hold up with this one.

It is a crook melodrama that has as its two principal characters a couple of young crooks, boy and girl. The latter at the opening is employed as a maid at the home of a wealthy widow and has been framing for a month to knock off the jewel strong box. On the night she has the job set another crook invades the house bent on the same purpose.

The two meet, and after the girl has stuck him up, they decide that they'll split the take, when the cops come on the scene, having been called by the butler, who has seen the crook enter the house. He is taken and the girl quits and starts to spring him from the big house. She is successful in arranging his escape from the pen and for a time they live happily, having been married on the way from the prison. They then are taken by a couple of cons, one of those cases of cheating cheaters, and about the same time a bank detective walks in on the scene to take the husband back to the pen.

The girl traces the cons that have gypped them and gets the $10,000 that was the net on a bank job and pays off the "dick," the pay-off taking place on the train, which is taking the husband back to jail. The train is wrecked and the prisoner rescues the cop from sure death. For that he is willing to let him loose.

It is just another of those crook reformation tales, but well directed and fairly well played as far as the roles assigned Evelyn Brent and Bruce Gordon are concerned. *Fred.*

The Making of O'Malley

First National starring Milton Sills with Dorothy Mackaill featured. Story by Gerald Beaumont. Directed by Lambert Hillyer. Supervised by Earl Hudson. At the Strand, New York, week of June 21. Running time, 60 minutes.

O'Malley.....................Milton Sills
Lucille Thayer............Dorothy Mackaill
Margie...................Helen Rowland
Danny the Dude........Warner Richmond
Herbert Browne........Thomas J. Carrigan
Capt. Collins.............Claude King
The Doctor.................Allen Brander
Sgt. Patterson..........Charles Graham
Clerk......................Jack DeLacey

This feature is a great set up for Milton Sills. It gives him a relief from lumberjack roles. The story has the sort of drama that will appeal to all and the Sills fans in particular.

"The Making of O'Malley" glorifies the New York copper, yet escapes the category of a propaganda picture. It is brimful of heart interest, thrills and sob stuff, from which good drama is made, also sufficient suspense to keep the spectator's interest arrested throughout.

Jim O'Malley is an over-zealous copper for whom his captain sees great possibilities, providing his ministering of the law can be balanced with a quality of mercy, especially in regard to minor infractions. O'Malley's generosity with summons for minor violations has thrown his precinct in an uproar. A way out comes when Lucille Thayer, society girl-school teacher, applies for a traffic cop to guide her charges over a dangerous crossing. Despite a shortage of men, the captain gives O'Malley the assignment, hoping that his contact with the little ones will thaw out his icy determination to prosecute the law to the letter.

The change does the trick via O'Malley's interest in a little crippled girl whose smiles have done the thawing out trick. The copper arranges for an operation, which cures the youngster and then finds that it was he who sent her father up the river for refusing to turn state's evidence against a bootlegger's ring. For Margie's sake he signs the petition for the man's parole, but continues his determination to round up the higher ups at the instigation of the society girl-teacher. He is ultimately successful, only to find that it is the girl's fiance who is head of the ring, and rather than subject her to unpleasant publicity turns him loose. Later the convicted man, vengeful for having been double-crossed by his confederates who promised to care for his mother and little one if he took the rap and the stretch, spills the beans, which wins O'Malley back his shield and the love of the society girl.

Sills is superb as the "hard boiled" copper and equally good in the finer touches when his affection for the little cripple has given him a new outlook on life and a more friendly feeling for mankind. Dorothy Mackaill gives a charming portrayal of Lucille Thayer with little Helen Rowland sharing support honors as Margie, the cupid aid on crutches. The remainder of the support give adequate performances of their respective roles.

The film contains two thrill punches, a raid scene and a midair fight between Sills and Thomas Carrington suspended on a rope, swinging over the house tops.

All in all, absorbing drama that should appeal especially to the feminine trade. *Edba.*

LOST—A WIFE

Famous Players' production of the play "Banco," by Alfred Savoir. Adapted to the screen by Clara Beranger, with Adolphe Menjou, Greta Nissen and Robert Agnew featured. Directed by William DeMille. Reviewed at the Rivoli, New York, June 21. Running time, 70 minutes.

Tony Hamilton..............Adolphe Menjou
Charlotte Randolph............Greta Nissen
Dick........................Robert Agnew
Baron Deliquieres............Edgar Norton
George....................Mario Carillo
Duke de Val..............Genaro Spagnoli
Louis....................Eugenio di Liguoro
Mrs. Randolph.............Henrietta Floyd
Baroness...................Toby Claude
Julie, the maid..............Marcel Corday

The plot of this one is just a bit more sexy than they usually put on the screen, being a farce and handled by expert farceurs, it is quite innocent. Moreover, both the hero and heroine are drawn as such interesting characters that their little peccadilloes haven't a great deal of bearing on the subject.

In brief, the story concerns Tony Hamilton and Charlotte Randolph. Charlotte blows into a fashionable European hotel. Tony gets one flash at her and tells his friends he'll marry her. So at a ball announcing her engagement to another man Tony sweeps her off the well-known feet and slips the gold band on the fourth finger. Then they start on a honeymoon and Tony gets in the gambling Casino. His wife asks him to leave. He refuses and then she counters with the proposition that she will not leave the Casino until he leaves the gambling room. For nearly four days he holds out, and in the meantime she is courted by a booby looking old baron. And, to spite the husband, she goes off with him. Then the husband hides in their rooms and wins her back. That's the spice of it all—his hiding in their rooms.

But he really loved her, and it was their individual pigheadedness which caused the split.

Menjou's role is the best he has had since the Chancellor in "Forbidden Paradise" with Negri. He plays it to the limit for endless laughs, while Miss Nissen, who is what Webster must have thought of when he put that "beautiful" word in his dictionary, is the lady in the cast. As an actress and as an optical treat she is probably as big an acquisition as the screen has made this year. Here she deports herself attractively and, although the direction is apparent in her work, she has an expressive face, and not the usual dumb-doll appearance of some other screen beauties. And she can wear clothes as well as any other woman on the screen.

Her teaming with Menjou in this film is perfect, for his sophisticated manner is met by hers. Miss Nissen looked pretty enough at the Broadhurst last year, when she was playing in "Beggar on Horseback," and here the closeups are not disillusioning. She has a face and a figure and all that goes with it.

The others in the cast are excellent, particularly the foreign types. Direction good, settings good and photography up to par. Which, coupled with the story and the stars, makes it an entertainment cinch. *Sisk.*

How Baxter Butted In

Warner Bros. release, adapted for the screen by Owen Davis from Harold Titus' novel, "Stuff of Heroes." Matt Moore and Dorothy Devore starred. Directed by William Beaudine. Reviewed at the Piccadilly, New York, June 20. Running time, 70 mins.

Beulah Dyer, the stenographer..........Dorothy Devore
Henry Baxter, her bashful suitor......Matt Moore
Walter Higgins, the shrewd trickster....Ward Crane
R. S. Falk, the Big Chief....Wilfred Lucas
Emmy Baxter, the widowed sister-in-law..Adda Gleason
Jimmy Baxter................Turner Savage
Mary Baxter................Virginia Marshall
Amos Nichols..................Otis Harlan
Rags, the pup..................."Cameo"

It was in "The Narrow Street" that Matt Moore and Dorothy Devore made such a hit as a comedy team. It was found Moore's comedy forte was in portraying that mute, inglorious specimen of manhood who dreams of big things. So in "How Baxter Butted In" Warner Bros. have followed that general line and provided Moore (for he is really the works) with a story which fits him perfectly. Moore, in return, gives a performance which is at once funny and pathetic. The hero has all the sympathy in the world enlisted for himself, a big point for any hero to score.

Henry Baxter is a clerk in a newspaper business office. He loves Beulah Dyer, stenographer. Week by week he saves a little toward that day when they can get married. His rival is Ward Higgins, business manager of the paper, also his boss. The time for the marriage nearly comes when Henry's brother dies, and he is burdened with the widow and two children and a litter of about 12 puppies. This keeps his nose to the grindstone, and the man with the hero complex can only dream of daring, for, like Cyrano, he did dream of daring, though the odds were against it.

Finally the outside work which he has taken on to keep the wolf away from the door overcomes him, and he is confined to his bed for weeks. It is at this juncture that the Big Chief in the office finds out that Baxter has contributed some of the ideas which Higgins has appropriated, and also learns of the silent suffering which he has undergone to support the family of his brother.

When Baxter regains his health he is the honor guest at a valor award dinner given by the paper. As the medal is about to be pinned on him word is phoned in that fire has broken out in his home. Out he dashes, hangs to a hook and ladder truck and rescues the children and the puppies. The man who has dreamed of bravery all his life has had his opportunity and embraced it.

From then it is indicated that things will take a brighter turn for him, so the happy ending fadeout follows.

Moore gives a splendid performance throughout, and in the dream sequences, where he always pictures himself as defending his sweetheart against the villain, he drew laughs in plenty. Ward Crane as the villain also brought himself to favorable notice, while Miss Devore, the heroine, fitted neatly in. Additional comedy was furnished by the puppies of the children, but all this comedy was leavened and made to stand out more prominently by the gentle pathos of Baxter. This pathos pervaded the entire film, and blended so perfectly with the comedy one is compelled to use that trite expression, "a perfect blend of pathos and comedy."

Warners' have turned out a good film, fit for any first-run and any audience and produced nicely in every detail. It is high-grade product from the story to the cast and from then on to the direction.

Sisk.

LIGHT OF WESTERN STARS

Zukor-Lasky presentation, Paramount release of Zane Gray's novel, adapted by George C. Hull and Lucien Hubbard; directed by William K. Howard. Running time, 90 minutes. Seen at Rialto theatre.

Gene Stewart	Jack Holt
Madeline Hammond	Billie Dove
Brand	Noah Beery
Bonita	Alma Bennett
Al Hammond	William Scott
Billy Stillwell	George Nichols
Monty Price	Mark Hamilton
Melse	Robert Perry
Stub	Gene Pellette

A thoroughly workmanlike Western, maintaining interest largely through the shrewd direction of William K. Howard and the unusually fine acting, despite a story which, for Zane Gray, is thin. It is more than flimsy alone; it is short, running out of plot about two-thirds along in the film almost entirely.

But it could be strung along for another reel and would hold as long as Noah Beery and Jack Holt continued their fascinating contest of wits and manners (as manners go among the bad men), for here are two personalities which when ranged at two ends of any scene create suspense and drama.

Both have in equal plenitude the gift of realism—uncompromising, courageous fidelity to character and atmosphere. They never seem to hurry in that hectic movie fear that they may "drag"; their make-ups are neither prettied up to give them beauty nor smeared up to add ferocity. They look and act exactly like what they play, and that is as full a compliment as may be accorded an artist.

Holt is a combination heavy-hero. Starting as a drunk and disorderly two-gun rowdy, sinking to the depths among the Mexican riffraff, he braces up when "the girl" tells him she has "faith." That is pretty old stuff. So is the rest of the yarn, much of which unapologetically skips about through sure-fire twists without coherence or foundation.

But when Beery, the outlaw and woman grabber, comes into close and extended combat with Holt the story can stop and no one will miss it. The by-plays, the facial transitions, the ever-present sense of two fine fighting animals jockeying for an eyelash of advantage, keeps the action tense and the important element of "danger" throbbing.

Miss Dove is just a nice, pretty ingenue, making about as little of her part as she could without doing anything wrong; she just strolls through it, and whenever she seems least essential she comes in for a close-up and shows why she is in the picture business. She surely is palatable to look at, both as to features and figure, and in one black satin dress her physical attractions stand forth so vividly that one wonders whether Sennett hasn't been wrong all these years in taking so much off his beauts. Miss Dove, fully dressed, still reveals a sufficiency.

The big scene is an adobe city hall and jail in a border burg, seized by the bandits and used as a headquarters and prison for their dirty work. It's the usual dirty work—to rape the girl and kill the hero, and the intent is made clear enough. A rescue scene, when the hard-riding ranch crew clumps in just in time, gives it a whooping finale, as customary in such instances.

The present high-peak demand for Westerns should lose none of its pointed appeal through the release of "The Light of Western Stars" (whatever that may mean), for the acting of the two splendid character men redeems it from the market-run of just shooting, riding, dance-hall and ranch-house material. Gray's name should help this picture, even though this picture will not help Zane Gray's name.

Lait.

A MAN OF IRON

Chadwick production starring Lionel Barrymore. Story by Lawrence Marston, directed by Whitman Bennett. Reviewed in projection room, June 18. Running time, 63 minutes.

Philip Durban	Lionel Barrymore
Claire Durban	Mildred Harris
Martha Durban	Winnifred Barry
Mrs. Edith Bowdoin	Dorothy Kingdon
Hugh Bowdoin	Alfred Mack
Denis Callahan	J. Moy Bennett
Maybelle Callahan	Isobel DeLeon
Prince Novakian	Jean Del Val

According to information, this picture is 6,200 feet in length, and therefore a guess is made that it would take about 63 minutes to run it. In the projection room they ground it out in 40 minutes, which made it look like one of those old-timers, where everyone ran through the picture. There is nothing to make it stand out, even had it been run slow. Just a society melodrama along stereotyped lines and hardly probable any of the fans are going to go wild about Lionel Barrymore in the principal role with short cropped hair and seemingly suffering from an ailment that has affected his leg action.

It is a tale of a broken down society family on one hand, a wealthy iron master on the other, and in between a wealthy chocolate manufacturer. There is also a foreign prince as the bone of contention. The society girl without money and the chocolate man's daughter want him. The latter gets him, even though he was engaged to the former and she in a moment of pique accepts the Iron Man, whom she had rejected but a few minutes earlier.

After marriage he realizes that she has not married him for love and at the same time the chocolate girl tires of her prince and has her dad pay him off to the extent of $250,000. But the iron master's wife has learned to love her husband, although she cannot make him realize it. Finally she and mother take a trip to Europe. The prince follows with his fresh bankroll and then her husband also takes the trip with the usual result, a fight and a duel, with both geting shot, the prince being killed and the husband wounded.

To have had the picture a complete success, it might have been just as well to have shot both of them before they started making it.

For the small houses for a single day, yes.

Fred.

Beauty and the Bad Man

A Producers' Distributing Corporation release produced by Frank E. Woods. Story by Peter B. Kyne and adapted by Woods. Directed by William Worthington. Reviewed at the Cameo, New York, June 22. Running time, 65 minutes.

Cassie	Mabel Ballin
Modoc Bill	Forrest Stanley
Chuckawalla Bill	Russell Simpson
L. I. B. Hall	Andre de Beranger
Mayne	Edna Mae Cooper
Gold Hil Cassidy	James Gordon

This is the second of the current P. D. C. program to go into the Cameo on a rental, and it looks like a good thing the house is getting rent, for "Beauty and the Bad Man," although not a poor picture in itself, is one of those negative box office propositions. The featured people, Mabel Ballin and Forrest Stanley, have never been figured as box office cards, and the kick of the works isn't big enough to cause any excitement. It is, therefore, one of those fillers which serves its purpose satisfactorily if bought cheap, but as first run special or even as a heavily advertised feature it doesn't hold up.

The plot concerns Cassie, a girl in the West. Her voice is wonderful, and Modoc Bill, who has some money, hears her sing and loans her enough to cultivate the pipes. Cassie, however, fell temporarily for the church organist, Hall, and married him, but left him immediately, finding that he wasn't four square and a yard wide. So from then on the trails of Cassie and Modoc Bill part. Bill and his pal, Chuckawalla, strike it rich with gold, while Cassie conquers Europe with her voice. The wind-up, however, brings her back to the West, where her ex-husband tries to kill Modoc, who is saved by his pal in time for a clinch finish.

It isn't an uninteresting story and the production is good. But like many others it lacks the kick of a hit and it lacks the names of a "draw." So that qualifies it with the great rank and file of the market.

Sisk.

For Another Woman

Rayart (W. Ray Johnston) production (in association with Frank Talbot. Story by Pearl Doles Bell. Scenario by Agnes Christine Johnston and Frank Dazey. Directed by David Kirkland. Cast includes Kenneth Harlan, Kathryn Riddell, Florence Billings, Arnold Daly, Henry Sedley, Alan Hale, Mary Thurman and Tyrone Power. At the Stanley, New York, one day (June 16). Runs about 65 minutes.

Pearl Doles Bell, whose "Sandra" was voted one of this season's dreariest pictures, is the authoress of "For Another Woman." The latter is much more interesting and human than the Barbara La Marr vehicle, but there is a heavy-handed, sombre and at times even ugly theme that leaves the well-known dark brown taste in the mouths of an audience.

Rayart produced it well, however, in all respects but one. This is the photography, which is distinctly off in the tinting and mechanical processes. Thus certain lavish-looking scenes which should have been as colorful as the screen can make them have been almost spoiled by the lack of clarity and proper lighting in the celluloid. The producers spent a load of jack not only for the sets and atmosphere but for the cast, which is a line-up of "all-star" names.

The locale of Miss Bell's story is Canada, with French Canucks the majority of the characters. As the title implies it tells of the sacrifice of the heroine in shielding the reputation and baby of her friend who has "been led into trouble." Much of the sacrifice seems uncalled for and when, near the finish, it is learned that the deserted girl has been married to the villain the whole time (the producers evidently kow-towing to the censors, as it is doubtful if the original story is so ridiculous), there seems to have been no excuse for all the persecution, sob stuff and heroics that have been going on for more footage than one cares to remember. The plot is almost unrelieved by comic touches and several semi-religious, allegorical bits, badly done, serve only to intensify the heavy air about the film.

The director does not seem to have succeeded very well in his attempts to make the French Canadians picturesque and at the same time keep them true to life. Mary Thurman, who plays the village the village flapper, everybody, including the audience, thinks has gone wrong until the wedding ring hokum is pulled in the final five minutes, makes her role interesting but unreal. Kenneth Harlan has practically nothing to do, while Kathryn Riddell is powerless to accomplish much with the walking angel role of the heroine. Arnold Daly and Tyrone Power, legit luminaries, have little more than bits.

The Tiller Girl from the "Follies" are utilized in one of the big party shots and make a good showing with their clock-work terpsichorean efforts. This and several other scenes emphasize the sex stuff rather strongly, but the moral coating of the picture is so thick that the general average is of Sunday school mildness.

All things considered, "For Another Woman" is not a bad job, but the unpleasant subject matter will keep the box office score down.

THE KISS BARRIER

Fox production, starring Edmund Lowe. Story by Frederick and Fanny Hatton. Directed by R. William Neill. At Loew's New York, one day (June 16), as half the bill. Runs about hour.

Richard Marsh	Edmund Lowe
Marion Weston	Claire Adams
Suzette	Dina Miller
Connie	Marion Harlan
O'Hara	Thomas Mills
Colonel Hale	Charles Clary
The Widow	Grace Cunard
Mrs. Hale	Virginia Madison

Harmless enough and not exactly boring, "The Kiss Barrier" stands nevertheless as about the weakest feature made by Edmund Lowe since he became a Fox star. Lowe is generally known as, or at least the Fox concern would like him to be known as "that young romantic actor," and for that reason they have given him a highly mushy, sentimental and preposterous role to play.

He is cast as a young dramatic star who, while serving in France, meets a girl and steals a kiss in the middle of all the fighting. The war ends and he returns to treading the boards, unable, however, to forget the little cutie who had bridled up so savagely at his amatory advances. She of course turns out to be the niece of his life-long friend, and the remaining four reels lead him a merry chase in pursuit of her forgiveness and love. This is complicated by his leading woman, who is really infatuated with him, and by a particularly irritating flapper, who imagines she is. Never turning to strict farce the picture skims the edges with bachelor apartment comedy and scandal.

The war episodes are going to get the nannies of a lot of veterans because of their minor but aggravating discrepancies. For instance, the presence of a stunning little ambulance driver right in the thick of the fighting probably would have stopped the hostilities in those days. And when she takes the time to indulge in a flirtation with the gallant, immaculate aviator whose machine has just crashed down a couple of thousand feet that's carrying it much too far. Then there are such military irregularities as a colonel wearing a major's insignia, a trench scene which leads to still further appreciation of "What Price Glory," and others.

Lowe's profile is as gorgeous as ever and he has three pretty women to gaze soulfully at in the production. Thomas Mills contributes a very fair comedy valet characterization. In fact, the Hattons have inserted some of the sparkling servant comedy which featured their earlier stage successes.

In all other respects the film is only so-so, and it will mean little in establishing Lowe as a greater favorite or drawing card.

ENEMIES OF YOUTH

Produced by Atlas Film Co. and distributed by the Moeller Theatre Service. From a story by Stacy A. Van Betten and directed by Arthur Berlethet. Reviewed as half a double bill at Loew's New York, June 19. Running time, 55 minutes.

This one has all the earmarks of being political propaganda for either one town or for a flock of them, but it is fairly interesting. Gladys Walton and Mahlon Hamilton are starred, but neither of them are particularly vital to present-day box offices.

The story concerns a "model" town, Arcadia, where the old citizens have plastered with blue laws to such an extent that the youngsters are forced to seek their recreation by drinking moonshine, shooting crap in one of those "social clubs" —and get their vicarious kicks by picking up the girls. By the element which has brought this on, Tom Raymond, the demon district attorney, is nominated for mayor. But he sees the error of legislating morals into a community, so refuses his party's nomination and runs on a liberal platform. Governor Wallace, a noted liberal, is to aid his campaign with a speech, yet by getting to his chauffeur the other party has his car stalled.

But an aeroplane brought him to town in time and he delivered the oration which elected Tom.

For a big city this kind of film is the ideal fatal booking, as the average cosmopolitan audience will remain unmoved and uninterested.

Sisk.

THE GOLD RUSH

Los Angeles, June 26.

Charlie Chaplin Production, written and directed by Charlie Chaplin. Associate director, Charles F. Reisner. Photography by Roland H. Totheroh and Jack Wilson. At Grauman's Egyptian theatre, Hollywood, Cal., for indefinite run beginning June 26, 1925. Running time, 120 minutes.

The Lone Prospector	Charlie Chaplin
Big Jim McKay	Mack Swain
Black Larson	Tom Murray
Jack Cameron	Malcolm Waite
The Girl, Georgia	Georgia Hale
Hank Curtis	Henry Bergman
Miners, dance hall girls and habitues, etc.	

"The Gold Rush" is a distinct triumph for Charlie Chaplin from both the artistic and commercial standpoints, and is a picture certain to create a veritable riot at theatre box offices. It is the greatest and most elaborate comedy ever filmed, and will stand for years as the biggest hit in its field, just as "The Birth of a Nation" still withstands the many competitors in the dramatic class.

Billed as a dramatic comedy, the story carries more of a plot than has been the rule with the star's former offerings. There are spots where Charlie has developed dramatic situations bordering on tragedy, and these show the master hand and finesse of Chaplin's artistry. But taken on the whole, the public will accept "The Gold Rush" as an out and out comedy, and the greatest of all time. Innumerable gags and situations that score round after round of laughter are logically woven into the theme of the story. At no time is the plot lost to gain extra laughs that do not belong.

Alaska, with its dangers, hazards, sufferings and riches, forms the locale of the story. The opening shows an unending stream of prospectors negotiating the difficult Chilcoot Pass, and this is very beautiful in so far as scenery is concerned, but is tedious to an audience that has viewed similar scenes in the news weeklies and scenics many times before.

Charlie is presented as a tramp prospector in the wilds of Alaska, garbed in his old familiar derby, cane, baggy pants and shoes. He seeks refuge from a raging Arctic storm in the cabin of Black Lawson, hunted outlaw, and is allowed to stay by the latter.

Big Jim McKay, a husky prospector, discovers a huge vein of gold on his claim, but the storm uproots his tent and blows him to the hut of Larson. The latter objects to McKay's intrusion, and a struggle ensues between the two for possession of a rifle. Chaplin scores here with business in trying to keep out of line with the barrel of the gun. McKay finally subdues Larson and elects to stay till the storm subsides. But the blizzard continues for many days, and provisions give out. The trio cut the cards to select one who must brave the elements to secure food. Larson gets the assignment, and sets forth, but down the trail encounters two officers of the law and kills them both. He picks up their provisions and equipment and continues on his way, making camp at McKay's claim and discovering the rich gold strike.

Meantime Charlie and McKay feel the pangs of hunger back in the cabin, and the tramp gets over a wow when he cooks and serves one of his shoes. The unusual meal rings the bell. Finally the two decide to leave, McKay to relocate his claim and Charlie heading for town. The tramp secures food and lodging at the cabin of Hank Curtis on the outskirts and Curtis leaves him to take care of the place during a prospecting trip.

McKay surprises Larson at the claim. In the battle ensuing McKay is felled by a shovel, Larson dashing off down the trail. A thrilling and realistic spectacle is presented when the outlaw is engulfed in a mountain of snow and ice that breaks loose and crashes to the bottom of the canyon hundreds of feet below.

Charlie visits the dance hall and secretly admires Georgia, the favorite girl in the place. Jack Cameron, in love with the girl, heckles the tramp. Georgia selects Charlie to dance with her in preference to Cameron. On the dance floor Chaplin tops each succeeding gag with another even better.

A few days later a quartet of the dance hall girls headed by Georgia stumble on the cabin of Charlie. The girl decides to have some fun at his expense, and the quartet promise to be at the cabin for a New Year's Eve party, without thought of being serious. But the tramp makes elaborate preparations to entertain his dream girl. The sequence depicting the disappointment of Charlie in the cabin in the midst of his spread for the girl is undoubtedly one of the finest pieces of dramatic interpretation ever put on the screen.

McKay, stunned by the blow delivered by Larson, wanders back to town and is laughed at when he declares a mountain of gold was found, but he cannot relocate it unless he finds the cabin occupied by Larson. At the dance hall Georgia pens a note to Cameron declaring her love for him. Cameron laughs at it and passes the letter around the table. Seeing the lone tramp over in a corner he has the waiter deliver the note to Charlie. The latter is elated and dashes to find Georgia. McKay has entered the place and spies the tramp while standing at the bar. Cornering Charlie, he demands that the lone prospector accompany him to Larson's cabin, promising Charlie an equal share if the mine is found.

Arriving at the cabin the pair decide to stay until the following day and then search for the mine. During the night a heavy storm breaks, the cabin is dislodged and carried to the brink of a high cliff. The balancing cabin and the struggles of the pair to escape provide more than a reel of solid laughs that do not cease until the cabin crashes over the cliff with Charlie escaping at the last moment. McKay then discovers his lost claim within a few yards of the precipice.

The final scenes of Charlie and McKay journeying back to the States as multi-millionaires are unusual in that they show Chaplin out of his familiar attire. He is dressed in the height of fashion with evening dress and all the adornments. Seeing him this way will make the audiences like him more in the makeup that made him famous. On the boat the newly created millionaire discovers Georgia en route home in steerage, with a fadeout on the usual clutch.

Humor is the dominating force, with Chaplin reaching new heights as a comedian. Chaplin naturally carries practically the entire 10 reels of action and performs this task without difficulty. He transcends everything that has ever gone before in comedy production, and it will be a long time before any one displaces him as the genius of pantomime.

The 10 reels do not leave one bored at any time, for Chaplin has deftly interspersed his comedy action throughout a logically developed plot. At times, in unfolding the story, there seem a few moments of retarding interest, but Chaplin snaps these up with clever and unexpected gags.

The sequence showing Chaplin and Swain in the see-sawing cabin on the edge of the precipice surpasses anything ever before screened and provides one reel of continuous roars and howls.

The Far North settings are adequate, although they show plainly they were of studio construction in most instances. In this case, however, Chaplin is the main attraction, and he comes back in his old familiar part that will make "The Gold Rush" a much-played and greatly enjoyed picture everywhere.

The supporting cast includes Georgia Hale as the dance hall girl, who shows great promise with more experience before the camera. Mack Swain, Tom Murray, Malcom Waite and Henry Bergman compete the balance of the principals. *Wally.*

PATHS OF PARADISE

Famous Players' presentation, Clarence Badger production of Keene Thompson's adaptation of Paul Armstrong's play, "The Heart of a Thief." At Rivoli, New York, week June 28.

Molly	Betty Compson
Friend	Raymond Griffith
Callahan	Tom Santschi
Father	Bert Woodruff
Confederate	Fred Kelsey

Paul Armstrong's last play, his personal production, was "The Heart of a Thief." He opened it at the Criterion one Wednesday night in 1916, and it closed that Saturday night. That play broke his heart. He never wrote another line, and he died soon afterward.

But, could he come back to the Broadway, which made and killed him, he would sit in the Rivoli this week and know he had not lived in vain—perhaps he might think he died in vain.

"Paths to Paradise," which preserves the plot of "The Heart of a Thief," though it is far afield in treatment, is at times almost a Keystone. But it is a glittering masterpiece of entertainment, directed with a flashing sense of hmor, acted to the last drop of blood, a thing of high thrills and low laughs, and an all-around ace of comedy-drama feature-films.

Raymond Griffith, who is rising faster than any other individual in the screen world, still rises. In "The Night Club" he did a near-Chaplin of broad, eccentric funning; here he achieves a Douglas MacLean, and once or twice almost a Jack Barrymore of light amusing.

Betty Compson glories in a slick comedy-crook role, fully as distinguished as in her heavy parts of past seasons, runs him neck and neck.

An auto race—out and back—running not less than twenty full minutes, which is a long, long time for such action these days—is worked up with laugh effects and hair-raising escapades toward the end, coming as a complete surprise against the indoor atmosphere of the rest, which is confined to now-I-got-it-now-you-got-it with a diamond necklace.

The two crooks, man and girl, are after the bauble. They trick one another, they get together, they trick all the police of California, they are attracted, they make the wild getaway, they get remorse when they get true love, they race back, they return the necklace, they are heroes, the police are still the suckers, everybody is happy—especially the audience.

Rarely in a sophisticated theatre like the Riovli is there applause for a film. Monday night there was an uproar of handclapping—and the theatre was packed with twelve-deep of standees upstairs and down.

Great film for any theatre at almost any prices.

Lait.

Kivalina of the Ice Lands

Presented by B. C. R. Productions, Inc., and made by Earl Rossman in the Arctic regions. Acted by a cast of Esquimaux and directed by Mr. Rossman. At the Strand, New York, week June 28. Running time, 61 minutes.

The Hero	Aguvaluk
The Heroine	Kivalina
The Witch Doctor	Nashulik
Kivalina's Brother	Tooktoo
The Master Hunter	Nuwak

This one will long be remembered because of the magnificent scenes in color of the Aurora Borealis. These shots are as thrilling as a dozen ordinary movies and of such actual magnificence the audience was literally enthralled. That's strong trade paper talk, but it is deserved.

The spectacle of the ever-changing colors, their swift shooting variations and the bursting of large hunks of brilliant hues is unmatched by any man-made picture spectacle. The argument may be that the man in the street isn't interested particularly in seeing the Aurora Borealis, and that may be so, but the problem then is to create enough interest. Any man, having seen these shots, can't help but thrill at the realization that here, for the first time, they are definitely recorded in motion and in color, something never achieved before.

Kivalina, it seems, is beloved by Aguvaluk, who is a big man among the Esquimaux tribes. Wanting to marry Kivalina, the witch doctor of the tribe holds him up, saying that not until he catches 40 seals and the rare silver fox and thus discharges a debt of his father, can he marry the lady. Aguvaluk catches the seals and then starts for that silver fox. He gets that, after a far trip North, and so wins the lady.

In all this the various activities of the tribe are depicted. We see them making their boats of skin; harpooning the walrus and the seal; skinning reindeer; constructing their igloos; eating blubber and then making a giant wall of ice in which to corral their herd of reinmigrate with the seasons and always take their reindeer along.

Their village of Tavik is on the ocean and in one scene is the unique spectacle of watching that ocean freeze. In a close-up of the waves, Rossman has the surging body of water in the congealing process—another truly phenomenal thing inasmuch as his shot shows the waves becoming encrusted with ice as they move.

All of the hunting trips are graphic, while one shot is of a giant cake of ice literally blackened by huge walrus. These mammals are also seen in the water, and in some of the close shots they show to good advantage. Still another has the men of the village towing in a rare Beluga whale.

As an educational picture, "Kivalina" ranks among the highest, and has the added grace of possessing a story which holds. The titles, by Katherine Hilliker and H. H. Caldwell, are very bad. They seem greatly overwritten and detrimental to the action of the film. Rossman is hurt by some of these titles, for one or two of the scenes don't live up to the preceding caption.

Few pictures were ever more deserving of success than this one.

Sisk.

THE LUCKY DEVIL

Famous Players Production starring Richard Dix. Directed by Frank Tuttle from the story by Bryon Morgan. Screen play by Townsend Martin. Reviewed at the Rivoli, New York, July 5. Running time, 61 minutes.

Bill Phelps	Richard Dix
Doris Kent	Esther Ralston
Auntie McDee	Edna May Oliver
Franklyne, Sr.	Tom Findley
Franklyne, Jr.	Anthony Jowitt
The Professor	Joe Burke
Mrs. Hunt	Mary Foy
Sailor Sheldon	Gunboat Smith
Sheriff	Charles Sellon

With his last few productions Dix has been coming along like a comet, clicking at the box offices in the Broadway first runs and giving the audiences a big money's worth. Particularly was this true of "The Shock Punch," the predecessor to this film. It had loads of thrill stuff and some comedy, while this one is even better, holding all the thrill stuff to the last two reels and planting much comedy in the other spots. And when the thrill stuff comes along, there is comedy with it. So it makes a good vehicle for the star, and he handles his part nicely.

The story has him as a salesman in a department store. By a raffle he wins a car his heart has long desired. Striking out for the camping country, he meets Doris Kent and her aunt and it is one of those love at first sight things. But his car once belonged to Rudy Franklyne, a scandalous young man, and recognizing the car the auntie takes the hero for a scapegoat, and tells her niece to stay away. However, he overtakes them on the road, broken down in their car, and tows them into a small town. There he goes broke, as some one steals his purse, while Doris and her aunt get a shock when they discover the rich uncle they came to visit was in the booby hatch.

It is up to the hero to dig some money. After many vicissitudes, he enters his car in a cross country race at the country fair, and at that time the landlady sends the sheriff to keep his eye on the car. Phelps isn't to be kidded, so he takes the sheriff with him, and starts on the race. He is laps ahead on the last round when his gears strip. The sheriff, who by this time is interested, suggests he throw the car in reverse, and he does—winning the race by coming in backwards.

This race is all fine comedy and with the hick sheriff as a partner, it goes for more laughs. Esther Ralston is a sweet looking leading lady and a relief from some of these hard boiled mammas who play the dainty dimpled parts. Edna May Oliver does a typical Edna May Oliver impersonation as the aunt and draws laughs, while the star himself delivers all the way through.

"The Lucky Devil" is a first rate run and will live up to lots of boosting, particularly if the star happens to be strong in your neighborhood. It is much on the type of film that Tom Meighan used to put out before he struck the retrograde. A few more of this type for Dix will "make" him solidly, for the audience Sunday night in the Rivoli ate it up and wanted more. Following "Paths to Paradise" of last week wasn't an easy job, but this one stood up well.

Sisk.

THE WHITE DESERT

Reginald Barker's production of Courtney Riley Cooper's story, "The White Desert." Metro-Goldwyn-Mayer picture. Trio of players co-starred: Claire Windsor, Pat O'Malley and Robert Fraser. At the Capitol, New York, week of July 5. Running time, 76 minutes.

Robinette	Claire Windsor
Barry	Pat O'Malley
Keith	Robert Frazer
Saul MacFarlane	Frank Currier
Foster	William Eugene
Engineer	Roy Laidlaw
Dark Wing	David Dunbar
Chinese Cook	Sojin
Mrs. Foster	Priscilla Bonner
Runt	Snitz Edwards
Dr. Carter	Milton Rose
Camp Cook	Sidney Bracey
Mrs. Martin	Trixie Friganza
Podopholous	Bert Sprotte
Buck Carson	Mathew Betz

They reached the biggest climax too early, i.e., too early for the dramatic tension to carry along at the same high speed, once that snowslide had done its deadliest.

In this Reginald Barker production that bears the Metro-Goldwyn label, the story was in the midst of one of the most exciting snowslides the screen has seen in many a day. Cracking and drifting of the snow was done with tremendous camera effectiveness and Mr. Barker did some A1 work in working in its thrill.

It was tough to follow the big avalanche of snow that either swept everything before it or buried deep what it encountered.

However, the characters were then steeped in a food famine, while the main characters, especially "the fighting Irishman," Barry Houston, went through snow, blizzards and hell to bring food relief 100 miles or so away from the buried camp.

There is a romance running through and all the way through, the girl being Robinette MacFarlane (Claire Windsor). Two men loved her, Keith, chief construction engineer (Mr. Fraser), and Barry, superintendent (Mr. O'Malley). A snow plough, the latest rotary kind, backed up by steam, when hitting those heavy snowdrifts, is a slow-moving thing at best and when it was called upon to hurry to the camp's relief it seemed like eternity before it finally pulled in.

That baby—the Foster baby—was a great little actor and it put a touch of nature that is bound to make the whole film world kin through its naturalness.

"The White Desert" isn't a great picture, but it has thrills and a human heart thread of romance that will keep it from doing a nose dive in the neighborhood theatres.

That snowslide is worth seeing. The rest is the kind that one has seen in most any of the melodramatic films.

Mark.

THE LADY WHO LIED

First National Production. Directed by Edwin Carewe, who gets credit in the program as "presenting" the same. Adapted from Robert Hichens' novel, "Snake Bite." Cojointly features Lewis Stone, Virginia Valli and Nita Naldi. At the Strand week July 5. Running time, 75 minutes.

Horace Pierpont	Lewis Stone
Fay Kennion	Virginia Valli
Fifi	Nita Naldi
Dr. Allen Mortimer	Edward Earle
Merton	Leo White
Gen. Sir Henry Kennion	Louis Payne
Ahmed	Purnell Pratt
Saad Ben Youssof	Sam Appel
Zetta	Zalla Zarana
Mahmud	George Lewis

It took a long time for this picture to hit its dramatic stride, but when it finally swung into channels increasing its heart interest a story was unfolded that proved boring for the most part. It had scenes showing how caddish some of our men can be when the love of the same woman is concerned.

This First National picture may have looked like the triple-action baby in the reading, but in the making it slashed and sloshed around through footage that had the characters making themselves look foolish.

In the lights appear the names of Louis Stone, Virginia Valli and Nita Naldi. Considering the work he had to do when the principals, barring Nita, who was eliminated from the story early, landed on the sands of the great desert, Edward Earle was justly entitled to billing prominence. He has a thankless role, but got as much as he could out of it and finally was killed off in a hurry.

Through interminable footage went a story that showed Horace Pierpont all set to marry a refined lady named Fay Kennion. When Horace was having a quiet moment with his pipe the lady known as Fifi came right into his room and tried to vamp him all over the place.

Fifi remained all night and didn't take time to unclasp the pearls around her neck, but she later uncoiled her hair in time for Horace's prospective bride to see her.

Then came the beginning of the lies the lady was to tell. She gave Horace the air and started on a long trip into the desert to find an old flame, Dr. Mortimer.

Mort was down on his love luck, so to speak, and we find him a regular toper, while a dancing girl shakes her physical self close within his stupified vision.

Fay's cable sobers him and he comes out of his drunken stupor to shave, doll up and give her the welcome to the desert embrace.

Horace follows, and Horace being overburdened with money and a devil for traveling, spends it like a drunken sailor on Mortimer and his wife. Then Morty, still winning desert championships at lushing, comes to long enough to realize that Fay and Horace were more than platonic friends.

A viper bites Horace and the doctor (Morty was a doctor with a past master's degree at drinking) decides to let him die if his wife shows that she loves Pierpont.

But Morty saves Horace and he and his wife turn back, leaving Horace in a wheel chair. Finally Horace meanders back to Venice and there in the same garden spot, playing a lover's uke, or guitar, to be explicit, was Fay, waiting for Horace to come back from his snake bite siesta.

Then a cut-back showing how quickly Mortimer's life had been snuffed out by desert pirates.

It's a story that took a lot of jumping around and while it went at a camel's crawl through the desert scenes, the biggest thrill comes, perhaps, when that snake is crawling over to snip Morty on the ankle.

There are some corking shots. However, it's doubtful, extremely so, whether these fine and unusual photographic shots can save the picture.

Oh, yes, Nita Naldi got back in the final footage, but she didn't do enough in this film to take the mazuma without blushing.

Mark.

Cyrano de Bergerac

(In colors)

Produced by the Unione Cinematographica Italia and released here by Atlas Distributing Corporation. Made from Edmond Rostand's famous play and directed by Augusto Genina with Pierre Magnier starred. At the Colony, New York, July 5. Running time, 90 minutes.

Cyrano de Bergerac	Pierre Magnier
Roxanne	Linda Moglia
Christian de Neuvillette	Angelo Ferrari
DeGuiche	Umberto Casilini
Rageuneau	Alex Bernard
The Duenna	Gemma De Sanctis

Coquelin rode the peak of his fame playing Cyrano, while Mansfield and Walter Hampden, the latter recently, have both scored tremendous hits in the role. Walter Damrosch wrote an opera on the Rostand play, but it failed for the reason that the soul of Cyrano was the dialog of Rostand, and while the picture has its good moments, subtitles can never replace the lines of the play.

It has action aplenty, and there is a love story as sweet and poignant as any recorded. There is atmosphere and comedy, but it is a role which only the great ones of the stage dare attempt. Sarah Bernhardt played Roxanne to Coquelin's Cyrano—and of such casts must it be constructed. Pierre Magnier, who has the title role, is unquestionably a capable actor and does finely here. The English translation used mars things at times and completely kills the ballade composed by Cyrano during his duel. The producing company tries to render it more effective by inserting lines of it at the top of the pictures.

Cyrano was a magnificent man but his nose protruded several inches from his face and rendered him unsightly. That is the pathos of the play—that this fine specimen of manhood should be so marred.

Cyrano died, happy, having lived a life of freedom and gallantry and **though poor at the end, his last speeches proclaimed his happiness at having defeated falsehood, prejudice, compromise and cowardice.**

There are individual incidents of much beauty and power while others just as beautiful have been blurred and sputtered. An instance is where Cyrano described his methods of reaching the Moon.

First, with crystal vials filled with dew, which will be drawn aloft, Cyrano argued, as the sun arose to drink the mist of the dawn. Then secondly by sealing air in a chest and rarefying it by means of mirrors, placed in an icosahedron. Then, thirdly, to construct a rocke driven onward by discharges of saltpeter from the read, its method of procedure to be like that of a locust. Fourth, as smoke had a natural tendency to rise, blow enough in a globe to lift himself. Or, fifth, to follow the method of Diana, anoint himself with the marrow of bulls and goats. And sixth, to be seated in an iron plate and proceed by throwing a magnet into the air.

And then DeGuiche became as fascinated as this "learned idiot." Querying Cyrano, he found his method was to recline on the beach with his head to the moon. And as the ocean in its rising tide seeks the moon, the moisture in his own hair drew him upward.

The makers of the film attempted to illustrate three of these methods and in very brief flashes, it impressed as a botched job. It was trick photography but far below the standards employed here. The fights of Cyrano are also portrayed, while large mobs are used in the battle scenes and as a rule the whole thing is capably, if somewhat stolidly, produced. But the supporting cast is undistinguished and the coloring at times bad.

The picture doesn't bore and is titled capably on the whole. There are several opportunities overlooked, the biggest one of which would have gone for howl. That occurs when Cyrano, falling from the tree, feigned ignorance and inquired where he was. When told that a lady was waiting nearby, Cyrano exclaimed, "So this is Paris."

Although unexpected the film received applause at its finish. That can hardly be its ultimate fate, for although the play is invariably successful, the picture is a poor substitute. B. S. Moss is understood to have booked it for a run. If kept strictly on its box office merits, that will hardly be attained, for "Cyrano" will ultimately and deservedly be classed with some of those other foreign made spectacles. *Sisk.*

ONE YEAR TO LIVE

First National production made by M. C. Levee. Aileen Pringle, Antonio Moreno and Dorothy Mackaill starred. Adapted to the screen by John Hunter and directed by Irving Cummings. At the Piccadilly, July 4. Running time, 65 minutes.

Elise Duchanier............Aileen Pringle
Marthe..................Dorothy Mackaill
Dr. Lucien la Pierre.......Sam de Grasse
Lolette....................Rosemary Theby
Stage Manager...................Leo White
Maurice Brunel............Joseph Kilgour
Capt. Tom Kendrick........Antonio Moreno

This plot is variation of about 100,000 other movies, and in acting is played like a Blaney stock company. In brief, a dirty theatrical manager pursues a good girl; she **says that when she is a star she will listen to him, but on the night of his conquest, her true love walks in and she gets good again, leaving the dirty theatrical manager flat.** The locale is Paris and several of the scenes are in a theatre.

There is a famous dancer, Lolette, and the subtitles say that she is the rage of the city. Her dancing, say those titles, is incomparable. So when the time comes for Lolette to step her dogs, the scene shows a curtain of girls moving aside to give an entrance to the star. And Lolette enters, dressed like a Columbia burlesque prima donna at the start of the season. Then comes the routine, as mild as anything ever screened. Yet the audience in the picture got up and cheered.

This ridiculous scene, which made them laugh at the Piccadilly, is followed by quite a few others, principally one in which Lolette's maid, the heroine, puts on the clothes of her mistress and steps before a big ball to demonstrate that her mistress isn't one-two-three with her as a stepper. Matter of fact, she wasn't.

Rosemary Theby, one of the old timers, is Lolette, while Aileen Pringle was borrowed by Metro-Goldwyn to play Elise, the downtrodden maid, who was beloved by Capt. Kendrick of the U. S. A. Dorothy Mackaill plays the small role of a sick sister, while Joseph Kilgour leers as that dirty theatrical manager. He's the kind of a manager, incidentally, who stands in the wings all the time to applaud his actors.

In plot and situation, this is a tawdry film, and except for the theatre scenes, it doesn't look to be expensive. The real lowdown on it is that it is the fourth First National inside of a month to be kept out of the Strand, that house in the meantime playing some independent stuff. "White Monkey" went to the Colony, "Necessary Evil" and another film went for a one day's showing at Loew's New York for their metropolitan first run, while this one is shunted into the Piccadilly. It may do better than recent business there because of the stars but in week stands it is the kind of film that will be mercilessly roasted by the papers and wise patrons.

As a daily change program picture it may suffice, but not much more. *Sisk.*

THE HAPPY WARRIOR

J. Stuart Blackton Production, presented by A. E. Smith. From the story by A. S. M. Hutchinson. Directed by J. Stuart Blackton. Featuring Malcolm McGregor, Alice Calhoun, Wilfred North and Mary Alden. At the Rialto, N. Y., week July 5. Running time, 82 minutes.

Ralph ....Malcolm McGregor
Dora ....Alice Calhoun
Aunt Maggie ....Mary Alden
Stingo Hannaford ....Anders Randolf
Ima ....Olive Borden
Rollo ....Gardner James
Egbert ....Otto Mattieson
Mr. Letham ....Wilfrid North
Mrs. Letham ....Eulalie Jensen
Audrey ....Andree Tournier
Foxey Pinent....................Jack Herrick
Ralph, 9 years old..........Philippe deLacy
Rollo, 10 years old..........Bobby Gordon

Here is one of the best pictures from an entertainment standpoint that Vitagraph has turned out in a long while. It has a story well connected in the screen version and handled in such a manner as far as direction is concerned, that it will hold the audience. It is the nearest approach to a picture for the first-run houses that Vitagraph has turned out on its list of program production in a couple of years.

As for its money-getting chances, that is another story, for the drop-in audiences in the bigger houses seem to fight shy of the Vitagraph trademark productions. However, for the neighborhood houses and the smaller town theatres it should pass nicely.

It is a picture made to order for the English market, as the story and the manner of its screen treatment make it perfect for English audiences. It is an English story in the first place, one that puts the English youth of caste in front of the audiences in a manner that the rank and file of English want to see their nobility, and it is played and directed in a manner that will entertain in addition.

The story is that of the secret marriage of a young Baronet to a girl of the village, his death in India and the succession to the title of a distant relative. The wife of the latter, elated at stepping into a title the motto of which is "I Hold," decides to do that very thing when the unacknowledged widow of the late title holder comes on the scene with a babe in her arms. The widow is turned from the door, and as a result dies in a few hours later in the home of her sister. The boy in his early teens shows the disposition of "a happy warrior," he fights with a smile and rescues the youngster who is in the place in the world that he should rightly have had from the hands of the village bully. The boys become fast friends and later grow into young manhood together, both in love with the same girl. The years pass, and when the time comes for the rightful heir to the title to announce himself he renounces his right to both title and girl in favor of his youthful friend.

There is a corking prize fight scene in the picture, a lot of good hoak circus stuff, a portion of real comedy skillfully injected, and, above all, the photography is corking, with some really good exterior shots. *Fred.*

THE TEXAS TRAIL

Presented by Hunt Stromberg, starring Harry Carey. Adapted from the novel "Rangy Pete," by Guy Morton, directed by R. Scott Dunlop. Released by Producers' Dist. Corp. At the Cameo, New York, week July 5. Running time, 51 minutes.

Peter Grainger.................Harry Carey
Betty Foster..................Ethel Shannon
Fred Foster...................Charles French
Dan Merrill....................Claude Peyton
Ike Collander................Sidney Franklin

Very cheap western, when considered it is a starring production that has one of the top notch western stars in it. The picture is one of the caliber that will do more to cause the star to lose caste at the box office than anything else. The story is weak, the continuity laughable, the direction poor and likewise the editing and titling. If Hunt Stromberg is trying to kill off Harry Carey then he is taking the proper method to do so, and to succeed all he has to do is to continue with pictures of this quality. Carey ought to have foresight enough to protect himself when he is handed material of this sort.

It is a tale laid in the west with the usual mortgage on the ranch, which the heavy is about to foreclose. When he discovers that the rancher can meet the demand note he waylays the messenger who is carrying the money and steals it. The attempt to ship it out of the country in a box of dried apples supplies the plot. Of course, there is a girl. She is the niece of the rancher with the mortgage hanging over him. She discovers the plot to send the money away and leads the gang to recover it. In the end, with the assistance of the hero, the dough is brought back into the rightful hands and the girl and hero clinch.

Harry Carey and Ethel Shannon have the principal roles, with the girl overshadowing the star. There is also a puppy dog in the picture, which, at the opening, cannot be more than three weeks old, yet after the action of the picture is about over, and the period consumed is two days at the most, there is this same pup at the age of about three months, judging from appearances, yet she has a litter of her own pups romping about. They certainly work fast in pictures and this picture is one that was turned out fast.

Only for double feature bills is it worth considering. *Fred.*

WILD JUSTICE

Produced by John W. Considine, Jr., and to be distributed by United Artists. Story and scenario by C. Gardner Sullivan, and direction by Chester Franklin. Peter the Great, dog actor, starred. Reviewed at Loew's State July 6 as picture feature of combination bill. Running time, 63 minutes.

The plot is in the snow country of the north, and the protagonists are Dr. Wright, the hero; Jim Blake, the villain, and the heroine. The heroine, it happens, is the niece of a man who has been mysteriously murdered and at the time of his death she was on her way to make her home with him. A terrible blizzard, however, arises, and she takes refuge in the cabin of Jim Blake—really the cabin of the dead man, but taken over by Blake for a debt.

There Blake attacks her, but Dr. Wright has discovered the overturned sled and her clothing, so he holds a piece of it before the dog star and even though it is contrary to natural law, the dogs holds the scent over the snow and finds the girl as Blake is about to carry out what the novelists would call his nefarious purpose. After that, Blake is out to kill the dog and nearly succeeds, but the bullet he fired at the dog proves a boomerang, because the doctor compares it with the bullet that killed the girl's uncle, and they gee in all respects. Hence, villain is disposed of, dog is safe and the girl and hero marry.

The principal interest of the film naturally centers on the dog. And as dog stars go he stands up well, but not quite the equal of Rin-Tin-Tin. The picture, however, gives him some great opportunities and the humans in it are well directed by Chet Franklin. Some of the action stuff on skis is good and snappy, and while the bloody melodramatics of the plot seem far fetched and illogical, they provide the dog with many opportunities.

John W. Considine, Jr., produced this one independently, but it was announced early this week that United Artists would take it over for distribution. It doesn't rank, however, as a special of any kind and while its drawing power is negligible, being the dog's first vehicle, it suffices to hold up the entertainment end of a good program house. *Sisk.*

THE BOOMERANG

Gasnier Production presented by B. P. Schulberg. Adapted from the play by Winchell Smith and Victor Mapes. Directed by L. J. Gasnier. At Capitol, New York, week June 28. Running time, 76 minutes.

Virginia Zelza...............Anita Stewart
Dr. Gerald Sumner...............Bert Lytell
Budd Woodridge.............Donald Keith
Poulet ....Arthur Edmund Carew
Grace Tyler.................Mary McAllister
Preston Dewitt.............Philo McCollough
Bert Hanks ....Ned A. Sparks
Gordon ....Winter Hall

When they get around to picking the 10 best for 1925 it is a pipe that this won't be one of them. "The Boomerang" was a great show, but as a feature film it is a flop as far as the first run houses are concerned.

In the neighborhoods where there is a daily change of program and double features this one is about of the caliber to fit, but that is about all. No one need look to getting big box office returns with it. How it ever got into the Capitol is going to be one of life's great mysteries, but it's at the Capitol and therefore it must be judged by the standard of pictures that house plays. It is far from that standard.

There are three featured players, Anita Stewart, Bert Lytell and Donald Keith. Why the latter is included with the former pair is another mystery. Not that the others mean anything at the box office right now, for they have both slipped in the last year or so, but Keith doesn't mean a thing at the box office and in this picture he doesn't mean a thing on the screen.

Ned Sparks is the only one who really stands out, and his role is hardly more than a bit.

It is true Miss Stewart looks better in this picture than in any other in which she has been seen in some time and she does handle her role fairly well, but Anita never did mean a whole lot when it came to counting up the returns since the days when she was with Vitagraph.

The adaptation and the direction are not anything that people will rave about. Gasnier has made many better pictures. *Fred.*

PASSIONATE YOUTH

Truart Films presentation, directed by Dallas M. Fitzgerald. At Colony, New York, week June 28.

Mary Rand	Beverly Bayne
John Rand	Frank Mayo
Henrietta Rand	Pauline Garon
Corbin	Bryant Washburn
Peggy	Carmelita Geraghty
Matt Rutherford	Ralph McCullough
Jimmy Wellington	Ernest Wood

"Into each life some rain must fall,
Some days must be dark and
dreary."

Into the life of every picture reviewer must come now and then a "Passionate Youth." Then he gnashes his teeth and says to himself

"My duty to the readers suggests that I let loose a machine-gun loaded with adjectives—aye, superlatives.

"But, on the other hand, the function of the critic is to criticise, not to vilify."

So, what can one do with such a film?

"To err is only human," says one of the subtitles.

That isn't even a correctly quoted bromide—it's just a bromide. And it is typical of the whole of "Passionate Youth" as well as its sole alibi. If to err is human, "Passionate Youth" is superhuman.

It is a cumbersome, creaky, obsolete inter-involved set of triangles, tragedies, sex, woman triumphant, love victorious, villain foiled, masses and classes, tuxedos and mustaches "problem" play, the main problem being why it ever was made and the incidental problem being how it ever got to Broadway.

Perhaps on the title! An inspired bit of catch-nickel bunk and junk that is—look it over again, in all its majestic capitals, PASSIONATE YOUTH.

What chambermaid could resist it?

It has no more to do with the subject matter than would "Satan's Pajamas" or "The Duke's Revenge."

But, there it is, flaming along the Big Alley to hook in the yokels on false pretenses.

The story, stripped of about an hour of thick detail which is neither entertaining nor consistent, is this:

Mary Rand divorces her preacher husband. She's tired of slaving, and thinks her daughter is entitled to a fling. She goes back to law practice and she falls in love with her partner, who falls for daughter, daughter also being soft on partner. Partner makes love to both, and an old flame, besides, and toys with his waxy mustache as he filmflams the three. Before the end he's killed. Why not?

Meantime the mother has been elected District Attorney and the daddy, who once was a lawyer, defends the daughter, charged with murder. Daughter is not sent to the chair. Her father proves that the gun the great lover was croaked with wasn't the gun found on daughter. Happy blowoff. Any blowoff to such a story would be happy.

The acting is awful and the direction indescribably fierce. Bryant Washburn, noted hero, is the villain; Frank Mayo, noted villain, is the father-hero; Beverly Bayne is the mother, and she never acted worse in her distinguished career of bad screen acting; Pauline Garon, as the daughter, is just a flippant flapper, and Carmelita Geraghty, as the third of the villain's butterflies, is just pretty and dumb.

There is less action than even the above story would indicate, and a series of wild orgies dragged in during the daughter's crack at going to bow-wows doesn't fill much of the void.

Will probably get by as a program picture in melodrama and heavy sex-stuff houses, and may draw drop-ins on the title, if there are still some who believe such titles and of those if there are still some who crave what such titles imply if they are meant.

Such presentations serve to remind the public of the days which the film industry wants forgotten. *Lait.*

THE MAD WHIRL

Universal production of the novel "Here's How," by Richard Washburn Child. May McAvoy starred and William A. Seiter, director. At the Piccadilly, New York, June 27. Running time, 69 minutes.

Cathleen Gillis	May McAvoy
Jack Herrington	Jack Mulhall
His mother	Myrtle Stedman
His father	Alec B. Francis
Margie Taylor	Barbara Bedford
Benny Kingsley	Ward Crane
Martin Gillis	George Fawcett
Julia Sparling	Marie Astaire
Spivins	Joseph Singleton

One more good film to Universal's credit, and maybe U hasn't been making good ones recently. This one has a good sound story, its continuity is airtight, the cast all to the mustard and Seiter's direction mighty nifty. Seiter was formerly the Pathe serial director, but since branching out into the feature field, he has been delivering like an intelligent veteran.

The plot of this concerns both an argument pro and con on the relationship of parents with their children and a love affair between a boy and girl of different classes. The Herrington family is rich, and pa and ma at 50 adopt the jazz method of living to keep in touch with their kids. But the jazz method brought on some serious drinking and many all night parties (and they're not staged nonsensically, but accurately). The idea of the parents was that they kept in better touch with their children, but in reality they made them pretty wild.

The boy, Jack, was in love with Cathleen Gillis, whose father ran a small store in the town. She was a fine girl and loved Jack, but his drinking and general gayness disgusted her and embittered her father, who tried to keep them apart.

After some struggle she had Jack on the road to reformation, and they were married. That made her father sore and he delivered himself to the Herringtons and bawled them for a row of oratory. But it was evident that the two children had found themselves—so that shoved the parents in the background.

Miss McAvoy, in the lead, does mighty good work and George Fawcett, as her father, is just as fine as George Fawcett can be. That's some, too. Jack Mulhall is okeh as the hero, while everybody else in the cast, with no exception, came through. Seiter, the director, deserves a big share of praise, while the location man and the technical director also contributed largely by the attractiveness of the atmosphere which they created.

It is astonishing in a sense to figure that Universal is making program pictures that are on a par with the best. Not so long ago U was considered one of the cheaper concerns and its product wasn't used in the big houses. Serials of the "Broken Coin" and "Trey of Hearts" type were their forte at the start, then the Westerns and the cheap society dramas. But now U is taking stories that are good and producing them expensively and intelligently.

Which is a sign that times do change. *Sisk.*

THE AWFUL TRUTH

A Producers' Distributing Corporation release made by Peninsula Studios, Inc. Adapted from Arthur Richman's play of the same name and directed by Paul Powell with Agnes Ayres starred. At the Cameo, New York, June 27 week. Running time, 65 minutes.

Lucy Satterley	Agnes Ayres
Norman Satterley	Warner Bexter
Kempster	Phillips Smalley
Danny Leeson	Raymond Lowney
Josephine	Winifred Bryson
Mrs. Leesoh	Carrie Clarke Ward

This play was produced legitimately about three seasons ago by the Frohmans and had a fair run at Henry Miller's theatre with Ina Claire in the lead. The movie version has Agnes Ayres in the Claire role, and the fault with this is that Miss Ayres doesn't shine as a comedienne. What she does can probably be credited to the director, Paul Powell, who has turned out an entertaining program feature.

In plot the whole thing is as slim-waisted as they come, but Powell has maneuvered his various scenes with a delicacy that stretches them out a bit without impairing their dramatic value. The locale has been changed for reasons movie and an advantage has been gained. On the stage it was played in a smart interior set, but here the locale is a fashionable hotel in snowy Canada, where honeymooners go once in a while to look at the scenery.

Lucy Satterley, recently divorced from hubby Norman, has arrived. Danny Leeson, a sap-headed young millionaire, has proposed to her. His old aunt, however, won't hear of having a divorced woman in the family until she is sure that the divorce wasn't obtained for terrible reasons. So the ex-husband is called into consultation and he lies beautifully. While he is taking up for his ex-mate, she falls in love with him all over again. The rest of the picture portrays her whimsical conquest.

The cast supporting the star is excellent and the settings also good. They're much better than the sets usually found in the P. D. C. releases, which may mean that the technical department has been improved.

"The Awful Truth" may never be a box office wallop, nor can it be rated as a great film, but it qualifies as pleasing entertainment for the middle-class houses. *Sisk.*

TAMING THE WEST

Universal-Jewel starring Hoot Gibson. Adapted from the novel, "The Range Dwellers," by B. M. Bowers. Directed by Arthur Rosson. Reviewed at the Circle, New York, June 29, as half as a double bill. Running time, 61 minutes.

J. P. Carleton	Edmund Tilton
J. P. Carleton, Jr.	Hoot Gibson
Frosty Miller	Francis Ford
Lafe Connors	Albert J. Smith
Jerry Potter	Lewis Hippy
Beryl King	Marceline Day
Tom King	Herbert Prior

U this year made Hoot Gibson one of its leading stars and scheduled his releases to be included in the U-Jewel list, which takes in the features classed highest of their output. Previously Hoot had been doing straightaway westerns, but here lately they have held a strong comedy vein. Probably noting the star's aptitude for comedy, they decided to provide him with lively comedy yarns and push him in that direction. If all of Gibson's future vehicles are as swift and as funny as this and if U is successful in making the public dissociate him from straight cowboy parts, then they have another Denny on their hands.

Why they put a film like this on as half a double bill is a question, unless it can be that a house like the Circle depends upon a star name for a draw. Gibson can't be reckoned just now with the stars in so far as city reputation goes, but he's like Tom Mix in that when he strikes the smaller towns his stuff has box office pull. A film like this one could provide satisfactory first-run entertainment — provided the star was popular.

The plot of this concerns the rapscallion son of J. P. Carleton, a capitalist. J. P. started on a ranch, and when his boy steps too fast in the city the father buys him a one-way ticket to the ranch out west and puts him on his own. Out there he walks in as the city dude, but the fellows soon put him in his place. As luck would have it, he gets smitten with the daughter of old Tom King, who is his father's bitter enemy, and although denied access to the place he rides through on his horse ever so often just to give the King crowd a thrill. He has the gall of a ticket speculator, and some funny subtitles are put in his mouth, so his attempted courtship scenes are funny. There is a good fight or so, and at a dance he swears he'll trip around once with the King girl—and he does.

Then the blowoff comes when he kidnaps her in her own car and tells her that they're going to get married. For awhile she's doubtful, and thinking to kid him says that she'll have to say goodby to pop. It's all right with the boy, so they drive back and whiz by pop like a shell from a cannon. Then the girl is forced to hug him to keep in the car, and from then on the boy has things his way. Finally his father arrives on the scene, the two families patch it up, and after doing a few more tricks with the racing car the boy clinches for a fadeout.

There's action in every foot and comedy along with it. When Hoot isn't kidding somebody he's fighting; and when fighting slacks up he does some fancy riding; and when that palls he grabs a racer and does Chinese figures over the road. In the scenes which require acting he cashes in all okeh, while his support here upholds him at every move. Francis Ford, once upon a time U's ace serial star and dashing hero, here plays an old character role in which a tough beard hides his face. His work makes this role rank next to that of the star.

"Taming of the West" is about the best thing Hoot Gibson ever turned out. It has had about twice as much spent on it, from appearances as his usual vehicles, but most important of all, the director had a story that was ideal. *Sisk.*

HIS BUDDY'S WIFE

Associated Exhibitors' release directed by Tom Terriss. Adapted from a story by T. Howard Kelly. Glenn Hunter featured. July 2 at the New York Roof in pre-release showing. Running time, 70 minutes.

Intended as a sob story with a predominating war theme, this one shoots wide of the mark and becomes tiresome because of many unnecessary and hokumish scenes. Maybe these will be eliminated before it is released, for its present running time could stand some slicing without hurting the film.

At the start Jim Mullaney, a

young farmer, is at home with his wife and aged mother when the war starts. Jim volunteers and leaves for France, where he gets into the front line. One night, on a telephone extension in a shell hole, he is sent out to get dope on the location of enemy artillery and in so doing is killed. His buddy, Jim McMorrow, had promised that he would care for the mother and wife. with the war over Jim goes to the farm.

The mother dies shortly after, after getting herself the most prolific collection of old lady close ups yet shown. Then the inevitable happens, the young pair fall in love with each other and the village gossips start their tongues and jaws working on the overtime shift. The upshot is that Jim nearly strangles a fellow who spoke out of turn. For that he is haled before the local magistrate.

When things look badly because he won't justify himself, the girl appears in the middle of the aisle and pulls one of those "stop, you haven't heard my story." She tells the crowd she is proud of him and that they are to be married.

The day for the wedding arrives. The husband returns, for he wasn't killed but taken prisoner. And as he embraces his wife, Jim slips out the door, torn between love for the girl and duty—one of those things!

Glenn Hunter as Jim registers unevenly throughout, while Edna Murphy as the girl brings but little to the part. Of the cast, the various rural types stood out as being carefully chosen. Among them, incidentally, was Flora Finch, who is seen often now in small parts. The direction of Tom Terriss is good in spots and not so good in others.

The whole picture looks cheaply made. On that basis and on the fact it is so unoriginal in theme and direction, it cannot receive high rating. As a daily change for a small house it may suffice, but that lets it out. *Sisk.*

That Devil Quemado

F. B. O. production starring Fred Thomson and made from the story by Marvin Whilhite. Directed by Del Andrews. At the Stanley, New York, July 2, one day. Running time, 63 minutes.

Quemado	Fred Thomson
Juan Gonzalez	Robert Cantero
Jose Ramirez	Albert Piscoe
Conchita	Nola Lawford
Mace Saunders	Pat Harmon
Joanna Thatcher	Gloria Hope

Fred Thomson, like a few others, can stand the strain of acting as well as riding, while his humorous stuff usually registers.

This one has him as a bold bad bandit of the Robin Hood order, who helped the oppressed of Mexico in their struggle against the richer folk. Then he had a streak of the audacious in him and he puts a pleasant smile behind it.

He is first cussed and discussed by one Joanna Thatcher, daughter of a wealthy American visiting in Mexico. He pursues her and, much to her disgust, gets in solid with the old boy by making the dyspeptic son of the family hop out and get air into his lungs. It is proven that instead of being a bandit he is old Jim Fairfax, of Yale, and that in doing good he is merely letting the steam of the ancient Dons from his veins.

It is a smooth little plot nicely made and nicely told. The sets are sufficient and Thomson's white horse, labeled an Arab steed in the titles, makes a fine appearance. Of the supporting cast there was no outstanding work, it being adequate as a whole.

For a daily change "That Devil Quemado" holds up nicely. *Sisk.*

SCANDAL PROOF

William Fox production starring Shirley Mason. Story by Charles Kenyon and direction by Edmund Mortimer. Reviewed as half of a double bill at Loew's New York, June 19. Running time, 61 minutes.

Grace Whiting	Shirley Mason
Richard Thorbeck	Joseph Striker
Reed Hollister	Edward Martindel
Mrs. Hollister	Ruth King
Billy	Billy Seay
Monte Brandster	Freeman Wood
His Mother	Margaret Raymond
Thelma	Hazel Howell
Herbert Wyckoff	John Roche
His Sister	Clarissa Selwyn

Obviously made for the second runs and the daily change houses, this film fulfils its destiny excellently. The story is interesting and meaty, while the star works well and is supported by a good cast. Moreover, the direction is of a good grade, while all the sets are solid looking. Some tasteful exteriors add to the general effect. The only complaint is the leading man, John Roche, whose every impersonation, it seems, be it for Fox or Warners, is the same.

In plot this concerns a girl, Grace Whiting, innocently connected with the murder of Monte Brandster, a gad-about of Los Angeles, who was bumped off by a jealous sweetheart, Thelma. Grace is saved in court by the sympathetic testimony of Herbert Wyckoff. She leaves L. A. to start life anew and secures a position in New York as nurse girl in the wealthy Hollister family.

Then coincidence enters and Herbert Wyckoff comes east with his sister. By this time he has discovered he loves the girl. Telling her so, their pleasure is marred when his sister recognizes and exposes her. At this juncture Mrs. Hollister, with whom the Wyckoffs are visiting, is in a compromising situation with a young man who has carried his attentions too far. Grace immediately enters and by the time Mrs. Hollister's husband comes to the room, she is ready to assume the blame. Through the general denunciation which follows Wyckoff sticks to her for a pleasing and melodramatic finale, for he knew the truth.

The running time of this picture is assurance enough that it hasn't been overstretched in order to fill a program all by itself. So with allowance for the usual short subjects, it holds up strongly as the feature of the average bill. *Sisk.*

THE NECESSARY EVIL

First National production directed by George Archainbaud. Featuring Viola Dana and Ben Lyon. Supervised by Earl Hudson. From the story "Uriah's Son," by Stephen Vincent Benet. At Loew's New York, one day (June 25). Runs about 65 minutes.

Frank Jerome	Ben Lyon
Shirley Holmes	Viola Dana
Dick Jerome	Frank Mayo
David Devanant	Thomas Holding
Frances Jerome	Gladys Brockwell
Hattie	Mary Thurman
Belle	Betty Jewel
Esther	Martha Madison
Pug	Arthur Housman
Reggie	Beach Cooke

"The Necessary Evil" is only neighborhood stuff, it is true, but about twice as entertaining as "The Teaser" at the Strand recently, and a check-up would more than likely prove it to be well up to the average in both common sense and showmanship values of a great many pictures that play big Broadway houses.

It is adapted from a story by Stephen Benet, the rising young Yale novelist, whose books have delved deeply enough into the wrongdoings of the far-famed younger generation without overdoing the sex stuff.

The plot begins some score of years ago, but does not dwell for very long on the events at that time. The modern episodes concern a wild young college boy (Ben Lyon) who has inherited most of the bad traits of his worthless father and few of the angelic-like qualities of his mother. Upon the death of his parents David Devanant, who had loved the boy's mother, takes charge of him and consecrates his life to bringing the kid up, away from the evil influences prompted by paternal heredity. With Viola Dana's winsome assistance this is finally accomplished.

Miss Dana has very little to do, leaving the work to Lyon, who is much less insipid than usual in a difficult role. The balance of the cast is impressive in its "names" and more than satisfactory. Included is Gladys Brockwell, one of the original vampires but now playing a spotless part. The direction has allowed too many phantom figures of the dead parents to parade around, but has inserted plenty of color in some South Sea Island shots and accomplished its task well enough otherwise.

The picture ranks as a good one for the daily change houses and out in the sticks where they don't know such a theatre as the Strand exists they may accept it as in the same class with the heavily plugged first-run affairs.

SHATTERED LIVES

Weak stuff.

The plot of this concerns mistaken identity and also involves the long arm of coincidence. John Trent, a rich man, years ago left his wife and boy. Crooks, later learning that he was seeking the wife and son, faked proofs of the boys' identification and palmed him off on the mother, who was living in farmhouse obscurity.

Trent, however, falls into the crooks' hands and they try to polish him off. The hero, however, intervenes, and then takes the old man to his wife. The crook son, thus fronted, is taken in charge by a detective, while the real son is reunited to his father and mother.

And finding the heroine, who doesn't figure greatly in the story, he sits down on the woodpile with her and shows her how hugging should be done.

Cheaply made and filler for daily changes at best. *Sisk.*

Night Life of New York

Famous Players presents this Allan Dwan production by Paul Schofield; Julian Johnson, title editor; William LeBaron, film editor. At Rivoli, New York, week July 12.

Ronald Bentley	Rod La Rocque
John Bentley	Ernest Torrence
Meg	Dorothy Gish
Carrie Reed	Helen Lee Worthing
Jimmy	George Hackathorne
Jerry	Arthur Housman
William Workman	Riley Hatch

A light, bright "bright-light" picture is "Night Life of New York." It is enough "hokey" to make it generally appealing, possibly more so for the hinterland which will gape at and drink in the pseudo night-life stuff, wonder at the erotic and exotic aura of the supper clubs and secretly envy but hypocritically voice their conclusions in keeping with the hero's father-character who hates New York.

The old man has a grudge at the Big Burg because he was crossed in love there 25 years ago, and therefore swears by his Clay City, Iowa. Young Ronald Bentley (Rod La Rocque) on the contrary is the community's cutup and "fast" exponent. He is framed to go to New York on the theory he will become so thorougly disgusted with it he will yearn to return to Clay City. In a sense, despite he gets along swimmingly in fast company and wins a bride, he is willing to return home in the last reel, but Bentley, Sr., does an about-face and decides to go in for the bright light stuff more thoroughly.

In between, Bentley is thrown into the hoosegow on a criminal charge, his telephone operator-sweetheart (Dorothy Gish) apprehending the real crooks.

There isn't much substance to it all, but for the time and season, as likely as could be desired. It has action, La Rocque maintaining a fine pace that accelerates the action considerably. The "local color" stuff of shots at the various cafes including the El Fay and Texas Guinan (it's a pity all that free ad stuff is wasted with the El Fay now closed) is kayo for the average audience.

Ernest Torrence as the father does a nice bit of work. Helen Lee Worthing is the "Manhattan Follies" beaut who is young Bentley's original charmer and later makes his father also capitulate.

In summation, an obvious but well directed and well cast comedy-drama that should go well in the metropolitan neighborhoon houses and great in the hinterlands. *Abel.*

MARRIAGE WHIRL

First National release, starring Corinne Griffith, with Nita Naldi, Kenneth Harlan and Harrison Ford featured. From the Hartley Manners play, "The National Anthem." Directed by Al. Santell. Shown at the Strand, New York, week July 12, 1925. Running time, 81 minutes.

Marian Hale	Corinne Griffith
Arthur Carleton	Kenneth Harlan
Tom Carrol	Harrison Ford
John K. Carlton	E. J. Radcliffe
Ruben Hale	Charles Lane
Dick Mayne	Edgar Norton
Toinette	Nita Naldi

Here is another of those pictures setting forth the jazzy side of American social life. Possibly it is exactly one of the type that the English critics delight in taking a pan at, but at that it is a fairly interesting film exposition built to entertain without any great thought behind it. Corinne Griffith, who plays the lead in the picture, has a role that seems to fit her perfectly, and Harrison Ford, who plays the lead opposite her, scores and wins all the sympathy. As much cannot be said for Kenneth Harlan, who plays the heavy. From a box office standpoint the picture will measure up with the average program release intended for the pre-release houses and Corrine Griffith should prove a drawing card. That girl's popularity with the film fans seems to be growing with each picture as she goes along.

It is the story of a quiet girl who has the choice between two men and picks the wrong one for her happiness. In the end, however, the bad boy is forced out of the picture through the medium of an automobile wreck, while he is driving with her "sweetie" and then all works out well for the real lovers.

The story is well handled in the film. There is a symbolical touch at the opening that carries out the idea of the dance mad whirl that the country has been living in for the last decade, and there is considerable color to the film as a picture of modern life.

Fred.

PRETTY LADIES

Metro-Goldwyn production from the story by Adela Rogers St. John. Directed by Monta Bell with Zasu Pitts and Tom Moore featured. At the Capitol, New York, July 12.

Maggie Keenan ....Zasu Pitts
Al Cassidy ....Tom Moore
Ann Pennington............Ann Pennington
Selma Larson............Lilyan Tashman
Aaron Savage............Bernard Randall
Adrienne............Helen D'Algy
Maggie's Dream Lover......Conrad Nagel
Frances White ....Norma Shearer
Roger Van Horn........George K. Arthur
Bobby ....Lucille Leseur
Warren Hadley ....Paul Ellis
Paul Thompson............Roy D'Arcy
Fay ....Gwendolyn Lee
Diamond Tights Girl.....Dorothy Seastrom
Will Rogers............Lew Harvey
Frisco ....Chad. Huber
Mr. Gallagher............Walter Shumway
Mr. Shean............Dan Crimmins
Eddie Cantor............Jimmie Quinn

Two weeks ago Florenz Ziegfeld signed with Famous Players to make a series of glorified films.

This week the opposition, Metro-Goldwyn, issues an expensive film devoted primarily to plugging the "Follies," for it mentions that show by name many times. A night scene on Forty-second street has the old sign flashing, the celebrities of the show are imitated and the manager in the film is nearly a ringer for Zieggy.

However, the thing of interest is that a very reliable actress, Zasu Pitts, gets her first really big chance and comes through like a million dollars. Then Monta Bell, the Washington newspaper man who is heralded as a directorial genius, handled the film and, although he hasn't been backed up well technically, some of his ideas are excellent. But if he is responsible for the staging of the revue numbers in the film, especially that one based on "House Fly Blues," then Monta can look over a few more shows and learn a few more basic facts about the theatre.

In theme the story has great appeal, for it is the Pagliacci theme transposed to a woman. Here Maggie Keenan is a great comedienne with the world at her feet but loneliness at home. So when she goes home, at the table with her sits a dream lover—a delicate bit of fantasy. Maggie is plain in the face but bright looking—and Irish. Her romance comes one day when she meets the drummer with the show, Al Cassidy. From then on she backs him until he becomes established as a hit song writer and she deserts the stage to care for her children.

The pathetic Maggie had found happiness when Al got called to Atlantic City for the new show's opening. There the prima donna of the "Follies" got him in a hotel room and Al didn't feel like leaving **until morning. He felt ashamed of himself and Maggie, loving him so much, dismissed it as she knelt for prayer at her bed.** In the bed Al and the baby were sleeping, and Maggie looked, speaking:

"But oh, dear God, it must'nt happen again."

The fault with the film is that either Bell or the producers have tried to mix a spectacle of New York's theatrical with an absorbing human interest story. Either by itself would have been sufficient, but added to the theatrical stuff are many minor details which have been muffed.

Heavily advertised are the Broadway imitated stars. That, however, is the bunk. Most of the revue scenes are shown in color, but the impersonations aren't so good. Will Rogers is imitated for a brief second, while Norma Shearer appeared briefly doing a bad impression of Frances White. Eddie Cantor and others come in for momentary flashes that are unimpressive.

The film was made on the Coast. Consequently, when the New York shots were made (with one exception), they were faked. We have Al and Maggie riding atop a Fifth avenue bus, and the background is so faked and so badly pieced with the moving shots that it appears antiquated in a modern film. From Maggie's roof garden on her home is a view of New York electric light area—obviously a curtain. Living chandeliers and undressed ladies, usual revue adjuncts, are to be seen.

What is often beautiful and interesting is the story of Maggie Keenan. In that role Miss Pitts scores an emphatic personal success, but Bell's handling of the other stuff rather lessens his rating.

"Pretty Ladies" was probably made as an out of town clean up and as such it may go. But in the metropolitan areas of the East, where the people know anything about New York or shows, it can hardly be counted on as a sensation. Its start-off at the Capitol was decidedly weak despite much advance exploitation.

Sisk.

THE WOMAN HATER

A Warner Brothers' Production adapted from Dorothy Day's novel, "The Eleventh Virgin," by Ruby M. Ayres. Directed by John Flood with Helene Chadwick and Clive Brook starred. Reviewed at the Piccadilly, New York, June 13. Running time, 70 minutes.

Marie Laurent............Helene Chadwick
Miles Faversham............Clive Brook
Phillip Tranter............John Harron
Mrs. Tranter............Helen Dunbar
Marie Laurent's secretary......Dale Fuller

If "The Woman Hater" is illogical in spots, it is interesting most of the way because of its excellent direction and the appealing acting of Clive Brook, who is the Menjou opposite of the screen. Adolphe is a sophisticate with a sense of deviltry and humor, while Brook is also a sophisticate, but one to whom sophistication has meant a reversion to the basically good things of life—and nearly all of his roles are of this sort. And in his screen career here, Mr. Brook is apparently getting himself a sizeable feminine draw, and like Menjou, he also clicks with the men.

In this he is cast as a rich artist called upon by a wealthy New York woman to break off a match between her son and Marie Laurent, a famous French actress. Marie, it happened, had been his model once and he loved her, but he quit her when he saw a sable coat around her—and the girl was innocent.

Therefore, when he was reintroduced, there was a feeling that maybe he had done the girl wrong and so they began going out a bit. Phillip Tranter, her young sweetheart, however, grew very jealous and after the artist had professed his love in Marie's apartment, Phillip was seen by Marie with a pistol pointing from behind a curtain. So feigning ridicule, she mocked the artist out of her place and thereby saved him. But it took a wild auto ride through Riverside drive and Fifth avenue to reach his pier before the boat sailed, and before a dock full of folks, they went into a squashy kiss that lasted plenty long.

Helene Chadwick as the girl in the case is but fair, principally she is a bit hefty for such a part. Moreover, there is a ridiculous touch given, when to impress upon the audience her importance as an actress, she is announced in a gala farewell performance of "L'Aiglon." Just a few years before she had been a mere model, but since then she had risen to that point of stardom when she could essay probably the greatest feminine role in France as The Eaglet. Mr. Brook, on the other hand, is excellent, while Johnny Harron, brother of the late Bobbie Harron, does well as young Tranter. Dale Fuller as a maid also got laughs.

One serious technical fault is apparent when the faking of the race along the Drive and Fifth avenue is done. In this the outline is quite clear where the racing shot was put into the panorama of the streets, and in a picture of such manufacture, Warners, it looked out of place and unworthy.

However, insofar as story and direction goes, "The Woman Hater" qualifies as nice program material and despite the actress end of the theme, there is nothing even remotely suggestive nor is there anything in the film that would disqualify for either Sunday showing or the general family trade.

Sisk.

MARRY ME

Film adaptation of Ann Caldwell's play, "The Nest Egg," adapted by Walter Woods. Produced by Famous Players. Directed by James Cruze. Screen play by Anthony Coldewey. At the Rivoli, New York, week July 12. Running time, 66 minutes.

Hetty Gandy............Florence Vidor
John Smith No. 2..Edward Everett Horton
John Smith No. 1............John Roche
Sarah Hume............Helen Jerome Eddy
Granny............Fanny Midgley
Norman Frisbie............Ed. Brady
Jenkins............Z. Wall Covington
Mrs. Hume............Anna Schaefer
Jackson............Erwin Connelly

A routine program picture, directed by James Cruze, with Florence Vidor and Edward Everett Horton featured.

It is the conventional story of the trusting girl who has waited seven years after proposal for her sweetheart to follow her to the tank town whither she had gone after the proposal and whisk her away to matrimony. The story is planted in a conventional manner and carried along the same way.

With relatives and friends feeling that Helen Gandy, the girl, is bordering on certain oldmaidhood, a wire is received from John Smith, evidently the fiance, who announces he is coming on. The town friends make capital of the news for a celebration and shower for the bride elect. But it's all a false alarm. When John Smith arrives he is not the John that Hetty had been expecting.

In contrast to the expected romantic youth of her heart, Helen is confronted by a hypochondriac. He has located her through a marked egg intended for the other John. She left it for the latter when she left town seven years ago. It was dated and the intruder wants her testimony to convict a group of egg dealers for palming off ancient cold storage eggs on the public and himself in general, for which he blames for his imaginary ills.

Helen is about to tell her friends of the false alarm. Her aunt intervenes and suggests that they continue the masquerade until after Helen has testified at the trial and that she'll handle the matter after that. The couple start off presumably to be married in the other town. The supposed newlywed angle makes for several humorous situations. Before the final reel is spun out, Smith has won his case and also Helen.

Miss Vidor has the only opportunity role as Helen Gandy and handles it well. Mr. Horton is likeable as the imaginary invalid. Helen Jerome Eddy contributes a seriocomic portrait as a giddy bride.

Although capably directed, well-cast and equally well played, this one may stand up as a feature in neighborhoods, but not in the big houses, unless built up with other strong features.

Edba.

PRIVATE AFFAIRS

Gilbert Heyfron production made for Producers' Distributing Corporation and adapted from the "Saturday Evening Post" story, "The Ledger of Life," by George Patullo. Directed by Renaud Hoffman. At the Cameo, New York.

Agnes Bomar............Gladys Bomar
Frank Henley............Robert Agnew
Amy Lufkin............Mildred Harris
Lee Cross............David Butler
Alf Stacey............Arthur Hoyt
Irma Stacey............Betty Francisco
Howard Bomar............Willis Marks
Joe Hines............Charles Sellon
Andy Gillespie............Hardee Kirkland
John Maddox............J. Frank Glendon

A neat little film of small town life with more than the usual small town idiosyncrasies in the background sums up "Private Affairs."

The plot is concerned mostly with what might have been, for after the old postmaster dies, a five-year old packet of lost letters is found behind his desk. In that a lover sent for his sweetheart to come on and marry him; a drunkard was notified of a fortune left him; the postmaster himself was advised of a lapsing insurance policy, etc.

But the sweetheart didn't go and marry the lover, Lee Cross, for instead, Amy Lufkin married John Maddox and bore him children. And, so Cross came back to town, with his fortune made, but still the strutter at heart, and in an ill-fitting, but flashy suit. Swathed with barber shop cologne, he stepped from his hired Rolls-Royce and visited the old folks. Just before his arrival, the five-year old letter had been delivered to Amy, but after he had gone, she was ashamed that she had ever loved such a man and from then on she loved her husband all the more.

The juveniles of the film, Gladys Hulette and Bobbie Agnew, have attractive small town parts. In the end the old drunkard, Andy Gillespie, puts Bobbie in charge of his newly inherited factories and determines that they get the happiness he never saw. There's considerable optimism toward the end and of that kind that will find audience favor.

"Private Affairs," while not anything with which to stir the box office, will size up satisfactorily as a daily change, program feature. The cast names probably won't be of much help, but the exhibitor can be assured that in place of famous names, the director has furnished a capable group of players.

Enjoyable, if not notable.

Sisk.

THE FRESHMAN

Pathe release, starring Harold Lloyd. Directed by Sam Taylor and Fred Newmeyer. Story by Sam Taylor, John Grey, Ted Wilde and Tim Whelan. Photographed by Walter Lundin, chief, and Henry N. Kohler. Privately exhibited at invitation performance, New York Roof. Running time about 80 minutes.

The Freshman............Harold Lloyd
Peggy............Jobyna Ralston
College Cad............Brooke Benedict
College Hero............James Anderson
College Belle............Hazel Keener
College Tailor............Jos. Harrington
Football Coach............Pat Harmon

Harold Lloyd's "Freshman" is a cinch at the picture box office as a

Lloyd comedy and a laugh getter, but that is all that may be said for it. That's enough for the exhibitor and he needn't read anything else.

In story, however, it's the poorest devised of its kind ever put out. Whoever is responsible muffed a chance for a whale here and the biggest Lloyd ever has had, not excepting "Safety First," his best to date.

The entire fault is that Lloyd as a freshman at college been over-boobed, made the boobiest sort of a booby boob, and in that they overdid it.

All the rules of college life have been violated, all the rules of the athletic field as well, and whoever laid out the yarn must have had a course of his own at a business college as a guide.

The writers may seek to defend themselves upon the comedy angle, but it won't stand up. The laugh results would have been exactly the same with a logical story and the violations appear to be more a matter of ignorance than travesty.

This picture will appeal to every boy in the world and almost every girl and to their parents and grandparents, but there's a kick-back through the very foolishness that goes so far for laughs. Much of this is at the finish where in an impossible football game they attempt to make a hero of the boob and fail in both, merely making the boob more boobish.

Had the picture brought out Lloyd at the finale as a real gridiron warrior, this picture would have ended with a wallop that would have left Harold Lloyd indelibly upon the minds of the youths for recall whenever they afterward heard or read of football.

The football game finish in itself is a fine scene. It is the Berkley Bowl in California (actually) with the Lloyd insertion made between the first and second quarters of the game there last winter between the East and West. It's an enormous bowl. First glance says it's the Yale Stadium, denoting its magnitude.

This picture is full of laughable gags, some new and novel, some old, and some adapted. There are laughs from the outset, although the first ludicrous error is when Lloyd entering Tate College as a freshman, goes there with a white sweater and the letter "T" on it, without anyone noting a freshie is wearing the college letter. After that it will be applesauce for reality to any of the kids who know as much about college life as this freshman learned from the books he read.

The freshman in his clumsy stumbling way wins the football game and is placed on the college pedestal he dreamed of, after he had become the spendthrift of the school, living in a $3 room so he could live up to his self-imposed rep as a spender who called himself "Speedy."

To make a football player play with glasses on! Who thought of that? Or to take the rough stuff Lloyd did as the dummy tackle and with glasses on—even if they were painted on.

Mr. Lloyd needs a personal editor who isn't afraid of losing his job.

As a laugh picture "The Freshman" is fine—as a muffed opportunity, it's great. *Sime.*

Her Husband's Secret

First National production, directed by Frank Lloyd. Adapted by J. G. Hawks from May Edginton's Saturday Evening Post story, "Judgment." At the Stanley, New York, one day (June 25. Runs 77 minutes.)

Owen Elliot.................Antonio Moreno
Judy Brewster............Patsy Ruth Miller
Mrs. Ruth Pearce-Kent......Ruth Clifford
Ross Brewster.............David Torrence
Owen Elliot (boy)..........Frankie Darro
Leon Kent.................Walter McGrail
Pansy La Rue...............Phyllis Haver
Mrs Van Tuyler.............Pauline Neff

Miss Van Tuyler..........Frances Teague
Irene Farway...............Margaret Fielding
Tony Van Oren.............Joseph Girard

"Her Husband's Secret" is one of the comparatively few First Nationals that failed to make the first-run grade around New York. The reason is that it is draggy, unimportant, but fairly interesting in its story and treatment and surely no worse than a good many features seen at the best Broadway houses.

Frank Lloyd turned out the film from an adaptation of a "Saturday Evening Post" story by May Edginton. He has endeavored to produce a film without tricks, and the straightforward method of direction is convincing for the most part. But he erred in allowing the picture to run more than a quarter of an hour overtime, as it is the type of production, almost devoid of action, that would be bound to drag somewhat even in the regular 60 minutes' time quota.

The story opens 22 years ago, with the atmosphere apparently correct and made prticularly interesting by including a wild booze party of those pre-flapper days. The naughty actions of the girls seem incongruous as contrasted to their sedate and modest clothes, but Phyllis Haver, as a Victorian cutie manages to be very wicked and exciting.

The modern portion of the plot introduces a highly unsympathetic hero (Antonio Moreno), whose character is painted so black that there seems to be almost no possibility of happiness for the little girl (Patsy Ruth Miller) who worships him. When her father literally forces him to a suicide attempt as the only way out, the film, which has been gloomy all along, is somber enough to drive a good many sensitive people out of the theatre. However, it turns up that he has not really been killed and a year later finds him reformed and everything serene, excepting a squalling baby.

The leads give their usual adequate performances, while such troupers as David Torrence, Ruth Clifford, Walter McGrail and Phyllis Haver lend box office weight, as well as distinction to the picture. Miss Clifford, in particular, in the later sequences when she represents an old woman, shows some real ability, omitting all the trembling, forced poses and strained expressions usually accompanying such portrayals.

Although it will tire out most audiences before the finish, the film is better than average fare for the program houses where its high-class production can not fail to make an impression.

A Fool and His Money

Columbia Pictures production adapted from the George Barr McCutcheon novel. Adapted by D. Z. Doty and directed by Erle Kenton. Madge Bellamy and William Haines starred. Reviewed at the Circle, New York, June 29, as half of a double bill. Running time, 55 minutes.

Countess Von Pless.......Madge Bellamy
Count Von Pless...........Stuart Holmes
Annette Ritazy............Alma Bennett
"Mother"..................Eugenie Besserer
Mrs. Schmick.............Carrie Clark Ward
Mr. Schmick.............}
George Washington Stubbs } William Haines
John Smart..............}

There's a strain of Graustark running through this one, so its mixture of Old World villainy and heroics, and New World romance makes it an attractive theme. Moreover, Columbia has given it a nice production, really better than one would expect coming from one of the grade B independents. And as it frames up, the whole thing has action, plenty of heart interest, flocks of comedy and enough love interest to satisfy the women folks.

John Smart, writer, isn't doing so well with his typewriter, but when he gets $300,000 in cash left him, he hies to Europe and buys an old castle. And as he goes wandering through it one night, he finds a

luscious looking lady concealed in a hidden apartment. Looks like a piece of luck, but it develops that she is hiding from her villain husband, who wants the custody of the child. Smart, therefore, makes plans to get the woman out of the country, and would have succeeded had not a vamp, who had tried unsuccessfully to put the bee on him for some money, spied the countess on the balcony. And the vamp went to the count and sold her info, so the count dug himself up some gendarmes and they started to tear the castle apart. Smart, however, gets the girl out and has an aeroplane waiting to take her away. The pursuers get close, so he jumps on a bridge and pulls his sword, one with which his ancestors had fought in the Revolutionary, Civil and Spanish wars, and does one of those Horatius at the Bridge acts. He gets nicked, but the girl gets away, and the outcome is that the castle is taken from him by a crooked judge and he comes back to America broke, and muttering things about "a fool and his money." But the surprise comes when his colored servant arrives by a later boat. The servant, it seems, was locked in the wine cellar and got gloriously stewed. While down there, however, he stumbled across a treasure chest that appeared to hold, the crown jewels of Peggy Joyce and a few empresses. So he brings this back, and as heroine has to fled to America, they look well-heeled for their married life.

Miss Bellamy is very nice in this and Haines, although stiff once or twice, has a Harold Lloyd-like face that suits the role. Stuart Holmes and Alma Bennett, playing the heavies, were all right, and the rest of the cast stood up in proportions.

"Fool and His Money" is much better than the usual independent of its type, and appears strong enough to hold up the feature end of a daily change satisfactorily. *Bisk.*

FEARLESS LOVER

Perfection production distributed by Commonwealth. Story by Scott Dunlap. Directed by Henry McRae. Featuring William Fairbanks and Eva Novak. At Loew's, New York, one day (July 10) as half the bill. Runs about 63 minutes.

Patrick Michael Casey..William Fairbanks
Mrs. Casey.................Ruby Lafayette
Tom Dugan.................Tom Kennedy
Mrs. James Sexton.........Lydia Knott
Enid Sexton...............Eva Novak
Ted Sexton................Arthur Rankin
Frankie ....Frankie Darrow

Film producers are wise enough to realize that the American public, for all its ridicule of "bulls" and "coppers" as portrayed in the Keystone Comedies and crook shows, has a wholesome respect and admiration for the great majority of "the finest." The flash of a badge and a uniform will intimidate the toughest gangsters and the kid who at one time or another has not hoped to be a policeman when he grew up is very hard to find.

That explains, possibly, why since the beginning of the film industry there have been so many pictures with cop heroes and why so large a percentage of them have gone over at the box office. In spite of its wishy-washy title "The Fearless Lover," latest of this series, is quite a brisk and pleasant little program attraction.

The policeman is of course Irish, courageous, witty, acrobatic and, far from least, the son of old Sergeant Casey whose exploits on the force a score of years ago are still being raved about.

As played by William Fairbanks, always a good trouper, and in this case giving a particularly excellent performance, the cop is bound to

strike a responsive chord in all of us, particularly when on his first day on beat he strides up to Dugan, the greatly-feared gangster leader, and grabbing him masterfully by the collar, introduces himself as "Casey —Mr. Casey to you and no funny business either," or words to that effect.

But the patrolman's angle is not the only one to this interesting film. Eva Novak, Fairbanks' sidekick in several recent pictures, is one of the chief operators in the local telephone exchange. The action shows the girls overworked, crowded and hounded by impatient, unreasonable and cranky subscribers. For a time it looks as though someone has put across a bit of propaganda for the Bell System. The phone girls go out on strike and leave the exchange empty. Five minutes later a little boy neighbor of the heroine's is struck by an auto. The phone is not working and the youngster dies before a doctor can be reached, whereas quick medical attention might have saved him.

That puts a cloud upon the heroine for a time, but is quickly forgotten when her kid brother gets in bad with Dugan's gang. Casey comes to the rescue and while at it rounds up the gang for silk stealing. The fight scenes are a bit over-stretched but otherwise crammed with action. Director Henry McRae deserves much praise for his work with these and the quieter scenes alike.

Altogether, it is an unusual box office bet for the neighborhood theatres. A little more comedy would have made it even better.

HEARTS AND SPURS

Fox production starring Buck Jones. From the story, "The Outlaw," by Jackson Gregory. Scenario by John Stone. Directed by W. S. Van Dyke. At Loew's New York, one day (July 10), as half the bill. Runs about an hour.

Hal Emory...................Buck Jones
Sybil Estabrook............Carol Lombard
Victor Dyfresne............William Davidson
Oscar Estabrook............Freeman Wood
Celeste......................Jean Lamott
Sid Thomas..................J. Gordon Russell
Jerry Clark..................Walt Robbins
Sheriff.....................Charles Eldridge

"Hearts and Spurs" may be cataloged right in that pigeon hole of second flight westerns contributed during the past year or two by Jones, Gibson, Carey and more recently by Fred Thompson. Here once again there is practically no variation in the formula but it is a well turned-out picture of its type and should entertain the western rooters (try and count 'em) as much as any of its predecessors.

The story is even more commonplace than usual. Prescription: One hero; one pretty lady and one rakish gambler; add one weakling brother under the influence of the latter; throw in a couple of exaggerated comic characters for the laughs, and then mix the whole solution with a stage-coach hold-up, some cattle stealing, and the proper hand-to-hand fight for the girl, and you have the regulation plot.

The big kick comes when Buck shields his girl's brother by taking the blame for the stage-coach robbery himself, but that certainly is far from a new twist.

Where the film does rise above its story level is in the handling of the action. A couple of mountain slides with huge rocks apparently falling headlong on the actor is startling in realism. These and certain others featuring the hard riding and fighting will attract favorable attention. The photography is even finer than the high standard set in the recent better-class westerns.

Jones continues the loosening up improvement in his acting and even gets across a couple of laugh situations without seeming to force them. He is still primarily the serious-faced and slightly dull though thoroughly likeable cowboy gentleman, however. The heroine, Carol Lombard, a newcomer, is attractive looking, particularly in the fashionable eastern clothes she is permitted to wear, but as for expressiveness she might just as well have been labeled "For decorative purposes only."

Much more animated is Jean Lamott, the petite French maid, whose flirtation with the roughneck cowboy, Walt Robbins, accounts for several laughs. Freeman Wood, who usually plays one of the weightiest of the heavies, is only a weakling, and William Davidson, ordinarily a hero, makes a despicable villain, thanks largely to a big, bushy mustache.

The up-to-date exhibitor will know what to expect when he hears this is just one more average Buck Jones feature and he must arrange the exploitation accordingly.

FAIR PLAY

William Steiner production, starring Edith Thornton. Supervised by Charles Hutchinson and directed by Frank Crane. Scenario by J. F. Natteford. At Loew's New York one day (July 7) as half of bill. About 65 minutes.

Norma Keith................Edith Thornton
Bruce Elliot...................Lou Tellegen
Dickie Thane...................Gaston Glass
Rita Thane.................Betty Francisco
Bull Mong..................David Dunbar
Charlie Morse................Simon Greer

The Steiner series of independents featuring Edith Thornton have attracted quite a bit of favorable attention from trade reviewers in particular. While it is doubtful if "Fair Play" is one of the best of the series it is not at all a bad picture for the daily change houses.

Miss Thornton will never rate as one of the really beautiful women of the screen, but she is a colorful, industrious and appealing actress who knows how to play dramatics. In the present film Steiner secured no less a name than that of Lou Tellegen as her leading man. While there always has been a great difference of opinion over the French actor's thespian ability, most of the women at least will like him in this, a generally sympathetic role for one who almost always plays oily villians.

Tellegen has, it would seem, married the wrong woman, choosing the mercenary blonde schemer (Betty Francisco), instead of the faithful young secretary who has helped him up from obscurity to the position of a prominent criminal lawyer. When the wife accidentally dies and circumstantial evidence is pointing the way to the chair for him it is Miss Thornton who scoops around in the underworld for the dope to set him free.

The scenes between Tellegen and Miss Thornton are well directed and played. It is the bringing to the screen of that familiar type of situation so popular in the "True Stories" type of fiction wherein an innocent young girl finds herself in love with her married employer with no decent way out suggesting itself.

While not exactly lavish, the film is nicely set and the underworld shots show an interesting sort of atmosphere. Charles Hutchinson, who, presumably, is the same "Hutch" remembered for his whirlwind stunt features and serials, supervised the production with a sure touch. Some added comedy situations would have made it better than the pretty fair picture it is.

YOUTH'S GAMBLE

Rayart (W. Ray Johnston) production, starring Reed Howes. Supervised by Harry J. Brown and directed by Albert Rogell. Story and continuity by Henry Roberts Symonds and John Wesley Grey. Photographed by Ross Fisher. At Loew's New York one day (July 7) as half of bill. About 61 minutes.

William Ignatius Newton......Reed Howes
Addison Simms..........Jimmy Thompson
Hazel Dawn...........Margaret Morris
Harry Blaine.............Wilfred Lucas
Winifred Elaine Thomas.......Gale Henry
"Tombstone" Reilly......William Buckley
"Obituary" Blake............David Kirby

"Youth's Gamble" starts interestingly if none too original with a lovably worthless young man who inherits an auto, prize and a silver dime from his millionaire old man. This promising premise peters out unworthily as the film progresses, and, in spite of the pulchritudinous Reed Howes (of Arrow collar fame), the picture only measures up as fair program house material.

The picture suffers from the same fault, inconsistency, as have the others of the Howes series. There is the almost complete lack of emotional display by the hero when he learns his father is not dead. The stunt, fight and chase bits coming at the end are fairly well staged and shot, but have often been seen before. The handsome star is pleasantly earnest and likable without ever quite reaching the acting scale needed for even such a mild role. Others in the cast are capable.

A check-up of the last three Reed Howes' features indicates "Youth's Gamble" to be better than the clumsy "Lightning Romance," but not as entertaining as the brisk "Snob Buster." As half way between these two, it is just about acceptable stuff of its kind.

THE SCUTTLERS

Fox re-issue, starring William Farnum. Directed by J. G. Edwards. Story by Clyde Westover. Cast includes Hershell Mayall and Jacqueline Saunders. At the Stanley one day (June 29). Runs about an hour.

Both the billing and titles at the start are frank to admit this is a re-issue. It is just as well they do as the picture could hardly pass as a new release, not because of any particular unworthiness, but because the costumes and some of the atmosphere are much out of date. Just how long ago it was shot is a puzzle, but it is safe to say quite a few years. All the bunk about improvement in the film particularly in this class of program picture, is disproved as the production is no worse, though hardly any better either, than a hundred others turned out today.

In the photographic detail one might expect some serious defects, but the camera work is of surprisingly high grade and just as modern looking as in any similar feature of today. There has been little restraint used in the direction or acting, however, so that the film is overcrowded with hysterical dramatic scenes of the "Foiled again. Jack Dalton," variety.

The story is fairly interesting for a plot dealing almost exclusively with the rough life of commercial seamen. Scuttlers, it would seem, are sailors who sink their own ships to collect the insurance that comes after the disaster. Another trick of their trade is to carry cargoes filled only with water barrels instead of the valuable commodities also insured for their supposed worth and collectible when the boat goes to the bottom. McKinnery is hired by Lloyd's, the insurance people, to get the goods on a certain band of these scuttlers. After going through all sorts of dangers, not the least of which is nearly losing his girl because she happens to be the daughter of the scuttler sea captain, he emerges triumphant with the evidence and the lady.

The wreck scenes are well shot and there is a battle in a hold furiously filling with water, that packs a real thrill. William Farnum gives his usual careful performance and seems particularly spry in the fight scenes. He was considerably younger then, perhaps. So, too, was Miss Jackie Saunders, who plays the heroine, but not, unfortunately, any better an emotional actress than she is today. A few familiar faces are in the cast, not recognizable by name aside from Hershal Mayall.

As long as it is not noised around too much that this is an old baby, it should do as much at the box office as any other similar Farnum release. That the Fox star's name may still mean something was implied at the Stanley the night it was reviewed, since business, while far from big, was better than ordinarily.

George B. Seitz has been chosen to direct "The Vanishing American" for Paramount instead of William K. Howard, originally selected, with Howard transferred to direct Bebe Daniels in "Martinique." Seitz is a new member of the Paramount staff, having just concluded making his first picture "Wild Horse Mesa," a Zane Grey story.

A SLAVE OF FASHION

Hobart Henley production. From a story by Samuel Shipman. Directed by Hobart Henley. Co-starring Norma Shearer and Lew Cody. Presented by Metro-Goldwyn. Shown at the Capitol, N. Y., week July 19, 1925. Running time, 60 minutes.

Katherine Emerson.........Norma Shearer
Nicholas Wentworth...........Lew Cody
Dick Wayne.................William Haines
Mother Emerson...............Mary Carr
Father Emerson............James Corrigan
Aunt Sophie..................Vivia Ogden
Madeline....................Miss Dupont
Mayme....................Estelle Clark
Hobson....................Sidney Bracey

A sure-fire box office bet. It has everything film fans want. There is a beautiful star, a lot of romance in the story that also carries a great suspense thrill, clothes, laughs, and in addition a surprise in the fact that Lew Cody turns out to be a hero instead of a heavy, which is fair enough in itself.

Atop of all this the picture is directed with a score or more of deft touches on the part of Hobart Henley, who is now about at the top of the group that are labeled "commercial directors," for he is turning out pictures distinctly box office in value and doing it at a price within the cost mark. At that he manages to put the "kick" in the film where it will do the most good.

This one starts off with just that type of kick that is usually held for the big scene in a picture. It is a railroad smash-up, high in the air on a trestle, as a result of which the heroine of the story instead of landing in New York to hunt for work assumes the identity of a girl of pleasure who was one of the victims, takes over an apartment that a former admirer and protector has placed at her disposal while he is abroad, with the understanding that she is to leave before he returns.

Just think of the transition of a small town girl from the wilds of Io-way, where Jed Flanagan comes from, to a Park avenue duplex with a maid and a man servant, a Rolls and a charge account for everything from theatre tickets to clothes.

Does she step! And how! Why she just speeds and all is going along in great shape, for she has even copped herself a would-be pineapple who thinks she's a married woman with a lot of loose dough that she doesn't know what to do with, until the folks back home decide to hop into Henry and fliv their way east. That's a laugh, Henry chugging up to the Park avenue joint and parking front of the door.

Then things begin to happen. Aunt Sophie fears for the niece, who incidentally has accounted for her living in splendor by confessing to a secret marriage with her husband hurriedly called away to Europe, because the boy friend is very much on the job and it looks as though the niece might be compromised. So auntie suggests to mother that word be sent the husband and this is done. He does drop everything in Europe and dashes back to the good old U. S. A. because if he has a wife he wants to see who she is, and with his arrival the little heroine masquerader and fibber is in another jam. She wants to confess all to mother and the family when the "husband" decides that she might as well be the wife anyway and brings about a happy ending.

Norma Shearer looks like a million dollars, especially in a shower bath scene that'll make all the boys out in Io-way sore on themselves for ever letting her get to New York, and Cody handles himself like the master of acting that he is. Mary Carr as the mother is just her wistful charming screen self, and Vivia Ogden gets laugh after laugh.

The production looks like a lot of money, and the clothes display is corking. The title in itself suggests naturally a fashion show, which is always sure fire, but with this picture one doesn't need go after anything heavy in the way of a flash to go with it for it is certain to make 'em come. *Fred.*

LIGHTNIN'

William Fox presentation from the stage play by Winchell Smith and Frank Bacon; scenario by Frances Marion, directed by John Ford, released by a John Golden unit; seen at Strand.

Lightnin' Bill Jones	Jay Hunt
Millie	Madge Bellamy
John Marvin	Wallace MacDonald
Judge Townsend	J. Farrell MacDonald
Margaret Davis	Ethel Clayton
Raymond Thomas	Richard Travers
Sheriff	James Marcus
Zeb	Otis Harlan
Oscar	Peter Mazutis
Mother	Edythe Chapman
Hammond	Brandon Hurst

Next to the greatest stage success of all times, "Lightnin'", is a good but not great film.

The story does not dovetail on the screen as it did on the stage. Much of the classic comedy which fitted so snugly in the spoken drama appears dragged in, though it isn't, for the screen version closely follows the original script. But Frances Marion's scenario is amateurishly unskillful, despite her long experience and repute as the ranking movie adapter.

Jay Hunt, sloshing about in the ill-fitting shoes of the late Frank Bacon, muffs the spirit of the immortal role. He looks so much like Bacon that he would seem to be that revered artist, himself—until he begins to act, when the resemblance dims away. Lightnin' Bill was one of the funniest characters ever created in light comedy, and Hunt is one of the unfunniest screen actors who ever put on a makeup. He lacks as thoroughly the penchant for pathos, that getting a tear with a smile which Lightnin' had—and not alone Bacon produced it, several who followed him attained the effect. It is in the character, not alone in the playe. Hunt is not the character.

The producing and direction, however, cover a multitude of his sins. Seldom has a film conductor revealed a better touch for combined humor and drama than John Ford here develops. And when the shortcomings of the principal player and the disjointed continuity are not deadly, the action is sweet and amusing, as well as effectively touching at times.

The cast is a distinguished one, and the list is imposing. Otis Harlan, who plays the part of Lightnin's bozo pal, is a delight; had he been cast for the lead it would have been a far finer film, even though he does not look like Frank Bacon. Madge Bellamy is a confection as the daughter, and Edythe Chapman plays her mother down to the ground.

But the performing palm goes to Ethel Clayton as the divorce-seeking hooferess. Handling the vamp very much as Jane Oaker did in the New York run of the play, when she gave an account of herself that will not be soon forgotten, Miss Clayton translates all that Miss Oaker gave through the interpretative limitations of the celluloid. The scenario has fumbled her part, but it would take more than a scrap of paper to befumble Miss Clayton.

Richard Travers, also a star in his day, in a small bit stands forth with unction and distinction; Travers is still a good bet for a producer as judged by his work and appearance here.

To those who have not seen the stage edition of "Lightnin'" (if there be any) flaws and shortcomings of the screen conception may not be so conspicuous. But one who saw the great comedy cannot refrain from deploring the opportunities lost, for here was a native comedy destined to pass into folk-lore, screened without the spark and the flare which made it great.

Though many of Lightnin's famous fibs are in the titles, yet his whimsical personality as the most notorious and most harmless liar in Nevada does not gleam forth here. Lightnin's was not the creation of either Winchell Smith or Bacon—he is the beloved Tennessee's Pardner of Bret Harte, and he should breathe the soul of the sympathetic, Peterpanlike Bill of Harte, not the stilted stock-company character-man of Frances Marion as crippled up by Jay Hunt.

Commercially, "Lightnin'" may turn out a good investment. Its title should be a gold-mine of box office appeal, and the film will not displease, though it may disappoint many who remember the reactions of the play.

The love interest, which might have been amplified for the screen, is not warmed up, the undercurrent of melodrama is not inflated, leaving the feature dependant upon its comedy to give it backbone. That element cannot be lost in any version of "Lightnin'", but stacked against many funny pictures that come and go, "Lightnin'" will not rate as a high-power laughing effusion.

It will get by, and no more.

Lait.

Street of Forgotten Men

Herbert Brenon Production presented by Adolph Zukor and Jesse L. Lasky. From the story by George Kibbe Turner, adapted by John Russell, continuity by Paul Schofield. Shown at the Rivoli, N. Y., week July 19, 1925. Running time, 71 minutes.

Easy Money Charlie	Percy Marmont
Fancy Vanhern	Mary Brian
Philip Peyton	Neil Hamilton
Bridgeport White Eye	John Harrington
Portland Fancy	Juliet Brenon
Adolphe	A. Bargato
Dutch Dolly	Josephine Deffry
Diamond Mike	Riley Hatch
Adolphe's Assistant	Albert Roccardi
Widow McGee	Dorothy Walters

To those who read the George Kibbe Turner story in the "Satevepost" the picturization of "The Street of Forgotten Men" is going to come along as a disappointment more or less. It was a corking story. One cannot say as much for the picture. However, it will average up with the usual run of program attractions that Famous is turning out, but it won't be the box office knockout expected.

Three featured players: Percy Marmont, Mary Brian, and Neil Hamilton. The two former acquit themselves most creditably, while Hamilton does the best he can with a role that offers but little.

The trouble would seem to be in the film adaption. It does not follow the story in the principal theme and that detracts from the punch and unfortunately does not place victory into the hands of the hero who has won the audience's sympathy. In direction Herbert Brenon has done exceedingly well, even though he slurred over a few points early in the picture where "planting" was most necessary. Because of the fact that he did not plant his characters sufficiently well with his audience was another reason that the story was weakened.

New York of today and of the pre-prohibition period are the scenes in which the story is laid. It is a tale of the "dead house" on the Bowery, a combination saloon, dance hall and whatnot, with an adjunct given over to the outfitting of panhandlers, where whole men are changed to cripples with distorted bodies and seeming unseeing eyes in a jiffy to go out into the streets and prey on the public in the name of charity.

"Easy Money Charlie," played by Marmont, is the cleverest of all the panhandlers. He would go out and pick up $150 on a good day. Portland Fancy, one of the "fallen sisters," is in the last stages of the con and ready to pass on. She entrusts her little girl to the mercies of Charley, who rears her away from the Bowery and educates her in a fashionable boarding school. Later they live in a fashionable suburb where she meets with a young lawyer who wants to marry her. To make her happiness possible the guardian effaces himself and leads her to believe that he is dead, but way in the background he watches his former charge on the day that she weds.

The early Bowery days tingling with atmospheric touches, the scenes in the bar-room and the latter-day conversion of the bar to a quick lunch counter which also dispenses booze, are all very well done and carry conviction. Here Brenon has done some of his best work and he has handled a couple of fight scenes decidedly well.

Percy Marmont is doing probably his best work, and both Mary Brian and Juliet Brenon in the roles of daughter and mother, respectively, stand out. John Harrington as the heavy scores, while Riley Hatch, as the barkeep, looks the part to perfection.

"The Street of Forgotten Men" won't stand the crowds on their heads, but it will do to play in the bigger houses as well as the smaller ones. *Fred.*

RUGGED WATER

Adolph Zukor and Jesse L. Lasky present an Irvin Willat Production. From the novel by Joseph C. Lincoln. Screen play by James Shelley Hamilton. Co-featured are Lois Wilson, Wallace Beery, Warner Baxter and Phyllis Haver. A Paramount picture. At Rialto, New York, week July 19. Running time, 70 minutes.

Norma Bartlett	Lois Wilson
Capt. Bartlett	Wallace Beery
Calvin Homer	Warner Baxter
Myra Fuller	Phyllis Haver
Mrs. Fuller	Dot Farley
Supt. Kellogg	J. P. Lowrey
Wally Oaks	James Mason
Sam Bearse	William Cooley
Cook	Walter Ackerman
Jarvis	Knute Erickson
Gammon	Thomas Delmar
Orrin Hendricks	Jack Byron
Bloomer	Walter Rodgers
Josh Phinney	Warren Rodgers

Joseph C. Lincoln has written some corking stories of the sea. But despite a photographic draw on the mighty ocean the picture will not be classified as one of the great films of the year.

Famous Players bought on the strength of Lincoln's worth and popularity, yet as a film it doesn't skyrocket far from the beaten path.

Several climaxes are well staged, due to Irvin Willat, one of the best "big screen" directors. He has tried hard to make something fine out of "Rugged Water," yet the nature of its plain theme was too much even for a master hand like Willat.

The cast gives a lot of help. Lois Wilson is a subtle actress who makes much of her emotional moments. Wallace Beery, that rogue of the screen is invariably cast for a role that scatters villainy all over the sheet, yet here he is an old lifeguard who has gone plumb loco over religion.

There is a life-saving scene, and when one sees Cal Homer enact heroic tricks, one recalls the biggest scene in "The Courtship of Miles Standish," when Ray as the hero rescued a fellow Pilgrim in a storm at sea.

The picture will interest and entertain, going its way through the neighborhood houses, not banging over any boxoffice records, but giving satisfaction because the hero and heroine are brought together by a touch of nature that makes the world kin. *Mark.*

UNDER THE ROUGE

Associated Exhibitors' production, directed by Lewis H. Moomaw. Story and scenario by A. P. Younger. At the Colony, New York, week July 19. Runs about 62 mins.

Kitty	Eileen Percy
Whitey	Tom Moore
Skeeter	Eddie Phillips
Mal	James Mason
Daisy	Claire De Lorez
Doc Haskell	William V. Mong
Mr. Fleck	Chester Conklin
Mrs. Fleck	Aileen Manning
Jim Condon	Stanley Blystone
Maybelle	Peggy Prevost
Martha Maynard	Mary Alden
Evelyn	Carmelita Geraghty
Tommy	Bruce Guerin
Simmons	Frank Clarke
Fred Morton	Tom Gallery
Constable	William Dills

So much action has been jammed into "Under the Rouge" that a good deal of the incident leading from one fight to another has been left to the watcher's imagination. Too much so, in fact; for there are gaping holes in the continuity. It is never explained, for instance, how the hero gets himself out of jail, nor do we know until some 2,000 feet after it has happened that his buddy has been killed in an earlier scuffle so poorly lighted no one can tell what is happening.

A lesser fault is the triteness of the story, dealing with the same old regeneration theme in the same old, commonplace way. And yet, discounting the faulty continuity, it has been intelligently and refreshingly handled by both director and cast. The incessant action is due to the by-play of half a dozen different plots, chief of which is the gradual reformation of the crooks, Kitty and Whitey (Eileen Percy and Tom Moore).

Some shots in which the heroine, seeking to kill herself, propels her canoe down the rapids to be rescued by her lover at the brink of the giant falls are as tense and well staged as any of the innumerable similar ones in other pictures. The scenes in a cheap dance hall, rendezvous of the crooks, are also well handled.

An innovation is a heavy who, unlike the usual villain of today who at first has the hero groggy in the inevitable fight, is so yellow he refuses to battle at all, and is socked not only by the gentlemen of the cast, but by one of the young women he has been trifling with. As played by James Mason the role is particularly slimy.

That sterling actress, Mary Alden, dominates the production in the few moments allotted to her in a mother part, although Tom Moore's lovable crook is up to its usual standard. The beauteous Carmelita Geraghty has an unsympathetic role, but looks as well as ever, while the rest of the cast is dotted with the names of minor film celebrities.

The title, "Under the Rouge," might just as well have been "Quo Vadis" for all its relation to the story, but it sounds attractive for the box office. The picture is strictly of the program variety, although a good one of that category. Not good enough, however, to receive the necessary word-of-mouth boosts, and consequently it doesn't qualify as a first-run prospect for real money.

Tracked in Snow Country

Warner Bros.' production, featuring Rin-Tin-Tin. Directed by Herman Raymaker. Story by Edward Meagher. At the Piccadilly, New York, week starting July 18. Runs about 65 minutes.

Rin-Tin-Tin	Himself
Joan Hardy	June Marlow
Terry Moulton	David Butler
Jules Renault	Mitchell Lewis
Simon Hardy	Charles Sellon
Wah-Wah	Princess Lea

The most successful pictures featuring Rin-Tin-Tin, Strongheart and other dog actors have not played up the canine side too strongly, but have introduced it merely as interwoven with a plot of human beings that holds a good deal of interest in itself. "Tracked in the Snow Country" makes the mistake of focusing the spotlight on its animal actors, and its star in particular, to the almost total exclusion of the men and women in the cast. The result seems to be a certain amount of monotony.

Rin-Tin-Tin's suffering and adventures are almost analogous to those undergone in countless films by Bill Hart and others of the school of martyred, silent, western heroes. It is a wolf-dog, thoroughly domesticated and manageable when the picture begins. But when falsely accused of the murder of his master and forced to fight for his life the wolf blood in him becomes uppermost, and he wages a battle with man in truly primitive style. He mates with a widow wolf and becomes a leading figure of the pack, scoffing at those who try to capture him.

Rin's opportunity finally comes for vengeance on the man who really murdered his master and, vindicated himself, he once again becomes a gentleman pup, bidding adieu to his wolf instincts forever. The love interest, as far as the humans are concerned, meets no obstacles and almost passes unnoticed. The murder is the result of the heavy's desire to lay his hands on a gold mine. Otherwise the people of the picture just serve as background for Rinty's talented capers and posing.

The snow shots are, as might be expected, particularly beautiful, with the photographer's name omitted. Some storm scenes are startling in their realism, and effective pictorial use is made of the dark bodies of the wolves as contrasted with the white blankets of the Alaskan plains.

Rin-Tin-Tin shows himself to be as effective a canine actor as ever, shedding real tears when his master dies and portraying most effectively the mental torture of a poor animal pursued and hounded by those who had formerly loved him. The humans in the cast have very little to do, although June Marlow is attractive, David Butler manly and active, if somewhat of a dub on snow shoes, and Mitchell Lewis as sinister a French Canuck as always.

Dog fanciers and those particularly addicted to pictures of this type may really enjoy this film. All of us will find Rin-Tin-Tin likable and the story's setting impressive in a vast sense, but the majority will be slightly bored much of the time.

VIC DYSON PAYS

Ben Wilson production, released by Arrow. Directed by Jacques Jacard. Starring Ben Wilson and Neva Gerber. Shown at the Stanley, New York, one day, July 20, 1925. Running time, 60 minutes.

'Mad' Vic Dyson	Ben Wilson
Skip	Archie Ricks
Albert Stacey	Mel McCormick
Neva	Neva Gerber

Just another of those routine westerns turned out by the mile and cut into five reel lengths for the state right market at a price. There is very little story, not much more action and in all "Vic Dyson Pays" is one of those pictures that one could safely sleep through and not miss very much. In the very small houses in the likewise small towns it might get by on a double feature bill, but that is about all.

It is a range story with Vic Dyson in the heroic role. Vic is a cattleman embittered at the world because of a faction working against him. He, however, puts up a fight to retain his ranch, which the enemy want to take from him because it is to be the right of way for a railroad. In fighting he slams a couple of the enemy about a bit and finally causes the stenographer of the opposite side to fall over a cliff. She is engaged to the clerk of the leader of the gang who operate both in cattle and real estate. The fall causes the girl to lose the sight of her eyes because of a spinal infliction, and when the clerk runs out on her it is up to the ranchman to care for her. He does this and falls in love with her, and while she reciprocates this feeling, he does not know it. When she manages to recover fully he deeds her his ranch and starts to ride off, but she follows him and at the final fade out they are clinched.

For the greater part the picture is shot outdoors, so there was no great expense there.

The direction is only fair and there are some technical faults that are most glaring, but in the nickleodeons, where they like their film romance rough and ready and are willing to look at anything just so long as it moves on the screen, this will do. There is a portion of the picture that has been duped toward the end of the film and this stands out glaringly. *Fred.*

OVERLAND LIMITED

Sam Sax (Gotham) production distributed by Lumas Film Corp. Directed by Frank O'Neil and supervised by Renaud Hoffman. Story by James J. Tynan. At Loew's New York, one day (July 14), as half the bill. Runs about 62 minutes.

David Barton	Malcolm McGregor
Ruth Dont	Olive Borden
Violet Carlton	Alice Lake
Mrs. Barton	Ethel Wales
"Big Ed" Barton	Ralph Lewis
Brice Miller	John Miljan
Pat Madden	Roscoe Karns
Carson North	Emmett King
Schuyler Dont	Charles Mailes
"Bitterroot" Jackson	Charles West
"One Round" Farrell	Charles "Buddy" Post
Agnes Barton	Evelyn Jennings

This one is going to make them sit up in their chairs as straight as the vertical side of a cross-word puzzle all the way from Walla Walla to Canarsie. It fires thrills with rapidity, and at no time does the mechanism get clogged. It possesses, in addition to superlatively high-grade cast and direction, a story that while old and jammed with melodramatic hokum, has a tear, a smile and a wallop for every one of the several housand feet of film in its make-up.

Railroad stories when they are properly told and filmed always make good picture material. There are few thrills to be compared with the sight of a steel monster crowded with humanity rushing toward a bridge that has been tampered with and is ready to crash down when the weight of the engine reaches it. The heavy, for instance, no sooner has the destruction of the bridge planned than he learns his mother is a passenger on the train. The hero's father, crack engineer of the line, is at the throttle, the first to pass over the new bridge built under the direction of his boy. But his heart is heavy as his little girl is desperately ill at home and a red flag flying from his house as he speeds by shows her to have taken a turn for the worse.

To cap the climax a giant maniac breaks loose on the train and takes possession of the engine after knocking out the engineer. Nothing can stop the train and the engineer comes to just in time to uncouple the locomotive and apply the brakes to the first car, as the engine crashes down from the bridge.

In the reading all of this and the countless other strong situations sound as though it were all piled on too thickly, but the expert handling does away with that danger. The direction is credited to Frank O'Neil, but, although the press sheet fails to mention his name, Renaud Hoffman is given as supervisor in the preliminary titles, and his sure touch in the small-town commonplaces, pathos and humor, is clearly defined.

The entire cast is tremendously effective. Malcolm McGregor, who has been arriving like a sky-rocket, is excellent in the lead, as is the dainty Olive Borden, who plays opposite. Alice Lake successfully resists the temptation to overact as a vicious small-town flapper who tries to frame the hero, while Ralph Lewis, John Miljan and "Buddy" Post, as the engineer, heavy and maniac, respectively, are others who are outstanding.

It's a genuine pleasure, none the less, because it is surprising, to see an unheralded independent of this quality. According to announcement it is the first of a series of 12 productions to be made under the same banner, and if the rest average one half as good, Gotham will be the talk of the industry.

THE DANGER SIGNAL

Columbia Production distributed by Apollo. Cast includes Eva Novak, Dorothy Revier, Robert Gordon, Gaston Glass, Robert Edeson, Lincoln Stedman, Mayme Kelso, Lee Shumway. At the Broadway, New York, week July 20. Runs about 65 minutes.

"The Danger Signal" is not strictly a railroad picture although all characters are interwoven with the workings of a giant trunk line and the physical climax is reached with a runaway locomotive. The chief thing about the film is the story, which might just as well have taken place in any other industry or at any other locale. Incidentally it is an interesting and moderately original plot, interpreted by intelligent direction, a sagaciously chosen cast and backgrounded against the right sort of atmosphere and production.

The story starts in 1904 with the railroad president refusing to have anything to do with the widow of his son who had eloped the year before. He agrees, however, to bring up her baby, not knowing that she is the mother of twins. She gives one of them over to his keeping and changes her name.

Twenty years later finds both boys working for the railroad, the grandfather's ward, spoiled and shiftless, as a district assistant superintendent, and his brother, unbeknown to him, as a fireman at the same junction. The twins come to conflict over the girl in the case and the poorer one underservedly loses his job. Affairs are finally righted and the grandfather realizes that the boy brought up in poverty but with a mother's love has made a much better man than the one with everything in the world but maternal affection.

The big thrill comes when a runaway engine seems to be headed straight for the passenger express coming in the opposite direction. The hero (Robert Gordon, and it is really he doing the stunt) jumps on a motorcycle and cuts in front of the locomotive racing it down the tracks just a few yards in front of its snorting nose. Just in time he hurls himself off the cycle to the last switch between the two trains and collision, tackling it just as the crash seems unavoidable. The runaway rushes down a sideline and into a baggage car while the express goes its merry way unmolested.

Eva Novak is the featured name and she does well with the difficult role of a middle-aged mother. Her make-up, however, is bad. Dorothy Revier is handsome and reserved, while Gaston Glass makes the heavy not totally detestable. Bob Edeson is effective, as always, in the only other important part.

"The Danger Signal" is one more of the steadily increasing but still small list of better independents. It will do nicely for the majority of houses.

NOT SO LONG AGO

Famous Players presentation featuring Betty Bronson and Ricardo Cortez. Directed by Sidney Olcott. Adapted from Arthur Richman's play. Photography by James Howe. At Rivoli, New York, week July 26. Running time, 70 mins.

Betty Dover	Betty Bronson
Billy Ballard	Ricardo Cortez
Jerry Flint	Edwards Davis
Mrs. Ballard	Julia Swane Gordon
Sam Robinson	Laurance Wheat
Ursula Kent	Jacqueline Gadson
Michael Dover	Dan Crimmins

Extremely weak around the knees and a passive interlude sans any kick whatsoever. The story leaves the impression it was a mischosen script in that the little old New York theme falls short of the action and dramatic interest normally construed as a screen necessity.

Revolving around the horseless carriage age with Betty Dover's (Miss Bronson) father struggling on his steam contraption the sidelights are on Betty helping eke out an existence by becoming a seamstress for the aristocratic Ballards. The Ballard son (Mr. Cortez- is the Don Juan of the day and forced on an English heiress by his mother with that engagement broken by the couple themselves, whence Betty closes out the film by grabbing Billy for herself.

Meanwhile, the foreclosure of a note on Dover's steam cart by a money lender supplies what meagre interest the film contains. A race with the town braggart, who states he can beat the machine by walking, consummates a restricted thrill with the loud-mouthed person also a persistent suitor for the fair Betty.

As cameraed, Richman's play leaves little for either Miss Bronson or Cortez to do. The former looks like an absolute child among these costumed players and the contrast in that sense is so strong between the featured pair it has a detrimental effect. Through the small demand placed upon them cast honors are confined to Laurance Wheat as Sam Robinson, the local bulldozing champ. Wheat has turned in the performance of the picture. Other contributing members are equal to the occasion without particular prominence, although Dan Crimmins has made the role of Betty's father convincing.

Olcott has done much better work than the supervising with which he is herein credited. At the same time the tale must have had its limitations from the director's standpoint.

In toto "Not So Long Ago" is an actionless filming during which the characters and their trials do not provoke sufficient interest to overcome this becalmed adaptation. *Skig.*

Never the Twain Shall Meet

Cosmopolitan Production, distributed by Metro-Goldwyyn. From the story by Peter B. Kyne. Directed by Maurice Tourneur. Shown at the Capitol, N. Y., week July 26, 1925. Running time, 79 minutes.

Tamea	Anita Stewart
Dan Pritchard	Bert Lytell
Mark Mellengor	Huntley Gordon
Maisie	Justine Johnstone
James Muggridge	George Siegmann
Gaston Larrieau	Lionel Belmore
Butler	William Norris
Mrs. Pippy	Emily Fitzroy
Miss Smith	Princess Marie de Bourbon
Julia	Florence Turner
Capt. Hackett	Ernest Butterworth
Doctor	Ben Deeley

Up at the Capitol this week they are trying to figure out just what it is that is attracting the most unusual business which started at that house Sunday when this picture drew $13,997. The question is whether it is the picture, the advertising in the Hearst papers, that Roxy is no longer there, or just some freak in the minds of the public that made them want to come to the Capitol in droves this week. One theory is that the popularity the story achieved both in serial and novel form is responsible for the added box office receipts. At any rate, no matter what it is the Capitol is pulling toward a record week for this time of the year.

"Never the Twain Shall Meet" was a corking story. The same cannot be said for the picture, although it is directed most capably by Maurice Tourneur, who jammed it full of atmospheric shots, and even though Anita Stewart looks and acts like a million dollars, and Justine Johnstone looks like a couple of million, and by the same token Bert Lytell and Huntley Gordon give great performances. Still the suspense present in written word is lacking on the screen, as is also the quaint comedy that did so much to give an added kick to the tale.

As the title indicates, "Never the Twain Shall Meet" is an East is East-West is West tale of the South Seas and San Francisco. The heroine, a little half-breed, who is queen in her native island, is, after, all just another "Butterfly," only she seeks out her own fate and when finding her happiness is being won at the cost of that of the man she loves she willingly renounces him, sending him back to civilization and the girl he was really meant for.

On the screen the story becomes commonplace. Were it not for Tourneur's direction and the superb photography and locations that were shot the picture would be just one of those things. However, the direction does carry it along, and there are Tourneur touches in the island scenes that just about shave the back of the necks of the censors. There was a brief moment when it looked as though the director was going to show more of Anita than the law allowed, but they edited that out of the film.

Miss Stewart does make an altogether perfect Tamea, full of fire when it was required and soft and lovable in her other scenes. Lytell did not seem to impress particularly, although the rôle was more or less a thankless one, still the character registered in the story to greater advantage than on the screen. Huntley Gordon delivered 100 per cent, as did also George Siegmann as the heavy. Lionel Belmore, as the old sea captain, while only in the earlier portion of the picture, registered heavily. *Fred.*

THE HALF-WAY GIRL

First National Production, adapted from the original story by E. Lloyd Sheldon. Featuring Doris Kenyon, Lloyd Hughes and Hobart Bosworth. Directed by John Francis Dillon. Supervision of Earl Hudson. At the Strand, New York, week July 26. Running time, 77 minutes.

Poppy La Rue.......................Doris Kenyon
Philip Douglas.....................Lloyd Hughes
John Gutherie.....................Hobart Bosworth
The Crab...........................Tully Marshall
Jardine.................................Sam Hardy
Gibson..........................Charles Wellesley
Miss Brown.......................Martha Madison
Effie......................................Sally Crute

Good old fashioned meller with a burning steamer at sea as the great spectacular wallop. That burning steamer is exceedingly well done, and it burns with possibly the most lurid orange flames on the screen in some time. But it does make a mighty good hurrah for the latter end.

The story is of the Orient, its dives and the general line that go after easy pickings from the driftwood of civilization landing in the backwash of the China coast. From a box office angle it won't have the crowds breaking down the doors, but it is entertaining enough to please.

The hero and heroine are both regenerated by their love. That is the theme. The girl isn't too bad. She's just an actress who goes to the Orient with a show that strands, and she has to get along the best she can, so to work out her hotel bill she becomes one of the paid hostesses at the hotel. That is only about a step above the hostess, also for pay, that infest a quarter known as Malay street in Singapore. The boy is the son of the chief of the C. I. D. and the youngster has gone down to the bottom because of a woman, run away from his folks and is drinking himself to death.

After he has met up with the paid hostess, his father traces him and sees in the girl another of the vultures of the Orient who is only out to fleece the youngster. But when the boy gets in a jam, she sticks by, helps him to escape, straightens him out after the ship burns and sinks and brings him to a realization that there is something worth living for.

The story is well handled on the screen and in a certain class of house it will fill all the requirements of film food for the regulators. *Fred.*

A WOMAN'S FAITH

Universal production featuring Alma Rubens and Percy Marmont, adapted from Clarence Buddington Kelland's serial, "Miracle." Directed by Edward Laemmle. At Colony, New York, week beginning July 26. Running time, 65 minutes.

Neree Caron / Jean Dubal ....Alma Rubens
Donovan Steele.....................Percy Marmont
Francois.................................Hughie Mack
Cluny...................................Jean Hersholt
Leandre Turcott...............Andre de Beranger
Odillon Turcott.....................Cesare Gravin
Delima Turcott.....................Rose Rosanova
Blanche......................................Zasu Pitts
Xavier Caron.................William H. Turner
Ancelme...............................Calvin Roberts

Melodrama of the Canadian woods which gives Percy Marmont another of those trespassed upon roles and Alma Rubens another opportunity for emotionalism, although seldom permitting her to achieve similar heights to some of her previous screen roles.

Marmot is Donovan Steele, who because of being double-crossed in love has attempted to double-cross his God. Embittered, he goes into the Canadian woods to forget. Neree Caron (Miss Rubens) is also there as a fugitive from justice, wanted for murder, which she claims is a frame-up.

Although crude melodrama the film contains several flashes of beauty in architecture with the Cathedral scenes, of course, standing out. The fight between Marmont and Hersholt is also realistic and provides the only real action the story boasts.

"A Woman's Faith" may enjoy a measure of popularity among those who read the serial. Otherwise just a fair program picture. *Edba.*

EVE'S LOVER

Warner Bros. production, starring Irene Rich. Adapted from the novel by Mrs. W. K. Clifford. Directed by Roy Del Ruth. At the Piccadilly, New York, week July 25. Running time, 70 minutes.

Eve Burnside...........................Irene Rich
Baron Geraldo Maddox...............Bert Lytell
Rena.......................................Clara Bow
Austin Saarfield.....................Willard Louis

As a feature picture "Eve's Lover" doesn't amount to Adam.

It is just one of those business woman stories, where the business woman falls in love and marries a man who doesn't give a darn about her, but learns to love her, although she believes that he has wed her for her dough.

From a box office angle the picture hasn't a thing except the title.

Irene Rich does give a performance worth while, but she isn't starring material, at least not in this picture. Bert Lytell plays the Austrian Baron the same as George Beban played an Italian Count in musical comedy. Clara Bow is just a flapper trouble maker and Willard Louis works overtime in the picture advertising Bromo Seltzer and not getting laughs.

The plot revolves about two steel mills. One is controlled by the heroine and the other by a business rival. The Baron is a friend of the business rival and indebted to him, because his checks have been coming back with "no account" stamped on them. That gives the business rival a hold on the Baron to compel him to make love to the wealthy spinster and marry her. The idea being that after the wedding the Baron will convince his wife that she should sell out to her rival.

Then the Baron falls in love with the wife, but she overhears his former mistress bawl him out and threaten to expose the whole scheme and then she's broken hearted and remains so until hubby invades the steel works, blocks a strike and finally is held in her arms for the two to start honeymooning all over again. *Fred.*

Ranger of the Big Pines

Vitagraph Production. From the story "Cavanaugh, Forest Ranger," by Hamlin Garland. Directed by William Van Dyke. At the Rialto, New York, week July 26. Running time 69 minutes.

Ross Cavanaugh.................Kenneth Harlan
Lee Virginia Weatherford.Helene Costello
Lize Weatherford...............Eulalie Jensen
Sam Gregg...........................Will Walling
Joe Gregg.............................Lew Harvey
Redfield..........................Robert J. Garves

Just a western, possibly strong enough to place on a double feature bill in the average daily change of picture house, but it has no business on Broadway or any place else in a de luxe presentation theatre. The picture isn't strong enough for that and it is a certainty the box office returns at the Rialto this week are just going to add another back mark to the long list of box office flops bearing the Vitagraph trademark that have been presented here.

A love story, shooting, ride to the rescue and all the usual ingredients that go to make up the typical western. For the small theatre it will answer but that is the only type of house where it should play.

The story isn't compelling, interesting or even logical. The hero is a forest ranger, the heroine the daughter of the keeper of the cattle town hash house, but educated in the east, and the boy is also from the east. In the end she rides to his rescue when the cattlemen who have been feeding their herds on government land without paying the tax decide to kill him for running them off.

The picture is rather poorly directed and there are several spots where a little editing would have helped. *Fred.*

THE FIGHTING CUB

Phil Goldstone production with all star cast. Issued as a Truart and called Renown picture. At Broadway (Moss') New York (pop vaudeville), week July 27 Running time around 60 minutes (watch stopped at 5:25—picture caught at 7:20 show).

A very good independent picture and "independent" employed without intent to reflect. Through cast of known names, story and some interesting side lights, this picture may be shoved in during the summer by many of the larger program houses without fear of flopping any harder with it than some of the junk they have been using for the hot weather.

A considerable play could be made on the names here and they are not one-day names, but appear throughout the film's tale. In production cost the picture looks comparatively light. That is worth something for those "big producers" who produce for inside of $75,000 and say $300,000. This picture looks just as good to those who won't get the difference. No expensive sets, no expensive interiors, not even a rented one in Hollywood, and no extras. That no extras not so bad. Nowadays a picture of the bigger bunch without a mob scene on a street or cabaret must have been written by a tyro.

It's the story of a copy boy in a newspaper office who wants to become a reporter and does. He's quite free with the managing editor who promises him the reportorial job if he can interview the political boss of the town. This the boy does and tells the boss' daughter his mother does the washing for her family.

Several human touches redound to the credit of the director as well as the story writer.

Immediately after the boy makes good, gets the job, a raise in salary and an advance on his increased pay, he spends the advance to buy flowers for his washwoman mother. That was a dandy touch.

Melodramatic in a mild way and also romantic, reading like a boy hero or boy detective story well built and carried out.

Wesley Barry is the boy, giving a corking performance. This Goldstone formerly turned out some pretty slouchy pictures. Of late he has been doing much better. This "Fighting Cub" is an example of his best to date.

If the smaller independents could do one like this more often they wouldn't have so many squawks to utter. *Sime.*

O. U. WEST

F. B. O. release featuring "Lefty" Flynn. Directed by Harry Garson. Cast includes Milton Ross, Ann May, Evelyn Francisco, Fred Burns, Leonard Trainor and Raymond Turner. At the Stanley, New York, 1 day (July 24). Running time, 61 mins.

An ordinary western which staggers in and stops off at every port other films of the type have habitated since the first chaps were screened. The picture is spasmodic in sequence and overrates itself in its 61 minutes.

Flynn receives feature billing. Despite this the young man has done some creditable work as a secondary character in past major releases this bit of open atmosphere proves nothing for him other than he could formerly boot considerable football with that southpaw leg for Yale. But no 70-yard spiral could pull this bit of celluloid making out of the hole it soon digs for itself and it's two to one Flynn hasn't let one go from his instep in years. Whatever promise Flynn revealed in those other pictures is completely buried here, if for nothing else than the story lacks the substance to bring any latent talent forth.

Other cast members are at an equal disadvantage with the exception of a colored porter (Raymond Turner), who practically runs away with the footage because of the comedy angle. Ann May provides a listless heroine while Evelyn Francisco is a luke-warm and half-way villainess. The male roles are purely mechanical requisites.

In detail the yarn is of a young and wealthy heir westbound on a train in possession of a glorious "stew" which he ultimately shares with the porter. Upon reaching the ranch of his father's partner the youth, not too soon after, cleans out a gang of rustlers and wins the girl, the latter against his better judgement. It looks like that the way Flynn plays it and as presumably directed. Anyway, there is an under cover bet between the father and the ranch owner that the son will give his cowboy playmates "air" and the finish has both parents, the girl is the daughter of the partner, donating their checks as wedding gifts.

From the appearance of the settings the picture could play three houses and be clear of the production "nut" but that it will get a certain number of screenings in the main street film emporiums is reasonable to expect. *Skig.*

Brand of Cowardice

Phil Goldstone production, directed by John P. McCarthy. Story by the latter and Roger Pocock. Features Carmelita Geraghty and Bruce Gordon, with Cuyler Supplee, Ligio deGolconda, Harry Lonsdale, Charles McHugh, Mark Fenton and Sidney de Grey also in the cast. At Loew's New York one day (June 30) as half the bill. Runs about 62 minutes.

Metro produced a picture of similar title in 1916 with Lionel Barrymore featured in a story of Mexican adventure. The more recent release also concerns Mexico, or at least that southern part of California bordering on the Mexican country, but the plots are essentially different and by two separate authors.

The Goldstone brand of films has received more than a little praise recently in Variety as being superior types of independent releases, and "Brand of Cowardice," while it is no knockout, is a better than average western. The story is as conventional as the title is meaningless, but in all other respects—direction, acting, photography, continuity, atmosphere and general presentation—the picture maintains a sufficiently high standard.

The formula this time concerns the U. S. Marshal who poses as a bandit himself in order to trap a gang of outlaws after the jewels of a wealthy Mexican ranch owner. Naturally he has to beg the Mexican's lovely daughter to trust him no matter what happens. She is kept in doubt as to his moral worthiness until the finish, although the audience is let in on the secret that he is no ordinary robber right at the beginning.

A departure is the omission of practically all hand-to-hand battling, but there is plenty of pistol play, hard chases and wild riding in the moonlight included in the action. The pictorial photography is particularly fine, with the Mexican color cleverly introduced.

The film has also been fortunate in its leads, Bruce Gordon and Carmelita Geraghty. Miss Geraghty is not a great actress as yet, but with her looks she doesn't have to be, and though she may be more Geraghty than Carmelita she makes as dainty an Irish senorita as any one could wish. Gordon doesn't match her on looks. In fact, he is more or less of a homely looking individual, but his personality and acting skill are of high grade, and as an addition to the apparently limitless number of western stars he is to be welcomed heartily.

Incidentally every one will wonder where the cowardice comes in, as no one in the picture seems to have the slightest fear of any one else. The Goldstone name probably means nothing to the general public as yet, but observant exhibitors have probably noticed the improvement in this brand, and if they play "Brand of Cowardice" up right the favorable impression should be retained if not exactly strengthened.

FIGHTING DEMON

F. B. O. film made by A. Carlos and starring Richard Talmadge. Scenario by James Beck Smith and direction by Arthur Rosson. At Loew's New York June 26, as half of double bill. Running time, 60 minutes.

James Drake.............Richard Talmadge
Jackson Pierce...............Herbert Prior
Mr. D'Arcy...........Charles Hill Mailes
Dolores D'Arcy............Lorraine Eason
Dynamite Diaz...........Dick Sutherland

Peggy Shaw..........."Peaches" Delaware
Isaac Belden.................Stanton Heck

Apparently Talmadge pictures are catching on nicely, for this one is indicative of a money expenditure which shames some of the other stunt man films. The script is much better than usually provided for the dare devil heroes and with a competent cast and good settings, the whole thing works into a good program feature for the smaller houses. For the combination theatres it looks like a setup, for the vaude-picture emporiums are partial to these fast action babies.

In plot this concerns Jim Drake, a young safe engineer. A crowd of crooks lure him to South America on a phoney contract, their game being to force him to open a safe which he designed. This safe is in a bank owned by a Mr. D'Arcy.

D'Arcy has a good looking daughter and Jim meets her on the way down and they fall hard on the love stuff. Another woman on the boat, Peggy Shaw, has just married Dynamite Diaz, the famous fighter, but she likes to do a little flirting on the side. Her flirting with Jim got him in bad all around and furnished the excuse for some merry chases on ship-board. Once in South America, however, Jim outwits the crooks and has them locked up, and for good measure he goes into the ring against Dynamite Diaz, taps that gent on the tummy and walks out the hero.

And he marries the gal.

Talmadge, in differentiation from some other stunt men, is a pretty fair actor, while the productions with which he is being backed are gaining with each release. Some more like this one and his advance will be strong. *Sisk.*

SALLY OF SAWDUST

D. W. Griffith directed production, adapted by Forrest Halsey from the stage play "Poppy." Released by United Artists (the final picture of Griffith's for U. A., with his next to be made for Famous Players). This picture made on the Famous Players lot on Long Island lead to an impression it is Griffith's first F. P. release. First run in Chicago last week. Opened at Strand New York, Aug. 2—week. Running time 104 minutes.
Sally .... Carol Dempster
Prof. Eustace McGargle ....W. C. Fields
Peyton Lennox .... Alfred Lunt
Judge Henry L. Foster....Erville Alderson
Mrs. Foster .... Effie Shannon
Lennox, Sr. .... Charles Hammond
The Detective .... Roy Applegate
Miss Vinton ....Florence Fair
Society Leader ....Marie Shotwell

A cinch for the picture houses through its comedy, supplied mostly by W. C. Fields, with Carol Dempster's performance as Sally a delight.

D. W. Griffith is down to common picture making in this one. While it is strange to witness a Griffith film directed by him in a straight-away manner, so foreign to his far-advanced ideas and ideals for the average picture fan, still Griffith with all of this and all of what he must have suppressed or suffered in the making of this picture, has sent many a wallop across for first aid of the box office.

As W. C. Fields made his legit stage hit in the musical "Poppy" as the carnival showman, so does he here scream his screen debut as a film funny man in "Sally." Mr. Fields has put in bits of business and gags that will make the Chaplins and the Lloyds bawl out their gag writers. And Fields plays them as well as though on the stage. He gives a smoothness to his comedy stuff and his playing that can not be missed.

While that Miss Dempster in this picture is a dear. As Mr. Griffith so truthfully remarked at the end of the first showing Sunday at the Strand, when the two principals and himself made a personal appearance upon the stage:

"As to Miss Dempster, I would like to convey that in Sally, she is Sally and plays Sally, not playing a 'movie queen.'" As a large professional contingent was in that over-capacity audience, they all got Mr. Griffith's point. Miss Dempster was just Sally, a daughter of the circus, a little sprite with the exact spirit of the role and the big top.

"Sally" is not a great picture nor is it a great comedy, but it's a fine film comedy release, that must get over at any house, albeit the 104 minutes are much too long. Without the footage that must have been removed, there are still hundreds of feet that could go out.

Mr. Griffith from reports followed the stage story but sparsely. His picturization is nearly an original other than the characters. The director slipped in pathos and sentiment in his masterly manner without too much of either, but he allowed the comedy to go at full tilt. There are one or two bits that were "taking chances" but as the censors passed them, Griffith could.

One of the Fields' bit is among those two. When Charlie Chaplin sees it he will wonder why he didn't think of it, for it's a bear and messy enough in content to have been English.

Alfred Lunt is a so-so juvenile hero, not over-burdened and making no particular impression. Close ups were employed of Roy Appelgate as the detective, for no earthly reason. Effie Shannon was a sweetly and saintly looking mother, while Florence Fair conspicuously stood out as Miss Vinton.

Sally is an orphan, her mother, a gentlewoman from New England having married a theatrical man

against her parents' wishes. When her mother dies, Prof. Gargle takes charge of Sally, bringing her up as his daughter with the girl unaware of her parentage. The finale is the restoration of the girl to her grandparents as her grandfather, now wealthy and a judge in his home town, Green Meadows, is about to send her to a home for wayward girls. She was charged with being an accomplice of Gargle's in his three-shell gyp. Gargle could deal three-card or shake the shells or sell Indian medicine; nothing about a circus or carnival with a dishonest dollar in it that he couldn't do or get—but he brought up Sally faithfully and honestly.

In circus scenes no extensive matter was employed other than the equipment of a circus. Much of this apparently had been cut. Miss Dempster did a couple of scenes where doubling was probably utilized but skillfully.

The general atmosphere of the picture is pleasant and inviting.

Almost anyone who knew would say, "Attaboy, Dave" for Griffith when seeing this, knowing that at the least he will get some money for himself out of "Sally" and all of the other regular programers he will make while thinking only of the box office and not 25 years ahead as he usually has done. *Sime.*

THE UNHOLY THREE

Tod Browning Production released by Metro-Goldwyn. Lon Chaney starred, with Mae Busch and Matt Moore featured. Story by C. A. Robbins. Shown at the Capitol, N. Y., week Aug. 2. Running time, 69 minutes.
Echo, the Ventriloquist........Lon Chaney
Rosie O'Grady...................Mae Busch
Hector McDonald...............Matt Moore
Hercules..................Victor McLaglen
Tweedledee ....Harry Earles
Regan ....Matthew Betz
Announcer ....Walter Perry
Jeweler ....John Merkyl
John Arlington ....Charles Wellsley
Butler ....Percy Williams
Mrs. Arlington ....Marjorie Morton
Arlington Baby ....Violet Crane
Police Commissioner.........Lou Morrison
Judge ....Edward Connelly
Attorney for Defense...William Humphreys
Prosecuting Attorney........A. E. Warren

Here is about the best bet from a box office standpoint that has come along in a while. It's a picture that will compel the box office to get business on an enlarging scale as the days go along. That is saying a whole lot for any screen production, with the possible exception of the outstanding one or two a year that come along. This is one of the exceptions.

It's a picture that is going to be measured up to "The Miracle Man" by a lot of people who, the chances are, never saw "The Miracle Man" on the screen, and that includes a lot of reviewers of films in New York as well as elsewhere. This picture isn't a "Miracle Man" and it won't be a "Miracle Man" in the point of outstanding box office popularity in this day against productions that will contend with it for honors, it won't overwhelm the field as did the production of the late George Loane Tucker in its day, but it is going to be liked universally and it will get money for the exhibitor.

It is a wow of a story in the first place. One of those stories that one would expect to see the name of Train or some author of that ilk attached. It has everything—hoak, romance, crook stuff, murder, suspense, trick stuff and, above all, is as cleverly titled as has been any production in many moons. Why, they've even screenized a dirty story that is four or five years old, the one about the gal that couldn't hold out on her pineapple after which he told her that "money got that way didn't do anybody any good," but they have cleaned it up and utilized it in a manner that fits the story perfectly. It's a picture with a kick all right, all right.

And there's another thing about this picture, and that is that Lon Chaney stands out like a million dollars. He's done that before, but always with a more or less grotesque make-up. No make-up this time. He isn't all hunched up, he isn't legless, he isn't this, that or the other thing in deformities. He's just Lon Chaney, and he's great. He must have had a hard time convincing 'em that as just plain Lon Chaney he could be as great as though he was this, that or the other form of a cripple, but from now on it's going to be another story.

An' May Busch! Well, Mae has just gone out and done it, an' how? It certainly is a far cry from Mae at the old St. Francis on 47th street to Mae Busch in the "Unholy Three," but Mae was a great little gal then and she certainly is a great little actress now. This picture more than proves it. Matt Moore has the role with the majority of the sympathy, and he gives a performance worthy of the best screen traditions of the Moore family.

The story is just one of those accidents that come along and happen to be the thing that fits; that is, when it's properly handled as Tod Browning certainly did handle this.

It opens in a dime museum with the announcer presenting the freaks. There is the strong man, the ventriloquist, the midget, the cooch dancer and the rest of the "Weird Wonders of the World in Human Form." Chaney is Echo the ventriloquist and Mae Busch is his gal. She's a gun moll, and she fans the chumps in the crowds for everything from their turnips to their leathers, and slips her swag to her guy, and because he promises her a big steak for dinner slips him an extra watch that she had thought of holding out.

It's the midget that finally causes a fight in the joint which necessitates the cops being called in, and a general scramble for a getaway on the part of every one, with Echo slipping the swag back to his moll when the bulls come on the scene, but they all manage to get away clean. Then the frame. It's Echo that has the idea. He can ventril, so next he is seen as an "old dame" who has a parrot shop. All the birds talk when the old lady sells 'em. Get the idea?

But that is only the stall. When the birds get home to their purchasers they stop talking, and the old lady comes up to see about it. That gives Echo a chance to look the joint over, and later with the aid of his two confederates he returns to turn-off the place. The midget is great for the transoms, while the strong man can force the bars of a window open with all ease.

Meantime in the parrot shop, where Moore in the role of Hector is the sap clerk, he and the moll have fallen for each other. In the end when the sap is accused of murder, a crime which two of the "three" are responsible for, the moll to save him is willing to sacrifice herself and stick to Echo if he will save the boy. He finally consents, after the midget and the strong man lose their lives in a battle with a gorilla, and here is as pretty a piece of business as has been pulled yet. It's so good that it should not be disclosed, but it takes place in the usual conventional court room scene and makes even that worth while in the picture, and that's going some.

Of course, in the finish the regeneration of Echo is brought about, and he releases the girl from her promise so that she can go to the arms of the man she loves. The turning loose of Echo by the courts is about the only inconsistent fact in the whole darn yarn, for he certainly was an accessory before the fact in the murder if there ever was one, and the courts don't turn those boys out, especially after the two murderers are dead and out of the way without the courts having had a chance at them.

But, boys, it's a picture—and what a picture! *Fred.*

THE GOOSE WOMAN

Universal production of Rex Beach's story. Features Louise Dresser with Jack Pickford and Constance Bennett underlined. Directed by Clarence Brown. At Colony, New York, week Aug. 2. Running time, 75 mins.

Mary Holmes.................Louise Dresser
Gerald Holmes...............Jack Pickford
Hazel Woods............Constance Bennett
Jacob Riggs..............James O. Barrows
Reporter.....................George Cooper
Mr. Vogel.........Gustave von Seyffertitz
Detective Lopez..............George Nichols
Amos Ethridge...................MacDermott

A sweet picture which will principally become known for the performance of Louise Dresser. It's a murder mystery yarn capably pieced together, with the support of Jack Pickford and Constance Bennett enhancing the general value.

After viewing the film there is no doubt concerning the why of Miss Dresser's presence being emphasized in the billing. Her degraded opera star becomes a gin-drinking old hag who isolates herself in a dilapidated cottage on the outskirts of a town. It is nothing less than brilliant and unquestionably the peak of Miss Dresser's screen career to date.

In its latter stages the story permits Miss Dresser to emerge from the depths, whence she done modern regalia to panic a group of newspaper reporters. A break for her on appearance and a contrast to her earlier depiction which she handles equally well. Pickford is the second choice for prominence only because of the outstanding merit of Miss Dresser's characterization. A sympathetic role is the foundation of Pickford's advantage, upon which he immediately begins to construct a convincing piece of acting, mayhaps as surprising as it is convincing.

The film is under way with Mary Holmes (Miss Dresser) existing in squalor following 20 years of aimlessly dreaming of the past when she was a star among footlight celebrities, all of which she lost when the birth of an illegitimate son destroyed a marvelous voice. Resenting and ignoring her offspring, Gerald (Mr. Pickford), for that reason she provides for herself by conducting a flock of geese, ignoring the pleas of her son (who has the State agency of accessories for a lesser-priced automobile) to live with him.

She sees in a nearby murder the chance to again get her name in the press, and, refusing admittance to reporters, only tells what she knows to the State's attorney after proving to him who she really is and upon his promise that he will secure her the desired publicity. The attorney makes good by bringing her to a hotel where a police matron, manicurist and facial masseur do their bit previous to springing the bombshell upon the newspaper boys.

The former stage luminary basks in her regained prominence until suddenly her son is revealed as the man her manufactured evidence has compromised. The situation then straightens itself out when the real murderer gives himself up. Underlying this sequence is the love affair of Gerald with Hazel Woods (Miss Bennett), a local stock actress, to whom the murdered man has been attentive, inasmuch as he owns the company, and for which attentions he is killed by the stage door keeper.

Clarence Brown has directed without resorting to dramatic heroics. Besides which he has terminated the picture with a laugh, a corking twist in lieu of the preceding tension. Recognition should also be tendered the department of continuity, for the picture flows by smoothly and does not lost its sense of proportion.

Universal in this picture has a release capable of playing any regular program house in the country. It can certainly stand up for a week in the major theatres, and they'll like it where the box office tariff isn't so heavy.

Between the story and Miss Dresser it can't miss, and it marks a great send-off for the Colony on the Greater Movie Season propaganda, although the house seemingly is not paying any attention to that business-making idea. *Skig.*

KISS ME AGAIN

Ernst Lubitsch production presented by the Warner Bros. starring Marie Prevost and Monte Blue. Based on an original story by Hans Kraely. Shown at the Piccadilly, New York, week Aug. 1. Running time, 67 minutes.

Loulou Fleury................Marie Prevost
Gaston Fleury..................Monte Blue
Maurice Ferriere...............John Roche
Grizette.........................Clara Bow
Dr. Dubois..................Willard Louis

Another tribute to the art of farcical direction by Ernst Lubitsch. He has turned out a production that will delight all picture fans. It is just suggestive enough at times to make the flappers rave about it and contains sufficient comedy in spots to have them in roars of laughter. It is a picture that is designed principally for the sophisticated, but still broad enough in its humor to be appreciated almost by anyone. In the bigger towns it should be surefire at the box office.

One of its virtues is that it is enacted by a short cast with the principal trio of players always in the foreground. They are Marie Prevost, Monte Blue and John Roche. Clara Bow absolutely triumphs in the role of a lawyer's steno, and Willard Louis manages to exact much from the role of attorney.

The story is decidedly Parisian in its flavor. The Fleurys are married, the husband is a business man, the wife is somewhat fond of music, and Maurice, the musician, is fond of the wife. This brings about a flirtation, and finally the husband decides that he will not stand in the way of his wife's happiness, so he arranges for a divorce with his wife to receive his home and half his fortune. This naturally delights the musician, who will then marry her and have a made-to-order home and income at his disposal. But the wife in reality loves her husband and wants him back. It is the touch of arranging for the divorce evidence that creates much laughter.

The criss-crossing of the husband-who-is-to-be-free and the husband-that-is-to-be at the home of the wife is decidedly laughable. Also is the moment after the reconciliation is effected between the man and his wife and the pair repair to the chamber of the wife. There is a touch that will cause audiences to gasp when they get the suggestion of the two disrobing. It is cleverly done, and at the finish there is a touch that takes away all the suggestiveness.

It is well acted, delightfully directed and edited without a wasted foot of film, and on the whole is a picture that should get box office returns. *Fred.*

WILD, WILD SUSAN

Paramount feature starring Bebe Daniels and featuring Rod La Rocque. Adapted by Tom J. Geraghty from the story, "The Wild, Wild Child," by Steuart M. Emery. Directed by Edward Sutherland. Produced by Adolph Zukor and Jesse L. Lasky. At the Rialto, New York, week Aug. 2. Running time, 60 minutes.

Susan Van Dusen..............Bebe Daniels
Tod Waterbury...............Rod La Rocque
Peter Van Dusen.........Henry Stephenson
Edgar ....Jack Kane
Emily Dutton ....Helen Holcomb
M. Crawford Dutton........Osgood Perkins
Malcolm ....Ivan Simpson
Eustace Waterbury........Russell Medcroft
Chauncey Ames Waterbury....Warren Cook
Parker ....Joseph Smiley
Edgar's Sweetheart...........Mildred Ryan

This latest vehicle of Bebe Daniels is a trifle lightweight for the big feature houses despite its star's superb role and her ability to get everything possible out of it. It suffers mainly through lack of action in the early reels and a seeming premeditation to crowd them into the final spin-offs and never once taking it beyond the realm of a more or less conventional story.

Miss Daniels is cast as a harum-scarum debutante in search of thrills. Her quest has the fashionable household upset. Dad and brother promote a trip abroad for her with some friends. Brother has built up the son as a real shock absorber, but when Susan lamps him she does a leap from the departing Leviathan and practically into the arms of Tod Waterbury, the more virile brother of the departing Eustace. Tod has a literary complex and is driving a brown and white for local color.

For want of a better adventure Susan hires out as a sleuth with a detective agency and receives her first thrill by tracking a shoplifter. She is later given a tougher assignment to invade a rendezvous of gangsters and recover a precious bond. She enters and is subjectd to all sorts of spooky devices, including an audience with the hooded leaders, which winds up with them removing their hoods and being Eustace, her brother and her pseudo-detective chief. It is plain that the series of events had been stage managed to give Susan the desired thrills. The precious paper also turns out to be nothing more than an accident policy on Susan, taken out by the brother with the fixed idea that it would be a good investment at the pace Sis was going.

The film has suspense in sections, also considerable action, and in the melodrama, which provides a telling comedy wallop. It falls short, however, through obvious padding and a dragginess in the early reels.

Miss Daniels has a corking role and plays it well. Rod La Rocque is convincing as Tod Browning. Other members of the cast gave adequate portrayal of their respective roles.

Unless the star's name can sell this one to the big feature houses it looks as though it's doomed as a routine program picture. *Edba.*

The Trouble with Wives

Presented by Famous Players-Lasky. Story by Sada Cowan and Howard Higgin. Directed by Mal St. Clair. Featuring Florence Vidor, Tom Moore, Esther Ralston and Ford Sterling. At the Rivoli, New York, week Aug. 2. Running time, 67 minutes.

Grace Hyatt................Florence Vidor
William Hyatt..................Tom Moore
Dagmar......................Esther Ralston
Al Hennessy..................Ford Sterling
Grace's Mother...............Lucy Beaumont
Prey, detective...............Edward Kennedy
Maid...............................Etta Lee
Butler....................William Courtright

Well directed and because the script has much comedy relief and capably played by the quartet of featured artists gets over in great shape. The story is not particularly strong as to them, but the detail and manner of presentation make it stand out as a worth-while feature.

"The Trouble With Wives" is just what the title indicates. In a word, the average wife may start out with the best intentions in the world regarding her husband and the absolute trust she has in him, but before she goes around the corner she is going to be suspicious of him and, although he is innocent of any wrong-doing, anything that looks the least bit off is going to find hubby in a kettle of hot water that is prepared by wifie's fire. That's the story of this picture in a nutshell.

The manner in which it is exploited on the screen makes it a well-worth-while bit of film entertainment. Incidentally it takes Esther Ralston, who, although on the screen some time, and gives her an opportunity that make her for the future. She looks more like a real "comer" now than she ever did; and as for Ford Sterling—well, he's there 1,000 ways from the ace when it comes to putting over a comedy role, and without the aid of slapstick.

Mal St. Clair deserves a great measure of credit for this one.

Fred.

THE HOME MAKER

Universal production directed by King Baggot. Featuring Alice Joyce and Clive Brook. From the novel of the same name by Dorothy Canfield. Continuity by Mary O'Hara. Photographed by John Stumar. At the Colony, New York, week Aug. 9. Runs about 70 minutes.

Eva Knapp....................Alice Joyce
Lester Knapp..................Clive Brook
Stephen...............Billy Kent Schaeffer
Henry....................Maurice Murphy
Helen..................Jacqueline Wells
Harvey Bronson............Frank Newberg
Dr. Merritt.................George Fawcett
Aunt Mattie Farnum...Margaret Campbell
Mrs. Anderson..........Martha Mattox
John (Janitor)............Alfred Fisher
Miss West.................Alice Flowers
Mrs. Prouty...........Virginia Boardman
Nolly Prouty..............Elaine Ellis
Mrs. Hennessy.............Mary Gordon
Mr. Willings...............Lloyd Whitlock

As a study of middle-class domestic life there are moments when "The Home Maker" almost reaches the heights of greatness. Unfortunately, the general impression, handicapped by one thing or another, is only that of one more average feature picture. King Baggot's direction is thorough and workmanlike, but it is not human nor understanding enough to give the story the tremendous wallop it might have had. Perhaps had the plot not been so typically American, one of the highly touted foreign realistic directors might have done something big with it.

Miss Canfield is a novelist of almost distinguished reputation, and although "The Home Maker" is not one of her most popular books it has been highly praised by many as a searching study of family life. A husband and wife are central figures. Both are failures in their respective life tasks, chiefly because they detest the work alloted to them. He is an unpractical dreamer to whom office work is unbearable while she, though she keeps her home meticulously neat, cannot, with any efficiency, control the whims and tantrums of her three youngsters. Consequently, near-poverty and unhappiness reign in the home, a circumstance delicately hinted at when the two older children are shown taking the longest way home from school.

Finally the father loses his job and decides that suicide is the only way out. But even in this he is a dub and paralysis of the legs is the result. The wife has to support the family and in the business world her initiative and efficiency bring her success and happiness. Her husband on the other hand has found comfort and enjoyment in the company of his children and books and the ease of a life at home. The kids, too, are allowed to do as they please and become better youngsters because of it.

Then comes the genuine O. Henry twist. One night a curtain catches fire and in extinguishing the blaze the father discovers that under the stress of fear and excitement he has recovered the use of his legs. But realizing that such a condition means a return to the boredom and dissatisfaction of the old days he swears the friendly old doctor to secrecy and returns to the wheel chair for the rest of his life.

There is a good deal of delving into child psychology and it is here the picture gets definitely on the wrong track. Entirely too much of the "'ou wouldn't let 'em wash my teddy bear, would 'ou" type of stuff that makes much of the action seem either ridiculous or boresome. Incidentally an overdose of sub-titles give a talky effect to a film that otherwise leaves quite a bit to the imagination.

It would seem an error was made in the placing the roles of this distinctly middle-class couple in the hands of such patrician looking types as Alice Joyce and Clive Brook. Considering this limitation, however, both do excellently. Brook's performance in those scenes in which he discovers with mingled joy and dread that his legs are not worthless will rank as one of the best of its kind. Little Billy Kent Schaeffer as the youngest and most unmanageable of the children supplies the acting that will be most talked about, doing wonders with a role that is more genuinely nasty and irritating than cute and appealing. George Fawcett and Martha Mattox head a supporting cast of capable character actors.

"The Home Makers," then, is a serious effort at domestic naturalism. There will be a certain number of people who will think it splendid in a quiet and yet forceful way. They do not promise, however, to be numerous enough to make the picture a real box office attraction. That goes particularly for its commercial chances at the Colony this week, with Broadway providing all sorts of important opposition in the "Greater Movie Season" line.

WILD HORSE MESA

Famous Players production of the Zane Grey story. Directed by George B. Seitz and the screen story by Lucien Hubbard. Jack Holt, Noah Beery, Billy Dove and Douglas Fairbanks, Jr., featured. At the Rialto, New York, week Aug. 9. Running time, 75 minutes.

Chane Weymer..................Jack Holt
Bud McPherson.................Noah Beery
Sue Melberne..................Billie Dove
Chess Weymer......Douglas Fairbanks, Jr.
Bent Marerube...............George Magrill
Lige Melberne................George Irving
Grandma Melberne............Edith Yorke
Toddy Nokin..............Bernard Seigle
Josie.....................Margaret Morris

This western, produced on a de luxe scale, and photographed before settings that are probably among Nature's best, qualifies as a program attraction, but not among the real hits of that class.

The story concerns the expedition made by Lige Melberne and Bent Marerube to the canyon land where wild horses lived in multitudes. Bent had a scheme for trapping these horses in a natural corral and proposed to use barbed wire fences to keep from getting out of the passages which might free them. This murderous plan was stopped when Chane Weymer came upon the scene. Chane was a rider of the desert lands, friend of the Indians and born and bred in the open. He and Marerube got into a fight when the sole punch came as Weymer pushed Marerube against the barbs to let him get a feel of them.

The direction is loose and the continuity rather poor. Cutting isn't of the best, for many of the scenes could stand much elimination and some other are unnecessary and injected for comedy touches. They do nothing but impede the story.

Jack Holt stands out most prominently, with Billie Dove and Noah Beery in the order named. The remainder of the cast is capable, but even this cast and the majestic beauty of the scenery will not be enough to lift "Wild Horse Mesa" into the hit film class. It needed kicks and lots of them.

Bisk.

GOLD AND THE GIRL

A William Fox production starring Charles (Buck) Jones. Directed by Edmund Mortimer. Story by John Stone. At the Stanley, New York, Aug. 6. Running time, 62 minutes.

Usually the Jones pictures are pretty good and filled with action, but this one is the exception. Compared to the rest it doesn't rank at all.

The plot has Jones as a western detective and his victims are two fast working boys, one of whom has a beautiful niece while the other is just a bad boy with a yellow streak. Things work to the point where Jones falls in love with the girl and she falls for him. But the detective gets after the two bad boys and the girl risks her life to tell the hero "dick" they're after him. Anyway, the other bad boy kills the uncle and then he in turn is nailed, clearing the way for a kissy ending.

Produced economically and with a supporting cast that never supports, Jones bears the entire burden himself. Some of the locations are good, and the dog actor employed as the pal of the detective works for laughs. Decidedly a mediocre member of the Jones' series. *Bisk.*

The Girl Who Wouldn't Work

B. P. Schulberg presents "The Girl Who Wouldn't Work," by Gertie D. Wentworth-James. Adapted by Lois Hutchinson. Directed by Marcel De Sano. This picture reviewed in the Simplex projection room, Candler building, at 2:30 p. m. Monday, Aug. 10. The regular release date on this film is Aug. 15. Footage, 5,979 feet.

Gordon Kent..............Lionel Barrymore
Mary Hale........Marguerite De La Motte
William Hale........Henry B. Walthall
Greta Verlaine..............Lilyan Tashman
William Norworth.........Forrest Stanley
District Attorney..............Winter Hall
The "Rounder".........Thomas Ricketts

Thanks to a cast headed by Lionel Barrymore, this picture may meet the demands of the present-day film houses that thrive on dramatic subjects. The story is a "weak sister." At times it flares up and shows some semblance of life, but lacks the big punch.

Mr. Schulberg has done everything possible to make a big picture out of this commonplace story.

For a few minutes Lilyan Tashman took all the fancy door cinema play away from Barrymore when she went to her sweetie's home. She raged, ranted and fumed and hustled the other woman out in a hurry.

The picture was interminably slow in getting into dramatic action. When the time came for it to speed up it had little in reserve to make the picture stand up as a big, smack-'em-between-the-eyes hit.

Mark.

THE SPEED DEMON

All particulars missed, excepting that Kenneth McDonald is featured. Running time around 60 minutes.

Not to be judged through being on a one-day double bill at Loew's New York. The other half ("Dollar Down") was so bad it needed something stronger than usual to bring up the average.

"The Speed Demon" could and can stand by itself. It has two "thrills" in a horse race and an auto race. There isn't much of a thrill in either; but together in one picture they give it a swing for liveliness.

Kenneth McDonald as Speed Sherman, auto racer, does pretty driving in his racing car. That links in with some racetrack touts from New York going to extraordinary lengths to obtain a Kentucky filly through crooked means. The far-fetched story hurts it, but Mr. McDonald covers up a lot through his likeable playing way and personality. There's a girl heroine here, also of personality, while the low comedy that gets laughs is capably handled by Speed's side-kick. Besides which the captions are deserving for their laugh prowess. That caption writer has a sense of humor that should be worth much to him for the screen.

Not a bad one-day stand by itself, "The Speed Demon." Inexpensive, with the big scenes inserts, but well done. *Sime.*

DOLLAR DOWN

Truart picture, also marked Renown. Henry Walthour starred and Ruth Roland featured. Directed by Tod Browning. Other names missed through fast screening of opening slides. Running time, 65 minutes.

A poor picture.

The producer must have been deceived by the scenario. It's possible that this story looked quite good on paper. It doesn't work out that way. "Dollar Down" might have been sponsored by the associated savings banks, if that organization were in existence. It's propaganda for thrift, made doubly tiresome through inexpert cutting in the earlier sections. The picture picks up a bit toward its finale—then too late, of course.

This story abounds in inconsistencies in both ends of the contrast. It attempts to prove the evil of installment buying and the rewards of economy and saving. From that angle it might interest the high-living clerk as the preachment, for it is only that, could carry its lesson.

If 12 or 15 minutes were elided the film would be helped, but not much. To bring out the boresomeness, it could have been suggested in the editing room that all of the scenes, every one, with the children (couple contrast) in them should be removed. They are too silly for grown-ups (the scenes, not the children).

Henry Walthour hasn't much to do, so it was a walkaway for him. Ruth Roland doesn't look the part of the daughter alongside of Mayme Kelson as the mother (the dollars down). But the boy juvenile of the economy family gives a peachy performance. (His name was missed).

Any exhibitor may sidestep this with perfect safety. It's guaranteed to irritate any audience. Cheaply produced. *Sime.*

BORDER VENGEANCE

Sam Efrus production distributed by Aywon Films. Story by Forrest Sheldon. Directed by Harry Webb. Runs about 48 minutes.
Wes Channing................Jack Perrin
Bumps Jackson.............Vondell Darr
Mrs. Jackson................Mina Redman

A new Lochinvar has entered the western program house lists, attempting to take his place alongside of the countless fiery two-gun men who have come out of the west. Jack Perrin is his name, and his entrance, while inauspicious, is not entirely without promise.

Perrin's face looks slightly familiar, and it is probable he has played minor roles in various western films. "Border Vengeance" is his first starring vehicle that has come to the attention of this reviewer or, so far as can be ascertained, that has slipped into a house like the New York for a showing. He is pleasant looking and clean-cut without being handsome, and has that happy faculty given to so many other similar stars of getting away with the acting requirements without exerting himself with any real histrionic attempts. He is in addition an excellent horseman and can handle himself in a fist fight with the best of them, but is handicapped with a pistol by possessing what the cowboy fans will call "a bum draw."

As for the picture it may be dismissed briefly by saying it has a moderately pretty heroine, four or five heavies, ranging from a misguided weakling to a very demon of a despicable gambler, the proper amount of hard riding and fighting, a three-cornered battle for the girl, a mine that after many disappointments fairly spouts precious ore, and practically no comedy whatsoever.

The film breathes cheapness, and yet possibly no more so than others of its type which seldom reach even the most obscure New York city houses. The photography is all wet two ways, scenically and technically, and the ranch exteriors are, of the mouldiest possible variety. Jack Richardson is the only recognizable face or name in the cast, although little Josephine Hill, one of the tiniest of film leading ladies, has her moments of appeal. The director has permitted entirely too much exaggerated gesticulating by everybody concerned.

A weak buy for the metropolitan Loew picture house, but the film may not be considered so bad in the sticks, and at least it introduces a new glorified galloper. As a final recommendation, it is blessedly short.

THE GOLD RUSH

Charlie Chaplin production with producer starred and programmed as director and author. Associate director, Charles F. (Chuck) Reisner; assistant director, H. d'Abbadie d'Arrast. General manager, Alf Reeves. Released through United Artists. Runs 96 minutes in about eight reels. Opened at Strand, New York, Aug. 16-week at regular house scale, 85c top. Special performance Strand, Saturday, Aug. 15 midnight, at $3.30 top with balcony $2.20.
Lone Prospector ....Charlie Chaplin
Big Jim McKay.................Marl Swain
Black Larsen....................Tom Murray
Georgia ....Georgia Hale
Jack Cameron................Malcolm White
Hank Curtis.................Henry Bergman

A review in Variety July 1, last, on Chaplin's "Gold Rush" went into an ecstatic rave over this comedy drama, both as a comedy and a drama. It may have impressed friends of Chaplin's on the coast to that degree, but as shown at the Strand, New York, it does not live up to the rave from the west. It's just a good Chaplin comedy, a picture that's certain at the film theatres because of Chaplin's name.

More drama than comedy in "The Gold Rush," a lot of story with laughs spaced too far apart in the 96 minutes used up (106 minutes if the 10-minute intermission be retained).

Charlie Chaplin again is the beaten and buffeted creature, who escapes every jam with a laugh. Chaplin has the Geo. M. Cohan system of giving himself the worst of it. The world likes that. And in addition, Chaplin as a truly great pantomimist finds it as easy to handle the drama as the comedy. Here there are lots of pathos, sentiment and romance of a sort set amidst snow-capped Alaska, where Chaplin is presumed to have gone forth to prospect for gold, and alone. He meets many people and adventures, finding gold and a lady-love for the finish.

It's at the finish that about the funniest scene is revealed, when Mr. Chaplin and Georgia Hale are posed for a still photo. It's the old "family tintype" in life. The biggest laugh of the film is the rocking cabin set on the edge of a snow white precipice, the cabin balancing either way as the weight of one or both of the two men inside the cabin sway it. It finally topples into the canyon as Chaplin leaps forth to bare safety. This scene is a succession of laughs. It is adapted from the chair swaying bit atop of mounted tables as done by several vaudeville acts.

Another laugh bit is Chaplin doing a Sliding Billy Watson sliding step as he stands between the opposite open doors of another cabin in a howling wind storm. Ordered to leave, Chaplin attempts it but the incoming gale holds him stationery while he is trying to walk forward. Other funny bits will be familiar to show people but none of these strike the lay and paying-people from that angle. An entirely original gag is of two famished men making a meal of Chaplin's boots, stewed in a pan.

Miss Hale as a dance hall girl gives a pleasing performance, throwing just enough abandon and independence into the role, also causing the pathetic highlight when Chaplin, in love with her, sets the table in his cabin for her New Year's Eve dinner as she forgets about it and neglects to call.

A couple of mob scenes are in the dance hall but the picture is mainly out of doors with plenty of snow and several trick bits that puzzle.

"The Gold Rush" is at the Strand for at least two weeks, with the house reported paying $40,000 for the first run privilege in the hope it may remain four weeks. Four weeks are doubtful—three will be a long while. There is nothing in this picture to make people talk about it other than that it is a new Chaplin and he has been on the screen for quite a while.

But as a picture house attraction at the regular scale for the usual run, "The Gold Rush" in any kind of show weather will draw a heavy gross.

At the Saturday midnight performance Chaplin was there and made a short, very short speech. He had watched the picture from about the centre of the house in an aisle seat.

For picture houses the film is too long for the full number of usual performances if short reels are to be also given. It can stand cutting with judicious cutting bringing the laughs closer together. *Sime.*

The Lucky Horseshoe

Fox picture starring Tom Mix. Story by Robert Lord. Screen play by John Stone. J. G. Blystone production. At the Rialto, New York, week Aug. 16. Running time, 57 min.
Rand Foster.....................Tom Mix
Eleanor Hunt.................Billie Dove
Anita......................Ann Pennington
Denman...................Malcolm Waite
Mack...............J. Farrell MacDonald
Aunt Ruth...........Clarissa Selwynne
Denman's valet............J. Gunnis Davis

It is doubtful if Tom Mix ever worked harder in his camera life than he does in this film. A lavish producing hand also reaches out and gives Mix more of an animated and panoramic background than he is usually accustomed to.

The Fox people made a wise pick in placing Billie Dove opposite the star. Miss Dove is every inch the picture heroine. Mix and Miss Dove make a corking pair of leads and the former is all over the lot, air, ground and everywhere at the same time. You can stick a pin right here that this picture has enough thrilling climaxes to make a half dozen films.

It isn't so much the story as it is very much of the hackneyed stripe. Yet there is a passage wherein Mix dreams he is Don Juan and for a considerable stretch of celluloid the audience sees him outwitting riders, swordsmen and bodyguards in carrying off the fair lady.

Ann Pennington not only dances but handles what little photoplay work there is for her most proficiently. The dancing scene, in which Miss Pennington is the principal figure, is very well staged. Praise must be given J. F. MacDonald, who gives what comedy there is more than ordinary buoyancy.

Mix has been consistently adding to his popularity and in such a film as this appears to be striving to enhance his camera worth by going in heavier and stronger for work, expenditure and cast. There is no doubt that Miss Dove and Miss Pennington are a big feminine asset to Mix's general support.

It is not a horse racing story as the title might imply. The horseshoe is simply a lucky talisman the heroine gives to the hero. The main theme, as embodied in the reproduction of the costumed part is the Don Juan idea. On that the picture seems made to order for Mix and it should make him stronger than ever. *Mark.*

WINDS OF CHANCE

First National production of the Rex Beach novel. Directed by Frank Lloyd. Cast features Anna Q. Nilsson, Ben Lyon, Viola Dana, Hobart Bosworth, Victor McLaglen, Claude Gillingwater, John T. Murray and Philla McCullough. At the Piccadilly, New York, Aug. 16 week. Running time, 108 minutes.
Countess Courteau.........Anna Q. Nilsson
Pierce Philips.....................Ben Lyon
Rouletta Kirby.................Viola Dana
Sam Kirby..............Hobart Bosworth
'Poleon Doret............Victor McLaglen
Laure..................Dorothy Sebastian
Tom Linton............Claude Gillingwater
Jerry......................Charles Crockett
Frank McCaskey.........Laurence Fisher
Joe McCaskey................Fred Kohler
Jim McCaskey.............Wade Boteler
Count Courteau........Philo McCullough

Lucky Broad	John T. Murray
Kid Bridges	Fred Warren
Vigilante Chairman	George Nicholls
Sergeant Rock	Tom London

A tremendous production, massive in its scope of detail and the number of people employed, but trite in its story and lacking in a kicky punch which would probably have sent it over the top as a huge success. As it stands it boasts a great cast of experienced screen actors and many names, while its director, Frank Lloyd, is also recognized as one of the aces of the business. They're doing Lloyd an injustice, however, in billing this as his "greatest production," for he made "The Sea Hawk," which was certainly no slouch.

Rex Beach wrote the book from which this was made. In plot it centres about Pierce Phillips, a young prospector, who falls in love with a Countess Courteau. Still married, she told him love was impossible at the moment. Infuriated, he left her camp after he had helped her shoot perilous rapids in order to bring hotel equipment to Dawson.

Also Poleon Doret, French-Canadian guide, who helped Pierce through trouble when some bad men, the McCaskeys, tried to frame him. Pierce gets mixed up with Rouletta Kirby, a sweet little girl and the daughter of Sam Kirby, a gambler who got killed protecting his daughter. Her affection goes to Pierce for a while and his to her, for he considers the affair with Countess Courteau off.

But that affair isn't off, for the Count tries to frame the boy for theft. By trickery the Countess forces a confession of his "frame." Then the bad men, the McCaskeys, fall out with the Count and kill him, while 'Poleon brings them to justice, and Pierce sees that the Countess really loves him. And as Sam Kirby's daughter loves 'Poleon, it all works around to a happy finish.

The running time is at least 30 minutes too much. Moreover, the claims and pretentions made for the picture in no way hold up, for although Lloyd's program notice of the hardships encountered in the making are probably true, those hardships are not reproduced on the screen; nor is anything epoch-making or unusually entertaining shown as a result of those hardships.

So it looks like a big effort missing fire.

The cast is one of the best First National or any other company has ever furnished a film of this type. That also goes for the locations and much of the physical action, particularly the shooting of the rapids. Of the individual performances, Victor McLaglen, as the French-Canadian, stands out most prominently, having turned hero after so many heavy parts. Miss Nilsson and Miss Dana, the two heroines, are fine, while Ben Lyon drops the delicate look and shows up finely as the hero. What comedy relief there is Claude Gillingwater and Charles Crockett, as a team of old-timers, furnish, with the aid of lengthy subtitles.

For the average exhibitor this film will be suitable as a program picture, but as a special it does not measure up. All the thousands used in it fail to make it anything more than another picture of North Woods romance.

Sisk.

SUN-UP

A Metro-Goldwyn production directed by Edmund Goulding. Adapted by Goulding and Arthur Statter from the play by Lulu Vollmer. Reviewed at the Capitol, New York, week Aug. 16, 1925. Running time, 63 minutes.

Widow Cagle	Lucille LaVerne
Emmy Todd	Pauline Starke
Rufe Cagle	Conrad Nagel
Sheriff Weeks	Sam de Grasse
Stranger	George K. Arthur
Bud	Arthur Rankin
Pap Todd	Edward Connelly
Bob	Bainard Beckwith

Heretofore, Edmund Goulding has been known principally as an adaptor or a writer of originals for the screen. He has always had the letch to direct, and finally this young Englishman has achieved his ambition. And what a good job he has done of it, too! One can now readily realize why a director could take a Goulding story and make a good picture, no matter who the director might be. And there have been some mighty good Goulding adaptations screened in the past. This picture in itself is more or less of a peculiar one. In the big cities it will get a little flash; in the small cities less, and in the tiny towns the chances are that they won't know what it's all about, except possibly those small hill-billy settlements on the life of which the story itself is based.

There is, however, this to it—it is entertainment. It is a story with sufficient strength to make the average movie-goer sit on the edge of his seat and wonder what is going to happen next.

The only guy that really is "next" is possibly the original author. There wasn't enough in "Sun-Up" to really make it a picture but Goulding has padded it and protected it from the censors, though it really was open to censorship prejudices in its theme and action. Goulding takes a matter of fact, more or less, story of a hill-billy who packs himself off to war. There are a couple of gags here about where France is, which really don't matter, but which serve probably to plant more firmly in the minds of those viewing the picture the exact mental and educational status of the average hill-billy. This boy, played by Conrad Nagle, does portray the role of the ignorant kid who is tired of feuds and who tramps off to war in a magnificent manner. His mother thinks he is dead, but he comes back home and surprises his mother harboring one of a tribe of their worst enemies. Mother doesn't realize what she has done, but when she does, she wants the boy to do more killin'. He, however, is fed up on feuds and says that he has done all his killing abroad. But there is a sheriff who is a bad boy and he "don't do right by our Nell." Just for that he is conveniently beaten up and jailed by the hero, who is in love with the girl, and who conveys to the minds of his ignorant fellow hill-billy that the law must have its way.

Aside from the directorial triumph which goes to Goulding through his having left something to the imagination of those in the audience (especially in one fight scene), the honors of the performance are attended to by Lucille La Verne, Pauline Starke and Conrad Nagel. Miss LaVerne, playing the role which she took in the stage production, is superb as the old mother, while Miss Starke (a ringer for Gilda Gray, by the way) and Mr. Nagel give excellent support.

Fred.

WHERE WAS I?

Universal-Jewel, presented by Carl Laemmle. From the story by Edgar Franklin. Directed by George Seiter. At the Colony, N. Y., week Aug. 16. Running time, 75 mins.

Thomas S. Bedford	Reginald Denny
Alicia Stone	Marion Nixon
Claire	Pauline Garon
Henry	Lee Moran
George Stone	Tyrone Power
Bennett	Otis Harlan
Elmer	Chester Conklin

Rather conveniently constructed for Reginald Denny, and very well suited to his likewise convenient talents. At least that is the way it would appear when one notes the manner in which Denny works through this picture. Denny tries to dominate at all times, and gets away with it, excepting where Otis Harlan takes it away from him with comedy. The picture is one that must be designated more or less as a filler for the average run of houses where there is almost a daily change of program. It is far from being sufficiently strong to stand up for a full week at one of Broadway's de luxe presentation houses.

The story is of a farcical nature, with a series of complications being built that has the hero on the wing until the final few hundred feet. Denny is cast in the role of a young business man who has taken over his father's plant and is running it successfully. He has wiped out all of the firm's competitors excepting one, and at the opening of the picture becomes engaged to the daughter of the head of the rival firm. The girl's dad becomes furious and decides to break off the match. He engages a vamp to act as his agent, and she manages to keep both the audiences and players guessing as to her acting purpose, it not being disclosed who she actually is until almost the end of the picture.

She claims that the hero married her on a certain date, and his troubles commence when he tries to disprove her assertion that he was with her on the date that she alleges the ceremony took place. A wild taxi ride, full of thrills and narrow escapes, fills in a goodly portion of the picture. Then there is an in-and-out sequence of the most approved although routine farce nature that fills the balance of the picture. The titles do not get any great amount of laughter, and what comedy there is comes through the speed of the action.

Opposite Denny is Marion Nixon, with no great opportunity. Pauline Garon, as the vamping queen, walks away with practically all honors.

Fred.

FIGHTING FLAMES

Columbia production of the story by Douglas Zoty. William Haines, Dorothy Devore and David Torrence featured. At the Broadway, New York, Aug. 17 week. Running time, 65 minutes.

Judge Manly	David Torrence
His son	William Haines
Alice	Dorothy Devore
Blackie	Sheldon Lewis
Mickey	Frankie Darro

Fires, with the flames done in natural colors; the regeneration of a wild youth, and the wistfulness of a crook's little son form the chief attraction of "Fighting Flames." For entertainment it holds up nicely, for it has action enough for half a dozen films and to work out this action an excellent cast has been employed.

A young drunkard, son of a judge, meets up with the small boy of a crook, and taking a liking to each other, they put their money together to start housekeeping. Gradually, the little boy's good qualities tell on the young man, and he begins taking pride, not only in himself, but in keeping the tot up to scratch in appearance. Then the girl across the hall enters.

Meantime, the youth joins the fire department. In a series of finely filmed fires, he distinguishes himself. His father hears of this and is proud, but the big point comes when Blackie, father of the little boy, comes home to get his child and teach him the crook's ways. Trapping the boy in the room of the girl across the hall, he locks her in a closet and tries to take the kid out. But the kid was tough and kicked and dodged long enough to keep the father busy for a long time. Then a fire broke out—in that house.

Enter hero, who saves heroine and small boy. The end is a rich and happy father looking on his regenerated son happy with the little boy and the sweetheart.

Haines shows up very well as a leading man here, but the picture goes to Frankie Darro as the kid. No doubt he was well directed, but then he handled himself better than the usual child would—even with good direction. There's considerable hoak attached to the kid episodes—but his manner of looking on the fireman as his pal, and his jealousy when the fireman and the girl get thick makes interesting footage.

"Fighting Flames" may not draw much on its cast or title but for the houses where they want entertainment primarily, this will satisfy more completely than a dozen of the high hat society melos.

Sisk.

SHE WOLVES

Fox production, with Alma Rubens starred. Adapted from the stage play, "A Man in Evening Clothes." Directed by Maurice Elvey. At the Stanley, New York, Aug. 13. Running time, 65 mins.

Germaine	Alma Rubens
Lucien, her husband	Jack Mulhall
Andre Landal	Bertram Grassby

The stage play from which this picture was made, "A Man in Evening Clothes," ran about nine nights last winter at Henry Miller's theatre, with Mr. Miller starred. Shortly after that Fox bought it for films and as produced it looks as if the story has been greatly altered and the woman's part brought to the fore as a concession to the star, Alma Rubens.

The picture is tawdry, both in theme and production, and contains more old-fashioned emoting than the screen has seen in a long time. The plot concerns a country gentleman and his new wife. The country man was a greater hunter, and his wife complained that he smelled of games and horses too much, and she wished that he would learn how to be charming and gentlemanly. So straightaway he goes to Paris to cultivate the art of wearing stiff collars and hard shirts. He hadn't been there long, however, before the wife wrote him that their marriage was a mistake and that she loved another. Then she came to Paris and found him at the end of his resources. And because her new lover poked fun at her husband she revolted and went back to him, patching up the family fortune and settling down happily.

The production is skimpy and the direction accorded one character is deplorable, notably the way Judy King is made to act as a cabaret dancer. What was meant for poignant pathos has been made ludicrous. Miss Rubens is lifeless, but Mulhall as the man is excellent. The others are in keeping with the tone of the picture.

"She Wolves" hardly qualifies for the better class houses, but for the cheaper ones it may barely pull through.

Sisk.

HER SISTER FROM PARIS

Jos. M. Schenck presentation and First National picture starring Constance Talmadge. Sidney Franklin, director, with story by Hans Kraly. At the Capitol, New York, week August 23. Running time, 74 mins.

Helen Weyringer	Constance Talmadge
Lola—"La Perry"	Constance Talmadge
Joseph Weyringer	Ronald Colman
Robert Well	George K. Arthur
Bertha	Margaret Mann

Understood to have riled the censors of Ohio this latest Connie Talmadge release appears to have been judiciously trimmed in various passages but the omission of the "dirt," if any, hasn't hurt, for it's a rollicking farce that holds beaucoup entertainment.

Ronald Colman is underlined and, opposite to Miss Talmadge, gives an excellent performance as a bewildered husband amidst twin sisters. George Arthur is another laugh provider. Between the trio there's plenty of giggles for a picture house audience, and a Sunday matinee crowd gave that prediction authority.

Miss Talmadge is in a dual role, that of a wedded and old fashioned girl and a lone dancing star. Located in Vienna the tale opens with a comedy battle between the husband and wife. The latter pulls stakes out halts at the railway station upon viewing the arrival of her sister, ballyhooed by picture cameras, flowers, attendants, "Johns" and whatnot. A heart to heart talk brings the resultant hair bobbing and similar likeness between the girls with the wife out to give her husband a run as "La Perry," the dancer.

A fast and furious courtship has the wife taking the unknowing husband off his feet to the point where he develops a timidity that's surefire screen material, when his spouse finally induces him to the same hotel and room where he spent his honeymoon. His final begging off to go back to his wife precedes the appearance of the real "La Perry" when the two girls are together and hubby tumbles to the situation.

There is obviously much double photography, expertly handled. In fact, it's an outstanding example of this type of camera work, smooth and with enough fast twists of Miss Talmadge in the two characters (neat cutting) to make it puzzling.

Miss Talmadge flits through the story to stamp herself as an ideal exponent of this manner of screen farce. She is closely trailed by Colman who seemingly takes to the comedy thing as readily as Conrad Nagle. Colman won consistent laughs for himself with pantomiming, ofttimes without a "situation" George Arthur also contributes more than the usual quota obtained from a secondary role.

A theatrical performance had Miss Talmadge before a Russian "production" number more legitimate han 90 per cent of film stage presentations. However, Franklin succumbed to the inevitable by having every member in the audience applauding both at the finish of the "number" and at the opening. If there were as much applause in Broadway legit houses as there is the way they film it they'd issue ear muffs with the tickets around here.

The picture is a well constructed celluloid farce from any angle. It should do much for Miss Talmadge and that it can sustain itself in the better houses, whether they're addicted to this girl or not, is unquestioned.

Skig.

Man Who Found Himself

Famous Players production, starring Thomas Meighan. Virginia Valli featured. Story by Booth Tarkington. Directed by Alfred Green. At the Rivoli, New York, Aug. 23. Running time, 75 mins.

Tom Macaulay	Thomas Meighan
Nora Brooks	Virginia Valli
Lon Morris	Frank Morgan
Edwin Macaulay, Jr.	Ralph Morgan
Edwin Macaulay, Sr.	Charles Stephenson
Evelyn Corning	Julia Hoyt
Mrs. Macaulay, Jr.	Lynn Fontanne
Polly Brooks	Mildred Ryan
Hoboken William	Hugh Cameron
Humpty Dumpty Smith	Victor Moore
Tom Macaulay, Jr.	Russell Griffin
Commodore Branding	Norman Trevor
Warden of Sing Sing	John Harrington

Almost but not quite good enough to belong to that group of pictures which made Thomas Meighan a great picture star. That Meighan's recent slump has hurt was evidenced by the lack of a box office rush Sunday night. A few more like this will do much toward putting Meighan back in the favorite's place he once held.

This story once more concerns a small town; once more Tom takes the blame for something he didn't do; once more he endures ignominy to save some one else, and, as inevitably happens, he gets the girl after vicissitudes, worries and humiliation.

No who is the son of a bank president in Riverview, N. Y. His brother goes South with some money, and because the brother is married Tom takes the blame. It seems the head of a rival bank (also Tom's rival in love) framed the whole thing, and so Tom is sent to the old-fashioned prison on the Hudson while the rival marries the girl.

But in the jailhouse he meets two crafty birds, Hoboken William and Humpty Dumphy Smith, and when their terms have expired they skip into Riverview and do the same thing to the rival bank president that he did to Tom's brother, namely, tipping off the bank inspectors that there was a shortage. The difference, however, was that Tom had his gangsters go into the bank and take it, then plant the bills in the man's room. The news, however that there is a shortage in his bank panics the rival and he immediately tarts jumping to South America. So he goes over to the bank first to get fare down, but in coming out he is shot by a night watchman. So his widow is left free for the man she loves and her story to him is that although she married his rival she never lived with him. And then Tom, apparently forgetting that the rival had all but ruined his entire family, says that such being the case, he can even forgive the miscreant. All of which looks like Booth Tarkington, in compounding this hokum tale, spread the revenge stuff on so thick he had to show tenderness in the hero's makeup, even though that tenderness bordered on silliness.

In direction this one trumps anything Meighan has turned out in some time. It was Green who made the series which "made" Meighan. The cast is good, having two excellent actors in Frank and Ralph Morgan. Frank (from "The Firebrand" cast) plays the villain, while Ralph (last with "Cobra") is the weak brother. Virginia Valli (loaned by Universal) is the girl, while Lynn Fontanne, well-known legit star makes her cinema debut in a small part which showed that Miss Fontanne's place is in the speakies. The Lambs' Club was well treated in several of the small reparts, for Shepherd Meighan had Norman Trevor, Hugh Cameron, Victor Moore and the Morgans with him. Julia Hoyt also appears, but in a part so small that her much publicized face doesn't even get a full camera flash.

The cast, holding so many legit people, probably won't mean much to the fans, but Meighan's familiar work and the interior (and authentic) shots of Sing Sing should be interesting all over the country. Then the action is good and the continuity smooth and airtight.

All in all, "Man Who Lost Himself" qualifies. Its faults are to be placed with the illogical sequences of the story rather than on the star.

Sisk.

IN THE NAME OF LOVE

Paramount picture adapted from the play, "The Lady of Lyons," by Bulwer Lytton. Directed by Howard Higgin. At the Rialto, New York, week Aug. 23. Running time, 66 mins.

Raoul Melnotte	Ricardo Cortez
Marie Dufrayne	Greta Nissen
M. Glavis	Wallace Beery
Marquis de Beauseant	Raymond Hatton
Mother Dufrayne	Lillian Leighton
Mother Melnotte	Edythe Chapman
Damas Dufrayne	Richard Arlen
Butler	William Kelly
Florist	Arthur Hoya

"In the Name of Love" has a cast enacting its principal characters that can't miss. Mr. Cortez and Miss Nissen are the "lovers" and come up to all requirements, although the character of Marie Dufrayne is that of a selfish, snobbish "society" girl who does not melt the audience until the last hundred feet or so. It ends happily for those who like their pictures that way.

Mr. Hatton hasn't much to do compared with other stories, but he handles the role of the Marquis adequately, while the comedy interpretation of Mr. Beery is a gem.

The Dufraynes are of a poor neighborhood, but become fabulously rich through the death of the head of the family. Riches, however, fail to bring them the society glad hand. Then Marie determines to wed a title. Her boyhood sweetie, Raoul, comes back from America and in his home town settles down and buys a garage, which he puts on a modern plane.

Marie turns down the Count, the Marquis, and also bawls out Raoul over the 'phone. Then the Count and the Marquis, with Raoul, plan revenge on Marie. Raoul is palmed off as the Prince of Como, who goes through with the deception even to where he marries the girl. Then he packs her off to his peasant home, where he tells her the truth. There is a big scene, with Marie slapping her husband and locking herself in an upstairs room.

Through a knothole in the floor she sees hubby telling his mother the truth, and she realizes through the locket she had given him with the "mon prince" on its heart-shaped back that he is her old sweetheart and that she still loves him.

She comes downstairs in time to stop her irate brother from pumping holes into Raoul with his —— and then bids Damas good-bye and is again carried across the threshold by her husband. This carrying "bit" becomes important, as it follows an old peasant belief that such a performance will never bring about a separation of the pair.

The story is more or less incidental to keeping the main characters in a humorous, romantic light, especially the males, as evidenced by the work of Cortez, Beery and Hatton in the make-believe prince plot.

The story is airy, containing some capital comedy "bits" which registered heavily at the Rialto Sunday afternoon.

Mark.

LADY ROBIN HOOD

F. B. O. production, starring Evelyn Brent. Directed by Ralph Ince. Story by Clifford Howard and Burke Jenkins. Continuity by Fred Myton. At Loew's New York, one day (Aug. 14) as half the bill. Runs about 65 minutes.

La Ortiga / Senorita Catalina	Evelyn Brent
Hugh Winthrop	Robert Ellis
Cabraza	Boris Karloff
Governor	William Humphrey
Padre	Darcy Corrigan
Raimundo	Robert Cauterio

Evelyn Brent, famed for her crook roles, is this time a female Spanish desperado (or would it be desperada?) As a result "Lady Robin Hood" is more colorful than most of her recent releases, but for one reason or another not nearly as interesting.

The story suggests to a great extent Fairbanks' "Mark of Zorro." Here, however, it is a girl who roams the countryside avenging the injustices of a tyrannical government. The heroine's particular Nemesis is Cabraza, the corrupt power behind the weakling Spanish governor. Not until she horsewhips him a few times and has him socked in the jaw by her American sweetie does she emerge victorious.

It would seem F. B. O. expended neither as much money nor as much care on "Lady Robin Hood" as it has in the earlier productions of this series. A good many of the Spanish exteriors are obviously faked and most of the action takes place in a none too pretentious Castillian castle. Miss Brent's performance is again a high-light. Her type of beauty suggests particularly a Spanish charmer and she is very much at home in the fiery role of the lady insurgent. Opposite her, Robert Ellis, as the only American in the cast, resists the temptation to overdo the heroics called for. The balance of the cast is just about fair.

Miss Brent's showing at the Capitol, New York, some weeks ago, as well as at other theatres, proves her to possess a draw. This newest release won't impress as have some of her earlier ones, but it should bring good patronage to most of the neighborhood houses.

WILD BULL'S LAIR

F. B. O. production starring Fred Thompson. Directed by Del Andrews. Story by Marion Jackson. At Loew's New York one day (Aug. 14) as half bill. Runs about 1 hour.

Dan Allen	Fred Thompson
Eleanor Harbison	Catherine Bennett
James Harbison	Herbert Prior
Henry Harbison	Tom Carr
Eagle Eye	Frank Hagney
Yuma	Frank Abbott

The boom in Fred Thompson westerns continues unabated. The praiseworthy thing about this F. B. O. series seems to be that every one is slightly different. Marion Jackson, who writes most of them, is one of the few authors apparently who can get away from the stereotyped formula stuff in cowboy stories.

Thus the last one dealt with Thompson and a baby and played up the comedy side to splendid advantage. "The Wild Bull's Lair" features a savage beast and is successful in maintaining a consistent entertainment.

James Harbison, western ranch owner, enjoys a hobby of crossing cattle breeds. Upon one occasion he mates a bison and a Durham (can that be where the famous tobacco derives its name?) and the result is a brute animal of ferocious strength and savage disposition. Near this same ranch is a supposedly haunted mountain, and from it emanates all sorts of trouble to the white men in the district. It is inhabited by a tribe of Indians (not the nice, wild old injuns of former days, but a group of college trained redskins who want to reclaim their land from the "palefaces.") The red men utilize the savage bull to lead their fight against the white usurpers and raise enough cane to start a sugar plantation.

Thompson is the secret service agent who solves the mystery of the mountain and foils the plans of the Indians. His biggest feat is taming the wild bull. The animal is a demoniacal looking one and the scenes in which Fred tackles it and finally throws it after an astonishingly strenuous wrestling bout have seldom been equalled in thrills of this kind. The beautiful "Silver King" again proves himself to be Mix's Tony's only rival among western horses.

The love interest is not particularly emphasized but there are, particularly in the beginning, some amusing comedy scenes. The photography is excellent and the supporting cast something less than that.

'Wild Bull's Lair' should bring box office business as one of the all-too-few better westerns.

GOING THE LIMIT

Gerson production, presented by B. Berger. Directed by Duke Worne, and starring Richard Holt. Cast includes Ruth Dwyer, Garry O'Dell, Miriam Fouche, Robert Cosgrif, Hal Stephens. At Loew's New York, one day, as half the bill. Runs about 52 minutes.

"Going the Limit" stands as about the worst of the Richard Holt series. What that means can only be appreciated by those who have seen the earlier ones of these Gerson productions.

When Holt is quiet he may be called charitably an incompetent actor and nothing worse, but when he dances around and tries to get athletic, the temptation is strong to label him "clumsy." Certainly no one with his avoirdupois and awkwardness should go in for the Fairbanks rough-house stuff.

The billing lists the players mentioned above as a distinguished supporting cast. If the exhibitor finds anyone who has ever heard of one of them he should donate free admission. Miss Dwyer is pretty and whoever plays the heavy has a dirty-looking black mustache, but aside from that just how they are "distinguished" isn't quite plain.

The story bothers its cumbersome stuff with clairvoyants and swindlers and other mysterious folk. Young Holt breaks up all their plots and plans, more by means of beef than brains. The last quarter of the picture features a long chase, reminiscent of those staged in the old Keystone comedies, but not one-tenth as funny. There are a few laughs in this but no real thrills, and the general impression is one of faked, slow-moving sequences.

If Berger didn't make some money on these it is unlikely he would continue to produce them, but this one possibly sets a new record for stupidity.

THE THOROBRED

Truart picture releasing through Renown. Cast includes Carter DeHaven, Maclyn Arbuckle and Gladys Hewlett. At Loew's New York as half double bill, August 21. Directed by Oscar Apfel.

A comedy-drama with Carter De-Haven responsible for what merit it contains. Otherwise the narration is pretty much of the cut and dried type minus any ingredient to lift it above its many relatives.

DeHaven, as the broke out social hanger-on, gives the film a fair smattering of laughs to definitely surpass any other cost number. The story contains a horse race in which the heroine's entry actually loses, and Apfel has seen fit to play an assault scene away from the ordinary by giving it a restrained touch that demands attention.

Gladys Hewlett is the show girl for whom a wealthy western youth falls, despite his having been sent east by an uncle to "crash" society. De Haven is the pilot for the youth and when the uncle comes on the complications ensue. The girl's father being in a money jam, lows the hero to make good the coin although the check comes back when his uncle cancels the bank account because of the chorus angle.

The windup is the usual joyful routine with DeHaven staking the wealthy relative to a party with the choristers as a "squarer."

Lightweight entertainment, but capable of prying loose laughs from the audiences for which it is aimed. Not a bad effort on the director's part and a distinct piece of work for DeHaven, who looks a though he is capable of carrying the comedy thing up to a plane where the requirements are more rigid. *Skig.*

BEFORE MIDNIGHT

William Russell Production, starring William Russell. Directed by J. Adolfe. At Loew's New York as half double bill Aug. 21. Cast includes Brinsley Shaw, Alan Rossere, Barbara Bedford, Rex Lease. Running time, 55 mins.

A release weakling much in need of a co-operating feature to make a one day's bill stand up. In the smallest of the small houses the film will suffice, but it can never hope to overreach that mark. Russell is starred and is correspondingly prominent throughout. Not being the best-looking boy in the world, he has something to surmount as regards appearance, but, if given suitable stories, should be able to relegate the handicap.

During this particular 55 minutes Russell is most concerned with being a wealthy youngster who assists in the unveiling of a private detective agency which has made a practice of blackmailing crooks instead of haling 'em before a judge. Meanwhile the girl, through her brother, is threatened into helping the hokus-pokus sleuth snare an outfit reported to be sneaking a priceless emerald into the country. Suspicion naturally points to the hero, with the resultant complications but happy ending.

Not an overabundance of action and no deviation from the prescribed rules places the picture in the ordinary class, with the production cost evidently cut to a minimum. Barbara Bedford is the young woman in the case, meeting such demands as there are without quailing. Brinsley Shaw in a minor role played with reserve, and for that reason made his secret service valet stand out. Others in the cast carry the story.

In this release Russell suffers from too frail a story. He needs action and a yarn which will keep him away from parlors and evening dress. *Skig.*

EVERYMAN'S WIFE

Fox production, directed by Maurice Elvey. Story by Ethel Hill and Enid Hibbard. Scenario by Lillie Hayward. At Loew's Circle, New York, one day. Runs about an hour.
Mrs. Randolph.........Elaine Hammerstein
Mr. Randolph............Herbert Rawlinson
Mr. Bradin.................Robert Cain
Mrs. Bradin..............Dorothy Phillips
Emily.......................Diana Miller

Starting at the top of the brief cast above is the jealous wife, the misjudged husband, the guilty husband, the neglected wife and the gossipy friend. Further discussion of the plot is hardly necessary.

Consequently it is a very ordinary release, redeemed only by the competence of the cast, and possibly for the feminine picture-goers, by the dressy gowns worn by the women players. The British director, Maurice Elvey, has handled the unimportant story with some smoothness, but with none of the essential touches that relieve such a film of much of its triteness.

Scarcely one of the stupid, over-familiar situations seen in these pictures of early married life has been omitted.

The players, competent troupers though they are, can do little to make this mess convincing. The editing of the film has not been particularly careful, and one "bull" wherein a book has a different title on the cover than inside can hardly fail to be noticed. These are small matters, of course, but when observed they flatter the critical powers of the film fan and lower his estimation of the picture.

"Everyman's Wife," with its theme of "tit for tat" in marital infidelity, is very similar to "What Women Do," one of the most recent and distressing of Broadway's legit flops. It is almost bad enough to have been an adaptation of that limping little play, and certainly it stands as one of the most insipid Fox pictures in months.

Greater Than a Crown

One's imagination doesn't have to be powerful to visualize just about what this picture is like when it is learned it deals with a princess of the mythical kingdom of Livadia and a romantic young American adventurer. Yet, for all of that, it is thoroughly pleasant entertainment all the way, and it provides Edmund Lowe with one of the best vehicles he has had since becoming a star.

Most of the action takes place in London, although the plot concerns the intrigues and court affairs of the above-mentioned Livadia. The hero hails from Yonkers and his name is Tony Conway. The film opens with some shots in a London oyster bar, with some fine cockney local color given and the general atmosphere suggestive of "Knocked 'Em in the Old Kent Road" and other "limey" ditties.

This is all too short lived. Soon there is a maelstrom of Livadian political affairs. The men in power have arranged a wedding between King Danilo and the Princess Isabel. Both parties are unwilling, however, Isabel because she loves the go-getter from Yonkers, and his majesty because he is having a little affair of his own with an American actress, who also hails from that much-maligned town.

A twist comes when it is learned that the king is really married to the American charmer, a concession to the censors, it is safe to say, that was not in the original novel. This doesn't stop the wicked prime minister, however, and both the prospective bride and groom are kidnaped and brought to Livadia. Only a last-minute substitution of the actress for the princess saves the day, and the king is remarried to his true love, while the other couple escape across the border.

Roy Neill's direction is largely straightforward, but there are moments when some delicate satirical touches illuminate the almost preposterous action. At these times the film is at its best. The interior photographic shots are most striking, and artistically the picture is of a very high grade.

Lowe is his usual suave self, and Margaret Livingston has no trouble with the role of the actress who is so much misjudged until she drags out the royal marriage license. Maurice Costello's daughter Dolores makes her first appearance since she has grown up, and gives an appealing, wistful performance. In appearance and mannerism she rather suggests Constance Bennett. Incidentally Maurice himself was prominent in and around the New York most of the day on which the picture was shown there.

While many may consider it light weight, none can really be bored by "Greater Than a Crown," and it should draw business in any but the first-run houses.

THE MERRY WIDOW

Metro-Goldwyn picture. Eric Von Stroheim production, starring Mae Murray. Adapted from Franz Lehar's operetta of the same name. Directed by Von Stroheim, with Oliver Marsh the photographer. Features John Gilbert. Opened new Embassy, New York, Aug. 26, indefinitely. Running time, 107 mins.

The Widow	Mae Murray
The Prince	John Gilbert
Crown Prince	Roy D'Arcy
Queen Milena	Josephine Crowell
King Nikita	George Fawcett
Baron Sadoja	Tully Marshall

Give Von Stroheim a uniform symbolic of a comic opera country, a girl determined to remain good, and the officer just as stubborn only with the reverse moral twist and it's a "set-up." Not being able to recall the exact book of "The Merry Widow" as a stage presentation it is nevertheless logical to suppose Von Stroheim has taken manifold liberties with the original writing to insert a sex angle that consumes the first 50 minutes.

That means it takes the Prince 10 minutes short of an hour to realize the little road show dancer actually believes in her college yell of "No."

Following that it's a series of complications and misunderstandings.

Before proceeding let it be understood that Von Stroheim has turned out Miss Murray in the most gorgeous production she has yet had and a film that is a leader among program leaders.

Miss Murray, in all her screen career, has not been backed by the splendor which herein abounds. To add to this is a coronation scene in natural color as a climax that carries a terrific punch, especially as there is no inkling that it is to come other than an early "shot" of a mammoth rose bouquet. In fact this picture rates a second viewing to fully absorb the extensiveness of the scenic splurge.

All of which wouldn't have meant a thing without the superlative camera work Oliver Marsh has turned in. Miss Murray has never previously looked as well as she does before Marsh's camera. Some of her close-ups are nothing less than superb, while the lighting, practically throughout the entire picture, is a revelation. Outside of meaning added prestige for Von Stroheim, Miss Murray, Mr. Gilbert and Mr. D'Arcy (for they are the predominating component personalities) the film is a distinct band for Marsh's hat and is an outstanding example of what a camera man can mean to a picture.

Gilbert and D'Arcy reek with the Von Stroheim military schooling. D'Arcy can give Lowell Sherman something to worry about by the manner in which he maneuvers a monocle. It's all very much to the point and in tune with the close-cropped hair cuts which the male contingent has assumed.

Other than this Von Stroheim has eliminated a number of subtitles by symbolizing, a commendable adjunct expertly handled. Distinct credits are the freezing of rain upon a window to denote the passing of time, a royal funeral suggested through a corps of muffled drums descending a long flight of stairs, and the brilliant silhouetting of gems adorning Miss Murray to the exclusion of her face and figure when gazed upon by the mercenary Prince. The latter bit is a corking and probably a technical credit for Marsh.

Miss Murray's work is far superior to any of her previous efforts, and with the support she is receiving from all angles her characterization of the title role should do much to re-establish her in this country. In Germany, where she is a prime favorite, this picture should be sensational, and it should be equally well received on most all foreign shores, due to the Continental military mannerisms with which the director has flooded the action. Its acceptability over here is assured.

Gilbert and D'Arcy are splendid foils for the star with, perhaps, a slight edge in favor of the latter, due to his intolerable Crown Prince in which he has instilled an invaluable comedy vein. Josephine Crowell is restricted to brief footage, while the two errors of the picture seem to be in the overplaying of George Fawcett as the enraged King and the proneness of Miss Murray to overdress when the locale is Paris.

Von Stroheim has seen fit to end the feature with a laugh through having the newly crowned King and Queen, Sally and Danilo, address each other in undertones as "Sally" and "Pete" as they exit up the aisle. Dynamited into the gorgeous surroundings of the moment it handily serves its purpose.

As to the Embassy, Broadway's newest picture theatre. It has the diminutive capacity of 600 on one floor, possesses soothing interior decorations in gold, green and red, has an orchestra of 15 pieces besides an organ, and for this showing is minus any prolog presentation other than the playing of the Lehar score into which the picture abruptly breaks.

For the current twice daily showing the price scale lists a straightaway $1 for matinees, with evening performances graduating from there to $1.50 and $2. There are no loges.

"The Merry Widow" should mark a great start for the Embassy. Were it in the Capitol it would be a sure hold-over. *Skig.*

THE COAST OF FOLLY

Famous Players production with Gloria Swanson starred in three roles. Adapted from Conings by Dawson story by James Creelman and scenario by Forrest Halsey. Directed by Allan Dwan. At the Rivoli, New York, week August 30. Running time, 80 minutes.

Nadine Gathaway	Gloria Swanson
Joyce Gathaway	Gloria Swanson
Larry Fay	Anthony Jowitt
Count de Tauro	Alec B. Francis
Constance Fay	Dorothy Cummings
Cholly Knickerbocker	Jed Prouty
Nanny	Eugenie Besserer
Reporter	Arthur Hausman

For the box office this picture will be saved by the Swanson name. It's probably safe to play at the usual rental for that reason, but it belongs in the daily change houses, with or without Gloria Swanson.

All it has is Miss Swanson, excepting the titles. Titles like these on a Famous Players star production! another 27. It was easier to count the words than read them. Nearly 30 percent of the running time in captions. The entire story is threaded out by the captions, with the audience reading more than seeing. It wouldn't have been a bad idea to have scrapped the picture and given away the book instead. The book must have been vastly more interesting, for in that surely one did not have to watch how Gloria Swanson thinks an old woman should act or look.

Miss Swanson as the old woman is very bad. And it must be very bad for a director necessarily directing a star who may insist upon this or that. Surely Allan Dwan never called for the many closeups of Miss Swanson as the aged adventuress. Maybe Miss Swanson after seeing them herself will regret them with the audience. In houses where the Swanson bug hasn't been as strongly developed as on Broadway, some of those closeups will get plenty of laughs. Still in those neighborhoods or cities where the Swanson name can't draw alone, it will be as well to pass up this picture. It can't do business by itself.

And the moral of this picture:
"The wages of sin"—is marrying a count!

Nothing else to the film, one of those mother-love things with Nadine Cathaway suddenly getting remorse after years of adventure with men when seeing her daughter on the brink of a scandal. Nadine fixed that too, so the woman suing the daughter for alienation agreed to divorce her husband in order that he could marry the daughter. Nadine's daughter, the innocent, starting off right well for her, it might be said.

No action and all interiors, with those having anything else to do not getting enough time to do it because the captions busted in on them—but not on Miss Swanson's work. Sometimes her closeups were held so long that one would almost swear in different scenes as the old woman Miss Gloria must have used two make-ups.

But there is a Gloria Swanson rep. The box office records of the past attest to that. And Gloria needs some rep to stand off a picture like this. Its only claim for attention is the matter of the adventuress. Miss Swanson had better side step old women roles, whether playing dually or not. They are not for her—yet.

And what the picture playing bunch will say about her makeup as the Mme. Sans Gene imitator!

While Miss Swanson's Joyce Cathaway, as the daughter, didn't mean a thing beyond the baby stare that was as vacant as it sounds.

Famous may have stood in on this production to the extent of keeping down the production cost, probably figuring Miss Swanson's salary was enough in itself. And Miss Swanson's clothes. And Monday a hot day! They should have been held back until the week before Christmas when the fur shops would have paid for the display.

"Larry Fay" is one of the characters on the billing. If the picture had had Larry's night club in it, there would have been at least that much ginger to it. *Sime.*

THE MYSTIC

Metro-Goldwyn production directed by Tod Browning and made from his story. Scenario by Waldemar Young and Conway Tearle, featured with Aileen Pringle. At Capitol, New York, week August 30. Running time, 70 minutes.

Zara	Aileen Pringle
Michael Nash	Conway Tearle
Poppa Zazarack	Mitchell Lewis
Anton	Robert Ober
Carlo	Stanton Heck
Bradshaw	David Torrence
Doris Merrick	Gladys Hulette
Police Inspector	DeWitt Jennings

The usual thing to happen when a director announces one of his own stories is that he turns out a grand frost. Here, however, there is nothing of the kind, and if his picture stood up in the middle as it does at both ends, Tod Browning would have landed with a whale. As it is, however, "The Mystic" is an interesting piece of melodrama which has been made carefully and with the exception of Gladys Hulette, cast to perfection.

The opening scenes are in Hungary, where an itinerant carnival troupe numbers among its performers one Zara, a peach to look upon and a professed medium whose stunts are awesome to the ignorant villagers. Michael Nash, a suave American crook sees the girl and persuades her guardian and assistant that they could make a killing in America if they set up the right kind of shop, so the next sequence finds the pair operating for heavy money in a swell Manhattan layout. The assistant is the phantom spirit; Nash is the outside man with the electrical apparatus, while her guardian is the "professor," with Zara herself doing the medium and trance routine. The police get after them on the start-off, but they're smart enough to work sharp and keep the skirts clean.

Into their hands, however, walks a Mr. Bradshaw, who has been using his niece's legacy to manipulate the stock market, and the gang starts to clean him out. They scare him to death by making the spirit of his niece's brother return and give him a note. After that, they get to the girl and because she is gullible, tell her, among other things, she should entrust her securities and jewels to them.

As Nash is about to take them, he is conscience stricken at such an easy haul from a trusting girl. The rest of the gang accuse him of being in love with the kid, and although he isn't, he has to fight them to prove it.

Zara then steps in and determines to take the valuables herself, and so takes the girl to her home. Traced by the police, all are surprised when an inspector and several bluecoats stop a battle between Nash and the other fakirs. Nash in reality was trying to return the valuables but he couldn't convince the police. While they're all standing around with guns pointed to their tummies, he makes a well photographed grab for a gun, gets it and holds the crew up while he grabs the jewels and escapes. Darting through a door, he hides in a secret panel used in the fake spiritual manifestations and so eludes the coppers. Next he is seen delivering the jewels to the little girl, while the Hungarians are being deported. The fadeout, however, has him back in Hungary with Zara, whom he followed for thousands of miles to convince her that if she would play sheba to his sheik, everything would be candy.

Conway Tearle and Aileen Pringle in the leads are fine, while Mitchell Lewis also comes in for good applause. The scenes are particularly well directed and the only sequences which suffer a lack of interest are those played by Gladys Hulette, sadly out of place in the film. Aside from this, a slight scenario weakness in spots, "The Mystic" qualifies as a fast action melo and as such should hold up.

Its basic idea has never been used on the stage in this form, and if any producer cares to buy a piece which carries with it no potential movie rights, "The Mystic" looks like a cinch. It would not be hard to confine this one to the far side of the footlights and with the action and dialogue paced and well directed, it is almost impossible to see why it wouldn't be an outstanding stage melodrama. *Sisk.*

THE LIMITED MAIL

Warner Bros.' production, featuring Monte Blue. Adapted and scenarioed by Daryl Francis Zanuck from the Elmer E. Vance melodrama. At Warner's theatre (formerly Piccadilly), New York, week starting (at house) Aug. 29. Running time not taken. Entire length of performance, including stage show and short reels, two hours.

Bob Snobson	Monte Blue
Bob Wilson	Monte Blue
Caroline Dale	Vera Reynolds
Joe "Bub" Potts	Willard Louis
Jim Fowler	Tom Gallery
Bobby Fowler	Master Jack Huff
"Spike" Nelson	Edward Gribbon
Mr. Joffrey	Otis Harlan
Mrs. O'Leary	Lydia Yeamans Titus

A melodramatic thrill. Several of them. After wrecking a couple of trains with a head-on collision, a tunnel caves in while a little boy is swiftly flowing down the rapids. Mixed in 'twixt love and duty, Monte Blue saves the next oncoming while an escaped convict rescues the child. Then Blue and his sweetie find out their errors, the convict gets conscience stricken, returning to jail; and as the only guy that seemed liable to jam the plot was killed in the wreck, there was nothing left to do but end the picture.

As a thriller "The Limited Mail" is there. It's the best railroad picture since "The Great Train Robbery," and although "The Great Train Robbery" made its mark long ago, no one has since touched it.

The Warners have done more, however, in the straight thrilling way in this film of theirs. There is plenty of railroad stuff in it. And who doesn't like to see pictures of the steel rods? Fast expresses and slow freights, three tramps at the start and two at the finish, sentiment, conniving, that little boy and a darn nice girl, and others, including Lydia Yeamans Titus playing a landlady, and well, and Otis Harlan doing an elderly swell with a cheating wife.

Plenty here, with not a little comedy, one scene quite broad, but neatly handled by Edward Gribbon, as the escaped convict. While on a train and in the prison car, he is seated next to a pretty boy manicuring his fingers. Mr. Gribbon looks the youth over, takes a smell of his hair, then gives a look that can't be mistaken, adding other comedy upon top of it. For the wise bunch it's a wow, and for the others just kidding, so it's safe.

Mr. Blue is one of the tramps who falls in with a messenger on the Mail. The bums prevent a wreck, with Bob Wilson (Mr. Blue) eventually gaining a job engineering the freight, with five years elapsing before making the engine of the Limited, which runs on a single-track road through a dandy range of mountains. The scenic end, including moving trains, is always pretty and effective.

The first night Wilson ran the Limited he ran it into a head-on, made better here even than the one they prepared for weeks at the old Brighton track years ago. That certainly is a smash in the Warners' picture. But it will get the bird from railroaders. The freight with double-headed engines going down a grade is running wild, says the engineer in the first engine, through the brakes not working. Everybody, including dispatchers, let it run wild, with everybody forgetting all about the second engine, that may have had its brakes working, if anyone had inquired. Still that's regular, too, for probably it was the only break to make the colish.

Mr. Blue takes hold of a hard-working role here and does quite well with it. He looks the engineer better than the tramp. Willard was the bear tramp, although Mr. Gribbon must be given full credit for an all-around performance.

Among the women Vera Reynolds caught right on. Whether new or not, she should be given a role with a little more action to it. That girl appears to hold possibilities, judging her more by her screen personality than what she had to do, but Miss Reynolds has expression besides looks. The other principal woman is not programed, though prominent. Anyway, she is so blondy her hair suggests a wig instead of her own. These blondy blondes on the screen might be toned down somewhat. She is a better actress than looker in this picture, and that doesn't tell what kind of an actress she is, either.

Master Jack Huff was the kidlet. He's a cute kid and also the cause of one thrill that took the breath away from the women patrons who surely thought an onrushing train would demolish him. It passed by, however, on the other track. Neat direction—something to be noted throughout, with the director also unprogramed.

A very good melodrama—one of the best. It can stand a lot of exploitation. Given something to make it draw for those not enticed by the title, "The Limited Mail" will stand up and do business anywhere.

Sime.

THE LOVE HOUR

Vitagraph production featuring Huntly Gordon, Louise Fazenda, Ruth Clifford and Willard Louis. Directed by Herman Raymaker. Scenaric and adaptation by Bess Meredyth. At Rialto, New York, week August 30. Running time, 75 minutes.

Rex Westmore ....Huntly Gordon
Jennie Tibbs ....Louise Fazenda
Gus Yerger ....Willard Louis
Betty Brown ....Ruth Clifford
Ward Ralston ....John Roche
Kid Lewis ....Charles Farrell
Attorney ....Gayne Whitman

Rather an inconsequential picture, this, fortunate to find itself on Broadway. It is drawn thin in all the essentials that make for appeal, creaks and wobbles along for the most part, and ranks far down in the scale of picture making.

The first reel, with the atmosphere of a summer park to lend zest, contains more interest than anything that follows. As the film turns to its story-telling, awkward direction, further retarded by inferior acting and atrociously written titling, smother it completely.

The heroine's husband is advised by his physician an operation is imperative. He must go to Switzerland to have it performed. There are no funds. His wife is desperate. Scheming villain offers necessary aid.

Many times "The Love Hour" betrays an amateurishness that could hardly be expected from such an old institution as Vitagraph.

"The Love Hour" is the last Vitagraph picture to be seen at the Rialto. It hasn't a chance, even as a program release.

Samuel.

SEVEN DAYS

Al Christie feature, starring Lillian Rich. Adapted from stage farce by Mary Roberts Rinehart and Avery Hopwood. Directed by Scott Sidney. Released by Producers' Distributing Corp. At the Colony, New York, week Aug. 30. Running time, 75 minutes.

Kit Eclair.....................Lillian Rich
James Wilson..............Creighton Hale
Bella Wilson..............Lilyan Tashman
Anne Brown..........Mabel Julienne Scott
Dallas Brown.................William Austin
Tom Harrison...............Hallam Cooley
Aunt Salina.........................Rosa Gore
The Cop..........................Tom Wilson
The Burglar.....................Eddie Gribbon
The Seer.........................Charles Clary

Much in favor of this Al Christie picture getting the booking attention of the exhibitors. "Seven Days" has its Broadway record as a stage farcical success. Then, again, it has the names of Mary Roberts Rinehart and Avery Hopwood as writers. But it doesn't line up strong enough for comparison with "Charlie's Aunt," Christie's other comedy.

There is much horseplay, with the main comedy prop the burglar whose liveliest minutes were in dodging the cop who is also locked up in the quarantined house. Some laugh-getting stuff is done, but it is not sufficient to carry the whole picture along.

There is hardly a "bit" or scene that hasn't been done in some manner before the camera, and even the memory of the success of "Seven Days" upon the stage will not be able to lift it high and mighty as one of the biggest comedy gems of the present season.

Miss Rich is starred, or, at least, given unusual billing prominence. She is Kit Eclair, the girl who is introduced as the wife of Jim Wilson, but who in reality is in love with Jim Harrison, and as a whole makes it a pleasing characterization throughout. Creighton Hale is an acceptable Jim Wilson, who finally rewins the love of his divorced wife, played by Miss Tashman.

Some of the captions have resurrected some old, old wheezes, good in the main for laughs at the Colony.

"Seven Days" will suffice in the houses where they are not so exacting and where horseplay considerably stretched through interminable footage is a cinema riot.

kansas. *Mark.*

THE POLICE PATROL

Gotham Production produced by Sam Sax and released by Lumas. Directed by Burton King with James Kirkwood and Edna Murphy featured. Reviewed at Loew's New York, August 28, as half a double bill. Running time, 57 minutes.

Jim Ryan ....James Kirkwood
Alice Bennett ....Edna Murphy
Dorothy Stone ....Edna Murphy
Lieut. Burke ....Edmund Breese
Maurice Ramon ....Robert McKim

A good hoak story of the New York police force in which mistaken identity plays a large share. The hero, Jim Ryan, is much in love with Alice Bennett, who happens to be the counterpart of Dorothy Stone, the leader of a notorious criminal gang.

The film has been well produced and some river chase stuff counts in the exciting moments. Several shots of police parades and the annual field games are also worked in, while added to the love interests of the principals is a little boy, brother of the girl, who acts well.

James Kirkwood and Miss Murphy carry their roles well, while Edmund Breese is rightfully severe as the police lieutenant.

As an independent release and program picture, this one stacks up satisfactorily. Its scenario is well constructed and the scenes are of the type which neither call for nor merit an extravagant outlay. Particularly in the smaller theatres will this go well. Although crook stuff is involved, it is of the type safe to set before children. Matter of fact, the kids like this one and the older folks, too.

Sisk.

HIGH AND HANDSOME

F. B. O. production starring Maurice ("Lefty") Flynn. From the Red Book Magazine story by Gerald Beaumont. Produced and directed by Harry Garson. At Loew's New York, Aug. 26, as half the bill. Runs about an hour.

Joe Hanrahan......Maurice "Lefty" Flynn
Mrs. Hanrahan ....Lydia Knott
Jim Burke.............................Jean Perry
Marie Le Doux.............Kathleen Myers
Battling Kennedy.............Tom Kennedy
Myrt Riley..................Marjorie Bonner
Jimmy Le Doux.................John Gough

"High and Handsome" is the latest of a cycle of cop pictures. It's as good as most of them and probably quite a lot better when it comes to the star.

Flynn is "there," whatever role he is given to play. His gridiron experience at Yale stands him in good stead when it comes to the rough-house stuff, and he doesn't make the role of the copper too high-hat. Besides, "Lefty" has a full share of good looks.

The policeman he plays is scrupulously honest, and because he won't accept a bribe from a boxing promoter whose arena is unsafe, is framed and suspended from the force. The cop is incidentally the champ boxer of the department, which makes his fistic victory over the promoter's pet heavyweight more logical than otherwise. The fight scenes are well staged, both in the ring action and in the shots of the various types of spectators.

Just at the finish of the battle the faulty balcony crashes down and the hero's earlier accusations are vindicated. This scene, while not exactly the height of realism, is well directed and cleverly photographed.

The love interest is provided by pretty Kathleen Myers, and the usual comedy bits of Irish blarney are present in full force. Tom Kennedy is an able heavy, but rather too literally that in weight to make as formidable a ring figure as he is supposed to be.

There must be a good reason for this sudden influx of police pictures. If, as seems probable, the public demand for them is strong, "High and Handsome" is a worthy one of its type.

WAS IT BIGAMY?

William Steiner production starring Edith Thornton. Story by Forrest Sheldon. Directed by Charles Hutchinson. At Loew's New York, Aug. 25, as half the bill. Runs about 58 minutes.

Ruth Steele.................Edith Thornton
Carleton......................Earle Williams
Judge Gaynor.............Thomas Picketts
Harvey Gaynor.................Charles Crux
Attorney......................Wilfsed Lucas

After seeing "Was It Bigamy?" there is sympathy for the recent $5,000 offer to endow a chair in one of the larger universities to improve the status of the motion picture. If ever a film needed some sort of intelligent guidance this is it. Mr. Steiner seems to have turned out an even less worthy affair than usual.

In the first place it looks as if several hundred feet of film in the middle of the picture have been cut without due explanation. Thus the heroine is married, the old character actor dead and a series of events have transpired about which the audience is given no inkling. Not that the faulty continuity has materially hurt, for if the cast played it backwards, it could hardly be more senseless.

The heroine marries in the first few hundred feet and then, although it is totally unnecessary, takes unto herself another spouse soon after in the hope of getting her guardian out of a mess. Realizing she's got two husbands on her hands, she sets out to get a divorce from one of them (the one she really loves) by making him think she's a bold, bad woman. The finish drags to a faked looking Central American set and sees the wicked hubby put out of the way by a jealous native rival.

Miss Thornton, as always, tries hard but can do little with her preposterous role. Opposite is no other than Earle Williams, who must remember his former triumphs regretfully when he was forced to play in such junk as this.

September 9, 1925

Phantom of the Opera

Universal production featuring Lon Chaney, Mary Philbin and Norman Kerry. Directed by Rupert Julian. Adapted from the novel of the same name by Gaston Leroux. At the Astor, New York, for run starting Sept. 6. Running time, 101 mins.

The Phantom....................Lon Chaney
Christine Dane..................Mary Philbin
Raoul de Chagny..............Norman Kerry
Ledoux.............Arthur Edmund Carewe
Simon Buquet...............Gibson Gowland
Philip de Chagny............John Sainpolis
Florine Papillon..............Snitz Edwards

Universal has turned out another horror.

This newest of U specials is probably the greatest inducement to nightmare that has yet been screened. If the picture equals in dollars the sleepless hours it will cause the children who view it, U has a money film on its hands—and it's reported the production cost approached $1,000,000, including over $50,000 for retakes, far above the firm's expectations.

It's not a bad film from a technical viewpoint, but revolving around the terrifying of all inmates of the Grand Opera House in Paris by a criminally insane mind behind a hideous face, the combination makes a welsh rarebit look foolish as a sleep destroyer.

Lon Chaney is again the "goat" in the matter, no matter if it is another tribute to his character acting. His makeup as the hunchback within the Notre Dame Cathedral was morbid enough, but this is infinitely worse, as in this instance his body is normal with a horrible face solely relied upon for the effect

Following the "Hunchback" thing it becomes a moot question whether or not Chaney's name in connection with a picture is going to keep children away from a theatre. Any number of "Unholy Threes" cannot erase the impression of these two makeups. While adults may throw off the hideous film characterizations it leaves an aftermath that can't be too favorable for Chaney as a general draw.

Assuredly it is ruinous to any juvenile appeal.

Universal is evidently out to establish itself as the champ ghost story telling firm among film producers. There can be no question of its supremacy after seeing this one. Late in the footage it is learned the Phantom is an escaped inmate of an asylum for the criminally insane. This explains his fiendish means to gain any desired end, and a musical twist in the degenerate brain allows for his taking up an abode in the cellars of the opera house.

The love angle is encountered in the persons of an understudy (Miss Philbin) whom the Phantom cherishes while she is also the sole thought of her military lover (Mr. Kerry).

The girl is twice abducted by the Phantom to his cellar retreat, and the finish is built up by the pulling of levers, concealed buttons, etc., to make active secret doors, heat chambers, flooding passages and other appropriate devices. To add to the general cheerfulness it is revealed that the Phantom sleeps in a coffin flanked by two enormous candles.

However, the kick of the picture is in the unmasking of the Phantom by the girl. Told she is in no peril while his mask remains untouched, the girl satisfies the audience's curiosity by lifting it from behind. The resultant "shot" is from the front. Between Chaney's horrible facial makeup and the expression thereon it's a wallop that can't miss its objective.

There is actually no work for the cast inasmuch as the story carries the picture, neither is there any comedy to relieve. Kerry is a colorless hero in this instance, Miss Philbin contents herself with being pretty and becoming terrorized at the Phantom, and Chaney is either behind a mask or grimacing through his fiendish makeup. It's rather a costume picture, with uniforms abounding and the women assuming attire made famous by family albums.

Julian has done well enough with his directing. An operatic ballet is a well-staged bit, while views of the auditorium of the opera house, entrance and foyer have been done in natural colors. Also included in this is a masque ball.

There's plenty of melodramatic "hoke," while the climax is ridiculous. Following 100 minutes of gruesomeness, terminating with a mob beating out the brains of the Phantom on a wharf, is shown the girl and her officer in the proverbial clinch preceded by a subtitle explaining it's the honeymoon. That addition can go right out, for it is impossible in the face of the previously established morale and the picture can stand cutting.

It's understood that the time taken, money spent and the retakes necessary for this release are what sent Carl Laemmle to Europe. Undoubtedly a big effort for Universal, the "Phantom" will appeal to those addicted to gruesome narrations.

How many will wish they hadn't seen it is something else again.

There has been no doubt in the trade for some time that the bunch knew they had a bad boy in this one, but were helpless after the money poured in and had to go through with it. Shown some time **ago in San Francisco to obtain a line on what they had, what they had didn't please them nor San Francisco. It was then retakes were ordered, with some attempt to insert comedy. Exploitation was the final point decided to push over the picture. There has been much of that in and around New York. Placing the picture as a special on Broadway may tend to fool some exhibitors, but every exhibitor solicited or persuaded or intending to play this picture should either see it first in person or have some member of his family see it before presenting this horrifier before his patronage.**

It's impossible to believe there are a majority of picturegoers who prefer this revolting sort of a tale on the screen. It is better for any exhibitor to pass up this film or 100 like it than to have one patron pass up his theatre through it. *Skig.*

GRAUSTARK

First National Production by Joseph M. Schenck with Norma Talmadge starred. Adapted to screen by Frances Marion from George Barr McCutcheon's novel. Directed by Dimitri Buchowetski. At the Capitol, New York, Sept. 6, week. Running time, 70 minutes.

Princess Yetive.............Norma Talmadge
Grenfall Lorry................Eugene O'Brien
Prince Gabriel..............Marc McDermott
Dangloss..........................Roy D'Arcy
Count Halfont.......................Albert Gran
Countess Halfont..........Lillian Lawrence
Captain Quinnox............Michael Vavitch
King Ferdinand.................Frank Currier
The American Ambassador.....Winter Hall
Countess Dagmar...........Wanda Hawley

"Graustark" tells the familiar tale of an American love for a royal princess. Because it is all romance with never a tinge of sexiness, "Graustark" is in itself a great relief from the usual run of photoplays. Added to whatever worth there is in the story is the production accorded the film by Joseph M. Schenck. It is safe to say that few regular features have had such sumptuous settings and that few have been made with so much attention to intricate detail. As a program picture "Graustark" is 100 per cent suitable to any house.

The story opens when the hero, Grenfall Lorry, sees Princess Yetive sitting in a dining car window—in the train opposite. Immediately he boards her train, and on the transcontinental journey is ignorant of her royal blood, but conscious of his love. And she loves him, too, so when she is forced home to consummate a marriage for state reasons, it is hard for both of them. Still, Lorry hasn't learned that she's a princess, for in America she was traveling incognito as Miss Guggenslocker.

He knew she lived in Graustark and once there he had the American ambassador help him locate the girl. At a court ball he scanned a thousand faces, and finally stopped in his tracks when he saw his Miss Guggenslocker in regal robes, descending a grand staircase with her father, King Ferdinand.

The latter part of the film is a detail of how they outwitted the villain, who wanted to marry her.

Norma Talmadge, as the princess, never looked so beautiful. Her gowns are all creations and eye smashing.

In her support Eugene O'Brien, Marc McDermott and Albert Gran are notable, and everybody else is excellent.

The settings are heavy, impressive and artistically done, while in several instances straight line effects are used for what seems to be futuristic stuff. But futuristic in its intent or not, the whole thing is as handsome as the Kohinoor diamond.

Buchowetski, the director, is the same man who made such a flop of "The Swan" in pictures by rearranging the story. Here he has taken no such liberties and with competent people to direct, he has handled them well. *Sisk.*

GREAT SENSATION

Produced by Perfection Pictures, Inc., and released by Columbia. William Fairbanks starred and direction by Jay Marchant. Scenario by Douglas Z. Zoty. At Loew's New York, Aug. 28, as half a double bill. Running time, 55 minutes.

A more or less typical William Fairbanks picture, with his thrill stuff featured against a background of melodramatic action. He is the son of a rich family, but because he loves a girl in the neighborhood, hires out as her chauffeur, and she doesn't recognize him for the first 3,000 feet. The girl, Peggy Howell, is saved by him several times, once in swimming, and to do this Fairbanks takes a good high dive that photographed well.

Then he thwarts two crooks who had their eyes on her mama's jewelry, and after administering them a real fight the girl begins razzing him by treating him like a low-down menial. But he wins out in the end, and it's all safe for the happiness angle.

Fairbanks as the hero is good, and Pauline Garon plays the heroine, making her comeback to pictures after a long period of inactivity. Her part here is purely a flapper role, and she plays it as such; but Pauline makes everything too cute for words, and after playing the cutie-cutie girl goes in for some bathing-suit stuff that could have stood some brassiere assistance.

The picture on the whole rates as good program stuff for the smaller houses, and as it wasn't intended for anywhere else, it fills the bill. *Sisk.*

September 16, 1925

THE PONY EXPRESS

Famous-Players picture made from the story by Henry James Forman and Walter Woods. Directed by James Cruze and released as a special, being given day and date showings at the Rivoli and Rialto. Betty Compson, Ricardo Cortez, Wallace Beery and Ernest Torrence featured. At the Rivoli, New York, week of Sept. 13. Running time, 110 mins.

Molly Jones......................Betty Compson
Jack Weston......................Ricardo Cortez
"Ascension" Jones.........Ernest Torrence
"Rhode Island" Red.........Wallace Beery
Jack Slade.....................George Bancroft
Charlie Bent.....................Frank Lackteen
Billy Cody............................John Fox, Jr.
William Russell ....William Turner
Senator Glen................................Al Hart
Sam Clemens...................Charles Gerson
Aunt.................................Rose Tapley
Baby..................................Vondell Barr

Patriotic, expensive, pretentious, verbose and just fair—that describes "The Pony Express."

This long one, rushed into instant distribution in an effort to beat out an opposition company is being heralded more than any F-P release of the year, not excepting "The Wanderer." Given a day and date showing at the Rivoli and Rialto, it was advertised heavily all last week, while this week huge flags bearing the picture's title cover the front of the two houses. In addition a ballyhoo in front of the Putnam building is being run off regularly, while good sized ads were carried in the dailies yesterday and Monday.

But even all that exploitation and advertising will never make the regular picturegoer believe that "The Pony Express" is one-two-three alongside of "The Covered Wagon." It isn't half as good as either "North of 36" or "The Thundering Herd."

In plot this concerns the machinations of Senator Glen of California, and his attempt to establish an empire of that state and Sonora, Mexico. To this end, he plots to have the new pony express system "fixed" at Julesberg, Miss., so that any political news from the east which would have a bearing on his plans might be delayed.

In Sacramento he had told his men to get Frisco Jack, a gambler and gunman, because Jack had made disparaging remarks concerning the senator. But it happens when the senator leaves town, Jack goes after him. Instead of killing him, he happens along in time to avert a holdup, and the senator, in Julesburg, tells him he is desired for the pony express, so Jack falls in line, having in mind a system to "fix" the politician.

In Julesburg is Molly Jones, the girl of the film, and her father, a psalm singing blacksmith called "Ascension" Jones. There is also a poker playing bum called "Rhode Island" Red, and with Red as an ally, Jack is soon able to let Jack Slade, the Overland express agent and tool of Glen, know that he is on to their tricks.

From that time on it becomes a battle between the pair, with Jack finally winning. Other intrigues include an Indian spy, Charlie Bent, who brings his people down in a murderous attack just as "Ascension" Jones has completed his new church. But while the Indians are scrapping, the troops ride back and that is finished nicely.

The end has Jack defeating the aim of Glen by riding through with the messages which proclaimed Lincoln's election, and when this news reached California it made that state cast its lot with the Union in the civil war. The windup has Jack and Molly marrying, while "Rhode Island" Red enlists as a private—and everybody is happy.

"The Pony Express" has all the atmosphere in the world. Its production has been careful and elaborate, but the scenario and story are weak. Were it not for the comedy relief of Torrence and Beery, the whole thing would be tiresome. Cortez has a good role here and plays it well, while Betty Compson and George Bancroft are others of the cast who do well.

The film has its moments, but 110

minutes of running time is long.

To the exhibitor who has bought "The Pony Express" the only thing to do is to follow the lead of the company which produced it—exploit it as you never exploited a picture before. A "natural" doesn't have to be boosted so much. *Sisk.*

SOULS FOR SABLES

Tiffany Production starring Claire Windsor and Eugene O'Brien. From the story Garlan and Co. by David Graham Phillips. Directed by James McKay. Shown at the Colony, New York, week Sept. 14, 1925. Running time, 82 minutes.

Alice Garlan	Claire Windsor
Fred Garlan	Eugene O'Brien
Helen Ralston	Claire Adams
Mrs. Kendall	Edith Yorke
Mr. Nelson	George Fawcett
Esther Hamilton	Eileen Percy

Mighty good program feature, all the more surprisingly so because it is an independently-made production. It has a fairly strong story theme and is very well directed and cast. In regard to the latter it seemingly has names that should mean something at the box office in the regular run of film houses. The picture is one of those middle class society yarns that usually please the women and the shop girls.

The story in itself is that of a struggling young business man whose wife wants a sable coat. She manages to get one and almost pays the price to the heavy, who is after her, but in the end she manages to escape his clutches, but not until after her girl friend, who also fell for the sable wrap thing, is bumped off by her hubby, who gets wise to the manner in which she got the coat.

Eugene O'Brien plays the young business man and if not making faces all over the lot he might have gotten away with the role. Claire Windsor as the foolish young wife who is out to make the fashionable flash with clothes and furs she manages to fill the picture in rather satisfactory manner. The balance of the cast measures up nicely.

The photography is particularly clean cut and snappy, and the lightings are also well handled.

At a price the picture is worth while for the average run of houses, although it does not stand up as strong enough to be given a full week in one of Broadway's de luxe presentation houses. *Fred.*

SHORE LEAVE

First National release made by Inspiration Pictures, Inc. Adapted by Josephine Lovett from the play by Hubert Osborne. Directed by John S. Robertson. At the Strand, New York, week of Sept. 13. Running time, 74 minutes.

"Bilge" Smith	Richard Barthelmess
Connie Martin	Dorothy Mackaill
"Bat" Smith	Ted McNamara
Capt. Bimby Martin	Nick Long
Mrs. Schuyler-Payne	Marie Shotwell
Mr. Schuyler-Payne	Arthur Metcalf
Admiral Metcalf	Warren Cooke
Chief Petty Officer	Samuel Hines

In so far as the average audience is concerned this is very close to being the best picture Barthelmess has yet turned out. It has good comedy, pathos, and a plot that neither sags nor prolongs itself. Added to this is the good characterization Barthelmess gives to his role, that of "Bilge" Smith, a sailor in the U. S. navy.

"Bilge" was pretty much like sailors are supposed to be—rough and uncouth, but with a fairly definite set of morals. Women didn't mean a whole lot to him. Landed at Wautucket in New England, "Bilge" met a sweet little dressmaker, a girl whose forebears had been seagoing folks. To "Bilge" it didn't mean so much, for he ate a big supper at her house and said good-bye, promising to come back some time. The girl had fallen in love with him.

When he left, however, the girl had an old schooner salvaged, and by the time he returned again to port she hoped he would get out of the navy and be the skipper of her schooner—so she could be the skipper's wife. But "Bilge" came back, and although she gave a party for all the Smiths in the fleet, he was late in showing up, and when he did he'd forgotten all about her. After he remembered her and proposed it struck him that as she owned this vessel she must be a wealthy woman. And so he left.

The fleet struck Buenos Aires and "Bilge" was smitten. Shortly there came 50 letters to the 50 Smiths of the fleet, all of them from Connie and all telling that she was poor again and was sewing for a living. So "Bilge" tells the captain he won't re-enlist and works his way back to Wautucket. There he and Connie have an understanding, and the fade-out is as happy as only fade-outs can be.

Barthelmess has put over a rather uncompromising characterization of his sailor. There is no bid for sympathy made until nearly at the end of the picture—unless it can be that his code of morals forbid his marrying a woman for her money. Dorothy Mackaill, as the little dressmaker, is also very fine, ranking almost with the star for a sincere and consistent performance. The others are good, with the comedy honors going to Ted McNamara as an Irish sailor.

"Shore Leave" is a cinch, and in the week stand places the bet is that business increases daily instead of slumping. It's that kind of a picture—the kind with which people are entertained and satisfied. And if a picture does that much, they tell their friends.

Sisk.

COMING OF AMOS

Producers' Distributing Corp. release produced by Cecil B. DeMille for the Cinema Corp. Adapted from the story by William J. Locke and directed by Paul Sloane. At the Colony, New York, Sept. 6, week. Running time, 75 minutes.

Amos Burden	Rod LaRocque
Princess Nadia Ramiroff	Jetta Goudal
Ramon Garcia	Noah Beery
David Fontenay	Richard Carle
Bendyke Hamilton	Arthur Hoyt
Duchess of Perth	Trixie Friganza
Pedro Valdez	Clarence Burton
The Nurse	Ruby Lafayette

This, the second of DeMille's new series of P. D. C., is a good film from almost any angle. Its interesting story is fully matched by a lavish and well-ordered production. Directed by the experienced Paul Sloane, the works move along with precision and pace, while the leading players, Rod LaRocque and Miss Goudal, form an excellent love-making pair. DeMille, incidentally, has made a star of LaRocque, and the young leading man fills his new shoes comfortably.

Cast as a young ranch owner in Australia and deft in the hurling of a boomerang, Amos Burden is suddenly transplanted to the French Riviera. In this new atmosphere he is out of place, but is taken in hand and polished. He falls in love with Princess Nadia, an exiled Russian, also pursued by Ramon Garcia, a dirty dog, whose villainy is trumped only by his manners.

In their several encounters Ramon comes off the top hand, but Garcia finally gets Nadia to his castle and there begins a gentle torture system to make her acquiesce to those dirty ideas only villains have.

On comes Amos, and, landing at Garcia's pier, he breaks off the handle of two boathooks until they become boomerangs, and, hurling them at Garcia's gunmen, he dispatches in succession a "kiss for Cinderella" and a "message to Garcia." After a brutal fight he rescues Nadia from a dungeon filled with water, and plunges the villain into his own death device.

LacRocque is breezy, natural and quick in all his actions. Miss Goudal looks the Russian princess, and is gowned in some creations that will "get" the women. These gowns, incidentally, are so unusual that they form a good publicity or exploitation angle. As the villain Noah Beery is true to the screen tradition of his family, while Trixie Friganza and Richard Carle in lesser roles turn in laughs.

"Coming of Amos" is a handsomely produced proposition filled with good photography and screen novelties. Having, as it does, a good story, it seems like an audience satisfier; and getting the audience in is the only thing left. That's up to the exhibitor, for this picture will please.

Sisk.

The Wife That Wasn't Wanted

A Warner Bros. production with Irene Rich starred. From the novel Gertie Wentworth-James, adapted by Bess Meredyth. Directed by James Flood. Shown at the Piccadilly, New York, week Sept. 5, 1925. Running time, 71 minutes.

Mrs. John Mannering	Irene Rich
John Mannering	Huntly Gordon
Bob Mannering	John Harron
Jerome Wallace	Gayne Whitman
Mary Patterson	June Marlowe
"Slick Jennings	Edward Piel
John Graham	Winifred Lucas
Diane Graham	Elinor Fair
Greta	Gertrude Astor

This is a rather lengthy meller that has everything, but the kitchen stove drawn in by the hair to attempt a kick. The result is just a melodrama of society and politics that means little or nothing as far as the box office is concerned. On the screen, however, it will pass as fair entertainment.

The picture is a little too long at present, draggy in spots. The possibility of its draw depends entirely on the fact of whether or not your audiences are anxious to see Irene Rich in another film version of a story that is much like a dozen others she has turned out heretofore.

The story is that of the wife of a district attorney who is willing to compromise herself in order that her husband is defeated for re-election, because their son is under arrest charged with manslaughter because of an automobile accident in which a woman was killed. The father is torn between love and duty and the mother is actuated only by mother love. She wants her boy freed, and she is willing to go to any length to secure his freedom. A forest fire and a few other like thrills are injected into the picture.

Miss Rich and Huntly Gordon give performances that are worthy of extended comment. She particularly is good in the mother role, although overacting in one or two scenes. The heavy handled by Gayne Whitman was a neat piece of acting. This trio managed to carry the brunt of the task of telling the story. The balance of the cast merely filled the picture.

If anyone can find out where the title, "The Wife That Wasn't Wanted," came from as far as the story is concerned they should be given a prize. *Fred.*

THE SCARLET WEST

Frank J. Carroll production, released and distributed by First National. Made with the co-operation of various Colorado civic and historical societies. Story by A. B. Heath. Directed by John G. Adolphi. At the Broadway, New York, week Sept. 7. Runs about 70 minutes.

Gen. Kinnard	Robert Edeson
Harriet	Martha Francis
Miriam	Clara Bow
Lieut. Parkman	Johnnie Walker
Lieut. Harper	Walter McGrail
Mrs. Harper	Florence Crawford
Cardelanche	Robert Fraser
Neshna	Helen Ferguson
Mrs. Custer	Ruth Stonehouse
Capt. Howard	Gaston Glass

"The Scarlet West" for the program houses is a bear. Any Yankee kid who sees it and doesn't get a big thrill has the wrong color of blood. Every school with a projection machine should get a hold of it, as it will do more to instill patriotic spirit than months of lecturing.

But it is not only for the youngsters. At the Broadway a hard-boiled audience apparently enjoyed every minute of it, and conclusively showed their approval at the finish.

Produced with the aid of several Colorado historical and civic societies, from the standpoint of authenticity it is probably as carefully presented as any of the big historical westerns. Besides its stirring story of Custer's last stand and the other incidents of the redskin uprisings in the 70's, the story tells a genuinely absorbing tale of life and love in a frontier army garrison. This picture only falls a bit under in comedy relief and expert scenario.

The Indians as a race are the villains of the film, but one of their number is the real hero. He is Cardelanche, educated, intelligent and holding a captain's commission in the army. He falls in love with the flirtatious daughter of the post commander, but realizes, when trouble breaks out between the whites and reds, that he is still a member of the latter people. After a struggle with himself he decides his place is with his own tribes, and, although he first saves the garrison from a treacherous Indian attack, he gives the girl to the young white liteutenant, who worships her, and returns to the haunts of his forefathers.

Incidental to the plot, but strikingly done, are the scenes in which Custer and his men make their last glorious stand. It is very effectively screened, with several thousand Indians circling around the ever-decreasing detachment, and the four photographers employed by the producer earned whatever was paid them. Unfortunately, however, the dust from the myriad horses' hoofs raised clouds that sometimes blur the action.

A glance at the cast shows some seven or eight really notable screen names. Robert Fraser is astonishingly good as the Indian hero, probably the best part he has yet had. Such well-known players as Ruth Stonehouse and Gaston Glass have merely bits. The name of the actor playing Custer is not given—just as well, since he is the only unimpressive one in the cast. McGrail, Edeson and the Misses Bow and Ferguson do sterling work.

First National evidently knew what it was doing when it took over this independent. The small share of comedy and the rather jerky and badly cut scenario are going to handicap it, of course, but there is plenty there to make it a box-office wow if exploited properly. Any list of better present-day pictures should include it, as it treats a worthy American subject in clear, direct and meritorious fashion.

THE WHITE OUTLAW

Universal production starring Jack Hoxie. Directed by Cliff Smith. Story by Isadore Bernstein. Photographed by William Noble. At Loew's New York one day (Sept. 1) as half the bill. Runs about 55 minutes.

Jack Lupton	Jack Hoxie
Mary Gale	Marceline Day
Malcolm Gale	William Welsh
James Hill	Duke Lee
Cook	Floyd Shackelford
Sheriff	Charles Brinley

Universal bills this one as a "Blue Streak Western." That holds good partially, because the action is at top speed, but unfortunately enough the dizzy pace is about the only commendable thing about this otherwise stupid picture.

The white outlaw is not Hoxie,

but his horse, "Scout," the latest cinema steed to run wild and wage warfare against man. The hero gets the blame for the animal's misdeeds, but in the end not only clears himself, but reforms the savage "Scout" as well.

"Bunk," an Australian shepherd dog, also is in the plot. There are some well-directed scenes in which a bear attacks "Scout's" young colt and is driven off by the fiery white horse. The love interest is the conventional one of the girl who sticks to the falsely accused hero. . The comic relief is sadly microscopic and unfunny.

The big thrill comes when a herd of wild steeds led by "Scout" stampede the heroine and she is saved at the last second by being thrust into a small washout by her cowboy sweetie. This is rather exciting, more than can be said for the fight scenes between the ranchers and rustlers.

Hoxie is his usual pleasant and placid self, while the rest of the cast have little opportunity to demonstrate whether or not they have talent. The photography is of high-grade and the scenic locale of the picture splendid in its beauty. That, however, is nothing extraordinary for present-day westerns.

"The White Outlaw" is more an animal picture than a straight western, and that may prove to be bait for some people. On the whole, it registers as an inferior effort, even for a Hoxie program release.

MAKERS OF MEN

Bud Barsky production with Kenneth MacDonald starred. Story by William E. Wing and direction by Forrest Sheldon. At the Stanley, New York, September 4. Running time, 70 minutes.
Hiram Renfrew............William Burton
Jimmie Jones..........Kenneth MacDonald
Lillian Gilman................Clara Horton
Steppling ....William Loewry
"Shift'ess" Poole ....Ethan Laidlow
Sergt. Dan Banks........J. P. MacGowan

An idle preachment, this, with the late war as its background. The moralizing is done by a group of Keystone comedy rubes seated around a general store stove, while the town philosopher relates the legend of how the war made a new man of Jimmie Jones.

Jimmie had a nervous affliction which made him shudder at a sudden noise or crash. Because of this his best girl thought he was a coward and his rival helped that idea grow. But the war came. With the help of Sergt. Banks Jimmie overcame his nervousness and proved himself quite a hero.

Coming back home, he was still afraid to broach the marriage question to the girl and it took the sergeant's help to put this over. To top it all off, the sergeant and Jimmie put the dukes all over the rival's physiognomy.

The slender and maudlin tale is related with the aid of cut-backs. While the production end of it is well handled the scenario is so twisted and inept that the good acting of J. P. MacGowan as the sergeant and that of Clara Horton goes to waste. The star, Kenneth MacDonald, is the Corse Payton of pictures, and at that Corse probably knows a lot more about acting.

For the cheap grind houses where they buy film for the purpose of using so much footage per day, this one may slide by, but in intelligent neighborhoods they'd laugh it off the screen. The story itself has a good idea but so badly is it developed, acted and directed that it doesn't stand a chance. In all the chaos, J. P. MacGowan and Miss Horton emerge triumphant, and of the two, MacGowan leads because of a thoroughly professional piece of acting. *Sisk.*

CIRCUS CYCLONE

Western feature released through Universal but made by Al Rogell. Art Acord starred. Half double bill at Loew's New York, Sept. 11. Running time, 56 minutes.

Typical western, with the cowboy doing the finest of heroics.

In this instance he is in love with the daughter of a circus clown. When a gang of crooks frame the old man so that it appears the clown robbed a bank, the cowboy rides hard and fast to bring back both the crooks and their money.

To build up suspense, a mob is ready to lynch the clown while the cowboy is riding after the crooks. After regaining the money and the crooks have driven their machine over a cliff, he gets back just in time to stop serious trouble.

Art Acord is nice enough in this one. It is cheaply produced and ought to sell for a small nickel. It will hardly hold up a bill by itself in any except the smallest houses. *Sisk.*

WRECKAGE

Banner Production made by Ben Verschleiser and distributed by Henry Ginsberg. Directed by Scott Dunlap, with May Allison starred. At Loew's New York, Sept. 12. Running time, 70 minutes.
Rene Jordan....................May Allison
Maurice Dysart...............John Miljan
Stuart Ames.................Holmes Herbert
Grant Demarest...........James Morrison
Margot.....................Rosemary Theby

This story holds a nasty villain and a hero under suspicion for a murder. The hero, Stuart Ames, really didn't kill Grant Demarest, but it took him a lot of money to convince the courts, so he naturally left the land to keep away from an unpleasant atmosphere. On the boat he met Rene Jordan, blonde and nifty. When Maurice Dysart and his villainy became too obnoxious, Ames thwarted the bad man.

Then came a great sea storm, put on in studio fashion with some moments of good work and some glaring discrepancies. To save the girl Ames jumps overboard with her. Though waves are lashing the ship brutally, they jump into water as calm as that of a lake. Minor detail.

The villain is later disclosed as a phoney count and lures the girl to a mountain cabin on pretext of giving her news of her father. Just as he is forcing her to participate in a little bedroom scene, Ames appears. The two start in a battle which ends when the villain is tossed over a few thousand feet of cliffs.

The film is well produced with a good cast. Direction is good, but the scenario is garbled in spots, while several little inconsistencies have been allowed to creep through. This ranks a little over the usual independent output and will probably hold up its end of a program in the smaller houses. *Sisk.*

THE LOVE GAMBLE

Banner Production made by Ben Verschleiser and distributed by Henry Ginsberg. Directed by Edward LeSaint and scenario by Harry O. Hoyt. At Loew's New York as half double bill Sept. 11. Running time, 65 minutes.
Peggy Mason.................Lillian Rich
Douglas Wyman...........Robert Frazer
Jennie Howard.............Pauline Garon
Jack Mason...............Arthur Rankin
Titi...................Kathleen Clifford
Peggy's Grandfather........James Marcus
Joe Wheeler.............Brooks Benedict

Well made and interesting—and that sums up this new one of the Banner list, which holds 13 in all.

The story tells of Peggy Mason, dissatisfied with her prospects in life and who invests a $1,000 legacy in a tea room venture which proves successful. In the tea room she meets Douglas Wyman, wealthy and

bored with life. Although loving him very much, the voice of rumor sticks itself in occasionally and it is revealed that Doug in the past hasn't gone to Sunday school in the spare time. She sticks to him and lets her old sweetheart, Joe Wheeler, go, because Doug is really square and they understand things better before the six reels of this one have been used up.

The cast is uniformly good, the production excellent, and the continuity as smooth as they come. In addition Frazer and Rich make a nice pair, while Kathleen Clifford and Pauline Garon chip in a little comedy relief as waitresses who serve the long hairs of Bohemia.

As a program feature for the intermediate houses this one should please. Some money has been spent and a maximum of result has been achieved. *Sisk.*

THE CIRCLE

Metro-Goldwyn production from the play by W. Somerset Maugham. Directed by Frank Borzage. At the Capitol, New York, week of Sept. 20. Running time, 66 min.
Elizabeth ....Eleanor Boardman
Edward Luton...........Malcolm McGregor
Lord Olive Choney............Alec Francis
Lady Catherine...........Eugenie Besserer
Portias ....George Fawcett
Mrs. Spenstone..............Eulalie Jensen
Arnold ....Creighton Hale
Dorkin ....Otto Hoffman

"The Circle," the W. Somerset Maugham play for which an all star cast was employed in the stage presentation, has a good cast but not one that can be compared with those who were selected for the stage presentation. No one is starred or featured. If anyone were, the honors should go to Eugenie Besserer, as she fairly walks away with the honors.

As a play "The Circle" was delightfully complete. As a screen entertainment it has been so adapted that it will meet with the approval of the rank and file of the screen house audiences. That is to say, the logical and happy ending has been switched to one that will appease the censors who undoubtedly would find it unpassable if the young wife skipped off with the man she really loved and left her sappy husband.

Frank Borzage deserves a vote of thanks for having filmed the play so faithfully that the switch became necessary to please the Woolworth picture audiences. He has turned out a screen version of the play that holds interest and has handled his players perfectly.

There is always something in favor of a short cast story so that the average viewer can follow the story easily. That is exactly the case here. Incidentally, it is also difficult for any player in a short cast to put over anything that is going to stand out above the others, but that is exactly what Eugenie Besserer does in this instance. She plays the Leslie Carter role to a fare-thee-well. She, George Fawcett and Alec Francis so far overshadow the youngsters in the film that the latter never have a chance.

Creighton Hale rather overplayed the sappy husband and it was a laugh to think what Malcolm McGregor could have done ha' he unleashed himself in the scrap scene written to fill in the desired ending.

"The Circle" is not going to be a boxoffice knockout by any means, but it is a picture that will pleasingly entertain in the bigger towns. In some of the small ones they are going to wonder what it is all about. *Fred.*

BELOW THE LINE

Warner Bros. production with Rin-Tin-Tin starred, June Marlowe and John Harron featured. Story and adaptation by Charles A. Logue. Directed by Herman Raymaker. At Warner's, New York, Sept. 19. Running time, 67 mins.
Rin-Tin-Tin ....Rin-Tin-Tin
Donald Cass...................John Harron
May Barton..................June Marlowe
Jamber Niles................Pat Hartigan
"Cuckoo" Niles.............Victor Potel
Deputy Sheriff....Charles (Heinie) Conklin
Rev. Barton...............Gilbert Clayton
Mrs. Cass....................Edith Yorke
The Sheriff.................Taylor Duncan

This is one of the best pictures starring a police dog that has come along in a year or so. The question now remains whether or not the public is tiring of dog stars. That seems to be the general impression in the trade as far as Class A houses are concerned. However, in the localities where they still go in for this type of picture the audiences will eat this one up.

There are a few minor details that should be looked to. There is one title which informs that the scene is laid in Louisiana and a little later there is a reward offered in Kentucky. Of course, if the action took place in Kentucky it wouldn't have been possible to have the alligators in the swamps, so it's quite possible the Louisiana title will have to stand and the producers will have to just hope that folks wont notice the difference in locale. Despite that, and other slipshod bits here and there, the story certainly has suspense and Rin-Tin-Tin does work. He isn't a dog that would ever get a thing in the show-ring, being short in body and a little low, but he does make a good flash in this picture. However, in his fight with the dogs the stuffed animals used in certain shots were all too noticeable.

The story is that of a trained dog shipped south to head a pack of blood hounds in trailing criminals. The crate in which he is shipped falls from the baggage car and lies in a swamp for three days with the 'gators prowling around it. Thus is the dog's spirit broken. It is further broken by the brutal trainer who takes him in hand and tries to beat him into doing his will. Then comes the change. It is through love that a new master brings back the animal's self confidence and in the end the dog saves his life, the church funds with which he has been entrusted, kills the villain and finally fights off the pack of savage blood hounds who would attack his beloved master and mistress.

June Marlowe and John Harron carry the juvenile love story along nicely. The acting honors go to Victor Potel in the role of the half-wit brother of the heavy, the latter played by Pat Hartigan. A comedy role is well handled by Charles Conklin who secured a lot out of a leaking roof scene and also in a dog training bit. *Fred.*

TESSIE

Arrow production made by Dallas M. Fitzgerald from Sewell Ford's story. May McAvoy starred. Direction by Mr. Fitzgerald. Reviewed in projection room Sept. 18. Running time, 65 mins.

Tessie ....May McAvoy
Roddy Welles.................Bobby Agnew
Barney Taylor....................Lee Moran
Mrs. Rodney Welles.......Myrtle Stedman
Mame McGuire.............Gertrude Short
Aunt Maggie....................Mary Gordon
Uncle Dan......................Frank Perry

Good little farcical comedy based on a "Saturday Evening Post" story and made in good fashion.

The story tells of a little candy counter girl, Tessie, and of her errant sweetheart, Barney, who threw the bologna and caught himself a society sweetie and left poor Tessie flat. Whereupon the son of the society sweetie sets out to take up the duties of the man who is soon to become his step-father. Mother, of course, misunderstands and thinks that Tessie is vamping the darling boy, while Tessie says little and gets a little revenge in razzing her ex-sweetie who is tied up with society for a short term.

The ending has the sappy son of the idle rich marrying the pretty daughter of the Irish and, in a good technical touch, the taxi in which they are riding fades right off the roadway into nothingness.

Miss McAvoy as Tessie gives a corking performance and Myrtle Stedman as the mother is also above par. Lee Moran is miscast as Barney, while Bobby Agnew dons a pair of cheaters and gets by with the rich son role. Frank Wood as an Irish father, introduced by a title as "Ireland's gift to evolution," is excellent, while several minor types are well taken.

The important thing about "Tessie" is that it is the first of many features lined up by Arrow for the new season and that it is mercifully free from the pathos and bunk which have permeated so many features from the independent market.

This one is a breezy and ingratiating little comedy able to hold up the feature end of a program in the intermediate and neighborhood houses. *Sisk.*

OFF THE HIGHWAY

Producers Distributing Corporation release directed by Tom Forman and made by the Hunt Stromberg unit. Scenarized from the novel, "Tatterly." At Loew's New York, Sept. 17. Running time, 65 mins.

Ella Tarrant......Marguerite De La Motte
Caleb Fry—Tatterly......William V. Mong
.........................William V. Mong
Donald Fry.....................John Bowers
Kiddon.......................Charles Gerrard
Castro.........................Josef Swickard
Barridio........................Gene Corrado

A funny combination of story, this picture, and yet very interesting because of a dual characterization and the strength of the theme.

Caleb Fry is an old man, wealthy but miserly. His nephew, Donald, is a struggling artist. And when the mandate comes from his uncle to either give up art or his share of an inheritance, the boy sticks to art and Ella Tarrant, his sweetheart. So the fortune is left to a spendthrift nephew, Kiddon, who immediately begins squandering the money.

But Caleb Fry has not died. Instead his manservant, Tatterly, who looked enough like him to have been his twin, fell over the desk and then Fry decided to fool his relatives, for he assumed the guise of Tatterly and let them bury "Caleb Fry." The usual happens for the spendthrift nephew who talks too much and the real Caleb Fry overhears. And the nephew who spurned the money lives sensibly.

The love interest is nice and the story fully justifies its running time. In production the casting has been well done with Mong shining brilliantly in the dual role. The photography in these scenes is apparently so well done that it defies detection in any detail. The female star, De La Motte is also good, as is John Bowers. Some artists' studio scenes will need shears, but aside from that, okay.

As a program feature for the intermediate houses, "Off the Highway" qualifies. *Sisk.*

SPOOK RANCH

Universal production, starring Hoot Gibson. Directed by Edward Laemmle. Story by Raymond Schrock and Edward Sedgwick. Photographed by Harry Neumann. At Loew's New York one day (Sept. 15) as half the bill. Runs about an hour.

Bill Bangs.......................Hoot Gibson
George Washington Black.....Jules Cowles
Navarre........................Tote Ducrow
Elvira.........................Helen Ferguson
Don Ramies...................Robert McKim
Sheriff............................Frank Rice

The Hoot Gibson series are now billed as Jewel productions, somewhat of a distinction over the pictures made by Jack Hoxie, Art Accord, Josie Sedgwick and other Universal cowboy stars, which are known only as Blue Streak Westerns. In spite of the Jewel label, however, "Spook Ranch," first of the new Gibson series, measures up as considerably below this breezy star's general average.

The blame rests where it so often does; on the poor, woe-begone plot. True, a ranch has been substituted for the usual haunted house, but the situations employ the same old bits. Bill Bangs, a hobo cowboy, breaks a plate over the head of the Chink, who refuses him a free meal and after quite a chase goes to jail for it. He is freed on the condition he investigate the haunted ranch and rid the community of its unholy fear. He finds it, of course, the rendezvous of the usual gang of outlaws and while cleaning things up meets and falls in love with the pretty girl held as prisoner there.

The comedy relief is provided, as it has been in dozens of films from Griffith's "One Exciting Night," down by the colored pal of the hero, who is ossified with fear throughout half the picture. His antics during the more spooky scenes are fairly funny, but a good deal more might have been done with the comedy situations.

It is in the fight scenes that "Spook Ranch" is least convincing. The photography and continuity are up to scratch, but Edward Laemmle's direction does not show any distinctive qualities of imagination Gibson is his usual manly hero, but does not go in for the clown stuff very strongly, leaving most of that to Jules Cowles as the coon, who does fairly well with the role. Helen Ferguson is very appealing as the girl.

Just about satisfactory for the neighborhood houses. Those who have seen Gibson before will expect something better.

The Outlaw's Daughter

Universal production starring Josie Sedgewick. Leading man is Edward Hearn. All other information missed at film's projection, and press sheet not ready as yet. Runs about hour.

The Josie Sedgewick series of Universals have been steadily improving and she stands now as the only real woman western star. This picture, "The Outlaw's Daughter," is as good and probably better than the majority of all western pictures. It is refreshing to say the least, to see the cowboy villains tamed by a trim little figure in the smartest tailored bull-dogger outfit imaginable.

Miss Sedgwick is a little fool on a horse, with a lightning draw on a gun, and even when she uses her sturdy fists as persuasive arguments. Reported to be the daughter of a notorious outlaw, a conscientious mining executive gives her a chance to show she's on the level in this picture. After many temptations she not only accomplishes that but proves to the world her old man also had been innocent.

There is a pippin of a fight near the end of the picture and a new thrill when the hero and heavy battle each other in one of those aerial cars suspended by wires over a deep chasm. The former is played by the likable Edward Hearn, best remembered as "The Man Without a Country," but not, for some reason, very prominent either before or since that Fox release.

The balance of the cast, direction, comic relief, photography and scenario are all good and the film should do very well in the neighborhood houses.

WITH THIS RING

Preferred Pictures distributed by B. P. Schulberg Productions. Suggested by the novel by Fanny Heaslip Lea. Directed by Fred C. Windemere. Privately shown in projection room Sept. 4. Runs about 62 minutes.

Cecille Vaughn....................Alyce Mills
John Wendell...............Forrest Stanley
Maid.............................Joan Standing
Tabitha Van Buren.........Eulalie Jensen
Rufus Van Buren.............Lou Tellegen
Donald Van Buren..........Donald Keith
Luella Van Buren..........Martha Mattox
Portuguese..................Dick Sutherland

While it is thoroughly trashy all the way through, "With This Ring," manages to be consistently entertaining. The plot holds a full share of action and possesses, in addition, the box office virtue of being spicy with super-sexed.

The film has several glaring deficiencies. The worst seem to be the titles, about as clumsily written a set as might be imagined. The one in which the heroine's second husband, coming suddenly upon his predecessor whom he has believed dead for the longest while, exclaims "Will wonders never cease!" may be accepted as a sample. Lou Tellegen has probably never been more disastrously miscast than as the prudish hypocrite he attempts here.

The story tells of a couple shipwrecked on the usual barren island and deciding to become married "in the sight of God" because they feel the chances of rescue are almost nil. Thinking that her pseudo-husband has been killed in a battle with the only other human on the island she accepts a chance to be saved by visiting pearl fishers. On her return to this country she is spurned by her lover's narrow-minded family but secretly and dishonorably courted by his scurvy older brother. In desperation she marries the hero's old friend and lawyer, chiefly to give her baby a name.

Then the illegitimate young husband, who naturally hasn't really been killed, comes on the scene, and the old Enoch Arden twist makes its appearance. The mess is straightened out when the noble lawyer explains that he "has never really been her husband in the full sense of the word," and agrees to an annulment.

Thus it may be seen that the plot, for all its sensationalism, holds the elements of interest. It has been handled moderately well by the director but there might have been considerable more comedy. There are several discrepencies, such as when after the titles have announced the heroine is returning to the three-a-day she is shown working in a regular legitimate musical show.

Aside from Tellegen the cast is very adequate. Alyce Mills makes up for in appearance what she lacks in emotional ability and in the desert island scenes seems to be as scantily clad as "Aloma." One sequence shows her bathing "au natural," but as she wears her hair very long, employs skin tights and is apparently 100 yards from the camera one misses thrills. Donald Keith is a likable juvenile, and such sterling character actresses as Eulalie Jensen and Martha Mattox have only bits.

Exhibitors might exploit the idea behind the title "With This Ring," indicating that the principals perform the wedding ceremony themselves instead of the more conventional way.

LORRAINE OF THE LIONS

Universal production directed by Edward Sedgewick. Story by Isadore Bernstein. Cast headed by Norman Kerry and Patsy Ruth Miller and also includes Philo Mc Cullough, Joseph J. Dowling, Harry Todd and Doreen Turner. At Loew's New York one day (Sept. 18) as half the bill. Runs about 65 minutes.

"Lorraine of the Lions" is one of the features of Universal's Second White List, which means it will be given a special plug in exploitation and salesmanship. From a strictly audience point of view (and assuming that that audience is not too discriminating) it should be quite a box office success.

Because, though utterly ridiculous, it is very well done for the most part and never becomes stupid or boring. It will profit by the current interest in South Sea Island stuff and also, though only in those larger cities where the show has played, by the renewed interest in gorilla life brought about by the successful legitimate comedy bearing the title of that ferocious animal.

Lorraine (Patsy Ruth Miller) has been wrecked as a child on a desert island, and there is solitude and with a gorilla for her only companion she has grown to beautiful, though very wild, young womanhood. Finally her whereabouts are discerned and a rescuing party headed by her grandfather and the handsome young tutor he has engaged for the girl take her from the island. After a strenuous complaint, she is allowed to bring the gorilla with her to civilization.

After the usual amusing incidents attending her transformation from a savage to a perfect lady she becomes thoroughly tamed and genteel. But not so the big monk, and finally when even Loraine loses her controlling and soothing influence on him, he goes off on a rampage and makes it merry for everybody concerned. These scenes, taken in a driving rainstorm and showing a fierce struggle between the ape and the hero (Norman Kerry) are particularly effective. The chase finally leads to a roof and from there the gorilla jumps to a window awning, where, finally at bay, he is shot to the ground in a realistic and powerfully directed bit.

The man who plays the animal (the billing does not divulge his name) gives an uncanny performance throughout. Perhaps his imitation of a gorilla is not the most lifelike in the world, but it is always horrible and convincing. Neither is Miss Miller's acting a true interpretation of how a girl who has been brought up with lions and monkeys would disport herself, but she is always cute and appealing. In the island scenes she makes an entrancing picture in a carefully planned, abbreviated costume and later in the civilized sequences she manages to be very amusing.

Kerry is as handsome a figure as ever, but has little to do other than attempt to battle the gorilla. The balance of the cast, the photography and the general atmosphere of the film serve to give it a dash of "class" not found in the ordinary program picture.

LONDON FILM REVIEWS

THE ONLY WAY

London, Sept. 4.

This First National-Herbert Wilcox picture marks a gigantic forward movement in British film production. No picture made in this country by British or American producers has ever been received with such genuine enthusiasm as was this one on its initial public screening at the Hippodrome Aug 28. Never in the history of a picture shown in this country has an audience deliberately refused to leave a theatre and called insistently for the leading actor and the producer as they did in this case.

The success of "The Only Way" is more remarkable from the fact that it has been somewhat of a dark horse. It was known First National was backing Herbert Wilcox and that Sydney Carton, a role he has played in the theatres since 189..

Herbert Wilcox has kept with reverential care to Freeman Willis' dramatization of Charles Dickens' "Tale of Two Cities." He has tried no "playing about" with the dramatic possibilities which are so rich in this story. For the general public he has made a "super," which will in every way justify the confidence of his backers.

The story requires no re-telling. Sir John Martin-Harvey has appeared in pictures before and has failed, notably in the screen version of "The Breed of the Treshams," made a few years ago. His performance of Sydney Carton now proves his previous screen failure was a matter of inferior direction. His performance here is a revelation. Harvey is no longer a young man, and has all the traditions of a stage career to fight against, but in this picturization of his most fa-

mous play he gives a remarkable performance. His Carton will live as a screen classic.

The casting of the support has, in the majority of cases, been exceedingly well judged. Fisher White, Ben Webster and Frederick Cooper all give fine performances. Frank Stanmore is good, but miscast as Mr. Joly. Out of a great number of clever small part shows, Gib McLaughlan stands out. Judd Green is also capital.

The women are not as good as the men. Madge Stewart is capable, and in the building up of this character Wilcox has taken one of his few liberties. Betty Faire does not show sincerity, but Mary Brough is excellent and could have had more to do. The mob work is excellent, and it's a great picture. *Gore.*

THE RAT

London, Sept. 7.

Adapted from the stage play by Ivor Novello and Constance Collier and presented by W. & F., "The Rat" is a masterpiece of sordid realism and animalism. If ever a picture depicted life in the rough, its unrestrained passion and animalism, this one is that one. And these things are accentuated by some of the best screen acting and direction seen over here.

Some of the episodes have never even been touched even by von Ströheim. To enumerate would be the gradual seduction of the Apache lad by the wealthy courtesan, and the attempted seduction of the pure young girl by the courtesan's "friends."

Zelie de Chaumet, a courtesan, falls in love with 'The Rat." He, however, has a little friend, a pure affair, and for a time he resists Zelie. He yields at last and only returns to his old allegiance when he learns his Odile is in danger from the villain, Stetz. Arriving in the nick of time, he kills this man. Odile is arrested for the crime and sooner than give the Rat away allows herself to be thought guilty. She is, however, acquitted by a sympathetic jury, and the couple start a new life.

The staging of this feature is extremely good, including all sets. Many scenes of a revue at the Folies Bergere are shown in discreet "long shots." Graham Cutts, the director, has done his work exceedingly well, but his use of a traveling camera, which seems never still, is annoying to the eyes.

Ivor Novello shows surprising sincerity and power in the title role and Isabel Jeans possesses not only seductive beauty of face and figure, but she can act. Mae Marsh is not good as Odile, and her performance is marred by her persistent use of mannerisms. "The Rat" will do well at the box office. *Gore.*

THE SHE DEVIL

London, Sept. 5.

This sequel to the "Nibelungs" is being given a premier run at the Capitol. It is the first picture put out by the newly solidified firm of Grangers Exclusives. The only wonder is that such an established firm should have thought of acquiring such an impossibility from the showman's point of view. Nothing in the history of the screen has ever reached the appalling morbidity and unrelieved gloom of this heavy German feature.

From first to last it is nothing but a mad piling up of horror and throughout its entire length there is not one struggling ray of brightness.

It has the heaviness of a catacomb and however fine are its scenic properties it is of little or no use o the average exhibitor.

After Hagen has killed Siegfried, beloved husband of Kriemhielda, she receives an offer of marriage from Attila, the Hun, and upon his swear-

ing to avenge her beloved's death becomes his queen. A child is born and Attila's adoration of the infant knows no bounds. Kriemhielda asks her relatives to visit the court of Attila with a view to having them slaughtered. This is done with all the genius of Germanic production, and having no one else to do to death Kriemhielda dies herself.

Several remarkable performances are given, notably by Rudolph Klein-Rogge and Margaret Schon, while every minor part is played with artistry. However, "The She Devil" will cast her gloom over any cinema she enters. *Gore.*

FORBIDDEN CARGOES

London, Sept. 5.

Handled by "W. & F.," a firm which seldom handles anything beyond American and Colonial features but has recently started looking for good native material, this picture is of the supposedly good old English type replete with heroes and villains in Hessian boots, long riding coats, and all the romance of two centuries ago.

It is a very ordinary penny novelette type of story without logic or dramatic strength. The interior scenes are well done, and the exteriors, made at Polperro, in Cornwall, are much too good for the poor story.

The cast has little acting pull. Peggy Hyland is the typical "pretty leading lady," Guy Tilden Wright is the type of amateur who has helped to bring the British film trade into its present perilous condition, and Clifford McLaglen gives a very ordinary performance. As is usual in this class of British picture the best performances come from small part but good actors, such as James Barber and Bob Vallis. The photography is good.

This film has been hanging about for some time, having been made with capital greatly subscribed by one of its ambitious players, and now that it has been shown it will make but little difference to the upward or downward trend of home production. *Gore.*

MAN ON THE BOX

Warner Bros. production starring Syd Chaplin. From the novel and play by Harold McGrath. Directed by Charles Reisner. Shown at Warner's New York City, week April 26, 1925. Running time 80 minutes.

Bob Warburton	Syd Chaplin
Bob's Brother-in-Law	David Butler
Betty Annesly	Alice Calhoun
Mrs. Lampton (Inventor's wife)	Kathleen Calhoun
Mr. Lampton (Inventor)	Theodore Lorch
Bob's Sister	Helene Costello
Col. Annesly	E. J. Ratcliffe
Badkoff ..Count's Spy)	Charles F. Reisner
Count Karaloff	Charles Gerrard
Warburton, Sr.	Henry Barrowes

The Warner Brothers gave a special trade and press showing of "The Man On The Box" at their theatre early last Saturday morning. Those invited got a number of titters and a few laughs out of the picture, but the screen production is far from being an uproarious farce. It is funny and Syd Chaplin is quite as good as he was in "Charley's Aunt" in a role that is practically the same in its general contour, for it gives him the same opportunity to appear straight and as a dame as in the previous characterization.

However, "The Man On The Box" isn't a "Charley's Aunt" either its laughs, action or box office power that it will have. "Charley's Aunt" was a laugh and box office wow. "The Man on the Box" isn't nearly as laughable nor does it seem to carry the kick. It is, nevertheless, a good entertaining picture. A little long, perhaps, and draggy in spots and would be improved if anywhere from 10 to 20 minutes were eliminated as shown.

The biggest laugh in the picture is one that will have to be taken out in several states to pass the censors. It is the scene where Chaplin, in trying to escape from a cop, who is chasing him, runs into the bushes in the park with the copper in full pursuit. A startled couple dash out of the bushes as they dash in.

The story of "The Man On The Box" is a little too well known generally to need extended explanation here. The picture had previously been done with Max Figman by the Lasky Co. about 11 years ago. Previous to that it had been played on the stage with Henry E. Dixey as the star. The present version is somewhat changed from the former screen presentation.

Chaplin as Bob Warburton is the son of a man of wealth and he is backing an invention which has to do with air planes. A representative of the United States wants to purchase the plans and the inventor agrees to turn them over, he being jealous of the youthful backer who seems to have made a hit with the inventor's wife. There are other elements in the race and a count from Continental Europe is trying to secure the plans for his country. He calls the inventor from his home so that his spy may enter and steal the papers. The inventor on finding that the phone call has been a hoax suspects the young backer as trying to get him out of the way so that he may make love to the wife.

On his return when he finds the young man in the wife's bedroom and the woman in a swoon, believes the worst. In reality the wife has summoned the young man to rid the room of the spy, who is under her bed. Follows a series of hand-to-hand tussles, chases and all the usual comedy tricks. They are mildly laughable, but not screamingly funny.

Syd Chaplin is funny, but the balance of the cast is not, with the exception of Charles Reisner, who in addition to playing the principal low comedy spy, also directed the picture. Reisner and Chaplin are a funny pair and they might be teamed up to advantage, providing of course, that they get a real script that they can do things with. In this one it is easily seen what was in the script and what the director furnished and the odds are all in the favor of Reisner, for he has certainly gagged the picture as much as it was possible to do.

The two Calhoun girls are in the picture, Alice, who plays the ingenue lead fairly well, and Kathleen, who plays the inventor's wife.

"The Man On The Box" will get some money, but it won't ever prove to be a world-beater. *Fred.*

THE TOWER OF LIES

Metro-Goldwyn production adapted from Selma Lagerlof's novel "The Emperor of Portugallia" by Agnes Christine Johnson and Max Marcin. Directed by Victor Seastrom with Norma Shearer and Lon Chaney starred. Reviewed at the Capitol, New York, Sept. 27 week. Running time, about 80 minutes.

Glory, daughter of Jan....Norma Shearer
Jan....Lon Chaney
Lars Gunnerson....Ian Keith
Katrina, Jan's Wife....Claire McDowell
August....William Haines
Erik Gunnerson....David Torrence

Notwithstanding that "Tower of Lies" is a sincerely made picture and excellent from the artistic and literary viewpoints, it is too heavy for the picture audiences. When finished the impression left is that one more prostitute has reformed and been forgiven.

Norma Shearer and Lon Chaney are co-starred and this will probably give it some draught; also that Victor Seastrom, who made "He Who Gets Slapped" with Shearer and Chaney, also made this one will count—but in the final analysis "Tower of Lies" can't measure up.

The thread of fantasy in the theme is well planted by the director and the acting of Chaney goes a long way toward making it bearable, but the theme itself is ponderous and in its scenario form advanced largely by means of subtitles. Getting down to points, the fault with the whole thing is that it isn't a movie story by any stretch of the imagination.

The locale is apparently some Scandinavian country. Jan, a rough farmer, finds love playing an important part in his life when a baby daughter is born. She grows to be his pride but when the nephew of their former landlord gets bad over back rents, the girl goes to the city to make money.

She doesn't come back for many years. Finally, she does after rumors that she had turned prostitute had preceded her to town. By this time her father's mind had been dimmed and her mother ashamed. Moreover, the good people of the town ordered her to leave. So she packed off again, her demented father chasing. But she got to the boat before he did—and he ran off the pier and drowned. A moment later the man responsible for her downfall was also drowned—which put two deaths close together. The windup had the girl back on the farm, sowing wheat behind furrows made by a childhood sweetheart. And for the fadeout, Seastrom had the lovers pose together against a sunset effect much in the manner of a Millet painting.

The fantasy concerned enters where the father, when the girl was young, called her his Empress of Portugallia, a land where everything was as we wished it. As he grew demented, he imagined himself the Emperor and still thought of the daughter as his Empress.

Primarily, the fault with the story itself is its illogical explanation of how the girl went wrong. That a woman, well bred, with parental love always about her, would turn prostitute for purely pecuniary reasons is silly. Furthermore, if she had gone into the business for that purpose she would have stopped immediately she had raised enough dough to raise the mortgage on the old homestead. Why she stayed in the city so long is unexplained, and another silly thing is that the villagers should march in a body (for that sort of stuff is strictly the hokum from Hohokus) and tell her to hop. One more funny thing is that the cast is almost entirely brunette, while the Scandinavian people are usually blondes.

The acting is aces and the direction masterful. But with all this, "Tower of Lies" can never be anything more than a soggy picture made bearable by the leavening forces of Seastrom, Chaney and Shearer. *Sisk.*

WHAT FOOLS MEN

First National picture directed by George Archainbaud. Adapted from a novel by H. K. Webster. At the Cameo, New York, week Sept. 27. Running time, around 65 minutes.

Joseph Greer....Lewis Stone
Beatrice....Shirley Mason
Jennie McArthur....Barbara Bedford
Vi Williamson....Ethel Grey Terry
George Burns....Hugh Allan
Lancing Ware....John Patrick
John Williamson....David Torrence
"Handsome"....Tom Wilson
Henry Craven....Lewis Dayton

Nicely produced picture but no smash in the story to lift it above being an intermediate release. Lewis Stone's name and the production give it a major house rating but it's one of those films that slip by and is never thought of again.

Located in Chicago the story relates of Greer (Stone) who comes north from South America to instal his money saving invention with a powerful company. Widowed or divorced, he sends to the Coast for his daughter (Miss Mason) who, being motherless, is socially guided by the concern's president's wife, as the latter has a yearning for Greer. Meanwhile, the daughter wins the good looking chauffeur (Hugh Allan) with the pilot pulling her away from a wild party to get himself fired. Flying for the air mail service the former chauffeur marries the girl but Greer is now financially broke as a result of the president's wife having exaggerated their affair to her husband after Greer has lessened in his attentions. The finish has the daughter and the new son-in-law reviving their dad's spirit in a low caste boarding house.

Archainbaud has given the picture little inspiration and it plays along, tells its story and closes out. Comedy is inserted for more or less value at widely separated points with the character of the daughter not evoking a great deal of sympathy. There is more interest surrounding Greer's feminine secretary (Barbara Bedford) who is obviously in love with her boss. The presumption is that they marry but you can't prove it by the picture.

Stone gives his usual capable performance while Miss Mason is as flighty as required in the no-mother-to-guide-her characterization. Allan is a good looking youngster impressing as capable of better material. Barbara Bedford was prominent enough to head the feminine players.

Nice and neat, but no kick. *Skig.*

SON OF HIS FATHER

Famous Players production of Harold Bell Wright's story. Adapted to the screen by Anthony Coldeway and directed by Victor Fleming. Bessie Love, Warner Baxter and Raymond Hatton featured. At the Rialto, New York, Sept. 27, week. Running time, 75 minutes.

Nora....Bessie Love
"Big Boy" Morgan....Warner Baxter
Charlie Grey....Raymond Hatton
Holdbrook....Walter McGrail
Zobester....Carl Stockdale
Larry....Billy Eugene
Indian Pete....James Farley
Pablo....Charles Stevens
Dolores....Valentina Semina
Wing....George Kuwa

One more of Harold Bell Wright's handsome hero and dirty villain stories, localed in the West and actionless for the greater part. This time the western stuff is liberally sprinkled with shamrock, for the heroine (Bessie Love) is Irish and straight from the old country with a brogue thick enough to be cut with a knife.

The villain in this is a smuggler over the Mexican border, his business being to supply guns to rebels, and he is aiming to take the hero's ranch away because aforementioned hero's father owed him some money. And although the son offered to pay it, mean villain demanded his ranch as per agreement. And although villain came near winning, love and justice triumphed for a sugary ending.

Fleming's direction and excellent injection of nice bits saved the while business from being a loss. Raymond Hatton, in one of those pill eating, hypochondriac roles injected for comedy relief, was very unfunny. The other principals, however, did nicely, with Miss Love taking the acting honors.

"Son of His Father" is hardly first class movie stuff and unless the community happens to be mad on Harold Bell Wright, and so far his movies haven't started any riots, there is no other classification for this one than just a western and not so exciting at that. *Sisk.*

LENA RIVERS

Arrow production directed and adapted by Whitman Bennett from Mary J. Holmes' novel of the same name. At the Stanley, New York, one day (Sept. 25). Runs about 70 minutes.

Henry Rivers Grahme....Earle Williams
Durward Belmont....Johnny Walker
Lena Rivers....Gladys Hulette
Carrie Nichols....Edna Murphy
Granny Nichols....Marcia Harris
Mathilde Nichols....Doris Rankin
Anna Nichols....Irma Harrison
Henry Grahme, Sr.....Frank Sheridan
Capt. Atherton....Herman Lieb
The old sea dog....Harlan Knight
John Nichols....William P. Hayes
Grandfather Nichols....Frank Andrews

As a popular novel a couple of decades ago "Lena Rivers" was one of those million-copy affairs and as a stock and road show its success was almost proportional.

As a film it is nothing less than terrible. If there ever has been a worse collection of cheap heroics, obvious melodramatics and dull sob stuff in one picture before, it is hard to remember when.

The severe criticism goes for the cast, too, as the acting is almost as bad as the scenario, with this qualification that the blame apparently rests more upon the director than on the individual players.

With such experienced troupers as Earle Williams, Gladys Hulette, Johnny Walker, Doris Rankin, Edna Murphy, Marcia Harris and others, only Miss Hulette gives a half-way adequate performance. The coaching of the cast is not the only way in which the direction has fallen down as the action is sluggish, the atmosphere amateurish and pretty nearly everything else is wrong.

The story, of thoroughly familiar pattern, tells of a New England Cinderella, who manages to be a little Miss Fix-it, a ray of sunshine and a pain in the neck all in one.

In spite of the potent appeal behind its title it is almost inconceivable that "Lena Rivers" will get by as a box office attraction. It is of the vintage of 1910, and a poor specimen at th...

FIGHTING YOUTH

Perfection production released by Columbia and distributed by Apollo. Story by Paul Archer. Directed by Reeves Eason and photographed by George Meehan. Features William Fairbanks and Pauline Garon. At the Stanley, New York, one day (Sept. 22). Runs 56 minutes.

Dick Covington....William Fairbanks
Jean Manley....Pauline Garon
Judge Manley....George Periolat
Harold Brennty....William Norton Bailey
Paddy O'Ryan....Pat Harmon
"Murdering" Mooney....Frank Hagney
Gangster....Tom Carr
Referee....Jack Britton

Practically every bit that has ever been used in boxing pictures is present in all its triteness in "Fighting Youth." Even with this handicap it manages to be a breezy and moderately bright little program attraction. These stories about amateur prize fighters, just like those about Irish cops and demure little chorus girls, seem to hold an audience appeal that not all the hackneyed teamment in the world can obliterate.

The hero this time, Dick Covington, is a young society man who can control neither his temper nor his fists. Consequently his fiance, Jean, threatens to break off their engagement unless he promises to become more pacific. He vows never to battle again but is inveigled by an unscrupulous rival into accepting a challenge bout at a charitable function.

Jean, of course, is very angry until she is insulted by the big roughneck professional who is to fight her sweetie. She then forgives the latter and entreats him to mop up the bully.

But the slick rival has not used up all his (and the movies') bag of tricks yet. On the day of the fight he has Dick kidnapped and taken to a lonely spot way out in the country. The hero hammers his way through the three guards and by an incredible voyage of automobile, aeroplane and even swimming arrives at the arena just as the white feather is, figuratively, being awarded to him.

In the first round Dick, winded and weary, receives a severe beating. He is saved by the bell. During the moment's intermission before the second round dainty little Jean, as countless picture heroines before her have done, sneaks up to his corner and beseeches him to knock the "champeen" for a row of pink elephants. He does and then takes the young lady to his manly, though somewhat bare, chest.

It's the applesauce, but countless other films of this type have been liked and there's no reason why this one shouldn't be.

William Fairbanks is a smooth and muscular hero, while Pauline Garon is as deliciously and precociously petite as ever. The balance of the cast, direction and photography are satisfactory and, though the fight scenes are not remarkable for their realism, they are exciting enough to please the gullible.

WITHOUT MERCY

P. D. C. release made by Metropolitan Pictures and directed by George Melford. Scenario by Monte Katterjohn. Dorothy Phillips featured. At Loew's New York, Sept. 25, as half double bill. Running time, 58 minutes.

Sir Melmuth Craven....Rockliffe Fellowes
John Orme....Robert Ames
Enid Garth....Dorothy Phillips
Marguerite Garth....Vera Reynolds
Mrs. Gordon....Tempe Piggett

Good program picture made from a story which is interesting and also a bit far fetched. Its emotional elements are original and the theme sticks closely to relating how one woman revenged herself on a man who had years before treated her shamefully.

In the Argentine the family of Enid Garth discovered valuable mines. Melmuth Craven, to learn their location, apparently kidnaped Enid and flogged her into insensibility. Years later Enid Garth became the head of a great London banking house and the same Craven came into London society as Sir Melmuth Craven. He sought her daughter and also sought loans from her bank. Enid refused him the daughter, but the loan was made on her own terms and before she had finished with him, he had been taken away by the London police as a murderer.

Good acting features this celluloid strip, with Miss Phillips and Mr. Fellowes counting strongly. Vera Reynolds as the young daughter looked nicely, while Robert Ames as the lover who eventually got the girl, screened very well. This legit actor certainly conducted himself professionally before the lenses.

"Without Mercy" is good intermediate theatre fodder and its well ordered production, competent direction and acting make it an okeh feature bet.

THE FEAR FIGHTER

Rayart release produced by Harry Brown. Billy Sullivan starred with direction by Al Rogell. Story by Grover Jones. At Loew's New York, Sept. 25, as half double bill. Running time, 65 minutes.

Billy Griffin........................Billy Sullivan
Catherine Curtis ....Ruth Dwyer
James Curtis....................J. P. MacGowan

Corking independent comedy, with boxing as background and a nice love story. Billy Griffin, it seems, loved the daughter of James Curtis, boxing manager, and the father said that if Billy wanted his daughter he'd have to fight for her.

Billy didn't know how to fight, yet to shake off suspicion of a yellow streak, he put on the gloves and they were still on him after one of papa's dukes had smacked him for a fadeout.

This fadeout made Billy lose his memory and soon he was in jail. His cell-mate was a former champ, played by Gunboat Smith, who soon discovered that the boy had a natural punch. Before the 90 day was up Billy had a punch like a pile driver. So, once more out (and the memory still gone) he began knocking over fighters right and left and gained so much fame he was matched to meet the lightweight champ. Just about that time, he regained his memory and couldn't recall a thing about being a fighter.

It took a lot of coaxing to get him into the ring on the fight night. For the first few rounds he looked ridiculous. Finally his sweetie called at him and hollered that he was yellow, which made him so sore he mopped up the champ, received a lot of applause and then didn't speak to her. It all came around to the happy finish point—after a rousing motorcycle chase.

Sullivan, apparently a good stunt man who is good looking, athletic and not a bad actor, flashes as a new one and looks good. *Sisk.*

EXCHANGE OF WIVES

Metro-Goldwyn release, produced by Hobart Henley. Adapted by Frederic and Fanny Hatton from the story by Cosmo Hamilton. At the Capitol, New York, Oct. 4 week. Running time, 60 minutes.

Margaret Rathburn ....Eleanor Boardman
John Rathburn ....Lew Cody
Ellen Moran........................Renee Adoree
Victor Moran ....Creighton Hale

Probably one of the best farce-comedies ever turned out by any firm, yet made economically with a cast of four and by a director who has inserted a laugh for almost every minute. It is rich, rare and as racy as you'd care to see in spots, and although some of this naughtiness may be eliminated by the censors in Ohio, Pennsylvania and Maryland there will still be left a sure-fire picture.

The story is very simple. A tame man marries a woman who is continually crying out loud for loving and petting. A tame woman marries a man who likes to trot around a bit and who doesn't appreciate his wife. They live side by side. What happens is that the wild wife and the wild husband meet, while the tame husband and the tame wife meet. And things go along until the tame wife gets them all at a mountain camp, and there decrees that there shall be an exchange of wives and that her husband shall have the other man's wife and that she shall have the other man. This is all done nicely, with no hint of suggestiveness, for the rules had the men living in the big house and the women sleeping in separate cabins. But each woman was to cook for her man, and that eventually smoothed out affairs, for the wild man had a rapacious appetite while the wild woman was good only in opening canned soups, etc. On the other hand, the tame wife was a great cook and the tame husband was appreciative of good grup, so he got along well. Before it was all over, the tame husband had tamed his wild wife by turning her across the knee to deliver a few blows to the rear, while the tame wife had her wild husband on his knees begging for mercy and lots of it.

Henley's raciness in direction creeps out in handling Miss Adoree, for she is a woman with much sex appeal, and he photos it all. In the interests of family audiences and the houses playing Sunday films in the territories where there is sentiment against such a practice she should have worn a brassier constantly, and Henley shouldn't have been so anxious to show off the outlines of the lady's breasts. Maybe it's good stuff for big city crowds, but, notwithstanding, it is T. N. T. for the church elements, which are working for stringent censorship.

However, that is a phase concerned purely with the producers, and if they wanted to take the chance it's their business, insomuch as the reflection will be on them. It's likely to get some of the smaller exhibitors in bad with his clientele, however.

On the whole, though, it is a finely made film which reflects much credit on Henley, for he hasn't spent a lot of money on this one, and what lavish effects he used are confined solely to bedrooms.

For first-runs a sure thing; for the smaller houses, dependent on length of run and the seriousness with which the community takes morality. *Sisk.*

THANK YOU

John Golden Production presented by William Fox. From the play of the same title by Winchell Smith and Tom Cushing. Directed by John Ford. At the Rialto, New York, week of Oct. 4. Running time, 75 mins.

Kenneth Jamieson...........George O'Brien
Diane.........................Jacqueline Logan
David Lee.........................Alec Francis
Andy..............J. Farrell MacDonald
Mr. Jones.....................Cyril Chadwick
Mrs. Jones...................Edith Bostwick
Miss Blodgett....................Vivian Ogden
Dr. Cobb..........................James Neill
Sweet, Jr..........................Billy Rinaldi
Willie Jones...............Maurice Murphy
Sweet, Sr...................Robert Milasch
Jamieson, Sr..............George Fawcett
Millie Jones..................Marion Harlan
Gossip.................................Ida Moore
Gossip..........................Frankie Bailey

"Thank You" as a play was a corking comedy drama. It may not have been a tremendous box office wallop, but it went along for a number of months in New York and got some money. As a screen entertainment it has lost much of the value it had on the stage and the only place that the blame can be laid is at the doorsteps of the adaptor and the director. The material was "there" in the original script; in the picture, it is missing. The result is "just another picture" where it might have been a classic.

It is, however, a picture that each and every exhibitor can go to the ministers and get their support, as it is an open and shut bid for better wages for preachers.

"Thank You" cannot be counted on to do miracles at the box office. It will satisfy, for the most part, the average audience, but it is somewhat too long in its present shape. It could have at least 10 minutes dropped from the running time and the story would still get over.

It is well played, particularly in the roles handled by Alec Francis, Jacqueline Logan, J. Farrell MacDonald, George O'Brien and Vivia Ogden. The cast looks as though a try was being made for an all star aggregation on the Fox lot when they went after this one. In addition to the above names also is listed George Fawcett and James Neill. Francis, Fawcett and Miss Ogden carry away the honors in the character roles, while Miss Logan and O'Brien supply the love interest.

For an exploitation stunt the exhibitor might work out a "Politeness Day" or week, as the case might be, with one of the local dailies. Possibly a 'dollar man," similar to the old Raffles stunt used by the papers as a circulation builder, might be worked out. The idea here is that you get a dollar providing you say "Thank You" to the right person for some favor accorded you. It would undoubtedly promote interest and get word-of-mouth publicity at slight cost. The chances are the paper hooked up with would stand the biggest part of the expense. *Fred.*

GO STRAIGHT

A. B. P. Schulberg production featuring Owen Moore and Gladys Hulette. Reviewed at the Broadway, New York, where it was shown as the picture part of a combination bill. Running time, 63 minutes.

Gilda Hart.......................Gladys Hulette
Mrs. Rhodes..........................Mary Carr
Billy Rhodes.......................Owen Moore

Another of Schulberg's new product and a fair piece of product for the combination and neighborhood houses.

The story concerns a girl who was once mixed up with a gang of crooks. With them she was the lure but after a time, she decided to go straight. Getting a job in a bank, she fell in love with her employer, the manager.

Therefore, when the crooks put it up to her that she must help them in a payroll theft, she refused and sneaking to the bank, took the payroll to the manager's home leaving it with his mother. But the manager, hearing rumors of a robbery, was in the bank and when the burglars came, was knocked out. The detectives on the job arrive at the nest of the crooks only to find the girl there. She had been pleading for the whereabouts of the hero. When a telephone call is made to his house and it is discovered that the payroll is safe, they go into the clinch fadeout.

Owen Moore plays his part well, while Gladys Hulette also does okeh, except that in spots her makeup is bad. Directly, this refers to her nose makeup, for in some full face views, that organ shows up badly, being darker on the end that the rest of the face. Mary Carr does the mother part well, and the burglar roles are well handled.

Scenario is fast a direction good with the comedy relief well cared for. *Sisk.*

A LOVER'S OATH

Astor Distribution Corp. production starring Ramon Novarro, with Kathleen Key featured. Directed by Ferdinand P. Earle Edited by Milton Sills. Photographed by George Benoit. At Loew's New York, one day (Sept. 29), as half the bill. Runs 70 minutes.

Ben Ali..........................Ramon Novarro
Sherin..............................Kathleen Key
Hassen ben Sabbath..........Edwin Stevens
Omar Khayyam...............Frederick Warde
Hassan's Wife...............Hedwig Reicher
Omar's Servant..............Shitz Edwards
Commander of the Faithful.Charles A. Post
Prince Yussuf.....Arthur Edmund Carewe
Sheik Rustum....................Paul Wigel
His Son.......................Phillippe de Lacy
Haja..............................Warren Rodgers

In certain respects "A Lover's Oath" almost qualifies as a program house edition of "The Thief of Bagdad" while in others it is distinctly ordinary film fare. If the very considerable amount of money spent in bringing this fantasy, based on the "Rubaiyat of Omar Khayyam," to the screen had been more judiciously distributed a better picture would have been forthcoming.

The principal fault lies in the editing and handling of the scenario. Since Milton Sills, the actor, is credited with the supervision he and the director, Ferdinand Earle, must share the blame. The continuity is wretched, and the action so jerky and disconnected it becomes almost a task to follow the story.

On the other hand the sets are bizarre, imaginative and very often beautiful, rivalling any ever seen in such productions. Unfortunately the technical end of the photographic work has not kept pace, so that the magnificently handsome and unique scenery does not always look as impressive as it should. Earle has also gone in for several fantastic pictorial shots, chiefly of the sky and the clouds, but though they are impressive they lose by not being introduced properly.

Against this unusual background the rather common-place handling of the story seems almost ludicrous in spots. Particularly unfortunate is the comedy relief, consisting of such glaring bits as a parrot's continued chirping "Thou speakest a mouthful."

The plot introduces Omar as a leader of his people but deals rather with the love of his nephew, Ben Ali, for the fairest daughter of the tribe. The last expression sounds like a quotation from one of the titles, which manage to be rather sickeningly gushy when they do not quote directly from the "Rubaiyat."

The cast is an excellent one but it is laboring under difficulties. The Apolloesque Novarro has little to do but loll around and murmur such love words as "O moon of my delight! I will build for thee the alabaster palaces of my dreams—for thee, beloved, I will conquer the seven kingdoms of the earth," and so on nux vomica.

Miss Key is astonishingly pretty and such sterling players as Frederick Warde, Hedwig Reicher, Edwin Stevens and Paul Wigel lend a legitimate classical atmosphere.

For the neighborhood stands the film impresses as a novelty. Though it may bore at times, its splendid sets and the serious effort to put across something better class than usual should cause it to be favorably received.

SOME PUN'KINS

I. E. Chadwick production starring Charles Ray. Directed by Jerome Storm. Story by Bert Woodruff and Charles E. Banks. Photographed by Phillip Tannura and James Brown. At Loew's New York one day (Sept. 29) as half the bill. Runs about 64 minutes.

Lem Blossom....................Charles Ray
Pa Blossom....................George Fawcett
Ma Blossom....................Fanny Midgely
Mary Griggs....................Duane Thompson
Josh Griggs....................Bert Woodruff
Tom Perkins....................Hallam Cooley
Constable....................William Courtreight
Gossip....................Ida Lewis

A glance at the characters listed above indicates that this is another rural film, almost identical to some dozen others in which Charles Ray has appeared. The Chadwick company makes no bones about it for its press-staff sheet screams in its most prominent headline "Charles Ray is the Same Old Hick in 'Some Pun'kins.'"

That brings up the interesting question as to whether Ray's at-one-time substantial popularity waned because he so strictly held to type. Certainly "Miles Standish" in which he played a similarly bashful but otherwise totally different sort of youth, did anything but prove that a switch would bring him back in the spotlight.

It would seem that Chadwick is on the right track if all it is looking for is a very pleasing program picture. Their first Ray film won't do for the big houses, but as general entertainment, regardless of how many times Ray has been seen doing exactly the same kind of characterization, it is a much better bet than four-fifths of the neighborhood theatre fuel released by independents and the big babies alike.

This time, Ray emerges from sapdom to glory in his home town by putting across a deal in which he outwits an unscrupulous concern that is trying to gyp the farmers out of the proper returns for their pumpkin crop. Incidentally, as chief of the fire department, he extinguishes a blaze almost single-handed by using a trick invention of his that had previously been the joke of the village. He saves his father from going to jail as a bootlegger, recoups the family fortune and wins the one and only from the city slicker who has done all the dirt.

The best scenes, as in the old Ray releases, are in those sequences in church and at a party, wherein Lem, the hero, suffers acutely from the usual rustic inferiority complex in regard to his city rival. The love bits are directed most skillfully and with Duane Thompson, a charming newcomer, playing opposite, Ray is once more at his best.

While it is not exactly a rural idyll or anything remotely resembling that, there are many people throughout the country who will like "Some Pun'kins" a great deal.

HELL'S HIGHROAD

Cecil B. DeMille production released by Producers Distributing Corporation. Starring Leatrice Joy. Directed by Rupert Julian. From the novel by Ernest Pascal. Adapted by Leonore Coffee and Eve Unsell. At Loew's New York one day (Oct. 1). Runs about 70 minutes. Generally released about three weeks ago.

Judy Nichols....................Leatrice Joy
Ronald McKane....................Edmund Burns
Sanford Gillespie....................Robert Edeson
Anne Broderick....................Julia Faye
Dorothy Harmon....................Helene Sullivan

"Hell's Highroad," judged strictly as to its quality, doesn't rate among the leaders, but many worse productions have been screened at the biggest Broadway houses. But that does not say the first DeMille independent is a good feature, but rather that the first run standard is pretty low.

The unfortunate part is that "Hell's Highroad" is far from being a wow for the neighborhood theatres. It is not typical DeMille stuff nor is there an adequate portion of action. It stands as an "in-between" society drama, preaching the time-worn sermon of gold versus happiness.

The film opens in the squalid room of a Chicago shop girl, Judy Nichols. She is obsessed with a hatred for poverty and for this reason refuses to marry Ronald McKane, the struggling engineer who has nothing to boast of but his ambitions. Judy received word of a bequest from a deceased uncle and in her joy promises to become McKane's wife. The first of several good twists comes when she learns the legacy is $9.43 or something very near that.

The young couple marry anyhow and Judy sets about getting a wealthy admirer of hers interested in her husband. The latter, aided by this influence, becomes a successful broker and catches his wife's lust for dough. Finally he becomes so bad that she entreats the influential heavy to break him. The villain agrees after exhorting the usual promise from her in return. The finish finds both of the young pair with their eyes opened, and since the third angle of the triangle does not insist upon his payment everything is Jake.

One very broad situation that will attract attention features the events happening on the first night of the honeymoon. Just in the nick of time the ardent husband is called away upon a business deal as part of his rival's campaign to have the marital arrangement in an uproar from the first. Three or four silly and far-fetched incidents are going to irritate those with any sense of balance.

Miss Joy is competent, but her part does not permit much real acting. Edmund Burns is a likeable leading man. Honors go to the veteran, Robert Edeson, as the elderly Lothario. The settings are never lavish but fairly rich-looking and sightly.

Altogether it is not a bad affair, but one expects something much more worth while or at least entertaining from Mr. DeMille. The only thing most film-goers will carry away with them will be the memory of that unmentionable outfit worn by Julia Faye as she does her daily dozen.

THE MIDSHIPMAN

Metro-Goldwyn-Mayer picture starring Ramon Novarro. Directed by Christy Cabanne and produced under the supervision of the U. S. Navy Department. At the Capitol, New York, week Oct. 11. Running time, 74 mins.

Midshipman Randall ....Ramon Novarro
Patricia Lawrence ......Harriet Hammond
Ted Lawrence ....Wesley Barry
Mrs. Randall ....Margaret Seddon
Basil Courtney ....Crawford Kent
"Fat" ....Maurice Ryan
"Tex" ....Harold Goodwin
Midshipman "Spud" ....William Boyd

The follow up on Richard Barthelmess' "Classmates" (sanctioned by and produced under the supervision of the West Point authorities) and as good propaganda for the Middies as "Classmates" was for the Cadets. Both are corking pictures and each picturesque.

The story told is a secondary consideration as it's the Naval Academy, the student corps, the inside angle on the routine of the Government institution and the comedy evolved that make the picture. It closely follows the comedy inserts which "Classmates" had in the arrival of the plebes, their difficulties and the horseplay they must undergo at the will of upper classmen. However, this tale stays within the limits of Annapolis while "Classmates" took a leap to South America before again reaching the Point and its climax.

Cabanne, the director, throws the spirit behind this nautical school into an audience chiefly because of the principal boys in the cast, the situations and setting. The women are woefully weak albeit there are only a couple of any importance. Novarro makes a good looking undergraduate and plays both naturally and easily to convince. In this respect Harold Goodwin provided more than average support as the boy with whom Randall (Novarro) continually crosses swords during their four years at the Academy. Wesley Barry, now so grown as to be genuinely acceptable as a student in a major institution, also does well in a secondary role while Crawford Kent as the film's civilian villain suffices.

High lights are two parade flashes, an actual mess hall scene, an authentic June Ball and the graduating exercises with Secretary of the Navy Wilbur, giving out the diplomas. The latter scene is the one which caused some controversy in Washington at the time when it was proposed that President Coolidge should enter the picture in giving away the sheepskins inasmuch as the film was ostensibly propaganda for the Navy. Permission was willingly granted the celluloid company to have Novarro take his place with the graduating class so that he might march up and receive an unsigned diploma. The smiling faces of the officials on the rostrum in this scene may probably be taken two ways.

It's a clean picture, scrupulously clean. So much so that when the villain abducts the girl on his yacht the purpose is marriage. It is here that the Navy Department throws in a couple of pursuing destroyers and a 'plane for good measure. Previously, and at the opening of the film, a couple of inserts from the weeklies reveal the "first line of defense" steaming along and at target practice.

They laughed plenty over the comedy in this release at the Capitol Sunday afternoon. Cabanne has seemingly taken no liberties to send the photoplay beyond the realm of probability. If some of the action does become exaggerated it assuredly comes within the classification of screen license. The story is ordinary. It simply tells of young Randall who has entered the academy because his father was a Navy man before him and gave his life in action. The "jam" comes on the eve of graduation through the girl's brother (Barry) being circumstantially made to look as if he had violated an Academy regulation. Randall, officer of the day, is goaded by the girl until he is on the verge of resigning so that, presumably, the blame will fall upon him. Cabanne has not made this passage any too clear. However, the practical joke framing of the civilian villain is ultimately disclosed and the finish has Randall dragging his sweetheart into the chapel for a marriage ceremony.

Harriet Hammond is colorless as the heroine and in a role which carries none too much sympathy, in that while urging Randall to do anything to save her brother she was made to appear to less advantage. Cabanne's only indiscretion surround Miss Hammond and Margaret Seddon, as Randall's mother, the latter not impressing with her pathos.

It's a good picture and will be of general interest simply on the strength of the Naval Academy settings. That it possesses enough class for any of the better houses is admitted without saying. The only regret, and this includes "Classmates" as well, is that both pictures completely passed up the annual Army-Navy football classic. Had it been a consideration in either film, or even just a revived snatch from the weeklies, it would have been a great kick. However, both of these Government supervised releases were "shot" in the spring, so the fall sport thing may have been out of thought.

Anyway, where the Army previously had the Navy one film down, it's now all square. Anytime the picture companies, capable of handling the subject care to delve into either of these institutions for material it should be financially profitable as well as a boost for the schools. The Cadets and Middies are surefire subjects, always have been and always will be. *Skig.*

Lovers in Quarantine

Paramount picture presented by Adolph Zukor and Jesse L. Lasky with Bebe Daniels starred. From the play by F. Tennyson Jesce, adapted by Townsend Martin and Luther Reed. Directed by Frank Tuttle. At Rivoli, New York, week Oct. 11, 1925. Running time, 73 minutes.

Diana....................Bebe Daniels
Anthony Blunt....................Harrison Ford
Mackintosh Josephs....................Alfred Lunt
Pamela Gordon....................Eden Gray
Amelia Pincent....................Edna May Oliver
Lola....................Diana Kane
The Silent Passenger....................Ivan Simpson
Mrs. Burroughs....................Marie Shotwell

In adapting this play for the screen a num · of liberties have been taken with the original, but the result proves rather tiresome instead of entertaining. It seems too bad that poor Bebe Daniels has to be the sufferer, but in this instance she has been handed a role that, try as she would, she could do nothing with.

The picture is just one of those long drawn out, draggy affairs that start nowhere and after almost an hour and 15 minutes fails to arrive at any place. It is far and away below the average standard of the Paramount productions, and the chances are that the audiences will be thoroughly dissatisfied with the picture after viewing it.

In adapting the story Martin and Reed have tried to make a hoydenish younger sister of Miss Daniels. She is the girl that worships her sister's beau from afar. When he returns from an exploring expedition to South Africa, just at the moment that the invitations are being sent out for the wedding of the older sister, the young girl determines to save the young man from eloping with the girl engaged to another man.

There is but one sequence that rouses anything like laughter; that is on ship board when the star is going about the ship's deck on her hands and knees hooked to the cane of the hero, and he looking everywhere for her, except down at his feet, where she is.

All of the laughs originally in the bungalow scene are lost in the picture. There is instead a lot of slapstick gagging, most ineffective for laughs.

To Edna May Oliver must go the honors for the best performance. Without her work there would be nothing in the film to talk about. In casting a mess was made in the selection of Eden Gray as the older sister. She just doesn't fit. Alfred Lunt was also rather sorry in his role.

It would be just as well to pass this picture up entirely. *Fred.*

The Everlasting Whisper

Fox production starring Tom Mix. From the novel by Jackson Gregory. Directed by A. J. G. Blystone. At the Rialto, New York, week Oct. 11. Runs about 65 minutes.

Mark King....................Tom Mix
Gloria Gaynor....................Alice Calhoun
Gratton....................Robert Cain
Old Honeycutt....................George Berrell
Swin Brody....................Walter James
Mrs. Gaynor....................Virginia Madison
Jarrold....................Karl Dane

"The Everlasting Whisper" starts just like most the westerns and ends like all of them, but in between there are several unique twists. That's what makes Mix the undisputed czar of the cowboys; this faculty of turning out productions that have everything the western fans demand and still manage to be just a wee bit different. This new release doesn't give it to 'em in comedy or in any particular thrills but in a dramatic turn or two in the story.

Thus the hero gets the girl when the film is about half over only to discover that she has married him to spite someone else and apparently does not care in the least for him.

Instead of being the usual regulation rancher, Mix is this time a young prospector seeking gold in the Rocky Mountain region. He starts the action off right by rescuing the heroine from catastrophe on a run-away horse. She becomes grateful but not sufficiently interested in him to resist using his love for her to her own advantage. It is not until he is in danger from a gang of ruffians seeking to drive him from his newly discovered goldmine that she realizes how much he means to her. So she pitches in the general battle and aids him in disposing of the assorted half dozen heavies he has been fighting single-handed. The last 10 minutes of the picture see no less than four villains shot, strangled or thrown over cliffs, an enviable record even for such a renowned mixer as Mr. Mix.

The photographic shots are particularly lovely, although that is expected in this superior brand of Fox westerns. The latest in the long procession of Mix's leading women is Alice Calhoun, who carries off with charm and distinction a role that is quite thankless until the final few moments. The above-mentioned dearth of comedy is damaging, but is made up for in some degree by a plentitude of action.

There is a startling scene in which Tony and his master most realistically fight off a pack of wolves, and several chase and struggle bits in the deep mountain snows that are pictorially effective and exciting.

The title is not typical of the series and may figure to some slight degree in lessening the draw, although it is doubtful if the majority of Mix enthusiasts ever get further in the reading matter than the name of their idol. For the first-run houses it is assuredly no smash, but it should knock them aflutter in the neighborhood theatres from here to Walla Walla and back again. *Herb.*

SATAN IN SABLES

Warner Brothers' production starring Lowell Sherman. Adapted from the story by Bradley King. Directed by James Flood. At Warner's, New York, week October 10. Running time 72 minutes.

Michael Lyev Yervedoff....Lowell Sherman
Paul Yervedoff....................John Harron
Colette Breton....................Pauline Garon
Dolores Sierra....................Gertrude Astor
Victor....................Frank Butler
Emilie....................Francis J. MacDonald
Sophia, Ex-Grand Duchess, Frances Raymond
Sergius ....Otto Hoffman
Billee....................Richard Botsford
Student....................Richard Barry
Student....................Don Alvarado

Just where the title "Satan In Sables" comes in as applied to this picture is a mystery. It doesn't mean a thing as far as the picture is concerned. As a matter of fact the picture itself doesn't mean so much either. It is far from having the required class, outside of the star and a good cast, that qualifies it for a run on Broadway in a de luxe presentation house. Possibly in the neighborhood houses where there is a daily change of program it will get by on one of the double feature days. That is about as strong as it is.

The story is about as mixed up an affair as one could conceive. It is told in a haphazard manner and very badly titled. In the latter regard there hasn't been the slightest attempt to hold to the atmosphere of the locale of the tale, which is Paris. The titles are just flip slum stuff that one would hear in New York.

"Satan In Sables" relates the tale of a Russian grand duke living in Paris, who becomes enamoured of a good-looking blonde on whom he showers gifts. For no visible reason his love grows cold and he casts her off.

She swears vengeance and ensnares the Grand Duke's younger brother. The G. D. himself falls in love with a gamin of the slums and elevates her to an apartment. His affair with this girl, however, is one of the heart only. He becomes jealous of her when discovering an Apache is visiting her, but when he later discovers that it is her brother-in-law it is all okay with him.

Meantime the younger brother has fallen for the vamp and she, to be revenged on the G. D., relates to the boy that she was formerly the mistress of his older brother. The youngster then virtually commits suicide in a racing car, the older brother chasing him in another car and also tumbling over an open bridge. The young man dies in his older brother's arms. As the Grand Duke is about to leave Paris the gamin comes to him and asks that he take her with him.

Just a lot of old hoke cooked up for the cheap houses, and rather badly cooked up at that.

Supporting Lowell Sherman, who gives a rather finished performance, are John Harron as the younger brother and Pauline Garon as the gamin. She handles her role to decided advantage, but the producers would do well to cut the couple of close-ups that there are of her in the latter portion of the picture. Gertrude Astor plays the vamp and looks like a million dollars. *Fred.*

THE LIVE WIRE

C. C. Burr presentation releasing through First National and starring Johnny Hines. Directed by Charles Hines. Cast includes Ed Breese, Mildred Ryan, J. Barney Sherry and Bradley Barker. At the Broadway, New York, week Oct. 12. Running time, better than 70 mins.

Too much footage to get the full value out of the story sums the main indiscretion. Running well over an hour, the picture becomes an in-and-outer as to laughs, with most of the real comedy spotted early. Deft cutting, plentifully attended to, would have given this Hines release a neat kick which in its present form it lacks. Toward the finish the dramatic action has a tendency to become on the level, and it nullifies the previous morale. And that despite a fight between Hines and a gang which is hoked up to a fare-thee-well.

It's a circus scenario that starts out with Hines, a well-known tent performer who loses caste in the eyes of circus patrons and becomes a hobo. Previously, however, he has seen Dorothy Langdon and a mud hole on a dirt road, the girl's car becoming embedded therein, and the rescue gives him the chance to renew the acquaintance. Ultimately Hines becomes a salesman for Dorothy's father and aids her in putting over an amusement park.

Betwixt and between the action gets away from the love interest to permit of Hines frolicking about with a hobo quartet and also a fake bouncer in a saloon before reaching the offices of the girl's pater. There's a goodly amount of laughs in these passages in which the subtitles aid. Hines is at his best witn the low comedy bits and throws in a neat Charleston for good measure.

A masque ball is worked in towards the finish for a production flash while the opening circus atmosphere is again hinted at in the amusement park angle.

The supporting cast about meets demands, with Mildred Ryan commendably playing the heroine minus the usual frills.

As stated, the glaring fault is the length. As projecting the film will make them laugh in a majority of the houses, but it just misses being a corking comedy due to that twice mentioned fact. *Skig.*

A, REGULAR FELLOW

Famous Players picture, Paramount release, starring Raymond Griffith. Mary Brian featured. Directed by Edward Sutherland. At the Rivoli, New York, week Oct. 4. Running time, 58 mins.

Prince ....Raymond Griffith
Girl ....Mary Brian
King ....Tyrone Power
Prince's Valet....................Edgar Norton
Revolutionist ....Nigel de Bruliere
Prime Minister.....Gustav Von Seyffertitz
Princess ....Jacqueline Gadsen
Lover ....Jerry Austin

Another light comedy interlude led by Raymond Griffith, with the first reel so strong in laughs the remaining footage can't follow it on an equal plane. Extremely light and airy, this film may almost be classed as a "gag" unit. But it will amuse as many witnesses as it fails to impress. It's one of those pictures. Some will like and some won't, the latter because of the improbability of the story.

Griffith has already established himself as a light comedian, and he again scores here, although, to transgress into the past, it's doubtful if this boy has or ever will turn in a better piece of work than he did in Mickey Neilan's "Fools First" of some years ago. "Fools First" was a comedy-drama, and how! It was probably the initial big push in Griffith's film career Now that promotion has come to where his name is above the title it gives every indication of remaining at that point. There is little or no question that Griffith is fully capable of meeting the responsibility.

"A Regular Fellow" is an out-and-out satire on the publicity campaign which England wages with the Prince of Wales as its figurehead. The laughs are fast and furious during this opening reel when Griffith, as the Prince, flies from one ceremony to another as a matter of routine and for which he changes uniform each time while tearing along in a limousine.

"Hoke" here is plentiful, while the formalities include the launching of a ship which sinks upon striking the water; the laying of a cornerstone that falls upon the Prince, and the lighting of the first fire in a fire engine, which explodes. The action is furious during the time this is going on, after which the speed slackens when the love interest angle becomes a necessity.

Mary Brian is the girl whom the heir to the throne gets a flash at when he has managed to slip his noose for a brief period. He doesn't see her again until he lands in the adjoining musical comedy country, previous to which the lover of the princess to whom the Prince is betrothed parachutes from an aeroplane to leave his royal nibs to figure out air currents and the mechanics for himself.

A wild and exaggerated air ride, finishing with a crash, puts the Prince on terra firma again, where no one recognizes him. The general belief is that he is out of his head through insisting he is the Prince.

This passage climaxes in jail, where he sees the girl for the second time. She is being detained because of a lost passport. Both eventually reach the royalty member's native heath. A coronation scene, the King having died, goes into low comedy via a revolutionist, bomb throwing and a dog always returning the explosive sphere.

The film leads into its finish with the Prince propositioning the revolutionist to establish a republic so that he can marry the girl. The "gag" finale has him first dethroned and then elected president of the new republic by the rabid reds.

Eddie Sutherland can direct light comedies and handle Griffith. He proves it here if nowhere alse. That the opening minutes are so strong as to belittle the later reels is not necessarily his fault. The late moments of the picture are certainly not weak; it's that the momentum is so fast at the opening which gives the impression of descent.

Griffith receives capable support from Gustav Von Seyffertitz, his advisor and shadow, but otherwise carries the entire burden himself outside of the situations constructed for him. Miss Brian looks good as the girl and Nigel de Bruliere registers an adequate political fanatic. The remaining cast members are negligible. Tyrone Power does little more than a bit.

"A Regular Fellow" is a good picture for both Griffith and Sutherland. It's almost vehemently clean (mayhaps to show it can be done), and whether they like it or not they'll laugh. That goes for any house that owns a projection machine. *Skig.*

THE DARK ANGEL

First National release produced by Sam Goldwyn with George Fitzmaurice director. Ronald Colman and Vilma Banky featured. Adapted from the stage play of same name by H. B. Trevelyan. Scenario by Frances Marion. At Strand, New York, Oct. 11, week. Running time, 75 minutes.

Hilary Trent ....Ronald Colman
Kitty Vane ....Vilma Banky
Gerald Shannon ....Wyndham Standing
Lord Beaumont....................Frank Elliott
Miss Pindle....................Helen Jerome Eddy
Roma....................Florence Turner
Sir Evelyn Brent....................Charles Lane

A rare, fine up and outstanding audience feature; produced with taste and care, and in its two leading roles, cast ideally.

Interest in this one naturally centers about Vilma Banky, a German actress brought over by Sam Goldwyn and who has been touted to the heavens as the greatest ever. Apparently Goldwyn has had a crew of press agents working on her publicity, for the trade has been flooded and that goes for the dailies.

Funniest of all, is that Miss Banky is as good as Goldwyn claimed. A blonde, she has hair which is not bobbed but light, and soft-eyes that are expressive, and set of good looks such as one rarely views. In other words, the girl is there all around and her acting here is as sure and as professional as if she had been used to American studios for years.

The plot is one of those wistful and pathetic things which has been improved greatly by filming. As produced in New York last year by Robert Milton and his associates, "The Dark Angel" was rated a good play but failed to click. Hilary Trent and Kitty Vane are in love and on the eve of the war, they go to Dover to marry. Arriving too late to secure a special license, they spend one night together in an inn—the last night before Hilary joined his regiment. And after that she went back to her people and he went to France. But Hilary did not come back, and she gave him up for lost. Truth was he had been blinded and fearing to become a burden on her, removed himself to the north of England and in obscurity wrote juvenile tales under a non-de-plume. Kitty, on the eve of her marriage to another man, heard that he was still alive and hastened to him, but her father reached Hilary before the daughter, and between them they arranged to deceive her.

Arranging things around the room so that the blind man knew their exact location, they awaited Kitty. When she entered, Hilary stepped to greet her, commented on the color of her dress and did other things which threw Kitty off the track. He explained that he had been badly shell shocked and didn't want to marry and Kitty accepted his conversation. Leaving the room, she remained outside a few moments, while Hilary in his heartbroken state, dug into a closet and brought forth a small bust of Kitty, and laying his head beside the one of marble, felt every outline of her face, caressed the features and wept. But Kitty had not left and returned. She saw in a glance what a sacrifice he had made and the clinch followed.

That's a good story in itself and the last few scenes are rather compelling bits of drama. Fitzmaurice has also injected several directorial touches which add to the film. One of these has the troops coming back from war, and when brought to a halt, the bereaved parents are shown sadly looking into the depleted ranks. Slowly figures of the dead soldiers arise, resplendent in white uniforms. This effect is corking, as is the phantom of the dark angel, Death, flying over the battlefields and then into the quiet English home of Kitty.

A great comedy gag shows a soldier coming home and meeting his wife, who has a baby in her arms. The soldier stops with surprise on every feature and then slowly counts on his fingers. Then a smile and an embrace.

Colman, as the man, gives a bang-up performance, while Helen Jerome Eddy also chips in with a nice show. The comedy relief in spots is bad and there are times when the direction lags, but on the whole, 'The Dark Angel" has such fine moments it can be heartily recommended. The exhibitor can also depend on this one as not being a hocus-pocus proposition which appeals to critics only. It has a whale of a punch and heart interest. Moreover, it has been produced lavishly and with all these attributes, is almost a cinch for satisfying any audience. *Sisk*.

UNNAMED WOMAN

Embassy Picture produced by Arthur F. Beck and released by Arrow Pictures Corp. Written by Charles E. Blaney and directed by Harry O. Hoyt. Privately screened Oct. 9 in projection room. Runs about 65 mins.
Flora Brookes..........Katherine McDonald
Donald Brookes.........Herbert Rawlinson
Doris Gray ....Wanda Hawley
Billie Norton...................Leah Baird
Archie Wesson................John Miljan

Another of the long line of films in which circumstantial evidence makes things look mighty black for the virtuous wife falsely accused of infidelity. Her husband just won't believe her story about the burglar, and as he's a lawyer who has previously declared that all women who figure in divorce cases are worthless, he can do nothing else than act the unforgiving brute. "The Unnamed Woman" wades through seven reels of that sort of foam and emerges an average program production in almost every detail.

The film is unusual in that it holds in its cast three actresses who were stars in their own right some time ago—Wanda Hawley, Katherine McDonald and, to go back even farther, Leah Baird. Miss Hawley and Miss Baird play gold diggers, and do it well, while Miss McDonald, grown somewhat stouter but still charming, is the grossly abused heroine, Herbert Rawlinson, also no tyro, is the husband, and John Miljan takes the honors in the fat role of a villain with a streak of the right stuff in him. Mike Donlin also appears in a bit.

The film is full of typical movie wild parties, in which the hint of something really daring is never quite fulfilled. One situation that might have been quite risque has been handled with kid gloves. This is when the heavy awakens one morning to find he has been married the night before in a drunken stupor. Glancing over to the other twin bed he finds the gold digger who has roped him sleeping in all tranquillity. Just why twin beds in the bachelor's room is not explained, although that could happen in real life.

It is difficult to say how this pale pink society story will be received. Money has been spent on it, with the result that the cast, settings and direction are all above the average.

SUBSTITUTE WIFE

Whitman Bennett production released by Arrow Picture Corp. featuring Jane Novak. Story by Katherine Smith. Directed by Wilfred Noy. Privately screened Oct. 9 in projection room. Runs about hour.
Hilda Nevers................Jane Novak
Laurence Sinton............Niles Welch
Victor Bronson............Colt Albertson
Evelyn Wentworth..........Louise Carter
Dr. Kitchell.............Gordon Standing
Dr. De Longe.............Mario Majeroni

The natural tragedy of blindness overtaking a person provides a splendid theme for dramatic situations, whether in fiction, plays or pictures. "The Substitute Wife" shows nothing new in elaborating upon this situation, but if film fans are ready to overlook the preposterous premise to the whole plot they will undoubtedly be moderately entertained.

This time it is Laurence Sinton blinded by burglars on his wedding evening. His bride, unbeknown to him, is an unscrupulous gold-digger, caring only for his money and secretly enamored of a villianous young doctor. The guilty couple decide to go away for some weeks while the husband is recuperating. With this in view they hire a pretty trained nurse, Hilda Nevers, who happens to have a speaking voice identical with that of the wife, to pose as the latter.

Hilda of course grows to care for Laurence and he, in his turn observes qualities in her which he had never noticed in his wife. The big situation comes when Hilda learns that his eyesight can be restored by a delicate operation. This, she feels, will sing the swan-song for her love, but believing Laurence will be **happy with his wife, she makes the usual film martyr of herself. He regains his sight, learns of his spouse's infidelity and welcomes to his heart the other girl.**

Miss Novak gives a tender, moving performance as the nurse, standing head and shoulders above the rest of the somewhat ordinary cast. The picture is entirely devoid of comedy relief attempts, a deficiency better, however, than the usual unfunny nibbling for the elusive laughs. Some of the exterior photographic shots are very beautiful.

It is all very typical neighborhood house stuff, made, perhaps a little better by a story that is more gripping than most.

The Vanishing American

Paramount production presented by Adolph Zukor and Jesse L. Lasky. From the story by Zane Grey, adapted by Lucien Hubbard and script by Ethel Doherty. Directed by George B. Seitz. Featuring Richard Dix, Lois Wilson, Noah Beery and Malcolm McGregor. At the Criterion, N. Y., Oct. 15, for a run. Running time, 132 mins.
Nophaie.....................Richard Dix
Marion Warner..............Lois Wilson
Booker...........................Noah Beery
Capt. Earl Ramsdall....Malcolm McGregor
Shoie.....................Charles Stevens
Nasja.................Son of Man Hammer
Nocki.....................George Magrill
Gekin Yashi.................Shannon Day
Amos Halliday............Charles Crockett
Bart Wilson.................Bert Woodruff
Do Etin.....................Bernard Siegel
Kit Carson....................Guy Oliver
Jay Lord......................Joe Ryan
Rhur......................Bruce Gordon
Glendon.................Richard Howard
Naylor................John Webb Dillon

"The Vanishing American," a Paramount production that has been widely and widely heralded as the "picture of pictures," failed to live up to the advance work done for it. While it proves to be a picture that will undoubtedly get money in the first houses it does not give indication of possessing the possibilities that will make it stand out as a box office winner on a special run. With cutting the picture should improve, and it certainly can stand scissoring, as the first part is exceedingly draggy.

It is a "western," but there is no big moment that will stir. In the occasional spots where there was a possibility the film might be lifted with the aid of an inspiring orchestral arrangement, the music was lamentably lacking.

The second half of the picture does, however, pick up and the ending will have a tear effect on the women. Whether it is that the story stirred them or the fact that their hero, Richard Dix, as the Indian, does not live to marry the White Desert Rose (Lois Wilson) is an open question. This angle may make the women want to see this, for to them the idea of having a good cry means a corking time.

The story itself calls attention to the vanishing of the real American, the Indian, off the face of the North American continent. Nothing is said about the Indians who are living in Oklahoma at this time and drawing down a weekly royalty of about $1,750 and riding around in sedans which they discard immediately after a tire blows, so as to get a new car.

The scene is an Indian reservation which is in the care of an agent who, while a whale for details and filing cases, doesn't know what it is all about and his assistant, with the aid of a couple of rough necks, is cleaning up on the outside. He has an arrangement to judge the horses of the Indians, infected and impound them, thence paying the Redskins $25 each for their stock out of the Government funds to sell them for an average of $100.

On the reservation as a teacher in the Indian school is Marion Warner (Lois Wilson) with whom Nophaie (Dix) falls in love. He is the leader of his particular clan and the other leaders respect his judgment in all matters. At the same time the heavy is trying to win the girl and when he attacks her the Indian comes to her rescue. There is a corking free-for-all at this point between the Indian, the heavy and several of the latter's cronies. The result is that the Indian is compelled to hide in the hills and he remains there until the call comes for the World War. Not only does he prevail upon his people to produce their horses for the use of the Government, but he lines up the young bucks to enlist, going overseas with them at the head of a machine gun unit.

He serves at the front with valor and distinction, but when he and his comrades return to the reservation they find that the kindly old agent has been removed and in his stead the heavy has been appointed. He has appropriated all of the Indians' land and driven the old men, squaws and youngsters into the Bad Lands, where they are slowly dying off. An uprising occurs and the swarthy hero warns the whites who flee to a block house, where they make a stand. The hero, who is with them, goes forth to try to pacify his people, but a returned Indian soldier, crazed by shell shock, fires and kills him. This brings about the weepy ending and prevents the necessity of closing the story with an inter-marriage.

Dix gives a corking performance as the Indian leader, although at times he appeared to be laughing at himself in the role. Lois Wilson was sincere and an altogether charming heroine. Noah Berry was the heavy, somewhat overplaying at times.

The direction of Sietz leaves much to be desired. His handling of the war stuff especially fell short, while the gathering Indians' clans was overlooked for picturesque effectiveness.

"The Vanishing American" is a big picture in the sense of those houses where it might do sufficient business to hold over for a second week, but it falls short of qualifying as an attraction destined for a long run.

At the Criterion it's doubtful if it will stand up more than six weeks.

Fred.

Little Annie Rooney

United Artists release starring Mary Pickford. From an original story by Katherine Hennessey, adapted for the screen by Hope Loring and Louis Leighton. Directed by William Beaudine. At the Strand, New York, week beginning October 18. Running time, 95 min.

Little Annie Rooney........Mary Pickford
Joe Kelly..................William Haines
Officer Rooney..............Walter James
Tim Rooney.................Gordon Griffith
Tony...........................Carlo Schipa
Abie.......................Spec O'Donnell
Spider.............................Hugh Fay
Mamie...............................Vola Vale
Mickey....................Joe Butterworth
Humidor....................Eugene Jackson
Athos.........................Oscar Rudolph

"Our Mary" is back again in "Little Annie Rooney." Gone are the long velvet robes, the flowing plumes, the brocades and white powdered wigs, and Mary is again a smudgy-faced gamin of the streets. She's dirty-hands, dirty-face and all that sort of things, and the fans are going to love her to death. This is a picture-house picture, the kind that made Mary a big star and made dollars for the exhibitors. Mary can go right along now and turn out about three or four of these a year, and she will not only be enhancing her own value as a star again, but will also make it possible for the exhibitor to make money, and reestablish herself in the hearts of the public. Mary got away from the idea of being just "Mary." Ambition is to be lauded, but when one gets to the point where "finer" means nothing but "costume" plays, one has to side with the exhibitor who said, "The French Revolution is raising hell at the box office.

But "Little Annie Rooney" is going to make Mary the favorite of the masses again. New York, especially, is going to love this picture. It is a New York story. A story of that New York which lies south of Fourteenth street and east of "Thoid" aveneo in the day when the Irish ruled the section. It is the east side of twenty-five years ago.

No one would like to intimate that the author responsible for this "original" story may have read "Haunch, Paunch and Jowl," but it is that same east side which was depicted in that bit of literature. Incidentally, they have a reporter in this picture who is a reporter. He is a ringer for the dean of police reporters in New York, "Bill" Reitmeier of the "World," who has been covering the Tenderloin for years.

"Little Annie Rooney" runs an hour and thirty-five minutes. The picture could be cut in a couple of spots to advantage. With a little snapping this picture would be the answer to the exhibitor's prayer.

There is a kid in this picture who, although a little older than Jackie Coogan was when he got his first chance in "The Kid," is going to make his mark on the strength of his screen performance here. As a matter of fact, Spec O'Donnell gives Mary a run for honors in certain spots.

Then there is Walter James. The same Walter that was at the Circle and the American theatres years agone. Walter plays Mary's dad, who is "on the force," and he is a copper to the last touch. Walter likewise got a chance here, and the chances are that he'll be a cop for the rest of his life, as far as pictures are concerned. The lead opposite the star is played by William Haines. He registers well enough, as does Gordon Griffith as her brother. To Hugh Fay go the comedy honors among the adults. The "Tony" of Carlo Schipa also stands out as a clever characterization.

The story is of the two children of Rooney, the cop. Mary is the daughter, who is about 12, and her brother is around 18 or so. The kids of the neighborhood taunt Mary with "Little Annie Rooney is My Sweetheart" and she starts a battle, part of the gang being lined up with her and part against her. Abie has to stay home and can't fight 'cause it's a holiday, but when the battle gets too hot you can't keep Abie out and he goes to Annie's aid. It is great kid stuff and the director made the most of his chances. The older brother of the leader of the faction opposed to Mary steps in and separates the kids and on learning the reason for the melee whistles "Little Annie Rooney," and it takes on an entirely different meaning for the girl.

The boys have a social club and give a blowout in one of the "halls" to get a little ready cash in case one of the mob should get jammed. At that blow-out Tony grabs a rod and lets fly at Joe, but instead of Joe getting it the bullet hits Rooney, the cop, as he comes into the hall to quell the disturbance. It's his birthday, and at home Annie is waiting for her dad, but instead a brother officer comes in and tells her the sad news. Weeks later the cops haven't been able to land the killer, but Spider tells Annie's brother that it was Joe that fired the shot, and the brother goes gunning for Joe, gets him, and then Annie saves his life in the blood transfusion that takes place. The real killer is revealed and the picture jumps to a hurried close, with young Rooney a traffic cop, with Annie and Joe and all the rest out on his auto-truck for a Sunday picnic.

This one is "in." *Fred.*

FLOWER OF NIGHT

A Paramount production presented by Adolph Zukor and Jesse L. Lasky. From the story by Joseph Hergesheimer, adapted by Willis Goldbeck. Directed by Paul Bern. At the Rivoli, New York, week beginning Oct. 18. Running time, 67 mins.

Carlotta y Villalan..................Pola Negri
Don Geraldo y Vilalon......Joseph Dowling
John Basset............Youcca Troubeszkoy
Luke Rand.......................Warner Oland
Derck Bylandt.................Edwin J. Brady
Servant.........................Cesare Gravina
Mrs. Bylandt....................Eulalie Jensen
Vigilante Leader.....Gustav von Seyffertitz
Josefa..................Helen Lee Worthing

Just what is Famous Players trying to do? Are they aiming to achieve a record of turning out the most inconsistent product of any of the bigger producers? Or is it possible that they figure they do not have to trouble about theatres to play their product in so that they can turn out anything they want to and get away with it? Whichever of the three ideas it may be they are all wrong.

For the record of motion picture sales says that the profit isn't in the first runs, they only bring back the production cost, after that the profit has to come out of the subsequent runs. True Famous have their own "A," "B" and "C" grades of houses but even these are first runs, for in the majority the product that can't play the "A" house is shifted to either of the two others and it is a certainty that the independent exhibitor following their first run isn't going to play the flops.

"Flower of Night" is a flop judged by all the standards of F. P. in the past. The only redeeming feature is that it has Pola Negri, and all that Pola would have to do is to star in about two more pictures as bad as this one to find herself washed-up as a boxoffice card in those few sections where she has developed a following over here. It is a picture that had it been turned out by an independent producing firm would be generally panned by the trade.

Taken point by point "Flower of Night" is a story that would have made a fairly good two reeler. Secondly: The cast is about as badly a picked aggregation as has ever been assigned roles in a Paramount production. Thirdly: It is poorly directed without the slightest idea of holding suspense and the characters wander through the tale in a purely mechanical manner. Fourthly: Technically it is about on the same plane as the average Universal of three years ago.

Once Famous Players productions were the ultimate in lighting. This one is lighted so that a fly-by-night producer of westerns would be ashamed of it. Imagine in a Famous Players picture a tinted night scene that has everything else done on broaddaylight? That's exactly what one gets in this picture.

Pola, herself, gives a terrible performance. Bad as to make-up, with possibly one or two flashes of what she may be able to do, and then atop of the faulty make-up there is regretable photography. These faults are enough to kill any star.

Warner Oland is the only one who gives a performance that is in keeping with the usual F. P. standard. Joseph Dowling is horribly miscast.

A bad picture. *Fred.*

THE BEST PEOPLE

Famous-Players production adapted from the stage play by David Gray and Avery Hopwood. Produced and directed by Sidney Olcott from scenario by Bernard McConville. At the Rialto, New York, Oct. 18 week. Running time, 70 minutes.

Henry Morgan ....Warner Baxter
Alice O'Neil ....Esther Ralston
Mrs. Bronson Lenox......Kathlyn Williams
Bronson Lenox ....Edward Davis
Arthur Rockmere ....William Austin
George Grafton ....Larry Steers
Millie Montgomery ....Margaret Livingston
Bertie Lenox ....Joseph Striker
Marian Lenox ....Margaret Morris
Taxi Driver ....Ernie Adams

Another weak sister and made so by deplorable casting.

Taking from last year's stage play, the adaptation sticks fairly close to the original but the cast is lacking in real names and two of the leading roles are taken by some of Paramount's newcomers, who in this instance, don't come anywhere near qualifying.

The plot concerns the Bronson Lenoxes, a rich family, the son of which falls in love with a good chorus girl, while the daughter falls for their chauffeur. Of course various interested parties try to prevent the matches, but they go through as per schedule and both are apparently good marriages.

Into this muddle is such a choice bit of entertainment as an illuminating discussion upon who are 'the best people,' the folks who inherited their money or the people who do an honest day's work, etc. This is brought into the story for rah-rah purposes, the audiences being looked forward to as ready to thrill inwardly at such mawkish sentiments. For comedy relief there is a chorus girl role which attained almost stellar proportions as Florence Johns played it on the stage and which is the one bright spot of the film.

Edward Davis, a good actor, is miscast as the kind father, being more suited to villainous roles, while Margaret Morris and Joseph Striker as the daughter and son, respectively, are also out of the picture. Striker is the great offender by posing continually with a serious look which might be taken to mean that he is responsible for the cares of the world. Warner Baxter is nice as the chauffeur and Margaret Livingston handles the chorus girl role well.

In selecting costumes for the women principals, someone erred in garbing Miss Morris in knee-length dresses, while Kathlyn Williams as the mother was fearfully over-dressed in several scenes. Altogether, it is hard to believe that Sidney Olcott was altogether wholly behind this one, although he is so credited.

Sisk.

FINE CLOTHES

Adapted from Ferenc Molnar's play, "Fashions For Men," by Benjamin Glazer. A First National production presented by Louis B. Mayer and directed by John M. Stahl. At the Capitol, New York, Oct. 18 week. Running time, 65 minutes.

Earl of Denham..............Lewis S. Stone
Peter Hungerford..........Percy Marmont
Paula ....Alma Rubens
Oscar ....Raymond Griffith
Adele ....Eileen Percy
Philip ....William V. Mong
Receiver ....John Merkyl

If they had made this one in 20 reels there would still have been enough subtitles left to go around. As it is, "Fine Clothes" is nothing more than a story told entirely by subtitles and illustrated with motion pictures of its characters.

Louis B. Mayer, for a long time with Metro, is listed as presenting this one, while it is called a John M. Stahl production. Probably it has been held back for some time, as Raymond Griffith, now an F-P star, has a minor part, but for all that he is in the lights on the downtown side of the Capitol's marquee. Why it should have been held back is understandable, but why it should have ever been put out in the belief that it could be a potential money maker is beyond belief.

What was a brilliant stage play (but hardly a commercial success), is here a prize bunch of dullness acted by a cast more or less indifferently directed. It has all been Anglicized and what was once Hungary becomes England, etc., with the usual results.

The plot tells of a shop-keeper who was too generous, and by his loose ways of doing business, he lost his store and his wife to the chief clerk. Forced to work for a noble, he takes his stenographer with him, as he is in love with her. The stenog, however, went along to become mistress of the noble. Toward the end the horizon began to clear, so that he regained his store, had the pleasure of seeing his deceitful chief clerk hard up and also got back his stenog as a wife. And from then on, he lost his lax business ways and became hard boiled.

Percy Marmont wears his poker face through the role of Peter, which O. P. Heggie distinguished in the legit, while Lewis Stone was seen once in a while as the noble

Griffith made whimsical job of the deceitful clerk, while Alma Rubens and Eileen Percy can be entered on the red ink side.

Toward the end, there are a few spicy subtitles calculated for laughs around this territory but which will be sliced by the censors once they get into Ohio, Pa., Maryland Free State and other sections where the scissors holders look upon spiciness as vulgarity.

For the ordinary exhibitor, this one is just a filler, and for the fellow who might be inclined to book it on a Sunday, the answer is that its moral tone hardly qualifies it for showing then. In other words, the whole thing is more or less of a 'dud.' *Sisk.*

PRIDE OF THE FORCE

B. Berger production released through Rayart (Independent). Tom Santschi starred. Story by Arthur Hoerl. Directed by Duke Worne. Loew's Circle, New York, as half of a double bill, Oct. 19. Running time, about 58 mins.

Patrolman Danny Moore......Tom Santschi
His Wife..................Edyth Chapman
Mary Moore................Gladys Hulette
Jim Moore.................James Morrison
George Weldon..............Cruford Kent

Here is one of the hokiest films ever. Combines the tear jerkers of every show that ever played the Stair and Havlin time; its hero is as pure a hero as any one ever created; its mother bears what sorrows Job left over, while the errant son is not only errant but equipped with a backbone of muffin-like consistency. In other words, it bears the same relation to the average movie that newspaper boiler plate stuff bears to a first page lead story set by linotype, which makes it less, even for exhibs.

Dan Moore is a policeman, just a patrolman, and wears a long, old-fashioned coat which comes down to his knees. Slated for promotion, it happens that on his beat a holdup occurs, and while he and his brother officers are chasing the thugs a little girl is run over. Off the car hops Danny Moore, fondles the child in his arms, comments on how it is better to save the life of one little child than to put three thugs behind the bars, and then meets his captain, who tells him that in the first place he had no right to let a holdup happen and that in the second place he should get the thieves.

Home goes Danny, crestfallen. When he gets there he finds a cake waiting, one of those fancy things with sergeant's stripes painted on top, but he sorrowfully tells the gathering that he isn't to be promoted, and he is then placed on desk duty in the station house.

His weak son, really in business with a crooked gambler, is trying to make his sister marry the crook, but Sis has herself a real rich young fellow, who is so noble and upright that Sis thinks he's grand. The crook and the young brother plan a robbery at the rich boy's home, and they pull it off.

Hearing that it is to come off through one of the funniest looking stool pigeons who ever took dough for being deceitful, Danny goes out to clear his record. Rich young man grabs the brother and keeps him from police. Danny chases the villain to his gambling house and shoots him full of holes. Then finds his daughter with villain. Of course, laughter was innocent, and after they both had a good crying spell Danny turns stoic and turns daughter over to another copper to be locked up.

The whole thing is poorly acted. Santschi has an ill-fitting uniform and a pistol so long it looks ridiculous. The rich young man, unnamed on film, looks too handsome for words, but can't act at all, while the rest of the troupe is just fair.

For a bunch of police reporters who haven't laughed in years this is one of the best things ever made. Maybe in the country towns they'd accept it as a great moral preachment, but in the cities where people know wooden nickels when they see them, it doesn't stand a chance. At the Circle when reviewed the balcony crowd roared at certain parts and snickered like the deuce when the maudling sentimentality of the finale was shown. *Sisk.*

HIS MASTER'S VOICE

Gotham production, releasing through Lumas Films and featuring "Thunder," the dog. Directed by Renand Hoffman. Cast includes George Hackathorne, Marjorie Daw, Mary Carr, Will Walling and Brooks Benedict. At Loew's, New York, as half the bill, Oct. 16. Running time, around 70 minutes.

A dog and war picture in the first person; that is, Thunder, the featured canine, is depicted as telling the yarn to one of his pups. And that's the kick of the picture, for this particular pup has a trick of holding his head on one side while registering a bewildered expression that is good for a laugh on every insert. Otherwise "His Master's Voice" is pretty much of an out-and-out "meller," and for other than the smallers houses needs a bolstering companion film.

The scenario relates of a small town weakling who "finds" himself through the war, and having won the girl in France (she is a Red Cross attache), comes back to thrash the town bully. A majority of the action is no the battlefield, with the dog prominent in the heroic passages. Thunder goes over the top to drag his wounded master to safety and the latter makes the connection on the all-important wire which explodes the mine and saves the left sector.

Neither George Hackathorne or Marjorie Daw, in the love interest roles, particularly distinguish themselves. The same may be said of the remaining players. It's material that has oft been done, and for that reason carries a restricted appeal. The dog is not strong enough to lift it above its shortcomings, and while the battle stuff has been fairly well done, it suffers from wandering over a well-worn trail. *Skig.*

ROMANCE ROAD

Granada Production (Independent) released in this territory through Renown Exchanges. Directed by Fred Windemere with Raymond McKee starred. At the Stanley, New York, Oct. 20. Running time, 60 mins.

Pat O'Brien..............Raymond McKee
Mary VanTassle.........Marjorie Meadows
Pat's Mother...............Gertrude Claire
Mary's Aunt..................Alice Manning
Arthur.........................Dick Gordon
Pat's Buddy..................Billy Fletcher

A nice little picture of no great pretense, but honest in its entertainment value. A familiar theme, that of the poor boy in the village and the rich girl who lived in the house on the hill. Same hill. Done with a sense of humor and McKee in the male lead is good enough to carry it along to a neat conclusion.

Pat O'Brien leaves a hospital to which he was sent during the war and starts the homeward trudge of 40 miles. On the way back Mary VanTassle, a little girl when the war began but grew up over likes him in the car. Against the wishes of a fiance somebody wished on her, she gives Pat a lift. From then on the romance develops, although he has to work hard for his living.

Sugar all the way and granted, but with McKee doing nice work, also helped along by the leading lady, Marjorie Meadows, a newcomer, who plays breezily. The others are more or less typical except for Gertrude Claire, who scores definitely as Pat's mother.

Quiet comedy in this one and while names are lacking it manages to provide entertainment. As a program picture for the neighborhoods, it qualifies with respect to keeping the interest, but its lack of names will probably need something else to draw 'em in. *Sisk.*

THE UNWRITTEN LAW

Columbia Pictures production. Directed by E. J. Lesaint; supervised by Harry Cohen. Elaine Hammerstein and Forrest Stanley featured. At Loew's, New York, half of double bill, one day, Oct. 16. Running time, 62 minutes.

Another of those unfortunate Southern colonels with nothing left but a beautiful daughter, a black cigar and whiskers.

Not hard to build a story therefrom, but this story runs pretty rocky; also draggy in the first part. Picking up toward the centre when action goes to work, it does rather better after that, finishing to a conclusion that it can get over in the neighborhoods.

Some nice little bits of direction crop out now and then, and there is a laugh toward the finale.

The colonel's daughter is a stenog in a busy man's office, but the man is not too busy to notice her. She loves another, but her daddy is broke, and he needs a haircut besides, so the busy man frames him, also the daughter and also the young man she loves.

Then the busy man confesses the frames after he had married the girl. To permit the girl to marry her returned sweetheart, the housekeeper accommodatingly kills the busy man, the boy marries the girl and daddy gets his haircut—or should. *Sime.*

CRACK O' DAWN

Rayart picture, starring Reed Howes. Produced by Harry J. Brown; directed by Al Rogell. At the Stanley, New York, Oct. 16. Running time, 55 minutes.

Young Thorpe.................Reed Howes
Old Thorpe...............J. P. MacGowan
Etta Thompson..................Ruth Dwyer
Her Father...............William Barrows

Reed Howes gained his fame as the model for the collar advertisements, and on this basis was taken into the movies. Notwithstanding this, Rayart has built him into a real stunt star, and his pictures, without exception, have been crammed with action and daring stuff. Moreover, his good looks have made the love interest plausible, while his dexterity has also stood him in good stead.

This latest of his series is directed by Al Rogell, who has made hundreds of independent action pictures and apparently knows his business thoroughly. The theme concerns a feud between two former partners in an automobile manufacturing business and how they are reunited by the love of their children. In this screening both children are interested in auto racing, and when a cross-country race for endurance is announced, they team in constructing a machine from the plans of the old partners. The machine wins after a series of exciting episodes which constitute the greater part of the film.

The race stuff is well filmed and comedy relief nicely planted. With Howes doing his stuff in good shape and the narrow escapes well photographed, this one is above the usual release and calculates to thoroughly satisfy as a program picture. *Sisk.*

7 KEYS TO BALDPATE

Cleveland, Oct. 16.

"Seven Keys to Baldpate" in its newest cinema form, had a premiere here this week at the Allen that has seldom been accorded the initial showing of a regular release.

A general feeling that this latest improvement of George M. Cohan's comedy will put the film across in great style has been somewhat tempered by the doubtful tactics used by Douglas MacLean, the Famous Players-Lasky star, in expressing various emotions, especially that of surprise.

In the new version, a series of amusing circumstances supplant to a large degree the mystery angles which in its earlier form rendered "Seven Keys" comparable with recent "mystery plays." This change is regarded as compatible with the general tenor of the plot and the resulting addition of humorous incidents are such as to keep audience in constant rippling good humor.

The box receipts, it is said, will total well above the average for this play. The Allen, one of Cleveland's "Big Three" has had a rather plump average in years gone by. The surprise ending, comedy of the lighter sort and a certain element of mystery ever in the background and breaking forth here and there—all of these contrive to make the plot inviting to those who deligh in even-tempered entertainment.

The actors generally are but fair. MacLean, whose early individuality and sense of the ridiculous placed him eventually upon a pedestal as a "polite comedian," is grating to an appreciative sense of well-defined emotions. He raises his eyebrows and expects the reaction of the audience to be varying degrees of surprise, anger, despair or what not. It isn't being done—in that way alone or by him.

Otherwise, MacLean, who plays William Halowell Magee, is his usual likeable self, fluttering, in this case, to Baldpate to write his masterpiece and there encountering serious distractions of mind and body.

Edith Roberts, the cause of MacLean's wild effort to write a book within 24 hours, is the kind of heroine you would expect, injecting into the part a personality that satisfies without intruding.

Probably William Orlamonde, as the hermit leaves with you a clearer impression than do the other members of the cast. But, characters aside, the "Seven Keys" in the last analysis, is bound to create a disturbance somewhere along the line.

Its rolls of celluloid arrived here direct from Los Angeles, tightly sealed in galvanized iron carriers. Nowhere, outside the studio, had the picture been run on the screen before. Even blase New York must wait this time. After witnessing the effect of the picture here, it is safe to predict that "blase New York" will find in it just as much to laugh about as did the movie fans of the Fifth City who saw it last week. *Gregg.*

DIE POSTMEISTERIN

("THE POSTMISTRESS")

Bronx, N. Y., Oct. 15.

"Die Postmeisterin," the operetta by August Neidhart, with music by Leon Jessel, which Rudolph Bach presented Wednesday at the Yorkville theatre for the first time in this country, is so excellent a work of its kind that one wonders how its production came about in this country in the original German.

Certainly, the work compares favorably with any of the German put on Broadway in English versions.

The program announces the operetta had a three-year run at the Thalia, Berlin before produced at the Yorkville. Obviously then, Bach acquired the American rights long ago, for the German piece could not help have been noticed by others bent on securing German entertainment for American audiences.

The story is simple, but contains much of the sparkling dialog of Strauss, von Suppe, Milloceker and other German masters.

It tells of an attractive young woman, a wife in name only, who assumes the duties of a postmaster after her husband has left for the war. He returns suddenly and unexpectedly when not wanted and there is some good drama.

The music is superb. An exquisite duet, "Langsam, Langsam," in the first act and a love song, "Reich Mir die Leibe," in the second, are gems. There is also a topical song, "Ja, ja, der Storch," which, if in English, should be a second "Oh Katherina."

Bach has given the operetta a good production and, what is more, an excellent cast. Erni Belian, imported from Berlin to head the company plays the postmistress. Gustave Jahrbeck is the prince, Kurt Schlegel, the comedian, and Willy Bolle, a lovable old priest. *Teil.*

GO WEST

A Joseph M. Schenck production, starring Buster Keaton, released by Metro-Goldwyn. Shown at the Capitol, N. Y., week Oct. 25, 1925. Running time, 69 minutes.
The Drifter...................Buster Keaton
Owner of Ranch........Howard Truesdale
His Daughter..............Kathleen Myers
A Cow.......................Brown Eyes

This latest comedy has Buster Keaton slipping over a series of comedy stunts that cause but mild laughter. Buster in this particular instance is treading on the toes of the western stars in a burlesque that has with him a cow. Tom Mix has "Tony," Bill Hart his "Pinto," so along comes Buster with his "Brown Eyes." Pretty name for a cow, isn't it? The only thing the Capitol needed was Jimmy Durante's "Perfect Lady" song. You know the one about "She's not a dame, she's just a cow." That would have gone great with Buster's "Brown Eyes" and at the same time it would have killed any possible suspicion that the name of "Brown Eyes" was applied to the cow as a plug for the number that is being issued by a New York song publishing house.

Anyhow, Buster has a comedy in which the cow is the whole show. However it was written (the chances are that it wasn't) and whoever did the job was certainly long on memory and short on invention. The result is there in the picture, for the laughs are few and far between. Buster starts as a drifter, purse snatcher who is finally inspired by the famed speech of Horace Greeley's "Go West, Young Man"; in fact, there is a double of a Greeley statue in one of the scenes.

Buster manages to hop a freight car on the A. T. & S. F. It is a car loaded with barrels of potatoes and he starts a barrel slide through a little phoney-baloney risley work. That was good for a laugh, as was also the scene when Buster was flopped out of the car himself into the Arizona desert. Then his troubles began. He got a job as a cow hand and makes a pet of "Brown Eyes," one of the milch cows in the herd. The ranch owner decides to ship 1,000 head to market and includes the cow, but when the hand tries to save her he is paid off. No chance for the youngster to get ahead at all.

A rival rancher objecting to the early sale of the live stock because he is holding out for a price on his beeves, tries to wreck the train and cause the shipment to be lost, but it is the comic cow hand that saves the day. He is the only one on the train and climbs into the engineer's cabin in time to stop the train just as it pulls into the passenger station with the steers.

Then comes the trick of getting them to the stock yards, so the comic takes his "Brown Eyes" as the bell-cow for the steers. He leads them through the town, which gives a chance for a lot of old fashioned Keystoning and not a bet overlooked.

In the end he gets the shipment safely to its destination, but only after wrecking a department store, a barber shop and invading a Turkish bath and a few other little stunts like calling out the fire department and the police. They didn't have the old Keystone Cops, that was the one left to Sennett.

In the end, with the rancher, the cow hand and the daughter of the former all ranged on the platform at the stock yards. The hero has saved the day and the rancher offers him anything in his house and home and the hero points behind him, stating "I want her." To the audience it looks as though it's the daughter, but they are all wrong,

"It's not the dame, it's just the cow."

The trouble with the picture is that too much of it is shot in the distance and the audience does not get a chance to watch the action sufficiently close to get the benefit of whatever laughs there might have been in those shots, if there were any. The Capitol audience that jammed the house Sunday afternoon missed them if there.

Fred.

THE KING ON MAIN STREET

Famous Players picture starring Adolphe Menjou and Greta Nissen and Bessie Love featured. From the play by G. A. de Caillavet, Rbert de Flers and Samuel Arene. Adapted by Dough. Doty. Directed by Monta Bell. At the Rivoli, New York, Oct. 25. Running time, 68 minutes.
Serge IV, King of Molvania..Adolph Menjou
Gladys Humphries...........Bessie Love
Terese Manix...............Greta Nissen
John Rockland..............Oscar Shaw
Arthur Trent...............Joseph Kilgour
Jensen.....................Edgar Norton
Mrs, Nash..................Carlotta Monterey
Aunt Tabitha...............Marcia Harris
Bourdier...................Edouard Durand

Here is the comedy box office wow of the Famous program thus far this year. It is going to clean up. The women are going to love it and they are going to like Adolphe Menjou all the more for it. This is one that the exhibitor can't possibly go wrong on for it is sure to mop.

It is a sophisticated comedy, or rather was as a play, and with Leo Dietrichstein in the title role just about suited the better classes, but with the adaptation has broadened to such an extent that the high, the low and the in between are all bound to fall for it.

But, all in all, it is Menjou. The manner in which he plays the role of the king is going to stir the hearts and pull the laughs.

In Molvania, where he is the ruling monarch, the treasury needs replenishing. There are two ways to accomplish this. Either marry the princess of a neighboring ruling house who looks as though she had worked as a hostess in a night club, day and night for 40 years or so, or go to America to arrange a loan on the oil lands of the country. The king, who has worked up a reputation as a Romeo, doesn't take long to decide. It's a trip to America for the boys. But Paris first. He has a sweetie in Paris and wants to spend the evening, the night and part of the morning with her first. He does that little thing and the way in which it is handled in the direction is complete. There isn't a single thing that anyone could take offense at, yet there isn't a single thing left to the imagination. Then a few hours later, when the sweetie is shown phoning the king in his apartments, it is also quite evident that another sweetie came in and caught her, for she has a "lovely eye."

The question is how to meet her request to "take her to America" without causing a scandal, so the private secretary is pressed into service and compelled to wed the lady in question. Then America! New York, Times Square and finally Coney Island with its parks, the roller coaster and the hot dog stands, and finally a meeting with a little American girl. The same girl, who in Paris at the king's hotel in her excitement threw a cream puff instead of a bouquet at him and hit him in the eye with it. Then romance. At first the king is just philandering again, but after he has passed up an important date with the bankers in order to spend a week-end in the "biggest house in Little Falls," shows himself to the audience as a gentleman after all, even though it necessitates his signing away the oil lands to the banker who virtually blackmails him out of them. But in so doing he saves the good name of the little American girl.

She in turn marries the young American go-getter that she is en-

gaged to; and the king returns to Molvania to marry the ugly princess and retain his throne. The latter shots are shown in color, which is an effective ending.

Bessie Love, as the little American girl, shines in this, while Greta Nissen, as the gay Parisienne, does nothing that distinguishes her. Carlotta Monterey, as an American society woman who tries to snub the king because of his Romeo-ing rep and finally falls, is a bit that is cleverly handled and Carlotta looks like a million dollars of haughty society spilled into a gown. She's a Nita Naldi, only there is so much of her, if you get what is meant.

Oscar Shaw is the go-getter and he proves it and does it real well. Edgar Norton handles a comedy role as the secretary and delivers it with a wallop. Joseph Kilgour is the banking heavy.

This is a picture bet that shouldn't be overlooked anywhere. *Fred.*

THE KNOCKOUT

First National production, starring Milton Sills. Adapted from M. D. C. Crawford's story, "The Comeback," by Frances Marion, and directed by Lambert Hillyer. At the Rialto, F-P house, New York, Oct. 25 week. Running time, about 65 mins.
Sandy Donlin..................Milton Sills
Jeannie Farot...............Lorna Duveen
Mac Macmahon................Jed Prouty
J. VanDyke Parker...........Claude King
Black Jack..................John Kolb
Mike Leary..................Edward Lawrence
Steve McKenna...............Harry Cording
Dr. Natter..................Warren Cook
John Farot..................Harlan Knight

A he-man-outdoor special will probably be the press agent's appraisal of "The Knockout." Except for the "special" part of it, the p. a. may be right, for in this Sills plays another of those sturdy and honest he-men without which no picture of his or of Tommy Meighan's could exist.

This time Sills is a gentleman prize fighter, light-heavyweight champ, even if he does keep the works of Epictetus in his library. After his scrap, in which the right arm was incapacitated, but in which he kayoed his opponent with the left, a wealthy lumberman engages him to go to Canada and manage his lumber properties. Up there he discovers that the wealthy man has a bunch of double-crossers working who are trying to take the land and lumber held by Jeannie Farot and her invalid father. Being in the employ of their enemy, he has a hard time to break ice with Jeannie, but he sells himself so well that eventually he is breaking not only ice but bread. His lieutenants, however, do some dirty tricks which throw suspicion on him, and the dirtiest blow of all comes when they dynamite the Farot dam, causing a jam of millions of logs, maybe not the same logs, but it's the same old dam-jam.

The hero, to prove he isn't a double-crosser, tries to dynamite the jam, but is unsuccessful. But he proves himself true blue by allying with the girl, and they outwit the crooked New York lumberman, who wanted things his own way. So you see the old dam-jam still works in the same old way.

There is good action in the film. In the first reel Sills has a championship fight in which he uses only the left hand. Later on the forming of the log jam furnishes a kick, while Sills' attempt to dynamite it is another kick.

The star performs as always, gritting his teeth and looking determined. This time he has a new leading lady, Lorna Duveen, apparently taking the place of Doris Kenyon in the Sills pictures. Miss Duveen is a brunet and shows up nicely, particularly so as an outdoor girl type. Rest of the cast is there, and the whole thing frames up as a satisfactory example of that type of film in which Sills usually appears. *Sisk.*

KEEPER OF THE BEES

F. B. O. production called a "Gold Bond Special." Adapted to the screen from the Gene Stratton Porter novel and directed by James Leo Meehan. Robert Frazer, Clara Bow and Alyce Mills featured. At the Cameo, New York, Oct. 25. Running time, about 75 minutes.

James Lewis McFarlane....Robert Frazer
The Bee Master............Josef Swickard
Margaret Cameron..........Martha Mattox
Alice Louise Cameron..........Clara Bow
Molly Cameron..................Alyce Mills
Jean Meredith................Gene Stratton

This is the one about the girl who sinned and the fellow who took the blame. As usual, the fellow gets the devil bawled out of him by a self-sacrificing and tear stained mother, who later says she "understands." Truth of it all is that the older sister of "the girl" knew her predicament and married herself to the man under "the girl's" name so that the child would have a name.

All of which is hokey-pokey hoke and done in precisely the cheap manner which such stuff deserves.

The hero, James Lewis McFarlane, is in a government hospital and when he hears the medicos say he will probably be tubercular (and that's a nice thing to throw in the face of an audience) he skips from the hospital and walks for days to the sea. There he meets an old Bee Master who is ill and who asks the boy to stay at his place while he's in the hospital. The boy does, and there meets the sister of "the girl" who is to have the child. That same girl's mother nurses him back to health.

Eventually the sister tricks him into marriage under the name of the sister who sinned, and after the sinning sister does a Camille on the deathbed (minus coughing), the hero picks up the newly born babe, carries it out into the world and takes it home. Here the mother misunderstands, for the whole thing hadn't been explained to her, and it is only when the sister who actually married him 'fesses up, does the mater relent. Then the sister and the hero meet by the side of the sea and go into a clinch.

Robert Frazer and Alyce Mills of the cast are good, but Clara Bow acts all over the lot and aside from weeping and swirling around, does little. Direction medium and production itself looks like a cheap proposition.

As a business getter, it doesn't look to be in the running. *Sisk.*

COMPROMISE

Warner Brothers' production, starring Irene Rich. Adapted from the novel by Jay Glazer; directed by Alan Crosland. At Warner's, N. Y., week of Oct. 24. Running time, 69 mins.

Jean Trevore......................Irene Rich
Alan Thayer....................Clive Brook
Hilda..........................Louise Fazenda
Nathalie.......................Pauline Garon
Cholly......................Raymond McKee
Catherine....................Helen Dunbar
Joan's Father..................Winter Hall
James..........................Lynn Cowan
Commodore Smithson...Edward Martindale

Here is one that they have everything in except possibly that well-known old "kitchen stove." There is a wallop in a terrific cyclone which knocks down a prop town, but does it in a manner that seems convincing. Why it was worked into the story and how the yachting party managed to get on the scene on horseback is going to be one of those things hard to dope out. But who cares?

Irene Rich has the role of the elder daughter who has been neglected for the younger. She manages to capture the male prize of their particular set, while the younger daughter is abroad securing a divorce. The younger girl returns just after the wedding ceremony is completed and decides that she'd like to have her brother-in-law for herself and starts out to get him. She does manage to land him through getting him aboard a financier's yacht on a two weeks' cruise.

Then, just to let the elder sister know that she was the winner, she marches her captive up to their country place from the yacht, arriving just as the cyclone does. In the end the husband and wife are reconciled, and that's that.

There is some comedy in the picture, due to the efforts of Louise Fazenda, but the bits seem to be over-gagged and dragged in simply to work a laugh into the story.

Miss Rich, however, gives a corking performance opposite Clive Brook, who manages to handle himself perfectly.

Incidentally Raymond McKee, in a comedy role which he overplays at times, looks like a bet for the future, especially if he is handled right and a line of stories given him. *Fred.*

WANDERING FOOTSTEPS

A Banner Production adapted from the story "A Wise Son." Directed by Phil Rosen. Released in the independent market. Shown on double feature bill at Loew's, New York, Oct. 23. Running time, 59 minutes.

Hal Whitney............Bryant Washburn
Tim Payne...............Alec B. Francis
Helen Maynard...............Estelle Taylor
Matilda........................Ethel Wales
Mrs. Whitney...........Eugenie Besserer
Horace Maynard............Phillips Smalley

A mighty entertaining little picture that will get by in most of the neighborhood houses. That also goes for some of the bigger ones where there is a daily change of program and an occasional double feature. Its showing at Loew's New York, together with "The Boomerang," made an exceptionally strong bill.

With the names of Bryant Washburn and Estelle Taylor the exhibitor has something to work on as a boxoffice card and the picture manages to stand up. It is well directed and there are a couple of exceedingly funny bits of business in the visualization of the story.

It is the tale of a young society man who likes his booze a little too well. He has nothing to do except spend dough and he manages to do that by buying booze. On one of his sprees he picks up with an old bum whom he has adopt him as his father. This loses the girl he is engaged to, for he had promised to go on the "wagon" and this escapade proves he's not riding. In the end, however, the adopted father manages to straighten out the boy and they are both in business. The girl is won again and the old man marries the boy's mother. They had been sweethearts years before.

Not much to the story as a whole, but the manner in which it is presented makes it worth while. *Fred.*

PROUD HEART

Universal-Jewell, featuring Rudolph Schildkraut. Story by Isadore Bernstein. Adapted by Charles Whittaker. Scenario by Alfred Cohen. Musical score by Dr. Edward Kilenyi. Directed by Edward Sloman. At the Astor, New York, Nov. 1, for two weeks. Running time, 90 minutes.

David Cominsky.......Rudolph Schildkraut
Rose Cominsky.............Rose Rosanova
Sammy Cominsky............George Lewis
Child.......................Bobby Gordon
Morris Cominsky...........Arthur Lubin
Child.....................Albert Busholano
Mamie Shannon..........Blanche Mehaffey
Child......................Jean Johnson
Kate Shannon.....................Kate Price
Ruth Stein...........Virginia Brown Faire
Chaim Barowitz......................Nat Carr
Judge Nathan Stein.....Bertram Marburgh
Thomas Nolan..............Edgar Kennedy

Those who rallied to "Humoresque" will find every whit as potent a heart wallop in this Universal picture. Also an equally good story that gives the elder Schildkraut his best opportunity since swinging over from legit to the flicker drama. Also a support which for both types and ability could not have possibly been improved upon. The combination should attract business for the two weeks' run it will have at this house.

From a picture standpoint it packs everything that "Abie's Irish Rose" has been selling a legit clientele for nearly four years, and will undoubtedly be labeled as balderdash by the same group of sophisticates who wouldn't have hazarded $500 for a half interest in the Anne Nichols bonanza at any time during the first four weeks of its four-year (or longer) run.

Set in the drab shadow of the lower east side of New York, "Proud Heart," not unlike "Humoresque" is a story of parental sacrifice, with the emphasis this time upon the paternal branch of the household. There is also a tinge of Jewish family devotion that the former had, but this is handled with a dissimilar twist.

Rudolph Schildkraut is David Cominsky, a brilliant scholar in his native country, who has been unable to market his learning here and consequently is compelled to bring up his sons in New York's ghetto. Morris, the eldest, is the favored son with the father. By dint of the latter's sales from a merchandise pushcart and the younger brother Sammy's earnings from selling papers, Morris is given an education that eventually graduates him from law school.

Morris's rise has so elated the old man he is totally blind to the sacrifices of Sammy, despite the mother's natural bent for her baby to attempt to win him recognition from his dad. As a kid Sammy learned to scrap perforcedly in taking his brother's part in street fights, despite the latter never showing him an iota of appreciation for the many "shiners" and claret-smeared faces he had endangered to protect him. Morris was permitted to keep his earnings to keep up a front in his position, while Sammy found the intake of coppers from newspaper sales inadequate, and decided to add to his earnings as a boxer.

This, of course, had to be kept subrosa from his parents, because he knew the proud old father would never be reconciled to a pugilist son (or a "box fighter," as the father called it); but the secret is dropped when a handbill announcing a neighborhood combat and with Sammy's picture resting above the caption of Battling Rooney. This sufficiently arouses the ire of the father to disown him.

Practically simultaneously Morris decides to pull from the family hearth for a more classy berth uptown. That momentarily staggers the old man, but he willingly sacrifices his feelings when he understands that the change of quarters may help the boy to success. But as a matter of fact Morris has proposed to the daughter of his employer, Judge Stein, and rather than admit his humble parentage is posing as an orphan.

Prior to the betrothal dinner at the fashionable Stein menage, Morris makes a demand upon his father for the price of a dress suit. He hasn't the money, but pawns his overcoat or, rather, exchanges it for a dress suit which is a hand-me-down not classy enough for Morris and which he eventually deposits in an ashcan.

The old man's trip through the sleet has taken its toll. He is practically upon his deathbed and calling for Morris, the apple of his eye. Despite a telegraphic appeal, Morris prefers the company of his fiancee. Sammy is summoned and palmed off in a dark room as the favored son when it is thought the old man is about to pass over. After the visit he rallies, and during the convalescent period a friend shows him an announcemnt of the Cominsky-Stein betrothal.

The orphan angle of the yarn bewilders him. He decides to find out for himself, only to be denied by the son for whom he had pledged his very existence, while at the same hour Sammy is facing a possible fatal lambasting in a squared arena, having substituted for a more experienced fighter in a championship match to earn $1,000 which is to send his father to a different climate to save his life.

Sammy takes an unmerciful beating, but scores a knockout on a fluke punch. When he learns of his brother's ingratitude he makes for the Stein home and drags his brother back to the tenements to apologize for having been ashamed of his parents. Forgiveness all around reunites the family, at least temporarily, for Sammy is contemplating matrimony with Mamie Shannon, the girl across the hall, with the nuptials being a culmination of a kid romance which furnishes the love interest.

Schildrkraut gives a masterful impersonation of a heart-torn father. His performance is a gem and a personal film triumph sufficient in itself to warrant the success of this picture. Rose Rosanova is splendid also as the indulgent mother, giving to it a human touch that is far-reaching. George Lewis also comes in for capital honors through his splendid Sammy, while Arthur Lubin is the snobbish Morris in a manner making the role adequately despicable. Blanche Mehaffey makes Mamie Shannon a worthy incentive for Sammy's struggles, bringing to the role a poignant freshness and acting ability when given the opportunity. Nat Carr, Virginia Browne Faire and Kate Price also did well in less important roles.

"Proud Heart" can't miss as a program picture. It has a comedy blend that lightens its more tragic moments, an irresistible heart wallop, a star and supporting cast that are a credit to its director. Though Jewish in play and character mainly, its heart appeal is universal, also rebounding to the able direction of Edward Sloman. *Edba.*

Seven Keys to Baldpate

Douglas MacLean Production presented by Famous Players. Adapted from the George M. Cohan comedy and Earl Derr Biggers novel. Directed by Fred Newmeyer. At the Rivoli, New York, week Nov. 1. Running time, 66 minutes.

Wm. Hallowell Magee....Douglas MacLean
Mary Norton..................Edith Roberts
J. K. Norton.............Anders Randolph
Bentley...........................Crauford Kent
Bland...............................Ned Sparks
The Hermit...........William Orlamonde
Cargan............................Wade Boteler
Lou Max..........................Edwin Sturgis
Myra Thornhill............Betty Francisco
Mrs. Rhodes....................Maym Kelso
Sheriff............................Fred Kelsey
Quimby...........................Fred Lockney
Mrs. Quimby....................Edith Rorke

A comedy choc-a-block with laughs. A really remarkable thing about it all is that on this occasion Douglas MacLean did not resort to injecting something not in the original to get his comedy over. There is no chase or like stunt to give the final comedy wallop, but the star goes along in the role of the author in a straightaway manner that hits the audience right between the eyes for laughs.

This is the first Douglas MacLean-Famous Players release, and the comedian has gotten away from the style he used in clowning through the releases that he made for Associated Exhibitors, but he does his work in a business-like fashion and proves himself a greater comedian than his previous pictures suggested.

"Seven Keys to Baldpate" makes an ideal vehicle for Doug, and he tackles the job with a winning smile and a snappy style.

At the Rivoli on Sunday afternoon the house was jammed, and those there laughed their heads off.

The forepart is practically all MacLean, but once the Baldpate Inn sequence is reached everyone gets a chance to shine, and they all do. There are a couple of shots in color and they are most effective.

At the opening is a sub-title requesting those in the audience who have seen the picture previously not to disclose the ending to the first timers. Some of those in Sunday's audience must have thought that was comedy, for they started in to laugh at it.

There is a string of laughs in the radiograms at the start of the story, and a good gag is the scene showing the long line of messenger boys at the home of the hero's fiancee delivering his messages to her.

Edith Roberts plays the lead opposite the star and registers nicely. Anders Randolph as the publisher stood out in the earlier scenes. William Orlamonde as the Hermit got any number of laughs.

The story of the attempt to turn out a novel in 24 hours by a young author who goes to a deserted summer hotel and the subsequent events taking place are just as screamingly funny on the screen as they were on the stage.

Doug MacLean has turned out a sure-fire box office picture as his first production under the new association. *Fred.*

NEW BROOMS

William deMille Production presented by Famous Players. From the play by Frank Craven, adapted by Clara Beranger. Featuring Bessie Love, Neil Hamilton and Phyllis Haver. At the Rialto, New York, week Nov. 1 Running time, 57 minutes.

Thomas Bates, Jr. .... Neil Hamilton
Geraldine Marsh .... Bessie Love
Florence Levering .... Phyllis Haver
Thomas Bates, Sr. .... Robert McWade
Williams .... Fred Walton
Margaret .... Josephine Crowell
George Morrow .... Larry Steers

"New Brooms" was not very successful as a play. On the screen it makes a rather interesting little entertainment, although a great deal of the humor of the play is lost in the transition.

Of course, "New Brooms" won't be a great big box office clean-up, but it is a picture that will get by with any audience. Neil Hamilton, Bessie Love and Phyllis Haver are featured, but the best performance is by Robert McWade, playing the role he created in the stage production, the grouchy old broom manufacturer who turns his business over to his son to prove to the youngster that he wasn't quite as smart as he thought he was.

Miss Love as the little orphaned girl who comes into the Bates family as their housekeeper and finally wins the heart of the son, played with far greater appeal than it was endowed with on the stage. Miss Haver as the haughty ward of the family fitted fairly well, although she did nothing that will particularly distinguish her. Neil Hamilton rather overplayed at times.

Fred Walton as the butler impressed, although what he had to do was rather limited. His pantomime was perfect, and he got over a couple of laughs in a manner most clever. *Fred.*

BOBBED HAIR

Warner Brothers feature directed by Alan Crosland. Adapted from the novel of the same title which had 20 famous authors as collaborators. Co-starring Marie Prevost and Kenneth Harlan. Shown at Warner's, New York, week Oct. 31. Running time 74 minutes.

Connemara Moore .... Marie Prevost
David Lacy .... Kenneth Harlan
"Sweetie" .... Louise Fazenda
Saltonstall Adams .... John Roche
Aunt Cellmena Moore .... Emily Fitzroy
Bingham Carrington .... Reed Howes
The "Swede" .... Walter Long
"Pooch" .... Francis McDonald
Mr. Brewster .... Tom Ricketts
"Pal" .... The Dog

A mighty formidable list of names attached to this screen version of what the program terms "popular novel." Those listed as responsible are Carolyn Wells, Sophie Kerr, Alexander Woollcott, Robert Gordon Anderson, Louis Bromfield, Gerald Mygatt, Elsie Janis, Kermit Roosevelt, Edward Streeter, Bernice Brown, George Barr McCutcheon, Wallace Irwin, George Agnew Chamberlain, Frank Craven, Meade Minningerose, Rube Goldberg, Dorothy Parker, John V. A. Weaver, H. C. Witwer and George Palmer Putnam. They should mean something at the box office, but the chances are that they won't. The story itself that they have jointly turned out is just a hodge-podge affair that resolves itself into a cheap thriller.

All the hoke in the world in the feature. Gag follows gag. When out of gags they insert a good old reliable "chase" which has been a sure fire footage eater ever since pictures started to be made. There is an auto chase, a couple of motor boat chases, and finally a chase with a dog.

The story is supposed to be a mystery yarn anent bobbed hair and bootleggers, hi-jackers and just plain crooks. There is a certain measure of love interest thrown in, and atop of that is Louise Fazenda, who contributes comedy, sometimes rough and ready and at other times really clever.

Marie Prevost plays Connemara Moore who has two suitors. One wants her to bob her hair and the other doesn't. She cannot make up her mind which of the two she really likes best, so on the night of a masquerade ball at the home of her aunt when she has to announce which of the boys she is going to accept, she runs away from home. On the road she meets Kenneth Harlan, who is driving a car to keep an appointment with the smugglers. As the story develops, each believes that the other is a gangster. Harlan in reality is aiding the Government officers to trap the gang.

For four and a half reels or more there follows a wild auto ride with three cars chasing each other, a grand smashup of one of the cars and then aboard a yacht, with three motor boats chasing each other, the hero and the heroine having the gangsters after them because the hero has grabbed $50,000 in dough from the gang and the gang are trying to get it back.

Finally when the officers take the crooks in charge and the true identity of the two principal characters are revealed in their true light, the young lady decides that she will give both of her former suitors the air and accept the young man who has been shot at, smashed up in an auto wreck, doused in the bay and beat over the head in her company during an exciting couple of hours that have preceded the final disclosure of who is who.

It is a lot of hoke—the kind of hoke they will eat up in the small daily change of program houses.

Marie Prevost looks stunning in her masquerade costume as a sister of charity, and Harlan is a likeable hero. The best actor in the picture, however, is the trained bull terrier who goes flying through the chase with Miss Fazenda. The dog proves a great comedy foil for her. *Fred.*

Lights of Old Broadway

Cosmopolitan Production released through Metro-Goldwyn. Marion Davies starred Directed by Monta Bell. Story adapted by Carey Wilson from Laurence Eyre's play, "Merry Wives of Gotham." At the Capitol, New York, week Nov. 1. Running time, 77 minutes.

Dirk DeRhonde .... Conrad Nagel
Lambert DeRhonde .... Frank Currier
Andy .... George K. Arthur
Shamus O'Tandy .... Charles McHugh
Fely }
Anne } .... Marion Davies
Mrs. O'Tandy .... Eleanor Lawson
Mrs. DeRhonde .... Julia Swayne Gordon
Baby Blue .... Matthew Betz
Fowler .... Wilbur Higby
Widow Gorman .... Bodil Rosing
Tony Pastor .... George Bunny
Joe Weber .... George Harris
Lew Fields .... Bernard Berger
Thomas A. Edison .... Frank Glendon
Young Theodore Roosevelt .... Buck Black
Roosevelt's Father .... Karl Dane
DeRhonda's Butler .... Billie DeVaull

A corking picture from almost every angle. As a first-run proposition it is entirely suitable; for the places where the star stands strong it offers lots to look at, and for the numerous cities and villages overridden with critics who are concerning themselves needlessly about the artistic state of the movies, this one offers a rebuke, as it has been intelligently produced in every foot of celluloid.

Because of that, a bow in the direction of Monta Bell.

This story is adapted from "Merry Wives of Gotham," a stage play which featured Grace George and Laura Hope Crews, and these two players, in their elderly roles, were the chief interest in the legit version. For movies, however, the startoff shows how two deserted babies were adopted aboard ship, one by Mrs. DeRhonde, an aristocrat, and the other by Mrs. Shamus O'Tandy, wife of a scrapping Irishman. Miss Davies takes the dual role of the daughter of the rich and the gamin child of the poor Irish folks who lived in Shantytown, at 59th street and 5th avenue.

And such quirks as this make the picture. Old 14th street is shown rather accurately in all its glory. We have Tony Pastor's theatre, with the varieties impresario standing before his lobby questioning applicants for jobs. Up walked two young fellows, who showed their dancing and comedy wares to Tony. He asked their names. They were Weber and Fields. As he turned them down, one of them (probably Joe Weber) turned to the other and remarked that when he did hire them it would cost him twice as much.

Then there is a shot of young Teddy Roosevelt running home with his report card, which carried a very low mark in deportment. Thomas A. Edison and the introduction of electric lights in practical use—these and many other things of interest not only in New York but all over the country. Bell has been wise in this, for while the picture is fascinating to the average resident of New York, he has fixed it so that the appeal carries farther than just this one city.

The story proper concerns the love with the step-brother of the Irish gamin's real sister for the [illegible] in Shantytown, and of how Shamus O'Tandy, whose wife said he spent more for linament than he did for groceries, grew rich with his electric light stocks, and of how the aristocrat grew poor because of his heavy investments in the gas works.

The free adaptation was entirely justified, for much has been made of it. Miss Davies in the gamin role is excellent, while as the rich girl she is suitable enough. But it is in playing rough slapstick that she excels, for her make-ups are good and the comedy, although rough, is effective with the audience. The support here is unusually good, while not enough can be said of the production, which shows interiors of Tony Pastor's theatre, 14th street, as it was, and other things of equal interest.

This film aimed at a high mark and struck the bull's eye. Little more need be said. *Sisk.*

THREE IN EXILE

Truart Production, released in New York territory through Renown Exchange. Story by George Hively, with direction by Fred Windemere. Reviewed at the Stanley, New York, Oct. 30. Running time, 45 minutes.

The Dog .... Rex, "the wonder dog"
The Horse .... Blackie
Art Flanders .... Art Acord
Lorraine Estes .... Louise Lorraine

Rather cheaply made western, which obviously tries to combine the best features of the horse picture turned out by Pathe and the dog pictures made by Warners and others. It is unsuccessful, for the animals used are too obviously nothing but trained performers working under cues all the time.

The plot tells of a cowboy who takes to the desert after a fight; a dog driven from a town because people thought he was mad, and a wild horse which bounded out of its corral. The three meet, and as they are all about to die of thirst they come upon a desert house run by the daughter of the late John Estes, a prospector, who for years worked a claim in the desert.

It seems that a bad man is going to take the claim away from the little girl, but the cowboy does the manual labor requisite to getting the land officer's okeh for further possession, while the dog and the horse bring the cowboy back once again to apprehend agents of the villain who were trying to dynamite the mine. Aforementioned villain and his agents are punished, while one of those "year later" sub-titles shows the hero and heroine with a baby, the dog with a litter of pups, while the poor horse is monkeying around with the baby's hobby horse.

The animal stuff may get over in a few places, but the love-interest is negligible and the whole plot so patently obvious that little suspense is developed.

Strictly for the shooting galleries. *Sisk.*

THE BIG PARADE

King Vidor's Production, presented by Metro-Goldwyn. From the story by Laurence Stallings. Directed by King Vidor. Starring John Gilbert with Rene Adoree. World premiere for indefinite run at Grauman's Egyptian, Hollywood, Nov. 5. Running time, 150 minutes.

James Apperson	John Gilbert
Melisande	Renee Adoree
Mr. Apperson	Hobart Bosworth
Mrs. Apperson	Claire McDowell
Justyn Reed	Claire Adams
Harry	Robert Ober
Bull	Tom O'Brien
Slim	Karl Dane
French Mother	Rosita Marstini

Jeff McCarthy's prophecy that "The Big Parade" is a road show proposition, destined to get big money, is verified in the production that King Vidor made of Laurence Stallings' tale of what he visualized as incidents of the war, or possibly a tale close to home itself, so far as he is concerned, with respect to the dramatic touches and story components.

Stallings in a prolific and light vein outlined an interesting yarn of three youths, each from a different station in life, who were thrown together during the war and stuck together until "death did part them." Of course his big punches—or, at least, those of the film's, so far as the public will be concerned—are the battle sequences. There have been signal corps and other war pictures shown in the past, but nothing evoked the interest in the past along these lines as this picture will, due to its story, nicely woven and well told.

This picture can only be judged from an entertainment standpoint, and as such should bring plenty of profit, possibly with cost productions taken into consideration more than "Ben-Hur." However, if one wanted to perform a post-mortem from the military technical standpoint plenty of fault can be found with it; but so far as the lay mind is concerned these details either exaggerated or wrongly executed will not be noticed, nor will they detract.

That the views of Stallings on war are reflected in the picture is obvious by the titles used. The swear language is liberally resorted to in expressing thought, and no doubt modification or elimination will have to be made in communities where the censors hold forth.

Vidor can be credited with having executed the best job of his career in the making of this picture. He had a tough subject to deal with. He knew that he would have to show the horrors of war, and therefore worked his story out in such a manner that it had plenty of comedy relief and a love sequence that will impress those who view it in such a manner that they will carry the performance of Renee Adoree and John Gilbert in these scenes in their minds for a long time to come.

Instead of an officer and soldier fighting over a French girl as they do in "What Price Glory," Stallings worked this story out so that a buck private, after his corporal and another man were turned down, had a clear field with the French peasant girl. This private, John Gilbert, who joined the forces at the outbreak of war rather than toil in his father's mills, hooks up with Bull, a former bartender from the Bowery, and Slim, who was an ironworker and riveter. They get into the same company. Bull, on account of his ways, is made a corporal. They get to the other side, and the girl appears. Slim and Bull try to make her, but she cuts them short and falls for Jimmie. Then her Jimmie forgets about his American sweetheart and professes love for her.

The outfit is ordered to the front. The girl hears about it as the last contingent is leaving town. She hurries to find her boy. He is located on a motor truck. He jumps off.

Then the big love scene. It is beautiful and heartrending as this girl clings to him as he caresses her, then when he tries to make his getaway on the truck, clings to his leg until she is pushed away and then grabs hold of a chain and hangs to the truck as it goes along the road for a distance until she is knocked off. A pathetic and lovable sight as she stands in the middle of the road as the troops disappear from sight. It is the big punch of the first portion of the picture, which is rather draggy and could easily be chopped 1,000 or more feet.

The boys get to the front. They stick together, with Slim replacing Bull as the corporal, for the latter had, for some reason or other, booted an officer when he saw him reading mail. They are pals throughout. They get lost during a battle, and finally get into a shell-hole. Word from the company commander comes that one must take a machine gun nest which is knocking off men by the wholesale. All want to go, but they decide to spit for the honor. Slim, being a tobacco chewer, wins, and goes over the top. The other two men remain in suspense waiting for Slim to come back.

Slim meantime takes the nest, k.'s the two gunners and starts to cra l back with their helmets as trophies. On the way he is spotted, made a target and fatally wounded. The other boys get a touch of the powder odor, go wild, and decide they will bring back Slim.

Bull is knocked off, and then Jim goes it alone. He finds Slim, gasping his last breath. There is a scene there as realistic and touching as any death scene imaginable. It was heart-reaching, and had the majority of the audience in tears.

After Slim has gone to the Great Beyond, Jimmie does a bit of crawling and is shot in the leg by a sniper. The latter crawls after him, and Jim gets him above the heart. Then the boche sniper tries to get back to his shell-hole, with Jim following. He makes it, and Jim is right on top of him.

Comes as beautiful a touch of directing as has ever been done—the death scene of the boche. Jim has his bayonet and is about to stick the German when the latter sneers at him and asks for a cigaret. Jim's heart is touched, and he gives the dying man the fag. The latter takes a few puffs and passes out. Jim takes the lighted cigaret from the dead man's mouth, touches it to his mouth and face. Seeing no response he knows the man is dead, and proceeds to finish smoking.

Of course Jim is rescued by his comrades, who have advanced, and taken to a hospital. While there he hears from another soldier that the town his sweetheart resides in has been bombed and destroyed. In his hysterical moments he escapes from the hospital, commands a truck to halt and is taken to the town. The enemy bombard it, and when it is over the Americans find him again, taking him once more to the hospital, where his leg is amputated (as was that of Stallings). He is sent back to America, discharged, received in the home as a hero, but finds that his girl has changed her affections to his brother. In another heart-touching scene with his mother he tells her his love is in France and he will not be happy until claiming her. He returns to France, with a wooden leg, finds the girl, and all is serene.

Everything one can expect from real war is in this picture. One sees the various branches of artillery in action, plenty of hand-grenade and machine-gun warfare, gas attacks, tractors, etc. Also men marching over the dead in the fields and men dropping right and left. There are air attacks and maneuvers, and not a detail lacking that occurred in the big affray.

It was obvious that a good portion of the long shots and battles, so far as big guns, barrages, etc., were stock material—in some instances used for double exposures. Whether or not this stuff came from the signal corps' large stock of film, the picture as put together is surefire entertainment and cannot miss, no matter where. It may be a bit morbid; folks may object, but it is one of the greatest pieces of propaganda ever launched against war.

Gilbert in the starring role worked hard, but he did not seem to be at ease at any time. He had plenty of hard work to do and did it well. Miss Adoree had the chance of her life and made good in the farewell scene just as her lover was leaving for the front. That one moment alone entitles her to a niche in the screen hall of fame.

Tom O'Brien as Bull and Karl Dane as Slim did remarkable characterization, and actually go through the roles as though living their life that way. Both are sterling character actors and should not miss at whatever they try in their respective lines. The balance of the principals did nobly in their endeavors.

With all credit for the entire epic to be cast in the direction of Vidor.

Ung.

THE EAGLE

United Artists Production presented by John W. Considine, Jr. Starring Rudolph Valentino with Vilma Banky and Louise Dresser featured. Screen play by Hans Kraly based on the Russian classic "Dubrovsky" by Alexander Pushkin. Directed by Clarence Brown. Shown at the Strand, New York, week Nov. 8, 1925. Running time, 72 minutes.

Vladmir Bubrovsky	Rudolph Valentino
Mascha Troekuroff	Vilmy Banky
The Czarina	Louise Dresser
Kuschka	Albert Conti
Kyrilla Troekouroff	James Marcus
Judge	George Nichols
Aunt Aurelia	Carrie Clark Ward

Rudolph Valentino as a Russian Robin Hood of more modern times. In "The Eagle" the sheik, who says he is tired of being dubbed as strictly a ladies' man, really goes out and does some "he-man" stuff and rides in a manner that is going to make Tom Mix and a couple of the riding boys look to their laurels. But with Valentino as their star there must also be a lot of credit bestowed on the two feature supports, Vilma Banky and Louise Dresser.

That Louise Dresser girl as the Czarina certainly does handle herself superbly. She is the old girl of the Russians who liked the boys. Whenever a good looking young lieutenant or captain of her guard appealed to her she usually made him a general after he had spent an evening or a night in the royal suite. Miss Dresser conveys this all in the picture and there is a great laugh toward the end of it when all of her "boy friends" are lined up with their imposing decorations. But Rudy as the Lieut. Dubrovsky, who ran out on her when she tried to "make" him, was too much for the old girl and she signed his death warrant because he refused to fall.

That's the spot where he opened up the Robin Hood store and started on a career of crime. He had an added incentive, for Kyrilla had dispoiled his father of his estate and took possession of the place, lock, stock and barrel. He was a playful sort of a bird, Kyrilla. When tiring of anyone he usually slipped them the key to his wine cellar to let them pick out the best bottle. In the wine cellar was a ferocious bear held captive by a long chain. When once one entered the cellar and the door closed behind him the bear could be counted on to take care of things.

Vladmir decides to go after Kyrilla to even things up, but falls in love with the old boy's daughter and can't carry out his plan of vengence. Kyrilla doesn't want whom he supposes is a French traitor to grab off the prize of his family and he sends him to the wine cellar, but the girl steps in in time to save the day.

In the finish Vladmir is captured by the troops of the Czarina and taken to the palace to be executed, but the old girl still has a bit of love for him and through her latest "general" arranges for his departure from the country, although in prison just prior to the moment that he believes is to be his execution, he weds the daughter of his enemy.

The picture is skillfully handled and there are many moments of a light variety where there are laughs and there is enough suggestion in the scenes with the Czarina to make the money come to the box office. Whether they will be able to get away with these scenes and what they imply in certain censor spots remains to be seen.

But Rudy is doing considerable of a come-back with this picture and if Joe Schenck can follow it with another as good, the chances and that he will have this star right on the real road to popularity.

Vilma Banky as the daughter makes a most charming heroine opposite the star, but that Louise Dresser is about as much the picture as the star himself. *Fred.*

NEW COMMANDMENT

First National production presented by Robert T. Kane. From the novel, "Invisible Wounds," by Col. Frederick Palmer, adapted by Sada Cowan and Howard Higgin. Directed by Howard Higgin. At the Rialto, New York, week Nov. 8. Running time, 73 minutes.

Rene Darcourt	Blanche Sweet
Billy Morrow	Ben Lyon
William Morrow	Holbrook Blinn
Mrs. Parr	Clara Eames
Marquis de la Salle	Effie Shannon
Countess Stoll	Dorothy Cummings
Picard	Pedro de Cordova
Red	George Cooper
Ethel	Diana Kane
Henri Darcourt	Lucius Henderson

A love scene in this picture between Blanche Sweet and Ben Lyon is about the most intense ever screened. Can you imagine an audience right in the middle of a picture breaking into applause as the scene finishes. That is just what those in the Rivoli did Sunday night. And boy, how they applauded! And how the girls snickered to cover up—and how they chattered after the scene finished. That love scene alone is worth the price of admission.

In addition to that, "The New Commandment" is a good picture, a little draggy in spots but it can easily be snapped up and then it will be about as good a picture as any of the average program features.

It is a war story to a certain degree and has some corking battle stuff toward the latter portion. Incidentally there is proof positive that the picture must have cost a pretty penny. No cheating on this one except for a few shots where it is possible the U. S. Signal Corps pictures taken in France during the war were utilized to add to the thrill. These however are so skillfully blended they are almost as though especially made. There is one bit of color film most effective and playing the picture on Broadway during Armistice Week was a clever stroke of booking, for it is right in the atmosphere.

The story opens in New York with Tammany Young acting as a lecturer on a rubberneck wagon. It closes the same way, except for the years that have lapsed. Two homes are shown of the Darcourts and the Morrows. Darcourt is an old Frenchman who has written a book. He cannot get a publisher and decides to go to France to have his work printed.

The Morrow family also goes abroad, principally because Mrs. Parr who is Morrow's sister, would like to have her stepdaughter marry Billy. Billy manages to escape and in a cafe meets Rene Darcourt, who is being shown the sights of Paris by a party including an artist for whom she posed after the death of her father. A wow of a fight scene here that will have most audiences on the edge of their chairs while it is in progress. It is to escape arrest as a result of the fight that Billy Morrow accompanied by Red, a New York taxi-chauffeur, and the girl escape into the country, arriving at the home of the Marquis de la Salle.

There are complications and the young lovers are parted. Then the war and in a hospital they are reunited.

Blanche Sweet looks great and handles herself wonderfully well and how she did eat up that love scene. Ben Lyon is a likeable enough hero, but George Cooper walks off with the comedy honors, and Holbrook Blinn for acting.

In directing, Howard Higgin put over a couple of clever touches. That little bit of business with Diana Kane as the stepdaughter, looking over the boys, thrice repeated, got to be one of the wow touches as far as the audience was concerned. Clara Eames as the match-making mother scored most effectively.

If Bob Kane continues to put 'em over along the lines of this one, he is going to be in the big money.

Fred.

CLASSIFIED

First National release, produced by Asher, Small & Rogers. Directed by Al Santell, with Corrine Griffith starred. Jack Mulhall and Charles Murray featured. At Strand, New York, week Nov. 2. Running time about 65 minutes.

Babs Comet	Corrine Griffith
Lloyd Whiting	Jack Mulhall
Spencer Clark	Ward Crane
Mart Comet	Carroll Nye
Old Man Comet	Charles Murray
"Maw" Comet	Edythe Chapman
Jeanette Comet	Jacqueline Wells
Weinstein	George Sidney
Bernstein	Bernard Randall

This story by Edna Ferber may have been published, and if as on the screen, probably in one of those true story magazines. But it is doubtful if Miss Ferber wrote it as it is screen-played, for it's scenarioed right down to the picture level, perhaps below, made broad and tiresome at times, with even Corinne Griffith's over-wise flapper-character aiding in this.

As a picture house comedy of the general release standard, it's enough, for it slapsticks the story sufficiently in its action and tale to amuse mildly the Griffith admirers. The real and best laughs come from the captions. Many are quite snappy and several are bright in humor.

It is really the dramatization of the story of the girl who had to walk home from her auto ride. There's nothing else to it excepting that, in the picture. The rest is freshness on the part of the flapper who works in the classified department of a daily.

She flirts to get an auto ride downtown every morning, tells her mother she doesn't like the "joint" the family lives in, and the story or plot of a girl who remains out late at night, but "can take care of herself" has been recited more than once in pictures.

It's when the "millionaire from 5th avenue" takes her autoing that she walks home as another of her wise wheezes, besides the pantomime that went with it, when the machine broke down, as Babs Comet saw Lloyd Whiting inspect a convenient road house right in front of them. That is when she walked, getting back home via milk wagon at 7 a. m. to express neither sympathy nor regret over the fact that her folks had remained up all night waiting for her.

This kind of stuff for picture is about the worst kind of trash that can be put upon the screen for young girls and boys. It's too fresh and it's too wise; it's too loose and it's too careless. It's the worst kind of an example to set before **the youth who attend pictures and it's tiresome to anyone with an intellect.**

And yet and again no doubt it fits the picture house audiences. It fits them because such pictures as this, perhaps a little better and not much worse, are constantly being fed to the American picture house audience.

Technically, the best thing about this film, next to the captions, is its continuity. The direction is fair enough for the material unfolded. In acting Miss Griffith cannot come first, for she overplayed, although making a great looking little flapper. Jack Mulhall did a dandy juvenile, but Charles Murray as the tad father showed nothing to hold up his feature billing.

George Sidney and Bernard Randall were a couple of P. & P. cloak and suiters, who were involved in one scene that somehow passed the censors. It was raw and pushed in to follow up laughs in the sequence.

Carroll Nye did a neat little bit as Babs' brother. That boy seems expressive. Ward Crane had the heavy, doing an in and out piece of work. Edythe Chapman carried a mother role very well.

The First National exhibitors need not be afraid of this one, but it will be far from a riot and possibly drive away some of the class trade —if there is any picture house left with any class patronage. *Sime.*

ROSE OF THE WORLD

Warner Brothers production, directed by Harry Beaumont. Patsy Ruth Miller featured. Adapted from the Kathleen Norris novel. At Warner's, New York, week Nov. 7. Running time, around 70 minutes.

Rose Kirby	Patsy Ruth Miller
Jack Talbot	Alan Forrest
Edith Rodgers	Pauline Garon
Clyde Bainbridge	Rockliffe Fellowes
Cecelia Kirby	Barbara Luddy
"Gramp" Tallifer	Alec Francis
Mrs. John Talbot	Helen Dunbar
Mrs. Kirby	Lydia Knott
The Boy	Edward Piel, Jr.
Sally Towsey	Carrie Clark Ward

A real reliable program feature that will make itself especially interesting to women. It's full of sentimental intrigue, has some types without in character dress, weaves in and out of plot and schemes, with an overdose of love interest, also kissing—but it's clean.

Men may say it is padded out too long but that is not so although excellent direction fell into the error now and then of too much detail. That the women will like it is enough.

While the action is meagre, the many twists to the tale upholds continued interest. It's the most perfectly cast picture in New York for a long while. Every player fits in, even to the boy and cute little girl of the company. Special commendation might be slipped to Alan Forrest as Jack Talbot on his make up. In a most unsympathetic role at the outset, the part of a weakling lover easily weaned away and always falling for a girl who would kiss him, Mr. Forrest, with a slight mustache, as the youthful idiot, as the years passed grew older with them in a workmanly quiet manner. Probably technical for the lays but it does display thought and application. As the player of the role, Mr. Forrest did about all that could have been done; he must have hated it, too

Patsy Ruth Miller, featured, is the mushy country girl, engaged to the son of the village social tiger and expected to bridge the high life gap. Miss Miller was outstripped for performance by Pauline Garon as the young society girl who comes home to find her youthful swain about to marry the other girl, and she cuts her out. The other girl was Miss Miller. Later as his wife and the social leader in the burg, Miss Garon gave a fine impersonation of a beautiful dumbell.

In this picture they had to kill two young people to get them out of the path of the sweet finish. That was no light job and it seemed to take a long while. But at last one died of heart disease and the other was thrown into a gulley. That permitted Miss Miller and Mr. Forrest to return to their first love tryst and marry, each having unsatisfactorily mated meantime.

There's a player unprogrammed who did about the most artistic "death" that has been seen on the stage or screen. He is elderly and was the Jack Talbot's father. Taken by an apoplectic stroke in his office, this unknown fell off his chair and he seemed to become rigid on the way to the floor. This man put a lot of acting into a very minute bit and should be worth watching for character roles.

Another finger of appreciation going to Harry Beaumont is for resisting any sex stuff temptation and running through it wholesomely as he did. There are several spots where the box office would come first to the mind of any director of Mr. Beaumont's experience but he never allowed a move to get off side. That was fine, for it would have hurt instead of helping.

Nice settings, several neat interjections, extremely pretty outdoor shots, and in general one of those regular releases they all would like to make all of the time, instead of in and outers. *Sime.*

ANCIENT HIGHWAY

Famous Players picture featuring Jack Holt, Billie Done and Montague Love. Irwin Willat production, directed by Willat. Adapted from James Oliver Curwood's story. Alfred Gilks, photographer. At Rialto, New York, week Nov. 8. Running time, 60 mins.

Cliff Brant	Jack Holt
Antoinette St. Ives	Billie Dove
Ivan Hurd	Montague Love
Gaspard St. Ives	Stanley Taylor
John Denis	Lloyd Whitlock
Ambrose	William A. Carroll
Angel Fanchon	Marjorie Bonner
George Bolden	Christian J. Frank

Another of those tried and true lumber camp tales but entertaining for all of that. The narrative includes the inevitable log jam, the blocking of the stream by the villain and the dynamiting to free the timber after which Jack Holt must rescue Billie Dove from the turbulent torrent.

The picture starts out with plenty of action in an enthusiastic fistic encounter between Holt and Montague Love before ten minutes have elapsed. Famous has staged the office and home interiors with customary splendor, although the major portion of the footage is out of doors and supposedly north of Quebec. The story covers a number of months but Willat has reduced the footage by depicting a couple of passing seasons by means of "shots" at the foliage.

A program feature consuming but around 60 minutes is an oddity these days, and that this release has been so cut as to curtail the running time is much in its favor. This film could easily have become a screen bore if permitted to run at large due to its much used plot, a fact which someone evidently realized.

Ivan Hurd has the Canadian lumber situation in his lap. So much so the inherited forest tracts of Antoinette St. Ives are almost lost to her with Hurd's price to cease his oppression being marriage. Cliff Brant disrupts a conference between the girl and Hurd in the latter's office by a call which terminates in Brant administering a terrific beating to the lumber monarch. This is in retaliation for Hurd having ruined young Brant's father and causing the pater's death (told by subtitle). Antoinette is in the next room while the hand to hand warfare is going on but gets a glimpse of Brant as he departs.

A sprained ankle of the heroine's brother paves the way for the entrance of Brant into the St. Ives home where the girl's cousin, managing her interests, hails Brant as his overseas captain believed dead. The combination of these two interests to fight Hurd follows.

Changing to the tree country the spring drive is ready when the dirty work commences. Brant starts the logs down stream but Hurd's men blast out a side of a hill to halt the flow. Brant and the cousin make a frantic trip in a canoe to reply by exploding the resultant jam. They light the fuse but the cousin becomes imprisoned among the logs and to complicate matters Antoinette selects this moment to become remorseful over her previous attitude toward Brant and rushes out to seek her lover's forgiveness. The fuse finally reaches its destination and the trio are hurled into the mad rush of water and timber. A rescue is finally effected with the usal clinch finish.

William Carroll gets comedy into the sequence although some of the bits designed for him are out-and-out hoke. Holt convinces as the very masculine hero while Love is obligingly and sufficiently underhanded to become appropriately disliked. Miss Love's appearance is a pleasing study regarding her previous appearance in comedies while her performance fits all requirements of the script. Other cast support is efficient.

Nothing great about this release but suitable program fare, helped by the cast names, and as the houses grow smaller its entertaining capabilities will increase.

Skig.

THE LAST EDITION

F. B. O. production made by Emory Johnson and starring Ralph Lewis. Story and continuity by Emilie Johnson. At the Cameo, New York, Nov. 8 week. Running time, 60 minutes.

Tom MacDonald	Ralph Lewis
Mary MacDonald	Lila Leslie
Ray MacDonald	Ray Hallor
Polly MacDonald	Frances League
Clarence Walker	Rex Lease
George Hamilton	Lou Payne
"Red" Moran	David Kirby
Mike Fitzgerald	Wade Boteler
Gerald Fuller	Cuyler Supplee
Aaron Hoffman	Leigh Willard
Sam Blotz	Will Frank

Emory Johnson, who put this one on, has made a specialty for the past few years of turning out melodramas, filled with more hokum than any small time vaudeville show and usually glorifying some underpaid group, such as the firemen, the policemen, the mail carriers. Now he comes to the newspapermen, who deserve, if one is to judge from his subtitles, all the glory in this world and a large part of that in the next. He really meant newspapermen, although in his zeal he made a reference to "journalism," that somewhat mysterious occupation pursued by **fellows who don't cut so much of a flash in their own city rooms but who put on the dog outside.**

His hero is a reporter—and what a reporter. One of the kind with his own car, a flivver, but funniest of all, a big sign which labels his machine as the "Press Car." The reporter, being somewhat of a sleuth, takes the sign off when he gets after a big story, and being a good reporter, he never follows a man unless he creeps along the side of a wall in stooping posture, a la Sheerluck Bones.

The story proper concerns a young district attorney whose father is assistant foreman of the press room in the San Francisco "Chronicle" office. The boy is framed by the villains and thrown into jail. Immediately the paper gets a flash on the yarn, the time being about 5 a. m. But the city room men were still working and by the time the yarn hit the composing room, a full union force was there also, which must indicate one of two things—that the Frisco "Chronicle" is a very wealthy paper to stand such an expense, or Emory Johnson's zeal ıs-ness is much greater than his knowledge of newspaper work. However, when the yarn gets to the press room, the assistant foreman sees that his boy is implicated and he goes mad, threatening to stop the presses. He breaks up to the publisher's office, and even at that early hour, the boss is still in. Asking that the story be killed, he is refused.

A few moments later the boiler explodes and the entire building burns, bringing out the fire department and the crowds, while Johnson, has the building cave in—a huge skyscraper tumbling because of fire. The falling business was done in miniature and well handled, however.

Of course the old foreman is accused of the damage but all the time his accusers reckoned without the bright young reporter, who had overheard a big political boss laying the plot; revealed that a henchman went to the boiler room and got the firemen so drunk they engaged in a coal heavi g contest, which agitated the boilers. Then the old foreman was made boss of the press room and the bright young reporter married the daughter of the boss.

From a newspaperman's standpoint, the whole thing is dotted with silly errors, which, if Mr. Johnson should insist, will be enumerated. For the mugs it may be great stuff, but it is the type of thriller which is shooting gallery stuff and suitable for the picture side of the small time vaudeville houses. As first run stuff it will never do.

At the Cameo Sunday afternoon there were some folks present who apparently knew their newspaper business and whenever the reporter got very brave or whenever the title writer pulled a particularly maudlin title, they would applaud vigorously. Apparently someone in authority knew something about the newspaper business too, for he called out to an usher:

"Go down there and ask those people to stop kidding this picture."

So the usher walked himself down, sent over an austere look and turned around again.

To get back to the film:

It is cheaply done with a poor cast. The story is that F. B. O. has made terrific grosses by exploiting these hokum specials of Johnson's. That being true, their line of exploitation is easily understood, for the lobby signs termed "The Last Edition" a "dramatic thunderbolt."

Sisk.

The Pace That Thrills

First National release. Original by Byron Morgan; directed by Webster Campbell. Shown at the Broadway, New York, week Nov. 9. Running time, 62 minutes.

Danny Wade.................Ben Lyon
Doris.................Mary Astor
Duke LeBaron.................Charles Beyer
Hezekiah Sims.................Tully Marshall
Jack Van Loren.................Warner Richmond
Mrs. Van Loren.................Evelyn Walsh Hall
Mr. Van Loren.................Thomas Holding
Paula.................Fritzi Brunette
Toreador.................Paul Ellis

Can't say whether it was the pace or not, but in this case it isn't thrills, it's "kills." This picture really hasn't a chance outside of the smallest houses and then it will get by principally on double feature bills or with some other added attraction. At the Broadway it has seven acts of vaudeville to back it up. The vaudeville was good; the picture wasn't.

There are some names in the cast and that is about the principal asset. The story itself isn't convincing, nor has it been handled in the direction to lead any audience to believe that any of it was on the level. The featured male lead, Ben Lyon, is the most unconvincing of them all. The boy was miscast in this one. Even Tammany Young in a little bit is better than Lyon in any of his scenes.

The story itself is one that combines society, picture producing and an auto race. Lyon as the hero is the son of a Van Loren. His dad married a girl from the chorus, and the Van Lorens, when the father comes home soused and accidently causes his own death, accuse his wife of having committed the crime and with the aid of servants convict her. The baby is placed in an orphanage, but gets a chance in pictures and finally becomes the Valentino of the day, thus earning sufficient to wage a battle to have his mother pardoned. Meantime he has a double work all his daring stunts and gets the reputation of being a coward. He loves the daughter of the producer for whom he is working and is loved by her in return, but the heavy instills in her mind that the favored one isn't game. An auto race for a society charity is on and the picture star is scheduled to drive in it. The same day the pardon hearing comes up, but he manages to make the scene of the race in time to start driving. He doesn't win but proves he's game and wins the girl.

All of the action worked up to that auto race and then it flopped all over the place.

Mary Astor, as the heroine, got about all that she could out of the role assigned her and Tully Marshall, as her dad, pulled secondary acting honors. Warner Richmond, who was in but a few scenes at the opening of the picture, seemed to have far the best of it as far as acting honors go.

Fred.

OLD CLOTHES

Metro-Goldwyn production starring Jackie Coogan. Written by Willard Mack and directed by Eddie Cline. At the Capitol, New York, Nov. 8 week. Running time, 65 mins.

Max Ginsberg.................Max Davidson
Mrs. Burke.................Lillian Elliott
Mary Riley.................Joan Crawford
Nathan Burke.................Alan Forrest
Dapper Dan.................James Mason
The Adjuster.................Stanton Heck
"Dynamite".................The Horse
Timothy Kelly.................Jackie Coogan

Max Ginsberg, an old man, and little Timothy Kelly are partners in the old clothes business. Mary Riley and a boy named Nathan are in love. Max, Timothy and Mary live together in comparative poverty, while Nathan is a rich uptown man. And the reason that Max and Timothy are poor is that they invested their money in Vista Copper.

So in walks the boy Nathan toward the finish of the last reel, bemoaning his fate and saying that if only he could corner Vista Copper he wouldn't go broke and could marry Mary. Timothy walks him upstairs and shows him a room papered with the stock which makes everybody rich and happy.

It doesn't take a great deal of imagination to figure out the plot, the names being what they are. Furthermore, the titles coming from Ginsberg run like this:

"From me you should do this, oi, oi."

Little Coogan as the Irishman wears a big derby hat, walks with his hand behind his back and is generally grownup. The others fulfill their roles satisfactorily, and to the credit of Eddie Cline, the director, it must be said that he has injected clever business at spots.

Inasmuch as the recent Coogan films haven't done so well, and as this one is cheaply produced, it doesn't seem to be in the stars that "Old Clothes" will be a mop-up for anybody.

Sisk.

CALL OF COURAGE

Universal production, starring Art Accord. From the novel "Red Dawn," by Harold Shumate. Directed by Clifford S. Smith. Runs about 58 minutes.

Steve Caldwell.................Art Accord
Sam.................D. R. Lee
Jimmy.................Turner Savage
June Hazleton.................Olive Hasbrouck

Probably the most preposterous, tiresome and aggravating of all Universal's westerns. The best thing in it is the leading lady's rather pretty profile.

Accord has done much better things than this, and rather than appear in this piece of junk he should have forfeited his contract. It will ruin whatever popularity he has achieved with those unlucky enough to see it.

As travesty it might be more bearable. The heavy is the hero's brother, and up to a certain point is not pictured as such a bad fellow. But, without motivation, he suddenly shoots his employer, the ranch owner, and places the blame on his younger brother. The most peculiar thing about it is that he hasn't really killed the old man, but severely wounded him and placed him in a vault in the mine. It is never made clear whether he expected him to starve to death or merely keep on existing while the brother gets put out of the way at the hand of justice.

Usual chase scenes, but badly done. The comedy relief is blaah, the love-interest mushy, and only the horsemanship and photography at all adequate. "The Call of Courage" is food for morons.

Herb.

UNKNOWN LOVER

Vitagraph production starring Elsie Ferguson. Supervised by Victor Hugo Halperin. At Loew's New York, one day (Oct. 30) as half bill. Runs about hour.

Ken Billings.................Frank Mayo
Gale Norman.................Mildred Harris
Gladys.................Peggy Kelly
Fred Wagner.................Leslie Austin
Elaine Kent.................Elsie Ferguson

Another Vitagraph "bad boy." Still for the program theatres it isn't so very bad as far as the business possibilities go because Elsie Ferguson's name should be some draw in picture houses and there is a lot of sex stuff in the picture that will be talked about. This consists of some undress scenes and of a rather risque honeymoon situation. The nudity comes in a sculptor's studio and later on in some cabaret sequences where living curtain girls are employed. Nothing very startling but enough to give the boys a thrill.

Otherwise it's the usual masterpiece about a woman who sets out to reform her husband. The one twist comes when after he has had a nervous break-down and must, according to the doctor either quit work or die, his wife purposely ruins his business to save his life.

Miss Ferguson has not much of an opportunity but is charming though there are far too many clear close-ups that disclose too much. Frank Mayo does little with an unsympathetic part and Mildred Harris has just a bit. The best is Leslie Austin, who seems to be a promising newcomer.

The production was expensive and it is doubtful if Vitagraph gets it's money back. For Miss Ferguson it marks another unlucky break, or poor judgment in taking any job offered.

Herb.

STELLA DALLAS

Samuel Goldwyn production directed by Henry King. Adapted from Olive H. Prouty's novel of the same name by Frances Marion. Cameraed by Arthur Edeson. At the Apollo, New York, for special run beginning Nov. 16. Running time, 108 mins.

Stella Dallas.................Belle Bennett
Stephen Dallas.................Ronald Colman
Helen Morrison.................Alice Joyce
Ed Munn.................Jean Hersholt
Laurel Dallas.................Lois Moran
Richard Grovesnor..Douglas Fairbanks, Jr.
Miss Philiburn.................Vera Lewis
Mrs. Grovesnor.................Beatrix Prior

A mother picture. Not a great picture, but a great mother picture.

Samuel Goldwyn undoubtedly has the gem of its type the screen has produced to date in "Stella Dallas." Its sentiment is terrific. Henry King has told his story simply and directly without dramatics, gauging the extent to which he can play upon such an emotional subject to a nicety. In this he has been held up in reaching his objective by two magnificent performances by Belle Bennett and Lois Moran.

"Stella Dallas" is "a woman's picture." Women will love it. Men will respect it if nothing else, for the film demands and will get that recognition. This picture is hardly original in any way. King has even delved into the lore of D. W. to accomplish a beautiful love scene and has carried the Griffith idea of restraint into the entire footage. It's effective, of course.

Watching this picture is similar to witnessing a small cast play. If ever there were a two-character picture this is it. Both characters are women, mother and daughter. At least it's the closest filmdom has ever come to a two-people film. On that basis the strength of the story may be imagined when it can sustain a tremendous interest in these same two women for an hour and three quarters. True, the sequence gets away to a slow start and at no time is there superlative action, but the story is certainly the thing here.

Not having read the book, it cannot be said how closely the celluloid follows the original. However, the novel had an impressive vogue and it doesn't seem possible that the picture can have harmed or detracted from Miss Prouty's work. Its appeal is to the heart and but tells of a mother who eliminates herself so that her child may enjoy the advantages of which the girl will not partake while knowing that her mother has no one to whom she can turn. To gain this end the mother, Stella Dallas (Miss Bennet) finally goes to her husband's boyhood sweetheart and offers to divorce him so that they may marry and take Laurel, the daughter, (Miss Moran).

The child rejects the luxury, despite an idolizing father (Mr. Colman) and an understanding stepmother (Miss Joyce), upon learning of the manner in which she has gained, returning to her uneducated, slovenly and grossly dressed mother, who is incapable of attaining the "class" instinct of her baby. The mother finally gains her end, after contemplating suicide, by marrying a drunken horse trainer who has been her suitor for years but for whom she cares nothing.

Early passages are concerned with Stephen Dallas outlawing himself from his own set because of a father embezzler who shot himself as a way out. Hiding away in a mill town, Stephen learns of his sweetheart's marriage, whence follows his taking the small town girl to wife. The inevitable separation takes place when their baby is around four years of age.

Sentimental wallops are a birthday party which the mother gives for her baby, then 10, with none of the children attending, because of the school head 's seeing the mother go to a neighboring city with Ed Munn (Mr. Hersholt), the horse trainer; a fashionable summer hotel as cause for further humiliation for the girl now a young woman, due to her being a popular item amidst the youngsters whose members ridicule an exaggeratedly dressed guest, not knowing that it is Laurel's

Following this, King has made a touching thing of a scene between the mother and daughter in a lower berth after both have overheard a conversation describing the parent as a millstone around the youngster's neck. Other standouts are the scenes between the mother and the prospective step-mother of the girl, the mother and father, the witnessing of her daughter's marriage through a window (the finish and excellently directed) and the loyalty and mother-love of the two principal characters.

This picture should do for Miss Moran what "The Birth of a Nation" did for Mae Marsh, what "Merry-Go-Round" did for Mary Philbin, what "Humoresque" did for Vera Gordon, and what one picture here or there has done for other individuals. Miss Moran convinces in what practically amounts to three roles, as she plays the daughter at 10, 13 and as a young woman. Excellent in each, her performance was something of a revelation to those who had never seen her before. There can be no doubt that Miss Moran has the advantage of what might almost be termed an actor-proof role, but that is not meant to detract from her performance, for the same might be said of the story and Miss Bennet. However, to the skeptical Miss Moran will have to prove herself in other assignments sustaining less sympathy as there have been too many one-role luminaries whose light dwindles with subsequent characterizations. But if ever a girl seemed to be "in," it's Miss Moran.

The same goes for Miss Bennett, who is doing something of a cinema comeback in this release. More latterly playing in stock on the Coast, Miss Bennett has here supplied the equal of any personal portrayal the screen has revealed during the past year. Much credit unquestionably belongs to King for the way he has handled this actress, and she is all of that, but the ability to quicken the pulse, throb the throat and ache the heart is majorly her own.

Miss Joyce makes a splendid contrast, while Ronald Colman is limited in his activities. Jean Hershort is prominent among the secondary players, with young Fairbanks acquitting himself creditably in his brief footage.

In is understood the picture will release through United Artists and that Goldwyn brought it into the Apollo for the purpose of giving it a whoop sendoff, maybe also figuring on roadshowing it. The idea of a special New York display bears out the reasoning upon the viewing, for the picture should draw corking notices and the word- f-mouth billing it will get should be plentiful and sufficient to keep it in at the special price scale for at least a moderate run. As a road show "Stella Dallas" looks to have more than a good chance if the price is right, at about $1.50 top.

It's bound to create ta.k, it's clean and superbly done from all angles. It is a surety as a program feature, for it's far better than such a classification signifies. The film is subtle enough to suit the fastidious and yet its obviousness does not detract while safeguarding it against a lower intellect.

To that end it appears this film can't miss. *Skig.*

LORD JIM

Famous Players present Joseph Conrad's novel adapted by John Russell. Percy Marmont, Shirley Mason, Noah Beery and Raymond Hatton featured. Directed by Victor Fleming. At the Rialto, New York, week Nov. 15. Running time, 67 minutes.

Lord Jim....................Percy Marmont
Jewel.......................Shirley Mason
Capt. Brown...................Noah Beery
Cornelius..................Raymond Hatton
Stein.......................Joseph Dowling
Dain Waris..................George Magrill
Sultan........................Nick de Ruiz
Scroggings................J. Gunnis Davis

"Lord Jim" gave every indication at the beginning it was going to be a big picture but fell down as it passed in review. A real start did not hold to the pace, so that the best that can be said for it is that it stands out as a little above the average program feature Famous is turning out. What it will do at the box office is more or less of a problem. There are four names that should have some drawing power, but an unhappy ending is going to leave rather a bad taste.

Percy Marmont is giving a fine performance as Lord Jim. He gets over in great shape. And if anyone thinks that Shirley Mason doesn't make good all they have to do is to take one squint at this picture and they'll change their minds. True, there were moments in closeups when Shirley overshot the mark a little, but these were minor.

As for Noah Beery and Raymond Hatton one does not have to go beyond saying that their performances were up to their usual standard.

A great piece of work here by Nick de Ruiz, who gave a character performance as the Sultan that will be hard to beat. This bit of work alone should place him in demand for a long while. Joseph Dowling handled the part of the gentle old man willing to give a chance to a down and outer in a manner that won him the audience.

As to the picture itself, Victor Fleming, who directed, handled his subject nicely and sustained the interest. The trick stuff with the steamer in the earlier shots was fitted into the story cleverly, and the scenes on board the boat itself were corkingly done.

The later battle stuff did not stand up so well, although his directing of the passing out of Lord Jim was done in such fashion as to make it as easy on the audience as possible.

"Lord Jim" won't pull big money but in the majority of houses it will prove pleasing. *Fred.*

MORALS FOR MEN

Tiffany Production released in the State-right market. Suggested by the Gouverneur Morris story, "The Lucky Serum." Co-featuring Conway Tearle and Agnes Ayres at head of cast, including Alyce Mills, Otto Matieson, Robert Ober and John Miljan. Directed by Bernie Hyman under the supervision of A. P. Younger. At Broadway, New York, week Nov. 16. Running time, 70 minutes.

Independent picture that looks like something as far as title and cast are concerned, but which falls down on the story and its directorial handling. It is just a picture worthy of filling in on the double feature bills in the daily change houses, and that simply because it has Conway Tearle and Agnes Ayres co-featured

There was a real story here somewhere, for even the horrible handling that it received in direction, cutting and editing do not entirely cover that fact.

The theme is regeneration of a man and a woman. The man, an engineer, who has fallen as low as the estate of "mackerel" through drink, is living off of the earnings of a girl bootlegger. She, believing he has stolen money from her, leaves him flat and takes to manicuring, meeting another man whom she loves but who is a bad boy. She finally commits suicide.

The man manages to win the love of a society girl whom he saves from drowning, through regaining his self respect and making a success of his profession. The wife is insanely jealous and suspects her husband. The woman, who lives in the next apartment, is none other than the former lady "boot," but all between the two is the husband's desire to aid an old friend in distress. When the truth is known the wife condemns herself for having mistrusted hubby and winds her arms around his neck.

Had the director handled the story so that the audience had any idea of how the affairs of the principal characters developed to bring about certain situations it would have been a much better picture.

Conway Tearle makes an altogether forceful hero, but there are certain scenes where the lighting and camera work did about all they could do to hurt him. Agnes Ayres isn't quite as youthful as she once was and shows it on the screen, and in this particular picture it cannot be said that she distinguishes herself particularly. Possibly it was the fault of direction and camera in her case also. But there is a find in the girl that plays the wife of Tearle in the picture. She can troupe and looks like a million dollars. Possibly she is Alyce Mills.

In casting there was a bit of faulty selection displayed in taking two men who looked so similar that it was hard to distinguish for a time that there were really two different personages, for the husband of the lady "boot" looked decidedly like the lawyer who wanted to make the hero's wife.

One doesn't want to bank too much on this one other than the names of the featured players. *Fred.*

BRIGHT LIGHTS

Metro-Goldwyn-Mayer release featuring Charles Ray and Pauline Starke. Robert Z. Leonard production directed by Leonard. Adapted from Liberty Magazine story authored by Richard Connell. John Arnold, the photographer. At the Capitol, New York, week Nov. 15. Running time, 65 mins.

Tom..........................Charles Ray
Patsy......................Pauline Starke
Gwendolyn..................Lilyan Tashman
Marty.....................Lawford Davidson
Barney........................Ned Sparkes

A lightweight comedy with Charles Ray as his familiar awkward, rural youngster. Such an outline may not hold much promise on paper but the value increases upon the viewing for Ray has turned out a corking performance in the character which long ago brought him feature billing. It is Ray's picture completely.

A Sunday matinee audience at the Capitol thoroughly enjoyed it. Though the plot is obvious upon the entrance of Ray into the running, the astuteness of Robert Z. Leonard in weaving comedy touches into the narrative and the playing of Ray will hold it up for pleasing and clean program fare.

The locale divides itself between the city and a Jersey farm in telling of a cabaret girl (Pauline Starke) who goes back to the farm to help her mother and there meets Tom (Mr. Ray), the first boy in her life she doesn't have to be afraid of.

A misunderstanding between the two sends the girl back to the city whence Tom follows, much overdressed in swagger wearing apparel. His misconceived idea of the man he thinks Patsy wants him to be causes another brief separation during which the heroine's girl friend informs Tom "to be himself"—after which follows the happy ending.

Very frothy, to be sure, but the comedy side issues are sufficient to hold up the story while it must be remembered Ray is not without pathos in these assignments. It has been so long since Ray has been around in overalls that his work is almost new, and if not that, it's good enough to stand in bold relief over similar attempts by other screen artists.

M.-G. has given the production substantial interiors as called for, although the only splash in this direction is a cabaret scene. Beyond that there is little else than the farm, the old homestead and the New York flat of the girls. The outlay for a hotel lobby passage is appropriately dodged by closeups.

In directing, Robert Z. Leonard has made much use of a traveling tripod and to this end has achieved a number of effective "suspense shots." One solid laugh is gained through coloring Ray's face a light green after he has delved into a box of cigars.

Mr. Ray convinces all the way as the farm boy for the best piece of screen work he has donated in some time. It is when he steps out of a rural role that this boy is not sure of his ground, but here he is entirely at home and his work bears out the confidence he must have when intrusted with such an assignment. Miss Starke does nicely as the on the level chorister and provides a neat share of laughs. The support for this couple suffices, while the titling is an asset in that it sparkles here and there. *Skig.*

RIDIN' THE WIND

Fred Thomson production. Starring Fred Thomson and featuring his horse, Silver King. Story by Marion Jackson. Directed by Del Andrews. Presented and distributed by Film Booking Offices of America, Inc. At Stanley, New York, one-day presentation, Nov. 12. Running time, 57 minutes.

Jim Harkness...............Fred Thomson
May Lacy..................Jacqueline Gadson
Dick Harkness..............Lewis Sargent
Black Hat gang leader....David Dunbar
Dolly Dutton..................Betty Scott
Sheriff Lacy......................Red Kirby

Meller. Western. As customary with pictures having cowboys as the central figures there's riding gun play and chases. In shooting this one no bets were overlooked in digging up some of the oldest scenes known to shooting cameras.

Fred Thomson stars and barring the opening, where two boys are used, he is in, about and over the picture, being aided and abetted in his riding and shooting by his horse, Silver King. This horse is a beauty, both on looks and in action. A lot of horse sense, too. Magnificently trained. Silver King can stand right up and stand comparison with either Bill Hart's or Tom Mix's celebrated film ponies.

The story was about as connected as a jackrabbit's tail after being blown to pieces by a shotgun. There was a robbery, fire and fights, with Thomson pulling one that was done by some of the old comedies in style of execution. Thomson as the riding hound who loves the school marm and his hoss is cornered by five desprit men and he overpowers and makes captive of each much to the edification of even a small crowd at the Stanley that was looking for a little relief from a hard rain outside the theatre.

Thomson is a well-set up young man, not bad to look upon and a hard worker. He shows his horse off wonderfully well and that horse is sure to tickle the kids of any neighborhood. While a bit strong in the imagination that bit where the horse pushes the apparently empty auto out into the country and sends it crashing down a steep embankment is one of the features. Thomson applies the thrill needles in several scenes.

As an independent, not so bad. Story off balance. Direction good in spots. Photographically it's an excellent job. Thomson is certain to become more of a box office tag when his stories are stronger. And that fine bit of horseflesh can't miss.

It might be a good tip for Mr. Thomson to place several good women in his support. This isn't meant as a slam at the two who worked in this one, but neither added the feminine punch that a star of this calibre deserves. *Mark.*

THE BEAUTIFUL CITY

First National release made by Inspiration Pictures, starring Richard Barthelmess. From story by Edmund Goulding and directed by Kenneth Webb. Dorothy Gish featured. At the Strand, New York, Nov. 22. Running time, 70 minutes.

Tony Gillardi	Richard Barthelmess
Mollie	Dorothy Gish
Nick di Silva	William Powell
Car'o Gillardi	Frank Puglia
Mamma Gillardi	Florence Auer

A fair story and release, but far below the recent standards set by Barthelmess, who "delivered" in "Classmates," "Shore Leave" and "The Enchanted Cottage." "The Beautiful City" is not a bad picture, but, on the other hand, it is not of the type expected from a star who ranks so high.

The story is laid in New York's ghetto, and has Barthelmess as an Italian pushcart peddler; but he doesn't do a Bevan, for his loves are not the little children, but his mother and an Irish girl named Mollie O'Connor. Early in the picture he goes to jail for a crime committed by his brother, and after he gets out his efforts are devoted toward freeing his brother from the influence of one Nick di Silva, a crook who has been under the master mind in several operations in which Tony's brother figured. Finally he catches di Silva and, in his chasing, the villain is killed, so the field is free for Tony, and he marries his Irish sweetheart and they grab a vessel of the Iron Steamship Co. and make that trip around the Battery to Coney Island.

In so far as atmosphere goes it is good, and the cast is also good. The villain, di Silva, is manager of a Chinese theatre, and the screen shots show it to be the one owned by Jennie Moscowitz, the Yiddish actress playing in "Kosher Kitty Kelly." Interesting scenes of a Chinese play in progress are given. but these few moments are more or less sunk by some of the obvious stuff which follows.

Lighting and photography just fair and direction weak. But the star gives a good performance and Miss Gish is likeable in her part, so that may save the day. *Sisk.*

IRISH LUCK

Victor Heerman Production, presented by Adolph Zukor and Jesse L. Lasky, with Thomas Meighan starred. Adapted from Norman Venner's "The Imperfect Impostes," by Thomas J. Geraghty. Directed by Victor Heerman. At Rivoli, New York, week Nov. 22. Running time, 71 minutes.

Tom Donahue }	Thomas Meighan
Lord Fitzhugh }	
Lady Gwendolyn	Lois Wilson
Douglas	Cecil Humphreys
Solicitor	Claude King
Earl	Ernest Lawford
Doctor	Charles Hammond
Aunt	Louise Grafton
Uncle	S. B. Carrickson
Denis MacSwiney	Charles McDonald
Kate MacSwiney	Mary Foy

"The Imperfect Imposter" was originally a "Sat. Eve. Post" story and had its locale in England. In the film version the scene of action is located in Ireland, in itself a very good idea, as it did give Thomas Meighan the Irish background that he so dearly loves, and it will have an added attraction for those of Irish birth or extraction a chance to view the historic spots of Ireland in a sort of a travelogue with the added attraction with being a film star en route.

While the change of scene may prove a help to the picture it is just as certain that the treatment of the story effaced all of the suspense element present in the original, and it certainly did not add to the dramatic value.

In direction the picture has one of the best double exposure shots disclosed in some time where there is a star playing a dual role. The one trick shot in particular is that where Meighan hands himself a light from one cigarette to another.

Heerman ought to get a hand for that one.

As for the rest it turned out, as adapted, as just meller and for the box office Thomas Meighan is going to be the greatest asset next to the Irish scenery.

Lois Wilson is a noble Irish lady, while Meighan has the roles of Sir Fitzhugh, her brother, and Tom Donahue, a New York cop back on a visit to Ireland. On the way over he goes broke and, landing in Ireland, walks onto a race course where a bookie, mistaking him for the Lord, lays him a finger bet on a horse which wins at 10 to 1. But Tom, the copper, can't collect, the bookie saying that he'll send him a check in the morning. Then the New York copper seeks out the Irish Lord and the two are struck by each other's resemblance to one another.

Meantime back in Killarney the Earl, uncle of his lordship, is dying and wants to see the boy. There is a heavy, another nephew who is looking to step into the picture, the title, and the dough, so he is trying to forestall the return of the uncle's favorite, and while the sister is motoring to the city to fetch the brother he is on his way by train in response to a telegram, only to be waylaid by the hired sluggers of heavy. The girl walks in on her brother's double for a corking comedy scene, and then finally, when her brother is among the missing, she impresses the double into service to enact her brother before the dying man.

Then for the finish. The heavy is cornered, the brother is aided to escape from his confinement, the double is right on the job to take the girl in his arms, and then there is a final fadeout. All fine for the Meighan fans, and on Broadway they liked it Monday night.

Miss Wilson handles what she has to do nicely. The heavy, enacted by Cecil Humphreys, seemed rather prone to overdo things, while Claude King as a crooked lawyer seemed much more at ease in his role. Charles McDonald and Mary Foy, playing a couple of Irish peasants who were persuaded to help the heavy, carry themselves nicely in unsympathetic roles. The former is a huge man who looks as though he could put up a whale of a fight if called on. *Fred.*

STAGE STRUCK

Famous Players production starring Gloria Swanson. Story by Frank R. Adams and scenario by Forrest Halsey. Directed by Allan Dwan. At Rivoli, New York, Nov. 15. Running time, 70 minutes.

Jennie Hagen	Gloria Swanson
Orme Wilson	Lawrence Gray
Lillian Lyons	Gertrude Astor
Hilda Wagner	Marguerite Evans
Buck	Ford Sterling
Mrs. Wagner	Carrie Scott
Mr. Wagner	Emil Hoch
Soubrette	Margery Whittington

Women will laugh and men will writhe at "Stage Struck" and Gloria Swanson. Not all men nor all women. Some of each may walk out on it. But women in general, those who go to pictures as a regular thing out of town and in the big city neighborhoods, will laugh. There's plenty to laugh at, whichever way you see it.

As a Famous Players feature release it's a fine piece of hoke. The inside of this Allan Dwan-directed comic is said to be that it was made in three weeks, whereby Mr. Dwan drew down a bonus. Just as a matter of opinion, F. P. should have paid Dwan more if it had not been made at all.

And what took three weeks to make? Perhaps it needed a week or so to build the Ohio River. And any time saved should go to the title writer with whom Dawn might split the side coin. Watching the picture after the second of the six reels, you try to figure how this ever got past for over two reels. It's one of the old time Keystone models, padded out. Ford Sterling has a role in it, and it must have been Ford who recalled the gags, even to Miss Swanson, when in trousers, allowing them to fall down. A laugh, though!

Another laugh was when she tried to make up as an actress. And another after her prize fight when she jumped overboard to be saved from drowning by her pants catching on a nail on the side of the "Water Queen," a river boat, probably bought with the river.

At that, though, the "Water Queen" was the best actor in the picture—at least the boat didn't try to be funny. Next to the boat, barring his comedy, Lawrence Gray gave rather a good performance in the juvenile role, and barring Miss Swanson's material, she is not at all bad as a comedienne.

The story is flat, flatter than the batter so important to the comedy.

A colored display of clothes is at the opening, apologized for in dream style, since it holds no relation to the picture itself, and color comes out again at the finale. The only thing missing was an old Mammy, some picks and a levee scene. Probably Mr. Dwan didn't want to miss his bonus.

As her final picture under the direction of Mr. Dwan for F. P. Miss Swanson may recall it as one of her worst, despite that her personal work in it is worthy of much more credit than it ever will receive from those who ever passed the fifth grade at school.

But her waitress in a beanery and Gray's cake making antics should draw all of the waitresses and all of the batterers from all of the eating places—and that's a lot.

And yet, "Stage Struck" will likely draw, because its comedy can't be muffed and it has Gloria Swanson.

Attaboy, kick 'em again! *Sime.*

THE ONLY THING

Elinor Glyn production, directed by Jack Conway. Released by Metro-Goldwyn. Story by Elinor Glyn and picture made under her personal supervision. At Capitol, New York, week Nov. 22. Running time, 62 minutes.

Princess Thyra	Eleanor Boardman
Duke of Chevenix	Conrad Nagel
The King	Edward Connelly
Sir Charles Vane	Louis Payne
Gigberto	Arthur Edmund Carew
Princess Erek	Vera Lewis
Princess Anne	Carrie Clarke Ward
Countess Arline	Constance Wylie
Governess	Dale Fuller
Gitson	Ned Sparks
Prime Minister	Mario Carillo
Kalkur	David Mir
Captain of the Guards	Michael Pleschkoff
Young Arnold	Buddy Smith
Young Lady Catherine	Joan Crawford
Young Porteous	Frank Braidwood
Young Cheney	Derek Glynne
Thyra's Maid	Mary Hawes

The only thing that Elinor Glyn missed was the Bible itself. She has everything else. A little "Graustark" and possibly some or all of the other novels of a like ilk written regarding those mythical kingdoms in the Balkans, a little of "The Tale of Two Cities" given a little modern Russian Red touch. These she has taken and shaken well, adding a little of "Three Weeks" to top it off. Net result: one picture. Not good, but still not bad.

With the name of Elinor Glyn added, Elinor practically directing what a handsome young leading man shall do under a given set of circumstances, concocted by the red-headed lady from merry old England, well, mebbe the flapper will want to take a peek. But it doesn't look like real money at the box office outside of that.

Miss Glyn has for her formula the marriage of a princess, young and beautiful, to a doddering old king. Then a handsome young English duke steps in the picture and falls in love with her, takes all sorts of chances to let her know it and finally enters her chamber the night before the wedding begging her to fly with him. But she, though returning his love, insists that she cannot betray her own country. Then next day the wedding ceremony. At the same time a revolution and the death of the king, the final escape of the lovers after the Tribunal of the Reds has decreed that the princess shall be sent to death, bound in the arms of their own leader who has stated that he was willing to betray his own cause for her love, and the change of places in the prison cell by the duke with the red leader so that the lovers are arm in arm as they are sent out to drown on a leaky barge.

Conrad Nagel is a handsome enough young duke, but Eleanor Boardman steals the picture from him. That girl is sure on her way to the very top and this picture proves it as much as anything. Edward Connelly as the king is a distinct triumph in a character role that required real thought and work. Arthur Edmund Carew was the leader of the Reds, looking the p[art]. Vera Lewis handled the role of the sister of the king for laughs and got them and there were a couple of character kids as the twin offspring of the king's first marriage that did as much to save the picture as anything. Those kids were a happy thought and whoever stuck them in should get a raise.

In directing Conway did not particularly distinguish himself, but it is easy to assume that he may have been working under a handicap.

Fred.

HOGAN'S ALLEY

Warner Bros.' production, starring Monte Blue. Story by Gregory Rogers. Directed by Roy Del Ruth. Scenario by Darryl Francis Zanuck. At the Warner's, New York, week of Nov. 21. Runs about 70 minutes.

Lefty O'Brien....................Monte Blue
Michael Ryan....................Willard Louis
Patsy Ryan..............Patsy Ruth Miller
Dolly.........................Louise Fazenda
A Stranger........................Ben Turpin
Jewish Clothier..................Max Davidson
"The Texas Kid".Herbert Spencer Griswold
Battling Savage................Frank Hagney
Dr. Emmett Franklin.............Nigel Barrie
Mother Ryan......................Mary Carr
Al Murphy........................Frank Bond

Not even a particularly good supporting bill, including no less an attraction than Chaplin's "A Dog's Life," one of his very best, can lend anything but a cheap neighborhood-theatre atmosphere to "Hogan's Alley." But that does not necessarily mean that audiences in the daily-change houses are not going to like it.

It is safe as far as these latter stands are concerned, because every possible sort of hoke has been crowded into it, with more than a fair share of low comedy and a cast studded with the names of lesser film luminaries. Still at times the picture is so ludicrous and artificial that even the gangs will resent it.

"Hogan's Alley" is supposedly an east side street, inhabited by the Irish and Heebs, and a fitting battle ground for their fruit-throwing feuds. Here events surprisingly similar to some in Miss Pickford's "Annie Rooney" take place, but they are slapped on with an exaggeration and tawdriness that makes that earlier film seem like a jewel in comparison.

The hero (Monte Blue) is a prize-fighter who eventually gets to be world's champion but still resides in the delightful alley. Mr. Blue has little chance for acting but a good deal for fighting, and though he seems to be slightly flabby acquits himself with great agility in a championship battle that bristles with action. A more important role falls to Patsy Ruth Miller as the Irish terror of the neighborhood, who grows into such a beauty overnight that she is kidnaped by the scheming, wealthy doctor from uptown.

The comedy is intrusted to Willard Louis in a familiar and not particularly well-done "Bring Up Father" characterization and Max Davidson, Master Coogan's side-kick recently. Louise Fazenda has just a bit, and neither Ben Turpin nor his famous eyes, though programed, were observed.

Miss Miller is unquestionably cute at moments, and her charm will do much to overbalance many of the crude bits that are introduced. But neither she nor anything else can make "Hogan's Alley" other than a typical program film.

Herb.

SIMON THE JESTER

Production by Metropolitan Pictures, with a Frances Marion adaptation from novel by William J. Locke. Featuring Lillian Rich and Eugene O'Brien. Directed by George Melford. Released by P. D. C. At Cameo, New York, week May 15. Running time, about 60 minutes.

Simon de Gex................Eugene O'Brien
Lola Brandt.......................Lillian Rich
Dale Kennerly..................Edmund Burns
Brandt...................Henry B. Walthall
Midget..........................William Platt

Whatever the Locke volume-story was, it must have contained more action than this screen version does. Yet the Eugene O'Brien followers are going to enjoy Mr. O'Brien bowling over mobs, one by one, as he does a couple of times, safely escaping. In one of the scenes of kayoing in gross he makes Douglas Fairbanks look like a featherweight.

As a program release, however, and with Lillian Rich, besides Henry B. Walthall as the light heavy, along with some circus scenes, this picture will mildly in erest, because of its sentiment and cleanliness. Cleanliness is clung to all through, with any doubt removed through titles.

Mr. Walthall as the villain and separated husband from his circus-owning wife came all of the way from Tangiers to London to kill a horse. He killed it. It was the performing pet of his wife's. While on the opposite, was Mr. O'Brien as **Simon, told by his physician to be restful to save his life, going to Tangiers into more excitement than he ever had had in his life, and having his life saved through it.**

In between is much of lit le, some love making and a dandy bachelor dinner scene at the outset, where it is explained how Simon de Gex got his nom-de-plume, through cynicism. He overcame being a cynic when meeting Lola Brandt and finally married her, shortly after the midget clown killed her husband for killing the horse, leaving the score 90-10.

William Platt as the midget gave far and away the best performance. Mr. Walthall's role called for about an hour's work, net, including dressing. The hardest work he did was to take a punch delivered by Mr. O'Brien.

Necessarily one can't rave over the George Melford direction. A part of the story may have been played while Mr. Melford was out to lunch. Yet some of the blame should be placed against Frances Marion's record for the adaptation. Maybe Miss Marion is lending her name only to some of the independent films.

Circus end of the story good for matinee via children. There is a travesty bit with a horse and mule in it that will make the children laugh.

Sime.

THE BIG PARADE

Metro-Goldwyn-Mayer picture, directed by King Vidor, from the story by Laurence Stallings. Stars John Gilbert and features Renee Adoree. Musical score by David Mendoza and William Axt. John Arnold, photographer. At the Astor, New York, for run. Opened Nov. 19. Running time, 130 minutes.

James Apperson................John Gilbert
Melisande......................Renee Adoree
Mr. Apperson..............Hobart Bosworth
Mrs. Apperson.............Claire McDowell
Justyn Reed.....................Claire Adams
Harry..............................Robert Ober
Bull................................Tom O'Brien
Slim.................................Karl Dane
French Mother..............Rosita Marstini

An opening week's gross of around $20,000 and a big advance sale speaks for itself. That's the tipoff on the merit of this one, and that it will continue to do tremendous business seems assured. It's the best of the war pictures.

The first Sunday night (Nov. 22) saw them standing six deep in the Astor, and they've been on their feet to view it ever since. Last Friday an inquiry at the box office for Sunday night seats brought a "sold out" answer, and this despite the management vehemently denies that it is selling to the specs. (The big ticket agencies are handling Astor tickets). However, specs or no specs, it's a cinch Jeff McCarthy knew what he was talking about when he took one flash at this picture long before it was finished and said "road show."

Coming in the same week as "Stella Dallas," the contrast was striking, the former being very much of a woman's film and the "Parade" having a strong masculine appeal. The difference in the manner in which the two premieres were received was also interesting in that "Stella Dallas" brought cheers, while this one drew a few calls at the end of the first half, but closed out to just applause. Distinctive "picture" audiences greeted both films.

A hearsay comparison to the Coast showing of the "Parade" (at Grauman's Egyptian in Hollywood) states that a few of the "swear" subtitles were deleted for New York, while the bit of Gilbert touching a lighted cigaret to the face of a dead German to verify that belief is also absent.

Other snatches here and there also may be out, but where the western opinion was that the film was around 3,000 feet too long, there is no such fault to find on this end. One overheard audience remark at the conclusion was that "it isn't long enough," and the picture is running two hours and 10 minutes, exclusive of the intermission.

The Astor presentation is devoid of anything resembling a prolog, an 8:36 start blasting right into the footage, with the continuity planting the story at a terrific clip and within the first 500 feet—a noteworthy achievement and a decided advantage. After that it's all "meat," the first half probably holding more laughs than any other "special" Broadway has seen, while the after portion is the intense war stuff.

Gilbert's performance is a superb thing, while Renee Adoree, as the little French peasant, figuratively lives the role. The same may as well be said for Karl Dane and Tom O'Brien, for it is the excellent work of all these players and the manner in which King Vidor has handled them that lifts this production far above the ordinary. Dane's performance will probably do for him what "Tol'able David" did for Ernest Torrence. The picture is nothing less than a triumph for Vidor. His handling of "scenes" is great, while the "inside" army stuff that Stallings has slipped him consummates a flavoring vein ever present. Team work has made this picture. It makes 'em laugh, cry, and it thrills—plenty. Besides which the subtitling (captions) may be pointed to as an example and a lesson of how it should be done.

The continuity is replete with bits. Little things that ordinarily wouldn't draw attention, but have been so planted here that they must register. For example, while a company of infantry is advancing a German machine gun opens up and sprays the line. Four or five men drop and the middle private of the group becomes rooted to the ground in terror, with his knees trembling. This is a distant "shot" with action before and behind it, yet it stands out.

Backstage effects are much on the principle as for "The Birth of a Nation," while the musical score, perhaps, outranks anything of its kind since that Griffith masterpiece. Both Mendoza and Axt deserve a world of credit for their work in this, as it's an essential contribution—in this case a mighty one.

Jeff McCarthy's contention is that "The Big Parade" is the nearest thing to the "Nation" that the screen has divulged to date—and he's right.

Skig.

ROAD TO YESTERDAY

First personally directed film by Cecil DeMille since allying with P. D. C. Adapted by Jeanie McPherson from the stage play by J. E. Sutherland and Beulah Marie Dix. At the Rivoli, New York, week of Nov. 29. Running time, about 100 minutes.

Kenneth Paulton........Joseph Schildkraut
Malena Paulton.................Jetta Goudal
Beth Tyrell....................Vera Reynolds
Jack Moreland..................William Boyd
Dolly Foules.......................Julia Faye
Adrian Tompkins.........Casson Ferguson
Harriet Tyrell.............Trixie Friganza
Hugh Armstrong...........Clarence Burton
Anne Veneer..............Josephine Norman
Watt Earnshaw.................Charles West

This is Cecil DeMille's first personally directed release through his new alliance with Producers' Distributing, although two other films made by the DeMille unit have preceded "Road to Yesterday." Of his own special it may be said that it qualifies as first run stuff, lavishly made, furnished with beautiful backgrounds and settings and cast competently in every spot. To top off the generally pleasing tone of the film, DeMille has provided the greatest train wreck scene ever shot.

And—to make that scene more effective—it is preceded by a single shot of a long train of sleepers on the prairie at night, rushing through space at 75 miles an hour and reproducing to a remarkable degree the eerie phantom of a great express leaving the countryside behind in its swift and accurate rush to a given point. This scene aided greatly in building up the other, for when the wreck came, the engine of one train ploughed through a sleeper car, with the heroine, Malena Paulton, clinging in fright and horror to its tender.

Rails, dislodged by the impact and twisted out of shape, thrust themselves through the floor and every imaginable feature of an on-the-level wreck is reproduced. It's a whale in itself and whether the picture is remembered twenty years from now or not, you'll not forget that wreck.

The plot is one of those reincarnation things, beginning with a modern sequence of a newly wed pair, and winding up with this same pair as medieval personages. The wife feels that somewhere, at sometime in a previous life, her husband has hurt her, but is never able to explain her aversion to him.

After the wreck, which comes when a general domestic split-up had ensued, the scene shifts back to the Merrie England of long ago, and the husband is revealed as a knight and the wife as a gypsy girl.

Joseph Schildkraut and Jetta Goudal are in the leading roles, both admirable types, with the wisdom in such casting all the more apparent with the beginning of the old English sequence.

Trixie Friganza is installed for comedy purposes and gets plenty of laughs, while Vera Reynolds and Casson Ferguson are two other sweethearts who also appear in the later sequence.

But it is William Boyd, apparently a newcomer, who takes the cake and icing away from everyone else. As a minister who falls in love with Miss Reynolds, he plays much in the old Wallace Reid manner, and what is more, looks a great deal like Reid. Of good build, Boyd has light hair and a clean, bright face with a personality which walks off the screen. DeMille, it is understood, is figuring on Boyd as a real bet, and after seeing his performance in "Road to Yesterday," that is easy to understand.

One fault—the film is too long. The reviewer saw it several weeks ago at a pre-showing in the Embassy late one night and then it ran many minutes overtime. At the Rivoli Sunday it was so long the rest of the program was materially chopped. Many minutes might be sliced out to good effect, although it is really hard to see where the slicing can be done. Whether difficult or not, cutting is important, through the present length, 100 minutes.

"Road to Yesterday" shapes up as high class product, directed in the true DeMille manner and filled with his fine touches. Either you like him or you don't (and many of the high art boys don't) but the public will enjoy this one. *Sisk.*

THE BEST BAD MAN

Fox picture starring Tom Mix. From the novel by Max Brand and directed by J. G. Blystone. A Blystone production. At the Rialto, New York, week Nov. 29. Running time, 53 minutes.

Hugh Nichols.................Tom Mix
Hank Smith...............Buster Gardner
Frank Dunlap.............Cyril Chadwick
Peggy Swain....................Clara Bow
Dan Ellis....................Tom Kennedy
Mr. Swain.......................Frank Beal
Molly Jones......................Judy King
Sam, the butler...............Tom Wilson
Sheriff.........................Paul Panzer

Just an ordinary picture for Tom Mix that will neither hurt nor improve his standing among the enthusiasts. Extremely faulty projection failed to help the presentation at this house Sunday afternoon. Everyone's eyes were swimming. This was due to a poor focus which must have gone uncorrected for around 500 feet. A bad "break" for any film, and especially deplorable in a Broadway house.

Mix frolics through this screen epic as a wealthy heir whose hobby is musical instruments. Having been left a Colorado land tract he investigates when informed his manager is getting in some underhand work. The cleaning out of the schemers, while hiding his own identity, takes up a majority of the running time, during which he wins the daughter of the most oppressed rancher.

The action opens in New Orleans with flashes of the Mardi Gras after which the locale is the west, much riding during chases and the exploding of a dam for a water finish.

Opposite Mix is Clara Bow, not too convincing as the steel-nerved western girl. Other than the star the picture really belongs to Tom Wilson, as Mix's colored butler, who holds up the chain of events when the story indicates a weakness. Were it not for the comedy angle the picture would be decidedly anemic.

Fairly fast after it once gets away, this release should fill the requirements of Mix fans. He's turned out better and worse than this. *Skig.*

Clothes Make the Pirate

Sam Rork production for First National with Leon Errol and Dorothy Gish starred. Authorship not credited, but whatever source adapted and scenarized by Marion Fairfax. Directed by Maurice Tourneur. At Strand, New York, Nov. 30, week. Running time, 75 mins.

Trem Tidd.....................Leon Errol
Betsy Tidd...................Dorothy Gish
Madame LaTour..................Nita Naldi
Scute, the Baker............Tully Marshall
Lieut. Cavendish............James Rennie
Nancy Downs..................Edna Murphy
Jennison.....................George Marion
Dixie Bull, the Pirate..........Walter Law
The Innkeeper...................Frank Lalor
Capt. Montague...........Reginald Barlow

Leon Errol registers as a screen comedian. If somebody will exert a little brainwork on a good story and arrange it into a scenario which builds as it progresses, it is likely the funny man with the creaky knee will register a decisive hit.

"Clothes Make the Pirate" is his first effort alone, for in "Sally" he supported Colleen Moore. Here he is the central figure. Sometimes the picture is good and sometimes not. The only time when it is very funny are when Errol is participating in some choice bits of slapstick.

The story concerns a henpecked husband in 1771 in Boston. The husband was a tailor who had a hankering to be a pirate. That life, he thought, would at least take him away from a shrewish wife. The tailor wasn't a youngster, being an old fellow with whiskers, but by some stroke of poor casting, Dorothy Gish was given the shrewish role of his wife.

However, pirates do come to town and he, on a lark, is dressed in his pirate suit when they mistake him for their chief and shove him aboard the vessel.

The remainder of the story concerns his mishaps, his craven cowardice in the face of battle and of how his wife happened to be taken prisoner by his own crew.

Then comes some real fun. Having shaved off his whiskers, his wife doesn't recognize him, so he is free to slap her around and flirt with a hoity-toity vamp who shot warm glances from beneath a white wig. The windup shows a completely changed man. His piratical experience has made him master in his home.

Tourneur, in directing, has done excellently with his characters, but his characters have not always done well by him. James Rennie (husband of Miss Gish) is an unimpressive juvenile, while Nita Naldi, though featured, has little to do.

While Miss Gish is miscast, Errol is suited. If the scenario had been formed with any degree of originality, it is more than likely a corking film would have resulted. The film is but so-so and shows evidences all around of being produced for a not overly large sum. Children seem to like it best.

In other words, it will suffice, but will hardly arouse undue enthusiasm among those who believed Errol would click decisively once left to himself on the screen. As it is, Errol clicks, but the picture doesn't. *Sisk.*

THE MASKED BRIDE

Metro-Goldwyn-Mayer production, directed by Christy Cabanne, starring Mae Murray. At the Capitol, New York, week of Nov. 29. Running time, 68 minutes.

Gaby.............................Mae Murray
Bruce Gordon..........Francis X. Bushman
Prefect of Police...................Roy D'Arcy
Antoine...........................Basil Rathbone
Miss Gordon......................Pauline Neff
Vibout...............................Fred Warren

Just a picture, nothing more or less. The chances are that if it had been turned out by any company other than Metro-Goldwyn it never would have seen the inside of the Capitol theatre even with Mae Murray. It is melodrama of the hoakiest kind. Away from the Capitol there should be some doubt as to its ability to attract business.

The story is made to order for Miss Murray. It gives her an opportunity to display pretty much all of her very dainty figure and likewise an opportunity to shine in what was her original field of endeavor in entertaining—dancing. She does three dances during the picture. The first is a novelty in a cabaret scene with a series of circular drapes employed, one enveloping another until the dancer, who is standing in the center, is entirely blotted from view. Later she does her Apache and finally a Spanish number. Miss Murray incidentally looks very well in a black wig.

The scene of the story is laid in Paris with the star as a cabaret entertainer and at the head of a band of jewel thieves. The hero is an American millionaire bent on reforming her. He finally succeeds and marries her. Interwoven with the love theme is a lot of crook stuff, a plot to relieve him of the diamond necklace that once belonged to the Czarina and a few little things like that.

Francis X. Bushman plays the male lead. He seems rather bulky for the role, and in the earlier scenes failed to get over. Later in dress clothes he improved somewhat. Basil Rathbone is the heavy, the dancing partner of Miss Murray, and handled himself to advantage in a role that was far from being sympathetic. The others in the cast were just runners-up.

The picture to all appearances was made in a rush. No great production cost evident. *Fred.*

The Timber Wolf

William Fox production starring Buck Jones. Story by Jackson Gregory, directed by W. S. Van Dyke. At the Stanley, N. Y. (25c grind house), one day, Nov. 30. Running time, 59 minutes.

Bruce Standing..................Buck Jones
Renee Brooke......................Ellnor Fair
Babe Deverll......................David Dyas
Joe Terry............................Sam Allen
Sheriff.........................William Walling
The Boy............................Jack Craig
Billy Winch.....................Robert Mack

As a regular release aimed at the house where a daily change of program is the order of things, this picture will be counted above the average run of westerns that come along. It is a meller full of action and fight with the usual riding and chase stuff. Where the houses run better than a two-bit admission it will fit on the double feature bills.

Buck Jones plays one of those devil-may-care characters who runs his lumber camp with the idea that booze is bad for his men. The town is run by one Deverll who sells hooch and who occasionally sends a runner into the lumber camp with it. In the end Buck bests the heavy and incidentally wins his girl away from him, but not until Buck receives a bullet wound at her hand and had the task of taming her.

The girl is played by Elinor Fair, who, at times, registers fairly well, and then again, not so well. To a certain extent photography is responsible for this. The heavies are unusually well handled by David Dyas and William Walling. The former puts up a corking fight with the star along about the third reel. Two old men, character types, divided honors with the star. One was an old prospector played by Sam Allen and the other Robert Mack. Looks as though these two might be teamed up to advantage in a series of characters.

There are a few thrills earlier with falling timber and a fight between the star and a bootlegger. The riding stuff shows off Jones' white charger to advantage. That horse certainly can slide down the side of a mountain as easily as though he was going along on the level.

In all, it is a very fair western on the strength of the constant action that the picture contains. *Fred.*

SPEED MADNESS

Hercules production, distributed by Peter Kanellos. Starring Frank Merrill. Written by William E. Wing. Directed by Bruce Mitchell. Cast includes Clara Horton, Evelyn Sherman, Garry O'Dell, Joe Girard, Jimmy Quinn and Geno Corrado. Runs approximately an hour.

A lot of unintentional laughs in this one if you're in the right humor. It's a rare example of the stunt picture at its worst.

Frank Merrill, a comparatively new stunt man, is featured. When young boys have grown just a trifle too old for fairy tales and have not yet had their interest awakened in the naughty novels of today their favorite reading if it is not the "Rover Boys" is certain to be "Frank Merriwell." The implication is obvious and just so "Speed Madness" is aimed at 11-year-old intelligences. The dear old homestead mortgaged to the mustachioed, foreign villain. And the kindly but weak old mother who consents to her daughter's marrying the cur to save the farm. And finally the hero who says "Nay" and nearly breaks his neck selling his auto valve patent, chasing the heavy all around the place and finally crushing the little lady to his athletic bosom.

Merrill sets a record in this picture. Never once does he take an ordinary step where he can jump, hop, hurdle or vault instead. Instead of running straight through an open gate he goes way out of his way to leap over the fence. For some reason he never drives the auto himself, always intrusting that duty to his partner in invention, whose driving is much better than his comedy attempts.

Clara Horton endeavors valiantly to be appealing and sweet in the love scenes, and perhaps it was not her fault if in one brightly illuminated bit she did not wear quite enough underskirts or petticoats or whatever the women called those obsolete mysteries. Incidentally, she might have registered a kick for not having been given a prettier wardrobe entirely.

But that's only one of hundreds of faults. But "Speed Madness" is not the kind that irritates or displeases violently since it is such a simple effort. *Herb.*

WE MODERNS

First National production, starring Colleen Moore. Presented by John McCormick and adapted from Israel Zangwill's stage play. Directed by John Francis Dillon. At the Strand, New York, Dec. 6. Running time, 75 minutes.

Mary Sundale	Colleen Moore
John Ashlar	Jack Mulhall
Oscar Pleat	Carl Miller
Sir Robert Sundale	Claude Gillingwater
Lady Kitty Sundale	Clarissa Selwyn
Dick Sundale	Cleve Moore
Theodosia	Marcella Corday
Beamish	Tom McGuire
Johanna	Blanche Payson

One big punch may put this picture over—and without the punch it would be strictly in the so-so class.

Along about the 60th minute of the running time, things have worked to the point where the heroine is on a party aboard a dirigible, and as they are sailing through the clouds an airplane swoops up and smacks the blimp in the kisser—and the airplane catches fire, falling to the ground in a great tail spin. The blimp also catches fire, but apparently burns very slowly and gives the heroine plenty of time to escape the wreck. The wreck stuff was all faked, but rather well, and registered distinctly. For added effect the flame stuff was 'inted and showed up well.

The rest of the picture concerns Mr. Zangwill's silly play of "We Moderns," so cordially panned by everyone when it stayed a few weeks at the Gaiety (legit) in New York a season or so ago. In it Zangwill got worried about the state of our younger generation, and after putting his heroine through a series of paces wherein her wings were nearly scorched. Of course, the airship wreck brings her around and she runs home to papa and mama and tells them that at last she realizes and she won't ever be bad again and will marry her true love without fooling around.

The story is neither logical nor especially interesting, and what picture value it attains will be solely due to the marvelous personality of Colleen Moore, which is at once breezy, sweet and magnetic. Her performance here isn't any great shakes, but it would have been impossible for any star to have given a good performance under the circumstances. Jack Mulhall is the hero and goes well, while Carl Miller also deserves a hand for his work as the heavy.

Many of the scenes were taken in London. Several of the more famous spots are woven logically into the story. But London scenes or not, if "We Moderns" ever does anything extraordinary in the way of business, it will be because of Miss Moore and the wreck scenes. Otherwise it is in the dubious class and exhibitors will do well to screen it before they begin promising too much. *Sisk.*

Sally, Irene and Mary

Metro-Goldwyn-Mayer picture and an Edmund Goulding production. Adapted from the musical show of that name, and directed by Goulding. Photographed by John Arnold. At the Capitol, New York, week Dec. 6. Running time, 58 minutes.

Sally	Constance Bennett
Irene	Joan Crawford
Mary	Sally O'Neil
Jimmy Dugan	William Haines
Marcus Morton	Henry Kolker
Mrs. Dugan	Kate Price
Tom O'Dare	Sam De Grasse

Transplanted to the screen, this book for a musical show projects as rather trashy chorus-girl stuff that the "sticks" may eat up. It's not a good picture.

Dealing with Broadway's backstage angle, the script doesn't ring true. Some of the subtitles carry a hurrah flourish, but with it all the rurals are liable to take it verbatim, and it won't improve the general lay impression of chorus girls. Goulding has given the production one lavish stage setting for a full-stage Charleston number, but has fallen into the pitfall of having every member of the audience applaud as soon as the curtain starts to ascend. Any musical show is a panic in pictures, and this one is anything but an exception.

"Sally, Irene and Mary," as a show, had a successful road career. Whether the cast, music, comedy or production held it up is for those who saw it to say. It doesn't seem as though there could have been much of a book or comedy. If so, Goulding has lost a great deal in the migration to a scenario form or has made his characters too broad. Sally is the "kept woman" of the trio; Irene can't make up her mind whether to choose a "chaser" or a boy with honorable intentions, and Mary is the innocent miss who nearly loses Sally her de luxe flat when the latter's money man takes a tumble in her favor.

It's somewhat difficult to separate this triumvirate as Goulding has started them off, but it ends with Mary returning to her east side boy friend, Sally regaining her "dough boy," while Irene is finally rejected by the "chaser" when he learns she is a "good girl," walks out of the apartment and into the car of her other suitor, only to be killed en route to a "spite" marriage.

Not exactly what would be termed a wholesome tale, but not convincing enough to be taken seriously. Therefore the conclusion that where they like any sort of an "inside" on the choristers this release will fill the bill, but it will never appease a major house gathering.

Constance Bennett gives the one genuine performance in the picture as Sally, and suffers because of an unsympathetic role. Joan Crawford makes a silly girl of Irene, with whom interest is lost when she falls for he of the evil intent, and it's doubtful if there ever has been a chorus girl such as Sally O'Neill has been instructed to play in depicting Mary, fresh and too dizzy. Kolker makes a fair money man who seemingly has nothing to do but attend loose-moraled teas in apartments and wait at stage doors, with Haines doing little more than becoming indignant when seeing the scarcity of costume his Mary is wearing across the footlights—which isn't enough to demand censorship.

The best thing Goulding has done as the adapter and director of this one is the working up of the impending automobile tragedy and having picked John Arnold as his photographer. Arnold has been prominent on Broadway screens of late, especially at the Capitol, and is amassing a neat reputation in these parts, or should be. He now has two "specials" on the street—"Merry Widow" and "The Big Parade," either of which is a special recommendation in itself. A corking crank spinner, this boy, who gives a film every kind of a photographic "break" and rates more than passing mention on such consistent performances. *Skig.*

LAZYBONES

William Fox production, directed by Frank Borzage, with screen adaptation by Frances Marion from comedy-drama by Owen Davis. Starring Buck Jones and featuring Madge Bellamy, also Jane Novak. At Loew's New York, one-half double bill, one day, Dec. 4. Running time, about 60 minutes.

Nothing much to say about this picture unless to kid it.

Owen Davis could not possibly have written as poor a play as Frances Marion's adaptation. If it isn't the fault of the adaptation, Frank Borzage had better set up his defense.

But it looks like the Marion end. While her name is attached as the adapter, it doesn't run along her work. It's an old trick of writers to lend their names or money, willing to stand for it, and then engage some hack to perform the actual work. It's common in lyrical, musical and book lines. If it has crept into pictures, it should be kicked out.

Otherwise this picture is full of dullness, platitudes and maybe unconscious humor, such as when the girl at private school, commanded by her mother to return home, did so with her unacknowledged baby, attempting suicide into the river near the homestead instead of jumping in near the school and saving the carfare.

Or when the mother, curious about the baby she had heard of by accident, was told by her daughter of a marriage, and informing the daughter she was "a liar" (that kind of a mother), neither thought to mention the minister who had married or even excuse the missing evidence by stating the town and church records had been destroyed by fire.

It was funny to see the women's clothes of 1905 or before; also instead of cabaret scene, a country dance in the woods.

Buck Jones played "Lazybones" and the title must have gotten into the story and picture. Jane Novak was the girl who married and lost a sailor, but hung onto the baby.

The grownup granddaughter gave the best performance, although there was a rushing river shown that never was made in the studio. You will have to think a lot of Buck Jones to forget this one. *Sime.*

SEVEN SINNERS

Warner Bros. production from an original by Louis Milestone and Darryl Francis Zanuck, directed by Louis Milestone. Marie Prevost and Clive Brook featured. At Warners, New York, Dec. 5. Running time, 68 minutes.

Molly Brian	Marie Prevost
Jerry Winters	Clive Brook
Handsome Joe Hagney	John Patrick
Daylight Saunders	Charles Conklin
Pious Joe McDowell	Claude Gillingwater
Mamie McDowell	Mathilde Brundage
Policeman	Fred Kelsey

Above the average of the program product the Warners have been turning out. It is a crook comedy that only slows up in the last 500 feet or so when the regeneration of two pairs of crooks is brought about.

Had the comedy vein been maintained to the last the picture would have stood up with anything of its kind that has been along in a long while. As it is, the box office value should be above the average and the entertainment value on a par with the pictures that are being turned out by some of the bigger competitors of the Warners.

Marie Prevost and Clive Brook give performances that will please the fans. Miss Prevost is a female crook, while Brook is also of the soft dough breed, although from a good family. In all there are eight characters. Seven are crooks and the other is a policeman.

The scene is on Long Island in an exclusive colony where the private police have gone on strike. This news printed in the paper seems to have attracted all the safe workers to the spot. Brook is evidently first to arrive. He is followed by Miss Prevost and John Patrick, her partner in crime. As the two are cleaning the safe Brook arrives, covers them with a revolver, and while Patrick escapes he corners the girl who is under the impression he is the guardian of the home. He offers to let her go free if she can open the safe. As she leaves he proceeds to stuff the jewels in his pocket. But as he starts out of the door she is back on the job and covers him with her gun, takes the jewels away and locks him in a closet.

She, in turn, is trapped by two elderly crooks who pose as friends of the owner, there on a visit while he is abroad. The twist comes when the young woman crook announces to them that she is the new housekeeper who arrived that day with a new butler, releasing Brook from the closet to pose in the role she assigned.

From that point the complications continue with the introduction of a couple of rough working crooks, the return of Miss Prevost's original partner who then poses as the cook. They are all locked in the home through the policeman arriving and setting the alarm so that no one can leave.

In the finish when the youngsters are caught as they are escaping, the older crooks decide to turn square and give themselves up if the D. A. will be lenient to the youngsters.

Charles Conklin has a wow of a comedy role as a hick crook, while Claude Gillingwater, as the smooth old-timer, stands out like a diamond.

The direction is working, which may be accounted for through Milestone being co-author of the story and knowing what it was all about.

From a cost standpoint the picture does not appear a whole lot, but it should on the strength of its laughs be one of the big moneymakers of the year for the Warners. *Fred.*

PRIMROSE PATH

Independent picture, produced by Arthur F. Beck from original story by Leah Baird. Released by Arrow. Clara Bow and Wallace McDonald featured. At Loew's New York, with Miss Bow starred on picture's paper. One-half double bill, one day, Dec. 4, at Loew's New York. Running time, about 60 minutes.

Too good a picture to have been split up on a Loew's New York's double bill, although the other half of the program certainly did need assistance. Written and looking like an original story by Leah Baird, Miss Baird, a former picture star, seemed to put, besides ingenuity, much of the maternal instinct into the plot.

It's a sympathetic picture, even for the boy who went wrong. Also there is a silent grieving mother who instills good feeling into both of her sons, with the older having been the cause of the younger's crippled leg, obliging the smaller boy to wear a brace. That accident, not shown (and unnecessary to show, chopping out "detail") was caused through the older boy drinking. All of the older boy's jams came through drinking primarily. One of them brought him to court on the charge of murder.

The entire show business should thank Miss Baird for making Miss Bow a clean, good, lovable girl of a cabaret, who stuck to her boy to the finish. That seemed so nice and different from the usual scenarist who wants to give another branch of the show business, whether musical comedy or cabaret or circus, a wallop whenever that can be done, to make it a little stronger for the box office.

Good names in this cast, some corkers, besides those featured, but on a double picture day at the New York it's get 'em in and out. You're lucky to be able to read captions, let alone a string of names.

Good continuity in this story, too, of a story without mush, plenty of action, and some nice working out of secret service methods in the attempt to catch a smuggler, the tool of a gambler who is the cabaret's proprietor.

Miss Baird worked a shift of detachable canes very neatly. It was on the dock. The drinking youth, to prevent his arrest for bad checks given at gambling with the proprietor, was obliged to go to the dock, exchanging walking sticks as the smuggler came off of the boat. This was safely accomplished but led, up to the murder charge through one of the mob killing the chief gambler.

It may have been the author's thought that the cane switching was a good way, and it was—it has been done, with drugs as well as diamonds.

There are a couple of laughs, but it's not a comedy drama, more like a velvety melodrama, and as such can stand up.

Great picture for the drys but won't be resented by the wets. No propaganda in it.

Miss Bow looked cute and Mr. McDonald did very well as the juvenile. Besides intelligent direction all through, there is a trial scene in court here as well handled in a straightforward way as anything similar seen on the screen.

Stuart Holmes was the villain-gambler who first got bumped off and he did his death scene with much finesse. And now, if Stuart ever will consent to stop parting his hair in the middle, he can go into the heaviest of the heavy classes, for he can look any glossy, villain-our role, besides acting it.

Too bad other names were allowed to escape. That English made-up smuggler did some excellent work, also the crippled boy, the latter especially, if not actually lame, and the mother was a peach.

This is a very interesting picture, just that, which may be more for those who prefer a reliable. *Sime.*

SPEED MAD

Perfection Pictures production releasing through Apollo Exchange. Features Edith Roberts, with William Fairbanks included in cast. Story by Dorothy Howell. Directed by Jay Marchant. At the Stanley, New York, one day (Dec. 4). Running time, 49 minutes.

Ostensibly an independent follow up on the program automobile race pictures in evidence early last fall. The late Wallace Reid and Theodore Roberts made corking comedy films out of the same material, hence the terra firma which this script covers is a much cultivated area.

William Fairbanks is the reckless, shiftless and speed-crazed son to whom the father finally gives "air." On his own until college opens, a month hence, the boy "hocks" his car for the entrance fee of a road race, is abducted by the villain but gets back to the track in time to win and save the girl's homestead from folding up.

The picture is light on production, while the race stuff might be termed pot shots at a road race with track "lifts" from a weekly or some such film. The continuity is not too bad, although the motive power is inclined to be jumpy. A freckled face youth is the comedy sidelight, while the cuteness and reasoning powers of a dog appear to have been too much emphasized for the good of the picture.

Miss Roberts is called upon for no marked acting, while Fairbanks simply drives a car as his principal contribution. Can't be classed much higher than a filler for the smaller houses. *Skig.*

Fighting the Flames

Independent production released through Commonwealth. Directed by Reeves Beacon. At Loew's New York, one day, Dec. 2. Running time, 62 minutes.

Hoak fire-fighting melodrama that appears to have come out of Joe Miller's joke book. For the small time neighborhood houses it may get by, but it isn't strong enough even for the bigger daily change houses. The New York Roof audience on Wednesday practically laughed it off the screen. That's a pretty wise Broadway audience that slips up there of an evening, and they should know better than to try to slip them this kind of junk.

Why they even go so far as to pull the oldest of Joe Miller's on the screen in this one. It's the apple-sauce gag: "How can you divide two apples equally among five children?" That's a sample.

The story concerns the wild son of a wealthy man who is turned out by the latter. The boy meets up with a kiddie in the jailhouse where he is lodged as a souse. When the two get out he takes care of the kid and the youngster brings about his regeneration.

The young man immediately goes into the Fire Department training school and right after he is a full-fledged fire fighter on the job. He rescues the girl he loves from a burning building which gives an excuse for the final clinch.

William Haines does the best he can in an impossible role, and the same might be said for Dorothy DeVore. *Fred.*

JOANNA

First National picture, directed by Edwin Carewe. A Carewe production. Features Dorothy Mackaill and Jack Mulhall. Adapted from the newspaper serial story of the same name authored by H. L. Gates, at the Strand, New York, week Dec. 13. Running time, 76 minutes.

Joanna Manners..........Dorothy Mackaill
John Wilmore..............Jack Mulhall
Frank Brandon............Paul Nicholson
Andrew Eggleston........George Fawcett
James Grayson............Edward Davis
Carlotta de Silva........Dorothy del Rio
Teddy Dorminster........John T. Murray
Georgie Leach............Rita Carewe

A newspaper serial yarn that must have been eaten up in many a kitchen. Its a story of a shopgirl who suddenly gains command of a million dollars. With that knowledge on tap, fill in your own scenario, for you can't be entirely wrong.

The story screens very much as it must have read, and will be thoroughly snubbed by the clientele which likes the "worth-while" things. Major city balcony trade should accept it as satisfying, and as and where illiteracy percentage mount so will the entertaining qualities of "Joanna." It's strictly for the back-door insiders.

Joanna comes into her million because a bank president takes exception to a newspaper editorial belittling the modern girl. The old boy is so steamed up that, having a loose ten hundred thousand doing not a thing but roll up interest, he wagers it that a normal present-day girl will still have a spotless character after burning up the money and won't sell herself because of having become accustomed to luxury. Of course, the individual accepting this sporting proposition can hardly be said to be starving to death. And what's a million in a sub-title? A thousand or so feet later is revealed the why of Joanna being "it." The bank pres. knew her mother.

Well lubricated with the oil concerning "money cannot buy love," one thing leads to another, with the audience always 100 feet ahead of the action, until Joanna loses and regains her struggling architect (Jack Mulhall), while the bank's head is so overjoyed to see his million come back he adopts Joanna as his daughter during the time it will take her to get her blueprint interpreter before an altar.

The film is overboard with wild and gay parties, elaborate cabaret scenes and anything interiorly that enters the imagination along with the thought of a million bucks. Incidentally the author has seen fit to allow Joanna a little over two years in which to consume the "roll." Most of that period is spent abroad by means of a caption, but there is revealed the girl's joyous plunge into check signing, while the depiction of a bank president laughing himself to death at the sight of five-figure drafts on his "dough" for automobiles, etc., is a new angle on a banker's sense of humor.

The playwrights who are squawking against the stage producers affiliating themselves with the big film concerns should take a look at this release and then celebrate. They could turn out one of these things daily for a month and then lay off for the remaining 11 months. The evident hookup between the paper or papers, which ran this serial and First National must have been a bitter pill for someone to have downed after gleaning the substance of the tale.

At that Miss Mackaill contributes a nice performance. She looks good and wears an abundance of clothes, while Carewe has slipped in a midnight negligee bathing party so as to be sure nothing would be missed. There is also a laugh here and there. Mulhall convinces as the hero with old-fashioned ideas, with Paul Nicholson still "tight," according to this screening. He's either been "chasing" or "stewed" for the past year as seen in picture houses around here.

"Joanna' should and probably will draw that public which followed it in print. The costly looking production donated indicates that the author's readers will be appeased at his brain-child in celluloid form. But the money spent on it is out of all proportion to the actual worth of the lightweight theme. That would "go" if this were a "nickel" production—and it isn't. *Skig.*

WHY WOMEN LOVE
(The Sea Woman)

First National release produced and directed by Edwin Carewe. Adapted from the play "The Sea Woman" by Willard Robertson. Blanche Sweet starred. Titles by Ralph Spence. Reviewed at the Broadway, New York, Dec. 14. Running time, 65 minutes.

Molla......................Blanche Sweet
Ira Meers, the Engineer......Edward Earle
Rodney O'Malley, the Captain......
......................Robert Frazer
Olaf Hansen................Bert Sprotte
Pearl....................Dorothy Sebastian
Jerry....................Charles Murray

First the title is flashed.

Then the fact that it was adapted from the "Sea Woman"; that so and so did the adaptation; that Ralph Spence wrote the titles.

Then that Edwin Carewe personally directed this one.

That he was deeply indebted to the staff for their assistance.

Then the seal of the M. P. P. D. A., the Hays organization, was shown.

Then that this was a First National picture.

Then the censor board's approval. Then two titles.

And after that, the picture.

At the conclusion it was once more called to attention that First National made the picture and that First National was a member of the M. P. P. D. A. All of which must have been very interesting to an audience of laymen.

Aside from the clutter of credits, "Why Women Love" is a good picture, even if the title hasn't anything to do with the film itself. It is being released, however, both as "Why Women Love" and as "The Sea Woman."

The story concerns the daughter of a Norwegian sea captain. After she, Molla, had been rescued through a sea of burning oil by an old lighthouse keeper, she pledged that she would look after his wayward daughter, Pearl. This meant giving up the idea of marrying her sweetheart, Rodney O'Malley, captain of a large freighter. But she stayed on at the lighthouse until one day, the captain came back and they were packing to get married, when a letter arrived from the town doctor, the purport of which was that Pearl had arrived in an "interesting condition."

So Molla chose between love and duty, and although her lover's ship was sailing, she told him she'd have to stay and find the man connected with Pearl and make them marry.

The big scenes show the sinking of a large schooner laden with oil which catches fire and burns over the water. Another scene is that of the burning lighthouse, nicely done. The scene of the schooner breaking up, however, is badly done in miniature, a procedure so obviously cheap looking it is surprising a real picture firm will resort to it.

Blanche Sweet has the leading role, and is fine, once more convincing most of the spectators that if she isn't the most beautiful woman on the screen she's near it. Charlie Murray, Robert Frazer and Edward Earle give good performances, while the production details, aside from the miniature shot, are excellent.

All in all, "Why Women Love" is a good audience film, thanks mostly to Blanche Sweet, who fits the part ideally. *Sisk.*

TIME, THE COMEDIAN

Metro-Goldwyn production adapted by Frederic and Fanny Hatton from the novel by Kate Jordan. Directed by Robert Z. Leonard with Lew Cody and Mae Busch starred. At Capitol, New York, week of Dec. 13. Running time, 60 minutes.

Nora Dakon....................Mae Busch
Larry Brundage....................Lew Cody
Ruth Dakon..............Gertrude Olmstead
Ruth Dakon (child)..............Rae Ethelyn
Michael Lawlor..................Roy Stewart
Mrs. St. Germaine..........Paulette Duval
Tom Cautley................Creighton Hale
Aunt Abbey........Nellie Parker Spaulding
Anthony Dakon..................Robert Ober
Count de Brissac..................David Mir
Prince Strotoff.................Templar Saxe
Swedish Maid..............Mildred Vincent

This is the first really poor picture Metro has turned out in a long time.

The plot, reduced to its essentials, tells the story of a male vampire, of his love for one woman and his ultimate throwing her over for her daughter. In the end the daughter packs up, leaves home and determines to go to the male vamp, and when she arrives she finds her mother in his arms.

Which brings the customary accusations, but the mother feels that she has triumphed because she has kept the daughter from the bad man's clutches.

All of this is punctuated by intermittent glimpses of Theodore Kosloff, arrayed as a clown playing Time, a comedian who romps hither and thither laughing at the foibles of people. There are many shots of Kosloff in his panto makeup. After the entire plot has been told, he erases a blot from the book of Time, climbs up a large pendulum and disappears into a clock. Whatever symbolism this procedure may have aimed at it lost because of the picture itself, which is badly made, both as regards acting and the technical end. There are too many long shots throughout the picture, and particularly in a theatre as large as the Capitol, where the great majority of the audience sits far away from the screen, the effect on the eyes is bad. Moreover, whatever facial expressions are registered by the actors are lost in these far away shots.

Mae Busch, Lew Cody and Gertrude Olmstead have the leading roles with nobody contributing anything out of the ordinary.

The pre-Christmas slump period is a good time to slip this one into the Capitol, and even if it had gone in during the good weeks it is doubtful if it would have held up.

Sisk.

THE GOLDEN COCOON

Warner Bros.' production from the novel of Ruth Cross, adapted by Hope Loring and Louis Lighton. Directed by Millard Webb. Shown at Warners, New York, week Dec. 14, 1925. Running time, 75 minutes.

Gregory Cochrane............Huntly Gordon
Molly Shannon.............Helene Chadwick
Mr. Renfro...................Richard Tucker
Split-Ticket Dillworth......Frank Campeau
Mrs. Shannon..............Margaret Seddon
Mrs. Parker.............Carrie Clarke Ward
Mr. Shannon...............Charles McHugh
The Baby..........................Violet Kane

Pretty good melodrama of love and politics that would have been a whole lot better had it not been permitted to run to so much footage. With about 15 minutes lopped off the picture would have been far more entertaining.

The story does give Helene Chadwick a corking chance to strut her stuff, and the manner in which that young woman runs the gamut from young girlhood to wife shows that all she needs is a chance in a really great role to prove how great she is.

The picture itself isn't a bad one nor is it one that stands out as particularly good. Classifying it as a fair program picture would be about safe.

It is the story of a small-town girl in Texas who educates herself and wins a scholarship at an eastern university. While there one of the professors makes love and promises to marry her, then runs off with the heiress daughter of the chief of the vice element of the town. This drives the youngster practically out of her mind, and she returns home.

In time the man who donated the scholarship which she won—a judge—has become so interested in her he follows her home and marries her. They return to the city. Five years later, when he is a candidate for Governor, his opponent, being the head of the vice ring and the father-in-law of his wife's former lover, tries to frame a story to the effect that she was once an inmate of one of his dives. They threaten to make the accusation public unless she has her husband withdraw from the race. Instead she disappears, leaving the impression she has been drowned.

Fate in the form of her old lover overtakes her in the subway, and he threatens to expose her disappearance in the papers as a trick framed between herself and her husband for sympathy. She prevents him from doing so at the point of a revolver. In the struggle for its possession he is shot and dies, but not until he confesses the plot.

Huntly Gordon as the philanthropically inclined Judge and husband gave his usual studied performance, while Richard Tucker was all that could be asked as a villain. Lew Cody will have to look to his laurels as an insincere lover if this boy plays a few more love scenes as he did the once in the summer house in this picture. Frank Campeau as the vice king slips over the role as one real "hard guy."

There is nothing about the direction to distinguish it particularly, and there are a couple of ballroom shots that appear to have been rather badly handled.

Fred.

THE SPLENDID CRIME

Famous Players release, produced, directed and written by William DeMille. Bebe Daniels starred, and Neil Hamilton featured. Scenario by Violet Clark. At the Rialto, week Dec. 13. Running time, 65 minutes.

Jenny..........................Bebe Daniels
Bob Van Dyke..................Neil Hamilton
Beth Van Dyke...............Anne Cornwall
John Norton..................Anthony Jowitt
Dugan............................Fred Walton
Kelly...........................Lloyd Corrigan
The Kid........................Mickey McBan
Mary.........................Josephine Crowell
Madam Denise...............Marcelle Corday

"The Splendid Crime" is poor stuff all the way through. It seems Famous Players isn't giving Bebe Daniels much help in the way of stories.

William DeMille, who directed this, also wrote it, which shows, among other things, that his mind isn't given to holding anything which smacks of originality. His most recent pieces of directorial work for F-P, such as "New Brooms," "Icebound" and "The Splendid Crime," have shown him to be a consistent producer of box office flops and in his most recent effort he has again kept down to his record. Thus "The Splendid Crime" is the combination of a poor story, a star whose recent work has been marked by flops, and a director whose box office success list is very small of late.

This time ("The Splendid Crime") DeMille's story, to be original, tells of a poor girl who lived with crooks and who was a crook, but who reformed and became very honest—so honest that she kept the boy she loved (an aristocrat with golf pants and everything) from temporarily appropriating money entrusted to him. When he says he must take the money to save himself from ruin, she goes back to her old pals and gets them to crack his safe and take the money, which she intends to keep until he changes his mind.

The early part has Miss Daniels in dirty clothes and acting generally like a hard-boiled dame who gives them lots of gestures, some plain and fancy gum chewing, and little real acting. Her support includes Neil Hamilton, a good actor who does well as the poor hero.

But the surprise of the whole film to the initiate is that Anthony Jowitt, Gloria Swanson's leading man in "The Coast of Folly," has a part here. Corse Payton could teach him volumes about acting, for Jowitt hasn't even learned the elementals yet—such things as walking, lifting a hand, bowing, etc. The crook types are well handled, and Josephine Crowell plays an old housekeeper role well.

As far as the exhibitors are concerned, nothing beyond ordinary business is to be expected on the strength of this film.

Sisk.

WANDERING FIRES

Arrow Pictures release and Maurice Campbell production, directed by Campbell. Adapted from a Warner Fabian story. Cast includes Constance Bennett, Wallace MacDonald, George Hackathorne, Henrietta Crosman, Effie Shannon. Running time, 48 minutes.

Warner Fabian's name is allotted most of the billing in that he turned out "Flaming Youth" and is also the pen parent of this one. Whether a novel or not doesn't make much difference, for Campbell has cluttered up the film by permitting Wallace MacDonald to wax overly dramatic, often and consistently. The film's best personal bet is Connie Bennett, and her assignment here amounts to little more than setting up exercises.

It's a story of a serious minded youth who falls in love with a society miss with a blemish against her name. The dark spot is revealed in a flashback, the girl having remained in the apartment of her love the night before he sailed for France to fight.

Reported dead and accused as a traitor, the girl cleared his name by proving an alibi when admitting she had been with him that night, and all night.

The besmirched warrior comes back a shell-shock victim; two niched piano keys restore his memory, and after MacDonald has heaved and acted all over the screen worrying whether his wife still craves her former fiance he learns she still dotes on him, so it's okay.

The picture is a bantamweight principally because of the manner in which Campbell has handled it. A subtitle, "The Vacant Chair," preceded a scene of the mother of the supposedly dead soldier dining at a table with her son's picture and his two medals glowing at her from an opposite plate. Touching with grapefruit? Hardly.

Hackathorne is the demented A. E. F. member for an average performance, Miss Bennett rides in on her appearance, and MacDonald is handicapped by the manner in which he has been directed. The remaining characters are secondary.

Limited to the smaller houses, one dayers or double features.

Skig.

A Woman of the World

Presented by Famous Players, starring Pola Negri. Adapted by Pierre Collings from the novel by Carl Van Vechten. Directed by Malcolm St. Clair. At the Rivoli, New York, week Dec. 14. Running time, 67 minutes.

Countess Elnora Natatorini......Pola Negri
Gareth Johns........Charles Emmett Mack
Richard Granger............Holmes Herbert
Lennie Porter.............Blanche Mehaffey
Sam Poore..................Chester Conklin
Lou Poore.......................Lucille Ward
Judge Porter.......................Guy Oliver
Mrs. Bierbauer......................Dot Farley
Mrs. Fox..........................May Foster
Annie....................Dorothea Wolbert

Poor Pola! Wonder what they are trying to do to her, anyway? It's a dead certainty that Famous isn't giving her this type of picture on purpose and taking a chance of wasting the money they are putting into her productions. Then what is the trouble?

If they can't pick stories any better than this they should get someone who can; or if it is a case of Pola selecting her own, then they had better stop her.

If something isn't done, then Pola Negri's value as a box-office attraction in the spots where that does exist is going to be wiped out. This picture is just another horrible example of what she should not do. It doesn't look as though it was going to be worth a nickel at the box office.

Possibly Carl Van Vechten's novel had some kick in it as written, but as screened it isn't even a fair story. There is nothing to it that would make any one want to walk farther than half a block to see it, providing there was no charge for admission.

Pola plays a countess who has an unfortunate love affair abroad and decides to come to America to forget. She joins relatives who are typical of a hundred thousand families in any of our smaller midwest towns. Here her gowns and her foreign customs cause any amount of stir and consternation.

It is one of those towns that is in the throes of an anti-vice campaign, with the district attorney as the leading crusader. The countess on the night of her arrival runs afoul of him, and determines to bring him to her feet for his attitude when he meets her. In the long run she falls in love with him and he with her, but not until the two have had several clashes.

Charles Emmett Mack is programed as the juvenile lead, but Holmes Herbert as the D. A. takes all of the honors away from him. The picture really belongs to Chester Conklin in a comedy role. He just about walks away with the entire production, and if it wasn't for him the whole picture would be a sorry affair.

Pola has a new bob, and it is the type that is not going to endear her, particularly to the women, evident through the comment made by women in the audience at the Rivoli at the final show Sunday night. Pola seemed to get on their nerves.

The picture doesn't look as though it was very costly in production and there is nothing about the direction that distinguishes it. It is just a small-time picture that might have been turned out by any dink independent.

Fred.

TUMBLEWEEDS

United Artists release, starring Wm. S. Hart. Hal G. Evart's story, directed by King Baggot. A Wm. S. Hart production. At the Strand, New York, week of Dec. 20. Running time, 76 mins.

Don Carver.............William S. Hart
Molly Lassiter............Barbara Bedford
Kentucky Rose............Lucien Littlefield
Noll Lassiter.............J. Gordon Russell
Bill Freel.................Richard R. Neill
Bart Lassiter.................Jack Murphy
Mrs. Riley.................Lillian Leighton

"Tumbleweeds" marks Bill Hart's return to the screen following his long lapse in picture making, brought about through a disagreement with Famous Players over policy.

It's a welcome return.

Bill Hart still means the West on the screen and he is seen here under a new banner, a new hat and on a new horse. It's a picture that rates a hearing in the more imposing program houses.

This is a typical Hart western, although the story carries something of a different angle on the open country. Its punch is a stampede of homesteaders to claim-stake the Cherokee strip, an area undoubtedly famed in the annals of the old west, as Hart is fastidious on the authenticity of his pictures.

The mad real estate boom is brought about by the government, which chases the cattle herds off this territory, between Oklahoma and Kansas, so that it may be opened to the settlers. The resultant "jam" is such that cavalry is detailed to patrol the borders with the official start, by cannon, from a lineup of all manner of horse-drawn vehicles. Thence the kick of the wild rush with Hart getting away late, but sweeping past the opposition to stake out the ranch, of which he had been foreman, for the girl.

The girl (Barbara Bedford) has a scheming half-brother in league with an equally "shady" pal. Hart hounds both throughout the action. Only one death in the picture, a soldier.

The heroine, not getting into any serious difficulties, has eliminated the need of any ultra-heroic measures to save her and for that matter, the love theme of the tale may be said to be secondary to its historical interest.

Hart's wild ride, for many feet of film and at a full gallop, allowed for excellent camera work. Some "shots" of this hectic jaunt ahorse were of a calibre to draw applause from a Monday night audience that well nigh filled Joe Plunkett's Strand. It is a splendid piece of photography no denying that.

Supporting players are capable if not particularly prominent. Miss Bedford suffices as the girl of the script and more closely conforms to Hart's physique than many other miniatures he has appeared opposite. J. Gordon Russell and Richard B. Neill consummate lukewarm villains, while there is a certain amount of that ever desired ingredient present, comedy relief, for more or less results.

Pictorially, the film has its moments, with pretty landscape backgrounds, etc.

Hart gives a strong performance. Judging from his reception at this house he has lost no prestige during his absence. As in the majority of cases, it's simply a matter of stories and direction. King Baggott has done nicely with this latter assignment.

Mix and Hart are unquestionably alone at this type of character delineation and with the never ceasing demand for better grade westerns there is as much room on the screen for both as there always has been.

Bill Hart's pictures have a long standing reputation for being clean, always great for the kids and if they didn't appeal to adults it was most always a case of inferior material or an occasional tendency to overreach on the director, possibly causing over-acting.

The reference to cleanliness and the appeal to children is also true of Tom Mix.

It is to be sincerely hoped that both Bill Hart and Tom Mix will go on making their westerns until neither is physically capable of throwing a leg over a horse.

Because these two actors typify something to the youth—the heroic, the story book, the brave, the honest and the true—in short, the example—and as it is a good example always with either—what could be better on the screen. *Skig.*

STEEL PREFERRED

Metropolitan Picture distributed by Producers' Dist. Corp. From the "Sat. Eve. Post" stories by H. S. Hall, entitled "The Adventures of Wally Gay," adapted by Elliott J. Clawson. Directed by James Hogan. At Warner's, New York, week Dec. 19. Running time, 67 minutes.

Amy Creeth.................Vera Reynolds
Wally Gay...................William Boyd
James Creeth..............Hobart Bosworth
Goofy.........................Walter Long
Nicker....................William V. Mong
Dicker.....................Charlie Murray
Waldron......................Nigel Barrie
Mrs. Creeth...............Helene Sullivan
Bartender.......................Ben Turpin

One that has everything. Comedy that is great, a love story that stands up, melodrama that thrills, and, above all, a cast that is a cast. It is a picture that should get money anywhere, the de luxe house and shooting gallery alike. There is but one trouble, and that is in trying to hold down the footage there are a couple of spots in the latter part of the picture where the scenes are cropped rather close. Imagine complaining of that! It only goes to prove that the picture is so good that when it is over you wish there was more of it, and pictures of that kind are darn few and far between.

The comedy end is one of the features that makes it stand out as a sure-fire winner. Can you see Ben Turpin playing a bartender and putting the glasses where he's looking, and Charlie Murray and William V. Mong as a couple of steel mill souses? Shake the three up together and you have laughs that come from the heels.

As for story, there is enough in this one to satisfy anybody. The scenes are laid in Steelburg at the Creeth Mills. Wally Gay, a product of the town's gully, where all the steel workers live, has worked himself into the engineering department of the mills, but because he has seen fit to argue with the chief over the plans for new furnaces, has been demoted to the ranks of the puddlers as helper to Goofy. As a further punishment he is later put on the hot metal train, and here he gets the chance to save the life of the mill owner's daughter.

In the end he marries her. But not until he has been invited to the owner's home for dinner, at which he makes a sap of himself at first with the table ware, but later wins out when he explains his plans for the new furnaces.

To block their success the chief engineer fixes a walk-out of the men through rumors that the new furnaces are unsafe. The youngster fights their ringleader, who is in the pay of the chief, and through whipping him gets the men to go back. That fight is a sweet one and as good as any screened in some time. Of course, when the men go back the coast is clear for the final happy ending.

But it is the comedy that Turpin, Murray and Mong handle early in the story that sends that portion along. Then the meller stuff that Goofy pulls with the chief in the clutches of the metal carrier over the blazing furnaces that gives a kick, and atop of that, the fight adds another wallop.

William Boyd is corking as the hero. He handles himself to show that he was not camera-struck when he got on the lot and acquits himself to make certain he is going to be a screen success. Vera Reynolds didn't have very much to do and did that only passingly well. Nigel Barrie, as the heavy, delivered right, while Hobart Bosworth, who can always be counted on for a corking performance, did not disappoint. Walter Long as Goofy, a half-witted steel worker, stood out, but the honors after all have to go to those three vets, Turpin, Murray and Mong.

The picture is well directed, and Jimmie Hogan deserves a full measure of credit for that.

"Steel Preferred" looks as though it is going to be one of the outstanding successes of the P. D. C. program. *Fred.*

HIS SECRETARY

Metro-Goldwyn picture, starring Norma Shearer and featuring Lew Cody. Hobart Henley production, directed by Henley. Story by Carey Wilson. At the Capitol, New York, week of Dec. 20. Running time, 73 mins.

Ruth Lawrence.............Norma Shearer
David Colman....................Lew Cody
John Sloden..................Willard Louis
Janitor.........................Karl Dane
Clara Bayne......................Gwen Lee
Mrs. Sloden.............Mabel Van Buren
Minnie.........................Estelle Clark
Head Clerk....................Ernest Gillen

A neat, well played light comedy that should plentifully amuse in all of the better class houses. They'll understand this one, high or low. It gives Norma Shearer an opportunity to do something other than merely look good.

It tells of a stenographer old-fashioned in ideas and frumpy as to dress (Miss Shearer), who falls for the Colman half of the law firm (Cody) and sets out to snare him after overhearing his remark that he wouldn't kiss a face like hers on a bet. Sloden, the senior partner of the firm, and possessed of a jealous wife, is framed by Colman to take the hatchet-faced typist to Washington on a business trip instead of the "doll" he had picked. Ruth, the stenog, gets an idea in the Capitol, drops into a beauty parlor for a factory-rebuilt job, whence is seen Miss Shearer as is. After that it's a friendly contest between the law partners for the services of the previously abominated shorthand specialist.

There is abundance of comedy all through the story, with personal honors divided between Miss Shearer and Willard Louis, as the broadminded husband. Miss Shearer does exceptionally well during the first half of the film when bedecked in a mannish business suit, straw sailor, cotton stockings and glasses. She plays it for all it's worth, as well, and when given the chance to be herself looks plenty gorgeous. Louis overshadows Cody in this celluloid opus as regards a scoring total, although the major share of laughs is gained through "situation" giggle getters. Cody plays both easily and nicely as the bachelor, the matrimonial angle giving Louis the edge on the story end.

The results of "The Big Parade" are beginning to show in the Metro-Goldwyn program features, for but a couple of weeks ago Tom O'Brien appeared in a picture at the Capitol and this one has Karl Dane as a janitor. Seen but briefly in this instance, Dane nevertheless leaves a marked impression.

Appropriate interiors lend a distinct tone to the picture, while Henley, directing, has kept the players in a light mood throughout. The subtitling is also a valuable aid, many of the captions drawing laughs on their own. Extremely airy, "His Secretary" is nothing to ponder over, but will pleasingly annihilate an hour and a quarter.

It found no trouble in entertaining a Sunday matinee audience at the Capitol, and for the second afternoon show they were standing downstairs and waiting for vacancies upstairs. *Skig.*

SIEGFRIED

UFA production, made in Germany with German cast. Based on the Nibelungenleid and directed by Fritz Lang. Handled here by UFA-USA. At the Rialto, New York, Dec. 20 week. Running time, 110 minutes.

No programs at the Rialto this week, the ushers telling applicants **that they are "out" for the seven days.**

The legend, which is the basis of "Siegfried" is one of the old German folk tales—the story of how young Siegfried, son of Siegmund the Wise, on the beautiful Kreimhild and was then done to death by the wish of the scheming Brunhilde.

Consequently the picture is purely artistic and holds but few things to interest the average picturegoer of today.

It's an artistic but not a commercial film.

This reviewer purposely caught the picture on its first showing Sunday afternoon, so that he could witness the film without the accompaniment of a large orchestra handling a compiled Wagnerian score, and the conclusion is that the film needs the score to put it over.

When the film was shown at the Century earlier in the year for four weeks, Dr. Hugo Reisenfeld was prevailed upon to "score" the film with Wagnerian music taken from the "Ring" operas. That he did a good job of it almost goes without saying, for Dr. Reisenfeld knows his music and has an almost uncanny sense of fitting tunes to the screen. With his accompaniment it furnishes at least satisfactory entertainment.

The point is that in the really first-class theatres, with an orchestra of 30 or more men, it will be satisfactory entertainment, but shown **to the accompaniment of the pipe organ it is almost deadly dull. The UFA billing on the Rialto marquee is "A music photodrama."**

Paul Richter plays the title role, and does a magnificent job of it at most times, although there are moments when the portrayal grows too effeminate. That seemed to be a great fault with some of the other actors, while the woman who played Brunhilde, although an excellent actress, was as masculine as a bottle of bay rum in a barber shop.

The rave about these German pictures is that the directors are artists to their fingertips (so forth). But after looking at "Siegfried" the only conclusion is that their artistry consists in playing the film story before settings of a very stagey nature and in playing the various scenes in a slow and stodgy pace, not only tiresome to an American audience, but ruinous to the picture.

"Siegfried" will barely get by with an orchestra, is this reviewer's guess, and without decent music it will drive the audience out in droves.

Just an "artistic success," which doesn't mean 10 cents in Mexican money. *Sisk.*

Somebody's Darling

London, Dec. 10.

Betty Balfour is the only real British film "star" and probably the only player in British pictures whose name and work are certain to insure a substantial box office return. At the moment she appears to be passing backward and forward from one set of producers to another.

"Somebody's Darling" is a Gau-

mont feature directed by George A. Cooper from a newspaper serial by Sydney Morgan. The story is neither particularly original nor strong, but it is capital entertainment on comedy lines which at times almost approach burlesque.

Cooper has gone out to provide really good, clean entertainment, without suggestive incident or episode, and in this he has succeeded. Under his direction Miss Balfour has cast aside many of the Squibb-like mannerisms which have marred much of her work since George Pearson raised her to box office stellar position in the series of comedy-dramas written around the adventures of the Cockney heroine, Squibbs. She has learned that acting can be restful at times and not a mere matter of waving hands and restless feet. Her new repose adds to her power and enhances the eccentricity she loves when the action of the plot gives a plausible excuse for its introduction.

The story tells, over a length of footage which could easily be cut still further, how Joan Meredith, the **granddaughter of a village publican, is in the habit of receiving cheques from an unknown source upon her birthday. Then, one day, she comes into a fortune.**

She immediately becomes an object of great interest to the unscrupulous Jordan, who plans her marriage to his worthless son, Oliver. She leaves the old home and embarks on a metropolitan whirl of pleasure, aided by the Jordans.

Meanwhile her true love leaves the village and comes to London to become a great author, etc.

The chief support is Forrester Harvey, who gives a good eccentric performance. He is somewhat over-weighted, however, and there are signs that some of his best work has been tampered with lest it should injure the position of the "star." Harvey makes good, however, and should have a screen future.

A fine "cameo" of pure comedy comes from Jack Harris, a weird-looking youth who would be a find of the Larry Semon type in three months if an American showman got hold of him. Rex O'Malley is painfully immature and youthful as the hero.

British producers have a fixed idea that heroes must be fair of face and frail of form. They object strongly to any man who looks over 21 and who possesses physical attributes which would help him to overcome the machinations of villainy. O'Malley is at his best as the musical-comedy nursing sister. Fred Raynham gives an excellent rendering of a new-style villain and contributes much to the success of the all-pervading comedy. Small parts are well played by Fisher White, Clarence Blakiston, Clifton Boyne, Bromley Devomport and Minna Grey.

Throughout Cooper's work is admirable, and he gets every ounce out of his story. The photography is very good and many of the opening "shots" are of rare artistic beauty.

If all British films were half so good as this, we should not have need for a trade revival.   *Gore.*

WHEN THE DOOR OPENED

William Fox production of a James Oliver Curwood story, directed by Reginald Barker. Scenario by Bradley King. At Loew's New York, Dec. 17, one day. Running time, 74 minutes.
Teresa de Fontenac.......Jacqueline Logan
Clive Grenfel.............Walter McGrail
Mrs. Grenfel.........Margaret Livingston
John Fredericks................Robert Cain
Grandfather de Fontenac....Frank Keenan
O'Flaherty...................Roy Laidlaw

This picture deserved a better fate than just coming on Broadway in a daily change house. A couple of years ago when any story, no matter how picturized, carried the name of Curwood, it was certain of a deluxe presentation on Broadway. Why this one wasn't must have been because of a flock of super-pictures coming along, but as yet they haven't been seen by the reviewer. It may have been, however, that they said that the Northwest mounted pictures have lost their vogue. Possibly Curwood suspected this, for there is but one brief flash of a Mountie, and that is near the end. He has taken a love story and made it stand up in fine shape, with the cast holding sufficient names to make it worth while for any box office.

The story tells of a young Canadian husband returning to his home in Montreal after a week's business trip and finding his wife in the arms of another man. He gets his revolver and shoots, escaping into the night. He wanders away under the belief that he is a murderer. Some time later he meets the granddaughter of a Frenchman of the old school living in a timber fastness. She loves him and he loves her, and their love is finally rewarded.

Directing the story Reginald Barker started out with all the speed in the world, and the first couple of reels flashed by as though this was going to be a whale, but toward the end it began to drag a little, and there were spots where judicious cutting would have improved matters. At least 10 minutes should have been clipped. Otherwise the direction is corking, and the trick camera stuff in the flood scenes so good it gives the audience an awful kick.

A surprise in the casting is Walter McGrail in a heroic role. He plays the lead and handles it excellently. McGrail should get away from heavies on the strength of his work here. Jacqueline Logan also did corking work. In a couple of scenes she stood out like a house afire. Robert Cain was the heavy, while that excellent actor, Frank Keenan, lent dignity and poise as the old Frenchman. One important member of the cast goes unnamed. It is the police dog, with a pretty good head outside of a drooping ear. The dog does good work in the picture.

"When the Door Opened" is a darn good picture, far above the average of Fox program release, and it should pull some money.
Fred.

MAY 1 9 1988   N

MAY 1 9 1988   N